MORNINGSTAR®
Stocks500™

Annual Sourcebook
2003 Edition

Introduction by
Mark Sellers III,
Editor

Editor
Mark Sellers III

Managing Editor
Kelli A. Stebel

Contributing Editor
Amy C. Arnott

Editor-in-Chief, Morningstar
Haywood Kelly

Director of Stock Analysis
Pat Dorsey

Stock Analysts
Sanjay Ayer
Rachel Barnard
Joe Beaulieu
Todd Bernier
Rozilyn Bryant
Damon Ficklin
Tom Goetzinger
Michael Hodel
Fritz Kaegi
Jill Kiersky
Paul Larson
Todd Lebor
Jeremy Lopez
David Kathman
Rich McCaffery
T.K. MacKay
Nicolas Owens
Travis Pascavis
Josh Peters
Mike Porter
Dan Quinn
Dan Schick
Matt Scholz
Jonathan Schrader
Carl Sibilski
Mike Trigg
Debbie Wang
Aaron Westrate
Craig Woker

Content Editor
Sylvia Hauser

Copy Editors
Jason Phillip
Jason Stipp
Karen Wallace

Director of Technology
Fred Wong

Programmers
Jennifer Billows
Eider Deleoz
Scott Kauffman
Vickly Mork
Christine Tan
Dongsheng Wu

Data Analysts
William Danford
P.J. Goodrum
Julie Lyczak
Katherine Nasser
Jeffrey Manczko
Joanna Trzcinska

Director of Design
David Williams

Designer
Jason Ackley

Project Manager
Claudia Sohn

Product Manager
Erica Moor

President
Catherine Gillis Odelbo

Managing Directors
Tim Armour
Don Phillips

Chairman and CEO
Joe Mansueto

For general information on our other products and services, or technical support, please contact our Customer Care Department within the United States at 800-762-2974, outside the United States at 317-572-3993 or fax 317-572-4002.

For general information about Morningstar's other products and services, please contact Morningstar's product sales line at 800-735-0700 or visit www.morningstar.com.

Wiley also publishes its books in a variety of electronic formats. Some content that appears in print may not be available in electronic books.

For more information about Wiley products, visit our web site at www.wiley.com.

ISBN: 0-471-399663
ISBN: 0-471-269611

Printed in the United States of America
10 9 8 7 6 5 4 3 2 1

Table of Contents

2   The Year in Review

5   How to Use the Morningstar Stocks 500

8   The Four Principles of Profitable Investing

14   Understanding Fair Value

16   Improving the Morningstar Rating for Stocks

18   Keeping It Simple Isn't Stupid

19   Morningstar's Two Stock Portfolios:
The Tortoise and the Hare

Index and Tables

23   Morningstar Stocks 500 Index

32   Benchmark Performance

34   Industry Performance

36   Industry Averages

38   Top and Bottom Performing Stocks

40   Stocks with Highest and
Lowest Morningstar Ratings

41   Most Attractive and Least Attractive Stocks

42   Stocks with Low Risk Measure

43   Stocks with High Risk Measure

44   Highest Market Capitalization and Sales

45   Highest Return on Equity and Return on Assets

46   Highest Dividend Yield and Cash Return

47   Highest and Lowest Price Multiples

49   Companies with Wide Economic Moat

50   Companies with No Economic Moat

Report Pages

53   Stock Reports

User's Guide

555   User's Guide

Welcome to the 2003 edition of the *Morningstar Stocks 500*.

For many stock investors, 2002 was nothing short of depressing. The S&P 500 lost 23.4% and the Nasdaq lost 31.5%. The average U.S. diversified mutual fund lost 22.6%. And it was the first time since the 1930s—and just the second time ever—that the U.S. stock market declined for a third consecutive year. Once again, bonds outperformed stocks, and despite several short-lived rallies, stock investors spent most of the year navigating their way through a perfect storm. There were several ingredients that formed this year's bear market soup.

For starters, by the time 2002 rolled around the Federal Reserve's options were limited. This was the same Fed that cut interest rates a record 11 times in 2001. In 2002, the Fed's powder was pretty much dry, so it was forced to watch from the sidelines as business spending stagnated. There was a glut of excess capacity in the technology and capital goods sectors, and when there's excess capacity, companies delay spending no matter how cheap credit is.

The same thing can't be said of American consumers, though, who joyfully backed up their pickup trucks and loaded them with... more trucks! And more cars, and more new homes, and more credit cards. Rock-bottom mortgage rates and credit gimmicks such as zero percent financing, cash rebates, or other derivations of the "buy now, pay later" variety were seen just about everywhere in 2002 as retail companies competed fiercely for consumer dollars. Economics 101 tells us that when the price of something—including credit—goes down (other things equal), there will be more demand for it, so it's not much of a surprise that the mortgage, auto, and consumer lending markets stayed red hot in 2002. Consumers were merely doing what's logical when things go on sale: borrowing from tomorrow to pay for today. In the end, the Fed's 2001 easing of monetary policy had the desired effect on the U.S. economy in 2002.

But in 2002, a far more ominous concern was a loss of trust: in CEOs, in auditors, in analysts, in Martha Stewart, and in ourselves. Perhaps 2002, and not 2000, was the year the bubble finally burst. After all, part of what created the excesses of the late 1990s in the first place was an almost unwavering trust that the system was fair, that corporate management teams had every incentive to do right by shareholders. It turns out that's often not the case.

We can learn a few lessons from 2002. First, blindly trusting a company's management team is a recipe for disaster. Investors and analysts must do their homework by digging through proxy statements, reading and understanding the financial statements, and asking tough questions of management.

A second lesson is that human beings often behave in very predictable ways based on the financial incentives they're given. If you offer someone $100 million in options to pump his company's stock price through any means possible, and then let that person cash out at his earliest convenience, then by golly, many people will do just that. The solution is for analysts and investors to take an active role in assessing executive compensation. Company incentive plans should reward managers for taking a long-term approach to the business instead of fostering a "get rich quick" mentality. For some reason, we thought human nature had changed in the 1990s because stock prices were going up.

But the biggest lesson from 2002 is a reminder of Benjamin Graham's old adage: In the short run, the market is a voting machine, but in the long run, it's a weighing machine. Companies with strong balance sheets, conservative management teams, and wide economic moats do well over the long term—they're "heavy." By contrast, companies that play fast and loose with the books, make aggressive financial projections, and issue press releases designed solely to pump up their own stock prices are sucker bets.

Your job as an investor, then, boils down to this: Avoid the sucker bets. If you can do that, everything else will take care of itself.

Sincerely,

Mark Sellers III
Editor
Morningstar Stocks 500

How to Use the *Morningstar Stocks 500*

Get the most value from this book by following these tips.

by Amy C. Arnott
Contributing Editor,
Morningstar
Stocks 500

We've designed the *Morningstar Stocks 500* to be an essential resource for investors, whether you're looking for promising new stocks to add to your portfolio or you just want to keep a close eye on stocks you already own. Here are some of the key elements of the book, and information on how you can get the most value from each one.

Insightful Articles about Stocks

At the beginning of this book, you'll find several articles by Morningstar analysts and editors that give important guidance on how to invest in stocks. If you want to learn more about Morningstar's approach to investing, this is a great place to start. These articles shed light on recent changes to Morningstar's stock star rating, explain how to use fair value estimates to make better investing decisions, and more.

Indexes and Tables

If you want to find essential statistics about the leading companies in the *Stocks 500*, the indexes and tables at the beginning of the book are the place to go. The Company Index contains some of the most important information at a glance: the company's name, industry, star rating, risk profile, fundamentals, and Morningstar grades for Growth, Profitability, and Financial Health.

The Benchmark Performance page on Page 32 is a great reference for performance on market benchmarks in every major asset class. Use this page to find out which areas of the market performed best and worst in 2002, as well as in previous years.

On Page 33, we show total returns for the average mutual fund in each of the nine squares of the Morningstar style box, as well as stock performance by sector. Comparing a stock's performance to an appropriate benchmark can be helpful—if a stock's performance is dramatically different from that of other stocks in the same sector or style box, it's worthwhile to find out why. In this section, you'll also find benchmark

averages for each one of Morningstar's roughly 130 industries.

The next several pages highlight the best and worst of the *Morningstar Stocks 500* universe. You'll find tables showing the best and worst performers over various time periods, stocks with the highest and lowest Morningstar ratings, the most and least attractive stocks, and companies with the best and worst risk profiles. This section also shows companies that stand out based on a variety of fundamental measures, including total sales, market capitalization, profitability measures like return on equity and return on assets, dividend yield, cash returns, and price multiples. If you've already crafted an investment strategy based on specific value or growth measures, these pages will help you find investment ideas that might be worthy of further investigation.

Report Pages

These pages are the heart of the *Morningstar Stocks 500*. Each page packs in a lot of information, but don't be intimidated: You'll find lots of data on each company, but we've also provided plenty of written material from our analysts that helps place all the numbers in context.

Here's an overview of all the sections covered on each page. We'll start at the top of the page and go on a counterclockwise tour of all the different information covered. If you're looking for a more specific definition of any data point on the page, refer to the User's Guide at the back of the book for more information.

Company Profile
This section gives an overview of the company's major lines of business. This is a good place to start if you want to learn more about a company's operations; it also gives an update on any recent corporate events, such as mergers or acquisitions.

Management
This section details the analyst's opinion about the company's management team. Here we discuss our thoughts on the strengths and weaknesses of the company's top managers, and offer insight on how key players are influencing the company's strategic direction. If there's anything notable about the company's compensation practices or key executives' stock ownership, we'll cover that here, too.

Strategy

The strategy section sheds light on the thinking behind the company's current direction. You'll find out where management is finding the best opportunities for growth and how it aims to give the company a competitive edge. We'll also cover how management plans to deal with financial challenges, technological developments in the industry, or emerging competitive threats.

Morningstar Grades

For a quick summary of the company's financial strengths and weaknesses, look at the letter grades for Growth, Profitability, and Financial Health. The text below each grade explains what's been driving trends in the numbers.

Growth: Has the company been increasing its sales, earnings, book value, and dividends over the past several years? All else being equal, an upward trend is generally a good sign. Since these numbers are expressed in percentage terms, it's easy to see how the trends have changed each year. Just watch out for extremely high numbers here—they're typically not sustainable. And there's no guarantee that a company that has generated impressive historical growth will continue to deliver in the future.

Profitability: How successful has the company been in converting top-line sales into profits after expenses? This section summarizes the annual change in return on assets and shows the company's free cash flow in dollars. Free cash flow is the amount of money a company generates from its operations, minus the amount it invests back in the business. Unlike items such as reported earnings (which can be subject to accounting quirks or deliberate attempts by management to make things look better than they really are), free cash flow generally gives a reliable picture of a company's financial health. If a company consistently generates healthy free cash flows, that's a very good sign. To see how things stack up, divide the free cash flow in dollars by revenue for the same year. If it's over 5%, that's a reassuring sign.

Financial Health: With the implosions we've seen at **WorldCom** WCOEQ, **Global Crossing** GBLXQ, **UAL** UAL, and scores of other companies, financial health has taken on newfound importance for many investors. Check this section to see the company's long-term debt in dollars and compare it with total equity. A debt/equity ratio of 0.3 or less is generally pretty good, although this number can vary considerably by industry.

Morningstar's Take

This is where we tell you exactly what we think about each individual company in the *Morningstar Stocks 500* universe—good or bad. The written analysis sums up whether we think the company's shares are worth investing in, gives our take on the company's future prospects, and explains the rationale behind our fair value estimate on the shares. We'll also discuss any recent developments or potential risks that could affect the company's value. Morningstar has a staff of 30 analysts who are responsible for analyzing stocks, and much of their time is devoted to valuing companies and writing reports on individual companies. Because Morningstar isn't beholden to investment-banking revenue, we're free to offer strong opinions on the companies we cover—both positive and negative.

Valuation Ratios

This section shows how expensive the stock is compared with earnings, book value, sales, and cash flow. These measures can help you approximate whether a stock is cheap or pricey. You can also compare the stock's valuation ratios to the market and industry averages to see how they stack up. If the stock's valuation is higher than the norm, watch out. To justify paying a higher-than-average price, you'd have to be very confident that the company will deliver a high enough growth rate to sustain the hefty price tag. Some firms can do that, but the market often overestimates the growth prospects of companies with innovative new products or impressive business plans. If they fall short of earnings targets, their stock prices can quickly drop.

Major Fund Holders

Check the list of fund holders to see if there are any names you recognize—are they big diversified funds, or more specialized players? If you see a well-respected fund in the list, that's generally a good sign (though it's not a guarantee that the stock is worth buying).

Historical Financial Statements

Below the stock's historical price graph, you'll find some of the most important items from the company's income statement and balance sheet over the past six years. Here, you'll find the company's revenue in dollars, net income, earnings per share, and shares outstanding. The data shown are based on restated numbers, which means that the most recent financial statements override all historical statements. If the company restates earnings for previous years, we'll use the revised numbers instead of the originally reported data.

The advantage of using restated numbers is that they allow for purely operational growth calculations. For example, when AOL and Time Warner merged, AOL's revenues jumped from $7.7 billion to more than $38 billion. The huge $30.5 billion increase (based on as-originally-reported numbers) tells you nothing about how revenues were impacted by core business growth during the year, while a $2 billion increase (based on restated numbers) would tell you that operating activities generated revenue growth of about 6%. The same comparison can be made for all income statement, balance sheet, and cash flow items.

This section also shows the return on equity for each of the past six years. The three lines that follow—net margin, asset turnover, and financial leverage—are the key drivers that determine the company's return on equity. Check here to find out what's driving the company's profitability. If it's showing steady increases in net margins or asset turnover, that's generally a good sign. But if the company is pumping up profits by taking on more debt (shown in the financial leverage line), that's cause for concern.

Price Volatility
The graph toward the top of the page shows the stock's price volatility from year to year. Check here to find out where the stock price has landed in the past. The top of the graph shows the stock's highest and lowest price during the year, which can give you an idea of how volatile it has been over time. The solid line below the stock's price chart shows the stock's strength relative to the s&p 500. When this line is upward sloping, that means it has been performing better than the market. A downward-sloping line means it has been falling behind.

Competition
Near the top of the page, we show key data about the company's primary competitors. The companies featured are those that we think the company competes with most directly; they typically have similar products or lines of business. Note: Although there's room for up to three competi-

tors for each company, we won't always list three if we think the company has a smaller number of direct competitors. We also include close competitors that are privately held; in those cases, the key financial data is not available.

Summary
The top of the page gives some key information that can can help you determine how a stock might fit in with the rest of your portfolio if you're considering a potential investment. The second line down shows the company's industry, investment style, stock type, and sector. Before you make a new purchase, make sure these key characteristics don't overlap too much with stocks or funds that you already own.

At the top of the page, you'll find the stock's Morningstar Rating, Risk profile, Moat Size, and Fair Value estimate. You'll also find the latest closing price (as of the publishing date), and the dividend yield the company has paid out over the past 12 months expressed in percentage terms. The star rating sums up how attractive we think the stock is based on our estimate of the present value of the company's future cash flows. The most attractive stocks are those with ratings of 5 stars, while the least attractive are those with ratings of 1 star. The star rating also incorporates risk and our assessment of its economic moat.

The concept of economic moats is a key part of Morningstar's approach to investing. One of the main things that separates a great company from a mediocre one is the size of the moat, or competitive barrier, a company builds around itself. The larger the moat, the greater the shareholder value a company is able to create. For each company in the *Morningstar Stocks 500*, we classify the Moat Size as wide, narrow, or none. A high-risk stock with a narrow moat must sell at a bigger discount to our fair value to earn an above-average star rating. A low-risk stock with a wide moat, on the other hand, requires a smaller discount to fair value.

One important note: The fair values shown in the *Morningstar Stocks 500* incorporate our best assessment of the company's value as of the date this book was published. Our analysts continuously monitor their valuation models and change them as conditions warrant. For the most up-to-date fair values and star ratings, visit www.morningstar.com. ⁣

The Four Principles of Profitable Investing

Use the techniques of great investors to improve your own stock-picking.

by Mark Sellers III
Editor, *Morningstar*
Stocks 500

Warren Buffett. Peter Lynch. Bill Miller. Bill Nygren.

These are some of the greatest stock market investors of the past 30 years—investors who have beaten the S&P 500 index year in and year out. If you'd invested just $945 in three shares of Warren Buffett's holding company, **Berkshire Hathaway** BRK.B, at the beginning of 1980, today you'd have more than $213,000. And Bill Miller, manager of the **Legg Mason Value Trust Fund** LMVTX, has beaten the S&P 500 benchmark in each of the past 12 years—the only fund manager ever to do so.

Why is it that some investors are able to rise far above the crowd? Are they smarter than everyone else? Do they have access to "inside" information that others don't? Or maybe they're statistical anomalies with nothing in common except luck. (This is the explanation thousands of eager young business school students are taught year after year.)

Of course, none of these explanations holds much water. Sure, all these guys are smart, but so are the legions of Harvard- and Stanford-trained MBAs who fail to beat the market every year. So what do these investors have that others don't?

To find out, Morningstar looked back at hundreds of interviews we've done with elite stock market investors over the past 15 years. Because Morningstar talks to great investors every day, we're uniquely qualified to delve into their investment styles and strategies. And what we found was fascinating. On the surface, many of these managers don't have much in common. They grew up in different places, came from different educational backgrounds, manage different kinds of funds, and hold different stocks within different industries.

In fact, there's really only one obvious trait shared by many of the great stock market investors we talk to. What is it? It's a methodology for uncovering great stocks at reasonable prices. It's designed to generate above-average returns while minimizing taxes and risk. We've named this methodology the Four Principles of Profitable Investing:

1. *Find economic moats.*
2. *Have a margin of safety.*
3. *Use the magic of compounding.*
4. *Know when to sell.*

Principle 1: Find Economic Moats

What separates a bad company from a good one? Or a good company from a great one? In large part, it's the size of the "economic moat," or competitive barrier, a company builds around itself. We've identified four main types of economic moats:

1. *High customer switching costs*
2. *Economies of scale*
3. *Intangible assets*
4. *The network effect*

If the meanings of these terms seem a bit fuzzy at first, don't worry—I'll give you an example of each.

High Customer Switching Costs
If a business sells you something you can't get elsewhere—at least not easily—then that business has high customer switching costs. For example, if you have only one grocery store in your neighborhood, and you don't own a car, you'd be willing to pay extra to buy your food there. To get to another store, you'd have to walk a long way. Thus, there are high "costs" to switching to a different grocery store. In this scenario, the grocery store can charge higher prices and generate excess profits.

Let's look at an example from the stock market.

More than 30 years ago, **Paychex** PAYX founder Tom Galisano anticipated the upcoming boom in outsourced payroll-processing services and began aggressively targeting small and medium-sized businesses, which he saw (correctly) as a willing but underserved customer base. Today, the company generates about $900 million in annual revenue and has grown earnings per share by an average of more than 30% annually over the past decade. If you had jumped in and bought 100 shares of Paychex at $31 each 15 years ago and held them until today, you'd now have 5,767 shares (after splits) worth about $140,000. If you had allocated the same amount of money to an S&P 500 index fund, you'd have caught one of the greatest bull market periods in stock market history—but even so, you'd still have only $16,968 today. That's a tremendous difference. How could you have spotted Paychex early enough to get in on the action?

The best way would have been to recognize one of the common traits of a company building an economic moat: high customer switching costs.

Paychex does payroll processing for other businesses that don't want to hire and train a staff of people for this function. Since Paychex is a specialist in payroll and tax processing and has developed proprietary software for this purpose, it can offer the same as an in-house staff of payroll employees, but at a lower cost, more quickly, and with fewer errors. For small companies without the resources to hire a staff of payroll employees and accountants, Paychex is a boon.

What happens if a company decides it wants to forgo using Paychex's services and bring the job in-house? Well, it's looking at hiring payroll employees and training them, buying computers, buying software, and dealing with IRS audits and employee complaints because of frequent errors. Not many small businesses would willingly make this trade-off unless the cost savings of bringing the job in-house were enormous. Thus, Paychex enjoys very high customer switching costs. This is a type of economic moat that makes great stock investors giddy.

Economies of Scale
In commodity industries such as oil, industrial chemicals, steel, and personal computers, economic moats are very difficult to create. Take the airline industry—please! Most travelers are looking for the lowest fare, regardless of the airline. That forces airlines to compete aggressively on price to generate business, which translates into small profits when the economy is hot but large losses when it's not. In fact, according to Buffett, in the entire 100-year history of the airline industry (since the Wright Brothers' famous flight at Kitty Hawk in 1903), not one net dollar of profit has been made.

I said earlier that an economic moat is a barrier against competition. When price is the only thing to compete on, there is only one form of barrier—the ability to offer lower prices than your competitors.

For those rare companies that thrive on being the low-cost provider in a commodity industry, profits are plentiful. In the airline industry, that low-cost provider is **Southwest Airlines** LUV. Southwest's entire mission is centered on offering cheaper flights than competitors without shirking on service. By thriving in an environment that forces many other airlines to take large losses or declare bankruptcy (including United Airlines, US Air, TWA, National, Legend, PanAm, and Eastern Airlines), Southwest has been able to increase its earnings per share more than 1,400% over the past 10 years. During that same period, its stock has risen about 760%, compared with a rise of 163% for the S&P 500.

Dell Computer DELL is another low-cost provider in an industry that is rapidly becoming commodified—the PC industry. Selling computers directly to consumers was a novel concept when Michael Dell founded the company out of his college dorm room in 1984. The advantages of this kind of business model may seem obvious now, but back in the 1980s and early 1990s, people thought the average consumer would never buy a computer without assistance from a salesperson. Of course, they were wrong.

It turns out a significant percentage of consumers will buy a computer from a catalog (or over the Internet) if that means getting a great machine at a good price. Because Dell builds to order and sells directly to consumers, it's able to keep prices low, while producing and selling computers at a much lower cost than competitors. And that means it has a sustainable economic moat allowing it to generate more profit than competitors on every sales dollar. With the industry rapidly shifting to a slow-growth commodity industry, Dell should continue to squash the other box makers because it can offer lower prices and still make a profit.

Intangible Assets
Some companies have an advantage over competitors because of unique nonphysical, or "intangible," assets. Intangibles are things such as intellectual property rights (patents, trademarks, and copyrights), government approvals, brand

names, a unique company culture, or a geographic advantage.

In some cases, whole industries derive huge benefits from intangible assets. These industries, such as drugs and software, are exactly the opposite of commodity industries. Companies in these industries live and die by their ability to generate intellectual property (IP) rights such as patents, copyrights, and governmental agency approvals. The great thing about IP rights is that they are protected by law, which means a company that owns a lot of patents or copyrights can raise prices without fear of being undercut by competitors. This can be one of the strongest types of economic moats because it virtually guarantees a monopoly on a product until the IP rights expire.

For example, **Pfizer** PFE holds patents on more than 25 drugs currently on the market, including three of the top 10 in the world. These patents allow the company to charge high prices for new drugs for years after they hit the market. With little competition during the life of the patent, profits and cash flows are huge. That's why Pfizer's average return on equity over the past five years has been greater than 30%, and its net profit margins are north of 25% (compared with around 6% for the average S&P 500 company). That's also why it's been a great stock to own. In fact, many of the major pharmaceutical players, including **Amgen** AMGN, **Johnson & Johnson** JNJ, **Merck** MRK, **Abbott Labs** ABT, and **Eli Lilly** LLY have outperformed the S&P 500 over the past 10 years because of the economic moats inherent in this industry.

Another example of a company that benefits from intellectual property rights is **Microsoft** MSFT. In fact, all software companies rely on IP laws to protect their investments in new products from competitors. Because of this protection, leading software companies can generate huge profits and cash flows. Along with Microsoft, which sports an unbelievable net profit margin of more than 40%, other notable industry examples include **Oracle** ORCL, **Adobe** ADBE, **Intuit** INTU, **DST Systems** DST, and **SunGard Data Systems** SDS. The average net profit margin for the software industry as a whole is about 15%, well above the S&P 500 average.

The Network Effect
Perhaps the strongest type of economic moat is the network effect. For those rare companies that successfully take advantage of this phenomenon, the reward is often a legal monopoly. A common trait among these types of companies is that they are the first, or one of the first, to enter an emerging communications industry or business niche.

Let's take a trip back to March 7, 1876, the day Alexander Graham Bell was awarded a patent on a new invention called the telephone. (Elisha Gray would have been known to us as the inventor of the telephone, but Bell got to the patent office a few hours before Gray.) Even though this marked one of the most important inventions in the history of the world, many people saw it as a mere curiosity. Since few people had access to a telephone, there was no one to call.

But slowly, more and more people gained access to a telephone, giving them the ability to communicate with friends, family, and associates.

The more people gained access to telephones, the more valuable telephones became—and the faster phone usage grew. This is a classic example of the network effect (or winner-take-all effect): The more people who are "plugged in" to a communication network, the more valuable the network becomes to each person in the network.

The network effect also explains the incredible exponential growth of the Internet (and e-mail) over the past decade. A prominent example is **eBay** EBAY. Given our discussion about the network effect thus far, it should be easy to understand why eBay has a monopoly in online auctions. EBay was the first to connect individual buyers and sellers over the Internet in an auction-like format, so it grew very quickly. As more rare baseball cards and vintage posters came up for auction on eBay, more buyers were attracted to the Web site to bid on those items. Those extra bidders attracted still more sellers, and it created a virtuous circle that fed on itself.

By the time competitors like **Yahoo** YHOO and **Amazon.com** AMZN got into the auction game, it was too late. There were already too many bidders on eBay for sellers to want to jump to a new, smaller auction service (where they might get a lower price for their wares because of fewer bids on each item), and there were so many items for sale on eBay, the bidders weren't interested in going anywhere either. Thus, eBay gained a critical mass and, today, a near-monopoly position in the online-auction market.

Of course, the stock hasn't done too poorly either, rising more than 800% since its IPO in fall 1998. Investors realized that eBay was on its way to a monopoly due to network economics, and they bid the stock up accordingly in the greatest auction of all, the U.S. stock market.

How could you have gotten in on eBay's stock before its meteoric rise from $7 to $42 in late 1998? By recognizing that the leading company in an industry dominated by network economics will often gain a monopoly position and be highly profitable. Industries made up of companies that enable communication or commerce between individuals are the Petri dishes of network economics. The online-auction industry certainly meets those criteria.

Below are some companies and organizations that have tried to take advantage of network economics. Some of these companies currently have monopolies, while others are former monopolies. I've also listed a few companies that have failed recently in their attempts to dominate competitors by using the network effect.

Some Organizations Have Created Partial or Full Monopolies by Using the Network Effect, While Others Have Failed

Successful
Microsoft, The NASDAQ stock exchange, Visa/Mastercard, American Express (credit cards), AOL, eBay, U.S. Postal Service,

Former
AT&T (before its breakup), New York Stock Exchange, NBC

Failed
Ariba, Commerce One, Free Markets, VerticalNet, Palm

Final Thought
One final thought about economic moats: It is possible for some companies to have more than one type of economic moat. For example, many companies that use the network effect can also benefit from economies of scale, because these companies tend to grow so large that they dwarf smaller competitors.

Principle 2: Have a Margin of Safety
Okay, so you've uncovered a company that has at least one good-sized economic moat. Unfortunately, your work is only half done at this point. You can't just go out and pay whatever the market is asking for this stock until you cal-culate what it's worth. Otherwise, you might end up having to hold the stock for many, many years to get a decent return on your money. And in some cases, you might never get one.

Are the people who paid $212 for Yahoo in January 2000 are ever going to get their money back? Yahoo's a good company, but it may take a very long time for the stock to get back to that price. The same could be said of many other technology companies with moats around them that got clobbered when the bull market came crashing to a halt.

So the question is: How do I make sure this doesn't happen to me? The answer: Have a strict valuation discipline so that you incorporate a margin of safety into the price you pay. That way, if you later realize you overestimated the company's prospects, you won't regret paying too much for the shares.

This is tough for many people because they're worried that if they don't buy today, they might miss the boat forever on the stock. That's almost never the case, though. If you wait long enough, almost any stock will sell at a big discount to fair value at one time or another. So treat investing like baseball: If the pitcher doesn't throw one right down the middle, don't swing. The good thing about investing, unlike baseball, is that you can let as many knuckleballs and curveballs go by as you want and only swing at pitches that come right down the middle.

Successful investors spend a great deal of time calculating the fair value of a stock before they consider buying it. And they'll only buy stocks that they're confident are undervalued. How can you follow this plan? There are a few ways.

One way is to read *Morningstar StockInvestor* every month. In it, we present two model portfolios and give our analysts' fair value estimates for each stock. We also give you information on stocks to stay away from because they're selling above our fair value estimates.

If you want to do it yourself, though, another way to value a stock is to look at its historical price/earnings ratio over the past five years or so. If you can get 10 years of data, even better. If a stock is currently selling at a P/E of 30, and its range over the past 10 years has been between 15 and 33, you're obviously buying in at the high end of historical norms. To justify paying today's price, you have to be plenty confident that the company's outlook is better today than it was over the past 10 years. Occasionally, this is the case, but most of the time when a company's valuation is higher now than in the past, watch out. The market is probably overestimating growth prospects and you may be left with a stock that underperforms the market over the coming years. An even more complicated, but also more precise, way to value a stock is to learn how to do a discounted cash flow (DCF) valuation. Most of the great investors use some form of DCF model to value stocks. I won't go into the specifics of doing a DCF model here, but suffice it to say you need to be able to estimate three things: the company's current-year free cash flow, its future growth rate, and its level of risk.

But whichever method you use to place a value on a stock, one thing is certain: If you don't use a lot of discipline and conservatism in figuring out the prices you're willing to pay for stocks, you'll regret it eventually. You might be able to sell some of your overvalued shares to some sucker who is willing to pay an even more inflated price, but in the end, this kind of speculating is the investing equivalent of musical chairs, with the last one holding the stock the loser. Don't let it be you. Buy at a price below fair value and sleep well at night.

Principle 3: Exploit the Magic of Compounding

Why are there no billionaire day traders? Because the mathematics of investing mean that the value of an investment compounds over time. Thus, mathematically speaking, it's far better to hold stocks for long periods of time than it is to trade in and out of them often. This concept is often called the magic of compounding.

Unfortunately, the magic of compounding can work against you, too. If you trade a lot, you'll rack up taxes, commissions, and other expenses which, over time, compound. Every $1 you spend on commissions today could have been turned into $30 if you had invested that dollar at 12% for 30 years. Spend $500 today and you could be giving up $15,000 30 years hence.

The math gets even worse if you make lots of trades year after year. If you spend $500 every year on commissions, by the end of the 30 years you'll be $121,000 behind where you would have been if you had instead invested that $500 each year and gotten a 12% return on the money.

But that's just the beginning of the story, because frequent trading also dramatically increases the taxes you pay. Let's take another example by assuming you invest $10,000 in a group of 10 stocks today (this example assumes a 12% pretax investment return and 28% short-term and 20% long-term capital-gains tax rates). If you put $10,000 into these stocks and they rise at an annual rate of 12% for 30 years, and then you sell them all and pay taxes on the gain, your original investment will turn into about $239,000, an 11.17% aftertax return. But by selling your stocks once per year, paying taxes on your realized gains, reinvesting what's left for another year, and repeating this process each year for 30 years, the same $10,000 will turn into just $120,000, an 8.6% aftertax return. That's another $119,000 you've just left on the table, along with the $121,000 you lost by spending $500 a year in commissions.

Think of it this way: Suppose I offered you a loan at 0% interest and told you I expected you to pay me eventually, but only when you choose. Until then, you could use the money in any way you wanted. Would you take that loan? Of course you would—you'd be a fool not to. Well, guess what: Both your stockbroker and Uncle Sam are offering you this deal every day. When you hold a stock for a long period of time and its value compounds, you're really getting a no-interest loan that you have to pay only when you sell the stock at a time and price of your choosing.

What a deal.

I hope I've done a good job of convincing you to be a long-term investor. All things considered, the mathematical benefits are just too big to ignore.

Principle 4: Know When to Sell

Despite the examples I highlighted above about the mathematical advantages of being a long-term investor, there's something I didn't mention: Most successful investors are really good at knowing when to sell. As Kenny Rogers sang in his popular song "The Gambler," "You gotta know when to hold 'em, and know when to fold 'em." He was referring to a game of poker, but the same could be said of stocks.

Knowing when to sell is difficult. Time and again at Morningstar, we hear from investors telling us they want to know when to sell a stock as much as when to buy one. The problem: Investors are inundated with advice about which stocks to buy, but sell recommendations are far less common then enthusiastic buy opinions.

Knowing when to sell is especially important in a down market. The talking heads on financial news channels and the Wall Street pitchmen aren't going to help. They can be good sources for gathering information, but by the time something's on television, it's way too late to profit from it.

But there is hope: By studying the writings, interviews, and investment styles of great investors, Morningstar has gleaned some powerful insights into this dilemma. We think there are really only four good reasons to sell a stock:

1. *You realize you made a mistake buying it in the first place.*
2. *The stock is wildly overvalued.*
3. *The fundamentals of the company are deteriorating.*
4. *You need the money for a specific purpose, such as a new house or being laid off from your job.*

Before I elaborate further on the reasons for selling a stock, though, I want to point out some of the wrong reasons to sell a stock. First, just because a stock has gone up doesn't mean you should sell it. A whole host of factors go into this decision, such as tax considerations and your personal financial situation. Suffice it to say that in most cases it's better to hold on to a stock that's gone up than to sell it.

Also, you should try to avoid the mistake most beginning investors make: Selling their winning stocks while holding on to their losers. Human psychology comes into play here. We humans hate to admit when we've made a mistake. Therefore, lots of investors hold on to stocks that have gone down with the hope of selling them as soon as they get back to the "break even" point. If they need to raise cash, they sell one of their winners instead.

Unfortunately, in most cases selling your winners is exactly the opposite of what you should do. The U.S. tax code gives you a write-off for realizing a loss, so why not take advantage of Uncle Sam's generosity whenever you can?

The thing to always keep in mind is that it doesn't matter what a stock has done since you bought it; there's nothing you can do to change the past. But you can change your future by selling a dud and taking the tax write-off. Hold on to those winners, though, because in most cases the reason they're winners is that they've beaten expectations, and this is often a sign that the company is building an economic moat.

Sometimes, though, you do have to sell even your winners. For example, if the fundamentals of a company deteriorate, you may want to consider getting out of the stock.

Gap GPS is a good example of this. This company has increased its debt load at the same time its returns on capital and profit margins have fallen steadily during the past few years. In other words, the fundamentals are deteriorating (though they're still not too bad compared with those of a lot of other retailers). If I owned this stock, I would definitely consider selling it despite the fact that it has risen more than 9,000% over the past 20 years. I certainly wouldn't expect such returns in the future.

You might also want to sell a stock if the price has gone up so much that it's wildly overvalued by any reasonable metric. For example, in early 2000 when Yahoo was selling for around $200 per share (close to 200 times sales), it was nearly impossible to make a logical argument that the stock was fairly valued. Investors who held the stock as it went from $2 to $200 were crazy not to take some money off the table.

An important point here is to not worry about missing a stock's peak. No matter how savvy you are, there's no way you can consistently pick the top (or bottom) of the market. There's a saying on Wall Street: The only person who always buys at the bottom and sells at the top is a liar. ▮

Understanding Fair Value

Why it makes sense to buy stocks at a discount.

by Amy C. Arnott
Contributing Editor,
*Morningstar
Stocks 500*

When you own a stock, you own a piece of a business. This idea is at the heart of how Morningstar evaluates stocks. To figure out the fair value of a company's shares, we focus on the financial performance of the company we're analyzing. We don't look at share-price momentum, investor sentiment, or technical indicators. In other words, our fair value estimates are meant to pin down the actual value of the company's shares—not what we think the market may pay for them.

The reason for this is simple: Although market sentiment and many other factors can affect stock prices in the short term, over the long run, share prices are driven by the performance of the underlying business. It's tough—if not impossible—to guess whether a stock will be "in favor" or "out of favor" six months from now. But over long periods of time, a stock's price should ultimately reflect the true worth of the company's underlying business.

Does our strong emphasis on valuation mean we're "value" investors? You bet. But does that mean we like only stocks with low price-to-earnings and low price-to-book ratios? Not at all. If a company has great long-term prospects and earns high returns on invested capital, it can be a great value—even if the P/E or P/B looks high relative to those of other companies. Conversely, a stock can still be overvalued even if it looks cheap based on its P/E ratio. We think investors are better served paying a fair price for a company with great long-term prospects—one that creates economic value—than a "cheap" price for a wealth-destroying company.

To calculate a stock's fair value, Morningstar analysts estimate the company's future financial performance using a detailed cash-flow model that factors in five-year projections for the company's income statement, balance sheet, and cash-flow statement. We then figure out the total value of the company's future cash flows and discount the value to reflect its worth in today's dollars. The result is an analyst-driven estimate of the stock's fair value. We look carefully to see whether companies are growing by simply pumping capital into their business at low rates of return, or whether they are growing by wisely allocating shareholders' capital to earn positive economic returns.

Using Morningstar's Fair Value Estimates
Although we don't change our fair value estimates every day or without careful consideration, we do make changes to a company's fair value if we think its prospects have fundamentally changed. Our analysts are responsible for monitoring the companies they follow on a daily basis. For each company we cover, we'll revisit the fair value estimate at least once every three months to make sure it's still on target. You can find the most up-to-date fair values on www.morningstar.com. You can also find out more about the assumptions behind each company's fair value estimate by reading the Analyst Report.

Our fair value numbers can be a useful way to generate watch lists for your future investments. Check out *Morningstar Stocks 500* to find solid companies you'd be interested in owning at the right price. When the stock's price drops below the fair value estimate, it might be worth closer consideration. You can also use fair value to figure out which stocks in your portfolio are candidates for selling. If you buy a stock because it looks cheap relative to its fair value, it's logical to consider selling it if it rises above fair value.

Fair Value and the Morningstar Rating for Stocks
Our fair value estimates are an integral part of the Morningstar Rating for stocks. Generally speaking, stocks trading at large discounts to our analysts' fair value estimates will receive higher (4 or 5 stars) ratings, and stocks trading at large premiums to their fair value estimates will receive lower (1 or 2 stars) ratings. Stocks that are trading very close to our analysts' fair value estimates will usually get 3-star ratings.

A stock with a lower risk score and a wider economic moat (or competitive advantage) will receive a higher star rating than a stock with a higher risk score and a smaller economic moat, given an equal discount (or premium) to their fair value estimates.

For example, a low-risk stock with a wide economic moat needs only a 20% discount to our fair value estimate to receive a rating of 5 stars, while a high-risk stock with no economic moat needs a 60% discount to its fair value estimate to receive the same rating.

Remember, the single greatest determinant of a stock's return in your portfolio is the price you pay for it. As important as it is to understand the quality of a company—its growth prospects, competitive position, and so forth—it's even more vital that you pay a fair price for that firm's shares. You'll make a lot more money buying decent firms with low valuations than by paying premium prices for premium companies. Why? Because the future is uncertain, and low valuations leave a lot more room for error.

The bottom line: If you're not careful about the price you pay for a stock, you'll probably regret it eventually. You might be able to sell some of your overvalued shares to someone who's willing to pay an even more inflated price, but that only works when the market is in an optimistic mood. To be safe, focus on buying stocks at a price below fair value with an adequate margin of safety. This strategy should not only lead to better returns for your portfolio, but should also help you sleep better at night. **M**

Improving the Morningstar Rating for Stocks

We've made some changes to better incorporate quality and risk.

by Mark Sellers III
Editor, *Morningstar Stocks 500*

In *The Intelligent Investor*, value investor Benjamin Graham wrote, "To distill the secret of sound investment into three words, we venture the motto, Margin of Safety." With those three words in mind, we made some changes to the Morningstar Rating for stocks in 2002.

Why? Well, all companies are not created equal—and neither are all stocks. Some are riskier than others, of course. Thus, we changed the way we calculate our star ratings to better include risk in the equation. Previously, any stock selling more than 30% below its fair value estimate was rated with 5 stars. With the new methodology, however, we added a risk adjustment to the star rating. To get a 5-star rating now, a risky stock such as **Americredit** ACF will have to fall further below its fair value estimate than a low-risk stock such as **Federated Investors** FII.

We made another change by incorporating the size of a company's economic moat into our calculation. "Economic moat" is a term used by Warren Buffett to describe the predictability of a company's future profits. Companies with big competitive advantages in mature industries (e.g., **Pfizer** PFE or **Gillette** G) are fairly predictable, so we rate them as "wide" moat companies, while companies with no competitive advantages

(e.g., **DaimlerChrysler** DCX or **Advanced Micro Devices** AMD) by definition have no economic moats. Most large-cap companies fall in between and get a "narrow" moat rating.

A New Way of Seeing Stars

As a result of these changes, the hurdle a stock has to clear before it qualifies as a 5-star holding depends on its risk and moat. The higher the risk, and the weaker the moat, the bigger the hurdle. Practically speaking, the changes had the following effects:

1. A company's quality is better reflected in its star rating.
The new rating system rewards high-quality companies because they can earn a 5-star rating with a smaller discount to their fair value estimates than in the past. A wide-moat, low-risk stock need only be 20% below our fair value estimate to receive 5 stars.

By the same token, we think requiring a larger margin of safety for riskier stocks is prudent. So, we've incorporated that idea into our calculation. Now a high-risk, no-moat stock requires a 60% discount to reach 5-star status—a much larger margin of safety than a wide-moat, low-risk stock would require. Additionally, stocks with no moats can become 1-star holdings more easily. After all, these types of stocks aren't long-term keepers; they're short-term valuation plays—stocks Buffett calls "cigar butts" because they may have only one puff left in them. If one of these stocks is 10% overvalued, we'll rate it with 1 star.

2. There are fewer 5-star stocks.
Because of these changes, fewer stocks qualify for 5-star ratings than under our previous methodology, and the quality of our typical 5-star stock is higher. We think readers would rather have a few really good picks—only our very best ideas—than a longer list of 5-star stocks we aren't as confident in.

No-Moat/High-Risk Stocks

Some stocks were affected more than others under this new star-rating methodology. As previously mentioned, stocks with no economic moats and high risk ratings experienced the most significant changes.

To illustrate, consider these 10 high-risk stocks (left), with their old and new star ratings. Note: The star ratings and fair value estimates

Ten High-Risk Stocks: Old and New Morningstar Ratings

Company	Size of Moat	Fair Value ($)	Price ($)	Old Rating	New Rating
Nextel NXTL	None	12.00	7.44	★★★★★	★★★
EchoStar Comm DISH	None	27.00	17.51	★★★★★	★★★
Tyco TYC	None	28.00	15.75	★★★★★	★★★
Advanced Micro Devices AMD	None	7.00	6.25	★★★★	★★
El Paso EP	Narrow	21.00	12.20	★★★★★	★★★★
Check Point Software CHKP	Narrow	23.00	15.53	★★★★★	★★★★
Apple Computer AAPL	None	20.00	14.72	★★★★	★★★
Genzyme GENZ	Narrow	35.00	21.42	★★★★★	★★★★
Goodyear Tire & Rubber GT	None	26.00	10.59	★★★★★	★★★★
ICOS ICOS	None	48.00	21.99	★★★★★	★★★★

Prices as of September 22, 2002.

Wide Moat Stocks: Old and New Morningstar Ratings

Company	Risk Rating	Fair Value ($)	Price ($)	Old Rating	New Rating
Eli Lilly LLY	Low	70.00	55.63	★★★★	★★★★★
PepsiCo PEP	Low	48.00	37.50	★★★★	★★★★★
UPS UPS	Low	55.00	62.80	★★	★★★
Berkshire Hathaway BRK.B	Low	3,015.00	2,400.00	★★★★	★★★★★
American Express AXP	Low	43.00	31.22	★★★★	★★★★★
American Intl Group AIG	Medium	80.00	56.23	★★★★	★★★★★
Gentex GNTX	Medium	35.00	27.91	★★★★	★★★★★
Blackrock BLK	Low	53.00	41.99	★★★★	★★★★★
Bank of New York BK	Medium	39.00	28.65	★★★★	★★★★★
Freddie Mac FRE	Low	78.00	58.24	★★★★	★★★★★

Prices as of September 22, 2002.

shown in this table are as of September 2002, when we first changed the star-rating methodology.

Wide-Moat Stocks

The changes also helped award a higher star rating to some wide-moat stocks. Stocks with this moat rating are the highest-quality companies we cover—the type of stocks we'd feel comfortable buying and holding on to for long periods of time. Because their earnings and cash flows are more predictable, they require a lower margin of safety to earn a 5-star rating.

Shown above are some of the wide-moat stocks that earned higher ratings as a result of the changes. Note: The star ratings and fair value estimates shown in this table are also as of September 2002, when we first changed the star-rating methodology.

All 10 of these companies have big competitive advantages in their respective industries and a relatively high degree of earnings predictability. In 10 years, they will still exist in one form or another—something I can't predict about the stocks on the no-moat/high-risk list, at least not with any degree of confidence.

Fair Value Estimates Unchanged

It's worth noting one more important aspect of the new star ratings: They didn't affect our fair value estimates. If a stock had a fair value estimate of $50 before the changes, it still had a fair value estimate of $50 immediately after the change in methodology.

As before, only two things can cause us to change a stock's fair value estimate:

1. We change our estimate of a company's future cash flows.
2. We change our estimate of the appropriate discount rate. (Discount rate is determined by a company's business risk, the risk-free rate, and the general riskiness of stocks versus Treasury bonds.)

We think these stock star-rating changes are a big improvement over our previous "one size fits all" methodology. We expect them to make the Morningstar Rating for stocks a better, more meaningful tool for investors. ▌

Keeping It Simple Isn't Stupid

Consider these three things before buying a stock.

by Mark Sellers III
Editor, *Morningstar*
Stocks 500

Seventeenth-century French philosopher Blaise Pascal once said, "All man's miseries derive from not being able to sit quietly in a room alone." I can't think of better words to describe investing.

As I write this, the S&P 500 Index stands at around 900, the same level as in July 1997. That means most investors' portfolios have gone nowhere, on average, over the past five years. Sure, there have been moments of euphoria and, lately, despair. But on average, an investor who stuffed his or her money under a mattress and "sat quietly in a room" for the past five years would have been no worse off than those of us who scrutinize every nook and cranny of the stock market.

Times like this remind me just how simple stock investing is. When the talking heads start to blather on about unemployment numbers, the falling U.S. dollar, or the direction of interest rates, do yourself a favor and hit the "mute" button. These things are just noise.

When thinking about whether to buy a stock, there are only three main considerations.

Economic Moats

First, you need to determine if a company has what Warren Buffett calls an "economic moat." An economic moat is a long-term competitive advantage, and the wider the moat, the better the quality of the company.

How do you determine the size of a company's moat? By considering two important things: the attractiveness of the industry and the company's competitive position within that industry. Sickly industries, such as steel manufacturing or the airlines, will have few companies with wide moats. By contrast, the pharmaceutical and data-processing industries, which have very attractive long-term economics, include numerous companies with wide moats, such as **Merck** MRK, **Pfizer** PFE, **Automatic Data Processing** ADP, and **First Data** FDC. Just being in a good industry isn't

enough, though—a company must also have a strong position within that industry. Still, a mediocre data processor probably has a wider moat than **Nucor** NUE, the best steel company.

Margin of Safety

The second critical factor in making the "buy" decision is valuation. Specifically, you need to determine whether a stock's price is far enough below its intrinsic value to give you an acceptable margin of safety.

Why is a margin of safety so important? Because we all make mistakes from time to time. You may calculate **Johnson & Johnson**'s JNJ valuation to be $70 per share, when in reality it may be worth only $49 a share. If you buy the stock at $70, there's a decent probability the stock could fall and take several years to get back to your purchase price. But if you require, say, a 30% margin of safety before buying, you'd wait until it fell below $49 before jumping in. In other words, a margin of safety mitigates your valuation risk.

This method isn't perfect, and it virtually guarantees you'll miss out on some great opportunities. **Microsoft** MSFT, for example, always looked overvalued during its meteoric runup in the 1980s and 1990s. But investors who refused to buy unless they had an acceptable margin of safety were selling stocks, not buying them, during the latter part of the 1990s and in early 2000. Those people, including Warren Buffett, look pretty smart right now.

Your Time Horizon

Finally, to do well in the stock market, you need another kind of patience: the ability to wait out bear markets without panicking. If your time horizon is anything less than three to five years, you probably shouldn't be buying stocks in the first place. If you're buying stocks with money you'll need next year, the year after, or anytime before the next five years, you're playing with fire. Sure, things may work out well, but as we're seeing now, markets can go nowhere for stretches of five years or longer.

So there you have it—three simple questions to ask yourself before buying a stock: Does the company have an economic moat? Is there an acceptable margin of safety? Am I willing to wait for the stock to perform as expected? If the answer to all of these questions is yes, it's time to buy the stock. If the answer to any of these is no, sitting on the sidelines is a better idea. ▥

Morningstar's Two Stock Portfolios: The Tortoise and the Hare

Here are some of our favorite picks for investors, both conservative and aggressive.

by Mark Sellers III
Editor, *Morningstar*
Stocks 500

At Morningstar, we put our money where our mouths are. If we're really confident about our opinions on the stocks we cover, we shouldn't be afraid to make buy and sell decisions for our own account based on those opinions. So, in June 2001, we created two stock portfolios, the Tortoise and the Hare. I manage these portfolios, with a lot of input from an investment committee comprised of senior stock analysts and editors.

The portfolios are designed for investors with varying levels of risk tolerance. As the names imply, the Tortoise Portfolio is designed for conservative stock investors, while the Hare Portfolio is intended for those who are willing to stomach a lot of volatility. Because most investors don't fall neatly into one of these two categories, we expect that most readers will pick and choose stocks from each portfolio based on their personal risk tolerance and investment goals.

Our goal for each portfolio is to outperform the S&P 500, considered a proxy for the performance of the market, over a long-term basis. We consider long-term to be at least three to five years.

Although they are portfolios, we do not mean to imply that investors should attempt to precisely duplicate them by purchasing shares in each company listed. Although some investors may choose to do this, most investors will benefit by picking a few stocks from each portfolio that they consider to be the most compelling.

We manage the two portfolios based on the investment strategy we call the "Four Principles of Profitable Investing." (For a complete description of this strategy, see Pages 8-14.) In a nutshell, this means we look for companies with sustainable competitive advantages, or "economic moats," selling far below our estimates of their fair value. Unless we feel a stock is significantly undervalued, we will not add it to one of the portfolios. Because of this discipline, only a fraction of the more than 8,000 publicly traded companies are worthy of consideration for the portfolios at any one time. We consider small-cap, mid-cap, and large-cap stocks for the portfolio.

Some other aspects of the Morningstar Stock Portfolios:

- Each portfolio began with $50,000 on June 18, 2001. Every month, we add $2,000 to each portfolio.

- Our brokerage firm is Ameritrade. Using Ameritrade.com, each limit order trade costs us $13. This commission is included in the cost basis of each stock.

- We only buy stocks listed on one of the three major U.S. exchanges.

- We assume a 28% tax rate on all short-term capital gains, and a 20% tax rate on long-term capital gains. If we end a calendar year with a net loss, we carry over the net loss to the following year, rather than realizing a tax "benefit."

- We do not short-sell stocks or purchase bonds, options, futures, or other types of financial instruments. The portfolios do not use margin loans.

- Cash balances in the portfolios generate 3.5% annualized interest income.

- The weighting of the stocks in the portfolios generally signifies the degree of confidence we have in each stock. For example, we have more confidence in a stock that makes up 10% of a portfolio than one that makes up only 5%.

- We may sell a stock at any time, or we may choose to hold on to a stock, even if we feel it's overvalued, because of tax considerations or other reasons.

If you'd like to get updated information about all the stocks in these portfolios, including immediate notification of any transactions we make, subscribe to our monthly newsletter, *Morningstar StockInvestor*. In addition to getting regular updates on the portfolios, each month you'll get a list of 50 stocks to buy and hold, read bull/bear discussions of controversial stocks, see a listing of stocks we think you should avoid, and more. To subscribe, call 800-735-0700. ▥

The Tortoise Portfolio

Stock Name	Star Rating	Risk Rating	Fair Value ($)	Consider Buying	Consider Selling	Size of Moat	Dividend Yield (%)	Growth	Profitability	Financial Health
Berkshire Hathaway BRK.B	★★★★	Low	2900	2320	3770	Wide	0.00	A	B	A
American Express AXP	★★★	Low	37.00	30.00	48.00	Wide	1.13	C-	B+	A
Capital One Financial COF	★★★★★	High	50.00	35.00	60.00	Wide	0.36	A+	A+	A
Home Depot HD	★★★★★	Med	36.00	29.00	47.00	Wide	0.57	A	A+	A+
Pfizer PFE	★★★★	Low	37.00	30.00	48.00	Wide	1.65	C+	A+	A
Jones Apparel Group JNY	★★	Med	35.00	18.00	39.00	None	0.00	A	A-	A
Washington Mutual WM	★★★	Med	47.00	28.00	56.00	Narrow	3.07	A	C	A
Moody's MCO	★★★★★	Low	52.00	42.00	68.00	Wide	0.44	A	A+	A
Colgate-Palmolive CL	★★★	Low	45.00	36.00	59.00	Wide	1.37	C+	A+	B-
J.P. Morgan Chase & Co. JPM	★★★	High	36.00	18.00	40.00	Narrow	5.40	D-	D	B
Kimberly-Clark KMB	★★★	Med	57.00	34.00	68.00	Narrow	2.53	B	A	A-
White Mountains Ins WTM	★★★	Med	440.00	264.00	528.00	Narrow	0.31	A+	A	C+
Robert Half International RHI	★★★	Low	20.00	14.00	24.00	Narrow	0.00	D+	A	A+
PepsiCo PEP	★★★★	Low	48.00	38.00	62.00	Wide	1.41	B-	A+	A+
General Motors GM	★★★	High	73.00	29.00	80.00	None	5.04	C	C	C
SBC Communications SBC	★★★	Med	36.00	22.00	43.00	Narrow	3.93	D	A	A-
Northern Trust NTRS	★★★★★	Med	50.00	40.00	65.00	Wide	1.94	D+	B	B
Wal-Mart Stores WMT	★★★	Low	53.00	42.00	69.00	Wide	0.59	A	A	B+
Kemet KEM	★★★★★	Med	15.00	9.00	18.00	Narrow	0.00	D-	B+	A
Humana HUM	★★★★	Med	15.00	9.00	18.00	Narrow	0.00	C-	C+	B

Morningstar ratings, fundamentals, and Morningstar grades as of 11-30-02. Portfolio inception date: 6-18-01.

The Hare Portfolio

Stock Name	Star Rating	Risk Rating	Fair Value ($)	Consider Buying	Consider Selling	Size of Moat	Dividend Yield (%)	Growth	Profitability	Financial Health
Boston Scientific BSX	★★	Med	34.00	27.00	44.00	Wide	0.00	C-	B	A
Abercrombie & Fitch A ANF	★★★★	Med	30.00	18.00	36.00	Narrow	0.00	B	A	A+
Paychex PAYX	★★★★★	Low	40.00	32.00	52.00	Wide	1.51	A-	A	A
Amgen AMGN	★★★	High	55.00	39.00	66.00	Wide	0.00	B	A	A
First Data FDC	★★★★	Low	40.00	32.00	52.00	Wide	0.17	B+	A-	C+
IDEC Pharmaceuticals IDPH	★★★★★	Med	49.00	39.00	64.00	Wide	0.00	A+	A-	B+
Cytyc CYTC	★★★	Med	11.00	7.00	13.00	Narrow	0.00	A	B	A+
Dell Computer DELL	★★★	Med	28.00	22.00	36.00	Wide	0.00	A	A+	B+
Applied Materials AMAT	★★★	Med	14.00	11.00	18.00	Wide	0.00	C-	A	A+
First Health Group FHCC	★★★	Med	30.00	18.00	36.00	Narrow	0.00	C+	A	A
IMS Health RX	★★★★★	Med	28.00	22.00	36.00	Wide	0.48	C	A+	A-
Concord EFS CE	★★★	Med	19.00	11.00	23.00	Narrow	0.00	A+	A	A+
Autodesk ADSK	★★★★	Med	16.00	13.00	21.00	Wide	1.05	C	A	A
Learning Tree Intl LTRE	★★★	Med	17.00	10.00	20.00	Narrow	0.00	F	A	A
Intel INTC	★★★	Med	15.00	12.00	20.00	Wide	0.51	C	A+	A+
Adobe Systems ADBE	★★★	Med	22.00	18.00	29.00	Wide	0.15	C	A+	A+
Automatic Data Prcssing ADP	★★★★★	Low	54.00	43.00	70.00	Wide	1.19	B	A	A
Linear Technology LLTC	★★★	Med	24.00	19.00	31.00	Wide	0.74	D	A+	A+

Morningstar ratings, fundamentals, and Morningstar grades as of 11-30-02. Portfolio inception date: 6-18-01.

Index and Tables

This section serves as an overview of the companies included in the Morningstar Stocks 500.

Pg	Company	Industry	Star Rating	Risk Measure	Fair Value ($)	Market Cap ($Mil)	Revenue ($Mil)	Price/ Earnings	Dividend Yield %	Growth	Profitability	Financial Health
53	1-800 Flowers.com	Online Retail	★★★★	High	12.00	410	507	--	0.0	B	D	D+
54	3M Company	Chemicals	★★★	Low	115.00	48,111	16,075	26.5	2.0	C+	A+	A+
55	Abbott Laboratories	Drugs	★★★	Low	38.00	62,502	17,290	22.6	2.3	C+	A	A-
56	Abercrombie & Fitch A	Clothing Stores	★★★★	Med	30.00	1,990	1,528	12.4	0.0	B+	A	A+
57	Accenture	Consultants	★★★	Med	19.00	17,231	13,105	32.1	0.0	B-	A	A
58	Adobe Systems	Development Tools	★★★	Med	22.00	5,860	1,135	32.2	0.2	C	A+	A
59	Advance PCS	Managed Care	★★★	Med	30.00	1,997	14,250	18.8	0.0	A+	B+	C+
60	Advanced Micro Devices	Semiconductors	★★	High	6.00	2,219	2,962	--	0.0	C	B-	B+
61	Aegon NV ADR	Insurance (Life)	★★★	Med	18.00	18,248	28,441	8.2	5.9	A+	C	B-
62	Aetna	Insurance (Life)	★★	Med	44.00	6,190	21,201	--	0.1	C	D	A
63	AFC Enterprises	Restaurants	★★	High	23.00	597	642	26.6	0.0	D	C+	B
64	Affiliated Computer Services	Business Support	★	Med	40.00	6,958	3,306	29.9	0.0	A+	A	A
65	AFLAC	Insurance (Life)	★★★	Med	30.00	19,509	9,995	20.0	0.8	C	A-	A+
66	AG Edwards	Securities	★★★	Med	46.00	2,605	2,312	37.5	1.9	D-	A-	A+
67	Albertson's	Groceries	★★★	Low	26.00	8,440	37,185	18.1	3.4	C-	B	B-
68	Alcan	Aluminum	★★	Med	29.00	9,485	12,397	--	2.0	A+	C+	B-
69	Alcatel SA ADR A	Wireline Equipment	★	Med	3.90	5,615	17,080	--	2.6	B-	C	C
70	Alcide	Chemicals	★	High	11.00	39	22	22.7	0.0	B+	B	B
71	Alcoa	Aluminum	★★★	Med	29.00	19,232	20,631	38.6	2.6	B	B	B+
72	Alcon	Drugs	★★★★	Low	45.00	11,835	2,748	--	0.0	D+	--	A
73	Allergan	Drugs	★★★	Med	62.00	7,455	1,895	81.2	0.6	B-	A-	A
74	Alliance Capital Management	Money Management	★★★★	Med	36.00	2,360	184	14.6	7.4	D-	A-	A+
75	Allied Capital	Finance	★★	High	21.00	2,237	315	10.3	10.1	A+	A+	A+
76	Alltel	Wireless Service	★★★	Med	56.00	15,837	7,837	17.7	3.1	C-	A	B
77	Altera	Semiconductors	★★★	Med	14.00	4,720	694	176.3	0.0	D	A	A+
78	Amazon.com	Online Retail	★	Med	13.00	7,206	3,620	--	0.0	A-	F	F
79	AMB Property	REITS	★★★	Low	30.00	2,293	640	22.1	6.0	B+	A-	C
80	Ambac Financial Group	Insurance (General)	★★★	Med	72.00	5,960	816	12.6	0.7	A	A	A+
81	American Axle & Mfg Holdings	Auto Parts	★★★	Med	27.00	1,165	3,361	7.8	0.0	B	B	C
82	American Express	Finance	★★★	Low	37.00	46,839	23,482	20.7	1.1	C-	B	A
83	American International Group	Insurance (Property)	★★★★★	Med	80.00	150,907	66,823	20.4	0.3	A	B	A
84	American Power Conversion	Electric Equipment	★★	Med	15.00	2,970	1,309	36.1	0.0	C+	A	A+
85	Americredit	Finance	★★★★★	High	25.00	664	1,248	2.0	0.0	A+	A+	A
86	AmerisourceBergen	Medical Goods & Services	★★★	Med	73.00	5,788	45,235	17.2	0.2	A+	B+	B
87	Amgen	Biotechnology	★★★	High	55.00	61,986	4,881	--	0.0	B	A+	A
88	AMR	Air Transport	UR	High	--	1,030	16,913	--	0.0	C-	B-	C
89	AmSouth Bancorporation	Regional Banks	★★★	Low	22.00	6,870	3,067	11.7	4.6	D-	C+	B
90	Amvescap PLC ADR	Money Management	★★★	Med	16.00	4,940	2,336	23.5	2.7	A+	A-	A+
91	Analog Devices	Semiconductors	★★★	Med	32.00	8,748	1,675	99.5	0.0	C+	A	A
92	Andrx Group	Drugs	★	Med	10.00	1,041	753	14.5	0.0	B+	B+	A
93	Anheuser-Busch Companies	Alcoholic Drinks	★★★	Low	52.00	41,426	13,362	22.6	1.6	B	A+	B
94	AnnTaylor Stores	Clothing Stores	★★★	Med	25.00	916	1,400	30.6	0.0	B	B	A-
95	Anthem	Insurance (Life)	★★★	Low	66.00	8,884	11,954	15.3	0.0	A+	B+	A+
96	AOL Time Warner	Media Conglomerates	★★★	High	15.00	56,278	41,024	--	0.0	--	--	--
97	Apartment Investment & Mgmt.	REITS	★★★	Med	39.00	3,493	1,573	30.5	8.8	A	D	D
98	Apple Computer	Computer Equipment	★★★	High	20.00	5,029	5,742	79.6	0.0	B	A-	A+
99	Applied Materials	Semiconductor Equipment	★★★	Med	14.00	21,473	4,881	--	0.0	C-	A	A+
100	Applied Micro Circuits	Semiconductors	★★★	High	5.00	1,114	131	--	0.0	D	B+	B
101	Aramark	Restaurants	★★	Low	21.00	1,462	8,770	17.5	0.0	B+	B+	B
102	Archstone-Smith Trust	REITS	★★★	Low	24.00	4,254	1,040	17.4	7.2	B	A	A
103	AstraZeneca PLC ADR	Drugs	★★★★★	Med	45.00	61,408	16,663	20.8	2.0	C-	A+	A
104	AT&T	Telecommunication Services	★★	Med	25.00	20,115	48,821	--	2.9	D	B	B+
105	AT&T Wireless Services	Wireless Service	★★★	High	8.00	15,300	15,112	--	0.0	B-	B-	B-
106	Autodesk	Business Applications	★★★★	Med	16.00	1,622	883	17.9	1.0	C	A	A
107	Automatic Data Processing	Data Processing	★★★★★	Low	54.00	23,506	7,043	22.4	1.2	B	A	A
108	AutoNation	Auto Retail	★★★★	Low	16.00	3,951	20,106	13.2	0.0	C+	B-	B
109	AutoZone	Auto Retail	★★★	Low	80.00	6,881	5,368	17.7	0.0	B	A	B-
110	Aventis SA ADR	Drugs	★★★	Low	65.00	43,115	20,457	32.2	0.7	B	C+	C+
111	Avon Products	Household & Personal Prod.	★★★	Med	50.00	12,672	6,123	29.6	1.5	B	A+	B+
112	AVX	Components	★★★★★	Med	19.00	1,706	1,170	--	1.5	D	A	A+

Company Index

Pg	Company	Industry	Morningstar Ratings		Company Fundamentals					Morningstar Grades		
			Star Rating	Risk Measure	Fair Value ($)	Market Cap ($Mil)	Revenue ($Mil)	Price/ Earnings	Dividend Yield %	Growth	Profitability	Financial Health
113	Baker Hughes	Oil & Gas Services	★	Med	18.00	10,806	5,272	37.0	1.4	D+	C	B
114	Ballard Power Systems	Electric Equipment	UR	High	--	1,166	106	--	0.0	A	--	D
115	Bank of America	International Banks	★★	Med	64.00	104,505	46,628	12.8	3.5	D	C+	B
116	Bank of New York	Money Management	★★★★	Med	29.00	17,396	6,017	15.5	3.2	D	B+	B+
117	Bank One	Super Regional Banks	★★★	Med	39.00	42,636	22,444	14.4	2.3	D	D+	A-
118	Barnes & Noble	Specialty Retail	★★★★	Med	27.00	1,167	5,238	19.2	0.0	A-	C	C+
119	Barr Laboratories	Drugs	★★★★	Low	91.00	2,855	1,057	14.1	0.0	A	A	A+
120	Barra	Business Applications	★★★	Med	35.00	604	144	5.8	0.0	C-	A+	A+
121	Bausch & Lomb	Medical Equipment	★	Low	29.00	1,942	1,828	61.0	1.8	C-	B	B+
122	Baxter International	Medical Equipment	★★★★	Med	41.00	16,905	8,210	25.2	2.1	B-	A-	B+
123	BB&T	Super Regional Banks	★★★	Med	42.00	17,771	5,891	14.1	3.0	B-	B	A
124	BEA Systems	Development Tools	★	High	7.00	4,708	916	--	0.0	A-	B	B-
125	Bear Stearns Companies	Securities	★★	Med	56.00	5,711	7,184	9.6	1.0	D	D	B
126	Bed Bath & Beyond	Furniture Retail	★	Med	25.00	10,104	3,318	46.7	0.0	A+	A+	A+
127	BellSouth	Telecommunication Services	★★★	Med	35.00	48,170	22,961	30.1	3.0	D	A	A-
128	Berkshire Hathaway B	Insurance (General)	★★★★	Low	2900.00	111,526	39,133	34.8	0.0	A	B+	A
129	Best Buy	Electronics Stores	★★★	Med	30.00	7,766	21,330	13.6	0.0	A+	B+	A
130	Biogen	Biotechnology	★★	High	40.00	5,972	1,128	28.2	0.0	B-	A+	A+
131	Biomet	Medical Equipment	★★★	Med	28.00	7,445	1,237	32.6	0.3	B	A+	A+
132	BJ's Wholesale Club	Discount Stores	★★★	Med	25.00	1,270	5,730	16.5	0.0	B+	A	B+
133	Black & Decker	Electric Equipment	★★	Med	44.00	3,455	4,444	24.7	1.1	C	C-	C+
134	Blackrock	Money Management	★★★★★	Low	53.00	2,554	569	20.1	0.0	A-	A+	A+
135	Blockbuster	Rental & Repair Services	★★★	Med	18.00	2,196	5,342	--	0.7	B-	D-	C+
136	BMC Software	Systems & Security	★	Med	13.00	4,029	1,249	--	0.0	D+	A-	A
137	Boeing	Aerospace & Defense	★★★	Med	42.00	27,691	56,071	--	2.1	B	B-	B-
138	Borders Group	Specialty Retail	★★★	Med	20.00	1,273	3,470	15.2	0.0	C+	B	B+
139	BorgWarner	Auto Parts	★★★★	Med	84.00	1,356	2,613	--	1.2	B-	C+	A
140	Boston Scientific	Medical Equipment	★★	Med	34.00	17,341	2,782	51.9	0.0	C-	B	A
141	BP PLC ADR	Oil & Gas	★★	Med	40.00	152,063	175,389	19.1	3.5	A-	A-	A
142	Brinker International	Restaurants	★★★	Med	36.00	3,124	2,988	21.2	0.0	A	A	B+
143	Bristol-Myers Squibb	Drugs	★★★★★	Low	33.00	44,843	17,588	16.1	6.0	D	A+	A
144	Broadcom	Semiconductors	★	High	11.00	4,154	1,014	--	0.0	A	D-	C
145	Brocade Communications Systems	Systems & Security	UR	High	--	970	526	--	0.0	A	C	B+
146	Brunswick	Recreation	★★★	Med	25.00	1,790	3,502	32.6	2.5	C-	C	B-
147	Cablevision Systems A	Cable TV	UR	High	--	5,054	4,517	10.7	0.0	C+	C+	D
148	Cadbury Schweppes PLC ADR	Food Mfg.	★★★	Low	27.00	13,106	7,957	16.6	2.6	A+	A-	A
149	Callaway Golf	Recreation	★	High	11.00	877	774	12.3	2.1	C-	A-	A
150	Campbell Soup	Food Mfg.	★★★	Med	24.00	9,633	6,109	18.3	3.4	B-	A	C
151	Capital One Financial	Finance	★★★★★	High	50.00	6,594	9,099	8.1	0.4	A+	A+	A
152	Cardinal Health	Medical Goods & Services	★★★	Med	65.00	26,192	52,687	25.7	0.2	B-	A	B
153	Caremark RX	Managed Care	★★★	Med	18.00	3,709	6,440	15.5	0.0	A	C	D-
154	Carnival	Recreation	★★★	Med	35.00	14,640	4,292	15.6	1.7	A-	B	C
155	Caterpillar	Construction Machinery	★★★	Med	47.00	15,736	19,871	24.1	3.1	C	A+	A+
156	CDW Computer Centers	Electronics Stores	★★★	Med	58.00	3,680	4,199	21.5	0.0	A-	A	B-
157	Cedar Fair LP	Recreation	★★★	Med	23.00	1,193	493	18.4	7.0	C+	A	B-
158	Celestica	Contract Manufacturers	★★★	Med	16.00	3,239	10,004	--	0.0	A	C+	A
159	Cendant	Business Support	★★★	High	14.00	10,862	13,069	47.6	0.0	A+	B-	B+
160	Centurytel	Telecommunication Services	★★★	Med	35.00	4,190	2,259	5.2	0.7	C	A	B
161	Ceridian	Data Processing	★★★	Med	16.00	2,140	1,174	24.9	0.0	C+	A	A
162	Charles Schwab	Securities	★	Med	9.00	14,579	4,198	83.5	0.4	D	B	A+
163	Charter Communications	Cable TV	★	High	1.00	348	4,522	--	0.0	A-	C	F
164	Checkfree	Systems & Security	★★	Med	17.00	1,419	504	--	0.0	B	C	C+
165	Check Point Software Technologies	Business Applications	★★★	High	15.00	3,174	439	12.4	0.0	B+	A+	A+
166	ChevronTexaco	Oil & Gas	★★★	Med	75.00	71,011	93,451	--	4.2	D+	B	A
167	Chico's FAS	Clothing Stores	★★	Med	18.00	1,605	494	37.5	0.0	A+	A	A+
168	Chiron	Biotechnology	★★	Med	40.00	7,073	1,238	45.9	0.0	B	A-	A+
169	Chubb	Insurance (Property)	★★★	Med	70.00	8,929	8,685	46.6	2.7	C+	B	A-
170	Cigna	Managed Care	★★★	Med	55.00	5,732	19,958	--	3.2	C-	B+	C
171	Cintas	Business Support	★★	Med	37.00	7,774	2,372	33.6	0.5	B+	A+	A
172	Circuit City Stores	Electronics Stores	★★★	Med	11.00	1,559	10,035	8.1	0.9	D+	B	A+

Pg	Company	Industry	Star Rating	Risk Measure	Fair Value ($)	Market Cap ($Mil)	Revenue ($Mil)	Price/ Earnings	Dividend Yield %	Growth	Profitability	Financial Health
173	Cisco Systems	Data Networking	★★	Med	13.00	94,649	19,312	52.4	0.0	B+	A	A
174	CIT Group	Finance	★★★★	Med	30.00	4,147	2,595	--	0.6	D	D-	D
175	Citigroup	International Banks	★★★	Med	37.00	177,948	106,096	11.0	2.0	C+	B	A-
176	Citizens Communications	Telecommunication Services	★★★	High	13.00	2,968	2,676	--	0.0	B	C+	C+
177	Clear Channel Communications	Radio	★★	Med	35.00	22,849	8,073	--	0.0	A	D+	C-
178	Clorox	Household & Personal Prod.	★★★	Med	47.00	9,076	4,124	30.1	2.1	B-	A	A
179	Coca-Cola	Beverage Mfg.	★★★	Low	46.00	108,635	21,554	33.5	1.8	B	A	A+
180	Coca-Cola Enterprises	Beverage Mfg.	★★	Med	20.00	9,742	16,678	25.6	0.7	A-	D+	D+
181	Colgate-Palmolive	Household & Personal Prod.	★★★	Low	45.00	28,221	9,546	25.1	1.4	C+	A+	B-
182	Comcast A	Cable TV	★★★★	Med	28.00	22,319	10,789	--	0.0	A	B-	B+
183	Comerica	Regional Banks	★★★	Low	51.00	7,555	3,703	13.0	4.4	D	A	A
184	Computer Associates International	Systems & Security	★	High	10.00	7,739	3,056	--	0.6	D	B	B+
185	Computer Sciences	Consultants	★★	Med	32.00	5,929	11,444	17.1	0.0	B+	A-	A-
186	Compuware	Systems & Security	★★	Med	5.00	1,814	1,555	--	0.0	D	A-	A
187	Concord EFS	Data Processing	★★★	Med	19.00	8,007	2,045	27.6	0.0	A+	A	A+
188	ConocoPhillips	Oil & Gas	UR	Med	--	18,492	46,828	166.9	3.1	A+	B	C+
189	Continental Airlines B	Air Transport	UR	High	--	470	8,102	--	0.0	D+	B	C+
190	Cooper Industries	Electric Equipment	★★★	Med	49.00	3,398	3,965	15.6	3.8	C	A	A-
191	Corning	Optical Equipment	★	Med	2.60	3,800	3,605	--	0.0	C-	C-	D
192	Costco Wholesale	Discount Stores	★★★★	Med	42.00	12,788	38,763	19.0	0.0	A-	B+	B+
193	Countrywide Financial	Savings & Loans	★	Med	44.00	6,528	--	13.3	0.8	A+	A	B
194	Cox Communications A	Cable TV	★★★	Med	33.00	17,611	4,646	--	0.0	A	B	C+
195	Cummins Engine	Auto Parts	★★★	High	35.00	1,167	5,902	41.4	4.3	D	D+	D+
196	CVS	Specialty Retail	★★★	Med	26.00	9,809	23,787	26.6	0.9	A-	B	A-
197	Cytyc	Medical Equipment	★★★	Med	11.00	1,182	233	--	0.0	A	B	A+
198	DaimlerChrysler AG	Auto Makers	★★★	Med	45.00	30,750	136,142	--	2.9	C	C	C
199	Dana	Auto Parts	★★★	High	14.00	1,747	10,472	--	0.3	D	C-	C-
200	Danaher	Electric Equipment	★★★	Low	75.00	10,013	4,221	60.8	0.1	A	A	A+
201	Deere & Company	Agricultural Machinery	★	Med	38.00	10,970	13,947	34.5	1.9	B	C	B-
202	Dell Computer	Computer Equipment	★★★	Med	28.00	68,968	33,730	58.1	0.0	A	A+	B+
203	Delphi	Auto Parts	★★★	Med	12.00	4,495	26,836	47.4	3.5	C-	C-	C
204	Delta Air Lines	Air Transport	UR	High	--	1,493	12,860	--	0.8	D	B	C
205	Deutsche Bank AG	International Banks	★★★	Med	57.00	27,916	25,501	188.5	0.0	C	F	B
206	Diageo PLC ADR	Alcoholic Drinks	★★★	Low	47.00	35,203	16,283	15.6	3.3	C	A-	A
207	Dillard's	Department Stores	★★★	Low	21.00	1,343	8,304	18.7	1.0	D+	C	B-
208	Dollar General	Discount Stores	★★★	Med	15.00	3,983	5,927	19.3	1.1	A	A	A
209	Dollar Tree Stores	Discount Stores	★★★	Med	33.00	2,805	2,217	19.5	0.0	A	A+	A+
210	Dow Chemical	Chemicals	★★	Med	33.00	27,060	26,866	63.2	4.5	C+	B-	C
211	Dow Jones & Company	Media Conglomerates	★★★	Low	37.00	3,608	1,594	16.7	2.3	D	C	C-
212	DST Systems	Data Processing	★★★	Low	37.00	4,255	1,648	20.2	0.0	A-	A	A
213	DuPont De Nemours E.I.	Chemicals	★★	Med	45.00	42,120	24,013	18.4	3.3	C+	A	A
214	E*Trade Group	Securities	★	High	4.00	1,757	1,322	--	0.0	A-	F	F
215	Eastman Kodak	Photography & Imaging	★	Med	28.00	10,224	12,759	22.8	5.1	C-	C+	B
216	Eaton Vance	Money Management	★★★★★	Med	40.00	1,955	514	15.9	1.1	A	A+	A
217	eBay	Online Retail	★	Med	47.00	18,804	1,020	102.8	0.0	A	B	A+
218	EchoStar Communications	Cable TV	★★★	High	28.00	10,673	4,646	--	0.0	A	D	D
219	Ecolab	Chemicals	★	Low	30.00	6,408	3,109	32.6	1.1	A+	A+	B+
220	El Paso	Pipelines	★★★★	High	12.00	4,160	12,207	5.7	12.5	C	C	C
221	Electronic Arts	Entertainment/Educ. Media	★★★	Med	54.00	7,220	2,088	70.1	0.0	A-	A	A
222	Electronic Data Systems	Consultants	★★	High	20.00	8,774	22,127	7.8	3.3	B+	A	A-
223	Eli Lilly & Company	Drugs	★★★	Low	62.00	71,334	10,951	27.0	2.0	C	A	A
224	EMC	Computer Equipment	★★	High	6.00	13,507	5,462	--	0.0	C	A	A+
225	Emerson Electric	Electric Equipment	★★★	Med	57.00	21,400	13,824	175.4	3.1	D+	B+	A
226	ENI SpA ADR	Oil & Gas	★★	Med	72.00	62,812	44,449	8.9	3.0	A-	A	--
227	Equity Office Properties Trust	REITS	★★★	Low	27.00	10,284	3,562	16.2	8.0	A	A-	A
228	Equity Residential	REITS	★★★	Low	27.00	6,780	2,137	19.5	7.0	B+	A-	A
229	Ericsson Telephone ADR B	Wireless Equipment	★	High	--	10,767	18,112	--	0.0	B	B	C
230	Estee Lauder A	Household & Personal Prod.	★★	Low	24.00	6,158	4,791	37.7	1.1	B	B+	A
231	Ethan Allen Interiors	Appliance & Furn. Makers	★★★	Low	37.00	1,318	902	16.7	0.6	C+	A	A+
232	Expedia	Online Retail	★	High	53.00	3,876	508	85.8	0.0	A	D-	B-

Morningstar Stocks 500
Company Index

Pg	Company	Industry	Star Rating	Risk Measure	Fair Value ($)	Market Cap ($Mil)	Revenue ($Mil)	Price/ Earnings	Dividend Yield %	Growth	Profitability	Financial Health
233	Expeditors International of WA	Transportation - Misc	★★★	Med	36.00	3,399	1,866	34.4	0.4	B	A+	A+
234	Express Scripts	Managed Care	★★★	Med	52.00	3,757	12,188	21.3	0.0	A	A−	B
235	ExxonMobil	Oil & Gas	★★★	Low	41.00	235,108	196,513	23.8	2.6	D+	A	A+
236	Family Dollar Stores	Discount Stores	★★	Med	30.00	5,410	4,163	25.0	0.8	A	A+	A+
237	Fannie Mae	Finance	★★★★	Low	90.00	72,629	52,478	12.0	2.1	A	D+	D
238	Federated Department Stores	Department Stores	★★★	Med	38.00	5,470	15,550	--	0.0	D+	C	B
239	Federated Investors B	Money Management	★★★★★	Low	41.00	2,889	722	15.3	0.9	B	A+	A
240	FedEx	Transportation - Misc	★★	Med	50.00	16,189	21,015	23.2	0.3	B+	A	A
241	Fifth Third Bancorp	Super Regional Banks	★★★	Low	54.00	33,873	6,272	21.8	1.7	C+	A−	A
242	First Data	Data Processing	★★★★	Low	40.00	26,633	7,118	23.5	0.2	B+	B+	C+
243	First Health Group	Managed Care	★★★	Med	30.00	2,470	715	20.5	0.0	B−	A	A
244	Fiserv	Data Processing	★★★	Med	35.00	6,508	2,180	26.3	0.0	A	B+	A
245	FleetBoston Financial	Super Regional Banks	★★★★	Med	35.00	25,459	16,036	59.3	5.8	D−	C	A
246	Flextronics International	Contract Manufacturers	★★★	High	10.00	4,239	13,217	--	0.0	A	C+	D
247	Ford Motor	Auto Makers	★★★	High	14.00	17,066	163,518	--	4.3	C	C−	C+
248	Forest Laboratories	Drugs	★	Med	54.00	17,702	1,882	54.0	0.0	A	A+	A+
249	Franklin Resources	Money Management	★★★	Med	37.00	8,789	2,519	20.7	0.8	C	A	A+
250	Freddie Mac	Finance	★★★★	Low	78.00	40,934	8,986	7.9	1.5	A+	D+	B
251	Freemarkets	Business/Online Services	★★★	High	8.00	271	167	--	0.0	A	D+	C−
252	Gabelli Asset Management	Money Management	★★★	Med	36.00	905	216	16.2	0.0	B−	A	A
253	Gannett	Media Conglomerates	★★★	Low	73.00	19,190	6,354	18.2	1.3	B−	A	A
254	Gap	Clothing Stores	★	High	8.00	13,718	13,894	--	0.6	B−	A−	B
255	Gateway	Computer Equipment	UR	High	--	1,017	4,250	--	0.0	D	C+	C+
256	Genentech	Biotechnology	★★★	High	32.00	17,067	2,541	--	0.0	A	B	A
257	General Dynamics	Aerospace & Defense	★★★★★	Med	110.00	15,948	13,429	16.0	1.5	A+	A+	A
258	General Electric	Electric Equipment	★★★	Med	28.00	242,308	130,295	16.2	3.0	A−	B	B
259	General Mills	Food Mfg.	★★★	Med	50.00	17,278	8,540	35.0	2.3	A+	A−	C
260	General Motors	Auto Makers	★★★	High	73.00	20,658	184,057	16.8	5.4	C	C	C
261	Gentex	Auto Parts	★★★	Med	34.00	2,407	368	30.7	0.0	A−	A+	A+
262	Genuine Parts	Auto Retail	★★★	Low	38.00	5,379	8,213	--	3.8	C	A	A
263	Genzyme Corp. General Division	Biotechnology	★★★	High	35.00	6,345	1,296	140.8	0.0	B+	B+	A−
264	Getty Images	Business Support	★	High	22.00	1,634	447	--	0.0	B	D+	D−
265	Gilead Sciences	Biotechnology	★	High	24.00	6,687	396	40.0	0.0	A	B−	C−
266	Gillette	Household & Personal Prod.	★★★	Med	30.00	41,593	9,219	30.1	2.1	C−	A	A−
267	GlaxoSmithKline PLC ADR	Drugs	★★★★	Low	42.00	57,810	29,541	26.0	3.1	C+	A+	A
268	GlobespanVirata	Semiconductors	★★★	High	6.00	576	238	--	0.0	A−	F	C
269	Golden West Financial	Savings & Loans	★★★	Low	67.00	11,020	3,809	12.1	0.4	B+	B−	B
270	Goldman Sachs Group	Securities	★★★	Med	75.00	32,608	23,924	17.2	0.7	C	C	B+
271	Goodyear Tire & Rubber	Rubber Products	★★★	High	12.00	1,194	13,792	--	7.0	C	C	C−
272	Graco	Machinery	★	Med	26.00	1,364	480	18.5	1.0	C	A+	A+
273	Groupe Danone ADR	Food Mfg.	★★★	Low	28.00	18,873	12,903	158.0	1.4	C+	C	C+
274	Guidant	Medical Equipment	★★★	Med	30.00	9,458	3,063	14.5	0.0	C+	A	--
275	H & R Block	Personal Services	★★★★	Med	48.00	7,182	3,518	17.4	1.7	A	A	B+
276	Halliburton	Oil & Gas Services	★	Med	11.00	8,158	12,396	--	2.7	D+	A	A+
277	Harley-Davidson	Recreation	★★★	Low	43.00	13,982	4,134	25.7	0.3	A+	A+	A+
278	Harrah's Entertainment	Gambling/Hotel Casinos	★★★	Med	48.00	4,426	4,108	19.0	0.0	A−	C+	B−
279	Hasbro	Toys/Hobbies	★★★	Med	14.00	2,000	2,808	--	1.0	D	C−	C
280	HCA-The Healthcare Company	Hospitals	★★★	Med	50.00	21,270	19,243	23.5	0.2	C−	B	C+
281	Health Management Associates	Hospitals	★★	Med	17.00	4,673	2,263	18.5	0.1	B+	A+	A−
282	Health Net	Physicians	★★★	Low	27.00	3,269	10,038	13.9	0.0	C	B−	A
283	Healthsouth	Physicians	★★★	High	5.00	1,661	4,502	8.2	0.0	C	B+	B
284	Heinz HJ	Food Mfg.	★★★	Med	37.00	11,549	9,712	13.9	4.9	B−	A−	C
285	Hershey Foods	Food Mfg.	★★	Med	56.00	9,197	4,537	40.9	1.9	C+	A	A
286	Hewlett-Packard	Computer Equipment	★★	High	19.00	34,321	49,416	--	1.8	A−	A	B
287	Home Depot	Home Supply	★★★★★	Med	36.00	56,498	58,522	18.6	0.9	A+	A+	A+
288	Honeywell International	Aerospace & Defense	★★★	Med	33.00	19,705	22,272	14.4	3.1	C	B	A
289	Hormel Foods	Food Mfg.	★★★	Med	24.00	3,235	4,166	17.3	1.7	B+	A	A
290	Hotels.com A	Online Retail	★	Med	35.00	3,158	814	53.6	0.0	A	C	A
291	Household International	Finance	★★	High	30.00	12,649	14,924	7.2	3.5	A	A	C
292	Hughes Electronic H	Cable TV	★★★	High	18.00	14,233	8,743	--	0.0	A−	C	B

Morningstar Stocks 500

Company Index

Pg	Company	Industry	Star Rating	Risk Measure	Fair Value ($)	Market Cap ($Mil)	Revenue ($Mil)	Price/ Earnings	Dividend Yield %	Growth	Profitability	Financial Health
293	Human Genome Sciences	Biotechnology	★★★	High	10.00	1,134	4	--	0.0	F	C	C
294	Humana	Managed Care	★★★★	Med	15.00	1,673	11,029	9.4	0.0	C-	C+	B
295	IBM	Computer Equipment	★★★	Med	77.00	130,982	82,442	27.8	0.8	B	A+	B
296	IDEC Pharmaceuticals	Biotechnology	★★★★★	Med	49.00	5,916	362	43.1	0.0	A+	A-	B+
297	Illinois Tool Works	Machinery	★★★	Low	65.00	19,875	9,319	29.4	1.4	B	A+	A+
298	IMS Health	Data Processing	★★★★★	Med	28.00	4,502	1,387	27.1	0.5	C	A+	B+
299	Ingersoll-Rand A	Machinery	★★★	Med	52.00	7,285	9,968	--	1.6	A	B	B-
300	Intel	Semiconductors	★★★	Med	15.00	103,151	26,587	41.0	0.5	C	A+	A+
301	International Flavors & Fragrances	Food Mfg.	★★	Med	34.00	3,311	1,804	20.2	1.7	B+	B+	C+
302	International Game Tech	Gambling/Hotel Casinos	★★	Med	72.00	6,578	1,621	24.0	0.0	A	A	A
303	International Paper	Paper	★★	Med	33.00	16,774	24,940	--	2.9	C	C-	D-
304	International Speedway A	Recreation	★★★	Med	35.00	1,983	543	--	0.2	A	C+	B
305	Internet Security Systems	Systems & Security	★	High	11.00	889	238	--	0.0	B+	B	A
306	Interpublic Group of Companies	Advertising	★★★	Med	16.00	5,422	6,205	17.6	2.7	C-	C+	B-
307	Intuit	Business Applications	★★	Med	37.00	9,630	1,413	73.3	0.0	A-	A	A
308	Investors Financial Services	Money Management	★★	Med	23.00	1,769	528	27.8	0.2	A+	A	B-
309	J.C. Penney	Department Stores	★★	Med	22.00	6,174	32,340	88.5	2.2	C	D+	B+
310	J.P. Morgan Chase & Co.	International Banks	★★★	High	36.00	47,901	42,911	28.9	5.7	D	D	B
311	Jabil Circuit	Contract Manufacturers	★★	Med	17.00	3,550	3,545	105.4	0.0	B	A-	B+
312	JD Edwards & Company	Business Applications	★	Med	10.00	1,347	904	29.7	0.0	C	B+	B-
313	JDS Uniphase	Optical Equipment	★★	High	2.40	3,494	963	--	0.0	B-	C+	C
314	JetBlue Airways	Air Transport	★★	Med	23.00	1,706	543	--	0.0	--	C-	D
315	Jo-Ann Stores A	Specialty Retail	★★	Med	21.00	448	1,654	--	0.0	B-	C-	C-
316	Johnson & Johnson	Drugs	★★★	Low	58.00	159,452	35,807	26.1	1.5	B-	A+	A
317	Johnson Controls	Auto Parts	★★★★	Low	105.00	7,132	20,103	12.6	1.7	A	B	B
318	Jones Apparel Group	Apparel Makers	★★	Med	35.00	4,572	4,246	16.0	0.0	A-	A-	A
319	Kellogg	Food Mfg.	★★★	Low	37.00	13,991	9,525	21.8	2.9	A	B+	C
320	Kemet	Components	★★★★★	Med	15.00	753	472	--	0.0	D-	B+	A
321	Kimberly-Clark	Household & Personal Prod.	★★★	Med	57.00	24,416	14,809	15.1	2.5	B	A	A-
322	Kinder Morgan	Pipelines	★★★★	Med	51.00	5,145	1,014	16.6	0.7	F	C-	D+
323	Kinder Morgan Energy Partners	Pipelines	★★★★	Med	39.00	4,548	3,559	19.0	6.7	A+	B	C-
324	King Pharmaceuticals	Drugs	★★★★	Med	26.00	4,139	1,111	15.6	0.0	A	A	A+
325	KLA-Tencor	Semiconductor Equipment	★	Med	27.00	6,674	1,510	32.2	0.0	C+	A	A
326	Knight Ridder	Publishing	★★	Med	58.00	5,209	2,816	22.8	1.6	D	A	B+
327	Knight Trading Group	Securities	★★	High	5.00	567	548	--	0.0	F	A-	B+
328	Kohl's	Discount Stores	★★	Med	48.00	18,865	8,660	38.6	0.0	A+	A	--
329	Kraft Foods	Food Mfg.	★★	Med	36.00	45,853	34,063	--	1.4	A-	B	B
330	Krispy Kreme Doughnut	Restaurants	★	Med	24.00	1,898	472	75.0	0.0	A	B	A-
331	Kroger	Groceries	★★★	Med	21.00	11,791	51,418	12.3	0.0	C	B	B-
332	Laboratory Corp of America	Diagnostics	UR	Med	--	3,435	2,421	7.9	0.0	B-	B	A
333	Lam Research	Semiconductor Equipment	★	High	8.00	1,353	801	--	0.0	D	C+	C+
334	Lattice Semiconductor	Semiconductors	★	High	7.00	985	224	--	0.0	D	B-	A-
335	Lear	Auto Parts	★★★★★	Med	56.00	2,188	14,069	--	0.0	B+	C	C
336	Learning Tree International	Education	★★★	Med	17.00	241	174	8.3	0.0	F	A-	A
337	Legg Mason	Money Management	★★★	Med	60.00	3,144	1,638	21.7	0.9	B	A	A+
338	Lehman Brothers Holdings	Securities	★★★	Med	74.00	12,738	16,947	16.5	0.7	D	D	B-
339	Level 3 Communications	Telecommunication Services	★★★	High	9.00	2,043	2,529	--	0.0	A	D+	D-
340	Lexmark International	Computer Equipment	★★	Med	57.00	7,605	4,328	27.9	0.0	A	A+	B
341	Liberty Media	Cable TV	UR	Med	--	23,114	2,069	--	0.0	B+	D+	C
342	Limited Brands	Clothing Stores	★★★	Med	16.00	7,287	9,260	11.7	2.2	D	A-	A+
343	Linear Technology	Semiconductors	★★★	Med	24.00	8,024	534	42.9	0.7	D	A+	A
344	Liz Claiborne	Apparel Makers	★	Med	26.00	3,162	3,610	14.7	0.8	A	A	A
345	Lockheed Martin	Aerospace & Defense	★★	Med	56.00	26,512	26,132	--	0.8	B	D+	B
346	Lowe's Companies	Home Supply	★★	Med	35.00	29,285	25,627	28.9	0.2	A+	A	B
347	LSI Logic	Semiconductors	★★★	High	10.00	2,146	1,743	--	0.0	C	C	D+
348	Lucent Technologies	Wireline Equipment	★	High	0.60	4,545	12,321	--	0.0	D	F	F
349	M & T Bank	Regional Banks	★★	Med	78.00	7,290	2,377	16.5	1.3	A	B-	A-
350	Macromedia	Development Tools	★	High	8.00	642	318	--	0.0	C+	C	C+
351	Mandalay Resort Group	Gambling/Hotel Casinos	★★	Med	29.00	2,019	2,417	43.1	0.0	C	C	C+
352	Manpower	Employment	★★★	Med	41.00	2,448	10,309	24.9	0.6	C	A-	B-

Morningstar Stocks 500

Company Index

Pg	Company	Industry	Star Rating	Risk Measure	Fair Value ($)	Market Cap ($Mil)	Revenue ($Mil)	Price/ Earnings	Dividend Yield %	Growth	Profitability	Financial Health
353	Marathon Oil	Oil & Gas	★★★	Med	24.00	6,599	29,905	--	4.3	C	C+	A-
354	Markel	Insurance (Property)	★★★	Med	240.00	1,928	1,647	--	0.0	A	D	D+
355	Marsh & McLennan Companies	Insurance (General)	★★★	Med	46.00	24,818	10,164	21.5	2.4	C	A+	A+
356	Martha Stewart Living Omnimedia A	Media Conglomerates	★	High	7.00	485	307	31.8	0.0	C	A	A
357	Marvell Technology	Semiconductors	★	High	16.00	2,266	437	--	0.0	A+	C	C+
358	Masco	Building Materials	★★	Med	21.00	10,357	9,103	19.9	2.6	A+	A-	A
359	Mattel	Toys/Hobbies	★	Med	15.00	8,373	4,893	46.7	2.0	C	D+	C
360	Maxim Integrated Products	Semiconductors	★★★	Med	32.00	10,584	1,072	45.3	0.1	C-	A+	C
361	Maytag	Appliance & Furn. Makers	★★★	Med	40.00	2,224	4,776	13.5	2.5	A-	B	C
362	MBIA	Insurance (General)	★★★	Med	59.00	6,365	1,191	10.5	1.6	B+	A+	A
363	MBNA	Finance	★★	High	18.00	24,301	10,348	14.3	1.4	A+	A+	A+
364	McDonald's	Restaurants	★★★★★	Low	29.00	20,411	15,278	13.7	1.5	B-	A	A
365	McGraw-Hill Companies	Publishing	★★★★	Low	75.00	11,713	4,730	26.5	1.7	B-	A	A
366	MedImmune	Biotechnology	★★	High	28.00	6,820	759	--	0.0	A-	B	A+
367	Medtronic	Medical Equipment	★★★	Low	40.00	55,637	6,989	57.0	0.7	B	A	A
368	Mellon Financial	Money Management	★★★★	Med	38.00	11,252	4,350	9.1	1.9	D	A	A-
369	Merck	Drugs	★★★	Med	50.00	127,121	50,430	18.1	2.5	B	A+	A-
370	Mercury General	Insurance (Property)	★★★	Med	40.00	2,042	1,697	28.9	3.2	B+	A	A
371	Mercury Interactive	Development Tools	★	Med	20.00	2,499	373	42.3	0.0	A-	A	B+
372	Merrill Lynch & Company	Securities	★★★	Med	40.00	32,806	30,635	53.5	1.7	D	D	B+
373	Metropolitan Life Insurance	Insurance (Life)	★★	Med	30.00	18,936	33,057	25.8	0.8	C-	D	B-
374	MGM Mirage	Gambling/Hotel Casinos	★★★	Med	38.00	5,111	3,970	19.0	0.0	A-	C+	C
375	Micron Technology	Semiconductors	★★★	High	11.00	5,872	2,589	--	0.0	D	C	C
376	Microsoft	Business Applications	★★★	Med	52.00	276,411	29,985	36.7	0.0	B+	A+	A+
377	Monsanto Company	Agrochemical	★★★	Med	23.00	5,032	4,662	--	2.5	C	D+	A
378	Moody's	Business Support	★★★★★	Low	52.00	6,239	972	23.6	0.4	A	A+	A
379	Morgan Stanley	Securities	★★★	Med	52.00	43,977	32,954	14.2	2.3	B-	C+	C+
380	Motorola	Wireless Equipment	★★	Med	9.00	19,903	26,576	--	1.9	C	C+	D-
381	Mylan Laboratories	Drugs	★★★★★	Low	50.00	4,275	1,175	17.1	0.5	B	A+	A+
382	National City	Super Regional Banks	★★★	Low	34.00	16,717	10,419	10.8	4.4	C	A-	B
383	National Processing	Data Processing	★★★	Med	18.00	836	461	15.4	0.0	C+	B	A+
384	National Semiconductor	Semiconductors	★★★	Med	17.00	2,716	1,576	--	0.0	C-	C	B-
385	Navistar International	Truck Makers	★★★	High	30.00	1,659	6,784	--	0.0	C-	D	D+
386	NCR	Computer Equipment	★★★	Med	35.00	2,316	5,604	--	0.0	B-	B+	B-
387	Neiman-Marcus Group A	Department Stores	★★	Med	33.00	1,458	3,001	14.6	0.0	C-	B+	A
388	Network Associates	Systems & Security	★★	High	15.00	2,517	966	59.6	0.0	B-	B	D+
389	New York Times A	Media Conglomerates	★★★	Low	45.00	6,924	3,019	26.4	1.2	D	A+	A-
390	Nextel Communications	Wireless Service	★★★	High	13.00	11,124	8,464	--	0.0	B	C-	D+
391	Nike B	Shoes	★★★	Med	46.00	11,798	10,076	18.2	1.1	B-	A	A+
392	Nokia ADR	Wireless Equipment	★★	Med	14.00	73,432	27,814	37.8	1.5	A	A	A
393	Nortel Networks	Wireline Equipment	★	High	1.10	6,182	11,496	--	0.0	D+	B-	F
394	Northern Trust	Money Management	★★★★★	Med	50.00	7,498	2,817	17.6	1.9	D+	B	B
395	Northrop Grumman	Aerospace & Defense	★★★	Med	135.00	10,977	17,067	--	1.6	A+	C	B
396	Northwest Airlines	Air Transport	UR	High	--	630	9,135	--	0.0	D+	B-	B
397	Novartis AG ADR	Drugs	★★★★★	Low	48.00	105,974	18,933	22.9	1.2	D	A+	A+
398	Novellus Systems	Semiconductor Equipment	★★	Med	24.00	4,015	822	112.3	0.0	C+	A-	A+
399	Nucor	Steel/Iron	★★★	Med	45.00	3,229	4,315	22.2	1.8	C	A-	A
400	NVIDIA	Semiconductors	★	High	10.00	1,815	1,944	11.2	0.0	A+	A-	A-
401	Oakley	Recreation	★★	High	11.00	703	477	16.3	0.0	A	A	B
402	Occidental Petroleum	Oil & Gas	★★★	Med	34.00	10,724	11,151	25.9	3.5	C-	C+	A
403	Office Depot	Specialty Retail	★★★	Med	17.00	4,554	11,369	16.2	0.0	C	B	A
404	Omnicom Group	Advertising	★	High	53.00	12,149	7,388	19.9	1.2	A	A-	B
405	Oracle	Business Applications	★	Med	7.00	57,845	9,459	27.7	0.0	C	A+	A
406	Oxford Health Plans	Managed Care	★★★	Med	45.00	3,209	4,623	11.5	0.0	C-	B	B
407	Paccar	Truck Makers	★★★	Low	53.00	5,346	6,826	17.8	1.7	D	B+	B+
408	PacifiCare Health Systems	Managed Care	★	Med	14.00	1,004	11,288	--	0.0	C-	B-	B+
409	Parker Hannifin	Machinery	★★	Med	43.00	5,445	6,259	41.2	1.6	A	B+	A-
410	Paychex	Data Processing	★★★★★	Low	40.00	10,493	973	38.2	1.6	A	A	A
411	PeopleSoft	Business Applications	★★	Med	17.00	5,728	1,931	32.7	0.0	B-	A-	A+
412	Pepsi Bottling Group	Beverage Mfg.	★★★	Med	26.00	7,247	8,898	150.3	0.2	A-	C	B

Pg	Company	Industry	Star Rating	Risk Measure	Fair Value ($)	Market Cap ($Mil)	Revenue ($Mil)	Price/ Earnings	Dividend Yield %	Growth	Profitability	Financial Health
413	PepsiAmericas	Beverage Mfg.	★★	Med	13.00	2,016	3,266	33.6	0.3	A+	C-	B-
414	PepsiCo	Beverage Mfg.	★★★★	Low	48.00	73,589	28,044	24.0	1.4	B-	A+	A+
415	Pfizer	Drugs	★★★★	Low	37.00	188,377	34,407	23.5	1.7	C+	A+	A
416	Philip Morris Companies	Tobacco	★★★★	Med	50.00	84,290	90,561	7.6	6.0	A-	A+	B
417	Philips Electronics NV ADR	Audio/Video Equipment	★★	Med	19.00	22,527	28,837	--	1.8	D	B	B
418	Pier 1 Imports	Furniture Retail	★★	Med	21.00	1,748	1,661	18.2	1.0	B	A+	A+
419	Pitney Bowes	Office Equipment	★★★	Low	35.00	7,725	4,336	15.6	3.6	B+	A+	B
420	Playboy Enterprises B	Publishing	★	High	8.00	264	285	--	0.0	D-	C-	D
421	PMC-Sierra	Semiconductors	★★	High	6.00	930	213	--	0.0	D	D	D
422	PNC Financial Services Group	Super Regional Banks	★★★	Med	50.00	11,900	6,095	23.8	4.6	D	B-	A
423	Procter & Gamble	Household & Personal Prod.	★★★	Med	75.00	111,662	41,268	27.8	1.8	B	A	A
424	Progressive	Insurance (Property)	★★★★	Med	59.00	10,804	8,738	7.6	0.2	A	A	A
425	Protein Design Labs	Biotechnology	★★★	High	10.00	757	78	--	0.0	B	B-	B
426	Providian Financial	Finance	★★★	High	9.00	1,877	4,271	--	0.0	A-	B	A+
427	Prudential Financial	Insurance (Life)	★★	Med	32.00	18,553	26,992	--	1.3	D+	F	B
428	Qualcomm	Wireless Equipment	★	High	24.00	28,569	3,040	82.7	0.0	B	B	A+
429	Quest Diagnostics	Diagnostics	UR	Med	--	5,561	3,985	19.4	0.0	B	B	A-
430	Quiksilver	Apparel Makers	★★	High	27.00	630	676	23.2	0.0	A	A-	D+
431	Qwest Communications International	Telecommunication Services	★★★	High	6.00	8,375	19,013	--	0.0	C	B	B
432	RadioShack	Electronics Stores	★★★	Med	23.00	3,181	4,595	18.6	1.2	C-	A-	A
433	Raytheon	Aerospace & Defense	★★★★	Med	45.00	12,481	17,341	--	2.6	B	D+	B
434	Reebok International	Shoes	★	Med	26.00	1,760	3,030	16.2	0.0	C	B-	B
435	Reuters Group PLC ADR	Publishing	★★★	High	22.00	4,105	5,460	62.1	5.1	B-	A	A+
436	RF Micro Devices	Semiconductors	★★	High	7.00	1,239	425	--	0.0	A	B	B
437	RJ Reynolds Tobacco Holdings	Tobacco	★★★	Med	57.00	3,741	8,602	38.6	8.8	A	C+	B+
438	Robert Half International	Employment	★★★	Low	20.00	2,743	1,937	134.3	0.0	D+	A+	A+
439	Ross Stores	Clothing Stores	★★	Low	40.00	3,287	3,415	22.2	0.4	A-	A+	A-
440	Royal Caribbean Cruises	Recreation	★★★	Med	19.00	3,204	3,309	11.8	1.6	A-	B-	C
441	Royal Dutch Petroleum ADR	Oil & Gas	★★★	Low	49.00	93,615	135,759	16.9	3.6	C-	A	A+
442	RR Donnelley & Sons	Printing	★★★★	Med	32.00	2,467	4,835	43.5	4.5	D+	B+	B+
443	Sabre Holdings	Online Retail	★★★	Med	21.00	2,579	2,006	18.3	0.0	C-	B+	A+
444	Safeway	Groceries	★★★	Med	35.00	13,376	34,757	20.3	0.0	B	A-	C+
445	SanDisk	Semiconductors	★	High	16.00	1,400	453	33.3	0.0	B+	C+	B-
446	Sanofi-Synthelabo ADR	Drugs	★★★	Low	35.00	44,512	5,785	36.3	0.0	A	A+	A+
447	SAP AG ADR	Business Applications	★	Med	15.00	24,556	6,546	47.3	0.7	A	A+	A-
448	Sara Lee	Food Mfg.	★★★	Med	25.00	17,551	17,914	18.3	2.7	C+	B+	B
449	SBC Communications	Telecommunication Services	★★★	Med	36.00	90,011	43,824	19.2	3.9	D	A	A-
450	Schering-Plough	Drugs	UR	Med	--	32,567	10,311	18.1	3.0	C	A	A+
451	Schlumberger	Oil & Gas Services	★	Med	30.00	24,440	13,553	45.8	1.8	B	B	B
452	Scientific-Atlanta	Wireline Equipment	★★	Med	13.00	1,828	1,573	18.0	0.3	C	A+	A+
453	SCP Pool	Recreation	★★	Med	27.00	682	958	18.3	0.0	A+	A	C-
454	Sealed Air	Packaging	★	Med	33.00	3,131	3,140	17.9	0.0	B	C+	C
455	Sears Roebuck	Department Stores	★★★	High	28.00	7,576	41,156	7.6	3.8	C-	B-	C
456	Sepracor	Drugs	★	High	--	814	197	--	0.0	A+	D	F
457	ServiceMaster	Personal Services	★★	Med	10.00	3,342	3,664	29.2	2.7	B	B	A
458	Shell Transport & Trading ADR	Oil & Gas	★★★	Low	41.00	63,236	135,211	14.6	3.4	C-	A	A+
459	Siebel Systems	Business Applications	★★★	Med	9.00	3,539	1,692	15.1	0.0	B+	A	A
460	Simon Property Group	REITS	★★★	Low	36.00	6,384	2,130	19.9	6.4	B-	B	B
461	SLM	Finance	★★★	Low	96.00	15,947	2,898	22.4	0.8	D	C+	B+
462	Smithfield Foods	Food Mfg.	★★	Med	20.00	2,170	8,008	11.2	0.0	A+	B	C
463	Solectron	Contract Manufacturers	★	High	2.50	2,928	12,276	--	0.0	C+	C	D+
464	Sony ADR	Audio/Video Equipment	★★	Med	43.00	38,122	60,413	--	0.4	B	C-	B
465	Southern	Electric Utilities	★★★	Low	26.00	20,256	10,252	16.0	4.8	D+	B+	A
466	Southtrust	Regional Banks	★★★	Low	29.00	8,619	3,391	13.8	2.7	C-	C+	A
467	Southwest Airlines	Air Transport	★★★	Med	17.00	10,768	5,359	42.1	0.1	C+	A	A
468	Sovereign Bancorp	Savings & Loans	★★★	Med	16.00	3,725	2,481	11.9	0.7	A	D-	B+
469	Sprint	Telecommunication Services	★★★	High	19.00	12,953	15,951	--	3.5	D	A	B
470	Sprint PCS Group	Wireless Service	★	High	3.00	4,376	11,782	--	0.0	A	C-	F
471	SPX	Electric Equipment	★★★	Med	51.00	3,016	4,981	26.1	0.0	A+	B-	B-
472	St. Jude Medical	Medical Equipment	★	Med	30.00	7,053	1,529	28.6	0.0	B-	A	A+

Pg	Company	Industry	Morningstar Ratings		Company Fundamentals					Morningstar Grades		
			Star Rating	Risk Measure	Fair Value ($)	Market Cap ($Mil)	Revenue ($Mil)	Price/Earnings	Dividend Yield %	Growth	Profitability	Financial Health
473	Stanley Works	Metal Products	★★★	Med	35.00	3,064	2,577	17.6	2.9	C	B+	A+
474	Staples	Specialty Retail	★★	Med	18.00	8,608	11,190	45.8	0.0	B	B	A
475	Starbucks	Restaurants	★★	Med	17.00	7,912	3,289	37.7	0.0	A+	A	A+
476	State Street	Money Management	★★★★★	Med	50.00	12,649	4,947	18.1	1.2	C	C	B
477	Stilwell Financial	Money Management	★★★	Med	17.00	2,907	1,231	29.7	0.4	B-	A	A-
478	Stryker	Medical Equipment	★★★	Med	64.00	13,276	2,892	43.0	0.2	B	A	A
479	Student Loan	Finance	★★★★	Low	135.00	1,956	1,039	11.1	2.9	B+	D+	D
480	Sun Microsystems	Computer Equipment	★★★★	High	7.00	9,687	12,382	--	0.0	C	A-	A-
481	SunTrust Banks	Super Regional Banks	★★★	Low	64.00	16,225	7,631	12.1	3.0	C-	B	B
482	SuperValu	Food Wholesale	★★★★	Low	24.00	2,206	19,606	10.8	3.4	D	B-	B
483	Symantec	Systems & Security	★	Med	31.00	5,797	1,242	--	0.0	A	A	A
484	Sysco	Food Wholesale	★★★	Low	30.00	19,417	23,946	29.5	1.6	B	A	A-
485	T Rowe Price Group	Money Management	★★★	Med	30.00	3,337	940	18.2	2.4	D-	A	A+
486	Taiwan Semiconductor Manufacturing	Semiconductors	UR	--	--	25,567	3,709	57.8	0.0	A+	A+	A+
487	Target	Discount Stores	★★★	Med	40.00	27,263	43,138	20.0	0.8	A-	B+	C
488	TCF Financial	Savings & Loans	★★★	Med	45.00	3,238	1,133	14.3	2.6	C+	A	B
489	Tellabs	Wireline Equipment	★★★	Med	9.00	2,995	1,474	--	0.0	D	A	A+
490	Tenet Healthcare	Hospitals	UR	Med	--	7,990	14,319	10.5	0.0	B-	B+	B
491	Teradyne	Semiconductor Equipment	★	High	11.00	2,382	1,109	--	0.0	D	B+	B
492	Teva Pharmaceutical Industries ADR	Drugs	★	Med	27.00	9,891	2,077	37.9	0.4	A-	A	B
493	Texas Instruments	Semiconductors	★★★	Med	16.00	25,982	8,024	--	0.6	C	B+	A
494	Tiffany	Jewelry/Accessories	★★	Med	21.00	3,471	1,653	20.8	0.7	B	A	A
495	Timberland	Shoes	★★	Med	30.00	1,312	1,175	14.0	0.0	B+	A+	A+
496	TJX Companies	Clothing Stores	★★	Med	18.00	10,250	11,684	21.7	0.6	A-	A+	A
497	Tommy Hilfiger	Apparel Makers	★★★	Med	9.00	630	1,887	4.7	0.0	C+	B	A
498	Total Fina Elf SA ADR	Oil & Gas	★★	Med	71.00	100,949	93,914	14.5	2.0	A+	B+	A+
499	Total System Services	Data Processing	★★★	Med	13.00	2,660	693	22.5	0.5	A-	A+	A+
500	Toys R Us	Specialty Retail	★★★	Med	14.00	2,124	11,195	30.3	0.0	D+	C	C
501	Transocean	Oil & Gas Services	★	Med	18.00	7,406	2,757	--	0.3	A+	B+	A-
502	Travelers Property Casualty	Insurance (Property)	★★★	Med	18.00	14,704	13,294	--	0.0	B	A	A+
503	Tribune	Media Conglomerates	★★★	Low	42.00	13,856	5,273	78.4	1.0	B	B	B
504	Triquint Semiconductor	Semiconductors	★★★	High	8.00	562	260	--	0.0	C	A-	A-
505	Tuesday Morning	Department Stores	★★★	High	26.00	686	705	18.0	0.0	B	B	B
506	Tyco International	Electric Equipment	★★★	High	25.00	34,087	35,644	--	0.3	A	D+	C
507	Tyson Foods A	Food Mfg.	★★★	Med	16.00	3,959	23,367	10.4	1.4	A+	C	C
508	UAL	Air Transport	UR	High	--	95	13,768	--	0.0	--	--	A
509	United Parcel Service B	Transportation - Misc	★★★	Low	55.00	70,397	31,337	29.8	1.2	B	A	A
510	United States Cellular	Wireless Service	★★★	High	32.00	2,155	2,082	--	0.0	C	A-	B+
511	United Technologies	Aerospace & Defense	★★★★	Low	70.00	29,339	27,971	15.3	1.6	B+	A	A
512	UnitedHealth Group	Managed Care	★★★★	Low	94.00	25,235	24,358	21.9	0.0	C	A-	B+
513	Universal Health Services B	Hospitals	★★★	Med	49.00	2,726	3,148	21.6	0.0	B	A	B
514	Urban Outfitters	Clothing Stores	★	Med	20.00	454	409	27.4	0.0	A-	A	A-
515	US Bancorp	Super Regional Banks	★★★	Med	28.00	40,630	15,324	13.0	3.7	C-	B	A
516	USA Interactive	Media Conglomerates	★	Med	17.00	10,290	4,231	5.5	0.0	A+	B-	B
517	VeriSign	Systems & Security	★★	High	8.00	1,902	1,230	--	0.0	A+	C-	C
518	Verizon Communications	Telecommunication Services	★★★	Med	45.00	106,011	67,422	--	4.0	C-	B+	B
519	Vertex Pharmaceuticals	Biotechnology	★★★	High	22.00	1,206	169	--	0.0	B-	C	D+
520	Viacom B	Broadcast TV	★★	Low	40.00	71,391	23,868	--	0.0	A-	C	B-
521	Vishay Intertechnology	Components	★★★	Med	16.00	1,786	1,745	--	0.0	C+	B	A-
522	Visteon	Auto Parts	★★★	Med	8.00	912	18,345	--	3.4	A-	C	C+
523	VISX	Medical Equipment	★★★	Med	13.00	495	138	24.6	0.0	D-	A	A+
524	Vivendi ADR	Media Conglomerates	UR	High	--	17,500	51,149	--	4.7	A+	C-	D+
525	Vodafone Group PLC ADR	Wireless Service	★	Med	16.00	123,471	22,323	--	1.3	A+	D	B+
526	Wachovia	Super Regional Banks	★★★	Med	37.00	50,032	24,107	14.3	2.7	D+	D	B
527	Wal-Mart Stores	Discount Stores	★★★	Low	53.00	222,949	241,163	33.9	0.6	A	A	B
528	Walgreen	Specialty Retail	★★★	Med	32.00	29,917	28,681	29.5	0.5	A	B+	A
529	Walt Disney	Media Conglomerates	★★★★	Low	21.00	33,308	25,329	27.2	1.3	C	B	A-
530	Washington Mutual	Savings & Loans	★★★	Med	47.00	32,933	18,011	8.7	3.1	A	C	A
531	Washington Post	Media Conglomerates	★★	Low	650.00	7,018	2,522	56.6	0.8	C+	A-	A
532	Waste Management	Waste Management	★★★★★	Low	35.00	13,950	11,121	19.3	0.0	C-	C+	D

Benchmark Performance

Morningstar Universe

Category	Annual Total Return %					Annualized Total Return%		
	2002	2001	2000	1999	1998	3-Year	5-Year	10-Year

Index Benchmarks

Morningstar Indexes

Category	2002	2001	2000	1999	1998	3-Year	5-Year	10-Year
Morningstar U.S. Market	−22.16	−11.88	−7.02	19.79	23.86	−13.92	−1.10	8.68
Morningstar U.S. Growth	−33.20	−26.32	−28.45	44.51	39.76	−29.38	−6.59	—
Morningstar U.S. Core	−21.18	−9.31	7.10	14.67	17.75	−8.52	0.67	—
Morningstar U.S. Value	−13.68	−0.68	10.06	−1.27	14.13	−1.91	1.24	—
Morningstar Large Cap	−23.47	−15.10	−11.38	21.05	30.73	−16.81	−1.84	8.68
Morningstar Large Growth	−33.15	−29.07	−33.51	42.59	51.23	−31.94	−7.43	—
Morningstar Large Core	−23.82	−14.35	4.24	17.81	23.18	−12.06	−0.26	—
Morningstar Large Value	−15.05	−3.38	5.66	0.57	17.85	−4.64	0.55	—
Morningstar Mid Cap	−18.06	−4.63	6.94	15.55	6.01	−5.81	0.47	8.30
Morningstar Mid Growth	−32.54	−21.59	−11.10	52.46	9.49	−22.23	−4.73	—
Morningstar Mid Core	−12.42	6.05	14.77	1.89	2.87	2.15	2.24	—
Morningstar Mid Value	−10.00	5.06	24.59	−6.83	5.85	5.61	3.05	—
Morningstar Small Cap	−20.36	5.26	7.66	17.78	−6.01	−3.36	−0.02	7.85
Morningstar Small Growth	−36.87	−12.92	−12.10	46.80	−6.55	−21.53	−7.89	—
Morningstar Small Core	−14.16	14.60	23.21	16.74	−7.55	6.62	5.52	—
Morningstar Small Value	−8.24	18.58	18.65	−5.19	−3.67	8.89	3.35	—

Domestic Stock

Category	2002	2001	2000	1999	1998	3-Year	5-Year	10-Year
Dow Jones Industrial	−15.01	−5.44	−4.85	27.21	18.13	−8.55	2.82	12.00
Dow Jones Utility	−23.38	−26.27	50.76	−6.02	18.88	−5.21	−0.99	4.58
Dow Jones Transportation	−11.48	−9.30	0.40	−4.52	−2.45	−6.93	−5.57	6.25
NASDAQ Composite	−31.53	−21.05	−39.29	85.59	39.63	−31.02	−3.19	7.03
Standard & Poor's 500	−22.09	−11.88	−9.10	21.04	28.58	−14.55	−0.58	9.34
Russell Top 200 Value	−18.03	−8.79	2.31	10.95	21.24	−8.54	0.57	10.82
Russell Top 200 Growth	−27.98	−20.50	−24.52	29.68	45.10	−24.40	−4.05	7.09
Standard & Poor's Midcap 400	−14.53	−0.60	17.49	14.72	19.11	−0.06	6.40	11.95
Russell Midcap Value	−9.65	2.34	19.19	−0.10	5.09	3.29	2.96	11.06
Russell Midcap Growth	−27.40	−20.16	−11.75	51.30	17.87	−20.02	−1.82	6.71
Wilshire 4500	−17.81	−9.30	−15.77	35.49	8.63	−14.37	−1.57	7.31
Wilshire 5000	−20.85	−10.89	−10.93	23.56	23.43	−14.36	−0.86	8.75
Russell 2000	−20.48	2.49	−3.03	21.26	−2.55	−7.54	−1.36	7.16
Russell 2000 Value	−11.42	14.02	22.81	−1.48	−6.43	7.45	2.72	10.85
Russell 2000 Growth	−30.27	−9.23	−22.43	43.09	1.23	−21.11	−6.59	2.62
Wilshire REIT	3.60	12.36	31.04	−2.57	−17.00	15.11	4.29	10.41

International Stock

Category	2002	2001	2000	1999	1998	3-Year	5-Year	10-Year
MSCI EAFE ID	−17.52	−22.61	−15.21	25.27	18.23	−18.50	−4.33	2.44
MSCI World ID	−21.06	−17.83	−14.05	23.56	22.78	−17.69	−3.29	4.77
MSCI Europe ID	−20.11	−21.23	−9.66	14.12	26.53	−17.16	−3.87	5.93
MSCI Pacific IL	−18.27	−17.10	−18.41	43.21	−8.91	−17.93	−6.33	−2.66
MSCI EMF Latin America ID	−24.79	−4.31	−18.39	55.48	−38.04	−16.25	−10.77	0.90
MSCI EMF ID	−7.97	−4.91	−31.80	63.70	−27.52	−15.81	−6.67	−0.75

Bonds

Category	2002	2001	2000	1999	1998	3-Year	5-Year	10-Year
Lehman Brothers Aggregate Bond	10.27	8.42	11.63	−0.83	8.67	10.10	7.54	7.51
Lehman Brothers Corp Bond	10.53	10.40	9.40	−1.94	8.46	10.11	7.26	7.85
CSFB High Yield	3.11	5.78	−5.21	3.28	0.58	1.11	1.44	6.51

Miscellaneous

Category	2002	2001	2000	1999	1998	3-Year	5-Year	10-Year
3 Month T-Bill	1.68	3.67	6.32	4.87	5.01	3.87	4.30	4.54
Consumer Price Index	2.60	1.55	3.39	2.68	1.61	2.51	2.37	2.48
JSE Gold (USD)	130.33	29.65	−38.19	25.95	−10.08	22.67	15.89	2.89

Morningstar Stocks 500
Company Index

Pg	Company	Industry	Morningstar Ratings		Company Fundamentals					Morningstar Grades		
			Star Rating	Risk Measure	Fair Value ($)	Market Cap ($Mil)	Revenue ($Mil)	Price/ Earnings	Dividend Yield %	Growth	Profitability	Financial Health
533	Waters	Medical Equipment	★★★	Med	30.00	2,824	882	27.9	0.0	C	A	A+
534	Watson Pharmaceuticals	Drugs	★★	Med	27.00	3,021	1,188	17.0	0.0	B	A	A-
535	WellPoint Health Networks	Managed Care	★★★	Low	69.00	10,372	16,180	16.5	0.0	A+	A	A-
536	Wells Fargo	Super Regional Banks	★★★	Med	50.00	79,608	28,119	15.7	2.3	C	B-	B
537	Wendy's International	Restaurants	★★★	Med	34.00	3,125	2,634	14.6	0.9	B	A	A
538	Weyerhaeuser	Forestry/Wood	★★	Med	50.00	10,774	17,267	109.4	3.3	A	B-	C-
539	Whirlpool	Appliance & Furn. Makers	★★★	Med	72.00	3,561	10,718	168.5	2.6	C	C	B+
540	White Mountains Insurance	Insurance (Property)	★★★	Med	440.00	2,676	4,384	5.2	0.3	A+	A	--
541	Whole Foods Market	Groceries	★★	Med	52.00	3,045	2,690	37.7	0.0	A+	B+	A
542	Williams Companies	Pipelines	UR	High	--	1,395	8,895	--	15.6	C	D+	C-
543	Williams-Sonoma	Furniture Retail	★	Med	22.00	3,154	2,280	20.9	0.0	A	A	A-
544	Winn-Dixie Stores	Groceries	★★★	Med	20.00	2,151	12,359	24.7	1.3	D+	C	B
545	Wm. Wrigley Jr.	Food Mfg.	★★	Med	45.00	12,360	2,673	32.1	1.5	A	A+	A+
546	Wyeth	Drugs	★★★★	Low	52.00	49,579	14,598	13.5	2.5	C	B	C
547	Xerox	Office Equipment	★★★	High	11.00	5,909	15,985	--	0.0	C-	C-	C
548	Xilinx	Semiconductors	★★★	Med	22.00	6,944	1,069	--	0.0	B-	A	A+
549	Yahoo!	Media Conglomerates	★	High	8.00	9,661	856	--	0.0	B	C	B+
550	Yum Brands	Restaurants	★★★	Med	29.00	7,169	7,498	13.0	0.0	C-	A	B-
551	Zimmer Holdings	Medical Equipment	★★	Med	35.00	8,092	1,314	--	0.0	B-	A+	B+
552	Zions Bancorporation	Regional Banks	★★★	Med	40.00	3,587	1,837	15.1	2.0	B	C	A-

Benchmark Performance

Morningstar Universe

Category	Annual Total Return %					Annualized Total Return%		
	2002	2001	2000	1999	1998	3-Year	5-Year	10-Year
Mutual Fund Benchmarks								
Domestic Stock								
Large Value	−18.92	−4.51	8.29	5.48	11.73	−6.01	−0.54	8.63
Large Blend	−22.02	−12.29	−5.20	19.61	21.79	−13.53	−1.47	7.85
Large Growth	−27.73	−22.26	−14.06	39.67	33.37	−21.65	−2.72	6.22
Mid-Cap Value	−12.91	6.92	18.42	7.43	2.11	2.54	3.17	10.26
Mid-Cap Blend	−17.08	−0.57	7.62	21.05	8.91	−4.17	2.75	9.79
Mid-Cap Growth	−27.53	−21.05	−5.08	62.33	16.87	−18.97	−1.09	6.54
Small Value	−10.25	16.73	18.67	4.01	−7.14	7.32	2.86	10.28
Small Blend	−16.17	9.50	12.82	15.28	−4.63	0.97	2.10	7.97
Small Growth	−28.42	−8.85	−4.05	58.87	4.88	−14.72	−1.10	6.25
Stock Benchmarks								
Sectors								
Information Economy								
Software	−34.58	3.75	−48.73	289.76	24.63	−47.44	−19.21	−5.94
Hardware	−39.33	−4.18	−14.75	194.57	6.46	−34.30	−14.42	0.73
Media	−27.82	4.63	−30.90	85.52	35.11	−29.29	−10.45	4.18
Telecommunications	−35.54	3.35	−45.10	140.82	47.37	−46.58	−22.48	2.36
Service Economy								
Health Care	−21.66	36.01	28.35	72.11	21.74	−10.43	−8.83	−1.12
Consumer Services	−6.15	51.00	−9.09	10.10	16.82	−6.29	−5.43	1.97
Business Services	−19.40	17.78	−27.08	77.62	9.33	−25.81	−15.25	0.62
Financial Services	13.03	26.04	7.47	−1.74	−4.21	9.42	0.24	10.94
Manufacturing Economy								
Consumer Goods	2.05	25.43	−10.26	10.56	3.13	−7.92	−8.70	2.66
Industrial Materials	−3.90	13.53	−9.72	25.46	−12.08	−10.97	−12.08	1.88
Energy	−4.82	−2.41	68.28	30.45	−37.33	6.56	−6.11	6.30
Utilities	−14.97	−4.75	36.62	−1.88	11.76	0.89	−0.42	5.41

Industry Performance

128 Industries, 6300 Stocks

Industry	Annual Total Return %					Annualized Total Return%		
	2002	2001	2000	1999	1998	3-Year	5-Year	10-Year
Advertising	-26.90	8.83	-16.41	73.82	38.36	-17.72	5.57	22.01
Aerospace & Defense	-2.72	-16.76	50.65	2.64	6.96	9.67	2.25	9.18
Agricultural Machinery	7.06	-2.52	8.10	34.86	-42.32	2.41	-2.15	14.75
Agriculture	-12.12	1.91	32.38	-24.61	-16.21	6.39	-5.41	1.97
Agrochemical	7.77	-0.15	0.62	27.60	-31.62	9.07	2.30	9.16
Air Transport	-24.70	-17.25	102.03	6.74	38.38	2.66	6.22	13.75
Alcoholic Drinks	5.29	1.01	30.51	-12.05	42.15	7.90	11.07	8.80
Aluminum	-34.59	7.86	-18.02	125.88	8.13	-14.32	4.69	11.85
Apparel Makers	6.84	10.38	18.67	-5.59	2.57	13.18	2.53	5.64
Appliance & Furniture Makers	-6.29	16.75	-24.54	-4.09	26.13	-0.77	1.91	12.69
Assisted Living	-21.51	14.96	28.91	-45.53	-27.02	6.68	-16.37	5.48
Audio/Video Equipment	-12.57	-35.11	-50.92	195.40	0.84	-24.22	1.99	9.94
Auto Makers	-10.95	-5.24	-35.06	26.54	-6.94	-12.56	-0.63	9.07
Auto Parts	-2.40	43.52	-22.46	-2.36	4.91	3.43	1.64	11.51
Auto Retail	-1.60	105.50	-11.80	-23.13	1.51	21.76	7.71	13.67
Beverage Mfg.	-5.55	-21.45	5.99	-12.17	1.32	1.37	-2.26	9.07
Biotechnology	-14.35	-11.73	6.45	129.77	93.18	-6.16	22.95	18.53
Broadcast TV	-7.68	-5.56	-22.65	-18.33	78.58	-10.34	-1.43	-4.05
Building Materials	-12.05	5.63	-12.03	-10.34	14.86	-3.50	-0.69	7.37
Business Applications	-21.99	52.78	-62.85	68.36	114.60	-22.89	10.13	25.50
Business Support	-4.19	56.04	18.73	2.22	15.22	7.71	8.30	17.66
Business/Online Services	-18.56	22.78	-69.48	-18.47	28.54	-20.47	3.73	20.27
Cable TV	-32.24	-12.86	-13.71	100.56	80.31	-23.04	10.11	8.54
Chemicals	2.95	-9.14	-13.22	39.88	-0.98	-3.16	2.03	12.77
Clothing Stores	-1.50	-12.01	-19.18	23.21	69.61	4.18	11.39	13.06
Components	-25.29	-12.54	-46.21	198.26	16.34	-24.95	-1.79	6.14
Computer Equipment	-35.47	43.00	-20.84	39.37	77.48	-19.20	6.44	21.23
Construction Machinery	-9.81	13.73	4.15	4.69	-3.06	-0.21	0.25	15.55
Consultants	-33.17	12.85	-12.82	34.82	15.94	-15.41	-6.25	-4.38
Contract Manufacturers	-65.86	-15.83	-2.25	104.70	87.41	-30.20	0.96	4.27
Data Networking	-27.66	-52.65	-28.59	130.84	149.72	-36.48	5.81	28.19
Data Processing	-19.78	-5.09	18.28	35.36	31.68	3.04	13.40	15.46
Department Stores	-29.68	16.86	-21.82	-23.39	1.16	-4.42	-8.02	3.83
Development Tools	-25.52	-29.45	14.58	141.67	21.43	-23.50	8.52	10.30
Diagnostics	-20.65	1.00	152.74	71.57	5.56	31.33	37.70	-5.89
Discount Stores	-11.76	8.94	-22.79	70.44	107.55	-4.60	18.41	12.86
Distributors	8.89	21.25	-22.32	2.24	-7.34	8.06	1.88	7.06
Drugs	-17.56	-12.49	38.08	-17.73	41.22	0.84	3.81	15.77
Education	46.63	37.26	145.16	-40.77	7.54	56.43	22.54	20.77
Electric Equipment	-37.71	-15.07	-6.00	53.56	41.00	-15.88	0.44	15.37
Electric Utilities	-4.59	-5.36	51.61	-18.02	16.82	6.75	2.94	8.81
Electronics Stores	-45.34	92.68	-33.26	63.91	84.05	-14.07	12.65	27.26
Employment	-28.79	-10.74	-18.06	50.43	11.25	-10.28	-2.13	11.91
Engineering & Construction	-23.62	28.62	39.73	-20.25	29.44	14.94	6.74	10.18
Entertainment/Education Media	-16.98	40.65	1.49	49.66	48.43	1.37	18.11	17.05
Environmental Control	4.27	38.36	7.49	17.35	-6.04	15.34	8.30	12.19
Film & TV Production	-40.64	19.87	-15.19	78.67	-5.34	-5.89	5.40	3.54
Finance	-17.64	-6.95	41.48	-10.77	31.72	3.89	6.23	18.91
Food Mfg.	8.48	-4.75	23.19	-16.25	32.62	8.31	4.70	11.86
Food Wholesale	15.54	-11.70	53.47	45.63	22.17	17.94	19.91	17.97
Forestry/Wood	-6.30	9.73	-27.04	45.16	7.07	-4.23	0.11	6.16
Furniture Retail	1.86	51.51	28.78	1.83	77.28	24.10	22.69	31.04
Gambling/Hotel Casinos	11.16	40.32	12.31	68.52	-19.63	30.68	18.33	11.98
Gold & Silver	52.60	27.47	-22.29	16.38	-22.97	21.46	10.57	1.13
Groceries	-27.42	-22.88	-15.74	-18.15	36.28	-21.93	-5.69	15.50
Home Building	3.02	48.68	88.69	-25.83	29.53	41.25	20.07	13.03
Home Health	-1.43	0.41	17.25	-14.49	35.06	7.03	7.36	23.56
Home Supply	-52.74	12.07	-33.32	68.98	108.45	-12.06	11.95	8.26
Hospitals	5.42	-12.25	50.52	25.18	-16.18	12.81	4.96	12.21
Hotels	-17.65	-3.16	34.74	6.02	-34.47	6.30	-6.00	7.65
Household & Personal Products	11.32	3.14	-12.73	21.57	15.89	-2.13	2.53	14.54
Insurance (General)	-4.04	7.26	28.63	-22.13	52.70	8.00	7.24	14.89
Insurance (Life)	-13.97	-23.92	3.68	-0.03	72.95	-8.81	0.62	15.19
Insurance (Property)	-26.94	-19.29	36.98	40.16	33.61	4.30	4.35	17.18
Insurance (Title)	47.87	-25.04	161.36	-51.79	8.68	36.07	8.07	19.25

Industry Performance

128 Industries, 6300 Stocks

Industry	Annual Total Return %					Annualized Total Return%		
	2002	2001	2000	1999	1998	3-Year	5-Year	10-Year
International Banks	-15.30	-5.47	6.29	31.58	-1.61	-1.22	3.52	18.91
Jewelry/Accessories	8.49	0.09	-22.34	136.76	17.00	-6.60	16.96	19.40
Land Transport	2.64	38.21	18.49	-1.51	-9.17	13.98	3.81	7.45
Machinery	-2.91	15.31	-10.66	17.60	-2.67	3.87	2.69	15.50
Managed Care	18.04	15.37	131.18	5.71	-13.29	33.82	18.34	19.43
Manufacturing - Misc.	-0.39	24.12	-9.54	-1.01	6.44	4.37	3.75	12.11
Media Conglomerates	-17.29	-7.76	-22.44	45.04	18.84	-19.22	4.85	13.83
Medical Equipment	-10.35	13.30	49.08	-1.50	42.11	12.81	12.11	15.29
Medical Goods & Services	-8.32	-2.51	108.42	-36.79	51.69	25.24	7.59	23.74
Metal Products	-13.72	52.96	6.68	7.79	-26.26	5.23	-2.44	7.96
Mining (Nonferrous & Nonmetals)	5.34	6.72	-17.69	90.64	-15.46	-0.38	5.96	6.63
Money Management	-24.53	-17.75	51.37	5.03	21.48	3.30	3.15	14.85
Natural Gas Utilities	4.03	-1.57	40.70	-19.63	0.15	14.20	5.06	10.28
Office Equipment	-14.41	60.11	-29.25	-25.55	49.60	-11.47	-11.44	6.94
Oil & Gas	-8.86	-2.17	6.42	29.81	11.01	1.88	4.94	12.08
Oil & Gas Services	-6.46	-26.75	43.90	38.03	-56.56	4.43	-2.74	7.02
Oil/Gas Products	4.88	8.16	24.36	24.94	-22.52	16.55	5.50	14.60
Online Retail	1.38	102.73	-47.28	55.67	966.36	-9.06	21.12	--
Optical Equipment	-46.08	-79.06	-29.18	293.14	23.67	-44.78	-18.68	-9.40
Packaging	22.03	34.85	-1.08	-5.62	-12.02	13.60	3.31	5.89
Paints/Coatings	4.90	7.12	28.41	-27.14	7.50	14.34	3.97	8.12
Paper	-3.63	1.43	-23.25	33.24	6.14	-5.35	2.73	2.90
Personal Services	-8.69	120.09	-2.40	-15.39	2.49	13.74	2.36	10.07
Photography & Imaging	5.60	4.47	-16.74	89.58	-7.36	-6.51	1.94	13.50
Physicians	14.99	-9.15	163.51	-16.31	-44.37	28.72	-3.30	-4.41
Pipelines	-0.68	14.03	46.38	-14.20	0.83	13.36	2.46	14.45
Plastics	-36.03	31.85	40.61	-29.51	-7.45	5.12	0.49	6.29
Printing	4.56	23.67	3.48	-23.27	11.97	14.89	1.74	6.91
Publishing	0.71	5.70	14.85	3.86	9.75	0.54	2.36	10.25
REITS	7.68	17.13	33.61	-2.53	-9.89	19.20	6.66	14.30
Radio	-26.75	5.10	-45.73	63.76	37.21	-18.88	2.78	36.75
Real Estate	-24.82	-16.20	4.27	-1.80	-21.93	-6.82	2.49	13.83
Recreation	-9.77	35.60	-16.11	0.78	74.65	-0.62	10.07	13.29
Regional Banks	10.32	14.26	13.86	-10.23	-3.48	16.47	4.99	15.49
Reinsurance	-14.99	6.96	73.74	-28.58	21.13	18.76	5.38	15.43
Rental & Repair Services	3.61	37.06	-21.53	-37.60	7.20	8.36	2.69	6.91
Research Services	-9.41	22.30	12.04	-60.50	46.54	31.27	3.46	8.31
Restaurants	-6.54	5.66	6.95	1.08	61.77	6.74	8.05	5.95
Rubber Products	-1.74	7.97	-13.55	-29.06	-14.52	0.08	-9.67	-2.67
Savings & Loans	15.63	7.01	78.90	-22.77	-7.98	29.82	8.30	16.39
Securities	-26.12	-22.71	14.11	93.40	-7.35	-6.75	4.96	19.57
Security Services	-16.01	151.67	-54.85	-33.34	-20.58	17.32	-2.87	12.14
Semiconductor Equipment	-35.01	5.01	-39.71	196.78	41.69	-22.42	7.67	28.58
Semiconductors	-50.31	4.89	-26.86	84.97	69.03	-26.65	3.90	19.36
Shoes	-20.11	1.86	13.97	23.32	5.07	8.38	3.24	9.10
Specialty Retail	-12.93	-19.20	43.56	-15.50	87.81	2.27	6.01	17.59
Steel/Iron	9.30	35.52	-51.31	109.05	-9.54	-12.87	-1.61	1.48
Super Regional Banks	5.20	0.55	27.45	-28.61	6.45	9.15	1.32	12.66
Systems & Security	-35.71	-29.23	-44.06	120.35	35.81	-33.28	-1.85	8.76
Telecommunication Services	-17.75	-16.06	-18.91	24.85	37.85	-21.61	-2.69	8.35
Textiles	3.77	100.48	3.79	-37.30	91.74	12.13	6.45	19.68
Tobacco	-6.78	9.12	105.92	-54.66	22.87	28.78	6.04	9.98
Toys/Hobbies	-37.75	12.96	-6.58	77.16	-2.95	-3.56	-3.31	2.07
Transport Equipment	-6.81	12.40	-9.25	-27.22	-4.47	1.27	-7.50	4.20
Transportation - Misc	17.19	-6.09	-13.75	-8.20	46.06	1.69	12.86	14.84
Truck Makers	4.18	11.75	-33.22	13.58	-11.76	1.79	4.27	9.81
Waste Management	-28.14	15.04	61.54	-63.12	18.84	15.04	-6.58	4.71
Water Transport	0.08	1.05	123.53	-5.56	-24.06	22.80	4.33	4.15
Water Utilities	11.40	4.48	8.24	-29.34	26.99	17.41	8.05	16.57
Wireless Equipment	-36.10	-43.04	-8.70	219.52	250.84	-33.24	18.12	51.04
Wireless Service	-28.44	-27.73	-27.30	54.35	123.57	-30.08	7.05	17.39
Wireline Equipment	-35.01	-22.87	0.63	104.09	9.42	-34.42	-9.51	6.54

Industry Averages

128 Industries, 6300 Stocks

Industry	% of US Economy (Revenue)	Industry Averages Market Cap ($Mil)	Revenue ($Mil)	Price/ Book	Price/ Sales	Price/ Earnings	Dividend Yield %	Morningstar Industry Grade Average Growth	Profitability	Financial Health
Advertising	0.30	177	334	2.50	1.64	17.60	1.2	C+	C+	C+
Aerospace & Defense	1.56	99	24	2.54	0.90	15.29	1.6	C+	C-	C-
Agricultural Machinery	0.28	38	58	3.47	0.79	34.47	1.9	C+	C-	C
Agriculture	0.27	157	136	1.19	0.32	16.53	1.8	C+	B-	B-
Agrochemical	0.20	90	146	1.60	0.90	25.06	2.1	C+	C+	C+
Air Transport	0.93	202	570	2.49	2.01	42.12	0.1	C+	B-	C+
Alcoholic Drinks	0.53	455	651	3.81	2.16	19.87	1.6	B-	B-	B-
Aluminum	0.36	293	261	1.80	0.93	38.61	2.6	C	C+	C
Apparel Makers	0.25	147	414	2.03	0.88	16.04	0.0	C+	C+	C+
Appliance & Furniture Makers	0.35	136	322	2.25	0.47	13.51	2.3	C	B-	B-
Assisted Living	0.08	162	93	1.33	0.63	20.68	0.0	C+	C+	C
Audio/Video Equipment	0.98	177	111	1.66	0.63	—	0.4	C	C+	B-
Auto Makers	6.08	234	306	1.74	0.60	16.26	0.7	C+	C+	B-
Auto Parts	1.18	70	140	1.70	0.40	12.63	0.0	C+	C	C
Auto Retail	0.53	203	802	2.57	0.66	16.51	0.0	C+	C	C
Beverage Mfg.	0.63	1,059	1,163	9.36	5.04	33.45	1.8	B	C+	C+
Biotechnology	0.16	73	9	3.51	12.70	45.85	0.0	C+	D+	C-
Broadcast TV	0.23	248	266	1.14	2.99	—	0.0	C	C-	C-
Building Materials	0.42	287	450	1.74	0.95	15.86	1.8	B	B-	B-
Business Applications	0.54	41	43	5.17	9.22	30.77	0.0	C	C+	C+
Business Support	0.30	143	206	3.21	2.11	28.16	0.0	B-	B-	B-
Business/Online Services	0.22	20	38	2.25	2.77	23.33	0.0	C	D+	C-
Cable TV	0.41	247	539	1.60	3.21	10.73	0.0	B	C	D+
Chemicals	1.88	381	692	4.90	1.86	22.04	2.2	C+	C+	B-
Clothing Stores	0.54	375	574	4.05	0.89	18.42	0.6	B-	B+	B+
Components	0.34	869	928	1.67	1.92	49.40	0.4	C	B+	B
Computer Equipment	3.03	48	61	5.93	1.59	27.78	0.8	C+	C	C
Construction Machinery	0.18	117	620	2.63	0.79	24.06	3.1	C	B-	C
Consultants	0.51	138	188	3.52	1.32	20.67	0.0	C	C+	B-
Contract Manufacturers	0.42	64	279	0.95	0.32	105.41	0.0	C+	B-	C
Data Networking	0.22	63	99	3.32	4.90	35.41	0.0	C+	C	C
Data Processing	0.22	1,008	470	4.95	3.34	23.45	0.2	B	B	B+
Department Stores	1.04	1,015	2,005	1.22	0.29	16.08	2.2	C	B-	B
Development Tools	0.10	78	57	4.43	4.23	39.68	0.0	C+	C+	C+
Diagnostics	0.08	51	24	3.32	1.64	22.83	0.0	C	C+	C+
Discount Stores	2.92	1,403	3,510	5.86	0.92	29.20	0.6	B	B	B-
Distributors	0.11	1,266	842	2.93	1.02	23.22	0.1	C	B	B-
Drugs	2.48	175	62	7.22	3.94	23.52	1.7	C+	B-	B-
Education	0.05	189	170	12.73	4.82	50.58	0.0	B	C+	B-
Electric Equipment	2.60	48	69	3.89	1.86	16.23	3.0	C	C	C+
Electric Utilities	5.44	1,642	3,562	1.42	0.82	12.33	4.4	C+	C	C+
Electronics Stores	0.38	42	323	3.26	0.36	35.67	0.0	C-	C	C+
Employment	0.32	78	413	3.66	0.55	59.93	0.6	C	B-	B
Engineering & Construction	0.34	42	170	1.82	0.37	18.84	0.0	C	B-	C+
Entertainment/Education Media	0.05	16	45	5.19	3.46	29.80	0.0	B-	C	C
Environmental Control	0.20	45	86	4.13	0.67	16.64	0.9	C	B-	C+
Film & TV Production	0.03	9	31	1.56	2.30	32.12	0.0	C	C	C
Finance	1.05	65	90	3.35	2.00	11.98	1.5	C+	C+	C+
Food Mfg.	2.73	115	329	4.26	1.46	21.01	1.5	B-	C+	C+
Food Wholesale	0.65	225	2,659	8.85	0.81	28.37	1.6	B-	C+	C
Forestry/Wood	0.38	271	521	1.70	0.60	109.36	3.3	C+	C+	C-
Furniture Retail	0.08	294	616	8.16	3.05	40.15	0.0	B	B	B
Gambling/Hotel Casinos	0.20	180	257	2.51	1.29	19.04	0.0	C	C	C
Gold & Silver	0.07	160	34	2.16	4.39	78.46	0.9	C+	D	C
Groceries	2.13	275	2,023	3.13	0.39	20.31	0.6	C+	C+	C+
Home Building	0.42	248	570	1.34	0.43	7.50	0.3	C+	B	B-
Home Health	0.09	55	119	2.85	1.78	18.40	0.0	C	B-	C
Home Supply	0.63	25	779	2.81	0.97	15.36	0.9	C	B-	C+
Hospitals	0.37	473	677	3.52	1.11	23.45	0.1	C+	B	C+
Hotels	0.21	332	379	2.13	1.25	28.89	0.8	C-	C	C
Household & Personal Products	0.92	516	932	8.84	2.71	25.73	1.8	C+	C+	C+
Insurance (General)	1.15	548	523	1.78	2.85	34.84	0.0	B	B-	B
Insurance (Life)	2.22	655	710	1.12	0.69	19.95	1.3	C+	C-	B
Insurance (Property)	2.24	543	537	1.87	2.26	20.44	0.3	B-	C+	B
Insurance (Title)	0.09	512	1,887	1.49	0.68	7.19	1.2	A	B+	A

Industry Averages
128 Industries, 6300 Stocks

Industry	% of US Economy (Revenue)	Industry Averages Market Cap ($Mil)	Revenue ($Mil)	Price/ Book	Price/ Sales	Price/ Earnings	Dividend Yield %	Morningstar Industry Grade Average Growth	Profitability	Financial Health
International Banks	4.26	25,320	17,580	2.24	1.68	12.77	3.5	B	C	C+
Jewelry/Accessories	0.10	47	192	2.23	3.81	27.67	0.5	C	C	C+
Land Transport	0.54	278	394	1.44	1.23	13.55	1.4	C	B	B-
Machinery	0.45	73	160	2.51	1.27	29.35	1.4	C	B-	B-
Managed Care	0.95	180	715	5.54	0.69	21.26	0.0	B-	B	C+
Manufacturing - Misc.	0.10	86	102	2.36	1.04	20.40	2.2	C+	B-	B-
Media Conglomerates	1.23	8,339	2,771	1.42	2.20	27.18	0.2	C+	B	B
Medical Equipment	0.56	68	29	6.59	4.59	31.15	0.3	C	C+	C+
Medical Goods & Services	1.25	120	292	4.12	0.50	23.12	0.2	C+	B	B-
Metal Products	0.34	83	190	1.71	0.63	18.96	2.9	C	C+	C+
Mining (Nonferrous & Nonmetals)	1.15	896	660	2.97	1.53	21.24	2.3	B-	C+	C+
Money Management	0.29	2,338	528	2.65	2.66	17.61	1.9	C	B+	B+
Natural Gas Utilities	1.89	792	1,184	1.94	0.84	18.41	4.6	C-	C+	C-
Office Equipment	0.42	18	456	3.04	0.37	15.55	0.0	C	C-	C-
Oil & Gas	8.49	215	116	2.21	1.08	19.09	3.0	C+	C	C
Oil & Gas Services	0.51	605	456	2.62	2.05	33.59	0.3	C+	B-	B-
Oil/Gas Products	0.48	339	1,012	2.70	1.05	22.42	1.9	C	B-	C+
Online Retail	0.09	27	31	10.31	7.62	102.76	0.0	C+	D-	D+
Optical Equipment	0.10	86	40	1.68	1.43	37.90	0.0	C	C	C
Packaging	0.27	401	983	3.17	0.83	17.85	0.7	C-	C-	C-
Paints/Coatings	0.07	22	62	3.35	0.82	37.17	2.1	C+	B-	B-
Paper	0.70	271	820	1.65	0.80	19.77	2.9	B-	C+	C
Personal Services	0.16	147	335	3.37	2.04	17.15	1.7	C	C+	C+
Photography & Imaging	0.43	42	89	2.84	1.25	26.14	0.5	C	C-	C
Physicians	0.17	89	198	1.92	0.37	13.90	0.0	C+	B	B
Pipelines	0.42	892	754	2.03	1.97	16.58	6.6	C+	C+	C
Plastics	0.09	32	77	0.87	0.25	16.98	3.9	C	C	C-
Printing	0.11	201	459	2.90	0.58	13.31	3.5	C	B	B
Publishing	0.34	434	466	4.60	2.48	26.51	1.7	C-	B-	B
REITS	0.39	356	140	1.54	3.33	17.44	7.2	C+	B	C+
Radio	0.08	393	144	1.63	2.83	54.31	0.0	B-	C	C+
Real Estate	0.09	85	72	0.88	6.29	13.37	2.9	C	B-	B-
Recreation	0.23	87	157	2.01	3.38	17.29	1.6	C+	C+	C
Regional Banks	0.86	134	65	2.11	2.22	14.16	2.8	C+	C	C
Reinsurance	0.11	893	1,021	1.71	2.56	19.33	0.6	B+	C+	B-
Rental & Repair Services	0.22	45	149	8.88	2.24	15.12	0.0	C-	C	C
Research Services	0.04	154	68	3.73	1.75	27.12	0.0	C+	B-	B
Restaurants	0.52	56	178	2.55	1.34	14.55	0.1	C+	C+	C+
Rubber Products	0.16	37	123	1.19	0.34	19.43	2.7	C	B-	C+
Savings & Loans	0.44	73	40	1.63	2.23	12.07	2.4	C	C-	C-
Securities	1.04	87	92	1.73	1.33	17.15	0.9	C-	C-	B-
Security Services	0.04	31	76	2.11	0.63	48.92	0.0	C	B-	C-
Semiconductor Equipment	0.13	159	94	2.73	4.40	—	0.0	C	C+	B-
Semiconductors	0.62	205	96	2.92	3.88	40.97	0.2	C+	B-	B-
Shoes	0.16	170	294	3.21	1.17	29.07	1.1	C+	B-	B
Specialty Retail	1.16	141	432	3.53	0.77	29.49	0.5	C	C-	C
Steel/Iron	0.52	128	695	1.20	0.75	7.29	1.7	C	C	C
Super Regional Banks	1.08	21,615	9,025	2.05	2.13	14.39	2.7	D+	C+	A-
Systems & Security	0.15	153	76	2.26	3.73	64.45	0.0	C+	C+	C+
Telecommunication Services	4.93	138	343	2.76	1.57	15.43	3.5	C	C+	B-
Textiles	0.11	42	472	1.99	0.90	13.43	0.0	C-	C-	C-
Tobacco	1.02	2,349	3,535	3.95	0.93	7.60	6.0	B-	B	B
Toys/Hobbies	0.11	26	79	2.03	3.22	14.81	0.9	C-	C	C+
Transport Equipment	0.04	41	271	2.46	0.90	25.22	0.3	C	C	C+
Transportation - Misc	0.59	121	260	6.43	2.25	29.76	1.2	B-	B	B-
Truck Makers	0.33	137	414	2.10	0.61	13.50	1.7	C	C+	C
Waste Management	0.17	8	71	2.58	1.25	19.26	0.0	C	C	C
Water Transport	0.04	227	214	1.18	1.38	14.28	0.0	C+	B	C+
Water Utilities	0.05	146	95	2.14	1.70	18.77	3.5	C	B-	C-
Wireless Equipment	0.65	37	58	6.80	2.64	37.81	1.5	B-	C+	C
Wireless Service	1.05	79	393	2.71	2.64	12.11	0.0	C+	C	C
Wireline Equipment	1.02	54	57	1.66	0.49	12.90	1.6	C	C	C

Top/Bottom Performing Stocks
Morningstar Stocks 500 Universe

Last 12 Months

Pg	Company	Industry	Return (%)
Top Performers			
315	Jo-Ann Stores A	Specialty Retail	221.26
426	Providian Financial	Finance	82.82
140	Boston Scientific	Medical Equipment	76.29
408	PacifiCare Health Systems	Managed Care	75.63
78	Amazon.com	Online Retail	74.58
232	Expedia	Online Retail	64.81
430	Quiksilver	Apparel Makers	55.00
276	Halliburton	Oil & Gas Services	47.23
351	Mandalay Resort Group	Gambling/Hotel Casinos	43.04
167	Chico's FAS	Clothing Stores	42.89
445	SanDisk	Semiconductors	40.97
531	Washington Post	Media Conglomerates	40.53
551	Zimmer Holdings	Medical Equipment	35.95
264	Getty Images	Business Support	32.94
439	Ross Stores	Clothing Stores	32.78
226	ENI SpA ADR	Oil & Gas	30.63
193	Countrywide Financial	Savings & Loans	27.29
95	Anthem	Insurance (Life)	27.07
543	Williams-Sonoma	Furniture Retail	26.57
492	Teva Pharmaceutical Industries ADR	Drugs	25.86
215	Eastman Kodak	Photography & Imaging	25.52
479	Student Loan	Finance	25.13
62	Aetna	Insurance (Life)	24.77
461	SLM	Finance	24.72
345	Lockheed Martin	Aerospace & Defense	24.67
Bottom Performers			
163	Charter Communications	Cable TV	-92.82
508	UAL	Air Transport	-89.41
542	Williams Companies	Pipelines	-89.01
145	Brocade Communications Systems	Systems & Security	-87.50
229	Ericsson Telephone ADR B	Wireless Equipment	-87.09
220	El Paso	Pipelines	-83.46
456	Sepracor	Drugs	-83.05
400	NVIDIA	Semiconductors	-82.80
470	Sprint PCS Group	Wireless Service	-82.06
92	Andrx Group	Drugs	-79.16
517	VeriSign	Systems & Security	-78.92
393	Nortel Networks	Wireline Equipment	-78.53
85	Americredit	Finance	-75.47
348	Lucent Technologies	Wireline Equipment	-75.16
480	Sun Microsystems	Computer Equipment	-74.72
425	Protein Design Labs	Biotechnology	-74.19
293	Human Genome Sciences	Biotechnology	-73.87
421	PMC-Sierra	Semiconductors	-73.85
459	Siebel Systems	Business Applications	-73.55
251	Freemarkets	Business/Online Services	-73.14
69	Alcatel SA ADR A	Wireline Equipment	-72.94
222	Electronic Data Systems	Consultants	-72.57
189	Continental Airlines B	Air Transport	-72.34
313	JDS Uniphase	Optical Equipment	-71.71
283	Healthsouth	Physicians	-71.66

Last 3 Years

Pg	Company	Industry	Avg. Annual Return (%)
Top Performers			
167	Chico's FAS	Clothing Stores	65.38
302	International Game Tech	Gambling/Hotel Casinos	55.19
429	Quest Diagnostics	Diagnostics	54.99
434	Reebok International	Shoes	53.13
86	AmerisourceBergen	Medical Goods & Services	53.02
153	Caremark RX	Managed Care	47.51
248	Forest Laboratories	Drugs	47.32
512	UnitedHealth Group	Managed Care	46.56
412	Pepsi Bottling Group	Beverage Mfg.	46.16
119	Barr Laboratories	Drugs	46.00
418	Pier 1 Imports	Furniture Retail	45.55
437	RJ Reynolds Tobacco Holdings	Tobacco	44.69
406	Oxford Health Plans	Managed Care	42.16
345	Lockheed Martin	Aerospace & Defense	39.90
540	White Mountains Insurance	Insurance (Property)	39.59
282	Health Net	Physicians	38.50
472	St. Jude Medical	Medical Equipment	37.31
461	SLM	Finance	36.56
453	SCP Pool	Recreation	36.31
332	Laboratory Corp of America	Diagnostics	36.09
265	Gilead Sciences	Biotechnology	35.95
513	Universal Health Services B	Hospitals	35.82
439	Ross Stores	Clothing Stores	34.14
465	Southern	Electric Utilities	34.01
308	Investors Financial Services	Money Management	33.74
Bottom Performers			
251	Freemarkets	Business/Online Services	-73.38
508	UAL	Air Transport	-73.25
348	Lucent Technologies	Wireline Equipment	-71.82
313	JDS Uniphase	Optical Equipment	-68.71
393	Nortel Networks	Wireline Equipment	-68.25
229	Ericsson Telephone ADR B	Wireless Equipment	-65.37
517	VeriSign	Systems & Security	-65.24
255	Gateway	Computer Equipment	-64.81
163	Charter Communications	Cable TV	-62.22
339	Level 3 Communications	Telecommunication Services	-60.88
421	PMC-Sierra	Semiconductors	-58.91
463	Solectron	Contract Manufacturers	-57.90
549	Yahoo!	Media Conglomerates	-57.72
191	Corning	Optical Equipment	-57.34
480	Sun Microsystems	Computer Equipment	-56.85
470	Sprint PCS Group	Wireless Service	-55.95
145	Brocade Communications Systems	Systems & Security	-54.60
69	Alcatel SA ADR A	Wireline Equipment	-53.47
542	Williams Companies	Pipelines	-53.08
327	Knight Trading Group	Securities	-52.95
144	Broadcom	Semiconductors	-52.00
489	Tellabs	Wireline Equipment	-51.62
224	EMC	Computer Equipment	-51.44
100	Applied Micro Circuits	Semiconductors	-51.23
431	Qwest Communications International	Telecommunication Services	-51.17

Top/Bottom Performing Stocks

Morningstar Stocks 500 Universe

Last 5 Years

Pg	Company	Industry	Avg. Annual Return (%)
	Top Performers		
167	Chico's FAS	Clothing Stores	90.69
218	EchoStar Communications	Cable TV	60.44
248	Forest Laboratories	Drugs	51.44
429	Quest Diagnostics	Diagnostics	46.48
428	Qualcomm	Wireless Equipment	42.57
296	IDEC Pharmaceuticals	Biotechnology	42.08
332	Laboratory Corp of America	Diagnostics	40.24
453	SCP Pool	Recreation	38.63
308	Investors Financial Services	Money Management	36.87
436	RF Micro Devices	Semiconductors	36.62
371	Mercury Interactive	Development Tools	34.64
64	Affiliated Computer Services	Business Support	31.96
129	Best Buy	Electronics Stores	31.48
366	MedImmune	Biotechnology	30.62
73	Allergan	Drugs	30.40
78	Amazon.com	Online Retail	30.34
392	Nokia ADR	Wireless Equipment	30.09
483	Symantec	Systems & Security	29.82
478	Stryker	Medical Equipment	29.47
126	Bed Bath & Beyond	Furniture Retail	29.11
87	Amgen	Biotechnology	29.00
265	Gilead Sciences	Biotechnology	28.88
233	Expeditors International of WA	Transportation - Misc	28.11
277	Harley-Davidson	Recreation	28.05
307	Intuit	Business Applications	27.82
	Bottom Performers		
508	UAL	Air Transport	-56.24
348	Lucent Technologies	Wireline Equipment	-38.99
542	Williams Companies	Pipelines	-35.10
271	Goodyear Tire & Rubber	Rubber Products	-33.76
393	Nortel Networks	Wireless Equipment	-31.85
229	Ericsson Telephone ADR B	Wireless Equipment	-31.64
189	Continental Airlines B	Air Transport	-31.52
283	Healthsouth	Physicians	-31.45
396	Northwest Airlines	Air Transport	-31.27
69	Alcatel SA ADR A	Wireline Equipment	-28.73
255	Gateway	Computer Equipment	-28.13
204	Delta Air Lines	Air Transport	-27.08
547	Xerox	Office Equipment	-25.12
220	El Paso	Pipelines	-24.83
70	Alcide	Chemicals	-24.72
88	AMR	Air Transport	-24.64
184	Computer Associates International	Systems & Security	-23.73
489	Tellabs	Wireline Equipment	-22.76
191	Corning	Optical Equipment	-22.57
199	Dana	Auto Parts	-21.84
186	Compuware	Systems & Security	-21.40
159	Cendant	Business Support	-21.15
500	Toys R Us	Specialty Retail	-20.47
435	Reuters Group PLC ADR	Publishing	-20.07
339	Level 3 Communications	Telecommunication Services	-19.83

Last 10 Years

Pg	Company	Industry	Avg. Annual Return (%)
	Top Performers		
392	Nokia ADR	Wireless Equipment	51.04
96	AOL Time Warner	Media Conglomerates	49.75
202	Dell Computer	Computer Equipment	42.96
428	Qualcomm	Wireless Equipment	37.71
177	Clear Channel Communications	Radio	36.75
296	IDEC Pharmaceuticals	Biotechnology	36.68
119	Barr Laboratories	Drugs	35.86
543	Williams-Sonoma	Furniture Retail	34.09
360	Maxim Integrated Products	Semiconductors	33.46
233	Expeditors International of WA	Transportation - Misc	33.19
405	Oracle	Business Applications	31.45
77	Altera	Semiconductors	31.39
126	Bed Bath & Beyond	Furniture Retail	31.04
328	Kohl's	Discount Stores	31.03
410	Paychex	Data Processing	30.81
438	Robert Half International	Employment	30.73
430	Quiksilver	Apparel Makers	29.56
162	Charles Schwab	Securities	29.50
346	Lowe's Companies	Home Supply	29.25
513	Universal Health Services B	Hospitals	29.01
216	Eaton Vance	Money Management	28.94
272	Graco	Machinery	28.93
99	Applied Materials	Semiconductor Equipment	28.58
187	Concord EFS	Data Processing	28.37
173	Cisco Systems	Data Networking	28.19
	Bottom Performers		
508	UAL	Air Transport	-23.39
69	Alcatel SA ADR A	Wireline Equipment	-14.33
500	Toys R Us	Specialty Retail	-12.97
271	Goodyear Tire & Rubber	Rubber Products	-12.54
393	Nortel Networks	Wireline Equipment	-10.73
207	Dillard's	Department Stores	-10.26
191	Corning	Optical Equipment	-9.40
88	AMR	Air Transport	-7.42
294	Humana	Managed Care	-6.93
204	Delta Air Lines	Air Transport	-6.89
98	Apple Computer	Computer Equipment	-6.70
544	Winn-Dixie Stores	Groceries	-6.05
332	Laboratory Corp of America	Diagnostics	-5.89
426	Providian Financial	Finance	-5.88
408	PacifiCare Health Systems	Managed Care	-5.79
542	Williams Companies	Pipelines	-5.21
220	El Paso	Pipelines	-4.83
283	Healthsouth	Physicians	-4.41
222	Electronic Data Systems	Consultants	-4.38
199	Dana	Auto Parts	-3.67
60	Advanced Micro Devices	Semiconductors	-3.33
435	Reuters Group PLC ADR	Publishing	-3.21
507	Tyson Foods A	Food Mfg.	-2.89
547	Xerox	Office Equipment	-2.81
351	Mandalay Resort Group	Gambling/Hotel Casinos	-2.10

Stocks with Highest and Lowest Morningstar Ratings

Morningstar Stocks 500 Universe

Morningstar Rating

Pg	Company	Industry	Risk Measure
	Highest: ★★★★★		
83	American International Group	Insurance (Property)	Medium
85	Americredit	Finance	High
103	AstraZeneca PLC ADR	Drugs	Medium
107	Automatic Data Processing	Data Processing	Low
112	AVX	Components	Medium
134	Blackrock	Money Management	Low
143	Bristol-Myers Squibb	Drugs	Low
151	Capital One Financial	Finance	High
216	Eaton Vance	Money Management	Medium
239	Federated Investors B	Money Management	Low
257	General Dynamics	Aerospace & Defense	Medium
287	Home Depot	Home Supply	Medium
296	IDEC Pharmaceuticals	Biotechnology	Medium
298	IMS Health	Data Processing	Medium
320	Kemet	Components	Medium
335	Lear	Auto Parts	Medium
364	McDonald's	Restaurants	Low
378	Moody's	Business Support	Low
381	Mylan Laboratories	Drugs	Low
394	Northern Trust	Money Management	Medium
397	Novartis AG ADR	Drugs	Low
410	Paychex	Data Processing	Low
476	State Street	Money Management	Medium
532	Waste Management	Waste Management	Low
	Lowest: ★		
64	Affiliated Computer Services	Business Support	Medium
69	Alcatel SA ADR A	Wireline Equipment	Medium
70	Alcide	Chemicals	High
78	Amazon.com	Online Retail	Medium
92	Andrx Group	Drugs	Medium
113	Baker Hughes	Oil & Gas Services	Medium
121	Bausch & Lomb	Medical Equipment	Low
124	BEA Systems	Development Tools	High
126	Bed Bath & Beyond	Furniture Retail	Medium
136	BMC Software	Systems & Security	Medium
144	Broadcom	Semiconductors	High
149	Callaway Golf	Recreation	High
162	Charles Schwab	Securities	Medium
163	Charter Communications	Cable TV	High
184	Computer Associates International	Systems & Security	High
191	Corning	Optical Equipment	Medium
193	Countrywide Financial	Savings & Loans	Medium
201	Deere & Company	Agricultural Machinery	Medium
214	E*Trade Group	Securities	High
215	Eastman Kodak	Photography & Imaging	Medium
217	eBay	Online Retail	Medium
219	Ecolab	Chemicals	Low
229	Ericsson Telephone ADR B	Wireless Equipment	High
232	Expedia	Online Retail	High
248	Forest Laboratories	Drugs	Medium
254	Gap	Clothing Stores	High
264	Getty Images	Business Support	High
265	Gilead Sciences	Biotechnology	High
272	Graco	Machinery	Medium
276	Halliburton	Oil & Gas Services	Medium

Pg	Company	Industry	Risk Measure
	Lowest: ★ (cont.)		
290	Hotels.com A	Online Retail	Medium
305	Internet Security Systems	Systems & Security	High
312	JD Edwards & Company	Business Applications	Medium
325	KLA-Tencor	Semiconductor Equipment	Medium
330	Krispy Kreme Doughnut	Restaurants	Medium
333	Lam Research	Semiconductor Equipment	High
334	Lattice Semiconductor	Semiconductors	High
344	Liz Claiborne	Apparel Makers	Medium
348	Lucent Technologies	Wireline Equipment	High
350	Macromedia	Development Tools	High
356	Martha Stewart Living Omnimedia A	Media Conglomerates	High
357	Marvell Technology	Semiconductors	High
359	Mattel	Toys/Hobbies	Medium
371	Mercury Interactive	Development Tools	Medium
393	Nortel Networks	Wireline Equipment	High
400	NVIDIA	Semiconductors	High
404	Omnicom Group	Advertising	High
405	Oracle	Business Applications	Medium
408	PacifiCare Health Systems	Managed Care	Medium
420	Playboy Enterprises B	Publishing	High
428	Qualcomm	Wireless Equipment	High
434	Reebok International	Shoes	Medium
445	SanDisk	Semiconductors	High
447	SAP AG ADR	Business Applications	Medium
451	Schlumberger	Oil & Gas Services	Medium
454	Sealed Air	Packaging	Medium
456	Sepracor	Drugs	High
463	Solectron	Contract Manufacturers	High
470	Sprint PCS Group	Wireless Service	High
472	St. Jude Medical	Medical Equipment	Medium
483	Symantec	Systems & Security	Medium
491	Teradyne	Semiconductor Equipment	High
492	Teva Pharmaceutical Industries ADR	Drugs	Medium
501	Transocean	Oil & Gas Services	Medium
514	Urban Outfitters	Clothing Stores	Medium
516	USA Interactive	Media Conglomerates	Medium
525	Vodafone Group PLC ADR	Wireless Service	Medium
543	Williams-Sonoma	Furniture Retail	Medium
549	Yahoo!	Media Conglomerates	High

Most Attractive and Least Attractive Stocks
Based on Morningstar Rating and Risk Measure

Most Attractive (High Rating/Low Risk)

Pg	Company	Industry	Rating
107	Automatic Data Processing	Data Processing	★★★★★
134	Blackrock	Money Management	★★★★★
143	Bristol-Myers Squibb	Drugs	★★★★★
239	Federated Investors B	Money Management	★★★★★
364	McDonald's	Restaurants	★★★★★
378	Moody's	Business Support	★★★★★
381	Mylan Laboratories	Drugs	★★★★★
397	Novartis AG ADR	Drugs	★★★★★
410	Paychex	Data Processing	★★★★★
532	Waste Management	Waste Management	★★★★★
72	Alcon	Drugs	★★★★
108	AutoNation	Auto Retail	★★★★
119	Barr Laboratories	Drugs	★★★★
128	Berkshire Hathaway B	Insurance (General)	★★★★
237	Fannie Mae	Finance	★★★★
242	First Data	Data Processing	★★★★
250	Freddie Mac	Finance	★★★★
267	GlaxoSmithKline PLC ADR	Drugs	★★★★
317	Johnson Controls	Auto Parts	★★★★
365	McGraw-Hill Companies	Publishing	★★★★
414	PepsiCo	Beverage Mfg.	★★★★
415	Pfizer	Drugs	★★★★
479	Student Loan	Finance	★★★★
482	SuperValu	Food Wholesale	★★★★
511	United Technologies	Aerospace & Defense	★★★★
512	UnitedHealth Group	Managed Care	★★★★
529	Walt Disney	Media Conglomerates	★★★★
546	Wyeth	Drugs	★★★★

Least Attractive (Low Rating/High Risk)

Pg	Company	Industry	Rating
70	Alcide	Chemicals	★
124	BEA Systems	Development Tools	★
144	Broadcom	Semiconductors	★
149	Callaway Golf	Recreation	★
163	Charter Communications	Cable TV	★
184	Computer Associates International	Systems & Security	★
214	E*Trade Group	Securities	★
229	Ericsson Telephone ADR B	Wireless Equipment	★
232	Expedia	Online Retail	★
254	Gap	Clothing Stores	★
264	Getty Images	Business Support	★
265	Gilead Sciences	Biotechnology	★
305	Internet Security Systems	Systems & Security	★
333	Lam Research	Semiconductor Equipment	★
334	Lattice Semiconductor	Semiconductors	★
348	Lucent Technologies	Wireline Equipment	★
350	Macromedia	Development Tools	★
356	Martha Stewart Living Omnimedia A	Media Conglomerates	★
357	Marvell Technology	Semiconductors	★
393	Nortel Networks	Wireline Equipment	★
400	NVIDIA	Semiconductors	★
404	Omnicom Group	Advertising	★
420	Playboy Enterprises B	Publishing	★
428	Qualcomm	Wireless Equipment	★
445	SanDisk	Semiconductors	★
456	Sepracor	Drugs	★
463	Solectron	Contract Manufacturers	★
470	Sprint PCS Group	Wireless Service	★
491	Teradyne	Semiconductor Equipment	★
549	Yahoo!	Media Conglomerates	★
60	Advanced Micro Devices	Semiconductors	★★
63	AFC Enterprises	Restaurants	★★
75	Allied Capital	Finance	★★
130	Biogen	Biotechnology	★★
222	Electronic Data Systems	Consultants	★★
224	EMC	Computer Equipment	★★
286	Hewlett-Packard	Computer Equipment	★★
291	Household International	Finance	★★
313	JDS Uniphase	Optical Equipment	★★
327	Knight Trading Group	Securities	★★
363	MBNA	Finance	★★
366	MedImmune	Biotechnology	★★
388	Network Associates	Systems & Security	★★
401	Oakley	Recreation	★★
421	PMC-Sierra	Semiconductors	★★
430	Quiksilver	Apparel Makers	★★
436	RF Micro Devices	Semiconductors	★★
517	VeriSign	Systems & Security	★★

Stocks with Low Risk Measure
Morningstar Stocks 500 Universe

Pg	Company	Industry	Rating
107	Automatic Data Processing	Data Processing	★★★★★
134	Blackrock	Money Management	★★★★★
143	Bristol-Myers Squibb	Drugs	★★★★★
239	Federated Investors B	Money Management	★★★★★
364	McDonald's	Restaurants	★★★★★
378	Moody's	Business Support	★★★★★
381	Mylan Laboratories	Drugs	★★★★★
397	Novartis AG ADR	Drugs	★★★★★
410	Paychex	Data Processing	★★★★★
532	Waste Management	Waste Management	★★★★★
72	Alcon	Drugs	★★★★
108	AutoNation	Auto Retail	★★★★
119	Barr Laboratories	Drugs	★★★★
128	Berkshire Hathaway B	Insurance (General)	★★★★
237	Fannie Mae	Finance	★★★★
242	First Data	Data Processing	★★★★
250	Freddie Mac	Finance	★★★★
267	GlaxoSmithKline PLC ADR	Drugs	★★★★
317	Johnson Controls	Auto Parts	★★★★
365	McGraw-Hill Companies	Publishing	★★★★
414	PepsiCo	Beverage Mfg.	★★★★
415	Pfizer	Drugs	★★★★
479	Student Loan	Finance	★★★★
482	SuperValu	Food Wholesale	★★★★
511	United Technologies	Aerospace & Defense	★★★★
512	UnitedHealth Group	Managed Care	★★★★
529	Walt Disney	Media Conglomerates	★★★★
546	Wyeth	Drugs	★★★★
54	3M Company	Chemicals	★★★
55	Abbott Laboratories	Drugs	★★★
67	Albertson's	Groceries	★★★
79	AMB Property	REITS	★★★
82	American Express	Finance	★★★
89	AmSouth Bancorporation	Regional Banks	★★★
93	Anheuser-Busch Companies	Alcoholic Drinks	★★★
95	Anthem	Insurance (Life)	★★★
102	Archstone-Smith Trust	REITS	★★★
109	AutoZone	Auto Retail	★★★
110	Aventis SA ADR	Drugs	★★★
148	Cadbury Schweppes PLC ADR	Food Mfg.	★★★
179	Coca-Cola	Beverage Mfg.	★★★
181	Colgate-Palmolive	Household & Personal Prod.	★★★
183	Comerica	Regional Banks	★★★
200	Danaher	Electric Equipment	★★★
206	Diageo PLC ADR	Alcoholic Drinks	★★★
207	Dillard's	Department Stores	★★★
211	Dow Jones & Company	Media Conglomerates	★★★
212	DST Systems	Data Processing	★★★
223	Eli Lilly & Company	Drugs	★★★
227	Equity Office Properties Trust	REITS	★★★
228	Equity Residential	REITS	★★★
231	Ethan Allen Interiors	Appliance & Furn. Makers	★★★
235	ExxonMobil	Oil & Gas	★★★
241	Fifth Third Bancorp	Super Regional Banks	★★★
253	Gannett	Media Conglomerates	★★★

Pg	Company	Industry	Rating
262	Genuine Parts	Auto Retail	★★★
269	Golden West Financial	Savings & Loans	★★★
273	Groupe Danone ADR	Food Mfg.	★★★
277	Harley-Davidson	Recreation	★★★
282	Health Net	Physicians	★★★
297	Illinois Tool Works	Machinery	★★★
316	Johnson & Johnson	Drugs	★★★
319	Kellogg	Food Mfg.	★★★
367	Medtronic	Medical Equipment	★★★
382	National City	Super Regional Banks	★★★
389	New York Times A	Media Conglomerates	★★★
407	Paccar	Truck Makers	★★★
419	Pitney Bowes	Office Equipment	★★★
438	Robert Half International	Employment	★★★
441	Royal Dutch Petroleum ADR	Oil & Gas	★★★
446	Sanofi-Synthelabo ADR	Drugs	★★★
458	Shell Transport & Trading ADR	Oil & Gas	★★★
460	Simon Property Group	REITS	★★★
461	SLM	Finance	★★★
465	Southern	Electric Utilities	★★★
466	Southtrust	Regional Banks	★★★
481	SunTrust Banks	Super Regional Banks	★★★
484	Sysco	Food Wholesale	★★★
503	Tribune	Media Conglomerates	★★★
509	United Parcel Service B	Transportation - Misc	★★★
527	Wal-Mart Stores	Discount Stores	★★★
535	WellPoint Health Networks	Managed Care	★★★
101	Aramark	Restaurants	★★
230	Estee Lauder A	Household & Personal Prod.	★★
439	Ross Stores	Clothing Stores	★★
520	Viacom B	Broadcast TV	★★
531	Washington Post	Media Conglomerates	★★
121	Bausch & Lomb	Medical Equipment	★
219	Ecolab	Chemicals	★

Stocks with High Risk Measure
Morningstar Stocks 500 Universe

Pg	Company	Industry	Rating	Pg	Company	Industry	Rating
85	Americredit	Finance	★★★★★	363	MBNA	Finance	★★
151	Capital One Financial	Finance	★★★★★	366	MedImmune	Biotechnology	★★
53	1-800 Flowers.com	Online Retail	★★★★	388	Network Associates	Systems & Security	★★
220	El Paso	Pipelines	★★★★	401	Oakley	Recreation	★★
480	Sun Microsystems	Computer Equipment	★★★★	421	PMC-Sierra	Semiconductors	★★
87	Amgen	Biotechnology	★★★	430	Quiksilver	Apparel Makers	★★
96	AOL Time Warner	Media Conglomerates	★★★	436	RF Micro Devices	Semiconductors	★★
98	Apple Computer	Computer Equipment	★★★	517	VeriSign	Systems & Security	★★
100	Applied Micro Circuits	Semiconductors	★★★	70	Alcide	Chemicals	★
105	AT&T Wireless Services	Wireless Service	★★★	124	BEA Systems	Development Tools	★
159	Cendant	Business Support	★★★	144	Broadcom	Semiconductors	★
165	Check Point Software Technologies	Business Applications	★★★	149	Callaway Golf	Recreation	★
176	Citizens Communications	Telecommunication Services	★★★	163	Charter Communications	Cable TV	★
195	Cummins Engine	Auto Parts	★★★	184	Computer Associates International	Systems & Security	★
199	Dana	Auto Parts	★★★	214	E*Trade Group	Securities	★
218	EchoStar Communications	Cable TV	★★★	229	Ericsson Telephone ADR B	Wireless Equipment	★
246	Flextronics International	Contract Manufacturers	★★★	232	Expedia	Online Retail	★
247	Ford Motor	Auto Makers	★★★	254	Gap	Clothing Stores	★
251	Freemarkets	Business/Online Services	★★★	264	Getty Images	Business Support	★
256	Genentech	Biotechnology	★★★	265	Gilead Sciences	Biotechnology	★
260	General Motors	Auto Makers	★★★	305	Internet Security Systems	Systems & Security	★
263	Genzyme Corp. General Division	Biotechnology	★★★	333	Lam Research	Semiconductor Equipment	★
268	GlobespanVirata	Semiconductors	★★★	334	Lattice Semiconductor	Semiconductors	★
271	Goodyear Tire & Rubber	Rubber Products	★★★	348	Lucent Technologies	Wireline Equipment	★
283	Healthsouth	Physicians	★★★	350	Macromedia	Development Tools	★
292	Hughes Electronic H	Cable TV	★★★	356	Martha Stewart Living Omnimedia A	Media Conglomerates	★
293	Human Genome Sciences	Biotechnology	★★★	357	Marvell Technology	Semiconductors	★
310	J.P. Morgan Chase & Co.	International Banks	★★★	393	Nortel Networks	Wireline Equipment	★
339	Level 3 Communications	Telecommunication Services	★★★	400	NVIDIA	Semiconductors	★
347	LSI Logic	Semiconductors	★★★	404	Omnicom Group	Advertising	★
375	Micron Technology	Semiconductors	★★★	420	Playboy Enterprises B	Publishing	★
385	Navistar International	Truck Makers	★★★	428	Qualcomm	Wireless Equipment	★
390	Nextel Communications	Wireless Service	★★★	445	SanDisk	Semiconductors	★
425	Protein Design Labs	Biotechnology	★★★	456	Sepracor	Drugs	★
426	Providian Financial	Finance	★★★	463	Solectron	Contract Manufacturers	★
431	Qwest Communications International	Telecommunication Services	★★★	470	Sprint PCS Group	Wireless Service	★
435	Reuters Group PLC ADR	Publishing	★★★	491	Teradyne	Semiconductor Equipment	★
455	Sears Roebuck	Department Stores	★★★	549	Yahoo!	Media Conglomerates	★
469	Sprint	Telecommunication Services	★★★				
504	Triquint Semiconductor	Semiconductors	★★★				
505	Tuesday Morning	Department Stores	★★★				
506	Tyco International	Electric Equipment	★★★				
510	United States Cellular	Wireless Service	★★★				
519	Vertex Pharmaceuticals	Biotechnology	★★★				
547	Xerox	Office Equipment	★★★				
60	Advanced Micro Devices	Semiconductors	★★				
63	AFC Enterprises	Restaurants	★★				
75	Allied Capital	Finance	★★				
130	Biogen	Biotechnology	★★				
222	Electronic Data Systems	Consultants	★★				
224	EMC	Computer Equipment	★★				
286	Hewlett-Packard	Computer Equipment	★★				
291	Household International	Finance	★★				
313	JDS Uniphase	Optical Equipment	★★				
327	Knight Trading Group	Securities	★★				

Highest Market Capitalization and Sales
Morningstar Stocks 500 Universe

Market Capitalization

Pg	Company	Industry	$Mil
376	Microsoft	Business Applications	276,411
258	General Electric	Electric Equipment	242,308
235	ExxonMobil	Oil & Gas	235,108
527	Wal-Mart Stores	Discount Stores	222,949
415	Pfizer	Drugs	188,377
175	Citigroup	International Banks	177,948
316	Johnson & Johnson	Drugs	159,452
141	BP PLC ADR	Oil & Gas	152,063
83	American International Group	Insurance (Property)	150,907
295	IBM	Computer Equipment	130,982
369	Merck	Drugs	127,121
525	Vodafone Group PLC ADR	Wireless Service	123,471
423	Procter & Gamble	Household & Personal Prod.	111,662
128	Berkshire Hathaway B	Insurance (General)	111,526
179	Coca-Cola	Beverage Mfg.	108,635
518	Verizon Communications	Telecommunication Services	106,011
397	Novartis AG ADR	Drugs	105,974
115	Bank of America	International Banks	104,505
300	Intel	Semiconductors	103,151
498	Total Fina Elf SA ADR	Oil & Gas	100,949
173	Cisco Systems	Data Networking	94,649
441	Royal Dutch Petroleum ADR	Oil & Gas	93,615
449	SBC Communications	Telecommunication Services	90,011
416	Philip Morris Companies	Tobacco	84,290
536	Wells Fargo	Super Regional Banks	79,608
414	PepsiCo	Beverage Mfg.	73,589
392	Nokia ADR	Wireless Equipment	73,432
520	Viacom B	Broadcast TV	71,391
223	Eli Lilly & Company	Drugs	71,334
166	ChevronTexaco	Oil & Gas	71,011
509	United Parcel Service B	Transportation - Misc	70,397
202	Dell Computer	Computer Equipment	68,968
458	Shell Transport & Trading ADR	Oil & Gas	63,236
226	ENI SpA ADR	Oil & Gas	62,812
55	Abbott Laboratories	Drugs	62,502
87	Amgen	Biotechnology	61,986
103	AstraZeneca PLC ADR	Drugs	61,408
405	Oracle	Business Applications	57,845
267	GlaxoSmithKline PLC ADR	Drugs	57,810
287	Home Depot	Home Supply	56,498
96	AOL Time Warner	Media Conglomerates	56,278
367	Medtronic	Medical Equipment	55,637
526	Wachovia	Super Regional Banks	50,032
546	Wyeth	Drugs	49,579
127	BellSouth	Telecommunication Services	48,170
54	3M Company	Chemicals	48,111
310	J.P. Morgan Chase & Co.	International Banks	47,901
82	American Express	Finance	46,839
329	Kraft Foods	Food Mfg.	45,853
143	Bristol-Myers Squibb	Drugs	44,843

Median Market Capitalization ($Mil)	**6,597**

Sales

Pg	Company	Industry	$Mil
527	Wal-Mart Stores	Discount Stores	241,163
235	ExxonMobil	Oil & Gas	196,513
260	General Motors	Auto Makers	184,057
141	BP PLC ADR	Oil & Gas	175,389
198	DaimlerChrysler AG	Auto Makers	136,142
441	Royal Dutch Petroleum ADR	Oil & Gas	135,759
458	Shell Transport & Trading ADR	Oil & Gas	135,211
258	General Electric	Electric Equipment	130,295
175	Citigroup	International Banks	106,096
498	Total Fina Elf SA ADR	Oil & Gas	93,914
166	ChevronTexaco	Oil & Gas	93,451
416	Philip Morris Companies	Tobacco	90,561
295	IBM	Computer Equipment	82,442
518	Verizon Communications	Telecommunication Services	67,422
83	American International Group	Insurance (Property)	66,823
464	Sony ADR	Audio/Video Equipment	60,413
287	Home Depot	Home Supply	58,522
137	Boeing	Aerospace & Defense	56,071
152	Cardinal Health	Medical Goods & Services	52,687
331	Kroger	Groceries	51,418
524	Vivendi ADR	Media Conglomerates	51,149
369	Merck	Drugs	50,430
286	Hewlett-Packard	Computer Equipment	49,416
104	AT&T	Telecommunication Services	48,821
188	ConocoPhillips	Oil & Gas	46,828
115	Bank of America	International Banks	46,628
86	AmerisourceBergen	Medical Goods & Services	45,235
226	ENI SpA ADR	Oil & Gas	44,449
449	SBC Communications	Telecommunication Services	43,824
487	Target	Discount Stores	43,138
310	J.P. Morgan Chase & Co.	International Banks	42,911
423	Procter & Gamble	Household & Personal Prod.	41,268
455	Sears Roebuck	Department Stores	41,156
96	AOL Time Warner	Media Conglomerates	41,024
128	Berkshire Hathaway B	Insurance (General)	39,133
192	Costco Wholesale	Discount Stores	38,763
67	Albertson's	Groceries	37,185
316	Johnson & Johnson	Drugs	35,807
506	Tyco International	Electric Equipment	35,644
444	Safeway	Groceries	34,757
415	Pfizer	Drugs	34,407
329	Kraft Foods	Food Mfg.	34,063
202	Dell Computer	Computer Equipment	33,730
373	Metropolitan Life Insurance	Insurance (Life)	33,057
379	Morgan Stanley	Securities	32,954
309	J.C. Penney	Department Stores	32,340
509	United Parcel Service B	Transportation - Misc	31,337
372	Merrill Lynch & Company	Securities	30,635
376	Microsoft	Business Applications	29,985
353	Marathon Oil	Oil & Gas	29,905

Median Sales ($Mil)	**4,813**

Highest Return on Equity and Return on Assets

Morningstar Stocks 500 Universe

Return on Equity (Trailing 12 Months)

Pg	Company	Industry	%
211	Dow Jones & Company	Media Conglomerates	327.62
181	Colgate-Palmolive	Household & Personal Prod.	241.60
505	Tuesday Morning	Department Stores	107.90
550	Yum Brands	Restaurants	107.88
298	IMS Health	Data Processing	102.22
551	Zimmer Holdings	Medical Equipment	79.89
361	Maytag	Appliance & Furn. Makers	78.98
448	Sara Lee	Food Mfg.	60.13
319	Kellogg	Food Mfg.	59.82
109	AutoZone	Auto Retail	59.56
239	Federated Investors B	Money Management	59.49
406	Oxford Health Plans	Managed Care	55.87
57	Accenture	Consultants	55.83
419	Pitney Bowes	Office Equipment	55.62
546	Wyeth	Drugs	54.91
416	Philip Morris Companies	Tobacco	53.87
93	Anheuser-Busch Companies	Alcoholic Drinks	50.05
461	SLM	Finance	44.62
415	Pfizer	Drugs	43.40
496	TJX Companies	Clothing Stores	42.53
202	Dell Computer	Computer Equipment	42.49
266	Gillette	Household & Personal Prod.	42.06
369	Merck	Drugs	40.61
275	H & R Block	Personal Services	40.50
267	GlaxoSmithKline PLC ADR	Drugs	40.49
368	Mellon Financial	Money Management	39.79
284	Heinz HJ	Food Mfg.	39.17
423	Procter & Gamble	Household & Personal Prod.	36.34
405	Oracle	Business Applications	35.86
216	Eaton Vance	Money Management	35.39
414	PepsiCo	Beverage Mfg.	33.35
331	Kroger	Groceries	32.67
439	Ross Stores	Clothing Stores	32.48
265	Gilead Sciences	Biotechnology	32.17
272	Graco	Machinery	32.00
484	Sysco	Food Wholesale	31.84
101	Aramark	Restaurants	31.45
223	Eli Lilly & Company	Drugs	30.83
103	AstraZeneca PLC ADR	Drugs	30.32
274	Guidant	Medical Equipment	29.85
242	First Data	Data Processing	29.83
178	Clorox	Household & Personal Prod.	29.80
250	Freddie Mac	Finance	28.90
301	International Flavors & Fragrances	Food Mfg.	28.87
410	Paychex	Data Processing	28.83
316	Johnson & Johnson	Drugs	28.61
226	ENI SpA ADR	Oil & Gas	28.42
512	UnitedHealth Group	Managed Care	27.98
432	RadioShack	Electronics Stores	27.92
179	Coca-Cola	Beverage Mfg.	27.90
	Average Return on Equity (%)		**10.89**

Return on Assets (Trailing 12 Months)

Pg	Company	Industry	%
378	Moody's	Business Support	43.81
239	Federated Investors B	Money Management	38.95
551	Zimmer Holdings	Medical Equipment	26.50
153	Caremark RX	Managed Care	22.19
167	Chico's FAS	Clothing Stores	21.80
272	Graco	Machinery	21.77
119	Barr Laboratories	Drugs	20.15
56	Abercrombie & Fitch A	Clothing Stores	20.00
165	Check Point Software Technologies	Business Applications	19.84
405	Oracle	Business Applications	19.75
265	Gilead Sciences	Biotechnology	19.20
248	Forest Laboratories	Drugs	19.17
545	Wm. Wrigley Jr.	Food Mfg.	19.03
274	Guidant	Medical Equipment	18.60
216	Eaton Vance	Money Management	18.54
415	Pfizer	Drugs	18.33
406	Oxford Health Plans	Managed Care	18.28
211	Dow Jones & Company	Media Conglomerates	18.28
181	Colgate-Palmolive	Household & Personal Prod.	17.61
156	CDW Computer Centers	Electronics Stores	17.09
495	Timberland	Shoes	16.93
58	Adobe Systems	Development Tools	16.80
131	Biomet	Medical Equipment	16.65
103	AstraZeneca PLC ADR	Drugs	16.50
316	Johnson & Johnson	Drugs	16.34
134	Blackrock	Money Management	16.18
120	Barra	Business Applications	16.14
381	Mylan Laboratories	Drugs	16.12
499	Total System Services	Data Processing	15.80
369	Merck	Drugs	15.04
243	First Health Group	Managed Care	14.90
277	Harley-Davidson	Recreation	14.67
496	TJX Companies	Clothing Stores	14.64
439	Ross Stores	Clothing Stores	14.35
505	Tuesday Morning	Department Stores	14.17
485	T Rowe Price Group	Money Management	14.03
446	Sanofi-Synthelabo ADR	Drugs	13.91
267	GlaxoSmithKline PLC ADR	Drugs	13.89
209	Dollar Tree Stores	Discount Stores	13.83
111	Avon Products	Household & Personal Prod.	13.72
126	Bed Bath & Beyond	Furniture Retail	13.69
261	Gentex	Auto Parts	13.64
472	St. Jude Medical	Medical Equipment	13.57
93	Anheuser-Busch Companies	Alcoholic Drinks	13.52
223	Eli Lilly & Company	Drugs	13.46
418	Pier 1 Imports	Furniture Retail	13.43
202	Dell Computer	Computer Equipment	13.42
546	Wyeth	Drugs	13.38
416	Philip Morris Companies	Tobacco	13.37
414	PepsiCo	Beverage Mfg.	13.34
	Average Return on Assets (%)		**3.56**

Highest Dividend Yield and Cash Return

Morningstar Stocks 500 Universe

Dividend Yield

Pg	Company	Industry	%
542	Williams Companies	Pipelines	**15.60**
220	El Paso	Pipelines	**12.50**
75	Allied Capital	Finance	**10.10**
97	Apartment Investment & Mgmt.	REITS	**8.80**
437	RJ Reynolds Tobacco Holdings	Tobacco	**8.80**
227	Equity Office Properties Trust	REITS	**8.00**
74	Alliance Capital Management	Money Management	**7.40**
102	Archstone-Smith Trust	REITS	**7.20**
157	Cedar Fair LP	Recreation	**7.00**
271	Goodyear Tire & Rubber	Rubber Products	**7.00**
228	Equity Residential	REITS	**7.00**
323	Kinder Morgan Energy Partners	Pipelines	**6.70**
460	Simon Property Group	REITS	**6.40**
416	Philip Morris Companies	Tobacco	**6.00**
143	Bristol-Myers Squibb	Drugs	**6.00**
79	AMB Property	REITS	**6.00**
61	Aegon NV ADR	Insurance (Life)	**5.90**
245	FleetBoston Financial	Super Regional Banks	**5.80**
310	J.P. Morgan Chase & Co.	International Banks	**5.70**
260	General Motors	Auto Makers	**5.40**
215	Eastman Kodak	Photography & Imaging	**5.10**
435	Reuters Group PLC ADR	Publishing	**5.10**
284	Heinz HJ	Food Mfg.	**4.90**
465	Southern	Electric Utilities	**4.80**
524	Vivendi ADR	Media Conglomerates	**4.70**
422	PNC Financial Services Group	Super Regional Banks	**4.60**
89	AmSouth Bancorporation	Regional Banks	**4.60**
442	RR Donnelley & Sons	Printing	**4.50**
210	Dow Chemical	Chemicals	**4.50**
183	Comerica	Regional Banks	**4.40**
382	National City	Super Regional Banks	**4.40**
353	Marathon Oil	Oil & Gas	**4.30**
195	Cummins Engine	Auto Parts	**4.30**
247	Ford Motor	Auto Makers	**4.30**
166	ChevronTexaco	Oil & Gas	**4.20**
518	Verizon Communications	Telecommunication Services	**4.00**
449	SBC Communications	Telecommunication Services	**3.90**
262	Genuine Parts	Auto Retail	**3.80**
190	Cooper Industries	Electric Equipment	**3.80**
455	Sears Roebuck	Department Stores	**3.80**
515	US Bancorp	Super Regional Banks	**3.70**
419	Pitney Bowes	Office Equipment	**3.60**
441	Royal Dutch Petroleum ADR	Oil & Gas	**3.60**
115	Bank of America	International Banks	**3.50**
291	Household International	Finance	**3.50**
469	Sprint	Telecommunication Services	**3.50**
402	Occidental Petroleum	Oil & Gas	**3.50**
203	Delphi	Auto Parts	**3.50**
141	BP PLC ADR	Oil & Gas	**3.50**
150	Campbell Soup	Food Mfg.	**3.40**
	Average Dividend Yield (%)		**0.79**

Cash Return (Free Cash Flow/Market Cap)

Pg	Company	Industry	%
135	Blockbuster	Rental & Repair Services	**56.25**
158	Celestica	Contract Manufacturers	**53.66**
463	Solectron	Contract Manufacturers	**47.21**
69	Alcatel SA ADR A	Wireline Equipment	**38.54**
497	Tommy Hilfiger	Apparel Makers	**38.13**
452	Scientific-Atlanta	Wireline Equipment	**36.53**
435	Reuters Group PLC ADR	Publishing	**30.10**
535	WellPoint Health Networks	Managed Care	**22.10**
459	Siebel Systems	Business Applications	**21.44**
136	BMC Software	Systems & Security	**17.81**
165	Check Point Software Technologies	Business Applications	**17.46**
186	Compuware	Systems & Security	**17.19**
406	Oxford Health Plans	Managed Care	**15.77**
271	Goodyear Tire & Rubber	Rubber Products	**15.21**
215	Eastman Kodak	Photography & Imaging	**14.92**
184	Computer Associates International	Systems & Security	**14.90**
282	Health Net	Physicians	**14.87**
286	Hewlett-Packard	Computer Equipment	**14.47**
490	Tenet Healthcare	Hospitals	**14.47**
437	RJ Reynolds Tobacco Holdings	Tobacco	**14.04**
432	RadioShack	Electronics Stores	**13.92**
246	Flextronics International	Contract Manufacturers	**13.62**
403	Office Depot	Specialty Retail	**13.33**
344	Liz Claiborne	Apparel Makers	**13.05**
146	Brunswick	Recreation	**12.82**
521	Vishay Intertechnology	Components	**12.55**
458	Shell Transport & Trading ADR	Oil & Gas	**12.51**
94	AnnTaylor Stores	Clothing Stores	**12.41**
84	American Power Conversion	Electric Equipment	**12.36**
506	Tyco International	Electric Equipment	**12.28**
311	Jabil Circuit	Contract Manufacturers	**12.21**
118	Barnes & Noble	Specialty Retail	**12.11**
279	Hasbro	Toys/Hobbies	**12.10**
359	Mattel	Toys/Hobbies	**11.99**
489	Tellabs	Wireline Equipment	**11.97**
377	Monsanto Company	Agrochemical	**11.89**
267	GlaxoSmithKline PLC ADR	Drugs	**11.74**
495	Timberland	Shoes	**11.65**
251	Freemarkets	Business/Online Services	**11.23**
101	Aramark	Restaurants	**11.16**
356	Martha Stewart Living Omnimedia A	Media Conglomerates	**11.09**
434	Reebok International	Shoes	**10.99**
544	Winn-Dixie Stores	Groceries	**10.60**
312	JD Edwards & Company	Business Applications	**10.57**
56	Abercrombie & Fitch A	Clothing Stores	**10.56**
407	Paccar	Truck Makers	**10.53**
309	J.C. Penney	Department Stores	**10.49**
469	Sprint	Telecommunication Services	**10.46**
534	Watson Pharmaceuticals	Drugs	**10.30**
342	Limited Brands	Clothing Stores	**10.22**
	Average Cash Return		**1.39**

Highest & Lowest Price Multiples

Morningstar Stocks 500 Universe

Price/Earnings Ratio (Trailing 12 Months)*

Pg	Company	Industry	Ratio
	Highest		
91	Analog Devices	Semiconductors	**99.46**
309	J.C. Penney	Department Stores	**88.50**
232	Expedia	Online Retail	**85.81**
162	Charles Schwab	Securities	**83.46**
428	Qualcomm	Wireless Equipment	**82.71**
73	Allergan	Drugs	**81.16**
98	Apple Computer	Computer Equipment	**79.61**
503	Tribune	Media Conglomerates	**78.38**
330	Krispy Kreme Doughnut	Restaurants	**75.04**
307	Intuit	Business Applications	**73.31**
221	Electronic Arts	Entertainment/Educ. Media	**70.10**
210	Dow Chemical	Chemicals	**63.19**
435	Reuters Group PLC ADR	Publishing	**62.09**
121	Bausch & Lomb	Medical Equipment	**61.02**
200	Danaher	Electric Equipment	**60.83**
388	Network Associates	Systems & Security	**59.59**
245	FleetBoston Financial	Super Regional Banks	**59.27**
202	Dell Computer	Computer Equipment	**58.13**
486	Taiwan Semiconductor Manufacturing	Semiconductors	**57.79**
367	Medtronic	Medical Equipment	**57.00**
531	Washington Post	Media Conglomerates	**56.64**
248	Forest Laboratories	Drugs	**53.97**
290	Hotels.com A	Online Retail	**53.56**
372	Merrill Lynch & Company	Securities	**53.45**
173	Cisco Systems	Data Networking	**52.40**
140	Boston Scientific	Medical Equipment	**51.85**
	Lowest		
85	Americredit	Finance	**2.00**
497	Tommy Hilfiger	Apparel Makers	**4.66**
540	White Mountains Insurance	Insurance (Property)	**5.18**
160	Centurytel	Telecommunication Services	**5.19**
516	USA Interactive	Media Conglomerates	**5.54**
220	El Paso	Pipelines	**5.66**
120	Barra	Business Applications	**5.77**
291	Household International	Finance	**7.21**
416	Philip Morris Companies	Tobacco	**7.60**
455	Sears Roebuck	Department Stores	**7.60**
424	Progressive	Insurance (Property)	**7.63**
81	American Axle & Mfg Holdings	Auto Parts	**7.78**
222	Electronic Data Systems	Consultants	**7.81**
332	Laboratory Corp of America	Diagnostics	**7.87**
250	Freddie Mac	Finance	**7.94**
172	Circuit City Stores	Electronics Stores	**8.07**
151	Capital One Financial	Finance	**8.08**
61	Aegon NV ADR	Insurance (Life)	**8.22**
283	Healthsouth	Physicians	**8.24**
336	Learning Tree International	Education	**8.30**
530	Washington Mutual	Savings & Loans	**8.70**
226	ENI SpA ADR	Oil & Gas	**8.89**
368	Mellon Financial	Money Management	**9.10**
294	Humana	Managed Care	**9.35**
125	Bear Stearns Companies	Securities	**9.60**
75	Allied Capital	Finance	**10.30**
	Average Price/Earnings Ratio		**33.11**

Price/Book Ratio

Pg	Company	Industry	Ratio
	Highest		
181	Colgate-Palmolive	Household & Personal Prod.	**60.61**
211	Dow Jones & Company	Media Conglomerates	**54.68**
412	Pepsi Bottling Group	Beverage Mfg.	**29.52**
298	IMS Health	Data Processing	**27.72**
505	Tuesday Morning	Department Stores	**19.42**
57	Accenture	Consultants	**17.94**
390	Nextel Communications	Wireless Service	**15.89**
202	Dell Computer	Computer Equipment	**15.43**
550	Yum Brands	Restaurants	**14.05**
319	Kellogg	Food Mfg.	**13.06**
265	Gilead Sciences	Biotechnology	**12.87**
266	Gillette	Household & Personal Prod.	**12.64**
448	Sara Lee	Food Mfg.	**12.05**
410	Paychex	Data Processing	**11.36**
93	Anheuser-Busch Companies	Alcoholic Drinks	**11.32**
248	Forest Laboratories	Drugs	**11.22**
167	Chico's FAS	Clothing Stores	**11.01**
109	AutoZone	Auto Retail	**10.97**
361	Maytag	Appliance & Furn. Makers	**10.67**
217	eBay	Online Retail	**10.64**
330	Krispy Kreme Doughnut	Restaurants	**10.55**
354	Markel	Insurance (Property)	**10.55**
267	GlaxoSmithKline PLC ADR	Drugs	**10.52**
73	Allergan	Drugs	**10.44**
415	Pfizer	Drugs	**10.21**
405	Oracle	Business Applications	**10.07**
	Lowest		
508	UAL	Air Transport	**0.06**
163	Charter Communications	Cable TV	**0.15**
137	Boeing	Aerospace & Defense	**0.20**
431	Qwest Communications International	Telecommunication Services	**0.23**
542	Williams Companies	Pipelines	**0.27**
522	Visteon	Auto Parts	**0.29**
220	El Paso	Pipelines	**0.36**
271	Goodyear Tire & Rubber	Rubber Products	**0.38**
189	Continental Airlines B	Air Transport	**0.39**
283	Healthsouth	Physicians	**0.42**
497	Tommy Hilfiger	Apparel Makers	**0.42**
104	AT&T	Telecommunication Services	**0.43**
158	Celestica	Contract Manufacturers	**0.46**
85	Americredit	Finance	**0.49**
207	Dillard's	Department Stores	**0.50**
524	Vivendi ADR	Media Conglomerates	**0.50**
521	Vishay Intertechnology	Components	**0.51**
204	Delta Air Lines	Air Transport	**0.52**
105	AT&T Wireless Services	Wireless Service	**0.54**
135	Blockbuster	Rental & Repair Services	**0.54**
437	RJ Reynolds Tobacco Holdings	Tobacco	**0.54**
88	AMR	Air Transport	**0.55**
191	Corning	Optical Equipment	**0.57**
463	Solectron	Contract Manufacturers	**0.58**
96	AOL Time Warner	Media Conglomerates	**0.60**
172	Circuit City Stores	Electronics Stores	**0.60**
	Average Price/Book Ratio		**3.74**

* Excludes companies with P/E ratios above 100.

Highest & Lowest Price Multiples

Morningstar Stocks 500 Universe

Price/Cash Flow Ratio (Trailing 12 Months)

Pg	Company	Industry	Ratio
	Highest		
265	Gilead Sciences	Biotechnology	154.69
546	Wyeth	Drugs	83.55
333	Lam Research	Semiconductor Equipment	62.84
98	Apple Computer	Computer Equipment	58.14
232	Expedia	Online Retail	55.91
330	Krispy Kreme Doughnut	Restaurants	54.67
412	Pepsi Bottling Group	Beverage Mfg.	51.58
217	eBay	Online Retail	50.97
78	Amazon.com	Online Retail	48.35
357	Marvell Technology	Semiconductors	43.13
248	Forest Laboratories	Drugs	42.76
131	Biomet	Medical Equipment	42.38
549	Yahoo!	Media Conglomerates	41.74
53	1-800 Flowers.com	Online Retail	40.68
191	Corning	Optical Equipment	40.40
229	Ericsson Telephone ADR B	Wireless Equipment	38.86
313	JDS Uniphase	Optical Equipment	38.75
492	Teva Pharmaceutical Industries ADR	Drugs	38.56
366	MedImmune	Biotechnology	38.09
256	Genentech	Biotechnology	35.90
328	Kohl's	Discount Stores	35.30
516	USA Interactive	Media Conglomerates	35.29
367	Medtronic	Medical Equipment	35.27
99	Applied Materials	Semiconductor Equipment	35.05
296	IDEC Pharmaceuticals	Biotechnology	34.76
410	Paychex	Data Processing	34.54
	Lowest		
163	Charter Communications	Cable TV	0.44
137	Boeing	Aerospace & Defense	0.78
260	General Motors	Auto Makers	0.80
247	Ford Motor	Auto Makers	0.89
522	Visteon	Auto Parts	1.13
271	Goodyear Tire & Rubber	Rubber Products	1.16
463	Solectron	Contract Manufacturers	1.30
135	Blockbuster	Rental & Repair Services	1.51
69	Alcatel SA ADR A	Wireline Equipment	1.59
104	AT&T	Telecommunication Services	1.66
158	Celestica	Contract Manufacturers	1.67
547	Xerox	Office Equipment	1.75
497	Tommy Hilfiger	Apparel Makers	1.78
172	Circuit City Stores	Electronics Stores	1.94
283	Healthsouth	Physicians	1.96
198	DaimlerChrysler AG	Auto Makers	2.16
207	Dillard's	Department Stores	2.18
431	Qwest Communications International	Telecommunication Services	2.43
118	Barnes & Noble	Specialty Retail	2.69
199	Dana	Auto Parts	2.72
482	SuperValu	Food Wholesale	2.82
435	Reuters Group PLC ADR	Publishing	3.22
470	Sprint PCS Group	Wireless Service	3.24
81	American Axle & Mfg Holdings	Auto Parts	3.37
507	Tyson Foods A	Food Mfg.	3.39
490	Tenet Healthcare	Hospitals	3.57
	Average Price/Cash Flow Ratio		**14.49**

Price/Sales Ratio (Trailing 12 Months)

Pg	Company	Industry	Ratio
	Highest		
293	Human Genome Sciences	Biotechnology	318.05
217	eBay	Online Retail	19.03
265	Gilead Sciences	Biotechnology	16.99
343	Linear Technology	Semiconductors	16.54
296	IDEC Pharmaceuticals	Biotechnology	15.73
74	Alliance Capital Management	Money Management	12.85
549	Yahoo!	Media Conglomerates	11.51
360	Maxim Integrated Products	Semiconductors	11.44
248	Forest Laboratories	Drugs	11.39
341	Liberty Media	Cable TV	11.14
410	Paychex	Data Processing	10.99
87	Amgen	Biotechnology	10.98
114	Ballard Power Systems	Electric Equipment	10.63
376	Microsoft	Business Applications	10.12
425	Protein Design Labs	Biotechnology	10.11
428	Qualcomm	Wireless Equipment	9.79
366	MedImmune	Biotechnology	9.03
367	Medtronic	Medical Equipment	8.75
256	Genentech	Biotechnology	8.52
232	Expedia	Online Retail	8.46
446	Sanofi-Synthelabo ADR	Drugs	7.69
307	Intuit	Business Applications	7.57
77	Altera	Semiconductors	7.55
165	Check Point Software Technologies	Business Applications	7.53
80	Ambac Financial Group	Insurance (General)	7.52
357	Marvell Technology	Semiconductors	7.47
	Lowest		
508	UAL	Air Transport	0.01
137	Boeing	Aerospace & Defense	0.04
522	Visteon	Auto Parts	0.05
189	Continental Airlines B	Air Transport	0.06
163	Charter Communications	Cable TV	0.07
396	Northwest Airlines	Air Transport	0.07
88	AMR	Air Transport	0.08
260	General Motors	Auto Makers	0.08
271	Goodyear Tire & Rubber	Rubber Products	0.08
408	PacifiCare Health Systems	Managed Care	0.09
247	Ford Motor	Auto Makers	0.10
482	SuperValu	Food Wholesale	0.11
204	Delta Air Lines	Air Transport	0.12
86	AmerisourceBergen	Medical Goods & Services	0.13
294	Humana	Managed Care	0.15
542	Williams Companies	Pipelines	0.15
172	Circuit City Stores	Electronics Stores	0.16
203	Delphi	Auto Parts	0.16
207	Dillard's	Department Stores	0.16
335	Lear	Auto Parts	0.16
59	Advance PCS	Managed Care	0.17
199	Dana	Auto Parts	0.17
507	Tyson Foods A	Food Mfg.	0.17
544	Winn-Dixie Stores	Groceries	0.17
195	Cummins Engine	Auto Parts	0.18
500	Toys R Us	Specialty Retail	0.18
	Average Price/Sales Ratio		**3.04**

Companies with Wide Economic Moat
Morningstar Stocks 500 Universe

Pg	Company	Industry	Rating
83	American International Group	Insurance (Property)	★★★★★
103	AstraZeneca PLC ADR	Drugs	★★★★★
107	Automatic Data Processing	Data Processing	★★★★★
134	Blackrock	Money Management	★★★★★
143	Bristol-Myers Squibb	Drugs	★★★★★
151	Capital One Financial	Finance	★★★★★
216	Eaton Vance	Money Management	★★★★★
257	General Dynamics	Aerospace & Defense	★★★★★
287	Home Depot	Home Supply	★★★★★
296	IDEC Pharmaceuticals	Biotechnology	★★★★★
298	IMS Health	Data Processing	★★★★★
364	McDonald's	Restaurants	★★★★★
378	Moody's	Business Support	★★★★★
394	Northern Trust	Money Management	★★★★★
397	Novartis AG ADR	Drugs	★★★★★
410	Paychex	Data Processing	★★★★★
476	State Street	Money Management	★★★★★
72	Alcon	Drugs	★★★★
74	Alliance Capital Management	Money Management	★★★★
106	Autodesk	Business Applications	★★★★
116	Bank of New York	Money Management	★★★★
128	Berkshire Hathaway B	Insurance (General)	★★★★
182	Comcast A	Cable TV	★★★★
242	First Data	Data Processing	★★★★
267	GlaxoSmithKline PLC ADR	Drugs	★★★★
275	H & R Block	Personal Services	★★★★
322	Kinder Morgan	Pipelines	★★★★
323	Kinder Morgan Energy Partners	Pipelines	★★★★
365	McGraw-Hill Companies	Publishing	★★★★
414	PepsiCo	Beverage Mfg.	★★★★
415	Pfizer	Drugs	★★★★
416	Philip Morris Companies	Tobacco	★★★★
424	Progressive	Insurance (Property)	★★★★
511	United Technologies	Aerospace & Defense	★★★★
512	UnitedHealth Group	Managed Care	★★★★
54	3M Company	Chemicals	★★★
55	Abbott Laboratories	Drugs	★★★
58	Adobe Systems	Development Tools	★★★
65	AFLAC	Insurance (Life)	★★★
82	American Express	Finance	★★★
87	Amgen	Biotechnology	★★★
93	Anheuser-Busch Companies	Alcoholic Drinks	★★★
96	AOL Time Warner	Media Conglomerates	★★★
99	Applied Materials	Semiconductor Equipment	★★★
111	Avon Products	Household & Personal Prod.	★★★
131	Biomet	Medical Equipment	★★★
157	Cedar Fair LP	Recreation	★★★
175	Citigroup	International Banks	★★★
179	Coca-Cola	Beverage Mfg.	★★★
181	Colgate-Palmolive	Household & Personal Prod.	★★★
202	Dell Computer	Computer Equipment	★★★
211	Dow Jones & Company	Media Conglomerates	★★★
223	Eli Lilly & Company	Drugs	★★★
233	Expeditors International of WA	Transportation - Misc	★★★
241	Fifth Third Bancorp	Super Regional Banks	★★★

Pg	Company	Industry	Rating
244	Fiserv	Data Processing	★★★
256	Genentech	Biotechnology	★★★
261	Gentex	Auto Parts	★★★
266	Gillette	Household & Personal Prod.	★★★
274	Guidant	Medical Equipment	★★★
277	Harley-Davidson	Recreation	★★★
295	IBM	Computer Equipment	★★★
300	Intel	Semiconductors	★★★
304	International Speedway A	Recreation	★★★
316	Johnson & Johnson	Drugs	★★★
343	Linear Technology	Semiconductors	★★★
355	Marsh & McLennan Companies	Insurance (General)	★★★
360	Maxim Integrated Products	Semiconductors	★★★
367	Medtronic	Medical Equipment	★★★
369	Merck	Drugs	★★★
376	Microsoft	Business Applications	★★★
419	Pitney Bowes	Office Equipment	★★★
423	Procter & Gamble	Household & Personal Prod.	★★★
461	SLM	Finance	★★★
465	Southern	Electric Utilities	★★★
478	Stryker	Medical Equipment	★★★
499	Total System Services	Data Processing	★★★
509	United Parcel Service B	Transportation - Misc	★★★
527	Wal-Mart Stores	Discount Stores	★★★
528	Walgreen	Specialty Retail	★★★
536	Wells Fargo	Super Regional Banks	★★★
140	Boston Scientific	Medical Equipment	★★
171	Cintas	Business Support	★★
285	Hershey Foods	Food Mfg.	★★
307	Intuit	Business Applications	★★
545	Wm. Wrigley Jr.	Food Mfg.	★★
217	eBay	Online Retail	★
264	Getty Images	Business Support	★
428	Qualcomm	Wireless Equipment	★

Companies with No Economic Moat

Morningstar Stocks 500 Universe

Pg	Company	Industry	Rating	Pg	Company	Industry	Rating
480	Sun Microsystems	Computer Equipment	★★★★	168	Chiron	Biotechnology	★★
482	SuperValu	Food Wholesale	★★★★	210	Dow Chemical	Chemicals	★★
66	AG Edwards	Securities	★★★	213	DuPont De Nemours E.I.	Chemicals	★★
67	Albertson's	Groceries	★★★	236	Family Dollar Stores	Discount Stores	★★
86	AmerisourceBergen	Medical Goods & Services	★★★	301	International Flavors & Fragrances	Food Mfg.	★★
98	Apple Computer	Computer Equipment	★★★	303	International Paper	Paper	★★
100	Applied Micro Circuits	Semiconductors	★★★	309	J.C. Penney	Department Stores	★★
105	AT&T Wireless Services	Wireless Service	★★★	311	Jabil Circuit	Contract Manufacturers	★★
132	BJ's Wholesale Club	Discount Stores	★★★	318	Jones Apparel Group	Apparel Makers	★★
142	Brinker International	Restaurants	★★★	327	Knight Trading Group	Securities	★★
148	Cadbury Schweppes PLC ADR	Food Mfg.	★★★	351	Mandalay Resort Group	Gambling/Hotel Casinos	★★
158	Celestica	Contract Manufacturers	★★★	358	Masco	Building Materials	★★
159	Cendant	Business Support	★★★	366	MedImmune	Biotechnology	★★
169	Chubb	Insurance (Property)	★★★	373	Metropolitan Life Insurance	Insurance (Life)	★★
170	Cigna	Managed Care	★★★	380	Motorola	Wireless Equipment	★★
172	Circuit City Stores	Electronics Stores	★★★	387	Neiman-Marcus Group A	Department Stores	★★
190	Cooper Industries	Electric Equipment	★★★	388	Network Associates	Systems & Security	★★
198	DaimlerChrysler AG	Auto Makers	★★★	401	Oakley	Recreation	★★
203	Delphi	Auto Parts	★★★	417	Philips Electronics NV ADR	Audio/Video Equipment	★★
205	Deutsche Bank AG	International Banks	★★★	418	Pier 1 Imports	Furniture Retail	★★
207	Dillard's	Department Stores	★★★	421	PMC-Sierra	Semiconductors	★★
208	Dollar General	Discount Stores	★★★	427	Prudential Financial	Insurance (Life)	★★
209	Dollar Tree Stores	Discount Stores	★★★	430	Quiksilver	Apparel Makers	★★
246	Flextronics International	Contract Manufacturers	★★★	436	RF Micro Devices	Semiconductors	★★
247	Ford Motor	Auto Makers	★★★	439	Ross Stores	Clothing Stores	★★
260	General Motors	Auto Makers	★★★	452	Scientific-Atlanta	Wireline Equipment	★★
268	GlobespanVirata	Semiconductors	★★★	462	Smithfield Foods	Food Mfg.	★★
271	Goodyear Tire & Rubber	Rubber Products	★★★	464	Sony ADR	Audio/Video Equipment	★★
292	Hughes Electronic H	Cable TV	★★★	474	Staples	Specialty Retail	★★
293	Human Genome Sciences	Biotechnology	★★★	517	VeriSign	Systems & Security	★★
299	Ingersoll-Rand A	Machinery	★★★	538	Weyerhaeuser	Forestry/Wood	★★
331	Kroger	Groceries	★★★	64	Affiliated Computer Services	Business Support	★
338	Lehman Brothers Holdings	Securities	★★★	121	Bausch & Lomb	Medical Equipment	★
339	Level 3 Communications	Telecommunication Services	★★★	124	BEA Systems	Development Tools	★
342	Limited Brands	Clothing Stores	★★★	126	Bed Bath & Beyond	Furniture Retail	★
347	LSI Logic	Semiconductors	★★★	136	BMC Software	Systems & Security	★
375	Micron Technology	Semiconductors	★★★	144	Broadcom	Semiconductors	★
377	Monsanto Company	Agrochemical	★★★	149	Callaway Golf	Recreation	★
382	National City	Super Regional Banks	★★★	162	Charles Schwab	Securities	★
384	National Semiconductor	Semiconductors	★★★	184	Computer Associates International	Systems & Security	★
385	Navistar International	Truck Makers	★★★	191	Corning	Optical Equipment	★
403	Office Depot	Specialty Retail	★★★	193	Countrywide Financial	Savings & Loans	★
406	Oxford Health Plans	Managed Care	★★★	214	E*Trade Group	Securities	★
425	Protein Design Labs	Biotechnology	★★★	215	Eastman Kodak	Photography & Imaging	★
426	Providian Financial	Finance	★★★	229	Ericsson Telephone ADR B	Wireless Equipment	★
431	Qwest Communications International	Telecommunication Services	★★★	232	Expedia	Online Retail	★
435	Reuters Group PLC ADR	Publishing	★★★	254	Gap	Clothing Stores	★
444	Safeway	Groceries	★★★	290	Hotels.com A	Online Retail	★
497	Tommy Hilfiger	Apparel Makers	★★★	305	Internet Security Systems	Systems & Security	★
500	Toys R Us	Specialty Retail	★★★	312	JD Edwards & Company	Business Applications	★
502	Travelers Property Casualty	Insurance (Property)	★★★	333	Lam Research	Semiconductor Equipment	★
504	Triquint Semiconductor	Semiconductors	★★★	334	Lattice Semiconductor	Semiconductors	★
506	Tyco International	Electric Equipment	★★★	344	Liz Claiborne	Apparel Makers	★
507	Tyson Foods A	Food Mfg.	★★★	371	Mercury Interactive	Development Tools	★
510	United States Cellular	Wireless Service	★★★	393	Nortel Networks	Wireline Equipment	★
521	Vishay Intertechnology	Components	★★★	400	NVIDIA	Semiconductors	★
544	Winn-Dixie Stores	Groceries	★★★	420	Playboy Enterprises B	Publishing	★
547	Xerox	Office Equipment	★★★	454	Sealed Air	Packaging	★
60	Advanced Micro Devices	Semiconductors	★★	470	Sprint PCS Group	Wireless Service	★
62	Aetna	Insurance (Life)	★★	514	Urban Outfitters	Clothing Stores	★
63	AFC Enterprises	Restaurants	★★	516	USA Interactive	Media Conglomerates	★
125	Bear Stearns Companies	Securities	★★	525	Vodafone Group PLC ADR	Wireless Service	★
133	Black & Decker	Electric Equipment	★★				
164	Checkfree	Systems & Security	★★				
167	Chico's FAS	Clothing Stores	★★				

Report Pages

This section offers a full-page
report on each of the 500 stocks.

1-800 Flowers.com FLWS

	Rating	Risk	Moat Size	Fair Value	Last Close	Yield %
	★★★★	High	Narrow	$12.00	$6.25	0.0

Company Profile

1-800-Flowers.com sells flowers, food, and other home and garden products over the telephone and Internet. The company sells more than 1,500 varieties of fresh-cut and seasonal flowers, plants, and floral arrangements. It also sells more than 6,000 stock-keeping units of gifts, gourmet foods, and home and garden products like garden accessories and home and lifestyle furnishings. Flowers and plants account for about 72% of net revenue. 1-800-Flowers.com has online partnerships with America Online, Excite, and Microsoft Network.

Management

Jim McCann has been chairman and CEO of the company since its founding in 1976 as a chain of retail flower shops in the New York area. His younger brother Christopher is president.

Strategy

1-800-Flowers.com sells flowers and gifts through multiple channels, primarily the telephone and the Internet (each of which accounts for more than 40% of revenue). It uses partnerships with such Web sites as AOL and Yahoo to drive online sales, and a network of florists to deliver flowers. It has been trying to sell more gift items, since they have higher margins than flowers.

1600 Stewart Avenue
Westbury, NY 11590
www.1800flowers.com

Morningstar Grades

Growth [B]	1999	2000	2001	2002
Revenue %	32.8	29.6	16.5	12.4
Earnings/Share %	NMF	NMF	NMF	NMF
Book Value/Share %	—	—	NMF	-10.1
Dividends/Share %	NMF	NMF	NMF	NMF

The company has grown at an annual rate of better than 20% over the past seven years, but that growth slowed to 12% in fiscal 2002. We expect growth to reaccelerate to 15%-18% over the next few years.

Profitability [D]	2000	2001	2002	TTM
Return on Assets %	-29.8	-21.2	-0.7	0.1
Oper Cash Flow $Mil	-34	-13	12	5
- Cap Spending $Mil	22	16	12	12
= Free Cash Flow $Mil	-56	-28	0	-7

The company made a net profit for three quarters before losing money in the September 2002 period because of a lack of holidays. Because it's not a capital-intensive business, it should be able to expand margins as sales grow.

Financial Health [D+]	2000	2001	2002	09-02
Long-term Debt $Mil	9	13	12	11
Total Equity $Mil	159	118	124	117
Debt/Equity Ratio	0.1	0.1	0.1	0.1

Its cash position fell by $15 million in the fiscal first quarter, and stood at $25.1 million as of September 30. However, its balance sheet is healthy, with a debt/equity ratio of 0.1.

Industry	Investment Style	Stock Type	Sector
Online Retail	Small Growth	Classic Growth	Consumer Services

Competition	Market Cap $Mil	Debt/ Equity	12 Mo Trailing Sales $Mil	Price/Cash Flow	Return On Assets%	Total Return% 1 Yr	3 Yr
1-800 Flowers.com	410	0.1	507	77.9	0.1	-59.9	-17.6
EFTD	—	—	—	—	—	—	—
GIFTD	—	—	—	—	—	—	—

Price Volatility

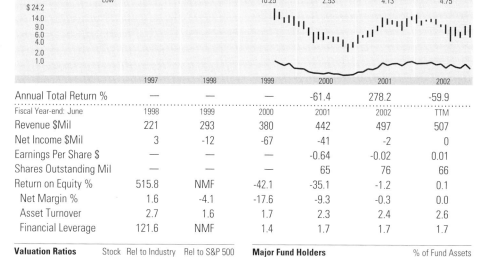

Monthly Price High/Low — Relative Strength to S&P 500

	1997	1998	1999	2000	2001	2002
Annual $Price High			23.19	12.88	16.50	17.86
Low			10.25	2.53	4.13	4.75
Annual Total Return %	—	—	—	-61.4	278.2	-59.9

Fiscal Year-end: June	1998	1999	2000	2001	2002	TTM
Revenue $Mil	221	293	380	442	497	507
Net Income $Mil	3	-12	-67	-41	-2	0
Earnings Per Share $	—	—	—	-0.64	-0.02	0.01
Shares Outstanding Mil	—	—	—	65	76	66
Return on Equity %	515.8	NMF	-42.1	-35.1	-1.2	0.1
Net Margin %	1.6	-4.1	-17.6	-9.3	-0.3	0.0
Asset Turnover	2.7	1.6	1.7	2.3	2.4	2.6
Financial Leverage	121.6	NMF	1.4	1.7	1.7	1.7

Valuation Ratios	Stock	Rel to Industry	Rel to S&P 500
Price/Earnings	625.0	6.1	26.6
Price/Book	3.5	0.3	1.1
Price/Sales	0.8	0.1	0.4
Price/Cash Flow	77.9	1.6	5.9

Major Fund Holders	% of Fund Assets
IDEX Munder Net50 A	1.88
Munder NetNet A	1.69
Oppenheimer Discovery A	1.59
JP Morgan U.S. Small Company Opp Sel	1.19

Morningstar's Take By David Kathman, 12-01-2002 Stock Price as of Analysis: $10.33

With consistent profitability just around the corner, 1-800-Flowers.com is one of the few e-commerce stocks worth serious attention from investors.

The company is in the middle of a major, successful transformation. Four years ago it was a profitable phone-based business; since then it has gradually moved its business to the Internet, losing a lot of money in the process. However, this risky move has paid off: 1-800-Flowers.com has started making money again, though its profits are still erratic because of the seasonal nature of the business. It made a net profit for three straight quarters before losing money in the September quarter, which lacks a major flower-giving holiday like Valentine's Day, Mother's Day, or Christmas. However, its quarterly loss declined from a year earlier, and it's still robustly profitable for the year as a whole.

We think profits will soon become permanent because 1-800-Flowers.com's business model is especially suited to e-commerce. The company farms out most of the orders it receives to independent florists in its network who do the actual delivery, so the firm hasn't had to spend too much money on expensive delivery infrastructure. Plus, flowers are almost always gifts, and are thus much less subject to returns than many other things sold online, like

clothing or electronics. Over the past two years, operating expenses as a percentage of revenue have shrunk from 53% to 37%. We think that trend should continue, pushing operating margins into the double digits by 2005.

Over the past few years, 1-800-Flowers.com has been beefing up its offerings of nonfloral gifts by acquiring such companies as Plow & Hearth, Greatfood.com, and The Popcorn Factory. Most of the items sold by these companies are held as inventory and shipped directly to customers, thus potentially diluting the benefits of 1-800-Flowers.com's business model by requiring more capital-intensive warehouses. On the other hand, these gift items have higher profit margins than flowers and are growing faster; in fact, nonfloral gifts have accounted for most of the company's growth in the past year, and are a major factor in the expanding margins.

We think 1-800-Flowers.com is in a good position to succeed long-term--its business model makes a lot of sense and has been executed very well. There are certainly risks involved, but if the price approached $6 (a 50% discount to our fair value estimate of $12), we think the stock would look quite appealing for investors who can stomach the volatility.

3M Company MMM

	Rating	Risk	Moat Size	Fair Value	Last Close	Yield %
	★★★	Low	Wide	$115.00	$123.30	2.0

Company Profile

Minnesota Mining and Manufacturing (3M) manufactures adhesive, coating, electronic, and health-care products. Its industrial and consumer division develops adhesive tapes, sealants, and lubricants; sandpaper and other abrasives; and automotive gaskets and moldings. The life sciences division manufactures personal-safety equipment, pharmaceuticals, medical equipment, and transdermal drug-delivery systems. 3M markets its products in the United States and abroad. Foreign sales account for about 52% of the company's total sales.

Management

James McNerney, a former General Electric executive and a finalist to replace Jack Welch, became CEO in December 2000. CFO Pat Campbell was director of finance for General Motors' European division before joining 3M.

Strategy

3M has made internal growth a priority, but is also looking for acquisitions to complement its existing operations. In anticipation, the firm has shuffled management and has been looking most likely in the beaten-down electronics and telecom sectors. 3M is well positioned for such activity. The firm's ultimate goal is to reduce volatility by diversifying its operations and improving efficiency.

3M Center
St. Paul, MN 55144
www.3m.com

Morningstar Grades

Growth [C+]	1998	1999	2000	2001
Revenue %	0.2	4.3	6.2	-3.9
Earnings/Share %	-43.1	50.7	2.5	-19.6
Book Value/Share %	2.9	6.4	5.3	-6.6
Dividends/Share %	3.8	1.8	3.6	3.4

Sales growth remains 3M's biggest challenge. The company's increased focus on technology-based products coincided with the collapse of the technology and telecom markets. New products, acquisitions, and an economic rebound should fuel growth.

Profitability [A+]	1999	2000	2001	TTM
Return on Assets %	12.7	12.3	9.8	11.7
Oper Cash Flow $Mil	3,081	2,326	3,078	2,811
- Cap Spending $Mil	1,050	1,115	980	744
= Free Cash Flow $Mil	2,031	1,211	2,098	2,067

While sales have remained flat with 2001, operating income has surged 12.5%. Cost-cutting initiatives and enhanced capital discipline have improved margins and cash flows. Returns on assets and equity have been exceptional.

Financial Health [A+]	1999	2000	2001	09-02
Long-term Debt $Mil	1,480	971	1,520	1,678
Total Equity $Mil	6,289	6,531	6,086	6,643
Debt/Equity Ratio	0.2	0.1	0.3	0.3

3M boasts a stellar balance sheet. Debt/capital is only 31% and cash flows are superb. Capital discipline should help maintain strong free cash flows: 2002 spending is projected to be around $800 million, down 45% from its 1998 peak of $1.45 billion.

Industry	Investment Style	Stock Type	Sector
Chemicals	Large Core	Cyclical	Industrial Mats

Competition	Market Cap $Mil	Debt/ Equity	12 Mo Trailing Sales $Mil	Price/Cash Flow	Return On Assets%	Total Return% 1 Yr	3 Yr
3M Company	48,111	0.3	16,075	17.1	11.7	6.4	13.3
Johnson & Johnson	159,452	0.1	35,120	18.0	16.3	-7.9	8.0
Avery Dennison	6,707	—	4,014	—	—		

Price Volatility

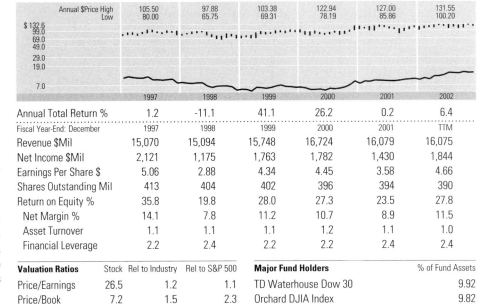

	Monthly Price High/Low		Relative Strength to S&P 500			
Annual $Price High Low	105.50 80.00	97.88 65.75	103.38 69.31	122.94 78.19	127.00 85.86	131.55 100.20

	1997	1998	1999	2000	2001	2002
Annual Total Return %	1.2	-11.1	41.1	26.2	0.2	6.4
Fiscal Year-End: December	1997	1998	1999	2000	2001	TTM
Revenue $Mil	15,070	15,094	15,748	16,724	16,079	16,075
Net Income $Mil	2,121	1,175	1,763	1,782	1,430	1,844
Earnings Per Share $	5.06	2.88	4.34	4.45	3.58	4.66
Shares Outstanding Mil	413	404	402	396	394	390
Return on Equity %	35.8	19.8	28.0	27.3	23.5	27.8
Net Margin %	14.1	7.8	11.2	10.7	8.9	11.5
Asset Turnover	1.1	1.1	1.1	1.2	1.1	1.0
Financial Leverage	2.2	2.4	2.2	2.2	2.4	2.4

Valuation Ratios	Stock	Rel to Industry	Rel to S&P 500
Price/Earnings	26.5	1.2	1.1
Price/Book	7.2	1.5	2.3
Price/Sales	3.0	1.6	1.5
Price/Cash Flow	17.1	1.0	1.3

Major Fund Holders	% of Fund Assets
TD Waterhouse Dow 30	9.92
Orchard DJIA Index	9.82
Fidelity Select Chemicals	7.15
Strong Dow 30 Value	5.47

Morningstar's Take By Sanjay Ayer, 12-18-2002 Stock Price as of Analysis: $120.86

3M is evolving into a higher-growth company, but we believe the market has already priced the firm's improved prospects into the stock. We love this wide-moat firm and would gladly pick up some shares if they dropped 10% below our fair value estimate.

3M is a diversified powerhouse. Its scale is an enormous advantage: With several of its cyclical businesses struggling in the economic downturn, other segments have picked up the slack. For instance, 3M recently placed a big bet on technology-based products, just in time to watch the technology and telecommunication markets slump. However, strong performance in its health-care business (3M's largest and fastest-growing segment) has more than offset the weakness in telecom.

3M stock did not participate in the bull market of the late 1990s, when investors bailed out of slow-growth industrials in favor of high-flying tech stocks. But since James McNerney took the helm in early 2001, 3M's growth prospects--and stock price--have improved considerably. McNerney, who is a disciple of Jack Welch, wasted no time in attacking 3M's cost structure. Spending cuts, technology upgrades, capital discipline, and the implementation of the Six Sigma efficiency program should result in cost savings and added shareholder value for years to come.

While we applaud these cost-cutting efforts, we are anxious to see whether management can revitalize the firm's lackluster sales growth. One way 3M is trying to juice its top line is by emphasizing faster-growing products tied to hot industries, rather than the industrial products for which it's best known. Perhaps the most interesting development is management's willingness to embrace acquisitions as a source of growth; previous regimes often relied exclusively on internal growth. 3M's recent acquisition of Corning Lens Precision, the largest worldwide manufacturer of lens systems for rear-projection televisions, exemplifies the firm's strategic shift. If 3M can combine sound acquisitions with its reputation for product innovation, it might have the perfect recipe for creating and sustaining strong top-line growth.

As McNerney continues to unlock value for shareholders, 3M's stock price has surged, easily trumping the market over the past two years. Our fair value of $115 indicates the stock is currently overpriced. We'll keep 3M on our radar screen and wait patiently for the right time to invest.

MORNINGSTAR® Stocks 500

Abbott Laboratories ABT

	Rating	Risk	Moat Size	Fair Value	Last Close	Yield %
	★★★	Low	Wide	$38.00	$40.00	2.3

Industry	Investment Style	Stock Type	Sector
Drugs	▦ Large Core	↗ Classic Growth	◆ Healthcare

Company Profile

Abbott Laboratories manufactures and markets pharmaceuticals, hospital products, medical devices, and consumer health-care products. The company produces pharmaceuticals that treat conditions like respiratory infections, ulcers, epilepsy, HIV, and hypertension. It also makes diagnostic-imaging products and blood-screening tests. The company's consumer products include infant formulas sold under the Similac and Isomil names; adult nutritional liquids sold under the Ensure label; and personal-care products like Selsun Blue shampoo. Abbott has been around since 1888.

Management

CEO Miles White came up through the ranks after joining the company in 1984 at age 28. White's management style is supposedly aggressive, but the lack of a resolution regarding the Lake County diagnostic facility has us thinking the opposite.

Strategy

Abbott has reorganized its pharmaceutical business in an effort to get sales growth back to double digits. The firm is also trying to promote synergies between its drug division and diagnostic products. The purchase of Knoll Pharmaceutical built up Abbott's franchise in metabolic diseases and gave it a potential blockbuster drug, D2E7 for rheumatoid arthritis.

100 Abbott Park Road   www.abbott.com
Abbott Park, IL 60064-6400

Morningstar Grades

Growth [C+]	1998	1999	2000	2001
Revenue %	5.2	5.3	4.3	18.5
Earnings/Share %	13.6	4.7	13.4	-44.4
Book Value/Share %	15.6	29.0	14.9	5.6
Dividends/Share %	11.4	12.8	12.1	10.8

Abbott's internal top-line growth hasn't been anything to write home about lately, but it's been steady over the years. Pharmaceutical sales in 2002 were up 16.5% through September 30, thanks to the Knoll acquisition.

Profitability [A]	1999	2000	2001	TTM
Return on Assets %	16.9	18.2	6.7	11.8
Oper Cash Flow $Mil	3,035	3,100	3,567	3,871
- Cap Spending $Mil	987	1,036	1,164	1,272
= Free Cash Flow $Mil	2,048	2,064	2,403	2,599

Even though pharmaceutical products account for only 40% of sales, Abbott's net margins have kept pace with those of pure-play pharma companies. Margins have decreased from several years ago, but seem to be on the mend.

Financial Health [A-]	1999	2000	2001	09-02
Long-term Debt $Mil	1,337	1,076	4,335	4,456
Total Equity $Mil	7,428	8,571	9,059	10,547
Debt/Equity Ratio	0.2	0.1	0.5	0.4

Abbott doesn't carry a lot of cash, unlike many of the pure-play pharmaceutical companies. Its $6.9 billion debt load is manageable, though, especially when viewed alongside the company's solid cash flows.

Competition

	Market Cap $Mil	Debt/ Equity	12 Mo Trailing Sales $Mil	Price/Cash Flow	Return On Assets%	Total Return% 1 Yr	3 Yr
Abbott Laboratories	62,502	0.4	17,290	16.1	11.8	-26.7	7.6
Pfizer	188,377	0.2	34,407	21.1	18.3	-22.2	1.0
Johnson & Johnson	159,452	0.1	35,120	18.0	16.3	-7.9	8.0

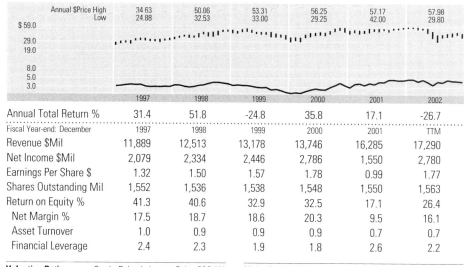

Price Volatility — Monthly Price High/Low — Relative Strength to S&P 500

Annual $Price High / Low	34.63 / 24.88	50.06 / 32.53	53.31 / 33.00	56.25 / 29.25	57.17 / 42.00	57.98 / 29.80
	1997	1998	1999	2000	2001	2002

Annual Total Return %	31.4	51.8	-24.8	35.8	17.1	-26.7

Fiscal Year-end: December	1997	1998	1999	2000	2001	TTM
Revenue $Mil	11,889	12,513	13,178	13,746	16,285	17,290
Net Income $Mil	2,079	2,334	2,446	2,786	1,550	2,780
Earnings Per Share $	1.32	1.50	1.57	1.78	0.99	1.77
Shares Outstanding Mil	1,552	1,536	1,538	1,548	1,550	1,563
Return on Equity %	41.3	40.6	32.9	32.5	17.1	26.4
Net Margin %	17.5	18.7	18.6	20.3	9.5	16.1
Asset Turnover	1.0	0.9	0.9	0.9	0.7	0.7
Financial Leverage	2.4	2.3	1.9	1.8	2.6	2.2

Valuation Ratios	Stock	Rel to Industry	Rel to S&P 500
Price/Earnings	22.6	1.0	1.0
Price/Book	5.9	0.8	1.9
Price/Sales	3.6	0.9	1.8
Price/Cash Flow	16.1	0.8	1.2

Major Fund Holders	% of Fund Assets
Hartford Global Health A	7.64
Fidelity Advisor Health Care A	6.85
Smith Barney Health Sciences B	6.74
Fidelity Select Medical Equip/Systems	6.42

Morningstar's Take By Todd N. Lebor, 12-03-2002 Stock Price as of Analysis: $42.18

Abbott is fading into mediocrity. Despite the company's product diversification and venerable record of consecutive dividends, we think there are better places to invest in health care.

Since the 1970s, when the firm started diversifying into nonpharmaceutical health-care fields like nutritionals and diagnostics, Abbott has enjoyed performance matched by only a handful of companies. From 1974 to 2000, Abbott stock bested the S&P 500 by 4.5 times. However, we think management has rested on its laurels lately, endangering a promising business.

Incidents like the Lupron pricing fine and an inability to resolve manufacturing troubles at the Lake County, Ill., diagnostic facility have us wondering if management is asleep at the wheel. Since signing a consent degree with the Food and Drug Administration in 1999 that came with a $100 million fine, Abbott has been prohibited from manufacturing certain diagnostic tests. Not only are these incidents embarrassing, but they cost the company millions in lost revenue and extra compliance and monitoring.

We view Abbott's diversified product offering, established distribution network, and vast client base as possible competitive advantages, but not enough to put the company on autopilot. Abbott does have a few bright stars, though. Its HIV protease inhibitor Kaletra is number one in the world, and the Knoll acquisition in early 2001 added several promising candidates, most especially D2E7, a fully human monoclonal antibody for the treatment of rheumatoid arthritis. Knoll also brought Synthroid, the standard treatment for hypothyroidism and the second-most prescribed drug in the United States.

The company pulls only 40% of revenue from pharmaceuticals, but after adding the 15%-20% of total net income that comes from its TAP Pharmaceutical joint venture, Abbott is sufficiently exposed to the drug industry. The remaining 60% of sales come in equal amounts from hospital products, nutritionals, and diagnostics. Pharmaceuticals is the most profitable unit with operating margins in the high 30s, followed by nutritionals (high 30s), hospital products (high 20s), and diagnostics (low teens). Abbott earns a return in the high 30s on TAP's sales, amounting to nearly 15% of its operating income.

Abbott Labs is no has-been, but management needs to resolve its manufacturing woes and revive the drive for excellence that made the company one to own in the 1970s and 1980s. We'd ask for a little extra protection before buying Abbott shares.

Abercrombie & Fitch A ANF

	Rating	Risk	Moat Size	Fair Value	Last Close	Yield %
	★★★★	Med.	Narrow	$30.00	$20.46	0.0

Company Profile

Abercrombie & Fitch is a specialty retailer of casual apparel for men and women between the ages of 15 and 50 through 350 stores nationwide. The company designs and sells all of its merchandise under its proprietary Abercrombie & Fitch brand name. In addition to men's and women's apparel, the company also sells accessories, including belts, socks, caps, boxer shorts and underwear, and personal-care products. Approximately 60% of the company's products are men's clothing and 40% are women's.

Management

CEO Michael Jeffries led the major shift in Abercrombie's image that started in 1992. He has served as the company's CEO since since then.

Strategy

Abercrombie & Fitch's strives to remain on the cutting edge of fashion trends for high school and college-aged men and women. It uses a bad-boy image in its advertising to appeal to this group. The retailer's popularity enables it to command higher prices for its merchandise than the majority of its rivals.

6301 Fitch Path   www.abercrombie.com
New Albany, OH 43054

Morningstar Grades

Growth [B+]	1999	2000	2001	2002
Revenue %	54.4	28.0	20.1	10.3
Earnings/Share %	104.3	44.8	11.5	6.5
Book Value/Share %	206.2	65.1	43.3	40.6
Dividends/Share %	NMF	NMF	NMF	NMF

Abercrombie's revenue growth has fallen significantly below its historic average as the economy has weakened and its stores have matured. Its new Hollister concept holds a lot of potential for future growth.

Profitability [A]	2000	2001	2002	TTM
Return on Assets %	32.7	26.8	21.9	20.0
Oper Cash Flow $Mil	153	151	233	275
- Cap Spending $Mil	73	153	127	90
= Free Cash Flow $Mil	79	-2	107	184

Thanks to the pricing power its brands command, Abercrombie's profitability tops most of its peers'. We believe its returns on assets will remain below historical highs, but continue to outpace those of rivals.

Financial Health [A+]	2000	2001	2002	10-02
Long-term Debt $Mil	0	0	0	0
Total Equity $Mil	311	423	595	655
Debt/Equity Ratio	0.0	0.0	0.0	0.0

Despite a history of rapid expansion, Abercrombie has no long-term debt on its balance sheet. Even after taking its lease commitments into account, we think the retailer generates sufficient cash to meet its obligations.

Industry	Investment Style	Stock Type	Sector
Clothing Stores	⊞ Mid Core	↗ Classic Growth	⊟ Consumer Services

Competition	Market Cap $Mil	Debt/ Equity	12 Mo Trailing Sales $Mil	Price/Cash Flow	Return On Assets%	Total Return% 1 Yr	3 Yr
Abercrombie & Fitch A	1,990	0.0	1,528	7.2	20.0	-22.9	-7.6
Gap	13,509	0.8	13,582	11.5	2.0	12.1	-27.7
American Eagle Outfitters	994	—	1,425	—	—	—	—

Price Volatility

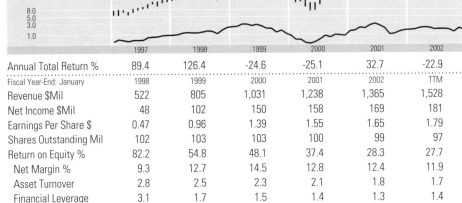

		I Monthly Price High/Low		— Relative Strength to S&P 500	
Annual $Price High	18.06	36.13	50.75	31.31	47.50	33.85
Low	6.25	14.44	21.00	8.00	16.21	15.00

	1997	1998	1999	2000	2001	2002
Annual Total Return %	89.4	126.4	-24.6	-25.1	32.7	-22.9

Fiscal Year-End: January	1998	1999	2000	2001	2002	TTM
Revenue $Mil	522	805	1,031	1,238	1,365	1,528
Net Income $Mil	48	102	150	158	169	181
Earnings Per Share $	0.47	0.96	1.39	1.55	1.65	1.79
Shares Outstanding Mil	102	103	103	100	99	97
Return on Equity %	82.2	54.8	48.1	37.4	28.3	27.7
Net Margin %	9.3	12.7	14.5	12.8	12.4	11.9
Asset Turnover	2.8	2.5	2.3	2.1	1.8	1.7
Financial Leverage	3.1	1.7	1.5	1.4	1.3	1.4

Valuation Ratios	Stock	Rel to Industry	Rel to S&P 500
Price/Earnings	11.4	0.6	0.5
Price/Book	3.0	0.8	1.0
Price/Sales	1.3	1.5	0.6
Price/Cash Flow	7.2	0.7	0.5

Major Fund Holders	% of Fund Assets
Buffalo Mid Cap	3.28
Legg Mason Opportunity Prim	3.11
Regions Morgan Keegan Select Agg Gr B	3.02
Summit Everest Fund	3.02

Morningstar's Take By Roz Bryant, 11-05-2002 Stock Price as of Analysis: $18.20

Abercrombie & Fitch's success illustrates just how far a smart branding strategy can go toward boosting a retailer's profits. Given the retailer's popularity and our belief that they know how to maintain it, we'd feel comfortable owning the shares at a 40% discount to our fair value estimate.

Using innovative marketing that targets the MTV generation, Abercrombie has developed quite a following. Abercrombie publishes its own lifestyle magazine, A&F Quarterly, which doubles as a catalog. Its racy content--and the controversy it generates--seems to work to the company's advantage. Customers are willing to pay a hefty premium for the Abercrombie brand. The retailer's gross margin has averaged 41% over the past five years, compared to Urban Outfitter's 35%.

Management remains committed to protecting those margins. Abercrombie has endured several quarters of negative same-store sales (or comps, which exclude sales from stores open less than a year) in order to maintain the brand's high-priced aspirational image. The company realizes how hard it is to restore a brand's image once it has been tarnished in the minds of customers, so markdowns are limited. This pricing discipline is possible because inventories are kept lean.

In addition, Hollister is shaping up to be a powerful revenue growth engine. The chain, which was introduced in 2000, sells West-Coast-inspired casual apparel for young men and women. Based on the warm customer response to date, the company plans to nearly triple the number of Hollister locations during fiscal 2002. Because Hollister's surfer image is different from the traditional Abercrombie look, we don't expect much cannibalization of existing Abercrombie revenues.

Even so, we think the company is likely to face gross margin pressure in the future. Hollister's prices are 20% below Abercrombie's, so it earns lower gross margins. As the stores grow and contribute a greater percentage of overall revenue, we expect margins to fall incrementally. Even Abercrombie store margins are vulnerable to an extent. If youthful tastes shift to other retailers, we think the stores would be hard pressed to sell $50 logo sweatshirts.

Thus far, however, Abercrombie has shown that it knows its customers well. We don't expect flawless execution, but we believe the firm will be able to successfully navigate its customers' fickle fashion preferences over the long haul. We'd feel comfortable buying the shares in the high teens.

MORNINGSTAR® Stocks 500

Accenture ACN

	Rating	Risk	Moat Size	Fair Value	Last Close	Yield %
	★★★	Med.	Narrow	$19.00	$17.99	0.0

Company Profile

Accenture provides management and technology consulting services and solutions to clients in industries such as communications and technology, financial services, products, resources and government. The company's professionals use industry knowledge, service offering expertise and insight into and access to existing and emerging technologies to deliver business and management consulting, technology, and outsourcing services through five global market units that comprise 18 industry groups.

Management

CEO Joe Forehand has been with Accenture since 1972. Accenture stock could be pressured by the many shares that become eligible for sale on each of the first eight anniversaries of the initial public offering.

Strategy

Accenture wants to use its longstanding customer relationships and expertise in consulting and systems integration to sell additional services, like outsourcing, to existing clients. The company also continues to invest in other areas of the world, like Asia Pacific.

Cedar House   www.accenture.com
Hamilton, HM12

Industry	Investment Style	Stock Type	Sector
Consultants	⊞ Large Core	➡ Slow Growth	🗎 Business Services

Competition	Market Cap $Mil	Debt/ Equity	12 Mo Trailing Sales $Mil	Price/Cash Flow	Return On Assets%	Total Return% 1 Yr	3 Yr
Accenture	17,231	0.0	13,105	16.2	4.5	-33.2	—
IBM	130,982	0.8	82,442	9.0	5.8	-35.5	-11.1
Hewlett-Packard	34,321	0.3	—	6.1	-3.5	-13.9	-24.7

Price Volatility

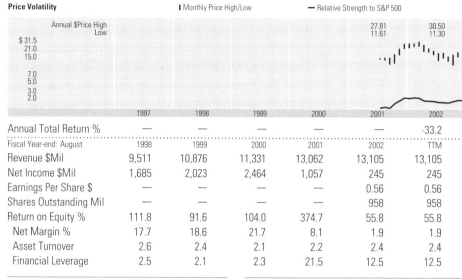

	1997	1998	1999	2000	2001	2002	TTM
Annual Total Return %	—	—	—	—	—	-33.2	
Fiscal Year-end: August	1998	1999	2000	2001	2002	TTM	
Revenue $Mil	9,511	10,876	11,331	13,062	13,105	13,105	
Net Income $Mil	1,685	2,023	2,464	1,057	245	245	
Earnings Per Share $	—	—	—	—	0.56	0.56	
Shares Outstanding Mil	—	—	—	—	958	958	
Return on Equity %	111.8	91.6	104.0	374.7	55.8	55.8	
Net Margin %	17.7	18.6	21.7	8.1	1.9	1.9	
Asset Turnover	2.6	2.4	2.1	2.2	2.4	2.4	
Financial Leverage	2.5	2.1	2.3	21.5	12.5	12.5	

Valuation Ratios	Stock	Rel to Industry	Rel to S&P 500
Price/Earnings	32.1	1.6	1.4
Price/Book	39.3	11.2	12.3
Price/Sales	1.3	1.0	0.7
Price/Cash Flow	16.2	1.4	1.2

Major Fund Holders	% of Fund Assets
Hartford Global Technology A	3.75
Goldman Sachs Research Select A	3.73
Baron iOpportunity	3.55
Security Technology A	3.49

Morningstar Grades

Growth [B-]	1999	2000	2001	2002
Revenue %	14.4	4.2	15.3	0.3
Earnings/Share %	NMF	NMF	NMF	NMF
Book Value/Share %	—	—	—	NMF
Dividends/Share %	NMF	NMF	NMF	NMF

The top line has averaged 9% growth over the past four years. Despite fewer consulting and systems integration contracts, Accenture has kept growing, albeit modestly, by winning more outsourcing deals.

Profitability [A]	2000	2001	2002	TTM
Return on Assets %	45.2	17.4	4.5	4.5
Oper Cash Flow $Mil	2,131	2,281	1,063	1,063
- Cap Spending $Mil	315	535	263	263
= Free Cash Flow $Mil	1,816	1,746	801	801

Although profitability will suffer as outsourcing becomes a larger portion of the sales mix, the firm plans to offset any margin erosion by cutting roughly $1 billion in pretax expenses this year.

Financial Health [A]	2000	2001	2002	08-02
Long-term Debt $Mil	99	1	3	3
Total Equity $Mil	2,368	282	439	439
Debt/Equity Ratio	0.0	0.0	0.0	0.0

Financial health is excellent; the firm has $1.3 billion in cash and less than $100 million in debt. Accenture repurchased more than $500 million in stock last year.

Morningstar's Take By Mike Trigg, 11-22-2002 Stock Price as of Analysis: $18.50

Accenture's transition from a partnership to a public company has been smooth, in our opinion. We think anywhere below $14 is an attractive price to buy the stock.

Like most computer services firms, Accenture has struggled with difficult economic conditions, earnings volatility among clients, and customers' reshuffling of priorities (consulting tends to take a backseat in a weak economy). The firm's problems have been compounded by a reliance on consulting and systems integration. Demand for these projects depends on software vendors selling new licenses, and key partners like Siebel Systems and SAP have struggled.

Still, Accenture has stayed highly profitable, generating returns on invested capital in the mid-30s. We attribute this to a business model that requires few capital requirements; employing a talented workforce is the key to generating profits. Accenture also has longstanding relationships with customers, a strong brand, and a diverse business across geographies and industries, all of which have benefited it in the downturn.

Accenture has smartly expanded into outsourcing, which is less profitable than consulting and systems integration, but provides badly needed revenue. Accenture has also mitigated margin erosion by

focusing on business process outsourcing (BPO), a hybrid of outsourcing that has the benefit of higher margins. Outsourcing is unlike BPO in that it involves farming out core IT functions, whereas BPO deals with handling business functions like human resources.

However, our enthusiasm is tempered. Accenture has historically benefited from close ties to software vendors because it plays a key role in recommending applications to clients. Also, software vendors want to protect their lofty profit margins by outsourcing as many low-margin services as possible. But with IT spending unlikely to improve soon, consulting and systems integration will probably remain stagnant.

Accenture also faces intense competition. Key rival IBM can offer lower prices by bundling hardware, software, and services. And with a long history of selling hardware and software, Big Blue has an extensive list of customers. Others like BearingPoint and EDS have struggled, but they have vast resources and brand awareness.

We think Accenture is a solid company. But given that economic conditions and IT spending show no signs of improving anytime soon, we wouldn't buy the stock until it fell 30% below our fair value estimate.

Adobe Systems ADBE

	Rating	Risk	Moat Size	Fair Value	Last Close	Yield %
	★★★	Med.	Wide	$22.00	$24.80	0.2

Company Profile

Adobe Systems provides graphic design, publishing, and imaging software for Web and print production. The company's products enable users to assemble illustrations, images, and text into formatted documents; send documents directly to printers; and distribute documents on paper, video, compact disc, the Internet, or private corporate networks. Adobe Systems' clients include graphic designers, publishers, and individual consumers.

Management

Adobe's recently retired co-founders were technology whizzes. Now the company is counting on the marketing savvy of CEO Bruce Chizen.

Strategy

Adobe's strategy is threefold: 1) gain more wallet share with creative professionals; 2) take advantage of the explosive demand for digital video and photography; 3) build an enterprise software business leveraging Acrobat that allow documents to be more tightly integrated with front- and back-office applications like enterprise resource planning (ERP) and customer relationship management (CRM).

345 Park Avenue   www.adobe.com
San Jose, CA 95110-2704

Industry	Investment Style	Stock Type	Sector
Development Tools	Mid Growth	Slow Growth	Software

Competition

	Market Cap $Mil	Debt/ Equity	12 Mo Trailing Sales $Mil	Price/Cash Flow	Return On Assets%	Total Return% 1 Yr	3 Yr
Adobe Systems	5,860	0.0	1,135	18.2	16.8	-20.0	-6.1
Macromedia	642	0.0	318	—	-27.6	-40.2	-48.0
Quark	—	—	—	—	—	—	—

Price Volatility

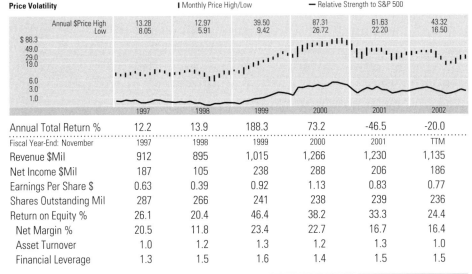

		1997	1998	1999	2000	2001	2002
Annual $Price High		13.28	12.97	39.50	87.31	61.63	43.32
Low		8.05	5.91	9.42	26.72	22.20	16.50

Monthly Price High/Low — Relative Strength to S&P 500

$ 88.3 / 49.0 / 29.0 / 19.0 / 6.0 / 3.0 / 1.0

	1997	1998	1999	2000	2001	2002
Annual Total Return %	12.2	13.9	188.3	73.2	-46.5	-20.0

Fiscal Year-End: November	1997	1998	1999	2000	2001	TTM
Revenue $Mil	912	895	1,015	1,266	1,230	1,135
Net Income $Mil	187	105	238	288	206	186
Earnings Per Share $	0.63	0.39	0.92	1.13	0.83	0.77
Shares Outstanding Mil	287	266	241	238	239	236
Return on Equity %	26.1	20.4	46.4	38.2	33.3	24.4
Net Margin %	20.5	11.8	23.4	22.7	16.7	16.4
Asset Turnover	1.0	1.2	1.3	1.2	1.3	1.0
Financial Leverage	1.3	1.5	1.6	1.4	1.5	1.5

Valuation Ratios	Stock	Rel to Industry	Rel to S&P 500
Price/Earnings	32.2	0.8	1.4
Price/Book	7.7	1.7	2.4
Price/Sales	5.2	1.2	2.6
Price/Cash Flow	18.2	1.0	1.4

Major Fund Holders	% of Fund Assets
Firsthand Technology Leaders	4.96
Fidelity Select Software & Comp	4.60
Firsthand e-Commerce	3.90
T. Rowe Price Developing Tech	3.62

Morningstar Grades

Growth [C]	1998	1999	2000	2001
Revenue %	-1.9	13.5	24.7	-2.9
Earnings/Share %	-38.5	137.4	22.8	-26.5
Book Value/Share %	-21.1	4.2	49.1	-15.7
Dividends/Share %	0.6	0.0	0.0	0.0

Growth has not been impressive. Even amid strong technology spending throughout the past five years, the top line averaged only 10% annual growth.

Profitability [A+]	1999	2000	2001	TTM
Return on Assets %	29.6	26.9	22.1	16.8
Oper Cash Flow $Mil	334	445	419	322
- Cap Spending $Mil	42	30	47	29
= Free Cash Flow $Mil	292	415	372	293

Management has done an excellent job of cutting costs. While profits may suffer in the near term, we expect operating margins will top out in the low 30s.

Financial Health [A]	1999	2000	2001	08-02
Long-term Debt $Mil	0	0	0	0
Total Equity $Mil	512	753	617	760
Debt/Equity Ratio	0.0	0.0	0.0	0.0

With cash and investments over $600 million and no debt, Adobe is in stellar financial shape. It also generates strong cash flow from operations.

Morningstar's Take   By Mike Trigg, 11-07-2002   Stock Price as of Analysis: $25.58

Adobe is our favorite name in the software industry. We think anywhere below $20 is a good entry point.

Our enthusiasm begins with Adobe's two economic moats. High switching costs make it tough for customers to get comparable products elsewhere or do their job without Adobe. In other words, since customers are trained early in their career to use Adobe applications, like Photoshop and Illustrator, it's nearly impossible for competitors to take meaningful market share. Adobe also benefits from the network effect; with over 500 million copies downloaded, Acrobat has become the standard for reading and creating documents electronically in PDF format.

Few software vendors have a wide moat, let alone two, because the competitive advantage periods in the industry are very short, given the rapid pace of technological change. In other words, today's leader can quickly become tomorrow's loser if a company can't reinvent itself. Also, Adobe has generated returns on invested capital near 100% because of the industry's favorable financial characteristics (high margins and few capital requirements). But because of Adobe's wide moats, we feel the company's excess returns should be sustainable for some time.

However, our enthusiasm is bounded. Adobe's top products are mature and have been updated several times. This is problematic because it becomes difficult to add enough new compelling features with each upgrade. But it also appears the company is releasing upgrades more frequently; the newest version of Photoshop came only 20 months after the last release, compared with 27 months before that. This is alarming because quick upgrades prevent Adobe from milking the current version as long as possible. Also, longer upgrade cycles typically create more demand.

Still, we see plenty of positives. Products like Illustrator and InDesign remain the consensus choice among creative professionals. And as the electronic sharing of documents becomes more popular, so too will Acrobat, which saves companies money by reducing paper flow. Adobe has also entered the enterprise software market with applications that allow documents to be tightly integrated with front- and back-office software like ERP and CRM. Lastly, growing demand around digital photography bodes well for products like Photoshop.

We think Adobe has a bright future. With two wide moats and plenty of growth opportunities, we'd buy the stock at a 20% discount to our fair value estimate.

MORNINGSTAR® Stocks 500

Advance PCS ADVP

	Rating	Risk	Moat Size	Fair Value	Last Close	Yield %
	★★★	Med.	Narrow	$30.00	$22.21	0.0

Company Profile

Advance PCS provides pharmacy benefit management services to health benefit plan sponsors. The company's services are designed to inform and educate these sponsors, as well as their members and participating physicians, on guidelines for various diseases. The services include clinical and benefit design consultation, formulary and rebate administration, electronic point-of-sale pharmacy claims processing, pharmaceutical distribution by mail, pharmacy network management, drug-utilization review, and data information reporting throughout the United States.

Management

David Halbert founded the company in 1986 and is chairman and CEO. In May 2000, he stepped down as president, handing those duties to David George. Together, they have overseen a smooth transition of the PCS acquisition.

Strategy

Advance PCS has grown through acquisitions to achieve a competitive advantage in size and services offered. The company is now focused on increasing its mail-order penetration rate and its specialty pharmaceutical business, which has been bolstered by recent joint ventures.

750 West John Carpenter Freeway   www.AdvancePCSrx.com
Irving, TX 75039

Morningstar Grades

Growth [A+]

	1999	2000	2001	2002
Revenue %	59.8	142.2	283.0	86.6
Earnings/Share %	71.0	39.6	-18.9	293.3
Book Value/Share %	33.6	36.0	219.6	59.7
Dividends/Share %	NMF	NMF	NMF	NMF

Over the past three years, acquisitions have provided explosive revenue growth. We project an average of 12% internal sales growth for the next three years with cross-selling of new services to existing customers and increased mail-order penetration.

Profitability [B+]

	2000	2001	2002	TTM
Return on Assets %	5.1	0.7	3.6	4.0
Oper Cash Flow $Mil	32	92	143	172
- Cap Spending $Mil	23	41	51	75
= Free Cash Flow $Mil	9	51	92	97

The best measure of profitability is EBITDA (earnings before interest, taxes, depreciation, and amortization) per prescription. We expect that growth in high-margin mail prescriptions will continue to support this metric despite industry pressures.

Financial Health [C+]

	2000	2001	2002	09-02
Long-term Debt $Mil	50	830	499	469
Total Equity $Mil	98	405	877	895
Debt/Equity Ratio	0.5	2.1	0.6	0.5

Advance PCS significantly improved its financial health in fiscal 2002. It reduced debt from $845 million to $501 million, dropping its debt/equity ratio from 2.0 to 0.6. The company also has $145 million in cash.

Industry	Investment Style	Stock Type	Sector
Managed Care	▦ Mid Growth	↑ Aggr. Growth	◉ Healthcare

Competition

	Market Cap $Mil	Debt/ Equity	12 Mo Trailing Sales $Mil	Price/Cash Flow	Return On Assets%	Total Return% 1 Yr	3 Yr
Advance PCS	1,997	0.5	14,250	11.6	4.0	-24.3	30.3
Merck	127,121	0.3	50,430	13.2	15.0	-1.3	-2.5
Express Scripts	3,757	0.6	12,188	9.3	5.8	2.7	15.6

Price Volatility | Monthly Price High/Low   — Relative Strength to S&P 500

Annual $Price High / Low	8.31 / 2.84	10.88 / 4.25	17.38 / 7.84	25.81 / 4.75	40.15 / 14.50	35.17 / 15.50
	1997	1998	1999	2000	2001	2002

Annual Total Return %	53.0	10.2	23.2	111.0	29.0	-24.3

Fiscal Year-end: March	1998	1999	2000	2001	2002	TTM
Revenue $Mil	474	757	1,834	7,024	13,107	14,250
Net Income $Mil	8	14	21	22	116	140
Earnings Per Share $	0.16	0.27	0.37	0.30	1.18	1.39
Shares Outstanding Mil	43	48	49	59	84	90
Return on Equity %	16.1	20.6	21.1	5.4	13.2	15.6
Net Margin %	1.7	1.9	1.1	0.3	0.9	1.0
Asset Turnover	2.7	2.5	4.5	2.3	4.1	4.1
Financial Leverage	3.5	4.4	4.1	7.4	3.7	3.9

Valuation Ratios	Stock	Rel to Industry	Rel to S&P 500
Price/Earnings	16.0	0.8	0.7
Price/Book	2.2	0.4	0.7
Price/Sales	0.1	0.2	0.1
Price/Cash Flow	11.6	1.2	0.9

Major Fund Holders	% of Fund Assets
Super Core A	4.66
Monterey Murphy New World Biotech	4.44
Villere Balanced	3.69
Credit Suisse Trust Glb Post-Vent Cap	3.30

Morningstar's Take By Damon Ficklin, 12-17-2002 Stock Price as of Analysis: $23.23

Advance PCS has made solid progress since the PCS acquisition, but it still has room to improve.

Despite its considerable share price volatility over the past year, we think Advance PCS remains a key player in a complex and narrowly dominated market. We would wait for a 40% discount to our fair value estimate before investing, though.

The pharmacy benefit management (PBM) business model aims to consolidate pharmaceutical buyers in order to extract large discounts from drug manufacturers and retailer pharmacies. Advance PCS' customers--large employers and health insurers--either don't have the critical mass to extract discounts from drugmakers on their own or can't justify the large investment required to bring distribution in-house.

If success proves to be a function of size, Advance PCS is nicely positioned. It has a much larger membership base than any of its competitors. We think this large base provides the firm with a great opportunity to boost profitability, despite low margins. Unlike Caremark RX, which will be hard-pressed to increase its mail-order penetration, Advance PCS has plenty of room for improvement.

In the low-margin PBM business, Advance PCS' lower exposure to the high-margin mail pharmacy business (which is 2-4 times more profitable than retail pharmacy distribution) has translated into smaller operating profits. At a 10% adjusted mail-order penetration rate (mail-order prescriptions are adjusted for size differences), the company is way behind its key competitors. Caremark RX leads with about 50% penetration, and Merck-Medco and Express Scripts have about 30% and 20%, respectively.

Analyzing the PBM business is difficult. Negotiations are closed, and PBM accounting can leave even the most adept financial statement reader wondering who paid what to whom. Forecasting can be a treacherous endeavor. Among the few distinguishing factors among PBMs are relative membership size, sales volume, operating margins, and the mix of retail versus mail pharmacy business. While Advance PCS has the largest membership base, it is well behind the pack in the last two categories.

We think the company has the best opportunity to expand its margins relative to its peers, but this is a highly competitive industry subject to heightened scrutiny. To account for the myriad risks the company faces, we would require a 40% margin of safety to our fair value estimate before investing.

Advanced Micro Devices AMD

	Rating	Risk	Moat Size	Fair Value	Last Close	Yield %
	★★	High	None	$6.00	$6.46	0.0

Industry	Investment Style	Stock Type	Sector
Semiconductors	Mid Core	Slow Growth	Hardware

Company Profile

Advanced Micro Devices designs and produces microprocessor chips and related semiconductor products. The firm's chips are primarily used in personal computers, but are also used in telecom, office automation, and computer networking applications. Its microprocessor products include the Athlon and Duron processor chips, which are marketed and sold to the original equipment manufacturers of computers, peripherals, and communication equipment. Francisco Partners acquired most of the company's communication chip operations in August 2000.

Management

Chairman and CEO W.J. Sanders co-founded the firm in 1969. AMD hired former Motorola executive Hector Ruiz as Sanders' successor.

Strategy

AMD's mission is to win share from Intel. Historically, AMD has focused on the lower end of the PC market. Its Athlon chip, however, is intended to compete with Intel's higher-performance chips. AMD also operates a flash memory unit and is making a bigger push to produce chips for corporate PCs, notebooks, and servers.

One AMD Place www.amd.com
Sunnyvale, CA 94088

Competition

	Market Cap $Mil	Debt/ Equity	12 Mo Trailing Sales $Mil	Price/Cash Flow	Return On Assets%	Total Return% 1 Yr	3 Yr
Advanced Micro Devices	2,219	0.4	2,962	18.4	-8.1	-59.3	-23.8
Intel	103,151	0.0	26,587	11.8	5.9	-50.3	-27.7

Price Volatility

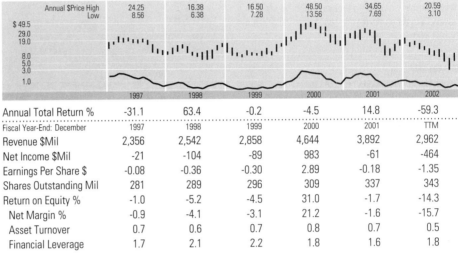

	1997	1998	1999	2000	2001	2002
Annual $Price High	24.25	16.38	16.50	48.50	34.65	20.59
Low	8.56	6.38	7.28	13.56	7.69	3.10
Annual Total Return %	-31.1	63.4	-0.2	-4.5	14.8	-59.3

Fiscal Year-End: December	1997	1998	1999	2000	2001	TTM
Revenue $Mil	2,356	2,542	2,858	4,644	3,892	2,962
Net Income $Mil	-21	-104	-89	983	-61	-464
Earnings Per Share $	-0.08	-0.36	-0.30	2.89	-0.18	-1.35
Shares Outstanding Mil	281	289	296	309	337	343
Return on Equity %	-1.0	-5.2	-4.5	31.0	-1.7	-14.3
Net Margin %	-0.9	-4.1	-3.1	21.2	-1.6	-15.7
Asset Turnover	0.7	0.6	0.7	0.8	0.7	0.5
Financial Leverage	1.7	2.1	2.2	1.8	1.6	1.8

Valuation Ratios

	Stock	Rel to Industry	Rel to S&P 500
Price/Earnings	NMF	—	—
Price/Book	0.7	0.2	0.2
Price/Sales	0.7	0.2	0.4
Price/Cash Flow	18.4	1.6	1.4

Major Fund Holders

	% of Fund Assets
ING Global Technology A	3.15
American Heritage Growth	2.96
Fidelity Value Strategies	2.47
Fidelity Select Electronics	2.37

Morningstar Grades

Growth [C]	1998	1999	2000	2001
Revenue %	7.9	12.4	62.5	-16.2
Earnings/Share %	NMF	NMF	NMF	NMF
Book Value/Share %	-3.8	-3.8	39.7	13.3
Dividends/Share %	NMF	NMF	NMF	NMF

AMD has more room to grow than Intel by virtue of its smaller size. But that doesn't mean growth will occur. After rising 63% in 2000, sales fell 16% in 2001. They will probably fall more than 30% in 2002.

Profitability [B-]	1999	2000	2001	TTM
Return on Assets %	-2.0	17.0	-1.1	-8.1
Oper Cash Flow $Mil	260	1,206	168	121
- Cap Spending $Mil	620	805	679	704
= Free Cash Flow $Mil	-360	400	-511	-583

AMD's margins have been inconsistent and inferior to Intel's, and returns on capital have not historically exceeded the cost of capital. Weak demand and falling chip prices have recently led to operating losses.

Financial Health [B+]	1999	2000	2001	09-02
Long-term Debt $Mil	1,427	1,168	673	1,197
Total Equity $Mil	1,979	3,172	3,555	3,241
Debt/Equity Ratio	0.7	0.4	0.2	0.4

AMD is in decent but not ideal health, with less than $1 billion in cash offsetting more than a billion in debt. The firm has secured additional financing, which should allow it to ride out the current weakness. Cost-cutting should help as well.

Morningstar's Take By Jeremy Lopez, 12-10-2002 Stock Price as of Analysis: $7.95

Advanced Micro has proved scrappy enough to keep Intel in check. But given its disadvantages relative to its rival, AMD is worth a look only at a considerable discount to our fair value estimate.

AMD has improved its market position by developing a reasonably competitive product lineup. Its Duron and Athlon chips offer solid performance at reasonable prices relative to Intel's products. AMD also generates around a third of its sales from flash memory chips, which are used in gadgets like cell phones. Here, AMD is also second behind Intel, but isn't as far away in share. A better PC chip mix and strong flash position have helped improve AMD's fundamentals; sales growth has averaged 15% over the past three years and margins, while inconsistent, have also improved.

But that's where the good news ends. In our view, Intel's dominance and competitive advantages will always severely limit AMD's investment appeal.

Any strides AMD can make by producing more-powerful PC chips are typically short-lived. In the chip business, size matters. Intel holds roughly 80% of the processor market, and its annual sales of $26 billion are 7 times those of AMD. Intel's 2001 research and development budget was about the same size as AMD's sales--a big advantage. Intel can always pour money into its products and marketing to stay ahead of AMD. Intel's manufacturing scale also gives it a considerable cost advantage.

AMD's margins have been consistently lower than Intel's for several reasons. An obvious one is that its average chip prices are 2-3 times lower than Intel's. One of Intel's key strategies has been to keep AMD at the lower end of the chip market; even when AMD has released higher-end products, Intel has driven down AMD's prices by accelerating its own product road map. Intel's scale also makes it a lower-cost producer than AMD, so if Intel wants to price its products aggressively--as it has for a while now--it has the pricing power to starve AMD from profits.

AMD serves a valuable role in the PC industry by keeping Intel from being too dominant. This is good for consumers, but not for investors. AMD's host of competitive disadvantages will always result in up-one-day-down-the-next fundamentals, in our view. The same will probably prove true for the stock, which is why we'd need a wide discount to our fair value estimate (at least 60%) to even consider investing.

M⚹RNINGSTAR® Stocks 500

Aegon NV ADR AEG

	Rating	Risk	Moat Size	Fair Value	Last Close	Yield %
	★★★	Med.	Narrow	$18.00	$12.83	5.9

Company Profile

Aegon provides insurance and financial services primarily in the United States, the Netherlands, and the United Kingdom. Close to 90% of Aegon's existing core business is life insurance, pensions, and related savings and investment products. The firm is also active in accident and health insurance, general insurance, and limited banking activities. Aegon's North American operations account for about 60% of total net income.

Management

We don't expect any major changes now that 30-year company veteran Don Shepard has replaced retiring chairman Kees Storm. Shepard has shrewdly run the U.S. operations since 1985 and has served on Aegon's executive board since 1992.

Strategy

Aegon's largest business segments are life insurance and related investment products, and the firm remains focused on them. The company operates across many countries and tailors its insurance products to local customers' needs. Aegon wants to increase profits by 10% a year; any acquisitions by the company will add to this target.

AEGONplein 50   www.aegon.com
The Hague, 2501 CE

Morningstar Grades

Growth [A+]	1998	1999	2000	2001
Revenue %	20.9	30.2	37.5	3.7
Earnings/Share %	20.5	18.9	23.0	12.9
Book Value/Share %	-6.4	61.2	-11.3	15.9
Dividends/Share %	20.2	18.8	23.3	12.2

Aegon's 23% three-year revenue growth exceeds the industry average and is due in part to the TransAmerica acquisition in 1999.

Profitability [C]	1999	2000	2001	TTM
Return on Assets %	0.7	0.8	0.9	0.9
Oper Cash Flow $Mil	23,131	2,807	609	—
- Cap Spending $Mil	108	148	173	—
= Free Cash Flow $Mil	—	—	—	—

Aegon's cost-conscious ways have allowed the firm to grow profitably over the years. Reserve hikes have chopped earnings per share by 35% year to date, however.

Financial Health [B-]	1999	2000	2001	12-01
Long-term Debt $Mil	—	—	—	—
Total Equity $Mil	13,543	12,117	13,533	13,533
Debt/Equity Ratio	—	—	—	—

Although Aegon's financial ratings from Moody's and Standard and Poor's remain intact, Moody's recently downgraded the firm's senior debt in response to erosion in the firm's capital position.

	Industry	Investment Style	Stock Type	Sector
	Insurance (Life)	▦ Large Value	⚡ High Yield	$ Financial Services

Competition

	Market Cap $Mil	Debt/ Equity	12 Mo Trailing Sales $Mil	Price/Cash Flow	Return On Assets%	Total Return% 1 Yr	3 Yr
Aegon NV ADR	18,248	—	28,441	—	0.9	-49.9	-33.5
American International Gr	150,907	—	66,823	—	1.4	-26.9	-4.0
ING Group NV ADR	33,183	—	54,424	—	—		

Price Volatility

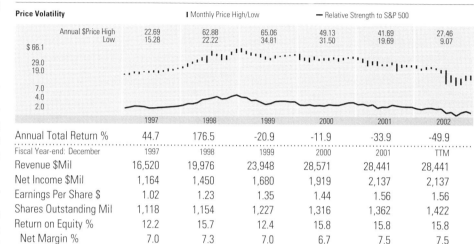

Annual $Price High Low	22.69 15.28	62.88 22.22	65.06 34.81	49.13 31.50	41.69 19.69	27.46 9.07
	1997	1998	1999	2000	2001	2002
Annual Total Return %	44.7	176.5	-20.9	-11.9	-33.9	-49.9

Fiscal Year-end: December	1997	1998	1999	2000	2001	TTM
Revenue $Mil	16,520	19,976	23,948	28,571	28,441	28,441
Net Income $Mil	1,164	1,450	1,680	1,919	2,137	2,137
Earnings Per Share $	1.02	1.23	1.35	1.44	1.56	1.56
Shares Outstanding Mil	1,118	1,154	1,227	1,316	1,362	1,422
Return on Equity %	12.2	15.7	12.4	15.8	15.8	15.8
Net Margin %	7.0	7.3	7.0	6.7	7.5	7.5
Asset Turnover	0.1	0.1	0.1	0.1	0.1	0.1
Financial Leverage	15.1	16.5	16.9	19.0	17.3	17.3

Valuation Ratios	Stock	Rel to Industry	Rel to S&P 500
Price/Earnings	8.2	0.4	0.3
Price/Book	1.3	1.2	0.4
Price/Sales	0.6	0.9	0.3
Price/Cash Flow	—	—	—

Major Fund Holders	% of Fund Assets
Wells Fargo Equity Value A	2.72
Sextant International	2.69
Wells Fargo Equity Income I	2.61
Alpha Analytics Value	1.61

Morningstar's Take By Aaron Westrate, 12-16-2002 Stock Price as of Analysis: $14.22

We clearly underestimated the impact that declining bond and equity markets would have on Aegon. After factoring in our more realistic full-year 2002 and 2003 assumptions, we're cutting our fair value estimate from $27 to $18. We are also viewing the business as riskier than before, so we'd wait to buy until the stock traded at $10 or below.

Choppy global equity markets have derailed Aegon's 19-year streak of growing earnings. Aegon has raised its bond-default provision twice in 2002, after raising it once in 2001, as several companies in its investment portfolio are on the verge of bankruptcy. Also, in the current low-interest-rate environment, Aegon's $130 billion fixed-income portfolio isn't yielding what it did a year ago. Longer term, Aegon's prospects look bright as its product offering is well-suited for the growing legions of baby boomers in the United States and Europe.

Unlike its more aggressive counterparts, Aegon isn't prone to the latest industry fads, and limits its riskier investments in startup businesses to just 3% of net income. These conservative principles have contributed to compound annual earnings-per-share growth of 15% in the past decade and 19 consecutive years of EPS growth.

The source of Aegon's constancy is that the giant

insurer sticks to what it knows best: life insurance. In fact, 91% of Aegon's pretax income in 2001 came from its life insurance operations while just 6% came from its property-casualty operations. Life insurance tends to produce very steady results because, unlike property-casualty insurance, it isn't subject to huge claims when a disaster occurs.

Another factor helping Aegon is its ability to maintain margins in the face of intense competition. Aegon's penny-pinching culture enables the firm to take steps like locating one of its main U.S. offices in Cedar Rapids, Iowa, instead of a major financial center. Aegon estimates this choice of location gives it a 30% cost advantage over competitors based in the Northeastern United States. As a result of Aegon's relentless cost-cutting, the company's gross margin--which includes interest, underwriting gains, and management fees--has grown to 41.5% from 30% in 1990.

Aegon will regain its footing by 2004, in our view, and should return to its winning ways. Nevertheless, even with that assumption incorporated into our fair value estimate, the shares look a bit pricey.

Aetna AET

	Rating	Risk	Moat Size	Fair Value	Last Close	Yield %
	★★	Med.	None	$44.00	$41.12	0.1

Company Profile

Aetna is one of the nation's largest health-care and related benefits organizations, providing a full spectrum of products and services including health care, dental, vision, pharmacy, group life, disability, and long-term care coverage. Aetna provides products and services to more than 15 million health-care and 13 million dental members, plus 11 million group insurance customers nationwide.

Management

John Rowe became president and CEO of Aetna in September 2000. In April 2001, he was named chairman as well. He was chosen to lead the company's turnaround after serving as president and CEO of Mount Sinai NYU Health.

Strategy

Aetna is focusing on the U.S. health-care market after selling its financial services and international units. Management seems to be following the successful HMO playbook: It is trying to push through large price increases, exiting Medicare and Medicaid markets, and dropping unprofitable commercial members.

151 Farmington Avenue   www.aetna.com
Hartford, CT 06156

Morningstar Grades

Growth [C]	1998	1999	2000	2001
Revenue %	13.0	33.3	21.3	-6.1
Earnings/Share %	-3.4	-12.6	-80.9	NMF
Book Value/Share %	5.8	-3.3	1.7	-3.8
Dividends/Share %	NMF	NMF	NMF	NMF

Aetna's top line has been on the decline for two years now, reflecting the reduction of its health-care membership from 19 million to about 14 million. We expect that revenue will stabilize in 2003 and resume 5% growth for 2004-06.

Profitability [D]	1999	2000	2001	TTM
Return on Assets %	1.4	0.3	-0.6	-7.2
Oper Cash Flow $Mil	1,666	1,527	-34	—
- Cap Spending $Mil	58	37	143	—
= Free Cash Flow $Mil	—	—	—	—

Aetna has markedly improved its medical loss ratio by paring unprofitable members. It reported a MLR of 86.1% at mid-2002. This is slightly worse than the industry average of about 85%, but much better than the 90% it reported for 2001.

Financial Health [A]	1999	2000	2001	09-02
Long-term Debt $Mil	—	—	—	—
Total Equity $Mil	10,703	10,127	9,890	7,629
Debt/Equity Ratio	—	—	—	—

With $1.6 billion in cash, Aetna has more than enough resources to manage its turnaround.

Industry	Investment Style	Stock Type	Sector
Insurance (Life)	▦ Mid Value	▧ Distressed	$ Financial Services

Competition	Market Cap $Mil	Debt/ Equity	12 Mo Trailing Sales $Mil	Price/Cash Flow	Return On Assets%	Total Return% 1 Yr	3 Yr
Aetna	6,190	—	21,201	—	-7.2	24.8	—
UnitedHealth Group	25,235	0.3	24,358	12.5	8.9	18.0	46.6
WellPoint Health Networks	10,372	0.3	16,180	7.9	6.0	21.8	29.5

Price Volatility | Monthly Price High/Low   — Relative Strength to S&P 500

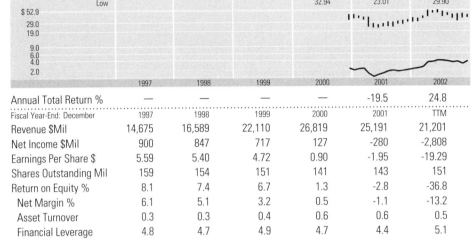

	Annual $Price High Low				42.38 32.94	42.69 23.01	51.91 29.90
		1997	1998	1999	2000	2001	2002

Annual Total Return %	—	—	—	—	-19.5	24.8

Fiscal Year-End: December	1997	1998	1999	2000	2001	TTM
Revenue $Mil	14,675	16,589	22,110	26,819	25,191	21,201
Net Income $Mil	900	847	717	127	-280	-2,808
Earnings Per Share $	5.59	5.40	4.72	0.90	-1.95	-19.29
Shares Outstanding Mil	159	154	151	141	143	151
Return on Equity %	8.1	7.4	6.7	1.3	-2.8	-36.8
Net Margin %	6.1	5.1	3.2	0.5	-1.1	-13.2
Asset Turnover	0.3	0.3	0.4	0.6	0.6	0.5
Financial Leverage	4.8	4.7	4.9	4.7	4.4	5.1

Valuation Ratios	Stock	Rel to Industry	Rel to S&P 500
Price/Earnings	NMF	—	—
Price/Book	0.8	0.7	0.3
Price/Sales	0.3	0.4	0.1
Price/Cash Flow	—	—	—

Major Fund Holders	% of Fund Assets
Quaker Mid-Cap Value A	7.61
Impact Management Investment Retail	6.08
Hillman Aggressive Equity	4.78
Sparrow Growth A	4.72

Morningstar's Take   By Damon Ficklin, 10-25-2002   Stock Price as of Analysis: $41.45

During the past two years Aetna has given itself a complete corporate makeover. It has sold its financial and international operations and taken drastic measures to put its health insurance business back on track. While we expect Aetna to regain footing in the next year or two, we would require a large margin of safety to buy into the turnaround.

Aetna has trimmed health insurance enrollment from 19 million to about 14 million during the past two years. It pushed through very aggressive price increases and dropped large blocks of unprofitable business. While we are glad to see Aetna's focus shift from sales growth to margin growth, we remain cautious because downsizing can be tricky.

One big concern is that Aetna's aggressive price increases may cause plan members to look for other options. Invariably, the healthy members will find other economical options, while the unhealthy or high-risk members will not. If Aetna loses too many healthy members, its membership base will become skewed. In the long term, a more expensive membership base can lead to a higher medical loss ratio (MLR), thereby offsetting any short-term improvements.

Aetna will also find it difficult to maintain its level of service while downsizing because it must cut selling, general, and administrative expenses as its sales decline. If it doesn't cut SG&A expenses enough, its operating margins will decline despite improvements in its MLR. On the other hand, if it cuts SG&A expenses too much, its service will suffer. We expect it will take Aetna another year or two to stabilize its membership base and strike the right balance. It is a couple of years behind the pack because competitors restructured earlier.

On a positive note, Aetna has significantly improved its mix of business through its downsizing. The vast majority of membership reductions have been risk-based members. Fee-based membership has remained fairly stable throughout the restructuring process. The net result has been an increase in the proportion of fee-based members from less than 50% at the end of 2000 to more than 60% in mid-2002. Though we think this mix shift is a one-time change rather than a trend, Aetna has decreased the risk of future cash flows.

We expect that Aetna will re-emerge as a stable player in the industry, but it still has some significant hurdles to clear. We would recommend investing in this turnaround only if its price provided a 35% margin of safety to our fair value estimate.

    MORNINGSTAR® Stocks 500

AFC Enterprises AFCE

	Rating	Risk	Moat Size	Fair Value	Last Close	Yield %
	★★	High	None	$23.00	$21.01	0.0

Company Profile

AFC Enterprises owns, operates, and franchises restaurants, bakeries, and cafes in the United States and overseas, under the names Popeyes Chicken & Biscuits, Church's Chicken, Cinnabon, Seattle's Best Coffee, and Torrefazione Italia. AFC operates and franchises more than 3,618 restaurants, bakeries, and cafes in 46 states, the District of Columbia, and 27 foreign countries. In addition, the company sells its premium specialty coffees through wholesale and retail distribution channels under its Seattle's Best Coffee brands.

Management

Chairman, CEO, and founder Frank Belatti is the mastermind behind AFC's successful growth. He's credited with making core chains Popeyes and Church's more profitable, enabling the company to attract more franchisees.

Strategy

AFC buys well-known restaurant chains, improves their profitability, and resells the chains' stores to franchisees. About 80% of its system is franchised, though it targets 90% as it sells company-operated units to franchisees. AFC also has expansion commitments from the franchisees of Cinnabon and Seattle's Best brands, which should lead to a greater store base.

6 Concourse Parkway   www.afc-online.com
Atlanta, GA 30328-5352

Morningstar Grades

Growth [D]	1998	1999	2000	2001
Revenue %	26.3	16.7	3.9	-4.5
Earnings/Share %	NMF	NMF	NMF	NMF
Book Value/Share %	—	—	—	NMF
Dividends/Share %	NMF	NMF	NMF	NMF

Near-term sales growth will remain weak because of the competitive fast-food environment. However, we expect sales growth to pick up as a result of favorable customer demographics in AFC's target markets.

Profitability [C+]	1999	2000	2001	TTM
Return on Assets %	2.2	5.1	7.0	5.1
Oper Cash Flow $Mil	55	62	71	94
- Cap Spending $Mil	53	51	56	46
= Free Cash Flow $Mil	1	11	15	48

Returns on assets should improve to the upper teens, about average for the peer group, as company stores are sold to franchisees.

Financial Health [B]	1999	2000	2001	09-02
Long-term Debt $Mil	264	292	174	164
Total Equity $Mil	101	130	224	200
Debt/Equity Ratio	2.6	2.3	0.8	0.8

The company has paid down debt, though capitalizing operating leases and technology contracts would effectively increase the debt load by $270 million, resulting in a less stable balance sheet.

Industry	Investment Style	Stock Type	Sector
Restaurants	Small Core	Slow Growth	Consumer Services

Competition	Market Cap $Mil	Debt/ Equity	12 Mo Trailing Sales $Mil	Price/Cash Flow	Return On Assets%	Total Return% 1 Yr	3 Yr
AFC Enterprises	597	0.8	642	6.3	5.1	-26.0	—
Starbucks	7,914	0.0	3,113	16.6	9.4	7.0	19.5
Yum Brands	7,169	4.3	7,498	6.9	11.1	-1.5	9.8

Price Volatility

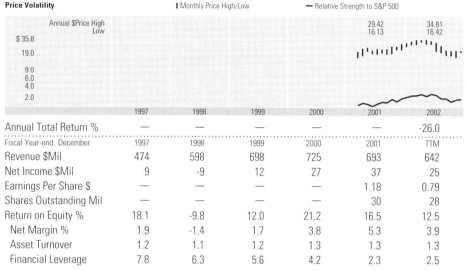

Annual Total Return %	—	—	—	—	—	-26.0
Fiscal Year-end: December	1997	1998	1999	2000	2001	TTM
Revenue $Mil	474	598	698	725	693	642
Net Income $Mil	9	-9	12	27	37	25
Earnings Per Share $	—	—	—	—	1.18	0.79
Shares Outstanding Mil	—	—	—	—	30	28
Return on Equity %	18.1	-9.8	12.0	21.2	16.5	12.5
Net Margin %	1.9	-1.4	1.7	3.8	5.3	3.9
Asset Turnover	1.2	1.1	1.2	1.3	1.3	1.3
Financial Leverage	7.8	6.3	5.6	4.2	2.3	2.5

Valuation Ratios	Stock	Rel to Industry	Rel to S&P 500
Price/Earnings	26.6	1.8	1.1
Price/Book	3.0	1.2	0.9
Price/Sales	0.9	0.7	0.5
Price/Cash Flow	6.3	0.9	0.5

Major Fund Holders	% of Fund Assets
Columbia Partners Equity	2.48
William Blair Small Cap Growth I	2.33
RS Partners	2.30
Elite Growth & Income	2.24

Morningstar's Take By Carl Sibilski, 12-05-2002 Stock Price as of Analysis: $21.33

AFC Enterprises faces an uphill battle against bigger and better-financed rivals. We think the shares would be attractive at a 60% discount to our fair value estimate, but given the company's characteristics, we wouldn't hold on to the stock very long after it rebounded.

AFC has come a long way since its bankruptcy and has the potential for better days, though not without jumping some significant hurdles. The company's performance is dominated by the Popeyes and Church's chicken concepts, which together equal about 3,000 stores. Compared with industry leader KFC's store base of nearly 12,000, AFC appears to be outgunned in terms of mass-market appeal. Accordingly, the company has targeted a niche of consumers who appreciate a well-seasoned bite of chicken. Its size may also afford it opportunities to buy and consolidate other small chicken shops into its operations, a practice that may be unsuitable for a larger organization.

We expect AFC to grow through improved customer demographics for its chicken business and expansion of its coffee products. AFC's chicken customers are now evenly split among lower-income Latin-, African- and Anglo-Americans; the stores are heavily concentrated in the South and in major metropolitan areas, and cater to family- as well as single-size servings. We also think the company has opportunities to expand the Seattle's Best Coffee business significantly from its current base of 176 stores, as it's the only nationwide alternative to Starbucks. However, it's probably destined to always play second fiddle to Starbucks.

While the company claims to be very franchisee-friendly, we're concerned that its control may be limited where the franchisees own the land and buildings. For example, remodeling the Popeye's stores tends to boost sales by 8%. It's easy to execute this in company-owned stores, but it may be a tough sell to get franchisees to invest in the idea too.

AFC is also very dependent on a few recently low-priced commodities, including chicken and coffee. At times coffee prices have risen sharply and circumstances surrounding depressed chicken prices may change. With a relatively undiversified product line, AFC could find itself in a tight spot. For these reasons, we'd seek a large margin of safety before buying the shares.

Affiliated Computer Services ACS

	Rating	Risk	Moat Size	Fair Value	Last Close	Yield %
	★	Med.	None	$40.00	$52.65	0.0

Company Profile

Affiliated Computer Services offers data-processing services to banks, insurers, and government agencies. The company's Dataplex subsidiary offers such information and image-management services as microfilm and microfiche processing. ACS sold its ATM-processing operations in 2000, using the proceeds to pay down debt. In addition, ACS acquired IMS, a data-processing unit of Lockheed Martin, in mid-2001.

Management

Jeff Rich, a Citibank veteran, joined ACS in 1989 and became CEO in 1999. Management has done a good job of mitigating integration problems throughout the company's acquisitive history.

Strategy

ACS targets government entities and the private sector. The company continues to develop long-term relationships that yield recurring revenues and expand its offering through acquisition, so it can sell additional services to existing clients. Most recently, ACS bought AFSA, an educational services company that has an $85 billion student loan portfolio.

2828 North Haskell
Dallas, TX 75204
www.acs-inc.com

Morningstar Grades

Growth [A+]	1999	2000	2001	2002
Revenue %	38.1	19.5	5.1	48.4
Earnings/Share %	49.6	24.1	19.4	43.1
Book Value/Share %	13.8	14.6	21.0	98.0
Dividends/Share %	NMF	NMF	NMF	NMF

Sales have averaged 28% growth over the past five years. Through additional acquisitions and internal growth, management believes the top-line can continue growing at least 20% annually.

Profitability [A]	2000	2001	2002	TTM
Return on Assets %	6.6	7.1	6.7	7.4
Oper Cash Flow $Mil	158	142	372	420
- Cap Spending $Mil	72	99	144	153
= Free Cash Flow $Mil	86	43	228	267

ACS is very profitable. Even with over half of its assets in intangible assets, it generates returns on invested capital in excess of 12%. This indicates ACS probably didn't overpay for its many acquisitions.

Financial Health [A]	2000	2001	2002	09-02
Long-term Debt $Mil	526	649	708	382
Total Equity $Mil	711	886	2,095	2,165
Debt/Equity Ratio	0.7	0.7	0.3	0.2

The balance sheet isn't great, with only $53 million in cash and $700 million in debt. Still, the company generates plenty of cash and has adequate access to the capital markets to continue growing.

Industry	Investment Style	Stock Type	Sector
Business Support	Mid Growth	Classic Growth	Business Services

Competition	Market Cap $Mil	Debt/ Equity	12 Mo Trailing Sales $Mil	Price/Cash Flow	Return On Assets%	Total Return% 1 Yr	3 Yr
Affiliated Computer Services	6,958	0.2	3,306	16.5	7.4	-0.8	35.2
IBM	130,982	0.8	82,442	9.0	5.8	-35.5	-11.1
Electronic Data Systems	8,774	0.7	22,127	4.5	6.6	-72.6	-32.5

Price Volatility

	Monthly Price High/Low		Relative Strength to S&P 500

Annual $Price High Low	15.13 9.75	22.50 11.19	26.50 15.88	31.31 15.50	53.63 26.81	57.05 32.79

	1997	1998	1999	2000	2001	2002
Annual Total Return %	-11.6	71.0	2.2	31.9	74.9	-0.8

Fiscal Year-End: June	1998	1999	2000	2001	2002	TTM
Revenue $Mil	1,189	1,642	1,963	2,064	3,063	3,306
Net Income $Mil	54	86	109	134	230	255
Earnings Per Share $	0.56	0.83	1.03	1.23	1.76	1.87
Shares Outstanding Mil	95	97	98	100	118	132
Return on Equity %	10.8	14.2	15.4	15.2	11.0	11.8
Net Margin %	4.6	5.3	5.6	6.5	7.5	7.7
Asset Turnover	1.3	1.3	1.2	1.1	0.9	1.0
Financial Leverage	1.9	2.0	2.3	2.1	1.6	1.6

Valuation Ratios	Stock	Rel to Industry	Rel to S&P 500
Price/Earnings	28.2	1.0	1.2
Price/Book	3.2	1.0	1.0
Price/Sales	2.1	1.0	1.0
Price/Cash Flow	16.5	1.0	1.2

Major Fund Holders	% of Fund Assets
Evergreen Technology A	8.33
Evergreen Premier 20 A	6.08
American Century Technology Inv	5.23
Fremont New Era Growth	4.47

Morningstar's Take By Mike Trigg, 11-12-2002 Stock Price as of Analysis: $47.75

Although computer services firms have generally struggled as corporate spending has declined, such has not been the case with Affiliated Computer Services. However, the lack of a sustainable competitive advantage and risks related to future growth necessitate at least a 40% discount to our fair value estimate before buying.

ACS differs from traditional outsourcers, such as EDS and Computer Sciences, because business process outsourcing (BPO) services make up the majority of its business (60% of sales). Outsourcing is unlike BPO in that it involves farming out core IT operations, whereas BPO deals more with handling business functions like accounting.

ACS is one of the most profitable firms in the computer services industry. Since BPO tends to be very customized, the typical deal has gross margins of 30%-40%, versus 18%-25% for outsourcing. For instance, running a company's accounting department is a more specialized process. But outsourcing involves offering the same service to every company, such as Web hosting, which leads to lower prices.

We credit much of ACS' success to management. When competitors were investing heavily in consulting and systems integration practices during the technology boom, management remained focused on BPO. This bet has paid off as those businesses have been some of the hardest hit by the IT slowdown.

But strong demand for BPO has drawn a crowd. Traditional outsourcers like Computer Sciences have greater brand awareness and financial resources. And with the acquisition of PricewaterhouseCoopers' consulting arm, IBM has become a formidable player. Our fear is that ACS lacks a sustainable competitive advantage. Although it was early to BPO, the first mover advantage won't last forever. Also, its size provides economies of scale, but most of the competition has the same advantage.

We are also concerned about growth. Although management has been able to successfully integrate acquisitions, the process will become more difficult. As ACS grows, it will be forced to buy larger companies in order to increase sales. Up until now, ACS has also been able to avoid the megacontracts that have hurt competitors like EDS. Eventually, ACS might be forced to go after these large deals to continue growing.

MORNINGSTAR® Stocks 500

AFLAC AFL

	Rating	Risk	Moat Size	Fair Value	Last Close	Yield %
	★★★	Med.	Wide	$30.00	$30.12	0.8

Company Profile

AFLAC sells supplemental health insurance in the United States and Japan. The company writes medical insurance policies, including policies for hospital intensive care, accident and disability, long-term care, home health care, and Medicare supplements. In addition, AFLAC offers several life insurance plans in the United States. Insurance operations in Japan, where AFLAC does business with 95% of the companies listed on the Tokyo Stock Exchange, account for approximately 80% of the company's revenue.

Management

Chief executive Daniel P. Amos has been with AFLAC since 1973 and in his current position since 1990. Another key figure for shareholders is Atsushi Yagai, the new marketing director brought on to revive AFLAC's struggling Japanese operations.

Strategy

Nearly 25% of all Japanese citizens buy insurance from AFLAC; the firm is focusing on keeping its hefty market share with constantly improved products and significant advertising spending. It's also trying to broaden its product line to include other types of insurance as Japanese deregulation allows, which could help accelerate sales growth.

1932 Wynnton Road   www.aflac.com
Columbus, GA 31999

Morningstar Grades

Growth [C]

	1998	1999	2000	2001
Revenue %	-2.0	21.6	12.3	-1.1
Earnings/Share %	-15.4	17.6	21.7	1.6
Book Value/Share %	11.7	2.9	22.8	17.4
Dividends/Share %	13.4	14.8	13.8	16.7

AFLAC's three-year growth of 11% is below the 13% peer average. Foreign exchange rates significantly affect reported sales, though; the yen has been weak for the past several years, which has depressed reported sales growth.

Profitability [A-]

	1999	2000	2001	TTM
Return on Assets %	1.5	1.8	1.8	1.9
Oper Cash Flow $Mil	2,803	3,245	2,849	—
- Cap Spending $Mil	14	26	45	—
= Free Cash Flow $Mil	—	—	—	—

The company's returns on equity are consistently in the top third of its peers. As AFLAC Japan's business mix shifts toward its new, higher-margin policies, returns on equity should remain robust.

Financial Health [A+]

	1999	2000	2001	09-02
Long-term Debt $Mil	—	—	—	—
Total Equity $Mil	3,868	4,694	5,425	6,104
Debt/Equity Ratio	—	—	—	—

AFLAC uses debt sparingly, and its Japanese operations maintain a strong AA rating, leading to the firm's excellent reputation among consumers there.

Industry	Investment Style	Stock Type	Sector
Insurance (Life)	⊞ Large Core	↗ Classic Growth	$ Financial Services

Competition

	Market Cap $Mil	Debt/ Equity	12 Mo Trailing Sales $Mil	Price/Cash Flow	Return On Assets%	Total Return% 1 Yr	3 Yr
AFLAC	19,509	—	9,995	—	1.9	23.6	12.2
Aetna	6,190	—	21,201	—	-7.2	24.8	—
Cigna	5,732	0.3	19,958	5.3	-0.3	-54.8	-18.0

Price Volatility

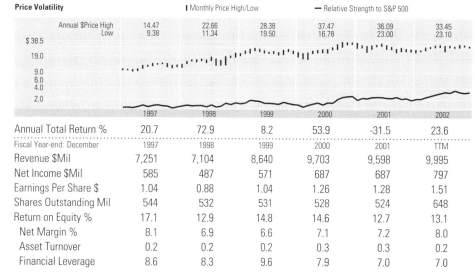

Annual $Price High Low	14.47 9.38	22.66 11.34	28.38 19.50	37.47 16.78	36.09 23.00	33.45 23.10
	1997	1998	1999	2000	2001	2002
Annual Total Return %	20.7	72.9	8.2	53.9	-31.5	23.6

Fiscal Year-end: December	1997	1998	1999	2000	2001	TTM
Revenue $Mil	7,251	7,104	8,640	9,703	9,598	9,995
Net Income $Mil	585	487	571	687	687	797
Earnings Per Share $	1.04	0.88	1.04	1.26	1.28	1.51
Shares Outstanding Mil	544	532	531	528	524	648
Return on Equity %	17.1	12.9	14.8	14.6	12.7	13.1
Net Margin %	8.1	6.9	6.6	7.1	7.2	8.0
Asset Turnover	0.2	0.2	0.2	0.3	0.3	0.2
Financial Leverage	8.6	8.3	9.6	7.9	7.0	7.0

Valuation Ratios	Stock	Rel to Industry	Rel to S&P 500
Price/Earnings	19.9	1.0	0.8
Price/Book	3.2	2.9	1.0
Price/Sales	2.0	2.8	1.0
Price/Cash Flow	—	—	—

Major Fund Holders	% of Fund Assets
Reserve Large-Cap Growth R	6.44
Credit Suisse Global Finan Serv Com	5.14
Oak Value	4.67
Nations Financial Services Investor A	4.64

Morningstar's Take   By Aaron Westrate, 11-14-2002   Stock Price as of Analysis: $32.45

AFLAC's dominance of the Japanese health insurance market has continued even after deregulation. When AFLAC began selling cancer insurance in Japan in 1974, it was one of the few firms targeting that niche because of the market's small initial size. Even as the market grew, strict regulation limited new entrants until 2001, when the health insurance sector was deregulated. Given that AFLAC generates three fourths of its pretax profits in Japan, this development was a crucial test of how well the firm's foundation had been laid. It's pretty solid, as it turns out.

From the beginning, AFLAC has structured its salesforce and claims-paying systems to efficiently sell low-premium cancer policies. Competitors seeking to make inroads into AFLAC's core market have, by and large, hit the highway instead as they found they couldn't compete with AFLAC on price. In fact, rather than compete head to head with AFLAC, one of its rivals, Dai-Ichi, opted to join AFLAC's reputation and product offering with its 50,000-strong salesforce, and both firms are better for it.

Although the threat from outside competition turned out to be overstated, AFLAC has been its own worst enemy at times. The firm introduced a new cancer product in early 2001, but the complexity of the offering confused consumers. Also, the rollout of a lower-premium substitution of its second-largest product, Rider Max, cut deeply into sales.

Management responded decisively to this adversity, though, revamping the organization by bringing sales, advertising, and product development under one roof. The cancer product was streamlined, and the success of two new products, a Rider Max whole life option and a standalone medical policy, Ever, has restored confidence in management's ability to deliver new products to market.

AFLAC's success in the land of the rising sun isn't the only bright spot, however. A popular ad campaign featuring the AFLAC spokesduck has increased brand awareness and the size of the firm's salesforce in the United States. The swelling ranks of producing agents every quarter is a harbinger of sales growth, as are several huge corporate account wins in 2001, including Wal-Mart. This successful push outside the insurer's traditional small- to midsize-business market should enable the AFLAC juggernaut to keep growing for years to come.

AG Edwards AGE

	Rating	Risk	Moat Size	Fair Value	Last Close	Yield %
	★★★	Med.	None	$46.00	$32.96	1.9

Company Profile

Financial services firm AG Edwards is primarily a retail brokerage and possesses one of the largest networks of brokers in the United States. The company is slowly trying to move from a commission-based model to a fee-based asset-management model, but more than 60% of revenue still comes from transactions and interest. AG Edwards has built up its asset-management business to more than 25% of revenue and has a growing investment bank.

Management

AG Edwards was run by successive generations of the Edwards family until Benjamin Edwards III retired in 2001. A 26-year veteran of the firm, Robert Bagby, is now CEO. Benjamin Edwards IV was named president in 2001.

Strategy

AG Edwards has suffered as trading commissions declined; it is seeking to take the volatility out of its revenue by moving to a portfolio management model in which customers pay recurring fees for the assets that AG Edwards manages. The firm is also building up its investment management business and is now among the top 20 equity underwriters in the United States.

One North Jefferson Avenue   www.agedwards.com
St. Louis, MO 63103

Industry	Investment Style	Stock Type	Sector
Securities	Mid Core	Slow Growth	Financial Services

Competition	Market Cap $Mil	Debt/ Equity	12 Mo Trailing Sales $Mil	Price/Cash Flow	Return On Assets%	Total Return% 1 Yr	3 Yr
AG Edwards	2,605	—	2,312	—	1.3	-24.1	4.3
Merrill Lynch & Company	32,806	—	36,032	—	0.2	-26.0	0.5
Legg Mason	3,149	—	1,613	—	3.0	-2.1	16.7

Price Volatility

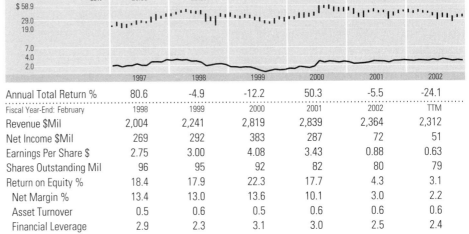

Annual $Price High Low	39.94 20.50	48.81 22.63	41.00 24.25	57.94 29.56	52.19 29.76	46.70 26.50
	1997	1998	1999	2000	2001	2002

Annual Total Return %	80.6	-4.9	-12.2	50.3	-5.5	-24.1

Fiscal Year-End: February	1998	1999	2000	2001	2002	TTM
Revenue $Mil	2,004	2,241	2,819	2,839	2,364	2,312
Net Income $Mil	269	292	383	287	72	51
Earnings Per Share $	2.75	3.00	4.08	3.43	0.88	0.63
Shares Outstanding Mil	96	95	92	82	80	79
Return on Equity %	18.4	17.9	22.3	17.7	4.3	3.1
Net Margin %	13.4	13.0	13.6	10.1	3.0	2.2
Asset Turnover	0.5	0.6	0.5	0.6	0.6	0.6
Financial Leverage	2.9	2.3	3.1	3.0	2.5	2.4

Valuation Ratios	Stock	Rel to Industry	Rel to S&P 500
Price/Earnings	52.3	3.0	2.2
Price/Book	1.6	0.9	0.5
Price/Sales	1.1	0.8	0.6
Price/Cash Flow	—	—	—

Major Fund Holders	% of Fund Assets
Performance Mid Cap Equity Instl	3.56
Fidelity Select Brokerage & Investmnt	3.38
UMB Scout Small Cap	3.03
Buffalo Mid Cap	2.84

Morningstar Grades

Growth [D-]	1999	2000	2001	2002
Revenue %	11.8	25.8	0.7	-16.7
Earnings/Share %	9.1	36.0	-15.9	-74.3
Book Value/Share %	11.9	9.4	6.1	4.5
Dividends/Share %	10.0	9.1	6.7	0.0

Fiscal 2002, which ended in February, was a difficult year for the company. Revenue dropped 17%, pulling down the five-year compound annual growth rate to 6.7%. Revenue was down 4% for the first half of fiscal 2003.

Profitability [A-]	2000	2001	2002	TTM
Return on Assets %	7.2	5.9	1.7	1.3
Oper Cash Flow $Mil	-407	690	926	—
- Cap Spending $Mil	131	296	191	—
= Free Cash Flow $Mil	—	—	—	—

Return on assets fell from 7.2% in 2000 to 1.7% in fiscal 2002. Similar troubles throughout the brokerage industry have reduced competitors' ROA as well, giving Edwards an average performance.

Financial Health [A+]	2000	2001	2002	08-02
Long-term Debt $Mil	—	—	—	—
Total Equity $Mil	1,717	1,626	1,648	1,627
Debt/Equity Ratio	—	—	—	—

AG Edwards has very little debt and one of the strongest balance sheets in the brokerage industry. Its financial leverage ratio of 2.4 is extremely low compared with its peers'.

Morningstar's Take By Rachel Barnard, 12-11-2002 Stock Price as of Analysis: $33.88

Like most retail brokerages, AG Edwards has lost revenue as trading volume has declined. But we believe investors underestimate the company's longer-term potential and the value of financial advice as the economy recovers. We believe the shares are worth $46, although we would demand a wider discount to our fair value estimate before buying.

AG Edwards' recent performance has been uninspiring. As the stock market tumbled, individual investors lost their zeal for investing, which had driven high securities trading volume in the late 1990s. Less trading meant less revenue for commission-based brokerages like AG Edwards.

In response, AG Edwards is attempting to lessen its dependence on commission revenue and move to a model in which the company charges a fee to manage client assets. Such fees now make up more than one fourth of Edwards' revenue and they have grown steadily. This has not been enough to offset the sharp decline in commission revenue, however, and last year the company eliminated 460 jobs, cut bonuses, and froze salaries.

In addition, the company is re-evaluating its technology initiative, which includes its online investing capability. This means that the online investing product--something its competitors already have--has been postponed. Edwards took a $48 million charge to write off some of its technology investment.

Given its recent troubles, AG Edwards was forced to rethink its strategy, but its vision of the future looks much like the past. Edwards has opted to stick with the service-oriented broker model and says its customers show little interest in online trading. The gradual shift to asset-based fees will continue to emphasize the role of the broker as an investment advisor as Edwards targets customers who desire some hand-holding.

This retro strategy should appeal strongly to investors who want professional advice after losing money in the markets. Already, mutual fund companies are seeing a shift to sales through financial advisors. Plus, the asset-based fee model serves to align the interest of investors (more assets) with the interest of brokers (bigger fees) and discourages churning a customer's portfolio to generate trading commissions.

This brokerage certainly has a future. However, for this stock to look like a very attractive buying opportunity, it must fall below $23.

  MORNINGSTAR® Stocks 500

Albertson's ABS

	Rating	Risk	Moat Size	Fair Value	Last Close	Yield %
	★★★	Low	None	$26.00	$22.26	3.4

Company Profile

Albertson's operates the second-largest chain of retail food and drug stores in the United States with locations in 36 states, primarily under the Albertson's, Jewel, Osco, Acme, and Sav-On names. The company operates 2,533 stores, including combination food and drug stores, conventional supermarkets, and stand-alone drug stores. Retail operations are supported by company-owned distribution centers. Albertson's merged with American Stores in 1999.

Management

Larry Johnston was named CEO in April 2001; he's a former head of GE Appliances and had no experience in the grocery trade. That makes veteran COO Peter Lynch a key figure. We're pleased that Lynch, who was passed over for CEO, has joined the board.

Strategy

With store closings aimed at improving profitability largely complete, Albertson's is now focusing on growth. The company plans to spend on opening and remodeling stores in an effort to boost its standing in key markets. It also intends to expand its combination food and drug stores.

250 Parkcenter Blvd.   www.albertsons.com
Boise, ID 83726

Morningstar Grades

Growth [C-]	1999	2000	2001	2002
Revenue %	6.0	4.5	-1.9	3.2
Earnings/Share %	1.1	-50.0	92.6	-32.8
Book Value/Share %	129.5	2.4	1.6	6.6
Dividends/Share %	6.3	5.9	5.6	0.0

Sales growth has been on par with that of other large grocers, though it trails that of smaller, nimbler chains.

Profitability [B]	2000	2001	2002	TTM
Return on Assets %	2.6	4.8	3.1	4.2
Oper Cash Flow $Mil	1,418	1,791	2,092	2,356
- Cap Spending $Mil	1,837	1,771	1,487	1,429
= Free Cash Flow $Mil	-419	20	605	927

Operating and net margins are thinner than those of competitors, but Albertson's is hoping to improve them through restructuring efforts. We don't think these efforts will be successful in the long term.

Financial Health [B-]	2000	2001	2002	10-02
Long-term Debt $Mil	4,990	5,942	5,336	4,953
Total Equity $Mil	5,702	5,694	5,915	5,535
Debt/Equity Ratio	0.9	1.0	0.9	0.9

Debt/equity is lower than that of the company's peers, and operations generate solid free cash flows. Albertson's has reduced long-term debt over the past year using cash generated from asset sales.

Industry	Investment Style	Stock Type	Sector
Groceries	Large Value	High Yield	Consumer Services

Competition	Market Cap $Mil	Debt/ Equity	12 Mo Trailing Sales $Mil	Price/Cash Flow	Return On Assets%	Total Return% 1 Yr	3 Yr
Albertson's	8,440	0.9	37,185	3.6	4.2	-27.4	-8.5
Wal-Mart Stores	223,388	0.5	233,651	18.9	8.0	-11.8	-7.3
Safeway	13,376	1.5	34,757	6.3	3.4	-44.1	-12.2

Price Volatility   ❙ Monthly Price High/Low   — Relative Strength to S&P 500

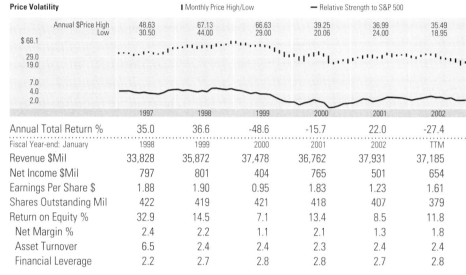

	1997	1998	1999	2000	2001	2002
Annual $Price High	48.63	67.13	66.63	39.25	36.99	35.49
Low	30.50	44.00	29.00	20.06	24.00	18.95
Annual Total Return %	35.0	36.6	-48.6	-15.7	22.0	-27.4

Fiscal Year-end: January	1998	1999	2000	2001	2002	TTM
Revenue $Mil	33,828	35,872	37,478	36,762	37,931	37,185
Net Income $Mil	797	801	404	765	501	654
Earnings Per Share $	1.88	1.90	0.95	1.83	1.23	1.61
Shares Outstanding Mil	422	419	421	418	407	379
Return on Equity %	32.9	14.5	7.1	13.4	8.5	11.8
Net Margin %	2.4	2.2	1.1	2.1	1.3	1.8
Asset Turnover	6.5	2.4	2.4	2.3	2.4	2.4
Financial Leverage	2.2	2.7	2.8	2.8	2.7	2.8

Valuation Ratios	Stock	Rel to Industry	Rel to S&P 500
Price/Earnings	13.8	0.7	0.6
Price/Book	1.5	0.5	0.5
Price/Sales	0.2	0.6	0.1
Price/Cash Flow	3.6	0.6	0.3

Major Fund Holders	% of Fund Assets
Legg Mason Value Prim	4.92
Legg Mason American Leading Co Prim	3.16
Aristata Equity	2.92
Capital Management Mid-Cap Instl	2.84

Morningstar's Take   By David Kathman, 12-20-2002   Stock Price as of Analysis: $21.88

Albertson's is vulnerable to the threat of supercenters, and we're skeptical of its long-term prospects. We'd require a 30% margin of safety to our fair value estimate to buy in.

With its market share and margins threatened by competitors ranging from Wal-Mart to Whole Foods, Albertson's has gone into retrenchment mode. Since the summer of 2001, it has closed more than 200 stores, including a wholesale withdrawal from some major but underperforming markets. To offset these closings the company has cautious plans to expand in geographic areas where it's already strong, like Los Angeles and Dallas-Fort Worth. Also, it has tightened inventory control and reduced merchandise theft in its remaining stores, causing the gross margin to widen to 29.3% in the fiscal third quarter of 2002 from 28.4% a year earlier.

Albertson's modest expansion involves not just opening new stores, but expanding existing ones to make them more like superstores. In some cases, this involves co-branded stores with its drug store chains (mainly Osco and Sav-On), one factor that distinguishes Albertson's from rivals Safeway and Kroger. The firm is also opening more stand-alone Osco stores and trying to boost prescription drugs at its supermarkets, in pursuit of the wider gross

margins that prescriptions bring. But here it faces competition from Walgreen and CVS, which have proved to be skillful protectors of market share.

One thing that worries us about the company's ability to compete in this rough-and-tumble environment is its margin structure. The firm's operating margin has averaged 3.8% over the past three years, lower than Kroger's 4.3% and Safeway's 7.2%, offering less room to maneuver with strategic price cuts. Furthermore, most recent earnings growth has come from the gross margin line, whereas Kroger's and Safeway's gross margins are trending down because of lower prices on items. This suggests that Albertson's is not competitive enough in its pricing, raising the possibility that it might be sacrificing long-term share for short-term profit gains.

In our opinion, some of the firm's strategic moves (like the increased emphasis on drug stores) are good, but we think Albertson's will continue to be hurt along with other traditional grocers by the trends transforming the industry. To compensate, we'd need at least a 30% discount to our fair value estimate before looking at the stock.

Alcan AL

	Rating	Risk	Moat Size	Fair Value	Last Close	Yield %
	★★	Med.	None	$29.00	$29.52	2.0

Company Profile

Alcan manufactures aluminum and fabricated aluminum products. The company is involved in bauxite mining and aluminum refining, manufacturing, marketing, and recycling. Its primary markets include the container, packaging, electrical, and construction industries. Alcan operates on six continents, with its primary mining and alumina-processing operations in Canada, Ireland, and Jamaica.

Management

Travis Engen, former chief executive of ITT Industries, became Alcan's CEO in March 2001. Geofferey Merszei, former treasurer of Dow Chemical, was appointed CFO in June 2001. Engen's cash compensation in 2001 was valued at nearly $2.3 million.

Strategy

Alcan's unlikely to get much bigger because of regulatory barriers, so its focus has shifted to diversifying operations, cutting costs, and improving profitability. The company announced in late 2002 that would acquiring VAW Packaging to expand its international product packaging business. It has also been taking ownership stakes in high-efficiency smelters, which should reduce costs as well.

1188 Sherbrooke St. West
Montreal, QC H3A 3G2
www.alcan.com

Morningstar Grades

Growth [A+]	1998	1999	2000	2001
Revenue %	0.2	-6.0	24.9	38.0
Earnings/Share %	-18.2	20.5	18.9	NMF
Book Value/Share %	9.9	4.3	45.4	-19.5
Dividends/Share %	0.0	0.0	0.0	0.0

Alcan's internally generated growth hasn't been impressive. We believe average annual growth of 3%-4% (compared with 5%-6% for Alcoa) is probably as good as investors should expect, given Alcan's record and the industries the firm serves.

Profitability [C+]	1999	2000	2001	TTM
Return on Assets %	4.6	3.3	0.0	-0.1
Oper Cash Flow $Mil	1,182	1,066	1,387	1,695
- Cap Spending $Mil	1,169	1,491	1,110	806
= Free Cash Flow $Mil	13	-425	277	889

Alcan's profitability hasn't been impressive. Between 1997 and 2001, Alcan's average returns on assets and equity trailed Alcoa's by 3.4 and 7.5 percentage points, respectively. Alcan hasn't come close to earning its cost of capital, either.

Financial Health [B-]	1999	2000	2001	09-02
Long-term Debt $Mil	1,011	3,195	2,884	3,042
Total Equity $Mil	5,381	8,867	8,631	8,366
Debt/Equity Ratio	0.2	0.4	0.3	0.4

Alcan took on a big slug of debt to finance the Algroup deal, but its balance sheet can handle the additional leverage. The firm has recently improved free cash flow by keeping a lid on capital expenditures.

Industry	Investment Style	Stock Type	Sector
Aluminum	Large Value	Hard Assets	Industrial Mats

Competition

Competition	Market Cap $Mil	Debt/ Equity	12 Mo Trailing Sales $Mil	Price/Cash Flow	Return On Assets%	Total Return% 1 Yr	3 Yr
Alcan	9,485	0.4	12,397	5.6	-0.1	-16.3	-9.0
Alcoa	19,232	0.7	20,631	11.4	1.7	-34.6	-16.1
Pechiney ADR A	2,829	—	11,437	—	—	—	—

Price Volatility

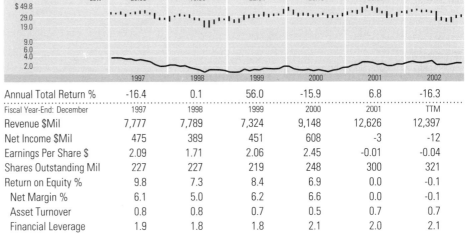

		1997	1998	1999	2000	2001	2002
Annual $Price High		40.31	34.50	42.00	45.94	48.75	41.97
Low		26.06	18.69	22.94	28.19	28.00	23.15
Annual Total Return %		-16.4	0.1	56.0	-15.9	6.8	-16.3

Fiscal Year-End: December	1997	1998	1999	2000	2001	TTM
Revenue $Mil	7,777	7,789	7,324	9,148	12,626	12,397
Net Income $Mil	475	389	451	608	-3	-12
Earnings Per Share $	2.09	1.71	2.06	2.45	-0.01	-0.04
Shares Outstanding Mil	227	227	219	248	300	321
Return on Equity %	9.8	7.3	8.4	6.9	0.0	-0.1
Net Margin %	6.1	5.0	6.2	6.6	0.0	-0.1
Asset Turnover	0.8	0.8	0.7	0.5	0.7	0.7
Financial Leverage	1.9	1.8	1.8	2.1	2.0	2.1

Valuation Ratios	Stock	Rel to Industry	Rel to S&P 500
Price/Earnings	NMF	—	—
Price/Book	1.1	0.6	0.4
Price/Sales	0.8	0.8	0.4
Price/Cash Flow	5.6	0.5	0.4

Major Fund Holders	% of Fund Assets
Fidelity Select Industrial Materials	8.35
Oppenheimer Quest Opportunity Value A	3.65
PIMCO PEA Value Instl	3.64
Quaker Mid-Cap Value A	3.33

Morningstar's Take By Daniel Quinn, 12-19-2002 Stock Price as of Analysis: $30.25

Without the low-cost position in the industry, Alcan is at a long-term competitive disadvantage to rival Alcoa, in our opinion. Consequently, we wouldn't be tempted to buy Alcan unless it traded at a wide discount to our fair value estimate.

Establishing the low-cost position is arguably the most important competitive advantage in commodity industries, like aluminum, where companies have little ability to differentiate their products or set prices. The firm with the lowest cost per unit will have higher margins, better returns, and increasing market share. In the aluminum industry, Alcoa has the low-cost position. Alcan's performance has displayed its second-class status. By our reckoning, Alcan's operating margins and returns on invested capital averaged 8.8% and 4.8% respectively, between 1997 and 2001. In comparison, Alcoa averaged 12% and 7.5%, respectively.

Alcan tried to level the playing field when it sought to merge with Pechiney and Algroup in 2000. The European Union stepped in with antitrust concerns and Pechiney was forced to drop out. Left only with Algroup, Alcan still has just about half Alcoa's market share and capacity. Rather than getting bigger, Alcan has focused recently on improving efficiency and seeking diversifying acquisitions. By squeezing costs, improving working capital management, and trimming capital spending, free cash flows should improve.

Alcan's performance has bested Alcoa's recently, but this is primarily a result of product mix. Alcoa sells heavily into the aerospace industry, which has been hurting lately. Alcan, on the other hand, depends more on the consumer market, including autos, which has been a source of economic strength. Longer term, aerospace will probably rebound, and the ability to produce low-cost aluminum will again give Alcoa the upper hand.

Further complicating things for Alcan is the threat posed by the fast-growing aluminum industry in developing regions. If China became a net exporter of aluminum, for example, the global supply balance would be altered and could lead to depressed prices and instability. In such a situation, we'd feel more comfortable being invested with the acknowledged industry leader, Alcoa.

While it may look as if Alcan is making headway, we think Alcoa will generate superior long-term returns for investors. We'd buy Alcan only if it traded at a wide margin of safety to our fair value estimate and at a discount to Alcoa's valuation.

MORNINGSTAR® Stocks 500

Alcatel SA ADR A ALA

	Rating	Risk	Moat Size	Fair Value	Last Close	Yield %
	★	Med.	None	$3.90	$4.44	2.6

Company Profile

Alcatel is one of the world's largest manufacturers of telecommunication equipment. The French company produces a wide range of network equipment including broadband access systems, transmission and switching equipment, data-networking gear, optical systems and fiber-optic cables, wireless infrastructure and handsets, and satellites. Sales to European customers accounted for 51% of the total in 2001 (the U.S. was 19%). The firm created a tracking stock for its optical components business in October 2000 and spun off its copper wire and cable business in early 2001.

Management

CEO Serge Tchuruk came to Alcatel in 1995 from French oil and gas firm Total Fina Elf. Considered a turnaround expert, Tchuruk deserves credit for focusing Alcatel on its core business--telecom equipment--and exiting various unrelated fields.

Strategy

Like Lucent and Nortel, Alcatel aims to be the leading telecom equipment vendor across a broad range of categories. But Alcatel supplies a wider range of components than Lucent or Nortel, including things like fiber optics and lasers. Alcatel hopes to use its European beachhead and first-rate technological base to build its share of the U.S. market .

54, rue La Boetie
Paris, 75008
www.alcatel.com

Morningstar Grades

Growth [B-]	1998	1999	2000	2001
Revenue %	-25.0	8.3	36.4	-19.3
Earnings/Share %	195.5	-73.8	73.9	NMF
Book Value/Share %	32.8	10.9	5.3	-35.5
Dividends/Share %	14.3	10.0	9.1	-66.7

Sales rise or fall with telecom capital spending, though government orders for Alcatel's aerospace business somewhat reduce this volatility. We expect sales to fall another 18%-20% in 2003 before rebounding maybe 10% in future years.

Profitability [C]	1999	2000	2001	TTM
Return on Assets %	2.0	3.0	-13.7	-17.4
Oper Cash Flow $Mil	1,152	-1,157	486	3,290
- Cap Spending $Mil	1,310	1,704	1,559	738
= Free Cash Flow $Mil	-158	-2,860	-1,073	2,553

Though margins should hold steady, we believe long-term operating margins will be only 5% because of greater industry price competition and the need to sell to more price-sensitive markets like China.

Financial Health [C]	1999	2000	2001	09-02
Long-term Debt $Mil	3,478	5,261	5,203	6,009
Total Equity $Mil	11,532	13,548	8,522	6,103
Debt/Equity Ratio	0.3	0.4	0.6	1.0

We expect Alcatel to reduce expenses to where it can break even on annual sales of $12 billion. The balance sheet is decent; debt of $6 billion is offset by $5 billion in cash.

Industry	Investment Style	Stock Type	Sector
Wireline Equipment	▦ Large Value	▨ High Yield	▦ Hardware

Competition

	Market Cap $Mil	Debt/ Equity	12 Mo Trailing Sales $Mil	Price/Cash Flow	Return On Assets%	Total Return% 1 Yr	3 Yr
Alcatel SA ADR A	5,615	1.0	17,080	1.7	-17.4	-72.9	-53.2
Cisco Systems	94,649	0.0	19,312	15.1	7.5	-27.7	-36.4
Nortel Networks	6,197	1.4	12,835	8.6	-29.6	-78.5	-67.5

Price Volatility

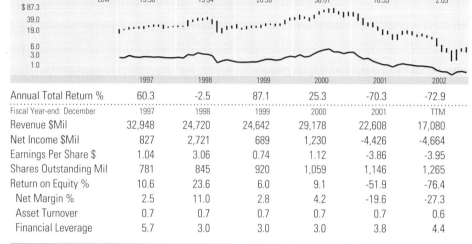

Annual $Price High Low	28.50 15.50	47.13 15.94	46.06 20.38	86.25 36.81	66.94 10.53	19.15 2.03

	1997	1998	1999	2000	2001	2002
Annual Total Return %	60.3	-2.5	87.1	25.3	-70.3	-72.9

Fiscal Year-end: December	1997	1998	1999	2000	2001	TTM
Revenue $Mil	32,948	24,720	24,642	29,178	22,608	17,080
Net Income $Mil	827	2,721	689	1,230	-4,426	-4,664
Earnings Per Share $	1.04	3.06	0.74	1.12	-3.86	-3.95
Shares Outstanding Mil	781	845	920	1,059	1,146	1,265
Return on Equity %	10.6	23.6	6.0	9.1	-51.9	-76.4
Net Margin %	2.5	11.0	2.8	4.2	-19.6	-27.3
Asset Turnover	0.7	0.7	0.7	0.7	0.7	0.6
Financial Leverage	5.7	3.0	3.0	3.0	3.8	4.4

Valuation Ratios	Stock	Rel to Industry	Rel to S&P 500
Price/Earnings	NMF	—	—
Price/Book	0.9	0.6	0.3
Price/Sales	0.3	0.7	0.2
Price/Cash Flow	1.7	0.4	0.1

Major Fund Holders	% of Fund Assets
Wells Fargo Specialized Technology A	2.34
PIMCO RCM Global Technology Instl	2.13
Fremont International Growth	1.43
Rydex Telecommunications Inv	1.38

Morningstar's Take By Fritz Kaegi, 12-30-2002 Stock Price as of Analysis: $4.40

We expect Alcatel to grow less quickly than peers, mainly because European telecom carriers account for half of its sales. We'd be buyers of this firm with no moat at a 40% discount to our fair value estimate.

In the telecom equipment business it is relatively easy to get more orders once you are a customer's supplier, but it's very hard to win new customers or orders for new products from existing customers. Alcatel has held a key position in Europe for decades, selling local carriers everything from switches to fiber to satellites. The rapid growth in Europe of wireless telephony provided a huge boost during the past decade. The near-monopoly status of the European wireline carriers made Alcatel's relationships with these firms doubly valuable: In addition to providing a good base of installed equipment, their dominant competitive position gave them little incentive to change vendors. Also, Alcatel has a leg up in the fast-growing telecom markets of Eastern Europe.

A bright spot for Alcatel is broadband access equipment. Though this business is growing less quickly than expected (less than 0.5% of European homes have digital subscriber lines), we expect good growth eventually as consumers learn the benefits of fast Internet service. Joint ventures, like the one with local Chinese telecom carriers (known as Shanghai

Bell), and local distributors will be a more effective way to build business in faster-growing developing markets.

But where does it go from here? Wireless telephony is nearing saturation in most of Europe and consumers are resisting paying for advanced functionality. European carriers are mired in debt--France Telecom has $70 billion--that will govern spending for years. Forces that spurred equipment spending in the United States--local wireline competition and Internet-led demand for broadband--are much weaker in Europe, where local phone calls are billed by the minute and computer ownership is low. For instance, only 30%-40% of homes in Italy and France have PCs. Also, economic conditions could be unfavorable over the next decade as Europe copes with a host of problems, including the European Union's caps on state spending. Gaining share in other regions will be extremely challenging because of Lucent's and Nortel's close relationship with local carriers and Cisco's superior ability to compete on price.

A company without an economic moat like Alcatel would need to become cheap--say, 40% below our fair value estimate--before we'd invest.

Alcide ALCD

	Rating	Risk	Moat Size	Fair Value	Last Close	Yield %
	★	High	Narrow	$11.00	$14.75	0.0

Company Profile

Alcide develops and markets unique biocidal products based on its patented technology. The company sells anti-infective products to the animal health market, and its Sanova system for controlling food-borne pathogens to the meat and produce industries. Alcide has approximately 35 employees and is based in Redmond, Washington.

Management

Alcide's optimistic projections don't always pan out, causing some to doubt management's credibility. Also, management has not courted the institutional investment community, so the stock is unknown to most large investors. Management controls about 30% of the outstanding shares.

Strategy

Alcide seeks to dominate the market for controlling food-borne pathogens while holding steady the sales of its animal health products. The company seeks to gain broad government agency approval to market its Sanova treatment system to the food industry, building a barrier to entry for competitors.

8561 154th Avenue NE
Redmond, WA 98052

www.alcide.com

Morningstar Grades

Growth [B+]	1999	2000	2001	2002
Revenue %	-13.7	10.9	44.4	22.4
Earnings/Share %	NMF	NMF	NMF	12.1
Book Value/Share %	-3.1	-1.5	13.5	10.0
Dividends/Share %	NMF	NMF	NMF	NMF

Sales of Sanova totaled $3.4 million in the August quarter, flat with the May quarter. We expect sales of animal health products (34% of total sales) to stay flat in coming years.

Profitability [B]	2000	2001	2002	TTM
Return on Assets %	-3.1	8.1	8.1	7.0
Oper Cash Flow $Mil	1	4	5	5
- Cap Spending $Mil	5	5	5	4
= Free Cash Flow $Mil	-4	-1	-1	0

In 1999 and 2000, profitability suffered because of distribution problems. In 2001 and 2002, it improved dramatically, but we're concerned that recent changes in third-party distribution relationships may devastate profits this year.

Financial Health [B]	2000	2001	2002	08-02
Long-term Debt $Mil	0	0	0	0
Total Equity $Mil	13	16	18	18
Debt/Equity Ratio	0.0	0.0	0.0	0.0

The company has a small debt load and generates lots of cash flow from operations. However, its grade is hurt by its small size and the high capital expenditures involved in expanding plant installations of the Sanova system.

Industry	Investment Style	Stock Type	Sector
Chemicals	▦ Small Core	▨ Spec. Growth	⚙ Industrial Mats

Competition	Market Cap $Mil	Debt/ Equity	12 Mo Trailing Sales $Mil	Price/Cash Flow	Return On Assets%	Total Return% 1 Yr	3 Yr
Alcide	39	0.0	22	8.7	7.0	-38.5	8.7
Rhodia SA ADR	1,506	—	6,892	—	—	—	—
SureBeam A	225	—	41	—	—	—	—

Price Volatility ❙ Monthly Price High/Low — Relative Strength to S&P 500

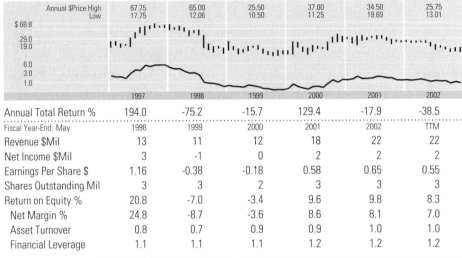

		1997	1998	1999	2000	2001	2002
Annual $Price High		67.75	65.00	25.50	37.00	34.50	25.75
Low		17.75	12.06	10.50	11.25	19.69	13.01

Annual Total Return %	194.0	-75.2	-15.7	129.4	-17.9	-38.5

Fiscal Year-End: May	1998	1999	2000	2001	2002	TTM
Revenue $Mil	13	11	12	18	22	22
Net Income $Mil	3	-1	0	2	2	2
Earnings Per Share $	1.16	-0.38	-0.18	0.58	0.65	0.55
Shares Outstanding Mil	3	3	2	3	3	3
Return on Equity %	20.8	-7.0	-3.4	9.6	9.8	8.3
Net Margin %	24.8	-8.7	-3.6	8.6	8.1	7.0
Asset Turnover	0.8	0.7	0.9	0.9	1.0	1.0
Financial Leverage	1.1	1.1	1.1	1.2	1.2	1.2

Valuation Ratios	Stock	Rel to Industry	Rel to S&P 500
Price/Earnings	26.8	1.2	1.1
Price/Book	2.1	0.4	0.7
Price/Sales	1.8	1.0	0.9
Price/Cash Flow	8.7	0.5	0.7

Major Fund Holders	% of Fund Assets
None	

Morningstar's Take By Mark A. Sellers, 10-15-2002 Stock Price as of Analysis: $13.52

Alcide's Sanova product is aimed at helping red meat- and poultry-processing plants reduce pathogens like E coli and salmonella. Sales of Sanova in the most recent quarter rose 25% year over year but were flat from the previous quarter. Although Alcide continues to slowly expand within the poultry-processing market, the low-hanging fruit seems to have been picked. And the company has had very little success to date entering the beef-processing market.

Alcide's other unit, which sells animal health products, has performed horribly, with sales and earnings declining rapidly. We think management has done a rotten job of running this division in recent years, frequently rejiggering product distributors in a seemingly willy-nilly fashion. This constant reconfiguring causes sales and earnings to be highly unpredictable from one quarter to the next. This is one company that consistently overpromises and underdelivers--the hallmark of a poor management team, in our opinion.

As a result of the recent slowdown in both divisions, as well as our flagging faith in management's ability to expand the company over the long term, we're lowering our estimates of Alcide's future cash flows. We were too optimistic in our previous analyses because we believed the food safety unit would be able to grow much more quickly than it has. At this point, we think growth in the food safety division could slow to around 10% in 2003 and decline from there over the next few years. Including zero growth from the animal health division (an optimistic assumption), Alcide's overall revenue growth should average somewhere around 8% over the next five years. Factoring this assumption into our valuation model, we estimate a fair value for the shares of $11.

 MORNINGSTAR® Stocks 500

Alcoa AA

	Rating	Risk	Moat Size	Fair Value	Last Close	Yield %
	★★★	Med.	Narrow	$29.00	$22.78	2.6

Company Profile

Alcoa produces primary aluminum and semi-fabricated and finished aluminum products. It also produces alumina and alumina-based chemicals, other finished products, and components and systems for various applications. Alcoa's customers include the international packaging, transportation, building, and industrial industries. Alcoa acquired Reynolds Metals, Cordant Technologies, and Howmet International in 2000.

Management

After more than two decades in Alcoa's management, Alain Belda took the reins from Paul O'Neill in May 1999. Belda wanted to double Alcoa's revenue in five years, but poor pricing, weak demand, and antitrust restrictions make that unlikely.

Strategy

Alcoa's operations are among the most efficient, given the scale it enjoys as the world's biggest aluminum company. Growth has been bolstered by acquisitions and joint ventures, but antitrust issues make future large-scale mergers unlikely. Future deals will probably involve smaller "bolt-on" acquisitions or additions to nonaluminum segments like consumer packaging.

201 Isabella Street   www.alcoa.com
Pittsburgh, PA 15212-5858

Morningstar Grades

Growth [B]	1998	1999	2000	2001
Revenue %	14.9	5.4	40.5	-0.3
Earnings/Share %	4.8	16.5	27.7	-41.7
Book Value/Share %	35.9	-1.6	64.6	-11.4
Dividends/Share %	53.9	7.4	24.1	20.0

Over the past two economic cycles, Alcoa's growth averaged about 4% per year (excluding acquisitions). Because of poor industry fundamentals and an uncertain economic outlook, we assume a more conservative 3% long-term growth rate in our model.

Profitability [B]	1999	2000	2001	TTM
Return on Assets %	6.2	4.7	3.2	1.7
Oper Cash Flow $Mil	2,381	2,851	2,411	1,692
- Cap Spending $Mil	920	1,121	1,177	1,220
= Free Cash Flow $Mil	1,461	1,730	1,234	472

Alcoa's gotten bigger, but looks like it's getting better as well. During the past two business cycles, average operating margin and return on assets improved by about a third, and average return on equity by almost half.

Financial Health [B+]	1999	2000	2001	09-02
Long-term Debt $Mil	2,657	4,987	6,388	7,938
Total Equity $Mil	6,262	11,366	10,558	10,673
Debt/Equity Ratio	0.4	0.4	0.6	0.7

Moody's cut Alcoa's rating to A2 in response to the company's acquisitive growth strategy and weak industry fundamentals. But A2 isn't bad, and Alcoa still generates healthy free cash flows most years, which adds to its financial strength.

Industry	Investment Style	Stock Type	Sector
Aluminum	Large Value	High Yield	Industrial Mats

Competition

	Market Cap $Mil	Debt/ Equity	12 Mo Trailing Sales $Mil	Price/Cash Flow	Return On Assets%	Total Return% 1 Yr	3 Yr
Alcoa	19,232	0.7	20,631	11.4	1.7	-34.6	-16.1
Alcan	9,485	0.4	12,397	5.6	-0.1	-16.3	-9.0
Pechiney ADR A	2,829	—	11,437	—	—		

Price Volatility

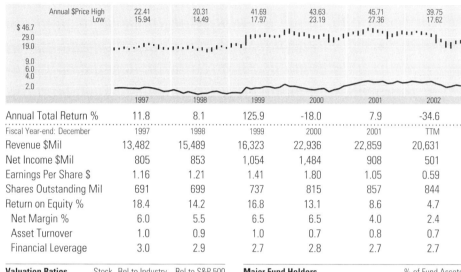

Annual Total Return %	11.8	8.1	125.9	-18.0	7.9	-34.6
Fiscal Year-end: December	1997	1998	1999	2000	2001	TTM
Revenue $Mil	13,482	15,489	16,323	22,936	22,859	20,631
Net Income $Mil	805	853	1,054	1,484	908	501
Earnings Per Share $	1.16	1.21	1.41	1.80	1.05	0.59
Shares Outstanding Mil	691	699	737	815	857	844
Return on Equity %	18.4	14.2	16.8	13.1	8.6	4.7
Net Margin %	6.0	5.5	6.5	6.5	4.0	2.4
Asset Turnover	1.0	0.9	1.0	0.7	0.8	0.7
Financial Leverage	3.0	2.9	2.7	2.8	2.7	2.7

Valuation Ratios	Stock	Rel to Industry	Rel to S&P 500
Price/Earnings	38.6	1.0	1.6
Price/Book	1.8	1.0	0.6
Price/Sales	0.9	1.0	0.5
Price/Cash Flow	11.4	1.0	0.9

Major Fund Holders	% of Fund Assets
Rydex Basic Materials Inv	5.96
MainStay Select 20 Equity A	5.49
ProFunds Ultra Basic Materials Inv	5.43
GAM American Focus A	4.75

Morningstar's Take By Daniel Quinn, 10-21-2002 Stock Price as of Analysis: $23.73

We think Alcoa is a solid core long-term holding at the right price.

Alcoa dominates the aluminum industry, with revenue and smelting capacity almost double those of Alcan, its closest rival. Alcoa also controls one fourth of the world's production of bauxite, the mineral from which aluminum is refined. As the industry's low-cost producer, Alcoa generates margins in its core aluminum smelting operations that are 4 percentage points higher than Alcan's, on average. We think it's unlikely Alcoa will lose its industry-leading position anytime soon. Alcan proposed a three-way merger in 2000 would have given it the size and heft of Alcoa, but the deal was rejected by European regulators because of antitrust concerns.

Alcoa's influence over the industry isn't absolute, though. We believe there are two big risks--one short-term and one long-term--that investors must weigh before investing in Alcoa. The core aluminum business is subject to economic cyclicality, and right now it's in a slump. Recent data from the London Metal Exchange suggest production has been outstripping demand, creating an imbalance that has depressed prices to about the lowest in 14 years. It will probably take a sustained industrial recovery to

eliminate the surplus and increase prices.

The long-term risk looms in emerging areas, particularly China. The Chinese industry has numerous small-scale producers, many of which are owned by local municipalities for whom tax revenue and employment are paramount concerns. Absent national regulation, it's possible these operators will overproduce. The Chinese government could also consolidate its massive industry and create a behemoth to rival Alcoa's global influence. When Russian producers flooded the international market with aluminum in the early 1990s, the Russian government stepped in and agreed to curb output. Now that China has become a member of the World Trade Organization, we hope it will be a responsible steward of industry health as well.

All of these issues have weighed heavily on Alcoa, with the shares losing more than 45% of their value in 2002. We've cut our fair value estimate from $35 to $29 in response to the short- and long-term risks we described. We think the shares would look attractive under $20.

Alcon ACL

	Rating	Risk	Moat Size	Fair Value	Last Close	Yield %
	★★★★	Low	Wide	$45.00	$39.45	0.0

Company Profile

Alcon is a global leader in developing, manufacturing, and selling ophthalmology drugs, supplies, and surgical devices. It also sells consumer eye-care products like contact lens cleaning solution. Alcon was part of global food king Nestle from the late 1970s until its partial IPO in 2002. Alcon has quietly become the largest eye-care company in the world, with one fourth of the $11 billion global market and three domains: pharmaceutical, surgical, and consumer products. Alcon operates in more than 75 countries and sells products in more than 180 nations.

Management

Tim Sear became CEO in 1997 after running the international business for 15 years. Many of the firm's top execs have spent the better part of their careers at Alcon. Nestle still controls three board seats, thanks to its 75% ownership of Alcon.

Strategy

It's all about the eye with Alcon. The former unit of Nestle makes surgical devices and solutions, consumer products, and drugs for the eye. By focusing solely on ophthalmology, Alcon has built a commanding market presence and is often the share leader. The company has a global perspective, selling goods in every major world market and generating half its revenue overseas.

Bosch 69
6331 Hunenberg,
www.alconlabs.com

Morningstar Grades

Growth [D+]	1998	1999	2000	2001
Revenue %	NMF	NMF	6.4	7.6
Earnings/Share %	NMF	NMF	NMF	NMF
Book Value/Share %	—	—	—	—
Dividends/Share %	NMF	NMF	NMF	NMF

Revenue growth has been consistently in the high single digits for the past five years. The bulk of this growth is coming from new pharmaceuticals, but the purchase of Summit Autonomous Technologies has also boosted surgical revenue.

Profitability [NA]	1999	2000	2001	TTM
Return on Assets %	NMF	8.5	7.8	7.8
Oper Cash Flow $Mil	452	393	529	529
- Cap Spending $Mil	99	117	127	127
= Free Cash Flow $Mil	352	276	401	401

Alcon's margins are very healthy. Gross margins of 70% reflect the strong demand for Alcon's products, and operating margins in the mid- to low 20s are representative of its dominant industry position.

Financial Health [A]	1999	2000	2001	12-01
Long-term Debt $Mil	—	700	697	697
Total Equity $Mil	—	1,101	1,390	1,390
Debt/Equity Ratio	—	0.6	0.5	0.5

The price of Alcon's freedom from Nestle was a $1.4 billion debt load and only $200 million in cash. Over the past few years, though, Alcon has generated more than enough free cash flow to cover the additional interest expense.

Industry	Investment Style	Stock Type	Sector
Drugs	▦ Large Growth	➡ Slow Growth	🌀 Healthcare

Competition	Market Cap $Mil	Debt/ Equity	12 Mo Trailing Sales $Mil	Price/Cash Flow	Return On Assets%	Total Return% 1 Yr	Total Return% 3 Yr
Alcon	11,835	0.5	2,748	22.4	7.8	—	—
Allergan	7,455	0.6	1,895	29.2	5.5	-19.0	7.8
Bausch & Lomb	1,942	0.5	1,828	9.1	1.1	-2.7	-16.3

Price Volatility   ❙ Monthly Price High/Low   ▬ Relative Strength to S&P 500

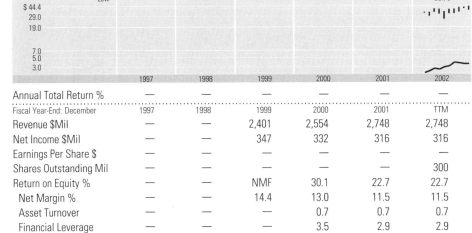

	1997	1998	1999	2000	2001	2002
Annual Total Return %	—	—	—	—	—	—

Fiscal Year-End: December	1997	1998	1999	2000	2001	TTM
Revenue $Mil	—	—	2,401	2,554	2,748	2,748
Net Income $Mil	—	—	347	332	316	316
Earnings Per Share $	—	—	—	—	—	—
Shares Outstanding Mil	—	—	—	—	—	300
Return on Equity %	—	—	NMF	30.1	22.7	22.7
Net Margin %	—	—	14.4	13.0	11.5	11.5
Asset Turnover	—	—	—	0.7	0.7	0.7
Financial Leverage	—	—	—	3.5	2.9	2.9

Valuation Ratios	Stock	Rel to Industry	Rel to S&P 500
Price/Earnings	—	—	—
Price/Book	8.5	1.2	2.7
Price/Sales	4.3	1.1	2.1
Price/Cash Flow	22.4	1.1	1.7

Major Fund Holders	% of Fund Assets
IPO Plus Aftermarket	7.47
Simms International Equity	5.32
Pax World Growth	4.54
INVESCO Health Sciences Inv	3.90

Morningstar's Take By Todd N. Lebor, 12-13-2002 Stock Price as of Analysis: $38.67

Alcon is a dominant player in the eye health-care market, and we'd be buyers at the right price.

Market dominance isn't something that comes easily, especially when you're dealing with high-tech equipment and finicky customers. But thanks to its focused approach on ophthalmology, Alcon has leading share in most of its markets. Best of all, the high transfer costs--the costly and time-consuming retraining--for doctors to switch from one medical device to another help Alcon maintain its share. We believe this focused strategy and product excellence will enable Alcon to stay competitive.

With nearly half of the global market in cataract surgery, Alcon's devices and equipment are a mainstay for ophthalmologists. As the population ages, cataracts--the cause behind 40% of blindness worldwide--are becoming more prevalent, fueling Alcon's sales in this area. In a bid to extend its presence in eye surgeries, Alcon acquired Summit Autonomous in 2000. Summit brought the world's number-two laser refractive surgical device to Alcon, opening up a fast-growing market. Alcon has only a fraction of the share of industry leader VISX, leaving plenty of room for growth. But since laser eye surgery is expensive and isn't reimbursed by most insurance plans, it's very sensitive to economic cycles. As a

result, Alcon has seen little upside from its acquisition. The company hopes to grab more share with its new LADARVision surgery system once the economy is back on track.

Another growth driver for Alcon is pharmaceuticals. Drugs offer high margins, patent protection, and the greatest platform for advancements. Until recently, physicians didn't have the tools to study such a delicate body part as the eye, but newfound knowledge is leading to new discoveries, especially in the pharmaceutical arena. We expect pharmaceuticals to lead Alcon's growth over the next few years.

Alcon's focus on eyes has led to a dominant position, but scientific advancements threaten this position every day, creating inherent risk in the business model. Investors need to be prepared for a shock should something happen to one of the company's main revenue streams. Also a bit disconcerting is the firm's debt. As a result of the Nestle spin-off, Alcon's debt/equity ratio is higher than we'd like, near 2.0. However, the company produces plenty of free cash flow (cash flow from operations less capital expenditures) to meet its obligations and pay down debt over the next decade.

M🌀RNINGSTAR® Stocks 500

Allergan AGN

	Rating	Risk	Moat Size	Fair Value	Last Close	Yield %
	★★★	Med.	Narrow	$62.00	$57.62	0.6

Industry	Investment Style	Stock Type	Sector
Drugs	Mid Growth	↗ Classic Growth	Healthcare

Company Profile

Allergan manufactures specialty pharmaceutical products. Its prescription ophthalmic products include treatments for allergies, glaucoma, inflammation, infection, and ophthalmic muscle disorders. The company generates approximately 20% of its revenue from the drug Botox. Allergan plans to spin off its medical device business--consisting of the eye care, surgical, and contact lens product lines--by mid-2002. The new company will be called Advanced Medical Optics.

Management

Chairman and chief executive David Pyott joined Allergan in 1998 and remains the top executive after the spin-off. Biotech bigwig Herbert Boyer, a founder of Genentech, has been on Allergan's board since 1994 and vice chairman since 2001.

Strategy

Allergan hopes to capitalize on the high-margin pharmaceutical business, now that it's spun off the contact lens and eye-care divisions into a separate company. The specialty pharmaceutical firm will focus on research and development and in-licensing technology to keep its product pipeline full and fend off the effects of increasing generic competition.

2525 Dupont Drive   www.allergan.com
Irvine, CA 92612

Competition

Competition	Market Cap $Mil	Debt/ Equity	12 Mo Trailing Sales $Mil	Price/Cash Flow	Return On Assets%	Total Return% 1 Yr	3 Yr
Allergan	7,455	0.6	1,895	29.2	5.5	-19.0	7.8
Alcon	11,835	0.5	2,748	22.4	7.8	—	—
Bausch & Lomb	1,942	0.5	1,828	9.1	1.1	-2.7	-16.3

Price Volatility

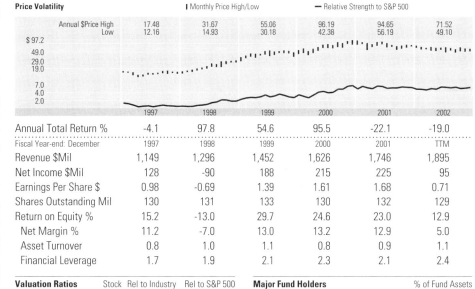

		Monthly Price High/Low		— Relative Strength to S&P 500		
Annual $Price High	17.48	31.67	55.06	96.19	94.65	71.52
Low	12.16	14.93	30.18	42.38	56.19	49.10
	1997	1998	1999	2000	2001	2002

	1997	1998	1999	2000	2001	2002
Annual Total Return %	-4.1	97.8	54.6	95.5	-22.1	-19.0

Fiscal Year-end: December	1997	1998	1999	2000	2001	TTM
Revenue $Mil	1,149	1,296	1,452	1,626	1,746	1,895
Net Income $Mil	128	-90	188	215	225	95
Earnings Per Share $	0.98	-0.69	1.39	1.61	1.68	0.71
Shares Outstanding Mil	130	131	133	130	132	129
Return on Equity %	15.2	-13.0	29.7	24.6	23.0	12.9
Net Margin %	11.2	-7.0	13.0	13.2	12.9	5.0
Asset Turnover	0.8	1.0	1.1	0.8	0.9	1.1
Financial Leverage	1.7	1.9	2.1	2.3	2.1	2.4

Valuation Ratios	Stock	Rel to Industry	Rel to S&P 500
Price/Earnings	81.2	3.5	3.4
Price/Book	10.1	1.4	3.2
Price/Sales	3.9	1.0	2.0
Price/Cash Flow	29.2	1.4	2.2

Major Fund Holders	% of Fund Assets
Jundt Growth I	5.53
Montgomery U.S. Focus	4.85
American Eagle Twenty	4.84
Jundt Twenty-Five A	4.57

Morningstar Grades

Growth [B-]	1998	1999	2000	2001
Revenue %	12.8	12.1	11.9	7.4
Earnings/Share %	NMF	NMF	15.8	4.3
Book Value/Share %	-16.7	-12.0	39.6	11.6
Dividends/Share %	0.0	7.7	14.3	12.5

The slow-growing optical device business has been a drag on sales in recent years. With the company focused on specialty pharmaceuticals and Botox sales soaring, revenue is expected to take a sharp turn upward over the next few years.

Profitability [A-]	1999	2000	2001	TTM
Return on Assets %	14.1	10.9	11.0	5.5
Oper Cash Flow $Mil	254	354	361	255
- Cap Spending $Mil	63	67	90	79
= Free Cash Flow $Mil	191	287	271	176

Allergan's gross margins improved to nearly 83% after the spin-off of its low-margin businesses. The company's return on equity hasn't been stellar when compared with the pharmaceutical industry, but the mid-20s is nothing to sneeze at.

Financial Health [A]	1999	2000	2001	09-02
Long-term Debt $Mil	209	585	521	445
Total Equity $Mil	635	874	977	738
Debt/Equity Ratio	0.3	0.7	0.5	0.6

Allergan is in good financial health. The company had $750 million in cash at the end of September 2002 and shifted nearly three fourths of its debt to the new entity.

Morningstar's Take By Jill Kiersky, 12-10-2002 Stock Price as of Analysis: $58.52

Now that Allergan has spun off its low-margin medical device business, the company can focus solely on high-margin specialty pharmaceuticals. The latter is a more attractive business model, but involves riskier projects and higher regulatory hurdles, which means we'd buy shares only at a reasonable discount to our fair value estimate.

Allergan is building on its success with treatments for glaucoma--the buildup of pressure in the eye--with several recently approved drugs. Alphagan P is the company's patent-protected derivative of its original Alphagan product, and causes fewer allergic reactions. Together, the Alphagan products have captured 15% of the $2 billion market. Allergan ceased selling the original product in mid-2002 and now markets only the patented version, but with generics close to market and several substitute treatments available, Alphagan sales are declining.

That's where Lumigan comes in. Launched in early 2002, this glaucoma treatment has been shown to reduce intraocular pressure more than the Alphagan series has. As a result, Lumigan is used for more-serious glaucoma cases, which may help boost Allergan's already strong penetration of the market.

The company's eye-care products are only the beginning. Allergan has captured more than 80% of the neurotoxin market with Botox, a treatment for everything from eye twitches to wrinkles. Since the aging population doesn't mind spending cash to look a few years younger, and physicians can earn as much as $84,000 per year in profit by giving Botox injections for cosmetic use--a newly approved indication--sales are expected to surge. Cosmetic use currently accounts for only 40% of the drug's sales. Allergan is investigating other uses like pain management, so even if the wrinkle-reduction use is short-lived, Botox should continue to be a strong seller.

Margins have already shown signs of improvement since the company spun off its device and contact lens product business, which had many competitors and price-sensitive buyers. Gross margins have reached nearly 83%, 10 percentage points higher than in 2000. That's far better than those of companies like Bausch & Lomb and Alcon, which make devices and therapeutics, and more in line with those of big pharmaceutical firms. Increased selling costs from new product introductions have somewhat offset savings. But the company still generates plenty of free cash flow (cash from operations minus capital expenditures) to cover its interest expense and provide investors with a decent dividend.

Alliance Capital Management Holding LP AC

		Risk	Moat Size	Fair Value	Last Close	Yield %
Rating ★★★★		Med.	Wide	$36.00	$31.00	7.4

Company Profile

Alliance Capital Management Holding is a diversified global investment advisor. It provides investment-management services to institutional investors, in the form of employee pension funds and endowment funds, and to individual investors through various investment vehicles, including a broad line of mutual funds, money market funds, deposit accounts, and certificates of deposit. Alliance Capital acquired Sanford C. Bernstein, a value-oriented manager of institutional assets, in October 2000.

Management

CEO Bruce Calvert joined Alliance in 1973 as a portfolio manager and worked his way up the ranks, earning the top executive job in 1999. The board named him chairman in May 2001.

Strategy

With more than $380 billion in assets under management, Alliance is one of the world's largest asset managers and can exploit economies of scale. A full menu of investment products, including growth, value, and fixed-income, makes Alliance a one-stop investment shop. The firm is particularly well situated to serve institutional and international investors.

1345 Avenue of The Americas   www.alliancecapital.com
New York, NY 10105

Morningstar Grades

Growth [D-]	1998	1999	2000	2001
Revenue %	35.8	12.6	-83.6	-25.7
Earnings/Share %	124.3	52.4	15.8	-28.3
Book Value/Share %	6.8	-28.1	839.5	-2.3
Dividends/Share %	24.5	29.4	53.6	-10.7

Revenue has increased at a compound annual rate of 31% over the past three years, buoyed by acquisitions. But market depreciation has taken a heavy toll on revenue in 2002. We expect a decline of 11%-12% for the year.

Profitability [A-]	1999	2000	2001	TTM
Return on Assets %	140.7	17.7	12.9	13.1
Oper Cash Flow $Mil	259	229	210	—
- Cap Spending $Mil	50	—	—	—
= Free Cash Flow $Mil	—	—	—	—

Alliance has only a tepid commitment to expense management. Expense growth outpaced revenue growth in 2001, leading to a 25% decrease in earnings per share. The same problem in 2002 has decreased operating margins to 29% from 34% a year ago.

Financial Health [A+]	1999	2000	2001	09-02
Long-term Debt $Mil	—	—	—	—
Total Equity $Mil	265	1,259	1,220	1,224
Debt/Equity Ratio	—	—	—	—

With $400 million worth of senior debt and commercial paper outstanding, Alliance has a debt/equity ratio of only 18% with a fairly low interest rate. This indicates a good financial position following the Sanford C. Bernstein acquisition.

Industry	Investment Style	Stock Type	Sector
Money Management	⊞ Mid Core	→ Slow Growth	💲 Financial Services

Competition	Market Cap $Mil	Debt/ Equity	12 Mo Trailing Sales $Mil	Price/Cash Flow	Return On Assets%	Total Return% 1 Yr	3 Yr
Alliance Capital Management Holding LP	2,360	—	184	—	13.1	-31.7	8.2
Franklin Resources	8,929	—	2,519	—	6.7	-2.6	3.8
Amvescap PLC ADR	4,858	—	2,478	—	3.9	-55.8	-15.8

Price Volatility ▮ Monthly Price High/Low   — Relative Strength to S&P 500

	1997	1998	1999	2000	2001	2002
Annual $Price High	19.94	29.00	34.00	56.69	59.35	50.81
Low	12.00	18.75	24.00	29.31	37.40	23.20
Annual Total Return %	62.6	37.9	25.3	81.8	0.9	-31.7

Fiscal Year-End: December	1997	1998	1999	2000	2001	TTM
Revenue $Mil	975	1,324	1,491	245	182	184
Net Income $Mil	129	293	383	224	159	162
Earnings Per Share $	0.74	1.66	2.53	2.93	2.10	2.12
Shares Outstanding Mil	170	171	147	68	74	76
Return on Equity %	32.4	68.1	144.3	17.8	13.1	13.2
Net Margin %	13.2	22.1	25.7	91.4	87.5	87.9
Asset Turnover	1.2	1.2	5.5	0.2	0.1	0.2
Financial Leverage	2.0	2.6	1.0	1.0	1.0	1.0

Valuation Ratios	Stock	Rel to Industry	Rel to S&P 500
Price/Earnings	14.6	0.8	0.6
Price/Book	1.9	0.7	0.6
Price/Sales	12.8	4.8	6.4
Price/Cash Flow	—	—	—

Major Fund Holders	% of Fund Assets
Royce Trust & GiftShares Inv	2.65
Royce Select	1.87

Morningstar's Take By Rachel Barnard, 12-10-2002 Stock Price as of Analysis: $33.00

A broad diversity of products and investment styles makes Alliance Capital an attractive asset manager to own at the right price.

Diversity is a real competitive advantage for asset-management companies, and that has never been more crucial than in the recent bear market. Alliance has done a good job of putting together a mix of fixed-income, value equity, and growth equity products that have helped prop up revenue during the stock market plunge. The firm also sells to both retail and institutional investors while nurturing a growing wealth-management business that now accounts for 10% of assets under management (AUM).

Even so, this giant was helpless in the face of a large drop in the equity markets, which decreased the value of its AUM. With more than 50% of assets in equity funds, some damage was inevitable.

This caused investors, mostly on the retail side, to yank money from Alliance funds. But the firm managed to add net new money on both the institutional and private-client sides over the past 12 months--an impressive achievement. Because the firm has not been hemorrhaging assets like some of its competitors, a market rebound will go a long way toward restoring lost revenue.

We are still worried about the firm's cost structure, however. We believe revenue will take a long time to build up again, especially if the economic recovery is a slow one. This means Alliance will be stuck with lower margins unless it takes a harder line on costs--something it doesn't seem to have the stomach for. We believe Alliance will continue to lag its money-management peers in profitability.

The real bright spot for Alliance has been its institutional research and trading business, which grew 13% in the first nine months of 2002. Since the firm doesn't have an investment bank, its research is free of the taint that has affected Wall Street analysts. We believe the market's hunger for independent research, coupled with a growing European franchise, will drive further growth in Alliance's research arm.

Size, diversity, and an international reach help to make Alliance an attractive investment. The shares aren't usually a bargain, but some bad calls by Alliance portfolio managers--notably investments in Enron and WorldCom--have generated negative publicity. The resulting dips in Alliance's stock price afforded investors a good buying opportunity, and we would keep an eye out for these in the future. We think the shares are attractive below $29.

 MRNINGSTAR® **Stocks 500**

Allied Capital ALD

	Rating	Risk	Moat Size	Fair Value	Last Close	Yield %
	★★	High	Narrow	$21.00	$21.83	10.1

Company Profile

Allied Capital is a business-development (sometimes called venture capital or private equity) firm that provides funding to small and midsize companies. It makes loans or invests in the equity of its portfolio companies and shepherds them along with help and advice as they grow. This type of funding is particularly critical for startups or small companies, which have a difficult time finding other sources of financing. Allied profits from the long-term growth of its portfolio companies, cashing out when they no longer need venture funds.

Management

William L. Walton has been chairman and CEO since 1997 and a board member since 1986. Previously a managing director for Butler Capital, Walton has extensive experience in venture capital and private equity.

Strategy

Allied Capital aims to pay a substantial and growing dividend to its shareholders. To make this happen, the firm reinvests its capital, borrows money, and raises new capital to invest in private companies and commercial mortgage-backed securities. The company pays no state or federal taxes as long as it follows government guidelines, including distributing 90% of its income to shareholders.

1919 Pennsylvania Avenue N.W.   www.alliedcapital.com
Washington, DC 20006

Morningstar Grades

Growth [A+]	1998	1999	2000	2001
Revenue %	9.6	32.2	49.9	36.6
Earnings/Share %	21.0	9.3	18.3	11.3
Book Value/Share %	11.1	17.7	25.7	4.2
Dividends/Share %	-18.1	14.3	13.8	10.4

Interest and fee income--the primary source of dividend funds--has grown strongly over the past three years, increasing at a compound annual rate of 39%. An industry downturn has slowed growth this year and more income is coming from capital gains.

Profitability [A+]	1999	2000	2001	TTM
Return on Assets %	7.6	7.7	8.2	8.6
Oper Cash Flow $Mil	-332	-332	-344	—
- Cap Spending $Mil	—	—	—	—
= Free Cash Flow $Mil	—	—	—	—

The firm returned 9% on assets in 2001, surpassing its peers in the finance industry. Return on invested capital has averaged an impressive 15% over the past five years. Profitability could be threatened by severe economic conditions.

Financial Health [A+]	1999	2000	2001	09-02
Long-term Debt $Mil	—	—	—	—
Total Equity $Mil	668	1,030	1,352	1,422
Debt/Equity Ratio	—	—	—	—

Regulations prohibit excessive leverage for business-development firms like Allied, but the company still borrows money to enhance its investment returns. Debt is now at a manageable 70% of equity.

Industry	Investment Style	Stock Type	Sector
Finance	▦ Mid Core	⬛ High Yield	$ Financial Services

Competition

	Market Cap $Mil	Debt/ Equity	12 Mo Trailing Sales $Mil	Price/Cash Flow	Return On Assets%	Total Return% 1 Yr	3 Yr
Allied Capital	2,237	—	315	—	8.6	-8.0	19.5
CIT Group	3,920	—	—	—	-15.7	—	—
LNR Property	1,179	—	476	—	—	—	—

Price Volatility

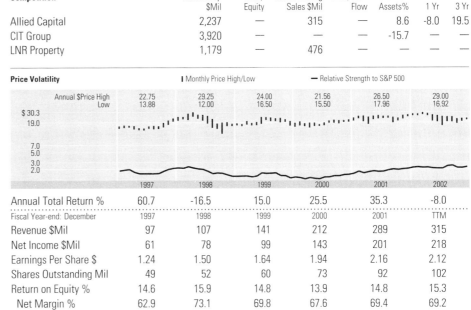

| | Monthly Price High/Low | | | Relative Strength to S&P 500 | | |

Annual $Price High Low	22.75 13.88	29.25 12.00	24.00 16.50	21.56 15.50	26.50 17.96	29.00 16.92

	1997	1998	1999	2000	2001	2002
Annual Total Return %	60.7	-16.5	15.0	25.5	35.3	-8.0

Fiscal Year-end: December	1997	1998	1999	2000	2001	TTM
Revenue $Mil	97	107	141	212	289	315
Net Income $Mil	61	78	99	143	201	218
Earnings Per Share $	1.24	1.50	1.64	1.94	2.16	2.12
Shares Outstanding Mil	49	52	60	73	92	102
Return on Equity %	14.6	15.9	14.8	13.9	14.8	15.3
Net Margin %	62.9	73.1	69.8	67.6	69.4	69.2
Asset Turnover	0.1	0.1	0.1	0.1	0.1	0.1
Financial Leverage	1.9	1.7	1.9	1.8	1.8	1.8

Valuation Ratios	Stock	Rel to Industry	Rel to S&P 500
Price/Earnings	10.3	0.9	0.4
Price/Book	1.6	0.5	0.5
Price/Sales	7.1	3.6	3.5
Price/Cash Flow	—	—	—

Major Fund Holders	% of Fund Assets
FAM Equity-Income	5.23
Phoenix-Seneca Real Estate Secs A	5.13
Green Century Balanced	4.41
Hillman Total Return	4.05

Morningstar's Take By Rachel Barnard, 10-08-2002 Stock Price as of Analysis: $19.52

Allied Capital pays terrific dividends. However, these juicy returns come from potentially volatile investments in small private companies and junk bonds. Only investors with a high risk tolerance should consider this stock.

This little company has been dragged through the limelight because many investors are betting that it is headed for a fall. We believe these fears have been blown out of proportion, but the publicity has served to highlight real risks in Allied Capital's business that investors should understand and weigh carefully before jumping on board.

Allied Capital derives its income from a portfolio of investments valued at $2.4 billion. Of this, 70% is invested in private companies and the remaining 30% is in noninvestment-grade commercial mortgage-backed securities (CMBS). These are high-yield investments because a typical bank won't touch them. Small companies, searching for the capital to grow, often cannot get enough funding from a bank because their businesses are too speculative. This is where Allied Capital steps in and makes a loan or buys an equity stake. The loans carry high interest payments, yielding around 14% on the private debt and 15% on CMBS.

But the high return carries with it a high likelihood of default. With the economy in marginal shape, many small businesses are struggling and those closer to the edge are more apt to run into trouble. If this happened with a significant portion of its investments, Allied would not have the earnings to support its dividend and would be forced to cut it. This would affect its shares, which largely trade on the dividend yield.

It would help if Allied's portfolio could be independently valued, but because there is little or no information available about private companies, an outside estimate would be mainly conjecture. This hasn't stopped investors from trying, however. One hedge fund manager remains convinced that Allied's portfolio is grossly overvalued and publicly announced his short sale of the stock, causing a wave of controversy and spurring investor lawsuits.

We believe the valuation of Allied's investments is a key risk factor. Over the past 40 years the firm has done a good job of making investments and valuing them appropriately. But while we don't see any reason to doubt current management's ability to continue this tradition, we do see some real risks to the portfolio, given the shaky economy, and think investors should seek a substantial margin of safety before investing.

Alltel AT

	Rating	Risk	Moat Size	Fair Value	Last Close	Yield %
	★★★	Med.	Narrow	$56.00	$51.00	3.1

Company Profile

Alltel provides a variety of telecom services. About 25% of revenue comes from traditional local phone services. The company services about 2.6 million local customers, primarily in the Southeast. Alltel is also the sixth-largest wireless company in the United States with about 6.6 million subscribers. The wireless business generates about half of total revenue. In addition to telecom services, the company also has an information services business, which provides software, information processing, and outsourcing services, primarily to the financial industry.

Management

Chairman Joe Ford, with Alltel since 1959, relinquished the CEO post to his son Scott in July 2002. Scott has been president since 1997 and had served as COO since 1998. The Fords own less than 1% of shares outstanding.

Strategy

Alltel is expanding its wireless subscriber base by offering regional and nationwide calling plans. It is trying to cut costs and increase margins by consolidating its diverse operations into three regions. Alltel is working to integrate the lines acquired from Verizon and wireless customers from Centurytel. The company also makes small acquisitions to augment its existing territories.

One Allied Drive   www.alltel.com
Little Rock, AR 72202

Morningstar Grades

Growth [C-]	1998	1999	2000	2001
Revenue %	17.8	13.9	10.2	4.8
Earnings/Share %	-7.1	26.7	146.2	-44.1
Book Value/Share %	19.3	13.1	21.0	10.4
Dividends/Share %	5.4	5.1	4.5	3.1

The local phone business can be counted on for about 3% growth. Wireless growth has slowed considerably, hurt by falling roaming rates and fewer customer additions. Though acquisitions may indicate otherwise, Alltel is a slow grower.

Profitability [A]	1999	2000	2001	TTM
Return on Assets %	7.3	15.8	8.5	5.5
Oper Cash Flow $Mil	1,500	1,496	2,071	2,428
- Cap Spending $Mil	1,106	2,205	1,449	1,506
= Free Cash Flow $Mil	394	-708	621	922

Alltel is solidly profitable. The local phone business generates operating margins near 40%. Other units aren't as profitable but still turn in respectable results. Once recent acquisitions are integrated, increased scale should help margins some.

Financial Health [B]	1999	2000	2001	09-02
Long-term Debt $Mil	3,750	4,612	3,862	6,391
Total Equity $Mil	4,205	5,095	5,565	5,846
Debt/Equity Ratio	0.9	0.9	0.7	1.1

Although leverage has increased to finance acquisitions, Alltel is among the strongest firms in the industry. Cash flow covers interest expense about 8 times over and the company has a history of paying down debt quickly after making acquisitions.

Industry	Investment Style	Stock Type	Sector
Wireless Service	Large Core	High Yield	Telecom

Competition

	Market Cap $Mil	Debt/ Equity	12 Mo Trailing Sales $Mil	Price/Cash Flow	Return On Assets%	Total Return% 1 Yr	3 Yr
Alltel	15,837	1.1	7,837	6.5	5.5	-14.7	-11.1
Verizon Communications	106,011	1.4	67,422	4.7	-0.1	-15.2	-9.8
SBC Communications	90,011	0.6	43,824	6.1	5.1	-28.3	-12.8

Price Volatility

▌ Monthly Price High/Low   — Relative Strength to S&P 500

Annual $Price High Low	41.63 29.75	61.38 38.25	91.81 56.31	82.94 47.75	68.69 49.43	63.25 35.33

$ 92.8
49.0
29.0
19.0
8.0
5.0

	1997	1998	1999	2000	2001	2002
Annual Total Return %	35.2	49.5	40.7	-22.8	1.1	-14.7

Fiscal Year-End: December	1997	1998	1999	2000	2001	TTM
Revenue $Mil	4,907	5,781	6,583	7,254	7,599	7,837
Net Income $Mil	651	602	783	1,929	1,067	899
Earnings Per Share $	2.10	1.95	2.47	6.08	3.40	2.88
Shares Outstanding Mil	307	306	313	315	312	311
Return on Equity %	21.3	16.6	18.6	37.9	19.2	15.4
Net Margin %	13.3	10.4	11.9	26.6	14.0	11.5
Asset Turnover	0.5	0.6	0.6	0.6	0.6	0.5
Financial Leverage	3.0	2.8	2.6	2.4	2.3	2.8

Valuation Ratios	Stock	Rel to Industry	Rel to S&P 500
Price/Earnings	17.7	1.5	0.8
Price/Book	2.7	1.0	0.8
Price/Sales	2.0	0.8	1.0
Price/Cash Flow	6.5	0.6	0.5

Major Fund Holders	% of Fund Assets
ProFunds Ultra Wireless Inv	21.95
Fidelity Select Wireless	10.56
Scudder Flag Communications A	10.16
Flex-funds Total Return Utilities	6.78

Morningstar's Take By Michael Hodel, 12-05-2002 Stock Price as of Analysis: $50.90

Alltel is one of our favorite telecom companies. Should the stock trade below $40, we'd deem it attractive enough to buy.

As much of the telecom world crashes around it, Alltel keeps moving forward. On August 1, 2002, the company completed the acquisitions of Centurytel's CTL 800,000 wireless customers and Verizon's VZ 600,000 local phone customers. The Centurytel deal expands Alltel's wireless unit by about 11%, adding scale in an industry where bigger is increasingly proving better. The deal also fills some gaps in Alltel's existing footprint. Centurytel's wireless operations had been struggling, with customer growth flattening and margins shrinking. As a result, Alltel was able to acquire the business for a fair price. Alltel will be able to offer these acquired customers nationwide and regional calling plans at reasonable prices, improving profitability and growth.

The Verizon deal increases the size of Alltel's local phone unit by 22%. The acquired customers, like Alltel's existing base, reside predominantly in rural areas. While the rural markets don't provide a ton of growth opportunities, they have the benefit of stability; they simply aren't big enough to attract much competition. While the more urban-focused regional Bells have seen lines in service fall 5% or

more over the past year, Alltel's lines have held steady--not bad, given the state of the economy. Alltel is a skilled local phone operator, generating margins near the top of the industry. Adding lines should give the firm another source of steady cash flow to support capital spending and debt reduction.

Alltel's current financial position is strong. Free cash flow will probably top $1 billion (more than $3 per share) this year. The company has a history of using cash flow to pay down debt following acquisitions, a trend we expect to continue. Debt reduction in this manner boosts earnings growth and positions the firm to take advantage of acquisition opportunities when they arise.

We've granted Alltel a narrow economic moat rating because it derives half of its revenue from the wireless business. While the wireless business offers protection over the long term if wireless substitution starts to erode Alltel's local phone business, wireless is very competitive. The company derives another fourth of its revenue from the far lower-margin information services business. Narrow-moat stocks require a larger margin of safety to our fair value estimate than wide-moat stocks do. Should Alltel shares fall 30% below our fair value estimate, though, we'd be very interested.

 **M**ORNINGSTAR® **Stocks 500**

Altera ALTR

	Rating	Risk	Moat Size	Fair Value	Last Close	Yield %
	★★★	Med.	Narrow	$14.00	$12.34	0.0

Company Profile

Altera develops and produces programmable logic semiconductor devices. The company offers programmable logic chips with architectures that provide varied levels of logic integration and performance. Its customers in the telecommunication, industrial, office automation and peripherals, military, and aerospace markets use the company's software or other industry-standard software to configure and program these chips for a wide variety of end uses. Altera sells its chips in the United States and abroad. Foreign sales account for approximately 44% of the company's revenue.

Management

After running Altera since 1983, Rodney Smith retired as president and CEO in November 2000; he remains chairman. Former LSI Logic executive John Daane is now president and CEO.

Strategy

Altera is focused on increasing its market share in the programmable logic device industry, and is also looking to expand its presence beyond traditional PLD applications, which would usually use preprogrammed chips. The firm believes that the time-to-market advantages of PLDs will lead to broader acceptance over preprogrammed chips, as per-unit costs of PLDs decrease.

101 Innovation Dr.   www.altera.com
San Jose, CA 95134

Morningstar Grades

Growth [D]	1998	1999	2000	2001
Revenue %	3.7	27.9	64.6	-39.0
Earnings/Share %	13.9	38.5	120.4	NMF
Book Value/Share %	61.7	21.0	10.9	-6.3
Dividends/Share %	NMF	NMF	NMF	NMF

Following 30% average growth from 1998 to 2000, Altera's sales plummeted 39% in 2001 because of a massive industry downturn. We expect the firm's growth to outpace the industry over the long term, but sales are on track to fall sharply again in 2002.

Profitability [A]	1999	2000	2001	TTM
Return on Assets %	15.6	24.8	-2.9	2.2
Oper Cash Flow $Mil	403	550	-118	256
- Cap Spending $Mil	30	88	66	15
= Free Cash Flow $Mil	373	463	-184	241

Net margins--usually 25%-30%--are tops in the PLD industry, even higher than Xilinx's, and generally better than most other chipmakers'. Altera remains solidly profitable despite the impact of falling sales on margins.

Financial Health [A+]	1999	2000	2001	09-02
Long-term Debt $Mil	—	—	—	—
Total Equity $Mil	1,118	1,248	1,115	1,085
Debt/Equity Ratio	—	—	—	—

Altera is debt-free and free cash flow positive, and has enough cash and investments (about $850 million) to cover liabilities more than 3 times.

Industry	Investment Style	Stock Type	Sector
Semiconductors	▦ Mid Growth	➡ Slow Growth	▣ Hardware

Competition	Market Cap $Mil	Debt/ Equity	12 Mo Trailing Sales $Mil	Price/Cash Flow	Return On Assets%	Total Return% 1 Yr	3 Yr
Altera	4,720	—	694	18.5	2.2	-41.9	-20.9
Xilinx	6,944	0.0	1,069	20.3	5.3	-47.3	-23.3
Lattice Semiconductor	985	0.3	224	24.8	-5.6	-57.4	-26.9

Price Volatility

I Monthly Price High/Low — Relative Strength to S&P 500

Annual $Price High / Low	16.44 / 7.59	15.47 / 7.06	34.28 / 11.97	67.13 / 19.63	34.69 / 14.66	26.18 / 8.32

	1997	1998	1999	2000	2001	2002
Annual Total Return %	-8.8	83.8	62.8	6.2	-19.4	-41.8

Fiscal Year-end: December	1997	1998	1999	2000	2001	TTM
Revenue $Mil	631	654	837	1,377	839	694
Net Income $Mil	133	154	224	497	-40	30
Earnings Per Share $	0.34	0.39	0.54	1.19	-0.10	0.07
Shares Outstanding Mil	353	377	393	398	398	383
Return on Equity %	24.9	17.5	20.0	39.8	-3.6	2.7
Net Margin %	21.1	23.6	26.8	36.1	-4.7	4.3
Asset Turnover	0.7	0.6	0.6	0.7	0.6	0.5
Financial Leverage	1.8	1.2	1.3	1.6	1.2	1.2

Valuation Ratios	Stock	Rel to Industry	Rel to S&P 500
Price/Earnings	176.3	4.3	7.5
Price/Book	4.4	1.5	1.4
Price/Sales	6.8	1.8	3.4
Price/Cash Flow	18.5	1.6	1.4

Major Fund Holders	% of Fund Assets
Firsthand Technology Leaders	3.90
Phoenix-Seneca Mid-Cap Edge A	3.56
Alliance Select Investor Technology A	3.30
AFBA Five Star Science & Technology A	3.12

Morningstar's Take By Jeremy Lopez, 10-29-2002 Stock Price as of Analysis: $11.43

We like Altera's fundamentals and long-term prospects. However, we'd buy the stock only at a wide--roughly 40%--discount to our fair value estimate.

As a producer of programmable logic devices (PLDs), Altera operates in one of the chip industry's more attractive niches. Since 1990, PLD sales growth has outpaced the chip industry's 10% average by about 6 percentage points. Part of this performance has been driven by the growth in end-market products that use PLDs, like telecom/wireless infrastructure, storage gear, and consumer electronics. Since PLDs are more customizable than preprogrammed ASIC chips, customers can save time designing their products with PLDs and therefore get their products to market more quickly. This flexibility has historically resulted in PLDs gaining share on ASICs, which is a trend we expect to continue.

The PLD industry is essentially a two-horse race, with Altera and rival Xilinx controlling roughly three fourths of the market. The rest of the niche consists of lower-end, marginal players--like Lattice and Actel--that do not present a big competitive threat. Xilinx has most recently had an edge on Altera, as its Virtex PLD family led to better top-line growth over the past chip cycle. But Xilinx and Altera have been

duking it out for years for the leading spot in PLDs, and we think it's only a matter of time before Altera narrows this gap. In fact, Altera should be in great shape heading into the next cycle with its heavily refreshed product mix, including its new Stratix, Excalibur, and Cyclone chip families.

Of course, Altera's outlook is far from perfect. A huge slump in tech spending has limited the firm's near-term prospects, and telecom/wireless infrastructure providers--the hardest-hit in the current downturn--have historically been some of the biggest PLD users. However, PLDs are used in nearly all major tech segments, and Altera's competitive position is improving. Also, Altera avoids the burden of capital spending by outsourcing its chip production. This "fabless" model, combined with the limited rivalry in PLDs, contributes to relatively strong and stable fundamentals, in our view. The firm's gross margins are typically above 60% and it's not uncommon for operating margins to hover above 30%.

The best time to buy Altera, or any other chipmaker, is usually during an industry slump, when the market is overly pessimistic on the stock. The industry is certainly in a slump, but we'd wait for a 40% discount to our fair value estimate before considering Altera's valuation attractive.

Amazon.com AMZN

	Rating	Risk	Moat Size	Fair Value	Last Close	Yield %
	★	Med.	Narrow	$13.00	$18.89	0.0

Company Profile

Amazon.com markets books, videos, music recordings, and other products over the Internet. It sells more than 4.7 million book, video, and music titles, including mystery, computer, business, science fiction, children's, and fiction books, as well as textbooks. In addition, the company discounts books on select bestseller lists and on certain company-selected books. Amazon.com also sells products such as electronics, toys, tools, autos, and software. In addition, it offers auction services.

Management

CEO Jeff Bezos founded Amazon.com in 1994 after developing computer systems for Bankers Trust and investment firm D.E. Shaw.

Strategy

Amazon.com is by far the leading retailer on the Internet, selling everything from books to toys to consumer electronics. The company has made an effort to move toward profitability over the past couple of years, finally achieving its first-ever profit in the fourth quarter of 2001. It's also hoping for more bricks-and-clicks partnerships modeled after its deals with Toys 'R' Us and Borders.

1200 12th Avenue South   www.amazon.com
Seattle, WA 98144-2734

Morningstar Grades

Growth [A-]	1998	1999	2000	2001
Revenue %	312.6	168.9	68.4	13.1
Earnings/Share %	NMF	NMF	NMF	NMF
Book Value/Share %	NMF	73.9	NMF	NMF
Dividends/Share %	NMF	NMF	NMF	NMF

Growth slowed dramatically in 2001 but has started to accelerate again. Revenue increased 25% in the first nine months of 2002 (compared with 11% a year earlier), and should grow at a comparable rate in the fourth quarter.

Profitability [F]	1999	2000	2001	TTM
Return on Assets %	-29.2	-66.1	-34.6	-9.8
Oper Cash Flow $Mil	-91	-130	-120	151
- Cap Spending $Mil	287	135	50	31
= Free Cash Flow $Mil	-378	-265	-170	120

After its first-ever net profit in the fourth quarter of 2001, Amazon has lost money again in each of the past three quarters. But it made a pro forma operating profit in each of those quarters, and is generating positive free cash flow.

Financial Health [F]	1999	2000	2001	09-02
Long-term Debt $Mil	—	2,127	2,156	2,265
Total Equity $Mil	266	-967	-1,440	-1,478
Debt/Equity Ratio	—	ELB	ELB	NMF

The firm is highly leveraged, with more than $2 billion in long-term debt. Working capital (current assets minus current liabilities) has stabilized after fears of a credit crunch.

Industry	Investment Style	Stock Type	Sector
Online Retail	▦ Mid Growth	▦ Spec. Growth	▤ Consumer Services

Competition

	Market Cap $Mil	Debt/ Equity	12 Mo Trailing Sales $Mil	Price/Cash Flow	Return On Assets%	Total Return% 1 Yr	3 Yr
Amazon.com	7,206	NMF	3,619	47.8	-9.8	74.6	-38.7
eBay	18,804	0.0	1,020	49.4	9.1	1.4	2.0
Barnes & Noble.com	50	—	410	—	—	—	—

Price Volatility

⎮ Monthly Price High/Low   — Relative Strength to S&P 500

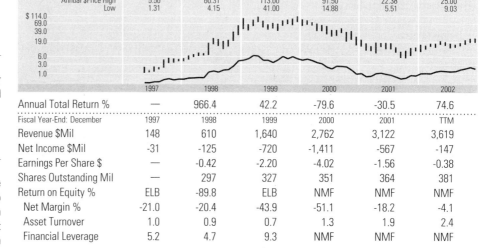

Annual $Price High Low	5.50 1.31	60.31 4.15	113.00 41.00	91.50 14.88	22.38 5.51	25.00 9.03

	1997	1998	1999	2000	2001	2002
Annual Total Return %	—	966.4	42.2	-79.6	-30.5	74.6

Fiscal Year-End: December	1997	1998	1999	2000	2001	TTM
Revenue $Mil	148	610	1,640	2,762	3,122	3,619
Net Income $Mil	-31	-125	-720	-1,411	-567	-147
Earnings Per Share $	—	-0.42	-2.20	-4.02	-1.56	-0.38
Shares Outstanding Mil	—	297	327	351	364	381
Return on Equity %	ELB	-89.8	ELB	NMF	NMF	NMF
Net Margin %	-21.0	-20.4	-43.9	-51.1	-18.2	-4.1
Asset Turnover	1.0	0.9	0.7	1.3	1.9	2.4
Financial Leverage	5.2	4.7	9.3	NMF	NMF	NMF

Valuation Ratios	Stock	Rel to Industry	Rel to S&P 500
Price/Earnings	NMF	—	—
Price/Book	—	—	—
Price/Sales	2.0	0.3	1.0
Price/Cash Flow	47.8	1.0	3.6

Major Fund Holders	% of Fund Assets
Legg Mason Focus	11.94
Legg Mason Opportunity Prim	7.77
ProFunds Ultra Internet Inv	7.33
Legg Mason Value Prim	6.02

Morningstar's Take By David Kathman, 11-12-2002 Stock Price as of Analysis: $19.82

Amazon.com's delicate balancing act is working well, helping the e-tail giant combine rejuvenated growth with improved margins. While we're impressed with the way Amazon is executing its game plan, we'd be wary of paying too much for it.

After reaching the holy grail of profitability in the fourth quarter of 2001, Amazon has spent 2002 trying to rejuvenate its top line without causing too much erosion to its hard-won margin gains. One of its key strategies has been a series of price cuts and offers of free shipping on orders over a certain amount. The free-shipping offer was designed to lure new online shoppers intimidated by high delivery costs while also getting existing customers to buy more per order.

This strategy has succeeded in doubling Amazon's top-line growth to 25% in the first three quarters of 2002, compared with 12% in the same period a year earlier. The core U.S. book-movie-video business has improved from flat sales in 2001 to 10% growth in the first nine months of 2002, and unit volume in the electronics-kitchen-tool (ETK) segment has been helped significantly by the free-shipping offer. Also, Amazon's international operations have been growing better than 70% each quarter and now account for 36% of the company's revenue.

Yet this growth revival has not hurt Amazon's bottom line too much. Fulfillment costs, or the cost of storing and shipping goods, have stayed steady as a percentage of sales despite the free-shipping promotion. Although it has lost money on a net basis ever since its surprise profit at the end of 2001, Amazon has consistently posted operating profits each quarter, and we expect operating margins to improve significantly as the company leverages the infrastructure it has built up.

True, the ETK division is still losing money, and we continue to have our doubts that this business will ever be a significant moneymaker. But this is partially offset by the profitable services division, which includes the sites Amazon builds and runs for such bricks-and-mortar partners as Toys 'R' Us and Circuit City. We also like the increasing use of Amazon as a platform for third-party sellers (now representing 23% of U.S. units sold on the site), which takes a page from eBay's inventory-free (and very profitable) business model.

We think Amazon will continue to thrive as a company, but we'd want a 30% margin of safety to our fair value estimate before buying the stock.

MORNINGSTAR® Stocks 500

AMB Property AMB

	Rating	Risk	Moat Size	Fair Value	Last Close	Yield %
	★★★	Low	Narrow	$30.00	$27.36	6.0

Company Profile

AMB is a self-administered, self-managed real estate investment trust that owns, manages, and develops industrial property in the United States. The REIT owns approximately 80 million square feet of industrial space and just more than a million square feet of retail space. Its properties are concentrated in 26 major U.S. markets, including Atlanta, Chicago, Dallas, greater New York, and Northern and Southern California. Before going public in 1997, AMB was a private institutional real estate money manager.

Management

CEO Hamid Moghadam helped found AMB's predecessor firm in the early 1980s. Some managers have investments in other real estate ventures; although these don't appear material, they could cause a conflict of interest.

Strategy

AMB's strategy is to own and manage high-throughput distribution centers near busy transportation hubs, like international passenger cargo airports and seaports that focus on container shipping. The REIT likes to team up with institutional investors in joint ventures. AMB usually retains at least a 20% ownership interest in these ventures and manages the properties.

Pier 1
San Francisco, CA 94111
www.amb.com

Morningstar Grades

Growth [B+]

	1998	1999	2000	2001
Revenue %	540.2	24.9	7.1	25.1
Earnings/Share %	NMF	54.0	-30.4	8.9
Book Value/Share %	NMF	3.9	-0.7	-2.3
Dividends/Share %	922.4	2.2	5.7	6.8

Including our projection for 2002, revenue will have grown about 16% annually since 1998, which is impressive considering that this growth has been generated internally via capital recycling.

Profitability [A-]

	1999	2000	2001	TTM
Return on Assets %	4.6	2.6	2.6	2.1
Oper Cash Flow $Mil	190	261	289	—
- Cap Spending $Mil	400	605	402	—
= Free Cash Flow $Mil	—	—	—	—

AMB's operating margin of roughly 76% is relatively high for a REIT. Dividends have grown at about a 5% annual rate over the past three years.

Financial Health [C]

	1999	2000	2001	09-02
Long-term Debt $Mil	—	—	—	—
Total Equity $Mil	1,733	1,672	1,656	1,642
Debt/Equity Ratio	—	—	—	—

Standard & Poor's recently affirmed AMB's BBB debt rating, which is investment-grade. Debt/total market capitalization is roughly 36%, about average for an industrial REIT.

Industry	Investment Style	Stock Type	Sector
REITS	▦ Mid Value	▦ Hard Assets	💲 Financial Services

Competition	Market Cap $Mil	Debt/ Equity	12 Mo Trailing Sales $Mil	Price/Cash Flow	Return On Assets%	Total Return% 1 Yr	3 Yr
AMB Property	2,293	—	640	—	2.1	11.5	19.0
ProLogis Trust	4,476	—	554	—	—	—	—
CenterPoint Properties	1,318	—	165	—	—	—	—

Price Volatility

▌ Monthly Price High/Low — Relative Strength to S&P 500

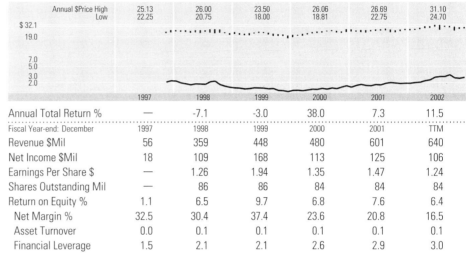

Annual $Price High	25.13	26.00	23.50	26.06	26.69	31.10
Low	22.25	20.75	18.00	18.81	22.75	24.70

	1997	1998	1999	2000	2001	2002
Annual Total Return %	—	-7.1	-3.0	38.0	7.3	11.5
Fiscal Year-end: December	1997	1998	1999	2000	2001	TTM
Revenue $Mil	56	359	448	480	601	640
Net Income $Mil	18	109	168	113	125	106
Earnings Per Share $	—	1.26	1.94	1.35	1.47	1.24
Shares Outstanding Mil	—	86	86	84	84	84
Return on Equity %	1.1	6.5	9.7	6.8	7.6	6.4
Net Margin %	32.5	30.4	37.4	23.6	20.8	16.5
Asset Turnover	0.0	0.1	0.1	0.1	0.1	0.1
Financial Leverage	1.5	2.1	2.1	2.6	2.9	3.0

Valuation Ratios	Stock	Rel to Industry	Rel to S&P 500
Price/Earnings	22.1	1.3	0.9
Price/Book	1.4	0.9	0.4
Price/Sales	3.6	1.1	1.8
Price/Cash Flow	—	—	—

Major Fund Holders	% of Fund Assets
Delaware REIT A	4.86
Undiscovered Managers REIT Inst	4.84
Fidelity Real Estate High-Income II	4.73
Security Capital U.S. Real Estate	4.72

Morningstar's Take By Matthew Scholz, 12-10-2002 Stock Price as of Analysis: $28.24

AMB is doing a great job of executing its focused investment and management strategy. Our net asset value estimate is $30 per share.

Although the predecessor firm dates to 1983, AMB is a fairly new real estate investment trust (REIT). At AMB's 1997 initial public offering, the property portfolio was roughly two thirds industrial and one third retail.

In 1999, management chose to focus on industrial properties that it calls high-throughput distribution (HTD) facilities. Unlike run-of-the-mill warehouses that are used mainly to store products, HTD facilities are near hubs of international trade and see above-average production or inventory flow.

Since 1999, AMB has sold nearly all of its retail properties, totaling approximately $1 billion, and recycled this capital into HTD properties. Eight hub and gateway markets are key to the HTD strategy. These eight cities form a transportation nexus for international trade, and account for 69% of AMB's net operating income.

Warehousing facilities near places like O'Hare International airport and the Port of Los Angeles may not have a lot of sex appeal, but they are critical to a lot of firms, even during what has been a sharp downturn in industrial leasing demand. As of

September 30, AMB's occupancy level was above 94%, which compares with the industrial average of about 90%. Even though AMB has been cautious with the rates it charges on new leases, the higher occupancy has resulted in above-average growth in net operating income.

Most of AMB's clients are large, logistics-oriented firms that require a distribution presence in multiple markets. Since AMB has facilities and development capabilities in most large North American distribution markets, the company has a competitive advantage over most of its rivals. With so many of its clients engaged in international trade, AMB is seeking to expand its competitive advantage by developing a presence in select international locales. Singapore, which is home to the world's third-busiest cargo airport and seaport, is one place AMB plans to go.

AMB is a core industrial REIT holding that trades at a discount to our net asset value. We don't look for much appreciation until demand for industrial properties gets boosted by increased capital spending and job growth. But until then, AMB sports a healthy 6% dividend yield.

Ambac Financial Group ABK

	Rating	Risk	Moat Size	Fair Value	Last Close	Yield %
	★★★	Med.	Narrow	$72.00	$56.24	0.7

Company Profile

Ambac Financial guarantees the timely payment of principal and interest on municipal and corporate bonds and asset-backed securities in the United States and abroad. Any issue insured by the firm is assigned Ambac's AAA rating, lowering the cost of capital for the issuer. With its capital backing the issue, Ambac substantially cuts the default risk for investors and provides price stability in the secondary market. Ambac's Cadre Financial Services subsidiary offers investment advisory services to school districts, hospitals, health organizations, and municipalities.

Management

Phillip Lassiter has been chairman and CEO since 1991, the same year Ambac went public. He is Ambac's largest individual shareholder, with 1.6% of the outstanding shares. No other insider owns more than 1%.

Strategy

Ambac is looking to the international financial guaranty markets to achieve its targeted 15% annual earnings growth. The firm has made progress in expanding its revenue stream beyond its slow-growing core business of insuring muni bonds: During 2001, earned premiums from international operations constituted 23% of the firm's total, up from just 6% in 1997.

One State Street Plaza
New York, NY 10004

www.ambac.com

Industry	Investment Style	Stock Type	Sector
Insurance (General)	▦ Mid Core	↗ Classic Growth	💲 Financial Services

Competition	Market Cap $Mil	Debt/ Equity	12 Mo Trailing Sales $Mil	Price/Cash Flow	Return On Assets%	Total Return% 1 Yr	Total Return% 3 Yr
Ambac Financial Group	5,960	—	816	—	3.3	-2.2	20.2
General Electric	242,308	2.2	130,295	8.2	2.7	-37.7	-18.9
American International Gr	150,907	—	66,823	—	1.4	-26.9	-4.0

Price Volatility

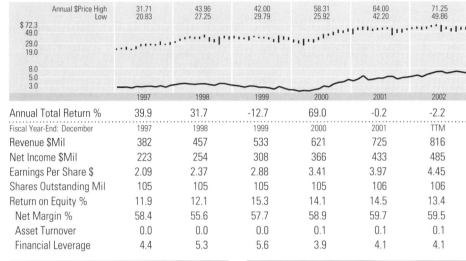

Annual $Price High / Low	31.71 / 20.83	43.96 / 27.25	42.00 / 29.79	58.31 / 25.92	64.00 / 42.20	71.25 / 49.86
	1997	1998	1999	2000	2001	2002
Annual Total Return %	39.9	31.7	-12.7	69.0	-0.2	-2.2

Fiscal Year-End: December	1997	1998	1999	2000	2001	TTM
Revenue $Mil	382	457	533	621	725	816
Net Income $Mil	223	254	308	366	433	485
Earnings Per Share $	2.09	2.37	2.88	3.41	3.97	4.45
Shares Outstanding Mil	105	105	105	105	106	106
Return on Equity %	11.9	12.1	15.3	14.1	14.5	13.4
Net Margin %	58.4	55.6	57.7	58.9	59.7	59.5
Asset Turnover	0.0	0.0	0.0	0.1	0.1	0.1
Financial Leverage	4.4	5.3	5.6	3.9	4.1	4.1

Valuation Ratios	Stock	Rel to Industry	Rel to S&P 500
Price/Earnings	12.6	0.4	0.5
Price/Book	1.6	0.9	0.5
Price/Sales	7.3	2.6	3.6
Price/Cash Flow	—	—	—

Major Fund Holders	% of Fund Assets
Oak Value	6.34
Navellier Large Cap Value	5.42
New Market	4.83
Orbitex Financial Service A	4.32

Morningstar Grades

Growth [A]	1998	1999	2000	2001
Revenue %	19.7	16.7	16.5	16.7
Earnings/Share %	13.7	21.4	18.4	16.4
Book Value/Share %	11.8	-3.6	28.1	13.2
Dividends/Share %	10.2	10.5	9.5	10.9

Ambac's three-year annual revenue growth exceeds 17%. Earned premiums--a key component of the firm's revenue--jumped 23% in the first nine months of 2002, thanks to robust growth in all three divisions.

Profitability [A]	1999	2000	2001	TTM
Return on Assets %	2.7	3.6	3.5	3.3
Oper Cash Flow $Mil	454	481	672	—
- Cap Spending $Mil	—	—	—	—
= Free Cash Flow $Mil	—	—	—	—

A strengthening pricing environment and a tight control on expenses should enable Ambac to maintain or slightly improve its 15% ROE.

Financial Health [A+]	1999	2000	2001	09-02
Long-term Debt $Mil	—	—	—	—
Total Equity $Mil	2,018	2,596	2,984	3,620
Debt/Equity Ratio	—	—	—	—

Ambac has $7.6 billion of total claims-paying resources and maintains a high level of loss provisioning. But the odds of huge payouts are slim, since Ambac's insured bonds are nearly all investment grade even without the firm's backing.

Morningstar's Take By Aaron Westrate, 12-16-2002 Stock Price as of Analysis: $58.79

Ambac is in good shape, and we maintain our fair value estimate of $72 per share. We'd buy if the shares dipped to $50 or less, a 30% discount to our fair value. Our required margin of safety flows from the moderate risk inherent in Ambac's leveraged business model countered by the barriers to entry in the financial guaranty business.

A high level of underwriting expertise is necessary to succeed in the bond-insurance industry. Another prerequisite is a strong reputation in the minds of investors who want to be assured of an insurer's claims-paying ability. A large part of this reputation is derived from the ratings of agencies that rate not only the issues Ambac insures, but Ambac itself.

Virtually all of the issues--municipal and asset-backed--are rated investment-grade without Ambac's guaranty, so the firm isn't wrapping junk credit in its AAA label. Although the net debt service (principal and interest obligations in the event of a default) of its insured portfolio is 69 times larger than its total claims-paying resources, the quality of its insured portfolio is extremely high. Ambac has had a minuscule loss ratio (a measure of default frequency) over the past decade, never exceeding 6% of earned premiums.

Ambac's AAA rating from the major rating agencies also bolsters our view that the firm is financially solid. The rating agencies run each of Ambac's insured credits through a depression-type scenario that assumes an unprecedented level of defaults. Garnering a top mark suggests that the firm can fulfill its obligation to make interest and principal payments on the defaulted securities and remain a going concern.

We anticipate solid growth for the financial guaranty industry and for Ambac in particular. Low interest rates have spurred new issues of municipal bonds, and investors clamoring for safer issues have increased the percentage of those new issues that carry insurance. Over the long term, though, it is Ambac's asset-backed and international businesses that should drive growth.

Ambac and several competitors apparently agree with our assessment of the industry's prospects because they added significant amounts of capital in 2001. Ambac proactively raised capital by issuing debt in a low-interest-rate environment, enabling it to write more business. (An insurer's capital base restricts how much business it can write.)

Its AAA rating, growth prospects, and solid competitive position make Ambac a stock to watch at current levels.

MORNINGSTAR® Stocks 500

American Axle & Mfg Holdings AXL

	Rating	Risk	Moat Size	Fair Value	Last Close	Yield %
	★★★	Med.	Narrow	$27.00	$23.42	0.0

Company Profile

American Axle and Manufacturing Holdings produces automotive, sport-utility vehicle, and light-truck components. Its products include rear and front axles, propeller shafts, steering-linkage assemblies, and stabilizer bars. In addition, the company manufactures forged products such as axle shafts, differential gears, pinions, relay rods, hubs, struts, trunnions, and wheel spindles. American Axle and Manufacturing Holdings markets its products to vehicle producers. Sales to General Motors account for approximately 86% of the company's total sales.

Management

Chairman and CEO Richard Dauch, 59, founded Axle in 1994. His background includes stints at GM and Volkswagen; as Chrysler's manufacturing chief in the 1980s he helped make the firm the industry's low-cost producer. He owns 14% of AAM stock.

Strategy

This is the largest public company in America that still has the word "manufacturing" in its name, which speaks volumes about American Axle's focus. The company's passion for quality, precision, efficiency, and cost control is becoming a Detroit legend. Already riding the wave of GM's resurgence, Axle is aggressively going after new drivetrain business with other automakers.

1840 Holbrook Avenue   www.aam.com
Detroit, MI 48212-3488

Morningstar Grades

Growth [B]	1998	1999	2000	2001
Revenue %	-5.0	44.7	3.9	1.2
Earnings/Share %	NMF	NMF	NMF	-9.2
Book Value/Share %	—	—	NMF	46.7
Dividends/Share %	NMF	NMF	NMF	NMF

Axle's fortunes are closely tied to GM's--and that's not bad these days. Even given our conservative auto industry outlook, GM's popular truck programs and the new heavy-duty Dodge Ram should result in healthy top-line growth over the next few years.

Profitability [B]	1999	2000	2001	TTM
Return on Assets %	6.9	6.8	5.3	6.5
Oper Cash Flow $Mil	310	252	233	359
- Cap Spending $Mil	302	381	376	262
= Free Cash Flow $Mil	9	-129	-143	97

After spending more than $1 billion on expanded plant capacity in the past few years, Axle is seeing new business roll in. Its returns on capital already surpass those of peers like Dana, and we expect them to at least stabilize at 2002's level.

Financial Health [C]	1999	2000	2001	09-02
Long-term Debt $Mil	775	817	878	823
Total Equity $Mil	264	372	535	692
Debt/Equity Ratio	2.9	2.2	1.6	1.2

With enormous investment in new capacity, AAM hasn't been free cash flow positive since 1999. But as spending tails off, cash flow is rising, and several stock offerings have reduced the debt/capital ratio sharply in the past few years.

Industry	Investment Style	Stock Type	Sector
Auto Parts	Small Value	Cyclical	Consumer Goods

Competition

	Market Cap $Mil	Debt/ Equity	12 Mo Trailing Sales $Mil	Price/Cash Flow	Return On Assets%	Total Return% 1 Yr	3 Yr
American Axle & Mfg Holdings	1,165	1.2	3,361	3.2	6.5	9.5	23.9
Delphi	4,495	0.9	26,836	3.8	0.5	-39.6	-16.6
Dana	1,747	2.0	10,472	2.7	-4.7	-15.1	-23.1

Price Volatility

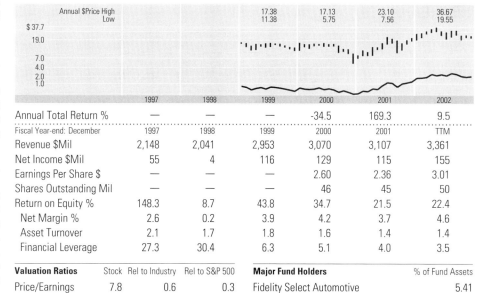

	1997	1998	1999	2000	2001	2002
Annual $Price High			17.38	17.13	23.10	36.67
Low			11.38	5.75	7.56	19.55
Annual Total Return %	—	—	—	-34.5	169.3	9.5

Fiscal Year-end: December	1997	1998	1999	2000	2001	TTM
Revenue $Mil	2,148	2,041	2,953	3,070	3,107	3,361
Net Income $Mil	55	4	116	129	115	155
Earnings Per Share $	—	—	—	2.60	2.36	3.01
Shares Outstanding Mil	—	—	—	46	45	50
Return on Equity %	148.3	8.7	43.8	34.7	21.5	22.4
Net Margin %	2.6	0.2	3.9	4.2	3.7	4.6
Asset Turnover	2.1	1.7	1.8	1.6	1.4	1.4
Financial Leverage	27.3	30.4	6.3	5.1	4.0	3.5

Valuation Ratios	Stock	Rel to Industry	Rel to S&P 500
Price/Earnings	7.8	0.6	0.3
Price/Book	1.7	0.1	0.5
Price/Sales	0.3	0.0	0.2
Price/Cash Flow	3.2	0.1	0.2

Major Fund Holders	% of Fund Assets
Fidelity Select Automotive	5.41
ARK Social Issues Capital Growth Inst	2.61
Evergreen Select Sm Cap Grth Instl	1.86
Advantus Venture A	1.85

Morningstar's Take By Josh Peters, 11-15-2002 Stock Price as of Analysis: $24.83

American Axle caters to the auto industry's sweet spot: General Motors' lineup of large trucks. Capital intensity is a concern, but we would find the shares attractive at $16 or lower.

AAM is one of modern-day Detroit's more remarkable success stories. Cobbled together in 1994 from GM's decrepit driveline plants by former Chrysler exec Richard Dauch, AAM has set standards of quality and productivity that few metal-bending suppliers can match. Product quality, for instance, improved from 13,400 defective parts per million shipped during the last half of 1994 to just 31 in the second half of 2001.

In our view, Dauch could scarcely have picked a better business. GM's 1999 redesign of its large-pickup and utility lineup brought about a boom that has driven solid market share gains for GM and strong sales growth for AAM. Not only is the entire large-truck and utility segment expanding with hot offerings from GM and Dodge, but refreshed versions of GM's pickups arriving in the fall of 2002 are poised to pick up still more share.

Its commitment to quality and close attention to operating cost have enabled AAM to start winning business from other automakers. For the supplier's first major business win outside GM, DaimlerChrysler

awarded AAM driveline contracts for the 2003 heavy-duty Dodge Ram. These powerful trucks, with their Texas-size grilles, began shipping in mid-2002 and are flying off dealer lots. AAM's contribution to the product's success sets the firm up for more DaimlerChrysler business down the road.

At its core, however, is a competitive anomaly that puts AAM practically in a class by itself. Owing to Dauch's original purchase agreements, AAM's long-term agreements with General Motors (some of which could last until 2015 and beyond) shield the company from the harsh competitive and price pressures faced by many other suppliers. This frees AAM to invest more in new product development and exacting quality standards--the keys to winning new business elsewhere.

Rebuilding AAM's manufacturing plants and investing in new driveline technologies hasn't come cheap. The company ran up a $1.9 billion tab for capital spending between 1995 and 2001, much of which was financed by borrowing. Free cash flow has been positive only once since 1996. However, as the company's investments start to pay off with strong cash flows in 2002, we believe AAM is establishing itself as one of the sector's more appealing players.

American Express AXP

	Rating	Risk	Moat Size	Fair Value	Last Close	Yield %
	★★★	Low	Wide	$37.00	$35.35	1.1

Company Profile

American Express provides travel and financial services. Its services include charge and credit cards, stored-value products, financial planning, investment products, insurance, and international banking. The company provides its credit cards, American Express Travelers Cheques, and other travel products and services through 1,700 offices in the United States and abroad. American Express also administers pension and other employee benefit plans, offers accounting and tax preparation to businesses, and provides financial education courses.

Management

Kenneth Chenault, who took over for former CEO Harvey Golub in April 2001, had a tough first year. We've said the jury is still out on his performance, but we're seeing good signs, like his decision to expense stock options.

Strategy

American Express wants to be a one-stop shop for all financial services. The company offers credit cards, financial advisory products, and online banking and brokerage services. It seeks to establish longtime relationships with its customers by offering products that a client can use at any point in his or her lifetime.

World Financial Center   www.americanexpress.com
New York, NY 10285

Morningstar Grades

Growth [C-]	1998	1999	2000	2001
Revenue %	7.7	11.2	11.3	-4.6
Earnings/Share %	11.6	17.3	14.4	-52.7
Book Value/Share %	5.1	5.6	16.6	4.5
Dividends/Share %	-25.0	33.3	5.0	1.6

After strong 11% growth in 2000, revenue fell 5% in 2001 as the weak economy and falling stock market took their toll. We forecast average revenue growth of 8% annually through 2006, in line with the company's target.

Profitability [B]	1999	2000	2001	TTM
Return on Assets %	1.7	1.8	0.9	1.6
Oper Cash Flow $Mil	6,443	6,353	5,324	—
- Cap Spending $Mil	737	919	859	—
= Free Cash Flow $Mil	—	—	—	—

Return on equity steadily improved this year as the company put a lousy 2001 in the rearview mirror. Its ROE of 18.1% for the first nine months of 2002, well above its cost of capital, meets the company's long-term goal.

Financial Health [A]	1999	2000	2001	09-02
Long-term Debt $Mil	—	—	—	—
Total Equity $Mil	10,095	11,684	12,037	13,978
Debt/Equity Ratio	—	—	—	—

The company's leverage is low for a financial services firm, which means its return on equity relative to peers is stronger than it looks. With good capital levels and credit quality, American Express is on firm financial footing.

Industry	Investment Style	Stock Type	Sector
Finance	▦ Large Core	→ Slow Growth	💲 Financial Services

Competition	Market Cap $Mil	Debt/ Equity	12 Mo Trailing Sales $Mil	Price/Cash Flow	Return On Assets%	Total Return% 1 Yr	3 Yr
American Express	46,839	—	23,482	—	1.6	0.2	-10.4
Citigroup	177,948	—	106,096	—	1.6	-24.2	1.1
Morgan Stanley	43,977	—	32,954	—	0.6	-27.2	-12.5

Price Volatility
❙ Monthly Price High/Low   — Relative Strength to S&P 500

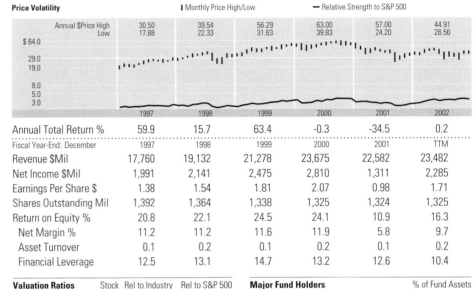

	1997	1998	1999	2000	2001	2002
Annual $Price High	30.50	39.54	56.29	63.00	57.00	44.91
Low	17.88	22.33	31.63	39.83	24.20	26.56
Annual Total Return %	59.9	15.7	63.4	-0.3	-34.5	0.2

Fiscal Year-End: December	1997	1998	1999	2000	2001	TTM
Revenue $Mil	17,760	19,132	21,278	23,675	22,582	23,482
Net Income $Mil	1,991	2,141	2,475	2,810	1,311	2,285
Earnings Per Share $	1.38	1.54	1.81	2.07	0.98	1.71
Shares Outstanding Mil	1,392	1,364	1,338	1,325	1,324	1,325
Return on Equity %	20.8	22.1	24.5	24.1	10.9	16.3
Net Margin %	11.2	11.2	11.6	11.9	5.8	9.7
Asset Turnover	0.1	0.2	0.1	0.2	0.1	0.2
Financial Leverage	12.5	13.1	14.7	13.2	12.6	10.4

Valuation Ratios	Stock	Rel to Industry	Rel to S&P 500
Price/Earnings	20.7	1.7	0.9
Price/Book	3.4	1.0	1.0
Price/Sales	2.0	1.0	1.0
Price/Cash Flow	—	—	—

Major Fund Holders	% of Fund Assets
Davis Financial A	8.95
MassMutual Instl Large Cap Value S	8.04
Davis NY Venture A	7.83
Selected American	7.51

Morningstar's Take   By Richard McCaffery, 11-19-2002   Stock Price as of Analysis: $37.25

We've dropped our fair value estimate for Amex to $37, and think the stock is fully valued. Long term, we still think the firm's business model is one of the most attractive in the financial services world. Investors had a great chance to buy shares in October when they fell under $27, and we think this stock would be very attractive under $30.

Amex is one of the few finance companies with a built-in competitive advantage. Most finance companies with an edge, like Fifth Third, have operational advantages rather than something inherent that creates high returns.

We look at Amex's competitive advantage as a stool with three legs. First, it operates a closed-loop system. This means Amex earns money issuing cards as well as processing transactions. It also means Amex has access to information on both sides of the transaction, from customers and from merchants, whereas bank card companies aren't privy to all the data acquisitors collect. Amex uses this information to better target marketing.

Second, Amex's high-spending card members allow the company to charge merchants a premium. The discount rate has fallen significantly over the past decade, and we expect it will keep falling as consumers use their cards at gas stations and

such--everyday places where it's hard for Amex to justify charging more. Overall, however, the 2.63% rate is significantly higher than the roughly 1.4% discount rate most credit card companies collect, and we expect Amex will be able to continue charging a premium in places where higher-spending card members make a difference.

Finally, Amex has one of the few cards that's more than a commodity. Many people want to hang on to their American Express card--some for the rewards programs, others for the prestige, others because it was the first card they owned. It's pretty hard to differentiate the typical Visa or MasterCard, and we think this gives Amex a durable edge. Customers with multiple relationships--say, those who own Amex charge and credit cards--have lower attrition and loss rates, pay their bills faster, and tend to spend more than those with just one card. This greatly increases their profitability and gives Amex a number of growth channels.

In combination with Amex Financial Advisors, its retail advisory force that sells mutual funds and other financial products to consumers, American Express has the product depth and geographic reach to generate strong returns on invested capital, in our opinion.

M RNINGSTAR® Stocks 500

American International Group AIG

	Rating	Risk	Moat Size	Fair Value	Last Close	Yield %
	★★★★★	Med.	Wide	$80.00	$57.85	0.3

Company Profile

AIG specializes in property-casualty and life insurance coverage and offers its products and services in 130 countries. AIG's property-casualty operations contribute about 20% of the firm's operating income, life insurance generates 50%, and financial services and asset management provide the remaining 30%. The company's noninsurance operations include commodities trading, equipment financing, private banking, retirement products, aircraft leasing, mutual fund management, and interest rate and currency swaps.

Management

Chief executive Maurice Greenberg, 76, is one of the most influential managers in the insurance industry. There is a succession plan--which isn't yet publicly disclosed--but Greenberg doesn't seem ready to retire anytime soon.

Strategy

AIG wants to dominate the insurance industry on a global scale by being the low-cost provider. It's trying to expand revenue by tailoring its products to each region's needs and by attracting new policyholders to the security of its rock-solid balance sheet. It also aims to generate an underwriting profit with its conservative policies.

70 Pine Street   www.aigcorporate.com
New York, NY 10270

Morningstar Grades

Growth [A]	1998	1999	2000	2001
Revenue %	11.3	11.8	11.2	9.4
Earnings/Share %	17.1	21.9	7.7	-19.8
Book Value/Share %	12.4	1.3	20.1	9.1
Dividends/Share %	11.9	11.5	11.9	12.1

Net premiums written--a key indicator of future growth--grew 42% in the third quarter. Given reports from AIG and other insurers of very strong, double-digit premium hikes, we think AIG has solid prospects for top-line growth through at least 2003.

Profitability [B]	1999	2000	2001	TTM
Return on Assets %	1.6	1.6	1.1	1.4
Oper Cash Flow $Mil	12,643	9,081	7,710	—
- Cap Spending $Mil	3,967	4,465	5,115	—
= Free Cash Flow $Mil	—	—	—	—

Losses and acquisition charges in 2001 knocked returns on equity to 10% from 14% in 2000. Premium hikes and tight expense controls should enable the firm to post midteen returns on equity on a consistent basis, though.

Financial Health [A]	1999	2000	2001	09-02
Long-term Debt $Mil	—	—	—	—
Total Equity $Mil	39,641	47,439	52,150	58,783
Debt/Equity Ratio	—	—	—	—

AIG sports a huge capital position of $58.7 billion. Heavy losses in 2001 didn't seriously dent the firm's combined ratio, and we expect a return in 2002 to profitable underwriting levels, unusual in the industry.

Industry	Investment Style	Stock Type	Sector
Insurance (Property)	▦ Large Core	↗ Classic Growth	$ Financial Services

Competition

	Market Cap $Mil	Debt/ Equity	12 Mo Trailing Sales $Mil	Price/Cash Flow	Return On Assets%	Total Return% 1 Yr	Total Return% 3 Yr
American International Group	150,907	—	66,823	—	1.4	-26.9	-4.0
Berkshire Hathaway B	111,526	—	39,133	—	1.9	-4.0	12.5
Allianz AG ADR	23,469	—	71,394	—	—	—	—

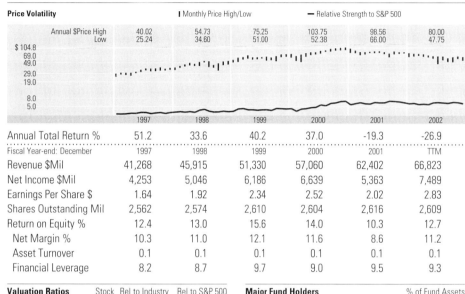

Price Volatility   ▌Monthly Price High/Low   — Relative Strength to S&P 500

Annual $Price High Low	40.02 25.24	54.73 34.60	75.25 51.00	103.75 52.38	98.56 66.00	80.00 47.75

$104.8 / 69.0 / 49.0 / 29.0 / 19.0 / 8.0 / 5.0

1997 1998 1999 2000 2001 2002

Annual Total Return %	51.2	33.6	40.2	37.0	-19.3	-26.9
Fiscal Year-end: December	1997	1998	1999	2000	2001	TTM
Revenue $Mil	41,268	45,915	51,330	57,060	62,402	66,823
Net Income $Mil	4,253	5,046	6,186	6,639	5,363	7,489
Earnings Per Share $	1.64	1.92	2.34	2.52	2.02	2.83
Shares Outstanding Mil	2,562	2,574	2,610	2,604	2,616	2,609
Return on Equity %	12.4	13.0	15.6	14.0	10.3	12.7
Net Margin %	10.3	11.0	12.1	11.6	8.6	11.2
Asset Turnover	0.1	0.1	0.1	0.1	0.1	0.1
Financial Leverage	8.2	8.7	9.7	9.0	9.5	9.3

Valuation Ratios	Stock	Rel to Industry	Rel to S&P 500
Price/Earnings	20.4	1.0	0.9
Price/Book	2.6	1.4	0.8
Price/Sales	2.3	1.0	1.1
Price/Cash Flow	—	—	—

Major Fund Holders	% of Fund Assets
Scudder Dreman Financial Services A	11.15
Century Shares Trust	10.62
Fidelity Select Insurance	8.20
Conseco 20 A	8.15

Morningstar's Take By Aaron Westrate, 11-22-2002 Stock Price as of Analysis: $65.50

We think AIG has some of the best economics and management in the insurance industry. This leading player is well worth owning at the right price and should be watched closely by investors, especially if the stock slips to a 20% discount to our fair value estimate.

AIG's mix of complex and far-flung businesses isn't easily understood. The firm's operations span property-casualty insurance to mortgage guaranty and life insurance to airplane leasing. AIG is also geographically diverse, doing business in more than 130 countries. Although this complexity is nothing new, investors won't hesitate to mark down what they don't understand in the present environment.

While it's far from clear when AIG will escape the penalty box, we're confident that it will. The conservative fiscal philosophy evident in AIG's general (nonlife) insurance operations--exacting standards have resulted in an unparalleled record of underwriting profitability--extends throughout the organization, in our view. Despite AIG's diverse operations, the entire firm operates within chairman and industry legend Maurice Greenberg's framework of fiscal discipline.

An 11-year review of AIG's general insurance reserve adjustments suggests that the firm is astute

at measuring risk and conservative in its reserving practices. We compared the initial reserve estimate at the end of each year since 1991 with the December 2001 estimate of that same block of reserves and found that, on average, AIG had to raise its reserve estimate only 2% per year. For all but three of those years, reserves at year-end 2001 were within 3% of the initial reserve estimate.

Not only are AIG's conservative underwriting standards a good practice for all seasons, but they will stand the firm in especially good stead in the current environment. At a time when many competitors are using higher premiums to repair deficient loss reserves instead of increase profits, more of AIG's underwriting profits will fall to the bottom line.

The attention AIG dedicates to its balance sheet is also evident by its triple A rating (the highest possible). This financial strength has become a competitive advantage since clients have begun paying attention to their insurer's ability to pay massive and unexpected claims.

We consider AIG shares to be worth $80. Given the firm's long record of excellence and strong financial position, we'd be buyers if the stock fell below $64.

American Power Conversion APCC

	Rating	Risk	Moat Size	Fair Value	Last Close	Yield %
	★★	Med.	Narrow	$15.00	$15.15	0.0

Company Profile

American Power Conversion manufactures uninterruptible power-supply (UPS) products, electrical-surge-protection devices, and related products for use with personal computers, engineering workstations, file servers, and communication equipment. Its UPS products provide protection from disturbances in the flow of power as well as automatic backup power when power is lost. The company also develops automatic-shutdown and power-management software for a variety of computer systems. Foreign sales account for approximately 43% of the company's total sales.

Management

CEO Rodger Dowdell, 53, joined APC in 1985; his background includes degrees in electrical engineering and a stint as a Navy engineer. Co-founders Neil Rasmussen and Emanuel Landsman are still with the firm as vice presidents. Officers own 16% of APC.

Strategy

APC dominates the market for desktop-size UPS units; it's now looking to exploit its strong brand name with larger systems. Through heavy research and development spending and several acquisitions, APC has introduced products that aim to capture share in the mature data center market. The firm is also an efficient manufacturer, with most of its production now sourced from low-cost plants in Asia.

132 Fairgrounds Road
West Kingston, RI 02892
www.apc.com

Industry	Investment Style	Stock Type	Sector
Electric Equipment	▦ Mid Core	→ Slow Growth	✿ Industrial Mats

Competition

	Market Cap $Mil	Debt/ Equity	12 Mo Trailing Sales $Mil	Price/Cash Flow	Return On Assets%	Total Return% 1 Yr	3 Yr
American Power Conversion	2,970	0.0	1,309	9.4	5.4	4.8	-17.1
Emerson Electric	21,411	0.5	13,838	11.8	0.8	-8.3	-1.1
Invensys	—	—	—	—	—	—	—

Price Volatility

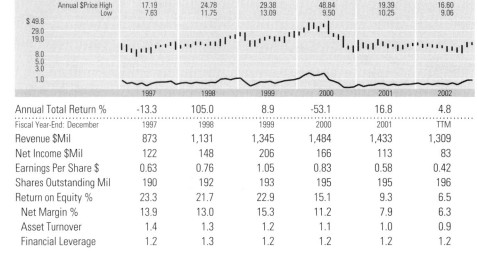

	1997	1998	1999	2000	2001	2002
Annual $Price High	17.19	24.78	29.38	48.84	19.39	16.60
Low	7.63	11.75	13.09	9.50	10.25	9.06
Annual Total Return %	-13.3	105.0	8.9	-53.1	16.8	4.8

Fiscal Year-End: December	1997	1998	1999	2000	2001	TTM
Revenue $Mil	873	1,131	1,345	1,484	1,433	1,309
Net Income $Mil	122	148	206	166	113	83
Earnings Per Share $	0.63	0.76	1.05	0.83	0.58	0.42
Shares Outstanding Mil	190	192	193	195	195	196
Return on Equity %	23.3	21.7	22.9	15.1	9.3	6.5
Net Margin %	13.9	13.0	15.3	11.2	7.9	6.3
Asset Turnover	1.4	1.3	1.2	1.1	1.0	0.9
Financial Leverage	1.2	1.3	1.2	1.2	1.2	1.2

Valuation Ratios	Stock	Rel to Industry	Rel to S&P 500
Price/Earnings	36.1	2.2	1.5
Price/Book	2.3	0.6	0.7
Price/Sales	2.3	1.2	1.1
Price/Cash Flow	9.4	1.2	0.7

Major Fund Holders	% of Fund Assets
Mosaic Foresight	4.27
Matrix Advisors Value	3.82
Managers Capital Appreciation	3.46
Navellier Mid Cap Growth	3.13

Morningstar Grades

Growth [C+]	1998	1999	2000	2001
Revenue %	29.5	18.9	10.3	-3.4
Earnings/Share %	20.6	38.2	-21.0	-30.1
Book Value/Share %	30.0	30.9	19.7	13.7
Dividends/Share %	NMF	NMF	NMF	NMF

APC's product markets have matured and are unlikely to match the growth of technology spending in general. However, we expect the firm to gain share in large systems and think mid-double-digit growth in the next five years is reasonable.

Profitability [A]	1999	2000	2001	TTM
Return on Assets %	18.6	12.6	8.0	5.4
Oper Cash Flow $Mil	278	17	117	315
- Cap Spending $Mil	36	74	48	21
= Free Cash Flow $Mil	242	-57	69	294

Combining technological leadership with low-cost production has made APC solidly profitable--though not immune to a downturn. Operating margins dropped from 20% to 12% last year, but we expect margins to return to the high teens when sales rebound.

Financial Health [A+]	1999	2000	2001	09-02
Long-term Debt $Mil	0	0	0	0
Total Equity $Mil	902	1,097	1,221	1,280
Debt/Equity Ratio	0.0	0.0	0.0	0.0

With zero debt and substantial cash reserves, APC's balance sheet is rock-solid. Free cash flow, though somewhat erratic, has averaged an impressive 8% of sales since 1997.

Morningstar's Take By Josh Peters, 10-15-2002 Stock Price as of Analysis: $10.03

Long the leader in small backup power systems, American Power Conversion is looking to extend its strength into larger systems. We like APC's chances and count ourselves as fans of the stock.

APC virtually invented the market for small uninterruptible power supply (UPS) units--the backup batteries used for desktop PCs, servers, and other small users of electric power. Its competitive edge is built on technological leadership, dominant share (upward of 50% in its core small UPS product line), and highly flexible, low-cost production sourced out of Southeast Asia. Until the downturn in corporate tech spending put a damper on results, APC's return on invested capital routinely topped 20%.

The timing of a recovery in corporate information technology spending is anyone's guess; right now, we're not counting on a rebound until 2004. Over the long run, however, we expect the small-systems business can grow at approximately the rate of IT spending in general--around 10%-15% annually. The UPS unit itself is relatively low-tech, but the increasing sensitivity of electronics to power hiccups should increase the need for backups.

However, we believe APC's new push into large power-conditioning systems can bring about a new generation of rapid growth. Between AC power systems (primarily servers and storage), DC systems (network equipment), and precision air conditioning, this is a $7-$8 billion global business that APC has barely scratched. APC's newest entry into this segment, PowerStruXure, has all the looks of a game changer. It brings all of these systems into a single, stackable architecture, thus minimizing the entry cost of a backup system while leaving the eventual scope of the system up to the user.

Duplicating its dominance of small systems won't be easy for APC. PowerStruXure will compete with some entrenched electrical giants, including Emerson's Liebert division. But as IT customers start to recover, we believe PowerStruXure's flexible features can win a significant share of this market.

With all the gloom in tech, we think APC's strong growth potential is being ignored. Our fair value estimate of $15 is based on growth averaging 14% in 2003-06, with a healthy rebound in margins accompanying larger volume and a swing to profitability in the large-systems segment. Given APC's healthy financial position and modest risk profile compared with most tech firms, we'd accumulate the shares at a 30% discount to our fair value estimate--at $10.50 or less.

MORNINGSTAR® Stocks 500

Americicredit ACF

Rating	Risk	Moat Size	Fair Value	Last Close	Yield %
★★★★★	High	Narrow	$25.00	$7.74	0.0

Company Profile

Americredit finances automobile loans for consumers who don't meet the credit requirements of traditional lenders. Targeting this high-risk segment of consumers gives the company a higher percentage of loan losses, which means that they typically charge higher rates for their loans. Americredit is an indirect lender, marketing to dealers who then pass on their customers' loan applications. If approved, Americredit makes the loan and assumes the risk of default. By securitizing the majority of its loan portfolio, Americredit finances its continued lending operations.

Management

President and CEO Michael R. Barrington took the reins from Clifton Morris Jr. in July 2000. Barrington leads a team of executives that have worked together for nearly a decade creating the largest company in their market niche.

Strategy

Americredit focuses on a specialized segment of the market: subprime auto financing. It lends to car customers who have questionable credit. Though individual car buyers are the ultimate customers, Americredit sells its services directly to car dealers, who pass on loan applications. It has also built relationships with prime lenders to offer one-stop loan shopping for dealers.

801 Cherry Street   www.americredit.com
Fort Worth, TX 76102

Morningstar Grades

Growth [A+]	1999	2000	2001	2002
Revenue %	60.2	51.9	60.5	45.5
Earnings/Share %	46.1	33.3	75.7	48.8
Book Value/Share %	25.6	50.1	39.0	29.0
Dividends/Share %	NMF	NMF	NMF	NMF

Americredit's loan volume has grown at an average annual rate of 50% the past four years. Management is slowing the growth rate to about 15% to reduce risk, decrease leverage, and increase control over funding.

Profitability [A+]	2000	2001	2002	TTM
Return on Assets %	6.1	6.6	8.2	7.8
Oper Cash Flow $Mil	-531	-990	-375	—
- Cap Spending $Mil	10	34	12	—
= Free Cash Flow $Mil	—	—	—	—

Return on managed assets has declined over the last year as loss rates increased, but remains very strong at 2.72%. As long as loss rates remain within expectations, profits should remain high.

Financial Health [A]	2000	2001	2002	09-02
Long-term Debt $Mil	—	—	—	—
Total Equity $Mil	689	1,060	1,432	1,501
Debt/Equity Ratio	—	—	—	—

Financial leverage, at 13 times equity on a managed basis, is at the high end, but not unusual for a financial services company. Still, rating agencies want to see it reduced.

Industry	Investment Style	Stock Type	Sector
Finance	◧ Small Core	⬆ Aggr. Growth	$ Financial Services

Competition

	Market Cap $Mil	Debt/ Equity	12 Mo Trailing Sales $Mil	Price/Cash Flow	Return On Assets%	Total Return% 1 Yr	3 Yr
Americredit	664	—	1,248	—	7.8	-75.5	-22.2
Household International	12,649	—	14,924	—	1.8	-50.7	-5.6
Capital One Financial	6,594	—	9,099	—	2.3	-44.8	-11.6

Price Volatility

I Monthly Price High/Low   — Relative Strength to S&P 500

Annual $Price High Low	17.22 5.94	18.66 6.63	18.94 9.81	31.13 10.63	64.90 14.00	46.93 5.92
	1997	1998	1999	2000	2001	2002
Annual Total Return %	35.1	-0.2	33.9	47.3	15.8	-75.5

Fiscal Year-end: June	1998	1999	2000	2001	2002	TTM
Revenue $Mil	209	335	510	818	1,190	1,248
Net Income $Mil	49	75	115	223	347	339
Earnings Per Share $	0.76	1.11	1.48	2.60	3.87	3.80
Shares Outstanding Mil	60	63	73	80	85	86
Return on Equity %	16.1	18.7	16.6	21.0	24.3	22.6
Net Margin %	23.6	22.3	22.5	27.2	29.2	27.2
Asset Turnover	0.3	0.3	0.3	0.2	0.3	0.3
Financial Leverage	2.4	2.7	2.7	3.2	3.0	2.9

Valuation Ratios	Stock	Rel to Industry	Rel to S&P 500
Price/Earnings	2.0	0.2	0.1
Price/Book	0.4	0.1	0.1
Price/Sales	0.5	0.3	0.3
Price/Cash Flow	—	—	—

Major Fund Holders	% of Fund Assets
Wasatch Core Growth	8.59
Weitz Hickory	4.53
Wasatch Small Cap Value	4.05
Quaker Mid-Cap Value A	4.01

Morningstar's Take   By Richard McCaffery, 09-19-2002   Stock Price as of Analysis: $7.15

As long as Americredit keeps making smart loans and properly pricing risk, we think it's deeply undervalued. We believe its credit-scoring model is an advantage in a large, fragmented market. That said, we consider it a high-risk stock.

It all comes down to credit quality. Americredit has been making subprime auto loans for more than a decade, and was one of the few to emerge from an industry meltdown in 1996 and 1997 when competition led to bad underwriting. Surviving wasn't a fluke. The company established a credit-scoring methodology in 1994 and has steadily improved its methods. It's now implementing its fourth-generation model, which draws on more than 150 customer characteristics from credit bureaus, loan applications, and loan structure data. The company maintains a credit profile scorecard for every customer to whom it has made a loan.

The best lenders have models that rigorously test account data for behavioral clues. This drives improvement in risk and pricing models. This is what Capital One does with credit cards, what Fannie Mae does with mortgages, what Berkshire Hathaway's Geico does with auto insurance. Americredit's attention to credit quality is on par with what we've seen at the best lenders.

An analysis of securitized loans underscores our belief that the company's underwriting keeps improving. In 1996 and 1997, net loss rates in the company's worst-performing loan pools topped 13%. Today, loss rates in its oldest loan pools are at 10.68%--well below the 11.89% compliance rate required.

Besides, the company prices its loans to make a good profit even at higher loss rates. In a recent $1.3 billion securitization (sale of loans), the excess spread at issuance was about 12.11%. So after paying investors, fees, and providing for credit enhancement (which protects debt investors), the company will realize a healthy return as long as loss rates don't greatly exceed projections. This is just what has happened in the past. Cash generated from trusts increased to $418 million in fiscal 2002 from $384 million in 2001 and $265 million in 2000.

With its dedication to credit quality, Americredit earns healthy returns. With just 1% share of a $146 billion new-car market and 7% share of an $82 billion used-car market, the company has room to grow.

Data as of 12-31-02

AmerisourceBergen ABC

	Rating	Risk	Moat Size	Fair Value	Last Close	Yield %
	★★★	Med.	None	$73.00	$54.31	0.2

Company Profile

In August 2001, Amerisource Health and Bergen Brunswig merged to create AmerisourceBergen, the largest pharmaceutical distribution company in the United States. It is the leading distributor of pharmaceutical products and services to the hospital systems/acute-care market, alternative-care facilities, and independent community pharmacies. The company is based in Valley Forge, Pennsylvania, and employs more than 13,000 people serving more than 20,000 customers.

Management

Amerisource's R. David Yost stayed on as president and CEO of the merged firm, while Bergen's Robert Martini is chairman. The rest of senior-level management is filled with former Amerisource personnel, a clear positive.

Strategy

AmerisourceBergen is focusing on combining Amerisource's Eastern U.S. operations with Bergen's Western U.S. operations. This integration will cut costs by reducing overlapping distribution centers, personnel, and product lines. At the same time, management will strive to maintain its high standards of customer service.

1300 Morris Drive   www.amerisourcebergen.net
Chesterbrook, PA 19087-5594

Morningstar Grades

Growth [A+]	1999	2000	2001	2002
Revenue %	3.2	18.7	39.0	179.4
Earnings/Share %	44.0	45.0	10.5	50.5
Book Value/Share %	116.7	67.8	788.9	-36.9
Dividends/Share %	NMF	NMF	NMF	NMF

On a restated basis, AmerisourceBergen's combined net income has grown at a mid-double-digit rate for the past five years. Favorable demographics and increased pharmaceutical spending should support low- to mid-double-digit growth for the next five.

Profitability [B+]	2000	2001	2002	TTM
Return on Assets %	4.0	1.2	3.1	3.1
Oper Cash Flow $Mil	217	-46	536	536
- Cap Spending $Mil	17	23	64	64
= Free Cash Flow $Mil	200	-69	472	472

AmerisourceBergen's operating margin of 1.9% is much lower than Cardinal Health's 2.8% margin in its pharmaceutical distribution segment. But increased economies of scale and merger cost savings should provide for some improvement.

Financial Health [B]	2000	2001	2002	09-02
Long-term Debt $Mil	413	1,597	1,756	1,756
Total Equity $Mil	282	2,839	3,316	3,316
Debt/Equity Ratio	1.5	0.6	0.5	0.5

The company's debt/equity ratio of 0.48 is still a little higher than the industry average, but the balance sheet has improved considerably in the past year. Amerisource was highly leveraged before the merger.

	Industry	Investment Style	Stock Type	Sector
	Medical Goods & Services	▦ Mid Growth	⬆ Aggr. Growth	Healthcare

Competition	Market Cap $Mil	Debt/ Equity	12 Mo Trailing Sales $Mil	Price/Cash Flow	Return On Assets%	Total Return% 1 Yr	3 Yr
AmerisourceBergen	5,788	0.5	45,235	10.8	3.1	-14.4	55.4
Cardinal Health	26,192	0.4	52,687	18.1	7.2	-8.3	22.3
McKesson	7,847	—	53,513	—	—		

Price Volatility

ι Monthly Price High/Low   — Relative Strength to S&P 500

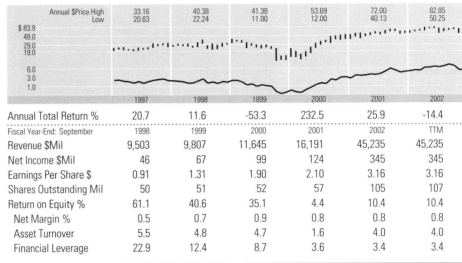

Annual $Price High Low	33.16 20.63	40.38 22.24	41.38 11.00	53.69 12.00	72.00 40.13	82.85 50.25

	1997	1998	1999	2000	2001	2002
Annual Total Return %	20.7	11.6	-53.3	232.5	25.9	-14.4

Fiscal Year-End: September	1998	1999	2000	2001	2002	TTM
Revenue $Mil	9,503	9,807	11,645	16,191	45,235	45,235
Net Income $Mil	46	67	99	124	345	345
Earnings Per Share $	0.91	1.31	1.90	2.10	3.16	3.16
Shares Outstanding Mil	50	51	52	57	105	107
Return on Equity %	61.1	40.6	35.1	4.4	10.4	10.4
Net Margin %	0.5	0.7	0.9	0.8	0.8	0.8
Asset Turnover	5.5	4.8	4.7	1.6	4.0	4.0
Financial Leverage	22.9	12.4	8.7	3.6	3.4	3.4

Valuation Ratios	Stock	Rel to Industry	Rel to S&P 500
Price/Earnings	17.2	0.7	0.7
Price/Book	1.7	0.4	0.5
Price/Sales	0.1	0.3	0.1
Price/Cash Flow	10.8	0.6	0.8

Major Fund Holders	% of Fund Assets
CDC Nvest Targeted Equity A	6.14
Merrill Lynch Focus Twenty A	5.12
Choice Long-Short A	4.63
Merrill Lynch Healthcare A	4.34

Morningstar's Take By Damon Ficklin, 11-20-2002 Stock Price as of Analysis: $60.34

AmerisourceBergen's merger has been a success so far, and we think the company could be a solid play in the pharmaceutical distribution industry. Although this high-volume, low-margin business is not flashy, the company's continuing integration should provide some tangible benefits and drive marginal profit improvements for the next few years.

Size doesn't guarantee success in the pharmaceutical and medical supply distribution market, but it sure helps. After its merger in mid-2001, AmerisourceBergen vaulted to the top spot with 31% market share, followed by Cardinal Health at 30% and McKesson at 28%, according to IMS Health. Although AmerisourceBergen is not the low-cost leader, its merger provides the scale it needs to improve its cost structure. It has consolidated seven facilities and will consolidate another six in fiscal 2003, eventually paring 40% of its distribution facilities.

AmerisourceBergen is also increasing the automation, efficiency, and average size of its facilities and has already migrated its procurement activities to a single system. These and other improvements should yield $150 million of cost savings by fiscal 2004. Given the firm's operating income of $718 million in fiscal 2002, the

improvements should have a meaningful impact on the bottom line.

AmerisourceBergen has a more diverse customer base than its competitors, which has been a double-edge sword. Its focus on regional and independent retail pharmacy chains leaves it less dependent on any given retail account, but the more concentrated national pharmacy chains like CVS have been growing faster than the industry average and the company may be missing out on that added growth. (This has been a factor behind higher sales growth at Cardinal, but that firm is also exposed to Kmart.) We think AmerisourceBergen has a good, balanced position. We expect its sales growth to shadow industry growth of 11%-14% over the next several years.

AmerisourceBergen's size is its greatest advantage and we expect that it will continue to focus on improving its economies of scale. With its focus on one core business and favorable industry trends helping it along, the company doesn't have to deliver exceptional performance to support investor expectations. We don't expect AmerisourceBergen to dazzle anyone, but at a 40% margin of safety to our fair value estimate, we think it could be a solid investment.

MORNINGSTAR® Stocks 500

Amgen AMGN

	Rating	Risk	Moat Size	Fair Value	Last Close	Yield %
	★★★	High	Wide	$55.00	$48.34	0.0

Industry	Investment Style	Stock Type	Sector
Biotechnology	Large Growth	Classic Growth	Healthcare

Company Profile

Amgen develops and manufactures biotechnology therapies. Its products Epogen and Aranesp spur the production of red blood cells to treat anemia associated with chronic renal failure and chemotherapy. Neupogen and Neulasta stimulate white blood cell production in patients undergoing chemotherapy or receiving bone marrow transplants. In addition, the company is developing products that may treat conditions like arthritis, cancer, obesity, and Parkinson's disease. Its $17 billion purchase of biotech firm Immunex is expected to close in mid-2002.

Management

CEO Kevin Sharer has been trying to implement a team-based management style; to that end, he has brought in some top-level executives from outside and appointed four vice presidents in key areas.

Strategy

Amgen is looking to new products Aranesp and Neulasta as well as recently acquired Enbrel to drive sales growth while it focuses on developing treatments for cancer, inflammatory diseases, neurological problems, and metabolic disorders. The company is broadening its research strategy to include antibodies and small-molecule drugs in addition to injectable proteins.

One Amgen Center Drive   www.Amgen.com
Thousand Oaks, CA 91320-1799

Morningstar Grades

Growth [B]

	1998	1999	2000	2001
Revenue %	13.2	22.9	8.7	10.6
Earnings/Share %	39.0	24.4	2.9	-1.9
Book Value/Share %	24.2	15.6	41.5	20.6
Dividends/Share %	NMF	NMF	NMF	NMF

Amgen's sales growth has picked up once again thanks to stronger-than-expected Neulasta sales. Including Enbrel, new drug approvals, and Aranesp's approval in oncology, we expect sales to increase 34% in 2002 (over 2001 pre-Immunex sales).

Profitability [A+]

	1999	2000	2001	TTM
Return on Assets %	26.9	21.1	17.4	-7.1
Oper Cash Flow $Mil	1,227	1,635	1,480	1,954
- Cap Spending $Mil	304	438	442	533
= Free Cash Flow $Mil	923	1,197	1,038	1,421

Amgen is among the most profitable healthcare companies. On a pro-forma basis, the combined firm's free cash flow (cash from operations minus capital spending) is 17% of sales, on par with that of most large pharmaceutical firms.

Financial Health [A]

	1999	2000	2001	09-02
Long-term Debt $Mil	223	223	223	3,040
Total Equity $Mil	3,024	4,315	5,217	17,665
Debt/Equity Ratio	0.1	0.1	0.0	0.2

Amgen boasts $4 billion in cash and securities and $3 billion in convertible debt. The company plans to use its recently-acquired borrowings to pay for acquisition-related expenses and a share-repurchase plan.

Competition

	Market Cap $Mil	Debt/ Equity	12 Mo Trailing Sales $Mil	Price/Cash Flow	Return On Assets%	Total Return% 1 Yr	3 Yr
Amgen	61,986	0.2	4,881	31.7	-7.1	-14.4	-6.0
Johnson & Johnson	159,452	0.1	35,120	18.0	16.3	-7.9	8.0
Genentech	17,067	0.0	2,541	28.3	0.2	-38.9	-19.2

Price Volatility

| Monthly Price High/Low   — Relative Strength to S&P 500 |

Annual $Price High / Low	17.34 / 11.22	27.25 / 11.66	66.44 / 25.69	80.44 / 50.00	75.06 / 32.00	62.94 / 30.57
	1997	1998	1999	2000	2001	2002
Annual Total Return %	-0.5	93.2	129.8	6.5	-11.7	-14.4

Fiscal Year-end: December	1997	1998	1999	2000	2001	TTM
Revenue $Mil	2,401	2,718	3,340	3,629	4,016	4,881
Net Income $Mil	644	863	1,096	1,139	1,120	-1,685
Earnings Per Share $	0.59	0.82	1.02	1.05	1.03	-1.52
Shares Outstanding Mil	1,056	1,016	1,025	1,026	1,046	1,282
Return on Equity %	30.1	33.7	36.3	26.4	21.5	-9.5
Net Margin %	26.8	31.8	32.8	31.4	27.9	-34.5
Asset Turnover	0.8	0.7	0.8	0.7	0.6	0.2
Financial Leverage	1.5	1.4	1.3	1.3	1.2	1.3

Valuation Ratios	Stock	Rel to Industry	Rel to S&P 500
Price/Earnings	NMF	—	—
Price/Book	3.5	1.0	1.1
Price/Sales	12.7	1.0	6.3
Price/Cash Flow	31.7	1.0	2.4

Major Fund Holders	% of Fund Assets
Smith Barney Biotechnology A	21.97
ProFunds Ultra Biotechnology Inv	21.75
Rydex Biotechnology Inv	18.63
Franklin Biotechnology Discovery A	11.66

Morningstar's Take   By Jill Kiersky, 11-05-2002   Stock Price as of Analysis: $48.36

The ability to deliver blockbuster drugs has distinguished Amgen from most of its peers. But we'd like to see a 25%-30% margin of safety to our fair value estimate because the shares are susceptible to Aranesp's success in oncology, pipeline setbacks, and dips in the broader biotech market.

In many ways, Amgen looks more like a pharmaceutical company than a typical speculative biotech. It spends lots of money on research and development, but reaps the rewards by delivering gross margins in the mid-80s and net profits--which most biotech's don't have--averaging 30% over the past five years. Furthermore, the company rains free cash flow, around 22% of sales.

But Amgen has a big ax to grind. The company is trying to prove it deserves the high growth rates and price multiples associated with young, innovative companies, yet it's grappling with slowing sales growth and declining R&D expenditures as a percentage of sales--two traits often associated with big pharma. This indicates that earnings might expand more slowly than in previous years.

Within the next decade, Amgen will begin to look more like Pfizer or Merck, with slower sales growth and less risk (requiring a lower discount to our fair value estimate). But the end of Amgen's innovation is not yet in sight. The company's biologic pipeline holds more uncertainty than most big pharma firms, yet it's had three products approved since last summer, two of which should garner more than $1 billion in sales. And Amgen has products in late-stage testing to treat large-market diseases like non-Hodgkin's lymphoma, a $3 billion annual market.

In the near term, we expect anemia drug Aranesp, a longer-lasting version of Amgen's flagship Epogen, to steal the show. Aranesp, approved to treat patients in kidney failure, was recently given the thumbs-up to treat patients with chemotherapy-induced anemia--a huge market currently dominated by J&J's Procrit, which raked in $3 billion last year. Rheumatoid arthritis drug Enbrel will also bolster near-term sales, but the drug's supply constraints have allowed J&J's competing product, Remicade, to steal share. Amgen will have to provide a quick fix for Enbrel's supply problems if it wants to realize value from its $10 billion merger with Immunex.

Despite the risks inherent to drug development, Amgen's financial strength and strong pipeline give us confidence in the company's ability to continue delivering profitable products. As long as this doesn't change, we would consider adding shares if they fell to the $30s.

AMR AMR

	Rating	Risk	Moat Size	Fair Value	Last Close	Yield %
	UR	High	None	UR	$6.60	0.0

Company Profile

AMR is the parent company of American Airlines and other aviation companies. American Airlines accounts for more than 82% of the company's revenue; it provides passenger and cargo service to about 180 destinations in the United States and abroad, and sells reservation- and data-processing services to travel vendors. American Eagle, a subsidiary, also owns three regional airlines and provides services including consulting and leasing to the aviation industry. AMR acquired most of Trans World Airlines' assets in 2001.

Management

AMR has one of the most experienced management teams in the industry, led by CEO Donald Carty. He owns more than 2% of the company, so his interests should be clearly aligned with shareholders'.

Strategy

AMR's strategy at this point is survival. It has scaled back unprofitable routes to preserve cash and begun to focus on flying the best ones.

4333 Amon Carter Blvd
Ft. Worth, TX 76155
www.amrcorp.com

Industry	Investment Style	Stock Type	Sector
Air Transport	Small Value	Slow Growth	Business Services

Competition	Market Cap $Mil	Debt/ Equity	12 Mo Trailing Sales $Mil	Price/Cash Flow	Return On Assets%	Total Return% 1 Yr	3 Yr
AMR	1,030	4.8	16,913	—	-12.0	-70.4	-38.1
Southwest Airlines	10,768	0.4	5,359	16.8	2.9	-24.7	10.7
Delta Air Lines	1,493	3.2	12,860	—	-6.9	-58.4	-37.0

Price Volatility

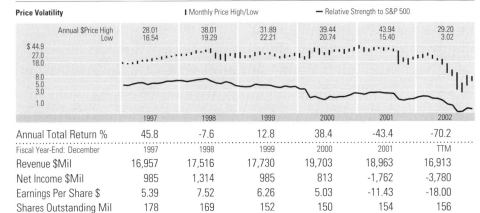

		Monthly Price High/Low		— Relative Strength to S&P 500	
Annual $Price High Low	28.01 16.54	38.01 19.29	31.89 22.21	39.44 20.74	43.94 15.40	29.20 3.02

	1997	1998	1999	2000	2001	2002
Annual Total Return %	45.8	-7.6	12.8	38.4	-43.4	-70.2

Fiscal Year-End: December	1997	1998	1999	2000	2001	TTM
Revenue $Mil	16,957	17,516	17,730	19,703	18,963	16,913
Net Income $Mil	985	1,314	985	813	-1,762	-3,780
Earnings Per Share $	5.39	7.52	6.26	5.03	-11.43	-18.00
Shares Outstanding Mil	178	169	152	150	154	156
Return on Equity %	15.8	19.6	14.4	11.3	-32.8	ELB
Net Margin %	5.8	7.5	5.6	4.1	-9.3	-22.4
Asset Turnover	0.8	0.8	0.7	0.8	0.6	0.5
Financial Leverage	3.4	3.3	3.6	3.7	6.1	12.5

Valuation Ratios	Stock	Rel to Industry	Rel to S&P 500
Price/Earnings	NMF	—	—
Price/Book	0.4	0.2	0.1
Price/Sales	0.1	0.0	0.0
Price/Cash Flow	—	—	—

Major Fund Holders	% of Fund Assets
Fidelity Select Air Transportation	4.65
ING Midcap Value A	2.24
Fidelity Select Transportation	1.43
PIMCO PEA Value Instl	1.03

Morningstar Grades

Growth [C-]	1998	1999	2000	2001
Revenue %	3.3	1.2	11.1	-3.8
Earnings/Share %	39.5	-16.8	-19.6	NMF
Book Value/Share %	12.7	13.7	1.9	-21.5
Dividends/Share %	NMF	NMF	NMF	NMF

Last year's acquisition of TWA's assets made growth seem better than it really was. The industry, and this airline, are actually shrinking. No revenue or profit growth is likely over the next couple of quarters.

Profitability [B-]	1999	2000	2001	TTM
Return on Assets %	4.0	3.1	-5.4	-12.0
Oper Cash Flow $Mil	2,264	3,142	511	-1,267
- Cap Spending $Mil	3,539	3,678	3,640	2,118
= Free Cash Flow $Mil	-1,275	-536	-3,129	-3,385

Returns on equity have been below average, and there will probably be no profits over the next year or so.

Financial Health [C]	1999	2000	2001	09-02
Long-term Debt $Mil	5,689	5,474	9,834	11,931
Total Equity $Mil	6,858	7,176	5,373	2,511
Debt/Equity Ratio	0.8	0.8	1.8	4.8

While the company does have more than $2.8 billion in cash and plenty of assets that it can sell or borrow against, its situation is perilous: 88% of its capital is already borrowed.

Morningstar's Take By Nicolas Owens, 11-10-2002 Stock Price as of Analysis: $6.28

Due to the unsustainable nature of its business model, we don't see any good reason to invest in the shares of AMR.

Our overarching concern is that AMR's strategy is not viable over the long term. Generally speaking, there are two types of strategy that a company can successfully pursue. The first is to offer a differentiated product for which customers are willing to pay a premium. The other approach is to be the low-cost provider in a particular market. Unfortunately, AMR has seen its price premium evaporate as low-cost carriers have successfully entered its markets and undercut prices. Competition within the airline industry is increasingly based upon price, making air travel a commodity. The success of Southwest over the years has been based on its low cost structure, which allows it to charge less than its competition, and make money. The fact that AMR's unit costs are 41% higher than Southwest's--and 6% higher than the industry average--leaves it at a great disadvantage.

Another fundamental issue we have with AMR is the volatility of its operating results. Because of the company's dependence on business travelers, particularly in the domestic market, its earnings are very sensitive to the business cycle. In 1999, AMR made $1 billion in profit on almost $18 billion in sales. In 2000, it made $813 million on $20 billion in sales, and last year the company lost $1.76 billion on $19 billion in sales. This continues a pattern of large profits and losses that has persisted every decade since the 1940s. Since deregulation in 1978, the airline industry as a whole has lost an aggregate $8.5 billion. Given the current structure of the industry, we don't see this pattern ending anytime soon.

The most pressing reason to avoid investing in AMR--and most of its rivals--is its significant leverage. AMR has high operating leverage--a result of high fixed costs--which can be very good when business is booming, but terrible when business is in the dumps. More importantly, the firm has taken on loads of debt in the past in order to buy newer, more efficient aircraft. And recently, AMR has been using this debt to fund losses in its operations. The result of this financial leverage is to exacerbate the poor operating performance of the airline, resulting in enormous net losses.

Most airline stocks--including AMR--are bad long-term investments. Wild swings in share price can make for tempting speculative trades, but over the long haul airlines have a terrible record for shareholders, and that isn't about to change.

 MORNINGSTAR® Stocks 500

AmSouth Bancorporation ASO

	Rating	Risk	Moat Size	Fair Value	Last Close	Yield %
	★★★	Low	Narrow	$22.00	$19.20	4.6

Company Profile

AmSouth Bancorporation is the holding company for bank subsidiaries that operate approximately 660 banking offices in Alabama, Mississippi, Louisiana, Tennessee, Arkansas, Kentucky, Georgia, Florida, and Virginia. The banks provide savings, checking, money market, and individual retirement accounts. In addition, the banks offer credit cards and computer banking services. Its banks originate real-estate, business, and consumer loans. Real-estate loans account for approximately 52% of the company's total loan portfolio.

Management

CEO C. Dowd Ritter has been in control since 1996, leading the bank through the First American acquisition and the current restructuring. AmSouth brought in a new team, led by the former head of Citigroup's private bank, to strengthen its wealth-management unit.

Strategy

In 2000, AmSouth drafted a set of strategic initiatives to encourage faster revenue and profit growth across its three reporting segments: consumer banking, commercial banking, and wealth management. In response to the firm's costly experience with the First American merger, AmSouth's goal is to generate growth internally, especially in Florida.

1900 Fifth Avenue North   www.amsouth.com
Birmingham, AL 35203

Morningstar Grades

Growth [D-]

	1998	1999	2000	2001
Revenue %	8.9	3.8	-1.1	-9.6
Earnings/Share %	1.7	-28.3	0.0	68.6
Book Value/Share %	7.6	-7.9	-1.7	8.7
Dividends/Share %	11.8	24.7	14.6	4.9

AmSouth had more assets in 1999--before certain asset dispositions and the recent recession--than it does today. Bank assets will finally show a couple of percentage points of growth this year after two years of decline.

Profitability [C+]

	1999	2000	2001	TTM
Return on Assets %	0.8	0.9	1.4	1.5
Oper Cash Flow $Mil	345	856	882	—
- Cap Spending $Mil	2	51	185	—
= Free Cash Flow $Mil	—	—	—	—

Return on assets, which was 1.53% in the third quarter, has been steadily improving for two years. The net interest margin, however, compressed by 25 basis points to 4.36% in the third quarter.

Financial Health [B]

	1999	2000	2001	09-02
Long-term Debt $Mil	—	—	—	—
Total Equity $Mil	2,959	2,813	2,955	3,123
Debt/Equity Ratio	—	—	—	—

The balance sheet has improved. We have concerns about credit quality, but net charge-offs declined to 0.66% in the third quarter. AmSouth has raised equity/assets from less than 7% in 1999 to about 8%.

Industry	Investment Style	Stock Type	Sector
Regional Banks	▦ Mid Value	☒ High Yield	$ Financial Services

Competition

	Market Cap $Mil	Debt/ Equity	12 Mo Trailing Sales $Mil	Price/Cash Flow	Return On Assets%	Total Return% 1 Yr	3 Yr
AmSouth Bancorporation	6,870	—	3,067	—	1.5	6.0	7.7
SunTrust Banks	16,225	—	7,631	—	1.2	-6.7	-0.4
Southtrust	8,619	—	3,391	—	1.3	3.4	18.1

Price Volatility

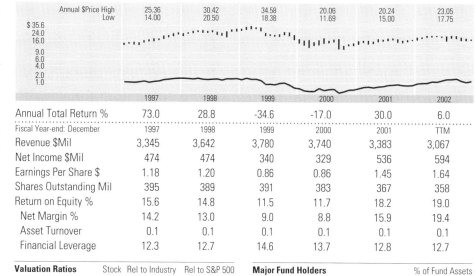

I Monthly Price High/Low   — Relative Strength to S&P 500

Annual $Price High / Low	25.36 / 14.00	30.42 / 20.50	34.58 / 18.38	20.06 / 11.69	20.24 / 15.00	23.05 / 17.75

	1997	1998	1999	2000	2001	2002
Annual Total Return %	73.0	28.8	-34.6	-17.0	30.0	6.0

Fiscal Year-end: December	1997	1998	1999	2000	2001	TTM
Revenue $Mil	3,345	3,642	3,780	3,740	3,383	3,067
Net Income $Mil	474	474	340	329	536	594
Earnings Per Share $	1.18	1.20	0.86	0.86	1.45	1.64
Shares Outstanding Mil	395	389	391	383	367	358
Return on Equity %	15.6	14.8	11.5	11.7	18.2	19.0
Net Margin %	14.2	13.0	9.0	8.8	15.9	19.4
Asset Turnover	0.1	0.1	0.1	0.1	0.1	0.1
Financial Leverage	12.3	12.7	14.6	13.7	12.8	12.7

Valuation Ratios	Stock	Rel to Industry	Rel to S&P 500
Price/Earnings	11.7	0.8	0.5
Price/Book	2.2	1.0	0.7
Price/Sales	2.2	1.0	1.1
Price/Cash Flow	—	—	—

Major Fund Holders	% of Fund Assets
Stratton Growth	2.12
Scudder Contrarian A	1.78
Federated Large Cap Growth A	1.66
John Hancock Regional Bank B	1.58

Morningstar's Take By Matthew Scholz, 11-27-2002 Stock Price as of Analysis: $19.15

AmSouth has made progress, but we still have concerns. Our fair value estimate is $22 per share.

In 2000, following a costly merger with Tennessee-based First American Corporation and problems with certain syndicated loans, management introduced a three-year initiative to put AmSouth's house in order. One key purpose is to instill a deeper, bankwide sales culture; AmSouth wants to generate higher revenue through better ongoing sales efforts with more cross-selling. Florida is key to AmSouth's growth plans. Of the 30 or so branches AmSouth plans to add in 2003, most will be in the Sunshine State. Florida is a focal point because its wealthy, growing population provides ample cross-selling opportunities for AmSouth's commercial, consumer, and private bankers.

These restructuring efforts have yielded impressive results in recent quarters. As of September 30, AmSouth's efficiency ratio was about 50%, return on equity was near 20%, and equity/assets ratio was close to 8%. We're worried, however, about the bank's ability to sustain such performance.

Our chief concern is with the credit quality of AmSouth's consumer loan portfolio. For the first nine months of 2002, net charge-offs were 0.75% of total loans. This is lower than in the same period last year, but above the regional bank average. Management says that following a tightening of credit standards, the average credit quality of its consumer loans has risen and the number of older problem loans will fall. This may happen, but given the high level of overall consumer leverage, softness in the Southeastern property market, and AmSouth's spotty record of credit control, we'll take a wait-and-see approach.

We also wonder whether the company can grow as rapidly as management seems to think is possible. We forecast that the net interest margin will compress another 15-20 basis points over the next year. Most loan growth has been in residential mortgages and equity lines of credit, which will probably fall off when interests rates rise. Florida is an expanding market, but with so many competing financial institutions there we're unclear how AmSouth will differentiate itself. The branch buildout will also result in higher expenses.

AmSouth has an attractive footprint, but given our concerns about consumer loan credit quality and the bank's ability to generate sustainable growth, we're advocating that investors sit tight.

Amvescap PLC ADR AVZ

	Rating	Risk	Moat Size	Fair Value	Last Close	Yield %
	★★★	Med.	Narrow	$16.00	$12.60	2.7

Company Profile

Amvescap PLC is an international investment management firm. The company manages equity, balanced, fixed-income, money market, and real estate investments for institutional and retail investors. Institutional assets make up the bulk of Amvescap's holdings. As of March 2002, the company had $400 billion in funds under management. Amvescap owns the Invesco Funds Group, a mutual fund company based in Denver, as well as the AIM and Atlantic Trust brands.

Management

Executive chairman Charles Brady founded Invesco along with eight other partners in 1978. Ten years later, a merger created Amvescap and he has led the conglomerate in his current role since 1993.

Strategy

Amvescap aims to have a major presence in all significant international markets and to offer a broad product line. The firm has recently accomplished this through strategic acquisitions that bring either new products or new distribution channels.

30 Finsbury Square
London, EC2A 1AG
www.amvescap.com

Industry	Investment Style	Stock Type	Sector
Money Management	▦ Mid Value	⚡ High Yield	💲 Financial Services

Competition	Market Cap $Mil	Debt/ Equity	12 Mo Trailing Sales $Mil	Price/Cash Flow	Return On Assets%	Total Return% 1 Yr	3 Yr
Amvescap PLC ADR	4,940	—	2,336	—	3.9	-55.8	-15.8
Franklin Resources	8,929	—	2,519	—	6.7	-2.6	3.8
Stilwell Financial	2,907	—	1,231	—	3.4	-51.9	—

Price Volatility ❘ Monthly Price High/Low — Relative Strength to S&P 500

	1997	1998	1999	2000	2001	2002
Annual $Price High	17.25	24.90	23.40	51.10	48.00	31.80
Low	8.60	8.60	14.40	20.60	16.20	7.62
Annual Total Return %	98.1	-9.5	49.1	94.4	-32.6	-55.8

Fiscal Year-End: December	1997	1998	1999	2000	2001	TTM
Revenue $Mil	874	1,331	1,736	2,478	2,336	2,336
Net Income $Mil	195	166	294	458	223	223
Earnings Per Share $	0.69	0.52	0.88	1.29	0.54	0.54
Shares Outstanding Mil	258	301	320	339	403	392
Return on Equity %	NMF	30.0	41.7	14.4	6.8	6.8
Net Margin %	22.3	12.4	16.9	18.5	9.6	9.6
Asset Turnover	1.3	0.5	0.6	0.4	0.4	0.4
Financial Leverage	NMF	4.9	4.2	1.8	1.7	1.7

Valuation Ratios	Stock	Rel to Industry	Rel to S&P 500
Price/Earnings	23.5	1.3	1.0
Price/Book	1.5	0.6	0.5
Price/Sales	2.1	0.8	1.1
Price/Cash Flow	—	—	—

Major Fund Holders	% of Fund Assets
Smith Barney Financial Services B	1.60
Federated Global Financial Services A	1.34

Morningstar Grades

Growth [A+]	1998	1999	2000	2001
Revenue %	51.2	33.7	51.9	-0.5
Earnings/Share %	-25.7	74.4	55.5	-56.0
Book Value/Share %	NMF	26.6	357.8	-8.5
Dividends/Share %	14.3	12.5	11.1	10.0

Acquisitions account for much of the growth in recent years, though internal growth had been strong until 2001, when revenue fell by half a percentage point for the year. We expect 2002 revenue to be off more than 15%.

Profitability [A-]	1999	2000	2001	TTM
Return on Assets %	10.0	7.8	3.9	3.9
Oper Cash Flow $Mil	592	891	766	—
- Cap Spending $Mil	—	—	—	—
= Free Cash Flow $Mil	—	—	—	—

Amvescap's operating margin fell to 18% in 2001, well behind peers. Profitability has slipped further in 2002. The company has finally come around to the necessity of cutting staff, which should improve margins beginning in 2003.

Financial Health [A+]	1999	2000	2001	12-01
Long-term Debt $Mil	—	—	—	—
Total Equity $Mil	704	3,179	3,306	3,306
Debt/Equity Ratio	—	—	—	—

Amvescap is slowly paying down the debt from its acquisition spree. Long-term debt on the balance sheet now totals 33% of equity. Financial leverage of 1.7 times equity is slightly above the asset-management peer average.

Morningstar's Take By Rachel Barnard, 12-05-2002 Stock Price as of Analysis: $13.93

It took a punishing third quarter to get Amvescap to wake up and smell the coffee. The firm is finally downsizing its staff--a move we think is long overdue.

Last year was another tough one for asset managers as the stock market's travails sent investors scurrying to safer havens and market depreciation depressed asset levels. Amvescap, however, managed to hang onto most of its assets under management (AUM) and even showed modest AUM growth in the first quarter of 2002.

However, revenue has fallen since the heyday of 2000 and net income has dropped off dramatically. In early 2002, investors responded to the declining equity markets by moving assets among Amvescap funds. This kept AUM higher, but investors increasingly sought more-conservative products like bond and money market funds, which charge lower fees.

Then investors began to flee equity funds in droves and Amvescap reported net outflows in every one of its businesses except Invesco Global, which comprises Amvescap's business outside North America. AUM dropped a staggering 19% in the first nine months of 2002.

Even though revenue and income were falling,

Amvescap was determined not to cut compensation--the firm's largest expense by far. Management wanted to hang on to all of its staff and wait for a market turnaround. The bear market third quarter, however, forced Amvescap to announce one set of layoffs after another, culminating in a 10% workforce reduction announced in November. Thus far, the workforce is 6% lighter than at the beginning of 2002.

As we mentioned in a previous analysis, Amvescap needed to take a harder line on costs much earlier, when profitability began to fall. The company lost time and money by dragging its feet. While we think these cuts are necessary to restore margins and profitability, we are not convinced that management will be able to implement timely cost-cutting measures if they are necessary in the future. As a consequence, we believe other asset managers will continue to outperform Amvescap.

We still believe Amvescap will be a profitable company well into the future. Though it will probably grow more slowly than its peers, its attractive product mix and international presence make it a solid company to own and we would consider the shares attractive below $10.

 **M✪RNINGSTAR®** Stocks 500

Analog Devices ADI

	Rating	Risk	Moat Size	Fair Value	Last Close	Yield %
	★★★	Med.	Narrow	$32.00	$23.87	0.0

Company Profile

Analog Devices manufactures integrated circuit products. Its products include analog, mixed-signal, and digital integrated circuits for use in signal-processing applications. The company also makes multichip and printed circuit board modules. Analog Devices markets its products to original equipment manufacturers in the defense, aerospace, computer, telecommunication, and consumer electronics industries in the U.S. and abroad. Sales outside North America account for about 54% of revenue. Analog Devices operates facilities in the U.S. and overseas.

Management

Chairman Ray Stata has been with the company for more than 30 years. Jerry Fishman is Stata's successor as president and CEO. Combined, management owns almost 3% of the firm.

Strategy

Analog Devices' goal is to achieve above-average growth and returns on equity of 20%-25%. The firm has focused its product lines on its analog and DSP chip segments and has chosen its niches wisely, rather than taking on segments dominated by other producers. The firm will also align itself with strategic partners, like Intel, to take on larger competitors.

One Technology Way   www.analog.com
Norwood, MA 02062-9106

Morningstar Grades

Growth [C+]	1998	1999	2000	2001
Revenue %	-1.0	17.9	77.7	-11.7
Earnings/Share %	-51.9	120.0	189.1	-41.5
Book Value/Share %	7.8	31.9	33.6	23.0
Dividends/Share %	NMF	NMF	NMF	NMF

Sales grew 78% in fiscal 2000, but in classic cyclical fashion fell 12% in 2001 and 25% in 2002. However, the firm held up better than most other chipmakers and is poised to outperform most rivals going into the next upcycle.

Profitability [A]	1999	2000	2001	TTM
Return on Assets %	8.9	13.8	7.3	1.9
Oper Cash Flow $Mil	442	705	844	328
- Cap Spending $Mil	78	275	297	60
= Free Cash Flow $Mil	365	430	546	268

Analog generates relatively high and stable margins, leading to double-digit returns on equity. But there is still room for improvement: Analog's margins trail slightly those of other key analog chipmakers, like Linear Technology.

Financial Health [A]	1999	2000	2001	07-02
Long-term Debt $Mil	16	1,213	1,206	1,232
Total Equity $Mil	1,616	2,304	2,843	2,961
Debt/Equity Ratio	0.0	0.5	0.4	0.4

Analog is in good financial health with cash of nearly $3 billion and a debt/equity of 0.4.

Industry	Investment Style	Stock Type	Sector
Semiconductors	▦ Large Growth	→ Slow Growth	▥ Hardware

Competition

	Market Cap $Mil	Debt/ Equity	12 Mo Trailing Sales $Mil	Price/Cash Flow	Return On Assets%	Total Return% 1 Yr	3 Yr
Analog Devices	8,748	0.4	1,675	26.7	1.9	-46.2	-17.7
Texas Instruments	25,982	0.1	8,024	12.8	0.9	-46.2	-32.5
Motorola	19,903	0.7	26,576	13.0	-12.9	-41.7	-42.2

Price Volatility

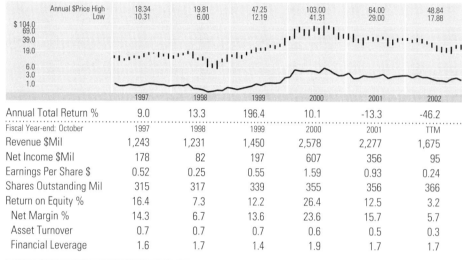

Annual Total Return %	9.0	13.3	196.4	10.1	-13.3	-46.2
Fiscal Year-end: October	1997	1998	1999	2000	2001	TTM
Revenue $Mil	1,243	1,231	1,450	2,578	2,277	1,675
Net Income $Mil	178	82	197	607	356	95
Earnings Per Share $	0.52	0.25	0.55	1.59	0.93	0.24
Shares Outstanding Mil	315	317	339	355	356	366
Return on Equity %	16.4	7.3	12.2	26.4	12.5	3.2
Net Margin %	14.3	6.7	13.6	23.6	15.7	5.7
Asset Turnover	0.7	0.7	0.7	0.6	0.5	0.3
Financial Leverage	1.6	1.7	1.4	1.9	1.7	1.7

Valuation Ratios	Stock	Rel to Industry	Rel to S&P 500
Price/Earnings	99.5	2.4	4.2
Price/Book	3.0	1.0	0.9
Price/Sales	5.2	1.3	2.6
Price/Cash Flow	26.7	2.3	2.0

Major Fund Holders	% of Fund Assets
Ariston Convertible Securities	13.01
IDEX Great Companies-Technology A	7.56
Fidelity Select Electronics	6.63
Kelmoore Strategy C	5.01

Morningstar's Take By Jeremy Lopez, 12-17-2002 Stock Price as of Analysis: $26.91

In the low $20s, Analog Devices would be one of our better chip investment ideas.

Analog has held up relatively well throughout the chip industry's worst year ever. The firm's sales fell only 25% in 2002 (ending in October), which is generally less than the pain felt at close peers like Linear Technology. Unlike most chipmakers, Analog has remained profitable in each quarter of the current downturn.

Analog Devices can thank the appealing economics of the analog chip industry, the company's niche, for the outperformance. The firm has leading share in high-performance data converters and amplifiers, both key markets within the analog realm. Because of the custom engineering required to develop most analog products, the chips tend to be more proprietary in nature. Not only does the lack of direct substitutes mean the typical analog chip enjoys a long, stable product cycle, but it tends to generate high profits and does not attract much price competition compared with other semiconductor niches. Finally, analog engineering talent tends to be scarce, which raises the barriers to entry.

Analog also has product diversity on its side. Sales are not heavily weighted in any particular sector: industrial applications account for 40% of

sales, followed by communication (30%), PCs (20%), and consumer electronics (10%). About 20% of the firm's sales come from selling digital signal processors (DSPs). Analog Devices is a distant second behind industry giant Texas Instruments, but it has done well gaining share in general-purpose applications. Since customers often need both analog and DSP chips, Analog can cross-sell them, an ability matched only by TI.

There are a few other reasons we like Analog Devices. First, the firm has some new products that haven't been out long enough to gain traction, like its Othello chipset for cell phones, which combines a few key components into one product. Also, Analog should continue to gain share in DSPs. Finally, margins could improve; the company's margins are below those of other analog chipmakers. By rationalizing some manufacturing and overhead inefficiencies, the firm may see a nice improvement in margins when the chip market rebounds.

Andrx Group ADRX

	Rating	Risk	Moat Size	Fair Value	Last Close	Yield %
	★	Med.	Narrow	$10.00	$14.67	0.0

Industry	Investment Style	Stock Type	Sector
Drugs	▦ Small Core	▪ Spec. Growth	◉ Healthcare

Company Profile

Andrx Group primarily develops and produces generic pharmaceutical products. The company is developing proprietary controlled-release drug-delivery technologies for use in generic versions of products like Cardizem, Dilacor, Prilosec, Tiazac, and Naprelan. Andrx has one branded product on the market and is beefing up research and development efforts. In addition, Andrx markets generic drugs manufactured by other companies to independent pharmacies, pharmacy chains, and wholesalers. Its Cybear subsidiary develops health-care Internet applications.

Management

Andrx hired Richard Lane as CEO shortly after he was fired from Bristol-Myers Squibb in March 2002. Lane was blamed for using aggressive price incentives to sell more drugs than were demanded, resulting in write-downs at Bristol.

Strategy

Andrx distributes generic drugs and manufactures and sells oral controlled-release generic and branded drugs. Its concentration on complex, hard-to-manufacture controlled-release drugs minimizes competition. The firm relies on legal expertise to challenge branded drugs' patents. Andrx also has an Internet-based unit, Cybear, that markets drugs directly to doctors.

4955 Orange Drive
Davie, FL 33314
www.andrx.com

Competition

Competition	Market Cap $Mil	Debt/ Equity	12 Mo Trailing Sales $Mil	Price/Cash Flow	Return On Assets%	Total Return% 1 Yr	3 Yr
Andrx Group	1,041	—	753	—	-8.2	-79.2	-10.1
Mylan Laboratories	4,275	0.0	1,175	14.9	16.1	-6.4	15.2
Watson Pharmaceuticals	3,021	0.2	1,188	7.8	6.8	-9.9	-5.9

Price Volatility

| Monthly Price High/Low — Relative Strength to S&P 500

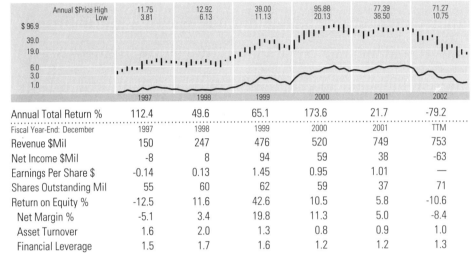

Annual $Price High / Low	11.75 / 3.81	12.92 / 6.13	39.00 / 11.13	95.88 / 20.13	77.39 / 38.50	71.27 / 10.75
	1997	1998	1999	2000	2001	2002
Annual Total Return %	112.4	49.6	65.1	173.6	21.7	-79.2

Fiscal Year-End: December	1997	1998	1999	2000	2001	TTM
Revenue $Mil	150	247	476	520	749	753
Net Income $Mil	-8	8	94	59	38	-63
Earnings Per Share $	-0.14	0.13	1.45	0.95	1.01	—
Shares Outstanding Mil	55	60	62	59	37	71
Return on Equity %	-12.5	11.6	42.6	10.5	5.8	-10.6
Net Margin %	-5.1	3.4	19.8	11.3	5.0	-8.4
Asset Turnover	1.6	2.0	1.3	0.8	0.9	1.0
Financial Leverage	1.5	1.7	1.6	1.2	1.2	1.3

Valuation Ratios	Stock	Rel to Industry	Rel to S&P 500
Price/Earnings	14.5	0.6	0.6
Price/Book	1.7	0.2	0.5
Price/Sales	1.4	0.4	0.7
Price/Cash Flow	—	—	—

Major Fund Holders	% of Fund Assets
RS Partners	4.61
Monterey Murphy New World Biotech	3.41
Schroder Small Capitalization Val Inv	3.34
Columbia Partners Equity	2.88

Morningstar Grades

Growth [B+]	1998	1999	2000	2001
Revenue %	65.0	92.7	9.2	44.1
Earnings/Share %	NMF	EUB	-34.5	6.3
Book Value/Share %	0.7	203.1	166.7	91.8
Dividends/Share %	NMF	NMF	NMF	NMF

Even though Andrx lost the Prilosec case, costing it hundreds of millions in sales for 2003, we think revenue should still increase 20%-25%. Success with Altocor and an expected launch of generic Wellbutrin are the main drivers.

Profitability [B+]	1999	2000	2001	TTM
Return on Assets %	26.3	8.7	4.8	-8.2
Oper Cash Flow $Mil	49	57	28	-61
- Cap Spending $Mil	22	45	75	93
= Free Cash Flow $Mil	27	12	-47	-154

Strong growth from the low-margin distribution business and new sales from high-margin Altocor are whipsawing gross margins. Operating margins are at the lower end of peer averages, mostly because of Cybear's costs.

Financial Health [A]	1999	2000	2001	09-02
Long-term Debt $Mil	—	—	—	—
Total Equity $Mil	221	560	648	596
Debt/Equity Ratio	—	—	—	—

Andrx has plenty of cash and carries no debt. It'll need the additional resources as it moves into the branded drug arena. The firm doesn't generate a lot of cash, though, and any excess usually goes to buying new products.

Morningstar's Take By Todd N. Lebor, 10-15-2002 Stock Price as of Analysis: $13.98

Andrx's future is only slightly more predictable than the 1992 Florida hurricane the firm was named after. We'd require a steep margin of safety before investing.

Andrx has several principal businesses. Its generic distribution unit brings in two thirds of total revenue. Revenue growth for this unit averaged 29% annually from 1997 to 2001, but margins are wafer-thin. We view the distribution business as a solid base for Andrx to build on, but not a driver of value.

Applying its expertise in manufacturing controlled-release (CR) versions of drugs has been much better to Andrx; we view this as a competitive advantage because not every drugmaker, generic or not, can manufacture CR substances. Although revenue growth hasn't been as strong, CR generic drugs generate operating margins between 40% and 60% compared with 5%-10% from the distribution business and 20%-30% for the non-CR generic drugs.

In search of even higher operating margins, Andrx has recently begun applying its CR technology to generic drugs that were previously sold only as immediate-release drugs. Studies have shown releasing a drug into the human body on a more consistent basis can mitigate side effects, making the drug safer. Andrx is trying to capitalize on this with its 10 patented CR technologies. It has built a small sales team and launched its first branded CR drug, Altocor, a version of Merck's cholesterol-lowering Mevacor. The anticholesterol market is enormous (more than $18 billion in sales in 2001), so even a small percentage of the market could bode well for Andrx.

But slapping a brand on a CR version of a generic drug is still an unproven strategy for Andrx. It has only one CR-branded drug on the market and one other in late-stage development. We're not expecting branded drugs to change the company's profitability overnight, but over the next five years, they could drive major margin improvements.

Over the past decade, Andrx's management has shown that it can successfully navigate, adapt to, and profit from a changing generic drug industry, and that carries some weight. However, it needs new skills to succeed in the branded drug business. Andrx will have to prove its mettle against some of the best marketers in the world, like Pfizer and Merck. We think investors should look for a 40% discount before buying Andrx shares, given the firm's volatile margins.

 MORNINGSTAR® Stocks 500

Anheuser-Busch Companies BUD

	Rating	Risk	Moat Size	Fair Value	Last Close	Yield %
	★★★	Low	Wide	$52.00	$48.40	1.6

Company Profile

Anheuser-Busch, the world's largest brewer by total sales, also operates theme parks. Its beer brands, which include Budweiser, Michelob, Busch, Red Wolf, Hurricane, King Cobra, and ZiegenBock, are produced at 12 breweries in the United States. The company's nonalcoholic beer brands include O'Doul's and Busch NA. Anheuser-Busch also owns a stake in Redhook Ale Brewery. In addition, the company also operates Busch Gardens theme parks in Florida and Virginia, Discovery Cove in Florida, and Sea World theme parks in California, Florida, Texas, and Ohio.

Management

In July 2002, Patrick Stokes, a 33-year company veteran who had been CEO of brewery operations, succeeded CEO August Busch III, who remains as chairman. August Busch IV, 38, succeeded Stokes as chief of beer operations.

Strategy

Anheuser-Busch aims to extend its domestic dominance overseas by licensing brewers to manufacture its beer, which keeps international capital expenditures to a minimum, and buying stakes in foreign counterparts like Grupo Modelo and Tsingtao, the largest brewers in Mexico and China respectively.

One Busch Place   www.anheuser-busch.com
St. Louis, MO 63118

Industry	Investment Style	Stock Type	Sector
Alcoholic Drinks	▦ Large Core	→ Slow Growth	⬠ Consumer Goods

Competition

	Market Cap $Mil	Debt/ Equity	12 Mo Trailing Sales $Mil	Price/Cash Flow	Return On Assets%	Total Return% 1 Yr	3 Yr
Anheuser-Busch Companies	41,426	1.6	13,362	15.9	13.5	8.6	13.1
Diageo PLC ADR	37,348	0.6	18,658	12.1	8.2	-2.6	14.3
Adolph Coors B	2,219	—	3,354	—	—	—	—

Price Volatility

Monthly Price High/Low — Relative Strength to S&P 500

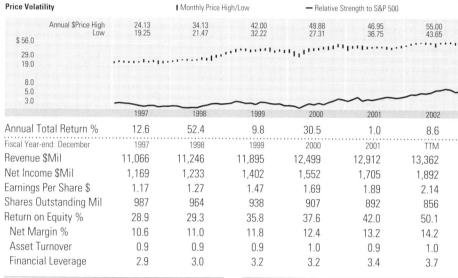

	1997	1998	1999	2000	2001	2002
Annual $Price High	24.13	34.13	42.00	49.88	46.95	55.00
Low	19.25	21.47	32.22	27.31	36.75	43.65
Annual Total Return %	12.6	52.4	9.8	30.5	1.0	8.6

Fiscal Year-end: December	1997	1998	1999	2000	2001	TTM
Revenue $Mil	11,066	11,246	11,895	12,499	12,912	13,362
Net Income $Mil	1,169	1,233	1,402	1,552	1,705	1,892
Earnings Per Share $	1.17	1.27	1.47	1.69	1.89	2.14
Shares Outstanding Mil	987	964	938	907	892	856
Return on Equity %	28.9	29.3	35.8	37.6	42.0	50.1
Net Margin %	10.6	11.0	11.8	12.4	13.2	14.2
Asset Turnover	0.9	0.9	0.9	1.0	0.9	1.0
Financial Leverage	2.9	3.0	3.2	3.2	3.4	3.7

Valuation Ratios	Stock	Rel to Industry	Rel to S&P 500
Price/Earnings	22.6	1.1	1.0
Price/Book	11.0	2.9	3.4
Price/Sales	3.1	1.4	1.5
Price/Cash Flow	15.9	1.1	1.2

Major Fund Holders	% of Fund Assets
Navellier Top 20 A	6.73
Fidelity Congress Street	5.85
Fidelity Select Food & Agriculture	5.29
Navellier Large Cap Value	4.93

Morningstar Grades

Growth [B]	1998	1999	2000	2001
Revenue %	1.6	5.8	5.1	3.3
Earnings/Share %	8.1	16.2	15.0	11.8
Book Value/Share %	6.9	-4.9	9.4	0.1
Dividends/Share %	8.0	7.4	8.6	9.5

Sales growth has been steady, with volume increases supplemented by higher revenue per barrel. Net sales grew 4.5% over the first nine months of 2002, with an excellent balance between volume and pricing growth.

Profitability [A+]	1999	2000	2001	TTM
Return on Assets %	11.1	11.9	12.3	13.5
Oper Cash Flow $Mil	2,136	2,258	2,361	2,608
- Cap Spending $Mil	865	1,075	1,022	824
= Free Cash Flow $Mil	1,271	1,183	1,339	1,784

Anheuser-Busch has consistently posted double-digit earnings growth each quarter, and its return on equity is above 30%. Its margins have expanded steadily over the past several years.

Financial Health [B]	1999	2000	2001	09-02
Long-term Debt $Mil	4,881	5,363	5,984	6,041
Total Equity $Mil	3,922	4,129	4,062	3,781
Debt/Equity Ratio	1.2	1.3	1.5	1.6

Although the company has added debt to expand its share-repurchase program, cash from operations more than covers the added interest expense.

Morningstar's Take By David Kathman, 11-01-2002 Stock Price as of Analysis: $53.22

As the 800-pound gorilla of the U.S. beer industry, Anheuser-Busch remains one of our favorite food and beverage stocks. It doesn't require a very large margin of safety to be appealing.

Anheuser-Busch has been a rock of stability in trying economic times. The brewing giant has achieved sixteen straight quarters of double-digit earnings growth through the third quarter of 2002, and those earnings have been of generally high quality. Its gross margin has increased steadily from 36% in 1995 to 43% in the first nine months of 2002, and its operating margin has improved from 16% to 26% during the same period. Its steady sales growth has been driven by a balance of volume and pricing which competitors such as Miller and Coors have been unable to match.

How is Anheuser-Busch able to raise prices so consistently without alienating customers? For one thing, it has nearly 50% market share in the U.S., and its outstanding marketing ensures that it won't be relinquishing that leadership anytime soon. Its distribution system is also second to none; more than 60% of its volume is sold through distributors who handle Anheuser-Busch products exclusively, while less than 10% of Miller's and Coors' volume is through exclusive distributors. This muscle makes it

easier for Anheuser-Busch to support its brands and also introduce new products like Bacardi Silver, which has performed quite well since its introduction in early 2002.

Anheuser-Busch has also pursued a smart strategy overseas. Rather than trying to force Budweiser too hard on other countries with different tastes, it has bought stakes in successful overseas brewers who know what the locals like. Its purchase of 50% of Mexico's largest brewery, Grupo Modelo, has been a great success, and the company recently upped its stake in China's leading brewer, Tsingtao. Volume from these equity partner brands has increased almost 5% so far in 2002--faster than the firm's domestic operations. Income from its equity investments has been growing at double-digit rates.

As a company, Anheuser-Busch has long been one of the steadiest performers in the beverage industry, and its stock has generally held up well in the volatile market of the past few years. That makes it an appealing pick for long-term investors seeking stable growth rather than huge gains. If it dipped more than 20% below our fair value estimate of $52, we'd snap up shares.

AnnTaylor Stores ANN

	Rating	Risk	Moat Size	Fair Value	Last Close	Yield %
	★★★	Med.	None	$25.00	$20.42	0.0

Company Profile

AnnTaylor Stores operates a chain of about 480 retail women's-clothing stores in 42 states, primarily in downtown areas and shopping malls, with the largest concentration in California. The stores primarily offer merchandise sold under the Ann Taylor brand name, including career separates, dresses, tops, weekend wear, shoes, and accessories. The company purchases merchandise from about 235 vendors, about 45% of which are located in China. Its single largest merchandise group--separates--accounted for about 31% of net sales in fiscal 1999.

Management

The firm reorganized its management structure in 2001. In place of a companywide president, it now has two presidents--one for the AnnTaylor division and one for AnnTaylor Loft--who report to CEO J. Patrick Spainhour.

Strategy

AnnTaylor is seeking a same-store sales recovery with its return to more-classic styling after suffering from fashion missteps in 2000 and 2001. Meanwhile, the retailer continues to expand its store base with its AnnTaylor Loft stores, which sell more-casual attire.

142 West 57th Street   www.anntaylor.com
New York, NY 10019

Industry	Investment Style	Stock Type	Sector
Clothing Stores	▦ Small Core	↗ Classic Growth	🏛 Consumer Services

Competition	Market Cap $Mil	Debt/ Equity	12 Mo Trailing Sales $Mil	Price/Cash Flow	Return On Assets%	Total Return% 1 Yr	3 Yr
AnnTaylor Stores	916	0.2	1,400	5.6	6.4	-12.5	0.2
Talbots	1,652	—	1,589	—	—	—	—
Chico's FAS	1,580	0.0	451	15.1	21.8	42.9	73.0

Price Volatility

▮ Monthly Price High/Low — Relative Strength to S&P 500

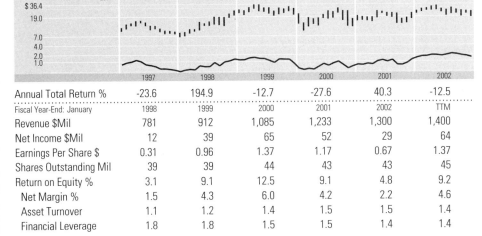

Annual $Price High	16.83	26.83	35.38	29.92	26.17	33.19
Low	8.67	7.50	20.79	10.00	14.07	19.25

	1997	1998	1999	2000	2001	2002
Annual Total Return %	-23.6	194.9	-12.7	-27.6	40.3	-12.5

Fiscal Year-End: January	1998	1999	2000	2001	2002	TTM
Revenue $Mil	781	912	1,085	1,233	1,300	1,400
Net Income $Mil	12	39	65	52	29	64
Earnings Per Share $	0.31	0.96	1.37	1.17	0.67	1.37
Shares Outstanding Mil	39	39	44	43	43	45
Return on Equity %	3.1	9.1	12.5	9.1	4.8	9.2
Net Margin %	1.5	4.3	6.0	4.2	2.2	4.6
Asset Turnover	1.1	1.2	1.4	1.5	1.5	1.4
Financial Leverage	1.8	1.8	1.5	1.5	1.4	1.4

Valuation Ratios	Stock	Rel to Industry	Rel to S&P 500
Price/Earnings	14.9	0.8	0.6
Price/Book	1.3	0.3	0.4
Price/Sales	0.7	0.7	0.3
Price/Cash Flow	5.6	0.6	0.4

Major Fund Holders	% of Fund Assets
Value Line Leveraged Growth Investors	2.24
Brazos Small Cap Y	2.20
Chesapeake Aggressive Growth	2.18
Golden Oak Small Cap Value Instl	2.03

Morningstar Grades

Growth [B]	1999	2000	2001	2002
Revenue %	16.8	18.9	13.7	5.4
Earnings/Share %	213.0	42.4	-14.2	-43.2
Book Value/Share %	6.0	3.4	17.8	9.0
Dividends/Share %	NMF	NMF	NMF	NMF

A rapid pace of new store openings is mostly responsible for AnnTaylor's respectable average revenue growth. At the individual store level, growth is typically volatile from year to year because of changes in the economy and fashion tastes.

Profitability [B]	2000	2001	2002	TTM
Return on Assets %	8.4	6.2	3.3	6.4
Oper Cash Flow $Mil	102	77	79	163
- Cap Spending $Mil	53	83	84	55
= Free Cash Flow $Mil	48	-6	-5	108

With a sales mix heavily reliant on women's careerwear, AnnTaylor's profitability depends nearly as much on the health of the job market as it does on the perceived stylishness of its merchandise. Margins are likely to continue fluctuating.

Financial Health [A-]	2000	2001	2002	10-02
Long-term Debt $Mil	114	116	118	121
Total Equity $Mil	516	574	612	696
Debt/Equity Ratio	0.2	0.2	0.2	0.2

With much heavy capital spending on remodeling behind the firm, we expect free cash flow to perk up. The balance sheet currently carries a modest amount of debt that helps fund store remodeling and expansion.

Morningstar's Take By Roz Bryant, 11-22-2002 Stock Price as of Analysis: $23.90

We believe there will be some bright spots in AnnTaylor's future. But given the firm's mixed past performance, we'd look for a 40% margin of safety to our fair value estimate before buying the shares.

AnnTaylor has a checkered past. The retailer spent the first half of the 1990s laden with debt after being acquired in a leveraged buyout. During the mid-1990s, management's decision to increase the average store size to 6,000 square feet from 3,500 was out of step with customer demand. Sales per square foot tumbled 17% between 1995 and 1996. The stores were subsequently "right-sized," which helped same-store sales (a measure of growth in stores open at least a year) perk up in 1998 and 1999. The firm slipped up again in 2000, when a shift from its classic careerwear roots toward more trendy styling left loyal customers out in the cold. Same-store sales have been in the red since as the clothing chain has tried to win back customers.

We think AnnTaylor may have a tough row to hoe in this regard. One reason is that rivals like Chico's have become a force in the marketplace. Chico's has a growing number of satisfied customers and a strategy to keep them loyal. The two chains serve roughly the same middle-age female demographic and have about the same number of stores, so

AnnTaylor appears to be fighting an uphill battle from a competitive standpoint. For a retailer, that disadvantage often means increased marketing spending and price concessions that lead to lower margins.

We predict that Chico's will emerge as the likely victor in that market share fight, but we also believe AnnTaylor's other retail concept will boost top-line growth. The AnnTaylor Loft division, which sells relaxed apparel at more moderate prices, has grown to nearly 200 stores from 27 in 1998. We like that the concept takes advantage of the trend toward casual workplace attire and offers apparel that is both appealing and attainable for younger customers.

Moreover, we expect capital spending to decline slightly as a percentage of sales over the next several years, which should benefit free cash flow. To boost its image, AnnTaylor has invested heavily in remodeling to update the look of its stores. Approximately 56% of the company's stores were either opened or have been remodeled within the past five years.

Although we think that there are more-reliable apparel retailers out there, we also think that AnnTaylor is far from being dead in the water. We'd consider the shares if they fell to the low teens.

MORNINGSTAR® Stocks 500

Data as of 12-31-02

Anthem ATH

Rating ★★★	**Risk** Low	**Moat Size** Narrow	**Fair Value** $66.00	**Last Close** $62.90	**Yield %** 0.0

Company Profile

Anthem provides health care benefits and services to over 7.8 million people and is a Blue Cross and Blue Shield licensee in eight states. The firm's product portfolio includes many health benefits products, including HMO, POS, PPO, and traditional indemnity products. Anthem's product portfolio also includes specialty products such as group life, disability, prescription management, and dental and vision. Under self-funded and partially insured products, the firm charges a fee for services, and the employer or plan sponsor reimburses all or most of the health care costs.

Management

Larry Glasscock has been president and CEO since July 2001, and has worked at Anthem since 1998. He has a decade of experience with a variety of BCBS firms and is familiar with statewide regulatory issues governing them.

Strategy

Anthem is constantly looking to expand into new states through acquisitions of other Blue Cross Blue Shield plans. The company has successfully entered markets in the Northeast and West with six acquisitions in the past five years. The Trigon acquisition, completed in July 2002, will serve as a beachhead in the populous Southeast.

120 Monument Circle   www.anthem.com
Indianapolis, IN 46204

Morningstar Grades

Growth [A+]	1998	1999	2000	2001
Revenue %	6.6	10.3	39.9	19.1
Earnings/Share %	NMF	NMF	407.0	51.4
Book Value/Share %	—	NMF	16.4	7.3
Dividends/Share %	NMF	NMF	NMF	NMF

Over the past five years, Anthem has more than doubled its membership and revenue by acquiring various BCBS plans. We expect growth will slow as the firm relies more on the internal expansion of its products in its current coverage areas.

Profitability [B+]	1999	2000	2001	TTM
Return on Assets %	0.9	4.0	5.5	3.8
Oper Cash Flow $Mil	220	685	655	—
- Cap Spending $Mil	97	73	70	—
= Free Cash Flow $Mil	—	—	—	—

Like most managed-care companies, Anthem has pushed through aggressive premium increases to offset rising health-care costs. Its medical loss ratio has typically hovered around the industry average of about 85%.

Financial Health [A+]	1999	2000	2001	09-02
Long-term Debt $Mil	—	—	—	—
Total Equity $Mil	1,661	1,920	2,060	5,325
Debt/Equity Ratio	—	—	—	—

Even after its slew of acquisitions, Anthem has a strong balance sheet. With a debt/total capital ratio of 0.28, consistent operating cash flow, and an investment portfolio that exceeds policy liabilities by about $3 billion, it is in good shape.

Industry	Investment Style	Stock Type	Sector
Insurance (Life)	Large Core	Classic Growth	Financial Services

Competition	Market Cap $Mil	Debt/ Equity	12 Mo Trailing Sales $Mil	Price/Cash Flow	Return On Assets%	Total Return% 1 Yr	3 Yr
Anthem	8,884	—	11,954	—	3.8	27.1	—
UnitedHealth Group	25,235	0.3	24,358	12.5	8.9	18.0	46.6
WellPoint Health Networks	10,372	0.3	16,180	7.9	6.0	21.8	29.5

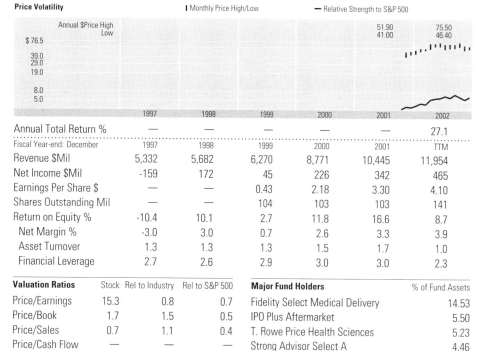

Price Volatility — Monthly Price High/Low — Relative Strength to S&P 500

	1997	1998	1999	2000	2001	2002
Annual Total Return %	—	—	—	—	—	27.1

Fiscal Year-end: December	1997	1998	1999	2000	2001	TTM
Revenue $Mil	5,332	5,682	6,270	8,771	10,445	11,954
Net Income $Mil	-159	172	45	226	342	465
Earnings Per Share $	—	—	0.43	2.18	3.30	4.10
Shares Outstanding Mil	—	—	104	103	103	141
Return on Equity %	-10.4	10.1	2.7	11.8	16.6	8.7
Net Margin %	-3.0	3.0	0.7	2.6	3.3	3.9
Asset Turnover	1.3	1.3	1.3	1.5	1.7	1.0
Financial Leverage	2.7	2.6	2.9	3.0	3.0	2.3

Valuation Ratios	Stock	Rel to Industry	Rel to S&P 500
Price/Earnings	15.3	0.8	0.7
Price/Book	1.7	1.5	0.5
Price/Sales	0.7	1.1	0.4
Price/Cash Flow	—	—	—

Major Fund Holders	% of Fund Assets
Fidelity Select Medical Delivery	14.53
IPO Plus Aftermarket	5.50
T. Rowe Price Health Sciences	5.23
Strong Advisor Select A	4.46

Morningstar's Take By Damon Ficklin, 12-09-2002 Stock Price as of Analysis: $61.65

Anthem has propelled itself into the top echelon of managed care through targeted acquisitions that have ambitiously expanded the reach of its Blue Cross Blue Shield (BCBS) franchise over the past few years. We would look for a 30% margin of safety to our fair value estimate before buying.

Anthem operates under the recognized BCBS franchise. It has an exclusive BCBS license in nine states and commands the leading share in all but one of them. Although other companies operate within the BCBS franchise, Anthem is the only publicly traded, multistate managed-care company other than WellPoint Health Networks WLP. Because only a BCBS licensee is able to acquire another BCBS plan, Anthem is one of only two major players likely to benefit from BCBS consolidation.

Anthem has delivered exceptionally strong revenue growth. While a good portion of this has been driven by acquisitions, it masks the 8% internal membership growth the firm has posted for the past few years. This is quite impressive compared with the industry average of 3%-4%.

With the help of the Blue Card Plan (a service that allows any BCBS plan member to acquire services from any BCBS network), Anthem's national account membership base has been growing in the middouble

digits for several years now. National accounts are primarily fee-based accounts (as opposed to risk-based), so this strong growth has not only been supporting overall membership growth, it has been improving the company's risk profile. Fee-based members have increased from 46% of Anthem's total membership mix in 1999 to more than 51% as of September 2002.

Over the past several years, Anthem has maintained its medical loss ratio (medical expenses divided by premium revenue) at or below the industry average of about 85% and has consistently improved its administrative loss ratio (selling, general, and administrative costs divided by operating revenue). Driven by cost containment and an expanding revenue base, Anthem decreased its administrative loss ratio from 26.6% in 1997 to 19.5% at September 2002. These improvements have led to higher operating margins over the past few years, and we expect Anthem to continue to drive margins higher as it realizes additional scale benefits from the Trigon acquisition.

We think Anthem is well positioned, but considerable integration efforts lie ahead. We would look to buy at a 30% margin of safety to our fair value estimate.

AOL Time Warner AOL

Rating	Risk	Moat Size	Fair Value	Last Close	Yield %
★★★	High	Wide	$15.00	$13.10	0.0

Company Profile

AOL Time Warner provides media services and products. Its America Online business offers Internet services to its subscribers. In addition, the company publishes magazines like Time, Fortune, People, and Sports Illustrated. It also produces and licenses compact discs and music videos. In addition, the company makes and distributes motion pictures, television shows, and video recordings under various names, and owns cable television networks like HBO. AOL Time Warner also operates television networks, including CNN and the WB Network.

Management

The firm is now largely run by former Time Warner managers. Richard Parsons is calling the shots, while Jeff Bewkes and Don Logan head up AOL's two businesses. Former AOL chief Steve Case acts as an advisor to Parsons.

Strategy

AOL Time Warner wants to establish itself as the world's primary media conglomerate. To get there, it will cross-sell media products to its users. Most of its online customers use dialup modems, but AOL is aggressively expanding into the broadband market.

75 Rockefeller Plaza
New York, NY 10019   www.aoltimewarner.com

Industry	Investment Style	Stock Type	Sector
Media Conglomerates	⊞ Large Core	—	🎤 Media

Competition	Market Cap $Mil	Debt/ Equity	12 Mo Trailing Sales $Mil	Price/Cash Flow	Return On Assets%	Total Return% 1 Yr	3 Yr
AOL Time Warner	56,278	0.3	41,024	8.1	-34.6	-59.2	-44.6
Microsoft	276,411	0.0	29,985	16.0	13.2	-22.0	-22.9
Walt Disney	32,923	0.5	24,550	14.6	2.5	-20.3	-19.1

Price Volatility   ▌Monthly Price High/Low   — Relative Strength to S&P 500

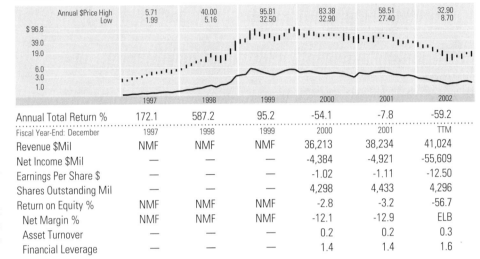

	1997	1998	1999	2000	2001	2002
Annual $Price High Low	5.71 1.99	40.00 5.16	95.81 32.50	83.38 32.90	58.51 27.40	32.90 8.70
Annual Total Return %	172.1	587.2	95.2	-54.1	-7.8	-59.2

Fiscal Year-End: December	1997	1998	1999	2000	2001	TTM
Revenue $Mil	NMF	NMF	NMF	36,213	38,234	41,024
Net Income $Mil	—	—	—	-4,384	-4,921	-55,609
Earnings Per Share $	—	—	—	-1.02	-1.11	-12.50
Shares Outstanding Mil	—	—	—	4,298	4,433	4,296
Return on Equity %	NMF	NMF	NMF	-2.8	-3.2	-56.7
Net Margin %	NMF	NMF	NMF	-12.1	-12.9	ELB
Asset Turnover	—	—	—	0.2	0.2	0.3
Financial Leverage	—	—	—	1.4	1.4	1.6

Valuation Ratios	Stock	Rel to Industry	Rel to S&P 500
Price/Earnings	NMF	—	—
Price/Book	0.6	0.4	0.2
Price/Sales	1.4	0.6	0.7
Price/Cash Flow	8.1	0.5	0.6

Major Fund Holders	% of Fund Assets
Rydex Internet Inv	11.77
Dessauer Global Equity	8.97
SunAmStySel Focused Growth & Inc A	7.58
New York Equity	7.48

Morningstar Grades

Growth [NA]	1998	1999	2000	2001
Revenue %	—	—	NMF	5.6
Earnings/Share %	—	—	NMF	NMF
Book Value/Share %	—	—	NMF	-6.5
Dividends/Share %	NMF	NMF	NMF	NMF

Future revenue growth is likely to be unimpressive. We expect the top line to increase at an 8% clip over the next five years, largely thanks to strong performance at Time Warner Cable and increased revenue from broadband customers.

Profitability [NA]	1999	2000	2001	TTM
Return on Assets %	NMF	-2.0	-2.4	-34.6
Oper Cash Flow $Bil	—	4.6	5.3	7.0
- Cap Spending $Bil	—	3.6	3.6	3.4
= Free Cash Flow $Bil	—	1.1	1.7	3.6

Past profitability was skewed by large charges for goodwill amortization. We expect operating margins to increase as more revenue comes from the higher-margin cable business.

Financial Health [NA]	1999	2000	2001	09-02
Long-term Debt $Bil	—	21.3	22.8	28.2
Total Equity $Bil	—	157.6	152.1	98.0
Debt/Equity Ratio	—	0.1	0.2	0.3

Past AOL transactions have led to above-average financial leverage. The company's debt has been downgraded, and there is a chance that it could be cut to junk status. This would significantly increase AOL's cost of borrowing.

Morningstar's Take By Jonathan Schrader, 11-13-2002 Stock Price as of Analysis: $15.22

Although we enjoy hits like The Sopranos and Curb Your Enthusiasm from its HBO network, we just can't get excited about AOL Time Warner.

We aren't normally lukewarm about companies with wide economic moats, but AOL is a special case: It is one of a handful of firms with a wide economic moat and high risk. The vast majority of our wide-moat stocks generate fat excess profits, which the firms generally use to maintain a strong balance sheet. AOL, however, has suffered deteriorating financial health because of bad deal making over the past couple of years. The company's bottom line will probably suffer for quite some time as AOL makes substantial interest payments to its creditors.

It's not just AOL's poor financial health that prompts the high risk rating. We are also concerned about the firm's accounting. AOL has said that financial statements for 2000 and 2001 can "no longer be relied upon" as a result of improper booking of advertising revenue. This issue--and the possibility of others--has attracted the interest of the Securities and Exchange Commission. It isn't the first time that AOL's accounting has come under scrutiny. The company has long been aggressive in its reporting, leading to large charges to earnings--and calling into question the quality of those earnings.

To us, AOL's management lacks credibility. When initially confronted with the most recent accounting concerns, management defended the practices as "appropriate and accurate." Just as troublesome, AOL has consistently overpromised and underperformed since the merger with Time Warner. We now question nearly everything that comes out of the firm's New York headquarters.

If it weren't for AOL's excellent media properties, we'd demand an even larger discount to our fair value estimate before buying. America Online is still the dominant player in the Internet world. This business enjoys the benefits of the "network effect," economies of scale, and high switching costs.

We think that over the long haul, AOL will generate a significant amount of cash flow. But it would have taken decades to recover the shareholder wealth that was destroyed by the merger; AOL admitted as much with its $55 billion charge to write down goodwill. We expect similar charges in the future.

MORNINGSTAR® Stocks 500

Data as of 12-31-02

Apartment Investment & Management AIV

	Rating	Risk	Moat Size	Fair Value	Last Close	Yield %
	★★★	Med.	Narrow	$39.00	$37.48	8.8

Company Profile

Apartment Investment and Management Company (AIMCO) is one of the largest public real estate investments trusts in the United States. It owns, controls, or has an interest in more than 335,000 apartments units in 47 states, the District of Columbia, and Puerto Rico. AIMCO owns outright approximately half those properties, making it the second-largest apartment REIT in the country. AIMCO's largest markets are Washington, D.C., Los Angeles, Chicago, Houston, and Atlanta. AIMCO is an unlimited partnership REIT and self-managed.

Management

Terry Considine has been chairman and CEO since 1994 and owns approximately 7% of AIMCO. He is also chairman and CEO of another real estate investment trust, but claims to allocate the majority of his time to AIMCO.

Strategy

AIMCO's basic strategy is to realize the scale economies that result from operating a large and diverse portfolio of apartments in locations where population and employment growth are above the national average. Part of the firm's stated strategy is to acquire properties below replacement cost. Acquisitions are essential to the company's growth.

2000 South Colorado Blvd.   www.aimco.com
Denver, CO 80222-7900

Morningstar Grades

Growth [A]	1998	1999	2000	2001
Revenue %	92.3	43.8	90.6	34.2
Earnings/Share %	-25.9	-52.5	36.8	-55.8
Book Value/Share %	-37.3	9.1	-5.9	-10.5
Dividends/Share %	21.8	11.1	12.0	11.4

Revenue in 2002 will be about flat with 2001. The additional revenue from the new Casden and Flatley properties will be offset by lower rental rates and increased expenses across the entire portfolio.

Profitability [D]	1999	2000	2001	TTM
Return on Assets %	0.4	0.5	0.2	1.0
Oper Cash Flow $Mil	253	400	494	—
- Cap Spending $Mil	217	334	374	—
= Free Cash Flow $Mil	—	—	—	—

Operating margins for the rental property business (90% of AIMCO's total revenue) fluctuate between the mid-50s and low 60s. Third-quarter operating margins were 57.0%. We calculate that 2002 growth in funds from operations will be flat at about $4.60 per share.

Financial Health [D]	1999	2000	2001	09-02
Long-term Debt $Mil	—	—	—	—
Total Equity $Mil	1,618	1,664	1,592	2,285
Debt/Equity Ratio	—	—	—	—

AIMCO has $5.9 billion in debt, primarily mortgage debt secured by its properties at an average interest rate of 6.70%, on top of $1.1 billion in preferred stock costing 9.25% per year. With a heavy fixed-charge burden like that, Standard & Poor's rates AIMCO's debt BB+, which is junk status.

Industry	Investment Style	Stock Type	Sector
REITS	▦ Mid Value	▦ Hard Assets	💲 Financial Services

Competition	Market Cap $Mil	Debt/ Equity	12 Mo Trailing Sales $Mil	Price/Cash Flow	Return On Assets%	Total Return% 1 Yr	3 Yr
Apartment Investment & Management	3,493	—	1,573	—	1.0	-11.5	7.3
Equity Residential	6,780	—	2,137	—	2.9	-8.6	12.5
Archstone-Smith Trust	4,254	—	1,040	—	2.6	-4.2	12.1

Price Volatility

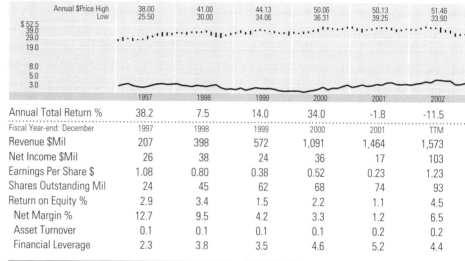

		▌ Monthly Price High/Low		— Relative Strength to S&P 500		
Annual $Price High	38.00	41.00	44.13	50.06	50.13	51.46
Low	25.50	30.00	34.06	36.31	39.25	33.90
	1997	1998	1999	2000	2001	2002

Annual Total Return %	38.2	7.5	14.0	34.0	-1.8	-11.5
Fiscal Year-end: December	1997	1998	1999	2000	2001	TTM
Revenue $Mil	207	398	572	1,091	1,464	1,573
Net Income $Mil	26	38	24	36	17	103
Earnings Per Share $	1.08	0.80	0.38	0.52	0.23	1.23
Shares Outstanding Mil	24	45	62	68	74	93
Return on Equity %	2.9	3.4	1.5	2.2	1.1	4.5
Net Margin %	12.7	9.5	4.2	3.3	1.2	6.5
Asset Turnover	0.1	0.1	0.1	0.1	0.2	0.2
Financial Leverage	2.3	3.8	3.5	4.6	5.2	4.4

Valuation Ratios	Stock	Rel to Industry	Rel to S&P 500
Price/Earnings	30.5	1.7	1.3
Price/Book	1.5	1.0	0.5
Price/Sales	2.2	0.7	1.1
Price/Cash Flow	—	—	—

Major Fund Holders	% of Fund Assets
Fidelity Real Estate High-Income II	8.97
PBHG REIT PBHG	7.07
Fidelity Real Estate Investment	5.92
Security Capital U.S. Real Estate	5.23

Morningstar's Take By Matthew Scholz, 11-22-2002 Stock Price as of Analysis: $37.70

We would want to see reduced leverage and a further streamlining of AIMCO's many limited partnership interests before recommending the stock. We estimate its net asset value at $39.

One of the basic assumptions of the real estate investment trust (REIT) business model is that scale provides certain advantages. Although scale economies often provide only a tenuous competitive advantage, we think there is good logic behind the scale argument as it applies to real estate operating companies. For example, AIMCO can lower general and administrative costs by managing a large number of apartment units in a particular geographic area from a single administrative office. The firm's heft also allows it to bargain hard for low rates on utility services like cable TV.

AIMCO has a strong record of growing via internally developed projects and acquisitions since its 1994 initial public offering. The recent $500 million Flatley acquisition in the Boston area and the $1.1 billion Casden acquisition in Southern California last year serve one of AIMCO's strategic goals--to increase its presence in markets with high barriers to entry.

But despite its attractive business model and record of growth, AIMCO just isn't as solid a firm as industry leader Equity Residential. Look no further than the balance sheets to see the difference: As of September 30, AIMCO's ratio of debt to total market capitalization was 54%, compared with Equity Residential's 40%. AIMCO's fixed coverage charge ratio (its margin of safety for satisfying its interest and preferred dividend payments) is also smaller than Equity's.

Roughly half of AIMCO's apartment ownership interests are in limited partnerships. While there isn't necessarily anything wrong with this structure, it is more difficult to ascertain what exactly is in the company's portfolio. The firm also lacks wiggle room with regard to its common stock dividend if the apartment market doesn't recover quickly. The ratio of funds available for distribution to the common stock dividend is close to 100%, which means that after taking into account nonrecurring items and capital expenditures, nearly all of AIMCO's free cash is used to pay its common stock dividend.

AIMCO is a work in progress. We have concerns about above-average leverage, lower dividend coverage, and a complicated investment structure, and we will monitor this REIT for improvements in its fundamentals.

Apple Computer AAPL

	Rating	Risk	Moat Size	Fair Value	Last Close	Yield %
	★★★	High	None	$20.00	$14.33	0.0

Company Profile

Apple Computer designs and produces personal computer hardware, software, and peripherals. The company makes its Macintosh and iMac personal and PowerBook and iBook portable computers, which use Apple's proprietary operating system. It also sells operating systems and applications software. In addition, Apple offers Internet services that it markets under the iTools brand name. The company markets its products in the United States and abroad. Microsoft owns a stake in nonvoting Apple stock. Foreign sales account for about 45% of the company's total sales.

Management

CEO and co-founder Steve Jobs is compensated through his holdings in Apple stock, so his interests are much in line with investors'.

Strategy

Having been stuck with 5% market share for some time, Apple's key goal is to raise awareness of its products. It is adding retail stores to increase its exposure and lure new customers; advertising heavily; and rolling out proprietary software for the Mac. These efforts appear to be working, although given the weak state of the PC industry, it is too early for conclusive results.

1 Infinite Loop
Cupertino, CA 95014
www.apple.com

Morningstar Grades

Growth [B]	1999	2000	2001	2002
Revenue %	3.2	30.1	-32.8	7.1
Earnings/Share %	72.4	20.4	NMF	NMF
Book Value/Share %	75.5	25.7	-1.8	3.3
Dividends/Share %	NMF	NMF	NMF	NMF

Fiscal 2001 was tough for Apple, and 2002, although a bit stronger, posed challenges as well. However, we think revenue growth in the very low teens is achievable. Management's number-one priority now is gaining share, even at the expense of margins.

Profitability [A-]	2000	2001	2002	TTM
Return on Assets %	11.6	-0.4	1.0	1.0
Oper Cash Flow $Mil	868	185	89	89
- Cap Spending $Mil	142	232	174	174
= Free Cash Flow $Mil	726	-47	-85	-85

Management met its promise to return to profitability in the March 2001 quarter after earnings disappointments in the second half of 2000. Apple has managed to stay profitable since then, and we do not anticipate a return to the red.

Financial Health [A]	2000	2001	2002	09-02
Long-term Debt $Mil	300	317	316	316
Total Equity $Mil	4,031	3,920	4,095	4,095
Debt/Equity Ratio	0.1	0.1	0.1	0.1

Apple has more than $4 billion in cash and investments--nearly $12 per share. The company carries little debt and has plenty of room to maneuver.

Industry	Investment Style	Stock Type	Sector
Computer Equipment	⊞ Mid Core	→ Slow Growth	▣ Hardware

Competition	Market Cap $Mil	Debt/ Equity	12 Mo Trailing Sales $Mil	Price/Cash Flow	Return On Assets%	Total Return% 1 Yr	3 Yr
Apple Computer	5,029	0.1	5,742	56.5	1.0	-34.6	-34.6
Dell Computer	69,252	0.1	32,054	20.1	13.4	-1.6	-16.9
Hewlett-Packard	34,321	0.3	—	6.1	-3.5	-13.9	-24.7

Price Volatility   ▌ Monthly Price High/Low   — Relative Strength to S&P 500

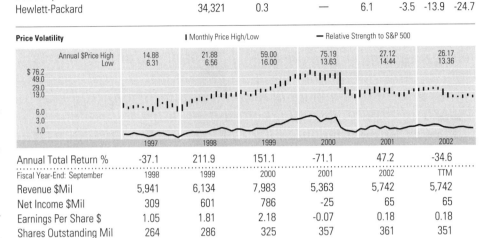

Annual $Price High / Low	14.88 / 6.31	21.88 / 6.56	59.00 / 16.00	75.19 / 13.63	27.12 / 14.44	26.17 / 13.36
	1997	1998	1999	2000	2001	2002

Annual Total Return %	-37.1	211.9	151.1	-71.1	47.2	-34.6

Fiscal Year-End: September	1998	1999	2000	2001	2002	TTM
Revenue $Mil	5,941	6,134	7,983	5,363	5,742	5,742
Net Income $Mil	309	601	786	-25	65	65
Earnings Per Share $	1.05	1.81	2.18	-0.07	0.18	0.18
Shares Outstanding Mil	264	286	325	357	361	351
Return on Equity %	20.7	20.3	19.5	-0.6	1.6	1.6
Net Margin %	5.2	9.8	9.8	-0.5	1.1	1.1
Asset Turnover	1.4	1.2	1.2	0.9	0.9	0.9
Financial Leverage	2.9	1.7	1.7	1.5	1.5	1.5

Valuation Ratios	Stock	Rel to Industry	Rel to S&P 500
Price/Earnings	79.6	2.9	3.4
Price/Book	1.2	0.2	0.4
Price/Sales	0.9	0.6	0.4
Price/Cash Flow	56.5	6.3	4.3

Major Fund Holders	% of Fund Assets
Fidelity Select Computers	8.71
Fidelity Select Software & Comp	4.34
Cutler Value	4.25
Cutler Core	3.41

Morningstar's Take By Joseph Beaulieu, 10-24-2002 Stock Price as of Analysis: $14.69

To merit our fair value estimate of $20, Apple doesn't have to become the next Dell. We merely assume that the company will achieve modest market share gains and small margin improvements, and we don't project it returning to fiscal 2000 revenue and margin levels even five years out.

Although we are confident in its long-term prospects, Apple does face significant risks. We believe the assumptions we use in our discounted cash flow model are conservative, but the economy is still a wild card. Management is understandably unwilling to give revenue projections for the full fiscal year (ending September 2003), so we think a conservative approach is appropriate. Still, if the company doesn't achieve modest revenue growth or if margins fall substantially, we'd have to lower our fair value estimate.

In addition to an uncertain economy and consumer demand issues, Apple faces company-specific risks. More than that of the "clone" PC makers like Dell, Apple's revenue growth is driven largely by new product cycles. The company's core customers are accustomed to seeing brand-new products, rather than modest upgrades, on a regular basis. And if the new products aren't a big success, Apple can be up a creek until the next cycle.

Having said that, we are impressed by Apple's latest product offerings, and believe that even a modest economic recovery will help the company ship more iMacs and PowerMacs to both consumers and companies. We think that the "Switchers" ad campaign will continue to build on its current success, and that the increased cross-platform compatibility provided by Jaguar (the latest version of Apple's OSX operating system) will entice more PC users to purchase Macs.

We remain optimistic about the company's long-term strategy of increasing market share through its chain of retail stores, targeted marketing campaigns, and product innovation. We think this strategy will lead to the low-single-digit market share gains that would support our $20 fair value estimate.

The stock can still be had for just a few dollars more than the company's cash per share. Given the risks facing Apple, we would typically want at least a 40% discount (and preferably 50%) to our fair value estimate, but since the company has nearly $12 per share in cash, we'd only expect that discount on the remaining $8 per share that is attributable to future cash flows. Therefore, we'd consider the stock below $16.

MORNINGSTAR® Stocks 500

Applied Materials AMAT

	Rating	Risk	Moat Size	Fair Value	Last Close	Yield %
	★★★	Med.	Wide	$14.00	$13.03	0.0

Company Profile

Applied Materials manufactures systems that produce silicon wafer circuits using several different technologies, including chemical vapor deposition, physical vapor deposition, and electroplating. It makes etching, ion implantation, chemical mechanical polishing, and wafer and reticle inspection systems, as well as critical dimension and defect scanning electron microscopes. It also produces flat-panel display systems. Sales outside North America account for about 66% of the company's total sales. The firm acquired Etec Systems in March 2000.

Management

James Morgan has been CEO since 1977 and chairman since 1987. His team of managers has little turnover and a long history in the semiconductor industry. This firm is very well managed.

Strategy

Applied Materials uses its product depth and market share to appeal to customers as a one-stop shop across several equipment areas. Research and development is a high priority for Applied; this keeps the firm at the forefront of new technological trends. With its deep industry expertise, the company wants to exploit its ability to offer customers more consulting and support services.

3050 Bowers Avenue   www.appliedmaterials.com
Santa Clara, CA 95054-3299

Morningstar Grades

Growth [C-]	1998	1999	2000	2001
Revenue %	0.3	17.7	87.7	-23.2
Earnings/Share %	-48.5	160.0	163.7	-75.0
Book Value/Share %	5.9	31.2	48.4	8.8
Dividends/Share %	NMF	NMF	NMF	NMF

Applied's rising market share has led to a growth rate exceeding the industry average over the past five years. A sharp tech downturn hurt sales in fiscal 2001 and 2002; it is possible Applied ceded some share during this period.

Profitability [A]	1999	2000	2001	TTM
Return on Assets %	10.7	19.6	5.2	0.4
Oper Cash Flow $Mil	1,081	1,652	1,580	733
- Cap Spending $Mil	220	383	711	531
= Free Cash Flow $Mil	861	1,269	870	202

Applied is one of the more profitable chip equipment makers, with net margins and returns on assets usually among the top 20% of the industry. It is impressive that Applied has stayed profitable during the current slowdown.

Financial Health [A+]	1999	2000	2001	07-02
Long-term Debt $Mil	584	573	565	579
Total Equity $Mil	4,575	7,104	7,607	7,857
Debt/Equity Ratio	0.1	0.1	0.1	0.1

With debt/equity of 0.1, the firm has a modest debt load. Positive cash flows and more than $4.8 billion in cash and investments allow Applied to invest in R&D or make acquisitions despite tough times.

Industry	Investment Style	Stock Type	Sector
Semiconductor Equipment	Large Growth	→ Slow Growth	Hardware

Competition	Market Cap $Mil	Debt/ Equity	12 Mo Trailing Sales $Mil	Price/Cash Flow	Return On Assets%	Total Return% 1 Yr	3 Yr
Applied Materials	21,473	0.1	4,881	29.3	0.4	-35.0	-24.3
KLA-Tencor	6,674	0.0	1,510	20.3	6.7	-28.6	-12.0
Novellus Systems	4,015	—	822	21.2	1.7	-28.8	-11.6

Price Volatility

	Annual $Price High Low	13.55 4.34	11.75 5.39	32.25 10.67	57.50 17.06	29.55 13.30	27.95 10.26

$ 58.5 / 29.0 / 19.0 / 8.0 / 5.0 / 3.0 / 1.0

1997   1998   1999   2000   2001   2002

Annual Total Return %	67.6	41.7	196.8	-39.7	5.0	-35.0

Fiscal Year-end: October	1997	1998	1999	2000	2001	TTM
Revenue $Mil	4,315	4,330	5,096	9,564	7,343	4,881
Net Income $Mil	533	278	748	2,064	508	39
Earnings Per Share $	0.34	0.18	0.46	1.20	0.30	0.02
Shares Outstanding Mil	1,567	1,543	1,558	1,612	1,638	1,648
Return on Equity %	17.0	8.2	16.3	29.0	6.7	0.5
Net Margin %	12.4	6.4	14.7	21.6	6.9	0.8
Asset Turnover	0.8	0.8	0.7	0.9	0.7	0.5
Financial Leverage	1.7	1.6	1.5	1.5	1.3	1.3

Valuation Ratios	Stock	Rel to Industry	Rel to S&P 500
Price/Earnings	651.5	4.3	27.7
Price/Book	2.7	1.0	0.9
Price/Sales	4.4	1.0	2.2
Price/Cash Flow	29.3	1.0	2.2

Major Fund Holders	% of Fund Assets
Fidelity Advisor Electronics A	8.23
Rydex Electronics Inv	7.90
Marketocracy Technology Plus Fund	7.53
White Oak Growth Stock	7.27

Morningstar's Take By Jeremy Lopez, 11-19-2002 Stock Price as of Analysis: $15.07

Accounting for almost a fifth of total chip equipment sales in 2001, Applied Materials is the industry heavyweight. It remains one of our favorite semiconductor names.

In general, the industry is segmented, with the competitive lines drawn across the individual categories of equipment required for chip production. The market within each niche can be oligopolistic, as suppliers tend to specialize in one or a few product areas. Applied, however, breaks the mold with a dominant presence in many categories. For example, the firm holds strong share in deposition (a $5 billion market in 2001) and both etch and clean (also crucial markets at about $3 billion each in sales last year).

Led by James Morgan--the industry's most seasoned and respected veteran, in our view--Applied has a superb legacy of financial performance. The industry is notorious for its booms and busts; most chip equipment firms teeter in and out of profitability during the course of a cycle. But Applied Materials not only has an outstanding record of above-average margins and returns on capital, but it also has remained profitable and cash flow positive through the worst of market downturns, including the current one. Applied's balance sheet is among the strongest in the industry.

A strong position and performance give Applied several competitive edges. A healthy balance sheet allows the firm to keep spending on research and development during market downturns, further distancing itself from weaker rivals. And while Applied might not always make the best products in each category, it is the closest thing to a one-stop shop for chip equipment. This minimizes the number of suppliers customers have to deal with and allows Applied to easily integrate its products. The firm is also able to offer its customers leading support, spare parts, service, and consistent product innovation. Customers value these qualities, which we think point to the firm's keeping or widening its lead.

But even the industry heavyweight can't avoid a major downturn. Applied will continue to suffer alongside peers as long as capital spending remains weak--and it'll probably remain soft well into fiscal 2004. But usually the best time to load up on industry leaders like Applied is when market conditions are poor. Applied continues to be one of the chip equipment horses we'd bet on long term, and the stock would look attractive to us at around a 30% discount to our fair value estimate.

Applied Micro Circuits AMCC

	Rating	Risk	Moat Size	Fair Value	Last Close	Yield %
	★★★	High	None	$5.00	$3.69	0.0

Company Profile

Applied Micro Circuits produces semiconductors for the communication sector. The firm makes digital, mixed signal, and analog integrated circuits for use in the Internet's infrastructure in optical-networking equipment. Applied Micro also makes chips used in corporate networking applications. The firm markets its products in the United States and overseas. Sales outside North America account for about 24% of the company's total sales. Applied Micro Circuits' customers include Nortel and Cisco. The company acquired MMC Networks in October 2000.

Management

David Rickey has been president and CEO since 1996. Before joining Applied in 1993, Rickey spent eight years running Nortel's chip-production operations. Management owns almost 5% of the firm.

Strategy

Applied Micro aims to meet the custom needs of telecom equipment makers by producing a broad line of semiconductor products for all layers of the telecom network. By outsourcing as well as doing some of its own chip production, Applied is able to provide a good mix of high-performance and low-cost chips.

6290 Sequence Drive
San Diego, CA 92121
www.amcc.com

Industry	Investment Style	Stock Type	Sector
Semiconductors	▦ Small Growth	→ Slow Growth	▣ Hardware

Competition

	Market Cap $Mil	Debt/ Equity	12 Mo Trailing Sales $Mil	Price/Cash Flow	Return On Assets%	Total Return% 1 Yr	3 Yr
Applied Micro Circuits	1,114	0.0	131	—	-44.3	-67.4	-50.8
PMC-Sierra	930	1.2	213	—	-44.3	-73.9	-57.9
Triquint Semiconductor	562	0.4	260	13.9	-6.9	-65.4	-46.7

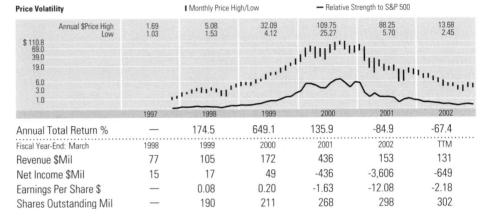

Price Volatility

| | Monthly Price High/Low | — Relative Strength to S&P 500 |

Annual $Price High / Low	1.69 1.03	5.08 1.53	32.09 4.12	109.75 25.27	88.25 5.70	13.68 2.45

$110.8 / 69.0 / 39.0 / 19.0 / 6.0 / 3.0 / 1.0

1997 1998 1999 2000 2001 2002

Annual Total Return %	—	174.5	649.1	135.9	-84.9	-67.4
Fiscal Year-End: March	1998	1999	2000	2001	2002	TTM
Revenue $Mil	77	105	172	436	153	131
Net Income $Mil	15	17	49	-436	-3,606	-649
Earnings Per Share $	—	0.08	0.20	-1.63	-12.08	-2.18
Shares Outstanding Mil	—	190	211	268	298	302
Return on Equity %	16.6	14.1	4.8	-8.3	ELB	-46.1
Net Margin %	19.9	16.3	28.2	ELB	ELB	ELB
Asset Turnover	0.7	0.7	0.2	0.1	0.1	0.1
Financial Leverage	1.2	1.2	1.0	1.0	1.0	1.0

Valuation Ratios	Stock	Rel to Industry	Rel to S&P 500
Price/Earnings	NMF	—	—
Price/Book	0.8	0.3	0.2
Price/Sales	8.5	2.2	4.2
Price/Cash Flow	—	—	—

Major Fund Holders	% of Fund Assets
Firsthand Technology Innovators	3.21
Firsthand Technology Value	2.19
Pioneer Growth A	2.04
Wireless	1.96

Morningstar Grades

Growth [D]	1999	2000	2001	2002
Revenue %	37.0	64.1	152.7	-64.9
Earnings/Share %	NMF	150.0	NMF	NMF
Book Value/Share %	NMF	633.8	369.4	-69.7
Dividends/Share %	NMF	NMF	NMF	NMF

Growth of 153% in fiscal 2001 (ending March 2001) was fantastic, but yielded to a huge slowdown in telecom spending in 2002 as sales fell more than 60%.

Profitability [B+]	2000	2001	2002	TTM
Return on Assets %	4.6	-8.0	ELB	-44.3
Oper Cash Flow $Mil	65	200	-36	-70
- Cap Spending $Mil	23	79	31	16
= Free Cash Flow $Mil	43	122	-67	-86

Applied Micro's products generate solid gross margins, but business has been so decimated that R&D costs exceed sales. The firm recently announced cost-cutting measures that should help matters.

Financial Health [B]	2000	2001	2002	12-02
Long-term Debt $Mil	5	2	1	1
Total Equity $Mil	1,014	5,238	1,771	1,406
Debt/Equity Ratio	0.0	0.0	0.0	0.0

With solid cash flows, minimal debt, and more than $1 billion in cash on its balance sheet, Applied is in good health. This is a competitive advantage because Applied can ride out the business storm, while rivals may struggle to stay afloat.

Morningstar's Take By Jeremy Lopez, 12-17-2002 Stock Price as of Analysis: $3.80

In this awful telecom capital spending environment, about the only thing Applied Micro Circuits has going for it is the $1 billion in cash on its balance sheet.

The main strike against Applied Micro is that its prospects are inextricably linked to telecom capital spending. Demand for telecom equipment is paltry and unlikely to significantly improve for some time, given the speculative excesses spent on infrastructure during the Internet bubble. Also, the bulk of Applied's chip products are focused at the core of telecom networks, where demand is weakest. And because sales have fallen so far so fast, R&D costs now exceed total sales. Even assuming strong growth for several years, it is going to take a very long time for Applied to create shareholder wealth again, or generate a return on capital greater than its cost of capital.

But with a very strong balance sheet, Applied Micro has a distinct competitive advantage. The firm has more than $1 billion in net cash (cash and investments minus debt), a luxury most others do not have. For example, Vitesse Semiconductor, whose balance sheet is much weaker, plans to exit a few key product areas, which we interpret as an effort to conserve cash. If there is a silver lining to this market turmoil, it is that Applied has the resources to

maintain its strong competitive position. Without an urgent need to radically slash key R&D projects, Applied should be in better shape than most when market conditions improve.

Considering Applied has $3.50 per share in net cash, the stock has some redeeming value. Certainly we expect the firm will burn through some of it this year, and perhaps next year as well. But it's unlikely Applied will use much of it in light of past meager losses; it had a free cash flow loss of only $67 million in 2001. This year's cash burn should be lower thanks to management's aggressive cost cutting and reduced capital spending. Our fair value estimate assumes $3 per share in cash and $2 for Applied's ongoing operations.

MORNINGSTAR® Stocks 500

Aramark RMK

	Rating	Risk	Moat Size	Fair Value	Last Close	Yield %
	★★	Low	Narrow	$21.00	$23.50	0.0

Company Profile

Aramark is one of the largest food-service providers in the world. The firm operates on-site restaurants and executive dining rooms for corporations, concession stands at stadiums and convention centers, and dining rooms at universities, among other venues. The firm is also the second-largest player in the uniform rental industry, behind Cintas. Aramark was a private company from 1984 until its initial public offering at the end of 2001.

Management

Joseph Neubauer has been CEO since 1983. The next year, he helped lead a management buyout of the firm. After the recent IPO, employees and management still own a sizable portion of the firm's equity.

Strategy

Aramark focuses on providing food and support services, as well as uniform rentals. Aramark seeks to increase revenue by convincing new customers to outsource and by selling current clients additional services. The firm holds down costs by benefiting from its size, saving money in areas like food purchases. It recently made a large acquisition of ServiceMaster's facilities-management business.

1101 Market St.   www.aramark.com
Philadelphia, PA 19107

Morningstar Grades

Growth [B+]	1999	2000	2001	2002
Revenue %	1.6	7.7	7.2	12.6
Earnings/Share %	NMF	NMF	NMF	NMF
Book Value/Share %	—	—	—	NMF
Dividends/Share %	NMF	NMF	NMF	NMF

Aramark is riding worldwide outsourcing trends. Although growth is not turbocharged, we expect the firm to internally increase revenue at 4%-5%, a rate that could be boosted by acquisitions.

Profitability [B+]	2000	2001	2002	TTM
Return on Assets %	5.3	5.5	6.3	6.3
Oper Cash Flow $Mil	407	497	631	631
- Cap Spending $Mil	207	219	267	267
= Free Cash Flow $Mil	200	278	364	364

Operating margins are around 5.9%. Aramark should be able to slowly--and slightly--boost margins as it benefits from its size and increases its efficiency at managing its labor costs.

Financial Health [B]	2000	2001	2002	09-02
Long-term Debt $Mil	1,778	1,636	1,836	1,836
Total Equity $Mil	131	247	858	858
Debt/Equity Ratio	13.5	6.6	2.1	2.1

Although Aramark has a substantial debt load, operating income easily covers interest expense. Because the firm generates a lot of free cash flow, we would expect it to reduce leverage over time.

Industry	Investment Style	Stock Type	Sector
Restaurants	▣ Mid Core	↗ Classic Growth	⊟ Consumer Services

Competition

	Market Cap $Mil	Debt/ Equity	12 Mo Trailing Sales $Mil	Price/Cash Flow	Return On Assets%	Total Return% 1 Yr	3 Yr
Aramark	1,462	2.1	8,770	2.3	6.3	-12.6	—
Cintas	7,774	0.4	2,372	20.1	9.4	-4.2	11.6
Sodexho Alliance	—		—				

Price Volatility

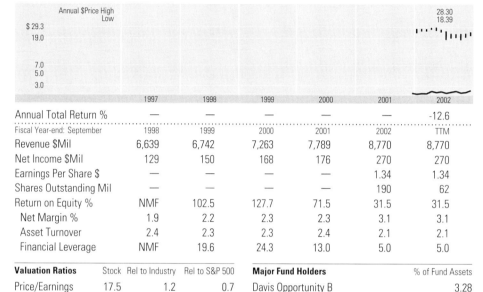

▮ Monthly Price High/Low	━ Relative Strength to S&P 500

	1997	1998	1999	2000	2001	2002
Annual Total Return %	—	—	—	—	—	-12.6

Fiscal Year-end: September	1998	1999	2000	2001	2002	TTM
Revenue $Mil	6,639	6,742	7,263	7,789	8,770	8,770
Net Income $Mil	129	150	168	176	270	270
Earnings Per Share $	—	—	—	—	1.34	1.34
Shares Outstanding Mil	—	—	—	—	190	62
Return on Equity %	NMF	102.5	127.7	71.5	31.5	31.5
Net Margin %	1.9	2.2	2.3	2.3	3.1	3.1
Asset Turnover	2.4	2.3	2.3	2.4	2.1	2.1
Financial Leverage	NMF	19.6	24.3	13.0	5.0	5.0

Valuation Ratios	Stock	Rel to Industry	Rel to S&P 500
Price/Earnings	17.5	1.2	0.7
Price/Book	1.7	0.7	0.5
Price/Sales	0.2	0.1	0.1
Price/Cash Flow	2.3	0.3	0.2

Major Fund Holders	% of Fund Assets
Davis Opportunity B	3.28
CRM Mid Cap Value Instl	3.15
Diversified Mid-Cap Value Instl	3.10
Diversified Mid-Cap Value Inv	3.10

Morningstar's Take By Dan Schick, 12-13-2002 Stock Price as of Analysis: $22.73

A worldwide leader in outsourced services, Aramark should benefit from modest and stable growth for years. Given the difficulty of stealing Aramark's customers, as well as the firm's size and scale advantages over competitors, we grant the company a narrow moat rating and would buy its shares at a 30% discount to our fair value estimate.

Continuing the age-old trend of division of labor and driven by cost considerations and a desire to provide quality services, organizations are choosing to outsource more noncore functions. Yet a large percentage of businesses, educational institutions, sports and entertainment venues, and health-care facilities remain self-operators. As the second-largest domestic provider of outsourced food and facility support services--and one of the largest globally--Aramark is operating in a favorable stage of industry growth, in our opinion.

Despite a poor economic climate, the firm continues to win new clients at a good rate, adding nearly 10% to its revenue base in new sales volume. Because the decision to outsource to Aramark is driven by quality concerns as much as price considerations, the company rarely loses a customer, either to competition or an insourcing initiative. Aramark boasts customer-retention rates in the

mid-90s; its average customer stays with the firm for close to 20 years. Aramark treats its customers as long-term partners.

Being big also helps. Aramark purchases most of its food-related products through Sysco; as one of that company's largest customers, Aramark negotiates volume-based discounts that give it a cost advantage over smaller players. Size helps in other ways: With national reach, Aramark can win the food-service business of geographically dispersed organizations that want to work with one supplier.

Another attractive aspect of Aramark is its position in the uniform rental industry. Although the firm lags the profitability of chief competitor Cintas, the segment does well. The uniform rental industry is profitably structured. For example, the firm's distribution network, which serves 300,000 customer locations in 39 states from more than 200 locations, is a powerful barrier to entry.

These advantages allow the firm to earn profits above the cost of the capital needed to run the business. By our calculations, Aramark generates returns on capital greater than 12%, well above its cost. Given the durability of its advantages, at the right price Aramark would be a rewarding investment, in our view.

Archstone-Smith Trust ASN

	Rating	Risk	Moat Size	Fair Value	Last Close	Yield %
	★★★	Low	Narrow	$24.00	$23.54	7.2

Company Profile

Archstone-Smith Trust acquires, develops, and operates income-producing real-estate properties in markets across the United States with high barriers to entry. As of June 2001, the company owned, operated, or developed 53,585 multifamily units; 3,440 of those are in the development pipeline. In May 2001, Archstone and Charles E. Smith announced their plan to merge in a deal scheduled to close in October 2001.

Management

President and CEO Scot Sellers, architect of the firm's capital-reallocation strategy, joined Archstone in 1994. He previously worked for Archstone's founder, Security Capital Group.

Strategy

The firm wants to build a national portfolio of apartments in metro areas with high barriers to entry. Roughly 80% of Archstone's net operating income comes from these protected markets. The firm continues to recycle its capital out of what it considers less desirable property locations into more protected areas. Archstone purchased its first apartment building in Manhattan earlier this year.

9200 E. Panorama Circle   www.archstonecommunities.com
Englewood, CO 80112

Morningstar Grades

Growth [B]	1998	1999	2000	2001
Revenue %	44.4	29.9	8.4	0.8
Earnings/Share %	129.2	-2.0	21.9	0.6
Book Value/Share %	25.6	-16.8	-6.9	76.8
Dividends/Share %	6.9	6.5	4.1	6.5

Funds from operation will decline to about $2.08 per share in 2002, and we expect they will continue to erode in 2003. For the first nine months of 2002, same-store net operating income was down 1.9% because of slightly lower rental rates and increased expenses.

Profitability [A]	1999	2000	2001	TTM
Return on Assets %	3.9	4.7	2.8	2.6
Oper Cash Flow $Mil	296	322	309	—
- Cap Spending $Mil	769	671	531	—
= Free Cash Flow $Mil	—	—	—	—

Archstone has an above-average operating margin of 66%. However, the firm does spend roughly 4% of property revenue on general and administrative expenses, which is more than the peer average.

Financial Health [A]	1999	2000	2001	09-02
Long-term Debt $Mil	—	—	—	—
Total Equity $Mil	2,312	2,038	3,576	3,580
Debt/Equity Ratio	—	—	—	—

With debt/total market capitalization of 42%, Archstone has a below-average amount of financial leverage for an apartment REIT. The firm has good access to capital because its Standard & Poor's BBB+ rating is relatively high for a REIT.

Industry	Investment Style	Stock Type	Sector
REITS	Mid Value	Hard Assets	Financial Services

Competition	Market Cap $Mil	Debt/ Equity	12 Mo Trailing Sales $Mil	Price/Cash Flow	Return On Assets%	Total Return% 1 Yr	3 Yr
Archstone-Smith Trust	4,254	—	1,040	—	2.6	-4.2	12.1
Equity Residential	6,780	—	2,137	—	2.9	-8.6	12.5
Apartment Investment & Ma	3,493	—	1,573	—	1.0	-11.5	7.3

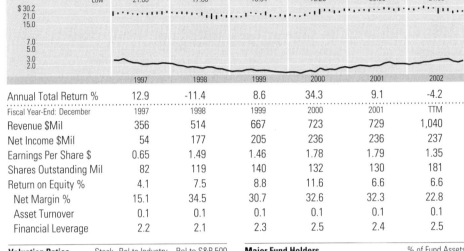

Price Volatility   I Monthly Price High/Low   — Relative Strength to S&P 500

	1997	1998	1999	2000	2001	2002
Annual $Price High	25.13	24.50	24.09	26.56	27.85	29.19
Low	21.00	17.88	18.94	19.25	23.00	21.33
Annual Total Return %	12.9	-11.4	8.6	34.3	9.1	-4.2

Fiscal Year-End: December	1997	1998	1999	2000	2001	TTM
Revenue $Mil	356	514	667	723	729	1,040
Net Income $Mil	54	177	205	236	236	237
Earnings Per Share $	0.65	1.49	1.46	1.78	1.79	1.35
Shares Outstanding Mil	82	119	140	132	130	181
Return on Equity %	4.1	7.5	8.8	11.6	6.6	6.6
Net Margin %	15.1	34.5	30.7	32.6	32.3	22.8
Asset Turnover	0.1	0.1	0.1	0.1	0.1	0.1
Financial Leverage	2.2	2.1	2.3	2.5	2.4	2.5

Valuation Ratios	Stock	Rel to Industry	Rel to S&P 500
Price/Earnings	17.4	1.0	0.7
Price/Book	1.2	0.8	0.4
Price/Sales	4.1	1.2	2.0
Price/Cash Flow	—	—	—

Major Fund Holders	% of Fund Assets
Undiscovered Managers REIT Inst	5.89
Fremont Real Estate Securities	5.87
Security Capital U.S. Real Estate	5.77
Scudder RREEF Real Estate Sec Instl	5.49

Morningstar's Take   By Matthew Scholz, 11-22-2002   Stock Price as of Analysis: $23.48

Having successfully executed its plan to build an apartment portfolio in protected metropolitan areas, Archstone-Smith has transformed itself into a high-grade apartment real estate investment trust (REIT). We estimate its net asset value at $24.

Archstone's evolution over the past few years demonstrates one of the advantages of the REIT structure: the ability to largely self-fund property portfolio changes through "capital recycling." In 1995, roughly 85% of Archstone's properties were in Texas, Arizona, and New Mexico--nice places to live, but generally not the best places to own apartment buildings because the states' wide-open spaces make it easy to build gobs of new apartments and houses. CEO Scot Sellers has led an extensive capital-reallocation program, and now more than 80% of Archstone's net operating income comes from metropolitan areas with high barriers to entry, like Southern California and Boston.

The 2001 merger with Charles E. Smith was a logical decision because it supports Archstone's strategy of focusing on protected markets. Charles E. Smith's high-rise portfolio dovetails nicely with Archstone's collection of garden apartments. Archstone should also benefit from the high-rise expertise of the old Smith employees, as the

combined company expands in its core markets and enters select new markets, like New York City.

Archstone has maintained above-average occupancy in the current economic downturn. For the quarter ended September 30, the average occupancy of its portfolio was 95.9%, which is a couple of percentage points above most peers. Part of this success can be explained by the fact that Archstone is heavily exposed to some of the country's strongest apartment markets, like Washington, D.C. Although it will take more time to know for certain, the high occupancy may also be explained in part by Archstone's new inventory-management software, which helps the company price its apartments more effectively.

Archstone-Smith is a bit of a hybrid. It is a national operator, but its portfolio is concentrated in only a few metropolitan areas. Archstone is well run, and the urban areas in which it has a presence should provide superior long-term growth in net operating income. Archstone is a high-quality, long-term REIT investment, in our opinion.

MORNINGSTAR® Stocks 500

AstraZeneca PLC ADR AZN

Rating	Risk	Moat Size	Fair Value	Last Close	Yield %
★★★★★	Med.	Wide	$45.00	$35.09	2.0

Company Profile

Astrazeneca is the result of a 1999 merger between Astra AB of Sweden and Zeneca Group PLC of the United Kingdom. It ranks number one in gastrointestinal (ulcer) sales worldwide and has a strong showing in cancer, respiratory and heart medicines as well. Astrazeneca's top-selling drugs are Prilosec/Nexium (ulcers), Seloken/Toprol (cardio), Zestil (cardio), Zoladex (cancer), and Seroquel (antipsychotic). The company has half a dozen drugs with $500 million or better in worldwide sales and several grossing $1 billion-plus. It sells products in more than 100 countries.

Management

Tom McKillop came up the ranks at Zeneca and became CEO just before the 1999 merger with Astra. His background is in research and development.

Strategy

AstraZeneca, which was formed from the merger of two European drug companies in April 1999, is focusing on the high-margin pharmaceutical business. It recently spun off its agricultural unit. The company's major areas of concentration are gastrointestinal, cardiovascular, cancer, and respiratory therapies.

15 Stanhope Gate   www.astrazeneca.com
London, W1Y 6LN

Morningstar Grades

Growth [C-]	1998	1999	2000	2001
Revenue %	NMF	13.2	-1.9	-8.9
Earnings/Share %	1.4	-56.2	125.0	17.4
Book Value/Share %	14.2	-5.6	-6.4	3.2
Dividends/Share %	—	NMF	0.0	0.0

AstraZeneca's revenue growth remains strong--up 10% in the first half of 2002--thanks to legal efforts to hold back generic Prilosec. On average, we expect revenue to increase 7% annually through 2006.

Profitability [A+]	1999	2000	2001	TTM
Return on Assets %	5.8	13.8	16.5	16.5
Oper Cash Flow $Mil	3,113	4,183	3,762	3,762
- Cap Spending $Mil	1,490	1,347	1,385	1,385
= Free Cash Flow $Mil	1,623	2,836	2,377	2,377

Operating margins were steady and on par with industry peers over the past several years. Gross margins for the first half of 2002 were 73.9%, while operating margins improved from 25.4% a year ago to 26.8% in the first half of 2002.

Financial Health [A]	1999	2000	2001	12-01
Long-term Debt $Mil	739	631	635	635
Total Equity $Mil	10,302	9,521	9,786	9,786
Debt/Equity Ratio	0.1	0.1	0.1	0.1

The balance sheet is extremely healthy, with very little debt and adequate cash. At of June 30, 2002, the company had less than $1 billion in debt and more than $4 billion in cash and equivalents.

Industry	Investment Style	Stock Type	Sector
Drugs	⊞ Large Growth	→ Slow Growth	Healthcare

Competition

	Market Cap $Mil	Debt/ Equity	12 Mo Trailing Sales $Mil	Price/Cash Flow	Return On Assets%	Total Return% 1 Yr	3 Yr
AstraZeneca PLC ADR	61,408	0.1	16,663	16.3	16.5	-23.4	-1.7
Pfizer	188,377	0.2	34,407	21.1	18.3	-22.2	1.0
Merck	127,121	0.3	50,430	13.2	15.0	-1.3	-2.5

Price Volatility

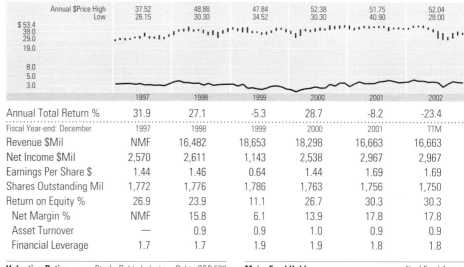

		Monthly Price High/Low			Relative Strength to S&P 500	
Annual $Price High Low	37.52 26.15	48.88 30.30	47.84 34.52	52.38 30.30	51.75 40.90	52.04 28.00

$53.4 / 39.0 / 29.0 / 19.0 / 8.0 / 5.0 / 3.0

	1997	1998	1999	2000	2001	2002
Annual Total Return %	31.9	27.1	-5.3	28.7	-8.2	-23.4

Fiscal Year-end: December	1997	1998	1999	2000	2001	TTM
Revenue $Mil	NMF	16,482	18,653	18,298	16,663	16,663
Net Income $Mil	2,570	2,611	1,143	2,538	2,967	2,967
Earnings Per Share $	1.44	1.46	0.64	1.44	1.69	1.69
Shares Outstanding Mil	1,772	1,776	1,786	1,763	1,756	1,750
Return on Equity %	26.9	23.9	11.1	26.7	30.3	30.3
Net Margin %	NMF	15.8	6.1	13.9	17.8	17.8
Asset Turnover	—	0.9	0.9	1.0	0.9	0.9
Financial Leverage	1.7	1.7	1.9	1.9	1.8	1.8

Valuation Ratios	Stock	Rel to Industry	Rel to S&P 500
Price/Earnings	20.8	0.9	0.9
Price/Book	6.3	0.9	2.0
Price/Sales	3.7	0.9	1.8
Price/Cash Flow	16.3	0.8	1.2

Major Fund Holders	% of Fund Assets
Fidelity Select Pharmaceuticals	5.03
Hartford Global Health A	4.86
Vanguard Health Care	3.25
Hartford Growth L	2.84

Morningstar's Take By Todd N. Lebor, 10-18-2002 Stock Price as of Analysis: $37.35

AstraZeneca has very few drugs that go off patent in the near future, several blockbusters in late-stage development, and a healthy number of newly launched drugs. We think the company can improve its position in the global pharmaceutical market over the next few years. We'd require only a 20% margin of safety before snapping up shares of this Anglo-Swedish giant.

Even though Prilosec, AstraZeneca's biggest-selling drug by far (one third of 2001 revenue), is under attack from generic drug companies, the company's anti-ulcerant franchise isn't in immediate danger. In October 2002, AstraZeneca successfully fended off challenges to Prilosec's formulation patents from all but one generic company. The result, assuming the U.S. court ruling isn't overturned on appeal, is that Prilosec will face only one direct competitor until 2007. We think this will keep pricing pressure to a minimum, but more important, it buys AstraZeneca more time to convert Prilosec patients to Nexium, its next-generation heartburn pill. So far, the company's execution has been textbook. Nexium sales hit nearly $1.5 billion in the first 18 months on the market, snagging 20% of the proton-pump inhibitor market.

It is execution like this that should allow AstraZeneca to maintain its dominant position in the gastrointestinal market. But it's the cardio segment where we think AstraZeneca will really make a move. AstraZeneca's Atacand, with only $400 million in worldwide sales, was found to be more effective than Merck's Cozaar, the leading angiotension II receptor blocker with $2 billion in worldwide sales. Then there's Crestor, a cholesterol-lowering drug that demonstrated superior efficacy to Pfizer's Lipitor. It's under review by the Food and Drug Administration with an expected launch in 2004. The $18 billion statin market is so large that only a 10% piece of the pie is worth billions. We expect Crestor be a strong contender because of AstraZeneca's experience in marketing Zestril to cardiologists, despite intense marketing resistance from Pfizer and Merck.

AstraZeneca also has an admirable lineup of cancer drugs on the market, including Arimidex and Faslodex for breast cancer, Zoladex for prostate cancer, and Iressa (recommended but not approved in the United States) for lung cancer.

There's more to a drug company than its drugs, and AstraZeneca's management of patent expiration exposure, productive research department, and consistently strong operating margins make the stock a good buy at the right price.

AT&T T

	Rating	Risk	Moat Size	Fair Value	Last Close	Yield %
	★★	Med.	None	$25.00	$26.11	2.9

Industry	Investment Style	Stock Type	Sector
Telecommunication Services	▦ Large Core	▨ High Yield	▣ Telecom

Company Profile

AT&T provides telecommunication services, including voice, data, and video services to businesses, individuals, and government entities. The company's consumer unit is currently the largest provider of long-distance phone services to consumers and also provides Internet access. AT&T's business services unit generates about half of its revenue from long-distance services, with the rest coming from data services like Web hosting and data transport. The company also serves about 16 million cable subscribers.

Management

Michael Armstrong, who joined AT&T in 1997 and orchestrated the firm's push into cable, left to become chairman of Comcast. Telecom veteran David Dorman is now AT&T's chairman and CEO.

Strategy

AT&T is working to shore up declining revenue and shrinking profit margins by expanding beyond long-distance voice services. The company is pushing into the local phone business and expanding its ability to offer high-end data services around the globe.

32 Avenue of Americas
New York, NY 10013-2412
www.att.com

Competition

Competition	Market Cap $Mil	Debt/ Equity	12 Mo Trailing Sales $Mil	Price/Cash Flow	Return On Assets%	Total Return% 1 Yr	3 Yr
AT&T	20,115	0.8	48,821	1.8	-10.9	-27.7	-28.2
Verizon Communications	106,011	1.4	67,422	4.7	-0.1	-15.2	-9.8
SBC Communications	90,011	0.6	43,824	6.1	5.1	-28.3	-12.8

Price Volatility

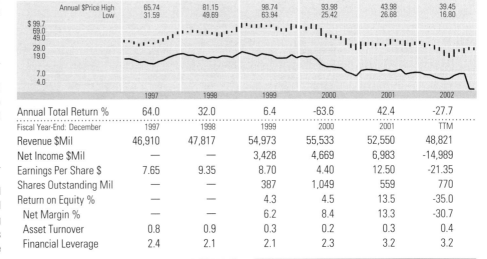

Annual $Price High / Low	65.74 / 31.59	81.15 / 49.69	98.74 / 63.94	93.98 / 25.42	43.98 / 26.68	39.45 / 16.80
	1997	1998	1999	2000	2001	2002
Annual Total Return %	64.0	32.0	6.4	-63.6	42.4	-27.7

Fiscal Year-End: December	1997	1998	1999	2000	2001	TTM
Revenue $Mil	46,910	47,817	54,973	55,533	52,550	48,821
Net Income $Mil	—	—	3,428	4,669	6,983	-14,989
Earnings Per Share $	7.65	9.35	8.70	4.40	12.50	-21.35
Shares Outstanding Mil	—	—	387	1,049	559	770
Return on Equity %	—	—	4.3	4.5	13.5	-35.0
Net Margin %	—	—	6.2	8.4	13.3	-30.7
Asset Turnover	0.8	0.9	0.3	0.2	0.3	0.4
Financial Leverage	2.4	2.1	2.1	2.3	3.2	3.2

Valuation Ratios	Stock	Rel to Industry	Rel to S&P 500
Price/Earnings	NMF	—	—
Price/Book	0.5	0.2	0.1
Price/Sales	0.4	0.3	0.2
Price/Cash Flow	1.8	0.4	0.1

Major Fund Holders	% of Fund Assets
ProFunds Ultra Telecommunications Inv	10.88
Hartford Global Communications A	10.41
Fidelity Select Telecommunications	9.58
SunAmerica Focused Large Cap Value A	7.01

Morningstar Grades

Growth [D]

	1998	1999	2000	2001
Revenue %	1.9	15.0	1.0	-5.4
Earnings/Share %	22.2	-7.0	-49.4	184.1
Book Value/Share %	—	NMF	-51.4	-4.9
Dividends/Share %	0.0	0.0	-20.7	-78.5

Thanks to the declining long-distance business, overall growth is paltry. Revenue has fallen about 11% thus far in 2002 as data and local phone growth hasn't been enough to offset the drop in long-distance sales.

Profitability [B]

	1999	2000	2001	TTM
Return on Assets %	2.1	2.0	4.2	-10.9
Oper Cash Flow $Bil	10.5	11.7	10.6	11.0
- Cap Spending $Bil	11.9	11.5	9.3	7.9
= Free Cash Flow $Bil	-1.4	0.2	1.3	3.2

AT&T continues to see margins erode as highly profitable long-distance phone revenue falls and is replaced by less profitable data revenue.

Financial Health [B+]

	1999	2000	2001	09-02
Long-term Debt $Bil	35.7	33.1	40.5	36.4
Total Equity $Bil	78.9	103.2	51.7	42.9
Debt/Equity Ratio	0.5	0.3	0.8	0.8

Comcast assumed a big chunk of AT&T's debt load and all its preferred stock. AT&T now has $16.6 billion in debt, net of $7.5 billion in cash (adjusted for the firm's $3.5 billion AT&T Canada obligation). Current cash flow easily meets this burden.

Morningstar's Take
By Michael Hodel, 12-27-2002 Stock Price as of Analysis: $26.75

With the cable business spun off, AT&T's remaining businesses aren't attractive, in our opinion. The company should initially throw off decent cash flow, but this stream will probably decline. Given AT&T's relatively weak position in a tough industry, estimating the extent of this decline is difficult. We'd consider the shares only at a steep--40% or greater--discount to our fair value estimate.

AT&T's remaining operations are struggling. AT&T Consumer has seen revenue fall more than 20% thus far in 2002. The unit has had some success in the local phone business, and it now serves about 2 million customers. The company is able to serve these customers as a result of regulations that force the regional Bells, like Verizon, to offer services on their networks at wholesale rates. Over the long term, though, we have serious doubts about AT&T Consumer's ability to compete effectively. The Federal Communications Commission is reviewing the rules governing local phone services, and an unfavorable change would hurt AT&T's prospects.

More important to AT&T Consumer's long-term competitive position, the Bells continue to generate huge, fairly steady cash flows while the AT&T unit's cash flow declines at an increasing rate. Compounding this issue, the Bells will be able to replicate AT&T's long-distance capabilities far more cheaply after they receive nationwide long-distance approvals than AT&T can replicate the Bell's local capabilities.

AT&T Business, on the other hand, has brighter prospects today than it did a couple of quarters ago. The fraud and bankruptcy of WorldCom will drive customers to more-stable providers, and AT&T fits this bill as well as anyone. AT&T has already been performing better than its peers, and adding a few large business customers could widen the gulf. Changing telecom providers is a complex proposition for large businesses, though, so new business probably won't hit the top line until sometime next year. The biggest knock against this unit is its heavy exposure to the long-distance phone business, which still accounts for nearly half of revenue.

The Bells' entry into the long-distance market will have a disproportionately large impact on AT&T. Many states, including California, have only recently granted their local Bell long-distance authority; a handful more will do so in 2003. As bad as the decline in AT&T's revenues has been thus far, the worst may be yet to come.

MORNINGSTAR® Stocks 500

AT&T Wireless Services AWE

	Rating	Risk	Moat Size	Fair Value	Last Close	Yield %
	★★★	High	None	$8.00	$5.65	0.0

Company Profile

AT&T Wireless is the third-largest wireless carrier in the United States, behind Verizon Wireless and Cingular Wireless. Along with its partners and affiliates like TeleCorp PCS (which it has acquired), AT&T Wireless has licenses to cover 98% of the U.S. population; this allows it to offer popular calling plans like Digital One Rate (one rate anywhere in the States). The firm was a tracking stock of AT&T before being spun off in 2001. Japanese wireless giant NTT DoCoMo owns 16%.

Management

Led by chairman and CEO John Zeglis, a wireless industry veteran, the management team is topnotch. However, the firm's highly respected president, Mohan Gyani, recently announced his retirement; losing someone as talented as Gyani is never a good thing.

Strategy

As the third-largest wireless carrier in the States, AT&T Wireless wants to provide voice and mobile Internet services to the best customers available in every major market of North America. The firm is spending aggressively on its network to improve capacity and launch next-generation services, like mMode.

7277 164th Avenue N.E.   www.attws.com
Redmond, WA 98052

Morningstar Grades

Growth [B-]

	1998	1999	2000	2001
Revenue %	NMF	41.1	37.0	30.3
Earnings/Share %	NMF	NMF	NMF	NMF
Book Value/Share %	—	—	—	NMF
Dividends/Share %	NMF	NMF	NMF	NMF

Growth numbers are skewed by acquisitions, but market saturation will limit 2002 subscriber growth to the midteens. Competition is keeping a lid on phone rates, ensuring that gains will be muted.

Profitability [B-]

	1999	2000	2001	TTM
Return on Assets %	-2.0	1.5	-2.3	-7.5
Oper Cash Flow $Mil	913	1,786	2,734	2,648
- Cap Spending $Mil	2,135	3,601	5,205	4,737
= Free Cash Flow $Mil	-1,222	-1,815	-2,471	-2,089

Although EBITDA grew 65% in 2001, it is projected to move up roughly 20% this year. It is encouraging that EBITDA growth is substantially outpacing sales growth, which shows that the firm is gaining economies of scale.

Financial Health [B-]

	1999	2000	2001	09-02
Long-term Debt $Mil	3,558	1,800	6,617	11,033
Total Equity $Mil	12,997	21,877	26,945	27,492
Debt/Equity Ratio	0.3	0.1	0.2	0.4

The firm is rated BBB by S&P, a solid rating for any wireless carrier; its credit statistics are stellar. The company is flush with cash, which it will need to make hefty capital expenditures. We expect free cash flow will finally turn positive in 2003.

Industry	Investment Style	Stock Type	Sector
Wireless Service	Large Growth	Spec. Growth	Telecom

Competition

	Market Cap $Mil	Debt/ Equity	12 Mo Trailing Sales $Mil	Price/Cash Flow	Return On Assets%	Total Return% 1 Yr	3 Yr
AT&T Wireless Services	15,300	0.4	15,112	5.8	-7.5	-60.7	—
Verizon Communications	106,011	1.4	67,422	4.7	-0.1	-15.2	-9.8
Nextel Communications	11,124	23.4	8,464	5.9	-7.5	5.4	-37.6

Price Volatility

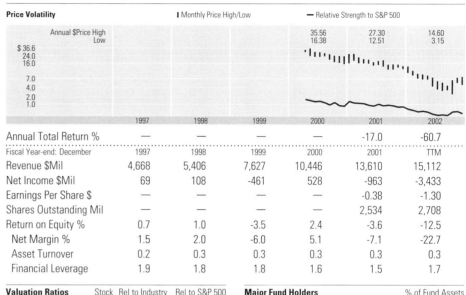

Annual Total Return %	—	—	—	—	-17.0	-60.7

Fiscal Year-end: December	1997	1998	1999	2000	2001	TTM
Revenue $Mil	4,668	5,406	7,627	10,446	13,610	15,112
Net Income $Mil	69	108	-461	528	-963	-3,433
Earnings Per Share $	—	—	—	—	-0.38	-1.30
Shares Outstanding Mil	—	—	—	—	2,534	2,708
Return on Equity %	0.7	1.0	-3.5	2.4	-3.6	-12.5
Net Margin %	1.5	2.0	-6.0	5.1	-7.1	-22.7
Asset Turnover	0.2	0.3	0.3	0.3	0.3	0.3
Financial Leverage	1.9	1.8	1.8	1.6	1.5	1.7

Valuation Ratios

	Stock	Rel to Industry	Rel to S&P 500
Price/Earnings	NMF	—	—
Price/Book	0.6	0.2	0.2
Price/Sales	1.0	0.4	0.5
Price/Cash Flow	5.8	0.5	0.4

Major Fund Holders

	% of Fund Assets
ProFunds Ultra Wireless Inv	20.23
Cutler Value	4.45
Cutler Core	4.41
Fidelity Select Telecommunications	4.15

Morningstar's Take By Todd P. Bernier, 12-23-2002 Stock Price as of Analysis: $6.75

Despite decent fundamentals, AT&T Wireless cannot escape a sick wireless industry. We would buy the stock only at a very wide discount--roughly 50%--to our fair value estimate.

We've always been impressed by AT&T. The company's executive team is professional and disciplined; the company won't chase substandard customers simply in the name of growth. And because the firm went public when wireless valuations peaked, its balance sheet is flush with cash, the reason for its investment-grade debt rating. Finally, AT&T's spectrum portfolio is the best in the industry, which eliminates the need to overpay at future spectrum auctions.

However, a fundamentally flawed wireless industry and persistent negative free cash flow dog AT&T Wireless.

The U.S. market for new customers is shrinking, and six major carriers are clamoring for growth. To attract new customers and keep existing ones, the wireless players just keep offering more minutes per month at the same price. This has caused prices to plummet; the average price per minute was $0.56 in 1995, roughly 5 times the current level. Although overall wireless usage has nearly quadrupled over that period, from 119 billion to 456 billion minutes,

carriers have failed to capitalize. It's as though the wireless firms learned nothing from their long-distance cousins, who hung themselves with a rope called nickel minutes.

AT&T's other big problem is a network that requires substantial reconstruction. Years ago the company opted for TDMA as its second-generation air interface of choice, instead of rival technologies CDMA and GSM. However, future third-generation (3G) standards have been developed on the latter two protocols, forcing AT&T to overlay GSM equipment on its network. This has meant big capital spending: more than $5 billion in both 2001 and 2002, and another $4 billion planned in 2003.

Like all other domestic carriers (save Nextel), AT&T is betting that customers will embrace advanced 3G services. But we're not convinced that subscribers, who already complain about high monthly bills, will shell out for expensive services. Should 3G disappoint, which we believe is likely, the carriers will have taken on unnecessary debt.

Only if the shares became unavoidably cheap would we buy AT&T Wireless.

Autodesk ADSK

	Rating	Risk	Moat Size	Fair Value	Last Close	Yield %
	★★★★	Med.	Wide	$16.00	$14.30	1.0

Industry	Investment Style	Stock Type	Sector
Business Applications	▦ Mid Core	➡ Slow Growth	◪ Software

Company Profile

Autodesk provides digital systems and software that help develop computer images. The company's Discreet Logic subsidiary assists with creating visual effects, three-dimensional animation, and broadcasting. Discreet's tools are used to create moving pictures for video, feature films, broadcast graphics, interactive games, and Web sites. Autodesk's other customers for its design-related software include architects, engineers, construction firms, designers, and drafters. It also markets design software under the AutoCAD name.

Management

CEO Carol Bartz has been with the company since 1992 and serves on the boards of Cisco Systems and BEA Systems. Alfred Castino, former CFO of PeopleSoft, recently came on board as CFO.

Strategy

The two keys to Autodesk's strategy are branching out into new industries--entertainment, broadcasting, and video games--and smoothing out its revenue by moving to a subscription-based model and incremental updates to its software.

111 McInnis Parkway
San Rafael, CA 94903
www.autodesk.com

Competition	Market Cap $Mil	Debt/ Equity	12 Mo Trailing Sales $Mil	Price/Cash Flow	Return On Assets%	Total Return% 1 Yr	3 Yr
Autodesk	1,622	—	883	13.1	5.2	-22.5	-2.6
Dassault Systemes SA ADR	2,483	—	587	—	—	—	—
Parametric Tech	658	—	754	—	—	—	—

Price Volatility | Monthly Price High/Low — Relative Strength to S&P 500

Annual $Price High Low	25.88 14.00	25.03 10.81	24.72 8.50	28.03 9.72	21.10 12.09	23.69 10.18

	1997	1998	1999	2000	2001	2002
Annual Total Return %	33.0	16.2	-20.3	-19.6	39.4	-22.5

Fiscal Year-End: January	1998	1999	2000	2001	2002	TTM
Revenue $Mil	786	894	848	936	947	883
Net Income $Mil	56	97	10	93	90	47
Earnings Per Share $	0.47	0.82	0.08	0.80	0.80	0.41
Shares Outstanding Mil	112	113	123	114	109	113
Return on Equity %	NMF	18.1	1.6	20.3	17.1	8.1
Net Margin %	7.2	10.9	1.2	10.0	9.5	5.3
Asset Turnover	1.1	1.1	0.9	1.2	1.1	1.0
Financial Leverage	—	1.5	1.5	1.8	1.7	1.5

Valuation Ratios	Stock	Rel to Industry	Rel to S&P 500
Price/Earnings	35.3	1.1	1.5
Price/Book	2.8	0.5	0.9
Price/Sales	1.8	0.2	0.9
Price/Cash Flow	13.1	0.8	1.0

Major Fund Holders	% of Fund Assets
Westcore Select	7.39
STI Classic Small Cap Equity Tr	3.79
Seligman Communications&Information A	3.49
DEM Equity Institutional	3.39

Morningstar Grades

Growth [C]	1999	2000	2001	2002
Revenue %	13.7	-5.1	10.4	1.2
Earnings/Share %	74.5	-90.2	900.0	0.0
Book Value/Share %	NMF	8.3	-19.7	18.9
Dividends/Share %	0.0	0.0	0.0	0.0

The top line averaged 15% annual growth over the past five years, but has slowed significantly as key industries like manufacturing and construction have reduced spending in a soft economy.

Profitability [A]	2000	2001	2002	TTM
Return on Assets %	1.1	11.5	10.0	5.2
Oper Cash Flow $Mil	108	196	210	124
- Cap Spending $Mil	15	32	45	37
= Free Cash Flow $Mil	93	164	165	87

Autodesk generates enough cash to repurchase stock and pay a dividend. We expect margins to improve slightly as the firm sells more software over the Internet and on a subscription basis.

Financial Health [A]	2000	2001	2002	10-02
Long-term Debt $Mil	—	—	—	—
Total Equity $Mil	602	460	529	586
Debt/Equity Ratio	—	—	—	—

With $407 million in cash and no debt, financial health is excellent. However, cash has dropped because of acquisitions and stock repurchases.

Morningstar's Take By Mike Trigg, 10-09-2002 Stock Price as of Analysis: $11.67

We think Autodesk will generate above-average returns when the economy improves. Investors buying the stock below $13 could profit handsomely.

Autodesk dominates architecture and construction design software with its market-leading AutoCAD product. With more than 4 million loyal users, the firm has a wide economic moat--high switching costs make it tough for customers to get comparable products elsewhere or do their job without Autodesk. Since customers are trained early to use Autodesk software, it's nearly impossible for competitors to take meaningful market share.

Autodesk's software is also relatively affordable, making the firm more immune to a miserable economy. While some software costs millions of dollars, Autodesk's products cost much less; the initial price of AutoCAD is a little over $3,000. This makes Autodesk less susceptible to cutbacks in information technology spending. In addition, using its software reduces expenses by shortening the design, testing, and manufacturing processes.

Management has made great strides in reducing the firm's dependence on AutoCAD and "big release" updates of key products, both of which have historically made financial results (and the stock price) very volatile. Instead, Autodesk has begun offering industry-specific and multimedia design software, more-frequent updates, new functionality through add-on modules, and a subscription-based sales model. The last, in particular, should make business more predictable by generating recurring revenue.

Our enthusiasm is tempered by concerns over the size of Autodesk's addressable market. Some liken the computer-aided design (CAD) market to the graphic design industry of the 1980s, which was transformed by software like Adobe's PhotoShop and Illustrator. But we think it is a stretch to assume that CAD software will be as big. Graphic design software appeals to consumers as well as professionals, while CAD applications are used only by designers and architects for complex drawings and models.

We think Autodesk has a bright future, even though business has struggled as spending in key industries, like construction and manufacturing, has slowed. Management has cut AutoCAD sales to 30%-40% of total revenue, and as the subscription model gains traction, business will be more predictable. While uncertainty remains regarding Autodesk's efforts to expand its market, a wide economic moat and loyal customer base ease our concerns.

MO RNINGSTAR® **Stocks 500**

Automatic Data Processing ADP

	Rating	Risk	Moat Size	Fair Value	Last Close	Yield %
	★★★★★	Low	Wide	$54.00	$39.25	1.2

Company Profile

Automatic Data Processing is the world's largest provider of payroll services, including processing checks for businesses and maintaining human resources records. The firm offers a comprehensive range of services including payroll tax depositing and reporting, 401(k) record-keeping, and unemployment compensation management. The firm also operates a securities transaction division that handles stock trades and processes proxies. In addition, ADP has dealer and claims services divisions that maintain and sell data to car dealers and the insurance industries.

Management

Arthur Weinbach became CEO in 1996 and added the title of chairman in 1998. He has been with the company since 1980. Honorary chairman Henry Taub founded the firm in 1949.

Strategy

ADP operates in growing markets with substantial barriers to entry. The firm tries to capitalize on this enviable position by getting and keeping more clients and selling add-on services to those clients. Strategic acquisitions have given ADP some of these add-on services and allowed the firm to expand outside its core payroll market.

One ADP Boulevard   www.adp.com
Roseland, NJ 07068

Morningstar Grades

Growth [B]	1999	2000	2001	2002
Revenue %	12.5	11.3	11.1	2.2
Earnings/Share %	12.2	19.1	9.9	21.5
Book Value/Share %	14.2	12.9	2.5	11.1
Dividends/Share %	15.1	14.8	16.6	13.3

Fiscal 2002 was difficult; 2003 will be, too. But once the firm gets past the next couple of years, we think it should meet its goals of double-digit revenue growth.

Profitability [A]	2000	2001	2002	TTM
Return on Assets %	5.0	5.2	6.0	7.1
Oper Cash Flow $Mil	1,070	1,491	1,532	1,388
- Cap Spending $Mil	166	185	146	140
= Free Cash Flow $Mil	904	1,306	1,386	1,248

ADP is amazingly profitable. It generated more than $1 billion of free cash flow in fiscal 2002, thanks to low capital spending needs and high operating margins.

Financial Health [A]	2000	2001	2002	09-02
Long-term Debt $Mil	132	110	91	84
Total Equity $Mil	4,583	4,701	5,114	4,749
Debt/Equity Ratio	0.0	0.0	0.0	0.0

There isn't much to complain about here since ADP has little debt and strong cash flows. The bloated asset and liability accounts on the balance sheet pertain to payroll taxes the firm collects and submits for its clients.

Industry	Investment Style	Stock Type	Sector
Data Processing	⊞ Large Growth	↗ Classic Growth	▤ Business Services

Competition	Market Cap $Mil	Debt/ Equity	12 Mo Trailing Sales $Mil	Price/Cash Flow	Return On Assets%	Total Return% 1 Yr	3 Yr
Automatic Data Processing	23,506	0.0	7,043	16.9	7.1	-32.7	-8.2
Paychex	10,493	—	973	29.9	9.1	-19.2	5.3
DST Systems	4,255	0.3	1,648	10.1	8.3	-28.7	-0.8

Price Volatility

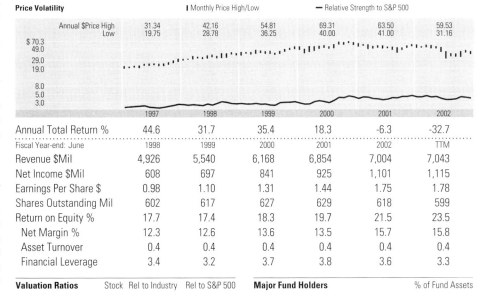

		Monthly Price High/Low		— Relative Strength to S&P 500		
Annual $Price High	31.34	42.16	54.81	69.31	63.50	59.53
Low	19.75	28.78	36.25	40.00	41.00	31.16

	1997	1998	1999	2000	2001	2002
Annual Total Return %	44.6	31.7	35.4	18.3	-6.3	-32.7

Fiscal Year-end: June	1998	1999	2000	2001	2002	TTM
Revenue $Mil	4,926	5,540	6,168	6,854	7,004	7,043
Net Income $Mil	608	697	841	925	1,101	1,115
Earnings Per Share $	0.98	1.10	1.31	1.44	1.75	1.78
Shares Outstanding Mil	602	617	627	629	618	599
Return on Equity %	17.7	17.4	18.3	19.7	21.5	23.5
Net Margin %	12.3	12.6	13.6	13.5	15.7	15.8
Asset Turnover	0.4	0.4	0.4	0.4	0.4	0.4
Financial Leverage	3.4	3.2	3.7	3.8	3.6	3.3

Valuation Ratios	Stock	Rel to Industry	Rel to S&P 500
Price/Earnings	22.1	0.9	0.9
Price/Book	5.0	1.0	1.5
Price/Sales	3.3	1.0	1.7
Price/Cash Flow	16.9	1.0	1.3

Major Fund Holders	% of Fund Assets
AmSouth Select Equity B	7.73
Berger Information Technology Instl	6.54
Berger Information Technology Inv	6.54
Huntington Growth Tr	6.16

Morningstar's Take By Dan Schick, 11-29-2002 Stock Price as of Analysis: $43.47

A sterling record of growth, strong competitive positions in its markets, and a fortresslike balance sheet make Automatic Data Processing a rare company. We believe the stock is worth buying at a 20% discount to our fair value estimate.

Low interest rates, rising unemployment, and a weak equity market have made times tough for ADP recently. But even in tough times, ADP produces results many companies would envy. The firm just racked up its 165th quarter of growth in revenue and earnings per share and is on track to produce a billion dollars of free cash flow this year. We attribute ADP's success to its strong competitive position. Like General Electric, ADP is a leader in its markets.

ADP commands the pole position serving the payroll-processing needs of medium and large companies, while running neck-and-neck with Paychex for the attentions of smaller firms. The firm earns about 60% of its revenue from the payroll business, a market where we believe ADP's lead should endure. First, economies of scale place smaller firms at a disadvantage. Because a startup processor is necessarily small, new entrants are deterred. Second, the large and fragmented nature of ADP's customer base works in the firm's favor. None of its more than 450,000 payroll customers contribute

a big portion of revenue, so they are not in a good position to bargain away its profits.

ADP's brokerage services group accounts for about one fourth of the company's revenue. The part of the unit that processes trades for the securities industry is suffering from the weak stock market. However, it is a leader in the business and long-term trends toward further outsourcing and increased trade volume are still favorable. Within brokerage services, ADP also earns revenue providing communication services to investors on behalf of corporations. This area is also suffering from the feeble market as growth in individual stock positions has increased at a slower rate. Nevertheless, ADP has a commanding market share in this area and has acquired a broad line of service offerings, becoming a one-stop shop for corporations' investor communication needs. We view this as a significant competitive advantage.

Finally, ADP's dealer services group contributes 10% of revenue and operates in a duopoly with Reynolds & Reynolds. Although it hasn't been growing much, this business throws off a lot of cash flow. Thanks to the lack of competition, ADP's outlook here is good and we think growth should reaccelerate in this segment.

AutoNation AN

	Rating	Risk	Moat Size	Fair Value	Last Close	Yield %
	★★★★	Low	Narrow	$16.00	$12.56	0.0

Company Profile

AutoNation is the largest automotive dealer in the United States. Its 368 dealerships are located in 17 states, primarily in large metropolitan areas and the Sunbelt. Sales of new vehicles account for approximately 60% of revenue; the company also sells used vehicles, parts, and repair services, as well as auto financing. Formerly known as Republic Industries, the company spun off its waste-management unit (Republic Services) in 1999 and its car-rental businesses (ANC Rental) in 2000. Its AutoNation.com unit is the nation's largest online car retailer.

Management

CEO Michael J. Jackson joined AutoNation in October 1999, replacing the founder, Miami entrepreneur Wayne Huizenga. Jackson was previously president and CEO of Mercedes-Benz USA and has nearly three decades of industry sales experience.

Strategy

After increasing its size sevenfold between 1996 and 1999, AutoNation is now working to integrate its vast network of acquired dealerships into a consistent, more profitable whole. With thin margins on new car sales, the company is focusing on more-lucrative service and financial operations to expand profitability.

110 S.E. 6th Street
Ft. Lauderdale, FL 33301
www.autonation.com

Morningstar Grades

Growth [C+]	1998	1999	2000	2001
Revenue %	106.8	58.8	2.4	-3.0
Earnings/Share %	3.9	-37.7	37.9	-24.2
Book Value/Share %	42.4	-6.7	-1.3	7.3
Dividends/Share %	NMF	NMF	NMF	NMF

A buying binge that ended two years ago left AutoNation a little hung over: Revenue rose just 2.4% in 2000 and fell 3% in 2001. We expect sluggish industry sales and a much smaller acquisition program will keep revenue growth modest for a few years.

Profitability [B-]	1999	2000	2001	TTM
Return on Assets %	3.0	3.7	2.9	3.8
Oper Cash Flow $Mil	47	431	540	473
- Cap Spending $Mil	242	139	164	177
= Free Cash Flow $Mil	-195	293	377	296

AutoNation has become more profitable in recent quarters by dumping unprofitable stores, improving inventory turnover, and expanding its financial and repair businesses. A surge of new car sales in late 2001 also helped boost margins.

Financial Health [B]	1999	2000	2001	09-02
Long-term Debt $Mil	836	850	647	638
Total Equity $Mil	4,601	3,843	3,828	4,020
Debt/Equity Ratio	0.2	0.2	0.2	0.2

The company's balance sheet is much more conservative than those of its publicly traded peers. Management has been putting AutoNation's substantial free cash flow into debt reduction and share repurchases.

Industry	Investment Style	Stock Type	Sector
Auto Retail	▦ Mid Core	➡ Slow Growth	🖳 Consumer Services

Competition	Market Cap $Mil	Debt/ Equity	12 Mo Trailing Sales $Mil	Price/Cash Flow	Return On Assets%	Total Return% 1 Yr	3 Yr
AutoNation	3,951	0.2	20,106	8.3	3.8	1.9	17.0
Sonic Automotive	697	—	7,008	—	—	—	—
CarMax	663	—	3,461	—	—	—	—

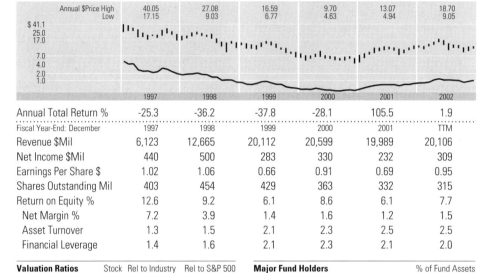

Price Volatility
▮ Monthly Price High/Low   — Relative Strength to S&P 500

	1997	1998	1999	2000	2001	2002
Annual $Price High	40.05	27.08	16.59	9.70	13.07	18.70
Low	17.15	9.03	6.77	4.63	4.94	9.05
Annual Total Return %	-25.3	-36.2	-37.8	-28.1	105.5	1.9

Fiscal Year-End: December	1997	1998	1999	2000	2001	TTM
Revenue $Mil	6,123	12,665	20,112	20,599	19,989	20,106
Net Income $Mil	440	500	283	330	232	309
Earnings Per Share $	1.02	1.06	0.66	0.91	0.69	0.95
Shares Outstanding Mil	403	454	429	363	332	315
Return on Equity %	12.6	9.2	6.1	8.6	6.1	7.7
Net Margin %	7.2	3.9	1.4	1.6	1.2	1.5
Asset Turnover	1.3	1.5	2.1	2.3	2.5	2.5
Financial Leverage	1.4	1.6	2.1	2.3	2.1	2.0

Valuation Ratios	Stock	Rel to Industry	Rel to S&P 500
Price/Earnings	13.2	0.8	0.6
Price/Book	1.0	0.4	0.3
Price/Sales	0.2	0.3	0.1
Price/Cash Flow	8.3	0.8	0.6

Major Fund Holders	% of Fund Assets
CGM Mutual	4.82
CGM Capital Development	4.68
CDC Nvest Targeted Equity A	3.18
Neuberger Berman Regency Inv	2.64

Morningstar's Take By Josh Peters, 11-21-2002 Stock Price as of Analysis: $11.72

We think the nation's number-one car dealer is more profitable and less risky than most investors realize. We'd consider the shares at $11 or less.

A car dealership has pretty good economics. Dealers have protected sales territories and are shielded from abusive automakers by state regulation. Costs are largely variable (unlike the automakers' high fixed costs), making a well-run dealership a relatively low-risk business. AutoNation says it could break even if U.S. industry sales plunged to 10 million--a level not seen since 1970. New car sales may provide 60% of the top line, but they account for only 30% of total gross profits--the more stable (and much more profitable) used car, parts and service, and financing operations contribute the rest.

As a group, publicly traded dealers have done their best to ruin these advantages by making too many acquisitions, paying too much, and ignoring the basics. These "roll-ups" are playing with an inherently flimsy business model.

But AutoNation's current aim--as opposed to its roll-up days--is to maximize the profitability of existing dealerships with a focus on best practices, not revolutionary strategy. CEO Mike Jackson, a successful former dealer himself, has imposed much-needed discipline on the dealerships: tighter cost controls, better inventory management, and a focus on profitability before growth. Gone are the used car superstores, in-house financing operations, and volatile volume-based dealerships.

This newfound discipline is flooding AutoNation's coffers with cash. We forecast free cash flow of $300-$400 million over the next several years, close to 100% of income. Debt is only 14% of capital, but management doesn't plan to go back into roll-up mode. Instead, the firm plans to spend only its free cash by carefully adding dealerships or buying back stock--whichever is cheaper.

But since AutoNation is still proving it can operate its past acquisitions effectively, some skepticism is warranted. Of particular concern is lagging same-store sales performance. In each of the past seven quarters, AutoNation has lagged the industry's year-to-year change--in one case by 10 percentage points. Thus far, we attribute this gap to a focus on per-unit profitability rather than maximum volume, and gross profit per new car has improved. But declining share isn't a trend we'd like to see continue.

In most respects, though, we think AutoNation's management is doing a fine job of maximizing the value of this former roll-up. We think the shares are worth $16.

MORNINGSTAR® Stocks 500

AutoZone AZO

	Rating	Risk	Moat Size	Fair Value	Last Close	Yield %
	★★★	Low	Narrow	$80.00	$70.65	0.0

Industry	Investment Style	Stock Type	Sector
Auto Retail	▥ Mid Growth	↗ Classic Growth	⊟ Consumer Services

Company Profile

AutoZone operates the largest chain of do-it-yourself auto parts stores in North America. It owns approximately 3,000 retail stores in 44 U.S. states and Mexico. The stores typically range from 4,000 to 7,000 square feet and carry 19,000-22,000 items. The company doesn't offer services or installations, but does supply independent repair garages through its commercial sales program. AutoZone acquired Auto Palace, Chief Auto Parts, and 100 Pep Express locations in 1998 and sold heavy-truck part retailer TruckPro in December 2001. Its fiscal year ends in August.

Management

Steve Odland, 43, became chairman and CEO in January 2001; his last position was chief operating officer of Dutch grocer Ahold's U.S. operations. He introduced a more intense focus on creating shareholder value; early results look good.

Strategy

AutoZone hopes to dominate the do-it-yourself segment in auto maintenance the way Home Depot rules home improvement. The company's marketing aims to increase drivers' awareness of their cars' need for maintenance. AutoZone is looking to strengthen its toehold in Mexico and expand its commercial business with independent repair garages.

123 South Front Street   www.autozone.com
Memphis, TN 38103

Competition

Competition	Market Cap $Mil	Debt/ Equity	12 Mo Trailing Sales $Mil	Price/Cash Flow	Return On Assets%	Total Return% 1 Yr	3 Yr
AutoZone	6,881	1.7	5,368	9.9	12.4	-1.6	32.4
Sears Roebuck	7,576	3.3	41,156	—	2.1	-48.6	-6.5
Genuine Parts	5,379	0.3	8,213	24.4	-2.4	-13.2	13.5

Price Volatility

		I Monthly Price High/Low	— Relative Strength to S&P 500

Annual $Price High Low	32.81 19.50	38.00 20.50	37.31 22.56	32.50 21.00	79.90 24.42	89.34 59.20

$ 90.3
49.0
29.0
19.0
7.0
4.0
2.0

	1997	1998	1999	2000	2001	2002
Annual Total Return %	5.5	13.6	-1.9	-11.8	151.9	-1.6

Fiscal Year-end: August	1998	1999	2000	2001	2002	TTM
Revenue $Mil	3,243	4,116	4,483	4,818	5,326	5,368
Net Income $Mil	228	245	268	176	428	449
Earnings Per Share $	1.48	1.63	2.00	1.54	4.00	4.28
Shares Outstanding Mil	152	149	133	113	104	97
Return on Equity %	17.5	18.5	27.0	20.3	62.1	59.6
Net Margin %	7.0	5.9	6.0	3.6	8.0	8.4
Asset Turnover	1.2	1.3	1.3	1.4	1.5	1.5
Financial Leverage	2.1	2.5	3.4	4.0	5.0	4.8

Valuation Ratios	Stock	Rel to Industry	Rel to S&P 500
Price/Earnings	16.5	1.0	0.7
Price/Book	9.1	3.5	2.9
Price/Sales	1.3	2.0	0.6
Price/Cash Flow	9.9	1.0	0.7

Major Fund Holders	% of Fund Assets
Fidelity Select Automotive	6.11
Stratus Growth Inst	4.23
Fremont New Era Growth	4.03
Brandywine Blue	3.76

Morningstar Grades

Growth [B]	1999	2000	2001	2002
Revenue %	26.9	8.9	7.5	10.5
Earnings/Share %	10.1	22.7	-23.0	159.7
Book Value/Share %	4.3	-15.9	2.5	-15.3
Dividends/Share %	NMF	NMF	NMF	NMF

The top line has risen an average of 19% annually since 1991. Growth has slowed in recent years to a more sustainable high-single-digit rate. Booming same-store results bode well for results this year, though.

Profitability [A]	2000	2001	2002	TTM
Return on Assets %	8.0	5.1	12.3	12.4
Oper Cash Flow $Mil	513	459	739	696
- Cap Spending $Mil	250	169	117	131
= Free Cash Flow $Mil	263	290	622	565

Margins have remained fairly stable over the years, but sagging inventory turns reduced returns on invested capital during the 1990s. Returns are rebounding, though, as overall asset efficiency has improved sharply under Odland's watch.

Financial Health [B-]	2000	2001	2002	11-02
Long-term Debt $Mil	1,250	1,225	1,195	1,313
Total Equity $Mil	992	866	689	754
Debt/Equity Ratio	1.3	1.4	1.7	1.7

Borrowings soared between 1998 and 2001 because of huge share buybacks. But those purchases have paid off handsomely without damaging the company's financial flexibility: Operating income covered interest charges nearly 10 times in fiscal 2002.

Morningstar's Take By Josh Peters, 10-23-2002 Stock Price as of Analysis: $87.76

With a good chance of dominating the fragmented retail auto part business, AutoZone is "in the zone." We believe the stock is a buy at $56 or less.

In the past two years, AutoZone has turned a good growth business into a potentially great one. Though we wouldn't describe the company as troubled in the late 1990s, there was room for improvement. Mostly it's been a matter of getting little things right, like optimizing inventory mix and selectively raising prices. The company is using new, innovative marketing, like its Loan-A-Tool program and access to computer diagnostic tools, to drive higher store traffic. AutoZone is also using its existing store base to pick up commercial accounts (independent repair shops and the like), a huge market segment it had until recently ignored.

These seemingly small improvements have made AutoZone a much more profitable enterprise. After declining steadily in the late 1990s and bottoming in 1999 at 12.5%, returns on invested capital improved (by our reckoning) to more than 18% last year.

Our chief fear regarding AutoZone--and the largest risk to our forecast--lies in the sustainability of the company's recent gains. Until last year, AutoZone's highest operating margin as a public company was 1994's 12.6%. In fiscal 2002, margins shot up 3.2

points to 14.5% while net investment in the business, by our estimate, was either flat or down slightly.

We see few competitive threats on the horizon. Not only has the retail auto part industry shown few destructive cyclical tendencies, but it looks ripe for the emergence of a dominant player. AutoZone, though it operates fewer than 3,100 of the industry's 39,000 stores, is by far the most promising candidate. Much of the industry is still in the hands of old mom-and-pop operators, often located on the wrong side of the tracks, while newer locations like AutoZone's capture the industry's growth. General discounters like Wal-Mart pose only a modest threat; among other factors, they're unlikely to stock the 22,000 or so separate parts in their stores that an AutoZone does. And unlike number-two Advance Auto Parts, AutoZone operates under a single store banner nationwide and faces no merger-integration issues.

If AutoZone's gains prove sustainable, we think the firm has a shot at joining retail's elite club of high-profit category-killers like Home Depot and Walgreen. We'd like to see its returns sustained for a while longer before assigning AutoZone a wide economic moat, but even so, we think it belongs on investors' watch lists.

Aventis SA ADR AVE

	Rating	Risk	Moat Size	Fair Value	Last Close	Yield %
	★★★	Low	Narrow	$65.00	$54.19	0.7

Company Profile

Aventis was created in December 1999 when Hoechst and Rhone-Poulenc merged. Since then it has been selling noncore investments in an attempt to become a pure-play pharmaceutical giant. By the end of 2002, 90% of revenue will come from prescription drug and vaccine sales; 37% of 2001 core sales came from the United States. Aventis has treatments for allergies, heart disease, cancer, arthritis, multiple sclerosis, and diabetes, among others. Vaccines and therapeutic proteins, like those used to treat bleeding disorders, also contribute to total revenue.

Management

Igor Landau is chairman of the management board (comparable to a U.S. CEO). He previously was chairman of Rhone-Poulenc and sat on the advisory board of Hoechst, the two companies that combined to form Aventis.

Strategy

Aventis has transformed itself from an agrochemical and drug business into a pure-play pharmaceutical company. It's building a strategy around key brands like allergy drug Allegra and aggressively going after the U.S. market, although sales in countries like France, Germany, and Japan remain important. Cancer, heart disease, allergies, and diabetes are all major therapeutic targets.

1, avenue de L'Europe www.aventispharma-us.com
Strasbourg, 67300

Morningstar Grades

Growth [B]	1998	1999	2000	2001
Revenue %	-3.5	-4.8	77.0	2.9
Earnings/Share %	NMF	NMF	NMF	NMF
Book Value/Share %	-10.9	30.2	-48.7	11.1
Dividends/Share %	5.3	-25.0	11.1	16.0

Historical revenue growth is all over the charts as a result of acquisitions and dispositions. Core revenue growth for the first nine months of 2002 was 7.3%. This is in line with what we expect revenue growth will be over the next few years.

Profitability [C+]	1999	2000	2001	TTM
Return on Assets %	-2.5	-0.3	3.9	3.9
Oper Cash Flow $Mil	626	1,181	2,776	2,776
- Cap Spending $Mil	1,476	2,324	1,544	1,544
= Free Cash Flow $Mil	-850	-1,144	1,232	1,232

Excluding goodwill amortization (still a regular expense for European companies), operating margins are in line with peers. They averaged 25.4% for the first nine months of 2002, continuing their incremental climb since the restructuring began.

Financial Health [C+]	1999	2000	2001	12-01
Long-term Debt $Mil	6,437	7,751	4,117	4,117
Total Equity $Mil	10,019	9,631	10,327	10,327
Debt/Equity Ratio	0.6	0.8	0.4	0.4

Aventis has shed billions in debt through divestitures. At June 30, 2002, debt was around $6 billion, down from $13 billion at the end of 2001. Although debt/equity of 0.5 is higher than the peer average, it's still low relative to the S&P 500.

Industry	Investment Style	Stock Type	Sector
Drugs	▦ Large Growth	◈ Spec. Growth	◩ Healthcare

Competition

	Market Cap $Mil	Debt/ Equity	12 Mo Trailing Sales $Mil	Price/Cash Flow	Return On Assets%	Total Return% 1 Yr	3 Yr
Aventis SA ADR	43,115	0.4	20,457	15.5	3.9	-23.3	-1.3
GlaxoSmithKline PLC ADR	116,607	0.3	27,512	6.2	13.9	-22.8	-9.3
Novartis AG ADR	105,974	0.1	18,933	24.4	10.4	1.8	2.3

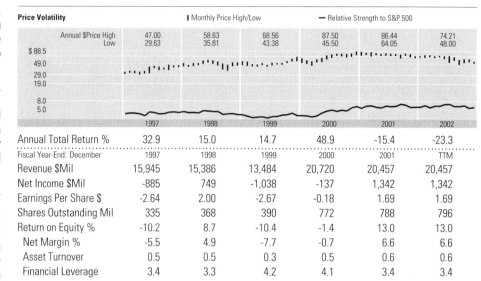

Price Volatility ▌ Monthly Price High/Low — Relative Strength to S&P 500

Annual $Price High / Low	47.00 / 29.63	58.63 / 35.81	68.56 / 43.38	87.50 / 45.50	86.44 / 64.05	74.21 / 48.00

$ 88.5 / 49.0 / 29.0 / 19.0 / 8.0 / 5.0

	1997	1998	1999	2000	2001	2002
Annual Total Return %	32.9	15.0	14.7	48.9	-15.4	-23.3

Fiscal Year-End: December	1997	1998	1999	2000	2001	TTM
Revenue $Mil	15,945	15,386	13,484	20,720	20,457	20,457
Net Income $Mil	-885	749	-1,038	-137	1,342	1,342
Earnings Per Share $	-2.64	2.00	-2.67	-0.18	1.69	1.69
Shares Outstanding Mil	335	368	390	772	788	796
Return on Equity %	-10.2	8.7	-10.4	-1.4	13.0	13.0
Net Margin %	-5.5	4.9	-7.7	-0.7	6.6	6.6
Asset Turnover	0.5	0.5	0.3	0.5	0.6	0.6
Financial Leverage	3.4	3.3	4.2	4.1	3.4	3.4

Valuation Ratios	Stock	Rel to Industry	Rel to S&P 500
Price/Earnings	32.2	1.4	1.4
Price/Book	4.2	0.6	1.3
Price/Sales	2.1	0.5	1.0
Price/Cash Flow	15.5	0.7	1.2

Major Fund Holders	% of Fund Assets
Fidelity Select Pharmaceuticals	4.95
Nuveen European Value A	4.39
Saratoga International Equity I	3.98
Sextant International	3.64

Morningstar's Take By Todd N. Lebor, 12-24-2002 Stock Price as of Analysis: $52.92

Aventis is new and improved. It has shed noncore assets and boasts margins comparable with those of its global pharmaceutical peers. But that doesn't make Aventis anything more than average. We'd want a 30% discount to our fair value estimate before jumping in.

After ridding itself of its crop science, animal nutrition, therapeutic protein, and industrial gas units, Aventis has less debt and margins in line with its peers'. It no longer looks like a European conglomerate, but rather a streamlined, pure-play drug company. Core revenue growth is solid, and few products face near-term patent expiration. That said, Aventis isn't all that different from its peers. It is better suited to compete since its transformation, but we don't see any advantages that could allow it to break away from the pack.

Aventis does offer good sector diversification, something missing from giants like Pfizer and Merck. Aventis may derive 90% of its revenue from pharmaceuticals, but no more than 20% of its revenue comes from any one therapeutic area. The company pulls between 10% and 20% of its sales from four areas: cardiovascular, oncology, respiratory, and diabetes/metabolism. Anti-infectives aren't far behind the 10% mark, thanks to newcomer Ketek.

Aventis' highest-grossing drug--allergy treatment Allegra--provides around 14% of total revenue; its top five drugs supply just 38% of sales. Relative to Pfizer, which derives 20% of total revenue from one drug (Lipitor) and more than 50% of sales from its top five drugs, Aventis is shielded from large drops in sales of individual drugs, like the one we forecast for Allegra.

Aventis comes with the standard big pharma competitive advantages like patent protection, a global distribution and sales network, established brands, and a highly skilled labor force. But a weak late-stage pipeline offsets some of these advantages, so management's ambitious growth objectives will have to be achieved partially through acquisitions. Several recently launched products, like respiratory tract infection medicine Ketek and synthetic insulin Lantus, are fueling a revenue growth spurt now, but one or two products with similar potential are needed each year to help a company of Aventis' size to grow.

Aventis is well positioned within its industry but has yet to really prove itself. We wouldn't invest unless it traded at a 30% discount to our fair value estimate.

MORNINGSTAR® Stocks 500

Avon Products AVP

	Rating	Risk	Moat Size	Fair Value	Last Close	Yield %
	★★★	Med.	Wide	$50.00	$53.87	1.5

Industry	Investment Style	Stock Type	Sector
Household & Personal Products	Large Core	Slow Growth	Consumer Goods

Company Profile

Avon is the world's largest direct seller of cosmetics; its famed "Avon ladies" now number 3.5 million. Avon also sells its products over the Internet and in retail stores, although representatives generate most of the revenue by conducting business in homes and workplaces. About 75% of sales come from the United States and Europe. Avon produces most of its own products.

Management

CEO Andrea Jung was credited with reinvigorating Avon's product line three years ago as head of global marketing. Her soft touch will be valuable in soothing the concerns of Avon's sales representatives about the new distribution strategy.

Strategy

Avon seeks to widen its operating margin by 2.5 percentage points by 2004, partly by redrawing its global regions to market efficiently. To increase revenue, it is expanding distribution into retail outlets and onto the Internet. It's also hiking research and development spending by more than $100 million over the next three years to ensure its cosmetics advancements do not lag those of rivals.

1345 Avenue of the Americas   www.avon.com
New York, NY 10105-0196

Competition

Competition	Market Cap $Mil	Debt/ Equity	12 Mo Trailing Sales $Mil	Price/Cash Flow	Return On Assets%	Total Return% 1 Yr	3 Yr
Avon Products	12,672	NMF	6,123	21.5	13.7	17.7	22.4
Procter & Gamble	111,662	0.9	41,268	13.3	11.0	11.3	-4.5
Unilever NV ADR	35,272	—	46,553	—	—	—	—

Price Volatility

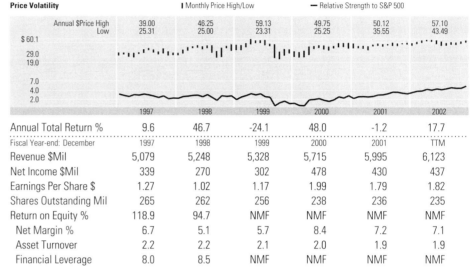

Monthly Price High/Low					Relative Strength to S&P 500	
Annual $Price High Low	39.00 25.31	46.25 25.00	59.13 23.31	49.75 25.25	50.12 35.55	57.10 43.49

	1997	1998	1999	2000	2001	2002
Annual Total Return %	9.6	46.7	-24.1	48.0	-1.2	17.7

Fiscal Year-end: December	1997	1998	1999	2000	2001	TTM
Revenue $Mil	5,079	5,248	5,328	5,715	5,995	6,123
Net Income $Mil	339	270	302	478	430	437
Earnings Per Share $	1.27	1.02	1.17	1.99	1.79	1.82
Shares Outstanding Mil	265	262	256	238	236	235
Return on Equity %	118.9	94.7	NMF	NMF	NMF	NMF
Net Margin %	6.7	5.1	5.7	8.4	7.2	7.1
Asset Turnover	2.2	2.2	2.1	2.0	1.9	1.9
Financial Leverage	8.0	8.5	NMF	NMF	NMF	NMF

Valuation Ratios

Valuation Ratios	Stock	Rel to Industry	Rel to S&P 500
Price/Earnings	29.6	1.2	1.3
Price/Book	—	—	—
Price/Sales	2.1	0.8	1.0
Price/Cash Flow	21.5	1.6	1.6

Major Fund Holders

Major Fund Holders	% of Fund Assets
William Blair Large Cap Growth I	3.20
Bremer Growth Stock	3.08
Stratus Growth Inst	3.03
Fairport Growth & Income	2.89

Morningstar Grades

Growth [B]	1998	1999	2000	2001
Revenue %	3.3	1.5	7.3	4.9
Earnings/Share %	-19.7	14.7	70.1	-10.1
Book Value/Share %	0.8	NMF	NMF	NMF
Dividends/Share %	7.9	5.9	2.8	2.7

Avon continues to exceed its midsingle-digit sales growth target, excluding the effects from currency translation. We expect the firm to continue this pace with the occasional setback from troubled economies like those in Latin America.

Profitability [A+]	1999	2000	2001	TTM
Return on Assets %	12.0	16.9	13.5	13.7
Oper Cash Flow $Mil	449	324	755	590
- Cap Spending $Mil	203	194	155	124
= Free Cash Flow $Mil	245	130	600	466

We expect Avon's net profit margins to increase to 10% in 2006. That would be up from past years' upper-single-digit growth, thanks to plans for cutting product costs and general corporate overhead.

Financial Health [B+]	1999	2000	2001	09-02
Long-term Debt $Mil	701	1,108	1,236	1,300
Total Equity $Mil	-406	-216	-75	-63
Debt/Equity Ratio	ELB	ELB	ELB	NMF

Earnings before interest and taxes are nearly 12 times interest expense, leaving us confident that the dividend will not be in jeopardy.

Morningstar's Take By Carl Sibilski, 12-15-2002 Stock Price as of Analysis: $53.82

We think steady sales growth and cost-cutting opportunities will help Avon Products continue its strong earnings growth. We're concerned, though, about the long-term viability of the company's sales model, and would buy the shares only at a 40% discount to our fair value estimate.

International success is boosting Avon's sales growth. European and Asian sales have been increasing 25% annually in local currencies, and we think there's more in store. Like other multinational companies, Avon's sales measured in U.S. dollars have been hurt in recent years by a strengthening dollar. With signs that the dollar's beginning to level off against other currencies, we think Avon will be able to increase sales in dollars at a 7% clip annually.

Avon's direct selling distribution system is responsible for maintaining customer relationships and recruiting new product users and sales representatives. The number of representatives has grown to 3.5 million worldwide. Moreover, this sales system has built-in career advancement pathways. An experienced representative can become a leadership representative, for example, with more responsibilities for recruiting and training others. Many traditional representatives are women who would like to earn money part-time.

While this system has had success historically, evolving societal norms may render the direct-sales system obsolete. Many busy women would prefer to visit a department store cosmetics counter and try products when it's convenient for them, rather than making an appointment with an Avon representative. Avon has responded by building an Internet site to peddle its products. The site is helpful for placing orders and providing product information, but hasn't been a huge success commercially.

Managing its myriad products has also been a big challenge for Avon. Representatives have a difficult time satisfying customers when a favorite product isn't available in a current sales campaign. Additionally, the company ties up resources by holding enough inventory for 100 days of sales. We think this problem will be alleviated by Avon's recent product line initiatives, which involve fewer and simplified sales brochures.

Because so many current customers depend daily on Avon products, we think this stock could be a good buy, but only if it sold off substantially.

AVX AVX

	Rating	Risk	Moat Size	Fair Value	Last Close	Yield %
	★★★★★	Med.	Narrow	$19.00	$9.80	1.5

Company Profile

AVX, a 75%-owned subsidiary of Kyocera, manufactures passive electronic components and related products. A substantial portion of the company's passive electronic component sales are of ceramic and tantalum capacitors, both in the leaded and surface-mount versions. Capacitors are used in nearly all electronic products to store, filter, and regulate electric energy. The company also makes and sells electronic connectors, and distributes passive components and connectors manufactured by Kyocera.

Management

Former COO John Gilbertson succeeded Benedict Rosen as CEO in July 2001; Rosen remains chairman. Kyocera Corporation of Japan owns 70% of AVX shares.

Strategy

AVX tries to balance its high-volume commodity capacitor production with higher-margin, custom-designed products. The firm has also pursued vertical integration to help with costs; it is the only U.S. manufacturer that makes its own ceramic raw materials.

801 17th Avenue South
Myrtle Beach, SC 29577

www.avxcorp.com

Industry	Investment Style	Stock Type	Sector
Components	■ Mid Core	→ Slow Growth	▣ Hardware

Competition	Market Cap $Mil	Debt/ Equity	12 Mo Trailing Sales $Mil	Price/Cash Flow	Return On Assets%	Total Return% 1 Yr	3 Yr
AVX	1,706	—	1,170	11.8	-0.4	-58.0	-24.2
Vishay Intertechnology	1,786	0.2	1,745	5.6	-0.6	-42.7	-16.7
Kemet	753	0.1	472	20.5	-4.4	-50.8	-25.2

Price Volatility | Monthly Price High/Low — Relative Strength to S&P 500

	1997	1998	1999	2000	2001	2002
Annual $Price High	19.81	11.69	25.22	50.00	24.40	25.40
Low	8.84	6.75	6.28	15.13	14.51	7.31
Annual Total Return %	-13.5	-6.8	198.3	-34.1	45.1	-58.0

Fiscal Year-End: March	1998	1999	2000	2001	2002	TTM
Revenue $Mil	1,268	1,245	1,630	2,608	1,250	1,170
Net Income $Mil	135	42	157	568	-7	-6
Earnings Per Share $	0.76	0.24	0.90	3.22	-0.04	-0.04
Shares Outstanding Mil	177	173	174	175	181	174
Return on Equity %	15.8	5.0	16.0	37.7	-0.5	-0.4
Net Margin %	10.6	3.3	9.6	21.8	-0.6	-0.5
Asset Turnover	1.2	1.2	1.2	1.4	0.7	0.7
Financial Leverage	1.2	1.3	1.3	1.3	1.1	1.1

Valuation Ratios	Stock	Rel to Industry	Rel to S&P 500
Price/Earnings	NMF	—	—
Price/Book	1.1	0.7	0.4
Price/Sales	1.5	0.8	0.7
Price/Cash Flow	11.8	1.4	0.9

Major Fund Holders	% of Fund Assets
Third Avenue Value	3.65
SunAmerica Focused Multi-Cap Value A	2.91
SunAmerica Focused 2000 Value A	2.20
Heartland Select Value	1.80

Morningstar Grades

Growth [D]	1999	2000	2001	2002
Revenue %	-1.8	30.9	60.0	-52.1
Earnings/Share %	-68.4	275.0	257.8	NMF
Book Value/Share %	0.0	17.3	51.6	-4.4
Dividends/Share %	8.3	1.9	5.7	7.1

Sales growth over the long term has been strong, driven by the growth of the electronics business, but very cyclical. AVX is now suffering one of the worst downturns in the capacitor industry's history.

Profitability [A]	2000	2001	2002	TTM
Return on Assets %	12.0	30.1	-0.4	-0.4
Oper Cash Flow $Mil	178	585	302	145
- Cap Spending $Mil	172	227	75	41
= Free Cash Flow $Mil	6	357	227	104

Margins are in the dumps because of overcapacity and weak demand. We think AVX will earn relatively attractive profits averaged over a full cycle. From 1995 to 2001, average operating margins were well above 13%.

Financial Health [A+]	2000	2001	2002	09-02
Long-term Debt $Mil	18	14	—	—
Total Equity $Mil	982	1,505	1,476	1,506
Debt/Equity Ratio	0.0	0.0	—	—

AVX is in good financial health, with about $715 million in cash and little long-term debt. The firm is using its balance sheet strength to repurchase some of its stock.

Morningstar's Take By Dan Schick, 11-12-2002 Stock Price as of Analysis: $9.52

We think that the capacitor industry, currently reaching for the bottom in a dreadful cycle, is attractive for the long term, and that leading player AVX is worth owning. In our opinion, investors should use the current slump to get in at a wide discount to our fair value estimate.

Like rivals Kemet and Vishay, AVX was bruised by the one of the worst downturns ever in the capacitor industry. AVX's sales in fiscal 2002, which ended in March, plummeted 52% from 2001 and the company recorded its first operating loss since the mid-1980s.

The poor near-term outlook is nothing new. The capacitor industry is notoriously cyclical, and AVX has weathered the downturns before and should again. The firm is in good financial health, with more than $715 million in cash and investments, less than $20 million in debt, and only $210 million in total balance sheet liabilities at the end of September. Despite the operating losses, AVX continues to generate free cash flow. Capital spending has fallen sharply as depressed component demand gives little reason to expand capacity.

We believe the relentless progress of electronics will drive the growth of the capacitor industry. Virtually all electronic devices contain capacitors, so capacitor growth dovetails with that of the electronics market. Turbocharging that growth is the shrinking size of electronic devices--smaller and more advanced devices actually use more capacitors. For example, a new CDMA phone requires about 480 components in AVX's catalog, compared with 330 in a traditional phone.

AVX spends relatively heavily on research and development, which differentiates it from more commodity-driven competitors and ensures participation in industrywide growth. AVX is reaping the rewards of its technical edge in advanced passive component sales. These custom-designed products earn higher margins than typical capacitors, while helping the company forge better relationships with its customers. AVX also differentiates itself by distributing Kyocera's line of products (the Japanese firm owns 70% of AVX). This allows AVX to offer one-stop shopping to its customers. Finally, the company's connector division, while contributing only about 9% of revenue, is more profitable than the capacitor division and less capital-intensive.

With the capacitor industry in the doldrums, there is the risk of a protracted downturn in AVX's results. However, we think a 40% margin of safety compensates for this risk.

M○RNINGSTAR® Stocks 500

Baker Hughes BHI

	Rating	Risk	Moat Size	Fair Value	Last Close	Yield %
	★	Med.	Narrow	$18.00	$32.19	1.4

Company Profile

Houston-based Baker Hughes is one of the premier providers to the oil patch, selling products and services related to finding, drilling, and producing oil and gas. Baker Hughes specializes in downhole tool technologies and is the leading provider of drill bits and related systems. Roughly two thirds of Hughes' revenue is generated outside the United States.

Management

Michael Wiley heads Baker Hughes. He was president of Atlantic Richfield before it was acquired by BP in early 2000. The company is divided and managed along seven separate business lines.

Strategy

Baker Hughes' goal is to create value for oil and gas producers by researching and providing practical technology that will make finding and producing oil cheaper. The company aims to keep a competitive edge by focusing on niche markets where it has a technological lead that cannot be easily replicated.

3900 Essex Lane
Houston, TX 77027-5177
www.bakerhughes.com

Morningstar Grades

Growth [D+]	1998	1999	2000	2001
Revenue %	47.5	-37.4	6.0	2.8
Earnings/Share %	NMF	NMF	210.0	319.4
Book Value/Share %	-7.3	-8.6	0.1	7.0
Dividends/Share %	26.1	-20.7	0.0	0.0

Like the rest of those servicing the oil patch, Baker Hughes sees its demand fluctuate wildly with commodity prices. After dropping 37% in 1999, revenue has been relatively flat. Profits have grown nicely, however.

Profitability [C]	1999	2000	2001	TTM
Return on Assets %	0.5	1.6	6.6	4.5
Oper Cash Flow $Mil	543	564	721	769
- Cap Spending $Mil	640	599	319	326
= Free Cash Flow $Mil	-97	-36	402	443

After a tumultuous 1998 that saw Baker Hughes in the red, profit margins have grown steadily and impressively. Though vastly improved, last year's return on invested capital was only 8.7%, slightly below Hughes' cost of capital.

Financial Health [B]	1999	2000	2001	09-02
Long-term Debt $Mil	2,706	2,050	1,682	1,446
Total Equity $Mil	3,071	3,047	3,328	3,450
Debt/Equity Ratio	0.9	0.7	0.5	0.4

Baker Hughes has focused on reducing debt, and it has been quite successful at this through paring capital expenditures and selling noncore businesses. Debt/equity has gone from 0.9 at year-end 1999 to 0.5 currently.

Industry	Investment Style	Stock Type	Sector
Oil & Gas Services	▦ Large Growth	▦ Hard Assets	◉ Energy

Competition	Market Cap $Mil	Debt/ Equity	12 Mo Trailing Sales $Mil	Price/Cash Flow	Return On Assets%	Total Return% 1 Yr	3 Yr
Baker Hughes	10,806	0.4	5,272	14.0	4.5	-10.4	18.3
Schlumberger	24,304	0.8	13,942	12.1	3.2	-22.2	-6.9
Halliburton	8,158	0.3	12,396	5.5	-2.1	47.2	-19.9

Price Volatility		▮ Monthly Price High/Low		— Relative Strength to S&P 500		
Annual $Price High Low	49.63 32.63	44.13 15.00	36.25 15.00	43.38 19.63	45.25 25.76	39.95 22.60
	1997	1998	1999	2000	2001	2002

Annual Total Return %	27.9	-59.0	21.7	100.2	-11.1	-10.4
Fiscal Year-end: December	1997	1998	1999	2000	2001	TTM
Revenue $Mil	5,344	7,883	4,937	5,234	5,382	5,272
Net Income $Mil	25	-182	33	102	438	296
Earnings Per Share $	0.08	-0.58	0.10	0.31	1.30	0.87
Shares Outstanding Mil	318	319	333	320	334	336
Return on Equity %	0.7	-5.7	1.1	3.4	13.2	8.6
Net Margin %	0.5	-2.3	0.7	2.0	8.1	5.6
Asset Turnover	0.8	1.0	0.7	0.8	0.8	0.8
Financial Leverage	2.0	2.5	2.3	2.1	2.0	1.9

Valuation Ratios	Stock	Rel to Industry	Rel to S&P 500
Price/Earnings	37.0	1.1	1.6
Price/Book	3.1	1.2	1.0
Price/Sales	2.1	1.0	1.0
Price/Cash Flow	14.0	1.2	1.1

Major Fund Holders	% of Fund Assets
Rydex Energy Services Inv	9.25
Fidelity Select Energy Service	4.22
INVESCO Energy Inv	3.88
AXP Global Growth A	3.79

Morningstar's Take By Paul Larson, 10-15-2002 Stock Price as of Analysis: $27.90

We're content to fish for investment ideas elsewhere until Baker Hughes comes down significantly in price.

Baker Hughes is one of the oil patch's leading suppliers of products and services, providing such critical components as advanced drill bits, drilling fluids, submersible pumps, and well-measurement devices. Specializing in so-called "downhole" equipment, Baker Hughes enjoys a dominant position in both share and technology in several niche markets for advanced drilling systems.

In the short run, demand for drilling services and equipment tends to be highly volatile and dependent on commodity oil and gas prices. When oil prices are high--like they were in 2000--Baker Hughes' phones are ringing off the hook with oil producers scrambling to drill more wells so they can get more oil to market while profits are high. But when oil prices tank to near $10 a barrel--like they did in 1998--demand can quickly evaporate and come to a grinding halt. Budgets for new drilling are often the first to be cut when oil companies are operating with lean cash flow.

Luckily for Baker Hughes, long-run demand for advanced oil services should only increase as oil companies have to dig in more-difficult places and at deeper depths to find and produce from fresh oil

fields. While there will inevitably be some bumps along the road when oil prices are low, we expect modest long-term growth for the overall oil services field, and Baker Hughes should be able to maintain its share, given its positioning.

Things have gotten better at Baker Hughes after a traumatic 1998. Highlighting just how cyclical oil services can be, the company saw its operating margin fall from 11.8% in 1997 to 3.7% in 1999. Since then, Baker Hughes has gotten rid of unprofitable lines of business while focusing on improving its balance sheet. Over the past four years, Baker Hughes has retired more than a third of its debt--$1 billion worth--while cutting costs to get profitability back to a respectable level. Excluding goodwill, returns on invested capital should be close to 10% for 2002.

Though we think Baker Hughes has a relatively bright future, the market has bid the shares up to nosebleed levels in anticipation of the company's continued turnaround. Valuation remains our main gripe with the stock. We wouldn't mind owning Baker Hughes at the right price, but it would take quite a drop for the shares to trade enough below our $18 fair value estimate to interest us.

Ballard Power Systems BLDP

	Rating	Risk	Moat Size	Fair Value	Last Close	Yield %
	UR	High	None	UR	$11.07	0.0

Company Profile

Ballard Power Systems develops and commercializes fuel cells. A fuel cell is an environmentally clean power generator that converts hydrogen fuel directly, without combustion, into electricity with water and heat as the only byproducts. The company's clients are located throughout Canada, the United States, Europe, and Japan. Principal customers include Dow Chemical, General Motors, Mazda, and Nissan. The Ballard Advanced Materials subsidiary conducts research on proton-exchange membranes for fuel cells, batteries, and other electrochemical devices.

Management

Firoz Rasul has been chief executive since 1988 and chairman since 1999. His degree in industrial engineering and experience in marketing and sales should help Ballard bring new products to market.

Strategy

Although Ballard's fuel cells have only a handful of commercial applications thus far, the company has a number of strategic alliances to develop mass-market products. By partnering with carmakers to develop electric cars, Ballard aims to lock in demand for its fuel cells and boost sales.

9000 Glenlyon Parkway   www.ballard.com
Burnaby, BC V5J 5J9

Industry	Investment Style	Stock Type	Sector
Electric Equipment	—	⚡ Cyclical	⚙ Industrial Mats

Competition	Market Cap $Mil	Debt/ Equity	12 Mo Trailing Sales $Mil	Price/Cash Flow	Return On Assets%	Total Return% 1 Yr	3 Yr
Ballard Power Systems	1,166	0.0	106	—	-17.9	-62.6	-28.9
Toyota Motor ADR	97,652	—	118,527	—	—	—	—
General Motors	20,658	9.7	184,057	1.1	0.3	-20.8	-16.9

Price Volatility

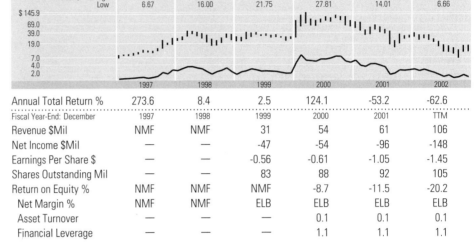

Price Volatility	I Monthly Price High/Low			— Relative Strength to S&P 500		
Annual $Price High Low	27.50 6.67	44.17 16.00	40.50 21.75	144.94 27.81	78.94 14.01	38.50 6.66

$ 145.9 / 69.0 / 39.0 / 19.0 / 7.0 / 4.0 / 2.0

1997   1998   1999   2000   2001   2002

Annual Total Return %	273.6	8.4	2.5	124.1	-53.2	-62.6
Fiscal Year-End: December	1997	1998	1999	2000	2001	TTM
Revenue $Mil	NMF	NMF	31	54	61	106
Net Income $Mil	—	—	-47	-54	-96	-148
Earnings Per Share $	—	—	-0.56	-0.61	-1.05	-1.45
Shares Outstanding Mil	—	—	83	88	92	105
Return on Equity %	NMF	NMF	NMF	-8.7	-11.5	-20.2
Net Margin %	NMF	NMF	ELB	ELB	ELB	ELB
Asset Turnover	—	—	—	0.1	0.1	0.1
Financial Leverage	—	—	—	1.1	1.1	1.1

Valuation Ratios	Stock	Rel to Industry	Rel to S&P 500
Price/Earnings	NMF	—	—
Price/Book	1.6	0.4	0.5
Price/Sales	11.0	5.9	5.5
Price/Cash Flow	—	—	—

Major Fund Holders	% of Fund Assets
Winslow Green Growth	1.59
Green Century Balanced	1.34
Fidelity Select Environmental	1.21
Portfolio 21	1.04

Morningstar Grades

Growth [A]	1998	1999	2000	2001
Revenue %	—	NMF	74.9	13.1
Earnings/Share %	—	NMF	NMF	NMF
Book Value/Share %	—	NMF	NMF	31.0
Dividends/Share %	NMF	NMF	NMF	NMF

Revenue has been growing quickly--nearly tripling through the first three quarters of 2002. Several acquisitions made during 2001 account for the majority of the sales increase; sales of Ballard fuel cell systems are still severely limited.

Profitability [NA]	1999	2000	2001	TTM
Return on Assets %	NMF	-8.1	-10.0	-17.9
Oper Cash Flow $Mil	-41	-37	-55	-129
- Cap Spending $Mil	16	20	18	23
= Free Cash Flow $Mil	-57	-58	-73	-153

Ballard expects to burn through $122-$142 million in cash during 2002. Gross profits from product sales have turned negative this year, reflecting steep costs associated with limited-quantity production of its systems.

Financial Health [D]	1999	2000	2001	09-02
Long-term Debt $Mil	—	4	8	9
Total Equity $Mil	—	616	837	733
Debt/Equity Ratio	—	0.0	0.0	0.0

After issuing $100 million in stock in December 2002, Ballard had about $375 million in cash and investments and relatively modest liabilities. But with these resources being depleted by operating losses, additional funding may be necessary.

Morningstar's Take   By Josh Peters, 12-20-2002   Stock Price as of Analysis: $11.85

With technologies that are far from commercial viability and with no earnings in sight, Ballard Power Systems should be avoided, in our opinion.

Ballard believes its fuel cell technology is the answer to demands for more and cheaper energy with lower emissions. Fuel cells, which generate electricity when hydrogen and oxygen molecules react, are clean (the only exhaust is water vapor), quiet, and efficient. But thus far, they're not powerful or even remotely affordable--Ballard's first commercially available fuel cell, offered in partnership with Coleman Powermate, can be had for $5,995 and provides a single kilowatt of power. Coleman's closest gasoline-powered match goes for around $200.

It will take a lot of additional research to make fuel cells commercially viable, but Ballard can at least claim a lead over most of its competitors--it's been developing fuel cell technologies since 1983 and has more than 1,200 patents to its credit. Ballard can also lean on a pair of strong partners in Ford and DaimlerChrysler.

But Ballard is hardly the only alternative energy game in town. A number of companies, including several well-heeled automakers, are working on fuel cell technologies that could render Ballard's technology outdated. And it isn't as if fuel cells are guaranteed to solve the world's energy problems; like a number of electric vehicle projects before it, this technology might never pan out.

In the meantime, the company is burning through large sums of cash to fund its research--more than $70 million in 2001 and well over $100 million in 2002. In late 2002, Ballard announced a plan meant to reduce 2003's cash outflow to $80 million and stretch cash reserves through 2007. By then the company believes it can turn an operating profit, but the formidable challenges it faces don't give us much confidence in this goal.

With so much uncertainty surrounding Ballard's ability to build a self-supporting, profitable business before its capital-raising ability runs out, we aren't giving the stock a fair value estimate or star rating. At the very least, we believe getting Ballard to the point of profitability will require substantially more capital funding, which would dilute current shareholders' interest in whatever technological progress the company achieves.

MORNINGSTAR® Stocks 500

Bank of America BAC

	Rating	Risk	Moat Size	Fair Value	Last Close	Yield %
	★★	Med.	Narrow	$64.00	$69.57	3.5

Company Profile

Bank of America is a financial services holding company that provides commercial, retail, and foreign banking services; originates home mortgage loans; and operates full-service and discount securities businesses. It also issues credit cards and provides computer banking services. The company offers securities underwriting and other investment banking services to corporations. Bank of America operates approximately 4,500 banking offices and supermarket branches throughout the United States.

Management

Chairman and CEO Ken Lewis has committed to focusing on profits rather than size. He earned his current job in 2001, succeeding his mentor, Hugh McColl, who had headed NationsBank and merged it with Bank of America.

Strategy

Bank of America is the nation's only true coast-to-coast retail bank network. Now its priority is to create a world-class investment bank. This is a very expensive goal, which it seeks to accomplish through small acquisitions and internal growth. The bank is also shoring up its balance sheet by selling off its less profitable loans in order to focus on its most profitable lending customers.

Bank of America Corporate Center   www.bankofamerica.com
Charlotte, NC 28255

Morningstar Grades

Growth [D]	1998	1999	2000	2001
Revenue %	4.9	-0.8	12.4	-8.8
Earnings/Share %	-19.7	54.5	0.9	-7.5
Book Value/Share %	5.0	-2.5	13.4	4.3
Dividends/Share %	16.1	16.4	11.4	10.7

Revenue has been flat for the past two years. Bank of America is one of the largest institutions in a very mature industry. Even factoring in higher interest rates--which boost revenue--we're assuming only midsingle-digit growth.

Profitability [C+]	1999	2000	2001	TTM
Return on Assets %	1.2	1.2	1.1	1.3
Oper Cash Flow $Mil	9,823	3,734	-12,826	—
- Cap Spending $Mil	465	642	835	—
= Free Cash Flow $Mil	—	—	—	—

Bank of America promises to focus on profits rather than balance sheet size. As such, the firm boosted its return on assets to 1.36% in the first nine months of 2002, compared with 0.98% a year earlier. We believe the stronger returns will continue.

Financial Health [B]	1999	2000	2001	09-02
Long-term Debt $Mil	—	—	—	—
Total Equity $Mil	44,355	47,556	48,455	48,179
Debt/Equity Ratio	—	—	—	—

Bank of America has wisely repositioned its balance sheet. After shedding some weak-performing assets, the firm now has stronger core capital levels and is using more deposits to fund loans. In addition, it seems to have adequate loan-loss reserves.

	Industry	Investment Style	Stock Type	Sector
	International Banks	Large Value	High Yield	Financial Services

Competition	Market Cap $Mil	Debt/ Equity	12 Mo Trailing Sales $Mil	Price/Cash Flow	Return On Assets%	Total Return% 1 Yr	Total Return% 3 Yr
Bank of America	104,505	—	46,628	—	1.3	14.5	19.8
Citigroup	177,948	—	106,096	—	1.6	-24.2	1.1
Wells Fargo	79,608	—	28,119	—	1.5	10.3	10.4

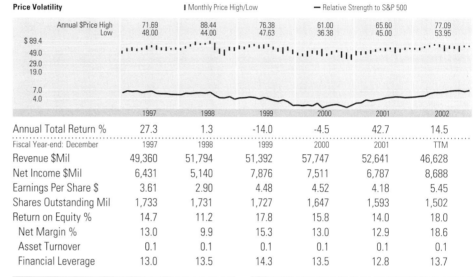

Price Volatility — Monthly Price High/Low — Relative Strength to S&P 500

Annual $Price High / Low	71.69 / 48.00	88.44 / 44.00	76.38 / 47.63	61.00 / 36.38	65.60 / 45.00	77.09 / 53.95

	1997	1998	1999	2000	2001	2002
Annual Total Return %	27.3	1.3	-14.0	-4.5	42.7	14.5

Fiscal Year-end: December	1997	1998	1999	2000	2001	TTM
Revenue $Mil	49,360	51,794	51,392	57,747	52,641	46,628
Net Income $Mil	6,431	5,140	7,876	7,511	6,787	8,688
Earnings Per Share $	3.61	2.90	4.48	4.52	4.18	5.45
Shares Outstanding Mil	1,733	1,731	1,727	1,647	1,593	1,502
Return on Equity %	14.7	11.2	17.8	15.8	14.0	18.0
Net Margin %	13.0	9.9	15.3	13.0	12.9	18.6
Asset Turnover	0.1	0.1	0.1	0.1	0.1	0.1
Financial Leverage	13.0	13.5	14.3	13.5	12.8	13.7

Valuation Ratios	Stock	Rel to Industry	Rel to S&P 500
Price/Earnings	12.8	1.0	0.5
Price/Book	2.2	1.0	0.7
Price/Sales	2.2	1.3	1.1
Price/Cash Flow	—	—	—

Major Fund Holders	% of Fund Assets
Rydex Banking Inv	14.94
Prudential Financial Services A	7.92
ICAP Select Equity	7.81
Profunds Ultra Banking Inv	7.44

Morningstar's Take By Craig Woker, 10-17-2002 Stock Price as of Analysis: $68.58

Bank of America is the largest pure-play bank in the nation, with a coast-to-coast branch network that has 40% more locations than its nearest rival and a domestic deposit base 80% bigger than the number-two institution. But size and a widely known brand are irrelevant if they don't translate into a healthy return for shareholders, and on this count, we believe Bank of America will fall short.

Our fair value estimate is $64 per share, and we would not start to find this stock an attractive buying opportunity unless it slipped to the mid-$40s. The cash flow model we use to derive this value makes Bank of America's past problem glaringly apparent: The firm has spent too much time getting big rather than boosting profits. Since 1997, its balance sheet has expanded 27% per year on average through a series of acquisitions. During that period, Bank of America often earned a return on invested capital below its cost of capital.

Bank of America contends that it plans to focus on boosting profits and, it hopes, shareholder value. The firm has been expanding its investment banking and brokerage operations, picking up Wall Street talent in a weak market. Plus, Bank of America's core capital ratio--a measure of its financial health--is near the top of the industry, which signals that it can either lend more, should the economy improve, or increase share buybacks, if it doesn't. However, we've accounted for some of this promised improvement in our model already, and in our opinion, the bank must do even more to offer investors a healthy return.

The linchpin for Bank of America will be how much it can widen its interest spread. Unlike most large competitors, this bank has significantly more deposits than loans, with a loan/deposit ratio in the mid-80s; most peers hover around 100%. We've modeled for Bank of America to steadily retool its balance sheet more in line with better-performing competitors. We've also assumed a corresponding increase of about 10-15 basis points per year in the interest rate spread it earns from the subpar 3.6% it chalked up in 2001 and the 3.78% it delivered through the first nine months of 2002.

Should Bank of America make faster progress or generate more net interest income than we've assumed, our fair value estimate will prove conservative. However, given the company's record of falling short of its potential, this isn't a bet we're willing to make.

Bank of New York BK

	Rating	Risk	Moat Size	Fair Value	Last Close	Yield %
	★★★★	Med.	Wide	$29.00	$23.96	3.2

Company Profile

Bank of New York is a bank holding company with operations worldwide. Its bank subsidiaries provide retail banking services in New York, New Jersey, and Connecticut; the banks also operate 30 banking offices abroad. Its Bank of New York subsidiary is the largest securities processing provider in the U.S. The company also originates real-estate, business, consumer, and foreign loans; issues credit cards; and provides trust services. Bank of New York provides investment banking and financial advisory services to many U.S. companies.

Management

Thomas Renyi, chairman and CEO, is leading the company's new business strategy. A former credit officer, Renyi has been pushing Bank of New York to get rid of questionable and unprofitable loans and focus on fee-generating activities.

Strategy

Bank of New York is limiting some traditional banking activities that generate interest income to focus more heavily on services that generate fee income. The company has been building up its top sources of fees--securities processing and trust management--through acquisitions in recent years.

One Wall Street   www.bankofny.com
New York, NY 10286

Morningstar Grades

Growth [D]	1998	1999	2000	2001
Revenue %	1.7	20.2	7.5	-4.4
Earnings/Share %	12.5	48.4	-15.4	-5.7
Book Value/Share %	12.6	-4.0	23.1	3.0
Dividends/Share %	10.2	7.4	13.8	9.1

We expect bad loans and portfolio losses to erase any gains in the securities business for 2002. Longer term, growth will be driven by the core business of securities processing.

Profitability [B+]	1999	2000	2001	TTM
Return on Assets %	2.3	1.9	1.7	1.4
Oper Cash Flow $Mil	-982	-2,166	5,966	—
- Cap Spending $Mil	97	106	165	—
= Free Cash Flow $Mil	—	—	—	—

The company's returns on assets and equity rank among the best in the banking industry, thanks to its focus on high-margin businesses. But operating margins have suffered amid the stock market downturn.

Financial Health [B+]	1999	2000	2001	09-02
Long-term Debt $Mil	—	—	—	—
Total Equity $Mil	5,142	6,151	6,317	6,633
Debt/Equity Ratio	—	—	—	—

An equity/assets ratio of 12% is safely within banking industry norms. The company's drive to pare its riskier loans should result in higher credit grades and a less risky portfolio in the long term.

Industry	Investment Style	Stock Type	Sector
Money Management	▦ Large Value	▨ High Yield	$ Financial Services

Competition	Market Cap $Mil	Debt/ Equity	12 Mo Trailing Sales $Mil	Price/Cash Flow	Return On Assets%	Total Return% 1 Yr	3 Yr
Bank of New York	17,396	—	6,017	—	1.4	-39.9	-11.1
Citigroup	177,948	—	106,096	—	1.6	-24.2	1.1
J.P. Morgan Chase & Co.	47,901	—	42,911	—	0.2	-30.7	-17.5

Price Volatility

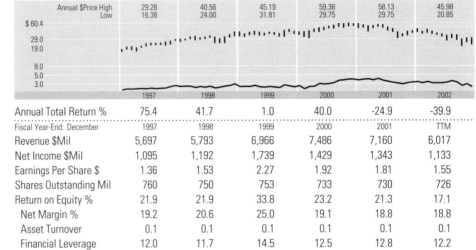

	Monthly Price High/Low		Relative Strength to S&P 500			
Annual $Price High Low	29.28 16.38	40.56 24.00	45.19 31.81	59.38 29.75	58.13 29.75	45.98 20.85
	1997	1998	1999	2000	2001	2002

Annual Total Return %	75.4	41.7	1.0	40.0	-24.9	-39.9
Fiscal Year-End: December	1997	1998	1999	2000	2001	TTM
Revenue $Mil	5,697	5,793	6,966	7,486	7,160	6,017
Net Income $Mil	1,095	1,192	1,739	1,429	1,343	1,133
Earnings Per Share $	1.36	1.53	2.27	1.92	1.81	1.55
Shares Outstanding Mil	760	750	753	733	730	726
Return on Equity %	21.9	21.9	33.8	23.2	21.3	17.1
Net Margin %	19.2	20.6	25.0	19.1	18.8	18.8
Asset Turnover	0.1	0.1	0.1	0.1	0.1	0.1
Financial Leverage	12.0	11.7	14.5	12.5	12.8	12.2

Valuation Ratios	Stock	Rel to Industry	Rel to S&P 500
Price/Earnings	15.5	0.9	0.7
Price/Book	2.6	1.0	0.8
Price/Sales	2.9	1.1	1.4
Price/Cash Flow	—	—	—

Major Fund Holders	% of Fund Assets
Salomon Brothers Opportunity	9.81
Lake Forest Core Equity	5.87
Granum Value	5.26
Fifth Third Quality Growth Inv A	4.22

Morningstar's Take By Rachel Barnard, 12-20-2002 Stock Price as of Analysis: $24.28

Bad loans will keep Bank of New York from achieving the full potential of its lucrative securities business.

The bank derives the majority of its revenue from fees it charges for securities processing, asset management, foreign-exchange trading, and other related services. This is the core of its business, and the bank is focused on increasing its already dominant presence in this market.

Bank of New York is the world's leading custodian, with $6.6 trillion in assets under custody around the globe. As a custodian, the bank takes over many back-office processing tasks for financial institutions, like mutual funds and brokerages, which oversee large securities portfolios. Custodians rely on economies of scale to be profitable; they charge tiny fees based on the assets under custody, which can add up to a hefty chunk of fee income when assets reach into the trillions. As the largest global processor, Bank of New York can leverage its scale to boost profitability and attract new business around the world. This gives the bank a significant competitive advantage.

The bank also has its foot in the door of the lucrative asset-management and private banking market. It already manages $80 billion for wealthy customers, and has been aggressively acquiring new boutique firms whose products appeal to the high-net-worth market. Recent purchases include a hedge fund manager, an equity manager, and a provider of separately managed accounts. Separate accounts have been popular among wealthy investors who want the diversification of a mutual fund with the tax advantages of holding individual securities. All these wealth-management products typically come with the premium fees that Bank of New York covets. So the company is shaking off the old-fashioned image of banking that is tied to interest income and concentrating on earning fee income.

Although the wisdom of this move is especially obvious in the current economic climate, Bank of New York's commercial loan portfolio--heavy in media and telecom--has been an albatross that the firm is trying to throw off its neck. The bank decided to end its exposure to 24 emerging telecom companies last year by disposing of the loans and credit lines and taking a substantial charge. Even so, the bank has been stung repeatedly by bad loans to a variety of industries, including cable, telecom, and airlines. We believe the remaining loan portfolio may contain some more losers, and our fair value estimate of $29 reflects this.

 **MORNINGSTAR®** Stocks 500

Bank One ONE

	Rating	Risk	Moat Size	Fair Value	Last Close	Yield %
	★★★	Med.	Narrow	$39.00	$36.55	2.3

Company Profile

Bank One is the holding company for bank subsidiaries that operate about 2,000 banking offices primarily in the Midwestern and Western United States. It also operates commercial banking offices overseas. The company offers corporate and mortgage banking, bank card, computer banking, and trust management services. Bank One also operates mutual funds. Its nonbank subsidiaries provide data-processing, merchant and investment banking, venture-capital, and insurance services. Business loans make up approximately 57% of the company's total loan portfolio.

Management

Jamie Dimon, former president of Citigroup, was named chairman and CEO in March 2000. At the end of 2001, he exercised a large block of stock options, a bullish sign.

Strategy

Bank One aims to be the best-run bank in the United States by improving its service, boosting its business lending, and expanding its capital markets business. Its First USA credit card unit is stepping up acquisitions as money is made through greater card volume. Bank One is also seeking greater consumer market share by beefing up wealth management and other financial advisory services.

1 Bank One Plaza
Chicago, IL 60670
www.bankone.com

Morningstar Grades

Growth [D]	1998	1999	2000	2001
Revenue %	5.6	1.5	-3.1	-2.5
Earnings/Share %	NMF	NMF	NMF	NMF
Book Value/Share %	—	NMF	-6.3	8.6
Dividends/Share %	10.0	10.5	-25.0	-33.3

Growth has been stunted for the past two years as Bank One turned away unprofitable customers to build share in more-lucrative business segments. The firm now looks ready to grow, perhaps by going on the hunt for a small acquisition.

Profitability [D+]	1999	2000	2001	TTM
Return on Assets %	1.3	-0.2	1.0	1.1
Oper Cash Flow $Mil	3,634	16,824	2,375	—
- Cap Spending $Mil	593	533	169	—
= Free Cash Flow $Mil	—	—	—	—

Returns on equity had been low--or negative--as a result of acquisition charges and declining credit quality. However, Bank One has tightened lending standards and slashed costs, which has led to recent profitability improvement.

Financial Health [A-]	1999	2000	2001	09-02
Long-term Debt $Mil	—	—	—	—
Total Equity $Mil	19,900	18,445	20,226	21,925
Debt/Equity Ratio	—	—	—	—

The firm's balance sheet is much improved. Bank One's Tier 1 capital ratio of 9.5% is above the 8.7% average of the nation's top 25 banks. Plus, loss reserves equal 3% of outstanding loans, much higher than the 2.1% average of its peers.

Industry	Investment Style	Stock Type	Sector
Super Regional Banks	Large Value	Slow Growth	Financial Services

Competition

	Market Cap $Mil	Debt/ Equity	12 Mo Trailing Sales $Mil	Price/Cash Flow	Return On Assets%	Total Return% 1 Yr	3 Yr
Bank One	42,636	—	22,444	—	1.1	-4.4	9.4
Citigroup	177,948	—	106,096	—	1.6	-24.2	1.1
Wells Fargo	79,608	—	28,119	—	1.5	10.3	10.4

Price Volatility

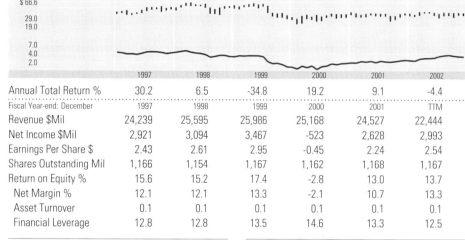

Annual $Price High	54.43	65.63	63.56	39.00	41.50	42.87
Low	35.68	36.06	29.75	23.19	27.00	31.60

	1997	1998	1999	2000	2001	2002
Annual Total Return %	30.2	6.5	-34.8	19.2	9.1	-4.4

Fiscal Year-end: December	1997	1998	1999	2000	2001	TTM
Revenue $Mil	24,239	25,595	25,986	25,168	24,527	22,444
Net Income $Mil	2,921	3,094	3,467	-523	2,628	2,993
Earnings Per Share $	2.43	2.61	2.95	-0.45	2.24	2.54
Shares Outstanding Mil	1,166	1,154	1,167	1,162	1,168	1,167
Return on Equity %	15.6	15.2	17.4	-2.8	13.0	13.7
Net Margin %	12.1	12.1	13.3	-2.1	10.7	13.3
Asset Turnover	0.1	0.1	0.1	0.1	0.1	0.1
Financial Leverage	12.8	12.8	13.5	14.6	13.3	12.5

Valuation Ratios	Stock	Rel to Industry	Rel to S&P 500
Price/Earnings	14.4	1.0	0.6
Price/Book	1.9	0.9	0.6
Price/Sales	1.9	0.9	0.9
Price/Cash Flow	—	—	—

Major Fund Holders	% of Fund Assets
Fidelity Select Banking	8.05
Rydex Banking Inv	7.39
UC Investment	5.20
Legg Mason Value Prim	4.91

Morningstar's Take By Craig Woker, 01-02-2003 Stock Price as of Analysis: $37.55

After two difficult years of restructuring, Bank One is finally poised to start growing again; however, we think the market has already priced the firm's improving prospects into the stock. We would wait for a larger discount to our fair value estimate of $39 per share before jumping in.

To climb back from its troubled past, Bank One has followed a straightforward strategy: Slash costs and make profitable loans. Since CEO Jamie Dimon took the helm in 2000, he put the firm on a crash diet, cutting noninterest costs by 8% annually on average and tightening lending standards. Dimon also appears to have learned a key lesson that made his one-time mentor, Citigroup CEO Sandy Weill, successful: Whip the back office into shape and build capital during the good times. That way, the firm has the capacity--operationally as well as financially--to either steal market share or expand through acquisition when competitors stumble and can be had for cheap.

As a result of what we view as a widening economic moat, this is a stock we'd love to buy if the price were right. However, plenty of work lies ahead before the firm is operating fully from a position of strength. In particular, we believe Bank One is likely to continue shrinking some portions of its commercial banking portfolio, an area where credit losses had spiked. The bank also has said it will eliminate its exposure to two already pared-down businesses: auto leasing and brokered home equity.

Those problems aside, Bank One is improving in other areas. Most important, credit quality is getting better, in our view. Bad-debt charge-offs are trending down, and nonperforming assets have leveled off. Plus, the credit card unit--the bank's second-largest division and long its biggest headache--has slowly become one of the lowest-cost producers in the industry.

Longer term, retail and small-business banking look like particularly bright spots to us. Bank One is offering more tack-on services to help businesses grow, a strategy reminiscent of the one that made many of the firm's predecessor banks successful before rolling up into the current conglomerate. On the retail front, Bank One has launched basic initiatives like approving customers for credit cards when they open new checking accounts and trolling its data to see if different accounts might make more sense for long-time customers.

Initiatives like these are transforming Bank One into a stronger firm. However, we prefer to buy quality at a bargain price.

Barnes & Noble BKS

	Rating	Risk	Moat Size	Fair Value	Last Close	Yield %
	★★★★	Med.	Narrow	$27.00	$18.07	0.0

Company Profile

Barnes & Noble is the largest bookseller in the United States. Its superstore operations consist of 582 book superstores under the Barnes & Noble, Bookstop, and Bookstar trade names. Its mall bookstores consist of about 328 stores under the B. Dalton Bookseller, Doubleday Book Shops, and Scribner's Bookstore trade names. The company owns a 35% share of BN.com and a 63% share of Gamestop, which it spun off in early 2002.

Management

Chairman Leonard Riggio took over Barnes & Noble in 1971 and built it into the nation's largest bookseller by pioneering the book superstore concept. His younger brother Stephen, a board member since 1993, was named CEO in February 2002.

Strategy

Barnes & Noble has grown by building giant stores with coffee bars and other amenities. Now that it has spun off GameStop (keeping a 63% stake in the company), management will focus once again on the core bookstore business. Given that growth in the book business is unlikely to crack the double digits, key goals are gaining market share and cutting costs.

122 Fifth Avenue www.barnesandnobleinc.com
New York, NY 10011

Industry	Investment Style	Stock Type	Sector
Specialty Retail	Small Core	Classic Growth	Consumer Services

Competition

	Market Cap $Mil	Debt/ Equity	12 Mo Trailing Sales $Mil	Price/Cash Flow	Return On Assets%	Total Return% 1 Yr	Total Return% 3 Yr
Barnes & Noble	1,167	0.5	5,238	3.1	2.3	-39.0	-2.4
Wal-Mart Stores	223,388	0.5	233,651	18.9	8.0	-11.8	-7.3
Target	27,252	1.2	42,275	21.5	5.7	-26.5	-3.9

Price Volatility

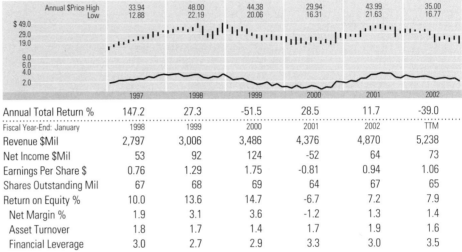

Annual $Price High	33.94	48.00	44.38	29.94	43.99	35.00
Low	12.88	22.19	20.06	16.31	21.63	16.77
	1997	1998	1999	2000	2001	2002

Annual Total Return %	147.2	27.3	-51.5	28.5	11.7	-39.0

Fiscal Year-End: January	1998	1999	2000	2001	2002	TTM
Revenue $Mil	2,797	3,006	3,486	4,376	4,870	5,238
Net Income $Mil	53	92	124	-52	64	73
Earnings Per Share $	0.76	1.29	1.75	-0.81	0.94	1.06
Shares Outstanding Mil	67	68	69	64	67	65
Return on Equity %	10.0	13.6	14.7	-6.7	7.2	7.9
Net Margin %	1.9	3.1	3.6	-1.2	1.3	1.4
Asset Turnover	1.8	1.7	1.4	1.7	1.9	1.6
Financial Leverage	3.0	2.7	2.9	3.3	3.0	3.5

Valuation Ratios	Stock	Rel to Industry	Rel to S&P 500
Price/Earnings	17.0	0.6	0.7
Price/Book	1.3	0.4	0.4
Price/Sales	0.2	0.3	0.1
Price/Cash Flow	3.1	0.2	0.2

Major Fund Holders	% of Fund Assets
Bear Stearns S&P Stars Opp A	3.48
Bear Stearns S&P Stars Opp B	3.48
Buffalo Large Cap	3.48
Bear Stearns S&P Stars A	3.44

Morningstar Grades

Growth [A-]	1999	2000	2001	2002
Revenue %	7.5	16.0	25.5	11.3
Earnings/Share %	69.7	35.7	NMF	NMF
Book Value/Share %	24.7	25.5	1.9	7.7
Dividends/Share %	NMF	NMF	NMF	NMF

Sales growth was artificially inflated by acquisitions in fiscal 2001. We expect stable growth in the midsingle digits for the bookstore business, and mid- to low-teens growth in the video game business, for a combined mid-single-digit growth rate.

Profitability [C]	2000	2001	2002	TTM
Return on Assets %	5.2	-2.0	2.4	2.3
Oper Cash Flow $Mil	187	81	457	382
- Cap Spending $Mil	146	134	169	204
= Free Cash Flow $Mil	41	-54	289	178

Book retailing is a low-margin business; the company's operating margin was 5.7% in fiscal 2002. Barnes & Noble is at the end of a big round of expansion and is cutting costs, so we expect gradual, moderate margin improvements.

Financial Health [C+]	2000	2001	2002	10-02
Long-term Debt $Mil	432	667	449	444
Total Equity $Mil	846	778	888	925
Debt/Equity Ratio	0.5	0.9	0.5	0.5

The balance sheet is still solid, thanks in part to the GameStop spin-off, but the company reported negative free cash flows for fiscal 2001. Fiscal 2002 free cash flows were back in positive territory because of better operating results.

Morningstar's Take By Joseph Beaulieu, 12-19-2002 Stock Price as of Analysis: $17.45

The video game explosion has the potential to put a bit more spring into Barnes & Noble's revenue growth through subsidiary GameStop, but the risks to investors are now a bit higher.

While the bookstore business isn't a particularly attractive one, it carries fairly low risk as a stable, slow-growing business with steady margins. But a look at Barnes & Noble's financial statements (or those of competitor Borders) speaks volumes about the difficulty of the industry. It is asset-intensive, making it difficult to generate high returns on invested capital. In Barnes & Noble's case, book inventory makes up more than half of total assets, and inventory turns over just 2.5 times per year. At least books are not a rapidly depreciating asset.

Meanwhile, consolidation in the publishing industry and intense price competition keep a lid on margins. Barnes & Noble's operating margins have been stuck in the midsingle digits and are unlikely to move much above 6%.

Barnes & Noble's 63%-owned subsidiary GameStop (the amalgamation of Barnes & Noble acquisitions Funco and Babbages) is turning in impressive growth, as the latest cycle of home video games nears its top. While computer games aren't quite as cyclical as console video games (i.e., games for the Xbox, GameCube, or PlayStation), console games are a big growth driver, so we expect growth to slow after the 2002 Christmas season.

We had originally valued the company with a sum-of-the-parts analysis, using a discounted cash flow (DCF) analysis on the bookstore business, and attributing 63% of GameStop's market cap to B&N shareholders. However, given the recent volatility of GameStop shares, and our concern that the video game business is much more cyclical than books, we are treating B&N and GameStop as a consolidated company in our DCF.

Unfortunately, this makes the story a bit more complicated. We think Barnes & Noble has a significant economic moat in its bookstore business, but we don't feel the same way about GameStop, which competes with retailing powerhouses like Wal-Mart, Target, and Best Buy. The risk of increased cyclicality, combined with the exposure to much tougher competitors, led us to lower our economic moat rating for B&N.

We'd consider buying B&N shares at a 30% discount to our fair value estimate of $27, but because of the increased risk of the video game business, we wouldn't consider the shares a bargain until they reached a 40% discount.

 **MORNINGSTAR® Stocks 500**

Barr Laboratories BRL

	Rating	Risk	Moat Size	Fair Value	Last Close	Yield %
	★★★★	Low	Narrow	$91.00	$65.09	0.0

Company Profile

Barr Laboratories develops, manufactures, and sells generic drugs. It also has a few proprietary drugs in late-stage clinical trials, like Seasonale, a female oral contraceptive, and Cypat, which treats symptoms of prostate cancer. Barr recently acquired Duramed, which increased its generic product count to 120 as well as enhanced its stature in the hormone-replacement and oral contraceptive markets. Barr also concentrates on oncology drugs and generates much of its revenue from tamoxifen, a generic version of Astrazeneca's breast cancer drug.

Management

Three of the top five execs at Barr are lawyers, emphasizing the importance of legal expertise to the company, which is constantly challenging the validity of patents. CEO and chairman Bruce Downey is a former patent attorney.

Strategy

Barr Labs mostly manufactures and sells generic drugs, but is attempting to add several proprietary drugs to its offerings. These drugs are aimed at the female health-care and oncology markets. It acquired Duramed in October 2001 to get access to the firm's sales team and enhance its female health-care lineup. Barr aggressively challenges the validity of patents to create new revenue opportunities.

Two Quaker Road
Pomona, NY 10970-0519
www.barrlabs.com

Morningstar Grades

Growth [A]

	1999	2000	2001	2002
Revenue %	19.2	5.4	20.8	100.5
Earnings/Share %	166.7	-74.0	460.0	230.7
Book Value/Share %	23.7	22.1	18.4	57.4
Dividends/Share %	NMF	NMF	NMF	NMF

Fiscal 2002 revenue was up 133% from a year ago, mostly because of the $367 million in sales from generic Prozac. We expect annual revenue growth around 15% for next few years.

Profitability [A]

	2000	2001	2002	TTM
Return on Assets %	1.9	9.4	23.7	20.1
Oper Cash Flow $Mil	12	48	230	184
- Cap Spending $Mil	18	19	47	60
= Free Cash Flow $Mil	-5	28	183	124

Generic Prozac sales pumped up fiscal 2002 operating margins to 27.4%, compared with 16.8% in fiscal 2001. We expect operating margins to drop to the low 20s in fiscal 2003 and remain there for several years.

Financial Health [A+]

	2000	2001	2002	09-02
Long-term Debt $Mil	574	66	43	42
Total Equity $Mil	325	417	667	713
Debt/Equity Ratio	1.8	0.2	0.1	0.1

The balance sheet is flush with cash, thanks to Barr's success with generic Prozac. Debt is low, at less than $45 million. Fiscal 2002 was a record year for free cash flow (cash flow from operations less capital expenditures).

Industry	Investment Style	Stock Type	Sector
Drugs	Mid Growth	Aggr. Growth	Healthcare

Competition

	Market Cap $Mil	Debt/ Equity	12 Mo Trailing Sales $Mil	Price/Cash Flow	Return On Assets%	Total Return% 1 Yr	3 Yr
Barr Laboratories	2,855	0.1	1,057	15.5	20.1	-18.0	47.8
Teva Pharmaceutical Indus	9,891	0.7	2,077	36.2	8.0	25.9	32.8
Mylan Laboratories	4,275	0.0	1,175	14.9	16.1	-6.4	15.2

Price Volatility

	Monthly Price High/Low		Relative Strength to S&P 500			
Annual $Price High Low	33.25 10.95	33.17 16.42	32.38 18.88	80.13 20.00	90.60 44.50	79.99 49.40
	1997	1998	1999	2000	2001	2002

Annual Total Return %	101.7	40.7	-34.6	248.7	8.8	-18.0

Fiscal Year-end: June	1998	1999	2000	2001	2002	TTM
Revenue $Mil	391	466	491	593	1,189	1,057
Net Income $Mil	14	38	10	63	210	182
Earnings Per Share $	0.36	0.96	0.25	1.40	4.63	3.99
Shares Outstanding Mil	37	38	40	42	43	44
Return on Equity %	6.9	14.9	3.2	15.0	31.5	25.5
Net Margin %	3.6	8.2	2.1	10.5	17.7	17.2
Asset Turnover	1.0	1.1	0.9	0.9	1.3	1.2
Financial Leverage	1.9	1.7	1.7	1.6	1.3	1.3

Valuation Ratios	Stock	Rel to Industry	Rel to S&P 500
Price/Earnings	16.3	0.7	0.7
Price/Book	4.0	0.6	1.3
Price/Sales	2.7	0.7	1.3
Price/Cash Flow	15.5	0.7	1.2

Major Fund Holders	% of Fund Assets
RS Contrarian	5.11
Sextant Growth	4.68
Profit Value	3.91
Schroder MidCap Value Inv	3.42

Morningstar's Take By Todd N. Lebor, 12-15-2002 Stock Price as of Analysis: $63.74

Competitive advantages are tough to come by in the fiercely competitive, low-margin generic drug industry. Despite its best efforts, we think Barr falls short in this regard, causing us to require a 40% discount to our fair value estimate before investing.

Barr has tried to distance itself from the competition with its legal expertise. The firm has a strong record of Paragraph IV wins, topped off by its Prozac success. (Paragraph IV of the Hatch-Waxman Act gives the first company to file an abbreviated new drug application--i.e., a generic drug application--180 days of market exclusivity from other generics.) But while Barr's record of Paragraph IV wins is solid, it's not much better than those of its top three or four competitors, so we see no sustainable competitive advantage.

Another way to separate from the pack is to develop proprietary drugs. Like many of its peers that started as pure-play generic drugmakers, Barr is trying to develop more-profitable branded pharmaceuticals. It jump-started its branded franchise with Cenestin, a hormone-replacement therapy acquired with the Duramed purchase in 2001. Simply adding branded drugs to its lineup doesn't differentiate Barr, so the company has decided to focus on products that should take less time to

develop and gain approval. But even that strategy won't create sustainable competitive advantages, in our opinion. There are a number of specialty drug companies targeting the same smaller-market ($10-$150 million per year) drugs. Rejuvenating the scraps from big pharma isn't novel, either.

That said, Barr has built a reputable position in the oral contraceptive market and has several promising late-state proprietary products. Oral contraceptive Seasonale, in Phase III testing, will try to redefine the female menstrual cycle from monthly to quarterly. CyPat and BRL3 are cancer treatments that could, if approved, start adding revenue by 2004. On the other hand, Barr's success as a deft legal adversary and efficient producer of generic drugs may not translate well to the branded pharma arena, and that gives us pause.

Generic drugs are poised for a period of strong growth and Barr is well positioned within the industry. However, its business model provides few advantages over its peers. While we expect Barr to outperform the entire market thanks to its industry, we expect only mediocrity relative to its peers. Unless Barr is trading at a healthy discount to our fair value estimate we see little reason to invest.

Barra BARZ

	Rating	Risk	Moat Size	Fair Value	Last Close	Yield %
	★★★	Med.	Narrow	$35.00	$30.33	0.0

Company Profile

Barra provides computer software and services for the global investment industries. Its core software products analyze and conduct risk modeling on equity, fixed-income, currency, and other financial instruments in international financial markets. The company also offers consulting services, information services, and trading-related software. Its clients in 42 worldwide markets include active and passive equity managers, global managers, fixed-income managers, pension funds, investment consultants, securities traders, and master custodians.

Management

Kamal Duggirala joined Barra in 1984 and has been CEO since 1999. He was instrumental in dividing the business into two groups: core and venture.

Strategy

Barra sells risk-management software. The company hopes to expand beyond portfolio-management products to the corporate level, where large investment firms can analyze risk companywide, and sell cheaper versions of its software over the Web. The company has sold noncore businesses.

2100 Milvia Street
Berkeley, CA 94704-1113
www.barra.com

Industry	Investment Style	Stock Type	Sector
Business Applications	▦ Small Core	→ Slow Growth	⬚ Software

Competition

	Market Cap $Mil	Debt/ Equity	12 Mo Trailing Sales $Mil	Price/Cash Flow	Return On Assets%	Total Return% 1 Yr	3 Yr
Barra	604	—	144	87.6	16.1	-35.6	17.2
FactSet Research Systems	955	—	206	—	—	—	—
Advent Software	447	—	176	—	—	—	—

Price Volatility

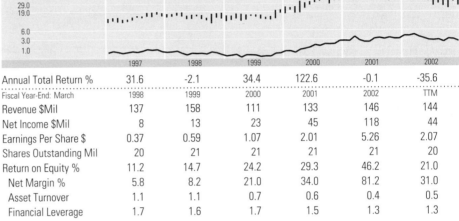

Monthly Price High/Low — Relative Strength to S&P 500

Annual $Price High	19.83	19.33	22.00	50.13	61.50	61.38
Low	10.89	10.42	11.67	17.83	35.36	23.60
	1997	1998	1999	2000	2001	2002

Annual Total Return %	31.6	-2.1	34.4	122.6	-0.1	-35.6

Fiscal Year-End: March	1998	1999	2000	2001	2002	TTM
Revenue $Mil	137	158	111	133	146	144
Net Income $Mil	8	13	23	45	118	44
Earnings Per Share $	0.37	0.59	1.07	2.01	5.26	2.07
Shares Outstanding Mil	20	21	21	21	21	20
Return on Equity %	11.2	14.7	24.2	29.3	46.2	21.0
Net Margin %	5.8	8.2	21.0	34.0	81.2	31.0
Asset Turnover	1.1	1.1	0.7	0.6	0.4	0.5
Financial Leverage	1.7	1.6	1.7	1.5	1.3	1.3

Valuation Ratios

	Stock	Rel to Industry	Rel to S&P 500
Price/Earnings	14.7	0.5	0.6
Price/Book	2.9	0.6	0.9
Price/Sales	4.2	0.5	2.1
Price/Cash Flow	87.6	5.5	6.6

Major Fund Holders

	% of Fund Assets
Transamerica Premier Growth Opp Inv	6.51
IDEX Transamerica Growth Opport A	6.51
Calvert New Vision Small Cap A	4.71
Transamerica Premier Aggr Grth Inv	3.77

Morningstar Grades

Growth [C-]

	1999	2000	2001	2002
Revenue %	15.1	-29.5	19.5	9.4
Earnings/Share %	61.8	80.3	87.9	161.7
Book Value/Share %	22.6	9.8	55.4	66.0
Dividends/Share %	NMF	NMF	NMF	NMF

Sales growth averaged 9% annually over the past five years, but was held back by slower-growing noncore businesses. We expect growth rates to increase now that these businesses have been sold.

Profitability [A+]

	2000	2001	2002	TTM
Return on Assets %	13.9	20.0	36.4	16.1
Oper Cash Flow $Mil	29	68	29	7
- Cap Spending $Mil	4	3	3	3
= Free Cash Flow $Mil	25	64	26	4

Barra is extremely profitable. Strong pricing power and a 13% stake in an electronic trading platform joint venture, where margins are near 90%, produce superb returns on equity (29% in 2001).

Financial Health [A+]

	2000	2001	2002	09-02
Long-term Debt $Mil	—	—	—	—
Total Equity $Mil	97	155	256	211
Debt/Equity Ratio	—	—	—	—

With $11 per share in cash and investments and no debt, the balance sheet is pristine. Barra has used excess cash to repurchase stock.

Morningstar's Take By Mike Trigg, 10-03-2002 Stock Price as of Analysis: $26.04

Risk is good for Barra.

For more than 25 years, Barra has helped institutional investors mitigate risk. Its risk-management software can analyze a portfolio and provide buy/sell recommendations depending on a manager's risk tolerance. This long record has given the company more than 1,200 customers, including the world's 10 largest asset managers and 75 of the 100 biggest global investment-management firms.

But the face of Barra has changed in recent years. Whereas the strategy was once to sell additional offerings like pension fund consulting services, Barra has refocused solely on risk management, selling four noncore businesses in 2002. This leaves just POSIT (10%-15% of revenue), an electronic trading platform joint venture with Investment Technology Group; it is clearly worth keeping, considering that it generates operating margins near 90%.

Barra has two economic moats: a dominant brand and a proprietary database. These create significant barriers to entry. Given the importance of risk management, asset managers are unlikely to consider any firm other than Barra, which is unanimously recognized as the industry leader. With 25 years of data on most of the world's publicly traded securities from 150 sources, Barra has a wealth of data that's nearly impossible to reproduce.

Barra is unlike other software firms. Like many, it's extremely profitable; operating margins are in the mid-30s. But it does not depend on closing most of its deals in the final days of a quarter; subscriptions constitute at least 80% of sales, making the company somewhat immune to a deteriorating economy.

Our only major concern is the size of Barra's market. To combat the consolidation among asset managers, Barra has expanded beyond portfolio risk management to the corporate level, where firms can analyze risk companywide. This requires a large commitment from firms to employ a common risk strategy. Also, Barra is trying to expand its market by selling software over the Web to smaller asset managers who have been unable to afford the hefty price tag. But this business model is unproven, and is hampered by worries over reliability and security.

With a profitable, recurring business model and an emphasis on risk management, in which the company has sustainable competitive advantages, Barra will continue to prosper, in our opinion. Using some conservative assumptions in our discounted cash flow model, we think that the stock is worth $35 per share and that anywhere in the mid-$20s is an attractive entry point for investors.

MORNINGSTAR® Stocks 500

Bausch & Lomb BOL

	Rating	Risk	Moat Size	Fair Value	Last Close	Yield %
	★	Low	None	$29.00	$36.00	1.8

Company Profile

Bausch & Lomb primarily manufactures optical products, including contact lenses, lens-care and eye-care solutions, and eye drops. The company also produces OptiPranolol, a beta blocker used to fight glaucoma; Lotemax, an ophthalmic steroid; and products for use in optical surgical procedures. Bausch & Lomb markets its products in the United States and internationally. Foreign sales account for approximately 56% of the company's total sales. Bausch & Lomb operates facilities in the United States and overseas.

Management

Ronald Zarrella, who's been CEO since November 2001, admitted to having misleading information on his resume. Bausch's board took away his 2002 bonus but sanctioned him as the right man for the job, citing the company's turnaround under his watch.

Strategy

Bausch & Lomb is fighting off rivals like CIBA, Johnson & Johnson, and VISX to remain atop the eye-care industry. In response to falling volume, the firm has focused on cutting manufacturing costs in mature businesses like contacts and contact-cleaning products. It's also investing heavily in its laser surgery products and drug development, two areas that offer stronger growth prospects.

One Bausch & Lomb Place
Rochester, NY 14604-2701
www.bausch.com

Morningstar Grades

Growth [C-]	1998	1999	2000	2001
Revenue %	44.7	10.0	0.5	-3.4
Earnings/Share %	-49.4	EUB	-80.0	-74.3
Book Value/Share %	2.3	39.5	-10.0	-5.3
Dividends/Share %	0.0	0.0	0.0	0.0

Pharmaceuticals are leading the company's revenue growth, but constitute just one fourth of the firm's sales. Surgical unit sales and lens-care products continue to sputter along. We expect top-line sales growth only in the midsingle digits.

Profitability [B]	1999	2000	2001	TTM
Return on Assets %	13.6	2.6	0.7	1.1
Oper Cash Flow $Mil	223	335	183	213
- Cap Spending $Mil	156	95	96	101
= Free Cash Flow $Mil	68	240	87	112

Operating margins have improved in the past few quarters as restructuring efforts begin to pay dividends. That said, operating margins are still only 10%-12%, below 1999 levels. We've modeled operating margins to remain at 8%-9%.

Financial Health [B+]	1999	2000	2001	09-02
Long-term Debt $Mil	977	763	703	509
Total Equity $Mil	1,234	1,039	975	999
Debt/Equity Ratio	0.8	0.7	0.7	0.5

The company has dramatically improved its balance sheet since year-end 1998 by using the proceeds from the sale of businesses to pay down debt. Debt/equity is a respectable 0.76, but the company's debt rating remains junk at BB1.

Industry	Investment Style	Stock Type	Sector
Medical Equipment	Mid Core	Slow Growth	Healthcare

Competition

	Market Cap $Mil	Debt/ Equity	12 Mo Trailing Sales $Mil	Price/Cash Flow	Return On Assets%	Total Return% 1 Yr	3 Yr
Bausch & Lomb	1,942	0.5	1,828	9.1	1.1	-2.7	-16.3
Johnson & Johnson	159,452	0.1	35,120	18.0	16.3	-7.9	8.0
Novartis AG ADR	105,974	0.1	18,933	24.4	10.4	1.8	2.3

Price Volatility

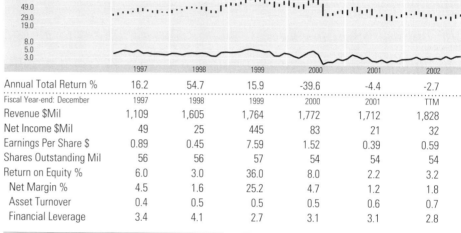

		Monthly Price High/Low			Relative Strength to S&P 500		
Annual $Price High Low	47.88 32.50	60.00 37.75	84.75 51.38	80.88 33.56	54.93 27.20	44.80 27.16	
	1997	1998	1999	2000	2001	2002	
Annual Total Return %	16.2	54.7	15.9	-39.6	-4.4	-2.7	

Fiscal Year-end: December	1997	1998	1999	2000	2001	TTM
Revenue $Mil	1,109	1,605	1,764	1,772	1,712	1,828
Net Income $Mil	49	25	445	83	21	32
Earnings Per Share $	0.89	0.45	7.59	1.52	0.39	0.59
Shares Outstanding Mil	56	56	57	54	54	54
Return on Equity %	6.0	3.0	36.0	8.0	2.2	3.2
Net Margin %	4.5	1.6	25.2	4.7	1.2	1.8
Asset Turnover	0.4	0.5	0.5	0.5	0.6	0.7
Financial Leverage	3.4	4.1	2.7	3.1	3.1	2.8

Valuation Ratios	Stock	Rel to Industry	Rel to S&P 500
Price/Earnings	61.0	2.0	2.6
Price/Book	1.9	0.3	0.6
Price/Sales	1.1	0.2	0.5
Price/Cash Flow	9.1	0.4	0.7

Major Fund Holders	% of Fund Assets
MainStay Equity Income A	3.79
Osterweis	3.34
Heartland Value Plus	3.06
TCW Galileo Diversified Value N	2.98

Morningstar's Take By Todd N. Lebor, 12-11-2002 Stock Price as of Analysis: $35.83

Bausch & Lomb has brand recognition and a global presence in eye care, but has failed to execute over the past few years. Until management shows sustained operational improvement, we'd buy the stock only at a 40%-50% discount to our fair value estimate.

Bausch relies on the contact lens market for 55% of revenue--30% from lenses and 25% from lens-care products like ReNu solution. The contact lens market is big, growing, and dominated by a small number of companies; the $2.8 billion global industry is expanding around 6% annually, and manufacturing advances have made contacts an option for a whole new group of patients. For example, toric and multifocal contact lenses are drawing in the 40- to 64-year-olds, who represent the fastest-growing segment of the market. However, Bausch & Lomb has been behind the technology curve for some time and is simply following in the footsteps of nimbler and more innovative competitors. We can't see any sustainable competitive advantages in this business segment.

Bausch has been retooling its operations for several years now, booking more than $150 million in restructuring costs since 1999. So far, these efforts have only moved the firm from the cellar back to

mediocrity. Margins have shown some improvement, but they're not even back to 1999 levels. Also, our confidence in CEO Ron Zarrella is tenuous. The revelation that his resume was inaccurate (he doesn't have an MBA from New York University, but his resume read as if he did) brings his integrity into question. While Zarrella's apology seemed sincere and the loss of $1.1 million in bonus may help prevent future lapses in judgment, we still think investors should require a slightly larger margin of safety, given this incident.

The other 45% of Bausch & Lomb's revenue comes from surgical products and pharmaceuticals. Sales of laser surgery equipment and procedures continue to suffer with the economy, but drugs offer a glimmer of hope. Higher-margin drug sales have increased 11% annually since 1999 and now represent 23% of total sales, up from 17% in 1999, helping boost profitability. We think Bausch & Lomb's industry has promise, and we like the company's counterbalancing business units--the laser surgery unit is a logical hedge against possible declines in the contact lens unit. However, too many miscues over the past several years and mediocre profitability lead us to look for better investments.

Baxter International BAX

	Rating	Risk	Moat Size	Fair Value	Last Close	Yield %
	★★★★	Med.	Narrow	$41.00	$28.00	2.1

Company Profile

Baxter International make health-care products used in hospitals and other health-care settings. The company's fast-growth businesses are related to blood products and vaccines. It also produces medication-delivery products, like IV fluids, and is a leading provider of hemodialysis machines and dialyzers. Foreign sales account for about 52% of the company's total sales. Baxter produces bulk smallpox vaccine for its partner, Acambis, on behalf of the U.S. Department of Health and Human Services.

Management

CEO Harry Kraemer added the chairman title in January 2000. Since 1982, Kraemer has held several positions within the company. His experience in the banking industry should help him keep Baxter focused on cash flow generation.

Strategy

Baxter is striving to be the leading global provider of critical therapies for individuals with life-threatening conditions, like hemophilia and kidney failure. It is investing heavily to develop new products, expand its overseas market share, and shift to higher-margin products outside the United States. It aims to leverage its capabilities across various segments of the health-care industry.

One Baxter Parkway   www.baxter.com
Deerfield, IL 60015-4633

Morningstar Grades

Growth [B-]	1998	1999	2000	2001
Revenue %	8.5	11.8	8.1	11.1
Earnings/Share %	2.8	23.9	-8.1	-19.4
Book Value/Share %	NMF	-42.3	-21.4	37.8
Dividends/Share %	2.2	0.0	0.0	0.0

Excluding divestitures, sales have increased 10% annually since 1997. With the renal division hurting from dialyzer recalls in 2001 and slower growth in biosciences, Baxter is unlikely to meet its expected midteens growth in 2002.

Profitability [A-]	1999	2000	2001	TTM
Return on Assets %	8.3	8.5	5.9	6.2
Oper Cash Flow $Mil	977	1,233	1,149	1,205
- Cap Spending $Mil	631	648	787	872
= Free Cash Flow $Mil	346	585	362	333

Baxter's profitability has been erratic over the past five years, owing to one-time charges from acquisitions and divestitures. Returns on equity and assets would be more stable without these effects.

Financial Health [B+]	1999	2000	2001	09-02
Long-term Debt $Mil	2,601	1,726	2,486	2,935
Total Equity $Mil	3,348	2,659	3,757	4,358
Debt/Equity Ratio	0.8	0.6	0.7	0.7

Baxter has slowly decreased debt/total capital from 0.54 in 1998 to 0.42 at the end of 2001. Its long-term target capital structure is 40% debt. It has been generating strong cash from operations, and we expect that to continue.

Industry	Investment Style	Stock Type	Sector
Medical Equipment	⊞ Large Core	⬈ Classic Growth	⊗ Healthcare

Competition	Market Cap $Mil	Debt/ Equity	12 Mo Trailing Sales $Mil	Price/Cash Flow	Return On Assets%	Total Return% 1 Yr	3 Yr
Baxter International	16,905	0.7	8,210	14.0	6.2	-46.7	0.7
Medtronic	55,399	0.3	6,669	34.6	11.4	-10.4	10.3
Wyeth	49,579	1.1	14,598	83.0	13.4	-37.9	-0.4

Price Volatility

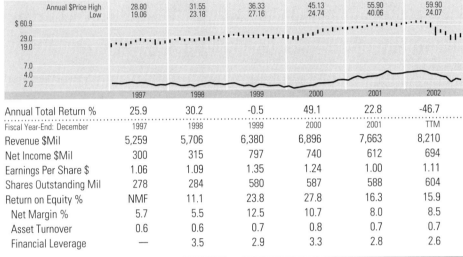

		Monthly Price High/Low			— Relative Strength to S&P 500	
Annual $Price High Low	28.80 19.06	31.55 23.18	36.33 27.16	45.13 24.74	55.90 40.06	59.90 24.07
	1997	1998	1999	2000	2001	2002

Annual Total Return %	25.9	30.2	-0.5	49.1	22.8	-46.7
Fiscal Year-End: December	1997	1998	1999	2000	2001	TTM
Revenue $Mil	5,259	5,706	6,380	6,896	7,663	8,210
Net Income $Mil	300	315	797	740	612	694
Earnings Per Share $	1.06	1.09	1.35	1.24	1.00	1.11
Shares Outstanding Mil	278	284	580	587	588	604
Return on Equity %	NMF	11.1	23.8	27.8	16.3	15.9
Net Margin %	5.7	5.5	12.5	10.7	8.0	8.5
Asset Turnover	0.6	0.6	0.7	0.8	0.7	0.7
Financial Leverage	—	3.5	2.9	3.3	2.8	2.6

Valuation Ratios	Stock	Rel to Industry	Rel to S&P 500
Price/Earnings	25.2	0.8	1.1
Price/Book	3.9	0.6	1.2
Price/Sales	2.1	0.4	1.0
Price/Cash Flow	14.0	0.6	1.1

Major Fund Holders	% of Fund Assets
Monetta Blue Chip	6.17
Fidelity Select Medical Equip/Systems	4.69
MainStay Select 20 Equity A	4.51
Stratton Growth	4.45

Morningstar's Take By Damon Ficklin, 12-19-2002 Stock Price as of Analysis: $28.70

Despite its recent setbacks, we think Baxter has a convincing growth story, given the favorable demographic trends and market leadership in its biggest areas of opportunity. While there are risks to owning this stock, weakness in the price could provide a chance to invest.

A mix of commodity products, like intravenous solutions, and high-margin equipment and biopharmaceutical therapies has led Baxter to become the top seller among medical device companies. It has achieved economies of scale by spreading its salesforce over a larger product base, leading to high-teens selling and general expenses as a percentage of sales--5 percentage points lower than those of peers like Medtronic. Margins aren't sensational, but they're consistent enough to provide decent returns on capital.

But Baxter's kidney and plasma (blood) businesses are maturing. The firm's recent retrenchment in the renal-care services business indicates the lack of growth and profit potential in that segment. Also, recent pricing pressure in plasma products has caused Baxter to miss its sales growth target in the bioscience division.

We're optimistic about the company's prospects, however. Baxter derives higher revenue per liter of

input (plasma) than its competitors because it produces more than 20 products per liter, while most of its competitors produce fewer than five. This is an important advantage in a maturing market.

Baxter is also developing new products to maintain its growth rates. It is well ahead of the pack with recombinant factor VIII, a hemophilia treatment that is a safer and more profitable substitute for the low-margin plasma version. Baxter has captured a majority of the market for factor VIII products because it's been more successful at obtaining approval from the Food and Drug Administration for new production facilities.

It looks as if Baxter will be first to market with the next-generation factor VIII product as well. The worldwide market is expected to increase from $2 billion today to $5 billion in 2005, and Baxter plans to have the capacity to service 70% of that market. If approved, the treatment could bring in $2 billion in revenue by 2005.

While we believe Baxter's growth prospects, improving margins, and strong financial health will provide strong returns on invested capital, the risks tell us we want a 30%-40% margin of safety to our fair value estimate before investing. We'd be buyers in the mid-$20s.

MORNINGSTAR® Stocks 500

BB&T BBT

	Rating	Risk	Moat Size	Fair Value	Last Close	Yield %
	★★★	Med.	Narrow	$42.00	$36.99	3.0

Company Profile

BB&T is the holding company for bank subsidiaries that operate more than 900 banking offices in the East and South. The banks provide savings, checking, money market, and individual retirement accounts. They also offer credit cards and trust services and make real-estate, business, and consumer loans. BB&T has acquired more than 50 insurance agencies to create one of the largest retail insurance agencies in the United States. BB&T agreed to acquire FirstSpartan Financial, Century South Banks, F&M National, and Virginia Capital Bancshares in 2001.

Management

John Allison has been with the bank since 1971 and has served as BB&T's chairman and CEO since 1989. He has been the driving force behind the bank's successful acquisition strategy.

Strategy

BB&T has been buying up small banks in the Carolinas, Georgia, Maryland, West Virginia, and most recently Kentucky to gain market share and fuel earnings growth. It has also bought more than 50 small insurance companies and 16 nonbank financial firms as a way to boost fee income. BB&T is now looking to expand its brokerage business and enter the large Florida market.

200 West Second Street
Winston-Salem, NC 27101
www.bbandt.com

Morningstar Grades

Growth [B-]	1998	1999	2000	2001
Revenue %	11.4	10.4	14.5	2.7
Earnings/Share %	27.0	6.9	-10.5	38.6
Book Value/Share %	12.3	-0.7	16.5	12.8
Dividends/Share %	13.8	13.6	14.7	14.0

Growth has been strong as a result of BB&T's ingrained sales culture and many acquisitions. The company's five-year annualized revenue growth rate easily bests the peer average of 10.5%.

Profitability [B]	1999	2000	2001	TTM
Return on Assets %	1.3	1.1	1.4	1.6
Oper Cash Flow $Mil	1,984	300	94	—
- Cap Spending $Mil	156	170	190	—
= Free Cash Flow $Mil	—	—	—	—

Although BB&T has had periods of below-average profitability, its returns on average assets and equity have been above average for at least the past six quarters.

Financial Health [A]	1999	2000	2001	09-02
Long-term Debt $Mil	—	—	—	—
Total Equity $Mil	4,640	5,420	6,150	7,535
Debt/Equity Ratio	—	—	—	—

BB&T is generally quite conservative in its financial operations. Charge-offs remain below average and have decreased for two consecutive quarters.

Industry	Investment Style	Stock Type	Sector
Super Regional Banks	▦ Large Core	⚡ High Yield	$ Financial Services

Competition

	Market Cap $Mil	Debt/ Equity	12 Mo Trailing Sales $Mil	Price/Cash Flow	Return On Assets%	Total Return% 1 Yr	3 Yr
BB&T	17,771	—	5,891	—	1.6	5.7	17.4
Wachovia	50,032	—	24,107	—	1.0	19.5	9.8
SunTrust Banks	16,225	—	7,631	—	1.2	-6.7	-0.4

Price Volatility

Annual $Price High Low	32.50 17.50	40.75 26.25	40.63 27.06	38.25 21.69	38.84 30.25	39.47 31.03

	1997	1998	1999	2000	2001	2002
Annual Total Return %	81.5	28.5	-30.7	40.7	-0.5	5.7

Fiscal Year-end: December	1997	1998	1999	2000	2001	TTM
Revenue $Mil	4,222	4,702	5,192	5,945	6,106	5,891
Net Income $Mil	565	721	779	698	974	1,244
Earnings Per Share $	1.26	1.60	1.71	1.53	2.12	2.63
Shares Outstanding Mil	438	442	448	451	453	480
Return on Equity %	13.8	15.6	16.8	12.9	15.8	16.5
Net Margin %	13.4	15.3	15.0	11.8	15.9	21.1
Asset Turnover	0.1	0.1	0.1	0.1	0.1	0.1
Financial Leverage	12.0	11.8	12.8	12.3	11.5	10.4

Valuation Ratios	Stock	Rel to Industry	Rel to S&P 500
Price/Earnings	14.1	1.0	0.6
Price/Book	2.4	1.2	0.7
Price/Sales	3.0	1.4	1.5
Price/Cash Flow	—	—	—

Major Fund Holders	% of Fund Assets
Banknorth Large Cap Value	6.61
Pitcairn Select Value	5.49
Leonetti Growth	4.13
Expedition Equity Income Instl	3.18

Morningstar's Take By Richard McCaffery, 12-16-2002 Stock Price as of Analysis: $38.13

BB&T won't ever have the geographic reach of Citigroup or the brand of American Express, but it has a host of solid bank qualities. It is large enough to realize economies of scale as it expands market share and improves technology, and it has an efficient operating platform that allows it to earn a decent return on plain-vanilla lending products like home mortgages, which gives it a foot in the door for selling higher-margin services.

We also like its niche focus on community banking, which centers on making loans to small businesses. There are about 5.5 million businesses with fewer than 500 people in the United States, and they provide about 75% of the new jobs, according to the Small Business Administration. BB&T's growing branch network will allow the bank to continue tapping this lucrative market, which is getting more attention from bigger players such as American Express, a company that started buying small accounting firms years ago because it's a smart way to gain access to this market.

BB&T itself has acquired more than 60 banks and more than 50 insurance companies in the past 15 years, and the firm has more than doubled its asset base in the past five years. So far in the fourth quarter of 2002, the company has announced plans to buy an insurance company in Georgia and a small thrift in Florida. These are typical BB&T acquisitions: small companies that can be quickly integrated and that add to the firm's product depth and reach.

Overall, BB&T has added significant shareholder value by acquiring rivals that are less well run and then increasing returns on equity. We think this is a sound strategy in a fragmented banking industry, and one that has turned BB&T into a bank with high credit quality and above-average growth.

This strategy brings some risk, though. The bank could stumble on a tough acquisition, overpay for a target, or fail to find appropriate candidates. However, BB&T reduces acquisition risk by targeting smaller banks with $250 million to $10 billion in assets. It doesn't acquire banks that need an overhaul, and it looks to retrain existing employees in an effort to maintain a close connection with the local community.

Banks with solid credit quality and good revenue prospects are often sound investments. BB&T is a company we would keep on the radar screen.

BEA Systems BEAS

	Rating	Risk	Moat Size	Fair Value	Last Close	Yield %
	★	High	None	$7.00	$11.47	0.0

Company Profile

BEA Systems designs and develops software that helps large organizations support their business processes. The company's Tuxedo software engine manages transactions and communications for enterprisewide applications. Its clients are primarily in the telecommunication, finance, manufacturing, retail, technology, and transportation industries. Customers include AT&T, China Telecom, Discover Card, Gap, FedEx, Fidelity Investments, McKesson, and Motorola.

Management

Recent departures include Bill Coleman (chairman), Matt Green (president of worldwide sales), and Ivan Koon (president of new technologies). Co-founder and CEO Alfred Chuang owns 2% of the company.

Strategy

Because it has acquired key technologies like the highly successful WebLogic application server, BEA has been referred to as "Built Entirely by Acquisition." The company sells key products, like portal and integration software, that leverage the leadership of WebLogic.

2315 North First Street
San Jose, CA 95131

www.bea.com

Industry	Investment Style	Stock Type	Sector
Development Tools	Mid Growth	Spec. Growth	Software

Competition	Market Cap $Mil	Debt/ Equity	12 Mo Trailing Sales $Mil	Price/Cash Flow	Return On Assets%	Total Return% 1 Yr	3 Yr
BEA Systems	4,708	0.8	916	26.1	3.4	-25.5	-31.2
Microsoft	276,411	0.0	29,985	16.0	13.2	-22.0	-22.9
IBM	130,982	0.8	82,442	9.0	5.8	-35.5	-11.1

Price Volatility

Monthly Price High/Low — Relative Strength to S&P 500

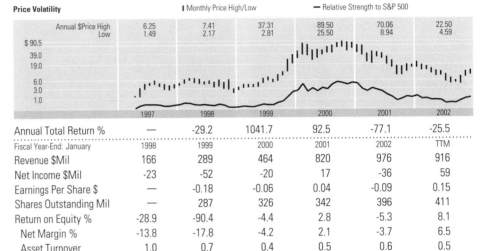

Annual $Price High Low	6.25 1.49	7.41 2.17	37.31 2.81	89.50 25.50	70.06 8.94	22.50 4.59

	1997	1998	1999	2000	2001	2002
Annual Total Return %	—	-29.2	1041.7	92.5	-77.1	-25.5

Fiscal Year-End: January	1998	1999	2000	2001	2002	TTM
Revenue $Mil	166	289	464	820	976	916
Net Income $Mil	-23	-52	-20	17	-36	59
Earnings Per Share $	—	-0.18	-0.06	0.04	-0.09	0.15
Shares Outstanding Mil	—	287	326	342	396	411
Return on Equity %	-28.9	-90.4	-4.4	2.8	-5.3	8.1
Net Margin %	-13.8	-17.8	-4.2	2.1	-3.7	6.5
Asset Turnover	1.0	0.7	0.4	0.5	0.6	0.5
Financial Leverage	2.2	7.1	2.8	2.6	2.5	2.4

Valuation Ratios	Stock	Rel to Industry	Rel to S&P 500
Price/Earnings	76.5	1.9	3.3
Price/Book	6.4	1.4	2.0
Price/Sales	5.1	1.2	2.6
Price/Cash Flow	26.1	1.4	2.0

Major Fund Holders	% of Fund Assets
Fifth Third Technology Instl	5.86
ProFunds Ultra Internet Inv	5.53
Phoenix-Engemann Aggressive Growth A	5.22
Fidelity Select Software & Comp	5.20

Morningstar Grades

Growth [A-]	1999	2000	2001	2002
Revenue %	73.7	60.7	76.5	19.0
Earnings/Share %	NMF	NMF	NMF	NMF
Book Value/Share %	NMF	585.0	4.1	19.8
Dividends/Share %	NMF	NMF	NMF	NMF

Sales averaged 50% growth over the past three years, but those heady days are over. Now, growth hinges on selling integration and portal software that complements BEA's market-leading application server.

Profitability [B]	2000	2001	2002	TTM
Return on Assets %	-1.6	1.1	-2.1	3.4
Oper Cash Flow $Mil	95	225	225	181
- Cap Spending $Mil	18	35	56	35
= Free Cash Flow $Mil	77	190	169	146

We are impressed that BEA has maintained midteen operating margins despite the IT slowdown. The company's past GAAP profits are skewed by various noncash charges.

Financial Health [B-]	2000	2001	2002	10-02
Long-term Debt $Mil	578	564	553	554
Total Equity $Mil	445	606	674	733
Debt/Equity Ratio	1.3	0.9	0.8	0.8

The balance sheet is quite good, with roughly $1 billion in cash and investments and $500 million in debt. Also, the company generates lots of free cash flow.

Morningstar's Take By Mike Trigg, 12-17-2002 Stock Price as of Analysis: $11.50

There are storm clouds on the horizon at BEA Systems.

BEA is the leading vendor of application servers, the layer that sits between front-end applications you access with a browser and back-end systems like databases. This market has exploded in recent years as firms moved internal and external business processes like procurement and sales to the Web. We expect strong demand to continue as companies build more Web applications that link to data in older systems.

However, strong demand has led to intensified competition. IBM, Sun Microsystems, and Oracle are all going after the market with vigor because application servers eliminate many of the previous advantages of their high-end servers and databases. Microsoft too is including some application server functionality in its Windows server operating system. However, we are concerned that application servers are becoming commodities, like the database market years ago. Whereas BEA's competitive advantage has historically been superior technology, rivals--particularly IBM--have been closing this gap. This has resulted in BEA's losing market share to Big Blue, which is on the verge of overtaking the market's top spot.

We expect IBM and others to succeed because they can offer lower prices by bundling services, software, and hardware. In some cases, companies are willing to give away the application server for nothing to generate sales. In the current environment some firms are willing to forgo a better product for a cheaper alternative that meets their needs.

BEA's strategy is to leverage the success of its application server by offering ancillary applications like portal and integration software. However, it remains to be seen whether these new products will be viewed by customers as anything other than mere add-on features, and whether they will generate meaningful revenue.

Stiff competition from the world's most dominant technology companies and the commodification of application servers make us skeptical about BEA's prospects. The company's only real competitive advantage--superior technology--has been mitigated in recent years, proving less of a buying incentive for customers.

MORNINGSTAR® Stocks 500

Bear Stearns Companies BSC

	Rating	Risk	Moat Size	Fair Value	Last Close	Yield %
	★★	Med.	None	$56.00	$59.40	1.0

Company Profile

Bear Stearns provides financial services including investment banking, securities trading, and brokerage, through offices in the U.S. and overseas. The company underwrites share issues and provides assistance in mergers, acquisitions, restructurings, and securities clearance. Bear Stearns trades mainly U.S. government obligations, institutional equities, corporate fixed-income securities, and mortgage-related instruments on the major U.S. commodities and stock exchanges, including the New York Stock Exchange.

Management

Chief executive James Cayne has suggested he would consider selling the firm for about 4 times book value--a steep price, given that similar firms were acquired for less than 3.5 times book value in 2000.

Strategy

Bear Stearns' focus has been primarily at the institutional level; it's one of the leading underwriters of corporate debt and has an active merger and acquisition team. Its strategy is to leverage its expertise in certain areas and thereby offer a broader array of products based on client needs.

383 Madison Avenue   www.bearstearns.com
New York, NY 10179

Industry	Investment Style	Stock Type	Sector
Securities	Mid Value	Slow Growth	Financial Services

Competition

	Market Cap $Mil	Debt/ Equity	12 Mo Trailing Sales $Mil	Price/Cash Flow	Return On Assets%	Total Return% 1 Yr	3 Yr
Bear Stearns Companies	5,711	—	7,184	—	0.4	2.3	16.6
Citigroup	177,948	—	106,096	—	1.6	-24.2	1.1
Morgan Stanley	43,977	—	32,954	—	0.6	-27.2	-12.5

Price Volatility

Monthly Price High/Low — Relative Strength to S&P 500

Annual $Price High Low	44.05 23.22	58.05 23.58	50.48 31.91	72.50 36.50	64.45 40.65	67.55 50.50
	1997	1998	1999	2000	2001	2002
Annual Total Return %	81.9	-20.1	27.7	20.0	17.0	2.3

Fiscal Year-end: November	1997	1998	1999	2000	2001	TTM
Revenue $Mil	6,077	7,980	11,352	10,277	8,701	7,184
Net Income $Mil	589	629	903	734	580	806
Earnings Per Share $	3.81	4.17	6.05	5.35	4.27	6.19
Shares Outstanding Mil	155	151	149	137	129	96
Return on Equity %	20.8	18.0	21.8	15.1	12.0	15.3
Net Margin %	9.7	7.9	8.0	7.1	6.7	11.2
Asset Turnover	0.1	0.1	0.1	0.1	0.0	0.0
Financial Leverage	42.8	44.2	39.1	34.7	38.4	35.2

Valuation Ratios	Stock	Rel to Industry	Rel to S&P 500
Price/Earnings	9.6	0.6	0.4
Price/Book	1.1	0.6	0.3
Price/Sales	0.8	0.6	0.4
Price/Cash Flow	—	—	—

Major Fund Holders	% of Fund Assets
Fidelity Select Brokerage & Investmnt	6.64
Citizens Value	4.57
Permanent Portfolio Aggressive Growth	4.42
Chicago Asset Management Value	4.22

Morningstar Grades

Growth [D]	1998	1999	2000	2001
Revenue %	31.3	42.3	-9.5	-15.3
Earnings/Share %	9.5	44.9	-11.5	-20.2
Book Value/Share %	26.2	19.8	27.6	0.6
Dividends/Share %	3.4	55.9	-35.1	9.1

Net revenue dropped 10% in 2001. Despite strong growth in the fixed-income markets, net revenue was up only 5.7% through the first three quarters of fiscal 2002. Debt markets must remain steady and equities must improve for Bear Stearns to see better results.

Profitability [D]	1999	2000	2001	TTM
Return on Assets %	0.6	0.4	0.3	0.4
Oper Cash Flow $Mil	-1,225	-7,012	6,552	—
- Cap Spending $Mil	252	192	185	—
= Free Cash Flow $Mil	—	—	—	—

Profit margins have been erratic over the past five years, but have generally averaged out in the midteens. We assume that they'll hover around 14%-15% over the next five years, meaning that Bear Stearns must focus on cost control.

Financial Health [B]	1999	2000	2001	08-02
Long-term Debt $Mil	—	—	—	—
Total Equity $Mil	4,142	4,854	4,829	5,262
Debt/Equity Ratio	—	—	—	—

The brokerage industry is balance-sheet-intensive, and most firms employ large amounts of leverage. Bear Stearns' financial leverage has been trending downward, but is still higher than the industry average.

Morningstar's Take By Craig Woker, 11-19-2002 Stock Price as of Analysis: $61.13

This just might be as good as it gets for Bear Stearns. Unfortunately, that's not saying much.

With the fixed-income sector booming, Bear Stearns is reveling in the strong growth of its biggest business line. The firm has been one of the few investment banks to post year-over-year gains in revenue and earnings throughout fiscal 2002 (ending in November). That was entirely due to a 19% jump in fixed-income trading and a 48% rise in investment banking revenue through the fiscal third quarter, most of which was attributable to bond and asset-backed securities underwriting, in our view.

It's going to be difficult--if not impossible--to keep beating rivals by such a wide margin. The stars have aligned to allow this rampant growth. The foremost driver is that the equity markets have become impervious to all but a handful of new share issuances. Therefore, firms that otherwise would raise capital in the equity markets have turned to the debt sector. Some high-grade issuers have taken advantage of low rates to refinance. Further, AAA grade asset-backed securities--mortgages, credit card receivables, or other debt--have been in hot demand, and issuers have complied by bringing these to market.

Even if this unbridled fixed-income growth continues, it won't necessarily translate to rapid bottom-line increases for Bear Stearns. Steep declines in other business lines--clearing services, equities, and wealth management--have worked to counter much of the fixed-income gains.

Overall, our forecast, which yields a fair value estimate of $56 per share, calls for average annual revenue growth in the upper-single-digit range over the next five years and net margins in the midteens, in line with historical numbers. Given Bear Stearns' weaker competitive position compared with larger rivals, we would need a sizable margin of safety before we'd buy this stock.

After all, despite its strong recent performance, Bear Stearns has generated subpar growth and returns on equity over the past five years. To achieve even this level of profitability, the firm has needed to focus on cost control, an area where it has shown some prowess. As of the third quarter, the firm's workforce was down 5.9% from a year earlier. In addition to holding down compensation expense, Bear Stearns has cut marketing and consulting expenditures by more than 20%.

However, because Bear Stearns can't shrink its way to greatness, we'd take a pass on this stock unless it becomes a better value.

Bed Bath & Beyond BBBY

	Rating	Risk	Moat Size	Fair Value	Last Close	Yield %
	★	Med.	None	$25.00	$34.53	0.0

Company Profile

Bed Bath & Beyond is a chain of retail stores that sells domestic merchandise and home furnishings. Domestic merchandise includes bed linens, bath accessories, and kitchen textiles; home furnishings include cookware, dinnerware, glassware, and basic housewares. Brand-name merchandise is generally offered. As of December 2000, the company operated 311 stores in 43 states. This number includes superstores that offer domestic merchandise and home furnishings and 4 smaller stores offering domestic merchandise. The company also sells its products over the Internet.

Management

Leonard Feinstein and Warren Eisenberg, who co-founded the company in 1971, remain co-CEOs and co-chairmen. Each has extensive experience in the retail industry. Insiders have been aggressively selling shares during 2002.

Strategy

Bed Bath & Beyond is rapidly expanding its store base, seeking to capitalize on the fragmented linens and housewares market. A more centralized distribution system (reducing the number of vendor deliveries made directly to individual stores) may become necessary to improve supply-chain efficiency and boost margins.

650 Liberty Avenue   www.bedbathandbeyond.com
Union, NJ 07083

Morningstar Grades

Growth [A+]	1999	2000	2001	2002
Revenue %	29.6	34.4	29.0	22.2
Earnings/Share %	33.3	33.8	29.7	25.4
Book Value/Share %	39.4	35.0	44.7	31.5
Dividends/Share %	NMF	NMF	NMF	NMF

Bed Bath & Beyond's growth record has been excellent. We expect more of the same, though growth is decelerating from its historical pace.

Profitability [A+]	2000	2001	2002	TTM
Return on Assets %	15.2	14.4	13.3	13.7
Oper Cash Flow $Mil	136	198	338	353
- Cap Spending $Mil	90	140	122	129
= Free Cash Flow $Mil	46	58	216	224

The retailer follows a strategy of everyday low pricing, so its stores don't hold sales. The policy has helped gross margins remain between 41% and 42% over the past 10 years.

Financial Health [A+]	2000	2001	2002	08-02
Long-term Debt $Mil	—	—	—	—
Total Equity $Mil	559	817	1,094	1,238
Debt/Equity Ratio	—	—	—	—

Despite heavy capital spending to fund expansion, Bed Bath & Beyond's free cash flow just keeps rolling in. The balance sheet is debt-free and the company has plenty of cash with which to open stores.

Industry	Investment Style	Stock Type	Sector
Furniture Retail	▦ Large Growth	⬆ Aggr. Growth	▱ Consumer Services

Competition

	Market Cap $Mil	Debt/ Equity	12 Mo Trailing Sales $Mil	Price/Cash Flow	Return On Assets%	Total Return% 1 Yr	3 Yr
Bed Bath & Beyond	10,104	—	3,318	28.6	13.7	1.9	30.7
J.C. Penney	6,167	0.9	32,197	3.8	1.5	-12.3	8.6
Linens 'N Things	994	—	2,049	—	—		

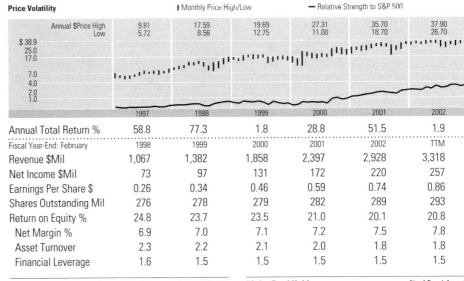

Price Volatility			I Monthly Price High/Low		— Relative Strength to S&P 500	
Annual $Price High	9.81	17.59	19.69	27.31	35.70	37.90
Low	5.72	8.56	12.75	11.00	18.70	26.70

	1997	1998	1999	2000	2001	2002
Annual Total Return %	58.8	77.3	1.8	28.8	51.5	1.9

Fiscal Year-End: February	1998	1999	2000	2001	2002	TTM
Revenue $Mil	1,067	1,382	1,858	2,397	2,928	3,318
Net Income $Mil	73	97	131	172	220	257
Earnings Per Share $	0.26	0.34	0.46	0.59	0.74	0.86
Shares Outstanding Mil	276	278	279	282	289	293
Return on Equity %	24.8	23.7	23.5	21.0	20.1	20.8
Net Margin %	6.9	7.0	7.1	7.2	7.5	7.8
Asset Turnover	2.3	2.2	2.1	2.0	1.8	1.8
Financial Leverage	1.6	1.5	1.5	1.5	1.5	1.5

Valuation Ratios	Stock	Rel to Industry	Rel to S&P 500
Price/Earnings	40.2	1.0	1.7
Price/Book	8.2	1.0	2.6
Price/Sales	3.0	1.0	1.5
Price/Cash Flow	28.6	1.0	2.2

Major Fund Holders	% of Fund Assets
Strong Advisor Focus A	6.97
PBHG Large Cap 20 PBHG	6.63
Strong Growth 20 Inv	6.13
Morgan Stanley Cap Opportunities B	5.84

Morningstar's Take By Roz Bryant, 12-23-2002 Stock Price as of Analysis: $34.86

Bed Bath & Beyond's operating strategy yields superior growth and profitability, and the shares are retail favorites. Still, we think they're currently priced for perfection and overvalued, and wouldn't invest until they hit the midteens.

Bed Bath & Beyond has arch rival Linens 'N Things beat: It's averaged 33% annual sales growth since 1995 compared with Linens' 24%. For consumers, the appeal of both chains is their broad assortment of name-brand bed linens and below-department-store pricing. But the former's stores consistently achieve higher sales productivity: Sales per square foot were $199 in 2001 compared with Linens' $152.

Much of the difference can be tied to the fact that Bed Bath & Beyond's store managers possess a great deal of autonomy in making purchasing decisions. To ensure that each store's merchandise assortment reflects local trends, reordering is conducted at the store level. Apparently, regional style preferences for textiles and home furnishings vary enough for this practice to benefit sales.

Largely because of its superior growth, Bed Bath & Beyond is also more profitable than Linens 'N Things. Solid sales growth enables the company to better cover fixed costs like rent expense and employee salaries. Also, the retailer doesn't use

distribution centers, as 10%-15% of each store is dedicated to receiving and processing. Merchandise is delivered directly to individual stores, which lowers freight costs.

However, direct-to-store shipments appear to be losing their cost-effectiveness as Bed Bath & Beyond increases its store base; gross margins are trending slightly downward. We think the company will probably need to construct distribution centers to maintain its margins as well as the efficient flow of merchandise from vendors to its growing network of stores.

Also, we're concerned that Bed Bath & Beyond's relatively loose strategy leaves senior management with less control over what's stocked in its growing number of stores. Without skilled store managers and appropriate oversight, this entrepreneurial procurement method could be a recipe for trouble. Skilled retail store managers can be tough to come by, possibly hindering the company's expansion progress.

For these reasons, we'd require a margin of safety to our fair value estimate before investing in this continuing growth story.

MORNINGSTAR® Stocks 500

BellSouth BLS

	Rating	Risk	Moat Size	Fair Value	Last Close	Yield %
	★★★	Med.	Narrow	$35.00	$25.87	3.0

Company Profile

BellSouth, a regional Bell holding company, provides communication and information services. It delivers local and long-distance phone service to about 67% of the population in 10 Southeastern states. It also provides cellular phone, e-mail, credit card validation, and paging services in the United States and abroad. In addition, the company publishes approximately 500 telephone directories. The company has ownership interests in foreign telecommunication companies throughout Europe, Asia, and South America.

Management

Chairman and CEO F. Duane Ackerman has served in various positions at the company since 1964. He was elevated to the top spot in 1997.

Strategy

Known for local phone service, BellSouth now wants to meet all of its customers' telecom needs, be they voice or data. The company is expanding and improving its wireless and data services, while striving for regulatory approval to offer long-distance services. Cost-cutting is also at the forefront.

1155 Peachtree Street N.E.   www.bellsouth.com
Atlanta, GA 30309-3610

Morningstar Grades

Growth [D]	1998	1999	2000	2001
Revenue %	12.5	9.1	3.7	-7.7
Earnings/Share %	8.5	1.1	23.9	-39.0
Book Value/Share %	6.6	-4.9	15.6	10.1
Dividends/Share %	1.4	4.1	0.0	0.0

Growth turned negative in 2002. The slow economy has compounded the effects of growing competition in the phone business. Maturation of the wireless market and weak corporate spending on new data services have hindered these former growth drivers.

Profitability [A]	1999	2000	2001	TTM
Return on Assets %	7.9	8.3	4.9	3.3
Oper Cash Flow $Mil	8,199	8,590	7,998	8,170
- Cap Spending $Mil	6,200	6,995	5,997	4,136
= Free Cash Flow $Mil	1,999	1,595	2,001	4,034

Reported profitability looks better than it actually is because of pension credits and asset write-downs. But even when these are taken into account, BellSouth is solidly profitable, with operating margins around 25% and returns on equity of 20%.

Financial Health [A-]	1999	2000	2001	09-02
Long-term Debt $Mil	9,113	12,463	15,014	12,287
Total Equity $Mil	14,815	16,912	18,597	17,435
Debt/Equity Ratio	0.6	0.7	0.8	0.7

Debt has risen sharply over the past few years to fund share buybacks and capital spending. Still, BellSouth generates plenty of cash to meet interest payments. A recent drop in capital spending has led to improved free cash flow.

Industry	Investment Style	Stock Type	Sector
Telecommunication Services	▦ Large Value	📈 High Yield	🏢 Telecom

Competition

	Market Cap $Mil	Debt/ Equity	12 Mo Trailing Sales $Mil	Price/Cash Flow	Return On Assets%	Total Return% 1 Yr	Total Return% 3 Yr
BellSouth	48,170	0.7	22,961	5.9	3.3	-30.4	-14.8
AT&T	20,115	0.8	48,821	1.8	-10.9	-27.7	-28.2
Alltel	15,837	1.1	7,837	6.5	5.5	-14.7	-11.1

Price Volatility

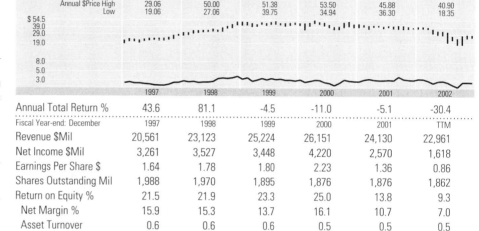

I Monthly Price High/Low — Relative Strength to S&P 500

Annual $Price High Low	29.06 19.06	50.00 27.06	51.38 39.75	53.50 34.94	45.88 36.30	40.90 18.35
	1997	1998	1999	2000	2001	2002

Annual Total Return %	43.6	81.1	-4.5	-11.0	-5.1	-30.4
Fiscal Year-end: December	1997	1998	1999	2000	2001	TTM
Revenue $Mil	20,561	23,123	25,224	26,151	24,130	22,961
Net Income $Mil	3,261	3,527	3,448	4,220	2,570	1,618
Earnings Per Share $	1.64	1.78	1.80	2.23	1.36	0.86
Shares Outstanding Mil	1,988	1,970	1,895	1,876	1,876	1,862
Return on Equity %	21.5	21.9	23.3	25.0	13.8	9.3
Net Margin %	15.9	15.3	13.7	16.1	10.7	7.0
Asset Turnover	0.6	0.6	0.6	0.5	0.5	0.5
Financial Leverage	2.4	2.4	2.9	3.0	2.8	2.9

Valuation Ratios	Stock	Rel to Industry	Rel to S&P 500
Price/Earnings	30.1	1.9	1.3
Price/Book	2.8	1.0	0.9
Price/Sales	2.1	1.3	1.0
Price/Cash Flow	5.9	1.1	0.4

Major Fund Holders	% of Fund Assets
Smith Barney Telecomm Income	23.56
ProFunds Ultra Telecommunications Inv	10.29
Fidelity Advisor Telecomm&Util Gr A	9.29
Fidelity Utilities	8.95

Morningstar's Take By Michael Hodel, 11-18-2002 Stock Price as of Analysis: $25.58

BellSouth faces several unknowns on the regulatory, technological, and competitive fronts. But the company owns an attractive set of assets that generate solid cash flow. Though the future won't look like the past, the stock is worth owning, in our opinion.

BellSouth's primary attributes stem from its huge local phone network, which is unrivaled in its ubiquity in the markets the company serves. Most homes and businesses still use traditional phones, and true competitive options are few because of the difficulty of replicating a network. Providing phone service thus generates fantastic cash flow. BellSouth's network is a direct connection to its customers; the company could use it to deliver other services down the road. The combination of a network that's difficult to replicate and the huge financial resources available to invest in that network makes for a big competitive advantage.

Competition is growing, though. Current regulation allows competitors like AT&T to buy services from BellSouth at wholesale rates. Also, a few cable companies have upgraded their networks to provide phone and Internet services, bypassing the local phone network entirely. After decades of steady growth, the number of BellSouth's retail phone lines in service has shrunk about 5% over the past year. Wholesale lines make up part of this decline, but line losses are pulling revenue lower, forcing BellSouth to cut operating expenses to maintain margins.

Operating cash flow hasn't grown much recently, but free cash flow has risen sharply, thanks to a reduction in capital spending. The company has used this cash flow to strengthen its financial position. However, the recent cuts have us wondering what the appropriate level of capital spending might be to maintain the business. The answer to this question is a huge determinant of BellSouth's fair value estimate. While the excessive spending of 1999 and 2000 (nearly 30% of fixed-line revenue) isn't likely to return, we doubt the current level (about 15% of revenue) is sustainable as markets become increasingly competitive.

BellSouth's other major unit, the Cingular Wireless venture with SBC, is a good business in a tough industry. Cingular's size allows it to earn decent margins today, but strong competition has hurt growth and profits. However, Cingular and its parents have the resources to make it through the current storm and generate value for shareholders.

Berkshire Hathaway B BRK.B

	Rating	Risk	Moat Size	Fair Value	Last Close	Yield %
	★★★★	Low	Wide	$2900.00	$2423.00	0.0

Company Profile

Berkshire Hathaway engages in various enterprises and investments through its subsidiaries. Its insurance and reinsurance business is conducted through 47 international subsidiaries including National Indemnity. Its Geico subsidiary writes private-passenger automobile insurance. Other subsidiaries underwrite multiple lines of casualty coverage, mainly for commercial accounts. Its investments include ownership interests in Coke and Gillette. Berkshire Hathaway and Leucadia offered to purchase 51% of troubled finance company Finova in the first quarter of 2001.

Management

Warren Buffett heads the firm and allocates capital to its subsidiaries. Operating decisions are made by the respective managers of those businesses. Buffett makes investment decisions in consultation with Charles Munger, the vice chairman.

Strategy

Berkshire Hathaway's long-term goal is to maximize the average annual increase in intrinsic business value. The company does not measure success by its size but by per-share progress. It seeks to increase per-share value faster than the average large U.S. company. Buffett uses book value as a good proxy for success. This has increased 22.6% on average over the past 36 years.

1440 Kiewit Plaza   www.berkshirehathaway.com
Omaha, NE 68131

Morningstar Grades

Growth [A]	1998	1999	2000	2001
Revenue %	32.6	73.7	41.5	10.8
Earnings/Share %	19.0	-54.7	113.1	-76.2
Book Value/Share %	45.9	-17.1	6.6	-6.3
Dividends/Share %	NMF	NMF	NMF	NMF

Sales have grown rapidly over the past five years, thanks to the 1998 acquisition of General Re. Price hikes and more insurance policies--as well as acquisitions--should boost sales further.

Profitability [B+]	1999	2000	2001	TTM
Return on Assets %	1.2	2.5	0.5	1.9
Oper Cash Flow $Mil	2,200	2,947	6,574	—
- Cap Spending $Mil	—	—	—	—
= Free Cash Flow $Mil	—	—	—	—

Berkshire's quarterly net income is a meaningless measure of performance because of the timing of investment gains. The businesses Berkshire owns are extremely profitable, however, and boast returns on equity in excess of 15%.

Financial Health [A]	1999	2000	2001	09-02
Long-term Debt $Mil	—	—	—	—
Total Equity $Mil	57,761	61,724	57,950	62,617
Debt/Equity Ratio	—	—	—	—

This powerhouse sports the 22nd-largest equity base among U.S. companies--based on market value of equity--and has little debt. It finances most of its investments through the float--that is, the premiums received before paying out claims.

	Industry	Investment Style	Stock Type	Sector
	Insurance (General)	▦ Large Growth	↗ Classic Growth	$ Financial Services

Competition

	Market Cap $Mil	Debt/ Equity	12 Mo Trailing Sales $Mil	Price/Cash Flow	Return On Assets%	Total Return% 1 Yr	3 Yr
Berkshire Hathaway B	111,526	—	39,133	—	1.9	-4.0	12.5
American International Gr	150,907	—	66,823	—	1.4	-26.9	-4.0
Allstate	26,004	—	29,350	—	—	—	—

Price Volatility

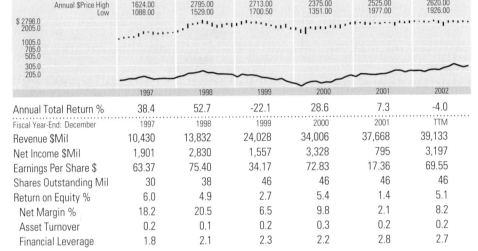

Monthly Price High/Low — Relative Strength to S&P 500						
Annual $Price High Low	1624.00 1088.00	2795.00 1529.00	2713.00 1700.50	2375.00 1351.00	2525.00 1977.00	2620.00 1926.00
	1997	1998	1999	2000	2001	2002

Annual Total Return %	38.4	52.7	-22.1	28.6	7.3	-4.0

Fiscal Year-End: December	1997	1998	1999	2000	2001	TTM
Revenue $Mil	10,430	13,832	24,028	34,006	37,668	39,133
Net Income $Mil	1,901	2,830	1,557	3,328	795	3,197
Earnings Per Share $	63.37	75.40	34.17	72.83	17.36	69.55
Shares Outstanding Mil	30	38	46	46	46	46
Return on Equity %	6.0	4.9	2.7	5.4	1.4	5.1
Net Margin %	18.2	20.5	6.5	9.8	2.1	8.2
Asset Turnover	0.2	0.1	0.2	0.3	0.2	0.2
Financial Leverage	1.8	2.1	2.3	2.2	2.8	2.7

Valuation Ratios	Stock	Rel to Industry	Rel to S&P 500
Price/Earnings	34.8	1.0	1.5
Price/Book	1.8	1.0	0.6
Price/Sales	2.9	1.0	1.4
Price/Cash Flow	—	—	—

Major Fund Holders	% of Fund Assets
New Market	28.45
Fairholme Fund, The	23.82
Midas Special Equities	13.39
RS Contrarian	6.02

Morningstar's Take By Travis Pascavis, 12-10-2002 Stock Price as of Analysis: $2351.00

Berkshire Hathaway is a collection of wide-moat companies, and we would be buyers of the shares at just a 20% discount to our fair value estimate.

The most important businesses to Berkshire Hathaway are property and casualty insurance for consumers as well as other insurance companies (known as reinsurance). Although these types of insurance can produce lumpy results, their economics are excellent. Insurance companies can invest the so-called float generated from receiving premiums in advance of any payout of claims.

In this regard, Berkshire has a structural advantage over many other insurance companies. The company has special regulatory approval from the Nebraska insurance department to invest its float in equities. Berkshire received this preferential treatment because of its great investing record and its very low reliance on debt. It would take a long time before another competitor could duplicate this performance record, so we feel comfortable that this competitive advantage will continue.

However, it isn't enough for Berkshire to be able to invest its float in high-returning equities relative to bonds (most insurance companies' investment of choice). It must also obtain this float at a reasonable cost. The cost of float (underwriting expenses divided by premiums earned) has been the black eye at Berkshire for the past couple of years at unacceptable levels of 12.8% in 2001 and 6% in 2000. We think a return to more conservative underwriting should help lead these costs back to around zero. Moreover, the company is now charging for terrorism risks.

Operating companies (as opposed to insurance companies and investments) are also a big part of Berkshire's business, accounting for nearly 43% of revenue in 2001, up from 21% in 1996. A fine example of one of its operating businesses with a wide economic moat is NetJets, a sort of time-share for private jets. NetJets accounts for about half of the fractional jet ownership industry, making it the most attractive option in the business for a number of reasons. For example, the company has 300 planes throughout the United States that can be ready for use by a customer on very short notice.

Although Berkshire's businesses may produce uneven results every now and then, its competitive advantages should help it earn excess returns over the long haul. Berkshire also has a number of excellent managers who are aligned with shareholders, and Buffett himself has more than 99% of his net worth invested in Berkshire stock.

MᴏRNINGSTAR® Stocks 500

Best Buy BBY

	Rating	Risk	Moat Size	Fair Value	Last Close	Yield %
	★★★	Med.	Narrow	$30.00	$24.15	0.0

Company Profile

Best Buy is a consumer electronics discount retailer. The company's approximately 413 stores, primarily located in the central United States, offer name-brand video and audio equipment, including mobile electronics; personal computers and other home office products; major appliances; and entertainment software, like compact discs, prerecorded audio and video cassettes, and computer software. In addition, the company operates an in-house advertising agency. Best Buy acquired Musicland Stores in 2001.

Management

Management has a lot of industry experience. Richard M. Schulze founded Best Buy in 1966 and is chairman. He stepped down as CEO in June 2002 and was succeeded by president Brad Anderson, who has been with the company since 1973.

Strategy

Best Buy provides a huge selection of electronics and related products at discount prices. Noncommissioned store personnel assist with complex items but leave simple products to self-service. Efficient inventory management has been a top priority, and has paid off for the firm. Recently, the company has expanded externally by acquiring Musicland and Future Shop.

7075 Flying Cloud Drive   www.bestbuy.com
Eden Prairie, MN 55344

Morningstar Grades

Growth [A+]	1999	2000	2001	2002
Revenue %	20.7	24.1	22.7	27.9
Earnings/Share %	123.9	58.3	14.1	42.7
Book Value/Share %	57.2	4.5	66.3	37.2
Dividends/Share %	NMF	NMF	NMF	NMF

Sales growth has been explosive, even with consumer spending weak throughout most of the economy. However, we expect growth to slow over the next few years. Growth comes primarily from new stores.

Profitability [B+]	2000	2001	2002	TTM
Return on Assets %	11.6	8.2	7.7	3.1
Oper Cash Flow $Mil	776	808	1,578	835
- Cap Spending $Mil	361	658	627	809
= Free Cash Flow $Mil	415	150	951	26

Best Buy is substantially more profitable than its closest peer, Circuit City CC. Management has turned its attention to cutting costs to compensate for weaker consumer spending. There is still fat to be trimmed from recent acquisitions, too.

Financial Health [A]	2000	2001	2002	08-02
Long-term Debt $Mil	15	181	813	821
Total Equity $Mil	1,096	1,822	2,521	2,381
Debt/Equity Ratio	0.0	0.1	0.3	0.3

Best Buy's balance sheet is still fairly healthy despite the accumulation of substantial debt during fiscal 2002. An extended downturn in consumer spending could hamper the company's ability to add stores without piling on more debt.

Industry	Investment Style	Stock Type	Sector
Electronics Stores	Large Core	↗ Classic Growth	Consumer Services

Competition	Market Cap $Mil	Debt/ Equity	12 Mo Trailing Sales $Mil	Price/Cash Flow	Return On Assets%	Total Return% 1 Yr	3 Yr
Best Buy	7,766	0.3	21,330	9.3	3.1	-51.4	-14.2
Amazon.com	7,206	NMF	3,620	47.8	-9.8	74.6	-38.7
RadioShack	3,181	0.9	4,595	5.3	8.0	-37.1	-29.2

Price Volatility | Monthly Price High/Low   — Relative Strength to S&P 500

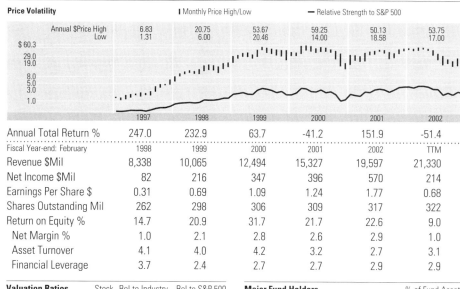

	Annual $Price High Low	6.83 1.31	20.75 6.00	53.67 20.46	59.25 14.00	50.13 18.58	53.75 17.00
		1997	1998	1999	2000	2001	2002

Annual Total Return %	247.0	232.9	63.7	-41.2	151.9	-51.4
Fiscal Year-end: February	1998	1999	2000	2001	2002	TTM
Revenue $Mil	8,338	10,065	12,494	15,327	19,597	21,330
Net Income $Mil	82	216	347	396	570	214
Earnings Per Share $	0.31	0.69	1.09	1.24	1.77	0.68
Shares Outstanding Mil	262	298	306	309	317	322
Return on Equity %	14.7	20.9	31.7	21.7	22.6	9.0
Net Margin %	1.0	2.1	2.8	2.6	2.9	1.0
Asset Turnover	4.1	4.0	4.2	3.2	2.7	3.1
Financial Leverage	3.7	2.4	2.7	2.7	2.9	2.9

Valuation Ratios	Stock	Rel to Industry	Rel to S&P 500
Price/Earnings	35.7	1.0	1.5
Price/Book	3.3	1.0	1.0
Price/Sales	0.4	1.0	0.2
Price/Cash Flow	9.3	1.0	0.7

Major Fund Holders	% of Fund Assets
Fidelity Advisor Strategic Growth A	4.85
MassMutual Instl Focused Value S	4.15
IPS IFund	3.96
Dreyfus MidCap Value Plus	3.44

Morningstar's Take By Joseph Beaulieu, 11-19-2002 Stock Price as of Analysis: $23.09

Assuming that Best Buy continues on its current course, we think its shares are worth about $30.

The company dominates home electronics and entertainment software retailing; an investment in Best Buy is an implicit bet on the continued growth of these two businesses. We think this is a pretty good bet. Americans have a long record of embracing new gadgetry and entertainment technology, and no company is doing a better job of capitalizing on that trend. Since 1997, Best Buy has nearly doubled its number of stores, from 272 to around 550, and revenue has nearly tripled. (A small part of this revenue growth is from acquisitions, but more than 90% of the company's revenue comes from Best Buy stores.)

Sales at existing stores are showing low-single-digit growth. This means the company will have to rely on expansion of the Best Buy chain and on acquisitions for revenue and earnings growth.

In the near term, growth will probably come from expansions. Suffering from a slight case of indigestion from its recent buying binge (Sam Goody/Musicland and Canadian consumer electronics chain Future Shop), management has announced an acquisition moratorium. But even though management has indicated that it is going to cut back

on spending, it still intends to open new Best Buy stores near its historical pace.

Best Buy will probably find it difficult to substantially increase revenue by adding stores. For one thing, the law of diminishing returns is at work: Adding 60 stores per year on the firm's current base will make for less growth than when that base was much smaller. Also, it is likely that management will have to consider less-ideal locations for new stores and open smaller stores; there is already some evidence of this. We expect the average annual revenue of new stores to fall below the current per-store average of $38 million.

There are many things that could go wrong with the Best Buy story. Management could go overboard with acquisitions. Long-term economic weakness could keep a lid on consumer confidence and spending. Another terrorist attack could deal a sharp blow to consumer spending. But assuming no major economic or geopolitical shocks in the immediate future, we expect Best Buy to continue on its current track.

Biogen BGEN

	Rating	Risk	Moat Size	Fair Value	Last Close	Yield %
	★★	High	Narrow	$40.00	$40.06	0.0

Industry	Investment Style	Stock Type	Sector
Biotechnology	Mid Growth	Classic Growth	Healthcare

Company Profile

Biogen develops and manufactures pharmaceuticals through genetic engineering. The company produces Avonex, the leading multiple sclerosis drug in the United States. Biogen is also developing drugs for congestive heart failure, psoriasis, inflammatory diseases, autoimmune diseases, and transplant rejection. The company markets its products in the United States and overseas. Avonex revenue accounts for nearly all of the company's revenue, with royalties from several other drugs marketed by Merck, GlaxoSmithKline, and Schering-Plough making up the balance.

Management

CEO James Mullen, the successor of James Vincent, assumed leadership of the firm in June 2000 and became chairman of the board in 2002. Mullen oversaw the launch of Avonex in Europe. Three fourths of the board is outside directors.

Strategy

Biogen is striving to wrest as much growth as possible out of blockbuster multiple sclerosis drug Avonex. It's counting on two late-stage drugs--psoriasis treatment Amevive and second-generation MS treatment Antegren--to provide growth beyond 2003. The company is also looking to in-license products to fill its new-drug pipeline.

14 Cambridge Center   www.biogen.com
Cambridge, MA 02142

Competition

Competition	Market Cap $Mil	Debt/Equity	12 Mo Trailing Sales $Mil	Price/Cash Flow	Return On Assets%	Total Return% 1 Yr	Total Return% 3 Yr
Biogen	5,972	0.0	1,128	26.6	11.5	-30.2	-18.2
Amgen	61,986	0.2	4,881	31.7	-7.1	-14.4	-6.0
Genentech	17,067	0.0	2,541	28.3	0.2	-38.9	-19.2

Price Volatility

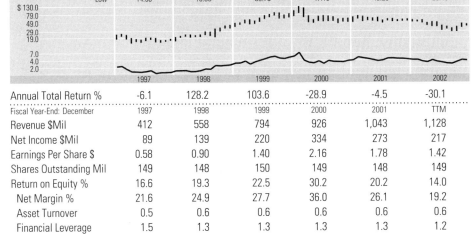

	1997	1998	1999	2000	2001	2002
Annual $Price High	26.38	43.75	90.44	129.00	75.00	58.30
Low	14.50	16.38	38.75	47.13	48.29	28.43
Annual Total Return %	-6.1	128.2	103.6	-28.9	-4.5	-30.1

Fiscal Year-End: December	1997	1998	1999	2000	2001	TTM
Revenue $Mil	412	558	794	926	1,043	1,128
Net Income $Mil	89	139	220	334	273	217
Earnings Per Share $	0.58	0.90	1.40	2.16	1.78	1.42
Shares Outstanding Mil	149	148	150	149	148	149
Return on Equity %	16.6	19.3	22.5	30.2	20.2	14.0
Net Margin %	21.6	24.9	27.7	36.0	26.1	19.2
Asset Turnover	0.5	0.6	0.6	0.6	0.6	0.6
Financial Leverage	1.5	1.3	1.3	1.3	1.3	1.2

Valuation Ratios

Valuation Ratios	Stock	Rel to Industry	Rel to S&P 500
Price/Earnings	28.2	0.6	1.2
Price/Book	3.9	1.1	1.2
Price/Sales	5.3	0.4	2.6
Price/Cash Flow	26.6	0.8	2.0

Major Fund Holders

Major Fund Holders	% of Fund Assets
Fidelity Advisor Biotechnology A	11.05
Fidelity Select Biotechnology	10.97
PIMCO RCM Biotechnology D	5.11
John Hancock Biotechnology A	4.61

Morningstar Grades

Growth [B-]	1998	1999	2000	2001
Revenue %	35.4	42.5	16.6	12.6
Earnings/Share %	55.2	55.6	54.3	-17.6
Book Value/Share %	33.7	33.4	15.2	22.9
Dividends/Share %	NMF	NMF	NMF	NMF

Avonex has driven Biogen's annual sales past $1 billion, but new competition and high inventory levels at wholesalers have slowed revenue growth. The company is depending on new-product launches to reach sales of $2 billion by 2005 or 2006.

Profitability [A+]	1999	2000	2001	TTM
Return on Assets %	17.3	23.3	15.8	11.5
Oper Cash Flow $Mil	364	366	316	225
- Cap Spending $Mil	83	194	191	221
= Free Cash Flow $Mil	281	172	126	3

Operating margins have been in the mid-30s, placing Biogen in the upper echelon of profitable biotechs. While margins will decline through 2003 as the company brings new products to market, we expect profits to remain strong.

Financial Health [A+]	1999	2000	2001	09-02
Long-term Debt $Mil	52	47	42	39
Total Equity $Mil	980	1,106	1,349	1,543
Debt/Equity Ratio	0.1	0.0	0.0	0.0

With very little debt and $830 million in cash and securities, the company is in excellent financial health. Free cash flow (cash from operations minus capital spending) has been greater than 16% of sales for the past five years in a row.

Morningstar's Take By Jill Kiersky, 11-25-2002 Stock Price as of Analysis: $46.23

Now that Biogen's Crohn's treatment has failed in clinical trials and sales growth of multiple sclerosis drug Avonex has come to a halt, we'd like the stock to trade at a big discount to our fair value estimate before we would consider investing.

While not the most innovative biotech company, Biogen is among the more successful. Its flagship product, Avonex, has enjoyed impressive 66% compound annual sales growth over the past five years and surpassed $1 billion in sales in 2001--one of a handful of biotech drugs to reach this level. Gross margins remained strong at 87% over the same period. Operating margins have hovered around 35%, but have slipped recently as the company attempts to fend off new competition and beef up research and development.

Avonex lost its pseudomonopoly in March 2002, and competition from Serono's Rebif is coming on strong. Rebif has 30% of the European multiple sclerosis market and is making headway in the U.S. market, where Biogen's share has dropped more than 10 percentage points since Rebif's approval. In addition, margins could slip as Biogen works to prove it's not a one-hit wonder.

The company now has the opportunity to repeat its success with two late-stage products. The first is

Antegren, a new type of treatment that we expect to continue Biogen's strong MS franchise. Biogen is also gearing up for Amevive, its psoriasis treatment. With the Food and Drug Administration advisory committee's recent recommendation for approval, Amevive should be the first drug approved to treat patients in the $2 billion psoriasis market.

But neither of these drugs is a slam dunk. Even if Antegren is approved, it won't help profits until 2005, and Biogen will split the profits with partner Elan. As for Amevive, with substitute products and similar therapies like Amgen's Enbrel and Johnson & Johnson's Remicade already on the market for other indications, Biogen will have to put up quite a fight to achieve the strong sales it projects.

If either product falters, the company doesn't have much to cushion the blow. Aside from these drugs, Biogen is down to a handful of therapies in early-stage testing, since its Crohn's treatment, CDP-571, proved disappointing in clinical trials. The company has enough cash to purchase or in-license late-stage products, but with this much risk, we'd like a significant margin of safety before buying shares.

MORNINGSTAR® Stocks 500

Biomet BMET

	Rating	Risk	Moat Size	Fair Value	Last Close	Yield %
	★★★	Med.	Wide	$28.00	$28.66	0.3

Industry	Investment Style	Stock Type	Sector
Medical Equipment	Mid Growth	Classic Growth	Healthcare

Company Profile

Biomet manufactures products used in orthopedic surgery and therapy. Its products include reconstructive equipment, trauma-treatment devices, orthopedic supports, surgical instruments, arthroscopic devices, and general operating-room supplies. The company's Electro-Biology subsidiary manufactures electrical bone-growth and spinal-fusion stimulators, which generate pulsed electromagnetic signals to aid in healing fractures. Biomet markets its products under brand names like Biomet, AOA, Arthrotek, Walter Lorenz, and EBI in the United States and abroad.

Management

Three of the four founders are still managing the firm, including Dane Miller, president and CEO. Miller's compensation totaled around $500,000 (far less than his peers' compensation) in the year ended May 2002, and he doesn't receive bonus options.

Strategy

Biomet is spending aggressively to continue developing innovative products. It's also attempting to expand the range of medical conditions its products can treat. That way, the company will maintain its above-average net margins, as its products compete on design and quality rather than on price.

56 East Bell Drive
Warsaw, IN 46582

www.biomet.com

Competition

	Market Cap $Mil	Debt/ Equity	12 Mo Trailing Sales $Mil	Price/Cash Flow	Return On Assets%	Total Return% 1 Yr	Total Return% 3 Yr
Biomet	7,445	—	1,237	36.0	16.7	-6.9	22.0
Johnson & Johnson	159,452	0.1	35,120	18.0	16.3	-7.9	8.0
Stryker	13,276	0.4	2,892	26.3	11.6	15.2	25.9

Price Volatility

Annual $Price High Low	12.00 6.33	18.31 10.50	20.33 10.95	27.83 12.06	34.36 20.46	33.26 21.75

	1997	1998	1999	2000	2001	2002
Annual Total Return %	70.3	57.7	-0.3	49.4	17.1	-6.9

Fiscal Year-end: May	1998	1999	2000	2001	2002	TTM
Revenue $Mil	706	831	924	1,031	1,192	1,237
Net Income $Mil	128	125	174	198	240	250
Earnings Per Share $	0.49	0.47	0.65	0.73	0.88	0.92
Shares Outstanding Mil	259	260	263	267	269	260
Return on Equity %	19.2	15.7	18.4	17.2	20.4	22.1
Net Margin %	18.1	15.0	18.8	19.2	20.1	20.2
Asset Turnover	0.8	0.7	0.8	0.7	0.8	0.8
Financial Leverage	1.3	1.4	1.3	1.3	1.3	1.3

Valuation Ratios	Stock	Rel to Industry	Rel to S&P 500
Price/Earnings	31.2	1.0	1.3
Price/Book	6.6	1.0	2.1
Price/Sales	6.0	1.3	3.0
Price/Cash Flow	36.0	1.5	2.7

Major Fund Holders	% of Fund Assets
Fidelity Select Medical Equip/Systems	6.06
State Farm Growth	4.82
Brandywine Blue	3.99
Waddell & Reed Adv New Concepts A	3.69

Morningstar Grades

Growth [B]	1999	2000	2001	2002
Revenue %	17.7	11.2	11.6	15.6
Earnings/Share %	-3.4	38.3	12.3	20.5
Book Value/Share %	17.8	17.9	20.0	2.0
Dividends/Share %	14.1	12.6	22.2	22.8

Biomet's revenue growth in the past five years has been average relative to its peers, but is showing signs of revival. The faster growth rate is in part due to new product innovations and price hikes.

Profitability [A+]	2000	2001	2002	TTM
Return on Assets %	14.3	13.3	15.8	16.7
Oper Cash Flow $Mil	138	191	184	207
- Cap Spending $Mil	43	35	62	60
= Free Cash Flow $Mil	95	155	122	146

Thanks to its generous and stable margins, Biomet is one of the most profitable companies in the medical equipment industry. Its gross margins exceed 70% and the net margin surpassed 20% in the year ending May 2002.

Financial Health [A+]	2000	2001	2002	08-02
Long-term Debt $Mil	—	—	—	—
Total Equity $Mil	943	1,146	1,176	1,129
Debt/Equity Ratio	—	—	—	—

Biomet is in top financial condition. It has little debt and cash on hand covers its current liabilities. In addition, the company generates positive free cash flow despite increasing capital expenditures.

Morningstar's Take By Jill Kiersky, 11-22-2002 Stock Price as of Analysis: $29.29

Biomet's strong competitive position has led to topnotch returns on invested capital, averaging 16% over the past five years. We think that the firm can continue this, and that the stock could be a good bet if it dropped 30% below our fair value estimate.

Biomet's superior financial performance stems from the company's ability to charge hefty prices for the artificial joints--hips, elbows, knees--that it manufactures. In fact, the firm has been flexing its pricing power over its customers as of late. In the year ending May 2002, the average selling price for the company's reconstructive products--which make up 60% of sales--rose about 5% over the prior year, and we expect 3%-4% price increases over the next several years.

Thanks to the high price tag for its products, Biomet's gross margins exceed 70% and operating margins have topped 30%. This is in part due to the company's high-margin product mix relative to competitors like Stryker and Zimmer, whose operating margins are in the mid-20s. We expect the company to maintain its superior profitability in the near term as Zimmer, the company's largest pure-play orthopedic device rival, spends its cash to develop or acquire additional products that will compete with Biomet's full orthopedic product line.

Biomet and the entire orthopedic industry should continue to benefit from an aging population. People older than 65 need joint-replacement products--Biomet's specialty--nearly 3 times more often than younger folks do. While this trend gives a boost to the entire industry, we think Biomet has been stealing share from a struggling rival, Sulzer Medica, now a part of Centerpulse and rumored to be on the selling block. However, most of the low-hanging fruit seems to have already been plucked, and further share gains may be more challenging.

The company is looking for additional growth to come from its expansion into Japan, a large and growing market once thought to provide high margins. However, the country is cracking down on excessive medical spending. As Biomet's selling, general, and administrative expenses have increased substantially, making money on its investment may prove challenging. The company's ability to generate strong profits using its own salesforce does give us some confidence, though.

We think Biomet's experienced management team can handle the challenges ahead. But to be sure, we would want a moderate discount to our fair value estimate before investing.

BJ's Wholesale Club BJ

	Rating ★★★	Risk Med.	Moat Size None	Fair Value $25.00	Last Close $18.30	Yield % 0.0

Company Profile

BJ's Wholesale Club operates 118 warehouse club stores in the Eastern United States. The stores sell brand-name merchandise at prices that are generally lower than those at traditional wholesalers, discount retailers, supermarkets, and specialty retail operators. The stores have an average size of 112,000 square feet and carry an average of approximately 5,000 active stock-keeping units. Food sales account for about 59% of total sales.

Management

Most of the current top management has been with BJ's for at least 10 years. President and CEO John Nugent has held his titles since 1997, and has been with the company since 1993.

Strategy

The company is the smallest of the three big players in the warehouse club market. It seeks to differentiate itself by offering a much greater variety of goods than its competitors, and by focusing on the retail customer more than the small-business customer. It has positioned itself as a grocery store alternative.

One Mercer Road
Natick, MA 01760
www.bjs.com

Morningstar Grades

Growth [B+]	1999	2000	2001	2002
Revenue %	10.1	18.4	17.3	7.0
Earnings/Share %	NMF	79.3	20.4	-37.3
Book Value/Share %	NMF	20.0	17.2	3.4
Dividends/Share %	NMF	NMF	NMF	NMF

Five-year sales growth has averaged about 13% annually. Net income growth over that time has been double that. We don't believe sales and earnings growth can get to that level any longer, however.

Profitability [A]	2000	2001	2002	TTM
Return on Assets %	9.8	10.7	5.8	8.9
Oper Cash Flow $Mil	206	156	212	145
- Cap Spending $Mil	87	99	166	149
= Free Cash Flow $Mil	118	57	46	-4

Given its business model, BJ's is surprisingly profitable. Its returns on equity around 20% are most likely gone for good, and will probably be around 12%.

Financial Health [B+]	2000	2001	2002	10-02
Long-term Debt $Mil	2	2	64	17
Total Equity $Mil	577	665	687	694
Debt/Equity Ratio	0.0	0.0	0.1	0.0

The balance sheet is in excellent shape, with no debt to speak of.

Industry Discount Stores	Investment Style Small Core	Stock Type Classic Growth	Sector Consumer Services

Competition	Market Cap $Mil	Debt/ Equity	12 Mo Trailing Sales $Mil	Price/Cash Flow	Return On Assets%	Total Return% 1 Yr	3 Yr
BJ's Wholesale Club	1,270	0.0	5,730	8.8	8.9	-58.5	-18.5
Wal-Mart Stores	223,388	0.5	233,651	18.9	8.0	-11.8	-7.3
Costco Wholesale	12,788	0.2	38,763	12.6	6.0	-36.8	-12.6

Price Volatility   ▌ Monthly Price High/Low   — Relative Strength to S&P 500

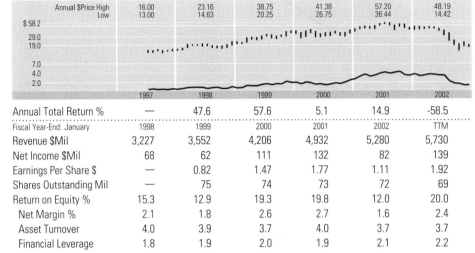

Annual $Price High Low	16.00 13.00	23.16 14.63	38.75 20.25	41.38 26.75	57.20 36.44	48.19 14.42

	1997	1998	1999	2000	2001	2002
Annual Total Return %	—	47.6	57.6	5.1	14.9	-58.5

Fiscal Year-End: January	1998	1999	2000	2001	2002	TTM
Revenue $Mil	3,227	3,552	4,206	4,932	5,280	5,730
Net Income $Mil	68	62	111	132	82	139
Earnings Per Share $	—	0.82	1.47	1.77	1.11	1.92
Shares Outstanding Mil	—	75	74	73	72	69
Return on Equity %	15.3	12.9	19.3	19.8	12.0	20.0
Net Margin %	2.1	1.8	2.6	2.7	1.6	2.4
Asset Turnover	4.0	3.9	3.7	4.0	3.7	3.7
Financial Leverage	1.8	1.9	2.0	1.9	2.1	2.2

Valuation Ratios	Stock	Rel to Industry	Rel to S&P 500
Price/Earnings	9.5	0.3	0.4
Price/Book	1.8	0.3	0.6
Price/Sales	0.2	0.2	0.1
Price/Cash Flow	8.8	0.5	0.7

Major Fund Holders	% of Fund Assets
Oppenheimer MidCap A	4.77
Eaton Vance Small-Cap Value A	2.62
Eaton Vance Tax-Mgd Small-Cap Value C	2.31
Old Westbury Capital Opportunities	2.24

Morningstar's Take   By Mike Porter, 12-24-2002 Stock Price as of Analysis: $17.29

As the small-fry in the world of warehouse clubs, BJ's Wholesale Club is finding the going increasingly tough. We'd want close to a 50% discount to our fair value estimate before investing.

Like rivals Costco and Wal-Mart's Sam's Club, BJ's has made its name by selling goods--mainly in bulk--at a low price. Pay your annual fee, and you can get groceries, electronics, jewelry, tires, and lots of other things on the cheap. The warehouse club format has proved very popular over the years, and all three companies have had a good deal of success with it.

Until now, BJ's has done an admirable job differentiating itself from its bigger competitors, knowing that it had to do so to survive. It has mainly marketed itself as a grocery store alternative, a claim neither of its rivals can make. Whereas a trip through the aisles at Costco can look very different from week to week, not a lot changes at a typical BJ's store. The company stocks a few thousand more items, or stock-keeping units, than other warehouse clubs (though not nearly as many items as most grocery chains) with the same number of square feet.

For the number of stores BJ's has now, this strategy works. We're concerned about its viability over the long term, however. We're not sure how broad the appeal is in paying an annual fee to be able to buy groceries in bulk at a discount, especially among individual consumers, whom BJ's targets. (Its rivals go after small-business customers in addition to individuals.)

About 50% of BJ's clubs are in close proximity to those of competitors, and that percentage is almost certain to increase. As it moves into more markets where it is not known and where Costco and Sam's Club already have a presence, BJ's will have to give folks a reason to switch allegiances. One method for enticing people is to offer a one-year free membership. That's a big deal, as membership fees go straight to the bottom line at the warehouse clubs, and are an important component of the business model. In fact, these fees make up about 70% of BJ's operating income. Profitability could continue to get squeezed if this trend continues.

At some price, almost any stock can look attractive. We put BJ's in that category. It will never be the market leader, but then it won't be going out of business anytime soon, either. We'd be interested in the shares in the $13-$14 range.

MORNINGSTAR® Stocks 500

Black & Decker BDK

	Rating	Risk	Moat Size	Fair Value	Last Close	Yield %
	★★	Med.	None	$44.00	$42.89	1.1

Industry	Investment Style	Stock Type	Sector
Electric Equipment	☒ Mid Core	⟳ Cyclical	✿ Industrial Mats

Company Profile

Black & Decker is the world's largest manufacturer of power tools and accessories, primarily sold under the Black & Decker and DeWalt trademarks. The firm is also a leading maker of lawn and garden equipment, as well as plumbing products (under the Price Pfister brand), security hardware (Kwikset) and fasteners, mostly for the automotive industry (Emhart). The firm's power tools segment constituted 72% of total sales in 2001, and 65% of overall revenue was generated in the United States. Black & Decker sold its household, recreational, and glass product businesses in 1998.

Management

Chairman and CEO Nolan Archibald, 58, has been running Black & Decker since 1985. In that time, he's turned the company around twice, with a large, unfortunate acquisition (Emhart) between. He plans to remain firmly in charge until age 65.

Strategy

Black & Decker has built a reputation for continually introducing new products, supported by aggressive marketing, to gain market share. Its highly profitable DeWalt brand has grabbed a huge share of the domestic tool market since 1992, a feat the company now hopes to replicate abroad. The firm is relocating and reducing its manufacturing capacity to improve profitability.

701 East Joppa Road   www.bdk.com
Towson, MD 21286

Morningstar Grades

Growth [C]	1998	1999	2000	2001
Revenue %	-7.7	-0.9	0.9	-5.0
Earnings/Share %	NMF	NMF	-1.8	-60.2
Book Value/Share %	-66.3	45.1	-9.6	12.8
Dividends/Share %	0.0	0.0	0.0	0.0

Growth in core products has been solid in recent years, averaging in the midsingle digits. Last year's recession and inventory rollbacks by retailers cut sales 5%, but improved results in the second quarter point to a resumption of growth.

Profitability [C-]	1999	2000	2001	TTM
Return on Assets %	7.5	6.9	2.7	3.2
Oper Cash Flow $Mil	376	350	379	513
- Cap Spending $Mil	171	200	135	105
= Free Cash Flow $Mil	204	150	244	408

Amid declining sales in 2001, Black & Decker's gains in profitability of the late 1990s came under assault. However, unexpected sales increases in the second and third quarters led to better plant utilization and substantially higher earnings.

Financial Health [C+]	1999	2000	2001	09-02
Long-term Debt $Mil	847	799	1,191	927
Total Equity $Mil	801	692	751	919
Debt/Equity Ratio	1.1	1.2	1.6	1.0

Black & Decker's debt/capital of 58% is a tad high by industrial standards, but this is mostly the result of heavy share buybacks. Free cash flow has improved sharply in the past two years, thanks to falling receivable and inventory levels.

Competition

	Market Cap $Mil	Debt/ Equity	12 Mo Trailing Sales $Mil	Price/Cash Flow	Return On Assets%	Total Return% 1 Yr	3 Yr
Black & Decker	3,455	1.0	4,444	6.7	3.2	14.9	-3.5
Emerson Electric	21,411	0.5	13,838	11.8	0.8	-8.3	-1.1
Masco	10,357	0.7	9,103	9.4	4.6	-12.1	-2.8

Price Volatility

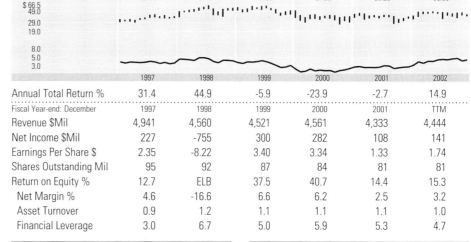

	Monthly Price High/Low			— Relative Strength to S&P 500		
Annual $Price High	43.44	65.50	64.63	52.38	46.95	50.50
Low	29.63	37.94	41.00	27.56	28.26	35.00
	1997	1998	1999	2000	2001	2002

Annual Total Return %	31.4	44.9	-5.9	-23.9	-2.7	14.9
Fiscal Year-end: December	1997	1998	1999	2000	2001	TTM
Revenue $Mil	4,941	4,560	4,521	4,561	4,333	4,444
Net Income $Mil	227	-755	300	282	108	141
Earnings Per Share $	2.35	-8.22	3.40	3.34	1.33	1.74
Shares Outstanding Mil	95	92	87	84	81	81
Return on Equity %	12.7	ELB	37.5	40.7	14.4	15.3
Net Margin %	4.6	-16.6	6.6	6.2	2.5	3.2
Asset Turnover	0.9	1.2	1.1	1.1	1.1	1.0
Financial Leverage	3.0	6.7	5.0	5.9	5.3	4.7

Valuation Ratios	Stock	Rel to Industry	Rel to S&P 500
Price/Earnings	24.6	1.5	1.0
Price/Book	3.8	1.0	1.2
Price/Sales	0.8	0.4	0.4
Price/Cash Flow	6.7	0.8	0.5

Major Fund Holders	% of Fund Assets
CDC Nvest Select A	4.23
Diamond Hill Focus A	3.26
Ariel Appreciation	3.17
Excelsior Value & Restructuring	3.15

Morningstar's Take   By Josh Peters, 12-12-2002   Stock Price as of Analysis: $42.00

Despite a stable of attractive brand names, Black & Decker fails to earn good returns on investment. Restructuring may keep returns from sinking further, but we'd consider buying only at a 50% or larger discount to our fair value estimate.

Black & Decker made something of a comeback in the late 1990s. It improved operating margins by shedding a diverse group of underperforming businesses and redirecting investment to its core business of power tools. Reacting to weak financial returns, it squeezed funds out of working capital to generate record free cash flow.

But while Black & Decker has established a strong customer following with the DeWalt brand and a slew of innovative new products, we have trouble identifying a sustainable competitive advantage for the firm as a whole. Return on invested capital averaged a pitiful 8% between 1997 and 2001, a strong period for unit volume growth generally--and that excludes $300 million in restructuring charges.

The consumer hardware and tool industry has also become quite unfavorable, in our view, with much of the power now in the hands of big-box home-improvement retailers, led by Home Depot. Their soaring market share enables them to dictate price, payment terms, and inventory levels at manufacturers' expense. And when the big-box retailers aren't pressuring their suppliers for cutbacks, they're taking products off their shelves entirely to make room for private-label products from Asia. Black & Decker's recently announced loss of $50 million in Price Pfister business at Home Depot (a bit more than 1% of total revenue) is typical of the new realities manufacturers must accommodate.

So Black & Decker is restructuring. Price deflation of 1%-2% annually is eating away at revenue while a number of costs (wages and health care, for example) are rising, so the company is moving production to low-wage regions in Asia and Eastern Europe. We view this kind of restructuring as less of a current expense than an investment. But as long as the company is giving up ground on unit prices, acceptable returns on any kind of investment will be hard to maintain--and any lift in margins as a result of restructuring could well prove temporary.

A rebound in orders boosted unit sales and the stock price in mid-2002, and we suppose an economic recovery will be of short-term benefit to Black & Decker as well. But in the long term, the home-improvement industry is unfavorable to suppliers; we'd generally prefer to seek opportunities elsewhere.

Blackrock BLK

	Rating	Risk	Moat Size	Fair Value	Last Close	Yield %
	★★★★★	Low	Wide	$53.00	$39.40	0.0

Company Profile

Blackrock is an asset manager that caters primarily to institutional clients, but also sells mutual funds to individual investors. Its portfolios include domestic and international equity, taxable fixed-income, municipal bond, and money market funds. Its alternative investment products include real-estate financing, domestic and offshore fixed-income hedge funds, and high-yield securities. Blackrock has a growing business providing risk-management services and products to financial companies.

Management

Laurence D. Fink has been chairman and CEO of Blackrock since its formation in 1988. The company's board is dominated by executives connected to PNC Financial Services, which owns 70% of Blackrock.

Strategy

Blackrock's core strength is in fixed-income products geared toward institutions. In this market niche, it is part of an oligopoly that dominates the landscape. Alternative investments have been growing robustly and the company is concentrating on attracting more high-net-worth clientele. Blackrock also maintains a growing risk-management business for institutional clients.

40 E. 52nd Street
New York, NY 10022
www.blackrock.com

Industry	Investment Style	Stock Type	Sector
Money Management	▦ Mid Growth	↑ Aggr. Growth	💲 Financial Services

Competition	Market Cap $Mil	Debt/ Equity	12 Mo Trailing Sales $Mil	Price/Cash Flow	Return On Assets%	Total Return% 1 Yr	3 Yr
Blackrock	2,554	—	569	—	16.2	-5.5	35.4
Allianz AG ADR	23,469	—	71,394	—	—	—	—
Legg Mason	3,149	—	1,613	—	3.0	-2.1	16.7

Price Volatility

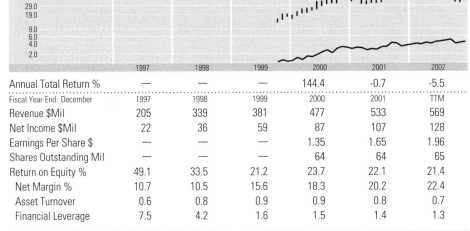

	Monthly Price High/Low				Relative Strength to S&P 500
Annual $Price High Low			19.38 12.50	48.00 15.00	44.50 30.76	47.60 33.55

	1997	1998	1999	2000	2001	2002
Annual Total Return %	—	—	144.4	-0.7	-5.5	

Fiscal Year-End: December	1997	1998	1999	2000	2001	TTM
Revenue $Mil	205	339	381	477	533	569
Net Income $Mil	22	36	59	87	107	128
Earnings Per Share $	—	—	—	1.35	1.65	1.96
Shares Outstanding Mil	—	—	—	64	64	65
Return on Equity %	49.1	33.5	21.2	23.7	22.1	21.4
Net Margin %	10.7	10.5	15.6	18.3	20.2	22.4
Asset Turnover	0.6	0.8	0.9	0.9	0.8	0.7
Financial Leverage	7.5	4.2	1.6	1.5	1.4	1.3

Valuation Ratios	Stock	Rel to Industry	Rel to S&P 500
Price/Earnings	20.1	1.1	0.9
Price/Book	4.3	1.6	1.3
Price/Sales	4.5	1.7	2.2
Price/Cash Flow	—	—	—

Major Fund Holders	% of Fund Assets
IDEX Transamerica Growth Opport A	3.91
Transamerica Premier Growth Opp Inv	3.84
Morgan Stanley Financial Services B	3.18
Selected Special	3.09

Morningstar Grades

Growth [A-]	1998	1999	2000	2001
Revenue %	65.2	12.2	25.2	11.8
Earnings/Share %	NMF	NMF	NMF	22.2
Book Value/Share %	—	—	NMF	31.2
Dividends/Share %	NMF	NMF	NMF	NMF

With 57% of assets under management in fixed income, and 33% in liquidity (money market), Blackrock has benefited from the flight out of equities. Revenue increased at a compound annual rate of 16% since 1998 and rose 12% in 2001.

Profitability [A+]	1999	2000	2001	TTM
Return on Assets %	13.3	16.3	15.7	16.2
Oper Cash Flow $Mil	116	109	167	—
- Cap Spending $Mil	19	33	40	—
= Free Cash Flow $Mil	—	—	—	—

Blackrock increased earnings per share at a compound annual rate of 36% since 1998 and operating margins have improved to 32%. Return on assets of 18% puts the company among the top one fourth of asset managers.

Financial Health [A+]	1999	2000	2001	09-02
Long-term Debt $Mil	—	—	—	—
Total Equity $Mil	281	368	486	596
Debt/Equity Ratio	—	—	—	—

Blackrock is rock-solid financially. With healthy cash flows and very low leverage, the company is the gold standard among asset managers.

Morningstar's Take By Rachel Barnard, 09-24-2002 Stock Price as of Analysis: $40.79

Volatile equity markets have been a boon for Blackrock, feeding investor demand for the stable fixed-income products that are the firm's bread and butter. The combination of its prosperous fixed-income business and some new diversity plays makes Blackrock one of the more attractive buys in asset management.

Bond funds may not be sexy, but demand for them is large and growing. Blackrock has a good chunk of the institutional fixed-income market sewn up as part of an oligopoly of bond managers that manage large blocks of pension assets. The recent losses in equity products have made many pension managers skittish, sending them to Blackrock for less risky alternatives.

Not surprisingly, fixed-income is the growth engine for Blackrock now, driving the addition of $12.8 billion in net new funds in the second quarter of 2002 alone. Liquidity offerings--like money market funds--have also come on strong as equity prices have fallen. But Blackrock is not just a company for bear markets. It has proved its ability to prosper in different environments, with 36% compound annual earnings growth since 1998.

Not resting on its laurels, Blackrock has undertaken a cautious expansion plan that begins by targeting the rich. High-net-worth business is the fastest-growing area of asset management and Blackrock currently has a measly $500 million share of the wealth market. The firm recently lured a team of wealth-management specialists away from Goldman Sachs Asset Management to spearhead its effort.

Blackrock is also on a mission to bolster its fledgling domestic equity business. With dismal returns in recent quarters, money has been flowing out of its equity offerings, but Blackrock is forging ahead. It hired a small-cap growth team from MFS and plans to diversify into equities despite the hurdles.

Combined with its proven fixed-income business, we think Blackrock's growth plans are a smart move. The company is targeting focused, high-value areas to expand and it should be able to leverage its strong brand. We are expecting assets under management to increase around 16% in 2002, resulting in some of the most impressive growth in the asset-management industry.

MORNINGSTAR® Stocks 500

Blockbuster BBI

	Rating	Risk	Moat Size	Fair Value	Last Close	Yield %
	★★★	Med.	—	$18.00	$12.25	0.7

Company Profile

Blockbuster, a subsidiary of Viacom, is a retailer of videocassettes, DVDs, and video games. The company had a total of about 7,520 stores in the United States and 26 other countries as of September 2000. Blockbuster's store formats are either 4,800, 2,500 to 3,000, or 1,000 to 2,000 square feet in size. About 21% of its revenues are generated outside the U.S. The company intends to open additional stores throughout the United States in 2000 and 2001. Blockbuster had about 90 million U.S. member accounts and 8 million Canadian member accounts as of December 1999.

Management

Following a period of management turmoil, Blockbuster hired John Antioco as chairman, president, and CEO in 1997. Antioco has turned the tide at Blockbuster, just as he previously engineered a turnaround at Circle K.

Strategy

Blockbuster strives for dominant store presence by aggressively opening new units while minimizing cannibalization of existing stores. Blockbuster aims to capitalize on the growing demand for DVDs and introductions of new gaming platforms. The firm recently rearranged store layouts to feature more DVDs for sale and rental while paring down VHS videos, and conducted a series of game promotions.

1201 Elm Street   www.blockbuster.com
Dallas, TX 75270

Morningstar Grades

Growth [B-]	1998	1999	2000	2001
Revenue %	17.5	14.6	11.1	4.0
Earnings/Share %	NMF	NMF	NMF	NMF
Book Value/Share %	—	—	NMF	-3.7
Dividends/Share %	NMF	NMF	300.0	0.0

Blockbuster's 4% revenue growth in 2001 was relatively weak, especially compared with double-digit increases a few years ago. After reconfiguring stores to highlight DVDs and video games, Blockbuster is poised for high-single-digit growth.

Profitability [D-]	1999	2000	2001	TTM
Return on Assets %	-0.8	-0.9	-3.1	-27.9
Oper Cash Flow $Mil	1,143	1,321	1,395	1,472
- Cap Spending $Mil	374	222	93	110
= Free Cash Flow $Mil	768	1,099	1,302	1,361

Blockbuster's profitability has lagged that of its key competitors. New emphasis on higher-margin DVDs should help considerably, but we expect the high costs of operating stores will continue to eat into profit margins.

Financial Health [C+]	1999	2000	2001	09-02
Long-term Debt $Mil	1,138	1,137	546	335
Total Equity $Mil	6,125	6,008	5,749	4,124
Debt/Equity Ratio	0.2	0.2	0.1	0.1

Blockbuster's financial underpinnings are rather precarious. Viacom's VIA purchase and spin-off of Blockbuster created a huge goodwill asset that artificially lowered the firm's financial leverage, making it appear healthier than it really is.

	Industry	Investment Style	Stock Type	Sector
	Rental & Repair Services	▦ Mid Value	➡ Slow Growth	🛒 Consumer Services

Competition

	Market Cap $Mil	Debt/ Equity	12 Mo Trailing Sales $Mil	Price/Cash Flow	Return On Assets%	Total Return% 1 Yr	3 Yr
Blockbuster	2,196	0.1	5,342	1.5	-27.9	-51.2	2.5
Hollywood Entertainment	889	—	1,445	—	—	—	—
Movie Gallery	357	—	440	—	—	—	—

Price Volatility

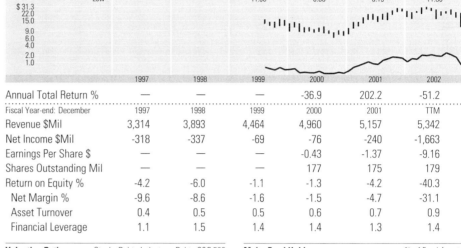

Annual $Price High Low			17.25 11.38	14.88 6.88	28.65 8.19	30.25 11.80

	1997	1998	1999	2000	2001	2002
Annual Total Return %	—	—	—	-36.9	202.2	-51.2

Fiscal Year-end: December	1997	1998	1999	2000	2001	TTM
Revenue $Mil	3,314	3,893	4,464	4,960	5,157	5,342
Net Income $Mil	-318	-337	-69	-76	-240	-1,663
Earnings Per Share $	—	—	—	-0.43	-1.37	-9.16
Shares Outstanding Mil	—	—	—	177	175	179
Return on Equity %	-4.2	-6.0	-1.1	-1.3	-4.2	-40.3
Net Margin %	-9.6	-8.6	-1.6	-1.5	-4.7	-31.1
Asset Turnover	0.4	0.5	0.5	0.6	0.7	0.9
Financial Leverage	1.1	1.5	1.4	1.4	1.3	1.4

Valuation Ratios	Stock	Rel to Industry	Rel to S&P 500
Price/Earnings	NMF	—	—
Price/Book	0.5	0.1	0.2
Price/Sales	0.4	0.2	0.2
Price/Cash Flow	1.5	0.4	0.1

Major Fund Holders	% of Fund Assets
CDC Nvest Jurika & Voyles Rel Val Y	4.13
Rice, Hall James Small/Mid Cap	3.36
Heritage Aggressive Growth A	3.32
Montgomery Mid Cap Focus R	3.28

Morningstar's Take By Debbie Wang, 12-12-2002 Stock Price as of Analysis: $21.41

We like Blockbuster's nimbleness and management's vigilant efforts to counter competitive threats. However, considering the substantial uncertainty surrounding the firm, we'd stay on the sidelines for now.

Though the video rental business is always vulnerable to changes in the underlying audiovisual technology, CEO John Antioco's deft maneuvering has allowed Blockbuster to thrive despite earlier predictions of the firm's demise at the hands of long-awaited video-on-demand services. Video on demand is still some years away. In the meantime, Blockbuster has focused on growing demand for DVD rental and sales, launched its own DVD mail rental to compete with Netflix, and created an alliance to sell DirecTV satellite systems through its retail locations. In covering all the bases, Blockbuster has better positioned itself for growth no matter where that growth might come from.

However, several risks may significantly influence Blockbuster's performance. The company's strong sales growth in the late 1990s was primarily driven by opening 200-300 new stores a year. With more than 5,400 stores domestically, Blockbuster may soon reach saturation in the United States, which accounts for 80% of its revenue.

Developments in technology will probably force Blockbuster away from its traditional business model into new territories. As consumers move to DVDs, they are more likely to buy the lower-priced discs than rent them. This means Blockbuster must compete for DVD sales with the likes of Wal-Mart. Longer term, Blockbuster must keep its eye on the movie studios. Tired of Blockbuster's market power and revenue-sharing agreements, movie studios would love to diminish the chain's influence, and they view video on demand as an opportunity to cut out Blockbuster's middleman role altogether.

Finally, Blockbuster must improve profit margins. Its 2.9% profit margin is anemic compared with those of closest peers Hollywood Entertainment (12.2%) and Movie Gallery (6.8%). We believe the firm has pursued market share at the expense of profitability. In Blockbuster's case, small changes in gross and operating margins can make a big difference in financial performance. Thus far, we have not seen any improvement in operating margins, and would require a 40% discount to our fair value estimate before we'd be interested in the stock.

BMC Software BMC

	Rating	Risk	Moat Size	Fair Value	Last Close	Yield %
	★	Med.	None	$13.00	$17.11	0.0

Company Profile

BMC Software develops systems software for use in transaction-intensive computing environments. Its products function with IBM's mainframe operating, database management, and data communication systems. The company's products include programming and performance tools and utilities. It also offers data compression and networking products. The company's Masterplan products automate administrative tasks and perform operating tasks for its DB2 database management systems. BMC Software acquired OptiSystems Solutions in August 2000.

Management

Max Watson stepped down as CEO in 2001 and was replaced Robert Beauchamp, former senior vice president of product management and development. Beauchamp has been with BMC since 1988.

Strategy

BMC sells software that increases the efficiency of mainframes. To lessen its dependence on this slow-growing market, it has placed more emphasis on software for distributed systems--networks that combine mainframes, desktops, and servers--and high-growth segments like storage and security.

2101 CityWest Boulevard
Houston, TX 77042-2827
www.bmc.com

Morningstar Grades

Growth [D+]	1999	2000	2001	2002
Revenue %	32.3	31.9	-12.2	-14.6
Earnings/Share %	89.6	-34.2	-82.3	NMF
Book Value/Share %	49.9	31.2	3.2	-15.7
Dividends/Share %	NMF	NMF	NMF	NMF

Tough IT spending conditions and declining demand for mainframe software have crimped sales growth. It is unclear whether BMC will succeed in new markets like distributed systems software.

Profitability [A-]	2000	2001	2002	TTM
Return on Assets %	8.2	1.4	-6.9	-3.0
Oper Cash Flow $Mil	367	579	523	622
- Cap Spending $Mil	148	183	64	42
= Free Cash Flow $Mil	219	397	459	581

Even though BMC has done a better job of cutting costs, profitability has declined. Increased competition and pricing pressure mean the days of 25%-30% operating margins are probably history.

Financial Health [A]	2000	2001	2002	09-02
Long-term Debt $Mil	—	—	—	—
Total Equity $Mil	1,781	1,815	1,507	1,411
Debt/Equity Ratio	—	—	—	—

The balance sheet is solid, with $1.2 billion in cash and no debt. The company also throws off plenty of free cash flow.

Industry	Investment Style	Stock Type	Sector
Systems & Security	▦ Mid Core	➡ Slow Growth	◩ Software

Competition	Market Cap $Mil	Debt/ Equity	12 Mo Trailing Sales $Mil	Price/Cash Flow	Return On Assets%	Total Return% 1 Yr	3 Yr
BMC Software	4,029	—	1,249	6.5	-3.0	4.5	-39.4
IBM	130,982	0.8	82,442	9.0	5.8	-35.5	-11.1
Computer Associates Inter	7,739	0.4	3,056	5.8	-5.3	-60.7	-41.5

Price Volatility

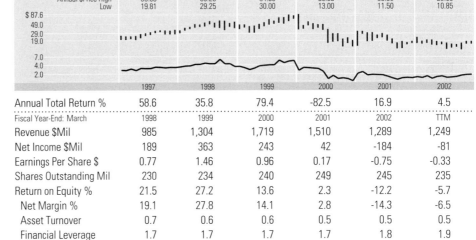

| Monthly Price High/Low — Relative Strength to S&P 500

Annual $Price High Low	35.63 19.81	60.25 29.25	84.06 30.00	86.63 13.00	33.00 11.50	23.00 10.85

	1997	1998	1999	2000	2001	2002
Annual Total Return %	58.6	35.8	79.4	-82.5	16.9	4.5

Fiscal Year-End: March	1998	1999	2000	2001	2002	TTM
Revenue $Mil	985	1,304	1,719	1,510	1,289	1,249
Net Income $Mil	189	363	243	42	-184	-81
Earnings Per Share $	0.77	1.46	0.96	0.17	-0.75	-0.33
Shares Outstanding Mil	230	234	240	249	245	235
Return on Equity %	21.5	27.2	13.6	2.3	-12.2	-5.7
Net Margin %	19.1	27.8	14.1	2.8	-14.3	-6.5
Asset Turnover	0.7	0.6	0.6	0.5	0.5	0.5
Financial Leverage	1.7	1.7	1.7	1.7	1.8	1.9

Valuation Ratios	Stock	Rel to Industry	Rel to S&P 500
Price/Earnings	NMF	—	—
Price/Book	2.9	1.3	0.9
Price/Sales	3.2	0.9	1.6
Price/Cash Flow	6.5	0.6	0.5

Major Fund Holders	% of Fund Assets
Cambiar Opportunity Inst	6.16
Alpha Analytics Value	3.98
UMB Scout Technology	3.89
ING Technology A	2.73

Morningstar's Take By Mike Trigg, 12-09-2002 Stock Price as of Analysis: $15.52

Unless BMC Software re-emerges as a high-growth, high-margin software company, the only reason to buy the stock is if it becomes sickly cheap.

We attribute BMC's struggles to two factors: A punk economy has made IT executives wary of investing in software, and demand for additional computing power in mainframes--BMC's primary source of revenue--has slowed because companies already have excess capacity. While management has done a better job of cutting costs, it makes little sense why BMC is struggling to break even when it has historically enjoyed operating margins of 25%-30%.

BMC is a dominant seller of software for mainframes, large computers that store vast amounts of data. Among other things, the firm's software helps maintain the performance and reliability of the database that sits on a mainframe. The beauty of the business is that there are high switching costs; customers are locked into using BMC software and are even forced to pay additional fees when the size of the mainframe increases.

Although mainframe software carries high margins, the market is maturing. Hence, BMC has turned its sights to faster-growing areas like software for distributed systems, storage, and

security. (A distributed system might store data on multiple servers in multiple locations; a mainframe would store data in one place.) However, these markets are filled with other technology stalwarts, like Sun Microsystems and EMC; success is anything but guaranteed.

At this point BMC is still all about mainframes, its largest revenue source. BMC expects that additional upgrades and new IBM mainframes should provide steady growth, albeit at a slower rate than the distributed systems market. Big Blue is also pushing Linux technology for mainframes, which could drive additional demand. However, BMC's close proximity to the mainframe market suggests that BMC really does stand for Big Mainframe Company.

We think BMC is a decent company and is addressing many of its earlier problems. However, we are taking a wait-and-see approach to the company's efforts beyond mainframes. We would buy the stock only if it became unavoidably cheap.

M🌟RNINGSTAR® Stocks 500

Boeing BA

	Rating	Risk	Moat Size	Fair Value	Last Close	Yield %
	★★★	Med.	Narrow	$42.00	$32.99	2.1

Company Profile

Boeing manufactures aerospace products for government and commercial use. Its commercial-aircraft models include the 747, 757, 767, and 777. The company also produces versions of its civilian products for military use. Boeing is a major contractor for the U.S. Space Station and manufactures the V-22 Osprey and AH-64 Apache helicopters; F-22 fighter planes; F-15 Eagle, C-17 Globemaster, and AWACS planes; electronic systems; and missiles for military use. The company sells its products in the U.S. and abroad. Foreign sales account for about 40% of Boeing's total sales.

Management

CEO Phil Condit's bio reads like a higher-education shopping list: UC Berkeley, Princeton, MIT, and even the Science University of Tokyo. His and senior management's know-how will be tested as Boeing transforms into a GE-like conglomerate.

Strategy

Boeing shares the market for large-frame aircraft with European rival Airbus. It has pursued growth opportunities in defense, space, and communication, diversifying away from commercial aviation and thereby reducing its cyclicality. Sales unrelated to commercial aviation have climbed to about 45% of revenue.

100 North Riverside www.boeing.com
Chicago, IL 60606-1596

Morningstar Grades

Growth [B]	1998	1999	2000	2001
Revenue %	22.6	3.3	-11.5	13.4
Earnings/Share %	NMF	116.5	-2.0	39.8
Book Value/Share %	-3.5	-2.3	2.2	3.3
Dividends/Share %	0.0	0.0	0.0	21.4

Revenue is set to fall about 5% in 2002 from last year, mostly because of a large decrease in commercial aircraft deliveries. Revenue will probably drop again next year, as aircraft deliveries stagnate.

Profitability [B-]	1999	2000	2001	TTM
Return on Assets %	6.4	5.0	5.8	0.0
Oper Cash Flow $Mil	6,224	5,942	3,814	2,809
- Cap Spending $Mil	1,236	932	1,068	942
= Free Cash Flow $Mil	4,988	5,010	2,746	1,867

While profit margins improved in 2001 thanks to increasing operating efficiency, the downturn in the commercial jet business has hurt margins this year and is likely to continue to do so for at least the next few quarters.

Financial Health [B-]	1999	2000	2001	09-02
Long-term Debt $Mil	5,980	7,567	10,866	11,988
Total Equity $Mil	11,462	11,020	10,825	10,903
Debt/Equity Ratio	0.5	0.7	1.0	1.1

The balance sheet is in pretty good shape, but we are watching the growth of Boeing Capital's financing portfolio very closely. A few bad lending decisions and the declining value of some in-service airplanes could hurt Boeing's financial position.

Industry	Investment Style	Stock Type	Sector
Aerospace & Defense	▦ Large Value	⭙ Cyclical	✦ Industrial Mats

Competition	Market Cap $Mil	Debt/ Equity	12 Mo Trailing Sales $Mil	Price/Cash Flow	Return On Assets%	Total Return% 1 Yr	3 Yr
Boeing	27,691	1.1	56,071	9.9	0.0	-13.4	-4.9
Lockheed Martin	26,512	0.9	26,132	11.2	-2.3	24.7	47.9
Raytheon	12,481	0.6	17,341	14.9	-3.0	-3.0	8.8

Price Volatility

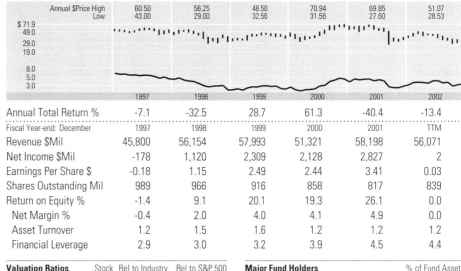

Annual $Price High	60.50	56.25	48.50	70.94	69.85	51.07
Low	43.00	29.00	32.56	31.56	27.60	28.53

	1997	1998	1999	2000	2001	2002
Annual Total Return %	-7.1	-32.5	28.7	61.3	-40.4	-13.4

Fiscal Year-end: December	1997	1998	1999	2000	2001	TTM
Revenue $Mil	45,800	56,154	57,993	51,321	58,198	56,071
Net Income $Mil	-178	1,120	2,309	2,128	2,827	2
Earnings Per Share $	-0.18	1.15	2.49	2.44	3.41	0.03
Shares Outstanding Mil	989	966	916	858	817	839
Return on Equity %	-1.4	9.1	20.1	19.3	26.1	0.0
Net Margin %	-0.4	2.0	4.0	4.1	4.9	0.0
Asset Turnover	1.2	1.5	1.6	1.2	1.2	1.2
Financial Leverage	2.9	3.0	3.2	3.9	4.5	4.4

Valuation Ratios	Stock	Rel to Industry	Rel to S&P 500
Price/Earnings	EUB	—	—
Price/Book	2.5	1.0	0.8
Price/Sales	0.5	0.5	0.2
Price/Cash Flow	9.9	1.0	0.7

Major Fund Holders	% of Fund Assets
Strong Dow 30 Value	7.54
Fidelity Select Defense & Aerospace	7.41
Fidelity Select Air Transportation	5.42
Oppenheimer Quest Opportunity Value A	4.87

Morningstar's Take By Nicolas Owens, 12-04-2002 Stock Price as of Analysis: $33.93

Competition and diversification into new businesses mean Boeing no longer has a wide moat.

Historically, Boeing's competitive advantage was its ability to design and build big jet planes; huge capital investments staved off likely rivals. But Airbus started in 1970 to build a competing European franchise that now hampers Boeing's ability to reap economies of scale. As a result, we haven't seen the financial returns from Boeing that we might otherwise expect in the concentrated jet industry. Today, Boeing's competitive advantage resides in its ability to innovate, a lower barrier to rivals. To reflect this, we downgraded Boeing's moat rating from wide to narrow.

For growth, Boeing is looking outside the volatile and increasingly competitive commercial jet business. We expect growth to come from a rebound in commercial aircraft, two to five years hence; increased revenue through innovation in existing products, including defense projects and air traffic control systems; and new businesses, including aircraft financing and satellite communication. Some of these are unproven ground for Boeing, and each comes with its own set of risks.

Even if most airlines turn a profit again by 2004, as we assume, they may not rush to order tons of new planes: they have thousands of aircraft parked in the desert, ready to go. If airlines opt to fly these jets rather than order new ones, Boeing's aircraft sales could languish for years.

Boeing's defense business has risks, too. One is that Congress funds defense projects annually. Rising cost estimates for the Comanche helicopter program triggered rumblings about cutting back or killing it. Budget concerns also fueled debate about trimming Boeing's Super Hornet fighter jet program. Still, the firm has had several key defense wins, positioning it as a leading integrator of complex military projects, and it has improved its operating efficiency.

Another risk is that Boeing's brand-new lines of business could fail. General Electric and ILFC, an arm of American International Group, already dominate aircraft financing, leaving Boeing to prove that it can finance planes as profitably. New uses for satellites like fast Internet service aboard planes and beaming movies to digital theaters are cool, but commercially unproved. Working in Boeing's favor is its record of engineering and strategic thinking.

Boeing has weathered turmoil before, and we think its long-term prospects remain strong. We would buy the shares at a 40% discount to our $42 fair value estimate.

Data as of 12-31-02

Borders Group BGP

Rating	Risk	Moat Size	Fair Value	Last Close	Yield %
★★★	Med.	Narrow	$20.00	$16.10	0.0

Industry	Investment Style	Stock Type	Sector
Specialty Retail	Small Core	Slow Growth	Consumer Services

Company Profile

Borders Group is the second-largest operator of book superstores and the largest operator of mall-based bookstores in the United States, on the basis of sales and number of stores. Each superstore carries an average of 128,000 stock-keeping units of books and 50,000 SKUs of music. As of January 2001, the company operated more than 330 book and music superstores under the Borders name, approximately 900 mall-based and other bookstores under the Waldenbooks name, and 31 bookstores under the Books etc. name in the United States and overseas.

Management

Greg Josefowicz became president and CEO of Borders in November 1999, after serving as president of grocery chain Jewel-Osco. He replaced Philip Pfeffer, who left after only six months on the job.

Strategy

In two cost-cutting moves, Borders outsourced Borders.com to Amazon and turned over fulfillment of special orders and online sales to Ingram. Book retailing is a mature business, so management has been adding additional products, like DVDs, to its sales mix to spur growth. This is an area of minor concern, as the strategy has backfired on Borders in the past.

100 Phoenix Drive
Ann Arbor, MI 48108
www.borders.com

Morningstar Grades

Growth [C+]	1999	2000	2001	2002
Revenue %	14.5	14.4	10.2	3.6
Earnings/Share %	14.3	0.9	-52.2	96.3
Book Value/Share %	19.0	15.5	4.4	9.9
Dividends/Share %	NMF	NMF	NMF	NMF

Declining sales at Waldenbooks are dragging down growth at Borders' superstores. While there is certainly room for improvement, book retailing will never be a high-growth industry. We expect long-term sales growth in the mid- to high single digits.

Profitability [B]	2000	2001	2002	TTM
Return on Assets %	4.7	2.1	4.0	4.9
Oper Cash Flow $Mil	173	139	264	247
- Cap Spending $Mil	144	139	91	120
= Free Cash Flow $Mil	30	0	174	128

With growth prospects fairly small, management is focusing on cutting costs. The company is cutting back on the addition of retail space, has outsourced running Borders.com to Amazon, and has outsourced online fulfillment to Ingram.

Financial Health [B+]	2000	2001	2002	10-02
Long-term Debt $Mil	16	15	50	50
Total Equity $Mil	803	847	950	925
Debt/Equity Ratio	0.0	0.0	0.1	0.1

Borders sports a healthy balance sheet with little long-term debt. The firm generates enough operating cash flow to support its capital expenditures.

Competition

	Market Cap $Mil	Debt/ Equity	12 Mo Trailing Sales $Mil	Price/Cash Flow	Return On Assets%	Total Return% 1 Yr	3 Yr
Borders Group	1,273	0.1	3,470	5.2	4.9	-18.9	0.9
Barnes & Noble	1,217	0.5	5,103	3.1	2.3	-39.0	-2.4

Price Volatility

■ Monthly Price High/Low — Relative Strength to S&P 500

Annual $Price High Low	32.31 17.06	41.75 17.88	25.75 11.75	17.88 10.88	24.43 11.00	24.49 14.68

	1997	1998	1999	2000	2001	2002
Annual Total Return %	74.6	-20.4	-34.8	-28.1	69.7	-18.9

Fiscal Year-End: January	1998	1999	2000	2001	2002	TTM
Revenue $Mil	2,266	2,595	2,968	3,271	3,388	3,470
Net Income $Mil	80	92	90	44	87	115
Earnings Per Share $	0.98	1.12	1.13	0.54	1.06	1.40
Shares Outstanding Mil	76	77	78	78	81	79
Return on Equity %	13.4	12.9	11.3	5.2	9.2	12.4
Net Margin %	3.5	3.5	3.0	1.3	2.6	3.3
Asset Turnover	1.5	1.5	1.6	1.6	1.6	1.5
Financial Leverage	2.6	2.5	2.4	2.4	2.3	2.5

Valuation Ratios	Stock	Rel to Industry	Rel to S&P 500
Price/Earnings	11.5	0.4	0.5
Price/Book	1.4	0.4	0.4
Price/Sales	0.4	0.5	0.2
Price/Cash Flow	5.2	0.4	0.4

Major Fund Holders	% of Fund Assets
Corbin Small-Cap Value	3.88
Scudder Dreman High Return Equity A	2.58
AFBA Five Star Small Cap A	2.36
Buffalo Small Cap	2.30

Morningstar's Take By Joseph Beaulieu, 12-12-2002 Stock Price as of Analysis: $17.90

As much as we like spending time (and money) in bookstores, we don't think they make for an attractive business model. It's a mature business, with industrywide revenue growth likely to stick in the mid- to high single digits; inventory turns over only a couple of times a year; and given the consolidation of the publishing industry, there isn't really much room for gross margin improvements.

But within the constraints of the industry, Borders is doing many of the right things, in our opinion. It took an important step in outsourcing Borders.com to Amazon, although since the site is still losing money, we'd prefer to see it shut down altogether. Its decision to outsource special orders and online fulfillment to Ingram (which also entailed a transfer of some inventory) was another smart cost-saving move.

Ironically, the success of the big bookstore chains and their megastores has caused some problems for Borders and Barnes & Noble, as both companies own chains of smaller mall-based stores. The Borders-owned Waldenbooks chain has suffered as book buyers have become spoiled by the megastores, which offer a much more comprehensive selection of books, chairs for reading, cafes, live music, reading groups, and even story time for kids. Waldenbooks'

sales (which account for about a third of Borders' sales) have been contracting over the past several years. The lack of amenities has allowed Waldenbooks stores to boast higher per-square-foot sales than the Borders megastores, but we'd still like to see some stabilization in this business.

Assuming that Borders can achieve revenue growth in the midsingle digits over the next several years, wring out some cost efficiencies from its Amazon and Ingram relationships, and shave just a point or two from its selling, general, and administrative expense (bringing it back to 1997-98 levels), we think the shares are worth about $20.

While we don't think the book retailing business model is all that attractive, it is very stable, and that is why we would strongly consider buying the shares in the low to mid-teens. We think the biggest risk is that management may be tempted to go overboard in stocking nonbook merchandise to spur growth. This is something we will watch very closely.

138

©2003 Morningstar, Inc. All rights reserved. Intended for United States residents only, this report is for information purposes and should not be considered a solicitation to buy or sell any security. Visit www.morningstar.com for your research.

Morningstar® Stocks 500

BorgWarner BWA

	Rating	Risk	Moat Size	Fair Value	Last Close	Yield %
	★★★★	Med.	Narrow	$84.00	$50.42	1.2

Company Profile

BorgWarner is a global supplier of drivetrain components and systems for passenger cars, trucks, and industrial equipment. Its products include engine management systems, turbochargers, transmission components, and four- and all-wheel-drive systems. The company acquired Kuhlman Corporation and the fluid power division of Eaton Corporation in 1999; it sold its fuel systems and climate control operations during 2000. Ford Motor accounted for 30% of BorgWarner's revenue in 2001, with DaimlerChrysler and General Motors furnishing 21% and 12%, respectively.

Management

CEO John Fiedler, 63, is among the industry's most respected executives. He joined BorgWarner in 1994 after 29 years with Goodyear. Fiedler will probably cede the CEO title to president and COO Tim Manganello next year.

Strategy

BorgWarner is focused on the powertrain, a capital-intensive area of the vehicle with plenty of room for technological advancement. After years of investing heavily in new products and expanding capacity, the company has developed a lineup to meet the needs of North American automakers (four- and all-wheel-drive systems, lower emissions) and their European counterparts (better fuel economy).

200 South Michigan Avenue   www.bwauto.com
Chicago, IL 60604

Morningstar Grades

Growth [B-]	1998	1999	2000	2001
Revenue %	4.0	33.9	7.6	-11.1
Earnings/Share %	-7.2	26.8	-30.2	-29.1
Book Value/Share %	13.3	23.4	1.0	2.0
Dividends/Share %	0.0	0.0	0.0	0.0

BorgWarner's revenue doubled between 1994 and 2000, but weak production in North America sent sales 11% lower in 2001. The company's backlog is among the best in the business and should set the stage for several years of double-digit growth.

Profitability [C+]	1999	2000	2001	TTM
Return on Assets %	4.5	3.4	2.4	-5.9
Oper Cash Flow $Mil	345	292	196	181
- Cap Spending $Mil	143	167	141	129
= Free Cash Flow $Mil	201	124	55	52

Margins have been trending higher, but returns on invested capital have averaged less than 8% in recent years. Moderating capital spending should help mitigate this problem, but pricing pressures from automakers make margin improvement a challenge.

Financial Health [C+]	1999	2000	2001	09-02
Long-term Debt $Mil	846	740	701	648
Total Equity $Mil	1,058	1,087	1,104	985
Debt/Equity Ratio	0.8	0.7	0.6	0.7

Free cash flow has been applied to debt reduction since several acquisitions in 1999; rising free cash flows in the next few years should drive debt lower still. BorgWarner is one of a handful of suppliers to sport an investment-grade credit rating.

Industry	Investment Style	Stock Type	Sector
Auto Parts	Mid Value	Cyclical	Consumer Goods

Competition	Market Cap $Mil	Debt/ Equity	12 Mo Trailing Sales $Mil	Price/Cash Flow	Return On Assets%	Total Return% 1 Yr	3 Yr
BorgWarner	1,356	0.7	2,613	7.5	-5.9	-2.4	10.7
Honeywell International	19,705	0.5	22,272	8.7	5.6	-27.3	-22.9
Delphi	4,495	0.9	26,836	3.8	0.5	-39.6	-16.6

Price Volatility | Monthly Price High/Low   — Relative Strength to S&P 500

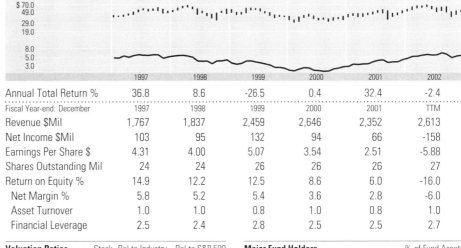

Annual $Price High Low	61.50 38.38	68.38 33.06	60.00 36.75	45.00 29.75	55.19 34.20	68.95 38.38

	1997	1998	1999	2000	2001	2002
Annual Total Return %	36.8	8.6	-26.5	0.4	32.4	-2.4
Fiscal Year-end: December	1997	1998	1999	2000	2001	TTM
Revenue $Mil	1,767	1,837	2,459	2,646	2,352	2,613
Net Income $Mil	103	95	132	94	66	-158
Earnings Per Share $	4.31	4.00	5.07	3.54	2.51	-5.88
Shares Outstanding Mil	24	24	26	26	26	27
Return on Equity %	14.9	12.2	12.5	8.6	6.0	-16.0
Net Margin %	5.8	5.2	5.4	3.6	2.8	-6.0
Asset Turnover	1.0	1.0	0.8	1.0	0.8	1.0
Financial Leverage	2.5	2.4	2.8	2.5	2.5	2.7

Valuation Ratios	Stock	Rel to Industry	Rel to S&P 500
Price/Earnings	NMF	—	—
Price/Book	1.4	0.1	0.4
Price/Sales	0.5	0.0	0.3
Price/Cash Flow	7.5	0.1	0.6

Major Fund Holders	% of Fund Assets
ABN AMRO/Talon Mid Cap N	4.04
Eaton Vance Tax-Mgd Small-Cap Value C	3.16
Eaton Vance Small-Cap Value A	3.02
Transamerica Premier Balanced Inv	2.64

Morningstar's Take By Josh Peters, 11-15-2002 Stock Price as of Analysis: $46.23

Innovative powertrain systems have positioned BorgWarner for a turn into profitable growth. We think the shares are attractively priced at $50 or less.

A rare find in the dysfunctional auto industry, BorgWarner has proved adept at what it calls "catching technology waves." The firm has long dedicated itself to innovative engineering, which has repeatedly put BorgWarner in technological sweet spots like four- and all-wheel-drive systems, turbochargers, and engine timing systems. At the same time, the company has shed metal-bending businesses like manual transmissions that had few opportunities for technology-driven growth. We believe this combination of engineering prowess and focused strategy constitutes a narrow but sustainable competitive advantage.

Catching these waves has created an impressive backlog of new business, estimated to total $1.2 billion annually by 2005. This alone sets the stage for annual volume growth in the neighborhood of 13% in the next three years. The quality of BorgWarner's customer base, which traditionally centered on Ford, is also improving: The new business is disproportionately weighted toward automakers that are well positioned to expand their worldwide market share, including General Motors and, better yet, Honda and Korea's fast-growing Hyundai.

Most of the investments necessary to support these new supply programs are already in place. Capital spending, 7.6% of sales as recently as 1997, is planned to fall below 5% annually in the next several years. By increasing the utilization of existing investments in manufacturing capacity, we think BorgWarner will be able to preserve its operating margins despite the relentless pricing pressures.

With all of these pieces in place, we believe BorgWarner's returns on invested capital are about to rise. This hasn't been a bright spot--ROIC has averaged only 8.6% since 1994, short of our 9% cost of capital estimate. The costly plant and equipment needed to support BorgWarner's product lineup makes the midteen returns of sector leader Johnson Controls unlikely. But if BorgWarner can improve its asset utilization while preserving margins--which we believe it will--returns should move toward a healthy 10%-11% by middecade.

The company faces risks in the form of a probable decline in industry auto production, continued deflation, and a heavy reliance on troubled Ford. But we view BorgWarner as well-prepared to meet these challenges; we'd consider the shares at a 40% or better discount to our fair value estimate.

Boston Scientific BSX

	Rating	Risk	Moat Size	Fair Value	Last Close	Yield %
	★★	Med.	Wide	$34.00	$42.52	0.0

Company Profile

Boston Scientific produces medical devices. It manufactures products for use in angioplasty, blood clot filtration, catheter-directed ultrasound imaging, electrophysiology diagnosis, catheters, wound-treatment implants, forceps, upper gastrointestinal tract tests, and treatment of kidney stones, incontinence, and enlarged prostates. The company markets its devices to health-care professionals and institutions in the United States and overseas. Foreign sales account for approximately 39% of Boston Scientific's total sales.

Management

Founder Pete Nicholas is still active as chairman. James Tobin, known as a forthright manager, has been president and CEO since March 1999, and gained experience from posts at Baxter International.

Strategy

Boston Scientific seeks to dominate its niche in the less-invasive medical equipment market on a global scale. It is bent on developing a broad and deep product line through research and development and acquisitions to maintain its leadership position.

One Boston Scientific Place   www.bsci.com
Natick, MA 01760-1537

Industry	Investment Style	Stock Type	Sector
Medical Equipment	▦ Large Growth	→ Slow Growth	▨ Healthcare

Competition

	Market Cap $Mil	Debt/ Equity	12 Mo Trailing Sales $Mil	Price/Cash Flow	Return On Assets%	Total Return% 1 Yr	3 Yr
Boston Scientific	17,341	0.4	2,782	24.7	7.8	76.3	22.1
Johnson & Johnson	159,452	0.1	35,120	18.0	16.3	-7.9	8.0
Medtronic	55,399	0.3	6,669	34.6	11.4	-10.4	10.3

Price Volatility

| Monthly Price High/Low   — Relative Strength to S&P 500

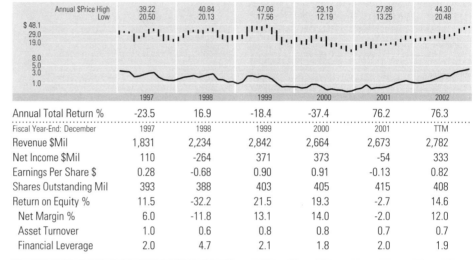

Annual $Price High Low	39.22 20.50	40.84 20.13	47.06 17.56	29.19 12.19	27.89 13.25	44.30 20.48
	1997	1998	1999	2000	2001	2002
Annual Total Return %	-23.5	16.9	-18.4	-37.4	76.2	76.3

Fiscal Year-End: December	1997	1998	1999	2000	2001	TTM
Revenue $Mil	1,831	2,234	2,842	2,664	2,673	2,782
Net Income $Mil	110	-264	371	373	-54	333
Earnings Per Share $	0.28	-0.68	0.90	0.91	-0.13	0.82
Shares Outstanding Mil	393	388	403	405	415	408
Return on Equity %	11.5	-32.2	21.5	19.3	-2.7	14.6
Net Margin %	6.0	-11.8	13.1	14.0	-2.0	12.0
Asset Turnover	1.0	0.6	0.8	0.8	0.7	0.7
Financial Leverage	2.0	4.7	2.1	1.8	2.0	1.9

Valuation Ratios	Stock	Rel to Industry	Rel to S&P 500
Price/Earnings	51.9	1.7	2.2
Price/Book	7.6	1.2	2.4
Price/Sales	6.2	1.4	3.1
Price/Cash Flow	24.7	1.0	1.9

Major Fund Holders	% of Fund Assets
Exeter Life Sciences A	9.03
Fidelity Select Medical Equip/Systems	7.85
Fountainhead Special Value	5.73
Liberty Acorn Twenty Z	5.57

Morningstar Grades

Growth [C-]	1998	1999	2000	2001
Revenue %	22.0	27.2	-6.3	0.3
Earnings/Share %	NMF	NMF	1.1	NMF
Book Value/Share %	-13.2	97.8	12.9	2.8
Dividends/Share %	NMF	NMF	NMF	NMF

Sales growth has averaged about 6% over the past three years, below the industry average of 17%. We expect sales and earnings growth to get back to the midteens in 2003 thanks to new product approvals.

Profitability [B]	1999	2000	2001	TTM
Return on Assets %	10.4	10.9	-1.4	7.8
Oper Cash Flow $Mil	776	739	490	702
- Cap Spending $Mil	80	76	121	114
= Free Cash Flow $Mil	696	663	369	588

Returns on equity and assets are erratic. This is partly because of one-time charges for purchased in-process research and development from 1996 through 1998. Without these charges, returns would be good.

Financial Health [A]	1999	2000	2001	09-02
Long-term Debt $Mil	688	574	973	840
Total Equity $Mil	1,724	1,935	2,015	2,286
Debt/Equity Ratio	0.4	0.3	0.5	0.4

The company's acquisition strategy has resulted in more debt on the balance sheet: Debt/equity was 0.4 in the September quarter. This is still a modest use of debt, and is down significantly from fiscal 1998.

Morningstar's Take By Travis Pascavis, 12-12-2002 Stock Price as of Analysis: $42.20

Boston Scientific has spent over $671 million in research and development over the past three years, and it has paid off handsomely. Most of the company's products are inserted in to the human body through natural openings or small cuts in the skin and can be guided to areas in need. This type of treatment benefits the patient in the form of a shorter recovery time, and the medical insurer in the form of a less costly treatment option. In fact, Boston Scientific's sales have increased from $1.8 million in 1979 to over $2.7 billion in 2001, a 39% compound annual growth rate.

Prior to 1999, Boston Scientific relied on a privately owned company called Medinol for much of its research and development. One of the first things that chief executive Jim Tobin did was to move its R&D in-house in 1999. This move was painful in the short term, leading to declining earnings in 2000 and 2001. But in the end, Boston Scientific should be able to bring new products to market in a more timely fashion. The strategy is already bearing fruit with the approval of a new bare-metal stent. These devices prop open blood vessels after they are cleaned through angioplasty. The company launched its Express2 stent in the United States during the third quarter of 2002. We think this new device will help

Boston Scientific's U.S. market share in stents, which had once fallen to less than 10%.

In fact, the best is yet to come from Boston Scientific's next generation of stents. Several studies have shown that drug-coated stents can dramatically reduce the chance of blood vessels reclogging. Johnson & Johnson JNJ is in the lead for regulatory approval so far, and will most likely take the leading market position by mid-2003. Still, Boston Scientific's device has had similar clinical results to J&J's, and we are confident that it will gain share in the fourth quarter of 2003. These new stents will cost patients nearly twice as much as noncoated stents--about $2,400 per device--so sales and earnings should get a boost even if volume stays the same or shrinks.

While we think that Boston Scientific's turnaround is for real, we can't get excited about the shares. Competition will likely keep a lid on the company's market share, and the firm isn't likely to gain first-mover advantage, given Johnson & Johnson's lead. Even after giving the company the benefit of more than 20% average earnings per share growth over the next five years, we can't justify the share price.

MORNINGSTAR® **Stocks 500**

BP PLC ADR BP

	Rating	Risk	Moat Size	Fair Value	Last Close	Yield %
	★★	Med.	Narrow	$40.00	$40.65	3.5

Company Profile

London-based BP is the second-largest oil company on the planet, trailing only ExxonMobil in size. Formed by the 1998 merger of British Petroleum and Amoco, BP boasts proven reserves of 15 billion oil equivalent barrels. BP can also refine 2.9 million barrels a day and sells petroleum through its roughly 29,000 service stations around the globe. BP stock trades on the New York Stock Exchange as an ADR.

Management

John Browne has been BP's CEO since 1995. Browne has been the driving force behind the company's numerous mergers and acquisitions as well as its expansion into natural gas.

Strategy

BP seeks to increase profits by expanding production, reducing unit costs, and diversifying its revenue stream. It has shifted its exploration emphasis to natural gas in order to increase total production at annual rate of 6% through 2006; it hopes this greater volume will reduce unit costs. BP also continues to seek acquisitions.

Britannic House | www.bpamoco.com
London, EC2M 7BA

Morningstar Grades

Growth [A-]	1998	1999	2000	2001
Revenue %	-22.9	20.8	59.9	8.4
Earnings/Share %	-42.4	53.9	112.1	-34.9
Book Value/Share %	1.5	0.8	51.8	-2.2
Dividends/Share %	10.0	1.0	2.5	7.3

BP has been an aggressive acquisitor in recent years. As with the rest of the industry, short-term growth can quickly rise and fall with commodity oil and gas prices. Revenue growth should remain choppy from year to year.

Profitability [A-]	1999	2000	2001	TTM
Return on Assets %	5.6	8.2	5.7	5.7
Oper Cash Flow $Mil	10,290	20,416	22,409	22,409
- Cap Spending $Mil	6,534	10,101	12,214	12,214
= Free Cash Flow $Mil	3,756	10,315	10,195	10,195

BP has been a consistent performer and hasn't had an unprofitable year in more than a decade. Returns on capital employed have averaged in the high teens in recent years, well above the firm's cost of capital.

Financial Health [A]	1999	2000	2001	12-01
Long-term Debt $Mil	11,889	18,614	15,413	15,413
Total Equity $Mil	43,260	73,395	74,346	74,346
Debt/Equity Ratio	0.3	0.3	0.2	0.2

Even with all its mergers, BP has kept debt down. Total interest-bearing debt is roughly $21 billion, modest for a company with a market capitalization approaching $200 billion. Leverage remains low and the balance sheet is healthy.

Industry	Investment Style	Stock Type	Sector
Oil & Gas	Large Value	Hard Assets	Energy

Competition	Market Cap $Mil	Debt/ Equity	12 Mo Trailing Sales $Mil	Price/Cash Flow	Return On Assets%	Total Return% 1 Yr	3 Yr
BP PLC ADR	152,063	0.2	175,389	6.8	5.7	-9.9	-9.2
ExxonMobil	235,108	0.1	196,513	12.0	6.7	-8.9	-0.9
Total Fina Elf SA ADR	100,949	0.3	93,914	9.2	8.7	3.7	5.2

Price Volatility

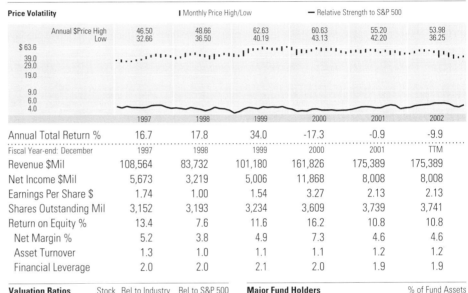

| | Monthly Price High/Low | Relative Strength to S&P 500 |

Annual $Price High Low	46.50 32.66	48.66 36.50	62.63 40.19	60.63 43.13	55.20 42.20	53.98 36.25

$ 63.6 / 39.0 / 29.0 / 19.0 / 9.0 / 6.0 / 4.0

	1997	1998	1999	2000	2001	2002
Annual Total Return %	16.7	17.8	34.0	-17.3	-0.9	-9.9
Fiscal Year-end: December	1997	1998	1999	2000	2001	TTM
Revenue $Mil	108,564	83,732	101,180	161,826	175,389	175,389
Net Income $Mil	5,673	3,219	5,006	11,868	8,008	8,008
Earnings Per Share $	1.74	1.00	1.54	3.27	2.13	2.13
Shares Outstanding Mil	3,152	3,193	3,234	3,609	3,739	3,741
Return on Equity %	13.4	7.6	11.6	16.2	10.8	10.8
Net Margin %	5.2	3.8	4.9	7.3	4.6	4.6
Asset Turnover	1.3	1.0	1.1	1.1	1.2	1.2
Financial Leverage	2.0	2.0	2.1	2.0	1.9	1.9

Valuation Ratios	Stock	Rel to Industry	Rel to S&P 500
Price/Earnings	19.1	1.0	0.8
Price/Book	2.0	0.9	0.6
Price/Sales	0.9	0.8	0.4
Price/Cash Flow	6.8	1.0	0.5

Major Fund Holders	% of Fund Assets
Amana Mutual Funds Trust Income	7.17
Banknorth Large Cap Value	6.24
Putnam Global Natural Resources A	6.11
ProFunds Europe 30 Svc	6.11

Morningstar's Take By Paul Larson, 11-13-2002 Stock Price as of Analysis: $37.95

BP has a lot going for it, and we'd be tempted to buy the shares at the right price.

Oil is a highly profitable business. The OPEC cartel has great influence, limiting supply to keep commodity prices above its costs and maintain industrywide profitability. This helps explain why BP has not had an unprofitable year in decades and, subsequently, has a balance sheet with a nominal amount of debt for BP's size, even as the company has been paying out a healthy dividend and repurchasing shares.

Part of BP's strength comes courtesy of its size--it's the fourth-largest public company in the world on the basis of sales. BP has proved that larger oil companies can operate more efficiently and profitably than the little guys. Much of its size results from its 1998 marriage to Amoco, which started the manic race of major mergers in the oil industry. Since then the firm has made additional acquisitions, increasing its size and producing billions in cost savings.

Because of these acquisitions, BP's sales and profit growth has been quite strong over the past few years. However, the company is not content to increase earnings solely through acquisitions; it also has set aggressive production growth targets. The

firm aims to increase output at an annual rate of about 6% over the next five years, with the majority of this increase coming from natural gas. While the company has had near-term difficulties that will make it fall short of this goal for 2002, the long-term target, if achieved, is roughly double that of its peers.

Many of the factors that influence BP's--as well as the entire industry's--profitability remain outside the company's control. Most important is the price of commodity oil and gas. Economic weakness or overproduction can depress prices, which can sap revenue and profits. In the oil patch, risks like war, higher taxes, and oil spills are ever present. Any of these could cause actual results to differ materially from our assumptions.

That said, BP remains an innovative operator and financial performer, and we think the firm has solid prospects. We are attracted by the structural characteristics of big oil created by OPEC, BP's long history of profitability and dividends, and a balance sheet composed of a nominal amount of debt against an enormous portfolio of hard assets. It's a firm certainly worth keeping on the radar, in our opinion.

Brinker International EAT

	Rating	Risk	Moat Size	Fair Value	Last Close	Yield %
	★★★	Med.	None	$36.00	$32.25	0.0

Industry	Investment Style	Stock Type	Sector
Restaurants	▦ Mid Growth	↗ Classic Growth	▭ Consumer Services

Company Profile

Brinker International operates more than 1,100 restaurants across North America, Europe, Southeast Asia, and Australia. The company operates and develops the Southwestern-themed Chili's Grill & Bar, as well as Maggiano's, Romano's Macaroni Grill, Big Bowl, Eatzi's, Corner Bakery, On the Border Mexican Grill, Rockfish Seafood, and Cozymel's restaurants. Of the restaurants, more than 800 are Chili's establishments.

Competition

	Market Cap $Mil	Debt/ Equity	12 Mo Trailing Sales $Mil	Price/Cash Flow	Return On Assets%	Total Return% 1 Yr	3 Yr
Brinker International	3,124	0.4	2,988	7.8	8.7	8.4	27.8
Yum Brands	7,169	4.3	7,498	6.9	11.1	-1.5	9.8
Darden Restaurants	3,495	—	4,470	—	—	—	—

Management

Brinker's brand heads either worked their way up from low positions at the firm or joined as seasoned restaurant executives. CEO Ron McDougall is constantly sniffing out new restaurant ideas--the reason Brinker has so many brands.

Strategy

Brinker has raised prices as a way to offset a decline in customer visits in some of its restaurants, and it's repositioning its lackluster Macaroni Grill and On the Border brands. We think Brinker would see greater long-term returns if it invested more in its Big Bowl and Corner Bakery chains. The company is mitigating risk by betting on a much larger number of brands than rivals.

6820 LBJ Freeway
Dallas, TX 75240
www.brinker.com

Price Volatility

	Monthly Price High/Low	— Relative Strength to S&P 500

Annual $Price High Low	11.92 7.08	19.50 10.00	20.42 13.25	28.83 13.83	31.30 21.30	36.00 24.07

	1997	1998	1999	2000	2001	2002
Annual Total Return %	0.0	80.5	-16.5	75.1	5.7	8.4

Fiscal Year-End: June	1998	1999	2000	2001	2002	TTM
Revenue $Mil	1,574	1,871	2,100	2,407	2,887	2,988
Net Income $Mil	69	79	118	145	153	158
Earnings Per Share $	0.68	0.77	1.17	1.42	1.52	1.58
Shares Outstanding Mil	99	99	98	99	98	97
Return on Equity %	11.6	11.9	15.5	16.1	15.6	15.8
Net Margin %	4.4	4.2	5.6	6.0	5.3	5.3
Asset Turnover	1.6	1.7	1.8	1.7	1.6	1.6
Financial Leverage	1.6	1.6	1.5	1.6	1.8	1.8

Valuation Ratios	Stock	Rel to Industry	Rel to S&P 500
Price/Earnings	20.4	1.4	0.9
Price/Book	3.1	1.2	1.0
Price/Sales	1.0	0.8	0.5
Price/Cash Flow	7.8	1.1	0.6

Major Fund Holders	% of Fund Assets
Brundage, Story & Rose Equity	3.38
Bramwell Focus	3.23
Papp Small & Mid-Cap Growth	3.06
Capital Management Mid-Cap Instl	3.05

Morningstar Grades

Growth [A]	1999	2000	2001	2002
Revenue %	18.8	12.3	14.6	20.0
Earnings/Share %	13.7	51.3	21.4	7.0
Book Value/Share %	11.0	16.6	16.4	10.4
Dividends/Share %	NMF	NMF	NMF	NMF

Brinker should be able to replicate its 15% sales growth from the past three years in 2003 and 2004. But this growth rate will be tough to maintain in the long term, especially if less successful concepts become a larger portion of the store base.

Profitability [A]	2000	2001	2002	TTM
Return on Assets %	10.1	10.0	8.6	8.7
Oper Cash Flow $Mil	269	247	390	402
- Cap Spending $Mil	165	205	371	402
= Free Cash Flow $Mil	104	42	19	1

The company has consistently earned an average net profit margin of 5.5%, which we expect to slightly increase because of economies of scale.

Financial Health [B+]	2000	2001	2002	09-02
Long-term Debt $Mil	110	236	427	439
Total Equity $Mil	762	900	977	1,003
Debt/Equity Ratio	0.1	0.3	0.4	0.4

Including the effects of capitalized operating leases, Brinker sports a hefty debt/equity ratio of 1.24. This financial leverage could become a problem if same-store sales growth decreased for a significant period.

Morningstar's Take By Carl Sibilski, 12-04-2002 Stock Price as of Analysis: $29.16

The successful Chili's restaurant chain has helped carry the day for Brinker, though we'd seek a 40% discount to our fair value estimate before buying the shares.

Contributing 60% of revenue and 70% of operating profits, Chili's dominates the company's financial performance. Most of Brinker's double-digit sales growth can be attributed to the expansion of Chili's. Given the company's long-term plans to increase the number of Chili's restaurants to 1,500 from the current base of more than 800, we believe double-digit sales growth will continue for several years.

Brinker has performed admirably while other restaurant companies have experienced difficulties. Same-store sales (sales at stores open more than 12 months) for the year ending June 2002 were up 1.5%. For the five weeks ending in October, Brinker's same-store sales rose 3.4%. Chili's experienced same-store sales growth of 5.0%, which included a 1.9% price increase. These kinds of results warrant additional expansion of Chili's, in our view.

We're concerned about Brinker's eight other restaurant concepts, though. Same-store sales at On the Border decreased 1.3% and Macaroni Grill's increased a mere 0.7% during the October period.

The company continues to remodel its On the Border stores, but we think the Mexican food concept will have difficulty gaining a strong foothold outside the Southwestern United States. Italian concept Macaroni Grill has been eclipsed by Darden's lower-priced Olive Garden, which has attained national brand recognition. Brinker responded by lowering Macaroni Grill's prices, but we think it may be too little too late.

Brinker has several potentially successful concepts, like Big Bowl Asian Kitchen and Corner Bakery Cafe, that it could expand. The challenge is to determine which concepts to invest in and, more important, which ones to cut. Brinker has done a good job of spreading business risk over several different types of restaurants. However, the current number of concepts is a real mouthful compared with rivals, which generally have four or fewer.

We think Brinker will be able to ride the success of Chili's long enough to give it time to work out many of these issues and come up with another red-hot restaurant idea down the road. We'd be buyers of the stock in the low $20s.

MORNINGSTAR® Stocks 500

Bristol-Myers Squibb BMY

	Rating	Risk	Moat Size	Fair Value	Last Close	Yield %
	★★★★★	Low	Wide	$33.00	$23.15	6.0

Industry	Investment Style	Stock Type	Sector
Drugs	▦ Large Value	▨ High Yield	◉ Healthcare

Company Profile

Bristol-Myers Squibb produces pharmaceuticals and medicines. Its major areas of expertise are oncology, diabetes, HIV/AIDS, and cardiovascular. The firm's top-selling drugs are Pravachol for high cholesterol, Glucophage for Type 2 diabetes and Plavix, an anticlotting medicine. Bristol also sells brand-name products including Enfamil infant formula, Bufferin, and Excedrin pain relievers. Two thirds of sales come from the United States. Bristol sold Clairol to Procter & Gamble and spun off its Zimmer business in 2001.

Management

CEO Peter Dolan is playing musical chairs with his executive team. Since April, he has fired his COO and hired a new CFO and head of research. With Bristol stock in the gutter, Dolan's job is rumored to be on the line.

Strategy

Bristol-Myers Squibb is putting more of its eggs in its pharmaceutical basket. In 2001, it spun off its Zimmer orthopedic implant business, bought DuPont's pharmaceutical unit, and sold its Clairol hair-care business. Bristol is pushing for megablockbuster ideas and making more use of joint ventures, co-promotions, and licensing agreements.

345 Park Avenue   www.bms.com
New York, NY 10154-0037

Competition

Competition	Market Cap $Mil	Debt/ Equity	12 Mo Trailing Sales $Mil	Price/Cash Flow	Return On Assets%	Total Return% 1 Yr	3 Yr
Bristol-Myers Squibb	44,843	0.6	17,588	19.2	11.3	-52.4	-23.7
Pfizer	188,377	0.2	34,407	21.1	18.3	-22.2	1.0
Merck	127,121	0.3	50,430	13.2	15.0	-1.3	-2.5

Price Volatility

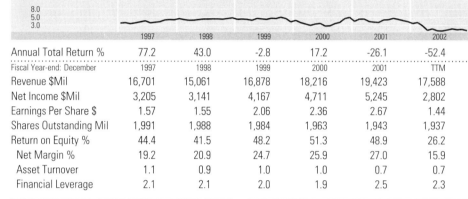

						Monthly Price High/Low — Relative Strength to S&P 500
Annual $Price High Low	46.71 25.34	64.35 42.02	75.40 54.47	71.25 40.38	70.35 48.50	51.90 19.50

$76.4 / 49.0 / 29.0 / 19.0 / 8.0 / 5.0 / 3.0

	1997	1998	1999	2000	2001	2002
Annual Total Return %	77.2	43.0	-2.8	17.2	-26.1	-52.4

Fiscal Year-end: December	1997	1998	1999	2000	2001	TTM
Revenue $Mil	16,701	15,061	16,878	18,216	19,423	17,588
Net Income $Mil	3,205	3,141	4,167	4,711	5,245	2,802
Earnings Per Share $	1.57	1.55	2.06	2.36	2.67	1.44
Shares Outstanding Mil	1,991	1,988	1,984	1,963	1,943	1,937
Return on Equity %	44.4	41.5	48.2	51.3	48.9	26.2
Net Margin %	19.2	20.9	24.7	25.9	27.0	15.9
Asset Turnover	1.1	0.9	1.0	1.0	0.7	0.7
Financial Leverage	2.1	2.1	2.0	1.9	2.5	2.3

Valuation Ratios	Stock	Rel to Industry	Rel to S&P 500
Price/Earnings	16.1	0.7	0.7
Price/Book	4.2	0.6	1.3
Price/Sales	2.6	0.6	1.3
Price/Cash Flow	19.2	0.9	1.4

Major Fund Holders	% of Fund Assets
Ameristock Focused Value	11.37
Thompson Plumb Select	7.89
Fidelity Select Pharmaceuticals	5.97
Thompson Plumb Growth	5.50

Morningstar Grades

Growth [D]	1998	1999	2000	2001
Revenue %	-9.8	12.1	7.9	6.6
Earnings/Share %	-1.3	32.9	14.6	13.1
Book Value/Share %	5.7	14.3	7.6	18.8
Dividends/Share %	-23.5	47.0	14.0	12.2

We estimate revenue will drop 12% in 2002, but the company should return to positive growth in 2003 and beyond. We expect below-industry-average revenue growth of 6% for 2003-06.

Profitability [A+]	1999	2000	2001	TTM
Return on Assets %	24.3	26.8	19.4	11.3
Oper Cash Flow $Mil	4,224	4,652	5,402	2,339
- Cap Spending $Mil	709	589	1,023	1,089
= Free Cash Flow $Mil	3,515	4,063	4,379	1,250

The loss of market exclusivity for key drugs has taken its toll on Bristol. As a result, gross and operating margins are well below normal. Until the company releases restated financials for 2000-02, we are conservatively estimating margins.

Financial Health [A]	1999	2000	2001	06-02
Long-term Debt $Mil	1,342	1,336	6,237	6,140
Total Equity $Mil	8,645	9,180	10,736	10,714
Debt/Equity Ratio	0.2	0.1	0.6	0.6

Bristol took on $5 billion in debt to purchase the DuPont pharmaceutical unit, but its debt/equity ratio of 0.6 is still healthy. Despite slowing sales and dismal cash flow in 2002, Bristol's credit rating remains only a notch below triple A.

Morningstar's Take   By Todd N. Lebor, 12-03-2002   Stock Price as of Analysis: $26.48

We think Bristol will pull out of its death spiral and reward patient investors.

Bristol's troubles run deep. The Securities and Exchange Commission is investigating the company's inventory and pricing practices, leading Bristol to restate revenue from 2000 through 2002. (Although revenue will be restated, we expect cumulative sales for that time to remain constant. Revenue will simply be moved from earlier periods to later periods.) Bristol failed to do proper due diligence before investing more than $1 billion in Imclone Systems, embroiling it in one of 2002's nastiest trading scandals. Sales growth evaporated as three blockbusters lost patent protection. On top of it all, CEO Peter Dolan is scrambling to rebuild his management team after cleaning out most of the executive suite. But all of these troubles are surmountable, in our opinion; Bristol just needs time.

This isn't a cash-starved, debt-laden startup. It's a financially healthy, global pharmaceutical company with hundreds of products. Bristol has a solid product lineup headed by hypertension drug Avapro, anticlotting pill Plavix, and cholesterol-lowering med Pravachol. Each of these drugs has double-digit growth potential, and the company is putting every resource behind achieving that. The November 2002

approval of Abilify, Bristol's first shot at the antipsychotic market, also offers blockbuster potential. Even Eli Lilly, maker of the leading antipsychotic drug Zyprexa, recognizes the potential of Abilify and has lowered its forecasts as a result of the approval. Bristol also has Atazanavir, a protease inhibitor for HIV that has shown promise in late-stage trials. Atazanavir fits well in Bristol's effective HIV franchise, which includes Sustiva, Zerit, and Videx.

These drugs will only stem the bleeding, though. Bristol needs to crank up the productivity in its research unit. To do this, Bristol hired a new research chief and is consolidating several facilities. We think these are steps in the right direction. While the company is rebuilding, it can lean on its nonpharmaceutical units for stable cash flow. About 20% of the company's revenue comes from nutritionals like infant formula Enfamil, wound-care products, and over-the-counter medicines like Excedrin and Bufferin.

Bristol has dug itself into a hole, but a solid balance sheet and an armada of globally branded products should be enough to see it through while it slowly climbs out. We think Bristol stock requires only a 20% discount to our fair value estimate to look attractive, thanks to the firm's fiscal health.

Broadcom BRCM

	Rating	Risk	Moat Size	Fair Value	Last Close	Yield %
	★	High	None	$11.00	$15.06	0.0

Company Profile

Broadcom develops custom semiconductors that enable high-speed data transmission to consumer and business users. The firm's products are used in cable set-top boxes, cable modems, high-speed networking, and direct-broadcast satellites. The firm only designs its chips, and then outsources 100% of its semiconductor manufacturing to third parties. Broadcom's customers include 3Com, Cisco Systems, Motorola, and Scientific-Atlanta.

Management

President and CEO Henry Nicholas co-founded Broadcom with Henry Samueli in 1991; they have 70% of the firm's voting power. Broadcom's management team is topnotch and very aggressive.

Strategy

Broadcom targets the most promising communication chip markets, especially those related to high-speed Internet access, including chips for cable modems, set-top boxes, and home networking. Broadcom works hard to set industry standards, staying at the cutting edge of technology. When attacking markets, the firm tries to be the lowest-cost producer.

16215 Alton Parkway   www.broadcom.com
Irvine, CA 92618-3616

Morningstar Grades

Growth [A]	1998	1999	2000	2001
Revenue %	411.9	140.5	110.3	-12.3
Earnings/Share %	NMF	210.0	NMF	NMF
Book Value/Share %	606.5	110.7	821.1	-38.0
Dividends/Share %	NMF	NMF	NMF	NMF

Broadcom has outperformed rivals. Sales growth of 100% in 2000 was followed by a 12% contraction in 2001, though that was much better than peers'. The firm has grown sequentially in each of the past five quarters.

Profitability [D-]	1999	2000	2001	TTM
Return on Assets %	11.9	-14.7	-75.7	-21.4
Oper Cash Flow $Mil	109	162	49	-32
- Cap Spending $Mil	31	81	71	37
= Free Cash Flow $Mil	78	81	-22	-69

After posting decent margins in 2000, the firm spent almost half of its sales on research and development in 2001. Given the risk of slowing growth, the chipmaker could remain in the red until the end of 2003.

Financial Health [C]	1999	2000	2001	09-02
Long-term Debt $Mil	—	—	4	2
Total Equity $Mil	517	4,475	3,207	3,211
Debt/Equity Ratio	—	—	0.0	0.0

Financial health is sound. Broadcom has minimal debt and generates operating cash flow. As of September 2002, the firm had enough cash and investments on its balance sheet to cover all of its liabilities.

	Industry	Investment Style	Stock Type	Sector
	Semiconductors	▦ Mid Growth	◪ Spec. Growth	▣ Hardware

Competition	Market Cap $Mil	Debt/ Equity	12 Mo Trailing Sales $Mil	Price/Cash Flow	Return On Assets%	Total Return% 1 Yr	3 Yr
Broadcom	4,154	0.0	1,014	—	-21.4	-63.3	-51.0
Texas Instruments	25,982	0.1	8,024	12.8	0.9	-46.2	-32.5
National Semiconductor	2,716	0.0	1,576	20.0	-2.9	-51.3	-29.6

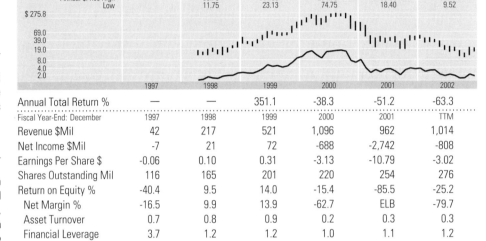

Price Volatility   I Monthly Price High/Low   — Relative Strength to S&P 500

Annual $Price High / Low	33.75 / 11.75	144.50 / 23.13	274.75 / 74.75	139.50 / 18.40	53.35 / 9.52

$275.8
69.0
39.0
19.0
8.0
4.0
2.0

1997   1998   1999   2000   2001   2002

Annual Total Return %	—	—	351.1	-38.3	-51.2	-63.3

Fiscal Year-End: December	1997	1998	1999	2000	2001	TTM
Revenue $Mil	42	217	521	1,096	962	1,014
Net Income $Mil	-7	21	72	-688	-2,742	-808
Earnings Per Share $	-0.06	0.10	0.31	-3.13	-10.79	-3.02
Shares Outstanding Mil	116	165	201	220	254	276
Return on Equity %	-40.4	9.5	14.0	-15.4	-85.5	-25.2
Net Margin %	-16.5	9.9	13.9	-62.7	ELB	-79.7
Asset Turnover	0.7	0.8	0.9	0.2	0.3	0.3
Financial Leverage	3.7	1.2	1.2	1.0	1.1	1.2

Valuation Ratios	Stock	Rel to Industry	Rel to S&P 500
Price/Earnings	NMF	—	—
Price/Book	1.3	0.4	0.4
Price/Sales	4.1	1.1	2.0
Price/Cash Flow	—	—	—

Major Fund Holders	% of Fund Assets
Red Oak Technology Select	7.44
Fidelity Select Network & Infrastruct	4.39
SunAmerica Focused Technology A	3.92
Black Oak Emerging Technology	3.83

Morningstar's Take By Jeremy Lopez, 10-22-2002   Stock Price as of Analysis: $11.51

While Broadcom has been a strong relative performer, we remain uninterested in the stock.

Despite a huge cyclical downturn, Broadcom continues to outperform its peers. The firm remains the dominant supplier of cable modem and set-top box chips--two markets that have held up relatively well despite the carnage in other tech areas. Broadcom has also done well by its early lead in a new corporate networking standard (gigabit Ethernet). And the firm recently entered wireless networking, another attractive market. Broadcom has not only had a knack for identifying strong growth opportunities, but also tended to win big, early leads in markets.

There are good reasons for Broadcom's success. Few communication chipmakers can match the firm's rich trove of intellectual property. Its past acquisitions have been controversial, but Broadcom has benefited greatly from the acquired technologies. Also, management's business acumen has been beneficial. Many chipmakers can develop good technology, but Broadcom thinks more about how to develop products that are reasonably priced so they will be widely adopted by customers.

But we lose interest in Broadcom once we consider the vulnerability of its growth. Like sharks

that smell blood in the water, other firms have been quick to enter Broadcom's promising chip niches. Marvell Technology, for example, has recently taken share from Broadcom in networking. And even if competitors fail to take share, they'll certainly make life difficult for Broadcom. The product cycles in these niches tend to be short, making the barriers to entry fairly low. More competition is likely to lead to commodification, pricing pressures, and lower margins, not to mention more research and development spending to stay ahead of the pack. We suspect all of these factors will govern returns on capital, thus limiting the benefit of growth to investors.

We like Broadcom's long-term growth prospects (although there's a good chance growth could weaken in the short term), but we're not particularly fond of its lack of economic moat. Also, Broadcom doesn't have the cleanest accounting record; the past repricing of employee stock options is Exhibit A. We think the firm will be a leading communication chip supplier for years to come, and would make a good investment at the right price. Given the firm's high risk level, we would require a fairly wide discount to our fair value estimate--at least 40%-50%--before liking the stock.

    MORNINGSTAR® Stocks 500

Data as of 12-31-02

Brocade Communications Systems BRCD

	Rating	Risk	Moat Size	Fair Value	Last Close	Yield %
	UR	High	None	UR	$4.14	0.0

Company Profile

Brocade Communications Systems provides switching hardware for storage area networks. The company's switches enable clients to manage growth in their storage capacity, improve performance between their servers and storage systems, and increase the size and scope of their SANs. Brocade Communications' customers are storage system and server original equipment manufacturers.

Management

CEO Gregory Reyes has been with Brocade since 1998 and owns more than 1% of the outstanding shares. COO Michael Byrd recently stepped down.

Strategy

As the leader in storage networking hardware, Brocade wants to rule SANs. The company has developed tight partnerships with leading storage hardware and software vendors, creating sizable barriers to entry, and expanded into the high-end storage switch market, which McData leads.

1745 Technology Drive
San Jose, CA 95110
www.brocade.com

Morningstar Grades

Growth [A]	1998	1999	2000	2001
Revenue %	185.9	183.3	379.0	55.9
Earnings/Share %	NMF	NMF	NMF	-96.4
Book Value/Share %	—	—	NMF	17.2
Dividends/Share %	NMF	NMF	NMF	NMF

The top line averaged triple-digit annual growth during the past five years, but those days are over. Lackluster spending on storage and the high cost of deploying SANs won't make life any easier for Brocade.

Profitability [C]	1999	2000	2001	TTM
Return on Assets %	2.1	14.9	0.4	-0.7
Oper Cash Flow $Mil	16	70	112	121
- Cap Spending $Mil	3	41	82	84
= Free Cash Flow $Mil	13	29	29	37

Since EMC's gross margins have plummeted, we have little faith that Brocade's margins will hold steady at 60%. We think it is only a matter of time before Brocade's margins start declining as well.

Financial Health [B+]	1999	2000	2001	07-02
Long-term Debt $Mil	—	—	—	574
Total Equity $Mil	84	391	538	668
Debt/Equity Ratio	—	—	—	0.9

The balance sheet is okay, with nearly $300 million in net cash (after deducting long-term debt). But free cash flow isn't great because of high capital expenditures.

Industry	Investment Style	Stock Type	Sector
Systems & Security	Small Growth	Spec. Growth	Software

Competition	Market Cap $Mil	Debt/ Equity	12 Mo Trailing Sales $Mil	Price/Cash Flow	Return On Assets%	Total Return% 1 Yr	3 Yr
Brocade Communications Systems	970	0.9	526	8.0	-0.7	-87.5	-52.4
Qlogic	3,224	—	379	—	—	—	—
Emulex	1,519	—	272	—	—	—	—

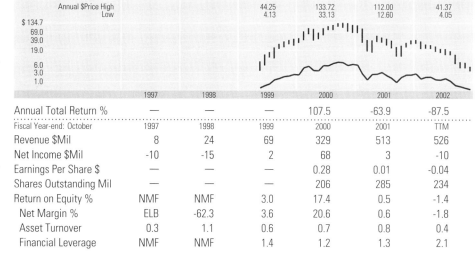

Price Volatility				
Annual $Price High / Low	44.25 / 4.13	133.72 / 33.13	112.00 / 12.60	41.37 / 4.05

	1997	1998	1999	2000	2001	2002
Annual Total Return %	—	—	—	107.5	-63.9	-87.5

Fiscal Year-end: October	1997	1998	1999	2000	2001	TTM
Revenue $Mil	8	24	69	329	513	526
Net Income $Mil	-10	-15	2	68	3	-10
Earnings Per Share $	—	—	—	0.28	0.01	-0.04
Shares Outstanding Mil	—	—	—	206	285	234
Return on Equity %	NMF	NMF	3.0	17.4	0.5	-1.4
Net Margin %	ELB	-62.3	3.6	20.6	0.6	-1.8
Asset Turnover	0.3	1.1	0.6	0.7	0.8	0.4
Financial Leverage	NMF	NMF	1.4	1.2	1.3	2.1

Valuation Ratios	Stock	Rel to Industry	Rel to S&P 500
Price/Earnings	NMF	—	—
Price/Book	1.5	0.6	0.5
Price/Sales	1.8	0.5	0.9
Price/Cash Flow	8.0	0.7	0.6

Major Fund Holders	% of Fund Assets
Black Oak Emerging Technology	4.94
Conseco Science & Technology Y	4.00
Oppenheimer Enterprise A	3.90
Oppenheimer Emerging Technologies A	3.35

Morningstar's Take By Mike Trigg, 12-20-2002 Stock Price as of Analysis: $4.46

Brocade is well positioned in the one of the fastest-growing areas of storage, but concerns over pricing pressure limit our enthusiasm. We'd need a 50% discount to our fair value estimate before buying.

Brocade dominates the market for storage switches, which connect servers and storage boxes to create the backbone of a storage area network (SAN). SANs have many advantages over storage that connects directly to servers. The problem with the latter is that if a particular server goes down, the data attached to it can't be accessed. SANs also support increased physical distance; the servers and storage can be located in different rooms or buildings.

Like most technology companies, Brocade has struggled as IT spending has declined. Problems have been compounded by overcapacity, since many businesses bought too much storage during the late 1990s. That said, long-term demand for storage is good, particularly for SANs. As firms depend more on the Internet and software to run business processes like sales and marketing, data will need to be stored and accessed quickly. And in the wake of 9/11, companies understand more than ever the importance of backing up critical information.

Our biggest worry is that increased competition will diminish Brocade's pricing power, hurting margins. We've already seen this happen to EMC. It's also possible that Brocade's success will encourage hardware vendors like IBM to enter the fray by either developing their own switches or acquiring a smaller competitor. That would be disastrous, since Brocade depends on partnerships to generate the majority of its revenue, and it can't match Big Blue's broad product offering.

For now, most of the pricing pressure is coming from McData, the number-two player. But Cisco Systems has also set its sights on Brocade's market with the recent acquisition of Andiamo. Cisco has greater financial resources, a huge installed base of existing customers, and the ability to undercut any company on price by bundling products.

We think Brocade has decent growth prospects, but significant competition should wring out excess profits (60% gross margins) over the long term. With Brocade's best days possibly over, we wouldn't buy the stock until it became unavoidably cheap.

Brunswick BC

	Rating ★★★	Risk Med.	Moat Size None	Fair Value UR	Last Close $19.86	Yield % 2.5

Company Profile

Brunswick produces and markets recreational products. The company's consumer brands include Mercury and Mariner outboard engines; Mercury Mercruiser sterndrives and inboard engines; and Sea Ray, Bayliner, Baja, and Boston Whaler pleasure boats. Its brands also include Life Fitness, Hammer Strength, and ParaBody fitness equipment; Brunswick bowling centers, equipment, and consumer products; and Brunswick billiards tables.

Management

Former COO George Buckley became CEO when predecessor Peter Larson was ousted in June 2000. Buckley has sold many of the acquisitions Larson made, and will focus on tightening up Brunswick's operations to restore profitability.

Strategy

Brunswick's previous CEO had made an aggressive series of acquisitions to diversify the firm's operations in leisure products. However, some of these proved to be costly mistakes, and current management has sold underperforming assets to focus on the core businesses of fitness equipment, bowling, billiards, and boat and marine engines.

One North Field Court   www.brunswick.com
Lake Forest, IL 60045-4811

Industry	Investment Style	Stock Type	Sector
Recreation	▦ Mid Value	⚡ High Yield	⌂ Consumer Goods

Competition

	Market Cap $Mil	Debt/ Equity	12 Mo Trailing Sales $Mil	Price/Cash Flow	Return On Assets%	Total Return% 1 Yr	3 Yr
Brunswick	1,790	0.5	3,502	4.9	1.6	-6.5	0.7
AMF Bowling	2	—	702	—	—	—	—
Genmar	—	—	—	—	—	—	—

Price Volatility

| Monthly Price High/Low | — Relative Strength to S&P 500

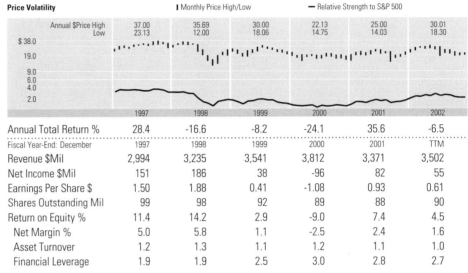

	1997	1998	1999	2000	2001	2002
Annual $Price High	37.00	35.69	30.00	22.13	25.00	30.01
Low	23.13	12.00	18.06	14.75	14.03	18.30
Annual Total Return %	28.4	-16.6	-8.2	-24.1	35.6	-6.5

Fiscal Year-End: December	1997	1998	1999	2000	2001	TTM
Revenue $Mil	2,994	3,235	3,541	3,812	3,371	3,502
Net Income $Mil	151	186	38	-96	82	55
Earnings Per Share $	1.50	1.88	0.41	-1.08	0.93	0.61
Shares Outstanding Mil	99	98	92	89	88	90
Return on Equity %	11.4	14.2	2.9	-9.0	7.4	4.5
Net Margin %	5.0	5.8	1.1	-2.5	2.4	1.6
Asset Turnover	1.2	1.3	1.1	1.2	1.1	1.0
Financial Leverage	1.9	1.9	2.5	3.0	2.8	2.7

Valuation Ratios

	Stock	Rel to Industry	Rel to S&P 500
Price/Earnings	32.6	1.9	1.4
Price/Book	1.4	0.7	0.5
Price/Sales	0.5	0.2	0.3
Price/Cash Flow	4.9	0.4	0.4

Major Fund Holders

	% of Fund Assets
Fidelity Advisor Small Cap A	3.85
Excelsior Small Cap	3.60
Marshall Mid-Cap Growth Inv	3.51
Diamond Hill Focus A	3.21

Morningstar Grades

Growth [C-]	1998	1999	2000	2001
Revenue %	8.1	9.5	7.6	-11.6
Earnings/Share %	25.3	-78.2	NMF	NMF
Book Value/Share %	1.0	6.3	-14.5	5.0
Dividends/Share %	0.0	0.0	0.0	0.0

Brunswick has increased sales about 6% annually since 1992, but the weak consumer environment and discontinued operations sent the top line down 12% in 2001. Things could improve in 2003, however, if consumer demand picks up by the end of the year.

Profitability [C]	1999	2000	2001	TTM
Return on Assets %	1.2	-3.0	2.6	1.6
Oper Cash Flow $Mil	299	257	331	363
- Cap Spending $Mil	167	156	111	104
= Free Cash Flow $Mil	132	101	219	259

Brunswick acquired several businesses that earned lower profit margins than its traditional operations, reducing overall profitability. Strict cost controls will help bring operating margins back toward historical levels, but pricing remains key.

Financial Health [B-]	1999	2000	2001	09-02
Long-term Debt $Mil	623	602	600	598
Total Equity $Mil	1,300	1,067	1,111	1,237
Debt/Equity Ratio	0.5	0.6	0.5	0.5

Because the firm financed much of its acquisition spree with cash, its balance sheet is in good shape. The company has fairly low debt and generates good amounts of free cash flow.

Morningstar's Take   By T.K. MacKay, 11-10-2002   Stock Price as of Analysis: $19.11

Brunswick's venerable brands make a nice long-term investment, but we'd only buy if the stock fell into 5-star territory.

Brunswick's 20% share of the boating industry and 40% share of the marine engine business is the company's golden goose and Achilles' Heel rolled into one. 77% of Brunswick's sales come from marine and boating-related products, making it nearly impossible for the firm to hedge itself against the cyclical nature of boating. The boating industry's tide is slow to come in and out, with two to three years spanning between tops and bottoms of each cycle. We're currently in the middle of a slump that started in late 2000, and many dealers are gun-shy about taking on significant inventory until signs of a turnaround are clear.

In a sour economy, a $50,000 boat won't sell itself. Consumers are holding off on purchasing many of the big-ticket consumer items Brunswick offers until things brighten up and people see their stock portfolios heading north instead of south. Brunswick's introduction of the Bayliner 175 at a retail price of $9,999 is a smart move to attract otherwise timid boat buyers, but it may only capture a small percentage of first time boat buyers that would otherwise be shopping in the plentiful used boat market.

To account for our concerns about Brunswick's reliance on the boating industry, we've built some conservative sales and profit growth assumptions into our model. Price discounts led to a five-percentage-point reduction in gross margins in 2001 compared with 2000, and unless sales spike in upcoming quarters, these discounts are likely to continue for the foreseeable future. We think weaker-than-normal operating margins will probably stand pat at their current level of around 6% of sales, about 2 percentage points below Brunswick's average operating margin over the past five years.

This depressed level of profitability generates a return on invested capital below Brunswick's cost of capital. This won't change until Brunswick can boost operating profits. The company has already shut down manufacturing facilities, implemented hiring and salary freezes and has reduced bonuses, so we think the only way for margins to improve from here is through better pricing. We have yet to see convincing enough evidence that the boating industry is in recovery mode to get excited about better margins, and would require a 50% margin of safety before we jumped aboard Brunswick's shares.

M✪RNINGSTAR® Stocks 500

Cablevision Systems A CVC

	Rating	Risk	Moat Size	Fair Value	Last Close	Yield %
	UR	High	None	UR	$16.74	0.0

Company Profile

Cablevision Systems consists of two companies, the Cablevision NY Group (CVC) and the Rainbow Media Group (RMG), both of which are publicly traded stocks. CVC comprises cable television operations serving approximately 3 million subscribers in the New York metropolitan area, as well as ownership in Madison Square Garden's assets. RMG is a tracking stock that represents Cablevision Systems' national programming networks--the Sports Channel, Prime Sports Channel, Bravo, and American Movie Classics channels--as well as its non-New York regional sports services.

Management

Chairman Charles Dolan founded Cablevision in 1973. His son, James, is the CEO. Like many other cable companies, Cablevision is controlled via supervoting stock by insiders (mainly the Dolan family).

Strategy

Unlike other cable operators, Cablevision owns both cable pipes and content. It also owns Madison Square Garden as well as other New York-based assets. Cablevision has been selling all its cable networks that are not clustered around New York City.

1111 Stewart Avenue
Bethpage, NY 11714-3581
www.cablevision.com

Morningstar Grades

Growth [C+]

	1998	1999	2000	2001
Revenue %	67.5	20.8	11.9	-0.1
Earnings/Share %	NMF	NMF	NMF	529.2
Book Value/Share %	NMF	NMF	NMF	NMF
Dividends/Share %	NMF	NMF	NMF	NMF

Growth has slowed from past levels, when the top line was juiced by various acquisitions. Cablevision expects to lose at least 1% of its cable subscriber base in 2002.

Profitability [C+]

	1999	2000	2001	TTM
Return on Assets %	-11.2	2.8	9.9	-6.9
Oper Cash Flow $Mil	274	125	-222	-142
- Cap Spending $Mil	871	1,326	1,385	1,249
= Free Cash Flow $Mil	-597	-1,201	-1,608	-1,392

Complex bookkeeping distorts profits in the cable industry; what matters is operating cash flow. On this front, Cablevision is posting just average results, with annual growth of 10%-12%.

Financial Health [D]

	1999	2000	2001	09-02
Long-term Debt $Mil	—	6,455	6,978	7,956
Total Equity $Mil	-3,067	-2,530	-1,586	-1,890
Debt/Equity Ratio	—	ELB	ELB	NMF

Cablevision's balance sheet is a joke; debt makes up most of the company's capitalization. The firm could face a cash shortfall of as much as $1 billion in 2003.

Industry	Investment Style	Stock Type	Sector
Cable TV	Mid Core	Slow Growth	Media

Competition

	Market Cap $Mil	Debt/ Equity	12 Mo Trailing Sales $Mil	Price/Cash Flow	Return On Assets%	Total Return% 1 Yr	3 Yr
Cablevision Systems A	5,054	NMF	4,517	—	-6.9	-64.7	-36.1
AOL Time Warner	56,278	0.3	41,024	8.1	-34.6	-59.2	-44.6
Hughes Electronic H	14,233	0.3	8,743	19.8	-2.8	-30.7	-31.0

Price Volatility

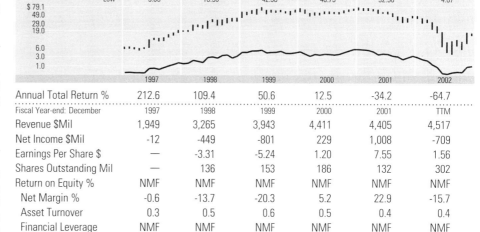

		Monthly Price High/Low				— Relative Strength to S&P 500	
Annual $Price High Low	20.87 5.85	42.69 18.50	78.06 42.38	73.81 46.73	77.74 32.50	48.25 4.67	
	1997	1998	1999	2000	2001	2002	

	1997	1998	1999	2000	2001	TTM
Annual Total Return %	212.6	109.4	50.6	12.5	-34.2	-64.7
Fiscal Year-end: December	1997	1998	1999	2000	2001	TTM
Revenue $Mil	1,949	3,265	3,943	4,411	4,405	4,517
Net Income $Mil	-12	-449	-801	229	1,008	-709
Earnings Per Share $	—	-3.31	-5.24	1.20	7.55	1.56
Shares Outstanding Mil	—	136	153	186	132	302
Return on Equity %	NMF	NMF	NMF	NMF	NMF	NMF
Net Margin %	-0.6	-13.7	-20.3	5.2	22.9	-15.7
Asset Turnover	0.3	0.5	0.6	0.5	0.4	0.4
Financial Leverage	NMF	NMF	NMF	NMF	NMF	NMF

Valuation Ratios	Stock	Rel to Industry	Rel to S&P 500
Price/Earnings	10.7	1.0	0.5
Price/Book	—	—	—
Price/Sales	1.1	0.3	0.6
Price/Cash Flow	—	—	—

Major Fund Holders	% of Fund Assets
MassMutual Instl Focused Value S	8.48
Gabelli Value A	4.37
Goldman Sachs Internet Tollkeeper A	4.34
ASAF Gabelli All-Cap Value A	3.30

Morningstar's Take By Todd P. Bernier, 12-02-2002 Stock Price as of Analysis: $17.10

Cablevision must reduce leverage and focus solely on cable before we'd be interested in it.

Despite wonderful fundamentals, including 3 million subscribers clustered in the most lucrative cable market in America, Cablevision has severely mismanaged its balance sheet. Total debt exceeds $9 billion; the ratio of net debt/EBITDA, above 6, is near covenant limitations. But things are only going to get worse in 2003, as cash losses are projected to be in the neighborhood of $1 billion.

Management has plans to limit the cash shortfall by selling noncore assets and slashing capital spending. The company has put Clearview Cinemas up for auction and plans to shutter most of its money-losing The Wiz electronic stores. Budgeted capital spending for 2003 is half the level of 2002. We applaud these moves, but think it is a case of too little too late.

It isn't Cablevision's weak balance sheet in isolation that concerns us; many companies have too much debt. But Cablevision's excessive leverage is the result of too many initiatives, few of which have paid dividends. The firm has interests in such superfluous realms as satellite, wireless telecom, movie theaters, and electronics retail. Any attempts at improving the balance sheet must involve the sale

of these assets--providing the capital desperately needed for cable system upgrades. Only one third of Cablevision's coverage footprint is digitized, which explains why the firm has lost basic analog customers to satellite-service providers that can offer more extensive programming. As a result, Cablevision's penetration of digital cable service is a fraction of the industry average.

The valuation divide between this firm and the cable industry elite is surprisingly narrow, despite the threat of insolvency hanging like Damocles' sword over Cablevision. We agree that Cablevision has attractive assets--foremost is its valuable Rainbow programming unit--that it can use to pare leverage. But finding a buyer willing to pay cash, as opposed to common equity (as was the case in recent transactions), for those assets is another story. Until that day comes, we'd avoid the headache that is Cablevision and opt for a more financially stable, better-managed cable operator like Cox or Comcast.

Cadbury Schweppes PLC ADR CSG

	Rating	Risk	Moat Size	Fair Value	Last Close	Yield %
	★★★	Low	None	$27.00	$25.61	2.6

Company Profile

Cadbury Schweppes produces food and beverage products. Its products include Canada Dry, Crush, 7 UP, Dr Pepper, A&W, Sunkist, and Squirt soft drinks; Schweppes tonic waters and carbonated beverages; Hawaiian Punch, Motts, Oasis, Vibe, and Capri-Sun fruit drinks; Energade sports drinks, and Cadbury's Dairy Milk and Flake chocolate. Cadbury Schweppes markets its products in the United Kingdom and overseas. Sales outside the United Kingdom account for about 75% of the company's total sales. The company acquired Triarc's Snapple operations in 2000.

Management

John Sunderland, a longtime Cadbury veteran, will become chairman in May 2003 after nearly seven years as chief executive. He will be replaced as CEO by Todd Stitzer, an American who has served as the company's chief strategy officer.

Strategy

Cadbury sold most of its international beverage business to Coca-Cola in 1999, then purchased Snapple as part of its increasing emphasis on high-margin noncarbonated beverages. It has been working to revive growth in its European candy business, particularly in the United Kingdom, and its purchase of Adams Gum makes it a much bigger player in the North American confectionery market.

25 Berkeley Square   www.cadburyschweppes.com
London, W1J 6HB

Morningstar Grades

Growth [A+]	1998	1999	2000	2001
Revenue %	-2.7	4.7	6.4	20.6
Earnings/Share %	-49.9	85.2	-21.7	9.0
Book Value/Share %	9.0	22.0	19.1	9.1
Dividends/Share %	5.6	5.3	5.0	4.8

Cadbury's sales increased 21% in 2001, but only 4% excluding currency effects and the acquisition of Snapple. North American beverage comparable volume was down slightly in the first half of 2002, but pricing helped boost revenue.

Profitability [A-]	1999	2000	2001	TTM
Return on Assets %	13.0	7.6	7.3	7.3
Oper Cash Flow $Mil	1,334	1,382	1,587	1,587
- Cap Spending $Mil	207	192	345	345
= Free Cash Flow $Mil	1,126	1,190	1,243	1,243

Cadbury's net margin of 9.6% in the first half of 2002 was up from 9.1% a year earlier. This margin is about half of Coca-Cola's, though different accounting standards make comparisons difficult.

Financial Health [A]	1999	2000	2001	12-01
Long-term Debt $Mil	502	622	2,028	2,028
Total Equity $Mil	3,613	3,930	4,174	4,174
Debt/Equity Ratio	0.1	0.2	0.5	0.5

Cadbury is as solid as they come financially, with less than half the financial leverage of the average stock in the S&P 500 Index and strong free cash flow.

Industry	Investment Style	Stock Type	Sector
Food Mfg.	▦ Large Growth	◪ High Yield	⬡ Consumer Goods

Competition	Market Cap $Mil	Debt/ Equity	12 Mo Trailing Sales $Mil	Price/Cash Flow	Return On Assets%	Total Return% 1 Yr	3 Yr
Cadbury Schweppes PLC ADR	13,106	0.5	7,957	8.3	7.3	2.0	2.7
Coca-Cola	108,635	0.2	21,554	24.3	12.8	-5.6	-6.4
Nestle SA ADR	85,869	—	50,054	—	—	—	—

Price Volatility   ▌Monthly Price High/Low   ━ Relative Strength to S&P 500

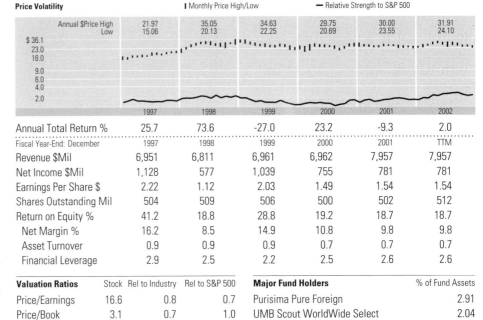

		1997	1998	1999	2000	2001	2002
Annual $Price High / Low		21.97 / 15.06	35.05 / 20.13	34.63 / 22.25	29.75 / 20.69	30.00 / 23.55	31.91 / 24.10

	1997	1998	1999	2000	2001	2002
Annual Total Return %	25.7	73.6	-27.0	23.2	-9.3	2.0

Fiscal Year-End: December	1997	1998	1999	2000	2001	TTM
Revenue $Mil	6,951	6,811	6,961	6,962	7,957	7,957
Net Income $Mil	1,128	577	1,039	755	781	781
Earnings Per Share $	2.22	1.12	2.03	1.49	1.54	1.54
Shares Outstanding Mil	504	509	506	500	502	512
Return on Equity %	41.2	18.8	28.8	19.2	18.7	18.7
Net Margin %	16.2	8.5	14.9	10.8	9.8	9.8
Asset Turnover	0.9	0.9	0.9	0.7	0.7	0.7
Financial Leverage	2.9	2.5	2.2	2.5	2.6	2.6

Valuation Ratios	Stock	Rel to Industry	Rel to S&P 500
Price/Earnings	16.6	0.8	0.7
Price/Book	3.1	0.7	1.0
Price/Sales	1.6	1.1	0.8
Price/Cash Flow	8.3	0.7	0.6

Major Fund Holders	% of Fund Assets
Purisima Pure Foreign	2.91
UMB Scout WorldWide Select	2.04
Bear Stearns Alpha Growth Portfolio A	1.88
UMB Scout WorldWide	1.73

Morningstar's Take   By David Kathman, 12-30-2002   Stock Price as of Analysis: $25.29

Despite some recent glitches in its beverage business, we remain cautiously optimistic about Cadbury Schweppes' prospects. However, we'd only feel comfortable buying the stock under $20.

Though the deal to purchase Adams Gum from Pfizer has garnered the headlines recently, Cadbury's North American beverage business is its largest and most profitable division, with more than a third of overall sales and operating margins near 30%. The Dr Pepper and 7 UP brands are the cornerstone of these beverage operations, but sales have been stagnant in the past couple of years. Cadbury is trying to rejuvenate these key brands through new products, most notably Dr Pepper Red Fusion and dnL, a fruit-flavored green soft drink, but it remains to be seen how these products will fare in the long run.

Matters weren't helped over the summer when Pepsi Bottling Group and PepsiAmericas both dumped 7 UP in favor of PepsiCo's Sierra Mist, forcing Cadbury to find new distributors for the brand. Despite the short-term disruption, this change should actually be a long-term positive for Cadbury, since it has forced the company to re-examine its reliance in many areas on bottlers who primarily handle Coke and Pepsi products. Cadbury has strengthened its relationship with Dr Pepper-7 UP Bottling, and is

otherwise building up a network of bottlers that won't be beholden to its rivals.

Cadbury has also been building up a strong portfolio of noncarbonated beverages through its $1.4 billion purchase of Snapple and more recent purchases like Nantucket Nectars. Cadbury now gets nearly half of its North American beverage revenue from noncarbonated drinks--a much greater percentage than rivals Coke or Pepsi. That's a good thing, because noncarbs have generally been growing much faster in recent years than carbonated soft drinks, and should continue to do so. Plus, Cadbury got an excellent distribution system in the Snapple purchase, which it can use to help the other noncarb brands it's been buying.

Cadbury's newly enlarged beverage business has become highly profitable; the North American beverage division's 29% operating margin in the first half of 2002 was nearly twice that of Cadbury's other main divisions. A companywide efficiency initiative has helped margins, and should continue to do so through 2005. Although the Adams purchase is likely to hurt margins in the short term, Cadbury looks good for the long run, and we'd be happy to buy the stock at the right price.

 **MORNINGSTAR®** Stocks 500

Callaway Golf ELY

	Rating	Risk	Moat Size	Fair Value	Last Close	Yield %
	★	High	None	$11.00	$13.25	2.1

Company Profile

Callaway Golf manufactures golf clubs. It sells its line of Big Bertha, Great Big Bertha, and Biggest Big Bertha oversized metal woods and conventional-style metal woods, irons, wedges, and putters. These clubs, as well as those marketed under other trademarks, are sold to intermediate and advanced golfers at premium prices through retailers of professional-quality golf clubs in the United States and overseas. Sales of metal woods account for approximately 60% of the company's total sales. Foreign sales account for about 45% of Callaway Golf's total sales.

Management

Founder Ely Callaway's death in 2001 left a cloud of uncertainty over the firm's future. But we are confident that his successor, Ronald Drapeau, will follow in Ely's footsteps by doing exactly what Ely did: develop premium, cutting-edge golf equipment.

Strategy

The company has expanded its product line into accessories and two series of performance golf balls in an effort to capitalize on its powerful brand name.

2180 Rutherford Road   www.callawaygolf.com
Carlsbad, CA 92008-8815

Morningstar Grades

Growth [C-]	1998	1999	2000	2001
Revenue %	-16.6	2.3	16.5	-2.6
Earnings/Share %	NMF	NMF	44.9	-27.4
Book Value/Share %	-3.4	8.8	1.3	1.2
Dividends/Share %	0.0	0.0	0.0	0.0

Annual growth rates have been choppy over the past few years because of product changes and the varying popularity of golf. Sales will likely grow in the low single digits over the next few years as the industry matures and competition intensifies.

Profitability [A-]	1999	2000	2001	TTM
Return on Assets %	9.0	12.8	9.0	9.6
Oper Cash Flow $Mil	166	91	100	113
- Cap Spending $Mil	56	28	35	35
= Free Cash Flow $Mil	110	63	65	78

Callaway's strong brand name has helped the company maintain 45%-50% gross margins on its products. Free cash flows have been strong over the years, despite wavering sales.

Financial Health [A]	1999	2000	2001	06-02
Long-term Debt $Mil	—	—	3	—
Total Equity $Mil	500	512	514	557
Debt/Equity Ratio	—	—	0.0	0.0

The company has a strong balance sheet, with plenty of cash and zero debt. Free cash flows were up about 4% in 2001 from 2000, and should top $50 million in 2002.

Industry	Investment Style	Stock Type	Sector
Recreation	▦ Small Value	⭫ Cyclical	🖾 Consumer Goods

Competition	Market Cap $Mil	Debt/ Equity	12 Mo Trailing Sales $Mil	Price/Cash Flow	Return On Assets%	Total Return% 1 Yr	3 Yr
Callaway Golf	877	0.0	774	7.7	9.6	-29.6	-6.0
Nike B	11,798	0.2	10,076	11.6	6.5	-20.1	0.3

Price Volatility

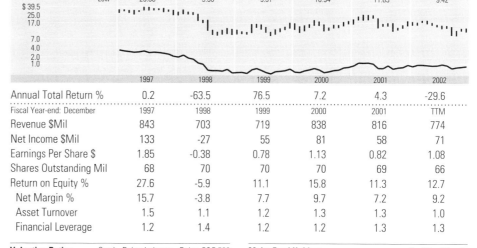

	Monthly Price High/Low	— Relative Strength to S&P 500

Annual $Price High / Low	38.50 / 25.88	33.94 / 9.38	18.19 / 9.31	20.81 / 10.94	27.18 / 11.83	20.68 / 9.42

	1997	1998	1999	2000	2001	2002
Annual Total Return %	0.2	-63.5	76.5	7.2	4.3	-29.6

Fiscal Year-end: December	1997	1998	1999	2000	2001	TTM
Revenue $Mil	843	703	719	838	816	774
Net Income $Mil	133	-27	55	81	58	71
Earnings Per Share $	1.85	-0.38	0.78	1.13	0.82	1.08
Shares Outstanding Mil	68	70	70	70	69	66
Return on Equity %	27.6	-5.9	11.1	15.8	11.3	12.7
Net Margin %	15.7	-3.8	7.7	9.7	7.2	9.2
Asset Turnover	1.5	1.1	1.2	1.3	1.3	1.0
Financial Leverage	1.2	1.4	1.2	1.2	1.3	1.3

Valuation Ratios	Stock	Rel to Industry	Rel to S&P 500
Price/Earnings	12.3	0.7	0.5
Price/Book	1.6	0.8	0.5
Price/Sales	1.1	0.3	0.6
Price/Cash Flow	7.7	0.7	0.6

Major Fund Holders	% of Fund Assets
Pitcairn Select Value	2.27
Pacific Advisors Small Cap A	2.19
Sterling Capital Small Cap Val Instl	2.13
Principal Inv Ptr SmallCap Val AdvPfd	2.04

Morningstar's Take By T.K. MacKay, 12-17-2002 Stock Price as of Analysis: $11.95

We're believers in the Callaway brand name, but would look for a substantial margin of safety before considering the shares.

The exclusive brand name in golf has driven Callaway from nothing to nearly $1 billion in annual sales in just 20 years. Sales growth, though, could be a thing of the past. The popularity of the sport over the past decade deserves much credit for the firm's success, but intense competition and a mature golf industry will probably keep a lid on substantial sales expansion. The golf industry, including golf courses and amateur players, has grown around 2% annually over the past decade. A continued shaky economy could slow this rate to zero.

We think Callaway's name will persist, regardless of the industry's growth rate, putting it in a position to capitalize on the nation's 75 million baby boomers preparing to retire. The company has top share in woods, irons, and putters, commanding roughly a third of the market in each of these club categories. This dominance is reflected in Callaway's return on equity, which tops 12%. The company also generates plenty of free cash flow, which it has used to repurchase about 7 million of its shares since August 2001. Callaway carries no debt, which should allow it to buy back even more shares.

Maintaining that dominance won't be an easy putt for Callaway, though. Nike is heading full steam into the golf market with its own clubs and sponsored players (including Tiger Woods). For Callaway to maintain its leading share in golf clubs, advertising will be essential. Our model incorporates fairly high marketing costs relative to historical levels to reflect Callaway's increased advertising. Callaway's profit margins aren't what they used to be, in part because of increased competition, and a brand name won't carry itself in a sport when Nike enters the fray.

We believe Callaway's returns on investment will remain attractive, despite increased competition. The company is exploring ways to revive (or possibly sell) its golf ball business, and has also employed a cost-cutting program that has resulted in a 30% reduction in per-club production costs since 2001.

Callaway won't be the growth machine it once was, but its brand name is second to none. The company continues to generate substantial free cash flow, which could lead to a significant share buyback program. Callaway is a great way to invest in the consumer product industry, but we would consider its shares only at a 60% or better discount to our fair value estimate.

Campbell Soup CPB

	Rating	Risk	Moat Size	Fair Value	Last Close	Yield %
	★★★	Med.	Narrow	$24.00	$23.47	3.4

Company Profile

Campbell Soup manufactures prepared foods. Its products include Campbell's canned soups and pasta sauces, Swanson broths, V-8 vegetable juice, Franco-American pasta products, Prego sauce, Pace Mexican foods, and Pepperidge Farm baked goods. Campbell Soup sells its products to grocery chains and other retailers, wholesale food-service distributors, institutional customers, and government agencies in the United States and abroad. The company also makes Godiva chocolates and operates Godiva retail shops.

Management

The board appointed Doug Conant as CEO in January 2001. He has 25 years' experience in the food business with General Mills, Kraft, and most recently, as president of Nabisco for six years.

Strategy

Campbell is trying to boost its revenue and strengthen its product lines, with its biggest problem being its lackluster soup business. It recently introduced Soup at Hand for convenience-loving consumers, and over the next three years it will slowly roll out a line of flavor-enhanced condensed soups. It's also spending marketing dollars to get Godiva and other nonsoup brands back on track.

Campbell Place
Camden, NJ 08103-1799
www.campbellsoup.com

Industry	Investment Style	Stock Type	Sector
Food Mfg.	▦ Large Value	▨ High Yield	⌂ Consumer Goods

Competition

	Market Cap $Mil	Debt/ Equity	12 Mo Trailing Sales $Mil	Price/Cash Flow	Return On Assets%	Total Return% 1 Yr	3 Yr
Campbell Soup	9,633	620.0	6,109	10.2	8.2	-19.0	-10.6
Kraft Foods	45,853	0.5	34,063	11.1	5.3	16.1	—
General Mills	17,278	1.5	8,540	17.8	2.7	-7.6	14.6

Price Volatility

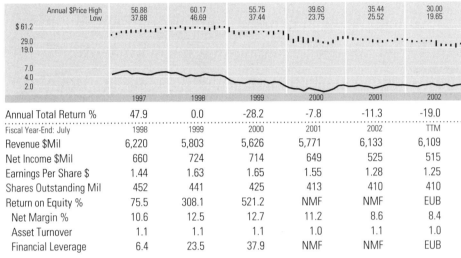

Annual $Price High Low	56.88 37.68	60.17 46.69	55.75 37.44	39.63 23.75	35.44 25.52	30.00 19.65

	1997	1998	1999	2000	2001	2002
Annual Total Return %	47.9	0.0	-28.2	-7.8	-11.3	-19.0

Fiscal Year-End: July	1998	1999	2000	2001	2002	TTM
Revenue $Mil	6,220	5,803	5,626	5,771	6,133	6,109
Net Income $Mil	660	724	714	649	525	515
Earnings Per Share $	1.44	1.63	1.65	1.55	1.28	1.25
Shares Outstanding Mil	452	441	425	413	410	410
Return on Equity %	75.5	308.1	521.2	NMF	NMF	EUB
Net Margin %	10.6	12.5	12.7	11.2	8.6	8.4
Asset Turnover	1.1	1.1	1.1	1.0	1.1	1.0
Financial Leverage	6.4	23.5	37.9	NMF	NMF	EUB

Valuation Ratios

	Stock	Rel to Industry	Rel to S&P 500
Price/Earnings	18.8	0.9	0.8
Price/Book	EUB	—	—
Price/Sales	1.6	1.1	0.8
Price/Cash Flow	10.2	0.9	0.8

Major Fund Holders

	% of Fund Assets
SunAmerica Focused Multi-Cap Value A	2.98
American Century Value Inv	2.26
SunAmerica Value A	2.02
American Century Equity Income Inv	2.01

Morningstar Grades

Growth [B-]

	1999	2000	2001	2002
Revenue %	-6.7	-3.1	2.6	6.3
Earnings/Share %	13.2	1.2	-6.1	-17.4
Book Value/Share %	-72.3	-40.2	NMF	NMF
Dividends/Share %	7.5	1.7	0.0	-30.0

A declining condensed soup business has hurt sales growth in recent years. Net sales grew 6% in fiscal 2002, but almost all of that increase came from an acquisition in the European soup business.

Profitability [A]

	2000	2001	2002	TTM
Return on Assets %	13.7	11.0	9.2	8.2
Oper Cash Flow $Mil	1,165	1,106	1,017	941
- Cap Spending $Mil	200	200	269	282
= Free Cash Flow $Mil	965	906	748	659

Earnings were down 18% in fiscal 2002. We expect only modest profit growth in 2003 as Campbell continues restructuring.

Financial Health [C]

	2000	2001	2002	10-02
Long-term Debt $Mil	1,218	2,243	2,449	1,860
Total Equity $Mil	137	-247	-114	3
Debt/Equity Ratio	8.9	ELB	ELB	620.0

With negative shareholders' equity at the end of fiscal 2002, Campbell's balance sheet is not pretty. However, ample operating cash flow alleviates our concern over the heavy debt load.

Morningstar's Take By David Kathman, 12-06-2002 Stock Price as of Analysis: $24.17

For the past year, Campbell has been trying to deal with the changing dynamics of the soup business. We can't get too excited about the stock right now, at least not until the company backs up its promises with real results.

Campbell's biggest problem is fixing its ailing soup division, the company's largest segment and the one most associated with it in the public mind. Shipments of traditional condensed soups, where Campbell is still dominant, declined 5% in fiscal 2002 as part of a long downward trend. Consumers have been flocking instead to ready-to-serve soups like Campbell's Chunky and Select, which are heartier and easier to prepare. Campbell's ready-to-serve shipments in the United States were up 9% in fiscal 2002, but here it faces strong competition from Progresso, where shipments have been growing at double-digit rates. New owner General Mills has already expanded Progresso's product line and has a formidable marketing machine.

In an effort to jump-start soup sales and exploit the trend toward convenient foods that can be eaten on the go, Campbell recently introduced Soup at Hand, which can be microwaved and eaten with one hand. Longer-term, the firm's also using "cold blend technology" to develop condensed soups with greatly enhanced flavors. These have tested well with consumers, but they will be rolled out slowly, most not until late 2003.

Campbell's nonsoup businesses are a key part of the restructuring, since they account for about half of revenue, but the company's plans here are considerably less focused. In the biscuits and confectionery division, sales have been growing in all three businesses (Pepperidge Farm, Godiva chocolate, and Arnott's biscuits), but profits have been down because of increased marketing and infrastructure spending. Similarly, sales in North American sauces and beverages grew slightly in fiscal 2002, with some strong performers (Pace) partially offset by some disappointments (V-8 Splash). But profits fell 20% for the year, with higher marketing spending a contributing factor.

Campbell's turnaround is still very far from complete, and the success of its newer initiatives remains up in the air. We think the company is moving in the right direction, but has not yet made enough progress to make an attractive investment. We'd want to see at least a 30% discount to our fair value estimate of $24 before we'd be interested in the stock.

MORNINGSTAR® Stocks 500

Capital One Financial COF

	Rating	Risk	Moat Size	Fair Value	Last Close	Yield %
	★★★★★	High	Wide	$50.00	$29.72	0.4

Industry	Investment Style	Stock Type	Sector
Finance	Mid Core	Aggr. Growth	Financial Services

Company Profile

Capital One Financial is one of the 10 largest issuers of Visa and MasterCard credit cards in the United States. The company markets its products to potential customers by examining credit records for credit risk and usage characteristics. Depending on a potential customer's credit record, Capital One offers credit cards that have low introductory interest rates, are secured by a collateral accounts, or have a balance-transfer option.

Management

CEO Richard Fairbank and COO Nigel Morris joined Signet Bank in the early 1990s to boost the credit card business. Their strategy worked so well that Signet--now part of Wachovia--spun off Capital One in 1994.

Strategy

Capital One is choosy about its customers: It wants just the best. Unlike niche-oriented rivals, the firm targets the gamut of consumers, from subprime borrowers to the affluent. Within each segment, it uses proprietary technology to lure only clients it believes will be the most profitable.

2980 Fairview Park Drive   www.capitalone.com
Falls Church, VA 22042-4525

Competition

Competition	Market Cap $Mil	Debt/ Equity	12 Mo Trailing Sales $Mil	Price/Cash Flow	Return On Assets%	Total Return% 1 Yr	3 Yr
Capital One Financial	6,594	—	9,099	—	2.3	-44.8	-11.6
Citigroup	177,948	—	106,096	—	1.6	-24.2	1.1
Bank One	42,636	—	22,444	—	1.1	-4.4	9.4

Price Volatility

Monthly Price High/Low — Relative Strength to S&P 500

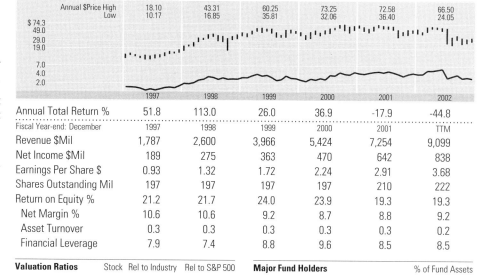

Annual $Price High Low	18.10 10.17	43.31 16.85	60.25 35.81	73.25 32.06	72.58 36.40	66.50 24.05

	1997	1998	1999	2000	2001	2002
Annual Total Return %	51.8	113.0	26.0	36.9	-17.9	-44.8

Fiscal Year-end: December	1997	1998	1999	2000	2001	TTM
Revenue $Mil	1,787	2,600	3,966	5,424	7,254	9,099
Net Income $Mil	189	275	363	470	642	838
Earnings Per Share $	0.93	1.32	1.72	2.24	2.91	3.68
Shares Outstanding Mil	197	197	197	197	210	222
Return on Equity %	21.2	21.7	24.0	23.9	19.3	19.3
Net Margin %	10.6	10.6	9.2	8.7	8.8	9.2
Asset Turnover	0.3	0.3	0.3	0.3	0.3	0.2
Financial Leverage	7.9	7.4	8.8	9.6	8.5	8.5

Valuation Ratios	Stock	Rel to Industry	Rel to S&P 500
Price/Earnings	8.1	0.7	0.3
Price/Book	1.5	0.5	0.5
Price/Sales	0.7	0.4	0.4
Price/Cash Flow	—	—	—

Major Fund Holders	% of Fund Assets
Neuberger Berman Focus Inv	10.97
Weitz Hickory	7.43
First Funds Growth & Income I	5.14
Pitcairn Select Growth	5.05

Morningstar Grades

Growth [A+]	1998	1999	2000	2001
Revenue %	45.5	52.5	36.8	33.7
Earnings/Share %	41.9	30.3	30.2	29.9
Book Value/Share %	38.9	17.8	30.4	60.9
Dividends/Share %	0.0	-0.2	0.1	0.1

After increased managed loans 40%-50% in the past two years, the company will slow growth to 20%-25%, more in line with its historical average and at a rate that should make investors less nervous.

Profitability [A+]	1999	2000	2001	TTM
Return on Assets %	2.7	2.5	2.3	2.3
Oper Cash Flow $Mil	1,273	1,443	1,268	—
- Cap Spending $Mil	351	374	327	—
= Free Cash Flow $Mil	—	—	—	—

Largely by avoiding bad debt, Capital One has grown quickly and added shareholder value. Return on average managed equity increased to 23.4% in the third quarter, and return on managed assets increased to 1.6%.

Financial Health [A]	1999	2000	2001	09-02
Long-term Debt $Mil	—	—	—	—
Total Equity $Mil	1,516	1,963	3,323	4,336
Debt/Equity Ratio	—	—	—	—

The firm operates in a highly leveraged sector, but it has actually decreased leverage over the past year.

Morningstar's Take   By Richard McCaffery, 12-01-2002   Stock Price as of Analysis: $35.83

The core of Capital One's competitive advantage is its information strategy. For more than 10 years the company has been testing products, processes, and consumer behavior, and using the results to guide strategy. Its move into the subprime market in 1996, for example, wasn't a rush to beat earnings estimates, but a decision made after four years of testing secured cards.

Testing allowed the firm to mass-customize products--an unusual ability in a scale business. It's not easy. Small differences in credit lines and yields are the difference between charge-off rates of 5% and 15%. Because testing drives the strategy, the company doesn't market products that will undermine credit quality. It doesn't research products that won't sell. It's a good system, with credit, operations, and marketing functioning as part of one unit.

This made Capital One very responsive, which is why it's grown so fast. When the company thought it could make money in the prime market with teaser rates in the early 1990s, it did so. In 1997, when competition heated up and returns fell below the company's 20% hurdle rate, Capital One left the prime segment and didn't return until late 2000, when pricing rationalized. It pushed into superprime when its scoring methodology and efficiency allowed

it to underprice rivals. While some have criticized the company for growing too fast, we think it's been opportunistic.

Of course, there are risks. Most high-flying lenders that blew up at one time impressed investors with their credit skills. Capital One has never been tested in a severe consumer downturn. There's an unknown risk with every loan portfolio, especially one that's grown fast and includes subprime credits.

But given its credit line management, charge-off rates, reserving methodology, and revenue-recognition policies, we think management is conservative. And we think the business model is profitable enough and flexible enough to bend with the times. On a managed basis over the past five years, for example, Capital One generated on average an 18% return on invested capital, well above its cost of capital. New regulations and competition will reduce these returns, but some of that will be offset as new ventures like auto lending turn a profit.

We think Capital One's abilities, like those of Southwest Airlines allowed the firm to expand the definition of the typical customer. We think it's a business with a sustainable advantage.

Cardinal Health CAH

	Rating	Risk	Moat Size	Fair Value	Last Close	Yield %
	★★★	Med.	Narrow	$65.00	$59.19	0.2

Company Profile

Cardinal Health distributes health- and beauty-care products. The company distributes pharmaceuticals, surgical and hospital supplies, and various other items sold by retail drugstores, hospitals, alternative-care centers, and the pharmacy departments of supermarkets and mass merchandisers. It also offers support services like in-pharmacy computer systems. In addition, the company operates specialty wholesaling businesses including a pharmaceutical-repackaging program for independent and chain customers. It acquired Bindley Western Industries in 2001.

Management

Robert Walter has been chairman and CEO since Cardinal's creation in 1971. He transformed Cardinal from a pure pharmaceutical distribution company into a vertically integrated firm servicing a variety of needs in the health-care supply chain.

Strategy

To supplement internal revenue and earnings growth, Cardinal acquires strong companies that are first or second in their respective industries. Using acquisition synergies to cut costs and cross-sell products, Cardinal has become a vital link in the supply chain between health-care manufacturers and providers.

7000 Cardinal Place www.cardinal.com
Dublin, OH 43017

Morningstar Grades

Growth [B-]	1999	2000	2001	2002
Revenue %	15.3	17.2	25.0	6.6
Earnings/Share %	4.7	42.9	17.5	22.3
Book Value/Share %	14.2	12.3	21.5	16.8
Dividends/Share %	29.9	10.4	21.4	17.6

Cardinal has been increasing sales faster than its competitors thanks to its larger mix of retail buyers. Regardless of whether it continues to trump competitors, strong prescription drug demand should continue to fuel low- to mid-teen sales growth.

Profitability [A]	2000	2001	2002	TTM
Return on Assets %	6.0	5.9	6.4	7.2
Oper Cash Flow $Mil	504	872	984	1,451
- Cap Spending $Mil	331	341	285	298
= Free Cash Flow $Mil	173	531	699	1,153

Cardinal's cost-cutting efforts and expansion into nondistribution businesses have increased its operating margin. We model additional improvements over the next few years, but expect longer-term margin expansion will be increasingly difficult.

Financial Health [B]	2000	2001	2002	09-02
Long-term Debt $Mil	1,525	1,871	2,207	2,238
Total Equity $Mil	4,400	5,437	6,393	6,354
Debt/Equity Ratio	0.3	0.3	0.3	0.4

Cardinal's debt/equity ratio of 0.35 is lower than the industry average and still declining. With expected operating cash flows of about $1 billion in fiscal 2003, the company will have no problem servicing its debt.

Industry	Investment Style	Stock Type	Sector
Medical Goods & Services	Large Growth	Classic Growth	Healthcare

Competition	Market Cap $Mil	Debt/ Equity	12 Mo Trailing Sales $Mil	Price/Cash Flow	Return On Assets%	Total Return% 1 Yr	3 Yr
Cardinal Health	26,192	0.4	52,687	18.1	7.2	-8.3	22.3
McKesson	7,847	—	53,513	—	—	—	—
AmerisourceBergen	5,750	0.5	39,518	10.8	3.1	-14.4	55.4

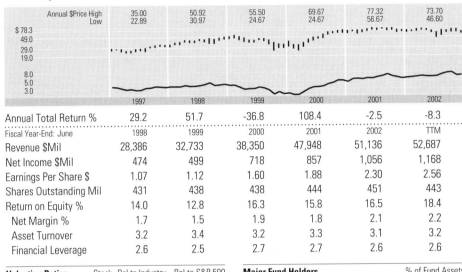

Price Volatility — Monthly Price High/Low — Relative Strength to S&P 500

	1997	1998	1999	2000	2001	2002
Annual $Price High	35.00	50.92	55.50	69.67	77.32	73.70
Low	22.89	30.97	24.67	24.67	56.67	46.60
Annual Total Return %	29.2	51.7	-36.8	108.4	-2.5	-8.3

Fiscal Year-End: June	1998	1999	2000	2001	2002	TTM
Revenue $Mil	28,386	32,733	38,350	47,948	51,136	52,687
Net Income $Mil	474	499	718	857	1,056	1,168
Earnings Per Share $	1.07	1.12	1.60	1.88	2.30	2.56
Shares Outstanding Mil	431	438	438	444	451	443
Return on Equity %	14.0	12.8	16.3	15.8	16.5	18.4
Net Margin %	1.7	1.5	1.9	1.8	2.1	2.2
Asset Turnover	3.2	3.4	3.2	3.3	3.1	3.2
Financial Leverage	2.6	2.5	2.7	2.7	2.6	2.6

Valuation Ratios	Stock	Rel to Industry	Rel to S&P 500
Price/Earnings	23.1	1.0	1.0
Price/Book	4.1	1.0	1.3
Price/Sales	0.5	1.0	0.2
Price/Cash Flow	18.1	1.0	1.4

Major Fund Holders	% of Fund Assets
Live Oak Health Sciences	8.87
Fidelity Dividend Growth	7.41
Parnassus	6.90
Wayne Hummer Growth	6.83

Morningstar's Take By Damon Ficklin, 11-20-2002 Stock Price as of Analysis: $65.00

Cardinal Health is a leading health-care company that distributes pharmaceutical products and provides services that span the entire pharmaceutical product life cycle. We would look to buy shares at a 30% margin of safety to our fair value estimate.

Cardinal's cost structure is a big competitive advantage. Although the company is much more operationally diversified than its competitors, pharmaceutical distribution still provides about 82% of sales and 51% of operating income. In this high-volume, low-margin business, cost control is the name of the game. With sales approaching $40 billion and an operating margin of less than 3%, a 10-basis-point cost advantage translates into $40 million of marginal profits in this segment.

While competitors Amerisource Bergen and McKesson are not far behind, Cardinal has consistently improved its operating leverage and we are confident that it will remain the low-cost leader. This is a business driven by marginal improvements, so catching the leader is a slow process.

Cardinal's diversity is also a competitive advantage. The company has successfully expanded into high-growth markets in pharmaceuticals, medical products and services, and automation and information services. It holds a number-one or -two position in each of its major lines, and each business segment has been growing faster than the market in which it competes. Its breadth of products and services in concentrated markets enables Cardinal to interact with its customers more regularly than its competitors can. This strengthens its relationships and provides more cross-selling opportunities.

Although Cardinal is expanding its other business segments (more than 70% of capital expenditures have gone into its nondistribution segments over the past three years), pharmaceutical distribution will continue to dominate the mix for the next several years. We expect Cardinal to continue to realize scale benefits and deliver small operating margin improvements as it spreads its fixed costs over a growing sales base. In the long term, however, Cardinal will have to increase the proportion of more-profitable nondistribution segments to notably improve its operating margins.

Cardinal is a market leader that will be hard to catch. Nevertheless, as its business continues to grow in size and complexity, meeting the high earnings growth expectations that its success has fostered will be increasingly difficult. We would require a 30% margin of safety to our fair value estimate before buying shares.

MORNINGSTAR® Stocks 500

Caremark RX CMX

Rating	Risk	Moat Size	Fair Value	Last Close	Yield %
★★★	Med.	Narrow	$18.00	$16.25	0.0

Company Profile

Caremark RX is one of the largest pharmaceutical services companies in the United States. The company's primary services involve the design and administration of programs aimed at reducing the costs and improving the safety and convenience of prescription drug use. Caremark dispenses drugs through its own mail-distribution network as well as through all major retail pharmacies. Major customers include sponsors of health benefit plans like employers, managed-care companies, and government agencies.

Management

Mac Crawford became president, CEO, and chairman in 1998, when the company was known as MedPartners. In 2000, James Dickerson Jr. replaced Crawford as president. Together, they have turned Caremark into a focused pure-play PBM.

Strategy

Now that Caremark has exited the physician practice management market, it is focusing on its pharmacy benefit management and specialty distribution businesses. Caremark continues to improve services through customized benefit plan options and the best prescription drug mail-delivery system in the industry.

3000 Galleria Tower
Birmingham, AL 35244
www.caremark.com

Industry	Investment Style	Stock Type	Sector
Managed Care	Mid Growth	Spec. Growth	Healthcare

Competition

	Market Cap $Mil	Debt/ Equity	12 Mo Trailing Sales $Mil	Price/Cash Flow	Return On Assets%	Total Return% 1 Yr	3 Yr
Caremark RX	3,709	NMF	6,440	9.8	22.2	-0.4	53.4
Merck	127,121	0.3	50,430	13.2	15.0	-1.3	-2.5
Express Scripts	3,757	0.6	12,188	9.3	5.8	2.7	15.6

Price Volatility

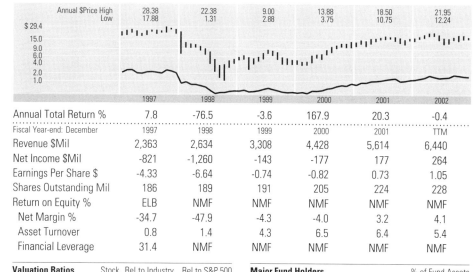

Monthly Price High/Low — Relative Strength to S&P 500

Annual $Price High Low	28.38 17.88	22.38 1.31	9.00 2.88	13.88 3.75	18.50 10.75	21.95 12.24
	1997	1998	1999	2000	2001	2002
Annual Total Return %	7.8	-76.5	-3.6	167.9	20.3	-0.4

Fiscal Year-end: December	1997	1998	1999	2000	2001	TTM
Revenue $Mil	2,363	2,634	3,308	4,428	5,614	6,440
Net Income $Mil	-821	-1,260	-143	-177	177	264
Earnings Per Share $	-4.33	-6.64	-0.74	-0.82	0.73	1.05
Shares Outstanding Mil	186	189	191	205	224	228
Return on Equity %	ELB	NMF	NMF	NMF	NMF	NMF
Net Margin %	-34.7	-47.9	-4.3	-4.0	3.2	4.1
Asset Turnover	0.8	1.4	4.3	6.5	6.4	5.4
Financial Leverage	31.4	NMF	NMF	NMF	NMF	NMF

Valuation Ratios

	Stock	Rel to Industry	Rel to S&P 500
Price/Earnings	15.5	0.7	0.7
Price/Book	—	—	—
Price/Sales	0.6	0.8	0.3
Price/Cash Flow	9.8	1.0	0.7

Major Fund Holders

	% of Fund Assets
Reserve Small-Cap Growth R	5.31
Turner Healthcare & Biotechnology	4.73
Fidelity Select Medical Delivery	4.60
Pax World Growth	4.59

Morningstar Grades

Growth [A]

	1998	1999	2000	2001
Revenue %	11.5	25.6	33.9	26.8
Earnings/Share %	NMF	NMF	NMF	NMF
Book Value/Share %	NMF	NMF	NMF	NMF
Dividends/Share %	NMF	NMF	NMF	NMF

While rival PBMs have been growing via acquisitions, Caremark has grown internally. Sales increased an impressive 27% in 2001, and we expect growth in mail services and specialty drug distribution to drive 20% growth in 2002 and 2003.

Profitability [C]

	1999	2000	2001	TTM
Return on Assets %	-18.6	-25.8	20.3	22.2
Oper Cash Flow $Mil	86	221	285	380
- Cap Spending $Mil	20	23	40	44
= Free Cash Flow $Mil	66	198	245	335

Its mail-focused business model generates the best margins in the industry. EBITDA (earnings before interest, taxes, depreciation, and amortization) per prescription is much higher than competitors', and we don't see that changing anytime soon.

Financial Health [D-]

	1999	2000	2001	09-02
Long-term Debt $Mil	1,230	733	696	696
Total Equity $Mil	-1,281	-969	-772	-557
Debt/Equity Ratio	ELB	ELB	ELB	NMF

Caremark's financial health is improving. The firm reduced long-term debt from $1.73 billion in 1998 to $700 million as of September 2002. It also has about $250 million in cash and is generating improved operating cash flows.

Morningstar's Take By Damon Ficklin, 12-17-2002 Stock Price as of Analysis: $16.37

Caremark RX is the most profitable pharmacy benefit manager (PBM). Although we think it has the best business model in the industry, the company is still working to clean up its balance sheet, and the shares look about fully valued.

The PBM business model aims to consolidate pharmaceutical buyers in order to extract large discounts from drug manufacturers and retailer pharmacies. Caremark's customers--large employers and health insurers--don't have the critical mass needed to negotiate these discounts on their own. Although Caremark has fewer members and lower volume than its competitors, it is by far the most profitable. Its operating margins have averaged 5% for the past few years, while Express Scripts and Advance PCS posted margins around 3% and 2%, respectively.

Caremark has delivered industry-leading margins because it has the highest mail penetration rate and a larger mix of corporate clients. The mail pharmacy business is roughly 2-4 times more profitable than the retail pharmacy business, and Caremark leads the pack with about 50% penetration. Merck-Medco, Express Scripts, and Advance PCS have about 30%, 20%, and 10%, respectively.

Caremark's corporate client focus is also a differentiating factor. These accounts are more profitable than managed-care accounts (given Caremark's better negotiating position with small groups), and corporate clients don't switch providers nearly as often. Caremark has retained more than 95% of its clients in the past couple of years.

Caremark also operates the nation's largest specialty distribution business, which further boosts margins. Specialty distribution involves managing and delivering biopharmaceutical products to patients with chronic diseases, like hemophilia. All of the PBMs are trying to push further into this market now because the robust pipeline of biotech products suggests it may be a future growth engine.

Analyzing the PBM business is difficult. Negotiations are closed, and PBM accounting can leave even the most adept financial statement reader wondering who paid what to whom. Forecasting can be a treacherous endeavor. In addition, in an apparent conflict of interest, PBMs often receive rebates from the very drugmakers from which they extract price discounts.

We think that Caremark is poised for continued growth, but given the many risks, we'd require a 40% margin of safety to our fair value estimate before investing.

Carnival CCL

	Rating	Risk	Moat Size	Fair Value	Last Close	Yield %
	★★★	Med.	Narrow	$35.00	$24.95	1.7

Company Profile

Carnival is the world's largest multiple-night cruise line on the basis of number of passengers and revenue. It serves the cruise market through Carnival Cruise Lines, the premium market through Holland America Line, and the luxury market through Windstar Cruises and Seabourn Cruise Line. The lines' itineraries include the Caribbean, Mexican Riviera, South Pacific, Mediterranean, and the Far East. The company also operates the Holland America Westours tour business, 14 hotels, and two luxury day boats. In 2000, 84% of Carnival's sales came from the United States.

Management

Micky Arison, son of Carnival founder Ted Arison, started out as a bingo operator on a cruise ship, and has been at the helm since 1990. The Arisons still control nearly half of the shares. Management continues to expand the firm aggressively, paying little heed to the economy.

Strategy

It's already the world's largest cruise operator, so Carnival aims to grow by becoming a consumer marketing company. It's expanding its distribution with Internet marketing and retail "vacation stores" and adding ports of call, making cruises easily accessible to more of the population. The firm has also been increasing its presence in Europe, where the cruise industry is still in its infancy.

3655 N.W. 87th Avenue
Miami, FL 33178-2428

www.carnivalcorp.com

Industry	Investment Style	Stock Type	Sector
Recreation	Large Core	↗ Classic Growth	Consumer Goods

Competition

	Market Cap $Mil	Debt/ Equity	12 Mo Trailing Sales $Mil	Price/Cash Flow	Return On Assets%	Total Return% 1 Yr	3 Yr
Carnival	14,640	0.4	4,292	11.2	7.7	-9.8	-17.3
P&O Princess Cruises ADR	4,803	—	2,450	—	—	—	—
Royal Caribbean Cruises	3,204	1.4	3,309	5.1	2.6	4.6	-26.6

Price Volatility

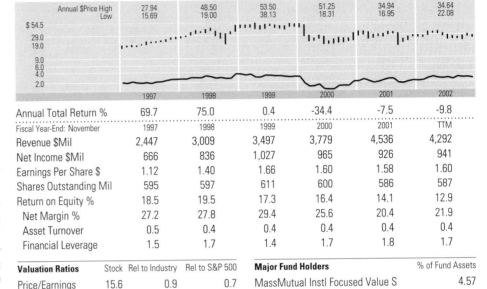

	1997	1998	1999	2000	2001	2002
Annual $Price High	27.94	48.50	53.50	51.25	34.94	34.64
Low	15.69	19.00	38.13	18.31	16.95	22.08
Annual Total Return %	69.7	75.0	0.4	-34.4	-7.5	-9.8

Fiscal Year-End: November	1997	1998	1999	2000	2001	TTM
Revenue $Mil	2,447	3,009	3,497	3,779	4,536	4,292
Net Income $Mil	666	836	1,027	965	926	941
Earnings Per Share $	1.12	1.40	1.66	1.60	1.58	1.60
Shares Outstanding Mil	595	597	611	600	586	587
Return on Equity %	18.5	19.5	17.3	16.4	14.1	12.9
Net Margin %	27.2	27.8	29.4	25.6	20.4	21.9
Asset Turnover	0.5	0.4	0.4	0.4	0.4	0.4
Financial Leverage	1.5	1.7	1.4	1.7	1.8	1.7

Valuation Ratios	Stock	Rel to Industry	Rel to S&P 500
Price/Earnings	15.6	0.9	0.7
Price/Book	2.0	1.0	0.6
Price/Sales	3.4	1.0	1.7
Price/Cash Flow	11.2	1.0	0.8

Major Fund Holders	% of Fund Assets
MassMutual Instl Focused Value S	4.57
Rydex Leisure Inv	4.37
GE Instl Premier Growth Equity Inv	3.89
WPG Large Cap Growth	3.84

Morningstar Grades

Growth [A-]	1998	1999	2000	2001
Revenue %	23.0	16.2	8.0	20.0
Earnings/Share %	25.0	18.6	-3.6	-1.3
Book Value/Share %	18.4	33.5	1.5	15.6
Dividends/Share %	31.3	19.0	12.0	0.0

The cruise industry is growing by about 10% annually, thanks to Carnival's aggressive 17% capacity increase over the next year, not including the acquisition of Princess. We think revenue will expand by about 10% over the next several years.

Profitability [A]	1999	2000	2001	TTM
Return on Assets %	12.4	9.8	8.0	7.7
Oper Cash Flow $Mil	1,330	1,280	1,239	1,302
- Cap Spending $Mil	873	1,003	827	1,136
= Free Cash Flow $Mil	457	276	412	166

The company has maintained excellent returns on assets, and operating margins are quickly recovering to historical levels in the mid-20s. Pricing pressures could keep a lid on profits if consumer sentiment turns sour again.

Financial Health [A]	1999	2000	2001	08-02
Long-term Debt $Mil	868	2,099	2,955	3,044
Total Equity $Mil	5,931	5,871	6,591	7,292
Debt/Equity Ratio	0.1	0.4	0.4	0.4

The company is in good financial shape with more than $3.3 billion in liquidity, half of which is in cash. There's plenty of money to spend on new ships and capital improvements across the board.

Morningstar's Take By T.K. MacKay, 11-11-2002 Stock Price as of Analysis: $28.32

We think Carnival's acquisition of Princess is a good move, but we would only consider Carnival's shares attractive below $21 per share.

In the 1990s, the cruise industry had the wind at its back. Steadily increasing numbers of retirees with above-average disposable income, combined with the greatest economic boom in history, gave cruise operators a green light to build new ships. Carnival's passenger capacity expanded more than 250% between 1990 and 2001 as it doubled its ship base. The ease with which Carnival filled its cabins allowed the company to generate near 30% operating margins in the latter half of the decade.

The future could entail rockier seas for Carnival, though. The firm has 15 ships scheduled for delivery over the next four years, not including the 19 it will acquire through Princess. In 2003 alone, passenger capacity will increase 17%, ahead of the industry's growth rate of 10%. The ability to react quickly to economic conditions still makes Carnival the most profitable cruise line in the world, with operating margins 5 percentage points ahead of the next largest operator, Royal Caribbean. However, we worry that growth may outpace demand in coming years, especially if the country enters a sustained economic slump.

Despite this risk, we are confident in Carnival's ability to quickly integrate new cruise ships. We believe sales will expand by 10% annually over the next few years, primarily because of new ships coming on line and a slow but steady return to the pricing power that the cruise industry had just before 9/11. Another benefit we see in bringing new ships online is cost savings. For cruise lines, costs per berth day (as opposed to revenue per berth day) go down as more ships join the fleet, because shoreside costs are spread over a larger base of vessels. Carnival's no-frills, low-cost structure should allow the company to make these savings a reality, bringing operating margins back toward 26% from their current level of about 20%, but still below historical levels.

We're excited about Carnival's planned acquisition of Princess, and think a formal deal will close in early 2003. We think the combined Carnival/Princess has the makings of a solid investment in the leisure industry, but there is a risk that Carnival could hit any number of speed bumps while integrating Princess' fleet, which has historically been a less-profitable operator than Carnival by about 5 percentage points. For this reason, we'd look for a 40% margin of safety before considering Carnival's shares for the long haul.

MORNINGSTAR® Stocks 500

Caterpillar CAT

	Rating	Risk	Moat Size	Fair Value	Last Close	Yield %
	★★★	Med.	Narrow	$47.00	$45.72	3.1

Company Profile

Caterpillar manufactures earthmoving, construction, and materials-handling machinery and engines. Its products include track and wheel tractors, lift trucks, track and wheel excavators, off-highway trucks, dump trucks, paving equipment, log loaders, and truck components. The company also makes engines used in earthmoving and construction machines; locomotives; and marine, petroleum, agricultural, and industrial applications. Caterpillar also offers financing and insurance services. Approximately 49% of the company's total sales are derived overseas.

Management

Glen Barton has been chairman and CEO since February 1999. He brings an international focus from two overseas stints with the company. He has a broad background in civil engineering and marketing and also has experience working with dealers.

Strategy

Cat's primary strategy is to dominate its current markets through consistent investment in research and development and reductions in capital spending and operating costs. The firm also aims to diversify its customer base through new product development. Cat has put substantial resources behind its financial subsidiary, which has grown in recent years. It uses excess cash for share buybacks.

100 NE Adams Street
Peoria, IL 61629-7310
www.cat.com

Morningstar Grades

Growth [C]	1998	1999	2000	2001
Revenue %	10.7	-6.1	2.4	1.4
Earnings/Share %	-6.0	-36.0	14.8	-23.2
Book Value/Share %	13.5	9.0	5.7	0.7
Dividends/Share %	22.2	13.6	6.4	3.8

Growth has been notoriously cyclical, but product diversification seems to have softened the impact of the current downturn. Sales are running just 5.5% below the last peak. We expect Cat's mature business lines to hold growth to about 4% annually.

Profitability [B]	1999	2000	2001	TTM
Return on Assets %	3.5	3.7	2.6	2.0
Oper Cash Flow $Mil	2,590	2,059	1,987	1,844
- Cap Spending $Mil	1,403	1,593	1,968	1,934
= Free Cash Flow $Mil	1,187	466	19	-90

Cat can be wildly profitable. During the late 1990s, returns on invested capital hit 14%, and returns on equity exceeded 30%. Returns are currently below our estimate of the firm's cost of capital, but we expect that to change as demand recovers.

Financial Health [C]	1999	2000	2001	09-02
Long-term Debt $Mil	9,928	11,334	11,291	12,435
Total Equity $Mil	5,465	5,600	5,611	5,978
Debt/Equity Ratio	1.8	2.0	2.0	2.1

Much of Cat's $18 billion debt load is supported by the financing operation's portfolio of trade and finance receivables and equipment leases. The manufacturing arm is in sound shape, with debt slightly under 40% of total capital.

Industry	Investment Style	Stock Type	Sector
Construction Machinery	▦ Large Value	▨ High Yield	✿ Industrial Mats

Competition

	Market Cap $Mil	Debt/ Equity	12 Mo Trailing Sales $Mil	Price/Cash Flow	Return On Assets%	Total Return% 1 Yr	3 Yr
Caterpillar	15,736	2.1	19,871	8.5	2.0	-9.8	1.6
Deere & Company	10,940	2.8	13,639	5.8	1.3	7.1	4.6
CNH Global NV	569	—	10,014	—	—	—	—

Price Volatility

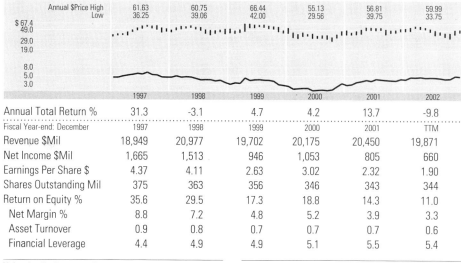

Annual $Price High Low	61.63 36.25	60.75 39.06	66.44 42.00	55.13 29.56	56.81 39.75	59.99 33.75
	1997	1998	1999	2000	2001	2002
Annual Total Return %	31.3	-3.1	4.7	4.2	13.7	-9.8

Fiscal Year-end: December	1997	1998	1999	2000	2001	TTM
Revenue $Mil	18,949	20,977	19,702	20,175	20,450	19,871
Net Income $Mil	1,665	1,513	946	1,053	805	660
Earnings Per Share $	4.37	4.11	2.63	3.02	2.32	1.90
Shares Outstanding Mil	375	363	356	346	343	344
Return on Equity %	35.6	29.5	17.3	18.8	14.3	11.0
Net Margin %	8.8	7.2	4.8	5.2	3.9	3.3
Asset Turnover	0.9	0.8	0.7	0.7	0.7	0.6
Financial Leverage	4.4	4.9	4.9	5.1	5.5	5.4

Valuation Ratios	Stock	Rel to Industry	Rel to S&P 500
Price/Earnings	24.1	1.0	1.0
Price/Book	2.6	1.0	0.8
Price/Sales	0.8	1.0	0.4
Price/Cash Flow	8.5	1.0	0.6

Major Fund Holders	% of Fund Assets
Hennessy Leveraged Dogs	5.44
Payden Growth & Income R	5.04
Willamette Value	4.82
Edgar Lomax Value	4.41

Morningstar's Take By Michael Hodel, 10-25-2002 Stock Price as of Analysis: $41.45

Massive economies of scale and a powerful brand name give Caterpillar a strong competitive position. We'd buy the stock at a 25% discount to our fair value estimate.

Demand for Cat's products depends on a host of factors tied to general economic conditions. Heavy construction equipment demand, for example, depends in part on state and local government spending, which is in turn tied to tax receipts. In addition, the pace of residential and commercial construction activity affects equipment demand. Commodity prices also influence customer decisions, as prospects for profit in the natural resource industries spur or limit capital spending by firms in those businesses.

Cat's long history of producing topnotch heavy equipment has kept its brand name strong. What turns that brand and product strength into a sustainable competitive advantage, in our view, is an extensive dealer network, which provides sales and high-quality customer service around the world. Thanks to its distribution network, Cat can get replacement parts into customers' hands quickly, keeping machines and engines up and running. For customers whose livelihood often depends on the equipment they use, this level of service is necessary,

and Cat can typically charge a premium for it.

Cat faces its share of risks. A global economic downturn would hurt Cat's value. This is a competitive business, and when demand weakens, pricing power erodes. High fixed costs also hurt profits when capacity utilization is low. And competition requires research and development spending and continual capital improvement.

Still, Cat seems to have learned from the recessions of the early 1980s and 1990s, and has diversified its revenue mix over the past decade. The firm has built up its engine capabilities in recent years, often via acquisitions, and has developed new product lines. Cat Financial has steadily boosted earnings over the past decade, and now contributes meaningfully to overall earnings. This business earns a steady interest spread, and charge-offs have been relatively low.

Demand for Cat equipment should remain strong, particularly in areas like Eastern Europe, Asia, and Latin America. The firm has shown it can earn attractive returns on its investments over the course of a cycle. We believe that at the right price--say, a 25% discount to our fair value estimate--Cat could deserve a place in investors' portfolios.

CDW Computer Centers CDWC

	Rating	Risk	Moat Size	Fair Value	Last Close	Yield %
	★★★	Med.	Narrow	$58.00	$43.85	0.0

Company Profile

CDW Computer Centers sells MS-DOS/Microsoft Windows-based microcomputer hardware and peripherals, accessories, networking products, and software. Its microcomputer products include desktop computers, notebooks, and laptops. The company is also authorized to sell the Apple line through its two Chicago-area retail showrooms and to offer Apple-compatible peripherals made by other manufacturers through inbound telemarketing. Currently, the company offers more than 40,000 products at discount prices and generally ships customer orders on a same-day basis.

Management

CEO John A. Edwardson succeeded founder Michael Krasny in January 2001. Before joining CDW, Edwardson was president and CEO of Burns International Services Corporation and president and COO of UAL and United Airlines.

Strategy

CDW's goal is to improve upon its 3% market share by adding new corporate accounts, selling more goods to existing ones, and pushing into the governmental and educational markets. It serves consumers and 80% of the Fortune 500, but small and midsize businesses are the company's bread and butter. CDW tends to sell at the departmental level, rather than the corporate level.

200 N. Milwaukee Ave.   www.cdw.com
Vernon Hills, IL 60061

Morningstar Grades

Growth [A-]	1998	1999	2000	2001
Revenue %	35.8	47.8	50.0	3.1
Earnings/Share %	28.8	46.1	61.3	5.6
Book Value/Share %	35.2	41.6	58.6	24.3
Dividends/Share %	NMF	NMF	NMF	NMF

CDW has shrugged off the sluggish economy to some extent and posted strong earnings and revenue growth relative to its peers. Its historical growth rates are very impressive, and we think the company is well positioned for future growth.

Profitability [A+]	1999	2000	2001	TTM
Return on Assets %	19.4	21.7	18.0	17.1
Oper Cash Flow $Mil	23	142	302	293
- Cap Spending $Mil	9	33	22	9
= Free Cash Flow $Mil	13	109	280	284

CDW's structure has provided returns on assets that should be the envy of companies in just about any industry, and certainly companies that do direct marketing. The firm has done a great job of managing its working capital.

Financial Health [A+]	1999	2000	2001	09-02
Long-term Debt $Mil	0	0	0	0
Total Equity $Mil	391	636	779	862
Debt/Equity Ratio	0.0	0.0	0.0	0.0

No worries here. The company has no debt on its books and generates healthy cash flow.

Industry	Investment Style	Stock Type	Sector
Electronics Stores	▦ Mid Growth	↑ Aggr. Growth	▱ Consumer Services

Competition	Market Cap $Mil	Debt/ Equity	12 Mo Trailing Sales $Mil	Price/Cash Flow	Return On Assets%	Total Return% 1 Yr	3 Yr
CDW Computer Centers	3,680	0.0	4,199	12.6	17.1	-18.4	9.4
Ingram Micro	1,860	—	22,712	—	—	—	—
Insight Enterprises	351	—	2,082	—	—	—	—

Price Volatility

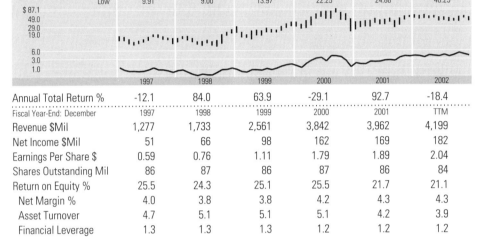

	1997	1998	1999	2000	2001	2002
Annual $Price High	19.50	25.97	40.00	86.13	56.88	60.00
Low	9.91	9.00	13.97	22.25	24.88	40.25
Annual Total Return %	-12.1	84.0	63.9	-29.1	92.7	-18.4

Fiscal Year-End: December	1997	1998	1999	2000	2001	TTM
Revenue $Mil	1,277	1,733	2,561	3,842	3,962	4,199
Net Income $Mil	51	66	98	162	169	182
Earnings Per Share $	0.59	0.76	1.11	1.79	1.89	2.04
Shares Outstanding Mil	86	87	86	87	86	84
Return on Equity %	25.5	24.3	25.1	25.5	21.7	21.1
Net Margin %	4.0	3.8	3.8	4.2	4.3	4.3
Asset Turnover	4.7	5.1	5.1	5.1	4.2	3.9
Financial Leverage	1.3	1.3	1.3	1.2	1.2	1.2

Valuation Ratios	Stock	Rel to Industry	Rel to S&P 500
Price/Earnings	21.5	0.6	0.9
Price/Book	4.3	1.3	1.3
Price/Sales	0.9	2.4	0.4
Price/Cash Flow	12.6	1.4	0.9

Major Fund Holders	% of Fund Assets
Bender Growth C	4.13
ING Technology A	3.43
Alliance Growth B	2.94
William Blair Growth I	2.51

Morningstar's Take By Joseph Beaulieu, 12-02-2002 Stock Price as of Analysis: $50.66

Information technology spending has been in a slump for quite a while, but CDW's steady performance in the current downturn suggests to us that the company is well positioned to ride out the bad times--and to be a big beneficiary of a future recovery.

There are three reasons we think investors might consider CDW shares. First, the company has plenty of growth opportunities. It has only 3% of a very fragmented market. CDW's growth thus far has been entirely internal; the company continues to add new customers and incremental sales to existing accounts. Additionally, the standardization of computer hardware has increased the percentage of IT products that can be purchased off the shelf. This should allow the company to take additional market share from value-added resellers of IT equipment.

Second, we think CDW's product mix and customer mix provide a great deal of stability relative to computer equipment manufacturers and consumer-oriented electronics retailers. This stability is the result of a number of factors. Consumer sales account for just 3% of CDW's revenue, and no single corporate customer generates a significant percentage of sales. Also, since CDW tends to make smaller sales to its customers at the departmental level (rather than large orders through corporations' headquarters), the company doesn't depend on large deals that get negotiated downward--or are canceled or delayed in the face of IT budget cuts.

Finally, the company has demonstrated operational excellence over the past several years. The company turns its inventories approximately every 15 days, and typically ships orders the day they are received.

We're fairly confident that the company can achieve average revenue growth of 15%-20% over the next five years. This assumes that management meets its targeted market share gains as well as its goal of beating overall IT spending growth by 10 percentage points. (We think that IT spending is likely to achieve long-term growth in the 5%-10% range.)

These growth assumptions, combined with only minor margin improvements generated by economies of scale, give us an estimated fair value estimate of $58 per share for CDW. Given the cyclicality of the IT industry and the competitiveness of computer equipment sales, we'd want a 30% discount before considering the shares.

MORNINGSTAR® Stocks 500

Cedar Fair LP FUN

	Rating	Risk	Moat Size	Fair Value	Last Close	Yield %
	★★★	Med.	Wide	$23.00	$23.60	7.0

Company Profile

Cedar Fair, L.P. owns and operates six amusement parks and five water parks across the United States, including Cedar Point, on Lake Erie between Cleveland and Toledo; Knott's Berry Farm in Buena Park, California, near Los Angeles; Dorney Park & Wildwater Kingdom near Allentown, Pennsylvania; Valleyfair near Minneapolis-St. Paul; Worlds of Fun, in Kansas City, Missouri; and Michigan's Adventure near Muskegon. Cedar Fair also operates Camp Snoopy at the Mall of America in Bloomington, Minnesota, under a management contract.

Management

CEO Richard Kinzel's top priority at his company's parks is safety. He and the rest of the firm's officers own about 5% of the partnership's units.

Strategy

Cedar Fair strives to boost its dividend while buying back company units. The firm always has its eyes open to acquisition opportunities, but not at the cost of partner interests.

One Cedar Point Drive   www.cedarfair.com
Sandusky, OH 44870-5259

Morningstar Grades

Growth [C+]

	1998	1999	2000	2001
Revenue %	58.8	4.4	8.0	0.9
Earnings/Share %	7.5	3.2	-8.0	-24.7
Book Value/Share %	6.0	2.7	-4.5	-5.7
Dividends/Share %	2.0	10.5	7.4	4.6

Cedar Fair relies on attendance, ticket price increases, and in-park spending to expand revenue. We believe revenue will increase 3.5% annually over the long term as a result of modest price increases and slow but steady attendance growth.

Profitability [A]

	1999	2000	2001	TTM
Return on Assets %	12.0	10.2	7.1	7.9
Oper Cash Flow $Mil	124	114	125	133
- Cap Spending $Mil	80	93	48	50
= Free Cash Flow $Mil	44	21	77	83

The prize for conservative growth has been solid profitability. Cedar Fair earns returns on invested capital near the top of the leisure industry, and generates ample free cash flows to pay dividends and develop new rides.

Financial Health [B-]

	1999	2000	2001	09-02
Long-term Debt $Mil	261	300	373	338
Total Equity $Mil	344	325	303	332
Debt/Equity Ratio	0.8	0.9	1.2	1.0

Positive free cash flows have kept the balance sheet free of significant debt, unlike at Six Flags. However, a major acquisition may require debt financing.

Industry	Investment Style	Stock Type	Sector
Recreation	Small Value	Slow Growth	Consumer Goods

Competition

	Market Cap $Mil	Debt/ Equity	12 Mo Trailing Sales $Mil	Price/Cash Flow	Return On Assets%	Total Return% 1 Yr	3 Yr
Cedar Fair LP	1,193	1.0	493	8.9	7.9	2.2	15.2
Six Flags	529	—	1,038	—	—	—	—

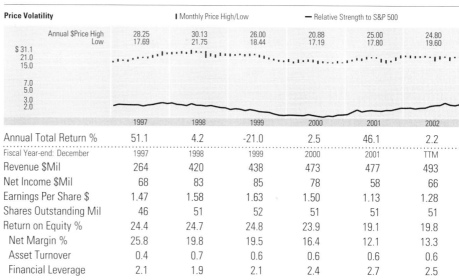

Price Volatility | Monthly Price High/Low   — Relative Strength to S&P 500

Annual $Price High Low	28.25 17.69	30.13 21.75	26.00 18.44	20.88 17.19	25.00 17.80	24.80 19.60

	1997	1998	1999	2000	2001	2002
Annual Total Return %	51.1	4.2	-21.0	2.5	46.1	2.2
Fiscal Year-end: December	1997	1998	1999	2000	2001	TTM
Revenue $Mil	264	420	438	473	477	493
Net Income $Mil	68	83	85	78	58	66
Earnings Per Share $	1.47	1.58	1.63	1.50	1.13	1.28
Shares Outstanding Mil	46	51	52	51	51	51
Return on Equity %	24.4	24.7	24.8	23.9	19.1	19.8
Net Margin %	25.8	19.8	19.5	16.4	12.1	13.3
Asset Turnover	0.4	0.7	0.6	0.6	0.6	0.6
Financial Leverage	2.1	1.9	2.1	2.4	2.7	2.5

Valuation Ratios	Stock	Rel to Industry	Rel to S&P 500
Price/Earnings	18.4	1.1	0.8
Price/Book	3.6	1.8	1.1
Price/Sales	2.4	0.7	1.2
Price/Cash Flow	8.9	0.8	0.7

Major Fund Holders	% of Fund Assets
Rochdale Alpha	6.37
Pioneer Equity-Income A	1.93
Morgan Stanley Next Generation A	1.36

Morningstar's Take   By T.K. MacKay, 10-15-2002   Stock Price as of Analysis: $22.05

A wide economic moat and consistent free cash flows make Cedar Fair an outstanding long-term investment, in our opinion. We would buy the stock below $20 per share.

The primary reason we like Cedar Fair is its wide economic moat. The local-oriented businesses of Cedar Point, Knott's Berry Farm, and Cedar Fair's nine other parks have a great competitive advantage. They are insulated from competition because consumers are choosing between going to the park and some other activity, rather than an alternative amusement park. The parks' focus on local markets makes them much less susceptible to changes in travel spending than a place like Disney World.

Cedar Fair has a long history of generating fat profits. Free cash flows as a percentage of sales have averaged 15% over the past decade, and operating margins are 60% higher than those of Six Flags. One reason is Cedar Fair's attention to customers' spending habits. For example, popular rides like the Millennium Force might require waiting times of an hour or more on weekends. By having more than a dozen soda and candy machines nearby, Cedar Fair keeps customers spending money even when they're just waiting in line. Also, express lines for popular rides limit wait times, allowing for more per-capita

spending on food and sundries.

Another reason we like Cedar Fair is that the weak economy could play right into the company's hands. A family of four may find it much less painful to part with $250 for a weekend at an amusement park like Cedar Point than to spend thousands on a big vacation. While a sustained economic slump could keep a lid on significant revenue growth for Cedar Fair, which we conservatively estimate to be 3.5% annually over the next several years, we are confident in the company's ability to generate attractive returns on its assets.

Cedar Fair's healthy dividend sweetens its charm as an investment. Its yield has averaged about 6.7% over the past decade, and in that period the company has raised its dividend about 7% annually. We assume slightly more moderate annual dividend growth of 6% over the next several years, but are confident that Cedar Fair will continue to generate the cash necessary to make its dividend payment, which its status as a limited partnership requires. We believe Cedar Fair operates the finest amusement parks in the country, and believe the stock is worth considering at a 20% discount to our estimated fair value.

Celestica CLS

	Rating	Risk	Moat Size	Fair Value	Last Close	Yield %
	★★★	Med.	None	$16.00	$14.10	0.0

Company Profile

Celestica provides electronic manufacturing services to original equipment manufacturers. The company's services include design, component selection and procurement, product assurance, assembly, failure analysis, supply-chain management, distribution, and sales support. It also provides memory and power products. Celestica's customers are primarily in the computer and communication sectors. Clients include Cisco Systems, Dell Computer, EMC, Fujitsu, Hewlett-Packard, IBM, Silicon Graphics, and Sun Microsystems.

Management

The highly regarded management team is led by president and CEO Eugene Polistuk. He led the 1996 spin-off from IBM Canada's Toronto manufacturing and technology center. A Canadian private equity firm (Onex) funded the spin-off and owns 25% of equity.

Strategy

Celestica focuses on core electronics manufacturing services--design, assembly, testing, and repair--without getting into peripheral activity like component fabrication. It hopes that a focus on higher-end networking and computing equipment will attract service-oriented and less-price-sensitive clients. Celestica is moving a major chunk of capacity to low-cost countries.

12 Concorde Pl.
Toronto, ON M3C 3R8
www.celestica.com

Morningstar Grades

Growth [A]

	1998	1999	2000	2001
Revenue %	61.9	63.0	84.1	2.6
Earnings/Share %	NMF	NMF	145.0	NMF
Book Value/Share %	—	NMF	69.7	88.5
Dividends/Share %	NMF	NMF	NMF	NMF

We expect sales to fall roughly 18% in 2002 and another 10% in 2003, worse than the rest of the EMS industry, because of Celestica's exposure to poor sales of networking gear. Over a longer period, sales should grow 16%-17% per year.

Profitability [C+]

	1999	2000	2001	TTM
Return on Assets %	2.6	3.5	-0.6	-0.6
Oper Cash Flow $Mil	-94	-85	1,291	1,291
- Cap Spending $Mil	212	283	199	199
= Free Cash Flow $Mil	-306	-368	1,091	1,091

Gross margins have held steady at 7%. While we expect margins to decline for most EMS firms, Celestica's marketing niche and operational strategy should keep longer-term margins closer to 8%.

Financial Health [A]

	1999	2000	2001	12-01
Long-term Debt $Mil	132	131	137	137
Total Equity $Mil	1,658	3,469	4,746	4,746
Debt/Equity Ratio	0.1	0.0	0.0	0.0

Celestica has $854 million of convertible debt (classified as equity), $360 million in operating lease obligations, and $147 million in straight debt. However, cash of $1.8 billion and solid operating cash flow put the firm in good shape.

Industry	Investment Style	Stock Type	Sector
Contract Manufacturers	Mid Value	Spec. Growth	Hardware

Competition

	Market Cap $Mil	Debt/ Equity	12 Mo Trailing Sales $Mil	Price/Cash Flow	Return On Assets%	Total Return% 1 Yr	3 Yr
Celestica	3,239	0.0	10,004	2.5	-0.6	-65.1	-33.1
Flextronics International	4,239	0.2	13,217	5.1	-0.1	-65.9	-26.4
Jabil Circuit	3,542	0.2	3,545	6.4	1.4	-21.1	-17.8

Price Volatility

Annual $Price High Low		13.75 5.19	57.00 12.06	87.00 35.50	76.40 20.69	47.08 9.89
	1997	1998	1999	2000	2001	2002

Annual Total Return %	—	—	349.6	-2.3	-25.5	-65.1

Fiscal Year-End: December	1997	1998	1999	2000	2001	TTM
Revenue $Mil	2,007	3,249	5,297	9,752	10,004	10,004
Net Income $Mil	-7	-48	68	207	-40	-40
Earnings Per Share $	—	—	0.40	0.98	-0.26	-0.26
Shares Outstanding Mil	—	—	167	205	153	230
Return on Equity %	-1.9	-5.6	4.1	6.0	-0.8	-0.8
Net Margin %	-0.3	-1.5	1.3	2.1	-0.4	-0.4
Asset Turnover	1.5	2.0	2.0	1.6	1.5	1.5
Financial Leverage	3.7	1.9	1.6	1.7	1.4	1.4

Valuation Ratios	Stock	Rel to Industry	Rel to S&P 500
Price/Earnings	NMF	—	—
Price/Book	0.7	0.7	0.2
Price/Sales	0.3	1.0	0.2
Price/Cash Flow	2.5	0.5	0.2

Major Fund Holders	% of Fund Assets
Neuberger Berman Focus Inv	4.41
Scudder Flag Communications A	3.28
Van Eck Mid Cap Value A	1.86
Lazard Mid Cap Instl	1.78

Morningstar's Take By Fritz Kaegi, 12-20-2002 Stock Price as of Analysis: $14.56

Celestica's focus on manufacturing networking and computing equipment is currently out of favor with investors. But we think the firm will earn above-average returns in the electronics manufacturing services (EMS) industry, and may have the early makings of an economic moat.

Original equipment manufacturers (OEMs) like Cisco Systems that outsource production choose their EMS partners on the basis of price and quality--traits like stability, operational excellence, specialized skills, and reputation are important. Also, it depends on what the OEM is having manufactured, be it disk drives or supercomputers. OEMs selling more-expensive complex gear, like telecom carrier switches or enterprise storage systems, tend to pay up for top quality.

Celestica caters to two product categories with these characteristics: high-end computing and networking firms. By producing higher-priced goods, Celestica weeds out less discriminating OEMs that may bolt for a better price. Instead, Celestica gains valuable knowledge about the needs of quality-sensitive OEMs and strengthens its relationship with those companies. This creates substantial switching costs for the OEMs, should they want to select an alternate EMS firm. Celestica's

long-standing role as leading contract manufacturer for Sun Microsystems, for instance, means the company can serve Sun's needs far better than other EMS firms; a new entrant would have a much harder time getting this business right than assembling circuit boards for PCs at a slightly cheaper price.

By sticking to core EMS functions like design, assembly, testing, and repair, Celestica stands in contrast to the vertical strategy adopted by Flextronics and Solectron; these firms own complementary segments, like component assembly and logistics. We think Celestica's strategy is superior because it conserves capital, reduces fixed operating costs, and focuses on the core business.

We think Celestica's niche strategy will overcome EMS' cyclical weaknesses. We expect sales will fall 18% in 2002 and another 10% in 2003 after 38% annual growth since 1996. Yet the heavy decline has had little impact on gross margins or overhead as a percentage of sales, and the company has strong operating cash flow. We believe Celestica has a good handle on fixed costs and pricing, and is well positioned to take advantage of long-term growth in high-end networking and computing. We'd be buyers 30%-40% below our fair value estimate.

MORNINGSTAR® Stocks 500

Cendant CD

	Rating	Risk	Moat Size	Fair Value	Last Close	Yield %
	★★★	High	None	$14.00	$10.48	0.0

Industry	Investment Style	Stock Type	Sector
Business Support	▦ Large Core	◈ Spec. Growth	🗎 Business Services

Company Profile

Cendant provides travel, real-estate, hospitality, and financial services. The company facilitates vacation time-share exchanges, manages corporate and government vehicle fleets, franchises real-estate brokerage businesses, and provides home buyers with mortgages. Most of its revenue derives from franchises that include Century 21, Days Inn, Avis, and Jackson Hewitt Tax Service. Cendant purchased two travel-services firms, Galileo International and Cheap Tickets, in October 2001.

Management

Henry Silverman is Cendant's CEO, chairman, and president. As the head of high-flying HFS Inc., Silverman was adored by Wall Street. The spectacular failure of the merger between HFS and CUC International tarnished his image, however.

Strategy

In the wake of accounting issues at the former CUC International, Cendant focused on internal growth and strengthening the balance sheet. Recent purchases highlight the company's shift to a growth-by-acquisition strategy that should lead to accelerated growth, increased market share, and more cross-selling opportunities.

9 West 57th Street
New York, NY 10019
www.cendant.com

Morningstar Grades

Growth [A+]

	1998	1999	2000	2001
Revenue %	21.3	-7.7	-23.3	92.1
Earnings/Share %	NMF	NMF	NMF	-49.4
Book Value/Share %	12.0	-48.6	32.9	102.2
Dividends/Share %	NMF	NMF	NMF	NMF

The acquisitions of Trendwest and NRT should boost revenue over the next several years, but growth relies on Cendant stock trading at high enough levels to make acquisitions without diluting the shares.

Profitability [B-]

	1999	2000	2001	TTM
Return on Assets %	-0.4	4.0	1.1	0.9
Oper Cash Flow $Mil	3,032	1,417	2,784	1,063
- Cap Spending $Mil	277	246	349	368
= Free Cash Flow $Mil	2,755	1,171	2,435	695

As the travel market rebounds, Cendant will regain lost pricing power. Free cash flows have been strong over the past few years, and are likely to top $2 billion, or $1.90 per share, in 2002.

Financial Health [B+]

	1999	2000	2001	09-02
Long-term Debt $Mil	5,159	3,988	15,575	16,300
Total Equity $Mil	2,206	2,774	7,068	9,137
Debt/Equity Ratio	2.3	1.4	2.2	1.8

Cendant has sold operations like its fleet-management service and used the proceeds to pay down debt and repurchase its stock. Future free cash flows will help the company handle additional acquisitions.

Competition

	Market Cap $Mil	Debt/ Equity	12 Mo Trailing Sales $Mil	Price/Cash Flow	Return On Assets%	Total Return% 1 Yr	3 Yr
Cendant	10,862	1.8	13,069	10.2	0.9	-46.6	-23.3
Wells Fargo	79,608	—	28,119	—	1.5	10.3	10.4
Washington Mutual	32,933	—	18,011	—	1.4	8.8	33.2

Price Volatility

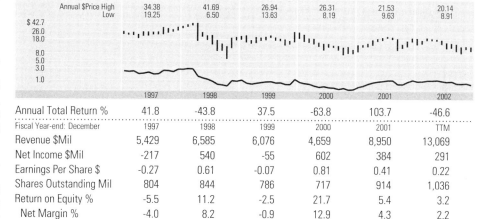

Annual $Price High	34.38	41.69	26.94	26.31	21.53	20.14
Low	19.25	6.50	13.63	8.19	9.63	8.91

	1997	1998	1999	2000	2001	2002
Annual Total Return %	41.8	-43.8	37.5	-63.8	103.7	-46.6

Fiscal Year-end: December	1997	1998	1999	2000	2001	TTM
Revenue $Mil	5,429	6,585	6,076	4,659	8,950	13,069
Net Income $Mil	-217	540	-55	602	384	291
Earnings Per Share $	-0.27	0.61	-0.07	0.81	0.41	0.22
Shares Outstanding Mil	804	844	786	717	914	1,036
Return on Equity %	-5.5	11.2	-2.5	21.7	5.4	3.2
Net Margin %	-4.0	8.2	-0.9	12.9	4.3	2.2
Asset Turnover	0.4	0.3	0.4	0.3	0.3	0.4
Financial Leverage	3.6	4.2	6.9	5.4	4.7	3.5

Valuation Ratios	Stock	Rel to Industry	Rel to S&P 500
Price/Earnings	47.6	1.7	2.0
Price/Book	1.2	0.4	0.4
Price/Sales	0.8	0.4	0.4
Price/Cash Flow	10.2	0.6	0.8

Major Fund Holders	% of Fund Assets
Dessauer Global Equity	13.55
ICAP Select Equity	6.79
Westcore Select	5.47
Oak Value	5.37

Morningstar's Take By T.K. MacKay, 12-17-2002 Stock Price as of Analysis: $11.09

Cendant is moving away from its hyperacquisitive strategy, but we're not too excited about its existing businesses. We'd stay away from the stock unless it traded substantially below our estimated fair value.

The average traveler is likely to cross paths with one of Cendant's businesses. Consider this scenario: A family is considering buying a vacation home. The family members book a flight on Cheaptickets.com and rent a car from Avis when they arrive at their destination. They stay at a Days Inn while they explore time-share opportunities offered by Trendwest/WordMark and visit homes for sale through Century 21. They buy a home and employ Jackson-Hewitt to prepare their more complicated tax return the following year.

Cendant owns every brand in this scenario. No other travel-related firm offers such wide-ranging services. Many of its 30-plus businesses are negatively correlated with the interest rate cycle, which keeps revenue relatively steady over long periods. But a broad brush doesn't always paint an appealing picture. Some of Cendant's brands could face an uphill battle over the next few years.

A bigger share of the car-rental business doesn't guarantee fatter profits. Avis generates the lowest EBITDA (earnings before interest, taxes, depreciation,

and amortization) margins of all Cendant's businesses, and a consumer-led recession would severely limit Cendant's ability to revive Budget, whose operations are more closely tied to leisure travel than Avis' are.

Rising interest rates could stall Cendant's real estate business. Homeowners are taking advantage of low interest rates to refinance mortgages or buy homes--a boon to Cendant Mortgage and Century 21. But if rates rise, this activity will slow, putting a lid on growth in these businesses.

Cendant's travel distribution businesses, which include Cheaptickets.com and computer reservation system Galileo, could also be pressured. The Department of Transportation has proposed changes to the rules for airlines' participation in competing computer reservation systems that could take business from Cendant. Cheaptickets also faces intense competition from other online ticket agents like Expedia and Travelocity.

Also, Cendant's tarnished past makes us worried that the market may never fully value the company on the basis of the cash flows that it will generate over the course of its life. Because of this, we wouldn't consider the stock unless it traded 50% or more below our fair value estimate.

Centurytel CTL

	Rating	Risk	Moat Size	Fair Value	Last Close	Yield %
	★★★	Med.	Narrow	$35.00	$29.38	0.7

Company Profile

Centurytel is the eighth-largest local phone company and eighth-largest wireless carrier in the United States. At the end of 2001, the company served about 1.8 million local phone lines and about 800,000 wireless customers in 21 states. The firm is purchasing an additional 675,000 phone lines in Missouri and Alabama from Verizon for $2.2 billion. CenturyTel is selling all of its wireless assets to Alltel for an estimated $1.3 billion after taxes. Both deals should close later this year. CenturyTel also provides long-distance and Internet access services.

Management

President and CEO Glen Post became chairman in June 2002 after the death of founder and chairman Clarke Williams. Post has been with Centurytel since 1976 and has been CEO since 1992.

Strategy

Centurytel had hoped to bundle wireline and wireless phone services into comprehensive telecom packages, but the economics of the wireless business favor larger operators. The firm has sold its wireless business, using the proceeds to expand its wireline business through acquisitions. Centurytel is working to improve its networks' technology and efficiency to increase revenue per customer.

100 CenturyTel Drive www.centurytel.com
Monroe, LA 71203

Morningstar Grades

Growth [C]	1998	1999	2000	2001
Revenue %	74.9	6.3	10.1	14.7
Earnings/Share %	-12.1	3.7	-4.1	47.9
Book Value/Share %	15.9	19.5	9.3	14.8
Dividends/Share %	5.4	3.9	5.6	5.3

Acquisitions have been the primary means of growth. Internally, access lines in service have been falling, limiting local phone revenue growth to about 3%. Combined with long-distance and data services, growth should average about 5% per year.

Profitability [A]	1999	2000	2001	TTM
Return on Assets %	5.1	3.6	5.4	10.0
Oper Cash Flow $Mil	409	562	665	843
- Cap Spending $Mil	390	450	507	446
= Free Cash Flow $Mil	19	113	159	398

At about 6%, returns on assets are decent given the firm's acquisition activity. Spending to improve networks and integrate acquired phone lines will probably hurt profitability, but the firm's 30% operating margins are superb.

Financial Health [B]	1999	2000	2001	09-02
Long-term Debt $Mil	2,078	3,050	2,088	3,650
Total Equity $Mil	1,840	2,024	2,329	3,056
Debt/Equity Ratio	1.1	1.5	0.9	1.2

The wireless sale greatly improved Centurytel's financial position. Debt following the Verizon line acquisition is only $500 million (or 17%) greater than before. Cash flows should cover interest expenses about 4 times.

	Industry	Investment Style	Stock Type	Sector
	Telecommunication Services	Mid Core	Classic Growth	Telecom

Competition	Market Cap $Mil	Debt/ Equity	12 Mo Trailing Sales $Mil	Price/Cash Flow	Return On Assets%	Total Return% 1 Yr	3 Yr
Centurytel	4,190	1.2	2,259	5.0	10.0	-9.8	-11.7
Verizon Communications	106,011	1.4	67,422	4.7	-0.1	-15.2	-9.8
SBC Communications	90,011	0.6	43,824	6.1	5.1	-28.3	-12.8

Price Volatility | Monthly Price High/Low — Relative Strength to S&P 500

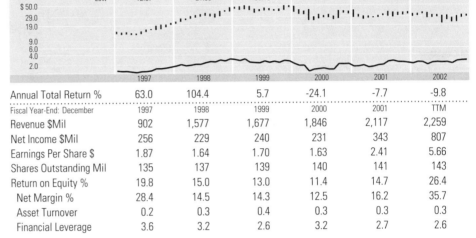

Annual $Price High Low	22.42 12.67	45.17 21.56	49.00 35.13	47.31 24.25	39.38 25.45	35.50 21.13
	1997	1998	1999	2000	2001	2002

Annual Total Return %	63.0	104.4	5.7	-24.1	-7.7	-9.8

Fiscal Year-End: December	1997	1998	1999	2000	2001	TTM
Revenue $Mil	902	1,577	1,677	1,846	2,117	2,259
Net Income $Mil	256	229	240	231	343	807
Earnings Per Share $	1.87	1.64	1.70	1.63	2.41	5.66
Shares Outstanding Mil	135	137	139	140	141	143
Return on Equity %	19.8	15.0	13.0	11.4	14.7	26.4
Net Margin %	28.4	14.5	14.3	12.5	16.2	35.7
Asset Turnover	0.2	0.3	0.4	0.3	0.3	0.3
Financial Leverage	3.6	3.2	2.6	3.2	2.7	2.6

Valuation Ratios	Stock	Rel to Industry	Rel to S&P 500
Price/Earnings	5.2	0.3	0.2
Price/Book	1.4	0.5	0.4
Price/Sales	1.9	1.2	0.9
Price/Cash Flow	5.0	1.0	0.4

Major Fund Holders	% of Fund Assets
Lindner Communications Inv	5.03
Gabelli Global Telecommunications	4.65
Flex-funds Total Return Utilities	4.15
Ariel Appreciation	3.66

Morningstar's Take By Michael Hodel, 12-05-2002 Stock Price as of Analysis: $29.70

We think Centurytel shares are very stable relative to those of the other telecom firms we follow. We would require only a 20% discount to our fair value estimate before considering investment.

The rural phone business isn't exciting. Unlike its urban brethren, who spend their days wiring up huge businesses with ever-greater communication capacity, Centurytel generates the vast majority of its revenue from plain old phone service. What the rural phone business does have, though, is stability. A small market isn't lucrative enough to encourage the big boys of the industry to spend millions of dollars building networks or marketing their service. So while the more urban-focused regional Bells have seen retail lines in service fall 5% or more over the past year, Centurytel has seen lines fall less than 1%--not too bad given the state of the economy. Centurytel's margins have also remained very strong, and not because of any major cost-cutting.

Centurytel is working to improve the quality of its networks to allow new services, most notably high-speed Internet access. Adding services boosts revenue growth a bit and further insulates the firm from competition. Unlike the Bells, Centurytel can also offer customers long-distance services throughout its territory. Long-distance isn't a great business, but it can tack additional dollars onto each customer's monthly bill. Centurytel has become a skillful acquiror of unwanted rural Bell lines, boosting revenue per customer.

We think Centurytel's decision to sell its wireless business to Alltel was smart. Centurytel's wireless revenue and margins had been declining for some time. The business didn't have the scale to compete effectively over the long term. Also, cash raised from the sale kept debt levels in check following the $2.2 billion Verizon line acquisition earlier in 2002. We've been impressed with Centurytel's disciplined use of cash flow to repay debt and acquire assets that generate solid cash flow and have a strong competitive advantage in their markets.

The lack of a wireless business does introduce some risks, though. The biggest long-term threat to Centurytel's franchise is the substitution of wireless for wireline service. Still, we think the company is taking the necessary steps, like investing in the wireline network, to keep it viable. We think Centurytel is a fine investment at the right price.

Ceridian CEN

	Rating	Risk	Moat Size	Fair Value	Last Close	Yield %
	★★★	Med.	Narrow	$16.00	$14.42	0.0

Company Profile

Ceridian provides human resources outsourcing to a variety of companies and financial transaction services to trucking firms. The HR business provides payroll preparation, tax-filing services, benefits administration, and retirement plan services. The trucking division, Comdata, allows companies to transfer money to truck drivers and pay for fuel and supplies on the road, as well as other services.

Management

Ron Turner took over as CEO in January 2000 after longtime chief Lawrence Perlman retired. Perlman and Turner transformed Control Data, a dying computer manufacturer, into Ceridian in the early 1990s.

Strategy

Ceridian spun off its Arbitron unit in 2001 to concentrate on its human resource services and transaction-processing businesses. The human resources segment mainly targets the payroll needs of large businesses with its Source 500 product and smaller businesses with its Powerpay offering. The transaction-processing unit is the dominant processor of payments made by long-haul truck drivers.

3311 East Old Shakopee Road   www.ceridian.com
Minneapolis, MN 55425

Industry	Investment Style	Stock Type	Sector
Data Processing	Mid Core	Slow Growth	Business Services

Competition	Market Cap $Mil	Debt/ Equity	12 Mo Trailing Sales $Mil	Price/Cash Flow	Return On Assets%	Total Return% 1 Yr	3 Yr
Ceridian	2,140	0.2	1,174	10.4	4.3	-23.1	-11.8
Automatic Data Processing	23,506	0.0	7,043	16.9	7.1	-32.7	-8.2
Paychex	10,493	—	973	29.9	9.1	-19.2	5.3

Price Volatility

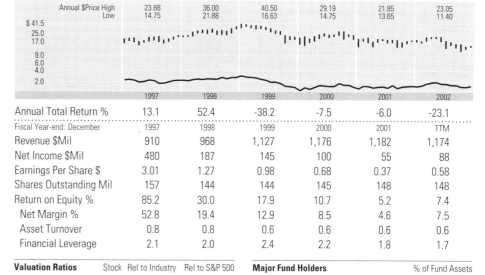

	1997	1998	1999	2000	2001	2002
Annual $Price High	23.88	36.00	40.50	29.19	21.85	23.05
Low	14.75	21.88	16.63	14.75	13.65	11.40
Annual Total Return %	13.1	52.4	-38.2	-7.5	-6.0	-23.1

Fiscal Year-end: December	1997	1998	1999	2000	2001	TTM
Revenue $Mil	910	968	1,127	1,176	1,182	1,174
Net Income $Mil	480	187	145	100	55	88
Earnings Per Share $	3.01	1.27	0.98	0.68	0.37	0.58
Shares Outstanding Mil	157	144	144	145	148	148
Return on Equity %	85.2	30.0	17.9	10.7	5.2	7.4
Net Margin %	52.8	19.4	12.9	8.5	4.6	7.5
Asset Turnover	0.8	0.8	0.6	0.6	0.6	0.6
Financial Leverage	2.1	2.0	2.4	2.2	1.8	1.7

Valuation Ratios	Stock	Rel to Industry	Rel to S&P 500
Price/Earnings	24.9	1.1	1.1
Price/Book	1.8	0.4	0.6
Price/Sales	1.8	0.5	0.9
Price/Cash Flow	10.4	0.6	0.8

Major Fund Holders	% of Fund Assets
PF Janus Strategic Value A	4.84
Janus Adviser Strategic Value	4.35
Oakmark Global I	3.47
Janus Aspen Strategic Value Instl	3.30

Morningstar Grades

Growth [C+]	1998	1999	2000	2001
Revenue %	6.4	16.5	4.3	0.6
Earnings/Share %	-57.8	-22.8	-30.6	-45.6
Book Value/Share %	19.7	29.5	16.0	13.0
Dividends/Share %	NMF	NMF	NMF	NMF

Ceridian's human resources division has badly lagged those of ADP and Paychex. However, a renewed focus on customer service and an augmented salesforce selling additional services to current customers might portend better times.

Profitability [A]	1999	2000	2001	TTM
Return on Assets %	7.3	4.8	2.9	4.3
Oper Cash Flow $Mil	198	269	183	206
- Cap Spending $Mil	107	97	94	85
= Free Cash Flow $Mil	91	172	89	121

Unusual charges have hurt Ceridian the past several years. Excluding them, the firm earns operating margins well over 10%, even when penalized by the poor performance of its human resources business. Improvements here would drive big profit gains.

Financial Health [A]	1999	2000	2001	09-02
Long-term Debt $Mil	611	500	236	192
Total Equity $Mil	812	936	1,061	1,187
Debt/Equity Ratio	0.8	0.5	0.2	0.2

Ceridian is in good financial shape. It has about $50 million in net debt, less than half a year's worth of operating income. Operating cash flow easily covers interest expense and funds capital investment and software development.

Morningstar's Take By Dan Schick, 10-28-2002 Stock Price as of Analysis: $13.15

Ceridian is trying to reinvigorate its business. We think it will succeed; however, the market is not sufficiently skeptical of the company's prospects to present a buying opportunity. Given our required margin of safety, we wouldn't be interested unless the shares traded near $11, about a 30% discount to our estimated fair value of $16.

Ceridian generates about 50% of its revenue from the payroll-processing business. Like its peers Automatic Data Processing and Paychex, Ceridian benefits from the stable and steady nature of the payroll business. People always work and always get paid, and someone must process the checks. Unlike its peers, though, Ceridian isn't making money hand over fist with its payroll business. ADP reports a payroll segment operating margin greater than 20%; Paychex scrapes the sky with close to 50%. Ceridian, on the other hand, topped out in recent years at 14% in 1998. Currently, its margins are in the single digits.

Smaller size and a different market focus explain Ceridian's lower profitability. Ceridian has $850 million in revenue compared with ADP's $4 billion. It is thus less able to reap the economies of scale inherent in the payroll-processing business. Also, Paychex's average client employs 14 people, while Ceridian's average client employs several hundred.

We think Paychex's core market is more profitable because there are many more small businesses than large, small businesses have fewer resources to devote to processing themselves, and fewer big players compete in the market. All of this means Paychex has more pricing power.

Ceridian's Comdata segment is on much stronger competitive footing. It boasts greater than 50% share in its core business of providing fuel and cash access cards to the over-the-road trucking industry. The Comdata card is more than a payment system; it gives trucking companies strict control over and real-time data on their employees' expenditures, features that credit cards lack. With a big market share and a differentiated product, Comdata produces around 30% operating margins and high returns on capital for Ceridian.

While we think payroll will improve and Comdata will maintain its margins, we doubt whether Ceridian can expand its business internally at very high rates. In the past, the firm has succumbed to the siren song of acquisitions. We think shareholders would be better off if Ceridian played the hand it holds and distributed its free cash flow to investors.

Charles Schwab SCH

	Rating	Risk	Moat Size	Fair Value	Last Close	Yield %
	★	Med.	None	$9.00	$10.85	0.4

Company Profile

Charles Schwab offers brokerage and investment services, and is the largest player in the discount brokerage arena. In addition, its Schwab Capital Markets subsidiary offers trade-execution services to institutional clients and broker-dealers, and its Charles Schwab Investment Management unit serves as investment advisor for its mutual funds. Through its MutualFund OneSource service, clients trade mutual funds without brokerage fees

Management

Co-CEO and founder Charles Schwab owns about 19% of the firm. Schwab became more involved in daily operations after the acquisitions and Internet strategy engineered by co-CEO David Pottruck did not pay off as well as expected.

Strategy

Schwab continues to duke it out with other discount brokerages in a dwindling market, but the company is now focusing on fee-based private client accounts and mutual fund products. Its U.S. Trust business, which caters to wealthy investors, may help Schwab in shedding its cut-rate image. It will need all the help it can get against larger, more-established rivals like Merrill Lynch.

120 Kearny Street   www.schwab.com
San Francisco, CA 94108

Morningstar Grades

Growth [D]	1998	1999	2000	2001
Revenue %	18.9	41.2	29.0	-24.8
Earnings/Share %	29.2	58.1	4.1	-72.5
Book Value/Share %	22.9	49.9	58.5	-2.5
Dividends/Share %	15.8	3.3	9.1	8.4

Founded in 1971, Schwab has enjoyed generally explosive growth for decades. However, trading volume evaporated in 2001, causing net revenue to drop 25%. Growth has been stagnant in 2002 with little hope for improvement.

Profitability [B]	1999	2000	2001	TTM
Return on Assets %	1.9	1.9	0.5	0.5
Oper Cash Flow $Mil	1,094	2,916	-584	—
- Cap Spending $Mil	370	705	301	—
= Free Cash Flow $Mil	—	—	—	—

Schwab's margins have been under increasing pressure because of the precipitous fall in trading volume. The operating margin dipped to only 3% in 2001, but cost cuts should help it recover to around 14% in 2002.

Financial Health [A+]	1999	2000	2001	09-02
Long-term Debt $Mil	—	—	—	—
Total Equity $Mil	2,576	4,230	4,163	4,143
Debt/Equity Ratio	—	—	—	—

Schwab operates in an industry that requires a large amount of leverage; however, the firm carries less debt than most. Its equity/assets ratio is about 10% compared with midsingle digits for most rivals.

Industry	Investment Style	Stock Type	Sector
Securities	▦ Large Growth	➡ Slow Growth	💲 Financial Services

Competition	Market Cap $Mil	Debt/ Equity	12 Mo Trailing Sales $Mil	Price/Cash Flow	Return On Assets%	Total Return% 1 Yr	3 Yr
Charles Schwab	14,579	—	4,198	—	0.5	-29.6	-23.4
Merrill Lynch & Company	32,806	—	36,032	—	0.2	-26.0	0.5
Bank of Montreal	13,559	—	11,220	⊢	—	—	—

Price Volatility

⎮ Monthly Price High/Low   — Relative Strength to S&P 500

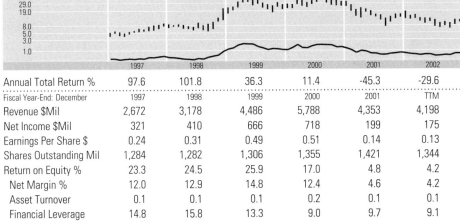

	1997	1998	1999	2000	2001	2002
Annual $Price High	9.83	22.83	51.67	44.75	33.00	19.00
Low	4.50	6.17	16.96	22.46	8.13	7.22
Annual Total Return %	97.6	101.8	36.3	11.4	-45.3	-29.6

Fiscal Year-End: December	1997	1998	1999	2000	2001	TTM
Revenue $Mil	2,672	3,178	4,486	5,788	4,353	4,198
Net Income $Mil	321	410	666	718	199	175
Earnings Per Share $	0.24	0.31	0.49	0.51	0.14	0.13
Shares Outstanding Mil	1,284	1,282	1,306	1,355	1,421	1,344
Return on Equity %	23.3	24.5	25.9	17.0	4.8	4.2
Net Margin %	12.0	12.9	14.8	12.4	4.6	4.2
Asset Turnover	0.1	0.1	0.1	0.2	0.1	0.1
Financial Leverage	14.8	15.8	13.3	9.0	9.7	9.1

Valuation Ratios	Stock	Rel to Industry	Rel to S&P 500
Price/Earnings	83.5	4.9	3.5
Price/Book	3.5	2.0	1.1
Price/Sales	3.5	2.6	1.7
Price/Cash Flow	—	—	—

Major Fund Holders	% of Fund Assets
Sextant Growth	7.04
Baron Asset	6.17
Pin Oak Aggressive Stock	6.05
Fidelity Select Brokerage & Investmnt	5.13

Morningstar's Take   By Rachel Barnard, 12-11-2002   Stock Price as of Analysis: $10.78

Schwab needs a turnaround strategy, but its recent attempts are more like a shot in the dark than a shot in the arm.

It's a tough time to be a brokerage firm. Investors, bitten by stock market losses, are now shy about going back into the water. But Schwab's solution to this dilemma is not nearly as innovative as we'd expect from the swashbuckling revolutionary that helped transform the world of Wall Street brokerages. The firm that brought investors discount trading now brings us advice for the wealthy.

To be fair, this is a very lucrative business, but it is a crowded field, filled with competitors who have years of expertise in this area--the likes of Northern Trust, Merrill Lynch, and Neuberger Berman. Schwab is not equipped to be in this business, and it will have a difficult time retooling.

The firm plans to offer advice to clients with at least $500,000 in assets who want professional direction but like to maintain control of their portfolios. This is a middle ground between its wealth-management division, U.S. Trust, and the discount brokerage. But this plan requires a significant staff of advisors, which Schwab doesn't have. It also siphons business from the financial advisors who use Schwab's custody and trading

services for their clients' assets. This could bring on a mutiny among the 5,900 advisor clients, who could leave for the likes of TD Waterhouse or other competitors and take their clients with them.

Schwab's other initiative is in mutual funds. Sensing investors' anxiety about tainted equity research, Schwab has rolled out a mutual fund that relies on computer-generated research--no conflicts of interest here--to pick winning stocks. The same computer will drive a product that will be able to take long and short positions in the market. Such products are normally only sold to the wealthy because they are very risky--blowups are common--and wealthy investors can afford to lose a chunk of their assets if their hedge fund implodes. Will average investors see things this way? Schwab seems to think so.

In our opinion, Schwab doesn't have the next big thing. We foresee a continuing struggle as long as trading remains sluggish. When investors return to stock trading, Schwab will certainly benefit, but we think its glory days are gone.

MORNINGSTAR® Stocks 500

Charter Communications CHTR

Rating	Risk	Moat Size	Fair Value	Last Close	Yield %
★	High	Narrow	$1.00	$1.18	0.0

Company Profile

Serving nearly 7 million subscribers, Charter Communications is the nation's fourth-largest cable provider. Charter was once just a small cable player but has grown significantly through acquisitions. The company has spent mightily upgrading its networks, enabling them to deliver broadband services like digital cable and high-speed Internet. Microsoft co-founder Paul Allen--the man behind the dream of a "wired world"--maintains roughly 94% of Charter's voting control.

Management

Ownership of Class B supervoting shares gives Paul Allen near total control of Charter. New CEO Carl Vogel is a serious cable guy, revered by Wall Street. The CFO and COO recently signed four-year employment contracts.

Strategy

Charter was once a small cable company, but has since grown through acquisitions. Although it has 6.7 million subscribers across 40 states, Charter focuses mainly on the less-competitive suburban markets. A recent management change has shifted Charter's strategy from basic subscriber growth to rolling out higher-margin broadband services.

12405 Powerscourt Drive   www.charter.com
St. Louis, MO 63131

Morningstar Grades

Growth [A-]

	1998	1999	2000	2001
Revenue %	236.3	EUB	127.5	21.7
Earnings/Share %	NMF	NMF	NMF	NMF
Book Value/Share %	—	—	NMF	-23.2
Dividends/Share %	NMF	NMF	NMF	NMF

Acquisitions account for Charter's torrid past growth. On a "same-store" basis, sales are growing roughly 12%-14% annually (they rose 13% in the September quarter). New broadband services--digital cable and high-speed data--are the catalyst for growth.

Profitability [C]

	1999	2000	2001	TTM
Return on Assets %	-0.3	-3.6	-4.7	-3.3
Oper Cash Flow $Mil	480	1,131	519	758
- Cap Spending $Mil	742	2,825	3,027	2,566
= Free Cash Flow $Mil	-262	-1,694	-2,508	-1,808

Charter is a typical cable operator: It never produces profits or free cash flow. Although operating cash flow was up 6% in the September quarter and should rise roughly 10% in 2002, free cash flow will be in the black no sooner than 2004.

Financial Health [F]

	1999	2000	2001	09-02
Long-term Debt $Mil	8,936	13,060	16,343	18,452
Total Equity $Mil	3,011	3,123	2,862	2,197
Debt/Equity Ratio	3.0	4.2	5.7	8.4

Debt continues to rise--$18.5 billion at the end of September--and now constitutes most of the firm's total value. Although Charter's cash needs are declining, insolvency remains a very real concern.

Industry	Investment Style	Stock Type	Sector
Cable TV	Small Value	Distressed	Media

Competition

	Market Cap $Mil	Debt/ Equity	12 Mo Trailing Sales $Mil	Price/Cash Flow	Return On Assets%	Total Return% 1 Yr	3 Yr
Charter Communications	348	8.4	4,522	0.5	-3.3	-92.8	-61.9
Liberty Media	22,975	0.2	2,065	—	-22.4	-35.3	-29.4
Comcast A	22,319	0.7	10,789	13.6	-1.5	-34.5	-18.3

Price Volatility

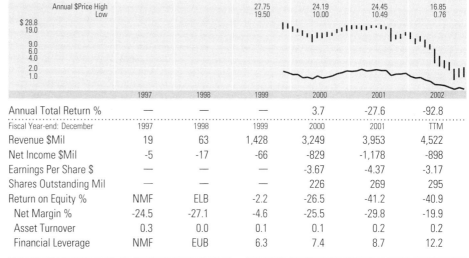

Annual $Price High/Low				27.75 / 19.50	24.19 / 10.00	24.45 / 10.49	16.85 / 0.76

	1997	1998	1999	2000	2001	2002	
Annual Total Return %	—	—	—	3.7	-27.6	-92.8	

Fiscal Year-end: December	1997	1998	1999	2000	2001	TTM
Revenue $Mil	19	63	1,428	3,249	3,953	4,522
Net Income $Mil	-5	-17	-66	-829	-1,178	-898
Earnings Per Share $	—	—	—	-3.67	-4.37	-3.17
Shares Outstanding Mil	—	—	—	226	269	295
Return on Equity %	NMF	ELB	-2.2	-26.5	-41.2	-40.9
Net Margin %	-24.5	-27.1	-4.6	-25.5	-29.8	-19.9
Asset Turnover	0.3	0.0	0.1	0.1	0.2	0.2
Financial Leverage	NMF	EUB	6.3	7.4	8.7	12.2

Valuation Ratios

	Stock	Rel to Industry	Rel to S&P 500
Price/Earnings	NMF	—	—
Price/Book	0.2	0.1	0.0
Price/Sales	0.1	0.0	0.0
Price/Cash Flow	0.5	0.0	0.0

Major Fund Holders

	% of Fund Assets
Weitz Hickory	4.65
Oak Value	4.50
Jundt Growth I	3.38
Jundt Twenty-Five A	2.86

Morningstar's Take By Todd P. Bernier, 12-19-2002 Stock Price as of Analysis: $1.26

Charter got big fast, with little thought to the consequences. Now, miserly capital markets have changed the rules midgame. As a result, Charter's shareholders are probably going to lose everything.

Charter grew by acquiring smaller operators and investing heavily to upgrade the networks. This capital spending is finally beginning to bear fruit, witnessed by the incredible growth of broadband subscribers. The main benefit, besides added revenue, is greater customer loyalty; disconnection rates drop with the addition of incremental services.

Charter is a leader in digital cable, mainly because it can offer this service to nearly all of its customers. More than one third of its homes take digital service, the highest penetration rate among major cable operators. This is significant because digital service carries a cash flow margin of roughly 65%.

The firm is also making strides in high-speed data, thanks to a more ubiquitous network and a clever multitier pricing strategy. Although the cash flow margin here doesn't match digital cable's, it is quickly closing the gap. Internet access is a huge opportunity for Charter: 80% of American Internet users still rely on dialup connections, and many will migrate to a faster connection as bandwidth-hogging applications become more mainstream.

With free cash flow just around the corner, logic suggests investors would flock to Big Cable. But the implosion at Adelphia, the nation's sixth-largest operator, has caused investors to eschew capital-intensive firms, particularly those valued on EBITDA multiples (as cable stocks are)--the implication is that firms have overstated EBITDA by booking operating expenses as capital spending. It is true that Charter, like all cable operators, accounts for certain charges as capital expenses.

But it is Charter's balance sheet that investors should fear. Charter will end 2002 with debt topping $18 billion, which implies a debt/EBITDA ratio of 9. Charter won't produce free cash flow until at least 2004; considering how uncooperative the high-yield debt markets are (Charter is one of the largest issuers of junk debt), we question how the firm will repay $750 million in senior notes maturing in 2005. We suspect Charter will gain some breathing room by swapping its debt for equity, resulting in massive shareholder dilution.

Aggressively assuming cable subscriber are worth $3,000 each (they're not), Charter is worth roughly $1 billion--near its current market value. Unless it receives an equity infusion, Charter has little intrinsic worth, in our view.

Checkfree CKFR

	Rating	Risk	Moat Size	Fair Value	Last Close	Yield %
	★★	Med.	None	$17.00	$16.00	0.0

Industry	Investment Style	Stock Type	Sector
Systems & Security	▦ Mid Growth	▦ Spec. Growth	▲ Software

Company Profile

Checkfree is the leading provider of electronic-bill-payment services. Through a number of operating subsidiaries, CheckFree designs, develops, and markets services that enable consumers to receive and pay bills over the Internet. Generally, Checkfree depends on its bank, brokerage, and Internet portal partners to market the service and then Checkfree services their customers. Nearly five million consumers pay their bills on Checkfree's systems.

Management

CEO Peter Kight founded the company in 1981 as a back-office transaction processor for banks. Kight, who owns more than 6.4% of the outstanding shares, launched Checkfree's flagship Internet billing product in 1997.

Strategy

Checkfree aims to do just what its name implies: make this a check-free society. The firm seeks to dominate the market for paying bills via the Internet by providing back-end systems to banks, which in turn offer the service to their customers. The firm also needs to build a big base of firms that present bills over Checkfree's systems.

4411 East Jones Bridge Road www.checkfree.com
Norcross, GA 30092

Morningstar Grades

Growth [B]	1999	2000	2001	2002
Revenue %	7.0	24.0	39.7	13.2
Earnings/Share %	NMF	NMF	NMF	NMF
Book Value/Share %	-7.4	161.6	154.5	-30.3
Dividends/Share %	NMF	NMF	NMF	NMF

Of Checkfree's three segments, the one to watch is the electronic commerce division, which provides electronic billing services. In this segment, revenue grew almost 14% in the first quarter and 17% last year.

Profitability [C]	2000	2001	2002	TTM
Return on Assets %	-4.5	-16.6	-26.9	-23.0
Oper Cash Flow $Mil	21	0	46	71
- Cap Spending $Mil	39	42	22	25
= Free Cash Flow $Mil	-18	-42	24	46

Checkfree's business model thrives on transaction growth. Ideally, the firm will process more and more transactions, spreading the fixed cost of its systems over a bigger revenue base and driving rapid profit growth.

Financial Health [C+]	2000	2001	2002	09-02
Long-term Debt $Mil	173	177	175	180
Total Equity $Mil	446	1,732	1,306	1,294
Debt/Equity Ratio	0.4	0.1	0.1	0.1

Free cash flow has been negative for several years as the firm invested heavily to build its business. We predict a rapid increase in free cash flow starting this year, though, which should enable Checkfree to remain in decent health.

Competition

	Market Cap $Mil	Debt/ Equity	12 Mo Trailing Sales $Mil	Price/Cash Flow	Return On Assets%	Total Return% 1 Yr	3 Yr
Checkfree	1,419	0.1	504	19.9	-23.0	-11.1	-44.6
Marshall & Ilsley	5,750	—	2,624	—	—	—	—

Price Volatility

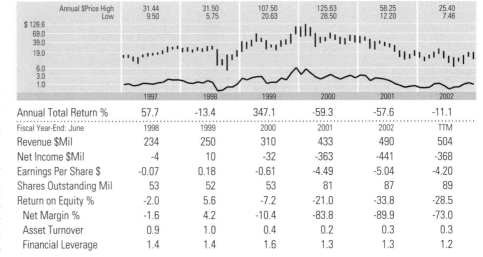

Annual $Price High	31.44	31.50	107.50	125.63	58.25	25.40
Low	9.50	5.75	20.63	28.50	12.20	7.46

I Monthly Price High/Low — Relative Strength to S&P 500

	1997	1998	1999	2000	2001	2002
Annual Total Return %	57.7	-13.4	347.1	-59.3	-57.6	-11.1

Fiscal Year-End: June	1998	1999	2000	2001	2002	TTM
Revenue $Mil	234	250	310	433	490	504
Net Income $Mil	-4	10	-32	-363	-441	-368
Earnings Per Share $	-0.07	0.18	-0.61	-4.49	-5.04	-4.20
Shares Outstanding Mil	53	52	53	81	87	89
Return on Equity %	-2.0	5.6	-7.2	-21.0	-33.8	-28.5
Net Margin %	-1.6	4.2	-10.4	-83.8	-89.9	-73.0
Asset Turnover	0.9	1.0	0.4	0.2	0.3	0.3
Financial Leverage	1.4	1.4	1.6	1.3	1.3	1.2

Valuation Ratios	Stock	Rel to Industry	Rel to S&P 500
Price/Earnings	NMF	—	—
Price/Book	1.1	0.5	0.3
Price/Sales	2.8	0.8	1.4
Price/Cash Flow	19.9	1.8	1.5

Major Fund Holders	% of Fund Assets
Gintel	8.55
Jundt U.S. Emerging Growth B	2.85
UM Small Cap Growth Instl	2.72
ABN AMRO/TAMRO Small Cap N	2.66

Morningstar's Take By Dan Schick, 12-18-2002 Stock Price as of Analysis: $15.61

Checkfree's electronic billing and payment services are interesting, and selling these services could be very profitable. But decent potential does not necessarily equate to a good investment. We believe the market already assumes Checkfree will be a success; to provide a margin of safety, we'd purchase shares only at a 40% discount to our fair value estimate.

Checkfree is getting interesting as its business begins to mature. The firm has always had vast potential. According to a Federal Reserve study, U.S. consumers pay at least 8.5 billion bills annually by writing checks. In theory, paying electronically would be more convenient and less costly for consumers. Firms would also benefit by presenting bills and receiving payment for them electronically.

The problem is that Checkfree has been unable to win over consumers as quickly as it would like--only 7 million have initiated payments using its systems. And despite a great deal of legwork and investment, the company has managed to convince a mere 267 firms to issue bills over its systems; moreover, only 657 organizations permit consumers to view and pay bills online through Checkfree. Billers and most financial institutions seem to be waiting for greater adoption by consumers before implementing electronic bill payment and presentment themselves.

Nevertheless, these metrics are showing substantial growth, as is the number of transactions Checkfree processes. That means that once consumers try the service, they seem to like it.

Changing consumer preferences and behavior is difficult, though. The best incentive to spur adoption seems to be giving away the services. That's what Bank of America, the nation's largest bank, has done; now Checkfree is experiencing subscriber growth of 30% from that bank's customers.

With increasing adoption comes falling per-transaction costs for Checkfree. The firm expects its cost per transaction to drop 20% this year alone. Because cost appears to be a big impediment to consumer adoption, the firm is passing on some of these scale economies to its customers in an attempt to win more users. If successful, this would define a virtuous circle.

Because of growing consumer acceptance and Checkfree's ability to gain processing efficiencies, the firm is generating free cash flow. The stock is no longer way overvalued as it was between 1999 and 2001, when it traded above $40. We'd still look for a discount to our fair value estimate before buying, though.

MORNINGSTAR® Stocks 500

Check Point Software Technologies CHKP

Rating	Risk	Moat Size	Fair Value	Last Close	Yield %
★★★	High	Narrow	$15.00	$12.97	0.0

Company Profile

Check Point Software Technologies develops software that organizes a computer network's security policy. The company's FireWall family of products integrates authentication, encryption, and remote access across multiple gateways and servers. Its technology also allows for private, encrypted communication over public networks, like the Internet, and with remote offices, business partners, and customers. Check Point Software has an original equipment manufacturer agreement with SunSoft, a subsidiary of Sun Microsystems.

Management

Founder Gil Shwed has chairman and CEO of Check Point since its inception. President Jerry Ungerman is responsible for worldwide sales.

Strategy

Check Point's goal is to dominate the VPN and firewall software market. As those markets mature, growth hinges on emerging areas like wireless Internet and selling to small and medium-size businesses.

3A Jabotinsky Street www.checkpoint.com
Ramat-Gan, 52520

Morningstar Grades

Growth [B+]	1998	1999	2000	2001
Revenue %	64.4	54.7	93.7	24.1
Earnings/Share %	74.4	29.3	115.4	48.8
Book Value/Share %	73.2	57.0	75.1	70.5
Dividends/Share %	NMF	NMF	NMF	NMF

While the top line averaged 55% growth over the past three years, those days are gone. We still expect sales can grow as fast as 20% because of strong demand for security products.

Profitability [A+]	1999	2000	2001	TTM
Return on Assets %	24.3	28.4	28.2	19.8
Oper Cash Flow $Mil	144	316	347	347
- Cap Spending $Mil	6	9	10	10
= Free Cash Flow $Mil	138	307	337	337

Check Point generates returns on invested capital in excess of 200%. This is explained in part by the company's operating margins, which are near 60%.

Financial Health [A+]	1999	2000	2001	09-02
Long-term Debt $Mil	0	0	0	0
Total Equity $Mil	293	549	916	1,121
Debt/Equity Ratio	0.0	0.0	0.0	0.0

The balance sheet is pristine, with no debt and $1 billion in cash and investments. The company also generates tons of free cash flow, providing ample liquidity to fund any business expansion.

Industry	Investment Style	Stock Type	Sector
Business Applications	Mid Growth	Aggr. Growth	Software

Competition	Market Cap $Mil	Debt/ Equity	12 Mo Trailing Sales $Mil	Price/Cash Flow	Return On Assets%	Total Return% 1 Yr	3 Yr
Check Point Software Technologies	3,174	0.0	439	9.1	19.8	-67.5	-26.8
Cisco Systems	94,649	0.0	19,312	15.1	7.5	-27.7	-36.4
Symantec	5,797	0.4	1,242	9.9	4.1	22.0	14.3

Price Volatility — Monthly Price High/Low — Relative Strength to S&P 500

	1997	1998	1999	2000	2001	2002
Annual $Price High	8.42	7.96	37.25	118.58	113.33	49.47
Low	2.71	1.81	3.83	29.08	19.56	10.37
Annual Total Return %	87.4	12.4	333.8	168.8	-55.2	-67.5

Fiscal Year-end: December	1997	1998	1999	2000	2001	TTM
Revenue $Mil	86	142	220	425	528	439
Net Income $Mil	40	70	96	221	322	268
Earnings Per Share $	0.17	0.30	0.39	0.84	1.25	1.05
Shares Outstanding Mil	205	213	223	233	240	245
Return on Equity %	39.5	39.8	32.7	40.3	35.2	23.9
Net Margin %	45.8	49.2	43.6	52.0	61.0	60.9
Asset Turnover	0.7	0.7	0.6	0.5	0.5	0.3
Financial Leverage	1.2	1.2	1.3	1.4	1.2	1.2

Valuation Ratios	Stock	Rel to Industry	Rel to S&P 500
Price/Earnings	12.4	0.4	0.5
Price/Book	2.8	0.5	0.9
Price/Sales	7.2	0.8	3.6
Price/Cash Flow	9.1	0.6	0.7

Major Fund Holders	% of Fund Assets
Conseco Science & Technology Y	5.57
ProFunds Ultra Internet Inv	4.93
Red Oak Technology Select	4.71
Bender Growth C	3.33

Morningstar's Take By Mike Trigg, 10-23-2002 Stock Price as of Analysis: $13.45

Check Point is a leading player in security software, but that doesn't make for a secure investment. We'd require at least a 30% discount to our fair value estimate before buying this high-risk name.

Check Point dominates the firewall and virtual private network (VPN) software markets. Firewalls keep unauthorized users from accessing a network; a VPN is a secure connection over the Internet. The company's economic moat, albeit narrow, is superior technology; few firms can offer market-leading, integrated firewall and VPN products. Bundling the two makes sense, because once you're past the firewall you need a secure connection to the network.

Check Point has produced tremendous financial results, with operating margins near 60% and returns on invested capital in excess of 200%. Even a software vendor as successful as Microsoft cannot match Check Point's profitability. This is explained by the fact that most of Check Point's products are developed in Israel, where the cost of doing business is cheap and taxes are low; also, the company relies on a network of resellers, rather than employing a costly direct salesforce.

However, Check Point faces stiff competition from Cisco Systems, Symantec, and NetScreen. Cisco has a large base of customers loyal to its products, while

Symantec has a more diversified offering that includes antivirus and intrusion-detection software. NetScreen has been growing by selling a security appliance that is cheap and easy to install. Check Point has partnered with 15 hardware vendors to sell a competing solution, but it remains to be seen how many of these relationships will translate into significant revenue. Thus far, Nokia generates nearly all of Check Point's hardware revenue.

Our concern is that Check Point's competitive advantage is unsustainable. Although Check Point is regarded as having superior technology, competitors have been closing this gap. Also, its software is the most expensive, which is problematic because right now many businesses are willing to forgo a better product for a cheaper one that meets their needs. At the very least, we expect Check Point's pricing power will diminish, leading to lower margins and ROIC.

Check Point is a well-run company with superior financials, but the lack of a wide economic moat and increasing competition leave the sustainability of its results in doubt. Although we think the stock is worth $15, we wouldn't become interested until it fell to $11.

ChevronTexaco CVX

	Rating	Risk	Moat Size	Fair Value	Last Close	Yield %
	★★★	Med.	Narrow	$75.00	$66.48	4.2

Company Profile

ChevronTexaco was formed by the 2001 merger of Chevron and Texaco to create the second-largest American oil company, trailing only ExxonMobil in size. ChevronTexaco has operations across all segments of the oil and gas industry, but its reputation is that of a premier upstream operator superb at finding and producing oil. The company boasts reserves totaling 11.5 billion barrels, the capacity to refine 2.7 million barrels a day, and 25,000 service stations.

Management

Chevron veteran David O'Reilly continued as chairman and CEO following the merger. O'Reilly rose through the Chevron ranks for 34 years and was a vice president for most of the 1990s.

Strategy

ChevronTexaco has bet that bigger is better--the marriage of Chevron and Texaco was consummated to increase efficiency and save billions. Beyond benefiting from lower costs, the firm hopes to leverage its success as one of the best exploration and production outfits in oil. Growth is expected to come from investments in natural gas and in the Caspian Sea, West Africa, and Far Eastern Russia.

575 Market Street
San Francisco, CA 94105-2586
www.chevrontexaco.com

Morningstar Grades

Growth [D+]	1998	1999	2000	2001
Revenue %	-28.4	17.0	39.0	-10.8
Earnings/Share %	-68.1	71.4	140.3	-57.1
Book Value/Share %	-5.9	4.5	12.1	3.4
Dividends/Share %	7.0	1.6	4.8	1.9

Like the rest of the oil patch, ChevronTexaco will see revenue rise and fall with changes in commodity oil prices. The firm is especially sensitive because a high percentage of its revenue comes from production activities.

Profitability [B]	1999	2000	2001	TTM
Return on Assets %	4.3	10.0	4.2	-3.0
Oper Cash Flow $Mil	7,771	13,467	11,457	7,938
- Cap Spending $Mil	7,895	7,629	9,713	9,477
= Free Cash Flow $Mil	-124	5,838	1,744	-1,539

The combined firm's return on capital employed has averaged in the low teens. While well above its cost of capital, this figure puts ChevronTexaco at the lower end of its peer group.

Financial Health [A]	1999	2000	2001	09-02
Long-term Debt $Mil	13,145	12,821	8,989	11,337
Total Equity $Mil	29,791	33,069	33,958	32,121
Debt/Equity Ratio	0.4	0.4	0.3	0.4

ChevronTexaco has a modest amount of debt, and its leverage is in line with its peers. The company has ample free cash flow that it will probably use to reduce debt as well as increase already juicy dividend payments in the coming years.

Industry	Investment Style	Stock Type	Sector
Oil & Gas	Large Value	Hard Assets	Energy

Competition

	Market Cap $Mil	Debt/ Equity	12 Mo Trailing Sales $Mil	Price/Cash Flow	Return On Assets%	Total Return% 1 Yr	3 Yr
ChevronTexaco	71,011	0.4	93,451	8.9	-3.0	-23.1	-4.4
ExxonMobil	235,108	0.1	196,513	12.0	6.7	-8.9	-0.9
BP PLC ADR	152,063	0.2	175,389	6.8	5.7	-9.9	-9.2

Price Volatility

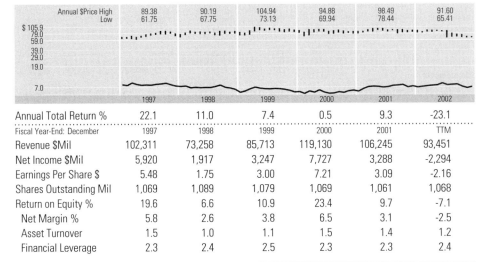

| | Monthly Price High/Low | — Relative Strength to S&P 500 |

Annual $Price High Low	89.38 61.75	90.19 67.75	104.94 73.13	94.88 69.94	98.49 78.44	91.60 65.41
	1997	1998	1999	2000	2001	2002

Annual Total Return %	22.1	11.0	7.4	0.5	9.3	-23.1
Fiscal Year-End: December	1997	1998	1999	2000	2001	TTM
Revenue $Mil	102,311	73,258	85,713	119,130	106,245	93,451
Net Income $Mil	5,920	1,917	3,247	7,727	3,288	-2,294
Earnings Per Share $	5.48	1.75	3.00	7.21	3.09	-2.16
Shares Outstanding Mil	1,069	1,089	1,079	1,069	1,061	1,068
Return on Equity %	19.6	6.6	10.9	23.4	9.7	-7.1
Net Margin %	5.8	2.6	3.8	6.5	3.1	-2.5
Asset Turnover	1.5	1.0	1.1	1.5	1.4	1.2
Financial Leverage	2.3	2.4	2.5	2.3	2.3	2.4

Valuation Ratios	Stock	Rel to Industry	Rel to S&P 500
Price/Earnings	NMF	—	—
Price/Book	2.2	1.0	0.7
Price/Sales	0.8	0.7	0.4
Price/Cash Flow	8.9	1.3	0.7

Major Fund Holders	% of Fund Assets
Rydex Energy Inv	13.95
Fidelity Select Energy	10.70
Fidelity Select Natural Resources	9.02
ProFunds Ultra Energy Inv	8.61

Morningstar's Take By Paul Larson, 11-26-2002 Stock Price as of Analysis: $66.28

We like big oil and think that ChevronTexaco, while it has its problems, is worth considering at the right price.

The late 2001 marriage of Chevron and Texaco brought together two of the oil patch's larger second-tier players to create one of oil's new big five. Economy of scale is one of the few ways to gain a competitive advantage in the commodity oil and gas industry, and ChevronTexaco anticipates it can duplicate the success enjoyed by its already-merged peers to the tune of $2.2 billion in annual savings within a year. This new economy of scale is primarily behind the narrow economic moat rating we've assigned the firm.

These savings should add to the company's long history of profitability and high dividends. Chevron has not had an unprofitable year in decades and has earned at least $1 per share in 19 of the past 20 years. While earnings vary a great deal with volatile commodity oil and gas prices, the company has historically stayed profitable even through cyclical troughs.

It has also paid a high dividend for decades, and the shares currently yield more than 4%. The company should be able to continue generating copious free cash flow for the foreseeable future,

which supports our belief that this dividend is safe from being cut. Plus, the balance sheet is in good shape, with less than a fourth of its mammoth $77 billion asset base supported by debt.

One factor in the company's success is the OPEC cartel, which has great influence in the oil patch, limiting supply from its member countries to keep commodity prices above the costs to maintain industrywide profitability. This is a fundamental strength that we do not see changing anytime soon.

All is not perfect at ChevronTexaco. Its recent expensive divorce from Dynegy shows that management can make missteps. The company is also not nearly as profitable as its essentially debt-free larger competitors, and the promised merger savings have been slow to appear. Plus, even though its dividend yield is high relative to its peers, its payout ratio is also higher. We would not pay as much for ChevronTexaco as we would for ExxonMobil, BP, or Royal Dutch-Shell. But even with its faults, ChevronTexaco is still a solid operation that has enriched, and should continue to enrich, its shareholders over the long term. At a sufficient discount to our estimated fair value, it would be worth buying, in our opinion.

MORNINGSTAR® Stocks 500

Chico's FAS CHS

	Rating	Risk	Moat Size	Fair Value	Last Close	Yield %
	★★	Med.	None	$18.00	$18.91	0.0

Company Profile

Chico's is a retailer of private-label casual clothing and accessories. Virtually all of the clothing offered at Chico's stores is designed by the company's in-house staff and bears the Chico's trademark. The private-label clothing is only available at the Chico's stores. Primary customers are women in the 30- to 60-year age group. In the United States, the company's store system consists of 265 stores, of which 254 are owned and 11 are franchised.

Management

Marvin J. Gralnick and his wife, Helene B. Gralnick, founded Chico's in 1983. Except for a few years in the early 1990s, Marvin Gralnick has been CEO the entire time.

Strategy

Chico's sells private-label casual clothing and accessories for women over 35. Revenue growth comes from increases in customer traffic as much as it comes from new store openings. The retailer aims to obtain repeat business by offering special discounts to customers through an affinity program.

11215 Metro Parkway   www.chicos.com
Fort Myers, FL 33912

Morningstar Grades

Growth [A+]	1999	2000	2001	2002
Revenue %	41.7	45.2	67.4	45.7
Earnings/Share %	200.0	62.5	76.9	46.4
Book Value/Share %	45.4	47.1	56.5	65.6
Dividends/Share %	NMF	NMF	NMF	NMF

Thanks to its loyal customers, Chico's has consistently posted explosive growth. We expect the retailer's sales to increase 27% annually over the next five years.

Profitability [A+]	2000	2001	2002	TTM
Return on Assets %	22.0	24.1	22.6	21.8
Oper Cash Flow $Mil	17	39	65	106
- Cap Spending $Mil	15	40	37	60
= Free Cash Flow $Mil	2	-1	28	47

Chico's is one of the most profitable companies in apparel retailing, with gross margins approaching 60%. We expect the company to outstrip its peers' profitability over the next several years.

Financial Health [A+]	2000	2001	2002	10-02
Long-term Debt $Mil	7	7	8	5
Total Equity $Mil	53	85	143	221
Debt/Equity Ratio	0.1	0.1	0.1	0.0

Chico's generates plenty of cash to fund expansion. Also, the retailer is better positioned to weather a sales downturn than many of its peers because the bulk of its leases are cancelable if sales don't meet minimum expectations.

Industry	Investment Style	Stock Type	Sector
Clothing Stores	Mid Growth	Aggr. Growth	Consumer Services

Competition	Market Cap $Mil	Debt/ Equity	12 Mo Trailing Sales $Mil	Price/Cash Flow	Return On Assets%	Total Return% 1 Yr	3 Yr
Chico's FAS	1,605	0.0	494	15.1	21.8	42.9	73.0
Talbots	1,652	—	1,589	—	—	—	—
AnnTaylor Stores	916	0.2	1,400	5.6	6.4	-12.5	0.2

Price Volatility

I Monthly Price High/Low   — Relative Strength to S&P 500

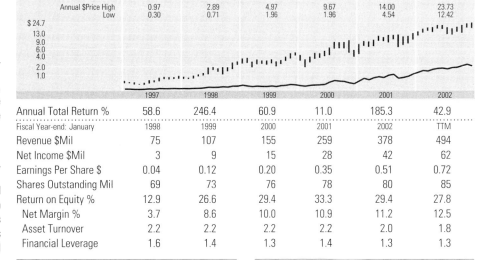

Annual $Price High Low	0.97 0.30	2.89 0.71	4.97 1.96	9.67 1.96	14.00 4.54	23.73 12.42
	1997	1998	1999	2000	2001	2002
Annual Total Return %	58.6	246.4	60.9	11.0	185.3	42.9

Fiscal Year-end: January	1998	1999	2000	2001	2002	TTM
Revenue $Mil	75	107	155	259	378	494
Net Income $Mil	3	9	15	28	42	62
Earnings Per Share $	0.04	0.12	0.20	0.35	0.51	0.72
Shares Outstanding Mil	69	73	76	78	80	85
Return on Equity %	12.9	26.6	29.4	33.3	29.4	27.8
Net Margin %	3.7	8.6	10.0	10.9	11.2	12.5
Asset Turnover	2.2	2.2	2.2	2.2	2.0	1.8
Financial Leverage	1.6	1.4	1.3	1.4	1.3	1.3

Valuation Ratios	Stock	Rel to Industry	Rel to S&P 500
Price/Earnings	26.4	1.4	1.1
Price/Book	7.3	1.8	2.3
Price/Sales	3.2	3.7	1.6
Price/Cash Flow	15.1	1.5	1.1

Major Fund Holders	% of Fund Assets
Oberweis Emerging Growth	7.96
Boyle Marathon	6.77
Oberweis Mid-Cap	5.73
Fairport Emerging Growth	4.38

Morningstar's Take By Roz Bryant, 11-18-2002 Stock Price as of Analysis: $20.19

Chico's FAS is a powerful growth and profit engine that has shown few signs of slowing. Given the retailer's wide base of loyal customers, we'd buy the shares with a 40% margin of safety instead of the 50% we require for most specialty retailers.

With its flexible sizing and mature yet fashionable apparel, Chico's targets women over 35. Customers in this demographic generally have more disposable income and less-fickle fashion preferences, so they can afford higher prices and are easier to satisfy consistently. The retailer promotes customer loyalty with its Passport Club, through which shoppers receive a permanent 10% discount once they make $500 in purchases. Program participants account for 60% of overall revenue.

Management estimates that its stores have penetrated just 10% of the firm's target market, so we believe prospects for growth are promising. With operating cash flow standing at 17.5% of sales and minimal debt, Chico's has the financial strength to continue funding its expansion. Despite increasing capital requirements associated with store expansions and remodeling, the firm has posted positive free cash flow in four of the past five years. Not even growing retail powerhouse Kohl's can boast such an achievement.

Thanks to its brand strength, Chico's delivers a level of profitability few other retailers can match. Chico's gross margins are nearly 60% compared with rival Talbots' 40%. We think Chico's will become even more profitable as it expands, thanks to recent infrastructure investments. We expect new supply-chain and inventory-management software to enable more-informed buying decisions, helping to weed out undesirable merchandise before it hits store shelves. A second distribution center in Atlanta, which is scheduled to become fully functional in 2003, should also help lower freight costs, a major expense for Chico's, which ships merchandise to stores daily.

Still, as other apparel makers and retailers eye the fat margins at Chico's, we expect competition for its customers to heat up. After all, a retailer can't patent a look, even if it invents it--just ask Gap. Companies like J. Jill, Christopher & Banks, and Talbots now peacefully coexist with Chico's while serving a similar age demographic, but that won't always be the case as the stores encroach on one another's territories more and more.

Given its ability to attract and retain customers, we are confident that Chico's will deliver superior returns for investors who buy in at the right price.

Chiron CHIR

	Rating	Risk	Moat Size	Fair Value	Last Close	Yield %
	★★	Med.	None	$40.00	$37.60	0.0

Company Profile

Chiron develops and produces biopharmaceutical products, vaccines, and blood tests. Its biopharmaceutical products emphasize treatments for cancer and infection. The firm's drug TOBI, which treats lung infections caused by cystic fibrosis, was acquired with Chiron's purchase of Pathogenesis in 2000. It makes vaccines to prevent conditions like meningitis, influenza, and hepatitis. Through partnerships with Gen-Probe and Johnson & Johnson subsidiary Ortho-Clinical Diagnostics, it develops blood-screening tests to detect HIV and hepatitis. Novartis owns 42% of the firm.

Management

Sean Lance, a former Glaxo executive, was hired as president and CEO in 1998. Lance has helped restructure the firm to focus on its three divisions and has cut less promising research efforts to boost earnings. Novartis owns 42% of Chiron.

Strategy

Chiron lowers risk by diversifying its product development over three areas--biopharmaceuticals, vaccines, and blood testing--rather than just drug development. The firm is focused on expanding uses, delivery methods, and geographic coverage of its existing products. Look for Chiron to boost its drug lineup via acquisition, as it did with Pathogenesis in 2000 and Matrix Pharmaceuticals in 2002.

4560 Horton Street   www.chiron.com
Emeryville, CA 94608

Morningstar Grades

Growth [B]

	1998	1999	2000	2001
Revenue %	28.2	3.5	27.5	17.3
Earnings/Share %	625.0	-70.3	-95.3	EUB
Book Value/Share %	74.3	5.6	-2.1	11.7
Dividends/Share %	NMF	NMF	NMF	NMF

Revenue has increased 17% annually since 1997; it's on pace to come in slightly lower in 2002. There's little in Chiron's near-term pipeline, so increases in the mid- to high teens are probably not sustainable beyond 2004.

Profitability [A-]

	1999	2000	2001	TTM
Return on Assets %	6.6	0.3	6.3	5.4
Oper Cash Flow $Mil	21	373	262	346
- Cap Spending $Mil	65	54	65	97
= Free Cash Flow $Mil	-44	319	197	249

Chiron is rebounding from declining profitability. Lower R&D costs in biopharmaceuticals have turned around operating margins in that division. Blood testing sales, which have higher margins, are increasing and contributing more to the bottom line.

Financial Health [A+]

	1999	2000	2001	09-02
Long-term Debt $Mil	97	3	409	415
Total Equity $Mil	1,686	1,881	1,932	2,022
Debt/Equity Ratio	0.1	0.0	0.2	0.2

The company has positive cash from operations and $1.3 billion in cash and marketable securities as of September 30--plenty to cover its obligations.

	Industry	Investment Style	Stock Type	Sector
	Biotechnology	Mid Growth	Classic Growth	Healthcare

Competition

	Market Cap $Mil	Debt/ Equity	12 Mo Trailing Sales $Mil	Price/Cash Flow	Return On Assets%	Total Return% 1 Yr	3 Yr
Chiron	7,073	0.2	1,238	20.5	5.4	-14.2	-2.6
Amgen	61,986	0.2	4,881	31.7	-7.1	-14.4	-6.0
MedImmune	6,820	0.1	759	37.9	-55.7	-41.4	-15.4

Price Volatility   ▮ Monthly Price High/Low   — Relative Strength to S&P 500

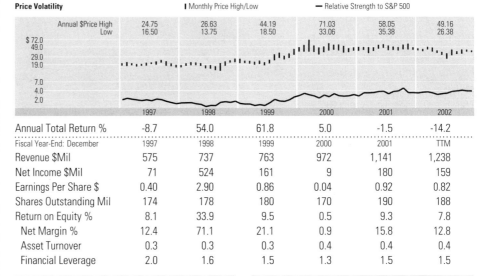

Annual $Price High / Low	24.75 / 16.50	26.63 / 13.75	44.19 / 18.50	71.03 / 33.06	58.05 / 35.38	49.16 / 26.38

	1997	1998	1999	2000	2001	2002
Annual Total Return %	-8.7	54.0	61.8	5.0	-1.5	-14.2

Fiscal Year-End: December	1997	1998	1999	2000	2001	TTM
Revenue $Mil	575	737	763	972	1,141	1,238
Net Income $Mil	71	524	161	9	180	159
Earnings Per Share $	0.40	2.90	0.86	0.04	0.92	0.82
Shares Outstanding Mil	174	178	180	170	190	188
Return on Equity %	8.1	33.9	9.5	0.5	9.3	7.8
Net Margin %	12.4	71.1	21.1	0.9	15.8	12.8
Asset Turnover	0.3	0.3	0.3	0.4	0.4	0.4
Financial Leverage	2.0	1.6	1.5	1.3	1.5	1.5

Valuation Ratios	Stock	Rel to Industry	Rel to S&P 500
Price/Earnings	45.9	1.0	1.9
Price/Book	3.5	1.0	1.1
Price/Sales	5.7	0.5	2.8
Price/Cash Flow	20.5	0.6	1.5

Major Fund Holders	% of Fund Assets
Smith Barney Aggressive Growth A	5.52
Alliance Select Investor Biotech A	5.15
Kinetics Medical Fund	5.13
ING Biotechnology A	5.06

Morningstar's Take By Jill Kiersky, 11-18-2002   Stock Price as of Analysis: $40.04

Chiron needs to decide what it wants to be when it grows up. Until then, its shares won't be very compelling.

The firm's roots are in developing vaccines and testing for infectious diseases like hepatitis and HIV. Unlike most biotech firms that focus solely on developing drugs, Chiron remains diversified. While this strategy can shield the company from idiosyncratic events in any one business, it can also spread resources too thin.

At first glance, it seems the diversification strategy has worked. Sales have increased an average of 17% annually since 1997 and have provided enough cash to cover some drug-development costs. Chiron's sales growth comes not from breakthrough drug development, however, but from acquisitions and nonrecurring payments like collaborative research. Sales of the once top-producing cancer drug Proleukin have been flat and are showing only moderate signs of revival, and vaccine sales, which provided 53% of operating income in 2001, have declined this year.

Chiron's most promising drug is TOBI, the only inhaled therapy for infections in cystic fibrosis patients. We think TOBI will enjoy moderate sales growth, but the market is small, and other treatments

are in clinical testing. Further hopes were shattered when Chiron's next potential growth engines, cardiovascular drug FGF-2 and sepsis treatment TFPI, did not meet testing standards. The company has halted several other trials this year.

Chiron's inability to develop profitable drugs isn't for lack of trying. The firm spends more than twice what other established biotech firms do on research and development. Chiron's biopharmaceutical segment now spends about 60% of its product sales on R&D, and that's down from 80% in 2001; its five closest rivals spend 27% on average. Given these statistics and Chiron's lab failures, we would like better proof of the firm's drug-development capabilities before we put our money at stake.

Chiron's next-best growth opportunity is Procleix, a blood test for HIV and hepatitis C, which is already used in 75% of all blood donations in the United States. Thanks in large part to the Food and Drug Administration's approval of the test in February, Procleix sales for the first nine months of this year were $84 million--triple those of the year-ago period.

Thanks to restructuring efforts and a more profitable sales mix, Chiron has improved its operating margins. But with its business model so shaky, we'd require a large discount before investing.

MORNINGSTAR®   **Stocks 500**

Chubb CB

	Rating	Risk	Moat Size	Fair Value	Last Close	Yield %
	★★★	Med.	None	$70.00	$52.20	2.7

Company Profile

Chubb's subsidiaries underwrite property and casualty insurance and reinsurance policies. The firm markets its insurance products through approximately 5,000 independent insurance agents and brokers worldwide. Chubb announced in November 2001 that it will team with AIG and Goldman Sachs to form a Bermuda-based company, Allied World Assurance Co. Ltd., to underwrite worldwide commercial property-casualty insurance and reinsurance.

Management

Former GMAC chief John Finnegan is replacing Dean O'Hare, chairman and chief executive officer since 1988. Long-time Chubb director Joel Cohen will take over board leadership. Given the split in power, we expect few strategic changes from Chubb.

Strategy

Chubb aims to aggressively write new commercial business to take advantage of rising commercial premium rates. The firm relies on its reputation as a premium-service insurer, with no-hassle claims service, to attract affluent homeowners and the corporate elite to its personal property and executive protection policies.

15 Mountain View Road   www.chubb.com
Warren, NJ 07061-1615

Morningstar Grades

Growth [C+]	1998	1999	2000	2001
Revenue %	-4.7	6.0	7.8	6.9
Earnings/Share %	-4.6	-12.6	9.6	-84.3
Book Value/Share %	3.6	10.5	6.0	-5.9
Dividends/Share %	6.9	3.4	2.9	3.0

Since the terrorist attacks, demand for commercial insurance and reinsurance has spiked while available capital has shrunk. This bodes extremely well for Chubb's premium growth over the next several years.

Profitability [B]	1999	2000	2001	TTM
Return on Assets %	2.6	2.9	0.4	0.6
Oper Cash Flow $Mil	1,339	964	1,011	—
- Cap Spending $Mil	98	139	185	—
= Free Cash Flow $Mil	—	—	—	—

Return on equity slumped in 2001 because of unprecedented claims related to 9/11 and Enron. Chubb's profitability should improve unless loss trends weaken dramatically.

Financial Health [A-]	1999	2000	2001	09-02
Long-term Debt $Mil	—	—	—	—
Total Equity $Mil	6,272	6,982	6,525	6,901
Debt/Equity Ratio	—	—	—	—

The company remains on solid financial footing with a capital position of $7 billion. Debt is just 16% of total capitalization.

Industry	Investment Style	Stock Type	Sector
Insurance (Property)	☐ Large Core	▨ High Yield	$ Financial Services

Competition	Market Cap $Mil	Debt/ Equity	12 Mo Trailing Sales $Mil	Price/Cash Flow	Return On Assets%	Total Return% 1 Yr	Total Return% 3 Yr
Chubb	8,929	—	8,685	—	0.6	-22.7	2.1
American International Gr	150,907	—	66,823	—	1.4	-26.9	-4.0
Berkshire Hathaway B	111,526	—	39,133	—	1.9	-4.0	12.5

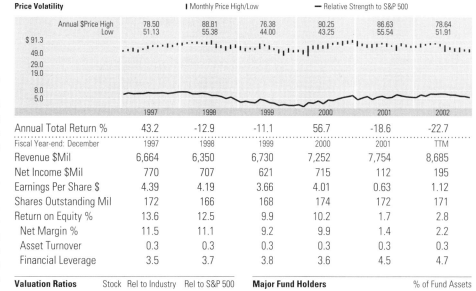

Price Volatility ▎Monthly Price High/Low — Relative Strength to S&P 500

Annual $Price High Low	78.50 51.13	88.81 55.38	76.38 44.00	90.25 43.25	86.63 55.54	78.64 51.91

$91.3 / 49.0 / 29.0 / 19.0 / 8.0 / 5.0

	1997	1998	1999	2000	2001	2002
Annual Total Return %	43.2	-12.9	-11.1	56.7	-18.6	-22.7
Fiscal Year-end: December	1997	1998	1999	2000	2001	TTM
Revenue $Mil	6,664	6,350	6,730	7,252	7,754	8,685
Net Income $Mil	770	707	621	715	112	195
Earnings Per Share $	4.39	4.19	3.66	4.01	0.63	1.12
Shares Outstanding Mil	172	166	168	174	172	171
Return on Equity %	13.6	12.5	9.9	10.2	1.7	2.8
Net Margin %	11.5	11.1	9.2	9.9	1.4	2.2
Asset Turnover	0.3	0.3	0.3	0.3	0.3	0.3
Financial Leverage	3.5	3.7	3.8	3.6	4.5	4.7

Valuation Ratios	Stock	Rel to Industry	Rel to S&P 500
Price/Earnings	46.6	2.3	2.0
Price/Book	1.3	0.7	0.4
Price/Sales	1.0	0.5	0.5
Price/Cash Flow	—	—	—

Major Fund Holders	% of Fund Assets
Salomon Brothers Opportunity	11.64
Choice Balanced Fund	8.16
Vontobel U.S. Value	4.76
GAMerica Capital A	4.37

Morningstar's Take By Aaron Westrate, 11-27-2002 Stock Price as of Analysis: $57.30

Chubb's outstanding premium growth has been offset by troubling reserve deficiencies and loss trends. As a result, we've cut our fair value estimate to $70 from $87 after lowering our profitability assumptions. We're also raising our risk rating to medium to reflect our uncertainty about Chubb's future economics, so we'd steer clear of the stock until it trades at a 40% discount to our fair value estimate.

Chubb should be a primary beneficiary of the hard market (i.e., rising rates). Its solid balance sheet has attracted a growing number of clients who are more concerned about an insurer's ability to pay than with who offers the best pricing. Premium growth has been in the low 30s, well beyond our expectations. Even better, Chubb has been able to reduce the coverage terms on many of its commercial policies, so it is collecting a higher premium for less risk than before.

Chubb's existing book of business, however, appears to be another story. The property-casualty business can be very unforgiving on the cost side since insurers set a price for their product well before they know its true costs. A recent $625 million charge to boost inadequate asbestos reserves reveals that even good underwriters like Chubb aren't immune to making large mistakes. The size of the charge, a

$2.38 per-share aftertax hit to earnings, caught us by surprise because it shows that Chubb has a much larger exposure to asbestos than we had believed.

Chubb's sterling claims service distinguishes it from several of its competitors in the personal lines segment. We don't anticipate much erosion of this business from outside threats, and the growing affluent class should help premiums grow nicely over time. However, rising mold claims have wracked its largest personal line, homeowners. Although Chubb has secured rate increases from state regulators for this line, mold costs may outrun Chubb's ability to raise rates.

Because Chubb is one of the largest writers of director and officer litigation coverage, the spate of shareholder lawsuits don't bode well either. The firm is now posting an underwriting loss in this previously very profitable line even as premiums have risen dramatically.

The new chief executive, John Finnegan, is another major uncertainty. While Finnegan arrives with a solid reputation built at GMAC, we are reluctant to give any newcomer to the notoriously difficult property-casualty industry the benefit of the doubt.

Cigna CI

	Rating	Risk	Moat Size	Fair Value	Last Close	Yield %
	★★★	Med.	None	$55.00	$41.12	3.2

Company Profile

Cigna provides insurance and related financial services. It offers health, group life, accident, and disability insurance, and pension and retirement products and services. The company's revenue is mainly derived from insurance premiums, fees, and investments, which include equity securities, mortgage loans, real estate, and fixed-maturity instruments. Cigna serves approximately 14 million health insurance members and about 13 million dental members in the United States.

Management

H. Edward Hanway was named president in January 1999, CEO in January 2000, and chairman in December 2000. He has been with the company for 22 years and was picked by former head Wilson Taylor.

Strategy

Cigna has sold its individual life, property-casualty, and reinsurance businesses to concentrate on group benefits (health care, group life, and pension). The company is focused on increasing profitability in its health-care operations by using a more disciplined pricing strategy to ensure that premium increases exceed medical cost trends.

One Liberty Place   www.cigna.com
Philadelphia, PA 19192-1550

Industry	Investment Style	Stock Type	Sector
Managed Care	▦ Mid Value	⚡ Distressed	Healthcare

Competition	Market Cap $Mil	Debt/ Equity	12 Mo Trailing Sales $Mil	Price/Cash Flow	Return On Assets%	Total Return% 1 Yr	3 Yr
Cigna	5,732	0.3	19,958	5.3	-0.3	-54.8	-18.0
UnitedHealth Group	25,235	0.3	24,358	12.5	8.9	18.0	46.6
WellPoint Health Networks	10,372	0.3	16,180	7.9	6.0	21.8	29.5

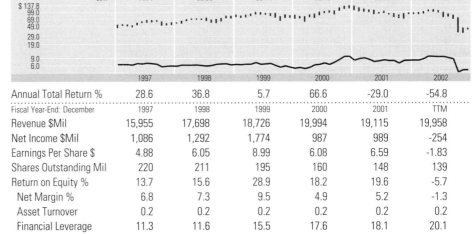

Price Volatility | Monthly Price High/Low — Relative Strength to S&P 500

Annual $Price High Low	66.92 44.71	82.38 56.00	98.63 63.44	136.75 60.75	134.95 69.90	111.00 34.20

	1997	1998	1999	2000	2001	2002
Annual Total Return %	28.6	36.8	5.7	66.6	-29.0	-54.8

Fiscal Year-End: December	1997	1998	1999	2000	2001	TTM
Revenue $Mil	15,955	17,698	18,726	19,994	19,115	19,958
Net Income $Mil	1,086	1,292	1,774	987	989	-254
Earnings Per Share $	4.88	6.05	8.99	6.08	6.59	-1.83
Shares Outstanding Mil	220	211	195	160	148	139
Return on Equity %	13.7	15.6	28.9	18.2	19.6	-5.7
Net Margin %	6.8	7.3	9.5	4.9	5.2	-1.3
Asset Turnover	0.2	0.2	0.2	0.2	0.2	0.2
Financial Leverage	11.3	11.6	15.5	17.6	18.1	20.1

Valuation Ratios	Stock	Rel to Industry	Rel to S&P 500	Major Fund Holders	% of Fund Assets
Price/Earnings	NMF	—	—	ING Large Company Value A	3.15
Price/Book	1.3	0.2	0.4	ING MagnaCap A	3.13
Price/Sales	0.3	0.4	0.1	AIM Large Cap Basic Value A	2.47
Price/Cash Flow	5.3	0.5	0.4	Putnam New Value A	2.24

Morningstar Grades

Growth [C-]	1998	1999	2000	2001
Revenue %	10.9	5.8	6.8	-4.4
Earnings/Share %	24.0	48.6	-32.4	8.4
Book Value/Share %	8.7	-19.6	7.0	1.0
Dividends/Share %	3.6	4.6	3.3	3.2

Sales declined more than 4% in 2001, bringing several consecutive years of positive revenue growth to an end. We expect revenue growth to remain underwhelming for the next couple of years and resume at 5% by 2005.

Profitability [B+]	1999	2000	2001	TTM
Return on Assets %	1.9	1.0	1.1	-0.3
Oper Cash Flow $Mil	1,817	1,685	1,086	1,073
- Cap Spending $Mil	0	0	0	NMF
= Free Cash Flow $Mil	1,817	1,685	1,086	NMF

Despite recent trouble with sales growth, Cigna has maintained its operating margin with steady medical and administrative cost management. Its medical loss ratio has hovered around the industry average of about 85% for the past couple of years.

Financial Health [C]	1999	2000	2001	09-02
Long-term Debt $Mil	1,359	1,163	1,627	1,500
Total Equity $Mil	6,149	5,413	5,055	4,458
Debt/Equity Ratio	0.2	0.2	0.3	0.3

The balance sheet is taking some serious hits. While Cigna has the internal funds to weather the storm of charges for the current year, it will probably need to tap the debt or equity markets for capital in 2003.

Morningstar's Take By Damon Ficklin, 10-30-2002 Stock Price as of Analysis: $36.10

Cigna is restructuring its operations and it will be awhile before it increases sales again. Until we see that the firm can recharge its top line, we would consider buying its stock only if the price provided a 50% margin of safety to our fair value estimate.

Cigna faces intense competition from other large group insurers like UnitedHealth Group and the regional Blue Cross Blue Shield operators, and it doesn't offer any truly innovative products. That this is a significant competitive disadvantage was recently confirmed when Cigna announced that it had mispriced certain indemnity products. Its products weren't competitive so it made margin concessions to keep its clients. The result: Earnings plunged.

As further evidence of product weakness, Cigna's medical insurance enrollment has been declining, and we can expect more of the same during the restructuring. We project overall sales to fall 10% next year, remain flat in 2004, and grow 5% in 2005. It is going to take time to design more-competitive products and stabilize enrollment and pricing.

Despite its product problems, Cigna has an exceptionally attractive mix of health insurance business. More than 80% of its health insurance membership is fee-based (instead of risk-based). This compares quite favorably with the more typical 50/50

split of most insurers. In a fee-based plan, Cigna simply charges a flat fee for access to its network of hospitals and physicians, leaving the customer to bear the risk of paying for its employees' medical costs.

Barring its recent misstep with the indemnity products, Cigna has delivered steady cost management over the past few years. Its commercial medical loss ratio has hovered around the industry average of about 85%, and its administrative loss ratio has shown some improvement despite flat sales growth. These bright spots lead us to believe that Cigna's restructuring may be less severe than the average experience in the industry.

Cigna has its work cut out for it. It needs to design more-competitive products and improve its service while keeping tight controls over its costs. Given the current weakness of its product offerings, the intensity of competition, and the uncertainty about how long it will take Cigna to right its course, we would require a 50% margin of safety to our fair value estimate before investing.

MORNINGSTAR® Stocks 500

Cintas CTAS

	Rating	Risk	Moat Size	Fair Value	Last Close	Yield %
	★★	Med.	Wide	$37.00	$45.75	0.5

Company Profile

Cintas designs and manufactures corporate identity uniforms, which it then rents or sells to its customers. More than 4 million people wear a Cintas uniform to work. In conjunction with its uniform rental operations, Cintas provides sanitation supplies, first aid products, and entrance mat services. All these services are provided throughout the United States to 420,000 business customers, ranging in size from very small companies to large corporations.

Management

Chairman Richard Farmer founded Cintas in 1968 and owns 20.7% of the stock. The CEO has been with the firm from the start, too, and in his current position since 1995. Management trainees, hired fresh from college, are given responsibility quickly.

Strategy

Cintas strives to produce growth by expanding the market for its core uniform rentals. In 2002, 55% of new uniform rental customers were first-time users. Cintas also leverages its distribution networks and close customer contacts to market entrance mat services, hygiene products, and first aid products--businesses now accounting for about 30% of revenue.

6800 Cintas Blvd.   www.cintas.com
Cincinnati, OH 45262-5737

Morningstar Grades

Growth [B+]

	1999	2000	2001	2002
Revenue %	18.6	8.6	13.6	5.1
Earnings/Share %	3.8	39.0	14.0	4.6
Book Value/Share %	10.7	19.5	17.0	14.9
Dividends/Share %	22.3	27.3	17.8	13.6

Helped by acquisitions, Cintas has reported record earnings and revenue each year for the past 33 years. But with the firm's bigger share of the market, we project lower growth.

Profitability [A+]

	2000	2001	2002	TTM
Return on Assets %	12.2	12.7	9.3	9.4
Oper Cash Flow $Mil	258	247	377	387
- Cap Spending $Mil	161	147	107	96
= Free Cash Flow $Mil	97	100	270	291

Cintas' operating margins, near 17%, trounce those of its publicly traded rivals, G&K Services and UniFirst. Acquisitions hurt margins in 1998 and 1999, but we believe the integration of Omni will go more smoothly.

Financial Health [A]

	2000	2001	2002	08-02
Long-term Debt $Mil	254	221	703	664
Total Equity $Mil	1,043	1,231	1,424	1,486
Debt/Equity Ratio	0.2	0.2	0.5	0.4

Cintas has used its strong cash flows and healthy finances to consolidate the uniform industry. It recently made its largest purchase ever, which added a lot of debt to the balance sheet.

		Investment Style	Stock Type	Sector
Industry				
Business Support		▦ Large Growth	↗ Classic Growth	🗎 Business Services

Competition

	Market Cap $Mil	Debt/ Equity	12 Mo Trailing Sales $Mil	Price/Cash Flow	Return On Assets%	Total Return% 1 Yr	3 Yr
Cintas	7,774	0.4	2,372	20.1	9.4	-4.2	11.6
Aramark	1,462	2.1	7,951	2.3	6.3	-12.6	—
G & K Services A	733	—	626	—	—	—	—

Price Volatility

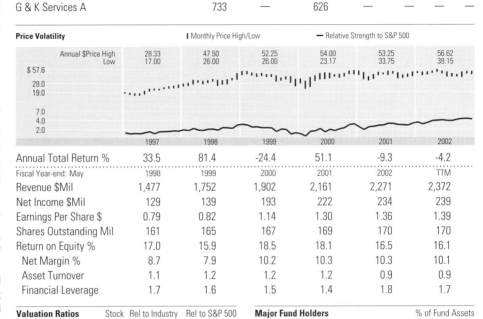

	Annual $Price High Low	28.33 17.00	47.50 26.00	52.25 26.00	54.00 23.17	53.25 33.75	56.62 39.15

		1997	1998	1999	2000	2001	2002
Annual Total Return %		33.5	81.4	-24.4	51.1	-9.3	-4.2

Fiscal Year-end: May	1998	1999	2000	2001	2002	TTM
Revenue $Mil	1,477	1,752	1,902	2,161	2,271	2,372
Net Income $Mil	129	139	193	222	234	239
Earnings Per Share $	0.79	0.82	1.14	1.30	1.36	1.39
Shares Outstanding Mil	161	165	167	169	170	170
Return on Equity %	17.0	15.9	18.5	18.1	16.5	16.1
Net Margin %	8.7	7.9	10.2	10.3	10.3	10.1
Asset Turnover	1.1	1.2	1.2	1.2	0.9	0.9
Financial Leverage	1.7	1.6	1.5	1.4	1.8	1.7

Valuation Ratios	Stock	Rel to Industry	Rel to S&P 500
Price/Earnings	32.9	1.2	1.4
Price/Book	5.2	1.6	1.6
Price/Sales	3.3	1.6	1.6
Price/Cash Flow	20.1	1.2	1.5

Major Fund Holders	% of Fund Assets
Cincinnati	5.70
MSB	3.68
Institutional Investors Capital Appr	3.58
Badgley Growth	3.51

Morningstar's Take By Dan Schick, 12-13-2002 Stock Price as of Analysis: $46.34

Cintas thrives in the profitable uniform rental business. Given the company's strong industry position, solid management, cash flows, and returns on capital, we'd purchase the shares at just a 20% discount to our fair value estimate.

The uniform rental industry is attractive for several reasons. For one, there is minimal threat of product substitution. For many employers, the choice between uniform or no uniform is an easy one; uniformed workers present a more coherent business image, like a brand. And once a business has decided to put its workers in uniform, the outsourcing decision is an easy sell for Cintas' aggressive salesforce. The first selling point is that Cintas has found that employees who wear rented uniforms would rather have them provided than have the cash used to pay for them. The second point is that by taking care of all the details like laundering, repairing, and replacing, the service is convenient and cost-effective for the employer.

Suppliers pose little danger to Cintas, because the company manufactures two thirds of its own products and the raw materials are easily obtainable commodities. Furthermore, Cintas' services are a small part of a company's cost of doing business, so customers are less motivated to bargain aggressively.

If Cintas keeps its customers happy, it keeps its customers, its profits, and its annual price increases.

These attractive industry characteristics would draw new rivals if the business were perfectly competitive. However, it's not: To protect its position Cintas has built barriers to entry, like its distribution network, which covers 90% of the U.S. population. This network helps Cintas provide superior services and also deters the emergence of a new nationwide competitor. A new entrant would have to bear the costs of duplicating the network as well as retaliation from Cintas. The network is also an asset that can be reutilized at low cost to generate additional sales. For example, Cintas' uniform delivery workers provide entrance mat services as well. Finally, through heavy investment and automation of new plants, Cintas has increased the amount of capital needed to compete, also deterring newcomers.

All these factors buffer Cintas from competitive onslaughts and protect its relatively stable, midteens returns on capital, well above the cost of the capital used in the business. Making a spread between the return on capital and its cost is the only formula for enduring value. We believe Cintas has learned this lesson, which makes it a good buy at the right price.

Circuit City Stores CC

	Rating	Risk	Moat Size	Fair Value	Last Close	Yield %
	★★★	Med.	None	$11.00	$7.42	0.9

Company Profile

Circuit City Stores is the largest specialty retailer of brand-name consumer electronics and appliances in the United States. The company operates 590 Circuit City Superstores (15,000-44,000 square feet in size) and 39 mall stores (2,000-4,000 square feet) operating under the Circuit City Express name. The stores sell video equipment, audio equipment, and other consumer electronic products like telephones and home computers. The company also owns a 74% stake in Circuit City Stores-CarMax Group, which sells cars and light-duty trucks in the United States.

Management

President and CEO W. Alan McCollough has been with the company since 1987. He has been president since 1997 and CEO since 2000.

Strategy

Circuit City Stores offers a broad selection of electronics at low prices. Margins are thin, and so sales volume is important. It also offers revolving credit to customers and profits on the interest of the loans.

9950 Mayland Drive
Richmond, VA 23233
www.circuitcity.pic.net

Industry	Investment Style	Stock Type	Sector
Electronics Stores	Mid Value	Slow Growth	Consumer Services

Competition	Market Cap $Mil	Debt/ Equity	12 Mo Trailing Sales $Mil	Price/Cash Flow	Return On Assets%	Total Return% 1 Yr	3 Yr
Circuit City Stores	1,559	0.0	10,035	26.0	4.8	-56.6	-35.9
Wal-Mart Stores	223,388	0.5	233,651	18.9	8.0	-11.8	-7.3
Target	27,252	1.2	42,275	21.5	5.7	-26.5	-3.9

Price Volatility — Monthly Price High/Low — Relative Strength to S&P 500

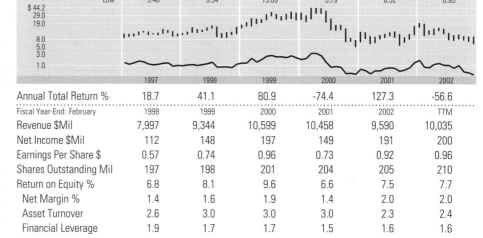

Annual $Price High Low	15.07 9.48	18.05 9.54	35.68 15.69	43.17 5.79	17.65 6.32	20.53 6.95

	1997	1998	1999	2000	2001	2002
Annual Total Return %	18.7	41.1	80.9	-74.4	127.3	-56.6

Fiscal Year-End: February	1998	1999	2000	2001	2002	TTM
Revenue $Mil	7,997	9,344	10,599	10,458	9,590	10,035
Net Income $Mil	112	148	197	149	191	200
Earnings Per Share $	0.57	0.74	0.96	0.73	0.92	0.96
Shares Outstanding Mil	197	198	201	204	205	210
Return on Equity %	6.8	8.1	9.6	6.6	7.5	7.7
Net Margin %	1.4	1.6	1.9	1.4	2.0	2.0
Asset Turnover	2.6	3.0	3.0	3.0	2.3	2.4
Financial Leverage	1.9	1.7	1.7	1.5	1.6	1.6

Valuation Ratios	Stock	Rel to Industry	Rel to S&P 500
Price/Earnings	7.7	0.2	0.3
Price/Book	0.6	0.2	0.2
Price/Sales	0.2	0.4	0.1
Price/Cash Flow	26.0	2.8	2.0

Major Fund Holders	% of Fund Assets
New Market	3.87
AXP Growth A	3.27
Cambiar Opportunity Inst	3.27
Capital Management Mid-Cap Instl	2.77

Morningstar Grades

Growth [D+]	1999	2000	2001	2002
Revenue %	16.9	13.4	-1.3	-8.3
Earnings/Share %	29.8	29.7	-24.0	26.0
Book Value/Share %	8.6	9.8	10.4	11.8
Dividends/Share %	0.0	0.0	0.0	0.0

Revenues have contracted over the last couple of years (partially due to Circuit City's exit from large-appliance sales), but recent comparable-store sales results have been mildly encouraging.

Profitability [B]	2000	2001	2002	TTM
Return on Assets %	5.6	4.3	4.6	4.8
Oper Cash Flow $Mil	662	149	795	60
- Cap Spending $Mil	177	275	173	146
= Free Cash Flow $Mil	485	-126	622	-86

The company is far less profitable than its competitors, with a return on assets of 3% and return on equity of 6%. Because of its low-price strategy and willingness to push low-margin items, profit margins are razor thin.

Financial Health [A+]	2000	2001	2002	08-02
Long-term Debt $Mil	128	33	14	12
Total Equity $Mil	2,055	2,257	2,560	2,606
Debt/Equity Ratio	0.1	0.0	0.0	0.0

Debt is minimal, and the company has almost $850 million in cash on its balance sheet. We'd like to see some improvements in working capital, though.

Morningstar's Take By Joseph Beaulieu, 12-12-2002 Stock Price as of Analysis: $8.39

Sluggish growth and a lack of significant competitive advantages keep us from getting too excited about Circuit City. We think that the stock is worth approximately $11 per share, but we'd want a substantial discount to that before buying the shares.

Now that Circuit City has spun off its ownership position in CarMax, it is much easier to compare the company to its biggest competitor, Best Buy. Looking at the two companies side by side, Circuit City doesn't look too bad, but a couple of small shortcomings add up to a big difference between the two. Until Circuit City shows significant operating improvements, we'd prefer to own Best Buy.

By far, the biggest difference between the two is operating margins. In fiscal 2002 (ended February of that year), Circuit City reported operating margins of 2.2%, compared with Best Buy's 4.8%. Best Buy is simply the leaner operator, and generates twice as much profit per dollar of revenue as Circuit City.

Inventories also tend to sit around on Circuit City shelves for about a week longer than they do at Best Buy. Circuit City also tends to pay its vendors about a week sooner than does Best Buy. With more than a billion dollars worth of inventories and another billion dollars due to suppliers at any given time, this represents a substantial difference in working capital use.

On the other hand, Circuit City has been doing a decent job of turning its fixed assets into sales, and actually beats Best Buy in this area. Best Buy's asset efficiency took a huge hit when it bought Musicland, but the core Best Buy stores remain more efficient than the Circuit City stores. We therefore think that Circuit City has room for improvement.

If over the course of the next few years Circuit City can trim costs to the point where it achieves Best Buy's 2002 operating margin level of 4.8%--through a combination of cutting costs and pushing more sales through their stores--we think that the stock would be worth just north of $20 per share. Until we see significant margin improvements, though, we won't be counting those chickens.

Over the next few quarters, as the company begins to report its results without CarMax, we expect to get a much better picture of where the company is going. For now, however, we only have three years of pro-forma financial data for Circuit City stores, so we'd want a 40% discount to our fair value estimate before considering the shares.

MORNINGSTAR® Stocks 500

Cisco Systems CSCO

Rating	Risk	Moat Size	Fair Value	Last Close	Yield %
★★	Med.	Narrow	$13.00	$13.10	0.0

Company Profile

Cisco Systems is the world's leading supplier of data networking equipment and software for the Internet. Its products include routers, switches, access equipment, and network management software that allow data communication among geographically dispersed computer networks. Customers outside North America account for approximately one third of total sales.

Management

Management is prudent and thinks for itself. Although acquisitions of small innovative competitors are key to its strategy, Cisco generally resists big splashy acquisitions and financial leverage--unlike many of its tech peers.

Strategy

As the growth of the Internet dramatically increases data traffic, telecom carriers are redesigning networks originally built for voice. Cisco aims to remain the networking equipment supplier of choice, while using its financial and research strength to make further inroads into telecom carriers' capital budgets. At the same time, it is tightening links to suppliers to reduce costs and risks.

170 West Tasman Drive
San Jose, CA 95134
www.cisco.com

Morningstar Grades

Growth [B+]	1999	2000	2001	2002
Revenue %	43.4	55.5	17.8	-15.2
Earnings/Share %	45.0	24.1	NMF	NMF
Book Value/Share %	56.6	111.2	4.7	1.1
Dividends/Share %	NMF	NMF	NMF	NMF

Although Cisco was once a growth machine, those days are over. We think structural problems in developed nations and the small size of developing economies will limit annual growth to 10%-12% during the next five years.

Profitability [A]	2000	2001	2002	TTM
Return on Assets %	8.1	-2.9	5.0	7.5
Oper Cash Flow $Mil	6,141	6,392	6,587	6,270
- Cap Spending $Mil	1,086	2,271	2,641	2,471
= Free Cash Flow $Mil	5,055	4,121	3,946	3,799

Cisco looks great on three fronts: Pricing has held steady, more savings have been squeezed from suppliers, and costs are more variable than fixed (giving Cisco flexibility). We expect average option-adjusted returns on equity of 10%.

Financial Health [A]	2000	2001	2002	10-02
Long-term Debt $Mil	0	0	0	0
Total Equity $Mil	26,497	27,120	28,656	28,546
Debt/Equity Ratio	0.0	0.0	0.0	0.0

With $21 billion of cash and investments and minimal debt, Cisco's balance sheet is a significant competitive weapon. Cash flow remains extremely solid and inventories are approaching normal levels after spiking last year.

Industry	Investment Style	Stock Type	Sector
Data Networking	▦ Large Growth	↗ Classic Growth	▣ Hardware

Competition	Market Cap $Mil	Debt/ Equity	12 Mo Trailing Sales $Mil	Price/Cash Flow	Return On Assets%	Total Return% 1 Yr	3 Yr
Cisco Systems	94,649	0.0	19,312	15.1	7.5	-27.7	-36.4
Nortel Networks	6,197	1.4	12,835	8.6	-29.6	-78.5	-67.5
Lucent Technologies	4,325	NMF	12,321	—	-67.2	-75.2	-71.8

Price Volatility

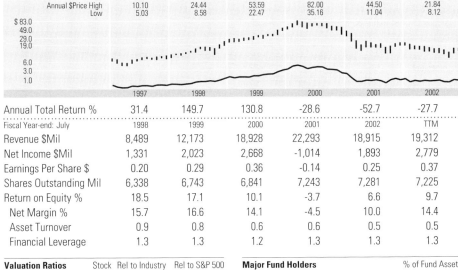

	Monthly Price High/Low			Relative Strength to S&P 500		
Annual $Price High	10.10	24.44	53.59	82.00	44.50	21.84
Low	5.03	8.58	22.47	35.16	11.04	8.12

$ 83.0 / 49.0 / 29.0 / 19.0 / 6.0 / 3.0 / 1.0

	1997	1998	1999	2000	2001	2002
Annual Total Return %	31.4	149.7	130.8	-28.6	-52.7	-27.7

Fiscal Year-end: July	1998	1999	2000	2001	2002	TTM
Revenue $Mil	8,489	12,173	18,928	22,293	18,915	19,312
Net Income $Mil	1,331	2,023	2,668	-1,014	1,893	2,779
Earnings Per Share $	0.20	0.29	0.36	-0.14	0.25	0.37
Shares Outstanding Mil	6,338	6,743	6,841	7,243	7,281	7,225
Return on Equity %	18.5	17.1	10.1	-3.7	6.6	9.7
Net Margin %	15.7	16.6	14.1	-4.5	10.0	14.4
Asset Turnover	0.9	0.8	0.6	0.6	0.5	0.5
Financial Leverage	1.3	1.3	1.2	1.3	1.3	1.3

Valuation Ratios	Stock	Rel to Industry	Rel to S&P 500
Price/Earnings	35.4	1.0	1.5
Price/Book	3.3	1.0	1.0
Price/Sales	4.9	1.0	2.4
Price/Cash Flow	15.1	1.0	1.1

Major Fund Holders	% of Fund Assets
Rydex Internet Inv	11.55
Fidelity Select Network & Infrastruct	11.37
Pin Oak Aggressive Stock	9.56
Reynolds Opportunity	8.76

Morningstar's Take By Fritz Kaegi, 11-20-2002 Stock Price as of Analysis: $14.38

Cisco's fundamentals are impressive, but we don't think earnings will grow fast enough to make the current share price compelling. Our fair value estimate is $13, and we'd buy if the stock traded below $10.

Voice and data telecom produces compelling benefits in time, reach, and efficiency. Networking equipment is thus a key economic input, especially for advanced countries where other productivity boosters (literacy, financial markets, and so on) are already in place. Demand for networking products will scale with growth in network traffic, since routers and switches have limited capacities.

Cisco is in a great competitive position. Equipment setup and maintenance are highly complex, so customers prefer bundled offerings (rewarding larger players) and well-established, trusted vendors. Thanks to Cisco's dominant market share in routers and switches, network engineers--who become key purchasing decision-makers--generally choose to become "certified" for Cisco products before others', and thus tend to prefer Cisco offerings. Cisco also has superior access to the capacity, buying power, and component supplies of contract manufacturers.

Cisco has the financial strength to capitalize on these advantages. With $21 billion in liquid assets and no debt, it maintains a research edge by acquiring small firms with promising technologies; a deal to buy a large peer would be out of character. It is also selectively cutting prices to make inroads into telecom carrier budgets.

How fast can Cisco grow? Only a robust rebound in North America, Europe, and Japan can deliver total sales growth of 15%-20%. Total Asia Pacific sales (excluding Japan) were $1.7 billion in 2002, less than half what is needed in coming years to attain these growth rates. Even under optimistic assumptions (say, new revenue rises in the same proportion to GDP that it did in the United States in 1999-2000), emerging market sales cannot grow by much more than $1 billion per year over the next five years.

We see serious obstacles to high growth in developed markets. In Europe, carriers have heavy debt loads and state budgets are severely constrained. Japan's budget deficit is unsustainable. In both regions, cultural and structural barriers (per-minute billing for local phone calls, for example) may prevent U.S.-style usage. In the United States, the Baby Bells have strong incentives to order from traditional suppliers like Lucent. Excess capacity and lower competition could spell years of subdued spending.

CIT Group CIT

	Rating	Risk	Moat Size	Fair Value	Last Close	Yield %
	★★★★	Med.	Narrow	$30.00	$19.60	0.6

Industry	Investment Style	Stock Type	Sector
Finance	⊞ Mid Core	➡ Slow Growth	$ Financial Services

Company Profile

CIT Group offers commercial and consumer financing primarily to smaller, middle-market, and larger businesses and individuals in the United States. The company specializes in factoring, equipment financing and leasing, recreation vehicle lending, commercial finance, sales finance, and home equity lending. Its principal clients are in the manufacturing, aerospace, construction, transportation, textiles, electronics, and railroad industries. Manufacturing comprises about 32% of CIT Group's financing and leasing assets. It acquired Newcourt Credit Group in November 1999.

Management

Albert Gamper, 60, has been president and CEO for more than 12 years. He's regarded as a steady, competent manager who understands the lending business and has guided CIT through a range of acquisitions and business cycles.

Strategy

Free from Tyco, CIT Group is restoring its credit rating and once again pursuing growth opportunities. It is also weeding out business lines that haven't fared well, like venture capital and manufactured housing loans.

1 CIT Drive
Livingston, NJ 07039
www.citgroup.com

Competition

	Market Cap $Mil	Debt/ Equity	12 Mo Trailing Sales $Mil	Price/Cash Flow	Return On Assets%	Total Return% 1 Yr	3 Yr
CIT Group	4,147	—	2,595	—	-15.7	—	—
General Electric	242,308	2.2	130,295	8.2	2.7	-37.7	-18.9
Citigroup	177,948	—	106,096	—	1.6	-24.2	1.1

Price Volatility

▮ Monthly Price High/Low　　— Relative Strength to S&P 500

Annual $Price High/Low

$25.1 / 19.0 / 8.0 / 6.0 / 4.0 / 3.0

24.05 / 13.80

	1997	1998	1999	2000	2001	2002
Annual Total Return %	—	—	—	—	—	—

Fiscal Year-End: September	1998	1999	2000	2001	2002	TTM
Revenue $Mil	2,271	2,917	2,381	1,891	2,595	2,595
Net Income $Mil	339	389	612	263	-6,699	-6,699
Earnings Per Share $	—	—	—	—	-31.66	-31.66
Shares Outstanding Mil	—	—	—	—	212	212
Return on Equity %	12.5	7.0	10.2	4.4	ELB	ELB
Net Margin %	14.9	13.4	25.7	13.9	ELB	ELB
Asset Turnover	0.1	0.1	0.0	0.0	0.1	0.1
Financial Leverage	9.0	8.1	8.1	8.6	9.0	9.0

Valuation Ratios

	Stock	Rel to Industry	Rel to S&P 500
Price/Earnings	NMF	—	—
Price/Book	0.9	0.3	0.3
Price/Sales	1.6	0.8	0.8
Price/Cash Flow	—	—	—

Major Fund Holders

	% of Fund Assets
John Hancock Classic Value A	3.71
ING Midcap Value A	3.69
Hotchkis and Wiley Large Cap Value I	3.25
Nuveen NWQ Multi-Cap Value	3.21

Morningstar Grades

Growth [D]

	1999	2000	2001	2002
Revenue %	28.5	-18.4	-20.6	37.2
Earnings/Share %	NMF	NMF	NMF	NMF
Book Value/Share %	—	—	—	NMF
Dividends/Share %	NMF	NMF	NMF	NMF

CIT has delivered solid growth during Gamper's reign. Since 1997, for example, net income increased from $310 million to roughly $731 million.

Profitability [D-]

	2000	2001	2002	TTM
Return on Assets %	1.3	0.5	-15.7	-15.7
Oper Cash Flow $Mil	1,905	1,027	1,360	—
- Cap Spending $Mil	2,458	1,451	1,877	—
= Free Cash Flow $Mil	—	—	—	—

Return on equity has been weak. In a more normal environment, the company can earn a mid-teens ROE.

Financial Health [D]

	2000	2001	2002	09-02
Long-term Debt $Mil	—	—	—	—
Total Equity $Mil	6,007	5,948	4,758	4,758
Debt/Equity Ratio	—	—	—	—

With reasonable leverage and good earnings power, CIT is in good health, and we expect its credit ratings will keep improving. But charge-offs are high and the company is exposed to volatile industries.

Morningstar's Take By Richard McCaffery, 12-10-2002 Stock Price as of Analysis: $20.35

CIT is no superstar, but we think its leading position in areas like factoring and capital finance makes it a well-positioned, durable company. Given its low returns and credit issues, though, we'd look for a wide margin of safety. We think it's a very good deal under $17, which is well below book value.

Our thesis is that CIT will gain share in a number of markets many mainstream lenders avoid. It has the scale, marketing know-how, and experience to make profitable loans to businesses and consumers across the credit spectrum. At the same time, banks and other lenders are pulling back from lending to companies with higher risk profiles.

CIT also has years of industry-specific experience. It's one of the largest lessors of airplanes, for example. This makes investors nervous, given the troubles in the airline industry. CIT has exposure here, but a look at its portfolio indicates to us that management knows what it's doing. CIT's focus is on narrow-body planes (it was wide-body planes that the airlines parked after 9/11). Its fleet of 193 aircraft has an average age of just 7.4 years, compared with an industry average above 10, and it's well diversified among North America, Europe, and Asia.

In every down cycle, investors fail to discriminate between firms engaged in riskier lending and those that lend recklessly. There's a big difference. While there are always a handful of lenders that blow up in a weak economy, they are usually the newer, most aggressive companies. CIT has been around for nearly a century and has an experienced management team. CEO Albert Gamper has run the business profitably for more than a dozen years.

The downside is that CIT's returns are nothing to crow about, and management has made some mistakes. The company earns a low- to mid-teens return on equity, mainly because margins are fairly low for a specialty financier. The combination of credit losses and high depreciation costs for the equipment it leases reduces profits.

In addition, ill-conceived entries into the venture capital industry, as well as unprofitable lines of lending like manufactured housing and trucking, worsened credit losses in the current cycle. The company is exiting these lines of business, but we think management needs to do a better job of allocating capital. Finally, losses in the core lines of business are at their highest in more than a decade. While we expect the company to weather the storm thanks to its strong earnings and good capital levels, risks remain.

MORNINGSTAR® Stocks 500

Citigroup C

	Rating	Risk	Moat Size	Fair Value	Last Close	Yield %
	★★★	Med.	Wide	$37.00	$35.19	2.0

Company Profile

Citigroup provides financial services worldwide. It offers commercial property and casualty, workers' compensation, life, and disability insurance. The company also operates banking offices in 101 countries. It provides real-estate and private, corporate, and mortgage banking services. In addition, the company offers managed health-care programs, investment management, trading services, and credit cards. Its Salomon Smith Barney subsidiary provides investment banking and asset-management services. The company acquired Associates First Capital in November 2000.

Management

Sanford Weill, the former head of Travelers, is chairman and CEO. Citi has realigned its management team to quell regulatory accusations, putting a deal-cutting lawyer in charge of the investment bank and hiring a corporate governance chieftain.

Strategy

Citigroup--the combination of insurance giant Travelers and banking giant Citibank--aims to be the global one-stop shop for corporate and consumer financial needs. It plans to target double-digit earnings growth every year by cross-selling its vast insurance, banking, and investment banking services.

399 Park Avenue
New York, NY 10043

www.citigroup.com

Morningstar Grades

Growth [C+]	1998	1999	2000	2001
Revenue %	6.7	9.9	18.5	0.2
Earnings/Share %	-7.7	65.6	20.7	3.8
Book Value/Share %	11.5	19.9	14.3	22.8
Dividends/Share %	38.8	45.9	28.4	15.4

Financial firms are not known for big revenue growth, but Citigroup's ability to post double-digit growth quarter after quarter proves the merits of cross-selling a variety of services.

Profitability [B]	1999	2000	2001	TTM
Return on Assets %	1.4	1.5	1.3	1.6
Oper Cash Flow $Mil	11,223	2,673	26,578	—
- Cap Spending $Mil	1,750	2,249	1,774	—
= Free Cash Flow $Mil	—	—	—	—

Profit growth has followed a consistent pattern: Buy a business, then cut costs and boost output. The firm's recent strong performance is due to margin expansion on the consumer side, which has made up for cyclical weakness elsewhere.

Financial Health [A-]	1999	2000	2001	09-02
Long-term Debt $Mil	—	—	—	—
Total Equity $Mil	56,395	64,461	79,722	79,366
Debt/Equity Ratio	—	—	—	—

Citigroup has an above-average default ratio because of its corporate loan and credit card exposure. The lagging effects of the recession are likely to keep defaults high in 2002, but strong earnings coverage and a big capital base make up for this.

	Industry	Investment Style	Stock Type	Sector
	International Banks	Large Core	Classic Growth	Financial Services

Competition	Market Cap $Mil	Debt/ Equity	12 Mo Trailing Sales $Mil	Price/Cash Flow	Return On Assets%	Total Return% 1 Yr	3 Yr
Citigroup	177,948	—	106,096	—	1.6	-24.2	1.1
Bank of America	104,505	—	46,628	—	1.3	14.5	19.8
J.P. Morgan Chase & Co.	47,901	—	42,911	—	0.2	-30.7	-17.5

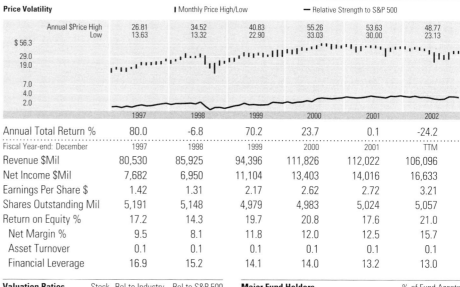

Price Volatility — Monthly Price High/Low — Relative Strength to S&P 500

Annual $Price High Low	26.81 13.63	34.52 13.32	40.83 22.90	55.26 33.03	53.63 30.00	48.77 23.13

	1997	1998	1999	2000	2001	2002
Annual Total Return %	80.0	-6.8	70.2	23.7	0.1	-24.2

Fiscal Year-end: December	1997	1998	1999	2000	2001	TTM
Revenue $Mil	80,530	85,925	94,396	111,826	112,022	106,096
Net Income $Mil	7,682	6,950	11,104	13,403	14,016	16,633
Earnings Per Share $	1.42	1.31	2.17	2.62	2.72	3.21
Shares Outstanding Mil	5,191	5,148	4,979	4,983	5,024	5,057
Return on Equity %	17.2	14.3	19.7	20.8	17.6	21.0
Net Margin %	9.5	8.1	11.8	12.0	12.5	15.7
Asset Turnover	0.1	0.1	0.1	0.1	0.1	0.1
Financial Leverage	16.9	15.2	14.1	14.0	13.2	13.0

Valuation Ratios	Stock	Rel to Industry	Rel to S&P 500
Price/Earnings	11.0	0.9	0.5
Price/Book	2.2	1.0	0.7
Price/Sales	1.7	1.0	0.8
Price/Cash Flow	—	—	—

Major Fund Holders	% of Fund Assets
Neuberger Berman Focus Inv	12.06
Merrill Lynch Global Financial Svcs B	11.19
Prudential Financial Services A	10.40
North Track Dow Jones US Fin 100 A	10.26

Morningstar's Take By Craig Woker, 10-23-2002 Stock Price as of Analysis: $35.49

Citigroup is a victim of the diversity paradox. We would pick up this conglomerate on the cheap when the stock dips to at least a 20% discount to our fair value estimate of $37 per share.

In a tough economic environment, like the current one, Citi can strut its stuff, boosting earnings at a steady pace and proving why its size and diverse product lineup give it an advantage over punier financial service rivals. Yet while that diversity has allowed this behemoth to increase core earnings per share 14% in the first nine months of 2002, it also has linked the company to almost every scandal that pops up anywhere in the industry. Business couldn't be better, but investors have dealt with a stomach-churning ride. On the bright side, the market turbulence creates buying opportunities.

It is likely that Citigroup's problems will continue to be political, legal, and regulatory, rather than operational. However, the laserlike focus placed on each new allegation is causing investors to miss the forest for the trees. Even if Citi is forced to change the way it does business in a few product lines, other units are likely to chug along just fine.

To put Citi's exposure into perspective, we've broken down the three biggest recent troublemakers weighing on the stock: (1) analysts' conflicts of interest with the investment banking business, (2) allegations of predatory lending, and (3) turmoil in Latin America. Because of Citi's scope and diversity, these three areas make up only a small percentage of the company's total business. For instance, investment banking is just 5.7% of net revenue and, we estimate, a slightly bigger portion of net income. The U.S. consumer finance unit--where the predatory accusations are centered--accounts for just 6.8% of net income. And Latin America is just 3.7% of Citi's total business.

Even if the profits from all three of these business lines were wiped out, Citigroup would still earn in excess of $13 billion in 2002, by our estimate. That would translate to a return on equity in the midteens, which by itself would be fairly good in this difficult environment.

Citi's strength doesn't end with its diversity, however. This company has a huge--and growing--equity base. Plus, the firm has a high level of operating earnings relative to bad debt charge-offs. If needed, the firm's earnings and capital could provide a massive cushion against potential losses. Together, these should insulate the company well if the economy once again slips into recession.

Citizens Communications CZN

	Rating	Risk	Moat Size	Fair Value	Last Close	Yield %
	★★★	High	Narrow	$13.00	$10.55	0.0

Company Profile

Citizens Communications is transforming itself from a natural gas, electric, and water utility into a telecommunication company. It currently owns about 2.5 million phone lines acquired from Global Crossing, Qwest, Verizon, and a handful of smaller companies. These lines are scattered across 27 states, with about one third of the total in New York. Citizens also owns 85% of Electric Lightwave, a competitive local phone company.

Management

Leonard Tow has been chairman and CEO since 1990. Scott Schneider replaced Rudy Graf as president and chief operating officer in July 2002. John H. "Jake" Casey is president and COO of the telecom segment.

Strategy

Citizens has taken advantage of the mergers among telecom giants, buying established local phone networks (usually in small markets) that the big guys no longer want. It hopes to improve returns on these assets by lavishing them with attention, upgrading the networks and offering new services. Citizens is selling assets and using cash flow to pay down debt incurred to finance its acquisitions.

3 High Ridge Park
Stamford, CT 06905
www.czn.net

Industry	Investment Style	Stock Type	Sector
Telecommunication Services	Mid Core	Spec. Growth	Telecom

Competition	Market Cap $Mil	Debt/ Equity	12 Mo Trailing Sales $Mil	Price/Cash Flow	Return On Assets%	Total Return% 1 Yr	3 Yr
Citizens Communications	2,968	4.0	2,676	4.8	-8.9	-1.0	-9.4
Verizon Communications	106,011	1.4	67,422	4.7	-0.1	-15.2	-9.8
SBC Communications	90,011	0.6	43,824	6.1	5.1	-28.3	-12.8

Price Volatility   ▌ Monthly Price High/Low   — Relative Strength to S&P 500

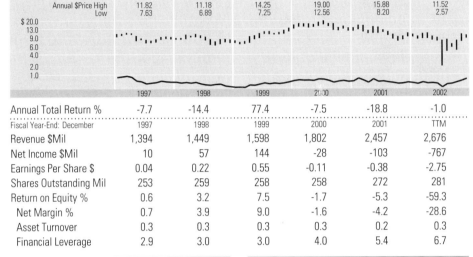

	1997	1998	1999	2000	2001	2002
Annual $Price High	11.82	11.18	14.25	19.00	15.88	11.52
Low	7.63	6.89	7.25	12.56	8.20	2.57
Annual Total Return %	-7.7	-14.4	77.4	-7.5	-18.8	-1.0

Fiscal Year-End: December	1997	1998	1999	2000	2001	TTM
Revenue $Mil	1,394	1,449	1,598	1,802	2,457	2,676
Net Income $Mil	10	57	144	-28	-103	-767
Earnings Per Share $	0.04	0.22	0.55	-0.11	-0.38	-2.75
Shares Outstanding Mil	253	259	258	258	272	281
Return on Equity %	0.6	3.2	7.5	-1.7	-5.3	-59.3
Net Margin %	0.7	3.9	9.0	-1.6	-4.2	-28.6
Asset Turnover	0.3	0.3	0.3	0.3	0.2	0.3
Financial Leverage	2.9	3.0	3.0	4.0	5.4	6.7

Valuation Ratios	Stock	Rel to Industry	Rel to S&P 500
Price/Earnings	NMF	—	—
Price/Book	2.3	0.8	0.7
Price/Sales	1.1	0.7	0.6
Price/Cash Flow	4.8	0.9	0.4

Major Fund Holders	% of Fund Assets
Hartford Global Communications A	11.26
Fidelity Utilities	4.67
MassMutual Instl Focused Value S	4.39
Fidelity Advisor Mid Cap B	3.68

Morningstar Grades

Growth [B]	1998	1999	2000	2001
Revenue %	3.9	10.3	12.8	36.3
Earnings/Share %	450.0	150.0	NMF	NMF
Book Value/Share %	3.9	5.7	-8.8	7.4
Dividends/Share %	NMF	NMF	NMF	NMF

Phone lines in service have declined slightly because of the sluggish economy. Although this line loss is milder than that of the Bells, sales growth has been limited to about 2%. We expect growth of about 4% over the long term.

Profitability [C+]	1999	2000	2001	TTM
Return on Assets %	2.5	-0.4	-1.0	-8.9
Oper Cash Flow $Mil	366	300	520	617
- Cap Spending $Mil	573	537	531	575
= Free Cash Flow $Mil	-207	-237	-10	42

The local phone business is very profitable, but restructuring charges and asset write-downs have decimated profits recently. Operating margins should typically exceed 20% at the incumbent local phone business.

Financial Health [C+]	1999	2000	2001	09-02
Long-term Debt $Mil	2,107	3,062	5,535	5,219
Total Equity $Mil	1,920	1,720	1,946	1,292
Debt/Equity Ratio	1.1	1.8	2.8	4.0

The company is finally starting to pull in some cash from asset sales. With the sale of the Hawaiian electric business in November, net debt should be about $4.6 billion at the end of 2002. Leverage remains higher than that of many peers.

Morningstar's Take By Michael Hodel, 12-09-2002 Stock Price as of Analysis: $9.61

Citizens isn't our favorite rural local phone company, but our interest in the shares is growing. We wouldn't buy the stock unless it offered a wide enough margin of safety relative to our fair value estimate. Alltel remains our favorite of the rural group.

Citizens is making progress in reducing debt. The bulk of the utility divestitures have closed, and management appears eager to finish the remaining sales. The company recently accepted a price below book value for its gas and electricity assets in Arizona. Assets for sale but not yet under contract were also written down because the sale prices, based on current negotiations, are also expected to be below book value. As a result, we've boosted our estimate of what the firm's debt load will be once all sales are completed. We think Citizens will be better off once it puts this drawn-out distraction behind it and can focus entirely on the telecom business.

Once Citizens finishes selling its utility assets, we think it will be left with an attractive business: providing telecom service for small towns. Serving these areas isn't particularly exciting; the majority of customers are consumers or small businesses whose telecom needs are growing slowly. What these markets do have, though, is stability. The market

opportunity isn't large enough to attract the level of competition seen in larger, densely populated areas. Data revenue has grown at the more urban-focused regional Bells in recent years, but retail phone lines in service fell at least 5% over the past year. Citizens' phone lines in service have held steady and have been a very profitable source of revenue.

We like a couple of Citizens' peers better. Alltel has a long operating history in rural wireline and wireless businesses, generating fantastic margins. We also think the wireless business offers protection, should this service increasingly serve as a substitute for the traditional phone line. Centurytel offers a rural local phone business similar in size to Citizens', but without as much debt or the distraction of nontelecom businesses. While we are gaining interest in Citizens as its restructuring progresses, we think there are better alternatives.

MORNINGSTAR® Stocks 500

Data as of 12-31-02

Clear Channel Communications CCU

Rating	Risk	Moat Size	Fair Value	Last Close	Yield %
★★	Med.	Narrow	$35.00	$37.29	0.0

Company Profile

Clear Channel Communications operates more than 1,200 radio stations and television stations in the United States (and has equity interests in more than 240 radio stations abroad). Additionally, the company owns approximately 770,000 outdoor advertising displays. Clear Channel's operations also encompass the concert promotion market.

Management

The firm is essentially family-managed. Members of the Mays family occupy the following top spots: CEO, president, chairman, director, CFO, and executive vice president.

Strategy

Clear Channel is focused on providing services to advertisers over the airwaves and through outdoor media like billboards and benches. Although its roots are in radio, the company has aggressively moved into TV, the Internet, and concert and sports promotion. After a recent acquisition spree, management is focusing more in internal growth.

200 East Basse Road
San Antonio, TX 78209-8328
www.clearchannel.com

Morningstar Grades

Growth [A]	1998	1999	2000	2001
Revenue %	93.8	98.2	99.6	49.1
Earnings/Share %	-33.3	0.0	159.1	NMF
Book Value/Share %	101.3	67.7	127.1	-27.8
Dividends/Share %	NMF	NMF	NMF	NMF

The company's strong numbers are overstated as a result of numerous buyouts, rather than internal expansion. Organic growth has been relatively flat, but acquisitions could provide high-single-digit revenue growth over the next several years.

Profitability [D+]	1999	2000	2001	TTM
Return on Assets %	0.4	0.5	-2.4	-60.0
Oper Cash Flow $Mil	639	755	610	1,509
- Cap Spending $Mil	239	496	598	518
= Free Cash Flow $Mil	401	260	11	992

As a result of heavy capital expenditures and weaker operating results, free cash flow dropped last year. But a gradual ad market recovery over the next year should provide a healthy boost to cash flow, which we estimate will top $1 billion in 2002.

Financial Health [C-]	1999	2000	2001	09-02
Long-term Debt $Mil	4,094	10,597	7,968	6,942
Total Equity $Mil	10,084	30,347	29,736	13,991
Debt/Equity Ratio	0.4	0.3	0.3	0.5

The company is in decent financial health, with roughly $200 million in cash. The firm has racked up debt as a result of its aggressive acquisition strategy. Its debt/equity ratio is 0.5, which still compares favorably with the S&P 500's 1.1.

Industry	Investment Style	Stock Type	Sector
Radio	Large Growth	Spec. Growth	Media

Competition	Market Cap $Mil	Debt/ Equity	12 Mo Trailing Sales $Mil	Price/Cash Flow	Return On Assets%	Total Return% 1 Yr	3 Yr
Clear Channel Communications	22,849	0.5	8,073	15.1	-60.0	-26.8	-23.9
Viacom B	71,391	0.2	23,868	20.3	0.0	-7.7	-8.8
Cox Communications A	17,611	0.8	4,646	16.3	-2.5	-32.2	-16.6

Price Volatility

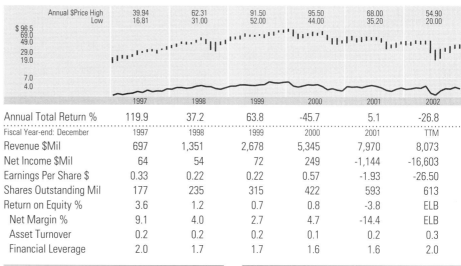

	1997	1998	1999	2000	2001	2002
Annual $Price High	39.94	62.31	91.50	95.50	68.00	54.90
Low	16.81	31.00	52.00	44.00	35.20	20.00
Annual Total Return %	119.9	37.2	63.8	-45.7	5.1	-26.8

Fiscal Year-end: December	1997	1998	1999	2000	2001	TTM
Revenue $Mil	697	1,351	2,678	5,345	7,970	8,073
Net Income $Mil	64	54	72	249	-1,144	-16,603
Earnings Per Share $	0.33	0.22	0.22	0.57	-1.93	-26.50
Shares Outstanding Mil	177	235	315	422	593	613
Return on Equity %	3.6	1.2	0.7	0.8	-3.8	ELB
Net Margin %	9.1	4.0	2.7	4.7	-14.4	ELB
Asset Turnover	0.2	0.2	0.2	0.1	0.2	0.3
Financial Leverage	2.0	1.7	1.7	1.6	1.6	2.0

Valuation Ratios	Stock	Rel to Industry	Rel to S&P 500
Price/Earnings	NMF	—	—
Price/Book	1.6	1.0	0.5
Price/Sales	2.8	1.0	1.4
Price/Cash Flow	15.1	1.0	1.1

Major Fund Holders	% of Fund Assets
Fidelity Select Multimedia	10.85
Gabelli Growth	6.54
MainStay Blue Chip Growth A	6.30
Gartmore U.S. Growth Leaders A	6.21

Morningstar's Take By T.K. MacKay, 12-19-2002 Stock Price as of Analysis: $37.75

Clear Channel boasts some of the best qualities of companies we like to buy: leading market share, increasing free cash flow, and a solid competitive advantage. However, we don't think it's quite worthy of our wide-moat rating, so we'd look for a 40% discount to our estimated fair value before investing.

Clear Channel rules the radio airwaves. With about 1,200 radio stations under its wing, the company owns 1 out of 10 radio stations in America, with a combined audience that tops 100 million--more than the next four largest broadcasters combined. The company's roughly 750,000 billboards and placards worldwide make it the largest outdoor advertiser, and its 2000 acquisition of SFX made Clear Channel the world's largest promoter of live entertainment, producing 26,000 events annually, including major acts like U2, Madonna, and Jerry Seinfeld.

In radio, which provides about 43% of Clear Channel's revenue, size gives the company bargaining power that smaller, locally owned radio stations don't have when it comes to negotiating advertising contracts. Clear Channel controls more than half of some of its markets, giving advertisers little choice with whom they do business. By adding billboards and concert venues to its media offerings,

Clear Channel makes itself producer, advertiser, and booking agent wrapped up in one.

Clear Channel's foray into new media hasn't come easy. Operating margins have declined to 19% from 28% five years ago, in part because of the lower-margin outdoor and entertainment businesses. However, free cash flow, a primary determinant of our estimated fair value for the company, has expanded 50% annually in that same period. With little capital expenditures necessary to maintain its assets (billboards don't fall down that often), the company should continue to generate strong free cash flow.

We don't think Clear Channel's hypergrowth of the past few years is sustainable, however. Politicians and industry players have voiced concerns about Clear Channel's size and market supremacy. We think the company will continue to pursue additional (albeit fewer) acquisitions, but predicting when and how large these acquisitions will be is guesswork.

Until we see this stock trading below $21, we're going to hold off.

©2003 Morningstar, Inc. All rights reserved.

MORNINGSTAR® Stocks 500   177

Clorox CLX

	Rating	Risk	Moat Size	Fair Value	Last Close	Yield %
	★★★	Med.	Narrow	$47.00	$41.25	2.1

Company Profile

Clorox mainly produces chlorine and nonchlorine bleaches, food products, and cleansers. The company also makes other well-known consumer products, including Pine Sol and Formula 409 household cleansers, S.O.S. soap pads, Glad plastic wrap, and Kingsford and Match Light charcoal products. In addition, it produces Hidden Valley Ranch salad dressings, K.C. Masterpiece barbecue sauce, Liquid-Plumr drain openers, Brita water filters, Armor All automotive-cleaning products, STP automotive additives, and Black Flag and Combat insecticides.

Management

Craig Sullivan has been CEO and chairman since 1992. He plans to sell about $30 million of his Clorox stake to diversify his holdings, though we wonder whether this is a signal that Sullivan, 62, may be planning to retire.

Strategy

Clorox is focused on improving profitability and shoring up market share for its expanded stable of brands, which now includes Glad bags, STP auto care, and Scoop Away cat litter after its First Brands purchase. It has stepped up promotions and advertising while offsetting those costs with savings from new supply-chain software and a manufacturing restructuring.

1221 Broadway   www.clorox.com
Oakland, CA 94612-1888

Morningstar Grades

Growth [B-]	1999	2000	2001	2002
Revenue %	3.3	2.7	-2.2	4.0
Earnings/Share %	-28.0	59.2	-17.7	1.5
Book Value/Share %	7.0	13.6	6.3	-27.5
Dividends/Share %	12.5	11.1	3.8	1.2

We expect the company to continue its focus on improving profitability, with sales growth a modest 3%-4% annually.

Profitability [A]	2000	2001	2002	TTM
Return on Assets %	9.1	8.1	8.9	11.2
Oper Cash Flow $Mil	681	747	876	868
- Cap Spending $Mil	158	192	177	184
= Free Cash Flow $Mil	523	555	699	684

Clorox consistently generates above-average 20% return on equity and has become more profitable thanks to cost-cutting.

Financial Health [A]	2000	2001	2002	09-02
Long-term Debt $Mil	590	685	678	501
Total Equity $Mil	1,794	1,900	1,354	1,302
Debt/Equity Ratio	0.3	0.4	0.5	0.4

The company's EBIT/interest expense ratio of nearly 14 in 2002 indicates that its balance sheet is very manageable.

Industry	Investment Style	Stock Type	Sector
Household & Personal Products	▦ Large Core	→ Slow Growth	⌂ Consumer Goods

Competition	Market Cap $Mil	Debt/ Equity	12 Mo Trailing Sales $Mil	Price/Cash Flow	Return On Assets%	Total Return% 1 Yr	3 Yr
Clorox	9,076	0.4	4,124	10.5	11.2	6.5	-2.7
Procter & Gamble	111,662	0.9	41,268	13.3	11.0	11.3	-4.5
Unilever NV ADR	35,272	—	46,553	—	—	—	—

Price Volatility

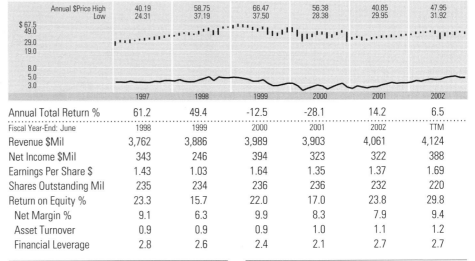

	Monthly Price High/Low			— Relative Strength to S&P 500		
Annual $Price High / Low	40.19 / 24.31	58.75 / 37.19	66.47 / 37.50	56.38 / 28.38	40.85 / 29.95	47.95 / 31.92
	1997	1998	1999	2000	2001	2002

Annual Total Return %	61.2	49.4	-12.5	-28.1	14.2	6.5

Fiscal Year-End: June	1998	1999	2000	2001	2002	TTM
Revenue $Mil	3,762	3,886	3,989	3,903	4,061	4,124
Net Income $Mil	343	246	394	323	322	388
Earnings Per Share $	1.43	1.03	1.64	1.35	1.37	1.69
Shares Outstanding Mil	235	234	236	236	232	220
Return on Equity %	23.3	15.7	22.0	17.0	23.8	29.8
Net Margin %	9.1	6.3	9.9	8.3	7.9	9.4
Asset Turnover	0.9	0.9	0.9	1.0	1.1	1.2
Financial Leverage	2.8	2.6	2.4	2.1	2.7	2.7

Valuation Ratios	Stock	Rel to Industry	Rel to S&P 500
Price/Earnings	24.4	0.9	1.0
Price/Book	7.0	0.8	2.2
Price/Sales	2.2	0.8	1.1
Price/Cash Flow	10.5	0.8	0.8

Major Fund Holders	% of Fund Assets
Papp America-Pacific Rim	7.40
Papp Stock	6.27
Papp Focus	4.93
SunAmerica Dogs of Wall Street A	3.84

Morningstar's Take By Carl Sibilski, 12-09-2002 Stock Price as of Analysis: $44.35

Clorox's products either wear out or get used up, so demand for them is there as long as things get messy. Clorox is a stock for the long haul, though we'd seek at least a 30% discount to our fair value estimate before investing.

Many kitchen or bathroom sink cabinets hold a healthy amount of Clorox products. These must-have brands like Formula 409, Glad bags, and Clorox bleach make it possible for the company to consistently earn above-average returns on equity of 20%. While Clorox will always be challenged to adapt its products to trends in use, it won't be forced to reinvent itself every couple of years like so many other firms have to. That should leave its managers with more time to focus on product enhancements, cut costs, and search for incremental growth.

Having an established brand helps the company quickly gain customer acceptance for its new products. For example, the Clorox Ready Mop was successfully selling off retail shelves only six weeks after production. We think the purpose of the new products will always be cleaning; the innovative aspect is finding a less painful way to do the job with a reasonably priced product.

Clorox is implementing cost-cutting technology that searches for inefficiencies in the supply chain, distribution, and inventories for its products. This has helped the firm reduce stock-keeping units 44%, by cutting less profitable or redundant product lines; that in turn increased inventory efficiency, lowering the time inventory is held to 41 days in 2002 from 61 in 2000. This frees resources to be put to better use in brand management and research. Working capital--the amount of money unprofitably tied up to keep the business operating--shrank to less than 1% of sales in 2002 from more than 9% of sales in 2000.

While we think the firm has more room to cut costs in the next couple of years, we're not convinced that it has found a way to increase sales faster than 3%-4% annually. However, at the right price we'd be happy buyers. The company has increased its dividend at an annualized rate of 11% over the past 15 years; given its rock-solid balance sheet and stable product lines, we see no reason to doubt the continuation of these dividend payments.

MORNINGSTAR® Stocks 500

Coca-Cola KO

	Rating	Risk	Moat Size	Fair Value	Last Close	Yield %
	★★★	Low	Wide	$46.00	$43.82	1.8

Company Profile

Coca-Cola Company is the world's largest producer of soft-drink concentrates, syrups, and juices. Its soft-drink brands include Coke, Diet Coke, Cherry Coke, Sprite, Tab, Nestea, and Barq's. The company sells about 59% of its concentrates and syrups to company-owned and independent bottlers in the United States and abroad, who distribute them to various end users. Coca-Cola also makes fruit juices that are sold under names like Minute Maid. Revenue outside North America accounts for approximately 62% of the company's revenue.

Management

Douglas Daft, a 30-year Coke veteran with lots of international experience, replaced Douglas Ivester in February 2000. Management shake-ups in 2001 resulted in the departure of two key senior executives and the reshuffling of others.

Strategy

Coca-Cola's restructuring plan, which includes more autonomy for regional management and significant layoffs, depressed earnings in 2000 and 2001 but should improve long-term growth and profitability. The company has increasingly relied on noncarbonated beverages, like juices and bottled water, but it's also trying to breathe renewed life into its core Coke brand.

One Coca-Cola Plaza   www.coca-cola.com
Atlanta, GA 30313

Industry	Investment Style	Stock Type	Sector
Beverage Mfg.	▦ Large Core	→ Slow Growth	⛝ Consumer Goods

Competition

	Market Cap $Mil	Debt/ Equity	12 Mo Trailing Sales $Mil	Price/Cash Flow	Return On Assets%	Total Return% 1 Yr	3 Yr
Coca-Cola	108,635	0.2	21,554	24.3	12.8	-5.6	-6.4
Nestle SA ADR	85,869	—	50,054	—	—	—	—
PepsiCo	73,589	0.2	28,044	14.3	13.3	-12.1	6.9

Price Volatility

I Monthly Price High/Low   — Relative Strength to S&P 500

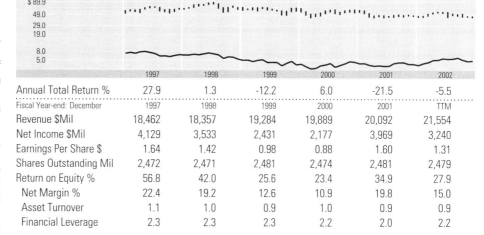

		1997	1998	1999	2000	2001	2002
Annual $Price	High	72.63	88.94	70.88	67.44	62.19	57.90
	Low	51.13	53.63	47.31	42.25	42.40	42.90
Annual Total Return %		27.9	1.3	-12.2	6.0	-21.5	-5.5

Fiscal Year-end: December	1997	1998	1999	2000	2001	TTM
Revenue $Mil	18,462	18,357	19,284	19,889	20,092	21,554
Net Income $Mil	4,129	3,533	2,431	2,177	3,969	3,240
Earnings Per Share $	1.64	1.42	0.98	0.88	1.60	1.31
Shares Outstanding Mil	2,472	2,471	2,481	2,474	2,481	2,479
Return on Equity %	56.8	42.0	25.6	23.4	34.9	27.9
Net Margin %	22.4	19.2	12.6	10.9	19.8	15.0
Asset Turnover	1.1	1.0	0.9	1.0	0.9	0.9
Financial Leverage	2.3	2.3	2.3	2.2	2.0	2.2

Valuation Ratios	Stock	Rel to Industry	Rel to S&P 500
Price/Earnings	33.5	1.0	1.4
Price/Book	9.4	1.0	2.9
Price/Sales	5.0	1.0	2.5
Price/Cash Flow	24.3	1.0	1.8

Major Fund Holders	% of Fund Assets
Rydex Consumer Products Inv	12.26
Wisdom Inv	9.98
W.P. Stewart & Co Growth	5.74
Fidelity Contrafund II	5.32

Morningstar Grades

Growth [B]	1998	1999	2000	2001
Revenue %	-0.6	5.1	3.1	1.0
Earnings/Share %	-13.4	-31.0	-10.2	81.8
Book Value/Share %	16.9	13.5	-1.8	21.7
Dividends/Share %	7.1	6.7	6.3	5.9

After several years of sluggish growth, Coke increased sales 11% in the first nine months of 2002, on solid 5% volume growth. Most of Coke's growth now comes from its noncarbonated beverages.

Profitability [A]	1999	2000	2001	TTM
Return on Assets %	11.2	10.4	17.7	12.8
Oper Cash Flow $Mil	3,883	3,585	4,110	4,462
- Cap Spending $Mil	1,069	733	769	823
= Free Cash Flow $Mil	2,814	2,852	3,341	3,639

Coke earned $0.47 per share in the third quarter, up 9% from a year ago. Its decision to expense the cost of stock options will damp earnings growth somewhat over the next few years.

Financial Health [A+]	1999	2000	2001	09-02
Long-term Debt $Mil	854	835	1,219	2,835
Total Equity $Mil	9,513	9,316	11,366	11,612
Debt/Equity Ratio	0.1	0.1	0.1	0.2

Coke achieves its profits internally, without taking on a lot of debt. Its financial leverage of 2.2 is healthy, especially for a company that generates such large and consistent cash flows.

Morningstar's Take   By David Kathman, 10-18-2002   Stock Price as of Analysis: $46.38

Coke's business appears to be on track, despite some minor setbacks so far in 2002. Given the company's large economic moat, we'd require only a 20% margin of safety to our fair value estimate to buy in.

We've always loved Coke as a business: It has a wide economic moat, including one of the best-known brands in the world, and it throws off tons of free cash flow ($3.3 billion in 2001, or 17% of revenue). These characteristics are what attracted superinvestor Warren Buffett, who is Coke's largest shareholder and a member of its board. Coke made headlines in July 2002 when it announced that it would start treating employee stock options as an expense; we're sure that this welcome move was influenced by Buffett, a longtime critic of traditional options accounting. The change will have a minimal effect on Coke's 2002 earnings, gradually rising to a $0.10-per-share impact in 2006.

Coke has done a good job of recovering from the problems that plagued it a few years ago. Improved relations between Coke and its bottlers, particularly Coca-Cola Enterprises, have set the stage for better pricing policies and improved profitability. Operating income grew 18% in the first nine months of 2002 from the year-ago period, and net income is growing in the high single digits. Successful new products like

Vanilla Coke and Diet Coke with Lemon have revived growth in the core cola business, recently written off by critics as moribund.

Noncarbonated beverages are the most important growth driver for Coke. Minute Maid juices and Powerade sports drinks have gained market share, and Dasani water is still growing strongly. In the spring of 2002, Coke announced deals to market and distribute several of Danone's bottled water brands in the United States. These deals give Coke super premium (Evian) and midrange (Dannon) water brands to complement Dasani and vault it ahead of PepsiCo in U.S. water market share.

Despite these positive signs, Coke has encountered a few snags in its recovery plan. Earnings for 2002 will fall slightly short of forecasts because of bad weather and other temporary factors. The Sprite brand has declined precipitously, and weakness has persisted in Latin America and Germany. None of these factors is debilitating by itself, but together they make us hesitant to become too aggressive in our growth projections. We're maintaining our fair value estimate of $46 per share, which is based on assumptions that we think are conservative but fair. We'd buy in below $40.

Coca-Cola Enterprises CCE

	Rating	Risk	Moat Size	Fair Value	Last Close	Yield %
	★★	Med.	Narrow	$20.00	$21.72	0.7

Company Profile

Coca-Cola Enterprises bottles Coca-Cola soft-drink products such as Coca-Cola, Diet Coke, Sprite, and Barq's. The company manufactures most of the bottled and canned Coca-Cola products sold in the United States from soft-drink concentrates and syrups that it purchases from Coca-Cola. It sells reconstituted products through company-owned coolers, dispensers, vending machines. In addition, the company markets syrups to fountain users in the United States and overseas. Coca-Cola Company owns a stake in the company.

Management

Lowry F. Kline became CEO in April 2001 upon the retirement of Summerfield Johnston, who remains chairman. Johnston's grandfather was a partner in the first Coca-Cola bottler more than 100 years ago.

Strategy

Coca-Cola Enterprises is still trying to recover from the troubles that plagued it in 1999. In an attempt to boost revenue, it raised prices for its North American products in 1999 and again in 2000. It agreed in December 2001 to work more closely with Coca-Cola on marketing, cost-cutting, and pricing, with Coke providing financial support if CCE meets volume targets.

2500 Windy Ridge Parkway, Suite 700 www.cokecce.com
Atlanta, GA 30339

Industry	Investment Style	Stock Type	Sector
Beverage Mfg.	▦ Large Core	→ Slow Growth	⌂ Consumer Goods

Competition

	Market Cap $Mil	Debt/ Equity	12 Mo Trailing Sales $Mil	Price/Cash Flow	Return On Assets%	Total Return% 1 Yr	3 Yr
Coca-Cola Enterprises	9,742	3.4	16,678	5.9	1.5	15.6	4.6
Pepsi Bottling Group	7,247	1.7	8,898	6.5	4.5	9.5	46.7
PanAmerican Beverages	2,526	—	2,651	—	—	—	—

Price Volatility

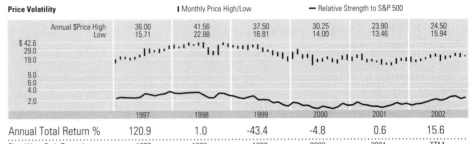

▌ Monthly Price High/Low — Relative Strength to S&P 500

		1997	1998	1999	2000	2001	2002
Annual $Price	High	36.00	41.56	37.50	30.25	23.90	24.50
	Low	15.71	22.88	16.81	14.00	13.46	15.94
Annual Total Return %		120.9	1.0	-43.4	-4.8	0.6	15.6

Fiscal Year-End: December	1997	1998	1999	2000	2001	TTM
Revenue $Mil	11,278	13,414	14,406	14,750	15,700	16,678
Net Income $Mil	169	141	56	233	-324	378
Earnings Per Share $	0.43	0.35	0.13	0.54	-0.75	0.85
Shares Outstanding Mil	384	392	431	416	432	449
Return on Equity %	9.3	5.9	1.9	8.4	-11.6	11.6
Net Margin %	1.5	1.1	0.4	1.6	-2.1	2.3
Asset Turnover	0.6	0.6	0.6	0.7	0.7	0.7
Financial Leverage	9.6	8.8	7.9	7.9	8.5	7.7

Valuation Ratios	Stock	Rel to Industry	Rel to S&P 500
Price/Earnings	25.6	0.8	1.1
Price/Book	3.0	0.3	0.9
Price/Sales	0.6	0.1	0.3
Price/Cash Flow	5.9	0.2	0.4

Major Fund Holders	% of Fund Assets
Turner Large Cap Value	2.65
Managers AMG Rorer Mid Cap	2.48
Navellier All Cap Growth A	2.31
DFA U.S. Large Cap Value	2.19

Morningstar Grades

Growth [A-]	1998	1999	2000	2001
Revenue %	18.9	7.4	2.4	6.4
Earnings/Share %	-18.6	-62.9	315.4	NMF
Book Value/Share %	28.5	12.6	-3.2	-0.4
Dividends/Share %	45.0	10.3	0.0	0.0

Revenue grew 8% over the first three quarters of 2002, helped by favorable currency translation. Case volume grew a solid 5% in the third quarter, recovering from a weak second quarter.

Profitability [D+]	1999	2000	2001	TTM
Return on Assets %	0.2	1.1	-1.4	1.5
Oper Cash Flow $Mil	1,402	1,469	1,114	1,661
- Cap Spending $Mil	1,480	1,181	972	1,028
= Free Cash Flow $Mil	-78	288	142	633

CCE's margins have improved significantly in the past year, but the bottom-line effect of these improvements has been artificially magnified by low interest rates.

Financial Health [D+]	1999	2000	2001	09-02
Long-term Debt $Mil	10,153	10,348	10,365	11,078
Total Equity $Mil	2,877	2,790	2,783	3,271
Debt/Equity Ratio	3.5	3.7	3.7	3.4

With more than $10 billion in long-term debt on its books, CCE is highly leveraged and capital-intensive, making it sensitive to relatively minor changes in macroeconomic conditions.

Morningstar's Take By David Kathman, 10-21-2002 Stock Price as of Analysis: $24.40

Coca-Cola Enterprises has made progress in recovering from the troubles that plagued it in recent years. But we'd still require at least a 30% margin of safety to our fair value estimate to account for possible future missteps.

To a casual observer, CCE's results in 2002 might look outstanding. After a tough 2001 in which it lost money and consistently fell short of expectations, CCE topped First Call earnings estimates in each of the first three quarters of 2002, raising its earnings forecasts each time. Yet its stock has been on a roller-coaster ride, falling on the day of each earnings announcement. There's good reason for the market's skepticism, because some problems lurk below the glossy surface of CCE's results.

We have to give CCE credit for dramatically lowering its selling, delivery, and administrative expenses over the past year. Its improved relationship with former parent Coca-Cola is a positive sign and is helping to keep down cost of goods sold, since Coke sets the price of the syrup that is one of CCE's key expenses. But another major contributor to CCE's earnings outperformance has been lower interest expense, a factor largely beyond the firm's control. The low interest rates of 2002 are virtually certain to rise over the next few years,

cutting significantly into CCE's profits.

More important, CCE still can't get the delicate balance between price and volume right in its core North American market. On a comparable basis, revenue per case fell 0.5% in North America over the first three quarters of 2002. CCE's originally stated goal of 2% pricing growth for the year now looks like a pipe dream. Volume growth was a solid 5% during the first three quarters, helped by the introduction of Vanilla Coke, but CCE needs to learn how to boost volume and price simultaneously to compete effectively with rival Pepsi Bottling Group.

We're wary of capital-intensive, low-margin businesses like this one; they're tough to make work. Rival Pepsi Bottling has become consistently profitable by doing lots of little things right, but CCE has continued to flounder through a series of ups and downs, making only fitful progress. After adjusting our model to account for the real strides that CCE has made (particularly in its dealings with Coke), we've bumped our fair value up to $20 per share. If the stock were to drop back into the low teens, we might become interested. But even then, we'd be cautious.

 MORNINGSTAR® Stocks 500

Colgate-Palmolive CL

	Rating	Risk	Moat Size	Fair Value	Last Close	Yield %
	★★★	Low	Wide	$45.00	$52.43	1.4

Company Profile

Colgate-Palmolive produces household consumer goods. Its brand-name products include Colgate oral-hygiene products, Speed Stick deodorant, Irish Spring bar soap, Softsoap, Protex antibacterial products, Palmolive dishwashing liquid, Murphy's oil soap, and Ajax household cleansers. The company also produces Hill's Science Diet pet food. Colgate markets its products in the United States and overseas. Household products sold in North America account for about a fourth of sales.

Management

There is no succession plan for chairman and CEO Reuben Mark, even though he is nearing retirement age. We would like to see him succeeded by COO Lois Juliber, who has demonstrated restructuring and leadership skills.

Strategy

Colgate increases profits by developing new products in its core brands and cutting costs. New products introduced within the past five years account for about 60% of U.S. sales. Meanwhile, 75% of the firm's operations are fitted with efficiency-boosting software, and that share is expected to rise to 90% in two years. This will extend margin expansion.

300 Park Avenue   www.colgate.com
New York, NY 10022

Morningstar Grades

Growth [C+]	1998	1999	2000	2001
Revenue %	-0.9	1.6	2.6	0.7
Earnings/Share %	15.0	12.6	15.6	11.2
Book Value/Share %	-4.8	-12.7	-22.9	-53.3
Dividends/Share %	3.8	7.3	6.8	7.1

Colgate's sales have grown an annualized 5% for the past 10 years. However, in recent years sales growth has been mediocre; we expect the next five years to average 3.6% growth, closer to the firm's long-term rate.

Profitability [A+]	1999	2000	2001	TTM
Return on Assets %	12.3	14.4	16.1	17.6
Oper Cash Flow $Mil	1,293	1,536	1,600	1,755
- Cap Spending $Mil	373	367	340	355
= Free Cash Flow $Mil	920	1,170	1,259	1,401

Net profit margins have increased markedly from their 7% in the early 1990s thanks to efficiencies discovered by using SAP software. We expect future net margins to be close to 15%.

Financial Health [B-]	1999	2000	2001	09-02
Long-term Debt $Mil	2,243	2,537	2,812	3,072
Total Equity $Mil	1,467	1,114	505	-2
Debt/Equity Ratio	1.5	2.3	5.6	6.1

Earnings before interest and taxes is 11 times interest expense, a safe coverage ratio for a firm of this stature.

Industry	Investment Style	Stock Type	Sector
Household & Personal Products	▦ Large Core	➡ Slow Growth	⌂ Consumer Goods

Competition	Market Cap $Mil	Debt/ Equity	12 Mo Trailing Sales $Mil	Price/Cash Flow	Return On Assets%	Total Return% 1 Yr	3 Yr
Colgate-Palmolive	28,221	6.1	9,546	16.1	17.6	-8.0	-3.6
Procter & Gamble	111,662	0.9	41,268	13.3	11.0	11.3	-4.5
Unilever NV ADR	35,272	—	46,553	—	—	—	—

Price Volatility   ▮ Monthly Price High/Low   — Relative Strength to S&P 500

	1997	1998	1999	2000	2001	2002
Annual $Price High	39.34	49.44	65.00	66.75	64.75	58.86
Low	22.50	32.53	36.56	40.50	48.50	44.05
Annual Total Return %	62.2	28.0	41.7	0.4	-9.4	-8.0

Fiscal Year-end: December	1997	1998	1999	2000	2001	TTM
Revenue $Mil	9,057	8,972	9,118	9,358	9,428	9,546
Net Income $Mil	719	828	916	1,043	1,125	1,220
Earnings Per Share $	1.14	1.31	1.47	1.70	1.89	2.09
Shares Outstanding Mil	590	589	584	576	557	538
Return on Equity %	40.1	48.4	62.5	93.6	222.7	241.6
Net Margin %	7.9	9.2	10.0	11.1	11.9	12.8
Asset Turnover	1.2	1.2	1.2	1.3	1.4	1.4
Financial Leverage	4.2	4.5	5.1	6.5	13.8	13.7

Valuation Ratios	Stock	Rel to Industry	Rel to S&P 500
Price/Earnings	25.1	1.0	1.1
Price/Book	55.9	6.3	17.5
Price/Sales	3.0	1.1	1.5
Price/Cash Flow	16.1	1.2	1.2

Major Fund Holders	% of Fund Assets
Vision Large Cap Growth A	5.18
Janus	4.73
Enterprise Growth A	4.67
ABN AMRO/Montag & Caldwell Growth N	4.43

Morningstar's Take   By Carl Sibilski, 12-17-2002   Stock Price as of Analysis: $52.41

Until we see the innovative category-killer products that Colgate promised, we'll avoid the shares.

Colgate generates more than a billion dollars in annual free cash flow, but we are concerned that the firm isn't putting it to good use. The company has a history of innovation, but recent me-too products like the Colgate Motion toothbrush and Simply White at-home tooth whitening system don't hold a candle to Colgate's cutting-edge products of the past. With its Crest SpinBrush and Crest Whitestrips, for example, Procter & Gamble has beaten Colgate to the punch several times.

This difference shows up in sales figures. Colgate's 10-year annualized sales growth is 5%; its five-year annualized sales growth is a mere 3%. By contrast, P&G's short- and long-term sales growth has been much more consistent at 5%. Yet both companies sport the same valuation using Zacks estimated 2003 earnings.

Colgate earned its premium valuation in the late 1990s by reorganizing its factories and using SAP technology to help spot areas where it could achieve greater operational efficiency. This increased net profit margins to 14% in 2001 from the midsingle digits of earlier years. Accordingly, most of Colgate's long-term earnings growth came from operational

changes within the past five years.

To continue increasing earnings, the company needs to focus on top-line sales growth. In particular, it needs to introduce a cutting-edge product that is capable of stealing market share. Earlier this year management promised that just this kind of product was in the pipeline, but we have yet to see it. And once the firm does have one, we think Colgate's recent lack of category-killer launches may result in rough execution. By launching several of these kinds of products annually, P&G has made the demanding legwork of coordinating retailers and suppliers into a regular routine.

While we believe Colgate will become slightly more efficient in the years ahead because of further SAP technology improvements, its current valuation can be justified only by assuming much higher sales growth. Right now, we think that's too much to hope for, and we would avoid the shares until we see visible proof.

Comcast A CMCSA

	Rating ★★★★	Risk Med.	Moat Size Wide	Fair Value $28.00	Last Close $23.57	Yield % 0.0

Company Profile

Comcast is the largest operator in the cable industry with 21 million subscribers, after purchasing AT&T Broadband in 2002. It owns cable, content, and electronic commerce assets. Comcast has benefited from the aggressive rollout of broadband services like digital cable and high-speed cable modem Internet access. Programming interests include stakes in electronic retailer QVC and E! Entertainment Television.

Management

Former AT&T CEO Michael Armstrong is a figurehead in the combined firm; Comcast is still led by the competent Roberts family, which controls 33% of Comcast. The board is split evenly between both firms' interests.

Strategy

Comcast is rapidly upgrading the networks of cable systems that it acquires, thus offering more-profitable digital services--digital cable TV and high-speed Internet access--across the same cable broadband pipe. The merger with AT&T Broadband vaults Comcast into cable telephony, which should augment growth.

1500 Market Street
Philadelphia, PA 19102-2148
www.comcast.com

Morningstar Grades

Growth [A]	1998	1999	2000	2001
Revenue %	15.3	20.5	25.9	17.7
Earnings/Share %	NMF	7.4	63.8	-70.4
Book Value/Share %	158.8	194.7	22.0	0.2
Dividends/Share %	0.0	NMF	NMF	NMF

Growth is driven by new broadband cable services and double-digit gains in the QVC commerce division. The cable industry is stagnant and facing tough competition from satellite; sales gains will be the result of higher penetration of advanced services.

Profitability [B-]	1999	2000	2001	TTM
Return on Assets %	3.6	5.6	1.6	-1.5
Oper Cash Flow $Mil	1,249	1,219	1,230	1,647
- Cap Spending $Mil	894	1,637	2,182	1,646
= Free Cash Flow $Mil	356	-418	-952	1

GAAP profits are skewed by many noncash charges; what matters most to cable investors is earnings before interest, taxes, depreciation, and amortization. On this front, Comcast is doing well, as the growth of EBITDA outpaces that of sales.

Financial Health [B+]	1999	2000	2001	09-02
Long-term Debt $Mil	8,707	10,517	11,742	9,928
Total Equity $Mil	9,772	14,027	14,473	13,942
Debt/Equity Ratio	0.9	0.8	0.8	0.7

The purchase of AT&T Broadband added debt of some $20 billion to Comcast's balance sheet, once the strongest in the cable industry. A key goal of management is to deleverage as quickly as possible and maintain the firm's investment-grade debt rating.

Industry	Investment Style	Stock Type	Sector
Cable TV	▦ Large Growth	↗ Classic Growth	🎤 Media

Competition	Market Cap $Mil	Debt/ Equity	12 Mo Trailing Sales $Mil	Price/Cash Flow	Return On Assets%	Total Return% 1 Yr	3 Yr
Comcast A	22,319	0.7	10,789	13.6	-1.5	-34.5	-18.3
Cox Communications A	17,611	0.8	4,646	16.3	-2.5	-32.2	-16.6
Hughes Electronic H	14,233	0.3	8,743	19.8	-2.8	-30.7	-31.0

Price Volatility   ▌Monthly Price High/Low   — Relative Strength to S&P 500

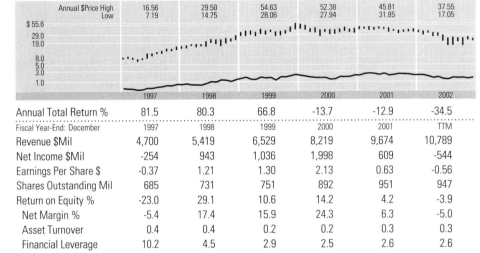

	1997	1998	1999	2000	2001	2002
Annual $Price High	16.56	29.50	54.63	52.38	45.81	37.55
Low	7.19	14.75	28.06	27.94	31.85	17.05
Annual Total Return %	81.5	80.3	66.8	-13.7	-12.9	-34.5

Fiscal Year-End: December	1997	1998	1999	2000	2001	TTM
Revenue $Mil	4,700	5,419	6,529	8,219	9,674	10,789
Net Income $Mil	-254	943	1,036	1,998	609	-544
Earnings Per Share $	-0.37	1.21	1.30	2.13	0.63	-0.56
Shares Outstanding Mil	685	731	751	892	951	947
Return on Equity %	-23.0	29.1	10.6	14.2	4.2	-3.9
Net Margin %	-5.4	17.4	15.9	24.3	6.3	-5.0
Asset Turnover	0.4	0.4	0.2	0.2	0.3	0.3
Financial Leverage	10.2	4.5	2.9	2.5	2.6	2.6

Valuation Ratios	Stock	Rel to Industry	Rel to S&P 500
Price/Earnings	NMF	—	—
Price/Book	1.6	1.0	0.5
Price/Sales	2.1	0.6	1.0
Price/Cash Flow	13.6	0.8	1.0

Major Fund Holders	% of Fund Assets
John Hancock Communications A	8.13
Neuberger Berman Socially Resp Inv	3.83
Smith Barney Aggressive Growth A	3.79
MassMutual Instl Large Cap Growth S	3.78

Morningstar's Take By Todd P. Bernier, 12-11-2002 Stock Price as of Analysis: $23.40

Comcast is unparalleled in the cable industry in terms of size and influence, which gives it a wide economic moat. We would buy the stock at a 20% discount to our fair value estimate.

After buying AT&T Broadband, Comcast has 21 million customers in 17 of the nation's 20 largest markets, up from 8.5 million subscribers before the merger. Comcast is nearly as large as the combined size of the next three largest cable companies--Time Warner Cable, Charter Communications, and Cox Communications. If content providers and advertisers aren't terrified at the prospect of Comcast controlling 30% of America's 70 million cable households, they should be.

But Comcast's buying AT&T Broadband is akin to restoring a vintage sports car: It will probably take lots of money and sweat before the investment pays off.

Comcast once had the best balance sheet in the cable business. Although it still has an investment-grade debt rating, Comcast's balance sheet is now encumbered with debt of $30 billion. Unless capital markets reopen for cable companies, this burden may be a concern down the road. Comcast does have plans to unwind its stake in Time Warner Entertainment and sell stock in AT&T and

Sprint PCS to raise cash and reduce debt by at least $5 billion in 2003. This would cut leverage to a reasonable 3.5 at year-end. After those initial divestitures, however, Comcast will need to cut debt the old-fashioned way--by generating free cash flow.

But that won't happen in 2003. Although Comcast's network spending is largely complete, that isn't the case at AT&T Broadband. Years of neglect have left Ma Bell's cable networks in desperate need of upgrading, which explains why its cable margins are far below those of existing Comcast properties. Comcast went through its upgrade cycle sooner than rivals, leading to a more robust network. As a result, Comcast will need to spend heavily to raise margins at the acquired systems. The ability to improve AT&T's EBITDA margin fundamentally underpins the calculus of this merger; otherwise, Comcast will have overpaid.

Management's challenge is to accelerate the launch of new services while improving the balance sheet. That won't be easy. Nonetheless, we like Comcast's wide moat and would be investors at just 20% below our fair value estimate.

     M⌀RNINGSTAR® Stocks 500

Comerica CMA

	Rating	Risk	Moat Size	Fair Value	Last Close	Yield %
	★★★	Low	Narrow	$51.00	$43.24	4.4

Company Profile

Comerica is the holding company for bank subsidiaries that operate 340 banking offices in Michigan, Texas, California, and Florida. The banks provide deposit accounts and computer banking services. In addition, the banks originate real-estate, business, foreign, and consumer loans. Business loans account for approximately 90% of the company's total loan portfolio. The company's nonbank subsidiaries offer insurance, mortgage banking, lease financing, investment-management, and international finance and trading services. Comerica acquired Imperial Bancorp in January 2001.

Management

Ralph Babb, Comerica's former CFO, assumed the titles of president, CEO, and chairman in 2002. Elizabeth Acton, who had been at Ford, was hired in March 2002 as the new CFO. The bank has two veteran vice chairmen, John Lewis and John Buttigieg.

Strategy

Comerica's main objective is to be a commercial lender to small and medium firms. As part of its effort to focus lending on high-growth urban areas, the bank bought California-based Imperial Bank in 2001, which had $7 billion of assets. Comerica also has a branch network in Florida that focuses mainly on private banking to transplanted retirees.

Comerica Tower at Detroit Center   www.comerica.com
Detroit, MI 48226-3509

Morningstar Grades

Growth [D]	1998	1999	2000	2001
Revenue %	2.9	8.0	17.9	-10.2
Earnings/Share %	12.9	17.7	4.4	-10.0
Book Value/Share %	12.2	16.9	15.1	12.9
Dividends/Share %	11.6	12.5	11.1	10.0

Most of the bank's recent asset growth can be attributed to the Imperial Bank acquisition. Earnings per share have declined from $4.38 in 2000 to a projected $3.40 this year. We don't forecast EPS to exceed the 2000 figure until at least 2005.

Profitability [A]	1999	2000	2001	TTM
Return on Assets %	1.6	1.6	1.4	1.1
Oper Cash Flow $Mil	1,153	940	1,001	—
- Cap Spending $Mil	56	46	68	—
= Free Cash Flow $Mil	—	—	—	—

Excluding items like merger expenses and the sorts of nonrecurring charges made during the third quarter of 2002, Comerica sports an impressive efficiency ratio. Before such charges, the September 30 efficiency ratio was about 46%.

Financial Health [A]	1999	2000	2001	09-02
Long-term Debt $Mil	—	—	—	—
Total Equity $Mil	3,698	4,250	4,807	4,870
Debt/Equity Ratio	—	—	—	—

The bank has a strong capital base. As of September 30, the Tier 1 common equity ratio stood at 7.3%. This exceeds management's goal of a minimum 7%.

Industry	Investment Style	Stock Type	Sector
Regional Banks	▦ Mid Value	⚡ High Yield	💲 Financial Services

Competition	Market Cap $Mil	Debt/ Equity	12 Mo Trailing Sales $Mil	Price/Cash Flow	Return On Assets%	Total Return% 1 Yr	3 Yr
Comerica	7,555	—	3,703	—	1.1	-21.9	3.5
Bank One	42,636	—	22,444	—	1.1	-4.4	9.4
Fifth Third Bancorp	33,873	—	6,272	—	2.1	-3.4	11.1

Price Volatility

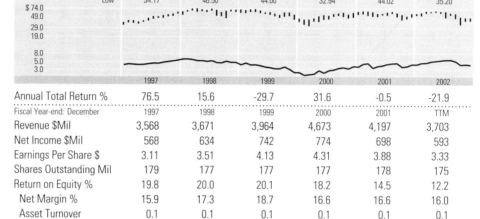

		Monthly Price High/Low		— Relative Strength to S&P 500	

Annual $Price High Low	61.88 34.17	73.00 46.50	70.75 44.00	61.13 32.94	65.15 44.02	66.09 35.20
	1997	1998	1999	2000	2001	2002

Annual Total Return %	76.5	15.6	-29.7	31.6	-0.5	-21.9
Fiscal Year-end: December	1997	1998	1999	2000	2001	TTM
Revenue $Mil	3,568	3,671	3,964	4,673	4,197	3,703
Net Income $Mil	568	634	742	774	698	593
Earnings Per Share $	3.11	3.51	4.13	4.31	3.88	3.33
Shares Outstanding Mil	179	177	177	177	178	175
Return on Equity %	19.8	20.0	20.1	18.2	14.5	12.2
Net Margin %	15.9	17.3	18.7	16.6	16.6	16.0
Asset Turnover	0.1	0.1	0.1	0.1	0.1	0.1
Financial Leverage	14.3	13.5	12.3	11.7	10.6	10.8

Valuation Ratios	Stock	Rel to Industry	Rel to S&P 500
Price/Earnings	13.0	0.9	0.6
Price/Book	1.6	0.7	0.5
Price/Sales	2.0	0.9	1.0
Price/Cash Flow	—	—	—

Major Fund Holders	% of Fund Assets
Orchard Value	3.31
Diamond Hill Bank & Financial A	3.28
Schroder MidCap Value Inv	2.99
FBR Financial Services	2.98

Morningstar's Take By Matthew Scholz, 12-10-2002 Stock Price as of Analysis: $44.01

Comerica is a pure play on middle-market commercial banking, but our concerns keep us from recommending the stock. Our fair value estimate is $51 per share.

After shedding most of its retail banking businesses over the past few years, Comerica is focusing on making loans to middle-market business. Comerica defines the middle market as companies with annual revenue of $5-$250 million. Despite the simplicity of the business model, we have concerns about the strategy and its execution.

Our most basic worry is that Comerica's success is highly leveraged to the health and capital needs of the middle-market manufacturing and service businesses. The commercial and industrial loans that are Comerica's bread-and-butter business have been one of the weakest areas of lending during the recent economic slowdown. This is a major reason for the rapid increase in nonperforming loans. As of September 30, Comerica's net charge-offs totaled $258 million, a whopping 2.44% of average total loans. This is bad enough, but by some measures, the bank still has poor reserves for its remaining nonperforming loans. The ratio of Comerica's loan-loss reserves to nonperformers stood at 1.25%, much lower than the third-quarter average 1.71% of

the 30 biggest banks.

There are problems with other areas of the loan portfolio, too. As recently as the end of 2001, Comerica's participation in the nationally syndicated loans of large companies accounted for 38% of the portfolio. A disproportionate number of Comerica's nonperforming loans have come from such syndicated loans. Comerica plans to reduce this portfolio below its current 20% weighting, and only participate in the syndicated loans of firms that do other business with the bank. Comerica also has about $700 million of loans to the Argentine and Brazilian operations of large multinationals. Comerica intends to exit Argentina and focus its foreign lending on its middle-market customers in the three NAFTA countries, but until this process is complete, the international portfolio constitutes a special pool of risk.

Given that Comerica will be reducing its exposure to syndicated and international loans, we're skeptical that the bank can find enough attractive middle-market lending opportunities to pick up the slack. We'd hold off on buying Comerica until we see evidence that the bank can restart asset growth without compromising credit quality.

Computer Associates International CA

	Rating	Risk	Moat Size	Fair Value	Last Close	Yield %
	★	High	None	$10.00	$13.50	0.6

Company Profile

Computer Associates International designs standardized software products for use with mainframe, midrange, and desktop computers. The software is designed to enable clients to use their data-processing resources more effectively. The company also develops and supports database-management, business applications, and graphics software for computers from various vendors, including IBM, Compaq, Apple, and Hewlett-Packard. Computer Associates acquired Sterling Software in April 2000.

Management

CEO Sanjay Kumar recently added the title of chairman, replacing founder Charles Wang. Management has a reputation for treating employees, customers, and shareholders poorly.

Strategy

CA is expanding beyond the slow-growing mainframe software market into high-growth areas like security, storage, and portals. The company has done so through acquisitions and internal development.

One Computer Associates Plaza   www.ca.com
Islandia, NY 11749

Industry	Investment Style	Stock Type	Sector
Systems & Security	▦ Mid Value	◪ Distressed	◪ Software

Competition	Market Cap $Mil	Debt/ Equity	12 Mo Trailing Sales $Mil	Price/Cash Flow	Return On Assets%	Total Return% 1 Yr	3 Yr
Computer Associates International	7,739	0.4	3,056	5.8	-5.3	-60.7	-41.5
IBM	130,982	0.8	82,442	9.0	5.8	-35.5	-11.1
BMC Software	4,029	—	1,249	6.5	-3.0	4.5	-39.4

Price Volatility

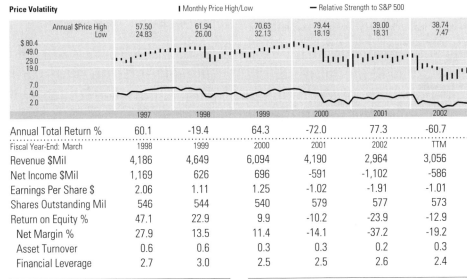

	1997	1998	1999	2000	2001	2002
Annual $Price High	57.50	61.94	70.63	79.44	39.00	38.74
Low	24.83	26.00	32.13	18.19	18.31	7.47
Annual Total Return %	60.1	-19.4	64.3	-72.0	77.3	-60.7

Fiscal Year-End: March	1998	1999	2000	2001	2002	TTM
Revenue $Mil	4,186	4,649	6,094	4,190	2,964	3,056
Net Income $Mil	1,169	626	696	-591	-1,102	-586
Earnings Per Share $	2.06	1.11	1.25	-1.02	-1.91	-1.01
Shares Outstanding Mil	546	544	540	579	577	573
Return on Equity %	47.1	22.9	9.9	-10.2	-23.9	-12.9
Net Margin %	27.9	13.5	11.4	-14.1	-37.2	-19.2
Asset Turnover	0.6	0.6	0.3	0.3	0.2	0.3
Financial Leverage	2.7	3.0	2.5	2.5	2.6	2.4

Valuation Ratios	Stock	Rel to Industry	Rel to S&P 500
Price/Earnings	NMF	—	—
Price/Book	1.7	0.8	0.5
Price/Sales	2.5	0.7	1.3
Price/Cash Flow	5.8	0.5	0.4

Major Fund Holders	% of Fund Assets
John Hancock Classic Value A	6.02
Hotchkis and Wiley Mid-Cap Value I	4.66
Hotchkis and Wiley Large Cap Value I	4.55
Nuveen NWQ Multi-Cap Value	3.76

Morningstar Grades

Growth [D]	1999	2000	2001	2002
Revenue %	11.1	31.1	-31.2	-29.3
Earnings/Share %	-46.1	12.6	NMF	NMF
Book Value/Share %	10.7	161.2	-21.1	-19.8
Dividends/Share %	9.6	0.0	0.0	0.0

Given the company's size, and the fact that most growth in recent years has come from acquisitions, CA is not a growth story. The move to a subscription-based business model won't help.

Profitability [B]	2000	2001	2002	TTM
Return on Assets %	4.0	-4.1	-9.0	-5.3
Oper Cash Flow $Mil	1,566	1,383	1,251	1,332
- Cap Spending $Mil	3,247	263	27	21
= Free Cash Flow $Mil	-1,681	1,120	1,224	1,311

The transition to a subscription-based sales model has deferred the recognition of revenue, thus killing near-term profits. Over time, profit margins should recover.

Financial Health [B+]	2000	2001	2002	09-02
Long-term Debt $Mil	4,527	3,629	3,334	1,838
Total Equity $Mil	7,037	5,780	4,617	4,536
Debt/Equity Ratio	0.6	0.6	0.7	0.4

The balance sheet is subpar; CA has a little more than $800 million in cash and $3.3 billion in debt. Financial health will be under greater strain in 2003 when debt of $1.3 billion comes due.

Morningstar's Take By Mike Trigg, 12-10-2002 Stock Price as of Analysis: $13.41

Questionable management, quirky accounting, an ongoing federal investigation, and deteriorating financial health make Computer Associates a highly speculative stock. We'd require at least a 50% discount to our fair value estimate before buying.

Our biggest anxiety is over the investigations by the Department of Justice and the Securities and Exchange Commission. The reason for the probe is unknown, but we suspect investigators may be looking at whether Computer Associates acquired companies and convinced those firms' existing customers to extend contracts. Computer Associates would then allegedly classify the money from those deals as license revenue and book it immediately, boosting sales.

Another worry is management, led by chairman and CEO Sanjay Kumar. Computer Associates may have used fancy bookkeeping to inflate its financial results and stock price to trigger a $1.1 billion stock grant in 1998 to the firm's top three executives by the board of directors (of which all three were members). Also, management paid disgruntled shareholder Sam Wyly $10 million to end his most recent effort--his second in as many years--to gain seats on the board of directors. In our mind, this equates to nothing more than greenmail that sends the wrong signal to dissident shareholders.

Financial health also concerns us. The company has more than $1.3 billion in debt coming due over the next year but has less than $800 million in cash. The best-case scenario has CA generating $1.25 billion from operations in fiscal 2003 (ending March 2003). While this hardly qualifies as a liquidity crunch, the company's financial flexibility is limited.

It's also worrisome that cash flow is being driven by the collection of account receivables that stem from the company's transition from a license- to subscription-based business model. In fiscal 2002, for example, Computer Associates collected $1.28 billion in receivables (billed under the old model), which was more than it reported for total operating cash flow. This is unsustainable, and indicates that the new business model isn't generating very much cash.

As if all of this weren't enough, Computer Associates is facing a downturn in IT spending. This, combined with a management team that we don't trust and the looming federal investigation, makes the stock extremely risky, in our opinion. Unless the shares fell below $5, we'd pass and sleep well at night.

MORNINGSTAR® Stocks 500

Computer Sciences CSC

	Rating	Risk	Moat Size	Fair Value	Last Close	Yield %
	★★	Med.	Narrow	$32.00	$34.45	0.0

Company Profile

Computer Sciences provides information technology consulting, systems integration, and outsourcing. Services include management consulting and education and research programs, and the design, engineering, installation, and operation of computer-based systems and communication systems. The company offers its services to financial, industrial, and service industries, and to many governmental agencies in United States and abroad. Contract services to the U.S. government account for about 24% of the company's revenue. The firm acquired Mynd in December 2000.

Management

Chairman and CEO Van Honeycutt has been with the company since 1975 and at the helm since 1995. He owns less than 1% of the outstanding stock.

Strategy

Computer Sciences has reduced its dependence on the government, which once made up 75% of sales, and expanded into the private sector and international markets. Its strategy is to increase its offerings and find cross-selling opportunities that leverage its mammoth customer base.

2100 East Grand Avenue
El Segundo, CA 90245
www.csc.com

Industry	Investment Style	Stock Type	Sector
Consultants	Mid Core	↗ Classic Growth	Business Services

Competition

	Market Cap $Mil	Debt/ Equity	12 Mo Trailing Sales $Mil	Price/Cash Flow	Return On Assets%	Total Return% 1 Yr	3 Yr
Computer Sciences	5,929	0.5	11,444	4.3	4.6	-29.7	-28.1
IBM	130,982	0.8	82,442	9.0	5.8	-35.5	-11.1
Accenture	17,231	0.0	13,105	16.2	4.5	-33.2	—

Price Volatility

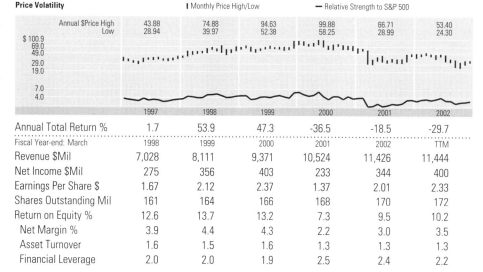

		1997	1998	1999	2000	2001	2002
Annual $Price High		43.88	74.88	94.63	99.88	66.71	53.40
Low		28.94	39.97	52.38	58.25	28.99	24.30
Annual Total Return %		1.7	53.9	47.3	-36.5	-18.5	-29.7

Fiscal Year-end: March	1998	1999	2000	2001	2002	TTM
Revenue $Mil	7,028	8,111	9,371	10,524	11,426	11,444
Net Income $Mil	275	356	403	233	344	400
Earnings Per Share $	1.67	2.12	2.37	1.37	2.01	2.33
Shares Outstanding Mil	161	164	166	168	170	172
Return on Equity %	12.6	13.7	13.2	7.3	9.5	10.2
Net Margin %	3.9	4.4	4.3	2.2	3.0	3.5
Asset Turnover	1.6	1.5	1.6	1.3	1.3	1.3
Financial Leverage	2.0	2.0	1.9	2.5	2.4	2.2

Valuation Ratios	Stock	Rel to Industry	Rel to S&P 500
Price/Earnings	14.8	0.7	0.6
Price/Book	1.5	0.4	0.5
Price/Sales	0.5	0.4	0.3
Price/Cash Flow	4.3	0.4	0.3

Major Fund Holders	% of Fund Assets
ING Technology A	2.87
Fidelity Select Business Serv&Outsrcg	2.78
Touchstone Enhanced 30 A	2.71
Security Mid Cap Value A	2.70

Morningstar Grades

Growth [B+]	1999	2000	2001	2002
Revenue %	15.4	15.5	12.3	8.6
Earnings/Share %	26.9	11.8	-42.2	46.7
Book Value/Share %	16.9	16.0	5.5	12.1
Dividends/Share %	NMF	NMF	NMF	NMF

Although annual sales growth averaged 12% over the past three years, it has hit a wall as consulting and systems integration has struggled. We estimate long-term sales growth in the high single digits.

Profitability [A-]	2000	2001	2002	TTM
Return on Assets %	6.9	2.9	4.0	4.6
Oper Cash Flow $Mil	946	854	1,305	1,376
- Cap Spending $Mil	586	897	672	617
= Free Cash Flow $Mil	361	-43	634	759

Returns on invested capital and profits margins are at the low end of the company's peer group. We don't expect meaningful improvement on either front.

Financial Health [A-]	2000	2001	2002	09-02
Long-term Debt $Mil	652	1,029	1,873	2,027
Total Equity $Mil	3,044	3,215	3,624	3,906
Debt/Equity Ratio	0.2	0.3	0.5	0.5

Since large outsourcing deals require significant up-front capital expenditures, free cash flow slows when sales, earnings, and bookings thrive. Conversely, free cash flow booms when those metrics slow.

Morningstar's Take By Mike Trigg, 11-26-2002 Stock Price as of Analysis: $33.25

Computer Sciences has performed relatively well during the slowdown. But we wouldn't buy the stock until it traded 30% below our fair value estimate.

Like most computer services firms, Computer Sciences has struggled because of difficult economic conditions and volatility among clients. Problems have been compounded by a reliance on the financial services industry (20% of revenue), which continues to struggle from apathy toward the equity markets and fears of an extended recession.

Consulting and systems integration, which constitute 50% of sales, has been the division hardest-hit. But outsourcing, which includes everything from running a company's Web site to managing noncore business processes like call centers, has performed slightly better. While outsourcing has kept overall growth positive, the downside is that profits have suffered; outsourcing has lower margins than consulting and systems integration.

Another area of business that has held up is the government, a market that Computer Sciences has catered to since the 1960s. We expect the firm's backlog of $29 billion in potential government contracts can keep growing as more resources are devoted to outsourcing and homeland security.

However, government deals are less profitable than private sector ones, which the company has struggled to close.

Still, our outlook for outsourcers like Computer Sciences and EDS is at an all-time low. We once considered the industry a safe haven among technology stocks because the companies have long-term contracts with predictable revenue, deep-rooted customer relationships, and brand awareness. However, outsourcing is becoming a commodity, in our opinion. Intense competition has made winning business tougher and lowered prices. This has forced firms to make adverse concessions to win deals, like contributing more capital up front before receiving any cash. Companies will struggle to earn returns that exceed the cost at which they can raise capital, be it debt or equity.

Although we've been encouraged by how Computer Sciences has performed in difficult conditions, our bearish outlook for outsourcing limits any enthusiasm. We wouldn't buy the stock until it fell below $23.

Compuware CPWR

	Rating	Risk	Moat Size	Fair Value	Last Close	Yield %
	★★	Med.	None	$5.00	$4.80	0.0

Company Profile

Compuware develops systems software products and offers data-processing services. Its systems software products and product options are used in the testing, debugging, implementation, and maintenance of application software for users of a wide range of operating systems. The company has licensed its products to more than 20,000 customers worldwide. It also provides business systems analysis, design, programming, software conversion, and systems planning services to corporate and public-sector clients.

Management

Most of senior management has been with Compuware for more than a decade. Peter Karmanos has been chairman since 1978 and CEO since 1987. COO Joseph Nathan joined the firm in 1981.

Strategy

Compuware's bread and butter is mainframe software. To lessen its dependence on this slow-growing market, the company is investing in software for distributed systems (networks that combine mainframes, desktops, and servers) and services.

31440 Northwestern Highway   www.compuware.com
Farmington Hills, MI 48334-2564

Morningstar Grades

Growth [D]	1999	2000	2001	2002
Revenue %	43.8	36.1	-9.9	-14.0
Earnings/Share %	74.0	4.6	-64.8	NMF
Book Value/Share %	47.0	15.9	18.9	-13.5
Dividends/Share %	NMF	NMF	NMF	NMF

Growth has continued to slow despite efforts to lessen dependence on a sluggish mainframe market by focusing on distributed systems software and services. These new markets have disappointed.

Profitability [A-]	2000	2001	2002	TTM
Return on Assets %	14.6	5.2	-12.3	-12.5
Oper Cash Flow $Mil	165	337	387	385
- Cap Spending $Mil	35	40	90	147
= Free Cash Flow $Mil	130	297	296	238

Historically, profitability has been quite good, but margins have contracted as business has slowed. As a result, Compuware's return on invested capital has been declining.

Financial Health [A]	2000	2001	2002	09-02
Long-term Debt $Mil	450	140	0	0
Total Equity $Mil	1,204	1,377	1,190	1,255
Debt/Equity Ratio	0.4	0.1	0.0	0.0

Repaying debt has improved Compuware's balance sheet. Despite recent struggles, cash flow remains very healthy.

Industry	Investment Style	Stock Type	Sector
Systems & Security	▦ Mid Core	→ Slow Growth	⬈ Software

Competition	Market Cap $Mil	Debt/ Equity	12 Mo Trailing Sales $Mil	Price/Cash Flow	Return On Assets%	Total Return% 1 Yr	3 Yr
Compuware	1,814	0.0	1,555	4.7	-12.5	-59.3	-48.4
IBM	130,982	0.8	82,442	9.0	5.8	-35.5	-11.1
Electronic Data Systems	8,774	0.7	22,127	4.5	6.6	-72.6	-32.5

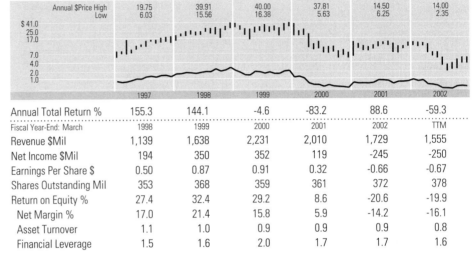

Price Volatility — Monthly Price High/Low — Relative Strength to S&P 500

Annual $Price High Low	19.75 6.03	39.91 15.56	40.00 16.38	37.81 5.63	14.50 6.25	14.00 2.35

	1997	1998	1999	2000	2001	2002
Annual Total Return %	155.3	144.1	-4.6	-83.2	88.6	-59.3

Fiscal Year-End: March	1998	1999	2000	2001	2002	TTM
Revenue $Mil	1,139	1,638	2,231	2,010	1,729	1,555
Net Income $Mil	194	350	352	119	-245	-250
Earnings Per Share $	0.50	0.87	0.91	0.32	-0.66	-0.67
Shares Outstanding Mil	353	368	359	361	372	378
Return on Equity %	27.4	32.4	29.2	8.6	-20.6	-19.9
Net Margin %	17.0	21.4	15.8	5.9	-14.2	-16.1
Asset Turnover	1.1	1.0	0.9	0.9	0.9	0.8
Financial Leverage	1.5	1.6	2.0	1.7	1.7	1.6

Valuation Ratios	Stock	Rel to Industry	Rel to S&P 500
Price/Earnings	NMF	—	—
Price/Book	1.4	0.6	0.5
Price/Sales	1.2	0.3	0.6
Price/Cash Flow	4.7	0.4	0.4

Major Fund Holders	% of Fund Assets
Fidelity Select Software & Comp	3.43
Turner Midcap Value	1.65
DLB Technology	1.33
Hotchkis and Wiley Small Cap Value I	1.23

Morningstar's Take By Mike Trigg, 12-05-2002 Stock Price as of Analysis: $5.17

Compuware's problems extend well beyond lousy IT spending. We wouldn't buy stock in Compuware, a company with no sustainable competitive advantage, until it traded 40% below our fair value estimate.

Along with BMC Software and Computer Associates, Compuware is a leading player in mainframe software. A mainframe is a large computer, typically made by IBM, that stores vast amounts of data. Compuware's software helps test, develop, and manage applications running on mainframes. Although this market is slow-growing, it provides a steady stream of cash that Compuware has used to fuel growth.

One opportunity for growth is software for distributed systems--networks that use multiple computers (e.g., desktops and servers) rather than one centralized system. Applications that can be downloaded from the Internet at any time and run on any computer are an example of distributed computing. This market is red hot with the advent of the Internet, but Compuware's mainframe prowess has been little help and business has struggled.

Another disappointment is professional services. Earlier this year, the company took a $500 million charge, most of which was impaired goodwill associated with acquisitions made to expand this business. The company has since launched a restructuring program, including layoffs and combining product sales with services to spur cross-selling opportunities. These moves were long overdue, in our view, considering that the business has repeatedly struggled to make money.

We'd be remiss if we didn't mention Compuware's lawsuit against IBM. Among other things, Compuware is charging IBM with copying its software, using anticompetitive practices, and providing limited access to source code. Although we can't assess the merits of the suit, we do know it could distract Compuware's management team from running the business and leave the company further cut off from IBM. The latter possibility has particular significance because roughly half of Compuware's business comes from IBM mainframes.

Our biggest knock on Compuware is its growth prospects. The bread-and-butter mainframe market is growing slowly, while distributed systems software and professional services have been a disappointment. Until the company proves it can kick-start growth and get its house in order, we wouldn't buy the stock unless it became unavoidably cheap.

MORNINGSTAR® Stocks 500

Concord EFS CE

	Rating	Risk	Moat Size	Fair Value	Last Close	Yield %
	★★★	Med.	Narrow	$19.00	$15.74	0.0

Company Profile

Concord EFS processes financial transactions for retailers, banks, and trucking companies. Concord's services include debit- and credit-card processing, ATM networking, and maintaining financial information for truck lines. Its computers process requests for information from the users. Concord also has a 57% interest in Network EFT, which sells electronic funds-transfer services to financial institutions through networks of terminals in retail stores.

Management

Dan Palmer has led Concord EFS as CEO and chairman since 1991 but will be stepping down as CEO in May 2003. President Edward Labry III, who started with Concord in 1985 as a salesman, will take the reins.

Strategy

Concord prides itself on spotting emerging trends in financial processing and then exploiting them. Concord focused on the emergence of electronic payments in supermarkets and gas stations and gained a leading position. So far this decade the firm has put together a nationwide debit network through a series of acquisitions to capture growth in PIN-based debit transactions.

2525 Horizon Lake Drive www.concordefs.com
Memphis, TN 38133

Morningstar Grades

Growth [A+]

	1998	1999	2000	2001
Revenue %	30.6	30.4	32.7	21.3
Earnings/Share %	48.4	17.4	55.6	0.0
Book Value/Share %	21.2	67.9	26.8	59.2
Dividends/Share %	NMF	NMF	NMF	NMF

Revenue has grown roughly 60% annually on average in the past five years. Much of that was due to acquisitions, but the firm also grows with debit and credit card use. We expect 20% average sales growth over the next five years.

Profitability [A]

	1999	2000	2001	TTM
Return on Assets %	9.9	11.5	7.9	9.6
Oper Cash Flow $Mil	199	405	662	747
- Cap Spending $Mil	68	87	137	154
= Free Cash Flow $Mil	131	317	525	592

The firm is able to process increasing numbers of transactions on its network, lowering its average cost per transaction. As a result, we are modeling Concord's operating margin to remain flat, despite the pricing pressure the company is facing.

Financial Health [A+]

	1999	2000	2001	09-02
Long-term Debt $Mil	89	110	119	142
Total Equity $Mil	855	1,133	1,859	2,154
Debt/Equity Ratio	0.1	0.1	0.1	0.1

Long-term debt is scant, cash flows are strong, and the firm has more than $1.8 billion in cash and investments. Concord is in outstanding shape.

Industry	Investment Style	Stock Type	Sector
Data Processing	▦ Large Growth	↑ Aggr. Growth	🖹 Business Services

Competition

	Market Cap $Mil	Debt/ Equity	12 Mo Trailing Sales $Mil	Price/Cash Flow	Return On Assets%	Total Return% 1 Yr	3 Yr
Concord EFS	8,007	0.1	2,045	10.7	9.6	-52.0	8.2
US Bancorp	40,630	—	15,324	—	1.8	5.2	11.7
First Data	26,633	0.8	7,118	16.5	4.6	-9.5	14.4

Price Volatility

❚ Monthly Price High/Low   — Relative Strength to S&P 500

	7.25 / 3.61	14.63 / 4.45	16.75 / 8.46	24.06 / 7.66	33.36 / 17.00	35.06 / 12.60

Annual $Price High / Low — $36.1, 23.0, 16.0, 7.0, 4.0, 2.0, 1.0

	1997	1998	1999	2000	2001	2002
Annual Total Return %	-11.9	155.5	-8.9	70.6	49.2	-52.0

Fiscal Year-end: December	1997	1998	1999	2000	2001	TTM
Revenue $Mil	623	813	1,060	1,407	1,707	2,045
Net Income $Mil	66	107	129	210	216	302
Earnings Per Share $	0.16	0.23	0.27	0.42	0.42	0.57
Shares Outstanding Mil	428	444	462	477	492	509
Return on Equity %	17.6	21.6	15.1	18.5	11.6	14.0
Net Margin %	10.7	13.1	12.2	14.9	12.7	14.7
Asset Turnover	0.8	0.8	0.8	0.8	0.6	0.6
Financial Leverage	2.1	2.0	1.5	1.6	1.5	1.5

Valuation Ratios	Stock	Rel to Industry	Rel to S&P 500
Price/Earnings	27.6	1.2	1.2
Price/Book	3.7	0.8	1.2
Price/Sales	3.9	1.2	1.9
Price/Cash Flow	10.7	0.7	0.8

Major Fund Holders	% of Fund Assets
Fidelity Select Business Serv&Outsrcg	5.43
Oppenheimer Enterprise A	5.06
Oppenheimer MidCap A	4.61
Scudder Flag Value Builder A	4.50

Morningstar's Take By Dan Schick, 11-01-2002 Stock Price as of Analysis: $15.10

Concord EFS is growing rapidly and producing substantial free cash flow. Given its strong balance sheet and competitive position, Concord is attractive at a 40% discount to our fair value estimate.

Rapid growth in PIN-based debit card transactions is driving revenue higher. We think PIN-based debit transactions--growing 30% annually at Concord in recent years--will continue gaining in popularity. Only one out of five retailers in the country that accept credit cards also accepts PIN-based debit cards. We see no reason the latter should not eventually be ubiquitous: PIN-based transactions involve a relatively small investment on the retailer's part, while greatly lowering processing costs relative to credit and signature debit transactions. After signing up Wal-Mart as a customer in 2001, Concord recently signed Dillard's, providing evidence that the PIN-based debit card is growing in popularity as a payment mechanism outside its original grocery store and gas station niches.

Concord is continuing its successful strategy of targeting niches where the low cost of PIN-based debit is particularly attractive. The firm is now pushing PIN-based debit in the fast-food market, which has characteristics similar to the grocery store and gas station markets--cash payments are

dominant and retailers' margins are relatively low. Concord should do well here.

Big-picture trends support Concord's growth prospects. According to Federal Reserve data on retail payments in the United States, consumers write 8-13 billion checks each year at the point of sale; these are prime candidates to be replaced by more-convenient debit transactions. The number of checks pales in comparison with the countless cash transactions for which a debit card could substitute.

Our biggest worry in our last report--Concord's "precharge operating income"--manifested itself recently. We now believe the various charges over the past four years relating to acquisitions and restructuring, which skewed earnings, also masked a lower profit margin. On the basis of the gross profit decline in the third quarter of 2002, we've reconsidered the actual operating profitability of the firm and lowered our fair value estimate.

Nevertheless, we believe Concord's potential growth and fortified balance sheet make the stock worth owning at the right price.

ConocoPhillips COP

	Rating	Risk	Moat Size	Fair Value	Last Close	Yield %
	UR	Med.	Narrow	UR	$48.39	3.1

Company Profile

Phillips Petroleum is an integrated petroleum company. It owns interests in about 16,180 wells worldwide, and hold proven reserves of approximately 958 million barrels of oil and about 6.3 trillion cubic feet of natural gas. The company operates refineries that primarily provide motor fuels to 6,500 Phillips 66 service stations, approximately 200 of which are company-operated. Many of the company's service stations include convenience stores and fast-food operations. Phillips Petroleum also produces chemicals and plastics.

Management

Management comes roughly equally from Conoco and Phillips. Chairman Archie Dunham was CEO of Conoco, while CEO James Mulva was CEO of Phillips. When Dunham retires in 2004, Mulva will take over as chairman.

Strategy

ConocoPhillips' focus over the next several quarters will be to cut redundant costs and improve efficiency to realize the potential financial benefits of the merger. The company may continue to buy select oil and gas assets to grow and gain additional economies of scale.

600 North Dairy Ashford Road
Houston, TX 77079
www.phillips66.com

Morningstar Grades

Growth [A+]	1998	1999	2000	2001
Revenue %	-23.2	32.4	47.2	16.4
Earnings/Share %	-74.8	162.6	203.8	-22.5
Book Value/Share %	-10.6	10.2	33.1	104.6
Dividends/Share %	1.5	0.0	0.0	2.9

Growth will ebb and flow as commodity oil and gas prices fluctuate. ConocoPhillips targets annual hydrocarbon production growth of 4%, and average long-term revenue growth (sans acquisitions) should be slightly higher than this.

Profitability [B]	1999	2000	2001	TTM
Return on Assets %	4.0	9.1	4.7	0.4
Oper Cash Flow $Mil	1,941	4,014	3,562	3,221
- Cap Spending $Mil	1,690	2,022	3,085	3,509
= Free Cash Flow $Mil	251	1,992	477	-288

Combining the historical results of Conoco and Phillips does not paint a pretty picture. Returns on invested capital have only been in the mid- to upper single digits, far lower than the results achieved by the company's new peers.

Financial Health [C+]	1999	2000	2001	09-02
Long-term Debt $Mil	4,271	6,622	8,645	17,850
Total Equity $Mil	4,549	6,093	14,340	29,991
Debt/Equity Ratio	0.9	1.1	0.6	0.6

ConocoPhillips has a tangible asset base of $59.4 billion, $20.0 billion of which is funded by debt. This is a high amount of leverage for its peer group, but is easily manageable given the company's free cash flow. We expect debt to fall over time.

Industry	Investment Style	Stock Type	Sector
Oil & Gas	Large Value	High Yield	Energy

Competition	Market Cap $Mil	Debt/ Equity	12 Mo Trailing Sales $Mil	Price/Cash Flow	Return On Assets%	Total Return% 1 Yr	Total Return% 3 Yr
ConocoPhillips	18,492	0.6	46,828	5.7	0.4	-17.4	5.7
Total Fina Elf SA ADR	100,949	0.3	93,914	9.2	8.7	3.7	5.2
ChevronTexaco	71,011	0.4	93,451	8.9	-3.0	-23.1	-4.4

Price Volatility

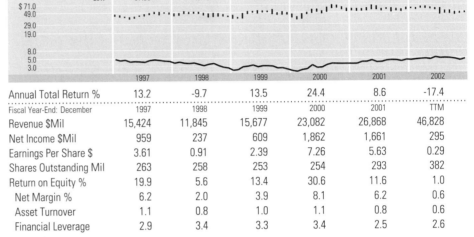

		52.25	53.25	57.25	70.00	68.00	64.10
Annual $Price High Low		37.38	40.19	37.69	35.88	50.00	44.05

	1997	1998	1999	2000	2001	2002
Annual Total Return %	13.2	-9.7	13.5	24.4	8.6	-17.4

Fiscal Year-End: December	1997	1998	1999	2000	2001	TTM
Revenue $Mil	15,424	11,845	15,677	23,082	26,868	46,828
Net Income $Mil	959	237	609	1,862	1,661	295
Earnings Per Share $	3.61	0.91	2.39	7.26	5.63	0.29
Shares Outstanding Mil	263	258	253	254	293	382
Return on Equity %	19.9	5.6	13.4	30.6	11.6	1.0
Net Margin %	6.2	2.0	3.9	8.1	6.2	0.6
Asset Turnover	1.1	0.8	1.0	1.1	0.8	0.6
Financial Leverage	2.9	3.4	3.3	3.4	2.5	2.6

Valuation Ratios	Stock	Rel to Industry	Rel to S&P 500
Price/Earnings	166.9	8.7	7.1
Price/Book	0.6	0.3	0.2
Price/Sales	0.4	0.4	0.2
Price/Cash Flow	5.7	0.8	0.4

Major Fund Holders	% of Fund Assets
Fidelity Select Energy	5.64
MainStay Select 20 Equity A	4.97
Fidelity Select Natural Resources	4.94
Fidelity Advisor Natural Res T	4.72

Morningstar's Take By Paul Larson, 10-15-2002 Stock Price as of Analysis: $48.04

A new major player was created in the oil patch when Conoco and Phillips finally merged. Though ConocoPhillips looks cheap, it's not cheap enough.

We have been big fans of this merger. Economies of scale have always played a major role in oil, with the big boys able to find, dig up, transport, and refine oil and gas cheaper than the small-fry. Getting bigger via merger has been extremely popular in the past four years, and ConocoPhillips is traversing well-tread ground toward reducing costs and improving its ability to create value. The company estimates it can find $750 million worth of synergy in the first year by getting rid of redundant costs and improving efficiency. We would not be surprised if the cost savings end up being higher.

Though we think the merger will advance ConocoPhillips' positioning and ability to create shareholder value, several problems make the company far less attractive than some of its peers.

First, there's the issue of anemic returns. Combining the historical performance of Conoco and Phillips, long-term returns on invested capital have averaged in the high single digits, near the new company's cost of capital. These returns are decidedly lower than what some of the company's peers were able to achieve before their mergers.

ConocoPhillips is still also substantially smaller than the likes of ExxonMobil. And the company is the largest domestic refiner, where oversupply is an ongoing concern and margins have recently been low. It follows that ConocoPhillips' returns will be lower than its peers', despite the merger's benefits.

The second issue is the debt on the balance sheet. While several oil heavies are essentially debt-free, ConocoPhillips has $20 billion of debt and a debt/equity ratio of 0.7. While ConocoPhillips should have more than adequate cash flow to pay this down, the financial leverage does raise risk.

We like big oil, largely because the OPEC cartel's influence remains strong, keeping industrywide profitability healthy. While we expect ConocoPhillips to improve its positioning in the industry, there are other oil companies with more attractive returns. There are reasons the stock trades at a lower valuation (P/E, price/book, etc.) than some of its peers, and even with expected merger-related savings, we don't see those reasons changing dramatically anytime soon. We'd want to see ConocoPhillips trading at bargain-basement prices before jumping in.

MORNINGSTAR® Stocks 500

Continental Airlines B CAL

	Rating	Risk	Moat Size	Fair Value	Last Close	Yield %
	UR	High	None	UR	$7.25	0.0

Company Profile

Continental Airlines is an air carrier that transports passengers, cargo, and mail. The company is the fifth-largest U.S. airline based on passenger traffic. Between Continental and Continental Express, the carrier serves more than 220 airports worldwide--with more than 130 domestic and 90 international destinations. Its Continental Micronesia subsidiary also provides service in the Western Pacific region.

Management

Gordon Bethune joined the airline in February 1994 as president and chief operating officer and became CEO in November 1994. He is considered one of the top CEOs in the industry.

Strategy

Continental is focusing on cutting costs and capturing as much business travel as possible out of its Newark hub. One step toward achieving this is the airline's recently formed alliance with Amtrak. Similar alliances may follow.

1600 Smith Street   www.flycontinental.com
Houston, TX 77002

Morningstar Grades

Growth [D+]

	1998	1999	2000	2001
Revenue %	10.2	9.0	14.6	-9.4
Earnings/Share %	0.6	23.5	-12.1	NMF
Book Value/Share %	31.0	38.8	-14.8	13.7
Dividends/Share %	NMF	NMF	NMF	NMF

The airline has experience negative growth for the last two years, as traffic and prices have declined.

Profitability [B]

	1999	2000	2001	TTM
Return on Assets %	5.5	3.7	-1.0	-4.5
Oper Cash Flow $Mil	776	904	567	-89
- Cap Spending $Mil	706	511	568	616
= Free Cash Flow $Mil	70	393	-1	-705

The airline is set to lose another half billion dollars in 2002, and we don't expect it to turn an annual profit until 2004 at the earliest.

Financial Health [C+]

	1999	2000	2001	09-02
Long-term Debt $Mil	3,055	3,374	4,198	5,133
Total Equity $Mil	1,593	1,160	1,161	1,126
Debt/Equity Ratio	1.9	2.9	3.6	4.6

The carrier's finances got a little boost from its spin-off of ExpressJet XJT in April 2002. However, leverage has gotten higher since then and the company is losing money.

Industry	Investment Style	Stock Type	Sector
Air Transport	Small Value	Slow Growth	Business Services

Competition

	Market Cap $Mil	Debt/ Equity	12 Mo Trailing Sales $Mil	Price/Cash Flow	Return On Assets%	Total Return% 1 Yr	3 Yr
Continental Airlines B	470	4.6	8,102	—	-4.5	-72.3	-44.9
Southwest Airlines	10,768	0.4	5,359	16.8	2.9	-24.7	10.7
Delta Air Lines	1,493	3.2	12,860	—	-6.9	-58.4	-37.0

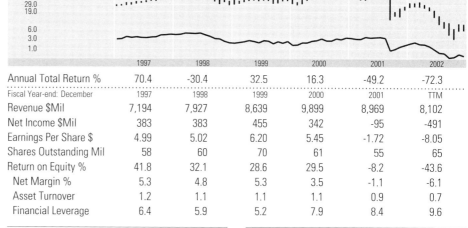

Price Volatility | Monthly Price High/Low   — Relative Strength to S&P 500

Annual $Price High Low	50.19 27.00	65.13 28.88	48.00 30.00	54.81 29.00	57.88 12.36	35.20 3.59

	1997	1998	1999	2000	2001	2002
Annual Total Return %	70.4	-30.4	32.5	16.3	-49.2	-72.3

Fiscal Year-end: December	1997	1998	1999	2000	2001	TTM
Revenue $Mil	7,194	7,927	8,639	9,899	8,969	8,102
Net Income $Mil	383	383	455	342	-95	-491
Earnings Per Share $	4.99	5.02	6.20	5.45	-1.72	-8.05
Shares Outstanding Mil	58	60	70	61	55	65
Return on Equity %	41.8	32.1	28.6	29.5	-8.2	-43.6
Net Margin %	5.3	4.8	5.3	3.5	-1.1	-6.1
Asset Turnover	1.2	1.1	1.1	1.1	0.9	0.7
Financial Leverage	6.4	5.9	5.2	7.9	8.4	9.6

Valuation Ratios	Stock	Rel to Industry	Rel to S&P 500
Price/Earnings	NMF	—	—
Price/Book	0.4	0.2	0.1
Price/Sales	0.1	0.0	0.0
Price/Cash Flow	—	—	—

Major Fund Holders	% of Fund Assets
Fidelity Select Air Transportation	3.59
Seligman Small Cap Value A	1.85
Fidelity Advisor Mid Cap B	1.60
Wilmington Large Cap Value Instl	1.11

Morningstar's Take By Nicolas Owens, 12-16-2002 Stock Price as of Analysis: $7.85

Given the unsustainable nature of Continental's business model, we don't see any good reason to invest in the shares.

One of our concerns is that Continental's strategy is not viable over the long term. Generally speaking, a company can pursue one of two strategies. The first is to offer a differentiated product for which customers are willing to pay a premium. The other approach is to be the low-cost provider in a particular market. Continental seems undecided--somewhere in between--in a market that does not allow for much differentiation or tolerate a slack cost structure. Competition in the airline industry revolves largely around price, making air travel a commodity. The success of Southwest over the years has been based on the carrier's low-cost structure, which allows it to charge less than its competition, profitably. The fact that Continental's unit costs are 20% higher than Southwest's--although they are 9% below the industry average--leaves the airline at a disadvantage in such a tight-margin business.

Another issue that we have with Continental is the volatility of its operating results. Because the company depends on business travelers, who have traditionally been less price-sensitive than leisure travelers, earnings are very sensitive to the business cycle. In 1999, Continental made $455 million in profit on almost $9 billion in sales. In 2000, it made $342 million on $10 billion in sales. Last year, it lost $95 million on $9 billion in sales. This continues a pattern of large profits and losses in the industry that has persisted every decade since the 1940s. Since deregulation in 1978, airlines have lost an aggregate $8.5 billion. Given the industry's current structure, we don't see this pattern ending anytime soon.

We think the most pressing reason to avoid investing in Continental--and most of its rivals--is the leverage. Continental has a lot of operating leverage; it has high fixed costs. This is great when business is booming, but it has the opposite effect when business is in the dumps. More important, the firm has taken on loads of new debt to buy newer, more efficient aircraft. Recently, Continental has even used this debt to fund losses in its operations. The result of this financial leverage is to exacerbate the poor operating performance of the airline, resulting in enormous net losses.

Most airline stocks--including Continental--are bad long-term investments. Wild swings in share price can make for tempting speculative trades, but over the long haul airlines have a terrible record for shareholders, and this isn't about to change.

Cooper Industries CBE

	Rating	Risk	Moat Size	Fair Value	Last Close	Yield %
	★★★	Med.	None	$49.00	$36.45	3.8

Company Profile

Cooper Industries manufactures electrical products, hand tools, and hardware. It produces electrical products like fuses, track lighting, fire-detection equipment, transformers, electrical plugs and connectors, and electrical outlet boxes. These products are used in power-distribution and lighting applications. Cooper Industries also produces power tools, screwdriver bits, pliers, saws, files, wrenches, and torches. The company markets its products in the United States and overseas. Foreign sales account for approximately 24% of operating revenue.

Management

H. John Riley has been in Cooper management since 1981, but upon becoming CEO in 1995 he dramatically changed corporate strategy. We like that he shrank Cooper with asset sales and share buybacks rather than pursuing haphazard acquisitions.

Strategy

In the past few years Cooper Industries has undone three decades of random conglomeration. Now that it focuses on electrical equipment and tools, Cooper pursues acquisitions like B-Line and Eagle Electric, which broaden its line of electrical products. It's also been relocating production facilities to Mexico and other low-cost regions to improve profitability.

600 Travis
Houston, TX 77002-1001
www.cooperindustries.com

Morningstar Grades

Growth [C]	1998	1999	2000	2001
Revenue %	6.9	6.0	15.3	-5.6
Earnings/Share %	13.2	-5.1	8.6	-35.8
Book Value/Share %	-38.5	34.8	10.1	5.4
Dividends/Share %	0.0	0.0	6.1	0.0

Most of Cooper's product lines have succumbed to the downturn in domestic industrial activity. Over the long haul, acquisitions should boost revenue growth, but Cooper isn't likely to expand internally at more than 2%-4% per year.

Profitability [A]	1999	2000	2001	TTM
Return on Assets %	8.0	7.5	5.0	4.8
Oper Cash Flow $Mil	402	503	422	450
- Cap Spending $Mil	166	175	115	67
= Free Cash Flow $Mil	236	328	307	384

What Cooper lacks in growth prospects it makes up for with strong profitability. It has moved quickly to cut operating costs in the face of a cyclical revenue decline, which we expect to boost earnings substantially when the economy rebounds.

Financial Health [A-]	1999	2000	2001	09-02
Long-term Debt $Mil	895	1,301	1,107	991
Total Equity $Mil	1,743	1,904	2,023	2,050
Debt/Equity Ratio	0.5	0.7	0.5	0.5

With free cash flow directed toward debt repayment rather than acquisitions, Cooper's leverage has declined nicely. With debt now at comfortable levels, the company is returning most of its cash to investors through stock buybacks.

Industry	Investment Style	Stock Type	Sector
Electric Equipment	▦ Mid Value	◪ High Yield	✦ Industrial Mats

Competition	Market Cap $Mil	Debt/ Equity	12 Mo Trailing Sales $Mil	Price/Cash Flow	Return On Assets%	Total Return% 1 Yr	3 Yr
Cooper Industries	3,398	0.5	3,965	7.5	4.8	8.4	1.6
Danaher	10,013	0.4	4,221	13.5	2.7	9.1	13.8
Rockwell Automation	3,848	—	3,901	—	—	—	—

Price Volatility

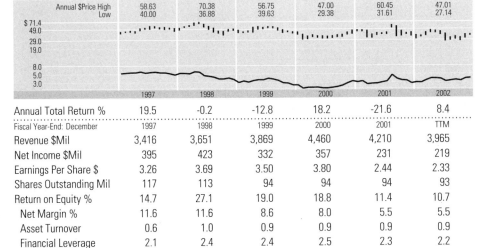

	Monthly Price High/Low			— Relative Strength to S&P 500		
Annual $Price High / Low	58.63 / 40.00	70.38 / 36.88	56.75 / 39.63	47.00 / 29.38	60.45 / 31.61	47.01 / 27.14

	1997	1998	1999	2000	2001	2002
Annual Total Return %	19.5	-0.2	-12.8	18.2	-21.6	8.4
Fiscal Year-End: December	1997	1998	1999	2000	2001	TTM
Revenue $Mil	3,416	3,651	3,869	4,460	4,210	3,965
Net Income $Mil	395	423	332	357	231	219
Earnings Per Share $	3.26	3.69	3.50	3.80	2.44	2.33
Shares Outstanding Mil	117	113	94	94	94	93
Return on Equity %	14.7	27.1	19.0	18.8	11.4	10.7
Net Margin %	11.6	11.6	8.6	8.0	5.5	5.5
Asset Turnover	0.6	1.0	0.9	0.9	0.9	0.9
Financial Leverage	2.1	2.4	2.4	2.5	2.3	2.2

Valuation Ratios	Stock	Rel to Industry	Rel to S&P 500
Price/Earnings	15.6	1.0	0.7
Price/Book	1.7	0.4	0.5
Price/Sales	0.9	0.5	0.4
Price/Cash Flow	7.5	0.9	0.6

Major Fund Holders	% of Fund Assets
MainStay Select 20 Equity A	5.29
John Hancock Classic Value A	4.42
Eclipse Value Equity	3.36
MainStay Value B	3.33

Morningstar's Take By Josh Peters, 11-25-2002 Stock Price as of Analysis: $35.79

Cooper is hardly the best-performing industrial business we can think of, but it's getting better. With prodigious cash generation to support our valuation, we'd consider the shares in the mid-$20s.

It's hard to get excited about Cooper. A substantial portion of its wares are simply electrical commodities, we can't identify any clear leadership in product innovation or productivity, and the industrial economy's downturn and price deflation have cut deeply into profit margins.

Cooper also has a few legal skeletons in its closet. Its automotive operations, which were sold to Federal-Mogul in 1998, had asbestos liabilities that the buyer agreed to assume. But now that Federal-Mogul is in bankruptcy, a share of those liabilities may return to Cooper.

The company's reincorporation in Bermuda for tax reasons in early 2002 has also attracted a lot of negative press. This paper move will cut the firm's effective tax rate from 33% in 2001 to 22% in 2003, adding $8 per share in future value, by our estimate. But politicians and some high-profile institutional investors have howled, perhaps justifiably so, about this supposed lack of patriotism. Though unlikely, this criticism could eventually manifest itself in tax penalties or the loss of government business.

The story starts to turn when it comes to cash flows. By aggressively cutting capital expenditures and tightening inventories, free cash flow could exceed $350 million for 2002--$3.75 per share--better than the cash generated during Cooper's peak profit year (2000). The firm has been trending toward higher cash flows for several years, so we don't believe this is a one-time surge.

We also believe the current downturn is making a leaner manufacturer out of Cooper, setting the stage for better returns on investment when the economy improves. The firm has steadily trimmed staff since the downturn took hold in early 2001 while shifting production to lower-cost facilities in Mexico and China.

Cooper's results aren't likely to improve much until a rebound in industrial spending takes hold, but when conditions finally turn up, we believe the firm will be in fine shape to take full advantage. With the legal wild cards in mind, we'd find Cooper stock attractive at a 50% or greater discount to our fair value estimate.

MORNINGSTAR® Stocks 500

Corning GLW

	Rating	Risk	Moat Size	Fair Value	Last Close	Yield %
	★	Med.	None	$2.60	$3.31	0.0

Company Profile

Corning manufactures products made from specialty glass, ceramics, and related inorganic materials. The materials have properties of chemical stability, electrical resistance, heat resistance, light transmission, and mechanical strength. Its products include optical fiber, optical cable, hardware, and equipment, and emission-control substrates. Corning makes about 60,000 different products at 40 plants in 20 countries; 25 of its plants are in the United States. The company acquired NetOptix in May 2000.

Management

Corning's experienced, mostly homegrown management was reshuffled following the disastrous decisions of 2000. James Houghton, CEO from 1983 to 1996 and of Corning's founding family, is back at the helm. He's shown much skill in restructuring so far.

Strategy

Corning has evolved from a diversified industrial conglomerate into a more focused optical fiber and equipment producer. It is a leveraged bet on telecom capital spending. Corning's competitive edge ostensibly derives from its patents, human capital, scale, and sales relationships. The firm may not have the financial strength to emerge from the telecom downturn with these advantages intact, however.

One Riverfront Plaza
Corning, NY 14831-0001
www.corning.com

Industry	Investment Style	Stock Type	Sector
Optical Equipment	⊞ Mid Value	⇅ Cyclical	▣ Hardware

Competition	Market Cap $Mil	Debt/ Equity	12 Mo Trailing Sales $Mil	Price/Cash Flow	Return On Assets%	Total Return% 1 Yr	3 Yr
Corning	3,800	0.8	3,605	52.8	-10.2	-62.9	-55.0
Alcatel SA ADR A	5,615	1.0	17,080	1.7	-17.4	-72.9	-53.2
JDS Uniphase	3,494	0.0	963	—	ELB	-71.7	-69.3

Price Volatility

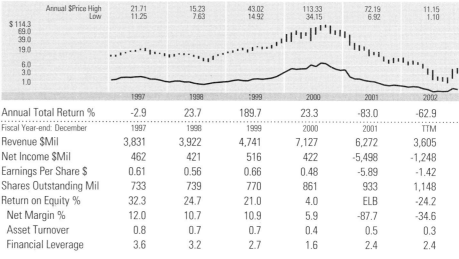

		1997	1998	1999	2000	2001	2002
Annual $Price	High	21.71	15.23	43.02	113.33	72.19	11.15
	Low	11.25	7.63	14.92	34.15	6.92	1.10

Annual Total Return %	-2.9	23.7	189.7	23.3	-83.0	-62.9

Fiscal Year-end: December	1997	1998	1999	2000	2001	TTM
Revenue $Mil	3,831	3,922	4,741	7,127	6,272	3,605
Net Income $Mil	462	421	516	422	-5,498	-1,248
Earnings Per Share $	0.61	0.56	0.66	0.48	-5.89	-1.42
Shares Outstanding Mil	733	739	770	861	933	1,148
Return on Equity %	32.3	24.7	21.0	4.0	ELB	-24.2
Net Margin %	12.0	10.7	10.9	5.9	-87.7	-34.6
Asset Turnover	0.8	0.7	0.7	0.4	0.5	0.3
Financial Leverage	3.6	3.2	2.7	1.6	2.4	2.4

Valuation Ratios	Stock	Rel to Industry	Rel to S&P 500
Price/Earnings	NMF	—	—
Price/Book	0.7	0.4	0.2
Price/Sales	1.1	0.7	0.5
Price/Cash Flow	52.8	3.0	4.0

Major Fund Holders	% of Fund Assets
New York Equity	10.83
Hillman Aggressive Equity	3.74
Dreyfus Premier Strategic Value A	2.10
Reserve Large-Cap Growth R	1.96

Morningstar Grades

Growth [C-]	1998	1999	2000	2001
Revenue %	2.4	20.9	50.3	-12.0
Earnings/Share %	-8.2	17.9	-27.3	NMF
Book Value/Share %	20.1	38.9	284.0	-52.0
Dividends/Share %	0.0	0.0	0.0	-50.0

The near-term outlook is actually worse than shown here because Corning recently sold its lens business--its fastest-growing unit. Growth will be directly geared to telecom capital spending. Long-term sales growth should be 10%-15%.

Profitability [C-]	1999	2000	2001	TTM
Return on Assets %	7.9	2.4	-43.0	-10.2
Oper Cash Flow $Mil	867	1,421	1,445	72
- Cap Spending $Mil	757	1,525	1,800	551
= Free Cash Flow $Mil	110	-104	-355	-479

Excess capacity is driving down prices. With manufacturing in-house, profits depend on utilization (which is a function of higher sales). Declining volume and a lower mix of long-haul fiber, which sells at a premium, have hurt profitability.

Financial Health [D]	1999	2000	2001	09-02
Long-term Debt $Mil	1,490	3,966	4,461	4,171
Total Equity $Mil	2,463	10,633	5,414	5,152
Debt/Equity Ratio	0.6	0.4	0.8	0.8

The optical fiber and cable business is profitable in good times but capital-intensive. Corning is saddled with debt from heavy investment in fiber during 2000, but will probably avoid bankruptcy. The challenge is to retire dilutive debt due in 2005.

Morningstar's Take By Fritz Kaegi, 12-05-2002 Stock Price as of Analysis: $3.95

We like Corning's long history and believe the firm will survive, but we fret about growing competition and the risk of equity dilution. We'd recommend shares in Corning, a company with no economic moat, at a 40% discount to our fair value estimate.

Corning's competitive edge comes from its knowledge base and size. The company's heavy investment in research on glass and related materials has allowed it to patent innovations in fiber optics, displays, life sciences gear, and catalytic converter materials. As with firms like 3M, this effort allowed it to attract the human capital necessary to harvest innovation. Corning's size and in-house production, meanwhile, permitted it to be a low-cost producer. These factors led to relatively high margins in ostensibly commodity businesses.

But two decisions have put Corning in a hole. First, it bet heavily on fiber during 2000 and 2001, spending $8.1 billion on acquisitions and $1.9 billion on telecom-related facilities. Second, it not only paid the bet mostly in cash (only 30% with stock), but also leveraged it with $4.1 billion of new debt. When telecom buildout came to a halt in 2001, the bets lost big.

The first law of holes is to stop digging, and so Corning has. James Houghton has returned as CEO,

and is orchestrating a virtuoso performance of corporate finance by deftly restructuring capacity, selling assets at good prices, and retiring debt at big discounts to face value. Bankruptcy is only a remote possibility. We expect Corning will enter 2004 with $1.2 billion in cash. Without more divestitures or refinancing, the remaining convertible debt due in 2005 ($800 million in face value, by our estimates) will probably have to be settled in common stock. In this case, Corning would have $2.1 billion in other debt, with $665 million due in 2008 and the rest evenly spread over 20 years. Barring a total breakdown in operating income, this would be a manageable burden.

Fiber demand over the very long term isn't bad: The global need for high-speed telecom access should spur carriers and cable operators to deploy fiber ever closer to homes and businesses and to light unused existing fiber, using Corning equipment. In an industry with few players and high barriers to entry, Corning should benefit. Yet by slashing research staff and capacity, Corning has eroded its competitive edge.

Costco Wholesale COST

	Rating	Risk	Moat Size	Fair Value	Last Close	Yield %
	★★★★	Med.	Narrow	$42.00	$28.06	0.0

Company Profile

Costco Wholesale operates a chain of cash-and-carry membership warehouses. The warehouses sell nationally branded and private-label merchandise to businesses for commercial use, personal use, or resale, and to individuals. Total inventories per warehouse are limited to approximately 3,700-4,500 active stock-keeping units. The company operates 350 warehouses in the United States, 59 in Canada, 11 in the United Kingdom, and 9 in Asia. Costco also operates 19 stores in Mexico through a 50%-owned joint venture.

Management

CEO James Sinegal and chairman Jeffrey Brotman co-founded the company in 1983. Most executives have been officers for at least 10 years. On the board of directors is Charlie Munger, Warren Buffett's investment partner at Berkshire Hathaway.

Strategy

Costco usually buys products directly from manufacturers instead of distributors, cutting out the middleman. The company carries only those products it can purchase at a significant discount to competitors. Because of its fast inventory turnover and low overhead, Costco can operate profitably at significantly lower gross margins than traditional retailers.

999 Lake Drive   www.costco.com
Issaquah, WA 98027

Morningstar Grades

Growth [A-]	1999	2000	2001	2002
Revenue %	13.1	17.1	8.2	11.4
Earnings/Share %	-14.9	57.0	-4.4	14.7
Book Value/Share %	17.4	18.6	15.4	15.1
Dividends/Share %	NMF	NMF	NMF	NMF

Revenue growth has been slow but consistent, averaging just under 11% during the past five years. Earnings per share have grown at a faster rate, albeit inconsistently.

Profitability [B+]	2000	2001	2002	TTM
Return on Assets %	7.3	6.0	6.0	6.0
Oper Cash Flow $Mil	1,070	1,033	1,018	1,018
- Cap Spending $Mil	1,228	1,448	1,039	1,039
= Free Cash Flow $Mil	-158	-415	-20	-20

Return on assets has averaged only 6% over the past five years, but that's not bad for discount retail. The company is more profitable than most of its competitors, but margins are still razor-thin.

Financial Health [B+]	2000	2001	2002	08-02
Long-term Debt $Mil	790	859	1,211	1,211
Total Equity $Mil	4,240	4,883	5,694	5,694
Debt/Equity Ratio	0.2	0.2	0.2	0.2

The company has an extremely strong balance sheet, with a debt/capital ratio of only 18%. Costco generates very strong cash flow from operations because of its quick inventory turnover, but free cash flow can drift into the red on occasion.

Industry	Investment Style	Stock Type	Sector
Discount Stores	▦ Large Core	↗ Classic Growth	▤ Consumer Services

Competition	Market Cap $Mil	Debt/ Equity	12 Mo Trailing Sales $Mil	Price/Cash Flow	Return On Assets%	Total Return% 1 Yr	3 Yr
Costco Wholesale	12,788	0.2	38,762	12.6	6.0	-36.8	-12.6
Wal-Mart Stores	223,388	0.5	233,651	18.9	8.0	-11.8	-7.3
Safeway	13,376	1.5	34,757	6.3	3.4	-44.1	-12.2

Price Volatility

Monthly Price High/Low — Relative Strength to S&P 500

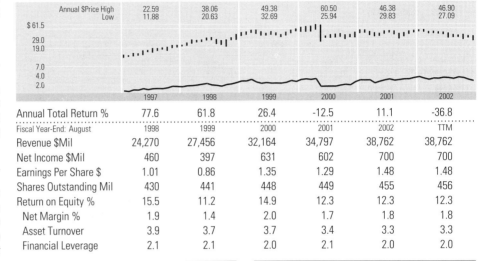

Annual $Price High / Low	22.59 / 11.88	38.06 / 20.63	49.38 / 32.69	60.50 / 25.94	46.38 / 29.83	46.90 / 27.09
	1997	1998	1999	2000	2001	2002
Annual Total Return %	77.6	61.8	26.4	-12.5	11.1	-36.8

Fiscal Year-End: August	1998	1999	2000	2001	2002	TTM
Revenue $Mil	24,270	27,456	32,164	34,797	38,762	38,762
Net Income $Mil	460	397	631	602	700	700
Earnings Per Share $	1.01	0.86	1.35	1.29	1.48	1.48
Shares Outstanding Mil	430	441	448	449	455	456
Return on Equity %	15.5	11.2	14.9	12.3	12.3	12.3
Net Margin %	1.9	1.4	2.0	1.7	1.8	1.8
Asset Turnover	3.9	3.7	3.7	3.4	3.3	3.3
Financial Leverage	2.1	2.1	2.0	2.1	2.0	2.0

Valuation Ratios	Stock	Rel to Industry	Rel to S&P 500
Price/Earnings	19.0	0.6	0.8
Price/Book	2.2	0.4	0.7
Price/Sales	0.3	0.4	0.2
Price/Cash Flow	12.6	0.7	0.9

Major Fund Holders	% of Fund Assets
Strategic Partners Focused Value A	5.78
First Funds Growth & Income I	5.17
Salomon Brothers Capital O	4.38
Permanent Portfolio Aggressive Growth	3.82

Morningstar's Take   By Mike Porter, 12-29-2002   Stock Price as of Analysis: $28.02

Costco Wholesale is the leader in its warehouse retailing niche. We would consider the shares at a 40% discount to our fair value estimate.

Costco--or, more accurately, Price Club, with which Costco merged--basically invented warehouse retailing in the mid-1970s. The key to the business model is the membership fee. Customers pay an up-front charge of around $50 annually in exchange for the privilege of shopping at Costco's warehouses. Both company and customer benefit from the arrangement: Costco gets close to 80% of its operating profit in the form of the fees, and shoppers get extremely low prices on all sorts of items, many of them sold in bulk. Consumers have embraced the concept. Sales at Costco have grown 10% annually on average over the past four years.

Recent results haven't been up to snuff, however. Monthly comparable-store sales growth (comps) has slipped into the low-single-digit range, after months in the high single digits. A sluggish economy and deflationary pressure on some product lines like groceries are mainly to blame for the weakness. Costco needs comps to be about 5% or greater to get any kind of sales, general, and administrative expense leverage. When comps growth is weak, operating margins suffer.

We're not too worried about this development right now. After all, it's not that customer traffic has slipped. If Costco wanted to prop margins up, it could slash costs through layoffs and other means that customers would notice. Costco realizes that cutting back on service and personnel would not make for a positive shopping experience. Instead, it's taking the bitter medicine of keeping up service and quality in tough times to help maintain customer loyalty. In the short term, though, profits could suffer.

We do have one concern. Cannibalization, or taking customers away from oneself, is something we'll be keeping a close eye on. The company says that, for the next few years, a smaller percentage of new store openings will come in brand-new markets; more will come from filling in stores where it already has a presence. That's good news, in a sense, because store opening costs will be lower: The company won't need to introduce itself to customers though expensive marketing campaigns. We expect lower operating costs as a result, but we could also see further pressure on comparable-store sales.

Costco is a company with a rich history of innovation, and we expect more of the same. We'd snap up shares in the mid-$20s.

MORNINGSTAR® Stocks 500

Countrywide Financial CFC

	Rating	Risk	Moat Size	Fair Value	Last Close	Yield %
	★	Med.	N/A	$44.00	$51.65	0.8

Company Profile

Countrywide Credit Industries is the third-largest mortgage issuer in the nation and fourth in servicing. The company's mortgage loans are principally first-lien mortgage loans secured for single-family residences. As its name suggests, Countrywide has retail branches nationwide and was one of the first mortgage lenders to jettison its sales staff in favor of advertising its rates directly to consumers. Through its subsidiaries, the company offers products and services complementary to its mortgage banking business, like insurance and banking products.

Management

Chairman and CEO Angelo Mozilo co-founded the company in 1969. He has a flexible vision that adjusts Countrywide's revenue mix in hard times. Mozilo also helped to found Indymac Bancorp, which was once part of Countrywide.

Strategy

Countrywide Credit is striving to maintain its prominence as a national mortgage banker while diversifying its revenue base to counteract the inherent cyclicality of the mortgage business. To this end, it is making forays into banking and insurance and increasing its presence in the capital markets, principally through securities underwriting.

4500 Park Granada
Calabasas, CA 91302
www.countrywide.com

Morningstar Grades

Growth [A+]	1998	1999	2000	2001
Revenue %	34.9	3.8	9.8	27.1
Earnings/Share %	6.5	7.0	-10.8	23.9
Book Value/Share %	15.0	15.2	20.5	9.5
Dividends/Share %	0.0	25.0	0.0	0.0

The company has a long history of solid growth. In the second quarter, net revenue grew 46% and net income soared 55% as strong mortgage volume and good hedging expanded the business. Growth will moderate as the housing boom slows.

Profitability [A]	1999	2000	2001	TTM
Return on Assets %	2.6	1.6	1.3	1.1
Oper Cash Flow $Mil	3,968	-3,304	-8,950	NMF
- Cap Spending $Mil	151	39	96	NMF
= Free Cash Flow $Mil	—	—	—	NMF

Earnings have grown at a compound annual rate of 17% over the past 10 years. The cyclical nature of the mortgage business begets fluctuations in profitability. Diversification should help stabilize this, though it has also boosted overhead costs.

Financial Health [B]	1999	2000	2001	09-02
Long-term Debt $Mil	—	—	—	—
Total Equity $Mil	2,888	3,559	4,088	4,904
Debt/Equity Ratio	—	—	—	—

Financial leverage has been creeping upward and now stands at 9 times equity. This is a healthy ratio for a company that needs a constant supply of money to fund loans.

Industry	Investment Style	Stock Type	Sector
Savings & Loans	⊞ Mid Core	↗ Classic Growth	$ Financial Services

Competition

	Market Cap $Mil	Debt/ Equity	12 Mo Trailing Sales $Mil	Price/Cash Flow	Return On Assets%	Total Return% 1 Yr	3 Yr
Countrywide Financial	6,528	—	0.44	—	1.1	27.3	29.3
Bank of America	104,505	—	46,628	—	1.3	14.5	19.8
Wells Fargo	79,608	—	28,119	—	1.5	10.3	10.4

Price Volatility

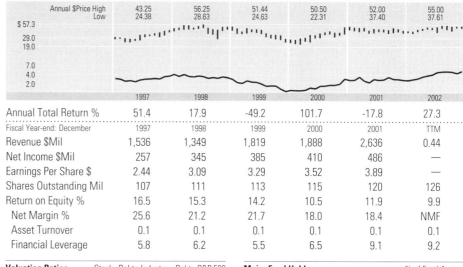

Annual $Price High Low	43.25 24.38	56.25 28.63	51.44 24.63	50.50 22.31	52.00 37.40	55.00 37.61
	1997	1998	1999	2000	2001	2002
Annual Total Return %	51.4	17.9	-49.2	101.7	-17.8	27.3

Fiscal Year-end: December	1997	1998	1999	2000	2001	TTM
Revenue $Mil	1,536	1,349	1,819	1,888	2,636	0.44
Net Income $Mil	257	345	385	410	486	—
Earnings Per Share $	2.44	3.09	3.29	3.52	3.89	—
Shares Outstanding Mil	107	111	113	115	120	126
Return on Equity %	16.5	15.3	14.2	10.5	11.9	9.9
Net Margin %	25.6	21.2	21.7	18.0	18.4	NMF
Asset Turnover	0.1	0.1	0.1	0.1	0.1	0.1
Financial Leverage	5.8	6.2	5.5	6.5	9.1	9.2

Valuation Ratios	Stock	Rel to Industry	Rel to S&P 500
Price/Earnings	13.3	1.1	0.6
Price/Book	1.3	0.8	0.4
Price/Sales	2.5	1.1	1.2
Price/Cash Flow	—	—	—

Major Fund Holders	% of Fund Assets
FMI AAM Palm Beach Total Return	5.85
Fountainhead Special Value	5.21
CGM Focus	4.86
CGM Capital Development	4.79

Morningstar's Take By Richard McCaffery, 10-07-2002 Stock Price as of Analysis: $42.61

Countrywide has the scale and hedging expertise to compete in a tough industry, but we like its business model less than those of its better-diversified competitors.

More than 80% of Countrywide's revenue comes from originating mortgages, the related gain-on-sale income recorded when these loans are sold to investors, and other fees. In other words, it doesn't make much from the lending side of its business. A company like Washington Mutual, on the other hand, makes most of its money as a lender. Lending isn't a perfect business; it's capital-intensive and volatile. This is why many banks have worked hard to generate more revenue from fee-based businesses, to smooth out the cyclicality associated with making loans.

But lending has some very attractive aspects. We cover plenty of well-run companies that have built valuable franchises by gathering deposits, selling these deposit customers new products, and making smart loans. A big part of the success of a bank like Fifth Third is in selling products and managing relationships.

We also like the management discipline that's always a byproduct of smart lending. It takes time to build a consistent credit culture, but once a company

has done so it has created, in our opinion, a critical intangible asset, one that tells us a lot about how management thinks and acts. So we don't really care that spread revenue is cyclical. We just want to find managers who are honest, know how to sell, know how to save, and know how to spot a good business opportunity.

Countrywide has made strides to diversify its revenue stream. In 2001 it bought a small bank and has expanded its asset base quickly. Its insurance and capital markets business is growing fast too, and increasingly contributing to the bottom line. We expect Countrywide's loan portfolio and other operations to become a bigger part of the business over time. But we don't think it has yet built a franchise based on its ability to attract and maintain customers.

We aren't convinced Countrywide will be as good as its best competitors at gathering deposits, selling add-on products, and keeping costs low. It does a lot of things well, but we aren't willing to bet that the market will start valuing it like a bank. The market doesn't value Washington Mutual like a bank, and WaMu is a lot further along in the transformation from thrift to bank than Countrywide is in making the transformation from mortgage lender to bank.

Cox Communications A COX

	Rating	Risk	Moat Size	Fair Value	Last Close	Yield %
	★★★	Med.	Narrow	$33.00	$28.40	0.0

Company Profile

Cox Communications is the cable operator that best defines the idea of convergence. Already the provider of cable service to 6.2 million homes, Cox is rapidly launching various broadband services like digital cable, high-speed Internet access, and cable-based telephony. Cox leads the cable industry in bundling. Also, Cox is an investor in several leading programming networks, including Discovery Channel and The Learning Channel, and is a stake holder in a variety of technology companies, like Sprint PCS. Media giant Cox Enterprises owns 68% of Cox Communications.

Management

CEO James Robbins has been in charge since 1988 and is widely respected in the industry. The Cox family has a significant stake in the firm; Cox Enterprises owns 65%. Bill Gates is Cox's largest single shareholder, with nearly 6% of the firm.

Strategy

Cox became the nation's fifth-largest cable company through acquisitions. An advanced digital cable network allows Cox to lead the industry in bundling--packaging digital video, voice, and data services.

1400 Lake Hearn Drive   www.cox.com
Atlanta, GA 30319

Morningstar Grades

Growth [A]	1998	1999	2000	2001
Revenue %	6.6	35.0	51.3	16.0
Earnings/Share %	NMF	-34.3	109.3	-60.8
Book Value/Share %	125.2	103.0	-23.4	5.1
Dividends/Share %	NMF	NMF	NMF	NMF

The cable industry may be boring, but it continues to grow thanks to the advent of broadband services and greater bundling. The top line gained 16% in the September quarter, and is projected to move up another 14%-15% in 2002.

Profitability [B]	1999	2000	2001	TTM
Return on Assets %	3.3	7.8	3.0	-2.5
Oper Cash Flow $Mil	402	306	799	1,078
- Cap Spending $Mil	1,155	2,188	2,205	2,037
= Free Cash Flow $Mil	-753	-1,882	-1,407	-958

GAAP profits are skewed by many noncash charges; what matters most to cable investors is EBITDA. On this front Cox is doing well, posting margins above 35%. In 2002, EBITDA should reach $2 billion--growth of 14%-15%--as more customers bundle services.

Financial Health [C+]	1999	2000	2001	09-02
Long-term Debt $Mil	6,376	8,544	8,418	7,967
Total Equity $Mil	11,531	9,211	9,671	9,414
Debt/Equity Ratio	0.6	0.9	0.9	0.8

Unlike those of other cable firms, Cox's balance sheet is solid and getting better. The firm has sold securities in an effort to reduce debt. Although free cash flow will be negative this year, that should change in 2003; operating cash flow is climbing while capital spending is declining.

Industry	Investment Style	Stock Type	Sector
Cable TV	Large Growth	Spec. Growth	Media

Competition	Market Cap $Mil	Debt/ Equity	12 Mo Trailing Sales $Mil	Price/Cash Flow	Return On Assets%	Total Return% 1 Yr	3 Yr
Cox Communications A	17,611	0.8	4,646	16.3	-2.5	-32.2	-16.6
Hughes Electronic H	14,233	0.3	8,743	19.8	-2.8	-30.7	-31.0
EchoStar Communications	10,673	NMF	4,646	17.2	-3.4	-19.0	-21.4

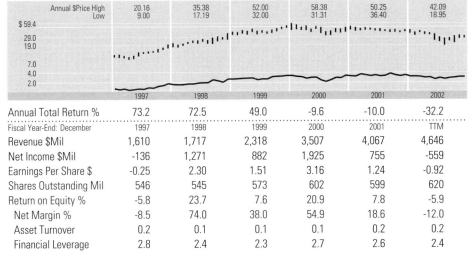

Price Volatility | Monthly Price High/Low   — Relative Strength to S&P 500

Annual $Price High / Low	20.16 / 9.00	35.38 / 17.19	52.00 / 32.00	58.38 / 31.31	50.25 / 36.40	42.09 / 18.95
	1997	1998	1999	2000	2001	2002
Annual Total Return %	73.2	72.5	49.0	-9.6	-10.0	-32.2

Fiscal Year-End: December	1997	1998	1999	2000	2001	TTM
Revenue $Mil	1,610	1,717	2,318	3,507	4,067	4,646
Net Income $Mil	-136	1,271	882	1,925	755	-559
Earnings Per Share $	-0.25	2.30	1.51	3.16	1.24	-0.92
Shares Outstanding Mil	546	545	573	602	599	620
Return on Equity %	-5.8	23.7	7.6	20.9	7.8	-5.9
Net Margin %	-8.5	74.0	38.0	54.9	18.6	-12.0
Asset Turnover	0.2	0.1	0.1	0.1	0.2	0.2
Financial Leverage	2.8	2.4	2.3	2.7	2.6	2.4

Valuation Ratios	Stock	Rel to Industry	Rel to S&P 500
Price/Earnings	NMF	—	—
Price/Book	1.9	1.2	0.6
Price/Sales	3.8	1.2	1.9
Price/Cash Flow	16.3	1.0	1.2

Major Fund Holders	% of Fund Assets
Fidelity Select Multimedia	6.99
Shelby	5.52
Fidelity Select Telecommunications	4.76
Rochdale Alpha	4.58

Morningstar's Take   By Todd P. Bernier, 12-22-2002   Stock Price as of Analysis: $29.44

Cox is one of two cable operators--Comcast is the other--that we would want to own. However, we'd wait to buy Cox, a firm with a narrow economic moat, at a 30% discount to our fair value estimate.

More than any other cable operator, Cox is defined by bundling. Roughly 25% of Cox customers--1.5 million households--combine either data or telephony services with a video product, by far the highest rate in the cable industry. Because bundling can run as high as 50% in some markets, Cox still has room to stretch its legs. In addition to greater customer loyalty, bundling leads to higher cash flow per subscriber because the incremental cost of adding a second and third service is very small to Cox. Bundling was the reason cable companies frantically upgraded systems over the past decade.

Cable telephony is the linchpin of Cox's bundling strategy. Although phone industry execs were quick to dismiss the voice-over-cable threat, they aren't laughing now; Cox's telephony subscribers well exceed half a million. For consumers, the biggest benefit is lower prices and a consolidated invoice. The Baby Bells still control 90% of the local phone market, but regulation prevents them from offering discounts in specific markets. Big Cable has exploited this loophole by promoting cheap phone service in order to win market share.

Logic suggests that such good news would bloat stock prices in the cable industry. But the bankruptcies at Adelphia and WorldCom have caused investors to eschew all highly leveraged companies, especially those valued primarily on multiples of earnings before interest, taxes, depreciation, and amortization (EBITDA), as cable stocks are. The key difference between Cox and the Adelphias of the world is found on the balance sheet. Cox has one of the best balance sheets in the cable industry, as well as an investment-grade debt rating. The ratio of debt/EBITDA is very manageable at around 4 and interest coverage is safely above 3. Considering that EBITDA is rising and capital spending is falling, it would be very difficult for Cox to misappropriate operating costs. We expect the firm to finally generate positive free cash flow in early 2003.

Although investors are currently eschewing cable stocks, we suspect Cox will brave the market's skepticism and be among the first out of the gates once perspective returns.

MORNINGSTAR® Stocks 500

Cummins Engine CUM

Rating	Risk	Moat Size	Fair Value	Last Close	Yield %
★★★	High	None	$35.00	$28.13	4.3

Company Profile

Cummins Engine manufactures diesel and gasoline engines and engine-related components and power systems for trucks, buses, light commercial vehicles including delivery trucks and vans, and other heavy equipment. The company's main North American markets are the heavy-duty and midrange truck industries; its other customers include manufacturers of equipment for construction, mining, agriculture, and various industrial uses. Cummins Engine's Fleetguard subsidiary makes heavy-duty and specialty filters.

Management

Theodore Solso has been chairman and CEO since 2000; he has been with Cummins since 1988.

Strategy

With demand for its engines falling, Cummins has focused on cost-cutting recently, implementing a program to improve efficiency. The company hopes these efforts will position it to benefit when the U.S. economy improves. Investments to improve engine performance are continual. Cummins is working to expand its products into new end markets like mining and rail.

500 Jackson Street   www.cummins.com
Columbus, IN 47202-3005

Morningstar Grades

Growth [D]	1998	1999	2000	2001
Revenue %	11.4	6.0	-0.6	-13.9
Earnings/Share %	NMF	NMF	-95.2	NMF
Book Value/Share %	-9.4	10.7	-9.5	-20.0
Dividends/Share %	2.3	2.3	6.7	0.0

Historically, growth has been decent--about 7% annually. But with truck engine demand slumping since 1999 and power generation hitting a wall recently, revenue has been declining for the past couple of years and now sits well below peak levels.

Profitability [D+]	1999	2000	2001	TTM
Return on Assets %	3.4	0.2	-2.4	0.6
Oper Cash Flow $Mil	307	388	144	119
- Cap Spending $Mil	215	228	206	102
= Free Cash Flow $Mil	92	160	-62	17

Profitability has been erratic and generally in decline since peaking in the mid-1990s, the result of restructuring charges and the drop in demand. Cost-cutting has helped the firm weather the current downturn better than that of the early 1990s.

Financial Health [D+]	1999	2000	2001	09-02
Long-term Debt $Mil	1,092	1,032	915	795
Total Equity $Mil	1,429	1,336	1,025	1,052
Debt/Equity Ratio	0.8	0.8	0.9	0.8

While earnings have been erratic, operating cash flow has remained narrowly in the black. Debt has risen sharply in recent years and the downturn has left interest coverage thin.

Industry	Investment Style	Stock Type	Sector
Auto Parts	Small Value	High Yield	Consumer Goods

Competition

	Market Cap $Mil	Debt/ Equity	12 Mo Trailing Sales $Mil	Price/Cash Flow	Return On Assets%	Total Return% 1 Yr	3 Yr
Cummins Engine	1,167	0.8	5,902	9.8	0.6	-24.4	-12.2
DaimlerChrysler AG	30,750	2.1	136,142	2.2	-0.3	-25.0	-23.0
Caterpillar	15,736	2.1	19,871	8.5	2.0	-9.8	1.6

Price Volatility

| Monthly Price High/Low   — Relative Strength to S&P 500

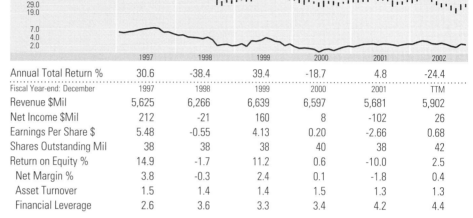

Annual $Price High	83.00	62.75	65.69	50.00	45.50	50.29
Low	44.25	28.31	34.56	27.06	28.00	19.60
	1997	1998	1999	2000	2001	2002

Annual Total Return %	30.6	-38.4	39.4	-18.7	4.8	-24.4

Fiscal Year-end: December	1997	1998	1999	2000	2001	TTM
Revenue $Mil	5,625	6,266	6,639	6,597	5,681	5,902
Net Income $Mil	212	-21	160	8	-102	26
Earnings Per Share $	5.48	-0.55	4.13	0.20	-2.66	0.68
Shares Outstanding Mil	38	38	38	40	38	42
Return on Equity %	14.9	-1.7	11.2	0.6	-10.0	2.5
Net Margin %	3.8	-0.3	2.4	0.1	-1.8	0.4
Asset Turnover	1.5	1.4	1.4	1.5	1.3	1.3
Financial Leverage	2.6	3.6	3.3	3.4	4.2	4.4

Valuation Ratios	Stock	Rel to Industry	Rel to S&P 500
Price/Earnings	41.4	3.3	1.8
Price/Book	1.1	0.1	0.3
Price/Sales	0.2	0.0	0.1
Price/Cash Flow	9.8	0.2	0.7

Major Fund Holders	% of Fund Assets
Tocqueville Small Cap Value	4.12
SYM Select Growth	2.65
TCW Galileo Value Opportunities I	1.78
Westcore Mid-Cap Opportunity	1.58

Morningstar's Take By Michael Hodel, 12-17-2002 Stock Price as of Analysis: $29.50

Cummins has a nice stable of products, but as a smaller player in a world of giants, the firm faces several challenges. We'd buy the shares only at a 40% discount to our fair value estimate.

Cummins' engine segment--the company's largest business--has built a strong reputation and a base of loyal end customers (truck drivers and fleet operators). Many truck buyers look for a make with a specific engine. Big rigs are heavily customized, and drivers are loath to part with the familiar. Similarly, fleet operators often have expertise in servicing a particular engine; introducing another engine type increases switching costs. Cummins engines power about one fourth of the heavy-duty trucks on the road.

Cummins' products aren't sold directly to drivers, though, and we think the firm's ability to milk its brand loyalty is limited. Many of the truckmakers whose products contain Cummins engines, like DaimlerChrysler's Freightliner unit and Volvo/Mack, also produce engines for their trucks. They're unlikely to drop Cummins as an option soon, but they aren't beholden to the engine maker and probably have the upper hand in negotiating prices.

Cummins' other businesses sell to a broader base of customers and offset the cyclical engine unit. Filtration products offer steady revenue and decent

returns on assets. The power generation business grew smartly during 2000 and 2001 with high returns on investment. It has suffered as a result of the tech bust, but it offers good growth potential.

Cummins has been a leader in meeting the Environmental Protection Agency's new emissions standards, getting its first engine certified six months before the October 2002 deadline. While it will take awhile for engine sales to reach levels seen before the deadline, Cummins has had more time than the competition to get its engines into the hands of customers for testing. This could help the firm win some share.

Cummins' profitability hasn't been great. Net income in recent years hasn't come close to its 1994 peak, as a result of falling gross margins and a string of restructuring charges. Combine that with heavy spending on new equipment in the mid-1990s and it's easy to see why returns on invested capital have been weak, averaging 3.7% annually since the peak. The firm also labors under a hefty debt load and an underfunded pension plan. Cost-cutting and reorganization should make Cummins more efficient when demand rebounds, but we're not sure the firm can hold on to these gains over the long term.

CVS CVS

	Rating ★★★	Risk Med.	Moat Size Narrow	Fair Value $26.00	Last Close $24.97	Yield % 0.9

Company Profile

CVS operates about 4,100 retail drugstores, primarily in the Northeast and Eastern United States. The company is replacing many of its strip-mall retail stores with more-profitable freestanding corner locations. Sales of prescription drugs constitute nearly two thirds of revenue. CVS is the successor to Melville Corporation's reorganization in 1995; the company acquired Revco D.S. in 1997 and Arbor Drugs in 1998. CVS also purchased the nation's largest specialty pharmacy operation (Stadtlander) in 2000, which it has since renamed CVS ProCare.

Management

CEO Thomas Ryan started with CVS as a pharmacist and rose through the ranks. Though questions arose about CVS' accounting and quality of earnings in 2000, management defended the firm's reporting and the issue hasn't resurfaced.

Strategy

CVS aims to improve the location and condition of its store base. The firm is selectively opening some new stores in new markets, relocating stores in existing markets to better freestanding spots, and renovating others to improve their appearance and selection. The company also continues efforts to curb shrinkage (lost merchandise via theft or inventory mismanagement).

One CVS Drive   www.cvs.com
Woonsocket, RI 02895

Morningstar Grades

Growth [A-]	1998	1999	2000	2001
Revenue %	11.1	18.5	11.0	10.7
Earnings/Share %	400.0	63.2	18.1	-45.4
Book Value/Share %	3.5	17.3	18.8	7.0
Dividends/Share %	2.3	2.2	0.0	0.0

Though CVS posted sales growth near 11% in 2000 and 2001, we expect annual growth for 2002-04 to average closer to 10%. Cheaper priced generics are becoming a bigger piece of prescription drug sales and could hold growth down some.

Profitability [B]	1999	2000	2001	TTM
Return on Assets %	8.5	9.2	4.6	4.1
Oper Cash Flow $Mil	726	780	681	1,002
- Cap Spending $Mil	723	695	714	1,045
= Free Cash Flow $Mil	4	85	-33	-43

Drugstores earn very small profit margins--in the neighborhood of 3%-4%. CVS has been less profitable than Walgreen because of operational missteps and fewer freestanding stores, which are about 30% more lucrative than mall-based sites.

Financial Health [A-]	1999	2000	2001	09-02
Long-term Debt $Mil	559	537	810	808
Total Equity $Mil	3,404	4,037	4,306	4,799
Debt/Equity Ratio	0.2	0.1	0.2	0.2

CVS' balance sheet is okay, but it doesn't sparkle like Walgreen's. CVS' debt/capital (debt plus equity) ratio of 0.2 is understated by the use of operating leases worth $7 billion. Capitalizing these leases pushes debt/capital to 0.6.

Industry Specialty Retail	Investment Style ▦ Large Core	Stock Type ↗ Classic Growth	Sector 🛒 Consumer Services

Competition	Market Cap $Mil	Debt/ Equity	12 Mo Trailing Sales $Mil	Price/Cash Flow	Return On Assets%	Total Return% 1 Yr	3 Yr
CVS	9,809	0.2	23,787	9.8	4.1	-15.0	-12.1
Walgreen	29,892	—	28,681	20.3	10.3	-12.9	2.4
Rite Aid	1,262	—	15,551	—	—	—	—

Price Volatility

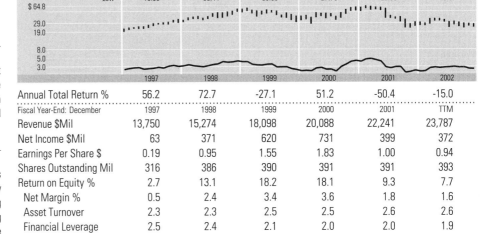

	▌Monthly Price High/Low	— Relative Strength to S&P 500

Annual $Price High/Low	35.00 / 19.50	56.00 / 30.44	58.38 / 30.00	60.44 / 27.75	63.75 / 22.90	35.70 / 23.03
	1997	1998	1999	2000	2001	2002

	1997	1998	1999	2000	2001	
Annual Total Return %	56.2	72.7	-27.1	51.2	-50.4	-15.0

Fiscal Year-End: December	1997	1998	1999	2000	2001	TTM
Revenue $Mil	13,750	15,274	18,098	20,088	22,241	23,787
Net Income $Mil	63	371	620	731	399	372
Earnings Per Share $	0.19	0.95	1.55	1.83	1.00	0.94
Shares Outstanding Mil	316	386	390	391	391	393
Return on Equity %	2.7	13.1	18.2	18.1	9.3	7.7
Net Margin %	0.5	2.4	3.4	3.6	1.8	1.6
Asset Turnover	2.3	2.3	2.5	2.5	2.6	2.6
Financial Leverage	2.5	2.4	2.1	2.0	2.0	1.9

Valuation Ratios	Stock	Rel to Industry	Rel to S&P 500
Price/Earnings	26.6	0.9	1.1
Price/Book	2.0	0.6	0.6
Price/Sales	0.4	0.5	0.2
Price/Cash Flow	9.8	0.7	0.7

Major Fund Holders	% of Fund Assets
Fidelity Select Retailing	5.97
Cambiar Opportunity Inst	3.98
Saratoga Large Capitalization Value I	3.88
Timothy Plan Large/Mid-Cap Value A	3.72

Morningstar's Take By Tom Goetzinger, 10-24-2002   Stock Price as of Analysis: $27.44

CVS is improving the location and layout of its store base, but still lags rival Walgreen in sales growth and profitability. We'd thus require a sizable discount to our fair value estimate before picking up the shares.

Since announcing its so-called action plan in 2001, CVS has done a nice job of improving its store base. The drugstore chain is closing underperforming stores, relocating some stores in existing markets to more-lucrative freestanding sites, and entering new markets. These moves are aimed at driving more traffic into CVS' stores while making the shopping experience more enjoyable once patrons are inside. Surveys indicate that store location and convenience are valued most by drugstore customers, followed by service, product selection, and finally price. CVS' strategy appears right on target.

However, much of CVS' action plan for the past year has focused on improving and relocating existing stores. Plans to enter new markets outside the beachhead of stores it has built on the East Coast will prove riskier and more cumbersome, in our opinion. Stores in new cities usually take three to four years to turn a profit, while "fill-in" stores or relocations within existing cities might take only half that long. The heavy lifting for CVS remains, and the firm might occasionally struggle to execute.

In addition to the growing pains, which could cause some volatility in sales and earnings growth, CVS also faces an industrywide trend of margin decline because of pharmacy pricing pressure. More than 90% of CVS' prescription payments come from third-party payers like pharmacy benefit managers, who work to lower drug costs for health insurers. These payers have been squeezing drugstores for years and aren't likely to let go anytime soon. CVS' operating margin has shrunk from 6.3% in 1999 to 5.0% so far in 2002. Prescription drug sales have increased from 59% to 68% of revenue in that time. We expect prescriptions to reach 75% of revenue by 2005, so margins should continue to slide.

Another potential problem for CVS is the shortage of qualified pharmacists in the United States. This has forced drugstores to ante up even more on recruitment and salaries, which further depresses margins. Given the pressures specific to CVS' pharmacy business and the challenges likely to pop up during its expansion over the next couple of years, we'd require at least a 30% margin of safety to our fair value estimate to buy in.

 **MORNINGSTAR® Stocks 500**

Cytyc CYTC

	Rating	Risk	Moat Size	Fair Value	Last Close	Yield %
	★★★	Med.	Narrow	$11.00	$10.20	0.0

Company Profile

Cytyc designs, develops, manufactures, and markets medical diagnostic systems for women's health. Its ThinPrep system is a more accurate screening method than conventional Pap smears. Cytyc has co-marketing agreements with Quest Diagnostics and Digene for promoting ThinPrep with other diagnostic tests such as human papillomavirus. The company is seeking approval for co-marketing ThinPrep with Roche Diagnostic tests for sexually transmitted diseases. The 2001 merger with Pro-Duct Health adds breast cancer risk evaluation tools to Cytyc's portfolio.

Management

Patrick Sullivan joined Cytyc in 1991 as vice president of sales and marketing and became president and CEO in 1994. Sullivan previously worked at Abbott Labs and McKinsey & Co.

Strategy

Now that ThinPrep sales have taken off, Cytyc is focused on evaluating additional diagnostic uses and enhancing the system's productivity through advanced imaging. The company also seeks to gain foreign market share. Recent acquisitions, like Pro-Duct Health, have added breast cancer risk evaluation and other women's health products.

85 Swanson Road www.cytyc.com
Boxborough, MA 01719

Morningstar Grades

Growth [A]	1998	1999	2000	2001
Revenue %	68.0	83.2	75.2	55.6
Earnings/Share %	NMF	NMF	540.0	-68.8
Book Value/Share %	-15.3	4.6	46.4	124.9
Dividends/Share %	NMF	NMF	NMF	NMF

Sales increased an average of 70% annually between 1998-2001. An inventory backlog hurt 2002 growth, but we expect sales to pick up to around 10% or 15% through 2006, as Cytyc expands foreign market share and increases its product line.

Profitability [B]	1999	2000	2001	TTM
Return on Assets %	5.0	22.3	3.3	-1.8
Oper Cash Flow $Mil	2	26	92	95
- Cap Spending $Mil	4	11	9	8
= Free Cash Flow $Mil	-2	15	82	86

Gross and net margins have improved to 80% and 21%, respectively. These could decline as the firm increases its sales and marketing efforts, and expands research and development and manufacturing capabilities.

Financial Health [A+]	1999	2000	2001	09-02
Long-term Debt $Mil	0	0	0	0
Total Equity $Mil	95	147	350	348
Debt/Equity Ratio	0.0	0.0	0.0	0.0

As of September 2002, the company had no debt and $174 million in cash and securities. With positive operating cash flow, Cytyc is currently able to fund operations internally.

Industry	Investment Style	Stock Type	Sector
Medical Equipment	▦ Small Growth	◈ Spec. Growth	◪ Healthcare

Competition

	Market Cap $Mil	Debt/ Equity	12 Mo Trailing Sales $Mil	Price/Cash Flow	Return On Assets%	Total Return% 1 Yr	3 Yr
Cytyc	1,182	0.0	233	12.5	-1.8	-60.9	-0.7
Chiron	7,073	0.2	1,238	20.5	5.4	-14.2	-2.6
Tripath Imaging	100	—	33	—	—	—	—

Price Volatility

Annual $Price High	5.25	4.65	10.39	23.48	30.22	27.99
Low	2.42	1.23	1.67	7.94	13.63	5.73

I Monthly Price High/Low — Relative Strength to S&P 500

	1997	1998	1999	2000	2001	2002
Annual Total Return %	-7.9	3.5	137.1	104.9	25.2	-60.9
Fiscal Year-end: December	1997	1998	1999	2000	2001	TTM
Revenue $Mil	26	44	81	142	221	233
Net Income $Mil	-22	-12	6	38	13	-7
Earnings Per Share $	-0.22	-0.11	0.05	0.32	0.10	-0.07
Shares Outstanding Mil	101	107	106	112	115	116
Return on Equity %	-22.9	-13.7	5.9	26.0	3.6	-2.0
Net Margin %	-83.8	-26.5	7.0	26.9	5.7	-3.0
Asset Turnover	0.2	0.5	0.7	0.8	0.6	0.6
Financial Leverage	1.1	1.1	1.2	1.2	1.1	1.1

Valuation Ratios	Stock	Rel to Industry	Rel to S&P 500
Price/Earnings	NMF	—	—
Price/Book	3.4	0.5	1.1
Price/Sales	5.1	1.1	2.5
Price/Cash Flow	12.5	0.5	0.9

Major Fund Holders	% of Fund Assets
Monterey Murphy New World Biotech	4.16
Polynous Growth A	3.61
MFS Instl Mid-Cap Growth	3.45
MFS Mid-Cap Growth B	3.29

Morningstar's Take By Jill Kiersky, 12-15-2002 Stock Price as of Analysis: $9.74

Cytyc has become a market leader in women's health products. If it proves it can expand the business beyond innovative liquid pap tests, Cytyc could be in the game for the long haul. Given its narrow economic moat and the work that lies ahead, though, we'd want a 40% discount to our fair value estimate before we'd take the plunge.

With sales growth averaging 75% annually since launching its ThinPrep cervical cancer screening system in 1997, Cytyc has been the star of its class. ThinPrep has quickly captured 58% of the U.S. market for pap tests. While it's more expensive than conventional pap smears, this liquid-based pap test provides for much better accuracy in detecting abnormalities and is quickly gaining acceptance among physicians. Case in point is the U.S. Army, Navy, and Air Force, which have inked contracts to use ThinPrep in all worldwide screening centers.

Sales growth has been losing steam, but we expect that recurring sales from disposables, as well as Food and Drug Administration approval of its imaging system to automate more of the cervical screening process, will give sales a boost. The next opportunity is Cytyc's FirstCyte Ductal Lavage breast cancer risk-screening test. Payers have been slow to reimburse for the exam, but leading women's health groups advocate the screen for one in eight high-risk women. At $565 per exam, the U.S. market for the test could reach $3 billion. Because of the reimbursement challenges, we forecast just 1% market share by 2006.

Cytyc's operating margins, at 33% (excluding one-time charges), have surpassed those of its peers, and the company's free cash flow (cash from operations minus capital expenses, excluding $41 million in tax benefits from stock options) was 19% of sales in 2001. Even better, Cytyc has achieved this level of growth without taking on debt, making for worry-free financial health.

The company's failed merger attempt with Digene could be indicative of an increasingly competitive environment. Digene's testing portfolio would have provided Cytyc with a virtual monopoly on certain cervical screening tests. With more tests being developed, the firms will be fighting for the larger lab customers. This, combined with Cytyc's several earnings revisions in 2002, has given us less confidence in the firm's ability to accurately forecast underlying demand and maintain high sales growth rates. Still, if the shares dropped below $7, the margin of safety would be big enough.

DaimlerChrysler AG DCX

	Rating	Risk	Moat Size	Fair Value	Last Close	Yield %
	★★★	Med.	None	$45.00	$30.65	2.9

Company Profile

DaimlerChrysler is the world's third largest motor vehicle concern. Its Mercedes-Benz brand, based in Germany, is the leading global luxury nameplate and made up 35% of DCX' 2001 revenue. 47% of sales were generated by Chrysler, based in Michigan, which produces cars and light trucks under the Chrysler, Dodge and Jeep brands. DaimlerChrysler also has significant financial services operations and, through Mercedes-Benz and Freighliner, is the world's top maker of commercial vehicles. The company is the result of the 1998 merger of Daimler-Benz AG and Chrysler Corporation.

Management

It didn't turn out to be a merger of equals; the firm is now dominated by Daimler-Benz veterans. Juergen Schrempp, 57, has been chairman of the board of management (equivalent to a U.S. CEO) since 1995. Dieter Zetsche is head of Chrysler Group.

Strategy

While its core Mercedes-Benz brand continues to perform well, DaimlerChrysler is restructuring just about everything else. Large cost and capital-spending cuts will continue at Chrysler and Freightliner. A positive offshoot of these troubles is the company's increasing focus on the car business; loads of noncore assets and investments either have been or will be sold.

Epplesstrasse 225   www.daimlerchrysler.com
Stuttgart, 70546

Morningstar Grades

Growth [C]	1998	1999	2000	2001
Revenue %	12.1	13.8	8.3	-6.0
Earnings/Share %	-27.6	15.9	37.1	NMF
Book Value/Share %	6.8	15.4	17.4	-7.2
Dividends/Share %	NMF	0.0	0.0	-57.4

Daimler-Benz expanded quickly in the 1990s with large acquisitions, most notably Chrysler. However, the manic buying wasn't accompanied by higher profits. Falling market share and vehicle prices will keep pressure on the top line in 2003.

Profitability [C]	1999	2000	2001	TTM
Return on Assets %	3.5	3.9	-0.3	-0.3
Oper Cash Flow $Mil	19,291	14,880	14,218	14,218
- Cap Spending $Mil	30,832	27,860	24,524	24,524
= Free Cash Flow $Mil	11,541	-12,980	-10,306	-10,306

Only Mercedes-Benz has shown stable earnings lately. Chrysler lost 5.3 billion euros in 2001, including restructuring. The firm expects modest profits for Chrysler and Freightliner this year, but we suspect they may slip back into the red in 2003.

Financial Health [C]	1999	2000	2001	12-01
Long-term Debt $Mil	49,450	65,425	72,022	72,022
Total Equity $Mil	36,060	40,008	34,517	34,517
Debt/Equity Ratio	1.4	1.6	2.1	2.1

With consolidated leverage of 4.6, DCX's balance sheet is better than that of U.S. rivals--though hardly as robust as Toyota's TM. Net liquidity (cash and securities less debt) in the industrial businesses, now positive, has sharply improved.

	Industry	Investment Style	Stock Type	Sector
	Auto Makers	Large Value	Distressed	Consumer Goods

Competition	Market Cap $Mil	Debt/ Equity	12 Mo Trailing Sales $Mil	Price/Cash Flow	Return On Assets%	Total Return% 1 Yr	3 Yr
DaimlerChrysler AG	30,750	2.1	136,142	2.2	-0.3	-25.0	-23.0
Toyota Motor ADR	97,652	—	118,527	—	—	—	—
Honda Motor ADR	35,196	—	58,319	—	—	—	—

Price Volatility ꞁ Monthly Price High/Low — Relative Strength to S&P 500

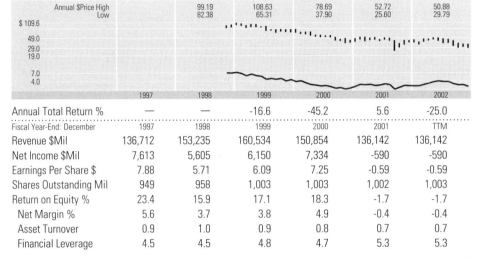

	1997	1998	1999	2000	2001	2002
Annual $Price High			99.19	108.63	78.69	52.72	50.88
Low			82.38	65.31	37.90	25.60	29.79

	1997	1998	1999	2000	2001	TTM
Annual Total Return %	—	—	-16.6	-45.2	5.6	-25.0
Fiscal Year-End: December	1997	1998	1999	2000	2001	TTM
Revenue $Mil	136,712	153,235	160,534	150,854	136,142	136,142
Net Income $Mil	7,613	5,605	6,150	7,334	-590	-590
Earnings Per Share $	7.88	5.71	6.09	7.25	-0.59	-0.59
Shares Outstanding Mil	949	958	1,003	1,003	1,002	1,003
Return on Equity %	23.4	15.9	17.1	18.3	-1.7	-1.7
Net Margin %	5.6	3.7	3.8	4.9	-0.4	-0.4
Asset Turnover	0.9	1.0	0.9	0.8	0.7	0.7
Financial Leverage	4.5	4.5	4.8	4.7	5.3	5.3

Valuation Ratios	Stock	Rel to Industry	Rel to S&P 500
Price/Earnings	NMF	—	—
Price/Book	0.9	0.5	0.3
Price/Sales	0.2	0.4	0.1
Price/Cash Flow	2.2	0.3	0.2

Major Fund Holders	% of Fund Assets
None	

Morningstar's Take By Josh Peters, 10-24-2002 Stock Price as of Analysis: $35.59

DaimlerChrysler's strength in Europe makes the stock less risky than its North American peers, but its turnaround efforts remain vulnerable to economic trends. We'd look for a minimum 40% discount to our fair value estimate before buying.

To say the 1999 merger of Daimler-Benz and Chrysler destroyed shareholder value would be an understatement. In the worst spirit of empire building, the deal morphed a solid business (Mercedes-Benz) into an unwieldy behemoth. As with so many global mergers, the combined entity fell on hard times. Chrysler alone swung from a 5 billion-euro operating profit in 1999 to a 5 billion-euro loss in 2001.

With the firm finally reacting to its strategic errors, a turnaround seems to be taking shape. After reducing its workforce by more than 20% and extracting steep discounts from suppliers, Chrysler is back to break-even. The Freightliner and Sterling heavy-truck businesses have been restructured as well to stanch cyclical losses. And despite the mess of the past several years, Mercedes has continued to grow and generate impressive cash flows--although the benefits have gone to subsidize restructuring activities elsewhere.

Our worry is that weakening trends in the auto industry--both in the United States and abroad--could stop this slow-gathering turnaround dead in its tracks. Chrysler's problems thus far can be attributed primarily to its own missteps with respect to quality, product appeal, and market share, rather than a traditional industry downturn. But even though it now seems to be recovering, another downshift in U.S. auto sales could quickly return the group to losses. Conditions seem unlikely to get much worse for Freightliner (industry sales of Class 8 tractors have been cut in half since their 1999 peak), but the shaky U.S. economy and the impact of new engine emission standards could easily forestall a rebound. Although Mercedes has thus far dodged the industry's downturn in Europe, even that unit could prove vulnerable in a still-weaker 2003.

We doubt that DaimlerChrysler will ever regain the kind of competitive advantages or investor esteem that Daimler-Benz enjoyed as a stand-alone entity. As the world's top-selling luxury brand, Mercedes could probably earn a narrow economic moat rating if it stood alone--something we're reluctant to grant any automaker. But that unit's appeal is heavily diluted by underperformers elsewhere; we doubt that the whole can create more economic value than the sum of its parts.

M✩RNINGSTAR® Stocks 500

Dana DCN

	Rating	Risk	Moat Size	Fair Value	Last Close	Yield %
	★★★	High	None	$14.00	$11.76	0.3

Company Profile

Dana produces vehicle and industrial components. Its products include axles, driveshafts, transmissions, piston rings, pistons, filters, brake assemblies, engine components, vehicular frames, side rails, pumps, seals, control valves, and hydraulic cylinders. The company's products are sold to vehicular, industrial, and mobile off-highway original-equipment markets in the United States and overseas. Foreign sales account for approximately 28% of Dana's total sales. Sales to Ford Motor make up about 16% of the company's total sales.

Management

CEO Joseph Magliochetti, who has significant experience in Dana's international expansion, took the helm in early 1999. Most of the firm's executives have been with Dana for decades.

Strategy

Dana's long-term strategy of integrating individual components into larger, higher-value modules is a sound one. We also approve of the company's recent decision to focus on its foundation businesses--driveshafts, axles, frames, and chassis parts. More sales of noncore businesses are in the works, including Dana Commercial Credit.

4500 Dorr Street
Toledo, OH 43615
www.dana.com

Industry	Investment Style	Stock Type	Sector
Auto Parts	Mid Value	Cyclical	Consumer Goods

Competition	Market Cap $Mil	Debt/ Equity	12 Mo Trailing Sales $Mil	Price/Cash Flow	Return On Assets%	Total Return% 1 Yr	3 Yr
Dana	1,747	2.0	10,472	2.7	-4.7	-15.1	-23.1
Delphi	4,495	0.9	26,836	3.8	0.5	-39.6	-16.6
American Axle & Mfg Holdi	1,165	1.2	3,361	3.2	6.5	9.5	23.9

Price Volatility | Monthly Price High/Low — Relative Strength to S&P 500

		1997	1998	1999	2000	2001	2002
Annual $Price High		54.38	61.50	54.06	33.25	26.90	23.20
Low		30.63	31.25	25.31	12.81	10.25	9.28

	1997	1998	1999	2000	2001	2002
Annual Total Return %	49.5	-11.8	-24.3	-45.9	-4.9	-15.1

Fiscal Year-end: December	1997	1998	1999	2000	2001	TTM
Revenue $Mil	12,402	12,839	13,353	12,691	10,469	10,472
Net Income $Mil	320	534	513	334	-298	-471
Earnings Per Share $	1.94	3.20	3.08	2.18	-2.01	-3.17
Shares Outstanding Mil	162	165	165	152	148	149
Return on Equity %	12.3	18.2	17.3	12.7	-15.2	-28.2
Net Margin %	2.6	4.2	3.8	2.6	-2.8	-4.5
Asset Turnover	1.3	1.3	1.2	1.1	1.0	1.0
Financial Leverage	3.7	3.4	3.8	4.3	5.2	6.0

Valuation Ratios	Stock	Rel to Industry	Rel to S&P 500
Price/Earnings	NMF	—	—
Price/Book	1.0	0.1	0.3
Price/Sales	0.2	0.0	0.1
Price/Cash Flow	2.7	0.1	0.2

Major Fund Holders	% of Fund Assets
Tocqueville Small Cap Value	4.12
Vanguard Selected Value	1.78
Smith Barney Peachtree Growth A	1.72
Lord Abbett Mid-Cap Value A	1.60

Morningstar Grades

Growth [D]	1998	1999	2000	2001
Revenue %	3.5	4.0	-5.0	-17.5
Earnings/Share %	64.9	-3.8	-29.2	NMF
Book Value/Share %	11.7	0.8	-3.4	-23.0
Dividends/Share %	9.6	8.8	0.0	-24.2

Acquisitions and expanding market share helped Dana grow in the 1990s, but falling auto and heavy-truck production have hit sales hard. An industry rebound thus far in 2002 has helped results, but the next few years could be grim.

Profitability [C-]	1999	2000	2001	TTM
Return on Assets %	4.6	3.0	-2.9	-4.7
Oper Cash Flow $Mil	608	984	639	642
- Cap Spending $Mil	807	662	425	371
= Free Cash Flow $Mil	-199	322	214	271

Dana didn't just take its eye off the ball on costs; with results comparable to those of Delphi and Visteon VC, it lost the ball entirely. Huge restructuring efforts are under way, but the road back to acceptable margins will be rough.

Financial Health [C-]	1999	2000	2001	09-02
Long-term Debt $Mil	2,732	2,649	3,008	3,303
Total Equity $Mil	2,957	2,628	1,958	1,673
Debt/Equity Ratio	0.9	1.0	1.5	2.0

Although Dana has paid off $1 billion in debt over the past two years, much of which was related to its commercial financing portfolio, its balance sheet is still one of the sector's most leveraged.

Morningstar's Take By Josh Peters, 12-02-2002 Stock Price as of Analysis: $13.34

We view turnaround attempts in the deflationary auto industry skeptically. In our opinion, the jury is still out on Dana's restructuring, so we take a cautious attitude toward the shares.

Dana spent most of its 98 years in business as one of the auto industry's most successful independent suppliers, but its business model has had trouble adapting to today's deflationary pressures. As automakers' demands for price reductions mounted, Dana waited too long to restructure. Productivity fell quickly as auto production weakened. Overpaying for a large acquisition (Echlin) and the collapse of heavy-truck demand didn't help, either. In just two years, 1999-2001, Dana's operating margin plunged nearly 8 points.

The company has responded with a massive restructuring plan, aimed primarily at its bloated fixed costs. The strategy, which resembles that of BorgWarner, is to outsource commodity-oriented production (metal bending) and concentrate on higher-margin, higher-tech components. A number of noncore businesses, like Dana Commercial Credit and a variety of small, nonautomotive industrial businesses, are being sold. The restructuring will probably continue well into 2003, but the early results--particularly in the company's large aftermarket parts business--have been quite respectable.

While we believe Dana is finding its way toward the right track, we also think investors would do well to adopt a "prove it" stance. This is a company that hasn't published an income statement free of nonrecurring charges since 1996--since then, such charges have averaged a dollar per share annually. Restructuring isn't cheap, either: Cash outflows associated with this restructuring could exceed 2% of sales in 2002. And Dana's debt load, though declining because of asset sales, still limits the firm's financial flexibility. A probable decline in auto production next year leaves the company little room for error.

Even after its restructuring is complete, we're not sure what the firm's key competitive advantages will be. Dana invests considerably less in research and development as a share of revenue than peers like Delphi and BorgWarner. The company has also suffered some notable program losses, like the axle for the 2003 heavy-duty Dodge Ram. That went to the nimbler American Axle, which is aggressively pursuing more business.

Assuming Dana's restructuring hits no major snags, we'd still demand a wide (60%) discount to our fair value estimate before considering the shares.

Danaher DHR

	Rating	Risk	Moat Size	Fair Value	Last Close	Yield %
	★★★	Low	Narrow	$75.00	$65.70	0.1

Company Profile

Danaher is a diversified manufacturing firm. Its environmental and process controls segment, which accounts for about 69% of sales, includes network test equipment, motion control products (motors) and electronic testing and control devices. Its tools division includes the Sears Craftsman line of hand tools and Delta pickup truck boxes. The firm acquired network test equipment maker Fluke Corp. in 1998, electric motor manufacturer Kollmorgen in 2000, and thermal control maker Lifschultz Industries in 2001. In 2001, 31% of revenue was generated outside the United States.

Management

In May 2001, longtime CEO George Sherman passed the reins to 39-year-old H. Lawrence Culp, who has been part of Danaher's management team since Sherman became CEO in 1990. The company encourages a tight-knit, collaborative culture.

Strategy

Danaher essentially manages a portfolio of industrial businesses with the aim of generating maximum free cash flow. Rather than returning free cash to shareholders, the firm feeds on a steady diet of bolt-on acquisitions. It then makes new operations more profitable by implementing its highly efficient Danaher Business System.

2099 Pennsylvania Ave. NW   www.danaher.com
Washington, DC 20006-1813

Morningstar Grades

Growth [A]	1998	1999	2000	2001
Revenue %	16.3	4.9	18.2	0.1
Earnings/Share %	1.5	34.6	24.6	-9.9
Book Value/Share %	18.9	20.6	14.3	12.6
Dividends/Share %	10.0	9.1	16.7	14.3

Danaher's industries tend to be slow-growing, so most growth has come from acquisitions, not unlike Illinois Tool Works ITW. The company expects its internal growth and acquisition activities to double revenue within four years.

Profitability [A]	1999	2000	2001	TTM
Return on Assets %	8.6	8.0	6.2	2.7
Oper Cash Flow $Mil	419	512	608	744
- Cap Spending $Mil	89	89	81	66
= Free Cash Flow $Mil	330	424	528	678

Excellent returns on equity and invested capital illustrate that Danaher's disciplined management approach creates value for shareholders. However, economic weakness finally started to pressure margins in 2002.

Financial Health [A+]	1999	2000	2001	09-02
Long-term Debt $Mil	341	714	1,119	1,143
Total Equity $Mil	1,709	1,942	2,229	2,884
Debt/Equity Ratio	0.2	0.4	0.5	0.4

The company is highly disciplined regarding capital usage. It works hard to minimize reinvestment in existing businesses, which leads to strong free cash flow. A low debt load probably indicates that more large acquisitions are ahead.

Industry	Investment Style	Stock Type	Sector
Electric Equipment	▦ Large Growth	↻ Cyclical	✿ Industrial Mats

Competition	Market Cap $Mil	Debt/ Equity	12 Mo Trailing Sales $Mil	Price/Cash Flow	Return On Assets%	Total Return% 1 Yr	3 Yr
Danaher	10,013	0.4	4,221	13.5	2.7	9.1	13.8
Tyco International	34,082	0.7	35,773	4.8	-14.2	-70.9	-22.1
Emerson Electric	21,411	0.5	13,838	11.8	0.8	-8.3	-1.1

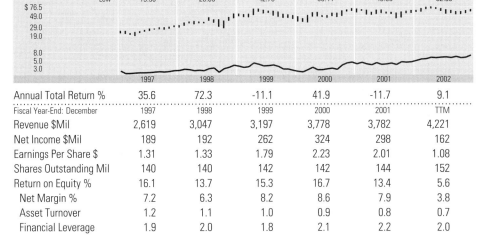

Price Volatility   ▌Monthly Price High/Low   — Relative Strength to S&P 500

Annual $Price High Low	32.00 19.50	55.25 28.00	69.00 42.75	69.75 36.44	68.69 43.90	75.46 52.60
	1997	1998	1999	2000	2001	2002

Annual Total Return %	35.6	72.3	-11.1	41.9	-11.7	9.1
Fiscal Year-End: December	1997	1998	1999	2000	2001	TTM
Revenue $Mil	2,619	3,047	3,197	3,778	3,782	4,221
Net Income $Mil	189	192	262	324	298	162
Earnings Per Share $	1.31	1.33	1.79	2.23	2.01	1.08
Shares Outstanding Mil	140	140	142	142	144	152
Return on Equity %	16.1	13.7	15.3	16.7	13.4	5.6
Net Margin %	7.2	6.3	8.2	8.6	7.9	3.8
Asset Turnover	1.2	1.1	1.0	0.9	0.8	0.7
Financial Leverage	1.9	2.0	1.8	2.1	2.2	2.0

Valuation Ratios	Stock	Rel to Industry	Rel to S&P 500
Price/Earnings	60.8	3.7	2.6
Price/Book	3.5	0.9	1.1
Price/Sales	2.4	1.3	1.2
Price/Cash Flow	13.5	1.6	1.0

Major Fund Holders	% of Fund Assets
Fidelity Select Construction&Housing	4.37
Delaware Core Equity A	3.21
Alliance Growth B	2.84
Neuberger Berman Socially Resp Inv	2.81

Morningstar's Take By Josh Peters, 12-10-2002 Stock Price as of Analysis: $61.74

Industrial conglomerates have become unpopular, but Danaher has a formula for making its whole worth more than the sum of its purchased parts. In our view, this stock is worth buying in the low $50s.

Most serial acquisitors--particularly those of the Tyco model--don't add much value to the firms they buy. Danaher goes after businesses with dominant products in niche fields, but specifically those lacking the talent to manufacture their products efficiently. To such businesses Danaher adds its Danaher Business System, a discipline based on Toyota's legendary practices. DBS strips waste--excess inventory, excess labor, wasted floor space--from the manufacturing process and imposes a culture of continuous improvement that keeps operations lean over the long run.

Danaher has made its model even better by adding more growth to the portfolio. The company's most recognizable business--hand tools--is decidedly low-tech and low-growth. In 1995, the tools and components segment was twice the size of process/environmental controls; now, the reverse is true. Operations like Gilbarco and Veeder-Root (petroleum-handling equipment), Hach (water-testing equipment), and Fluke (network test gear) sell to markets with strong long-term internal growth

prospects: mid- to high-single-digit annual growth, in our estimation, compared with the low to nonexistent growth of more mature industrial markets.

Danaher puts more distance between itself and the conglomerate pack with a pristine balance sheet and remarkably consistent cash flows. Even though the industrial economy has been hurting for three years, the company's operating margins have remained strong.

The economy is a wet blanket on the firm's near-term outlook, with industrial spending likely to remain depressed. With the high expectations (and a similarly lofty P/E) that Danaher has bred over the years, a bungled acquisition is also a threat.

Mitigating these fears are Danaher's tough acquisition standards (it passed on Cooper Industries in 2001 because of an asbestos taint) and a very strong management team. Acquisitors have become frequent targets of accounting criticism, but the fact that founders Steve and Mitchell Rales still hold 23% of the shares gives us extra confidence in the firm's practices. The economy is a wild card and we're sensitive to the shares' valuation, but on the merits of the business alone, Danaher is our top industrial pick.

  M⊙RNINGSTAR® Stocks 500

Deere & Company DE

	Rating	Risk	Moat Size	Fair Value	Last Close	Yield %
	★	Med.	Narrow	$38.00	$45.85	1.9

Company Profile

Deere & Company manufactures agricultural, industrial, and lawn-care equipment. The company's products include tractors, harvesters, sprayers, soil-preparation machinery, riding and walk-behind mowers, snowblowers, leaf blowers, excavators, loaders, diesel engines, utility-transport vehicles, and machinery components. Its primary industrial machine products include construction, earthmoving, and forestry equipment, and cranes and trucks. Deere & Company's credit subsidiaries provide financing services for businesses and consumers in the United States and abroad.

Management

Robert Lane became chairman and CEO in 2000 after longtime head Hans Becherer retired. Lane has been with Deere since 1982, following a stint with First National Bank. Directors and officers own less than 1% of the shares outstanding.

Strategy

Deere still depends on agriculture, and the firm aims to improve performance throughout the cycles of this business by increasing asset efficiency and keeping a tight rein on costs and inventories. Deere is also expanding its presence in landscaping and lawn-care via acquisition. Heavy investment in new product development is a priority.

One John Deere Place
Moline, IL 61265

www.deere.com

Morningstar Grades

Growth [B]	1999	2000	2001	2002
Revenue %	-15.0	11.8	1.2	4.9
Earnings/Share %	-75.5	102.0	NMF	NMF
Book Value/Share %	5.1	4.5	-7.7	-21.7
Dividends/Share %	0.0	0.0	0.0	0.0

When times are good in agriculture, growth can be impressive. Equipment sales rose a healthy 13% annually between 1992 and 1998. Sales declined sharply in 1999, though, and Deere has yet to eclipse 1998's record sales, despite recent acquisitions.

Profitability [C]	2000	2001	2002	TTM
Return on Assets %	2.4	-0.3	1.3	1.3
Oper Cash Flow $Mil	1,080	1,113	1,878	1,878
- Cap Spending $Mil	427	491	359	359
= Free Cash Flow $Mil	653	622	1,520	1,520

When agricultural equipment sales were hot in the mid- to late 1990s, profitability was solid, and operating margins exceeded 12%. Returns have been poor since, though, and the firm has failed to earn its cost of capital over the past four years.

Financial Health [B-]	2000	2001	2002	10-02
Long-term Debt $Mil	4,764	6,561	8,950	8,950
Total Equity $Mil	4,302	3,992	3,163	3,163
Debt/Equity Ratio	1.1	1.6	2.8	2.8

Deere is working to improve asset efficiency on the equipment side; this and rising demand have helped cash flow. Manufacturing debt, which excludes debt on the financing side, has risen recently, but is offset by a large cash position.

	Industry	Investment Style	Stock Type	Sector
	Agricultural Machinery	Large Core	Cyclical	Industrial Mats

Competition

	Market Cap $Mil	Debt/ Equity	12 Mo Trailing Sales $Mil	Price/Cash Flow	Return On Assets%	Total Return% 1 Yr	Total Return% 3 Yr
Deere & Company	10,970	2.8	13,947	5.8	1.3	7.1	4.6
Caterpillar	15,736	2.1	19,871	8.5	2.0	-9.8	1.6
Kubota ADR	3,736	—	7,611	—	—	—	—

Price Volatility

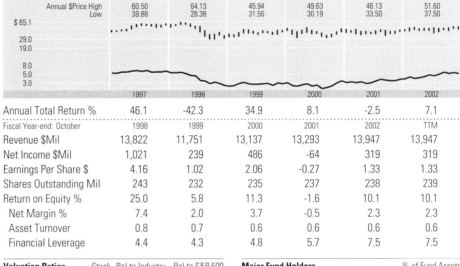

	Monthly Price High/Low		Relative Strength to S&P 500

	1997	1998	1999	2000	2001	2002
Annual $Price High	60.50	64.13	45.94	49.63	46.13	51.60
Low	39.88	28.38	31.56	30.19	33.50	37.50
Annual Total Return %	46.1	-42.3	34.9	8.1	-2.5	7.1

Fiscal Year-end: October	1998	1999	2000	2001	2002	TTM
Revenue $Mil	13,822	11,751	13,137	13,293	13,947	13,947
Net Income $Mil	1,021	239	486	-64	319	319
Earnings Per Share $	4.16	1.02	2.06	-0.27	1.33	1.33
Shares Outstanding Mil	243	232	235	237	238	239
Return on Equity %	25.0	5.8	11.3	-1.6	10.1	10.1
Net Margin %	7.4	2.0	3.7	-0.5	2.3	2.3
Asset Turnover	0.8	0.7	0.6	0.6	0.6	0.6
Financial Leverage	4.4	4.3	4.8	5.7	7.5	7.5

Valuation Ratios	Stock	Rel to Industry	Rel to S&P 500
Price/Earnings	34.5	1.0	1.5
Price/Book	3.5	1.0	1.1
Price/Sales	0.8	1.0	0.4
Price/Cash Flow	5.8	1.0	0.4

Major Fund Holders	% of Fund Assets
ARK Social Issues Capital Growth Inst	3.95
CDC Nvest Jurika & Voyles Rel Val Y	3.89
Capital Management Mid-Cap Instl	3.56
TCW Galileo Diversified Value N	3.30

Morningstar's Take By Michael Hodel, 10-18-2002 Stock Price as of Analysis: $47.25

Deere dominates agricultural equipment, but we don't think the stock is attractive right now.

Deere's profits, and its stock price, are still tied to the cyclical ag equipment market. The need to replace old, inefficient equipment drives demand, especially in the mature U.S. and European markets. The timing of this replacement cycle takes its cue from current and prospective farm income, which depends largely on government aid and the price of commodities like corn. During 1997 and 1998, a great time for equipment demand, Deere's ag business drove operating income sharply higher, taking the stock price up as well. With a ton of new equipment recently hitting the soil and commodity prices relatively low, demand--and Deere's profits and stock price--have yet to return to levels seen during those years.

Deere is well positioned in the ag industry. The firm's two primary competitors, Agco and CNH Global, are amalgamations of brand names, many of which have changed hands or restructured repeatedly over the years. The Deere brand, on the other hand, has weathered the industry's darkest days, giving it a continuity that has left the company with the strongest operations and financial position in the business and a solid dealer network. Deere's

operating margins at the top of the cycle were a full 5 percentage points higher than its closest competitor's. Deere's ability to spend on product development and new equipment outstrips that of rivals, helping the firm launch several new products recently.

Deere's other equipment operations aren't as well positioned, in our view. Its commercial and consumer division has exited the unprofitable handheld equipment business, but continues to operate at a loss. Weak demand has also pushed the construction and forestry equipment segment into the red. These businesses compete with entrenched firms like Toro and Caterpillar. The consumer business also sells to large retailers, like Home Depot, which are capable of extracting large discounts. These businesses have provided little to offset the currently weak ag business: Deere hasn't earned its cost of capital in four years.

Deere is working to cut costs and reduce inventories in an effort to boost returns throughout the ag cycle. Thus far, though, we haven't seen much improvement. Until Deere can earn a more consistent return on investment, we'd require a hefty discount to our fair value estimate before getting excited about the stock.

Dell Computer DELL

	Rating	Risk	Moat Size	Fair Value	Last Close	Yield %
	★★★	Med.	Wide	$28.00	$26.74	0.0

Company Profile

Dell Computer manufactures computer systems. The company markets its products directly to its customers, which include corporate, government, and education accounts, as well as small businesses and individuals. Dell Computer also sells its products through mass merchants and over the Internet. In addition to computer systems, the company produces network-storage and -server products, software, peripherals, and service and support programs. Dell Computer markets its products in the United States and overseas. Foreign sales account for about 33% of the company's total sales.

Management

Michael Dell built this firm from the ground up and, in many ways, wrote the book on how to run a PC company. He currently owns about 12% of Dell; his stake has decreased over the past year.

Strategy

Dell's direct-sales build-to-order strategy keeps costs and working-capital requirements low, even during periods of rapid growth. We expect the firm to increase its foreign sales and focus on expanding further into server and storage products. Dell is eyeing a move into the printer and handheld organizer markets, as well as a further push into services to support its enterprise hardware business.

One Dell Way   www.dell.com
Round Rock, TX 78682

Industry	Investment Style	Stock Type	Sector
Computer Equipment	▦ Large Growth	⬈ Classic Growth	◪ Hardware

Competition

	Market Cap $Mil	Debt/ Equity	12 Mo Trailing Sales $Mil	Price/Cash Flow	Return On Assets%	Total Return% 1 Yr	3 Yr
Dell Computer	68,968	0.1	33,730	20.1	13.4	-1.6	-16.9
IBM	130,982	0.8	82,442	9.0	5.8	-35.5	-11.1
Hewlett-Packard	34,321	0.3	—	6.1	-3.5	-13.9	-24.7

Price Volatility

Price Volatility	▮ Monthly Price High/Low	— Relative Strength to S&P 500

Annual $Price High / Low	12.99 / 3.12	37.91 / 9.92	55.00 / 31.38	59.69 / 16.25	31.32 / 16.01	31.06 / 21.90

	1997	1998	1999	2000	2001	2002
Annual Total Return %	216.2	248.5	39.4	-65.8	55.9	-1.6

Fiscal Year-End: January	1998	1999	2000	2001	2002	TTM
Revenue $Mil	12,327	18,243	25,265	31,888	31,168	33,730
Net Income $Mil	944	1,460	1,666	2,177	1,246	1,975
Earnings Per Share $	0.32	0.53	0.61	0.79	0.46	0.74
Shares Outstanding Mil	2,622	2,517	2,524	2,592	2,596	2,579
Return on Equity %	73.0	62.9	31.4	38.7	26.5	42.5
Net Margin %	7.7	8.0	6.6	6.8	4.0	5.9
Asset Turnover	2.9	2.7	2.2	2.3	2.3	2.3
Financial Leverage	3.3	3.0	2.2	2.4	2.9	3.2

Valuation Ratios	Stock	Rel to Industry	Rel to S&P 500
Price/Earnings	36.1	1.3	1.5
Price/Book	14.8	2.5	4.6
Price/Sales	2.0	1.3	1.0
Price/Cash Flow	20.1	2.2	1.5

Major Fund Holders	% of Fund Assets
Alliance Select Investor Technology A	8.74
Credit Suisse Glb New Technology Comm	7.65
Northern Technology	7.48
Smith Barney Technology A	7.03

Morningstar Grades

Growth [A]	1999	2000	2001	2002
Revenue %	48.0	38.5	26.2	-2.3
Earnings/Share %	65.6	15.1	29.5	-41.8
Book Value/Share %	92.2	130.7	5.0	-15.1
Dividends/Share %	NMF	NMF	NMF	NMF

Growth has held up fairly well, but is still losing steam because of the company's size and the PC market's maturity. Dell expects to partially make up for slower PC sales growth through overseas growth and a push to higher-end products.

Profitability [A+]	2000	2001	2002	TTM
Return on Assets %	14.5	15.9	9.2	13.4
Oper Cash Flow $Mil	3,926	4,195	3,797	3,434
- Cap Spending $Mil	401	482	303	313
= Free Cash Flow $Mil	3,525	3,713	3,494	3,121

In a cutthroat industry, Dell's overall cost structure is lower than its peers', providing a huge competitive advantage. Even in a weak-demand environment, Dell is still generating lots of cash.

Financial Health [B+]	2000	2001	2002	10-02
Long-term Debt $Mil	508	509	520	514
Total Equity $Mil	5,308	5,622	4,694	4,648
Debt/Equity Ratio	0.1	0.1	0.1	0.1

Dell's balance sheet is rock-solid, with $4 billion in cash, $4.7 billion in long-term investments, and just over half a billion dollars in long-term debt.

Morningstar's Take By Joseph Beaulieu, 11-18-2002   Stock Price as of Analysis: $28.92

Dell is one of the few computer hardware companies that we would be enthusiastic about owning--at the right price.

Having achieved near-total domination of the PC market--forcing Compaq to merge with competitor Hewlett-Packard, and driving Gateway deep into the red--Dell is moving further into enterprise hardware and eyeing the printer and handheld organizer markets.

Dell's dominance of the PC market is based primarily on the company's build-to-order direct-sales business model. Dell doesn't have to worry about sharing profits with retailers, getting stuck with rapidly depreciating inventories, or supporting a chain of retail stores. This means Dell can profitably sell a personal computer for a lower price than its competitors can.

Dell's not sacrificing profitability to push products, though. In fact, the firm has continued to improve both gross and operating margins while increasing unit volume and revenue in a tough environment.

Growth hasn't slowed as much as we had expected, thanks to market share gains, but we still expect a gradual slowdown. The company's ability to generate substantial revenue growth will depend on its ability to gain share in the enterprise hardware

business. Dell continues to make big advances at the low end of this market (and perhaps a bit into the midrange), but we think it is going to have a harder time pushing past that.

Midrange to high-end enterprise hardware isn't the commodity that PCs and low-end servers are, and price is not the sole focus of competition. Therefore, Dell is going to have to develop more expertise in selling these products (which it is doing in storage as a part of its partnership with EMC), or work toward commodifying the midrange.

In the absence of enterprise hardware market gains, we think Dell would be worth about $21 per share. However, we believe Dell can gain substantial share in the low end and midrange of the enterprise hardware market, and this assumption brings us to a fair value estimate of $28.

Dell's business model and strong management team provide the company with a wide economic moat. While the cyclicality of the IT industry carries risks of its own, Dell's enormous cash flows and strong balance sheet help mitigate those risks. We would therefore consider buying the shares if they traded 10% below our fair value estimate, but we wouldn't deem them a true bargain until they hit a 20% discount.

MORNINGSTAR® Stocks 500

Delphi DPH

	Rating	Risk	Moat Size	Fair Value	Last Close	Yield %
	★★★	Med.	None	$12.00	$8.05	3.5

Company Profile

Delphi manufactures automotive components. Its products include audio systems, powertrain and engine-control modules, collision-warning and security systems, and antilock-brake controllers. In addition, the company produces door modules, airbag systems, power sliding doors, and climate-control, brake, steering, and lighting systems. Delphi sells its products in the United States and overseas. It was spun off from General Motors in February 1999; sales to GM currently account for about two thirds of Delphi's revenue.

Management

Chairman and CEO J.T. Battenberg, 59, spent 41 years with GM before the spin-off, but isn't saddled with a business-as-usual approach. He aims to remake Delphi into a high-tech company with interests beyond the automotive industry.

Strategy

Delphi Automotive is making the best of its independence from GM to create a less cyclical, more innovative business model. The company is aggressively pursuing business beyond GM and offering auto components and electronic enhancements that carry higher profit margins. It has also shed many underperforming operations, enhancing profitability and reducing fixed costs.

5725 Delphi Drive
Troy, MI 48098

www.delphiauto.com

Morningstar Grades

Growth [C-]	1998	1999	2000	2001
Revenue %	-9.4	2.5	-0.2	-10.5
Earnings/Share %	NMF	NMF	NMF	NMF
Book Value/Share %	—	—	NMF	-38.1
Dividends/Share %	NMF	NMF	33.3	0.0

Rebounding auto production has blessed Delphi with a more favorable revenue outlook this year. However, as divestitures and product line shutdowns continue, we expect little growth until 2005.

Profitability [C-]	1999	2000	2001	TTM
Return on Assets %	5.9	5.7	-2.0	0.5
Oper Cash Flow $Mil	-1,214	268	1,360	1,172
- Cap Spending $Mil	1,200	1,272	1,057	1,033
= Free Cash Flow $Mil	-2,414	-1,004	303	139

Delphi's operating margins have stabilized this year, as growth in non-GM sales and higher GM production volume boosted capacity utilization. However, without an industry rebound, we can't expect much additional improvement.

Financial Health [C]	1999	2000	2001	09-02
Long-term Debt $Mil	1,640	1,623	2,083	2,062
Total Equity $Mil	3,200	3,766	2,312	2,352
Debt/Equity Ratio	0.5	0.4	0.9	0.9

Delphi's debt/capital ratio is now 60%--double the post-spin-off leverage. Cash flows have been generally quite strong (seven straight quarters of positive free cash flow), though most of this cash has gone to settle various legacy costs.

	Industry	Investment Style	Stock Type	Sector
	Auto Parts	▦ Mid Value	📈 High Yield	🚗 Consumer Goods

Competition

	Market Cap $Mil	Debt/ Equity	12 Mo Trailing Sales $Mil	Price/Cash Flow	Return On Assets%	Total Return% 1 Yr	3 Yr
Delphi	4,495	0.9	26,836	3.8	0.5	-39.6	-16.6
Johnson Controls	7,117	0.5	20,103	7.2	5.3	0.9	17.0
Dana	1,747	2.0	10,472	2.7	-4.7	-15.1	-23.1

Price Volatility

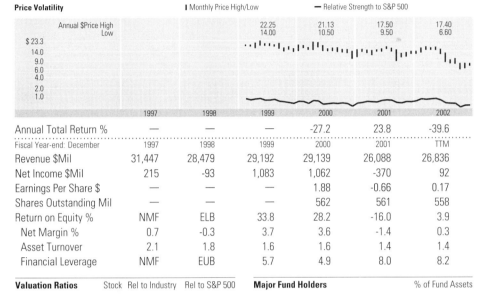

Annual Total Return %	—	—	—	-27.2	23.8	-39.6
Fiscal Year-end: December	1997	1998	1999	2000	2001	TTM
Revenue $Mil	31,447	28,479	29,192	29,139	26,088	26,836
Net Income $Mil	215	-93	1,083	1,062	-370	92
Earnings Per Share $	—	—	—	1.88	-0.66	0.17
Shares Outstanding Mil	—	—	—	562	561	558
Return on Equity %	NMF	ELB	33.8	28.2	-16.0	3.9
Net Margin %	0.7	-0.3	3.7	3.6	-1.4	0.3
Asset Turnover	2.1	1.8	1.6	1.6	1.4	1.4
Financial Leverage	NMF	EUB	5.7	4.9	8.0	8.2

Valuation Ratios	Stock	Rel to Industry	Rel to S&P 500
Price/Earnings	47.4	3.8	2.0
Price/Book	1.9	0.1	0.6
Price/Sales	0.2	0.0	0.1
Price/Cash Flow	3.8	0.1	0.3

Major Fund Holders	% of Fund Assets
Fidelity Select Automotive	5.51
Transamerica Premier Core Equity Inv	3.62
Transamerica Premier Balanced Inv	2.96
New Alternatives	2.72

Morningstar's Take By Josh Peters, 12-02-2002 Stock Price as of Analysis: $8.50

Delphi faces big opportunities and big challenges. The next few years could be rough, so we'd consider the stock only at an attractive discount to our fair value estimate--$6 or thereabouts.

It's bad enough that Delphi wrestles with the same stagnant-to-declining global auto production and relentless price pressure that all suppliers face, but it also bears special burdens related to its former life as General Motors' in-house parts operation. Delphi's U.S. workforce is covered by UAW contracts (similar to GM's) that restrict its efforts to reduce fixed costs. GM also stuck Delphi with the pension and postretirement health-care liabilities for these employees--the funding costs of which are beginning to skyrocket.

These legacy costs are likely to strip shareholders of an impressive amount of value in coming years. Unless the financial markets stage a miraculous recovery, Delphi's pension deficit of $2.4 billion at year-end 2001 is likely to exceed $3 billion by year-end 2002. Because of government funding requirements, the pension could sap $1-$2 billion from the firm's free cash flow by middecade. Future retiree health-care costs (with a present value of $5.4 billion) will require far smaller cash payments in the next few years, but rampant health-care inflation

means this liability could swallow Delphi's equity if not brought under control.

But all is not lost for Delphi. By virtue of its size and a deliberate focus on electronics, the company is a technological powerhouse. Its 2001 spending on research and development ($1.7 billion) was equal to that of the next three largest suppliers combined. This investment is yielding proprietary technologies for key business areas, like steering (Quadrasteer), and engine management (common-rail diesel systems) and entertainment (XM Satellite Radio receivers). We view this as crucial, giving Delphi a sense of purpose that many suppliers lack.

These innovations are leading to impressive growth in Delphi's non-GM business, which has expanded more than 50% since the spin-off and should continue growing at double-digit rates for several more years to come. In contrast to the GM days, when it was little more than captive manufacturing capacity, Delphi is winning new customers with the best technology, cost, and quality.

Delphi still has to contend with a shrinking base of GM revenue and substantial legacy claims on its cash flows. We'd thus require a 50% or greater discount to our fair value estimate before considering the stock for purchase.

Delta Air Lines DAL

	Rating	Risk	Moat Size	Fair Value	Last Close	Yield %
	UR	High	None	UR	$12.10	0.8

Company Profile

Delta Air Lines offers passenger and freight air-transportation services. It provides flights to 205 U.S. cities in 45 states, the District of Columbia, Puerto Rico, and the U.S. Virgin Islands; the airline also has service to 44 cities in 28 countries. Passenger transportation generates about 91% of the airline's total revenue. International passenger transportation makes up 19% of total revenue. The airline's hubs include Atlanta, Dallas-Fort Worth, Los Angeles, and Frankfurt, Germany. The company acquired Comair Holdings in January 2000.

Management

Chairman and CEO Leo Mullin has held the top post since 1997. Mullin, the management team, and the company have garnered well-earned recognition for their efforts to improve Delta's financial performance.

Strategy

To counter the weak pricing environment, Delta is focusing on keeping costs as low as possible in order to stem the cash drain. The airline has cut staff and flights and has taken on a new regional jet partner to take advantage of its lower cost structure.

Hartsfield Atlanta International Airport   www.delta-air.com
Atlanta, GA 30320

Morningstar Grades

Growth [D]	1998	1999	2000	2001
Revenue %	3.2	4.0	12.5	-17.1
Earnings/Share %	14.1	18.6	-22.9	NMF
Book Value/Share %	18.3	27.4	23.1	-25.6
Dividends/Share %	0.0	0.0	0.0	0.0

Delta is the third-largest airline in terms of revenue, yet it has managed to post decent growth compared with its biggest competitors. However, revenue performance will probably remain very weak over the next few quarters.

Profitability [B]	1999	2000	2001	TTM
Return on Assets %	6.0	3.7	-5.2	-6.9
Oper Cash Flow $Mil	2,647	2,898	236	-290
- Cap Spending $Mil	3,055	4,060	2,793	1,731
= Free Cash Flow $Mil	-408	-1,162	-2,557	-2,021

In general, Delta is more profitable than its rivals, particularly American AMR and United UAL. However, we don't expect the airline to turn a yearly profit until 2004.

Financial Health [C]	1999	2000	2001	09-02
Long-term Debt $Mil	4,144	5,896	8,347	9,214
Total Equity $Mil	4,908	5,343	3,769	2,845
Debt/Equity Ratio	0.8	1.1	2.2	3.2

The company has taken on additional debt to keep the planes flying, to the point that 85% of its capital is debt. It will be years before it can dig out of this financial hole.

Industry	Investment Style	Stock Type	Sector
Air Transport	▦ Mid Value	→ Slow Growth	▤ Business Services

Competition

	Market Cap $Mil	Debt/ Equity	12 Mo Trailing Sales $Mil	Price/Cash Flow	Return On Assets%	Total Return% 1 Yr	3 Yr
Delta Air Lines	1,493	3.2	12,860	—	-6.9	-58.4	-37.0
Southwest Airlines	10,768	0.4	5,359	16.8	2.9	-24.7	10.7
AMR	1,030	4.8	16,913	—	-12.0	-70.4	-38.1

Price Volatility

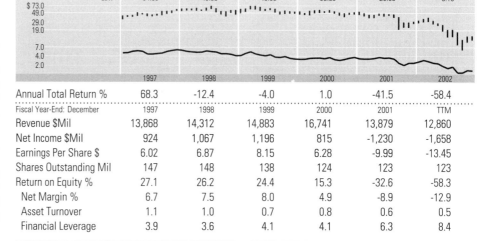

		Monthly Price High/Low			— Relative Strength to S&P 500	
Annual $Price High Low	60.31 34.63	71.81 40.88	72.00 45.69	58.31 39.63	52.94 20.00	38.69 6.10

	1997	1998	1999	2000	2001	2002
Annual Total Return %	68.3	-12.4	-4.0	1.0	-41.5	-58.4

Fiscal Year-End: December	1997	1998	1999	2000	2001	TTM
Revenue $Mil	13,868	14,312	14,883	16,741	13,879	12,860
Net Income $Mil	924	1,067	1,196	815	-1,230	-1,658
Earnings Per Share $	6.02	6.87	8.15	6.28	-9.99	-13.45
Shares Outstanding Mil	147	148	138	124	123	123
Return on Equity %	27.1	26.2	24.4	15.3	-32.6	-58.3
Net Margin %	6.7	7.5	8.0	4.9	-8.9	-12.9
Asset Turnover	1.1	1.0	0.7	0.8	0.6	0.5
Financial Leverage	3.9	3.6	4.1	4.1	6.3	8.4

Valuation Ratios	Stock	Rel to Industry	Rel to S&P 500
Price/Earnings	NMF	—	—
Price/Book	0.5	0.2	0.2
Price/Sales	0.1	0.1	0.1
Price/Cash Flow	—	—	—

Major Fund Holders	% of Fund Assets
Fidelity Select Air Transportation	6.73
Fidelity Select Transportation	1.98
ING Midcap Value A	1.89
DLB Value	1.70

Morningstar's Take By Nicolas Owens, 11-19-2002 Stock Price as of Analysis: $11.17

Given the unsustainable nature of Delta's current business model, we don't see any good reason to invest in the shares.

One of our concerns is that Delta's strategy is not viable over the long term. Generally speaking, a company can pursue one of two strategies. The first is to offer a differentiated product for which customers are willing to pay a premium. The other approach is to be the low-cost provider in a particular market. Delta seems undecided--somewhere in between--in a market that does not allow for much differentiation or tolerate a slack cost structure. Competition in the airline industry revolves largely around price, making air travel a commodity. The success of Southwest over the years has been based on the carrier's low cost structure, which allows it to charge less than its competition, profitably. The fact that Delta's unit costs are 40% higher than Southwest's--and 6% higher than the industry average--leaves Delta at a disadvantage in such a tight-margin business.

Another issue that we have with Delta is the volatility of its operating results. Because of the company's dependence on business travelers, earnings are very sensitive to the business cycle. In 1999, Delta made $1 billion in profit on almost $15 billion in sales. In 2000, it made $800 million on $17 billion in sales. Last year, it lost $1.25 billion on $14 billion in sales. This continues a pattern of large profits and losses in the industry that has persisted in every decade since the 1940s. Since deregulation in 1978, airlines have lost an aggregate $8.5 billion. Given the current structure of the industry, we don't see this pattern ending anytime soon.

But we think the most pressing reason to avoid investing in Delta--and most of its rivals--is the leverage. Delta has a lot of operating leverage, which basically means that the company has high fixed costs. This is a very good thing when business is booming, but it has the opposite effect when business is in the dumps. More important, the firm has taken on loads of new debt to buy newer, more efficient aircraft. Recently, Delta has even used this debt to fund losses in its operations. The result of this financial leverage is to exacerbate the poor operating performance of the airline, resulting in enormous net losses.

Most airline stocks--including Delta--are bad long-term investments. Wild swings in share price can make for tempting speculative trades, but over the long haul airlines have a terrible record for shareholders, and this isn't about to change.

MORNINGSTAR® Stocks 500

Data as of 12-31-02

Deutsche Bank AG DB

	Rating ★★★	Risk Med.	Moat Size None	Fair Value $57.00	Last Close $45.43	Yield % 2.6

Company Profile

Deutsche Bank AG is the largest bank in the European euro zone, with more than 93,000 employees in 60 countries. It offers an array of financial services, including traditional banking, online banking, and investment banking. It has been building up its investment banking division through acquisitions; during the past decade, it acquired Morgan Grenfell in the United Kingdom and Bankers Trust and Alex. Brown in the United States. It boosted its U.S. retail presence by acquiring online broker National Discount Brokers.

Management

Josef Ackermann came from the investment banking division to take the top spot at Deutsche Bank in the second quarter of 2002. Former CEO Rolf Breuer remains as chairman of the board.

Strategy

Deutsche Bank, Germany's largest bank, aims to be a world-leading financial services provider. Its strategy mandates aggressive cost-cutting and staff reductions to trim its bloated expense base. The firm is divesting itself of noncore businesses, including insurance and securities services, and focusing on its eight core businesses, including asset management and investment banking.

Taunusanlage 12
Frankfurt, 60262
www.deutsche-bank.de

Morningstar Grades

Growth [C]	1998	1999	2000	2001
Revenue %	-4.1	49.2	39.9	-15.9
Earnings/Share %	-76.8	407.4	692.7	-98.8
Book Value/Share %	17.2	6.6	27.8	-7.5
Dividends/Share %	0.0	21.7	2.7	13.0

Net revenue grew at a compound annual rate of 21% over the past three years, with most of that coming from a series of acquisitions. Net revenue fell 5% in the first half of 2002, hurt by the ailing economy.

Profitability [F]	1999	2000	2001	TTM
Return on Assets %	0.2	1.4	0.0	0.0
Oper Cash Flow $Mil	-8,661	-30,969	-11,781	—
- Cap Spending $Mil	3,565	2,010	3,290	—
= Free Cash Flow $Mil	—	—	—	—

Measures of profitability for this bank are miserable. Its five-year return on assets is a third of the banking industry average. Its 2001 efficiency ratio (operating expenses as a percentage of net revenue) of 87% is ridiculously high compared with its peers'.

Financial Health [B]	1999	2000	2001	12-01
Long-term Debt $Mil	—	—	—	—
Total Equity $Mil	32,351	41,210	35,569	35,569
Debt/Equity Ratio	—	—	—	—

Deutsche Bank deserves this poor grade. Financial leverage is far higher than that of its peers at 23 times equity. And excessive leverage has not translated into profitability; the bank's return on equity is well below the industry average.

Industry International Banks	Investment Style ▦ Large Value	Stock Type ⤢ Classic Growth	Sector 🛢 Financial Services

Competition	Market Cap $Mil	Debt/ Equity	12 Mo Trailing Sales $Mil	Price/Cash Flow	Return On Assets%	Total Return% 1 Yr	Total Return% 3 Yr
Deutsche Bank AG	27,916	—	25,501	—	0.0	-35.2	-17.2
Citigroup	177,948	—	106,096	—	1.6	-24.2	1.1
HSBC Holdings PLC ADR	101,913	—	49,861	—	—	—	—

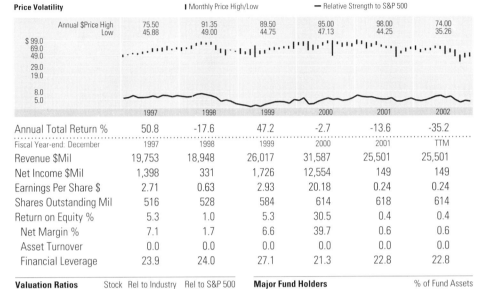

Price Volatility		Monthly Price High/Low		— Relative Strength to S&P 500		
Annual $Price High	75.50	91.35	89.50	95.00	98.00	74.00
Low	45.88	49.00	44.75	47.13	44.25	35.26
	1997	1998	1999	2000	2001	2002

	1997	1998	1999	2000	2001	2002
Annual Total Return %	50.8	-17.6	47.2	-2.7	-13.6	-35.2

Fiscal Year-end: December	1997	1998	1999	2000	2001	TTM
Revenue $Mil	19,753	18,948	26,017	31,587	25,501	25,501
Net Income $Mil	1,398	331	1,726	12,554	149	149
Earnings Per Share $	2.71	0.63	2.93	20.18	0.24	0.24
Shares Outstanding Mil	516	528	584	614	618	614
Return on Equity %	5.3	1.0	5.3	30.5	0.4	0.4
Net Margin %	7.1	1.7	6.6	39.7	0.6	0.6
Asset Turnover	0.0	0.0	0.0	0.0	0.0	0.0
Financial Leverage	23.9	24.0	27.1	21.3	22.8	22.8

Valuation Ratios	Stock	Rel to Industry	Rel to S&P 500
Price/Earnings	188.5	14.8	8.0
Price/Book	0.8	0.4	0.2
Price/Sales	1.1	0.7	0.5
Price/Cash Flow	—	—	—

Major Fund Holders	% of Fund Assets
TCW Galileo Select Intl Eq I	2.34
AXP European Equity A	2.00
Nuveen International Growth R	1.73

Morningstar's Take By Rachel Barnard, 09-06-2002 Stock Price as of Analysis: $59.50

By international standards, Deutsche Bank is a mess. Though its program of reform looks promising, we'd steer clear of this bank at the current price.

Deutsche Bank is embarking on an ambitious course of cost-cutting and reorganization, which it desperately needs. While Deutsche may be in the big leagues in terms of size, its profitability scores make it a long-shot for the pee-wee league. Return on equity, a major indicator of banking profitability, has languished around 4% or worse over the past five years. Compare this with major competitor Citigroup, whose ROE topped 17%. Deutsche Bank's efficiency ratio in 2001 indicates that 87% of net revenue went to pay operating expenses, a higher proportion than any U.S. bank. The upshot is that Deutsche Bank is making very little hay with its considerable resources.

Enter Josef Ackermann and his iron determination to turn the business around. He took the helm in early 2002 while the bank was already struggling to meet its target of cutting $2 billion in costs by the end of 2003. He announced further reductions in June, bringing the job-cutting target to 3,770, not including the 1,500 jobs that will go as a result of integrating investment firm Scudder and 1,000 more from IT outsourcing. If these ambitious goals are met, the cuts will go a long way toward reducing Deutsche's bloated cost structure and boosting profitability. However, it may be some time before this program is fully implemented; European labor laws make it difficult and expensive to cut staff.

Deutsche has also begun a major reorganization. The plan is to focus on the bank's eight core businesses: global markets, global equities, global corporate finance, global transaction banking, asset management, private wealth management, private and business clients, and corporate investments. This basically boils down to corporate banking and asset management, two areas that have proved lucrative in the past. Deutsche Bank is therefore looking to divest itself of its other "noncore" businesses, which include insurance, securities services, and French branch banking. The bank has started executing on this plan. It sold its insurance business to Zurich in 2001 and its custody assets are on the block. The bank is also seeking buyers for around 60% of its private equity portfolio.

We are big fans of these restructuring plans, but our outlook is still cautious. This type of major surgery--while necessary--will be difficult and painful for Deutsche Bank, not to mention costly. For now, we would steer clear of the shares.

Diageo PLC ADR DEO

	Rating	Risk	Moat Size	Fair Value	Last Close	Yield %
	★★★	Low	Narrow	$47.00	$43.80	3.3

Company Profile

Diageo produces alcoholic beverages and operates restaurants. Its beverage brand-name products include Guinness and Harp beers, Tanqueray and Gordon's gins, Bailey's Original Irish Cream liqueur, and Johnnie Walker scotch. The company also operates about 10,500 Burger King fast-food restaurants in the U.S. and abroad. It sold its Pillsbury food unit to General Mills in October 2001.

Management

Paul Walsh has been CEO since September 2000, after a decade of running the Pillsbury division.

Strategy

Having sold Pillsbury to General Mills and Burger King to a group of three private equity firms led by Texas Pacific Group, Diageo has completed its transformation from a sluggish conglomerate into a streamlined spirits-marketing machine. The addition of several top brands from Seagram's liquor business will enhance Diageo's leadership position vs. U.K. rival Allied Domecq.

8 Henrietta Place   www.diageo.com
London, W1M 0NB

Morningstar Grades

Growth [C]	1999	2000	2001	2002
Revenue %	-1.9	0.6	8.0	-12.0
Earnings/Share %	15.8	10.2	22.7	36.4
Book Value/Share %	-5.9	22.7	10.5	19.3
Dividends/Share %	-16.3	7.7	6.2	6.7

Diageo posted organic sales growth of 8% in fiscal 2002, and it aims to keep sales growing 8%-10% a year, which we think is a reachable goal.

Profitability [A-]	2000	2001	2002	TTM
Return on Assets %	6.4	7.1	8.2	8.2
Oper Cash Flow $Mil	3,243	3,312	2,898	2,898
- Cap Spending $Mil	868	639	844	844
= Free Cash Flow $Mil	2,375	2,673	2,054	2,054

Shedding Pillsbury and Burger King should help Diageo's profits. The premium drinks segment is more profitable on its own than either of those two businesses were.

Financial Health [A]	2000	2001	2002	06-02
Long-term Debt $Mil	5,630	5,759	5,785	5,785
Total Equity $Mil	7,067	7,215	9,232	9,232
Debt/Equity Ratio	0.8	0.8	0.6	0.6

Diageo generates more than enough cash flow to cover its interest expense. The $3.8 billion it received for Pillsbury partially offsets the $5 billion it paid for part of Seagram.

Industry	Investment Style	Stock Type	Sector
Alcoholic Drinks	▦ Large Growth	✓ High Yield	Consumer Goods

Competition	Market Cap $Mil	Debt/ Equity	12 Mo Trailing Sales $Mil	Price/Cash Flow	Return On Assets%	Total Return% 1 Yr	3 Yr
Diageo PLC ADR	35,203	0.6	16,283	12.1	8.2	-2.6	14.3
Brown-Forman B	4,471	—	2,210	—	—	—	—
AED	—	—	—	—	—	—	—

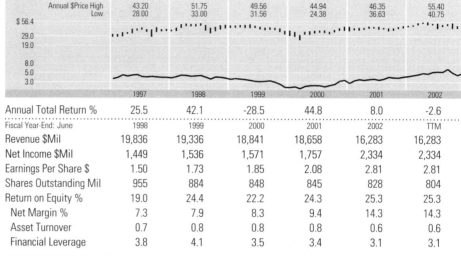

Price Volatility

Monthly Price High/Low — Relative Strength to S&P 500

Annual $Price High / Low	43.20 / 28.00	51.75 / 33.00	49.56 / 31.56	44.94 / 24.38	46.35 / 36.63	55.40 / 40.75

$56.4 / 29.0 / 19.0 / 8.0 / 5.0 / 3.0

	1997	1998	1999	2000	2001	2002
Annual Total Return %	25.5	42.1	-28.5	44.8	8.0	-2.6

Fiscal Year-End: June	1998	1999	2000	2001	2002	TTM
Revenue $Mil	19,836	19,336	18,841	18,658	16,283	16,283
Net Income $Mil	1,449	1,536	1,571	1,757	2,334	2,334
Earnings Per Share $	1.50	1.73	1.85	2.08	2.81	2.81
Shares Outstanding Mil	955	884	848	845	828	804
Return on Equity %	19.0	24.4	22.2	24.3	25.3	25.3
Net Margin %	7.3	7.9	8.3	9.4	14.3	14.3
Asset Turnover	0.7	0.8	0.8	0.8	0.6	0.6
Financial Leverage	3.8	4.1	3.5	3.4	3.1	3.1

Valuation Ratios	Stock	Rel to Industry	Rel to S&P 500
Price/Earnings	15.6	0.8	0.7
Price/Book	3.8	1.0	1.2
Price/Sales	2.2	1.0	1.1
Price/Cash Flow	12.1	0.8	0.9

Major Fund Holders	% of Fund Assets
ICAP Euro Select Equity	4.59
ICAP Select Equity	4.44
Nuveen European Value A	4.36
AssetMark International Equity	4.00

Morningstar's Take By David Kathman, 12-19-2002 Stock Price as of Analysis: $42.09

Now that Diageo has achieved its longstanding goal of shedding Burger King, it should be a significantly stronger company. However, we'd rather wait for concrete results from the new Diageo before getting too optimistic about the stock.

Nearly two years after announcing that it wanted to focus on premium alcoholic drinks (its fastest-growing and most profitable segment), Diageo has finally completed its transformation plan. Having already sold Pillsbury, in July 2002 Diageo announced plans to shed its other unwanted appendage, Burger King, to a consortium of private equity firms led by Texas Pacific Group. It finally completed the deal in December, even though it had to slash the price from $2.26 billion to $1.5 billion because of Burger King's continuing weakness.

Even as it has been shedding the deadwood, Diageo has been beefing up its already impressive portfolio of alcoholic drinks. It teamed up with Pernod Ricard SA to buy most of Seagram's liquor brands for a total of $8.15 billion, a deal that gave Diageo a leg up on fierce rival Allied Domecq and made it a clear number one among spirits firms. It started the flavored malt beverage craze in 2001 with the highly successful Smirnoff Ice, which looks like it will be one of the few long-term survivors (along with

Anheuser-Busch's Bacardi Silver) once the crowded field of entrants thins out.

This new focus on alcohol is a smart move for Diageo, because alcohol has been by far its best and most profitable business. Its premium drinks segment had an operating margin of 20% in fiscal 2002, up from 17% three years earlier; in contrast, Burger King's operating margin fell from 21% to 14% in the same period, with few immediate prospects for revival. The Seagram acquisition is looking like a winner so far: Not only did those brands post an operating profit of 29% in their first six months under Diageo's wing, but their consolidation into Diageo's North American distribution system should help boost profitability even more.

The main question is just how much more efficient Diageo can be now that it has rid itself of its excess baggage. Innovation will have to be a key driver if Diageo is to meet its growth targets, but the failure of Captain Morgan Gold as a follow-up to Smirnoff Ice shows that the company is not immune to missteps. We think decent growth and some margin improvement are in the cards over the next few years, but we'll wait for more results before projecting beyond that. We'd need a 20% discount to our $47 fair value estimate before considering the shares.

MORNINGSTAR® Stocks 500

Dillard's DDS

	Rating	Risk	Moat Size	Fair Value	Last Close	Yield %
	★★★	Low	None	$21.00	$15.86	1.0

Company Profile

Dillard Department Stores operates approximately 338 retail department stores primarily in 29 Southwestern, Southeastern, and Midwestern states. All of the company's stores are owned or leased from a wholly owned subsidiary or from third parties. These stores offer branded apparel and home furnishings. In addition, the company has a private label, Roundtree & Yorke.

Management

The next generation of Dillards, including brothers Bill (chairman and CEO) and Alex (president), has run the firm since 1998. Four siblings are on the board, and three brothers own the Class B shares that allow them to elect two thirds of the directors.

Strategy

Dillard's seeks to enter or strengthen its presence in markets where it can become the dominant traditional department store. It is pursuing a twofold strategy of keeping inventory fresh by turning it over faster (which involved overcoming the firm's long-standing reluctance to mark down slow-moving merchandise), and building a strong private-label program.

1600 Cantrell Road   www.dillards.com
Little Rock, AR 72201

Morningstar Grades

Growth [D+]	1999	2000	2001	2002
Revenue %	17.4	11.8	-1.2	-4.9
Earnings/Share %	-45.5	23.0	NMF	NMF
Book Value/Share %	5.4	1.3	0.6	17.1
Dividends/Share %	0.0	0.0	0.0	0.0

Top-line sales growth is still anemic, despite efforts to adjust the merchandise mix. We do not expect any dramatic changes.

Profitability [C]	2000	2001	2002	TTM
Return on Assets %	2.1	-0.1	1.0	-5.0
Oper Cash Flow $Mil	712	797	616	416
- Cap Spending $Mil	247	226	271	262
= Free Cash Flow $Mil	465	572	345	154

Though the firm's margins have historically trailed those of peers, we see some progress in profitability. Despite lower sales, Dillard's protected margins by emphasizing more-profitable private labels and closing underperforming stores.

Financial Health [B-]	2000	2001	2002	10-02
Long-term Debt $Mil	2,919	2,397	2,145	2,214
Total Equity $Mil	2,833	2,630	2,668	2,194
Debt/Equity Ratio	1.0	0.9	0.8	1.0

Dillard's continues to generate healthy cash flow and has wisely used some of it to pay down debt early. If the firm is conservative with its capital spending and resists any large-scale acquisitions, its financial footing will grow stronger.

Industry	Investment Style	Stock Type	Sector
Department Stores	▦ Mid Value	➜ Slow Growth	▣ Consumer Services

Competition	Market Cap $Mil	Debt/ Equity	12 Mo Trailing Sales $Mil	Price/Cash Flow	Return On Assets%	Total Return% 1 Yr	3 Yr
Dillard's	1,343	1.0	8,304	3.2	-5.0	-0.1	-6.8
Kohl's	18,851	0.4	8,277	31.0	9.8	-20.6	18.3
May Department Stores	6,623	—	14,111	—	—	—	—

Price Volatility   I Monthly Price High/Low   — Relative Strength to S&P 500

	1997	1998	1999	2000	2001	2002
Annual $Price High	44.75	44.50	37.44	20.81	22.50	31.20
Low	28.00	26.50	17.75	9.44	11.44	12.94
Annual Total Return %	14.7	-19.1	-28.4	-40.7	36.8	-0.1

Fiscal Year-end: January	1998	1999	2000	2001	2002	TTM
Revenue $Mil	6,795	7,978	8,921	8,818	8,388	8,304
Net Income $Mil	258	135	164	-6	72	-369
Earnings Per Share $	2.31	1.26	1.55	-0.06	0.85	-4.31
Shares Outstanding Mil	111	107	106	98	84	85
Return on Equity %	9.2	4.8	5.8	-0.2	2.7	-16.8
Net Margin %	3.8	1.7	1.8	-0.1	0.9	-4.4
Asset Turnover	1.2	1.0	1.1	1.2	1.2	1.1
Financial Leverage	2.0	2.9	2.8	2.7	2.7	3.3

Valuation Ratios	Stock	Rel to Industry	Rel to S&P 500
Price/Earnings	NMF	—	—
Price/Book	0.6	0.5	0.2
Price/Sales	0.2	0.6	0.1
Price/Cash Flow	3.2	0.8	0.2

Major Fund Holders	% of Fund Assets
FBP Contrarian Equity	2.88
Kirr Marbach Partners Value	2.13
FBP Contrarian Balanced	1.98
ING Smallcap Value A	1.47

Morningstar's Take   By Debbie Wang, 12-09-2002   Stock Price as of Analysis: $16.18

We do not see a turnaround taking hold at Dillard's, despite management's best efforts. The retailer continues along its path of mediocre performance, with sales growth lagging the competition's. Further, Dillard's is disregarding the larger consumer trend toward shopping at off-mall and discount store locations. For these reasons, we would consider investing only if the shares fell 40% below our fair value estimate.

Dillard's started 2002 with signs of hope in the form of rising profitability and rumors that the retailer was for sale following the death of founder William Dillard in February. These two factors propelled a 90% runup in the stock price. By summer, sales growth had not recovered and management, composed of William Dillard's sons, quashed any talk of selling the firm. The stock runup reversed itself.

Since William Dillard II and his brother Alex assumed day-to-day operations of the retailer in 1998, management has implemented several sound strategic moves to turn the company around. Over the past two years, Dillard's has largely succeeded in reducing inventory, keeping merchandise fresher by marking down slow-moving items, and raising profitability through greater emphasis on private-label lines. However, these micro-level

initiatives have not been enough to spawn the hoped-for turnaround, especially in the face of larger consumer shopping trends.

Dillard's must devise a new strategy to compete, given the fundamental shift in consumer behavior that has resulted in shoppers leaving malls for off-mall specialty stores and discount retailers like Kohl's KSS and Wal-Mart WMT. With so many alternatives, consumers have developed new expectations for selection and standards of value.

We do not see any evidence that Dillard's is retooling to compete with this larger group of rivals. In fact, even as mall traffic dwindles, the company is rolling out more doubleheader stores (two Dillard's stores with different departments in the same mall). We are not confident that management possesses the vision or resolve to make the far-reaching changes necessary for a true turnaround.

Sales for the 10 months ending November 30, 2002, were down 2% from the same period last year. We do not expect to see any improvement in the near future. With the company's efforts falling short thus far, we maintain a bearish outlook on Dillard's stock.

Dollar General DG

	Rating	Risk	Moat Size	Fair Value	Last Close	Yield %
	★★★	Med.	None	$15.00	$11.95	1.1

Company Profile

Dollar General is a discount retailer. The company owns and operates about 5,000 general merchandise stores in 25 Midwestern and Southeastern states, from Delaware to Nebraska. Serving primarily low-, middle-, and fixed-income families in small communities, its Dollar General Stores offer general merchandise at discount price points including $1, $5, $10, and multiples thereof, such as 2 for $1 and 2 for $5. The typical store has approximately 6,000 square feet of selling space. Sales of hardgoods make up most of the company sales.

Management

Dollar General made some changes to its management team in 2001, adding Don Shaffer as president and COO. He has since been promoted to interim CEO; he'll probably be named to the post permanently in 2003.

Strategy

Dollar General targets families with annual incomes below $30,000. The company offers deep-discount private-label and brand-name products. Its low-cost strategy includes spending little on advertising, locating in low-rent areas, increasing its store count each year, and locating new stores near its major distribution centers and warehouses to increase logistics efficiencies.

100 Mission Ridge   www.dollargeneral.com
Goodlettsville, TN 37072

Morningstar Grades

Growth [A]	1999	2000	2001	2002
Revenue %	NMF	20.7	17.0	17.0
Earnings/Share %	NMF	22.2	-61.8	195.2
Book Value/Share %	NMF	23.9	2.9	21.5
Dividends/Share %	25.8	18.2	24.9	11.1

Dollar General's expansion plan now targets 10% new store growth per year, so we expect sales to increase in the low to mid-teens over the next five years.

Profitability [A]	2000	2001	2002	TTM
Return on Assets %	9.7	3.1	8.1	10.5
Oper Cash Flow $Mil	197	216	266	352
- Cap Spending $Mil	142	217	125	130
= Free Cash Flow $Mil	55	-1	140	222

For a discount retailer, Dollar General has posted very strong returns on equity and assets. Its net margin has been declining, but that's part of the plan of boosting exposure to less-profitable consumable goods and driving more customer traffic.

Financial Health [A]	2000	2001	2002	10-02
Long-term Debt $Mil	514	721	339	502
Total Equity $Mil	845	862	1,042	1,190
Debt/Equity Ratio	0.6	0.8	0.3	0.4

Dollar General is in solid financial health, even considering the restatement of its financials for the past few years. Operating cash flow has increased an average of 15% over the past three years and covers the spending needed for new stores.

Industry	Investment Style	Stock Type	Sector
Discount Stores	▦ Mid Growth	↗ Classic Growth	▭ Consumer Services

Competition	Market Cap $Mil	Debt/ Equity	12 Mo Trailing Sales $Mil	Price/Cash Flow	Return On Assets%	Total Return% 1 Yr	3 Yr
Dollar General	3,983	0.4	5,927	11.3	10.5	-19.1	-11.6
Wal-Mart Stores	223,388	0.5	233,651	18.9	8.0	-11.8	-7.3
Family Dollar Stores	5,410	0.0	4,163	13.4	12.4	5.0	25.4

Price Volatility   ▌ Monthly Price High/Low   — Relative Strength to S&P 500

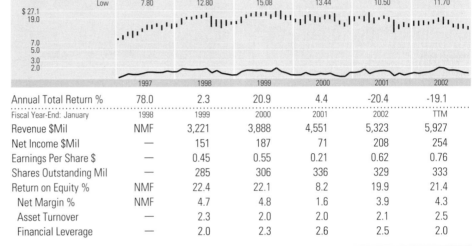

	Annual $Price High Low	16.38 7.80	24.19 12.80	26.10 15.08	23.19 13.44	24.05 10.50	19.95 11.70

		1997	1998	1999	2000	2001	2002
Annual Total Return %		78.0	2.3	20.9	4.4	-20.4	-19.1

Fiscal Year-End: January	1998	1999	2000	2001	2002	TTM
Revenue $Mil	NMF	3,221	3,888	4,551	5,323	5,927
Net Income $Mil	—	151	187	71	208	254
Earnings Per Share $	—	0.45	0.55	0.21	0.62	0.76
Shares Outstanding Mil	—	285	306	336	329	333
Return on Equity %	NMF	22.4	22.1	8.2	19.9	21.4
Net Margin %	NMF	4.7	4.8	1.6	3.9	4.3
Asset Turnover	—	2.3	2.0	2.0	2.1	2.5
Financial Leverage	—	2.0	2.3	2.6	2.5	2.0

Valuation Ratios	Stock	Rel to Industry	Rel to S&P 500
Price/Earnings	15.7	0.5	0.7
Price/Book	3.3	0.6	1.0
Price/Sales	0.7	0.7	0.3
Price/Cash Flow	11.3	0.6	0.9

Major Fund Holders	% of Fund Assets
FMI AAM Palm Beach Total Return	5.55
Oppenheimer Quest Capital Value A	2.49
Saratoga Large Capitalization Value I	2.23
Nicholas	2.09

Morningstar's Take   By Tom Goetzinger, 12-16-2002   Stock Price as of Analysis: $12.78

Dollar General's strategy of being a snack to Wal-Mart's five-course meal has proved successful. Though we like the business, the stock doesn't offer a large enough margin of safety right now. An attractive price would be $8-$9.

Dollar General is a neighborhood-driven chain--customers live within three to five miles of a store and most earn less than $30,000 annually. The company strictly adheres to its everyday low price strategy and doesn't run off-price promotions or employ a chainwide advertising program. The price you see is the best price you can get.

Customers appreciate this and have been loyal. Comparable-store sales growth (at stores open at least a year) has increased 6% on average over the past five years, and the number of stores has doubled without acquisitions. Future expansion plans are more modest, with square-footage growth at 10% per year (compared with 16% over the past five); we don't expect store saturation to be an issue.

The company isn't just increasing square footage, it's also changing the way that space is used. A new format with aisles from front to back instead of left to right has been well received. The layout provides greater shelf space and increased customer traffic through stores, as patrons pass more merchandise while they shop.

Another goal is to increase frequency of visits to boost total sales. The average bill at Dollar General is just under $9, which makes sense: Few people go to a dollar store with a shopping list, but rather a few items in mind that they need plus an impulse buy or two. This isn't likely to change much, so the company has added refrigerators in many stores stocked with milk, eggs, and other consumables, in the hope that customers will think of Dollar General as more of a convenience store. This should make consumables--already 60% of sales--an even more important source of revenue.

However, consumables are generally lower-margin, higher-turnover products than Dollar General's other goods, and require pinpoint inventory management--something the firm has struggled with in the past. Also, Dollar General's net profit margin has been on the slide, averaging 4.3% over the past five years compared with Family Dollar's 5.1% and Dollar Tree's 7.2%. Dollar General has less margin for error, given its consumables strategy.

While we like the company, it faces some challenges, and so we're looking for a much lower price before buying.

M⊙RNINGSTAR®   **Stocks 500**

Dollar Tree Stores DLTR

Rating	Risk	Moat Size	Fair Value	Last Close	Yield %
★★★	Med.	None	$33.00	$24.57	0.0

Company Profile

Dollar Tree Stores operates discount variety stores that offer merchandise that costs a dollar. The stores stock housewares, toys, seasonal goods (like wrapping paper and back-to-school products), food, stationery, health and beauty aids, books, party goods, hardware, and other consumer items. Dollar Tree Stores leases and operates approximately 1,780 stores in 36 states.

Management

Macon Brock has been CEO since 1993 and a director and president since 1986, when he founded the company with Douglas Perry and Ray Compton. Brock directs the company's overall operations.

Strategy

Dollar Tree seeks to increase revenue and earnings primarily through mergers and acquisitions with smaller rivals and by expanding its retail presence in new markets. Its latest twist on this strategy is to increase the size of most new stores.

500 Volvo Parkway
Chesapeake, VA 23320
www.DollarTree.com

Industry	Investment Style	Stock Type	Sector
Discount Stores	Mid Growth	Classic Growth	Consumer Services

Competition

	Market Cap $Mil	Debt/ Equity	12 Mo Trailing Sales $Mil	Price/Cash Flow	Return On Assets%	Total Return% 1 Yr	3 Yr
Dollar Tree Stores	2,805	0.0	2,217	20.5	13.8	-20.5	-8.9
Family Dollar Stores	5,410	0.0	4,163	13.4	12.4	5.0	25.4
Dollar General	3,983	0.4	5,927	11.3	10.5	-19.1	-11.6

Price Volatility

Monthly Price High/Low — Relative Strength to S&P 500

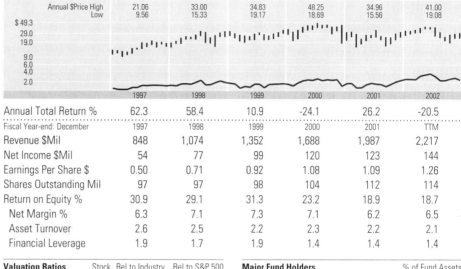

		21.06	33.00	34.83	48.25	34.96	41.00
Annual $Price High Low		9.56	15.33	19.17	18.69	15.56	19.08
		1997	1998	1999	2000	2001	2002
Annual Total Return %		62.3	58.4	10.9	-24.1	26.2	-20.5

Fiscal Year-end: December	1997	1998	1999	2000	2001	TTM
Revenue $Mil	848	1,074	1,352	1,688	1,987	2,217
Net Income $Mil	54	77	99	120	123	144
Earnings Per Share $	0.50	0.71	0.92	1.08	1.09	1.26
Shares Outstanding Mil	97	97	98	104	112	114
Return on Equity %	30.9	29.1	31.3	23.2	18.9	18.7
Net Margin %	6.3	7.1	7.3	7.1	6.2	6.5
Asset Turnover	2.6	2.5	2.2	2.3	2.2	2.1
Financial Leverage	1.9	1.7	1.9	1.4	1.4	1.4

Valuation Ratios	Stock	Rel to Industry	Rel to S&P 500
Price/Earnings	19.5	0.7	0.8
Price/Book	3.7	0.6	1.1
Price/Sales	1.3	1.4	0.6
Price/Cash Flow	20.5	1.1	1.5

Major Fund Holders	% of Fund Assets
Delaware Pooled Mid-Cap Growth Equity	3.20
Delaware Growth Opportunities A	3.19
Fidelity OTC	3.18
UBS PACE Small/Medium Company Gr Eq P	2.87

Morningstar Grades

Growth [A]	1998	1999	2000	2001
Revenue %	26.7	25.9	24.9	17.7
Earnings/Share %	42.0	29.6	17.4	0.9
Book Value/Share %	50.6	20.6	58.6	23.9
Dividends/Share %	NMF	NMF	NMF	NMF

Dollar Tree has grown at a pretty good clip, averaging 23% sales growth from 1998 to 2002. However, comparable-store sales averaged just 3.6% over that time. The company has become more dependent on new stores and larger store formats to fuel growth.

Profitability [A+]	1999	2000	2001	TTM
Return on Assets %	16.2	16.1	13.6	13.8
Oper Cash Flow $Mil	129	107	179	137
- Cap Spending $Mil	55	95	122	128
= Free Cash Flow $Mil	74	12	57	9

Net margins have hovered near 7% for the past decade, easily beating the industry average of 3.5% and comparing favorably with deep-discount rivals. Dollar Tree's returns on equity and assets also stack up well, but have been declining.

Financial Health [A+]	1999	2000	2001	09-02
Long-term Debt $Mil	78	43	34	24
Total Equity $Mil	316	519	652	767
Debt/Equity Ratio	0.2	0.1	0.1	0.0

The company has an extremely low debt/equity ratio and generates positive free cash flow, despite the sizable capital expenditures needed for new stores, remodeling of existing stores, and additional distribution centers.

Morningstar's Take By Tom Goetzinger, 12-16-2002 Stock Price as of Analysis: $26.92

Dollar Tree's stores appear to be getting bigger much faster than they're getting better.

The company has evolved since its inception in 1986. Back then, the stores were relatively small (2,000-3,000 square feet) shops in enclosed malls. Now, they are more often much larger (5,000-10,000 square feet) convenience stores in strip malls and shopping centers anchored by big-box retailers (like Wal-Mart or Kmart) or large grocery stores. This makes sense: Its core low- to middle-income customers frequent those strip malls often, and can pop into Dollar Tree to pick up a few things.

Over the past five years, the company has doubled its store base to 2,200, moved into 10 more states (38 at last count), and increased average square footage by 250% with larger, freestanding stores. The idea behind the bigger stores is to widen the array of products the company sells, and boost the percentage of goods that fall into the consumable category, like food, leading to more frequent customer visits.

The main appeal of Dollar Tree, though, is that it isn't a gigantic warehouse like Wal-Mart. As its stores get bigger, Dollar Tree loses some of the small-store convenience that dollar-store shoppers prefer. Moreover, we think the overall quality of merchandise could suffer. The company is testing some 12,000- to 18,000-square-foot stores in larger markets, but how much stuff can Dollar Tree reasonably (and profitably) sell for $1?

As the stores swell in size, inventory management (which the company has struggled with in recent years) also becomes more important. Dollar Tree is upgrading technology in this area. Point-of-sale (POS) scanners and registers are in 35% of stores so far, with 100% targeted over the next few years. Stores benefit because they can identify fast-selling items much more quickly and keep them from being out of stock. POS also leads to better merchandise ordering and the elimination of cumbersome and frequently erroneous manual inventory counts. This should help Dollar Tree cut down on labor costs, which have been increasing at a faster pace than sales over the past couple of years and eating into profits.

We're taking a cautious approach to the company's aggressive expansion. Square-footage growth of 20%-25% is twice that of rivals Dollar General and Family Dollar, and could lead to more operational hiccups. We'd wait for the shares to dip to around $20 before investing.

Dow Chemical DOW

	Rating	Risk	Moat Size	Fair Value	Last Close	Yield %
	★★	Med.	None	$33.00	$29.70	4.5

Company Profile

Dow Chemical manufactures plastic materials and chemicals. Sales of plastics like thermoplastics, epoxy products, adhesives, sealants, resins, polyurethanes, and fabricated products generate about 48% of the company's total sales. In addition, the company produces chemicals like polymer, food gums, and latex coatings. Dow Chemical also produces agricultural products like herbicides and insecticides. The company markets its products in the United States and abroad. Foreign sales account for about 60% of total sales. Dow acquired Union Carbide in 2001.

Management

Bill Stavropoulous is back as CEO after Michael Parker was fired for poor financial performance. Stavropoulous was Dow's CEO from 1995 to 2000 before retiring and becoming chairman. He orchestrated the merger with Union Carbide and now is responsible for its difficult integration.

Strategy

Dow's basic chemical unit produces chemicals that are used as raw materials for the firm's performance plastic and chemical divisions. This core strategy of vertical integration yields a very efficient cost structure. Dow is focused on building its specialty and agricultural businesses to reduce its vulnerability to the chemical cycle.

2030 Dow Center   www.dow.com
Midland, MI 48674

Industry	Investment Style	Stock Type	Sector
Chemicals	▦ Large Core	🗲 High Yield	⚙ Industrial Mats

Competition	Market Cap $Mil	Debt/ Equity	12 Mo Trailing Sales $Mil	Price/Cash Flow	Return On Assets%	Total Return% 1 Yr	3 Yr
Dow Chemical	27,060	1.1	26,866	10.1	1.2	-8.2	-8.1
BASF AG ADR	111,488	—	28,981	—	—	—	—
DuPont De Nemours E.I.	42,120	0.4	24,013	21.9	6.8	3.0	-10.5

Price Volatility

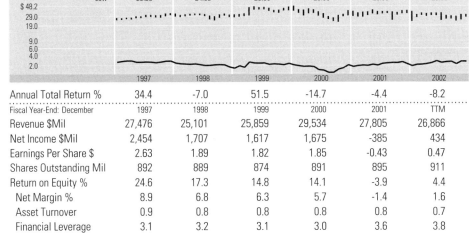

	1997	1998	1999	2000	2001	2002
Annual $Price High	34.21	33.83	46.00	47.17	39.67	37.00
Low	25.25	24.90	28.50	23.00	25.06	23.68
Annual Total Return %	34.4	-7.0	51.5	-14.7	-4.4	-8.2

Fiscal Year-End: December	1997	1998	1999	2000	2001	TTM
Revenue $Mil	27,476	25,101	25,859	29,534	27,805	26,866
Net Income $Mil	2,454	1,707	1,617	1,675	-385	434
Earnings Per Share $	2.63	1.89	1.82	1.85	-0.43	0.47
Shares Outstanding Mil	892	889	874	891	895	911
Return on Equity %	24.6	17.3	14.8	14.1	-3.9	4.4
Net Margin %	8.9	6.8	6.3	5.7	-1.4	1.6
Asset Turnover	0.9	0.8	0.8	0.8	0.8	0.7
Financial Leverage	3.1	3.2	3.1	3.0	3.6	3.8

Valuation Ratios	Stock	Rel to Industry	Rel to S&P 500
Price/Earnings	63.2	2.9	2.7
Price/Book	2.8	0.6	0.9
Price/Sales	1.0	0.5	0.5
Price/Cash Flow	10.1	0.6	0.8

Major Fund Holders	% of Fund Assets
Rydex Basic Materials Inv	8.92
Fidelity Select Chemicals	7.69
ProFunds Ultra Basic Materials Inv	6.46
Banknorth Large Cap Value	5.19

Morningstar Grades

Growth [C+]	1998	1999	2000	2001
Revenue %	-8.6	3.0	14.2	-5.9
Earnings/Share %	-28.1	-3.7	1.6	NMF
Book Value/Share %	2.3	12.6	6.2	-14.7
Dividends/Share %	3.6	0.0	0.0	1.2

Dow's five-year average sales growth of 7% outpaces many of its chemical peers', largely because of acquisitions. With the addition of Union Carbide, sales are even more subject to cyclical economic factors.

Profitability [B-]	1999	2000	2001	TTM
Return on Assets %	4.8	4.7	-1.1	1.2
Oper Cash Flow $Mil	3,562	1,691	1,789	2,684
- Cap Spending $Mil	2,176	1,808	1,587	1,675
= Free Cash Flow $Mil	1,386	-117	202	1,009

Earnings have disappointed this year, pressured by rising raw material costs. Given the difficulty of generating sales growth in this challenging environment, Dow has focused on cleaning up its cost structure to ensure bottom-line growth.

Financial Health [C]	1999	2000	2001	09-02
Long-term Debt $Mil	—	6,613	9,266	10,360
Total Equity $Mil	10,940	11,840	9,993	9,772
Debt/Equity Ratio	—	0.6	0.9	1.1

A flurry of recent acquisitions has stretched Dow's balance sheet. Debt/capital is 50% and free cash flows are negative. In turn, the firm has implemented an aggressive cost-cutting plan, aiming to improve cash flows by more than $1 billion in 2003.

Morningstar's Take By Sanjay Ayer, 12-14-2002 Stock Price as of Analysis: $30.36

Dow Chemical stock has a solid dividend yield and the potential to benefit greatly from an economic recovery. The timing and extent of a recovery are difficult to predict, though, and we'd require a larger discount to our fair value estimate to compensate for economic and company-specific risks.

When Dow merged with Union Carbide in 2001, the company figured to reap the benefits of enhanced global reach and substantial cost savings. Instead, these benefits have been masked by the inheritance of increased cyclicality, asbestos liabilities, massive debt, and a host of merger-related expenses. Union Carbide primarily produces commodity chemicals, demand for which is closely tied to cyclical economic factors. Dow is now even more sensitive to swings in the economy, and with industrial production in a prolonged slump, the company has been scorched by anemic demand, weak pricing, and record-low plant operating rates.

The merger should provide Dow with some added upside upon an economic recovery, however, especially once the economies of scale kick in. Dow is now the largest, lowest-cost producer of commodity chemicals. Integrating Union Carbide has yielded significant cost savings, which should allow Dow to fully capitalize on an upturn in demand. We

expect this recovery to be more gradual than previous surges toward cyclical peaks. High operating rates are the main catalyst for increased pricing power, and with rates emerging from historical lows, it will take several consecutive quarters of strong demand before margins improve.

While Dow stock had been fairly resilient to this industrial recession, it fell victim to asbestos concerns stemming from Union Carbide's former business activities, plunging 30% last January. Given Dow's sizable insurance coverage and the possibility of congressional asbestos legislation, we believe the firm's asbestos story packs far less punch than the bold headlines that have spooked investors. Nevertheless, headline risk will probably produce some stock price volatility in the short term.

While we believe Dow is slightly undervalued, we are concerned about the firm's dependence on an economy recovery and vulnerability to geopolitical uncertainty (war in the Middle East could spike energy prices). A pullback in the stock to around $23--particularly on investor overreaction to asbestos news--would present a nice buying opportunity, in our opinion.

M🔴RNINGSTAR® Stocks 500

Dow Jones & Company DJ

	Rating	Risk	Moat Size	Fair Value	Last Close	Yield %
	★★★	Low	Wide	$37.00	$43.23	2.3

Company Profile

Dow Jones & Company provides business information services. Its publications include The Wall Street Journal, Barron's, The Far Eastern Economic Review, and more than 30 community newspapers. The company's Dow Jones News Service division supplies real-time market information for print and electronic publications. In addition, Dow Jones provides radio and television financial news programming.

Management

CEO Peter Kann started as an intern in 1963. He has held several positions, including one as a reporter in Vietnam. He is also the editorial director of the Dow Jones publications, so he has control over both business decisions and editorial content.

Strategy

As one of the largest distributors of business and financial news and information, Dow Jones seeks to increase awareness of its brands and products by pursuing a larger circulation base and expanding its electronic media offerings, particularly WSJ.com.

200 Liberty Street
New York, NY 10281
www.dowjones.com

Industry	Investment Style	Stock Type	Sector
Media Conglomerates	Mid Core	Slow Growth	Media

Competition	Market Cap $Mil	Debt/ Equity	12 Mo Trailing Sales $Mil	Price/Cash Flow	Return On Assets%	Total Return% 1 Yr	3 Yr
Dow Jones & Company	3,608	1.5	1,594	19.0	18.3	-19.2	-11.1
Gannett	19,190	0.7	6,354	16.2	8.1	8.1	-1.1
McGraw-Hill Companies	11,713	0.3	4,730	9.8	8.3	0.7	4.5

Price Volatility

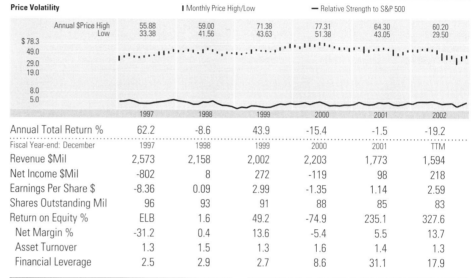

	1997	1998	1999	2000	2001	2002
Annual $Price High	55.88	59.00	71.38	77.31	64.30	60.20
Low	33.38	41.56	43.63	51.38	43.05	29.50
Annual Total Return %	62.2	-8.6	43.9	-15.4	-1.5	-19.2

Fiscal Year-end: December	1997	1998	1999	2000	2001	TTM
Revenue $Mil	2,573	2,158	2,002	2,203	1,773	1,594
Net Income $Mil	-802	8	272	-119	98	218
Earnings Per Share $	-8.36	0.09	2.99	-1.35	1.14	2.59
Shares Outstanding Mil	96	93	91	88	85	83
Return on Equity %	ELB	1.6	49.2	-74.9	235.1	327.6
Net Margin %	-31.2	0.4	13.6	-5.4	5.5	13.7
Asset Turnover	1.3	1.5	1.3	1.6	1.4	1.3
Financial Leverage	2.5	2.9	2.7	8.6	31.1	17.9

Valuation Ratios	Stock	Rel to Industry	Rel to S&P 500
Price/Earnings	16.7	0.6	0.7
Price/Book	54.1	38.1	16.9
Price/Sales	2.3	1.0	1.1
Price/Cash Flow	19.0	1.2	1.4

Major Fund Holders	% of Fund Assets
Oak Value	3.89
Westcore Mid-Cap Opportunity	2.30
Scudder Development S	2.10
Scudder Aggressive Growth A	2.08

Morningstar Grades

Growth [D]	1998	1999	2000	2001
Revenue %	-16.1	-7.2	10.0	-19.5
Earnings/Share %	NMF	EUB	NMF	NMF
Book Value/Share %	-32.6	10.8	-70.3	-73.1
Dividends/Share %	0.0	0.0	4.2	0.0

The company has been hit hard by the economic slowdown because of its high exposure to business-to-business advertising. We expect that a pickup in growth--both in sales and profits--is just around the bend.

Profitability [C]	1999	2000	2001	TTM
Return on Assets %	18.0	-8.7	7.6	18.3
Oper Cash Flow $Mil	297	446	342	190
- Cap Spending $Mil	191	187	129	96
= Free Cash Flow $Mil	106	259	213	93

Because of the fixed nature of the firm's cost structure, the decline in advertising revenue has walloped profit margins. As the economy recovers over the next few years, however, we expect improvement in this area.

Financial Health [C-]	1999	2000	2001	09-02
Long-term Debt $Mil	150	151	174	97
Total Equity $Mil	553	159	42	67
Debt/Equity Ratio	0.3	1.0	4.2	1.5

Dow Jones' share-repurchase program makes the company seem more risky than it is. We are quite comfortable with the firm's financial position: Even in a depressed operating environment, operating income is still almost 20 times interest expense.

Morningstar's Take By Jonathan Schrader, 12-11-2002 Stock Price as of Analysis: $42.84

Dow Jones is not our favorite company in the publishing industry. The volatility of its cash flows really bothers us, and so--despite its wide moat--we'd wait for the stock to fall below $28 before buying.

You would think that the publisher of The Wall Street Journal and Barron's would be a great company in which to invest. However, poor management over the past few years has meant poor results for DJ's equityholders. Over the past five- and ten-year periods, DJ shares have woefully underperformed the leading U.S. indexes, as well as peers like Gannett, New York Times, and Washington Post. We're not sure investors will do any better in the future, either.

We like to consider a company's economic moat before investing. DJ might seem to be an obvious candidate for wide-moat status--our best rating--given its strong collection of assets. After all, The Wall Street Journal and Barron's are arguably the most respected sources of information in American business and finance. Additionally, the company has a collection of community newspapers that generally face little in the way of competition. This often leads to attractive profit margins and high returns on invested capital.

We could not overlook DJ's competitive advantages, and we thus decided to allow the firm's wide moat rating to remain--with some reservations. We're leery of giving such a rating to a company that loses 20% of its revenue base in just one year, as DJ did between 2000 and 2001. This kind of performance flies in the face of what a wide economic moat stands for: sustainable, defensible profits and cash flow. It's also difficult to get a fix on the company's historical financial performance. Charges, divestitures, and economic weakness have combined to make historical financials extremely messy. On top of all that, the firm's exposure to the increasingly volatile business-to-business advertising market makes Dow Jones a medium-risk investment, despite its solid financial position.

Because we don't believe that management can maximize the potential of DJ's assets, we would want to see a 25% discount to our fair value estimate--rather than our usual 20% for a wide-moat, medium-risk firm--before investing.

DST Systems DST

	Rating	Risk	Moat Size	Fair Value	Last Close	Yield %
	★★★	Low	Narrow	$37.00	$35.55	0.0

Company Profile

DST acts as a data-processing backbone for mutual fund companies, insurance providers, and other financial service organizations. The company's main services are automated record-keeping and accounting for mutual fund shareholder accounts. DST also provides bill-payment processing services for industries like cable television, life insurance, and managed health care.

Management

Thomas McDonnell has been DST's CEO since 1984 and president since 1973. Fellow Kansas City Southern spin-off Stilwell Financial owns about a third of DST shares.

Strategy

In its core mutual fund processing business, DST differentiates itself by sustained investment in technology. The firm has put its data-processing knowledge to work by entering similar markets, like bill-processing services for cable companies and utilities. DST also purchased EquiServe in an attempt to expand its corporate securities processing business.

333 West 11th Street www.dstsystems.com
Kansas City, MO 64105

Morningstar Grades

Growth [A-]

	1998	1999	2000	2001
Revenue %	17.8	9.7	11.0	21.9
Earnings/Share %	-8.9	89.3	57.5	8.4
Book Value/Share %	26.5	23.2	7.9	-3.6
Dividends/Share %	NMF	NMF	NMF	NMF

With the downturn in the equity markets, DST has had a rough time ginning up growth. After more than five years of double-digit increases, revenue (excluding reimbursables) hit a wall in 2002.

Profitability [A]

	1999	2000	2001	TTM
Return on Assets %	5.9	8.5	8.4	8.3
Oper Cash Flow $Mil	252	334	367	421
- Cap Spending $Mil	139	176	194	229
= Free Cash Flow $Mil	113	158	173	192

Revenue growth benefits data processors by spreading the fixed system costs over a bigger sales base. DST is no exception; we expect operating margins, already impressive at 19%, to improve a bit as the firm processes more fund accounts.

Financial Health [A]

	1999	2000	2001	09-02
Long-term Debt $Mil	44	69	243	422
Total Equity $Mil	1,464	1,566	1,472	1,331
Debt/Equity Ratio	0.0	0.0	0.2	0.3

DST had about $470 million of debt at the end of September. This figure isn't much bigger than the firm's annual operating cash flow and is dwarfed by its $850 million available-for-sale investment portfolio. So, we have no worries.

	Industry	Investment Style	Stock Type	Sector
	Data Processing	Mid Growth	Classic Growth	Business Services

Competition

	Market Cap $Mil	Debt/ Equity	12 Mo Trailing Sales $Mil	Price/Cash Flow	Return On Assets%	Total Return% 1 Yr	Total Return% 3 Yr
DST Systems	4,255	0.3	1,648	10.1	8.3	-28.7	-0.8
Bank of New York	17,396	—	6,017	—	1.4	-39.9	-11.1
SunGard Data Systems	6,679	—	2,414	—	—		

Price Volatility

| Monthly Price High/Low — Relative Strength to S&P 500

	1997	1998	1999	2000	2001	2002
Annual $Price High	22.72	35.28	38.19	74.94	69.94	51.15
Low	12.13	17.00	25.47	25.81	36.25	24.14
Annual Total Return %	36.1	33.7	33.7	75.6	-25.6	-28.7

Fiscal Year-End: December	1997	1998	1999	2000	2001	TTM
Revenue $Mil	950	1,119	1,228	1,362	1,660	1,648
Net Income $Mil	79	72	138	216	228	215
Earnings Per Share $	0.62	0.56	1.06	1.67	1.81	1.76
Shares Outstanding Mil	127	126	127	125	123	120
Return on Equity %	8.5	6.1	9.4	13.8	15.5	16.1
Net Margin %	8.4	6.4	11.3	15.8	13.7	13.0
Asset Turnover	0.6	0.6	0.5	0.5	0.6	0.6
Financial Leverage	1.7	1.6	1.6	1.6	1.8	2.0

Valuation Ratios	Stock	Rel to Industry	Rel to S&P 500
Price/Earnings	20.2	0.9	0.9
Price/Book	3.2	0.6	1.0
Price/Sales	2.6	0.8	1.3
Price/Cash Flow	10.1	0.6	0.8

Major Fund Holders	% of Fund Assets
PBHG Focused Value	6.06
Selected Special	4.24
Alliance Technology A	3.31
Schroder MidCap Value Inv	2.94

Morningstar's Take By Dan Schick, 12-19-2002 Stock Price as of Analysis: $35.22

DST's leadership of the mutual fund account processing market is protected by a huge competitive advantage. However, that business accounts for less than half of the firm's revenue, and DST seems inclined to further cloud the value of its gem. As a result, we'd wait for a 30% discount to our fair value estimate before buying this stock.

On the strength of its proprietary mutual fund record-keeping and processing system, DST processes 78.4 million mutual fund accounts in the United States, a whopping 32% of the 247.8 million accounts that the Investment Company Institute reports existed at the end of 2001.

The firm traces its roots to 1969, when Kansas City Southern put the technology it had developed for the railroad industry to use in the fledgling mutual fund market, which at the time consisted of fewer than 400 funds and 11 million accounts. As one of the first companies dedicated to processing accounts, DST developed a wealth of technology and expertise with which to win over customers. Coupling the superior technology with the typical data-processing economies of scale that began to arise as DST processed more and more accounts, the firm increased its market share.

Once DST wins a customer, the two are bound tight. After all, a fund outsources accounting to DST to save on aggravations and expenses. Switching to a competitor's system would take time, cause hassles, and cost money. Furthermore, there is little incentive for a customer to switch. As long as DST provides good service, it keeps its customers.

If DST were only a mutual fund account processor, it would receive our widest moat rating. But the firm insists on investing in businesses that are much less attractive. For example, in 1998 it used stock to purchase its way into the customer management business that mainly serves cable and telephone companies. Whatever high hopes DST had for this move haven't been realized. The segment's revenue is declining, it has suffered losses recently, and big customers have gone elsewhere. Furthermore, because DST used its stock to buy its way into this business, it was tantamount to the firm's trading the family jewels for something much less valuable.

Despite having diluted the fund processing business, DST generates returns on capital greater than 20%. Thanks to its dominance in the fund processing market and the fact that its other divisions are poor only in comparison, shareholders would do well to own DST at the right price.

MORNINGSTAR® Stocks 500

DuPont De Nemours E.I. DD

	Rating	Risk	Moat Size	Fair Value	Last Close	Yield %
	★★	Med.	None	$45.00	$42.40	3.3

Company Profile

DuPont manufactures chemicals and related products, including refrigerants, engineered materials, pharmaceutical chemicals, white-pigment chemicals, textiles, carpets, coatings, industrial polymers, and acrylics. DuPont also produces herbicides and hybrid-seed and soy products. The company markets its products in the United States and internationally. Foreign sales account for about 49% of the company's total sales.

Management

Chad Holliday has been CEO since 1997. He is the architect of DuPont's shift toward specialty chemicals and life sciences. It's a strategy loaded with potential, but it's been tough finding the best way to realize that potential.

Strategy

DuPont has reorganized itself into five strategic business units: electronic and communication technologies; performance materials; coatings and color technologies; safety and protection; and agriculture and nutrition. Management believes that high-growth areas like electronics, biotechnology, material sciences, and safety and security will drive sustainable growth.

1007 Market Street   www.dupont.com
Wilmington, DE 19898

Morningstar Grades

Growth [C-]	1998	1999	2000	2001
Revenue %	2.6	8.3	4.7	-13.1
Earnings/Share %	87.5	79.2	-68.7	90.0
Book Value/Share %	25.1	-3.8	7.6	10.2
Dividends/Share %	11.0	2.6	0.0	0.0

Chemical companies have struggled to generate top-line growth, and DuPont is no exception. Improved volume across all segments has been offset by weak pricing. DuPont believes that its portfolio realignment will revitalize growth.

Profitability [A]	1999	2000	2001	TTM
Return on Assets %	18.9	5.9	10.8	6.8
Oper Cash Flow $Mil	4,840	5,070	2,419	1,919
- Cap Spending $Mil	2,055	1,925	1,494	1,335
= Free Cash Flow $Mil	2,785	3,145	925	584

DuPont has enjoyed topnotch returns on capital, but the recession has deeply affected all of its segments. The firm's extensive cost-cutting and restructuring initiatives have boosted operating margins in 2002.

Financial Health [A]	1999	2000	2001	09-02
Long-term Debt $Mil	6,625	6,658	5,350	4,810
Total Equity $Mil	12,638	13,062	14,215	11,334
Debt/Equity Ratio	0.5	0.5	0.4	0.4

DuPont sports the most attractive balance sheet of the major chemical companies. The firm is in the enviable position of having strong free cash flows and low debt. DuPont is the only company in the chemical industry with an AA- credit rating.

Industry	Investment Style	Stock Type	Sector
Chemicals	Large Core	High Yield	Industrial Mats

Competition

	Market Cap $Mil	Debt/ Equity	12 Mo Trailing Sales $Mil	Price/Cash Flow	Return On Assets%	Total Return% 1 Yr	Total Return% 3 Yr
DuPont De Nemours E.I.	42,120	0.4	24,013	21.9	6.8	3.0	-10.5
BASF AG ADR	111,488	—	28,981	—	—	—	—
Dow Chemical	27,060	1.1	26,866	10.1	1.2	-8.2	-8.1

Price Volatility

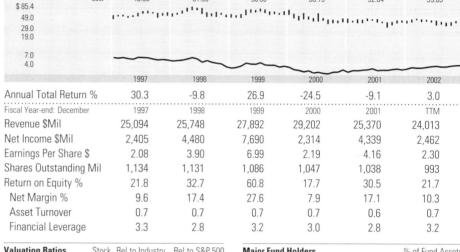

Annual $Price High	69.75	84.44	77.94	74.00	49.88	49.80
Low	46.38	51.69	50.06	38.19	32.64	35.03

	1997	1998	1999	2000	2001	2002
Annual Total Return %	30.3	-9.8	26.9	-24.5	-9.1	3.0

Fiscal Year-end: December	1997	1998	1999	2000	2001	TTM
Revenue $Mil	25,094	25,748	27,892	29,202	25,370	24,013
Net Income $Mil	2,405	4,480	7,690	2,314	4,339	2,462
Earnings Per Share $	2.08	3.90	6.99	2.19	4.16	2.30
Shares Outstanding Mil	1,134	1,131	1,086	1,047	1,038	993
Return on Equity %	21.8	32.7	60.8	17.7	30.5	21.7
Net Margin %	9.6	17.4	27.6	7.9	17.1	10.3
Asset Turnover	0.7	0.7	0.7	0.7	0.6	0.7
Financial Leverage	3.3	2.8	3.2	3.0	2.8	3.2

Valuation Ratios	Stock	Rel to Industry	Rel to S&P 500
Price/Earnings	18.4	0.8	0.8
Price/Book	3.7	0.8	1.2
Price/Sales	1.8	0.9	0.9
Price/Cash Flow	21.9	1.3	1.7

Major Fund Holders	% of Fund Assets
Rydex Basic Materials Inv	13.49
ProFunds Ultra Basic Materials Inv	11.48
Hennessy Leveraged Dogs	6.11
Payden Growth & Income R	5.99

Morningstar's Take   By Sanjay Ayer, 12-13-2002   Stock Price as of Analysis: $42.56

DuPont appears poised to capitalize on an economic recovery, but we believe the stock price already reflects the firm's growth prospects.

No stranger to strategic revision, DuPont has reinvented itself again. The company has spent $50 billion on acquisitions and divestitures over the past five years, with mixed results. Its venture into the pharmaceutical market was short-lived, as the firm was ill-equipped to compete with industry giants; it later sold the unit to Bristol-Myers Squibb. In 1999, the firm overpaid for Pioneer Hi-Bred International, the leading provider of seed products, as evidenced by a recent write-down of impaired goodwill (the amount paid for a company above its book value). The purchase also coincided with an emerging public backlash against genetically engineered foods.

Despite that checkered record, we applaud management's recent decision to sell the firm's textiles and interiors unit by the end of 2003. The once-stellar business has a rich portfolio of well-known brands (like Stainmaster and Lycra) and contributes 25% of sales, but global competition has pressured margins and crimped the segment's profitability. Separating the textiles unit will enhance the firm's chances of achieving its targets of 6% annual revenue growth and 10% earnings growth.

Success will ultimately be determined by DuPont's ability to innovate. While the company continues to pour money into its celebrated research and development platform, blockbuster products--once a hallmark of DuPont--haven't been forthcoming. Management aims to derive 33% of revenue from products developed in the previous five years (it's currently 24%). The company has touted several products in its pipeline, but we will remain skeptical until we see some positive results.

After a difficult 2001, DuPont has been a top performer in the chemical industry this year, posting strong earnings in the face of rising energy costs and weak pricing. Improving fundamentals in a cyclical industry emerging from a trough traditionally suggests a stock with considerable upside. In DuPont's case, however, we believe an economic recovery is already priced into the stock. If the company shows a renewed ability to produce lucrative products, we may consider raising our intrinsic value estimate. In the meantime, we'll wait for a deeper discount to our estimate before investing.

E*Trade Group ET

	Rating	Risk	Moat Size	Fair Value	Last Close	Yield %
	★	High	None	$4.00	$4.86	0.0

Industry	Investment Style	Stock Type	Sector
Securities	▦ Mid Growth	✦ Spec. Growth	$ Financial Services

Company Profile

E*Trade Group provides personal financial services over the Internet 24 hours a day. Originally an online brokerage firm, E*Trade has embarked on a major effort to diversify its revenue streams, acquiring a string of companies. It now offers a range of branchless banking services, financial products, brokerage services, news, and portfolio tools to the individual investor. Brokerage transaction revenue now accounts for about 30% of Internet revenue. The recent boom in mortgage refinancing helped E*Trade to make up for shrinking transaction volume in 2001.

Management

Christos Cotsakos has been CEO since 1996 and was instrumental in taking the company public. His $80 million pay package made him the highest-paid CEO on Wall Street in 2001, though the subsequent outcry prompted him to return $23 million.

Strategy

Once an online broker, E*Trade is diversifying away from its trading business in favor of steady and recurring revenue sources like mortgage lending. The company now wants to be an online one-stop financial shop and is focusing on cross-selling and up-selling current customers on additional products rather than on fighting over the dwindling pool of online traders.

4500 Bohannon Drive   www.etrade.com
Menlo Park, CA 94025

Competition

Competition	Market Cap $Mil	Debt/ Equity	12 Mo Trailing Sales $Mil	Price/Cash Flow	Return On Assets%	Total Return% 1 Yr	3 Yr
E*Trade Group	1,757	—	1,322	—	-1.1	-52.6	-43.8
Charles Schwab	14,579	—	4,198	—	0.5	-29.6	-23.4
Ameritrade Holding	1,224	—	439	—	—	—	—

Price Volatility

	Monthly Price High/Low			Relative Strength to S&P 500		
Annual $Price High Low	11.97 2.75	16.25 2.50	72.25 11.70	34.25 6.66	15.38 4.07	12.64 2.81

	1997	1998	1999	2000	2001	2002
Annual Total Return %	100.0	103.4	123.4	-71.8	39.0	-52.6

Fiscal Year-End: December	1997	1998	1999	2000	2001	TTM
Revenue $Mil	254	361	671	1,702	1,275	1,322
Net Income $Mil	18	0	-57	21	-242	-201
Earnings Per Share $	0.11	-0.01	-0.21	0.06	-0.73	-0.55
Shares Outstanding Mil	153	40	270	342	331	361
Return on Equity %	5.2	0.0	-3.9	1.2	-15.4	-13.7
Net Margin %	7.2	-0.1	-8.5	1.2	-18.9	-15.2
Asset Turnover	0.1	0.1	0.1	0.1	0.1	0.1
Financial Leverage	6.5	5.2	5.5	10.2	11.6	12.5

Valuation Ratios	Stock	Rel to Industry	Rel to S&P 500
Price/Earnings	NMF	—	—
Price/Book	1.2	0.7	0.4
Price/Sales	1.3	1.0	0.7
Price/Cash Flow	—	—	—

Major Fund Holders	% of Fund Assets
Jacob Internet	5.51
UM Small Cap Growth Instl	4.68
Munder NetNet A	4.50
Calvert Large Cap Growth I	4.30

Morningstar Grades

Growth [A-]	1998	1999	2000	2001
Revenue %	42.1	86.0	153.5	-25.1
Earnings/Share %	NMF	NMF	NMF	NMF
Book Value/Share %	896.3	-74.7	-4.9	-7.1
Dividends/Share %	NMF	NMF	NMF	NMF

Revenue growth was explosive until 2001, when net revenue fell 7% from the previous fiscal year. Without E*Trade's many acquisitions, this decline would have been steeper. We expect 2002 revenue to fall a further 10%.

Profitability [F]	1999	2000	2001	TTM
Return on Assets %	-0.7	0.1	-1.3	-1.1
Oper Cash Flow $Mil	24	-48	-255	—
- Cap Spending $Mil	154	246	130	—
= Free Cash Flow $Mil	—	—	—	—

Including the cost of stock options, E*Trade has not been profitable for the past three years. A $300 million goodwill write-down will damp earnings in 2002, though cost and compensation cuts are having a positive effect on operating profits.

Financial Health [F]	1999	2000	2001	09-02
Long-term Debt $Mil	—	—	—	—
Total Equity $Mil	1,452	1,746	1,571	1,465
Debt/Equity Ratio	—	—	—	—

Financial leverage has been creeping up and now stands at 12.5 times equity. That is high for the securities industry, but close to average for banks. Negative free cash flow has dogged E*Trade for the past five years.

Morningstar's Take By Rachel Barnard, 09-27-2002 Stock Price as of Analysis: $4.45

Between E*Trade's meager prospects and its record of poor corporate governance, we think there is little reason to consider investing in this stock.

E*Trade needs to get serious about shedding the vestiges of Internet-boom excesses and start looking out for its shareholders. From the scandal over the CEO's fat paycheck--while the stock price plummeted--to the scrutiny of the company's board, E*Trade's dirty laundry has gotten a much-needed airing. The picture that emerges is of well-paid executives and board members fiddling while watching Rome burn, leaving investors with the ashes. The company has addressed many of the glaring abuses, but given its record, investors should be wary.

Abuses aside, E*Trade is finally lumbering toward something that looks like profitability and permanence. With $300 million in goodwill write-downs, 2002 doesn't look to be profitable. But in 2003 and beyond, we expect the firm to be in the black even after the expense of stock options.

The improved outlook is due to a combination of diversification and expense management. Brokerage revenue still outstrips banking revenue, but E*Trade is having success in selling its brokerage customers all sorts of things, like mortgages, insurance, and car loans. The company's new strategy focuses on a wide breadth of products for customers willing to bank and trade online.

E*Trade's cross-selling and marketing strategy looks promising, too. The firm uses a database of customer attributes and economic indicators to focus on which products to push and when. Rates going down? Push mortgages. Just bought a house? We'll sell you insurance.

There are some hints of a successful strategy here, though it is still untested. But the online brokerage business and the banking business are both extremely competitive markets, and E*Trade will have to go well beyond its promising beginnings to succeed in the long term.

We believe most of the company's worth is captured in our $4 fair value estimate, giving the shares very little potential upside. We believe there are better bargains on more solid companies out there, and we think investors should put their money elsewhere.

MORNINGSTAR® Stocks 500

Eastman Kodak EK

	Rating	Risk	Moat Size	Fair Value	Last Close	Yield %
	★	Med.	None	$28.00	$35.04	5.1

Company Profile

Eastman Kodak manufactures imaging and information systems. The company produces film, photographic papers, photographic chemicals, cameras and projectors, photographic plates and processing equipment, as well as other imaging products that are sold under the Kodak name. Its commercial products include graphic-arts films, microfilm products, digital- and health-imaging products, copiers, and other business equipment. Foreign sales account for approximately 52% of Eastman Kodak's total sales. The company acquired Lumisys in December 2000.

Management

Daniel Carp became CEO in January 2000 and was named chairman in December 2000. In January 2002 he assumed the duties of chief operating officer Patricia Russo, who left after only nine months to become CEO of Lucent.

Strategy

In October 2001, Kodak announced its second major restructuring in six months, trying to minimize damage from the economic slowdown while positioning itself for an eventual recovery. At the same time, it's struggling to leverage its expertise and brand into digital photography without cannibalizing its traditional film sales.

343 State Street
Rochester, NY 14650
www.kodak.com

Morningstar Grades

Growth [C-]	1998	1999	2000	2001
Revenue %	-7.8	5.1	-0.7	-5.4
Earnings/Share %	EUB	2.1	6.0	-94.3
Book Value/Share %	92.4	0.0	-8.1	-11.5
Dividends/Share %	0.0	0.0	0.0	0.6

Revenue fell 5% in 2001, and we expect flat to down revenue in 2002. While digital photography revenue is likely to grow, we expect this to be offset by a continued decline in traditional film sales and processing.

Profitability [C+]	1999	2000	2001	TTM
Return on Assets %	9.7	9.9	0.6	3.3
Oper Cash Flow $Mil	1,933	982	2,065	2,199
- Cap Spending $Mil	1,127	945	743	574
= Free Cash Flow $Mil	806	37	1,322	1,625

Earnings have been clobbered by the slowing economy, falling 95% in 2001. Even excluding myriad restructuring charges, they were down by half. Margins have improved in recent quarters, however, as a result of aggressive restructuring.

Financial Health [B]	1999	2000	2001	09-02
Long-term Debt $Mil	936	1,166	1,666	1,227
Total Equity $Mil	3,912	3,428	2,894	3,390
Debt/Equity Ratio	0.2	0.3	0.6	0.4

Kodak's debt is relatively high for a company with such unpredictable earnings. Free cash flow has been consistently positive but lower than reported earnings.

Industry	Investment Style	Stock Type	Sector
Photography & Imaging	Large Value	High Yield	Consumer Goods

Competition	Market Cap $Mil	Debt/ Equity	12 Mo Trailing Sales $Mil	Price/Cash Flow	Return On Assets%	Total Return% 1 Yr	3 Yr
Eastman Kodak	10,224	0.4	12,759	4.6	3.3	25.5	-14.2
Fuji Photo Film ADR	16,504	—	12,996	—	—	—	

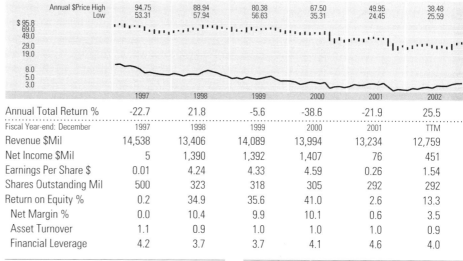

Price Volatility — Monthly Price High/Low — Relative Strength to S&P 500

Annual $Price High	94.75	88.94	80.38	67.50	49.95	38.48
Low	53.31	57.94	56.63	35.31	24.45	25.59

	1997	1998	1999	2000	2001	2002
Annual Total Return %	-22.7	21.8	-5.6	-38.6	-21.9	25.5

Fiscal Year-end: December	1997	1998	1999	2000	2001	TTM
Revenue $Mil	14,538	13,406	14,089	13,994	13,234	12,759
Net Income $Mil	5	1,390	1,392	1,407	76	451
Earnings Per Share $	0.01	4.24	4.33	4.59	0.26	1.54
Shares Outstanding Mil	500	323	318	305	292	292
Return on Equity %	0.2	34.9	35.6	41.0	2.6	13.3
Net Margin %	0.0	10.4	9.9	10.1	0.6	3.5
Asset Turnover	1.1	0.9	1.0	1.0	1.0	0.9
Financial Leverage	4.2	3.7	3.7	4.1	4.6	4.0

Valuation Ratios	Stock	Rel to Industry	Rel to S&P 500
Price/Earnings	22.8	0.9	1.0
Price/Book	3.0	1.1	0.9
Price/Sales	0.8	0.6	0.4
Price/Cash Flow	4.6	0.5	0.4

Major Fund Holders	% of Fund Assets
Hennessy Leveraged Dogs	6.73
Willamette Value	6.36
Navellier Large Cap Value	5.49
Edgar Lomax Value	5.18

Morningstar's Take By Joseph Beaulieu, 11-12-2002 Stock Price as of Analysis: $33.84

The struggling economy and fewer vacation photos in a post-9/11 world have contributed to Kodak's recent weakness, but the long-term shift from traditional to digital photography creates larger risks for the company.

Kodak has been attempting to adapt to an increasingly digital world, but the transition hasn't been easy. Sales in the company's professional division have been decimated over the past year by mass defections to digital cameras, and a similar defection is in its early stages among consumers. Trying to cover all the bases, Kodak is investing in a wide range of digital projects, from digital cameras to online photo finishing. Management expects combined digital initiatives to generate a profit by the end of 2003, but we doubt that the firm will be able to capitalize on digital trends enough to both offset traditional photography declines and show respectable revenue and earnings growth.

Even if the company meets its goal of regaining the market share in film that it has lost over the past year because of aggressive pricing from Fuji and the implosion of Kmart, we think it is going to be hard-pressed to make up for faltering consumer film sales and processing. Whereas users of traditional consumer cameras are accustomed to purchasing and

developing 24- or 36-exposure rolls of film and throwing away or storing all but a handful, digital camera users can be much more picky about which photos they have printed. Printing a few digital photos won't generate as much revenue as developing 24 or 36 photos at a time. So even if Kodak manages to gain share in the digital arena, it is not a certainty that the revenue trade-off will be even.

While almost 30% of Kodak's revenue comes from outside photography (health imaging and commercial imaging), the company is going to have a very difficult time generating substantial earnings and revenue growth without at least midsingle-digit revenue growth from the photography business. Nothing we have seen so far makes us think this is likely.

We are therefore basing our fair value estimate of $28 on the assumption that Kodak's photography revenue continues a very slow slide as film and photo processing wanes, and that both health imaging and commercial imaging show midsingle-digit growth. The company's dividend sweetens the pot, but it isn't enough to tempt us into buying the shares without a substantial margin of safety.

Eaton Vance EV

	Rating	Risk	Moat Size	Fair Value	Last Close	Yield %
	★★★★★	Med.	Wide	$40.00	$28.25	1.1

Company Profile

Eaton Vance manufactures, markets, and manages investment assets. Historically, Eaton Vance specialized in fixed-income funds but has since distinguished itself in tax-managed funds (both fixed income and equity) and in separate accounts, which allow wealthy investors to own a basket of managed investments, much like a mutual fund, in their own accounts. Eaton Vance recently purchased two equity asset-management firms and now has 59% of its assets under management in equity products. The firm's strategic priority is to expand the separate accounts business.

Management

Chairman and CEO James Hawkes began his career with Eaton Vance in the 1970s and came up through the ranks. A small group of company executives owns 100% of the voting shares, giving these insiders complete control of the firm's governance.

Strategy

Once known as a stodgy municipal bond shop, Eaton Vance now aims to have half of all new assets flow into its separate account products by 2006. The company also seeks to round out its offerings by buying or partnering with an international equity manager. Tax-managed funds will continue to be a profitable specialty.

255 State Street   www.eatonvance.com
Boston, MA 02109

Morningstar Grades

Growth [A]

	1998	1999	2000	2001
Revenue %	24.4	39.6	23.1	13.2
Earnings/Share %	-22.1	-48.1	652.4	1.3
Book Value/Share %	-3.9	-8.1	34.4	19.6
Dividends/Share %	21.4	25.5	26.6	24.7

Revenue climbed 4% in fiscal 2002, a good result in a challenging year for most asset managers. Revenue has grown at a compound annual rate of 21% in the past five years, helped along by two acquisitions.

Profitability [A+]

	1999	2000	2001	TTM
Return on Assets %	4.4	26.8	17.2	18.5
Oper Cash Flow $Mil	22	74	140	—
- Cap Spending $Mil	12	3	3	—
= Free Cash Flow $Mil	—	—	—	—

In 2001, Eaton Vance beat its average peer in profitability, with a return on assets of 17%. The firm expanded this to 19% in fiscal 2002. Operating margins around 35% are among the best in the industry.

Financial Health [A]

	1999	2000	2001	07-02
Long-term Debt $Mil	—	—	—	—
Total Equity $Mil	194	255	301	364
Debt/Equity Ratio	—	—	—	—

$117 million of convertible debt bumps Eaton Vance's financial leverage to 1.7 times equity, above most of its asset-management peers. The company is wise to take advantage of this low-cost financing while it lasts.

Industry	Investment Style	Stock Type	Sector
Money Management	Mid Growth	Classic Growth	Financial Services

Competition

	Market Cap $Mil	Debt/ Equity	12 Mo Trailing Sales $Mil	Price/Cash Flow	Return On Assets%	Total Return% 1 Yr	3 Yr
Eaton Vance	1,955	—	514	—	18.5	-19.8	16.6
Marsh & McLennan Companie	24,818	—	10,164	—	9.2	-12.0	2.8
Franklin Resources	8,929	—	2,519	—	6.7	-2.6	3.8

Price Volatility

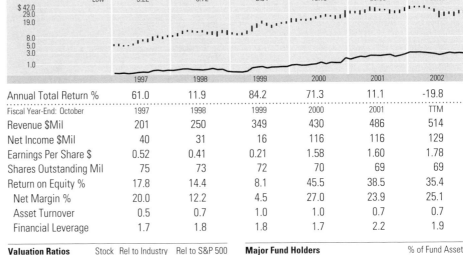

	1997	1998	1999	2000	2001	2002
Annual $Price High	9.56	12.55	20.00	32.94	39.22	41.00
Low	5.22	8.72	9.34	18.13	26.50	22.55
Annual Total Return %	61.0	11.9	84.2	71.3	11.1	-19.8

Fiscal Year-End: October	1997	1998	1999	2000	2001	TTM
Revenue $Mil	201	250	349	430	486	514
Net Income $Mil	40	31	16	116	116	129
Earnings Per Share $	0.52	0.41	0.21	1.58	1.60	1.78
Shares Outstanding Mil	75	73	72	70	69	69
Return on Equity %	17.8	14.4	8.1	45.5	38.5	35.4
Net Margin %	20.0	12.2	4.5	27.0	23.9	25.1
Asset Turnover	0.5	0.7	1.0	1.0	0.7	0.7
Financial Leverage	1.7	1.8	1.8	1.7	2.2	1.9

Valuation Ratios	Stock	Rel to Industry	Rel to S&P 500
Price/Earnings	15.9	0.9	0.7
Price/Book	5.4	2.0	1.7
Price/Sales	3.8	1.4	1.9
Price/Cash Flow	—	—	—

Major Fund Holders	% of Fund Assets
Fidelity Select Brokerage & Investmnt	3.21
Stratton Small-Cap Value	2.96
Bear Stearns S&P Stars A	2.94
Orbitex Financial Service A	2.75

Morningstar's Take   By Rachel Barnard, 12-02-2002   Stock Price as of Analysis: $31.92

We believe that Eaton Vance is one of the best values in asset management. The firm has a focused strategy and a diverse mix of assets that should allow it to prosper in a variety of market conditions. We wouldn't hesitate to scoop this one up from the bargain bin.

Eaton Vance has transformed itself into a profitable asset-management boutique with a whole array of investment products. The firm is focusing its efforts on the two groups of investors that it believes will be most profitable.

First, it intends to expand its client base of large institutions (universities, pension funds, and the like). Such clients typically come with a large portfolio of sticky assets. Second, it is focusing on separate account products, which allow wealthy investors to invest in a basket of funds, but also allow a small degree of customization to minimize tax liabilities. This has been a growth area in money management and Eaton Vance already has a considerable presence in the market. The firm's reputation for quality tax-managed funds should help differentiate its products in an increasingly crowded field.

The building blocks of this strategy are already in place and the company aims to increase separate account assets by $6 billion before the end of 2004.

The separate account sales force now numbers 15--up from two in 2001. And Eaton Vance is working with distributors to get additional visibility, or shelf space, for its products.

The firm has held up better than most of its peers during the recession. But the bear market has been no picnic for Eaton Vance's competitors and management has hinted that it might take advantage of its relatively good financial position to make some acquisitions on the cheap. With $150 million in cash, the firm could easily afford to bulk up. CEO Jim Hawkes has stated that the firm is looking at international acquisitions in particular.

With asset managers trading at low valuations, we think this would be the best use Eaton Vance could make of its capital. Strategic acquisitions now could position the firm well for the economic rebound and though Eaton Vance is well diversified, it does lack a portfolio of international offerings to round out its current funds.

Our fair value estimate remains at $40 per share and we are bullish on Eaton Vance. The shares would be an outstanding value below $28.

 MORNINGSTAR® Stocks 500

Data as of 12-31-02

eBay EBAY

Rating	Risk	Moat Size	Fair Value	Last Close	Yield %
★	Med.	Wide	$47.00	$67.82	0.0

Industry	Investment Style	Stock Type	Sector
Online Retail	Large Growth	Aggr. Growth	Consumer Services

Company Profile

EBay provides online person-to-person trading for buyers and sellers of personal items. These items include antiques, coins, collectibles, computers, memorabilia, stamps, and toys. Its service permits sellers to list items for sale and buyers to bid on items. As of December 31, 2001, the company had about 42.4 million registered users and had auctions listed in more than 18,000 categories. The company has entered into a marketing relationship with AOL. EBay also owns two auction-house subsidiaries. In addition, it operates a marketplace for small businesses.

Management

Founder Pierre Omidyar is chairman and owns about a third of the company. Day-to-day operations are run by CEO Meg Whitman, who came to eBay from Hasbro and was previously a brand manager for Procter & Gamble.

Strategy

EBay is expanding beyond its traditional base of relatively inexpensive collectibles into higher-end fare like cars, and it added a fast-growing fixed-price marketplace through its purchase of Half.com. It's also expanding overseas through both acquisitions and homegrown sites, giving it leading auction sites in Great Britain, Germany, France, and Taiwan.

2145 Hamilton Avenue
San Jose, CA 95125
www.ebay.com

Morningstar Grades

Growth [A]	1998	1999	2000	2001
Revenue %	108.2	160.9	92.0	73.6
Earnings/Share %	NMF	NMF	325.0	88.2
Book Value/Share %	—	NMF	-0.1	41.7
Dividends/Share %	NMF	NMF	NMF	NMF

Third-quarter revenue grew 49% from the year-earlier period, an acceleration from the second quarter despite slowdowns in noncore revenue. The company's goal of $3 billion in annual revenue by 2005 is a tall order but achievable.

Profitability [B]	1999	2000	2001	TTM
Return on Assets %	1.0	4.1	5.4	9.1
Oper Cash Flow $Mil	63	532	252	381
- Cap Spending $Mil	87	50	57	108
= Free Cash Flow $Mil	-24	482	195	273

Returns on capital have been consistently positive, which is rare for an Internet company. EBay's net margin was 20% in the first nine months of 2002, up from 12% a year earlier. It achieved its goal of a 30% operating margin ahead of schedule.

Financial Health [A+]	1999	2000	2001	09-02
Long-term Debt $Mil	15	11	12	9
Total Equity $Mil	854	1,014	1,429	1,823
Debt/Equity Ratio	0.0	0.0	0.0	0.0

Debt leverage has remained low, as the company has had no need to borrow money. It has $850 million in cash and short-term investments on its balance sheet, and it generates plenty of free cash flow.

Competition

Competition	Market Cap $Mil	Debt/ Equity	12 Mo Trailing Sales $Mil	Price/Cash Flow	Return On Assets%	Total Return% 1 Yr	3 Yr
eBay	18,804	0.0	1,020	49.4	9.1	1.4	2.0
AOL Time Warner	56,278	0.3	41,024	8.1	-34.6	-59.2	-44.6
Yahoo!	9,661	—	856	40.9	-0.4	-7.8	-58.1

Price Volatility

			1997	1998	1999	2000	2001	2002
Annual Total Return %			—	—	55.7	-47.3	102.7	1.4

Fiscal Year-end: December	1997	1998	1999	2000	2001	TTM
Revenue $Mil	41	86	225	431	749	1,020
Net Income $Mil	7	7	10	48	90	189
Earnings Per Share $	—	—	0.04	0.17	0.32	0.66
Shares Outstanding Mil	—	—	239	254	266	277
Return on Equity %	72.6	7.2	1.1	4.8	6.3	10.4
Net Margin %	17.1	8.4	4.3	11.2	12.1	18.5
Asset Turnover	0.7	0.6	0.2	0.4	0.4	0.5
Financial Leverage	6.4	1.5	1.1	1.2	1.2	1.1

Valuation Ratios	Stock	Rel to Industry	Rel to S&P 500
Price/Earnings	102.8	1.0	4.4
Price/Book	10.3	1.0	3.2
Price/Sales	18.4	2.4	9.2
Price/Cash Flow	49.4	1.0	3.7

Major Fund Holders	% of Fund Assets
Amerindo Internet B2B A	31.51
Amerindo Technology D	26.82
TCW Galileo Aggressive Growth Eq I	8.27
ProFunds Ultra Internet Inv	6.92

Morningstar's Take By David Kathman, 10-21-2002 Stock Price as of Analysis: $63.02

EBay is a great company that has executed its business plan flawlessly, but we'd want to see a 20% discount to our fair value estimate before buying the stock.

EBay is the unquestioned leader of the online auction industry. It has easily fended off challenges from such heavy hitters as Amazon.com and Yahoo, and it's hardly been affected by the slow economy; in fact, eBay seems to thrive in tough economic times, as more people search for bargains. Its core auction business has grown better than 70% annually, and should grow 50% annually in the near future. Operating margins have expanded beyond 30%. Overseas operations have been profitable for the past year, and now account for 24% of revenue.

To maintain its dominance, eBay has had to continually evolve and reinvent itself. For one thing, it has been moving beyond collectibles and into more practical items with much larger potential customer bases. EBay's largest category in terms of gross merchandise sales is now eBay Motors, which has shown excellent growth; its next-largest categories are computers and consumer electronics, many of them sold directly by manufacturers like IBM and Palm. It's also relying more on fixed-price sales, which now account for 22% of gross merchandise

sales through such features as BuyItNow and Half.com. A new option allows sellers to set a fixed price for any item and not bother with auctions at all.

EBay's $1.5 billion purchase of online payment platform PayPal should benefit both companies. For years, eBay has been trying to establish an effective online payment system that would make transactions easier for the small buyers and sellers who still make up the bulk of its users. EBay's own system, Billpoint, was never really able to challenge PayPal's dominance, so buying out the leader in the field makes a lot of sense.

While the stock is well off the highs it reached at the height of the Internet bubble, eBay remains quite expensive by just about any measure. We love the company's business model, and are impressed by how well it has adapted to maintain its competitive advantage. However, at some point the firm will have to slow down, which is why we're reluctant to get too aggressive in our projections. Our best estimate of eBay's fair value is $47 per share, and we would gladly buy the stock if it fell 20% or more below that.

©2003 Morningstar, Inc. All rights reserved. Intended for United States residents only, this report is for information purposes and should not be considered a solicitation to buy or sell any security. Visit www.morningstar.com for your research.

MORNINGSTAR® Stocks 500   217

EchoStar Communications DISH

	Rating	Risk	Moat Size	Fair Value	Last Close	Yield %
	★★★	High	Narrow	$28.00	$22.26	0.0

Company Profile

EchoStar Communications provides satellite television broadcasting services. The company operates six direct broadcast satellites that transmit digital satellite signals to the company's 5 million-plus subscribers throughout the United States. EchoStar provides approximately 300 channels of video and audio programming, including basic cable channels like ESPN, CNN, The Disney Channel, and USA Network; premium cable channels like HBO, Cinemax, and Showtime; and pay-per-view programming.

Management

EchoStar is a well-managed firm. Chairman and CEO Charles Ergen and director James DeFranco co-founded EchoStar in 1980. Their extensive experience and entrepreneurial spirit are major pluses for shareholders.

Strategy

EchoStar is focused on expanding its customer base, launching local channel service, and increasing the amount each subscriber spends. It's working to expand local programming in the 60 metro areas--holding about 65% of the U.S. population--where it already has a major presence and can offer services like Internet access and video on demand.

5701 S. Santa Fe Drive
Littleton, CO 80120
www.echostar.com

Morningstar Grades

Growth [A]	1998	1999	2000	2001
Revenue %	105.8	63.1	69.4	47.4
Earnings/Share %	NMF	NMF	NMF	NMF
Book Value/Share %	NMF	NMF	NMF	NMF
Dividends/Share %	NMF	NMF	NMF	NMF

Since the start of 2000, EchoStar's customer base has doubled, leading to impressive top-line growth; sales rose 47% in 2001 and will grow another 20% in 2002. Despite slowing subscriber growth, EchoStar should post double-digit sales gains for the next few years.

Profitability [D]	1999	2000	2001	TTM
Return on Assets %	-20.5	-14.1	-3.3	-3.4
Oper Cash Flow $Mil	-59	-119	489	620
- Cap Spending $Mil	91	331	637	500
= Free Cash Flow $Mil	-150	-450	-148	120

The amount spent on equipment subsidies and marketing began to fall in 2001, vastly improving profitability. Greater operational scale will bring substantial margin gains, as fixed costs are spread over a wider sales base.

Financial Health [D]	1999	2000	2001	09-02
Long-term Debt $Mil	3,031	4,000	5,700	5,997
Total Equity $Mil	-94	-668	-778	-994
Debt/Equity Ratio	ELB	ELB	ELB	NMF

EchoStar steadily raised cash to fund the now-defunct Hughes deal, leading to swelled debt levels. That said, interest coverage is handily above 1; insolvency isn't a major concern. We expect 2003 will be the inflection year for free cash flow.

	Industry	Investment Style	Stock Type	Sector
	Cable TV	Large Growth	Spec. Growth	Media

Competition	Market Cap $Mil	Debt/ Equity	12 Mo Trailing Sales $Mil	Price/Cash Flow	Return On Assets%	Total Return% 1 Yr	3 Yr
EchoStar Communications	10,673	NMF	4,646	17.2	-3.4	-19.0	-21.4
Liberty Media	22,975	0.2	2,065	—	-22.4	-35.3	-29.4
Comcast A	22,319	0.7	10,789	13.6	-1.5	-34.5	-18.3

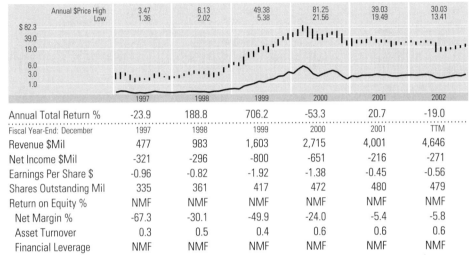

Price Volatility — Monthly Price High/Low — Relative Strength to S&P 500

Annual $Price High / Low	3.47 / 1.36	6.13 / 2.02	49.38 / 5.38	81.25 / 21.56	39.03 / 19.49	30.03 / 13.41
	1997	1998	1999	2000	2001	2002

Annual Total Return %	-23.9	188.8	706.2	-53.3	20.7	-19.0
Fiscal Year-End: December	1997	1998	1999	2000	2001	TTM
Revenue $Mil	477	983	1,603	2,715	4,001	4,646
Net Income $Mil	-321	-296	-800	-651	-216	-271
Earnings Per Share $	-0.96	-0.82	-1.92	-1.38	-0.45	-0.56
Shares Outstanding Mil	335	361	417	472	480	479
Return on Equity %	NMF	NMF	NMF	NMF	NMF	NMF
Net Margin %	-67.3	-30.1	-49.9	-24.0	-5.4	-5.8
Asset Turnover	0.3	0.5	0.4	0.6	0.6	0.6
Financial Leverage	NMF	NMF	NMF	NMF	NMF	NMF

Valuation Ratios	Stock	Rel to Industry	Rel to S&P 500
Price/Earnings	NMF	—	—
Price/Book	—	—	—
Price/Sales	2.3	0.7	1.1
Price/Cash Flow	17.2	1.1	1.3

Major Fund Holders	% of Fund Assets
Fidelity Leveraged Company Stock	18.75
Fidelity Advisor Leveraged Co Stk A	9.76
Jundt Twenty-Five A	6.07
Morgan Stanley Cap Opportunities B	5.22

Morningstar's Take By Todd P. Bernier, 12-10-2002 Stock Price as of Analysis: $21.09

Even without Hughes, EchoStar is the pre-eminent satellite operator in the States. We would buy shares in EchoStar, a firm with a narrow economic moat, at a 40% discount to our fair value estimate.

EchoStar has added 8 million subscribers since launching commercial service in 1995, driving revenue up 68% annually. If the satellite industry follows the same course as cable--as we expect--EchoStar's earnings before interest, taxes, depreciation, and amortization (EBITDA) should grow much faster than sales, leading to fatter margins. Indeed, margins are improving every quarter.

One of EchoStar's key competitive advantages is relatively low capital spending. Similar-size cable operators spend roughly 4 times what EchoStar does. Also, most of EchoStar's capital expenses are in the form of equipment leased by customers, something that can be slowed if necessary. Not only has low capital spending led to positive free cash flow, but it is a primary reason EchoStar can promote cheap service to win customers while cable rivals atrophy.

Scale is the reason EchoStar (fruitlessly) pursued its key rival, Hughes; profits soar as fixed costs are spread over a larger user base. Also, EchoStar wanted to prevent Hughes from falling into the hands of News Corp, a company that could inflict

substantial pain on EchoStar. But regulators prevented the marriage, arguing the coupling would hurt consumers. We disagree; we believe Big Satellite is the last defense against Big Cable. Nevertheless, we expect EchoStar to remain focused on improving operating leverage, gaining new customers, and launching local channels in more markets. In our view, local programming is the key to EchoStar's success because it makes satellite an attractive alternative to cable for more people.

Although the Hughes debacle ate up precious time and resources, including a $600 million breakup fee, it wasn't a complete waste. By temporarily scaring away Hughes' only other suitor and getting a long look at its strategies, EchoStar has made strides on its rival. For instance, EchoStar has beefed up its distribution network, gaining access to big retailers. Getting into RadioShack, once the exclusive domain of Hughes, is important because that is where Hughes gets roughly 10%-20% of its new subscribers; EchoStar's subscriber and profits gains should remain well ahead of Hughes.

We believe EchoStar has as bright a future as the cable companies, but without the onerous capital requirements. We'd buy the stock at a 40% discount to our fair value estimate.

MORNINGSTAR® Stocks 500

Ecolab ECL

	Rating	Risk	Moat Size	Fair Value	Last Close	Yield %
	★	Low	Narrow	$30.00	$49.50	1.1

Company Profile

Ecolab provides cleaning, sanitizing, and maintenance products and related services. Its products include water-treatment, vehicle-care, and infection-control products, as well as detergents. The company also offers pest-control and kitchen equipment repair services. Its customers include the food-service, lodging, health-care, dairy, and textile industries. It acquired full control of its joint venture with German-based Henkel in late 2001. Foreign sales account for about 23% of the company's total sales.

Management

Allan Schuman has a four-decade tenure at Ecolab and has been CEO since 1995. He owns 1.2% of the company's stock. His salary was $875,000 in 2001, with a $1.2 million bonus and 350,000 options, or 13.3% of 2001's total grant.

Strategy

Ecolab adds significant value to its product lineup with its 10,000 sales and customer-service representatives. This salesforce engenders tremendous brand loyalty through regularly scheduled sales and support calls. Frequent customer contact enables Ecolab to generate practical ideas for new products and product improvements.

370 Wabasha Street North   www.ecolab.com
St. Paul, MN 55102-1390

Morningstar Grades

Growth [A+]	1998	1999	2000	2001
Revenue %	15.1	10.2	8.9	4.0
Earnings/Share %	44.0	-9.0	19.1	-7.1
Book Value/Share %	25.4	9.9	0.9	18.4
Dividends/Share %	16.4	11.5	12.6	7.1

Growth has averaged 9.4% over the past decade, thanks mainly to the salesforce, a productive R&D platform, and acquisitions. Acquisitions are the real wild card in forecasting Ecolab's growth.

Profitability [A+]	1999	2000	2001	TTM
Return on Assets %	11.1	12.0	7.5	7.1
Oper Cash Flow $Mil	293	315	364	497
- Cap Spending $Mil	146	150	158	185
= Free Cash Flow $Mil	148	165	207	312

Ecolab's been consistently profitable: Returns on assets and equity have averaged 16.8% and 24.8%, respectively, over the past five years. The firm has kept margins fat by carefully managing costs and charging premium prices for its goods.

Financial Health [B+]	1999	2000	2001	09-02
Long-term Debt $Mil	169	234	512	540
Total Equity $Mil	762	757	880	1,053
Debt/Equity Ratio	0.2	0.3	0.6	0.5

Ecolab's balance sheet remains strong. Debt incurred from Henkel-Ecolab will still be quite manageable. Operations should continue to throw off strong free cash flow, as they have for the past decade.

Industry	Investment Style	Stock Type	Sector
Chemicals	Mid Growth	Cyclical	Industrial Mats

Competition	Market Cap $Mil	Debt/ Equity	12 Mo Trailing Sales $Mil	Price/Cash Flow	Return On Assets%	Total Return% 1 Yr	3 Yr
Ecolab	6,408	0.5	3,109	12.9	7.1	24.5	11.9
ServiceMaster	3,342	0.6	3,664	11.3	3.5	-17.5	0.9

Price Volatility

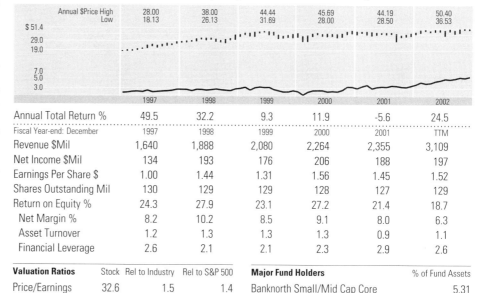

		Monthly Price High/Low		— Relative Strength to S&P 500	

Annual $Price High / Low	28.00 / 18.13	38.00 / 26.13	44.44 / 31.69	45.69 / 28.00	44.19 / 28.50	50.40 / 36.53
	1997	1998	1999	2000	2001	2002

Annual Total Return %	49.5	32.2	9.3	11.9	-5.6	24.5
Fiscal Year-end: December	1997	1998	1999	2000	2001	TTM
Revenue $Mil	1,640	1,888	2,080	2,264	2,355	3,109
Net Income $Mil	134	193	176	206	188	197
Earnings Per Share $	1.00	1.44	1.31	1.56	1.45	1.52
Shares Outstanding Mil	130	129	129	128	127	129
Return on Equity %	24.3	27.9	23.1	27.2	21.4	18.7
Net Margin %	8.2	10.2	8.5	9.1	8.0	6.3
Asset Turnover	1.2	1.3	1.3	1.3	0.9	1.1
Financial Leverage	2.6	2.1	2.1	2.3	2.9	2.6

Valuation Ratios	Stock	Rel to Industry	Rel to S&P 500
Price/Earnings	32.6	1.5	1.4
Price/Book	6.1	1.2	1.9
Price/Sales	2.1	1.1	1.0
Price/Cash Flow	12.9	0.8	1.0

Major Fund Holders	% of Fund Assets
Banknorth Small/Mid Cap Core	5.31
Fidelity Select Environmental	4.13
Badgley Growth	3.85
Delaware Core Equity A	3.57

Morningstar's Take By Daniel Quinn, 10-01-2002 Stock Price as of Analysis: $43.61

Given its long history of increasing shareholder value, we think Ecolab is a great company. This greatness comes at too steep a price, however.

Unlike its peers, who largely rely on retailers and other third parties to sell their products, Ecolab has a salesforce that aggressively markets its cleaning systems directly to customers, including hotels, restaurants, and hospitals. Monthly sales calls build strong customer relationships and foster brand loyalty. Ecolab can quickly react to the needs of its customers, who are willing to pay a premium price for this topnotch customer service. What's more, constant customer contact generates ideas for product lines and improvements.

While internal product development has been key to Ecolab's growth over the years, the company frequently fills holes in its lineup via acquisition. Between 1996 and 2001, revenue grew 9% annually. Exclude acquisitions, though, and that growth rate drops to 5.5%. Acquisitions will probably continue to be a part of the firm's growth strategy, so there is a risk that Ecolab could make a poor purchase or overpay for a company.

Management has largely avoided acquisition mistakes thus far. The company has increased earnings per share 9.4% annually since 1996--faster than revenue growth. Returns on assets averaged 16.6% during the same period, well in excess of Ecolab's cost of capital. The recent buyout of the Henkel-Ecolab joint venture has hurt returns recently, though, and it will take some time to see if this move will pay off. Still, Ecolab's performance has been impressive: Over the past 10 years the stock has returned 19.4% annually, compared with 7.8% for the S&P 500.

We do see some risk facing Ecolab. Given the firm's success, a larger, more diversified chemical company, like Dow Chemical, could use its resources to mimic Ecolab's customer-service strategy. Also, if the economy continues to worsen and Ecolab's clients continue looking for places to cut costs, they could choose cheaper substitute products.

As long as customer-service levels remain high, management prudently evaluates acquisition opportunities, and research and development is used to meet customer needs, Ecolab should prosper. However, the stock's recent performance has left the valuation stretched, in our view. We would require a generous margin of safety to our fair value estimate of $30 before getting excited about the shares.

El Paso EP

	Rating	Risk	Moat Size	Fair Value	Last Close	Yield %
	★★★★	High	Narrow	$12.00	$6.96	12.5

Company Profile

El Paso is a diversified energy company with four primary operating segments. Its pipeline business operates 60,000 miles pipelines in the United States and accounts for 34% of El Paso's operating income. Its merchant energy segment, a wholesale power generator and trader, makes up 32% of operating income. The company's field services and production business lines, which include exploration, gathering, processing, and storage of natural gas and oil, account for a combined 34% of El Paso's operating earnings. El Paso acquired Coastal in 2001.

Management

William Wise--CEO since 1990--has led the company's change from a local pipeline operator into a major energy company. Recent incidents concerning off-balance-sheet debt, reporting false trade data, and alleged earnings manipulation concern us.

Strategy

Like many other merchant energy companies, El Paso has seen its financial condition weaken because of its heavy debt load and energy trading shenanigans. In response, the company has stopped focusing on growth and has worked to improve its balance sheet by selling assets and paying off debt. It is also shuttering its trading business.

El Paso Building
Houston, TX 77002
www.elpaso.com

Morningstar Grades

Growth [C]	1998	1999	2000	2001
Revenue %	-25.1	2.9	32.0	4.8
Earnings/Share %	-78.6	44.1	424.5	-93.0
Book Value/Share %	-5.0	0.0	15.6	13.3
Dividends/Share %	4.8	4.6	3.0	3.2

Revenue has fallen 13.7% so far this year, mostly the result of much lower trading volume as well as a transfer of assets to El Paso Energy Partners EPN. Asset sales will keep revenue growth stuck in reverse.

Profitability [C]	1999	2000	2001	TTM
Return on Assets %	0.8	2.8	0.2	1.3
Oper Cash Flow $Mil	1,267	99	4,120	485
- Cap Spending $Mil	2,867	3,448	4,079	3,923
= Free Cash Flow $Mil	-1,600	-3,349	41	-3,438

Profitability has suffered in recent quarters because of the post-Enron meltdown in the merchant energy industry as well as a laundry list of write-offs El Paso has taken elsewhere. Penalties in California also greatly overhang profitability.

Financial Health [C]	1999	2000	2001	09-02
Long-term Debt $Mil	10,021	11,946	13,184	16,449
Total Equity $Mil	6,884	8,119	9,356	10,236
Debt/Equity Ratio	1.5	1.5	1.4	1.6

El Paso is making good on its plan to improve financial health. This year, it has issued $2.5 billion worth of stock and announced or completed $3.6 billion in asset sales. Next year, it plans to sell another $1.5-$2.0 billion worth of assets.

Industry	Investment Style	Stock Type	Sector
Pipelines	▦ Mid Value	⚡ High Yield	🔥 Energy

Competition

Competition	Market Cap $Mil	Debt/ Equity	12 Mo Trailing Sales $Mil	Price/Cash Flow	Return On Assets%	Total Return% 1 Yr	3 Yr
El Paso	4,160	1.6	12,207	8.6	1.3	-83.9	-41.2
Kinder Morgan	5,145	1.1	1,014	12.4	3.1	-23.5	24.5
Sempra Energy	4,844	—	5,936	—	—		

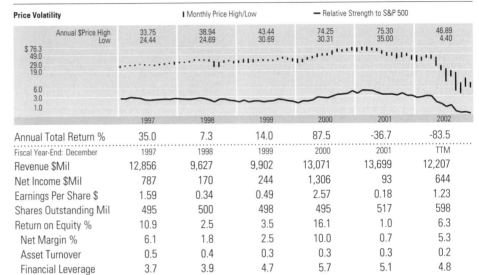

Price Volatility | Monthly Price High/Low — Relative Strength to S&P 500

Annual $Price High / Low	33.75 / 24.44	38.94 / 24.69	43.44 / 30.69	74.25 / 30.31	75.30 / 35.00	46.89 / 4.40
	1997	1998	1999	2000	2001	2002

Annual Total Return %	35.0	7.3	14.0	87.5	-36.7	-83.5

Fiscal Year-End: December	1997	1998	1999	2000	2001	TTM
Revenue $Mil	12,856	9,627	9,902	13,071	13,699	12,207
Net Income $Mil	787	170	244	1,306	93	644
Earnings Per Share $	1.59	0.34	0.49	2.57	0.18	1.23
Shares Outstanding Mil	495	500	498	495	517	598
Return on Equity %	10.9	2.5	3.5	16.1	1.0	6.3
Net Margin %	6.1	1.8	2.5	10.0	0.7	5.3
Asset Turnover	0.5	0.4	0.3	0.3	0.3	0.2
Financial Leverage	3.7	3.9	4.7	5.7	5.1	4.8

Valuation Ratios	Stock	Rel to Industry	Rel to S&P 500
Price/Earnings	5.7	0.3	0.2
Price/Book	0.4	0.2	0.1
Price/Sales	0.3	0.2	0.2
Price/Cash Flow	8.6	1.2	0.6

Major Fund Holders	% of Fund Assets
PBHG Clipper Focus PBHG	4.06
Clipper	3.88
FBR American Gas Index	3.48
PIMCO PEA Value Instl	3.23

Morningstar's Take By Paul Larson, 11-26-2002 Stock Price as of Analysis: $8.63

El Paso faces huge uncertainties as it moves forward in a troubled industry. We'd require a large discount to our fair value estimate before investing.

El Paso hasn't escaped the tumult in energy this year. Enron's debacle sparked it all, bringing to light bogus energy trading and the highly leveraged balance sheets propping up the industry. In Enron's wake, the credit-rating agencies required energy traders, including El Paso, to maintain much greater liquidity to keep their ratings. When many had problems coming up with the required cash, their credit ratings were chopped to junk status, further damaging already delicate finances.

Until recently, El Paso was one of the few energy traders to maintain an investment-grade credit rating. To avert a liquidity crunch, management has been frenetically acting to decrease debt. The company has sold $3.6 billion in assets, issued $2.5 billion in equity, and gotten creditors to ease covenants on $4 billion worth of debt. El Paso is also closing down its trading operations, which has eased liquidity requirements.

Even with these improvements, El Paso isn't out of the woods. Problems regarding El Paso's involvement in the California energy crisis have left stockholders and bondholders skittish. The recent rating downgrade is not fatal, since El Paso has removed essentially all of its rating triggers from its debt, but it does affect the market's confidence in the company, and subsequently its cost of capital.

A large part of El Paso's debt-reduction plan requires selling assets in a depressed environment. We have some concerns about the cash inflows from these sales. A great amount of uncertainty remains over El Paso's attempts to right its balance sheet.

Though the industry meltdown decimated El Paso's energy trading business, forcing it to be shut down, the core pipeline business remains rock-solid. The barriers to entry are high in the pipeline business, the service contracts tend to be of long duration, and demand is fairly steady. El Paso's pipeline business alone should generate $1.4 billion in operating income this year; it remains stable, predictable, and cash flow positive. While other parts of the company are crashing or being sold off, this pipeline network underpins El Paso's intrinsic value.

MORNINGSTAR® Stocks 500

Electronic Arts ERTS

	Rating	Risk	Moat Size	Fair Value	Last Close	Yield %
	★★★	Med.	Narrow	$54.00	$49.77	0.0

Company Profile

Electronic Arts creates and distributes interactive entertainment software for a variety of hardware platforms. The company markets more than 100 of its own titles and distributes more than 25 titles developed by other software publishers. The company develops products for multiple computer hardware platforms, including the PC, Apple, and PlayStation 2 video game system. The company is also producing games for the upcoming Microsoft Xbox and Nintendo GameCube systems.

Management

CEO Lawrence Probst has been with Electronic Arts since 1984. John Riccitiello, who joined the firm in 1997, is president and COO.

Strategy

Electronic Arts has invested heavily in developing games for the PlayStation 2, Xbox, and GameCube consoles. Between EA.com and the exclusive game channel on AOL, EA hopes to capitalize on gamers' thirst for networked gaming platforms.

209 Redwood Shores Parkway   www.ea.com
Redwood City, CA 94065-1175

Morningstar Grades

Growth [A-]	1999	2000	2001	2002
Revenue %	34.4	16.2	-6.9	30.4
Earnings/Share %	-2.5	51.7	NMF	NMF
Book Value/Share %	14.1	31.9	7.3	16.5
Dividends/Share %	NMF	NMF	NMF	NMF

EA operates in a highly cyclical business, and is approaching the top of the cycle. Even at the bottom, however, we expect at least 15%-20% annual growth.

Profitability [A]	2000	2001	2002	TTM
Return on Assets %	9.8	-0.8	6.0	12.8
Oper Cash Flow $Mil	78	194	285	453
- Cap Spending $Mil	135	120	52	45
= Free Cash Flow $Mil	-57	74	233	408

Gross margins hover around 50% and operating margins are around 9%, well above the competition's.

Financial Health [A]	2000	2001	2002	09-02
Long-term Debt $Mil	0	0	0	0
Total Equity $Mil	923	1,034	1,243	1,392
Debt/Equity Ratio	0.0	0.0	0.0	0.0

The company has plenty of room to maneuver, with $900 million in cash and no debt on its balance sheet. Cash flows have consistently been positive, but could fluctuate significantly with aggressive online and development spending.

Industry	Investment Style	Stock Type	Sector
Entertainment/Education Media	Mid Growth	Classic Growth	Software

Competition	Market Cap $Mil	Debt/ Equity	12 Mo Trailing Sales $Mil	Price/Cash Flow	Return On Assets%	Total Return% 1 Yr	3 Yr
Electronic Arts	7,220	0.0	2,088	15.9	12.8	-17.0	3.7
Activision	977	—	897	—	—	—	—
Take-Two Interactive Soft	924	—	700	—	—	—	—

Price Volatility

Annual $Price High	20.13	28.56	62.22	57.94	66.92	72.44
Low	9.63	16.63	19.00	24.50	34.50	49.47

	1997	1998	1999	2000	2001	2002
Annual Total Return %	26.3	48.4	49.7	1.5	40.6	-17.0

Fiscal Year-end: March	1998	1999	2000	2001	2002	TTM
Revenue $Mil	909	1,222	1,420	1,322	1,725	2,088
Net Income $Mil	73	73	117	-11	102	237
Earnings Per Share $	0.60	0.58	0.88	-0.08	0.71	1.67
Shares Outstanding Mil	118	121	126	123	112	145
Return on Equity %	12.9	11.0	12.6	-1.1	8.2	17.0
Net Margin %	8.0	6.0	8.2	-0.8	5.9	11.4
Asset Turnover	1.2	1.4	1.2	1.0	1.0	1.1
Financial Leverage	1.3	1.4	1.3	1.3	1.4	1.3

Valuation Ratios	Stock	Rel to Industry	Rel to S&P 500
Price/Earnings	29.8	1.0	1.3
Price/Book	5.2	1.0	1.6
Price/Sales	3.5	1.0	1.7
Price/Cash Flow	15.9	1.0	1.2

Major Fund Holders	% of Fund Assets
Northern Technology	7.61
Strong Growth 20 Inv	6.99
Super Core A	6.34
Rydex Leisure Inv	5.69

Morningstar's Take By Joseph Beaulieu, 12-12-2002 Stock Price as of Analysis: $61.34

This has been a banner year for the video game industry, and we think Electronic Arts will continue to benefit. Even so, we think the shares are fairly valued.

Fiscal 2003 (ending in March of that year) started off with a bang, with revenue growing 82% year over year in the June quarter and another 89% in September. The late 2001 launch of two new game consoles (Microsoft's Xbox and Nintendo's GameCube) and the sustained popularity of Sony's PlayStation 2 and the venerable PlayStation are big reasons for this success. We expect the console boom to continue, though not at quite that pace.

While the console war has focused investors' attention on the PlayStation, Xbox, and GameCube, it is important to remember that EA is the top dog in the PC game market. EA spent much of the 1990s snapping up many smaller game publishers, and its efforts have paid off. The Sims, with its five expansion packs (plus the upcoming online version), has become the top-selling computer game in the history of the industry, and still has some life in it.

We expect sales growth for the current fiscal year to come in near 40%. We think that the December quarter of calendar 2002 will be the peak of the video game cycle (although a strong list of new releases in

the March quarter should provide decent year-over-year growth) and that top-line growth will slide back toward the midteens.

One area of minor concern is the company's online division, EA.com, which is still losing money. EA's balance sheet is blemish-free, and online gaming could be an enormous market, so EA.com afford to lose money for now. But if the eagerly awaited Sims Online doesn't stem the red ink, we'll cut our fair value estimate by at least a small amount to account for the potential for ongoing losses in this business.

Our long-term outlook for EA is very positive. While we are concerned about the effect of the industry's cyclicality on the shares, we are confident that the company will continue to successfully navigate the up and down cycles as it has done for more than a decade. With the shares trading right around our fair value estimate of $54, we'd suggest waiting for a lower price--preferably a 30% discount--before buying.

Electronic Data Systems EDS

Rating	Risk	Moat Size	Fair Value	Last Close	Yield %
★★	High	Narrow	$20.00	$18.43	3.3

Company Profile

Electronic Data Systems provides information technology services, including managing computers, networks, information systems, information-processing facilities, and related business operations. The company's A.T. Kearney subsidiary provides business-management and marketing strategy and global sourcing and logistics-management services. Electronic Data Systems clients are primarily in the manufacturing, financial services, government, communications, transportation, health, and energy fields.

Management

Ross Perot founded EDS in 1962. CEO Dick Brown came on board in 1999 after serving as a telecom executive and CEO of H&R Block. Management has been very aggressive in expanding the business.

Strategy

Under CEO Dick Brown, EDS has performed well, cutting excess costs and expanding the business through acquisition and billion-dollar deals. Now, with the company under pressure for controversial accounting, exposure to risky contracts, and lackluster IT spending conditions, EDS' focus will turn to restoring investor confidence.

5400 Legacy Drive
Plano, TX 75024 -319
www.eds.com

Morningstar Grades

Growth [B+]	1998	1999	2000	2001
Revenue %	13.2	8.6	2.6	12.0
Earnings/Share %	1.4	-43.3	182.4	17.1
Book Value/Share %	11.0	-23.3	17.9	23.2
Dividends/Share %	0.0	0.0	0.0	0.0

Historical sales growth is skewed by past divestitures as part of a reorganization. Still, EDS is not a growth story; we project long-term sales growth at no better than 5% annually.

Profitability [A]	1999	2000	2001	TTM
Return on Assets %	3.4	9.0	8.3	6.6
Oper Cash Flow $Mil	1,936	1,559	1,722	1,962
- Cap Spending $Mil	685	768	1,285	1,119
= Free Cash Flow $Mil	1,251	791	437	843

Profitability has improved, thanks to cost-cutting. However, we expect additional margin gains to be minimal because nearly every excess cost has been cut.

Financial Health [A-]	1999	2000	2001	09-02
Long-term Debt $Mil	2,216	2,585	4,692	5,141
Total Equity $Mil	4,535	5,139	6,446	7,006
Debt/Equity Ratio	0.5	0.5	0.7	0.7

The balance sheet has worsened, with debt doubling in the past two years. Also, free cash flow has slowed because of up-front costs on large deals.

Industry	Investment Style	Stock Type	Sector
Consultants	⊞ Large Value	⬀ High Yield	▤ Business Services

Competition	Market Cap $Mil	Debt/ Equity	12 Mo Trailing Sales $Mil	Price/Cash Flow	Return On Assets%	Total Return% 1 Yr	3 Yr
Electronic Data Systems	8,774	0.7	22,127	4.5	6.6	-72.6	-32.5
IBM	130,982	0.8	82,442	9.0	5.8	-35.5	-11.1
Accenture	17,231	0.0	13,105	16.2	4.5	-33.2	—

Price Volatility

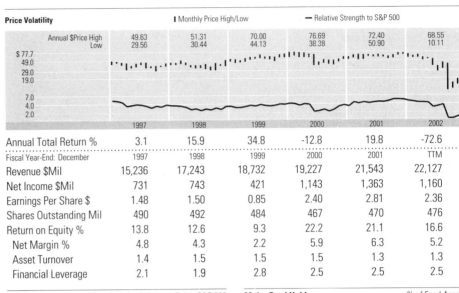

		Monthly Price High/Low		── Relative Strength to S&P 500	
Annual $Price High	49.63	51.31	70.00	76.69	72.40	68.55
Low	29.56	30.44	44.13	38.38	50.90	10.11

	1997	1998	1999	2000	2001	2002
Annual Total Return %	3.1	15.9	34.8	-12.8	19.8	-72.6

Fiscal Year-End: December	1997	1998	1999	2000	2001	TTM
Revenue $Mil	15,236	17,243	18,732	19,227	21,543	22,127
Net Income $Mil	731	743	421	1,143	1,363	1,160
Earnings Per Share $	1.48	1.50	0.85	2.40	2.81	2.36
Shares Outstanding Mil	490	492	484	467	470	476
Return on Equity %	13.8	12.6	9.3	22.2	21.1	16.6
Net Margin %	4.8	4.3	2.2	5.9	6.3	5.2
Asset Turnover	1.4	1.5	1.5	1.5	1.3	1.3
Financial Leverage	2.1	1.9	2.8	2.5	2.5	2.5

Valuation Ratios	Stock	Rel to Industry	Rel to S&P 500
Price/Earnings	7.8	0.4	0.3
Price/Book	1.3	0.4	0.4
Price/Sales	0.4	0.3	0.2
Price/Cash Flow	4.5	0.4	0.3

Major Fund Holders	% of Fund Assets
Thompson Plumb Select	8.24
Fidelity Select Business Serv&Outsrcg	5.58
PBHG Clipper Focus PBHG	4.94
Clipper	4.69

Morningstar's Take By Mike Trigg, 12-17-2002 Stock Price as of Analysis: $19.16

Although the firm's long-term outsourcing contracts generate predictable and recurring revenue, we no longer consider EDS a safe haven among technology stocks.

Despite drastic cuts in IT spending, EDS has performed well in recent years under CEO Dick Brown. The company has benefited from healthy demand for outsourcing and long-term customer relationships, an economic moat that's created barriers to entry for the competition. Brown also led an ambitious restructuring program that's cut $3 billion in excess costs.

But EDS grew in booming times by signing contracts with the companies that have since blown up, including the now-bankrupt WorldCom and US Airways. Although EDS could not have foreseen the demise of these behemoths, it signed other risky megacontracts that required significant up-front investments. These huge contracts have boosted revenue and earnings, but drained free cash flow. In many cases, EDS has been forced to make large capital expenditures before receiving any cash from customers. Also, revenue on these deals is usually recognized on a percentage-of-completion basis, which allows EDS to recognize some revenue before billing (that is known as unbilled revenue).

Buyers of EDS today are assuming that exposure to additional risky deals is limited and cash flow will improve when startup costs on large contracts decline. However, neither is a foregone conclusion. EDS has other risky contracts with airlines and troubled firms like Xerox. And to prime the growth pump, EDS will most likely be forced into more megacontracts that pressure free cash flow.

We conservatively peg EDS' intrinsic value at $20 per share. However, accounting concerns, the possibility of further problematic contracts, and the continued inability to generate meaningful free cash flow make EDS a risky bet. Despite the firm's decent-size economic moat in long-term customer relationships, we wouldn't buy the stock until it traded well under $12 per share. Until then, we'll sit safely on the sidelines.

MORNINGSTAR® Stocks 500

Eli Lilly & Company LLY

	Rating	Risk	Moat Size	Fair Value	Last Close	Yield %
	★★★	Low	Wide	$62.00	$63.50	2.0

Company Profile

Eli Lilly & Company produces pharmaceuticals for human and animal use. Its products include antibiotics, anti-infectives, diabetic-care products, and central nervous system and oncolytic drugs used to treat cancer. The company's major drugs include antidepressant Prozac, schizophrenia treatment Zyprexa, and Humulin insulin. Eli Lilly also manufactures products for animal use, like Tylan, an antibiotic for cattle, swine, and poultry. The company markets its products in the United States and overseas. Foreign sales account for about 36% of the company's total sales.

Management

Spanish-born Sidney Taurel is chairman and CEO. He's been with Lilly since 1971 in various roles and with various international divisions. Taurel started at Lilly as a marketing associate, and will take only $1 in salary for 2002.

Strategy

To drive growth and help launch a bevy of new drug candidates, Eli Lilly has nearly doubled its U.S. sales team and added 4,000 sales reps worldwide. Accompanying this personnel expansion is an increase in marketing dollars. The company's research strategy emphasizes breakthrough treatments for unmet needs that can claim to be the best in a given therapeutic class.

Lilly Corporate Center www.lilly.com
Indianapolis, IN 46285

Morningstar Grades

Growth [C]	1998	1999	2000	2001
Revenue %	15.6	8.3	8.6	6.3
Earnings/Share %	NMF	31.6	13.4	-8.6
Book Value/Share %	-3.7	14.8	21.7	18.1
Dividends/Share %	8.1	15.0	13.0	7.7

Given Prozac's demise, Lilly's revenue has held up fairly well. Year-to-date sales decreased 7% through September. Excluding Prozac, sales increased 8% over the same period. Several new products should fuel revenue growth over the next few years.

Profitability [A]	1999	2000	2001	TTM
Return on Assets %	21.2	20.8	16.9	13.5
Oper Cash Flow $Mil	2,742	3,732	3,662	2,456
- Cap Spending $Mil	528	678	884	1,053
= Free Cash Flow $Mil	2,214	3,054	2,778	1,403

Eli Lilly isn't as profitable as it used to be, but gross margins are still above 80% and operating margins are hovering around 30%. We expect Lilly's operating margins to sag over the next few years as it launches several new drugs, and then bounce back.

Financial Health [A]	1999	2000	2001	09-02
Long-term Debt $Mil	2,812	2,634	3,132	4,363
Total Equity $Mil	5,013	6,047	7,104	8,262
Debt/Equity Ratio	0.6	0.4	0.4	0.5

Lilly is very healthy, with an equal amount of cash and debt. Free cash flow (cash flow from operations less capital expenditures) as a percentage of revenue for the 12 months ended June 30, 2002, was a hearty 36%.

Industry	Investment Style	Stock Type	Sector
Drugs	⊞ Large Core	➡ Slow Growth	Healthcare

Competition

	Market Cap $Mil	Debt/ Equity	12 Mo Trailing Sales $Mil	Price/Cash Flow	Return On Assets%	Total Return% 1 Yr	3 Yr
Eli Lilly & Company	71,334	0.5	10,951	29.0	13.5	-17.6	1.8
Merck	127,121	0.3	50,430	13.2	15.0	-1.3	-2.5
Bristol-Myers Squibb	44,843	0.6	17,588	19.2	11.3	-52.4	-23.7

Price Volatility   ❙ Monthly Price High/Low   — Relative Strength to S&P 500

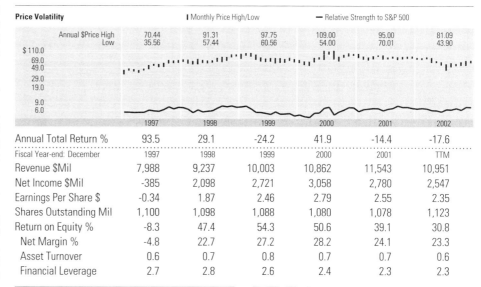

	1997	1998	1999	2000	2001	2002
Annual $Price High	70.44	91.31	97.75	109.00	95.00	81.09
Low	35.56	57.44	60.56	54.00	70.01	43.90
Annual Total Return %	93.5	29.1	-24.2	41.9	-14.4	-17.6

Fiscal Year-end: December	1997	1998	1999	2000	2001	TTM
Revenue $Mil	7,988	9,237	10,003	10,862	11,543	10,951
Net Income $Mil	-385	2,098	2,721	3,058	2,780	2,547
Earnings Per Share $	-0.34	1.87	2.46	2.79	2.55	2.35
Shares Outstanding Mil	1,100	1,098	1,088	1,080	1,078	1,123
Return on Equity %	-8.3	47.4	54.3	50.6	39.1	30.8
Net Margin %	-4.8	22.7	27.2	28.2	24.1	23.3
Asset Turnover	0.6	0.7	0.8	0.7	0.7	0.6
Financial Leverage	2.7	2.8	2.6	2.4	2.3	2.3

Valuation Ratios	Stock	Rel to Industry	Rel to S&P 500	Major Fund Holders	% of Fund Assets
Price/Earnings	27.0	1.1	1.1	One Group Health Sciences A	7.36
Price/Book	8.6	1.2	2.7	Matterhorn Growth	6.76
Price/Sales	6.5	1.7	3.2	Papp America-Pacific Rim	6.23
Price/Cash Flow	29.0	1.4	2.2	Smith Barney Health Sciences B	5.93

Morningstar's Take By Todd N. Lebor, 11-15-2002 Stock Price as of Analysis: $61.30

Oversize research spending--and its results--place Lilly near the top of our drug company pick list. We'd require only a 20% discount to our fair value estimate before investing.

Lilly's venerable new product lineup is primarily the result of a well-fed and productive research department. From 1997 to 2001, Lilly spent 18% of its revenue on research and development, while its peers spent only 13% on average. The result is Xigris, the first severe sepsis drug to be approved by the Food and Drug Administration; Cymbalta, a medicine for treatment-resistant depression; and Strattera, a pill for attention deficit hyperactivity disorder. These drugs are just beginning their marketed lives, so Lilly's revenue growth prospects look good. The Indianapolis-based company also has osteoporosis drug Forteo and Viagra competitor Cialis waiting in the wings.

But Lilly needs to figure out how to appease the FDA inspectors. Several of Lilly's most promising prospects, like Cymbalta, Forteo, and Zyprexa IntraMuscular, won't see the light of day until the FDA approves the company's factories, which have been under scrutiny since 2001. While we'd be happier if the inspections hadn't turned up problems, we think Lilly's response has been honest and

appropriate. In 2001, the company spent $50 million to upgrade manufacturing quality assurance and control, and added nearly 1,000 people to quality-control areas. Despite the product launch delays these unresolved manufacturing issues have caused, we think Lilly's product lineup is worth the gamble.

Lilly has also distinguished its research efforts by borrowing a page from the biotech playbook. Rather than directing all its attention to small-molecule drugs that can be sold in pill form (the common pharmaceutical approach), Lilly also focuses on large-molecule drugs like proteins that usually are administered by injection. Xigris, Forteo, and anticoagulant ReoPro are all results of this strategy, which often produces more targeted therapies and fewer direct competitors.

Lilly was built on the back of Prozac and still counts on neuroscience drugs for 40% of revenue, but over the years it has also built up a dominant position in the insulin market and offers competitive products for osteoporosis and cancer. Management has been forthright and taken corrective action regarding its manufacturing troubles, so we believe this won't be a recurring problem. We think Lilly is a good drug company to invest in at the right price.

EMC EMC

	Rating	Risk	Moat Size	Fair Value	Last Close	Yield %
	★★	High	Narrow	$6.00	$6.14	0.0

Company Profile

EMC is the leading storage hardware vendor. The company sells its products directly to end users (primarily large enterprises), through selected distributors, and through original equipment manufacturer agreements. During the year ending December 31, 2000, 70% of revenue came from the sales of storage hardware, 16% came from storage software, and 7% came from services.

Management

CEO Joseph Tucci joined EMC in early 2000 and is greatly responsible for the emphasis on software. Chairman Michael Ruettgers adds managerial depth.

Strategy

As demand for high priced storage hardware has slowed, EMC has moved into new markets. Also, it is betting heavily on storage software; the company's last eight acquisitions have been software companies. EMC is cutting costs aggressively and lowering prices to preserve market share.

35 Parkwood Drive
Hopkinton, MA 01748
www.emc.com

Morningstar Grades

Growth [C]	1998	1999	2000	2001
Revenue %	21.1	23.5	32.1	-20.1
Earnings/Share %	8.9	50.8	71.7	NMF
Book Value/Share %	25.8	29.6	60.8	-5.0
Dividends/Share %	NMF	NMF	NMF	NMF

Sales growth has plummeted alongside woes in IT spending. We expect new products and software to kick-start growth.

Profitability [A]	1999	2000	2001	TTM
Return on Assets %	14.1	16.9	-5.1	-1.3
Oper Cash Flow $Mil	1,390	2,109	1,631	1,567
- Cap Spending $Mil	542	858	889	502
= Free Cash Flow $Mil	847	1,250	742	1,065

EMC has struggled from a bloated cost structure and pricing pressure. Although expense cutting and high-margin software revenue should increase profits, the days of 25% operating margins are gone.

Financial Health [A+]	1999	2000	2001	09-02
Long-term Debt $Mil	687	0	0	0
Total Equity $Mil	4,952	8,177	7,601	7,434
Debt/Equity Ratio	0.1	0.0	0.0	0.0

The balance sheet is solid, with nearly $6 billion in cash and no long-term debt. EMC is using its healthy free cash flow to repurchase stock.

Industry	Investment Style	Stock Type	Sector
Computer Equipment	▦ Large Growth	➡ Slow Growth	▣ Hardware

Competition

	Market Cap $Mil	Debt/ Equity	12 Mo Trailing Sales $Mil	Price/Cash Flow	Return On Assets%	Total Return% 1 Yr	3 Yr
EMC	13,507	0.0	5,462	8.6	-1.3	-54.3	-50.9
IBM	130,982	0.8	82,442	9.0	5.8	-35.5	-11.1
Hitachi ADR	12,434	—	75,941	—	—	—	—

Price Volatility

ᛁ Monthly Price High/Low   — Relative Strength to S&P 500

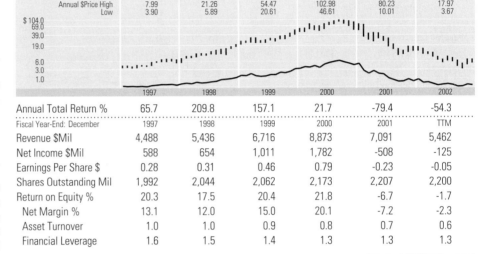

Annual $Price High Low	7.99 3.90	21.26 5.89	54.47 20.61	102.98 46.61	80.23 10.01	17.97 3.67
	1997	1998	1999	2000	2001	2002

	1997	1998	1999	2000	2001	2002
Annual Total Return %	65.7	209.8	157.1	21.7	-79.4	-54.3

Fiscal Year-End: December	1997	1998	1999	2000	2001	TTM
Revenue $Mil	4,488	5,436	6,716	8,873	7,091	5,462
Net Income $Mil	588	654	1,011	1,782	-508	-125
Earnings Per Share $	0.28	0.31	0.46	0.79	-0.23	-0.05
Shares Outstanding Mil	1,992	2,044	2,062	2,173	2,207	2,200
Return on Equity %	20.3	17.5	20.4	21.8	-6.7	-1.7
Net Margin %	13.1	12.0	15.0	20.1	-7.2	-2.3
Asset Turnover	1.0	1.0	0.9	0.8	0.7	0.6
Financial Leverage	1.6	1.5	1.4	1.3	1.3	1.3

Valuation Ratios	Stock	Rel to Industry	Rel to S&P 500
Price/Earnings	NMF	—	—
Price/Book	1.8	0.3	0.6
Price/Sales	2.5	1.6	1.2
Price/Cash Flow	8.6	1.0	0.7

Major Fund Holders	% of Fund Assets
Red Oak Technology Select	5.86
Conseco Science & Technology Y	5.02
IDEX Great Companies-Technology A	4.30
Fremont New Era Value	4.25

Morningstar's Take By Mike Trigg, 12-16-2002 Stock Price as of Analysis: $6.40

EMC's problems extend well beyond lackluster IT spending conditions. We wouldn't buy the stock until it traded 40% below our fair value estimate.

Like most tech companies, EMC has struggled as IT spending has slowed. Problems have been compounded by overcapacity, since businesses bought too much storage in the late 1990s. That said, long-term demand for storage is good. As businesses depend on the Internet and software to run business processes like sales and marketing, data will need to be stored and accessed quickly. And in the wake of September 11, companies understand more than ever the importance of backing up critical information.

In our opinion, superior technology is EMC's economic moat. In the late 1990's, the firm made a fortune selling storage boxes that were superior to the competition. This translated into high prices, which led to lofty profit margins and returns on invested capital exceeding 20%. And because there is a lack of common standards in the storage industry, which prevents products from different vendors from working well together, the company had a lock on customers once they settled on EMC's proprietary platform.

But EMC's moat has narrowed. IBM and Hitachi have been closing the technological gap, yet offer

lower prices. For example, Big Blue can bundle hardware, software, and services together, and practically give the storage away for free. And in the current environment, many businesses are willing to forego a superior product for one that meets their basic needs. Despite lowering prices, cutting costs, and moving into new markets through its reseller partnership with Dell, EMC still struggles to earn a profit.

The key to the company's new strategy is an emphasis on software. EMC is developing software that allows companies to manage storage regardless of the hardware vendor. For instance, EMC software is able to look into an IBM box and see how much room is left. This is significant in light of the industry's lack of standards. But it also risks making hardware a commodity should software be used to better manage storage needs.

EMC remains dominant in storage and has recently taken some positive actions. However, we wouldn't buy the stock until it traded well below our fair value estimate, mainly because stiff competition isn't going away and EMC's bet on software has yet to pay dividends.

MORNINGSTAR® Stocks 500

Emerson Electric EMR

	Rating	Risk	Moat Size	Fair Value	Last Close	Yield %
	★★★	Med.	Narrow	$57.00	$50.85	3.1

Company Profile

Emerson manufactures electrical and electronic products and components. The company's products include computer power supplies, electrical-testing equipment, valves, switches, heating, ventilating, and air-conditioning equipment, and electric motors. In addition, Emerson produces saws, grinders, battery-powered screwdrivers, drills, and sanders, which are sold under such brand names as Bosch, Sears, and Skil. Foreign sales account for about 40% of the company's total sales. It agreed to acquire Ericsson Telephone's energy systems operations in 2000.

Management

Emerson is renowned for its strong leadership and decentralized operating policies. David Farr, a 21-year company veteran, became CEO in late 2000. He succeeded Chuck Knight, who'd led the company since 1973 and remains chairman.

Strategy

Known for innovative products and rigorous planning, Emerson is shifting its business mix into faster-growing markets like electronic components and network power supply equipment. While this probably couldn't have come at a worse time given the collapse of telecom, we don't expect the firm's balanced approach to costs and product innovation will change.

8000 West Florissant Avenue   www.gotoemerson.com
St. Louis, MO 63136

Morningstar Grades

Growth [D+]

	1999	2000	2001	2002
Revenue %	6.1	8.9	-0.4	-10.7
Earnings/Share %	8.3	10.0	-27.3	-87.9
Book Value/Share %	7.9	5.2	-4.3	-4.0
Dividends/Share %	10.2	10.0	7.0	1.3

Plodding growth is often cited as Emerson's Achilles' heel--revenue hasn't expanded much faster than nominal GDP in the past decade. A shift in strategy aims to generate faster growth, which runs the risk of diluting profitability.

Profitability [B+]

	2000	2001	2002	TTM
Return on Assets %	9.4	6.9	0.8	0.8
Oper Cash Flow $Mil	1,840	1,708	1,818	1,818
- Cap Spending $Mil	692	554	384	384
= Free Cash Flow $Mil	1,148	1,154	1,434	1,434

Emerson's margins and returns on equity have been remarkable for any business, let alone an industrial component manufacturer. This owes to a deliberate focus on margins during the 1980s and 1990s rather than high growth.

Financial Health [A]

	2000	2001	2002	09-02
Long-term Debt $Mil	2,248	2,256	2,990	2,990
Total Equity $Mil	6,403	6,114	5,741	5,741
Debt/Equity Ratio	0.4	0.4	0.5	0.5

The company has shown a willingness to take on more debt in recent years to fund acquisitions. Debt/capital was 44% at fiscal year-end, above historical levels but well supported by strong operating income and free cash flow.

Industry	Investment Style	Stock Type	Sector
Electric Equipment	Large Value	High Yield	Industrial Mats

Competition

	Market Cap $Mil	Debt/ Equity	12 Mo Trailing Sales $Mil	Price/Cash Flow	Return On Assets%	Total Return% 1 Yr	3 Yr
Emerson Electric	21,400	0.5	13,824	11.8	0.8	-8.3	-1.1
General Electric	242,308	2.2	130,295	8.2	2.7	-37.7	-18.9
Siemens AG ADR	37,222	—	75,745	—	—	—	—

Price Volatility

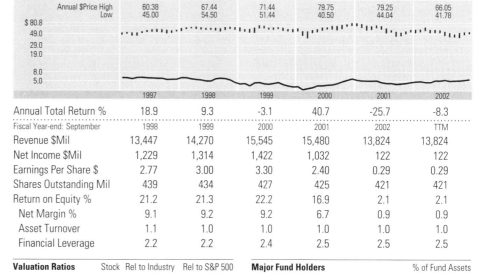

	1997	1998	1999	2000	2001	2002
Annual $Price High	60.38	67.44	71.44	79.75	79.25	66.05
Low	45.00	54.50	51.44	40.50	44.04	41.78
Annual Total Return %	18.9	9.3	-3.1	40.7	-25.7	-8.3

Fiscal Year-end: September	1998	1999	2000	2001	2002	TTM
Revenue $Mil	13,447	14,270	15,545	15,480	13,824	13,824
Net Income $Mil	1,229	1,314	1,422	1,032	122	122
Earnings Per Share $	2.77	3.00	3.30	2.40	0.29	0.29
Shares Outstanding Mil	439	434	427	425	421	421
Return on Equity %	21.2	21.3	22.2	16.9	2.1	2.1
Net Margin %	9.1	9.2	9.2	6.7	0.9	0.9
Asset Turnover	1.1	1.0	1.0	1.0	1.0	1.0
Financial Leverage	2.2	2.2	2.4	2.5	2.5	2.5

Valuation Ratios	Stock	Rel to Industry	Rel to S&P 500
Price/Earnings	175.3	10.8	7.5
Price/Book	3.7	1.0	1.2
Price/Sales	1.5	0.8	0.8
Price/Cash Flow	11.8	1.4	0.9

Major Fund Holders	% of Fund Assets
Fidelity Select Industrial Equipment	5.54
RSI Retirement Trust Core Equity	5.19
Jensen	4.99
Enterprise Growth and Income Y	4.79

Morningstar's Take By Josh Peters, 11-26-2002 Stock Price as of Analysis: $49.17

Emerson isn't as rock-solid as it used to be, but we think it would be attractive around $40.

In our view, Emerson is one of the strongest players in the electrical equipment industry. Though it's known for being tight with operating costs, the firm has a long history of wise investments in innovation. Its Copeland scroll compressor technology (used primarily in refrigeration and air-conditioning applications) is the class of the industry; it's one of the few businesses we know of that is operating at full capacity and still growing. The PlantWeb network platform for Emerson's lineup of industrial controls has been another home run, helping it gain share in the shrinking factory equipment market.

But Emerson reached out for faster growth at almost exactly the wrong time, making heavy investments in electronic, networking, and telecom-related fields just as the tech bubble was about to burst. Though the company has done an admirable job of just keeping these operations in the black, this still was the largest single factor in ending Emerson's 43-year streak of higher earnings. Use of debt has also risen in recent years, with borrowings as a share of total capital a moderately high 44%.

The real challenge Emerson faces isn't in its immediate control: Corporate capital spending is likely to stay depressed for some time. One reason that Emerson's own free cash flows have hit new records is that it's cut back its own investments in capacity (down 45% from fiscal 2000's peak) and inventory (down 20%). Trouble is, virtually every other manufacturer is employing the same strategy--which means they're not buying Emerson's factory controls, industrial motors, and network power equipment.

We don't expect corporate capital spending to deteriorate much further, but it will take quite a rebound in economic activity to get manufacturers spending again. Capacity utilization, which averaged 82% in the 1990s, is presently a weak 75%. Total output of manufactured goods will have to rise substantially before investment in new factories will be needed. Until then, Emerson's top line is likely to remain well below 2000's record.

Still, we think strong cash flows make Emerson worth owning at an appropriate price. It's repurchased $4 billion worth of stock in the last decade, and in early November, it raised its annual dividend rate for the 47th consecutive year. This strong cash performance offsets our concerns about the firm's debt load and underscores the modest fundamental risk we find in Emerson's diversified mix of businesses.

ENI SpA ADR E

	Rating	Risk	Moat Size	Fair Value	Last Close	Yield %
	★★	Med.	Narrow	$72.00	$78.49	3.0

Company Profile

Rome-based ENI explores for and produces oil and natural gas in Italy and abroad. The company holds proven reserves of 6.9 billion equivalent barrels of oil and gas, has the ability to refine nearly 900,000 barrels a day, and owns 11,700 retail service stations. One of the more diversified major energy companies, ENI also has operations in oil field services, petrochemicals, natural gas distribution and electricity generation. The company's shares trade on the NYSE as American Depository Receipts.

Management

Vittorio Mincato has risen through the ranks of the firm since joining in 1957 and became CEO in 1998.

Strategy

ENI is trying to improve its stance in the international oil industry by aggressively expanding and buying companies outside its Italian home turf. ENI also hopes to gain cost efficiencies and reduce commodity price exposure by staying vertically integrated instead of relying on contractors for services like drilling.

Piazzale Enrico Mattei, 1   www.eni.it/english/home.html
Rome, 1-00144

Morningstar Grades

Growth [A-]	1998	1999	2000	2001
Revenue %	-9.2	9.9	52.8	2.1
Earnings/Share %	-12.1	24.1	100.0	37.5
Book Value/Share %	5.2	15.2	20.6	25.6
Dividends/Share %	7.3	16.8	17.1	76.9

Even with lower oil prices, ENI managed to increase sales last year, a feat unmatched by its oil patch peers. ENI's expansion in upstream exploration and production should make growth more cyclical and lumpy than before.

Profitability [A]	1999	2000	2001	TTM
Return on Assets %	6.6	10.1	12.4	12.4
Oper Cash Flow $Mil	7,981	8,828	9,832	9,832
- Cap Spending $Mil	4,845	4,739	4,033	4,033
= Free Cash Flow $Mil	3,136	4,089	5,799	5,799

ENI's profitability has been great, even with low commodity prices. In 1998, when most oil companies were in the red, ENI managed a 9.8% return on assets. Returns on capital were 21.5% last year, though we expect weaker results in the future.

Financial Health [NA]	1999	2000	2001	12-01
Long-term Debt $Mil	4,787	4,826	5,384	5,384
Total Equity $Mil	18,398	21,133	24,321	24,321
Debt/Equity Ratio	0.3	0.2	0.2	0.2

While not sitting on a mound of cash, ENI has only a modest amount of debt. Its long-term debt/equity ratio is 0.5, down from 0.9 in 1997. Total debt has risen with recent acquisitions, but so have equity and cash flow.

Industry	Investment Style	Stock Type	Sector
Oil & Gas	▦ Large Core	▦ Hard Assets	◈ Energy

Competition	Market Cap $Mil	Debt/ Equity	12 Mo Trailing Sales $Mil	Price/Cash Flow	Return On Assets%	Total Return% 1 Yr	3 Yr
ENI SpA ADR	62,812	0.2	44,449	6.4	12.4	30.6	17.5
ExxonMobil	235,108	0.1	196,513	12.0	6.7	-8.9	-0.9
BP PLC ADR	152,063	0.2	175,389	6.8	5.7	-9.9	-9.2

Price Volatility

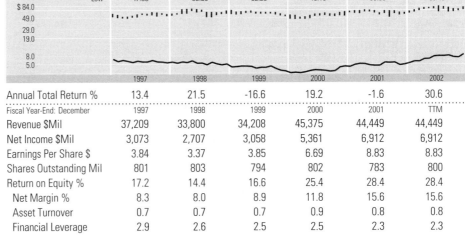

| | Monthly Price High/Low | — Relative Strength to S&P 500 |

Annual $Price High	63.94	74.50	69.75	65.00	70.25	83.05
Low	47.88	50.38	52.25	46.13	50.50	60.46

	1997	1998	1999	2000	2001	2002
Annual Total Return %	13.4	21.5	-16.6	19.2	-1.6	30.6

Fiscal Year-End: December	1997	1998	1999	2000	2001	TTM
Revenue $Mil	37,209	33,800	34,208	45,375	44,449	44,449
Net Income $Mil	3,073	2,707	3,058	5,361	6,912	6,912
Earnings Per Share $	3.84	3.37	3.85	6.69	8.83	8.83
Shares Outstanding Mil	801	803	794	802	783	800
Return on Equity %	17.2	14.4	16.6	25.4	28.4	28.4
Net Margin %	8.3	8.0	8.9	11.8	15.6	15.6
Asset Turnover	0.7	0.7	0.7	0.9	0.8	0.8
Financial Leverage	2.9	2.6	2.5	2.5	2.3	2.3

Valuation Ratios	Stock	Rel to Industry	Rel to S&P 500
Price/Earnings	8.9	0.5	0.4
Price/Book	2.6	1.2	0.8
Price/Sales	1.4	1.3	0.7
Price/Cash Flow	6.4	0.9	0.5

Major Fund Holders	% of Fund Assets
AssetMark International Equity	3.73
Hennessy Cornerstone Value	2.92
Vanguard Energy	2.67
INVESCO Energy Inv	2.65

Morningstar's Take By Paul Larson, 12-16-2002 Stock Price as of Analysis: $75.18

ENI appears to be making strides in its evolution from an Italian natural gas monopoly into an integrated international oil company. ENI wants to greatly increase its stature in the oil patch outside Italy; it's taken major stakes in gas distributors operating in Spain, Portugal, and Argentina, diversifying geographically.

Meanwhile, the firm has beefed up its upstream exploration and production by aggressively bidding for new properties around the globe and scooping up select oil companies, like British firm Lasmo. ENI's goal is to produce 1.6 million barrel equivalents of oil and gas per day by next year, up from the 1.3 million barrels it was doing at the end of last year. This translates to 23% growth over two years, which would make ENI's production growth the highest among its peers.

While ENI's relatively small size in oil affords heady growth, its diminutive stature will also make keeping unit costs in line with the oil supermajors an uphill battle. ENI remains a second-tier player in an industry where size and economies of scale matter. BP and Royal Dutch, for example, each produce nearly triple the amount of oil and gas that ENI does. While ENI has been a well-managed company, we would label its competitive position in oil as solidly mediocre.

Becoming more efficient is one of ENI's major goals. The company is selling portions of its low-margin petrochemical business while reinvesting the capital in areas like international oil production, where it hopes to achieve higher returns. With OPEC maintaining its strong influence over oil prices and keeping industrywide profitability high, this is probably a good strategy for ENI.

ENI is much more than just oil; the company still has its core gas and power distribution businesses in Europe. These legacy businesses are quite profitable, pushing returns on invested capital above 20% in 2000. As the firm gets into the more competitive oil business, though, we expect returns to fall from these lofty levels.

We wouldn't mind owning this stock at the right price, but that price is a bit lower than some of ENI's peers, all else equal. Aside from its weaker competitive position, the Italian company is tough to track and its future even tougher to predict. ENI stock is cheaper than some of the others in oil, but we don't see that discount disappearing soon.

MORNINGSTAR® Stocks 500

Equity Office Properties Trust EOP

	Rating	Risk	Moat Size	Fair Value	Last Close	Yield %
	★★★	Low	Narrow	$27.00	$24.98	8.0

Company Profile

Equity Office Properties Trust is a real-estate investment trust. The company owns or has an interest in 669 office properties containing approximately 125 million rentable square feet of office space. At the end of September 2001, 94% of the company's available space was occupied. No single tenant accounts for more than 2% of its annualized rent. Equity Office Properties Trust acquired Spieker Properties in July 2001.

Management

Former CFO Richard Kincaid was promoted to president and CEO in November 2002, which filled the void left when the former CEO resigned abruptly in April. Founder and real estate legend Sam Zell says he will remain an active chairman.

Strategy

Equity Office is making the transition from aggressive acquisitor to efficient operator and provider of value-added real-estate-related services. This strategy depends on Equity Office's scale and good tenant relationships. The company concentrates on high-end office properties in major markets, which means high rents and high barriers to entry.

Two North Riverside Plaza   www.equityoffice.com
Chicago, IL 60606

Morningstar Grades

Growth [A]	1998	1999	2000	2001
Revenue %	123.3	15.6	16.6	38.2
Earnings/Share %	NMF	19.4	2.7	2.0
Book Value/Share %	NMF	-4.5	10.8	7.7
Dividends/Share %	146.4	14.5	10.1	9.2

Since Equity Office's 1997 IPO, growth has been driven by the purchase of three other large office REITs, but management plans to become less acquisitive. A greater share of revenue growth is expected to come from services and well-timed asset sales.

Profitability [A-]	1999	2000	2001	TTM
Return on Assets %	2.7	2.3	2.2	2.5
Oper Cash Flow $Mil	721	907	1,242	—
- Cap Spending $Mil	297	294	360	—
= Free Cash Flow $Mil	—	—	—	—

Operating margins have improved over the years, thanks to the firm's ability to spread costs over its huge asset base. The operating margin for the quarter ended September 30 was 68.1%, more than 100 basis points higher than in 2000.

Financial Health [A]	1999.	2000	2001	09-02
Long-term Debt $Mil	—	—	—	—
Total Equity $Mil	6,213	7,457	10,445	10,444
Debt/Equity Ratio	—	—	—	—

Equity Office's debt/total market capitalization is 49%, about even with the industry average. The fixed-charge coverage ratio is adequate at more than 2.5 times, and the firm's senior unsecured debt is rated investment-grade.

Industry	Investment Style	Stock Type	Sector
REITS	▦ Large Value	▦ Hard Assets	$ Financial Services

Competition	Market Cap $Mil	Debt/ Equity	12 Mo Trailing Sales $Mil	Price/Cash Flow	Return On Assets%	Total Return% 1 Yr	3 Yr
Equity Office Properties Trust	10,284	—	3,562	—	2.5	-10.8	7.6
Boston Properties	3,348	—	1,144	—	—	—	—
Mack-Cali Realty	1,747	—	579	—	—	—	—

Price Volatility

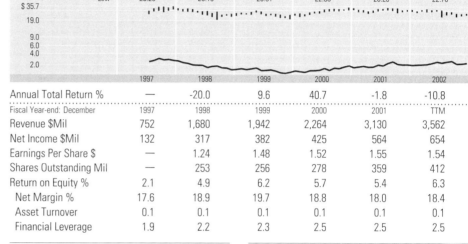

		1997	1998	1999	2000	2001	2002
Annual $Price High Low		34.69 25.25	32.00 20.19	29.44 20.81	33.50 22.88	33.08 26.20	31.36 22.78
Annual Total Return %		—	-20.0	9.6	40.7	-1.8	-10.8

Fiscal Year-end: December	1997	1998	1999	2000	2001	TTM
Revenue $Mil	752	1,680	1,942	2,264	3,130	3,562
Net Income $Mil	132	317	382	425	564	654
Earnings Per Share $	—	1.24	1.48	1.52	1.55	1.54
Shares Outstanding Mil	—	253	256	278	359	412
Return on Equity %	2.1	4.9	6.2	5.7	5.4	6.3
Net Margin %	17.6	18.9	19.7	18.8	18.0	18.4
Asset Turnover	0.1	0.1	0.1	0.1	0.1	0.1
Financial Leverage	1.9	2.2	2.3	2.5	2.5	2.5

Valuation Ratios	Stock	Rel to Industry	Rel to S&P 500
Price/Earnings	16.2	0.9	0.7
Price/Book	1.0	0.6	0.3
Price/Sales	2.9	0.9	1.4
Price/Cash Flow	—	—	—

Major Fund Holders	% of Fund Assets
Gabelli Westwood Realty AAA	8.33
Delaware Pooled Real Estate Inv Tr II	7.98
Delaware REIT A	7.96
Fidelity Real Estate Investment	7.63

Morningstar's Take By Matthew Scholz, 12-16-2002 Stock Price as of Analysis: $25.45

Equity Office Properties faces a difficult leasing environment that may get worse before it gets better, but this blue-chip real estate investment trust (REIT) should safely weather the current economic storm. Our net asset value is $27 per share.

Commercial office real estate fundamentals have deteriorated markedly over the past year. As of September 30, the national office vacancy rate was 16.8%, the highest since the recession of the early 1990s. However, REITs are in a far better position today than they were during the previous recession; over the past decade the best REITs, as exemplified by Equity Office, have become sophisticated operating companies led by professional managers. The overall level of REITs' debt is lower and there is less speculative building.

An important point, given the tough conditions, is that the weighted average term of Equity Office's leases is over five years. The relatively predictable and stable stream of cash flows generated by these leases helps Equity Office steer through the worst troughs of the business cycle.

Equity Office is 3 times the size of the next-biggest office REIT, and is the largest or second-largest landlord in nine of its top ten markets. All of this heft gives the firm scale advantages that

few other REITs have. Besides a good bargaining position with its suppliers, this scale provides Equity Office with a competitive advantage over its rivals: a superior client-servicing position. No other firm can offer a tenant as broad a range of property types and leasing options across major metropolitan markets.

Another reason to stick with Equity Office is its 7.7% dividend yield. Assuming the company doesn't cut its dividend--a highly unlikely event, given the strength of its balance sheet--long-term investors get paid a hearty dividend to wait for the office market to recover.

However, we don't anticipate much share appreciation over the next couple of years. Besides being buffeted by a sharp contraction in demand, Equity Office is a maturing company. Its vast scale means that it can no longer generate value simply by acquiring or developing properties; operating efficiencies and efforts to service and retain tenants are now increasingly critical.

Equity Residential EQR

	Rating	Risk	Moat Size	Fair Value	Last Close	Yield %
	★★★	Low	Narrow	$26.00	$24.58	7.0

Company Profile

Equity Residential is a real-estate investment trust. The company owns 1,077 multifamily residential properties that contain 225,250 apartment units throughout the United States. The properties have an average occupancy rate of 94.5%. Equity Residential is the largest apartment REIT and the second-largest overall REIT by market capitalization.

Management

Legendary real estate investor Sam Zell founded Equity Residential in 1969, took the firm public in 1993, and is chairman of the board.

Strategy

Equity Residential's strategy is to expand and improve its large and geographically diverse portfolio of apartments. To increase profitability, Equity Residential manages its mutual-fund-like portfolio by selling properties in slower-growth markets, like Memphis and Greensboro, while acquiring or developing properties in markets with high barriers to entry, like Washington, D.C., and Boston.

Two North Riverside Plaza   www.eqr.com
Chicago, IL 60606

Industry	Investment Style	Stock Type	Sector
REITS	▦ Mid Value	▦ Hard Assets	$ Financial Services

Competition

	Market Cap $Mil	Debt/ Equity	12 Mo Trailing Sales $Mil	Price/Cash Flow	Return On Assets%	Total Return% 1 Yr	3 Yr
Equity Residential	6,780	—	2,137	—	2.9	-8.6	12.5
Archstone-Smith Trust	4,254	—	1,040	—	2.6	-4.2	12.1
Apartment Investment & Ma	3,493	—	1,573	—	1.0	-11.5	7.3

Price Volatility

| Monthly Price High/Low   — Relative Strength to S&P 500

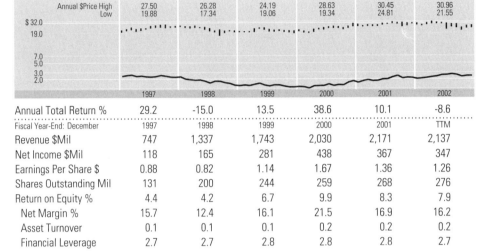

Annual $Price High / Low	27.50 / 19.88	26.28 / 17.34	24.19 / 19.06	28.63 / 19.34	30.45 / 24.81	30.96 / 21.55
	1997	1998	1999	2000	2001	2002
Annual Total Return %	29.2	-15.0	13.5	38.6	10.1	-8.6

Fiscal Year-End: December	1997	1998	1999	2000	2001	TTM
Revenue $Mil	747	1,337	1,743	2,030	2,171	2,137
Net Income $Mil	118	165	281	438	367	347
Earnings Per Share $	0.88	0.82	1.14	1.67	1.36	1.26
Shares Outstanding Mil	131	200	244	259	268	276
Return on Equity %	4.4	4.2	6.7	9.9	8.3	7.9
Net Margin %	15.7	12.4	16.1	21.5	16.9	16.2
Asset Turnover	0.1	0.1	0.1	0.2	0.2	0.2
Financial Leverage	2.7	2.7	2.8	2.8	2.8	2.7

Valuation Ratios	Stock	Rel to Industry	Rel to S&P 500
Price/Earnings	19.5	1.1	0.8
Price/Book	1.5	1.0	0.5
Price/Sales	3.2	1.0	1.6
Price/Cash Flow	—	—	—

Major Fund Holders	% of Fund Assets
Fremont Real Estate Securities	7.08
Lend Lease U.S. Real Estate Secs K	5.54
AssetMark Real Estate Securities	5.50
Wells S&P REIT Index A	5.07

Morningstar Grades

Growth [B+]	1998	1999	2000	2001
Revenue %	79.0	30.3	16.5	6.9
Earnings/Share %	-7.4	39.9	46.5	-18.6
Book Value/Share %	-2.5	-11.9	-0.6	-2.8
Dividends/Share %	6.8	8.1	7.1	6.7

Equity Residential has grown through both individual property purchases and developments, and a series of large acquisitions since 1997.

Profitability [A-]	1999	2000	2001	TTM
Return on Assets %	2.4	3.6	3.0	2.9
Oper Cash Flow $Mil	789	843	890	—
- Cap Spending $Mil	—	—	—	—
= Free Cash Flow $Mil	—	—	—	—

A net operating margin of 61% puts the firm at the midpoint of the REIT industry. Reported GAAP net income can fluctuate significantly from one quarter to the next based on the timing of property sales.

Financial Health [A]	1999	2000	2001	09-02
Long-term Debt $Mil	—	—	—	—
Total Equity $Mil	4,195	4,436	4,447	4,393
Debt/Equity Ratio	—	—	—	—

Leverage is lower than the industry average of 50% and isn't likely to increase dramatically. The firm funds most of its capital needs through the sale of properties in slower-growth markets, rather than by adding large amounts of debt or equity.

Morningstar's Take By Matthew Scholz, 11-07-2002 Stock Price as of Analysis: $24.27

Geographic diversity, a strong balance sheet, and a long, steady record of growth in funds from operations make Equity Residential a low-risk real estate investment trust (REIT) and an attractive investment for those looking for apartment sector exposure.

Equity Residential's geographically diverse portfolio is composed mostly of suburban apartment communities that attract people who are renters by necessity--those who generally can't yet afford a single-family house. With 1,059 properties in 36 states, Equity Residential is one of the only apartment owners with national scale. This gives the firm advantages like bargaining power with suppliers and deep market intelligence in the less liquid world of real estate.

Equity Residential is working to increase the percentage of its properties in markets with high barriers to entry: those with good job growth, pricey single-family homes, and limitations--because of the amount of available land or zoning laws--on how many new residences can be developed. Equity Residential prefers to purchase buildings in these areas with the proceeds from sales of less desirable properties. This capital recycling generally allows Equity Residential to move into or out of markets faster than if it had to build new apartments.

Another source of stability for Equity Residential is its solid balance sheet. As of September 30, debt constituted only 40% of total market capitalization. No more than 12% of this debt comes due in any one year.

For potential investors in any REIT, determining dividend sustainability is crucial. We think Equity Residential's dividend is safe. Our estimate of funds available for distribution, a measure of REIT free cash flow, is $2.07 per share this year. With an estimated annual dividend payment of $1.73 per share, this means that the ratio of dividend payments to funds available for distribution is 84%--pretty good, given the recent pressure on rental rates.

We think this is a solid low-risk investment. Like all REITs, Equity Residential offers the diversification that real estate exposure brings to equity portfolios. Equity Residential trades below our fair value estimate of $26, but given the continued weak apartment market, it is best to focus on the firm's 7%-plus dividend yield and ability to generate 6%-8% long-term growth in funds from operations.

MORNINGSTAR® Stocks 500

Ericsson Telephone ADR B ERICY

	Rating	Risk	Moat Size	Fair Value	Last Close	Yield %
	★	High	None	$0.00	$6.74	0.0

Company Profile

Ericsson is the most dominant supplier of wireless telecom equipment, supplying network operators and service providers globally with products like antennae and transmitters. Roughly three fourths of sales in 2001 came from the sale of network infrastructure gear. Ericsson is number three in mobile handsets, trailing Nokia and Motorola. The company formed a joint venture to co-produce handsets with consumer electronics giant Sony, to help stem losses in this money-losing division.

Management

Two big Swedish companies control 78% of Ericsson through supervoting class A shares, though they own just 11% of the equity. The board is filled with insiders and Sweden's corporate elite. CEO Kurt Hellstrom has been with Ericsson for many years, but management is not a strong suit.

Strategy

Ericsson is in a joint venture with Sony to co-produce mobile phones, with the goal of stemming losses in this segment. As a result, Ericsson is focusing more on its market-leading wireless infrastructure equipment segment, which is also ailing.

Telefonaktiebolaget LM   www.ericsson.com
Stockholm, S-126 25

Morningstar Grades

Growth [B]	1998	1999	2000	2001
Revenue %	10.0	16.8	27.0	-15.3
Earnings/Share %	9.5	-7.3	71.7	NMF
Book Value/Share %	20.2	9.2	31.4	-24.9
Dividends/Share %	14.2	0.0	0.0	-12.0

Growth is a thing of the past. The wireless carriers are struggling to stay viable and have slowed spending on wireless equipment, which accounts for 90% of sales. September-quarter revenue fell 28% on an apples-to-apples basis.

Profitability [B]	1999	2000	2001	TTM
Return on Assets %	5.9	8.2	-8.5	-5.3
Oper Cash Flow $Mil	1,227	-1,545	137	137
- Cap Spending $Mil	1,116	1,384	845	845
= Free Cash Flow $Mil	111	-2,929	-708	-708

Ericsson has become a money pit; operations continue to gush red ink. Although management has cut costs recently, it won't be enough to restore profitability before 2003 at the earliest.

Financial Health [C]	1999	2000	2001	06-02
Long-term Debt $Mil	2,692	2,148	4,361	4,074
Total Equity $Mil	8,119	9,733	6,489	6,464
Debt/Equity Ratio	0.3	0.2	0.7	0.6

Ericsson's health is poor, thanks to excessive debt and deepening operating losses. However, the firm should have enough cash after a recent equity issuance to make it through 2003.

Industry	Investment Style	Stock Type	Sector
Wireless Equipment	▦ Large Growth	➡ Slow Growth	▪ Hardware

Competition	Market Cap $Mil	Debt/ Equity	12 Mo Trailing Sales $Mil	Price/Cash Flow	Return On Assets%	Total Return% 1 Yr	3 Yr
Ericsson Telephone ADR B	10,767	0.6	18,112	78.4	-5.3	-87.1	-64.9
Nokia ADR	73,432	0.0	27,814	12.6	9.9	-36.1	-28.5
Motorola	19,903	0.7	26,576	13.0	-12.9	-41.7	-42.2

Price Volatility   ▌ Monthly Price High/Low   — Relative Strength to S&P 500

Annual $Price High / Low	63.28 / 35.94	85.00 / 37.50	168.13 / 51.25	263.13 / 103.75	135.00 / 30.50	60.00 / 3.40

	1997	1998	1999	2000	2001	2002
Annual Total Return %	24.9	29.5	177.5	-31.7	-52.9	-87.1

Fiscal Year-end: December	1997	1998	1999	2000	2001	TTM
Revenue $Mil	22,232	23,223	26,049	29,943	22,449	18,112
Net Income $Mil	1,583	1,642	1,467	2,300	-2,059	-1,252
Earnings Per Share $	2.02	2.10	1.87	2.90	-2.61	-1.58
Shares Outstanding Mil	785	783	786	787	790	1,597
Return on Equity %	23.8	21.1	18.1	23.6	-31.7	-19.4
Net Margin %	7.1	7.1	5.6	7.7	-9.2	-6.9
Asset Turnover	1.2	1.1	1.1	1.1	0.9	0.8
Financial Leverage	2.9	2.7	3.1	2.9	3.8	3.7

Valuation Ratios	Stock	Rel to Industry	Rel to S&P 500
Price/Earnings	NMF	—	—
Price/Book	1.7	0.2	0.5
Price/Sales	0.6	0.2	0.3
Price/Cash Flow	78.4	6.2	5.9

Major Fund Holders	% of Fund Assets
Papp America-Abroad	6.86
Rydex Telecommunications Inv	1.91
Choice Long-Short A	1.01

Morningstar's Take By Todd P. Bernier, 10-23-2002   Stock Price as of Analysis: $6.38

We question why investors would hitch their horse to a firm without an economic moat, particularly one whose future hinges on telecom capital spending.

The 1990s were the golden age at Ericsson. Revenue grew fivefold from 1991 to 2001, compound annual growth of 17.5%. Increased wireless penetration and usage forced carriers to spend heavily on their networks. After buying Qualcomm's infrastructure business in 1999, which provided expertise in the CDMA air-interface protocol, Ericsson was the dominant vendor of wireless gear.

But things are golden no more. Sickly capital spending among cash-strapped, debt-laden wireless service providers--Ericsson's customers--is the problem. The carriers are slashing spending to stay viable; spending heavily on their networks is not a priority. Further, the lifeline that Ericsson had been counting on--the launch of third-generation networks--is fading. Many carriers are nearly bankrupt as a result of overbidding at spectrum auctions and making questionable acquisitions. In response, they have deferred or canceled 3G plans and ceased buying equipment. There may be a day when ultraquick wireless data networks are ubiquitous, but that day is a long way off. In our opinion, the fundamentals in the wireless networking industry are bad and getting worse.

Ericsson formed a handset joint venture with Sony in 2001, with the goal of marrying Ericsson's phone expertise with Sony's dominance in consumer electronics. For Ericsson the goal was to stop handset losses. But the bleeding continues and Ericsson remains as irrelevant as ever in mobile phones.

Problems have been exacerbated by an executive team slow to respond to the industry's downturn. While some firms bolstered their cash stockpile by raising money at the peak of telecom valuations, ongoing losses and poor working-capital management have exhausted Ericsson's liquidity. Debt markets remain closed to ailing telecom suppliers. Running out of cash and lacking an investment-grade debt rating, Ericsson was forced to issue equity in 2002--the most inopportune time to raise new capital.

Ericsson has no economic moat, and its business model is broken. Unless capital spending by the wireless service providers recovers in a hurry, or the firm receives aid from the Swedish government, Ericsson is finished. We see no reason to buy this stock at any price.

Data as of 12-31-02

Estee Lauder A EL

	Rating	Risk	Moat Size	Fair Value	Last Close	Yield %
	★★	Low	Narrow	$24.00	$26.40	1.1

Industry	Investment Style	Stock Type	Sector
Household & Personal Products	▦ Mid Core	→ Slow Growth	Consumer Goods

Company Profile

Estee Lauder manufactures skin-care and cosmetic products. The company produces lipsticks, foundations, mascaras, eyeshadows, and blushes that are sold under brand names like Estee Lauder, Clinique, Prescriptives, jane, and Origins. It also makes skin-care and fragrance products for men that are sold mainly under the Aramis brand name. Estee Lauder's women's fragrances include Beautiful, White Linen, Pleasures, and Clinique Happy. It sells its products to department stores, perfumeries, pharmacies, and inflight and duty-free shops in the United States and abroad.

Management

Fred Langhammer became CEO in 2000; his various positions during his 25 years with the company make him a seasoned industry pro. Still, the savvy chairman, Leonard Lauder, has the last say, given his family's 92% voting control of the firm.

Strategy

Estee Lauder is expanding beyond its department store boutiques and should have 500 makeup and skin-care stores open within the next couple of years. This will allow the firm to expand its brands' sales while preserving their high-end cachet, which it could not do if it were to start selling in lower-end department stores. The new-product focus will be on the skin-care and makeup segments.

767 Fifth Avenue
New York, NY 10153
www.elcompanies.com

Morningstar Grades

Growth [B]	1999	2000	2001	2002
Revenue %	9.5	12.1	5.1	1.6
Earnings/Share %	15.7	16.5	-3.3	-39.7
Book Value/Share %	31.4	25.5	16.2	9.1
Dividends/Share %	4.4	12.7	0.0	0.0

The company averaged 7.6% sales growth over the past five years, though we expect the next five years' average to be 3.5%.

Profitability [B+]	2000	2001	2002	TTM
Return on Assets %	9.6	8.8	4.9	4.9
Oper Cash Flow $Mil	443	305	518	626
- Cap Spending $Mil	181	192	203	189
= Free Cash Flow $Mil	262	113	315	436

We expect average net profit margins to decrease to 6% during the next five years, from an average 6.25% over the past five years. We expect average return on equity for the next five years of 15%, down from the 25% average over the past five years.

Financial Health [A]	2000	2001	2002	09-02
Long-term Debt $Mil	418	411	404	404
Total Equity $Mil	1,160	1,352	1,462	1,386
Debt/Equity Ratio	0.4	0.3	0.3	0.3

Earnings before interest and taxes is 8 times interest expense, including the effect of capitalized operating leases. While we aren't currently concerned, this ratio could deteriorate as more freestanding stores are opened.

Competition	Market Cap $Mil	Debt/ Equity	12 Mo Trailing Sales $Mil	Price/Cash Flow	Return On Assets%	Total Return% 1 Yr	3 Yr
Estee Lauder A	6,158	0.3	4,791	9.8	4.9	-16.8	-17.9
Procter & Gamble	111,662	0.9	41,268	13.3	11.0	11.3	-4.5
L'Oreal ADR	5,087	—	11,507	—	—	—	—

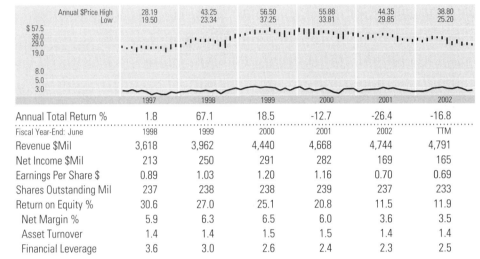

Price Volatility — Monthly Price High/Low — Relative Strength to S&P 500

Annual $Price High Low	28.19 19.50	43.25 23.34	56.50 37.25	55.88 33.81	44.35 29.85	38.80 25.20
	1997	1998	1999	2000	2001	2002
Annual Total Return %	1.8	67.1	18.5	-12.7	-26.4	-16.8

Fiscal Year-End: June	1998	1999	2000	2001	2002	TTM
Revenue $Mil	3,618	3,962	4,440	4,668	4,744	4,791
Net Income $Mil	213	250	291	282	169	165
Earnings Per Share $	0.89	1.03	1.20	1.16	0.70	0.69
Shares Outstanding Mil	237	238	238	239	237	233
Return on Equity %	30.6	27.0	25.1	20.8	11.5	11.9
Net Margin %	5.9	6.3	6.5	6.0	3.6	3.5
Asset Turnover	1.4	1.4	1.5	1.5	1.4	1.4
Financial Leverage	3.6	3.0	2.6	2.4	2.3	2.5

Valuation Ratios	Stock	Rel to Industry	Rel to S&P 500
Price/Earnings	38.3	1.5	1.6
Price/Book	4.4	0.5	1.4
Price/Sales	1.3	0.5	0.6
Price/Cash Flow	9.8	0.7	0.7

Major Fund Holders	% of Fund Assets
Fremont New Era Value	3.83
Exeter Pro-Blend Maximum Term A	2.46
Reserve Blue Chip Growth R	2.46
Dreyfus Founders Growth F	2.36

Morningstar's Take By Carl Sibilski, 12-18-2002 Stock Price as of Analysis: $26.80

We don't like Estee Lauder's growth strategy, and given the deteriorating long-term business fundamentals, we'd avoid the shares.

Estee Lauder owns some of the classiest and best-known cosmetic brands, like Clinique, Prescriptives, and MAC, which are typically sold through upscale department stores. These brands help the company generate more than $300 million in annual free cash flow, but we're not happy with the firm's reinvestment plans. In our opinion, the company's efforts to keep its 50-year streak of consecutive sales growth alive will come at the expense of lower margins and increased business risk.

In an attempt to increase sales faster and keep up with consumer trends away from department stores, the company is opening hundreds of freestanding boutique cosmetic stores. We think this strategy will result in flat--if not lower--margins and higher capital expenditures, resulting in lower free cash flow. These new sales outlets have a higher cost structure than traditional cosmetic counters, but we doubt consumers will be willing to pay higher prices. Operational expenses increased to 61.9% of sales in 2002 from 60.5% in 2001. And if a brand doesn't work out, the shutdown costs will be higher.

In our opinion, the firm's plan to improve inventory management by reducing stock-keeping units (SKUs) 15%-18% by 2007 doesn't go far enough for department stores, which are focusing on keeping inventory low and turnover high. With still too many sizes and variations, Estee Lauder's products will probably take up more shelf space than those of a small upstart cosmetic company. As a result, Estee Lauder may lose favor with retailers, which account for the lion's share of sales.

We think the company should come to terms with its size and start acting more like a mature slow-growth firm. The company could increase shareholder value by investing in technologies that aim to substantially improve margins through lower costs and better internal processing. This would involve dramatically reducing SKUs and committing much less capital to opening freestanding stores.

Estee Lauder has some terrific brands, but until management comes to terms with reality we think investors will be disappointed by the stock's performance.

230   ©2003 Morningstar, Inc. All rights reserved. Intended for United States residents only, this report is for information purposes and should not be considered a solicitation to buy or sell any security. Visit www.morningstar.com for your research.

MORNINGSTAR® Stocks 500

Ethan Allen Interiors ETH

	Rating	Risk	Moat Size	Fair Value	Last Close	Yield %
	★★★	Low	Narrow	$37.00	$34.37	0.6

Company Profile

Ethan Allen Interiors has broadened its product lines to include more casual and contemporary styles. It operates 18 facilities that produce wooden furniture like tables, chairs, and shelving; upholstered pieces that include sofas, love seats, and chairs; and furnishing accessories like lamps, clocks, rugs, and carpets. In addition, the company operates approximately 93 retail showrooms and oversees 219 dealer-owned stores that sell Ethan Allen products exclusively.

Management

Farooq Kathwari, who has been with Ethan Allen since 1973, became CEO in 1985 and led a leveraged buyout of the firm in 1989. He's also chairman, president, and chief operating officer and a major determinant of the firm's success or failure.

Strategy

Ethan Allen is well positioned for an economic recovery, but isn't waiting for one to get under way to improve stagnant sales. After aggressive cost-cutting during fiscal 2002, the company is lowering its prices on select items to boost customer reach and sales volume.

Ethan Allen Drive   www.ethanallen.com
Danbury, CT 06811

Morningstar Grades

Growth [C+]	1999	2000	2001	2002
Revenue %	12.2	12.3	5.6	-1.3
Earnings/Share %	19.3	14.6	-10.0	4.0
Book Value/Share %	16.4	14.6	21.8	10.8
Dividends/Share %	33.5	49.8	0.0	0.0

As a high-end furniture dealer, Ethan Allen is a cyclical company with fluctuating growth. Its merchandise is highly desired by consumers, so its growth booms during times of economic strength.

Profitability [A]	2000	2001	2002	TTM
Return on Assets %	16.7	12.9	11.9	12.3
Oper Cash Flow $Mil	105	88	125	136
- Cap Spending $Mil	42	39	31	32
= Free Cash Flow $Mil	63	49	94	104

Ethan Allen has some of the best margins in its industry, thanks to its premium-price merchandise and continuous cost-cutting. Margins should remain wide, but are unlikely to reach historical highs because of higher employee medical costs.

Financial Health [A+]	2000	2001	2002	09-02
Long-term Debt $Mil	9	9	9	10
Total Equity $Mil	391	465	511	507
Debt/Equity Ratio	0.0	0.0	0.0	0.0

Ethan Allen is in strong financial shape with virtually no debt, thanks to healthy operating cash flow that funds expansion.

Industry	Investment Style	Stock Type	Sector
Appliance & Furniture Makers	Mid Core	Cyclical	Consumer Goods

Competition

	Market Cap $Mil	Debt/ Equity	12 Mo Trailing Sales $Mil	Price/Cash Flow	Return On Assets%	Total Return% 1 Yr	3 Yr
Ethan Allen Interiors	1,318	0.0	902	9.7	12.3	-16.9	6.3
La-Z-Boy	1,360	—	2,201	—	—	—	—
Furniture Brands Internat	1,327	—	2,279	—	—	—	—

Price Volatility

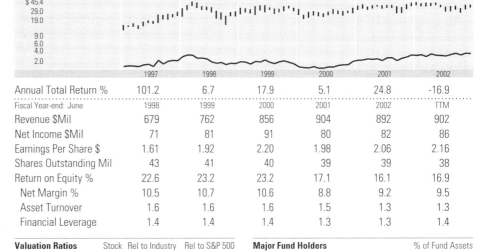

	Monthly Price High/Low				Relative Strength to S&P 500	
Annual $Price High Low	28.58 12.33	44.42 15.75	37.75 24.67	33.75 20.50	42.30 26.51	43.45 27.15

	1997	1998	1999	2000	2001	2002
Annual Total Return %	101.2	6.7	17.9	5.1	24.8	-16.9

Fiscal Year-end: June	1998	1999	2000	2001	2002	TTM
Revenue $Mil	679	762	856	904	892	902
Net Income $Mil	71	81	91	80	82	86
Earnings Per Share $	1.61	1.92	2.20	1.98	2.06	2.16
Shares Outstanding Mil	43	41	40	39	39	38
Return on Equity %	22.6	23.2	23.2	17.1	16.1	16.9
Net Margin %	10.5	10.7	10.6	8.8	9.2	9.5
Asset Turnover	1.6	1.6	1.6	1.5	1.3	1.3
Financial Leverage	1.4	1.4	1.4	1.3	1.3	1.4

Valuation Ratios	Stock	Rel to Industry	Rel to S&P 500
Price/Earnings	15.9	1.2	0.7
Price/Book	2.6	1.2	0.8
Price/Sales	1.5	3.1	0.7
Price/Cash Flow	9.7	1.1	0.7

Major Fund Holders	% of Fund Assets
Buffalo Balanced	3.80
Excelsior Small Cap	3.56
WesMark Small Company Growth	3.42
Mosaic Mid-Cap	3.38

Morningstar's Take By Roz Bryant, 10-21-2002 Stock Price as of Analysis: $32.15

Ethan Allen is armed with prudent management and a highly sought-after brand. We think these strengths separate the company from its peers. However, we would need a 40% discount to our fair value estimate before investing, to compensate for the fluctuating demand for high-end furniture and the added risk of the firm's overseas outsourcing efforts.

CEO Farooq Kathwari saved Ethan Allen from irrelevance when he led a leveraged buyout of the company in 1989. Kathwari has remained focused since then on improving profitability, and the company's earnings history proves he is a nimble operator. Under his leadership, the furniture maker closed or consolidated several manufacturing plants and tightened the reins on its independent dealers' practices before going public in 1993. Since 1995, net income has averaged 20.5% growth (with average sales growth of 9.5%).

The fact that Kathwari is still at the helm is one reason we have such confidence in the Ethan Allen's prospects. Last year, the company began outsourcing about 10% of its manufacturing to overseas vendors with lower labor costs. This enabled management to consolidate three domestic company-owned plants and lower overall production costs enough to eke out 1.6% profit growth in fiscal 2002 despite a sales decline.

In addition, Ethan Allen's design focus has broadened from its stodgy New England colonial-style roots, so the appeal of its merchandise has widened. Younger furniture buyers are now interested in the brand, which is virtually synonymous with high-quality, stylish furniture. The firm's consumer credit plan, which has been offered for about two years, is also boosting revenue. Customers who would normally balk at buying a $5,000 bed warm up to the idea when they can stretch payments out over five years.

A couple of challenges could trip Ethan Allen up in the near term, though. First, stylish designs and credit offers notwithstanding, its merchandise is expensive, and sales growth may not live up to its potential if the economy stays in a funk. Plus, the looming labor standoff at West Coast U.S. ports threatens Ethan Allen's ability to deliver customer orders. Further port slowdowns could stifle revenue because some of the firm's popular new items are Asian imports.

We wouldn't hesitate to buy Ethan Allen at the right price. The company faces significant near-term risks, so we'd stay out of the shares until they fell to the low $20s.

Expedia EXPE

	Rating	Risk	Moat Size	Fair Value	Last Close	Yield %
	★	High	None	$53.00	$66.93	0.0

Company Profile

Expedia provides travel help through its Web site. The site offers travel shopping and reservation services, including information on more than 450 airlines, 65,000 hotels, and major car-rental companies. Customers, primarily leisure and small-business travelers, can search and book the offerings of vacation packagers, cruise lines, and specialty lodging providers and buy travel merchandise from online retailers. The company licenses components of its technology and editorial content to selected airlines and American Express as a platform for their Web sites.

Management

Expedia founder Richard Barton remained CEO and president and USA's Barry Diller became chairman after the merger closed in February 2002. USA designees now control Expedia's board.

Strategy

USA Interactive's purchase of Microsoft's 70% stake in Expedia broadens the travel site's strategic options. Expedia can use USA's former television assets (being run for Vivendi by chairman Barry Diller) to bring television viewers to its Web site. In turn, Expedia can spotlight USA's other assets, both online and offline.

13810 SE Eastgate Way   www.expedia.com
Bellevue, WA 98005

Morningstar Grades

Growth [A]	1998	1999	2000	2001
Revenue %	179.9	144.5	134.8	-27.4
Earnings/Share %	NMF	NMF	NMF	NMF
Book Value/Share %	—	—	NMF	8.1
Dividends/Share %	NMF	NMF	NMF	NMF

Expedia is the fastest-growing online ticket agency. Revenue and profit growth has outpaced the company's closest competitors, and should continue to expand dramatically over the next several years as more tickets are booked online.

Profitability [D-]	1999	2000	2001	TTM
Return on Assets %	-43.3	-20.0	0.1	6.1
Oper Cash Flow $Mil	-31	63	77	NMF
- Cap Spending $Mil	5	17	12	NMF
= Free Cash Flow $Mil	-36	46	64	NMF

Expedia's merchant business, which generates gross margins 13 percentage points higher than those on agency revenue, has been growing faster than any other segment. This has translated into strong free cash flows.

Financial Health [B-]	1999	2000	2001	09-02
Long-term Debt $Mil	2	1	0	0
Total Equity $Mil	207	231	249	440
Debt/Equity Ratio	0.0	0.0	0.0	0.0

With no debt, half a billion dollars in cash, and solid free cash flows, Expedia is in a good position to explore new growth opportunities and spend on marketing.

Industry	Investment Style	Stock Type	Sector
Online Retail	▦ Mid Growth	◆ Spec. Growth	▱ Consumer Services

Competition

	Market Cap $Mil	Debt/ Equity	12 Mo Trailing Sales $Mil	Price/Cash Flow	Return On Assets%	Total Return% 1 Yr	3 Yr
Expedia	3,876	0.0	508	—	6.1	64.8	23.0
Cendant	10,862	1.8	13,069	10.2	0.9	-46.6	-23.3
Hotels.com A	3,142	0.0	814	16.6	7.0	18.8	—

Price Volatility

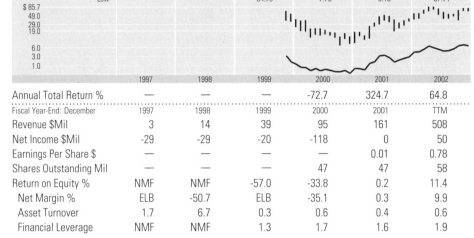

I Monthly Price High/Low   — Relative Strength to S&P 500

				65.88 / 34.75	40.38 / 7.75	51.84 / 9.13	84.65 / 37.71
	1997	1998	1999	2000	2001	2002	

Annual Total Return %	—	—	—	-72.7	324.7	64.8

Fiscal Year-End: December	1997	1998	1999	2000	2001	TTM
Revenue $Mil	3	14	39	95	161	508
Net Income $Mil	-29	-29	-20	-118	0	50
Earnings Per Share $	—	—	—	—	0.01	0.78
Shares Outstanding Mil	—	—	—	47	47	58
Return on Equity %	NMF	NMF	-57.0	-33.8	0.2	11.4
Net Margin %	ELB	-50.7	ELB	-35.1	0.3	9.9
Asset Turnover	1.7	6.7	0.3	0.6	0.4	0.6
Financial Leverage	NMF	NMF	1.3	1.7	1.6	1.9

Valuation Ratios	Stock	Rel to Industry	Rel to S&P 500
Price/Earnings	85.8	0.8	3.6
Price/Book	8.8	0.9	2.8
Price/Sales	7.6	1.0	3.8
Price/Cash Flow	—	—	—

Major Fund Holders	% of Fund Assets
Amerindo Technology D	20.83
Amerindo Internet B2B A	15.91
IDEX Transamerica Growth Opport A	7.22
Transamerica Premier Growth Opp Inv	6.57

Morningstar's Take By T.K. MacKay, 12-03-2002 Stock Price as of Analysis: $74.37

Expedia is a premier vendor of airline tickets and hotel rooms, but we think the commodity business it operates will severely limit long-term profitability. We'd require a 60% discount to our fair value estimate before considering investment.

We are having a difficult time coming up with a good reason why Expedia will continue to be a choice destination for travel bookings, despite its lead over the competition. We are concerned that over the long term, the profits that agent and merchant revenue generates for Expedia could shrink. The U.S. Department of Transportation's recently proposed changes to the rules for airline ticket distribution via the four major computer reservation systems could make it difficult for online travel agents like Expedia to stay competitive without jeopardizing profits.

The DOT's proposal would make it possible for the airlines to negotiate exclusive deals with individual sites like Orbitz. This proposal, combined with fewer seats available on airplanes and dramatically reduced fares, could make it extremely difficult to make money selling airline tickets. Expedia has built a distinctive brand name over the past few years, has a captive audience, and has links with a premier media company (USA Interactive) and a well-known service provider (Microsoft's MSN). We fail to see, however, how these alliances would preserve Expedia's industry-leading profit margins in the face of deregulation.

Borrowing a phrase from J. Scott Kirby, America West's executive vice president of marketing, we think the online ticket industry is a game that leads to inexorably lower prices. We don't doubt that the amount of airline seats, hotels, and vacation packages booked online will increase substantially over the long term. We've made some aggressive sales and profit growth assumptions for Expedia to account for this trend. However, Expedia's reliance on the commoditylike products sold in the travel industry, especially airline tickets, could pressure the company's ability to expand profits.

The online ticket industry is young enough that growth prospects for companies like Expedia can change overnight. Using our best estimates of how quickly the market for Web fares is growing (currently, about 20% of all fares are booked online) and how much of that market Expedia will capture over the long term, we estimate Expedia's fair value to be $53 per share. Given the intensely competitive and rapidly changing online booking landscape, we would require a wide margin of safety before buying this stock.

M⊙RNINGSTAR® Stocks 500

Expeditors International of WA EXPD

	Rating	Risk	Moat Size	Fair Value	Last Close	Yield %
	★★★	Med.	Wide	$36.00	$32.65	0.4

Company Profile

Expeditors International of Washington is a freight-shipping company. Its main source of revenue is air freight; it also provides ocean freight and import services. The air freight business generates about 41% of revenue. The company's air freight forwarding business primarily involves shipments to and from Asia, the United States, and Europe through its offices and international service centers in 28 countries. Operations in the United States account for about 33% of revenue. The company has developed its own electronic data interface, Contact, to track cargo.

Management

CEO Peter Rose and his fellow executives receive low base salaries--Rose's has been $110,000 since 1992--but share in a bonus pool composed of 10% of operating income. This gives management a very strong incentive to increase the bottom line.

Strategy

Expeditors is a rare bird in the transportation industry: It doesn't own any planes or ships. Instead, it buys cargo space in bulk from shippers and then resells the space to its customers. Management is adamant about maintaining this business model.

1015 Third Avenue   www.expditors.com
Seattle, WA 98104

Morningstar Grades

Growth [B]	1998	1999	2000	2001
Revenue %	11.5	35.8	17.3	-2.5
Earnings/Share %	21.9	23.6	38.2	16.4
Book Value/Share %	25.2	28.4	26.2	14.0
Dividends/Share %	40.0	42.9	40.0	42.9

Expeditors' long-term growth has been very strong, but has slowed along with the global economy. When assessing top-line growth, be sure to look at net revenue, rather than the gross revenue reported in the firm's SEC filings.

Profitability [A+]	1999	2000	2001	TTM
Return on Assets %	11.1	12.5	14.1	12.5
Oper Cash Flow $Mil	53	154	168	120
- Cap Spending $Mil	27	26	37	27
= Free Cash Flow $Mil	27	129	130	93

Expeditors is a free cash flow machine and allocates capital wisely--return on invested capital is around 22%. Because the firm does not have to maintain expensive transportation assets, its capital-spending needs are low.

Financial Health [A+]	1999	2000	2001	09-02
Long-term Debt $Mil	0	0	0	0
Total Equity $Mil	282	362	415	493
Debt/Equity Ratio	0.0	0.0	0.0	0.0

As good as it gets: no long-term debt, and $287 million in cash on the balance sheet. Expeditors has no worries on this front.

Industry	Investment Style	Stock Type	Sector
Transportation - Misc	▦ Mid Growth	↗ Classic Growth	▤ Business Services

Competition	Market Cap $Mil	Debt/ Equity	12 Mo Trailing Sales $Mil	Price/Cash Flow	Return On Assets%	Total Return% 1 Yr	3 Yr
Expeditors International of WA	3,399	0.0	1,866	28.4	12.5	15.1	15.8
United Parcel Service B	70,397	0.3	31,337	19.1	9.2	17.2	0.3
FedEx	16,189	0.3	21,015	6.8	5.4	4.8	9.4

Price Volatility — Monthly Price High/Low — Relative Strength to S&P 500

Annual $Price High/Low	12.19 5.16	12.06 6.22	23.19 10.16	30.06 16.31	32.96 20.98	34.44 21.38
	1997	1998	1999	2000	2001	2002
Annual Total Return %	67.9	9.5	109.3	22.9	6.5	15.1

Fiscal Year-end: December	1997	1998	1999	2000	2001	TTM
Revenue $Mil	954	1,064	1,445	1,695	1,653	1,866
Net Income $Mil	38	47	59	83	97	104
Earnings Per Share $	0.37	0.45	0.55	0.76	0.89	0.95
Shares Outstanding Mil	98	98	100	103	104	104
Return on Equity %	22.4	21.8	21.0	23.0	23.5	21.0
Net Margin %	4.0	4.4	4.1	4.9	5.9	5.6
Asset Turnover	2.8	2.5	2.7	2.6	2.4	2.2
Financial Leverage	2.0	1.9	1.9	1.8	1.7	1.7

Valuation Ratios	Stock	Rel to Industry	Rel to S&P 500
Price/Earnings	34.4	1.2	1.5
Price/Book	6.9	1.1	2.2
Price/Sales	1.8	0.8	0.9
Price/Cash Flow	28.4	1.5	2.1

Major Fund Holders	% of Fund Assets
Papp America-Pacific Rim	8.57
IDEX Transamerica Growth Opport A	6.56
Transamerica Premier Growth Opp Inv	6.08
Transamerica Premier Aggr Grth Inv	5.70

Morningstar's Take By Pat Dorsey, 12-13-2002 Stock Price as of Analysis: $34.10

Expeditors International has built a very attractive business that has largely variable costs, requires little capital spending, and throws off gobs of free cash flow. The firm also generates high returns on capital, and has compounded earnings at 25% per year over the past 10 years without large acquisitions or debt. (Expeditors' CEO on acquisitions: "Why buy what you can kill?")

Since profits invariably attract competition, we have to ask what would prevent a well-financed predator from moving in. We think Expeditors has two key advantages: a large global network of offices that would be very difficult to replicate, and a unique, incentive-based company culture.

At Expeditors, all employees receive a low base salary plus a bonus based on the firm's pretax profits. Expeditors' individual offices each retain about 20% of their operating profits, which are then redistributed to each office's staff, while executives receive a set percentage of the company's profits.

As an example of what this decentralized, branch-based compensation system can accomplish, consider Expeditors' success in reducing its accounts receivable balance in 2001. (Reducing receivables lowers a company's working-capital needs, which improves cash flow.) Rather than send out a bunch of

memos on the importance of the timely collection of receivables, Expeditors' management reserved past-due accounts receivable against the operating profits of the relevant branch. Since most Expeditors employees receive the bulk of their compensation from monthly bonuses based on branch-level operating income, they started to focus an awful lot of energy on making sure customers paid their bills quickly. As a result, the company's accounts receivable balance as a percentage of net revenue plunged from 63% in 2000 to 46% in 2001. The relationship is clear: Employees are motivated to treat the company's finances as their own.

In a service industry like freight forwarding, motivated employees are the factor that keeps a firm ahead of its peers. Our discussions with some of Expeditors' customers indicate that the firm is widely regarded as having the best service in the industry, and is a benchmark for other forwarders.

At the moment, Expeditors' valuation is too rich for us. Due to its high profit margins and returns on capital, it's unlikely that the shares will ever look cheap on a price-to-earnings or price-to-book basis, but we estimate the shares are worth $36 based on a discounted cash flow model. We'd be buyers at a 20% discount to this, which works out to $29.

Express Scripts ESRX

	Rating ★★★	Risk Med.	Moat Size Narrow	Fair Value $52.00	Last Close $48.04	Yield % 0.0

Company Profile

Express Scripts provides pharmacy benefit management services to managed-care firms, third-party administrators, large employers, and union-sponsored benefit plans. For its 50 million members, the company coordinates the distribution of outpatient pharmaceuticals through a combination of benefit services. These include retail drug card programs, Internet service, and mail pharmacy services.

Management

Barrett Toan became president in 1990, CEO in 1992, and chairman in 2000. He led the integration of large acquisitions that have sparked phenomenal growth at Express over the past five years.

Strategy

Express Scripts is attempting to increase generic drug sales and sales through its mail-order pharmacy, both of which earn higher margins. It is enhancing its Internet strategy to increase connectivity among doctors, patients, and their prescriptions, which will lower costs and increase profits. The firm is also continuing its disciplined approach to acquisitions in order to increase membership.

13900 Riverport Dr. www.express-scripts.com
Maryland Heights, MO 63043

Industry	Investment Style	Stock Type	Sector
Managed Care	☷ Mid Growth	↑ Aggr. Growth	🗾 Healthcare

Competition

	Market Cap $Mil	Debt/ Equity	12 Mo Trailing Sales $Mil	Price/Cash Flow	Return On Assets%	Total Return% 1 Yr	3 Yr
Express Scripts	3,757	0.6	12,188	9.3	5.8	2.7	15.6
Merck	127,121	0.3	50,430	13.2	15.0	-1.3	-2.5
Caremark RX	3,709	NMF	6,440	9.8	22.2	-0.4	53.4

Price Volatility

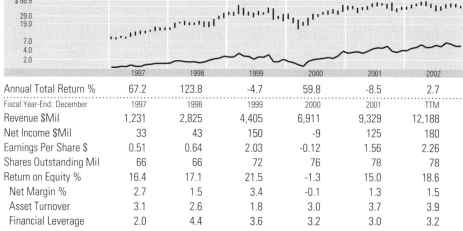

Annual $Price High / Low	16.19 / 7.81	34.50 / 13.50	52.75 / 22.19	53.50 / 14.25	61.45 / 34.84	65.90 / 38.66
	1997	1998	1999	2000	2001	2002
Annual Total Return %	67.2	123.8	-4.7	59.8	-8.5	2.7

Fiscal Year-End: December	1997	1998	1999	2000	2001	TTM
Revenue $Mil	1,231	2,825	4,405	6,911	9,329	12,188
Net Income $Mil	33	43	150	-9	125	180
Earnings Per Share $	0.51	0.64	2.03	-0.12	1.56	2.26
Shares Outstanding Mil	66	66	72	76	78	78
Return on Equity %	16.4	17.1	21.5	-1.3	15.0	18.6
Net Margin %	2.7	1.5	3.4	-0.1	1.3	1.5
Asset Turnover	3.1	2.6	1.8	3.0	3.7	3.9
Financial Leverage	2.0	4.4	3.6	3.2	3.0	3.2

Valuation Ratios	Stock	Rel to Industry	Rel to S&P 500
Price/Earnings	21.3	1.0	0.9
Price/Book	3.9	0.7	1.2
Price/Sales	0.3	0.4	0.2
Price/Cash Flow	9.3	1.0	0.7

Major Fund Holders	% of Fund Assets
Pin Oak Aggressive Stock	13.91
FMI AAM Palm Beach Total Return	6.54
Rochdale Alpha	6.00
Live Oak Health Sciences	5.75

Morningstar Grades

Growth [A]

	1998	1999	2000	2001
Revenue %	129.5	55.9	56.9	35.0
Earnings/Share %	25.7	219.7	NMF	NMF
Book Value/Share %	20.7	154.4	-1.9	12.2
Dividends/Share %	NMF	NMF	NMF	NMF

Over the past five years, Express Scripts has increased revenue at a compound rate of 65% with the help of acquisitions. The NPA acquisition should drive 40% revenue growth in 2002, and we expect internal growth of about 15% from 2003 to 2005.

Profitability [A-]

	1999	2000	2001	TTM
Return on Assets %	6.0	-0.4	5.0	5.8
Oper Cash Flow $Mil	214	246	281	403
- Cap Spending $Mil	37	80	57	53
= Free Cash Flow $Mil	177	166	224	350

Express Scripts has steadily increased operating profit per claim (prescription) from $0.70 in 1996 to more than $1.00 in 2002. The 46% compound average growth in higher-margin mail pharmacy prescriptions has helped fuel the improvement.

Financial Health [B]

	1999	2000	2001	09-02
Long-term Debt $Mil	636	396	346	621
Total Equity $Mil	699	705	832	971
Debt/Equity Ratio	0.9	0.6	0.4	0.6

Express Scripts reduced its debt/total capital ratio from 0.65 in 1998 to 0.29 in 2001. Even after the NPA acquisition in April 2002, the balance sheet remains strong, and the firm produces more than enough cash flow to manage its debt load.

Morningstar's Take By Damon Ficklin, 12-12-2002 Stock Price as of Analysis: $49.37

Express Scripts is a top-tier pharmacy benefit manager (PBM). The company has steadily increased revenue and operating income in the past several years, and we think it is well positioned to continue to benefit from pharmaceutical price inflation. But until we see more-comprehensive financial disclosure from Express Scripts (and other PBMs), we would like a 40% margin of safety to our fair value estimate before buying.

In general, PBMs have a reputation for providing limited financial disclosure. While their strategy is easy to understand--consolidate buyers to increase purchasing power and extract discounts from drug manufacturers--the complex accounting and closed negotiations that allow PBMs to capture more value make it very difficult to gain real insight into the business. This lack of visibility has led to sharp reactions to news and high price volatility in the past.

Despite these concerns, we think Express Scripts' earnings are of high quality. Although we can't forecast earnings with a high degree of certainty, we caution investors not to confuse poor visibility with low quality. Over the past five years, Express Scripts' operating cash flows have increased in tandem with operating earnings, matching them almost dollar for dollar even after subtracting capital expenditures.

Even though we can't always see exactly how it generates earnings, Express Scripts has consistently collected the cash to back those earnings.

Express Scripts is working to improve profitability by expanding its mail pharmacy business. We estimate the mail pharmacy business is 2-4 times more profitable than the retail pharmacy business, depending on the drug prescribed. Express Scripts' mail order penetration rate (about 20% of adjusted claims) is much lower than Caremark's and Merck-Medco's rates of about 50% and 30%, respectively. Although this may put Express Scripts at a disadvantage in negotiating current contracts, it offers a real opportunity to improve profitability.

Express Scripts' average revenue per claim has been increasing roughly in line with pharmaceutical prices, and we expect this trend to continue over the longer term. PBM's revenue is a function of rapidly rising pharmaceutical prices, and although pharmaceutical price inflation has slowed substantially in the past few years, we still expect prices to increase at a double-digit pace for the foreseeable future.

MORNINGSTAR® Stocks 500

ExxonMobil XOM

	Rating	Risk	Moat Size	Fair Value	Last Close	Yield %
	★★★	Low	Narrow	$35.00	$34.94	2.6

Company Profile

The product of the 1999 marriage of energy giants Exxon and Mobil, ExxonMobil is the largest in the oil and gas industry. Last year, ExxonMobil held the number-one spot in the Fortune 500. But sagging oil prices dropped the company to number two in early 2002, now trailing Wal-Mart in sales. ExxonMobil does business in almost every segment of oil industry, from wells to pipelines to refineries to gas stations. A truly global company, ExxonMobil has a presence in more than 200 countries around the world and boasts proven reserves of 22 billion barrels.

Management

Chairman and CEO Lee R. Raymond has nearly 40 years of experience in the oil patch. Raymond was the driving force behind Exxon's merger with Mobil, a marriage that has been a raging success thus far.

Strategy

ExxonMobil is focused on generating best-in-class returns on capital. To achieve its lofty profitability targets, the company relies on its size to squeeze efficiencies from its businesses. Technology also plays a large role in cutting costs and increasing proven reserves. As a mature firm, ExxonMobil has been returning value to its shareholders via dividends and share repurchases.

5959 Las Colinas Blvd.   www.exxon.mobil.com
Irving, TX 75039-2298

Morningstar Grades

Growth [D+]	1998	1999	2000	2001
Revenue %	-15.9	9.4	25.5	-8.3
Earnings/Share %	-30.5	-1.8	125.0	-12.3
Book Value/Share %	-1.8	3.7	12.0	4.9
Dividends/Share %	0.9	1.8	5.4	3.4

Revenue and profits are highly cyclical because of the company's dependence on oil prices. For example, 25% sales growth in 2000 was followed by a 9% decline in 2001. Vacillations of this magnitude should continue.

Profitability [A]	1999	2000	2001	TTM
Return on Assets %	5.5	11.9	10.7	6.7
Oper Cash Flow $Mil	15,013	22,937	22,889	19,579
- Cap Spending $Mil	10,849	8,446	9,989	11,273
= Free Cash Flow $Mil	4,164	14,491	12,900	8,306

ExxonMobil has done a stellar job of cutting costs and finding efficiencies after the merger. As a result, its returns on assets are the envy of the oil patch. Returns have also been remarkably stable, considering the cyclical nature of oil.

Financial Health [A+]	1999	2000	2001	09-02
Long-term Debt $Mil	8,402	7,280	7,099	7,110
Total Equity $Mil	63,466	70,757	73,161	74,690
Debt/Equity Ratio	0.1	0.1	0.1	0.1

The company has had an AAA credit rating for more than 80 years and has one of the healthiest balance sheets in oil. Less than 8% of its $148 billion asset base is funded by debt. This financial strength makes ExxonMobil an attractive partner.

Industry	Investment Style	Stock Type	Sector
Oil & Gas	Large Value	Hard Assets	Energy

Competition	Market Cap $Mil	Debt/ Equity	12 Mo Trailing Sales $Mil	Price/Cash Flow	Return On Assets%	Total Return% 1 Yr	3 Yr
ExxonMobil	235,108	0.1	196,513	12.0	6.7	-8.9	-0.9
BP PLC ADR	152,063	0.2	175,389	6.8	5.7	-9.9	-9.2
Total Fina Elf SA ADR	100,949	0.3	93,914	9.2	8.7	3.7	5.2

Price Volatility — Monthly Price High/Low — Relative Strength to S&P 500

| Annual $Price High | 33.63 | 38.66 | 43.63 | 47.72 | 45.84 | 44.54 |
| Low | 24.13 | 28.31 | 32.16 | 34.94 | 35.01 | 29.86 |

	1997	1998	1999	2000	2001	2002
Annual Total Return %	28.4	22.4	12.6	10.2	-7.6	-8.9

Fiscal Year-end: December	1997	1998	1999	2000	2001	TTM
Revenue $Mil	201,746	169,642	185,527	232,748	213,488	196,513
Net Income $Mil	11,732	8,074	7,910	17,720	15,320	10,050
Earnings Per Share $	1.64	1.14	1.12	2.52	2.21	1.47
Shares Outstanding Mil	7,067	7,021	6,939	6,949	6,870	6,729
Return on Equity %	18.6	13.2	12.5	25.0	20.9	13.5
Net Margin %	5.8	4.8	4.3	7.6	7.2	5.1
Asset Turnover	1.4	1.2	1.3	1.6	1.5	1.3
Financial Leverage	2.3	2.3	2.3	2.1	2.0	2.0

Valuation Ratios	Stock	Rel to Industry	Rel to S&P 500
Price/Earnings	23.8	1.2	1.0
Price/Book	3.1	1.4	1.0
Price/Sales	1.2	1.1	0.6
Price/Cash Flow	12.0	1.8	0.9

Major Fund Holders	% of Fund Assets
ProFunds Ultra Energy Inv	25.82
Rydex Energy Inv	19.98
UMB Scout Energy	19.63
ING Corporate Leaders Trust	14.75

Morningstar's Take By Paul Larson, 11-12-2002 Stock Price as of Analysis: $34.04

In an industry where economy of scale is an important advantage, oil titan ExxonMobil is off the charts. The company is the largest in the oil patch with a $148 billion asset base, nearly 23 billion barrels in reserves, and the capacity to refine more than 6 million barrels a day--all stats that are head and shoulders above the competition.

The combination of Exxon and Mobil has been a major success, significantly boosting earnings in recent years. Between cutting redundancies and increasing efficiency, ExxonMobil estimates that it added almost $6 billion to its bottom line in 2001. To put that in perspective, Microsoft MSFT earned $6 billion last year in total. ExxonMobil expects merger-related savings will only increase as it identifies and exploits additional efficiencies.

These savings are appreciated, since cost is one of the only ways to compete in a commodity market. Oil patch results tend to be volatile because of uncontrollable changes in commodity oil and gas prices. However, ExxonMobil has managed to keep its bottom line in the black through all the recent cycles. The company has not had an unprofitable year in decades and has earned at least $1 per share in each of the past 10 years. In 2000, when the economy was humming and oil was consistently

above $30 a barrel, ExxonMobil earned $2.52 per share.

Years of positive, if variable, profitability and solid management have given ExxonMobil one of the most impressive balance sheets around. Even though the company operates in an extremely capital-intensive industry, less than 8% of its enormous asset base is funded with debt. If we back out cash on hand and inventory, ExxonMobil is essentially debt-free. This should allow the firm to ride out a downturn better than most.

Management has put its excess cash flow to good use by returning value to shareholders via dividends and share repurchases. Without raising debt, ExxonMobil is on track to repurchase $5 billion worth of stock this year (roughly 2% of shares outstanding), and the shares currently have a juicy 2.5% dividend yield.

If we had to choose our favorite company in the energy industry regardless of price, ExxonMobil would be at the top of the list. However, price does matter, so we are merely keeping the company on the radar for now and waiting for a dip before buying.

Family Dollar Stores FDO

	Rating	Risk	Moat Size	Fair Value	Last Close	Yield %
	★★	Med.	None	$30.00	$31.21	0.8

Company Profile

Family Dollar Stores offer inexpensive basic merchandise in more than 3,830 small, easily accessible stores to a target customer whose median family income is below $25,000. The company's stores are located in 39 states, with a concentration in the South. Nationally advertised brand merchandise accounts for approximately 30% of sales. Family Dollar label merchandise accounts for about 5%, and merchandise sold under other labels, or unlabeled, makes up the balance. The typical store is 6,000-8,000 square feet in total area.

Management

CEO and president Howard Levine is the son of chairman and company founder Leon Levine. Howard Levine returned to the firm in 1996 after an eight-year hiatus and became CEO in 1997. Leon Levine still owns a sizeable number of Family Dollar shares.

Strategy

The company's neighborhood discount stores are low-overhead, no-frills operations in rural, small-town, and urban markets. Low rent, combined with easy accessibility, allow Family Dollar stores to compete with big-box chains such as Wal-Mart.

P.O. Box 1017, 10401 Old Monroe Road   www.familydollar.com
Charlotte, NC 28101-1017

Morningstar Grades

Growth [A]	1999	2000	2001	2002
Revenue %	16.5	13.9	17.0	13.6
Earnings/Share %	35.0	23.5	10.0	13.6
Book Value/Share %	18.9	16.2	20.0	19.6
Dividends/Share %	11.8	10.5	9.5	8.7

Family Dollar's 16% average sales growth rate from 1998-2002, while impressive, trails those of competitors Dollar General at 18% and Dollar Tree at 23%. Still, it looks to be sustainable, while the others are slowing.

Profitability [A+]	2000	2001	2002	TTM
Return on Assets %	13.8	13.5	12.4	12.4
Oper Cash Flow $Mil	184	166	403	403
- Cap Spending $Mil	172	163	187	187
= Free Cash Flow $Mil	12	3	216	216

Returns on assets and equity have been consistent with those of other discount stores, thanks to efficient store operations. With a profit margin of just 5%, Family Dollar must continue to be efficient or results could suffer.

Financial Health [A+]	2000	2001	2002	08-02
Long-term Debt $Mil	0	0	0	0
Total Equity $Mil	798	959	1,155	1,155
Debt/Equity Ratio	0.0	0.0	0.0	0.0

The balance sheet is debt-free. The company has never had long-term debt, and consistently finances its aggressive store expansion with internally generated cash. It has increased its dividend each year for more than 25 years.

	Industry	Investment Style	Stock Type	Sector
	Discount Stores	▦ Mid Growth	↗ Classic Growth	▭ Consumer Services

Competition	Market Cap $Mil	Debt/ Equity	12 Mo Trailing Sales $Mil	Price/Cash Flow	Return On Assets%	Total Return% 1 Yr	3 Yr
Family Dollar Stores	5,410	0.0	4,163	13.4	12.4	5.0	25.4
Wal-Mart Stores	223,388	0.5	233,651	18.9	8.0	-11.8	-7.3
Dollar General	3,983	0.4	5,927	11.3	10.5	-19.1	-11.6

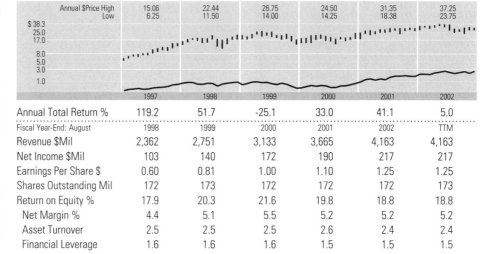

Price Volatility ▮ Monthly Price High/Low — Relative Strength to S&P 500

Annual $Price High Low	15.06 6.25	22.44 11.50	26.75 14.00	24.50 14.25	31.35 18.38	37.25 23.75

$ 38.3 / 25.0 / 17.0 / 8.0 / 5.0 / 3.0 / 1.0

	1997	1998	1999	2000	2001	2002
Annual Total Return %	119.2	51.7	-25.1	33.0	41.1	5.0

Fiscal Year-End: August	1998	1999	2000	2001	2002	TTM
Revenue $Mil	2,362	2,751	3,133	3,665	4,163	4,163
Net Income $Mil	103	140	172	190	217	217
Earnings Per Share $	0.60	0.81	1.00	1.10	1.25	1.25
Shares Outstanding Mil	172	173	172	172	172	173
Return on Equity %	17.9	20.3	21.6	19.8	18.8	18.8
Net Margin %	4.4	5.1	5.5	5.2	5.2	5.2
Asset Turnover	2.5	2.5	2.5	2.6	2.4	2.4
Financial Leverage	1.6	1.6	1.6	1.5	1.5	1.5

Valuation Ratios	Stock	Rel to Industry	Rel to S&P 500
Price/Earnings	25.0	0.9	1.1
Price/Book	4.7	0.8	1.5
Price/Sales	1.3	1.4	0.6
Price/Cash Flow	13.4	0.7	1.0

Major Fund Holders	% of Fund Assets
Franklin Rising Dividends A	4.18
Papp Small & Mid-Cap Growth	3.00
Oppenheimer MidCap A	2.81
Oppenheimer Enterprise A	2.67

Morningstar's Take By Tom Goetzinger, 12-20-2002 Stock Price as of Analysis: $30.74

Shopping at a Family Dollar store is like going to a garage sale: Everything's cheap, and you only find out about it by driving by or from a neighbor. The stock now trades close to our fair value estimate of $30. To ensure an adequate margin of safety, we'd wait for the shares to drop below $20 before investing.

Family Dollar, like many of its deep-discount peers, earns darn good returns. Its stores somehow make 5 cents of profit on each dollar's worth of toothpaste or toys they sell. Discount giants Wal-Mart and Target pull in little more than half that. Even new Family Dollar stores are generally profitable within a year of opening. They require minimal start-up capital for the lease payment, merchandise inventory, and a handful of employees.

It's no surprise, then, that 4,600 stores (and counting) have opened since Family Dollar was founded in 1959. Each store is financed using internally generated cash. Over the past decade alone, 2,500 new stores have been added. This has made for remarkably steady sales growth, averaging 15% annually (growth has registered between 10% and 18% in nine of the past ten years).

Future prospects also look good. More people are visiting dollar stores in general--the percentage of the populace has risen from 47% to 59% over the

past four years--and Family Dollar is incorporating improved technology to find areas with favorable demographics and little competition for new stores. It is also using the technology for "sister-store" profiling, which helps new store managers better plan the initial merchandise mix based on sales patterns at similar stores. First-year store sales increased to 87% of the chainwide average in fiscal 2002, up from 81% in 2001.

However, consistent growth usually breeds competition, and there is certainly no shortage of it in deep-discount retailing. Our biggest concern with Family Dollar isn't company-specific; it applies to the entire industry. Family Dollar, like peers Dollar General and Dollar Tree, operates in a low-margin, labor-intensive business, where everyone is doing just about the same thing. Though that statement applies to most retailers, it is particularly true for dollar stores. The skill level of a manager can determine the profitability of his or her store. A manager must closely monitor inventory and employees to ensure success--a lot to ask of one person. One reason we require a 30% margin of safety is that new stores could underperform given these pressures.

M✪RNINGSTAR® Stocks 500

Fannie Mae FNM

	Rating	Risk	Moat Size	Fair Value	Last Close	Yield %
	★★★★	Low	Narrow	$90.00	$64.33	2.1

Company Profile

Fannie Mae is a federally chartered, stockholder-owned company and is the largest secondary buyer of real-estate mortgages in the United States. It was chartered by the U.S. government to help provide low- and moderate-income-family housing by purchasing mortgage loans from lenders, thereby replenishing their funds for additional lending. The company also issues mortgage-backed securities in exchange for pools of mortgage loans from lenders. Fannie Mae's income is mainly derived from the difference between interest rates on mortgages and borrowed money.

Management

Franklin Raines took over as chairman and CEO in January 1999, after spending two years as director of the Office of Management and Budget.

Strategy

Fannie Mae is a government-sponsored enterprise and the chief buyer of mortgages from banks. Thus, it helps provide banks the capital they need to offer mortgages. Fannie Mae is increasing its market dominance with new loan products and extending its reach into underserved segments, like subprime borrowers.

3900 Wisconsin Avenue, NW   www.fanniemae.com
Washington, DC 20016-2892

Morningstar Grades

Growth [A]	1998	1999	2000	2001
Revenue %	13.4	17.4	19.3	15.2
Earnings/Share %	14.1	15.2	15.3	33.3
Book Value/Share %	13.9	15.0	16.1	-14.6
Dividends/Share %	14.3	12.5	3.7	7.1

Fannie Mae has shown strong, steady revenue growth over the past five years. Its low-teen revenue growth rate is on par with the finance industry average, though growth exploded recently because of low interest rates.

Profitability [D+]	1999	2000	2001	TTM
Return on Assets %	0.7	0.6	0.7	0.7
Oper Cash Flow $Mil	12,843	13,391	14,701	—
- Cap Spending $Mil	—	—	—	—
= Free Cash Flow $Mil	—	—	—	—

Fannie's return on assets is low because the mortgage business is extremely asset-intensive. It earns high returns on equity because it's highly leveraged.

Financial Health [D]	1999	2000	2001	09-02
Long-term Debt $Mil	—	—	—	—
Total Equity $Mil	16,329	18,560	15,815	14,964
Debt/Equity Ratio	—	—	—	—

Fannie is highly leveraged because its business involves issuing debt to purchase mortgages. There is added risk in added leverage, but we think Fannie has enough equity to support its asset base.

Industry	Investment Style	Stock Type	Sector
Finance	Large Value	Classic Growth	Financial Services

Competition	Market Cap $Mil	Debt/ Equity	12 Mo Trailing Sales $Mil	Price/Cash Flow	Return On Assets%	Total Return% 1 Yr	3 Yr
Fannie Mae	72,629	—	52,478	—	0.7	-17.6	5.5
Freddie Mac	41,058	—	—	—	0.8	-8.4	12.0
Lehman Brothers Holdings	12,738	—	1,291	—	0.3	-19.7	13.3

Price Volatility

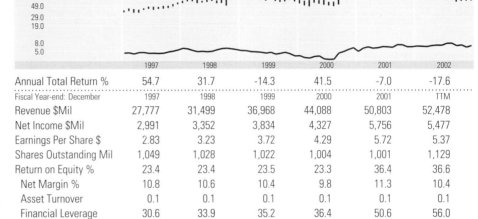

Annual $Price High Low	57.31 36.13	76.19 49.56	75.88 58.56	89.25 47.88	87.94 72.08	84.10 59.00

	1997	1998	1999	2000	2001	2002
Annual Total Return %	54.7	31.7	-14.3	41.5	-7.0	-17.6

Fiscal Year-end: December	1997	1998	1999	2000	2001	TTM
Revenue $Mil	27,777	31,499	36,968	44,088	50,803	52,478
Net Income $Mil	2,991	3,352	3,834	4,327	5,756	5,477
Earnings Per Share $	2.83	3.23	3.72	4.29	5.72	5.37
Shares Outstanding Mil	1,049	1,028	1,022	1,004	1,001	1,129
Return on Equity %	23.4	23.4	23.5	23.3	36.4	36.6
Net Margin %	10.8	10.6	10.4	9.8	11.3	10.4
Asset Turnover	0.1	0.1	0.1	0.1	0.1	0.1
Financial Leverage	30.6	33.9	35.2	36.4	50.6	56.0

Valuation Ratios	Stock	Rel to Industry	Rel to S&P 500
Price/Earnings	12.0	1.0	0.5
Price/Book	4.9	1.4	1.5
Price/Sales	1.4	0.7	0.7
Price/Cash Flow	—	—	—

Major Fund Holders	% of Fund Assets
Scudder Dreman Financial Services A	8.60
SunAmStySel Focused Growth & Inc A	7.10
Vontobel U.S. Value	6.57
Prudential Financial Services A	6.44

Morningstar's Take By Richard McCaffery, 12-06-2002 Stock Price as of Analysis: $63.82

Fannie's strong secular growth potential, along with its expertise at managing risk and keeping costs low, puts the company in a position to reward shareholders. But Fannie often trades at a discount to its earnings power because of interest rate risk, credit risk, and political risk. We'll address these one at a time.

For 15 years, Fannie's hedging strategy has proved effective as earnings grew at a double-digit pace despite wide changes in interest rates. Fannie's use of derivatives and callable debt allows it to ensure a profitable spread between earning assets and the liabilities that fund them. These instruments are well understood, and we see little reason why Fannie's hedging strategy, in which it invests billions, won't continue to safeguard income.

Regarding credit risk, Fannie has a deep database used to evaluate risk, one that becomes more powerful as more lenders use its underwriting software. Statistical models can't tell you everything, but access to good data is critical for managing risk.

Credit losses as a percentage of the company's book of business were just 0.004% through the first nine months of 2002. Such low loss rates stem from the secure nature of the typical mortgage loan, extensive credit insurance, and a workout program

aimed at minimizing losses. Loss rates won't stay this low forever, but Fannie is structured to absorb deeper losses, and its loss prevention strategies should keep credit quality sound.

Finally, Fannie's status as a government-sponsored enterprise (GSE) makes it a political target. While the company has powerful critics, support for the low-cost financing it provides is widespread among Democrats and Republicans. A proposed bill that would have required Fannie to register its securities with the Securities and Exchange Commission, a move that would have increased the company's funding costs, found little support and was denounced by the Bush administration.

Given Fannie's central position in the housing market and the housing market's central position in the economy, we think it's unlikely there will be material changes to its charter. It's possible, however, the government could issue other charters to increase competition and spread risk. Uncertainty surrounding the charter is the primary reason we've changed Fannie's moat from wide to narrow. It's just too hard to predict politics, so we've erred on the side of being conservative. That said, we think Fannie's strengths run deep and that the company will continue rewarding shareholders.

Federated Department Stores FD

Rating	Risk	Moat Size	Fair Value	Last Close	Yield %
★★★	Med.	None	$38.00	$28.76	0.0

Company Profile

Federated Department Stores operates 440 department stores across the United States. Its stores sell men's, women's, and children's apparel and accessories, cosmetics, home furnishings, and other consumer goods. The company's stores are generally located at urban or suburban sites. Federated Department Stores conducts its business through six retail operating divisions: Macy's East/Macy's West, Bloomingdale's, The Bon Marche, Burdines, Rich's/Lazarus/Goldsmith's, and Stern's. The company acquired Fingerhut Companies in March 1999.

Management

James Zimmerman has been a director with Federated since 1988 and became CEO in May 1997. Terry Lundgren, the current COO, is expected to assume the top post after Zimmerman retires.

Strategy

Having stripped underperforming units from its operations, Federated is investing in the future of its remaining stores. It has shut down its Fingerhut catalog unit and Stern's stores. Now, the company is revamping its existing Macy's stores and opening new smaller ones in an effort to improve the customer experience and find a more profitable store format.

151 West 34th Street   www.federated-fds.com
New York, NY 10001

Morningstar Grades

Growth [D+]

	1999	2000	2001	2002
Revenue %	1.0	4.3	3.8	-5.9
Earnings/Share %	22.8	22.3	NMF	NMF
Book Value/Share %	8.0	16.9	-4.5	-2.3
Dividends/Share %	NMF	NMF	NMF	NMF

Federated has been losing share to non-mall-based discount retailers for years; as a result, same-store sales growth has been poor. We expect the trend to continue, so growth is likely to rely even more on expansion and acquisitions.

Profitability [C]

	2000	2001	2002	TTM
Return on Assets %	5.0	-1.2	-1.8	0.2
Oper Cash Flow $Mil	1,735	1,332	1,372	1,388
- Cap Spending $Mil	745	720	615	594
= Free Cash Flow $Mil	990	612	757	794

In the past, Federated's profits were weighed down by losses in its now-defunct Fingerhut unit. The unit has been closed, but we think the company will continue to earn less than its cost of capital.

Financial Health [B]

	2000	2001	2002	10-02
Long-term Debt $Mil	3,801	3,845	3,859	3,410
Total Equity $Mil	6,552	5,822	5,564	5,680
Debt/Equity Ratio	0.6	0.7	0.7	0.6

Federated's debt leverage is higher than that of many retailers, but manageable. We expect free cash flow generation to remain solid.

Industry	Investment Style	Stock Type	Sector
Department Stores	Mid Value	Slow Growth	Consumer Services

Competition

	Market Cap $Mil	Debt/ Equity	12 Mo Trailing Sales $Mil	Price/Cash Flow	Return On Assets%	Total Return% 1 Yr	3 Yr
Federated Department Stores	5,470	0.6	15,550	3.9	0.2	-29.7	-16.2
May Department Stores	6,623	—	14,111	—	—	—	—
Nordstrom	2,563	—	5,772	—	—	—	—

Price Volatility

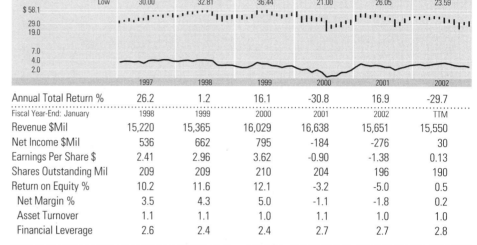

	Monthly Price High/Low		Relative Strength to S&P 500			
Annual $Price High Low	48.88 30.00	56.19 32.81	57.06 36.44	53.88 21.00	49.90 26.05	44.26 23.59

	1997	1998	1999	2000	2001	2002
Annual Total Return %	26.2	1.2	16.1	-30.8	16.9	-29.7

Fiscal Year-End: January	1998	1999	2000	2001	2002	TTM
Revenue $Mil	15,220	15,365	16,029	16,638	15,651	15,550
Net Income $Mil	536	662	795	-184	-276	30
Earnings Per Share $	2.41	2.96	3.62	-0.90	-1.38	0.13
Shares Outstanding Mil	209	209	210	204	196	190
Return on Equity %	10.2	11.6	12.1	-3.2	-5.0	0.5
Net Margin %	3.5	4.3	5.0	-1.1	-1.8	0.2
Asset Turnover	1.1	1.1	1.0	1.1	1.0	1.0
Financial Leverage	2.6	2.4	2.4	2.7	2.7	2.8

Valuation Ratios	Stock	Rel to Industry	Rel to S&P 500
Price/Earnings	221.2	13.8	9.4
Price/Book	1.0	0.8	0.3
Price/Sales	0.4	1.2	0.2
Price/Cash Flow	3.9	1.0	0.3

Major Fund Holders	% of Fund Assets
Salomon Brothers Capital O	3.01
Cutler Value	2.96
Prudential 20/20 Focus A	2.92
Credit Suisse Instl Large Cap Value	2.79

Morningstar's Take   By Roz Bryant, 12-10-2002   Stock Price as of Analysis: $30.41

We expect slow growth from Federated because the department store chain is essentially stuck with its lower market share. We'd require at least a 40% discount to our fair value estimate before investing.

Federated has had its share of problems over the past few years, many of which it created. The purchase of catalog operator Fingerhut in 1999 cost the company dearly. The unit's credit losses began to mount soon after the acquisition, marring Federated's earnings. After recording asset-impairment and restructuring charges in excess of $1 billion in 2000 and 2001, Federated disposed of the division altogether.

Federated's market share losses have been equally staggering. Sales growth has averaged just 0.6% over the past five years while more popular chains have flourished, and competition from Kohl's in the Northeast forced Federated to shutter its value-oriented Stern's department stores in that area.

Federated remains focused on its core high-end department store business. However, we think the prospects for that business are relatively dim. Like many old-line department store chains, Federated is battling both value-oriented retailers like Kohl's and upscale boutique-type stores like Chico's, trying to stem market share losses and stoke revenue growth.

So far, that's a battle the venerable old retailer is losing. Federated's same-store sales fell 2.6% through the first nine months of fiscal 2002, compared with increases of 8.1% for Kohl's and 14.4% for Chico's, as customers continued to move away from the company's traditional store format. This trend is likely to continue, in our opinion, leaving the company destined for slow growth.

Federated hasn't lost hope, though, and it still has a few irons in the fire. For one thing, the firm is relying on one of the most well-known names in retailing for growth--Macy's. Also, smaller store formats are being tested and fitted with new lighting and sound systems to attract younger shoppers. Both efforts could provide some modest revenue growth over the next several years if customer traffic picks up.

Still, we don't expect favorable growth, given the shift away from traditional department stores. We'd buy the stock only at $20 or less.

MORNINGSTAR® Stocks 500

Federated Investors B FII

	Rating	Risk	Moat Size	Fair Value	Last Close	Yield %
	★★★★★	Low	Narrow	$41.00	$25.37	0.9

Company Profile

Federated Investors provides investment-management products and related financial services. The company sponsors, markets, and provides investment advisory, distribution, and administrative services. It distributes its products through banks, brokers, and other investment advisers whose customers include retail investors, corporations, and retirement plans. As of December 31, 1999, Federated provided investment advisory services to 129 mutual funds. This total includes money-market funds, fixed-income funds, and equity funds.

Management

Federated is run by members of the Donahue family, who control all of the voting stock. Founder John Donahue is still with the company as chairman. He handed the CEO title to his son J. Christopher Donahue in 1998.

Strategy

Federated seeks to increase its assets under management through further penetration of the institutional, bank, and broker markets. The firm is always on the lookout for acquisitions that will increase its presence in the fixed-income and equity-management markets.

Federated Investors Tower   www.federatedinvestors.com
Pittsburgh, PA 15222-3779

Industry	Investment Style	Stock Type	Sector
Money Management	▦ Mid Growth	↗ Classic Growth	$ Financial Services

Competition

	Market Cap $Mil	Debt/ Equity	12 Mo Trailing Sales $Mil	Price/Cash Flow	Return On Assets%	Total Return% 1 Yr	Total Return% 3 Yr
Federated Investors B	2,889	—	722	—	38.9	-19.8	27.0
Bank of America	104,505	—	46,628	—	1.3	14.5	19.8
Blackrock	2,550	—	569	—	16.2	-5.5	35.4

Price Volatility

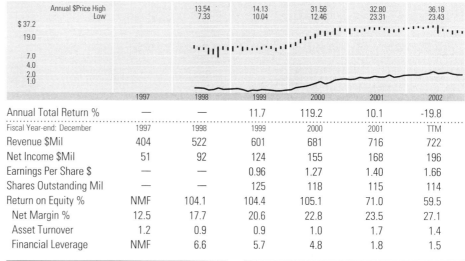

			Monthly Price High/Low	— Relative Strength to S&P 500		
Annual $Price High Low			13.54 7.33	14.13 10.04	31.56 12.46	32.80 23.31	36.18 23.43

$ 37.2
19.0
7.0
4.0
2.0
1.0

	1997	1998	1999	2000	2001	2002
Annual Total Return %	—	—	11.7	119.2	10.1	-19.8

Fiscal Year-end: December	1997	1998	1999	2000	2001	TTM
Revenue $Mil	404	522	601	681	716	722
Net Income $Mil	51	92	124	155	168	196
Earnings Per Share $	—	—	0.96	1.27	1.40	1.66
Shares Outstanding Mil	—	—	125	118	115	114
Return on Equity %	NMF	104.1	104.4	105.1	71.0	59.5
Net Margin %	12.5	17.7	20.6	22.8	23.5	27.1
Asset Turnover	1.2	0.9	0.9	1.0	1.7	1.4
Financial Leverage	NMF	6.6	5.7	4.8	1.8	1.5

Valuation Ratios

	Stock	Rel to Industry	Rel to S&P 500
Price/Earnings	15.3	0.9	0.6
Price/Book	8.8	3.3	2.7
Price/Sales	4.0	1.5	2.0
Price/Cash Flow	—	—	—

Major Fund Holders

	% of Fund Assets
Morgan Stanley Financial Services B	4.19
Fidelity Select Brokerage & Investmnt	3.59
Tweedy, Browne American Value	3.54
Citizens Emerging Growth Stndrd	3.46

Morningstar Grades

Growth [B]	1998	1999	2000	2001
Revenue %	29.3	15.1	13.3	5.1
Earnings/Share %	NMF	NMF	32.3	10.2
Book Value/Share %	—	NMF	31.4	63.0
Dividends/Share %	NMF	116.0	26.9	26.2

Revenue growth has been impressive, increasing at an annual rate of 17% over the past five years. The market downturn has hurt equity asset levels, but it has also sent money pouring into safer money market and bond funds, the firm's specialty.

Profitability [A+]	1999	2000	2001	TTM
Return on Assets %	18.4	22.0	39.0	38.9
Oper Cash Flow $Mil	132	170	281	—
- Cap Spending $Mil	17	12	7	—
= Free Cash Flow $Mil	—	—	—	—

Net margins increased to 23.5% in 2001 from 12.5% in 1997, largely because of the rise in assets under management. Rising profit margins have allowed earnings-per-share growth to outpace revenue growth.

Financial Health [A+]	1999	2000	2001	09-02
Long-term Debt $Mil	—	—	—	—
Total Equity $Mil	119	148	237	329
Debt/Equity Ratio	—	—	—	—

Federated boasts a squeaky-clean balance sheet, with no debt and plenty of cash. The firm should have no problem paying for share buybacks and future acquisitions.

Morningstar's Take By Rachel Barnard, 12-16-2002 Stock Price as of Analysis: $25.95

Managing primarily money market funds, Federated is one of the more defensive asset managers. We would be happy to own a piece of this growing business at the right price. We think that the shares are worth $41 and that they are a bargain below $25.

More than 75% of the assets that Federated manages are in money market products. While they are neither the most exciting nor the most profitable investment products, they are a staple for institutions and individuals who need a place to put their cash. Plus, the recent turmoil in the equity markets has made cash-management products increasingly attractive.

The firm offers a dizzying array of money market products. Federated covers the waterfront with products for banks, insurers, corporations, and individuals that invest in particular states and specific securities. But while selection is wide, margins are slim: Federated makes an average of 0.25% on money market assets. So although these offerings account for more than 75% of assets under management, they bring in only 47% of the revenue.

This business offers great economies of scale, though. The company can easily handle additional money market dollars with little additional cost. Federated's competitive advantage is evidenced by the recent cut in interest rates, which lowered the federal funds rate 50 basis points. Some money market rivals are considering exiting the business because yields on money fund assets are at the point where many broker-sold funds, which carry large sales fees, are not profitable to run. Firms across the industry have slashed fees to keep money funds from "breaking the buck" (shares falling below the $1 level). But Federated has only one fund, and a small one at that, that is presently in danger of having a negative yield. Most of its fund assets have lower expenses and are therefore safer from falling yields.

Instead of sounding a retreat, Federated is looking to buy up struggling competitors, since it can run the money at a lower cost. This will help the firm meet its double-digit growth goal for its money fund business. It also is eager to buy equity fund managers, which are now out of favor and might be going cheap. With plenty of cash and a hunger for diversification, Federated appears to have a winning strategy, positioning it to benefit from a resurgence in the equity markets. This also would help mitigate the risk of rising interest rates, which could accompany a market upturn and make many bonds more attractive than low-yielding money market products.

FedEx FDX

	Rating	Risk	Moat Size	Fair Value	Last Close	Yield %
	★★	Med.	Narrow	$50.00	$54.22	0.3

Company Profile

FedEx provides air-delivery services. It offers overnight and second-day delivery for heavy freight, packages, and documents in the United States and abroad. FedEx sells its services under the FedEx, International Priority, FedEx Ground, and FedEx Priority Overnight service marks. Its service network includes more than 660 aircraft and 49,000 vehicles, sorting facilities, and service centers. Foreign sales account for 28% of the company's total sales. It acquired American Freightways in 2001.

Management

Chairman and CEO Fred Smith founded the company in 1971; he still owns more than 7% of the outstanding stock. Under his leadership, FedEx has consistently been named one of the most admired companies in the world.

Strategy

FedEx hopes to increase growth by expanding its core service of business-to-business delivery into international markets, and by challenging rival UPS' lock on the business-to-consumer market through its FedEx Home Delivery unit and an alliance with the U.S. Postal Service.

942 South Shady Grove Road   www.fedex.com
Memphis, TN 38120

Morningstar Grades

Growth [B+]	1999	2000	2001	2002
Revenue %	5.7	8.8	7.5	5.0
Earnings/Share %	24.3	10.5	-14.2	17.6
Book Value/Share %	16.6	4.0	24.7	7.3
Dividends/Share %	NMF	NMF	NMF	NMF

FedEx's top-line growth has been okay, but not spectacular, over the past few years. The firm hopes its international service along with the newer segments--FedEx Ground and FedEx Global Logistics--will drive growth.

Profitability [A]	2000	2001	2002	TTM
Return on Assets %	6.0	4.4	5.1	5.4
Oper Cash Flow $Mil	1,625	2,044	2,228	2,381
- Cap Spending $Mil	1,627	1,893	1,615	1,651
= Free Cash Flow $Mil	-2	151	613	730

Profit margins are much lower than those of its rival UPS. However, FedEx's aggressive move into home delivery and international shipments should lead to increasing profitability over the next few years.

Financial Health [A]	2000	2001	2002	08-02
Long-term Debt $Mil	1,776	1,900	1,800	1,775
Total Equity $Mil	4,785	5,900	6,545	6,657
Debt/Equity Ratio	0.4	0.3	0.3	0.3

Operating cash flows are strong, enabling FedEx to keep its financial leverage ratio from expanding. However, the firm does have substantial off-balance-sheet debt because of its operating leases for aircraft.

Industry	Investment Style	Stock Type	Sector
Transportation - Misc	▦ Large Core	→ Slow Growth	▤ Business Services

Competition	Market Cap $Mil	Debt/ Equity	12 Mo Trailing Sales $Mil	Price/Cash Flow	Return On Assets%	Total Return% 1 Yr	3 Yr
FedEx	16,189	0.3	21,015	6.8	5.4	4.8	9.4
United Parcel Service B	70,397	0.3	31,337	19.1	9.2	17.2	0.3
FedEx	16,189	0.3	21,015	6.8	5.4	4.8	9.4

Price Volatility   ▌ Monthly Price High/Low   — Relative Strength to S&P 500

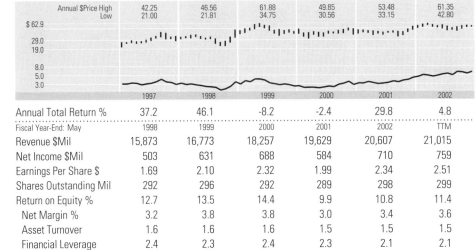

Annual $Price High	42.25	46.56	61.88	49.85	53.48	61.35
Low	21.00	21.81	34.75	30.56	33.15	42.80
	1997	1998	1999	2000	2001	2002

Annual Total Return %	37.2	46.1	-8.2	-2.4	29.8	4.8

Fiscal Year-End: May	1998	1999	2000	2001	2002	TTM
Revenue $Mil	15,873	16,773	18,257	19,629	20,607	21,015
Net Income $Mil	503	631	688	584	710	759
Earnings Per Share $	1.69	2.10	2.32	1.99	2.34	2.51
Shares Outstanding Mil	292	296	292	289	298	299
Return on Equity %	12.7	13.5	14.4	9.9	10.8	11.4
Net Margin %	3.2	3.8	3.8	3.0	3.4	3.6
Asset Turnover	1.6	1.6	1.6	1.5	1.5	1.5
Financial Leverage	2.4	2.3	2.4	2.3	2.1	2.1

Valuation Ratios	Stock	Rel to Industry	Rel to S&P 500
Price/Earnings	21.6	0.7	0.9
Price/Book	2.4	0.4	0.8
Price/Sales	0.8	0.3	0.4
Price/Cash Flow	6.8	0.4	0.5

Major Fund Holders	% of Fund Assets
Rydex Transportation Inv	10.57
Vanguard Primecap	6.47
Longleaf Partners	6.41
Vanguard Capital Opportunity	4.91

Morningstar's Take By Jonathan Schrader, 11-22-2002   Stock Price as of Analysis: $52.74

FedEx has a solid franchise in the express delivery market, but given the risk that its high leverage brings, we would want at least a 30% discount to our fair value estimate before we'd invest.

FedEx basically created the market for overnight delivery in the United States. Because of this, it gained first-mover advantage, and used this edge to dominate the market in the early years. Over time, though, competition--especially from United Parcel Service--chipped away at FedEx's franchise. While FedEx still delivers more overnight packages than any of its rivals, its lead over UPS has grown smaller. Over the past five years, FedEx's overnight volume has essentially been flat, while UPS' has increased 14% annually.

Despite this deterioration, we still think that FedEx has some moatlike traits; thus, we have assigned it a narrow moat rating (as opposed to no moat). It is not cheap or easy to build a network that can compete with it and UPS. It requires a large investment in aircraft, distribution systems, delivery vehicles, and people. And since there are already two strong players in the field, most potential rivals would shy away from entering the fray. We think FedEx's strong network and high barriers to entry should allow the firm to maintain its current level of profitability over

an extended period, while also benefiting from any market growth.

Despite its solid position in the express market, FedEx hasn't rested on its laurels. It has used the profits from this unit to move into higher-margin markets, including the less-than-truckload freight industry. While FedEx is still assimilating these businesses, the early results are promising. Also, FedEx is making a big push into the home delivery market, where UPS and the U.S. Postal Service have dominated. This market should provide the firm with higher-margin growth for years to come.

We do have an issue with FedEx's financial position. The company basically began life as an airline. It still relies heavily on operating leases to acquire aircraft, which translates into higher leverage than the balance sheet would imply. While the firm's financial position has been improving over the past few years, we are still somewhat leery, as net debt/total capital (including capitalized operating leases) remains around 65%.

We would buy this stock if it traded at a considerable discount to our fair value estimate, but all things being equal, we would probably opt for UPS instead.

M⚹RNINGSTAR® Stocks 500

Fifth Third Bancorp FITB

	Rating	Risk	Moat Size	Fair Value	Last Close	Yield %
	★★★	Low	Wide	$54.00	$58.55	1.7

Company Profile

Fifth Third Bancorp operates 17 bank affiliates with 965 banking offices in Ohio, Kentucky, Indiana, Michigan, Florida, Arizona, and Illinois. The banks provide a variety of financial services, including retail and commercial banking, trust, and investment banking. Fifth Third's Midwest Payment Systems subsidiary processes transactions for banks and other financial companies.

Management

CEO George Schaefer Jr. is at the heart of Fifth Third's style and culture--conservative, play-by-the-numbers banking. The company raises its own talent and does not pay up to attract outside managers.

Strategy

Fifth Third's strategy is based on increasing revenue and reducing costs, but few banks have had as much success with this simple formula. The firm operates as 16 separate bank affiliates to keep managers close to customers. Recently, Fifth Third has focused on expanding market share in Chicago and Detroit, where it has just a small percentage of total deposits.

Fifth Third Center   www.53.com
Cincinnati, OH 45263

Morningstar Grades

Growth [C+]	1998	1999	2000	2001
Revenue %	7.8	6.1	16.1	1.2
Earnings/Share %	3.7	16.9	19.3	-6.1
Book Value/Share %	7.1	3.2	18.5	12.4
Dividends/Share %	24.8	24.0	19.3	18.6

Fifth Third's revenue growth has been robust over the past few years, and we think the purchase of Old Kent will keep revenue growth healthy.

Profitability [A-]	1999	2000	2001	TTM
Return on Assets %	1.5	1.6	1.5	2.1
Oper Cash Flow $Mil	2,600	787	956	—
- Cap Spending $Mil	141	132	128	—
= Free Cash Flow $Mil	—	—	—	—

Fifth Third's return on assets of 2.20% is well above the industry average. Cost control and consistent growth of fee income have boosted profitability.

Financial Health [A]	1999	2000	2001	09-02
Long-term Debt $Mil	—	—	—	—
Total Equity $Mil	5,563	6,653	7,630	8,376
Debt/Equity Ratio	—	—	—	—

Its Tier 1 capital ratio (a key measure of its ability to lend) and loan default rate are much better than all of its peers'.

Industry	Investment Style	Stock Type	Sector
Super Regional Banks	▦ Large Growth	↗ Classic Growth	$ Financial Services

Competition

	Market Cap $Mil	Debt/ Equity	12 Mo Trailing Sales $Mil	Price/Cash Flow	Return On Assets%	Total Return% 1 Yr	3 Yr
Fifth Third Bancorp	33,873	—	6,272	—	2.1	-3.4	11.1
Bank One	42,636	—	22,444	—	1.1	-4.4	9.4
US Bancorp	40,630	—	15,324	—	1.8	5.2	11.7

Price Volatility

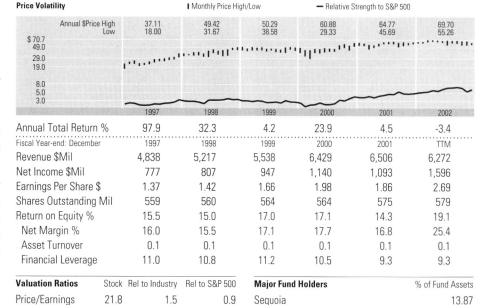

Annual $Price High Low	37.11 18.00	49.42 31.67	50.29 38.58	60.88 29.33	64.77 45.69	69.70 55.26

	1997	1998	1999	2000	2001	2002
Annual Total Return %	97.9	32.3	4.2	23.9	4.5	-3.4

Fiscal Year-end: December	1997	1998	1999	2000	2001	TTM
Revenue $Mil	4,838	5,217	5,538	6,429	6,506	6,272
Net Income $Mil	777	807	947	1,140	1,093	1,596
Earnings Per Share $	1.37	1.42	1.66	1.98	1.86	2.69
Shares Outstanding Mil	559	560	564	564	575	579
Return on Equity %	15.5	15.0	17.0	17.1	14.3	19.1
Net Margin %	16.0	15.5	17.1	17.7	16.8	25.4
Asset Turnover	0.1	0.1	0.1	0.1	0.1	0.1
Financial Leverage	11.0	10.8	11.2	10.5	9.3	9.3

Valuation Ratios	Stock	Rel to Industry	Rel to S&P 500
Price/Earnings	21.8	1.5	0.9
Price/Book	4.0	2.0	1.3
Price/Sales	5.4	2.5	2.7
Price/Cash Flow	—	—	—

Major Fund Holders	% of Fund Assets
Sequoia	13.87
FMI AAM Palm Beach Total Return	7.22
Cincinnati	7.01
Fidelity Select Banking	6.15

Morningstar's Take By Richard McCaffery, 11-22-2002 Stock Price as of Analysis: $57.13

Fifth Third remains one of the best-run banks in the country, and although it deserves a premium valuation, we think it's fully priced. That said, we wouldn't need much of a discount to get excited about the shares.

Fifth Third falls into the category of companies that create value through great execution. Just like Wal-Mart, Fifth Third knows how to sell products and cut costs. Fee income has grown at a compound annual rate of 19% over the past five years and now represents more than 40% of total revenue, above the industry average. This fee-based revenue stream means the company is able to produce more in revenue per dollar of assets than the typical bank, which drives up return on assets and equity. Meanwhile, operating expenses have fallen to about 43% of total revenue from 55% in 1996.

While credit losses almost doubled last year, credit quality remains strong. In the third quarter, charge-offs for bad loans were just 0.39% of average loans, well below the industry average. On top of that, the company continues building the balance sheet, increasing its capital ratio (a measure of financial strength) to 11.11%. Few banks in the country have earned higher credit ratings from the rating agencies. A healthy balance sheet, strong

credit ratings, and easy access to debt markets provide the company with a great deal of financial flexibility.

Put low operating costs, high margins, good sales growth, and low charge-offs together, and Fifth Third stands above its peers. The company has the business model every bank wants.

With less than 10% deposit market share in its core operating area, Fifth Third has plenty of room to expand. In Chicago and Detroit, for example, Fifth Third has less than a 3% share of customer deposits. Given its ability to attract low-cost deposits (last year demand deposits grew 55%), it's not a stretch to see the company's footprint expanding in its core five-state area of Ohio, Indiana, Kentucky, Illinois, and Michigan.

Still, competition is improving. Bank One CEO Jamie Dimon won't let Fifth Third march into Chicago and Detroit unchecked, and Citigroup has its eye on Chicago as well. Fifth Third will lose some battles, but overall we expect double-digit profit growth to continue. The company's low-cost model and focus on strong revenue growth are sustainable competitive advantages.

First Data FDC

	Rating	Risk	Moat Size	Fair Value	Last Close	Yield %
	★★★★	Low	Wide	$40.00	$35.41	0.2

Industry	Investment Style	Stock Type	Sector
Data Processing	Large Core	Classic Growth	Business Services

Company Profile

First Data moves money: Some $2 trillion a year to be exact. The company provides a wide host of financial processing services for retailers and banks. The company serves as an outsourced clearinghouse, crunching billions of credit card, debit card, and check transactions annually. In addition, First Data's Western Union subsidiary allows consumers to wire funds to more than 100,000 locations in 186 countries and territories.

Management

Long-time CEO Henry "Ric" Duques retired at the end of 2001. Replacing him was Charlie Fote, who has been with First Data or its predecessors since 1975 and has worked in all three of the firm's main divisions.

Strategy

First Data has pared its business units in recent years in order to focus on its three market-leading segments: providing money transfers to consumers, servicing credit card issuers, and processing credit card purchases for merchants. In the money transfer business, First Data is expanding its worldwide agent base; its two other units have big market share to exploit economies of scale.

6200 South Quebec Street   www.firstdatacorp.com
Greenwood Village, CO 80111

Competition

Competition	Market Cap $Mil	Debt/ Equity	12 Mo Trailing Sales $Mil	Price/Cash Flow	Return On Assets%	Total Return% 1 Yr	Total Return% 3 Yr
First Data	26,633	0.8	7,118	16.5	4.6	-9.5	14.4
Viad	1,994	—	1,637	—	—	—	—
National Processing	836	0.0	461	10.4	10.6	-50.6	22.4

Price Volatility

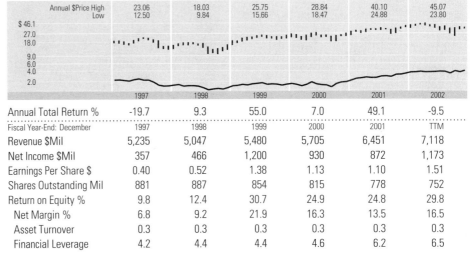

	1997	1998	1999	2000	2001	2002
Annual $Price High	23.06	18.03	25.75	28.84	40.10	45.07
Low	12.50	9.84	15.66	18.47	24.88	23.80
Annual Total Return %	-19.7	9.3	55.0	7.0	49.1	-9.5

Fiscal Year-End: December	1997	1998	1999	2000	2001	TTM
Revenue $Mil	5,235	5,047	5,480	5,705	6,451	7,118
Net Income $Mil	357	466	1,200	930	872	1,173
Earnings Per Share $	0.40	0.52	1.38	1.13	1.10	1.51
Shares Outstanding Mil	881	887	854	815	778	752
Return on Equity %	9.8	12.4	30.7	24.9	24.8	29.8
Net Margin %	6.8	9.2	21.9	16.3	13.5	16.5
Asset Turnover	0.3	0.3	0.3	0.3	0.3	0.3
Financial Leverage	4.2	4.4	4.4	4.6	6.2	6.5

Valuation Ratios

Valuation Ratios	Stock	Rel to Industry	Rel to S&P 500
Price/Earnings	23.5	1.0	1.0
Price/Book	6.8	1.4	2.1
Price/Sales	3.7	1.1	1.9
Price/Cash Flow	16.5	1.0	1.2

Major Fund Holders

Major Fund Holders	% of Fund Assets
Fidelity Select Business Serv&Outsrcg	12.07
Berger Information Technology Instl	7.64
Berger Information Technology Inv	7.64
Evergreen Technology A	7.29

Morningstar Grades

Growth [B+]	1998	1999	2000	2001
Revenue %	-3.6	8.6	4.1	13.1
Earnings/Share %	31.6	165.4	-18.5	-2.2
Book Value/Share %	3.6	7.2	0.4	-1.6
Dividends/Share %	0.0	0.0	0.0	0.0

Impressive performance at Western Union has been driving First Data's internal growth, while the merchant processing business is pitching in some acquisition-based growth. Holding the firm back is the card issuing group.

Profitability [B+]	1999	2000	2001	TTM
Return on Assets %	7.1	5.4	4.0	4.6
Oper Cash Flow $Mil	1,319	1,181	1,408	1,616
- Cap Spending $Mil	244	149	187	236
= Free Cash Flow $Mil	1,076	1,032	1,221	1,381

First Data has consistently earned operating margins greater than 20% and produced robust free cash flow. We expect it to produce returns on capital well above the rate investors demand, thanks to the strong position it has in each of its businesses.

Financial Health [C+]	1999	2000	2001	09-02
Long-term Debt $Mil	1,578	1,830	3,102	3,160
Total Equity $Mil	3,908	3,728	3,520	3,933
Debt/Equity Ratio	0.4	0.5	0.9	0.8

First Data generated about $1 billion of free cash flow in 2001 and we expect the firm will best that performance in 2002. With a debt load of $3 billion that is relatively small in relation to its stable cash-generating ability, First Data is fine.

Morningstar's Take By Dan Schick, 10-23-2002 Stock Price as of Analysis: $34.00

First Data looms large over the card and merchant processing and international money transfer businesses. We believe the firm's advantages in these markets will continue to sustain its high returns, so we would purchase shares at just a 20% discount to our fair value estimate of $40.

Economies of scale are important in the merchant processing business, so big size is a benefit. And First Data is big. It processes about 40% of the purchases made in the United States with Visa and MasterCard plastic, more than 3 times the volume of its nearest competitor. Spreading the fixed costs of computer systems and processing software over this huge transaction volume gives First Data a cost advantage over rivals that should last. Furthermore, because a brand-new processor would lack scale, First Data shouldn't be seeing new competition.

First Data's Western Union subsidiary dominates money transfer for two reasons. For one, First Data's marketing ensures that Western Union is a well-known brand. People worldwide know that they can send money safely using Western Union. Second, Western Union now boasts 135,000 locations worldwide. Western Union's main rival, MoneyGram (a Viad subsidiary), has just 55,000.

Because a network's worth grows with the amount of members, Western Union's large agent base creates huge value. Although Western Union's distribution network is just 2.5 times as large as MoneyGram's, we estimate Western Union rakes in about 8 times more revenue and operating profit than its rival. Western Union is boosting its lead by building its international agent base, adding 20,000 locations in India and China by the end of 2003. With its growing, valuable network, Western Union should thrive for a long time.

Compared with Western Union and the merchant processing segment, First Data's third big business--processing for card issuers--looks bad. Card issuing has lost several big contracts in the past few years, causing anemic revenue growth. Its technology has also been outgunned by TSYS' more advanced processing platform, pressuring prices. Despite these impediments, First Data still earns attractive returns thanks to its scale as the biggest processor. We also applaud management's shareholder-friendly attitude. CEO Fote has raised the possibility of a spin-off or sale of card issuing if sales goals cannot be met.

Market-leading businesses, strong cash flows, and a management team acting in shareholders' interests make First Data an attractive investment at the right price.

MORNINGSTAR® Stocks 500

First Health Group FHCC

	Rating	Risk	Moat Size	Fair Value	Last Close	Yield %
	★★★	Med.	Narrow	$30.00	$24.35	0.0

Company Profile

First Health Group provides medical cost management services. The company's networks are chains of hospitals, physicians, and outpatient-care providers that facilitate the delivery of care at fixed, negotiated rates. COMPARE Medical Review Programs are the company's utilization management programs, which facilitate the delivery of care and identify treatment alternatives. The OUCH Systems provide computer-assisted bill review and audit, fee schedule review, and claims pricing services.

Management

Edward Wristen joined First Health in 1990 and has held management positions in several of the firm's divisions. He was named president in January 2001 and CEO in January 2002.

Strategy

First Health's PPO network is the largest network of directly contracted health-care providers in the United States. The company derives more than 60% of revenue from its PPO and uses the network to cross-sell other products and services, including medical claims administration, pharmacy benefit management, and disease-management programs to benefit subscribers.

3200 Highland Avenue
Downers Grove, IL 60515
www.firsthealth.com

Morningstar Grades

Growth [B-]	1998	1999	2000	2001
Revenue %	29.3	-8.9	10.5	17.0
Earnings/Share %	EUB	-2.9	22.1	20.5
Book Value/Share %	-43.0	-22.5	114.1	80.9
Dividends/Share %	NMF	NMF	NMF	NMF

First Health has posted strong revenue growth for the past two years, and the CCN acquisition and recent contract wins should add fuel to the fire. We expect revenue growth of 21% and 18% in 2002 and 2003, respectively.

Profitability [A]	1999	2000	2001	TTM
Return on Assets %	14.2	16.8	13.2	14.9
Oper Cash Flow $Mil	112	171	151	238
- Cap Spending $Mil	50	62	64	54
= Free Cash Flow $Mil	62	109	88	183

Because of its efficient hospital and physician network, First Health has the industry's top EBITDA (earnings before interest, taxes, depreciation, and amortization) margin. It improved from 33% in 1999 to 37% in 2001 and early 2002.

Financial Health [A]	1999	2000	2001	09-02
Long-term Debt $Mil	240	128	0	104
Total Equity $Mil	87	181	339	446
Debt/Equity Ratio	2.8	0.7	0.0	0.2

Its financial health is sound. First Health paid down $100 million in debt in the first half of the year and produces more than enough operating cash flow to pay down remaining obligations.

Industry	Investment Style	Stock Type	Sector
Managed Care	Mid Growth	Classic Growth	Healthcare

Competition

	Market Cap $Mil	Debt/ Equity	12 Mo Trailing Sales $Mil	Price/Cash Flow	Return On Assets%	Total Return% 1 Yr	3 Yr
First Health Group	2,470	0.2	715	10.4	14.9	-1.6	24.4
UnitedHealth Group	25,235	0.3	24,358	12.5	8.9	18.0	46.6
Aetna	6,190	—	21,201	—	-7.2	24.8	—

Price Volatility

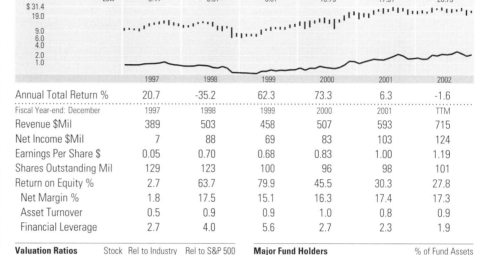

		I Monthly Price High/Low		— Relative Strength to S&P 500		
Annual $Price High	16.39	15.44	13.84	24.81	30.40	30.15
Low	9.41	6.81	6.81	10.75	17.31	20.79

	1997	1998	1999	2000	2001	2002
Annual Total Return %	20.7	-35.2	62.3	73.3	6.3	-1.6
Fiscal Year-end: December	1997	1998	1999	2000	2001	TTM
Revenue $Mil	389	503	458	507	593	715
Net Income $Mil	7	88	69	83	103	124
Earnings Per Share $	0.05	0.70	0.68	0.83	1.00	1.19
Shares Outstanding Mil	129	123	100	96	98	101
Return on Equity %	2.7	63.7	79.9	45.5	30.3	27.8
Net Margin %	1.8	17.5	15.1	16.3	17.4	17.3
Asset Turnover	0.5	0.9	0.9	1.0	0.8	0.9
Financial Leverage	2.7	4.0	5.6	2.7	2.3	1.9

Valuation Ratios	Stock	Rel to Industry	Rel to S&P 500
Price/Earnings	20.5	1.0	0.9
Price/Book	5.5	1.0	1.7
Price/Sales	3.5	5.0	1.7
Price/Cash Flow	10.4	1.1	0.8

Major Fund Holders	% of Fund Assets
Liberty Acorn Twenty Z	7.40
Liberty Acorn USA Z	5.12
Chesapeake Aggressive Growth	4.07
Oakmark Global I	3.72

Morningstar's Take By Damon Ficklin, 11-13-2002 Stock Price as of Analysis: $24.26

First Health is the only pure-play fee-based preferred provider organization (PPO) in the managed-care industry. We really like its business model, and would buy the shares at a 30% margin of safety to our fair value estimate.

First Health has the largest PPO network in the country. With more than 4,000 hospitals and almost 400,000 physicians across all 50 states, it can provide in-network access to about 98% of the U.S. population. Since most other PPOs have much smaller networks that are often regionally or locally focused, First Health has a real competitive advantage in attracting large national accounts--especially those with employees across the country. Employees benefit from the size of its network because their doctors are more likely to be included, and employers benefit because less out-of-network care means lower costs.

While First Health hasn't exactly built its network one provider at a time, it has avoided contracting with large provider groups. This makes First Health more important to the providers than the individual providers are to First Health, thereby increasing its bargaining power. Its 96% provider retention rate indicates that it is a good business partner as well.

First Health also has a much lower risk profile than its competitors. While the average managed-care company writes a roughly even mix of fee-based and risk-based business, First Health only writes fee-based business (with small exceptions). It does not underwrite policies for its members and it is not at risk for rising health-care costs. It simply charges its customers a fee for the use of its network, and the customers manage--and are at risk for--their own medical costs. With medical costs seeing double-digit growth and insurance premiums rising even faster, more and more employers are exploring self-funding options. First Health stands ready to gain.

First Health can provide more seamless service than most of its competitors because it owns and controls a unified information system. While many competitors are struggling with multiple platforms and outsourcing integration, First Health manages all customer data and processes in-house on one system. The company believes that this is the only way to truly control and enhance the customer experience.

We think First Health has a very attractive business model and we would buy shares at a 30% discount to our fair value estimate.

Data as of 12-31-02

Fiserv FISV

| | Rating ★★★ | Risk Med. | Moat Size Wide | Fair Value $35.00 | Last Close $33.95 | Yield % 0.0 |

Company Profile

Fiserv provides data-processing and information management services to financial institutions, serving a client base of more than 5,000 banks, credit unions, mortgage firms, savings institutions, and financial intermediaries. Its account and transaction services range from ATM, card management, and facilities management to performance analysis, self-directed retirement plan processing, and software development.

Management

Co-founder Leslie Muma has been with Fiserv since it formed in 1984 from the merger of two data-processing firms, one of which he ran. Muma was COO until 1999, when he became CEO.

Strategy

Fiserv wants to provide the financial services industry with one-stop shopping for information services. The company has made more than 100 acquisitions since its formation, providing it with new services to sell to its existing customers and new customers to sell its existing services to. We expect acquisitions to continue.

255 Fiserv Drive
Brookfield, WI 53045
www.fiserv.com

Morningstar Grades

Growth [A]

	1998	1999	2000	2001
Revenue %	26.6	14.1	17.5	14.3
Earnings/Share %	19.1	21.1	28.4	16.8
Book Value/Share %	9.0	23.6	14.8	27.3
Dividends/Share %	NMF	NMF	NMF	NMF

Fiserv targets 8%-10% annual revenue growth, before the effect of acquisitions. Including acquisitions, management's goal is 18%-20% annual earnings growth, helped along by profitability improvements.

Profitability [B+]

	1999	2000	2001	TTM
Return on Assets %	2.6	3.2	3.9	4.4
Oper Cash Flow $Mil	178	584	442	446
- Cap Spending $Mil	70	73	68	97
= Free Cash Flow $Mil	108	511	374	349

By getting bigger, Fiserv has reaped the economies of scale inherent in data processing. By driving revenue growth over its fixed cost base, Fiserv has increased operating margins more than 50% over the past eight years.

Financial Health [A]

	1999	2000	2001	09-02
Long-term Debt $Mil	473	335	343	261
Total Equity $Mil	1,091	1,252	1,605	1,769
Debt/Equity Ratio	0.4	0.3	0.2	0.1

Fiserv has more debt than many of its data-processing peers, a result of its acquisition strategy. But when compared with the firm's annual cash flow, the level is not troublesome.

| Industry Data Processing | Investment Style Mid Growth | Stock Type Classic Growth | Sector Business Services |

Competition

	Market Cap $Mil	Debt/ Equity	12 Mo Trailing Sales $Mil	Price/Cash Flow	Return On Assets%	Total Return% 1 Yr	3 Yr
Fiserv	6,508	0.1	2,180	14.6	4.4	-19.8	12.8
First Data	26,633	0.8	7,118	16.5	4.6	-9.5	14.4
Marshall & Ilsley	5,750	—	2,624	—	—	—	—

Price Volatility

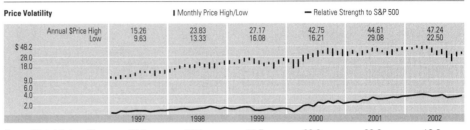

Annual $Price High/Low	15.26 9.63	23.83 13.33	27.17 16.08	42.75 16.21	44.61 29.08	47.24 22.50
	1997	1998	1999	2000	2001	2002
Annual Total Return %	33.7	57.1	11.7	23.8	33.8	-19.8

Fiscal Year-End: December	1997	1998	1999	2000	2001	TTM
Revenue $Mil	974	1,234	1,408	1,654	1,890	2,180
Net Income $Mil	91	114	138	177	208	251
Earnings Per Share $	0.50	0.60	0.73	0.93	1.09	1.29
Shares Outstanding Mil	175	184	185	184	188	192
Return on Equity %	11.8	12.9	12.6	14.1	13.0	14.2
Net Margin %	9.3	9.3	9.8	10.7	11.0	11.5
Asset Turnover	0.3	0.3	0.3	0.3	0.4	0.4
Financial Leverage	4.7	4.5	4.9	4.5	3.3	3.2

Valuation Ratios

	Stock	Rel to Industry	Rel to S&P 500
Price/Earnings	26.3	1.1	1.1
Price/Book	3.7	0.7	1.2
Price/Sales	3.0	0.9	1.5
Price/Cash Flow	14.6	0.9	1.1

Major Fund Holders

	% of Fund Assets
FMI AAM Palm Beach Total Return	7.14
Papp Focus	4.43
Alliance Technology A	3.80
Lindner Large-Cap Growth Inv	3.58

Morningstar's Take By Dan Schick, 12-18-2002 Stock Price as of Analysis: $32.16

Fiserv is a leading data processor for financial institutions. Given the firm's strong finances, cash flows, and returns on capital, we'd buy the stock at a 30% discount to our fair value estimate.

Fiserv should get stronger and make more money as its industry grows. Banks are spending more on technology as they try to cut operating costs and as their customers demand more services. These pressures are leading banks to outsource functions like account, check, and loan processing. A large number of banks still perform these functions in-house, providing Fiserv with many potential new contracts. Fiserv's broad portfolio of services and current customers also helps the company in the sales process. Calling on an existing customer to sell it another service is easier than prospecting for new customers. Also, as the banking, securities, and insurance markets blur together, banks will require additional processing services, which Fiserv is positioning itself to profit from.

Although profits are nice, cash is the lifeblood of any business. Ongoing capital expenditures are not high in the data-processing business, and Fiserv has abundant free cash flow. Capital spending has been running at less than 4% of revenue, and we believe this percentage should continue its long-term

downward trend as the firm gains more economies of scale and data-processing costs fall. Without big capital needs, the firm has been putting its free cash to work to broaden the range of services it offers. Since being founded in 1984, Fiserv has completed more than 100 acquisitions. The firm's ultimate goal is to offer a complete set of data-processing services to the entire financial services industry. CEO Leslie Muma maintains that the acquisition pipeline remains robust, and we expect more purchases. In fact, Fiserv just became a top five electronic fund transfer processor by taking over a business unit from EDS.

Acquisitions also help the firm gain scale in its core operations. With new customer relationships as well as new services sold to old customers, Fiserv drives more revenue through its processing centers. Leveraging the largely fixed costs of data processing, Fiserv has increased its operating margin (excluding reimbursable revenue items) by more than 6 percentage points since 1995, from 12.5% to 19%.

These favorable financial characteristics have led to stable returns on invested capital in the 12%-14% range, well above the cost of capital. Because of the economies of scale required to compete in the processing business, we don't think new entrants will diminish Fiserv's returns.

Morningstar® Stocks 500

FleetBoston Financial FBF

Rating	Risk	Moat Size	Fair Value	Last Close	Yield %
★★★★	Med.	Narrow	$35.00	$24.30	5.8

Company Profile

FleetBoston is the seventh-largest bank in the United States, based on asset size. The firm provides deposit, ATM, and computer banking services, primarily in the Northeast. Business loans account for more than half of the firm's loan portfolio. However, Fleet also originates real-estate, business, and consumer loans. The company's nonbank subsidiaries provide brokerage, municipal securities underwriting, and student loan processing services

Management

Charles Gifford, former head of BankBoston, recently took the helm as CEO. He succeeds Terrence Murray, who had been a driving force for growth. Gifford's success will be defined by how well he refocuses the firm on its profitable core franchise.

Strategy

FleetBoston plans to shed operations to focus on its core business: regional banking. The firm already is a powerhouse with a large presence in New England. To build its focus on consumer and small- and midsize-business banking, the firm sold its student loan operation and shut down its investment bank. It also plans to scale back venture-capital and corporate lending.

100 Federal Street
Boston, MA 02110-2010
www.fleet.com

Morningstar Grades

Growth [D-]	1998	1999	2000	2001
Revenue %	12.0	71.6	13.5	-26.0
Earnings/Share %	6.6	-10.7	63.0	-76.4
Book Value/Share %	8.3	9.3	5.9	-6.9
Dividends/Share %	6.9	10.4	10.8	8.9

Fleet's net revenue dropped 18% last year, and we forecast another 6% fall in 2002. After that, we assume revenue growth in the low double digits as the firm gets back to its historical asset turnover performance in the 6.5%-7.5% range.

Profitability [C]	1999	2000	2001	TTM
Return on Assets %	1.1	1.8	0.4	0.2
Oper Cash Flow $Mil	6,212	2,255	2,416	—
- Cap Spending $Mil	889	634	675	—
= Free Cash Flow $Mil	—	—	—	—

Fleet's return on equity--generally in line with industry averages--collapsed last year because of the firm's many problems. We believe that this represents a bottom and that ROE will steadily improve as Fleet focuses on steadier banking businesses.

Financial Health [A]	1999	2000	2001	09-02
Long-term Debt $Mil	—	—	—	—
Total Equity $Mil	18,074	18,795	17,337	16,595
Debt/Equity Ratio	—	—	—	—

Because of rising bad debt and investment banking losses, the ratio of earnings coverage to loan loss provisions dropped to 1.7 from 5.8 the prior year. However, the firm still expanded its equity base, boosting its ability to weather losses.

Industry	Investment Style	Stock Type	Sector
Super Regional Banks	Large Value	High Yield	$ Financial Services

Competition

	Market Cap $Mil	Debt/ Equity	12 Mo Trailing Sales $Mil	Price/Cash Flow	Return On Assets%	Total Return% 1 Yr	3 Yr
FleetBoston Financial	25,459	—	16,036	—	0.2	-30.2	-4.6
Citigroup	177,948	—	106,096	—	1.6	-24.2	1.1
Wachovia	50,032	—	24,107	—	1.0	19.5	9.8

Price Volatility

| Monthly Price High/Low   — Relative Strength to S&P 500

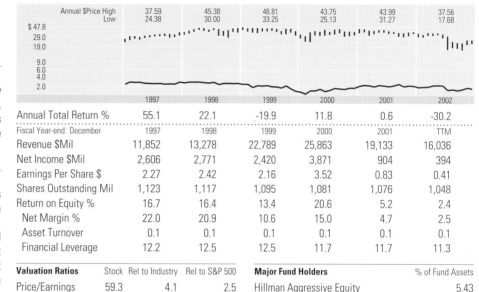

Annual $Price High Low	37.59 24.38	45.38 30.00	46.81 33.25	43.75 25.13	43.99 31.27	37.56 17.68
	1997	1998	1999	2000	2001	2002

Annual Total Return %	55.1	22.1	-19.9	11.8	0.6	-30.2
Fiscal Year-end: December	1997	1998	1999	2000	2001	TTM
Revenue $Mil	11,852	13,278	22,789	25,863	19,133	16,036
Net Income $Mil	2,606	2,771	2,420	3,871	904	394
Earnings Per Share $	2.27	2.42	2.16	3.52	0.83	0.41
Shares Outstanding Mil	1,123	1,117	1,095	1,081	1,076	1,048
Return on Equity %	16.7	16.4	13.4	20.6	5.2	2.4
Net Margin %	22.0	20.9	10.6	15.0	4.7	2.5
Asset Turnover	0.1	0.1	0.1	0.1	0.1	0.1
Financial Leverage	12.2	12.5	12.5	11.7	11.7	11.3

Valuation Ratios	Stock	Rel to Industry	Rel to S&P 500
Price/Earnings	59.3	4.1	2.5
Price/Book	1.5	0.7	0.5
Price/Sales	1.6	0.7	0.8
Price/Cash Flow	—	—	—

Major Fund Holders	% of Fund Assets
Hillman Aggressive Equity	5.43
IDEX Transamerica Value Balanced B	4.67
IDEX Transamerica Value Balanced A	4.67
Fidelity Select Banking	4.10

Morningstar's Take By Craig Woker, 10-08-2002 Stock Price as of Analysis: $18.73

FleetBoston isn't the greatest bank in the world, but it deserves a lot more respect from the stock market than it has been receiving.

Fleet is the dominant bank in New England, one of the country's most demographically attractive regions. Many of the states where Fleet holds a leading market share are also among the wealthiest on a per-capita income basis. Fleet hasn't screwed up this natural advantage. Its personal financial services division--which includes the retail bank--has held its own in a difficult economic environment, generating returns on equity in the midteens.

Outside this core strength, however, Fleet has behaved more like a childhood piano prodigy handed a tuba. The natural skill might be there to learn a new talent, but no matter what, it's going to be ugly for a while. For instance, Fleet's Latin American business has been an aggravation, with Argentina spurring Fleet to take charges in two of the past three quarters. The firm also ran its Robertson Stephens investment bank into the ground, writing off what just two years ago was one of the 10 largest investment banks in the world. Plus, the venture-capital portfolio has been a drag on earnings.

The biggest near-term risk, in our view, is the potential for further problems in Latin America. The leading candidate in Brazil's presidential race has in the past espoused a moratorium on the country's foreign debt, though he has backed off such drastic economic policies more recently. Fleet prudently restructured the government security portion of this portfolio to reduce risk, but a default would still hurt.

For investors who can tolerate this uncertainty, the stock is ridiculously cheap. Fleet is trading just above its book value of $16 per share. Because banks' balance sheets consist mostly of financial assets with varying degrees of liquidity, this means the market is pricing in almost no future growth or fee income from capital markets businesses. We assume Fleet turns itself around over the next two or three years, and come up with a fair value estimate of $35.

Granted, it will take time for Fleet to regain the market confidence that will lead to a much higher stock price. In the meantime, investors can pacify themselves with a 7.5% dividend yield. We view this payout as safe as long as Brazil doesn't default. Fleet's solid core capital levels plus its on-balance-sheet reserves--equal to 3% of loans outstanding--should be enough to weather almost any other problem.

We remain believers in Fleet's turnaround plan and this stock.

Flextronics International FLEX

	Rating	Risk	Moat Size	Fair Value	Last Close	Yield %
	★★★	High	None	$10.00	$8.19	0.0

Industry	Investment Style	Stock Type	Sector
Contract Manufacturers	▦ Mid Value	◈ Spec. Growth	▢ Hardware

Company Profile

Flextronics International provides electronic manufacturing services including the fabrication and assembly of plastic and metal enclosures, printed circuit boards, backplanes, and complete products and systems. The firm has established fully integrated, high volume industrial parks in low-cost regions (e.g. China, Hungary and Mexico) near customers' locations. In addition, Flextronics has set up numerous product introduction centers to provide engineering expertise. Customers include Ericsson, Cisco, Motorola, and Microsoft. The company acquired Dii Group in April 2000.

Management

Michael Marks has been CEO since 1994, and most other executives have been with the company since then (or come from acquired companies). Managers and directors have borrowed $19 million from the firm and own only 4% of equity.

Strategy

Flextronics provides a full range of electronics manufacturing services to leading global electronics original equipment manufacturers. It operates a number of large industrial parks in low-cost locations near big consumer markets. Flextronics hopes the advantages of these sites--cost savings and convenience--will sustain its leadership position in the EMS industry.

36 Robinson Road, #18-01   www.flextronics.com
Singapore, 06887

Competition

Competition	Market Cap $Mil	Debt/ Equity	12 Mo Trailing Sales $Mil	Price/Cash Flow	Return On Assets%	Total Return% 1 Yr	3 Yr
Flextronics International	4,239	0.2	13,217	5.1	-0.1	-65.9	-26.4
Jabil Circuit	3,542	0.2	3,545	6.4	1.4	-21.1	-17.8
Celestica	3,239	0.0	10,004	2.5	-0.6	-65.1	-33.1

Price Volatility

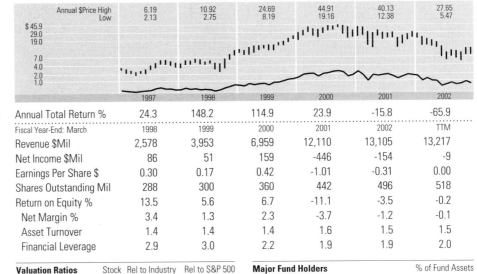

Annual $Price High	6.19	10.92	24.69	44.91	40.13	27.65
Low	2.13	2.75	8.19	19.16	12.38	5.47

	1997	1998	1999	2000	2001	2002
Annual Total Return %	24.3	148.2	114.9	23.9	-15.8	-65.9

Fiscal Year-End: March	1998	1999	2000	2001	2002	TTM
Revenue $Mil	2,578	3,953	6,959	12,110	13,105	13,217
Net Income $Mil	86	51	159	-446	-154	-9
Earnings Per Share $	0.30	0.17	0.42	-1.01	-0.31	0.00
Shares Outstanding Mil	288	300	360	442	496	518
Return on Equity %	13.5	5.6	6.7	-11.1	-3.5	-0.2
Net Margin %	3.4	1.3	2.3	-3.7	-1.2	-0.1
Asset Turnover	1.4	1.4	1.4	1.6	1.5	1.5
Financial Leverage	2.9	3.0	2.2	1.9	1.9	2.0

Valuation Ratios	Stock	Rel to Industry	Rel to S&P 500
Price/Earnings	NMF	—	—
Price/Book	0.9	1.0	0.3
Price/Sales	0.3	1.0	0.2
Price/Cash Flow	5.1	1.0	0.4

Major Fund Holders	% of Fund Assets
Pioneer Science and Technology B	6.53
Red Oak Technology Select	6.44
Conseco Science & Technology Y	5.52
Neuberger Berman Focus Inv	4.79

Morningstar Grades

Growth [A]	1999	2000	2001	2002
Revenue %	53.3	76.1	74.0	8.2
Earnings/Share %	-43.3	147.1	NMF	NMF
Book Value/Share %	37.1	106.3	45.0	-1.6
Dividends/Share %	NMF	NMF	NMF	NMF

Flextronics is riding the outsourcing wave in the electronics industry. Despite no growth in 2002, sales have improved at a compound annual rate of 38% in the past five years. We expect sales growth to slow to 16%-17% over the next five years.

Profitability [C+]	2000	2001	2002	TTM
Return on Assets %	3.1	-5.9	-1.8	-0.1
Oper Cash Flow $Mil	-34	-470	859	835
- Cap Spending $Mil	462	711	330	208
= Free Cash Flow $Mil	-497	-1,181	529	627

Given that the risk of obsolete inventory is borne by the OEMs, Flextronics' five-year average gross margin of 7% doesn't look so bad. We expect returns on capital to be 8%-10%.

Financial Health [D]	2000	2001	2002	09-02
Long-term Debt $Mil	645	917	863	865
Total Equity $Mil	2,377	4,030	4,455	4,485
Debt/Equity Ratio	0.3	0.2	0.2	0.2

In addition to the $850 million in debt on the books, Flextronics has $630 million in off-balance-sheet commitments. It has the cash to keep operating, but making a major acquisition would probably require additional capital.

Morningstar's Take By Fritz Kaegi, 12-19-2002 Stock Price as of Analysis: $8.31

The electronics industry continues to move to outsourced production. This trend should benefit Flextronics, the largest electronics manufacturing services (EMS) firm.

Flextronics' industry-leading size is a competitive advantage, as is the scope of its product offerings. Also, the company tries to lock in customers by building factories in industrial parks that will attract lots of specialist providers and logistics firms, which augment Flextronics' core EMS function. Although price competition among contract manufacturers can be tough, the cost and convenience advantages of these parks tend to keep customers locked in once they're used to using them. Besides, it can be expensive, complicated, time-consuming, and risky for an original equipment manufacturer (OEM) to switch providers.

Most managers would recoil at Flextronics' 7% gross margins. Part of the reason for this low number is that OEMs bear the lion's share of inventory risk. Thus OEMs, and not their EMS suppliers, got stuck with the inventory bill when the electronics industry began its nosedive in 2001: Cisco alone took $2.9 billion in inventory charges in 2001, while the two largest EMS firms took just $110 million in inventory charges (on $52 billion of costs of goods sold). EMS

firms are selling manufacturing and logistical expertise. Flextronics bears the burden of paying for the production process, capacity, the workforce, and occasionally some inventory risk when it expects shortages of components.

The key threat to Flextronics is competition. Its labor cost advantages are being threatened by smaller Asia-based competitors, led by Hon Hai (based in Taiwan), some of whom are longtime suppliers to the electronics industry. Also, large rivals are also building new capacity in China. Producers like Jabil Circuit and Benchmark may create a cost edge in their specific niches. With wider service offerings, like logistics, Flextronics is starting to compete with firms like package-delivery specialist UPS. Flextronics should mostly hold its own in this contest, but improving on the roughly 7% gross margin it received during the previous five years will be out of the question, in our opinion.

MORNINGSTAR® Stocks 500

Ford Motor F

	Rating	Risk	Moat Size	Fair Value	Last Close	Yield %
	★★★	High	None	$14.00	$9.30	4.3

Company Profile

Ford Motor is the world's second-largest manufacturer of passenger vehicles. The company manufactures cars and light trucks under the Ford, Lincoln, and Mercury marquees. It also owns several luxury brands, including Range Rover, Jaguar, and Volvo, collectively known as the Premier Automotive Group. Through its Ford Credit subsidiary, the company offers vehicle financing, rental services through its Hertz unit, and other financial services. Ford spun off its consumer finance business (Associates) in 1998 and auto part operations (Visteon) in 2000.

Management

William Clay Ford Jr. became CEO last year. Though he has some midlevel management experience, his main qualification is the Ford family's 40% voting stake. He'll be leaning heavily on operations chief Nick Scheele, who helped turn Jaguar around.

Strategy

After the distraction of former CEO Jac Nasser's vision of Ford as a consumer product company, Henry Ford's great-grandson is leading a back-to-basics movement and spending heavily on new products. The company is attacking excess capacity with plans to close five plants in the next few years. It will sell or close noncore assets, like Kwik-Fit and nonvehicle lending units.

One American Road   www.ford.com
Dearborn, MI 48126

Morningstar Grades

Growth [C]	1998	1999	2000	2001
Revenue %	-6.1	12.1	5.8	-4.5
Earnings/Share %	216.0	-67.0	-60.8	NMF
Book Value/Share %	-24.2	18.2	-44.6	-65.3
Dividends/Share %	4.6	9.3	4.9	-16.3

Booming U.S. vehicle sales--particularly in Ford's sweet spot, light trucks--helped the company outpace General Motors GM by a wide margin in the 1990s. Inventory rebuilding has boosted results thus far in 2002, but the outlook for 2003 is grim.

Profitability [C-]	1999	2000	2001	TTM
Return on Assets %	2.7	1.2	-2.0	-2.1
Oper Cash Flow $Bil	27.5	34.2	22.8	19.1
- Cap Spending $Bil	7.7	8.3	7.0	7.5
= Free Cash Flow $Bil	19.9	25.9	15.8	11.6

Ford is challenged by heavy incentive spending (like 0% financing) and high production costs. Management sees a modest profit this year, but falling production next year could send Ford back into the red.

Financial Health [C+]	1999	2000	2001	09-02
Long-term Debt $Bil	152.2	167.9	170.7	167.6
Total Equity $Bil	27.6	18.6	7.8	10.0
Debt/Equity Ratio	5.5	9.0	21.9	16.8

The balance sheet is still among the industry's weakest, but January's issuance of convertible preferred cut Ford's leverage ratio from nearly 33 at year-end to 18.3 in September.

Industry	Investment Style	Stock Type	Sector
Auto Makers	Large Value	High Yield	Consumer Goods

Competition

	Market Cap $Mil	Debt/ Equity	12 Mo Trailing Sales $Mil	Price/Cash Flow	Return On Assets%	Total Return% 1 Yr	3 Yr
Ford Motor	17,066	16.8	163,518	0.9	-2.1	-38.9	-30.4
Toyota Motor ADR	97,652	—	118,527	—	—	—	—
Honda Motor ADR	35,196	—	58,319	—	—	—	—

Price Volatility

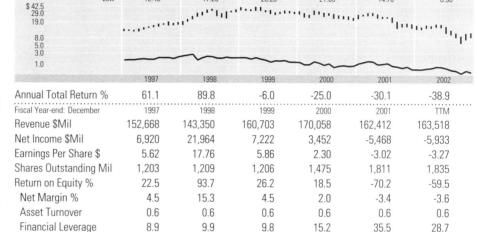

		1997	1998	1999	2000	2001	2002
Annual $Price High		20.36	37.57	41.51	35.00	31.42	18.23
Low		12.45	17.26	28.28	21.69	14.70	6.90

Annual Total Return %	61.1	89.8	-6.0	-25.0	-30.1	-38.9

Fiscal Year-end: December	1997	1998	1999	2000	2001	TTM
Revenue $Mil	152,668	143,350	160,703	170,058	162,412	163,518
Net Income $Mil	6,920	21,964	7,222	3,452	-5,468	-5,933
Earnings Per Share $	5.62	17.76	5.86	2.30	-3.02	-3.27
Shares Outstanding Mil	1,203	1,209	1,206	1,475	1,811	1,835
Return on Equity %	22.5	93.7	26.2	18.5	-70.2	-59.5
Net Margin %	4.5	15.3	4.5	2.0	-3.4	-3.6
Asset Turnover	0.6	0.6	0.6	0.6	0.6	0.6
Financial Leverage	8.9	9.9	9.8	15.2	35.5	28.7

Valuation Ratios	Stock	Rel to Industry	Rel to S&P 500
Price/Earnings	NMF	—	—
Price/Book	1.7	1.0	0.5
Price/Sales	0.1	0.2	0.1
Price/Cash Flow	0.9	0.1	0.1

Major Fund Holders	% of Fund Assets
Hillman Aggressive Equity	4.32
Seligman Large Cap Value A	3.28
Chicago Asset Management Value	2.37
Ameristock	1.98

Morningstar's Take By Josh Peters, 10-16-2002 Stock Price as of Analysis: $8.26

Ford's challenges have investors scared--and with good reason. At present we would consider the shares only at a 60% discount to our fair value estimate.

It didn't take long for mighty Ford to fall apart. With its leading lineup of large trucks and SUVs, Ford dominated the most profitable segments of the U.S. auto market for most of the 1990s. But the models got old, costs crept up, quality slipped (with some high-profile gaffes), and senior management became interested in anything but building and selling cars.

Now in the hands of Bill Ford Jr., the company has undertaken a revitalization plan aimed at restoring $7 billion in pretax profits by middecade. But in our view, the measures announced to date are unlikely to meet this goal. It seems to us that Ford is still blaming its suppliers for its troubles and demanding arbitrary price reductions. But reducing purchasing costs won't be enough--Ford needs to scale down its manufacturing costs to get a real turnaround under way. That won't be easy, either, given rising employee benefit costs and the UAW's staunch opposition to plant shutdowns.

Cost-cutting isn't the only challenge. Save for the Premier brands like Jaguar and Volvo, compelling new vehicles are notably absent from today's product lineup. As Ford attempts to keep production as high as possible, we expect its discounting will only escalate as competitors hit the market with more appealing cars and trucks.

And though we think it unlikely that U.S. industry auto sales are headed for a crash, a sudden downturn could turn today's modest losses into a balance sheet disaster. A deeper downturn might necessitate cuts in Ford's product-development budget, the setbacks from which could linger for years, or even another cut in the shares' still-attractive dividend.

A more serious squeeze in the auto operations would also threaten Ford's financial services operation, which has long been the firm's most stable and fastest-growing source of income. In 2000, Ford Credit, Hertz, and other units contributed more than a third of pretax profit, but those earnings are under pressure from poor credit risk management and rising borrowing costs. Additional credit-rating downgrades could squash Ford Credit's net interest margins.

Ford has always been a roller coaster, creating great buying opportunities at industry bottoms. But the unusual nature of this downturn demands extra caution, in our view. Unless the shares broached $6, we wouldn't feel the potential upside was worth the uphill fight.

Forest Laboratories FRX

	Rating	Risk	Moat Size	Fair Value	Last Close	Yield %
	★	Med.	Narrow	$54.00	$98.22	0.0

Company Profile

Forest Laboratories develops and manufactures brand-name, generic, and over-the-counter drugs. Its name-brand products include Celexa for depression; Aerobid for asthma; and Tiazac for hypertension and angina. Its generic products include drugs that treat hypertension and arthritis. The company markets its generic drug products through its Inwood Laboratories subsidiary. The Pharmax unit sells products outside the United States, predominantly in Ireland and the United Kingdom. U.S. sales account for 95% of revenue.

Management

Chairman and CEO Howard Solomon tells it like it is. He led the company to profitability by focusing on highly specialized niche products. He's also credited with building an extremely effective management team as well as an outstanding salesforce.

Strategy

Although Forest Labs has its roots as a generic drugmaker, the company is almost completely about branded products now. Instead of developing its own products, Forest typically licenses product rights from other firms. Lately, Forest has been concentrating on diversifying its product lineup beyond Celexa, which provides nearly two thirds of revenue.

909 Third Avenue
New York, NY 10022-4731
www.forestlaboratories.com

Morningstar Grades

Growth [A]	1999	2000	2001	2002
Revenue %	31.4	44.1	34.0	32.9
Earnings/Share %	104.5	42.2	84.4	54.2
Book Value/Share %	17.8	15.9	33.4	30.5
Dividends/Share %	NMF	NMF	NMF	NMF

Forest Labs' sales growth has been phenomenal, averaging 21.3% over the past five years, thanks to Celexa. Celexa and its follow-up drug, Lexapro, are expected to power revenue growth over the next few years as well.

Profitability [A+]	2000	2001	2002	TTM
Return on Assets %	10.0	14.9	17.3	19.2
Oper Cash Flow $Mil	196	180	426	489
- Cap Spending $Mil	35	31	36	55
= Free Cash Flow $Mil	161	149	390	434

Gross, operating, and net margins reached all-time highs in the third quarter; operating margins were 34.6%. However, we expect higher marketing costs over the next few years to slow margin improvement.

Financial Health [A+]	2000	2001	2002	09-02
Long-term Debt $Mil	0	0	0	0
Total Equity $Mil	885	1,222	1,625	1,926
Debt/Equity Ratio	0.0	0.0	0.0	0.0

Forest has kept debt off the balance sheet for more than five years, thanks to the cash flow provided from its blockbuster depression med, Celexa. With plenty of cash and securities and no debt, the firm has an outstanding balance sheet.

Industry	Investment Style	Stock Type	Sector
Drugs	▦ Large Growth	↑ Aggr. Growth	◉ Healthcare

Competition

	Market Cap $Mil	Debt/ Equity	12 Mo Trailing Sales $Mil	Price/Cash Flow	Return On Assets%	Total Return% 1 Yr	3 Yr
Forest Laboratories	17,702	0.0	1,882	36.2	19.2	19.9	49.7
Pfizer	188,377	0.2	34,407	21.1	18.3	-22.2	1.0
Eli Lilly & Company	71,334	0.5	10,951	29.0	13.5	-17.6	1.8

Price Volatility

▌ Monthly Price High/Low — Relative Strength to S&P 500

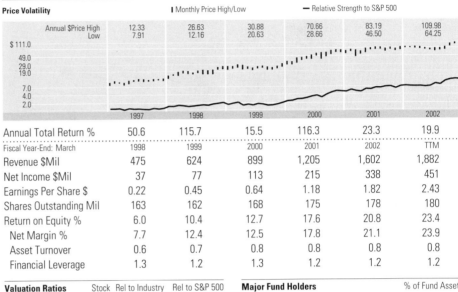

Annual $Price High Low	12.33 7.91	26.63 12.16	30.88 20.63	70.66 28.66	83.19 46.50	109.98 64.25
	1997	1998	1999	2000	2001	2002

Annual Total Return %	50.6	115.7	15.5	116.3	23.3	19.9

Fiscal Year-End: March	1998	1999	2000	2001	2002	TTM
Revenue $Mil	475	624	899	1,205	1,602	1,882
Net Income $Mil	37	77	113	215	338	451
Earnings Per Share $	0.22	0.45	0.64	1.18	1.82	2.43
Shares Outstanding Mil	163	162	168	175	178	180
Return on Equity %	6.0	10.4	12.7	17.6	20.8	23.4
Net Margin %	7.7	12.4	12.5	17.8	21.1	23.9
Asset Turnover	0.6	0.7	0.8	0.8	0.8	0.8
Financial Leverage	1.3	1.2	1.3	1.2	1.2	1.2

Valuation Ratios	Stock	Rel to Industry	Rel to S&P 500
Price/Earnings	40.4	1.7	1.7
Price/Book	9.2	1.3	2.9
Price/Sales	9.4	2.4	4.7
Price/Cash Flow	36.2	1.7	2.7

Major Fund Holders	% of Fund Assets
Smith Barney Aggressive Growth A	8.06
Strong Advisor Focus A	7.24
Strong Growth 20 Inv	7.14
Waddell & Reed Adv Tax Managed Eq A	6.42

Morningstar's Take By Todd N. Lebor, 11-21-2002 Stock Price as of Analysis: $104.65

We think investors in Forest Labs need a higher margin of safety than we'd normally require for a healthy pharmaceutical company, because two thirds of the firm's revenue comes from one drug.

Depression drug Celexa has put Forest Labs on the map, taking the company from $300 million in total revenue in 1993 to $1.5 billion in annual revenue from that drug alone. Forest's 21.3% compound annual revenue growth over the past five years has rewarded investors and opened doors for the once-insignificant company. The stock's five-year return has trounced that of the S&P 500. But the easy part is over, in our opinion.

With Celexa expected to lose patent protection in early 2004--after a six-month pediatric exclusivity period--Forest's ascent is nearing its end, although we don't expect the firm to lie down and die. Forest has an exciting late-stage pipeline as well as Lexapro, an improved version of Celexa. However, the 30%-50% top-line growth we've seen over the past few years is over.

Historically, Forest has relied on others--mostly small European drug companies like Lundbeck, which discovered Celexa--to do the heavy lifting in research and development. We believe Forest is going to need more homegrown research on top of a successful licensing program to maintain a healthy list of profitable drugs. As the revenue base grows, maintaining current profitability will become harder and harder. Celexa was a home run, but we think a repeat is unlikely, given the lull in new drugs from the global pharmaceutical pipeline and competitive threats from other major drug companies looking for hidden gems in the same places.

Forest has done an excellent job of licensing promising candidates, though. The company plans to bring a popular European Alzheimer's drug to the United States and is attempting to follow up Tiazac's success in the cardiovascular arena with Benicar and lercanidipine. There's also acamprosate, a treatment for alcohol dependency that has been marketed in Europe for more than a decade.

We think Forest will succeed in transforming itself from a company dependent on one drug into a broad-based company with multiple products. It has shown an ability to discover profitable drugs that others ignored, and then market them effectively. But until Forest builds a more diverse revenue base, we would demand a significant discount to our fair value estimate before investing.

M RNINGSTAR® Stocks 500

Franklin Resources BEN

	Rating	Risk	Moat Size	Fair Value	Last Close	Yield %
	★★★	Med.	Narrow	$37.00	$34.08	0.8

Company Profile

Asset manager Franklin Resources serves retail (64%), institutional (32%), and high-net-worth (4%) clients with mutual fund and separate account products. Franklin sells its retail products exclusively through advisor channels but has a direct salesforce for institutional products. Franklin Templeton mutual funds, which account for 70% of the company's managed assets, specialize in fixed-income, hybrid, and value-oriented equity funds. Franklin's acquisition of Fiduciary Trust significantly augments its institutional and high-net-worth businesses.

Management

Franklin has been run by the Johnson family for more than 50 years. The family still owns more than 30% of the stock and holds four of nine board positions. Charles B. Johnson is chairman and CEO.

Strategy

Franklin aims its offerings at affluent and high-net-worth investors who buy investment products through brokers and financial advisors. Large institutional accounts make up a third of the firm's business. Franklin has a significant presence in the international market with global Templeton funds and a large body of international clients.

One Franklin Parkway   www.frk.com
San Mateo, CA 94403

Morningstar Grades

Growth [C]	1999	2000	2001	2002
Revenue %	-12.2	3.4	0.6	7.0
Earnings/Share %	-14.6	34.9	-16.2	-13.6
Book Value/Share %	16.6	14.3	30.3	3.8
Dividends/Share %	10.0	9.1	-18.8	41.0

Two of Franklin's core strengths--value investing and international funds--have been out of favor in recent years. With these categories gaining new popularity, revenue growth outpaced most rivals in the September-ending fiscal year, at 7%.

Profitability [A]	2000	2001	2002	TTM
Return on Assets %	13.9	7.7	6.7	6.7
Oper Cash Flow $Mil	702	553	737	—
- Cap Spending $Mil	108	107	53	—
= Free Cash Flow $Mil	—	—	—	—

Franklin is still struggling with growing expenses, and the EBITDA (earnings before interest, taxes, depreciation, and amortization) margin dropped significantly in fiscal 2002. Its returns on assets and equity lag those of asset manager peers.

Financial Health [A+]	2000	2001	2002	09-02
Long-term Debt $Mil	—	—	—	—
Total Equity $Mil	2,965	3,978	4,267	4,267
Debt/Equity Ratio	—	—	—	—

Franklin has relatively low financial leverage and the business generates healthy cash flows that the company has been using to buy back shares following the Fiduciary Trust acquisition.

Industry	Investment Style	Stock Type	Sector
Money Management	▦ Large Core	➜ Slow Growth	$ Financial Services

Competition	Market Cap $Mil	Debt/ Equity	12 Mo Trailing Sales $Mil	Price/Cash Flow	Return On Assets%	Total Return% 1 Yr	3 Yr
Franklin Resources	8,789	—	2,519	—	6.7	-2.6	3.8
Marsh & McLennan Companie	24,818	—	10,164	—	9.2	-12.0	2.8
Amvescap PLC ADR	4,858	—	2,478	—	3.9	-55.8	-15.8

Price Volatility

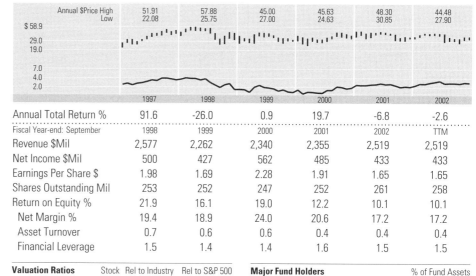

	❙ Monthly Price High/Low	— Relative Strength to S&P 500

Annual $Price High / Low	51.91 / 22.08	57.88 / 25.75	45.00 / 27.00	45.63 / 24.63	48.30 / 30.85	44.48 / 27.90

	1997	1998	1999	2000	2001	2002
Annual Total Return %	91.6	-26.0	0.9	19.7	-6.8	-2.6

Fiscal Year-end: September	1998	1999	2000	2001	2002	TTM
Revenue $Mil	2,577	2,262	2,340	2,355	2,519	2,519
Net Income $Mil	500	427	562	485	433	433
Earnings Per Share $	1.98	1.69	2.28	1.91	1.65	1.65
Shares Outstanding Mil	253	252	247	252	261	258
Return on Equity %	21.9	16.1	19.0	12.2	10.1	10.1
Net Margin %	19.4	18.9	24.0	20.6	17.2	17.2
Asset Turnover	0.7	0.6	0.6	0.4	0.4	0.4
Financial Leverage	1.5	1.4	1.4	1.6	1.5	1.5

Valuation Ratios	Stock	Rel to Industry	Rel to S&P 500
Price/Earnings	20.7	1.2	0.9
Price/Book	2.1	0.8	0.6
Price/Sales	3.5	1.3	1.7
Price/Cash Flow	—	—	—

Major Fund Holders	% of Fund Assets
Chicago Asset Management Value	4.23
T. Rowe Price Financial Services	3.79
Oppenheimer Value A	3.24
Atlanta Capital Large-Cap Growth I	2.92

Morningstar's Take By Rachel Barnard, 11-11-2002 Stock Price as of Analysis: $32.59

Bonds and value funds play well in a bear market and Franklin has benefited. Shares of this solid performer have remained fairly expensive, but we'd jump at the chance to own them at a 40% discount to our fair value estimate.

Franklin has been a wallflower for the past three years, sitting by while popular fund groups like Janus got all the attention. But now the bear market is playing Franklin's song. The declining stock market has put two of Franklin's strongest product lines in the limelight--value stocks and bond funds. Plus, the company sells its funds through the advisor channel, and shell-shocked investors have been clamoring for professional advice ever since the market turned sour. Suddenly, this neglected company is getting noticed.

Investors have certainly been paying attention to Franklin's fund lineup. Assets under management, the key driver of revenue, increased 5% in the first five months of 2002 alone. Though Franklin got hit by the market dips in the third quarter, it faired better than its average peer. Even as equity values sank, new assets poured into its bond funds, helping to stabilize assets under management. As the largest municipal bond fund manager in the world, Franklin benefited from investors' search for funds with positive returns.

Tax-free municipal bonds have fit the bill for many.

Franklin faces a few challenges, though. Persistently poor returns for international equity have caused Templeton, Franklin's large international investment arm, to languish. International returns have been slightly more attractive lately, but Templeton hasn't seen much investor interest and assets under management are up only slightly. The firm is undertaking a major advertising push to drum up business.

The firm needs to focus on cost-cutting since operating expenses have grown almost as quickly as revenue. Management has talked about cutting costs and outsourcing some back-office and support functions to India, where labor is cheaper. But it is also reinstating salaries for employees whose pay was cut last fall. As a result, we probably won't see the necessary improvement in margins very soon.

Fiscal 2002 operating income was up 14% on higher average assets under management, but net income fell as a result of investment write-downs. While this is not good news, it is too small to affect our fair value estimate, which remains $37.

Freddie Mac FRE

	Rating	Risk	Moat Size	Fair Value	Last Close	Yield %
	★★★★	Low	Narrow	$78.00	$59.05	1.5

Industry	Investment Style	Stock Type	Sector
Finance	⊞ Large Core	↑ Aggr. Growth	$ Financial Services

Company Profile

Freddie Mac is a shareholder-owned, U.S. government-sponsored enterprise that provides stability in the secondary market for residential mortgages. Freddie Mac purchases and securitizes conventional, residential mortgages from mortgage-lending institutions. Freddie Mac is one of two major sources of secondary-market funding for conventional mortgages, and has financed one out of every six homes in the United States.

Management

Leland Brendsel is chairman and CEO. President and vice chairman David Glenn is second in command.

Strategy

Freddie has an almost monopolistic dominance of the mortgage financing market, and it's aiming to boost its share further. Freddie is stepping up sales of its underwriting software to brokers; its broker ties also undermine the market influence of banks that compete with it. Elsewhere, it's buying subprime and home-improvement loans, both relatively new markets for Freddie.

8200 Jones Branch Drive   www.freddiemac.com
McLean, VA 22102-3110

Competition	Market Cap $Mil	Debt/ Equity	12 Mo Trailing Sales $Mil	Price/Cash Flow	Return On Assets%	Total Return% 1 Yr	3 Yr
Freddie Mac	40,934	—	8,986	—	0.8	-8.4	12.0
Fannie Mae	72,629	—	52,478	—	653.8	-17.6	5.5
Lehman Brothers Holdings	12,738	—	1,291	—	0.3	-19.7	13.3

Price Volatility

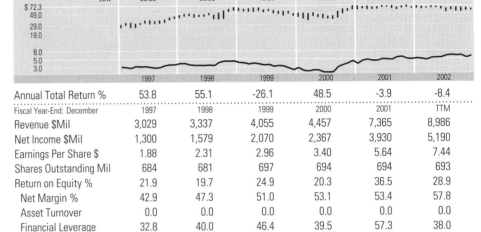

Annual $Price High Low	44.56 26.69	66.38 38.69	65.25 45.00	70.13 36.88	71.25 58.75	69.50 52.60

	1997	1998	1999	2000	2001	2002
Annual Total Return %	53.8	55.1	-26.1	48.5	-3.9	-8.4

Fiscal Year-End: December	1997	1998	1999	2000	2001	TTM
Revenue $Mil	3,029	3,337	4,055	4,457	7,365	8,986
Net Income $Mil	1,300	1,579	2,070	2,367	3,930	5,190
Earnings Per Share $	1.88	2.31	2.96	3.40	5.64	7.44
Shares Outstanding Mil	684	681	697	694	694	693
Return on Equity %	21.9	19.7	24.9	20.3	36.5	28.9
Net Margin %	42.9	47.3	51.0	53.1	53.4	57.8
Asset Turnover	0.0	0.0	0.0	0.0	0.0	0.0
Financial Leverage	32.8	40.0	46.4	39.5	57.3	38.0

Valuation Ratios	Stock	Rel to Industry	Rel to S&P 500
Price/Earnings	7.9	0.7	0.3
Price/Book	2.3	0.7	0.7
Price/Sales	4.6	2.3	2.3
Price/Cash Flow	—	—	—

Major Fund Holders	% of Fund Assets
Matthew 25	10.29
Scudder Dreman Financial Services A	9.81
Oppenheimer Quest Opportunity Value A	9.34
PBHG Clipper Focus PBHG	8.59

Morningstar Grades

Growth [A+]	1998	1999	2000	2001
Revenue %	10.2	21.5	9.9	65.2
Earnings/Share %	22.9	28.1	14.9	65.9
Book Value/Share %	36.9	1.4	40.4	-7.5
Dividends/Share %	20.0	25.0	13.3	17.6

Revenue growth has been impressive. On average, we expect double-digit revenue growth through 2006, though it will certainly slow from its recent pace.

Profitability [D+]	1999	2000	2001	TTM
Return on Assets %	0.5	0.5	0.6	0.8
Oper Cash Flow $Mil	-1,471	14,627	17,774	—
- Cap Spending $Mil	—	—	—	—
= Free Cash Flow $Mil	—	—	—	—

Freddie generates low returns on assets because the secondary mortgage market is extremely capital-intensive, but an inherent cost advantage and high leverage allow the company to generate strong returns on equity.

Financial Health [B]	1999	2000	2001	09-02
Long-term Debt $Mil	—	—	—	—
Total Equity $Mil	8,330	11,642	10,777	17,957
Debt/Equity Ratio	—	—	—	—

Freddie's financial leverage is more than twice the finance industry average, but the company is structured to carry much higher levels of debt than the average bank. Freddie has a three-month cash cushion and top credit ratings.

Morningstar's Take By Richard McCaffery, 09-13-2002 Stock Price as of Analysis: $62.52

Fears about everything from a housing bubble to derivatives exposure and political risk are weighing on Freddie's stock price. We think the shares are worth $78.

Given strong long-term trends in home ownership and Freddie's low cost of funds, the company can virtually manufacture shareholder value. This may upset opponents, or those who believe Freddie's cost advantage represents government interference in the markets, but the stock is still undervalued.

Political risk is part of the terrain for Freddie and Fannie Mae. But given the economic importance of a liquid housing market and the political support for home ownership, we don't think the risk is grave.

On average, we expect Freddie to increase assets 15% annually through 2006, which is conservative given its 29% growth since 1996. The company's balance sheet is huge, but its lean structure and access to inexpensive debt channel profits right to the bottom line. Freddie can easily increase equity fast enough to keep capital levels strong even as the balance sheet expands.

There's nothing inherently wrong with a big balance sheet. The mortgage business is capital-intensive, so it requires a lot of assets to generate profits. Freddie and Fannie generate strong returns on equity despite low returns on assets because they're highly leveraged, the benefit of their status as government-sponsored enterprises. As long as Freddie has the equity capital to support its asset base, and underwrites wisely, the balance sheet can keep growing, just as the number of people who own homes keeps growing.

Freddie expects its market will grow 7%-9% annually through 2010. The duopoly it shares with Fannie means the company should be able to grow faster than this. The National Association of Home Builders expects to see 18 million homes built from 2000 to 2010. This will require billions in mortgage capital, which Freddie provides by issuing debt and buying mortgages.

There are risks besides the political. For example, Freddie is highly leveraged. However, it is structured to carry more debt than the average bank. This makes sense, not only because of its government charter, but because its losses are much lower than those of a typical bank or thrift. Also, Freddie has $83 billion in liquid assets to support its higher debt levels. We think concerns are overblown, and the shares are a good investment.

MORNINGSTAR® Stocks 500

Freemarkets FMKT

	Rating	Risk	Moat Size	Fair Value	Last Close	Yield %
	★★★	High	Narrow	$8.00	$6.44	0.0

Company Profile

Freemarkets creates customized business-to-business online auctions for buyers of industrial parts, raw materials, and commodities. The company has created online auctions for more than 30 clients in more than 70 product categories, including injection-molded plastic parts, commercial machinery, metal fabrications, chemicals, printed circuit boards, corrugated packaging, and coal. Freemarkets' customers include United Technologies, Quaker Oats, Emerson Electric, Honeywell International, and the Commonwealth of Pennsylvania.

Management

Chairman and CEO Glen Meakem started Freemarkets in 1995 based on an idea that was rejected when he pitched it to his former employers at General Electric. Meakem owns about 8.5% of the company.

Strategy

Unlike many business-to-business vendors who want to offer a full spectrum of services and software, Freemarkets' sole focus is on Internet-based B2B auctions. Freemarkets provides all of the technological infrastructure and expertise for running these auctions, giving customers an intriguing alternative to setting up their own B2B infrastructure.

Freemarkets Center   www.freemarkets.com
Pittsburgh, PA 15222

Morningstar Grades

Growth [A]	1998	1999	2000	2001
Revenue %	337.5	167.7	299.1	77.1
Earnings/Share %	NMF	NMF	NMF	NMF
Book Value/Share %	—	—	NMF	-66.2
Dividends/Share %	NMF	NMF	NMF	NMF

The company's once-rapid growth is slowing as the economy founders. Growth from quarter to quarter can be volatile, as Freemarkets' customer base is somewhat concentrated, but we think growth in the low to mid-teens is reasonable.

Profitability [D+]	1999	2000	2001	TTM
Return on Assets %	-9.4	-33.8	ELB	-9.3
Oper Cash Flow $Mil	-16	-40	-15	26
- Cap Spending $Mil	10	40	17	9
= Free Cash Flow $Mil	-26	-80	-32	17

Management has done a great job of cutting expenses, even as revenue grows. Since the company's expenses are largely fixed, earnings can grow more quickly than revenue.

Financial Health [C-]	1999	2000	2001	09-02
Long-term Debt $Mil	3	1	3	2
Total Equity $Mil	219	417	150	154
Debt/Equity Ratio	0.0	0.0	0.0	0.0

Freemarkets has plenty of cash and little debt on its balance sheet, and it generates positive free cash flows. We expect the balance sheet to show continued improvement as the business scales and profitability grows.

Industry	Investment Style	Stock Type	Sector
Business/Online Services	Small Growth	Spec. Growth	Business Services

Competition

	Market Cap $Mil	Debt/ Equity	12 Mo Trailing Sales $Mil	Price/Cash Flow	Return On Assets%	Total Return% 1 Yr	3 Yr
Freemarkets	271	0.0	167	10.4	-9.3	-73.1	-71.5
Ariba	659	—	229	—	—	—	—
Commerce One	80	—	142	—	—	—	—

Price Volatility

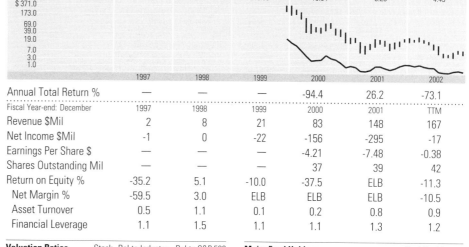

Annual $Price High Low			367.88 218.88	370.00 16.94	27.00 6.25	29.09 4.49

	1997	1998	1999	2000	2001	2002
Annual Total Return %	—	—	—	-94.4	26.2	-73.1

Fiscal Year-end: December	1997	1998	1999	2000	2001	TTM
Revenue $Mil	2	8	21	83	148	167
Net Income $Mil	-1	0	-22	-156	-295	-17
Earnings Per Share $	—	—	—	-4.21	-7.48	-0.38
Shares Outstanding Mil	—	—	—	37	39	42
Return on Equity %	-35.2	5.1	-10.0	-37.5	ELB	-11.3
Net Margin %	-59.5	3.0	ELB	ELB	ELB	-10.5
Asset Turnover	0.5	1.1	0.1	0.2	0.8	0.9
Financial Leverage	1.1	1.5	1.1	1.1	1.3	1.2

Valuation Ratios	Stock	Rel to Industry	Rel to S&P 500
Price/Earnings	NMF	—	—
Price/Book	1.8	0.8	0.5
Price/Sales	1.6	0.6	0.8
Price/Cash Flow	10.4	0.8	0.8

Major Fund Holders	% of Fund Assets
Jacob Internet	4.25
Dreyfus Premier Small Company Gr B	1.28
Managers AMG Essex Aggressive Gr Inv	1.05
WesMark Small Company Growth	1.05

Morningstar's Take By Dan Schick, 12-19-2002 Stock Price as of Analysis: $6.48

Born in the Internet bubble, Freemarkets looks like one of the survivors. However, because of the immaturity of the company's business and our doubt over whether it has a sustainable competitive advantage, we wouldn't purchase the shares unless they traded at a 50% discount to our fair value estimate.

While Freemarkets is typically labeled a tech firm, it is best understood as a services company. Its stability in recent quarters, during which much of the tech sector struggled, can be attributed to two key points in its business model. First, Freemarkets provides all of the technological infrastructure and industry expertise that its customers need to conduct Internet-based auctions for raw materials, components, and finished goods. Freemarkets does not depend on large capital expenditures from its customers.

Second, Freemarkets' customers typically sign contracts for one year or longer. Customers pay Freemarkets a fee based on the total value of goods they expect to purchase through the firm's auctions. If a company exceeds that estimate, Freemarkets gets an additional fee.

While we're enamored with Freemarkets' success so far, some risks are worth noting. Growth in new customers has slowed dramatically. Additionally, as a pure-play procurement auction provider, the firm could eventually face tougher competition from some of the more comprehensive business-to-business (B2B) or supply-chain management vendors. Finally, the company offers software that allows customers to essentially run their own auctions, and this product has been eating into Freemarkets' higher-margin full-service offerings. We cannot say whether this is a long-term trend or merely the result of customers' opting for the lowest-cost solution during tough economic times.

While Freemarkets has done well as other B2B companies have fallen by the wayside, its business model does have a couple of potential disadvantages. Since the company must invest heavily in both personnel and infrastructure, its business model isn't quite as scalable as that of some other vendors. Also, as we noted before, its procurement auction focus could hurt Freemarkets in competing with firms that offer more-comprehensive services.

Though we believe the firm is here to stay, we'd want a sizable discount to our fair value estimate before investing.

Gabelli Asset Management GBL

	Rating	Risk	Moat Size	Fair Value	Last Close	Yield %
	★★★	Med.	Narrow	$36.00	$30.04	0.0

Company Profile

Gabelli Asset Management manages money for institutions, mutual fund investors, and individual high-net-worth clients. The majority of Gabelli's assets under management are invested in equities, both in the United States and abroad. Fixed-income securities account for 10% of assets. Gabelli also has a growing hedge fund business. Two recent issuances of convertible debt are earmarked to fund expansion into Europe and additional hedge fund products.

Management

Star fund manager Mario Gabelli has been chairman, CEO, and chief investment officer of the company and its predecessors since its inception in 1976. He controls the firm through a private company, which owns more than 80% of Gabelli Asset Management stock.

Strategy

Gabelli casts a wide net, vying with other asset managers for the investment dollars of mutual fund investors, wealthy individuals, and institutions. The firm seeks to distinguish itself by investment performance first and foremost, but also seeks the right product mix to attract affluent investors in an increasingly crowded field.

One Corporate Center
Rye, NY 10580-1422

www.gabelli.com

Morningstar Grades

Growth [B-]	1998	1999	2000	2001
Revenue %	31.3	27.6	32.7	-4.1
Earnings/Share %	NMF	NMF	NMF	4.6
Book Value/Share %	—	—	NMF	35.2
Dividends/Share %	NMF	NMF	NMF	NMF

Revenue has grown at a compound annual rate of 18% over the past three years, but 2002 is shaping up to be disappointing. We expect assets under management--the main driver of revenue--to fall 8% for the year. Growth will remain tied to the market.

Profitability [A]	1999	2000	2001	TTM
Return on Assets %	7.6	18.2	12.6	10.0
Oper Cash Flow $Mil	-13	-2	140	—
- Cap Spending $Mil	—	—	—	—
= Free Cash Flow $Mil	—	—	—	—

Expense discipline has resulted in a 47% operating margin and a 19% return on equity, putting the firm near the top of the asset-management heap.

Financial Health [A-]	1999	2000	2001	09-02
Long-term Debt $Mil	—	—	—	—
Total Equity $Mil	148	202	275	317
Debt/Equity Ratio	—	—	—	—

Gabelli recently raised $190 million in two convertible debt offerings to fund its expansion plans. This debt will eventually be converted into shares, leaving shareholders to worry more about share dilution than Gabelli's debt burden.

Industry	Investment Style	Stock Type	Sector
Money Management	▦ Small Core	↗ Classic Growth	$ Financial Services

Competition	Market Cap $Mil	Debt/ Equity	12 Mo Trailing Sales $Mil	Price/Cash Flow	Return On Assets%	Total Return% 1 Yr	3 Yr
Gabelli Asset Management	905	—	216	—	10.0	-30.5	23.9
Franklin Resources	8,929	—	2,519	—	6.7	-2.6	3.8
Northern Trust	7,498	—	2,817	—	1.1	-40.9	-8.4

Price Volatility

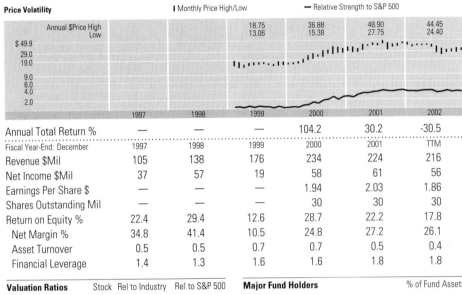

					18.75 13.06	36.88 15.38	48.90 27.75	44.45 24.40

Annual $Price High/Low · Monthly Price High/Low — Relative Strength to S&P 500

	1997	1998	1999	2000	2001	2002
Annual Total Return %	—	—	—	104.2	30.2	-30.5

Fiscal Year-End: December	1997	1998	1999	2000	2001	TTM
Revenue $Mil	105	138	176	234	224	216
Net Income $Mil	37	57	19	58	61	56
Earnings Per Share $	—	—	—	1.94	2.03	1.86
Shares Outstanding Mil	—	—	—	30	30	30
Return on Equity %	22.4	29.4	12.6	28.7	22.2	17.8
Net Margin %	34.8	41.4	10.5	24.8	27.2	26.1
Asset Turnover	0.5	0.5	0.7	0.7	0.5	0.4
Financial Leverage	1.4	1.3	1.6	1.6	1.8	1.8

Valuation Ratios	Stock	Rel to Industry	Rel to S&P 500
Price/Earnings	16.2	0.9	0.7
Price/Book	2.9	1.1	0.9
Price/Sales	4.2	1.6	2.1
Price/Cash Flow	—	—	—

Major Fund Holders	% of Fund Assets
Phoenix-Engemann Small & MidCap Gr A	3.96
AFBA Five Star Small Cap A	1.48
Buffalo Small Cap	1.35
Baron Small Cap	1.33

Morningstar's Take By Rachel Barnard, 12-10-2002 Stock Price as of Analysis: $32.15

Gabelli has most of its eggs in the equity basket, so it needs a little market momentum to outperform other asset managers.

With more than 85% of its assets under management in equity securities, Gabelli is subject to the ebb and flow of the stock market. But Mario Gabelli's longstanding commitment to value investing has really paid off in the recent bear market. What has been a bloodbath for many equity managers was only a mild setback for Gabelli.

Still, market depreciation took its toll on Gabelli funds in the third quarter of 2002--a nasty one for asset managers--and revenue fell 16%. Profits have been weaker this year as well, because of higher interest expense on the company's $185 million of convertible debt and a sharp decline in investment income.

Gabelli is still very profitable, however. The firm maintained a 47% operating margin during the first nine months of 2002. This beats most of its peers and comes in well above competitors in the equity fund business like Amvescap and Stilwell. We believe the firm can continue to keep a lid on costs while investing selectively in new growth areas and increasing its celebrated research team.

In recent months, Gabelli has invested in two small acquisitions to expand its fund lineup. The firm acquired Woodland Partners, a small-cap equity manager with $250 million in assets under management. It also added a partnership with a small energy hedge fund, Grove Investment Advisors, which will expand its growing list of alternative investment options.

Alternative investments (hedge funds), which seek double-digit growth regardless of market conditions, have been a bright spot for Gabelli. Assets have continued to roll into these funds, which generate large fees--including lucrative performance fees. The firm is committed to being a larger presence in the hedge fund market, which has been growing quickly and attracting wealthy investors as equity values have plummeted. In our opinion, this strategy makes a lot of sense for Gabelli and should position it to pick up a bigger chunk of the high-net-worth market.

We believe the prospect of a market rebound, combined with Gabelli's solid lineup of investment products, could make the stock a compelling investment at the right price. Following the Gabelli value investing philosophy, we would prefer to buy the shares at a discount to our fair value estimate and think they would be a great deal below $22.

MORNINGSTAR® Stocks 500

Gannett GCI

	Rating	Risk	Moat Size	Fair Value	Last Close	Yield %
	★★★	Low	Narrow	$73.00	$71.80	1.3

Company Profile

Gannett provides news, entertainment, and information services throughout North America and the United Kingdom. It publishes USA Today, which has a weekday circulation of about 2.3 million. Additionally, Gannett publishes nearly 300 domestic newspapers and publications. The company operates 22 network-affiliated television stations in the United States.

Management

Douglas H. McCorkindale became CEO in June 2000; he started with Gannett as general counsel in 1971. The former Army officer leads by example and isn't the stereotypical swashbuckling media mogul.

Strategy

Gannett is focused on financial results. While other media companies often pursue acquisitions for the sake of getting big, Gannett has been willing to sell business units at the right price. Publishing has become its core focus, particularly after the sale of its cable and radio properties in recent years.

7950 Jones Branch Drive   www.gannett.com
McLean, VA 22107

Morningstar Grades

Growth [B-]	1998	1999	2000	2001
Revenue %	9.3	8.2	22.1	2.0
Earnings/Share %	40.0	-2.9	88.5	-51.3
Book Value/Share %	14.1	18.0	15.8	13.1
Dividends/Share %	5.4	5.1	4.9	4.7

Expansion rates have slipped in recent years as a result of the cyclical downturn and a maturing publishing industry. But Gannett's revenue and earnings growth rates have slightly exceeded the industry averages.

Profitability [A]	1999	2000	2001	TTM
Return on Assets %	10.6	13.2	6.3	8.1
Oper Cash Flow $Mil	1,147	502	1,319	1,183
- Cap Spending $Mil	258	351	325	285
= Free Cash Flow $Mil	888	152	994	898

Return on equity has averaged more than 24% for the past five years. The company is aggressively cutting costs now but has suffered a slight decline in profits over the past year.

Financial Health [A]	1999	2000	2001	09-02
Long-term Debt $Mil	2,463	5,748	5,080	4,326
Total Equity $Mil	4,630	5,103	5,736	6,521
Debt/Equity Ratio	0.5	1.1	0.9	0.7

Recent acquisitions have pushed up leverage. The company now has a debt/equity ratio of 1 and $5 billion in debt, but its steady free cash flow will allow Gannett to gradually pay off that debt.

Industry	Investment Style	Stock Type	Sector
Media Conglomerates	Large Core	Classic Growth	Media

Competition	Market Cap $Mil	Debt/ Equity	12 Mo Trailing Sales $Mil	Price/Cash Flow	Return On Assets%	Total Return% 1 Yr	3 Yr
Gannett	19,190	0.7	6,354	16.2	8.1	8.1	-1.1
Tribune	13,856	0.6	5,273	15.2	1.3	22.7	-2.8
Washington Post	7,018	0.2	2,522	15.3	3.5	40.5	12.8

Price Volatility

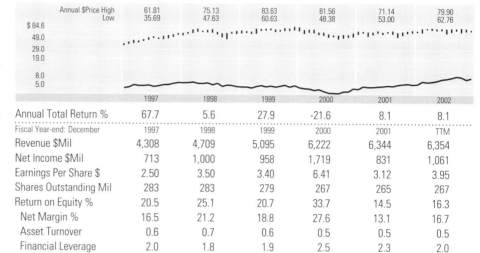

	Monthly Price High/Low		Relative Strength to S&P 500			
Annual $Price High	61.81	75.13	83.63	81.56	71.14	79.90
Low	35.69	47.63	60.63	48.38	53.00	62.76

	1997	1998	1999	2000	2001	2002
Annual Total Return %	67.7	5.6	27.9	-21.6	8.1	8.1

Fiscal Year-end: December	1997	1998	1999	2000	2001	TTM
Revenue $Mil	4,308	4,709	5,095	6,222	6,344	6,354
Net Income $Mil	713	1,000	958	1,719	831	1,061
Earnings Per Share $	2.50	3.50	3.40	6.41	3.12	3.95
Shares Outstanding Mil	283	283	279	267	265	267
Return on Equity %	20.5	25.1	20.7	33.7	14.5	16.3
Net Margin %	16.5	21.2	18.8	27.6	13.1	16.7
Asset Turnover	0.6	0.7	0.6	0.5	0.5	0.5
Financial Leverage	2.0	1.8	1.9	2.5	2.3	2.0

Valuation Ratios	Stock	Rel to Industry	Rel to S&P 500
Price/Earnings	18.2	0.7	0.8
Price/Book	2.9	2.1	0.9
Price/Sales	3.0	1.4	1.5
Price/Cash Flow	16.2	1.1	1.2

Major Fund Holders	% of Fund Assets
Westcore Select	5.51
Jensen	4.69
MSB	4.43
AmSouth Select Equity B	4.37

Morningstar's Take By T.K. MacKay, 11-22-2002 Stock Price as of Analysis: $73.00

Gannett sets the gold standard for the publishing industry.

More than a year ago, we called Gannett the gem of the publishing industry. We still think it is. The proof is in the pudding--over the past several years, Gannett has substantially outperformed its average peer in operating margins, free cash flow generation, and a host of other financial metrics.

The company is best known for publishing USA Today, the daily national newspaper that boasts the industry's highest circulation. Beyond this widely recognized brand name, Gannett owns nearly 100 community newspapers. These properties are mostly leaders in midsize and small markets and face limited competition. The company also owns 19 TV stations, most of which rank among the top two (as measured by ratings) in their respective markets.

Gannett management boasts a great record of mergers and acquisitions, which is very important in a consolidating industry. Among its many shrewd deals, Gannett sold its cable division to Cox Communications COX at the market peak in 2000. Although some observers initially questioned management's decision to abandon such a hot market, Gannett scored an enormous gain on the transaction and cable valuations have since crashed.

The company also managed to avoid capital spending on cable system upgrades. Gannett is likely to flex its deal-making muscles now that a recent easing in regulations could spark a new wave of media mergers.

Relative to other media companies, Gannett has moderate growth prospects and low risk. This is partly a function of its diverse businesses. Much of Gannett's ad revenue comes from local ads in its community papers, in the form of classified ads or promotions and coupons. This kind of advertising generates relatively steady performance during market swings. Rivals like Dow Jones have greater exposure to national advertising, branding campaigns, and financial advertising, all of which are highly cyclical.

Gannett's excellent franchises, strong management, and steady performance make the stock worth watching. We think its strong performance this year leaves the stock fully valued, but investors should be ready to buy on any major dips.

Gap GPS

	Rating	Risk	Moat Size	Fair Value	Last Close	Yield %
	★	High	None	$8.00	$15.52	0.6

Company Profile

Gap is a specialty retailer that operates stores selling casual apparel for men, women, and children under private-label brand names. These brands are marketed under Gap, GapKids, babyGap, GapShoes, and Banana Republic names. The company operates 3,542 stores including 2,505 Gap, 389 Banana Republic, and 648 Old Navy Clothing Co. stores throughout the United States, United Kingdom, Canada, France, Germany, and Japan. Virtually all stores are leased; no stores are franchised or operated by others. About 78% of its merchandise is imported from overseas vendors.

Management

Management has been in a state of flux over the past several years. Co-founder Mickey Drexler recently stepped down as president and CEO. Disney veteran Paul Pressler took Gap's reins in September.

Strategy

Gap is struggling to maintain profitability and a reasonable growth rate. It has had a hard time producing sales increases anywhere near the explosive growth of previous years. Management is focusing on improving margins by increasing sell-through rates on full-price items and narrowing its product offerings.

Two Folsom St.
San Francisco, CA 94105
www.gap.com

Morningstar Grades

Growth [B-]	1999	2000	2001	2002
Revenue %	39.1	28.5	17.5	1.3
Earnings/Share %	56.9	38.5	-20.6	NMF
Book Value/Share %	0.9	43.7	33.7	16.2
Dividends/Share %	0.0	0.0	0.0	0.0

We're pretty confident that Gap's high-flying growth is a thing of the past. Future growth will depend on the company's ability to right each of its three businesses.

Profitability [A-]	2000	2001	2002	TTM
Return on Assets %	21.7	12.5	-0.1	2.0
Oper Cash Flow $Mil	1,478	1,291	1,318	1,193
- Cap Spending $Mil	1,239	1,859	940	345
= Free Cash Flow $Mil	239	-567	378	848

Margins have been falling since 1999. Gap is relying on more full-price selling for profit growth, but we think returns on assets will remain well beneath the historical average.

Financial Health [B]	2000	2001	2002	10-02
Long-term Debt $Mil	785	780	1,961	2,876
Total Equity $Mil	2,233	2,928	3,010	3,389
Debt/Equity Ratio	0.4	0.3	0.7	0.8

Gap is free cash flow positive, but only because capital spending has been slashed dramatically. Leverage has also crept up to historically high levels, as the company has been forced to finance more and more of its inventory purchases with debt.

Industry	Investment Style	Stock Type	Sector
Clothing Stores	Large Growth	Slow Growth	Consumer Services

Competition	Market Cap $Mil	Debt/ Equity	12 Mo Trailing Sales $Mil	Price/Cash Flow	Return On Assets%	Total Return% 1 Yr	3 Yr
Gap	13,718	0.8	13,894	11.5	2.0	12.1	-27.7
Target	27,252	1.2	42,275	21.5	5.7	-26.5	-3.9
Limited Brands	7,283	0.1	9,184	7.7	7.7	-3.7	-9.6

Price Volatility

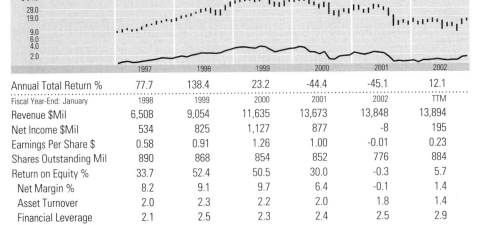

Annual $Price High Low	17.15 8.26	40.92 15.31	52.69 30.81	53.75 18.50	34.98 11.12	17.14 8.35

	1997	1998	1999	2000	2001	2002
Annual Total Return %	77.7	138.4	23.2	-44.4	-45.1	12.1

Fiscal Year-End: January	1998	1999	2000	2001	2002	TTM
Revenue $Mil	6,508	9,054	11,635	13,673	13,848	13,894
Net Income $Mil	534	825	1,127	877	-8	195
Earnings Per Share $	0.58	0.91	1.26	1.00	-0.01	0.23
Shares Outstanding Mil	890	868	854	852	776	884
Return on Equity %	33.7	52.4	50.5	30.0	-0.3	5.7
Net Margin %	8.2	9.1	9.7	6.4	-0.1	1.4
Asset Turnover	2.0	2.3	2.2	2.0	1.8	1.4
Financial Leverage	2.1	2.5	2.3	2.4	2.5	2.9

Valuation Ratios	Stock	Rel to Industry	Rel to S&P 500
Price/Earnings	67.5	3.7	2.9
Price/Book	4.0	1.0	1.3
Price/Sales	1.0	1.1	0.5
Price/Cash Flow	11.5	1.1	0.9

Major Fund Holders	% of Fund Assets
MassMutual Instl Focused Value S	5.96
Chicago Asset Management Value	4.17
Citizens Value	3.88
Matrix Advisors Value	3.67

Morningstar's Take By Roz Bryant, 10-21-2002 Stock Price as of Analysis: $10.31

Gap's story sounds a lot like the classic tale of a retail has-been. A successful turnaround may still be possible, but we think it's a long shot. To offset the odds, we'd need a 60% margin of safety to our fair value estimate before buying in.

Throughout the mid- to late 1990s, Gap had a good thing going. The apparel retailer averaged 10% growth in same-store sales (or comps) from 1995 to 1999. Management opened stores at a rapid pace during that period, netting 1,338 new locations over the five-year span, and averaged 23% annual growth in overall sales. But a massive inventory pileup followed, which, along with an ill-conceived change in fashion direction, resulted in an onslaught of markdowns in Gap stores. Earnings slid more than 20% in 2000, and the firm went on to post a loss in 2001 as well.

So far in 2002, comps are still firmly negative. The company is finding it difficult to convince shoppers to buy its clothing at full price after years of markdowns. Management has acknowledged that it could take a long time for the full-price message to sink in with shoppers, but we're even more skeptical. Alternative sources of high-quality basic clothing are more numerous than when Gap was enjoying its heyday--and many rivals offer lower prices. Plus, a

stalled economy won't ease the firm's efforts. We think the Gap brand's pricing power is largely gone, and we expect the company's gross margins to remain well below their historical average.

Management has recognized the severity of its problems, though, and we like that the retailer has focused on a key task: differentiating its Banana Republic, Old Navy, and Gap brands. We're cautiously optimistic that the retailer can pull this off. Already, the distinct identity of each brand has become more clear. Shoppers are now more likely than in the past to go to Banana Republic for sophisticated casual and tailored apparel, Gap for moderately priced casualwear, and Old Navy for fun designs at value prices.

With consumer spending teetering on the brink of decline, clothing retailers are fighting for their lives, and we view Gap as a wounded competitor. We think it's unlikely that the retailer will return to its historical profitability. We view its shares as risky, and wouldn't touch them until they hit $3.

MORNINGSTAR® Stocks 500

Gateway GTW

	Rating	Risk	Moat Size	Fair Value	Last Close	Yield %
	UR	High	None	UR	$3.14	0.0

Company Profile

Gateway develops and manufactures desktop and portable personal computers. The company's PCs are custom-configured with various memory and storage capacities, and other options specified by customers. Customers include consumers, businesses, government agencies, and educational institutions. Sales of desktop PCs and accompanying peripheral items to consumers make up most of the company's unit volume.

Management

Chairman and founder Ted Waitt reclaimed his position as CEO in January 2001, one year after stepping down.

Strategy

Gateway's new strategy is to build market share, even at the expense of profitability. Its hybrid strategy of combining online sales and a limited retail presence worked well during the PC boom, but when things turned sour in late 2000, the company started closing stores and focusing on high-end PCs. In another shift, Gateway is increasing its focus on the mass market and low-end PCs.

14303 Gateway Place   www.gateway.com
Poway, CA 92064

Industry	Investment Style	Stock Type	Sector
Computer Equipment	Small Value	Distressed	Hardware

Competition

	Market Cap $Mil	Debt/ Equity	12 Mo Trailing Sales $Mil	Price/Cash Flow	Return On Assets%	Total Return% 1 Yr	3 Yr
Gateway	1,017	0.1	4,250	EUB	-8.6	-61.0	-63.2
Dell Computer	69,252	0.1	32,054	20.1	13.4	-1.6	-16.9
Hewlett-Packard	34,321	0.3	—	6.1	-3.5	-13.9	-24.7

Price Volatility

Annual $Price High / Low	23.13 11.78	34.38 15.50	84.00 25.59	75.13 16.48	24.20 4.24	10.26 2.61
	1997	1998	1999	2000	2001	2002
Annual Total Return %	22.3	56.3	181.6	-75.0	-55.3	-60.9

Fiscal Year-end: December	1997	1998	1999	2000	2001	TTM
Revenue $Mil	6,461	7,703	8,965	9,601	6,080	4,250
Net Income $Mil	110	346	428	241	-1,034	-228
Earnings Per Share $	0.35	1.09	1.32	0.73	-3.20	-0.70
Shares Outstanding Mil	309	312	315	322	323	324
Return on Equity %	11.8	25.8	21.2	10.1	-75.7	-20.3
Net Margin %	1.7	4.5	4.8	2.5	-17.0	-5.4
Asset Turnover	3.2	2.7	2.3	2.3	2.0	1.6
Financial Leverage	2.2	2.2	2.0	1.8	2.2	2.4

Valuation Ratios	Stock	Rel to Industry	Rel to S&P 500
Price/Earnings	NMF	—	—
Price/Book	0.9	0.2	0.3
Price/Sales	0.2	0.2	0.1
Price/Cash Flow	EUB	—	—

Major Fund Holders	% of Fund Assets
Ameristock Focused Value	14.15
Hotchkis and Wiley Mid-Cap Value I	2.92
ING Smallcap Value A	2.80
American Heritage Growth	2.66

Morningstar Grades

Growth [D]	1998	1999	2000	2001
Revenue %	19.2	16.4	7.1	-36.7
Earnings/Share %	211.4	21.1	-44.7	NMF
Book Value/Share %	42.7	47.1	15.7	-41.3
Dividends/Share %	NMF	NMF	NMF	NMF

Gateway hit a wall in the December quarter of 2000 and has yet to recover. The combination of a maturing PC market, an economic downturn, and intense price competition has devastated revenue growth.

Profitability [C+]	1999	2000	2001	TTM
Return on Assets %	10.8	5.8	-34.6	-8.6
Oper Cash Flow $Mil	731	289	-270	1
- Cap Spending $Mil	338	315	199	83
= Free Cash Flow $Mil	393	-26	-470	-83

The PC price war, lower sales volume, and the cost of maintaining retail stores have hammered profit margins for more than a year now. After a brief return to profitability in December 2001, the firm will be in the red for all of 2002 at least.

Financial Health [C+]	1999	2000	2001	09-02
Long-term Debt $Mil	0	0	0	74
Total Equity $Mil	2,017	2,380	1,365	1,120
Debt/Equity Ratio	0.0	0.0	0.0	0.1

Gateway carries more than $3 per share in cash and investments, but that figure is falling as the company burns through cash. Investors shouldn't depend on this as a floor for the stock.

Morningstar's Take   By Joseph Beaulieu, 10-21-2002   Stock Price as of Analysis: $2.98

We have our doubts that Gateway's current business model is sustainable, and we wouldn't buy the stock at any price. Although Gateway trades below its cash per share of more than $3, the company continues to burn cash and destroy shareholder value, so we don't think current cash holdings represent a dependable floor for the stock.

The root of Gateway's problems is that the company's high fixed costs do not mix well with current industry conditions, where Dell, the low-cost provider, has a vast advantage. PCs are almost pure commodities--plastic cases full of third-party components (an Intel processor, a Creative Technology SoundBlaster sound card, an NVIDIA video card, and an IBM hard drive, for example), a Microsoft Windows operating system, and perhaps some third-party software applications. When consumers shop for PCs, the key point of comparison is price, and because the major vendors offer "build your own PC" options on their Web sites, customers (and competitors) have nearly perfect information and can easily spot the best deal.

Gateway's operating structure is leaner after the most recent round of restructuring, but still much more bloated than Dell's. In our opinion, the recent cuts still won't put Gateway in a position where competing with Dell on price is a viable long-term strategy. While Gateway has made market share gains offering some rock-bottom prices on PCs, we think these gains will evaporate the moment Dell offers a better deal.

We still cannot predict whether Gateway will return to profitability. Until management articulates a convincing business strategy, we would continue to avoid the shares at any price.

Genentech DNA

	Rating	Risk	Moat Size	Fair Value	Last Close	Yield %
	★★★	High	Wide	$32.00	$33.16	0.0

Company Profile

Genentech, a subsidiary of Roche Holdings, develops and produces pharmaceuticals. Its products include Herceptin and Rituxan, antibodies that treat breast cancer and non-Hodgkin's lymphoma; Protropin, a growth hormone used to alter short stature associated with genetic disorders in children; Activase, a declotting enzyme used to treat strokes; Pulmozyme, which manages cystic fibrosis; and Nutropin, a growth hormone for use in children and adults. The company is also developing drugs to treat conditions like cancer, cardiovascular diseases, and neurodegenerative diseases.

Management

Genentech is one of the oldest biotech firms and is headed by Arthur Levinson, who is credited with helping the company develop a diverse product pipeline. Swiss drug giant Roche owns 59% of Genentech and holds a third of its board seats.

Strategy

Genentech is aggressively building its pipeline of products in order to deliver strong, sustainable earnings growth. The company creates products in-house and co-develops and markets drugs with smaller biotech players. Two of the company's dominant franchises are protein therapies in oncology and growth hormones.

1 DNA Way
South San Francisc, CA 94080-4990
www.gene.com

Morningstar Grades

Growth [A]

	1998	1999	2000	2001
Revenue %	13.2	21.7	23.9	27.4
Earnings/Share %	NMF	NMF	NMF	NMF
Book Value/Share %	—	—	NMF	3.1
Dividends/Share %	NMF	NMF	NMF	NMF

Thanks to Rituxan, annual sales have increased an average of 22% since 1998. We expect sales growth to slow as existing products mature, but we believe new products and product expansion will boost sales by 15% annually through 2006.

Profitability [B]

	1999	2000	2001	TTM
Return on Assets %	-17.7	-1.1	2.1	0.2
Oper Cash Flow $Mil	-7	194	481	603
- Cap Spending $Mil	95	113	213	339
= Free Cash Flow $Mil	-102	81	267	264

Excluding the accounting impact of Roche's stock redemption, Genentech is approaching its goal of 25% net margins by 2005. But a $500 million charge for the City of Hope lawsuit damages makes the goal impossible this year.

Financial Health [B-]

	1999	2000	2001	09-02
Long-term Debt $Mil	150	150	0	0
Total Equity $Mil	5,270	5,674	5,920	5,301
Debt/Equity Ratio	0.0	0.0	0.0	0.0

Genentech is financially solid. The company holds no debt and has $2 billion in cash and investments as of September 30. In addition, free cash flow is strong.

Industry	Investment Style	Stock Type	Sector
Biotechnology	Large Growth	Spec. Growth	Healthcare

Competition

	Market Cap $Mil	Debt/ Equity	12 Mo Trailing Sales $Mil	Price/Cash Flow	Return On Assets%	Total Return% 1 Yr	3 Yr
Genentech	17,067	0.0	2,541	28.3	0.2	-38.9	-19.2
Johnson & Johnson	159,452	0.1	35,120	18.0	16.3	-7.9	8.0
Amgen	61,986	0.2	4,881	31.7	-7.1	-14.4	-6.0

Price Volatility

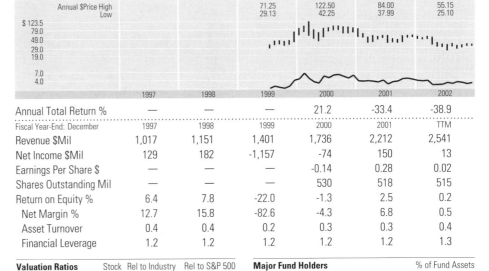

Annual $Price High / Low			71.25 / 29.13	122.50 / 42.25	84.00 / 37.99	55.15 / 25.10

	1997	1998	1999	2000	2001	2002
Annual Total Return %	—	—	—	21.2	-33.4	-38.9

Fiscal Year-End: December	1997	1998	1999	2000	2001	TTM
Revenue $Mil	1,017	1,151	1,401	1,736	2,212	2,541
Net Income $Mil	129	182	-1,157	-74	150	13
Earnings Per Share $	—	—	—	-0.14	0.28	0.02
Shares Outstanding Mil	—	—	—	530	518	515
Return on Equity %	6.4	7.8	-22.0	-1.3	2.5	0.2
Net Margin %	12.7	15.8	-82.6	-4.3	6.8	0.5
Asset Turnover	0.4	0.4	0.2	0.3	0.3	0.4
Financial Leverage	1.2	1.2	1.2	1.2	1.2	1.3

Valuation Ratios

	Stock	Rel to Industry	Rel to S&P 500
Price/Earnings	EUB	—	—
Price/Book	3.2	0.9	1.0
Price/Sales	6.7	0.5	3.3
Price/Cash Flow	28.3	0.9	2.1

Major Fund Holders

	% of Fund Assets
Pitcairn Select Growth	7.68
Parnassus	5.13
John Hancock Biotechnology A	5.01
Eaton Vance Worldwide Health Sci A	4.88

Morningstar's Take By Jill Kiersky, 11-12-2002 Stock Price as of Analysis: $35.20

With novel cancer treatments on the market and product revenue surpassing $2 billion, Genentech is the second-largest biotech firm in the United States. But companies are only worth the cash flows they can produce in the future, and Genentech's past successes alone won't sustain earnings growth for long.

Genentech relies on its two cancer therapies, Rituxan and Herceptin, for two thirds of its revenue. These products bring in $1.5 billion annually and don't cost much to produce (gross margins were 83% in 2001). Rituxan, which accounts for nearly half of sales, is the leader in its class and should continue to earn a nice profit until its patents expire--which won't be for another decade. But the mid-20s sales growth of the past will soon start to shrink as competing products enter the market. To be on par with Amgen, which has returns on capital above 30%, Genentech has to deliver new products.

The company is in as good a position as any drug developer to do just that. It has 10 new drugs in human testing. The most promising among these products includes Xolair, a completely new form of asthma treatment that gets to the heart of the disease rather than treating symptoms; Raptiva, one of several similar products targeting the psoriasis

market; and two innovative cancer treatments, Avastin and Tarceva, which could both generate large sums of cash. Indeed, each of these drugs has a multibillion-dollar market, and, if approved, could help the company glide over its next development hurdles.

Three of these drugs are in Phase III (with about 60% chance of reaching the market), and one awaits Food and Drug Administration approval (once here, drugs have a 70% chance of being approved). Any setbacks typically lead to big drops in the stock price, but more important, also reduce the chances for long-term success unless the company can keep its pipeline full.

Genentech has done a good job of stuffing its pipeline and improving its operating costs. Excluding costs to rearrange its relationship with parent firm Roche Holding, operating margins improved 7 percentage points from 1998 to 2001. But biotech investing is all about probabilities, and none of Genentech's products under development are guaranteed to earn revenue. As such, we'd like a wide margin of safety before taking on such big risks in our stock portfolio.

 **MORNINGSTAR® Stocks 500**

General Dynamics GD

	Rating	Risk	Moat Size	Fair Value	Last Close	Yield %
	★★★★★	Med.	Wide	$110.00	$79.37	1.5

Company Profile

General Dynamics is a leading defense and aerospace manufacturer with strong market positions in marine systems, combat systems, information systems, and business jets. The Electric Boat division builds nuclear submarines for the U.S. Navy, and Bath Iron Works produces naval destroyers. Land Systems makes battle tanks for the U.S. Army and foreign governments, including the M1 Series Abrams tank. The company also produces undersea-surveillance systems and Gulfstream commercial aircraft. The U.S. government accounted for 60% of sales in 2000.

Management

One reason for GD's extraordinary performance is its management team, ably led by CEO Nicholas Chabraja. The distinguished board of directors includes former Marine Corps Commandant Carl Mundy and retired General George Joulwan, former Supreme Allied Commander, Europe.

Strategy

General Dynamics seeks to increase revenue and profits at a consistent double-digit rate through both internal growth and acquisition. Recently, the company has found acquisition opportunities abroad.

3190 Fairview Park Drive   www.generaldynamics.com
Falls Church, VA 22042-4523

Industry	Investment Style	Stock Type	Sector
Aerospace & Defense	⊞ Large Core	⇅ Cyclical	✪ Industrial Mats

Competition	Market Cap $Mil	Debt/ Equity	12 Mo Trailing Sales $Mil	Price/Cash Flow	Return On Assets%	Total Return% 1 Yr	3 Yr
General Dynamics	15,948	0.1	13,429	15.5	8.3	1.0	17.6
Boeing	27,691	1.1	56,071	9.9	0.0	-13.4	-4.9
Lockheed Martin	26,512	0.9	26,132	11.2	-2.3	24.7	47.9

Price Volatility   ▮ Monthly Price High/Low   — Relative Strength to S&P 500

Annual $Price High Low	45.75 31.56	62.00 40.25	75.44 46.19	79.00 36.25	96.50 60.50	111.18 73.40

	1997	1998	1999	2000	2001	2002
Annual Total Return %	25.3	38.6	-9.2	50.6	3.6	1.0

Fiscal Year-end: December	1997	1998	1999	2000	2001	TTM
Revenue $Mil	5,966	7,398	8,959	10,356	12,163	13,429
Net Income $Mil	559	589	880	901	943	1,006
Earnings Per Share $	2.73	2.91	4.36	4.48	4.65	4.95
Shares Outstanding Mil	200	200	200	200	201	201
Return on Equity %	27.8	24.4	27.8	23.6	20.8	19.6
Net Margin %	9.4	8.0	9.8	8.7	7.8	7.5
Asset Turnover	1.1	1.2	1.2	1.3	1.1	1.1
Financial Leverage	2.8	2.6	2.5	2.1	2.4	2.4

Valuation Ratios	Stock	Rel to Industry	Rel to S&P 500
Price/Earnings	16.0	1.0	0.7
Price/Book	3.1	1.2	1.0
Price/Sales	1.2	1.3	0.6
Price/Cash Flow	15.5	1.6	1.2

Major Fund Holders	% of Fund Assets
Fidelity Select Air Transportation	6.05
Janus Aspen Capital Apprec Instl	4.98
Edgar Lomax Value	4.88
Rochdale Magna	4.30

Morningstar Grades

Growth [A+]	1998	1999	2000	2001
Revenue %	24.0	21.1	15.6	17.4
Earnings/Share %	6.6	49.8	2.8	3.8
Book Value/Share %	21.7	31.6	20.9	17.6
Dividends/Share %	5.5	8.7	8.5	7.8

Annual sales growth has averaged 30% since 1998. Acquisitions have boosted this rate, but the firm has also shown decent internal growth. The company should generate double-digit sales growth in 2003 and beyond. We project double-digit profit growth beyond 2003, as well.

Profitability [A+]	1999	2000	2001	TTM
Return on Assets %	11.3	11.3	8.5	8.3
Oper Cash Flow $Mil	1,016	1,071	1,103	1,032
- Cap Spending $Mil	197	288	356	265
= Free Cash Flow $Mil	819	783	747	767

General Dynamics has consistently returned more than 20% on its equity over the past five years, placing it near the top of its peer group. We expect comparable performance in the coming years.

Financial Health [A]	1999	2000	2001	09-02
Long-term Debt $Mil	169	173	724	728
Total Equity $Mil	3,170	3,820	4,528	5,121
Debt/Equity Ratio	0.1	0.0	0.2	0.1

Its solid balance sheet gives the firm a competitive advantage and has been the foundation of its recent acquisition strategy.

Morningstar's Take By Nicolas Owens, 12-05-2002 Stock Price as of Analysis: $81.37

We are bullish on General Dynamics.

In each of the past 10 years, GD delivered at least 15% return on equity, averaging over 25%. Despite slowing U.S. spending on defense programs since 1997, the firm has increased its sales at a 20% compound annual rate. Rapid growth, both internally and through strategic acquisitions, has not harmed overall profitability: Since 1997, GD's operating profit margin has improved from 11% to 12.4%.

Over the next five years, U.S. defense spending is set to increase as much as 6% annually. While the war on terrorism accounts for some of the increase, there's a bigger motivation: Years of defense budget cuts have left U.S. weapons systems--including aircraft and ships--in need of replacement and repair. Plus, initiatives under way to transform the military mean more money for new equipment that will make the United States more capable of responding quickly to threats around the globe.

GD is positioned to take advantage of higher defense and security spending. It is one of two firms--the other is Northrop Grumman--that will meet the shipbuilding needs of the U.S. Navy. This should provide several years of high profits and steady cash flow. GD also recently won a large contract to equip the Coast Guard with a new communication system to aid search and rescue operations.

GD benefits from the military's transformation as well. It already has a mandate to convert four Trident-class submarines into delivery platforms for cruise missiles and special operations forces. It's also part of the team building the Army's next-generation Stryker Interim Armored Vehicle. Finally, with a development contract for the Army's tactical Warfighter Information Network, GD has a strong foothold in information systems, the vital links between all of the military's transformational efforts. Spending in this area should be very strong over the next decade.

By acquiring Gulfstream Aviation, GD has diversified its cash streams and acquired a business with higher margins than its defense business. This strategy seems to mirror Boeing's extension of its defense business away from commercial aviation. The crucial difference is that even in this economic downturn, sales of small jets like Gulfstreams are healthier than sales of large-frame jets like Boeing's, which have declined sharply.

We believe GD remains poised for strong growth. Its strong defense franchise leads us to require only a 20% margin of safety to our fair value estimate to invest.

General Electric GE

	Rating	Risk	Moat Size	Fair Value	Last Close	Yield %
	★★★	Med.	Narrow	$28.00	$24.35	3.0

Company Profile

General Electric provides financial and broadcasting services and produces industrial products, power-generation and medical systems, aerospace systems, home appliances, locomotives, and engineered materials. The company offers financial and equipment-management services through its GE Capital subsidiary. In addition, it owns the National Broadcasting Company, which includes the broadcast network and cable television interests. Foreign sales make up about 32% of General Electric's revenue.

Management

Jeffrey Immelt took over the roles of chairman and CEO from Jack Welch in September 2001. Thus far, he has done a fine job of leading GE through rough terrain. He has been aided by a deep management team steeped in operating experience.

Strategy

General Electric uses its solid balance sheet to make prudent acquisitions that add to the top and bottom lines. The firm has been very willing to part with any business that does not have either strong profitability or good growth prospects. Much of GE's growth will come through increasing the assets of its financial services businesses.

3135 Easton Turnpike   www.ge.com
Fairfield, CT 06431-0001

Morningstar Grades

Growth [A-]	1998	1999	2000	2001
Revenue %	10.6	11.1	16.3	-3.0
Earnings/Share %	12.0	15.1	18.7	7.9
Book Value/Share %	11.6	9.2	18.5	9.0
Dividends/Share %	15.7	16.8	17.1	15.8

GE's top line has increased at a 9% clip over the past five years. Power systems revenue has been the biggest driver in the past couple of years. With this business expected to fall off, short-cycle businesses like NBC will need to pick up the slack.

Profitability [B]	1999	2000	2001	TTM
Return on Assets %	2.6	2.9	2.8	2.7
Oper Cash Flow $Bil	24.6	22.7	32.2	29.6
- Cap Spending $Bil	15.5	14.0	15.5	12.2
= Free Cash Flow $Bil	9.1	8.7	16.7	17.4

GE's focus on efficiency has been fruitful; net profit margins have expanded from 9% in 1997 to 11.2% in 2001. But margin expansion may become more difficult, especially if financial services growth outpaces industrial growth.

Financial Health [B]	1999	2000	2001	09-02
Long-term Debt $Bil	71.4	82.1	79.8	134.0
Total Equity $Bil	42.6	50.5	54.8	62.3
Debt/Equity Ratio	1.7	1.6	1.5	2.2

GE's financial health is very good, as its AAA credit rating indicates. We have some concerns about the transparency of the firm's financial business, however, which prompt us to rate the stock medium risk.

Industry	Investment Style	Stock Type	Sector
Electric Equipment	▦ Large Core	▨ High Yield	✿ Industrial Mats

Competition

	Market Cap $Mil	Debt/ Equity	12 Mo Trailing Sales $Mil	Price/Cash Flow	Return On Assets%	Total Return% 1 Yr	3 Yr
General Electric	242,308	2.2	130,295	8.2	2.7	-37.7	-18.9
Siemens AG ADR	37,222	—	75,745	—	—	—	—
United Technologies	29,339	0.5	27,971	9.4	7.2	-2.7	2.5

Price Volatility

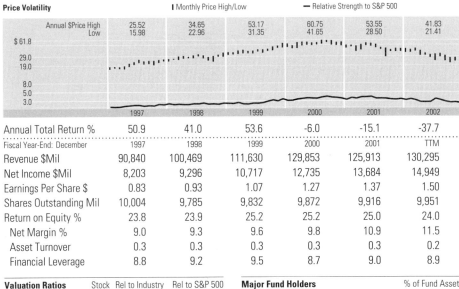

	▮ Monthly Price High/Low		— Relative Strength to S&P 500			
Annual $Price High Low	25.52 15.98	34.65 22.96	53.17 31.35	60.75 41.65	53.55 28.50	41.83 21.41
	1997	1998	1999	2000	2001	2002

Annual Total Return %	50.9	41.0	53.6	-6.0	-15.1	-37.7
Fiscal Year-End: December	1997	1998	1999	2000	2001	TTM
Revenue $Mil	90,840	100,469	111,630	129,853	125,913	130,295
Net Income $Mil	8,203	9,296	10,717	12,735	13,684	14,949
Earnings Per Share $	0.83	0.93	1.07	1.27	1.37	1.50
Shares Outstanding Mil	10,004	9,785	9,832	9,872	9,916	9,951
Return on Equity %	23.8	23.9	25.2	25.2	25.0	24.0
Net Margin %	9.0	9.3	9.6	9.8	10.9	11.5
Asset Turnover	0.3	0.3	0.3	0.3	0.3	0.2
Financial Leverage	8.8	9.2	9.5	8.7	9.0	8.9

Valuation Ratios	Stock	Rel to Industry	Rel to S&P 500	Major Fund Holders	% of Fund Assets
Price/Earnings	16.2	1.0	0.7	Schwab Financial Services Focus	11.20
Price/Book	3.9	1.0	1.2	Quaker Core Equity A	9.41
Price/Sales	1.9	1.0	0.9	Wayne Hummer CorePortfolio	8.49
Price/Cash Flow	8.2	1.0	0.6	IDEX Great Companies-America A	8.28

Morningstar's Take By Jonathan Schrader, 12-18-2002 Stock Price as of Analysis: $25.66

General Electric is a fine company and we would gladly buy its stock around $17. Any higher than that, though, and we would hold off.

One reason we like GE is its management team, which we think is one of the best in the world. The firm has always produced strong leaders, but the focus that former CEO and chairman Jack Welch placed on leadership training has taken GE to the next level. To stay there, the company spends about $1 billion annually on training and education. Jeff Immelt is a product of this training, and we are confident that he will make the tough choices and institute the policies necessary to maintain GE's leadership in its various markets.

Immelt has already made a couple of these moves: breaking GE Capital into four separate units and merging the appliance and lighting businesses. This second move was a clear cost-cutting measure, an area in which GE has excelled recently. Companywide efficiency efforts have prompted an increase in operating profit margins in the industrial businesses to almost 19% in 2001, up from less than 14% 10 years earlier. We expect that these margins will continue to improve as the company keeps implementing Six Sigma, reduces the amount of back-office staff, and globalizes its supplier and production base.

Higher profit margins have led to improved cash flow: The industrial businesses generated more than $17 billion in cash from operations in 2001. Capital investment takes up only a small portion of this cash; the rest is used for dividends, share repurchases, and acquisitions. Over the past decade, some of this cash has been used to increase GE's presence in financial services. Thanks to acquisitions and internal growth, GE's financial units now contribute more than 40% of the company's total revenue. However, this revenue tends to come with lower profit margins. If the financial side continues to increase its size at a faster rate than the industrial--which we expect--overall margins will probably be lower in the long run.

We don't expect GE's growth to be very impressive, given how large the revenue base is. However, we do like that the company generates so much cash and has such a strong balance sheet. This stock may not be a highflier, but it could make a sound long-term investment if purchased at the right price.

 MORNINGSTAR® Stocks 500

General Mills GIS

	Rating	Risk	Moat Size	Fair Value	Last Close	Yield %
	★★★	Med.	Narrow	$50.00	$46.95	2.3

Company Profile

General Mills produces packaged foods, including breakfast cereals, baking goods, snack and convenience foods, flour, frozen yogurt, and beverages. The company sells its products under trademarks like Lucky Charms, Cheerios, Total, Wheaties, Chex, Trix, Betty Crocker, Gold Medal, Hamburger Helper, Pop Secret, Bisquick, Bac*O's, Colombo, and Yoplait. General Mills has entered into a joint venture with Nestle to market its breakfast cereal abroad. Sales within the U.S. account for about 91% of the company's total sales. It acquired Pillsbury in 2001.

Management

Steve Sanger joined the company in 1974 and has been chairman and CEO since 1995. He previously ran Yoplait USA and Big G, the company's cereal division.

Strategy

General Mills has been expanding beyond cereal to faster-growing food categories, particularly convenience foods. The merger with Pillsbury has further reduced the firm's reliance on cereal while greatly expanding its presence in the food-service market and overseas. General Mills already has overseas joint ventures with Nestle and Frito-Lay.

One General Mills Boulevard   www.generalmills.com
Minneapolis, MN 55426-1348

Industry	Investment Style	Stock Type	Sector
Food Mfg.	▦ Large Core	↗ Classic Growth	🚗 Consumer Goods

Competition

	Market Cap $Mil	Debt/ Equity	12 Mo Trailing Sales $Mil	Price/Cash Flow	Return On Assets%	Total Return% 1 Yr	3 Yr
General Mills	17,278	1.5	8,540	17.8	2.7	-7.6	14.6
PepsiCo	73,589	0.2	28,044	14.3	13.3	-12.1	6.9
Kraft Foods	45,853	0.5	34,063	11.1	5.3	16.1	—

Price Volatility

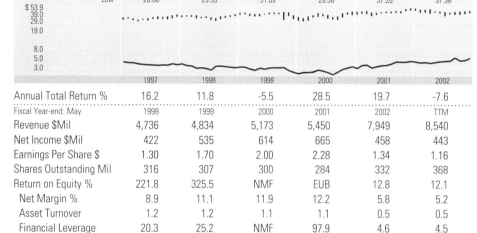

⌶ Monthly Price High/Low   — Relative Strength to S&P 500

	1997	1998	1999	2000	2001	2002
Annual $Price High	39.13	39.84	43.94	45.31	52.86	52.01
Low	28.88	29.59	31.09	29.38	37.26	37.38
Annual Total Return %	16.2	11.8	-5.5	28.5	19.7	-7.6

Fiscal Year-end: May	1998	1999	2000	2001	2002	TTM
Revenue $Mil	4,736	4,834	5,173	5,450	7,949	8,540
Net Income $Mil	422	535	614	665	458	443
Earnings Per Share $	1.30	1.70	2.00	2.28	1.34	1.16
Shares Outstanding Mil	316	307	300	284	332	368
Return on Equity %	221.8	325.5	NMF	EUB	12.8	12.1
Net Margin %	8.9	11.1	11.9	12.2	5.8	5.2
Asset Turnover	1.2	1.2	1.1	1.1	0.5	0.5
Financial Leverage	20.3	25.2	NMF	97.9	4.6	4.5

Valuation Ratios	Stock	Rel to Industry	Rel to S&P 500
Price/Earnings	40.5	1.9	1.7
Price/Book	4.7	1.1	1.5
Price/Sales	2.0	1.4	1.0
Price/Cash Flow	17.8	1.6	1.3

Major Fund Holders	% of Fund Assets
AmSouth Select Equity B	6.63
Mairs & Power Growth	4.01
M.S.D.&T. Equity Growth	2.77
Delaware Retirement Income A	2.65

Morningstar Grades

Growth [A+]	1999	2000	2001	2002
Revenue %	2.1	7.0	5.4	45.9
Earnings/Share %	30.8	17.6	14.0	-41.2
Book Value/Share %	-10.9	NMF	NMF	EUB
Dividends/Share %	1.9	1.9	0.0	0.0

Reported sales grew 46% in fiscal 2002, but most of that came from the Pillsbury acquisition. Comparable unit volume increased 2% in the most recent quarter after two quarters of declines.

Profitability [A-]	2000	2001	2002	TTM
Return on Assets %	13.4	13.1	2.8	2.7
Oper Cash Flow $Mil	725	740	916	971
- Cap Spending $Mil	268	307	506	536
= Free Cash Flow $Mil	457	433	410	435

General Mills' returns on assets have generally placed the firm in the top quintile of food companies. After two quarters of subpar earnings in early 2002 because of the Pillsbury integration, things now appear to be turning around nicely.

Financial Health [B-]	2000	2001	2002	08-02
Long-term Debt $Mil	1,760	2,221	5,591	5,547
Total Equity $Mil	-289	52	3,576	3,661
Debt/Equity Ratio	ELB	42.7	1.6	1.5

General Mills has had very high financial leverage for most of the past decade, and it assumed $5 billion of Pillsbury's debt in the merger. However, it generates plenty of free cash flow for paying down that debt.

Morningstar's Take By David Kathman, 12-13-2002 Stock Price as of Analysis: $43.49

We stuck with General Mills while it was struggling through its merger with Pillsbury, and we still like the company now that the merger problems are starting to fade.

In recent years, General Mills has been working to diversify away from its roots as a maker of breakfast cereal and expand faster-growing businesses with more potential, like yogurt and snack foods. The purchase of Pillsbury at the end of 2001 was another step in this direction, but the merger ran into more than its share of snags. Disruptions in combining the two companies' salesforces, plus a lack of new products during the transition, resulted in a couple quarters of disappointing sales and earnings. General Mills is now emerging from this tough period and showing real improvement, though most of the benefits of having Pillsbury in the fold have yet to materialize.

However, the difficult integration doesn't change our view that General Mills is a very solid company made stronger by Pillsbury. It already expected 2002 to be a transition year, with merger costs depressing earnings by $400 million, so the integration problems just made that transition a little bumpier. Even as the company warned of lower earnings during 2002, it raised its estimate of merger-related cost savings in

fiscal 2003 from $250 million to $350 million, which we think is realistic. Those savings, combined with the re-acceleration of sales growth after the recent merger-related snags, should help boost General Mills' net margin into the low double digits within the next couple of years.

In the long term, Pillsbury strengthens two growth avenues for General Mills: food service and international sales. Pillsbury gets about one fourth of its revenue from its food-service division and more than 20% from overseas, where General Mills had a limited presence before the merger. Pillsbury's solid business in Europe and Latin America will make it easier for General Mills to sell all its products in those regions. Terrible macroeconomic conditions in Latin America have temporarily hurt international sales overall, but the company's joint ventures in Europe are quite profitable and growing at double-digit rates.

General Mills remains one of our favorite food stocks and we'd gladly pick up shares at a 30% margin of safety to our fair value estimate.

General Motors GM

	Rating	Risk	Moat Size	Fair Value	Last Close	Yield %
	★★★	High	None	$73.00	$36.86	5.4

Company Profile

General Motors is the world's largest manufacturer of motor vehicles. Its brands include Buick, Cadillac, Chevrolet, GMC, Oldsmobile, Pontiac, and Saturn in the United States, plus Opel, Saab, Holden, and Vauxhall abroad. In 2000, North American automotive operations accounted for 61% of revenue, with foreign automotive sales contributing 19%. The remainder is earned by financial services subsidiary General Motors Acceptance Corporation (GMAC) and Hughes Electronics, which owns satellite broadcast carrier DirecTV. GM agreed to sell Hughes to EchoStar during 2001.

Management

Today's GM is shedding its tunnel vision and attacking problems head-on. CEO Rick Wagoner, 49, was the youngest of a group of junior executives who took control of GM in the early 1990s. Their leader was Jack Smith, who will soon retire as chairman.

Strategy

GM is getting leaner and--at least from the standpoint of its competitors--a lot meaner. Persistent cost-cutting has given GM the resources to wage a massive fight for market share while remaining profitable. The firm has also brought in the talent necessary to revive its long-lost design leadership and customer appeal. Assets not needed for the car business (like Hughes) are being sold.

300 Renaissance Center   www.gm.com
Detroit, MI 48265-3000

Morningstar Grades

Growth [C]	1998	1999	2000	2001
Revenue %	-9.9	13.6	4.6	-4.0
Earnings/Share %	-51.5	119.6	-27.2	-73.5
Book Value/Share %	-5.3	47.2	45.1	49.7
Dividends/Share %	0.0	0.0	0.0	0.0

Despite steady losses in market share through the 1990s, overall revenue growth managed to match the rate of inflation. If GM can maintain today's share (which we believe it will), it should achieve midsingle-digit growth over the long term.

Profitability [C]	1999	2000	2001	TTM
Return on Assets %	2.2	1.4	0.2	0.3
Oper Cash Flow $Bil	26.9	19.8	9.2	18.9
- Cap Spending $Bil	7.4	9.7	8.6	7.3
= Free Cash Flow $Bil	19.6	10.0	0.5	11.6

Right now, GM's modest profits look great next to the massive losses of rivals. Rising retiree benefit costs pose serious head winds, but we believe the company can continue to improve profitability even without a surge in industry demand.

Financial Health [C]	1999	2000	2001	09-02
Long-term Debt $Bil	129.7	142.4	163.9	185.1
Total Equity $Bil	20.6	30.2	19.7	19.1
Debt/Equity Ratio	6.3	4.7	8.3	9.7

GM's automotive net liquidity (cash less debt) ended the quarter at $2.6 billion, up $1.6 billion from the end of 2001. Gargantuan retiree obligations are our largest concern, but we consider the company's financial position sound at present.

	Industry	Investment Style	Stock Type	Sector
	Auto Makers	⊞ Large Value	⬓ High Yield	⌂ Consumer Goods

Competition	Market Cap $Mil	Debt/ Equity	12 Mo Trailing Sales $Mil	Price/Cash Flow	Return On Assets%	Total Return% 1 Yr	3 Yr
General Motors	20,658	9.7	184,057	1.1	0.3	-20.8	-16.9
Toyota Motor ADR	97,652	—	118,527	—	—	—	—
Honda Motor ADR	35,196	—	58,319	—	—	—	—

Price Volatility   ▎Monthly Price High/Low   — Relative Strength to S&P 500

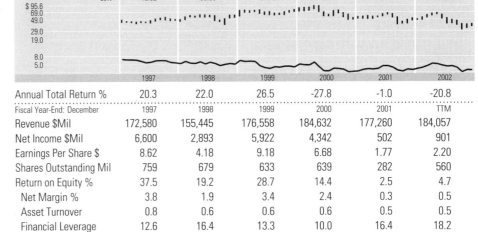

		1997	1998	1999	2000	2001	2002
Annual $Price	High	56.59	63.38	79.06	94.63	67.80	68.09
	Low	40.82	38.89	57.18	48.44	39.17	30.83
Annual Total Return %		20.3	22.0	26.5	-27.8	-1.0	-20.8

Fiscal Year-End: December	1997	1998	1999	2000	2001	TTM
Revenue $Mil	172,580	155,445	176,558	184,632	177,260	184,057
Net Income $Mil	6,600	2,893	5,922	4,342	502	901
Earnings Per Share $	8.62	4.18	9.18	6.68	1.77	2.20
Shares Outstanding Mil	759	679	633	639	282	560
Return on Equity %	37.5	19.2	28.7	14.4	2.5	4.7
Net Margin %	3.8	1.9	3.4	2.4	0.3	0.5
Asset Turnover	0.8	0.6	0.6	0.6	0.5	0.5
Financial Leverage	12.6	16.4	13.3	10.0	16.4	18.2

Valuation Ratios	Stock	Rel to Industry	Rel to S&P 500
Price/Earnings	16.8	1.0	0.7
Price/Book	1.1	0.6	0.3
Price/Sales	0.1	0.2	0.1
Price/Cash Flow	1.1	0.1	0.1

Major Fund Holders	% of Fund Assets
Payden Growth & Income R	5.70
Valley Forge	5.59
Hennessy Leveraged Dogs	5.49
Hillman Aggressive Equity	4.94

Morningstar's Take   By Josh Peters, 10-15-2002   Stock Price as of Analysis: $34.13

The risks posed by legacy costs are overshadowing General Motors' operating progress. We remain optimistic about the firm's ability to extend its gains in market share and profitability, but we demand a large discount to our fair value estimate before buying.

The turnaround at GM is finally under way. After a decade of downsizing, in which rival Ford set the agenda in the U.S. vehicle market, GM now has a sustainable cost advantage over its domestic competitors. The product lineup has caught up, too, and its plants can scarcely keep up with demand for hot trucks like the Chevrolet Tahoe and GMC Envoy.

These improved fundamentals are illustrated by this year's quick rebound in earnings. Not only has the massive increase in sales incentives failed to punish the bottom line, but it's actually enabled GM to increase market share, raise production, and score a healthy gain in profits. Even with $1 per share in increased pension expense, GM's earnings per share (excluding Hughes) could approach $7 this year compared with roughly $3 in 2001.

However, the gains GM has made in the basics of making and selling cars are threatened by adverse trends in pension and health-care costs. The legacy costs clinging to the world's largest automaker are staggering: In the United States, 459,000 retirees are being supported by just 177,000 active workers. A substantial pension deficit opened up in 2001 because of the equity markets' decline, and unfunded health-care benefits for retirees (net of tax benefits) total more than $50 per common share.

GM also faces an unfavorable trend in U.S. vehicle demand that we think could last another year or two. We don't expect a dramatic drop in industry sales, but any decline is sure to exacerbate the industry's excess capacity, leading to further price wars and additional pressure on earnings. Later in the decade we expect another peak with sales that could reach 20 million in the United States, but GM and its peers will have to slog through some tough times while still investing heavily for the future.

The difficulty in forecasting GM's cash flows with such an unpredictable outlook earns the stock our highest risk rating. Still, GM is capable of generating impressive amounts of cash in strong years and returning it to shareholders. The nature of pension liabilities also gives us comfort--they may destroy value, but are unlikely to cause liquidity problems, in our view. We would thus consider buying the stock, but only at a 50% or better discount to our fair value estimate.

MORNINGSTAR® Stocks 500

Data as of 12-31-02

Gentex GNTX

	Rating	Risk	Moat Size	Fair Value	Last Close	Yield %
	★★★	Med.	Wide	$34.00	$31.64	0.0

Company Profile

Gentex manufactures products using proprietary electro-optic technologies, primarily for the automotive industry. Its Night Vision Safety automatic-dimming rearview and exterior mirrors, which account for more than 90% of revenue, are used as standard or optional equipment on more than 100 new vehicle models worldwide. Operating out of four manufacturing facilities in western Michigan, Gentex also produces fire-detection equipment for commercial buildings. In 2001, General Motors accounted for 38% of sales, and approximately 44% of revenue was earned abroad.

Management

Chairman and CEO Fred Bauer, 58, founded Gentex in 1974 as a maker of fire-detection equipment. Bauer, who keeps Gentex focused on research and development, holds 4.6% of the stock. The firm encourages employee stock ownership.

Strategy

With growth prospects that far surpass the average part supplier, Gentex bills itself as an electronics company that happens to serve the automotive industry. By focusing on electro-optic product research, the company has maintained a huge lead over potential competitors while continually finding new opportunities to pack rearview mirrors with lucrative electronic features.

600 N. Centennial Street www.gentex.com
Zeeland, MI 49464

Morningstar Grades

Growth [A-]	1998	1999	2000	2001
Revenue %	19.3	17.9	13.5	4.3
Earnings/Share %	38.8	26.5	8.1	-7.5
Book Value/Share %	33.0	31.2	26.1	19.2
Dividends/Share %	NMF	NMF	NMF	NMF

Revenue expanded at an average of 22% between 1995 and 2000, but rose just 4% in 2001. Falling vehicle production and a temporary lull in new products were mostly to blame; double-digit growth is returning with a flourish in 2002.

Profitability [A+]	1999	2000	2001	TTM
Return on Assets %	19.2	16.5	12.9	13.6
Oper Cash Flow $Mil	74	79	81	98
- Cap Spending $Mil	22	22	45	32
= Free Cash Flow $Mil	52	57	36	66

Operating margins, which hit 32% in 1999, have been pressured by excess capacity and falling auto production. But Gentex looks wildly profitable compared with industry averages, and margins are ticking up nicely as double-digit growth resumes.

Financial Health [A+]	1999	2000	2001	09-02
Long-term Debt $Mil	0	0	0	0
Total Equity $Mil	317	402	479	542
Debt/Equity Ratio	0.0	0.0	0.0	0.0

Gentex hasn't owed a dime since 1992, and boasts more than enough resources to fund growth internally. Earnings are of exceptionally high quality for a fast-growing business, with two thirds of net income converted to free cash flow since 1995.

Industry	Investment Style	Stock Type	Sector
Auto Parts	Mid Growth	Cyclical	Consumer Goods

Competition	Market Cap $Mil	Debt/ Equity	12 Mo Trailing Sales $Mil	Price/Cash Flow	Return On Assets%	Total Return% 1 Yr	3 Yr
Gentex	2,407	0.0	368	24.5	13.6	18.4	7.0
Delphi	4,495	0.9	26,836	3.8	0.5	-39.6	-16.6
Magna International A	4,411	—	11,026	—	—	—	—

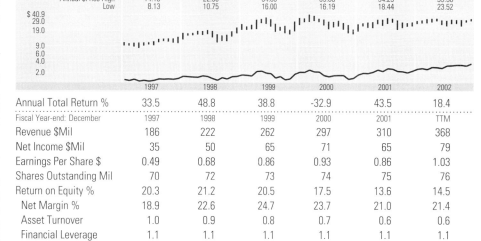

Price Volatility — Monthly Price High/Low — Relative Strength to S&P 500

Annual $Price High/Low	14.13 / 8.13	22.00 / 10.75	34.88 / 16.00	39.88 / 16.19	34.23 / 18.44	33.50 / 23.52
	1997	1998	1999	2000	2001	2002

Annual Total Return %	33.5	48.8	38.8	-32.9	43.5	18.4
Fiscal Year-end: December	1997	1998	1999	2000	2001	TTM
Revenue $Mil	186	222	262	297	310	368
Net Income $Mil	35	50	65	71	65	79
Earnings Per Share $	0.49	0.68	0.86	0.93	0.86	1.03
Shares Outstanding Mil	70	72	73	74	75	76
Return on Equity %	20.3	21.2	20.5	17.5	13.6	14.5
Net Margin %	18.9	22.6	24.7	23.7	21.0	21.4
Asset Turnover	1.0	0.9	0.8	0.7	0.6	0.6
Financial Leverage	1.1	1.1	1.1	1.1	1.1	1.1

Valuation Ratios	Stock	Rel to Industry	Rel to S&P 500
Price/Earnings	30.7	2.4	1.3
Price/Book	4.4	0.2	1.4
Price/Sales	6.5	0.2	3.3
Price/Cash Flow	24.5	0.5	1.8

Major Fund Holders	% of Fund Assets
Columbia Partners Equity	4.60
IDEX Transamerica Growth Opport A	4.56
Transamerica Premier Growth Opp Inv	4.31
WesMark Small Company Growth	3.83

Morningstar's Take By Josh Peters, 11-22-2002 Stock Price as of Analysis: $29.46

Gentex is arguably the best growth story the auto industry has to offer--but don't mistake that for faint praise. In our view, this small company has the potential to evolve into an electronics powerhouse.

Gentex has turned the humble rearview mirror into a gold mine. Its Night Vision Safety (NVS) rearview and side mirrors, which automatically dim when struck with another car's headlights, earn the industry's highest gross margins (40%) and returns on investment (we estimate 50% for 2002). Despite the fierce pressure automakers exert on pricing, they have shown themselves willing to pay up for Gentex's superior technology and quality, buttressed by more than 100 patents. As a result, Gentex dominates its lone competitor with about 80% of the business.

The technology is impressive, but so is Gentex's productivity growth. Since the mid-1990s the price of a basic NVS mirror has dropped 50%, but gross margins have remained essentially the same. A potential competitor would need to duplicate not only the product, but the quality and cost as well. When Toyota tries and fails, we can bet there are some pretty attractive economics at work.

These advantages have blessed debt-free Gentex with strong cash flows and $5 per share in cash and securities. These resources are available for new product development, helping secure the firm's value proposition with cost-conscious automakers.

After stagnating in the late 1990s, revenue growth is surging. NVS mirrors, once exclusive to luxury cars, are finding their way onto many more vehicles. Additional electronic content is another boon, much of it driven by safety (handheld cellular phones replaced by Gentex mirror-mounted microphones) and telematics (like General Motors' OnStar or Johnson Controls' HomeLink). More new products are on tap by middecade, including white LED lighting technology and the SmartBeam system, which automatically dims high beams at night.

We have only two concerns about the Gentex story. First, because our model forecasts double-digit growth in operating earnings for at least the next decade, we're assuming that unknown new products will pick up the slack as mirror-based growth slows. It's also possible that Gentex' lone competitor, recently sold to Magna, could now become a more formidable opponent.

These more distant concerns are offset by our confidence in Gentex's top-flight management and conservative approach. We believe the shares are worth $34.

Genuine Parts GPC

	Rating	Risk	Moat Size	Fair Value	Last Close	Yield %
	★★★	Low	Narrow	$38.00	$30.80	3.8

Company Profile

Genuine Parts is a distributor to independent retail stores. Its NAPA distribution centers sell to more than 6,000 auto parts stores, about 800 of which are company-owned. Motion Industries, its industrial parts division, distributes maintenance, repair, and operations supplies. The company also distributes office supplies and equipment and electrical components. Auto parts operations contribute half of the company's revenue. Less than 10% of Genuine Parts' business is done outside the United States.

Management

CEO Larry Prince, 62, has been with Genuine Parts since the 1970s. He and president and COO Thomas Gallagher, 52, have guided the firm's conservative performance since 1990. Both own a lot of company stock relative to their paychecks.

Strategy

Although its businesses are slow-growing, Genuine Parts is content to simply wring as much cash out of the company as possible and return it to shareholders with dividends and share buybacks. The firm hasn't strayed much from the distribution business; its last acquisition--a distributor of electronics equipment--has caused enough grief to keep management's energy focused.

2999 Circle 75 Parkway
Atlanta, GA 30339
www.genpt.com

Industry	Investment Style	Stock Type	Sector
Auto Retail	▦ Mid Value	✗ High Yield	⊟ Consumer Services

Competition

	Market Cap $Mil	Debt/ Equity	12 Mo Trailing Sales $Mil	Price/Cash Flow	Return On Assets%	Total Return% 1 Yr	3 Yr
Genuine Parts	5,379	0.3	8,213	24.4	-2.4	-13.2	13.5
AutoZone	6,962	1.7	5,326	9.9	12.4	-1.6	32.4
W.W. Grainger	4,714	—	4,634	—	—	—	—

Price Volatility

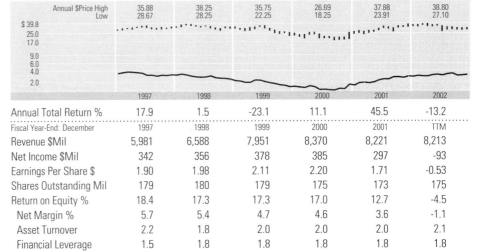

	1997	1998	1999	2000	2001	TTM
Annual $Price High	35.88	38.25	35.75	26.69	37.88	38.80
Low	28.67	28.25	22.25	18.25	23.91	27.10
Annual Total Return %	17.9	1.5	-23.1	11.1	45.5	-13.2

Fiscal Year-End: December

	1997	1998	1999	2000	2001	TTM
Revenue $Mil	5,981	6,588	7,951	8,370	8,221	8,213
Net Income $Mil	342	356	378	385	297	-93
Earnings Per Share $	1.90	1.98	2.11	2.20	1.71	-0.53
Shares Outstanding Mil	179	180	179	175	173	175
Return on Equity %	18.4	17.3	17.3	17.0	12.7	-4.5
Net Margin %	5.7	5.4	4.7	4.6	3.6	-1.1
Asset Turnover	2.2	1.8	2.0	2.0	2.0	2.1
Financial Leverage	1.5	1.8	1.8	1.8	1.8	1.8

Valuation Ratios	Stock	Rel to Industry	Rel to S&P 500
Price/Earnings	NMF	—	—
Price/Book	2.6	1.0	0.8
Price/Sales	0.7	1.0	0.3
Price/Cash Flow	24.4	2.5	1.8

Major Fund Holders	% of Fund Assets
Homestead Value	4.19
Vanguard Selected Value	3.34
SunAmerica Dogs of Wall Street A	3.01
Ave Maria Catholic Values	2.96

Morningstar Grades

Growth [C]	1998	1999	2000	2001
Revenue %	10.1	20.7	5.3	-1.8
Earnings/Share %	4.2	6.6	4.3	-22.3
Book Value/Share %	10.7	6.5	6.1	4.6
Dividends/Share %	4.2	4.0	5.8	3.6

Revenue has been stable, but internal growth has come at a snail's pace. On the basis of the company's sustainable growth ratio, we expect long-term expansion to approximate 3%-5% annually.

Profitability [A]	1999	2000	2001	TTM
Return on Assets %	9.6	9.3	7.1	-2.4
Oper Cash Flow $Mil	368	314	333	220
- Cap Spending $Mil	88	71	42	53
= Free Cash Flow $Mil	279	243	291	167

By keeping a tight rein on capital outlays and paying fat dividends, Genuine Parts has maintained solid returns on capital for an industrial firm. However, margins have dropped in the past few years, reflecting weak results in acquired businesses.

Financial Health [A]	1999	2000	2001	09-02
Long-term Debt $Mil	702	771	836	675
Total Equity $Mil	2,178	2,261	2,345	2,090
Debt/Equity Ratio	0.3	0.3	0.4	0.3

The company boasts a low debt/capital ratio of 26% and a current ratio of 3.3--both conservative marks for such a stable business. Debt rose after a few acquisitions in the late 1990s, but has been declining more recently thanks to strong cash flow.

Morningstar's Take By Josh Peters, 11-06-2002 Stock Price as of Analysis: $30.12

Few businesses match Genuine Parts' consistency. Until last year's recession put a damper on demand, this seemingly humdrum business racked up 51 years of continuously higher sales and 40 years of earnings increases. Even in a tough 2001, sales for Genuine Parts' core auto parts distribution business inched ahead 2%. Enormous buying power, an entrenched network of regional distribution centers, proprietary inventory management systems and the trusted NAPA brand all contribute to solid financial returns.

The modest declines in sales and profit that Genuine Parts has experienced can be attributed to its EIS segment, which distributes equipment used in electrical and electronic manufacturing. But even though this business has restrained the firm's overall performance, an eventual rebound in the electronics industry would give sales a nice boost.

And the most important streak at Genuine Parts, in our view, remains intact: The dividend has risen for 46 years straight, including a 2% boost in 2002. And unlike some firms with laudable dividend histories (i.e. Dana, until last year's cut), Genuine Parts' distributions are well supported by a strong balance sheet and healthy cash flows.

This generous payout doesn't come without a price. Between dividends and share repurchases,

Genuine Parts has distributed 72% of its net income to shareholders over the past six years. Given the low capital requirements and scarce investment opportunities of its businesses, this policy is a wise one, in our opinion. However, this means that Genuine Parts' sustainable growth ratio (return on equity--typically in the low teens--multiplied by the share of profits retained) is less than 5%. We wouldn't expect long-term growth to exceed that mark.

Yet we can't help but admire Genuine Parts' virtually bondlike cash flows and highly disciplined management. If anything, the EIS acquisition reinforced the company's aversion to risk. Consolidation in the industry, led by category killer AutoZone, poses a modest competitive threat, but NAPA is also expanding (conservatively) by expanding its company-owned base of stores and adding service bays to existing locations. Genuine Parts will probably never burn up the track or garner much of the limelight, but its consistency is a feature just about any investor can appreciate.

 MORNINGSTAR® Stocks 500

Genzyme Corporation General Division GENZ

	Rating	Risk	Moat Size	Fair Value	Last Close	Yield %
	★★★	High	Narrow	$35.00	$29.57	0.0

Industry	Investment Style	Stock Type	Sector
Biotechnology	Mid Growth	Spec. Growth	Healthcare

Company Profile

Genzyme General is one of the four divisions of Genzyme Corporation, a biotechnology company. Genzyme General develops and markets therapeutic products and diagnostic products and services. The division has four therapeutic products on the market and is developing other therapeutic products focused on the treatment of genetic disorders and other chronic debilitating diseases. Genzyme General also manufactures and markets diagnostic products, genetic testing services, and pharmaceutical intermediates.

Management

Henri Termeer has helped head up Genzyme for nearly 20 years. Before that, he was an executive at Baxter International. Termeer sits on the boards of BIO and PhRMA, the drug industry's leading lobbying organizations.

Strategy

Genzyme General--the largest of Genzyme Corporation's four divisions--is a tracking stock. Unlike most of its rivals, Genzyme General has a diagnostics division as well as a therapeutics division. The company's pipeline of new drugs focuses on rare genetic diseases--a unique niche. It recently acquired Novazyme, which ties in with its focus on lysosomal storage disorders.

One Kendall Square   www.genzyme.com
Cambridge, MA 02139

Morningstar Grades

Growth [B+]	1998	1999	2000	2001
Revenue %	16.5	8.9	17.0	35.5
Earnings/Share %	51.0	14.9	-20.0	-69.1
Book Value/Share %	11.9	7.7	57.8	1.0
Dividends/Share %	NMF	NMF	NMF	NMF

After a 30% sales increase in 2001, attempts to reduce Renagel inventory and a slowdown in end-user demand have led to dreary sales growth this year. This should pick up if Fabrazyme is approved, but will remain in the midsingle digits otherwise.

Profitability [B+]	1999	2000	2001	TTM
Return on Assets %	8.4	3.7	1.1	2.8
Oper Cash Flow $Mil	204	177	225	219
- Cap Spending $Mil	58	75	184	226
= Free Cash Flow $Mil	146	102	41	-7

Gross margins have been improving, but the company is spending aggressively on marketing and R&D. In addition, Genzyme has been on an acquisition spree that led to $120 million of in-process R&D charges. These ate into the bottom line last year.

Financial Health [A-]	1999	2000	2001	09-02
Long-term Debt $Mil	291	665	845	869
Total Equity $Mil	1,356	2,175	2,609	2,619
Debt/Equity Ratio	0.2	0.3	0.3	0.3

Genzyme can cover its $600 million in debt since it has nearly twice as much in cash and marketable securities. Also, the company generates more than $200 million (23% of sales) in cash from operations.

Competition

Competition	Market Cap $Mil	Debt/ Equity	12 Mo Trailing Sales $Mil	Price/Cash Flow	Return On Assets%	Total Return% 1 Yr	Total Return% 3 Yr
Genzyme Corporation General Division	6,345	0.3	1,296	29.0	2.8	-50.6	13.1
Amgen	61,986	0.2	4,881	31.7	-7.1	-14.4	-6.0
Genentech	17,067	0.0	2,541	28.3	0.2	-38.9	-19.2

Price Volatility

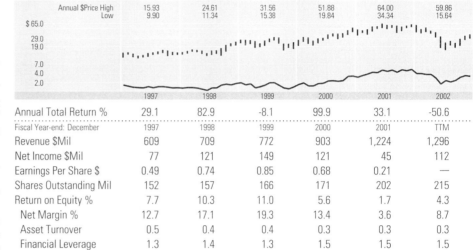

Annual $Price High / Low	15.93 / 9.90	24.61 / 11.34	31.56 / 15.38	51.88 / 19.84	64.00 / 34.34	59.86 / 15.64
	1997	1998	1999	2000	2001	2002
Annual Total Return %	29.1	82.9	-8.1	99.9	33.1	-50.6

Fiscal Year-end: December	1997	1998	1999	2000	2001	TTM
Revenue $Mil	609	709	772	903	1,224	1,296
Net Income $Mil	77	121	149	121	45	112
Earnings Per Share $	0.49	0.74	0.85	0.68	0.21	—
Shares Outstanding Mil	152	157	166	171	202	215
Return on Equity %	7.7	10.3	11.0	5.6	1.7	4.3
Net Margin %	12.7	17.1	19.3	13.4	3.6	8.7
Asset Turnover	0.5	0.4	0.4	0.3	0.3	0.3
Financial Leverage	1.3	1.4	1.3	1.5	1.5	1.5

Valuation Ratios	Stock	Rel to Industry	Rel to S&P 500
Price/Earnings	140.8	3.1	6.0
Price/Book	2.4	0.7	0.8
Price/Sales	4.9	0.4	2.4
Price/Cash Flow	29.0	0.9	2.2

Major Fund Holders	% of Fund Assets
Ariston Convertible Securities	9.68
Eaton Vance Worldwide Health Sci A	5.82
GenomicsFund	4.79
Fidelity Select Biotechnology	4.54

Morningstar's Take By Jill Kiersky, 09-26-2002   Stock Price as of Analysis: $21.37

Genzyme General has been able to do what virtually no other biotech company has done: build a profitable drug-development business model based on small-market diseases.

Because the cost of developing a single drug is so expensive (as much as $800 million) and highly subject to chance, most firms go after diseases that target large markets to provide more assurance of a return on their investment. But Genzyme's model is to target diseases like Gaucher disease, a genetic disorder that affects just 7,500 people worldwide. Most firms won't make the effort for such a small patient population, so Genzyme often has the only product available to treat its targeted diseases. This means it can charge a small fortune. Indeed, patients pay $80,000 a year for Cerezyme, the company's Gaucher drug.

The company also has three other marketed products and a slew of new drugs in late-stage testing, several of which build on its expertise in rare genetic diseases. Cerezyme generates more than $600 million in annual revenue. The company also generates $150 million in diagnostic product sales, and has extended its research into chronic debilitating diseases like Parkinson's and Huntington's diseases.

Genzyme has a leg up on possible competitors with its industry-leading recombinant technologies and enzyme-manufacturing processes. The company maintains gross margins around 75%--on par with its closest rivals, despite producing drugs for small patient populations. We expect margins to improve to 83%-85% as the company goes after more widespread diseases.

But Genzyme's novel drugs are beginning to face competition. The company is engaged in a fierce race with Transkaryotic Therapies for approval to market its treatment for Fabry's disease in the United States. It's not clear which firm will eventually win the fight in the United States--both products are already marketed in Europe--but if Genzyme falls behind, its chances to gain dominant share will be hurt. On top of that, the company could be facing a drop in the $175,000 annual price tag as a result of increased competition.

Any business model based on drug development holds significant risk. Genzyme is no exception, so we would need a 40% discount to our fair value estimate before believing the stock might provide an adequate risk-adjusted return.

Getty Images GYI

	Rating	Risk	Moat Size	Fair Value	Last Close	Yield %
	★	High	Wide	$22.00	$30.55	0.0

Company Profile

Getty Images provides visual content through its Web site and an international network of offices, agents, and distributors. Its offerings include stock film footage and sports, news, reporting, archival, and contemporary stock photographs. The company's clients include advertising agencies, newspapers, magazines, and broadcasters, traditional and new media publishers, and small businesses. The company has more than 70 million images and 30,000 hours of film footage.

Management

There's a lot of insider control. A group of people and entities connected to Getty Images executive chairman Mark Getty owns 21% of the firm, and five of the seven board members have close ties to management. There's also a poison pill provision.

Strategy

After growing quickly through acquisitions, Getty has shifted gears and is focused on generating profits and increasing cash flow. The company is investing in its sports and news segments, which are growing faster than its core business, and will eventually push to expand from stock photography into the larger market for commissioned images.

601 N. 34th Street   www.gettyimages.com
Seattle, WA 98103

Morningstar Grades

Growth [B]	1998	1999	2000	2001
Revenue %	83.6	33.9	95.6	-7.0
Earnings/Share %	NMF	NMF	NMF	NMF
Book Value/Share %	—	NMF	-35.6	-15.7
Dividends/Share %	NMF	NMF	NMF	NMF

Past sales growth was high because of scores of acquisitions. Growth slowed markedly amid a nasty advertising recession, and will probably peak no higher than 12%-15% when the ad market recovers.

Profitability [D+]	1999	2000	2001	TTM
Return on Assets %	-7.2	-15.4	-10.1	-2.4
Oper Cash Flow $Mil	5	38	45	87
- Cap Spending $Mil	52	79	73	43
= Free Cash Flow $Mil	-46	-41	-27	43

Merger and integration costs caused large GAAP losses, but Getty generates positive cash flow from operations and has begun to generate free cash flow. Returns on invested capital should be quite high (30% or more) over the next few years.

Financial Health [D-]	1999	2000	2001	09-02
Long-term Debt $Mil	102	274	256	259
Total Equity $Mil	746	684	599	653
Debt/Equity Ratio	0.1	0.4	0.4	0.4

Good, but not great. Acquisitions caused debt to rise substantially in the past few years, and the company's investments ate up a lot of cash. But with capital expenditures falling and acquisitions in the rearview mirror, Getty should be fine.

Industry	Investment Style	Stock Type	Sector
Business Support	▦ Mid Growth	▓ Spec. Growth	▤ Business Services

Competition	Market Cap $Mil	Debt/ Equity	12 Mo Trailing Sales $Mil	Price/Cash Flow	Return On Assets%	Total Return% 1 Yr	3 Yr
Getty Images	1,634	0.4	447	18.9	-2.4	32.9	-14.6
Corbis	—	—	—	—	—	—	—
Zefa	—	—	—	—	—	—	—

Price Volatility

| Monthly Price High/Low   — Relative Strength to S&P 500

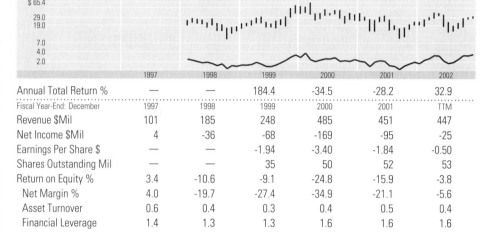

Annual $Price High / Low	28.25 / 8.63	56.13 / 15.88	64.38 / 21.25	37.25 / 9.15	38.48 / 13.19

$65.4 / 29.0 / 19.0 / 7.0 / 4.0 / 2.0

	1997	1998	1999	2000	2001	2002
Annual Total Return %	—	—	184.4	-34.5	-28.2	32.9

Fiscal Year-End: December	1997	1998	1999	2000	2001	TTM
Revenue $Mil	101	185	248	485	451	447
Net Income $Mil	4	-36	-68	-169	-95	-25
Earnings Per Share $	—	—	-1.94	-3.40	-1.84	-0.50
Shares Outstanding Mil	—	—	35	50	52	53
Return on Equity %	3.4	-10.6	-9.1	-24.8	-15.9	-3.8
Net Margin %	4.0	-19.7	-27.4	-34.9	-21.1	-5.6
Asset Turnover	0.6	0.4	0.3	0.4	0.5	0.4
Financial Leverage	1.4	1.3	1.3	1.6	1.6	1.6

Valuation Ratios	Stock	Rel to Industry	Rel to S&P 500
Price/Earnings	NMF	—	—
Price/Book	2.5	0.8	0.8
Price/Sales	3.7	1.7	1.8
Price/Cash Flow	18.9	1.1	1.4

Major Fund Holders	% of Fund Assets
Brown Advisory Small-Cap Growth I	7.29
Baron iOpportunity	4.79
Fremont U.S. Small Cap	3.90
Shaker Interm	3.38

Morningstar's Take By Pat Dorsey, 12-09-2002 Stock Price as of Analysis: $28.54

Getty Images is a great business, and we'd be enthusiastic buyers at the right price.

Getty has consolidated about 25% of the fragmented stock photography market into a single online distribution platform. The huge cost involved in creating this digital platform has created a large barrier to entry for any potential competitor, and this barrier grows with Getty's market share. Since photographers want to distribute their work to the largest possible group of potential customers, they have a strong incentive to work with Getty. The higher the number and quality of the images that Getty distributes, the more customers it will have, which then attracts more images.

Getty also has leverage over its customers and suppliers. The firm's suppliers--pro photographers--are a highly fragmented bunch who compete intensely with one another, limiting their bargaining power. For example, Getty essentially strong-armed them into signing a new contract in 2001 that lowered royalty rates. Getty's customers--marketing firms--are generally not sensitive to price increases. To them, having the perfect image is all that matters.

Finally, Getty's capital needs are relatively low. Although Getty does commission some pictures by paying a photographer to create an image, most of the pictures Getty sells are created by third-party photographers who front the cost themselves. So Getty often doesn't need to pay a photographer until it has been paid by the customer, which results in low working capital needs.

With low capital needs, low competitive threats, and solid pricing power, what's not to like?

Management. Five of the firm's seven directors are closely tied to company cofounder Mark Getty, and a group of insiders connected to Getty controls about 21% of the outstanding shares. Moreover, the firm has issued more than 8 million options over the past two years, a tremendous amount for a company with only 55 million shares outstanding. Finally, we think CEO Jonathan Klein's pay package is excessive: He received 900,000 options between 2000 and 2001, and now has a base salary of $1.1 million--very high for the CEO of a firm with $450 million in annual sales.

The strength of Getty's business outweighs our concerns about management's compensation--though we'd certainly prefer a different use of shareholders' capital. If Getty traded at a 30% discount to our fair value estimate of $22, we'd put it in our portfolio.

MORNINGSTAR® Stocks 500

Gilead Sciences GILD

	Rating	Risk	Moat Size	Fair Value	Last Close	Yield %
	★	High	Narrow	$24.00	$34.00	0.0

Company Profile

Gilead Sciences develops and produces human therapies based on nucleotides, the building blocks of DNA and RNA. Its research and development program focuses on researching small molecules, aptamers, and code blockers to develop potential agents that may treat certain types of vascular and inflammatory diseases, viral infections, and cancer. The company makes AmBisome, a liposome for treating systemic fungal infections. The company also makes Viread, a nucleotide reverse transcriptase inhibitor for slowing the growth of HIV.

Management

John Martin replaced Gilead's founder, Michael Riordan, as CEO in 1996. Martin was previously Bristol-Myers' director of antiviral chemistry. The board is filled with a variety of people, from a Nobel Prize winner to an ex-first lady of California.

Strategy

Gilead Sciences develops original drugs in-house and uses drug-delivery technologies to improve existing products, making them less toxic and more potent. The company has sold its oncology business and is focused on commercializing its largest drugs, Viread for HIV and Hespera for hepatitis B, and expanding the labels for existing products.

333 Lakeside Drive
Foster City, CA 94404
www.gilead.com

Morningstar Grades

Growth [A]	1998	1999	2000	2001
Revenue %	14.3	11.8	15.7	19.5
Earnings/Share %	NMF	NMF	NMF	NMF
Book Value/Share %	-10.8	-13.4	9.9	17.4
Dividends/Share %	NMF	NMF	NMF	NMF

Sales have finally picked up. Even with AmBisome revenue slowing, the company has shown decent 15% average growth over the past four years, and with Viread and Hespera on the market, Gilead should see sales increase rapidly through 2005.

Profitability [B-]	1999	2000	2001	TTM
Return on Assets %	-15.2	-8.4	6.6	19.2
Oper Cash Flow $Mil	-63	-38	-88	43
- Cap Spending $Mil	12	16	26	22
= Free Cash Flow $Mil	-75	-54	-114	21

Sales in 2002 will probably be greater than $400 million, so Gilead should finally reach profitability.

Financial Health [C-]	1999	2000	2001	09-02
Long-term Debt $Mil	92	258	255	250
Total Equity $Mil	297	351	452	523
Debt/Equity Ratio	0.3	0.7	0.6	0.5

The current long-term debt/equity ratio is around 0.5. Debt appears manageable because the firm had $625 million in cash and securities as of September 30. We also believe the company's operating cash flow could be positive at year-end.

Industry	Investment Style	Stock Type	Sector
Biotechnology	▦ Mid Growth	⚅ Spec. Growth	Healthcare

Competition	Market Cap $Mil	Debt/ Equity	12 Mo Trailing Sales $Mil	Price/Cash Flow	Return On Assets%	Total Return% 1 Yr	3 Yr
Gilead Sciences	6,687	0.5	396	153.8	19.2	3.5	36.3
GlaxoSmithKline PLC ADR	116,607	0.3	27,512	6.2	13.9	-22.8	-9.3
Schering-Plough	32,567	—	10,311	14.5	13.3	-36.4	-14.9

Price Volatility

| | | Monthly Price High/Low | | — Relative Strength to S&P 500 | | |

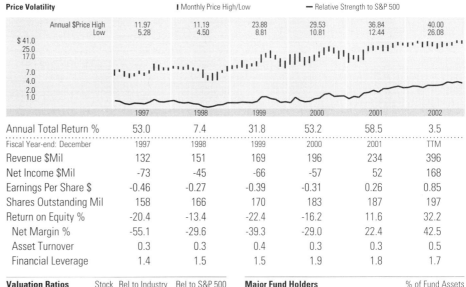

Annual $Price High Low	11.97 5.28	11.19 4.50	23.88 8.81	29.53 10.81	36.84 12.44	40.00 26.08
	1997	1998	1999	2000	2001	2002

Annual Total Return %	53.0	7.4	31.8	53.2	58.5	3.5
Fiscal Year-end: December	1997	1998	1999	2000	2001	TTM
Revenue $Mil	132	151	169	196	234	396
Net Income $Mil	-73	-45	-66	-57	52	168
Earnings Per Share $	-0.46	-0.27	-0.39	-0.31	0.26	0.85
Shares Outstanding Mil	158	166	170	183	187	197
Return on Equity %	-20.4	-13.4	-22.4	-16.2	11.6	32.2
Net Margin %	-55.1	-29.6	-39.3	-29.0	22.4	42.5
Asset Turnover	0.3	0.3	0.4	0.3	0.3	0.5
Financial Leverage	1.4	1.5	1.5	1.9	1.8	1.7

Valuation Ratios	Stock	Rel to Industry	Rel to S&P 500
Price/Earnings	40.0	0.9	1.7
Price/Book	12.8	3.6	4.0
Price/Sales	16.9	1.3	8.4
Price/Cash Flow	153.8	4.8	11.6

Major Fund Holders	% of Fund Assets
GenomicsFund	14.60
Fidelity Select Biotechnology	11.70
Fidelity Advisor Biotechnology A	10.14
Alliance Select Investor Biotech A	7.16

Morningstar's Take By Jill Kiersky, 11-14-2002 Stock Price as of Analysis: $37.58

Gilead Sciences has finally turned the corner to profitability. It has had several product wins over the past two years and has built a reputation for successfully developing anti-infective drugs. We would like the stock at the right price, but Gilead lacks a strong pipeline, so that price would have to provide a big discount to our fair value estimate to compensate investors for the firm's longer-term risks.

Gilead's main source of growth has been AmBisome, the dominant treatment for fungal infections. Its sales of nearly $180 million account for three fourths of the company's product revenue. But sales are slowing, and Gilead's four older commercial products, including influenza vaccine Tamiflu, have not provided remarkable revenue to date.

Now the company has Viread, approved in October 2001. The nucleotide reverse transcriptase inhibitor slows replication of HIV and is approved for all HIV-infected patients, not just those resistant to alternative medications. With a stronger resistance and safety profile, Viread has come on strong, gaining 13% market share with $200 million in sales.

Gilead's next big drug, Hespera, was approved in September 2002. It blocks the hepatitis B virus from reproducing in the body and has proved effective in patients resistant to GlaxoSmithKline's lamivudine,

which had sales of $225 million in 2001. Hespera could provide a similar revenue stream (or about one fourth of product sales) by 2006.

The issue plaguing Gilead isn't short-term sales growth; it's that the company has little else in its product pipeline to support long-term growth. The majority of its research is focused on expanding the uses for existing products and seeking approval in new markets, like Japan. The company recently ended its license agreement for pneumonia drug candidate Cidecin because the drug failed to reach primary goals. Gilead doesn't have much else in the works.

Now that Gilead's operating cash flow has turned positive, and free cash flow (cash from operations minus capital expenditures) should creep into the black in 2003, the company is in decent financial health. It also has enough cash to cover debt and operating expenses, leaving the company in a good position to acquire new products for its otherwise slim pipeline.

Gilead's new products should carry the firm for the next few years, but until the company has something that gives us more confidence in its long-term growth, we'd look for a big margin of safety before buying.

Gillette G

	Rating	Risk	Moat Size	Fair Value	Last Close	Yield %
	★★★	Med.	Wide	$30.00	$30.36	2.1

Company Profile

Gillette produces toiletry and health-care products. Its Braun division markets electric shavers and coffeemakers in Europe, North America, and Japan. The company also makes Right Guard, Soft & Dri, and Dry Idea deodorants; Gillette Sensor and Mach3 razors and blades; Oral-B dental-care products; Thermoscan ear thermometers; and Duracell batteries. Foreign sales account for about 60% of the company's sales. Gillette sold its stationery products operations to Newell Rubbermaid in December 2000.

Management

CEO James Kilts, who as Nabisco's former chief spearheaded that firm's turnaround, joined Gillette in February 2001. Interim head Ed DeGraan, who had led the company since Michael Hawley's ouster in October 2000, returned to his former post as COO.

Strategy

Gillette intends to focus on its high-margin shaving and Duracell units and boost profitability at its Braun business. Its strategy has always been to increase margins with higher-priced product reformulations that can be made more cheaply. Meanwhile, it is buying back stock to revive its earnings-per-share growth and is striving to decrease working capital.

Prudential Tower Building   www.gillette.com
Boston, MA 02199

Morningstar Grades

Growth [C-]

	1998	1999	2000	2001
Revenue %	0.7	-1.4	1.7	-2.9
Earnings/Share %	-23.4	20.0	-67.5	132.4
Book Value/Share %	-7.0	-31.2	-32.5	11.2
Dividends/Share %	18.8	16.3	11.4	2.4

Sales growth has suffered amid bloated inventories and a botched strategy for Duracell. Achieving historical annual sales growth of 5.5% is possible, though growth in profits will likely be well below the historical 10%.

Profitability [A]

	1999	2000	2001	TTM
Return on Assets %	10.7	3.8	9.1	10.7
Oper Cash Flow $Mil	1,427	1,604	2,092	2,332
- Cap Spending $Mil	889	793	624	453
= Free Cash Flow $Mil	538	811	1,468	1,879

Gillette consistently achieves above-average returns on equity of 35%. That may be lower in future years, but net margins should benefit from current restructuring plans.

Financial Health [A-]

	1999	2000	2001	09-02
Long-term Debt $Mil	2,931	1,650	1,654	1,852
Total Equity $Mil	2,975	1,924	2,137	2,544
Debt/Equity Ratio	1.0	0.9	0.8	0.7

Earnings before interest and taxes cover interest expense 10 times, making the company financially sound and its dividend safe.

Industry	Investment Style	Stock Type	Sector
Household & Personal Products	Large Core	→ Slow Growth	Consumer Goods

Competition

	Market Cap $Mil	Debt/ Equity	12 Mo Trailing Sales $Mil	Price/Cash Flow	Return On Assets%	Total Return% 1 Yr	3 Yr
Gillette	41,593	0.7	9,219	17.8	10.7	-7.3	-6.7
Procter & Gamble	111,662	0.9	41,268	13.3	11.0	11.3	-4.5
Unilever NV ADR	35,272	—	46,553	—	—	—	—

Price Volatility

	Monthly Price High/Low	— Relative Strength to S&P 500				
Annual $Price High Low	53.19 / 36.00	62.59 / 35.31	64.38 / 33.06	43.00 / 27.19	36.38 / 24.50	37.30 / 27.57
	1997	1998	1999	2000	2001	2002
Annual Total Return %	30.4	-3.9	-12.8	-10.7	-5.5	-7.3

Fiscal Year-End: December

	1997	1998	1999	2000	2001	TTM
Revenue $Mil	9,138	9,200	9,074	9,225	8,961	9,219
Net Income $Mil	1,427	1,081	1,260	392	910	1,070
Earnings Per Share $	1.24	0.95	1.14	0.37	0.86	1.01
Shares Outstanding Mil	1,124	1,126	1,096	1,059	1,058	1,370
Return on Equity %	29.5	24.3	42.4	20.4	42.6	42.1
Net Margin %	15.6	11.8	13.9	4.2	10.2	11.6
Asset Turnover	0.9	0.8	0.8	0.9	0.9	0.9
Financial Leverage	2.0	2.7	4.0	5.4	4.7	3.9

Valuation Ratios	Stock	Rel to Industry	Rel to S&P 500
Price/Earnings	30.1	1.2	1.3
Price/Book	16.4	1.8	5.1
Price/Sales	4.5	1.7	2.2
Price/Cash Flow	17.8	1.3	1.3

Major Fund Holders	% of Fund Assets
New Market	6.06
Smith Barney Large Cap Growth A	5.02
Shepherd Large Cap Growth	4.45
AmSouth Select Equity B	4.38

Morningstar's Take By Carl Sibilski, 12-15-2002 Stock Price as of Analysis: $30.37

Initial results have set high expectations for a successful turnaround at Gillette. Even so, we think investors should seek at least a 20% discount to our fair value estimate before buying the shares.

Gillette's razor business has been phenomenally successful. Despite having to pay a price 20% higher than on previous razor products, consumers have quickly accepted new razors like the Mach3 and Mach3 Turbo. It's these kinds of products that help the company consistently earn above-average returns on equity of 35%.

The company's other products would appear to have similar characteristics to the razors and blades business, but they haven't been as successful. This may be a simple case of poor execution. For example, like razors, Oral-B power toothbrushes use disposable brush tips. However, Gillette was late to market with its Oral-B product, and Procter & Gamble's early push of the Crest power toothbrush has gained more market share as a result.

Improving execution is a big part of Gillette's turnaround plan. The company has freed up working capital by improving efficiency in collections and inventory management. On average, Gillette now collects its trade receivables in 81 days, down from 110 in 2000. Similarly, it holds inventory for about

108 days, down from 122 in 2000. The company can use the resulting capital for more-productive uses like paying down debt or investing in product innovation.

The Duracell battery unit still poses a problem for the company. Once again, applying the razor model to another business hasn't taken hold. The company's attempt to shift battery consumers into the premium-price Duracell Ultra from the lower-price CopperTop resulted in lost market share and reduced overall profitability.

In our opinion, the battery business might just be a dud. The problem is that, unlike razors, consumers aren't very brand-loyal when it comes to batteries. Even a quick survey of Morningstar.com readers shows that consumer battery preferences are determined mostly by price. That sounds like a low-margin, commoditylike business to us, and at 27% of sales it's a heavy anchor for the company to drag as it seeks to achieve long-term profit growth.

Even though we believe Gillette will have operational success, because of the battery business it's hard for us to value this stock any higher than $30.

MORNINGSTAR® Stocks 500

GlaxoSmithKline PLC ADR GSK

	Rating	Risk	Moat Size	Fair Value	Last Close	Yield %
	★★★★	Low	Wide	$42.00	$37.46	3.1

Company Profile

GlaxoSmithKline develops and manufactures pharmaceuticals. It is the result of a 1999 merger between Glaxo Wellcome and SmithKline Beecham and is the second-largest pharmaceutical company in the world. It competes in a myriad of health-care sectors. Its major products are Paxil for depression, antibacterial Augmentin, Advair and Flovent for asthma, and Avandia for Type II diabetes. Glaxo also produces vaccines and consumer products like Aquafresh and Nicorette. Drug sales account for about 85% of revenue. Approximately 75% of revenue comes from outside Europe.

Management

Glaxo's board is a who's who of British elite. Christopher Hogg took the helm as chairman in May 2002. Before becoming CEO, Jean-Pierre Garnier headed SmithKline's U.S. pharmaceutical operations.

Strategy

GlaxoSmithKline is the number-two drugmaker based on sales. Scale and diversity play an important role in Glaxo's strategy. It has cut billions from operating costs as a result of the merger and is always eyeing acquisition candidates. Glaxo competes in a number of different therapeutic areas but is especially strong in the central nervous system, respiratory, and antiviral markets.

Glaxo Wellcome House   www.glaxosmithkline.com
Greenford, Middlesex, UB6 0NN

Morningstar Grades

Growth [C+]	1998	1999	2000	2001
Revenue %	1.8	5.0	7.6	13.3
Earnings/Share %	-15.6	17.5	46.2	-26.1
Book Value/Share %	28.2	22.9	42.0	-2.2
Dividends/Share %	2.9	2.8	2.7	2.6

Revenue growth is nothing to brag about, but given its size, Glaxo is holding its own. Revenue increased 7.4% in the first nine months of 2002. Scale and merger savings are helping Glaxo expand its net margins at a slightly faster pace.

Profitability [A+]	1999	2000	2001	TTM
Return on Assets %	15.3	19.6	13.9	13.9
Oper Cash Flow $Mil	7,795	8,280	9,382	9,382
- Cap Spending $Mil	3,627	498	2,565	2,565
= Free Cash Flow $Mil	4,168	7,782	6,817	6,817

Operating margins are improving but remain below peer averages. Even with a generic version of Augmentin introduced during the third quarter, operating margins for the first nine months of 2002, including restructuring costs, still averaged 27%.

Financial Health [A]	1999	2000	2001	12-01
Long-term Debt $Mil	3,297	2,827	3,330	3,330
Total Equity $Mil	8,813	11,509	10,894	10,894
Debt/Equity Ratio	0.4	0.2	0.3	0.3

Since Glaxo's corporate credit rating is only one notch below triple A, we're not worried about default on its $4 billion in long-term debt. The firm is also sitting on more than $3.6 billion in cash and $5 billion in long-term investments.

Industry	Investment Style	Stock Type	Sector
Drugs	Large Growth	High Yield	Healthcare

Competition	Market Cap $Mil	Debt/ Equity	12 Mo Trailing Sales $Mil	Price/Cash Flow	Return On Assets%	Total Return% 1 Yr	3 Yr
GlaxoSmithKline PLC ADR	57,810	0.3	29,541	6.2	13.9	-22.8	-9.3
AstraZeneca PLC ADR	61,408	0.1	16,663	16.3	16.5	-23.4	-1.7
Bristol-Myers Squibb	44,843	0.6	17,588	19.2	11.3	-52.4	-23.7

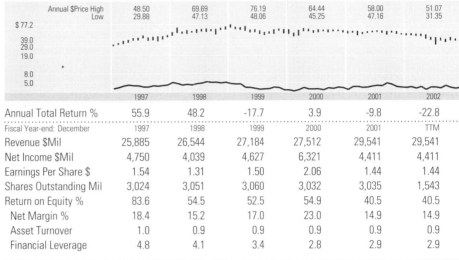

Price Volatility — Monthly Price High/Low — Relative Strength to S&P 500

	1997	1998	1999	2000	2001	2002
Annual $Price High	48.50	69.69	76.19	64.44	58.00	51.07
Low	29.88	47.13	48.06	45.25	47.16	31.35

Annual Total Return %	55.9	48.2	-17.7	3.9	-9.8	-22.8

Fiscal Year-end: December	1997	1998	1999	2000	2001	TTM
Revenue $Mil	25,885	26,544	27,184	27,512	29,541	29,541
Net Income $Mil	4,750	4,039	4,627	6,321	4,411	4,411
Earnings Per Share $	1.54	1.31	1.50	2.06	1.44	1.44
Shares Outstanding Mil	3,024	3,051	3,060	3,032	3,035	1,543
Return on Equity %	83.6	54.5	52.5	54.9	40.5	40.5
Net Margin %	18.4	15.2	17.0	23.0	14.9	14.9
Asset Turnover	1.0	0.9	0.9	0.9	0.9	0.9
Financial Leverage	4.8	4.1	3.4	2.8	2.9	2.9

Valuation Ratios	Stock	Rel to Industry	Rel to S&P 500
Price/Earnings	26.0	1.1	1.1
Price/Book	5.3	0.7	1.7
Price/Sales	2.0	0.5	1.0
Price/Cash Flow	6.2	0.3	0.5

Major Fund Holders	% of Fund Assets
Putnam Health Sciences A	5.74
ProFunds Europe 30 Svc	4.76
ICAP Euro Select Equity	4.43
Saratoga International Equity I	4.00

Morningstar's Take By Todd N. Lebor, 11-25-2002 Stock Price as of Analysis: $39.44

British drug juggernaut GlaxoSmithKline is like a nuclear submarine on cruise control: It's large but inconspicuous, has thousands of moving parts, and can withstand a blow or two. We think its diversified dullness makes it a low-risk choice in the global drug arena.

Glaxo's main appeal is its girth. It has a portfolio of 1,000-plus products sold in more than 140 countries. The firm doesn't depend on any one therapeutic area, either. Central nervous system and respiratory treatments are the main breadwinners, but they provide less than half of total pharmaceutical sales. Antivirals and antibacterials combine for another 25%, while vaccines contribute 6%-8% of total pharmaceutical sales.

Consumer products--15% of firmwide sales--also help stabilize Glaxo with steady, albeit slower-growing, revenue. The consumer unit, with products like Aquafresh and Nicorette, provides a respectable operating margin of 13%-15%.

We like how Glaxo's management team milks every penny out of the company's chemical entities, especially with respect to its HIV and respiratory franchises. These units have topnotch drugs that the company defends well with line extensions and combination products.

Glaxo's girth can also be a drawback, though. With more than $30 billion in annual revenue, the company has a hard time finding enough new products each year to sustain decent growth. That said, Glaxo doesn't need double-digit top-line growth to provide investors with an adequate risk-adjusted return. The company's restructuring is yielding cost savings that are boosting margins to competitive levels. For example, operating margins, excluding charges, for the nine months ended September 30, 2002, were 31.2% compared with 29.8% two years earlier. Also, as Glaxo increases its exposure to the United States (55% of sales in 2002 compared with 46% in 1999), where prices aren't restricted, we expect more margin improvement.

With less than 50% of total revenue coming from its top 10 drugs, Glaxo is one of the lowest-risk drug companies out there, in our opinion. Its staying power is bolstered by 17,000 sales reps and $4-$5 billion in annual free cash flow (cash flow from operations less capital expenditures). Glaxo isn't shy about using its cash to license promising drug candidates or partner with up-and-coming biotechs.

We think Glaxo is a good pharma to invest in, and would require only a 20% discount to our fair value estimate before buying.

GlobespanVirata GSPN

	Rating	Risk	Moat Size	Fair Value	Last Close	Yield %
	★★★	High	None	$6.00	$4.41	0.0

Company Profile

GlobespanVirata develops semiconductor products for telecom and networking gear that allows Web users to access the Internet with high-speed connections. The firm specializes in digital subscriber line technology and its products are highly programmable. Customers include Lucent and Cisco, while telecom providers like Qwest and Sprint ultimately deploy these DSL services. GlobespanVirata outsources the production of its products and markets them both in the United States and overseas.

Management

Globespan CEO Armando Geday heads the merged firm, while Virata CEO Charles Cotton is now executive chairman.

Strategy

GlobespanVirata looks to increase its leadership in the market for chips used in DSL equipment. To do this, it is trying to expand its product line and customer base, as well as increase the amount of technology and chip content it supplies in its customers' equipment. The company outsources its chip production.

100 Shulz Drive   www.globespan.net
Red Bank, NJ 07701

Industry	Investment Style	Stock Type	Sector
Semiconductors	Small Growth	Spec. Growth	Hardware

Competition

	Market Cap $Mil	Debt/ Equity	12 Mo Trailing Sales $Mil	Price/Cash Flow	Return On Assets%	Total Return% 1 Yr	3 Yr
GlobespanVirata	576	0.3	238	—	-96.1	-66.0	-43.7
Texas Instruments	25,982	0.1	8,024	12.8	0.9	-46.2	-32.5
STMicroelectronics NV	17,362	—	6,357	—	—	—	—

Price Volatility   ❙ Monthly Price High/Low   ━ Relative Strength to S&P 500

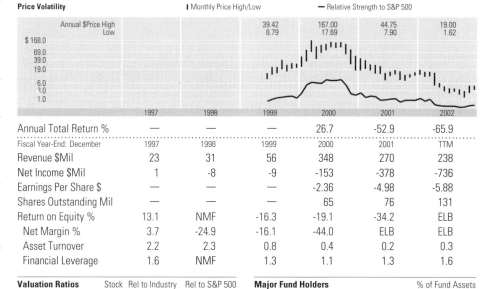

	1997	1998	1999	2000	2001	2002
Annual $Price High			39.42	167.00	44.75	19.00
Low			8.79	17.69	7.90	1.62

Annual Total Return %	—	—	—	26.7	-52.9	-65.9

Fiscal Year-End: December	1997	1998	1999	2000	2001	TTM
Revenue $Mil	23	31	56	348	270	238
Net Income $Mil	1	-8	-9	-153	-378	-736
Earnings Per Share $	—	—	—	-2.36	-4.98	-5.88
Shares Outstanding Mil	—	—	—	65	76	131
Return on Equity %	13.1	NMF	-16.3	-19.1	-34.2	ELB
Net Margin %	3.7	-24.9	-16.1	-44.0	ELB	ELB
Asset Turnover	2.2	2.3	0.8	0.4	0.2	0.3
Financial Leverage	1.6	NMF	1.3	1.1	1.3	1.6

Valuation Ratios	Stock	Rel to Industry	Rel to S&P 500
Price/Earnings	NMF	—	—
Price/Book	1.2	0.4	0.4
Price/Sales	2.4	0.6	1.2
Price/Cash Flow	—	—	—

Major Fund Holders	% of Fund Assets
Jacob Internet	3.37
Firsthand Technology Innovators	3.25
Schneider Small Cap Value	2.02
Black Oak Emerging Technology	1.71

Morningstar Grades

Growth [A-]	1998	1999	2000	2001
Revenue %	39.6	78.7	519.2	-22.5
Earnings/Share %	NMF	NMF	NMF	NMF
Book Value/Share %	—	—	NMF	17.6
Dividends/Share %	NMF	NMF	NMF	NMF

Sales grew 500% in 2000 to nearly $350 million, but dipped 23% in 2001 as the result of a massive slowdown in telecom capital spending. Sales will probably fall in 2002 despite the boost from last year's acquisition of Virata.

Profitability [F]	1999	2000	2001	TTM
Return on Assets %	-12.7	-16.9	-26.0	-96.1
Oper Cash Flow $Mil	-13	7	-11	-55
- Cap Spending $Mil	1	19	9	40
= Free Cash Flow $Mil	-14	-12	-19	-95

Gross margins are decent at more than 50%, but are falling because of declining average chip prices. The firm is unprofitable, but we think that will change as operating expenses decline as a percentage of sales.

Financial Health [C]	1999	2000	2001	09-02
Long-term Debt $Mil	0	3	132	130
Total Equity $Mil	55	804	1,104	483
Debt/Equity Ratio	0.0	0.0	0.1	0.3

With net cash of about $425 million, GlobespanVirata has a very strong balance sheet. This financial health will be handy, especially if the current downturn persists longer than expected.

Morningstar's Take By Jeremy Lopez, 12-17-2002 Stock Price as of Analysis: $4.39

GlobespanVirata looks undervalued, but not enough for us to recommend the stock.

Worldwide demand for digital subscriber line Internet services remains a positive for Globespan. Domestic DSL subscriber growth has been disappointing, thanks to anemic capital spending and competition from cable modem access. But growth abroad is strong, especially in Asia, where DSL service has penetrated 26% of all South Korean phone lines. Worldwide subscribers tripled in 2001 to roughly 19 million, and could nearly double in 2002. Because DSL penetration in technologically advanced countries like Japan and the United States is still relatively low, we think subscriber growth will continue at a nice pace in the coming years.

Globespan's position as a supplier of DSL equipment is strong. One of the firm's competitive advantages is its relatively large R&D budget dedicated solely to developing DSL chips. Few other chipmakers, if any, devote $140 million per year to DSL research and development; this keeps Globespan technologically ahead of peers. The firm also supplies DSL products for all the different flavors of DSL technology (standards are fragmented). This is very appealing to telecom carriers and equipment makers because they want to minimize their own R&D

efforts. The merger with Virata in 2001 has only strengthened the firm's product portfolio.

However, tough competition in DSL chips is a significant hurdle for Globespan. With large chipmakers like Texas Instruments, Analog Devices, and STMicroelectronics all breathing down the small chipmaker's neck, it will be a challenge for Globespan to generate strong, sustainable long-term margins and returns on capital. Competitors are already driving chip prices down and pressuring Globespan's market share. An inventory glut has exacerbated a fall in chip prices, but the competition is here to stay.

The negatives surrounding Globespan--competition, price erosion, and weak U.S. DSL demand--are no small matter. But the firm should partially offset these by jamming more chip content into its products and entering new niches. Also, Globespan has net cash of about $425 million, which represents more than 70% of its market capitalization. But given the risks of owning a small chipmaker like Globespan, investors should wait until the stock trades at a 50% discount to our fair value estimate before jumping in.

Morningstar® Stocks 500

Golden West Financial GDW

	Rating	Risk	Moat Size	Fair Value	Last Close	Yield %
	★★★	Low	Narrow	$67.00	$71.81	0.4

Company Profile

Golden West Financial is the holding company for bank subsidiaries that operate 414 savings and lending offices in 32 states. The banks provide savings, checking, money market, and individual retirement accounts, as well as certificates of deposit. In addition, the banks originate real-estate and consumer loans. Real-estate loans for single-family residences account for approximately 93% of the company's total loan portfolio. Certificates of deposit make up about 65% of the company's total deposits.

Management

Husband and wife Herbert and Marion Sandler are co-CEOs and built the bank practically from the ground up after buying it in 1963. They own 20% of the stock and are dedicated to staying independent, so a sale is unlikely.

Strategy

Golden West's business is primarily residential adjustable-rate mortgages, which have a floating rate typically after three to five years. It makes money on the difference between the mortgage yield and the cost of making the loan. The bank keeps costs at a minimum; for example, it encourages certificates of deposits, which are usually less costly than checking accounts to maintain.

1901 Harrison Street   www.gdw.com
Oakland, CA 94612

Morningstar Grades

Growth [B+]

	1998	1999	2000	2001
Revenue %	6.4	-4.2	33.3	12.4
Earnings/Share %	22.8	14.3	18.8	48.7
Book Value/Share %	15.9	5.9	20.6	16.0
Dividends/Share %	13.2	12.1	14.2	18.2

Growth is tied to the cyclicality of interest rates, which creates volatility in the revenue stream. But thrifts are judged more on profit growth and, in the past three years, Golden West's has been in the double digits.

Profitability [B-]

	1999	2000	2001	TTM
Return on Assets %	1.1	1.0	1.4	1.4
Oper Cash Flow $Mil	511	649	1,266	—
- Cap Spending $Mil	38	62	55	—
= Free Cash Flow $Mil	—	—	—	—

Return on equity is around 20%, very strong for a thrift. Low interest rates are part of the story as margins have widened, but further cost improvements have helped as well.

Financial Health [B]

	1999	2000	2001	09-02
Long-term Debt $Mil	—	—	—	—
Total Equity $Mil	3,195	3,687	4,284	4,794
Debt/Equity Ratio	—	—	—	—

Its financial leverage has decreased the past six quarters, making the high return on equity more impressive. Also, Golden West's nonperforming assets/total assets ratio, a measure of credit quality, is among the lowest in the industry.

Industry	Investment Style	Stock Type	Sector
Savings & Loans	▦ Large Core	↗ Classic Growth	$ Financial Services

Competition	Market Cap $Mil	Debt/ Equity	12 Mo Trailing Sales $Mil	Price/Cash Flow	Return On Assets%	Total Return% 1 Yr	3 Yr
Golden West Financial	11,020	—	3,809	—	1.4	22.6	34.1
Wells Fargo	79,608	—	28,119	—	1.5	10.3	10.4
US Bancorp	40,630	—	15,324	—	1.8	5.2	11.7

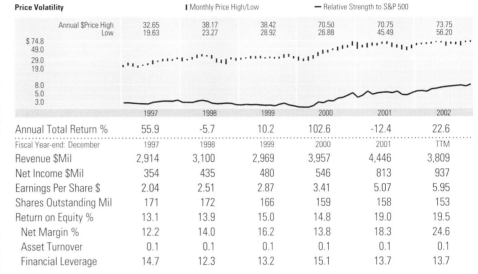

Price Volatility ▮ Monthly Price High/Low — Relative Strength to S&P 500

Annual $Price	High	32.65	38.17	38.42	70.50	70.75	73.75
	Low	19.63	23.27	28.92	26.88	45.49	56.20

	1997	1998	1999	2000	2001	2002
Annual Total Return %	55.9	-5.7	10.2	102.6	-12.4	22.6

Fiscal Year-end: December	1997	1998	1999	2000	2001	TTM
Revenue $Mil	2,914	3,100	2,969	3,957	4,446	3,809
Net Income $Mil	354	435	480	546	813	937
Earnings Per Share $	2.04	2.51	2.87	3.41	5.07	5.95
Shares Outstanding Mil	171	172	166	159	158	153
Return on Equity %	13.1	13.9	15.0	14.8	19.0	19.5
Net Margin %	12.2	14.0	16.2	13.8	18.3	24.6
Asset Turnover	0.1	0.1	0.1	0.1	0.1	0.1
Financial Leverage	14.7	12.3	13.2	15.1	13.7	13.7

Valuation Ratios	Stock	Rel to Industry	Rel to S&P 500
Price/Earnings	12.1	1.0	0.5
Price/Book	2.3	1.4	0.7
Price/Sales	2.9	1.3	1.4
Price/Cash Flow	—	—	—

Major Fund Holders	% of Fund Assets
Vontobel U.S. Value	4.87
FBR Financial Services	4.80
DEM Equity Institutional	4.54
Fidelity Select Home Finance	4.41

Morningstar's Take By Richard McCaffery, 09-30-2002 Stock Price as of Analysis: $62.18

Every happy thrift is alike; every unhappy thrift is unhappy in its own way.

Golden West, the second-largest thrift in the United States, has plenty to smile about. A well-run bank is a nicely profitable business. Management needs to instill a strong sales culture, control costs, and properly manage risk. Do that and you can achieve a decent average return on equity in a range of interest rate environments.

Golden West looks slightly undervalued at less than 11 times forward earnings. The company is a case study in how to run a business: strong credit quality, healthy capital levels, reasonable growth rates, clear presentation of financials, and a management team that owns a significant portion of the common stock.

Part of the secret for Golden West is its cost structure. Golden West's efficiency ratio, which measures how much it costs to produce $1 of revenue, is routinely less than 30%. Even highly regarded Washington Mutual, known for its lean cost structure, normally has an efficiency ratio in the mid-40s. It's not an exact comparison since WaMu is much more a full-service bank than Golden West, but the difference is telling.

Of course, just because it runs at the front of the

herd doesn't mean it's not one of the pack. Golden West faces the same risks and limitations as other thrifts. Most of its income comes from the spread earned on loans, which means interest rates strongly influence profitability. The bulk of the company's portfolio is composed of adjustable-rate mortgages, which reduces exposure to swings in interest rates, but there's still a lag effect visible on the bottom line. Also, return on assets is low because the business is extremely capital-intensive.

Golden West has done well of late, benefiting from the low rate environment, which has stretched margins, and the refinance boom, which has helped loan production. As management points out, the fact that it's been able to modestly expand the balance sheet in a period when everybody wants to buy fixed-rate loans says a lot about the company's sales culture.

There will be ups and downs in the housing market, but we believe the secular trend is strong as the number of American homeowners increases and the population ages. Golden West is well positioned to take advantage of this trend.

Goldman Sachs Group GS

	Rating ★★★	Risk Med.	Moat Size Narrow	Fair Value $75.00	Last Close $68.10	Yield % 0.7

Company Profile

Goldman Sachs Group provides investment banking and security services worldwide. The company's principal business lines include investment banking, trading and principal investments, as well as asset management and securities services. Its services include equity and debt underwriting, financial restructuring advisory, bank loans, commodities investment, currency investment, asset-management commissions, institutional asset management, margin lending, and real-estate advisory.

Management

Henry Paulson is in the top spot after Jon Corzine, who had led the company since 1994, stepped down when the firm went public. Paulson is aggressive about Goldman's having the size and scale to compete in the consolidating brokerage industry.

Strategy

Goldman Sachs plans to use its well-known brand and massive trading network to expand outside the United States. The other major strategy is to build areas that have stable yet growing revenue streams, like asset management, to reduce the volatility of earnings. Its acquisition of Spear, Leeds & Kellogg fits into this picture by providing recurring trading fees.

85 Broad Street
New York, NY 10004

www.gs.com

Industry	Investment Style	Stock Type	Sector
Securities	▦ Large Value	➡ Slow Growth	$ Financial Services

Competition

	Market Cap $Mil	Debt/ Equity	12 Mo Trailing Sales $Mil	Price/Cash Flow	Return On Assets%	Total Return% 1 Yr	3 Yr
Goldman Sachs Group	32,608	—	23,924	—	0.6	-26.1	-5.8
Citigroup	177,948	—	106,096	—	1.6	-24.2	1.1
Morgan Stanley	43,977	—	32,954	—	0.6	-27.2	-12.5

Price Volatility

▮ Monthly Price High/Low — Relative Strength to S&P 500

				94.81 55.19	133.63 65.50	120.00 63.27	97.25 58.57

$ 134.6
99.0
69.0
49.0
29.0
19.0
9.0
6.0

	1997	1998	1999	2000	2001	2002
Annual Total Return %	—	—	—	14.1	-12.8	-26.1

Fiscal Year-End: November	1997	1998	1999	2000	2001	TTM
Revenue $Mil	20,433	22,478	25,363	33,000	31,138	23,924
Net Income $Mil	2,746	2,428	2,708	3,067	2,310	2,106
Earnings Per Share $	—	—	—	6.00	4.26	3.97
Shares Outstanding Mil	—	—	—	485	510	479
Return on Equity %	45.0	38.5	26.7	18.6	12.7	11.2
Net Margin %	13.4	10.8	10.7	9.3	7.4	8.8
Asset Turnover	0.1	0.1	0.1	0.1	0.1	0.1
Financial Leverage	29.2	32.6	24.5	17.2	17.1	18.5

Valuation Ratios	Stock	Rel to Industry	Rel to S&P 500
Price/Earnings	17.2	1.0	0.7
Price/Book	1.7	1.0	0.5
Price/Sales	1.4	1.0	0.7
Price/Cash Flow	—	—	—

Major Fund Holders	% of Fund Assets
Kelmoore Strategy C	15.01
Fidelity Select Brokerage & Investmnt	5.70
Wells Fargo Large Co Growth I	5.22
John Hancock Financial Industries A	4.93

Morningstar Grades

Growth [C]	1998	1999	2000	2001
Revenue %	10.0	12.8	30.1	-5.6
Earnings/Share %	NMF	NMF	NMF	-29.0
Book Value/Share %	—	—	NMF	4.0
Dividends/Share %	NMF	NMF	100.0	0.0

Thanks to a strong market for stock offerings, Goldman's five-year revenue growth outshines most rivals'. But those days are over. We expect the firm's revenue in 2003 to be up only modestly from the weak performances of this year and last.

Profitability [C]	1999	2000	2001	TTM
Return on Assets %	1.1	1.1	0.7	0.6
Oper Cash Flow $Mil	-12,589	11,135	-15,176	—
- Cap Spending $Mil	656	1,552	1,370	—
= Free Cash Flow $Mil	—	—	—	—

The market downturn has eaten into profits. Last year, Goldman's return on equity slipped to 13% and it's up only modestly this year. But the firm shies away from long-term employment contracts, which gives it greater cost-cutting flexibility.

Financial Health [B+]	1999	2000	2001	08-02
Long-term Debt $Mil	—	—	—	—
Total Equity $Mil	10,145	16,530	18,231	18,844
Debt/Equity Ratio	—	—	—	—

Goldman employs a large amount of leverage, like other investment banks. But its equity base has been a bit bigger than most, primarily because of its recent money-raising IPO. We expect the firm's capital ratios to fall in line with the industry over time.

Morningstar's Take By Craig Woker, 10-28-2002 Stock Price as of Analysis: $73.58

Goldman Sachs is the investment bank that rivals aspire to be. The firm typically lands at the top of the underwriting and merger advisory league tables, the measuring stick of success in this industry. But Goldman's cachet and the firm's propensity to beat up on rivals are not reason enough to overpay for this investment. We would demand a much bigger discount to our fair value estimate before buying the stock.

We believe Goldman is worth about $75 per share. Before we would consider buying one of the most volatile stocks in a notoriously volatile industry, we would need a discount of at least 40% to this valuation estimate. Depending on the timing and strength of a recovery in the capital markets, it is very easy to arrive at wildly divergent values for this stock, easily $20 above or below our estimate.

Like other brokerage house stocks, Goldman has been under pressure for most of this year, primarily because of a series of regulatory investigations related to Wall Street conflicts of interest. However, Goldman is probably the best insulated of the large brokerages against allegations that sell-side analysts privately derided stocks that they pounded the table for publicly. Unlike Merrill Lynch--the initial target--or others like Morgan Stanley that have large retail

businesses, Goldman's focus long has been on serving institutions and sophisticated, wealthy investors. We believe such clients would have a hard time making a case that they'd been duped by the not-so-secret fact that most stocks are rated "buy" or "strong buy" by brokerages, regardless of analysts' actual opinions.

More important, business conditions facing Goldman and its rivals look weak. In the first nine months of 2002, Goldman's investment banking revenue dropped 29% from a year earlier and the trading division had a 34% decline. Together, these cyclical enterprises constitute about half of Goldman's revenue. We're not expecting much improvement through the remainder of the year or in 2003, either.

Longer term, we believe it will be difficult for Goldman to trounce rivals as easily as it did in the past. Goldman increasingly looks like a small-fry compared with giants like Citigroup and J.P. Morgan Chase. These financial services supermarkets threaten to capture more business because they can package bank loans with investment banking services to become a one-stop shop for major corporations. In our opinion, Goldman is not a compelling investment at the current price.

MORNINGSTAR® Stocks 500

Goodyear Tire & Rubber GT

	Rating	Risk	Moat Size	Fair Value	Last Close	Yield %
	★★★	High	None	$12.00	$6.81	7.0

Company Profile

Goodyear Tire & Rubber manufactures tires and rubber products, including run-flat tires and inner tubes. The company sells its products under brand names like Aquatread, Eagle, and Kelly. Goodyear Tire & Rubber also provides retreading services. In addition, the company produces natural- and synthetic-rubber automotive components, industrial belts and hoses, brake-shoe components, and chemicals. Goodyear Tire & Rubber markets its products in the United States and overseas. Foreign sales account for approximately 47% of the company's total sales.

Management

Samir Gibara, 62, has spent more than 30 years with Goodyear--mostly in its foreign operations--with the last six as chairman and CEO; he's widely expected to retire next year. Gibara's likely successor is Robert Keegan, recently of Eastman Kodak.

Strategy

104-year-old Goodyear has gone to great lengths to maintain its number-one share of the world tire industry. The company is investing heavily in new technologies (particularly run-flat tires) to maintain premium pricing for its lineup. On the manufacturing side, Goodyear is reducing its workforce and gradually retooling existing plants with faster, more efficient tire-making equipment.

1144 East Market Street www.goodyear.com
Akron, OH 44316-0001

Industry	Investment Style	Stock Type	Sector
Rubber Products	▦ Small Value	▨ High Yield	✦ Industrial Mats

Competition	Market Cap $Mil	Debt/ Equity	12 Mo Trailing Sales $Mil	Price/Cash Flow	Return On Assets%	Total Return% 1 Yr	3 Yr
Goodyear Tire & Rubber	1,194	1.0	13,792	1.3	-1.3	-70.4	-34.3
Cooper Tire & Rubber	1,114	—	3,265	—	—	—	—
Bandag	741	—	943	—	—	—	—

Price Volatility

| Monthly Price High/Low | — Relative Strength to S&P 500

	1997	1998	1999	2000	2001	TTM
Annual $Price High	71.25	76.75	66.88	31.63	32.10	28.85
Low	49.25	45.88	25.50	15.60	17.37	6.51

Annual Total Return %	26.3	-19.1	-43.0	-13.5	8.0	-70.4
Fiscal Year-end: December	1997	1998	1999	2000	2001	TTM
Revenue $Mil	13,502	13,082	13,355	14,417	14,147	13,792
Net Income $Mil	534	638	243	40	-204	-175
Earnings Per Share $	3.30	4.03	1.53	0.25	-1.27	-1.08
Shares Outstanding Mil	156	157	157	155	160	175
Return on Equity %	14.8	16.3	6.4	1.2	-7.1	-6.0
Net Margin %	4.0	4.9	1.8	0.3	-1.4	-1.3
Asset Turnover	1.3	1.2	1.0	1.1	1.0	1.0
Financial Leverage	2.8	2.7	3.5	3.9	4.7	4.6

Valuation Ratios	Stock	Rel to Industry	Rel to S&P 500
Price/Earnings	NMF	—	—
Price/Book	0.4	0.3	0.1
Price/Sales	0.1	0.3	0.0
Price/Cash Flow	1.3	0.3	0.1

Major Fund Holders	% of Fund Assets
ING Smallcap Value A	2.47
ING Midcap Value A	2.08
Nations Classic Value Investor A	1.35
Quaker Mid-Cap Value A	1.08

Morningstar Grades

Growth [C]	1998	1999	2000	2001
Revenue %	-3.1	2.1	8.0	-1.9
Earnings/Share %	22.1	-62.0	-83.7	NMF
Book Value/Share %	10.9	-3.7	-8.9	-17.8
Dividends/Share %	5.3	0.0	0.0	-15.0

Goodyear's long-term growth (about 2%) has been disappointing, but no worse than the industry's as a whole. Beyond an cyclical rebound in demand of uncertain timing, which might be worth around 10% of current sales, we don't expect much growth.

Profitability [C]	1999	2000	2001	TTM
Return on Assets %	1.8	0.3	-1.5	-1.3
Oper Cash Flow $Mil	635	510	1,267	952
- Cap Spending $Mil	805	615	435	413
= Free Cash Flow $Mil	-170	-105	831	539

The Dunlop acquisition has masked a deep slump in sales that is primarily to blame for weak profitability. Operating margins are as low as they've been in decades, but we find little cause for any rebound in 2003.

Financial Health [C+]	1999	2000	2001	09-02
Long-term Debt $Mil	2,348	2,350	3,204	2,944
Total Equity $Mil	3,793	3,503	2,864	2,909
Debt/Equity Ratio	0.6	0.7	1.1	1.0

With debt at 50% of total capital and a history of subpar cash flows, Goodyear is not in good shape--in fact, it lost its investment-grade credit ratings earlier this year. A substantial pension deficit adds to the company's effective leverage.

Morningstar's Take By Josh Peters, 11-15-2002 Stock Price as of Analysis: $6.95

Goodyear's lot in the business world is not been a pleasant one. MIT's Jim Womack, founder of the Lean Enterprise Institute, described it thusly: "I can't think of an industry I'd less like to be in." Virtually every advance in tire technology has ended in diminished replacement demand. Tire makers, Goodyear included, have been slow to adopt the lean production techniques now common elsewhere in the auto industry. And with virtually no growth in volume, the industry's productivity gains translate into excess capacity, which in turn wreaks havoc on pricing.

The company's legacy of decline has also left it with a bevy of problems that resemble those of General Motors. Its once-sterling reputation has flagged as France's Michelin has seized the high ground in consumers' minds--not unlike the intangible leadership GM has long since ceded to foreign automakers. The company has a massive pension deficit brought on by crumbling financial markets. Its cost structure is uncompetitive and ill-suited to its declining market power.

But unlike GM, we see little room for Goodyear to solve its problems anytime soon. GM can--and has--put better products on the road, sowing the seeds of a bonafide turnaround. Goodyear, by contrast, produces what could be the ultimate

commodity product. Few drivers ever think about their tires until there's a problem. Even the Ford-Firestone debacle, which ought to have heightened America's awareness of tire safety, failed to revive sales or pricing for Goodyear's premium brands.

The tire business has always been deeply cyclical, and this isn't the first time Goodyear has suffered a downturn. Because tires are more durable than ever, replacements are an easily deferred purchase that creates pent-up demand down the road. We can see a case for cyclical industry rebound--eventually--that will revive Goodyear's margins and aid in the firm's need for drastic balance sheet repair.

Unfortunately, we have no idea what will trigger this recovery, let alone if it will occur soon enough to save Goodyear from still deeper financial pain. In the meantime, Goodyear will wrestle with rising costs, underutilized facilities and enormous debt. We hope that incoming CEO Robert Keegan will give the company a much-needed shake up when he takes the reins next year. But until then, we are taking a conservative approach to our fair value estimate.

Graco GGG

	Rating	Risk	Moat Size	Fair Value	Last Close	Yield %
	★	Med.	Narrow	$26.00	$28.65	1.0

Company Profile

Graco manufactures specialized pumps, regulators, valves, meters, atomizing devices, and replacement parts that are used to dispense and apply paints, adhesives, sealants, and lubricants. The company produces portable painting and cleaning equipment that uses paint-circulating and fluid-application technologies for the construction market. Graco markets its products in the United States and overseas. Sales outside the Western hemisphere account for approximately 31% of the company's total sales.

Management

Graco has an independent-minded board--unable to find a satisfactory leader from within, the firm hired new CEO David Roberts in mid-2001 from the Marmon Group, a large diversified industrial. Corporate attorney Lee Mitau was named chairman.

Strategy

With slow-growing end markets, Graco expands internally with adaptations of existing technologies in new applications--it targets 5% of each year's sales to be in fields less than three years old. Graco's highly efficient manufacturing operation helps smooth cyclical bumps in sales. The company is scouting for a large acquisition within its fluid-handling mandate.

88 - 11th Avenue Northeast
Minneapolis, MN 55413

www.graco.com

Morningstar Grades

Growth [C]

	1998	1999	2000	2001
Revenue %	3.9	2.2	9.7	-4.4
Earnings/Share %	17.5	41.3	19.9	-8.8
Book Value/Share %	-93.4	660.7	78.8	53.5
Dividends/Share %	56.8	0.0	26.9	-1.7

Given Graco's concentration on internal growth instead of acquisitions, we consider its five-year annualized growth rate fairly healthy at 4%. The firm's aiming for $1 billion in sales by 2005 (double today's level), so we expect a few acquisitions.

Profitability [A+]

	1999	2000	2001	TTM
Return on Assets %	25.1	29.4	23.6	21.8
Oper Cash Flow $Mil	76	82	89	103
- Cap Spending $Mil	9	15	30	14
= Free Cash Flow $Mil	67	68	59	89

With gross margins hovering around 50% and a 40% return on invested capital, Graco's focus on core markets is paying off handsomely. Its efficient use of capital is also highlighted by free cash flows approaching 100% of net income.

Financial Health [A+]

	1999	2000	2001	09-02
Long-term Debt $Mil	66	18	0	0
Total Equity $Mil	63	111	174	233
Debt/Equity Ratio	1.0	0.2	0.0	0.0

Having paid off the debt incurred from a large share buyback in 1998, Graco is beginning to accumulate a lot of cash. A significant acquisition will probably necessitate some borrowing, but powerful cash flows should keep Graco's position strong.

Industry	Investment Style	Stock Type	Sector
Machinery	⊞ Mid Core	↻ Cyclical	⚙ Industrial Mats

Competition	Market Cap $Mil	Debt/ Equity	12 Mo Trailing Sales $Mil	Price/Cash Flow	Return On Assets%	Total Return% 1 Yr	3 Yr
Graco	1,364	0.0	480	13.2	21.8	11.3	26.6
Illinois Tool Works	19,875	0.2	9,319	14.5	6.5	-2.9	3.5
Ingersoll-Rand A	7,247	0.6	9,968	9.8	-2.4	4.6	-4.5

Price Volatility | Monthly Price High/Low — Relative Strength to S&P 500

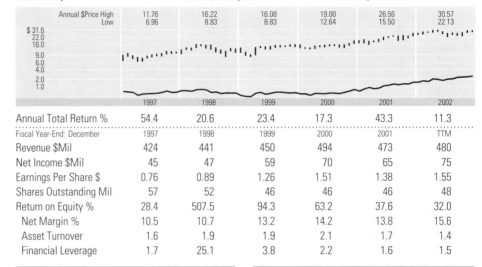

Annual $Price High Low	11.76 6.96	16.22 8.83	16.08 8.83	19.00 12.64	26.56 15.50	30.57 22.13
	1997	1998	1999	2000	2001	2002

Annual Total Return %	54.4	20.6	23.4	17.3	43.3	11.3
Fiscal Year-End: December	1997	1998	1999	2000	2001	TTM
Revenue $Mil	424	441	450	494	473	480
Net Income $Mil	45	47	59	70	65	75
Earnings Per Share $	0.76	0.89	1.26	1.51	1.38	1.55
Shares Outstanding Mil	57	52	46	46	46	48
Return on Equity %	28.4	507.5	94.3	63.2	37.6	32.0
Net Margin %	10.5	10.7	13.2	14.2	13.8	15.6
Asset Turnover	1.6	1.9	1.9	2.1	1.7	1.4
Financial Leverage	1.7	25.1	3.8	2.2	1.6	1.5

Valuation Ratios	Stock	Rel to Industry	Rel to S&P 500
Price/Earnings	18.5	0.6	0.8
Price/Book	5.8	2.3	1.8
Price/Sales	2.8	2.2	1.4
Price/Cash Flow	13.2	1.3	1.0

Major Fund Holders	% of Fund Assets
FPA Paramount	4.61
Mairs & Power Growth	3.84
Ariel	3.69
Mairs & Power Balanced	3.60

Morningstar's Take By Josh Peters, 12-20-2002 Stock Price as of Analysis: $28.10

An intense focus on customer and shareholder value makes Graco the most profitable machinery concern we know of. We don't expect much top-line growth, but we'd be willing to consider the shares around $18, a 30% discount to our fair value estimate of $26.

Flow control isn't the most appealing business, but this company makes the very most of it. Graco's machinery for pushing sticky substances through pipes and spray guns has won acclaim from customers worldwide. The company has also made a sizable commitment to innovation, investing 4% of sales in product development annually.

The company's narrow yet relentless focus has led to what we think are the best financial returns in capital goods. Gross margins have consistently registered around 50% for the past decade, signaling a triple play of top-shelf products, pricing power, and highly productive manufacturing capacity.

Another portion of Graco's outsize returns can be traced to old-fashioned cost control. Sales are 50% higher today than a decade ago, but in 2001 the company got by with $114 million in selling and general expenses--$12 million less than it spent in 1992--contributing to a ninefold increase in earnings. Furthermore, the quality of this profit growth has been impeccable--only $22 million in net investment

for $150 million in incremental sales.

With a clean balance sheet and a long record of returning cash to shareholders, Graco has just one problem that we can find: lack of growth. Most industrial companies with Graco's attractive financial characteristics grow via acquisition, and Graco itself has set a goal of $1 billion in revenue by 2005.

But Graco has been a very selective shopper at the acquisition store, which creates a dilemma. Such conservatism will help preserve existing profitability, but at some point quantity of profits must matter as much as quality. On the other hand, a large but poorly executed purchase could hurt results for years to come. In any event, we think returns on invested capital--around 40% since 1999--are unlikely to rise.

The company should have global economic winds at its back through middecade, as industrial capital spending recovers from its current three-year slump. But we doubt Graco will double itself by 2005 without engaging in an acquisition that could prove value-neutral at best; as a result, our fair value estimate of $26 assumes the firm will fall far short of its $1 billion goal.

M⟋RNINGSTAR® Stocks 500

Groupe Danone ADR DA

Rating	Risk	Moat Size	Fair Value	Last Close	Yield %
★★★	Low	Narrow	$28.00	$26.70	1.4

Company Profile

Groupe Danone produces food products. Its brand-name products include Evian, Dannon, and Sparklett mineral waters, Dannon yogurt, and LU cookies and biscuits. It also owns U.S.-based Lea & Perrins, a producer of sauces and condiments, and a stake in Italian cheese producer Galbani. Groupe Danone markets its products in Western Europe. Sales outside of France account for approximately 60% of the company's total sales. It disposed of its beer operations and most of its grocery business in early 2000.

Management

Franck Riboud presides over both the board of directors as chairman and the management team as chief executive officer, a position he has held since 1996.

Strategy

Danone's key brands--Evian and Dannon--are either first or second in France and the rest of the European Union. Not only is Danone extending these brands to faster-growing international markets, but it is buying other yogurt, water, and cookie brands that dominate their regions, rather than pursuing global brands that often carry a high price tag.

7, rue de Teheran
Paris, 75008
www.danonegroup.com

Industry	Investment Style	Stock Type	Sector
Food Mfg.	Large Growth	Slow Growth	Consumer Goods

Competition	Market Cap $Mil	Debt/ Equity	12 Mo Trailing Sales $Mil	Price/Cash Flow	Return On Assets%	Total Return% 1 Yr	Total Return% 3 Yr
Groupe Danone ADR	18,873	0.9	12,903	9.4	0.8	13.0	6.8
Nestle SA ADR	85,869	—	50,054	—	—	—	—
Kraft Foods	45,853	0.5	34,063	11.1	5.3	16.1	—

Price Volatility

I Monthly Price High/Low — Relative Strength to S&P 500

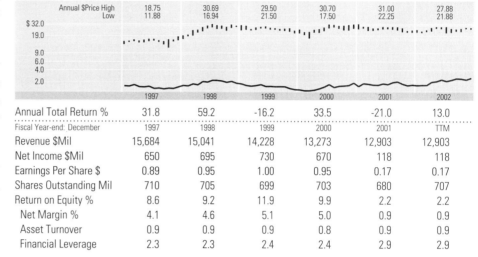

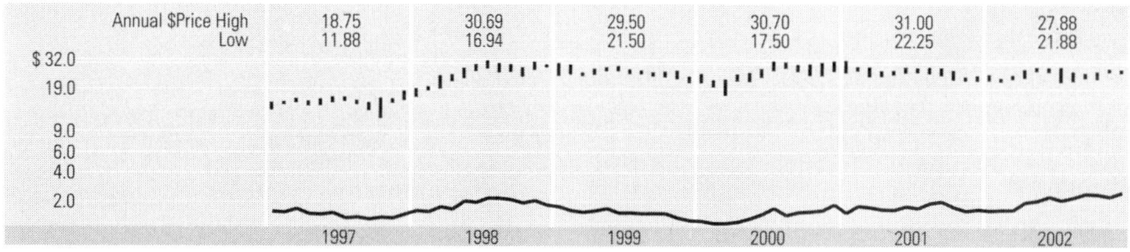
Annual $Price High
Low
18.75
11.88
30.69
16.94
29.50
21.50
30.70
17.50
31.00
22.25
27.88
21.88
$ 32.0
19.0
9.0
6.0
4.0
2.0
1997
1998
1999
2000
2001
2002

	1997	1998	1999	2000	2001	2002
Annual Total Return %	31.8	59.2	-16.2	33.5	-21.0	13.0

Fiscal Year-end: December	1997	1998	1999	2000	2001	TTM
Revenue $Mil	15,684	15,041	14,228	13,273	12,903	12,903
Net Income $Mil	650	695	730	670	118	118
Earnings Per Share $	0.89	0.95	1.00	0.95	0.17	0.17
Shares Outstanding Mil	710	705	699	703	680	707
Return on Equity %	8.6	9.2	11.9	9.9	2.2	2.2
Net Margin %	4.1	4.6	5.1	5.0	0.9	0.9
Asset Turnover	0.9	0.9	0.9	0.8	0.9	0.9
Financial Leverage	2.3	2.3	2.4	2.4	2.9	2.9

Valuation Ratios	Stock	Rel to Industry	Rel to S&P 500
Price/Earnings	158.0	7.5	6.7
Price/Book	3.6	0.8	1.1
Price/Sales	1.5	1.0	0.7
Price/Cash Flow	9.4	0.9	0.7

Major Fund Holders	% of Fund Assets
Navellier International Growth A	4.55
Purisima Pure Foreign	2.83
Phoenix-Kayne International X	2.60
CSI Equity Inv	2.14

Morningstar Grades

Growth [C+]	1998	1999	2000	2001
Revenue %	-4.1	2.8	7.5	1.3
Earnings/Share %	6.8	15.1	8.7	-81.4
Book Value/Share %	-0.2	-4.8	20.3	-15.8
Dividends/Share %	6.1	16.9	8.4	8.4

Danone posted strong 5.3% sales growth in the first nine months of 2002, including an excellent 7.8% in the third quarter. Unloading slow-growing business has helped the top line.

Profitability [C]	1999	2000	2001	TTM
Return on Assets %	4.9	4.1	0.8	0.8
Oper Cash Flow $Mil	1,418	1,340	1,997	1,997
- Cap Spending $Mil	752	741	773	773
= Free Cash Flow $Mil	666	598	1,224	1,224

Its operating margin has improved in recent years as Danone has shed some lower-margin businesses. This improvement continued through 2001 and 2002, despite the weak economy and disruptions in the water and biscuit businesses.

Financial Health [C+]	1999	2000	2001	12-01
Long-term Debt $Mil	3,507	3,935	4,801	4,801
Total Equity $Mil	6,146	6,782	5,263	5,263
Debt/Equity Ratio	0.6	0.6	0.9	0.9

Danone carries a reasonable level of debt, though it has increased in each of the past two years. Free cash flow (cash from operations minus capex) increased 31% in 2001 and represented a healthy 5.7% of sales.

Morningstar's Take By David Kathman, 12-16-2002 Stock Price as of Analysis: $26.29

Despite a few short-term glitches, we think Danone's long-term strategy is a winner. We'd be interested in the stock if it reached the low $20s.

While competitors Nestle and Unilever have grown bigger and more diversified recently, Danone has gone in the other direction. It has shed low-margin businesses and concentrated on bulking up the three areas in which it's a leader: fresh dairy, bottled water, and cookies, which now collectively make up 97% of company sales. While there have been some problems in the short term, we like the long-term strategy Danone has crafted.

Fresh dairy (mostly yogurt) is the largest of Danone's divisions, and it's also a cash cow whose margins have been expanding over the past decade. Not only does the dairy business have high barriers to entry due to the specialized distribution systems needed for milk, but Danone has been a leading innovator, exploiting trends toward convenience (with drinkable yogurt) and healthier eating (with Actimel, a yogurt-based health drink). Danone is the world's largest seller of fresh dairy products, yet the division is still growing at an impressive pace (8.7% in the first nine months of 2002).

Danone has also become the world's leader in bottled water, another area that has benefited from healthy-eating trends. It's a strong player in Europe and dominant in China and India, the two biggest bottled-water markets in the world. It struggled in the U.S. after Coca-Cola and PepsiCo aggressively entered the water market there, but in 2002 it inked a distribution deal with Coke that should give a boost to its Evian, Dannon, and Sparkletts brands.

In cookies and crackers, Danone takes the number two worldwide spot behind Kraft, though sales have been hurt over the past couple of years by snags in the integration of United Biscuits and labor disputes stemming from a reorganization in Europe. Yet the very reorganization that caused much of this turmoil has quietly helped profits, as the company has rid itself of inefficient product lines. Danone's dominance in fast-growing emerging markets, and innovations such as Taillefine/Vitalinea low-fat biscuits, make us optimistic about future growth.

Danone is the worldwide leader in two of its main product areas and takes second place in the other, giving it the kind of brand equity and economies of scale that we like to see. Its restructuring has resulted in five years of increasing operating margins, with more improvements likely. The recent problems do little to detract from Danone's long-term potential, and we'd gladly snap up the stock in the low $20s.

Guidant GDT

	Rating	Risk	Moat Size	Fair Value	Last Close	Yield %
	★★★	Med.	Wide	$30.00	$30.85	0.0

Company Profile

Guidant manufactures products for use in cardiac rhythm management and coronary artery disease intervention, as well as for other forms of minimally invasive surgery. It also designs and manufactures implantable pacemaker systems used in the treatment of slow or irregular arrhythmias. In addition, Guidant develops and manufactures products for access, vision, dissection, and retraction focusing on the laparoscopic market. The company also makes stents, catheters, and heart failure therapy devices. Foreign sales account for about 30% of the company's total sales.

Management

Ronald Dollens has been chief executive officer and president since the company was spun off from Eli Lilly in 1994. He had been with Eli Lilly since 1972. He receives nearly equal amounts of cash and options as compensation.

Strategy

Guidant is focused on blood vessel and heart products, the demand for which is increasing as populations age. It invests heavily in research and development to stay ahead of competitors like Medtronic, St. Jude, and Boston Scientific.

111 Monument Circle   www.guidant.com
Indianapolis, IN 46204-5129

Industry	Investment Style	Stock Type	Sector
Medical Equipment	Large Growth	Classic Growth	Healthcare

Competition	Market Cap $Mil	Debt/ Equity	12 Mo Trailing Sales $Mil	Price/Cash Flow	Return On Assets%	Total Return% 1 Yr	3 Yr
Guidant	9,458	0.2	3,063	9.3	18.6	-38.1	-11.7
Johnson & Johnson	159,452	0.1	35,120	18.0	16.3	-7.9	8.0
Medtronic	55,399	0.3	6,669	34.6	11.4	-10.4	10.3

Price Volatility

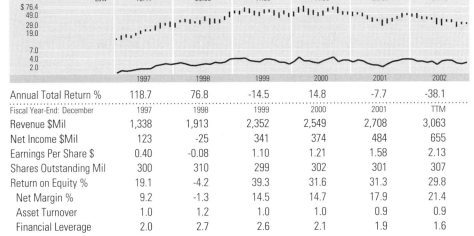

Annual $Price High	34.75	56.50	69.88	75.38	55.06	51.00
Low	13.41	25.50	41.00	44.00	26.90	25.15

Monthly Price High/Low — Relative Strength to S&P 500

	1997	1998	1999	2000	2001	2002
Annual Total Return %	118.7	76.8	-14.5	14.8	-7.7	-38.1

Fiscal Year-End: December	1997	1998	1999	2000	2001	TTM
Revenue $Mil	1,338	1,913	2,352	2,549	2,708	3,063
Net Income $Mil	123	-25	341	374	484	655
Earnings Per Share $	0.40	-0.08	1.10	1.21	1.58	2.13
Shares Outstanding Mil	300	310	299	302	301	307
Return on Equity %	19.1	-4.2	39.3	31.6	31.3	29.8
Net Margin %	9.2	-1.3	14.5	14.7	17.9	21.4
Asset Turnover	1.0	1.2	1.0	1.0	0.9	0.9
Financial Leverage	2.0	2.7	2.6	2.1	1.9	1.6

Valuation Ratios	Stock	Rel to Industry	Rel to S&P 500
Price/Earnings	14.5	0.5	0.6
Price/Book	4.3	0.7	1.3
Price/Sales	3.1	0.7	1.5
Price/Cash Flow	9.3	0.4	0.7

Major Fund Holders	% of Fund Assets
Marketocracy Medical Specialists	7.80
Kelmoore Strategy Eagle A	6.40
Cambiar Opportunity Inst	5.07
Alpha Analytics Value	4.66

Morningstar Grades

Growth [C+]	1998	1999	2000	2001
Revenue %	43.0	23.0	8.3	6.2
Earnings/Share %	NMF	NMF	10.0	30.6
Book Value/Share %	-8.3	45.9	36.8	31.9
Dividends/Share %	0.0	NMF	NMF	NMF

Guidant's three-year average revenue growth of 12% is below Medtronic's 18%. Sales growth could sputter in 2003 as sales of drug-eluting stents eclipse sales of bare-metal stents.

Profitability [A]	1999	2000	2001	TTM
Return on Assets %	15.2	14.8	16.6	18.6
Oper Cash Flow $Mil	401	647	683	1,022
- Cap Spending $Mil	—	—	—	—
= Free Cash Flow $Mil	—	—	—	—

In the past three years, the firm has generated returns on equity in excess of 30%. Returns on assets have generally increased over the same period. Gross margins so far in 2002 are 75%, lower than 2000's 76.2%.

Financial Health [NA]	1999	2000	2001	09-02
Long-term Debt $Mil	528	509	460	348
Total Equity $Mil	867	1,184	1,546	2,193
Debt/Equity Ratio	0.6	0.4	0.3	0.2

Guidant has increased its use of debt to fund its many acquisitions. Still, the firm had free cash flows after capital expenditures of $487 million in 2001, putting it in good financial shape.

Morningstar's Take By Travis Pascavis, 12-12-2002 Stock Price as of Analysis: $31.30

Guidant still has a strong franchise in heart products, so we would look to pick up shares in the mid $20s.

Guidant squares off against its competitors with state-of-the-art medical technology. Changes usually revolve around modest upgrades to existing technology, such as making pacemakers smaller or easier to implant. However, Guidant's record of keeping up with radical changes in its products is less than stellar, and highlights the risk of investing in medical device companies.

The company had a major miss in drug coated stents. With several court rulings in favor of Boston Scientific BSX, Guidant isn't likely to bring a drug-coated stent to market until perhaps 2005--nearly two years later than its rivals. Early in 2002, Guidant agreed to purchase privately-held Cook in order to develop and distribute Cook's paclitaxel-coated stents, but a court has barred Guidant from doing so. Although Cook is still appealing, we think it is prudent to not count on any sales from drug-eluting stents until 2005.

However, Guidant has had a big regulatory win in heart products. Guidant is one of only two companies--Medtronic is the other--selling a proven resynchronization device to help heart patients increase their physical activity. With this approval,

the company should be able to keep its leading market position in heart products, or even gain some share on companies like St. Jude that don't offer such a device. We think sales of these devices could increase in the low teens, and should help get Guidant's total sales back on the growth track by 2004. Progressive heart disease affects nearly 22 million people worldwide and more than 5 million people in the United States alone.

Although Guidant has its share of problems, the company still generates strong returns on invested capital. Guidant spends almost double the industry average on research and development as a percentage of sales, which should help keep it on top of the technological curve even if it falls behind in any given year. Moreover, the company's gross margins--the percentage of sales left over after cost of goods sold is subtracted--exceeded 75% in the latest quarter. We think the company will be able to continue charging a premium price for most of its products, thanks to the advantages outlined above.

MORNINGSTAR® Stocks 500

H & R Block HRB

	Rating	Risk	Moat Size	Fair Value	Last Close	Yield %
	★★★★	Med.	Wide	$48.00	$40.20	1.7

Company Profile

H&R Block is the largest tax-preparation company in the world. With offices in the United States, Canada, Australia, and the United States, H&R Block provides complete tax-preparation services to individual taxpayers. For more-independent taxpayers, the company sells tax-preparation software and runs an online tax service as well. H&R Block also operates a mortgage business and a retail financial advice business. The RSM McGladrey subsidiary provides tax-consulting services for business clients.

Management

Mark Ernst became CEO in early 2001. He joined Block as COO in 1998, coming over from American Express. Ernst became chairman in September 2002 when Frank Salizzoni stepped down.

Strategy

H&R Block, a company synonymous with tax preparation, is attempting to become a year-round financial services firm. The company wants to grow by expanding into banking services like mortgages, home equity loans, and credit cards along with brokerage and broader business accounting offerings.

4400 Main Street
Kansas City, MO 64111
www.hrblock.com

Morningstar Grades

Growth [A]	1999	2000	2001	2002
Revenue %	30.2	49.8	22.9	11.3
Earnings/Share %	-41.2	18.7	19.7	52.0
Book Value/Share %	-15.3	16.4	3.3	14.8
Dividends/Share %	18.8	13.3	9.3	7.1

Revenue grew a healthy 11% in fiscal 2002, which ended after tax season in April. Block's 25% compound annual growth over the past five years is largely the result of acquisitions.

Profitability [A]	2000	2001	2002	TTM
Return on Assets %	4.4	6.8	10.3	11.2
Oper Cash Flow $Mil	453	248	741	506
- Cap Spending $Mil	146	92	112	135
= Free Cash Flow $Mil	307	156	630	371

The tax business provides an annuitylike stream of profits, with pretax margins typically around 20%. Mortgages are currently very profitable, but rising rates will damp this. The investment services business is losing money in this weak market.

Financial Health [B+]	2000	2001	2002	10-02
Long-term Debt $Mil	872	871	868	830
Total Equity $Mil	1,219	1,174	1,369	1,102
Debt/Equity Ratio	0.7	0.7	0.6	0.8

Long-term debt has increased to 68% of equity, but the company has plenty of free cash flow available to pay this down. Financial leverage of 5.2 times equity reflects the changing business mix.

	Industry	Investment Style	Stock Type	Sector
	Personal Services	Mid Core	↗ Classic Growth	Consumer Services

Competition	Market Cap $Mil	Debt/ Equity	12 Mo Trailing Sales $Mil	Price/Cash Flow	Return On Assets%	Total Return% 1 Yr	3 Yr
H & R Block	7,182	0.8	3,518	14.2	11.2	-8.7	28.2
American Express	46,839	—	23,482	—	1.6	0.2	-10.4
Intuit	9,814	0.0	1,358	28.1	6.6	9.7	-8.3

Price Volatility

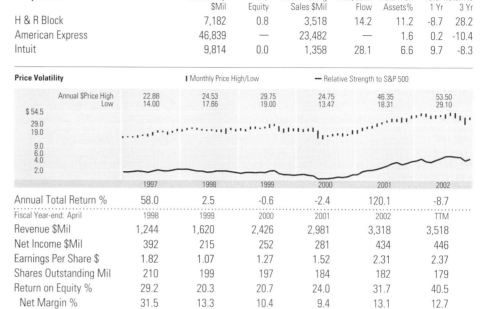

	1997	1998	1999	2000	2001	2002
Annual $Price High	22.88	24.53	29.75	24.75	46.35	53.50
Low	14.00	17.66	19.00	13.47	18.31	29.10
Annual Total Return %	58.0	2.5	-0.6	-2.4	120.1	-8.7

Fiscal Year-end: April	1998	1999	2000	2001	2002	TTM
Revenue $Mil	1,244	1,620	2,426	2,981	3,318	3,518
Net Income $Mil	392	215	252	281	434	446
Earnings Per Share $	1.82	1.07	1.27	1.52	2.31	2.37
Shares Outstanding Mil	210	199	197	184	182	179
Return on Equity %	29.2	20.3	20.7	24.0	31.7	40.5
Net Margin %	31.5	13.3	10.4	9.4	13.1	12.7
Asset Turnover	0.4	0.9	0.4	0.7	0.8	0.9
Financial Leverage	2.2	1.8	4.7	3.5	3.1	3.6

Valuation Ratios	Stock	Rel to Industry	Rel to S&P 500
Price/Earnings	17.0	1.0	0.7
Price/Book	6.5	1.9	2.0
Price/Sales	2.0	1.0	1.0
Price/Cash Flow	14.2	1.0	1.1

Major Fund Holders	% of Fund Assets
Oakmark Select I	8.63
Liberty Acorn Twenty Z	7.59
Runkel Value	6.24
Boyle Marathon	5.77

Morningstar's Take By Rachel Barnard, 11-11-2002 Stock Price as of Analysis: $33.63

H&R Block has built a great brand and a dominant franchise, giving it a wide moat and excellent prospects. A recent rash of lawsuits increases the risk, in our opinion, but our fair value estimate remains at $48 and we think the shares are attractive below $38.

H&R Block is best known for its tax services, and this business still generates the majority of revenue and growth. The firm's priority, however, is to diversify into other financial services, selling other products and services to its existing tax clients. So far the results have been mixed. Luckily for Block, its tax business has dominant market share in the United States and its experimentation hasn't affected that.

The 2002 tax season was successful. The average charge for tax preparation increased 9%, as a result of a 5% price hike and increasing complexity in the tax code, which means more work--and more money--for Block. The firm prepared 14% of all tax returns filed in the United States.

TaxCut, Block's tax-preparation software, has been successfully gaining on market leader Intuit's TurboTax product and has garnered critical praise for its built-in advice component, among other things.

But efforts to make H&R Block into more than a tax business have met with mixed results. The mortgage business was hot in 2002, thanks to low interest rates and heaps of refinancing. Revenue shot up 77% over the past year. We don't believe this is a sustainable pace, however, and as soon as rates rise we expect the mortgage engine to cool.

Results from the financial advice business are much worse. Revenue dropped 47% in the past year and the segment lost $55 million. So far, Block's grand scheme of upselling customers on financial advice has been a dud. Some clients have opened brokerage accounts, but the market environment meant that few of them felt like trading. The firm has realized that a fee-based advice model is much more profitable, but so far it has not succeeded in being the "financial partner" for its tax clients.

We applaud the company's quest for less-seasonal business, but so far we don't see much promise in its recent forays into financial services. The reason to invest in this company is the hegemony of its tax business, and that is stronger than ever. Solid core earnings make this an attractive investment below $38, in our opinion.

Halliburton HAL

	Rating	Risk	Moat Size	Fair Value	Last Close	Yield %
	★	Med.	Narrow	$11.00	$18.71	2.7

Company Profile

Dallas-based Halliburton operates in the energy and construction industries. Its energy services group, responsible for about two thirds of sales, makes drilling equipment and provides maintenance, testing, and data-processing services for oil and gas companies. Halliburton's construction group provides engineering, design, and construction services for projects like power and chemical plants. Halliburton has split its operations into two subsidiaries to try to protect its energy unit from ballooning asbestos litigation on the construction side.

Management

Former chief operating officer David Lesar became CEO and chairman after Dick Cheney resigned to run for vice president of the United States in August 2000. Cheney was CEO for five years before joining the Bush ticket.

Strategy

Halliburton is attempting to bookend its asbestos liabilities through a settlement with plaintiffs' attorneys that calls for creation of a trust from which all current and future claims will be paid. The company is also negotiating with its insurance carriers to get reimbursed for its asbestos liabilities. Once asbestos is behind it, management can focus again on its core businesses.

3600 Lincoln Plaza   www.halliburton.com
Dallas, TX 75201

Morningstar Grades

Growth [D+]	1998	1999	2000	2001
Revenue %	7.5	-15.1	-3.0	9.2
Earnings/Share %	NMF	NMF	13.1	67.9
Book Value/Share %	-17.9	19.3	-9.4	25.8
Dividends/Share %	0.0	0.0	0.0	0.0

Halliburton's growth has been nothing to crow about, contracting in 1999 and 2000 before finally expanding in 2001. This is a function of working in a mature and cyclical industry.

Profitability [B]	1999	2000	2001	TTM
Return on Assets %	4.5	4.9	7.4	-2.1
Oper Cash Flow $Mil	-58	-57	1,029	1,473
- Cap Spending $Mil	520	578	797	793
= Free Cash Flow $Mil	-578	-635	232	680

Showing returns on assets in the midsingle digits over the past three years, profitability has been mediocre but in line with Halliburton's peers. There'll be a large one-time charge against earnings if the proposed asbestos settlement is approved.

Financial Health [C]	1999	2000	2001	09-02
Long-term Debt $Mil	1,056	1,049	1,403	1,120
Total Equity $Mil	4,287	3,928	4,752	4,321
Debt/Equity Ratio	0.2	0.3	0.3	0.3

The proposed settlement calls for Halliburton to pay $2.8 billion in cash into a trust, which will dramatically increase the company's currently nominal debt. However, insurance claims should cover a large amount of this.

Industry	Investment Style	Stock Type	Sector
Oil & Gas Services	▦ Large Core	✗ High Yield	◓ Energy

Competition	Market Cap $Mil	Debt/ Equity	12 Mo Trailing Sales $Mil	Price/Cash Flow	Return On Assets%	Total Return% 1 Yr	3 Yr
Halliburton	8,158	0.3	12,396	5.5	-2.1	47.2	-19.9
Schlumberger	24,304	0.8	13,942	12.1	3.2	-22.2	-6.9
Baker Hughes	10,840	0.4	5,227	14.0	4.5	-10.4	18.3

Price Volatility

ǀ Monthly Price High/Low   — Relative Strength to S&P 500

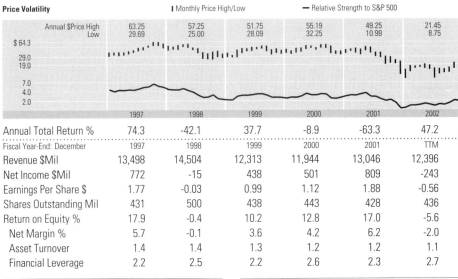

Annual $Price High Low	63.25 29.69	57.25 25.00	51.75 28.09	55.19 32.25	49.25 10.99	21.45 8.75
	1997	1998	1999	2000	2001	2002

Annual Total Return %	74.3	-42.1	37.7	-8.9	-63.3	47.2
Fiscal Year-End: December	1997	1998	1999	2000	2001	TTM
Revenue $Mil	13,498	14,504	12,313	11,944	13,046	12,396
Net Income $Mil	772	-15	438	501	809	-243
Earnings Per Share $	1.77	-0.03	0.99	1.12	1.88	-0.56
Shares Outstanding Mil	431	500	438	443	428	436
Return on Equity %	17.9	-0.4	10.2	12.8	17.0	-5.6
Net Margin %	5.7	-0.1	3.6	4.2	6.2	-2.0
Asset Turnover	1.4	1.4	1.3	1.2	1.2	1.1
Financial Leverage	2.2	2.5	2.2	2.6	2.3	2.7

Valuation Ratios	Stock	Rel to Industry	Rel to S&P 500
Price/Earnings	NMF	—	—
Price/Book	1.9	0.7	0.6
Price/Sales	0.7	0.3	0.3
Price/Cash Flow	5.5	0.5	0.4

Major Fund Holders	% of Fund Assets
Rydex Energy Services Inv	6.54
Van Kampen Value Opportunities A	4.66
Van Kampen Comstock A	4.51
PIMCO PEA Value Instl	3.65

Morningstar's Take By Paul Larson, 12-30-2002 Stock Price as of Analysis: $18.50

Halliburton's recent settlement of asbestos liabilities is positive for the company, but we still think the shares are overvalued.

The settlement calls for Halliburton to create a trust to pay all current and future asbestos claims. It will contribute $2.8 billion in cash and issue 59.5 million shares to the trust, about 10% of its equity. Operationally, it will be business as usual. The deal won't be final until the bankruptcy courts approve it and Halliburton can finance its contribution, but we think the chances of completion are high.

Now, instead of a never-ending legal saga with liabilities of unknown size, Halliburton's liabilities will be capped. While the price of the settlement is relatively steep--roughly $3,000 per claimant compared with about $400 the firm had been paying--the cost is fixed and won't spiral out of control. Halliburton's ultimate asbestos liability under the settlement, net of our estimate of insurance reimbursement, shouldn't be far from what we previously expected.

Though uncertainty has been greatly reduced, we still wouldn't buy the stock unless it traded at a deep discount to our fair value estimate. Halliburton has generated subpar returns on invested capital for years (typically 3%-8%). With returns merely at or below its cost of capital, Halliburton has not been creating much value for shareholders.

The oil services industry is capital-intensive and highly cyclical--demand for oil and construction services tends to depend on commodity oil prices as well as the state of the economy. Not one of the oil service companies we cover has earned its cost of capital for a sustained time. Profits in the booms have been modest and Halliburton has dipped into the red during the busts. The firm's best year was 1997, when Halliburton earned $1.77 per share and had a 10% return on assets. But the very next year, it lost $0.03 per share. It should only break even this year.

Being the largest in many areas of oil services, Halliburton does enjoy some modest economies of scale and topnotch industry connections, which is why we've given it a narrow economic moat rating. Beyond that, sustainable competitive advantages are tough to come by in oil services.

Halliburton doesn't have a business we are attracted to. It operates in a competitive, capital-intensive industry. Its historical returns have barely met its cost of capital. It would take a lot more than clearing the asbestos slate to interest us.

MʘRNINGSTAR® Stocks 500

Harley-Davidson HDI

	Rating	Risk	Moat Size	Fair Value	Last Close	Yield %
	★★★	Low	Wide	$43.00	$46.20	0.3

Company Profile

Harley-Davidson manufactures motorcycles and related parts and accessories. Its products include motorcycles having V-twin engines ranging from 883 to 1,450 cubic centimeters of displacement. The company markets its motorcycles under names like Softail, Sportster, Fat Boy, Low Rider, Road King, and Wide Glide, as well as the Buell brand. It also sells accessories for its motorcycles and clothing bearing the Harley-Davidson name. The Harley-Davidson Financial Services subsidiary offers financing for the company's customers.

Management

Jeff Bleustein has been with Harley-Davidson for more than two decades, first as an engineer and then as part of the management group that led the buyout of the firm from AMF. He has been CEO since late 1998.

Strategy

Harley-Davidson's brand name ensures rabid demand for its products and makes it difficult for competitors to crack the firm's market share for recreational and custom heavyweight motorcycles. Harley's near-term goal is for modest production increases. It also wants to build up its line of Buell performance motorcycles to bring younger and entry-level riders into the Harley-Davidson fold.

3700 West Juneau Avenue   www.harley-davidson.com
Milwaukee, WI 53208

Morningstar Grades

Growth [A+]	1998	1999	2000	2001
Revenue %	18.4	19.3	17.8	16.4
Earnings/Share %	21.1	24.6	31.4	26.5
Book Value/Share %	23.0	12.3	22.2	25.6
Dividends/Share %	14.7	12.2	12.0	17.3

Increasing unit sales have fueled double-digit revenue growth, though Harley-Davidson's market share has remained steady. Modest price increases for anniversary editions and continued capacity expansion should keep sales growth steady.

Profitability [A+]	1999	2000	2001	TTM
Return on Assets %	12.7	14.3	14.0	14.7
Oper Cash Flow $Mil	432	565	757	885
- Cap Spending $Mil	166	204	290	308
= Free Cash Flow $Mil	266	362	467	578

As befits its strong brand name, Harley earns outstanding profit margins, especially on its top-of-the-line custom bikes. A relatively debt-free balance sheet and efficient production process also help.

Financial Health [A+]	1999	2000	2001	09-02
Long-term Debt $Mil	280	355	380	380
Total Equity $Mil	1,161	1,406	1,756	2,128
Debt/Equity Ratio	0.2	0.3	0.2	0.2

Harley-Davidson is in great shape. It carries virtually no debt, aside from funding for its finance division, and generates loads of free cash flow. That means it can internally finance growth.

Industry	Investment Style	Stock Type	Sector
Recreation	▦ Large Growth	↻ Cyclical	⌂ Consumer Goods

Competition

	Market Cap $Mil	Debt/ Equity	12 Mo Trailing Sales $Mil	Price/Cash Flow	Return On Assets%	Total Return% 1 Yr	3 Yr
Harley-Davidson	13,982	0.2	4,134	15.8	14.7	-14.7	15.0
Honda Motor ADR	35,196	—	58,319	—	—	—	—
Ducati Motor Holding SpA	262	—	268	—	—	—	—

Price Volatility		Monthly Price High/Low		— Relative Strength to S&P 500		
Annual $Price High Low	15.63 8.34	23.75 12.47	32.03 21.38	50.63 29.53	55.98 32.00	57.25 42.69

$58.3
29.0
19.0
9.0
6.0
4.0
2.0

	1997	1998	1999	2000	2001	2002
Annual Total Return %	16.6	74.6	35.6	24.4	37.0	-14.7
Fiscal Year-end: December	1997	1998	1999	2000	2001	TTM
Revenue $Mil	1,830	2,167	2,586	3,047	3,545	4,134
Net Income $Mil	174	214	267	348	438	548
Earnings Per Share $	0.57	0.69	0.86	1.13	1.43	1.80
Shares Outstanding Mil	305	305	304	302	302	303
Return on Equity %	21.1	20.7	23.0	24.7	24.9	25.7
Net Margin %	9.5	9.9	10.3	11.4	12.3	13.3
Asset Turnover	1.1	1.1	1.2	1.3	1.1	1.1
Financial Leverage	1.9	1.9	1.8	1.7	1.8	1.8

Valuation Ratios	Stock	Rel to Industry	Rel to S&P 500
Price/Earnings	25.7	1.5	1.1
Price/Book	6.6	3.3	2.1
Price/Sales	3.4	1.0	1.7
Price/Cash Flow	15.8	1.4	1.2

Major Fund Holders	% of Fund Assets
Rydex Leisure Inv	7.95
Pitcairn Select Growth	7.66
Armada Tax Managed Equity I	7.45
Merrill Lynch Focus Twenty A	6.23

Morningstar's Take By T.K. MacKay, 10-23-2002 Stock Price as of Analysis: $54.59

Harley-Davidson is a well-oiled machine worth buying in the mid-$30s.

We're big believers in strong consumer brands, and find Harley-Davidson to be one of the most robust of all. Harley-Davidson easily meets one of Warren Buffett's foremost criteria for a sound investment: long-term competitive advantage. In 2003, the firm will be 100 years old, having dominated the American motorcycle industry the whole way. Harleys sell at or near their manufacturer's suggested retail price, and the company makes just enough bikes each year to retain this pricing power. By the end of 2002, Harley-Davidson will have produced 261,000 motorcycles for the year, and every single one will be sold.

Ensuring that demand constantly outweighs supply is the key to Harley's fat profits; it relieves the firm from much of the high costs of marketing that other manufacturers put into selling their bikes. For example, Harley's selling, general, and administrative expenses are 8 percentage points lower than those of venerable Italian motorcycle maker Ducati, at 17% of sales. Such cost savings afford Harley the highest operating margins in the industry. This superior profitability combined with a strong increase in

demand has resulted in annual free cash flow growth of 33% over the past decade. Harley carries more cash than debt on its balance sheet.

Harley puts part of its cash hoard to work each year by expanding its manufacturing capacity, the most recent project being a $145 million, 350,000-square-foot expansion at its York, Pennsylvania, plant that will come online in 2003. Capital projects like these paid off in spades during the 1990s as the country enjoyed one of its greatest periods of economic expansion. Harley was able to increase prices at the same time it increased output because demand always outweighed supply. This led to high-double-digit sales increases year after year. In less affluent times, however, increased supply could produce a lower return on investment than Harley hopes. We fear that aggressive capacity expansion in a slow-growing economy could lead to an imbalance of supply and demand, resulting in pricing pressure. This would jeopardize Harley's gross margins, which have historically topped 33%.

The prospect of lower returns makes it hard for us to put a premium valuation on Harley stock. We believe the company's wide economic moat makes Harley an attractive investment, but only at the right price.

Harrah's Entertainment HET

	Rating	Risk	Moat Size	Fair Value	Last Close	Yield %
	★★★	Med.	Narrow	$48.00	$39.60	0.0

Company Profile

Harrah's Entertainment operates riverboat and hotel casinos in 10 states. It owns and operates 5 land-based casinos and 10 riverboats under the Harrah's brand, as well as the Showboat in Atlantic City and the Rio in Las Vegas. The firm also manages 3 Native American casinos and Harrah's Jazz in New Orleans. In 2000, 82% of revenue was earned from gaming operations, with the balance derived mostly from hospitality and entertainment venues. Harrah's acquired Players International in March 2000 and announced plans to purchase Harvey's Casinos Resorts in April 2001.

Management

Chairman and CEO Phil Satre, a Harrah's veteran, has done a good job of developing the firm's core brand with effective use of technology and marketing, especially the loyalty program. His successor as CEO, Gary Loveman, should be a fine replacement.

Strategy

The repeat visitor is the driving force behind Harrah's marketing-focused strategy. The firm's goal is to increase brand loyalty among the 25 million members of its Total Rewards program--the only national program in the casino industry--through customized marketing programs.

One Harrah's Court
Las Vegas, NV 89119
www.harrahs.com

Morningstar Grades

Growth [A-]	1998	1999	2000	2001
Revenue %	23.8	44.4	15.1	11.4
Earnings/Share %	2.0	62.0	NMF	NMF
Book Value/Share %	15.1	38.4	-8.8	13.0
Dividends/Share %	NMF	NMF	NMF	NMF

The company offers a mixed growth picture. Same-store sales at the Harrah's branded properties have been excellent for several years, but overall revenue will probably grow around 9% because of underperforming noncore properties.

Profitability [C+]	1999	2000	2001	TTM
Return on Assets %	4.4	-0.2	3.4	3.9
Oper Cash Flow $Mil	490	548	774	815
- Cap Spending $Mil	340	421	530	439
= Free Cash Flow $Mil	150	126	244	376

Excluding write-offs, Harrah's has consistently led its industry in profitability. Its returns on equity (15% in 2001) and assets (4%) are significantly higher than its peers' and provide a cushion against economic uncertainty.

Financial Health [B-]	1999	2000	2001	09-02
Long-term Debt $Mil	2,540	2,836	3,719	3,533
Total Equity $Mil	1,486	1,270	1,374	1,497
Debt/Equity Ratio	1.7	2.2	2.7	2.4

Leverage has increased over the years, but is on par with peers'. Free cash flows jumped in the past few years, as the company has scaled back on spending to convert acquired casinos to the Harrah's brand name.

Industry	Investment Style	Stock Type	Sector
Gambling/Hotel Casinos	Mid Growth	Classic Growth	Consumer Services

Competition	Market Cap $Mil	Debt/ Equity	12 Mo Trailing Sales $Mil	Price/Cash Flow	Return On Assets%	Total Return% 1 Yr	3 Yr
Harrah's Entertainment	4,426	2.4	4,108	5.4	3.9	7.0	17.8
MGM Mirage	5,111	1.8	3,970	6.1	2.7	14.2	12.2
Park Place Entertainment	2,718	—	4,698	—	—	—	—

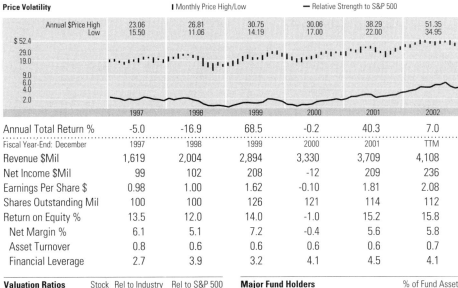

Price Volatility — Monthly Price High/Low — Relative Strength to S&P 500

Annual $Price High Low	23.06 15.50	26.81 11.06	30.75 14.19	30.06 17.00	38.29 22.00	51.35 34.95

	1997	1998	1999	2000	2001	2002
Annual Total Return %	-5.0	-16.9	68.5	-0.2	40.3	7.0

Fiscal Year-End: December	1997	1998	1999	2000	2001	TTM
Revenue $Mil	1,619	2,004	2,894	3,330	3,709	4,108
Net Income $Mil	99	102	208	-12	209	236
Earnings Per Share $	0.98	1.00	1.62	-0.10	1.81	2.08
Shares Outstanding Mil	100	100	126	121	114	112
Return on Equity %	13.5	12.0	14.0	-1.0	15.2	15.8
Net Margin %	6.1	5.1	7.2	-0.4	5.6	5.8
Asset Turnover	0.8	0.6	0.6	0.6	0.6	0.7
Financial Leverage	2.7	3.9	3.2	4.1	4.5	4.1

Valuation Ratios	Stock	Rel to Industry	Rel to S&P 500
Price/Earnings	19.0	1.0	0.8
Price/Book	3.0	1.2	0.9
Price/Sales	1.1	0.8	0.5
Price/Cash Flow	5.4	0.9	0.4

Major Fund Holders	% of Fund Assets
Heritage Capital Appreciation A	8.78
INVESCO Leisure Inv	7.90
Rydex Leisure Inv	4.26
ASAF Goldman Sachs Concentrated Gr A	3.95

Morningstar's Take By T.K. MacKay, 10-11-2002 Stock Price as of Analysis: $44.66

We are strong believers in the Harrah's business model and would consider the stock in the mid-20s.

When Harrah's sticks to what it does best--catering to America's "low-roller" gamblers--it's a winning bet. It has what we consider to be the most recognizable brand name and the most efficient loyalty program in the business. These two competitive advantages keep the company's 25 properties filled in good times and bad.

The combination of loyal players and geographic diversity has dealt Harrah's a winning hand. Operating margins have been in the midteens over the past several years and revenue has expanded more than 20% annually, thanks to smart acquisitions like Players International and Harvey's Casinos. The company is reviving profits at the struggling Rio Hotel & Casino in Las Vegas, and the Harvey's acquisition is adding significant revenue to the top line. We expect revenue to expand around 9% annually over the next several years, as Harrah's continues to benefit from the same-store sales growth that the loyalty program generates.

Geographic diversity gives Harrah's a cushion that Vegas-based operator's don't have; the firm receives only about 9% of its earnings before interest, taxes, depreciation, and amortization from the Strip. This strategy has its pros and cons. In the first half of this year, would-be Vegas vacationers opted to stay closer to home markets like Chicago, Iowa, and Mississippi, which helped boost revenue of non-Vegas operators. But as Vegas lures back customers with cheap flights, Harrah's misses out on the fat profits that Vegas-based operators generate because of its small presence in that region.

Harrah's appears determined to maximize the profits that it does receive from Las Vegas by reviving the underperforming Rio Hotel. Over the long term, we expect the company to continue to make prudent acquisitions while using excess cash to pay down debt and repurchase shares.

Harrah's is a great way for investors to tap into the casino industry without having all their chips in one basket, but because of the risk of higher gaming taxes across the nation and the firm's limited exposure to the growing Las Vegas market, we'd look for at least a 40% discount to our estimated fair value before placing our bet on the stock.

  MORNINGSTAR® Stocks 500

Hasbro HAS

	Rating	Risk	Moat Size	Fair Value	Last Close	Yield %
	★★★	Med.	Narrow	$14.00	$11.55	1.0

Company Profile

Hasbro primarily produces toys. The company sells its products in the United States and abroad under brand names that include Hasbro, Playskool, Tonka, Tiger, Milton Bradley, and Parker Brothers. Its products include Nerf toys, Furby interactive toys, Tinkertoys, GI Joe action figures, Tonka toy trucks, Mr. Potato Head, and the Monopoly, Parcheesi, Candy Land, Yahtzee, The Game of Life, and Scrabble board games. Hasbro also makes Pokemon products and interactive CD-ROM versions of several board games. Foreign sales account for about 36% of the company's revenue.

Management

Chairman and CEO Alan Hassenfeld is widely viewed as the creative visionary of Hasbro. While COO Herb Baum's departure is a loss to the company, the management team knows the toy industry well.

Strategy

Hasbro is focusing on cost reduction throughout its business. The company has cut its manufacturing facilities from 12 to three since 1997 and expects to discontinue unprofitable products and license agreements.

1027 Newport Avenue
Pawtucket, RI 02862

www.hasbro.com

Morningstar Grades

Growth [D]	1998	1999	2000	2001
Revenue %	3.6	28.1	-10.5	-24.6
Earnings/Share %	47.1	-7.0	NMF	NMF
Book Value/Share %	1.8	-1.9	-18.6	5.3
Dividends/Share %	4.3	9.3	3.0	-50.0

The rapid sales growth of the late 1990s is history. Sales will probably expand about 4% annually over the next several years as Hasbro focuses on profitability.

Profitability [C-]	1999	2000	2001	TTM
Return on Assets %	4.2	-3.8	1.8	-5.8
Oper Cash Flow $Mil	392	163	372	395
- Cap Spending $Mil	107	125	50	55
= Free Cash Flow $Mil	284	38	322	340

Hasbro's restructuring is already paying off. Operating profit was about 7.4% of sales in 2001; we think the company's cost-reduction efforts will help lift this margin to 12% by 2005.

Financial Health [B]	1999	2000	2001	09-02
Long-term Debt $Mil	421	1,168	1,166	856
Total Equity $Mil	1,879	1,327	1,353	1,139
Debt/Equity Ratio	0.2	0.9	0.9	0.8

Long-term debt is high at about two thirds of total equity, but free cash flows over the next year should easily take care of debt repayments as they come due.

Industry	Investment Style	Stock Type	Sector
Toys/Hobbies	▦ Mid Core	↻ Cyclical	🚗 Consumer Goods

Competition

	Market Cap $Mil	Debt/ Equity	12 Mo Trailing Sales $Mil	Price/Cash Flow	Return On Assets%	Total Return% 1 Yr	3 Yr
Hasbro	2,000	0.8	2,808	5.1	-5.8	-28.2	-11.5
Mattel	8,373	0.4	4,893	7.4	4.1	13.6	15.1

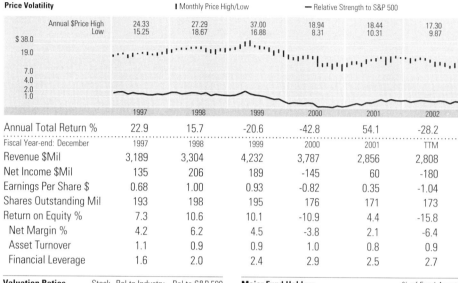

Price Volatility		Monthly Price High/Low		— Relative Strength to S&P 500		
Annual $Price High Low	24.33 15.25	27.29 18.67	37.00 16.88	18.94 8.31	18.44 10.31	17.30 9.87
	1997	1998	1999	2000	2001	2002

Annual Total Return %	22.9	15.7	-20.6	-42.8	54.1	-28.2
Fiscal Year-end: December	1997	1998	1999	2000	2001	TTM
Revenue $Mil	3,189	3,304	4,232	3,787	2,856	2,808
Net Income $Mil	135	206	189	-145	60	-180
Earnings Per Share $	0.68	1.00	0.93	-0.82	0.35	-1.04
Shares Outstanding Mil	193	198	195	176	171	173
Return on Equity %	7.3	10.6	10.1	-10.9	4.4	-15.8
Net Margin %	4.2	6.2	4.5	-3.8	2.1	-6.4
Asset Turnover	1.1	0.9	0.9	1.0	0.8	0.9
Financial Leverage	1.6	2.0	2.4	2.9	2.5	2.7

Valuation Ratios	Stock	Rel to Industry	Rel to S&P 500
Price/Earnings	NMF	—	—
Price/Book	1.8	0.9	0.5
Price/Sales	0.7	0.2	0.4
Price/Cash Flow	5.1	0.4	0.4

Major Fund Holders	% of Fund Assets
C&B Mid Cap Value	3.49
Mosaic Mid-Cap	3.25
ING Midcap Value A	2.97
C&B Large Cap Value	2.68

Morningstar's Take By T.K. MacKay, 12-03-2002 Stock Price as of Analysis: $12.76

Hasbro's great American brand names won't be fading anytime soon. The company is only a little more than half as profitable as it once was, however, and it is no longer a big-growth story. On top of that, the stock is susceptible to trends in retail spending, especially the whims of toy-crazy kids. We'd look for a decent margin of safety before investing in the shares.

Hasbro's competitive advantage stems from the strength of its products: Monopoly, Mr. Potato Head, Trivial Pursuit, and G.I. Joe are among the most venerable of Hasbro's 100-plus toy brands. These toys and games sell year after year, even as their age tops that of the parents who buy them for their children. With 80% of Hasbro's items priced below $20, the company is somewhat shielded from economic downturns. Returns on assets have topped 12% in recent years, and net margins have historically held steady at 7%.

But it isn't all fun and games for Hasbro. The company has stumbled financially in its effort to cope with "age compression" and the faddish nature of popular toys. Pricey license contracts for toys like Pokemon and Star Wars have made for drastically lower profit margins, despite bringing in additional sales dollars. To finance this rapid sales growth,

Hasbro dramatically increased its leverage: Debt/equity jumped ninefold between 1995 and 2000, and cash flows slid deep into negative territory.

Hasbro has since shifted its strategy away from licensed products, but still must undo the damage that rapid growth did to its balance sheet in the late 1990s. The company has closed 13 of its 23 factories and office properties since 1995, and has reduced head count by 38% (10% in 2002 alone). But will these strategies--a renewed focus on in-house toys and a leaner operation--translate into better operating profits?

It appears that the moves have paid off so far. Free cash flow is back in the black, allowing Hasbro to pay down debt. Operating margins--the most important lever in our fair value estimate for Hasbro--are improving with each quarter. We believe the company will eventually return to historical operating profit levels of about 12%.

Hasbro is a good long-term investment at the right price. We think investors could get a great deal if the stock fell below $10.

HCA-The Healthcare Company HCA

Rating	Risk	Moat Size	Fair Value	Last Close	Yield %
★★★	Med.	Narrow	UR	$41.50	0.2

Company Profile

HCA buys, sells, and owns general, acute-care, and specialty hospitals and related health-care facilities, primarily in fast-growing urban markets. The company's general and acute-care hospitals provide medical and surgical services, including inpatient care, intensive and cardiac care, diagnostic services, and emergency services. HCA also provides therapeutic programs for psychiatric and chemically dependent patients.

Management

Jack Bovender was named CEO in January 2001; he has been president since 1997. Former CEO Thomas Frist is chairman. Bovender has 20 years of service with the company in two separate stints.

Strategy

Now that HCA has sold the hospitals not in its core urban markets, it is launching an aggressive plan to expand services and improve its existing facilities. This coincides with HCA's shared services initiative that focuses on cutting costs by consolidating areas like supply ordering, technology, personnel, and billing and collecting.

One Park Plaza
Nashville, TN 37203
www.columbia-hca.com

Morningstar Grades

Growth [C-]	1998	1999	2000	2001
Revenue %	-0.7	-10.8	0.1	7.7
Earnings/Share %	NMF	88.1	-64.9	323.1
Book Value/Share %	7.9	-19.6	-17.3	13.1
Dividends/Share %	0.0	0.0	0.0	0.0

We forecast sales growth to remain strong for the next couple of years, but to fade a bit in the long-term. We expect that pricing power will decline under increasing health-care cost scrutiny. Increased volume should offset some of the decline.

Profitability [B]	1999	2000	2001	TTM
Return on Assets %	3.9	1.2	5.0	5.0
Oper Cash Flow $Mil	1,223	1,547	1,413	2,556
- Cap Spending $Mil	1,287	1,155	1,370	1,648
= Free Cash Flow $Mil	-64	392	43	908

HCA has steadily improved its EBITDA (earnings before interest, taxes, depreciation, and amortization) margin over the past two years. It was about 17% in early 2000 and is currently about 20% -- near the top of the urban hospital group.

Financial Health [C+]	1999	2000	2001	09-02
Long-term Debt $Mil	5,284	5,631	6,553	6,933
Total Equity $Mil	5,617	4,405	4,762	5,737
Debt/Equity Ratio	0.9	1.3	1.4	1.2

HCA has a total (short- and long-term) debt/equity ratio of 1.25--about twice the average of its competitors. However, HCA generates strong cash flow and should be able to handle the financial leverage and accompanying interest burden.

Industry	Investment Style	Stock Type	Sector
Hospitals	▦ Large Core	➡ Slow Growth	◔ Healthcare

Competition

	Market Cap $Mil	Debt/ Equity	12 Mo Trailing Sales $Mil	Price/Cash Flow	Return On Assets%	Total Return% 1 Yr	3 Yr
HCA-The Healthcare Company	21,270	1.2	19,243	8.3	5.0	7.9	13.4
Tenet Healthcare	7,990	0.6	14,319	3.2	7.0	-58.1	1.0
Universal Health Services	2,726	0.7	3,148	9.0	5.9	5.4	35.2

Price Volatility

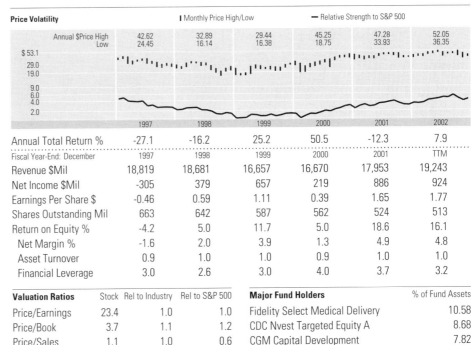

| | Monthly Price High/Low | — Relative Strength to S&P 500 |

Annual $Price High Low	42.62 24.45	32.89 16.14	29.44 16.38	45.25 18.75	47.28 33.93	52.05 36.35

	1997	1998	1999	2000	2001	2002
Annual Total Return %	-27.1	-16.2	25.2	50.5	-12.3	7.9
Fiscal Year-End: December	1997	1998	1999	2000	2001	TTM
Revenue $Mil	18,819	18,681	16,657	16,670	17,953	19,243
Net Income $Mil	-305	379	657	219	886	924
Earnings Per Share $	-0.46	0.59	1.11	0.39	1.65	1.77
Shares Outstanding Mil	663	642	587	562	524	513
Return on Equity %	-4.2	5.0	11.7	5.0	18.6	16.1
Net Margin %	-1.6	2.0	3.9	1.3	4.9	4.8
Asset Turnover	0.9	1.0	1.0	0.9	1.0	1.0
Financial Leverage	3.0	2.6	3.0	4.0	3.7	3.2

Valuation Ratios	Stock	Rel to Industry	Rel to S&P 500
Price/Earnings	23.4	1.0	1.0
Price/Book	3.7	1.1	1.2
Price/Sales	1.1	1.0	0.6
Price/Cash Flow	8.3	1.0	0.6

Major Fund Holders	% of Fund Assets
Fidelity Select Medical Delivery	10.58
CDC Nvest Targeted Equity A	8.68
CGM Capital Development	7.82
CGM Mutual	7.35

Morningstar's Take By Damon Ficklin, 11-10-2002 Stock Price as of Analysis: $36.93

Industry stalwart HCA is well positioned to continue to lead the industry. We'd buy this industry leader at a 30% discount to our fair value estimate.

With 181 hospitals and 78 ambulatory surgery centers, HCA runs the largest hospital network in the country. While size is not always a good thing, given the high fixed operating cost and the highly standardized nature of hospital services, it does provide advantages for HCA. By consolidating functions like purchasing and collections, and attacking broader issues such as hiring and nurse staffing shortages at regional or national levels HCA is able to reduce costs and develop more cost-effective solutions to some of its toughest challenges.

Even more important than its size as a whole is the strength of its parts. HCA operates hospitals in 16 of the 20 fastest growing markets in the country and maintains a number-one or -two position in each of its key markets. This translates into better bargaining and pricing power and positions it to reap the volume benefits of population growth. It also provides HCA with outstanding internal investment opportunities that are less risky than external acquisitions.

HCA's size, substantial cash flow, and demonstrated commitment to continued investment in its own facilities also make it an acquirer of choice. While HCA has been divesting more hospitals than it has been acquiring over the past several years, it still looks to acquire hospitals that complement its competitive strategy (hospitals that have market leading positions). And being an acquirer of choice means that it will nearly always be in the bidding. In the pending Health Midwest acquisition HCA out-muscled Tenet to obtain yet another market leading network of hospitals in a major market.

We look for internal expansion projects and selective acquisitions to continue to produce strong admissions, revenue, and earnings growth for HCA. With 7% fewer hospitals today than in 1990 and a growing and aging population, the demand for care should remain strong. To provide the supply, HCA spent an average of $1.3 billion annually from 1998 through 2001 and plans to spend $1.6 and $1.8 billion in 2002 and 2003, respectively. It is expanding high-acuity services, improving its facilities, and saturating its markets with investment. We expect margins to remain strong while revenue growth fades to a long-term rate of 5%.

MORNINGSTAR ® Stocks 500

Health Management Associates HMA

Rating	Risk	Moat Size	Fair Value	Last Close	Yield %
★★	Med.	Narrow	$17.00	$17.90	0.1

Company Profile

Health Management Associates provides general acute-care health services. Its hospitals are marketed toward communities of 40,000-300,000 people in the Southeastern and Southwestern United States. The company operates 42 facilities with more than 5,700 licensed beds. Its hospitals offer services including inpatient care, surgery, intensive and cardiac care, diagnostic services, and emergency services.

Management

In January 2001, Joseph Vumbacco was promoted from president to CEO, replacing William Schoen. Schoen, one of HMA's largest individual shareholders, remains as chairman.

Strategy

Health Management Associates aims to be the dominant provider of health care in nonurban areas (fewer than 400,000 people), primarily in the Southeast and Southwest. The company uses selective acquisition and cost-cutting to drive earnings growth.

5811 Pelican Bay Boulevard   www.hma-corp.com
Naples, FL 34108-2710

Morningstar Grades

Growth [B+]	1999	2000	2001	2002
Revenue %	19.0	16.4	19.1	20.4
Earnings/Share %	9.3	15.3	11.8	27.6
Book Value/Share %	17.4	19.1	17.0	8.5
Dividends/Share %	NMF	NMF	NMF	NMF

Sales growth declined from about 28% per year in 1996-98 to about 18% per year in 1999-2002. We expect that it will decline further over the next several years, from 15% in fiscal 2003 to 8% in fiscal 2006.

Profitability [A+]	2000	2001	2002	TTM
Return on Assets %	9.5	10.0	10.4	10.4
Oper Cash Flow $Mil	180	296	354	354
- Cap Spending $Mil	251	174	416	416
= Free Cash Flow $Mil	-72	122	-62	-62

HMA has long boasted the top EBITDA margin in the industry. We expect that it will maintain its edge through efficiency efforts, but improvements will be hard to come by, given the increasing size or number of acquisitions it will need to increase sales.

Financial Health [A-]	2000	2001	2002	09-02
Long-term Debt $Mil	520	429	650	650
Total Equity $Mil	1,030	1,254	1,347	1,347
Debt/Equity Ratio	0.5	0.3	0.5	0.5

HMA has about $124 million in cash (much more than is needed for working capital) and has consistently delivered a better-than-average return on equity. Its debt/total capitalization of about 0.33 is also much lower than the industry average.

Industry	Investment Style	Stock Type	Sector
Hospitals	Mid Growth	Classic Growth	Healthcare

Competition

	Market Cap $Mil	Debt/ Equity	12 Mo Trailing Sales $Mil	Price/Cash Flow	Return On Assets%	Total Return% 1 Yr	3 Yr
Health Management Associates	4,673	0.5	2,263	13.2	10.4	-2.6	6.6
HCA-The Healthcare Compan	21,270	1.2	19,243	8.3	5.0	7.9	13.4
Tenet Healthcare	7,990	0.6	14,319	3.2	7.0	-58.1	1.0

Price Volatility

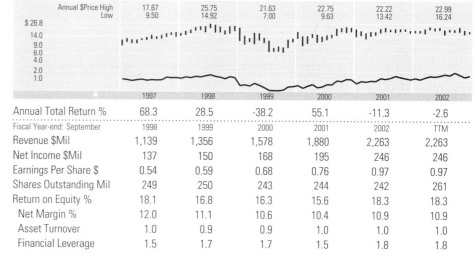

	Monthly Price High/Low			Relative Strength to S&P 500		
Annual $Price High Low	17.67 9.50	25.75 14.92	21.63 7.00	22.75 9.63	22.22 13.42	22.99 16.24

	1997	1998	1999	2000	2001	2002
Annual Total Return %	68.3	28.5	-38.2	55.1	-11.3	-2.6

Fiscal Year-end: September	1998	1999	2000	2001	2002	TTM
Revenue $Mil	1,139	1,356	1,578	1,880	2,263	2,263
Net Income $Mil	137	150	168	195	246	246
Earnings Per Share $	0.54	0.59	0.68	0.76	0.97	0.97
Shares Outstanding Mil	249	250	243	244	242	261
Return on Equity %	18.1	16.8	16.3	15.6	18.3	18.3
Net Margin %	12.0	11.1	10.6	10.4	10.9	10.9
Asset Turnover	1.0	0.9	0.9	1.0	1.0	1.0
Financial Leverage	1.5	1.7	1.7	1.5	1.8	1.8

Valuation Ratios	Stock	Rel to Industry	Rel to S&P 500
Price/Earnings	18.5	0.8	0.8
Price/Book	3.5	1.0	1.1
Price/Sales	2.1	1.9	1.0
Price/Cash Flow	13.2	1.6	1.0

Major Fund Holders	% of Fund Assets
Rochdale Alpha	6.24
AllianceBernstein Disciplined Val A	5.12
Fidelity Select Medical Delivery	4.74
American Century Life Sciences Inv	4.57

Morningstar's Take By Damon Ficklin, 12-04-2002 Stock Price as of Analysis: $18.85

Health Management Associates is one of the best at acquiring and rejuvenating struggling hospitals. Its prowess has driven strong revenue growth and the highest operating margins in the industry. But we expect that the company's size--revenue topped $2 billion in fiscal 2002--will slow its progress, so we'd look for a 30% margin of safety to our fair value estimate before buying shares.

HMA is focused on the underserved nonurban market. Not only is this market a little less competitive than the urban market, but the rural population is growing faster than the national average and HMA holds the sole or dominant position in almost all of the areas it serves. HMA tries to further insulate itself from competition by operating in states that require certificates of need. In essence, these certificates require proof that additional health-care need exists before new facilities can be built or existing ones can be expanded. This guards against overcapacity and can serve as a good barrier to competition. However, it can also be a barrier to growth.

HMA has driven its growth via acquisitions, buying small hospitals with 100-300 beds in nonurban areas of the United States. These acquisition targets are usually struggling with management inefficiency, high costs, and a lack of capital to improve their facilities. HMA provides new management, better billing and workflow systems, and much-needed capital to revamp facilities. The company has gotten so good at picking the right markets and managing its acquisitions that it has the top margins in the hospital industry. Its EBITDA (earnings before interest, taxes, depreciation, and amortization) margin has bested the peer average by more than 5 percentage points for several years now.

While we expect HMA to maintain its margin advantage, we think further margin expansion is unlikely, given the firm's need to make more or larger acquisitions to fight fading revenue growth. As the company has gotten larger, revenue growth has slowed, from about 28% per year in 1996-98 to about 18% per year for 1999-2002. Acquisitions have produced the majority of the growth in recent years. Stable margins and fading sales growth mean slower earnings growth.

Balancing concerns over slowing revenue and earnings growth against our confidence in HMA's business model and its position in the nonurban market, we would look to buy shares at a 30% margin of safety to our fair value estimate.

Health Net HNT

	Rating	Risk	Moat Size	Fair Value	Last Close	Yield %
	★★★	Low	None	$27.00	$26.40	0.0

Company Profile

Health Net is a managed health-care organization. The company provides services in the Western, Northwestern, and Eastern United States. Its health-maintenance organizations offer their members health-care services like ambulatory and outpatient physician care, hospital care, pharmacy and mental health services, eye care, and ancillary diagnostic and therapeutic services. Health Net provides these services through group, individual, Medicare risk, Medicaid, and other programs.

Management

Jay Gellert became president and CEO in 1998, after serving as COO for a year. We think he has done a solid job of moving Health Net into shared-risk plans from the capitation plans that were once so popular in California.

Strategy

Health Net is focusing on profitability over top-line growth. The company has been improving health insurance policy pricing to offset rising medical costs, and dropping customers unwilling to pay the higher premiums. It has also been selling its nonstrategic and unprofitable business segments and using the proceeds to pay down debt and improve its balance sheet.

21650 Oxnard Street
Woodland Hills, CA 91367

www.health.net

Morningstar Grades

Growth [C]	1998	1999	2000	2001
Revenue %	23.2	0.2	5.0	10.9
Earnings/Share %	NMF	NMF	14.7	-48.1
Book Value/Share %	-16.5	19.4	18.8	7.8
Dividends/Share %	NMF	NMF	NMF	NMF

Health insurance enrollment has declined as Health Net has instituted more-disciplined pricing, but we expect membership growth to resume at a modest pace now that the firm has dropped most of its less profitable accounts.

Profitability [B-]	1999	2000	2001	TTM
Return on Assets %	3.9	4.5	2.4	7.0
Oper Cash Flow $Mil	297	366	546	337
- Cap Spending $Mil	37	87	70	53
= Free Cash Flow $Mil	261	279	477	284

Over the past few years, Health Net has maintained a stable medical loss ratio just below the industry average. We expect that its disciplined pricing will result in more of the same.

Financial Health [A]	1999	2000	2001	09-02
Long-term Debt $Mil	1,039	766	594	399
Total Equity $Mil	891	1,061	1,166	1,346
Debt/Equity Ratio	1.2	0.7	0.5	0.3

Health Net's balance sheet looks secure, as the firm has used strong operating cash flow to retire debt and repurchase stock. It has reduced its debt/total capital ratio to under 23% from nearly 50% at the end of 2000.

Industry	Investment Style	Stock Type	Sector
Physicians	Mid Core	→ Slow Growth	Healthcare

Competition

	Market Cap $Mil	Debt/ Equity	12 Mo Trailing Sales $Mil	Price/Cash Flow	Return On Assets%	Total Return% 1 Yr	3 Yr
Health Net	3,269	0.3	10,038	9.7	7.0	21.2	41.9
UnitedHealth Group	25,235	0.3	24,358	12.5	8.9	18.0	46.6
WellPoint Health Networks	10,372	0.3	16,180	7.9	6.0	21.8	29.5

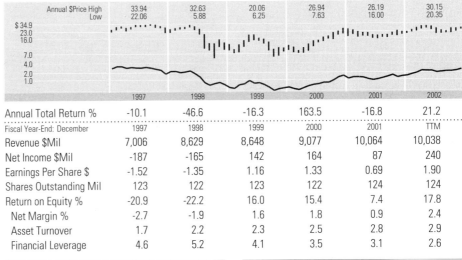

Price Volatility — Monthly Price High/Low — Relative Strength to S&P 500

Annual $Price High / Low	33.94 / 22.06	32.63 / 5.88	20.06 / 6.25	26.94 / 7.63	26.19 / 16.00	30.15 / 20.35

	1997	1998	1999	2000	2001	2002
Annual Total Return %	-10.1	-46.6	-16.3	163.5	-16.8	21.2

Fiscal Year-End: December	1997	1998	1999	2000	2001	TTM
Revenue $Mil	7,006	8,629	8,648	9,077	10,064	10,038
Net Income $Mil	-187	-165	142	164	87	240
Earnings Per Share $	-1.52	-1.35	1.16	1.33	0.69	1.90
Shares Outstanding Mil	123	122	123	122	124	124
Return on Equity %	-20.9	-22.2	16.0	15.4	7.4	17.8
Net Margin %	-2.7	-1.9	1.6	1.8	0.9	2.4
Asset Turnover	1.7	2.2	2.3	2.5	2.8	2.9
Financial Leverage	4.6	5.2	4.1	3.5	3.1	2.6

Valuation Ratios	Stock	Rel to Industry	Rel to S&P 500
Price/Earnings	13.9	1.0	0.6
Price/Book	2.4	1.3	0.8
Price/Sales	0.3	0.9	0.2
Price/Cash Flow	9.7	1.0	0.7

Major Fund Holders	% of Fund Assets
Legg Mason American Leading Co Prim	5.35
Morgan Stanley Inst Value	3.95
Van Kampen Value A	3.61
Morgan Stanley Value A	3.27

Morningstar's Take By Damon Ficklin, 11-18-2002 Stock Price as of Analysis: $26.23

Health Net has finally completed a long restructuring, divesting itself of unprofitable business and focusing on core markets. While its bottom line is starting to show the fruits of this strategy, we'd still wait for a 40% margin of safety to our fair value estimate before buying.

Health Net has emerged from its turnaround well positioned and financially sound. It has been dropping less-profitable Medicare accounts, where government reimbursements have trailed rising medical costs, as well as large commercial groups that refuse to pay higher premiums. It has diversified its customer base with a strong push into the small-group and individual market and is intensifying efforts in the midsize market as well.

Commercial small-group and individual enrollment now accounts for 27% of the mix, up from less than 20% just a couple of years ago. Health Net has shown particularly strong growth in this segment in California, where the exit of several competitors over the past 18 months has created plenty of room to grow. Although total enrollment is down 6% over the past 12 months, small-group and individual enrollment is up 20%. With most targeted cuts behind the company, we expect total enrollment growth to resume at 2%-3% by the end of 2002.

Health Net has done a great job of managing costs over the past few years. Its has delivered a stable medical loss ratio (medical costs paid divided by premiums collected) just below the industry average of 85%, and improved its selling, general, and administrative expense ratio (SG&A plus depreciation divided by premiums collected) from 16% in 1999 to about 13.5% in the current year. We expect the firm will continue to improve its service while maintaining administrative cost savings as it moves to a unified information system by the end of 2003.

Health Net has strengthened its balance sheet by using strong cash flows and the proceeds from business divestitures to retire debt and buy back shares. It has reduced debt/total capital from nearly 50% at the end of 2000 to less than 23% in October 2002. This is the first time it has been below the company's target of 30% (closer to, but still above, the industry average). Health Net has also repurchased about 2.5% of its outstanding stock since initiating its share-buyback plan in May.

While we don't think Health Net has many sustainable competitive advantages, it is entrenched in its target markets and doing everything necessary to maintain its position. We would buy the shares at a 40% discount to our fair value estimate.

MORNINGSTAR® Stocks 500

Healthsouth HRC

	Rating	Risk	Moat Size	Fair Value	Last Close	Yield %
	★★★	High	Narrow	$5.00	$4.20	0.0

Company Profile

Healthsouth provides rehabilitative health-care services. In its outpatient and inpatient rehabilitation facilities, it has established interdisciplinary programs to rehabilitate patients experiencing disability because of physical conditions like stroke, head injuries, and sports-related injuries. The company's rehabilitation services include physical therapy, sports medicine, neurorehabilitation, occupational and respiratory therapy, and speech-language pathology. The firm operates more than 2,000 locations in the United States, Canada, United Kingdom, and Australia.

Management

Richard Scrushy is out as CEO, though he remains as chairman. The promotion of Bill Owens to CEO is a decent choice, given his experience as president, controller, CFO, and COO, but he'll have a difficult time regaining employee and investor trust.

Strategy

Healthsouth had to suspend the spin-off of its surgery center segment because of a lack of investor interest stemming from the company's weak credibility. Now, the firm is trying to trim costs in tandem with the reduced reimbursements through staff reductions and a restructuring of its physical therapy business.

One Healthsouth Parkway   www.healthsouth.com
Birmingham, AL 35243

Morningstar Grades

Growth [C]	1998	1999	2000	2001
Revenue %	28.3	1.6	3.0	4.4
Earnings/Share %	-87.6	63.6	294.4	-28.2
Book Value/Share %	-5.3	-6.7	19.2	6.4
Dividends/Share %	NMF	NMF	NMF	NMF

Increases in patient volume and higher prices led to revenue growth of 4% in the first nine months of 2002 from the year-ago period. We expect growth to slow because of lower reimbursement rates for outpatient rehabilitation services.

Profitability [B+]	1999	2000	2001	TTM
Return on Assets %	1.1	3.8	2.7	2.6
Oper Cash Flow $Mil	705	797	670	857
- Cap Spending $Mil	474	584	440	713
= Free Cash Flow $Mil	230	213	230	145

Profitability is in question now that the company is restructuring. Given the unfavorable changes in Medicare reimbursements, we expect the EBITDA margin to fall from the 28% posted so far in 2002 to 25% in 2003.

Financial Health [B]	1999	2000	2001	09-02
Long-term Debt $Mil	3,077	3,169	3,005	2,836
Total Equity $Mil	3,206	3,526	3,797	3,964
Debt/Equity Ratio	1.0	0.9	0.8	0.7

Credit-rating agencies are worried about uncertain cash flows; we share their concerns. Although S&P has cut the firm's debt to junk status, we don't think Healthsouth faces an immediate liquidity crunch and has time to right its sinking ship.

Industry	Investment Style	Stock Type	Sector
Physicians	Mid Value	→ Slow Growth	Healthcare

Competition	Market Cap $Mil	Debt/ Equity	12 Mo Trailing Sales $Mil	Price/Cash Flow	Return On Assets%	Total Return% 1 Yr	3 Yr
Healthsouth	1,661	0.7	4,502	1.9	2.6	-71.7	-7.9
Lifepoint Hospitals	1,182	—	706	—	—	—	—
RehabCare Group	302	—	556	—	—	—	—

Price Volatility

	Monthly Price High/Low				— Relative Strength to S&P 500	
Annual $Price High Low	28.94 17.75	30.81 7.69	17.75 4.56	17.50 4.75	18.49 11.25	15.90 2.80
	1997	1998	1999	2000	2001	2002

Annual Total Return %	43.7	-44.4	-65.2	203.5	-9.2	-71.7
Fiscal Year-end: December	1997	1998	1999	2000	2001	TTM
Revenue $Mil	3,123	4,006	4,072	4,195	4,380	4,502
Net Income $Mil	343	47	77	278	202	204
Earnings Per Share $	0.89	0.11	0.18	0.71	0.51	0.51
Shares Outstanding Mil	365	423	403	387	389	395
Return on Equity %	10.4	1.4	2.4	7.9	5.3	5.1
Net Margin %	11.0	1.2	1.9	6.6	4.6	4.5
Asset Turnover	0.6	0.6	0.6	0.6	0.6	0.6
Financial Leverage	1.7	2.0	2.1	2.1	2.0	2.0

Valuation Ratios	Stock	Rel to Industry	Rel to S&P 500
Price/Earnings	8.2	0.6	0.4
Price/Book	0.4	0.2	0.1
Price/Sales	0.4	1.0	0.2
Price/Cash Flow	1.9	0.2	0.1

Major Fund Holders	% of Fund Assets
Polynous Growth A	4.12
HSBC Investor Mid Cap Tr	3.01
HSBC Investor Mid Cap A	3.01
Fidelity Advisor Asset Allocation A	2.67

Morningstar's Take By Tom Goetzinger, 12-04-2002 Stock Price as of Analysis: $3.98

Healthsouth may still be the nation's leading provider of rehabilitation and outpatient surgery services, but we'd require a large margin of safety to our fair value estimate and significantly more management credibility before purchasing the shares.

Healthsouth's restructuring of its outpatient physical therapy business--which brings in 20% of the company's revenue--stems from changes in the way Medicare reimburses providers for these rehabilitation services. Healthsouth estimates that the reimbursement rate change will reduce EBITDA (earnings before interest, taxes, depreciation, and amortization) by $175 million annually; we estimate a drop of more than $250 million because we think managed-care firms will demand rates for their patients that are in line with government patients'. We're disappointed by management's disclosure of the matter. Other physical therapy providers like Select Medical and RehabCare Group said they had known about the effects of the rule change for several months before Healthsouth revealed the impact on its operations.

Given this poor disclosure, the Securities and Exchange Commission is conducting an investigation into whether former CEO and current chairman Richard Scrushy and other senior managers delayed disclosure of the impact of the rate change so they could cash out before the bad news hit. We contend that the late-August press release date looks suspicious. (Scrushy sold 2.5 million shares in late July at $10 and 5.3 million shares in May at $14.) The rate change that precipitated the whole mess was first discussed in 1999, and was clarified and amended by the Centers for Medicare & Medicaid Services in May 2002 with an effective date of July 1. Because Healthsouth failed to include the anticipated negative impact of the rate change in its outlook during the year, we think some company insiders, including Scrushy, could face indictment at some point in 2003, once the investigation is concluded.

In the meantime, Healthsouth is trying to reduce operating costs in tandem with lower reimbursements and slower revenue growth. The company plans to trim its workforce, but that's the easy part. The heavy lifting involves improving the efficiency of its three main businesses--physical therapy, surgery, and diagnostics--and retaining its franchiselike appeal for patients and payers. So far, the firm hasn't communicated a concrete strategy to do so. With this much legal and organizational chaos, we'd stay on the sidelines.

Heinz HJ HNZ

	Rating	Risk	Moat Size	Fair Value	Last Close	Yield %
	★★★	Med.	Narrow	$37.00	$32.87	4.9

Company Profile

HJ Heinz produces consumer food products, including Heinz ketchup and other condiments, canned and frozen soups, canned meats, and baby food. The company's other products include StarKist canned tuna, Rosetto frozen pasta products, and Bagel Bites pizza snacks. Heinz markets its products in the United States and overseas. The company also manufactures pet foods under brand names that include 9Lives, Kibbles 'n Bits, and Snausages.

Management

Bill Johnson, only the sixth CEO in the company's 132-year history, led Heinz's marketing efforts as the head of the firm's pet products, StarKist, and Asia Pacific operations before he took over the top spot in 1998.

Strategy

In an effort to become a more focused, faster-growing company, Heinz spun off five of its underperforming businesses to Del Monte in December 2002. The firm is boosting the amount of money it spends on marketing its key remaining brands in an attempt to attract more customer awareness and increase sales.

600 Grant Street
Pittsburgh, PA 15219
www.heinz.com

Morningstar Grades

Growth [B-]	1999	2000	2001	2002
Revenue %	1.0	-3.9	-1.3	6.9
Earnings/Share %	-40.0	91.5	-44.9	73.5
Book Value/Share %	-17.5	-9.7	-11.7	24.5
Dividends/Share %	8.7	7.6	6.9	4.0

Heinz's 6.3% year-over-year sales growth in the first half of fiscal 2003 was due to price increases in the hyperinflationary markets of South America and Africa; volume actually fell 3%. We expect sales to grow 3%-4% annually after the spin-off.

Profitability [A-]	2000	2001	2002	TTM
Return on Assets %	10.1	5.3	8.1	6.8
Oper Cash Flow $Mil	543	506	891	1,059
- Cap Spending $Mil	452	411	213	186
= Free Cash Flow $Mil	91	95	678	873

A program to cut operating expenses has been slow to bear fruit. Base earnings per share fell 6% in fiscal 2002 and 17% in the first half of fiscal 2003, but will probably grow 8%-10% annually after the spin-off.

Financial Health [C]	2000	2001	2002	10-02
Long-term Debt $Mil	3,936	3,015	4,643	4,782
Total Equity $Mil	1,596	1,374	1,719	1,882
Debt/Equity Ratio	2.5	2.2	2.7	2.5

Heinz's long-term debt has increased more than 50% over the past year, to $4.6 billion, but the spin-off to Del Monte will reduce that debt by $1.1 billion. The company plans to continue reducing debt over the next three years.

Industry	Investment Style	Stock Type	Sector
Food Mfg.	Large Value	High Yield	Consumer Goods

Competition	Market Cap $Mil	Debt/ Equity	12 Mo Trailing Sales $Mil	Price/Cash Flow	Return On Assets%	Total Return% 1 Yr	3 Yr
Heinz HJ	11,549	2.5	9,712	10.9	6.8	-9.2	2.3
Nestle SA ADR	85,869	—	50,054	—	—	—	—
Kraft Foods	45,853	0.5	34,063	11.1	5.3	16.1	—

Price Volatility

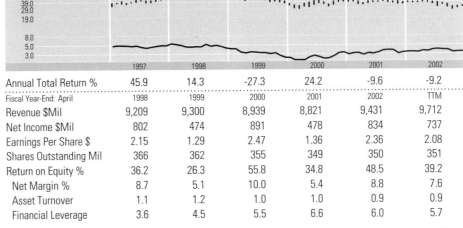

	Monthly Price High/Low			Relative Strength to S&P 500	
Annual $Price High / Low	52.49 / 32.64	57.18 / 44.91	54.45 / 36.57	44.44 / 28.53	44.39 / 34.17	40.26 / 27.41

	1997	1998	1999	2000	2001	2002
Annual Total Return %	45.9	14.3	-27.3	24.2	-9.6	-9.2

Fiscal Year-End: April	1998	1999	2000	2001	2002	TTM
Revenue $Mil	9,209	9,300	8,939	8,821	9,431	9,712
Net Income $Mil	802	474	891	478	834	737
Earnings Per Share $	2.15	1.29	2.47	1.36	2.36	2.08
Shares Outstanding Mil	366	362	355	349	350	351
Return on Equity %	36.2	26.3	55.8	34.8	48.5	39.2
Net Margin %	8.7	5.1	10.0	5.4	8.8	7.6
Asset Turnover	1.1	1.2	1.0	1.0	0.9	0.9
Financial Leverage	3.6	4.5	5.5	6.6	6.0	5.7

Valuation Ratios	Stock	Rel to Industry	Rel to S&P 500
Price/Earnings	15.8	0.8	0.7
Price/Book	6.1	1.4	1.9
Price/Sales	1.2	0.8	0.6
Price/Cash Flow	10.9	1.0	0.8

Major Fund Holders	% of Fund Assets
AmSouth Select Equity B	6.53
CDC Nvest Growth and Income A	3.26
Chicago Asset Management Value	3.10
Dobson Covered Call	2.54

Morningstar's Take By David Kathman, 12-30-2002 Stock Price as of Analysis: $32.91

Heinz's spin-off of five underperforming units to Del Monte is a potentially good move, but the company's history of lackluster restructuring attempts gives us pause. Until the effects of the deal become clearer, we remain wary of the stock.

Since he took the reins nearly four years ago, Heinz CEO Bill Johnson has struggled to boost the food conglomerate's lackluster performance. He's achieved some successes, like introducing Blastin' Green and Funky Purple ketchup for kids and leveraging other popular brands like Boston Market and T.G.I. Friday's in the frozen food division. But overall, sales growth has remained sluggish and earnings have been erratic.

In an effort to get off this treadmill of lackluster performance, Johnson announced a new restructuring plan in June 2002 designed to make Heinz leaner and more focused. The firm would spin off five underperforming businesses representing 20% of revenue--StarKist tuna, pet food, baby food, private-label soups, and College Inn Broth--and merging them into Del Monte Foods to create a "new" Del Monte 75% owned by Heinz shareholders. The new Heinz will be smaller but have better growth potential; sales in the spun-off businesses declined in fiscal 2002, whereas sales in the core divisions grew 10%.

But to reap those benefits, Heinz is going through a difficult "transition year" of wobbly growth and depressed earnings. One significant factor has been a chain reaction from a shift in marketing strategy. Heinz reduced the discounts it gives to retailers in favor of increased advertising and promotions aimed directly at consumers; retailers then cut back on new purchases in order to sell off the inventory they already had. This shift has caused considerable disruption, and its ultimate success will depend on the strength of Heinz's brands.

Given Heinz's unimpressive record with its previous restructurings, we'd prefer to see how this newest plan works before getting too excited about the stock. We also question where the new, smaller Heinz will fit into a market where most of its competitors have been getting bigger through acquisitions. These uncertainties mean that we'd want to see a significant discount to our $37 fair value estimate before we could recommend the stock.

MORNINGSTAR® Stocks 500

Hershey Foods HSY

	Rating	Risk	Moat Size	Fair Value	Last Close	Yield %
	★★	Med.	Wide	$56.00	$67.44	1.9

Company Profile

Hershey Foods manufactures food products, primarily chocolate. Its candy brands include Hershey's, Reese's, Kit Kat, Mounds, Almond Joy, Payday, Jolly Rancher, Milk Duds, 5th Avenue, Rolo, Skor, York, Whoppers, and Twizzlers. The company's grocery product division produces cocoa, chocolate syrup and milk, baking chocolate, and dessert toppings and beverages under the Hershey name, and peanut butter under the Reese's name. Hershey Foods markets its products in the United States and overseas. Sales to Wal-Mart account for about 15% of Hershey's total sales.

Management

The board of directors parted with tradition by appointing an outsider, Kraft veteran Rick Lenny, to lead the firm in 2000. He has done a great job of getting costs down, but has alienated some in the tradition-rich company.

Strategy

Hershey seeks to generate growth by introducing new products, like Jolly Rancher lollipops and Hershey Bites, and through acquisitions, like that of Nabisco's gum and mint division. The chocolatier has freed up marketing dollars to stimulate sales growth by cutting its distribution costs through improved logistics and enterprise software.

100 Crystal A Drive
Hershey, PA 17033
www.hersheys.com

Morningstar Grades

Growth [C+]	1998	1999	2000	2001
Revenue %	3.1	-10.5	6.3	8.0
Earnings/Share %	4.9	39.3	-25.8	-38.0
Book Value/Share %	26.5	8.7	9.2	-2.3
Dividends/Share %	9.5	8.7	8.0	7.9

Sales were basically flat in the first nine months of 2002 as a result of the strike in the second quarter and the abortive sale of the firm in the third quarter. Hershey will fall short of its original target of 3%-4% internal sales growth in 2002.

Profitability [A]	1999	2000	2001	TTM
Return on Assets %	13.8	9.7	6.4	6.6
Oper Cash Flow $Mil	318	412	706	595
- Cap Spending $Mil	115	138	160	120
= Free Cash Flow $Mil	203	274	546	476

Despite weak sales, Hershey beat First Call earnings estimates in the second and third quarters, since cost savings have been coming in ahead of schedule. Its double-digit net margin is very solid for a food company.

Financial Health [A]	1999	2000	2001	09-02
Long-term Debt $Mil	878	878	877	868
Total Equity $Mil	1,099	1,175	1,147	1,370
Debt/Equity Ratio	0.8	0.7	0.8	0.6

Hershey consistently generates strong free cash flow, and its financial leverage of 2.5 isn't especially high for the food industry.

Industry	Investment Style	Stock Type	Sector
Food Mfg.	Large Core	→ Slow Growth	Consumer Goods

Competition	Market Cap $Mil	Debt/ Equity	12 Mo Trailing Sales $Mil	Price/Cash Flow	Return On Assets%	Total Return% 1 Yr	3 Yr
Hershey Foods	9,197	0.6	4,537	15.4	6.6	1.4	17.0
Nestle SA ADR	85,869	—	50,054	—	—	—	—
Wm. Wrigley Jr.	12,360	—	2,673	28.2	19.0	8.5	13.4

Price Volatility

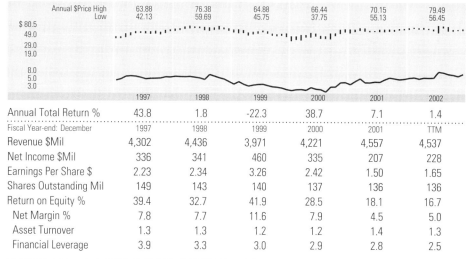

		Monthly Price High/Low		— Relative Strength to S&P 500		
Annual $Price High Low	63.88 42.13	76.38 59.69	64.88 45.75	66.44 37.75	70.15 55.13	79.49 56.45

	1997	1998	1999	2000	2001	2002
Annual Total Return %	43.8	1.8	-22.3	38.7	7.1	1.4
Fiscal Year-end: December	1997	1998	1999	2000	2001	TTM
Revenue $Mil	4,302	4,436	3,971	4,221	4,557	4,537
Net Income $Mil	336	341	460	335	207	228
Earnings Per Share $	2.23	2.34	3.26	2.42	1.50	1.65
Shares Outstanding Mil	149	143	140	137	136	136
Return on Equity %	39.4	32.7	41.9	28.5	18.1	16.7
Net Margin %	7.8	7.7	11.6	7.9	4.5	5.0
Asset Turnover	1.3	1.3	1.2	1.2	1.4	1.3
Financial Leverage	3.9	3.3	3.0	2.9	2.8	2.5

Valuation Ratios	Stock	Rel to Industry	Rel to S&P 500
Price/Earnings	40.9	1.9	1.7
Price/Book	6.7	1.6	2.1
Price/Sales	2.0	1.4	1.0
Price/Cash Flow	15.4	1.4	1.2

Major Fund Holders	% of Fund Assets
Fidelity Select Food & Agriculture	5.80
AmSouth Select Equity B	3.39
Chesapeake Core Growth	2.05
Enterprise Mergers & Acquisitions A	1.93

Morningstar's Take By David Kathman, 11-13-2002 Stock Price as of Analysis: $65.25

Though we like to munch on Hershey candy as much as the next guy, we wouldn't pick up shares unless they fell to the mid-$40s.

Since taking the reins at Hershey in early 2000, Rick Lenny has been a busy man. He broadened Hershey's product line by purchasing Nabisco's gum and mint business, and in the fall of 2001 he initiated an ambitious restructuring program designed to reduce costs by $75-$80 million a year, investing the proceeds in strengthening key brands. This program has already started to show results. Though overall sales have been essentially flat in recent quarters, sales of Hershey's core brands have been growing in the midsingle digits, helped by new products like Reese's Fast Break. Cost controls, along with a greater percentage of sales in higher-margin brands and channels, have resulted in significant improvement in both gross and operating margins.

But this improvement has not come without a price. The cost-cutting and restructuring were indirectly responsible for a six-week factory strike in the spring of 2002, as workers resisted company efforts to reduce employee benefits. The strike hurt Hershey's sales, but more important, it damaged employee morale as Hershey's strong sense of tradition and community was tested by the dispute.

That sense of community was tested in a different way in late July, when the Milton Hershey Trust, which owns 79% of the voting rights in Hershey, announced plans to sell the company in order to diversify the trust's portfolio. Furious opposition to the sale from employees and the surrounding community led the trust to reject a sweetheart offer from Wrigley and pull Hershey off the table at the last minute. That decision probably saved Lenny's job, since he was unlikely to stay on if Hershey was bought out.

Now Hershey's main job is to keep its legacy reasonably intact while hanging on to its productivity gains and charting a course for growth. Its 30% share of the U.S. candy market is nearly twice that of number-two Mars, but it gets almost no revenue from outside North America, limiting expansion possibilities. And while the trust now insists that Hershey management has a free hand to pursue whatever course it chooses, we can't help but remain a little nervous at having such a capricious controlling shareholder. There's still plenty to like about Hershey, but we'd need around a 20% margin of safety to our $56 fair value estimate before getting excited about the stock.

Hewlett-Packard HPQ

	Rating	Risk	Moat Size	Fair Value	Last Close	Yield %
	★★	High	Narrow	$19.00	$17.36	1.8

Company Profile

Hewlett-Packard manufactures computer products and provides related services. Its products include computer systems, computer peripherals like HP LaserJet and HP DeskJet printers, digital scanners, information-storage products, and computer systems that are compatible with IBM equipment. The company also provides installation and consulting services. HP recently agreed to purchase Compaq in an all-stock deal.

Management

CEO Carly Fiorina joined HP in 1999. She was initially greeted with enthusiastic press, but a string of earnings disappointments put her on the defensive. The apparent progress in integrating Compaq may salvage her reputation yet.

Strategy

The acquisition of Compaq is part of Hewlett-Packard's plan to push further into servers, storage, and consulting. This is especially important for HP, since the PC and printer markets will not be enough to sustain current growth and profitability levels. Management expects to achieve cost savings by reducing staff and consolidating product lines.

3000 Hanover Street   www.hp.com
Palo Alto, CA 94304

Morningstar Grades

Growth [A-]	1998	1999	2000	2001
Revenue %	11.2	7.7	15.3	-7.5
Earnings/Share %	-6.1	20.1	7.8	-88.3
Book Value/Share %	4.2	9.6	-21.0	3.8
Dividends/Share %	15.4	6.7	0.0	0.0

Growth has slowed over the past few years, thanks to a combination of the economic slowdown and HP's exposure to PCs and printers. We think long-term growth of 8%-10% (after an initial merger-related contraction) is reasonable.

Profitability [A]	1999	2000	2001	TTM
Return on Assets %	9.9	10.9	1.3	-3.5
Oper Cash Flow $Mil	3,096	3,705	2,561	5,657
- Cap Spending $Mil	1,134	1,737	1,527	1,333
= Free Cash Flow $Mil	1,962	1,968	1,034	4,324

A key goal of HP's acquisition of Compaq was to generate cost synergy. Management has cut costs and jobs well ahead of schedule, and the two money-losing businesses (PCs and enterprise hardware) are moving toward breaking even.

Financial Health [B]	1999	2000	2001	07-02
Long-term Debt $Mil	1,764	3,402	3,729	4,442
Total Equity $Mil	18,295	14,209	13,953	14,961
Debt/Equity Ratio	0.1	0.2	0.3	0.3

No reason for concern here. Cash and debt effectively balance each other, and cash flows remain strong.

Industry	Investment Style	Stock Type	Sector
Computer Equipment	▦ Large Value	➡ Slow Growth	▦ Hardware

Competition

	Market Cap $Mil	Debt/ Equity	12 Mo Trailing Sales $Mil	Price/Cash Flow	Return On Assets%	Total Return% 1 Yr	3 Yr
Hewlett-Packard	34,321	0.3	49,416	6.1	-3.5	-13.9	-24.7
IBM	130,982	0.8	82,442	9.0	5.8	-35.5	-11.1
Dell Computer	69,252	0.1	32,054	20.1	13.4	-1.6	-16.9

Price Volatility

I Monthly Price High/Low   — Relative Strength to S&P 500

Annual $Price High Low	28.49 18.80	32.18 18.38	46.27 24.76	69.00 29.13	37.95 12.50	24.12 10.75

	1997	1998	1999	2000	2001	2002
Annual Total Return %	25.6	11.0	68.0	-28.4	-34.0	-13.9

Fiscal Year-End: October	1997	1998	1999	2000	2001	TTM
Revenue $Mil	35,358	39,330	42,371	48,870	45,226	49,416
Net Income $Mil	3,119	2,945	3,491	3,697	408	-1,196
Earnings Per Share $	1.48	1.39	1.67	1.80	0.21	-0.23
Shares Outstanding Mil	2,107	2,059	2,018	1,977	1,943	1,977
Return on Equity %	19.3	17.4	19.1	26.0	2.9	-8.0
Net Margin %	8.8	7.5	8.2	7.6	0.9	-2.4
Asset Turnover	1.2	1.2	1.2	1.4	1.4	1.4
Financial Leverage	1.8	1.9	1.9	2.4	2.3	2.3

Valuation Ratios	Stock	Rel to Industry	Rel to S&P 500
Price/Earnings	NMF	—	—
Price/Book	2.3	0.4	0.7
Price/Sales	0.7	0.4	0.3
Price/Cash Flow	6.1	0.7	0.5

Major Fund Holders	% of Fund Assets
Security Technology A	5.16
Hartford Global Technology A	4.95
Kelmoore Strategy Liberty A	4.72
Thompson Plumb Growth	4.61

Morningstar's Take By Joseph Beaulieu, 11-21-2002 Stock Price as of Analysis: $18.99

We now have a second full quarter of results to show what Hewlett-Packard and Compaq look like as a combined company. We weren't impressed with the July quarter, but the October quarter looked good enough for us to boost our fair value estimate.

The printer business, which has kept HP in the black, is still going strong, with modest revenue growth and solid profit margins. Printing supplies (toner cartridges and such) are an extremely profitable recurring revenue stream, and now account for around half of printing revenue. Dell's expected entry into the printer market probably won't have an enormous impact on HP at first (if ever), but we would be concerned if Dell appeared to be gaining enough share to dilute HP's supply revenue.

PCs, servers, and storage are still losing money, but it seems that management is delivering cost cuts more quickly than promised; the businesses are moving toward break-even at a surprising pace. However, we still think the PC business is going to be a major challenge for HP. Dell continues to dominate the market for personal computers, and by some accounts has leading share. If HP is going to regain lost ground in the PC market, we suspect it will have to be through larger corporate deals in which the company provides PCs along with enterprise

hardware and services. Dell has an enormous advantage with individuals and small businesses that will be difficult to challenge.

The enterprise hardware business poses problems as well. The spending environment remains weak, and product integration could be difficult, given the large numbers of brands and product lines (Compaq's enterprise hardware business was mainly the product of acquisitions). Depressed IT spending and fierce competition aren't going to make HP's work any easier.

Management has a few quarters to go with the integration process, but the October-quarter results have made us reconsider our general pessimism about the merger's prospects. After making some minor adjustments to our discounted cash flow model (mostly on the margin side), we are raising our fair value estimate on the stock to $19 from $17. We would still require a substantial margin of safety (30%-40%) to account for the large integration, competitive, and macroeconomic risks facing the company.

If HP does deliver on all of its promises, we still think the stock could be worth more than $20. For now, though, we'll take a more cautious approach.

MORNINGSTAR® Stocks 500

Home Depot HD

	Rating	Risk	Moat Size	Fair Value	Last Close	Yield %
	★★★★★	Med.	Wide	$36.00	$23.96	0.9

Company Profile

Home Depot is a home-improvement retailer. The company operates stores that sell an assortment of building materials and home-improvement products. It operates more than 1,120 stores in the United States, Canada, and South America. The 40,000-50,000 items stocked in a typical store are name-brand merchandise. The largest segment of sales, approximately 25%, is from building materials, lumber, and millwork. In addition to these stores, the company's Depot Diners provide food services. Home Depot also offers home-improvement loans.

Management

Bernard Marcus and Arthur Blank founded Home Depot in 1978. General Electric veteran Robert Nardelli became chairman and CEO in December 2000, and is focused on improving operational efficiency.

Strategy

Home Depot is the archetypal category killer, a retailer that specializes in a niche and comes to dominate it. It has done this by offering the largest selection of home-improvement merchandise at prices equal to or below those of competitors. To keep growth strong, it is expanding its services business and going after professional contractors.

2455 Paces Ferry Road N.W.   www.homedepot.com
Atlanta, GA 30339-4024

Morningstar Grades

Growth [A+]	1999	2000	2001	2002
Revenue %	25.1	27.2	19.0	17.1
Earnings/Share %	36.5	40.8	10.0	17.3
Book Value/Share %	20.8	38.4	20.2	19.8
Dividends/Share %	21.0	47.8	41.1	6.3

Growth in the 1990s was fantastic: Sales and earnings increased about 30% per year, while square footage jumped 25% annually. As a mature firm with a slower pace of store openings, Home Depot will now have much slower sales growth.

Profitability [A+]	2000	2001	2002	TTM
Return on Assets %	13.6	12.1	11.5	11.8
Oper Cash Flow $Mil	2,446	2,796	5,963	6,394
- Cap Spending $Mil	2,581	3,558	3,393	2,793
= Free Cash Flow $Mil	-135	-762	2,570	3,601

Return on equity has been between 17% and 20% every year since 1990, even as Home Depot decreased its financial leverage. Steady asset turnover and margin expansion have allowed the firm to maintain its strong profitability.

Financial Health [A+]	2000	2001	2002	10-02
Long-term Debt $Mil	750	1,545	1,250	1,316
Total Equity $Mil	12,341	15,004	18,082	20,119
Debt/Equity Ratio	0.1	0.1	0.1	0.1

Home Depot is in excellent financial health. The firm sports a solid balance sheet and a plethora of cash, although its debt/equity ratio would be a little higher if off-balance-sheet operating leases were capitalized.

Industry	Investment Style	Stock Type	Sector
Home Supply	☐ Large Growth	↗ Classic Growth	Consumer Services

Competition	Market Cap $Mil	Debt/ Equity	12 Mo Trailing Sales $Mil	Price/Cash Flow	Return On Assets%	Total Return% 1 Yr	3 Yr
Home Depot	56,498	0.1	58,522	8.8	11.8	-52.7	-24.8
Lowe's Companies	29,242	0.5	24,666	11.0	8.7	-19.0	12.7
Sears Roebuck	7,576	3.3	41,156	—	2.1	-48.6	-6.5

Price Volatility

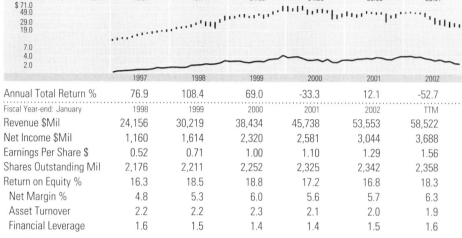

| | I Monthly Price High/Low | — Relative Strength to S&P 500 |

Annual $Price High / Low	20.17 / 10.61	41.33 / 18.44	69.75 / 34.58	70.00 / 34.69	53.73 / 30.00	52.60 / 23.01

	1997	1998	1999	2000	2001	2002
Annual Total Return %	76.9	108.4	69.0	-33.3	12.1	-52.7

Fiscal Year-end: January	1998	1999	2000	2001	2002	TTM
Revenue $Mil	24,156	30,219	38,434	45,738	53,553	58,522
Net Income $Mil	1,160	1,614	2,320	2,581	3,044	3,688
Earnings Per Share $	0.52	0.71	1.00	1.10	1.29	1.56
Shares Outstanding Mil	2,176	2,211	2,252	2,325	2,342	2,358
Return on Equity %	16.3	18.5	18.8	17.2	16.8	18.3
Net Margin %	4.8	5.3	6.0	5.6	5.7	6.3
Asset Turnover	2.2	2.2	2.3	2.1	2.0	1.9
Financial Leverage	1.6	1.5	1.4	1.4	1.5	1.6

Valuation Ratios	Stock	Rel to Industry	Rel to S&P 500
Price/Earnings	15.4	1.0	0.7
Price/Book	2.8	1.0	0.9
Price/Sales	1.0	1.0	0.5
Price/Cash Flow	8.8	1.0	0.7

Major Fund Holders	% of Fund Assets
Rydex Retailing Inv	10.07
Gartmore U.S. Growth Leaders A	5.81
W.P. Stewart & Co Growth	5.40
John Hancock U.S. Global Leaders Gr A	5.32

Morningstar's Take By Tom Goetzinger, 11-21-2002 Stock Price as of Analysis: $24.98

Home Depot has moved from aggressive growth into a more mature stage. The home-improvement titan needs to focus on operational efficiency and cost-cutting instead of rapid expansion to maintain respectable earnings and cash flow growth, and we think the firm's strategy so far looks appropriate. Still, we'd require at least a 25% margin of safety to our fair value estimate to buy in, given the potential for missteps from time to time.

Home Depot was one of the great growth stories of the 1990s. Annual sales and earnings growth averaged 30%, while square footage increased 25% per year. Its top line surged tenfold during the decade, from $4 billion to $40 billion. But with sales now approaching $60 billion, Home Depot's sustainable growth rate is much lower than it was. Sales growth slowed to 19% in 2000 and 17% in 2001, and is likely to settle around 10% for the next couple of years. The main culprit is store saturation. Home Depot has already constructed stores in the most lucrative urban and suburban markets. Fill-in stores in these markets--as well as stores in new, albeit less populated, markets--will be smaller and generate less sales growth.

Though the company hasn't given up on sales growth altogether, management has been focusing more on operational efficiency. Centralized purchasing gives Home Depot more buying power over suppliers and better payment terms on inventory purchases--60 days instead of 30, for example--helping the firm to extend its days payable over the past year. The result has been a more favorable cash conversion cycle and greater amounts of operating cash flow. As of the third quarter, Home Depot had a cash hoard of $2.7 billion, net of debt.

Another supply-chain improvement involves merchandise transportation. By building more transit facilities or distribution centers, Home Depot is reducing the number of less profitable partial truckloads making their way directly to individual stores. This lowers freight costs and helps margins.

Home Depot's operating margin has improved from 9% in 2000 and 2001 to more than 10% so far in 2002. We think it can increase to 11% in the next couple of years, and project earnings growth of 18% in 2003 and 2004, even with sales increasing just 9%-11%. Our margin assumptions (and thus valuation) depend on strong strategic execution, but we think the company is on the right track.

Honeywell International HON

	Rating	Risk	Moat Size	Fair Value	Last Close	Yield %
	★★★	Med.	Narrow	$33.00	$24.00	3.1

Company Profile

Honeywell is a leader in aerospace, automotive, power, and transportation products, as well as performance materials. Annual revenue regularly tops $20 billion. Honeywell's product portfolio includes Fram filters, Prestone antifreeze, Bendix brakes, turbochargers, avionics, flight safety equipment, engines, cooling and heating systems, and control systems.

Management

David Cote is CEO and chairman. Previously he was CEO of TRW and the appliance business of General Electric. He appears committed to the productivity efforts begun by former CEO and fellow GE alumnus Larry Bossidy.

Strategy

Honeywell is focused on increasing efficiency through workforce reductions and its proprietary Six Sigma Plus program. The company is also looking to sell noncore operations and seeking acquisitions to strengthen its aerospace business.

101 Columbia Road   www.honeywell.com
Morristown, NJ 07962-2497

Morningstar Grades

Growth [C]	1998	1999	2000	2001
Revenue %	4.7	0.8	5.4	-5.5
Earnings/Share %	17.0	-18.8	7.9	NMF
Book Value/Share %	20.4	6.7	13.1	-7.3
Dividends/Share %	15.4	13.3	10.3	0.0

Sales have declined almost 8% so far in 2002. More than one third of the company's sales are to the aerospace market, so revenue is likely to remain weak until the airline industry recovers from its troubles, which could be awhile.

Profitability [B]	1999	2000	2001	TTM
Return on Assets %	6.6	6.6	-0.4	5.6
Oper Cash Flow $Mil	2,374	1,989	1,996	2,265
- Cap Spending $Mil	986	853	876	708
= Free Cash Flow $Mil	1,388	1,136	1,120	1,557

Excluding major charges in the past two years, Honeywell has been profitable, but it doesn't earn enough to make up for its cost of capital.

Financial Health [A]	1999	2000	2001	09-02
Long-term Debt $Mil	2,457	3,941	4,731	4,708
Total Equity $Mil	8,599	9,707	9,170	10,372
Debt/Equity Ratio	0.3	0.4	0.5	0.5

The balance sheet is solid and improving. Debt continues to decline and interest payments aren't a problem.

Industry	Investment Style	Stock Type	Sector
Aerospace & Defense	Large Value	High Yield	Industrial Mats

Competition

	Market Cap $Mil	Debt/ Equity	12 Mo Trailing Sales $Mil	Price/Cash Flow	Return On Assets%	Total Return% 1 Yr	3 Yr
Honeywell International	19,705	0.5	22,272	8.7	5.6	-27.3	-22.9
DuPont De Nemours E.I.	42,120	0.4	24,013	21.9	6.8	3.0	-10.5
United Technologies	29,339	0.5	27,971	9.4	7.2	-2.7	2.5

Price Volatility

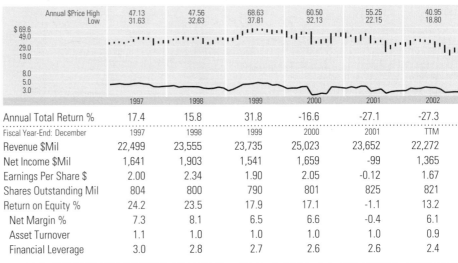

	Monthly Price High/Low				Relative Strength to S&P 500	
Annual $Price High	47.13	47.56	68.63	60.50	55.25	40.95
Low	31.63	32.63	37.81	32.13	22.15	18.80

	1997	1998	1999	2000	2001	2002
Annual Total Return %	17.4	15.8	31.8	-16.6	-27.1	-27.3
Fiscal Year-End: December	1997	1998	1999	2000	2001	TTM
Revenue $Mil	22,499	23,555	23,735	25,023	23,652	22,272
Net Income $Mil	1,641	1,903	1,541	1,659	-99	1,365
Earnings Per Share $	2.00	2.34	1.90	2.05	-0.12	1.67
Shares Outstanding Mil	804	800	790	801	825	821
Return on Equity %	24.2	23.5	17.9	17.1	-1.1	13.2
Net Margin %	7.3	8.1	6.5	6.6	-0.4	6.1
Asset Turnover	1.1	1.0	1.0	1.0	1.0	0.9
Financial Leverage	3.0	2.8	2.7	2.6	2.6	2.4

Valuation Ratios	Stock	Rel to Industry	Rel to S&P 500
Price/Earnings	14.4	0.9	0.6
Price/Book	1.9	0.7	0.6
Price/Sales	0.9	1.0	0.4
Price/Cash Flow	8.7	0.9	0.7

Major Fund Holders	% of Fund Assets
Marketocracy Technology Plus Fund	7.24
Howard Capital Appreciation	4.69
Fidelity Select Air Transportation	4.58
SunAmerica Focused Multi-Cap Value A	4.34

Morningstar's Take By Nicolas Owens, 12-11-2002 Stock Price as of Analysis: $24.81

We see Honeywell as a franchise of many smaller franchises, with a record of mixed results and big restructuring charges. Until it can translate the strength of its franchises to the bottom line, we don't think the results will be much to write home about.

Honeywell faces declining revenue as it restructures. Since its combination with AlliedSignal in 1999, more than one third of Honeywell's sales are to the aerospace market, which has been in the dumps for the past two years. We forecast a double-digit decline in sales for this segment in 2002, after a 3% deterioration in 2001.

A weak aerospace market isn't Honeywell's only challenge. On the basis of 2001 performance and the results so far this year, we estimate lower sales in each of the firm's four segments: We expect the transportation unit to experience a 9% drop; the automation and control unit to lose 4%; and the specialty materials segment to lose more than 5%. Year-over-year declines in 2001 were 2% in transportation, 3% in automation, and 18% in specialty materials.

Notably, productivity gains have maintained Honeywell's operating margins at 12% even in the downturn. Honeywell is applying an efficiency program, Six Sigma Plus, to examine and improve every aspect of its operations. A lot of the company's top management came from General Electric, where a similar program is in place. GE has shown that a diversified manufacturer like Honeywell can apply this kind of discipline to reap real efficiency gains. The program takes years to apply, though, and requires cooperation from everyone involved, from design to delivery.

For us to take notice, Honeywell has to improve its margins enough to earn more than its cost of invested capital. We like to measure a company's profitability by comparing its return on invested capital--the money invested in the firm over the years--with the cost of that investment. The difference between the two is economic profit. Because of the cyclical nature of Honeywell's cash flows and its financial structure, its cost of capital is higher than that of many peers. While Honeywell usually manages positive net income, its economic profit is quite meager. This prompts us to assign a relatively unattractive valuation to the shares.

Unless Honeywell makes surprising profitability gains in the near future, we don't think it will make a compelling investment. We would require a 40% margin of safety to our fair value estimate before we'd be interested.

MORNINGSTAR® Stocks 500

Hormel Foods HRL

	Rating	Risk	Moat Size	Fair Value	Last Close	Yield %
	★★★	Med.	Narrow	$24.00	$23.33	1.7

Company Profile

Hormel Foods produces food products for the consumer and industrial markets. Its fresh and frozen meat products include beef, pork, poultry, hot dogs, and bacon. The company makes Spam canned luncheon meats, Dinty Moore stews, Hormel chili and hash, Dubuque sausage links and hot dogs, Jennie-O turkey products, and Stagg chili. Hormel Foods also sells ethnic foods such as its Chi-Chi's line of Mexican food, its House of Tsang Asian foods, and its Marrakesh Express group of Mediterranean foods. The company markets its products in the United States and overseas.

Management

Joel Johnson has been president and CEO since 1993. Before coming to Hormel in 1991, he gained a reputation as a branding and marketing whiz at Kraft Foods, where he launched the popular Oscar Mayer Lunchables line.

Strategy

Hormel's main focus is still on being a leading producer of convenient, consumer-friendly meat products. Although Hormel is best known for pork, it has diversified into more beef and turkey products, as well as ethnic foods. Hormel has also become a significant producer of specialty health-care foods through its acquisitions of Cliffdale Farms and Diamond Crystal Brands.

1 Hormel Place
Austin, MN 55912-3680
www.hormel.com

Morningstar Grades

Growth [B+]	1998	1999	2000	2001
Revenue %	0.1	3.0	9.5	12.2
Earnings/Share %	30.1	19.4	8.1	8.3
Book Value/Share %	3.7	5.2	7.8	15.2
Dividends/Share %	3.2	3.1	6.1	5.7

After a double-digit gain in 2001, sales inched up less than 1% in fiscal 2002 because of a glut of meat caused by the Russian poultry ban. Long-term growth has been solid and reasonably consistent.

Profitability [A]	1999	2000	2001	TTM
Return on Assets %	9.7	10.4	8.4	8.7
Oper Cash Flow $Mil	240	151	320	303
- Cap Spending $Mil	79	100	77	59
= Free Cash Flow $Mil	160	51	243	244

Earnings per share increased 4% in fiscal 2002 despite the continuing effects of the meat glut, and the net profit margin improved slightly to 4.8%. Value-added pork products helped margins, and should help even more in the future.

Financial Health [A]	1999	2000	2001	07-02
Long-term Debt $Mil	185	146	462	421
Total Equity $Mil	841	874	996	1,077
Debt/Equity Ratio	0.2	0.2	0.5	0.4

Hormel's balance sheet is very solid. Long-term debt tripled after the Turkey Store acquisition in early 2001, but debt/equity and financial leverage are still lower than those of rival Smithfield Foods.

Industry	Investment Style	Stock Type	Sector
Food Mfg.	Mid Core	Slow Growth	Consumer Goods

Competition	Market Cap $Mil	Debt/ Equity	12 Mo Trailing Sales $Mil	Price/Cash Flow	Return On Assets%	Total Return% 1 Yr	3 Yr
Hormel Foods	3,235	0.4	4,166	10.7	8.7	-11.8	7.5
ConAgra Foods	13,431	—	27,085	—	—	—	—
Tyson Foods A	3,972	1.0	22,814	3.4	3.7	-1.6	-9.9

Price Volatility | Monthly Price High/Low — Relative Strength to S&P 500

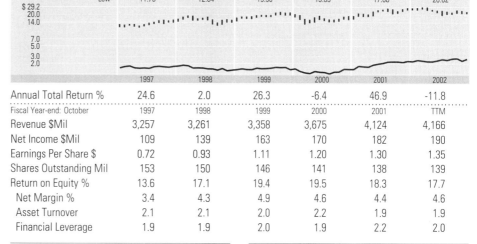

Annual $Price High Low	16.53 11.75	19.69 12.84	23.09 15.50	20.97 13.63	27.35 17.00	28.20 20.02
	1997	1998	1999	2000	2001	2002
Annual Total Return %	24.6	2.0	26.3	-6.4	46.9	-11.8

Fiscal Year-end: October	1997	1998	1999	2000	2001	TTM
Revenue $Mil	3,257	3,261	3,358	3,675	4,124	4,166
Net Income $Mil	109	139	163	170	182	190
Earnings Per Share $	0.72	0.93	1.11	1.20	1.30	1.35
Shares Outstanding Mil	153	150	146	141	138	139
Return on Equity %	13.6	17.1	19.4	19.5	18.3	17.7
Net Margin %	3.4	4.3	4.9	4.6	4.4	4.6
Asset Turnover	2.1	2.1	2.0	2.2	1.9	1.9
Financial Leverage	1.9	1.9	2.0	1.9	2.2	2.0

Valuation Ratios	Stock	Rel to Industry	Rel to S&P 500
Price/Earnings	17.3	0.8	0.7
Price/Book	3.0	0.7	0.9
Price/Sales	0.8	0.5	0.4
Price/Cash Flow	10.7	1.0	0.8

Major Fund Holders	% of Fund Assets
Mairs & Power Growth	3.41
Banknorth Small/Mid Cap Core	2.36
CDC Nvest Jurika & Voyles Rel Val Y	2.05
Security Mid Cap Value A	1.97

Morningstar's Take By David Kathman, 12-20-2002 Stock Price as of Analysis: $22.91

Hormel has overcome many of the limitations of the meat-processing business to become an appealingly steady and profitable company. We think it could be a solid long-term investment, but we'd want a sizable margin of safety to compensate for the inherent volatility of the business.

For many years, Hormel has been one of the leading U.S. producers of pork products, including its flagship brand, Spam. But like all meat processors, Hormel must deal with fluctuating commodity prices, which can cause sudden, unpredictable swings in sales and profits. One strategy it has tried is diversification: After its purchase of The Turkey Store in 2001, Hormel now gets more than 20% of its revenue from turkey, making it a bit less vulnerable to volatile hog prices. It has also used procurement contracts to hedge against price volatility, so it pays less than its competitors when hog prices rise, but more when those prices plunge.

Hormel has also focused on adding value to meat products, making them less of a commodity and more of a branded product that consumers will seek out. Fully cooked entrees and sliced meats, for instance, have been quite successful, and the firm's Always Tender pork is growing at double-digit rates. In April 2002, Hormel announced a joint venture with Cargill to extend the Always Tender brand to beef, which will add to the company's diversification and branding efforts. Hormel has recently stepped up spending to support its brands, which we consider a wise move given their importance to the company; 13 of Hormel's brands are ranked first or second in their categories.

This emphasis on adding value and brand-building has improved Hormel's profitability, as return on equity grew from 10.1% in 1996 to 19.5% in 2000. While a tough operating environment caused Hormel's ROE to dip to around 18% in 2001 and 2002, that figure was remarkably good under the circumstances, enough to rank Hormel in the top fourth of food companies. In contrast, meat rivals Smithfield and Tyson saw much wider swings in sales and ROE during the same period.

The ability to weather just about any economic storm makes Hormel appealing. However, it's still not immune to the meat industry's volatility, so we'd look for a discount to our $24 fair value estimate, say 30%, before we'd get really interested in the stock.

Hotels.com A ROOM

	Rating	Risk	Moat Size	Fair Value	Last Close	Yield %
	★	Med.	None	$35.00	$54.63	0.0

Company Profile

Hotels.com contracts with hotels in advance for volume purchases and then sells these rooms to consumers online and through a telephone call center for less than the published rate. As of March 2002, the company had supply relationships with about 6,000 hotels in 218 metropolitan markets, 146 in the United States and 72 overseas. It also had relationships with more than 25,000 affiliate Web sites through which its products are sold. In April 2002, the company changed its name from Hotel Reservations Network to Hotels.com.

Management

The firm was founded as a phone-based operation in 1991 by David Litman, now CEO, and Robert Diener, now president. They took the company to the Internet in 1995 and in 1999 sold it to USA Networks, which retains voting control.

Strategy

By purchasing rooms and then reselling them, Hotels.com generates higher margins than competitors who merely earn commissions. Its size is also a competitive advantage, giving the firm greater leverage over suppliers than other intermediaries. It recently launched a brand-building effort centered on its Hotels.com site.

8140 Walnut Hill Lane www.hoteldiscount.com
Dallas, TX 75231

Industry	Investment Style	Stock Type	Sector
Online Retail	▦ Mid Growth	◆ Spec. Growth	▭ Consumer Services

Competition	Market Cap $Mil	Debt/ Equity	12 Mo Trailing Sales $Mil	Price/Cash Flow	Return On Assets%	Total Return% 1 Yr	Total Return% 3 Yr
Hotels.com A	3,158	0.0	814	16.6	7.0	18.8	—
Cendant	10,862	1.8	13,069	10.2	0.9	-46.6	-23.3
Expedia	3,876	0.0	508	—	6.1	64.8	23.0

Price Volatility

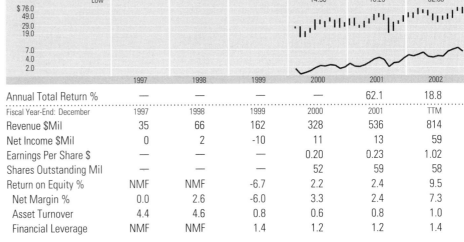

Annual Total Return %	—	—	—	62.1	18.8

Fiscal Year-End: December	1997	1998	1999	2000	2001	TTM
Revenue $Mil	35	66	162	328	536	814
Net Income $Mil	0	2	-10	11	13	59
Earnings Per Share $	—	—	—	0.20	0.23	1.02
Shares Outstanding Mil	—	—	—	52	59	58
Return on Equity %	NMF	NMF	-6.7	2.2	2.4	9.5
Net Margin %	0.0	2.6	-6.0	3.3	2.4	7.3
Asset Turnover	4.4	4.6	0.8	0.6	0.8	1.0
Financial Leverage	NMF	NMF	1.4	1.2	1.2	1.4

Valuation Ratios	Stock	Rel to Industry	Rel to S&P 500
Price/Earnings	53.6	0.5	2.3
Price/Book	5.1	0.5	1.6
Price/Sales	3.9	0.5	1.9
Price/Cash Flow	16.6	0.3	1.3

Major Fund Holders	% of Fund Assets
Baron iOpportunity	8.21
Eaton Vance Growth A	6.92
Eaton Vance Tax-Mgd Multi-Cap Opp A	6.48
Rockland Small Cap Growth	6.04

Morningstar Grades

Growth [A]	1998	1999	2000	2001
Revenue %	91.2	143.4	102.7	63.6
Earnings/Share %	NMF	NMF	NMF	15.0
Book Value/Share %	—	—	NMF	8.0
Dividends/Share %	NMF	NMF	NMF	NMF

The sagging hotel industry has played right into Hotels.com's hands by creating excess room inventory. Revenue should expand about 45% next year as the company takes advantage of excess room capacity across America's 40,000 hotel properties.

Profitability [C]	1999	2000	2001	TTM
Return on Assets %	-4.8	1.9	2.0	7.0
Oper Cash Flow $Mil	38	82	103	191
- Cap Spending $Mil	1	3	16	21
= Free Cash Flow $Mil	36	79	87	169

By using a merchant business model, Hotels.com generates about 30% gross margins on the hotel rooms that it buys in bulk and sells to its customers. Additional industry players could put pressure on these profits, however.

Financial Health [A]	1999	2000	2001	09-02
Long-term Debt $Mil	0	0	0	0
Total Equity $Mil	146	484	542	621
Debt/Equity Ratio	0.0	0.0	0.0	0.0

Hotels.com is generating strong cash flow, which has been piling up on the balance sheet. Liquidity is good (especially for a dot-com), but too much cash will eventually lower the company's return on assets.

Morningstar's Take By T.K. MacKay, 12-06-2002 Stock Price as of Analysis: $65.25

Intense competition and few barriers to entry in the online booking industry make Hotels.com shares an extremely risky investment.

A lack of business and leisure travel has resulted in above-average vacancies at the 40,000-plus hotel properties across America. Suppliers (hotel operators) are scrambling to find the most effective way to lure customers to their properties, and Hotels.com has been their solution. By employing a merchant business model, whereby Hotels.com purchases hotel room nights from suppliers in bulk then sells them to the public through its affiliated Web sites, Hotels.com sells excess inventory and makes a nice profit at the same time. Hotels.com makes about $0.30 for each dollar it sells in rooms through the merchant model, and can "return" the rooms it doesn't sell to the supplier. When the suppliers are hurting for business, Hotels.com is their knight in shining armor.

Several factors could hurt Hotels.com's success, however. In the wake of the airline industry's virtual meltdown, major online travel agencies, including Orbitz and Travelocity, are searching for alternative ways to expand revenue. Their first stop is hotel rooms. For example, Travelocity, which has an affiliate agreement with Hotels.com to sell its rooms,

recently purchased Site59.com, a last-minute hotel and vacation seller. If this venture meets with success, Travelocity's deal with Hotels.com, which makes up about 15% of Hotels.com's revenue, could vanish when the time comes to renew the contract in 2005.

The rapid expansion of ticket and room distribution is commodifying Hotels.com's business. Hotels.com alone is affiliated with more than 25,000 booking Web sites. Also, like the airline industry, suppliers have been taking the online ticketing process into their own hands. In May 2002, Starwood Hotels launched a program through its own Web sites that is designed to match any rate for one of its rooms found elsewhere on the Web.

The more participants there are, the more Hotels.com essentially becomes a commodity broker. Although Hotels.com has a good brand name and solid market share, we're wary of extrapolating the company's recent financial performance too far into the future. Our estimated fair value for the company is extremely sensitive to our sales and profit forecasts, and is based on very aggressive assumptions. We would not consider the stock unless it traded at a 60% discount to our fair value estimate.

MORNINGSTAR® Stocks 500

Household International HI

	Rating	Risk	Moat Size	Fair Value	Last Close	Yield %
	★★	High	Narrow	$30.00	$27.81	3.5

Company Profile

Household International provides consumer loan products. The company offers home equity loans, auto finance loans, MasterCard and Visa credit cards, private-label credit cards, tax refund anticipation loans, and other types of unsecured loans throughout the United States, United Kingdom, and Canada. It also offers credit life, credit accident, health, disability, term, and specialty insurance to its customers where applicable laws permit. Household International is the second-largest provider of third-party private-label credit cards in the United States.

Management

CEO William Aldinger joined Household in 1994 to restructure the firm by dumping brokerage, banking, and insurance operations to focus on home equity, credit card, auto finance, and personal lending across the credit spectrum.

Strategy

Household International seeks the customers that banks ignore. By targeting borrowers with spottier credit histories, Household can charge higher interest rates and face less competition in the consumer finance business. As part of HSBC, a better-capitalized institution with higher credit ratings and a global footprint, Household should see its strategy thrive.

2700 Sanders Road   www.household.com
Prospect Heights, IL 60070-2799

Morningstar Grades

Growth [A]	1998	1999	2000	2001
Revenue %	6.0	6.8	25.9	16.3
Earnings/Share %	-46.6	198.1	15.6	14.9
Book Value/Share %	-2.5	6.5	24.5	5.1
Dividends/Share %	11.1	13.3	8.8	14.9

Household's diversity allows the firm to lean on different areas to drive growth at different times. Growth will slow this year as the company works to build capital, but the trade-off of higher profits for safety is well worth it.

Profitability [A]	1999	2000	2001	TTM
Return on Assets %	2.4	2.2	2.1	1.8
Oper Cash Flow $Mil	3,254	4,188	5,518	—
- Cap Spending $Mil	140	174	175	—
= Free Cash Flow $Mil	—	—	—	—

A focus on lucrative, albeit risky, subprime clients has generated above-average returns. So far, Household has weathered the weak economy well. Strong consumer spending and low interest rates have played to its strengths.

Financial Health [C]	1999	2000	2001	09-02
Long-term Debt $Mil	—	—	—	—
Total Equity $Mil	6,451	7,951	8,203	8,438
Debt/Equity Ratio	—	—	—	—

Household has increased its long-term debt and employs quite a bit of leverage. But increasing the maturities of its debt allowed the company to reduce reliance on the volatile commercial paper market, improving liquidity.

Industry	Investment Style	Stock Type	Sector
Finance	▦ Large Value	％ High Yield	$ Financial Services

Competition	Market Cap $Mil	Debt/ Equity	12 Mo Trailing Sales $Mil	Price/Cash Flow	Return On Assets%	Total Return% 1 Yr	3 Yr
Household International	12,649	—	14,924	—	1.8	-50.7	-5.6
Citigroup	177,948	—	106,096	—	1.6	-24.2	1.1
Capital One Financial	6,594	—	9,099	—	2.3	-44.8	-11.6

Price Volatility

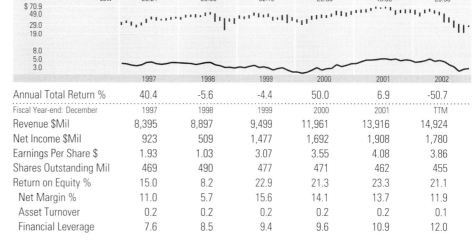

| | Monthly Price High/Low | | — Relative Strength to S&P 500 | | | |

Annual $Price High / Low	43.33 / 26.21	53.69 / 23.00	52.31 / 32.19	57.44 / 29.50	69.90 / 48.00	63.25 / 20.50

	1997	1998	1999	2000	2001	2002
Annual Total Return %	40.4	-5.6	-4.4	50.0	6.9	-50.7

Fiscal Year-end: December	1997	1998	1999	2000	2001	TTM
Revenue $Mil	8,395	8,897	9,499	11,961	13,916	14,924
Net Income $Mil	923	509	1,477	1,692	1,908	1,780
Earnings Per Share $	1.93	1.03	3.07	3.55	4.08	3.86
Shares Outstanding Mil	469	490	477	471	462	455
Return on Equity %	15.0	8.2	22.9	21.3	23.3	21.1
Net Margin %	11.0	5.7	15.6	14.1	13.7	11.9
Asset Turnover	0.2	0.2	0.2	0.2	0.2	0.1
Financial Leverage	7.6	8.5	9.4	9.6	10.9	12.0

Valuation Ratios	Stock	Rel to Industry	Rel to S&P 500
Price/Earnings	7.2	0.6	0.3
Price/Book	1.5	0.4	0.5
Price/Sales	0.8	0.4	0.4
Price/Cash Flow	—	—	—

Major Fund Holders	% of Fund Assets
Fairholme Fund, The	7.15
PIMCO PEA Value Instl	6.12
CDC Nvest Targeted Equity A	4.94
CGM Capital Development	4.94

Morningstar's Take By Richard McCaffery, 11-18-2002 Stock Price as of Analysis: $28.40

Subprime lending is a good business when run by a competent management team, and we think Household's experience, underwriting ability, and scale give this company an advantage.

Investors must know, however, that they're going to get a rough ride with a company like Household. First, subprime lending gets a lot of negative publicity. Second, when the economy weakens, bad loans rise and investors dump shares of companies with exposure to unsecured credits.

But the basis for our thesis isn't wishful thinking. Household earns a healthy, midsingle-digit return above its cost of capital, and it has a leading position in a valuable niche, serving customers who don't go to the typical bank. With about 1,400 branches in 46 states, only Citigroup has comparable reach.

Key issues in the current environment are charge-offs and funding. Management must underwrite good loans because bad debts can quickly destroy a company if they spiral out of control. The firm also must price for risk accordingly, and it can't ever get suckered into growing too fast or cutting corners on underwriting standards.

In the third quarter, Household's charge-offs reached 4.39%, up from 4.26% in the second quarter. This is well within the range of what management

expected, though higher charge-offs and delinquencies of real estate secured loans were worrisome. Management expects overall loss rates to stabilize in the fourth quarter.

The second issue is funding, since Household relies on access to capital to survive. Funding costs have increased as spreads in the debt markets widened, driven by economic fears and company-specific issues. Household did some things poorly, like waiting too long to tap its real estate portfolio as a source of asset-backed funding. While funding costs will be higher, Household has lowered liquidity risk by shifting its funding mix longer-term, mainly by reducing reliance on commercial paper. As a result, it expects the cash generated from maturing assets in the coming years to exceed liabilities that must be replaced, putting the company on sounder footing.

We also think Household's ability to lend across the credit spectrum--to prime and subprime borrowers--adds flexibility to the business and potential for growth. So while the economy will continue to be a challenge, we think Household is well positioned.

Hughes Electronic H GMH

	Rating	Risk	Moat Size	Fair Value	Last Close	Yield %
	★★★	High	None	$18.00	$10.70	0.0

Company Profile

The DirecTV division of General Motors Class H (Hughes Electronics) provides satellite-transmission services. Hughes Electronics also owns a 72% stake in PanAmSat, which operates a global satellite broadcast network. The company acquired Telocity in 2001.

Management

Michael Smith resigned in May 2001, ceding the CEO post to Jack Shaw, who has been with Hughes since 1987, recently serving as vice president of enterprise services. Hughes is a tracking stock, representing the satellite assets of General Motors.

Strategy

Now that the proposed merger with EchoStar is dead, Hughes' focus has shifted to maximizing profit. Hughes is working to improve customer loyalty through targeting higher-quality new customers and marketing new services to existing customers. Hughes is also working to lower the cost of acquiring customers and eliminate service theft.

200 North Sepulveda Boulevard
El Segundo, CA 90245
www.hughes.com

Morningstar Grades

Growth [A-]	1998	1999	2000	2001
Revenue %	22.6	59.8	31.1	13.4
Earnings/Share %	EUB	NMF	NMF	NMF
Book Value/Share %	EUB	15.9	-1.5	-9.4
Dividends/Share %	NMF	NMF	NMF	NMF

Sales have grown at a compound annual rate of 23% since 1997, driven by a near tripling in DirecTV's subscriber base. We expect the DBS industry to grow substantially faster than traditional cable.

Profitability [C]	1999	2000	2001	TTM
Return on Assets %	-1.7	3.8	-3.7	-2.8
Oper Cash Flow $Mil	380	1,091	190	720
- Cap Spending $Mil	506	939	799	603
= Free Cash Flow $Mil	-127	152	-609	117

Spending to sign up customers remains high, keeping a lid on margins. But the average amount consumers are spending is trending up and disconnection rates are falling, meaning the growth of profits should outpace that of sales.

Financial Health [B]	1999	2000	2001	09-02
Long-term Debt $Mil	1,586	1,292	989	2,391
Total Equity $Mil	10,194	10,830	9,574	9,551
Debt/Equity Ratio	0.2	0.1	0.1	0.3

Hughes repaid debt in 2000 after selling its satellite-manufacturing business to Boeing. However, free cash flow losses have caused debt to rise again to $2.5 billion (net). Hughes expects to need cash of approximately $700 million during 2002.

Industry	Investment Style	Stock Type	Sector
Cable TV	Large Growth	Spec. Growth	Media

Competition	Market Cap $Mil	Debt/ Equity	12 Mo Trailing Sales $Mil	Price/Cash Flow	Return On Assets%	Total Return% 1 Yr	3 Yr
Hughes Electronic H	14,233	0.3	8,743	19.8	-2.8	-30.7	-31.0
AOL Time Warner	56,278	0.3	41,024	8.1	-34.6	-59.2	-44.6
AT&T	20,115	0.8	48,821	1.8	-10.9	-27.7	-28.2

Price Volatility — Monthly Price High/Low — Relative Strength to S&P 500

Annual $Price High / Low	13.33 / 8.97	19.29 / 9.10	32.54 / 12.69	57.88 / 21.35	28.00 / 11.50	17.55 / 8.00

	1997	1998	1999	2000	2001	2002
Annual Total Return %	19.6	7.4	141.9	-28.1	-32.8	-30.7

Fiscal Year-End: December	1997	1998	1999	2000	2001	TTM
Revenue $Mil	2,838	3,481	5,560	7,288	8,262	8,743
Net Income $Mil	471	272	-321	733	-715	-528
Earnings Per Share $	0.01	0.23	-0.26	0.55	-0.55	-0.40
Shares Outstanding Mil	47,070	1,181	1,235	1,309	1,299	1,330
Return on Equity %	5.7	3.2	-3.2	6.8	-7.5	-5.5
Net Margin %	16.6	7.8	-5.8	10.1	-8.7	-6.0
Asset Turnover	0.2	0.3	0.3	0.4	0.4	0.5
Financial Leverage	1.5	1.5	1.8	1.8	2.0	2.0

Valuation Ratios	Stock	Rel to Industry	Rel to S&P 500
Price/Earnings	NMF	—	—
Price/Book	1.5	0.9	0.5
Price/Sales	1.6	0.5	0.8
Price/Cash Flow	19.8	1.2	1.5

Major Fund Holders	% of Fund Assets
Longleaf Partners	4.66
Torray	4.37
Torray Institutional	4.33
Oppenheimer Quest Balanced Value A	4.14

Morningstar's Take By Todd P. Bernier, 12-16-2002 Stock Price as of Analysis: $10.91

Now that regulators have called off the engagement with EchoStar, Hughes desperately needs a partner. We wouldn't invest in Hughes until it traded at a 50% discount to our fair value estimate.

Hughes Electronics began life as a humble division of Hughes Aircraft, a defense contractor and leading manufacturer of satellites. General Motors bought the company in 1985, believing the aircraft firm's technology could contribute to more-sophisticated vehicles. However, the General and Hughes didn't make sense together. GM sold Hughes' aircraft and military operations to Raytheon in 1997 and the satellite-manufacturing business to Boeing in 2000. Next on the chopping block was Hughes' crown jewel, DirecTV, the nation's largest direct broadcast satellite (DBS) company.

EchoStar outbid News Corp. for Hughes in 2001; consummation of the merger would have created a satellite provider with 17 million subscribers--bigger than any U.S. cable carrier. But the Federal Communications Commission vetoed the deal, saying it would crimp consumers' choice. The FCC's decision exacerbates the fundamental problem at Hughes: Despite its size advantage, the company has been outperformed by EchoStar. Hughes' sales growth, at 9% in 2002, is less than half that of EchoStar,

primarily because of weak subscriber growth. We expect EchoStar to gain about 30% more net new subscribers in 2002 than Hughes, which is impressive considering EchoStar's smaller size. There are a few reasons for this.

DirecTV has never been a separate company with a leader on scale with EchoStar's Charlie Ergen. Considering GM's history of mismanagement, the fact that it handpicked Hughes' CEO and controls the board is hardly the elixir for dynamism at the top. Also, EchoStar recently gained entry into new retail outlets, like Wal-Mart and RadioShack, with whom Hughes once had exclusivity. This is significant because RadioShack historically contributed 10%-20% of Hughes' new customers. Finally, Hughes has removed its sub-$30 offering, Select Choice, thereby kicking the door wide open for EchoStar to grab market share.

Despite negative free cash flow and soaring debt levels, Hughes' 11 million subscribers and network of satellites should be enough to induce a bid from Rupert Murdoch, News Corp.'s empire builder. We would be comfortable owning Hughes stock at a 50% discount to our fair value estimate.

MORNINGSTAR® Stocks 500

Human Genome Sciences HGSI

	Rating	Risk	Moat Size	Fair Value	Last Close	Yield %
	★★★	High	None	$10.00	$8.81	0.0

Company Profile

Human Genome Sciences researches proprietary drugs and diagnostic products. The company uses automated, large-scale gene sequencing together with its proprietary bioinformatics capabilities to rapidly identify novel genes. Bioinformatics refers to the use of computers to process, analyze, store, and retrieve biological information. The company is in a collaborative agreement with Isis Pharmaceuticals to create drugs based on genes discovered by the company that are known as antisense drugs.

Management

Leader William Haseltine is well known for aggressively pursuing gene patents. He has focused HGS' research on genes that are more promising targets, rather than sequencing the entire human genome like rival Craig Venter (formerly of Celera).

Strategy

Human Genome Sciences is striving to be the leading genomics-based drug developer. From its extensive analysis of genes and their functions, the firm provides research to other pharmaceutical companies and uses its research to develop drugs in-house. The company has also been one of the leading players in patenting genes--a potential (although uncertain) revenue source in the long term.

9410 Key West Avenue   www.hgsi.com
Rockville, MD 20850-3338

Morningstar Grades

Growth [F]	1998	1999	2000	2001
Revenue %	15.6	-17.1	-10.0	-41.9
Earnings/Share %	NMF	NMF	NMF	NMF
Book Value/Share %	-10.2	-21.3	566.9	-16.7
Dividends/Share %	NMF	NMF	NMF	NMF

At this point, HGS' revenue comes from licensing its intellectual property to drug companies, so income is small and growth is erratic. With no collaborative revenue in sight, we don't expect the company to bring in much cash.

Profitability [C]	1999	2000	2001	TTM
Return on Assets %	-8.0	-12.5	-6.3	-12.6
Oper Cash Flow $Mil	-39	-104	-73	-127
- Cap Spending $Mil	11	19	64	55
= Free Cash Flow $Mil	-50	-123	-137	-182

The company is many years away from profitability, and losses are widening considerably. HGS' operating loss was $170 million in 2001 and is expected to increase to more than $200 million in 2002.

Financial Health [C]	1999	2000	2001	09-02
Long-term Debt $Mil	326	533	504	504
Total Equity $Mil	169	1,363	1,304	1,161
Debt/Equity Ratio	1.9	0.4	0.4	0.4

HGS has more debt than many of its rivals. But the debt doesn't come due until 2007, and the company has plenty of cash--$1.5 billion in cash and securities as of September, 2002--to cover payments on this debt and fund operations for several years.

Industry	Investment Style	Stock Type	Sector
Biotechnology	Small Growth	Distressed	Healthcare

Competition	Market Cap $Mil	Debt/ Equity	12 Mo Trailing Sales $Mil	Price/Cash Flow	Return On Assets%	Total Return% 1 Yr	3 Yr
Human Genome Sciences	1,134	0.4	4	—	-12.6	-73.9	-36.6
Amgen	61,986	0.2	4,881	31.7	-7.1	-14.4	-6.0
Millennium Pharmaceutical	2,293	—	311				

Price Volatility

	1997	1998	1999	2000	2001	2002
Annual $Price High	12.25	11.47	43.14	116.38	77.00	34.40
Low	7.50	5.69	7.19	25.00	26.41	8.15
Annual Total Return %	-2.5	-10.5	329.2	81.7	-51.4	-73.9

Fiscal Year-end: December	1997	1998	1999	2000	2001	TTM
Revenue $Mil	26	30	25	22	13	4
Net Income $Mil	-21	-23	-42	-244	-117	-215
Earnings Per Share $	-0.25	-0.26	-0.46	-2.20	-0.92	-1.67
Shares Outstanding Mil	86	89	92	111	127	129
Return on Equity %	-9.6	-11.1	-24.9	-17.9	-9.0	-18.5
Net Margin %	-83.6	-78.3	ELB	ELB	ELB	ELB
Asset Turnover	0.1	0.1	0.0	0.0	0.0	0.0
Financial Leverage	1.1	1.2	3.1	1.4	1.4	1.5

Valuation Ratios	Stock	Rel to Industry	Rel to S&P 500
Price/Earnings	NMF	—	—
Price/Book	1.0	0.3	0.3
Price/Sales	317.9	25.0	158.2
Price/Cash Flow	—	—	—

Major Fund Holders	% of Fund Assets
Alliance Select Investor Biotech A	3.41
SYM Select Growth	2.86
Brown Capital Mgmt Small Co Instl	2.29
John Hancock Biotechnology A	2.02

Morningstar's Take By Jill Kiersky, 12-10-2002   Stock Price as of Analysis: $9.21

Human Genome Sciences is a biotech firm filled with top-notch scientists, a strong management team, and a great vision. But no matter how you splice the numbers, with no product revenue in its near future, this genomics-based drug research company is a highly speculative stock.

We believe our usual discounted cash flow approach to valuing the company leaves too much room for error. We feel more comfortable with a valuation based on the firm's cash (plus a little for its business). Our fair value estimate of $10 includes the firm's cash and future cash flow from commercialized products. HGS has about $1 billion, or $8 per share, in net cash (cash and securities minus debt). It currently burns through about $200 million per year, which means that the company can survive for several years without funding. But a year from now, if its products are no further along in testing, our fair value would drop by more than $1.

For HGS' future cash flow, we look at its current pipeline. Its most promising drug is Repifermin, which is in Phase II testing (with less than 30% chance of eventual approval) for treating skin wounds resulting from a variety of diseases, including cancer, mucositis, and irritable bowel disease. These diseases combined afflict more than 13 million people worldwide, a huge population. But even if the drug is approved, it won't hit the market until at least 2005--and even then, it will only be for a small subset of this population.

We assume that Repifermin and one of the seven other drugs in testing will eventually be approved (based on the 20% chance that drugs in the earliest testing phase have of commercialization). On average, we suppose each drug brings in $100 million in annual profits ($300 million in annual revenue and a 33% profit margin). The present value of those cash flows is about $800 million.

Subtract the $700 million or so the company will spend on research and administrative costs to get those drugs to market, and we have about $100 million (about $1 per share) in future cash flows. Tack on a small amount of royalty revenue from licensing its patents and platform technology, and we'll give HGS about $2 per share for its drug-discovery business. That's a total estimated fair value for the company of $10 per share.

HGS has an invaluable management team and industry-leading history. Our assumptions may seem conservative to those who believe that the technology works. But until positive cash flows are in sight, we believe the stock is too speculative.

Humana HUM

	Rating	Risk	Moat Size	Fair Value	Last Close	Yield %
	★★★★	Med.	Narrow	$15.00	$10.00	0.0

Company Profile

Humana provides health-benefit plans in the United States. The company owns and manages health-maintenance organizations and preferred-provider organizations that provide services to subscribers through contract agreements with approximately 440,000 physicians and about 4,300 hospitals. Humana's products are primarily sold to employers and other groups, as well as to Medicare-eligible individuals. The company also manages a dental-services subsidiary. Humana operates primarily in 15 states in the Midwest and Southeast.

Management

Chairman and co-founder David Jones was CEO of Humana from 1961 until 1997. In February 2000, Michael McCallister was named president and CEO. McCallister has led the company through recent restructuring efforts.

Strategy

In an effort to turn around operations, Humana has been exiting its least profitable Medicare and noncore businesses. In its remaining commercial and government HMO plans, Humana is pushing through premium increases and keeping only the most profitable members.

500 West Main Street   www.humana.com
Louisville, KY 40202

Industry	Investment Style	Stock Type	Sector
Managed Care	▣ Mid Core	→ Slow Growth	◩ Healthcare

Competition

	Market Cap $Mil	Debt/ Equity	12 Mo Trailing Sales $Mil	Price/Cash Flow	Return On Assets%	Total Return% 1 Yr	3 Yr
Humana	1,673	0.2	11,029	—	4.1	-15.2	9.5
UnitedHealth Group	25,235	0.3	24,358	12.5	8.9	18.0	46.6
Aetna	6,190	—	21,201	—	-7.2	24.8	—

Price Volatility

I Monthly Price High/Low   — Relative Strength to S&P 500

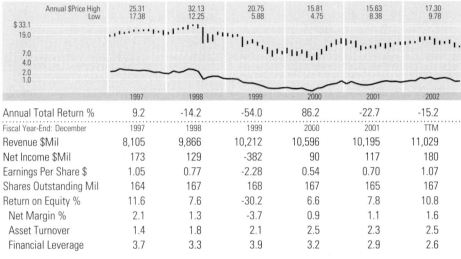

Annual $Price High Low	25.31 17.38	32.13 12.25	20.75 5.88	15.81 4.75	15.63 8.38	17.30 9.78
	1997	1998	1999	2000	2001	2002
Annual Total Return %	9.2	-14.2	-54.0	86.2	-22.7	-15.2

Fiscal Year-End: December	1997	1998	1999	2000	2001	TTM
Revenue $Mil	8,105	9,866	10,212	10,596	10,195	11,029
Net Income $Mil	173	129	-382	90	117	180
Earnings Per Share $	1.05	0.77	-2.28	0.54	0.70	1.07
Shares Outstanding Mil	164	167	168	167	165	167
Return on Equity %	11.6	7.6	-30.2	6.6	7.8	10.8
Net Margin %	2.1	1.3	-3.7	0.9	1.1	1.6
Asset Turnover	1.4	1.8	2.1	2.5	2.3	2.5
Financial Leverage	3.7	3.3	3.9	3.2	2.9	2.6

Valuation Ratios	Stock	Rel to Industry	Rel to S&P 500
Price/Earnings	9.3	0.4	0.4
Price/Book	1.0	0.2	0.3
Price/Sales	0.2	0.2	0.1
Price/Cash Flow	—	—	—

Major Fund Holders	% of Fund Assets
American Eagle Capital Appreciation	5.37
Tocqueville	3.92
Fairmont	3.47
Heartland Select Value	2.49

Morningstar Grades

Growth [C-]	1998	1999	2000	2001
Revenue %	21.7	3.5	3.8	-3.8
Earnings/Share %	-26.7	NMF	NMF	29.6
Book Value/Share %	10.9	-25.0	7.9	10.4
Dividends/Share %	NMF	NMF	NMF	NMF

Revenue was up 10% through the first nine months of 2002 compared with the year-ago period, thanks to strong industrywide premium pricing. Before 2002, Humana hadn't posted double-digit growth in any quarter for three years.

Profitability [C+]	1999	2000	2001	TTM
Return on Assets %	-7.8	2.1	2.7	4.1
Oper Cash Flow $Mil	218	40	149	-12
- Cap Spending $Mil	89	135	115	116
= Free Cash Flow $Mil	129	-95	34	-129

Humana's medical loss ratio should remain near the industry average. The company has a history of strict underwriting discipline and is unlikely to wander from this even for the sake of membership growth.

Financial Health [B]	1999	2000	2001	09-02
Long-term Debt $Mil	324	0	315	334
Total Equity $Mil	1,268	1,360	1,508	1,667
Debt/Equity Ratio	0.3	0.0	0.2	0.2

Humana's financial health is sound. The firm has plenty of cash and liquid investments and a manageable debt load of $600 million. Humana is also generating much more operating cash flow in 2002 than in previous years.

Morningstar's Take By Tom Goetzinger, 12-04-2002 Stock Price as of Analysis: $10.50

Humana's turnaround is progressing nicely, but the company isn't one of the best-run health insurers, in our opinion. We'd require about a 40% margin of safety to our fair value estimate to invest.

After spending the past two years culling its least profitable government (Medicare and Medicaid) and commercial HMO members and exiting noncore businesses, Humana is aiming for selective membership growth. The firm only wants to add members willing to accept its quoted premiums.

Though much of Humana's historical growth has come from winning new government contracts, the company isn't emphasizing them anymore. Government plans still constitute more than 50% of Humana's membership, but reimbursement rates for Medicare, Medicare + Choice, and Medicaid have not kept pace with rising medical costs the past few years, making these accounts less attractive.

Since Humana's fortunes are tied to the whims of the government in these plans, the company has shifted its focus to commercial (employer) plans. Commercial accounts allow health insurers to negotiate annual premiums to offset medical cost inflation, and are usually more profitable.

However, we think Humana's commercial growth prospects for 2003 and beyond are average at best.

The company is rolling out health benefit plans like Smart Suite, which give consumers more choices and responsibilities in determining their health-care options, but other insurers are doing the same. Moreover, Humana faces intense competition from well-respected Blue Cross Blue Shield plans in many of its primary commercial markets.

We also think Humana's days near the top of the industry in terms of medical cost management are over. Humana may have had a competitive advantage in administering government plans (where there were few players), but it has no such edge on the commercial side. As such, its medical loss ratio (medical costs paid as a percentage of premium revenue) has been inching up the past few quarters and is now very close to the industry average of 84%.

We see a widening gap between the best-run health insurers and the rest. For now, we think Humana belongs in the latter category. The company still needs to prove it can generate decent commercial membership growth without sacrificing medical cost management. We'd stay on the sidelines unless the shares fell below $10.

MORNINGSTAR® Stocks 500

IBM IBM

	Rating	Risk	Moat Size	Fair Value	Last Close	Yield %
	★★★	Med.	Wide	$77.00	$77.50	0.8

Company Profile

IBM designs computer systems, peripherals, and software, and provides related services. The company makes personal and mainframe computers, as well as networking systems. It also makes microprocessor chips, hard drives, fax boards, and keyboards for computers. IBM offers financing for its products and services. It also offers consulting services. The company sells its products under brand names like ThinkPad, PS/Note, Lotus, Tivoli, and PowerPC. Foreign sales make up approximately 57% of the company's revenue.

Management

Lou Gerstner retired March 1, 2002. He was replaced as CEO by former president and chief operating officer Samuel Palmisano, an IBM lifer.

Strategy

Whether it's consulting, support, hardware, software, or financing, IBM's goal is to give companies whatever technology they need to drive their businesses forward. Big Blue hasn't been shy about partnering with other software companies and either reselling or cross-selling their products when it makes sense.

One New Orchard Road   www.ibm.com
Armonk, NY 10504

Industry	Investment Style	Stock Type	Sector
Computer Equipment	Large Core	Slow Growth	Hardware

Competition

	Market Cap $Mil	Debt/ Equity	12 Mo Trailing Sales $Mil	Price/Cash Flow	Return On Assets%	Total Return% 1 Yr	3 Yr
IBM	130,982	0.8	82,442	9.0	5.8	-35.5	-11.1
Oracle	57,845	0.1	9,459	18.1	19.8	-21.8	-26.3
Hewlett-Packard	34,321	0.3	—	6.1	-3.5	-13.9	-24.7

Price Volatility

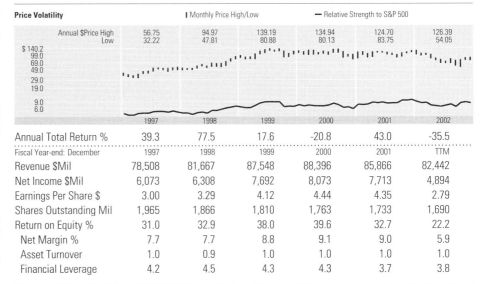

Annual $Price High / Low	56.75 / 32.22	94.97 / 47.81	139.19 / 80.88	134.94 / 80.13	124.70 / 83.75	126.39 / 54.05
	1997	1998	1999	2000	2001	2002
Annual Total Return %	39.3	77.5	17.6	-20.8	43.0	-35.5

Fiscal Year-end: December	1997	1998	1999	2000	2001	TTM
Revenue $Mil	78,508	81,667	87,548	88,396	85,866	82,442
Net Income $Mil	6,073	6,308	7,692	8,073	7,713	4,894
Earnings Per Share $	3.00	3.29	4.12	4.44	4.35	2.79
Shares Outstanding Mil	1,965	1,866	1,810	1,763	1,733	1,690
Return on Equity %	31.0	32.9	38.0	39.6	32.7	22.2
Net Margin %	7.7	7.7	8.8	9.1	9.0	5.9
Asset Turnover	1.0	0.9	1.0	1.0	1.0	1.0
Financial Leverage	4.2	4.5	4.3	4.3	3.7	3.8

Valuation Ratios

	Stock	Rel to Industry	Rel to S&P 500
Price/Earnings	27.8	1.0	1.2
Price/Book	5.9	1.0	1.9
Price/Sales	1.6	1.0	0.8
Price/Cash Flow	9.0	1.0	0.7

Major Fund Holders

	% of Fund Assets
Smith Barney Technology A	10.00
Scudder Technology Innovation S	9.87
One Group Technology A	8.62
Rydex Technology Inv	8.60

Morningstar Grades

Growth [B]	1998	1999	2000	2001
Revenue %	4.0	7.2	1.0	-2.9
Earnings/Share %	9.7	25.2	7.8	-2.0
Book Value/Share %	3.5	8.5	3.3	18.8
Dividends/Share %	11.0	9.3	8.5	7.8

It's not easy to increase a $90 billion top line. Although IBM will never blow the doors off smaller companies, its high-end server, storage, and software businesses have high-single-digit or low-double-digit growth potential.

Profitability [A+]	1999	2000	2001	TTM
Return on Assets %	8.8	9.1	8.7	5.8
Oper Cash Flow $Mil	10,111	9,274	14,265	14,615
- Cap Spending $Mil	5,959	5,616	5,660	5,083
= Free Cash Flow $Mil	4,152	3,658	8,605	9,532

Profitability has been improving, as margins have been on the rise in most areas of the company. Because of its sluggish top-line growth, IBM has been using cost-cutting and stock repurchases as its primary vehicles for earnings growth.

Financial Health [B]	1999	2000	2001	09-02
Long-term Debt $Mil	14,124	18,371	15,963	17,773
Total Equity $Mil	20,264	20,377	23,614	22,092
Debt/Equity Ratio	0.7	0.9	0.7	0.8

IBM carries some debt on its balance sheet, but this isn't a concern. Its earnings are more stable and reliable than most because of its large streams of recurring revenue, and the company generates enormous free cash flows.

Morningstar's Take By Joseph Beaulieu, 10-23-2002 Stock Price as of Analysis: $74.59

While none of IBM's individual businesses are particularly remarkable, they combine to create a formidable economic moat. We think that at the right price, IBM is a great stock to own for the long haul.

The big picture for Big Blue hasn't changed much over the past year. The services business has carried the company through the worst of the IT spending downturn. That business is much more stable than hardware or software sales, as contracts are typically long-term and less likely to be affected by economic hiccups.

We are pleased to see IBM finally showing even a little strength in its software business. IBM is making a successful push into the middleware market, and is going head-to-head with BEA Systems for this promising market. Given the potential for high margins in software, and the relatively small portion of IBM's revenue that comes from this business, we think investors would richly reward IBM for more consistent growth in this area.

Things aren't quite so cut and dried on the hardware side of the business. Total hardware revenue has shown a remarkable decline in recent quarters, but most of the shortfall has been in low-end servers and PCs. The company's push into storage appears to have legs, and our channel contacts tell us that IBM is aggressively bundling Shark, its high-end storage system, into large server/services deals at a low incremental cost to grab share from EMC. IBM's high-end server business appears to be performing admirably, much to the detriment of competitors Sun and Hewlett-Packard.

IBM's OEM technology business, which sells microelectronics and hard disk drives, has had a rough year, and IBM has announced plans to sell all of the hard disk drive business to Hitachi. We see hard disk drives as a commodity product, and anyway the business has lost $500 million thus far in 2002. Selling it is a smart move that will generate some cash for the company and eliminate a big source of volatility in quarterly results.

With its annuitylike revenue streams from its services business' long-term contracts, and its unique position of being able to sell enterprise hardware, software, services, and PCs to its corporate customers (and provide financing), IBM has a formidable economic moat that is worth paying for. We'd consider buying the shares at just a 20% discount to our fair value estimate.

IDEC Pharmaceuticals IDPH

	Rating	Risk	Moat Size	Fair Value	Last Close	Yield %
	★★★★★	Med.	Wide	$49.00	$33.17	0.0

Company Profile

IDEC Pharmaceuticals develops and manufactures immunotherapeutic products. Its antibody-based products are designed to harness a patient's own immune mechanisms to fight disease. The company developed Rituxan, a treatment for non-Hodgkin's lymphoma, which Genentech markets. It also developed and in 2002 will begin marketing Zevalin, an injectable radiation therapy for cancer treatment. IDEC is developing other biopharmaceuticals that may treat autoimmune and inflammatory diseases.

Management

Business acumen and scientific expertise are the name of the game for IDEC's executive team and board. William Rastetter, previously at Genentech, has been CEO since 1986. Herb Boyer, known as the father of biotechnology, serves on the board.

Strategy

IDEC is using its monoclonal antibody therapies, Rituxan and Zevalin, as a platform for growth. The company is leveraging its capabilities in immunology to research autoimmune and inflammatory diseases. IDEC has pursued partnerships for marketing and manufacturing its products and is looking to build on its expertise in proteins to develop, manufacture, and market monoclonal antibodies.

3030 Callan Road www.idecpharm.com
San Diego, CA 92121

Morningstar Grades

Growth [A+]	1998	1999	2000	2001
Revenue %	94.9	35.7	31.1	76.3
Earnings/Share %	NMF	93.3	3.4	96.7
Book Value/Share %	3.5	44.6	302.6	28.3
Dividends/Share %	NMF	NMF	NMF	NMF

Thanks to Rituxan, IDEC has been a great growth story. Sales have increased 56% annually since 1998, and should continue to climb in the mid- to high 20s as Rituxan takes hold and Zevalin makes its mark in oncology.

Profitability [A-]	1999	2000	2001	TTM
Return on Assets %	14.1	5.6	8.9	6.9
Oper Cash Flow $Mil	53	62	154	164
- Cap Spending $Mil	4	31	67	119
= Free Cash Flow $Mil	48	31	87	45

IDEC has been operating in the black since 1998, which sets it apart from most biotech companies. Having transferred Rituxan manufacturing to Genentech, its margins should continue to be strong despite increasing research and development spending.

Financial Health [B+]	1999	2000	2001	09-02
Long-term Debt $Mil	123	129	136	861
Total Equity $Mil	160	695	956	993
Debt/Equity Ratio	0.8	0.2	0.1	0.9

The company is in good financial health. It successfully raised $700 million in convertible debt this year for facilities expansions, has $1.5 billion in cash and securities (as of September 30), and generates plenty of free cash flow.

Industry	Investment Style	Stock Type	Sector
Biotechnology	Mid Growth	Aggr. Growth	Healthcare

Competition	Market Cap $Mil	Debt/ Equity	12 Mo Trailing Sales $Mil	Price/Cash Flow	Return On Assets%	Total Return% 1 Yr	3 Yr
IDEC Pharmaceuticals	5,916	0.9	362	36.1	6.9	-51.9	4.6
Johnson & Johnson	159,452	0.1	35,120	18.0	16.3	-7.9	8.0
Amgen	61,986	0.2	4,881	31.7	-7.1	-14.4	-6.0

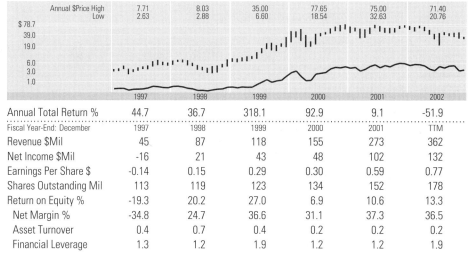

Price Volatility | Monthly Price High/Low | — Relative Strength to S&P 500

Annual $Price High	7.71	8.03	35.00	77.65	75.00	71.40
Low	2.63	2.88	6.60	18.54	32.63	20.76
	1997	1998	1999	2000	2001	2002

Annual Total Return %	44.7	36.7	318.1	92.9	9.1	-51.9
Fiscal Year-End: December	1997	1998	1999	2000	2001	TTM
Revenue $Mil	45	87	118	155	273	362
Net Income $Mil	-16	21	43	48	102	132
Earnings Per Share $	-0.14	0.15	0.29	0.30	0.59	0.77
Shares Outstanding Mil	113	119	123	134	152	178
Return on Equity %	-19.3	20.2	27.0	6.9	10.6	13.3
Net Margin %	-34.8	24.7	36.6	31.1	37.3	36.5
Asset Turnover	0.4	0.7	0.4	0.2	0.2	0.2
Financial Leverage	1.3	1.2	1.9	1.2	1.2	1.9

Valuation Ratios	Stock	Rel to Industry	Rel to S&P 500
Price/Earnings	43.1	0.9	1.8
Price/Book	6.0	1.7	1.9
Price/Sales	16.3	1.3	8.1
Price/Cash Flow	36.1	1.1	2.7

Major Fund Holders	% of Fund Assets
Fidelity Advisor Biotechnology A	7.07
Fidelity Select Biotechnology	6.90
Kinetics Medical Fund	6.28
Franklin Biotechnology Discovery A	5.95

Morningstar's Take By Jill Kiersky, 12-09-2002 Stock Price as of Analysis: $33.32

IDEC Pharmaceuticals has turned the corner. It's now a top-tier biotech company and a leading developer of cancer antibodies. But given the company's inherent drug-development risks and uncertainty about Zevalin's sales potential, we'd require a 30% discount to our fair value estimate to invest.

If a biotech firm's success is measured by its ability to develop multimillion-dollar drugs, IDEC is successful. Rituxan, the firm's non-Hodgkin's lymphoma drug, was the first monoclonal antibody approved to treat cancer and has become the standard for treating this disease, the fifth most common cause of cancer-related deaths. Rituxan sales have surpassed $1 billion (which IDEC shares with marketing partner Genentech) annually and continue to grow.

With the Food and Drug Administration clearing the way for Zevalin, IDEC is poised to continue strong top- and bottom-line growth. Zevalin is the first approved radioactive monoclonal antibody (it attaches itself to cancer cells and then blasts only the bad cells with radiation). It was approved for use in combination with Rituxan to treat non-Hodgkin's lymphoma patients.

We think the market for Zevalin, priced at $17,000 per dose, could be $500 million by 2006, based on current patient numbers. Even if rival drugs enter the market, Zevalin should help boost Rituxan sales because the two drugs work together. However, the strong sales we had originally anticipated have not yet materialized, because Medicare just began reimbursement in October and physicians have been slow to pick up the new therapy.

We're keeping our eye on IDEC's manufacturing capabilities. Producing monoclonal antibodies is no small feat, especially on a large scale. Partner Genentech currently manufactures Rituxan, so IDEC's gross margins have remained high. With a new manufacturing facility coming online in 2003, IDEC is hoping its smaller-scale clinical manufacturing prowess will translate into efficient mass production. If successful, not only should the company exhibit high returns on capital, but it could also fill a marketwide capacity void as more antibodies are commercialized.

Because the firm has two solid drugs set to drive revenue growth over the next few years, our confidence in IDEC's future cash flows is strengthened. The stock, slashed in half since the beginning of 2002, now looks priced to provide an adequate return for investors.

  MORNINGSTAR® **Stocks 500**

Illinois Tool Works ITW

	Rating	Risk	Moat Size	Fair Value	Last Close	Yield %
	★★★	Low	Narrow	$65.00	$64.86	1.4

Industry	Investment Style	Stock Type	Sector
Machinery	▦ Large Core	⚡ Cyclical	⚙ Industrial Mats

Company Profile

Illinois Tool Works is a diversified manufacturer, operating more than 600 largely autonomous subsidiaries in 43 countries. Product segments include engineered components (fasteners, metal and plastic parts, packaging), specialty systems (industrial machinery), and consumer products (appliances, cookware, ceramic tile). ITW's customer base is similarly diverse; target markets include the automotive, food service, construction, and general manufacturing industries. Foreign sales constituted 35% of revenue in 2000. ITW merged with Premark International in November 1999.

Management

W. James Farrell became CEO in 1995 after spending 30 years climbing the ranks. He has maintained ITW's traditionally passive approach to managing far-flung subsidiaries. But with five outside directorships, Farrell could be a bit too hands-off.

Strategy

Illinois Tool Works is a highly disciplined acquisition machine. It is perpetually on the prowl for small manufacturers that strengthen or expand its existing business lines. Once the deal is done, ITW management applies its considerable manufacturing expertise and economies of scale to increase production efficiencies and raise profit margins.

3600 West Lake Avenue
Glenview, IL 60025-5811
www.itw.com

Competition

Competition	Market Cap $Mil	Debt/ Equity	12 Mo Trailing Sales $Mil	Price/Cash Flow	Return On Assets%	Total Return% 1 Yr	3 Yr
Illinois Tool Works	19,875	0.2	9,319	14.5	6.5	-2.9	3.5
Danaher	10,013	0.4	4,221	13.5	2.7	9.1	13.8
Dover	5,900	—	4,248	—	—	—	—

Price Volatility

| Monthly Price High/Low — Relative Strength to S&P 500

	1997	1998	1999	2000	2001	2002
Annual $Price High	60.13	73.19	82.00	69.00	71.99	77.80
Low	37.38	45.19	58.00	49.50	49.15	55.03
Annual Total Return %	51.9	-2.7	17.6	-10.7	15.3	-2.9

Fiscal Year-end: December	1997	1998	1999	2000	2001	TTM
Revenue $Mil	7,149	7,898	8,840	9,512	9,293	9,319
Net Income $Mil	692	810	841	958	806	681
Earnings Per Share $	2.27	2.66	2.76	3.15	2.63	2.21
Shares Outstanding Mil	299	300	300	301	304	306
Return on Equity %	19.1	19.1	17.5	17.7	13.3	10.5
Net Margin %	9.7	10.3	9.5	10.1	8.7	7.3
Asset Turnover	1.0	1.0	1.0	1.0	0.9	0.9
Financial Leverage	2.0	1.9	1.9	1.8	1.6	1.6

Valuation Ratios	Stock	Rel to Industry	Rel to S&P 500
Price/Earnings	29.3	1.0	1.2
Price/Book	3.1	1.2	1.0
Price/Sales	2.1	1.7	1.1
Price/Cash Flow	14.5	1.5	1.1

Major Fund Holders	% of Fund Assets
Fidelity Select Industrial Equipment	9.29
Torray	5.80
Torray Institutional	5.41
Wayne Hummer Growth	4.75

Morningstar Grades

Growth [B]	1998	1999	2000	2001
Revenue %	10.5	11.9	7.6	-2.3
Earnings/Share %	17.2	3.8	14.1	-16.5
Book Value/Share %	17.5	13.4	12.4	11.0
Dividends/Share %	18.7	22.2	15.2	10.5

Beneath all those acquisitions (ITW doubled in size between 1996 and 2000), the company's internal growth has been tied to the fate of the industrial economy. Sales fell 2% in 2001 despite a 7% net boost from acquisitions.

Profitability [A+]	1999	2000	2001	TTM
Return on Assets %	9.4	10.1	8.2	6.5
Oper Cash Flow $Mil	1,037	1,116	1,351	1,374
- Cap Spending $Mil	336	306	257	256
= Free Cash Flow $Mil	701	810	1,094	1,118

Operating margins and returns on capital have risen as ITW has expanded, reaching levels well above industry averages. Both suffered during the downturn of the past two years, but should rebound when an economic recovery finally materializes.

Financial Health [A+]	1999	2000	2001	09-02
Long-term Debt $Mil	1,361	1,549	1,267	1,475
Total Equity $Mil	4,815	5,401	6,041	6,498
Debt/Equity Ratio	0.3	0.3	0.2	0.2

Modest use of debt (net of cash, just 11% of total capital), powerful free cash generation, and consistently high profitability place ITW's financial condition among the very strongest of U.S. industrials.

Morningstar's Take By Josh Peters, 12-10-2002 Stock Price as of Analysis: $66.05

We have some concerns about ITW's growth prospects, but its diversity and remarkable record make it an attractive industrial to watch.

Growth by acquisition isn't a unique strategy, but few firms have pulled it off with as much success or for as long a time as Illinois Tool Works. The company follows the 80/20 rule (80% of profits come from the top 20% of customers) to wring unprofitable activities and excess costs out of acquired businesses. Though it sounds simple, it requires a strong operating culture. ITW can boast one of the best--it was a bona fide "lean manufacturer" long before that became a corporate buzz phrase.

The kind of firms ITW generally acquires are another source of strength. A typical acquisition is small ($19 million in annual revenue, on average, for the 29 firms purchased during 2001) but caters to niche industrial markets with innovative products. ITW's skillful operating managers then add low-cost producer status to the newly acquired firm's natural competitive advantages. We give ITW a lot of credit for being able to create economic value with its acquisition strategy.

Also burnishing ITW's reputation is a pristine balance sheet. Among large industrials we follow, ITW's financial strength ranks second only to General

Electric's. Net out the company's investment portfolio (primarily mortgages and leases), and ITW earns double-digit returns on equity with no debt at all.

But as for virtually all manufacturers of capital goods, the industrial economy's dismal state has been a tough head wind. Persistent cost reductions have allowed profits to recover from 2001's 17% decline without a more favorable economic environment, but it will be tough to generate additional internal earnings growth without broader demand improvement.

We're also put off by the fact that ITW's acquisition engine, which doubled the firm's roster of operating units between 1995 and 2000, seems to be firing on just a cylinder or two. During the first nine months of 2002, ITW bought just 14 companies with a meager $107 million in revenue. Management is being selective--a crucial plus--but our fair value estimate depends on the firm bringing acquisition spending back to its annual goal of $800 million.

All else being equal, we prefer the smaller Danaher to ITW because of the former's faster-growing industrial markets. But if purchased at a 30% or greater discount to our fair value estimate, ITW is a worthy blue-chip holding, in our view.

IMS Health RX

	Rating	Risk	Moat Size	Fair Value	Last Close	Yield %
	★★★★★	Med.	Wide	$28.00	$16.00	0.5

Company Profile

IMS Health provides information to the pharmaceutical and health-care industries in 100 countries. Its services include market research for prescription and over-the-counter pharmaceutical products; sales-management information; and technology systems and services that support managed-care organizations. Market research services represents approximately 32% and sales management services constitute about 56% of the company's worldwide revenue.

Management

Former IBM manager David Thomas has been replacing many IMS executives with his own hires. He's paid a hefty salary and has a lot of perks, but also has 1 million options exercisable at $24.50, so he has a big incentive to get the stock price up.

Strategy

IMS owns 70% of the pharmaceutical data business and seeks to build on this by selling additional services to customers who purchase IMS' data. IMS is also seeking to spur growth by changing the company culture from being service-oriented to being sales-oriented, which will be a challenge.

1499 Post Road
Fairfield, CT 06430   www.imshealth.com

Industry	Investment Style	Stock Type	Sector
Data Processing	▦ Mid Growth	➡ Slow Growth	▤ Business Services

Competition

	Market Cap $Mil	Debt/ Equity	12 Mo Trailing Sales $Mil	Price/Cash Flow	Return On Assets%	Total Return% 1 Yr	3 Yr
IMS Health	4,502	1.1	1,387	13.9	11.0	-17.6	-13.4
Quintiles Transnational	1,424	—	1,596	—	—	—	—
NDCHealth	690	—	369	—	—	—	—

Price Volatility

| | Monthly Price High/Low — Relative Strength to S&P 500 |

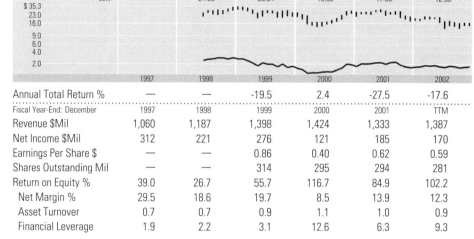

Annual $Price High Low			33.65 21.99	34.28 20.34	28.69 13.88	30.50 17.90	22.59 12.93

	1997	1998	1999	2000	2001	2002
Annual Total Return %	—	—	-19.5	2.4	-27.5	-17.6

Fiscal Year-End: December	1997	1998	1999	2000	2001	TTM
Revenue $Mil	1,060	1,187	1,398	1,424	1,333	1,387
Net Income $Mil	312	221	276	121	185	170
Earnings Per Share $	—	—	0.86	0.40	0.62	0.59
Shares Outstanding Mil	—	—	314	295	294	281
Return on Equity %	39.0	26.7	55.7	116.7	84.9	102.2
Net Margin %	29.5	18.6	19.7	8.5	13.9	12.3
Asset Turnover	0.7	0.7	0.9	1.1	1.0	0.9
Financial Leverage	1.9	2.2	3.1	12.6	6.3	9.3

Valuation Ratios	Stock	Rel to Industry	Rel to S&P 500
Price/Earnings	27.1	1.2	1.2
Price/Book	27.0	5.5	8.5
Price/Sales	3.2	1.0	1.6
Price/Cash Flow	13.9	0.8	1.0

Major Fund Holders	% of Fund Assets
Thompson Plumb Select	5.18
Oakmark Select I	4.13
Liberty Acorn Twenty Z	3.97
Members Capital Appreciation A	3.04

Morningstar Grades

Growth [C]	1998	1999	2000	2001
Revenue %	12.0	17.8	1.9	-6.4
Earnings/Share %	NMF	NMF	-53.5	55.0
Book Value/Share %	—	NMF	-77.8	113.0
Dividends/Share %	NMF	166.7	0.0	0.0

Top-line growth has been slow for a number of reasons, chief among them a decline in marketing spending by large drug companies as fewer new drugs hit the market. Growth will remain weak until industry conditions improve (our forecast is 2004).

Profitability [A+]	1999	2000	2001	TTM
Return on Assets %	18.0	9.2	13.6	11.0
Oper Cash Flow $Mil	347	170	325	324
- Cap Spending $Mil	33	33	34	31
= Free Cash Flow $Mil	314	136	291	293

IMS Health typically enjoys operating profit margins in the low 30s. We project a slight improvement in overhead costs and an eventual expansion in gross margins once sales growth improves.

Financial Health [B+]	1999	2000	2001	09-02
Long-term Debt $Mil	0	0	150	175
Total Equity $Mil	495	104	218	167
Debt/Equity Ratio	0.0	0.0	0.7	1.1

The balance sheet is strong. IMS has about $550 million in debt and $260 million in cash on hand. In addition, the company generates prodigious amounts of free cash flow.

Morningstar's Take By Pat Dorsey, 11-27-2002 Stock Price as of Analysis: $16.84

Long-term, IMS Health is in an enviable position. It owns a peerless database of information about prescription and over-the-counter pharmaceutical sales, generates solid free cash flow, and is well protected from potential rivals. Large pharmaceutical firms will continue to need IMS' data to help them maximize their return on the $500 million or so it takes to bring a new drug to market. Meanwhile, demand for prescription drugs continues to rise.

Moreover, the economics of database-driven businesses are good. It's tough for potential competitors to replicate the database, so pricing power tends to be strong and profit margins are high. Capital spending needs are also low, which means that database businesses generally generate large amounts of free cash flow. With operating margins in the mid-30s and free cash flow at about 15% of sales, IMS is in fine shape.

However, there's a dark side to dominating the drug data industry: When big pharmaceutical companies suffer from a dearth of new drug launches, IMS takes it on the chin as well. Until the pace of new drug rollouts picks up, IMS' sales growth is unlikely to move past 5%, and predicting the timing of this rebound is difficult. However, the fixed-cost nature of IMS' business means that any increase in

the top line will quickly drive margins higher. Also, IMS will still be the dominant player when drug companies' fortunes improve.

If IMS were simply an industry play, we would be only mildly enthusiastic about the shares. But a new management team has been investing considerable resources in new products and services, and we're cautiously optimistic that these efforts will add incremental growth over the next few years. Essentially, CEO Dave Thomas is trying to move IMS from being merely a data vendor to a provider of comprehensive services--the more tools and interpretive features that IMS can layer on top of its raw data, the more it can charge the relatively small pool of huge drug firms that are its primary clients.

While we're skeptical of any strategy involving "solutions," some of the new products do appear to be selling well. At the moment, we're factoring in minimal benefits from these new product rollouts, and view their success as more of an insurance policy against continued tough times for the industry than anything else. Assuming that industry conditions stay tough through 2004 and then rebound to more normal levels, we think IMS shares are worth $28, making them attractive anywhere below the low $20s.

MORNINGSTAR® Stocks 500

Ingersoll-Rand A IR

	Rating	Risk	Moat Size	Fair Value	Last Close	Yield %
	★★★	Med.	None	$52.00	$43.06	1.6

Company Profile

Ingersoll-Rand manufactures construction machinery and temperature-control systems. The company produces road-building equipment like excavators and loaders. In addition, Ingersoll-Rand makes temperature-control systems for use primarily in vehicles, golf carts, and steel doors. The company sold its Ingersoll-Dresser Pumps operations to Flowserve in August 2000. Ingersoll-Rand acquired Hussmann International in June 2000.

Management

Former Textron president Herbert Henkel became CEO in October 1999, replacing the retiring James Perrella. Henkel is trying to update the firm's image and enhance profitability by emphasizing the company's nonconstruction businesses.

Strategy

I-R has done a good job of reducing dependence on construction equipment, which now accounts for about one fourth of revenue. By selling underperforming businesses, concentrating on faster-growing sectors, and paying close attention to costs and capital allocation, the firm has dramatically improved its free cash flow over the past few years.

Clarendon House www.ingersoll-rand.com
Hamilton, HM 11

Industry	Investment Style	Stock Type	Sector
Machinery	Mid Core	Cyclical	Industrial Mats

Competition	Market Cap $Mil	Debt/ Equity	12 Mo Trailing Sales $Mil	Price/Cash Flow	Return On Assets%	Total Return% 1 Yr	3 Yr
Ingersoll-Rand A	7,285	0.6	9,968	9.8	-2.4	4.6	-4.5
United Technologies	29,339	0.5	27,971	9.4	7.2	-2.7	2.5
Emerson Electric	21,411	0.5	13,838	11.8	0.8	-8.3	-1.1

Price Volatility

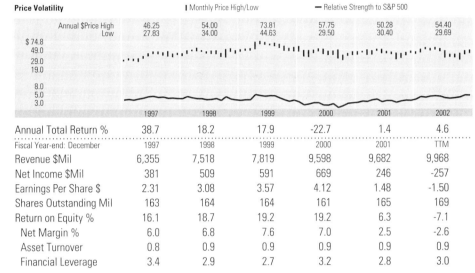

	Annual $Price High Low	46.25 27.83	54.00 34.00	73.81 44.63	57.75 29.50	50.28 30.40	54.40 29.69

		1997	1998	1999	2000	2001	2002
Annual Total Return %		38.7	18.2	17.9	-22.7	1.4	4.6
Fiscal Year-end: December		1997	1998	1999	2000	2001	TTM
Revenue $Mil		6,355	7,518	7,819	9,598	9,682	9,968
Net Income $Mil		381	509	591	669	246	-257
Earnings Per Share $		2.31	3.08	3.57	4.12	1.48	-1.50
Shares Outstanding Mil		163	164	164	161	165	169
Return on Equity %		16.1	18.7	19.2	19.2	6.3	-7.1
Net Margin %		6.0	6.8	7.6	7.0	2.5	-2.6
Asset Turnover		0.8	0.9	0.9	0.9	0.9	0.9
Financial Leverage		3.4	2.9	2.7	3.2	2.8	3.0

Valuation Ratios	Stock	Rel to Industry	Rel to S&P 500	Major Fund Holders	% of Fund Assets
Price/Earnings	NMF	—	—	MainStay Research Value A	3.47
Price/Book	2.0	0.8	0.6	JP Morgan Focus A	3.31
Price/Sales	0.7	0.6	0.4	Standish Tax-Sensitive Equity	3.00
Price/Cash Flow	9.8	1.0	0.7	Touchstone Value Plus A	2.83

Morningstar Grades

Growth [A]	1998	1999	2000	2001
Revenue %	18.3	4.0	22.7	0.9
Earnings/Share %	33.3	15.9	15.4	-64.1
Book Value/Share %	15.0	12.7	15.4	9.9
Dividends/Share %	4.7	6.7	6.3	0.0

Over the long term, I-R expects internal growth of 4%-6% annually; more acquisitions are likely. Sales will probably remain sluggish until the economy and capital spending stage a real recovery.

Profitability [B]	1999	2000	2001	TTM
Return on Assets %	7.0	6.1	2.2	-2.4
Oper Cash Flow $Mil	855	737	602	745
- Cap Spending $Mil	191	201	201	184
= Free Cash Flow $Mil	664	536	401	561

Operating margins, which approached 14% in 1999, fell to the midsingle digits in the face of weaker demand. Restructuring has led to an improvement in profits in 2002, but margins will probably remain below normal until sales rebound.

Financial Health [B-]	1999	2000	2001	09-02
Long-term Debt $Mil	2,113	1,540	2,901	2,166
Total Equity $Mil	3,073	3,481	3,917	3,601
Debt/Equity Ratio	0.7	0.4	0.7	0.6

I-R's $3.4 billion debt load is a concern, particularly with interest coverage running at a rather low 3-to-1 ratio. Strong cash flow and tight capital budgets are a plus, but the firm's leverage is still higher than peers'.

Morningstar's Take By Josh Peters, 12-13-2002 Stock Price as of Analysis: $41.52

Nothing sets Ingersoll-Rand apart from the diversified industrial pack. We'd be willing to own the shares, but only if acquired in the low $30s--a 40% discount to our fair value estimate.

Building on strength in rock drills and other construction equipment, I-R assembled a diversified portfolio of niche industrial businesses in the last decade. These operations are often among the brand leaders in their market segments, leading to high returns on tangible capital (excluding acquired goodwill). I-R also boasts good cash-generating characteristics: Capital spending equaled just 2.4% from 1997 to 2001, well below the 3%-4% of comparable capital goods firms.

But diversity alone doesn't make an industrial worth owning, in our view. To make a case for long-term value creation, we look for something that makes the whole worth more than the sum of its parts. Despite I-R's relatively strong product positioning in a number of niche markets, we don't find anything comparable to the Danaher Business System or Illinois Tool Works' "80/20" disciplines.

In fact, the best thing Ingersoll-Rand has done to improve its profitability is to relocate, at least on paper, to Bermuda. Its reincorporation, similar to that of Cooper Industries and similarly unpopular with

politicians and some institutional investors, reduced the company's effective tax rate to around 18% this year. We can't deny that the strategy results in legitimately higher reported profits and cash flows, but we wouldn't call it a high-quality means of achieving those ends, either.

We think I-R will continue to face weak markets across its businesses over the next several years. The firm's construction machinery, much of which relates to road building, will be hurt by contracting state and municipal government spending. Ongoing price wars in the retail grocery business will keep chains' capital spending depressed, constraining results at Hussman. The door and lock businesses are vulnerable to softening residential and commercial construction activity. Until capital spending picks up across the economy, we think I-R faces a flat top line at best and more restructuring charges. These challenges will probably be addressed by repositioning the portfolio. I-R recently announced the sale of its Torrington bearing business to Timken, the proceeds of which we expect to be used to reduce debt. But should I-R again enter the acquisition game, the poor returns of prior acquisitions keep us from having much enthusiasm.

Intel INTC

	Rating	Risk	Moat Size	Fair Value	Last Close	Yield %
	★★★	Med.	Wide	$15.00	$15.57	0.5

Company Profile

Intel produces personal computer semiconductor components and related products. The firm manufactures PC microprocessors, and markets them under the Pentium III, Pentium 4, Xeon, and Celeron trademarks in the United States and abroad. Intel also makes chipsets, memory chips, embedded processors, graphics accelerator chips, network and communication products, and digital imaging products. Foreign sales account for more than half of total sales, and the firm produces the bulk of its own semiconductors in its own chip plants spread across the globe.

Management

Andy Grove is renowned for his accomplishments in making Intel a technology bellwether. Today he is chairman, having passed the CEO title to Craig Barrett in 1998. Intel is well managed.

Strategy

Intel aims to maintain its dominance in semiconductor manufacturing for PCs while moving into the communication sector. The firm uses its enormous scale and the latest technologies to maximize performance and cost efficiencies. It also manages a large venture-capital unit to maintain relationships with firms in emerging technology areas.

2200 Mission College Blvd.   www.intel.com
Santa Clara, CA 95052-8119

Morningstar Grades

Growth [C]	1998	1999	2000	2001
Revenue %	4.8	11.9	14.8	-21.3
Earnings/Share %	-10.3	21.8	42.5	-87.4
Book Value/Share %	24.4	40.7	13.5	-1.4
Dividends/Share %	17.8	69.2	27.3	14.3

Slowing PC chip sales have hurt Intel; revenue fell 21% in 2001. In our view, Intel will be lucky to grow much at all this year in light of the soft demand for new computers.

Profitability [A+]	1999	2000	2001	TTM
Return on Assets %	16.7	22.0	2.9	5.9
Oper Cash Flow $Mil	12,134	12,827	8,654	8,768
- Cap Spending $Mil	3,403	6,674	7,309	1,171
= Free Cash Flow $Mil	8,731	6,153	1,345	7,597

Intel remains very profitable, but margins are below historical norms because of competition and weak demand. Gross margins were depressed in the second and third quarters, and will probably remain poor for some time.

Financial Health [A+]	1999	2000	2001	09-02
Long-term Debt $Mil	955	707	1,050	1,000
Total Equity $Mil	32,535	37,322	35,830	35,307
Debt/Equity Ratio	0.0	0.0	0.0	0.0

Intel generates lots of cash--nearly $9 billion in 2001 despite a poor year. Heavy capital spending erased most of this, but with minimal debt and $9 billion in cash, the firm is in excellent financial health.

Industry	Investment Style	Stock Type	Sector
Semiconductors	▦ Large Growth	➡ Slow Growth	▣ Hardware

Competition	Market Cap $Mil	Debt/ Equity	12 Mo Trailing Sales $Mil	Price/Cash Flow	Return On Assets%	Total Return% 1 Yr	3 Yr
Intel	103,151	0.0	26,587	11.8	5.9	-50.3	-27.7
Advanced Micro Devices	2,219	0.4	2,962	18.4	-8.1	-59.3	-23.8
NVIDIA	1,761	0.3	1,879	9.6	7.1	-82.8	0.4

Price Volatility   ❙ Monthly Price High/Low   — Relative Strength to S&P 500

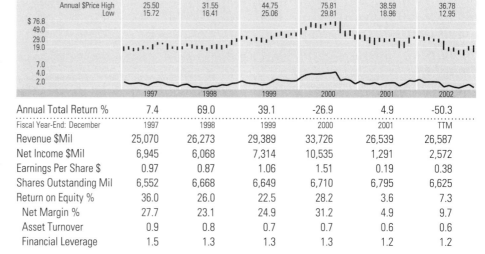

Annual $Price High / Low	25.50 / 15.72	31.55 / 16.41	44.75 / 25.06	75.81 / 29.81	38.59 / 18.96	36.78 / 12.95
	1997	1998	1999	2000	2001	2002
Annual Total Return %	7.4	69.0	39.1	-26.9	4.9	-50.3

Fiscal Year-End: December	1997	1998	1999	2000	2001	TTM
Revenue $Mil	25,070	26,273	29,389	33,726	26,539	26,587
Net Income $Mil	6,945	6,068	7,314	10,535	1,291	2,572
Earnings Per Share $	0.97	0.87	1.06	1.51	0.19	0.38
Shares Outstanding Mil	6,552	6,668	6,649	6,710	6,795	6,625
Return on Equity %	36.0	26.0	22.5	28.2	3.6	7.3
Net Margin %	27.7	23.1	24.9	31.2	4.9	9.7
Asset Turnover	0.9	0.8	0.7	0.7	0.6	0.6
Financial Leverage	1.5	1.3	1.3	1.3	1.2	1.2

Valuation Ratios	Stock	Rel to Industry	Rel to S&P 500
Price/Earnings	41.0	1.0	1.7
Price/Book	2.9	1.0	0.9
Price/Sales	3.9	1.0	1.9
Price/Cash Flow	11.8	1.0	0.9

Major Fund Holders	% of Fund Assets
ProFunds Ultra Semiconductor Inv	29.09
American Capital Exchange	12.41
Rydex Electronics Inv	9.50
Munder Future Technology Y	9.14

Morningstar's Take By Jeremy Lopez, 10-17-2002 Stock Price as of Analysis: $14.23

As the world's largest chipmaker, Intel enjoys several advantages. But competition and a mature PC market have eroded the chip giant's financial performance, and therefore some of its investment appeal.

Intel's scale and dominance have historically resulted in competitive advantages aplenty. The firm dwarfs all other chipmakers in size: With sales of more than $26 billion in 2001, Intel was 3.5 times larger than any other chipmaker. Its 2001 research and development budget of $3.8 billion was larger than the sales of all but the top 10 producers, and roughly equal to the sales of chief rival Advanced Micro Devices. This has helped keep competitors in check, as has Intel's huge marketing budget, which has helped build its ubiquitous brand name. The giant's size also gives it enormous manufacturing scale, and therefore a cost advantage. And 80% market share has given Intel a big influence on the direction of PC component standards, and has helped keep product pricing fairly stable.

This dominance and wide economic moat have been big drivers behind Intel's superb historical financial performance. Not only was the firm's growth impressive through most of the 1990s, but its returns on invested capital typically ranged between 30% and 50%. A lot has changed in recent years,

however, and not for the better.

The first problem is that Intel still derives 80% of its sales from a mature PC market. Without much room to gain share, Intel's PC business has mediocre growth prospects. Any growth probably needs to come from the foray into communication chips, or from new areas like the Itanium server chip. But neither of these has lived up to expectations. Also, Intel's margins and returns on capital have eroded in recent years. Part of this is due to a weak PC market, which we see as temporary. But we think part of this erosion is permanent. Stronger products from AMD have intensified competition, resulting in a faster drop in average chip prices and higher R&D costs--both of which hurt margins--and greater capital spending. The shift to cheaper PCs has also damaged Intel's pricing power, a trend that may not prove temporary.

Competition and mediocre prospects will probably result in permanently lower growth and ROIC. That said, Intel's size and manufacturing scale mean the firm still has several key competitive advantages. The stock could still be a solid investment at the right price; we'd find it attractive at a 20%-30% discount to our fair value estimate.

MORNINGSTAR® Stocks 500

International Flavors & Fragrances IFF

	Rating	Risk	Moat Size	Fair Value	Last Close	Yield %
	★★	Med.	None	$34.00	$35.10	1.7

Company Profile

International Flavors & Fragrances produces flavoring and fragrance agents for use in consumer goods. Its fragrance products are used in cosmetics and other personal-care products, soaps, detergents, and room fresheners. The company's flavors are used in processed foods, beverages, drugs, tobacco products, and animal food. The company makes synthetic and organic products, mainly from organic chemicals, fruits, vegetables, flowers, and woods. Sales outside North America account for about 68% of the company's total sales. It acquired Bush Boake Allen in 2000.

Management

Unilever's former U.S. head, Richard Goldstein, became chairman and CEO in 2000. Because Unilever was an IFF customer, Goldstein knows IFF client needs firsthand.

Strategy

International Flavors & Fragrances intends to grow internally, much as it always has, by investing in cutting-edge technology to create new flavors and fragrances. The company also seeks to expand globally, particularly in Asia.

521 West 57th Street
New York, NY 10019-2960

www.iff.com

Morningstar Grades

Growth [B+]	1998	1999	2000	2001
Revenue %	-1.4	2.3	1.6	26.0
Earnings/Share %	-4.5	-19.5	-20.3	-1.6
Book Value/Share %	-3.4	-8.0	-22.8	-13.4
Dividends/Share %	2.8	2.0	-15.1	-53.5

Sales growth over the past ten and five years has averaged 7% and 5%, respectively. Now that IFF is much larger, we expect long-term sales growth to be slower, around 3.5% annually.

Profitability [B+]	1999	2000	2001	TTM
Return on Assets %	11.6	4.9	5.1	7.5
Oper Cash Flow $Mil	196	269	182	246
- Cap Spending $Mil	104	61	52	77
= Free Cash Flow $Mil	92	208	129	169

IFF has historically achieved net profit margins in the middle teens. Although the firm stumbled in 2001, we expect it to return to historical levels over the next five years.

Financial Health [C+]	1999	2000	2001	09-02
Long-term Debt $Mil	4	417	939	1,054
Total Equity $Mil	858	631	524	575
Debt/Equity Ratio	0.0	0.7	1.8	1.8

Earnings before interest and taxes is 4 times interest expense. The company took on a lot of debt in its 2000 acquisition of Bush Boake Allen, but we expect strong operating cash flow to help improve its balance sheet.

Industry	Investment Style	Stock Type	Sector
Food Mfg.	▦ Mid Core	→ Slow Growth	🚘 Consumer Goods

Competition	Market Cap $Mil	Debt/ Equity	12 Mo Trailing Sales $Mil	Price/Cash Flow	Return On Assets%	Total Return% 1 Yr	Total Return% 3 Yr
International Flavors & Fragrances	3,311	1.8	1,804	13.4	7.5	20.3	3.0
BASF AG ADR	111,488	—	28,981	—	—	—	—
McCormick	3,246	—	2,422	—	—	—	—

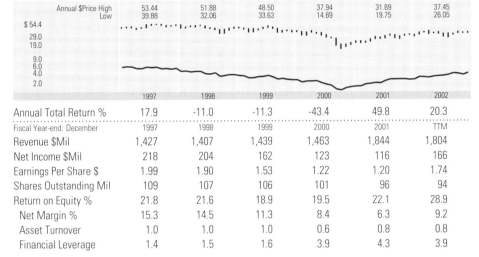

Price Volatility — Monthly Price High/Low — Relative Strength to S&P 500

Annual $Price High / Low	53.44 / 39.88	51.88 / 32.06	48.50 / 33.63	37.94 / 14.69	31.69 / 19.75	37.45 / 26.05

	1997	1998	1999	2000	2001	2002
Annual Total Return %	17.9	-11.0	-11.3	-43.4	49.8	20.3

Fiscal Year-end: December	1997	1998	1999	2000	2001	TTM
Revenue $Mil	1,427	1,407	1,439	1,463	1,844	1,804
Net Income $Mil	218	204	162	123	116	166
Earnings Per Share $	1.99	1.90	1.53	1.22	1.20	1.74
Shares Outstanding Mil	109	107	106	101	96	94
Return on Equity %	21.8	21.6	18.9	19.5	22.1	28.9
Net Margin %	15.3	14.5	11.3	8.4	6.3	9.2
Asset Turnover	1.0	1.0	1.0	0.6	0.8	0.8
Financial Leverage	1.4	1.5	1.6	3.9	4.3	3.9

Valuation Ratios	Stock	Rel to Industry	Rel to S&P 500
Price/Earnings	20.2	1.0	0.9
Price/Book	5.8	1.4	1.8
Price/Sales	1.8	1.3	0.9
Price/Cash Flow	13.4	1.2	1.0

Major Fund Holders	% of Fund Assets
Synovus Mid Cap Value C	4.61
Synovus Mid Cap Value Instl	4.61
AmSouth Select Equity B	4.55
Schroder MidCap Value Inv	3.90

Morningstar's Take By Carl Sibilski, 12-23-2002 Stock Price as of Analysis: $34.04

Although International Flavors & Fragrances' sales have increased and merger-related efficiencies have been realized ahead of time, this is still a show-us story. We'd seek at least a 40% discount to our fair value estimate before considering the shares.

The purchase of Bush Boake Allen, its biggest domestic rival, bolstered IFF's presence in food flavors and turned the company into the world's largest maker of flavors and fragrances. The industry had only a few players to begin with, and consolidation has led to fewer yet. In our opinion, IFF is making significant progress toward building an economic moat for itself. Its wide-ranging chemical production processes are difficult for competitors to imitate, and its negotiating position should improve as customers have fewer supply alternatives. While we believe additional cost savings and efficiencies are yet to come, the initial success is encouraging. If these trends continue, we could raise IFF's economic moat to narrow from none.

IFF is more than halfway through a major restructuring started by CEO Richard Goldstein almost two years ago. Goldstein has brought in senior-level talent, accelerated the share-repurchase program, and cut the dividend by 60% to free up additional cash for research and development. The reorganization could cost as much as $100 million but could also reduce annual expenses by $25-$30 million.

With some of these cost savings coming in ahead of schedule, we think IFF will be able to allocate capital more efficiently. We're particularly encouraged to see an increase in spending on research and development, which we expect to increase to 7.8% of sales from 7.2% in 2001. These intensified research efforts should result in a fuller pipeline of products several years hence. We're encouraged by a number of recent and upcoming new products, including fragrances for Estee Lauder, Calvin Klein, and Hugo Boss, which should help IFF gain share in the highly profitable perfume and cologne market.

While recent results show much improvement, the company has a lot on its plate. It faces further integration challenges, like improving customer service and finding more ways to boost top-line growth. However, as long as we see signs of fundamental improvement, we think the stock would be a good buy under $20.

International Game Tech IGT

	Risk	Moat Size	Fair Value	Last Close	Yield %
Rating ★★	Med.	Narrow	$72.00	$75.92	0.0

Company Profile

International Game Technology is the world's largest manufacturer of casino gaming machines and related systems. A majority of revenue comes from manufacturing gaming machines, driven by new casino development, casino expansion, and periodic machine replacement. IGT makes 70% of the casino games operating in North America. Recent innovations include games based on TV shows and cashless ticketing systems. Additional revenue comes from operating wide-area progressive jackpots. IGT is licensed to operate in every significant gaming jurisdiction worldwide.

Management

Longtime chairman Charles Mathewson retired as CEO in December 2000 and promoted CFO Tom Baker to the top job. Except for a short stint in casino management, Baker has been with IGT since 1988. Insiders hold about 8% of the stock.

Strategy

IGT's market dominance and emphasis on rapid innovation are changing the game machine industry. While the firm once relied on gaming expansion to create demand, its focus on developing new games and operating technologies reduces dependence on new casino development and shortens the product cycle. Highly profitable progressive slot operations also help IGT achieve more-consistent results.

9295 Prototype Drive www.igt.com
Reno, NV 89511

Morningstar Grades

Growth [A]	1998	1999	2000	2001
Revenue %	10.8	3.6	5.2	33.5
Earnings/Share %	17.7	-53.4	222.6	40.0
Book Value/Share %	10.3	-48.8	-49.1	214.6
Dividends/Share %	0.0	-50.0	NMF	NMF

We think the casino industry's aging base of slots and IGT's popular machines will keep product revenue growing. Lucrative participation games may grow slower than those machines that are sold outright, however.

Profitability [A]	1999	2000	2001	TTM
Return on Assets %	3.5	9.7	11.1	7.8
Oper Cash Flow $Mil	261	129	198	503
- Cap Spending $Mil	18	18	35	37
= Free Cash Flow $Mil	244	110	163	466

IGT's leading market share gives it pricing power, and participation games sweeten its margins even more. However, participation games, which carry significantly higher margins than regular slots, may fall out of favor if the economy doesn't pick up.

Financial Health [A-]	1999	2000	2001	06-02
Long-term Debt $Mil	990	992	985	1,217
Total Equity $Mil	242	97	296	1,361
Debt/Equity Ratio	4.1	10.3	3.3	0.9

IGT is in fine financial shape. EBITDA covers interest expense 4 times, and the company's current assets (which include $540 million in cash) are equal to total long-term debt.

	Industry	Investment Style	Stock Type	Sector
	Gambling/Hotel Casinos	⊞ Mid Growth	🗘 Cyclical	🖃 Consumer Services

Competition	Market Cap $Mil	Debt/ Equity	12 Mo Trailing Sales $Mil	Price/Cash Flow	Return On Assets%	Total Return% 1 Yr	3 Yr
International Game Tech	6,578	0.9	1,621	13.1	7.8	11.2	55.2
GTech Holdings	1,594	—	991	—	—	—	—
Alliance Gaming	830	—	611	—	—	—	—

Price Volatility | Monthly Price High/Low — Relative Strength to S&P 500

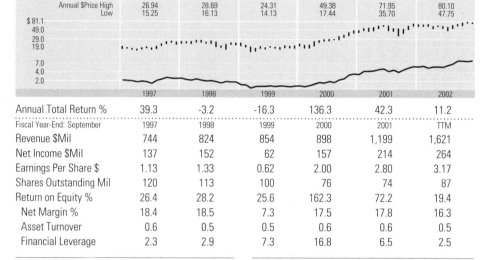

	1997	1998	1999	2000	2001	2002
Annual $Price High	26.94	28.69	24.31	49.38	71.95	80.10
Low	15.25	16.13	14.13	17.44	35.70	47.75

Annual Total Return %	39.3	-3.2	-16.3	136.3	42.3	11.2

Fiscal Year-End: September	1997	1998	1999	2000	2001	TTM
Revenue $Mil	744	824	854	898	1,199	1,621
Net Income $Mil	137	152	62	157	214	264
Earnings Per Share $	1.13	1.33	0.62	2.00	2.80	3.17
Shares Outstanding Mil	120	113	100	76	74	87
Return on Equity %	26.4	28.2	25.6	162.3	72.2	19.4
Net Margin %	18.4	18.5	7.3	17.5	17.8	16.3
Asset Turnover	0.6	0.5	0.5	0.6	0.6	0.5
Financial Leverage	2.3	2.9	7.3	16.8	6.5	2.5

Valuation Ratios	Stock	Rel to Industry	Rel to S&P 500
Price/Earnings	24.0	1.3	1.0
Price/Book	4.8	1.9	1.5
Price/Sales	4.1	3.2	2.0
Price/Cash Flow	13.1	2.1	1.0

Major Fund Holders	% of Fund Assets
Strong Growth 20 Inv	6.51
INVESCO Leisure Inv	6.34
Strong Advisor Focus A	5.92
Liberty Acorn Twenty Z	5.55

Morningstar's Take By T.K. MacKay, 12-26-2002 Stock Price as of Analysis: $75.30

International Game Technology's 70% share of the slot machine business is holding firm. The business plan--making great games--that built IGT into what it is now is the formula for the company's continued success. IGT is a good way to play the gaming industry without investing in an individual casino operator, but we'd be careful not to pay too high a price for its shares.

The most profitable way IGT exploits its skill at developing games is through the participation game market. Casinos lease participation slot machines, like Wheel of Fortune and Jeopardy, instead of buying them outright. IGT "participates" in leased machines by receiving a portion (about 20%) of the money gamblers lose in the machine on a daily basis. This generates an annuitylike stream of revenue for IGT that increases with each new participation game the company sells.

The benefit of participation games is evident in IGT's profit growth. Operating margins have expanded from 22% in 1995 to 33%. Casinos have a big incentive to continue to install participation games on their floors: Popular titles like Wheel of Fortune and Jeopardy are only available as participation games, and earn nearly twice as much as owned machines because they are usually linked

through progressive systems paying out larger jackpots, thus offering more appeal to players. If one casino has a popular slot on its floor, the casino next door probably has it too.

The greatest risk that IGT will face over the next several years is largely out of the company's control. Casino operators operate under various state legislation. In a weak economy, some states turn to the gaming industry to boost their income (about a dozen states allow commercially operated casinos). They either issue new gaming licenses, which lead to more casinos (and more space for slot machines), or they levy increased taxes on existing casinos. The former option would be a boon to IGT, but lately, states facing a budget crunch have opted for the latter. Capital expenditures--including budgets for new slot machines--are one of the first things casinos cut to cope with higher taxes.

Despite the risk that states will raise taxes before allowing more casinos to enter the industry, IGT is likely to maintain its stranglehold on the slot machine business. This affords the company a decent economic moat, thereby reducing the discount we'd like to see before investing. We think IGT shares would start to look attractive below $45.

MORNINGSTAR® Stocks 500

International Paper IP

	Rating	Risk	Moat Size	Fair Value	Last Close	Yield %
	★★	Med.	None	$33.00	$34.97	2.9

Company Profile

International Paper manufactures paper and forest products. The company operates more than 7 million acres of forestland and manages manufacturing plants in the United States and abroad. It produces bleached board for milk and food packaging, and white and colored business papers, including those marketed under the Hammermill, Strathmore, Beckett, and Springhill brand names. Other products include logs and other wood items. Foreign sales account for about 28% of the company's total sales. International Paper acquired Champion International in June 2000.

Management

John Dillon has been with IP since 1955 and took over as CEO in 1996. He's the driving force behind the firm's moves to cut costs, reduce capacity, and gain market share through acquisitions.

Strategy

International Paper is selling assets in an effort to focus on its core paper business. The firm is also streamlining operations and closing some mills to combat persistent overcapacity. Long-term, it seems IP wants garner enough market share to gain some control over paper prices, much as Alcoa has done in the aluminum industry.

400 Atlantic Street
Stamford, CT 06921
www.internationalpaper.com

Morningstar Grades

Growth [C]	1998	1999	2000	2001
Revenue %	-2.4	2.5	14.7	-6.4
Earnings/Share %	NMF	-26.7	-27.3	NMF
Book Value/Share %	-2.0	-5.0	9.5	-21.2
Dividends/Share %	0.0	0.0	0.0	0.0

Acquisitions have been IP's main growth vehicle. Including acquisitions, revenue has grown about 7% since 1995. Exclude the mergers, though, and that figure drops to 3%.

Profitability [C-]	1999	2000	2001	TTM
Return on Assets %	0.6	0.3	-3.2	-0.4
Oper Cash Flow $Mil	1,728	2,430	1,714	1,714
- Cap Spending $Mil	950	1,194	975	975
= Free Cash Flow $Mil	778	1,236	739	739

At the last cyclical peak in 1995, IP earned returns on assets and equity of 6% and 16%, respectively. Since then, these profitability measures have been dismal.

Financial Health [D-]	1999	2000	2001	09-02
Long-term Debt $Mil	7,520	12,648	12,457	11,926
Total Equity $Mil	10,304	12,034	10,291	10,159
Debt/Equity Ratio	0.7	1.1	1.2	1.2

Acquisitions have pumped debt up substantially, but almost $1 billion in cash sits on the balance sheet and cash flow has been solid. More asset sales are coming, the proceeds of which will probably be used to pay down debt.

Industry	Investment Style	Stock Type	Sector
Paper	▦ Large Value	▨ High Yield	✿ Industrial Mats

Competition	Market Cap $Mil	Debt/ Equity	12 Mo Trailing Sales $Mil	Price/Cash Flow	Return On Assets%	Total Return% 1 Yr	3 Yr
International Paper	16,774	1.2	24,940	9.8	-0.4	-11.1	-11.3
Smurfit-Stone Container	3,764	—	8,108	—	—	—	—
Georgia-Pacific Group	3,718	—	23,960	—	—	—	—

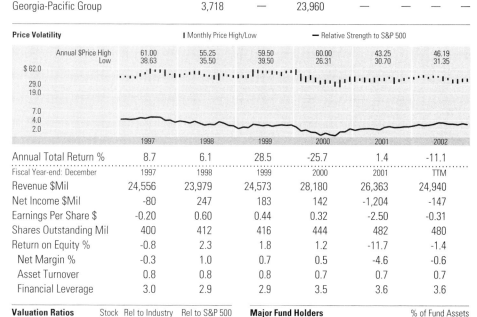

Price Volatility		▮ Monthly Price High/Low	— Relative Strength to S&P 500			
Annual $Price High / Low	61.00 / 38.63	55.25 / 35.50	59.50 / 39.50	60.00 / 26.31	43.25 / 30.70	46.19 / 31.35

	1997	1998	1999	2000	2001	2002
Annual Total Return %	8.7	6.1	28.5	-25.7	1.4	-11.1

Fiscal Year-end: December	1997	1998	1999	2000	2001	TTM
Revenue $Mil	24,556	23,979	24,573	28,180	26,363	24,940
Net Income $Mil	-80	247	183	142	-1,204	-147
Earnings Per Share $	-0.20	0.60	0.44	0.32	-2.50	-0.31
Shares Outstanding Mil	400	412	416	444	482	480
Return on Equity %	-0.8	2.3	1.8	1.2	-11.7	-1.4
Net Margin %	-0.3	1.0	0.7	0.5	-4.6	-0.6
Asset Turnover	0.8	0.8	0.8	0.7	0.7	0.7
Financial Leverage	3.0	2.9	2.9	3.5	3.6	3.6

Valuation Ratios	Stock	Rel to Industry	Rel to S&P 500
Price/Earnings	NMF	—	—
Price/Book	1.7	1.0	0.5
Price/Sales	0.7	0.8	0.3
Price/Cash Flow	9.8	1.0	0.7

Major Fund Holders	% of Fund Assets
Rydex Basic Materials Inv	7.03
Payden Growth & Income R	5.99
Strong Dow 30 Value	5.75
Fidelity Congress Street	5.32

Morningstar's Take By Daniel Quinn, 12-18-2002 Stock Price as of Analysis: $35.25

International Paper wants to dominate the paper industry. But given the industry's nature and the company's poor operating record, we'd avoid the stock unless it traded at a 50% discount to our $33 fair value estimate.

In recent years, IP's return on invested capital has been well below its cost of capital: Profits (as measured by operating income) have been less than the average return required by those who put up cash to fund the firm's assets (lenders and shareholders). Shareholder value has been destroyed and IP stock has languished for the past several years.

In an effort to rectify these past sins, IP seems to be taking a page from Alcoa's book, trying to dominate its industry enough to influence pricing and other fundamentals. For Alcoa, this strategy has paid off with a high return on invested capital and a stock that has returned 13% annually for the past decade. IP's ability to replicate this success in paper is highly uncertain.

In 1999 and 2000, two big acquisitions added about $12 billion in assets and $5 billion in annual revenue. While these enhanced the company's industry dominance, they have actually exacerbated IP's poor profitability. The asset base has grown 23% since 1998, yet sales are up only 7% over the same

period. What's worse, the firm turned in an operating loss in 2001, even after excluding restructuring charges. IP's assets aren't being used as efficiently as in the past, despite their growing size.

Another problem is that the paper industry remains highly fragmented and competitive. As a result, further consolidation on a sizable scale will probably be contentious and costly.

IP seems to recognize these conditions. It has been busy closing mills and taking excess capacity permanently offline. It has sold more than $3 billion in assets, using the proceeds to reduce debt. The firm has lowered interest expenses by refinancing some debt and has cut capital spending, both of which help improve the amount of free cash flow its operations generate.

We believe the shares are fairly valued at $33. Given the inherent uncertainty in predicting an economic rebound, the unattractive fundamentals of the paper industry, and IP's poor operating record over the past five or six years, we'd wait until the shares traded at a significant discount to this estimate.

International Speedway A ISCA

	Rating	Risk	Moat Size	Fair Value	Last Close	Yield %
	★★★	Med.	Wide	$35.00	$37.29	0.2

Company Profile

International Speedway promotes motorsports. The company owns or operates 15 race tracks across the United States, including the Daytona International Speedway in Florida, Talladega Superspeedway in Alabama, Michigan International Speedway, and Darlington Raceway in South Carolina. ISC also owns and operates MRN Radio, the nation's largest independent sports radio network, and Americrown Service Corporation, a provider of catering services and merchandise sales. ISC acquired Penske Motorsports in May 1999.

Management

The France family has an overwhelming controlling interest in the company, with 60% voting power. It also has a 40% economic interest in the shares, suggesting that its interests are aligned with shareholders'.

Strategy

By acquiring racetracks, International Speedway has established itself as the premier Nascar promoter in the United States. Through television deals and other marketing tactics, the company intends to drive attendance at and viewing of races.

1801 W. International Speedway Blvd. www.iscmotorsports.com
Daytona Beach, FL 32114-1243

Morningstar Grades

Growth [A]	1998	1999	2000	2001
Revenue %	33.7	58.1	47.4	20.0
Earnings/Share %	28.2	22.0	-22.1	73.7
Book Value/Share %	66.1	113.1	-7.9	8.8
Dividends/Share %	0.0	0.0	0.0	0.0

International Speedway's close relationship with Nascar, dominant market position, and share of television broadcasting fees should generate revenue growth north of 8% annually over the next several years.

Profitability [C+]	1999	2000	2001	TTM
Return on Assets %	3.5	3.0	5.1	-35.9
Oper Cash Flow $Mil	100	140	161	184
- Cap Spending $Mil	127	133	98	56
= Free Cash Flow $Mil	-26	7	62	129

Lucrative concession sales help keep International Speedway's operating margins above 30%, which is rare for a company in the consumer cyclical sector.

Financial Health [B]	1999	2000	2001	08-02
Long-term Debt $Mil	496	471	402	325
Total Equity $Mil	902	951	1,035	585
Debt/Equity Ratio	0.6	0.5	0.4	0.6

International Speedway may choose to spend the $100 million in free cash flow it will generate this year on building a new racetrack before it begins to pay down debt. Either way, the company is in great financial shape.

Industry	Investment Style	Stock Type	Sector
Recreation	▦ Mid Growth	↑ Aggr. Growth	⌂ Consumer Goods

Competition

	Market Cap $Mil	Debt/ Equity	12 Mo Trailing Sales $Mil	Price/Cash Flow	Return On Assets%	Total Return% 1 Yr	3 Yr
International Speedway A	1,983	0.6	543	10.8	-35.9	-4.5	-10.4
Speedway Motor Sports	1,088	—	385	—	—	—	—
Dover Downs Entertainment	—	—	—	—	—	—	—

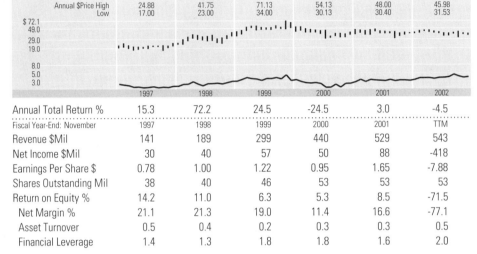

Price Volatility			▌ Monthly Price High/Low		— Relative Strength to S&P 500	
Annual $Price High	24.88	41.75	71.13	54.13	48.00	45.98
Low	17.00	23.00	34.00	30.13	30.40	31.53

	1997	1998	1999	2000	2001	2002
Annual Total Return %	15.3	72.2	24.5	-24.5	3.0	-4.5

Fiscal Year-End: November	1997	1998	1999	2000	2001	TTM
Revenue $Mil	141	189	299	440	529	543
Net Income $Mil	30	40	57	50	88	-418
Earnings Per Share $	0.78	1.00	1.22	0.95	1.65	-7.88
Shares Outstanding Mil	38	40	46	53	53	53
Return on Equity %	14.2	11.0	6.3	5.3	8.5	-71.5
Net Margin %	21.1	21.3	19.0	11.4	16.6	-77.1
Asset Turnover	0.5	0.4	0.2	0.3	0.3	0.5
Financial Leverage	1.4	1.3	1.8	1.8	1.6	2.0

Valuation Ratios	Stock	Rel to Industry	Rel to S&P 500
Price/Earnings	NMF	—	—
Price/Book	3.4	1.7	1.1
Price/Sales	3.7	1.1	1.8
Price/Cash Flow	10.8	1.0	0.8

Major Fund Holders	% of Fund Assets
FBR Small Cap Value A	5.13
FAM Equity-Income	4.70
Nicholas Limited Edition	3.88
Liberty Acorn Twenty Z	2.87

Morningstar's Take By T.K. MacKay, 10-23-2002 Stock Price as of Analysis: $37.40

International Speedway's wide economic moat and predictable revenue stream make for a great investment at the right price. We would gas up on the shares below $30.

We like International Speedway because of its competitive advantage. Through construction and acquisition, it has built a portfolio of 14 tracks, more than twice either competitor's. The company will host half of all Nascar Winston Cup races this year at the industry's most popular tracks, including the Daytona Motor Speedway, Talladega Speedway, and Michigan International Speedway. It costs $100 million or more to build a new track, making the barriers to entry very high for anyone wishing to compete in the auto-racing industry.

Chairman and CEO Bill France is in a position to ensure that these tracks maintain their popularity. He and COO James France also control Nascar, which creates the schedule for all races throughout the season. This relationship gives International Speedway a leg up on the competition by ensuring that the most popular races will always be held at the firm's tracks and under favorable terms.

Popular races will generate strong revenue growth for International Speedway over the next several years. In 1999, Nascar reached six- and eight-year

television broadcasting agreements with NBC and Fox, respectively. As a promoter, International Speedway receives 90% of the broadcast fees that the networks pay to air races held on its tracks. The total broadcast fees, which totaled $260 million in 2001, are structured to increase 17% annually through 2006, providing International Speedway with a predictable revenue stream.

Broadcast-fee-related revenue makes up nearly 50% of International Speedway's overall revenue, up from 33% in 1997. We believe slow growth in attendance and food sales, which expanded just 1% last year, will offset faster growth in broadcast fees, resulting in 8% annual sales growth over the long term. Part of the attraction of a Nascar event is that it is less frequent than, say, an NFL or NBA game. Nascar recognizes that substantial growth in races could chip away at its charm as a limited-event sport--and the premium price that networks pay to broadcast a race. It is likely to keep a lid on the number of new events it rolls out, and this inherently limits the internal growth prospects of the firm.

We are confident in International Speedway's ability to maintain its competitive advantage and would gladly pick up shares at a 20% discount to our estimated fair value.

MORNINGSTAR® Stocks 500

Internet Security Systems ISSX

	Rating	Risk	Moat Size	Fair Value	Last Close	Yield %
	★	High	None	$11.00	$18.33	0.0

Company Profile

Internet Security Systems provides total information security management. It has an end-to-end security management solution, SAFEsuite, that offers intrusion detection, vulnerability assessment, and policy enforcement. It also is a managed security services provider, offering 24-hour monitoring of information networks. The Atlanta-based company also provides education through SecureU, consulting services, and access to its team of security specialists.

Management

CTO Christopher Klaus is the founder and developed the firm's first product. CEO Tom Noonan, a seasoned technology executive, helped launch ISS in 1994.

Strategy

ISS wants to be synonymous with ID/VA software. In 2001, ISS acquired Network ICE, expanding its offering to include intrusion detection software for the desktop. The company also offers managed security services, allowing companies to outsource the management of their security infrastructure, including firewalls and virtual private networks.

6303 Barfield Road
Atlanta, GA 30328
www.iss.net

Morningstar Grades

Growth [B+]

	1998	1999	2000	2001
Revenue %	124.5	104.0	67.4	14.7
Earnings/Share %	NMF	NMF	141.2	NMF
Book Value/Share %	—	NMF	19.8	122.7
Dividends/Share %	NMF	NMF	NMF	NMF

The top line averaged 58% growth over the past three years, but those days are likely gone. We estimate ISS' long-term growth rate to be roughly 20%.

Profitability [B]

	1999	2000	2001	TTM
Return on Assets %	4.1	7.6	-3.1	0.7
Oper Cash Flow $Mil	12	21	39	45
- Cap Spending $Mil	6	20	32	14
= Free Cash Flow $Mil	5	0	8	31

Half of ISS' operating costs are salaries and benefits. ISS should be able to leverage these fixed costs as revenue grows, leading to hefty margin gains.

Financial Health [A]

	1999	2000	2001	09-02
Long-term Debt $Mil	0	0	0	0
Total Equity $Mil	155	188	427	453
Debt/Equity Ratio	0.0	0.0	0.0	0.0

The balance sheet is pristine, with $174 million in cash and no debt. However, days' sales outstanding are among the highest in the software industry.

Industry	Investment Style	Stock Type	Sector
Systems & Security	▦ Small Growth	▰ Spec. Growth	◩ Software

Competition

	Market Cap $Mil	Debt/ Equity	12 Mo Trailing Sales $Mil	Price/Cash Flow	Return On Assets%	Total Return% 1 Yr	3 Yr
Internet Security Systems	889	0.0	238	19.8	0.7	-42.8	-32.1
Cisco Systems	94,649	0.0	19,312	15.1	7.5	-27.7	-36.4
Symantec	5,797	0.4	1,242	9.9	4.1	22.0	14.3

Price Volatility

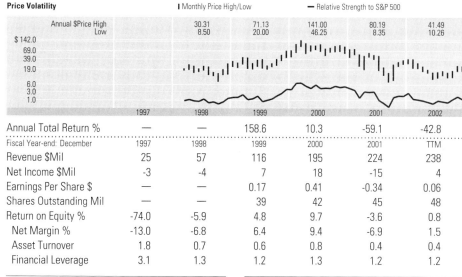

		1997	1998	1999	2000	2001	2002
Annual $Price High			30.31	71.13	141.00	80.19	41.49
Low			8.50	20.00	46.25	8.35	10.26
Annual Total Return %		—	—	158.6	10.3	-59.1	-42.8

Fiscal Year-end: December	1997	1998	1999	2000	2001	TTM
Revenue $Mil	25	57	116	195	224	238
Net Income $Mil	-3	-4	7	18	-15	4
Earnings Per Share $	—	—	0.17	0.41	-0.34	0.06
Shares Outstanding Mil	—	—	39	42	45	48
Return on Equity %	-74.0	-5.9	4.8	9.7	-3.6	0.8
Net Margin %	-13.0	-6.8	6.4	9.4	-6.9	1.5
Asset Turnover	1.8	0.7	0.6	0.8	0.4	0.4
Financial Leverage	3.1	1.3	1.2	1.3	1.2	1.2

Valuation Ratios	Stock	Rel to Industry	Rel to S&P 500
Price/Earnings	305.5	4.7	13.0
Price/Book	2.0	0.9	0.6
Price/Sales	3.7	1.0	1.9
Price/Cash Flow	19.8	1.8	1.5

Major Fund Holders	% of Fund Assets
RS Information Age	4.46
IDEX Munder Net50 A	4.34
RS Internet Age	4.17
Munder NetNet A	3.99

Morningstar's Take By Mike Trigg, 12-17-2002 Stock Price as of Analysis: $20.89

Internet Security Systems is an early leader in the red-hot security software industry. But without a sustainable competitive advantage and rising competition, the company's shares are very risky. We would avoid the stock until it is priced at least 50% below our fair value estimate.

We are bullish on the security industry because the progression of technology continues to drive strong demand. Even in the current environment, when businesses are slashing information technology budgets, security has remained a priority over other areas of software, like customer-focused applications. Because critical data like credit card numbers are being used online, companies demand solutions that protect their business.

ISS is the leader in an attractive niche, intrusion detection/vulnerability assessment (ID/VA), which identifies security violations on corporate networks and recommends actions to prevent such attacks. Market researchers like IDC expect this market will grow roughly 20% annually over the next five years. ISS is also an early entrant in managed security services, which allow companies to outsource their security needs.

Being the pioneer in an industry does not always translate into sustained success, however. The strong demand for ID/VA has spurred competition from Cisco, Check Point, and Symantec, all of which have greater financial resources and product offerings. While ISS still has the most functionality, we don't believe it has any sustainable competitive advantages that could keep rivals from overtaking its leading market position. In fact, the competition could hurt ISS' pricing power and margins.

Although we like the prospects of long-term demand for security, the lack of an economic moat makes it difficult to predict ISS' future. Thus, we'd need a large discount to our fair value estimate to recommend the stock. With the shares trading well above our fair value estimate, we'd pass and sleep well at night.

Interpublic Group of Companies IPG

	Rating	Risk	Moat Size	Fair Value	Last Close	Yield %
	★★★	Med.	Narrow	$16.00	$14.08	2.7

Company Profile

Interpublic Group primarily operates two advertising agencies: McCann-Erickson WorldGroup and The Lowe Group. It offers advertising agency services through arrangements with local agencies worldwide. The company conducts market research, telemarketing, and other related services through its DraftWorldwide subsidiary and conducts a media buying business through its Western International Media. It also conducts public relations, graphic design, market research, sales promotion, and interactive services.

Management

After several stumbles in 2002, CEO and chairman John Dooner Jr. is striving to restore management credibility. He has found a new CFO for McCann-Erickson, created a new chief risk officer position, and is trying to fill the COO post.

Strategy

As it is for the other three large agency holding companies, Interpublic's main source of revenue growth is acquisitions. In a departure from its previous focus on high-profile advertising agencies, the firm now seeks fewer but more selective acquisitions that offer specialized marketing services, thereby reducing vulnerability to volatile advertising revenue streams.

1271 Avenue of the Americas
New York, NY 10020 www.interpublic.com

Industry	Investment Style	Stock Type	Sector
Advertising	Mid Value	High Yield	Business Services

Competition	Market Cap $Mil	Debt/ Equity	12 Mo Trailing Sales $Mil	Price/Cash Flow	Return On Assets%	Total Return% 1 Yr	Total Return% 3 Yr
Interpublic Group of Companies	5,422	1.1	6,205	6.0	2.7	-51.5	-33.6
Omnicom Group	12,149	1.1	7,388	12.8	5.4	-26.9	-10.8
WPP Group PLC ADR	4,212	—	21,227	—	—		

Price Volatility | Monthly Price High/Low — Relative Strength to S&P 500

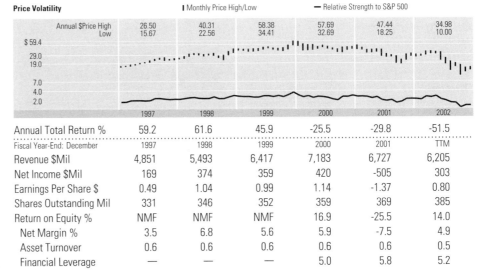

Annual $Price High / Low	26.50 / 15.67	40.31 / 22.56	58.38 / 34.41	57.69 / 32.69	47.44 / 18.25	34.98 / 10.00

	1997	1998	1999	2000	2001	2002
Annual Total Return %	59.2	61.6	45.9	-25.5	-29.8	-51.5

Fiscal Year-End: December	1997	1998	1999	2000	2001	TTM
Revenue $Mil	4,851	5,493	6,417	7,183	6,727	6,205
Net Income $Mil	169	374	359	420	-505	303
Earnings Per Share $	0.49	1.04	0.99	1.14	-1.37	0.80
Shares Outstanding Mil	331	346	352	359	369	385
Return on Equity %	NMF	NMF	NMF	16.9	-25.5	14.0
Net Margin %	3.5	6.8	5.6	5.9	-7.5	4.9
Asset Turnover	0.6	0.6	0.6	0.6	0.6	0.5
Financial Leverage	—	—	—	5.0	5.8	5.2

Valuation Ratios	Stock	Rel to Industry	Rel to S&P 500
Price/Earnings	17.6	1.0	0.7
Price/Book	2.5	1.0	0.8
Price/Sales	0.9	0.5	0.4
Price/Cash Flow	6.0	0.5	0.5

Major Fund Holders	% of Fund Assets
STI Classic Information & Tech Tr	6.11
MassMutual Instl Focused Value S	5.00
PBHG Clipper Focus PBHG	4.33
Oak Value	3.89

Morningstar Grades

Growth [C-]	1998	1999	2000	2001
Revenue %	13.2	16.8	11.9	-6.3
Earnings/Share %	112.2	-4.8	15.2	NMF
Book Value/Share %	NMF	NMF	NMF	-20.3
Dividends/Share %	15.2	13.8	12.1	2.7

The current ad spending slump and a few high-profile account losses have hit Interpublic hard over the past two years. As Interpublic eases up on acquisitions, we do not expect to see much positive revenue growth until 2004.

Profitability [C+]	1999	2000	2001	TTM
Return on Assets %	3.2	3.4	-4.4	2.7
Oper Cash Flow $Mil	769	607	149	908
- Cap Spending $Mil	250	260	268	197
= Free Cash Flow $Mil	520	348	-120	711

With profit margins that have trailed those of its peers, management recently stated intentions to make margin improvement a top priority and has taken major steps to align costs with lower revenue. We anticipate some improvement in this area.

Financial Health [B-]	1999	2000	2001	09-02
Long-term Debt $Mil	1,085	1,532	2,481	2,367
Total Equity $Mil	—	2,482	1,979	2,170
Debt/Equity Ratio	—	0.6	1.3	1.1

After tripling debt since 1999 to fund acquisitions, Interpublic has taken small steps toward cleaning up its balance sheet. Free cash flow was negative in 2001 because of huge restructuring charges, but we expect it to turn positive again in 2002.

Morningstar's Take By Debbie Wang, 12-15-2002 Stock Price as of Analysis: $13.50

Amid the worst advertising recession in 50 years, management's missteps have made a bad situation even worse for Interpublic. We are uncertain this management team can lead a turnaround, and remain lukewarm about the firm's prospects.

After gorging itself on acquisitions through the 1990s, Interpublic has a severe case of indigestion. Even though competitors also participated in the buying spree, Interpublic has had a particularly difficult time integrating new agencies, leading to a series of restructuring initiatives. Many of current management's headaches are due to ex-CEO Philip Geier Jr.'s decisions. However, current chairman and CEO John Dooner Jr. only exacerbated the situation when he engineered the huge acquisition of True North in 2001.

Now management struggles to control a vast conglomeration of large and small agencies, while unpleasant surprises keep cropping up in the form of lingering accounting irregularities at McCann-Erickson Europe, the loss of several high-profile accounts because of client conflicts, and substantial losses at the Octagon sports marketing unit. These and other glitches resulted in Interpublic's missing consensus earnings estimates by a wide margin two quarters in a row. Considering how often

unexpected problems have appeared over the last year, we wouldn't be surprised to see a few more.

With Interpublic stock down 60% from its 2002 high in April, CEO Dooner announced steps to rectify the situation, focusing on personnel changes, streamlining operations, and selling units that do not fit in the holding company's core competencies. While we believe this is the right path to follow, it is a large endeavor; given management's performance so far, we aren't yet convinced it'll be able to pull it off.

In the meantime, the firm must continue to tread water in a very soft advertising market and win new business. We do not see demand for communication and marketing services rebounding strongly anytime soon. We also do not believe Interpublic will be able to prop up revenue and earnings growth with acquisitions to the same degree it has. Thus, we have incorporated more conservative revenue growth of 5%-6% over the next five years in our financial model, and would be interested only if the shares fell to $10.

MORNINGSTAR® Stocks 500

Intuit INTU

	Rating	Risk	Moat Size	Fair Value	Last Close	Yield %
	★★	Med.	Wide	$37.00	$46.92	0.0

Company Profile

Intuit is well-known for its software products, like Quicken for managing personal finances, Quicken Turbo Tax for preparing tax returns, and Quickbooks for small-business accounting. The firm is further branching out into the small-business market, though, targeting additional needs of small businesses with its payroll service and industry-specific software offerings. The firm also offers mortgages through its Quicken Loans division.

Management

CEO Stephen Bennett, formerly of GE, has brought greater discipline and focus to Intuit. Bennett has brought in several GE execs to run major divisions. Co-founder Scott Cook remains on the board and is the public face of Intuit.

Strategy

Intuit has scrapped money-losing products, like insurance, to refocus on small-business customers. It's offering new products, like payroll processing and QuickBooks for accountants. We expect management to continue adding industry-specific software in areas like health care and manufacturing.

2535 Garcia Avenue
Mountain View, CA 94043
www.intuit.com

Morningstar Grades

Growth [A-]	1999	2000	2001	2002
Revenue %	42.4	23.1	10.7	18.3
Earnings/Share %	EUB	-24.9	NMF	NMF
Book Value/Share %	6.8	26.0	6.3	-3.1
Dividends/Share %	NMF	NMF	NMF	NMF

Intuit is counting on expanding its reach among small businesses with new products. We project midteen revenue growth for the next several years.

Profitability [A]	2000	2001	2002	TTM
Return on Assets %	10.9	-2.9	4.7	6.6
Oper Cash Flow $Mil	92	236	358	343
- Cap Spending $Mil	95	49	43	56
= Free Cash Flow $Mil	-3	188	316	287

Profitability is good, with returns on capital in excess of 20%. Intuit's business has large fixed costs, so it should generate more profits for each dollar of sales.

Financial Health [A]	2000	2001	2002	10-02
Long-term Debt $Mil	1	12	15	14
Total Equity $Mil	2,071	2,161	2,216	1,928
Debt/Equity Ratio	0.0	0.0	0.0	0.0

The balance sheet is solid, with more than $800 million in cash and minimal debt. Also, Intuit generates tons of free cash, which it often uses to repurchase stock.

Industry	Investment Style	Stock Type	Sector
Business Applications	▦ Large Growth	↗ Classic Growth	◣ Software

Competition	Market Cap $Mil	Debt/ Equity	12 Mo Trailing Sales $Mil	Price/Cash Flow	Return On Assets%	Total Return% 1 Yr	3 Yr
Intuit	9,630	0.0	1,413	28.1	6.6	9.7	-8.3
Microsoft	276,411	0.0	29,985	16.0	13.2	-22.0	-22.9
H & R Block	7,264	0.8	3,420	14.2	11.2	-8.7	28.2

Price Volatility

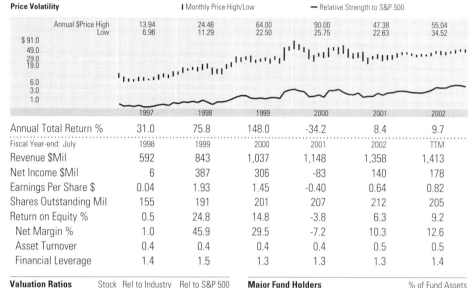

		▮ Monthly Price High/Low		— Relative Strength to S&P 500		
Annual $Price High Low	13.94 6.96	24.46 11.29	64.00 22.50	90.00 25.75	47.38 22.63	55.04 34.52

	1997	1998	1999	2000	2001	2002
Annual Total Return %	31.0	75.8	148.0	-34.2	8.4	9.7
Fiscal Year-end: July	1998	1999	2000	2001	2002	TTM
Revenue $Mil	592	843	1,037	1,148	1,358	1,413
Net Income $Mil	6	387	306	-83	140	178
Earnings Per Share $	0.04	1.93	1.45	-0.40	0.64	0.82
Shares Outstanding Mil	155	191	201	207	212	205
Return on Equity %	0.5	24.8	14.8	-3.8	6.3	9.2
Net Margin %	1.0	45.9	29.5	-7.2	10.3	12.6
Asset Turnover	0.4	0.4	0.4	0.4	0.5	0.5
Financial Leverage	1.4	1.5	1.3	1.3	1.3	1.4

Valuation Ratios	Stock	Rel to Industry	Rel to S&P 500	Major Fund Holders	% of Fund Assets
Price/Earnings	57.2	1.9	2.4	Northern Technology	7.79
Price/Book	5.0	1.0	1.6	American Eagle Capital Appreciation	7.29
Price/Sales	6.8	0.7	3.4	PBHG Focused Value	6.38
Price/Cash Flow	28.1	1.8	2.1	Rydex Internet Inv	5.52

Morningstar's Take By Mike Trigg, 12-12-2002 Stock Price as of Analysis: $48.24

Wide-moat companies, like Intuit, are what we love to own. We think anywhere below $30 is a good price to buy the stock.

Intuit dominates tax, personal finance, and small-business software. TurboTax has 65% market share in tax preparation software; QuickBooks has over 80% share in small-business software. And with 34 million tax returns still prepared manually and 5.5 million small businesses (fewer than 100 employees) in the United States, there's plenty of room for Intuit to stretch its legs.

Our enthusiasm begins with Intuit's wide economic moat--high switching costs make it difficult for customers to run their small businesses or pay taxes without software like QuickBooks and TurboTax. The data entry alone is cumbersome enough that users have little incentive to switch products. In our mind, this will make it difficult to displace Intuit's lead.

We believe few businesses have a moat as wide as Intuit's. For example, Intuit is one of only a handful of firms to fend off Microsoft, which attempted to compete in and later exited the personal finance and tax preparation software markets after achieving limited success. This prompted Microsoft to try buying Intuit, but the acquisition was killed by the Department of Justice.

Our biggest knock on Intuit is its inability to leverage the dominance of QuickBooks and TurboTax. Intuit made forays into loans and insurance, but these proved unsuccessful; these new areas are notoriously competitive yet have marginal relevance to the typical Intuit customer. New management led by CEO Stephen Bennett, formerly of General Electric, has switched gears at Intuit by selling noncore units, bringing in former GE managers to run major product divisions, and refocusing on small businesses. Like former GE CEO Jack Welch, Bennett wants Intuit to compete only in markets where it can be number one or two.

Since Intuit already dominates its core markets, its strategy is to extract more money from existing customers. For instance, Intuit has released industry-specific software and a Spanish-language version of TurboTax. One exciting area is payroll processing. Despite tough competition from firms like Paychex, this presents a great opportunity because it's an obvious extension of Intuit's small-business software.

With a defensible moat and loyal customers, Intuit has a bright future, in our opinion. We would buy the stock at a 20% discount to our fair value estimate.

Investors Financial Services IFIN

	Rating	Risk	Moat Size	Fair Value	Last Close	Yield %
	★★	Med.	Narrow	$23.00	$27.39	0.2

Company Profile

Investors Financial Services provides wholesale asset-administration services through its Investors Bank & Trust Company subsidiary. It serves asset-management clients including mutual funds, banks, and insurance companies who wish to outsource their back-office services. Investors Financial provides domestic and global custody, multicurrency accounting, institutional transfer agency, performance measurement, foreign exchange, securities lending, and mutual fund administration. About 95% of the firm's business is based in the United States.

Management

Investors Financial bought the financial products services division of the Bank of New England just before the bank's failure in 1990, and Kevin J. Sheehan came with it. Now chairman, CEO, and president, Sheehan shepherded the IPO in 1995.

Strategy

Investors Financial wants to be the back-office service provider for every company in the asset-management business--a global market with $51 trillion in assets. It has cast a wide net, focusing on upselling current customers as well as courting new ones. The company believes that its dedication to back-office services and technological innovation will convince asset managers to outsource.

200 Clarendon Street   www.investorsbnk.com
Boston, MA 02116

Morningstar Grades

Growth [A+]	1998	1999	2000	2001
Revenue %	18.1	30.8	43.0	44.1
Earnings/Share %	18.3	30.9	50.0	41.7
Book Value/Share %	15.7	43.6	24.2	81.6
Dividends/Share %	52.0	-1.3	100.0	33.3

Investors Financial has delivered impressive growth year after year as a result of strong demand for outsourcing services, superior technology, and responsive customer service. Management has targeted 25% annual growth.

Profitability [C]	1999	2000	2001	TTM
Return on Assets %	0.8	0.9	0.9	1.0
Oper Cash Flow $Mil	34	42	56	—
- Cap Spending $Mil	3	9	36	—
= Free Cash Flow $Mil	—	—	—	—

Return on equity has ranged between 14% and 19% for the past five years, coming in at 14.7% for 2001. This is lower than its larger global custody peers, which have more assets under custody and greater economies of scale.

Financial Health [B-]	1999	2000	2001	09-02
Long-term Debt $Mil	—	—	—	—
Total Equity $Mil	137	179	343	419
Debt/Equity Ratio	—	—	—	—

Though technically a bank, the firm does not make unsecured loans and has never had a credit loss. With $910 million of short-term borrowings and $24 million in trust preferred securities (akin to long-term debt), total debt is 2.7 times equity.

Industry	Investment Style	Stock Type	Sector
Money Management	▦ Mid Growth	↑ Aggr. Growth	$ Financial Services

Competition	Market Cap $Mil	Debt/ Equity	12 Mo Trailing Sales $Mil	Price/Cash Flow	Return On Assets%	Total Return% 1 Yr	3 Yr
Investors Financial Services	1,769	—	528	—	1.0	-17.1	37.1
J.P. Morgan Chase & Co.	47,901	—	42,911	—	0.2	-30.7	-17.5
Bank of New York	17,396	—	6,017	—	1.4	-39.9	-11.1

Price Volatility

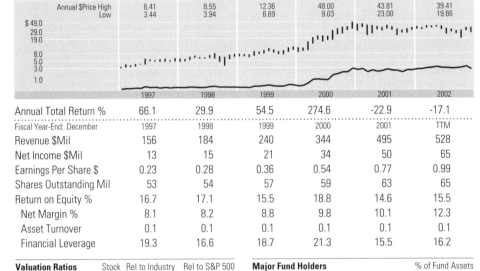

	Monthly Price High/Low	— Relative Strength to S&P 500

Annual $Price High Low	6.41 3.44	8.55 3.94	12.36 6.69	48.00 9.03	43.81 23.00	39.41 19.66

	1997	1998	1999	2000	2001	2002
Annual Total Return %	66.1	29.9	54.5	274.6	-22.9	-17.1
Fiscal Year-End: December	1997	1998	1999	2000	2001	TTM
Revenue $Mil	156	184	240	344	495	528
Net Income $Mil	13	15	21	34	50	65
Earnings Per Share $	0.23	0.28	0.36	0.54	0.77	0.99
Shares Outstanding Mil	53	54	57	59	63	65
Return on Equity %	16.7	17.1	15.5	18.8	14.6	15.5
Net Margin %	8.1	8.2	8.8	9.8	10.1	12.3
Asset Turnover	0.1	0.1	0.1	0.1	0.1	0.1
Financial Leverage	19.3	16.6	18.7	21.3	15.5	16.2

Valuation Ratios	Stock	Rel to Industry	Rel to S&P 500
Price/Earnings	27.8	1.6	1.2
Price/Book	4.2	1.6	1.3
Price/Sales	3.4	1.3	1.7
Price/Cash Flow	—	—	—

Major Fund Holders	% of Fund Assets
Orbitex Financial Service A	3.91
J&B Mid-Cap Aggressive Growth	3.84
Papp Small & Mid-Cap Growth	3.23
Strong Advisor U.S. Small/Mid Cp Gr C	3.00

Morningstar's Take   By Rachel Barnard, 09-19-2002 Stock Price as of Analysis: $26.95

The explosive growth at Investors Financial Services has barely been affected by sluggish equity markets, and we see robust growth ahead. If the shares dropped to around $18, we would jump at the chance to own this industry leader.

We think the money-management industry has robust long-term growth prospects. Global custody--which involves accounting and record-keeping for securities firms--is poised to benefit from the same trends we see in the larger world of money management. These include the growing popularity of mutual funds and retirement programs and the need for baby boomers to save for retirement. We estimate the industry can grow 12%-15% annually over the long haul.

The number of players in the custody industry is getting smaller because of the huge scale needed to compete profitably. We believe the successful ones, among them State Street, Bank of New York, and Investors Financial, have a long-term competitive advantage--and therefore a moat--because of the formidable barriers to entry. Significant investment in processing technology is required, but even then it takes years to build up a base of custody assets. With fees for asset processing around 0.03%, a company needs well more than $100 billion in

custody assets to operate profitably.

Investors Financial is the fastest-growing company in this industry. With only $835 billion in custody assets, it is dwarfed by the likes of Bank of New York, which processes nearly $7 trillion in assets. But Investors Financial has plenty of room to grow and is positioned to compete effectively for its share of the custody pie. In fact, the firm has been snapping up more than its share as a result of its reputation for quality service.

We think Investors Financial has an advantage in its customer service model, which assigns one representative as the dedicated point person for each customer. Clients have responded positively. In a survey of customers by Global Investor magazine, Investors Bank was ranked the best global custodian, ahead of larger rivals.

We believe Investors Financial can easily hit its target of 25% annual earnings growth if it continues to invest in customer service, though this investment will probably keep returns on equity lower than peers'. But the fact that other custodians would have to sacrifice profitability to beef up customer service gives Investors Financial an ace in the hole.

 MORNINGSTAR® Stocks 500

J.C. Penney JCP

	Rating	Risk	Moat Size	Fair Value	Last Close	Yield %
	★★	Med.	None	$22.00	$23.01	2.2

Company Profile

J.C. Penney operates department and drugstores. It operates about 1,080 J.C. Penney department stores and more than 2,650 drugstores across the United States. In addition, the company operates six catalog distribution centers. J.C. Penney conducts business under the J.C. Penney, Thrift Drug, Genovese, Fay's, and Eckerd names. The company also operates 50 Renner department stores in Brazil.

Management

J.C. Penney's management team of former outsiders has been charged with turning the company around. Retail expert Allen Questrom replaced James Oesterreicher as chairman and CEO in the fall of 2000.

Strategy

After years of outdated operating practices that hurt sales growth and profitability, J.C. Penney is centralizing decision-making to achieve a turnaround. The company is now focused on its core department store and catalog businesses. It sold its direct-marketing services business to Aegon in early 2001, and it may spin off its Eckerd drugstores in the future.

6501 Legacy Drive
Plano, TX 75024-3698

www.jcpenney.net

Morningstar Grades

Growth [C]	1999	2000	2001	2002
Revenue %	-0.1	6.7	0.3	0.5
Earnings/Share %	47.0	-47.0	NMF	NMF
Book Value/Share %	-0.4	0.2	-14.9	-2.6
Dividends/Share %	1.9	-11.8	-57.1	-39.4

Sales growth has been anemic at J.C. Penney for years because of a sizable disconnect between strategy and execution. We expect the company's turnaround to enable modest future growth.

Profitability [D+]	2000	2001	2002	TTM
Return on Assets %	1.4	-3.7	0.4	1.5
Oper Cash Flow $Mil	1,131	1,535	987	1,627
- Cap Spending $Mil	686	678	631	585
= Free Cash Flow $Mil	445	857	356	1,042

Returns on equity and assets declined in the past because of thin profit margins and poor asset turnover. Management hopes to reverse this trend by paring down inventory and improving product selection.

Financial Health [B+]	2000	2001	2002	10-02
Long-term Debt $Mil	5,844	5,448	5,179	5,169
Total Equity $Mil	6,782	5,860	5,766	5,879
Debt/Equity Ratio	0.9	0.9	0.9	0.9

Last year's sale of its direct-marketing business allowed the company to continue to pay down debt and shore up its balance sheet. With operational improvements, the company is poised to boost cash flow.

Industry	Investment Style	Stock Type	Sector
Department Stores	▣ Mid Core	➡ Slow Growth	⌂ Consumer Services

Competition	Market Cap $Mil	Debt/ Equity	12 Mo Trailing Sales $Mil	Price/Cash Flow	Return On Assets%	Total Return% 1 Yr	3 Yr
J.C. Penney	6,174	0.9	32,340	3.8	1.5	-12.3	8.6
Target	27,252	1.2	42,275	21.5	5.7	-26.5	-3.9
Sears Roebuck	7,576	3.3	41,156	—	2.1	-48.6	-6.5

Price Volatility

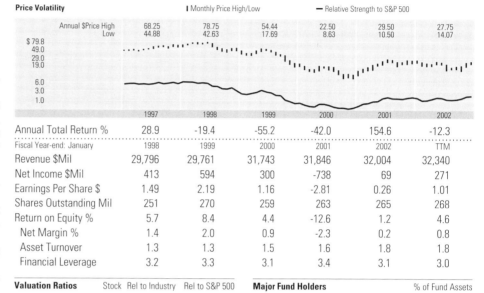

		Monthly Price High/Low		— Relative Strength to S&P 500		
Annual $Price High	68.25	78.75	54.44	22.50	29.50	27.75
Low	44.88	42.63	17.69	8.63	10.50	14.07

	1997	1998	1999	2000	2001	2002
Annual Total Return %	28.9	-19.4	-55.2	-42.0	154.6	-12.3
Fiscal Year-end: January	1998	1999	2000	2001	2002	TTM
Revenue $Mil	29,796	29,761	31,743	31,846	32,004	32,340
Net Income $Mil	413	594	300	-738	69	271
Earnings Per Share $	1.49	2.19	1.16	-2.81	0.26	1.01
Shares Outstanding Mil	251	270	259	263	265	268
Return on Equity %	5.7	8.4	4.4	-12.6	1.2	4.6
Net Margin %	1.4	2.0	0.9	-2.3	0.2	0.8
Asset Turnover	1.3	1.3	1.5	1.6	1.8	1.8
Financial Leverage	3.2	3.3	3.1	3.4	3.1	3.0

Valuation Ratios	Stock	Rel to Industry	Rel to S&P 500
Price/Earnings	22.8	1.4	1.0
Price/Book	1.1	0.9	0.3
Price/Sales	0.2	0.7	0.1
Price/Cash Flow	3.8	1.0	0.3

Major Fund Holders	% of Fund Assets
PIMCO PEA Value Instl	5.67
Impact Management Investment Retail	4.79
FMI Sasco Contrarian Value	4.79
Quaker Mid-Cap Value A	4.67

Morningstar's Take By Roz Bryant, 12-13-2002 Stock Price as of Analysis: $23.60

After years of decline, J.C. Penney's restructuring effort is finally producing some positive results. However, we think the old-line retailer will be little more than an also-ran even after stores are refurbished. We wouldn't consider the shares until they hit $10-$12.

J.C. Penney's new management team inherited a laundry list of problems to clean up. For years, there was little relationship between overall corporate strategy and store product selection. Individual managers handled store merchandising, a practice that resulted in unpredictable and oftentimes undesirable product offerings from store to store as well as slow inventory turnover. Meanwhile, its Eckerd drugstore chain was suffering from theft and unauthorized product discounting. Shoppers fled J.C. Penney's stores in droves and troubles at Eckerd mounted.

Enter CEO Allen Questrom and his team, who have done a nice job so far on J.C. Penney's turnaround. Since the retailer announced its restructuring plan in early 2001, operating margins have improved, moving from negative territory to 2.6%. Several underperforming stores have been closed, more fashionable merchandise is being stocked, and inventory management practices have been shored

up--all in an effort to improve store productivity. Same-store sales growth has returned as well; revenue from stores open more than a year increased 3% during the first nine months of fiscal 2002.

Even with these improvements, we're not optimistic about J.C. Penney's long-term prospects. The department store chain will have a tough time winning back alienated customers from Kohl's and Target, as middle-income shoppers have come to prefer the competing stores. As a result, we think it's likely that J.C. Penney will close even more department stores in the future. Plus, in light of rival Walgreen's aggressive expansion strategy, the Eckerd drugstore chain (which accounts for nearly 50% of Penney's total revenue) is unlikely to be able to offset mediocre growth in the department store division.

Furthermore, we expect the company's return on invested capital or ROIC (operating income divided by total capital invested) to peak at around 5% over the next couple years. While such results would certainly be an improvement from the retailer's negative ROIC in 2000, which led to the current restructuring, they're still well short of the firm's cost of capital--and we don't recommend a long-term investment in any firm that can't earn its cost of capital.

J.P. Morgan Chase & Co. JPM

	Rating	Risk	Moat Size	Fair Value	Last Close	Yield %
	★★★	High	Narrow	$36.00	$24.00	5.7

Company Profile

J.P. Morgan Chase is the holding company for subsidiaries that provide financial services through banking offices in New York, New Jersey, Connecticut, and Texas. The company also offers international banking offices throughout the world. In addition, J.P. Morgan Chase provides investment banking, security trading, consumer and real-estate financing, trust, discount brokerage, leasing, and computer banking services, as well as credit cards. It is one of the world's largest commercial lenders.

Management

Former Chase CEO William Harrison Jr. is chairman and CEO of the combined firm. Chase was the buyer and controls the show. Chase has eight seats on the board and J.P. Morgan has five.

Strategy

J.P. Morgan Chase aims to be a global financial services supermarket offering investment banking, asset management, credit cards, and retail banking. It plans to deepen Chase's corporate lending ties with high-margin capital markets business, and seeks to attract lucrative high-net-worth individuals with a greater range of asset-management tools.

270 Park Avenue   www.chase.com
New York, NY 10017

Industry	Investment Style	Stock Type	Sector
International Banks	▦ Large Value	🗲 High Yield	💲 Financial Services

Competition	Market Cap $Mil	Debt/ Equity	12 Mo Trailing Sales $Mil	Price/Cash Flow	Return On Assets%	Total Return% 1 Yr	3 Yr
J.P. Morgan Chase & Co.	47,901	—	42,911	—	0.2	-30.7	-17.5
Citigroup	177,948	—	106,096	—	1.6	-24.2	1.1
Bank of America	104,505	—	46,628	—	1.3	14.5	19.8

Price Volatility

I Monthly Price High/Low   — Relative Strength to S&P 500

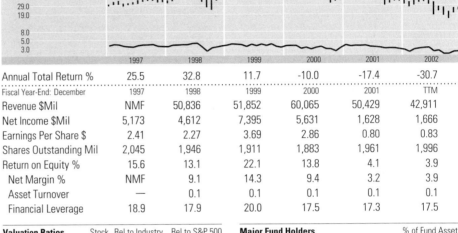

Annual $Price High Low	42.19 28.21	51.71 23.71	60.75 43.88	67.17 32.38	57.30 29.04	39.68 15.30
	1997	1998	1999	2000	2001	2002

Annual Total Return %	25.5	32.8	11.7	-10.0	-17.4	-30.7

Fiscal Year-End: December	1997	1998	1999	2000	2001	TTM
Revenue $Mil	NMF	50,836	51,852	60,065	50,429	42,911
Net Income $Mil	5,173	4,612	7,395	5,631	1,628	1,666
Earnings Per Share $	2.41	2.27	3.69	2.86	0.80	0.83
Shares Outstanding Mil	2,045	1,946	1,911	1,883	1,961	1,996
Return on Equity %	15.6	13.1	22.1	13.8	4.1	3.9
Net Margin %	NMF	9.1	14.3	9.4	3.2	3.9
Asset Turnover	—	0.1	0.1	0.1	0.1	0.1
Financial Leverage	18.9	17.9	20.0	17.5	17.3	17.5

Valuation Ratios	Stock	Rel to Industry	Rel to S&P 500
Price/Earnings	28.9	2.3	1.2
Price/Book	1.1	0.5	0.4
Price/Sales	1.1	0.7	0.6
Price/Cash Flow	—	—	—

Major Fund Holders	% of Fund Assets
Dessauer Global Equity	6.39
Fidelity Select Brokerage & Investmnt	5.33
First Funds Growth & Income I	5.23
PIMCO PEA Value Instl	4.95

Morningstar Grades

Growth [D]	1998	1999	2000	2001
Revenue %	NMF	2.0	15.8	-16.0
Earnings/Share %	-5.8	62.6	-22.5	-72.0
Book Value/Share %	11.9	-3.4	24.3	-5.0
Dividends/Share %	14.9	14.4	16.4	8.7

Net revenue dropped 12% in 2001 and is likely to end 2002 down as well. We assume that Morgan Chase doesn't return to its peak revenue levels reached in 2000 until 2004, implying a slow, arduous recovery.

Profitability [D]	1999	2000	2001	TTM
Return on Assets %	1.1	0.8	0.2	0.2
Oper Cash Flow $Mil	50	-13,676	-3,107	—
- Cap Spending $Mil	—	—	—	—
= Free Cash Flow $Mil	—	—	—	—

We have ratcheted down our near-term expectations because of problems with the firm's loan portfolio. Though our forecast of a 7% return on equity in 2002 is higher than last year's 4%, both of these performances are well below the firm's potential.

Financial Health [B]	1999	2000	2001	09-02
Long-term Debt $Mil	—	—	—	—
Total Equity $Mil	33,434	40,818	40,090	42,428
Debt/Equity Ratio	—	—	—	—

Because Morgan Chase is committed to maintaining a high dividend payout, it must be extremely disciplined to boost its equity base over the next several years. The firm's loss reserves are above average, but so is its bad-debt loss rate.

Morningstar's Take By Craig Woker, 11-27-2002 Stock Price as of Analysis: $25.19

J.P. Morgan Chase is not a stock for investors with weak stomachs. However, this is an investment that we remain strong believers in, should the price look compelling.

The uncertainty surrounding this company--and the share price volatility that it creates--have given investors opportunities recently to buy this stock at or below its tangible book value of about $17 per share. Because banks' balance sheets consist mostly of financial assets with varying degrees of liquidity, the amount of premium above book is a good proxy for how much growth and fee income is baked into a bank stock. In essence, the market expects very little from Morgan Chase.

We assume only moderate growth in our earnings model, and arrive at a fair value estimate of $36 per share, which we view as the bottom end of a reasonable range for this stock. After all, we assume fairly weak performance from Morgan Chase compared with most of the companies in its peer group, and we have discounted the firm's estimated future cash flows at 13% per year, a high rate for a large-cap company. Thus, our fair value estimate implies a return of 13% per year over the long term, plus the difference between the market price and our fair value estimate.

The lingering short-term risk associated with this company merits caution, however. The opaqueness of the derivatives portfolio, the exact value of the venture capital business, and the uncertainty over whether the firm can maintain its capital structure are just a few of those risks. Weighing these numerous factors, we would be eager buyers below $22 per share--about 1.3 times book value.

This company is walking a tightrope. Because of deterioration in the loan portfolio, we've assumed bad-debt provisions of about $4 billion this year. We had believed that Morgan Chase could lose its surety bond battle and sustain an Enron-size hit this year--or even a bunch of smaller ones--and still maintain its balance sheet size, capital structure, and dividend. With our provision estimate now exceeding last year's record $3.2 billion, Morgan Chase is near its breakpoint. Another near-term hit would force the firm to shrink its balance sheet, eat into its capital base, or reduce its dividend, in our view.

So while we believe in this company's long-term potential, investors must be patient, buy at a conservative price, and be prepared for a bumpy ride.

 MORNINGSTAR® Stocks 500

Jabil Circuit JBL

	Rating	Risk	Moat Size	Fair Value	Last Close	Yield %
	★★	Med.	None	$17.00	$17.92	0.0

Company Profile

Jabil Circuit provides turnkey manufacturing services for circuitboard assemblies, systems, and subsystems. Its services include circuit and production design; component selection, sourcing, and procurement; automated assembly; and repair. The company markets these services in the U.S. and abroad to companies that manufacture personal computers and work stations; disk drives and other peripherals; communications equipment; and automotive equipment and accessories. Jabil's top customers include Cisco Systems, Dell Computer, and Hewlett-Packard.

Management

Tim Main became CEO in 2000, and like most of top management has long tenure and line experience at Jabil. Chairman William Morean, whose family owns 29% of the firm's equity, helped build Jabil and expand it from its early focus on the auto market.

Strategy

Jabil's goal is to offer a complete range of electronic manufacturing services, from initial design through final assembly. The firm delivers these services to a select group of customers, mostly in telecom, computing, and consumer goods. Operations are unique in the EMS sector in that equipment is dedicated to individual customers, providing better service and lower unit costs.

10560 Ninth Street North   www.jabil.com
St. Petersburg, FL 33716

Morningstar Grades

Growth [B]	1999	2000	2001	2002
Revenue %	50.8	59.0	21.7	-18.1
Earnings/Share %	40.0	59.2	-24.4	-71.2
Book Value/Share %	92.2	103.8	3.5	4.8
Dividends/Share %	NMF	NMF	NMF	NMF

Although revenue fell 18% in 2002, the annual growth rate over the past five years is impressive at 25%. We expect growth in 2003 to be 5%-10% and roughly 17%-19% annually thereafter, thanks to the trend toward outsourcing.

Profitability [A-]	2000	2001	2002	TTM
Return on Assets %	7.2	5.0	1.4	1.4
Oper Cash Flow $Mil	35	183	554	554
- Cap Spending $Mil	333	309	85	85
= Free Cash Flow $Mil	-298	-126	469	469

Jabil's operating model has delivered the best returns on capital--an average of 12% over the past five years--in the EMS industry. Although we expect gross margins to fall as acquisitions are integrated, the firm should still top the industry.

Financial Health [B+]	2000	2001	2002	08-02
Long-term Debt $Mil	25	362	355	355
Total Equity $Mil	1,270	1,414	1,507	1,507
Debt/Equity Ratio	0.0	0.3	0.2	0.2

Jabil has $450 million in cash, $360 million in debt, and should generate more than $100 million from operations in 2003. It is in the best financial condition of the major EMS firms.

Industry	Investment Style	Stock Type	Sector
Contract Manufacturers	▦ Mid Growth	→ Slow Growth	▣ Hardware

Competition	Market Cap $Mil	Debt/ Equity	12 Mo Trailing Sales $Mil	Price/Cash Flow	Return On Assets%	Total Return% 1 Yr	3 Yr
Jabil Circuit	3,550	0.2	3,545	6.4	1.4	-21.1	-17.8
Flextronics International	4,239	0.2	13,217	5.1	-0.1	-65.9	-26.4
Celestica	3,239	0.0	10,004	2.5	-0.6	-65.1	-33.1

Price Volatility

	Monthly Price High/Low		Relative Strength to S&P 500			
Annual $Price High Low	18.00 3.84	18.72 5.75	38.13 14.25	68.00 18.63	40.80 14.00	26.75 11.13
	1997	1998	1999	2000	2001	2002
Annual Total Return %	98.8	87.4	96.0	-30.5	-10.5	-21.1

Fiscal Year-end: August	1998	1999	2000	2001	2002	TTM
Revenue $Mil	1,484	2,238	3,558	4,331	3,545	3,545
Net Income $Mil	57	85	146	119	35	35
Earnings Per Share $	0.35	0.49	0.78	0.59	0.17	0.17
Shares Outstanding Mil	160	166	180	191	193	198
Return on Equity %	20.2	14.7	11.5	8.4	2.3	2.3
Net Margin %	3.9	3.8	4.1	2.7	1.0	1.0
Asset Turnover	2.4	2.2	1.8	1.8	1.4	1.4
Financial Leverage	2.2	1.8	1.6	1.7	1.7	1.7

Valuation Ratios	Stock	Rel to Industry	Rel to S&P 500
Price/Earnings	105.4	1.0	4.5
Price/Book	2.4	2.5	0.7
Price/Sales	1.0	3.1	0.5
Price/Cash Flow	6.4	1.3	0.5

Major Fund Holders	% of Fund Assets
Pioneer Science and Technology B	4.90
Phoenix-Seneca Mid-Cap Edge A	3.96
Neuberger Berman Focus Inv	3.73
Harbor Mid Cap Value	3.16

Morningstar's Take By Fritz Kaegi, 12-19-2002 Stock Price as of Analysis: $18.29

Jabil is the best firm in the electronic manufacturing services (EMS) industry, and should enjoy strong growth in the coming decade.

Jabil has a distinct operating strategy. Most EMS firms structure operations on the "batch" model, where equipment is grouped by function (like making circuit boards) and customers' items are intermingled. This method usually makes sense because a single customer's demand is too volatile to dedicate a piece of equipment to it. Jabil takes on contracts with higher purchase commitments for goods with lower demand volatility. It can thus operate on the "continuous flow" model--seen in high-volume sectors like food processing and auto manufacturing--where products move continuously along a line to make a single product. This provides a faster production cycle with lower unit costs, which helps explain Jabil's top industry ranking over the past five years in inventory turns, gross margin, and returns on invested capital.

This operating model also allows Jabil to assign workers to "work cells" dedicated to a single customer, which tends to lead to greater ownership--and customer service--on the part of employees. This blends both sales and production roles. This is a key differentiating factor in a market

where buyers are risk-averse and engineers play a key role in choosing vendors. Customer satisfaction tends to bring in new business from current clients and build loyalty.

During the boom, Jabil abstained from buying customers' plants to gain order flow. With asset prices now depressed, Jabil has made several big deals, which should bring in sales of roughly $2 billion annually. However, transferring Jabil's production method will be a great challenge because it may not be suited for some items produced at these plants, like optical gear. But we're willing to believe Jabil will eventually succeed, considering that the chairman's family owns 29% of the company's equity, almost every Jabil executive has line experience, and operational strategy has been focused.

The continuous flow model is especially capital-intensive. Jabil needs to be conservative in booking business, managing its finances, and investing in equipment so that it is not too exposed during slumps. It has made money in each quarter of the current downturn, so this seems likely. Given that electronics firms will continue shifting to outsourced manufacturing, Jabil's future looks bright.

JD Edwards & Company JDEC

	Rating	Risk	Moat Size	Fair Value	Last Close	Yield %
	★	Med.	None	$10.00	$11.28	0.0

Company Profile

JD Edwards & Company develops software systems that are designed to enable users to change technology or business practices while minimizing costs and business interruptions. The company's software application suites support manufacturing, finance, distribution and logistics, and human resources operations for multisite and multinational organizations. Its systems operate on IBM midrange systems. The company's clients include Amgen, E&J Gallo Winery, Harley-Davidson Europe, Lexmark International, Mobil, Samsonite, and GlaxoSmithKline.

Management

There have been a lot of changes in management. Bob Dutkowsky, formerly of IBM and EMC, was named president and CEO in January 2002.

Strategy

With its end-to-end product suite, OneWorld, JD Edwards is expanding beyond the slow-growing ERP market into more high-growth segments, like CRM and SCM. Management is also aggressively targeting the midmarket because those customers generally want an integrated suite of software applications.

One Technology Way   www.jdedwards.com
Denver, CO 80237

Morningstar Grades

Growth [C]	1999	2000	2001	2002
Revenue %	1.2	4.8	-12.6	1.1
Earnings/Share %	NMF	NMF	NMF	NMF
Book Value/Share %	4.8	-23.5	-37.4	35.7
Dividends/Share %	NMF	NMF	NMF	NMF

Even during the tech boom, growth was not impressive. However, selling a revamped product suite to existing customers should improve results.

Profitability [B+]	2000	2001	2002	TTM
Return on Assets %	-1.6	-27.2	5.7	5.7
Oper Cash Flow $Mil	4	67	138	138
- Cap Spending $Mil	32	24	28	28
= Free Cash Flow $Mil	-28	43	110	110

After several years of posting losses, profitability has greatly improved. Still, we think the company's expectation for operating margins of 15%-18% over the next three years is too optimistic.

Financial Health [B-]	2000	2001	2002	10-02
Long-term Debt $Mil	0	0	0	0
Total Equity $Mil	471	299	442	442
Debt/Equity Ratio	0.0	0.0	0.0	0.0

The balance sheet is solid, with over $350 million in cash and investments and no debt. Faster collection of receivables has also boosted cash generation.

Industry	Investment Style	Stock Type	Sector
Business Applications	▦ Mid Core	➡ Slow Growth	▣ Software

Competition	Market Cap $Mil	Debt/ Equity	12 Mo Trailing Sales $Mil	Price/Cash Flow	Return On Assets%	Total Return% 1 Yr	3 Yr
JD Edwards & Company	1,347	0.0	904	9.8	5.7	-31.4	-27.6
Oracle	57,845	0.1	9,459	18.1	19.8	-21.8	-26.3
SAP AG ADR	24,556	0.0	6,546	27.8	9.5	-38.7	-25.0

Price Volatility   ▍ Monthly Price High/Low   — Relative Strength to S&P 500

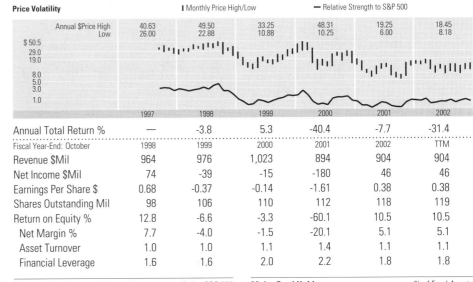

	1997	1998	1999	2000	2001	2002
Annual $Price High	40.63	49.50	33.25	48.31	19.25	18.45
Low	26.00	22.88	10.88	10.25	6.00	8.18
Annual Total Return %	—	-3.8	5.3	-40.4	-7.7	-31.4

Fiscal Year-End: October	1998	1999	2000	2001	2002	TTM
Revenue $Mil	964	976	1,023	894	904	904
Net Income $Mil	74	-39	-15	-180	46	46
Earnings Per Share $	0.68	-0.37	-0.14	-1.61	0.38	0.38
Shares Outstanding Mil	98	106	110	112	118	119
Return on Equity %	12.8	-6.6	-3.3	-60.1	10.5	10.5
Net Margin %	7.7	-4.0	-1.5	-20.1	5.1	5.1
Asset Turnover	1.0	1.0	1.1	1.4	1.1	1.1
Financial Leverage	1.6	1.6	2.0	2.2	1.8	1.8

Valuation Ratios	Stock	Rel to Industry	Rel to S&P 500
Price/Earnings	29.7	1.0	1.3
Price/Book	3.0	0.6	1.0
Price/Sales	1.5	0.2	0.7
Price/Cash Flow	9.8	0.6	0.7

Major Fund Holders	% of Fund Assets
FMI Focus	3.33
Van Wagoner Technology	2.57
Van Wagoner Emerging Growth	2.51
Phoenix-Engemann Focus Growth A	2.49

Morningstar's Take   By Mike Trigg, 12-17-2002   Stock Price as of Analysis: $12.16

We think JD Edwards is finally headed in the right direction after several years of missteps.

Despite 25 years of operation, JD Edwards struggled in recent years after forgetting what made it a success. Where it once battled SAP, PeopleSoft, and Oracle for larger deals in every industry, the company is now focusing on the midmarket (firms with revenue of $200 million to $5 billion) and sectors like manufacturing and construction, where it's performed well. It has also used the economic slowdown to trim organizational fat, so profits should outpace sales once corporate wallets reopen.

A revamped, integrated product suite is central to the turnaround. JD Edwards has expanded beyond the slow-growing enterprise resource planning (ERP) market, which caters to back-office operations like human resources, into high-growth, front-office areas like customer-relationship management (CRM) and supply-chain management (SCM). SCM in particular plays to the firm's strength because there's great demand for it from industries like manufacturing. JD Edwards should also succeed in selling the integrated suite to the midmarket, which lacks the resources to integrate software from different vendors.

Its 6,500 loyal customers are a competitive advantage; JD Edwards can rely on a certain level of

business from these users. Since most of the company's customers don't yet have CRM or SCM software, it is the perfect selling opportunity; they have been working with JD Edwards for years and can easily add new applications. In many cases, customers are so comfortable with the firm that they don't look at competing products. The only large challenge is getting firms to spend the money.

Our enthusiasm is bounded by the competition JD Edwards faces. SAP, PeopleSoft, and Oracle have similar end-to-end offerings and have identified the midmarket as a key source of growth. But our biggest worry is Microsoft, which added CRM to its already-formidable ERP offering by acquiring Navision. Thus far, Microsoft has set its sights on small companies (revenue less than $50 million), but we think it will eventually target larger firms.

We expect the turnaround to continue as JD Edwards sells its new applications to existing customers, but longer-term we have less confidence. The company can't tap the installed base forever, and it has no sustainable competitive advantage, which will make it difficult to win new business. With no economic moat and the risk of growing competition, we wouldn't become interested in buying the stock until it fell near $6 per share.

MORNINGSTAR® Stocks 500

JDS Uniphase JDSU

	Rating	Risk	Moat Size	Fair Value	Last Close	Yield %
	★★	High	Narrow	$2.40	$2.47	0.0

Company Profile

JDS Uniphase, formed by the merger of Uniphase and JDS Fitel in June 1999, manufactures a broad range of fiber-optic components, modules, and subsystems for the communication industry. Its products are deployed in advanced optical communication networks for the telecom and cable industries, generally in order to increase speed and traffic-handling capacity versus conventional electronic solutions. Customers include traditional telecom equipment vendors like Lucent, Nortel, and Alcatel, as well as a growing list of next-generation systems vendors like Ciena and Juniper.

Management

Though many observers may remember JDS for its expensive acquisitions during the boom years--and for $56 billion in asset write-downs during the bust--management strictly avoided debt when others, like Corning, did not.

Strategy

JDS Uniphase wants to offer one-stop shopping for optical components and subsystems. The company has used a string of acquisitions to expand its product line, maintain technology leadership, and enhance its market position. Keeping up with surging demand was the greatest challenge until 2001; now the focus has shifted to managing costs amid the severe industry downturn.

1768 Automation Parkway
San Jose, CA 95131
www.jdsuniphase.com

Industry	Investment Style	Stock Type	Sector
Optical Equipment	Mid Growth	Spec. Growth	Hardware

Competition

	Market Cap $Mil	Debt/ Equity	12 Mo Trailing Sales $Mil	Price/Cash Flow	Return On Assets%	Total Return% 1 Yr	3 Yr
JDS Uniphase	3,494	0.0	963	—	ELB	-71.7	-69.3
Corning	3,800	0.8	3,605	52.8	-10.2	-62.9	-55.0
New Focus	292	—	35	—			

Price Volatility

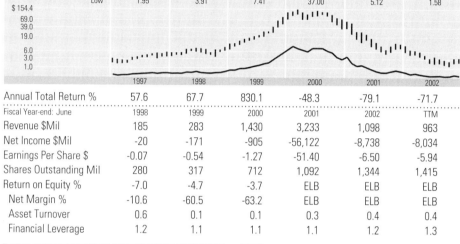

I Monthly Price High/Low   — Relative Strength to S&P 500

Annual $Price High Low	5.94 1.95	8.94 3.91	88.75 7.41	153.42 37.00	64.94 5.12	10.34 1.58

$154.4 / 69.0 / 39.0 / 19.0 / 6.0 / 3.0 / 1.0

1997 1998 1999 2000 2001 2002

Annual Total Return %	57.6	67.7	830.1	-48.3	-79.1	-71.7
Fiscal Year-end: June	1998	1999	2000	2001	2002	TTM
Revenue $Mil	185	283	1,430	3,233	1,098	963
Net Income $Mil	-20	-171	-905	-56,122	-8,738	-8,034
Earnings Per Share $	-0.07	-0.54	-1.27	-51.40	-6.50	-5.94
Shares Outstanding Mil	280	317	712	1,092	1,344	1,415
Return on Equity %	-7.0	-4.7	-3.7	ELB	ELB	ELB
Net Margin %	-10.6	-60.5	-63.2	ELB	ELB	ELB
Asset Turnover	0.6	0.1	0.1	0.3	0.4	0.4
Financial Leverage	1.2	1.1	1.1	1.1	1.2	1.3

Valuation Ratios

	Stock	Rel to Industry	Rel to S&P 500
Price/Earnings	NMF	—	—
Price/Book	1.8	1.1	0.6
Price/Sales	3.6	2.5	1.8
Price/Cash Flow	—	—	—

Major Fund Holders

	% of Fund Assets
John Hancock Communications A	4.46
Calvert Social Investment Tech A	3.96
Pin Oak Aggressive Stock	2.79
American Heritage Growth	2.38

Morningstar Grades

Growth [B-]	1999	2000	2001	2002
Revenue %	52.7	405.8	126.0	-66.0
Earnings/Share %	NMF	NMF	NMF	NMF
Book Value/Share %	EUB	204.5	-71.8	-81.3
Dividends/Share %	NMF	NMF	NMF	NMF

Optical component sales fell 71% in 2002, while sales for telecom applications fell 42% as telecom customers pare back capital spending. Sales will probably be extremely volatile, but over the long term should grow at 12%-14%.

Profitability [C+]	2000	2001	2002	TTM
Return on Assets %	-3.4	ELB	ELB	ELB
Oper Cash Flow $Mil	281	53	86	-38
- Cap Spending $Mil	275	735	133	95
= Free Cash Flow $Mil	6	-682	-47	-133

Earnings continue to be distorted by asset write-downs, while cash flow needs to be adjusted for cancellation fees (which are nonrecurring) and tax refunds. The firm is roughly breaking even on a cash basis.

Financial Health [C]	2000	2001	2002	09-02
Long-term Debt $Mil	41	0	6	0
Total Equity $Mil	24,779	10,707	2,471	1,939
Debt/Equity Ratio	0.0	0.0	0.0	0.0

Unlike many other equipment firms, like Lucent and Nortel NT, liquidity is not a major worry; JDS has no debt, $1.3 billion in cash, and is roughly breaking even.

Morningstar's Take By Fritz Kaegi, 12-22-2002 Stock Price as of Analysis: $2.56

JDS' position in the optical component industry should improve, thanks to favorable trends in product features, the firm's stable balance sheet, and continued spending on research and acquisitions. Downward pressure on component prices is our one major worry. We would buy stock in JDS, a company with a narrow moat, at roughly a 50% discount to our fair value estimate.

JDS aims to be the dominant optical component manufacturer. It operates as a "one-stop shop," offering customers bundled pricing and multiple functions for a wide range of parts. This approach is intended to appeal to buyers' strong preference for convenience, simplicity, and reliability. JDS' salesforce aims to gain the loyalty of engineers early in the equipment design process. A broad product line reduces JDS' exposure to category obsolescence, as numerous separate products are evolving into fewer, more multifunctional boxes. Another goal is to maintain a technological edge over competitors by investing in research and acquisitions.

As a supplier to equipment firms, JDS is in the most volatile segment of the telecom industry. To withstand the down years created by volatility, component suppliers need financial strength. They also need maximum flexibility in setting their

costs--the lower fixed costs are, the better, even at the expense of lower gross margins. JDS is in pretty good shape on both points. It has no debt, has avoided unnecessary cash outlays, is nearly cash flow neutral, and requires less working capital to do business than equipment makers, like Lucent, that need more time to sell. Thanks to JDS' concentrated customer base, the costs of maintaining a salesforce are relatively low. All of this should enable the firm to benefit from telecom equipment's good long-term growth prospects.

However, JDS does manufacturing in-house; aligning fixed costs with volatile demand is difficult. JDS has cut costs over six quarters, yet its restructuring is incomplete. We suspect the company has taken its time in making cuts to leverage its financial health and wait out a downturn with productive assets intact. Competitors have behaved similarly, which has resulted in desperate pricing conditions that have hurt profit margins. Continued competition, lack of product differentiation, and customers' strong bargaining power will probably prevent margins from returning to past levels.

JetBlue Airways JBLU

	Rating	Risk	Moat Size	Fair Value	Last Close	Yield %
	★★	Med.	Narrow	$23.00	$27.00	0.0

Company Profile

JetBlue is a low-cost passenger airline based at New York City's JFK airport. Operations began in 2000 with service to Florida and upstate New York. More recently, the airline set up a West Coast hub in Long Beach, California.

Management

The management team is excellent. CEO David Neeleman has a good record with two other startup carriers; other top execs held high-level positions at Continental, Southwest, and Neeleman's first airline, Morris Air.

Strategy

JetBlue's stated strategy is to stimulate demand, keep operating costs as low as possible, offer point-to-point service to overpriced markets, and differentiate its product offering. The airline is taking delivery of 53 A320 aircraft over the next few years to implement this strategy.

80-02 Kew Gardens Rd.   www.jetblue.com
Kew Gardens, NY 11415

Morningstar Grades

Growth [NA]	1998	1999	2000	2001
Revenue %	NMF	NMF	NMF	206.3
Earnings/Share %	NMF	NMF	NMF	NMF
Book Value/Share %	—	—	—	—
Dividends/Share %	NMF	NMF	NMF	NMF

Revenue doubled in 2002, after growing more than 200% in 2001. For the future, we have modeled five-year annual growth of 44%.

Profitability [C-]	1999	2000	2001	TTM
Return on Assets %	-13.3	-10.3	3.2	3.3
Oper Cash Flow $Mil	-7	3	111	199
- Cap Spending $Mil	12	206	234	429
= Free Cash Flow $Mil	-19	-203	-122	-230

Profit margins came under pressure in 2002, and we believe this will continue. We think the airline will manage to remain in the black, though, since its cost structure is still so low.

Financial Health [D]	1999	2000	2001	09-02
Long-term Debt $Mil	—	137	291	524
Total Equity $Mil	-19	-54	-32	392
Debt/Equity Ratio	—	ELB	ELB	1.3

JetBlue is well capitalized for a startup airline. However, net debt/capital is 50%, not including leases, which is higher than we'd like. It's unlikely this ratio will improve anytime soon, since the airline is taking delivery of so many planes.

Industry	Investment Style	Stock Type	Sector
Air Transport	—	⚅ Spec. Growth	🏢 Business Services

Competition	Market Cap $Mil	Debt/ Equity	12 Mo Trailing Sales $Mil	Price/Cash Flow	Return On Assets%	Total Return% 1 Yr	Total Return% 3 Yr
JetBlue Airways	1,706	1.3	543	8.6	3.3	—	—
Southwest Airlines	10,768	0.4	5,359	16.8	2.9	-24.7	10.7
Delta Air Lines	1,493	3.2	12,860	—	-6.9	-58.4	-37.0

Price Volatility

Annual $Price High/Low						36.77 / 19.83
$37.8 24.0 17.0 7.0 5.0 3.0						
	1997	1998	1999	2000	2001	2002
Annual Total Return %	—	—	—	—	—	—

Fiscal Year-End: December	1997	1998	1999	2000	2001	TTM
Revenue $Mil	—	0	0	105	320	543
Net Income $Mil	—	-1	-18	-35	22	40
Earnings Per Share $	—	—	—	—	—	—
Shares Outstanding Mil	—	—	—	—	—	63
Return on Equity %	—	NMF	NMF	NMF	NMF	10.2
Net Margin %	—	NMF	NMF	-33.9	6.7	7.4
Asset Turnover	—	0.0	0.0	0.3	0.5	0.5
Financial Leverage	—	NMF	NMF	NMF	NMF	3.1

Valuation Ratios	Stock	Rel to Industry	Rel to S&P 500
Price/Earnings	—	—	—
Price/Book	4.4	1.7	1.4
Price/Sales	3.1	1.6	1.6
Price/Cash Flow	8.6	0.5	0.6

Major Fund Holders	% of Fund Assets
Gartmore Worldwide Leaders A	3.68
SunAmerica Focused 2000 Growth A	2.94
Turner New Enterprise	2.25
Thornburg Core Growth A	1.79

Morningstar's Take By Nicolas Owens, 12-20-2002 Stock Price as of Analysis: $26.05

JetBlue is one of two airlines we'd consider investing in for the long term, but only at a significant discount to our fair value estimate.

Because the business cycle drives large swings in demand for air travel and the price of a ticket, only the airlines with the lowest cost structures are able to avoid huge losses. Like Southwest, JetBlue has built cost savings into every aspect of its business. By focusing on selective routes from New York's JFK to other second-tier airports, JetBlue gets much better use of its aircraft than conventional airlines do.

JetBlue also saves on pilot training and maintenance by using just one aircraft type--a brand-new fleet of Airbus A320s. All of its passengers fly ticketless, reducing the carrier's ticket-distribution expenses. And, most important, the company has very low compensation expenses compared with its peers. In aggregate, JetBlue's employees and other assets are much more productive than those at other airlines, which gives the airline the ability to price aggressively and still turn a profit.

For the time being, JetBlue's unit costs are even lower than Southwest's, but so is its unit revenue. Down the road, though, some of JetBlue's cost advantages are going to erode. Its new airplanes are cheap to operate now, but when they start going in for regular maintenance, JetBlue's costs will inch up. We also foresee unionization--and the higher wages that generally come with it--becoming a thorny issue for JetBlue over the next few years. Wage hikes would make JetBlue much more vulnerable to the inevitable downturns of the industry.

At this stage, JetBlue still has plenty of opportunity to increase its top line just by adding popular incremental routes, as it did from New York to Las Vegas in November. Its leather seats (cheaper to clean) and satellite TV (cheaper than food) are popular so far, too. But a stock is not necessarily a good investment simply because the company has a red-hot product. JetBlue operates in a very risky environment: The airline industry is subject to volatile fuel prices, cutthroat competition, unpredictable weather, powerful unions, heavy taxation, and economic downturns. While these factors may affect JetBlue less adversely because of its relative youth, the firm is not immune.

We like JetBlue's business model and growth prospects a lot, but it's an airline just the same. Because of the risks, we would hold off buying unless we saw a 40% discount to our fair value estimate.

MORNINGSTAR® Stocks 500

Jo-Ann Stores A JAS.A

	Rating	Risk	Moat Size	Fair Value	Last Close	Yield %
	★★	Med.	Narrow	$21.00	$22.97	0.0

Company Profile

Jo-Ann Stores is a fabric and craft retailer. The company operates more than 1,020 retail outlets in the United States, with stores operating under the Jo-Ann Fabrics and Crafts brand name. The stores feature such merchandise as fashion and decorator fabrics, related notions, crafts, floral, seasonal items, and other products. Approximately 47% of the company's sales are derived from fabric, about 21% from notions, and approximately 16% from crafts.

Management

President and CEO Alan Rosskamm has been with Jo-Ann Stores since 1978. He's a member of one of the company's founding families, and has held his current post for more than five years.

Strategy

Jo-Ann is focused on restructuring its operations. Stores are operating more efficiently, as investments in distribution and inventory management have begun to pay off. The company now expects to close another batch of underperforming stores by the end of this fiscal year, essentially completing its turnaround plan.

5555 Darrow Road
Hudson, OH 44236

www.joann.com

Morningstar Grades

Growth [B-]	1999	2000	2001	2002
Revenue %	27.5	11.2	7.4	5.9
Earnings/Share %	-56.5	106.0	NMF	NMF
Book Value/Share %	7.0	12.3	-1.9	-7.8
Dividends/Share %	NMF	NMF	NMF	NMF

Jo-Ann has put expansion plans on hold to focus on improving store operations. Growth in same-store sales has been strong throughout the restructuring, thanks to increased customer traffic and a refined selection of merchandise.

Profitability [C-]	2000	2001	2002	TTM
Return on Assets %	3.4	-1.8	-2.1	4.9
Oper Cash Flow $Mil	28	39	88	83
- Cap Spending $Mil	67	36	67	19
= Free Cash Flow $Mil	-40	3	22	64

Bloated operating costs and interest payments have hurt the bottom line in the past. Margins have improved substantially since the turnaround began, though, thanks to the company's focus on inventory management.

Financial Health [C-]	2000	2001	2002	10-02
Long-term Debt $Mil	245	240	224	276
Total Equity $Mil	259	249	233	260
Debt/Equity Ratio	0.9	1.0	1.0	1.1

Jo-Ann has relatively high leverage after borrowing heavily to finance an acquisition. Management plans to use the firm's strengthening cash flows to pay down debt and reduce interest expense.

Industry	Investment Style	Stock Type	Sector
Specialty Retail	Small Core	↗ Classic Growth	Consumer Services

Competition

	Market Cap $Mil	Debt/ Equity	12 Mo Trailing Sales $Mil	Price/Cash Flow	Return On Assets%	Total Return% 1 Yr	3 Yr
Jo-Ann Stores A	448	1.1	1,654	5.4	4.9	221.3	26.6
Michaels Stores	2,068	—	2,700	—	—	—	—
Hancock Fabrics	288	—	424	—	—	—	—

Price Volatility

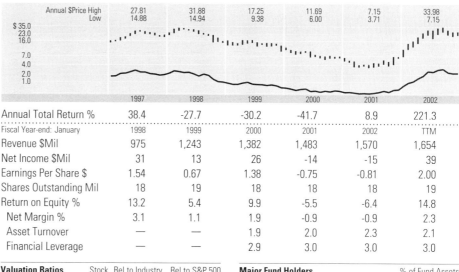

| | Monthly Price High/Low | — Relative Strength to S&P 500 |

		1997	1998	1999	2000	2001	2002
Annual $Price High		27.81	31.88	17.25	11.69	7.15	33.98
Low		14.88	14.94	9.38	6.00	3.71	7.15

Annual Total Return %	38.4	-27.7	-30.2	-41.7	8.9	221.3

Fiscal Year-end: January	1998	1999	2000	2001	2002	TTM
Revenue $Mil	975	1,243	1,382	1,483	1,570	1,654
Net Income $Mil	31	13	26	-14	-15	39
Earnings Per Share $	1.54	0.67	1.38	-0.75	-0.81	2.00
Shares Outstanding Mil	18	19	18	18	18	19
Return on Equity %	13.2	5.4	9.9	-5.5	-6.4	14.8
Net Margin %	3.1	1.1	1.9	-0.9	-0.9	2.3
Asset Turnover	—	—	1.9	2.0	2.3	2.1
Financial Leverage	—	—	2.9	3.0	3.0	3.0

Valuation Ratios	Stock	Rel to Industry	Rel to S&P 500
Price/Earnings	11.5	0.4	0.5
Price/Book	1.7	0.5	0.5
Price/Sales	0.3	0.4	0.1
Price/Cash Flow	5.4	0.4	0.4

Major Fund Holders	% of Fund Assets
Turner Micro Cap Growth	1.14

Morningstar's Take By Roz Bryant, 12-14-2002 Stock Price as of Analysis: $24.70

The recent surge in the popularity of arts and crafts activities will likely moderate in our opinion, so we'd wait for a 40% margin of safety to our fair value estimate for Jo-Ann Stores before investing.

Jo-Ann is the largest fabric retailer in the nation, and works in a niche with few formidable rivals. It competes with Michaels Stores and AC Moore in arts and crafts, but the fragmented fabrics retailing industry is largely made up of small stores and regional chains. Hancock Fabrics is Jo-Ann's largest competitor in this space, but generates only one fourth of Jo-Ann's annual revenue.

In the past, the company failed to fully exploit its competitive position, but management started turning things around in early 2001. Most of the company's troubles were related to bloated inventories and kinks in its distribution channels. To improve supply chain efficiency and lower freight costs, the company constructed its own distribution center to replace the one it had been contracting. Jo-Ann also modernized its inventory tracking system to improve ordering and weed out undesirable merchandise.

Jo-Ann is still improving inventory management by streamlining product offerings. In fiscal 2002, the retailer eliminated 10,000 stock-keeping units from its product lineup, enabling an 18% year-over-year

reduction in inventory. Customers have been impressed by the leaner, but better merchandise selections. Loyal patrons are making larger purchases on each shopping trip, and the number of new shoppers visiting stores is also up, thanks in part to a surge in arts and craft and home-decorating activities.

However, we believe Jo-Ann's sales growth will moderate over the next five years and return to the 5%-7% range, which it has hit in three of the past five years, as some of the popularity in arts and crafts wears off. Creating gifts and home accessories is less expensive than buying them, so many bargain-hunters affected by the slow economy have become crafters. But as consumer confidence picks up, we think some of these shoppers will shift more dollars back to finished goods.

With an existing base of more than 800 stores, we don't see Jo-Ann engaging in a rapid store-expansion plan anytime soon either. Rather, we believe it will open new stores at a moderate pace while spending heavily on store relocations and remodeling. We admire the company's turnaround progress over the past two years, but we'd only invest if the shares hit the low teens.

Johnson & Johnson JNJ

	Rating	Risk	Moat Size	Fair Value	Last Close	Yield %
	★★★	Low	Wide	$58.00	$53.71	1.5

Company Profile

Johnson & Johnson is a diversified health-care company with three divisions: pharmaceutical, professional, and consumer. Pharmaceutical is growing faster than the other two divisions and now represents 48% of total revenue. The professional segment, which makes medical devices and diagnostic equipment and supplies, represents 34% of revenue. The remaining 18% comes from the firm's well-known consumer health-care products like Band-Aids, Johnson's Baby Shampoo, and Tylenol. Approximately 63% of sales are from the United States. J&J sells products in more than 175 countries.

Management

After 12 years at the helm, Ralph Larsen stepped down as chairman and CEO. William Weldon, chairman of the company's worldwide pharmaceutical group, took over after the April 2002 board meeting.

Strategy

Johnson & Johnson is decentralized, with more than 190 operating companies. It has made pharmaceuticals its top priority but refuses to drop its slow-growing consumer segment because its brands inspire consumer trust. Consumer products also provide stability to the company's cash flow. J&J pursues acquisitions as part of its growth strategy.

One Johnson & Johnson Plaza
New Brunswick, NJ 08933
www.jnj.com

Morningstar Grades

Growth [B-]	1998	1999	2000	2001
Revenue %	5.5	14.8	6.6	10.6
Earnings/Share %	-7.5	-37.7	15.8	14.3
Book Value/Share %	NMF	NMF	25.7	18.7
Dividends/Share %	14.1	12.4	13.8	12.9

For a company J&J's size, revenue growth of 10.8% for the first nine months of 2002 is impressive. Drug sales led the way with a 15.4% increase year to date, followed by devices at 11.6% and consumer goods at negative 0.1%.

Profitability [A+]	1999	2000	2001	TTM
Return on Assets %	14.7	14.5	14.7	16.3
Oper Cash Flow $Mil	5,920	6,903	8,864	8,845
- Cap Spending $Mil	1,822	1,689	1,731	2,052
= Free Cash Flow $Mil	4,098	5,214	7,133	6,793

J&J is very profitable. Operating margins are in the high 20s, and net margins usually come in just below 20%. They're also slowly improving. Operating margins for the third quarter were 27.6%, up from 25.0% a year ago.

Financial Health [A]	1999	2000	2001	09-02
Long-term Debt $Mil	2,450	3,163	2,217	2,102
Total Equity $Mil	16,213	20,395	24,233	22,085
Debt/Equity Ratio	0.2	0.2	0.1	0.1

J&J remains one of a handful of companies with a triple A credit rating, thanks to its pristine balance sheet. The company had $7.2 billion in cash and securities and $4.5 billion in debt at September 30, 2002.

Industry	Investment Style	Stock Type	Sector
Drugs	Large Growth	↗ Classic Growth	Healthcare

Competition

	Market Cap $Mil	Debt/ Equity	12 Mo Trailing Sales $Mil	Price/Cash Flow	Return On Assets%	Total Return% 1 Yr	3 Yr
Johnson & Johnson	159,452	0.1	35,807	18.0	16.3	-7.9	8.0
Merck	127,121	0.3	50,430	13.2	15.0	-1.3	-2.5
Procter & Gamble	111,662	0.9	41,268	13.3	11.0	11.3	-4.5

Price Volatility

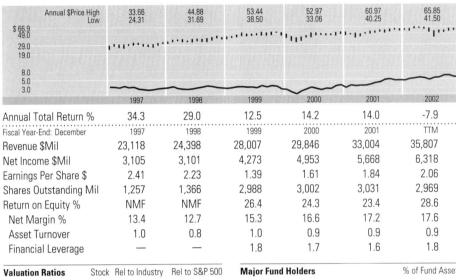

			Monthly Price High/Low		— Relative Strength to S&P 500	
Annual $Price High Low	33.66 24.31	44.88 31.69	53.44 38.50	52.97 33.06	60.97 40.25	65.85 41.50

	1997	1998	1999	2000	2001	2002
Annual Total Return %	34.3	29.0	12.5	14.2	14.0	-7.9

Fiscal Year-End: December	1997	1998	1999	2000	2001	TTM
Revenue $Mil	23,118	24,398	28,007	29,846	33,004	35,807
Net Income $Mil	3,105	3,101	4,273	4,953	5,668	6,318
Earnings Per Share $	2.41	2.23	1.39	1.61	1.84	2.06
Shares Outstanding Mil	1,257	1,366	2,988	3,002	3,031	2,969
Return on Equity %	NMF	NMF	26.4	24.3	23.4	28.6
Net Margin %	13.4	12.7	15.3	16.6	17.2	17.6
Asset Turnover	1.0	0.8	1.0	0.9	0.9	0.9
Financial Leverage	—	—	1.8	1.7	1.6	1.8

Valuation Ratios	Stock	Rel to Industry	Rel to S&P 500
Price/Earnings	26.1	1.1	1.1
Price/Book	7.2	1.0	2.3
Price/Sales	4.5	1.1	2.2
Price/Cash Flow	18.0	0.9	1.4

Major Fund Holders	% of Fund Assets
Schwab Health Care Focus	15.23
ProFunds Ultra Pharmaceuticals Inv	14.29
Rydex Health Care Inv	12.34
Papp America-Abroad	11.23

Morningstar's Take By Todd N. Lebor, 12-11-2002 Stock Price as of Analysis: $56.16

Year after year of double-digit revenue and EPS growth, dividend increases that you could set your watch by, and cash flow galore are all hallmarks of Johnson & Johnson. We see no end to this century-long run, and think investors should use any weakness in the shares to pick up this virtual health-care mutual fund.

J&J isn't slowing under its ever-increasing girth; it's actually getting stronger. In 10 years, J&J has improved its operating margins from 19.6% to 28.5%. We think these margins can continue to creep up as pharmaceuticals become a larger piece of the revenue pie. For a company its size--$33 billion in sales for 2001--J&J has shown a remarkable ability to increase revenue at a steady clip.

J&J's greatest feat is generating free cash flow (cash flow from operations less capital expenditures). It produced $7.2 billion in free cash flow in 2001 from $9.0 billion in cash flow from operations. Even more remarkable is that free cash flow has outpaced EPS growth. The compound annual growth rates for free cash flow and earnings per share for the five years ended December 31, 2001, were 23% and 12%, respectively.

With its cash drawers full and a triple A credit rating, J&J is a model of balance sheet fitness. It gets stability from its diversity as well. In the second quarter of 2002, it pulled 47% of revenue from pharmaceuticals, 35% from medical supplies and devices, and the remaining 18% from consumer products. Nearly 40% of sales came from overseas. While consumer operating margins can't stand up to those of pharmaceuticals, the segment provides solid cash flow, builds the J&J brand, and helps establish a distribution network. It also has seen significant margin improvement: In 1995, consumer operating margins were 5.1%; in 2001 they were 15.1%, only 2.8 percentage points below those of the professional division (medical devices and supplies).

J&J's real appeal lies in its drug portfolio. Rheumatoid arthritis and Crohn's disease treatment Remicade should easily top $1 billion in sales in 2002, while anemia drug Procrit/Eprex may top $4 billion worldwide. Pain patch Duragesic, epilepsy med Topamax, and antipsychotic drug Risperdal continue to post healthy growth rates. Antibiotic Levaquin is struggling to grow, but it's still bring home $1 billion a year in sales.

J&J's record of earnings growth and dividend increases is a tribute to its long-term business plan and execution. We'd require only a slight discount to our fair value before buying.

 MORNINGSTAR® Stocks 500

Johnson Controls JCI

	Rating	Risk	Moat Size	Fair Value	Last Close	Yield %
	★★★★	Low	Narrow	$105.00	$80.17	1.7

Company Profile

Johnson Controls manufactures automotive components and provides building control systems and services. Its automotive segment (71% of fiscal 2000 sales) produces seats, instrument panels, floor consoles, door panels, and other interior components to automakers, as well as batteries to aftermarket retailers. Controls, the other operating division, provides products and services related to heating, ventilation, energy management, and security systems. In 2000, 34% of sales were made outside North America. Johnson Controls employs approximately 110,000 people worldwide.

Management

JCI has done a fine job developing talent from within. Both James Keyes, who stepped aside as CEO in late 2002 and remains chairman, and incoming CEO John Barth are lifelong JCI employees. The firm has announced it will expense stock options in 2003.

Strategy

By pursuing a disciplined strategy of acquisitions and internal growth, Johnson Controls--which didn't enter the business until 1985--has become the world's second-largest interiors supplier. Its efficient, low-cost operating structure has made it a preferred supplier for automakers around the world. The firm has shed unrelated operations, retaining only its original building controls business.

5757 North Green Bay Avenue www.johnsoncontrols.com
Milwaukee, WI 53201

Morningstar Grades

Growth [A]	1999	2000	2001	2002
Revenue %	28.2	6.3	7.4	9.1
Earnings/Share %	23.3	11.7	1.0	9.7
Book Value/Share %	17.7	17.7	15.7	17.0
Dividends/Share %	8.7	12.0	10.7	6.5

Few industrial firms can match the company's record of internal growth. Sales have risen an average of 15% annually in the past decade; by our reckoning, at least two thirds of that was achieved internally (before the effect of acquisitions).

Profitability [B]	2000	2001	2002	TTM
Return on Assets %	5.5	5.4	5.3	5.3
Oper Cash Flow $Mil	790	973	989	989
- Cap Spending $Mil	547	622	496	496
= Free Cash Flow $Mil	244	352	493	493

JCI's operating margins are generally lower than its more cyclical peers during boom years, reflecting the firm's low fixed/high variable cost structure. But its returns on investment are solid for any industrial, let alone an auto parts supplier.

Financial Health [B]	2000	2001	2002	09-02
Long-term Debt $Mil	1,315	1,395	1,827	1,827
Total Equity $Mil	2,447	2,862	3,396	3,396
Debt/Equity Ratio	0.5	0.5	0.5	0.5

Strong cash generation and a flexible cost structure make JCI's debt load a relatively light one at 36% of total capital, earning JCI the sector's best credit rating.

Industry	Investment Style	Stock Type	Sector
Auto Parts	Mid Value	Cyclical	Consumer Goods

Competition

	Market Cap $Mil	Debt/ Equity	12 Mo Trailing Sales $Mil	Price/Cash Flow	Return On Assets%	Total Return% 1 Yr	3 Yr
Johnson Controls	7,132	0.5	20,103	7.2	5.3	0.9	17.0
Delphi	4,495	0.9	26,836	3.8	0.5	-39.6	-16.6
Magna International A	4,411	—	11,026	—	—	—	—

Price Volatility

	Monthly Price High/Low			— Relative Strength to S&P 500		
Annual $Price High Low	51.00 35.38	61.88 40.50	76.69 49.00	65.13 45.81	82.70 51.94	93.20 69.10

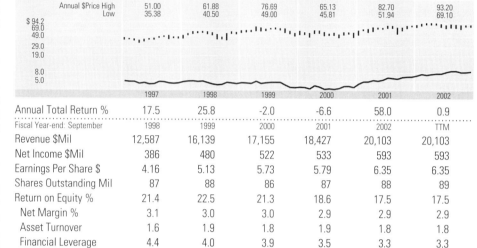

	1997	1998	1999	2000	2001	2002
Annual Total Return %	17.5	25.8	-2.0	-6.6	58.0	0.9

Fiscal Year-end: September	1998	1999	2000	2001	2002	TTM
Revenue $Mil	12,587	16,139	17,155	18,427	20,103	20,103
Net Income $Mil	386	480	522	533	593	593
Earnings Per Share $	4.16	5.13	5.73	5.79	6.35	6.35
Shares Outstanding Mil	87	88	86	87	88	89
Return on Equity %	21.4	22.5	21.3	18.6	17.5	17.5
Net Margin %	3.1	3.0	3.0	2.9	2.9	2.9
Asset Turnover	1.6	1.9	1.8	1.9	1.8	1.8
Financial Leverage	4.4	4.0	3.9	3.5	3.3	3.3

Valuation Ratios	Stock	Rel to Industry	Rel to S&P 500
Price/Earnings	12.6	1.0	0.5
Price/Book	2.1	0.1	0.7
Price/Sales	0.4	0.0	0.2
Price/Cash Flow	7.2	0.1	0.5

Major Fund Holders	% of Fund Assets
Banknorth Large Cap Value	5.49
ABN AMRO/Chicago Capital Growth N	3.48
Reserve Informed Investors Growth R	3.41
Orchard Value	3.12

Morningstar's Take By Josh Peters, 12-12-2002 Stock Price as of Analysis: $79.18

In the murky auto industry, Johnson Controls' financial performance stands out like stadium lights. We would consider buying shares in the low $70s.

Even though it's more profitable and less cyclical than the typical auto supplier, JCI rarely gets the kind of respect it deserves. But this perennial discount can lead to outsized returns: JCI has returned 17% annually over the past 10 years without the benefit of any expansion in its price-to-earnings ratio.

This begs the question: How does JCI keep its head so far above water in such a dysfunctional industry? For one thing, it has the right kind of products. Interior and electronic systems lend themselves easily to innovation and differentiation, allowing JCI to deliver proprietary products that earn above-average margins.

The company also has the right approach to manufacturing. JCI has positioned itself primarily as a final assembler of more complicated systems, rather than a commodity part producer. This means that JCI has lower fixed costs than its peers. Lower labor costs than those of its customers is another key advantage--in the case of the Big Three, much lower costs).

Perhaps most importantly, JCI boasts the right customer mix. Since it's only been in the auto parts

industry for seventeen years, JCI isn't bound by a long-standing dependency upon Detroit. It's had the flexibility to choose the best areas for investment; as a result, it's no surprise that JCI is a key supplier to Toyota and Nissan.

These strategies have led to high quality financial characteristics. Its return on invested capital is the best among the large diversified suppliers, preserved by a careful approach to acquisitions. And even while growing internally at the rate of 10% or thereabouts during the past decade, JCI still converted fully 83% of net income to free cash flow.

JCI may run laps around its supplier peers, but it's not perfect. An unusual gain will be offset by restructuring activity during 2003; though we think it unlikely, our esteem for the firm would diminish greatly if it climbed aboard the restructuring treadmill. Our expectations of lower industry production and continued price pressure are headwinds that affect all suppliers, JCI included.

Even so, between new business and the market share gains of its Japanese customers, we expect JCI to register higher automotive sales in fiscal 2003. The company's profitability and quality of market share set it apart from its peers--in the low 70s, we think the shares would be well worth a look.

Jones Apparel Group JNY

	Rating	Risk	Moat Size	Fair Value	Last Close	Yield %
	★★	Med.	None	$35.00	$35.44	0.0

Company Profile

Jones Apparel Group designs and produces women's sportswear, suits, dresses, and shoes. The company markets its products under the Jones New York, Jones*Wear, Saville, Rena Rowan for Saville, Evan-Picone, Todd Oldham, and Nine West names. The company sells its products through about 6,200 department stores, specialty retailer accounts, and direct-mail catalog companies throughout North America. It also operates approximately 1,000 domestic retail stores and 250 international ones.

Management

There have been shakeups in senior management recently. Former COO and president Jackwyn Nemerov resigned in March 2002, and Peter Boneparth, former head of McNaughton, was appointed as the new president and CEO.

Strategy

Jones Apparel has historically focused on the better apparel segment. Now the company is boosting its presence in the moderately priced clothing and accessories segment to spur growth and diversify its revenue stream. The firm recently acquired Gloria Vanderbilt Apparel and l.e.i., both designers of moderately priced casual apparel.

250 Rittenhouse Circle
Bristol, PA 19007
www.jny.com

Morningstar Grades

Growth [A-]	1998	1999	2000	2001
Revenue %	21.5	87.0	31.5	-1.7
Earnings/Share %	30.1	8.8	55.0	-26.6
Book Value/Share %	39.5	86.8	15.1	21.0
Dividends/Share %	NMF	NMF	NMF	NMF

Jones's growth has been largely driven by acquisitions over the past several years. We expect the apparel maker's pursuit of new brands to be the primary driver of growth.

Profitability [A-]	1999	2000	2001	TTM
Return on Assets %	6.7	10.1	7.0	7.5
Oper Cash Flow $Mil	248	339	562	878
- Cap Spending $Mil	30	47	375	375
= Free Cash Flow $Mil	218	292	188	503

Returns on assets have been erratic over the past couple of years, as the firm has taken on substantial amounts of goodwill. Still, tight cost controls should allow Jones to earn well above its cost of capital for the foreseeable future.

Financial Health [A]	1999	2000	2001	09-02
Long-term Debt $Mil	834	576	977	1,006
Total Equity $Mil	1,241	1,477	1,905	2,285
Debt/Equity Ratio	0.7	0.4	0.5	0.4

Jones Apparel generates solid operating cash flow. Capital requirements for existing business are relatively modest, but the apparel maker is spending aggressively to make acquisitions to foster growth.

Industry	Investment Style	Stock Type	Sector
Apparel Makers	Mid Core	Cyclical	Consumer Goods

Competition	Market Cap $Mil	Debt/ Equity	12 Mo Trailing Sales $Mil	Price/Cash Flow	Return On Assets%	Total Return% 1 Yr	3 Yr
Jones Apparel Group	4,572	0.4	4,246	5.2	7.5	6.8	12.4
Liz Claiborne	3,162	0.4	3,610	6.0	9.5	20.1	19.4

Price Volatility

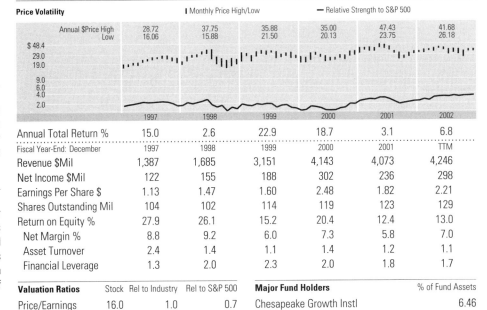

		28.72	37.75	35.88	35.00	47.43	41.68
Annual $Price High / Low		16.06	15.88	21.50	20.13	23.75	26.18
		1997	1998	1999	2000	2001	2002

Annual Total Return %	15.0	2.6	22.9	18.7	3.1	6.8
Fiscal Year-End: December	1997	1998	1999	2000	2001	TTM
Revenue $Mil	1,387	1,685	3,151	4,143	4,073	4,246
Net Income $Mil	122	155	188	302	236	298
Earnings Per Share $	1.13	1.47	1.60	2.48	1.82	2.21
Shares Outstanding Mil	104	102	114	119	123	129
Return on Equity %	27.9	26.1	15.2	20.4	12.4	13.0
Net Margin %	8.8	9.2	6.0	7.3	5.8	7.0
Asset Turnover	2.4	1.4	1.1	1.4	1.2	1.1
Financial Leverage	1.3	2.0	2.3	2.0	1.8	1.7

Valuation Ratios	Stock	Rel to Industry	Rel to S&P 500
Price/Earnings	16.0	1.0	0.7
Price/Book	2.0	1.0	0.6
Price/Sales	1.1	1.2	0.5
Price/Cash Flow	5.2	1.0	0.4

Major Fund Holders	% of Fund Assets
Chesapeake Growth Instl	6.46
Chesapeake Aggressive Growth	6.08
Jensen	5.71
Banknorth Small/Mid Cap Core	4.64

Morningstar's Take By Roz Bryant, 12-11-2002 Stock Price as of Analysis: $36.34

Jones Apparel and Liz Claiborne follow similar brand and product category diversification strategies, but we think Jones is better at integrating acquisitions and cutting costs. We'd gladly purchase the shares at a 40% discount to our fair value estimate.

Both Jones and Claiborne have diversified from a strict focus on traditional careerwear, but Jones is tapping the success of moderately priced apparel brands more aggressively and more successfully. Retailers offering value pricing, like Kohl's, have been stealing share from traditional department stores for years, so Jones has been on the prowl for clothing brands that appeal to value-focused retail chains. In 2002, Jones increased revenue derived from the fast-growing moderate segment to 24% of overall sales from 20% in 2001.

In 2002, Jones purchased the Gloria Vanderbilt and l.e.i. brands. Both are known for moderately priced casual apparel and count stores like Kohl's and Mervyn's (owned by Target) as customers. Given Jones' $4.1 billion in annual sales, the $400 million in additional sales from the small labels might seem like a drop in the bucket. However, we think the deals won Jones two nicely profitable businesses with potential for consistent double-digit sales growth--faster than its core careerwear brands deliver.

In addition to promoting growth, we think management has a knack for enhancing Jones' already superior operating performance. The company maintains a 400-basis-point lead in operating margin over Liz Claiborne, even though the latter's margins have improved markedly over the past few years. The primary reason: Jones has done a great job of reducing costs since its acquisition binge started with the 1999 purchase of Nine West.

Still, Jones' appetite for acquisitions increases its riskiness. Goodwill is the largest asset on the firm's balance sheet, and if it turns out that Jones has seriously misjudged the long-term prospects of any of its recently acquired brands, financial results could suffer. As Federated learned from its Fingerhut purchase, just one bad apple can do lots of damage to the batch. However, we still think Jones is a top apparel wholesaler and retailer, and we'd pick up shares at $20.

MORNINGSTAR® Stocks 500

Kellogg K

	Rating	Risk	Moat Size	Fair Value	Last Close	Yield %
	★★★	Low	Narrow	$37.00	$34.27	2.9

Company Profile

Kellogg produces ready-to-eat cereal products and other breakfast and convenience foods. Its breakfast cereals, which are sold under the Kellogg's brand name, include Corn Flakes, Rice Krispies, Special K, Nutri-Grain, Fruit Loops, Apple Jacks, Corn Pops, Frosted Mini-Wheats, and Frosted Flakes. The company also makes Nutri-Grain granola and fruit bars, Pop Tarts pastries, Rice Krispies Treats squares, and Eggo waffles. Foreign sales account for approximately 43% of the company's total sales. Kellogg acquired Keebler Foods in 2001.

Management

Carlos Gutierrez has been CEO of Kellogg since April 1999. In July 2002, David Vermylen, head of the key Keebler snacks division, left the company and was replaced by Paul Lustig, a veteran of Sara Lee.

Strategy

Management expects to achieve 4%-6% sales growth in the next couple of years by heavily marketing its core cereal brands and expanding its higher-growth health and convenience food offerings. Keebler's direct store distribution network will ensure that Kellogg's products get premium placement on store shelves.

One Kellogg Square Box 3599   www.kelloggs.com
Battle Creek, MI 49016-3599

Morningstar Grades

Growth [A]	1998	1999	2000	2001
Revenue %	-1.0	3.3	-0.4	27.3
Earnings/Share %	-6.8	-32.5	74.7	-20.0
Book Value/Share %	-9.7	-8.4	11.0	-3.6
Dividends/Share %	5.7	4.3	3.1	2.0

Kellogg's sales growth has been high in absolute terms because of the Keebler acquisition, but weak in comparable terms. Comparable sales growth has revived in recent quarters, and should be in the low to mid-single digits over the next few years.

Profitability [B+]	1999	2000	2001	TTM
Return on Assets %	7.0	12.0	4.6	6.3
Oper Cash Flow $Mil	795	881	1,132	1,348
- Cap Spending $Mil	266	231	277	259
= Free Cash Flow $Mil	529	650	856	1,089

Integration costs hurt Kellogg's margins in 2001, but there's been encouraging improvement more recently. Operating margins have improved by nearly 200 basis points in 2002, and the company should achieve a similar amount of savings in 2003.

Financial Health [C]	1999	2000	2001	09-02
Long-term Debt $Mil	1,613	709	5,619	4,594
Total Equity $Mil	813	898	872	1,094
Debt/Equity Ratio	2.0	0.8	6.4	4.2

The Keebler acquisition brought with it $5 billion in extra debt, but Kellogg has started using its strong cash flow to pay down that debt. It has also initiated a stock-buyback program.

Industry	Investment Style	Stock Type	Sector
Food Mfg.	Large Core	High Yield	Consumer Goods

Competition

	Market Cap $Mil	Debt/ Equity	12 Mo Trailing Sales $Mil	Price/Cash Flow	Return On Assets%	Total Return% 1 Yr	Total Return% 3 Yr
Kellogg	13,991	4.2	9,525	10.4	6.3	17.2	9.7
PepsiCo	73,589	0.2	28,044	14.3	13.3	-12.1	6.9
Kraft Foods	45,853	0.5	34,063	11.1	5.3	16.1	—

Price Volatility

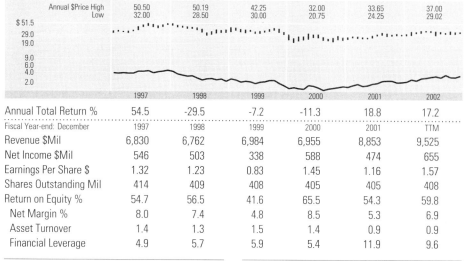

	I Monthly Price High/Low	— Relative Strength to S&P 500

Annual $Price High Low	50.50 32.00	50.19 28.50	42.25 30.00	32.00 20.75	33.65 24.25	37.00 29.02
	1997	1998	1999	2000	2001	2002

Annual Total Return %	54.5	-29.5	-7.2	-11.3	18.8	17.2
Fiscal Year-end: December	1997	1998	1999	2000	2001	TTM
Revenue $Mil	6,830	6,762	6,984	6,955	8,853	9,525
Net Income $Mil	546	503	338	588	474	655
Earnings Per Share $	1.32	1.23	0.83	1.45	1.16	1.57
Shares Outstanding Mil	414	409	408	405	405	408
Return on Equity %	54.7	56.5	41.6	65.5	54.3	59.8
Net Margin %	8.0	7.4	4.8	8.5	5.3	6.9
Asset Turnover	1.4	1.3	1.5	1.4	0.9	0.9
Financial Leverage	4.9	5.7	5.9	5.4	11.9	9.6

Valuation Ratios	Stock	Rel to Industry	Rel to S&P 500
Price/Earnings	21.8	1.0	0.9
Price/Book	12.8	3.0	4.0
Price/Sales	1.5	1.0	0.7
Price/Cash Flow	10.4	0.9	0.8

Major Fund Holders	% of Fund Assets
W.P. Stewart & Co Growth	3.60
Schroder MidCap Value Inv	3.49
Riverfront Large Company Select Inv A	3.43
Babson Value	2.98

Morningstar's Take By David Kathman, 12-06-2002 Stock Price as of Analysis: $33.59

Kellogg seems to be on the right track, starting to reap benefits from its merger with Keebler. We'd consider buying the stock below $30.

The purchase of Keebler in early 2001 was a major part of Kellogg's plan to diversify beyond breakfast foods while improving growth and profitability. Not only did the acquisition make Kellogg the number-two maker of cookies and crackers, it also gave Kellogg access to prime real estate in such important sales channels as convenience stores and vending machines through Keebler's direct store distribution (DSD) system.

Integrating Kellogg's snacks into the Keebler DSD system caused considerable disruption at first, as Kellogg eliminated lower-margin product lines and cut back on new products during the transition. But snack sales revived in 2002--from flat sales in the first quarter to 5% growth in the third--largely because of DSD. Sales of Rice Krispies Treats, Special K bars, and Nutri-Grain bars are up 30% year over year. Because these single-serve snacks tend to be higher-priced and more profitable than Kellogg's other products, this trend should help boost revenue for some time to come.

The increase in snack sales is just one part of the "volume-to-value" strategy that Kellogg has been implementing alongside the merger integration. Another part is increased marketing spending to support key brands, which we think is a good long-term strategy to maintain sales and profitability. The initial focus was in the U.S. cereal business, home of such iconic brands as Corn Flakes and Special K. Cereal sales increased a solid 7% in the first nine months of 2002, faster than those of rival General Mills, as Kellogg moved away from price promotions.

The combination of merger synergies and volume-to-value benefits has already helped Kellogg's margins. Its operating margin (excluding restructuring charges) improved to 17.6% in the first nine months of 2002 from 16% a year earlier. The company expects merger savings of $170 million in 2003 (representing 2% of sales), which we think is quite achievable given its record so far. The company has used some of its excess cash flow to pay down debt (from $6.8 billion to $5.8 billion since the start of 2001) and start a share-buyback program, both good moves to strengthen its financial health.

Kellogg's reshaping program is not over, but we're quite encouraged by the progress we've seen so far. Allowing for an appropriate margin of safety, we'd snap up the stock if it fell below $30.

Kemet KEM

	Rating	Risk	Moat Size	Fair Value	Last Close	Yield %
	★★★★★	Med.	Narrow	$15.00	$8.74	0.0

Company Profile

Kemet manufactures solid tantalum and multilayered ceramic capacitors. Its components are used in nearly all electronic applications and products. The company produces approximately 35,000 different types of capacitors to customer specifications. In fiscal 2000, Kemet shipped about 31.5 billion of these devices to customers. It markets its products under the Kemet brand name to manufacturers in the computer, communication, automotive, defense, and aerospace industries in the United States and abroad. Foreign sales account for approximately 50% of the total.

Management

Most of the top management team has been with the company for years. Chairman and CEO David Maguire has been with Kemet for 43 years.

Strategy

Kemet strives to produce a broad line of capacitors at competitive prices while maintaining high-quality service. It also attempts to build relationships with electronic manufacturing service providers like Flextronics to benefit from those firms' market share gains.

2835 Kemet Way
Simpsonville, SC 29681
www.kemet.com

Morningstar Grades

Growth [D-]	1999	2000	2001	2002
Revenue %	-15.3	45.4	71.0	-63.8
Earnings/Share %	-87.2	962.5	370.6	NMF
Book Value/Share %	4.9	62.6	51.6	-0.3
Dividends/Share %	NMF	NMF	NMF	NMF

Sales growth over the long term is strong but cyclical, driven by the growth of the electronics business. Kemet just suffered through one of the worst downturns in the capacitor industry's history.

Profitability [B+]	2000	2001	2002	TTM
Return on Assets %	7.6	25.8	-2.3	-4.4
Oper Cash Flow $Mil	187	392	-34	37
- Cap Spending $Mil	82	211	79	26
= Free Cash Flow $Mil	105	182	-113	10

Kemet's profits go up and down, depending on the capacitor manufacturing cycle. Over a full cycle, we believe the company should earn relatively attractive profits.

Financial Health [A]	2000	2001	2002	09-02
Long-term Debt $Mil	100	100	100	100
Total Equity $Mil	547	886	855	844
Debt/Equity Ratio	0.2	0.1	0.1	0.1

Despite the downturn, the firm remains net debt-free, with cash and investments of $235 million and $100 million in debt. This ensures Kemet will enter the next growth phase in strong shape.

Industry	Investment Style	Stock Type	Sector
Components	Small Core	Slow Growth	Hardware

Competition	Market Cap $Mil	Debt/ Equity	12 Mo Trailing Sales $Mil	Price/Cash Flow	Return On Assets%	Total Return% 1 Yr	3 Yr
Kemet	753	0.1	472	20.5	-4.4	-50.8	-25.2
Vishay Intertechnology	1,786	0.2	1,745	5.6	-0.6	-42.7	-16.7
AVX	1,708	—	1,170	11.8	-0.4	-58.0	-24.2

Price Volatility | Monthly Price High/Low   — Relative Strength to S&P 500

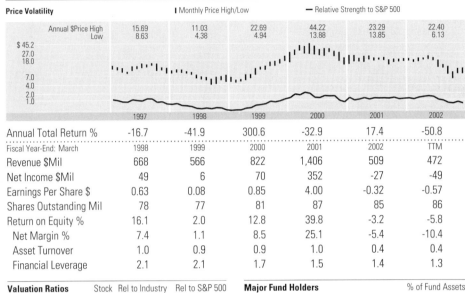

Annual $Price High Low	15.69 8.63	11.03 4.38	22.69 4.94	44.22 13.88	23.29 13.85	22.40 6.13

$45.2 27.0 18.0 7.0 4.0 2.0 1.0

	1997	1998	1999	2000	2001	2002
Annual Total Return %	-16.7	-41.9	300.6	-32.9	17.4	-50.8

Fiscal Year-End: March	1998	1999	2000	2001	2002	TTM
Revenue $Mil	668	566	822	1,406	509	472
Net Income $Mil	49	6	70	352	-27	-49
Earnings Per Share $	0.63	0.08	0.85	4.00	-0.32	-0.57
Shares Outstanding Mil	78	77	81	87	85	86
Return on Equity %	16.1	2.0	12.8	39.8	-3.2	-5.8
Net Margin %	7.4	1.1	8.5	25.1	-5.4	-10.4
Asset Turnover	1.0	0.9	0.9	1.0	0.4	0.4
Financial Leverage	2.1	2.1	1.7	1.5	1.4	1.3

Valuation Ratios	Stock	Rel to Industry	Rel to S&P 500
Price/Earnings	NMF	—	—
Price/Book	0.9	0.5	0.3
Price/Sales	1.6	0.8	0.8
Price/Cash Flow	20.5	2.5	1.5

Major Fund Holders	% of Fund Assets
ING Smallcap Value A	3.55
SunAmerica Focused Multi-Cap Value A	3.41
Meridian Growth	2.70
Third Avenue Small-Cap Value	2.41

Morningstar's Take By Dan Schick, 11-05-2002 Stock Price as of Analysis: $9.40

Though cyclical, the capacitor industry is attractive and will grow significantly over the long term, in our opinion. Kemet is a strong player in this industry, commanding large market share. We think buying Kemet and its peers at or near the bottom of a cycle, when they tend to trade well below reasonable fair value estimates, should be rewarding. But although Kemet is a solid holding that we would look to purchase at a 40% discount to our fair value estimate, we think AVX AVX is more attractive, with a stronger balance sheet and more diversified product line.

Like the capacitor industry, Kemet's business can be good, and it can be very bad. The industry saw sales and margins reach all-time highs in 2001, but Kemet's sales in fiscal 2002 (ending March) declined nearly 64%, to their lowest level since 1995. Swings in capacitor demand are common, but they typically aren't as short-lived or as dramatic as this. During the capital-spending bubble of 2000, some of Kemet's customers built inventory levels five times greater than normal to combat a perceived capacitor shortage. As demand for electronics slowed, these customers slashed orders to draw down inventory. Partially because these two years left such a hangover, and partially because the distance from the peak to the trough was so unprecedented, we doubt such dramatic swings will recur.

Over the long term, the relentless progress of the electronics industry should drive the growth of the capacitor industry. Virtually all electronic devices contain capacitors, so capacitor growth dovetails with that of the electronics market. Turbocharging that growth is the shrinking size and growing complexity of electronic devices--smaller and more-complex devices require more capacitors.

Kemet is well positioned to thrive as industry conditions return to normal. It claims the largest share of the tantalum capacitor market and is the fifth-largest maker of ceramic capacitors. This size is important, since unit costs are closely tied to economies of scale. Kemet also places greater emphasis on customer service than its peers, striving for 100% on-time delivery. Quality customer service is a necessity in meeting the needs of contract electronics manufacturers like Flextronics.

Kemet has the management and balance sheet to endure until the cycle turns up. Though we feel an investment in Kemet at a 40% discount to our fair value should be rewarding, we'd steer investors toward AVX first.

MORNINGSTAR® Stocks 500

Kimberly-Clark KMB

	Rating	Risk	Moat Size	Fair Value	Last Close	Yield %
	★★★	Med.	Narrow	$57.00	$47.47	2.5

Company Profile

Kimberly-Clark manufactures paper, synthetic, and health-care products. Its consumer products include Kleenex facial tissues; Cottonelle bathroom tissue; Huggies diapers, disposable swim pants, disposable wipes, and training pants; Kotex and New Freedom feminine-hygiene products; Depend adult undergarments; and Scott paper towels. The company also makes health-care products such as surgical gowns, face masks, and infection-control and respiratory products. Foreign sales account for about 45% of the company's total sales.

Management

Management has shown its dedication to profitability with several restructurings in the past decade. Thomas Falk, who as COO was the driving force behind major supply-chain initiatives, recently succeeded Wayne Sanders as CEO.

Strategy

The toilet paper and paper towel markets are mature, and by themselves offer only low-single-digit sales growth. Thus, Kimberly seeks technological advances in paper-derived consumer products for which it can charge more. The firm's expansion into medical supplies is an example of this. It also creates new product categories, like the paper-based beach towel launched in spring 2002.

P.O. Box 619100   www.kimberly-clark.com
Dallas, TX 75261-9100

Morningstar Grades

Growth [B]	1998	1999	2000	2001
Revenue %	-2.0	5.8	7.5	3.9
Earnings/Share %	11.2	55.3	7.1	-8.8
Book Value/Share %	-6.1	29.7	12.4	-0.1
Dividends/Share %	4.2	4.0	3.8	3.7

In 2001, Kimberly barely achieved its annual sales growth target, excluding currency translation, thanks to a global recession. With growth slower in the first half of this year, we think 2002 growth will fall beneath Kimberly's target.

Profitability [A]	1999	2000	2001	TTM
Return on Assets %	13.0	12.4	10.7	10.7
Oper Cash Flow $Mil	2,140	2,133	2,254	2,464
- Cap Spending $Mil	786	1,170	1,100	903
= Free Cash Flow $Mil	1,354	963	1,154	1,561

The company is consistently profitable, with annual return on assets typically in the upper teens. Strengthening foreign currencies should act like a tailwind and help prop up 2002 profitability in comparison with 2001's results.

Financial Health [A-]	1999	2000	2001	09-02
Long-term Debt $Mil	1,927	2,001	2,424	2,846
Total Equity $Mil	5,093	5,767	5,647	6,014
Debt/Equity Ratio	0.4	0.3	0.4	0.5

Kimberly's debt is very manageable, considering the company's strong cash flows. We don't foresee anything that might jeopardize the dividends paid to stockholders.

Industry	Investment Style	Stock Type	Sector
Household & Personal Products	Large Value	High Yield	Consumer Goods

Competition

	Market Cap $Mil	Debt/ Equity	12 Mo Trailing Sales $Mil	Price/Cash Flow	Return On Assets%	Total Return% 1 Yr	3 Yr
Kimberly-Clark	24,416	0.5	14,809	9.9	10.7	-19.0	-7.5
Johnson & Johnson	159,452	0.1	35,120	18.0	16.3	-7.9	8.0
Procter & Gamble	111,662	0.9	41,268	13.3	11.0	11.3	-4.5

Price Volatility — Monthly Price High/Low — Relative Strength to S&P 500

	1997	1998	1999	2000	2001	2002
Annual $Price High / Low	56.88 / 43.25	59.44 / 35.88	69.56 / 44.81	73.25 / 42.00	72.15 / 52.10	66.75 / 45.30
Annual Total Return %	5.5	12.8	22.3	10.1	-13.9	-19.0

Fiscal Year-end: December	1997	1998	1999	2000	2001	TTM
Revenue $Mil	12,547	12,298	13,007	13,982	14,524	14,809
Net Income $Mil	1,003	1,103	1,668	1,801	1,610	1,647
Earnings Per Share $	1.79	1.99	3.09	3.31	3.02	3.15
Shares Outstanding Mil	557	552	536	539	530	514
Return on Equity %	23.1	27.4	32.8	31.2	28.5	27.4
Net Margin %	8.0	9.0	12.8	12.9	11.1	11.1
Asset Turnover	1.1	1.1	1.0	1.0	1.0	1.0
Financial Leverage	2.6	2.9	2.5	2.5	2.7	2.6

Valuation Ratios	Stock	Rel to Industry	Rel to S&P 500
Price/Earnings	15.1	0.6	0.6
Price/Book	4.1	0.5	1.3
Price/Sales	1.6	0.6	0.8
Price/Cash Flow	9.9	0.7	0.7

Major Fund Holders	% of Fund Assets
AmSouth Select Equity B	6.31
SunAmerica Focused Multi-Cap Value A	5.51
Hartford Value A	4.95
Van Kampen Global Franchise A	4.69

Morningstar's Take By Carl Sibilski, 10-14-2002 Stock Price as of Analysis: $55.86

We think Kimberly-Clark is better positioned than its peers to cope with prolonged economic mediocrity. However, the company still faces strong competitors as well as consolidation in the retail industry. We would look for at least a 30% margin of safety to our fair value estimate before buying the stock.

Kimberly has a cost advantage in that it still owns enough raw material sites to produce 40% of the pulp used in the manufacturing of its products. While the company has plans to reduce the number of these sites (when it can get favorable prices for the land and facilities), it has not eliminated them completely like chief rival Procter & Gamble. If a period of inflation led to higher costs for raw materials, Kimberly could use this cost advantage and lag likely price increases by P&G.

With consumers paying more attention to prices, we think Kimberly's brand portfolio, consisting of generally lower-price products like Scott paper towels and bath tissues, will hold its own in terms of market share compared with P&G. We also think Kimberly can increase its overall share slightly through product innovations like the Neat Sheet.

In addition, Kimberly can use its brand recognition and market share to strengthen relationships with retailers and boost sales. The company can successfully introduce new products relatively quickly because brand awareness speeds customer acceptance. Also, by stocking the stores itself, Kimberly has an edge in the critical marketing battle for shelf space and product arrangement.

However, we believe that the company's annual sales growth is likely to be near the low end of its targeted 4%-6% range because it's fighting strong competition. Sales growth and profits also depend on the retail environment. Consolidation in the retail industry means that Kimberly will have fewer, albeit larger, customers. Wal-Mart already accounts for 10% of sales. While we think Kimberly's historical role in manufacturing and product placement on the store shelves will continue to win favor with retailers, we are a bit concerned that its buyers may be gaining bargaining power. Wal-Mart's reputation for having the upper hand in purchasing negotiations leads us to believe that Kimberly's margins may get squeezed in the years ahead. For these reasons we'd seek a 30% discount to our estimated fair value before buying the stock.

Kinder Morgan KMI

	Rating	Risk	Moat Size	Fair Value	Last Close	Yield %
	★★★★	Med.	Wide	$51.00	$42.27	0.7

Company Profile

Kinder Morgan is an integrated petroleum company with two major production susidiaries, KN Production and GASCO. The company operates pipelines to aggregate purchased gas with its own production, which it processes for use in its utility operations and for sale to other utility companies and municipal customers. Kinder Morgan provides natural gas utility service in Colorado, Nebraska, and Wyoming.

Management

CEO Richard Kinder and vice chairman Richard Morgan founded Kinder Morgan in 1997. Kinder was president and COO of Enron from 1990 to 1996, well before the funny business began. Kinder is the largest individual shareholder of KMI as well as KMP.

Strategy

One of KMI's goals is to increase cash flow at related company KMP. KMP is a leader in the business of transporting and processing energy commodities, and it is always looking for acquisitions to augment its operations. The company's other goal is to benefit from the energy industry's overall growth without taking on commodity price exposure.

500 Dallas
Houston, TX 77002
www.kindermorgan.com

Industry	Investment Style	Stock Type	Sector
Pipelines	Mid Growth	Hard Assets	Energy

Competition	Market Cap $Mil	Debt/ Equity	12 Mo Trailing Sales $Mil	Price/Cash Flow	Return On Assets%	Total Return% 1 Yr	3 Yr
Kinder Morgan	5,145	1.1	1,014	12.4	3.1	-23.5	24.5
El Paso	4,160	1.6	12,207	8.6	1.3	-83.9	-41.2
Williams Companies	1,395	2.4	8,895	—	-5.2	-89.0	-53.0

Price Volatility

Annual $Price High / Low	36.00 24.08	40.33 22.33	24.75 12.19	54.25 19.88	60.00 42.88	57.50 30.05

	1997	1998	1999	2000	2001	2002
Annual Total Return %	41.1	-30.9	-14.2	160.1	7.1	-23.5

Fiscal Year-End: December	1997	1998	1999	2000	2001	TTM
Revenue $Mil	341	1,660	1,836	2,680	1,055	1,014
Net Income $Mil	77	62	-260	152	225	314
Earnings Per Share $	1.63	0.96	-3.24	1.33	1.86	2.55
Shares Outstanding Mil	—	64	80	114	115	122
Return on Equity %	12.7	5.1	-15.6	8.6	10.0	13.4
Net Margin %	22.6	3.7	-14.2	5.7	21.3	30.9
Asset Turnover	0.1	0.2	0.2	0.3	0.1	0.1
Financial Leverage	3.8	7.9	5.6	4.7	4.2	4.3

Valuation Ratios	Stock	Rel to Industry	Rel to S&P 500
Price/Earnings	16.6	1.0	0.7
Price/Book	2.2	1.1	0.7
Price/Sales	5.1	2.6	2.5
Price/Cash Flow	12.4	1.8	0.9

Major Fund Holders	% of Fund Assets
Fidelity Select Natural Gas	6.90
Babson Growth	2.99
Osterweis	2.97
Aquila Rocky Mountain Equity A	2.84

Morningstar Grades

Growth [F]	1998	1999	2000	2001
Revenue %	387.3	10.6	45.9	-60.6
Earnings/Share %	-41.1	NMF	NMF	39.9
Book Value/Share %	47.7	9.8	-25.3	20.4
Dividends/Share %	4.6	-14.5	-69.2	0.0

Revenue fell in 2001 because of an accounting change, but operating and net income rose. Operating income has been flat in 2002, but the growth in contributions from KMP have been stout. We expect internally generated EPS growth next year of 15%-20%.

Profitability [C-]	1999	2000	2001	TTM
Return on Assets %	-2.8	1.8	2.4	3.1
Oper Cash Flow $Mil	321	167	437	413
- Cap Spending $Mil	93	86	124	189
= Free Cash Flow $Mil	228	81	313	225

KMI has generated steady, if uninspiring, returns the past three years. Its average return on invested capital during this time has been 6.3%. We suspect returns will not change much in coming years.

Financial Health [D+]	1999	2000	2001	09-02
Long-term Debt $Mil	3,293	2,479	2,405	2,631
Total Equity $Mil	1,670	1,778	2,260	2,333
Debt/Equity Ratio	2.0	1.4	1.1	1.1

KMI has $3.5 billion in debt against a tangible asset base of $9.0 billion. Debt at KMP is $3.6 billion, slightly more than half KMP's capital base. Solid cash flow is generated from hard assets at both companies. Liquidity is not a problem.

Morningstar's Take By Paul Larson, 12-16-2002 Stock Price as of Analysis: $42.88

We've liked Kinder Morgan Energy Partners (KMP) for some time, so it should be little surprise that we also like its parent company, Kinder Morgan (KMI). We would be buyers at today's price.

Slightly more than half of KMI's net income comes courtesy of the company's ownership in and management of KMP, one of the nation's largest operators of natural gas pipelines. KMI owns an 18% economic stake in KMP and 100% of the general partnership that manages KMP. In addition to getting 18% of KMP's quarterly cash distributions, KMI typically gets an additional third of the cash flow generated at KMP for its management services.

The other half of KMI's cash flow comes from assets it owns and operates outside KMP. More than three fourths of the earnings from these "independent" operations come from pipelines, tying nearly 90% of KMI's total earnings to this business. We've given KMI a wide-moat rating because pipelines are expensive to duplicate. Also, they are regulated businesses, with the Federal Energy Regulatory Commission setting rates and keeping competition at appropriate levels to maintain industrywide health. Plus, there are high switching costs--once a well, refinery, or power plant is physically hooked up to a pipeline, the physical costs

required to switch providers is often prohibitively high. Service contracts also tend to be long in duration.

In addition to being attracted to the stable nature of the cash flow KMI's assets generate, we also love the firm's management. Enron would have been a lot better off had it not strayed from its core businesses after parting ways with Richard Kinder. CEO Kinder is KMI's (as well as KMP's) largest shareholder and does not receive any compensation beyond his $1 annual salary. He got his 19% stake in the company the old-fashioned way--he bought it--and makes money purely from increasing the intrinsic value of KMI and the distributions at KMP. Few companies have management's and investors' interests so closely aligned.

Demand for moving energy is set to grow as the economy continues to expand. KMI is in an excellent position to benefit from economic growth as volume increases on its and KMP's systems. The company's core business is stable, predictable, and cash flow positive. With the stock at a sufficient discount to our fair value estimate, we would buy KMI.

Kinder Morgan Energy Partners KMP

	Rating	Risk	Moat Size	Fair Value	Last Close	Yield %
	★★★★	Med.	Wide	$39.00	$35.00	6.7

Company Profile

Houston-based Kinder Morgan Energy Partners is a master limited partnership that aims to be the leading consolidator of fixed assets used to transport energy-related commodities. The company owns and operates more than 25,000 miles of pipelines that primarily transport oil and gas. It also owns more than 70 processing terminals that can handle and store liquids, gases, and dry bulk materials like coal. As a partnership, Kinder Morgan Energy Partners pays no corporate income tax, but its tax burden flows through to individual stockholders.

Management

CEO Richard Kinder and vice chairman Richard Morgan founded Kinder Morgan in 1997. Kinder was president and COO of Enron from 1990 to 1996, well before the funny business began. Kinder is the largest individual shareholder.

Strategy

Aiming to leverage its tax-advantaged status and low cost of capital, Kinder Morgan Energy Partners is the premier rollup in the business of transporting and processing energy commodities. It buys (rolls up) cash-flow-generating assets, like pipelines, from other energy companies at discount prices and then aims to increase their utilization and efficiency.

500 Dallas Street
Houston, TX 77002
www.kindermorgan.com

Morningstar Grades

Growth [A+]	1998	1999	2000	2001
Revenue %	336.4	32.9	90.4	260.9
Earnings/Share %	71.6	47.4	3.5	16.9
Book Value/Share %	206.9	7.1	-8.5	22.4
Dividends/Share %	46.4	16.3	15.3	28.1

Growth has been astonishing in the past few years, but nearly all of it came from numerous acquisitions. We expect further purchases. Internally generated growth is expected to be 8%-10%.

Profitability [B]	1999	2000	2001	TTM
Return on Assets %	3.9	3.7	3.6	3.9
Oper Cash Flow $Mil	183	302	581	723
- Cap Spending $Mil	77	1,134	1,819	1,393
= Free Cash Flow $Mil	106	-833	-1,237	-670

Returns on invested capital have been lackluster for the past three years, but profitability has improved every year during this period. Adjusting for taxes, Kinder's ROIC last year was 6.5%.

Financial Health [C-]	1999	2000	2001	09-02
Long-term Debt $Mil	989	1,255	2,232	3,611
Total Equity $Mil	1,759	2,083	3,104	3,338
Debt/Equity Ratio	0.6	0.6	0.7	1.1

Thanks to asset purchases, debt has been growing and now stands at $3.6 billion against a total capital base of $7.0 billion. The firm aims to keep its debt/capital ratio under 50%. Kinder's hard assets provide ample positive cash flow.

Industry	Investment Style	Stock Type	Sector
Pipelines	▦ Mid Core	▦ Hard Assets	◐ Energy

Competition	Market Cap $Mil	Debt/ Equity	12 Mo Trailing Sales $Mil	Price/Cash Flow	Return On Assets%	Total Return% 1 Yr	3 Yr
Kinder Morgan Energy Partners	4,548	1.1	3,559	6.3	3.9	-0.7	27.7
El Paso Energy Partners L	1,226	—	366	—	—	—	—
Williams Energy Partners	184	—	76	—	—	—	—

Price Volatility

	Monthly Price High/Low		Relative Strength to S&P 500			
Annual $Price High Low	20.63 6.84	19.06 14.28	22.81 16.50	28.88 18.19	39.65 25.19	38.89 24.00
	1997	1998	1999	2000	2001	2002
Annual Total Return %	160.6	14.4	22.6	46.4	42.4	-0.7

Fiscal Year-end: December	1997	1998	1999	2000	2001	TTM
Revenue $Mil	74	323	429	816	2,947	3,559
Net Income $Mil	14	70	126	169	240	312
Earnings Per Share $	0.51	0.88	1.29	1.34	1.56	1.84
Shares Outstanding Mil	27	80	98	126	154	130
Return on Equity %	9.3	5.2	7.2	8.1	7.7	9.4
Net Margin %	18.5	21.7	29.4	20.7	8.2	8.8
Asset Turnover	0.2	0.2	0.1	0.2	0.4	0.4
Financial Leverage	2.1	1.6	1.8	2.2	2.2	2.4

Valuation Ratios	Stock	Rel to Industry	Rel to S&P 500
Price/Earnings	19.0	1.1	0.8
Price/Book	1.4	0.7	0.4
Price/Sales	1.3	0.6	0.6
Price/Cash Flow	6.3	0.9	0.5

Major Fund Holders	% of Fund Assets
Flex-funds Total Return Utilities	8.93
Oppenheimer Capital Income A	2.47
Scudder 21st Century Growth S	2.43
Liberty Newport Global Equity A	1.64

Morningstar's Take By Paul Larson, 10-20-2002 Stock Price as of Analysis: $32.16

We'd buy Kinder Morgan Energy Partners at today's prices.

It's not just the high yield that has attracted our attention. Kinder Morgan operates a solid portfolio of stable assets that generate substantial free cash flow and are largely insulated from swings in commodity prices.

As one of the premier "rollups" in the energy transportation and storage industries, Kinder Morgan is sitting in the catbird seat. As other energy companies--specifically the merchant energy traders--go through painful restructurings to avert bankruptcy, Kinder Morgan is one of the few buyers of energy assets. The acquisition opportunities are enormous, while the fire-sale prices potentially make the deals that much more beneficial.

We also love Kinder Morgan's management. Enron would have been a lot better off had it not strayed from its core businesses after parting ways with Richard Kinder. CEO Kinder is Kinder Morgan's largest shareholder and does not receive any compensation beyond his $1 annual salary. He got his 20% stake in the company the old-fashioned way--he bought it--and also makes money purely from increasing per-share cash flow and distributions. Few companies have management's and investors'

interests so closely aligned.

We've given Kinder Morgan a wide moat rating because pipelines are expensive to duplicate. Also, they are regulated businesses that have the Federal Energy Regulatory Commission setting rates and keeping competition at levels to maintain industrywide health. Plus, there are high switching costs--once a well, refinery, or power plant is physically hooked up to a pipeline, the physical capital required to switch providers is often prohibitively high. Service contracts also tend to be long in duration.

Demand for moving energy is set to grow as the economy continues to expand. Kinder Morgan is in an excellent position to benefit from economic growth as volume increases on its systems. The company's core business is stable, predictable, and cash flow positive. Even if the stock does not reach our fair value target anytime soon, the high and growing yield will make the wait profitable.

King Pharmaceuticals KG

	Rating	Risk	Moat Size	Fair Value	Last Close	Yield %
	★★★★	Med.	Narrow	$26.00	$17.19	0.0

Company Profile

King Pharmaceuticals does contract manufacturing for other pharmaceutical companies and markets its own brand-name products. Usually, King acquires drugs from major pharmaceutical companies that those companies determined were immaterial to their revenue. Its largest revenue driver is Altace, for hypertension. Its drug lineup is concentrated in four areas; cardiovascular, anti-infectives, critical care, and women's health. King is extremely acquisitive and spends very little on internal research and development. Other brand-name drugs are Levoxyl, Menest, and Nordette.

Management

Jeff Gregory took over as CEO from his brother John in January 2002. Four of his brothers and a sister-in-law occupy executive positions. The Gregorys have pared their company ownership to 8% by selling shares through a blind trust.

Strategy

King's strategy is to acquire small, neglected products that don't make a dent in the revenue of major pharmaceutical companies, but can be profitable to King. The company tries to boost sales by actively marketing the products to improve physician awareness. King acquires most of its drug technology through acquisitions and licensing agreements.

501 Fifth Street   www.kingpharm.com
Bristol, TN 37620

Morningstar Grades

Growth [A]

	1998	1999	2000	2001
Revenue %	87.9	74.1	21.0	40.6
Earnings/Share %	NMF	NMF	-38.3	220.7
Book Value/Share %	—	NMF	90.7	83.4
Dividends/Share %	NMF	NMF	NMF	NMF

Revenue growth is fueled by King's two top-selling drugs, Altace and Levoxyl. Altace was up 71% year over year for the first nine months of this year, and Levoxyl was up 90%. Top-line growth for 2002 should be around 35%.

Profitability [A]

	1999	2000	2001	TTM
Return on Assets %	8.5	5.0	8.7	10.1
Oper Cash Flow $Mil	148	181	280	354
- Cap Spending $Mil	13	25	40	69
= Free Cash Flow $Mil	135	156	239	286

King's margins are excellent. Gross margins topped 80% for the first three quarters of 2002, while operating margins have consistently topped 40% over the past 10-12 quarters. But free cash flow is negative because of high product acquisition costs.

Financial Health [A+]

	1999	2000	2001	09-02
Long-term Debt $Mil	553	99	346	346
Total Equity $Mil	495	988	1,908	1,971
Debt/Equity Ratio	1.1	0.1	0.2	0.2

With more than $900 million in cash and less than $350 million in debt, King's balance sheet is strong and in line with its peers'. Cash is essential because King buys, rather than develops, most of its new drugs.

Industry	Investment Style	Stock Type	Sector
Drugs	Mid Growth	⬆ Aggr. Growth	Healthcare

Competition

	Market Cap $Mil	Debt/ Equity	12 Mo Trailing Sales $Mil	Price/Cash Flow	Return On Assets%	Total Return% 1 Yr	3 Yr
King Pharmaceuticals	4,139	0.2	1,111	11.7	10.1	-59.2	-11.1
Forest Laboratories	17,702	0.0	1,882	36.2	19.2	19.9	49.7
Watson Pharmaceuticals	3,021	0.2	1,188	7.8	6.8	-9.9	-5.9

Price Volatility

I Monthly Price High/Low   — Relative Strength to S&P 500

Annual $Price High Low			9.58 3.54	34.00 6.46	41.63 14.81	46.05 24.79	42.13 15.00

$ 47.1 / 28.0 / 18.0 / 8.0 / 5.0 / 3.0 / 1.0

1997   1998   1999   2000   2001   2002

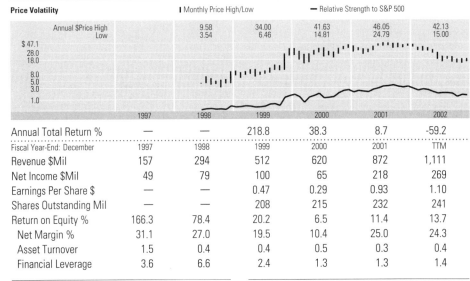

Annual Total Return %	—	—	218.8	38.3	8.7	-59.2

Fiscal Year-End: December	1997	1998	1999	2000	2001	TTM
Revenue $Mil	157	294	512	620	872	1,111
Net Income $Mil	49	79	100	65	218	269
Earnings Per Share $	—	—	0.47	0.29	0.93	1.10
Shares Outstanding Mil	—	—	208	215	232	241
Return on Equity %	166.3	78.4	20.2	6.5	11.4	13.7
Net Margin %	31.1	27.0	19.5	10.4	25.0	24.3
Asset Turnover	1.5	0.4	0.4	0.5	0.3	0.4
Financial Leverage	3.6	6.6	2.4	1.3	1.3	1.4

Valuation Ratios

	Stock	Rel to Industry	Rel to S&P 500
Price/Earnings	15.6	0.7	0.7
Price/Book	2.1	0.3	0.7
Price/Sales	3.7	0.9	1.9
Price/Cash Flow	11.7	0.6	0.9

Major Fund Holders

	% of Fund Assets
UC Investment	5.00
Credit Suisse Global Health Sci Comm	4.26
AIM Global Health Care A	3.81
Willamette Global Health Sciences	3.64

Morningstar's Take By Todd N. Lebor, 12-15-2002 Stock Price as of Analysis: $17.77

King's chart-busting margins come at a price: lots of product risk. Combine that with an unsustainable business model, and we require a 40% discount to our fair value estimate before scooping up this junior pharmaceutical company.

King's strategy is to selectively acquire branded drugs that it can reposition through revitalized marketing. But as the company grows, making a living off the discarded scraps of others will become more difficult, so we think its business model must change. To own drugs that can make meaningful contributions to its top line, King will have to develop its own or buy early-stage compounds, neither of which it has proved it can do. Its successes to date have built a financially strong company, but until it shows a little more independence by developing a drug or two on its own, we'd be hesitant to own this stock.

Few pharmaceuticals, big or small, can hold a candle to King, with its gross margins near 80%, operating margins comfortably above 40%, and net margins in the high 20s. (Industry average gross and operating margins are approximately 72% and 23%, respectively.) But these margins are a bit of a mirage. Rather than drop hundreds of millions on research and development, King prefers to buy its new

products from other drug firms. As a result, the real cost of its new products is kept off the income statement and appears on the cash flow statement as acquisitions. Therefore, we think the company's profitability shouldn't be judged by net income alone. It's important to look at adjusted free cash flow (cash flow from operations less capital expenditures less product acquisitions) along with net income. For example, while net income increased to more than $870 million from $21 million in five years, adjusted free cash flow was negative during all these years.

King's revenue growth comes mostly from two drugs--hence the product risk. Altace, an angiotensin-converting enzyme (ACE) inhibitor, makes up about 40% of revenue, and Levoxyl, a thyroid hormone-replacement drug, contributes another 15%-20%. This lack of diversification concerns us. If something should happen to these two revenue streams, King's financials would suffer more than most of its diversified peers'. That said, King has Altace and Levoxyl to thank for its spectacular revenue growth, which averaged 111.7% annually from 1997 to 2001.

King's business model isn't flawed, it's just worn out, in our opinion. It's time for the company to broaden its product base.

MORNINGSTAR® Stocks 500

KLA-Tencor KLAC

	Rating	Risk	Moat Size	Fair Value	Last Close	Yield %
	★	Med.	Narrow	$27.00	$35.37	0.0

Company Profile

KLA-Tencor designs and manufactures yield-management and process-monitoring systems for the semiconductor industry. The company's systems are used to analyze the manufacturing process at various steps in a product's development. Its laser-scanning products are used for wafer qualification, process monitoring, and equipment monitoring. KLA-Tencor also provides systems for optical metrology, e-beam metrology, as well as scanning-electron-microscope inspection systems.

Management

Ken Schroeder has been president and CEO since June 1999 and was president and COO of KLA since 1991. The management team owns almost 4% of the firm.

Strategy

Emerging technology is KLA-Tencor's strong suit. The company spends heavily on product development through research and development and acquiring smaller complementary firms. By focusing on a few niches, the firm has an extensive product line in its areas of specialty and can offer entire systems to its customers.

160 Rio Robles
San Jose, CA 95134   www.kla-tencor.com

Morningstar Grades

Growth [C+]	1999	2000	2001	2002
Revenue %	-27.7	77.8	40.4	-22.2
Earnings/Share %	-71.7	514.0	-74.2	223.5
Book Value/Share %	-0.4	31.5	1.0	15.1
Dividends/Share %	NMF	NMF	NMF	NMF

KLA's growth is better than most other chip equipment makers'. Sales growth of 78% in fiscal 2000 and 40% in 2001 is pretty impressive, and a decline of only 22% in 2002 is much better than that experienced by rivals, including Applied Materials.

Profitability [A]	2000	2001	2002	TTM
Return on Assets %	11.5	2.4	8.0	6.7
Oper Cash Flow $Mil	253	408	284	329
- Cap Spending $Mil	79	162	69	44
= Free Cash Flow $Mil	174	246	215	285

KLA's position in various high-margin segments leads to above-average profitability. Gross margins are usually 50% or higher, better than most peers'.

Financial Health [A]	2000	2001	2002	09-02
Long-term Debt $Mil	0	0	0	0
Total Equity $Mil	13	16	18	18
Debt/Equity Ratio	0.0	0.0	0.0	0.0

With no debt and flush with cash, KLA is in outstanding financial health. The firm has $1.3 billion in cash and investments on its balance sheet, representing almost half of total assets.

Industry	Investment Style	Stock Type	Sector
Semiconductor Equipment	Mid Growth	Slow Growth	Hardware

Competition

Competition	Market Cap $Mil	Debt/ Equity	12 Mo Trailing Sales $Mil	Price/Cash Flow	Return On Assets%	Total Return% 1 Yr	Total Return% 3 Yr
KLA-Tencor	6,674	0.0	1,510	20.3	6.7	-28.6	-12.0
Applied Materials	21,473	0.1	4,881	29.3	0.4	-35.0	-24.3
Hitachi ADR	12,434	—	75,941	—	—		

Price Volatility

		Monthly Price High/Low			Relative Strength to S&P 500	
Annual $Price High	38.44	24.00	56.56	97.75	61.00	70.58
Low	16.75	10.38	21.19	25.50	28.61	25.16
	1997	1998	1999	2000	2001	2002

	1997	1998	1999	2000	2001	2002
Annual Total Return %	8.8	12.3	156.8	-39.5	47.1	-28.6

Fiscal Year-end: June	1998	1999	2000	2001	2002	TTM
Revenue $Mil	1,166	843	1,499	2,104	1,637	1,510
Net Income $Mil	134	39	254	67	216	181
Earnings Per Share $	0.76	0.22	1.32	0.34	1.10	0.92
Shares Outstanding Mil	170	174	183	185	188	189
Return on Equity %	11.2	3.2	14.9	3.8	10.6	8.9
Net Margin %	11.5	4.7	16.9	3.2	13.2	12.0
Asset Turnover	0.8	0.5	0.7	0.8	0.6	0.6
Financial Leverage	1.3	1.3	1.3	1.6	1.3	1.3

Valuation Ratios	Stock	Rel to Industry	Rel to S&P 500
Price/Earnings	38.4	0.3	1.6
Price/Book	3.3	1.2	1.0
Price/Sales	4.4	1.0	2.2
Price/Cash Flow	20.3	0.7	1.5

Major Fund Holders	% of Fund Assets
Fidelity Advisor Electronics A	9.99
Monetta Select Technology	5.08
Van Kampen Technology A	4.86
Pioneer Science and Technology B	3.92

Morningstar's Take By Jeremy Lopez, 10-15-2002 Stock Price as of Analysis: $29.33

Accounting for roughly 7% of industry sales, KLA-Tencor was the world's third-largest chip equipment supplier in 2001. At a cheaper price, the stock could be one of the industry's better investment plays.

The chip equipment market is segmented; most firms specialize in products for just a few of the complex chipmaking steps. KLA's focus is on process diagnostics and control (PDC) equipment, which saves chipmakers money by increasing the percentage of chips made correctly. The PDC segment has become more important in recent years, mainly because of the growing complexity of smaller, faster semiconductor devices. PDC grew to more than 15% of total equipment sales in 2001, roughly 50% higher than a few years ago. What's more, total semiconductor capital spending dropped almost 30% last year, whereas PDC sales fell only 5%.

KLA may be dwarfed by Applied Materials in the overall chip equipment market, but it is a giant in PDC; it had more than 50% share of this $3 billion niche in 2001. Not only has KLA posted above-average growth relative to its peers, but its margins are also superior to those of its average rival. Gross margins, for example, have generally ranged between the high 40s and high 50s, much higher than the industry average. The firm's fat average selling prices and outsourced manufacturing strategy are two key reasons for this strong profitability. Given the intensive technology requirements to keep pace in PDC, KLA's deep research and development budget, and the firm's record of product innovation, KLA has a good shot at sustaining its market-leading position in PDC.

But even with a strong market position in a promising niche, there's something KLA can't do: avoid the manic capital-spending habits of chipmakers. Life is good when capital spending is strong. But when chipmakers close their wallets, KLA suffers like everyone else. Currently, overall spending is poor. But even if it remains so for a while, now might be the best time to put KLA on the radar screen--when the shares have taken it on the chin. The stock is pretty risky in the grand scheme of things, which means we require a wide margin of safety (30%-40%) before we'd recommend it. At its current price, KLA still has a long way to fall before we'd find it attractive. But one thing we don't question is the firm's ability to outperform when chip demand does eventually turn around.

Knight Ridder KRI

	Rating	Risk	Moat Size	Fair Value	Last Close	Yield %
	★★	Med.	Narrow	$58.00	$63.25	1.6

Company Profile

Knight Ridder publishes 32 daily newspapers and several nondaily newspapers in 28 U.S. markets. Its newspapers include The Philadelphia Inquirer, The Philadelphia Daily News, The Miami Herald, San Jose Mercury News, The Detroit Free Press, and The Kansas City Star. The company also invests in Internet and technology companies and two newsprint companies.

Management

P. Anthony Ridder has been chairman and CEO since 1995. He has more than 35 years of experience in the newspaper industry, and has spent almost half of his career with Knight Ridder.

Strategy

Shunning the diversified-conglomerate approach of its leading rivals, Knight Ridder wants to stick to its knitting--newspaper publishing. The firm is trying to increase its readership, with the help of acquisitions and investing in online ventures (its Real Cities Network and CareerBuilder online-recruitment joint venture).

50 W. San Fernando Street
San Jose, CA 95113
www.kri.com

Morningstar Grades

Growth [D]	1998	1999	2000	2001
Revenue %	7.8	4.8	5.9	-9.7
Earnings/Share %	-8.6	-6.4	1.1	-38.8
Book Value/Share %	10.6	7.9	-5.3	5.3
Dividends/Share %	0.0	11.3	3.4	8.7

Annual growth in sales as well as earnings per share has averaged an unimpressive 4% over the past decade. We assume that additional revenue from Knight Ridder Digital will help contribute to 4% annual revenue growth over the next several years.

Profitability [A]	1999	2000	2001	TTM
Return on Assets %	8.1	7.4	4.4	5.7
Oper Cash Flow $Mil	506	417	482	554
- Cap Spending $Mil	93	108	95	60
= Free Cash Flow $Mil	413	309	387	493

Both return on equity and return on assets have averaged in the top third of the industry over the past three years. Knight Ridder's exposure to the classified advertising market makes it very sensitive to changes in the ad market.

Financial Health [B+]	1999	2000	2001	09-02
Long-term Debt $Mil	1,261	1,592	1,573	1,500
Total Equity $Mil	1,779	1,540	1,559	1,532
Debt/Equity Ratio	0.7	1.0	1.0	1.0

With a debt/equity ratio of 1.0, Knight Ridder carries a lot less debt than most of its peers. It generates ample free cash flow to pay interest expenses and fund new projects.

Industry	Investment Style	Stock Type	Sector
Publishing	▦ Mid Core	→ Slow Growth	🎤 Media

Competition	Market Cap $Mil	Debt/ Equity	12 Mo Trailing Sales $Mil	Price/Cash Flow	Return On Assets%	Total Return% 1 Yr	3 Yr
Knight Ridder	5,209	1.0	2,816	9.4	5.7	-0.9	6.0
Gannett	19,190	0.7	6,354	16.2	8.1	8.1	-1.1
Dow Jones & Company	3,608	1.5	1,594	19.0	18.3	-19.2	-11.1

Price Volatility

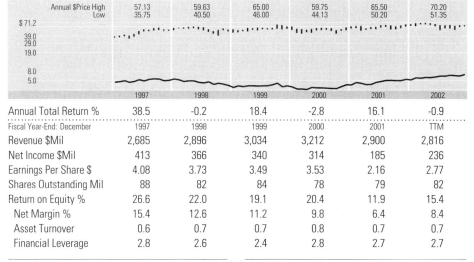

	1997	1998	1999	2000	2001	2002
Annual $Price High	57.13	59.63	65.00	59.75	65.50	70.20
Low	35.75	40.50	46.00	44.13	50.20	51.35
Annual Total Return %	38.5	-0.2	18.4	-2.8	16.1	-0.9

Fiscal Year-End: December	1997	1998	1999	2000	2001	TTM
Revenue $Mil	2,685	2,896	3,034	3,212	2,900	2,816
Net Income $Mil	413	366	340	314	185	236
Earnings Per Share $	4.08	3.73	3.49	3.53	2.16	2.77
Shares Outstanding Mil	88	82	84	78	79	82
Return on Equity %	26.6	22.0	19.1	20.4	11.9	15.4
Net Margin %	15.4	12.6	11.2	9.8	6.4	8.4
Asset Turnover	0.6	0.7	0.7	0.8	0.7	0.7
Financial Leverage	2.8	2.6	2.4	2.8	2.7	2.7

Valuation Ratios	Stock	Rel to Industry	Rel to S&P 500
Price/Earnings	22.8	0.9	1.0
Price/Book	3.4	0.7	1.1
Price/Sales	1.9	0.7	0.9
Price/Cash Flow	9.4	1.0	0.7

Major Fund Holders	% of Fund Assets
Fidelity Congress Street	5.13
CDC Nvest Select A	4.80
Undiscovered Managers Hidden Val Inst	4.26
Oakmark Select I	3.90

Morningstar's Take By T.K. MacKay, 12-05-2002 Stock Price as of Analysis: $61.89

Knight Ridder's reliance on print ads makes the shares less appealing to us than those of other publishing firms.

Unless you're Playboy Enterprises, publishing isn't a very sexy business to be in. While tremendously profitable, newspaper and magazine publishers are slow-growing businesses.

Knight Ridder increased revenue 4% annually between 1992 and 2000, through a combination of increased circulation, rising ad revenue, and rate increases. The advertising fallout of 2001 resulted in top-line growth of just 2% that year, and will result in about a 2% decline in overall revenue in 2002.

Classified advertising, from which Knight Ridder derives about 30% of revenue, takes much of the blame for the weak top-line performance. Lack of employment opportunities has led to double-digit revenue declines in this segment through 2002, and until the economy improves, the business will suffer. When the economy picks up steam, however, Knight Ridder's leverage to this segment should pay off. We believe the advertising market is improving, but this probably won't result in a significant jump in ad-related revenue for Knight Ridder until late 2003 at the earliest.

To cope with the slowdown, Knight Ridder is trying to boost circulation volume through rate reductions. This has improved circulation on a volume basis, but has resulted in weaker revenue overall. Circulation revenue has declined 4% in 2002, compared with industry average growth of 1%. We are also concerned that circulation volume growth could stall if Knight Ridder raises rates when business prospects improve. Fortunately for the company, it is still reaping the benefits of a 10% workforce reduction implemented in 2001, and it has taken advantage of recent declines in newsprint prices.

We're wary of when and by how much the advertising market (especially classified advertising) will improve. Because of this, we'd require a 40% margin of safety to our estimated fair value before considering Knight Ridder. This may be what other publishers are thinking, too. Knight Ridder has long been speculated as a takeover candidate because of its heavy exposure to classified advertising and its number-two position in newspaper circulation behind Gannett. We wouldn't buy the stock just for its attractiveness as a takeover candidate, however, and would wait for a decent discount before hopping aboard.

MORNINGSTAR® Stocks 500

Knight Trading Group NITE

	Rating	Risk	Moat Size	Fair Value	Last Close	Yield %
	★★	High	None	$5.00	$4.79	0.0

Company Profile

Knight Trading is the leading market-maker, with number-one market share, in Nasdaq stocks and over-the-counter trading of NYSE and Amex securities. A market-maker typically acts as principal and derives most of its revenue from the difference between the price paid when a security is bought and the price received when that security is sold. Knight also makes markets in options. Its asset-management wing, Deephaven Capital Management, operates a hedge fund. Operations abroad make Knight a significant player in international market-making.

Management

New CEO Thomas Joyce has his work cut out for him. He comes to Knight with a substantial background in trading operations, with 14 years at Merrill Lynch and a recent stint at Sanford C. Bernstein.

Strategy

Knight is at a crisis point and needs an in-depth examination of its strategy. The company has failed to make a profit because of low trading volume in the bear market and recently shuttered many of its once-promising international businesses. Knight intends to hunker down and focus on expense management while enhancing its customer relationships.

525 Washington Boulevard   www.knight-sec.com
Jersey City, NJ 07310

Morningstar Grades

Growth [F]	1998	1999	2000	2001
Revenue %	51.0	118.1	40.2	-45.5
Earnings/Share %	NMF	NMF	22.0	-84.9
Book Value/Share %	—	NMF	53.8	9.9
Dividends/Share %	NMF	NMF	NMF	NMF

Revenue has suffered severely amid a decline in equity prices and volume, falling 46% in 2001. This dragged the three-year compound annual growth rate down to 19%. We expect revenue to be off a further 22% in 2002.

Profitability [A-]	1999	2000	2001	TTM
Return on Assets %	13.7	10.3	1.2	-0.8
Oper Cash Flow $Mil	188	153	69	—
- Cap Spending $Mil	19	71	51	—
= Free Cash Flow $Mil	—	—	—	—

Though Knight had been profitable since its inception, it reported its first net loss in the third quarter of 2001. Knight lost another $0.33 per share in the first nine months of 2002, with little hope for profitability to recover soon.

Financial Health [B+]	1999	2000	2001	09-02
Long-term Debt $Mil	—	—	—	—
Total Equity $Mil	499	774	834	765
Debt/Equity Ratio	—	—	—	—

The balance sheet is highly leveraged, but this is reasonable and necessary for a market-maker. Knight has no debt on its sparkling clean balance sheet and typically finances its activities without borrowing.

Industry	Investment Style	Stock Type	Sector
Securities	⊞ Small Core	⚡ Distressed	$ Financial Services

Competition	Market Cap $Mil	Debt/ Equity	12 Mo Trailing Sales $Mil	Price/Cash Flow	Return On Assets%	Total Return% 1 Yr	3 Yr
Knight Trading Group	567	—	548	—	-0.8	-56.5	-52.9
Instinet Group LLC	1,052	—	1,146	—	—	—	—
Spear. Leeds, & Kellogg	—	—	—	—	—	—	—

Price Volatility

	Annual $Price High Low		13.38 2.25	81.63 10.00	60.06 13.88	24.50 7.25	13.97 3.46

	1997	1998	1999	2000	2001	2002
Annual Total Return %	—	—	284.3	-69.7	-20.9	-56.5

Fiscal Year-end: December	1997	1998	1999	2000	2001	TTM
Revenue $Mil	272	411	897	1,257	685	548
Net Income $Mil	77	96	211	260	39	-26
Earnings Per Share $	—	—	1.68	2.05	0.31	-0.22
Shares Outstanding Mil	—	—	121	123	124	118
Return on Equity %	124.3	46.5	42.3	33.6	4.6	-3.4
Net Margin %	28.2	23.3	23.6	20.7	5.6	-4.8
Asset Turnover	1.0	0.6	0.6	0.5	0.2	0.2
Financial Leverage	4.3	3.3	3.1	3.3	3.9	4.4

Valuation Ratios	Stock	Rel to Industry	Rel to S&P 500
Price/Earnings	NMF	—	—
Price/Book	0.7	0.4	0.2
Price/Sales	1.0	0.8	0.5
Price/Cash Flow	—	—	—

Major Fund Holders	% of Fund Assets
Merrill Lynch Mid Cap Value A	1.94
Martin Capital US Opportunity	1.49
Apex Mid Cap Growth	1.25
Merrill Lynch Small Cap Value A	1.21

Morningstar's Take By Rachel Barnard, 11-06-2002 Stock Price as of Analysis: $5.56

After prolonged losses at Knight Trading, management finally took a look under the hood to see if it could fix the engine. The solution: more duct tape. Without a major overhaul, we believe the firm's ability to compete in this market is seriously impaired, and we would steer clear of the shares.

The securities markets have fundamentally changed since Knight set up shop. The switch to decimalization means that spreads between the buy and sell prices of securities can now vary by only a penny. This has cut revenue for market-makers like Knight. Another revolution has ushered in increased competition from electronic trading networks, commonly known as ECNs. A brutal ECN price war this year cut trading prices to the bone.

Thanks to the declining equity markets and the resulting lack of trading volume on which revenue depends, Knight has been hammered. New CEO Thomas Joyce needs to engineer a turnaround strategy for this foundering market-maker that will be profitable and versatile, enabling Knight to make money in a variety of market conditions. This is no small task, since the firm faces nearly overwhelming challenges.

As if market conditions weren't enough to cope with, Knight suffered more blows this year. A software glitch that caused wild selling of Knight shares was enough to make investors jittery and probably contributed to the stock's decline on the following day when The Wall Street Journal reported alleged trading violations at Knight. The company is vigorously fighting these allegations, which are unsubstantiated, but the stock has not recovered.

Knight management has laid out a plan for slashing expenses and improving the quality of its services through enhanced relationships with its customers. While these are worthy ideas, we don't believe they will be enough to ensure profitability in the changing market environment, particularly with the low equity volume we've seen lately. This is a Band-Aid solution when we need major surgery. Consequently, we remain pessimistic on Knight's prospects.

Kohl's KSS

	Rating	Risk	Moat Size	Fair Value	Last Close	Yield %
	★★	Med.	Narrow	$48.00	$55.95	0.0

Company Profile

Kohl's operates 320 specialty department stores primarily in the Midwestern, mid-Atlantic, and Northeastern United States. Targeting middle-income customers, the stores feature moderately priced, nationally known brands of apparel, shoes, accessories, housewares, and soft home products like towels and pillows. In addition to Levi's, Lee, Nike, Reebok, Cannon, and other national brand merchandise, Kohl's stores also offer private-label merchandise in many departments, sold under several names. Approximately 61% of the company's sales are from apparel.

Management

CEO R. Lawrence Montgomery and president Kevin Mansell joined Kohl's in the 1980s. Combined, the two own less than 1% of the company's outstanding shares.

Strategy

With its innovative store format and value-priced branded merchandise, Kohl's has been far more successful in capturing market share than its traditional department store rivals. Now the company is focused on expanding its relatively small store base. Kohl's plans to open 150 stores over the next two years.

N56 W17000 Ridgewood Drive   www.kohls.com
Menomonee Falls, WI 53051-5660

Morningstar Grades

Growth [A+]	1999	2000	2001	2002
Revenue %	20.3	23.8	35.0	21.7
Earnings/Share %	31.1	30.5	42.9	31.8
Book Value/Share %	17.3	40.9	29.5	25.4
Dividends/Share %	NMF	NMF	NMF	NMF

The firm's growth has historically trounced that of competitors, thanks to new store openings and market share gains. Management plans to accelerate the pace of openings over the next few years, so we expect growth to remain robust.

Profitability [A]	2000	2001	2002	TTM
Return on Assets %	8.8	9.7	10.1	9.8
Oper Cash Flow $Mil	158	372	542	608
- Cap Spending $Mil	—	—	—	—
= Free Cash Flow $Mil	—	—	—	—

Profitability has improved steadily over the past five years as gross margins have benefited from a constant refinement of stores' merchandise mix. Operating margins stand to widen with economies of scale.

Financial Health [NA]	2000	2001	2002	10-02
Long-term Debt $Mil	495	803	1,095	1,237
Total Equity $Mil	1,686	2,203	2,791	3,227
Debt/Equity Ratio	0.3	0.4	0.4	0.4

Because Kohl's is spending heavily on expansion, free cash flow is negative. The retailer finances new store openings with a combination of operating cash flow, short-term trade credit, and debt secured by its credit card receivables.

Industry	Investment Style	Stock Type	Sector
Discount Stores	Large Growth	Aggr. Growth	Consumer Services

Competition	Market Cap $Mil	Debt/ Equity	12 Mo Trailing Sales $Mil	Price/Cash Flow	Return On Assets%	Total Return% 1 Yr	3 Yr
Kohl's	18,865	0.4	8,660	31.0	9.8	-20.6	18.3
Target	27,252	1.2	42,275	21.5	5.7	-26.5	-3.9
Sears Roebuck	7,576	3.3	41,156	—	2.1	-48.6	-6.5

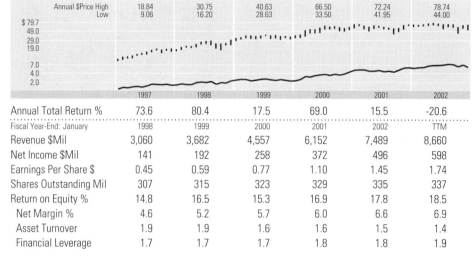

Price Volatility — Monthly Price High/Low — Relative Strength to S&P 500

Annual $Price High Low	18.84 9.06	30.75 16.20	40.63 28.63	66.50 33.50	72.24 41.95	78.74 44.00

	1997	1998	1999	2000	2001	2002
Annual Total Return %	73.6	80.4	17.5	69.0	15.5	-20.6

Fiscal Year-End: January	1998	1999	2000	2001	2002	TTM
Revenue $Mil	3,060	3,682	4,557	6,152	7,489	8,660
Net Income $Mil	141	192	258	372	496	598
Earnings Per Share $	0.45	0.59	0.77	1.10	1.45	1.74
Shares Outstanding Mil	307	315	323	329	335	337
Return on Equity %	14.8	16.5	15.3	16.9	17.8	18.5
Net Margin %	4.6	5.2	5.7	6.0	6.6	6.9
Asset Turnover	1.9	1.9	1.6	1.6	1.5	1.4
Financial Leverage	1.7	1.7	1.7	1.8	1.8	1.9

Valuation Ratios	Stock	Rel to Industry	Rel to S&P 500
Price/Earnings	32.2	1.1	1.4
Price/Book	5.8	1.0	1.8
Price/Sales	2.2	2.4	1.1
Price/Cash Flow	31.0	1.6	2.3

Major Fund Holders	% of Fund Assets
Strategic Partners Focused Gr A	7.69
Strong Advisor Focus A	7.32
Oppenheimer Growth A	6.41
Alliance Premier Growth A	6.09

Morningstar's Take By Roz Bryant, 11-18-2002 Stock Price as of Analysis: $64.57

We think a lot of growth lies ahead for Kohl's, thanks to its relatively small and young store base and successful business model. However, the retailer is likely to experience additional competition, so we'd need a 30% margin of safety to our fair value estimate before purchasing the stock.

Kohl's has changed the face of department store retailing, as its market share gains attest. Its sales growth has averaged 26.7% over the past three years, as the company has opened 169 new stores--a stark contrast to many traditional department store chains' low-single-digit growth. Kohl's eschews shopping malls and opts instead for stand-alone sites. The stores offer branded and private-label merchandise at moderate prices. Shoppers enjoy wide aisles, shopping carts, and centralized checkouts to help them get in and out quickly.

This store format has created loyal customers. Stores between two and four years old average annual sales growth between 10% and 15%, and 40% of the company's store base falls into this category. Moreover, we believe that Kohl's has yet to fully tap its expansion potential. Its store base of less than 500 pales in comparison to J.C. Penney's 1,000-plus stores. The company hasn't even entered some densely populated markets in California,

Nevada, and Arizona yet.

In addition to strong sales growth, Kohl's has been producing solid margin expansion: Its operating margin increased from 9.0% in 1999 to 11.4% in 2002. We expect the margin to reach 12.5% over the next couple of years as Kohl's can spread relatively fixed employee and infrastructure expenses over a larger store base and enjoy greater economies of scale.

However, desperate rivals fighting to regain share won't make it easy for Kohl's to significantly widen its margins. Already, several competing chains, including Sears and J.C. Penney, are incorporating elements of the Kohl's concept into their own stores. By acquiring Lands' End, Sears has shown how easy it is for rivals to copy the strategy of offering branded apparel. We think Kohl's may have to fight harder than it has to date--through lower prices and promotions--to win new customers, which will probably slow margin expansion.

Still, we think Kohl's will continue growing faster than its rivals, and in our opinion, the firm's most profitable days are ahead. For those reasons, we'd be happy to buy in around the low to mid-$30s.

MORNINGSTAR® Stocks 500

Kraft Foods KFT

	Rating	Risk	Moat Size	Fair Value	Last Close	Yield %
	★★	Med.	Narrow	$36.00	$38.93	1.4

Company Profile

Kraft Foods is more than mac and cheese; it is the largest branded food and beverage company based in the United States. Its brands are sold in more than 140 countries and used in 99.6% of U.S. households. Kraft's major brands are Kraft, Oscar Mayer, Maxwell House, Jacobs, and Philadelphia. Kraft also expanded its global presence by acquiring Nabisco, the largest manufacturer and marketer of cookies and crackers in the world. Philip Morris owns a controlling share of Kraft common stock.

Management

Kraft has two co-CEOs: Betsy Holden, who heads domestic operations, and Roger Deromedi, who is in charge of international operations. Both are company veterans, having joined Kraft predecessor General Foods in 1982 and 1977, respectively.

Strategy

Kraft focuses most of its energy on maintaining and expanding its biggest and best-known brands, 21 of which are the U.S. market share leaders in their categories. It's trying to increase its overseas presence as a way of lessening its dependence on the mature and slow-growing North American food market.

Three Lakes Drive
Northfield, IL 60093

Morningstar Grades

Growth [A-]	1998	1999	2000	2001
Revenue %	-1.4	-1.9	-1.0	27.7
Earnings/Share %	NMF	NMF	NMF	NMF
Book Value/Share %	—	—	—	—
Dividends/Share %	NMF	NMF	NMF	NMF

The strong dollar has caused Kraft's revenue to stagnate in recent years, though the acquisition of Nabisco increased the revenue base by 30%. Sales volume recovered in the third quarter after a weak spell, and pro forma revenue grew 2.1%.

Profitability [B]	1999	2000	2001	TTM
Return on Assets %	5.8	3.8	3.4	5.3
Oper Cash Flow $Mil	2,693	3,254	3,328	4,142
- Cap Spending $Mil	860	906	1,101	1,167
= Free Cash Flow $Mil	1,833	2,348	2,227	2,975

Kraft is more profitable than many of its food industry peers, with operating margins north of 15%. Its scale and brand recognition should allow it to maintain that advantage.

Financial Health [B]	1999	2000	2001	09-02
Long-term Debt $Mil	7,035	24,102	13,134	12,871
Total Equity $Mil	13,461	14,048	23,478	25,329
Debt/Equity Ratio	0.5	1.7	0.6	0.5

Kraft used proceeds from the IPO to pay down some of its massive debt load, reducing its debt/equity ratio from 1.84 to 0.60. Even so, it's still more heavily indebted than most food companies.

Industry	Investment Style	Stock Type	Sector
Food Mfg.	▦ Large Growth	→ Slow Growth	🚗 Consumer Goods

Competition

	Market Cap $Mil	Debt/ Equity	12 Mo Trailing Sales $Mil	Price/Cash Flow	Return On Assets%	Total Return% 1 Yr	3 Yr
Kraft Foods	45,853	0.5	34,063	11.1	5.3	16.1	—
Nestle SA ADR	85,869	—	50,054	—	—	—	—
Unilever PLC ADR	27,841	—	44,653	—	—	—	—

Price Volatility

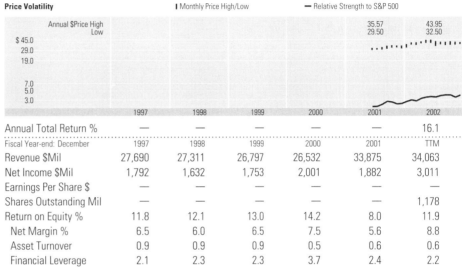

Monthly Price High/Low — Relative Strength to S&P 500

Annual Total Return %	1997	1998	1999	2000	2001	2002
	—	—	—	—	—	16.1

Fiscal Year-end: December	1997	1998	1999	2000	2001	TTM
Revenue $Mil	27,690	27,311	26,797	26,532	33,875	34,063
Net Income $Mil	1,792	1,632	1,753	2,001	1,882	3,011
Earnings Per Share $	—	—	—	—	—	—
Shares Outstanding Mil	—	—	—	—	—	1,178
Return on Equity %	11.8	12.1	13.0	14.2	8.0	11.9
Net Margin %	6.5	6.0	6.5	7.5	5.6	8.8
Asset Turnover	0.9	0.9	0.9	0.5	0.6	0.6
Financial Leverage	2.1	2.3	2.3	3.7	2.4	2.2

Valuation Ratios	Stock	Rel to Industry	Rel to S&P 500
Price/Earnings	—	—	—
Price/Book	1.8	0.4	0.6
Price/Sales	1.3	0.9	0.7
Price/Cash Flow	11.1	1.0	0.8

Major Fund Holders	% of Fund Assets
IPO Plus Aftermarket	7.77
Fidelity Select Food & Agriculture	5.31
Sparrow Growth A	4.49
Runkel Value	4.38

Morningstar's Take By David Kathman, 10-28-2002 Stock Price as of Analysis: $37.90

Kraft Foods has been an island of stability amid market turmoil, but we'd like to see a margin of safety of at least 30% before buying the stock.

Kraft was already the largest U.S.-based food company before its December 2000 merger with Nabisco, and it's been doing a fine job of leveraging the combined assets of the two companies. For one thing, Kraft is realizing positive synergies from such moves as marketing Nabisco crackers with Kraft cheese, and bringing improved marketing muscle to bear on a whole range of products. It's expanding the reach of its famous brands through such "line extensions" as Double Delight Oreos and Cheese Ritz crackers, and revitalizing old brands through packaging innovations like Jell-O Gel Sticks and Kool-Aid Jammers in pouches. Revenue from new products should exceed $1.3 billion in 2002, up from $1.1 billion in the year before.

The promised cost savings from the merger have been coming in ahead of schedule, and we don't think Kraft will have any trouble meeting its goal of $600 million in savings by the end of 2003. Fluctuating commodity costs (particularly for cocoa, cheese, and meat) have been a wild card, but Kraft has still been able to keep pro forma operating income growing in the 6%-7% range, and its

earnings per share growing in the solid double digits each quarter.

Despite its solid profitability, growth has been a sticking point for Kraft. Volume growth slowed in the first half of 2002 because of a variety of factors, including slow food-service sales and competition from cheap private-label products, before picking up in the second half. Making matters worse has been Kraft's inability to translate volume gains into revenue growth. Pro forma revenue (excluding the effects of acquisitions and divestitures) declined year over year in each of Kraft's first five quarters as a public company, though it did grow 2.1% in the third quarter of 2002. One factor dragging down revenue has been currency translation, since 25% of Kraft's sales come from overseas, but that should be less of a problem now that the dollar has weakened.

Kraft has quite a bit going for it, first and foremost its high profitability and wide-ranging array of great brands. Although we consider it an excellent company, its attractiveness as a stock is very much tied to its valuation. Our fair value estimate of $36 involves fairly generous growth and profitability assumptions, and we'd only get excited if the price fell to 30% below that level.

Krispy Kreme Doughnut KKD

	Rating	Risk	Moat Size	Fair Value	Last Close	Yield %
	★	Med.	Narrow	$24.00	$33.77	0.0

Company Profile

Krispy Kreme, founded in 1937, has turned its freshly baked doughnuts into a phenomenon. Many of its 75 company-owned stores and 143 franchised stores are in the South, although Krispy Kreme is accelerating its geographic expansion. The firm has agreements with its franchisees to open 62 new stores in fiscal 2003 and more than 200 new stores between fiscal 2003 and 2006. While its older stores double as wholesalers, which sell to major grocery chains, Krispy Kreme's new store format is smaller for urban areas and is strictly retail.

Management

Scott A. Livengood, an employee for 22 years, has been the chief executive officer since February 1998 and chairman since October 1999. Livengood and John N. McAleer, the vice chairman, are minority investors in several Krispy Kreme franchises.

Strategy

Krispy Kreme plans to expand into smaller U.S. cities and towns after targeting major metropolitan areas, and will rely increasingly on franchisees for expansion here and abroad. It is kicking off its international expansion in Canada. The company has maintained same-store sales growth by remodeling old stores and beefing up its menu, and has expanded its distribution into supermarkets.

370 Knollwood Street
Winston-Salem, NC 27103
www.krispykreme.com

Morningstar Grades

Growth [A]

	1999	2000	2001	2002
Revenue %	13.9	21.8	36.5	31.1
Earnings/Share %	NMF	NMF	NMF	NMF
Book Value/Share %	—	—	—	NMF
Dividends/Share %	NMF	NMF	NMF	NMF

With a relatively small store base it should be easy to achieve growth of around 25% for several years. The company is just beginning to tap its domestic market and may have significant opportunities to expand internationally.

Profitability [B]

	2000	2001	2002	TTM
Return on Assets %	5.7	8.6	10.3	9.6
Oper Cash Flow $Mil	8	32	36	39
- Cap Spending $Mil	11	26	37	73
= Free Cash Flow $Mil	-3	6	-1	-34

With a consistent return on equity of 14%, Krispy Kreme is a profitable growth company. We think it will become more profitable as it matures, with ROE increasing to 19% over the next five years.

Financial Health [A-]

	2000	2001	2002	10-02
Long-term Debt $Mil	21	—	4	51
Total Equity $Mil	48	126	188	254
Debt/Equity Ratio	0.4	—	0.0	0.2

Including the effect of capitalized operating leases, Krispy's debt/equity ratio is still just 0.45--conservative compared with peers.

	Industry	Investment Style	Stock Type	Sector
	Restaurants	▦ Mid Growth	↑ Aggr. Growth	▤ Consumer Services

Competition	Market Cap $Mil	Debt/ Equity	12 Mo Trailing Sales $Mil	Price/Cash Flow	Return On Assets%	Total Return% 1 Yr	3 Yr
Krispy Kreme Doughnut	1,898	0.2	472	48.8	9.6	-23.6	—
Wendy's International	—	—	—	—	—	—	—
Dunkin' Donuts	—	—	—	—	—	—	—

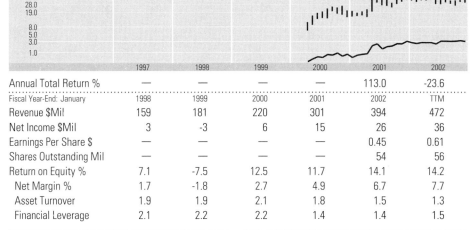

| Price Volatility | | Monthly Price High/Low | — Relative Strength to S&P 500 |

Annual Total Return %	—	—	—	—	113.0	-23.6

Fiscal Year-End: January	1998	1999	2000	2001	2002	TTM
Revenue $Mil	159	181	220	301	394	472
Net Income $Mil	3	-3	6	15	26	36
Earnings Per Share $	—	—	—	—	0.45	0.61
Shares Outstanding Mil	—	—	—	—	54	56
Return on Equity %	7.1	-7.5	12.5	11.7	14.1	14.2
Net Margin %	1.7	-1.8	2.7	4.9	6.7	7.7
Asset Turnover	1.9	1.9	2.1	1.8	1.5	1.3
Financial Leverage	2.1	2.2	2.2	1.4	1.4	1.5

Valuation Ratios	Stock	Rel to Industry	Rel to S&P 500
Price/Earnings	55.4	3.8	2.4
Price/Book	7.5	2.9	2.3
Price/Sales	4.0	3.0	2.0
Price/Cash Flow	48.8	6.7	3.7

Major Fund Holders	% of Fund Assets
Baron Growth	3.11
Delaware Trend A	2.80
UBS PACE Small/Medium Company Gr Eq P	2.77
Hodges	2.75

Morningstar's Take By Carl Sibilski, 11-14-2002. Stock Price as of Analysis: $34.95

New store openings may create a lot of local headlines and publicity for Krispy Kreme, but that's not enough to justify its high stock price. With a new, high-growth restaurant like this we'd consider buying if the stock price dipped 40% under our fair value estimate, but we'd be also be quick to sell once it rebounded.

Deliberate scarcity has helped create brand mystique for Krispy Kreme. By slowly opening new stores and accepting only the most experienced and financially well-heeled restaurant franchisees, Krispy Kreme has done an excellent job of creating a product and image that stands out from other doughnut makers like Dunkin' Donuts and Honey Dipped Doughnuts. Krispy Kreme intends to capitalize on this brand strength by gradually opening new stores and selling doughnuts through other outlets like grocery stores. Krispy's factory stores have a capacity of 4,000-10,000 dozen doughnuts daily, which could offer in-store grocery bakeries a less expensive alternative to making fresh doughnuts on site.

Krispy Kreme's growth outlook is superb. The company believes it can expand its number of stores to 1,300 from its current 200-plus. Because it's starting from such a small base we expect Krispy

Kreme to deliver annual sales growth averaging 25% for several years to come. We're also happy to see Krispy Kreme thinking more about beverage sales, which have higher gross margins than doughnuts. The company's 2001 acquisition of Digital Java should mean that consumers can look forward to both tasty doughnuts and high-quality coffee from the same store, a key to the success of chief rival Dunkin' Donuts.

Even though there's much to be excited about at the company, we think the stock could easily disappoint investors at the first hint of brand fatigue among consumers, or if sales slowed. For these reasons, we would take a very cautious and limited approach to investing in these shares.

As long as Krispy Kreme continues to make headlines with new store openings, we think investors would be right to buy in at prices 40% below our fair value estimate and follow a strict sell discipline after prices rebound. For now, though, we would just keep Krispy Kreme on the watch list.

MORNINGSTAR® Stocks 500

Kroger KR

	Rating	Risk	Moat Size	Fair Value	Last Close	Yield %
	★★★	Med.	None	$21.00	$15.45	0.0

Company Profile

Kroger is the largest retail grocery chain in the United States, operating 2,354 supermarkets in 31 states. About 1,200 supermarkets are operated under the Kroger name, while the rest are under nearly two dozen different banners including Fred Meyer, Ralph's, Fry's, King Soopers, Dillons, and QFC. It manufactures more than 3,000 grocery items under its Private Selection, Kroger, and FMV labels. It also operates more than 800 convenience stores under the Kwik Shop, Quik Stop, and Tom Thumb names, among others, as well as 389 fine jewelry stores.

Management

Since becoming CEO in 1990, Joseph Pichler, 60, has run Kroger as an acquisition machine, more than doubling its store count. The company's cost-consciousness and proven success at integrating acquisitions have been a big plus for shareholders.

Strategy

Competition has intensified in the grocery industry, where Kroger is contending with Wal-Mart's share gains and the threat of price wars from grocery rivals. To boost earnings in the face of slowing sales growth, the company is slashing operating costs and more aggressively lowering selected retail prices.

1014 Vine Street　　　　　www.kroger.com
Cincinnati, OH 45202

Morningstar Grades

Growth [C]	1998	2000	2001	2002
Revenue %	27.0	5.3	8.0	2.2
Earnings/Share %	-54.0	148.3	44.4	21.2
Book Value/Share %	82.1	39.0	16.5	15.5
Dividends/Share %	NMF	NMF	NMF	NMF

Kroger's revenue growth has been propped up by acquisitions. Same-store sales growth has been weakened by industry competition, but is holding up better than that of Kroger's rivals.

Profitability [B]	2000	2001	2002	TTM
Return on Assets %	3.4	4.8	5.5	6.2
Oper Cash Flow $Mil	1,462	2,359	2,347	2,366
- Cap Spending $Mil	1,691	1,623	2,139	2,046
= Free Cash Flow $Mil	-229	736	208	320

Competition in the grocery industry is likely to pressure gross margins over the next few years. The company is slashing costs in an effort to protect its earnings.

Financial Health [B-]	2000	2001	2002	10-02
Long-term Debt $Mil	8,422	8,210	8,412	8,205
Total Equity $Mil	2,678	3,089	3,502	3,770
Debt/Equity Ratio	3.1	2.7	2.4	2.2

Despite recent debt reductions, Kroger's leverage is still significantly higher than its peers'. Capital spending has generally been below that of other grocers, however, keeping free cash flows solid.

Industry	Investment Style	Stock Type	Sector
Groceries	Large Core	Classic Growth	Consumer Services

Competition	Market Cap $Mil	Debt/ Equity	12 Mo Trailing Sales $Mil	Price/Cash Flow	Return On Assets%	Total Return% 1 Yr	3 Yr
Kroger	11,791	2.2	51,418	5.0	6.2	-26.0	-7.6
Wal-Mart Stores	223,388	0.5	233,651	18.9	8.0	-11.8	-7.3
Safeway	13,376	1.5	34,757	6.3	3.4	-44.1	-12.2

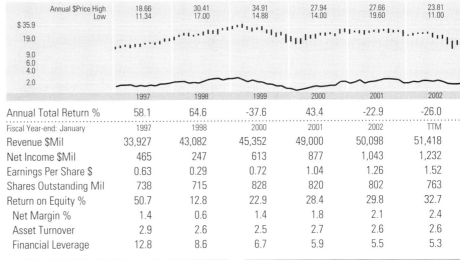

Price Volatility ┃ Monthly Price High/Low ── Relative Strength to S&P 500

Annual $Price High Low	18.66 11.34	30.41 17.00	34.91 14.88	27.94 14.00	27.66 19.60	23.81 11.00
	1997	1998	1999	2000	2001	2002

Annual Total Return %	58.1	64.6	-37.6	43.4	-22.9	-26.0
Fiscal Year-end: January	1997	1998	2000	2001	2002	TTM
Revenue $Mil	33,927	43,082	45,352	49,000	50,098	51,418
Net Income $Mil	465	247	613	877	1,043	1,232
Earnings Per Share $	0.63	0.29	0.72	1.04	1.26	1.52
Shares Outstanding Mil	738	715	828	820	802	763
Return on Equity %	50.7	12.8	22.9	28.4	29.8	32.7
Net Margin %	1.4	0.6	1.4	1.8	2.1	2.4
Asset Turnover	2.9	2.6	2.5	2.7	2.6	2.6
Financial Leverage	12.8	8.6	6.7	5.9	5.5	5.3

Valuation Ratios	Stock	Rel to Industry	Rel to S&P 500
Price/Earnings	10.2	0.5	0.4
Price/Book	3.1	1.0	1.0
Price/Sales	0.2	0.6	0.1
Price/Cash Flow	5.0	0.8	0.4

Major Fund Holders	% of Fund Assets
Cincinnati	4.93
Oppenheimer Quest Value A	4.64
Runkel Value	4.43
PBHG Clipper Focus PBHG	4.41

Morningstar's Take By David Kathman, 12-20-2002 Stock Price as of Analysis: $14.90

As the largest U.S. grocery chain, Kroger epitomizes the problems facing traditional grocers today. However, Kroger has some advantages that make it a potentially good buy, at the right price.

Like its peers Safeway and Albertson's, Kroger has faced increasing competition in recent years at the high end (from pricey niche grocers like Whole Foods) as well as the low end (from warehouse clubs and big-box retailers like Wal-Mart). With the pool of acquisition targets largely dried up after a buying binge in the late 1990s, the big three grocery chains have been forced to turn inward to keep earnings growing while defending market share.

Kroger's strategy has had mixed results. It's centralizing its merchandise purchasing and cutting 1,500 store-level and corporate positions, through which it hopes to save $500 million in the two years through 2003. However, it has acknowledged that it will probably fall short of its goal of achieving two thirds of that $500 million by the end of 2002.

Kroger has also cut prices in an effort to spur sales growth, and its success here has been mixed as well. Same-store sales have kept growing, but margins have been squeezed more deeply than the company expected, something Kroger can ill afford, given its relatively thin operating margins (4.3% over

the past three years, compared with 7.3% for Safeway and 3.8% for Albertson's). We're not too worried, though; Kroger's size is likely to provide significant pricing leverage with suppliers, which should help prevent gross margin erosion from becoming too bad.

We see Kroger's portfolio of stores as a long-term strategic advantage. More than 20% of its stores are convenience stores, less subject to the threats facing grocery stores, and its supermarket fuel centers have doubled in number over the past year, providing most of Kroger's recent same-store sales growth. It's expanding its Food4Less format, which challenges Wal-Mart and the discount clubs, and has put natural food departments in 800 of its 2,400 supermarkets, challenging Whole Foods at the high end.

We think that Kroger's growth and margins will be squeezed by competition, but that the firm will be able to compete relatively well under the circumstances. The stock might be worth taking a chance on if it falls more than 40% below our $21 fair value estimate.

Laboratory Corp of America LH

	Rating	Risk	Moat Size	Fair Value	Last Close	Yield %
	UR	Med.	Narrow	UR	$23.24	0.0

Company Profile

Laboratory Corporation of America offers clinical testing services through a network of 25 laboratories across the United States. The company's testing services are used by the medical profession in the diagnosis, monitoring, and treatment of disease. Office-based physicians constitute approximately 90% of the company's clients. The company's Roche Biomedical Laboratories subsidiary provides more than 1,700 clinical laboratory testing services to hospitals, laboratories, and physicians, primarily in the Midwestern, Southern, and Eastern United States.

Management

Thomas MacMahon has been chairman since April 1996 and president and CEO since January 1997. Before joining LabCorp, he was an executive at several Roche subsidiaries. Previously a significant shareholder, Roche now owns about 4% of the company.

Strategy

LabCorp uses its broad geographic reach and status as the second-largest diagnostic testing company as a competitive advantage. The company competes on the basis of speed, price, and quality of testing results. To improve profits, LabCorp is shifting its sales mix toward higher-margin specialized tests and improving its account collection.

358 South Main Street
Burlington, NC 27215
www.labcorp.com

Morningstar Grades

Growth [B-]	1998	1999	2000	2001
Revenue %	2.1	5.3	13.0	14.6
Earnings/Share %	NMF	-40.5	177.6	215.5
Book Value/Share %	17.9	10.0	168.6	68.5
Dividends/Share %	NMF	NMF	NMF	NMF

LabCorp executives are projecting revenue growth of 14% for 2002, including the impact of acquisitions. For the quarter ending Sept. 30, 2002, however, both volume growth and pricing power slowed somewhat from previous levels.

Profitability [B]	1999	2000	2001	TTM
Return on Assets %	0.9	4.6	9.3	9.1
Oper Cash Flow $Mil	181	247	316	390
- Cap Spending $Mil	69	56	88	84
= Free Cash Flow $Mil	111	191	228	306

Although LabCorp aims to boost margins by focusing on specialized tests, the firm's operating margin slipped to 14.7% for the quarter ending Sept. 30, down from 17.9% for the prior-year period. The company has suffered price and volume pressures in the South.

Financial Health [A]	1999	2000	2001	09-02
Long-term Debt $Mil	483	354	509	520
Total Equity $Mil	176	877	1,085	1,575
Debt/Equity Ratio	2.8	0.4	0.5	0.3

LabCorp recently took on some additional debt to finance acquisitions. Still, the company continues to generate ample free cash flows and earns an investment-grade credit rating.

Industry	Investment Style	Stock Type	Sector
Diagnostics	Mid Core	Classic Growth	Healthcare

Competition	Market Cap $Mil	Debt/ Equity	12 Mo Trailing Sales $Mil	Price/Cash Flow	Return On Assets%	Total Return% 1 Yr	Total Return% 3 Yr
Laboratory Corp of America	3,435	0.3	2,421	8.8	9.1	-42.5	38.5
Quest Diagnostics	5,561	0.5	3,985	10.8	8.4	-20.7	56.1
Ameripath	659	—	466	—	—		

Price Volatility

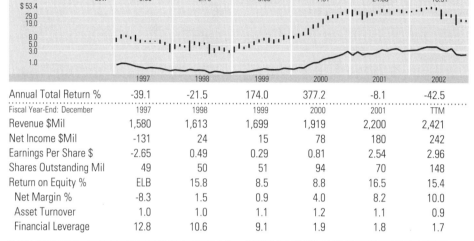

		Monthly Price High/Low			— Relative Strength to S&P 500	
Annual $Price High Low	9.79 3.06	6.73 2.76	9.69 3.06	45.75 7.81	45.68 24.88	52.38 18.51

$ 53.4 / 29.0 / 19.0 / 8.0 / 5.0 / 3.0 / 1.0

	1997	1998	1999	2000	2001	2002
Annual Total Return %	-39.1	-21.5	174.0	377.2	-8.1	-42.5

Fiscal Year-End: December	1997	1998	1999	2000	2001	TTM
Revenue $Mil	1,580	1,613	1,699	1,919	2,200	2,421
Net Income $Mil	-131	24	15	78	180	242
Earnings Per Share $	-2.65	0.49	0.29	0.81	2.54	2.96
Shares Outstanding Mil	49	50	51	94	70	148
Return on Equity %	ELB	15.8	8.5	8.8	16.5	15.4
Net Margin %	-8.3	1.5	0.9	4.0	8.2	10.0
Asset Turnover	1.0	1.0	1.1	1.2	1.1	0.9
Financial Leverage	12.8	10.6	9.1	1.9	1.8	1.7

Valuation Ratios	Stock	Rel to Industry	Rel to S&P 500
Price/Earnings	7.9	0.3	0.3
Price/Book	2.2	0.7	0.7
Price/Sales	1.4	0.9	0.7
Price/Cash Flow	8.8	0.5	0.7

Major Fund Holders	% of Fund Assets
Janus Aspen Global Life Sciences Inst	5.16
Reserve Blue Chip Growth R	4.27
Alliance Growth B	3.78
Dreyfus Premier Growth A	3.58

Morningstar's Take By Amy C. Arnott, 12-10-2002 Stock Price as of Analysis: $24.04

As one of the early players in genomic testing, LabCorp has long been a darling of the health-care sector. The stock gained 174% in 1999, followed by a 377% runup in 2000. But after dropping about 40% in 2002, the stock now looks relatively cheap based on most valuation ratios, and it's certainly less risky than it was a year or two ago.

LabCorp's revenue mix is heavily weighted toward routine diagnostic tests, which account for 80% of sales. Routine tests like blood or urine are simple procedures that can be done at a hospital or physician's office. It's a mature market characterized by slow growth, low margins, and a great deal of competition.

The real opportunity to spur earnings growth lies with the other 20% of LabCorp's revenue, esoteric testing. Esoteric tests include genetic testing and other nonroutine procedures. They involve complex equipment and highly skilled technicians to conduct and interpret results. The demand for these more-complicated tests is expected to rise steadily in coming years, driven by advances in biotechnology.

LabCorp is looking to its recent acquisition of Connecticut-based Dianon Systems to help drive future growth. Dianon has a strong presence in anatomic pathology and cancer screening, an area that LabCorp has identified as its most important growth opportunity over the next several years. In addition, Dianon's average price per test is higher than LabCorp's, so margins should improve after the merger is finalized in 2003.

LabCorp's size also gives it an advantage. As one of only two national diagnostic companies, LabCorp can perform more tests per facility than its smaller, regional competitors.

But LabCorp still carries its share of risk. Although many hospitals and physicians' offices choose to outsource tests to independent labs to avoid the expense of developing their own testing capabilities, LabCorp has recently lost some business in the South to hospitals offering their own tests. As a result, both testing volume and price per test came in lower than expected for the quarter ending Sept. 30, 2002. In addition, managed-care organizations and federal insurance programs continue to exert pressure on labs to drive prices lower.

Morningstar® Stocks 500

Lam Research LRCX

	Rating	Risk	Moat Size	Fair Value	Last Close	Yield %
	★	High	None	$8.00	$10.80	0.0

Company Profile

Lam Research manufactures semiconductor-processing equipment used in the fabrication of integrated circuits. Its products deposit specific films on a silicon wafer and selectively etch away parts of various films to create a circuit design. The company's products include multichamber systems that integrate up to four circuit chambers on a single platform, and chemical-vapor systems that expose a silicon wafer to various gases containing material to be deposited. Lam Research also produces four types of single-wafer plasma-etch systems.

Management

James Bagley has been CEO of Lam Research since 1997 and chairman since 1998. He was chairman and CEO of OnTrack Systems before the two firms merged. Stephen Newberry is president and COO.

Strategy

Like many chip equipment firms, Lam Research is focused on just a few niche segments in the industry. To regain a competitive edge, Lam has emphasized operational efficiency by reducing overhead expenses as well as the time it takes to deliver its products to customers, thereby increasing the productivity of its existing assets.

4650 Cushing Parkway
Fremont, CA 94538
www.lamrc.com

Industry	Investment Style	Stock Type	Sector
Semiconductor Equipment	Mid Core	Slow Growth	Hardware

Competition	Market Cap $Mil	Debt/Equity	12 Mo Trailing Sales $Mil	Price/Cash Flow	Return On Assets%	Total Return% 1 Yr	3 Yr
Lam Research	1,353	0.6	801	51.6	-7.5	-53.5	-33.0
Applied Materials	21,473	0.1	4,881	29.3	0.4	-35.0	-24.3
Novellus Systems	4,015	—	822	21.2	1.7	-28.8	-11.6

Price Volatility	Annual $Price High Low					
	22.48 7.79	11.00 2.79	37.49 5.94	56.81 13.00	55.00 14.19	29.98 6.63
	1997	1998	1999	2000	2001	2002
Annual Total Return %	4.0	-39.1	526.3	-61.0	60.1	-53.5

Fiscal Year-end: June	1998	1999	2000	2001	2002	TTM
Revenue $Mil	1,053	648	1,231	1,520	943	801
Net Income $Mil	-145	-113	205	52	-90	-95
Earnings Per Share $	-1.27	-0.98	1.53	0.39	-0.71	-0.75
Shares Outstanding Mil	114	115	121	124	127	125
Return on Equity %	-27.6	-27.6	32.2	7.3	-13.3	-15.3
Net Margin %	-13.7	-17.4	16.6	3.4	-9.5	-11.8
Asset Turnover	0.9	0.7	1.0	0.8	0.6	0.6
Financial Leverage	2.2	2.4	2.0	2.6	2.4	2.0

Valuation Ratios	Stock	Rel to Industry	Rel to S&P 500
Price/Earnings	NMF	—	—
Price/Book	2.2	0.8	0.7
Price/Sales	1.7	0.4	0.8
Price/Cash Flow	51.6	1.8	3.9

Major Fund Holders	% of Fund Assets
Calvert Social Investment Tech A	3.69
ING Technology A	3.34
Buffalo Science & Technology	2.90
Van Kampen Technology A	2.79

Morningstar Grades

Growth [D]	1999	2000	2001	2002
Revenue %	-38.4	89.9	23.5	-37.9
Earnings/Share %	NMF	NMF	-74.5	NMF
Book Value/Share %	-22.7	33.8	12.3	-0.2
Dividends/Share %	NMF	NMF	NMF	NMF

After solid growth in fiscal 2000 and 2001, sales fell 38% in fiscal 2002. On an average basis, Lam's sales have risen roughly 5 percentage points faster than the industry over the past three years.

Profitability [C+]	2000	2001	2002	TTM
Return on Assets %	16.4	2.8	-5.5	-7.5
Oper Cash Flow $Mil	120	261	22	26
- Cap Spending $Mil	50	64	11	12
= Free Cash Flow $Mil	69	197	11	14

All firms are suffering in the current downturn. Although it lost money in fiscal 2002, Lam had improved its bottom line smartly before that; net margins were 14% in fiscal 2000 and 10% in 2001.

Financial Health [C+]	2000	2001	2002	09-02
Long-term Debt $Mil	322	660	360	372
Total Equity $Mil	635	712	675	618
Debt/Equity Ratio	0.5	0.9	0.5	0.6

At the end of June 2002, the firm had more than $600 million in debt, about half of which was due in September 2002. But with almost $900 million in cash and investments on the balance sheet, Lam is in decent health.

Morningstar's Take By Jeremy Lopez, 10-11-2002 Stock Price as of Analysis: $8.41

Lam Research is not one of our favorite ideas in the chip equipment sector. Given the anemic state of capital spending, we would buy Lam only at a very hefty discount to our fair value estimate.

Chipmakers' capital spending will have the biggest impact on Lam's results, and currently, its outlook is very weak. After industry fundamentals improved in the first half of 2002, chipmakers retrenched their capital budgets in response to a further deterioration in their own businesses. Many major equipment spenders have trimmed their budgets recently, including Taiwan Semiconductor, STMicroelectronics, and United Microelectronics. Some estimate that equipment sales could fall another 25% in 2002 after falling roughly 35% in 2001. As long as chip demand and general tech spending remain sickly, this weakness could carry well into 2003.

Lam's position has improved since the last industry downturn, but the firm still faces stiff competition. The chipmaking process involves several complex types of equipment; usually a few specialized firms vie for market share in each of these product categories. Lam's specialties have been in etch and chemical mechanical planarization (CMP), and the firm has gained share in these key product categories in recent years. Future gains will probably be much harder, however. In etch, the two main players beside Lam are Applied Materials and Tokyo Electron. We certainly wouldn't bet against the former, which is the industry giant; the latter is scraping to regain the lost market share. Lam competes not only with Applied, but also with Novellus, a formidable player that entered CMP with the purchase of Speedfam-IPEC in August 2002.

Our investment bias is toward firms with big, defensible economic moats. In the chip equipment industry, that means those few companies that dominate the key market segments. In our view, the sector lends itself to the rich getting richer and the poor getting poorer, especially during market downturns. The larger, more dominant firms like Applied Materials are more likely to develop a sustainable competitive advantage over the long term. We don't believe Lam fits into this upper echelon of companies, given its volatile financial performance. Given its relative unattractiveness, we'd buy the stock only at a large discount--approximately 50%--to our fair value estimate.

Morningstar Stocks 500   333

Lattice Semiconductor LSCC

	Rating	Risk	Moat Size	Fair Value	Last Close	Yield %
	★	High	None	$7.00	$8.77	0.0

Company Profile

Lattice Semiconductor manufactures programmable logic devices (PLDs). The company markets its products to original equipment manufacturers of computers, computer peripherals, graphics systems, workstations, telecommunications systems, military systems, and industrial controls in the United States and abroad. Foreign sales account for about half of the company's sales.

Management

Cyrus Tsui has been president and CEO of Lattice since 1988. Most of the management team has been with the firm for several years and has considerable industry experience. About 7% of the firm is held by executives.

Strategy

Lattice makes programmable logic devices, a specialized niche in the chip industry. The firm has typically aimed for the low end of the market, which isn't necessarily a bad thing, given the high margins in PLDs. The firm has expanded its market presence via acquisition (it recently bought Agere's PLD unit) and outsources a portion of its own chip production.

5555 N.E. Moore Court
Hillsboro, OR 97124-6421
www.latticesemi.com

Morningstar Grades

Growth [D]	1998	1999	2000	2001
Revenue %	-18.6	34.8	110.5	-48.0
Earnings/Share %	-25.4	NMF	NMF	NMF
Book Value/Share %	11.7	-1.0	49.4	10.0
Dividends/Share %	NMF	NMF	NMF	NMF

After extremely strong growth in 2000, Lattice's sales, like those of almost all chipmakers, tanked in 2001, falling 48%. The firm's growth has typically been weaker than that of its closest peers; we expect sales to fall more than 20% this year.

Profitability [B-]	1999	2000	2001	TTM
Return on Assets %	-5.3	13.0	-9.3	-5.6
Oper Cash Flow $Mil	90	114	7	40
- Cap Spending $Mil	16	26	14	17
= Free Cash Flow $Mil	74	88	-7	23

Lattice's margins are generally solid and reasonably close to those of peers. But management has been unable to translate this into strong returns on capital, particularly when compared with Altera and Xilinx.

Financial Health [A-]	1999	2000	2001	09-02
Long-term Debt $Mil	260	260	260	227
Total Equity $Mil	483	856	894	791
Debt/Equity Ratio	0.5	0.3	0.3	0.3

The balance sheet isn't ideal, although the firm doesn't appear to be in any imminent financial trouble. With $226 million in debt, Lattice's net cash stands at only $63 million. We'd feel better if that number were higher.

Industry	Investment Style	Stock Type	Sector
Semiconductors	▦ Small Core	➜ Slow Growth	▣ Hardware

Competition	Market Cap $Mil	Debt/ Equity	12 Mo Trailing Sales $Mil	Price/Cash Flow	Return On Assets%	Total Return% 1 Yr	3 Yr
Lattice Semiconductor	985	0.3	224	24.8	-5.6	-57.4	-26.9
Xilinx	6,944	0.0	1,069	20.3	5.3	-47.3	-23.3
Altera	4,720	—	694	18.5	2.2	-41.9	-20.9

Price Volatility

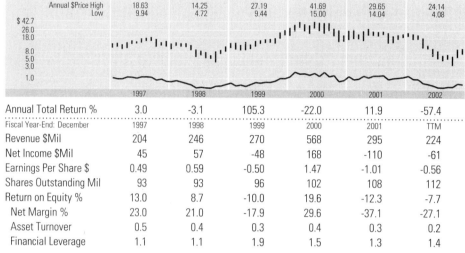

	I Monthly Price High/Low	— Relative Strength to S&P 500

Annual $Price High / Low	18.63 / 9.94	14.25 / 4.72	27.19 / 9.44	41.69 / 15.00	29.65 / 14.04	24.14 / 4.08

$42.7 / 26.0 / 18.0 / 8.0 / 5.0 / 3.0 / 1.0

	1997	1998	1999	2000	2001	2002
Annual Total Return %	3.0	-3.1	105.3	-22.0	11.9	-57.4
Fiscal Year-End: December	1997	1998	1999	2000	2001	TTM
Revenue $Mil	204	246	270	568	295	224
Net Income $Mil	45	57	-48	168	-110	-61
Earnings Per Share $	0.49	0.59	-0.50	1.47	-1.01	-0.56
Shares Outstanding Mil	93	93	96	102	108	112
Return on Equity %	13.0	8.7	-10.0	19.6	-12.3	-7.7
Net Margin %	23.0	21.0	-17.9	29.6	-37.1	-27.1
Asset Turnover	0.5	0.4	0.3	0.4	0.3	0.2
Financial Leverage	1.1	1.1	1.9	1.5	1.3	1.4

Valuation Ratios	Stock	Rel to Industry	Rel to S&P 500
Price/Earnings	NMF	—	—
Price/Book	1.2	0.4	0.4
Price/Sales	4.4	1.1	2.2
Price/Cash Flow	24.8	2.1	1.9

Major Fund Holders	% of Fund Assets
Harbor Mid Cap Value	3.69
UM Small Cap Growth Instl	3.41
Polynous Growth A	2.78
Merrill Lynch Global Value A	2.41

Morningstar's Take By Jeremy Lopez, 12-17-2002 Stock Price as of Analysis: $9.12

Lattice Semiconductor plays third fiddle in a struggling industry. We would continue to pass on the shares.

As a producer of programmable logic devices (PLDs), Lattice has had a less-than-stellar record over the past several quarters. Product demand has been weak overall; more than half the firm's sales originate from the struggling communication sector. Like other PLD makers, Lattice temporarily benefited from customers restocking their chip inventories. But this reprieve has proved short-lived because of a lack of end-market demand.

Even in a good market, Lattice isn't exactly the pick of the litter among PLD players. The reason requires a brief lesson in PLD acronyms: While Lattice derives most of its revenue from CPLDs (complex programmable logic devices), the firm has been well behind its peers in developing FPGA (field programmable gate array) products. This has put Lattice at a competitive disadvantage to firms like Xilinx and Altera because FPGAs are the more advanced product in the PLD niche, and therefore carry better growth prospects. To address this hole, the firm recently announced a long-awaited FPGA product, and also bought Agere's FPGA unit. But given the weak demand, coupled with the several

quarters it takes for PLDs to be designed and sold in volume, we don't expect much benefit from these moves anytime soon.

Lattice's inferiority is the reason the stock trades at just 4 times sales, a big discount to peers like Altera and Xilinx. It doesn't help that Lattice's balance sheet has deteriorated. Net cash (cash minus debt) has fallen to $63 million from $271 million at the start of 2002, primarily due to the acquisition of Agere.

Lattice's recent moves could pay off in the long run, despite the late entry into FPGAs. But until it demonstrates that it can compete with rivals, Lattice will remain at a competitive disadvantage to peers. This, coupled with weak tech demand that probably won't imminently improve, gives us little reason to own Lattice stock until it becomes unavoidably cheap.

MORNINGSTAR® Stocks 500

Lear LEA

	Rating	Risk	Moat Size	Fair Value	Last Close	Yield %
	★★★★★	Med.	Narrow	$56.00	$33.28	0.0

Company Profile

Lear is the fifth-largest supplier of components to the global automotive industry. The company focuses on interior parts and systems, like seats and seating systems (68% of revenue), headliners, door panels, instrument panels, and electrical distribution systems. With 309 facilities in 33 countries, including 53 just-in-time manufacturing plants, Lear is capable of supplying a complete interior module to an assembly plant. In 2001, 42% of sales were made outside the United States and Canada. General Motors, Ford, and DaimlerChrysler together account for 73% of sales.

Management

Lear boasts a tight-knit, highly experienced team led by chairman Ken Way (36-year veteran) and CEO Bob Rossiter (31 years). Both were part of the 1988 leveraged buyout and are known as hands-on managers. Officers and directors own 2.5% of the stock.

Strategy

After a 1990s acquisition binge that left the firm with an impressive portfolio of interior systems, Lear's focus is now on winning more business from existing customers. Its highly efficient business model is often compared with that of Dell. Still heavily dependent on the Big Three, Lear is also stepping up its marketing efforts with Asian automakers and their U.S. transplant operations.

21557 Telegraph Road
Southfield, MI 48086-5008
www.lear.com

	Industry	Investment Style	Stock Type	Sector
	Auto Parts	▦ Mid Core	↻ Cyclical	🚗 Consumer Goods

Competition	Market Cap $Mil	Debt/ Equity	12 Mo Trailing Sales $Mil	Price/Cash Flow	Return On Assets%	Total Return% 1 Yr	3 Yr
Lear	2,188	1.4	14,069	3.9	-2.0	-12.7	5.9
Johnson Controls	7,117	0.5	20,103	7.2	5.3	0.9	17.0
Delphi	4,495	0.9	26,836	3.8	0.5	-39.6	-16.6

Price Volatility

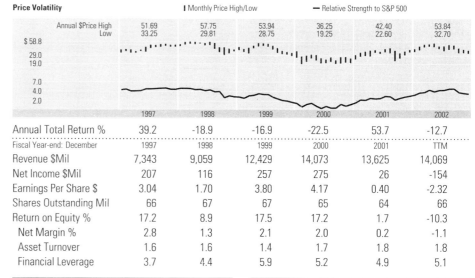

		1997	1998	1999	2000	2001	2002
Annual $Price High		51.69	57.75	53.94	36.25	42.40	53.84
Low		33.25	29.81	28.75	19.25	22.60	32.70
Annual Total Return %		39.2	-18.9	-16.9	-22.5	53.7	-12.7

Fiscal Year-end: December	1997	1998	1999	2000	2001	TTM
Revenue $Mil	7,343	9,059	12,429	14,073	13,625	14,069
Net Income $Mil	207	116	257	275	26	-154
Earnings Per Share $	3.04	1.70	3.80	4.17	0.40	-2.32
Shares Outstanding Mil	66	67	67	65	64	66
Return on Equity %	17.2	8.9	17.5	17.2	1.7	-10.3
Net Margin %	2.8	1.3	2.1	2.0	0.2	-1.1
Asset Turnover	1.6	1.6	1.4	1.7	1.8	1.8
Financial Leverage	3.7	4.4	5.9	5.2	4.9	5.1

Valuation Ratios	Stock	Rel to Industry	Rel to S&P 500
Price/Earnings	NMF	—	—
Price/Book	1.5	0.1	0.5
Price/Sales	0.2	0.0	0.1
Price/Cash Flow	3.9	0.1	0.3

Major Fund Holders	% of Fund Assets
PF Janus Strategic Value A	4.27
Montgomery Mid Cap Focus R	3.54
Janus Adviser Strategic Value	3.48
Leonetti Growth	3.39

Morningstar Grades

Growth [B+]	1998	1999	2000	2001
Revenue %	23.4	37.2	13.2	-3.2
Earnings/Share %	-44.1	123.5	9.7	-90.4
Book Value/Share %	8.0	13.2	12.2	-2.4
Dividends/Share %	NMF	NMF	NMF	NMF

The company, which had $13.6 billion in sales last year, set a goal of $25 billion annually by middecade. Management has backed away from that target recently, since another acquisition binge is unlikely, but we expect internal growth of 5%-7%.

Profitability [C]	1999	2000	2001	TTM
Return on Assets %	2.9	3.3	0.3	-2.0
Oper Cash Flow $Mil	560	753	830	559
- Cap Spending $Mil	391	322	267	283
= Free Cash Flow $Mil	169	431	563	276

Lower volume and price cuts led to lower margins in 2001, but Lear's pain was modest compared with that of with most suppliers. Price pressures combined with the lower margins on outsourcing contracts makes gently declining margins a long-term trend.

Financial Health [C]	1999	2000	2001	09-02
Long-term Debt $Mil	3,325	2,852	2,294	2,135
Total Equity $Mil	1,465	1,601	1,559	1,495
Debt/Equity Ratio	2.3	1.8	1.5	1.4

Though still lofty for such a cyclical industry, Lear's debt load is plummeting thanks to strong free cash flows. Debt fell to 60% of capital in the third quarter from more than 70% two years earlier, and should continue to decline this year.

Morningstar's Take By Josh Peters, 11-19-2002 Stock Price as of Analysis: $36.08

Lear should become profitable as it grows internally, rather than by acquisition. We consider the stock attractive at $34 or less.

In an industry not known for growth, Lear is a standout. The 2001 installment of the Fortune 500 named Lear as the ninth-fastest grower of the past 10 years, surpassing many well-known growth stocks like Home Depot and Amgen.

However, this rapid growth--coming primarily from acquisitions--hasn't been as big a boon for Lear shareholders. Though the company's return on invested capital excluding goodwill has averaged an astounding 28% in the past five years, ROIC including goodwill has been a much more modest 11%. This record pales in comparison with that of fellow seatmaker Johnson Controls, whose internal efforts have contributed about two thirds of its top-line expansion.

The company also seems to have bought more assets than it needed. Since the acquisition machine stopped in 1999 with the $2.3 billion purchase of United Technologies' part operation, Lear has sold $478 million worth of assets and recorded $338 million in restructuring and impairment charges.

We believe these recent rationalizations have brought Lear to a turning point. Now that it has the ability to deliver complete interior modules and electrical systems to automakers, the company has little reason to purchase anything else. Judging by management's backing away from a goal of $25 billion in revenue by 2005, we believe a more disciplined growth strategy is at hand--one that leverages Lear's excellent returns on tangible assets. This, combined with a global footprint, highly efficient cost structure, and good relations with the UAW, puts Lear in a great position to win new business.

Lear's story has a few drawbacks. In a business where product differentiation is crucial to maintaining control over pricing, we worry Lear could be skimping on new product innovation--its research and development spending as a percentage of sales lags JCI as well as most of the other suppliers we cover. Lear's reliance on the Big Three could also be a problem, since Japanese transplant manufacturers like Toyota continue to gain share.

However, we are confident in Lear's strategy of maximum plant productivity. Over the next few years we expect annual revenue growth to average 6%. Since this internal growth will exploit Lear's existing capacity, returns on capital should steadily rise. On the basis of this long-term trend, we estimate Lear's fair value at $56.

Learning Tree International LTRE

	Rating	Risk	Moat Size	Fair Value	Last Close	Yield %
	★★★	Med.	Narrow	$17.00	$13.70	0.0

Company Profile

Learning Tree International provides education and training for the maintenance of information technology throughout business and government organizations. The company is developing a proprietary library of course titles focused on client-server systems, computer networks, operating systems, databases, programming, graphical user interfaces, object-oriented technology, and IT management. Learning Tree International also tests and certifies IT professionals in 34 IT job functions. Its courses are offered in hotels, conference facilities, and customer sites.

Management

CEO and chairman David Collins and president Eric Garen founded Learning Tree in 1974 and together own 45% of the company's outstanding stock. As business has slowed, so has the growth of salaries and incentive bonuses for top executives.

Strategy

Learning Tree positions itself as an independent evaluator of hardware and software. The firm's training curriculum is also job-specific, so clients can immediately implement their training. With a global reach (Europe and Asia account for half of total revenue), Learning Tree aims to be a one-stop shop for its Fortune 1000 client base.

6053 West Century Boulevard www.learningtree.com
Los Angeles, CA 90045-0028

Morningstar Grades

Growth [F]	1999	2000	2001	2002
Revenue %	1.1	18.3	1.4	-23.4
Earnings/Share %	18.8	189.5	-28.5	39.8
Book Value/Share %	12.3	50.2	-32.8	304.0
Dividends/Share %	NMF	NMF	NMF	NMF

Revenue relies on corporate IT spending, which is highly discretionary, making year-to-year growth volatile. We forecast slower growth over the long term--around 10%--as we expect companies to continue watching their purse strings closely.

Profitability [A-]	2000	2001	2002	TTM
Return on Assets %	16.8	14.3	5.1	5.1
Oper Cash Flow $Mil	65	44	7	7
- Cap Spending $Mil	8	14	4	4
= Free Cash Flow $Mil	57	30	3	3

Because most expenses are relatively fixed, profit margins depend on overall revenue growth. In the current downturn, the firm has efficiently pared variable costs to help boost earnings.

Financial Health [A]	2000	2001	2002	09-02
Long-term Debt $Mil	—	—	—	—
Total Equity $Mil	133	84	77	77
Debt/Equity Ratio	—	—	—	—

The firm has no long-term debt (though some operating leases) and more than $100 million in cash on the books. Learning Tree generates plenty of free cash flow, and has recently used it to repurchase stock at depressed prices.

Industry	Investment Style	Stock Type	Sector
Education	▦ Small Growth	→ Slow Growth	▤ Consumer Services

Competition

	Market Cap $Mil	Debt/ Equity	12 Mo Trailing Sales $Mil	Price/Cash Flow	Return On Assets%	Total Return% 1 Yr	3 Yr
Learning Tree International	241	—	174	37.0	5.1	-50.9	-20.9
Apollo Group A	8,023	—	1,009	—	—	—	—
DeVry	1,161	—	657	—	—	—	—

Price Volatility

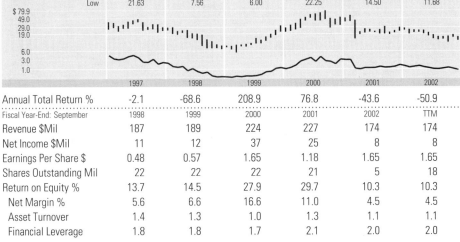

Annual $Price High	48.38	29.75	32.63	78.88	59.75	28.20
Low	21.63	7.56	6.00	22.25	14.50	11.68

	1997	1998	1999	2000	2001	2002
Annual Total Return %	-2.1	-68.6	208.9	76.8	-43.6	-50.9

Fiscal Year-End: September	1998	1999	2000	2001	2002	TTM
Revenue $Mil	187	189	224	227	174	174
Net Income $Mil	11	12	37	25	8	8
Earnings Per Share $	0.48	0.57	1.65	1.18	1.65	1.65
Shares Outstanding Mil	22	22	22	21	5	18
Return on Equity %	13.7	14.5	27.9	29.7	10.3	10.3
Net Margin %	5.6	6.6	16.6	11.0	4.5	4.5
Asset Turnover	1.4	1.3	1.0	1.3	1.1	1.1
Financial Leverage	1.8	1.8	1.7	2.1	2.0	2.0

Valuation Ratios	Stock	Rel to Industry	Rel to S&P 500
Price/Earnings	8.3	0.2	0.4
Price/Book	3.1	0.2	1.0
Price/Sales	1.4	0.3	0.7
Price/Cash Flow	37.0	1.0	2.8

Major Fund Holders	% of Fund Assets
MainStay Small Cap Value A	1.34

Morningstar's Take By Daniel Quinn, 09-23-2002 Stock Price as of Analysis: $14.99

The cold economic realities facing the information technology industry dictated that we lower our fair value estimate for Learning Tree. While we still think the company's long-term potential is solid, there's enough uncertainty in the industry to require a bigger cushion to our fair value estimate than the current price offers.

Firms with business connected to corporate IT spending have been brutalized in recent years. IT spending is closely tied to corporate earnings, and poor earnings and an uncertain outlook for improvement have left the IT industry in shambles. With less hardware and software sold, the demand for training services has suffered as well. So it's not surprising that Learning Tree's recent results have been ugly, with revenue down and earnings in the tank. Results could have been even worse if not for sound management and a flexible business model. Learning Tree has pared discretionary spending on sales and marketing and consequently hasn't had to lay off any employees.

Learning Tree has used its position between the creators and users of technology to build trust with Fortune 1000 companies and government agencies. Its strongest competition comes from the IT vendors themselves, like Microsoft and IBM, who sell training services along with their products. However, as an independent, Learning Tree can objectively discuss the relative strengths and weaknesses of the technology. In addition, Learning Tree can provide training across different platforms. It's unlikely a Microsoft trainer would comment meaningfully on a Dell DELL server, for example.

Learning Tree has maintained its competitive advantage during the current downturn. It is bolstering customer relationships and proprietary training materials while maintaining its global reach. Because Learning Tree has no debt and consistently produces free cash flow, it's been able to make these investments without overtaxing its resources, something startups and lesser-financed rivals can't do.

When and to what extent corporate IT spending will recover lends a good amount of uncertainty to any estimate of Learning Tree's fair value. We've tried to be conservative in our assumptions, but we'd still wait for a 30%-40% discount to our fair value estimate before making an investment, to allow for a sufficient margin of safety. At such a discount, we think Learning Tree would be a solid holding.

 **MORNINGSTAR** ® **Stocks 500**

Legg Mason LM

	Rating ★★★	Risk Med.	Moat Size Narrow	Fair Value $60.00	Last Close $48.54	Yield % 0.9

Company Profile

Legg Mason can now be classified as an asset manager, with more than 50% of net revenue coming from money-management fees. The firm manages fixed-income and equity funds for institutions, individual mutual fund investors, and wealthy private clients. Legg Mason maintains its regional brokerage business, which has historically been its focus, and has added investment banking capabilities. Legg Mason operates primarily in the United States, but has additional operations in Canada, Switzerland, and the United Kingdom.

Management

In 1962, Raymond "Chip" Mason founded Mason & Company, which merged with Legg and Company to form Legg Mason in 1970. He is chairman, president, and chief executive officer, and has been instrumental in Legg Mason's success.

Strategy

Legg Mason's main goal is to continue building the asset-management business. The revenue stream from asset management is more consistent and can offset volatility in the capital markets, investment banking, and brokerage businesses, which tend to be more cyclical. Building wealth management is also a priority because of the large margins on private client assets.

100 Light Street
Baltimore, MD 21202
www.leggmason.com

Morningstar Grades

Growth [B]	1999	2000	2001	2002
Revenue %	17.7	30.7	9.8	2.8
Earnings/Share %	24.4	53.4	1.3	-2.6
Book Value/Share %	12.4	28.2	17.4	16.3
Dividends/Share %	16.8	22.0	14.8	11.4

Net revenue grew 6.6% in fiscal 2002, which ended in March. Asset-management fees accounted for more than half of net revenue and were up 20% for the year. Investment banking revenue grew 55%. Five-year growth is solid at 20% annually.

Profitability [A]	2000	2001	2002	TTM
Return on Assets %	3.1	3.3	2.6	3.0
Oper Cash Flow $Mil	169	223	86	—
- Cap Spending $Mil	23	34	21	—
= Free Cash Flow $Mil	—	—	—	—

Return on assets of 3% is better than most brokers, but the large balance sheet necessary for a brokerage keeps ROA lower than asset managers'. Operating margins in the high teens reflect the high fixed costs associated with brokerages.

Financial Health [A+]	2000	2001	2002	09-02
Long-term Debt $Mil	—	—	—	—
Total Equity $Mil	771	928	1,085	1,168
Debt/Equity Ratio	—	—	—	—

Legg Mason's financial leverage ratio of 5.5 times equity is lower than its brokerage peers', reflecting its diversified business mix. Solid cash flow should allow the firm to quickly pay down its debt from numerous acquisitions.

Industry Money Management	Investment Style ⊞ Mid Core	Stock Type ↗ Classic Growth	Sector $ Financial Services

Competition	Market Cap $Mil	Debt/ Equity	12 Mo Trailing Sales $Mil	Price/Cash Flow	Return On Assets%	Total Return% 1 Yr	3 Yr
Legg Mason	3,144	—	1,638	—	3.0	-2.1	16.7
AG Edwards	2,605	—	2,312	—	1.3	-24.1	4.3
Neuberger Berman	2,337	—	669	—	—	—	—

Price Volatility

			Monthly Price High/Low		— Relative Strength to S&P 500

Annual $Price High Low	28.16 14.16	32.28 17.31	42.88 26.44	60.25 30.69	56.99 34.25	57.15 37.11

	1997	1998	1999	2000	2001	2002
Annual Total Return %	95.6	13.9	15.8	51.4	-7.5	-2.1

Fiscal Year-end: March	1998	1999	2000	2001	2002	TTM
Revenue $Mil	909	1,071	1,400	1,536	1,579	1,638
Net Income $Mil	75	93	150	156	153	182
Earnings Per Share $	1.19	1.48	2.27	2.30	2.24	2.64
Shares Outstanding Mil	60	59	62	64	65	65
Return on Equity %	14.7	16.3	19.5	16.8	14.1	15.5
Net Margin %	8.3	8.7	10.7	10.2	9.7	11.1
Asset Turnover	0.3	0.3	0.3	0.3	0.3	0.3
Financial Leverage	5.6	6.1	6.2	5.1	5.5	5.1

Valuation Ratios	Stock	Rel to Industry	Rel to S&P 500
Price/Earnings	18.4	1.0	0.8
Price/Book	2.7	1.0	0.8
Price/Sales	1.9	0.7	1.0
Price/Cash Flow	—	—	—

Major Fund Holders	% of Fund Assets
Managers AMG Rorer Mid Cap	4.62
Transamerica Premier Aggr Grth Inv	4.40
Fidelity Select Brokerage & Investmnt	4.24
Scudder Global Discovery S	4.23

Morningstar's Take By Rachel Barnard, 12-16-2002 Stock Price as of Analysis: $49.81

Legg Mason has a diversified stable of businesses that have helped to mitigate the effects of the market's decline, and we think the firm has robust growth prospects as the market recovers. Our fair value estimate is unchanged at $60 and we think the shares would be a bargain below $36.

Legg Mason has diversified its business mix without losing focus, and shareholders have benefited. Snapping up asset managers, most recently Private Capital Management and Royce Associates in 2001, has enabled Legg Mason to ride the asset-management wave; now 56% of net revenue comes from the recurring fees based on $177 billion of assets under management (AUM).

The firm has also zeroed in on the most profitable sector of money management: private wealth management. Currently 12% of AUM comes from wealthy private clients; this small proportion of assets generates 22% of fee revenue for Legg Mason. By contrast, institutional assets constitute 68% of AUM but generate only 43% of fees. By concentrating on selling higher-margin products to wealthy investors, the company should be able to increase its average fees on AUM.

The flip side of Legg Mason's diversity is its brokerage business, which has been struggling.

Retail investors have not been doing much trading since the market sank, and volume is still sluggish. The company has closed several offices and is focusing on cost management to stay above water. We don't expect brokerage to contribute much to the bottom line for the remainder of 2002, but when investors get back in the saddle, Legg Mason should be able to profit here.

Given the firm's diverse mix of businesses, there are several bright spots amid the gloom of the equity downturn. Investment banking has been a big winner for Legg Mason over the past several quarters. The firm's Western Asset Management subsidiary, which specializes in institutional fixed-income products, has also been a growth engine, increasing AUM as investors fled equities. And Royce Funds, one of Legg Mason's new acquisitions, has been among the best-selling fund groups in 2002.

Legg Mason has no further acquisitions in the works, which means that the heady days of 20% growth are probably at an end. But we believe the firm has an attractive mix of businesses and should be able to generate growth around 12% over the long haul.

Lehman Brothers Holdings LEH

	Rating	Risk	Moat Size	Fair Value	Last Close	Yield %
	★★★	Med.	None	$74.00	$53.29	0.7

Company Profile

Lehman Brothers Holdings is a holding company for Lehman Brothers investment bank. The company's businesses include raising capital through securities underwriting and direct placements, corporate finance advisory services, merchant banking, securities sales and trading, institutional asset management, research services, and the trading of foreign securities, commodities, and derivative products. It has offices across the United States, Europe, the Middle East, Latin America, and South America.

Management

Richard Fuld, who started with the company in 1969, has been chairman and CEO since 1994. He owns 2.7% of the company's outstanding shares and has attempted to improve profitability by focusing on consistent areas that offer good margins.

Strategy

Lehman Brothers' goal is to leverage its recently diversified business mix and further expand outside the United States. This will help the firm garner a larger percentage of total revenue from higher-margin businesses like investment banking and high-net-worth retail. The firm is looking to double its investment banking and equity capital market businesses in Europe.

745 Seventh Avenue
New York, NY 10019

www.lehman.com

Industry	Investment Style	Stock Type	Sector
Securities	▦ Large Value	➡ Slow Growth	$ Financial Services

Competition	Market Cap $Mil	Debt/ Equity	12 Mo Trailing Sales $Mil	Price/Cash Flow	Return On Assets%	Total Return% 1 Yr	3 Yr
Lehman Brothers Holdings	12,738	—	16,947	—	0.3	-19.7	13.3
Citigroup	177,948	—	106,096	—	1.6	-24.2	1.1
J.P. Morgan Chase & Co.	47,901	—	42,911	—	0.2	-30.7	-17.5

Price Volatility

| Monthly Price High/Low   — Relative Strength to S&P 500

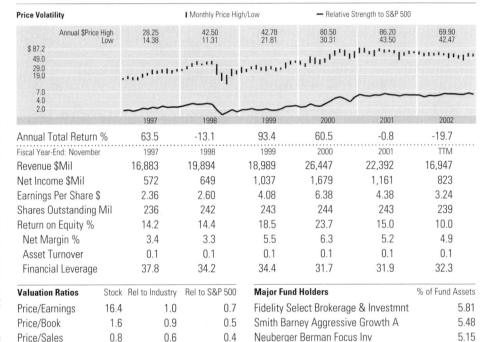

	1997	1998	1999	2000	2001	2002
Annual $Price High / Low	28.25 / 14.38	42.50 / 11.31	42.78 / 21.81	80.50 / 30.31	86.20 / 43.50	69.90 / 42.47
Annual Total Return %	63.5	-13.1	93.4	60.5	-0.8	-19.7

Fiscal Year-End: November	1997	1998	1999	2000	2001	TTM
Revenue $Mil	16,883	19,894	18,989	26,447	22,392	16,947
Net Income $Mil	572	649	1,037	1,679	1,161	823
Earnings Per Share $	2.36	2.60	4.08	6.38	4.38	3.24
Shares Outstanding Mil	236	242	243	244	243	239
Return on Equity %	14.2	14.4	18.5	23.7	15.0	10.0
Net Margin %	3.4	3.3	5.5	6.3	5.2	4.9
Asset Turnover	0.1	0.1	0.1	0.1	0.1	0.1
Financial Leverage	37.8	34.2	34.4	31.7	31.9	32.3

Valuation Ratios	Stock	Rel to Industry	Rel to S&P 500
Price/Earnings	16.4	1.0	0.7
Price/Book	1.6	0.9	0.5
Price/Sales	0.8	0.6	0.4
Price/Cash Flow	—	—	—

Major Fund Holders	% of Fund Assets
Fidelity Select Brokerage & Investmnt	5.81
Smith Barney Aggressive Growth A	5.48
Neuberger Berman Focus Inv	5.15
Credit Suisse Global Finan Serv Com	5.12

Morningstar Grades

Growth [D]	1998	1999	2000	2001
Revenue %	17.8	-4.5	39.3	-15.3
Earnings/Share %	10.0	57.0	56.6	-31.3
Book Value/Share %	8.7	22.1	22.4	8.8
Dividends/Share %	25.0	20.0	22.2	27.3

Lehman's revenue has been steadier than peers' because of the firm's diverse product lineup. For instance, with business weak in the equity markets, Lehman's fixed-income business has picked up the slack.

Profitability [D]	1999	2000	2001	TTM
Return on Assets %	0.5	0.7	0.5	0.3
Oper Cash Flow $Mil	6,341	-14,733	6,679	—
- Cap Spending $Mil	73	287	1,341	—
= Free Cash Flow $Mil	—	—	—	—

Returns on assets and equity are below the industry average because the firm focuses on lower-margin, more-consistent businesses. Recent strides to boost profits have been successful, and we believe the firm will continue to improve.

Financial Health [B-]	1999	2000	2001	08-02
Long-term Debt $Mil	—	—	—	—
Total Equity $Mil	5,595	7,081	7,759	8,209
Debt/Equity Ratio	—	—	—	—

Lehman operates in a very capital-intensive industry, and its heavy leverage reflects this. The firm recently has benefited from lower interest expenses, which helped cushion earnings in a weaker market environment.

Morningstar's Take By Craig Woker, 11-26-2002 Stock Price as of Analysis: $59.70

Lehman is transforming itself into a much stronger firm than it has been historically. However, there's little sense investing in a turnaround story--even though it's a story we believe in--when much of the upside has already been priced into the stock. We would need at least a 40% discount to our fair value estimate before we'd buy.

Since spinning off from American Express in 1994, Lehman has never generated the razzle-dazzle profits that characterize investment banks in boom years. During the 1990s, many large rivals posted returns on equity in the upper 30s and lower 40s; Lehman didn't come close to these levels. The long-bloated firm had other issues to deal with, like boosting revenue per employee through cost-cutting and improved output.

Lehman has steadily put its house in order. The firm now tracks its profits on a location-by-location basis to make better-informed decisions. This prudent management is a major reason that we believe Lehman's future performance should be much improved from its past. For instance, the firm's investment advisors are now the top producers in the industry with an average of $1.5 million each in commissions.

Another key to Lehman's recent success has been a focus on leveraging its strengths. For instance,

Lehman is a leader in the debt markets, ranking near the top in share of debt underwriting and bond trading. Because investors have rediscovered bonds after a long hiatus, Lehman has weathered the recent turbulence better than most rivals.

However, Lehman is not resting on its laurels. The firm has fought hard to gain market share in the higher-margin equity underwriting and merger advisory arenas. So far, Lehman is proving to be an increasing threat. The firm's global equity underwriting volume held steady in 2001 and so far in 2002, even though industrywide volume fell 32% last year and was down another 9% through the first three quarters of 2002, according to Bloomberg.

This increased focus on equities is a prudent strategy for Lehman. In our view, the recent industrywide dearth of equity work has created a backlog of potential merger and underwriting business, and given Lehman's increasing strength in this area, we believe the firm is well positioned to capture as much business as possible when the dam breaks. Plus, the diversity will prevent Lehman from being overly tied to fixed income.

All of this adds up to a solid future for Lehman. We'd just cautiously await the right price to be a part of it.

M⊙RNINGSTAR® Stocks 500

Level 3 Communications LVLT

	Rating	Risk	Moat Size	Fair Value	Last Close	Yield %
	★★★	High	None	$9.00	$4.90	0.0

Company Profile

Level 3 Communications is primarily a communication network provider. It has a 16,000-mile network in the United States, a 3,600-mile network in Europe, 36 data centers with more than 3 million square feet of space, and local networks in 36 markets. The company also owns a trans-Atlantic cable and is building an Asian network connecting Hong Kong, Korea, Japan, and Taiwan. Over these networks the company provides data transport, co-location, and other telecom services. Level 3 also owns coal-mining operations, a holdover from its former existence.

Management

Management is well regarded in the industry. CEO James Crowe was the head of MFS Communications before its merger with WorldCom. Chairman Walter Scott sits on the board of Berkshire Hathaway.

Strategy

Now that its network is substantially complete, Level 3 is working to win customers and boost revenue. The company is focused on minimizing costs to limit losses and makes the most of its cash reserves. Recently, the company has used cash to make a series of small acquisitions. Level 3 plans to maintain the most technologically advanced, lowest-cost network in the business.

1025 Eldorado Blvd   www.level3.com
Broomfield, CO 80021

Industry	Investment Style	Stock Type	Sector
Telecommunication Services	Mid Growth	Spec. Growth	Telecom

Competition

Competition	Market Cap $Mil	Debt/ Equity	12 Mo Trailing Sales $Mil	Price/Cash Flow	Return On Assets%	Total Return% 1 Yr	3 Yr
Level 3 Communications	2,043	NMF	2,529	—	-42.0	-2.0	-60.5
AT&T	20,115	0.8	48,821	1.8	-10.9	-27.7	-28.2
Qwest Communications Inte	8,375	0.6	19,013	2.4	-6.3	-64.6	-49.9

Price Volatility

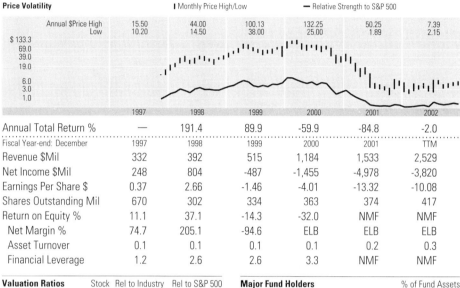

		1997	1998	1999	2000	2001	2002
Annual $Price High		15.50	44.00	100.13	132.25	50.25	7.39
Low		10.20	14.50	38.00	25.00	1.89	2.15
Annual Total Return %		—	191.4	89.9	-59.9	-84.8	-2.0

Fiscal Year-end: December	1997	1998	1999	2000	2001	TTM
Revenue $Mil	332	392	515	1,184	1,533	2,529
Net Income $Mil	248	804	-487	-1,455	-4,978	-3,820
Earnings Per Share $	0.37	2.66	-1.46	-4.01	-13.32	-10.08
Shares Outstanding Mil	670	302	334	363	374	417
Return on Equity %	11.1	37.1	-14.3	-32.0	NMF	NMF
Net Margin %	74.7	205.1	-94.6	ELB	ELB	ELB
Asset Turnover	0.1	0.1	0.1	0.1	0.2	0.3
Financial Leverage	1.2	2.6	2.6	3.3	NMF	NMF

Valuation Ratios	Stock	Rel to Industry	Rel to S&P 500
Price/Earnings	NMF	—	—
Price/Book	—	—	—
Price/Sales	0.8	0.5	0.4
Price/Cash Flow	—	—	—

Major Fund Holders	% of Fund Assets
Legg Mason Opportunity Prim	6.13
Weitz Hickory	4.41
Legg Mason Special Investment Prim	3.28
Fidelity Leveraged Company Stock	2.72

Morningstar Grades

Growth [A]	1998	1999	2000	2001
Revenue %	18.1	31.4	129.9	29.5
Earnings/Share %	618.9	NMF	NMF	NMF
Book Value/Share %	115.3	42.5	22.8	NMF
Dividends/Share %	NMF	NMF	NMF	NMF

The additions of CorpSoft and Software Spectrum make growth look very strong. Growth in the telecom business, which we believe is key to the firm's value, has been modest recently, with recurring service revenue flat year over year, by our estimate.

Profitability [D+]	1999	2000	2001	TTM
Return on Assets %	-5.5	-9.8	-53.4	-42.0
Oper Cash Flow $Mil	433	1,084	-329	-1,002
- Cap Spending $Mil	3,385	5,576	2,325	273
= Free Cash Flow $Mil	-2,952	-4,492	-2,654	-1,275

The telecom business has posted impressive margins recently. The much larger software business generates anemic margins. Here again, the telecom business must get bigger if the firm is to earn a decent return on invested capital.

Financial Health [D-]	1999	2000	2001	09-02
Long-term Debt $Mil	3,989	7,318	6,209	6,385
Total Equity $Mil	3,405	4,549	-65	-254
Debt/Equity Ratio	1.2	1.6	ELB	NMF

Level 3 has eliminated about $2 billion of debt through equity swaps and open-market purchases. It has also drastically reduced its cash-burn rate and now sits on about $1.5 billion in cash. The firm remains heavily leveraged, though.

Morningstar's Take By Michael Hodel, 12-24-2002 Stock Price as of Analysis: $5.01

Level 3 needs to prove it can grow into its debt load, making this a very speculative investment.

Level 3's primary advantage is its network. From its physical structure to the equipment and software that control it, the network was built to offer services at the lowest cost today and be easily upgraded to do the same tomorrow. The business Level 3 has won already generates gross margins around 80%, even as the company goes to market with lower prices than the competition.

Through two recent acquisitions, Level 3 has moved into software distribution and resale, and now derives about 75% of revenue from this extremely low-margin business. Although management claims this business holds strategic long-term value when combined with the telecom business, we think software sales add little to the company's ability to support its debt load. The business requires very little additional capital, though, so it shouldn't be a hindrance.

Level 3 has made acquisitions in its core business as well, most recently announcing a offer for Genuity. Genuity derives more than half of its revenue from two huge customers, Verizon and AOL. Genuity is horribly unprofitable, but because Level 3 can provide service on its own network at far lower costs, the acquired business should generate decent cash flow. Level 3 also expands its relationship with AOL and gets its foot in the door with Verizon.

Level 3 still needs to grow rapidly to meet its debt obligations. The company has done a great job of reducing debt, but the burden still sits at about $5 billion, net of cash. If the company can maintain telecom margins and generate a small profit in software, we estimate telecom revenue need to grow at least 50%, adjusted for Genuity, just to meet interest costs and capital needs.

With the industry in the dumps, recent growth has been modest, but there is reason to believe growth will return. Data traffic continues to increase and the old-line carriers, including AT&T and WorldCom, aren't in a great position to invest in their networks. The Bells (including Verizon) are also getting into long-distance and will need infrastructure to serve their customers. Level 3, as the low-cost infrastructure provider, should have opportunities to grow. It also has deep pockets with which to pursue other acquisitions. Until the company can translate this promise into reality, though, the stock remains very speculative.

Lexmark International LXK

Rating	Risk	Moat Size	Fair Value	Last Close	Yield %
★★	Med.	Narrow	$57.00	$60.50	0.0

Company Profile

Lexmark International manufactures laser and inkjet printers, as well as associated consumable supplies for the office and home markets. The company also sells serial wire matrix printers for printing single and multipart forms used by businesses. In addition to its core printer business, the company also manufactures other office imaging products including accessory supplies for IBM-brand printers, aftermarket supplies for original equipment manufacturer products, as well as typewriters and typewriter supplies that are sold under the IBM trademark.

Management

Chairman and CEO Paul Curlander leads a highly regarded management team. Curlander worked for IBM before the computer giant spun off Lexmark in 1991.

Strategy

Lexmark wants to build a large installed base of printer hardware that will drive a recurring stream of high-margin consumables sales. It has been successful in developing laser and inkjet printers with innovative features selling at attractive prices relative to leader Hewlett-Packard.

One Lexmark Centre Drive
Lexington, KY 40550
www.lexmark.com

Industry	Investment Style	Stock Type	Sector
Computer Equipment	Mid Growth	Classic Growth	Hardware

Competition

	Market Cap $Mil	Debt/ Equity	12 Mo Trailing Sales $Mil	Price/Cash Flow	Return On Assets%	Total Return% 1 Yr	3 Yr
Lexmark International	7,605	0.1	4,328	10.4	11.2	2.5	-12.3
Hewlett-Packard	34,321	0.3		6.1	-3.5	-13.9	-24.7
Canon ADR	32,267	—	25,882	—	—		

Price Volatility

I Monthly Price High/Low — Relative Strength to S&P 500

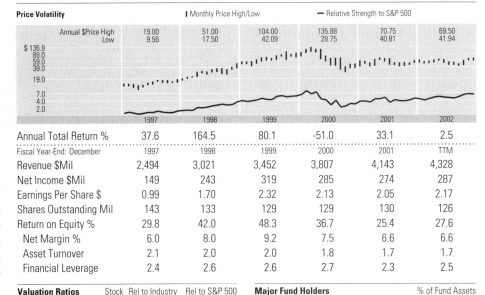

Annual $Price High Low	19.00 9.56	51.00 17.50	104.00 42.09	135.88 28.75	70.75 40.81	69.50 41.94

	1997	1998	1999	2000	2001	2002
Annual Total Return %	37.6	164.5	80.1	-51.0	33.1	2.5

Fiscal Year-End: December	1997	1998	1999	2000	2001	TTM
Revenue $Mil	2,494	3,021	3,452	3,807	4,143	4,328
Net Income $Mil	149	243	319	285	274	287
Earnings Per Share $	0.99	1.70	2.32	2.13	2.05	2.17
Shares Outstanding Mil	143	133	129	129	130	126
Return on Equity %	29.8	42.0	48.3	36.7	25.4	27.6
Net Margin %	6.0	8.0	9.2	7.5	6.6	6.6
Asset Turnover	2.1	2.0	2.0	1.8	1.7	1.7
Financial Leverage	2.4	2.6	2.6	2.7	2.3	2.5

Valuation Ratios	Stock	Rel to Industry	Rel to S&P 500
Price/Earnings	27.9	1.0	1.2
Price/Book	7.3	1.2	2.3
Price/Sales	1.8	1.1	0.9
Price/Cash Flow	10.4	1.2	0.8

Major Fund Holders	% of Fund Assets
Evergreen Technology A	8.18
Seligman Communications&Information A	5.70
Henderson Global Technology A	4.53
Hartford Global Technology A	4.39

Morningstar Grades

Growth [A]	1998	1999	2000	2001
Revenue %	21.1	14.3	10.3	8.8
Earnings/Share %	71.7	36.5	-8.2	-3.8
Book Value/Share %	21.6	18.7	20.8	39.0
Dividends/Share %	NMF	NMF	NMF	NMF

Lexmark delivered 9% revenue growth in 2001; we expect long-term growth of about that level. Increased competition and price pressure could keep a lid on hardware growth, but the company's printer supply business is in great shape.

Profitability [A+]	1999	2000	2001	TTM
Return on Assets %	18.7	13.8	11.2	11.2
Oper Cash Flow $Mil	448	476	196	731
- Cap Spending $Mil	220	297	214	116
= Free Cash Flow $Mil	228	180	-19	615

Despite aggressively pricing its printers, Lexmark has profitability that's well above average, since high-margin consumables are becoming a bigger percentage of sales.

Financial Health [B]	1999	2000	2001	09-02
Long-term Debt $Mil	149	149	149	149
Total Equity $Mil	659	777	1,076	1,040
Debt/Equity Ratio	0.2	0.2	0.1	0.1

The balance sheet is solid and cash flow has remained strong, even after last year's jump in capital spending (the company doubled inkjet capacity). Lexmark continues to buy back shares.

Morningstar's Take By Joseph Beaulieu, 11-18-2002 Stock Price as of Analysis: $62.25

We like Lexmark, but competitive shifts in the printing business create substantial risks for investors.

Revenue growth has been sluggish lately because of weak corporate IT spending, but we think Lexmark has decent long-term growth prospects. We concur with the firm that the number of pages printed on laser and inkjet printers could grow at a 7%-12% clip over the next decade, in part because the Internet is spurring demand from home and business users. Ink usage per page is going up as well, since Web pages often include graphics. Applications like digital photography also have the potential to fuel growth.

Partially offsetting our forecast of near-term weakness and slightly slower revenue growth is our assumption that as a larger percentage of revenue comes from higher-margin consumable supplies, gross and operating margins will improve once the IT spending downturn reverses. Although profit margins on printers (particularly inkjets) are likely to remain low, the large base of customers using its printers means that Lexmark should enjoy a recurring stream of high-margin replacement ink cartridge sales. Sales of printing supplies represent more than half of revenue and a larger share of profits, and we think this trend is sustainable.

With its focus on printing, Lexmark is in the enviable position of being both a technology leader and a low-cost producer. As a result, it has been able to maintain a price/performance advantage, despite being much smaller than Hewlett-Packard. However, with an increasing percentage of profits coming from printing, Hewlett-Packard is under a great deal of pressure to increase its focus on this area. This could increase competition over the next couple of years.

Two more sources of potential competitive pressure are Hewlett-Packard's acquisition of Compaq and Dell's anticipated entry into the printer market. Before it was bought by HP, Compaq offered Lexmark printers to its PC customers, so that leaves a sales gap. Lexmark is collaborating with Dell in the development of Dell's line of printers. Until it is ready to launch its new product line, Dell will be pushing Lexmark's printers. In the short run this is very good news for Lexmark, but once Dell is ready to sell its own printers, things could get tougher.

MORNINGSTAR® Stocks 500

Liberty Media L

	Rating	Risk	Moat Size	Fair Value	Last Close	Yield %
	UR	Med.	None	UR	$8.94	0.0

Company Profile

Liberty Media has ownership stakes in media and telecommunication operations. These markets include cable, broadcast television, and satellite networks. Liberty's ownership interests include Discovery Channel and QVC. AT&T spun off the company in August 2001.

Management

Chairman John Malone is the driving force behind Liberty. The former CEO of TCI (acquired by AT&T) is hailed as a consummate deal maker, engineering whiz, and financial genius.

Strategy

Liberty Media's strategy is to expand its portfolio of media assets through acquisitions and partnerships. The company's key areas of focus are television programming, cable, and interactive TV.

12300 Liberty Boulevard www.libertymedia.com
Englewood, CO 80112

Industry	Investment Style	Stock Type	Sector
Cable TV	Large Growth	Spec. Growth	Media

Competition

	Market Cap $Mil	Debt/ Equity	12 Mo Trailing Sales $Mil	Price/Cash Flow	Return On Assets%	Total Return% 1 Yr	3 Yr
Liberty Media	23,114	0.2	2,069	—	-22.4	-35.3	-29.4
AOL Time Warner	56,278	0.3	41,024	8.1	-34.6	-59.2	-44.6
Walt Disney	32,923	0.5	24,550	14.6	2.5	-20.3	-19.1

Price Volatility

| Monthly Price High/Low | — Relative Strength to S&P 500

Annual $Price High Low	6.09 2.95	11.55 5.47	28.13 10.84	30.42 10.64	17.86 9.65	14.85 6.10

	1997	1998	1999	2000	2001	2002
Annual Total Return %	90.4	90.6	146.7	-52.3	3.2	-35.2

Fiscal Year-end: December	1997	1998	1999	2000	2001	TTM
Revenue $Mil	1,225	1,359	964	1,526	2,059	2,069
Net Income $Mil	-470	622	-2,091	1,485	-6,203	-8,354
Earnings Per Share $	-0.18	0.24	-0.81	0.57	-2.40	-3.24
Shares Outstanding Mil	2,611	2,592	2,581	2,605	2,585	2,585
Return on Equity %	-10.0	7.1	-5.4	4.4	-20.6	-36.4
Net Margin %	-38.4	45.8	ELB	97.3	ELB	ELB
Asset Turnover	0.2	0.1	0.0	0.0	0.0	0.1
Financial Leverage	1.6	1.8	1.5	1.6	1.6	1.6

Valuation Ratios

	Stock	Rel to Industry	Rel to S&P 500
Price/Earnings	NMF	—	—
Price/Book	1.0	0.6	0.3
Price/Sales	11.2	3.5	5.6
Price/Cash Flow	—	—	—

Major Fund Holders

	% of Fund Assets
Janus Aspen Strategic Value Instl	7.44
Janus 2	7.31
Yacktman Focused	7.10
McCarthy	7.04

Morningstar Grades

Growth [B+]	1998	1999	2000	2001
Revenue %	10.9	-29.1	58.3	34.9
Earnings/Share %	NMF	NMF	NMF	NMF
Book Value/Share %	88.8	337.2	-12.0	-11.0
Dividends/Share %	NMF	NMF	NMF	NMF

The firm's key ownership interests are in Discovery Communications, Starz Encore, and QVC (the latter two aren't consolidated in Liberty's financials), which are growing faster than broadcast channels because of their limited ad exposure.

Profitability [D+]	1999	2000	2001	TTM
Return on Assets %	-3.6	2.7	-12.8	-22.4
Oper Cash Flow $Mil	26	199	26	-98
- Cap Spending $Mil	55	221	358	253
= Free Cash Flow $Mil	-29	-22	-332	-351

The company has had to write off huge chunks of its portfolio over the past few years due to declines in market value. This has led to large net losses.

Financial Health [C]	1999	2000	2001	09-02
Long-term Debt $Mil	2,723	5,269	4,764	4,389
Total Equity $Mil	38,408	34,109	30,123	22,923
Debt/Equity Ratio	0.1	0.2	0.2	0.2

Debt to equity ratios have risen as the company has taken on more debt and written down the value of its investment portfolio. We are watching the company's balance sheet closely, but we aren't too worried right now.

Morningstar's Take By Jonathan Schrader, 12-14-2002 Stock Price as of Analysis: $9.44

We're not sold on Liberty. The company has some great assets and a respected leader in John Malone, but it is tough to value accurately, and so we're going to pass on it for now.

Liberty does not operate businesses, rather it buys stakes in companies with good long-term prospects. Most of these investments--like BET and QVC--have done very well over time. As the value of Liberty's investments have increased, so has Liberty's share of the media market and Malone's standing within the media and investment communities. Malone--who built TCI into the largest cable company in the U.S. before selling it to AT&T--has used his influence, his intelligence, and the capital of those who believe in him to build a firm that owns large stakes in some of the most important and valuable media companies in the world, including News Corp., Viacom, and AOL Time Warner.

The problem with this is that Liberty is more like a mutual fund than a functioning business. (In fact, the SEC is considering making Liberty beholden to the Investment Act of 1940, which governs mutual funds.) Liberty does have some investments that it consolidates into its financials, but the value of these businesses is small relative to Liberty's total worth.

Most of Liberty's value comes from ownership stakes in companies in which Liberty does not exercise full control. As such, Liberty has limited access to these cash flows, and so a typical discounted cash flow model does not work. Thus, most investors rely upon the market to estimate the value of Liberty's public holdings, and comparable-multiple analysis to determine the value of its stake in private firms.

The problem with this is that the market often misprices these assets. Evidence of this would be the enormous swings in the market capitalizations of media companies over the past five years. Our old $13 fair value was based upon one of these sum of the parts valuations, using market prices and multiples. Given the large decline in value of Liberty's public holdings over the past few years, we think that this $13 estimate is probably a pretty conservative value for Liberty.

However, we think that we can do even better, so we are working on a new model based on the fair values of the various companies in which Liberty has invested. This is a time-consuming process, but one which we feel is worth the time. Until we determine this new estimate, we are going to pass on Liberty.

Limited Brands LTD

	Rating	Risk	Moat Size	Fair Value	Last Close	Yield %
	★★★	Med.	None	$18.00	$13.93	2.2

Company Profile

Limited Brands sells women's apparel and men's and children's apparel. The company sells its products through retail stores and mail-order catalog operations. Limited Brands operates about 5,100 stores, including the stores of Intimate Brands, of which Limited Brands owns 84%. It also has four catalog divisions. Its stores include Express, The Limited, Lerner New York, Lane Bryant, Victoria's Secret, Structure, Henri Bendel, Bath & Body Works, and Galyan's. Catalogs include Victoria's Secret, Lane Bryant Direct, Roaman's, and Lerner Direct.

Management

Founder and CEO Leslie Wexner is a hands-on leader. He recognized that Limited was losing sales to its competitors and has taken steps to improve the company's apparel lines to keep up with trends.

Strategy

Limited Brands has ditched its old name (Limited, Inc.) to underscore its focus on developing a strong portfolio of brands. In an effort to simplify its corporate structure, the retailer repurchased all publicly held shares in Intimate Brands in March. Now, its primary goals are to offer products that fit many different lifestyles and to keep up with the latest trends.

Three Limited Parkway
Columbus, OH 43216
www.limited.com

Morningstar Grades

Growth [D]	1999	2000	2001	2002
Revenue %	1.9	4.3	3.5	-7.3
Earnings/Share %	976.6	-75.9	-4.0	24.0
Book Value/Share %	18.0	6.2	11.5	21.1
Dividends/Share %	8.3	15.4	0.0	0.0

Sales growth at mature Limited Brands has trailed that of the younger, smaller clothing retailers for years. We expect growth to be a mixed bag, as customers' reactions to economic and fashion trends fluctuate.

Profitability [A-]	2000	2001	2002	TTM
Return on Assets %	11.2	10.5	11.0	7.7
Oper Cash Flow $Mil	599	498	969	941
- Cap Spending $Mil	365	469	348	261
= Free Cash Flow $Mil	234	29	621	680

Limited's historical returns on assets are inflated as a result of gains associated with three major spin-offs. Excluding these gains, profitability has varied greatly.

Financial Health [A+]	2000	2001	2002	10-02
Long-term Debt $Mil	400	400	250	248
Total Equity $Mil	2,147	2,316	2,744	4,526
Debt/Equity Ratio	0.2	0.2	0.1	0.1

Limited generates solid cash flows and its balance sheet carries a manageable level of debt. Management's tendency to reduce inventory during periods of slow sales helps preserve cash.

	Industry	Investment Style	Stock Type	Sector
	Clothing Stores	Mid Core	Slow Growth	Consumer Services

Competition	Market Cap $Mil	Debt/ Equity	12 Mo Trailing Sales $Mil	Price/Cash Flow	Return On Assets%	Total Return% 1 Yr	3 Yr
Limited Brands	7,287	0.1	9,260	7.7	7.7	-3.7	-9.6
Gap	13,509	0.8	13,582	11.5	2.0	12.1	-27.7
Abercrombie & Fitch A	1,997	0.0	1,463	7.2	20.0	-22.9	-7.6

Price Volatility

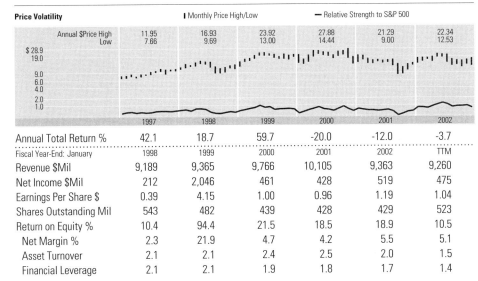

	1997	1998	1999	2000	2001	2002
Annual $Price High	11.95	16.93	23.92	27.88	21.29	22.34
Low	7.66	9.69	13.00	14.44	9.00	12.53
Annual Total Return %	42.1	18.7	59.7	-20.0	-12.0	-3.7

Fiscal Year-End: January	1998	1999	2000	2001	2002	TTM
Revenue $Mil	9,189	9,365	9,766	10,105	9,363	9,260
Net Income $Mil	212	2,046	461	428	519	475
Earnings Per Share $	0.39	4.15	1.00	0.96	1.19	1.04
Shares Outstanding Mil	543	482	439	428	429	523
Return on Equity %	10.4	94.4	21.5	18.5	18.9	10.5
Net Margin %	2.3	21.9	4.7	4.2	5.5	5.1
Asset Turnover	2.1	2.1	2.4	2.5	2.0	1.5
Financial Leverage	2.1	2.1	1.9	1.8	1.7	1.4

Valuation Ratios	Stock	Rel to Industry	Rel to S&P 500
Price/Earnings	13.4	0.7	0.6
Price/Book	1.6	0.4	0.5
Price/Sales	0.8	0.9	0.4
Price/Cash Flow	7.7	0.8	0.6

Major Fund Holders	% of Fund Assets
Rochdale Alpha	5.29
Managers AMG Rorer Mid Cap	3.42
Brandywine Advisors	3.35
Brandywine Blue	3.33

Morningstar's Take By Roz Bryant, 12-04-2002 Stock Price as of Analysis: $16.00

Limited Brands' diversification strategy has served investors well. But we expect growth to be slow over the next several years, and we'd require a 50% margin of safety to our fair value estimate before investing.

The company's diverse concepts shield its revenue from the volatility experienced by many one-format, one-brand specialty apparel chains. Sales are generated by several different store chains that sell men's and women's apparel, lingerie, and bath products; solid results in one or two divisions can offset poor performance in others. Also, newer chains can deliver a measure of square-footage growth to offset older concepts' lack of expansion opportunities. Limited Brands has posted positive sales growth in nine of the past ten years.

In the past, Limited Brands boosted profits with gains from sales of several of its retail concepts, including Abercrombie & Fitch and Galyans. More recently, the firm decided to part with Lerner New York/New York & Company. Lerner's sales productivity per square foot had been the lowest of all Limited's retail concepts, so we expect this divestiture to improve overall margins.

Limited Brands' fate is now largely in the hands of its Intimate Brands franchises. Victoria's Secret and Bath & Body Works, which constitute Intimate Brands, now produce more than 50% of Limited's total revenue. Both chains are far more profitable than Limited's other apparel stores, and are being expanded modestly. Intimate Brands' operating margins top 13% compared with apparel's 2%, and we expect its square footage to increase about 5% annually for the next couple of years.

However, the rest of Limited Brands' portfolio consists of mature retail concepts whose heydays were years ago. All of its apparel brands are more than 20 years old, which means that expansion opportunities have largely dried up. In fact, two of Limited's three apparel concepts experienced a decline in square footage in 2002. Barring a new smash-hit retail introduction, revenue growth will rely more heavily on customer traffic and transactions than in the past, which could lead to more sales volatility than the firm is accustomed to. Moreover, the spending required to reinvigorate customer interest is likely to be costly, and potentially ineffective.

We expect growth to slow over the next five years, and wouldn't buy the stock unless it traded well below our fair value estimate.

MORNINGSTAR® Stocks 500

Linear Technology LLTC

	Rating ★★★	Risk Med.	Moat Size Wide	Fair Value $24.00	Last Close $25.72	Yield % 0.7

Company Profile

Linear Technology manufactures analog semiconductors used in telecommunication equipment, computers, video equipment, industrial controls, automotive systems, and satellites. These chips monitor, condition, amplify, and transform continuous signals, like temperature, pressure, weight, light, sound, and speed. The company markets its products to customers in the United States and overseas. Linear operates plants in the United States and Malaysia.

Management

Founder and CEO Bob Swanson is an industry veteran, with long roots in the analog chip sector. Linear's consistent financial history speaks to how well the company is managed.

Strategy

Linear Technology has a disciplined and cost-conscious business model. The firm focuses on making standardized products for high-performance niches of the analog chip market. This doesn't mean its chips are commodities, however; Linear prides itself on designing proprietary products for myriad technology segments. The firm also manufactures its own chips.

1630 McCarthy Blvd.
Milpitas, CA 95035-7417
www.linear.com

Morningstar Grades

Growth [D]	1999	2000	2001	2002
Revenue %	4.5	39.3	37.8	-47.3
Earnings/Share %	5.2	44.3	46.6	-53.5
Book Value/Share %	17.5	42.0	33.1	0.6
Dividends/Share %	20.8	24.1	44.4	30.8

Linear is a paragon of consistent, above-average growth. Sales have risen each year over the past decade, except fiscal 2002 when sales dropped 47%. On average, however, sales have risen 18% per year over ten years--much faster than the industry.

Profitability [A+]	2000	2001	2002	TTM
Return on Assets %	19.1	21.2	9.9	10.8
Oper Cash Flow $Mil	442	560	257	279
- Cap Spending $Mil	80	128	18	12
= Free Cash Flow $Mil	362	432	239	267

Linear chooses its markets wisely and manages expenses shrewdly. Operating margins are usually north of 50% and gross margins are typically above 70%.

Financial Health [A+]	2000	2001	2002	09-02
Long-term Debt $Mil	—	—	—	—
Total Equity $Mil	1,322	1,782	1,781	1,702
Debt/Equity Ratio	—	—	—	—

With no debt on its balance sheet and about 75% of total assets in cash, Linear Technology is in great health. The firm is a cash cow, since it spends far less than peers on capital equipment.

Industry	Investment Style	Stock Type	Sector
Semiconductors	▦ Large Growth	➡ Slow Growth	▣ Hardware

Competition

	Market Cap $Mil	Debt/ Equity	12 Mo Trailing Sales $Mil	Price/Cash Flow	Return On Assets%	Total Return% 1 Yr	3 Yr
Linear Technology	8,024	—	534	28.8	10.8	-33.7	-11.1
Texas Instruments	25,982	0.1	8,024	12.8	0.9	-46.2	-32.5
Maxim Integrated Products	10,584	—	1,072	27.3	13.0	-37.0	-11.2

Price Volatility

		Monthly Price High/Low		— Relative Strength to S&P 500		
Annual $Price High Low	18.75 10.13	22.63 9.78	41.59 20.88	74.75 35.06	65.13 29.45	47.50 18.92

	1997	1998	1999	2000	2001	2002
Annual Total Return %	31.9	56.0	60.2	29.5	-15.3	-33.7

Fiscal Year-end: June	1998	1999	2000	2001	2002	TTM
Revenue $Mil	485	507	706	973	512	534
Net Income $Mil	181	194	288	427	198	206
Earnings Per Share $	0.58	0.61	0.88	1.29	0.60	0.63
Shares Outstanding Mil	307	304	310	317	319	312
Return on Equity %	23.9	21.4	21.8	24.0	11.1	12.1
Net Margin %	37.3	38.3	40.8	43.9	38.6	38.6
Asset Turnover	0.5	0.5	0.5	0.5	0.3	0.3
Financial Leverage	1.2	1.2	1.1	1.1	1.1	1.1

Valuation Ratios	Stock	Rel to Industry	Rel to S&P 500
Price/Earnings	40.8	1.0	1.7
Price/Book	4.7	1.6	1.5
Price/Sales	15.0	3.9	7.5
Price/Cash Flow	28.8	2.4	2.2

Major Fund Holders	% of Fund Assets
Marketocracy Technology Plus Fund	8.32
Phoenix-Kayne Large Cap X	5.30
Strong Advisor Technology A	4.86
Pin Oak Aggressive Stock	4.81

Morningstar's Take By Jeremy Lopez, 11-08-2002 Stock Price as of Analysis: $28.23

Linear Technology's fundamentals are among the best in the chip industry, but this performance has not gone unnoticed.

Few chipmakers have performed better than Linear over the past decade. With an average annual growth rate of 18% for ten years, Linear's has outperformed the industry average and its closest peers. More impressive is the consistency of this growth. Linear has managed to buck the notorious swings of the industry, increasing sales every year except 2001, while the industry has had several down years. Linear's profitability has also been stellar and consistent. Operating margins have averaged almost 50% over the past ten years, while gross margins have averaged more than 70%. Linear investors have certainly been rewarded, with the stock up 27% per year on average over the past decade.

Linear's track record has been outstanding for several reasons. The first is its niche in analog chips. Analog chips are used in many end-market applications, like PCs, telecom infrastructure, cell phones, cars, and even consumer appliances. Growth in these markets coupled with rising analog content per product has driven analog demand at a rate faster than the broader chip industry. Also overall analog chip prices and demand are not as volatile as other commodity products, like memory chips. This is all the more true for Linear since it focuses on high-end analog products, which are highly specialized, don't have direct substitutes, and enjoy long product cycles. Finally, the firm's margins and competitive position are protected by high barriers to entry in analog, which are a function of unique chip design challenges in the analog world and the resulting scarcity of analog engineering talent.

The main question with Linear as an investment is valuation. The market has historically given the stock one of the industry's richest multiples thanks to the factors mentioned above. If growth permanently slows, or competition proves to permanently crimp returns on capital, though, Linear could lose this premium. While we've historically been big fans of the stock, we've reevaluated our position. We've concluded that our outlook on the firm has been too optimistic, and that we've underestimated the size and length of the current downturn. While we continue to think Linear is a great company, we think investors should hold off on buying the stock until they are better compensated for the risk they are assuming. A 30% discount to our fair value estimate would meet this requirement.

Liz Claiborne LIZ

	Rating	Risk	Moat Size	Fair Value	Last Close	Yield %
	★	Med.	None	$26.00	$29.65	0.8

Company Profile

Liz Claiborne designs clothing and related items. Its products include women's apparel, accessories, and fragrances that are sold under brand names like Liz Claiborne, LizSport, LizWear, Villager, Elisabeth, dana b. & karen, Emma James, Claiborne, First Issue, Russ, JH Collectibles, and Dana Buchman. The company also makes women's jewelry and cologne and men's clothing and cologne. Liz Claiborne operates 113 retail stores under the Liz Claiborne, Elisabeth, Claiborne for Men, and Dana Buchman names in the United States and abroad. It also operates 102 outlet stores.

Management

CEO Paul Charron came to Liz Claiborne in 1994 after holding executive positions at apparel manufacturer VF Corporation. Senior vice president Robert Zane joined the firm in 1995 after operating his own textile manufacturing company.

Strategy

Liz Claiborne has developed a well-rounded portfolio of apparel brands. The company has historically focused on women's careerwear; but in recent years, it has used brands in other categories, like jeans, jewelry, and men's wear, to reach a wider audience and protect earnings against volatility.

1441 Broadway
New York, NY 10018
www.lizclaiborne.com

Morningstar Grades

Growth [A]	1998	1999	2000	2001
Revenue %	5.1	10.7	10.6	11.1
Earnings/Share %	-2.3	21.4	9.9	6.7
Book Value/Share %	13.4	-1.7	6.0	29.8
Dividends/Share %	-0.2	0.0	0.0	0.0

New brand acquisitions and licensing agreements have fueled Liz Claiborne's consistent year-over-year revenue growth. Growth relies heavily on the company's ability to make additional external purchases and introduce new product lines.

Profitability [A]	1999	2000	2001	TTM
Return on Assets %	13.6	12.2	9.8	9.5
Oper Cash Flow $Mil	301	268	329	526
- Cap Spending $Mil	75	67	82	87
= Free Cash Flow $Mil	226	201	247	438

Liz Claiborne's profitability has fluctuated over the years, but margins have consistently fallen short of Jones Apparel's performance. Acquisitions and new brands with higher cost structures have driven overhead expenses even higher in recent years.

Financial Health [A]	1999	2000	2001	09-02
Long-term Debt $Mil	116	269	387	454
Total Equity $Mil	902	834	1,056	1,229
Debt/Equity Ratio	0.1	0.3	0.4	0.4

Acquisitions haven't significantly marred the balance sheet. Liz Claiborne's debt/equity has crept up over the past few years, but free cash flow has remained solid.

Industry	Investment Style	Stock Type	Sector
Apparel Makers	▦ Mid Core	↻ Cyclical	🚗 Consumer Goods

Competition	Market Cap $Mil	Debt/ Equity	12 Mo Trailing Sales $Mil	Price/Cash Flow	Return On Assets%	Total Return% 1 Yr	3 Yr
Liz Claiborne	3,162	0.4	3,610	6.0	9.5	20.1	19.4
Jones Apparel Group	4,572	0.4	4,246	5.2	7.5	6.8	12.4
VF	3,903		5,305				

Price Volatility

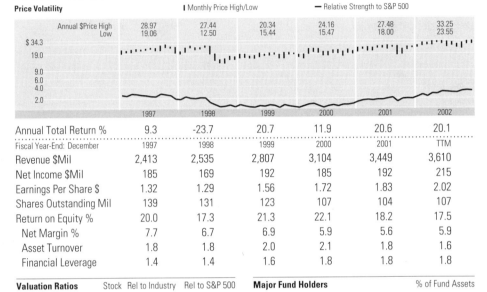

Annual $Price High Low	28.97 19.06	27.44 12.50	20.34 15.44	24.16 15.47	27.48 18.00	33.25 23.55

	1997	1998	1999	2000	2001	2002
Annual Total Return %	9.3	-23.7	20.7	11.9	20.6	20.1
Fiscal Year-End: December	1997	1998	1999	2000	2001	TTM
Revenue $Mil	2,413	2,535	2,807	3,104	3,449	3,610
Net Income $Mil	185	169	192	185	192	215
Earnings Per Share $	1.32	1.29	1.56	1.72	1.83	2.02
Shares Outstanding Mil	139	131	123	107	104	107
Return on Equity %	20.0	17.3	21.3	22.1	18.2	17.5
Net Margin %	7.7	6.7	6.9	5.9	5.6	5.9
Asset Turnover	1.8	1.8	2.0	2.1	1.8	1.6
Financial Leverage	1.4	1.4	1.6	1.8	1.8	1.8

Valuation Ratios	Stock	Rel to Industry	Rel to S&P 500
Price/Earnings	14.7	0.9	0.6
Price/Book	2.6	1.3	0.8
Price/Sales	0.9	1.0	0.4
Price/Cash Flow	6.0	1.2	0.5

Major Fund Holders	% of Fund Assets
Navellier Large Cap Value	5.78
Managers AMG Rorer Mid Cap	5.40
Electric City Value	4.52
FMI Common Stock	3.64

Morningstar's Take By Roz Bryant, 12-06-2002 Stock Price as of Analysis: $32.00

By placing its eggs in more than one basket, Liz Claiborne shields its earnings from fashion-driven volatility. However, the apparel maker still comes in second to rival Jones Apparel in terms of operating efficiency and profitability, and we'd wait for shares to dip to the low teens before picking them up.

Cooking in several pots has kept Liz Claiborne from becoming irrelevant. While the firm continues to nurture its core women's careerwear lines, its brand portfolio has widened to include jewelry and men's wear. The apparel maker has also expanded its reach both geographically and by channel, which has lessened its dependence on the health of the U.S. economy and department store market share. It now operates more than 400 retail stores, and thanks to last year's acquisition of European clothing maker Mexx, about one fourth of them are outside the United States.

Diversifying has helped insulate Liz Claiborne's financial performance against the volatility typical in the apparel industry, promoting steady growth. Its five-year annual sales growth average of 9.3% is not the result of drastic swings. Rather, top-line growth has been consistently positive over the past five years, amid a flurry of brand acquisitions and new licensing agreements. The addition of Mexx

illustrates the success of the company's diversification strategy. Strong performance in Mexx's wholesale and retail businesses has offset recent sales declines in Liz Claiborne's careerwear and accessories businesses, helping the firm post respectable sales growth.

However, Liz Claiborne has been less profitable than Jones Apparel for years, and we expect it to continue to deliver an inferior level of profitability. Both companies follow a similar diversification strategy, using acquisitions and licensing agreements as growth vehicles. But Claiborne's overhead expenses make up a larger percentage of sales than Jones'; since 1998 its operating margin has averaged 8.3%, compared with 14.1% for Jones. The disparity indicates that the Liz Claiborne hasn't kept as close an eye on costs, nor has it integrated acquisitions as successfully as its rival.

In our opinion, Jones Apparel holds the top slot among apparel wholesalers. Still, we admire Liz Claiborne's steady past performance and believe that diversification efforts will help offset the negative impact of fashion fluctuations and local economic cycles. With that in mind, we'd consider the shares if they fell to the low teens.

M⊙RNINGSTAR® Stocks 500

Lockheed Martin LMT

	Rating	Risk	Moat Size	Fair Value	Last Close	Yield %
	★★	Med.	Narrow	$56.00	$57.75	0.8

Company Profile

Lockheed Martin manufactures aerospace products that are marketed to government agencies in the United States and overseas. The company produces spacecraft, missiles, and launch vehicles, and jointly runs NASA's space shuttle program. Lockheed Martin also makes cargo and special-mission aircraft and tactical fighters. In addition, it provides nuclear-management services to the Department of Defense. U.S. government contracts account for approximately 71% of the company's revenue.

Management

CEO and chairman Vance Coffman has been with Lockheed since 1967. Former CFO Robert Stevens became president and COO in October 2000.

Strategy

Lockheed is focused on strong free cash flow and debt reduction, so it can invest in profitable long-term projects like the F-35 fighter jet. The company has been selling assets in an attempt to streamline its focus on defense, technology, and communication.

6801 Rockledge Drive
Bethesda, MD 20817-1877
www.lockheedmartin.com

Morningstar Grades

Growth [B]	1998	1999	2000	2001
Revenue %	-7.0	-3.1	-1.8	-2.2
Earnings/Share %	NMF	-62.4	NMF	NMF
Book Value/Share %	-99.9	2.2	8.0	-16.2
Dividends/Share %	2.5	7.3	-50.0	0.0

Revenue has declined an average of 4% over the past five years as a result of historically low defense spending and some divestitures. Revenue should rise over the next few years as the United States increases its annual defense budget.

Profitability [D+]	1999	2000	2001	TTM
Return on Assets %	1.3	-1.7	-3.8	-2.3
Oper Cash Flow $Mil	1,077	2,016	1,825	2,359
- Cap Spending $Mil	669	500	619	703
= Free Cash Flow $Mil	408	1,516	1,206	1,656

Profitability has suffered recently because of large one-time charges. However, operating margins have improved over the past year, and we expect margins to expand gradually.

Financial Health [B]	1999	2000	2001	09-02
Long-term Debt $Mil	11,427	9,065	7,422	6,693
Total Equity $Mil	6,361	7,160	6,443	7,700
Debt/Equity Ratio	1.8	1.3	1.2	0.9

Lockheed is using asset sales to shore up the balance sheet by slashing debt, which stands at $6.7 billion. If cash flow continues to be strong, as we expect, the firm should be able to reduce its debt even further.

Industry	Investment Style	Stock Type	Sector
Aerospace & Defense	▦ Large Core	◪ Distressed	✸ Industrial Mats

Competition

	Market Cap $Mil	Debt/ Equity	12 Mo Trailing Sales $Mil	Price/Cash Flow	Return On Assets%	Total Return% 1 Yr	3 Yr
Lockheed Martin	26,512	0.9	26,132	11.2	-2.3	24.7	47.9
Boeing	27,691	1.1	56,071	9.9	0.0	-13.4	-4.9
Honeywell International	19,705	0.5	22,272	8.7	5.6	-27.3	-22.9

Price Volatility

| | | Monthly Price High/Low | | | — Relative Strength to S&P 500 | |

Annual $Price High Low	56.72 39.13	58.94 41.00	46.00 16.38	37.11 16.50	52.00 31.00	71.50 45.85
	1997	1998	1999	2000	2001	2002

Annual Total Return %	9.5	-12.6	-46.9	58.0	39.0	24.7
Fiscal Year-end: December	1997	1998	1999	2000	2001	TTM
Revenue $Mil	27,764	25,809	24,999	24,541	23,990	26,132
Net Income $Mil	-1	1,001	382	-519	-1,046	-661
Earnings Per Share $	-1.56	2.63	0.99	-1.29	-2.42	-1.61
Shares Outstanding Mil	389	376	382	402	427	459
Return on Equity %	0.0	16.3	6.0	-7.2	-16.2	-8.6
Net Margin %	0.0	3.9	1.5	-2.1	-4.4	-2.5
Asset Turnover	1.0	0.9	0.8	0.8	0.9	0.9
Financial Leverage	5.5	4.7	4.8	4.2	4.3	3.8

Valuation Ratios	Stock	Rel to Industry	Rel to S&P 500
Price/Earnings	NMF	—	—
Price/Book	3.4	1.4	1.1
Price/Sales	1.0	1.1	0.5
Price/Cash Flow	11.2	1.1	0.8

Major Fund Holders	% of Fund Assets
Reserve Informed Investors Growth R	14.77
Fidelity Select Defense & Aerospace	10.98
Fidelity Select Air Transportation	10.54
PBHG Large Cap 20 PBHG	8.24

Morningstar's Take By Nicolas Owens, 12-15-2002 Stock Price as of Analysis: $50.42

Lockheed Martin is showing improvement, but we're still not sold on it as an investment.

Lockheed Martin has been mired in all types of issues in the past few years, most of them due to large acquisitions and poor investments. It appears, however, that a recovery is under way; one of the most important pieces of evidence is improving cash flow. Lockheed's recovery will probably get a boost from expected increases in defense spending over the next few years. We are still leery of investing, though, given the firm's lingering business and financial risk.

Lockheed Martin is the big daddy of defense contractors, and several of its programs--including the F-22 Raptor and F-35 Joint Strike Fighter jets--seem to have priority status at the Pentagon. But cost overruns and budget uncertainty have complicated these high-profile projects and mar the prospect of their profitability.

An important risk is that Congress must approve funding for defense projects every year. It isn't uncommon to see large-scale projects--like the B-2 bomber--dramatically cut because of spiraling costs or changes in military priorities. The F-22 program has been the subject of much debate for these very reasons. Some have questioned whether the F-22--a land-based fighter that would require bases close to the action--fits into future U.S. military strategy at all. If the top brass at the Pentagon starts to believe that it doesn't, the F-22 could be killed in order to shift funds to other projects.

The F-35 program has also been the topic of much debate, as the Navy and Marines have floated the idea of sharing aircraft resources. This would allow the branches to order fewer planes, probably reducing the overall size of the F-35 program. While this idea hasn't been embraced by the Pentagon, we have seen reductions in the estimated size of this program. This hurts Lockheed, because the more planes it can produce, the more easily it amortizes fixed costs over each plane.

Lockheed investors also must contend with the company's financial risk. Years of consolidation have left the balance sheet stretched pretty thin. While cash flow has been improving--which should help Lockheed pay down debt--the firm's debt is only two notches above junk status, and we are still leery of the company's overall financial health.

Given the risks and the stock's unattractive valuation, we wouldn't buy Lockheed Martin.

Lowe's Companies LOW

	Rating	Risk	Moat Size	Fair Value	Last Close	Yield %
	★★	Med.	Narrow	$35.00	$37.50	0.2

Company Profile

Lowe's is a specialty retailer serving the home decor, home electronics, and building contractor markets. The company operates more than 700 stores, predominantly across the Midwest, South Atlantic, and South Central regions of the United States. Each store combines the merchandise, sales, and service of a home-improvement center, a building contractor supply business, and a consumer durables retailer. The stores are divided into big, medium, and small size categories. Big stores, which have more than 100,000 square feet of selling space, account for 79% of company sales.

Management

Robert Tillman has been president and CEO since 1996 and chairman since 1998. He heads a very experienced senior management team--the top 20 executives average almost 20 years with the firm and have guided the firm's smooth expansion so far.

Strategy

Lowe's is expanding into large urban and suburban markets that were once thought to be proprietary to Home Depot. The company plans to open another 130-140 stores in both 2003 and 2004; new stores are roughly the same size as those of its chief rival. Lowe's is also emphasizing better service for professional contractors and installation services for do-it-for-me customers.

1605 Curtis Bridge Road
Wilkesboro, NC 28697
www.lowes.com

Morningstar Grades

Growth [A+]	1999	2000	2001	2002
Revenue %	20.0	19.3	18.1	17.7
Earnings/Share %	28.8	30.6	20.6	23.2
Book Value/Share %	37.3	26.0	17.2	18.5
Dividends/Share %	6.5	6.3	12.0	10.7

The march into Home Depot's territory has been successful. Bigger stores in the largest metropolitan markets have led to 21% growth in sales and 28% growth in net income over the past five years. We think strong growth still lies ahead.

Profitability [A]	2000	2001	2002	TTM
Return on Assets %	7.5	7.1	7.4	8.7
Oper Cash Flow $Mil	1,197	1,130	1,613	2,670
- Cap Spending $Mil	1,472	2,332	2,199	1,974
= Free Cash Flow $Mil	-275	-1,202	-586	696

Operating margins have improved from 7% in 1999 to 9% so far in 2002. We expect them to exceed 10% in the next couple years. Supply-chain initiatives, better inventory management, and fixed-cost leverage should continue pushing up profitability.

Financial Health [B]	2000	2001	2002	10-02
Long-term Debt $Mil	1,727	2,698	3,734	3,739
Total Equity $Mil	4,695	5,495	6,674	7,958
Debt/Equity Ratio	0.4	0.5	0.6	0.5

Lowe's is generating impressive earnings growth, which is translating into accelerating operating cash flow. However, the company is spending all of its cash on new stores, and probably won't generate positive free cash flow until 2006.

Industry	Investment Style	Stock Type	Sector
Home Supply	▦ Large Growth	↗ Classic Growth	▤ Consumer Services

Competition

	Market Cap $Mil	Debt/ Equity	12 Mo Trailing Sales $Mil	Price/Cash Flow	Return On Assets%	Total Return% 1 Yr	3 Yr
Lowe's Companies	29,285	0.5	25,627	11.0	8.7	-19.0	12.7
Home Depot	56,450	0.1	57,336	8.8	11.8	-52.7	-24.8
Sears Roebuck	7,576	3.3	41,156	—	2.1	-48.6	-6.5

Price Volatility

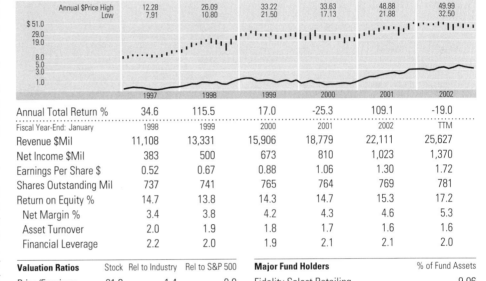

	Monthly Price High/Low	— Relative Strength to S&P 500				
Annual $Price High Low	12.28 7.91	26.09 10.80	33.22 21.50	33.63 17.13	48.88 21.88	49.99 32.50

$ 51.0
29.0
19.0
8.0
5.0
3.0
1.0

	1997	1998	1999	2000	2001	2002
Annual Total Return %	34.6	115.5	17.0	-25.3	109.1	-19.0

Fiscal Year-End: January	1998	1999	2000	2001	2002	TTM
Revenue $Mil	11,108	13,331	15,906	18,779	22,111	25,627
Net Income $Mil	383	500	673	810	1,023	1,370
Earnings Per Share $	0.52	0.67	0.88	1.06	1.30	1.72
Shares Outstanding Mil	737	741	765	764	769	781
Return on Equity %	14.7	13.8	14.3	14.7	15.3	17.2
Net Margin %	3.4	3.8	4.2	4.3	4.6	5.3
Asset Turnover	2.0	1.9	1.8	1.7	1.6	1.6
Financial Leverage	2.2	2.0	1.9	2.1	2.1	2.0

Valuation Ratios	Stock	Rel to Industry	Rel to S&P 500
Price/Earnings	21.8	1.4	0.9
Price/Book	3.7	1.3	1.2
Price/Sales	1.1	1.2	0.6
Price/Cash Flow	11.0	1.2	0.8

Major Fund Holders	% of Fund Assets
Fidelity Select Retailing	9.06
Sextant Growth	6.48
CDC Nvest Targeted Equity A	6.08
Fairport Growth	5.63

Morningstar's Take By Tom Goetzinger, 11-26-2002 Stock Price as of Analysis: $39.65

It's still full speed ahead for Lowe's and its aggressive expansion plan, but we'd require about a 30% discount to our fair value estimate to purchase shares in case the company starts to overheat.

Lowe's has produced some powerful results over the past five years. Its store base has swelled from fewer than 500 units at the end of 1997 to more than 800 now. Along the way, sales increased an average of 21% per year, while net income surged 28% annually. These tremendous gains were the result of an ambitious, somewhat risky, and successful foray into Home Depot's prized regions.

The incessant trespassing has allowed Lowe's to break up what once looked like a near monopoly by Home Depot, and turn it into a very competitive duopoly. Over the past five years, Lowe's has constructed about 65% of its new stores in the large urban and suburban areas that were once strictly the domain of Home Depot orange boxes. With plans to add another 250-300 stores over the next two years, Lowe's and its blue boxes are making their presence felt.

The big-city battle is important on a number of fronts for Lowe's. Its larger stores in the most populated urban and suburban areas generate double the sales of stores in rural areas or small towns, though they require just 50% more capital to build. They also produce wider margins because Lowe's is able to spread operating costs over a larger sales base. It's no surprise that returns on invested capital have improved from 10% five years ago to 13% today.

However, these operating margins and returns on capital still trail those of Home Depot, and aren't likely to catch up anytime soon, in our opinion. Moreover, Lowe's is continuing its mammoth expansion during a period of economic queasiness with a pretty sizable debt load on its books. Most of its recent store growth has been funded by operating cash flow, but a slowdown in sales and earnings would jeopardize this, forcing the firm to borrow even more.

We still forecast a few more fast laps around the track for Lowe's; we expect 15% annual sales growth and 18% annual earnings growth from 2003 to 2005. But given the state of the economy and competitive pressure from the formidable Home Depot, we'd look for a sizable margin of safety to our fair value estimate. We'd buy in around $25.

 MORNINGSTAR® Stocks 500

LSI Logic LSI

	Rating	Risk	Moat Size	Fair Value	Last Close	Yield %
	★★★	High	None	$10.00	$5.77	0.0

Company Profile

LSI Logic designs application-specific integrated circuits. Its products include customized chips and chipsets used in the electronics, computer, telecommunication, and entertainment industries in the United States and abroad. The company's circuits are used in direct-broadcast satellite equipment, digital video discs, cable television decoders, and networking applications. LSI Logic markets its products in the United States and overseas. Foreign sales account for approximately 63% of the company's revenue.

Management

CEO Wilf Corrigan co-founded LSI in 1981 and is one of the founders of the Semiconductor Industry Association; he owns about 4% of LSI shares. The flight of young managers raises a concern about succession planning (Corrigan is in his mid-60s).

Strategy

LSI Logic wants to tap into higher-growth markets of the chip sector--mainly communication--and use its specialized portfolio of technology to produce highly customized products. The firm can meet a customer's various needs thanks to a library of intellectual property and manufacturing capabilities.

1551 McCarthy Boulevard
Milpitas, CA 95035
www.lsilogic.com

Morningstar Grades

Growth [C]	1998	1999	2000	2001
Revenue %	14.7	37.7	31.0	-34.8
Earnings/Share %	NMF	NMF	204.3	NMF
Book Value/Share %	-2.3	18.6	16.3	-3.9
Dividends/Share %	NMF	NMF	NMF	NMF

LSI's sales have held up better than most chipmakers' because of acquisitions and the firm's exposure to consumer products, which have done well. LSI's sales growth has historically been decent, but below average.

Profitability [C]	1999	2000	2001	TTM
Return on Assets %	2.1	5.6	-21.4	-11.6
Oper Cash Flow $Mil	444	565	119	68
- Cap Spending $Mil	205	277	224	96
= Free Cash Flow $Mil	239	289	-105	-28

LSI could be profitable in this year's fourth quarter. Its margins and returns on capital tend to be below average relative to other chipmakers', mainly because of a lack of production scale and lower average selling prices for its chips.

Financial Health [D+]	1999	2000	2001	09-02
Long-term Debt $Mil	0	0	0	1,287
Total Equity $Mil	1,856	2,498	2,480	2,296
Debt/Equity Ratio	0.0	0.0	0.0	0.6

With a debt/equity ratio of 0.6, LSI's balance sheet isn't as strong as many other chipmakers'. But there's little cause for concern; its cash position is sufficient and cash flow has been spotty, but mainly positive.

Industry	Investment Style	Stock Type	Sector
Semiconductors	◨ Mid Core	➜ Slow Growth	▣ Hardware

Competition	Market Cap $Mil	Debt/ Equity	12 Mo Trailing Sales $Mil	Price/Cash Flow	Return On Assets%	Total Return% 1 Yr	3 Yr
LSI Logic	2,146	0.6	1,743	31.7	-11.6	-63.4	-43.3
IBM	130,982	0.8	82,442	9.0	5.8	-35.5	-11.1
STMicroelectronics NV	17,362	—	6,357	—	—	—	—

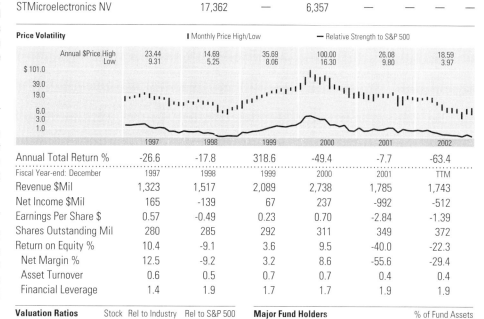

Price Volatility   ❙ Monthly Price High/Low   — Relative Strength to S&P 500

Annual $Price High Low	23.44 9.31	14.69 5.25	35.69 8.06	100.00 16.30	26.08 9.80	18.59 3.97

$ 101.0 / 39.0 / 19.0 / 6.0 / 3.0 / 1.0

	1997	1998	1999	2000	2001	2002
Annual Total Return %	-26.6	-17.8	318.6	-49.4	-7.7	-63.4

Fiscal Year-end: December	1997	1998	1999	2000	2001	TTM
Revenue $Mil	1,323	1,517	2,089	2,738	1,785	1,743
Net Income $Mil	165	-139	67	237	-992	-512
Earnings Per Share $	0.57	-0.49	0.23	0.70	-2.84	-1.39
Shares Outstanding Mil	280	285	292	311	349	372
Return on Equity %	10.4	-9.1	3.6	9.5	-40.0	-22.3
Net Margin %	12.5	-9.2	3.2	8.6	-55.6	-29.4
Asset Turnover	0.6	0.5	0.7	0.7	0.4	0.4
Financial Leverage	1.4	1.9	1.7	1.7	1.9	1.9

Valuation Ratios	Stock	Rel to Industry	Rel to S&P 500
Price/Earnings	NMF	—	—
Price/Book	0.9	0.3	0.3
Price/Sales	1.2	0.3	0.6
Price/Cash Flow	31.7	2.7	2.4

Major Fund Holders	% of Fund Assets
Dessauer Global Equity	6.55
Dean Large Cap Value A	2.67
Parnassus	2.58
Victory Diversified Stock A	2.13

Morningstar's Take By Jeremy Lopez, 12-17-2002   Stock Price as of Analysis: $6.19

We don't expect much more than average financial performance from LSI Logic. Because of this, we would need a pretty wide margin of safety to recommend the stock.

LSI Logic is a specialty shop, best known for making ASICs, or application-specific integrated circuits. The firm has a library of intellectual property at its customers' disposal to help them design custom parts for their own products. These custom chips are made for myriad tech applications, including consumer electronics, computer storage, and networking gear. Once a custom chip is designed into a customer's product, LSI keeps that customer for the life of the product. Its contract to produce key components for Sony's PlayStation 2 is a good example of locking into a product with nice prospects.

However, our enthusiasm for LSI is tempered by the tough competition in ASICs. Not only do ASIC makers compete with each other for design wins, but they also compete with makers of programmable logic devices (PLDs) like Xilinx and Altera. While ASICs are often cheaper and can perform better, they are being replaced more often by PLDs in certain tech applications because of the time-to-market advantages PLDs offer. So even assuming a more

solid long-term outlook for technology goods, ASIC makers may have a tough time growing faster than the broader chip market.

We're also not particularly fond of the economics of LSI's business. Besides designing its chips, the firm also manufactures the bulk of its products in proprietary plants, which can be capital-intensive. For a firm without the sufficient scale and production volume to make in-house manufacturing worthwhile (unlike larger chipmakers like Intel and Texas Instruments), the high equipment and fixed costs of operating a chip plant can be burdensome. Given LSI's small sales base, the lack of scale and volume contributes to below-average margins and returns on capital.

In other words, LSI is stuck in the middle: It isn't large enough to scale its business, but its products fail to generate high enough margins to compensate for a lack of scale. The firm plans to eventually outsource 40% of its chip production and its new RapidChip platform will help make it more competitive with PLD makers. But for now, given LSI's relative unattractiveness, we'd like to see at least a 40% discount to our fair value estimate before we'd consider investing.

Lucent Technologies LU

	Rating	Risk	Moat Size	Fair Value	Last Close	Yield %
	★	High	Narrow	$0.60	$1.26	0.0

Company Profile

Lucent Technologies is one of the world's largest suppliers of communication equipment software and services. The company, which was spun off from AT&T in 1996, is a leading supplier to AT&T and the regional Bell operating companies as well as many other global telecom carriers. While it continues to sell traditional central office voice switches, Lucent has become a leading provider of wireless infrastructure, optical systems, data networking gear, and network access equipment. The vaunted Bell Laboratories R&D organization continues to provide research support.

Management

Aggressive accounting, rosy guidance, and several rounds of restructurings are all strikes against management. The most crucial strategic issue, however, is the company's inability to shrink fixed costs to a level consistent with lower sales.

Strategy

As a soup-to-nuts telecom supplier, Lucent's fortunes have been hammered as demand for complex phone gear has vanished. As a result, the company is in survival mode, trying desperately to avoid bankruptcy and ride out the telecom slump (after which, presumably, growth will resume).

600 Mountain Avenue
Murray Hill, NJ 07974

www.lucent.com

Industry	Investment Style	Stock Type	Sector
Wireline Equipment	▦ Mid Value	◆ Distressed	▣ Hardware

Competition	Market Cap $Mil	Debt/ Equity	12 Mo Trailing Sales $Mil	Price/Cash Flow	Return On Assets%	Total Return% 1 Yr	3 Yr
Lucent Technologies	4,545	NMF	12,321	—	-67.2	-75.2	-71.8
Cisco Systems	94,649	0.0	19,312	15.1	7.5	-27.7	-36.4
Siemens AG ADR	37,222	—	75,745	—	—	—	—

Price Volatility

| Monthly Price High/Low — Relative Strength to S&P 500

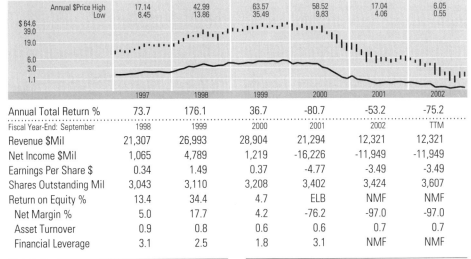

Annual $Price High Low	17.14 8.45	42.99 13.86	63.57 35.49	58.52 9.83	17.04 4.06	6.05 0.55
	1997	1998	1999	2000	2001	2002
Annual Total Return %	73.7	176.1	36.7	-80.7	-53.2	-75.2

Fiscal Year-End: September	1998	1999	2000	2001	2002	TTM
Revenue $Mil	21,307	26,993	28,904	21,294	12,321	12,321
Net Income $Mil	1,065	4,789	1,219	-16,226	-11,949	-11,949
Earnings Per Share $	0.34	1.49	0.37	-4.77	-3.49	-3.49
Shares Outstanding Mil	3,043	3,110	3,208	3,402	3,424	3,607
Return on Equity %	13.4	34.4	4.7	ELB	NMF	NMF
Net Margin %	5.0	17.7	4.2	-76.2	-97.0	-97.0
Asset Turnover	0.9	0.8	0.6	0.6	0.7	0.7
Financial Leverage	3.1	2.5	1.8	3.1	NMF	NMF

Valuation Ratios	Stock	Rel to Industry	Rel to S&P 500
Price/Earnings	NMF	—	—
Price/Book	—	—	—
Price/Sales	0.4	0.8	0.2
Price/Cash Flow	—	—	—

Major Fund Holders	% of Fund Assets
New York Equity	7.12
Gabelli Blue Chip Value AAA	3.91
American Heritage Growth	3.66
Salomon Brothers Capital O	2.54

Morningstar Grades

Growth [D]	1999	2000	2001	2002
Revenue %	26.7	7.1	-26.3	-42.1
Earnings/Share %	338.2	-75.2	NMF	NMF
Book Value/Share %	70.6	83.2	-59.2	NMF
Dividends/Share %	2.6	0.0	-25.0	NMF

Growth has gone from boom to bust alongside the plummet in telecom capital spending. Taking a long view, sales growth should significantly exceed GDP growth even in mature economies.

Profitability [F]	2000	2001	2002	TTM
Return on Assets %	2.6	-48.2	-67.2	-67.2
Oper Cash Flow $Mil	-703	-3,421	-756	-756
- Cap Spending $Mil	1,915	1,390	449	449
= Free Cash Flow $Mil	-2,618	-4,811	-1,205	-1,205

Lucent runs on operating leverage: research, manufacturing, and selling costs are largely fixed, meaning profits should outpace sales if this downturn reverses course. Despite cost cuts, Lucent remains built for larger sales volume.

Financial Health [F]	2000	2001	2002	09-02
Long-term Debt $Mil	3,030	3,274	3,236	3,236
Total Equity $Mil	26,172	11,023	-4,734	-4,734
Debt/Equity Ratio	0.1	0.3	ELB	NMF

Lucent has too much debt--$3.3 billion in straight debt (plus a $2.5 billion projected pension deficit)--resulting in a high debt/equity ratio of 0.8. Nonetheless, it doesn't need to begin repaying debt until 2006; most is not due until after 2027.

Morningstar's Take By Fritz Kaegi, 11-14-2002 Stock Price as of Analysis: $1.18

Lucent is a risky bet on the state of telecom spending, a wager we're not prepared to make.

After two years of foibles (and they've been doozies), it's easy to forget Lucent's considerable strengths: a great record of developing useful technologies; good long-term growth prospects; and decades-long relationships with carriers around the world. Despite much lower carrier spending, the pricing environment for Lucent products has been relatively benign.

Two competitive advantages create this price stability: It is expensive (and a hassle) for carriers to switch from Lucent's installed equipment, and it is hard for competitors to earn carriers' trust in their ability to provide fully compatible equipment for carriers' networks, which are often decades old.

Though long-term fundamentals like these can play a very positive role in our fair value estimate, cash position trumps all concerns. Cyclical, short-term factors that might normally be seen as chance events of little consequence assume central importance here. When you run out of money, there is no long term. And according to bondholders, the odds are better than even Lucent will fold.

Lucent will have $2 billion in cash by October 2003, given our expectations of a 25% drop in sales (in line with carriers' spending plans), a 25% gross margin, $600 million in interest and preferred dividends, $1.1 billion in cash restructuring expenses (compared with Lucent's forecast of $700 million), a bare-bones capital-expenditure budget of $400 million, and $2.6 billion in operating costs. From there, Lucent's fate will ride on sales and gross margins holding steady to roughly offset the $2.5 billion needed for annual operating costs and minimal capital expenditures. Then Lucent will hope long-term telecom tailwinds take over.

If that sounds like a lot of ifs, it is. Unforeseen sales or gross margin shortfalls or insufficient cost-cutting by 2005 could spell bankruptcy. Even a generous view of Lucent's abilities must allow for this chance. Lucent is a huge, lumbering organization that achieved its current size with great difficulty, and it remains 12,000 people above its claimed break-even level. Yet it has overshot toward optimism in its projections and budgeting, and the best estimate of telecom sales is only an educated guess. After all, if management had truly been able to project the declines of 2001 and 2002, it would have cut costs much sooner and not put the company at risk. The risk is that missing the new sales and cost projections could mean "game over" for stockholders.

 **M⌀RNINGSTAR®** Stocks 500

M & T Bank MTB

	Rating	Risk	Moat Size	Fair Value	Last Close	Yield %
	★★	Med.	Narrow	$78.00	$79.35	1.3

Company Profile

M&T Bank is the holding company for bank subsidiaries that operate more than 450 banking offices in New York, Pennsylvania, Maryland, West Virginia, and the Bahamas. The banks provide money market, checking, savings, and individual retirement accounts, as well as certificates of deposit. The banks originate residential and commercial real estate and business loans. Real estate loans account for approximately 58% of the company's total loan portfolio. M&T acquired Premier National Bancorp in February 2001.

Management

CEO Robert Wilmers headed M&T's predecessor bank, First Empire, and engineered the takeover of ONBANCorp, which created M&T. He became chairman as well in July 2000 when ONBANCorp's head retired.

Strategy

M&T's branches are located in midsize cities in western New York, the Hudson Valley, and Pennsylvania, where it focuses on community lending--both commercial and consumer. The bank has grown internally and through acquisitions.

One M&T Plaza
Buffalo, NY 14203
www.mandtbank.com

Morningstar Grades

Growth [A]

	1998	1999	2000	2001
Revenue %	29.0	8.5	19.1	23.0
Earnings/Share %	3.6	25.4	4.9	11.0
Book Value/Share %	36.5	10.1	46.3	-8.5
Dividends/Share %	18.8	18.4	38.9	60.0

Acquisitions and internal growth have combined to increase total revenue and net income at a compound annual rate of 21% since 1997. The company's stock has appreciated at a 24% compound annual rate since 1983.

Profitability [B-]

	1999	2000	2001	TTM
Return on Assets %	1.2	1.0	1.2	1.4
Oper Cash Flow $Mil	607	347	154	—
- Cap Spending $Mil	23	19	24	—
= Free Cash Flow $Mil	—	—	—	—

Amortization expenses from acquisitions booked as purchase transactions have artificially lowered returns on assets and equity. High net interest margins as a result of low leverage make the firm quite profitable.

Financial Health [A-]

	1999	2000	2001	09-02
Long-term Debt $Mil	—	—	—	—
Total Equity $Mil	1,797	2,700	2,939	3,059
Debt/Equity Ratio	—	—	—	—

M&T maintains lower leverage than many of its peers, and has a wider net interest margin. Asset quality has deteriorated with the weak economy, but remains better than the industry average.

Industry	Investment Style	Stock Type	Sector
Regional Banks	▣ Mid Core	↗ Classic Growth	$ Financial Services

Competition

	Market Cap $Mil	Debt/ Equity	12 Mo Trailing Sales $Mil	Price/Cash Flow	Return On Assets%	Total Return% 1 Yr	3 Yr
M & T Bank	7,290	—	2,377	—	1.4	10.3	28.0
Royal Bank of Canada	24,764	—	16,588	—	—	—	—
Bank of Montreal	13,559	—	11,220	—	—	—	—

Price Volatility

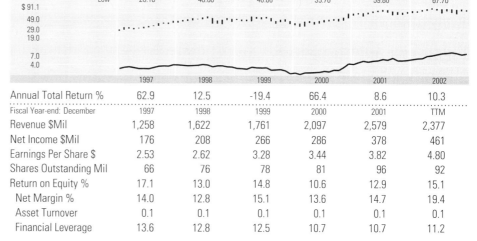

		I Monthly Price High/Low		— Relative Strength to S&P 500	
Annual $Price High	46.80	58.20	58.25	68.42	82.11	90.05
Low	28.10	40.00	40.60	35.70	59.80	67.70

$ 91.1 / 49.0 / 29.0 / 19.0 / 7.0 / 4.0

	1997	1998	1999	2000	2001	2002
Annual Total Return %	62.9	12.5	-19.4	66.4	8.6	10.3

Fiscal Year-end: December	1997	1998	1999	2000	2001	TTM
Revenue $Mil	1,258	1,622	1,761	2,097	2,579	2,377
Net Income $Mil	176	208	266	286	378	461
Earnings Per Share $	2.53	2.62	3.28	3.44	3.82	4.80
Shares Outstanding Mil	66	76	78	81	96	92
Return on Equity %	17.1	13.0	14.8	10.6	12.9	15.1
Net Margin %	14.0	12.8	15.1	13.6	14.7	19.4
Asset Turnover	0.1	0.1	0.1	0.1	0.1	0.1
Financial Leverage	13.6	12.8	12.5	10.7	10.7	11.2

Valuation Ratios

	Stock	Rel to Industry	Rel to S&P 500
Price/Earnings	16.5	1.2	0.7
Price/Book	2.4	1.1	0.7
Price/Sales	3.1	1.4	1.5
Price/Cash Flow	—	—	—

Major Fund Holders

	% of Fund Assets
Super Core A	6.13
Oppenheimer Quest Opportunity Value A	3.98
Morgan Stanley Financial Services B	3.26
Oppenheimer Quest Global Value A	2.99

Morningstar's Take By Richard McCaffery, 10-25-2002 Stock Price as of Analysis: $82.51

M&T is one of a small group of banks that consistently add shareholder value through organic growth, acquisitions, and good stewardship of capital. We wouldn't put it in the same category as Fifth Third, given its lower returns on invested capital, but it's still a top performer. Our thesis is that the bank, which is trading near our fair value estimate, will continue to be run much as it has been, and thus will continue to grow in value.

M&T has a community approach to banking, which means it focuses on building good relationships with customers. By keeping customers and selling them additional products, the company boosts revenue by securing new loans and adding a higher percentage of fee income to the mix. This close relationship with customers usually means better loan quality as well. It's a formula that works well in slow-growth areas like upstate New York, or faster-growth areas like Maryland.

We get some comfort, too, knowing that Warren Buffett has a 5.7% stake in M&T. An existing investment by Buffett doesn't tell us that a given stock is attractive, but it gives us an idea what kind of management team M&T has put together. It's well known that Buffett isn't interested in baby-sitting managers. His involvement, coupled with M&T's

record, gives us some evidence management knows what it's doing. Specifically, it adds to our comfort that M&T will continue to make smart loans, be opportunistic regarding growth, and conduct business in a manner friendly to shareholders.

In terms of raw performance, the biggest thing that separates M&T from Fifth Third or TCF is its percentage of fee income, which drives asset turnover, a key component of profitability. Noninterest income generates more than 40% of net revenue at TCF and Fifth Third and less than 30% at M&T, which means the first two banks generate higher revenue per dollar of assets employed. We aren't sure if M&T will make the jump to the next level, but more than 40% of net revenue at Allfirst comes from fees. In fact, the new M&T should have about $25.6 billion in fee-rich assets under management, up from just $7.7 billion at the old M&T. All told, 33% of net revenue will come from fees at the new M&T. We think the deal could give M&T a chance to improve an already impressive record.

Macromedia MACR

	Rating	Risk	Moat Size	Fair Value	Last Close	Yield %
	★	High	Narrow	$8.00	$10.65	0.0

Company Profile

Macromedia supplies software tools and services to manage digital content such as multimedia, graphic arts, and digital video applications. Macromedia's products are marketed under names including Fireworks, Dreamweaver, Flash, ColdFusion, and Spectra. The company acquired Allaire in March 2001.

Management

CEO Rob Burgess joined Macromedia in 1996 and quickly revived the company. Now he'll need to dust off his turnaround skills to fight the downturn.

Strategy

Macromedia wants to be all things to Web designers and developers. To achieve this goal, the company launched its MX initiative, a suite of software that bundles the necessary applications to run and create Web pages rich in graphics and motion.

600 Townsend Street
San Francisco, CA 94103
www.macromedia.com

Industry	Investment Style	Stock Type	Sector
Development Tools	Small Growth	Spec. Growth	Software

Competition

	Market Cap $Mil	Debt/ Equity	12 Mo Trailing Sales $Mil	Price/Cash Flow	Return On Assets%	Total Return% 1 Yr	3 Yr
Macromedia	642	0.0	318	—	-27.6	-40.2	-48.0
Microsoft	276,411	0.0	29,985	16.0	13.2	-22.0	-22.9
Adobe Systems	5,860	0.0	1,135	18.2	16.8	-20.0	-6.1

Price Volatility

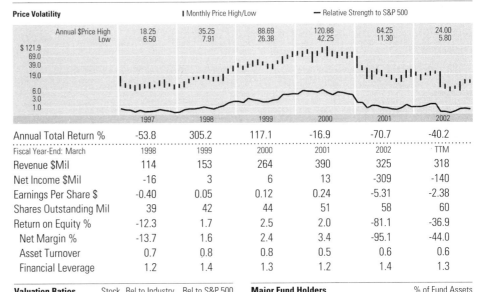

	18.25 / 6.50	35.25 / 7.91	88.69 / 26.38	120.88 / 42.25	64.25 / 11.30	24.00 / 5.80
Annual Total Return %	-53.8	305.2	117.1	-16.9	-70.7	-40.2

Fiscal Year-End: March	1998	1999	2000	2001	2002	TTM
Revenue $Mil	114	153	264	390	325	318
Net Income $Mil	-16	3	6	13	-309	-140
Earnings Per Share $	-0.40	0.05	0.12	0.24	-5.31	-2.38
Shares Outstanding Mil	39	42	44	51	58	60
Return on Equity %	-12.3	1.7	2.5	2.0	-81.1	-36.9
Net Margin %	-13.7	1.6	2.4	3.4	-95.1	-44.0
Asset Turnover	0.7	0.8	0.8	0.5	0.6	0.6
Financial Leverage	1.2	1.4	1.3	1.2	1.4	1.3

Valuation Ratios	Stock	Rel to Industry	Rel to S&P 500
Price/Earnings	NMF	—	—
Price/Book	1.7	0.4	0.5
Price/Sales	2.0	0.5	1.0
Price/Cash Flow	—	—	—

Major Fund Holders	% of Fund Assets
Firsthand e-Commerce	3.15
ABN AMRO/Veredus SciTech N	2.25
Orbitex Info-Tech & Communications A	2.00
TCW Galileo Value Opportunities I	1.99

Morningstar Grades

Growth [C+]	1999	2000	2001	2002
Revenue %	34.7	72.4	47.5	-16.6
Earnings/Share %	NMF	140.0	100.0	NMF
Book Value/Share %	-9.8	67.0	144.8	-45.4
Dividends/Share %	NMF	NMF	NMF	NMF

The growth of the Internet sent revenue soaring, but those days are over. New releases of Flash and Dreamweaver should kick-start growth.

Profitability [C]	2000	2001	2002	TTM
Return on Assets %	1.8	1.7	-59.6	-27.6
Oper Cash Flow $Mil	38	66	-42	-4
- Cap Spending $Mil	34	65	17	11
= Free Cash Flow $Mil	4	1	-59	-15

The Allaire acquisition and lower revenue have led to huge losses. However, tight cost controls have allowed the company to re-enter the black.

Financial Health [C+]	2000	2001	2002	09-02
Long-term Debt $Mil	0	0	0	0
Total Equity $Mil	254	668	381	379
Debt/Equity Ratio	0.0	0.0	0.0	0.0

Financial health isn't great. Although Macromedia has nearly $200 million in cash and no debt, it's barely generating operating cash flow.

Morningstar's Take By Mike Trigg, 11-13-2002 Stock Price as of Analysis: $11.04

Macromedia could be an attractive way to benefit from the long-term growth of the Internet. We think anywhere below $5 is a good price to buy the stock.

Like many software vendors, Macromedia has struggled as companies slash IT spending, particularly on Web design projects. Business has also suffered because customers have delayed purchases in anticipation of product upgrades, which Macromedia delayed to make more significant changes.

While we see few signs that spending is improving, Macromedia should benefit from a strong upgrade cycle. The company has released new versions of all its major products, including Flash, ColdFusion, and Dreamweaver, which together represent 75% of sales. Flash is the leading software for creating and viewing Web content that includes special effects and animation. We liken it to watching a movie on a PC, while HTML (the primary Web language) is akin to a slide show. ColdFusion creates simple Web applications, like employee directories, and Dreamweaver allows people to design Web pages without writing HTML.

The primary reason for our optimism is that Macromedia has an economic moat--the network effect. Having been downloaded on more than 98% of the world's PCs, the Flash player has become the standard for viewing Web content rich with sound, motion, and graphics. Web designers and developers have little choice but to use Flash, given the software's ubiquity on the Internet. Although the software is free to consumers, the tools needed to create Flash programs are not. This is similar to Adobe's Acrobat, the standard for creating and viewing documents electronically.

However, the network effect does not apply to all of Macromedia's products, which explains why its moat is narrow and not wide. ColdFusion competes in the crowded application server market with heavyweights BEA Systems and IBM. Even Dreamweaver, which is the dominant Web page development tool with 88% share, could someday be displaced by more innovative technology. Also, it's possible that Microsoft may someday challenge Flash, one of the few third-party technologies embedded in Windows XP.

Although we believe a strong upgrade cycle can buoy Macromedia's results, our enthusiasm is tempered by lackluster spending on Web design projects and the risk of competition from Microsoft and others. The stock would need to trade at least 40% below our fair value estimate before we'd buy.

MORNINGSTAR® Stocks 500

Mandalay Resort Group MBG

	Rating	Risk	Moat Size	Fair Value	Last Close	Yield %
	★★	Med.	None	$29.00	$30.61	0.0

Company Profile

Mandalay Resort Group operates 12 casino properties in Nevada, 10 of which are wholly owned. In early 1999 MBG completed its flagship development, the $1 billion Mandalay Bay resort casino. With Mandalay Bay, Luxor, Excalibur, and several secondary properties, the company controls 27% of the hotel rooms and several parcels of yet-undeveloped land on the Las Vegas Strip. More than 80% of the company's operating income comes from its Nevada markets. Mandalay also operates a dockside casino in Mississippi as well as joint ventures in Detroit and Elgin, Illinois.

Management

Michael Ensign, 62, has been CEO for three years; during his tenure cash flow has grown dramatically. Mandalay's interests should be well represented in Washington by the CEO's son, Sen. John Ensign. Insiders own 19% of the stock.

Strategy

Mandalay is betting heavily on continued growth in the Las Vegas casino, tourist, and convention businesses. Its strategy is to target all segments of the market, from the local market to the high end. With a stable of successful projects in place, the emphasis has shifted to increasing prices and per-customer revenue.

3950 Las Vegas Boulevard South www.mandalayresortgroup.com
Las Vegas, NV 89119

Morningstar Grades

Growth [C]	1999	2000	2001	2002
Revenue %	8.9	39.2	23.3	-1.4
Earnings/Share %	-4.3	-48.9	226.1	-52.7
Book Value/Share %	4.1	6.0	3.4	-6.0
Dividends/Share %	NMF	NMF	NMF	NMF

Revenue growth has averaged about 16% annually since 1998, but the bulk of this came with the opening of Mandalay Bay in 1999. Until the Mandalay Tower and convention center are complete, higher same-hotel results will have to drive top-line growth.

Profitability [C]	2000	2001	2002	TTM
Return on Assets %	1.0	2.8	1.3	1.5
Oper Cash Flow $Mil	225	436	358	356
- Cap Spending $Mil	352	110	157	249
= Free Cash Flow $Mil	-127	325	202	107

Its luxury properties earn Mandalay above-average operating margins, averaging about 17% annually. The planned all-suite Mandalay Tower will face pricing pressure if the weak economic climate persists, however.

Financial Health [C+]	2000	2001	2002	10-02
Long-term Debt $Mil	2,691	2,624	2,482	2,575
Total Equity $Mil	1,188	1,069	941	991
Debt/Equity Ratio	2.3	2.5	2.6	2.6

Mandalay has done an outstanding job of simultaneously financing new capital projects, paying down debt, and buying back stock. The firm has repurchased 30% of the outstanding stock since 1998 and plans to continue doing so.

	Industry	Investment Style	Stock Type	Sector
	Gambling/Hotel Casinos	▦ Mid Core	→ Slow Growth	🛒 Consumer Services

Competition

	Market Cap $Mil	Debt/ Equity	12 Mo Trailing Sales $Mil	Price/Cash Flow	Return On Assets%	Total Return% 1 Yr	3 Yr
Mandalay Resort Group	2,019	2.6	2,417	5.7	1.5	43.0	16.3
MGM Mirage	5,111	1.8	3,970	6.1	2.7	14.2	12.2
Harrah's Entertainment	4,426	2.4	4,108	5.4	3.9	7.0	17.8

Price Volatility

	Annual $Price High Low	36.50 20.00	26.50 7.13	26.31 11.31	28.38 12.88	27.88 13.90	36.90 21.12

Annual Total Return %	-40.4	-44.8	77.9	9.0	-2.5	43.0
Fiscal Year-end: January	1998	1999	2000	2001	2002	TTM
Revenue $Mil	1,336	1,454	2,025	2,496	2,462	2,417
Net Income $Mil	90	85	42	120	53	63
Earnings Per Share $	0.94	0.90	0.46	1.50	0.71	0.94
Shares Outstanding Mil	95	95	90	78	73	66
Return on Equity %	8.0	7.4	3.6	11.2	5.6	6.4
Net Margin %	6.7	5.9	2.1	4.8	2.2	2.6
Asset Turnover	0.4	0.4	0.5	0.6	0.6	0.6
Financial Leverage	2.9	3.3	3.6	4.0	4.3	4.3

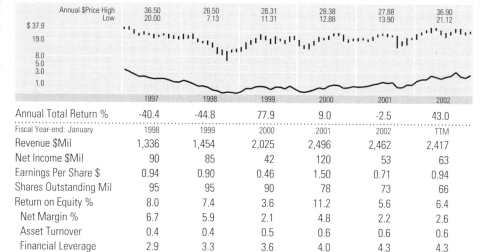

Valuation Ratios	Stock	Rel to Industry	Rel to S&P 500
Price/Earnings	32.6	1.7	1.4
Price/Book	2.0	0.8	0.6
Price/Sales	0.8	0.6	0.4
Price/Cash Flow	5.7	0.9	0.4

Major Fund Holders	% of Fund Assets
Legg Mason Special Investment Prim	4.56
Hotchkis and Wiley Small Cap Value I	2.88
Dreyfus Premier Strategic Value A	2.74
IDEX Janus Growth A	2.30

Morningstar's Take By T.K. MacKay, 10-11-2002 Stock Price as of Analysis: $30.19

Mandalay Resort Group is one of our favorite casino operators and we would consider investing in the company around $15.

We are excited about Mandalay's exposure to the Las Vegas market. Mandalay receives about 60% of its earnings before interest, taxes, depreciation, and amortization from its properties on the Strip, including Mandalay Bay, Luxor, and Circus Circus. We firmly believe that Las Vegas will continue to dominate the gaming industry, although recent history might suggest otherwise.

Mandalay has big plans to capitalize on the Strip's popularity. Over the next few years, nearly all of Mandalay's capital spending will focus on the Mandalay Bay Resort. Opened in 1999 at the cost of almost $1 billion, Mandalay Bay is about to get a big introduction to the convention market. The company is constructing a 1.3 million-square-foot convention center at the hotel, at a cost of about $235 million, and will soon begin construction of the $225 million Mandalay Tower, an all-suite 1,125-room hotel adjacent to the main resort. We believe these projects will contribute to Mandalay's growth, with revenue expanding by about 10% over the next several years.

This plan isn't a sure bet, however. Two major

capital projects in a questionable economic climate could turn out to be bad timing. Like the hospitality industry, casinos with convention facilities depend on business travel to keep room rates high, because conventioneers pay closer to the rack rate on rooms and spend more on dining. As long as corporate profitability is delayed, so is the high-margin business that corporate travel generates. Mandalay's planned minimum price of $200 per room in the new all-suite Tower could be a curse in this environment.

Our assumptions for Mandalay's future rely on Las Vegas seeing a continued rebound in occupancy and room rates (Mandalay generates 25% of its revenue from hotel rooms) over the next 12 months. The foundering airline industry and weak consumer spending pose a risk to this assumption. Nearly half of all visitors to Las Vegas travel by air, and increased airfares or fewer flights could send would-be Vegas vacationers to casinos closer to home, like those operated by Harrah's.

For these reasons, we would tread carefully when considering Mandalay shares. We think a substantial discount--about 50%--to our estimated fair value adequately addresses the risks we see, and we would consider the stock if it fell to that level.

Manpower MAN

	Rating	Risk	Moat Size	Fair Value	Last Close	Yield %
	★★★	Med.	Narrow	$41.00	$31.90	0.6

Company Profile

Manpower is a holding company for Manpower International, one of the largest nongovernmental employment services organization in the world. With more than 3,900 company-owned and franchised offices, Manpower's services include temporary help, contract services, and training and testing of temporary and permanent personnel. The company has offices in 61 countries, concentrating its operations in the United States, continental Europe, and the United Kingdom.

Management

Jeff Joerres came on as CEO in April 1999, replacing longtime CEO Mitchell Fromstein. Senior management has a long-term incentive program linked to economic profits, defined as operating profits less a charge for the capital that Manpower uses.

Strategy

Manpower has put aside its growth focus to emphasize profits. The company is investing in its specialty staffing businesses, like Manpower Professional, which deliver fatter margins. In 2001, Manpower bought Jefferson Wells, a provider of internal audit, accounting, technology and tax services. The firm is also rapidly expanding its newer international markets.

5301 N. Ironwood Road
Milwaukee, WI 53217
www.manpower.com

Morningstar Grades

Growth [C]	1998	1999	2000	2001
Revenue %	21.4	10.8	11.0	-3.3
Earnings/Share %	-52.8	105.4	16.2	-27.0
Book Value/Share %	10.7	0.8	15.9	10.4
Dividends/Share %	11.8	5.3	0.0	0.0

About 80% of revenue is foreign, so growth is affected by currency fluctuations. A strong U.S. dollar has hurt revenue during the past five years. Still, Manpower's geographic diversification has shielded it from the U.S. economic slowdown.

Profitability [A-]	1999	2000	2001	TTM
Return on Assets %	5.5	5.6	3.8	2.7
Oper Cash Flow $Mil	-1	158	136	149
- Cap Spending $Mil	75	83	87	61
= Free Cash Flow $Mil	-75	75	49	88

Manpower's business generates low margins. Operating margins have been below 3% for the past four fiscal years, significantly lower than those of the firm's top rival, Adecco ADO. Fierce competition should constrain margins in the future.

Financial Health [B-]	1999	2000	2001	09-02
Long-term Debt $Mil	358	492	811	848
Total Equity $Mil	651	740	814	926
Debt/Equity Ratio	0.5	0.7	1.0	0.9

Although working capital consumes a large portion of cash flow and debt has been growing, Manpower's financial health is reasonably strong and not imperiled.

Industry	Investment Style	Stock Type	Sector
Employment	Mid Core	→ Slow Growth	Business Services

Competition

	Market Cap $Mil	Debt/ Equity	12 Mo Trailing Sales $Mil	Price/Cash Flow	Return On Assets%	Total Return% 1 Yr	3 Yr
Manpower	2,448	0.9	10,309	16.5	2.7	-4.9	-3.8
Adecco SA ADR	7,410	1.1	16,102	9.02	-4.52	-28.8	-20.2
Kelly Services A	991	0	4,237	12.0	1.1	14.7	2.5

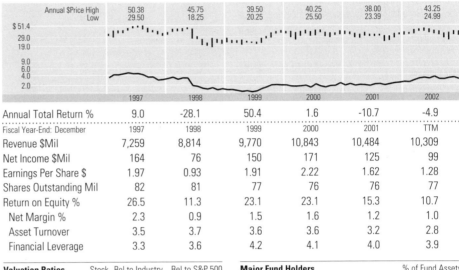

Price Volatility			Monthly Price High/Low		Relative Strength to S&P 500	
Annual $Price High / Low	50.38 / 29.50	45.75 / 18.25	39.50 / 20.25	40.25 / 25.50	38.00 / 23.39	43.25 / 24.99
	1997	1998	1999	2000	2001	2002
Annual Total Return %	9.0	-28.1	50.4	1.6	-10.7	-4.9

Fiscal Year-End: December	1997	1998	1999	2000	2001	TTM
Revenue $Mil	7,259	8,814	9,770	10,843	10,484	10,309
Net Income $Mil	164	76	150	171	125	99
Earnings Per Share $	1.97	0.93	1.91	2.22	1.62	1.28
Shares Outstanding Mil	82	81	77	76	76	77
Return on Equity %	26.5	11.3	23.1	23.1	15.3	10.7
Net Margin %	2.3	0.9	1.5	1.6	1.2	1.0
Asset Turnover	3.5	3.7	3.6	3.6	3.2	2.8
Financial Leverage	3.3	3.6	4.2	4.1	4.0	3.9

Valuation Ratios	Stock	Rel to Industry	Rel to S&P 500
Price/Earnings	24.9	0.4	1.1
Price/Book	2.6	0.7	0.8
Price/Sales	0.2	0.4	0.1
Price/Cash Flow	16.5	1.0	1.2

Major Fund Holders	% of Fund Assets
Ameristock Focused Value	5.06
Merrill Lynch Focus Twenty A	4.16
Principal Inv Ptr MidCap Value AdvPfd	2.80
ASAF Neuberger Berman Mid-Cap Value A	2.74

Morningstar's Take By Dan Schick, 12-17-2002 Stock Price as of Analysis: $33.16

Manpower and its geographically diverse portfolio of businesses should get a boost from a rebound in the global economy in the next two years. Although its market is brutally competitive, the firm has managed to deliver returns on capital above its cost in the good years, and remain solidly in the black in the bad. Because of the competitive forces, though, we'd purchase this leading temporary employment services firm only at a 40% discount to our fair value estimate.

Manpower's results depend on the state of the economy. When times are good and employment levels high, Manpower does well. But it can't control economic cycles, and when good times go bad, the firm suffers from greatly reduced demand. After all, one of the attractions of temporary employees is the flexibility to get rid of them.

However, Manpower has to stay ready to supply employees when the economy picks back up, so it must staff and keep its office network ready for action. So too must competitors. High fixed costs result from not being able to significantly reduce the network. And since a network of temp offices and the employees to run them is a specialized asset with no other use, firms are loath to exit the business. The end result of high fixed costs and barriers to exit is intense price competition as firms refuse to shrink and sacrifice margins to prop up volume.

It comes as no surprise, then, that holding the line on pricing and providing higher-margin services has been a main initiative for Manpower in recent years. The acquisitions of Elan in 2000 and Jefferson Wells in 2001 have boosted the firm's ability to provide specialized, higher-margin professional staff. Continued investments in the Empower Group and Manpower Professional should also raise gross margins when demand for professional-level workers returns.

These investments haven't been cost-free, though. Right now they're pressuring the bottom line: Manpower's operating margin has been running below 2% recently. Declining revenue has amplified the effect. However, we believe that maintaining a strong gross margin will benefit Manpower's shareholders. As revenue grows, solid gross margins will provide plenty of dollars to offset fixed costs. We think this will allow income to grow faster than sales, lifting Manpower's operating margins above 3% and sending returns on capital back above cost.

 **Stocks 500**

Marathon Oil MRO

	Rating	Risk	Moat Size	Fair Value	Last Close	Yield %
	★★★	Med.	Narrow	$24.00	$21.29	4.3

Company Profile

Marathon Oil is an integrated oil and gas company that separated from U.S. Steel in January 2002. Marathon Oil is one of the largest remaining companies in the industry not to have had a major merger. The company has roughly 1.3 billion barrels of oil of proven reserves concentrated in North America, the North Sea, and off the coast of West Africa. Through its partnership with Ashland, the company also owns a stake in seven major refineries, several major domestic pipelines, and nearly 6,000 retail gas stations.

Management

CEO Clarence Cazalot came to the company in 2000 from Texaco. He was head of production there and was brought on largely to improve Marathon's upstream performance. Cazalot has been CEO since the U.S. Steel split in January.

Strategy

Marathon knows that bigger is generally better in oil. A featherweight compared with heavies like ExxonMobil and BP, Marathon is trying to focus its operations in a select few geographic areas, becoming a large presence there while totally forgoing others. It also hopes its recent separation from U.S. Steel will improve efficiency.

5555 San Felipe Road
Houston, TX 77056-2723
www.marathon.com

Morningstar Grades

Growth [C]	1998	1999	2000	2001
Revenue %	37.9	9.6	42.8	-2.2
Earnings/Share %	-19.7	-46.2	-34.1	-12.2
Book Value/Share %	39.7	-44.4	10.3	67.9
Dividends/Share %	10.5	0.0	4.8	4.5

Oil has always been a cyclical industry held hostage by the swings in commodity prices, and recent quarters pale compared with the halcyon days of 2000. We expect Marathon to grow in the midsingle digits long-term.

Profitability [C+]	1999	2000	2001	TTM
Return on Assets %	3.9	2.4	1.0	-4.3
Oper Cash Flow $Mil	1,936	2,531	3,636	2,214
- Cap Spending $Mil	1,378	1,425	1,639	1,642
= Free Cash Flow $Mil	558	1,106	1,997	572

Marathon improved profitability in recent years, going from being a laggard to showing returns in line with industry norms, largely thanks to success at its downstream partnership with Ashland ASH. However, recent returns have been disappointing.

Financial Health [A-]	1999	2000	2001	09-02
Long-term Debt $Mil	3,320	1,937	3,432	4,579
Total Equity $Mil	6,856	6,762	4,940	5,013
Debt/Equity Ratio	0.5	0.3	0.7	0.9

Marathon is one of the more leveraged oil companies, but not terribly out of line with industry averages. Its free cash flow has been strong in recent years.

Industry	Investment Style	Stock Type	Sector
Oil & Gas	Mid Value	Hard Assets	Energy

Competition

	Market Cap $Mil	Debt/ Equity	12 Mo Trailing Sales $Mil	Price/Cash Flow	Return On Assets%	Total Return% 1 Yr	3 Yr
Marathon Oil	6,599	0.9	29,905	3.0	-4.3	-26.3	0.4
ChevronTexaco	71,011	0.4	93,451	8.9	-3.0	-23.1	-4.4
ConocoPhillips	18,492	0.6	46,828	5.7	0.4	-17.4	5.7

Price Volatility

	Monthly Price High/Low	— Relative Strength to S&P 500

Annual $Price High / Low	38.88 / 23.75	40.50 / 25.00	33.88 / 19.44	30.38 / 20.69	33.73 / 24.95	30.30 / 18.82
	1997	1998	1999	2000	2001	2002

Annual Total Return %	44.9	-8.4	-15.5	16.3	11.6	-26.3
Fiscal Year-end: December	1997	1998	1999	2000	2001	TTM
Revenue $Mil	15,670	21,602	23,666	33,799	33,066	29,905
Net Income $Mil	988	674	698	411	157	-752
Earnings Per Share $	4.88	3.92	2.11	1.39	1.22	-1.86
Shares Outstanding Mil	189	166	331	296	129	310
Return on Equity %	18.3	10.5	10.2	6.1	3.2	-15.0
Net Margin %	6.3	3.1	2.9	1.2	0.5	-2.5
Asset Turnover	1.3	1.3	1.3	2.0	2.1	1.7
Financial Leverage	2.3	2.6	2.6	2.5	3.3	3.5

Valuation Ratios	Stock	Rel to Industry	Rel to S&P 500
Price/Earnings	NMF	—	—
Price/Book	1.3	0.6	0.4
Price/Sales	0.2	0.2	0.1
Price/Cash Flow	3.0	0.4	0.2

Major Fund Holders	% of Fund Assets
Sparrow Growth A	4.64
UC Investment	4.10
Franklin Large Cap Value A	3.04
Fountainhead Special Value	2.92

Morningstar's Take By Paul Larson, 11-19-2002 Stock Price as of Analysis: $19.11

While Marathon does have a couple of warts, it retains our award for most eligible bachelor in an industry that is no stranger to marriage.

In oil, being a prime merger target is not something to brush off. Just look at the conglomeration of names leading the field--ExxonMobil, ChevronTexaco, and ConocoPhillips. Bigger oil companies are more efficient and can find, dig up, refine, and distribute oil more cheaply than the small-fry. Marathon will soon be the largest domestic oil company not bitten by the major merger bug. Though we typically don't try to guess the next takeover, we're wondering how long Marathon will go before getting hitched.

Marathon isn't waiting around for a merger, though, and is instead improving its fundamental positioning and performance. Marathon knows that economy of scale is a key competitive advantage, so it is focusing on areas where it can become the low-cost producer, beefing up in a few select geographic areas while selling other assets. For example, the firm recently sold its entire portfolio of properties in the San Juan Basin of New Mexico, where it had only a moderate presence and was not a leader. Meanwhile, it is aggressively acquiring properties where it can leverage its existing infrastructure to reduce costs, such as in the Powder River Basin in Wyoming. This recently enacted strategy has yet to yield benefits, but our discounted cash flow model does assume modest profitability improvement.

Oil itself is an attractive business, in our view, largely thanks to OPEC. The cartel keeps a lid on supply coming from its member countries in an attempt to keep commodity prices above costs and maintain industrywide profitability. Even with OPEC's members occasionally cheating on their quotas, profits over the long term have been strong across the industry.

Marathon has been tagged a financial laggard in the industry, a reputation it is trying to shake through solid execution. Recent quarterly results and watered-down production targets have done little to help, however. We have fairly low expectations to reflect the company's history of disappointing, but we would still be willing to buy Marathon if it got cheap enough.

Markel MKL

	Rating	Risk	Moat Size	Fair Value	Last Close	Yield %
	★★★	Med.	Narrow	$240.00	$205.50	0.0

Company Profile

Markel is an insurance holding company that, through its subsidiaries, underwrites specialty insurance products and programs. Its insurance products include professional and product liability, excess insurance, surplus insurance, medical malpractice, and other liability policies. Markel also offers reinsurance policies. Sales of excess-insurance and surplus-insurance premiums each account for approximately 69% of the company's total premium sales. The company operates facilities in the United States. Markel acquired Terra Nova Bermuda Holdings in March 2000.

Management

Markel boasts one of the best executive teams in the business, with a reputation for conservative accounting and delivering strong results. Directors and officers own about 15% of the outstanding shares.

Strategy

Management runs the business with a view toward building long-term intrinsic value, or book value per share. Markel aims to increase book value per share at least 20% annually by writing only profitable policies and earning above-average investment returns. A focus on specialty lines, which are less regulated than standard lines, allows pricing flexibility.

4521 Highwoods Parkway   www.markelcorp.com
Glen Allen, VA 23060-6148

Morningstar Grades

Growth [A]	1998	1999	2000	2001
Revenue %	1.7	23.1	108.7	27.7
Earnings/Share %	14.0	-29.2	NMF	NMF
Book Value/Share %	19.6	-10.0	60.1	16.9
Dividends/Share %	NMF	NMF	NMF	NMF

The acquisition of Terra Nova, Markel's largest-ever purchase, skews the three-year revenue figure. Markel's pricing and volume have jumped so far this year, evidenced by a 29% rise in written premiums.

Profitability [D]	1999	2000	2001	TTM
Return on Assets %	1.7	-0.5	-2.0	0.1
Oper Cash Flow $Mil	1	89	164	—
- Cap Spending $Mil	4	20	9	—
= Free Cash Flow $Mil	—	—	—	—

Large underwriting losses at Markel International hurt returns on equity in 2000 and 2001. Excluding these two years, ROE has averaged about 20% since 1992, and we believe a return to this rate is possible.

Financial Health [D+]	1999	2000	2001	09-02
Long-term Debt $Mil	—	—	—	—
Total Equity $Mil	383	752	1,085	1,135
Debt/Equity Ratio	—	—	—	—

Markel has a long record of posting a combined ratio below 100% and conservatively overestimating reserves. Its debt/total capital ratio is a reasonable 25%.

Industry	Investment Style	Stock Type	Sector
Insurance (Property)	▦ Mid Core	✦ Spec. Growth	$ Financial Services

Competition

	Market Cap $Mil	Debt/ Equity	12 Mo Trailing Sales $Mil	Price/Cash Flow	Return On Assets%	Total Return% 1 Yr	3 Yr
Markel	1,928	—	1,647	—	0.1	14.4	12.4
American International Gr	150,907	—	66,823	—	1.4	-26.9	-4.0
Berkshire Hathaway B	111,526	—	39,133	—	1.9	-4.0	12.5

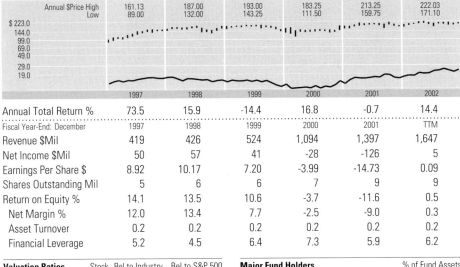

Price Volatility   ▌ Monthly Price High/Low   ▬ Relative Strength to S&P 500

Annual $Price High / Low	161.13 / 89.00	187.00 / 132.00	193.00 / 143.25	183.25 / 111.50	213.25 / 159.75	222.03 / 171.10

$223.0 / 144.0 / 99.0 / 69.0 / 49.0 / 29.0 / 19.0

	1997	1998	1999	2000	2001	2002
Annual Total Return %	73.5	15.9	-14.4	16.8	-0.7	14.4
Fiscal Year-End: December	1997	1998	1999	2000	2001	TTM
Revenue $Mil	419	426	524	1,094	1,397	1,647
Net Income $Mil	50	57	41	-28	-126	5
Earnings Per Share $	8.92	10.17	7.20	-3.99	-14.73	0.09
Shares Outstanding Mil	5	6	6	7	9	9
Return on Equity %	14.1	13.5	10.6	-3.7	-11.6	0.5
Net Margin %	12.0	13.4	7.7	-2.5	-9.0	0.3
Asset Turnover	0.2	0.2	0.2	0.2	0.2	0.2
Financial Leverage	5.2	4.5	6.4	7.3	5.9	6.2

Valuation Ratios	Stock	Rel to Industry	Rel to S&P 500
Price/Earnings	EUB	—	—
Price/Book	1.7	0.9	0.5
Price/Sales	1.2	0.5	0.6
Price/Cash Flow	—	—	—

Major Fund Holders	% of Fund Assets
FBR Small Cap Value A	17.79
New Market	11.91
Vontobel U.S. Value	7.62
Liberty Acorn Twenty Z	5.12

Morningstar's Take   By Aaron Westrate, 12-10-2002   Stock Price as of Analysis: $201.91

Markel is one of the best insurers we've ever seen. Rotten results in its international operations have obscured the firm's promise, but smart organizational moves and the best industry environment in a decade have Markel poised to deliver exceptional results. Investors accepting our view of Markel's future will find the stock reasonably priced, but not quite in bargain territory.

The acquisition of Terra Nova, now Markel International, in March 2000 has given management fits as losses exceeded expectations. To fix the mess, management consolidated underwriting units, cut roughly one fourth of the staff, discontinued unprofitable lines, and tied underwriters' bonuses to underwriting profit. The results are promising. Markel International's combined ratio improved from 115% in 2001 to 106% in the third quarter of 2002. It's worth noting that at the time of the acquisition, Terra Nova's premium volume was roughly equal to Markel's existing business. The stricter underwriting standards imposed overseas has had the effect of shrinking that business to about a third of Markel's overall written premiums today.

Over Markel's history, however, underwriting losses are the exception rather than the rule (insurers that generate consistent underwriting profits are exceedingly rare). In 12 of the past 16 years, Markel's overall combined ratio has been below 100%. Markel's core North American operations, net of acquisitions, have produced break-even or better underwriting results in 15 of the past 16 years. What makes this underwriting record all the more remarkable is that for the better part of the period Markel faced the head wind of soft premium rates. With rates and policy volume rising as competitors exit noncore lines, Markel should return to generating an underwriting profit by the end of 2003.

In addition to this underwriting discipline, Markel's ability to invest for total return makes it stand out. Although it invests policyholder funds (the reserves for future claims that it can invest until the claims are paid) in bonds, the rest of its portfolio (generally about 25% of invested assets) is often in higher-returning equities. Over the past decade, Markel has generated 17.5% equity returns compared with the S&P 500's 12.1%. At present, equities represent just 14% of invested assets, one of the lowest ratios in a decade, so Markel should have dry powder should any extraordinary investment opportunities emerge.

 M✪RNINGSTAR® Stocks 500

Marsh & McLennan Companies MMC

	Rating	Risk	Moat Size	Fair Value	Last Close	Yield %
	★★★	Med.	Wide	$46.00	$46.21	2.4

Company Profile

Marsh & McLennan provides insurance brokerage, consulting, and investment management services. It offers insurance and reinsurance services under the J & H Marsh & McLennan, Guy Carpenter, Sedgwick, and Seabury & Smith names. The Mercer Consulting Group subsidiary provides management consulting, especially in the areas of human resources. Marsh & McLennan also offers investment management for individual and institutional clients through its Putnam Investments subsidiary, which manages more than 100 mutual funds.

Management

Jeffrey Greenberg is chairman and chief executive officer. Greenberg started with Marsh in 1996, and is the eldest son and former protege of Maurice Greenberg, chairman of American International Group.

Strategy

Marsh differentiates itself from other insurance brokers by offering a broad product line. It wants to bring several financial businesses under one roof to create innovative solutions for its customers. Also, it's aiming to capitalize on a very strong pricing environment in the commercial insurance and reinsurance markets by forming a Bermuda-based underwriter as well as a crisis-consulting group.

1166 Avenue Of The Americas   www.mmc.com
New York, NY 10036

Morningstar Grades

Growth [C]	1998	1999	2000	2001
Revenue %	19.7	27.4	10.9	-2.1
Earnings/Share %	72.3	-12.1	56.5	-17.3
Book Value/Share %	6.3	9.9	20.6	-0.8
Dividends/Share %	15.8	16.0	11.8	8.4

A 15% drop in Putnam's revenue partially offset a 17% revenue increase in the brokerage division in the third quarter, leading to 6% total revenue growth. If Putnam's managed assets begin to grow again, Marsh's revenue should follow suit.

Profitability [A+]	1999	2000	2001	TTM
Return on Assets %	5.5	8.6	7.3	9.2
Oper Cash Flow $Mil	1,031	1,364	1,377	—
- Cap Spending $Mil	476	512	433	—
= Free Cash Flow $Mil	—	—	—	—

Returns on equity have been in the top 20% of the industry, with the exception of a dip in 1997 caused by an integration charge. Tight cost controls enabled the firm to post an excellent 14% net margin year to date.

Financial Health [A+]	1999	2000	2001	09-02
Long-term Debt $Mil	—	—	—	—
Total Equity $Mil	4,170	5,228	5,173	5,006
Debt/Equity Ratio	—	—	—	—

Marsh boasts steady cash flow and is capitalized with more equity than debt. The firm also has a hefty $675 million cash hoard that it may use to finance new opportunities or repurchase shares.

Industry	Investment Style	Stock Type	Sector
Insurance (General)	⊞ Large Core	↗ Classic Growth	$ Financial Services

Competition

	Market Cap $Mil	Debt/ Equity	12 Mo Trailing Sales $Mil	Price/Cash Flow	Return On Assets%	Total Return% 1 Yr	3 Yr
Marsh & McLennan Companies	24,818	—	10,164	—	9.2	-12.0	2.8
Franklin Resources	8,929	—	2,519	—	6.7	-2.6	3.8
Aon	5,156	—	8,492	—	—	—	—

Price Volatility

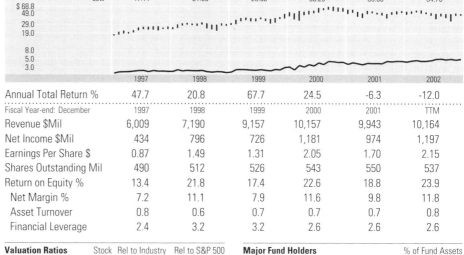

		▌Monthly Price High/Low		━ Relative Strength to S&P 500	

| Annual $Price High | 26.67 | 32.16 | 48.38 | 67.84 | 59.00 | 57.30 |
| Low | 17.11 | 21.69 | 28.56 | 35.25 | 39.50 | 34.70 |

	1997	1998	1999	2000	2001	2002
Annual Total Return %	47.7	20.8	67.7	24.5	-6.3	-12.0
Fiscal Year-end: December	1997	1998	1999	2000	2001	TTM
Revenue $Mil	6,009	7,190	9,157	10,157	9,943	10,164
Net Income $Mil	434	796	726	1,181	974	1,197
Earnings Per Share $	0.87	1.49	1.31	2.05	1.70	2.15
Shares Outstanding Mil	490	512	526	543	550	537
Return on Equity %	13.4	21.8	17.4	22.6	18.8	23.9
Net Margin %	7.2	11.1	7.9	11.6	9.8	11.8
Asset Turnover	0.8	0.6	0.7	0.7	0.7	0.8
Financial Leverage	2.4	3.2	3.2	2.6	2.6	2.6

Valuation Ratios	Stock	Rel to Industry	Rel to S&P 500
Price/Earnings	21.5	0.6	0.9
Price/Book	5.0	2.8	1.6
Price/Sales	2.4	0.9	1.2
Price/Cash Flow	—	—	—

Major Fund Holders	% of Fund Assets
Fifth Third Quality Growth Inv A	5.05
Managers AMG Rorer Large Cap	4.89
John Hancock U.S. Global Leaders Gr A	4.70
Orbitex Financial Service A	4.60

Morningstar's Take By Aaron Westrate, 12-10-2002 Stock Price as of Analysis: $47.45

We like Marsh's long-term competitive position in its two largest businesses. Our fair value estimate remains $46, and we'd be buyers if the stock fell below $37, giving us our required margin of safety.

Marsh dominates the insurance brokerage market. The global resources required to assess the risk of multinationals make this segment of the industry largely an oligopoly. Marsh's brokerage revenues are more than twice the combined brokerage revenue of the third- and fourth-largest firms. This size also facilitates strong relationships with insurance carriers since Marsh controls a large amount of the industry's premium dollars. We're less sanguine about Marsh's prospects for gaining share in the smaller-company market since risks in this segment are less complex and regional competitors are legion. Nevertheless, Marsh is well entrenched in its core business.

Marsh is benefiting as the insurance industry raises premium rates following substantial losses over the past couple of years. These anticipated rate increases prompted Marsh to form a Bermuda-based insurer, Axis. The venture's $1.6 billion capital base comes from Marsh and other institutional investors. This move is reminiscent of Marsh's formation of two other ventures in the mid-1980s to take advantage of

inadequate underwriting capacity. Marsh hasn't disclosed its long-term plans for Axis, but we wouldn't be surprised if it ended up in the public's hands, just as those earlier ventures became XL Capital XL and ACE ACE.

Marsh's asset-management business, Putnam, is struggling now, but should be a key driver of performance over time. Putnam ranks as one of the largest money managers, with $257 billion in assets under management and offering more than 100 mutual funds. This scale is important because it enables Putnam to spend heavily on marketing its stable of funds to its large network of independent brokers and planners. Depreciating stock values and net redemptions have hurt Putnam's profitability, but the division remains solidly in the black, with year-to-date operating margins of 27%.

Marsh belongs on anyone's list of excellent companies, given its solid competitive position in good industries, but until the stock falls to 80% or less of our fair value estimate, we think investors should pass.

Data as of 12-31-02

Martha Stewart Living Omnimedia A MSO

	Rating	Risk	Moat Size	Fair Value	Last Close	Yield %
	★	High	Narrow	$7.00	$9.87	0.0

Company Profile

Martha Stewart Living Omnimedia publishes magazines and books, produces television programming, and sells merchandise for the home. The company publishes Martha Stewart Living and Martha Stewart Weddings magazines and cooking, home-entertainment, gardening, wedding, and craft books. In addition, it produces weekly Martha Stewart-featured segments for CBS and daily Martha Stewart Living programming. Martha Stewart Living Omnimedia also sells home and garden products such as towels, latex paints, window treatments, and decorative fabrics.

Management

An unflattering biography and insider-trading allegations have recently hurt Martha Stewart, CEO since she founded the firm in 1996. The company's brand is built on Stewart's image and will suffer if her credibility diminishes.

Strategy

Martha Stewart wants to leverage content across multiple channels, including publishing, Internet/direct commerce, TV, and merchandising. The firm is looking for a new retail distributor after current partner Kmart filed for bankruptcy protection. The company is probably considering a contingency plan in case the Justice Department indicts Martha Stewart.

11 West 42nd Street
New York, NY 10036
www.marthastewart.com

Morningstar Grades

Growth [C]	1998	1999	2000	2001
Revenue %	35.6	29.0	23.0	3.5
Earnings/Share %	NMF	NMF	NMF	4.7
Book Value/Share %	—	—	NMF	15.2
Dividends/Share %	NMF	NMF	NMF	NMF

The soft advertising market has taken a toll on growth lately. Nevertheless, Martha Stewart has managed to register positive revenue growth in the past year, which cannot be said for many of its media rivals.

Profitability [A]	1999	2000	2001	TTM
Return on Assets %	9.1	7.2	7.0	4.6
Oper Cash Flow $Mil	28	40	19	41
- Cap Spending $Mil	6	25	17	6
= Free Cash Flow $Mil	22	15	2	35

The Internet/direct commerce segment is deep in the red, and the merchandising segment is feeling the pain of Kmart's bankruptcy. However, the company continues to generate positive operating cash flow.

Financial Health [A]	1999	2000	2001	09-02
Long-term Debt $Mil	—	—	—	—
Total Equity $Mil	199	196	222	236
Debt/Equity Ratio	—	—	—	—

Martha Stewart has no debt on its balance sheet and enjoys a growing cash balance totaling nearly $145 million. The company should scale down capital expenditures in the coming months, which would boost free cash flow.

Industry	Investment Style	Stock Type	Sector
Media Conglomerates	Small Growth	↗ Classic Growth	Media

Competition	Market Cap $Mil	Debt/ Equity	12 Mo Trailing Sales $Mil	Price/Cash Flow	Return On Assets%	Total Return% 1 Yr	3 Yr
Martha Stewart Living Omnimedia A	485	—	307	11.9	4.6	-40.0	-27.5
AOL Time Warner	56,278	0.3	41,024	8.1	-34.6	-59.2	-44.6
Walt Disney	32,923	0.5	24,550	14.6	2.5	-20.3	-19.1

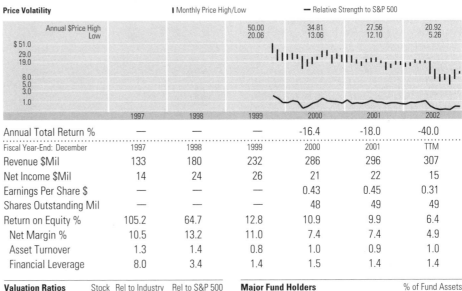

Annual Total Return %	—	—	—	-16.4	-18.0	-40.0
Fiscal Year-End: December	1997	1998	1999	2000	2001	TTM
Revenue $Mil	133	180	232	286	296	307
Net Income $Mil	14	24	26	21	22	15
Earnings Per Share $	—	—	—	0.43	0.45	0.31
Shares Outstanding Mil	—	—	—	48	49	49
Return on Equity %	105.2	64.7	12.8	10.9	9.9	6.4
Net Margin %	10.5	13.2	11.0	7.4	7.4	4.9
Asset Turnover	1.3	1.4	0.8	1.0	0.9	1.0
Financial Leverage	8.0	3.4	1.4	1.5	1.4	1.4

Valuation Ratios	Stock	Rel to Industry	Rel to S&P 500
Price/Earnings	31.8	1.2	1.4
Price/Book	2.1	1.5	0.6
Price/Sales	1.6	0.7	0.8
Price/Cash Flow	11.9	0.8	0.9

Major Fund Holders	% of Fund Assets
None	

Morningstar's Take By T.K. MacKay, 12-19-2002 Stock Price as of Analysis: $10.19

Drop the cookie cutters. Martha Stewart Living Omnimedia's business depends on its namesake CEO's reputation.

The controversy over Martha Stewart's December 2001 sale of her stake in Imclone is taking its toll on business. Advertisers are not committing to buying ad space in the company's flagship Martha Stewart Living magazine, and management is having difficulties negotiating with retailers to take over the lucrative merchandising business.

The success of these two businesses is vital to free cash flow generation. The publishing group contributes 62% of overall revenue and more than half of operating profits. Martha Stewart Living fuels the fire of the profitable merchandising segment, which contributes just 18% of revenue but nearly twice that amount in profits. The longer a cloud hangs over Martha Stewart's head, the more difficult it will be for the company to win back the favor of advertisers, who may already be seeking alternatives like Redbook and Ladies' Home Journal.

Merchandising is also feeling the impact of bankrupt Kmart, which sells the majority of Martha Stewart merchandise. Martha Stewart's name created an economic moat that allowed her firm to demand very generous terms when signing license agreements with retailers. Until last year, it received a royalty anytime Kmart made a wholesale purchase of Martha Stewart-branded goods. Kmart also reimbursed Martha Stewart for design and promotional costs for merchandise, resulting in a near-100% profit margin on these products.

The license agreement changed after Kmart declared bankruptcy. Now the firm only pays a royalty to Martha Stewart on sales of products to customers, and it no longer reimburses design and promotional costs. This has already hurt the fat margins Martha Stewart's merchandising business generates; the operating margin was 70% in the first nine months of 2002, compared with 91% last year.

Profits from this business increased 14% for the first nine months of 2002 when compared with the previous year because of higher sales, but they could decline if Martha Stewart can't strike a similar license agreement with another retailer like Wal-Mart or Target. Martha Stewart's charm and presentation skills have given Martha Stewart Living Omnimedia its economic moat. The federal investigation of Martha Stewart casts a black veil over these characteristics, greatly diminishing the economic moat they afford.

MORNINGSTAR® Stocks 500

Marvell Technology MRVL

	Rating	Risk	Moat Size	Fair Value	Last Close	Yield %
	★	High	None	$16.00	$18.86	0.0

Company Profile

Marvell Technology designs integrated circuits for communication applications. Its products use analog signals and digital information to store and transmit digital information. The company also creates products for the broadband data communication market that provide the interface between communication systems and data transmission media, and it is developing products for the gigabit Ethernet networking format. Its customers include Seagate Technology, Samsung, Hitachi, Fujitsu, and Toshiba. The company acquired Galileo Technology in January 2001.

Management

CEO Sehat Sutardja, CTO Pantas Sutardja, and executive vice president Weili Dai co-founded Marvell in 1995. The three men are related by birth or marriage. As of May 2002, management owned roughly 40% of the firm's stock.

Strategy

With a significant position in the market for chips used for computer storage, Marvell intends to leverage its high-performance technology into the communication market. The firm is already expanding into the market for corporate or data networking gear. Marvell outsources its chip production and works closely with customers to design customized products.

4th Floor, Windsor Place   www.marvell.com
Hamilton, HM 1179

Morningstar Grades

Growth [A+]	1999	2000	2001	2002
Revenue %	EUB	282.9	76.8	100.7
Earnings/Share %	NMF	NMF	NMF	NMF
Book Value/Share %	—	—	NMF	-51.1
Dividends/Share %	NMF	NMF	NMF	NMF

Growth is impressive; sales rose 78% in fiscal 2001 and 100% in 2002 thanks largely to market share gains. We anticipate sales will grow roughly 70% in fiscal 2003.

Profitability [C]	2000	2001	2002	TTM
Return on Assets %	28.1	-9.6	-19.9	-7.0
Oper Cash Flow $Mil	13	12	50	55
- Cap Spending $Mil	7	12	25	33
= Free Cash Flow $Mil	6	0	25	22

Marvell is both young and profitable, a big plus. At 55%, gross margins are on par with those of peers. But because Marvell is a small company, research and development and overhead costs made up half of fiscal 2002 sales.

Financial Health [C+]	2000	2001	2002	10-02
Long-term Debt $Mil	0	0	10	14
Total Equity $Mil	8	2,357	1,990	1,966
Debt/Equity Ratio	0.0	0.0	0.0	0.0

With no debt and about $250 million in cash and investments on the balance sheet, Marvell is in sound health.

Industry	Investment Style	Stock Type	Sector
Semiconductors	▦ Mid Growth	◈ Spec. Growth	▣ Hardware

Competition	Market Cap $Mil	Debt/ Equity	12 Mo Trailing Sales $Mil	Price/Cash Flow	Return On Assets%	Total Return% 1 Yr	3 Yr
Marvell Technology	2,266	0.0	437	41.1	-7.0	-47.4	—
Broadcom	4,154	0.0	1,014	—	-21.4	-63.3	-51.0
National Semiconductor	2,716	0.0	1,576	20.0	-2.9	-51.3	-29.6

Price Volatility

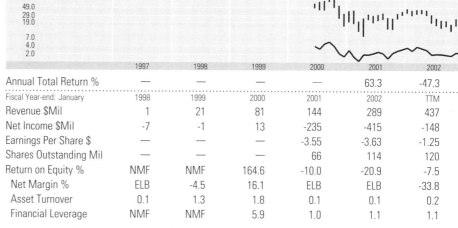

		Monthly Price High/Low	— Relative Strength to S&P 500		

Annual $Price High / Low

| | | | 109.75 / 15.38 | 42.00 / 7.94 | 46.24 / 11.27 |

$110.8
49.0
29.0
19.0
7.0
4.0
2.0

	1997	1998	1999	2000	2001	2002
Annual Total Return %	—	—	—	—	63.3	-47.3

Fiscal Year-end: January	1998	1999	2000	2001	2002	TTM
Revenue $Mil	1	21	81	144	289	437
Net Income $Mil	-7	-1	13	-235	-415	-148
Earnings Per Share $	—	—	—	-3.55	-3.63	-1.25
Shares Outstanding Mil	—	—	—	66	114	120
Return on Equity %	NMF	NMF	164.6	-10.0	-20.9	-7.5
Net Margin %	ELB	-4.5	16.1	ELB	ELB	-33.8
Asset Turnover	0.1	1.3	1.8	0.1	0.1	0.2
Financial Leverage	NMF	NMF	5.9	1.0	1.1	1.1

Valuation Ratios	Stock	Rel to Industry	Rel to S&P 500
Price/Earnings	NMF	—	—
Price/Book	1.2	0.4	0.4
Price/Sales	5.2	1.3	2.6
Price/Cash Flow	41.1	3.5	3.1

Major Fund Holders	% of Fund Assets
SunAmerica Focused Technology A	8.80
Black Oak Emerging Technology	8.07
PBHG Global Tech & Communications	5.44
RS Information Age	3.66

Morningstar's Take By Jeremy Lopez, 11-22-2002 Stock Price as of Analysis: $23.03

Marvell Technology is an outstanding growth story, but we think the firm's strong performance is already priced into the stock.

The firm's roots as a supplier of hard disk drive (HDD) components are hardly glamorous. This niche can be a ruthless area to operate in, considering that it tends to be mature, competitive, and price-sensitive. In fact, some incumbents like Texas Instruments and Cirrus Logic have exited altogether in recent years. Marvell has done well in HDD by gaining considerable market share from such competitors.

Marvell has also parlayed its success in HDD into the corporate networking market. Chips in this area are used in the gear that connects PCs; the newest standard is called gigabit Ethernet (gigE). Corporations have started adopting gigE as prices have fallen, and chips from firms like Marvell and Broadcom have helped enable this migration. Marvell has done better than most in gigE, mainly because it has better products, and has gained share from rivals like Broadcom. Marvell has also broadened its growth prospects with its recent move into wireless networking--one of the few semiconductor niches where growth has not skipped a beat.

Thanks to market share gains and a focus on the

right chip niches, Marvell's performance has stood out from most other chipmakers'. For example, sales doubled in fiscal 2002 (ended in January), and they could rise roughly 70% in 2003. Most other chipmakers have seen sales fall over this time. This performance is noticeable in the valuation of Marvell stock, which trades at a hefty 50 times First Call's expected earnings for fiscal 2003. The stock also trades at a wide premium to what we think is its intrinsic worth, on the basis of our projected cash flows for the firm.

We question whether this growth, market position, and valuation are sustainable. We're not too concerned about the long-term growth prospects in corporate networking. However, we are concerned that competition may limit Marvell's ability to benefit from its end-market prospects. Plenty of rivals are aiming for the growth in networking chips, and short product cycles could cause Marvell's thin lead to shrink. What's more, any blip in the firm's growth could easily send the stock's lofty valuation back to earth.

Unless Marvell stock becomes much cheaper--trading at big discount to our fair value estimate--we're content to watch the firm's marvelous growth from afar.

Masco MAS

	Rating	Risk	Moat Size	Fair Value	Last Close	Yield %
	★★	Med.	None	$21.00	$21.05	2.6

Company Profile

Masco manufactures building, home-improvement, and home-furnishings products, including faucets, plumbing supplies, shower items, and kitchen and bath cabinets. Products include Delta and Peerless single- and double-handle faucets and the Merillat, Kraftmaid, Starmark, and Fieldstone brands of custom kitchen and bath cabinets. Other specialty kitchen and bath consumer products include Thermador ovens and related cooking equipment. Home-furnishing products include Universal, Benchcraft, Henredon, Drexel, and Heritage wood and upholstered furniture.

Management

Richard Manoogian, 65, is the son of Masco founder Alex Manoogian. He's been with Masco since 1958 and CEO since 1985; he owns more than 2% of the stock. Overall, Masco's officers are fairly well along in years, with an average age of 59.

Strategy

Masco's strategy is built around acquisitions. The firm believes that to survive it must get bigger, broader, and more powerful relative to its big-box retail customers (chiefly Home Depot). Recent purchases have included hardware manufacturers as well as installation and contracting businesses--the latter of which are meant to open up new professional markets for Masco's products.

21001 Van Born Road
Taylor, MI 48180

www.masco.com

Morningstar Grades

Growth [A+]	1998	1999	2000	2001
Revenue %	17.1	19.5	14.8	15.4
Earnings/Share %	23.5	1.6	2.3	-67.9
Book Value/Share %	21.0	14.0	7.6	14.9
Dividends/Share %	41.0	4.7	8.9	7.1

Even by acquisitive industrial standards, Masco's growth rate (22% annually in the past five years) is pretty heady. The firm has a decades-long record of double-digit growth, but its size probably means slower expansion ahead.

Profitability [A-]	1999	2000	2001	TTM
Return on Assets %	8.6	7.6	2.2	4.6
Oper Cash Flow $Mil	491	734	967	1,104
- Cap Spending $Mil	351	388	274	735
= Free Cash Flow $Mil	140	346	692	370

Masco averaged a 19% return on equity between 1996 and 2000, but that hides the true cost associated with several acquisitions accounted for under the pooling method. A full accounting of Masco's purchases reveals declining returns.

Financial Health [A]	1999	2000	2001	09-02
Long-term Debt $Mil	2,431	3,018	3,628	3,964
Total Equity $Mil	3,137	3,426	4,120	5,336
Debt/Equity Ratio	0.8	0.9	0.9	0.7

With growth fueled by acquisitions, Masco has traditionally carried more debt than the average industrial. However, a recent stock offering should bring its debt/capital ratio below 40%, and coverage ratios have rebounded along with earnings.

Industry	Investment Style	Stock Type	Sector
Building Materials	▦ Large Core	◪ High Yield	✿ Industrial Mats

Competition

	Market Cap $Mil	Debt/ Equity	12 Mo Trailing Sales $Mil	Price/Cash Flow	Return On Assets%	Total Return% 1 Yr	Total Return% 3 Yr
Masco	10,357	0.7	9,103	9.4	4.6	-12.1	-2.8
Fortune Brands	6,942	—	5,806	—	—	—	—
American Standard Compani	5,148	—	7,669	—	—	—	—

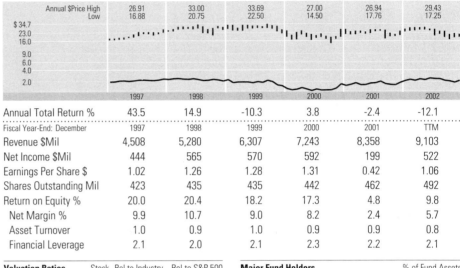

Price Volatility		Monthly Price High/Low		— Relative Strength to S&P 500		
Annual $Price High / Low	26.91 16.88	33.00 20.75	33.69 22.50	27.00 14.50	26.94 17.76	29.43 17.25

$ 34.7 / 23.0 / 16.0 / 9.0 / 6.0 / 4.0 / 2.0

	1997	1998	1999	2000	2001	2002
Annual Total Return %	43.5	14.9	-10.3	3.8	-2.4	-12.1

Fiscal Year-End: December	1997	1998	1999	2000	2001	TTM
Revenue $Mil	4,508	5,280	6,307	7,243	8,358	9,103
Net Income $Mil	444	565	570	592	199	522
Earnings Per Share $	1.02	1.26	1.28	1.31	0.42	1.06
Shares Outstanding Mil	423	435	435	442	462	492
Return on Equity %	20.0	20.4	18.2	17.3	4.8	9.8
Net Margin %	9.9	10.7	9.0	8.2	2.4	5.7
Asset Turnover	1.0	0.9	1.0	0.9	0.9	0.8
Financial Leverage	2.1	2.0	2.1	2.3	2.2	2.1

Valuation Ratios	Stock	Rel to Industry	Rel to S&P 500
Price/Earnings	19.9	1.3	0.8
Price/Book	1.9	1.1	0.6
Price/Sales	1.1	1.2	0.6
Price/Cash Flow	9.4	1.4	0.7

Major Fund Holders	% of Fund Assets
Fidelity Select Construction&Housing	5.18
Shepherd Large Cap Growth	3.67
CDC Nvest Growth and Income A	3.04
ABN AMRO/Montag & Caldwell Growth N	2.94

Morningstar's Take By Josh Peters, 10-16-2002 Stock Price as of Analysis: $19.00

Masco is building a bigger business with its acquisition strategy, but not necessarily a better one. We wouldn't take an interest in the shares unless they fell into the low teens.

The building products business is getting rough. Led by Home Depot, retailers are accumulating substantial power over their suppliers. Their dominant market share puts them in a position to extract price concessions--or, if met with resistance, to simply deny shelf space to incumbent brands and sell products from private-label manufacturers.

Already the nation's largest building product concern, Masco is attempting to meet these challenges by growing still larger. But despite the firm's strong product lines and impressive growth, we see several major flaws in this strategy.

First, while sales have more than doubled in the past five years, much less than half of that total is due to internal expansion. The balance has come from acquisitions, resulting in substantial dilution to Masco's return on invested capital.

Second, we suspect these acquisitions are costing Masco too much. Consider 2001: Masco bought two window manufacturers, an insulation installation business, and three other firms for $1.66 billion. These purchases yielded only $185 million in tangible

net assets--just $98 million of plants and equipment. The remaining 89% of its spending was assigned to goodwill and other intangibles. Those intangibles have some value, but in a cyclical industry threatened by powerful retailers, it could be tough to preserve Masco's original outlay.

But our biggest worry is this: Masco seems more interested in making acquisitions than running existing businesses. When asked at the annual meeting if the firm should be paying more attention to integrating the operations it already has, CEO Richard Manoogian replied, "I think that's a question we have to look at in a year or two." The sheer quantity of purchases also prompts us to wonder if unpleasant surprises might emerge--like the recent unfavorable class-action ruling against a 1999 acquisition, paint and stain maker Behr.

Despite its manic growth, we think it will be tough for Masco to preserve its competitive advantages in this environment. We're also reminded that a previous attempt by Masco to consolidate a fragmented industry--furniture--trashed a decade's worth of shareholder returns. Unfavorable economics merit a cautious stance toward the building product industry generally; even with the firm's remarkable record, we aren't making an exception for Masco.

MORNINGSTAR® Stocks 500

Mattel MAT

	Rating	Risk	Moat Size	Fair Value	Last Close	Yield %
	★	Med.	Narrow	$17.00	$19.15	2.0

Company Profile

Mattel manufactures children's toys and games and software products. Its products include the Barbie doll and related clothing and accessories, Fisher-Price toys and juvenile products, Hot Wheels and Matchbox toy vehicles and accessories, See 'N Say talking toys, Magna Doodle toys, Cabbage Patch and Polly Patch dolls, and Disney-licensed preschool and infant toys and large dolls. The company also produces family and educational games such as Uno and Scrabble. Mattel sold its Learning Company operations to an affiliate of Gores Technology Group· in October 2000.

Management

CEO Bob Eckert's salary seems more closely tied to stock performance than his predecessor's was, and his success at overseeing new-product launches at Kraft should carry over to this position.

Strategy

Mattel has undergone a massive effort to cut operating costs and rejuvenate its business. The company has closed its North American manufacturing facilities and is reducing the amount of license deals it signs with third parties, which cuts royalty expenses.

333 Continental Boulevard
El Segundo, CA 90245-5012

www.service.mattel.com

Morningstar Grades

Growth [C]	1998	1999	2000	2001
Revenue %	-1.7	-2.2	1.6	2.9
Earnings/Share %	NMF	NMF	NMF	NMF
Book Value/Share %	-4.6	-11.7	-27.7	20.3
Dividends/Share %	14.8	12.9	-22.9	-81.5

We believe Mattel can achieve midsingle-digit long-term revenue growth; real earnings growth will depend on the company's ability to cut costs and bring down interest expenses.

Profitability [D+]	1999	2000	2001	TTM
Return on Assets %	-1.8	-10.0	6.6	4.1
Oper Cash Flow $Mil	430	555	757	1,135
- Cap Spending $Mil	94	76	101	78
= Free Cash Flow $Mil	336	479	656	1,058

Mattel is doing exactly what it said it would in 2000: reducing expenses. Operating income was 12.5% of sales in 2001, and should continue to head toward 16% over the next several years.

Financial Health [C]	1999	2000	2001	09-02
Long-term Debt $Mil	983	1,242	1,021	640
Total Equity $Mil	1,963	1,403	1,738	1,832
Debt/Equity Ratio	0.5	0.9	0.6	0.4

The company paid down about 18% of its long-term debt in 2001, a big step toward bringing its capital structure in line with its goal of about 30% debt/capitalization. This ratio currently stands at about 40%.

Industry	Investment Style	Stock Type	Sector
Toys/Hobbies	Large Core	→ Slow Growth	Consumer Goods

Competition	Market Cap $Mil	Debt/ Equity	12 Mo Trailing Sales $Mil	Price/Cash Flow	Return On Assets%	Total Return% 1 Yr	3 Yr
Mattel	8,373	0.4	4,893	7.4	4.1	13.6	15.1
Hasbro	2,000	0.8	2,808	5.1	-5.8	-28.2	-11.5

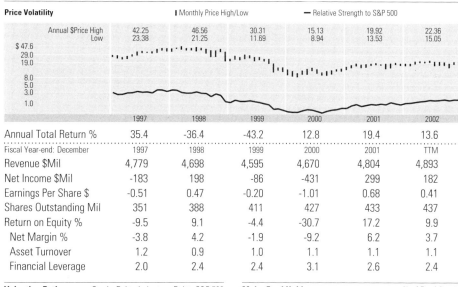

Price Volatility — Monthly Price High/Low — Relative Strength to S&P 500

Annual $Price High Low	42.25 23.38	46.56 21.25	30.31 11.69	15.13 8.94	19.92 13.53	22.36 15.05

	1997	1998	1999	2000	2001	2002
Annual Total Return %	35.4	-36.4	-43.2	12.8	19.4	13.6

Fiscal Year-end: December	1997	1998	1999	2000	2001	TTM
Revenue $Mil	4,779	4,698	4,595	4,670	4,804	4,893
Net Income $Mil	-183	198	-86	-431	299	182
Earnings Per Share $	-0.51	0.47	-0.20	-1.01	0.68	0.41
Shares Outstanding Mil	351	388	411	427	433	437
Return on Equity %	-9.5	9.1	-4.4	-30.7	17.2	9.9
Net Margin %	-3.8	4.2	-1.9	-9.2	6.2	3.7
Asset Turnover	1.2	0.9	1.0	1.1	1.1	1.1
Financial Leverage	2.0	2.4	2.4	3.1	2.6	2.4

Valuation Ratios	Stock	Rel to Industry	Rel to S&P 500
Price/Earnings	46.7	3.2	2.0
Price/Book	4.6	2.2	1.4
Price/Sales	1.7	0.5	0.9
Price/Cash Flow	7.4	0.6	0.6

Major Fund Holders	% of Fund Assets
INVESCO Leisure Inv	6.13
TCW Galileo Diversified Value N	4.79
Rydex Leisure Inv	4.78
Oakmark Select I	4.57

Morningstar's Take By T.K. MacKay, 10-31-2002 Stock Price as of Analysis: $18.35

Like competitor Hasbro, Mattel's advantage in the toy industry is the staying power of its brands. We're confident in the continued success of these products, but caution investors against getting too excited about Mattel's growth prospects.

Mattel is a turnaround story and classic growth story rolled into one. The economic prosperity of the past decade seduced the firm into overpaying for exceptional sales growth. Mattel's ill-fated $3.8 billion purchase of educational software developer The Learning Company in 1998 was one of the worst acquisitions ever; only recently has the company been able to shake the tarnished image the deal left. Mattel now aims to return to historical levels of profitability, even at the cost of sales dollars.

Mattel's brands--Barbie, Hot Wheels, Fisher-Price--have maintained their consumer appeal decade after decade. It is unlikely that the company's sales growth will exceed the low single digits over the long term, but it would take a pretty big industry shakeup to put a significant dent in that growth. Dolls, die-cast cars, and toys for infants are somewhat recession-proof, thanks in part to their low prices relative to other discretionary consumer goods.

The firm's goal to return to operating margins of 16%--a profitability level not seen since 1996--is

achievable, in our opinion. The driving force behind Mattel's turnaround is CEO Bob Eckert. Almost immediately after his arrival in 2000, the company initiated a massive restructuring, which included the sale of The Learning Company, the closure of Mattel's North American distribution and manufacturing facilities, and a reduction in license deals struck with third parties. As Eckert leads Mattel back to doing what it does best, margins should improve further.

It won't be an easy climb, though. The "on-demand" nature of popular toys is forcing Mattel to ship its products to retailers like Wal-Mart and Toys 'R' Us closer to the holidays than ever before. This increases the risk that Mattel could underproduce popular toys and overproduce toys that are out of favor in a given year, which could leave the company with worthless inventory at the end of the season--a manufacturer's nightmare.

Despite this risk, we think Mattel could make a good investment--at the right price. Its venerable brands earn Mattel an economic moat that is worth paying for at a 40% discount to our fair value estimate of $17.

Maxim Integrated Products MXIM

Rating	**Risk**	**Moat Size**	**Fair Value**	**Last Close**	**Yield %**
★★★	Med.	Wide	$32.00	$33.04	0.1

Company Profile

Maxim Integrated Products manufactures electronic circuits. It produces approximately 2,100 types of analog integrated circuits, about 75% of which are proprietary. The company's circuits are used mainly in test and measurement instrumentation, industrial controls and automation, data processing, and telecommunication. Maxim Integrated Products exports silicon wafers produced in the United States to several Asian countries for final assembly. Foreign sales account for about 57% of the company's total sales. It acquired Dallas Semiconductor in 2001.

Management

Jack Gifford has been president, chairman, and CEO since founding the firm in 1983. With tons of experience in relevant semiconductor fields, Gifford is a topnotch veteran. As of June 2002, management owned about 3% of company shares.

Strategy

As a specialist in high-performance analog chips, Maxim Integrated Products allocates its engineering resources to areas likely to generate the most profits. New product development and product diversity are hallmarks of the firm. Maxim produces chips in-house as well as outsourcing portions of its production.

120 San Gabriel Drive
Sunnyvale, CA 94086

www.maxim-ic.com

	Industry	Investment Style	Stock Type	Sector
	Semiconductors	Large Growth	Slow Growth	Hardware

Competition

	Market Cap $Mil	Debt/ Equity	12 Mo Trailing Sales $Mil	Price/Cash Flow	Return On Assets%	Total Return% 1 Yr	3 Yr
Maxim Integrated Products	10,584	—	1,072	27.3	13.0	-37.0	-11.2
Texas Instruments	25,982	0.1	8,024	12.8	0.9	-46.2	-32.5
STMicroelectronics NV	17,362	—	6,357	—	—	—	—

Price Volatility | Monthly Price High/Low   — Relative Strength to S&P 500

Annual $Price High	19.09	22.75	48.31	90.13	70.13	61.36
Low	10.53	11.16	19.94	41.50	32.20	20.75

$ 91.1 / 49.0 / 29.0 / 19.0 / 7.0 / 4.0 / 2.0

	1997	1998	1999	2000	2001	2002
Annual Total Return %	59.5	26.6	116.0	1.3	9.8	-37.0

Fiscal Year-End: June	1998	1999	2000	2001	2002	TTM
Revenue $Mil	904	1,003	1,376	1,577	1,025	1,072
Net Income $Mil	234	265	373	335	259	271
Earnings Per Share $	0.69	0.77	1.04	0.93	0.73	0.78
Shares Outstanding Mil	296	301	316	325	324	320
Return on Equity %	22.6	30.2	21.7	15.9	14.9	15.2
Net Margin %	25.9	26.5	27.1	21.2	25.3	25.3
Asset Turnover	0.7	1.0	0.7	0.6	0.5	0.5
Financial Leverage	1.2	1.2	1.2	1.2	1.2	1.2

Valuation Ratios

	Stock	Rel to Industry	Rel to S&P 500
Price/Earnings	42.4	1.0	1.8
Price/Book	5.9	2.0	1.9
Price/Sales	9.9	2.5	4.9
Price/Cash Flow	27.3	2.3	2.1

Major Fund Holders

	% of Fund Assets
Conseco 20 A	9.20
TCW Galileo Aggressive Growth Eq I	7.71
Pin Oak Aggressive Stock	6.70
TCW Galileo Technology N	6.66

Morningstar Grades

Growth [C-]	1999	2000	2001	2002
Revenue %	10.9	37.2	14.6	-35.0
Earnings/Share %	11.6	35.1	-10.6	-21.5
Book Value/Share %	-16.3	87.9	21.7	-15.9
Dividends/Share %	NMF	NMF	NMF	NMF

Maxim is the epitome of a consistent and rapid grower. It has posted positive sales growth in each of the past 10 years--not an easy feat in a cyclical industry. However, this streak ended in fiscal 2002 as sales dropped 35%.

Profitability [A+]	2000	2001	2002	TTM
Return on Assets %	17.9	13.8	12.9	13.0
Oper Cash Flow $Mil	666	810	404	388
- Cap Spending $Mil	292	337	90	103
= Free Cash Flow $Mil	374	473	313	284

By picking its spots wisely, Maxim sports some of the best margins in the analog industry. Its stable business model centers on profit-driven growth, as evidenced by its net margins, which tend to be above 30%.

Financial Health [A+]	2000	2001	2002	09-02
Long-term Debt $Mil	—	—	—	—
Total Equity $Mil	1,720	2,101	1,741	1,787
Debt/Equity Ratio	—	—	—	—

Maxim is in great health, with plenty of cash, no debt, and free cash flow. The firm doesn't have to load up on debt, since capital spending in the analog industry isn't as high as in other chip niches.

Morningstar's Take   By Jeremy Lopez, 12-12-2002   Stock Price as of Analysis: $37.02

Maxim Integrated Products is among the elite in the chip sector, but we'd hold off investing until the stock fell 30%-40% below our fair value estimate.

Few chipmakers rival Maxim's record. Not only has growth vastly outperformed the broader chip sector over the past 10 years, but the consistency of this growth is extraordinary. Besides fiscal 2002--when a huge downturn hurt all chipmakers--sales have risen every year over the past 10 years at an average rate of 28%. While this growth is partially skewed by the firm's Dallas Semiconductor acquisition in 2001, it is still impressive. Also, Maxim has remained profitable despite the booms and busts that characterize the chip industry. The firm's average margin are well above the average chipmaker's over the past 10 years.

A lot of Maxim's stellar performance is due to a focus on the analog market. Analog chips are used in many end-market applications, like notebook PCs, telecom infrastructure, cell phones, cars, and consumer appliances. Growth in these markets, coupled with rising analog content per product, has driven demand at a rate faster than the broader chip industry. Overall analog chip prices and demand are also not as volatile as commodity products, like memory chips. This is especially true for Maxim since it focuses on high-end analog products, which are highly specialized, lack direct substitutes, and enjoy long product cycles. The firm's competitive position is protected by high barriers to entry in analog, which are a function of unique chip design challenges and a scarcity of analog engineers.

Finally, we applaud the high quality of Maxim's financial statements--the firm rarely takes one-time charges--and the rock-solid balance sheet. Maxim's integration of Dallas Semi has also progressed well; the firm has reaped solid operating efficiencies. The only question from an investment standpoint is one of price--the stock has always commanded a premium and now is no exception. We'd recommend the shares only if they traded at a fairly large discount to our fair value estimate.

MORNINGSTAR® Stocks 500

Maytag MYG

	Rating	Risk	Moat Size	Fair Value	Last Close	Yield %
	★★★	Med.	Narrow	$40.00	$28.50	2.5

Company Profile

Maytag is the third-largest manufacturer of major home appliances in the United States. Its home appliances division makes washers, dryers, ranges, ovens, refrigerators, freezers, dishwashers, disposals, dehumidifiers, trash compactors and vacuum cleaners under the Maytag, Hoover, Jenn-Air, Admiral, and Magic Chef brands. Maytag also manufactures commercial-grade laundry equipment, restaurant equipment under the Jade name, and Dixie-Narco vending machines. Based in Newton, Iowa, Maytag does more than 90% of its business in North America.

Management

Maytag should feel much more comfortable with new CEO Ralph Hake than it did with the ousted Lloyd Ward. Hake spent 12 years with rival Whirlpool, rising to CFO before taking the same post at engineering concern Fluor in 1999.

Strategy

With aggressive product innovations and smart marketing, Maytag has staked a leading claim to the upper end of the domestic appliance market. After being distracted by a foray into lower-price appliances and the deterioration of some noncore businesses, the firm is reorienting itself around its core premium-price appliance lines and spending more on advertising and research and development.

403 West Fourth Street North   www.maytagcorp.com
Newton, IA 50208

Morningstar Grades

Growth [A-]	1998	1999	2000	2001
Revenue %	16.9	6.5	-1.4	8.2
Earnings/Share %	—	NMF	-33.3	-42.2
Book Value/Share %	—	NMF	-94.5	164.3
Dividends/Share %	6.3	5.9	0.0	0.0

By gaining share with its premium-price machines in the late 1990s, Maytag was able to beat its rivals and post healthy top-line growth. The Amana purchase is boosting sales comparisons right now, but the underlying trend is close to flat.

Profitability [B]	1999	2000	2001	TTM
Return on Assets %	12.5	7.5	1.5	5.2
Oper Cash Flow $Mil	447	382	400	343
- Cap Spending $Mil	135	153	146	201
= Free Cash Flow $Mil	312	229	255	142

Recovering from 2001's nadir, Maytag's operating margin rose 2.2 points to 9.3% in the first nine months of 2002. However, a more competitive landscape in premium-priced appliances makes a quick return to the 12%-14% margins of the past unlikely.

Financial Health [C]	1999	2000	2001	09-02
Long-term Debt $Mil	334	445	932	742
Total Equity $Mil	427	22	24	209
Debt/Equity Ratio	0.8	20.5	39.6	3.6

Huge share buybacks, the Amana purchase, and an underfunded pension plan have left Maytag highly leveraged. Rising operating profits mitigate our fears, but we still expect several years of debt repayment before share repurchases resume.

Industry	Investment Style	Stock Type	Sector
Appliance & Furniture Makers	▦ Mid Core	▨ High Yield	⬗ Consumer Goods

Competition

	Market Cap $Mil	Debt/ Equity	12 Mo Trailing Sales $Mil	Price/Cash Flow	Return On Assets%	Total Return% 1 Yr	3 Yr
Maytag	2,224	3.6	4,776	6.5	5.2	-6.3	-11.2
General Electric	242,308	2.2	130,295	8.2	2.7	-37.7	-18.9
Electrolux AB ADR	5,796	—	13,626	—	—		

Price Volatility   ▎Monthly Price High/Low   — Relative Strength to S&P 500

Annual $Price High Low	37.56 19.75	64.50 35.38	74.81 31.25	53.13 25.00	37.40 22.25	47.94 18.84

	1997	1998	1999	2000	2001	2002
Annual Total Return %	93.6	69.2	-21.9	-31.1	-1.8	-6.3

Fiscal Year-end: December	1997	1998	1999	2000	2001	TTM
Revenue $Mil	3,254	3,805	4,053	3,995	4,324	4,776
Net Income $Mil	—	—	329	201	48	165
Earnings Per Share $	1.83	3.00	3.66	2.44	1.41	2.11
Shares Outstanding Mil	—	—	86	78	77	78
Return on Equity %	—	—	76.9	927.1	202.7	79.0
Net Margin %	—	—	8.1	5.0	1.1	3.5
Asset Turnover	1.3	1.5	1.5	1.5	1.4	1.5
Financial Leverage	—	5.1	6.2	123.1	134.0	15.2

Valuation Ratios	Stock	Rel to Industry	Rel to S&P 500	Major Fund Holders	% of Fund Assets
Price/Earnings	13.5	1.0	0.6	Diamond Hill Focus A	4.03
Price/Book	10.7	4.7	3.3	Homestead Value	3.47
Price/Sales	0.5	1.0	0.2	Diamond Hill Large Cap A	3.15
Price/Cash Flow	6.5	0.7	0.5	Diamond Hill Small Cap A	3.01

Morningstar's Take By Josh Peters, 12-08-2002 Stock Price as of Analysis: $26.36

Now that it faces tougher competition in key market segments, Maytag is unlikely to scale new heights in profitability. But we think its new strategies put the firm on the right track, and would be willing to buy shares in the low $20s.

Long the appliance industry's leader in quality, innovation, and brand desirability, Maytag has traditionally earned the industry's highest profit margins. After a loss of strategic direction in 1999 and 2000 and a sharp drop in profits, Maytag is in full recovery mode. Gone are the Blodgett commercial oven business, a loss-making Chinese joint venture, and several oddball financing vehicles. In the place of these distractions has come accelerated investment in new product development, which should start to bear fruit in the form of a redesigned major appliance lineup in 2004.

Next on tap, we expect, will be some much-needed balance sheet repair. By accelerating its share-buyback program despite deteriorating cash flow, Maytag ran up $1.2 billion in debt. Meanwhile equity, depleted by the buybacks, a rising pension deficit, and the Amana acquisition, nearly dried up.

But once Maytag's debt load has been brought into a more appropriate balance, we believe the company will again return most of its free cash flow to shareholders. Between 1995 and 2001, the company disbursed $1.9 billion on dividends and stock buybacks--123% of the free cash flow earned during the period. We'd just as soon Maytag hadn't borrowed in the effort, but in an industry with few opportunities for profitable investment, we view this attitude as a plus.

Maytag is likely to fight an uphill battle against sluggish industry trends in 2003, as any decline in housing activity or a possible increase in interest rates could damp Americans' demand for new appliances. With Whirlpool's innovative new designs muscling Maytag aside in its most important product segment--premium-priced laundry machines--we think reaching 1999's peak operating margin of 14% is unlikely. We also worry about the industry's lack of pricing power: The Producer Price Index major appliance component has deflated 0.7% annually since 1990.

Despite strong cash flow, appliance stocks are notoriously cyclical. In keeping with our margin of safety guidelines, we would look to purchase Maytag shares at a 40% or greater discount to our fair value estimate of $40.

MBIA MBI

	Rating	Risk	Moat Size	Fair Value	Last Close	Yield %
	★★★	Med.	Narrow	$59.00	$43.86	1.6

Company Profile

MBIA provides financial-guarantee insurance for municipal bonds, asset-backed securities, and corporate obligations. This insurance provides an unconditional guarantee to pay the principal and interest on these bonds and securities. The company insures bonds sold in the primary and secondary markets, as well as those held in unit-investment trusts and by mutual funds. It also provides tax-revenue compliance and collection services to government agencies.

Management

Jay Brown, a protege of insurance legend Jack Byrne, overhauled MBIA's risk-assessment system when he became CEO in 1999. He refused a cash bonus in excess of $700,000 in 1999 and purchased more than 30,000 shares of MBIA with his own money in February 2000.

Strategy

MBIA is counting on the international bond insurance market, particularly in Europe, to drive much of its growth. Insuring U.S. asset-backed securities, which are growing at a much faster clip than the firm's traditional municipal bond business, is another growth driver. Meanwhile, MBIA is trying to boost its asset-management business, which, like bond insurance, offers solid recurring revenue.

113 King Street
Armonk, NY 10504
www.mbia.com

Morningstar Grades

Growth [B+]

	1998	1999	2000	2001
Revenue %	14.5	7.1	9.1	10.9
Earnings/Share %	4.9	-26.2	67.1	7.5
Book Value/Share %	10.9	-7.6	21.8	12.9
Dividends/Share %	2.6	1.9	1.9	9.7

MBIA's refusal to write policies with subpar profitability in 1999 and 2000 hurts its growth grade. Written premiums grew 26% through the first three quarters of 2002 as all of the firm's business lines expanded rapidly.

Profitability [A+]

	1999	2000	2001	TTM
Return on Assets %	2.6	3.8	3.5	3.3
Oper Cash Flow $Mil	443	640	722	—
- Cap Spending $Mil	59	16	6	—
= Free Cash Flow $Mil	—	—	—	—

Operating return on equity is about 13% for the trailing 12 months. This is solid but below the firm's 15% goal. Most new business meets profitability targets, but some less profitable business from earlier years remains on the books.

Financial Health [A]

	1999	2000	2001	09-02
Long-term Debt $Mil	—	—	—	—
Total Equity $Mil	3,513	4,223	4,783	5,482
Debt/Equity Ratio	—	—	—	—

MBIA's high level of provisioning for possible losses gives it a rock-solid balance sheet. Moreover, most of its business consists of investment-grade bonds, decreasing the chances that the firm will have to pay major claims.

	Industry	Investment Style	Stock Type	Sector
	Insurance (General)	▦ Mid Core	↗ Classic Growth	$ Financial Services

Competition

	Market Cap $Mil	Debt/ Equity	12 Mo Trailing Sales $Mil	Price/Cash Flow	Return On Assets%	Total Return% 1 Yr	3 Yr
MBIA	6,365	—	1,191	—	3.3	-17.1	11.7
General Electric	242,308	2.2	130,295	8.2	2.7	-37.7	-18.9
American International Gr	150,907	—	66,823	—	1.4	-26.9	-4.0

Price Volatility

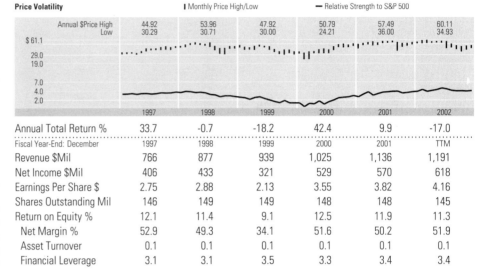

	Monthly Price High/Low	— Relative Strength to S&P 500

Annual $Price High Low	44.92 30.29	53.96 30.71	47.92 30.00	50.79 24.21	57.49 36.00	60.11 34.93

	1997	1998	1999	2000	2001	2002
Annual Total Return %	33.7	-0.7	-18.2	42.4	9.9	-17.0

Fiscal Year-End: December	1997	1998	1999	2000	2001	TTM
Revenue $Mil	766	877	939	1,025	1,136	1,191
Net Income $Mil	406	433	321	529	570	618
Earnings Per Share $	2.75	2.88	2.13	3.55	3.82	4.16
Shares Outstanding Mil	146	149	149	148	148	145
Return on Equity %	12.1	11.4	9.1	12.5	11.9	11.3
Net Margin %	52.9	49.3	34.1	51.6	50.2	51.9
Asset Turnover	0.1	0.1	0.1	0.1	0.1	0.1
Financial Leverage	3.1	3.1	3.5	3.3	3.4	3.4

Valuation Ratios

	Stock	Rel to Industry	Rel to S&P 500
Price/Earnings	10.5	0.3	0.4
Price/Book	1.2	0.7	0.4
Price/Sales	5.3	1.9	2.7
Price/Cash Flow	—	—	—

Major Fund Holders

	% of Fund Assets
Matthew 25	10.29
Century Shares Trust	6.13
Oppenheimer MidCap A	5.55
MassMutual Instl Focused Value S	5.10

Morningstar's Take By Aaron Westrate, 12-19-2002 Stock Price as of Analysis: $43.15

We maintain our $59 fair value estimate for MBIA, which represents an 18% premium to the company's adjusted book value. If the shares fell below $41, giving investors a 30% margin of safety, we'd be buyers.

The combination of MBIA's leverage and large potential losses because of the recession is pressuring the stock. At first glance, the very high leverage implied by $81 of net debt service insured for every $1 of claims-paying resources is disconcerting. An understanding of what MBIA insures should allay investors' concerns, however. MBIA's largest single issue is a New York City municipal bond with par value insured of $3.4 billion. In the event of a default, MBIA guarantees the timely payments to bondholders, but there is no cash balloon payment for the full par value insured. Furthermore, if New York City recovered from such an unlikely default, stringent terms would require it to repay MBIA for any claim payments and resume paying debt on the issue. Municipal bonds like this one, many of which are tax-backed or essential service revenue bonds, constitute 63% of MBIA's insured portfolio.

Nor does MBIA's leverage appear to be at odds with its triple A rating. The rating agencies run MBIA through a severe stress test that assumes an unprecedented level of losses. Garnering a top mark suggests that MBIA can sustain those depression-type losses and remain a going concern. Such a scenario would impair the firm's value materially, but the fact that MBIA could survive debunks the notion that its leverage has the company teetering on the brink of bankruptcy.

MBIA's stellar historical loss rate should further assuage investors' fears. In its 27 years of existence, MBIA has insured nearly 80,000 issues for $1.4 trillion in par value and incurred just 0.03% in losses on 54 of those issues. Such a minuscule loss ratio is the result of exacting underwriting standards. MBIA isn't lending its triple A rating to companies that would have junk-rated debt on a stand-alone basis. On the contrary, nearly all of the firm's insured portfolio is investment grade without MBIA's insurance.

We think overblown fears could give investors a compelling opportunity to own a bond insurer (the mention of which won't turn heads at cocktail parties) boasting a 67% pretax margin (the mention of which will turn heads). We'd invest if the shares fell below $41.

MORNINGSTAR® Stocks 500

Data as of 12-31-02

MBNA KRB

	Rating	Risk	Moat Size	Fair Value	Last Close	Yield %
	★★	High	Narrow	$18.00	$19.02	1.4

Company Profile

MBNA is a bank holding company and the parent company of MBNA America Bank. The bank issues standard and gold Visa and MasterCard credit cards, specializing in affinity credit cards marketed primarily to members of associations and financial institutions. MBNA also offers individual and second mortgage loans, money market deposit accounts, and certificates of deposit. The company operates two administrative and credit card facilities, two information-processing operations, and several telemarketing offices. MBNA is the world's second-largest issuer of bank credit cards.

Management

In June, 19-year MBNA veteran Bruce Hammonds was named CEO of MBNA America Bank, the company's primary business. Hammonds replaces Charlie Cawley, who will continue as company president. MBNA has a deep management team.

Strategy

MBNA seeks big profits in the credit card business by avoiding the "rags" and the "riches," so to speak. Through bank partnerships, the firm markets heavily to well-paid consumers who pose little credit risk, yet steers clear of clients so wealthy that they pay their bills on time to avoid interest charges. MBNA also seeks to expand through acquisitions and by increasing its foreign business.

1100 North King Street   www.mbna.com
Wilmington, DE 19884-0141

Morningstar Grades

Growth [A+]	1998	1999	2000	2001
Revenue %	14.8	28.9	19.5	26.7
Earnings/Share %	27.6	24.7	26.4	25.5
Book Value/Share %	24.2	66.0	55.7	14.4
Dividends/Share %	12.7	16.8	14.1	12.6

The firm's growth strategy involves originating new accounts as well as portfolio purchases and expansion into foreign markets. Given the size of its loan portfolio, however, growth is inevitably slowing.

Profitability [A+]	1999	2000	2001	TTM
Return on Assets %	3.3	3.4	3.7	3.5
Oper Cash Flow $Mil	1,556	-87	2,731	—
- Cap Spending $Mil	235	325	552	—
= Free Cash Flow $Mil	—	—	—	—

Earnings-per-share growth has averaged 25% annually for MBNA's 10 years as a public company. We forecast much slower growth going forward.

Financial Health [A+]	1999	2000	2001	09-02
Long-term Debt $Mil	—	—	—	—
Total Equity $Mil	4,199	6,627	7,799	8,542
Debt/Equity Ratio	—	—	—	—

Charge-offs rose a bit in the second quarter to 4.84%, but remain well below the industry average.

Industry	Investment Style	Stock Type	Sector
Finance	Large Core	Classic Growth	Financial Services

Competition	Market Cap $Mil	Debt/ Equity	12 Mo Trailing Sales $Mil	Price/Cash Flow	Return On Assets%	Total Return% 1 Yr	3 Yr
MBNA	24,301	—	10,348	—	3.5	-17.9	5.1
Citigroup	177,948	—	106,096	—	1.6	-24.2	1.1
American Express	46,839	—	23,482	—	1.6	0.2	-10.4

Price Volatility | Monthly Price High/Low — Relative Strength to S&P 500

Annual $Price High Low	13.59 7.96	17.25 9.00	22.17 13.88	26.75 12.96	26.38 15.62	26.27 12.95

	1997	1998	1999	2000	2001	2002
Annual Total Return %	-0.3	37.8	11.0	37.0	-3.7	-17.9
Fiscal Year-end: December	1997	1998	1999	2000	2001	TTM
Revenue $Mil	4,524	5,195	6,698	8,007	10,145	10,348
Net Income $Mil	623	776	1,024	1,313	1,694	1,751
Earnings Per Share $	0.51	0.65	0.81	1.02	1.28	1.33
Shares Outstanding Mil	1,168	1,153	1,220	1,246	1,290	1,278
Return on Equity %	31.6	32.5	24.4	19.8	21.7	20.5
Net Margin %	13.8	14.9	15.3	16.4	16.7	16.9
Asset Turnover	0.2	0.2	0.2	0.2	0.2	0.2
Financial Leverage	10.8	10.8	7.3	5.8	5.8	5.9

Valuation Ratios	Stock	Rel to Industry	Rel to S&P 500
Price/Earnings	14.3	1.2	0.6
Price/Book	2.8	0.8	0.9
Price/Sales	2.3	1.2	1.2
Price/Cash Flow	—	—	—

Major Fund Holders	% of Fund Assets
White Oak Growth Stock	9.29
Pin Oak Aggressive Stock	7.81
Alliance Select Investor Premier A	6.80
Alliance Premier Growth A	6.71

Morningstar's Take By Richard McCaffery, 12-16-2002 Stock Price as of Analysis: $20.10

MBNA has performed pretty well in a tough economy, but it's clear that growth is slowing and competition in the prime space is increasing. After putting the company into a more conservative model, which looks at return on invested capital and free cash flow, we've lowered our fair value to $18.

Our thesis on MBNA hasn't changed. The firm's a very capable lender, as evidenced by low charge-off rates, profitability, and good growth. Its affinity strategy, which markets cards to members of clubs and associations, is working well. The strategy distinguishes MBNA's marketing, improves the likelihood of consumers responding to new pitches, and perhaps even lowers attrition (switching to other card vendors) and default rates. MBNA is the largest independent credit card company, with $100 billion in total managed loans.

In addition, the company has aggressively moved overseas to extend its growth streak. Its August purchase of Alliance & Leicester's $1.2 billion portfolio gives MBNA about 10% market share in the United Kingdom, according to a recent PricewaterhouseCoopers' report. With operations in Ireland and Canada, about 11% of the company's managed loans are international accounts. In May, the company's application to market credit cards in

Spain was approved.

That said, we aren't willing to forecast a continuation of rapid growth from overseas markets. Credit card practices and behaviors are different in overseas markets, and regulatory issues abound. We think MBNA will find its niche, but we expect it will build gradually over time. We also see limits to the effectiveness of an affinity strategy, given the finite number of associations and near-superprime customers. More importantly, MBNA's focus on the upper end of the credit spectrum means it lacks the ability to look for more attractive accounts outside the prime and superprime markets, which limits flexibility. Of course, there are positive offsets to sticking with prime accounts, such as lower levels of needed capital, lower charge-offs and higher loan balances. Nevertheless, we think the ability to underwrite across the entire credit spectrum is a key advantage.

Although we think MBNA is a solid player, at present it's more than fully valued.

McDonald's MCD

	Rating	Risk	Moat Size	Fair Value	Last Close	Yield %
	★★★★★	Low	Wide	$29.00	$16.08	1.5

Company Profile

McDonald's is the world's largest fast-food chain, operating and franchising more than 30,000 of its restaurants. Its limited menu consists mainly of hamburgers and chicken sandwiches sold in combination with french fries. McDonald's has broadened into "fast-casual" dining with its Donatos pizzerias, Chipotle's Mexican restaurants, and Boston Market chain. These chains create a "sit-down" atmosphere and have more-diverse, higher-priced menus.

Management

Jack Greenberg knows the McDonald's system well from his long service with the company, including the past five years as CEO. However, the clock is running out in terms of investor patience with his turnaround efforts.

Strategy

As an increasingly mature franchise, McDonald's is focused on generating more sales and better profits from its current store base. With a new national advertising campaign (its first in five years), the company wants to reinvigorate brand awareness and spark sales. It also plans to remodel U.S. stores starting in 2003 to improve aesthetic appeal for customers and boost employee efficiency.

McDonald's Plaza   www.mcdonalds.com
Oak Brook, IL 60523

Morningstar Grades

Growth [B-]	1998	1999	2000	2001
Revenue %	8.9	6.7	7.4	4.4
Earnings/Share %	-4.3	26.4	5.0	-14.4
Book Value/Share %	8.4	2.4	-1.2	6.6
Dividends/Share %	9.2	8.6	12.3	4.7

McDonald's is the world's largest restaurant chain. Given the firm's market penetration, we think sales growth will average no better than the midsingle digits long term.

Profitability [A]	1999	2000	2001	TTM
Return on Assets %	9.3	9.1	7.3	6.4
Oper Cash Flow $Mil	3,009	2,752	2,688	2,821
- Cap Spending $Mil	1,868	1,945	1,906	1,949
= Free Cash Flow $Mil	1,141	806	782	872

Returns on assets have historically been higher than those of peers because of a rising number of franchised stores, which have limited operating expenses and higher profit margins. A drop in company-owned store margins pushed ROA beneath peers' in 2001.

Financial Health [A-]	1999	2000	2001	09-02
Long-term Debt $Mil	5,632	7,844	8,556	9,485
Total Equity $Mil	9,639	9,204	9,488	10,642
Debt/Equity Ratio	0.6	0.9	0.9	0.9

Its interest coverage ratio (earnings before interest and taxes over interest expense, including capitalized leases) of 3.0 bears watching. However, we think the steady nature of its business should keep McDonald's financially sound.

Industry	Investment Style	Stock Type	Sector
Restaurants	▦ Large Value	→ Slow Growth	▭ Consumer Services

Competition

	Market Cap $Mil	Debt/ Equity	12 Mo Trailing Sales $Mil	Price/Cash Flow	Return On Assets%	Total Return% 1 Yr	3 Yr
McDonald's	20,411	0.9	15,278	7.2	6.4	-38.4	-24.8
Yum Brands	7,169	4.3	7,498	6.9	11.1	-1.5	9.8
Wendy's International	3,125	0.5	2,634	7.7	8.4	-6.5	11.2

Price Volatility

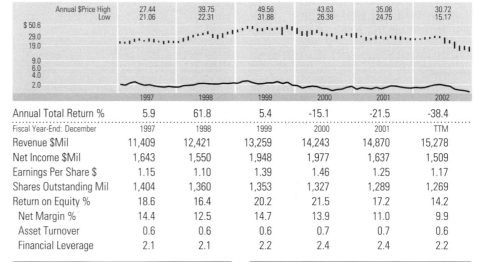

Annual Total Return %	5.9	61.8	5.4	-15.1	-21.5	-38.4

Fiscal Year-End: December	1997	1998	1999	2000	2001	TTM
Revenue $Mil	11,409	12,421	13,259	14,243	14,870	15,278
Net Income $Mil	1,643	1,550	1,948	1,977	1,637	1,509
Earnings Per Share $	1.15	1.10	1.39	1.46	1.25	1.17
Shares Outstanding Mil	1,404	1,360	1,353	1,327	1,289	1,269
Return on Equity %	18.6	16.4	20.2	21.5	17.2	14.2
Net Margin %	14.4	12.5	14.7	13.9	11.0	9.9
Asset Turnover	0.6	0.6	0.6	0.7	0.7	0.6
Financial Leverage	2.1	2.1	2.2	2.4	2.4	2.2

Valuation Ratios	Stock	Rel to Industry	Rel to S&P 500
Price/Earnings	13.7	0.9	0.6
Price/Book	1.9	0.8	0.6
Price/Sales	1.3	1.0	0.7
Price/Cash Flow	7.2	1.0	0.5

Major Fund Holders	% of Fund Assets
Rydex Leisure Inv	14.18
Reserve Large-Cap Growth R	5.72
Fidelity Select Food & Agriculture	5.10
Fidelity Select Retailing	4.97

Morningstar's Take By Carl Sibilski, 11-13-2002 Stock Price as of Analysis: $17.15

We think its planned improvements will help McDonald's remain the most powerful fast-food chain for years to come. Still, we'd look for at least a 20% margin of safety to our fair value estimate to account for operational hiccups that might pop up here or abroad.

Over the past decade, McDonald's has dealt with its share of drawbacks, including a strengthening dollar, concerns over mad cow disease, and transitional growth problems. Through all its travails, however, McDonald's hasn't flinched and remains a fundamentally strong company, in our opinion.

It appears that two of the firm's problems--currency translation and beef fears--have passed. After strengthening against the euro for the better part of the 1990s, the dollar appears to be holding steady or even weakening. For a company with 50% of sales coming from abroad and 20% from Europe (significantly more than its rivals), this is no small issue. With the more favorable exchange rates, McDonald's is able to convert its euro-denominated sales into more U.S. dollars.

The most recent hurdle for the company involves finding a way to stimulate sales and increase efficiency at its U.S. locations. McDonald's faces challenges like improving customer service and

designing healthier menu options at a time of increasing competition. The need for speed improvements is the most pressing issue affecting McDonald's and its customer service reputation. The company's Made for You system promises made-to-order food hot off the grill, but has stalled service time. Slower service means longer lines at the drive-through and counters, and could lead to lost sales as customers are turned off by the wait.

While these customer service challenges are great, none are new for a company that has evolved a great deal during its nearly 50-year history. We think its current struggles will provide the firm with a road map to handle the same issues in newly saturated foreign markets several years hence.

McDonald's continues to be one of the most recognized brands on the planet. It dominates the burger business with a 43% share of the market. In 2001, 46 million people per day ate in its stores. As one of the largest owners of real estate in the world, it already has exclusive rights to some of the best spots for selling food. Given these competitive strengths, we think McDonald's shares look like a real bargain below $20.

MORNINGSTAR® Stocks 500

McGraw-Hill Companies MHP

Rating	Risk	Moat Size	Fair Value	Last Close	Yield %
★★★★	Low	Wide	$75.00	$60.44	1.7

Company Profile

McGraw-Hill is an information services company. Its information and media services division operates ABC-affiliated television stations in four cities, publishes BusinessWeek magazine, and provides commercial directories to the construction and import-export industries. The financial services division includes Standard & Poor's, which provides consulting and analysis related to worldwide markets and securities. In addition, the company publishes textbooks and print and electronic information sources for legal, health, and business professionals.

Management

Harold W. (Terry) McGraw III leads the company that bears his family name. Since joining the firm in 1980, he has gradually moved up the ranks, becoming president in 1993, CEO in 1998, and chairman in 1999.

Strategy

McGraw-Hill uses the excellent cash flow from its financial services and media businesses to increase its presence in educational publishing, via acquisition and increased internal investment. This is a sound strategy, given that the educational publishing business benefits from additional scope and scale. The company is also focusing on increasing its international presence.

1221 Avenue Of The Americas   www.mcgraw-hill.com
New York, NY 10020

Morningstar Grades

Growth [B-]

	1998	1999	2000	2001
Revenue %	5.4	7.2	7.2	8.5
Earnings/Share %	13.7	28.9	-3.7	-6.8
Book Value/Share %	8.1	6.4	8.4	5.1
Dividends/Share %	8.3	10.3	9.3	4.3

The firm's top line has grown at an annual pace of almost 10% over the past 10 years, in part thanks to acquisitions in educational publishing. We assume more moderate growth in the future.

Profitability [A]

	1999	2000	2001	TTM
Return on Assets %	10.3	8.2	7.3	8.3
Oper Cash Flow $Mil	708	706	1,071	1,199
- Cap Spending $Mil	154	98	117	82
= Free Cash Flow $Mil	554	608	954	1,117

Operating profit margins have been on the rise over the past decade as the publishing unit has benefited from increased scale. Margins have also increased at the financial services unit.

Financial Health [A]

	1999	2000	2001	09-02
Long-term Debt $Mil	355	818	834	622
Total Equity $Mil	1,648	1,761	1,854	2,170
Debt/Equity Ratio	0.2	0.5	0.5	0.3

We're not concerned about the firm's financial health. Cash flow from operations in 2002 will be larger than the company's debt load. Also, operating income covers interest expense almost 40 times.

Industry	Investment Style	Stock Type	Sector
Publishing	Large Core	Slow Growth	Media

Competition

	Market Cap $Mil	Debt/Equity	12 Mo Trailing Sales $Mil	Price/Cash Flow	Return On Assets%	Total Return% 1 Yr	3 Yr
McGraw-Hill Companies	11,713	0.3	4,730	9.8	8.3	0.7	4.5
Vivendi ADR	17,447	0.8	39,593	4.4	-9.9	-69.3	-43.0
Reed Elsevier PLC ADR	11,056	—	3,034	—	—	—	—

Price Volatility

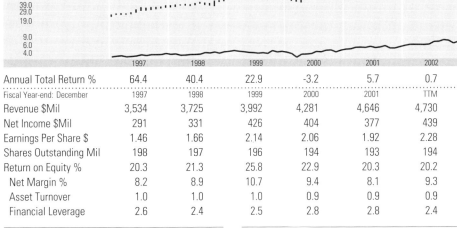

Annual $Price High / Low	37.69 / 22.44	51.66 / 34.25	63.13 / 47.13	67.69 / 41.88	70.87 / 48.70	69.70 / 50.71

	1997	1998	1999	2000	2001	2002
Annual Total Return %	64.4	40.4	22.9	-3.2	5.7	0.7

Fiscal Year-end: December	1997	1998	1999	2000	2001	TTM
Revenue $Mil	3,534	3,725	3,992	4,281	4,646	4,730
Net Income $Mil	291	331	426	404	377	439
Earnings Per Share $	1.46	1.66	2.14	2.06	1.92	2.28
Shares Outstanding Mil	198	197	196	194	193	194
Return on Equity %	20.3	21.3	25.8	22.9	20.3	20.2
Net Margin %	8.2	8.9	10.7	9.4	8.1	9.3
Asset Turnover	1.0	1.0	1.0	0.9	0.9	0.9
Financial Leverage	2.6	2.4	2.5	2.8	2.8	2.4

Valuation Ratios

	Stock	Rel to Industry	Rel to S&P 500
Price/Earnings	26.5	1.0	1.1
Price/Book	5.4	1.2	1.7
Price/Sales	2.5	1.0	1.2
Price/Cash Flow	9.8	1.0	0.7

Major Fund Holders

	% of Fund Assets
Berger Large Cap Value Inv	5.26
CDC Nvest Jurika & Voyles Rel Val Y	3.95
Enterprise Growth and Income Y	3.28
Transamerica Premier Balanced Inv	3.26

Morningstar's Take By Jonathan Schrader, 11-26-2002 Stock Price as of Analysis: $58.52

We love wide-moat companies; they're great long-term investments if purchased at the right price. McGraw-Hill possesses several competitive advantages that give it such an economic moat.

The company's education segment, its biggest in terms of revenue, benefits from economies of scale: Profitability tends to improve as market share increases. Since cash flow at the company is so strong, the education unit has easily increased its share through acquisitions and increased internal investment. As a result, operating margins now hover around 15%, up from 11% in 1992. This combination of share gains and margin increases has resulted in a quadrupling of operating profit in this segment over the past 10 years.

The financial services segment possesses some intangible assets that make it a great business as well. For one, Standard & Poor's is one of the most respected brands in the financial services arena. Whether in indexing, analysis, or ratings, this brand carries a cachet that allows the company to charge a premium to be associated with it. This cachet has served the firm particularly well over the past few years, as growth in exchange-traded funds based on S&P indexes has filled McGraw-Hill's coffers with extra cash.

S&P also benefits from government regulation. Because of the importance and complexity of evaluating credit risk, the Securities and Exchange Commission has developed a designation--Nationally Recognized Statistical Rating Organization--that a company must acquire before moving into the credit-rating market. This keeps competition at bay: Only three national firms--McGraw-Hill, Moody's, and Fitch--have the designation. This keeps margins high and cash flow strong, because this type of business requires little in the way of capital investment.

S&P has used its strong position in the United States and its great reputation to expand successfully into foreign markets. Much of this segment's growth will come from international business; the same goes for McGraw-Hill's education segment. With international exposure comes additional risk, but we are comfortable with the firm's international strategy.

We believe that McGraw-Hill's businesses are very attractive, and we'd be buyers as long as we could get in at a 20% discount to our fair value estimate.

MedImmune MEDI

	Rating	Risk	Moat Size	Fair Value	Last Close	Yield %
	★★	High	None	$28.00	$27.17	0.0

Company Profile

MedImmune develops and manufactures biopharmaceutical products and vaccines. It makes RespiGam and Synagis to prevent the respiratory syncytial virus in infants. The company also makes CytoGam, which prevents cytomegalovirus in major organ transplant patients. In addition, MedImmune makes Ethyol to reduce toxicity from cancer treatments. The company is developing vaccines that may prevent human papillomavirus, urinary tract infections, and psoriasis. In December 2001, MedImmune agreed to acquire Aviron, adding influenza vaccine FluMist to its late-stage product pipeline.

Management

CFO and vice chairman David Mott took over as CEO in October 2000. He's been with the company since 1992. Previously, he worked in investment banking at Smith Barney.

Strategy

MedImmune has three primary goals: Drive the growth of its first big-selling drug (Synagis), obtain approval for and commercialize influenza vaccine FluMist, and develop a continual stream of products in its pipeline. That pipeline includes vaccines to meet significant medical needs, like a vaccine for human papillomavirus, and drugs that aim to treat cancer and autoimmune diseases.

35 West Watkins Mill Rd   www.medimmune.com
Gaithersburg, MD 20878

Industry	Investment Style	Stock Type	Sector
Biotechnology	⊞ Mid Growth	↑ Aggr. Growth	◔ Healthcare

Competition

	Market Cap $Mil	Debt/ Equity	12 Mo Trailing Sales $Mil	Price/Cash Flow	Return On Assets%	Total Return% 1 Yr	3 Yr
MedImmune	6,820	0.1	759	37.9	-55.7	-41.4	-15.4
Merck	127,121	0.3	50,430	13.2	15.0	-1.3	-2.5
Amgen	61,986	0.2	4,881	31.7	-7.1	-14.4	-6.0

Price Volatility

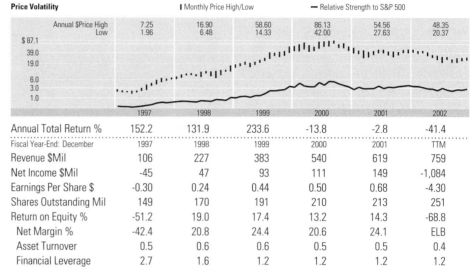

Annual $Price High Low	7.25 1.96	16.90 6.48	58.60 14.33	86.13 42.00	54.56 27.63	48.35 20.37

	1997	1998	1999	2000	2001	2002
Annual Total Return %	152.2	131.9	233.6	-13.8	-2.8	-41.4

Fiscal Year-End: December	1997	1998	1999	2000	2001	TTM
Revenue $Mil	106	227	383	540	619	759
Net Income $Mil	-45	47	93	111	149	-1,084
Earnings Per Share $	-0.30	0.24	0.44	0.50	0.68	-4.30
Shares Outstanding Mil	149	170	191	210	213	251
Return on Equity %	-51.2	19.0	17.4	13.2	14.3	-68.8
Net Margin %	-42.4	20.8	24.4	20.6	24.1	ELB
Asset Turnover	0.5	0.6	0.6	0.5	0.5	0.4
Financial Leverage	2.7	1.6	1.2	1.2	1.2	1.2

Valuation Ratios	Stock	Rel to Industry	Rel to S&P 500
Price/Earnings	NMF	—	—
Price/Book	4.3	1.2	1.4
Price/Sales	9.0	0.7	4.5
Price/Cash Flow	37.9	1.2	2.9

Major Fund Holders	% of Fund Assets
Amerindo Health & Biotechnology A	18.68
Smith Barney Biotechnology A	8.28
PIMCO RCM Biotechnology D	8.08
Turner Healthcare & Biotechnology	6.90

Morningstar Grades

Growth [A-]	1998	1999	2000	2001
Revenue %	114.9	68.7	41.0	14.5
Earnings/Share %	NMF	80.8	13.6	36.0
Book Value/Share %	118.6	97.5	49.9	25.6
Dividends/Share %	NMF	NMF	NMF	NMF

Annual sales growth, which averaged 60% between 1998 and 2001, is slowing. Total sales growth declined to 15% in 2001. A pop in Synagis demand and reacquired rights to Ethyol have boosted 2002 sales, but the company depends on FluMist for strong growth.

Profitability [B]	1999	2000	2001	TTM
Return on Assets %	14.4	11.0	12.2	-55.7
Oper Cash Flow $Mil	59	173	251	180
- Cap Spending $Mil	12	8	18	57
= Free Cash Flow $Mil	47	165	233	123

MedImmune is one of the few profitable biotechs. Operating margins reached 31% in 2001. An increase in research and development expenditures and a write-off of acquired R&D from Aviron will hurt earnings in 2002, but shouldn't affect cash.

Financial Health [A+]	1999	2000	2001	09-02
Long-term Debt $Mil	10	10	9	218
Total Equity $Mil	537	844	1,044	1,576
Debt/Equity Ratio	0.0	0.0	0.0	0.1

In addition to being able to fund operations internally, the company has $1.2 billion in cash and marketable securities--plenty to cover the little debt it has.

Morningstar's Take   By Jill Kiersky, 12-10-2002   Stock Price as of Analysis: $24.90

MedImmune has a strong position among mature biotechnology companies (ones that are actually profitable). The company should be able to maintain this status, but it's not without sizable risks. We think the stock would be worth the risk if it fell below $20 per share.

With several marketed drugs, MedImmune has been profitable since 1998. The firm has a blockbuster in Synagis, a monoclonal antibody therapeutic that prevents severe respiratory infections in high-risk infants. Sales of this drug improved 20% to $516 million in 2001, and were up 34% in the first nine months of 2002 from the year-ago period, primarily because of an increase in demand. With the drug's recent approval in Japan, patent protection until 2015, and a more potent formulation in testing, we expect sales to continue to increase, although not as rapidly.

With no new drugs ready for approval before 2005, most of MedImmune's sales growth will have to come from FluMist, an inhalable influenza vaccine acquired with MedImmune's purchase of Aviron in early 2002. The market for flu vaccines is large: 80 million doses of injectable flu vaccines were sold in 2000, and that number is expected to grow 10% annually. Three injectable vaccines are currently on

the market, and that number will drop to just two when Wyeth stops making its vaccine next year in favor of FluMist, which it will promote with MedImmune. As the only inhalable vaccine, FluMist could gain a large following.

There are plenty of roadblocks to achieving billion-dollar sales, however. In August 2001 and again in August 2002, the Food and Drug Administration raised questions about FluMist's safety, delaying the vaccine's approval at least until the 2003-04 flu season. Additional delays could destroy any momentum built up by the market's anticipation of the vaccine. Also, MedImmune intends to market FluMist as a low-volume, high-price vaccine. While FluMist offers an alternative to patients averse to injections, capturing a large segment of the market will be challenging, given the low-cost options already available.

We believe management is up to the task, however. The company keeps its spending in check and generates plenty of free cash flow from existing product sales. The balance sheet looks healthy, with very little debt and lots of cash to bring vaccines and drugs through the pipeline. The offsetting risks, however, necessitate a 40%-50% margin of safety to our fair value estimate before buying.

MORNINGSTAR® Stocks 500

Medtronic MDT

	Rating	Risk	Moat Size	Fair Value	Last Close	Yield %
	★★★	Low	Wide	$40.00	$45.60	0.7

Company Profile

Medtronic develops and manufactures therapeutic medical devices for cardiovascular and neurological applications. Its products include pacemakers, mechanical heart valves, implantable devices to treat urinary incontinence, and products for cardiopulmonary, vascular, and neurological and spinal stimulation. The company markets its products to health-care institutions and physicians in the United States and overseas. Foreign sales account for approximately 35% of the company's total sales.

Management

Arthur D. Collins Jr. gained the title of chief executive in May 2001 and the chairman's office in April 2002. Collins shares credit for broadening Medtronic's product lines.

Strategy

Medtronic is focused on combining implantable sensory technology with its medical devices that treat chronic diseases like heart disease. The firm hopes these products, which will allow doctors to monitor their patients in real time, will expand its revenue stream and maintain its annual sales growth rate of 15% in any five-year period.

710 Medtronic Parkway   www.medtronic.com
Minneapolis, MN 55432

Morningstar Grades

Growth [B]	1999	2000	2001	2002
Revenue %	23.6	18.5	10.7	15.5
Earnings/Share %	-22.0	128.2	-4.5	-5.9
Book Value/Share %	35.5	17.0	20.9	16.8
Dividends/Share %	18.2	23.1	25.2	14.8

Revenue growth has averaged 18% over the past five years, thanks to acquisitions and new product approvals. The MiniMed acquisition should continue the company's diversification strategy just in time to offset declines in the vascular business.

Profitability [A]	2000	2001	2002	TTM
Return on Assets %	19.0	14.9	9.0	11.4
Oper Cash Flow $Mil	1,026	1,832	1,590	1,610
- Cap Spending $Mil	343	440	386	368
= Free Cash Flow $Mil	684	1,392	1,204	1,243

Medtronic's gross margins are among the best in the industry, about 74%. Net income slipped in fiscal 2002 because of acquisition-related charges, but margins are still 4 percentage points above the industry average.

Financial Health [A]	2000	2001	2002	10-02
Long-term Debt $Mil	15	13	10	1,983
Total Equity $Mil	4,513	5,510	6,431	7,181
Debt/Equity Ratio	0.0	0.0	0.0	0.3

Medtronic took on more than $2.5 billion in debt to finance the MiniMed acquisition, raising its debt/equity ratio to 0.4, still far below the S&P 500 average. The company generates plenty of free cash flow to repay its obligations.

Industry	Investment Style	Stock Type	Sector
Medical Equipment	▦ Large Growth	↗ Classic Growth	◉ Healthcare

Competition	Market Cap $Mil	Debt/ Equity	12 Mo Trailing Sales $Mil	Price/Cash Flow	Return On Assets%	Total Return% 1 Yr	3 Yr
Medtronic	55,637	0.3	6,989	34.6	11.4	-10.4	10.3
Johnson & Johnson	159,452	0.1	35,120	18.0	16.3	-7.9	8.0
Boston Scientific	17,341	0.4	2,782	24.7	7.8	76.3	22.1

Price Volatility

Annual $Price High / Low	26.38 / 14.41	38.41 / 22.72	44.63 / 29.94	62.00 / 32.75	60.81 / 36.75	51.21 / 32.50

I Monthly Price High/Low — Relative Strength to S&P 500

	1997	1998	1999	2000	2001	2002
Annual Total Return %	55.2	42.1	-1.5	66.3	-14.8	-10.3

Fiscal Year-end: April	1998	1999	2000	2001	2002	TTM
Revenue $Mil	3,423	4,233	5,016	5,552	6,411	6,989
Net Income $Mil	588	467	1,084	1,046	984	1,301
Earnings Per Share $	0.50	0.39	0.89	0.85	0.80	1.06
Shares Outstanding Mil	1,152	1,167	1,191	1,202	1,215	1,220
Return on Equity %	21.4	12.3	24.0	19.0	15.3	18.1
Net Margin %	17.2	11.0	21.6	18.8	15.3	18.6
Asset Turnover	0.9	0.8	0.9	0.8	0.6	0.6
Financial Leverage	1.4	1.3	1.3	1.3	1.7	1.6

Valuation Ratios	Stock	Rel to Industry	Rel to S&P 500
Price/Earnings	43.0	1.4	1.8
Price/Book	7.7	1.2	2.4
Price/Sales	8.0	1.7	4.0
Price/Cash Flow	34.6	1.4	2.6

Major Fund Holders	% of Fund Assets
Conseco 20 A	12.86
Papp Stock	11.52
Papp America-Pacific Rim	7.75
Live Oak Health Sciences	7.42

Morningstar's Take By Travis Pascavis, 12-10-2002 Stock Price as of Analysis: $46.11

Medtronic is the largest medical device maker and the market leader in many of its product lines. We would need to see only a modest discount to our fair value estimate before purchasing shares.

A handful of companies dominate the medical device industry. Despite regulatory pressures that attempt to drive prices lower, firms have achieved economies of scale that provide decent margins and keep new competition at bay. Medtronic and its competitors defend their share primarily through product innovation and heavy-duty sales and marketing.

Medtronic's performance in both areas has paid off. The company makes better use of its research and development dollars; over the past three years, it spent an average 10% of sales on R&D while increasing sales an average 16%; rival Guidant spent 14% on R&D to gain 13% in sales over the same period. Medtronic is the clear cardiovascular device leader, with $6.4 billion in annual sales and more than 50% of the market for cardiac rhythm management devices like pacemakers and defibrillators. The company manages to turn about 20% of sales into free cash flow (cash from operations minus capital expenditures)--more to spend on development.

While Medtronic's grasp on cardiac rhythm management remains strong, the firm is losing ground in the vascular market. It lost about 15 percentage points ($200 million in sales) of its market share in perfusion delivery systems after dropping its license with Boston Scientific. Our bigger concern is its third-place position in the drug-coated stent race. Drug-coated stents, which effectively eliminate the reblocking of blood vessels, could cannibalize the market for bare-metal stents (which keep the blood flowing but often close up). Their entry could expand the total worldwide stent market to more than $4 billion by 2005, from $2.2 billion today.

Medtronic is developing a drug-coated product with Abbott, but we expect Johnson & Johnson, Boston Scientific, and possibly Guidant to have their versions on the market by the time Medtronic's is approved. As drug-coated stents are made available, we expect bare-metal stent prices to decline significantly, leaving Medtronic, which now sells about 15% of all bare-metal stents, in the lurch.

Given the challenges in the stent market and the constant need to enhance cardiac products, we'd want a 20% margin of safety to our fair value estimate before buying the shares.

Mellon Financial MEL

	Rating	Risk	Moat Size	Fair Value	Last Close	Yield %
	★★★★	Med.	Narrow	$38.00	$26.11	1.9

Company Profile

Mellon Financial is the holding company for subsidiaries that do private banking, consulting, asset management, and back-office management. Once a banking organization spanning the Northeast, the firm has dropped most of its retail banking operations to focus on nonlending financial businesses. The company's Boston Company subsidiary offers trust and investment-management services. Its Dreyfus subsidiary provides mutual fund and portfolio-management services.

Management

CEO Martin McGuinn has been battle-tested, both as a Marine and as a long-time Mellon corporate executive. His reign has been characterized by a radical restructuring of Mellon's business mix.

Strategy

Mellon is concentrating on fee-based businesses like asset management and global custody. It aims to take advantage of the expected growth of the private wealth-management market and the demand for corporate outsourcing of custody and accounting services. The firm also intends to drastically reduce its loan business to lessen its credit risk.

One Mellon Center   www.mellon.com
Pittsburgh, PA 15258-0001

Industry	Investment Style	Stock Type	Sector
Money Management	▦ Large Value	→ Slow Growth	$ Financial Services

Competition

	Market Cap $Mil	Debt/ Equity	12 Mo Trailing Sales $Mil	Price/Cash Flow	Return On Assets%	Total Return% 1 Yr	3 Yr
Mellon Financial	11,252	—	4,350	—	3.8	-29.5	-2.6
Bank of New York	17,396	—	6,017	—	1.4	-39.9	-11.1
State Street	12,649	—	4,947	—	0.9	-24.5	6.7

Price Volatility

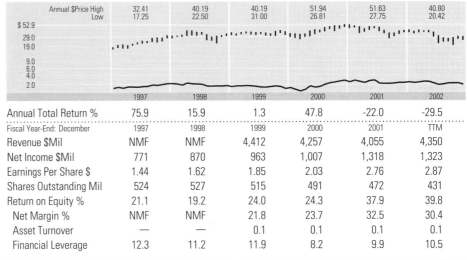

Annual $Price High Low	32.41 17.25	40.19 22.50	40.19 31.00	51.94 26.81	51.63 27.75	40.80 20.42
	1997	1998	1999	2000	2001	2002

	1997	1998	1999	2000	2001	2002
Annual Total Return %	75.9	15.9	1.3	47.8	-22.0	-29.5

Fiscal Year-End: December	1997	1998	1999	2000	2001	TTM
Revenue $Mil	NMF	NMF	4,412	4,257	4,055	4,350
Net Income $Mil	771	870	963	1,007	1,318	1,323
Earnings Per Share $	1.44	1.62	1.85	2.03	2.76	2.87
Shares Outstanding Mil	524	527	515	491	472	431
Return on Equity %	21.1	19.2	24.0	24.3	37.9	39.8
Net Margin %	NMF	NMF	21.8	23.7	32.5	30.4
Asset Turnover	—	—	0.1	0.1	0.1	0.1
Financial Leverage	12.3	11.2	11.9	8.2	9.9	10.5

Valuation Ratios	Stock	Rel to Industry	Rel to S&P 500
Price/Earnings	9.1	0.5	0.4
Price/Book	3.4	1.3	1.1
Price/Sales	2.6	1.0	1.3
Price/Cash Flow	—	—	—

Major Fund Holders	% of Fund Assets
Lake Forest Core Equity	6.36
Fifth Third Quality Growth Inv A	4.27
Berger Large Cap Value Inv	3.96
Heritage Value Equity A	3.40

Morningstar Grades

Growth [D]	1998	1999	2000	2001
Revenue %	—	NMF	-3.5	-4.7
Earnings/Share %	12.5	14.2	9.7	36.0
Book Value/Share %	23.4	-8.4	8.5	-12.9
Dividends/Share %	9.3	10.6	10.3	-4.7

Mellon's switch to a fee-based business strategy over the past three years was the right move, but a slowing economy and the need to sell noncore units hurt growth. Look for growth to improve as the economy picks up.

Profitability [A]	1999	2000	2001	TTM
Return on Assets %	2.0	2.9	3.8	3.8
Oper Cash Flow $Mil	-59	2,222	3,123	—
- Cap Spending $Mil	90	220	167	—
= Free Cash Flow $Mil	—	—	—	—

Returns on equity and assets have improved steadily over the past decade, though they declined last year with the slowing economy. Still, Mellon's business model has the ability to generate very attractive profits.

Financial Health [A-]	1999	2000	2001	09-02
Long-term Debt $Mil	—	—	—	—
Total Equity $Mil	4,016	4,152	3,482	3,325
Debt/Equity Ratio	—	—	—	—

Mellon's financial leverage has traditionally been lower than that of its banking peers, and declined over the past year. The company has more than $4 billion in cash on hand, which it has been spending on acquisitions and share repurchases.

Morningstar's Take By Rachel Barnard, 12-09-2002 Stock Price as of Analysis: $27.52

We think Mellon has laid the groundwork to be a successful money-management franchise.

Once a large lender to Pittsburgh's steel titans, Mellon has transformed itself into one of the world's largest global custodians and asset managers. The metamorphosis was swiftly and deftly executed by CEO Martin McGuinn, whose vision for the bank is coming to fruition. Mellon now brings in 86% of its revenue from investment-management and custody fees.

Mellon has aggressively expanded its custody business and now ranks as the world's fifth largest, hard on the heels of giants like State Street and Bank of New York. The custody business involves safekeeping and accounting services for financial firms with large numbers of securities to track. It has been a growth market as financial firms have sought to outsource this kind of back-office processing to specialists like Mellon, which now has more than $2 trillion in assets under custody.

Eyeing the overseas markets as well, Mellon has initiated a joint venture with Dutch bank ABN Amro and already has $250 billion in assets under custody. The venture will target markets around the world.

Mellon is also one of the world's fastest-growing asset managers, racking up 10% internal growth since 1998 and also acquiring numerous investment shops. Most recently, Mellon picked up a hedge fund, a separate account manager (which builds customized accounts for wealthy investors), and a wealth manager from Ohio--one if its key target markets for expanding its wealth-management business into the Midwest. Even so, Mellon is still sitting on a pile of cash left over from selling its retail banking business. We expect to see more acquisitions and share buybacks on the horizon.

We also see the potential for Mellon to combine its strength in money management and back-office processing with its pension consulting business to offer one-stop shopping for companies seeking pension and 401(k) management.

Mellon is downplaying corporate lending, but the business still exists to serve customers who buy other services like custody. With more loan losses possible, we're not betting that Mellon can achieve its aggressive targets for escalating returns on equity. But we do think the firm can maintain a return on equity above 20%, making it comparable to other asset managers and making the shares worth at least $38, in our opinion.

MORNINGSTAR® Stocks 500

Merck MRK

	Rating	Risk	Moat Size	Fair Value	Last Close	Yield %
	★★★	Med.	Wide	$53.00	$56.61	2.5

Company Profile

Merck produces pharmaceutical products and provides managed-care services. Its pharmaceutical products include cardiovascular therapeutics, antiulcerants, antibiotics, a male-pattern baldness treatment, HIV protease inhibitors, and hepatitis B and pediatric disease vaccines. The company also has drugs for conditions like asthma, arthritis, fungal infections, and osteoporosis. Its Merck-Medco pharmacy benefit manager division provides managed health-care and prescription-drug services and is slated to be spun off to shareholders by mid-2003.

Management

Since taking the helm in 1994, CEO Raymond Gilmartin has pushed the research division to produce marketable drugs faster. The Arcoxia withdrawal and changes in sales reporting have put management in an unfavorable light with us.

Strategy

With several of its key drugs coming off patent, Merck is focusing its marketing on newer products that it expects to drive growth. The company recently announced plans to separate its pharmacy benefit and pharmaceutical units in an effort to enhance value, provide more financial transparency, and rid itself of the conflict of interest between the units.

One Merck Drive   www.merck.com
Whitehouse Station, NJ 08889-0100

Morningstar Grades

Growth [B]	1998	1999	2000	2001
Revenue %	13.8	21.6	23.4	18.2
Earnings/Share %	15.0	14.0	18.4	8.3
Book Value/Share %	2.7	5.0	14.5	9.8
Dividends/Share %	8.6	18.5	12.5	9.5

In the past five years, much of Merck's revenue growth has come from Medco. Calendar 2002 is expected to produce no growth in earnings per share. Third-quarter revenue was up 8% from a year ago, but cost of goods sold increased twice as fast.

Profitability [A+]	1999	2000	2001	TTM
Return on Assets %	16.5	17.0	16.5	15.0
Oper Cash Flow $Mil	6,131	7,687	9,080	9,630
- Cap Spending $Mil	2,561	2,728	2,725	2,387
= Free Cash Flow $Mil	3,570	4,960	6,355	7,244

Merck's operating and net margins have been among the industry's best over the past six years, even with Medco in tow. Sans Medco, pro forma operating margins averaged 46.8% for the nine months ended September 30, 2002.

Financial Health [A-]	1999	2000	2001	09-02
Long-term Debt $Mil	3,144	3,601	4,799	4,870
Total Equity $Mil	13,242	14,832	16,050	17,533
Debt/Equity Ratio	0.2	0.2	0.3	0.3

Merck's balance sheet is well balanced, with $10 billion in debt and $11 billion in cash and investments. Given the $5-$6 billion in annual free cash flow (cash flow from operations less capex), we're not concerned about Merck's financial health.

Industry	Investment Style	Stock Type	Sector
Drugs	▦ Large Core	▨ High Yield	◪ Healthcare

Competition	Market Cap $Mil	Debt/ Equity	12 Mo Trailing Sales $Mil	Price/Cash Flow	Return On Assets%	Total Return% 1 Yr	3 Yr
Merck	127,121	0.3	50,430	13.2	15.0	-1.3	-2.5
Pfizer	188,377	0.2	34,407	21.1	18.3	-22.2	1.0
Eli Lilly & Company	71,334	0.5	10,951	29.0	13.5	-17.6	1.8

Price Volatility

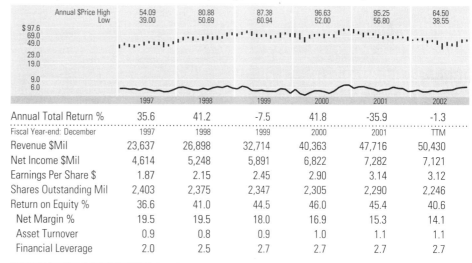

	1997	1998	1999	2000	2001	2002
Annual $Price High	54.09	80.88	87.38	96.63	95.25	64.50
Low	39.00	50.69	60.94	52.00	56.80	38.55
Annual Total Return %	35.6	41.2	-7.5	41.8	-35.9	-1.3

Fiscal Year-end: December	1997	1998	1999	2000	2001	TTM
Revenue $Mil	23,637	26,898	32,714	40,363	47,716	50,430
Net Income $Mil	4,614	5,248	5,891	6,822	7,282	7,121
Earnings Per Share $	1.87	2.15	2.45	2.90	3.14	3.12
Shares Outstanding Mil	2,403	2,375	2,347	2,305	2,290	2,246
Return on Equity %	36.6	41.0	44.5	46.0	45.4	40.6
Net Margin %	19.5	19.5	18.0	16.9	15.3	14.1
Asset Turnover	0.9	0.8	0.9	1.0	1.1	1.1
Financial Leverage	2.0	2.5	2.7	2.7	2.7	2.7

Valuation Ratios	Stock	Rel to Industry	Rel to S&P 500
Price/Earnings	18.1	0.8	0.8
Price/Book	7.3	1.0	2.3
Price/Sales	2.5	0.6	1.3
Price/Cash Flow	13.2	0.6	1.0

Major Fund Holders	% of Fund Assets
Papp America-Abroad	9.82
Fidelity Select Pharmaceuticals	9.66
ProFunds Ultra Pharmaceuticals Inv	9.48
Schwab Health Care Focus	8.54

Morningstar's Take By Todd N. Lebor, 10-31-2002 Stock Price as of Analysis: $54.24

Merck is not a company we'd throw money at right now.

It's no accident that Merck has a vaultlike balance sheet with $31 billion in retained earnings. It took decades to build up that kind of equity and we expect the company to add more over the next few decades; we just don't expect it in the next few quarters. In fact, we see too much risk in Merck because it's unclear how profitable the health-care bellwether will be once it sheds its prescription benefit manager (PBM) division.

Gross and operating margins are the key valuation triggers in a drug company. A percentage point here or there makes a huge difference in the company's cash flows. Cash flows dictate valuation, and since we are uncomfortable with Merck's pro forma (sans Medco) margins, the company's true value remains elusive.

Our suspicion is that Merck's extremely low selling, general, and administrative (SG&A) expenses are unsustainable. Excluding Medco, Merck is spending only 25%-28% of its revenue on SG&A. Even Pfizer, with 10 drugs producing more than $1 billion in annual sales, is spending 34%-38% of revenue on SG&A. Excluding Medco, Merck reported 47% operating margins in the third quarter of 2002.

Pfizer's were only 34%. We think these costs are so low because Merck has greatly benefited from Medco's buying its drugs in large quantities and at favorable prices. A Medco filing in April 2002 did state that Merck products are disproportionately represented (compared with the overall market) with Medco's customers. Once Medco is spun off, which we expect to occur before year-end 2003, this benefit will fade away, and Merck will have to build--and pay for--a salesforce commensurate with the competition.

Despite the uncertainty, we can see value in Merck. The company marches to its own drummer. In the 1990s, while peers were merging like crazy and spinning off their PBMs because of regulatory pressure, Merck stood pat. It increased sales internally and through joint ventures, and hung on to Medco, eventually turning it into the biggest PBM in the country. Also, its growth-driving drugs have enormous target audiences, just in the United States: Zocor has 50 million; Cozaar/Hyzaar, 40 million; Vioxx, 22 million; Fosamax, 25 million; and Singulair, 15 million.

Merck isn't financially troubled, but we question its profitability. Therefore, we'd require at least a 40% discount to our fair value estimate before buying the stock.

Mercury General MCY

	Rating	Risk	Moat Size	Fair Value	Last Close	Yield %
	★★★	Med.	Narrow	$40.00	$37.58	3.2

Company Profile

Mercury General writes automobile insurance. The company also offers its automobile policyholders coverage for bodily injury liability, property damage liability, and physical damage. Approximately 90% of the company's premiums are written for California residents, with the remainder for residents of Georgia, Oklahoma, Texas, Florida, and Illinois.

Management

George Joseph has been chairman and CEO since 1961. Insiders own 52% of outstanding shares, and the Joseph family owns 35%.

Strategy

Insuring preferred drivers--who constitute more than 70% of Mercury's California book of business--results in fewer claims and lower loss expenses. This core business gives the firm a solid base of profits, which it is using to gradually expand to other states like Virginia and New York.

4484 Wilshire Boulevard   www.mercuryinsurance.com
Los Angeles, CA 90010

Morningstar Grades

Growth [B+]	1998	1999	2000	2001
Revenue %	8.3	4.8	6.7	10.3
Earnings/Share %	13.8	-24.0	-17.2	-4.0
Book Value/Share %	15.0	0.1	14.9	3.3
Dividends/Share %	20.7	20.0	14.3	10.4

Adequate pricing has Mercury aggressively writing new business. In addition to writing more policies in its home state of California, Mercury is expanding its geographical reach to other high-growth states like Texas and Florida.

Profitability [A]	1999	2000	2001	TTM
Return on Assets %	7.0	5.1	4.5	2.8
Oper Cash Flow $Mil	189	153	199	—
- Cap Spending $Mil	9	8	18	—
= Free Cash Flow $Mil	—	—	—	—

Operating return on equity, normally 16%-25% over the past 10 years, slipped below 10% in 2001. If claim expenses remain in check, higher premium prices should boost ROE.

Financial Health [A]	1999	2000	2001	09-02
Long-term Debt $Mil	—	—	—	—
Total Equity $Mil	910	1,033	1,070	1,094
Debt/Equity Ratio	—	—	—	—

Mercury has a solid capital position, generates steady cash flow for its needs, and employs debt sparingly. Financial leverage stands at 2.2, much lower than the average property insurer's 9.5.

Industry	Investment Style	Stock Type	Sector
Insurance (Property)	▦ Mid Core	▨ High Yield	💲 Financial Services

Competition	Market Cap $Mil	Debt/ Equity	12 Mo Trailing Sales $Mil	Price/Cash Flow	Return On Assets%	Total Return% 1 Yr	3 Yr
Mercury General	2,042	—	1,697	—	2.8	-11.5	23.9
American International Gr	150,907	—	66,823	—	1.4	-26.9	-4.0
Berkshire Hathaway B	111,526	—	39,133	—	1.9	-4.0	12.5

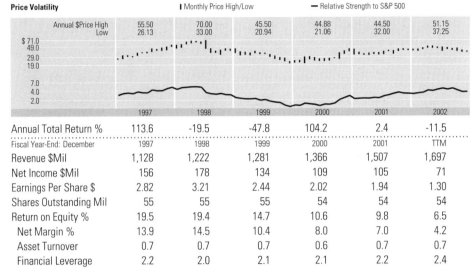

Price Volatility — Monthly Price High/Low — Relative Strength to S&P 500

Annual $Price High Low	55.50 26.13	70.00 33.00	45.50 20.94	44.88 21.06	44.50 32.00	51.15 37.25
	1997	1998	1999	2000	2001	2002
Annual Total Return %	113.6	-19.5	-47.8	104.2	2.4	-11.5

Fiscal Year-End: December	1997	1998	1999	2000	2001	TTM
Revenue $Mil	1,128	1,222	1,281	1,366	1,507	1,697
Net Income $Mil	156	178	134	109	105	71
Earnings Per Share $	2.82	3.21	2.44	2.02	1.94	1.30
Shares Outstanding Mil	55	55	55	54	54	54
Return on Equity %	19.5	19.4	14.7	10.6	9.8	6.5
Net Margin %	13.9	14.5	10.4	8.0	7.0	4.2
Asset Turnover	0.7	0.7	0.7	0.6	0.7	0.7
Financial Leverage	2.2	2.0	2.1	2.1	2.2	2.4

Valuation Ratios	Stock	Rel to Industry	Rel to S&P 500
Price/Earnings	28.9	1.4	1.2
Price/Book	1.9	1.0	0.6
Price/Sales	1.2	0.5	0.6
Price/Cash Flow	—	—	—

Major Fund Holders	% of Fund Assets
Nicholas	4.37
Boston Partners Mid Cap Value Inv	3.53
Nicholas Equity Income	3.30
Strong Multi-Cap Value	3.29

Morningstar's Take By Aaron Westrate, 12-17-2002 Stock Price as of Analysis: $38.08

Like its namesake, the Roman messenger god of cunning and commerce, Mercury has been outmaneuvering its rivals and earning excellent returns since its inception in 1962. Our message to investors is to put the stock on their watch lists, but not in their portfolios. The stock currently trades near our fair value estimate of $40. We'd wait for $28--a 30% discount to our estimate--before buying.

Mercury is one of the best auto insurers around. The firm has earned an underwriting profit in each of the past 10 years. Its average return on equity over that same period is nearly 18%. Much of the firm's success is attributable to being a niche player; Mercury sticks with auto insurance, rather than write multiple lines of insurance.

Another key factor in Mercury's success is its stringent underwriting standards. When cutthroat competition pushed premiums below Mercury's profitability threshold in 1999 and 2000, the firm put the brakes on writing new policies and filed for rate increases. Net premiums written inched up 5.4% and 5.5% in 1999 and 2000, respectively, as Mercury's higher prices were unattractive relative to rivals'. The tide turned in 2001, however, as profit-starved competitors also raised prices and Mercury enjoyed a 13.4% jump in net premiums written. Higher loss

trends and reduced investment yields have choked profits and precipitated the industrywide price hikes.

Not only do price hikes abound, but two of Mercury's largest rivals, State Farm and Allstate, have put a moratorium on new auto insurance in some of their regions. The large vacuum created by their retreat will enable Mercury to gain share at the same time that it is raising prices. Indeed, new policy applications for Mercury's standard and preferred auto lines in California skyrocketed 49% in the third quarter.

Mercury should enjoy outstanding premium growth through at least 2004. Because auto insurers are heavily regulated, achieving rate adequacy may take several years. Hypothetically, if an insurer requires a 12% increase in a given state, it may propose to raise premiums over two years, to ensure approval with the state's insurance commissioner.

Mercury's rosy prospects appear to be factored into the stock right now. If the stock fell enough to give us our required 30% margin of safety, though, we'd be buyers.

MORNINGSTAR® Stocks 500

Mercury Interactive MERQ

Rating	Risk	Moat Size	Fair Value	Last Close	Yield %
★	Med.	None	$20.00	$29.59	0.0

Company Profile

Mercury Interactive develops and supports a family of automated software quality products. These products automate testing and quality assurance for developers of client-server software and systems. Organizations use the company's products to identify software errors. Mercury's products are marketed under the XRunner, WinRunner, and LoadRunner names. XRunner runs under the UNIX multitasking operating system; WinRunner runs on personal computers running supported graphical environments; LoadRunner provides multi-user system testing.

Management

CEO Amnon Landan and COO Ken Klein have been at Mercury for a decade. Landan owns 4% of the stock.

Strategy

Mercury wants to help firms test, monitor, and manage Web sites and software to find weak spots before productivity suffers. To lessen its reliance on testing, Mercury has set its sights on performance monitoring and management, which allows companies to scrutinize software programs after they're live.

1325 Borregas Avenue   www.mercuryinteractive.com
Sunnyvale, CA 94089

Morningstar Grades

Growth [A-]

	1998	1999	2000	2001
Revenue %	57.8	55.1	63.6	17.6
Earnings/Share %	212.5	56.0	79.5	-45.7
Book Value/Share %	19.8	25.2	39.6	20.3
Dividends/Share %	NMF	NMF	NMF	NMF

Growth has been exceptional, with sales increasing 46% on average over the past five years. We peg long-term sales growth at no more than 20%.

Profitability [A]

	1999	2000	2001	TTM
Return on Assets %	11.2	6.6	3.7	6.4
Oper Cash Flow $Mil	61	130	83	120
- Cap Spending $Mil	24	45	22	9
= Free Cash Flow $Mil	37	85	61	111

The firm is highly profitable, with operating margins in the high teens. We expect margins will improve alongside sales growth, as fixed costs are more easily covered.

Financial Health [B+]

	1999	2000	2001	09-02
Long-term Debt $Mil	—	500	377	316
Total Equity $Mil	200	303	354	423
Debt/Equity Ratio	—	1.7	1.1	0.7

With nearly 2 times more cash than debt, financial health is solid. Mercury also generates lots of free cash flow.

Industry	Investment Style	Stock Type	Sector
Development Tools	Mid Growth	Aggr. Growth	Software

Competition	Market Cap $Mil	Debt/ Equity	12 Mo Trailing Sales $Mil	Price/Cash Flow	Return On Assets%	Total Return% 1 Yr	3 Yr
Mercury Interactive	2,499	0.7	373	20.8	6.4	-12.9	-15.2
Rational Software	2,028	—	657	—	—	—	—
Compuware	1,814	0.0	1,555	4.7	-12.5	-59.3	-48.4

Price Volatility

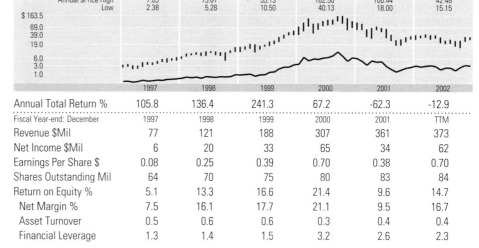

	Monthly Price High/Low		Relative Strength to S&P 500			
Annual $Price High Low	7.03 2.38	15.81 5.28	55.13 10.50	162.50 40.13	100.44 18.00	42.48 15.15

$ 163.5 / 69.0 / 39.0 / 19.0 / 6.0 / 3.0 / 1.0

	1997	1998	1999	2000	2001	2002
Annual Total Return %	105.8	136.4	241.3	67.2	-62.3	-12.9

Fiscal Year-end: December	1997	1998	1999	2000	2001	TTM
Revenue $Mil	77	121	188	307	361	373
Net Income $Mil	6	20	33	65	34	62
Earnings Per Share $	0.08	0.25	0.39	0.70	0.38	0.70
Shares Outstanding Mil	64	70	75	80	83	84
Return on Equity %	5.1	13.3	16.6	21.4	9.6	14.7
Net Margin %	7.5	16.1	17.7	21.1	9.5	16.7
Asset Turnover	0.5	0.6	0.6	0.3	0.4	0.4
Financial Leverage	1.3	1.4	1.5	3.2	2.6	2.3

Valuation Ratios	Stock	Rel to Industry	Rel to S&P 500
Price/Earnings	42.3	1.1	1.8
Price/Book	5.9	1.3	1.8
Price/Sales	6.7	1.6	3.3
Price/Cash Flow	20.8	1.1	1.6

Major Fund Holders	% of Fund Assets
John Hancock Technology A	3.95
T. Rowe Price Developing Tech	3.12
Van Kampen Technology A	3.05
John Hancock Mid Cap Growth A	2.75

Morningstar's Take By Mike Trigg, 12-04-2002 Stock Price as of Analysis: $30.87

Few software companies have performed as well as Mercury Interactive during the downturn in IT spending. However, the lack of a sustainable competitive advantage necessitates at least a 40% discount to our fair value estimate before we'd buy.

With roughly 50% market share according to industry researchers, Mercury is the dominant player in Web-testing products, which ensure Web-based software performs as it should. The importance of testing has grown considerably as companies use front- and back-office applications to run business processes like sales, marketing, and accounting. If an e-commerce site like Amazon.com crashed, for example, the firm could lose millions of dollars.

With products like WinRunner and LoadRunner on the market for nearly a decade, Mercury's prime advantage is superior technology. WinRunner analyzes the behavior of a Web site or application before deployment, while LoadRunner simulates real-world conditions (e.g., thousands of visitors to a Web site) to ensure adequate performance. Superior products and dominant market share have led to historical returns on invested capital around 30%.

Despite the strong long-term demand for testing, interest has waned as businesses have cut projects to develop new software programs. Thus, to expand beyond testing, Mercury has set its sights on performance monitoring and management; these products monitor programs after they've gone live. With companies trying to squeeze every dollar out of their existing technology, we expect these products will do well regardless of the economic conditions.

That said, we have concerns. Mercury's products are the most technologically superior, but also the most expensive; many businesses are willing to forgo a better product for a cheaper one that meets their needs. Also, as the company expands beyond testing, it's forced to compete with formidable companies, including Computer Associates and BMC Software, in markets where it's products aren't as superior.

The primary albatross around Mercury's neck remains the reluctance of software buyers to reopen their purses. In our view, it is too soon to declare a rebound in IT spending for new software projects. And achieving success will be tougher in performance management and monitoring, with stiff competition. We wouldn't buy the stock until it traded around $12.

Merrill Lynch & Company MER

	Rating	Risk	Moat Size	Fair Value	Last Close	Yield %
	★★★	Med.	Narrow	$40.00	$37.95	1.7

Company Profile

Merrill Lynch is one of the world's leading financial management and advisory companies, with offices in 38 countries. As an investment bank, Merrill is a leading global underwriter of debt and equity securities and a strategic advisor to corporations, governments, institutions, and individuals worldwide. Merrill also manages mutual funds, underwrites life insurance products, and is a primary dealer in equities, corporate debt, and U.S. government-issued obligations.

Management

Merrill COO Stanley O'Neal will become CEO in December, succeeding David Komansky. O'Neal, who will add the chairman title in April, did not rise through the ranks as a broker. He is expected to implement major changes at the firm.

Strategy

Merrill Lynch remains the world's largest brokerage firm, but its revenue is increasingly derived from recurring advisory fees. In its effort to ensure reliable double-digit profit growth, Merrill intends to boost its fee-based revenue. It's also able to use its broad array of financial products to retain its global leadership.

4 World Financial Center   www.ml.com
New York, NY 10080

Morningstar Grades

Growth [D]	1998	1999	2000	2001
Revenue %	10.7	1.4	26.9	-13.6
Earnings/Share %	-36.1	108.7	32.2	-86.1
Book Value/Share %	16.1	18.8	33.1	6.3
Dividends/Share %	22.7	14.1	15.2	5.8

Revenue has grown at a 13% compound annual rate since Merrill went public in 1971. We believe that 2002 represents a bottom in the capital markets, and that it will take until 2004 to return to the level of business achieved at its peak in 2000.

Profitability [D]	1999	2000	2001	TTM
Return on Assets %	0.9	0.9	0.1	0.2
Oper Cash Flow $Mil	880	1,304	6,421	—
- Cap Spending $Mil	1,090	1,150	663	—
= Free Cash Flow $Mil	—	—	—	—

Because Merrill has more banking assets than rivals, its return on assets--the key driver for this grade--is below average. Merrill is targeting improved earnings through cost-cutting, but capital-intensive lending businesses could pressure returns.

Financial Health [B+]	1999	2000	2001	09-02
Long-term Debt $Mil	—	—	—	—
Total Equity $Mil	12,579	17,879	19,583	21,874
Debt/Equity Ratio	—	—	—	—

Merrill is in a balance-sheet-intensive industry that employs large amounts of leverage. However, we expect Merrill to continue building equity capital--as it did last year--so it can expand rapidly once a recovery takes hold.

	Industry	Investment Style	Stock Type	Sector
	Securities	▦ Large Value	→ Slow Growth	$ Financial Services

Competition	Market Cap $Mil	Debt/ Equity	12 Mo Trailing Sales $Mil	Price/Cash Flow	Return On Assets%	Total Return% 1 Yr	Total Return% 3 Yr
Merrill Lynch & Company	32,806	—	30,635	—	0.2	-26.0	0.5
Citigroup	177,948	—	106,096	—	1.6	-24.2	1.1
Morgan Stanley	43,977	—	32,954	—	0.6	-27.2	-12.5

Price Volatility   ❙ Monthly Price High/Low   — Relative Strength to S&P 500

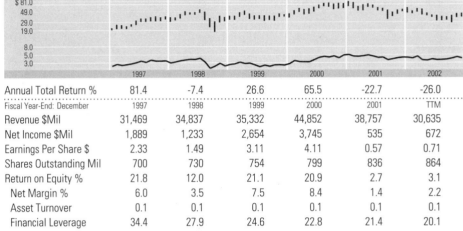

Annual $Price High / Low	39.09 / 19.63	54.56 / 17.88	51.25 / 31.00	74.63 / 36.31	80.00 / 33.50	59.32 / 28.21
	1997	1998	1999	2000	2001	2002

Annual Total Return %	81.4	-7.4	26.6	65.5	-22.7	-26.0

Fiscal Year-End: December	1997	1998	1999	2000	2001	TTM
Revenue $Mil	31,469	34,837	35,332	44,852	38,757	30,635
Net Income $Mil	1,889	1,233	2,654	3,745	535	672
Earnings Per Share $	2.33	1.49	3.11	4.11	0.57	0.71
Shares Outstanding Mil	700	730	754	799	836	864
Return on Equity %	21.8	12.0	21.1	20.9	2.7	3.1
Net Margin %	6.0	3.5	7.5	8.4	1.4	2.2
Asset Turnover	0.1	0.1	0.1	0.1	0.1	0.1
Financial Leverage	34.4	27.9	24.6	22.8	21.4	20.1

Valuation Ratios	Stock	Rel to Industry	Rel to S&P 500
Price/Earnings	53.5	3.1	2.3
Price/Book	1.5	0.9	0.5
Price/Sales	1.1	0.8	0.5
Price/Cash Flow	—	—	—

Major Fund Holders	% of Fund Assets
Neuberger Berman Focus Inv	5.88
Fidelity Select Brokerage & Investmnt	4.99
Kelmoore Strategy C	4.73
IDEX Great Companies-Global A	4.69

Morningstar's Take   By Craig Woker, 10-02-2002   Stock Price as of Analysis: $33.15

No financial company can claim to dominate the capital markets business, but Merrill Lynch comes the closest. Given the beating its stock has taken over the past year, Merrill is nearing value territory, but it's not there yet.

Merrill is the biggest brokerage, the third-largest equity underwriter and merger advisor, and a top-tier asset manager. This product span provides an important--and growing--competitive advantage. For instance, Merrill's retail brokerage and financial advisory channels provide attractive distribution outlets for its expanding mutual fund products. And because Merrill is growing larger as a bank, it can package loans with equity and debt underwriting for corporate clients.

As a result, Merrill is worth keeping on the radar screen. However, we would not start to consider the stock a reasonable buy unless it slipped to $30 per share--roughly 1.3 times book value and at a 25% discount to our fair value estimate of $40.

Patience and a long time horizon are prerequisites for investing in any brokerage stock because these firms are more volatile than the overall market. In Merrill's case, some political and legal risks remain. A handful of states have not yet signed on to the New York attorney general's settlement, something

we speculated would happen. Merrill believes the holdouts will eventually acquiesce. However, until every prosecutor signs on the dotted line, there remains risk that a holdout state will seek to extract another pound of flesh.

The more important factor to consider is that investment banking and trading business is way down, and we don't think it will return to 2000's peak until 2004. With a drought in equity underwriting and merger and acquisition work, one of the few segments propping up Merrill has been debt underwriting. However, fixed income's recent boom isn't sustainable. A large chunk of business is coming from high-grade companies taking advantage of ridiculously low rates, which won't last forever.

Some good is likely to come out of this drought. Merrill is tightening its belt in ways that should lead to a leaner cost structure over the long term. Through staff reductions and streamlining operations, Merrill targets operating margins of 24% by the fourth quarter of 2003, up from around 21% now.

Merrill is a stock we'd like to own, but only at the right price.

    Mᴏʀɴɪɴɢsᴛᴀʀ® **Stocks 500**

Metropolitan Life Insurance MET

Rating	Risk	Moat Size	Fair Value	Last Close	Yield %
★★	Med.	None	$30.00	$27.04	0.8

Company Profile

MetLife provides insurance and financial services to individual and institutional customers. The company primarily offers individual insurance, annuities, and investment products. It also provides group insurance and retirement and savings products and services to approximately 70,000 corporations that employ about 33 million individuals.

Management

Robert Benmosche is the company's chairman and chief executive. Benmosche arrived in 1995 to help with the assimilation of New England Financial, and was successful in integrating the two distinctly different distribution channels.

Strategy

MetLife wants to use its public ownership structure to tap the capital markets for funding acquisitions and expansion in the hopes of jump-starting sales. It has also overhauled agent compensation and added stock incentive plans to enhance productivity, while keeping a lid on costs. The company's goals include returns on equity of 13% by 2004 and 100 million customers by 2010.

One Madison Avenue
New York, NY 10010-3690

Industry	Investment Style	Stock Type	Sector
Insurance (Life)	▦ Large Value	➡ Slow Growth	💲 Financial Services

Competition

	Market Cap $Mil	Debt/ Equity	12 Mo Trailing Sales $Mil	Price/Cash Flow	Return On Assets%	Total Return% 1 Yr	3 Yr
Metropolitan Life Insurance	18,936	—	33,057	—	0.3	-14.0	—
Citigroup	177,948	—	106,096	—	1.6	-24.2	1.1
American International Gr	150,907	—	66,823	—	1.4	-26.9	-4.0

Price Volatility

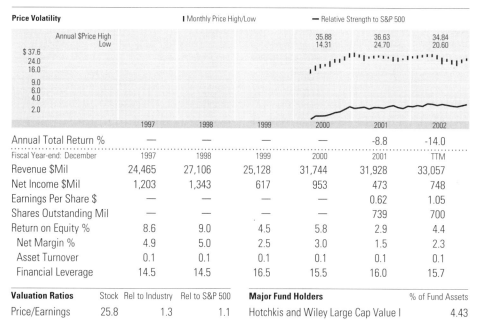

	Monthly Price High/Low	— Relative Strength to S&P 500

Annual $Price High/Low: 35.88/14.31, 36.63/24.70, 34.84/20.60

$37.6 24.0 16.0 9.0 6.0 4.0 2.0

	1997	1998	1999	2000	2001	2002
Annual Total Return %	—	—	—	—	-8.8	-14.0

Fiscal Year-end: December	1997	1998	1999	2000	2001	TTM
Revenue $Mil	24,465	27,106	25,128	31,744	31,928	33,057
Net Income $Mil	1,203	1,343	617	953	473	748
Earnings Per Share $	—	—	—	—	0.62	1.05
Shares Outstanding Mil	—	—	—	—	739	700
Return on Equity %	8.6	9.0	4.5	5.8	2.9	4.4
Net Margin %	4.9	5.0	2.5	3.0	1.5	2.3
Asset Turnover	0.1	0.1	0.1	0.1	0.1	0.1
Financial Leverage	14.5	14.5	16.5	15.5	16.0	15.7

Valuation Ratios	Stock	Rel to Industry	Rel to S&P 500
Price/Earnings	25.8	1.3	1.1
Price/Book	1.1	1.0	0.3
Price/Sales	0.6	0.8	0.3
Price/Cash Flow	—	—	—

Major Fund Holders	% of Fund Assets
Hotchkis and Wiley Large Cap Value I	4.43
Queens Road Large Cap Value	2.81
Federated Global Financial Services A	2.78
ICAP Equity	2.75

Morningstar Grades

Growth [C-]	1998	1999	2000	2001
Revenue %	10.8	-7.3	26.3	0.6
Earnings/Share %	NMF	NMF	NMF	NMF
Book Value/Share %	—	—	—	NMF
Dividends/Share %	NMF	NMF	NMF	0.0

The company's five-year compound growth rate is about 7%. Over the long term, this should be sustainable, though it could get a boost if MetLife's agents are successful in increasing the number of products purchased per client.

Profitability [D]	1999	2000	2001	TTM
Return on Assets %	0.3	0.4	0.2	0.3
Oper Cash Flow $Mil	3,883	1,299	4,799	—
- Cap Spending $Mil	—	—	—	—
= Free Cash Flow $Mil	—	—	—	—

MetLife's returns on equity land perennially in the bottom half of the industry. In 2001, myriad one-time charges hurt net income. Even excluding these charges, though, MetLife's ROE was 7.6% compared with 14% for the average life insurer.

Financial Health [B-]	1999	2000	2001	09-02
Long-term Debt $Mil	—	—	—	—
Total Equity $Mil	13,690	16,389	16,062	17,077
Debt/Equity Ratio	—	—	—	—

The company is in good financial shape. It boasts a solid equity base of $17 billion and has only $4.3 billion in debt. This gives MetLife the flexibility to add debt to finance an acquisition or two.

Morningstar's Take By Aaron Westrate, 12-06-2002 Stock Price as of Analysis: $26.63

We think MetLife has the right stuff to boost lagging return on equity closer to the life insurance industry average. Our fair value estimate remains at $30, and we'd require a 30% discount to that before buying shares.

Before April 2000, when it demutualized--shifting from policyholder ownership to stockholder ownership--MetLife was a sluggish behemoth with returns on equity well below the industry average. As a mutual insurance company, MetLife's owners were policyholders concerned mainly with capital strength and claims-paying ability. Now that it is publicly traded, its shareholders demand that in addition to these two priorities, the company earn a solid ROE. As a result, MetLife is attempting to raise its ROE to 13% by 2004.

To boost net income--a key component of ROE--MetLife trimmed expenses by reducing nonsales positions more than 20% and shuttering the same percentage of its offices since 1998. Despite these measures, though, MetLife's greatest opportunity to boost ROE is to sell more products to its existing customer base, and to add new customers.

MetLife has two extremely attractive assets: a massive customer base and wide product line. With 10 million households and 70,000 corporations (representing 33 million individual employees) as customers, MetLife can add high-margin revenue by selling additional products to these customers. And since MetLife offers a broad array of products--from life and health insurance to annuities and even banking products--it can meet many of its customers' needs without their turning to a competitor. This broad product offering is also an attractive asset because it positions MetLife to address consumer demand for retirement and estate planning, which is on the rise as the ranks of middle-age Americans nearing retirement swell.

It's worth noting, though, that MetLife isn't the only firm targeting wealthy and middle-age Americans. The competition from other financial service powerhouses like Merrill Lynch, Citigroup, and American Insurance Group will be fierce and could impede MetLife's sales growth and thus its ability to achieve higher returns on equity.

Given that MetLife stock isn't in bargain territory and considering the tough competition the firm will face, we'd recommend that investors put it on their radar screens, but not in their portfolios.

MGM Mirage MGG

	Rating ★★★	Risk Med.	Moat Size Narrow	Fair Value $38.00	Last Close $32.97	Yield % 0.0

Company Profile

MGM Mirage operates 18 resort casinos in the United States, Australia, and South Africa. Its flagship MGM Grand Hotel and Casino in Las Vegas is the world's largest hotel. Other major properties include Bellagio, New York-New York, and Mirage on the Las Vegas Strip, the Beau Rivage in Mississippi, and MGM Grand Detroit. About 60% of revenue comes from casino operations, with the balance derived from hotel, food and beverage, and entertainment venues. Controlled by billionaire investor Kirk Kerkorian, MGM acquired Primadonna Resorts in 1999 and Mirage Resorts in 2000.

Management

Kirk Kerkorian, 85, owns a 51% stake in MGM and has a long, illustrious record in the gaming industry. Chairman J. Terrence Lanni and co-CEOs John Redmond and Daniel Wade have made first-class acquisitions and have controlled costs effectively.

Strategy

MGM Mirage's resort casinos are targeted toward higher-income tourists and gamblers, a high-margin segment in which the company has commanding share. Management controls costs closely to maintain high free cash flow. Now the owner of the three most profitable properties in Nevada, MGM plans to expand its franchise in upscale gaming with two developments in Atlantic City.

3600 Las Vegas Boulevard South
Las Vegas, NV 89109
www.mgmmirage.com

Morningstar Grades

Growth [A-]

	1998	1999	2000	2001
Revenue %	-7.0	80.1	132.3	29.1
Earnings/Share %	-35.1	18.0	51.4	-2.8
Book Value/Share %	-9.0	2.0	88.7	-3.0
Dividends/Share %	NMF	NMF	NMF	NMF

MGM's growth story of the 1990s is history. We believe revenue will increase about 10% annually over the next several years, now that MGM's size has caught up with it.

Profitability [C+]

	1999	2000	2001	TTM
Return on Assets %	3.1	1.5	1.6	2.7
Oper Cash Flow $Mil	290	794	794	839
- Cap Spending $Mil	375	336	328	298
= Free Cash Flow $Mil	-85	458	466	541

Because casinos operate with high fixed costs, most of each dollar of lost sales will come out of operating income. But MGM's cost structure is already quite efficient, and EBITDA margins in excess of 30% will help cushion the blow.

Financial Health [C]

	1999	2000	2001	09-02
Long-term Debt $Mil	1,321	5,389	5,353	5,069
Total Equity $Mil	1,023	2,382	2,511	2,758
Debt/Equity Ratio	1.3	2.3	2.1	1.8

With debt at 70% of capital, MGM is about as leveraged as its peers. However, the company has put its $450 million in annual free cash flow toward paying down long-term debt.

Industry	Investment Style	Stock Type	Sector
Gambling/Hotel Casinos	▦ Mid Growth	⬆ Aggr. Growth	▤ Consumer Services

Competition

	Market Cap $Mil	Debt/ Equity	12 Mo Trailing Sales $Mil	Price/Cash Flow	Return On Assets%	Total Return% 1 Yr	3 Yr
MGM Mirage	5,111	1.8	3,970	6.1	2.7	14.2	12.2
Harrah's Entertainment	4,426	2.4	4,108	5.4	3.9	7.0	17.8
Park Place Entertainment	2,718	—	4,698	—	—	—	—

Price Volatility

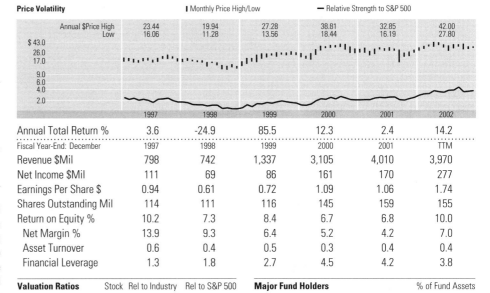

		Annual $Price High / Low	23.44 / 16.06	19.94 / 11.28	27.28 / 13.56	38.81 / 18.44	32.85 / 16.19	42.00 / 27.80

	1997	1998	1999	2000	2001	2002
Annual Total Return %	3.6	-24.9	85.5	12.3	2.4	14.2

Fiscal Year-End: December	1997	1998	1999	2000	2001	TTM
Revenue $Mil	798	742	1,337	3,105	4,010	3,970
Net Income $Mil	111	69	86	161	170	277
Earnings Per Share $	0.94	0.61	0.72	1.09	1.06	1.74
Shares Outstanding Mil	114	111	116	145	159	155
Return on Equity %	10.2	7.3	8.4	6.7	6.8	10.0
Net Margin %	13.9	9.3	6.4	5.2	4.2	7.0
Asset Turnover	0.6	0.4	0.5	0.3	0.4	0.4
Financial Leverage	1.3	1.8	2.7	4.5	4.2	3.8

Valuation Ratios

	Stock	Rel to Industry	Rel to S&P 500
Price/Earnings	18.9	1.0	0.8
Price/Book	1.9	0.7	0.6
Price/Sales	1.3	1.0	0.6
Price/Cash Flow	6.1	1.0	0.5

Major Fund Holders

	% of Fund Assets
Transamerica Premier Core Equity Inv	4.64
SunAmStySel Focused Growth & Inc A	4.56
Fidelity Select Leisure	3.09
Van Kampen Select Growth A	2.66

Morningstar's Take By T.K. MacKay, 10-10-2002 Stock Price as of Analysis: $32.55

If its stock were to fall into the low $20s, we'd be placing our long-term bets with MGM Mirage. The company's brand cachet and dominant market position in Las Vegas make it a great way to play the gaming industry.

MGM Mirage is leveraged like no other to the success of the Las Vegas tourist industry. The company generates 70% of its EBITDA--earnings before interest, taxes, depreciation, and amortization--from the Las Vegas Strip, compared with Mandalay Resort Group at 60%, Park Place at 43%, and Harrah's at 9%. And when it comes to capitalizing on tourism, MGM holds the winning hand. The luxurious Bellagio resort is the most profitable casino in the city; its glamorous clientele and lavish hotel rooms generate EBITDA margins of nearly 33%, 12 percentage points higher than those of the average hotel/casino. For visitors willing to sacrifice a bit of luxury, there's New York-New York, and for conventioneers, there's the MGM Grand, one of the largest hotels in the world.

In addition to bringing the Bellagio and the Mirage to its portfolio, MGM's 2000 acquisition of Mirage Resorts resulted in cost savings that afford MGM the highest EBITDA margins in Las Vegas, at about 30%. Consolidation of marketing and administrative costs

has saved MGM about $250 million on an annual basis, and the combined entity controls more than 35% of all gaming revenue generated on the Strip. This large share of the gaming market translates into strong pricing power for its hotel business as well.

With strong profits come solid cash flows. MGM's free cash flow has topped $450 million annually in each of the past two years. We believe that free cash flow will continue to be strong and that MGM will use this to pay down debt, which it has reduced by $1 billion since the Mirage acquisition. This lower leverage would translate into lower risk for equityholders.

We think MGM is one of the best names in the business, and we would be buyers in the low $20s. While this seems like a big drop from the current price, casino stocks often take big hits because of external events. However, such events tend to be temporary in nature, opening the door to a good investment. After all, gambling--like many vices--is a long-term growth opportunity, and we're confident that MGM is well positioned to profit from this growth.

MORNINGSTAR® Stocks 500

Micron Technology MU

	Rating	Risk	Moat Size	Fair Value	Last Close	Yield %
	★★★	High	None	$11.00	$9.74	0.0

Company Profile

Micron Technology produces memory chips for computers and other electronic devices. Most of the firm's business comes from selling dynamic random access memory chips to PC makers. Micron produces its DRAM chips in its own semiconductor plants across the world, and generates a large portion of its sales from Europe and Asia. The firm agreed to acquire the DRAM operations of Toshiba Corp. in December 2001.

Management

Steve Appleton has been president and CEO since 1989. Members of his management team have long histories with the firm. The team is very shrewd and arguably the best in the DRAM industry.

Strategy

Micron Technology is striving to increase its market share of the DRAM chip industry by achieving economies of scale through size and manufacturing efficiency. The firm will also expand share by acquiring weaker rivals.

8000 South Federal Way
Boise, ID 83716-9632
www.micron.com

Industry	Investment Style	Stock Type	Sector
Semiconductors	▣ Mid Core	◪ Distressed	▣ Hardware

Competition

	Market Cap $Mil	Debt/ Equity	12 Mo Trailing Sales $Mil	Price/Cash Flow	Return On Assets%	Total Return% 1 Yr	3 Yr
Micron Technology	5,872	0.1	2,589	10.2	-12.0	-68.6	-35.8
NEC ADR	6,118	—	37,090	—	—	—	—
SSNLF	—	—	—	—	—	—	—

Price Volatility

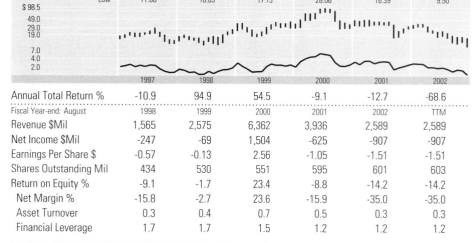

			Monthly Price High/Low		— Relative Strength to S&P 500	
Annual $Price High Low	30.03 11.00	27.81 10.03	44.00 17.13	97.50 28.06	49.52 16.39	39.50 9.50

$ 98.5
49.0
29.0
19.0
7.0
4.0
2.0

	1997	1998	1999	2000	2001	2002
Annual Total Return %	-10.9	94.9	54.5	-9.1	-12.7	-68.6

Fiscal Year-end: August	1998	1999	2000	2001	2002	TTM
Revenue $Mil	1,565	2,575	6,362	3,936	2,589	2,589
Net Income $Mil	-247	-69	1,504	-625	-907	-907
Earnings Per Share $	-0.57	-0.13	2.56	-1.05	-1.51	-1.51
Shares Outstanding Mil	434	530	551	595	601	603
Return on Equity %	-9.1	-1.7	23.4	-8.8	-14.2	-14.2
Net Margin %	-15.8	-2.7	23.6	-15.9	-35.0	-35.0
Asset Turnover	0.3	0.4	0.7	0.5	0.3	0.3
Financial Leverage	1.7	1.7	1.5	1.2	1.2	1.2

Valuation Ratios	Stock	Rel to Industry	Rel to S&P 500
Price/Earnings	NMF	—	—
Price/Book	0.9	0.3	0.3
Price/Sales	2.3	0.6	1.1
Price/Cash Flow	10.2	0.9	0.8

Major Fund Holders	% of Fund Assets
Fidelity Select Electronics	7.20
American Heritage Growth	5.51
PIMCO PEA Value Instl	5.06
Rydex Electronics Inv	4.80

Morningstar Grades

Growth [D]	1999	2000	2001	2002
Revenue %	64.6	147.1	-38.1	-34.2
Earnings/Share %	NMF	NMF	NMF	NMF
Book Value/Share %	20.0	46.4	9.5	-11.6
Dividends/Share %	NMF	NMF	NMF	NMF

Growth depends largely on the direction of DRAM prices, which are highly speculative and volatile. With DRAM prices weak for quite a long time, Micron's sales have fallen significantly in the past two years.

Profitability [C]	2000	2001	2002	TTM
Return on Assets %	16.0	-7.5	-12.0	-12.0
Oper Cash Flow $Mil	2,002	789	578	578
- Cap Spending $Mil	1,127	1,489	760	760
= Free Cash Flow $Mil	875	-700	-182	-182

Micron is one of the industry's low-cost producers. But low prices have killed profitability over the past two years and gross margins have at times even fallen into negative territory.

Financial Health [C]	2000	2001	2002	08-02
Long-term Debt $Mil	931	445	361	361
Total Equity $Mil	6,432	7,135	6,367	6,367
Debt/Equity Ratio	0.1	0.1	0.1	0.1

High capital spending and low chip prices have led to a big free cash flow loss, resulting in a declining cash balance (to just $658 million). While the firm has modest debt, it may have to assume more to finance its spending needs.

Morningstar's Take By Jeremy Lopez, 12-20-2002 Stock Price as of Analysis: $10.20

The unpredictability of Micron's earnings and cash flow necessitates a wide margin of safety to our fair value estimate before buying the shares.

One of the world's largest producers of DRAM (dynamic random-access memory) chips, Micron has not been dealt an easy hand. With little to differentiate one DRAM from another, Micron produces a commodity, and the market for its chips is extremely competitive. Chip prices are sensitive to factors like PC demand and chip supplies, which Micron has little control over. This lack of pricing power becomes an issue when PC demand is weak or chip supplies are abundant. In such a market, it's common for low chip prices to push operating margins (and even gross margins) deep into negative territory.

Micron is, at least, one of the industry's lowest-cost producers. With the manufacturing scale and efficiency to lower prices more than its peers, Micron should have a competitive advantage when times are tough. In a perfect world, the gap between the DRAM haves and have-nots should widen as strong firms like Micron reinvest in their businesses (becoming more price-competitive), while others cannot. But in recent years, Micron has not benefited much from this supposed advantage because foreign governments are subsidizing inefficient producers. This is particularly true in South Korea, where the government has propped up Micron's rival, Hynix Semiconductor.

The DRAM industry is structurally unattractive for many reasons-- it's cyclical, capital-intensive, ultracompetitive, and often unprofitable. Also, Micron must battle the protectionist trade policy of foreign governments. The International Trade Commission recently ruled in Micron's favor, but it's too early to predict whether the firm will benefit from this judgment. As a play on the direction of DRAM prices, Micron is a momentum trader's dream. But for longer-term, risk-averse investors, this stock has little appeal since it's anyone's guess where chip prices are heading. Thus, we'd pass on Micron stock unless it traded at a very large discount (at least 60%) to our fair value estimate.

Microsoft MSFT

	Rating	Risk	Moat Size	Fair Value	Last Close	Yield %
	★★★	Med.	Wide	$52.00	$51.70	0.0

Company Profile

Microsoft develops microcomputer software, mainly under the Windows name. Its businesses include operating systems for personal computers, office machines, and personal information devices; language and application programs; an online service; and personal computer books, hardware, and multimedia products. These products are available for all personal computers and computers running Intel microprocessors. It also operates the WebTV Internet access service. Foreign sales account for about 30% of total revenue. The company agreed to acquire Great Plains Software in 2001.

Management

CEO Steve Ballmer and chairman Bill Gates are some of the best executives in the business. Although much has been made of the brain drain at Microsoft, the company has a very deep bench of talented executives and programmers.

Strategy

Microsoft's strategy is to maintain its dominance of the PC market, expand its influence over the server market, and diversify into devices like game consoles, personal digital assistants, and set-top boxes. It is just beginning to roll out its promising Microsoft.NET strategy, which revolves around developing applications to deliver services to PCs, PDAs, and other devices via the Internet.

One Microsoft Way
Redmond, WA 98052-6399
www.microsoft.com

Morningstar Grades

Growth [B+]	1999	2000	2001	2002
Revenue %	29.4	16.3	10.2	12.1
Earnings/Share %	69.0	19.7	-22.4	6.8
Book Value/Share %	71.1	49.0	13.8	10.6
Dividends/Share %	NMF	NMF	NMF	NMF

The law of large numbers has taken hold, and long-term revenue growth has slowed to the low teens. Revenue growth is shifting away from the PC business and into enterprise software and consumer software and devices.

Profitability [A+]	2000	2001	2002	TTM
Return on Assets %	18.2	12.5	11.6	13.2
Oper Cash Flow $Bil	11.4	13.4	14.5	17.3
- Cap Spending $Bil	0.9	1.1	0.8	0.8
= Free Cash Flow $Bil	10.5	12.3	13.7	16.5

Microsoft's profitability is impressive, but much less so than in recent years. Margins have been declining in recent quarters, and we expect them to fall even further as the lower-margin consumer business increases as a percentage of revenue.

Financial Health [A+]	2000	2001	2002	09-02
Long-term Debt $Bil	0.0	0.0	0.0	0.0
Total Equity $Bil	41.4	47.3	52.2	53.5
Debt/Equity Ratio	0.0	0.0	0.0	0.0

Microsoft's portfolio has taken a big hit in the past year, but the company still has $39 billion in cash and short-term investments and $14 billion in equity investments. With no debt, Microsoft can afford to invest heavily in its future.

Industry	Investment Style	Stock Type	Sector
Business Applications	▦ Large Growth	↗ Classic Growth	◨ Software

Competition	Market Cap $Mil	Debt/ Equity	12 Mo Trailing Sales $Mil	Price/Cash Flow	Return On Assets%	Total Return% 1 Yr	3 Yr
Microsoft	276,411	0.0	29,985	16.0	13.2	-22.0	-22.9
IBM	130,982	0.8	82,442	9.0	5.8	-35.5	-11.1
Oracle	57,845	0.1	9,459	18.1	19.8	-21.8	-26.3

Price Volatility

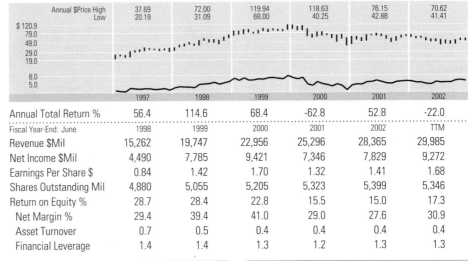

	Monthly Price High/Low		— Relative Strength to S&P 500			
Annual $Price High Low	37.69 20.19	72.00 31.09	119.94 68.00	118.63 40.25	76.15 42.88	70.62 41.41

$120.9 / 79.0 / 49.0 / 29.0 / 19.0 / 8.0 / 5.0

	1997	1998	1999	2000	2001	2002
Annual Total Return %	56.4	114.6	68.4	-62.8	52.8	-22.0

Fiscal Year-End: June	1998	1999	2000	2001	2002	TTM
Revenue $Mil	15,262	19,747	22,956	25,296	28,365	29,985
Net Income $Mil	4,490	7,785	9,421	7,346	7,829	9,272
Earnings Per Share $	0.84	1.42	1.70	1.32	1.41	1.68
Shares Outstanding Mil	4,880	5,055	5,205	5,323	5,399	5,346
Return on Equity %	28.7	28.4	22.8	15.5	15.0	17.3
Net Margin %	29.4	39.4	41.0	29.0	27.6	30.9
Asset Turnover	0.7	0.5	0.4	0.4	0.4	0.4
Financial Leverage	1.4	1.4	1.3	1.2	1.3	1.3

Valuation Ratios	Stock	Rel to Industry	Rel to S&P 500
Price/Earnings	30.8	1.0	1.3
Price/Book	5.2	1.0	1.6
Price/Sales	9.2	1.0	4.6
Price/Cash Flow	16.0	1.0	1.2

Major Fund Holders	% of Fund Assets
Fidelity Select Software & Comp	19.54
Schwab Technology Focus	19.16
Fidelity OTC	17.33
Profunds Ultra Technology Inv	15.44

Morningstar's Take By Joseph Beaulieu, 11-04-2002 Stock Price as of Analysis: $56.10

Microsoft's peak growth years may be behind it, but we think the company is still a formidable competitor that merits investors' attention.

Our long-term theme for Microsoft remains the slow, long-term shift in its revenue base away from the desktop PC software market toward enterprise software and other consumer products. Microsoft still owns the PC desktop, and there isn't a competitor in sight (although we do see Linux as a threat on the server side of the business). But the PC is no longer a growth market, and as years pass, PCs will represent a shrinking portion of Microsoft's business. For Microsoft to continue to grow, it is going to have to reap an increasing portion of its revenue in businesses where it faces real competition.

Management clearly understands this new reality, as it is dramatically increasing research and development and marketing spending to jump-start its efforts in non-PC-related areas and to revitalize long-term growth. The firm needs to invest heavily in these new areas, as it does not have anything resembling the massive advantage that it has in the PC software market. In fact, in several areas (video game platforms, online consumer services, and enterprise resource planning software), Microsoft is the hungry contender rather than the king of the hill.

While we think Microsoft is well positioned to move into new growth areas, we also think the heavier competition Microsoft will face in these areas will result in a gradual decline in margins and returns on invested capital. We expect Microsoft to continue to generate massive amounts of cash and to continue to create shareholder value with its investments in newer business areas. But investors should not expect the company to return to its glory days of 40% margins.

Given Microsoft's strong balance sheet and solid competitive position in its most important markets, and given the company's continued near-monopoly of the PC desktop, we would require only a small discount to our fair value estimate of $52 before buying the shares. We'd start to get interested in the shares in the mid-$40s.

Mᴏʀɴɪɴɢsᴛᴀʀ® Stocks 500

Monsanto Company MON

	Rating	Risk	Moat Size	Fair Value	Last Close	Yield %
	★★★	Med.	None	$23.00	$19.25	2.5

Company Profile

Monsanto manufactures agricultural and chemical products. The company produces agricultural herbicides that it markets under the Roundup, Lasso, Harness, and Maverick brand names. Monsanto also makes its Posilac recombinant bovine-growth hormone, which increases dairy cow milk production. In addition, the company produces genetic products that increase swine fertility. It also grows and harvests biotechnology-based corn, soybean, wheat, cotton, sunflower, sorghum, and canola seed products. Monsanto also researches other biotechnology-based agricultural products.

Management

Hendrik Verfaillie, a 26-year Monsanto veteran, abruptly resigned as CEO in December 2002. Chairman Frank AtLee will serve as interim CEO while the firm looks for a permanent successor. We expect no significant changes in the company's strategy.

Strategy

Monsanto has opened a dialog with the environmentalists and governments who have derided its business practices and questioned the safety of its genetically modified seeds. These negotiations are important because the company's cash cow--Roundup herbicide--has lost its patent protection, and the company is banking on its GM seed business for growth.

800 North Lindbergh Boulevard   www.monsanto.com
St. Louis, MO 63167

Industry	Investment Style	Stock Type	Sector
Agrochemical	▦ Mid Value	→ Slow Growth	✿ Industrial Mats

Competition

	Market Cap $Mil	Debt/ Equity	12 Mo Trailing Sales $Mil	Price/Cash Flow	Return On Assets%	Total Return% 1 Yr	3 Yr
Monsanto Company	5,032	0.2	4,662	5.3	-21.6	-41.8	—
DuPont De Nemours E.I.	42,120	0.4	24,013	21.9	6.8	3.0	-10.5
Dow Chemical	27,060	1.1	26,866	10.1	1.2	-8.2	-8.1

Price Volatility

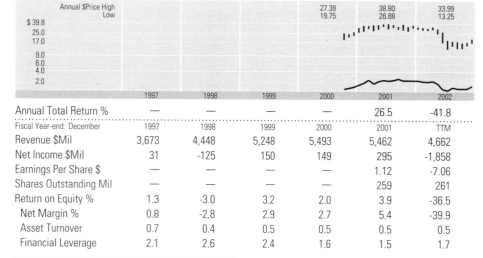

				27.38 / 19.75	38.80 / 26.88	33.99 / 13.25

I Monthly Price High/Low   — Relative Strength to S&P 500

	1997	1998	1999	2000	2001	2002
Annual Total Return %	—	—	—	—	26.5	-41.8

Fiscal Year-end: December	1997	1998	1999	2000	2001	TTM
Revenue $Mil	3,673	4,448	5,248	5,493	5,462	4,662
Net Income $Mil	31	-125	150	149	295	-1,858
Earnings Per Share $	—	—	—	—	1.12	-7.06
Shares Outstanding Mil	—	—	—	—	259	261
Return on Equity %	1.3	-3.0	3.2	2.0	3.9	-36.5
Net Margin %	0.8	-2.8	2.9	2.7	5.4	-39.9
Asset Turnover	0.7	0.4	0.5	0.5	0.5	0.5
Financial Leverage	2.1	2.6	2.4	1.6	1.5	1.7

Valuation Ratios	Stock	Rel to Industry	Rel to S&P 500
Price/Earnings	NMF	—	—
Price/Book	1.0	0.6	0.3
Price/Sales	1.1	1.2	0.5
Price/Cash Flow	5.3	0.8	0.4

Major Fund Holders	% of Fund Assets
ABN AMRO/Talon Mid Cap N	2.54
John Hancock Classic Value A	2.45
Fort Pitt Capital Total Return Fund	2.34
C&B Mid Cap Value	2.17

Morningstar Grades

Growth [C]	1998	1999	2000	2001
Revenue %	21.1	18.0	4.7	-0.6
Earnings/Share %	NMF	NMF	NMF	NMF
Book Value/Share %	—	—	—	NMF
Dividends/Share %	NMF	NMF	NMF	NMF

We forecast long-term sales growth around 8%. An economic recovery in South America and increasing European acceptance of GM crops would boost projections substantially.

Profitability [D+]	1999	2000	2001	TTM
Return on Assets %	1.4	1.3	2.6	-21.6
Oper Cash Flow $Mil	120	671	616	956
- Cap Spending $Mil	632	582	382	239
= Free Cash Flow $Mil	-512	89	234	717

After nearly doubling from 1999 to 2001, net margins have regressed this year, largely a result of pricing pressure on the firm's Roundup herbicide. Monsanto has turned to restructuring initiatives to boost operating efficiency and reduce costs.

Financial Health [A]	1999	2000	2001	09-02
Long-term Debt $Mil	4,278	962	893	1,134
Total Equity $Mil	4,645	7,341	7,483	5,096
Debt/Equity Ratio	0.9	0.1	0.1	0.2

When Monsanto merged with Pharmacia in 2000, more than $4 billion in debt was wiped from its balance sheet. As a result, Monsanto's liquidity improved dramatically. Free cash flows turned positive in 2001 and have been strong this year.

Morningstar's Take By Sanjay Ayer, 12-17-2002 Stock Price as of Analysis: $20.20

Monsanto is a lightning rod for controversy, so despite its solid growth prospects, we'd require a large discount to our fair value estimate before investing in the stock.

Genetically modified (GM) foods, the most promising source of growth for Monsanto, have sparked a raging debate. While scientific evidence testifies to the safety of GM foods, many environmental groups and governments have refused to accept them. In particular, Western Europe and Brazil--two regions rife with untapped agricultural growth opportunities--remain staunchly opposed to GM products.

Environmental and health concerns have fueled the resistance to GM foods, but we believe Monsanto's dubious record has intensified the opposition's rigid stance. Monsanto has a reputation of a dismissive behemoth seeking to impose its will on the very fabric of nature. New management has made minor strides toward repairing the firm's image, but gaining public acceptance will be a lengthy, painstaking process.

Monsanto's business has suffered several other setbacks this year. A wet planting season followed by droughtlike conditions in the Midwest wreaked havoc on Monsanto's seed and herbicide businesses.

Severe economic declines in Brazil and Argentina forced the company to adopt stricter credit policies to reduce bad debt. While tighter credit standards will enhance the firm's ability to collect outstanding customer receivables, total sales will decline as less creditworthy customers get the cold shoulder.

A variety of obstacles, some self-imposed, have prevented Monsanto from realizing its strong growth prospects. Despite all of its difficulties, however, Monsanto maintains a leading position in agricultural biotechnology, a niche with exciting potential. The firm's largest risk--slow adoption of genetically modified foods in Europe and Latin America--also represents its greatest opportunity. Unlocking these untapped global markets would provide an enormous sales boost, but management does not expect any progress here until at least 2005. Given the uncertainties swirling around the company, we require a 40% margin of safety to our fair value estimate of $23. We'd consider the shares if they dropped into the low teens.

Moody's MCO

	Rating	Risk	Moat Size	Fair Value	Last Close	Yield %
	★★★★★	Low	Wide	$52.00	$41.29	0.4

Company Profile

Moody's is a global credit-rating and research firm. It publishes credit opinions, research, and ratings on fixed-income securities, issuers of securities, and other credit obligations. Moody's maintains offices in 15 countries and is expanding into developing markets through joint ventures or affiliation agreements with local rating agencies. Its customers include corporate and governmental issuers of securities as well as investors, depositors, creditors, investment banks, commercial banks, and other financial intermediaries.

Management

Chief executive John Rutherfurd Jr., 62, has been with Moody's since 1995. Executives and board members own less than 1% of Moody's shares in aggregate, though Berkshire Hathaway owns 15.5% of the firm.

Strategy

Moody's is following an aggressive expansion strategy. It's moving into emerging markets directly or through joint ventures, and is also committed to extending its credit opinion franchise to the global bank counterparty universe. Moody's hopes to keep its net margins in the mid-20s by using the Internet and other electronic media, which should enhance client service as well.

99 Church Street
New York, NY 10007

www.moodys.com

Industry	Investment Style	Stock Type	Sector
Business Support	Mid Growth	Classic Growth	Business Services

Competition	Market Cap $Mil	Debt/ Equity	12 Mo Trailing Sales $Mil	Price/Cash Flow	Return On Assets%	Total Return% 1 Yr	Total Return% 3 Yr
Moody's	6,239	NMF	972	20.4	43.8	4.0	26.8
McGraw-Hill Companies	11,713	0.3	4,730	9.8	8.3	0.7	4.5

Price Volatility

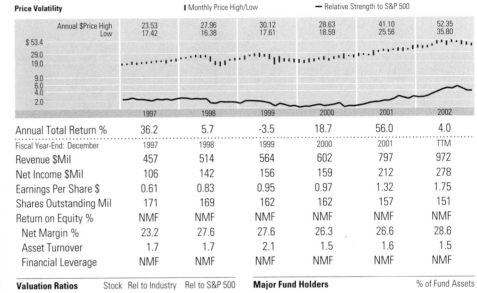

Annual $Price High Low	23.53 17.42	27.96 16.38	30.12 17.61	28.63 18.59	41.10 25.56	52.35 35.80
	1997	1998	1999	2000	2001	2002

I Monthly Price High/Low — Relative Strength to S&P 500

	1997	1998	1999	2000	2001	TTM
Annual Total Return %	36.2	5.7	-3.5	18.7	56.0	4.0
Fiscal Year-End: December	1997	1998	1999	2000	2001	TTM
Revenue $Mil	457	514	564	602	797	972
Net Income $Mil	106	142	156	159	212	278
Earnings Per Share $	0.61	0.83	0.95	0.97	1.32	1.75
Shares Outstanding Mil	171	169	162	162	157	151
Return on Equity %	NMF	NMF	NMF	NMF	NMF	NMF
Net Margin %	23.2	27.6	27.6	26.3	26.6	28.6
Asset Turnover	1.7	1.7	2.1	1.5	1.6	1.5
Financial Leverage	NMF	NMF	NMF	NMF	NMF	NMF

Valuation Ratios	Stock	Rel to Industry	Rel to S&P 500
Price/Earnings	23.6	0.8	1.0
Price/Book	—	—	—
Price/Sales	6.4	3.0	3.2
Price/Cash Flow	20.4	1.2	1.5

Major Fund Holders	% of Fund Assets
SEI Instl Mgd Capital Appreciation A	5.14
Oakmark Select I	5.13
Transamerica Premier Equity Inv	4.50
IDEX Transamerica Equity A	4.48

Morningstar Grades

Growth [A]	1998	1999	2000	2001
Revenue %	12.4	9.8	6.8	32.3
Earnings/Share %	36.1	14.5	2.1	36.1
Book Value/Share %	NMF	NMF	NMF	NMF
Dividends/Share %	-8.0	-8.6	-18.9	-70.0

Revenue growth over the past year has been impressive, thanks to strong international business and hot structured finance markets. Increased activity in Europe and emerging markets should help keep revenue humming in the long run.

Profitability [A+]	1999	2000	2001	TTM
Return on Assets %	56.6	39.8	42.0	43.8
Oper Cash Flow $Mil	198	68	306	306
- Cap Spending $Mil	13	14	15	15
= Free Cash Flow $Mil	185	53	292	292

Moody's is extremely profitable. Operating profit margins are above 50% and returns on invested capital are off the chart. Margins may decline as the lower-margin software business becomes a larger chunk of revenue.

Financial Health [A]	1999	2000	2001	09-02
Long-term Debt $Mil	—	300	300	300
Total Equity $Mil	-223	-283	-304	-181
Debt/Equity Ratio	—	ELB	ELB	NMF

Moody's is in great financial health. Debt is low and free cash flow is very strong.

Morningstar's Take By Jonathan Schrader, 12-18-2002 Stock Price as of Analysis: $40.21

The credit-rating franchise at Moody's is one of the best franchises we know of. If we could get the stock at a 20% discount to our fair value estimate, we'd gladly buy it and hold it.

Longtime readers know we're pretty fond of Warren Buffett, whose style of investing has been extraordinarily successful over the years. His Berkshire Hathaway owns shares in Moody's, and we think we know why: high profit margins, low capital investment, solid growth prospects, shareholder-friendly management, and oligopoly power.

Moody's plays an important role in the capital markets by evaluating the risk associated with borrowers and debt instruments. The rating process is hardly ever easy. The federal government has created a designation--Nationally Recognized Statistical Rating Organization--that a company must acquire before moving into the market. Achieving this designation is very challenging, meaning that the rating business is basically a government-sanctioned oligopoly.

The government protection Moody's enjoys is virtually priceless. Operating profit margins have climbed above 50% over the past year, thanks to growth in international and structured finance, where

pricing is especially sweet. We expect profitability to decline slightly over the coming years as an increasing percentage of revenue comes from the software segment, but we'd be satisfied with 48% margins.

These high margins lead to excellent cash flow from operations. The company requires very little in the way of capital investment, so its leverage is low, and free cash flow (cash flow from operations less capital investment) is strong. In the past, the company has used that cash to make some prudent acquisitions--including its biggest rival in risk-management software--and to enrich shareholders. The company recently concluded a $300 million stock-repurchase plan, and has begun a new $450 million repurchase program.

We think the company's best days are still ahead. Moody's is the leader in structured finance ratings, where we see many more years of excellent growth. And thanks to the introduction of the euro, the credit market in Europe is flourishing, opening up new opportunities for the firm. This is a great business to own, and we would do just that at the right price.

MORNINGSTAR® Stocks 500

Morgan Stanley MWD

	Rating	Risk	Moat Size	Fair Value	Last Close	Yield %
	★★★	Med.	Narrow	$52.00	$39.92	2.3

Company Profile

Morgan Stanley Dean Witter is a financial services company that provides nationally marketed credit and investment products. The company's credit services division issues the Discover and Private Issue credit cards; it also operates the Novus merchant and cash-access network. In addition, Morgan Stanley Dean Witter operates a full-service securities business and provides asset-management services in the United States and overseas. The company also offers research, foreign exchange, and securities underwriting, distribution, and trading services.

Management

In a high-profile power struggle, CEO and chairman Philip Purcell ousted president John Mack, an influential investment banker who came from Morgan Stanley. Purcell must gain the confidence of Mack's allies.

Strategy

Morgan Stanley is one of the largest and most diversified financial service firms, and it wants to stay that way. The firm is seeking near-term growth in its investment banking enterprise in Europe. But the firm also wants to build up its other offerings, like lending. In particular, the firm is looking to boost profits at its Discover unit and expand the card's acceptance beyond North America.

1585 Broadway
New York, NY 10036
www.msdw.com

Morningstar Grades

Growth [B-]	1998	1999	2000	2001
Revenue %	14.4	12.8	30.1	-2.8
Earnings/Share %	28.4	53.6	15.4	-34.2
Book Value/Share %	3.2	26.7	15.8	11.1
Dividends/Share %	42.9	20.0	66.7	15.0

After years of steady growth, revenue has dropped off a cliff in 2001 and 2002 because of a sectorwide collapse in demand for investment banking services and trading. We're forecasting net revenues to rise about 8.6% in 2003, coming off a weak base.

Profitability [C+]	1999	2000	2001	TTM
Return on Assets %	1.3	1.3	0.7	0.6
Oper Cash Flow $Mil	-28,945	-2,383	-24,091	—
- Cap Spending $Mil	—	—	—	—
= Free Cash Flow $Mil	—	—	—	—

Morgan Stanley reacted more quickly than other investment banks to the market downturn, being one of the first to cut jobs and other costs. However, it has not been as aggressive of late, and margins have suffered as a result.

Financial Health [C]	1999	2000	2001	08-02
Long-term Debt $Mil	—	—	—	—
Total Equity $Mil	16,344	18,726	20,371	21,416
Debt/Equity Ratio	—	—	—	—

Because it is in a balance-sheet-intensive industry, the company employs large amounts of leverage. Leverage has trended upward recently but is still reasonable. The firm also has an excellent risk-management record.

	Industry	Investment Style	Stock Type	Sector
	Securities	▦ Large Value	➡ Slow Growth	$ Financial Services

Competition	Market Cap $Mil	Debt/ Equity	12 Mo Trailing Sales $Mil	Price/Cash Flow	Return On Assets%	Total Return% 1 Yr	3 Yr
Morgan Stanley	43,977	—	32,954	—	0.6	-27.2	-12.5
Citigroup	177,948	—	106,096	—	1.6	-24.2	1.1
Merrill Lynch & Company	32,806	—	36,032	—	0.2	-26.0	0.5

Price Volatility

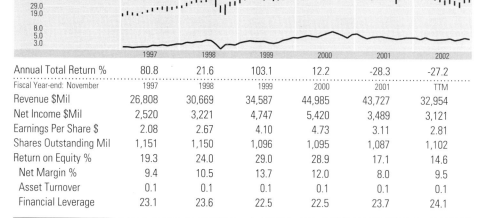

	Monthly Price High/Low			— Relative Strength to S&P 500		
Annual $Price High Low	29.75 16.38	48.75 18.31	71.44 35.41	110.00 58.63	90.40 35.75	60.00 28.85

	1997	1998	1999	2000	2001	2002
Annual Total Return %	80.8	21.6	103.1	12.2	-28.3	-27.2
Fiscal Year-end: November	1997	1998	1999	2000	2001	TTM
Revenue $Mil	26,808	30,669	34,587	44,985	43,727	32,954
Net Income $Mil	2,520	3,221	4,747	5,420	3,489	3,121
Earnings Per Share $	2.08	2.67	4.10	4.73	3.11	2.81
Shares Outstanding Mil	1,151	1,150	1,096	1,095	1,087	1,102
Return on Equity %	19.3	24.0	29.0	28.9	17.1	14.6
Net Margin %	9.4	10.5	13.7	12.0	8.0	9.5
Asset Turnover	0.1	0.1	0.1	0.1	0.1	0.1
Financial Leverage	23.1	23.6	22.5	22.5	23.7	24.1

Valuation Ratios	Stock	Rel to Industry	Rel to S&P 500
Price/Earnings	14.2	0.8	0.6
Price/Book	2.1	1.2	0.6
Price/Sales	1.3	1.0	0.7
Price/Cash Flow	—	—	—

Major Fund Holders	% of Fund Assets
White Oak Growth Stock	7.38
Conseco 20 A	6.76
Neuberger Berman Focus Inv	5.38
Fidelity Select Brokerage & Investmnt	5.29

Morningstar's Take By Craig Woker, 12-09-2002 Stock Price as of Analysis: $40.83

Morgan Stanley has found a happy medium, straddling the line between a financial-services supermarket and a focused capital markets player. We would find this stock attractively priced at a 30% discount to our $52 fair value estimate.

The future of the financial industry is often cast in two wildly divergent scenarios. One camp says that firms must transform into conglomerates like Citigroup to win; the other says specialized shops like Goldman Sachs will prevail. Morgan Stanley has hedged its bets. Though the firm is a leading investment bank, it has its toe in other services like credit cards and mutual funds.

This relative diversity has steadied results in the current market downturn. For instance, while net income fell 28% in the securities unit in the first nine months of fiscal 2002, Morgan Stanley had healthy results from Discover and the asset management group, which includes the Van Kampen fund family. As a result, Morgan Stanley's return on equity was 14.3% through the first three quarters of 2002. This keeps the firm in striking distance of achieving its long-term goal of averaging at least an 18% ROE through market cycles, especially considering that Morgan Stanley earned ROEs of 28% in the last peak years of 1999 and 2000.

Nonetheless, Morgan Stanley's stock--like those of other brokerages--has been under pressure, primarily because of a series of regulatory investigations related to Wall Street analysts' conflicts of interest. Like Merrill Lynch, the initial target of the New York attorney general, Morgan Stanley has the combination of a broad retail network and high-profile Internet and technology analysts that the prosecutor seems drawn to. However, we have accounted for this challenge--as well as other potential regulatory and legal problems--by squeezing Morgan Stanley's net margins over the next several years in our cash flow model as increasing legal expenses offset cost-cutting, which likely will come through further headcount reductions.

Legal action aside, Morgan Stanley is well positioned. The firm is a market share leader in mergers and acquisitions and has a heavy presence in Europe. We anticipate that demand for M&A services will far outpace the weak equities underwriting market in the near future, and we believe that Europe is likely to offer better prospects than the United States for the next several years.

Morgan Stanley has positioned itself to benefit from a market recovery, yet also cushion its profits from falling too far in a down cycle.

Motorola MOT

	Rating	Risk	Moat Size	Fair Value	Last Close	Yield %
	★★	Med.	None	$9.00	$8.65	1.9

Company Profile

Motorola is a company with many disparate businesses. It is the second-largest manufacturer (behind Nokia) of mobile phones, a segment that accounted for roughly one third of sales in 2001. It is also a big producer of embedded microprocessors as well as infrastructure gear for wireless and cable networks. The company has struggled recently, leading to severe personnel cuts; approximately one third of its workforce was slashed in 2001.

Management

Even though Chris Galvin--the latest member of the founding family to run Motorola--is still CEO, there has been much executive turnover, including the departure of highly regarded president and COO Ed Breen. Management isn't a strength at insular Motorola.

Strategy

Motorola tries to be a complete one-stop shop of technology. Its main business is selling wireless equipment (handsets and networking), semiconductors, and cable industry gear. In the slower economy, the firm is trying to become asset-light by increasingly outsourcing production and reducing capital expenditures.

1303 E. Algonquin Road
Schaumburg, IL 60196
www.motorola.com

Morningstar Grades

Growth [C]	1998	1999	2000	2001
Revenue %	-0.5	5.5	13.6	-20.2
Earnings/Share %	NMF	NMF	41.5	NMF
Book Value/Share %	-2.6	27.4	-4.8	-24.4
Dividends/Share %	0.0	0.0	0.0	0.0

September-quarter sales widely missed expectations, as suffering continued at each of the firm's businesses. Pressure won't ease anytime soon: Management projects just 4% sales growth in 2003. Motorola is hardly the stuff dreams are made of.

Profitability [C+]	1999	2000	2001	TTM
Return on Assets %	2.2	3.1	-11.8	-12.9
Oper Cash Flow $Mil	2,140	-1,164	1,976	1,533
- Cap Spending $Mil	2,388	3,957	1,307	655
= Free Cash Flow $Mil	-248	-5,121	669	878

Motorola finally put an end to its money-losing ways in the September quarter, generating a tiny profit for the first time in nearly two years. Management has done a superb job of cutting costs, thus keeping operating cash flow in the black.

Financial Health [D-]	1999	2000	2001	09-02
Long-term Debt $Mil	3,089	4,293	8,372	7,450
Total Equity $Mil	18,693	18,612	13,691	11,312
Debt/Equity Ratio	0.2	0.2	0.6	0.7

Financial health improves every quarter; management has kept a close eye on expenses, working capital, and capital spending. The goal is to use excess cash to repay debt, thereby raising the firm's debt rating further into investment-grade territory (it is now only BBB).

Industry	Investment Style	Stock Type	Sector
Wireless Equipment	▦ Large Value	➡ Slow Growth	▣ Hardware

Competition

	Market Cap $Mil	Debt/ Equity	12 Mo Trailing Sales $Mil	Price/Cash Flow	Return On Assets%	Total Return% 1 Yr	3 Yr
Motorola	19,903	0.7	26,576	13.0	-12.9	-41.7	-42.2
Nokia ADR	73,432	0.0	27,814	12.6	9.9	-36.1	-28.5
Ericsson Telephone ADR B	10,767	0.6	18,112	78.4	-5.3	-87.1	-64.9

Price Volatility

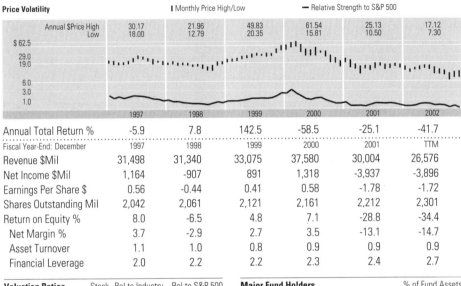

			I Monthly Price High/Low		— Relative Strength to S&P 500	
Annual $Price High Low	30.17 18.00	21.96 12.79	49.83 20.35	61.54 15.81	25.13 10.50	17.12 7.30

	1997	1998	1999	2000	2001	2002
Annual Total Return %	-5.9	7.8	142.5	-58.5	-25.1	-41.7

Fiscal Year-End: December	1997	1998	1999	2000	2001	TTM
Revenue $Mil	31,498	31,340	33,075	37,580	30,004	26,576
Net Income $Mil	1,164	-907	891	1,318	-3,937	-3,896
Earnings Per Share $	0.56	-0.44	0.41	0.58	-1.78	-1.72
Shares Outstanding Mil	2,042	2,061	2,121	2,161	2,212	2,301
Return on Equity %	8.0	-6.5	4.8	7.1	-28.8	-34.4
Net Margin %	3.7	-2.9	2.7	3.5	-13.1	-14.7
Asset Turnover	1.1	1.0	0.8	0.9	0.9	0.9
Financial Leverage	2.0	2.2	2.2	2.3	2.4	2.7

Valuation Ratios	Stock	Rel to Industry	Rel to S&P 500
Price/Earnings	NMF	—	—
Price/Book	1.8	0.3	0.6
Price/Sales	0.7	0.3	0.4
Price/Cash Flow	13.0	1.0	1.0

Major Fund Holders	% of Fund Assets
Rydex Electronics Inv	8.62
Fidelity Select Wireless	8.24
Fidelity Select Developing Comm	7.73
Dessauer Global Equity	6.74

Morningstar's Take   By Todd P. Bernier, 12-04-2002   Stock Price as of Analysis: $9.98

Motorola is akin to a cheap buffet: lots of different things to choose from, but nothing likable. For us to get excited about a firm like Motorola, which has no economic moat, its stock would need to trade at a 40%-50% discount to our fair value estimate.

The fundamental problem at Motorola--and the reason the firm is in decline--is a disparate and tired product line. Although management is quick to cite product diversification as a strength, we view it as a weakness: The firm is superb at nothing. Motorola's modus operandi may be product innovation, but the sad reality is that the company isn't dominant. If General Electric is number one or two in each of its markets, Motorola is the anti-GE. In none of its three largest business units--wireless phones, semiconductors, and wireless telecom infrastructure--is Motorola the top dog.

As the inventor of the cell phone, there is no reason Motorola shouldn't dominate the wireless landscape. But that hasn't been the case; Motorola has half the market share of Nokia. And the two firms couldn't be more different. Nokia views wireless phones the way a consumer would--fashion and image outweigh technology. Although it is changing slowly, Motorola typically promoted its products on the basis of their engineering prowess.

In semiconductors things have worsened over the years, mainly thanks to a chip industry that suffers from excess capacity and insufficient demand. Things aren't likely to improve anytime soon. Motorola has slashed capital spending at this unit, preferring to take an asset-light approach in which it outsources manufacturing capacity. However, it is possible that Motorola will fall further behind larger rivals, like Intel and Texas Instruments, whose sole corporate focus is chip production. Considering that Motorola has generated very low returns on its semiconductor investments, we question why it bothers to slug it out in the fiercely competitive commodity world of semiconductors.

Motorola's third major unit, wireless infrastructure, is also suffering. Many wireless service providers are on their deathbed, and have slashed spending as a result. That pain has rippled through the supplier food chain, including middle-of-the-pack Motorola. Once again, we question why Motorola is even slugging it out in a segment where potential returns on capital are low.

Motorola has no sustainable competitive advantage. And without an economic moat, Motorola would need to be unavoidably cheap before we'd buy.

MORNINGSTAR® Stocks 500

Mylan Laboratories MYL

	Rating	Risk	Moat Size	Fair Value	Last Close	Yield %
	★★★★★	Low	Narrow	$50.00	$34.90	0.5

Industry	Investment Style	Stock Type	Sector
Drugs	▦ Mid Growth	↗ Classic Growth	✛ Healthcare

Company Profile

Mylan Labs manufactures and markets generic and brand-name pharmaceuticals. While less than 20% of revenue comes from branded products, the company's long-term goal is a 50/50 split between generics and branded drugs. Mylan Labs has four divisions: Mylan Pharmaceuticals, which makes generic drugs; Mylan Technologies, which develops new and innovative drug-delivery methods; UDL Labs, which produces unit-dose forms of drugs; and Bertek Pharmaceuticals, which competes in the branded drug market. Mylan owns 50% of Somerset Pharmaceuticals, with partner Watson Pharmaceuticals.

Management

Founder, CEO, and chairman Milan Puskar has stacked the board in his favor; five of the eleven directors are considered insiders. Puskar is extremely well paid, pocketing $1 million in annual salary since 1996, regardless of company performance.

Strategy

Mylan Labs' generic drug unit manufactures nearly all its own drugs and concentrates on technologically hard-to-manufacture medicines, specifically transdermal patches--a specialty of the firm's drug-delivery unit. Mylan also has a branded drug unit and a formulating and packaging business. The firm's long-term goal is to generate half its sales from generics and half from branded drugs.

1030 Century Building   www.mylan.com
Pittsburgh, PA 15222

Morningstar Grades

Growth [B]	1999	2000	2001	2002
Revenue %	29.8	9.6	7.2	30.4
Earnings/Share %	11.0	29.7	-75.4	603.4
Book Value/Share %	38.0	10.2	-3.9	24.3
Dividends/Share %	0.0	0.0	0.0	0.0

Top-line growth has been strong over the past five years, averaging 20.4% through the fiscal year ended March 31, 2002. We estimate Mylan can growth at just above half that rate over the next five years.

Profitability [A+]	2000	2001	2002	TTM
Return on Assets %	11.5	2.5	16.1	16.1
Oper Cash Flow $Mil	119	66	346	287
- Cap Spending $Mil	30	25	21	27
= Free Cash Flow $Mil	89	41	326	260

Mylan has some of the best gross, operating, and net margins in the specialty pharmaceutical business. Gross margins have broken through the 50% mark, where we expect them to remain thanks to increased efforts in the branded drug arena.

Financial Health [A+]	2000	2001	2002	09-02
Long-term Debt $Mil	31	23	22	21
Total Equity $Mil	1,204	1,133	1,402	1,469
Debt/Equity Ratio	0.0	0.0	0.0	0.0

Mylan has no debt, plenty of cash, and generates most of its revenue growth internally. Cash and equivalents stood at $682 million at September 30, 2002.

Competition

	Market Cap $Mil	Debt/ Equity	12 Mo Trailing Sales $Mil	Price/Cash Flow	Return On Assets%	Total Return% 1 Yr	3 Yr
Mylan Laboratories	4,275	0.0	1,175	14.9	16.1	-6.4	15.2
Teva Pharmaceutical Indus	9,891	0.7	2,077	36.2	8.0	25.9	32.8
Watson Pharmaceuticals	3,021	0.2	1,188	7.8	6.8	-9.9	-5.9

Price Volatility

	I Monthly Price High/Low	— Relative Strength to S&P 500			
Annual $Price High / Low	25.31 / 11.50	35.94 / 17.06	32.00 / 17.06	32.25 / 16.00	38.12 / 20.20	37.50 / 25.10

	1997	1998	1999	2000	2001	2002
Annual Total Return %	27.1	51.3	-19.5	0.7	49.7	-6.4

Fiscal Year-end: March	1998	1999	2000	2001	2002	TTM
Revenue $Mil	555	721	790	847	1,104	1,175
Net Income $Mil	101	115	154	37	260	276
Earnings Per Share $	0.82	0.91	1.18	0.29	2.04	2.17
Shares Outstanding Mil	121	125	130	124	126	122
Return on Equity %	13.5	10.9	12.8	3.3	18.6	18.8
Net Margin %	18.1	16.0	19.5	4.4	23.6	23.5
Asset Turnover	0.7	0.6	0.6	0.6	0.7	0.7
Financial Leverage	1.1	1.1	1.1	1.3	1.2	1.2

Valuation Ratios	Stock	Rel to Industry	Rel to S&P 500
Price/Earnings	16.1	0.7	0.7
Price/Book	2.9	0.4	0.9
Price/Sales	3.6	0.9	1.8
Price/Cash Flow	14.9	0.7	1.1

Major Fund Holders	% of Fund Assets
TCW Galileo Income+Growth N	5.35
Fountainhead Special Value	4.43
Vanguard Selected Value	4.04
Henssler Equity	3.86

Morningstar's Take By Todd N. Lebor, 12-09-2002 Stock Price as of Analysis: $32.83

Mylan has some promise and the record to back it up. We'd be buyers of this specialty pharmaceutical company at the right price.

Mylan generates 85% of its revenue from generic drugs, but rather than compete in the cutthroat commodity generic drug arena, it focuses on products with high-barrier drug-delivery technologies, especially transdermal patches. This limits the competition and keeps gross margins above 50%, compared with the generic industry average of 40%.

Mylan's margins separate it from the pack. From 1997 to 2002, the company averaged 54%, 24%, and 16% gross, operating, and net margins, respectively. Only one other specialty pharmaceutical company--Watson Pharmaceuticals--posted better numbers, and Watson derives half of its revenue from branded products. We think the company's proprietary patch technology, specialized manufacturing capabilities, and industry reputation should keep it near the top of the group, financially and scientifically.

Like all generic drugmakers, Mylan relies on its patent team to uncover flaws in the patents of blockbuster branded drugs. While the company has grabbed its fair share in the first-to-file generic drug race, it's the future that holds the most promise for

Mylan. The company claims to have the six-month exclusivity rights to Johnson & Johnson's Levaquin and Duragesic. (It's only a claim because the Food and Drug Administration never confirms first-to-file information until the generic version of the drug is approved.) In 2001, these drugs posted U.S. sales of $990 million and $540 million, respectively. If Mylan can grab 50% of the market at 75% of the price (typical for a generic entrant) for these drugs for six months when they go off patent in 2004, that'll amount to $290 million in incremental sales. For a $1.1 billion company, that's quite a windfall.

Mylan also hopes to prop up its margins by pursuing more branded drug opportunities. Many of the company's so-called branded drugs are merely repackaged (with a new delivery method, for example) generics, so research costs and approval risks are low, while margins are better than with standard generics. Even so, this strategy isn't likely to produce many $100 million-plus drugs.

Mylan's erratic income is a concern. The unpredictable financial impact of first-to-file generic drugs is constantly wreaking havoc on margins, making it difficult to gauge true profitability. Therefore, we'd ask for a 30% margin of safety to our fair value estimate before investing.

National City NCC

	Rating	Risk	Moat Size	Fair Value	Last Close	Yield %
	★★★	Low	None	$34.00	$27.32	4.4

Company Profile

National City is a bank holding company. Its subsidiaries operate approximately 1,300 banking offices in Ohio, Michigan, Indiana, Illinois, Kentucky, and Pennsylvania. The company's National City Mortgage subsidiary operates about 154 mortgage-origination offices in 25 states. National City's other nonbank subsidiaries offer credit card, credit life insurance, brokerage, investment-management, leasing, trust, venture-capital, small-business, and community investment services.

Management

David A. Daberko has been chairman and CEO of National City since 1995. The bank typically develops its own executive talent, but in September 2000 it picked Peter Raskind, former vice chairman of US Bancorp, to run its consumer finance business.

Strategy

National City wants to diversify its revenue stream, which is dominated by lending and plain-vanilla consumer services. It has been investing in its higher-margin commercial banking, capital markets, and asset-management operations, which are still a much smaller part of overall revenue.

1900 East Ninth Street   www.nationalcity.com
Cleveland, OH 44114-3484

Morningstar Grades

Growth [C]	1998	1999	2000	2001
Revenue %	11.9	2.8	9.1	0.5
Earnings/Share %	-5.8	37.9	-4.1	6.6
Book Value/Share %	11.8	-14.2	22.5	9.5
Dividends/Share %	12.6	12.8	7.5	1.8

After years of weakness, growth picked up in 2001. Revenue grew 12% as the strong housing market drove better results at the company's mortgage unit. Revenue is up in 2002 as well, but mostly because of low interest expense.

Profitability [A-]	1999	2000	2001	TTM
Return on Assets %	1.6	1.5	1.3	1.4
Oper Cash Flow $Mil	1,990	1,180	-11,875	—
- Cap Spending $Mil	141	134	189	—
= Free Cash Flow $Mil	—	—	—	—

Return on equity slipped below 20% in 2001 and has declined the past three years because of lower margins. It will probably come in under 20% in 2002 as well.

Financial Health [B]	1999	2000	2001	09-02
Long-term Debt $Mil	—	—	—	—
Total Equity $Mil	5,698	6,740	7,381	8,157
Debt/Equity Ratio	—	—	—	—

National City's financial leverage is around 12.3, which is reasonable for a bank of its size. With an equity/assets ratio better than 8%, the bank carries plenty of capital, in our opinion.

Industry	Investment Style	Stock Type	Sector
Super Regional Banks	▦ Large Value	⊠ High Yield	⑤ Financial Services

Competition	Market Cap $Mil	Debt/ Equity	12 Mo Trailing Sales $Mil	Price/Cash Flow	Return On Assets%	Total Return% 1 Yr	3 Yr
National City	16,717	—	10,419	—	1.4	-2.6	14.0
US Bancorp	40,630	—	15,324	—	1.8	5.2	11.7
Fifth Third Bancorp	33,873	—	6,272	—	2.1	-3.4	11.1

Price Volatility

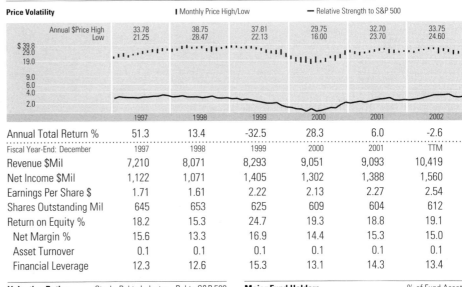

		1997	1998	1999	2000	2001	2002
Annual $Price High Low		33.78 21.25	38.75 28.47	37.81 22.13	29.75 16.00	32.70 23.70	33.75 24.60
Annual Total Return %		51.3	13.4	-32.5	28.3	6.0	-2.6

Fiscal Year-End: December	1997	1998	1999	2000	2001	TTM
Revenue $Mil	7,210	8,071	8,293	9,051	9,093	10,419
Net Income $Mil	1,122	1,071	1,405	1,302	1,388	1,560
Earnings Per Share $	1.71	1.61	2.22	2.13	2.27	2.54
Shares Outstanding Mil	645	653	625	609	604	612
Return on Equity %	18.2	15.3	24.7	19.3	18.8	19.1
Net Margin %	15.6	13.3	16.9	14.4	15.3	15.0
Asset Turnover	0.1	0.1	0.1	0.1	0.1	0.1
Financial Leverage	12.3	12.6	15.3	13.1	14.3	13.4

Valuation Ratios	Stock	Rel to Industry	Rel to S&P 500
Price/Earnings	10.8	0.7	0.5
Price/Book	2.0	1.0	0.6
Price/Sales	1.6	0.8	0.8
Price/Cash Flow	—	—	—

Major Fund Holders	% of Fund Assets
Huntington Income-Equity Tr	4.66
Rydex Banking Inv	3.58
Hartford Value A	3.04
Queens Road Large Cap Value	2.66

Morningstar's Take By Richard McCaffery, 12-09-2002 Stock Price as of Analysis: $27.02

We've lowered our fair value estimate for National City to $34 to reflect our more conservative valuation model. The bank still trades at a discount to this, but not enough of one to interest us.

National City has a broad consumer banking franchise and a strong middle-market corporate lending business that generates decent returns. Management runs a sound bank and gets high marks for good disclosure. It files its annual report with the Securities and Exchange Commission just 30 days after year-end, as fast as any company we know.

The bulk of business come from retail banking, corporate banking, and consumer finance. Over the past two years, management invested heavily to improve customer satisfaction in its retail branches through better training of sales staff, pay raises to attract and retain more qualified employees, and higher interest rates on savings accounts to increase deposit retention. These efforts should pay off, perhaps through improved growth rates, but certainly in a better experience for customers.

The company's aim to become a premier retail bank by improving service springs from weak growth over the past few years. Net revenue grew at a compound annual rate of 7% from 1997 through 2001 and income grew at just 5.4%, below the level

investors should expect from a bank with a broad franchise and established customer base.

While many of the recent measures are steps in the right direction, we see little reason to expect growth and profitability to take off, mainly because of the strength of the competition. The company, which operates primarily in Ohio, Pennsylvania, Illinois, Michigan, Indiana, and Kentucky, competes directly with rivals like Fifth Third and Charter One, a couple of the sharpest in the industry.

National City doesn't fit the mold of banks we think are likely to lead the consolidation wave and continue rewarding shareholders, because it doesn't really shine in its ability to grow or contain costs. The company's growth rates have been unimpressive, and its efficiency ratio, which measures operating costs as a percentage of net revenue, is typically well above 50%. Compared with Fifth Third or Charter One, National City has a long way to go.

So despite a good franchise, it's hard to see much upside beyond our estimate of the company's fair value. National City fits into a broad category of banks that do a lot of things pretty well, but nothing that really stands out.

  MORNINGSTAR® Stocks 500

National Processing NAP

	Rating	Risk	Moat Size	Fair Value	Last Close	Yield %
	★★★	Med.	Narrow	$18.00	$16.05	0.0

Company Profile

National Processing provides high-volume transaction processing services as well as customized processing solutions. The company's products and services include processing credit card and check transactions for merchants and other commercial businesses; outsourcing of administrative and financial functions for corporations seeking to reduce overhead costs; and ticket processing and settlement for providers of travel-related services. Merchant credit and debit card transactions represent approximately 60% of the company's revenues.

Management

Jon Gorney recently became chairman and CEO. He had worked at National City Corporation since 1973 and was responsible for information technology there. National City owns about 85% of National Processing.

Strategy

The business of credit card processing favors big firms, which reap economies of scale. To bulk up its market share, National Processing has made three acquisitions in the past three years. In recent years, the company has focused on improving its margins by generating more revenue from smaller, less price-sensitive merchants.

1231 Durrett Lane   www.npc.net
Louisville, KY 40213-2008

Morningstar Grades

Growth [C-]	1998	1999	2000	2001
Revenue %	19.1	-10.8	-0.9	10.8
Earnings/Share %	-28.6	NMF	NMF	18.8
Book Value/Share %	3.6	-9.8	13.2	8.3
Dividends/Share %	NMF	NMF	NMF	NMF

National is tagging along with the rise of credit and debit card payments. Because consumers are using these forms of payments in place of cash and checks, growth should be strong. Reported results are less impressive because of divested businesses.

Profitability [B]	1999	2000	2001	TTM
Return on Assets %	-8.7	10.0	11.0	10.6
Oper Cash Flow $Mil	59	45	50	81
- Cap Spending $Mil	17	14	20	19
= Free Cash Flow $Mil	42	31	30	62

Profits have been rising since the firm began going after higher-margin, smaller retailers. Operating margins are strong at about 18%.

Financial Health [A+]	1999	2000	2001	09-02
Long-term Debt $Mil	2	2	2	2
Total Equity $Mil	316	362	400	442
Debt/Equity Ratio	0.0	0.0	0.0	0.0

No debt, loads of cash on the balance sheet, and strong cash flows mean that investors have no worries here.

	Industry	Investment Style	Stock Type	Sector
	Data Processing	Small Core	Slow Growth	Business Services

Competition

	Market Cap $Mil	Debt/ Equity	12 Mo Trailing Sales $Mil	Price/Cash Flow	Return On Assets%	Total Return% 1 Yr	3 Yr
National Processing	836	0.0	461	10.4	10.6	-50.6	22.4
US Bancorp	40,630	—	15,324	—	1.8	5.2	11.7
First Data	26,633	0.8	7,118	16.5	4.6	-9.5	14.4

Price Volatility

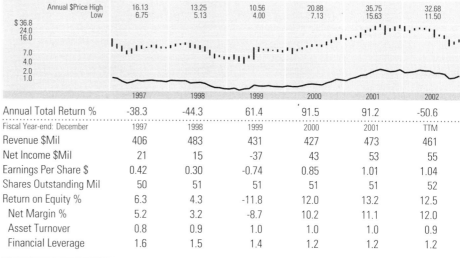

Annual $Price High Low	16.13 6.75	13.25 5.13	10.56 4.00	20.88 7.13	35.75 15.63	32.68 11.50
	1997	1998	1999	2000	2001	2002
Annual Total Return %	-38.3	-44.3	61.4	91.5	91.2	-50.6

Fiscal Year-end: December	1997	1998	1999	2000	2001	TTM
Revenue $Mil	406	483	431	427	473	461
Net Income $Mil	21	15	-37	43	53	55
Earnings Per Share $	0.42	0.30	-0.74	0.85	1.01	1.04
Shares Outstanding Mil	50	51	51	51	51	52
Return on Equity %	6.3	4.3	-11.8	12.0	13.2	12.5
Net Margin %	5.2	3.2	-8.7	10.2	11.1	12.0
Asset Turnover	0.8	0.9	1.0	1.0	1.0	0.9
Financial Leverage	1.6	1.5	1.4	1.2	1.2	1.2

Valuation Ratios	Stock	Rel to Industry	Rel to S&P 500
Price/Earnings	15.4	0.7	0.7
Price/Book	1.9	0.4	0.6
Price/Sales	1.8	0.5	0.9
Price/Cash Flow	10.4	0.6	0.8

Major Fund Holders	% of Fund Assets
Harbor Mid Cap Value	2.73
Fidelity Select Business Serv&Outsrcg	2.01
Lord Abbett Small-Cap Blend A	1.99
Alpha Select Target Select Equity	1.35

Morningstar's Take By Dan Schick, 12-16-2002 Stock Price as of Analysis: $15.98

National Processing has gotten its house in order, concentrating on the merchant-processing business. We'd buy shares of this solid contender at a 30% discount to our fair value estimate.

At National Processing's IPO in August 1996, the firm was a conglomeration, providing merchant processing, business process outsourcing, and data processing for the airline industry. At that time, the market valued National at nearly $1 billion. Now the market values a more focused, efficient, and strategically minded National at less than $850 million.

Soon after its IPO, National lost its biggest account to its main competitor, First Data. This spurred National, which prided itself on serving huge retailers, into action. A year later, it had improved its customer mix by acquiring an independent sales organization that specialized in selling processing services to small customers. Smaller customers produce lower transaction volume and revenue than big customers, but because they don't have pricing power, National earns much better margins serving them. In 1997, about one fourth of National's merchant-processing revenue was earned from smaller merchants and its processing margin was 11%. In 2001, with smaller merchants contributing

56% of processing revenue, that margin was 19%.

Besides reinvigorating the merchant business, National sold its business process outsourcing unit, reaping proceeds of more than $100 million that it reinvested in the processing business to boost its portfolio of small merchants. Furthermore, it decided to wind down its efforts directed at airlines. Though the airlines generated high transaction volume, they were low-margin customers and National received little revenue per transaction from them. Now that the firm is squarely focused on serving the card-processing needs of a diversified base of big and small clients, we like its prospects.

Consumers are substituting plastic cards, both debit and credit, for cash and checks at the point of sale. As one of the biggest merchant processors, National should continue on a growth track for the foreseeable future as transaction volume rises at double-digit rates. So long as the industry grows, we believe competition won't be brutal, and the scale required to enter the business will fend off any new entrants. We believe this will enable National to reward shareholders with solid growth and returns on capital.

National Semiconductor NSM

	Rating	Risk	Moat Size	Fair Value	Last Close	Yield %
	★★★	Med.	None	$17.00	$15.01	0.0

Company Profile

National Semiconductor manufactures semiconductor chips for various technology applications. The firm produces application-specific integrated analog and mixed-signal products for use in telecom and networking devices, notebook computers, and cellular phones. National Semi produces the bulk of its own semiconductors and markets its products in the United States and abroad.

Industry	Investment Style	Stock Type	Sector
Semiconductors	Mid Core	Slow Growth	Hardware

Competition	Market Cap $Mil	Debt/ Equity	12 Mo Trailing Sales $Mil	Price/Cash Flow	Return On Assets%	Total Return% 1 Yr	3 Yr
National Semiconductor	2,716	0.0	1,576	20.0	-2.9	-51.3	-29.6
Texas Instruments	25,982	0.1	8,024	12.8	0.9	-46.2	-32.5
STMicroelectronics NV	17,362	—	6,357	—	—		

Management

Brian Halla is National Semiconductor's president, chairman, and CEO. Before joining the company in 1996, Halla was an executive vice president at LSI Logic.

Price Volatility

	1997	1998	1999	2000	2001	2002
Annual $Price High	42.88	28.25	51.88	85.94	35.10	37.30
Low	21.63	7.44	8.88	17.13	19.70	9.95
Annual Total Return %	5.9	-48.0	217.1	-53.0	53.0	-51.3

Fiscal Year-End: May	1998	1999	2000	2001	2002	TTM
Revenue $Mil	2,537	1,957	2,140	2,113	1,495	1,576
Net Income $Mil	-99	-1,010	621	246	-122	-66
Earnings Per Share $	-0.60	-6.04	3.24	1.30	-0.69	-0.37
Shares Outstanding Mil	164	167	173	176	177	181
Return on Equity %	-5.3	ELB	37.8	13.9	-6.8	-3.7
Net Margin %	-3.9	-51.6	29.0	11.6	-8.2	-4.2
Asset Turnover	0.8	1.0	0.9	0.9	0.7	0.7
Financial Leverage	1.7	2.3	1.5	1.3	1.3	1.3

Strategy

As demand for wireless telecom products grows, National Semi is focusing on producing analog chips for this market and increasing the chip content per phone it supplies to customers. The firm also wants to be a major supplier of several components that go inside set-top boxes and Internet appliances. It continues to emphasize cutting costs and improving profitability.

2900 Semiconductor Drive   www.national.com
Santa Clara, CA 95052-8090

Valuation Ratios	Stock	Rel to Industry	Rel to S&P 500
Price/Earnings	NMF	—	—
Price/Book	1.5	0.5	0.5
Price/Sales	1.7	0.4	0.9
Price/Cash Flow	20.0	1.7	1.5

Major Fund Holders	% of Fund Assets
Oppenheimer Global Growth & Income A	7.04
TCW Galileo Value Opportunities I	3.92
Buffalo Mid Cap	3.76
Schroder MidCap Value Inv	3.50

Morningstar Grades

Growth [C-]	1999	2000	2001	2002
Revenue %	-22.9	9.4	-1.3	-29.2
Earnings/Share %	NMF	NMF	-59.9	NMF
Book Value/Share %	-52.4	59.2	9.1	7.8
Dividends/Share %	NMF	NMF	NMF	NMF

National Semi's three-year growth average of negative 8% lags the chip industry, in part because of past divestitures. We expect annual sales growth to be no greater than what is projected for the overall analog chip sector (roughly 12%).

Profitability [C]	2000	2001	2002	TTM
Return on Assets %	26.1	10.4	-5.3	-2.9
Oper Cash Flow $Mil	400	488	100	136
- Cap Spending $Mil	169	240	138	157
= Free Cash Flow $Mil	231	249	-38	-21

Gross margins have substantially improved since 1999, going from 21% to 37% in 2001. However, National Semi still has lots of room for improvement compared against pure analog players, like Linear Technology.

Financial Health [B-]	2000	2001	2002	08-02
Long-term Debt $Mil	49	26	20	22
Total Equity $Mil	1,643	1,768	1,781	1,767
Debt/Equity Ratio	0.0	0.0	0.0	0.0

The firm is in great financial health. By paying down most of its debt, National Semi has all but eliminated interest expenses and is in a position to weather the booms and busts of chip cycles far better than in the past.

Morningstar's Take By Jeremy Lopez, 12-17-2002 Stock Price as of Analysis: $17.10

There is nothing special or unique about National Semi. Only if the stock gets really cheap should investors be interested.

The chipmaker has evolved into a much better company from several years ago. Before the last chip cycle, the firm got itself into trouble by taking on Intel in PC processors. These efforts failed miserably, and took a toll on National Semi's balance sheet. But the firm has since sold its processor business and paid down debt. It has also focused more on producing analog chips, an area of the chip sector with higher, more stable margins. National Semi has better positioned itself for growth by focusing on hot end markets like notebook PCs, flat-panel displays, and cell phones.

While these changes have paid off--sales and profitability have fared much better in this downturn than in the last--National Semiconductor still isn't the pick of the chipmaking litter. It generates much lower gross margins and returns on capital than other analog players like Linear Technology, Maxim Integrated Products, and Analog Devices. We attribute part of this to the other firms' focus on the most attractive analog areas. Also, National Semi generates about 25% of its sales from peripheral, nonanalog businesses, which tend to carry lower margins.

We consider National Semiconductor to be a firm in sound financial health, but one with just average growth prospects and mediocre profitability relative to close rivals. Thus, it deserves to trade at a discount to its peers. The stock would have to be pretty cheap--at least 50% below our fair value estimate--for us to recommend it.

MORNINGSTAR® Stocks 500

Navistar International NAV

	Rating	Risk	Moat Size	Fair Value	Last Close	Yield %
	★★★	High	None	$30.00	$24.31	0.0

Company Profile

Navistar International manufactures diesel vehicles and replacement parts. The company produces diesel-powered medium and heavy trucks and buses, used by common carriers as well as by the passenger-transportation, leasing, construction, and energy/petroleum industries. It also manufactures diesel engines for use in its medium trucks and for sale to original-equipment manufacturers. The company's products are marketed in more than 70 countries. Navistar International operates 10 production plants in North America.

Management

John Horne, who has been with the firm since 1966, became CEO in 1995. Horne has led Navistar through a huge capital-investment and cost-cutting program. He will turn the reins over to current president and COO Daniel Ustian in February 2003 but remain chairman.

Strategy

Navistar has invested heavily in new manufacturing facilities during the past few years. Its goal is to reduce the labor needed to produce medium-duty trucks, limit the number of product variations to reduce costs, and offer better-designed, higher-quality products. The company continues to cut costs as it awaits a rebound in truck demand.

4201 Winfield Road, P.O.Box 1488
Warrenville, IL 60555
www.navistar.com

Morningstar Grades

Growth [C-]	1999	2000	2001	2002
Revenue %	9.4	-2.0	-20.2	0.7
Earnings/Share %	99.5	-68.5	NMF	NMF
Book Value/Share %	84.5	9.6	-10.4	-78.5
Dividends/Share %	NMF	NMF	NMF	NMF

The heavy-truck business is in a severe slump; sales are about half of their 1999 peak. Medium-duty truck sales have held up better, down only 25% from 1999. Growth has averaged about 7% over the past decade.

Profitability [D]	2000	2001	2002	TTM
Return on Assets %	2.3	-0.3	-7.7	-7.7
Oper Cash Flow $Mil	672	203	-74	-74
- Cap Spending $Mil	553	326	242	242
= Free Cash Flow $Mil	119	-123	-316	-316

The downturn has left the firm in the red, as high fixed costs bump up against lower sales, reducing operating margins. Restructuring and pension charges have decimated profits recently.

Financial Health [D+]	2000	2001	2002	10-02
Long-term Debt $Mil	2,148	2,468	2,398	2,398
Total Equity $Mil	1,310	1,123	247	247
Debt/Equity Ratio	1.6	2.2	9.7	9.7

Free cash flow has been negative because of new truck development and slow sales. The firm's credit rating was recently downgraded by S&P and Moody's, as recent profits have been inadequate to support the firm's debt load.

Industry	Investment Style	Stock Type	Sector
Truck Makers	▦ Mid Value	◪ Distressed	✿ Industrial Mats

Competition

	Market Cap $Mil	Debt/ Equity	12 Mo Trailing Sales $Mil	Price/Cash Flow	Return On Assets%	Total Return% 1 Yr	3 Yr
Navistar International	1,659	9.7	6,784	—	-7.7	-38.5	-18.7
DaimlerChrysler AG	30,750	2.1	136,142	2.2	-0.3	-25.0	-23.0
Volvo AB ADR B	6,576	—	14,236	—			

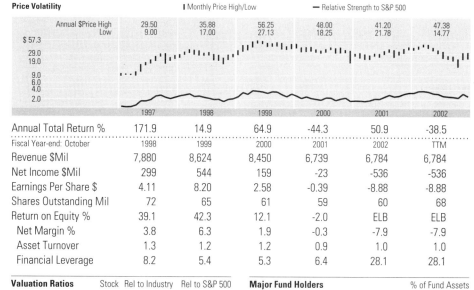

Price Volatility

Annual $Price High/Low	29.50 / 9.00	35.88 / 17.00	56.25 / 27.13	48.00 / 18.25	41.20 / 21.78	47.38 / 14.77

I Monthly Price High/Low — Relative Strength to S&P 500

	1997	1998	1999	2000	2001	2002
Annual Total Return %	171.9	14.9	64.9	-44.3	50.9	-38.5

Fiscal Year-end: October	1998	1999	2000	2001	2002	TTM
Revenue $Mil	7,880	8,624	8,450	6,739	6,784	6,784
Net Income $Mil	299	544	159	-23	-536	-536
Earnings Per Share $	4.11	8.20	2.58	-0.39	-8.88	-8.88
Shares Outstanding Mil	72	65	61	59	60	68
Return on Equity %	39.1	42.3	12.1	-2.0	ELB	ELB
Net Margin %	3.8	6.3	1.9	-0.3	-7.9	-7.9
Asset Turnover	1.3	1.2	1.2	0.9	1.0	1.0
Financial Leverage	8.2	5.4	5.3	6.4	28.1	28.1

Valuation Ratios	Stock	Rel to Industry	Rel to S&P 500
Price/Earnings	NMF	—	—
Price/Book	6.7	3.2	2.1
Price/Sales	0.2	0.4	0.1
Price/Cash Flow	—	—	—

Major Fund Holders	% of Fund Assets
Fidelity Select Automotive	13.20
MainStay Equity Income A	5.65
MainStay Select 20 Equity A	4.71
Eclipse Value Equity	3.71

Morningstar's Take By Michael Hodel, 12-16-2002 Stock Price as of Analysis: $24.45

Navistar has made improvements in recent years, but we think the negatives still outweigh the positives with this company. We wouldn't invest unless the shares traded at a 40% discount to our fair value estimate. We consider Paccar a far superior investment in the truck industry.

Navistar has historically been burdened by high fixed costs and substantial leverage. Given the deeply cyclical and highly competitive nature of the business, profitability has been both volatile and lackluster. Since the beginning of the 1990s, the firm has lost an average of about $1.80 per share annually, due in part to a series of restructurings. The company delivered great profits during the truck boom of the late 1990s, but the ensuing downturn has again sent earnings and cash flow into the red.

The company has been making improvements recently, though. Heavy spending on product development has led to a new line of medium-duty trucks that are distinctively styled and can be more efficiently produced. Navistar has also invested in new factory equipment, including a medium-duty truck plant in Ohio that includes some of the latest automation technology. Navistar's venture with Ford has also made the engine segment a much larger portion of sales, bringing the firm's products to the

hot market for diesel-powered pickup trucks. Finally, the company's new agreement with the UAW, reached after months of negotiations, should allow greater flexibility and reduce fixed labor costs.

The balance sheet contains significant debt and post-retirement benefit obligations. Navistar's pension plan ended fiscal 2002 with a $1 billion deficit, forcing the company to take a big charge against equity. Large cash contributions will be necessary in coming years. The company also recently transferred treasury shares to the plan, increasing shares outstanding by nearly 13%. Manufacturing debt (which excludes the financing unit) has risen sharply in recent years, as cash flows haven't covered the costs of the company's improvement plans. These demands on Navistar's resources won't make it any easier for the firm to compete for market share, especially given its limited profitability.

A rebound in truck demand could do wonders for Navistar's profitability and financial health, but we aren't convinced the company can generate decent returns for shareholders over the long term. We'd wait for Navistar to prove that it can translate recent efforts into actual profitability and cash flow before considering the stock.

NCR NCR

	Rating	Risk	Moat Size	Fair Value	Last Close	Yield %
	★★★	Med.	None	$35.00	$23.74	0.0

Company Profile

NCR designs, develops, and services information technology systems. The company's products include automated teller machines, checkout scanners, retail point-of-sale workstations, bar code scanning equipment, customized paper rolls, ink ribbons, automated ticket dispensers, business forms, and electronic payment devices. The firm also provides data-warehousing technology through its Teradata business.

Management

CEO Lars Nyberg led NCR out of AT&T's shadow with a spin-off in 1996. He has reinvigorated NCR by pushing toward data warehousing and away from the company's roots in retail automation equipment and an ill-fated venture into computer manufacturing.

Strategy

NCR traces its roots to 1884, when it was founded as the National Cash Register Co. It's milking its slow-growth businesses to fund Teradata, which provides data warehouses to companies. This is NCR's best growth opportunity and looks as if it might become a great business. The firm is also looking to boost the revenue it earns from providing technology-related services.

1700 South Patterson Blvd.　　www.ncr.com
Dayton, OH 45479

Industry	Investment Style	Stock Type	Sector
Computer Equipment	▦ Mid Core	➡ Slow Growth	▦ Hardware

Competition	Market Cap $Mil	Debt/ Equity	12 Mo Trailing Sales $Mil	Price/Cash Flow	Return On Assets%	Total Return% 1 Yr	3 Yr
NCR	2,316	0.2	5,604	15.4	-4.3	-35.6	-14.2
IBM	130,982	0.8	82,442	9.0	5.8	-35.5	-11.1
Oracle	57,845	0.1	9,459	18.1	19.8	-21.8	-26.3

Price Volatility

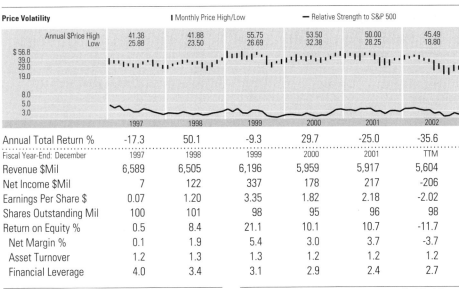

Monthly Price High/Low — Relative Strength to S&P 500

Annual $Price High Low	41.38 25.88	41.88 23.50	55.75 26.69	53.50 32.38	50.00 28.25	45.49 18.80
	1997	1998	1999	2000	2001	2002
Annual Total Return %	-17.3	50.1	-9.3	29.7	-25.0	-35.6

Fiscal Year-End: December	1997	1998	1999	2000	2001	TTM
Revenue $Mil	6,589	6,505	6,196	5,959	5,917	5,604
Net Income $Mil	7	122	337	178	217	-206
Earnings Per Share $	0.07	1.20	3.35	1.82	2.18	-2.02
Shares Outstanding Mil	100	101	98	95	96	98
Return on Equity %	0.5	8.4	21.1	10.1	10.7	-11.7
Net Margin %	0.1	1.9	5.4	3.0	3.7	-3.7
Asset Turnover	1.2	1.3	1.3	1.2	1.2	1.2
Financial Leverage	4.0	3.4	3.1	2.9	2.4	2.7

Valuation Ratios	Stock	Rel to Industry	Rel to S&P 500
Price/Earnings	NMF	—	—
Price/Book	1.3	0.2	0.4
Price/Sales	0.4	0.3	0.2
Price/Cash Flow	15.4	1.7	1.2

Major Fund Holders	% of Fund Assets
Dean Large Cap Value A	3.01
ING Midcap Value A	2.68
Summit Everest Fund	2.36
First Focus Core Equity Instl	2.12

Morningstar Grades

Growth [B-]	1998	1999	2000	2001
Revenue %	-1.3	-4.8	-3.8	-0.7
Earnings/Share %	EUB	179.2	-45.7	19.8
Book Value/Share %	5.2	11.5	13.3	13.3
Dividends/Share %	NMF	NMF	NMF	NMF

NCR hasn't grown in years. It is pinning its hopes on data warehousing, a business that is doing well in a tough tech-spending environment. In better times, this segment should grow fairly rapidly and help NCR post 5% revenue growth.

Profitability [B+]	1999	2000	2001	TTM
Return on Assets %	6.9	3.5	4.5	-4.3
Oper Cash Flow $Mil	607	171	146	150
- Cap Spending $Mil	291	324	258	211
= Free Cash Flow $Mil	316	-153	-112	-61

Some of NCR's businesses, like the ATM segment, are profitable. Others, like the retail automation division, are in the red. As Teradata contributes a bigger portion of the firm's sales, it should be a big boost to profitability.

Financial Health [B-]	1999	2000	2001	09-02
Long-term Debt $Mil	40	11	10	306
Total Equity $Mil	1,596	1,758	2,027	1,763
Debt/Equity Ratio	0.0	0.0	0.0	0.2

NCR is reasonably healthy, so we are not worried by its financial position. At the end of its second quarter, the firm had $461 million in cash and only $328 million in debt.

Morningstar's Take By Dan Schick, 11-26-2002 Stock Price as of Analysis: $28.11

NCR has done little for shareholders since it spun off from AT&T at the beginning of 1997. Given the firm's mishmash of businesses in slow-growing markets, strong competitors, and single-digit returns on capital, the stock's poor performance is not a surprise. While we think NCR has the potential to improve its returns--which we've factored into our fair value estimate--we would want a 50% discount to our fair value before investing.

NCR's biggest business right now is manufacturing and servicing ATMs; this accounts for about 27% of revenue. Although the business is growing slowly, it isn't a bad one. NCR is a leader in markets around the world and benefits from competing in a stable industry with relatively few players. While it has historically earned operating margins in the low teens, pricing pressures and a slowdown in Europe have hampered performance recently. We assume that NCR's cost-cutting, coupled with some small revenue growth, will put margins back on a comparable footing with its main competitor, Diebold.

Data warehousing will probably be NCR's biggest business in the not-too-distant future, though. The Teradata subsidiary provides about 23% of NCR's revenue, but it has the most growth potential. The division is a leading provider of the software, hardware, and consulting services needed to create the data warehouses that big businesses use to store huge volumes of data.

Since information is a valuable asset to businesses, Teradata's customers are willing to make significant investments to manage it and extract useful insights from it. The amount of business data is always growing, so eventually the initial capacity will run out, generating demand for upgrades. Teradata earns margins as high as 50% on these upgrades. As Teradata builds its base of customers and holds on to them because of the costs involved in switching providers, it should become a profitable business as more revenue consists of high-margin upgrades. NCR targets 15%-plus operating margins, which seems reasonable.

The rest of NCR's businesses are less inspiring, ranging from poor (the "other" segment) to so-so (the payment and imaging business, which enables banks to process check images), in our opinion. NCR seems to be milking these units' cash flows to fund Teradata, which we think is a smart use of capital.

Assuming that Teradata meets our expectations, we think NCR will see improving fortunes. However, we'd want a big discount before buying.

MORNINGSTAR® Stocks 500

Neiman-Marcus Group A NMG.A

	Rating	Risk	Moat Size	Fair Value	Last Close	Yield %
	★★	Med.	None	$33.00	$30.39	0.0

Company Profile

Neiman Marcus Group is a specialty retailer with three operating units. Its Neiman Marcus chain of 33 stores through the United States is a specialty retailer offering women's and men's apparel, jewelry, and home accessories. The company's NM Direct unit distributes the Neiman Marcus and Horchow catalogs. It owns two Bergdorf Goodman and Bergdorf Goodman Men stores in New York City. Harcourt General owns about 14% of the firm. About 83% of the company's revenue comes from its specialty retail stores and 17% from direct marketing.

Management

Burton Tansky, named CEO in 2001, has earned his stripes in the upscale retail world. In past posts at Bergdorf Goodman and Neiman Marcus stores, Tansky showed an acute instinct for the luxury goods market, leading to solid growth in those units.

Strategy

Neiman Marcus aims to solidify its high-end position by sharpening its focus on luxury designer goods and offering customers personal service. This should help improve margins as shoppers are more willing to pay full price for designer items. The company is also placing more emphasis on expanding distribution channels through its catalog and online unit.

1618 Main Street www.neimanmarcusgroup.com
Dallas, TX 75201

Morningstar Grades

Growth [C-]	1999	2000	2001	2002
Revenue %	10.4	13.4	3.0	-2.2
Earnings/Share %	-9.0	42.5	-17.8	-8.0
Book Value/Share %	14.2	13.0	17.0	11.2
Dividends/Share %	NMF	NMF	NMF	NMF

In a departure from the typical 5%-7% annual growth, sales declined in fiscal 2002 as a result of macroeconomic factors. However, we believe the retailer is in a stronger position than rival Saks Fifth Avenue to take advantage of an economic upturn.

Profitability [B+]	2000	2001	2002	TTM
Return on Assets %	7.6	6.0	5.2	5.2
Oper Cash Flow $Mil	255	132	212	191
- Cap Spending $Mil	89	120	149	155
= Free Cash Flow $Mil	166	12	63	35

Neiman Marcus has tried to keep its relatively high inventory levels down. This discipline will pay off in the form of increased margins because there will be less pressure to mark down merchandise just to get it out the door.

Financial Health [A]	2000	2001	2002	10-02
Long-term Debt $Mil	330	250	250	300
Total Equity $Mil	826	943	1,055	1,084
Debt/Equity Ratio	0.4	0.3	0.2	0.3

Neiman Marcus has steadily pared debt and now sports a very clean balance sheet. With solid cash flow from existing operations, the firm should be able to easily fund the development of two new stores planned for the next four years.

	Industry	Investment Style	Stock Type	Sector
	Department Stores	■ Mid Core	→ Slow Growth	Consumer Services

Competition

	Market Cap $Mil	Debt/ Equity	12 Mo Trailing Sales $Mil	Price/Cash Flow	Return On Assets%	Total Return% 1 Yr	3 Yr
Neiman-Marcus Group A	1,458	0.3	3,001	7.6	5.2	-2.2	4.8
Federated Department Stor	5,642	0.6	15,546	3.9	0.2	-29.7	-16.2
Nordstrom	2,563	—	5,772	—	—	—	—

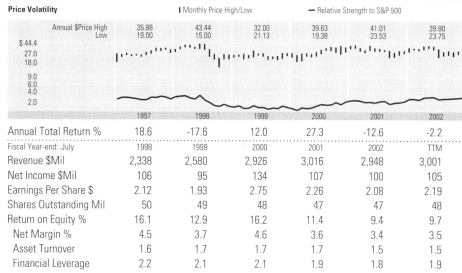

Price Volatility — Monthly Price High/Low — Relative Strength to S&P 500

Annual $Price High Low	35.88 19.00	43.44 15.00	32.00 21.13	39.63 19.38	41.01 23.53	39.80 23.75

	1997	1998	1999	2000	2001	2002
Annual Total Return %	18.6	-17.6	12.0	27.3	-12.6	-2.2

Fiscal Year-end: July	1998	1999	2000	2001	2002	TTM
Revenue $Mil	2,338	2,580	2,926	3,016	2,948	3,001
Net Income $Mil	106	95	134	107	100	105
Earnings Per Share $	2.12	1.93	2.75	2.26	2.08	2.19
Shares Outstanding Mil	50	49	48	47	47	48
Return on Equity %	16.1	12.9	16.2	11.4	9.4	9.7
Net Margin %	4.5	3.7	4.6	3.6	3.4	3.5
Asset Turnover	1.6	1.7	1.7	1.7	1.5	1.5
Financial Leverage	2.2	2.1	2.1	1.9	1.8	1.9

Valuation Ratios	Stock	Rel to Industry	Rel to S&P 500
Price/Earnings	13.9	0.9	0.6
Price/Book	1.3	1.1	0.4
Price/Sales	0.5	1.7	0.2
Price/Cash Flow	7.6	2.0	0.6

Major Fund Holders	% of Fund Assets
Ariel	4.06
Profit Value	3.36
Kenwood Growth & Income	2.32
Seligman Tax-Aware A	1.63

Morningstar's Take By Debbie Wang, 12-02-2002 Stock Price as of Analysis: $31.30

We believe Neiman Marcus Group is making the right moves to reinforce its standing in luxury retail. The firm will ultimately be in a stronger position to take advantage of an economic upturn, provided it weathers the near-term slowdown in consumer spending.

Under the leadership of CEO Burton Tansky, the retailer has adjusted its merchandise to focus on luxury and designer goods like Jil Sander and Ermenegildo Zegna, phasing out most of the private-label items that appealed to customers bent on saving a few dollars. Further, the company is continuing its emphasis on high-touch customer service by paying its salespeople on commission. We believe dedication to these efforts helped cushion the effects of the cyclical downturn in fiscal 2002. Comparable-store sales at Neiman Marcus Group decreased 4.6% for the year, while sales at rival Saks were down 7.8%.

With no clear economic upturn on the horizon, Neiman Marcus' primary near-term challenge is keeping costs under control, particularly inventory levels. Historically, this has been a bit of a weak point for the retailer, especially compared with competitors. We've recently seen some improvement, though, and believe this will lead to fewer markdowns and healthier margins.

In the longer term, we believe Neiman Marcus has the potential to outperform key rivals and dominate the upper echelon of the luxury realm by buckling down and continuing its emphasis on designer goods and personal service. The company kicked off a small but intriguing initiative to build alliances with up-and-coming designers, resulting in the purchase of controlling interests in Laura Mercier cosmetics and Kate Spade. Maintaining strong relationships with leading designers is important because retailers compete for quality merchandise; Neiman Marcus should reap benefits from its priority status with these two designers. It had to take a small impairment charge for several Kate Spade stores last fiscal year, but we don't anticipate any more write-downs from that business.

Still, the firm competes in a mature retail arena where single-digit growth is the norm. Thus, we conservatively estimate 3%-6% sales growth over the next five years. We believe the stock is fully valued, and would not buy until it traded at a 50% discount to our fair value estimate.

Network Associates NET

	Rating	Risk	Moat Size	Fair Value	Last Close	Yield %
	★★	High	None	$15.00	$16.09	0.0

Company Profile

Networks Associates develops and supports anti-virus software. The company also develops software used in the management of PC-based networks. Its primary product line, VirusScan, is a set of programs designed to detect, identify, and eradicate viruses from personal computers and networks. The company generates its revenue from licensing its products primarily to corporate, government, and institutional customers. Networks Associates also owns the majority of McAfee.com

Management

In a management shakeup, George Samenuk was hired as CEO in January 2001. He previously was general manager of IBM Americas.

Strategy

Under new leadership, Network Associates is focused on increasing profitability by eliminating noncore businesses and improving its salesforce. Over the past year, the company has shed more than 20 products once considered a drag on profits.

3965 Freedom Circle   www.nai.com
Santa Clara, CA 95054

Morningstar Grades

Growth [B-]	1998	1999	2000	2001
Revenue %	34.6	-30.9	9.1	11.9
Earnings/Share %	225.0	NMF	NMF	NMF
Book Value/Share %	39.3	-8.0	-21.3	-13.7
Dividends/Share %	NMF	NMF	NMF	NMF

Excluding the switch to a more conservative method of recognizing revenue, growth has been steady, in the midteens. We expect similar growth as the company expands its product offering.

Profitability [B]	1999	2000	2001	TTM
Return on Assets %	-10.8	-7.4	-6.2	2.1
Oper Cash Flow $Mil	-18	27	146	229
- Cap Spending $Mil	20	54	31	52
= Free Cash Flow $Mil	-39	-27	114	177

Profitability has not been impressive. At 13%, the firm's operating margins are half of Symantec's. But selling struggling businesses and gaining operating leverage should expand margins.

Financial Health [D+]	1999	2000	2001	09-02
Long-term Debt $Mil	—	396	579	356
Total Equity $Mil	660	519	445	700
Debt/Equity Ratio	—	0.8	1.3	0.5

Past losses have cut into shareholder equity, thus hurting leverage ratios. However, the balance sheet is in solid shape; cash doubles debt. Also, operating cash flow has significantly improved.

Industry	Investment Style	Stock Type	Sector
Systems & Security	▦ Mid Core	➡ Slow Growth	◪ Software

Competition	Market Cap $Mil	Debt/ Equity	12 Mo Trailing Sales $Mil	Price/Cash Flow	Return On Assets%	Total Return% 1 Yr	3 Yr
Network Associates	2,517	0.5	966	11.0	2.1	-37.8	-13.2
Computer Associates Inter	7,739	0.4	3,056	5.8	-5.3	-60.7	-41.5
Symantec	5,797	0.4	1,242	9.9	4.1	22.0	14.3

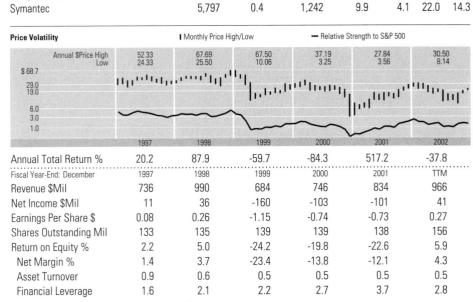

Price Volatility — Monthly Price High/Low — Relative Strength to S&P 500

Annual $Price High/Low	52.33 / 24.33	67.69 / 25.50	67.50 / 10.06	37.19 / 3.25	27.84 / 3.56	30.50 / 8.14
	1997	1998	1999	2000	2001	2002

Annual Total Return %	20.2	87.9	-59.7	-84.3	517.2	-37.8

Fiscal Year-End: December	1997	1998	1999	2000	2001	TTM
Revenue $Mil	736	990	684	746	834	966
Net Income $Mil	11	36	-160	-103	-101	41
Earnings Per Share $	0.08	0.26	-1.15	-0.74	-0.73	0.27
Shares Outstanding Mil	133	135	139	139	138	156
Return on Equity %	2.2	5.0	-24.2	-19.8	-22.6	5.9
Net Margin %	1.4	3.7	-23.4	-13.8	-12.1	4.3
Asset Turnover	0.9	0.6	0.5	0.5	0.5	0.5
Financial Leverage	1.6	2.1	2.2	2.7	3.7	2.8

Valuation Ratios	Stock	Rel to Industry	Rel to S&P 500
Price/Earnings	59.6	0.9	2.5
Price/Book	3.6	1.6	1.1
Price/Sales	2.6	0.7	1.3
Price/Cash Flow	11.0	1.0	0.8

Major Fund Holders	% of Fund Assets
Thurlow Growth	7.05
Fidelity Select Software & Comp	4.70
SunAmerica Focused Technology A	3.53
ING Technology A	2.98

Morningstar's Take   By Mike Trigg, 11-20-2002 Stock Price as of Analysis: $17.65

The turnaround at Network Associates has been impressive. But with a Securities and Exchange Commission investigation of the firm's accounting practices still looming, we wouldn't buy the stock until it traded 50% below our fair value estimate.

New management, led by CEO George Samenuk, has done a good job of restoring investor confidence after the previous leadership got in hot water over aggressive revenue-recognition policies. However, the SEC has yet to complete its investigation, and earlier this year the company discovered errors in its 1998, 1999, and 2000 financials, forcing another restatement.

The errors discovered are independent of the SEC probe, which is looking only at fiscal 2000, when Network Associates stuffed the channel--that is, gave distributors more inventory than could be sold in a reasonable time. This led to the dismissal of the firm's top three officers, a revenue-recognition change, and a restatement of financial results. But since the events predate current management, we fail to see how they will affect business prospects.

Management has also restored profitability by consolidating the company into four business units and selling underperforming products. Network Associates remains the leader in the corporate antivirus market with its McAfee software, despite losing share to Symantec while struggling to get its house in order. And while the antivirus market is growing slower than other areas of security, like virtual private networks, viruses like Code Red continue to cause damage and create demand.

Unlike previous initiatives, however, management plans on competing only in markets where it can leverage leadership in antivirus software. One promising area is McAfee.com, which provides individuals and small businesses access via the Web to antivirus software and related products that would otherwise be located on their PCs. McAfee.com is an attractive business with recurring subscription revenue.

Management has done a good job, but the turnaround isn't over. The focus now is execution, growing outside of antivirus software, and expanding margins; the company's 13% operating margin is half of that of Symantec. The uncertainty over this stage of the turnaround and the SEC investigation commands a large margin of safety. We wouldn't buy the stock until it fell below $8.

MORNINGSTAR® Stocks 500

New York Times A NYT

	Rating	Risk	Moat Size	Fair Value	Last Close	Yield %
	★★★	Low	Narrow	$45.00	$45.73	1.2

Company Profile

New York Times is a publishing, broadcasting, and information services company that operates throughout North America. Its primary newspaper, The New York Times, has an average weekday circulation exceeding 1 million. Additionally, the company publishes The Boston Globe, 21 regional newspapers, and magazines like Golf World and Golf Digest. The company also operates several television and radio stations.

Management

Arthur Sulzberger Jr. has been chairman since 1997. Russell Lewis became president in 1996 and CEO in 1997 after being president and general manager of The New York Times.

Strategy

The company seeks to dominate the publishing market with a stable of strong franchises, including The New York Times and The Boston Globe. It has also extended its business into the Internet, although plans to raise capital by spinning off its digital business died along with the IPO market.

229 West 43rd Street
New York, NY 10036
www.nytco.com

Morningstar Grades

Growth [D]	1998	1999	2000	2001
Revenue %	4.2	7.2	10.8	-10.6
Earnings/Share %	9.0	19.3	34.1	19.8
Book Value/Share %	-9.2	1.5	-7.5	-3.9
Dividends/Share %	15.6	10.8	9.8	8.9

Even in good economic times, sales growth was lackluster, averaging barely 6% annually in the past five years. But the firm has successfully managed costs, resulting in solid earnings growth.

Profitability [A+]	1999	2000	2001	TTM
Return on Assets %	8.9	11.0	12.9	7.6
Oper Cash Flow $Mil	601	590	471	324
- Cap Spending $Mil	73	85	90	130
= Free Cash Flow $Mil	528	505	381	194

In the face of weak demand, management has aggressively cut costs to protect the bottom line. Earnings have grown more than 25% annually in the past five years, but ad market woes have made the past couple of years ones to forget.

Financial Health [A-]	1999	2000	2001	09-02
Long-term Debt $Mil	—	637	599	778
Total Equity $Mil	1,449	1,281	1,150	1,263
Debt/Equity Ratio	—	0.5	0.5	0.6

The company's debt/equity ratio of 0.4 is quite low in an industry characterized by heavy leverage.

Industry	Investment Style	Stock Type	Sector
Media Conglomerates	▦ Mid Core	→ Slow Growth	🎙 Media

Competition	Market Cap $Mil	Debt/ Equity	12 Mo Trailing Sales $Mil	Price/Cash Flow	Return On Assets%	Total Return% 1 Yr	3 Yr
New York Times A	6,924	0.6	3,019	21.4	7.6	6.9	0.9
Gannett	19,190	0.7	6,354	16.2	8.1	8.1	-1.1
Tribune	13,856	0.6	5,273	15.2	1.3	22.7	-2.8

Price Volatility

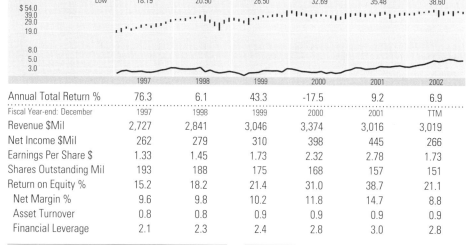

Annual $Price High Low		33.25 18.19	40.69 20.50	49.94 26.50	49.88 32.69	47.98 35.48	53.00 38.60

	1997	1998	1999	2000	2001	2002
Annual Total Return %	76.3	6.1	43.3	-17.5	9.2	6.9
Fiscal Year-end: December	1997	1998	1999	2000	2001	TTM
Revenue $Mil	2,727	2,841	3,046	3,374	3,016	3,019
Net Income $Mil	262	279	310	398	445	266
Earnings Per Share $	1.33	1.45	1.73	2.32	2.78	1.73
Shares Outstanding Mil	193	188	175	168	157	151
Return on Equity %	15.2	18.2	21.4	31.0	38.7	21.1
Net Margin %	9.6	9.8	10.2	11.8	14.7	8.8
Asset Turnover	0.8	0.8	0.9	0.9	0.9	0.9
Financial Leverage	2.1	2.3	2.4	2.8	3.0	2.8

Valuation Ratios	Stock	Rel to Industry	Rel to S&P 500
Price/Earnings	26.4	1.0	1.1
Price/Book	5.5	3.9	1.7
Price/Sales	2.3	1.0	1.1
Price/Cash Flow	21.4	1.4	1.6

Major Fund Holders	% of Fund Assets
W.P. Stewart & Co Growth	4.48
Van Kampen Global Franchise A	4.36
WST Growth Instl	2.76
MFS Instl Core Equity	2.55

Morningstar's Take By Jonathan Schrader, 11-26-2002 Stock Price as of Analysis: $46.77

New York Times is a good company, but we don't think it is worthy of a wide-moat rating. Because of this, we'd wait for a 30% discount to our fair value estimate before buying the stock.

With more than 20 newspapers in its stable, this media giant is best known for its flagship publication, The New York Times, which has a circulation that ranks third nationally among newspapers (trailing only USA Today and The Wall Street Journal). The Times boasts a great brand name and a Pulitzer-Prize-winning editorial staff. These attributes have allowed the company to increase weekday circulation at the flagship in each of the past three years--an impressive feat, given that overall newspaper circulation has declined during this period.

New York Times also owns several broadcasting stations, which constitute 5% of total sales. The company's bread and butter--publishing--accounts for roughly 93% of total revenue. Essentially a pure-play publishing firm, New York Times looks markedly different from rivals like Tribune, Washington Post, and Viacom, which own assets ranging from cable distribution to studios.

The focus on newspapers isn't necessarily bad. The company has thrown off more than $1.4 billion in free cash--cash flow from operations less capital spending--over the past three years, or 15% of revenue. This cash has been used for acquisitions, dividends, and share buybacks. The company has bought back 22% of its outstanding shares over the past three years.

Despite this great record of generating cash, we don't think New York Times deserves a wide moat rating. The New York Times is an excellent brand that attracts a lot of attention from the public and revenue from advertisers. However, the newspaper market in New York City is very competitive, with lower-price alternatives like the New York Post checking the growth of the Times. With many additional newspaper choices in New York and across the nation--especially USA Today--The New York Times, unlike many of its peers, hasn't been able to completely dominate its markets. Without this domination, New York Times merits only a narrow-moat rating.

Moat size matters, because the wider the moat, the less discount to fair value estimate we require on a stock. New York Times is a good company with solid long-term prospects. We'd be willing to buy and hold its stock, but we'd want a nice margin of safety before doing so.

Nextel Communications NXTL

	Rating	Risk	Moat Size	Fair Value	Last Close	Yield %
	★★★	High	Narrow	$13.00	$11.55	0.0

Company Profile

With 9.2 million customers in the United States, Nextel Communications is the fifth-largest wireless carrier. The company's Direct Connect feature allows to customers to instantly communicate--without a traditional dialup--as they would using a walkie-talkie. This feature is what mainly differentiates Nextel among business users, the company's bread-and-butter clientele. Motorola, the exclusive provider of iDEN handsets to Nextel, owns 14% of the company.

Management

Nextel's key shareholders are Motorola, asset manager Legg Mason, and wireless pioneer Craig McCaw. Insiders have been buying Nextel shares. COO Jim Mooney recently resigned after just one year with the firm.

Strategy

Nextel Communications targets mainly the high-end business user. This has resulted in a subscriber base that is one of the most profitable in the industry, with the highest monthly bills and the lowest churn rate. Part of the reason for Nextel's success is the Direct Connect feature, which functions much like a two-way radio.

2001 Edmund Halley Drive
Reston, VA 20191

www.nextel.com

Morningstar Grades

Growth [B]

	1998	1999	2000	2001
Revenue %	210.6	65.0	50.9	34.6
Earnings/Share %	NMF	NMF	NMF	NMF
Book Value/Share %	NMF	NMF	-35.6	NMF
Dividends/Share %	NMF	NMF	NMF	NMF

Nextel is a growth machine. Sales soared 26% in the September quarter, driven by 480,000 new users and the highest average revenue per user in the industry. Nextel now has 10.1 million subscribers, and projects 10.6 million at year's end.

Profitability [C-]

	1999	2000	2001	TTM
Return on Assets %	-8.3	-4.5	-13.0	-7.5
Oper Cash Flow $Mil	324	576	1,129	1,870
- Cap Spending $Mil	1,947	3,294	3,418	2,155
= Free Cash Flow $Mil	-1,623	-2,718	-2,289	-285

Nextel has been a money pit; however, shareholders should see a return in the next few years as strong sales growth and better operating efficiencies lead to profits. Nextel expects EBITDA to reach $3 billion in 2002--growth of 58% from 2001.

Financial Health [D+]

	1999	2000	2001	09-02
Long-term Debt $Mil	10,312	14,629	14,720	13,104
Total Equity $Mil	2,283	1,745	-865	561
Debt/Equity Ratio	4.5	8.4	ELB	23.4

Nextel has smartly repurchased deeply discounted debt using cash and equity; the violation of debt covenants is no longer an issue. The firm will burn through cash of less than $1 billion this year, meaning it will end 2002 with roughly $2 billion.

Industry	Investment Style	Stock Type	Sector
Wireless Service	▦ Large Growth	◆ Spec. Growth	◪ Telecom

Competition

	Market Cap $Mil	Debt/ Equity	12 Mo Trailing Sales $Mil	Price/Cash Flow	Return On Assets%	Total Return% 1 Yr	3 Yr
Nextel Communications	11,124	23.4	8,464	5.9	-7.5	5.4	-37.6
Verizon Communications	106,011	1.4	67,422	4.7	-0.1	-15.2	-9.8
AT&T Wireless Services	15,300	0.4	15,112	5.8	-7.5	-60.7	—

Price Volatility

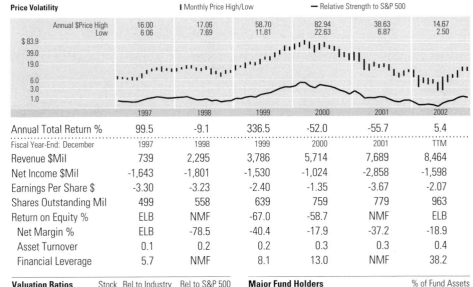

| | | Monthly Price High/Low | | | — Relative Strength to S&P 500 | |

Annual $Price High Low	16.00 6.06	17.06 7.69	58.70 11.81	82.94 22.63	38.63 6.87	14.67 2.50

$ 83.9 / 39.0 / 19.0 / 6.0 / 3.0 / 1.0

	1997	1998	1999	2000	2001	2002
Annual Total Return %	99.5	-9.1	336.5	-52.0	-55.7	5.4

Fiscal Year-End: December	1997	1998	1999	2000	2001	TTM
Revenue $Mil	739	2,295	3,786	5,714	7,689	8,464
Net Income $Mil	-1,643	-1,801	-1,530	-1,024	-2,858	-1,598
Earnings Per Share $	-3.30	-3.23	-2.40	-1.35	-3.67	-2.07
Shares Outstanding Mil	499	558	639	759	779	963
Return on Equity %	ELB	NMF	-67.0	-58.7	NMF	ELB
Net Margin %	ELB	-78.5	-40.4	-17.9	-37.2	-18.9
Asset Turnover	0.1	0.2	0.2	0.3	0.3	0.4
Financial Leverage	5.7	NMF	8.1	13.0	NMF	38.2

Valuation Ratios	Stock	Rel to Industry	Rel to S&P 500
Price/Earnings	NMF	—	—
Price/Book	19.8	7.3	6.2
Price/Sales	1.3	0.5	0.7
Price/Cash Flow	5.9	0.5	0.4

Major Fund Holders	% of Fund Assets
Legg Mason Focus	12.19
ProFunds Ultra Wireless Inv	9.47
Fidelity Leveraged Company Stock	6.50
Jundt Growth I	5.85

Morningstar's Take By Todd P. Bernier, 12-27-2002 Stock Price as of Analysis: $12.07

We attribute Nextel's strong showing in a soft economy to its focus on Corporate America and the popularity of Direct Connect. It is the only wireless carrier worth owning, in our opinion.

Unlike rivals obsessed with subscriber growth, Nextel doesn't wave a cell phone at every Tom, Dick, and Harry. Instead, it skims the cream of the crop: lucrative business customers who tend to be heavy cell phone users and who are more concerned with quality and features than price. As a result, Nextel's average revenue per user is the highest in the industry at roughly $70 per month. And because market saturation is making it increasingly difficult to find new, high-value subscribers, it is imperative for carriers to retain existing customers. While the Sprints of the world struggle with a customer exodus, Nextel has kept subscriber churn to roughly 2%, the lowest among the major wireless carriers.

Nextel's strong performance is due primarily to Direct Connect. No other operator can offer a similar push-to-talk service, which explains why 90% of Nextel's new subscribers come from another carrier. Nextel should add to its lead in push-to-talk technology in 2003 when it unveils the next generation of service, Nationwide Direct Connect, which will allow users in Boston, for example, to

reach those in San Francisco. In age when other carriers compete solely on price, Direct Connect is the unique service that gives Nextel a sizable economic moat.

Nextel's competitive advantage is sustainable, in our view. Although Sprint plans to someday offer a push-to-talk feature, liquidity issues will probably force it to scale back capital spending. And Nextel's exclusivity on qChat, Qualcomm's third-generation (3G) push-to-talk technology, protects the company from rivals who may be looking at the service.

As a result, Nextel need not frantically launch 3G upgrades to gain an edge on rivals. There is no timeline for when Nextel's network must migrate to the next digital standard. Rather, in 2003 Nextel will flip the switch on new vocoder compression software from Motorola that promises to double data-throughput rates and network capacity. We suspect 3G will be a big dud, leading to low returns on 3G investments. Thus, we applaud Nextel's deferral of 3G until demand warrants, protecting shareholder capital.

 MORNINGSTAR® Stocks 500

Nike B NKE

	Rating	Risk	Moat Size	Fair Value	Last Close	Yield %
	★★★	Med.	Narrow	$46.00	$44.47	1.1

Company Profile

Nike produces athletic and casual footwear, apparel, and accessories. The company sells its products to approximately 19,000 retail accounts in the United States and, through a combination of independent distributors, licensees, and subsidiaries, in 140 countries; it also operates about 60 retail outlets. In fiscal 2000, 56% of revenue was derived from domestic retail sales. Company products are sold under the Nike and other brand names, including Side 1 and i.e. footwear for women. Nike's Cole Haan division markets dress and casual footwear and accessories.

Management

Chairman and CEO Philip Knight founded Nike, but the firm's strategy rests with Charles Denson, co-president of Nike Brands, which accounts for the bulk of sales. Denson has 23 years with the firm and is credited with boosting sales in Europe.

Strategy

After lackluster sales the past few years, Nike hopes to spur a rebound in the United States by offering more midprice sneakers as well as establishing itself in the fast-growing equipment markets like golf, surfing, and skateboarding. Nike also seeks to expand margins with its new supply-chain software, which should better balance the firm's inventory with product demand.

One Bowerman Drive   www.nikebiz.com
Beaverton, OR 97005-6453

Morningstar Grades

Growth [B-]	1999	2000	2001	2002
Revenue %	-8.1	2.5	5.5	4.3
Earnings/Share %	16.3	31.8	4.3	13.0
Book Value/Share %	5.3	-3.3	14.2	10.3
Dividends/Share %	9.1	0.0	0.0	0.0

Annual sales growth averaged 23% from 1992 to 1997, but slumped to 2% from 1998 to 2002. In our opinion, Nike is now a mature firm, and its long-term target of high-single-digit sales growth appears unrealistic.

Profitability [A]	2000	2001	2002	TTM
Return on Assets %	9.9	10.1	10.3	6.5
Oper Cash Flow $Mil	700	657	1,082	1,020
- Cap Spending $Mil	420	318	283	269
= Free Cash Flow $Mil	280	339	799	751

Nike's operating margin declined from an average of 15% in 1992-97 to 11% in 1998-2002. However, its 11% margin is still twice that of rival Reebok RBK, and we think its improved supply chain can boost the margin to 13% over the next five years.

Financial Health [A+]	2000	2001	2002	08-02
Long-term Debt $Mil	470	436	626	736
Total Equity $Mil	3,136	3,495	3,839	3,673
Debt/Equity Ratio	0.2	0.1	0.2	0.2

The balance sheet remains healthy, thanks to the company's limited debt and history of strong operating cash flow. Nike has worked down its excess inventory, so operating cash flow should remain robust.

Industry	Investment Style	Stock Type	Sector
Shoes	Large Core	→ Slow Growth	Consumer Goods

Competition

	Market Cap $Mil	Debt/ Equity	12 Mo Trailing Sales $Mil	Price/Cash Flow	Return On Assets%	Total Return% 1 Yr	3 Yr
Nike B	11,798	0.2	10,076	11.6	6.5	-20.1	0.3
Reebok International	1,760	0.4	3,030	8.2	6.5	10.9	53.5
Timberland	1,340	—	1,175	7.8	16.9	-4.0	12.9

Price Volatility

Annual $Price High Low	76.38 37.75	52.69 31.00	66.94 38.75	57.00 25.81	60.06 35.50	64.28 38.53

	1997	1998	1999	2000	2001	2002
Annual Total Return %	-34.4	5.1	23.3	14.0	1.9	-20.1

Fiscal Year-end: May	1998	1999	2000	2001	2002	TTM
Revenue $Mil	9,553	8,777	8,995	9,489	9,893	10,076
Net Income $Mil	400	451	579	590	663	415
Earnings Per Share $	1.35	1.57	2.07	2.16	2.44	1.53
Shares Outstanding Mil	290	284	276	271	267	265
Return on Equity %	12.3	13.5	18.5	16.9	17.3	11.3
Net Margin %	4.2	5.1	6.4	6.2	6.7	4.1
Asset Turnover	1.8	1.7	1.5	1.6	1.5	1.6
Financial Leverage	1.7	1.6	1.9	1.7	1.7	1.7

Valuation Ratios	Stock	Rel to Industry	Rel to S&P 500
Price/Earnings	29.1	1.0	1.2
Price/Book	3.2	1.0	1.0
Price/Sales	1.2	1.0	0.6
Price/Cash Flow	11.6	1.0	0.9

Major Fund Holders	% of Fund Assets
Sparrow Growth A	3.74
Hartford Value A	2.71
MassMutual Instl Fundamental Value S	2.50
New Market	2.38

Morningstar's Take By Tom Goetzinger, 12-20-2002 Stock Price as of Analysis: $45.09

While we think Nike can eventually smooth out some of the volatility in its sales growth, we also think growth will remain challenged by fickle consumer tastes and the company's own market saturation. To compensate for potential zigzags in results, we'd look to buy shares at a 30% discount to our fair value estimate.

Nike no longer resembles the strong, quick, marquee athletes who don its gear. It's more like the weekend warrior on weary knees: good for short, explosive bursts from time to time, but mostly just huffing and puffing and trying to hold on. Over the past five years Nike has averaged 2% annual sales growth. One year growth might decline 8%; another it might increase 5%. This is hardly reminiscent of Nike's heyday of the 1980s and early 1990s. As recently as 1992-97, Nike averaged better than 20% annual sales growth.

Future growth will come from a number of different areas. International sales have become increasingly important to Nike's success and now represent 50% of revenue, up from 38% five years ago. International sales growth was more than triple domestic growth in the past two years--a trend that is likely to continue, in our opinion. Nike has also turned around its apparel segment. After posting a 10% sales decline in 2000, apparel sales increased 9% in 2001 and 5% in 2002, while footwear sales remained flat.

Nike's long-term goal is no longer sales growth, but profit growth. With U.S. sales stagnating, Nike has invested heavily in a supply-chain upgrade to lower material costs, improve logistics and transportation of products, and streamline manufacturing and design. Though it took Nike most of fiscal 2001 and 2002 to rectify problems with the new distribution system, everything appears on track now and inventory management is better than ever.

We think Nike's target for high-single-digit sales growth is probably unrealistic--we estimate sales will increase 5%-6% over the next five years. But we agree that its goal of midteen earnings growth is possible. Our model forecasts 11%-12% earnings growth for the next five years, with upside potential if more supply-chain efficiencies develop. Still, Nike has a lot to prove, and we'd thus require about a 30% margin of safety to buy in.

Nokia ADR NOK

	Rating	Risk	Moat Size	Fair Value	Last Close	Yield %
	★★	Med.	Narrow	$14.00	$15.50	1.5

Company Profile

Nokia the world's top maker of mobile phones, which accounted for roughly 75% of the firm's top line in 2001. At a time when the market for mobile phones is becoming saturated, Nokia is aggressively winning share from ailing rivals by cutting prices and launching many new models. The company's other main business is supplying telecom infrastructure gear to wireless carriers, a market segment that is currently dominated by Sweden's Ericsson. Nokia hopes to eventually have 30% share in this market.

Management

Chairman and CEO Jorma Ollila is credited with reversing Nokia's fortunes in the early 1990s by transforming it into a wireless-only company. Management is considered to be very stable, with most of the top positions dominated by veteran "Nokians."

Strategy

Nokia is the king of cell phones, capitalizing on its powerful brand to introduce desirable new phones. Thinking like a consumer-goods company, Nokia has segmented the market by providing different phones for different consumer categories. Management has put pressure on rivals who cannot match Nokia's marketing prowess and efficiency, in the process grabbing share.

Keilalahdentie 4   www.nokia.com
Espoo, 02150

Morningstar Grades

Growth [A]	1998	1999	2000	2001
Revenue %	50.6	48.4	53.6	2.7
Earnings/Share %	60.2	45.6	51.2	-43.9
Book Value/Share %	36.1	42.8	44.9	13.4
Dividends/Share %	54.8	66.7	40.0	-3.6

Market saturation and weak telecom capital spending have put the brakes on Nokia's growth; sales will decline roughly 4% this year. It is worrisome that phone users have yet to embrace Nokia's (or any other cell phone maker's) latest offerings.

Profitability [A+]	1999	2000	2001	TTM
Return on Assets %	19.3	19.5	9.9	9.9
Oper Cash Flow $Mil	3,320	3,260	5,838	5,838
- Cap Spending $Mil	1,394	1,468	928	928
= Free Cash Flow $Mil	1,927	1,792	4,910	4,910

An ability to charge premium prices, coupled with lean production expenses, has kept Nokia's margins high. In fact, Nokia's double-digit return on equity is in the top decile of its industry.

Financial Health [A]	1999	2000	2001	12-01
Long-term Debt $Mil	269	163	183	183
Total Equity $Mil	7,378	10,196	10,801	10,801
Debt/Equity Ratio	0.0	0.0	0.0	0.0

Nokia is a cash-generating machine and has the best balance sheet in the business; cash and investments are more than eight times debt. Unlike its peers struggling to stay afloat, Nokia throws off well more than $1 billion per quarter in operating cash flow.

Industry	Investment Style	Stock Type	Sector
Wireless Equipment	Large Growth	Spec. Growth	Hardware

Competition	Market Cap $Mil	Debt/ Equity	12 Mo Trailing Sales $Mil	Price/Cash Flow	Return On Assets%	Total Return% 1 Yr	3 Yr
Nokia ADR	73,432	0.0	27,814	12.6	9.9	-36.1	-28.5
Motorola	19,903	0.7	26,576	13.0	-12.9	-41.7	-42.2
Ericsson Telephone ADR B	10,767	0.6	18,112	78.4	-5.3	-87.1	-64.9

Price Volatility

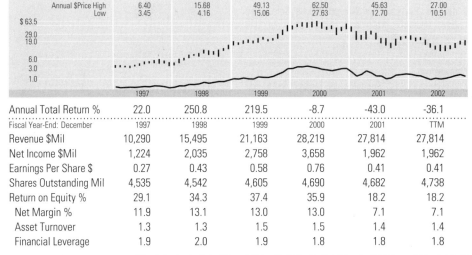

	Monthly Price High/Low		Relative Strength to S&P 500			
Annual $Price High	6.40	15.68	49.13	62.50	45.63	27.00
Low	3.45	4.16	15.06	27.63	12.70	10.51
	1997	1998	1999	2000	2001	2002

Annual Total Return %	22.0	250.8	219.5	-8.7	-43.0	-36.1
Fiscal Year-End: December	1997	1998	1999	2000	2001	TTM
Revenue $Mil	10,290	15,495	21,163	28,219	27,814	27,814
Net Income $Mil	1,224	2,035	2,758	3,658	1,962	1,962
Earnings Per Share $	0.27	0.43	0.58	0.76	0.41	0.41
Shares Outstanding Mil	4,535	4,542	4,605	4,690	4,682	4,738
Return on Equity %	29.1	34.3	37.4	35.9	18.2	18.2
Net Margin %	11.9	13.1	13.0	13.0	7.1	7.1
Asset Turnover	1.3	1.3	1.5	1.5	1.4	1.4
Financial Leverage	1.9	2.0	1.9	1.8	1.8	1.8

Valuation Ratios	Stock	Rel to Industry	Rel to S&P 500
Price/Earnings	37.8	1.0	1.6
Price/Book	6.8	1.0	2.1
Price/Sales	2.6	1.0	1.3
Price/Cash Flow	12.6	1.0	0.9

Major Fund Holders	% of Fund Assets
Rydex Telecommunications Inv	10.10
Wireless	8.29
Reynolds Blue Chip Growth	7.61
Thurlow Growth	6.88

Morningstar's Take By Todd P. Bernier, 12-12-2002 Stock Price as of Analysis: $17.19

The ubiquity of cell phones can largely be attributed to Nokia. But industry growth has hit a wall, rendering Nokia's hypergrowth as history. This is the key reason for our bearishness.

Nokia's brilliance in cell phones is the main reason to invest in the firm. One of Nokia's key strengths is its ability to combine a strong engineering culture with an emphasis on consumer marketing. Unlike its rivals, Nokia behaves like a consumer-product company by focusing on managing its valuable brand name. Nokia has repeatedly launched attractive and innovative phones--30 new models are scheduled for 2002--that it uses to segment the market into various classes, based on an individual's needs.

But waning demand, coupled with growing competition, is making life difficult for Nokia.

Global demand for cell phones is falling. Roughly the same number of phones will be sold this year as last (380 million). Carriers have cut handset subsidies in the quest for profits, and handset replacement cycles have lengthened. There is no compelling application on the horizon that will cause consumers to ditch their old phones and replace them with shiny new (and pricey) Nokia phones.

Competition is also intensifying. First, a retooled

Motorola is bent on grabbing share from Nokia, particularly in higher-end phones. And the Korean manufacturers, led by number-three player Samsung, are becoming increasingly dominant in CDMA phones. Also, several handset makers have announced plans to jointly develop phones. The marriages of Sony and Ericsson, NEC and Matsushita, and Mitsubishi and Toshiba create three formidable competitors, particularly for 3G units. Finally, Microsoft has made noise about creating a common design platform (with Intel producing the chips), hoping to broaden its PC dominance to cell phones. Although the software giant's quest to own the de facto wireless standard isn't being taken seriously yet, Microsoft's gargantuan resources and competitive fire are a major concern.

Nokia's other main business is wireless infrastructure, but capital spending among the debt-laden carriers is dropping like a lead zeppelin. In our opinion, the fundamentals in the wireless networking industry are bad and getting worse.

If we had to choose our favorite wireless company, Nokia would win. However, the wireless industry is in a funk and won't improve anytime soon. We'd stay away from Nokia until the shares trade at a big discount to our fair value estimate.

MORNINGSTAR® Stocks 500

Nortel Networks NT

	Rating	Risk	Moat Size	Fair Value	Last Close	Yield %
	★	High	None	$1.10	$1.61	0.0

Company Profile

Canada-based Nortel Networks is a leading manufacturer of telecommunication equipment for telecom service providers, cable network operators, corporations, governments, and universities. Its products include central office switching systems, optical-networking gear, and wireless infrastructure equipment. In 2001, sales by segment were as follows: metro and enterprise networks 50.6%, wireless networks 32.6%, optical long-haul networks 13.0%, and other 3.8%. By geography, the United States provided 49% of sales, Canada 5%, and international 46%.

Management

Management has mostly been promoted from within (CEO Frank Dunn has 25 years with Nortel). Management has done a good job of integrating Bay Networks and quickly restructuring the business to reflect the slowdown.

Strategy

Nortel Networks wants to remain a technology leader in optical networking while focusing on the most promising growth opportunities in its main business segments--optical, wireline, enterprise, and wireless infrastructure equipment. With restructuring largely complete, the emphasis in 2003 will be on rolling out new products, notching wins in key markets, and conserving cash.

8200 Dixie Road
Brampton, ON L6T 5P6
www.nortel.com

Morningstar Grades

Growth [D+]	1998	1999	2000	2001
Revenue %	16.1	19.8	45.0	-37.3
Earnings/Share %	NMF	NMF	NMF	NMF
Book Value/Share %	156.0	-9.1	102.7	-84.6
Dividends/Share %	0.0	0.0	0.0	-49.3

After several years of stellar growth, Nortel has been rocked by the downturn in telecom capital spending; sales could decline 20% in 2003. However, its long-term revenue growth rate should be higher than world GDP growth for a decade or more.

Profitability [B-]	1999	2000	2001	TTM
Return on Assets %	-1.5	-8.2	ELB	-29.6
Oper Cash Flow $Mil	1,617	824	425	722
- Cap Spending $Mil	795	1,876	1,300	654
= Free Cash Flow $Mil	822	-1,052	-875	68

Margins are mostly a function of sales volume, as most operating costs are fixed. Following restructuring, gross margins have recovered to 35%. We expect gross margins to improve alongside sales growth despite increased pricing pressure.

Financial Health [F]	1999	2000	2001	09-02
Long-term Debt $Mil	1,391	1,178	4,094	4,111
Total Equity $Mil	13,072	29,109	4,824	3,014
Debt/Equity Ratio	0.1	0.0	0.8	1.4

The downturn has strained finances and forced the firm to sell stock at low prices. Although Nortel should have sufficient liquidity until 2006, the bigger issue is whether it can refinance debt of roughly $3.5 billion between 2006 and 2008.

Industry	Investment Style	Stock Type	Sector
Wireline Equipment	Large Core	Distressed	Hardware

Competition

	Market Cap $Mil	Debt/ Equity	12 Mo Trailing Sales $Mil	Price/Cash Flow	Return On Assets%	Total Return% 1 Yr	3 Yr
Nortel Networks	6,182	1.4	11,496	8.6	-29.6	-78.5	-67.5
Cisco Systems	94,649	0.0	19,312	15.1	7.5	-27.7	-36.4
Ericsson Telephone ADR B	10,767	0.6	18,112	78.4	-5.3	-87.1	-64.9

Price Volatility

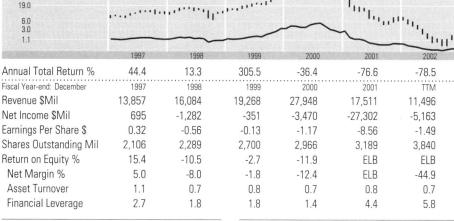

	1997	1998	1999	2000	2001	2002
Annual $Price High	14.24	17.31	55.03	86.00	40.49	8.76
Low	7.56	6.70	12.50	30.19	4.76	0.43
Annual Total Return %	44.4	13.3	305.5	-36.4	-76.6	-78.5

Fiscal Year-end: December	1997	1998	1999	2000	2001	TTM
Revenue $Mil	13,857	16,084	19,268	27,948	17,511	11,496
Net Income $Mil	695	-1,282	-351	-3,470	-27,302	-5,163
Earnings Per Share $	0.32	-0.56	-0.13	-1.17	-8.56	-1.49
Shares Outstanding Mil	2,106	2,289	2,700	2,966	3,189	3,840
Return on Equity %	15.4	-10.5	-2.7	-11.9	ELB	ELB
Net Margin %	5.0	-8.0	-1.8	-12.4	ELB	-44.9
Asset Turnover	1.1	0.7	0.8	0.7	0.8	0.7
Financial Leverage	2.7	1.8	1.8	1.4	4.4	5.8

Valuation Ratios	Stock	Rel to Industry	Rel to S&P 500
Price/Earnings	NMF	—	—
Price/Book	2.1	1.2	0.6
Price/Sales	0.5	1.1	0.3
Price/Cash Flow	8.6	1.8	0.6

Major Fund Holders	% of Fund Assets
American Heritage Growth	4.06
Calvert Social Investment Tech A	2.87
Turner Technology Instl	2.16
JP Morgan H&Q Technology A	1.75

Morningstar's Take By Fritz Kaegi, 12-03-2002 Stock Price as of Analysis: $2.24

Nortel should survive the telecom slump, and with a good product mix should outgrow most of its large peers. We would buy the stock at a 30% discount to our fair value estimate.

Nortel is built around a wide installed base of customers and the direct sales relationships that go with it, as well as years of spending on research and development. Like Cisco and Lucent, Nortel has an inherent advantage over rivals: A switch away from the dominant supplier is expensive and complex for customers. Also, Nortel gets an edge over niche vendors by bundling its offerings, which makes them more affordable.

Its vast product line is another strength. Nortel is the leading optical-networking vendor in the long-haul and metro markets. While this segment has poor near-term prospects, it should be a good source of growth because most new networks will eventually use these products at their core. For traditional circuit-based networks, Nortel leads in equipment for handling both voice and data, which is key to squeezing the most out of existing networks. Nortel has won notable next-generation wireless contracts in key European and Asian markets. Noncarrier clients, which account for 25% of sales, have provided stability and should be good customers

as they shift toward packet-based systems.

Having fired 50,000 workers and sold $1.5 billion in equity, Nortel has enough cash to avoid bankruptcy, though liquidity could be tight if sales remain flat over the next few years. We project a free cash flow loss of $2.2 billion in 2003 (ending the year with cash of $2 billion) and break-even the next year, assuming sales stay unchanged. However, Nortel will need to refinance debt--$1.7 billion in 2006 and $1.8 billion in 2008--should internally generated cash be insufficient.

Dilution is a concern. Roughly 600 million shares, the proceeds from which have already been received, will be issued before 2005. And in recent years Nortel has incurred $1.3-$1.6 billion in annual option expense. Though these options are now nearly worthless, this expense would equal 20% of Nortel's market value. We expect annual option expense of at least $400 million. Finally, Nortel has occasionally made acquisitions using its stock, including the 1998 purchase of Bay Networks. Although another large purchase is unlikely considering the deflated share price, acquisitive growth is a part of Nortel's DNA and can't be ruled out.

Northern Trust NTRS

	Rating	Risk	Moat Size	Fair Value	Last Close	Yield %
	★★★★★	Med.	Wide	$50.00	$35.05	1.9

Company Profile

Northern Trust began by specializing in asset management for affluent individuals. Today it is still committed to that mission and intends to expand the wealth-management side of its business aggressively in the coming years. Northern Trust also manages assets for institutions and corporations, specializing in retirement plan administration. While more than 70% of Northern Trust's income comes from fees, interest revenue makes up the rest, testifying to the company's full menu of banking services for individuals and businesses.

Management

Chairman and CEO William Osborn is a 30-year veteran of the bank and has been in his current position since 1995. The board of directors reads like a Who's Who of the Chicago business community.

Strategy

Northern Trust gears its services to those with lots of money to invest, including wealthy individuals, businesses, and institutions. It focuses on gathering assets that generate fee income and secondarily providing banking services to its clients. Expanding its share of the lucrative wealth-management market is a major priority.

50 South La Salle Street
Chicago, IL 60675
www.northerntrust.com

Morningstar Grades

Growth [D+]	1998	1999	2000	2001
Revenue %	13.6	8.9	26.5	-8.1
Earnings/Share %	14.3	14.5	19.5	1.4
Book Value/Share %	12.1	12.7	13.8	14.0
Dividends/Share %	16.0	13.8	13.1	13.4

After years of being in the double digits, sales growth ebbed to 3% in 2001. We expect 2002 revenue to be about flat, hurt by the declining stock market.

Profitability [B]	1999	2000	2001	TTM
Return on Assets %	1.4	1.3	1.2	1.1
Oper Cash Flow $Mil	607	371	726	—
- Cap Spending $Mil	196	247	263	—
= Free Cash Flow $Mil	—	—	—	—

Northern Trust straddles the fence between bank and asset manager, making its profitability measures harder to benchmark. But its average return on assets of 1.3% over the past five years is quite respectable.

Financial Health [B]	1999	2000	2001	09-02
Long-term Debt $Mil	—	—	—	—
Total Equity $Mil	2,055	2,342	2,654	2,825
Debt/Equity Ratio	—	—	—	—

Northern's Tier 1 capital ratio, a measure of lending ability, is solid at 10.9%. Charge-offs spiked in 2001, but the bank is adequately provisioned to handle an increase in credit losses.

Industry	Investment Style	Stock Type	Sector
Money Management	⊞ Mid Core	↗ Classic Growth	$ Financial Services

Competition	Market Cap $Mil	Debt/ Equity	12 Mo Trailing Sales $Mil	Price/Cash Flow	Return On Assets%	Total Return% 1 Yr	3 Yr
Northern Trust	7,498	—	2,817	—	1.1	-40.9	-8.4
J.P. Morgan Chase & Co.	47,901	—	42,911	—	0.2	-30.7	-17.5
Bank of New York	17,396	—	6,017	—	1.4	-39.9	-11.1

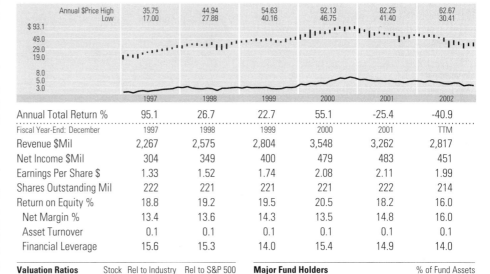

Price Volatility — ❙ Monthly Price High/Low — Relative Strength to S&P 500

Annual $Price High Low	35.75 17.00	44.94 27.88	54.63 40.16	92.13 46.75	82.25 41.40	62.67 30.41

	1997	1998	1999	2000	2001	2002
Annual Total Return %	95.1	26.7	22.7	55.1	-25.4	-40.9

Fiscal Year-End: December	1997	1998	1999	2000	2001	TTM
Revenue $Mil	2,267	2,575	2,804	3,548	3,262	2,817
Net Income $Mil	304	349	400	479	483	451
Earnings Per Share $	1.33	1.52	1.74	2.08	2.11	1.99
Shares Outstanding Mil	222	221	221	221	222	214
Return on Equity %	18.8	19.2	19.5	20.5	18.2	16.0
Net Margin %	13.4	13.6	14.3	13.5	14.8	16.0
Asset Turnover	0.1	0.1	0.1	0.1	0.1	0.1
Financial Leverage	15.6	15.3	14.0	15.4	14.9	14.0

Valuation Ratios	Stock	Rel to Industry	Rel to S&P 500
Price/Earnings	17.6	1.0	0.7
Price/Book	2.7	1.0	0.8
Price/Sales	2.7	1.0	1.3
Price/Cash Flow	—	—	—

Major Fund Holders	% of Fund Assets
Wayne Hummer Growth	4.30
SEI Instl Mgd Capital Appreciation A	4.28
MainStay Blue Chip Growth A	4.22
Gabelli Growth	4.13

Morningstar's Take By Rachel Barnard, 12-16-2002 Stock Price as of Analysis: $36.84

Northern Trust is one of the blue bloods of the wealth-management world.

Managing money for some of the country's wealthiest individuals and institutions, Northern Trust has established relationships that often span generations. Particularly in times of market turmoil, wealthy customers look for professional expertise and advice--something Northern Trust specializes in delivering with a personal touch.

But investment management is inherently affected by the market's ups and downs, and Northern Trust is no exception. Growth slowed to a crawl in 2001 and 2002. Still, the firm has done extraordinarily well in a bear market that has been much less kind to many of its competitors. Trust fees--Northern's largest source of income--have barely dipped in 2002 despite the market decline.

We believe that Northern Trust has an enviable position in the wealth-management market and that it is poised to gobble up a large chunk of future growth. The bank expects the high-net-worth segment (people with more than $1 million in investable assets) to increase at 9 times the rate of the overall population. With the baby boomers in their prime earning years and looking toward retirement, we think Northern is onto something.

We are concerned, however, about increasing competition. Other asset managers and banks have set their sights on this attractive and growing group of wealthy customers. Though Northern has been in the business for more than a century, the Johnny-come-latelys are attracting investors with a wide range of new and innovative offerings. Hedge funds are particularly effective competition now. These funds offer market-neutral returns that are attractive to investors whose portfolios have suffered in the sluggish economy.

Alternative investments like hedge funds tend to be more risky, however, and Northern can point to its conservative investment philosophy and a century of success. It isn't resting on its laurels, either. The bank recently hired a new director of fixed-income investments to expand and enhance its current offerings. Plus, the acquisition of Deutsche Bank's index fund business gives Northern $120 billion in new money and vaults it into the ranks of the top 10 asset managers in the country.

Given its large asset base and profitable niche, we're bullish on Northern Trust for the long term. We think that the shares are worth $50 and that they would be an excellent value below $40.

MORNINGSTAR® Stocks 500

Northrop Grumman NOC

	Rating	Risk	Moat Size	Fair Value	Last Close	Yield %
	★★★	Med.	Narrow	$135.00	$97.00	1.6

Company Profile

Northrop Grumman produces aircraft, special-purpose vehicles, and electronics for the defense and civilian applications. Its products include the B-2 Stealth bomber, components for F/A-22 fighter aircraft, and fuselage sections for Boeing aircraft. The company also manufactures missile-guidance systems, electronic sensors, radar systems, submarines, air-traffic-control systems, and electronic-targeting devices. Northrop Grumman acquired Litton Industries and Newport News Shipbuilding in 2001.

Management

Kent Kresa has been chairman and CEO since 1990. His 40 years of experience are a big plus. Former Litton president and COO Ronald Sugar assumed the same positions at Northrop.

Strategy

Northrop Grumman has grown through acquisitions to increase its access to U.S. military spending. Since the TRW acquisition has closed, we expect the firm will focus on improving the efficiency of its operations and reducing leverage.

1840 Century Park East   www.northropgrumman.com
Los Angeles, CA 90067-2199

Morningstar Grades

Growth [A+]	1998	1999	2000	2001
Revenue %	-19.5	3.4	0.0	78.0
Earnings/Share %	-53.3	139.8	28.3	-44.1
Book Value/Share %	6.4	13.8	18.5	50.2
Dividends/Share %	0.0	0.0	0.0	0.0

Acquisitions supercharged Northrop's revenue growth in 2001 and 2002. Increased defense spending should lead to rising revenue, albeit at more sustainable levels, for several years.

Profitability [B-]	1999	2000	2001	TTM
Return on Assets %	5.0	6.3	2.0	-0.1
Oper Cash Flow $Mil	1,207	1,010	817	1,557
- Cap Spending $Mil	201	274	393	458
= Free Cash Flow $Mil	1,006	736	424	1,099

Northrop's returns on assets have been about average for the defense industry, and they have trended downward since the firm made several large acquisitions. We will be watching margins for signs of postmerger hangover.

Financial Health [B]	1999	2000	2001	09-02
Long-term Debt $Mil	2,000	1,605	5,033	4,885
Total Equity $Mil	3,257	3,919	7,391	7,500
Debt/Equity Ratio	0.6	0.4	0.7	0.7

The firm has taken on more debt over the past year to finance acquisitions, leaving its balance sheet stretched. However, improving cash flow should allow Northrop to pay down this debt without any problem.

Industry	Investment Style	Stock Type	Sector
Aerospace & Defense	▦ Large Core	⚡ Cyclical	⚙ Industrial Mats

Competition

	Market Cap $Mil	Debt/ Equity	12 Mo Trailing Sales $Mil	Price/Cash Flow	Return On Assets%	Total Return% 1 Yr	3 Yr
Northrop Grumman	10,977	0.7	17,067	7.1	-0.1	-2.4	24.2
Boeing	27,691	1.1	56,071	9.9	0.0	-13.4	-4.9
Lockheed Martin	26,512	0.9	26,132	11.2	-2.3	24.7	47.9

Price Volatility

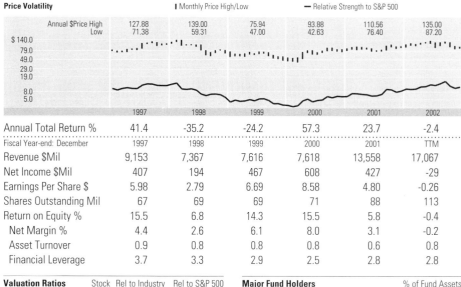

		1997	1998	1999	2000	2001	2002
Annual $Price High		127.88	139.00	75.94	93.88	110.56	135.00
Low		71.38	59.31	47.00	42.63	76.40	87.20

Annual Total Return %	41.4	-35.2	-24.2	57.3	23.7	-2.4
Fiscal Year-end: December	1997	1998	1999	2000	2001	TTM
Revenue $Mil	9,153	7,367	7,616	7,618	13,558	17,067
Net Income $Mil	407	194	467	608	427	-29
Earnings Per Share $	5.98	2.79	6.69	8.58	4.80	-0.26
Shares Outstanding Mil	67	69	69	71	88	113
Return on Equity %	15.5	6.8	14.3	15.5	5.8	-0.4
Net Margin %	4.4	2.6	6.1	8.0	3.1	-0.2
Asset Turnover	0.9	0.8	0.8	0.8	0.6	0.8
Financial Leverage	3.7	3.3	2.9	2.5	2.8	2.8

Valuation Ratios	Stock	Rel to Industry	Rel to S&P 500
Price/Earnings	NMF	—	—
Price/Book	1.5	0.6	0.5
Price/Sales	0.6	0.7	0.3
Price/Cash Flow	7.1	0.7	0.5

Major Fund Holders	% of Fund Assets
Fidelity Select Defense & Aerospace	11.31
ICAP Select Equity	7.12
Hartford Capital Appreciation A	5.50
Prudential 20/20 Focus A	5.07

Morningstar's Take By Nicolas Owens, 12-18-2002 Stock Price as of Analysis: $94.36

Although Northrop Grumman faces the near-term challenge of integrating TRW's defense assets, we think the deal holds promise.

On December 11, Northrop closed its acquisition of TRW for about $13 billion in stock and assumed debt. In early 2003, Northrop is set to sell the automotive piece of the business to The Blackstone Group, a prominent private equity fund, for around $4.75 billion. Most of our concerns about the TRW deal revolved around the automotive business, which, barring major developments, won't be Northrop's problem much longer.

So for just over $8 billion, Northrop has catapulted itself into a top-three spot in the defense industry and nicely rounded out its portfolio of businesses. The acquisition provides Northrop with exposure to one of the fastest-growing areas in the defense industry: national missile defense. President Bush has made an operational missile defense system a top priority. In the years ahead, annual U.S. spending on missile defense is likely to increase from its current $6.8 billion. TRW's space and electronics group is involved in several programs receiving these research and development funds from the Pentagon, including the ground-based midcourse defense segment and space-based infrared system low

programs.

With any acquisition, however, there are risks that can seriously hamper the performance of the acquiring company. These include overpaying for or poorly integrating the acquired firm. Northrop definitely had to pay up for TRW; whether it paid too much remains to be determined. Much depends on how the automotive closing goes and whether Northrop can improve the profitability of TRW's defense assets.

Because Northrop has done a very good job with its previous acquisitions--including Litton Industries and Newport News--its business was quite strong even before the TRW merger. As a key subcontractor on the F-35 Joint Strike Fighter, Northrop stands to gain from that program's continued development. Moreover, the company has a particular strength in producing the Global Hawk unmanned vehicle, which may play an increasing role in military and intelligence applications, as armed variants expand on its effectiveness as a surveillance tool.

We expect Northrop to shift from integrating acquisitions to improving its efficiency and paying off debt. We remain positive on the stock, and would consider buying with a 40% margin of safety to our fair value estimate.

Northwest Airlines NWAC

	Rating	Risk	Moat Size	Fair Value	Last Close	Yield %
	UR	High	None	UR	$7.34	0.0

Company Profile

Northwest Airlines operates the world's fourth-largest airline. It operates domestic and international route networks and directly serves more than 500 cities in 90 countries in North America, Africa, Australia, Asia, and Europe. Northwest has hubs at airports in Detroit, Minneapolis-St. Paul, and Tokyo, and has a trans-Atlantic alliance with KLM Royal Dutch Airlnes. Cargo accounts for approximately 7% of the company's operating revenue; the majority of cargo revenue is of Asian origination or destination.

Management

Richard Anderson assumed leadership of Northwest in February 2001 after being executive vice president and COO since December 1998. He is a lawyer by training and began his airline career in Continental Airlines' legal department.

Strategy

Although conditions have improved slightly over the past few months, Northwest is still focused on keeping costs low and pulling travelers back into its network. It will be quite awhile before the airline enters growth mode.

2700 Loan Oak Parkway
Eagan, MN 55121
www.nwa.com

Morningstar Grades

Growth [D+]	1998	1999	2000	2001
Revenue %	-11.9	13.5	10.9	-11.9
Earnings/Share %	NMF	NMF	-15.0	NMF
Book Value/Share %	NMF	NMF	NMF	NMF
Dividends/Share %	NMF	NMF	NMF	NMF

The airline has experience negative growth for the last two years, as traffic and prices have declined.

Profitability [C]	1999	2000	2001	TTM
Return on Assets %	2.8	2.3	-3.3	-3.9
Oper Cash Flow $Mil	1,259	893	646	-50
- Cap Spending $Mil	1,038	672	1,253	1,424
= Free Cash Flow $Mil	221	221	-607	-1,474

The airline is set to lose another half billion dollars in 2002, and we don't expect it to turn an annual profit until 2004 at the earliest.

Financial Health [B-]	1999	2000	2001	09-02
Long-term Debt $Mil	3,891	3,545	5,221	6,308
Total Equity $Mil	-52	231	-431	-738
Debt/Equity Ratio	ELB	15.3	ELB	NMF

The balance sheet is highly leveraged, making liquidity an important issue. The firm has more than $2 billion in cash, but it is burning through millions of dollars each day.

Industry	Investment Style	Stock Type	Sector
Air Transport	Small Value	Distressed	Business Services

Competition

	Market Cap $Mil	Debt/ Equity	12 Mo Trailing Sales $Mil	Price/Cash Flow	Return On Assets%	Total Return% 1 Yr	3 Yr
Northwest Airlines	630	NMF	9,135	—	-3.9	-53.3	-30.8
Southwest Airlines	10,768	0.4	5,359	16.8	2.9	-24.7	10.7
Delta Air Lines	1,493	3.2	12,860	—	-6.9	-58.4	-37.0

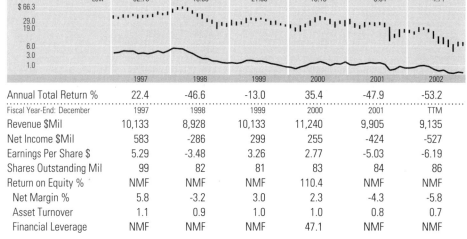

Price Volatility — Monthly Price High/Low — Relative Strength to S&P 500

Annual $Price High Low	49.75 32.75	65.31 18.63	35.50 21.50	39.00 16.13	33.06 9.04	20.92 4.71
	1997	1998	1999	2000	2001	2002

Annual Total Return %	22.4	-46.6	-13.0	35.4	-47.9	-53.2

Fiscal Year-End: December	1997	1998	1999	2000	2001	TTM
Revenue $Mil	10,133	8,928	10,133	11,240	9,905	9,135
Net Income $Mil	583	-286	299	255	-424	-527
Earnings Per Share $	5.29	-3.48	3.26	2.77	-5.03	-6.19
Shares Outstanding Mil	99	82	81	83	84	86
Return on Equity %	NMF	NMF	NMF	110.4	NMF	NMF
Net Margin %	5.8	-3.2	3.0	2.3	-4.3	-5.8
Asset Turnover	1.1	0.9	1.0	1.0	0.8	0.7
Financial Leverage	NMF	NMF	NMF	47.1	NMF	NMF

Valuation Ratios	Stock	Rel to Industry	Rel to S&P 500
Price/Earnings	NMF	—	—
Price/Book	—	—	—
Price/Sales	0.1	0.0	0.0
Price/Cash Flow	—	—	—

Major Fund Holders	% of Fund Assets
Fidelity Select Air Transportation	3.52
Columbia Partners Equity	1.72
John Hancock High-Yield Bond B	1.13
FMI Woodland Small Cap Value	1.09

Morningstar's Take By Nicolas Owens, 12-16-2002 Stock Price as of Analysis: $8.12

Given the unsustainable nature of Northwest's business model, we don't see any good reason to invest in the shares.

We don't think Northwest's strategy is viable over the long term. Generally speaking, a company can pursue one of two strategies. The first is to offer a differentiated product for which customers are willing to pay a premium. The other approach is to be the low-cost provider in a particular market. Northwest seems undecided--somewhere in between--in a market that does not allow for much differentiation or tolerate a slack cost structure. Competition in the airline industry revolves largely around price, making air travel a commodity. The success of Southwest over the years has been based on the carrier's low-cost structure, which allows it to charge less than its competition, profitably. The fact that Northwest's unit costs are 25% higher than Southwest's--although they are 6% below the industry average--leaves Northwest at a disadvantage in such a tight-margin business.

Northwest also has volatile operating results. Because the company depends on business travelers, earnings are very sensitive to the business cycle. In 1999, Northwest made $300 million in profit on more than $10 billion in sales. In 2000, it made $256

million on $11.4 billion in sales. Last year, it lost more than $400 million on $10 billion in sales. This continues a pattern of large profits and losses in the industry that has persisted every decade since the 1940s. Since deregulation in 1978, airlines have lost an aggregate $8.5 billion. Given the current structure of the industry, we don't see this pattern ending anytime soon.

We think the most pressing reason to avoid investing in Northwest--and most of its rivals--is the leverage. Northwest has a lot of operating leverage; it has high fixed costs. This is great when business is booming, but it has the opposite effect when business is in the dumps. More important, the firm has taken on loads of new debt to buy newer, more efficient aircraft. Recently, Northwest has even used this debt to fund losses in its operations. The result of this financial leverage is to exacerbate the poor operating performance of the airline, resulting in enormous net losses.

Most airline stocks--including Northwest's--are bad long-term investments. Wild swings in share price can make for tempting speculative trades, but over the long haul airlines have a terrible record for shareholders, and this isn't about to change.

MORNINGSTAR ® Stocks 500

Novartis AG ADR NVS

	Rating	Risk	Moat Size	Fair Value	Last Close	Yield %
	★★★★★	Low	Wide	$48.00	$36.73	1.2

Company Profile

Novartis produces pharmaceutical, general health-care, and vision products. Its primary breadwinners are oncology or cardiovascular drugs, but the company also makes drugs that treat allergies, arthritis, asthma, schizophrenia, diabetes, and more. Novartis has a consumer health-care division that sells under brand names like Ex-Lax, Maalox, Lamisil, and Gerber. In addition, Novartis makes disposable contact lenses as well as pharmaceuticals for domesticated animals and livestock. The company was forged in 1996 by the merger of two Swiss companies, Ciba-Geigy and Sandoz.

Management

Daniel Vasella, a Swiss native, has expressed his desire to Americanize many of Novartis' operations. At the same time, he has pushed other global pharmaceutical companies to offer more economically sensitive pricing models.

Strategy

Novartis is trying to revitalize growth by creating a more dynamic culture, increasing its exposure to the United States, and spinning off noncore businesses. The company pursues alliances to bolster its drug-development efforts and has increased the size of its U.S. salesforce. Pharmaceuticals are the company's most important business now.

Lichtstrasse 35   www.novartis.com
Basel, CH-4056

Morningstar Grades

Growth [D]	1998	1999	2000	2001
Revenue %	1.7	2.4	10.3	-10.5
Earnings/Share %	15.2	9.9	10.0	-1.1
Book Value/Share %	18.4	17.6	0.6	16.4
Dividends/Share %	16.0	10.3	6.3	5.9

The pharmaceutical division is powering Novartis' revenue growth. During the first three quarters of 2002, global prescription drug sales were up 11% (only 4% after negative currency effects).

Profitability [A+]	1999	2000	2001	TTM
Return on Assets %	10.9	11.9	10.4	10.4
Oper Cash Flow $Mil	4,617	4,531	4,339	4,339
- Cap Spending $Mil	918	805	798	798
= Free Cash Flow $Mil	3,699	3,726	3,540	3,540

Profitability is decent, but not as good as that of pure-play pharmaceutical peers. Third-quarter operating margins were 24.5%, up from 23.1% a year earlier. Novartis also generates significant free cash flow (cash flow from operations less capex).

Financial Health [A+]	1999	2000	2001	12-01
Long-term Debt $Mil	1,528	1,418	1,492	1,492
Total Equity $Mil	23,260	22,896	25,296	25,296
Debt/Equity Ratio	0.1	0.1	0.1	0.1

The firm follows the European tradition of conservative financial management, with little debt and ample cash reserves. Novartis is sitting on more than $10 billion in cash and is one of a handful of companies to hold a triple A credit rating.

Industry	Investment Style	Stock Type	Sector
Drugs	▦ Large Growth	→ Slow Growth	Healthcare

Competition	Market Cap $Mil	Debt/ Equity	12 Mo Trailing Sales $Mil	Price/Cash Flow	Return On Assets%	Total Return% 1 Yr	3 Yr
Novartis AG ADR	105,974	0.1	18,933	24.4	10.4	1.8	2.3
Pfizer	188,377	0.2	34,407	21.1	18.3	-22.2	1.0
Johnson & Johnson	159,452	0.1	35,120	18.0	16.3	-7.9	8.0

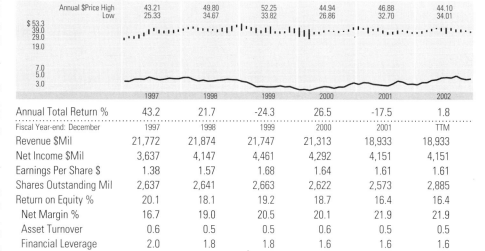

Price Volatility — ❙ Monthly Price High/Low — ▬ Relative Strength to S&P 500

Annual $Price High Low	43.21 25.33	49.80 34.67	52.25 33.82	44.94 26.86	46.88 32.70	44.10 34.01

$ 53.3 / 39.0 / 29.0 / 19.0 / 7.0 / 5.0 / 3.0

	1997	1998	1999	2000	2001	2002
Annual Total Return %	43.2	21.7	-24.3	26.5	-17.5	1.8

Fiscal Year-end: December	1997	1998	1999	2000	2001	TTM
Revenue $Mil	21,772	21,874	21,747	21,313	18,933	18,933
Net Income $Mil	3,637	4,147	4,461	4,292	4,151	4,151
Earnings Per Share $	1.38	1.57	1.68	1.64	1.61	1.61
Shares Outstanding Mil	2,637	2,641	2,663	2,622	2,573	2,885
Return on Equity %	20.1	18.1	19.2	18.7	16.4	16.4
Net Margin %	16.7	19.0	20.5	20.1	21.9	21.9
Asset Turnover	0.6	0.5	0.5	0.6	0.5	0.5
Financial Leverage	2.0	1.8	1.8	1.6	1.6	1.6

Valuation Ratios	Stock	Rel to Industry	Rel to S&P 500
Price/Earnings	22.9	1.0	1.0
Price/Book	4.2	0.6	1.3
Price/Sales	5.6	1.4	2.8
Price/Cash Flow	24.4	1.2	1.8

Major Fund Holders	% of Fund Assets
Kinetics Medical Fund	8.66
IDEX Great Companies-Global A	5.97
Fidelity Select Pharmaceuticals	5.93
Exeter World Opportunities A	4.74

Morningstar's Take By Todd N. Lebor, 11-19-2002 Stock Price as of Analysis: $38.23

Novartis is a keeper, in our opinion. The Swiss drug giant looks like a European version of Johnson & Johnson, with two thirds of its revenue coming from high-margin pharmaceuticals and the other third from health-care staples like vitamins, baby food, and foot fungus treatments. Novartis offers solid revenue growth with a healthy dose of stability, making it one of our favorites in the pharmaceutical industry.

Fueled by the success of drugs like hypertension medication Diovan and the potential of drugs like cancer therapy Gleevec and irritable bowel syndrome treatment Zelnorm, Novartis is climbing the drugmaker ladder. The company is also taking a more American approach (i.e., more attention to the bottom line) to business, which we think will lead to more-efficient operations, better margins, and industry-beating revenue growth over the next five years. Evidence of the success of this approach is visible in the climb in operating margins from the low 20s in 1998 to the mid-20s in 2002.

Like J&J, Novartis operates from a diverse base, with 44% of revenue coming from the United States, two thirds from pharmaceuticals, and nearly 10% from generic drugs. Novartis' generic drug unit is the second largest in the world and boasts an operating margin around 15%. Besides being one of the few big

pharma companies to have a prescription as well as generic presence, Novartis also stands out in its approach to drug pricing.

Management has been vocal about big pharma's need to deliver innovative pricing along with innovative therapies. Gleevec, the highly effective treatment for chronic myeloid leukemia, is a perfect example. The company priced Gleevec on a sliding scale tied to an individual's income in an attempt to make the drug available to all. This pioneering and practical pricing method backs up our thinking that Novartis will be a leader in the changing global drug industry.

In 2000 and 2001, Novartis pushed more drugs (nine) through the Food and Drug Administration than any of its peers. It has beefed up its U.S. salesforce, spun off its agribusiness, and moved key research facilities to the United States, where many researchers prefer to work because it's where the action and compensation are. Novartis has several blockbusters in waiting, like Prexige, a COX-2 inhibitor for arthritis, and Zelnorm. Novartis' fiscal health also makes it a favorite. We'd require only a nominal discount to our fair value estimate to account for the standard big pharma risks like early patent expiration or threats from better drugs.

Novellus Systems NVLS

	Rating	Risk	Moat Size	Fair Value	Last Close	Yield %
	★★	Med.	Narrow	$24.00	$28.08	0.0

Industry	Investment Style	Stock Type	Sector
Semiconductor Equipment	Mid Growth	Aggr. Growth	Hardware

Company Profile

Novellus Systems manufactures chemical and physical vapor deposition systems used in the production of integrated circuits. Its Concept One-Dielectric product deposits a variety of insulating films on semiconductor wafers. Its Concept Two product deposits both dielectric and conductive metal layers on semiconductor wafers. The company's Concept Three product processes wafers as large as 300 millimeters. Novellus Systems also produces physical vapor deposition systems that it sells under the Inova brand name. The company acquired Gasonics International in January 2001.

Management

Richard Hill has been CEO and on the board of directors since 1993. In 1996, he was appointed chairman. Novellus management owned about 2% of the firm's shares at the end of 2001.

Strategy

Novellus designs its chip equipment to maximize throughput--the amount of chips its equipment can spit out on a cost-per-wafer basis. The firm focuses on maintaining its leadership in chip technology and selling gear to larger chipmakers. By outsourcing its manufacturing, Novellus tries to keep fixed costs and capital spending low.

4000 North First Street
San Jose, CA 95134
www.novellus.com

Competition

	Market Cap $Mil	Debt/ Equity	12 Mo Trailing Sales $Mil	Price/Cash Flow	Return On Assets%	Total Return% 1 Yr	3 Yr
Novellus Systems	4,015	—	822	21.2	1.7	-28.8	-11.6
Applied Materials	21,473	0.1	4,881	29.3	0.4	-35.0	-24.3
Lam Research	1,353	0.6	801	51.6	-7.5	-53.5	-33.0

Price Volatility

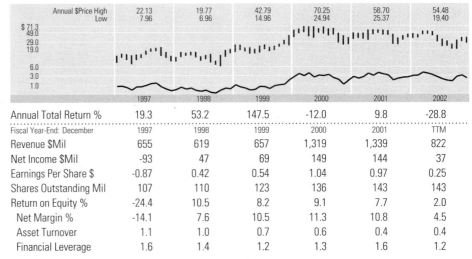

Monthly Price High/Low — Relative Strength to S&P 500

	1997	1998	1999	2000	2001	2002
Annual $Price High	22.13	19.77	42.79	70.25	58.70	54.48
Low	7.96	6.96	14.96	24.94	25.37	19.40

	1997	1998	1999	2000	2001	2002
Annual Total Return %	19.3	53.2	147.5	-12.0	9.8	-28.8

Fiscal Year-End: December	1997	1998	1999	2000	2001	TTM
Revenue $Mil	655	619	657	1,319	1,339	822
Net Income $Mil	-93	47	69	149	144	37
Earnings Per Share $	-0.87	0.42	0.54	1.04	0.97	0.25
Shares Outstanding Mil	107	110	123	136	143	143
Return on Equity %	-24.4	10.5	8.2	9.1	7.7	2.0
Net Margin %	-14.1	7.6	10.5	11.3	10.8	4.5
Asset Turnover	1.1	1.0	0.7	0.6	0.4	0.4
Financial Leverage	1.6	1.4	1.2	1.3	1.6	1.2

Valuation Ratios

	Stock	Rel to Industry	Rel to S&P 500
Price/Earnings	112.3	0.7	4.8
Price/Book	2.1	0.8	0.7
Price/Sales	4.9	1.1	2.4
Price/Cash Flow	21.2	0.7	1.6

Major Fund Holders

	% of Fund Assets
Conseco Science & Technology Y	6.27
Red Oak Technology Select	6.22
Tanaka Growth	4.60
Parnassus	4.24

Morningstar Grades

Growth [C+]

	1998	1999	2000	2001
Revenue %	-5.5	6.1	100.8	1.5
Earnings/Share %	NMF	28.6	92.6	-6.7
Book Value/Share %	12.6	63.8	73.6	10.0
Dividends/Share %	NMF	NMF	NMF	NMF

Market share losses limited past growth, but the firm has regained share recently. Sales growth was 134% in 2000, but came to a halt in 2001. Sales will easily fall 30% or more in 2002.

Profitability [B]

	1999	2000	2001	TTM
Return on Assets %	6.9	6.8	4.8	1.7
Oper Cash Flow $Mil	79	291	77	189
- Cap Spending $Mil	30	78	80	30
= Free Cash Flow $Mil	49	213	-3	159

Novellus is more profitable than the average chip equipment maker--its net margin is in the top 10% of the industry--because it sells high-margin equipment and keeps fixed costs low.

Financial Health [A+]

	1999	2000	2001	09-02
Long-term Debt $Mil	—	—	—	—
Total Equity $Mil	838	1,641	1,872	1,877
Debt/Equity Ratio	—	—	—	—

At the peak of the last cycle, Novellus floated $800 million in convertible debt at 0% interest. This puts the firm in great health with almost $2 billion in cash, which is especially important in light of the current downturn.

Morningstar's Take By Jeremy Lopez, 10-16-2002 Stock Price as of Analysis: $24.48

Novellus was the chip equipment industry's seventh-largest supplier in 2001 with about 4% market share. This share is growing, and the firm's solid performance and market position put Novellus on our short list of industry names worth owning--at the right price.

The chip equipment market is segmented, as most players specialize in products for just a few of the complex chipmaking steps. Novellus specializes in the deposition and clean steps, with strong share in both. Novellus' recent acquisition of SpeedFam-IPEC looks smart; it increases the firm's presence in clean, specifically in chemical mechanical polishing (CMP). This niche was roughly a billion-dollar market in 2001 and is expected to grow faster than most other market segments. Although Applied Materials is entrenched in CMP with more than 50% share, SpeedFam puts Novellus smack dab in middle of this market.

Novellus' strong profitability and technology make the company one of the industry's better performers. The firm has an inherently low cost structure, thanks to an emphasis on outsourcing product manufacturing. This helps Novellus generate gross margins typically in the mid-40s to mid-50s, or above those of most other equipment makers. Novellus is

also ahead of the curve in new materials like copper and low-k dielectrics. Chipmakers now demand gear that can make chips with copper wires, for example, because of the metal's speed and cost advantages. As a result of capitalizing on these trends, Novellus has produced growth much better than the industry average in recent years. We expect it will continue to do so.

Not everything is working in Novellus' favor, however. There is little the firm can do to circumvent anemic capital spending in the chip industry. And as long as chip demand remains weak--and we don't see it dramatically improving anytime soon--it's unlikely chipmakers will open their wallets en masse. Moreover, Novellus faces very strong competition; firms like Applied Materials will always make life difficult. But we believe Novellus has what it takes to be among the elite chip equipment makers over the long term, and we'd start to consider the shares attractive at a 30%-40% discount to our fair value estimate.

MORNINGSTAR® Stocks 500

Nucor NUE

	Rating	Risk	Moat Size	Fair Value	Last Close	Yield %
	★★★	Med.	Narrow	$45.00	$41.30	1.8

Company Profile

Nucor manufactures and sells steel products, principally hot-rolled, cold-rolled, and cold-finished steel; steel joists and joist girders; steel deck; and steel grinding balls. The company sells 85% of hot- and cold-rolled steel products to nonaffiliated customers. It sells hot-rolled, cold-rolled, and cold-finished steel to steel service centers, fabricators, and manufacturers. It sells its steel grinding balls primarily to the mining industry. The company sells steel joists and joist girders, and steel deck to general contractors and fabricators throughout the U.S.

Management

Dan DiMicco took Nucor's reins in September 2000. A longtime plant manager, DiMicco is known for encouraging innovation and employee rapport. His salary in 2001 was $423,000. He received no cash bonus, but did receive options valued at $442,000.

Strategy

Nucor seeks to beat rivals by using advanced processes to produce high-quality steel at cheap prices. Nucor's minimills are strategically located throughout the country, allowing for quick customer delivery. With bankruptcy rampant in the industry, Nucor has been picking up valuable assets at a discount. The company has been investigating new processing techniques to further lower costs.

2100 Rexford Road
Charlotte, NC 28211
www.nucor.com

Morningstar Grades

Growth [C]	1998	1999	2000	2001
Revenue %	-0.8	-3.4	14.4	-9.7
Earnings/Share %	-10.2	-6.6	35.6	-61.8
Book Value/Share %	10.8	9.9	0.5	8.5
Dividends/Share %	20.0	8.3	15.4	13.3

Growth screeched to a halt in 1998 when the industry was decimated by foreign competition. Nucor survived in good shape and made several acquisitions that will boost its top line when demand picks up in earnest.

Profitability [A-]	1999	2000	2001	TTM
Return on Assets %	6.6	8.4	3.0	3.6
Oper Cash Flow $Mil	605	819	495	494
- Cap Spending $Mil	375	415	261	208
= Free Cash Flow $Mil	230	403	234	286

Nucor has maintained profitability by streamlining operations and using efficient production techniques. Tough foreign competition lowered operating margins from 10% in 1997 to 4% in 2001, though, and could hurt profits again in the future.

Financial Health [A+]	1999	2000	2001	09-02
Long-term Debt $Mil	390	460	460	545
Total Equity $Mil	2,262	2,131	2,201	2,293
Debt/Equity Ratio	0.2	0.2	0.2	0.2

Nucor has one of the healthiest balance sheets around and is rated A1 by Moody's. Operating income easily services debt, operations throw off consistent free cash flow, and the firm has hundreds of millions in cash on its books.

Industry	Investment Style	Stock Type	Sector
Steel/Iron	◧ Mid Core	⚡ Cyclical	◆ Industrial Mats

Competition

	Market Cap $Mil	Debt/ Equity	12 Mo Trailing Sales $Mil	Price/Cash Flow	Return On Assets%	Total Return% 1 Yr	3 Yr
Nucor	3,229	0.2	4,315	6.5	3.6	-20.8	-7.0
United States Steel	1,340	—	6,569	—	—	—	—
AK Steel Holding	863	—	4,320	—	—	—	—

Price Volatility

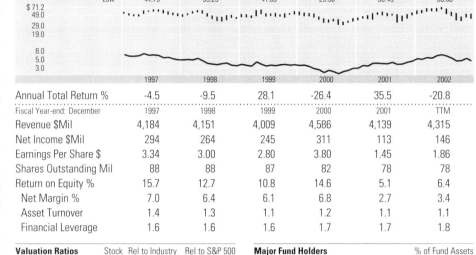

		Monthly Price High/Low		— Relative Strength to S&P 500	

Annual $Price High	62.94	60.63	61.81	56.44	56.20	70.15
Low	44.75	35.25	41.63	29.50	33.45	36.00

$71.2 / 49.0 / 29.0 / 19.0 / 8.0 / 5.0 / 3.0

	1997	1998	1999	2000	2001	2002
Annual Total Return %	-4.5	-9.5	28.1	-26.4	35.5	-20.8
Fiscal Year-end: December	1997	1998	1999	2000	2001	TTM
Revenue $Mil	4,184	4,151	4,009	4,586	4,139	4,315
Net Income $Mil	294	264	245	311	113	146
Earnings Per Share $	3.34	3.00	2.80	3.80	1.45	1.86
Shares Outstanding Mil	88	88	87	82	78	78
Return on Equity %	15.7	12.7	10.8	14.6	5.1	6.4
Net Margin %	7.0	6.4	6.1	6.8	2.7	3.4
Asset Turnover	1.4	1.3	1.1	1.2	1.1	1.1
Financial Leverage	1.6	1.6	1.6	1.7	1.7	1.8

Valuation Ratios	Stock	Rel to Industry	Rel to S&P 500
Price/Earnings	22.2	3.0	0.9
Price/Book	1.4	1.2	0.4
Price/Sales	0.7	1.0	0.4
Price/Cash Flow	6.5	1.9	0.5

Major Fund Holders	% of Fund Assets
Quaker Mid-Cap Value A	3.24
Harbor Mid Cap Value	2.97
Smith Barney Large Cap Value A	2.29
Smith Barney Premier Sel Large Cap A	2.01

Morningstar's Take By Daniel Quinn, 12-21-2002 Stock Price as of Analysis: $42.73

With its low-cost position, Nucor is the leader of the U.S. steel industry, and its stock typically trades at a premium valuation. Given the industry's poor condition, though, we'd require at least a 30% discount to our fair value estimate before investing.

Nucor is the most profitable, financially sound steel producer in the United States. Inefficient plants and huge legacy costs have kept margins razor-thin and balance sheets precariously leveraged for most other firms. When cheap foreign steel flooded the market in 1998, driving down steel prices, 40% of the industry was thrown into bankruptcy. But Nucor has weathered the storm unscathed.

Nucor has the most important competitive advantage available in a commodity industry: the low-cost position. Its minimills recycle steel scrap, producing steel slab more cheaply than making it from scratch. Old-line integrated producers like U.S. Steel haven't adopted this technology, putting them at a disadvantage. Between 1999 and 2001, Nucor's average gross margin was nearly double that of U.S. Steel: 11.8% compared with 6.5%. As a result, Nucor has remained profitable, generating a 7% average return on invested capital. While staying in the black in this environment is impressive, this return is below our estimate of Nucor's cost of capital.

Nucor's impressive growth through the 1990s was internal (not from acquisitions) and was financed using a healthy mix of free cash flow and debt. Nucor also lacks the crushing pension and other postretirement benefit obligations plaguing many in the industry. With a healthy balance sheet, Nucor has been able to cherry-pick prime assets from bankrupt firms at fire-sale prices. This added operational scale should contribute to the firm's cost advantage without the expense of building new plants.

In 2002, the steel industry has benefited from tariffs levied by the Bush administration on some types of foreign steel. We don't think tariffs are a long-term solution, however. Foreign governments are furious and we've already seen numerous exemptions awarded. We view the loss of tariff protection as inevitable, and Nucor will again have to compete with foreign companies, which often receive government subsidies. Without anything to keep global steel supply and demand in balance, the industry could suffer again. Despite Nucor's strong position, we'd still look for a sizable discount before buying the stock.

NVIDIA NVDA

	Rating	Risk	Moat Size	Fair Value	Last Close	Yield %
	★	High	None	$10.00	$11.51	0.0

Company Profile

NVIDIA designs graphics processors and related software that provide interactive 3D graphics for mainstream personal computers. Its chips are required across various PC and entertainment platforms, including workstations, arcade systems, and home-gaming consoles. The firm's products are used in Compaq, Dell, Gateway and IBM PCs, as well as Microsoft's Xbox game console. NVIDIA's customers also include motherboard and add-in board manufacturers, like ASUSTeK and Canopus. NVIDIA acquired 3dfx Interactive in 2001.

Management

CEO Jen-Hsun Huang co-founded Nvidia in 1993. Before that, he worked at LSI Logic and Advanced Micro Devices. His forward thinking has made Nvidia the leader in consumer 3D graphics.

Strategy

The firm's strategy is strikingly similar to Intel's in PC processors. Nvidia spends heavily on R&D to stay ahead of the pack in graphics chips, which allows it to charge a lot for high-end products. Once it comes out with new chips, it sells older versions at lower prices in the mainstream market. Nvidia is also targeting Xbox gaming systems and PC chipsets for additional growth opportunities.

2701 San Thomas   www.nvidia.com
Santa Clara, CA 95050

Morningstar Grades

Growth [A+]	1999	2000	2001	2002
Revenue %	490.2	118.3	96.3	86.3
Earnings/Share %	NMF	NMF	121.4	66.1
Book Value/Share %	—	NMF	194.3	73.5
Dividends/Share %	NMF	NMF	NMF	NMF

Nvidia's growth has been great in recent years and has bucked the current downturn. Sales of $1.3 billion in fiscal 2002 rose 87% from 2001. But growth is slowing: July-quarter sales fell 27% sequentially and did not improve in the most recent period.

Profitability [A-]	2000	2001	2002	TTM
Return on Assets %	20.2	9.7	11.8	7.1
Oper Cash Flow $Mil	16	268	161	188
- Cap Spending $Mil	12	36	97	73
= Free Cash Flow $Mil	4	232	64	115

A shift to low-end PCs is hurting margins; this may not be a short-term phenomenon. After coming in at 18% in fiscal 2002, operating margins will probably dip to 9% in 2003.

Financial Health [A-]	2000	2001	2002	10-02
Long-term Debt $Mil	1	300	306	300
Total Equity $Mil	127	407	764	879
Debt/Equity Ratio	0.0	0.7	0.4	0.3

Strong cash flows and plenty of cash on the balance sheet mean there is little to worry about with respect to financial health.

Industry	Investment Style	Stock Type	Sector
Semiconductors	▦ Mid Growth	↑ Aggr. Growth	▣ Hardware

Competition	Market Cap $Mil	Debt/ Equity	12 Mo Trailing Sales $Mil	Price/Cash Flow	Return On Assets%	Total Return% 1 Yr	3 Yr
NVIDIA	1,815	0.3	1,944	9.6	7.1	-82.8	0.4
Intel	103,151	0.0	26,587	11.8	5.9	-50.3	-27.7
ATI Technologies	1,067	—	1,060	—	—	—	—

Price Volatility

	Monthly Price High/Low	Relative Strength to S&P 500

				11.86 / 4.00	44.00 / 8.75	70.25 / 14.13	72.66 / 7.20

Annual $Price High / Low
$73.7 49.0 29.0 19.0 / 6.0 3.0 1.0

1997 1998 1999 2000 2001 2002

Annual Total Return %	—	—	—	39.5	308.6	-82.8	
Fiscal Year-End: January	1997	1999	2000	2001	2002	TTM	
Revenue $Mil	29	172	375	735	1,369	1,944	
Net Income $Mil	-4	5	41	98	177	116	
Earnings Per Share $	—	—	0.28	0.62	1.03	0.67	
Shares Outstanding Mil	—	—	120	131	143	158	
Return on Equity %	-52.1	8.5	32.1	24.2	23.2	13.2	
Net Margin %	-12.3	3.2	10.9	13.4	12.9	6.0	
Asset Turnover	1.2	1.5	1.8	0.7	0.9	1.2	
Financial Leverage	3.6	1.8	1.6	2.5	2.0	1.9	

Valuation Ratios	Stock	Rel to Industry	Rel to S&P 500
Price/Earnings	17.2	0.4	0.7
Price/Book	2.1	0.7	0.6
Price/Sales	0.9	0.2	0.5
Price/Cash Flow	9.6	0.8	0.7

Major Fund Holders	% of Fund Assets
DEM Equity Institutional	3.74
Calvert Social Investment Tech A	3.25
Navellier Mid Cap Growth	3.12
MassMutual Instl Mid Cap Growth Eq A	2.89

Morningstar's Take By Jeremy Lopez, 12-12-2002 Stock Price as of Analysis: $13.78

Nvidia has its attributes, but we see compelling reasons to avoid the stock.

With more than 50% of the desktop PC graphics chip market, Nvidia is well positioned. The firm is known for engineering talent, and few firms have the research and development budget to seriously challenge it. Nvidia has either bought rivals or put them out of business, with the exception of ATI Technologies. Nvidia has recently been gaining share in graphics chips; for example, it has steadily taken share from ATI in graphics chips used in mobile PCs

But if history serves as any guide, Nvidia's position is vulnerable to competition. Many firms have risen to the top of the graphic market only to succumb to rivals. Although there isn't a specific company to dethrone Nvidia, the odds are one will eventually arise. Nvidia's position in the stand-alone market is falling victim to the rise of integrated graphic processors (IGPs), which combine the graphics chip with other PC components. The firm has no presence in Intel-based IGPs, meaning it could continue to get squeezed out of the lower end of the PC market, where IGPs tend to be used. Finally, overall PC market remains mired in a tech slump and has limited long-term growth potential.

Given muted prospects in PCs and lots of competition, growth will not be easy. Nvidia hopes to boost the top line by producing graphic chips for gaming systems and IGPs of its own. Indeed, Nvidia already supplies the graphics chips for Microsoft's Xbox system; this business will deliver around $400 million in sales this fiscal year. But Nvidia must win the contract for the Xbox 2 for these sales to just hold up--let alone grow--over the next few years. This isn't a sure thing, considering Nvidia's current legal disputes with Microsoft. As for IGP, Nvidia has nForce for AMD-based PCs. Although it will win decent business from nForce over the next years, the upside is limited because Nvidia has little opportunity in Intel-based systems, which represent a majority of the PC market.

Also, management has lost a lot of credibility in our eyes over the past year. One decision--to replace underwater employee stock options with actual company shares in late 2002--is the sort of shareholder unfriendliness we loathe. With the stock trading above our fair value estimate, we see little reason to be bullish.

MORNINGSTAR® Stocks 500

Oakley OO

	Rating	Risk	Moat Size	Fair Value	Last Close	Yield %
	★★	High	None	$11.00	$10.27	0.0

Company Profile

Oakley manufactures high-performance athletic gear. The company's products currently include sunglasses, goggles, footwear, and watches. Its line of sunglasses includes products marketed under the M Frames, Zeros, Wires, Romeo, and eye jackets brand names. Oakley's targeted clientele are skiers, cyclists, runners, surfers, golfers, tennis players, and motorcyclists, as well as general fashion-oriented consumers. Foreign sales account for approximately half of Oakley's revenue.

Management

CEO Jim Jannard founded the company in 1975. Board members include Barnes & Noble director Irene Miller, Starbucks CEO and president Orin Smith, and basketball star Michael Jordan.

Strategy

Oakley is rapidly expanding its product line, putting its logo on wristwatches, clothing, and athletic shoes. The company has also introduced prescription sunglasses that carry higher margins than other models.

One Icon
Foothill Ranch, CA 92610

www.oakley.com

Morningstar Grades

Growth [A]	1998	1999	2000	2001
Revenue %	19.6	11.2	41.0	18.1
Earnings/Share %	21.4	-17.6	160.7	-1.4
Book Value/Share %	16.6	10.0	18.6	25.2
Dividends/Share %	NMF	NMF	NMF	NMF

New products are helping increase revenue at a quick pace, but the lousy consumer climate is mitigating that somewhat. We believe sales will expand 15% in 2002 as Oakley grows internationally and into product lines like footwear and apparel.

Profitability [A]	1999	2000	2001	TTM
Return on Assets %	8.3	16.9	13.9	11.2
Oper Cash Flow $Mil	39	28	30	82
- Cap Spending $Mil	25	27	45	35
= Free Cash Flow $Mil	14	1	-14	48

Gross margins have been declining because sales of sunglasses, which carry higher margins than products like clothes and shoes, have been falling as a percentage of overall sales.

Financial Health [B]	1999	2000	2001	09-02
Long-term Debt $Mil	19	16	16	15
Total Equity $Mil	178	208	261	294
Debt/Equity Ratio	0.1	0.1	0.1	0.1

Cash flows easily cover interest payments. Oakley has historically generated ample free cash flow, and has the capacity to institute a new share-repurchase program.

Industry	Investment Style	Stock Type	Sector
Recreation	Small Growth	Cyclical	Consumer Goods

Competition	Market Cap $Mil	Debt/ Equity	12 Mo Trailing Sales $Mil	Price/Cash Flow	Return On Assets%	Total Return% 1 Yr	3 Yr
Oakley	703	0.1	477	8.5	11.2	-36.8	23.1
Luxottica Group ADR	6,164	—	2,247	—	—	—	—

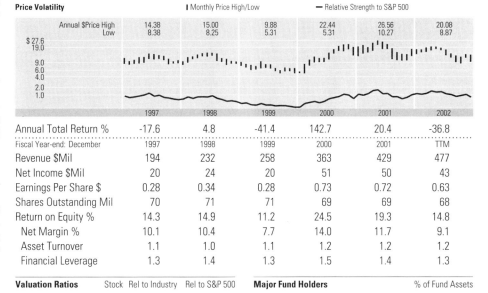

Price Volatility						
Annual $Price High / Low	14.38 / 8.38	15.00 / 8.25	9.88 / 5.31	22.44 / 5.31	26.56 / 10.27	20.08 / 8.87
	1997	1998	1999	2000	2001	2002

	1997	1998	1999	2000	2001	
Annual Total Return %	-17.6	4.8	-41.4	142.7	20.4	-36.8
Fiscal Year-end: December	1997	1998	1999	2000	2001	TTM
Revenue $Mil	194	232	258	363	429	477
Net Income $Mil	20	24	20	51	50	43
Earnings Per Share $	0.28	0.34	0.28	0.73	0.72	0.63
Shares Outstanding Mil	70	71	71	69	69	68
Return on Equity %	14.3	14.9	11.2	24.5	19.3	14.8
Net Margin %	10.1	10.4	7.7	14.0	11.7	9.1
Asset Turnover	1.1	1.0	1.1	1.2	1.2	1.2
Financial Leverage	1.3	1.4	1.3	1.5	1.4	1.3

Valuation Ratios	Stock	Rel to Industry	Rel to S&P 500
Price/Earnings	16.3	0.9	0.7
Price/Book	2.4	1.2	0.7
Price/Sales	1.5	0.4	0.7
Price/Cash Flow	8.5	0.8	0.6

Major Fund Holders	% of Fund Assets
Oakmark Small Cap I	2.11
Seligman Frontier A	1.48
Fremont U.S. Small Cap	1.31
Lazard Small Cap Instl	1.20

Morningstar's Take By T.K. MacKay, 10-23-2002 Stock Price as of Analysis: $11.28

Oakley's sunglasses are near the top of the heap in the eyewear business. The company is the only luxury consumer product manufacturer that develops eyewear for U.S. Army and Navy Special Forces, and is nestled between Ralph Lauren and Coach on Forbes' list of the world's top luxury brands. Oakley is leveraging this brand power through new product categories, opening a big avenue to sales growth, but it could jeopardize profits in the long run if it tries to grow too quickly. There is already some evidence of this happening, and we'd thus look for a substantial safety margin before considering Oakley shares.

CEO Jim Jannard is a brilliant marketer. He has consistently found ways to plug Oakley products in a highly visible and action-oriented way. Oakley products ran rampant throughout the 2002 Winter Olympics, found their way onto Lance Armstrong's head in the Tour de France, and are making their way toward the U.S. Elite Special Forces.

Oakley is putting its brand name to work. Shoes, shirts, and watches are among the newer product categories that the company has branched into, and overall sales have benefited greatly, expanding 18% annually over the past three years. Today, about one fourth of Oakley's sales come from new categories, and the percentage is likely to increase over the next

several years.

Oakley's quest for rapid sales growth is putting its high profit margins at risk, however. We estimate that some products in the new category group carry profit margins that are as much as 20% lower than those of sunglasses. The impact of these products on Oakley's results is already evident: Gross margins have been trailing historical averages by 4-5 percentage points in recent quarters. We think gross margins will decline further over the next several years as apparel and the like make up a greater percentage of overall sales. This would hurt Oakley's return on invested capital.

Investors need to separate a good product from a good stock. Oakley is a perfect example. Premium sunglasses come at a dear price--one that consumers are less willing to pay in a sour economy. Other product categories can't pick up the slack, and Oakley's overall profits in a given period can fluctuate wildly. There is a price at which we believe investors could earn an attractive return in Oakley shares, but it would have to be at a steep discount to our estimated fair value.

Occidental Petroleum OXY

	Rating ★★★	Risk Med.	Moat Size Narrow	Fair Value $34.00	Last Close $28.45	Yield % 3.5

Company Profile

Based in Los Angeles, Occidental Petroleum is an independent oil and gas producer with operations in the United States, the Middle East, and Latin America. Beyond finding and digging up hydrocarbons, Occidental also has a chemical manufacturing business. Occidental has 2.2 billion equivalent barrels of reserves in the ground.

Management

Ray R. Irani has been chairman and CEO since 1990; he was also president from 1984 through 1996. Dale R. Laurance, the former executive vice president of operations, succeeded Irani as president.

Strategy

Occidental is focused on producing and finding oil and gas in two areas: large, mature oil fields in America and new projects in the Middle East. The company hopes to exploit its expertise in extending the economic life of aging fields that already have proven reserves.

10889 Wilshire Boulevard
Los Angeles, CA 90024   www.oxy.com

Industry	Investment Style	Stock Type	Sector
Oil & Gas	▦ Large Value	▧ High Yield	◯ Energy

Competition

	Market Cap $Mil	Debt/ Equity	12 Mo Trailing Sales $Mil	Price/Cash Flow	Return On Assets%	Total Return% 1 Yr	3 Yr
Occidental Petroleum	10,724	0.7	11,151	5.4	2.6	11.0	16.3
Anadarko Petroleum	12,037	—	7,192	—	—	—	—
Unocal	7,482	—	4,942	—	—	—	—

Price Volatility

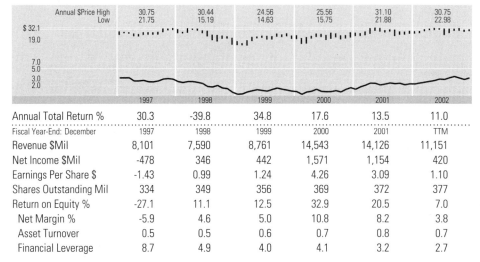

Monthly Price High/Low — Relative Strength to S&P 500

Annual $Price High Low	30.75 21.75	30.44 15.19	24.56 14.63	25.56 15.75	31.10 21.88	30.75 22.98
	1997	1998	1999	2000	2001	2002
Annual Total Return %	30.3	-39.8	34.8	17.6	13.5	11.0

Fiscal Year-End: December	1997	1998	1999	2000	2001	TTM
Revenue $Mil	8,101	7,590	8,761	14,543	14,126	11,151
Net Income $Mil	-478	346	442	1,571	1,154	420
Earnings Per Share $	-1.43	0.99	1.24	4.26	3.09	1.10
Shares Outstanding Mil	334	349	356	369	372	377
Return on Equity %	-27.1	11.1	12.5	32.9	20.5	7.0
Net Margin %	-5.9	4.6	5.0	10.8	8.2	3.8
Asset Turnover	0.5	0.5	0.6	0.7	0.8	0.7
Financial Leverage	8.7	4.9	4.0	4.1	3.2	2.7

Valuation Ratios	Stock	Rel to Industry	Rel to S&P 500
Price/Earnings	25.9	1.4	1.1
Price/Book	1.8	0.8	0.6
Price/Sales	1.0	0.9	0.5
Price/Cash Flow	5.4	0.8	0.4

Major Fund Holders	% of Fund Assets
Turner New Energy & Power Technology	5.99
Primary Trend	4.02
American Independence Stock Inst Svc	3.84
GMO Value III	3.44

Morningstar Grades

Growth [C-]

	1998	1999	2000	2001
Revenue %	-6.3	15.4	66.0	-2.9
Earnings/Share %	NMF	25.3	243.5	-27.5
Book Value/Share %	69.5	10.7	31.0	16.5
Dividends/Share %	0.0	0.0	0.0	0.0

Occidental's results are highly dependent on volatile, cyclical commodity prices. Severe sales spikes and declines are common. With oil prices coming off their winter 2000-01 highs, top-line shrinkage in recent quarters is not of long-term concern.

Profitability [C+]

	1999	2000	2001	TTM
Return on Assets %	3.1	8.1	6.5	2.6
Oper Cash Flow $Mil	1,044	2,401	2,652	1,970
- Cap Spending $Mil	601	952	1,401	1,333
= Free Cash Flow $Mil	443	1,449	1,251	637

Occidental's profit margins and returns are in line with those of midsize peers, but below those of the supermajors. Last year, Occidental's return on invested capital was 8.7%, in the same neighborhood as its cost of capital.

Financial Health [A]

	1999	2000	2001	09-02
Long-term Debt $Mil	4,368	5,185	4,065	4,141
Total Equity $Mil	3,523	4,774	5,634	6,021
Debt/Equity Ratio	1.2	1.1	0.7	0.7

Leverage is also in line with peers, but above that used by the larger companies in the industry. Occidental has been using free cash flow to pay down debt; long-term debt/equity is now at 0.7 compared with 1.7 in 1998.

Morningstar's Take By Paul Larson, 10-29-2002 Stock Price as of Analysis: $27.88

Occidental makes money by finding, digging up, and selling oil and gas. When commodity prices are above its costs, which are typically in the low to mid-teens per barrel, the company makes a profit.

Luckily for Occidental, the OPEC cartel works to ensure profits for its member countries, which greatly benefits the entire oil patch. OPEC exerts its control by limiting members' production, which ends up raising oil prices. This action typically maintains a nice spread between the price and cost per barrel of oil. Though OPEC members tend to cheat when prices are high, the cartel's influence is still strong.

Occidental is the largest producer of oil in Texas and is a major presence throughout the Southwest. The fields there tend to be large but have been drilled for decades, with all the easily available resources already mined. Though the oil can be costlier to get out of the ground, its proximity to domestic refineries and existence under Uncle Sam's stable control make these mature fields attractive. The typical American oil company of Occidental's size has 30%-40% of its reserves in the United States; Occidental has roughly 78%.

Balancing this staid group of assets are Occidental's operations in the lucrative but politically volatile Middle East. Nearly all of the firm's growth aspirations are pegged here. Occidental has exploration rights to 11% of the landmass of Yemen and also has significant operations in Qatar. Of specific interest is Occidental's 20% stake in one of the privatization consortia in Saudi Arabia. Negotiations are ongoing with the Saudi Arabian government, but it's notable that the firm has its foot in the door here and is working alongside much larger companies for this huge opportunity.

Although political risk is reduced by the heavy dominance of U.S. reserves, there are other forms of risk. Because of the nature of Occidental's portfolio of properties, its fixed cost structure is higher, which raises operational leverage and increases the volatility of profits as oil prices move. Plus, the firm has no significant refining and marketing operations to act as ballast when commodity prices are low. Throw in above-average financial leverage, and overall risk is relatively high for the oil patch.

Given the company's stable dividend and improving balance sheet, we'd be interested in buying Occidental at the right price, perhaps in the low $20s. But because it's trading not much below our fair value estimate, we're apathetic about the stock today.

MORNINGSTAR® Stocks 500

Office Depot ODP

	Rating	Risk	Moat Size	Fair Value	Last Close	Yield %
	★★★	Med.	None	$17.00	$14.76	0.0

Company Profile

Office Depot operates office supply warehouse stores in North America, with 888 office supply and furniture stores in the United States and Canada. The stores carry paper products, computer hardware and software, and office furniture sold at discounts ranging from 30% to 60% off list prices. Its stores also offer businesses a private-label credit card with revolving credit and other services, such as printing. The company has licensing agreements for the operation of its stores in Europe, Central America, and Asia. It plans to close 70 stores in North America in 2001.

Management

Industry veteran Bruce Nelson, former president of Viking, took the reins in 2000. In 2001, the company reorganized its management team, including hiring Jerry Colley as president of its North American operations (Office Depot's largest division).

Strategy

Office Depot is attempting to spark sales growth with a number of different store formats. New stores will be smaller (12,000 square feet instead of 20,000) and serve as fill-in locations in the company's most successful markets. The firm also expanding its presence near military bases and college campuses, where stores will face little competition from traditional foes.

2200 Old Germantown Road   www.officedepot.com
Delray Beach, FL 33445

Morningstar Grades

Growth [C]	1998	1999	2000	2001
Revenue %	11.2	14.0	12.6	-3.6
Earnings/Share %	-1.6	13.1	-76.8	312.5
Book Value/Share %	17.0	-3.7	1.6	16.8
Dividends/Share %	NMF	NMF	NMF	NMF

By focusing on costs, Office Depot has been able to boost earnings at a much faster pace than sales over the last several quarters. Top-line growth will be much tougher to come by, as the company has saturated the market and has fierce competitors.

Profitability [B]	1999	2000	2001	TTM
Return on Assets %	6.0	1.2	4.6	6.3
Oper Cash Flow $Mil	369	316	747	756
- Cap Spending $Mil	392	268	207	219
= Free Cash Flow $Mil	-23	49	540	537

Office Depot has managed to transfer many of its existing customers to the Web. By doing so, it has been able to improve returns on assets. As with many big-box retailers, net margins are very thin.

Financial Health [A]	1999	2000	2001	09-02
Long-term Debt $Mil	321	598	318	413
Total Equity $Mil	1,908	1,601	1,848	2,209
Debt/Equity Ratio	0.2	0.4	0.2	0.2

Office Depot has relatively little debt on the books, with a debt/equity ratio of about 0.2. Even if we capitalize off-balance-sheet operating leases, Office Depot has plenty of cash and operating cash flow to cover the debt burden.

Industry	Investment Style	Stock Type	Sector
Specialty Retail	▣ Mid Core	➡ Slow Growth	▣ Consumer Services

Competition

	Market Cap $Mil	Debt/ Equity	12 Mo Trailing Sales $Mil	Price/Cash Flow	Return On Assets%	Total Return% 1 Yr	3 Yr
Office Depot	4,554	0.2	11,369	6.0	6.3	-20.4	12.2
Staples	8,608	0.3	11,190	9.5	7.0	-2.1	-4.1
OfficeMax	674	—	4,653	—	—	—	—

Price Volatility

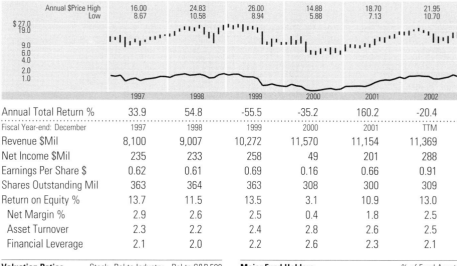

Annual $Price High / Low	16.00 8.67	24.83 10.58	26.00 8.94	14.88 5.88	18.70 7.13	21.95 10.70

I Monthly Price High/Low   — Relative Strength to S&P 500

	1997	1998	1999	2000	2001	2002
Annual Total Return %	33.9	54.8	-55.5	-35.2	160.2	-20.4
Fiscal Year-end: December	1997	1998	1999	2000	2001	TTM
Revenue $Mil	8,100	9,007	10,272	11,570	11,154	11,369
Net Income $Mil	235	233	258	49	201	288
Earnings Per Share $	0.62	0.61	0.69	0.16	0.66	0.91
Shares Outstanding Mil	363	364	363	308	300	309
Return on Equity %	13.7	11.5	13.5	3.1	10.9	13.0
Net Margin %	2.9	2.6	2.5	0.4	1.8	2.5
Asset Turnover	2.3	2.2	2.4	2.8	2.6	2.5
Financial Leverage	2.1	2.0	2.2	2.6	2.3	2.1

Valuation Ratios	Stock	Rel to Industry	Rel to S&P 500		Major Fund Holders	% of Fund Assets
Price/Earnings	16.2	0.6	0.7		Oakmark Select I	3.75
Price/Book	2.1	0.6	0.6		Matrix Advisors Value	3.61
Price/Sales	0.4	0.5	0.2		FPA Paramount	3.41
Price/Cash Flow	6.0	0.4	0.5		Mosaic Mid-Cap	3.39

Morningstar's Take By Tom Goetzinger, 12-10-2002 Stock Price as of Analysis: $15.06

The office supply retailing environment stinks; even industry leader Office Depot is hurting. We'd wait for shares to dip below $10 before investing.

Like peers Staples and Office Max, Office Depot is struggling to find growth. Low demand for big-ticket items like laptops, printers, digital cameras, and office furniture has crushed comparable-store sales growth, also known as comps (sales at stores open at least one year). Comps at North American retail stores (which contribute 50% of revenue) decreased 2% through the first nine months of 2002, while business service sales (at 35% of revenue) increased just 4%.

We're pessimistic about the company's growth prospects. Comps at retail stores have been flat over the past five years, indicating that the recent slumping economy isn't completely to blame for weak retail sales. The real culprits are intense price competition and market saturation. Given the small scraps of market share left to be had, Office Depot has pared its annual square-footage growth target to 3%-5% per year--down markedly from its historical average of 15%-20%.

Office Depot has a few things going for it, though. It has done a fantastic job of turning e-commerce hype into real dollars, with more than $2 billion in

Internet sales in 2002--double 2000's total and approaching 20% of total revenue. It's a nice example of what a lot of discount retailers would like to achieve: less overhead on existing sales.

It took Office Depot, an early e-commerce believer, a long time to get a critical mass of customers to make online efforts worthwhile. But like a mid-1990s dot-com fable come true, it stuck to its guns, and the effort has paid off. Office Depot has built the site, and the cost of maintaining it, unlike the stores, is minimal. As more customers use the Web, a higher percentage of revenue will make its way to the bottom line.

We also like Office Depot's international operations, which are growing at a double-digit clip. The company has little debt and generates plenty of cash, which it can invest in more profitable European and Asian operations. About 15% of sales comes from overseas, but more than 25% of operating income does.

Still, the bulk of sales come from the United States, where the firm is slumping (and showing no signs of breaking out). We'd pass on the shares unless they traded at a substantial discount to our fair value estimate of $17.

Omnicom Group OMC

	Rating	Risk	Moat Size	Fair Value	Last Close	Yield %
	★	High	Narrow	$53.00	$64.60	1.2

Company Profile

Omnicom Group operates advertising agencies through its subsidiaries. Its agencies include BBDO Worldwide, DDB Worldwide, and TBWA Worldwide. Omincom also operates marketing-service and specialty advertising companies.

Industry	Investment Style	Stock Type	Sector
Advertising	▦ Large Growth	↗ Classic Growth	▤ Business Services

Competition

	Market Cap $Mil	Debt/ Equity	12 Mo Trailing Sales $Mil	Price/Cash Flow	Return On Assets%	Total Return% 1 Yr	3 Yr
Omnicom Group	12,149	1.1	7,388	12.8	5.4	-26.9	-10.8
Interpublic Group of Comp	5,422	1.1	6,205	6.0	2.7	-51.5	-33.6
WPP Group PLC ADR	4,212	—	21,227	—	—		

Price Volatility

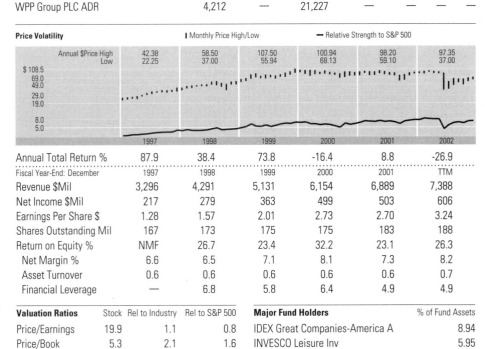

Annual $Price High Low	42.38 22.25	58.50 37.00	107.50 55.94	100.94 68.13	98.20 59.10	97.35 37.00
	1997	1998	1999	2000	2001	2002

Annual Total Return %	87.9	38.4	73.8	-16.4	8.8	-26.9
Fiscal Year-End: December	1997	1998	1999	2000	2001	TTM
Revenue $Mil	3,296	4,291	5,131	6,154	6,889	7,388
Net Income $Mil	217	279	363	499	503	606
Earnings Per Share $	1.28	1.57	2.01	2.73	2.70	3.24
Shares Outstanding Mil	167	173	175	175	183	188
Return on Equity %	NMF	26.7	23.4	32.2	23.1	26.3
Net Margin %	6.6	6.5	7.1	8.1	7.3	8.2
Asset Turnover	0.6	0.6	0.6	0.6	0.6	0.7
Financial Leverage	—	6.8	5.8	6.4	4.9	4.9

Management

John D. Wren, a former accountant, has been Omnicom's president and CEO since 1997. Management is decentralized; each firm in the holding company is run as an independent entity.

Strategy

Like its key competitors, Omnicom concentrates on acquiring subsidiary agencies that can expand its breadth of services and geographic reach. Omnicom is also aiming to strengthen relationships with and capture more marketing dollars from existing clients by offering a full range of services to meet every marketing need.

437 Madison Ave   www.omnicomgroup.com
New York, NY 10022

Valuation Ratios

	Stock	Rel to Industry	Rel to S&P 500
Price/Earnings	19.9	1.1	0.8
Price/Book	5.3	2.1	1.6
Price/Sales	1.6	1.0	0.8
Price/Cash Flow	12.8	1.0	1.0

Major Fund Holders

	% of Fund Assets
IDEX Great Companies-America A	8.94
INVESCO Leisure Inv	5.95
Hilliard Lyons Growth A	5.18
IDEX Great Companies-Global A	5.03

Morningstar Grades

Growth [A]	1998	1999	2000	2001
Revenue %	30.2	19.6	20.0	11.9
Earnings/Share %	22.7	28.0	35.8	-1.1
Book Value/Share %	NMF	46.1	-1.5	37.9
Dividends/Share %	16.7	19.0	12.0	10.7

Omnicom has a record of strong revenue growth relative to competitors. However, with the current industry slump and fewer first-tier agencies available for acquisition, we believe Omnicom is facing lower growth.

Profitability [A-]	1999	2000	2001	TTM
Return on Assets %	4.0	5.1	4.7	5.4
Oper Cash Flow $Mil	973	686	776	952
- Cap Spending $Mil	130	150	149	109
= Free Cash Flow $Mil	842	536	626	843

By placing greater emphasis on specialized marketing services that provide higher margins and less vulnerability to economic downturns than advertising, Omnicom is in a strong position to protect profitability.

Financial Health [B]	1999	2000	2001	09-02
Long-term Debt $Mil	712	1,245	1,340	2,509
Total Equity $Mil	1,553	1,548	2,178	2,308
Debt/Equity Ratio	0.5	0.8	0.6	1.1

Omnicom has positive operating cash flow, but it has nearly doubled its debt in the first six months of 2002 to fund its acquisition strategy. Off-balance-sheet liabilities stemming from earlier acquisitions present an added financial burden.

Morningstar's Take   By Debbie Wang, 11-22-2002   Stock Price as of Analysis: $66.58

Following a red-hot period of consolidation in the advertising industry, Omnicom's overvalued stock reflects expectations that the good times will continue. However, we believe growth will be harder to come by than before.

Like its competitors, Omnicom has been buying much of its growth via acquisition. The company is on track to meet its 2002 goal of 10% revenue growth. However, despite management's stated focus on shoring up internal growth, less than one third of year-to-date growth has been generated by existing operations.

To meet sales growth expectations, Omnicom must continue purchasing more subsidiary agencies. But nearly all the premier agencies have already been snatched up by various holding companies, leaving only smaller, less attractive prospects. While Omnicom has done a good job of searching for lesser-known sleeper agencies, we still anticipate a slowdown in growth by acquisition.

One red flag is Omnicom's long-term debt, which nearly doubled during the first six months of 2002. This, coupled with the possibility that credit-rating agencies could downgrade Omnicom's debt, has left the company very wary of doing anything that would raise its cost of borrowing. One way to avoid this is

to ease up on the acquisitions.

Another red flag is the byproduct of past purchasing activity in the form of earnouts. These long-term compensation deals with the acquired companies have resulted in an off-balance-sheet liability of $537 million that will be paid in increments through 2006. On this issue, Omnicom is well within the realm of GAAP accounting standards. However, we are taking the conservative approach and incorporating it in our model.

Omnicom's internal growth is suffering the same malaise as the entire industry. In an economic downturn, clients cut discretionary marketing budgets to the bare minimum. Thus, we do not expect much growth from existing operations until Omnicom's clients see their own sales numbers trending upward.

On the basis of these factors, we do not believe Omnicom will be able to sustain the double-digit sales growth of the 1990s. Instead, we expect growth to fall in the range of 6%-8% over the next five years. Considering that the stock price reflects more optimistic expectations than this, we'll take a pass until shares trade at a 25% discount to our fair value estimate.

MORNINGSTAR® Stocks 500

Oracle ORCL

	Rating	Risk	Moat Size	Fair Value	Last Close	Yield %
	★	Med.	Narrow	$7.00	$10.80	0.0

Company Profile

Oracle designs and supports computer software products. This software is used for database-management and network products, applications-development productivity tools, and end-user applications. The company's principal product, the Oracle relational database-management system, runs on supercomputers, mainframes, minicomputers, microcomputers, and personal computers. It also offers consulting, support, and systems-integration services for its customers. Foreign sales make up about 50% of revenue. The company acquired Carleton in January 2000.

Management

Founder Larry Ellison is one of Silicon Valley's most controversial CEOs. Ellison prefers the General Electric model of eight or nine strong managers, rather than a COO. Several successful technology firms (Siebel, PeopleSoft) are run by ex-Oracle executives.

Strategy

Oracle is the one-stop source for enterprise software. The company makes a strong argument that by purchasing all application and database software from one vendor--Oracle--customers can avoid integration headaches. Management is extremely aggressive in pursuing all potential avenues of growth.

500 Oracle Parkway   www.oracle.com
Redwood City, CA 94065

Morningstar Grades

Growth [C]

	1999	2000	2001	2002
Revenue %	23.6	15.9	7.1	-11.8
Earnings/Share %	61.1	382.8	-58.1	-11.4
Book Value/Share %	27.0	72.9	0.1	-0.5
Dividends/Share %	NMF	NMF	NMF	NMF

The top line averaged 12% growth over the past five years. As the database market matures, growth will depend on the success of the application business.

Profitability [A+]

	2000	2001	2002	TTM
Return on Assets %	48.2	23.2	20.6	19.8
Oper Cash Flow $Mil	2,923	2,179	3,243	3,196
- Cap Spending $Mil	263	313	278	209
= Free Cash Flow $Mil	2,660	1,866	2,965	2,987

Oracle is highly profitable and continues to cut excess costs. We think 40% operating margins are likely, but management's 50% goal is not.

Financial Health [A]

	2000	2001	2002	08-02
Long-term Debt $Mil	301	301	298	311
Total Equity $Mil	6,461	6,278	6,117	5,735
Debt/Equity Ratio	0.0	0.0	0.0	0.1

The balance sheet is excellent, with $6.4 billion in cash and only $300 million in debt. The company also generates lots of operating cash (20%-25% of sales).

Industry	Investment Style	Stock Type	Sector
Business Applications	▦ Large Growth	➡ Slow Growth	◨ Software

Competition

	Market Cap $Mil	Debt/ Equity	12 Mo Trailing Sales $Mil	Price/Cash Flow	Return On Assets%	Total Return% 1 Yr	3 Yr
Oracle	57,845	0.1	9,459	18.1	19.8	-21.8	-26.3
Microsoft	276,411	0.0	29,985	16.0	13.2	-22.0	-22.9
IBM	130,982	0.8	82,442	9.0	5.8	-35.5	-11.1

Price Volatility

| | Monthly Price High/Low | — Relative Strength to S&P 500 |

| Annual $Price High / Low | 7.02 / 3.49 | 7.48 / 2.94 | 28.34 / 5.25 | 46.47 / 21.50 | 35.00 / 10.16 | 17.50 / 7.25 |

$ 47.5 28.0 18.0 7.0 4.0 2.0 1.0

| | 1997 | 1998 | 1999 | 2000 | 2001 | 2002 |

| Annual Total Return % | -19.8 | 93.3 | 289.8 | 3.7 | -52.5 | -21.8 |

Fiscal Year-end: May	1998	1999	2000	2001	2002	TTM
Revenue $Mil	7,144	8,827	10,231	10,961	9,673	9,459
Net Income $Mil	814	1,290	6,297	2,561	2,224	2,056
Earnings Per Share $	0.14	0.22	1.05	0.44	0.39	0.36
Shares Outstanding Mil	5,896	5,784	5,673	5,567	5,560	5,356
Return on Equity %	27.5	34.9	97.5	40.8	36.4	35.9
Net Margin %	11.4	14.6	61.5	23.4	23.0	21.7
Asset Turnover	1.2	1.2	0.8	1.0	0.9	0.9
Financial Leverage	2.0	2.0	2.0	1.8	1.8	1.8

Valuation Ratios

	Stock	Rel to Industry	Rel to S&P 500
Price/Earnings	30.0	1.0	1.3
Price/Book	10.1	2.0	3.2
Price/Sales	6.1	0.7	3.0
Price/Cash Flow	18.1	1.1	1.4

Major Fund Holders

	% of Fund Assets
Kelmoore Strategy Liberty A	6.38
Hartford Global Technology A	5.87
Monetta Blue Chip	5.86
Security Technology A	5.69

Morningstar's Take By Mike Trigg, 12-17-2002 Stock Price as of Analysis: $11.00

Oracle is the second-largest and most profitable software company behind Microsoft. But uncertainty over the company's struggling application business necessitates a 30% discount to our fair value estimate before we'd consider buying the stock.

All companies have struggled as IT budgets have been slashed. Still, Oracle remains one of the most dominant technology firms on the globe. Its bread and butter is database software (70% of revenue), which collects and organizes data so that it can be easily accessed and updated. Oracle controls 35%-45% of this market, but IBM and Microsoft have challenged its lead. Oracle's competitive advantage is superior technology, but right now many companies are willing to forgo this for a cheaper alternative that meets their basic needs.

Although the database market is mature and unlikely to see more than high-single-digit growth over the long term, it generates tons of cash that Oracle can use to fund growth in new areas. For example, the firm now sells an application server, the layer that sits between front-end applications you access with a browser and back-end systems like databases. This market has exploded in recent years as firms move business processes like sales to the Web. We expect Oracle will succeed because it can

bundle an application server and database, an attribute very few firms can match.

The most important driver of Oracle's long-term growth is its application business. Along with PeopleSoft and SAP, Oracle is now selling an integrated suite of software that includes enterprise resource planning, customer-relationship management, and supply-chain applications that improve front- and back-office operations like sales, accounting, and procurement. Oracle is banking that customers will embrace the suite, which promises to reduce the time and money typically spent on integrating software from different vendors. However, this business has struggled because of technical problems, tough competition, and weak IT spending.

Even with price competition from IBM and Microsoft, Oracle should dominate databases. Companies are wed to this key piece of IT infrastructure, creating sizable barriers to entry for competition. But the soft application business tempers our enthusiasm. While Oracle has the advantage of more than 200,000 customers, all of which are solid sales candidates (the applications are built to run on its databases), licenses continue to plummet. Until this changes, we'll buy Oracle shares only when they become unavoidably cheap.

Oxford Health Plans OHP

	Rating	Risk	Moat Size	Fair Value	Last Close	Yield %
	★★★	Med.	None	$45.00	$36.45	0.0

Company Profile

Oxford Health Plans is a managed-care company providing health-benefit plans. Its products include point-of-service managed-care plans, health-maintenance organizations, third-party administration of employee-benefit plans, Medicare and Medicaid plans, and dental plans. Oxford sells these products through a direct salesforce, independent insurance agents under the Freedom Plan name, its Oxford Health HMO subsidiaries, and its Oxford Health Insurance subsidiary.

Management

Norm Payson joined Oxford in 1998 as CEO and was named chairman in 1999. He has been largely responsible for the health insurer's successful turnaround.

Strategy

Oxford's turnaround is essentially complete. The company has succeeded in cutting costs, upgrading information technology, dropping unprofitable customers, and focusing on core products. Oxford is now looking to selectively expand its commercial membership in New York and other geographic markets without disrupting improvements in profitability.

48 Monroe Turnpike   www.oxfordhealth.com
Trumbull, CT 06611

Morningstar Grades

Growth [C-]	1998	1999	2000	2001
Revenue %	11.0	-11.1	-2.0	7.5
Earnings/Share %	NMF	NMF	-38.0	58.9
Book Value/Share %	NMF	NMF	313.4	-5.0
Dividends/Share %	NMF	NMF	NMF	NMF

Oxford has posted respectable top-line growth for the past two years now that its restructuring is behind it. We expect modest sales growth over the next few years, gradually declining from 8% in 2003 to 5% in 2006.

Profitability [B]	1999	2000	2001	TTM
Return on Assets %	16.3	13.2	20.4	18.3
Oper Cash Flow $Mil	36	405	614	481
- Cap Spending $Mil	9	13	21	17
= Free Cash Flow $Mil	27	392	592	464

Oxford's medical loss ratio has improved from 83% in 1999 to 79% in 2001 and early 2002. This is significantly better than the industry average of 85%, as Oxford focuses on more-profitable small-employer accounts.

Financial Health [B]	1999	2000	2001	06-02
Long-term Debt $Mil	356	28	127	112
Total Equity $Mil	99	459	463	545
Debt/Equity Ratio	3.6	0.1	0.3	0.2

The balance sheet is getting stronger. The company has $200 million of cash on hand and has reduced debt to $150 million from $360 million at the start of its turnaround.

Industry	Investment Style	Stock Type	Sector
Managed Care	Mid Core	→ Slow Growth	Healthcare

Competition

	Market Cap $Mil	Debt/ Equity	12 Mo Trailing Sales $Mil	Price/Cash Flow	Return On Assets%	Total Return% 1 Yr	3 Yr
Oxford Health Plans	3,209	0.2	4,623	6.7	18.3	20.9	42.4
UnitedHealth Group	25,235	0.3	24,358	12.5	8.9	18.0	46.6
WellPoint Health Networks	10,372	0.3	16,180	7.9	6.0	21.8	29.5

Price Volatility | Monthly Price High/Low   — Relative Strength to S&P 500

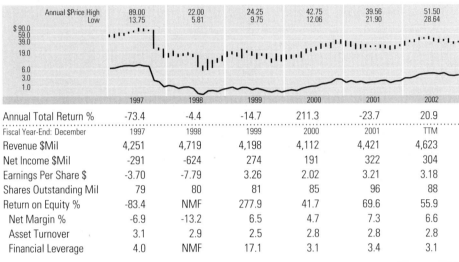

Annual $Price High Low	89.00 13.75	22.00 5.81	24.25 9.75	42.75 12.06	39.56 21.90	51.50 28.64
	1997	1998	1999	2000	2001	2002
Annual Total Return %	-73.4	-4.4	-14.7	211.3	-23.7	20.9

Fiscal Year-End: December	1997	1998	1999	2000	2001	TTM
Revenue $Mil	4,251	4,719	4,198	4,112	4,421	4,623
Net Income $Mil	-291	-624	274	191	322	304
Earnings Per Share $	-3.70	-7.79	3.26	2.02	3.21	3.18
Shares Outstanding Mil	79	80	81	85	96	88
Return on Equity %	-83.4	NMF	277.9	41.7	69.6	55.9
Net Margin %	-6.9	-13.2	6.5	4.7	7.3	6.6
Asset Turnover	3.1	2.9	2.5	2.8	2.8	2.8
Financial Leverage	4.0	NMF	17.1	3.1	3.4	3.1

Valuation Ratios	Stock	Rel to Industry	Rel to S&P 500
Price/Earnings	11.5	0.5	0.5
Price/Book	5.9	1.1	1.8
Price/Sales	0.7	1.0	0.3
Price/Cash Flow	6.7	0.7	0.5

Major Fund Holders	% of Fund Assets
Janus Aspen Global Life Sciences Inst	5.08
Undiscovered Managers Hidden Val Inst	3.72
Scudder Flag Equity Partners A	3.69
Hartford Value Opportunities N	3.46

Morningstar's Take   By Damon Ficklin, 11-12-2002 Stock Price as of Analysis: $34.00

Oxford Health Plans is a niche player in the managed-care industry. It is competitive in its target market, but has limited growth opportunities. We would require a 50% margin of safety to our fair value estimate before investing.

Oxford focuses on small- to medium-size employers that provide one choice of health insurance coverage to employees (the full replacement market). Independent insurance agents and brokers are the primary means of distributing health insurance products in this market segment and price is an important factor.

Oxford has built a competitive position with a strong network of sales agents, hospitals, and providers, and by maintaining consistent pricing over the past few years. It has posted steady sales and delivered stellar cost management. Its medical loss ratio (medical costs divided by premium revenue) of 79% is the best in the industry, and well below the average of about 85%. It has also cut unnecessary administrative expenses, steadily improving its administrative loss ratio (administrative expenses divided by operating revenue) from 17.6% in 1997 to 11.6% in the current year.

Oxford does not have the scale to invest heavily in technology like UnitedHealth Group and other competitors, so it has become an imitator. Rather than spend to develop technologies, it works to simplify processes that it believes will benefit from technology and then adopts standards that evolve. This is just one example of how it is managing its costs. Oxford also performs cost analysis at the product, cost category, and provider levels. Its business is built around cost management. While we expect its medical loss ratio to increase in the long term, it should remain below the industry average. We also expect Oxford will keep a tight lid on administrative expenses.

Although Oxford is strategically adept, it competes in a concentrated geography (80% of its members are in metropolitan New York) in a market segment that is particularly price-sensitive. It has entrenched itself with its strong network of sales agents, hospitals, and providers and is serious about cost management, but competition is fierce. While we expect that Oxford will continue to deliver respectable profits over the short term, pricing pressure will bring its margins down in the long term.

Given that Oxford does not have a long-term economic moat, we would look for a 50% margin of safety to our fair value estimate before buying.

   MORNINGSTAR® Stocks 500

Paccar PCAR

	Rating	Risk	Moat Size	Fair Value	Last Close	Yield %
	★★★	Low	Narrow	$53.00	$46.13	1.7

Company Profile

Paccar manufactures heavy-duty on- and off-road trucks, industrial machinery, and automotive parts. Its Peterbilt, Kenworth, Leyland DAF, and Foden trucks hold approximately 21% of the Class 8 diesel-truck market in the United States. Paccar also provides financing and leasing services to dealers and customers. The company operates manufacturing facilities in North America, Australia, and Europe.

Management

CEO Mark Pigott is the great-grandson of William Pigott, who founded the company in 1905. He took over the top spot in 1997 from his father, Charles, after holding several vice president positions in the firm. Pigott owns about 1% of the company.

Strategy

Paccar aims to keep its products at the forefront of the trucking industry in terms of quality, reliability, and technology. The company is working to gain market share in medium-duty trucks. Controlling costs is also a priority, especially during the current downturn in the United States. Paccar is using some excess cash to buy back shares.

777 - 106th Ave. N.E.   www.paccar.com
Bellevue, WA 98004

Morningstar Grades

Growth [D]

	1998	1999	2000	2001
Revenue %	16.7	14.3	-12.2	-23.1
Earnings/Share %	20.2	39.8	-22.7	-60.6
Book Value/Share %	17.0	19.5	8.9	0.5
Dividends/Share %	6.0	9.3	-8.5	-34.1

Geographic diversity and a smattering of other revenue (finance and parts) has helped smooth growth, but revenue can still vary wildly from year to year. The truck business in Paccar's primary markets is mature, limiting growth over the long term.

Profitability [B+]

	1999	2000	2001	TTM
Return on Assets %	7.4	5.3	2.2	3.5
Oper Cash Flow $Mil	955	667	626	935
- Cap Spending $Mil	406	368	309	363
= Free Cash Flow $Mil	549	300	316	572

When demand is high, as it was during 1999, Paccar's margins and returns on invested capital are typically fantastic. Though pricing pressure and manufacturing inefficiency limit performance during downturns, the company is still solidly profitable.

Financial Health [B+]

	1999	2000	2001	09-02
Long-term Debt $Mil	1,475	1,655	1,547	1,376
Total Equity $Mil	2,111	2,249	2,253	2,546
Debt/Equity Ratio	0.7	0.7	0.7	0.5

Paccar's balance sheet is solid, with $1 billion of cash, net of debt, sitting on the manufacturing business' books. Financial debt supports the firm's receivables and leasing portfolio. Cash flow has been very strong despite the U.S. downturn.

Industry	Investment Style	Stock Type	Sector
Truck Makers	▦ Mid Core	⤴ Cyclical	✿ Industrial Mats

Competition

	Market Cap $Mil	Debt/ Equity	12 Mo Trailing Sales $Mil	Price/Cash Flow	Return On Assets%	Total Return% 1 Yr	3 Yr
Paccar	5,346	0.5	6,826	5.7	3.5	9.0	23.0
DaimlerChrysler AG	30,750	2.1	136,142	2.2	-0.3	-25.0	-23.0
Volvo AB ADR B	6,576	—	14,236	—	—	—	—

Price Volatility   ▌Monthly Price High/Low   — Relative Strength to S&P 500

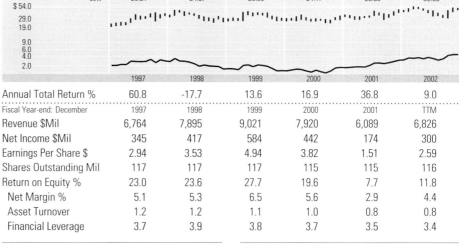

Annual $Price High Low	39.67 20.21	44.50 24.67	42.00 26.33	36.17 24.17	46.19 28.50	52.98 30.69
	1997	1998	1999	2000	2001	2002
Annual Total Return %	60.8	-17.7	13.6	16.9	36.8	9.0

Fiscal Year-end: December	1997	1998	1999	2000	2001	TTM
Revenue $Mil	6,764	7,895	9,021	7,920	6,089	6,826
Net Income $Mil	345	417	584	442	174	300
Earnings Per Share $	2.94	3.53	4.94	3.82	1.51	2.59
Shares Outstanding Mil	117	117	117	115	115	116
Return on Equity %	23.0	23.6	27.7	19.6	7.7	11.8
Net Margin %	5.1	5.3	6.5	5.6	2.9	4.4
Asset Turnover	1.2	1.2	1.1	1.0	0.8	0.8
Financial Leverage	3.7	3.9	3.8	3.7	3.5	3.4

Valuation Ratios	Stock	Rel to Industry	Rel to S&P 500	Major Fund Holders	% of Fund Assets
Price/Earnings	17.8	1.3	0.8	Pioneer Equity-Income A	3.53
Price/Book	2.1	1.0	0.7	WM West Coast Equity A	3.48
Price/Sales	0.8	1.3	0.4	Impact Management Investment Retail	3.35
Price/Cash Flow	5.7	0.8	0.4	Henssler Equity	3.32

Morningstar's Take By Michael Hodel, 12-17-2002 Stock Price as of Analysis: $46.63

With a long history of profitable operations in good times and bad, Paccar is the premier U.S.-based manufacturer of heavy-duty trucks, in our opinion. We'd be interested in Paccar shares at a 20% discount to our fair value estimate, smaller than our requirement for the peers (notably Navistar).

Paccar's primary competitive advantages are its relatively flexible cost structure and strong brand. The company's string of 63 consecutive profitable years speaks for itself, particularly in a business where sales volume can shrink 20% or more in a year and fixed costs are typically high. Paccar has done a great job of continuously improving its operations, eliminating the need to undertake costly restructuring when times get tough. During the current downturn, all of the company's primary competitors in the United States have undertaken restructurings or are otherwise trying to revamp their businesses. Beyond consistent profits, Paccar has generated free cash flow every year for the past decade, with an 11% average annual return on invested capital (including its large cash position).

When it comes to truck design, Paccar is at the industry fore. The company was a pioneer in developing efficient, aerodynamic trucks, yet its factories are equally capable of turning out the chrome-laden, square-nosed monsters that many drivers still desire. Market share fell in recent years when some competitors lowered prices, but with those rivals hurting today, Paccar's share has surged to about 23%.

Paccar is very conservative with its finances. The firm purchased European truckmaker DAF in 1996 for cash, taking on a small amount of debt in the process. Today, the debt is repaid, and Paccar owns a business with a growing share of the European truck market that provides some offset to volatility in North American truck demand. Paccar carries more than $1 billion in cash on its balance sheet. Finances shouldn't be a hindrance to making the right business decisions, in good times or bad.

The heavy-truck industry isn't terribly attractive. Besides huge swings in demand, two of the industry's biggest players, Freightliner and Volvo/Mack, are part of much larger organizations (DaimlerChrysler and Volvo). These companies can absorb losses in their truck units in an attempt to steal share and fund product development and capital spending. Given Paccar's solid finances and its history of successfully competing with these companies, though, we wouldn't avoid the stock because of this concern.

PacifiCare Health Systems PHSY

	Rating	Risk	Moat Size	Fair Value	Last Close	Yield %
	★	Med.	None	$14.00	$28.10	0.0

Industry	Investment Style	Stock Type	Sector
Managed Care	▦ Small Core	→ Slow Growth	⬡ Healthcare

Company Profile

PacifiCare Health Systems is a managed health-care services company. It delivers various health-care services including medical, dental, and behavioral care, primarily through its health-maintenance organizations. Users of the company's services include about 3.4 million commercial, Medicare, and Medicaid members. PacifiCare serves group employers through HMOs in 10 states and Guam. The company's programs are sold under the Secure Horizons brand name.

Management

Howard Phanstiel joined the firm in 2000 and was quickly named president and CEO. Despite the company's difficulties, we think Phanstiel has done a respectable job of leading PacifiCare through a forced change in its business model.

Strategy

PacifiCare has made two important strategic changes. First, it has reduced its heavy reliance on Medicare patients to avoid the higher medical costs and government reimbursement risk. Second, it has shifted away from capitated contracts to shared-risk contracts in order to become more competitive with other insurers.

3120 Lake Center Drive
Santa Ana, CA 92704
www.pacificare.com

Competition

	Market Cap $Mil	Debt/ Equity	12 Mo Trailing Sales $Mil	Price/Cash Flow	Return On Assets%	Total Return% 1 Yr	3 Yr
PacifiCare Health Systems	1,004	0.5	11,288	—	-21.6	75.6	-16.9
UnitedHealth Group	25,235	0.3	24,358	12.5	8.9	18.0	46.6
WellPoint Health Networks	10,372	0.3	16,180	7.9	6.0	21.8	29.5

Price Volatility

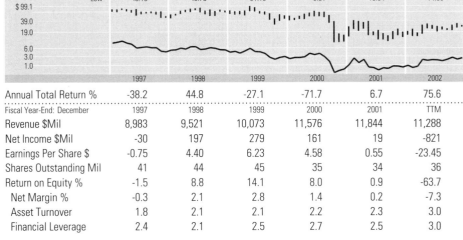

	1997	1998	1999	2000	2001	2002
Annual $Price High	85.63	88.88	98.13	72.31	40.50	33.66
Low	48.13	46.75	31.13	9.81	10.54	14.60
Annual Total Return %	-38.2	44.8	-27.1	-71.7	6.7	75.6

Fiscal Year-End: December	1997	1998	1999	2000	2001	TTM
Revenue $Mil	8,983	9,521	10,073	11,576	11,844	11,288
Net Income $Mil	-30	197	279	161	19	-821
Earnings Per Share $	-0.75	4.40	6.23	4.58	0.55	-23.45
Shares Outstanding Mil	41	44	45	35	34	36
Return on Equity %	-1.5	8.8	14.1	8.0	0.9	-63.7
Net Margin %	-0.3	2.1	2.8	1.4	0.2	-7.3
Asset Turnover	1.8	2.1	2.1	2.2	2.3	3.0
Financial Leverage	2.4	2.1	2.5	2.7	2.5	3.0

Valuation Ratios	Stock	Rel to Industry	Rel to S&P 500
Price/Earnings	NMF	—	—
Price/Book	0.8	0.1	0.2
Price/Sales	0.1	0.1	0.0
Price/Cash Flow	—	—	—

Major Fund Holders	% of Fund Assets
Stratton Growth	3.72
IMS Capital Value	3.68
Diamond Hill Focus A	3.31
Eaton Vance Growth A	3.01

Morningstar Grades

Growth [C-]	1998	1999	2000	2001
Revenue %	6.0	5.8	14.9	2.3
Earnings/Share %	NMF	41.6	-26.5	-88.0
Book Value/Share %	-1.5	-11.4	28.8	3.3
Dividends/Share %	NMF	NMF	NMF	NMF

An 8% decline in commercial membership (not all planned) and a 21% decline in Medicare + Choice membership (planned) led to a 6% decrease in third-quarter revenue from the year-ago period. We expect a 10% drop in commercial membership in 2002.

Profitability [B-]	1999	2000	2001	TTM
Return on Assets %	5.7	3.0	0.4	-21.6
Oper Cash Flow $Mil	570	631	39	-233
- Cap Spending $Mil	66	105	77	69
= Free Cash Flow $Mil	503	526	-38	-303

PacifiCare's medical loss ratio improved to 86% in the third quarter. However, the firm significantly trails the industry average of 84%, and we estimate it won't improve much in 2003.

Financial Health [B+]	1999	2000	2001	09-02
Long-term Debt $Mil	975	837	794	669
Total Equity $Mil	1,978	2,004	2,034	1,289
Debt/Equity Ratio	0.5	0.4	0.4	0.5

PacifiCare replaced 7% debt with 10.75% debt at a time when interest rates are at generational lows. The firm's lack of financing alternatives indicates mediocre health at best.

Morningstar's Take By Tom Goetzinger, 12-04-2002 Stock Price as of Analysis: $29.26

The list of reasons to shun PacifiCare stock remains a long one.

First and foremost, PacifiCare is engaged in a difficult and forced business model shift. While most managed-care companies have long focused on shared-risk contracts (where the health-maintenance organization shares the risk of rising medical costs with patients and providers), PacifiCare has historically relied on an unusual plan called capitation, in which it pays providers like hospitals and physicians a predetermined annual fee per patient. If the provider treats the patient for less than its set fee, it pockets the difference; if patient costs exceed the fee, the provider is stuck with the extra cost.

With health-care costs showing double-digit growth in 2000-02 and projected to increase another 12% or more in 2003, few providers now want anything to do with capitation. The market even dried up in California--home to 60% of PacifiCare's members--as several prominent physician groups declared bankruptcy because of medical cost inflation. At the start of 2000, hospitals covered 78% of PacifiCare's members under capitation; now, it's less than 50%.

As PacifiCare struggles to learn the shared-risk model, its competitors aren't sitting idle. Health plan membership has declined 8% so far in 2002 and 12% from last year's third quarter. Though PacifiCare claims all the losses are from culling unprofitable accounts, we disagree. PacifiCare is trying to push through aggressive price hikes to offset poor cost management, and its "healthier" members aren't biting. Instead, they're switching to more-experienced shared-risk firms like Health Net, UnitedHealth Group, and WellPoint that offer similar or better benefit plans at cheaper prices.

PacifiCare's strategic struggles are compounded by financial ones. With most of its debt coming due in 2003, the firm was forced to swap 7% notes for 10.75% debt with a later maturity. This isn't quite junk status, but it reflects the precarious nature of PacifiCare's finances. The move eliminates refinancing risk in 2003, but leaves the firm with the highest borrowing costs in the industry at a time when interest rates are near historical lows.

We still think PacifiCare shares are risky and expensive. Given the firm's declining membership and revenue and its industry-lagging medical cost management, we'd look elsewhere.

 MORNINGSTAR® Stocks 500

Parker Hannifin PH

	Rating	Risk	Moat Size	Fair Value	Last Close	Yield %
	★★	Med.	Narrow	$43.00	$46.13	1.6

Company Profile

Parker Hannifin manufactures motion-control products and replacement parts for the industrial and aerospace markets. The company sells its motion-control products, including fluid power systems and electromechanical controls, to the agricultural, construction, and food-processing equipment industries. Its aerospace products include hydraulic, pneumatic, and fuel systems and aircraft wheels and brakes. Sales outside North America account for about 26% of the company's revenue. Parker Hannifin acquired Wynn's International in July 2000.

Management

CEO Donald Washkewicz, 52, joined Parker 30 years ago as a mechanical engineer; he's spent his entire career with the firm. Washkewicz took the top job in July 2001 from Duane Collins, 65, who retired as CEO but remains Parker's chairman.

Strategy

Already a dominant player in motion control, Parker is out to consolidate its highly fragmented markets with a steady diet of small acquisitions. With its many purchases, the firm aims to become a one-stop shop for motion-control systems by combining components into higher-value systems and entering new markets. Newly acquired businesses are put through a rigorous cost-cutting process.

6035 Parkland Blvd.
Cleveland, OH 44124-4141
www.parker.com

Morningstar Grades

Growth [A]	1999	2000	2001	2002
Revenue %	7.6	8.0	11.0	2.8
Earnings/Share %	-0.7	17.0	-10.6	-62.2
Book Value/Share %	12.5	22.9	5.8	1.2
Dividends/Share %	6.7	6.3	2.9	2.9

Though Parker's top line expanded at better than 9% annually in the past decade, much of that is due to acquisitions. Washkewicz aims for 10% growth in years to come, but the company will have to overcome the current industrial recession first.

Profitability [B+]	2000	2001	2002	TTM
Return on Assets %	7.9	6.4	2.3	2.3
Oper Cash Flow $Mil	538	532	631	573
- Cap Spending $Mil	230	335	207	186
= Free Cash Flow $Mil	308	197	424	387

Profits have been crushed by weakness in Parker's end markets--the company's operating margin fell 6 percentage points, to 5.6%, between fiscal 2000 and 2002. Returns on invested capital have suffered mightily as well.

Financial Health [A-]	2000	2001	2002	09-02
Long-term Debt $Mil	702	857	1,089	955
Total Equity $Mil	2,309	2,529	2,584	2,613
Debt/Equity Ratio	0.3	0.3	0.4	0.4

Parker's debt ratio of 37%, though high compared with the firm's mid-1990s leverage, is not out of line with its industrial peers. Free cash flow has averaged a respectable 4.6% of sales over the past five years and rose smartly as profits fell.

Industry	Investment Style	Stock Type	Sector
Machinery	▦ Mid Core	⤴ Cyclical	⚙ Industrial Mats

Competition	Market Cap $Mil	Debt/ Equity	12 Mo Trailing Sales $Mil	Price/Cash Flow	Return On Assets%	Total Return% 1 Yr	3 Yr
Parker Hannifin	5,445	0.4	6,259	9.5	2.3	2.1	1.1
Honeywell International	19,705	0.5	22,272	8.7	5.6	-27.3	-22.9
ITT Industries	5,569	—	4,923	—	—	—	—

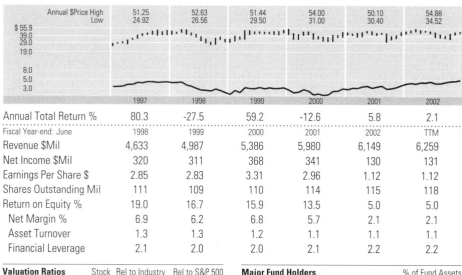

Price Volatility — Monthly Price High/Low — Relative Strength to S&P 500

Annual $Price High Low	51.25 24.92	52.63 26.56	51.44 29.50	54.00 31.00	50.10 30.40	54.88 34.52
	1997	1998	1999	2000	2001	2002

Annual Total Return %	80.3	-27.5	59.2	-12.6	5.8	2.1
Fiscal Year-end: June	1998	1999	2000	2001	2002	TTM
Revenue $Mil	4,633	4,987	5,386	5,980	6,149	6,259
Net Income $Mil	320	311	368	341	130	131
Earnings Per Share $	2.85	2.83	3.31	2.96	1.12	1.12
Shares Outstanding Mil	111	109	110	114	115	118
Return on Equity %	19.0	16.7	15.9	13.5	5.0	5.0
Net Margin %	6.9	6.2	6.8	5.7	2.1	2.1
Asset Turnover	1.3	1.3	1.2	1.1	1.1	1.1
Financial Leverage	2.1	2.0	2.0	2.1	2.2	2.2

Valuation Ratios	Stock	Rel to Industry	Rel to S&P 500
Price/Earnings	41.2	1.4	1.8
Price/Book	2.1	0.8	0.7
Price/Sales	0.9	0.7	0.4
Price/Cash Flow	9.5	1.0	0.7

Major Fund Holders	% of Fund Assets
Fidelity Select Industrial Equipment	3.67
Capital Management Mid-Cap Instl	3.00
Westcore Blue Chip	2.93
Lindner Large-Cap Growth Inv	2.85

Morningstar's Take By Josh Peters, 12-20-2002 Stock Price as of Analysis: $46.70

Parker Hannifin's acquisition strategy worked well in the industrial boom years, but it hasn't held through the bust. Without a quick turnaround in manufacturers' capital spending, we'd only take an interest in the shares in the $20s.

Parker's mission to dominate the motion-control industry has been successful. The industry, whose wide range of gear can be found everywhere from factory floors to roller coasters, is highly fragmented. This puts buyers of such equipment at a disadvantage; it's up to the customer to put together systems that may or may not be easily integrated in a particular industrial application. But by packaging such small and often disparate product lines into larger systems, Parker's consolidation builds a respectable competitive advantage for the firm.

Cost control has also been a plus. Despite spending $1.6 billion on acquisitions between 1995 and 2001, Parker managed to avoid diluting its historically strong results. Margins remained remarkably consistent in the 11%-12% range, contributing to a return on invested capital (including goodwill) that averaged a nice 14% in the late 1990s.

We like Parker's record, but profitability--generally quite appealing by diversified industrial standards--hasn't held up in the current industrial

downturn. Acquisitions continued to boost the top line in fiscal 2001 and 2002, but excluding acquired revenue, sales were flat and 9.5% lower in 2001 and 2002, respectively. This environment exposed some sharply negative operating leverage: Operating income declined 44% over this two-year period.

Parker has responded with a moratorium on acquisitions so it can instead focus on cutting costs in existing businesses, but it will be tough to recover the 6 percentage points of lost operating margin without a broad-based improvement in customer demand. That will probably take awhile--the late 1990s boom created a lot of excess capacity in manufacturing that will have to be filled first. Furthermore, the company's most profitable business segment (aerospace) is just starting to feel the effects of airline industry devastation.

At some point, an economic rebound should bail Parker out. As the economy recovered from the early 1990s slump in capital spending, the firm's sales rose at a 10% annual clip before acquisitions. However, we don't believe Parker is anywhere close to that kind of upturn, and the modest dividend yield doesn't pay enough for us to wait.

Paychex PAYX

Rating	Risk	Moat Size	Fair Value	Last Close	Yield %
★★★★★	Low	Wide	$40.00	$27.90	1.6

Company Profile

Paychex is a national payroll-processing and payroll tax-preparation company. Primarily serving small and midsize businesses, the company has more than 375,000 clients nationwide. In addition to its core computerized payroll accounting services business, the company provides human resource products and services, including cafeteria plans, employee handbook services, insurance services, and employee evaluation and testing tools.

Management

CEO B. Thomas Golisano, who founded the company in 1971, owns about 10.8% of outstanding shares. Top management doesn't draw obscene salaries.

Strategy

Paychex provides payroll outsourcing for small and midsize businesses that choose not to hire an internal staff and buy payroll software. Once a client becomes dependent on the outsourced payroll services, Paychex attempts to sell add-on services like benefits administration, 401(k) management, and electronic tax filing.

911 Panorama Trail South
Rochester, NY 14625-0397
www.paychex.com

Industry	Investment Style	Stock Type	Sector
Data Processing	▦ Large Growth	↗ Classic Growth	🗎 Business Services

Competition	Market Cap $Mil	Debt/ Equity	12 Mo Trailing Sales $Mil	Price/Cash Flow	Return On Assets%	Total Return% 1 Yr	Total Return% 3 Yr
Paychex	10,493	—	973	29.9	9.1	-19.2	5.3
Automatic Data Processing	23,506	0.0	7,043	16.9	7.1	-32.7	-8.2
Ceridian	2,140	0.2	1,174	10.4	4.3	-23.1	-11.8

Price Volatility

| Monthly Price High/Low — Relative Strength to S&P 500

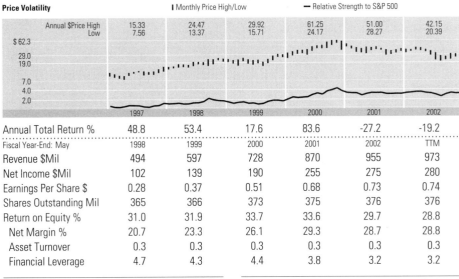

Annual $Price High	15.33	24.47	29.92	61.25	51.00	42.15
Low	7.56	13.37	15.71	24.17	28.27	20.39

	1997	1998	1999	2000	2001	2002
Annual Total Return %	48.8	53.4	17.6	83.6	-27.2	-19.2

Fiscal Year-End: May	1998	1999	2000	2001	2002	TTM
Revenue $Mil	494	597	728	870	955	973
Net Income $Mil	102	139	190	255	275	280
Earnings Per Share $	0.28	0.37	0.51	0.68	0.73	0.74
Shares Outstanding Mil	365	366	373	375	376	376
Return on Equity %	31.0	31.9	33.7	33.6	29.7	28.8
Net Margin %	20.7	23.3	26.1	29.3	28.7	28.8
Asset Turnover	0.3	0.3	0.3	0.3	0.3	0.3
Financial Leverage	4.7	4.3	4.4	3.8	3.2	3.2

Valuation Ratios	Stock	Rel to Industry	Rel to S&P 500
Price/Earnings	37.7	1.6	1.6
Price/Book	10.8	2.2	3.4
Price/Sales	10.8	3.2	5.4
Price/Cash Flow	29.9	1.8	2.3

Major Fund Holders	% of Fund Assets
Fidelity Select Business Serv&Outsrcg	7.55
New York Equity	5.43
The MP 63	4.87
Wells Fargo Large Co Growth I	4.24

Morningstar Grades

Growth [A-]	1999	2000	2001	2002
Revenue %	21.0	21.9	19.5	9.8
Earnings/Share %	35.5	36.6	33.3	7.4
Book Value/Share %	31.7	29.3	33.7	21.5
Dividends/Share %	49.8	50.0	50.0	27.3

Economic troubles will hold growth to 8%-10% in 2003, well below the 20% average annual growth that Paychex achieved during the past decade. When economic growth resumes, Paychex's growth should reaccelerate.

Profitability [A]	2000	2001	2002	TTM
Return on Assets %	7.7	8.8	9.3	9.1
Oper Cash Flow $Mil	249	305	304	352
- Cap Spending $Mil	34	45	54	70
= Free Cash Flow $Mil	215	260	249	282

Paychex makes a lot of money. Because of the fixed costs inherent in data processing, the firm benefits from massive operating leverage. This means that incremental revenue generates a lot of profits.

Financial Health [A]	2000	2001	2002	08-02
Long-term Debt $Mil	—	—	—	—
Total Equity $Mil	563	758	924	972
Debt/Equity Ratio	—	—	—	—

Paychex has virtually zero long-term debt, generates stellar cash flows, and has more than $450 million of cash and corporate investments on its balance sheet after paying for its Advantage acquisition.

Morningstar's Take By Dan Schick, 12-23-2002 Stock Price as of Analysis: $28.30

Paychex should be a rapidly growing money machine for the foreseeable future, thanks to a strong position in the payroll-processing industry. Given the firm's impressive profitability, conservative financial position, and formidable competitive advantages, we would consider purchasing the stock at only a 20% discount to our fair value estimate.

We think Paychex's simple growth formula--gaining new clients and selling ancillary services to current clients--will retain its potency. According to data gathered from the Small Business Administration, the firm ended fiscal 2002 with a 7% share of its market. Paychex's biggest competitor, Automatic Data Processing, boasts a similar share. The rest of the market is wide open, and Paychex has ample opportunity to win new business.

Once Paychex processes a new client's payroll, it has diverse tack-on services to sell. The firm's human resources and benefits segment--which includes services like 401(k) record-keeping and garnishment processing--has been growing better than 24% each year since 1996. Paychex tries hard to sell its clients on these services because they are extremely profitable. The processing is highly automated, reusing data Paychex has already collected. As a result, the company earns contribution margins as

high as 70% on these products.

These huge margins on incremental sales explain how Paychex has boosted operating margins to their current 40% from 25% five years ago. Since Paychex's business is service-oriented and not capital-intensive, the profits generate outsize returns on invested capital. By our calculations, Paychex has generated returns on capital as high as 127%, which it reached in 2001.

In a perfectly competitive marketplace, these returns would draw rabid competition. However, we believe the payroll-processing market is not perfectly competitive. First, economies of scale place smaller firms at a disadvantage. Because a startup processor is necessarily small, new entrants are deterred. Second, the large and fragmented nature of Paychex's customer base works in the firm's favor. None of its 440,000 customers contribute a big portion of revenue, so they are not in a good position to bargain away Paychex's profits.

We believe investors are ignoring Paychex's strong points. At more than a 20% discount to our fair value estimate, Paychex is a good deal, in our opinion.

MORNINGSTAR® Stocks 500

PeopleSoft PSFT

	Rating	Risk	Moat Size	Fair Value	Last Close	Yield %
	★★	Med.	Narrow	$17.00	$18.30	0.0

Company Profile

PeopleSoft sells software and services to corporations, educational institutions, and government agencies. It was originally founded as a client/server-based enterprise resource planning software vendor, focusing specifically on human resources and financial management applications. It has since expanded its product offering to include customer relationship management and supply-chain management software. In September 2000, it released its first Internet-based product suite, PeopleSoft 8.

Management

Chairman David Duffield founded PeopleSoft and remains the largest shareholder. CEO Craig Conway spent eight years at Oracle and is responsible for expanding PeopleSoft into areas like SCM.

Strategy

The newest version of PeopleSoft's software, PeopleSoft 8, includes internal applications, like human resources management, and external software, like CRM. PeopleSoft 8 is different from earlier client-server offerings because it's Internet-based, which makes it easier to install and use.

4460 Hacienda Drive   www.peoplesoft.com
Pleasanton, CA 94588

Morningstar Grades

Growth [B-]	1998	1999	2000	2001
Revenue %	58.2	-3.1	21.5	19.4
Earnings/Share %	35.1	NMF	NMF	22.9
Book Value/Share %	51.5	10.1	17.1	45.3
Dividends/Share %	NMF	NMF	NMF	NMF

The top line averaged 40% growth over the past five years, but those days are long gone. Sales should continue growing at a healthy clip, though, as PeopleSoft leverages its well of existing customers.

Profitability [A-]	1999	2000	2001	TTM
Return on Assets %	-10.6	7.3	7.5	6.8
Oper Cash Flow $Mil	-18	122	467	374
- Cap Spending $Mil	57	102	92	94
= Free Cash Flow $Mil	-75	20	375	279

Profitability trails that of similar-size enterprise software companies because low-margin service revenue makes up the majority of PeopleSoft's sales mix. Hefty margin expansion may be difficult.

Financial Health [A+]	1999	2000	2001	09-02
Long-term Debt $Mil	69	68	—	—
Total Equity $Mil	765	1,024	1,592	1,856
Debt/Equity Ratio	0.1	0.1	—	—

The balance sheet is pristine; PeopleSoft has $1.7 billion in cash and no debt. Working-capital management is also excellent; days' sales outstanding are some of the lowest in the software industry.

Industry	Investment Style	Stock Type	Sector
Business Applications	Mid Growth	Classic Growth	Software

Competition

	Market Cap $Mil	Debt/ Equity	12 Mo Trailing Sales $Mil	Price/Cash Flow	Return On Assets%	Total Return% 1 Yr	3 Yr
PeopleSoft	5,728	—	1,931	15.3	6.8	-54.5	-2.6
Oracle	57,845	0.1	9,459	18.1	19.8	-21.8	-26.3
SAP AG ADR	24,556	0.0	6,546	27.8	9.5	-38.7	-25.0

Price Volatility

Annual $Price High / Low	39.50 / 15.31	57.44 / 16.50	26.38 / 11.50	50.00 / 12.00	53.88 / 15.78	42.65 / 11.75

	1997	1998	1999	2000	2001	2002
Annual Total Return %	62.7	-51.4	12.5	74.5	8.1	-54.5

Fiscal Year-end: December	1997	1998	1999	2000	2001	TTM
Revenue $Mil	932	1,475	1,429	1,736	2,073	1,931
Net Income $Mil	101	140	-178	146	192	183
Earnings Per Share $	0.37	0.50	-0.67	0.48	0.59	0.56
Shares Outstanding Mil	241	250	265	280	299	313
Return on Equity %	21.4	19.1	-23.2	14.2	12.0	9.9
Net Margin %	10.9	9.5	-12.4	8.4	9.2	9.5
Asset Turnover	0.9	0.9	0.8	0.9	0.8	0.7
Financial Leverage	2.2	2.2	2.2	1.9	1.6	1.4

Valuation Ratios	Stock	Rel to Industry	Rel to S&P 500
Price/Earnings	32.7	1.1	1.4
Price/Book	3.1	0.6	1.0
Price/Sales	3.0	0.3	1.5
Price/Cash Flow	15.3	1.0	1.2

Major Fund Holders	% of Fund Assets
UMB Scout Technology	4.26
ING Global Technology A	4.02
Alliance Select Investor Technology A	3.36
Nuveen Innovation C	2.66

Morningstar's Take By Mike Trigg, 11-06-2002 Stock Price as of Analysis: $20.19

Few software vendors have navigated through the slowdown in information technology (IT) spending as well as PeopleSoft. However, the lack of a wide economic moat necessitates at least a 30% discount to our fair value estimate before buying the stock.

Like most software vendors, PeopleSoft has struggled as companies have slashed IT spending. The days of unabashed spending are over and customers are now buying in smaller increments. The downturn has been compounded by the fact that companies bought too much software in the late 1990s that still hasn't been implemented. Companies have had to finish existing software projects before investing in new ones.

PeopleSoft is a leading vendor of enterprise resource planning (ERP) software, which streamlines internal business processes like human resources, finance, and accounting. However, the ERP market is mature and slow growing; customers now demand software that improves external processes, like sales and marketing. This has led to the introduction of PeopleSoft 8, an end-to-end software suite that includes more popular applications like customer-relationship management (CRM) and supply-chain management (SCM).

PeopleSoft 8 has been successful because it leverages the company's competitive advantage: an installed base of 5,000 customers, all of which are solid candidates to buy the company's newest applications given their longstanding relationships. Only 30% of existing customers have upgraded to the suite, leaving lots of room for growth. Our concern, however, is that the firm's installed base is a static market, and so the opportunity will eventually dry up.

Hence, growth hinges on getting new business. But PeopleSoft and vendors with similar soup-to-nuts offerings, like Oracle and SAP, have had trouble. Many firms have already spent millions on other software and refuse to abandon those investments. While we think firms will eventually gravitate towards a suite because it reduces the resources that must be spent on integrating disparate pieces of software, this process will take time as firms choose to gradually buy individual applications.

PeopleSoft would make a good investment at the right price. We think the stock is worth $17 per share, but given the company's reliance on existing customers and uncertainty over the suite strategy, we wouldn't consider buying until it fell to the $12 range.

Pepsi Bottling Group PBG

	Rating	Risk	Moat Size	Fair Value	Last Close	Yield %
	★★★	Med.	Narrow	$26.00	$25.70	0.2

Company Profile

Pepsi Bottling Group manufactures and distributes beverages for PepsiCo in the United States and overseas. The company produces Pepsi-Cola soft drinks like Pepsi-Cola, Diet Pepsi, Pepsi One, Mountain Dew, and Slice. It also makes Lipton Brisk and Lipton's Iced Tea. In addition, Pepsi Bottling Group manufactures Frappuccino beverages for Starbucks. Sales within the United States account for approximately 87% of the company's total sales. The company operates manufacturing facilities in the United States and overseas. PepsiCo owns a 41% interest in the company.

Management

John Cahill was promoted to CEO in September 2001, with former CEO Craig Weatherup remaining as chairman. Cahill has been with PBG since its inception in 1998 and was an executive with former parent PepsiCo before that.

Strategy

Since being spun off from PepsiCo in March 1999, Pepsi Bottling Group has focused on improving its profitability while acquiring smaller Pepsi bottlers in North America. It has spurred growth by focusing on faster-growing products and faster-growing retail outlets, like convenience stores, and by combining price increases with volume growth.

One Pepsi Way
Somers, NY 10589

www.pbg.com

Morningstar Grades

Growth [A-]	1998	1999	2000	2001
Revenue %	6.8	6.6	6.4	5.8
Earnings/Share %	NMF	NMF	NMF	34.6
Book Value/Share %	—	—	NMF	-1.7
Dividends/Share %	NMF	NMF	33.3	0.0

Revenue growth was a solid 5.8% in 2001 and 7.6% in the first three quarters of 2002. Despite a volume slowdown, pricing remained solid.

Profitability [C]	1999	2000	2001	TTM
Return on Assets %	1.5	3.0	3.9	4.5
Oper Cash Flow $Mil	718	831	1,005	1,119
- Cap Spending $Mil	560	515	593	633
= Free Cash Flow $Mil	158	316	412	486

Operating income rose 15% in 2001 and 19% in the third quarter of 2002, continuing the company's run of steady profit growth. Its return on equity is significantly higher than those of other bottlers.

Financial Health [B]	1999	2000	2001	09-02
Long-term Debt $Mil	3,268	3,271	3,285	3,350
Total Equity $Mil	1,563	1,646	1,601	1,955
Debt/Equity Ratio	2.1	2.0	2.1	1.7

PBG has substantial debt, but its debt/equity ratio of 2.0 is much better than Coca-Cola Enterprises' 3.7. Healthy and growing free cash flow easily covers PBG's interest expense.

Industry	Investment Style	Stock Type	Sector
Beverage Mfg.	▦ Mid Core	➡ Slow Growth	🚗 Consumer Goods

Competition	Market Cap $Mil	Debt/ Equity	12 Mo Trailing Sales $Mil	Price/Cash Flow	Return On Assets%	Total Return% 1 Yr	3 Yr
Pepsi Bottling Group	7,247	1.7	8,898	6.5	4.5	9.5	46.7
Coca-Cola Enterprises	9,742	3.4	16,678	5.9	1.5	15.6	4.6
PanAmerican Beverages	2,526	—	2,651	—	—	—	—

Price Volatility

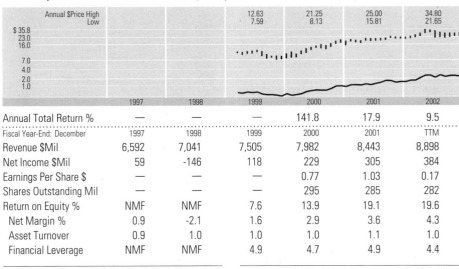

	1997	1998	1999	2000	2001	TTM
Annual Total Return %	—	—	—	141.8	17.9	9.5
Fiscal Year-End: December	1997	1998	1999	2000	2001	TTM
Revenue $Mil	6,592	7,041	7,505	7,982	8,443	8,898
Net Income $Mil	59	-146	118	229	305	384
Earnings Per Share $	—	—	—	0.77	1.03	0.17
Shares Outstanding Mil	—	—	—	295	285	282
Return on Equity %	NMF	NMF	7.6	13.9	19.1	19.6
Net Margin %	0.9	-2.1	1.6	2.9	3.6	4.3
Asset Turnover	0.9	1.0	1.0	1.0	1.1	1.0
Financial Leverage	NMF	NMF	4.9	4.7	4.9	4.4

Valuation Ratios	Stock	Rel to Industry	Rel to S&P 500
Price/Earnings	150.3	4.5	6.4
Price/Book	3.7	0.4	1.2
Price/Sales	0.8	0.2	0.4
Price/Cash Flow	6.5	0.3	0.5

Major Fund Holders	% of Fund Assets
Leonetti Growth	4.84
Sparrow Growth A	4.65
Brandywine Blue	3.98
Phoenix-Duff&Phelps Core Equity A	3.06

Morningstar's Take By David Kathman, 10-16-2002 Stock Price as of Analysis: $26.20

Pepsi Bottling Group is an outstanding company that has recently gone through some mild rough patches. The stock is definitely worth picking up for the long term if the price dips low enough.

PBG has achieved double-digit earnings growth in each of its first 15 quarters as a public company, and consistently beat earnings expectations during most of that time. It performed this remarkable feat by judiciously balancing price increases and volume growth, a combination that rival Coca-Cola Enterprises was consistently unable to achieve. Some signs of weakness began to appear in 2002, when constant-territory case volume growth slowed dramatically and the stock dropped on fears that the slowdown might be permanent. But we think that such pessimism is overblown, and that PBG is still in good shape for the long haul.

One reason for the volume slowdown was tough comparisons with the blockbuster introduction of Mountain Dew Code Red in 2001, one of the most successful soft-drink launches of the past 20 years. In that context, volume growth of 1% is actually not bad. Growth should be helped by new Pepsi Blue, which has been a big hit with teenagers and is now being rolled out to wider distribution channels. PBG's noncarbonated portfolio is still racking up

double-digit volume gains, led by Aquafina, the number-one bottled water. Aquafina volume growth accelerated in the third quarter to 40%, but the brand still accounts for less than 10% of PBG's revenue.

PBG's growth in revenue per case has remained reliably strong, helping to offset volume weakness. Pricing has been helped in particular by PBG's success in "cold-drink" channels like convenience stores and restaurants, where prices and profit margins are higher than in "take-home" channels like grocery stores. Though cold-drink volume did slow in mid-2002, revenue was kept up by double-digit volume growth in convenience stores, one of the more lucrative channels for pricing. Soon afterward, PBG successfully raised can prices in take-home channels, including large-format stores like Wal-Mart. It has consistently beaten Coca-Cola Enterprises in pricing, giving it a big competitive advantage.

We've been impressed with PBG's ability to balance the elements needed to succeed in the low-margin, capital-intensive bottling business. If the price dips 30% below our $26 fair value estimate, these shares are worth snapping up, in our opinion.

MORNINGSTAR® Stocks 500

PepsiAmericas PAS

	Rating	Risk	Moat Size	Fair Value	Last Close	Yield %
	★★	Med.	Narrow	$13.00	$13.43	0.3

Company Profile

PepsiAmericas manufactures and distributes beverage products. Its Pepsi-Cola General Bottlers subsidiary produces soft and sports drinks, juices, and bottled water. The company mainly uses concentrates purchased from PepsiCo and sells these products in 12 states, Russia, and Eastern Europe. The company makes beverages like Pepsi-Cola, Diet Pepsi, Pepsi One, Mountain Dew, Slice, Dr Pepper, All Sport, and Aquafina. It also distributes Starbucks Frappuccino, Sunny Delight, Hawaiian Punch, Lipton Iced Tea, and Ocean Spray juice drinks.

Management

CEO Bob Pohlad is a very capable industry veteran with 24 years of experience. He had held the top spot at the old PepsiAmericas since July 1998, and took over as CEO of the new company after the merger with Whitman in late 2000.

Strategy

After a string of acquisitions, PepsiAmericas trails only Pepsi Bottling Group as the world's largest independent Pepsi bottler. It has used mergers both to extend its geographic reach and to improve efficiency through synergies. It recently announced a renewed focus on the core Pepsi brands as the key to its success.

3880 Dain Rauscher Plaza
Minneapolis, MN 55402
www.pepsiamericas.com

Morningstar Grades

Growth [A+]	1998	1999	2000	2001
Revenue %	5.1	32.2	18.2	25.4
Earnings/Share %	950.0	NMF	NMF	-79.3
Book Value/Share %	-40.4	189.6	15.1	-13.2
Dividends/Share %	-55.6	-60.0	-50.0	0.0

Acquisitions have boosted reported revenue, making for a misleadingly high growth grade. Sales increased 3.9% in the first nine months of 2002, which is close to what we expect.

Profitability [C-]	1999	2000	2001	TTM
Return on Assets %	-0.3	2.4	0.6	1.7
Oper Cash Flow $Mil	182	326	317	299
- Cap Spending $Mil	165	165	219	220
= Free Cash Flow $Mil	16	161	98	79

PepsiAmericas' earnings stabilized in 2002 after a string of disappointments following the merger. However, its operating margin remained flat with a year ago because of higher costs in certain areas.

Financial Health [B-]	1999	2000	2001	09-02
Long-term Debt $Mil	809	860	1,083	1,080
Total Equity $Mil	1,142	1,450	1,430	1,493
Debt/Equity Ratio	0.7	0.6	0.8	0.7

High debt leverage characterizes the bottling industry, but PepsiAmericas' balance sheet is relatively solid. Its debt/equity ratio of 0.72 is much lower than Pepsi Bottling Group's 1.71, and operating cash flow easily covers capital investments.

Industry	Investment Style	Stock Type	Sector
Beverage Mfg.	Mid Core	Spec. Growth	Consumer Goods

Competition	Market Cap $Mil	Debt/Equity	12 Mo Trailing Sales $Mil	Price/Cash Flow	Return On Assets%	Total Return% 1 Yr	3 Yr
PepsiAmericas	2,016	0.7	3,266	6.7	1.7	-2.4	1.7
Coca-Cola Enterprises	9,742	3.4	16,678	5.9	1.5	15.6	4.6
Pepsi Bottling Group	7,247	1.7	8,898	6.5	4.5	9.5	46.7

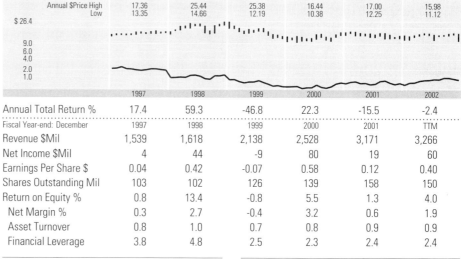

Annual $Price High/Low	17.36 / 13.35	25.44 / 14.66	25.38 / 12.19	16.44 / 10.38	17.00 / 12.25	15.98 / 11.12

	1997	1998	1999	2000	2001	2002
Annual Total Return %	17.4	59.3	-46.8	22.3	-15.5	-2.4

Fiscal Year-end: December	1997	1998	1999	2000	2001	TTM
Revenue $Mil	1,539	1,618	2,138	2,528	3,171	3,266
Net Income $Mil	4	44	-9	80	19	60
Earnings Per Share $	0.04	0.42	-0.07	0.58	0.12	0.40
Shares Outstanding Mil	103	102	126	139	158	150
Return on Equity %	0.8	13.4	-0.8	5.5	1.3	4.0
Net Margin %	0.3	2.7	-0.4	3.2	0.6	1.9
Asset Turnover	0.8	1.0	0.7	0.8	0.9	0.9
Financial Leverage	3.8	4.8	2.5	2.3	2.4	2.4

Valuation Ratios	Stock	Rel to Industry	Rel to S&P 500
Price/Earnings	33.6	1.0	1.4
Price/Book	1.4	0.1	0.4
Price/Sales	0.6	0.1	0.3
Price/Cash Flow	6.7	0.3	0.5

Major Fund Holders	% of Fund Assets
Longleaf Partners Small-Cap	3.10
Navellier Large Cap Value	2.92
C&B Large Cap Value	2.74
C&B Mid Cap Value	2.72

Morningstar's Take By David Kathman, 12-11-2002 Stock Price as of Analysis: $15.46

PepsiAmericas has started showing some progress, but it still has a ways to go to seriously threaten number-one Pepsi Bottling Group. We'd be inclined to buy the stock only at $9 or below.

Formed from the merger of the number-two and number-three Pepsi bottlers, PepsiAmericas struggled through a year of weak growth and merger-related charges in 2001 before showing signs of life in 2002. Volume has started growing nicely again, a strong 3.5% in the third quarter, after a feeble performance during the transition year. The main drivers behind this volume revival are new products like Pepsi Blue, a big hit with teenagers, and Mountain Dew Code Red, which has continued selling well since its introduction in 2001. Aquafina bottled water has contributed strong double-digit volume growth, 51% in the third quarter.

However, PepsiAmericas has had a tough time translating volume gains into consistent revenue growth, in contrast to rival PBG. One major reason for this difference is channel mix. PepsiAmericas sells an increasing amount of its products in channels like supermarkets, where people tend to buy 12-packs, two-liter bottles, and other cheaper formats. PBG, on the other hand, has been much more successful at selling through channels like convenience stores,

where people tend to buy single-serve bottles and other packages that generate higher revenue per case. This trend will cause PepsiAmericas to miss its original pricing forecast for 2002 by a significant margin, and we don't see an obvious remedy on the horizon.

On top of uninspiring sales growth resulting from weak pricing, PepsiAmericas' operating costs have risen despite the synergies that were supposed to result from the merger. One culprit has been higher employee benefit costs, a problem plaguing most consumer product companies, while investments in a new wireless purchasing system have also been a factor. The new purchasing system is supposed to improve supply-chain efficiencies, but not until after more spending in 2003.

PepsiAmericas has taken some positive steps toward becoming the company it wants to be, but it's not there yet. We expect operating expenses to improve eventually, but the company needs to get a handle on pricing before its sales growth and gross margin can get much better. We figure PepsiAmericas to be worth $13 per share, and would prefer a price at least 30% below that to provide an appropriate margin of safety.

PepsiCo PEP

	Rating	Risk	Moat Size	Fair Value	Last Close	Yield %
	★★★★	Low	Wide	$48.00	$42.22	1.4

Company Profile

PepsiCo produces beverages and snack foods. The company makes soft drinks, including Pepsi-Cola, Diet Pepsi, Pepsi One, Mountain Dew, Slice, and Mug, which it distributes to independent and company-owned bottlers. PepsiCo also produces Tropicana juice products and Aquafina bottled water products. The company's snack-food products include Fritos, Doritos, and Tostitos corn chips; Lay's and Ruffles potato chips; Cheetos cheese-flavored snacks; Rold Gold pretzels; and Cracker Jack candy-coated popcorn. PepsiCo acquired Quaker Oats in 2001.

Management

Steve Reinemund, a highly regarded Pepsi veteran who formerly headed Pepsi North America, took over as chairman and CEO from Roger Enrico in May 2001.

Strategy

Since 1997, Pepsi has spun off peripheral businesses to focus on soft drinks and snack foods. The firm hopes to rev its growth engine higher still by adding Quaker Oats' snack-food business and Gatorade brand, both of which will benefit from Pepsi's marketing muscle. It's also aggressively pursued exclusive contracts with the likes of United Airlines and the NFL.

700 Anderson Hill Road   www.pepsico.com
Purchase, NY 10577-1444

Morningstar Grades

Growth [B-]	1998	1999	2000	2001
Revenue %	4.9	-7.7	1.5	5.7
Earnings/Share %	—	NMF	2.9	3.5
Book Value/Share %	—	NMF	NMF	12.9
Dividends/Share %	5.1	3.9	3.7	3.6

After weak 2% second-quarter sales growth, PepsiCo improved its volume and pricing trends in the third quarter, resulting in a much-improved 4% increase in sales.

Profitability [A+]	1999	2000	2001	TTM
Return on Assets %	12.6	12.3	12.3	13.3
Oper Cash Flow $Mil	3,605	4,440	4,201	5,160
- Cap Spending $Mil	1,341	1,352	1,324	1,375
= Free Cash Flow $Mil	2,264	3,088	2,877	3,785

PepsiCo's third-quarter earnings per share increased 14% on a comparable basis, as margins remained robust. It has increased operating earnings at least 10% for 12 consecutive quarters.

Financial Health [A+]	1999	2000	2001	09-02
Long-term Debt $Mil	3,527	3,009	2,651	2,271
Total Equity $Mil	—	7,577	8,648	9,521
Debt/Equity Ratio	—	0.4	0.3	0.2

Financial leverage and long-term debt have fallen as the company has shed assets through spin-offs. Free cash flow remains strong, and the stock boasts a cash return of around 5%.

	Industry	Investment Style	Stock Type	Sector
	Beverage Mfg.	⊞ Large Core	→ Slow Growth	🚗 Consumer Goods

Competition	Market Cap $Mil	Debt/ Equity	12 Mo Trailing Sales $Mil	Price/Cash Flow	Return On Assets%	Total Return% 1 Yr	3 Yr
PepsiCo	73,589	0.2	28,044	14.3	13.3	-12.1	6.9
Coca-Cola	108,635	0.2	21,554	24.3	12.8	-5.6	-6.4
General Mills	17,278	1.5	8,540	17.8	2.7	-7.6	14.6

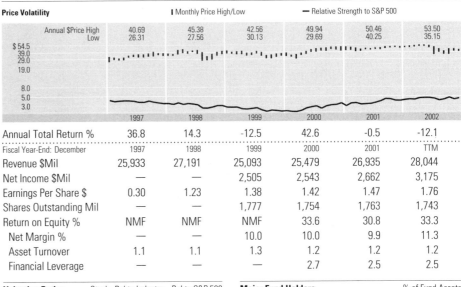

Price Volatility   ▌ Monthly Price High/Low   — Relative Strength to S&P 500

Annual $Price High Low	40.69 26.31	45.38 27.56	42.56 30.13	49.94 29.69	50.46 40.25	53.50 35.15

	1997	1998	1999	2000	2001	2002
Annual Total Return %	36.8	14.3	-12.5	42.6	-0.5	-12.1

Fiscal Year-End: December	1997	1998	1999	2000	2001	TTM
Revenue $Mil	25,933	27,191	25,093	25,479	26,935	28,044
Net Income $Mil	—	—	2,505	2,543	2,662	3,175
Earnings Per Share $	0.30	1.23	1.38	1.42	1.47	1.76
Shares Outstanding Mil	—	—	1,777	1,754	1,763	1,743
Return on Equity %	NMF	NMF	NMF	33.6	30.8	33.3
Net Margin %	—	—	10.0	10.0	9.9	11.3
Asset Turnover	1.1	1.1	1.3	1.2	1.2	1.2
Financial Leverage	—	—	—	2.7	2.5	2.5

Valuation Ratios	Stock	Rel to Industry	Rel to S&P 500
Price/Earnings	24.0	0.7	1.0
Price/Book	7.7	0.8	2.4
Price/Sales	2.6	0.5	1.3
Price/Cash Flow	14.3	0.6	1.1

Major Fund Holders	% of Fund Assets
Rydex Consumer Products Inv	8.48
Lake Forest Core Equity	7.05
Armada Tax Managed Equity I	5.33
Managers AMG Rorer Large Cap	4.65

Morningstar's Take   By David Kathman, 10-10-2002   Stock Price as of Analysis: $41.57

PepsiCo is an excellent company, made stronger by its acquisition of Quaker Oats. Its recent problems are minor and temporary, and we view a stock price decline below $40 as a buying opportunity.

PepsiCo is perhaps best known as the number-two soft-drink maker behind arch rival Coca-Cola, but in fact it gets less than 25% of its revenue from soft drinks. PepsiCo is also the dominant maker of salty snack foods through its Frito-Lay divisions (representing more than half of revenue), the dominant maker of sports drinks through Gatorade (which has a commanding 80% market share), and one of the top makers of juices and cereals.

Such diversification isn't always a recipe for success, but PepsiCo has done a good job of crafting a portfolio of strong businesses that complement one another. For example, in the two years after being acquired by PepsiCo in 1998, Tropicana boosted its growth and doubled its profits by exploiting Frito-Lay's direct-store distribution system, greatly expanding its presence in convenience stores and other high-traffic areas. The acquisition of SoBe in 2000 gave PepsiCo a fast-growing line of youth-oriented beverages with a healthier image than its traditional soft drinks.

PepsiCo's purchase of Quaker Oats has

encountered a few bumps in the road, but we're not too worried about these. Ironically, Tropicana was the main victim of the Quaker integration problems: the new Tropicana-Gatorade division stumbled in late 2001 as the two companies' combined salesforces struggled to become familiar with new product lines, and price tinkering exacerbated Tropicana's problems into 2002. Tropicana seems to be on its feet again, though, and hasn't suffered any lasting damage.

On the positive side, the Quaker merger continues to pay dividends. Snack-food items like granola bars were already one of Quaker's fastest-growing segments, and Frito-Lay's distribution network has given them a further boost. Although Gatorade is barred from Pepsi's bottling system for 10 years by the terms of the merger, it's still benefiting from PepsiCo's marketing muscle to achieve double-digit volume growth. Cost savings from the merger are coming in ahead of schedule, and are the main reason PepsiCo has been able to meet earnings expectations despite the sales weakness.

PepsiCo has been one of our favorite food and beverage companies for years, and recent events have done nothing to change that. It doesn't have to fall too far below our estimated fair value of $48 per share to be an attractive stock.

MORNINGSTAR® Stocks 500

Pfizer PFE

	Rating	Risk	Moat Size	Fair Value	Last Close	Yield %
	★★★★	Low	Wide	$37.00	$30.57	1.7

Industry	Investment Style	Stock Type	Sector
Drugs	Large Growth	Classic Growth	Healthcare

Company Profile

Pfizer manufactures health-care products. Its major pharmaceutical products include Lipitor, a cholesterol-lowering medicine; Zoloft, an antidepressant; Viagra, which treats impotence; Glucotrol XL, an antidiabetic drug; and Procardia XL, Norvasc, and Cardura, which regulate hypertension. Pfizer derives 15% of its revenue from consumer health-care products, including Visine eye drops, Ben-Gay ointment, Unisom sleep aids, and Plax dental rinse. Another 3% of revenue comes from its animal health division. Pfizer acquired Warner-Lambert in June 2000.

Management

CEO Henry McKinnell took over the top job when William Steere retired in January 2001. Karen Katen, who heads the pharmaceutical division, was recently promoted to executive vice president.

Strategy

Pfizer follows an aggressive-growth strategy, spending more dollars on research and a higher percentage of revenue on selling, general, and administrative expenses than its peers. Highly profitable megablockbuster drugs are Pfizer's forte. It actively pursues comarketing arrangements and mergers, like the pending merger with Pharmacia.

235 East 42nd Street
New York, NY 10017-5755
www.pfizer.com

Competition

Competition	Market Cap $Mil	Debt/ Equity	12 Mo Trailing Sales $Mil	Price/Cash Flow	Return On Assets%	Total Return% 1 Yr	3 Yr
Pfizer	188,377	0.2	34,407	21.1	18.3	-22.2	1.0
Merck	127,121	0.3	50,430	13.2	15.0	-1.3	-2.5
GlaxoSmithKline PLC ADR	116,607	0.3	27,512	6.2	13.9	-22.8	-9.3

Price Volatility

Monthly Price High/Low — Relative Strength to S&P 500

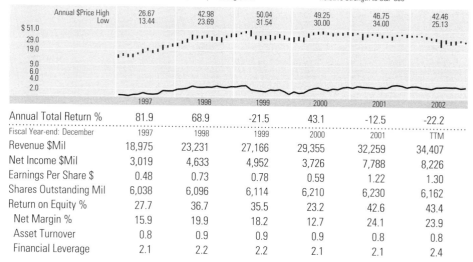

Annual $Price High / Low	26.67 / 13.44	42.98 / 23.69	50.04 / 31.54	49.25 / 30.00	46.75 / 34.00	42.46 / 25.13

	1997	1998	1999	2000	2001	2002
Annual Total Return %	81.9	68.9	-21.5	43.1	-12.5	-22.2

Fiscal Year-end: December	1997	1998	1999	2000	2001	TTM
Revenue $Mil	18,975	23,231	27,166	29,355	32,259	34,407
Net Income $Mil	3,019	4,633	4,952	3,726	7,788	8,226
Earnings Per Share $	0.48	0.73	0.78	0.59	1.22	1.30
Shares Outstanding Mil	6,038	6,096	6,114	6,210	6,230	6,162
Return on Equity %	27.7	36.7	35.5	23.2	42.6	43.4
Net Margin %	15.9	19.9	18.2	12.7	24.1	23.9
Asset Turnover	0.8	0.9	0.9	0.9	0.8	0.8
Financial Leverage	2.1	2.2	2.2	2.1	2.1	2.4

Valuation Ratios	Stock	Rel to Industry	Rel to S&P 500
Price/Earnings	23.5	1.0	1.0
Price/Book	9.9	1.4	3.1
Price/Sales	5.5	1.4	2.7
Price/Cash Flow	21.1	1.0	1.6

Major Fund Holders	% of Fund Assets
American Capital Exchange	16.73
Schwab Health Care Focus	16.17
ProFunds Ultra Pharmaceuticals Inv	15.77
Rydex Health Care Inv	13.65

Morningstar Grades

Growth [C+]	1998	1999	2000	2001
Revenue %	22.4	16.9	8.1	9.9
Earnings/Share %	52.1	6.8	-24.4	106.8
Book Value/Share %	14.7	10.5	15.9	12.6
Dividends/Share %	11.6	21.1	17.4	22.2

Pfizer generally sports one of the best EPS growth rates in the industry, even though top-line growth is nothing to phone home about. Revenue for the nine months ended September 30 was up 8.7% from the same period a year ago.

Profitability [A+]	1999	2000	2001	TTM
Return on Assets %	15.8	11.1	19.9	18.3
Oper Cash Flow $Mil	5,493	6,195	9,291	8,923
- Cap Spending $Mil	2,493	2,191	2,203	1,943
= Free Cash Flow $Mil	3,000	4,004	7,088	6,980

Margins improved dramatically over the past two years thanks to cost savings from the Warner-Lambert acquisition. Although gross and operating margins may come down a bit as a result of the Pharmacia merger, we think they will remain near current levels.

Financial Health [A]	1999	2000	2001	09-02
Long-term Debt $Mil	1,774	1,123	2,609	3,118
Total Equity $Mil	13,950	16,076	18,293	18,953
Debt/Equity Ratio	0.1	0.1	0.1	0.2

Pfizer is in excellent condition. Its debt burden isn't excessive and its cash pile keeps growing. The company boasts an AAA credit rating and is sitting on more than $16 billion in cash and long-term investments.

Morningstar's Take By Todd N. Lebor, 11-08-2002 Stock Price as of Analysis: $33.86

Pfizer is at the peak of its game, and buying Pharmacia should help it stay there a little longer. At the right price, Pfizer is a top choice in the drug industry.

Pfizer's drug portfolio is unequaled. Once the Pharmacia merger closes, which is expected by year-end 2002, Pfizer will have ten drugs with annual sales over $1 billion, including four drugs with more than $2 billion, and one drug (Lipitor) with more than $8 billion in annual sales. Those figures translate not only into high revenue, but high margins. Pfizer's gross and operating margins of approximately 84% and 33%, respectively, led the industry averages of around 72% and 23%. We believe the Pharmacia merger will help Pfizer sustain these margins thanks to cost-cutting, improved bargaining power against health-maintenance organizations and government buyers, and, most important, the addition of several new drugs with long patent lives.

Many of Pfizer's drugs command the top spot in their therapeutic areas. For example, Lipitor has more than 50% of the cholesterol-lowering market, nearly twice the share of Merck's Zocor. Erectile dysfunction pill Viagra, antifungal Diflucan, Alzheimer's treatment Aricept, antibiotic Zithromax, and incontinence drug Detrol are clear leaders in their markets.

Antidepressant Zoloft and osteoarthritis treatment Celebrex are also leaders, but have close competition.

This portfolio, the distribution network, and the sales teams pushing these drugs make Pfizer the partner of choice for struggling biotechs or foreign drug companies looking to back their novel therapies with marketing muscle. We view this as one of Pfizer's competitive advantages.

The major drawback to Pfizer's blockbuster-stacked drug lineup is its exposure to a single negative event. Should one of its major drugs fall victim to early patent termination or be found to cause a serious health risk, the company's revenue stream and profitability would be hurt worse than many of its peers'. And while the Pharmacia merger will help by spreading this risk over more drugs, we still think the risk is noteworthy.

Pfizer's management has displayed fine judgment with acquisitions in the past. The Warner-Lambert acquisition in 1999 gave Pfizer complete control over Lipitor and led to significant cost reductions (operating margins climbed from 25.3% in 1999 to 33.7% in 2001). Betting on the continuation of deft strategic planning by management is wise, in our opinion.

Philip Morris Companies MO

	Rating	Risk	Moat Size	Fair Value	Last Close	Yield %
	★★★★	Med.	Wide	$50.00	$40.53	6.0

Company Profile

Philip Morris produces tobacco, food, and beer products. Its tobacco division produces cigarettes under brand names like Marlboro, Merit, L&M, and Virginia Slims. Its Kraft General Foods subsidiary makes food products under brand names that include Kraft, General Foods, Nabisco, Jell-O, Tombstone, and Oscar Mayer. Philip Morris' Miller Brewing subsidiary brews beer sold under such brand names as Miller, Lowenbrau, Meister Brau, Icehouse, Red Dog, and Hamm's. Foreign revenue accounts for about 39% of the company's revenue.

Management

Chief financial officer Louis Camilleri succeeded Geoffrey Bible as CEO in April 2002 and became chairman in August. Camilleri quickly installed his own management team, including a senior vice president for mergers and acquisitions.

Strategy

Philip Morris said in November 2001 that it's changing its name to Altria in an effort to distance itself from tobacco taint as it fights tobacco-related lawsuits. Its Kraft divisions continue to grow both internally and through acquisitions.

120 Park Avenue
New York, NY 10017

www.philipmorris.com

Morningstar Grades

Growth [A-]	1998	1999	2000	2001
Revenue %	3.2	5.7	2.2	11.9
Earnings/Share %	-14.7	45.0	17.6	3.2
Book Value/Share %	8.7	-4.1	3.9	34.2
Dividends/Share %	5.0	9.5	9.8	9.9

Philip Morris' 12% revenue growth in 2001 was largely due to Kraft's acquisition of Nabisco. Revenue grew only 2.7% in the first nine months of 2002, held down by adverse currency translations and the effects of a tobacco tax hike.

Profitability [A+]	1999	2000	2001	TTM
Return on Assets %	12.5	10.8	10.1	13.4
Oper Cash Flow $Mil	11,375	11,044	8,893	10,943
- Cap Spending $Mil	2,431	2,547	2,882	3,012
= Free Cash Flow $Mil	8,944	8,497	6,011	7,931

Philip Morris is very profitable, with great returns on capital and stable net margins. It said in September that 2002 earnings growth will be only 3%-5%, rather than its earlier projection of 9%, but we think this slowdown is temporary.

Financial Health [B]	1999	2000	2001	09-02
Long-term Debt $Mil	12,226	19,154	18,651	18,386
Total Equity $Mil	15,305	15,005	19,620	21,345
Debt/Equity Ratio	0.8	1.3	1.0	0.9

Though it has relatively little cash on its balance sheet, Philip Morris generates billions of dollars annually in free cash flow.

Industry	Investment Style	Stock Type	Sector
Tobacco	Large Value	High Yield	Consumer Goods

Competition

	Market Cap $Mil	Debt/ Equity	12 Mo Trailing Sales $Mil	Price/Cash Flow	Return On Assets%	Total Return% 1 Yr	3 Yr
Philip Morris Companies	84,290	0.9	90,561	7.7	13.4	-6.8	26.8
British American Tobacco	21,178	—	16,610	—	—		
RJ Reynolds Tobacco Holdi	3,741	0.2	8,602	8.4	0.7	-19.9	43.7

Price Volatility

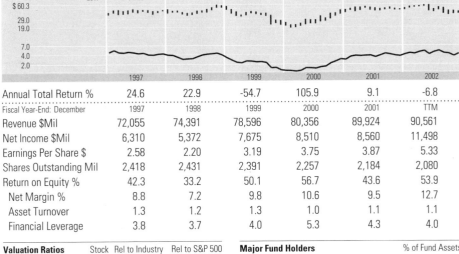

	Monthly Price High/Low				Relative Strength to S&P 500	
Annual $Price High Low	48.13 36.00	59.25 34.75	55.56 21.63	45.50 18.69	53.88 39.63	57.79 35.40
	1997	1998	1999	2000	2001	2002
Annual Total Return %	24.6	22.9	-54.7	105.9	9.1	-6.8

Fiscal Year-End: December	1997	1998	1999	2000	2001	TTM
Revenue $Mil	72,055	74,391	78,596	80,356	89,924	90,561
Net Income $Mil	6,310	5,372	7,675	8,510	8,560	11,498
Earnings Per Share $	2.58	2.20	3.19	3.75	3.87	5.33
Shares Outstanding Mil	2,418	2,431	2,391	2,257	2,184	2,080
Return on Equity %	42.3	33.2	50.1	56.7	43.6	53.9
Net Margin %	8.8	7.2	9.8	10.6	9.5	12.7
Asset Turnover	1.3	1.2	1.3	1.0	1.1	1.1
Financial Leverage	3.8	3.7	4.0	5.3	4.3	4.0

Valuation Ratios	Stock	Rel to Industry	Rel to S&P 500
Price/Earnings	7.6	1.0	0.3
Price/Book	3.9	1.0	1.2
Price/Sales	0.9	1.0	0.5
Price/Cash Flow	7.7	1.0	0.6

Major Fund Holders	% of Fund Assets
Fidelity Independence	19.55
Midas Special Equities	13.04
Scudder Dreman High Return Equity A	10.38
Fidelity Advisor Dynamic Cap App A	10.05

Morningstar's Take By David Kathman, 11-08-2002 Stock Price as of Analysis: $42.74

Philip Morris remains an undervalued stock that has shown an impressive ability to weather all kinds of storms.

Philip Morris is a cash machine. It generated $7 billion in free cash flow in 2001, with its domestic tobacco, international tobacco, and Kraft Foods divisions all contributing significantly. It recently sold struggling Miller Brewing to South African Breweries, creating a $1.7 billion windfall that it will use to accelerate its share-repurchase program. Yet its stock price does not reflect those fundamentals because of the challenges Philip Morris faces on a couple of different fronts, competitive and legal.

Philip Morris dominates the premium cigarette segment from which it gets 90% of its tobacco revenue, but it's being threatened from the lower end by deep-discount cigarette makers and online tobacco merchants. The company has responded by spending more to strengthen its key brands, which we consider a smart move despite the short-term hit to earnings. Smokers tend to be very brand-loyal, and Philip Morris has the best stable of cigarette brands in the business. Its customers have shown a willingness to pay up for these brands; a dozen price increases from 1998 to 2002 had little effect on Philip Morris' sales and profit growth.

On the legal front, Philip Morris still faces a plethora of tobacco lawsuits. But, fears that the company will be torpedoed by litigation are overblown, in our opinion. The $145 billion verdict in the Engle class-action lawsuit is unlikely to survive the appeal process, since the courts have not been very receptive lately to class-action tobacco suits. Philip Morris has lost a series of West Coast lawsuits by individual smokers, all of which are under appeal, but it has plenty of resources to handle such individual suits.

The 1998 master settlement agreement, in which the tobacco companies agreed to pay $206 billion to all 50 states, is actually a positive for Philip Morris. Although the tab is steep, the bill will be paid over 25 years, and a lot of uncertainty is removed. Even more important, the settlement gives the states a vested interest in keeping Philip Morris alive to pay the tab; thus, several state governments have moved to protect tobacco companies against potentially bankrupting lump-sum damage payments.

Even with all the challenges and risks Philip Morris faces, we think it is worth about $50 per share. It looks like a good buy below $40.

MORNINGSTAR® Stocks 500

Philips Electronics NV ADR PHG

	Rating	Risk	Moat Size	Fair Value	Last Close	Yield %
	★★	Med.	None	$19.00	$17.68	1.8

Company Profile

Philips Electronics primarily manufactures electronic products. It makes videocassette recorders, CD and DVD players, televisions, camcorders, personal computers, batteries, arena lighting systems, and medical and industrial systems. The company also assembles discrete semiconductors and makes LCD panels. Sales outside of Europe account for about 52% of Philips Electronics' revenue. In addition, it manufactures corded and cordless telephones and answering machines The company owns a 57% stake in MedQuist. It acquired ADAC Laboratories in December 2000.

Management

Gerard Kleisterlee, a company insider who was CEO of Philips Components, replaced Cor Boonstra as CEO in May 2001. His two top lieutenants are John Whybrow and Arthur van der Poel, who split responsibility for the main business units.

Strategy

Over the past few years, Philips Electronics had been getting rid of money-losing units, like music publisher PolyGram and a mobile phone joint venture with Lucent, and putting more resources into areas perceived as growth engines, particularly semiconductors. However, that backfired in 2001 and 2002, as the semiconductor and telecom markets went into free-fall.

The Rembrandt Tower   www.news.philips.com
Amsterdam, 1070 MX

Morningstar Grades

Growth [D]	1998	1999	2000	2001
Revenue %	2.7	3.3	20.4	-14.6
Earnings/Share %	127.9	-68.8	456.9	NMF
Book Value/Share %	55.8	6.3	53.7	-11.8
Dividends/Share %	22.3	8.7	20.0	20.0

Sales have increased for the past two quarters after six straight quarters of declines. However, the company is still exposed to some very volatile markets, including semiconductors, wireless phones, and digital networks.

Profitability [B]	1999	2000	2001	TTM
Return on Assets %	6.5	24.5	-6.8	-6.8
Oper Cash Flow $Mil	2,048	2,783	1,113	1,113
- Cap Spending $Mil	1,993	3,075	2,120	2,120
= Free Cash Flow $Mil	55	-292	-1,007	-1,007

Philips should post a net profit in 2003 after two disappointing years. We expect its more stable medical devices segment to lead the way. Many of the other businesses could be hurt by a prolonged slump in technology spending.

Financial Health [B]	1999	2000	2001	12-01
Long-term Debt $Mil	2,737	2,155	5,836	5,836
Total Equity $Mil	14,757	20,506	16,330	16,330
Debt/Equity Ratio	0.2	0.1	0.4	0.4

Philips' debt load has increased substantially over the past two years, but its balance sheet is still in decent shape. Despite negative earnings, the company continues to generate positive cash flow.

Industry	Investment Style	Stock Type	Sector
Audio/Video Equipment	▦ Large Growth	⟲ Cyclical	⛝ Consumer Goods

Competition

	Market Cap $Mil	Debt/ Equity	12 Mo Trailing Sales $Mil	Price/Cash Flow	Return On Assets%	Total Return% 1 Yr	3 Yr
Philips Electronics NV ADR	22,527	0.4	28,837	20.2	-6.8	-38.6	-18.3
General Electric	242,308	2.2	130,295	8.2	2.7	-37.7	-18.9
Sony ADR	38,122	0.4	60,413	6.5	0.2	-8.1	-32.4

Price Volatility

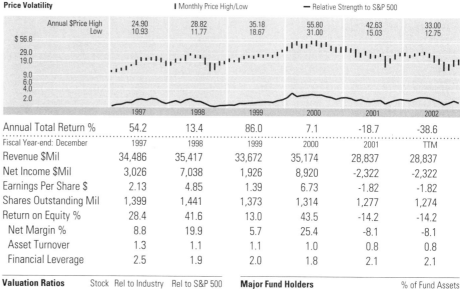

			Monthly Price High/Low		— Relative Strength to S&P 500	
Annual $Price High / Low	24.90 / 10.93	28.82 / 11.77	35.18 / 18.67	55.80 / 31.00	42.63 / 15.03	33.00 / 12.75

$ 56.8
29.0
19.0
9.0
6.0
4.0
2.0

	1997	1998	1999	2000	2001	2002
Annual Total Return %	54.2	13.4	86.0	7.1	-18.7	-38.6

Fiscal Year-end: December	1997	1998	1999	2000	2001	TTM
Revenue $Mil	34,486	35,417	33,672	35,174	28,837	28,837
Net Income $Mil	3,026	7,038	1,926	8,920	-2,322	-2,322
Earnings Per Share $	2.13	4.85	1.39	6.73	-1.82	-1.82
Shares Outstanding Mil	1,399	1,441	1,373	1,314	1,277	1,274
Return on Equity %	28.4	41.6	13.0	43.5	-14.2	-14.2
Net Margin %	8.8	19.9	5.7	25.4	-8.1	-8.1
Asset Turnover	1.3	1.1	1.1	1.0	0.8	0.8
Financial Leverage	2.5	1.9	2.0	1.8	2.1	2.1

Valuation Ratios	Stock	Rel to Industry	Rel to S&P 500
Price/Earnings	NMF	—	—
Price/Book	1.4	0.8	0.4
Price/Sales	0.8	1.2	0.4
Price/Cash Flow	20.2	2.8	1.5

Major Fund Holders	% of Fund Assets
Dessauer Global Equity	4.44
Salomon Brothers Opportunity	4.22
Longleaf Partners International	4.21
ICAP Euro Select Equity	3.04

Morningstar's Take   By Tom Goetzinger, 12-20-2002   Stock Price as of Analysis: $18.07

As Philips continues to struggle with the double whammy of broad economic weakness and a slumping semiconductor industry, we don't see much reason to get excited about the stock.

The economic weakness of the past couple of years has taken a heavy toll on Philips. Although the U.S. and European economies seem to be on the mend, Philips is still working to get on its feet. In the second quarter of 2002, the company was forced to take a 1.5 billion-euro write-down of its stake in troubled French media firm Vivendi.

To be fair, Philips is showing some improvement. After six straight quarters of declines in late 2000, 2001, and early 2002, overall sales actually increased in the second and third quarters of the past year, led by the medical systems division. Although revenue in the key consumer electronics division was down in both quarters in absolute terms, the comparable sales numbers looked better, helped by stronger sales of TVs and DVD players.

Offsetting these improvements, however, is continued weakness in Philips' other businesses. The lighting division is still struggling, and Philips' component and semiconductor divisions, which make parts for high-tech gadgets, are still in the throes of a brutal downturn. Component sales were down 50%

over this past summer as manufacturers were hesitant to spend money. Moreover, semiconductor sales look extremely unstable. The book/bill ratio, which measures future orders relative to current sales, dropped from 1.3 in the first quarter to 1.0 in the second to 0.7 in the third. This implies that demand is weakening.

Management has been cautious, saying that it expects conditions to improve in 2003, but we think the skies above many of Philips' businesses still look cloudy. We've factored in a modest recovery in 2003 into our fair value estimate of $19, but unless the tech sector stages a miraculous comeback or Philips' stock price plunges to around $10--thereby offering a better risk/return trade-off--we're content to take a pass on the shares.

Pier 1 Imports PIR

	Rating	Risk	Moat Size	Fair Value	Last Close	Yield %
	★★	Med.	None	$21.00	$18.93	1.0

Company Profile

Pier 1 Imports is the largest specialty retailer of imported home furnishings, gifts, and related items in North America. The company operates or franchises more than 800 stores in 47 states, the District of Columbia, Puerto Rico, Canada, Mexico, the United Kingdom, and Japan. Directly imported from more than 50 countries, its merchandise consists of more than 5,000 items, including casual living and dining area furniture, decorative home furnishings, dining and kitchen goods, and textiles.

Management

Marvin Girouard has been CEO for two years. He's had high-level posts for 15 years and helped oversee much of Pier 1's recent expansion efforts. He is focused on accelerating the firm's growth rate, even as the chain matures.

Strategy

Now that Pier 1 has refined its merchandising and pricing strategies, it's focused on growth. Management has accelerated new Pier 1 store openings in the United States, and over the next five to 10 years, the company has aggressive expansion plans for Cargo Furniture, a children's furniture retailer it bought in 2001.

301 Commerce Street
Fort Worth, TX 76102
www.pier1.com

Morningstar Grades

Growth [B]	1999	2000	2001	2002
Revenue %	5.9	8.1	14.7	9.7
Earnings/Share %	6.9	-2.6	29.3	7.2
Book Value/Share %	6.8	14.3	23.2	11.5
Dividends/Share %	33.1	2.8	25.0	6.7

Growth is driven primarily by Pier 1's ability to successfully predict consumer preferences and open new stores. Its stepped-up expansion efforts should boost overall revenue, but comparable-store sales will reflect merchandise hits or misses.

Profitability [A+]	2000	2001	2002	TTM
Return on Assets %	11.1	12.9	11.6	13.4
Oper Cash Flow $Mil	122	108	244	166
- Cap Spending $Mil	49	43	58	75
= Free Cash Flow $Mil	73	65	186	91

Pier 1 has consistently been more profitable than its peers, thanks to its long-standing relationships with overseas vendors. We expect profitability to improve further as the result of increasing economies of scale from expansion efforts.

Financial Health [A+]	2000	2001	2002	08-02
Long-term Debt $Mil	25	25	25	25
Total Equity $Mil	441	532	586	598
Debt/Equity Ratio	0.1	0.0	0.0	0.0

Pier 1 has historically expanded its store base more slowly than many of its rivals, so free cash flow has been kept strong and debt low. The retailer generates sufficient cash to fund even an accelerated pace of store openings.

Industry	Investment Style	Stock Type	Sector
Furniture Retail	Mid Core	Classic Growth	Consumer Services

Competition	Market Cap $Mil	Debt/ Equity	12 Mo Trailing Sales $Mil	Price/Cash Flow	Return On Assets%	Total Return% 1 Yr	3 Yr
Pier 1 Imports	1,748	0.0	1,661	10.5	13.4	10.3	48.5
Williams-Sonoma	3,148	0.3	2,214	9.6	9.9	26.6	8.7
Cost Plus	623	—	616	—	—	—	—

Price Volatility

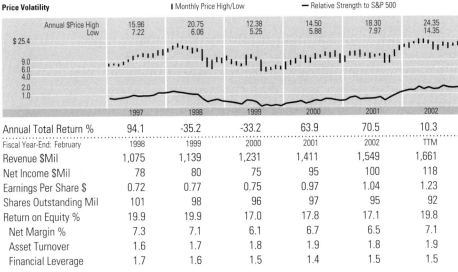

Annual $Price High	15.96	20.75	12.38	14.50	18.30	24.35
Low	7.22	6.06	5.25	5.88	7.97	14.35

	1997	1998	1999	2000	2001	2002
Annual Total Return %	94.1	-35.2	-33.2	63.9	70.5	10.3

Fiscal Year-End: February	1998	1999	2000	2001	2002	TTM
Revenue $Mil	1,075	1,139	1,231	1,411	1,549	1,661
Net Income $Mil	78	80	75	95	100	118
Earnings Per Share $	0.72	0.77	0.75	0.97	1.04	1.23
Shares Outstanding Mil	101	98	96	97	95	92
Return on Equity %	19.9	19.9	17.0	17.8	17.1	19.8
Net Margin %	7.3	7.1	6.1	6.7	6.5	7.1
Asset Turnover	1.6	1.7	1.8	1.9	1.8	1.9
Financial Leverage	1.7	1.6	1.5	1.4	1.5	1.5

Valuation Ratios	Stock	Rel to Industry	Rel to S&P 500
Price/Earnings	15.4	0.4	0.7
Price/Book	2.9	0.4	0.9
Price/Sales	1.1	0.3	0.5
Price/Cash Flow	10.5	0.4	0.8

Major Fund Holders	% of Fund Assets
Janus 2	4.82
Oppenheimer Enterprise A	4.04
Scudder Dynamic Growth A	3.20
Citizens Small Cap Core Growth	2.65

Morningstar's Take By Roz Bryant, 12-17-2002 Stock Price as of Analysis: $19.89

Pier 1 has endured because its merchandise changes to meet the needs of its customers. After 40 years in business, growth shows no sign of slowing. We'd consider shares at around $11.

Pier 1 knows how to keep growth on track. Over the past ten years, the retailer has averaged 6.7% same-store sales growth. This is quite an accomplishment for any retailer, particularly a 40-year-old home accessories chain.

We think this success can be attributed to Pier 1's constant tweaking of its product mix: It's always looking for the combination most appealing to its baby-boomer customer base. As baby boomers have matured from flower children to affluent homeowners, Pier 1's merchandise assortment has shifted from incense and love beads to high-quality, stylish home furnishings.

Pier 1 wants furniture to eventually comprise 60% of its sales mix, up from about 40% currently. We think furniture presents a unique growth opportunity for the retailer. Much of the furniture in Pier 1 stores has a style that appeals to Williams-Sonoma's Pottery Barn customers, but is less expensive. In making stylish furniture accessible to a less affluent customer base through an established brand, Pier 1 should be able to ensure demand for its products.

Its acquisition of the undercapitalized Cargo children's furniture chain may also help it move closer to this goal. Through Cargo, the company hopes to develop a national value-oriented children's furniture brand. Right now, there is no established leader in this niche; both Pottery Barn Kids and Ethan Allen's EA Kids carry pricier goods. Management intends to eventually expand the concept to 300 stores.

The jury's still out on Cargo's true growth potential. Because of their low prices, the stores will likely face competition from Sweden's IKEA. The rival home furnishings giant doesn't focus exclusively on children's products, but it sells them at lower prices than other stores can. Differentiation will thus be key to Cargo's success, and that may be tough to pull off at low prices.

It's the strength of Pier 1's core business that makes it an attractive business to us, though. We'd buy in at a 50% margin of safety to our fair value estimate.

MORNINGSTAR® Stocks 500

Pitney Bowes PBI

	Rating	Risk	Moat Size	Fair Value	Last Close	Yield %
	★★★	Low	Wide	$35.00	$32.66	3.6

Company Profile

Pitney Bowes provides equipment and supplies to business and government organizations. The company manufactures business equipment like mailing, copying, facsimile, and voice-processing systems. Pitney Bowes also provides facilities-management services. In addition, the company offers capital financing of large-ticket items. Pitney Bowes markets its products in the United States and overseas. Sales within the United States account for approximately 83% of total sales. The company spun off its office systems operation in 2001.

Management

Chairman and CEO Michael Critelli assumed his current position in 1997. Under his leadership, Pitney has shed noncore assets, improved its operating margins, and aggressively returned cash to shareholders.

Strategy

Pitney's dominant U.S. market position and recurring revenue stream generate large cash flows. Rather than drive growth for growth's sake, the company returns much of this cash to shareholders through stock buybacks and a healthy dividend. To expand, Pitney has made acquisitions in its international meter, outsourcing, and mailing and messaging technology businesses.

World Headquarters   www.pb.com
Stamford, CT 06926-0700

Morningstar Grades

Growth [B+]

	1998	1999	2000	2001
Revenue %	-9.0	8.9	1.8	6.2
Earnings/Share %	14.4	13.6	3.0	-18.3
Book Value/Share %	-5.9	1.7	-13.3	-21.5
Dividends/Share %	12.5	13.3	11.8	1.8

Pitney's main U.S. mail business is mature and shouldn't grow too much. To drive growth, the company has recently made acquisitions in the international mail, outsourcing, and document messaging technology businesses.

Profitability [A]

	1999	2000	2001	TTM
Return on Assets %	7.7	7.9	5.9	5.8
Oper Cash Flow $Mil	981	872	1,036	553
- Cap Spending $Mil	305	269	256	223
= Free Cash Flow $Mil	676	604	780	330

By focusing on cost reductions, Pitney has sustained operating margins near 20%. Return on assets, an attractive 11%, should be maintained thanks to the firm's strong competitive position.

Financial Health [B-]

	1999	2000	2001	09-02
Long-term Debt $Mil	1,998	1,882	2,419	2,380
Total Equity $Mil	1,934	1,593	1,200	916
Debt/Equity Ratio	1.0	1.2	2.0	2.6

Most of Pitney's debt relates to its finance operations. With maturities of debt matched up with maturities of finance receivables, as well as strong cash flow, Pitney can easily service its obligations.

Industry	Investment Style	Stock Type	Sector
Office Equipment	▦ Mid Core	▨ High Yield	✪ Industrial Mats

Competition

	Market Cap $Mil	Debt/ Equity	12 Mo Trailing Sales $Mil	Price/Cash Flow	Return On Assets%	Total Return% 1 Yr	3 Yr
Pitney Bowes	7,725	2.6	4,336	14.0	5.8	-10.4	-7.2
Neopost	—	—	—	—	—	—	—
Francotyp-Postalia	—	—	—	—	—	—	—

Price Volatility

I Monthly Price High/Low

	Annual $Price High Low					
$ 1.0	0.00 0.00	0.00 0.00	0.00 0.00	0.00 0.00	0.00 0.00	0.00 0.00

Annual Total Return %	68.0	49.6	-25.5	-29.3	19.8	-10.4
Fiscal Year-end: December	1997	1998	1999	2000	2001	TTM
Revenue $Mil	3,847	3,499	3,812	3,881	4,122	4,336
Net Income $Mil	526	576	636	623	488	510
Earnings Per Share $	1.80	2.06	2.34	2.41	1.97	2.10
Shares Outstanding Mil	289	274	267	256	245	237
Return on Equity %	24.2	29.5	32.9	39.1	40.7	55.6
Net Margin %	13.7	16.5	16.7	16.0	11.8	11.8
Asset Turnover	0.5	0.5	0.5	0.5	0.5	0.5
Financial Leverage	3.6	3.9	4.3	5.0	6.9	9.6

Valuation Ratios	Stock	Rel to Industry	Rel to S&P 500
Price/Earnings	15.6	1.0	0.7
Price/Book	8.4	2.8	2.6
Price/Sales	1.8	4.8	0.9
Price/Cash Flow	14.0	2.4	1.1

Major Fund Holders	% of Fund Assets
AmSouth Select Equity B	7.74
Evergreen Technology A	4.64
Stratton Growth	3.93
PBHG Clipper Focus PBHG	3.47

Morningstar's Take By Dan Schick, 12-12-2002 Stock Price as of Analysis: $34.77

Pitney Bowes dominates the mail meter industry. Given the firm's wide economic moat, strong, shareholder-oriented management, and healthy finances, we'd purchase this blue-chip at a 20% discount to our fair value estimate.

Pitney earns a wide moat rating because it nearly monopolizes the U.S. market for mail meters, from which it earns a little more than half of its revenue. The company claims about 80% of the mail meter market. New competition is limited because of postal service regulations--only two other firms compete in the United States, Neopost and Franco-Typ Postalia, and they're not a big threat.

Pitney has better products. Because of its much larger revenue base, Pitney can easily support a research and development budget as big as Neopost's operating profits and not much smaller than Franco-Typ's total revenue. These expenditures produce innovations that rivals can't match. Pitney's latest rollout is a line of networked digital meters offering services like mail tracking and delivery confirmation. Pitney also boasts a more extensive service network to keep its customers happy and a broader distribution network to sign up new customers.

This strong competitive position helps Pitney generate returns on invested capital of near 11%, well above our estimate of the firm's cost of capital. In a testament to management's discipline, Pitney never engaged in large-scale empire building. Under Michael Critelli's leadership, the firm has been selling what noncore assets it had. The latest move on this front is exiting part of its finance operations, which has freed up $400 million that will be recycled into the core meter business and used to pay down debt.

The only problem with Pitney's domination is that the meter market is mature. Because its core market isn't growing much, Pitney won't either. Worse, it is looking for growth in areas that are somewhat less attractive, like providing outsourcing services for corporations' document-related needs. Although growing more rapidly than the meter business, services have much lower operating margins. Mitigating the relatively poor profit performance is the paucity of capital that Pitney puts into services. Thus, these growth efforts won't stop Pitney from returning money to investors through a solid dividend and stock buybacks.

Playboy Enterprises B PLA

	Rating	Risk	Moat Size	Fair Value	Last Close	Yield %
	★	High	None	$8.00	$10.13	0.0

Company Profile

Playboy Enterprises publishes magazines and direct mail catalogs and provides entertainment and product marketing services. The company publishes Playboy magazine and operates businesses that include newsstand specials and calendars, foreign magazine editions, and direct mail catalogs. Playboy Enterprises' entertainment group develops and sells adult programming for the pay television and home video markets. The product marketing group manages licensing agreements for consumer products bearing the company's trademarks.

Management

Christie Hefner is chairman and CEO. Her father, Hugh Hefner, still controls the majority of the voting power through Playboy class A shares. His economic stake in Playboy equals 30% of the outstanding class B shares.

Strategy

Playboy is concentrating on its online and video businesses and working on ways to improve cost savings and sales growth. The company is putting a lid on its online unit's expenses to bring that business into profitable territory.

680 North Lake Shore Drive www.playboy.com
Chicago, IL 60611

Morningstar Grades

Growth [D-]	1998	1999	2000	2001
Revenue %	112.4	9.5	-11.5	-5.4
Earnings/Share %	320.0	NMF	NMF	NMF
Book Value/Share %	10.8	69.9	-32.4	-29.1
Dividends/Share %	NMF	NMF	NMF	NMF

Declining magazine sales have been offset by new business in the entertainment group. Overall sales have been flat since 1997. The company's newest ventures are much riskier than traditional publishing, which could make sales fluctuate.

Profitability [C-]	1999	2000	2001	TTM
Return on Assets %	-1.2	-12.3	-7.9	-5.9
Oper Cash Flow $Mil	16	-31	-8	-2
- Cap Spending $Mil	3	5	3	3
= Free Cash Flow $Mil	13	-36	-11	-4

EBITDA growth has been solid, thanks to the entertainment group, whose EBITDA jumped 64% in 2001 and should top $60 million in 2002. Interest and capital expenditures cut into profits, however, and cash flows have been choppy.

Financial Health [D]	1999	2000	2001	09-02
Long-term Debt $Mil	75	94	78	78
Total Equity $Mil	161	114	82	91
Debt/Equity Ratio	0.5	0.8	1.0	0.9

The company has less than $1 million in cash on hand and carries more than $70 million in long-term debt. Significant growth will have to be financed by additional equity or debt.

Industry	Investment Style	Stock Type	Sector
Publishing	▦ Small Value	◪ Distressed	🎙 Media

Competition	Market Cap $Mil	Debt/ Equity	12 Mo Trailing Sales $Mil	Price/Cash Flow	Return On Assets%	Total Return% 1 Yr	3 Yr
Playboy Enterprises B	264	0.9	285	—	-5.9	-40.0	-24.5
McGraw-Hill Companies	11,713	0.3	4,730	9.8	8.3	0.7	4.5
Reed Elsevier PLC ADR	11,056	—	3,034	—	—	—	—

Price Volatility   ▮ Monthly Price High/Low   — Relative Strength to S&P 500

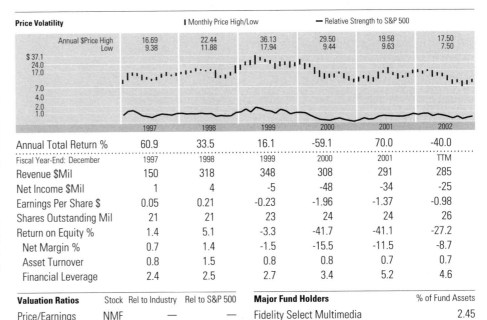

Annual $Price High Low	16.69 9.38	22.44 11.88	36.13 17.94	29.50 9.44	19.58 9.63	17.50 7.50

	1997	1998	1999	2000	2001	2002
Annual Total Return %	60.9	33.5	16.1	-59.1	70.0	-40.0

Fiscal Year-End: December	1997	1998	1999	2000	2001	TTM
Revenue $Mil	150	318	348	308	291	285
Net Income $Mil	1	4	-5	-48	-34	-25
Earnings Per Share $	0.05	0.21	-0.23	-1.96	-1.37	-0.98
Shares Outstanding Mil	21	21	23	24	24	26
Return on Equity %	1.4	5.1	-3.3	-41.7	-41.1	-27.2
Net Margin %	0.7	1.4	-1.5	-15.5	-11.5	-8.7
Asset Turnover	0.8	1.5	0.8	0.8	0.7	0.7
Financial Leverage	2.4	2.5	2.7	3.4	5.2	4.6

Valuation Ratios	Stock	Rel to Industry	Rel to S&P 500
Price/Earnings	NMF	—	—
Price/Book	2.9	0.6	0.9
Price/Sales	0.9	0.4	0.5
Price/Cash Flow	—	—	—

Major Fund Holders	% of Fund Assets
Fidelity Select Multimedia	2.45
Boyar Value	1.14
BlackRock Small Cap Grth Instl	1.12

Morningstar's Take By T.K. MacKay, 10-16-2002 Stock Price as of Analysis: $7.90

Playboy's brand name has potential, but we'd buy the stock only if it traded below $4.

Playboy's recent push into adult programming is generating sound profits, but it alone won't earn the firm an attractive return on investment. Playboy's acquisition of two adult networks has helped increase entertainment to about 44% of overall revenue from 30% five years ago, and so far has supplied the bulk of profits. Because of this, overall margins have improved dramatically over the past year, and we believe earnings will turn positive within a year.

But positive income doesn't mean attractive overall profits. The publishing group, including Playboy magazine, makes up about 38% of revenue, but has been just breaking even for several quarters. Declining newsstand sales, weak advertising (which contributes a third of the magazine's revenue), and slow subscriber growth relative to other men's magazines are making it difficult to turn this business around. We're excited about the hiring of ex-Maxim editor James Kaminsky as editorial director of Playboy, but believe it will take a lot more than one editor to make Playboy's name more appealing.

If Playboy can revive its brand name, which we believe has deteriorated, it can charge businesses more for using it. We would have more confidence in the company's ability to generate free cash flows if its licensing business were stronger. This business makes up just 7% of overall revenue, but we think it has the potential to generate profits similar to that of the entertainment business. Playboy currently generates slender 2%-3% royalties from the roughly $275 million worth of Playboy-branded merchandise, from T-shirts to martini glasses.

For this royalty stream to increase--which we'd like to see before getting excited about the company--we believe Playboy must distance itself from the explicit adult material for which it's known. We've seen evidence indicating Hugh Hefner's intention to do just that, but the company's recent hard-core network acquisitions could be a step in the opposite direction. If Playboy can alter its image without destroying it, the brand might gain more mass appeal, allowing it to demand higher royalties for licensed products. Combined with the decent profits that entertainment generates, this would break the trend of negative free cash flow and put the company back on a profitable track.

MORNINGSTAR® Stocks 500

PMC-Sierra PMCS

	Rating	Risk	Moat Size	Fair Value	Last Close	Yield %
	★★	High	None	$6.00	$5.56	0.0

Company Profile

PMC-Sierra develops integrated circuits for use in computer equipment. The company designs integrated circuits for use in asynchronous transfer mode, synchronous optical network, synchronous digital hierarchy, high-speed data control, T1 and T3 access, and Ethernet networks. Its products are used in voice and audio processing, Internet, caller identification, computer graphics display, music synthesis, and mass data storage applications. PMC-Sierra acquired Quantum Effect Devices in August 2000.

Management

Robert Bailey has been president and CEO since 1997. As of December 2001, management owned 6% of company shares.

Strategy

In light of the telecom sector's troubles, PMC-Sierra has most recently been focusing on cutting costs and on R&D projects with the greatest potential. It is also designing high-margin products with long product cycles in the telecom, wireless, and networking sectors. Another priority for PMC is to increase its chip content in existing customers' products.

3975 Freedom Circle   www.pmc-sierra.com
Santa Clara, CA 95054

Morningstar Grades

Growth [D]

	1998	1999	2000	2001
Revenue %	25.1	69.7	134.9	-53.5
Earnings/Share %	NMF	NMF	-8.9	NMF
Book Value/Share %	23.8	65.2	221.5	-64.7
Dividends/Share %	NMF	NMF	NMF	NMF

Sales have been decimated as a result of the meltdown in the telecom sector. After surging 135% in 2000, sales fell more than 50% in 2001, and will probably fall around 30% in 2002.

Profitability [D]

	1999	2000	2001	TTM
Return on Assets %	18.5	6.7	-74.7	-44.3
Oper Cash Flow $Mil	88	183	-53	-34
- Cap Spending $Mil	35	104	28	4
= Free Cash Flow $Mil	53	78	-81	-38

In a strong chip market, PMC generates outstanding margins. But the firm has not cut operating costs in line with the severe decline in sales. R&D costs, for example, are now more than half of sales.

Financial Health [D]

	1999	2000	2001	09-02
Long-term Debt $Mil	5	1	275	275
Total Equity $Mil	232	858	278	226
Debt/Equity Ratio	0.0	0.0	1.0	1.2

The balance sheet remains solid. PMC has almost $600 million in cash and investments (both short- and long-term) against convertible bonds of $275 million. Cash flow has been spotty but not terribly negative.

Industry	Investment Style	Stock Type	Sector
Semiconductors	▦ Small Growth	→ Slow Growth	💾 Hardware

Competition

	Market Cap $Mil	Debt/ Equity	12 Mo Trailing Sales $Mil	Price/Cash Flow	Return On Assets%	Total Return% 1 Yr	3 Yr
PMC-Sierra	930	1.2	213	—	-44.3	-73.9	-57.9
Applied Micro Circuits	1,114	0.0	131	—	-44.3	-67.4	-50.8
Vitesse Semiconductor	435	—	162	—	—		

Price Volatility

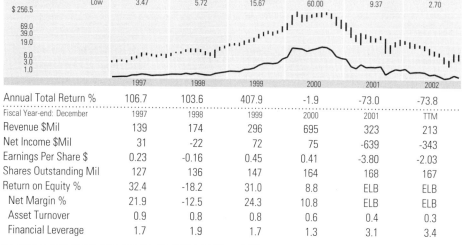

		8.72	16.41	80.56	255.50	111.75	26.80
Annual $Price High Low		3.47	5.72	15.67	60.00	9.37	2.70

	1997	1998	1999	2000	2001	2002
Annual Total Return %	106.7	103.6	407.9	-1.9	-73.0	-73.8

Fiscal Year-end: December	1997	1998	1999	2000	2001	TTM
Revenue $Mil	139	174	296	695	323	213
Net Income $Mil	31	-22	72	75	-639	-343
Earnings Per Share $	0.23	-0.16	0.45	0.41	-3.80	-2.03
Shares Outstanding Mil	127	136	147	164	168	167
Return on Equity %	32.4	-18.2	31.0	8.8	ELB	ELB
Net Margin %	21.9	-12.5	24.3	10.8	ELB	ELB
Asset Turnover	0.9	0.8	0.8	0.6	0.4	0.3
Financial Leverage	1.7	1.9	1.7	1.3	3.1	3.4

Valuation Ratios	Stock	Rel to Industry	Rel to S&P 500
Price/Earnings	NMF	—	—
Price/Book	4.1	1.4	1.3
Price/Sales	4.4	1.1	2.2
Price/Cash Flow	—	—	—

Major Fund Holders	% of Fund Assets
Calvert Social Investment Tech A	2.92
Wireless	2.51
Red Oak Technology Select	2.46
Conseco Science & Technology Y	1.85

Morningstar's Take By Jeremy Lopez, 11-11-2002 Stock Price as of Analysis: $4.54

PMC-Sierra is a solid firm, but awful industry conditions are a significant albatross around its neck.

The main cloud hanging over the company is a capital-spending void in the telecom industry, which still accounts for more than half of PMC's sales. Massive capital investment in telecom infrastructure during the Internet boom led to overcapacity and cutthroat pricing for telecom services. Many carriers still face distressed balance sheets or are working through bankruptcy, and now have little reason or ability to expand their infrastructure. This situation shows no sign of reversing anytime soon, leaving PMC's growth prospects lackluster at best.

At least PMC's prospects aren't as bad as some of its peers'. The firm's chips are primarily used at the edge of telecom networks, where carriers may be more apt to spend, given the subscriber growth in data services like DSL. This is in contrast to companies like Applied Micro Circuits, which are more dependent on spending on long-haul optical networks, where more overspending took place. PMC also targets the wireless infrastructure and corporate networking markets, where its prospects don't seem quite as bad.

But if PMC's sales mix shifts away from telecom, margins will suffer. Products designed for wireline infrastructure tend to have long, stable product cycles and generate exceptional margins. Illustrating this, the firm's gross margins hovered around 70% during the boom, which is outstanding for a chipmaker. But products sold outside the telecom market will have shorter product cycles and probably generate lower margins. Gross margins have already shown weakness, trending down to around 60% in recent quarters.

Management recognizes the dire demand outlook and has set a return to profitability as a top priority. Research and development and overhead costs have been trending down in recent quarters in absolute terms and as a percentage of sales. An outsourced manufacturing business model also allows PMC to avoid the big capital requirements and fixed depreciation costs of running a traditional chip business. The firm's modest cash burn (just a few million per quarter) and healthy balance sheet are a big plus. Still, PMC says it needs $75 million in quarterly sales to break even, but sales were only $59 million in the third quarter. With no hint of demand improving, we see no reason for investors to rush into the stock. We'd need a wide margin of safety before recommending PMC--at least 50% below our fair value estimate.

PNC Financial Services Group PNC

	Rating	Risk	Moat Size	Fair Value	Last Close	Yield %
	★★★	Med.	Narrow	$50.00	$41.90	4.6

Company Profile

PNC Financial Services Group is the holding company for subsidiaries that operate more than 700 banking offices in Pennsylvania, Delaware, Indiana, Kentucky, New Jersey, and Ohio. The banks provide deposit and computer banking services and also make real-estate, business, foreign, and consumer loans. Its nonbank subsidiaries provide brokerage, leasing, securities underwriting, and international banking services. The company's BlackRock subsidiary offers investment management services. The firm sold its residential mortgage operations to Washington Mutual in January 2001.

Management

Overseeing PNC's transformation is James Rohr, who has been with the firm since 1972. He became president in 1992. After being chief operating officer from 1998 to May 2000, he was named CEO, and became chairman a year later.

Strategy

This Pittsburgh-based company is transforming itself into a diversified financial services firm by adding asset-management and investment advisory capacity through Blackrock and Hilliard Lyons, respectively. Also, PNC is now a top mutual fund record-keeper through its acquisition of First Data Investor Services Group.

One PNC Plaza
Pittsburgh, PA 15265
www.pnc.com

Morningstar Grades

Growth [D]	1998	1999	2000	2001
Revenue %	1.8	39.5	8.4	-12.4
Earnings/Share %	9.8	15.3	3.9	-70.8
Book Value/Share %	16.2	-0.1	14.9	-13.2
Dividends/Share %	5.3	6.3	8.9	4.9

PNC's five-year revenue growth rate is well below the industry average. The company has focused on building scale in businesses where it can earn an attractive return, which has hurt revenue but will benefit shareholders in the long run.

Profitability [B-]	1999	2000	2001	TTM
Return on Assets %	1.8	1.8	0.5	0.7
Oper Cash Flow $Mil	1,772	3,048	1,266	—
- Cap Spending $Mil	—	—	—	—
= Free Cash Flow $Mil	—	—	—	—

Return on assets has greatly improved over the past five years as the company has expanded its asset-management and private banking businesses. This trend should continue as the firm keeps growing in these areas.

Financial Health [A]	1999	2000	2001	09-02
Long-term Debt $Mil	—	—	—	—
Total Equity $Mil	5,939	6,649	5,822	6,717
Debt/Equity Ratio	—	—	—	—

PNC's fee-based businesses aren't as balance-sheet-intensive as the lending business, so financial leverage has shrunk in recent years as the firm has focused on building its nonlending operations.

Industry	Investment Style	Stock Type	Sector
Super Regional Banks	▦ Large Value	⚡ High Yield	🅢 Financial Services

Competition	Market Cap $Mil	Debt/ Equity	12 Mo Trailing Sales $Mil	Price/Cash Flow	Return On Assets%	Total Return% 1 Yr	3 Yr
PNC Financial Services Group	11,900	—	6,095	—	0.7	-22.5	4.5
Fifth Third Bancorp	33,873	—	6,272	—	2.1	-3.4	11.1
Mellon Financial	11,252	—	4,350	—	3.8	-29.5	-2.6

Price Volatility

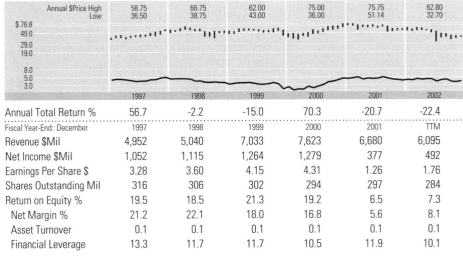

	1997	1998	1999	2000	2001	2002
Annual $Price High	58.75	66.75	62.00	75.00	75.75	62.80
Low	36.50	38.75	43.00	36.00	51.14	32.70
Annual Total Return %	56.7	-2.2	-15.0	70.3	-20.7	-22.4

Fiscal Year-End: December	1997	1998	1999	2000	2001	TTM
Revenue $Mil	4,952	5,040	7,033	7,623	6,680	6,095
Net Income $Mil	1,052	1,115	1,264	1,279	377	492
Earnings Per Share $	3.28	3.60	4.15	4.31	1.26	1.76
Shares Outstanding Mil	316	306	302	294	297	284
Return on Equity %	19.5	18.5	21.3	19.2	6.5	7.3
Net Margin %	21.2	22.1	18.0	16.8	5.6	8.1
Asset Turnover	0.1	0.1	0.1	0.1	0.1	0.1
Financial Leverage	13.3	11.7	11.7	10.5	11.9	10.1

Valuation Ratios	Stock	Rel to Industry	Rel to S&P 500
Price/Earnings	23.8	1.7	1.0
Price/Book	1.8	0.9	0.6
Price/Sales	2.0	0.9	1.0
Price/Cash Flow	—	—	—

Major Fund Holders	% of Fund Assets
Stratton Growth	4.70
Evergreen Capital Growth A	4.66
PBHG Large Cap Value PBHG	4.44
American Independence Stock Inst Svc	3.85

Morningstar's Take By Richard McCaffery, 12-16-2002 Stock Price as of Analysis: $42.18

PNC has made progress in transitioning to a higher-margin, fee-based revenue stream, and its leaner asset base has helped improve capital productivity. We think the company has done a good job looking for ways to add value. Still, given the operational and regulatory issues, we'd look for a wider margin of safety to our fair value estimate of $50 per share.

Since 1998, PNC has been restructuring the business away from lending toward more fee business. Just about every bank wants more fee income because it is higher margin and less capital intensive. The transition has been working, and fee income is expected to account for almost 60% of revenue this year, up from 44% in 1998.

Management has stressed the importance of expanding the balance sheet only when it's adding value to the business, not just feeding accounting profits. This is why it exited value-destroying businesses like credit cards where it doesn't have the skill or scale to earn a decent return. PNC has also made progress slimming down its institutional lending business, which proved a problem in 2001 as charge-offs soared. When it's functioning well, we think PNC is capable of yielding strong profits.

Recent challenges, however, have shaken

investors' confidence. The company mishandled the treatment of bad loans it was trying to scrub from its balance sheet, which led to a restatement of 2001 earnings. An accounting error discovered shortly after added to negative perceptions, and the roof came crashing in with the regulatory agreement last summer.

PNC is working things out with regulators, and is very close to compliance with the terms spelled out in last summer's regulatory agreement. The issues surrounding the company's problems are detailed in our previous analysis. We think the company has gone a long way toward fixing the problems that led to an earnings restatement and trouble with regulators, but we regard the operational problems that had to be addressed, which reached across the entire company, as very serious. It remains to be seen how well the company will execute under a new operational regime.

We believe PNC can move forward from here, but we wouldn't be excited about the shares unless they traded at a 40% discount to our fair value estimate.

MORNINGSTAR® Stocks 500

Procter & Gamble PG

	Rating	Risk	Moat Size	Fair Value	Last Close	Yield %
	★★★	Med.	Wide	$75.00	$85.94	1.8

Company Profile

Procter & Gamble is the world's largest consumer products company, and its stable of brands is among the most famous. While it has over 250 brands worldwide, there are 12 brands that each generate over $1 billion in annual sales and account for 50% of total sales. They include Bounty paper towels and Charmin toilet paper; Tide laundry detergent; Pantene shampoo; Iams pet food; Olay and Cover Girl cosmetics; Folgers coffee and Pringles potato chips. Almost 50% of total sales come from abroad.

Management

A.G. Lafley headed P&G's beauty-care business before replacing Durk Jager as CEO in June 2000. It's clear now that Lafley's appointment signaled P&G's strategic direction toward beauty care.

Strategy

Procter & Gamble aims to boost profit and sales growth by focusing marketing resources on core premium-price brands. Margins should widen amid 18,500 job cuts and greater global procurement after P&G reorganized its business according to product lines. It is also beefing up its more profitable and higher-growth beauty-care and drug businesses.

One Procter & Gamble Plaza   www.pg.com
Cincinnati, OH 45202

Morningstar Grades

Growth [B]	1999	2000	2001	2002
Revenue %	2.6	4.8	-1.8	2.5
Earnings/Share %	1.2	-4.6	-16.2	49.3
Book Value/Share %	0.4	4.4	0.2	15.8
Dividends/Share %	12.9	12.3	9.4	8.6

The move into the beauty-care and baby markets should help P&G continue to reach its modest sales growth targets of 4%-6%.

Profitability [A]	2000	2001	2002	TTM
Return on Assets %	10.0	8.1	10.4	11.0
Oper Cash Flow $Mil	4,675	5,804	7,742	8,423
- Cap Spending $Mil	3,018	2,486	1,679	1,608
= Free Cash Flow $Mil	1,657	3,318	6,063	6,815

P&G is an exceptionally profitable enterprise with consistently above-average returns on equity, in the mid-20s.

Financial Health [A]	2000	2001	2002	09-02
Long-term Debt $Mil	9,012	9,792	11,201	11,263
Total Equity $Mil	10,550	10,309	12,072	12,626
Debt/Equity Ratio	0.9	1.0	0.9	0.9

P&G has $11 billion in debt. However, its stable operating earnings can easily handle an interest coverage ratio (EBIT/interest expense) of 11.

Industry	Investment Style	Stock Type	Sector
Household & Personal Products	▥ Large Core	→ Slow Growth	⌂ Consumer Goods

Competition	Market Cap $Mil	Debt/ Equity	12 Mo Trailing Sales $Mil	Price/Cash Flow	Return On Assets%	Total Return% 1 Yr	3 Yr
Procter & Gamble	111,662	0.9	41,268	13.3	11.0	11.3	-4.5
Unilever NV ADR	35,272	—	46,553	—	—	—	—
Colgate-Palmolive	28,221	6.1	9,546	16.1	17.6	-8.0	-3.6

Price Volatility

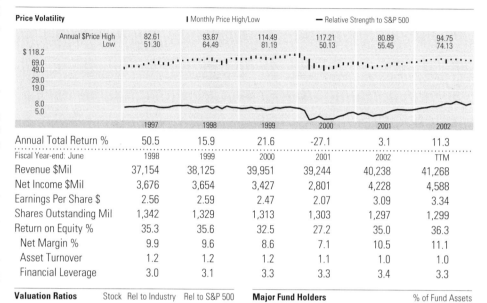

		1997	1998	1999	2000	2001	2002
Annual $Price High / Low		82.61 / 51.30	93.87 / 64.49	114.49 / 81.19	117.21 / 50.13	80.89 / 55.45	94.75 / 74.13
Annual Total Return %		50.5	15.9	21.6	-27.1	3.1	11.3

Fiscal Year-end: June	1998	1999	2000	2001	2002	TTM
Revenue $Mil	37,154	38,125	39,951	39,244	40,238	41,268
Net Income $Mil	3,676	3,654	3,427	2,801	4,228	4,588
Earnings Per Share $	2.56	2.59	2.47	2.07	3.09	3.34
Shares Outstanding Mil	1,342	1,329	1,313	1,303	1,297	1,299
Return on Equity %	35.3	35.6	32.5	27.2	35.0	36.3
Net Margin %	9.9	9.6	8.6	7.1	10.5	11.1
Asset Turnover	1.2	1.2	1.2	1.1	1.0	1.0
Financial Leverage	3.0	3.1	3.3	3.3	3.4	3.3

Valuation Ratios	Stock	Rel to Industry	Rel to S&P 500
Price/Earnings	25.7	1.0	1.1
Price/Book	8.8	1.0	2.8
Price/Sales	2.7	1.0	1.3
Price/Cash Flow	13.3	1.0	1.0

Major Fund Holders	% of Fund Assets
Rydex Consumer Products Inv	13.02
Lake Forest Core Equity	9.13
TD Waterhouse Dow 30	8.07
Orchard DJIA Index	7.98

Morningstar's Take By Carl Sibilski, 11-15-2002 Stock Price as of Analysis: $87.27

Procter & Gamble has emerged from its latest restructuring more efficient; we'd need just a 10% discount to our fair value estimate to buy into this wide-moat firm.

In our opinion, P&G is on track to achieve its modest long-term sales growth target of 4%-6% per year. The company is taking the right steps to position itself in growing markets like beauty care and baby products, and is finding ways to innovate and improve current products. Last year's purchase of Clairol was the start of a move into hair care and cosmetics, which now represent 20% of total sales. Globally these markets are growing 4% annually. Moreover, it's easier to be rewarded in the beauty-care business because minor product innovations often are all it takes to justify higher prices.

That higher pricing leverage results in better gross margins, which should help make up for the added marketing expenses involved with selling beauty-care products. Thanks to restructuring efforts and personnel outsourcing, we think gross margins in 2003 will improve to nearly 50%, up from 43% just five years ago. However, we also think the company has exhausted most of its cost-cutting opportunities, leaving little room for improvements in the years ahead.

It wouldn't surprise us if a major acquisition were on the horizon for P&G. The firm has quietly been building up cash reserves to $4.7 billion and free cash flow continues to increase over prior-year periods. Management will have to decide how to deploy those funds. Given the stock's rich valuation, we think a share-buyback program wouldn't be the best choice. Outside of paying out a substantially higher dividend, it appears that an acquisition is the only other reasonable choice.

Also on the horizon is consolidation in the retail industry, which means that P&G will have fewer, albeit larger, customers. Wal-Mart alone now accounts for 17% of 2002 sales, up from 10% in 1997. Given Wal-Mart's reputation for having the upper hand in purchasing negotiations, it's likely that P&G's selling position could weaken.

However, we think P&G's portfolio of dominant brands and large organizational resources will offset some of the pricing pressure from big discounters. Even Wal-Mart must satisfy consumer demands and needs vendors that can handle sophisticated inventory-management systems. Still, we believe investors should wait for a more attractive price before buying the shares.

Progressive PGR

	Rating	Risk	Moat Size	Fair Value	Last Close	Yield %
	★★★★	Med.	Wide	$59.00	$49.63	0.2

Company Profile

Progressive underwrites private and commercial auto insurance for 8 million customers and is the fourth-largest auto insurer in the United States. The company markets its policies through 30,000 independent insurance agencies in the United States and Canada and directly through the phone and Internet. Direct-marketed policies in force represented 31% and agent-marketed policies in force represented 69% of total in-force policies as of March 31, 2002.

Management

Chairman Peter Lewis transformed the company from a regional player to the country's fourth-largest auto insurer since he took the reins in 1965. Company veteran Glenn Renwick became CEO in 2001 and appears committed to the firm's principles.

Strategy

Progressive, the fourth-largest auto insurer, wants to surpass number-two Allstate and number-one State Farm by 2010. In addition to offering low-cost auto policies, Progressive plans to improve customer service by rapidly responding to claims. In addition, the company has implemented a profit-sharing plan and a decentralized management structure.

6300 Wilson Mills Road   www.progressive.com
Mayfield Village, OH 44143

Morningstar Grades

Growth [A]	1998	1999	2000	2001
Revenue %	14.8	15.7	10.6	10.6
Earnings/Share %	15.1	-35.2	-84.3	EUB
Book Value/Share %	20.7	7.9	4.5	236.5
Dividends/Share %	4.3	4.1	3.7	3.6

Solid customer service and a national advertising campaign have helped Progressive's three-year revenue growth beat the industry average. Net written premiums, an indicator of future growth, should continue to outpace the industry average handily.

Profitability [A]	1999	2000	2001	TTM
Return on Assets %	3.0	.0.5	3.7	5.0
Oper Cash Flow $Mil	795	822	1,235	—
- Cap Spending $Mil	148	130	75	—
= Free Cash Flow $Mil	—	—	—	—

Although the firm scores well here, its aggressive growth actually hampers current profitability, as new customers are less profitable than seasoned insurance policies. Returns on equity should improve once the portfolio matures.

Financial Health [A]	1999	2000	2001	09-02
Long-term Debt $Mil	—	—	—	—
Total Equity $Mil	2,753	2,870	3,251	3,538
Debt/Equity Ratio	—	—	—	—

Progressive uses debt moderately and has ample cash flows to service its needs. In addition, the firm regularly posts a solid underwriting profit, in contrast to its peers.

Industry	Investment Style	Stock Type	Sector
Insurance (Property)	⊞ Large Value	↗ Classic Growth	$ Financial Services

Competition	Market Cap $Mil	Debt/ Equity	12 Mo Trailing Sales $Mil	Price/Cash Flow	Return On Assets%	Total Return% 1 Yr	3 Yr
Progressive	10,804	—	8,738	—	5.0	-0.1	30.1
American International Gr	150,907	—	66,823	—	1.4	-26.9	-4.0
Berkshire Hathaway B	111,526	—	39,133	—	1.9	-4.0	12.5

Price Volatility

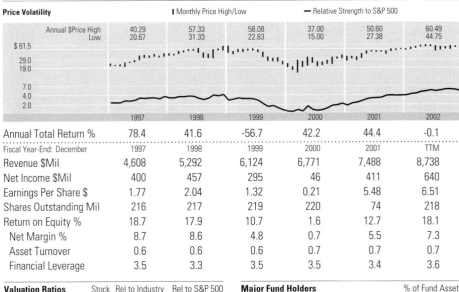

    | Monthly Price High/Low   — Relative Strength to S&P 500

Annual $Price High Low	40.29 20.67	57.33 31.33	58.08 22.83	37.00 15.00	50.60 27.38	60.49 44.75
	1997	1998	1999	2000	2001	2002
Annual Total Return %	78.4	41.6	-56.7	42.2	44.4	-0.1

Fiscal Year-End: December	1997	1998	1999	2000	2001	TTM
Revenue $Mil	4,608	5,292	6,124	6,771	7,488	8,738
Net Income $Mil	400	457	295	46	411	640
Earnings Per Share $	1.77	2.04	1.32	0.21	5.48	6.51
Shares Outstanding Mil	216	217	219	220	74	218
Return on Equity %	18.7	17.9	10.7	1.6	12.7	18.1
Net Margin %	8.7	8.6	4.8	0.7	5.5	7.3
Asset Turnover	0.6	0.6	0.6	0.7	0.7	0.7
Financial Leverage	3.5	3.3	3.5	3.5	3.4	3.6

Valuation Ratios	Stock	Rel to Industry	Rel to S&P 500
Price/Earnings	7.6	0.4	0.3
Price/Book	3.1	1.6	1.0
Price/Sales	1.2	0.5	0.6
Price/Cash Flow	—	—	—

Major Fund Holders	% of Fund Assets
TCW Galileo Select Equities I	11.77
Enterprise Equity B	11.11
Sequoia	10.08
AssetMark Large Cap Growth	6.27

Morningstar's Take By Aaron Westrate, 12-04-2002 Stock Price as of Analysis: $54.36

We're raising our assessment of Progressive's business value to account for extraordinary growth in net written premiums and higher-than-expected profitability in recent quarters. We'd require a 20% discount to our new $59 fair value estimate before buying the stock.

Over the past 10 years, Progressive's low cost structure, underwriting discipline, and flexible distribution approach have yielded outstanding economics. Progressive has generated 20% compound annual growth in net written premiums compared with the auto insurance industry average of 4%. Over that same period, it generated an average combined ratio in the mid-90s, meaning that, unlike the rest of the industry, it earned an underwriting profit.

The firm has long partnered with an independent agent network that in 2001 accounted for 64% of total net written premiums. Since the early 1990s, Progressive has simultaneously developed a very successful direct-marketing strategy. The firm was already one of the most efficient auto insurers before it began direct marketing, and the low variable costs of the direct channel will lower its cost structure still further. From 1999 to 2001, as net premiums written through the direct channel doubled, Progressive's

expense ratio (underwriting expenses divided by net written premiums) improved to 25.9% from 38.5%.

Geico, another low-cost auto insurer that uses direct channels exclusively, posted an average expense ratio of 18% between 1999 and 2001. While Progressive's overall expense ratio won't approach Geico's anytime soon because of its higher-cost independent agent network, we still think the firm can drive down its overall expense ratio to about 20% by 2006.

We expect Progressive's cost advantage to enable the firm to grow faster than the mature auto insurance market. Many competitors who had depended on strong investment returns to offset underwriting losses are now following Progressive's lead in hiking rates after many suffered painful investment losses. The incumbent carrier retains the advantage only until clients solicit bids (which occurs with increasing frequency during industrywide rate hikes), in which the low-cost provider will often gain the upper hand. Progressive's premium volume should rise as customers, disgruntled by rate increases, shop around.

Progressive's advantages make the stock a compelling pick if it becomes available at $47 or below.

 MORNINGSTAR® Stocks 500

Protein Design Labs PDLI

	Rating	Risk	Moat Size	Fair Value	Last Close	Yield %
	★★★	High	None	$10.00	$8.50	0.0

Company Profile

Protein Design Labs develops antibody-based pharmaceuticals. It designs artificial antibodies that bind to specific receptors on harmful cells to block the spread of disease or deliver toxins. The company is preclinically and clinically testing compounds that may treat autoimmune diseases, infectious diseases, and cancer. It licenses its products and collaborates on drug development with other biotech and pharmaceutical companies such as Genentech, MedImmune, and Wyeth.

Management

In a move to strengthen PDL's commercialization efforts, Laurence Korn, who had run the company since 1987, resigned in May 2002. Korn remains on the board; experienced biotech exec Mark McDade has taken the helm as CEO and director.

Strategy

Protein Design Labs is one of a handful of companies fighting to dominate the monoclonal antibody market. PDL research focuses on altering ("humanizing") mouse antibodies to combat illnesses like cancer and inflammatory diseases. The firm licenses its SMART (antibody humanization) technology to other companies and also uses it in-house to develop its own line of antibody therapies.

34801 Campus Drive   www.pdl.com
Fremont, CA 94555

Morningstar Grades

Growth [B]	1998	1999	2000	2001
Revenue %	52.2	16.0	76.4	26.1
Earnings/Share %	NMF	NMF	NMF	200.0
Book Value/Share %	-6.6	0.4	269.9	-23.3
Dividends/Share %	NMF	NMF	NMF	NMF

Revenue growth has ground to a halt as products from which PDL receives royalties become more mature and licensing revenue slows. Until its own products are on the market, the firm won't see blockbuster sales growth.

Profitability [B-]	1999	2000	2001	TTM
Return on Assets %	-5.7	0.1	0.4	-1.7
Oper Cash Flow $Mil	-11	7	3	1
- Cap Spending $Mil	19	3	9	28
= Free Cash Flow $Mil	-30	3	-6	-28

Interest income on PDL's huge cash stake pushed the firm to profitability in 2001. Operating income is still in the red, however, and will remain there over the next several years as the company spends more on R&D to develop its own products.

Financial Health [B]	1999	2000	2001	09-02
Long-term Debt $Mil	10	159	159	159
Total Equity $Mil	165	534	558	553
Debt/Equity Ratio	0.1	0.3	0.3	0.3

PDL had more than $5 per share in net cash (cash and investments minus debt) as of September 30, 2002. This leaves plenty of cash to fund operations for several years--and there might even be enough to in-license a late-stage molecule.

Industry	Investment Style	Stock Type	Sector
Biotechnology	Small Growth	Spec. Growth	Healthcare

Competition

	Market Cap $Mil	Debt/ Equity	12 Mo Trailing Sales $Mil	Price/Cash Flow	Return On Assets%	Total Return% 1 Yr	3 Yr
Protein Design Labs	757	0.3	78	EUB	-1.7	-74.2	-19.4
Abgenix	642	—	54	—	—	—	—
Medarex	298	—	47	—	—	—	—

Price Volatility

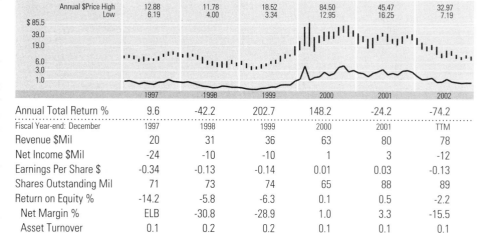

I Monthly Price High/Low		— Relative Strength to S&P 500

Annual $Price High / Low	12.88 / 6.19	11.78 / 4.00	18.52 / 3.34	84.50 / 12.95	45.47 / 16.25	32.97 / 7.19

	1997	1998	1999	2000	2001	2002
Annual Total Return %	9.6	-42.2	202.7	148.2	-24.2	-74.2

Fiscal Year-end: December	1997	1998	1999	2000	2001	TTM
Revenue $Mil	20	31	36	63	80	78
Net Income $Mil	-24	-10	-10	1	3	-12
Earnings Per Share $	-0.34	-0.13	-0.14	0.01	0.03	-0.13
Shares Outstanding Mil	71	73	74	65	88	89
Return on Equity %	-14.2	-5.8	-6.3	0.1	0.5	-2.2
Net Margin %	ELB	-30.8	-28.9	1.0	3.3	-15.5
Asset Turnover	0.1	0.2	0.2	0.1	0.1	0.1
Financial Leverage	1.0	1.1	1.1	1.3	1.3	1.3

Valuation Ratios	Stock	Rel to Industry	Rel to S&P 500
Price/Earnings	NMF	—	—
Price/Book	1.4	0.4	0.4
Price/Sales	9.7	0.8	4.8
Price/Cash Flow	EUB	—	—

Major Fund Holders	% of Fund Assets
GenomicsFund	3.85
Scudder Global Biotechnology A	3.15
Amerindo Health & Biotechnology A	3.11
Orbitex Growth A	2.34

Morningstar's Take By Jill Kiersky, 11-22-2002 Stock Price as of Analysis: $9.45

Protein Design Labs has been a strong contender, but the company is struggling to stay in the fight. We'd want a big margin of safety before holding PDL's risks.

Since 1986, PDL has worked hard to become a leader in developing technology to create humanized monoclonal antibodies (MAbs). The company has licensed its technology to 15 pharmaceutical and biotech companies that are working on nearly 40 possible MAb therapies. To date, its partners have developed four products with total sales near $1 billion--half the MAb market.

But PDL receives only a small stream of royalty revenue (we estimate 3%-5%) on these therapies because it gave up marketing rights early on in exchange for up-front payments. Thus, even if PDL's licensed technologies capture half the expected $5.2 billion MAb market by 2004, that amounts to only around $100 million in total revenue.

PDL will need its own successful therapies if it plans to become a drug powerhouse. But the company has not proved its ability in this arena yet. In late 2001, PDL announced that non-Hodgkin's lymphoma candidate Remitogen did not meet testing endpoints. In mid-2002, the company decided to discontinue studying Zenapax (currently on the

market for kidney transplants) for psoriasis. And PDL's most promising late-stage candidate, cancer drug Zamyl, is showing mixed results. These disappointments lead us to question whether PDL has the capabilities to develop its own therapies.

In a first step to make room for the expertise needed to bring drugs to market, 15-year PDL veteran Larry Korn stepped down from the head post in May 2002. The ability to commercialize products is a necessity, and we applaud the company for making such a difficult decision in light of Korn's past successes.

Our biggest concern about PDL lies with its core technology. PDL develops antibodies using an older technique that is thought to be less efficient than the technology used by newer competitors like Medarex and Abgenix. While there's no proof that PDL's technology will cease to provide viable antibodies, we still require a significant discount to fair value that takes into account this possibility, as well as the odds that the firm's drugs simply might not succeed.

Providian Financial PVN

	Rating	Risk	Moat Size	Fair Value	Last Close	Yield %
	★★★	High	None	$9.00	$6.49	0.0

Company Profile

Providian Financial issues Visas and MasterCards. The firm, which serves more than 17 million consumers, markets its cards primarily in the United States through direct mail, telemarketing, and the mass media. The firm also has operations in the United Kingdom and Argentina. In addition, Providian has a small home-equity loan business.

Industry	Investment Style	Stock Type	Sector
Finance	Mid Value	▪ Spec. Growth	$ Financial Services

Competition	Market Cap $Mil	Debt/ Equity	12 Mo Trailing Sales $Mil	Price/Cash Flow	Return On Assets%	Total Return% 1 Yr	3 Yr
Providian Financial	1,877	—	4,271	—	-1.6	82.8	-45.4
Citigroup	177,948	—	106,096	—	1.6	-24.2	1.1
Bank One	42,636	—	22,444	—	1.1	-4.4	9.4

Price Volatility

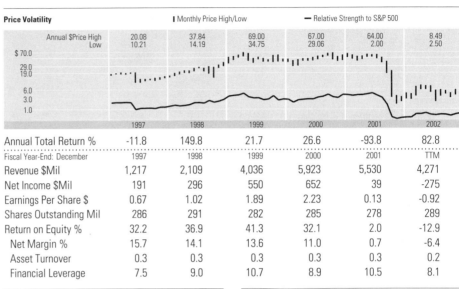

		1997	1998	1999	2000	2001	TTM
Annual Total Return %		-11.8	149.8	21.7	26.6	-93.8	82.8
Fiscal Year-End: December		1997	1998	1999	2000	2001	TTM
Revenue $Mil		1,217	2,109	4,036	5,923	5,530	4,271
Net Income $Mil		191	296	550	652	39	-275
Earnings Per Share $		0.67	1.02	1.89	2.23	0.13	-0.92
Shares Outstanding Mil		286	291	282	285	278	289
Return on Equity %		32.2	36.9	41.3	32.1	2.0	-12.9
Net Margin %		15.7	14.1	13.6	11.0	0.7	-6.4
Asset Turnover		0.3	0.3	0.3	0.3	0.3	0.2
Financial Leverage		7.5	9.0	10.7	8.9	10.5	8.1

Management

CEO Joe Saunders, hired last fall from FleetBoston, cleaned house. He overhauled the management team, structured a plan with regulators to keep the company alive, and exited the lowest trenches of the subprime industry.

Strategy

The firm's strategy of targeting subprime borrowers and charging them higher rates failed as bad debts spiraled out of control. Now, Providian will be more selective, targeting less-risky customers and growing much more slowly.

201 Mission Street
San Francisco, CA 94105 www.providian.com

Valuation Ratios	Stock	Rel to Industry	Rel to S&P 500
Price/Earnings	NMF	—	—
Price/Book	0.9	0.3	0.3
Price/Sales	0.4	0.2	0.2
Price/Cash Flow	—	—	—

Major Fund Holders	% of Fund Assets
Legg Mason Opportunity Prim	3.92
Legg Mason Special Investment Prim	3.46
Masters' Select Value	2.29
GE Small-Cap Value Equity B	1.99

Morningstar Grades

Growth [A-]	1998	1999	2000	2001
Revenue %	73.3	91.4	46.8	-6.6
Earnings/Share %	52.2	85.3	18.0	-94.2
Book Value/Share %	32.7	65.6	51.9	-8.3
Dividends/Share %	124.9	33.2	5.0	-14.3

Once a highflier, Providian couldn't sustain its growth rate as bad debts mounted last year. The sale of international and high-risk assets should clear a path for controlled growth.

Profitability [B]	1999	2000	2001	TTM
Return on Assets %	3.8	3.6	0.2	-1.6
Oper Cash Flow $Mil	1,783	2,462	1,458	—
- Cap Spending $Mil	91	91	77	—
= Free Cash Flow $Mil	—	—	—	—

Bad debts crushed returns on assets last year. As the company rebuilds, however, it believes it can earn returns in the 1%-1.5% range.

Financial Health [A+]	1999	2000	2001	09-02
Long-term Debt $Mil	—	—	—	—
Total Equity $Mil	1,332	2,032	1,908	2,131
Debt/Equity Ratio	—	—	—	—

Providian is regaining its footing as it exits the riskiest segments of the subprime industry. Charge-offs and delinquencies remain high, but the company is well reserved and has strong capital ratios.

Morningstar's Take By Richard McCaffery, 12-12-2002 Stock Price as of Analysis: $6.19

Providian is rising from the ashes as CEO Joseph Saunders reinvents the company. We think it will survive and that it's worth about $9. It's a highly risky stock with no economic moat, however, so investors should look for a wide margin of safety. The shares look attractive under $4.

Providian has to clear two hurdles to get to our $9 estimate. First, it must survive the crisis that forced a massive overhaul of its management team and loan portfolio. We've detailed these changes in our previous analyses.

Second, Saunders must forge a working business model, one that can compete against rivals with clear competitive advantages. For example, Providian will compete most directly with Capital One, which knows how to find profitable accounts and enjoys a strong cost advantage. That's a lot for Providian to overcome.

Still, the team working the turnaround is pretty much the same one that fixed Advanta's portfolio after the FleetBoston deal in 1998. Many of the challenges, which involved strengthening credit quality and repricing risk, are similar to what the team faces now, though not as extreme. So far, management has worked quickly to better match the products it offers customers with credit behavior.

These changes started paying off in the third quarter when net interest margins came in stronger than expected.

We also think Providian has decent in-house analytical skills that will help it pursue customers in the subprime sector. Before the company stepped off the path and revved up growth, its models worked pretty well in locating subprime customers who would actually pay their bills. We think companies that know how to price risk in the subprime market are well-positioned. As such, we hope Providian doesn't step too far away from its subprime base.

Finally, management has done a good job landing new accounts, which is critical for moving the business forward. The company expects to add two million new accounts this year. This won't offset the number lost from asset sales, attrition, and charge-offs, but the credit profile of new accounts is improved. The average credit profile of customers booked in the third quarter indicates the company is successfully attracting less risky borrowers, even in the face of stiff competition from established players.

Despite this progress, the recent runup in price has made the shares less attractive.

MORNINGSTAR® Stocks 500

Prudential Financial PRU

	Rating	Risk	Moat Size	Fair Value	Last Close	Yield %
	★★	Med.	None	$32.00	$31.74	1.3

Company Profile

Prudential provides financial services like asset management, life insurance, property-casualty insurance, and securities brokerage to more than 15 million individual and institutional customers in the United States and more than 30 foreign countries. Prudential had total assets under management of $590 billion and 20,800 sales representatives in its distribution network.

Management

Art Ryan became chairman and CEO in December 1994 after 22 years at Chase Manhattan Bank. Under his watch the firm has settled litigation related to illegal sales practices and exited a number of poor-performing businesses.

Strategy

Prudential aims to cut enough costs to boost its extremely poor operating return on equity to low double digits by 2004. The firm demutualized--converted from policyholder ownership to stockholder ownership--in December 2001, so now it can use its public ownership structure to add stock incentive compensation and access the capital markets to fund expansion.

751 Broad St.   www.prudential.com
Newark, NJ 07102

Morningstar Grades

Growth [D+]	1998	1999	2000	2001
Revenue %	2.1	-1.7	-0.2	2.5
Earnings/Share %	NMF	NMF	NMF	NMF
Book Value/Share %	—	—	—	—
Dividends/Share %	NMF	NMF	NMF	NMF

Prudential posted acquisition-aided 10% revenue growth in 2001 and 8% in the first half of 2002 compared with a year ago. It remains to be seen if the firm can generate top-line growth while cutting costs.

Profitability [F]	1999	2000	2001	TTM
Return on Assets %	0.3	0.1	-0.1	0.0
Oper Cash Flow $Mil	562	7,865	76	—
- Cap Spending $Mil	—	—	—	—
= Free Cash Flow $Mil	—	—	—	—

Over the trailing 12 months, operating return on equity, adjusted for demutualization costs, was a paltry 7%, far below the low-teen industry average. The firm hopes that cost cuts will enable it to match the industry average ROE by 2004.

Financial Health [B]	1999	2000	2001	09-02
Long-term Debt $Mil	—	—	—	—
Total Equity $Mil	19,291	20,608	20,453	21,841
Debt/Equity Ratio	—	—	—	—

Prudential is financially solid, with average financial leverage and a massive investment portfolio of $178 billion. To put that amount in perspective, Prudential's cost for the terrorist attacks after taxes and reinsurance was $30 million.

Industry	Investment Style	Stock Type	Sector
Insurance (Life)	⊞ Large Core	→ Slow Growth	$ Financial Services

Competition

	Market Cap $Mil	Debt/ Equity	12 Mo Trailing Sales $Mil	Price/Cash Flow	Return On Assets%	Total Return% 1 Yr	3 Yr
Prudential Financial	18,553	—	26,992	—	0.0	-3.1	—
American International Gr	150,907	—	66,823	—	1.4	-26.9	-4.0
AXA ADR	23,329	—	65,303	—	—	—	—

Price Volatility

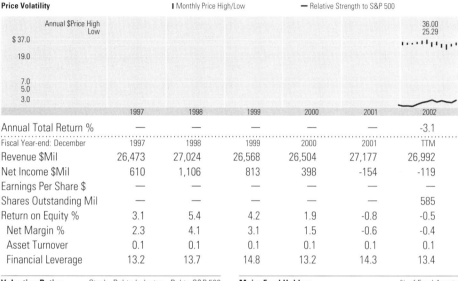

| I Monthly Price High/Low | — Relative Strength to S&P 500 |

	1997	1998	1999	2000	2001	2002
Annual Total Return %	—	—	—	—	—	-3.1

Fiscal Year-end: December	1997	1998	1999	2000	2001	TTM
Revenue $Mil	26,473	27,024	26,568	26,504	27,177	26,992
Net Income $Mil	610	1,106	813	398	-154	-119
Earnings Per Share $	—	—	—	—	—	—
Shares Outstanding Mil	—	—	—	—	—	585
Return on Equity %	3.1	5.4	4.2	1.9	-0.8	-0.5
Net Margin %	2.3	4.1	3.1	1.5	-0.6	-0.4
Asset Turnover	0.1	0.1	0.1	0.1	0.1	0.1
Financial Leverage	13.2	13.7	14.8	13.2	14.3	13.4

Valuation Ratios	Stock	Rel to Industry	Rel to S&P 500
Price/Earnings	—	—	—
Price/Book	0.8	0.8	0.3
Price/Sales	0.7	1.0	0.3
Price/Cash Flow	—	—	—

Major Fund Holders	% of Fund Assets
Burnham Financial Services A	4.29
Gartmore Global Financial B	3.47
Evergreen Capital Growth A	3.25
Members Growth & Income A	3.12

Morningstar's Take By Aaron Westrate, 10-25-2002 Stock Price as of Analysis: $30.01

Prudential is likely to face a lot of head wind on the turnaround trail, and the current stock price doesn't offer an adequate margin of safety to our fair value estimate of $32.

Before its demutualization in December 2001, Prudential was run primarily for the benefit of its policyholders, so the overriding concern was preserving financial strength, not profitability. Now that the firm is in public hands, it must also focus on using its resources efficiently. As a result, Prudential's overriding goal is to boost its poor operating return on equity from 7% to the industry average of 11%-12%.

One way Prudential aims to boost ROE is by increasing the productivity of its agents. The minimum commission bar has more than doubled to $23,500 since 1997, enabling the firm to prune unproductive career agents from 10,100 in 1997 to 4,551 at the end of June 2002. In addition, career agents are now selling to the affluent market, rather than the middle market Prudential has targeted in the past. This is hardly a novel strategy, however, and the big risk here is fierce competition.

Prudential's goal of consistent and adequate returns makes it likely that the firm will sell its sporadic-performing property-casualty operations.

We also believe the brokerage and research operation may be on the block: Near the end of 2001, Prudential indicated that it would give Prudential Securities until mid-2003 to attain a 10%-12% return on equity. We are fairly optimistic that shedding these underperformers will raise ROE significantly, since the capital supporting those operations will probably be redeployed to expand Prudential's valuable international empire.

Many competitors are attempting to gain a foothold on foreign soil because of the faster growth and higher profitability. Prudential's established position overseas--it generated 40% of its 2001 pretax operating income outside the United States--gives it a competitive edge. Naturally, the firm would love to extend its lead with a few select acquisitions.

That such a significant percentage of Prudential's profits come from international operations that are generating near 20% ROE only underscores just how bad the rest of the firm is performing, if overall returns are 7%. While there is often good money to be made in turnaround situations, we're skeptical that Prudential will be one of those cases.

Qualcomm QCOM

	Rating	Risk	Moat Size	Fair Value	Last Close	Yield %
	★	High	Wide	$24.00	$36.39	0.0

Company Profile

Qualcomm pioneered code division multiple access (CDMA) technology, a digital platform used in cellular phones, telecom equipment, and satellite base stations. As a result, Qualcomm is the world's leading designer and supplier of CDMA chipsets and system software; it licenses CDMA technology to more than 100 various device makers. The company's OmniTRACS systems provide satellite communication, position location, and location management for trucking fleets.

Management

Chairman, CEO, and founder Irwin Jacobs owns roughly 3% of the firm; the executive suite has other members of the Jacobs family. But insiders have feverishly sold shares since November, right around the time Qualcomm's stock price spiked.

Strategy

Qualcomm focuses on designing the chipsets and system software that go into CDMA products. Qualcomm also invests in companies that will spread the use of CDMA products, on which the company earns a royalty (thanks to an extensive patent portfolio).

5775 Morehouse Drive
San Diego, CA 92121-1714
www.qualcomm.com

Morningstar Grades

Growth [B]	1999	2000	2001	2002
Revenue %	17.6	-18.8	-16.2	13.4
Earnings/Share %	72.2	154.8	NMF	NMF
Book Value/Share %	179.0	56.7	-8.9	4.3
Dividends/Share %	NMF	NMF	NMF	NMF

Qualcomm was once a growth machine, but a soft wireless handset market has changed things. Sales in fiscal 2002 (ending September 30) were up 13%, only because of an abnormally strong fourth period. Management's growth forecast for 2003 of 19%-23% is probably too optimistic.

Profitability [B]	2000	2001	2002	TTM
Return on Assets %	10.3	-10.2	5.5	5.5
Oper Cash Flow $Mil	791	691	968	968
- Cap Spending $Mil	163	114	142	142
= Free Cash Flow $Mil	628	577	826	826

Qualcomm is a poster child for pro forma accounting, which hides the bad news while promoting the good. However, profit margins should steadily grow as royalty fees--roughly 90% profit--form a greater share of overall sales.

Financial Health [A+]	2000	2001	2002	09-02
Long-term Debt $Mil	0	0	94	94
Total Equity $Mil	5,468	4,812	5,392	5,392
Debt/Equity Ratio	0.0	0.0	0.0	0.0

Qualcomm's financial reporting may be laughable, but there is nothing funny about its rock-solid balance sheet. The company has $2.8 billion in cash and no debt.

Industry	Investment Style	Stock Type	Sector
Wireless Equipment	⊞ Large Growth	➡ Slow Growth	▣ Hardware

Competition	Market Cap $Mil	Debt/ Equity	12 Mo Trailing Sales $Mil	Price/Cash Flow	Return On Assets%	Total Return% 1 Yr	3 Yr
Qualcomm	28,569	0.0	3,040	29.5	5.5	-27.9	-39.2
Nokia ADR	73,432	0.0	27,814	12.6	9.9	-36.1	-28.5
Texas Instruments	25,982	0.1	8,024	12.8	0.9	-46.2	-32.5

Price Volatility

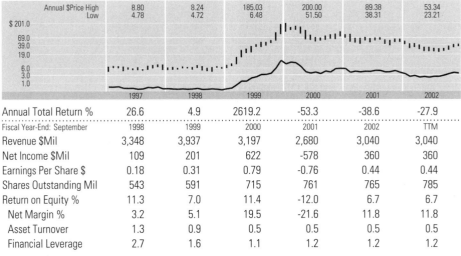

			Monthly Price High/Low		— Relative Strength to S&P 500	
Annual $Price High Low	8.80 4.78	8.24 4.72	185.03 6.48	200.00 51.50	89.38 38.31	53.34 23.21

	1997	1998	1999	2000	2001	2002
Annual Total Return %	26.6	4.9	2619.2	-53.3	-38.6	-27.9

Fiscal Year-End: September	1998	1999	2000	2001	2002	TTM
Revenue $Mil	3,348	3,937	3,197	2,680	3,040	3,040
Net Income $Mil	109	201	622	-578	360	360
Earnings Per Share $	0.18	0.31	0.79	-0.76	0.44	0.44
Shares Outstanding Mil	543	591	715	761	765	785
Return on Equity %	11.3	7.0	11.4	-12.0	6.7	6.7
Net Margin %	3.2	5.1	19.5	-21.6	11.8	11.8
Asset Turnover	1.3	0.9	0.5	0.5	0.5	0.5
Financial Leverage	2.7	1.6	1.1	1.2	1.2	1.2

Valuation Ratios	Stock	Rel to Industry	Rel to S&P 500
Price/Earnings	82.7	2.2	3.5
Price/Book	5.3	0.8	1.7
Price/Sales	9.4	3.6	4.7
Price/Cash Flow	29.5	2.3	2.2

Major Fund Holders	% of Fund Assets
Rydex Internet Inv	10.64
Ariston Convertible Securities	9.50
Wireless	7.13
Firsthand Technology Leaders	6.53

Morningstar's Take By Todd P. Bernier, 12-31-2002 Stock Price as of Analysis: $0.00

Qualcomm is a classic case of good company, lousy industry. With Qualcomm's wide economic moat, its stock would need to sell at a 20%-30% discount to our fair value estimate before we would invest.

Like Nokia, Ericsson, and Motorola, Qualcomm was once an integrated manufacturer of both wireless handsets and infrastructure equipment. But Qualcomm sold these businesses a few years ago, around the same time it spun off its fledgling wireless carrier, Leap Wireless. Qualcomm's sole focus now is on licensing the code-division multiple access, or CDMA, technology it pioneered and producing the chips that go into CDMA products.

In our view, Qualcomm's competitive advantage is its extensive trove of CDMA patents. Any handset maker licensing even one patent must pay a flat royalty rate. Like the gatekeeper on a bridge, Qualcomm collects a toll for nearly every CDMA phone sold. The same will hold true for third-generation, or 3G, wireless handsets.

The firm will benefit from the industry's migration to 3G, which comes in two flavors, Qualcomm's cdma2000 and W-CDMA. Both standards are rooted in CDMA, meaning Qualcomm will, in theory, collect the same royalty rate on every 3G handset sold. The firm has already signed licensing agreements with nearly every major manufacturer of 3G gear. This is the primary tenet of Qualcomm loyalists who equate ringing 3G cell phones with a ringing cash register.

But if Qualcomm is a proxy for 3G, it has a tough slog ahead--not because the firm is poorly positioned, but because the wireless industry is crumbling. The step from first- to second-generation technology was revolutionary, but the next step is minor. The ability to shuttle data at broadband speeds--the key benefit of 3G--will not be the industry's panacea: It is unclear whether users want (and will pay for) data-rich services. This explains why subscriber growth so far has been lukewarm. Also, debt-laden carriers lack the resources to roll out 3G. Several European wireless operators have announced plans to delay 3G implementation. Qualcomm's growth relies on the successful rollout of 3G and subsequent handset upgrades by consumers.

Despite being closely tied to a sick wireless industry, Qualcomm hasn't suffered as badly as rivals. In our view, too many stars need to align to justify the company's lofty valuation. Conservative investors should remain leery until the stock trades at a hefty discount to our fair value estimate.

MORNINGSTAR® Stocks 500

Quest Diagnostics DGX

	Rating	Risk	Moat Size	Fair Value	Last Close	Yield %
	UR	Med.	Narrow	UR	$56.90	0.0

Company Profile

Quest Diagnostics provides testing services used by the medical profession in the diagnosis, monitoring, and treatment of diseases and other medical conditions. The company's clinical laboratory testing network consists of 30 regional laboratories across the United States and an esoteric testing laboratory in California. In addition, Quest Diagnostics has 100 rapid-response laboratories and approximately 1,300 patient-testing service centers throughout the United States. Approximately 83% of the firm's revenue is derived from routine testing.

Management

Kenneth W. Freeman has been CEO since 1995 and chairman since 1996. He joined the financial department of former parent Corning in the 1970s. Corning spun off Quest as an independent company at the end of 1996.

Strategy

Quest Diagnostics became the largest national independent lab-testing company through its acquisition of SmithKline Beecham's clinical laboratory (SBCL) in 2000. The company plans to continue expanding its market share through acquisitions and shifting its product mix to higher-margin tests.

One Malcolm Avenue   www.questdiagnostics.com
Teterboro, NJ 07608

Morningstar Grades

Growth [B]

	1998	1999	2000	2001
Revenue %	-4.6	51.2	55.1	6.0
Earnings/Share %	NMF	NMF	NMF	53.7
Book Value/Share %	0.4	34.6	-13.6	25.3
Dividends/Share %	NMF	NMF	NMF	NMF

Quest's acquisition strategy has helped boost its growth rates, but organic growth is considerably slower. For the quarter ending Sept. 30, pro forma testing volume rose 5%, and revenue per test increased 2.9%.

Profitability [B]

	1999	2000	2001	TTM
Return on Assets %	-0.1	3.6	5.5	8.4
Oper Cash Flow $Mil	250	369	466	514
- Cap Spending $Mil	76	116	149	157
= Free Cash Flow $Mil	174	253	317	357

Quest is aiming for a 30% earnings growth rate in 2003, driven by merger synergies and improved efficiencies from its embrace of GE-style Six Sigma initiatives. Quest's free cash flows translate into about 9% of sales for the trailing 12 months.

Financial Health [A-]

	1999	2000	2001	09-02
Long-term Debt $Mil	1,171	761	820	797
Total Equity $Mil	862	1,031	1,336	1,678
Debt/Equity Ratio	1.4	0.7	0.6	0.5

Standard & Poor's recently upgraded Quest's debt to investment-grade. The company's debt levels are declining as a percentage of equity, and with more favorable interest rates as well as strong cash flows, debt is not a huge concern.

Industry	Investment Style	Stock Type	Sector
Diagnostics	Mid Growth	Spec. Growth	Healthcare

Competition	Market Cap $Mil	Debt/ Equity	12 Mo Trailing Sales $Mil	Price/Cash Flow	Return On Assets%	Total Return% 1 Yr	3 Yr
Quest Diagnostics	5,561	0.5	3,985	10.8	8.4	-20.7	56.1
Laboratory Corp of Americ	3,435	0.3	2,421	8.8	9.1	-42.5	38.5
Dianon Systems	589	—	182	—	—	—	—

Price Volatility | Monthly Price High/Low   — Relative Strength to S&P 500

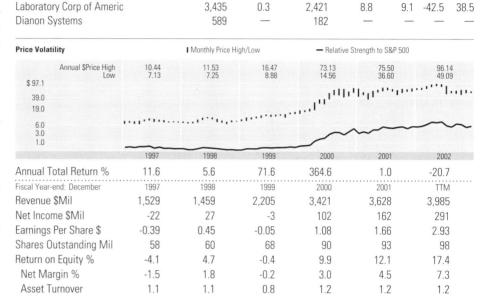

	Annual $Price High Low	10.44 7.13	11.53 7.25	16.47 8.88	73.13 14.56	75.50 36.60	96.14 49.09

	1997	1998	1999	2000	2001	2002
Annual Total Return %	11.6	5.6	71.6	364.6	1.0	-20.7

Fiscal Year-end: December	1997	1998	1999	2000	2001	TTM
Revenue $Mil	1,529	1,459	2,205	3,421	3,628	3,985
Net Income $Mil	-22	27	-3	102	162	291
Earnings Per Share $	-0.39	0.45	-0.05	1.08	1.66	2.93
Shares Outstanding Mil	58	60	68	90	93	98
Return on Equity %	-4.1	4.7	-0.4	9.9	12.1	17.4
Net Margin %	-1.5	1.8	-0.2	3.0	4.5	7.3
Asset Turnover	1.1	1.1	0.8	1.2	1.2	1.2
Financial Leverage	2.6	2.4	3.3	2.8	2.2	2.1

Valuation Ratios	Stock	Rel to Industry	Rel to S&P 500
Price/Earnings	19.4	0.9	0.8
Price/Book	3.3	1.0	1.0
Price/Sales	1.4	0.9	0.7
Price/Cash Flow	10.8	0.7	0.8

Major Fund Holders	% of Fund Assets
Super Core A	5.37
Nations Marsico Focused Eq Inv A	5.17
Marsico Focus	5.16
PBHG Large Cap 20 PBHG	4.97

Morningstar's Take By Amy C. Arnott, 12-11-2002 Stock Price as of Analysis: $59.00

Quest has plenty of opportunities to strengthen its leading position in the independent clinical lab industry, but its acquisition strategy carries considerable risk.

Quest is the top banana in the diagnostic testing industry: It boasts a leading market share in both routine clinical laboratory testing and more complex esoteric testing, including genetic testing. But because the clinical testing industry is highly fragmented, there's still share to be gained by the independent labs.

Over the past two years, Quest has been aggressive in buying smaller firms to increase its share of routine tests like blood, urine, and cervical pap tests. But this strategy of growing through acquisition will take the company only so far as the number of good acquisitions declines. We don't expect independents to grab much share from hospital counterparts that perform the same tests at the same or lower cost, driving the independent labs' margins down and eventually limiting sales growth. Rival Laboratory Corporation of America has already felt competitive pressure from some regional hospitals, and the same trends could eventually hurt Quest's business.

The opportunity lies with high-end laboratory tests, known as esoteric tests. Currently, 83% of Quest's revenue comes from routine tests. However, the market for esoteric tests like genetic testing is estimated at $1 billion and increasing 25% per year. With sophisticated equipment and highly skilled staff needed to perform these less frequent tests, independent labs have to devote more resources to this high-margin business. Quest views this market as a key area for growth, and it expanded its presence with a Feb. 2002 acquisition of American Medical Laboratories, a national provider of esoteric testing.

Even so, the company's strategy of acquiring firms and merging operations isn't fool-proof. Quest made a bid for Unilab Corporation back in April 2002, but the merger has yet to be consummated because the Federal Trade Commission raised antitrust concerns. The two companies plan to sell off some assets to address the issues raised and expect to complete the merger by January 2003.

If things don't go as planned, though, we think it could be tough for Quest to meet its aggressive goal of 30% growth in earnings per share. We'd recommend that investors hold off on the shares until some of the uncertainty is resolved.

Quiksilver ZQK

	Rating	Risk	Moat Size	Fair Value	Last Close	Yield %
	★★	High	None	$27.00	$26.66	0.0

Company Profile

Quiksilver designs and distributes activewear, primarily for young men and boys; it also makes snowboarding equipment. The company designs clothing like surfwear, swimwear, skiwear, and T-shirts, and arranges for its manufacture under brands that include Quiksilver, Quiksilver Roxy, and Que. Its Raisin subsidiary designs women's and girls' swimwear under the Raisins, Leilani, and Radio Fiji names. The company also makes snowboards, snowboard boots, and bindings. It sells its products to surf shops and specialty, company-operated, and department stores.

Management

CEO (and surfer) Robert McKnight founded Quiksilver in 1976. Management owns about 9% of the outstanding shares. Its compensation appears to be in line with that of management at other companies Quiksilver's size.

Strategy

Quiksilver has expanded its branding to different niches of the specialty retail market, including the Roxy and Hawk clothing lines. The company is aggressively expanding its retail presence by building and acquiring surf shops throughout the United States. Quiksilver hopes to gain better control over its inventory and pricing power through this retail channel.

15202 Graham Ave.   www.quiksilver.com
Huntington Beach, CA 92649

Morningstar Grades

Growth [A]	1998	1999	2000	2001
Revenue %	36.4	40.4	16.2	19.3
Earnings/Share %	36.7	39.0	20.2	-14.6
Book Value/Share %	19.1	21.2	17.5	18.3
Dividends/Share %	NMF	NMF	NMF	NMF

Sales have grown 25% annually since 1994, thanks to acquisitions and expansion into multiple product categories. Stand-alone store expansion, domestically and abroad, should greatly benefit Quiksilver's top-line growth.

Profitability [A-]	1999	2000	2001	TTM
Return on Assets %	10.2	8.9	6.7	6.1
Oper Cash Flow $Mil	5	-4	6	75
- Cap Spending $Mil	24	16	23	25
= Free Cash Flow $Mil	-19	-21	-17	50

Operating margins have remained steady at about 10% of sales, but could come under pressure if Quiksilver's owned-store expenses get out of control. Management must also carefully calculate demand to maintain healthy inventory levels.

Financial Health [D+]	1999	2000	2001	07-02
Long-term Debt $Mil	25	57	46	43
Total Equity $Mil	152	178	217	255
Debt/Equity Ratio	0.2	0.3	0.2	0.2

Operating profits cover interest expense 8 times, but as the company's retail presence expands, so will the costs associated with running stores. Quiksilver may need to issue debt or equity to fuel substantial retail growth.

Industry	Investment Style	Stock Type	Sector
Apparel Makers	Small Growth	Cyclical	Consumer Goods

Competition	Market Cap $Mil	Debt/ Equity	12 Mo Trailing Sales $Mil	Price/Cash Flow	Return On Assets%	Total Return% 1 Yr	3 Yr
Quiksilver	630	0.2	676	8.4	6.1	55.0	23.4
Nike B	11,798	0.2	10,076	11.6	6.5	-20.1	0.3
Tommy Hilfiger	629	0.3	1,887	2.0	-13.4	-49.5	-30.0

Price Volatility

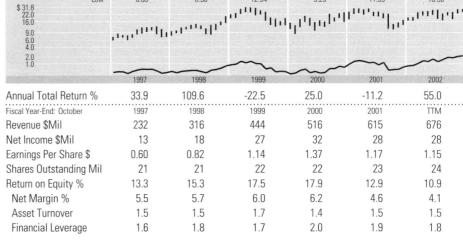

Monthly Price High/Low — Relative Strength to S&P 500

	1997	1998	1999	2000	2001	2002
Annual $Price High	13.17	20.83	30.83	24.50	29.15	28.51
Low	6.83	8.58	12.94	9.25	11.35	16.90
Annual Total Return %	33.9	109.6	-22.5	25.0	-11.2	55.0

Fiscal Year-End: October	1997	1998	1999	2000	2001	TTM
Revenue $Mil	232	316	444	516	615	676
Net Income $Mil	13	18	27	32	28	28
Earnings Per Share $	0.60	0.82	1.14	1.37	1.17	1.15
Shares Outstanding Mil	21	21	22	22	23	24
Return on Equity %	13.3	15.3	17.5	17.9	12.9	10.9
Net Margin %	5.5	5.7	6.0	6.2	4.6	4.1
Asset Turnover	1.5	1.5	1.7	1.4	1.5	1.5
Financial Leverage	1.6	1.8	1.7	2.0	1.9	1.8

Valuation Ratios	Stock	Rel to Industry	Rel to S&P 500
Price/Earnings	23.2	1.4	1.0
Price/Book	2.5	1.2	0.8
Price/Sales	0.9	1.1	0.5
Price/Cash Flow	8.4	1.6	0.6

Major Fund Holders	% of Fund Assets
WM Small Cap Stock A	2.97
Lord Abbett Developing Growth A	2.48
Lighthouse Opportunity	2.00
Westcore Small-Cap Growth	1.90

Morningstar's Take By T.K. MacKay, 12-13-2002 Stock Price as of Analysis: $25.99

Quiksilver's tight grip on the surfwear industry makes the stock an interesting play in the consumer goods sector, but we'd require a large margin of safety before riding its small-cap waves.

Quiksilver's brands go well beyond the wave logo found on neon shirts of the 1980s. Board shorts, jeans, and long-sleeve shirts emblazoned with the Quiksilver, Hawk, and Roxy brand names help generate 10%-plus operating margins, similar to those of big names like Tommy Hilfiger and Liz Claiborne. However, solid operating margins only materialize when the company gets its product out the door, and that hasn't always happened.

Inventory management has been a problem. Half of Quiksilver's customer base is surf shops; small, independent retailers like these aren't always financially stable, and can have erratic sales and purchasing practices. In each of the past three years, shaky demand and canceled orders left Quiksilver saddled with excess inventory; this prompted a $16 million hit to operating cash flows in 2001. The firm had to discount or write off its inventory, which directly affected gross margins.

To mitigate its inventory risk and gain better control over its product, Quiksilver is developing stand-alone retail locations dubbed Boardriders

Clubs, which now represent 30% of its domestic sales. Quiksilver licenses 80% of these stores to independent retailers and owns the rest. Rather than pay license fees, these owners agree to maintain Quiksilver's products at 80% of the store's inventory. Quiksilver has full control over the 20% of Boardriders Clubs that it owns outright, providing pricing power and a clearer picture of demand than it gets from smaller surf shops.

As Quiksilver expands its retail store ownership, the percentage of products it sells at higher gross margins will expand. Running a store isn't cheap, however. Selling, general, and administrative expenses are up about 2 percentage points over the past two years, primarily because of retail expansion, and aren't likely to decline as Quiksilver's retail presence grows. We believe gross margin expansion will outpace the increase in SG&A costs, though, resulting in better operating margins.

Quiksilver has cleaned up its inventory and is increasing its retail presence. That has paid off with substantially improved cash flow recently, but Quiksilver's history of negative free cash flows suggests this could be short-lived. We believe in Quiksilver's brands, but would carefully test the waters before jumping on the shares.

   Stocks 500

Qwest Communications International Q

	Rating	Risk	Moat Size	Fair Value	Last Close	Yield %
	★★★	High	None	$6.00	$5.00	0.0

Company Profile

Qwest Communications International provides communication services to businesses, consumers, and other telecom companies. The company acquired regional Bell US West in 2000, bringing a local phone network serving more than 18 million phone lines. Qwest also claims 908,000 wireless customers and 306,000 high-speed Internet access customers using DSL. Qwest is known for its next-generation long-distance network that covers the United States and Europe through a joint venture with KPN. Qwest serves more than 30 million customers worldwide.

Management

After a tumultuous few months, Qwest's board pulled the plug on Joe Nacchio and installed industry veteran Dick Notebaert as chairman and CEO. Company founder and majority owner Philip Anschutz also resigned as nonexecutive chairman.

Strategy

Qwest is working to pare debt via asset sales, cost and capital spending reductions, and debt swaps. The company is also evaluating its business lines, eliminating those not generating a profit. Winning regulatory approval to offer long-distance services, which would allow the firm to combine its local and long-distance capabilities for the first time, is also a priority.

1801 California Street   www.qwest.com
Denver, CO 80202

Morningstar Grades

Growth [C]	1998	1999	2000	2001
Revenue %	7.6	6.3	26.0	18.6
Earnings/Share %	NMF	-13.6	NMF	NMF
Book Value/Share %	NMF	NMF	EUB	-27.9
Dividends/Share %	NMF	NMF	NMF	NMF

Revenue is declining across all lines of business. Phone lines in service are falling, pulling local phone revenue down about 9% year over year. Growth should stabilize as exited businesses work through and long-distance approvals are gained.

Profitability [B]	1999	2000	2001	TTM
Return on Assets %	5.8	-0.1	-5.5	-6.3
Oper Cash Flow $Mil	4,546	3,681	4,034	3,428
- Cap Spending $Mil	3,944	6,597	8,543	6,796
= Free Cash Flow $Mil	602	-2,916	-4,509	-3,368

Profitability is dismal, with the firm running a bit below break-even. Huge goodwill and equipment write-offs in the fourth quarter of 2002 will reduce depreciation expense and invested capital, greatly improving reported returns.

Financial Health [B]	1999	2000	2001	03-02
Long-term Debt $Mil	10,189	15,421	20,197	21,427
Total Equity $Mil	1,255	41,304	36,655	35,969
Debt/Equity Ratio	8.1	0.4	0.6	0.6

Debt should fall to $18 billion after the directory business sale, but eliminating the directory cash flow will keep leverage high. Keeping free cash flow in the black will be crucial as Qwest attempts to trim debt and gain the trust of creditors.

	Industry	Investment Style	Stock Type	Sector
	Telecommunication Services	▦ Large Core	⑂ Distressed	▤ Telecom

Competition

	Market Cap $Mil	Debt/ Equity	12 Mo Trailing Sales $Mil	Price/Cash Flow	Return On Assets%	Total Return% 1 Yr	3 Yr
Qwest Communications International	8,375	0.6	19,013	2.4	-6.3	-64.6	-49.9
AT&T	20,115	0.8	48,821	1.8	-10.9	-27.7	-28.2
Sprint	12,903	0.3	15,811	2.8	0.1	-25.2	-37.5

Price Volatility

| | | Monthly Price High/Low | | — Relative Strength to S&P 500 | |

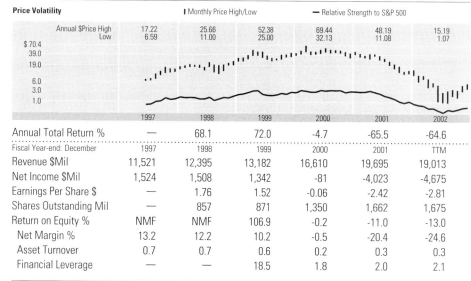

	Annual $Price High / Low	17.22 / 6.59	25.66 / 11.00	52.38 / 25.00	69.44 / 32.13	48.19 / 11.08	15.19 / 1.07

$ 70.4 / 39.0 / 19.0 / 6.0 / 3.0 / 1.0

	1997	1998	1999	2000	2001	2002
Annual Total Return %	—	68.1	72.0	-4.7	-65.5	-64.6

Fiscal Year-end: December	1997	1998	1999	2000	2001	TTM
Revenue $Mil	11,521	12,395	13,182	16,610	19,695	19,013
Net Income $Mil	1,524	1,508	1,342	-81	-4,023	-4,675
Earnings Per Share $	—	1.76	1.52	-0.06	-2.42	-2.81
Shares Outstanding Mil	—	857	871	1,350	1,662	1,675
Return on Equity %	NMF	NMF	106.9	-0.2	-11.0	-13.0
Net Margin %	13.2	12.2	10.2	-0.5	-20.4	-24.6
Asset Turnover	0.7	0.7	0.6	0.2	0.3	0.3
Financial Leverage	—	—	18.5	1.8	2.0	2.1

Valuation Ratios	Stock	Rel to Industry	Rel to S&P 500
Price/Earnings	NMF	—	—
Price/Book	0.2	0.1	0.1
Price/Sales	0.4	0.3	0.2
Price/Cash Flow	2.4	0.5	0.2

Major Fund Holders	% of Fund Assets
Fidelity Select Telecommunications	16.29
Thompson Plumb Select	10.58
Fidelity Leveraged Company Stock	4.27
Hartford Global Communications A	3.60

Morningstar's Take By Michael Hodel, 12-19-2002 Stock Price as of Analysis: $5.07

With the telecom industry shifting and Qwest still burdened with distractions, our estimate of the stock's worth has fallen drastically. We underestimated the size of the hole the firm dug for itself and the difficulty it would have climbing out. Given the uncertainties, we think the stock is worth about $6 and would consider buying only at a 50% or greater discount to this.

The review of Qwest's accounting practices is complete, but auditors still haven't signed off on the company's financials. As a result, financials haven't been filed with the Securities and Exchange Commission for the past two quarters. Qwest also remains under investigation by the SEC and the Justice Department.

Assuming Qwest can complete the second part of the directory business sale, net debt should fall to a shade under $18 billion. Qwest has offered to exchange some debt for new bonds with lower principal amounts and longer maturities but higher interest rates. The exchange could be positive for the company, but bondholders don't seem too interested--Qwest had to defend the offer in court.

Qwest's remaining (nondirectory) businesses are deteriorating, and we now doubt the firm's ability to manage its debt load and generate value for

shareholders. As with other Bells, phone lines in service are falling, but Qwest's local phone revenue is, by our estimate, declining substantially faster. The wireless business, small to begin with, has started to lose customers. Data revenue is also falling rapidly, as that business remains very competitive. Weakening revenue has pressured operating margins, and we estimate Qwest is operating in the red absent the directory business. The typical local phone business generates operating margins around 30%, so it is clear that the old Qwest business is still an albatross.

Like other phone companies, Qwest has cut capital spending sharply. While the Bells have generated huge amounts of free cash flow as a result, Qwest has merely managed to slightly break even. Here again, the firm sinks into the red without the directory business. Maintaining positive cash flow is critical as the firm tries to regain creditors' faith.

New management is starting to take steps to improve profitability, like the decision to shutter half the firm's data centers. Winning long-distance approval will also put an end to that costly process and provide a new growth avenue. But Qwest must bring its margins up to par if shareholders are to realize any value over the long term.

RadioShack RSH

	Rating	Risk	Moat Size	Fair Value	Last Close	Yield %
	★★★	Med.	Narrow	$23.00	$18.74	1.2

Company Profile

RadioShack is a retailer of consumer electronics. As of the end of 2000, RadioShack operated 5,109 company-owned stores throughout the world. Franchisees operated an additional 2,090 stores. These stores carry electronic parts and accessories, personal computers, telephones, audio and video equipment, digital satellite systems, weather radios, and other products. RadioShack stores average approximately 2,300 square feet in area.

Management

Leonard Roberts, president of the store division since 1993, took over as CEO in 1999. CFO Michael Newman, who joined the company in 2001, has been credited with putting into place some of the initiatives that have helped RadioShack's performance.

Strategy

Rather than just selling electronic products, RadioShack has focused on generating additional revenue from installation and repairs, as well as residual income from its partners when it sells wireless telephone, Internet, and satellite TV services. The company has also undertaken a supply-chain initiative to streamline operations, improve gross margins, and lower inventories.

100 Throckmorton Street   www.radioshack.com
Fort Worth, TX 76102

Morningstar Grades

Growth [C-]	1998	1999	2000	2001
Revenue %	-10.9	-13.8	16.2	-0.4
Earnings/Share %	-66.9	429.6	28.7	-53.8
Book Value/Share %	-15.4	4.2	8.1	-8.9
Dividends/Share %	0.0	2.5	7.3	-25.0

Sales growth has not been very strong--just 1.3% in 2001, and in the negative double digits in the late 1990s. It's tough to see where growth will come from longer term, unless the company changes its store format--something it is reluctant to do.

Profitability [A-]	1999	2000	2001	TTM
Return on Assets %	13.7	14.1	7.2	8.0
Oper Cash Flow $Mil	562	117	776	600
- Cap Spending $Mil	102	120	139	118
= Free Cash Flow $Mil	459	-3	637	482

Historically, the firm has had better net margins and returns on equity than its peers, thanks to its high-margin parts, batteries, and accessories business. Lately, this has been helped by residual income from partnerships with wireless providers.

Financial Health [A]	1999	2000	2001	09-02
Long-term Debt $Mil	319	303	565	590
Total Equity $Mil	779	812	714	662
Debt/Equity Ratio	0.4	0.4	0.8	0.9

RadioShack is in fine financial health. Although debt/equity is at the high end of its historical range, the company generates enough cash to keep on top of interest payments and buy back a meaningful number of shares.

Industry	Investment Style	Stock Type	Sector
Electronics Stores	▦ Mid Core	→ Slow Growth	▭ Consumer Services

Competition	Market Cap $Mil	Debt/ Equity	12 Mo Trailing Sales $Mil	Price/Cash Flow	Return On Assets%	Total Return% 1 Yr	3 Yr
RadioShack	3,181	0.9	4,595	5.3	8.0	-37.1	-29.2
Best Buy	7,766	0.3	21,330	9.3	3.1	-51.4	-14.2
Circuit City Stores	1,559	0.0	10,035	26.0	4.8	-56.6	-35.9

Price Volatility

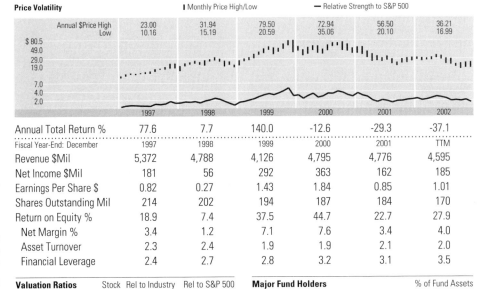

	▌ Monthly Price High/Low	— Relative Strength to S&P 500

Annual $Price High / Low	23.00 / 10.16	31.94 / 15.19	79.50 / 20.59	72.94 / 35.06	56.50 / 20.10	36.21 / 16.99

	1997	1998	1999	2000	2001	2002
Annual Total Return %	77.6	7.7	140.0	-12.6	-29.3	-37.1

Fiscal Year-End: December	1997	1998	1999	2000	2001	TTM
Revenue $Mil	5,372	4,788	4,126	4,795	4,776	4,595
Net Income $Mil	181	56	292	363	162	185
Earnings Per Share $	0.82	0.27	1.43	1.84	0.85	1.01
Shares Outstanding Mil	214	202	194	187	184	170
Return on Equity %	18.9	7.4	37.5	44.7	22.7	27.9
Net Margin %	3.4	1.2	7.1	7.6	3.4	4.0
Asset Turnover	2.3	2.4	1.9	1.9	2.1	2.0
Financial Leverage	2.4	2.7	2.8	3.2	3.1	3.5

Valuation Ratios	Stock	Rel to Industry	Rel to S&P 500
Price/Earnings	18.6	0.5	0.8
Price/Book	4.8	1.5	1.5
Price/Sales	0.7	1.9	0.3
Price/Cash Flow	5.3	0.6	0.4

Major Fund Holders	% of Fund Assets
IDEX Transamerica Growth Opport A	4.46
Transamerica Premier Growth Opp Inv	4.03
Seligman Large Cap Value A	3.35
SEI Instl Mgd Capital Appreciation A	3.34

Morningstar's Take By Joseph Beaulieu, 12-06-2002 Stock Price as of Analysis: $21.34

RadioShack is attempting to improve revenue growth and margins. We think the company will be successful in cutting costs and improving inventory management, but we aren't buying into its growth projections just yet. We think the shares are worth about $23, but because the company is in turnaround mode, we would want a substantial discount to that price before buying the stock.

RadioShack's ubiquitous stores and reputation as a one-stop source for batteries, cables, and adapters are the basis for the company's narrow economic moat. However, that moat doesn't encompass home electronics or wireless phone sales and service, where the company faces a great deal of competition from numerous companies including Amazon.com, Best Buy, and Circuit City.

We think products like digital cameras and DVD players will continue to provide incremental revenue, but not enough to make RadioShack a growth company. Management targets 2%-3% sales growth over the next several years, but given the company's recent record, we are skeptical of even that modest level of growth. (If management met the high end of that goal, our fair value estimate would increase to $28 from $23.)

Realizing that rapid growth just isn't in the cards,

management is focusing on improving profitability and reducing inventory. It is implementing wide-reaching initiatives that cut the number of suppliers the company uses (thereby increasing its leverage in negotiating prices and terms) and increase inventory turns. RadioShack is also at the tail end of a chainwide renovation project, and early tests suggest that the additional space the refitted stores have to display and demonstrate prime products could boost revenue slightly.

RadioShack's $4 billion revenue base, combined with small margin improvements and a small decline in working capital (mostly from reduced inventories), provides a great deal of leverage in the company's returns on invested capital, a key indicator of how well a company is using its investors' money--and a key driver of our valuation model.

Given the inherent riskiness of any turnaround story, we'd require a substantial margin of safety to our $23 fair value estimate before investing. We'd consider the shares at a 30% discount, but wouldn't consider them a true bargain unless they reached a 40% discount.

Ⓜ RNINGSTAR® Stocks 500

Raytheon RTN

	Rating	Risk	Moat Size	Fair Value	Last Close	Yield %
	★★★★	Med.	Narrow	$45.00	$30.75	2.6

Company Profile

Raytheon manufactures defense systems and electronic products. The company produces land, air, and water missile systems. It also makes electronic devices like radar, air traffic control, and autopilot systems, as well as integrated circuits. In addition, Raytheon produces jet aircraft. Sales to the U.S. government account for approximately 60% of the company's total sales. The firm is now trying to divest itself of noncore business units so it can focus on the defense business.

Management

Daniel Burnham was president and CEO of Raytheon from July 1998 to July 1999, when he was named chairman and CEO. He has a record of effective cost-cutting, having revived AlliedSignal's aerospace division in the early 1990s.

Strategy

Raytheon is focused on exploiting its market-leading positions in defense electronics, where it has particular expertise in radar, missiles, and air and missile defense systems. The company has been shedding nondefense businesses, most recently selling its aircraft integration business.

141 Spring Street
Lexington, MA 02421
www.raytheon.com

Industry	Investment Style	Stock Type	Sector
Aerospace & Defense	Large Value	High Yield	Industrial Mats

Competition

	Market Cap $Mil	Debt/ Equity	12 Mo Trailing Sales $Mil	Price/Cash Flow	Return On Assets%	Total Return% 1 Yr	3 Yr
Raytheon	12,481	0.6	17,341	14.9	-3.0	-3.0	8.8
Boeing	27,691	1.1	56,071	9.9	0.0	-13.4	-4.9
Lockheed Martin	26,512	0.9	26,132	11.2	-2.3	24.7	47.9

Price Volatility

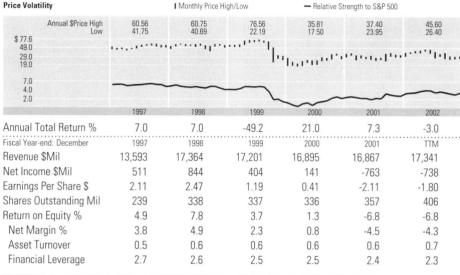

Annual $Price High	60.56	60.75	76.56	35.81	37.40	45.60
Low	41.75	40.69	22.19	17.50	23.95	26.40

	1997	1998	1999	2000	2001	2002
Annual Total Return %	7.0	7.0	-49.2	21.0	7.3	-3.0

Fiscal Year-end: December	1997	1998	1999	2000	2001	TTM
Revenue $Mil	13,593	17,364	17,201	16,895	16,867	17,341
Net Income $Mil	511	844	404	141	-763	-738
Earnings Per Share $	2.11	2.47	1.19	0.41	-2.11	-1.80
Shares Outstanding Mil	239	338	337	336	357	406
Return on Equity %	4.9	7.8	3.7	1.3	-6.8	-6.8
Net Margin %	3.8	4.9	2.3	0.8	-4.5	-4.3
Asset Turnover	0.5	0.6	0.6	0.6	0.6	0.7
Financial Leverage	2.7	2.6	2.5	2.5	2.4	2.3

Valuation Ratios	Stock	Rel to Industry	Rel to S&P 500
Price/Earnings	NMF	—	—
Price/Book	1.2	0.5	0.4
Price/Sales	0.7	0.8	0.4
Price/Cash Flow	14.9	1.5	1.1

Major Fund Holders	% of Fund Assets
Firsthand Technology Value	12.05
Firsthand Technology Leaders	7.74
Matterhorn Growth	5.70
Fidelity Select Defense & Aerospace	5.09

Morningstar Grades

Growth [B]

	1998	1999	2000	2001
Revenue %	27.7	-0.9	-1.8	-0.2
Earnings/Share %	17.1	-51.8	-65.5	NMF
Book Value/Share %	-26.6	2.2	-2.5	-0.8
Dividends/Share %	-20.0	0.0	0.0	0.0

Revenue has declined over the past five years, mostly through divestitures and weak performance in some of Raytheon's businesses. With the increase in U.S. military spending, we think the company will report stronger results over the next few years.

Profitability [D+]

	1999	2000	2001	TTM
Return on Assets %	1.5	0.5	-2.9	-3.0
Oper Cash Flow $Mil	-317	960	133	839
- Cap Spending $Mil	524	431	486	480
= Free Cash Flow $Mil	-841	529	-353	359

Profit margins declined through 2001, hurting overall profitability. Pretax return on assets was below 3% in 2001, the lowest in the past five years. The picture is brighter in 2002, with pretax ROA closer to 7%.

Financial Health [B]

	1999	2000	2001	09-02
Long-term Debt $Mil	7,298	9,054	6,875	6,088
Total Equity $Mil	10,959	10,823	11,290	10,842
Debt/Equity Ratio	0.7	0.8	0.6	0.6

The firm's financial position continued to improve in 2002. Debt/capital stands at 44%, down from its peak of 68% in 1997. Interest coverage has improved since 2001, when it came dangerously close to tripping some of the firm's debt covenants.

Morningstar's Take By Nicolas Owens, 12-17-2002 Stock Price as of Analysis: $28.60

We believe an increased focus on defense, strong product mix, and improving financial performance make Raytheon an attractive investment.

The last few years have been a muddle for Raytheon, but we believe the firm has begun to turn a corner by renewing its focus on defense. In 2002, it trimmed unprofitable parts of its consumer electronics division and sold its aircraft integration services unit. The remaining commercial aviation business continues to suffer from a very soft market for used aircraft. Revenue and profits were up in all of Raytheon's defense-related businesses, however.

Raytheon is involved with the military in long-range development as well as supplying high-tech ordnance and systems to meet its more immediate needs. Much of the expected increase in U.S. defense spending will be for missile technology, an area in which Raytheon is particularly strong. The firm is heavily involved in developing a ballistic missile defense system for the United States and its allies; tens of billions of dollars are likely to be spent on this project over the next decade.

So the future is bright at Raytheon and the present is shaping up nicely. While commitments from the engineering and construction business it sold in 2000 have sucked cash out of Raytheon's coffers, we think the worst is probably over. Cash flow from continuing operations improved in 2002, coming in at more than $1 billion. These results were masked by more than $800 million in outlays for discontinued operations, including the since-sold aircraft integration unit. In 2001, Raytheon generated $768 million from operations and dumped another $635 million in discontinued operations. Much of the improvement resulted from better working-capital management and good, old-fashioned sales growth--a rarity for Raytheon in recent years.

Raytheon stock does have risks. The most prominent issue is the depressed commercial aviation environment, which is not only robbing Raytheon of sales and profits, but also impairing some of its aviation assets. The firm also continues to meet costly legacy obligations from the engineering and construction business, and the cost to complete these projects could rise, eating up more cash and delaying the firm's debt-reduction plans.

Considering the risks and Raytheon's prospects, we believe a 40% margin of safety to our fair value estimate would make the shares worth a look.

Reebok International RBK

	Rating	Risk	Moat Size	Fair Value	Last Close	Yield %
	★	Med.	None	$26.00	$29.40	0.0

Industry	Investment Style	Stock Type	Sector
Shoes	▣ Mid Core	➡ Slow Growth	⌂ Consumer Goods

Company Profile

Reebok International manufactures footwear and leisure apparel and equipment. The company makes athletic shoes, apparel, and accessories under the Reebok and Avia names, and casual, dress, and walking shoes under the Rockport and Boks names. It sells these products worldwide through shoe stores, department stores, and company-owned specialty retail stores. The company also makes golf footwear and clothing under the Greg Norman name, sold mostly at golf pro shops and golf specialty stores. The majority of its products are produced by contractors in the Pacific Rim.

Management

Founder and chairman Paul Fireman took the helm again in 1999 after 12 years away from day-to-day operations. Since his return, the firm has cut costs considerably.

Strategy

In an effort to regain lost market share and boost profitability, Reebok has improved its product quality and is targeting a younger, hipper urban customer. The company is raising prices of selected revamped items and spending heavily to promote its basketball-related men's products. Reebok also plans to launch a new running shoe line in early 2003 to boost sales in that area.

1895 J.W. Foster Boulevard   www.reebok.com
Canton, MA 02021

Competition

Competition	Market Cap $Mil	Debt/ Equity	12 Mo Trailing Sales $Mil	Price/Cash Flow	Return On Assets%	Total Return% 1 Yr	Total Return% 3 Yr
Reebok International	1,760	0.4	3,030	8.2	6.5	10.9	53.5
Nike B	11,798	0.2	10,076	11.6	6.5	-20.1	0.3
Timberland	1,340	—	1,175	7.8	16.9	-4.0	12.9

Price Volatility

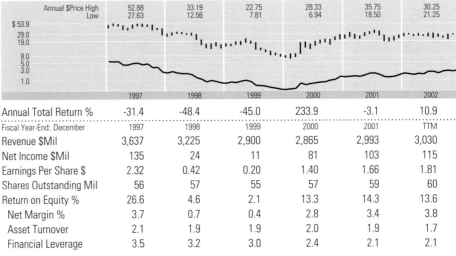

| | Monthly Price High/Low | Relative Strength to S&P 500 |

Annual $Price High Low	52.88 27.63	33.19 12.56	22.75 7.81	28.33 6.94	35.75 18.50	30.25 21.25
	1997	1998	1999	2000	2001	2002

Annual Total Return %	-31.4	-48.4	-45.0	233.9	-3.1	10.9

Fiscal Year-End: December	1997	1998	1999	2000	2001	TTM
Revenue $Mil	3,637	3,225	2,900	2,865	2,993	3,030
Net Income $Mil	135	24	11	81	103	115
Earnings Per Share $	2.32	0.42	0.20	1.40	1.66	1.81
Shares Outstanding Mil	56	57	55	57	59	60
Return on Equity %	26.6	4.6	2.1	13.3	14.3	13.6
Net Margin %	3.7	0.7	0.4	2.8	3.4	3.8
Asset Turnover	2.1	1.9	1.9	2.0	1.9	1.7
Financial Leverage	3.5	3.2	3.0	2.4	2.1	2.1

Valuation Ratios	Stock	Rel to Industry	Rel to S&P 500
Price/Earnings	16.2	0.6	0.7
Price/Book	2.1	0.6	0.7
Price/Sales	0.6	0.5	0.3
Price/Cash Flow	8.2	0.7	0.6

Major Fund Holders	% of Fund Assets
Navellier Large Cap Value	5.51
FPA Capital	3.25
Manor	2.90
Westcore Mid-Cap Opportunity	2.14

Morningstar Grades

Growth [C]	1998	1999	2000	2001
Revenue %	-11.4	-10.1	-1.2	4.5
Earnings/Share %	-81.9	-52.4	600.0	18.6
Book Value/Share %	5.7	4.0	9.9	10.6
Dividends/Share %	NMF	NMF	NMF	NMF

Sales declined an average of 5% over the past five years, while Nike averaged 2% growth. Reebok did post 4% growth in 2001, and is on track for modest growth in 2002. It has to scratch and claw for every scrap of market share gain, though.

Profitability [B-]	1999	2000	2001	TTM
Return on Assets %	0.7	5.5	6.7	6.5
Oper Cash Flow $Mil	264	183	176	214
- Cap Spending $Mil	51	29	27	25
= Free Cash Flow $Mil	212	154	149	189

Reebok has made great strides to improve profitability. Its profit margin has risen from less than 1% in 1998 and 1999 to 4% now. Better products and more effective marketing are the reasons for the margin expansion.

Financial Health [A]	1999	2000	2001	09-02
Long-term Debt $Mil	370	345	351	353
Total Equity $Mil	529	608	720	846
Debt/Equity Ratio	0.7	0.6	0.5	0.4

Reebok's debt load is manageable, and despite a weak top line, operating cash flow has historically held up well. Because its operations are not very capital-intensive, the company generates decent free cash flow.

Morningstar's Take By Tom Goetzinger, 10-31-2002 Stock Price as of Analysis: $28.25

Reebok's stock price history is one of vicious and frequent ups and downs. We'd require a significant margin of safety to our fair value estimate before strapping ourselves into the Reebok roller coaster for the long term.

The stock trades at roughly the same level it did a decade ago. Within the past five years alone, Reebok has seen its shares crest over $50 when it appeared the firm was stealing market share from rival Nike, and bottom out below $10 after Nike responded with an all-out marketing and product development blitz to protect and enhance its brand. Shares now hover in the middle of this range--right where they belong, in our opinion.

Reebok is still digging itself out of the dumps. Shaky inventory management and subpar products destroyed sales growth and profitability starting in the late 1990s. Confronted with an inventory pileup, Reebok turned to low-end retailers and price markdowns to move merchandise. In the process, Reebok damaged its brand, and consumer demand for its shoes and apparel quickly dried up.

Now Reebok is on the comeback trail, trying to revive the popularity of its brands with new licensing deals and heavy promotions. The firm is paying up for slick advertising and celebrity endorsements, hoping to woo customers--particularly the young male demographic, which spends more money on athletic gear than any other group. Thanks to NBA and NFL licensing contracts, the Reebok brand name is finally getting the exposure it needs to spark a sustainable sales recovery. After four years of negative sales growth from 1997 to 2000, Reebok posted positive 4% growth in 2001 and is on track for modest growth in 2002.

However, we think future growth will be challenging. Heavy promotional spending may temporarily boost Reebok's brand image--particularly for athletic footwear, which accounts for more than half of Reebok's revenue--but the firm must consistently and accurately predict customer tastes to drive long-term growth. Its record of doing so could hardly be worse. Given the fickle nature of the industry, the presence of a competitor with stronger finances and a history of better strategic execution, and Reebok's inability to hold on to market share gains over the long term, we'd pick up shares only if they traded at a 50% or greater discount to our fair value estimate.

MORNINGSTAR® Stocks 500

Reuters Group PLC ADR RTRSY

	Rating	Risk	Moat Size	Fair Value	Last Close	Yield %
	★★★	High	None	$22.00	$17.20	5.1

Company Profile

Reuters Group provides real-time financial data, news, historical databases, and information-management systems to businesses and the news media. Reuters Group offers electronic brokerage services like Instinet for equities and Dealing 2000-2 for foreign exchange. It provides U.S.-based Fox Broadcasting and U.K.-based Sky News with news programming.

Management

Tom Glocer became chief executive in July 2001. Glocer is not in the mold of previous leaders--he is the first American, and the first nonjournalist, to head the firm. He was paid more than $3 million in 2001 (including relocation).

Strategy

Reuters' main strategy in the current downturn is to cut costs faster than revenue declines. Reuters has targeted reductions of more than 2,500 employees out of its total of about 19,000. To maintain profit margins, the company is refusing to cut prices on its subscription services as aggressively as competitors.

85 Fleet Street   www.reuters.com
London, EC4P 4AJ

Morningstar Grades

Growth [B-]	1998	1999	2000	2001
Revenue %	5.2	3.1	14.9	5.4
Earnings/Share %	11.8	14.3	20.1	-91.2
Book Value/Share %	-71.6	57.8	74.7	-4.5
Dividends/Share %	10.8	1.4	9.6	-37.5

In 2002 sales will probably drop for the first time in more than a decade. In the first half of the year, revenue fell 12% (excluding currency moves, acquisitions, and such), largely because of a 40% decline in revenue at Instinet.

Profitability [A]	1999	2000	2001	TTM
Return on Assets %	16.1	13.7	1.0	1.0
Oper Cash Flow $Mil	1,329	1,297	1,279	1,279
- Cap Spending $Mil	414	417	398	398
= Free Cash Flow $Mil	914	880	881	881

Reuters has historically outperformed most peers, with net profit margins and returns on capital in the double digits. It will take a rebound in the financial sector, however, for profits to get back on track.

Financial Health [A+]	1999	2000	2001	12-01
Long-term Debt $Mil	458	463	499	499
Total Equity $Mil	1,069	1,721	1,607	1,607
Debt/Equity Ratio	0.4	0.3	0.3	0.3

Reuters' balance sheet is strong. Its debt/equity ratio is low for the industry. Until 2002, the company also generated consistently positive free cash flows.

Industry	Investment Style	Stock Type	Sector
Publishing	Mid Value	High Yield	Media

Competition

	Market Cap $Mil	Debt/ Equity	12 Mo Trailing Sales $Mil	Price/Cash Flow	Return On Assets%	Total Return% 1 Yr	3 Yr
Reuters Group PLC ADR	4,105	0.3	5,460	3.2	1.0	-70.6	-38.5
Reed Elsevier NV ADR	9,057	—	1,304	—	—	—	—
SunGard Data Systems	6,679	—	2,414	—	—	—	—

Price Volatility

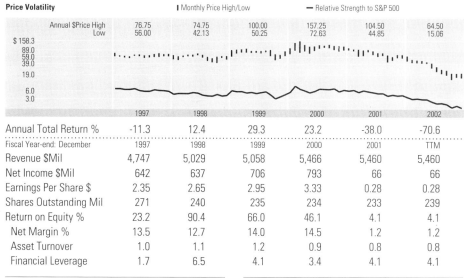

	Annual $Price High Low	76.75 56.00	74.75 42.13	100.00 50.25	157.25 72.63	104.50 44.85	64.50 15.06

I Monthly Price High/Low — Relative Strength to S&P 500

	1997	1998	1999	2000	2001	2002
Annual Total Return %	-11.3	12.4	29.3	23.2	-38.0	-70.6
Fiscal Year-end: December	1997	1998	1999	2000	2001	TTM
Revenue $Mil	4,747	5,029	5,058	5,466	5,460	5,460
Net Income $Mil	642	637	706	793	66	66
Earnings Per Share $	2.35	2.65	2.95	3.33	0.28	0.28
Shares Outstanding Mil	271	240	235	234	233	239
Return on Equity %	23.2	90.4	66.0	46.1	4.1	4.1
Net Margin %	13.5	12.7	14.0	14.5	1.2	1.2
Asset Turnover	1.0	1.1	1.2	0.9	0.8	0.8
Financial Leverage	1.7	6.5	4.1	3.4	4.1	4.1

Valuation Ratios	Stock	Rel to Industry	Rel to S&P 500
Price/Earnings	62.1	2.3	2.6
Price/Book	2.6	0.6	0.8
Price/Sales	0.8	0.3	0.4
Price/Cash Flow	3.2	0.3	0.2

Major Fund Holders	% of Fund Assets
Thompson Plumb Select	4.29
Nations International Value Prim A	2.20
Nations International Value Inv A	2.20
Thompson Plumb Growth	1.84

Morningstar's Take By Haywood Kelly, 12-23-2002 Stock Price as of Analysis: $17.73

The size of Reuters' economic moat is an open question.

Since Reuters went public in the 1980s, the market has never been this pessimistic about the firm's prospects. The shares peaked about the time the Nasdaq market did in March 2000, and have since crashed. As of December 2002, they were trading at the same price they fetched in 1991. The market now values Reuters at less than 1 times sales, compared with a norm of 2-3 times sales for most of the 1990s.

The troubles are one part cyclical, one part competitive. Brokerage firms, money managers, and investment banks are some of Reuters' biggest customers, and they're focused on their own bottom lines right now. One easy way for them to cut costs is to reduce their subscriptions to Reuters' data terminals. Owing largely to layoffs and budget cuts at major customers, Reuters' sales will almost certainly decline in 2002 and 2003.

The other chunk of Reuters' sales comes from Instinet, the electronic trading platform, and that's a deeply cyclical business. When Instinet will turn around depends on Nasdaq trading volume and how much share it loses to SuperMontage, the trading system recently launched by Nasdaq.

If Reuters' troubles were just cyclical, we'd be pounding the table on this stock. We're worried, though, that the great bull market of the 1990s masked an erosion in Reuters' competitive position in its core data business. The company generated high returns on capital going into the current slump, but that was during the greatest bull market in history, the likes of which we're unlikely to see again.

And in its core business of supplying data and news on securities, Reuters goes head to head with (among others) Bloomberg and Thomson Financial, two rivals that boast formidable product lineups of their own. All three companies are fighting for a shrinking pie right now, and Thomson in particular has been willing to boost business by offering low prices. Although price competition will ease with a cyclical rebound, it won't go away.

We're not giving Reuters the benefit of the doubt. We could be proved wrong, but Reuters may never achieve the kind of returns on capital it has in the past. We forecast a modest recovery in 2004 and only tepid sales growth thereafter. We're also lowering our moat rating to none until Reuters shows it can get back to high, sustainable returns on capital.

RF Micro Devices RFMD

	Rating	Risk	Moat Size	Fair Value	Last Close	Yield %
	★★	High	None	$7.00	$7.33	0.0

Company Profile

RF Micro Devices manufactures proprietary radio frequency integrated circuits for use in wireless communication. Its products include amplifiers, mixers, and modulators/demodulators for use in devices like cellular and cordless telephones, industrial radios, and wireless security. RF Micro Devices manufactures its products in-house and sells them worldwide both directly to customers and through a network of distribution firms.

Management

RF Micro was spun off from Analog Devices in the early 1990s. Many of the company's managers have previous experience at Analog. David Norbury has been president and CEO since 1992.

Strategy

RF Micro Devices has a concentrated mix of products, mostly for use in wireless telecom equipment. The company is seeking to diversify its product lineup and customer base as well as expand its manufacturing capabilities to take full advantage of demand. A unique manufacturing process gives RF Micro a competitive advantage.

7628 Thorndike Road   www.rfmd.com
Greensboro, NC 27409-9421

Morningstar Grades

Growth [A]	1999	2000	2001	2002
Revenue %	237.1	89.0	16.1	10.1
Earnings/Share %	NMF	123.1	-31.0	NMF
Book Value/Share %	NMF	14.4	22.7	5.5
Dividends/Share %	NMF	NMF	NMF	NMF

Sales growth has averaged 35% over the past three years. RF Micro has gained share in recent years, the key reason why it has outperformed peers.

Profitability [B]	2000	2001	2002	TTM
Return on Assets %	14.5	4.9	-2.8	2.0
Oper Cash Flow $Mil	20	56	69	64
- Cap Spending $Mil	107	90	52	55
= Free Cash Flow $Mil	-88	-33	17	8

Chip price declines and factory underutilization have hurt margins in fiscal 2002. In the three years before 2002, operating margins peaked at 25%--good for a small chipmaker.

Financial Health [B]	2000	2001	2002	09-02
Long-term Debt $Mil	8	296	294	295
Total Equity $Mil	303	376	390	401
Debt/Equity Ratio	0.0	0.8	0.8	0.7

The balance sheet is in good shape. The firm's $295 million in convertible debt (resulting in a debt/equity ratio of 0.75) isn't burdensome, since it carries a low interest rate. RF Micro has cash of $337 million on its balance sheet.

Industry	Investment Style	Stock Type	Sector
Semiconductors	▦ Small Growth	◈ Spec. Growth	▣ Hardware

Competition

	Market Cap $Mil	Debt/ Equity	12 Mo Trailing Sales $Mil	Price/Cash Flow	Return On Assets%	Total Return% 1 Yr	3 Yr
RF Micro Devices	1,239	0.7	425	19.4	2.0	-61.9	-42.2
Philips Electronics NV AD	22,527	0.4	28,837	20.2	-6.8	-38.6	-18.3
Triquint Semiconductor	562	0.4	260	13.9	-6.9	-65.4	-46.7

Price Volatility

| | Monthly Price High/Low | — Relative Strength to S&P 500 |

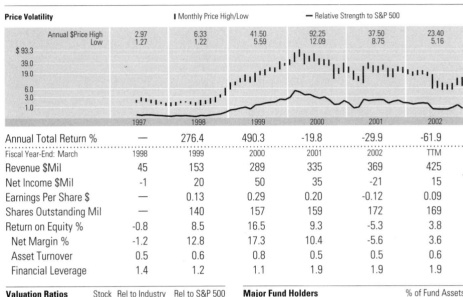

Annual $Price High / Low	2.97 / 1.27	6.33 / 1.22	41.50 / 5.59	92.25 / 12.09	37.50 / 8.75	23.40 / 5.16
	1997	1998	1999	2000	2001	2002

Annual Total Return %	—	276.4	490.3	-19.8	-29.9	-61.9
Fiscal Year-End: March	1998	1999	2000	2001	2002	TTM
Revenue $Mil	45	153	289	335	369	425
Net Income $Mil	-1	20	50	35	-21	15
Earnings Per Share $	—	0.13	0.29	0.20	-0.12	0.09
Shares Outstanding Mil	—	140	157	159	172	169
Return on Equity %	-0.8	8.5	16.5	9.3	-5.3	3.8
Net Margin %	-1.2	12.8	17.3	10.4	-5.6	3.6
Asset Turnover	0.5	0.6	0.8	0.5	0.5	0.6
Financial Leverage	1.4	1.2	1.1	1.9	1.9	1.9

Valuation Ratios	Stock	Rel to Industry	Rel to S&P 500
Price/Earnings	81.4	2.0	3.5
Price/Book	3.1	1.1	1.0
Price/Sales	2.9	0.8	1.5
Price/Cash Flow	19.4	1.6	1.5

Major Fund Holders	% of Fund Assets
John Hancock Communications A	4.79
Boyle Marathon	4.59
Wireless	3.41
Sentinel Mid-Cap Growth A	2.88

Morningstar's Take By Jeremy Lopez, 12-17-2002 Stock Price as of Analysis: $8.68

RF Micro has lots of promise, but the threat of a wireless industry hiccup necessitates a large discount to our fair value estimate before investing.

When considering RF Micro's prospects, it's impossible to ignore the cloudy outlook for the wireless industry. Wireless subscriber growth has recently hit a wall thanks to saturation in most of the world's major markets. This leaves RF Micro's growth prospects heavily dependent on users buying new cell phones, something that usually happens when people upgrade their phones or switch carriers. The Sprints of the world would argue that a major upgrade cycle is imminent, because customers will require an advanced phone to utilize new data-rich services. Given what we've seen so far, however, demand is shaky.

RF Micro has shown it can expand its business under tough industry conditions: Sales have risen each of the past two years despite brutal overall chip demand. The firm is arguably the strongest player in the radio frequency (RF) chip market, which supplies key components for cell phones. A big reason for the firm's above-average growth has been a close alliance with Nokia, the strongest handset maker, which accounts for more than half of RF Micro's sales.

We're glad RF Micro has begun to diversify its customer base. The firm was the first to bring RF power amplifier modules to market; these save cell phone makers time and money by combining several chips into one product. This has attracted new customers--Siemens, Samsung, and Motorola--and has allowed RF Micro to grab share from slower-moving peers.

RF Micro's product momentum and market share gains may be enough to drive growth despite a shaky near-term wireless market. However, this growth will come at a price. RF Micro's margins and returns on capital have suffered in recent quarters as a result of pricing pressures and underutilization of the firm's chip plants. It may take a few years for profitability to improve in line with historical levels, which puts a damper on our fair value estimate. RF Micro is a small chipmaker with lots of risk, and we'd need a 40%-50% discount to our fair value estimate before we would recommend it.

MORNINGSTAR® Stocks 500

RJ Reynolds Tobacco Holdings RJR

	Rating ★★★	Risk Med.	Moat Size Narrow	Fair Value $57.00	Last Close $42.11	Yield % 8.8

Company Profile

RJ Reynolds is the holding company for Reynolds Tobacco, which manufactures cigarettes. Reynolds Tobacco markets its cigarettes under brand names like Doral, Winston, Camel, and Salem. Reynolds Tobacco is also developing its Eclipse cigarette, which may reduce secondhand smoke. It also makes cigarettes for other companies. RJ Reynolds acquired Nabisco Group Holdings in December 2000 and Santa Fe Natural Tobacco, a privately held company, in January 2002.

Management

Andrew Schindler joined RJ Reynolds in 1974 and now is president, CEO, and chairman. He leads a group of tobacco industry veterans.

Strategy

After the sale of its international tobacco operations and Nabisco Foods in 1999-2000, RJ Reynolds paid down debt and became a pure domestic tobacco play. RJR places more stress than its rivals do on innovative new products, which it's using to battle the threat of generic cigarettes. Its acquisition of Santa Fe Natural Tobacco Company in 2002 gave it a fast-growing, profitable new brand.

401 North Main Street   www.rjrt.com
Winston-Salem, NC 27101-2866

Morningstar Grades

Growth [A]

	1998	1999	2000	2001
Revenue %	13.3	30.7	7.9	6.5
Earnings/Share %	NMF	NMF	NMF	-75.5
Book Value/Share %	—	—	NMF	-2.2
Dividends/Share %	NMF	NMF	100.0	6.5

RJR's reported sales growth has been artificially high because of acquisitions and restatements. Sales growth in the core U.S. cigarette business has been less than 5% annually, and will be hurt by price competition.

Profitability [C+]

	1999	2000	2001	TTM
Return on Assets %	16.3	11.7	2.9	0.7
Oper Cash Flow $Mil	929	590	626	444
- Cap Spending $Mil	55	60	74	104
= Free Cash Flow $Mil	874	530	552	340

RJR's earnings per share have been helped in recent quarters by share buybacks. Its operating margin and return on equity are lower than those for Philip Morris' tobacco business, and are likely to be squeezed further.

Financial Health [B+]

	1999	2000	2001	09-02
Long-term Debt $Mil	1,653	1,674	1,631	1,754
Total Equity $Mil	7,064	8,436	8,026	7,440
Debt/Equity Ratio	0.2	0.2	0.2	0.2

As of September 30, the firm held $3 billion in cash and short-term investments, and had $1.8 billion in long-term debt. It pays a hefty dividend and has been aggressively repurchasing shares.

Industry Tobacco	Investment Style Mid Value	Stock Type High Yield	Sector Consumer Goods

Competition

	Market Cap $Mil	Debt/ Equity	12 Mo Trailing Sales $Mil	Price/Cash Flow	Return On Assets%	Total Return% 1 Yr	3 Yr
RJ Reynolds Tobacco Holdings	3,741	0.2	8,602	8.4	0.7	-19.9	43.7
Philip Morris Companies	84,290	0.9	90,561	7.7	13.4	-6.8	26.8
British American Tobacco	21,178	—	16,610	—	—	—	—

Price Volatility

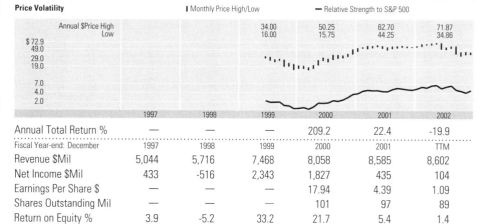

	∎ Monthly Price High/Low	— Relative Strength to S&P 500

Annual $Price High/Low			34.00 / 16.00	50.25 / 15.75	62.70 / 44.25	71.87 / 34.86

$72.9 / 49.0 / 29.0 / 19.0 / 7.0 / 4.0 / 2.0

	1997	1998	1999	2000	2001	2002
Annual Total Return %	—	—	—	209.2	22.4	-19.9

Fiscal Year-end: December	1997	1998	1999	2000	2001	TTM
Revenue $Mil	5,044	5,716	7,468	8,058	8,585	8,602
Net Income $Mil	433	-516	2,343	1,827	435	104
Earnings Per Share $	—	—	—	17.94	4.39	1.09
Shares Outstanding Mil	—	—	—	101	97	89
Return on Equity %	3.9	-5.2	33.2	21.7	5.4	1.4
Net Margin %	8.6	-9.0	31.4	22.7	5.1	1.2
Asset Turnover	0.2	0.3	0.5	0.5	0.6	0.6
Financial Leverage	1.8	2.0	2.0	1.8	1.9	2.1

Valuation Ratios	Stock	Rel to Industry	Rel to S&P 500
Price/Earnings	38.6	5.1	1.6
Price/Book	0.5	0.1	0.2
Price/Sales	0.4	0.5	0.2
Price/Cash Flow	8.4	1.1	0.6

Major Fund Holders	% of Fund Assets
Fidelity Advisor Dynamic Cap App A	14.72
Fidelity Independence	11.94
PIMCO NFJ Equity Income Admin	3.71
PIMCO NFJ Equity Income Instl	3.71

Morningstar's Take By David Kathman, 12-12-2002 Stock Price as of Analysis: $42.54

RJ Reynolds' hefty dividend yield is attractive, but its dependence on U.S. sales and nonpremium brands means the firm will have a tougher time than rival Philip Morris in meeting the challenges the tobacco industry faces. We'd need at least a 30% discount to our fair value estimate to buy the stock.

Lawsuits are not the only threat facing Big Tobacco these days; pricing power is also under siege. Over the past decade, the major tobacco companies have been able to raise prices repeatedly without hurting volume too much, helping offset increased litigation costs and declining demand. But an unusually large price hike in 1999 to help pay for the $250 billion master settlement agreement with the states has caused a proliferation of no-name "deep-discount" cigarettes whose sole attraction is price. Now the deep-discounters are stealing share from brand-name tobacco makers, who are being forced to fight back.

RJR faces a tougher fight than many of its competitors, particularly Philip Morris. For one thing, RJR gets nearly all of its sales from U.S. tobacco, where the deep-discounters are making their inroads and litigation is most active. Philip Morris gets only 25% of its sales from U.S. tobacco; in addition to a huge overseas business (from which most of its

growth is coming), it has stable, litigation-free Kraft Foods to lean on.

More important, Philip Morris gets 90% of its tobacco sales from premium brands; RJR gets 60%. While premium brands have started to feel the pinch from deep-discounters, branded discount cigarettes have been much harder-hit, with RJR's Doral (the largest U.S. discount brand) losing significant volume and market share in 2001. Philip Morris and RJR stepped up promotional spending in 2002 to support their brands, depressing profits. However, Philip Morris stands to benefit more in the long term from such spending, which tends to help premium brands like Big Mo's dominant Marlboro more than discount brands like Doral.

RJR has tried to beef up its brand portfolio by buying superpremium Santa Fe Natural Tobacco and introducing new Camel Turkish brands, which have boosted Camel's share. But Santa Fe represents less than 2% of RJR's volume, and the benefits from these innovations won't be enough in the long run to offset weakened pricing power. As a result, we expect RJR's sales growth to remain tepid and margins to be squeezed, and we'd want a substantial discount to our fair value estimate before taking a chance on the stock.

Data as of 12-31-02

Robert Half International RHI

	Rating	Risk	Moat Size	Fair Value	Last Close	Yield %
	★★★	Low	Narrow	$20.00	$16.11	0.0

Industry	Investment Style	Stock Type	Sector
Employment	▦ Mid Growth	➡ Slow Growth	▤ Business Services

Company Profile

Robert Half International is a worldwide provider of temporary and permanent placement services. It has more than 330 offices in the United States, Canada, and Europe and placed approximately 215,000 employees on temporary assignments in 2001. The company provides specialized staffing, including temporary and permanent professionals for accounting, finance, and information systems as well as for high-end general office, administrative, and legal services through its Accountemps, Robert Half, OfficeTeam, and Affiliates divisions.

Management

Harold Messmer has been CEO since 1987. Management and officers as a group own 12.8% of outstanding shares and are thus motivated to act in the interests of outside shareholders.

Strategy

Robert Half targets relatively small clients, which--unlike big Fortune 1000 companies--do not buy services in volume, and are thus less price-sensitive. Because of the investments the firm has made in branding, we believe Robert Half attracts higher-quality temporaries who have the skills to complete assignments more efficiently than less-experienced personnel.

2884 Sand Hill Road   www.rhii.com
Menlo Park, CA 94025

Competition	Market Cap $Mil	Debt/ Equity	12 Mo Trailing Sales $Mil	Price/Cash Flow	Return On Assets%	Total Return% 1 Yr	3 Yr
Robert Half International	2,743	0.0	1,937	14.9	2.3	-39.7	6.8
Manpower	2,448	0.9	10,309	16.5	2.7	-4.9	-3.8
Spherion	394	—	2,217	—	—		

Price Volatility

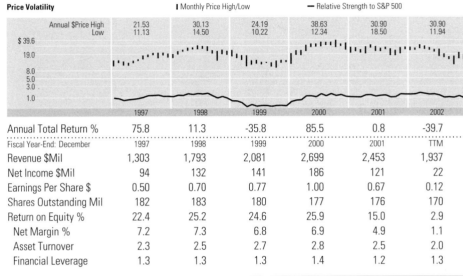

	1997	1998	1999	2000	2001	2002
Annual $Price High	21.53	30.13	24.19	38.63	30.90	30.90
Low	11.13	14.50	10.22	12.34	18.50	11.94
Annual Total Return %	75.8	11.3	-35.8	85.5	0.8	-39.7

Fiscal Year-End: December	1997	1998	1999	2000	2001	TTM
Revenue $Mil	1,303	1,793	2,081	2,699	2,453	1,937
Net Income $Mil	94	132	141	186	121	22
Earnings Per Share $	0.50	0.70	0.77	1.00	0.67	0.12
Shares Outstanding Mil	182	183	180	177	176	170
Return on Equity %	22.4	25.2	24.6	25.9	15.0	2.9
Net Margin %	7.2	7.3	6.8	6.9	4.9	1.1
Asset Turnover	2.3	2.5	2.7	2.8	2.5	2.0
Financial Leverage	1.3	1.3	1.3	1.4	1.2	1.3

Valuation Ratios	Stock	Rel to Industry	Rel to S&P 500
Price/Earnings	134.3	2.2	5.7
Price/Book	3.7	1.0	1.1
Price/Sales	1.4	2.6	0.7
Price/Cash Flow	14.9	0.9	1.1

Major Fund Holders	% of Fund Assets
IDEX Transamerica Growth Opport A	5.97
Transamerica Premier Growth Opp Inv	5.66
Seligman Global Growth A	4.01
Baron Asset	3.85

Morningstar Grades

Growth [D+]	1998	1999	2000	2001
Revenue %	37.6	16.1	29.7	-9.1
Earnings/Share %	39.0	10.1	30.7	-33.0
Book Value/Share %	23.5	12.9	23.9	15.4
Dividends/Share %	NMF	NMF	NMF	NMF

Economic problems are crimping Half's growth. Revenue increased 34% per year on average from 1995 to 2000, but it declined 9% in 2001 and will probably fall 23% in 2002. Longer term, growth should return, although not at the rate achieved when the firm was smaller.

Profitability [A+]	1999	2000	2001	TTM
Return on Assets %	18.2	19.2	12.2	2.3
Oper Cash Flow $Mil	157	267	276	185
- Cap Spending $Mil	53	74	85	52
= Free Cash Flow $Mil	105	193	191	133

Although we project that Half's profits will be minimal in 2002 because of the drop in sales, the firm has consistently exceeded 11% operating profit margins. This profitability places it in the top ranks of the staffing industry.

Financial Health [A+]	1999	2000	2001	09-02
Long-term Debt $Mil	3	3	2	2
Total Equity $Mil	576	719	806	749
Debt/Equity Ratio	0.0	0.0	0.0	0.0

Robert Half has more cash in the bank than the total amount of liabilities on the balance sheet. It also generates large free cash flows and buys back stock.

Morningstar's Take By Dan Schick, 11-22-2002 Stock Price as of Analysis: $20.15

There's a lot to like about Robert Half--a strong balance sheet, experienced, capable management, high returns on capital, and plenty of free cash flow. We'd buy the shares at a 30% discount to our fair value estimate to provide a margin of safety.

Half's balance sheet is a beauty, with more than $300 million in cash and less than $200 million in total liabilities. Such a strong financial position immunizes the firm against the vicissitudes of the economy, an advantage in an industry roped to the business cycle. Furthermore, healthy finances enable the firm to invest in its business as well as reward its owners. Half spent heavily in 2000 and 2001 on productivity enhancements that should pay off when employment demand returns. And since 2000, Half has repurchased almost $250 million worth of its shares.

The balance sheet full of cash and devoid of encumbrances points to management's capability. Cold cash is the measure of all management, and since 1995, Robert Half has produced nearly $700 million of free cash flow. Furthermore, almost all of the firm's growth from a $200 million revenue base in 1990 to a peak of $2.7 billion in 2000 was internally generated, a rarity in the often acquisitive temporary-labor supply industry. Half has a knack at

pursuing complementary lines of services, like its OfficeTeam administrative staffing group. It started the last decade with two divisions; it now has six. The four additions contribute 50% of revenue.

The latest seed sown by the company is its internal audit business, developed by taking over Arthur Andersen's internal audit and business risk consulting practice before the firm's demise. We believe Half should be able to expand Protiviti nicely, replicating its success with the other divisions that it has built from the ground up, like OfficeTeam. Furthermore, to get Protiviti going Half is investing only startup costs and a mere $16 million to release more than 50 ex-Andersen partners from their noncompete agreements. We think this is money well spent for a business that is already running at a rate of $60 million in annual revenue and once achieved operating margins near 10%.

Finally, Robert Half's experienced management team, led by CEO Harold Messmer, is maintaining the firm's strategic focus during this downturn. Half will continue to supply professional-level temporary staff mainly to smaller companies while pursuing internal growth. This formula served the firm and its shareholders well last decade. We believe the formula will prove successful this decade as well.

MORNINGSTAR® Stocks 500

Ross Stores ROST

	Rating	Risk	Moat Size	Fair Value	Last Close	Yield %
	★★	Low	None	$40.00	$42.39	0.4

Company Profile

Ross Stores operates a chain of 412 off-price retail apparel stores. The stores are located in 18 states across the West coast, Southwest, and Mid-Atlantic regions of the United States. The company offers its merchandise at generally 20% to 60% less than the prices of most department and specialty stores. Target customers are men and women ages 25 to 54. During fiscal 1999, women's apparel accounted for 34% of sales; men's apparel accounted for 21%. The remaining sales consisted of accessories, shoes, children's clothing, and fragrances and home decorations.

Management

Michael Balmuth joined Ross Stores in 1989 and has been CEO since 1996. James Peters, who was named president in July 2000, previously held the same post at the U.S. retail division of Staples.

Strategy

Ross Stores supplements its standard off-price retailing by opportunistically purchasing in-season closeouts for "packaways." In effect, it purchases merchandise very cheaply at the close of a season and stores it until the following year's season. The company has been expanding its merchandise mix beyond apparel with higher-margin items like home accents and accessories.

8333 Central Ave. www.rossstores.com
Newark, CA 94560-3433

Morningstar Grades

Growth [A-]	1999	2000	2001	2002
Revenue %	9.7	13.1	9.7	10.2
Earnings/Share %	19.1	17.1	11.0	4.9
Book Value/Share %	16.7	16.4	8.4	19.6
Dividends/Share %	22.2	18.2	15.4	13.3

A healthy pace of store openings and a rise in the number of bargain-hunting customers have produced strong revenue growth in a difficult economy.

Profitability [A+]	2000	2001	2002	TTM
Return on Assets %	15.8	15.6	14.3	14.3
Oper Cash Flow $Mil	183	143	243	373
- Cap Spending $Mil	74	82	86	105
= Free Cash Flow $Mil	109	61	157	268

Ross has been more profitable than larger rival TJX, thanks to its prudent buying practices. We think recent technology and supply-chain investments could boost profits even more.

Financial Health [A-]	2000	2001	2002	10-02
Long-term Debt $Mil	—	30	—	25
Total Equity $Mil	473	468	544	592
Debt/Equity Ratio	—	0.1	—	0.0

With no long-term debt and solid cash flow, Ross is financially healthy. However, its synthetic leases do heighten the firm's financial risk, as the retailer may have to use cash or assume debt to purchase the properties when the leases end.

Industry	Investment Style	Stock Type	Sector
Clothing Stores	Mid Growth	Classic Growth	Consumer Services

Competition	Market Cap $Mil	Debt/ Equity	12 Mo Trailing Sales $Mil	Price/Cash Flow	Return On Assets%	Total Return% 1 Yr	3 Yr
Ross Stores	3,287	0.0	3,415	8.8	14.3	32.8	37.6
TJX Companies	10,339	0.5	11,381	10.2	14.6	-1.5	27.4
Burlington Coat Factory	799	—	2,666	—	—	—	—

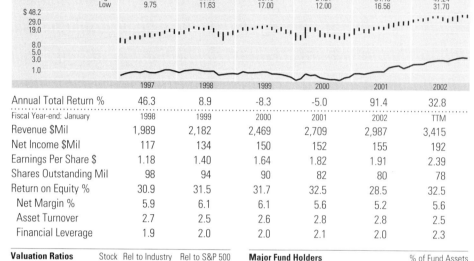

Price Volatility — Monthly Price High/Low — Relative Strength to S&P 500

Annual $Price High / Low	21.19 / 9.75	25.00 / 11.63	26.13 / 17.00	24.31 / 12.00	34.13 / 16.56	47.24 / 31.70

	1997	1998	1999	2000	2001	2002
Annual Total Return %	46.3	8.9	-8.3	-5.0	91.4	32.8

Fiscal Year-end: January	1998	1999	2000	2001	2002	TTM
Revenue $Mil	1,989	2,182	2,469	2,709	2,987	3,415
Net Income $Mil	117	134	150	152	155	192
Earnings Per Share $	1.18	1.40	1.64	1.82	1.91	2.39
Shares Outstanding Mil	98	94	90	82	80	78
Return on Equity %	30.9	31.5	31.7	32.5	28.5	32.5
Net Margin %	5.9	6.1	6.1	5.6	5.2	5.6
Asset Turnover	2.7	2.5	2.6	2.8	2.8	2.5
Financial Leverage	1.9	2.0	2.0	2.1	2.0	2.3

Valuation Ratios	Stock	Rel to Industry	Rel to S&P 500
Price/Earnings	17.7	1.0	0.8
Price/Book	5.5	1.4	1.7
Price/Sales	1.0	1.1	0.5
Price/Cash Flow	8.8	0.9	0.7

Major Fund Holders	% of Fund Assets
FPA Capital	6.20
Undiscovered Managers Hidden Val Inst	4.87
FAM Equity-Income	3.01
Schwartz Value	2.96

Morningstar's Take By Roz Bryant, 12-01-2002 Stock Price as of Analysis: $46.16

Off-price retailer Ross Stores has found a sweet spot in retailing. We admire the company's ability to ride out economic gyrations and use its capital wisely. We'd feel comfortable buying in at a smaller discount to our fair value estimate--say, 30%--than we would require for less-resilient retailers.

Ross Stores' consistent revenue growth has its department store rivals beat. Like many department stores, Ross offers recognizable brand names to attract shoppers, but it charges 20%-60% less than most department and specialty stores do for the same merchandise. A frequently changing selection helps keep customer traffic steady and strong during both good and bad economic times. As a result, Ross' five-year same-store sales growth average of 5.2% handily beats Federated's 1.2% and May's 1.0%.

We expect gross margins to expand as the retailer's investments in technology begin paying off. In an effort to lower costs, reduce customer wait times, and improve inventory management, Ross signed on with an enterprise software vendor in the summer of 2002 to roll out new point-of-sale, credit-settlement, and voucher-management systems in its stores. We think lower costs and increased customer traffic, driven by an improved in-store experience, will result in wider margins.

Ross is also benefiting from a careful expansion strategy. The retailer opens new stores to maintain leadership in existing markets or quickly match competitors in new markets, and avoids getting into uphill battles on rivals' turf. For example, Ross has steered clear of TJX's stronghold in the Midwest. The strategy is a way of ensuring that new stores achieve adequate profitability. We think it's working: Ross' return on invested capital has averaged 31% over the past five years--better than TJX's over that span.

We do think Ross' returns on capital and profit growth are likely to fall slightly as a result of rising employee benefit costs. Even so, a return on invested capital in the high 20s is still very attractive in this area of retail. We believe Ross' stable operating history and growth prospects would make the stock a compelling purchase around $28.

Royal Caribbean Cruises RCL

Rating	Risk	Moat Size	Fair Value	Last Close	Yield %
★★★	Med.	Narrow	$19.00	$16.70	1.6

Company Profile

Royal Caribbean Cruises operates 19 cruise ships with a total of 40,100 berths. The company's ships serve more than 200 destinations in the Caribbean, Bahamas, Mexico, Alaska, Europe, Bermuda, the Panama Canal, Hawaii, and East Asia. They range in capacity from 1,350 to 3,100 passengers and range in weight from 18,455 to 75,000 tons. The company expects to add an additional 10 cruise ships by the end of 2005.

Management

Under CEO Richard Fain, the firm has aggressively pursued expansion. But management credibility is at risk after the company pleaded guilty and was forced to pay fines for illegally dumping waste at sea two years in a row.

Strategy

Royal Caribbean's goals are to increase brand awareness and expand its fleet of ships to keep up with rising consumer demand. As the newly installed number-one cruise operator, Royal Caribbean offers a variety of cruises, from the price-conscious to luxury segments.

1050 Caribbean Way   www.royalcaribbean.com
Miami, FL 33132

Morningstar Grades

Growth [A-]	1998	1999	2000	2001
Revenue %	36.0	-3.4	12.6	9.7
Earnings/Share %	59.1	12.6	12.1	-42.9
Book Value/Share %	4.2	31.3	13.1	3.9
Dividends/Share %	17.2	17.6	20.0	8.3

Royal Caribbean has been adding ships and making acquisitions in recent years, and its shipbuilding program is accelerating quickly. However, industrywide oversupply and lower cabin prices are diminishing the returns from new ships.

Profitability [B-]	1999	2000	2001	TTM
Return on Assets %	6.0	5.7	2.5	2.6
Oper Cash Flow $Mil	583	703	634	634
- Cap Spending $Mil	972	1,286	1,737	1,737
= Free Cash Flow $Mil	-389	-582	-1,104	-1,104

Operating margins have been rising as new ships increase Royal Caribbean's economies of scale, but return on assets--a crucial measure of performance--has slid significantly since 1998.

Financial Health [C]	1999	2000	2001	12-01
Long-term Debt $Mil	2,214	3,300	5,408	5,408
Total Equity $Mil	3,089	3,616	3,757	3,757
Debt/Equity Ratio	0.7	0.9	1.4	1.4

The company has been financing its shipbuilding program with much heavier borrowing than its rivals, and long-term debt/capital now stands at 57%, well above Carnival's 29%.

Industry	Investment Style	Stock Type	Sector
Recreation	Mid Value	Classic Growth	Consumer Goods

Competition	Market Cap $Mil	Debt/ Equity	12 Mo Trailing Sales $Mil	Price/Cash Flow	Return On Assets%	Total Return% 1 Yr	3 Yr
Royal Caribbean Cruises	3,204	1.4	3,309	5.1	2.6	4.6	-26.6
Carnival	14,640	0.4	4,292	11.2	7.7	-9.8	-17.3
P&O Princess Cruises ADR	4,803	—	2,450	—	—	—	—

Price Volatility

Monthly Price High/Low — Relative Strength to S&P 500

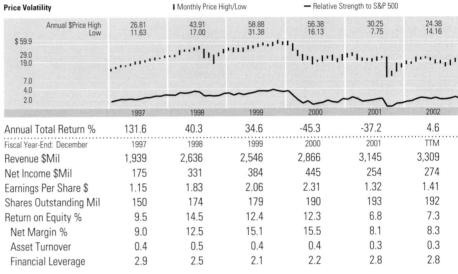

	1997	1998	1999	2000	2001	2002
Annual $Price High	26.81	43.91	58.88	56.38	30.25	24.38
Low	11.63	17.00	31.38	16.13	7.75	14.16
Annual Total Return %	131.6	40.3	34.6	-45.3	-37.2	4.6

Fiscal Year-End: December	1997	1998	1999	2000	2001	TTM
Revenue $Mil	1,939	2,636	2,546	2,866	3,145	3,309
Net Income $Mil	175	331	384	445	254	274
Earnings Per Share $	1.15	1.83	2.06	2.31	1.32	1.41
Shares Outstanding Mil	150	174	179	190	193	192
Return on Equity %	9.5	14.5	12.4	12.3	6.8	7.3
Net Margin %	9.0	12.5	15.1	15.5	8.1	8.3
Asset Turnover	0.4	0.5	0.4	0.4	0.3	0.3
Financial Leverage	2.9	2.5	2.1	2.2	2.8	2.8

Valuation Ratios	Stock	Rel to Industry	Rel to S&P 500
Price/Earnings	11.8	0.7	0.5
Price/Book	0.9	0.4	0.3
Price/Sales	1.0	0.3	0.5
Price/Cash Flow	5.1	0.4	0.4

Major Fund Holders	% of Fund Assets
Fountainhead Special Value	4.45
Buffalo Small Cap	3.82
Stonebridge Aggressive Growth	3.53
AFBA Five Star Small Cap A	3.37

Morningstar's Take By T.K. MacKay, 11-25-2002 Stock Price as of Analysis: $22.15

It appears that Royal Caribbean has failed to woo the Princess and may soon become a distant runner-up in the cruise industry. We favor Carnival as a long-term investment in the industry, and would consider Royal Caribbean only if it fell 40% below our fair value estimate.

Royal Caribbean's namesake cruise line and its luxurious Celebrity Cruises won't lose their appeal to vacationers in the wake of Carnival's seemingly successful acquisition of P&O Princess. However, we also believe that Royal Caribbean's high debt load and second-rate profitability won't change, either.

Royal Caribbean has a long history of subpar profitability compared with Carnival, whose 26% operating margins blow Royal Caribbean's 18% margins out of the water. Higher staff/guest ratios, luxury accommodations, and a less efficiently run fleet than Carnival make it difficult to compete with the larger operator. Even if the economy improves and customers become less price-sensitive, Carnival's acquisition of Princess' luxury brand could keep the pressure on Royal Caribbean's profit margins.

A weaker economy combined with double-digit capacity increases in the cruise industry over the next several years won't make this trend easy to change.

Royal Caribbean, Princess, and Carnival will be increasing capacity 40% overall through the next five years. Royal Caribbean has four ships on order, which will be paid for mostly with borrowed money--a worrisome condition, given the firm's already heavy debt load. Long-term debt makes up 57% of the company's total invested capital, compared with Carnival's debt/capital ratio of just 27%.

We worry that the cruise industry's growth in capacity may outpace demand in coming years, especially if the economy stays in a slump. Carriers, including Royal Caribbean, will be faced with similar scenarios to those in late 2001, and could be forced to lower rates to bring in customers. This is damaging to profitability and overall returns on investment, where Royal Caribbean's 8% return on invested capital has trailed Carnival by 5 percentage points over the past five years. We see little evidence that this trend will change, and would consider Royal Caribbean stock only if it fell 40% or more below our estimated fair value for the shares.

MORNINGSTAR® Stocks 500

Royal Dutch Petroleum ADR RD

	Rating	Risk	Moat Size	Fair Value	Last Close	Yield %
	★★★	Low	Narrow	$49.00	$44.02	3.6

Company Profile

Royal Dutch Petroleum is a holding company whose primary asset is its 60% interest in Royal Dutch/Shell Group (Shell), a century-old Anglo-Dutch combination that is one of the world's three largest integrated oil and gas companies. British company Shell Transport owns the other 40% of Shell. With operations spanning all aspects of oil, Shell has 13.7 billion barrels of reserves, the capacity to refine 3 million barrels a day, and some 46,000 service stations around the globe.

Management

Royal Dutch and Shell Transport jointly appoint directors to the Shell board and rotate the chairmanship among representatives of the two parent firms. Industry vet Phil Watts runs the operations at Shell.

Strategy

Spurred by the 1998 global economic slump, Shell has focused on improving internal efficiency, chopping underperforming lines, and reducing capital employed. Forgoing the megamerger game played by its peers caused Shell to lose its spot as the world's largest energy company, but recent purchases of Pennzoil-Quaker State and Britain's Enterprise Oil indicate a new urge to merge.

Carel Van Bylandtlaan 30   www.shell.com
HR The Haag, NL 2596

Morningstar Grades

Growth [C-]	1998	1999	2000	2001
Revenue %	-26.9	12.5	41.6	-9.3
Earnings/Share %	-93.7	EUB	79.8	-25.6
Book Value/Share %	27.7	-32.1	23.3	-14.2
Dividends/Share %	9.0	-10.1	11.2	-13.0

Sales grow and contract in spurts because of Shell's dependence on volatile commodity prices. Recent quarters saw commodity prices much lower than their 2000 peaks, and Shell's sales were down as a result. This is not a long-term concern.

Profitability [A]	1999	2000	2001	TTM
Return on Assets %	7.5	10.4	9.7	7.5
Oper Cash Flow $Mil	11,059	18,359	16,933	15,455
- Cap Spending $Mil	7,409	6,209	9,626	11,461
= Free Cash Flow $Mil	3,650	12,150	7,307	3,994

For years, Shell's been creating solid but unspectacular profitability. Recent efforts to cut costs and shed underperforming chemical units are aimed at bringing long-term returns on capital employed to 13%-15%.

Financial Health [A+]	1999	2000	2001	03-02
Long-term Debt $Mil	6,009	4,070	1,832	2,197
Total Equity $Mil	56,171	57,086	56,160	58,357
Debt/Equity Ratio	0.1	0.1	0.0	0.0

Sporting one of the healthiest balance sheets in the industry and an AAA credit rating, Shell has few liquidity concerns. Free cash flow has been reliably strong. Shell aims to leverage its financial health to acquire and shore up smaller firms.

	Industry	Investment Style	Stock Type	Sector
	Oil & Gas	Large Value	High Yield	Energy

Competition

	Market Cap $Mil	Debt/ Equity	12 Mo Trailing Sales $Mil	Price/Cash Flow	Return On Assets%	Total Return% 1 Yr	3 Yr
Royal Dutch Petroleum ADR	93,615	0.0	135,759	6.1	7.5	-7.3	-6.2
ExxonMobil	235,108	0.1	196,513	12.0	6.7	-8.9	-0.9
BP PLC ADR	152,063	0.2	175,389	6.8	5.7	-9.9	-9.2

Price Volatility

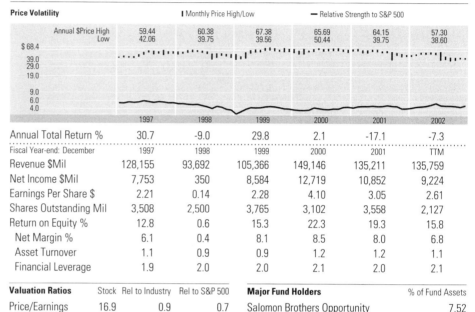

| | | | | | | Monthly Price High/Low | Relative Strength to S&P 500 |

Annual $Price High / Low	59.44 / 42.06	60.38 / 39.75	67.38 / 39.56	65.69 / 50.44	64.15 / 39.75	57.30 / 38.60

$ 68.4 / 39.0 / 29.0 / 19.0 / 9.0 / 6.0 / 4.0

	1997	1998	1999	2000	2001	2002
Annual Total Return %	30.7	-9.0	29.8	2.1	-17.1	-7.3

Fiscal Year-end: December	1997	1998	1999	2000	2001	TTM
Revenue $Mil	128,155	93,692	105,366	149,146	135,211	135,759
Net Income $Mil	7,753	350	8,584	12,719	10,852	9,224
Earnings Per Share $	2.21	0.14	2.28	4.10	3.05	2.61
Shares Outstanding Mil	3,508	2,500	3,765	3,102	3,558	2,127
Return on Equity %	12.8	0.6	15.3	22.3	19.3	15.8
Net Margin %	6.1	0.4	8.1	8.5	8.0	6.8
Asset Turnover	1.1	0.9	0.9	1.2	1.2	1.1
Financial Leverage	1.9	2.0	2.0	2.1	2.0	2.1

Valuation Ratios	Stock	Rel to Industry	Rel to S&P 500
Price/Earnings	16.9	0.9	0.7
Price/Book	1.6	0.7	0.5
Price/Sales	0.7	0.6	0.3
Price/Cash Flow	6.1	0.9	0.5

Major Fund Holders	% of Fund Assets
Salomon Brothers Opportunity	7.52
Rydex Energy Inv	4.76
Putnam Global Natural Resources A	4.59
UBS Strategy A	4.50

Morningstar's Take By Paul Larson, 11-26-2002 Stock Price as of Analysis: $42.23

Shell's integrated operations cover the entire spectrum in oil. Its upstream exploration and production business finds, digs up, transports, and sells crude oil and gas. When the prices of these commodities are above their cost to produce (typically in the low teens per barrel), Shell makes money. At the right price, Shell is a solid investment, in our opinion.

The OPEC cartel works to ensure profits for its member countries, which greatly benefits the entire oil patch. OPEC limits its members' production, which ends up raising oil prices. This action typically maintains a nice spread between the price and cost per barrel of oil. Though OPEC members tend to cheat when prices are high, the cartel's influence is still strong. The spread between the cost to produce and the price of a barrel of oil allows Shell to typically earn decent, though widely variable, margins in its exploration and production business.

Shell also has significant downstream refining and marketing operations. Its refineries get crude oil from the upstream business or on the open market and transform it into usable commodities, like heating oil and gasoline. Through the marketing business, Shell distributes these products to service stations around the globe, selling directly to consumers. Refining and marketing profit margins tend to remain healthy even when commodity prices are poor, providing a nice counterbalance to the upstream results that are so sensitive to commodity price swings.

Shell is highly profitable and has a long history of creating shareholder value. The company has not had an unprofitable year in decades and has enjoyed a healthy 13.0% return on its invested capital over the past three years. Free cash flow has also been strong, allowing the firm to pare its debt to $20 billion, a comparatively small amount considering Shell's $146 billion base of hard assets.

Though volatile commodity prices make for a bumpy road, we expect Shell will continue to generate free cash flow for many years to come, enriching its shareholders in the process. Royal Dutch-Shell is one of the leaders in energy; we'd love to own it at the right price and receive a chunk of the robust dividends it pays. We'd wait for the shares to drop below $40 to provide an adequate margin of safety.

RR Donnelley & Sons DNY

	Rating	Risk	Moat Size	Fair Value	Last Close	Yield %
	★★★★	Med.	Narrow	$32.00	$21.77	4.5

Company Profile

RR Donnelley & Sons is a commercial printer and supplier of print and digital information services. The company operates under contracts with customers that include publishers of commercial and trade magazines, textbooks, professional and reference books, telephone and other directories, merchandise catalogs, and computer equipment owner's manuals. In addition, RR Donnelley & Sons provides printing, binding, prepress, and electronic medium duplication services. Magazine and book publishing revenue accounts for approximately 42% of the company's revenue.

Management

William Davis has been CEO and chairman since 1997. Previously a vice president at Emerson Electric, Davis has led Donnelley's push beyond printing.

Strategy

To pump some life into its flatlining growth, RR Donnelley has attempted to move beyond its core printing services by offering communication and logistics services to current clients. This strategy has the company trying to become a supply-chain partner rather than just a printer. So far, it has met with limited success.

77 West Wacker Drive   www.rrdonnelley.com
Chicago, IL 60601

Morningstar Grades

Growth [D+]	1998	1999	2000	2001
Revenue %	6.6	3.8	6.4	-8.1
Earnings/Share %	133.7	14.4	-8.8	-90.3
Book Value/Share %	-15.3	-4.3	14.0	-25.5
Dividends/Share %	5.1	4.9	4.7	4.4

Growth-obsessed investors should look elsewhere: Donnelley's sales are declining. However, the firm should increase sales around 5% annually over the next several years, a respectable pace in this mature industry.

Profitability [B+]	1999	2000	2001	TTM
Return on Assets %	8.0	6.8	0.7	1.7
Oper Cash Flow $Mil	635	741	548	473
- Cap Spending $Mil	276	237	273	293
= Free Cash Flow $Mil	359	503	275	180

Although revenue fell only 8% in 2001, net income was sliced by a third. This reflects the firm's heavy fixed-cost base. We think improvements in the print division could bring operating margins back into the high single digits over time.

Financial Health [B+]	1999	2000	2001	09-02
Long-term Debt $Mil	748	739	881	775
Total Equity $Mil	1,138	1,233	888	850
Debt/Equity Ratio	0.7	0.6	1.0	0.9

Donnelley has taken on debt to finance new growth initiatives. But debt is low compared with other capital-intensive businesses. Moreover, the firm enjoys substantial free cash flow and a strong credit rating (A2 from Moody's).

	Industry	Investment Style	Stock Type	Sector
	Printing	▦ Mid Core	✓ High Yield	🗎 Business Services

Competition	Market Cap $Mil	Debt/ Equity	12 Mo Trailing Sales $Mil	Price/Cash Flow	Return On Assets%	Total Return% 1 Yr	3 Yr
RR Donnelley & Sons	2,467	0.9	4,835	5.2	1.7	-23.8	0.5
McGraw-Hill Companies	11,713	0.3	4,730	9.8	8.3	0.7	4.5
Quebecor World	3,262	—	6,347	—	—	—	—

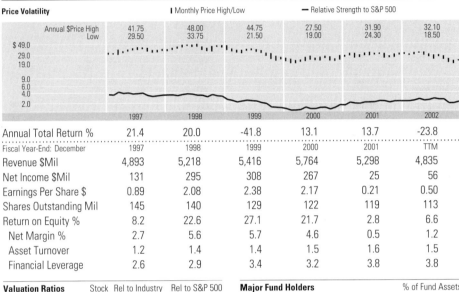

Price Volatility							
	❚ Monthly Price High/Low			▬ Relative Strength to S&P 500			
Annual $Price High Low	41.75 29.50	48.00 33.75	44.75 21.50	27.50 19.00	31.90 24.30	32.10 18.50	
	1997	1998	1999	2000	2001	2002	

	1997	1998	1999	2000	2001	2002
Annual Total Return %	21.4	20.0	-41.8	13.1	13.7	-23.8

Fiscal Year-End: December	1997	1998	1999	2000	2001	TTM
Revenue $Mil	4,893	5,218	5,416	5,764	5,298	4,835
Net Income $Mil	131	295	308	267	25	56
Earnings Per Share $	0.89	2.08	2.38	2.17	0.21	0.50
Shares Outstanding Mil	145	140	129	122	119	113
Return on Equity %	8.2	22.6	27.1	21.7	2.8	6.6
Net Margin %	2.7	5.6	5.7	4.6	0.5	1.2
Asset Turnover	1.2	1.4	1.4	1.5	1.6	1.5
Financial Leverage	2.6	2.9	3.4	3.2	3.8	3.8

Valuation Ratios	Stock	Rel to Industry	Rel to S&P 500
Price/Earnings	43.5	3.3	1.9
Price/Book	2.9	1.0	0.9
Price/Sales	0.5	0.9	0.3
Price/Cash Flow	5.2	1.0	0.4

Major Fund Holders	% of Fund Assets
UC Investment	3.74
STI Classic Mid Cap Value Eq Flex	2.23
Franklin Global Communications A	2.05
Huntington Income-Equity Tr	2.01

Morningstar's Take By T.K. MacKay, 12-16-2002 Stock Price as of Analysis: $21.97

We believe RR Donnelley's size makes for a solid economic moat. However, we'd still want a 40% discount to our fair value estimate before buying.

Donnelley's grip on the printing industry isn't letting up. The company is the world's third-largest commercial printer, printing Time magazine, a third of all textbooks used in America's classrooms, half of the books on The New York Times' bestseller list, and prospectuses and other financial documents for soon-to-be publicly traded companies. Of this business, 70% is done on a contractual basis, locking in long-term recurring revenue streams.

In addition, Donnelley has built a network of more than 60 printing facilities, digging a formidable economic moat around itself. A smaller competitor would have to spend billions of dollars to buy or build the facilities necessary to print and distribute enough materials to achieve the pricing power that Donnelley has built.

Donnelley also has a competitive advantage as one of the largest buyers of print and ink, which account for more than 40% of the company's cost of goods sold. This affords the company the bargaining power that many firms don't have, and has historically kept a lid on costs as the company has grown.

However, growth has been a challenge for Donnelley lately. To cope with the weak advertising market (which results in fewer pages in magazines) and the comatose market for initial public offerings, Donnelley has beefed up offerings in logistics (postal services), electronic directories, and Web site design. But these areas make up just 15% of the company's revenue, are less profitable than printing, and face tougher competition than Donnelley's core business.

To account for this, we forecast Donnelley's sales to expand a modest 5% annually over the next several years (coming off a 12% decline in 2002) as the advertising and financial markets improve. We assume that operating margins climb back to the high single digits as the company improves printing operations under Ron Daly, Donnelley's president of print solutions, who has helped close underperforming facilities and streamline printing operations.

We believe Donnelley will continue to generate substantial free cash flow, but we'd still want a 40% discount to our estimated fair value for the company before buying in.

MORNINGSTAR® Stocks 500

Sabre Holdings TSG

	Rating	Risk	Moat Size	Fair Value	Last Close	Yield %
	★★★	Med.	Narrow	$21.00	$18.11	0.0

Company Profile

Sabre Holdings is an electronic distributor of travel services. The company's proprietary Sabre system allows travel agencies, corporate travel departments, and individual consumers to access information on, and book reservations with, airlines and other providers of travel-related services. Sabre subscribers are able to book reservations with more than 450 airlines and make reservations with more than 50 car-rental properties and more than 230 hotel companies covering approximately 47,000 hotel properties worldwide. Sabre acquired GetThere in 2000.

Management

William Hannigan became CEO and president of Sabre in December 1999, just before it was spun off from AMR. He came from SBC Communications, where he had been considered a contender for the top spot.

Strategy

Sabre wants to be a leader in Internet travel booking, which is widely expected to continue cannibalizing the travel agent business that is still Sabre's bread and butter. Its purchase of GetThere in 2000 solidified its leadership in the nascent online business-to-business travel industry, and Travelocity, now 100% owned by Sabre again, is a leader in online travel services.

3150 Sabre Drive
Southlake, TX 76092
www.sabre.com

Morningstar Grades

Growth [C-]	1998	1999	2000	2001
Revenue %	-12.7	8.8	14.2	8.4
Earnings/Share %	16.3	42.7	-56.3	-78.4
Book Value/Share %	26.3	31.9	-36.9	31.4
Dividends/Share %	NMF	NMF	NMF	NMF

Revenue from Sabre's core business, its booking system, is slowly declining. Travelocity and GetThere face intense competition and have a tough fight to make up the difference. We expect high-single-digit sales growth over the next several years.

Profitability [B+]	1999	2000	2001	TTM
Return on Assets %	17.0	5.4	1.3	5.2
Oper Cash Flow $Mil	495	311	410	91
- Cap Spending $Mil	168	190	158	68
= Free Cash Flow $Mil	327	121	252	23

Cost-cutting and eliminating low-margin businesses have helped Sabre maintain profitability despite its growth problems. However, airfares are a commodity, and more competition threatens Sabre's 20% operating margins.

Financial Health [A+]	1999	2000	2001	09-02
Long-term Debt $Mil	—	149	400	435
Total Equity $Mil	1,262	791	1,042	1,659
Debt/Equity Ratio	—	0.2	0.4	0.3

An infusion of $670 million from the sale of its outsourcing business in 2001 allowed Sabre to reduce its debt load and improve its financial leverage. The company has plenty of cash on hand to finance its new businesses for an extended period.

	Industry	Investment Style	Stock Type	Sector
	Online Retail	▦ Mid Core	→ Slow Growth	⊟ Consumer Services

Competition

	Market Cap $Mil	Debt/ Equity	12 Mo Trailing Sales $Mil	Price/Cash Flow	Return On Assets%	Total Return% 1 Yr	3 Yr
Sabre Holdings	2,579	0.3	2,006	28.4	5.2	-57.2	-25.1
Cendant	10,862	1.8	13,069	10.2	0.9	-46.6	-23.3
Amadeus (Spain)	—	—	—	—	—	—	—

Price Volatility

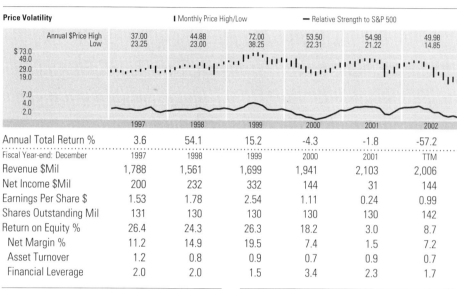

Annual $Price High		37.00	44.88	72.00	53.50	54.98	49.98
Low		23.25	23.00	38.25	22.31	21.22	14.85

Monthly Price High/Low — Relative Strength to S&P 500

	1997	1998	1999	2000	2001	2002
Annual Total Return %	3.6	54.1	15.2	-4.3	-1.8	-57.2

Fiscal Year-end: December	1997	1998	1999	2000	2001	TTM
Revenue $Mil	1,788	1,561	1,699	1,941	2,103	2,006
Net Income $Mil	200	232	332	144	31	144
Earnings Per Share $	1.53	1.78	2.54	1.11	0.24	0.99
Shares Outstanding Mil	131	130	130	130	130	142
Return on Equity %	26.4	24.3	26.3	18.2	3.0	8.7
Net Margin %	11.2	14.9	19.5	7.4	1.5	7.2
Asset Turnover	1.2	0.8	0.9	0.7	0.9	0.7
Financial Leverage	2.0	2.0	1.5	3.4	2.3	1.7

Valuation Ratios	Stock	Rel to Industry	Rel to S&P 500
Price/Earnings	18.3	0.2	0.8
Price/Book	1.6	0.2	0.5
Price/Sales	1.3	0.2	0.6
Price/Cash Flow	28.4	0.6	2.1

Major Fund Holders	% of Fund Assets
Hartford Global Technology A	4.01
Security Technology A	3.90
Fidelity Select Transportation	2.94
Seligman Communications&Information A	2.57

Morningstar's Take By T.K. MacKay, 12-15-2002 Stock Price as of Analysis: $17.30

Because Sabre faces a troubled airline industry and intense competition, we'd stay away from the stock unless it fell 40% or more below our estimated fair value.

Sabre's fortunes are intimately tied to those of the travel industry, so the precipitous decline in air travel after 9/11 has affected the firm deeply. Its core business is still the Sabre computer reservations system, which processes nearly 40% of worldwide travel reservations booked through travel agents. Sabre gets 80% of its revenue from this business, which had been a steady double-digit grower until the end of 2001.

The sharp decline in air travel in the fourth quarter of 2001 put a quick halt to this unit's growth prospects. According to the Air Transport Association, since Jan. 1, the average domestic coach fare has declined 11% from last year, and total available seat miles--a measure of airlines' total capacity--declined 8.5%. This is reducing the inventory available to companies like Travelocity to handle and make commissions from.

In addition to reducing flights and lowering fares, airlines are making their fares available through every distribution channel possible. Consumers can easily find rock-bottom rates on Expedia, Orbitz, and the airlines' own Web sites. With airlines posting billion-dollar losses each quarter, it seems unlikely that the trend of reduced rates, declining capacity, and increased distribution will change anytime soon.

This adds pressure to Sabre's newer businesses, including Travelocity and GetThere. Sabre sees these businesses as major growth drivers, but Travelocity has steadily lost market share to Expedia, airline-owned Orbitz, and Cendant's CD Trip.com, and quarterly revenue from this segment has slipped throughout 2002. Corporate online travel site GetThere is doing better, but makes up just 3% of Sabre's overall sales, and is growing at a slower pace than earlier in the year. Sabre's program offering a new pricing structure designed to lure corporations and suppliers to GetThere is promising but still unproved.

We are increasingly concerned that the combination of increased competition and the airlines' ongoing quest for cheaper distribution could squeeze Sabre's operating margins. Because of this, we would require at least a 40% margin of safety to our fair value estimate before we considered the stock attractive.

Safeway SWY

	Rating	Risk	Moat Size	Fair Value	Last Close	Yield %
	★★★	Med.	None	$35.00	$23.36	0.0

Company Profile

Safeway operates the nation's third-largest retail grocery chain with 1,688 stores, primarily in the Western United States, western Canada, and the Chicago and Washington, D.C., areas. It operates stores under the Safeway, Dominick's, Vons, Carr's, Randall's, and Tom Thumb names. In 1999, the company acquired Alaska's largest grocer, Carr-Gottstein, and Texas-based Randall's. Safeway also owns 42 private-label food manufacturing plants and a 49% interest in Casa Ley, which operates food/variety, clothing, and wholesale outlet stores in western Mexico.

Management

CEO Steve Burd has guided Safeway to industry-leading growth and profitability since coming aboard in 1992. But since he appears to be a hands-on executive without strong lieutenants, investors run the risk of betting on a one-man band.

Strategy

Safeway is getting its restructuring back on track while seeking to maintain its market share. The goal of centralizing some operations is to reduce costs, leaving the company more flexible to compete with rivals. But the effort has proved to be more complicated and expensive than expected, so the retailer is now focused on improving logistics.

5918 Stoneridge Mall Rd.   www.safeway.com
Pleasanton, CA 94588

Morningstar Grades

Growth [B]	1998	1999	2000	2001
Revenue %	8.9	17.9	10.8	7.3
Earnings/Share %	42.0	18.2	13.3	14.6
Book Value/Share %	40.7	30.2	32.9	9.0
Dividends/Share %	NMF	NMF	NMF	NMF

Positive sales growth in recent quarters has come mainly from new-store openings. Same-store sales declined more than 1% in each of the past two quarters, a worrisome trend.

Profitability [A-]	1999	2000	2001	TTM
Return on Assets %	6.5	6.8	7.2	3.4
Oper Cash Flow $Mil	1,488	1,901	2,231	2,108
- Cap Spending $Mil	1,334	1,573	1,793	1,668
= Free Cash Flow $Mil	155	329	438	439

Safeway is the third-largest grocer in terms of sales, but it has historically topped peers when it comes to profit margins. Competition has hurt margins recently, but we expect profitability to improve again within a couple of years.

Financial Health [C+]	1999	2000	2001	09-02
Long-term Debt $Mil	6,357	5,822	6,712	7,449
Total Equity $Mil	4,086	5,390	5,890	4,841
Debt/Equity Ratio	1.6	1.1	1.1	1.5

Safeway is a solid cash flow generator. The company is spending heavily to remodel stores and restructure operations, but still has had plenty of cash to repurchase shares.

	Industry	Investment Style	Stock Type	Sector
	Groceries	▦ Large Value	↗ Classic Growth	▭ Consumer Services

Competition	Market Cap $Mil	Debt/ Equity	12 Mo Trailing Sales $Mil	Price/Cash Flow	Return On Assets%	Total Return% 1 Yr	3 Yr
Safeway	13,376	1.5	34,757	6.3	3.4	-44.1	-12.2
Wal-Mart Stores	223,388	0.5	233,651	18.9	8.0	-11.8	-7.3
Kroger	11,946	2.2	51,105	5.0	6.2	-26.0	-7.6

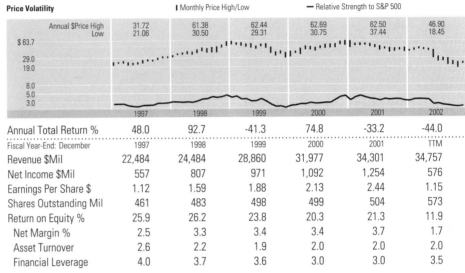

Price Volatility — Monthly Price High/Low — Relative Strength to S&P 500

	1997	1998	1999	2000	2001	2002
Annual $Price High	31.72	61.38	62.44	62.69	62.50	46.90
Low	21.06	30.50	29.31	30.75	37.44	18.45
Annual Total Return %	48.0	92.7	-41.3	74.8	-33.2	-44.0

Fiscal Year-End: December	1997	1998	1999	2000	2001	TTM
Revenue $Mil	22,484	24,484	28,860	31,977	34,301	34,757
Net Income $Mil	557	807	971	1,092	1,254	576
Earnings Per Share $	1.12	1.59	1.88	2.13	2.44	1.15
Shares Outstanding Mil	461	483	498	499	504	573
Return on Equity %	25.9	26.2	23.8	20.3	21.3	11.9
Net Margin %	2.5	3.3	3.4	3.4	3.7	1.7
Asset Turnover	2.6	2.2	1.9	2.0	2.0	2.0
Financial Leverage	4.0	3.7	3.6	3.0	3.0	3.5

Valuation Ratios	Stock	Rel to Industry	Rel to S&P 500
Price/Earnings	20.3	1.0	0.9
Price/Book	2.8	0.9	0.9
Price/Sales	0.4	1.0	0.2
Price/Cash Flow	6.3	1.0	0.5

Major Fund Holders	% of Fund Assets
PBHG Focused Value	6.49
PBHG Clipper Focus PBHG	5.05
Strategic Partners Focused Value A	4.33
Salomon Brothers Capital O	4.18

Morningstar's Take By David Kathman, 10-09-2002 Stock Price as of Analysis: $21.01

While Safeway's problems are certainly cause for concern, we can't agree with the worst-case scenario implied by the stock's price. We think the shares are worth picking up, though investors may need to be patient to reap the benefits.

Safeway has traditionally been the most profitable of the major grocery chains, and among the steadiest growers. But it, along with the rest of the industry, has been facing increased competition from big-box stores like Wal-Mart (now the nation's largest grocery retailer), warehouse clubs like Costco, and specialty grocers like Whole Foods. Not only have these upstarts cut into the market share of traditional grocers, they have sparked price wars that have eroded margins over the past year.

Safeway's efforts to adapt to these new realities have not always gone smoothly. Some of its efforts to drive volume through lower prices didn't work and were abandoned. Logistical kinks also surfaced as Safeway sought to centralize buying operations across its far-flung empire, creating product shortages and late deliveries. Some store managers stopped ordering items that were prone to spoilage or theft, but this narrowed product selection and alienated shoppers--something Safeway can ill afford to do in this cutthroat competitive environment.

However, we think Safeway's bottom line will eventually recover from its fumbles, given the company's record. Much of the recent margin shrinkage has resulted from investments designed to drive sales, some of which will take time to bear fruit. The excellent customer-oriented service that drove Safeway's historically industry-leading margins is still in place, despite the temporary glitches. Once the economy improves and consumers are less focused on price, Safeway stands to gain against such bare-bones competitors as Costco. Although full realization of restructuring benefits is likely to be further away than we first thought, we think substantial savings will start in a couple of years.

Safeway is certainly a riskier investment than it was a couple of years ago. The heightened competitive environment is likely to put a long-term dent in the company's growth and profitability, but even so, we estimate Safeway's fair value to be $35 per share. We'd want a substantial margin of safety before jumping in, but in the low $20s, this is definitely a stock worth owning.

MORNINGSTAR® Stocks 500

SanDisk SNDK

	Rating	Risk	Moat Size	Fair Value	Last Close	Yield %
	★	High	Narrow	$16.00	$20.30	0.0

Industry	Investment Style	Stock Type	Sector
Semiconductors	▦ Mid Growth	⬙ Spec. Growth	▤ Hardware

Company Profile

SanDisk manufactures data-storage products. Its flash memory products can be either inserted or embedded in computers, telephones, medical devices, cellular telephones, digital cameras, handheld terminals, voice and audio recorders, digital audio samplers, and other computer-based products. SanDisk makes data-storage products that can store up to 440 megabytes of memory. The company also produces flash memory products that are sold under private labels. Foreign revenue accounts for approximately 56% of the company's revenue.

Management

Founder Eli Harari is president and CEO. As of March 2002, he owned nearly 4% of the firm. Management as a whole, including Harari, owns about 6% of shares outstanding.

Strategy

SanDisk focuses on flash memory products for consumer-oriented uses, like digital cameras. The firm looks to drive industry standards for flash memory and partner with leading electronic device makers so its products will have mass appeal. SanDisk has historically outsourced its chip production, but is starting to take a more direct role in the actual manufacturing.

140 Caspian Court   www.sandisk.com
Sunnyvale, CA 94089

Morningstar Grades

Growth [B+]	1998	1999	2000	2001
Revenue %	8.4	81.9	143.7	-39.1
Earnings/Share %	-47.5	104.8	855.8	NMF
Book Value/Share %	-4.4	151.3	28.2	-16.6
Dividends/Share %	NMF	NMF	NMF	NMF

Sales have been very volatile, demonstrating the manic nature of the memory chip industry. After more than doubling in 2000, the honeymoon ended in 2001 when sales fell almost 40%. Sales are on pace in 2002 to rebound by more than 40%.

Profitability [C+]	1999	2000	2001	TTM
Return on Assets %	4.0	27.1	-32.0	4.4
Oper Cash Flow $Mil	17	85	-72	50
- Cap Spending $Mil	21	27	26	22
= Free Cash Flow $Mil	-4	58	-98	28

SanDisk earns fat margins on royalty sales, but overall margins are nothing to brag about since most of its sales come from actual memory cards, which are far less profitable. Operating margins have average 11% since 1995.

Financial Health [B-]	1999	2000	2001	09-02
Long-term Debt $Mil	—	—	125	150
Total Equity $Mil	572	863	675	608
Debt/Equity Ratio	—	—	0.2	0.2

SanDisk is in very solid health. Cash and investments of $550 million are greater than total liabilities by almost $200 million. Trailing-12-month free cash flows are also positive.

Competition

	Market Cap $Mil	Debt/ Equity	12 Mo Trailing Sales $Mil	Price/Cash Flow	Return On Assets%	Total Return% 1 Yr	3 Yr
SanDisk	1,400	0.2	453	28.1	4.4	41.0	-23.2
Sony ADR	38,122	0.4	60,413	6.5	0.2	-8.1	-32.4
Toshiba	9,979	—	54,858	—	—	—	—

Price Volatility

| | | ❙ Monthly Price High/Low | — Relative Strength to S&P 500 | | | |

Annual $Price High Low	20.00 4.44	13.13 2.56	50.31 6.63	169.63 27.50	48.69 8.61	29.20 9.60
$170.6 69.0 39.0 19.0 6.0 3.0 1.0						
	1997	1998	1999	2000	2001	2002

Annual Total Return %	108.3	-30.5	581.4	-42.3	-48.1	41.0
Fiscal Year-end: December	1997	1998	1999	2000	2001	TTM
Revenue $Mil	125	136	247	602	366	453
Net Income $Mil	20	12	27	299	-298	42
Earnings Per Share $	0.40	0.21	0.43	4.11	-4.37	0.61
Shares Outstanding Mil	46	51	55	67	68	69
Return on Equity %	10.4	5.7	4.6	34.6	-44.1	7.0
Net Margin %	15.8	8.7	10.7	49.6	-81.3	9.3
Asset Turnover	0.5	0.5	0.4	0.5	0.4	0.5
Financial Leverage	1.3	1.2	1.2	1.3	1.4	1.6

Valuation Ratios	Stock	Rel to Industry	Rel to S&P 500
Price/Earnings	33.3	0.8	1.4
Price/Book	2.3	0.8	0.7
Price/Sales	3.1	0.8	1.5
Price/Cash Flow	28.1	2.4	2.1

Major Fund Holders	% of Fund Assets
Firsthand Technology Innovators	7.34
AFBA Five Star Science & Technology A	6.04
Buffalo Science & Technology	5.34
Harris Insight Small Cap Agg Gr Inst	4.97

Morningstar's Take By Jeremy Lopez, 11-26-2002 Stock Price as of Analysis: $25.79

SanDisk's growth prospects are strong but already reflected in the stock, in our opinion.

With a focus on flash memory chips, SanDisk's growth prospects look solid. The firm's standardized memory cards are used in myriad consumer electronic devices, like digital cameras, music players, and Palm organizers. The sale of tech gadgets has been strong over the past year, as consumers have preferred smaller-ticket items over pricier ones. Given that the market for electronics isn't nearly as saturated as, say, the market for PCs, we think SanDisk will ride the coattails of strong demand for consumer electronics.

SanDisk's prospects are even more appealing considering the firm's defensible economic moat. The company's standardized memory cards are compatible with the products of most major digital music player and camera makers. This proliferation leads to what is commonly referred to as the network effect, which creates a high barrier to entry for any rival standard. The only other serious threat, in our view, comes from Sony's Memory Stick. But Sony's rivals are not likely to make their products compatible with a competitor's standard. Also, SanDisk has patented its cards, meaning chipmakers that make them must pay SanDisk a royalty.

However, there is a dark side to SanDisk's business. In addition to licensing its technology, the firm also competes with customers in making the physical memory cards. In many respects, this part of SanDisk's business can occasionally be unattractive. There's a lot of competition in memory cards and little--other than price--differentiates SanDisk-branded cards from other knock-off versions. Because 90% of SanDisk's sales come from memory cards, price competition has led to poor and volatile margins. Gross margins were nearly cut in half in 2001 from the prior year.

While SanDisk has decent growth prospects and a solid franchise, its appeal is limited by the volatile and oft-low margins in memory chips. As a result, we consider SanDisk a high-risk stock and would need around a 50% margin of safety to our fair value estimate before recommending it to investors.

Sanofi-Synthelabo ADR SNY

	Rating	Risk	Moat Size	Fair Value	Last Close	Yield %
	★★★	Low	Narrow	$35.00	$30.40	0.0

Company Profile

Sanofi-Synthelabo is a France-based global pharmaceutical company. It concentrates on four therapeutic areas: cardiovascular/thrombosis, central nervous system, internal medicine, and oncology. Sanofi sells in more than 100 countries and derives half its revenue from Europe and a third from the United States. Its top-selling drugs are Avapro, Plavix (both marketed by Bristol-Myers Squibb in the United States), and Ambien. Sanofi was listed on the NYSE in July 2002, signifying its attempt to build a stronger U.S. presence.

Management

Two French firms effectively control Sanofi: Total Fina Elf and L'Oreal have voting rights to 36% and 27%, respectively, of the stock. Jean-Francois Dehecq is chairman and CEO. He also is chairman of the European pharmaceutical lobbying group.

Strategy

Sanofi concentrates on four therapeutic areas: cardiovascular, central nervous system, internal medicine, and oncology. It markets drugs on its own where it can, but has partnered up, specifically in the United States, to market several of its best sellers. The company is trying to increase its U.S. presence.

174 Avenue de France
Paris, 75013
www.sanofi-synthelabo.fr

Industry	Investment Style	Stock Type	Sector
Drugs	⊞ Large Growth	◆ Spec. Growth	⚕ Healthcare

Competition	Market Cap $Mil	Debt/ Equity	12 Mo Trailing Sales $Mil	Price/Cash Flow	Return On Assets%	Total Return% 1 Yr	3 Yr
Sanofi-Synthelabo ADR	44,512	0.0	5,785	27.5	13.9	—	—
Merck	127,121	0.3	50,430	13.2	15.0	-1.3	-2.5
Novartis AG ADR	105,974	0.1	18,933	24.4	10.4	1.8	2.3

Price Volatility   ❙ Monthly Price High/Low   — Relative Strength to S&P 500

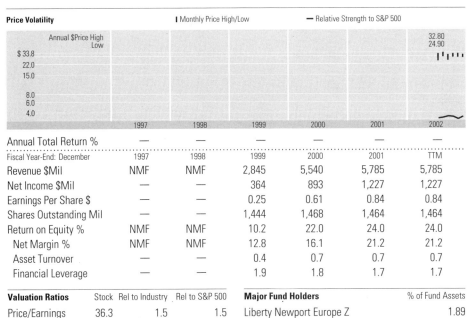

Annual Total Return %	—	—	—	—	—	—
Fiscal Year-End: December	1997	1998	1999	2000	2001	TTM
Revenue $Mil	NMF	NMF	2,845	5,540	5,785	5,785
Net Income $Mil	—	—	364	893	1,227	1,227
Earnings Per Share $	—	—	0.25	0.61	0.84	0.84
Shares Outstanding Mil	—	—	1,444	1,468	1,464	1,464
Return on Equity %	NMF	NMF	10.2	22.0	24.0	24.0
Net Margin %	NMF	NMF	12.8	16.1	21.2	21.2
Asset Turnover	—	—	0.4	0.7	0.7	0.7
Financial Leverage	—	—	1.9	1.8	1.7	1.7

Valuation Ratios	Stock	Rel to Industry	Rel to S&P 500
Price/Earnings	36.3	1.5	1.5
Price/Book	8.7	1.2	2.7
Price/Sales	7.7	2.0	3.8
Price/Cash Flow	27.5	1.3	2.1

Major Fund Holders	% of Fund Assets
Liberty Newport Europe Z	1.89
CitiStreet International Stock I	1.37
Dreyfus Premier Health Care A	1.35

Morningstar Grades

Growth [A]	1998	1999	2000	2001
Revenue %	NMF	NMF	124.3	8.8
Earnings/Share %	NMF	NMF	178.7	43.5
Book Value/Share %	—	NMF	18.6	34.3
Dividends/Share %	NMF	NMF	NMF	NMF

Sanofi's revenue growth should slightly outdo the competition's over the next five years, thanks to products like Plavix, Avapro, Ambien, and Eloxatine. We expect 10% compound annual growth through 2006.

Profitability [A+]	1999	2000	2001	TTM
Return on Assets %	5.3	12.1	13.9	13.9
Oper Cash Flow $Mil	545	1,114	1,621	1,621
- Cap Spending $Mil	240	346	504	504
= Free Cash Flow $Mil	305	768	1,117	1,117

Sanofi's margins have improved dramatically. Gross margins are now north of 80% and operating margins are in the low to mid-30s compared with gross margins below 70% and operating margins in the midteens in 1998.

Financial Health [A+]	1999	2000	2001	12-01
Long-term Debt $Mil	137	114	105	105
Total Equity $Mil	3,578	4,060	5,104	5,104
Debt/Equity Ratio	0.0	0.0	0.0	0.0

With approximately $3 billion in cash and less than $500 million in debt, Sanofi's balance sheet is very solid. The company also generates plenty of free cash flow (cash flow from operations less capital expenditures).

Morningstar's Take By Todd N. Lebor, 12-16-2002 Stock Price as of Analysis: $29.81

Sanofi-Synthelabo could be a terrific investment someday, but until it builds a global salesforce, we're not signing up unless it trades at a decent discount to our fair value estimate.

Sanofi has discovered some of the world's best-selling drugs, but because it hasn't built a sizable U.S. sales team, it has forgone hundreds of millions in profits from the world's most lucrative drug market. Until April 2002, Sanofi was sharing the profits on its three top-selling products. Bristol-Myers Squibb is still pocketing most of the U.S. revenue for anticoagulant Plavix and hypertension drug Avapro. Until April 2002, when Sanofi acquired the 51% of Lorex Pharmaceuticals it didn't own from Pharmacia, it was sharing the sales of sleep disorder drug Ambien. Sanofi now gets 100% of Ambien sales.

As of June 2002, Sanofi derived only 20% of its consolidated revenue (revenue it keeps from drugs it developed) from the U.S. market. Even if we add the unconsolidated U.S. sales from Plavix, Avapro, and Ambien, Sanofi's total U.S. revenue exposure would only be 35%-40%. Given the unrestricted pricing and the size of the U.S. market (it's half of the global drug market), Sanofi needs more exposure to the United States, in our opinion.

We believe the company could improve its margins as well. Sanofi is no slouch, with operating and net margins in the low 30s and mid-20s, respectively, but we believe it's leaving cash on the table. Assuming royalty income is between 10% and 20%, Sanofi could improve its margins by selling its own drugs that have product margins closer to 25%-30%, even after manufacturing, marketing, and distribution costs. We view the acquisition of Lorex as a step in the right direction, but not enough.

It's too bad the French drug concern has to share, because its labs have been some of the most productive over the past few years. In 2002, Sanofi obtained six new U.S. marketing authorizations and has also demonstrated a competent understanding of the Food and Drug Administration. We view Sanofi as an excellent candidate for a merger with a U.S.-based drug company. Bristol is the obvious choice, given the Plavix and Avapro comarketing relationship, but we're not holding our breath, given Bristol's troubles.

With a productive research department, several young drugs with blockbuster potential, and a healthy balance sheet, Sanofi has the makings of a global pharmaceutical powerhouse. However, we think it needs to be more self-sufficient.

MORNINGSTAR® Stocks 500

SAP AG ADR SAP

	Rating	Risk	Moat Size	Fair Value	Last Close	Yield %
	★	Med.	Narrow	$15.00	$19.50	0.7

Company Profile

SAP is a leading provider of e-business software. The mySAP.com platform covers applications like accounting, human resources, supply-chain management, customer-relationship management, enterprise portals, and electronic marketplaces. The company also offers consulting and training services. SAP has subsidiaries in Europe, the Americas, Australasia, Africa, and the Middle East. More than 15,000 companies in over 100 countries run more than 36,000 installations of SAP software.

Management

Co-founder and CEO Hasso Plattner is SAP. The company recently appointed William R. McDermott, former head of worldwide sales at Siebel, to head up its struggling North American operations.

Strategy

Through its end-to-end suite, mySAP, the company is expanding beyond the slow-growing enterprise resource planning market into customer-relationship and supply-chain management. Its strategy is to tap its installed base of 15,000 customers, all of which are solid candidates to buy its newer applications, and take market share from Siebel and i2.

Neurottstrasse 16   www.sap.com
Walldorf, 69190

Morningstar Grades

Growth [A]	1998	1999	2000	2001
Revenue %	42.8	18.4	22.6	17.2
Earnings/Share %	18.4	13.8	5.8	-8.0
Book Value/Share %	26.5	40.4	-1.2	-27.9
Dividends/Share %	8.3	0.0	9.6	1.8

The top line has averaged 32% over the past five years, but those days are over. We conservatively peg long-term sales growth at 10%.

Profitability [A+]	1999	2000	2001	TTM
Return on Assets %	7.8	6.5	9.5	9.5
Oper Cash Flow $Mil	569	632	882	882
- Cap Spending $Mil	379	265	337	337
= Free Cash Flow $Mil	190	367	545	545

Profitability has been outstanding. The company generates returns on invested capital and returns on equity in excess of 30% and 20%, respectively.

Financial Health [A-]	1999	2000	2001	12-01
Long-term Debt $Mil	1	4	6	6
Total Equity $Mil	2,559	2,375	2,752	2,752
Debt/Equity Ratio	0.0	0.0	0.0	0.0

The balance sheet is pristine, with more than $1 billion in cash and no debt. SAP also produces significant amounts of cash flow.

Industry	Investment Style	Stock Type	Sector
Business Applications	▦ Large Growth	↗ Classic Growth	↖ Software

Competition

	Market Cap $Mil	Debt/ Equity	12 Mo Trailing Sales $Mil	Price/Cash Flow	Return On Assets%	Total Return% 1 Yr	3 Yr
SAP AG ADR	24,556	0.0	6,546	27.8	9.5	-38.7	-25.0
Oracle	57,845	0.1	9,459	18.1	19.8	-21.8	-26.3
PeopleSoft	5,728	—	1,931	15.3	6.8	-54.5	-2.6

Price Volatility

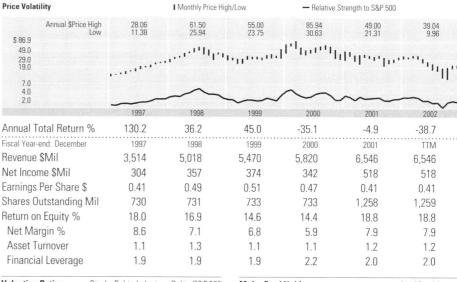

		Monthly Price High/Low			— Relative Strength to S&P 500	
Annual $Price High	28.06	61.50	55.00	85.94	49.00	39.04
Low	11.38	25.94	23.75	30.63	21.31	9.96

	1997	1998	1999	2000	2001	2002
Annual Total Return %	130.2	36.2	45.0	-35.1	-4.9	-38.7

Fiscal Year-end: December	1997	1998	1999	2000	2001	TTM
Revenue $Mil	3,514	5,018	5,470	5,820	6,546	6,546
Net Income $Mil	304	357	374	342	518	518
Earnings Per Share $	0.41	0.49	0.51	0.47	0.41	0.41
Shares Outstanding Mil	730	731	733	733	1,258	1,259
Return on Equity %	18.0	16.9	14.6	14.4	18.8	18.8
Net Margin %	8.6	7.1	6.8	5.9	7.9	7.9
Asset Turnover	1.1	1.3	1.1	1.1	1.2	1.2
Financial Leverage	1.9	1.9	1.9	2.2	2.0	2.0

Valuation Ratios	Stock	Rel to Industry	Rel to S&P 500
Price/Earnings	47.3	1.5	2.0
Price/Book	8.9	1.7	2.8
Price/Sales	3.8	0.4	1.9
Price/Cash Flow	27.8	1.7	2.1

Major Fund Holders	% of Fund Assets
Turner Concentrated Growth Instl	3.21
Gartmore Global Tech & Comm A	2.98
Wells Fargo Specialized Technology A	2.54
PIMCO RCM Europe D	2.33

Morningstar's Take By Mike Trigg, 10-21-2002 Stock Price as of Analysis: $19.10

Germany-based SAP isn't on the radar screens of most investors, but we think it should be. However, we wouldn't buy until the stock fell 25% below our fair value estimate, because the firm lacks a wide economic moat and IT spending remains dormant.

Like most software vendors, SAP has struggled as companies slashed IT spending in the wake of slowing profits. The days of unabashed spending are over and customers are now buying in smaller increments. The downturn has been compounded by the fact that companies bought too much software in the late 1990s that still hasn't been implemented. Companies have had to finish existing software projects before investing in new ones.

SAP dominates the market for enterprise resource planning (ERP) software, which streamlines internal operations like human resources and accounting. However, the ERP market is mature and slow-growing; customers now demand software that improves external processes, like sales and marketing. This led the company to introduce mySAP, an end-to-end software suite that includes more popular applications like customer-relationship management (CRM) and supply-chain management (SCM).

MySAP has been successful because it leverages SAP's competitive advantage: an installed base of 15,000 customers, all of which are solid candidates to buy the newest applications given their longstanding relationships. Management estimates 15% of current customers have upgraded to the suite, leaving lots of room for growth. Our only concern is that the installed base opportunity will eventually dry up.

Thus, growth hinges on new business and taking share from niche incumbents like Siebel Systems and i2 Technologies. However, SAP and other vendors with similar soup-to-nuts offerings, like Oracle and PeopleSoft, have had trouble. While we think more firms will gravitate toward suites because they reduce the time that must be spent on integrating software from different vendors, it hasn't happened yet. Many companies have already spent millions of dollars on other software and are unwilling to abandon those investments. Instead, we expect firms to buy individual applications and gradually build toward the suite over time.

SAP would make a good investment at the right price. We think the stock is worth $15 per share, but given that the company lacks a sustainable competitive advantage, which will make it tough to win new business, we wouldn't buy the stock until it fell to $11-$12.

Sara Lee SLE

	Rating	Risk	Moat Size	Fair Value	Last Close	Yield %
	★★★	Med.	Narrow	$25.00	$22.51	2.7

Company Profile

Sara Lee produces food products and consumer goods. Its brand-name products include Sara Lee frozen and baked goods, Hillshire Farms smoked sausage, Jimmy Dean sausages, and Ball Park hot dogs. The company also produces specialty coffees and teas and rice products. Its nonfood operations include Hanes hosiery and clothing, Playtex intimate apparel, L'eggs hosiery, and Kiwi leather-care products. Foreign sales account for approximately 43% of the company's total sales.

Management

Steve McMillan took the reins in July 2000. McMillan, a 26-year veteran of Sara Lee, had been chief operating officer since 1993.

Strategy

In an effort to simplify and focus, Sara Lee is getting rid of underperforming assets while beefing up its core food and apparel divisions. It has sold 16 businesses over the past two years, including PYA/Monarch food service and Coach leather goods, while strengthening its bakery division with the purchase of Earthgrains, the second-largest bakery in the United States.

Three First National Plaza
Chicago, IL 60602-4260
www.saralee.com

Morningstar Grades

Growth [C+]	1999	2000	2001	2002
Revenue %	-0.9	-4.7	1.1	6.0
Earnings/Share %	NMF	6.3	97.8	-53.6
Book Value/Share %	-34.0	0.9	-4.8	77.7
Dividends/Share %	8.9	8.2	7.5	4.4

Revenue grew 6% in fiscal 2002 and 7% in the first quarter of fiscal 2003, but most of that was due to the acquisition of Earthgrains. Excluding divestitures and acquisitions, sales declined 2%-3% over the same period.

Profitability [B+]	2000	2001	2002	TTM
Return on Assets %	10.5	22.3	7.3	7.9
Oper Cash Flow $Mil	1,540	1,496	1,735	2,073
- Cap Spending $Mil	647	532	669	706
= Free Cash Flow $Mil	893	964	1,066	1,367

Profitability is finally getting a boost after two years of lackluster results. Earnings per share grew 42% in the September quarter and operating income grew 25%. The company also raised its earnings forecasts for 2003.

Financial Health [B]	2000	2001	2002	09-02
Long-term Debt $Mil	2,248	2,640	4,326	3,957
Total Equity $Mil	1,007	899	1,534	1,791
Debt/Equity Ratio	2.2	2.9	2.8	2.2

Even though the company has used debt to fund share repurchases and recent acquisitions, its strong operating cash flow easily covers debt expense. Long-term debt ballooned in late 2001 because of the Earthgrains purchase.

Industry	Investment Style	Stock Type	Sector
Food Mfg.	▦ Large Value	📈 High Yield	🏠 Consumer Goods

Competition

	Market Cap $Mil	Debt/ Equity	12 Mo Trailing Sales $Mil	Price/Cash Flow	Return On Assets%	Total Return% 1 Yr	3 Yr
Sara Lee	17,551	2.2	17,914	8.5	7.9	4.2	5.2
Procter & Gamble	111,662	0.9	41,268	13.3	11.0	11.3	-4.5
Philip Morris Companies	84,290	0.9	90,561	7.7	13.4	-6.8	26.8

Price Volatility

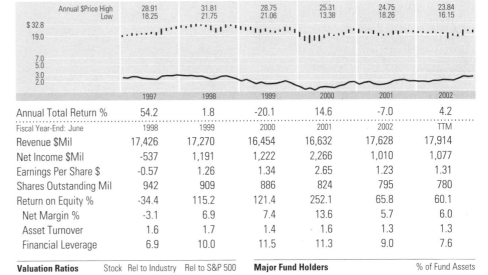

		1997	1998	1999	2000	2001	2002
Annual $Price High		28.91	31.81	28.75	25.31	24.75	23.84
Low		18.25	21.75	21.06	13.38	18.26	16.15
Annual Total Return %		54.2	1.8	-20.1	14.6	-7.0	4.2

Fiscal Year-End: June	1998	1999	2000	2001	2002	TTM
Revenue $Mil	17,426	17,270	16,454	16,632	17,628	17,914
Net Income $Mil	-537	1,191	1,222	2,266	1,010	1,077
Earnings Per Share $	-0.57	1.26	1.34	2.65	1.23	1.31
Shares Outstanding Mil	942	909	886	824	795	780
Return on Equity %	-34.4	115.2	121.4	252.1	65.8	60.1
Net Margin %	-3.1	6.9	7.4	13.6	5.7	6.0
Asset Turnover	1.6	1.7	1.4	1.6	1.3	1.3
Financial Leverage	6.9	10.0	11.5	11.3	9.0	7.6

Valuation Ratios	Stock	Rel to Industry	Rel to S&P 500
Price/Earnings	17.2	0.8	0.7
Price/Book	9.8	2.3	3.1
Price/Sales	1.0	0.7	0.5
Price/Cash Flow	8.5	0.8	0.6

Major Fund Holders	% of Fund Assets
Ameristock	5.15
Wells Fargo Equity Value A	4.62
GE Premier Value Equity A	4.54
Wells Fargo Equity Income I	4.41

Morningstar's Take By David Kathman, 11-21-2002 Stock Price as of Analysis: $23.48

Sara Lee's ambitious restructuring plan has finally started to show some encouraging results. We think Sara Lee will emerge as a stronger company, though we'd wait for the right price before buying.

Over the past two-plus years, Sara Lee has worked to transform itself from a lumbering conglomerate into a more nimble, focused firm. It sold or spun off 16 underperforming businesses, many of which fell outside its core areas of food and beverages, household products, and apparel. It also made a few key acquisitions to strengthen those core businesses, most notably its $2.8 billion purchase of number-two U.S. bakery Earthgrains. That deal beefed up the division most closely associated with Sara Lee in the public's mind, and Earthgrains' direct-store distribution system is expected to boost annual sales of Sara Lee products by $300 million within four years.

The results of this restructuring have been mixed so far, with the biggest problem being weak sales. The beverage division fell off a cliff in 2002, as coffee sales plunged in the face of stepped-up competition. Sales in the meat division have remained lackluster despite the introduction of new products and increased marketing spending on core brands. The intimates and underwear division continues to be

squeezed by the weak U.S. economy and price competition from Fruit of the Loom, resulting in flat sales. Even in the bakery division, sales have been declining when Earthgrains is factored out.

It's on the bottom line that the restructuring is finally having some positive effects. Sara Lee's meat and intimates and underwear divisions, its two largest in terms of revenue, have seen strong double-digit growth in operating profits despite the lackluster sales figures. Some of this improvement has been due to lower meat and cotton costs during most of 2002, but improved efficiencies have also been a major factor, especially in the streamlined meat division. The company boosted its earnings forecasts in October, making us more optimistic about its ability to maintain profit gains.

Sara Lee is not out of the woods yet, but we think it's on track to be a stronger company once the effects of its restructuring are in full force. We're bumping up our fair value estimate to $25, which assumes modest growth and profitability increases in the next few years. However, we'd be inclined to buy the stock only at a significant discount to that estimate--the high teens or lower.

MORNINGSTAR® Stocks 500

SBC Communications SBC

	Rating	Risk	Moat Size	Fair Value	Last Close	Yield %
	★★★	Med.	Narrow	$36.00	$27.11	3.9

Company Profile

SBC is the amalgamation of three regional Bells, the dominant local phone companies created by the breakup of AT&T in 1984. Southwestern Bell offers local phone service in Arkansas, Kansas, Missouri, Oklahoma, and Texas. Pacific/Nevada Bell provides service to California and Nevada. Ameritech offers service in Illinois, Michigan, Indiana, Ohio, and Wisconsin. Cingular Wireless, SBC's 60%-owned joint venture with BellSouth, provides wireless service to 20.5 million customers. The company also has extensive international investments and a directory publishing business.

Management

Chairman and CEO Edward Whitacre has been in the telecommunication industry since 1965 and in the top spot at SBC since 1990. Whitacre is also on the boards of several large corporations, including Anheuser-Busch.

Strategy

SBC has been hard-hit by the weak economy and regulations that force it to open its network to competition. The firm been lobbying for regulatory change, reducing costs (through layoffs), and cutting capital spending. Long-distance is also key to SBC's strategy--winning approval in all states will allow the firm to offer larger service bundles, adding to revenue and customer loyalty.

175 E. Houston
San Antonio, TX 78205-2933

www.sbc.com

Morningstar Grades

Growth [D]	1998	1999	2000	2001
Revenue %	7.2	7.2	3.7	-10.6
Earnings/Share %	85.8	5.8	-1.7	-8.2
Book Value/Share %	NMF	17.1	14.8	7.7
Dividends/Share %	4.4	4.3	4.1	1.8

Local phone revenue has been falling as lines in service decrease. Cingular Wireless and SBC's data operations (traditional growth drivers) haven't generated enough incremental revenue to offset this decline, pushing total revenue lower.

Profitability [A]	1999	2000	2001	TTM
Return on Assets %	9.8	8.1	7.5	5.1
Oper Cash Flow $Mil	16,674	14,066	14,805	14,821
- Cap Spending $Mil	10,304	13,124	11,189	8,091
= Free Cash Flow $Mil	6,370	942	3,616	6,730

SBC is solidly profitable, but not to the extent its reported financials indicate. A noncash pension credit inflated 2001's operating margin by 3 percentage points. Cost-cutting has offset a smaller pension credit and lower revenue in 2002.

Financial Health [A-]	1999	2000	2001	09-02
Long-term Debt $Mil	17,475	15,492	17,133	18,933
Total Equity $Mil	26,726	30,463	32,491	32,389
Debt/Equity Ratio	0.7	0.5	0.5	0.6

SBC maintains one of the strongest balance sheets in the industry. Its cash flow covers interest expenses more than a dozen times. Reduced spending on new equipment has vastly improved free cash flow.

Industry	Investment Style	Stock Type	Sector
Telecommunication Services	▦ Large Value	▨ High Yield	▯ Telecom

Competition

	Market Cap $Mil	Debt/ Equity	12 Mo Trailing Sales $Mil	Price/Cash Flow	Return On Assets%	Total Return% 1 Yr	3 Yr
SBC Communications	90,011	0.6	43,824	6.1	5.1	-28.3	-12.8
Verizon Communications	106,011	1.4	67,422	4.7	-0.1	-15.2	-9.8
AT&T	20,115	0.8	48,821	1.8	-10.9	-27.7	-28.2

Price Volatility

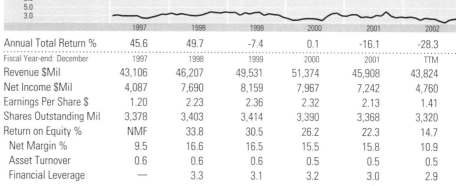

		Monthly Price High/Low		─ Relative Strength to S&P 500		
Annual $Price High Low	38.06 24.63	54.88 35.00	59.94 44.06	59.00 34.75	53.06 36.50	40.99 19.60
	1997	1998	1999	2000	2001	2002

Annual Total Return %	45.6	49.7	-7.4	0.1	-16.1	-28.3
Fiscal Year-end: December	1997	1998	1999	2000	2001	TTM
Revenue $Mil	43,106	46,207	49,531	51,374	45,908	43,824
Net Income $Mil	4,087	7,690	8,159	7,967	7,242	4,760
Earnings Per Share $	1.20	2.23	2.36	2.32	2.13	1.41
Shares Outstanding Mil	3,378	3,403	3,414	3,390	3,368	3,320
Return on Equity %	NMF	33.8	30.5	26.2	22.3	14.7
Net Margin %	9.5	16.6	16.5	15.5	15.8	10.9
Asset Turnover	0.6	0.6	0.6	0.5	0.5	0.5
Financial Leverage	—	3.3	3.1	3.2	3.0	2.9

Valuation Ratios	Stock	Rel to Industry	Rel to S&P 500
Price/Earnings	19.2	1.2	0.8
Price/Book	2.8	1.0	0.9
Price/Sales	2.1	1.3	1.0
Price/Cash Flow	6.1	1.2	0.5

Major Fund Holders	% of Fund Assets
Smith Barney Telecomm Income	24.15
ProFunds Ultra Telecommunications Inv	18.40
Rydex Telecommunications Inv	11.79
Schwab Communications Focus	9.75

Morningstar's Take By Michael Hodel, 12-06-2002 Stock Price as of Analysis: $26.43

Though it faces several challenges, SBC is still one of our favorites in telecom.

SBC is the second-largest local phone company in the United States, which is its key competitive advantage. The local phone network reaches millions of homes and businesses, making it extremely difficult to replicate. Because most businesses and consumers use wireline phone or data services and options are often limited, SBC maintains generous margins and returns on capital, keeping cash flow strong. With this network already in place, SBC is also in a position to invest its ample cash flow in the network to meet future needs of its customers.

Competition is heating up, though, and SBC has been particularly hard-hit. Regulations force incumbent local phone companies to lease access to their networks to rivals at wholesale rates. Rates are set on a state-by-state basis, and SBC faces some of the lowest in the nation. Compounding the problem, SBC has fallen behind in its effort to win regulatory approval to offer long-distance services--also granted on a state-by-state basis. With long-distance companies like AT&T combining resold local service with their existing long-distance offerings, SBC operates at a disadvantage in some states. As a result, SBC has been losing retail customer at

significantly faster clip than peers. While wholesale revenue makes up some of the lost business, SBC's growth rates have been among the worst in the local phone industry.

The telecom landscape is rapidly changing, though, and we think SBC is positioned to take advantage of this. Despite recent troubles, the company should win long-distance approval in all states by the end of 2003. Like its Bell peers, SBC will be able to use long-distance to generate additional revenue and cultivate customer loyalty. What sets SBC apart is its massive size and industry-best balance sheet. Financial flexibility should allow SBC to build or acquire the capability to offer a full line of services to all of its customers, large or small. Lower debt should allow SBC to better handle a continuing telecom downturn.

Despite falling revenue, SBC has greatly improved free cash flows recently. The biggest driver of this improvement has been capital spending cuts. While we don't think spending will return to the high levels seen during the telecom bubble, we think growing competition will prove current spending too low. Our fair value estimate is very sensitive to SBC's ultimate spending needs.

Schering-Plough SGP

	Rating	Risk	Moat Size	Fair Value	Last Close	Yield %
	UR	Med.	Wide	$30.00	$22.20	3.0

Industry	Investment Style	Stock Type	Sector
Drugs	▦ Large Core	◩ High Yield	◉ Healthcare

Company Profile

Schering-Plough manufactures pharmaceutical and health-care products, including prescription and over-the-counter drugs, and animal-health and foot-care products. Its best-selling product is prescription allergy drug Claritin. The company also sells Drixoral cold and decongestant medications, Gyne-Lotrimin feminine health-care products, Coppertone sun-protection products, Correctol laxatives, and Dr. Scholl's foot-care products. Pharmaceuticals account for 85% of total company sales; nearly 40% of revenue comes from overseas.

Management

Concerns over management integrity have arisen because of suspicion that material information was disclosed in private before it was released to the general public. Schering-Plough's management is not known for its openness.

Strategy

Schering-Plough was built on its allergy franchise. The company is expanding that franchise to the over-the-counter market and with related products like Nasonex and Asmanex. It recently retooled two plants to address serious manufacturing and quality-control problems and put systems in place to avoid similar debacles.

2000 Galloping Hill Road   www.schering-plough.com
Kenilworth, NJ 07033

Morningstar Grades

Growth [C]	1998	1999	2000	2001
Revenue %	18.4	13.6	7.7	-0.1
Earnings/Share %	21.6	20.3	15.5	-19.5
Book Value/Share %	41.9	29.3	19.2	16.9
Dividends/Share %	15.6	14.1	12.4	13.8

We forecast 4.4% annual revenue growth for 2003-06. Excluding Claritin, we expect revenue to increase 14% in 2003 and 10% in 2004, thanks mostly to strength in the hepatitis C franchise.

Profitability [A+]	1999	2000	2001	TTM
Return on Assets %	22.5	22.4	16.0	13.3
Oper Cash Flow $Mil	2,020	2,511	2,512	2,243
- Cap Spending $Mil	543	763	759	784
= Free Cash Flow $Mil	1,477	1,748	1,753	1,459

Gross and operating margins are coming down as Claritin loses its luster. First-half 2002 gross margins were 76.8%, 280 basis points lower than a year ago. Operating margins also declined 180 basis points to 29.7%.

Financial Health [A+]	1999	2000	2001	09-02
Long-term Debt $Mil	—	—	—	—
Total Equity $Mil	5,165	6,119	7,125	7,976
Debt/Equity Ratio	—	—	—	—

Schering-Plough rarely carries long-term debt, and it generates a hefty amount of free cash flow (cash flow from operations less capital expenditures). In 2001, it produced $1.3 billion in free cash flow on revenue of $9.8 billion.

Competition

Competition	Market Cap $Mil	Debt/ Equity	12 Mo Trailing Sales $Mil	Price/Cash Flow	Return On Assets%	Total Return% 1 Yr	3 Yr
Schering-Plough	32,567	—	10,311	14.5	13.3	-36.4	-14.9
Pfizer	188,377	0.2	34,407	21.1	18.3	-22.2	1.0
Roche Holding AG ADR	59,517	—	17,067	—	—		

Price Volatility

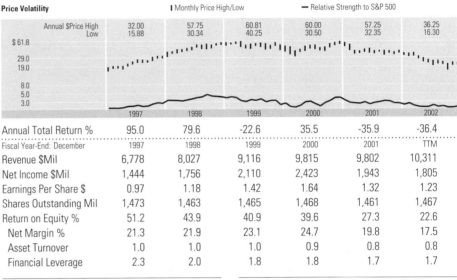

| | Monthly Price High/Low | | | | Relative Strength to S&P 500 | |

Annual $Price High Low	32.00 15.88	57.75 30.34	60.81 40.25	60.00 30.50	57.25 32.35	36.25 16.30
	1997	1998	1999	2000	2001	2002
Annual Total Return %	95.0	79.6	-22.6	35.5	-35.9	-36.4

Fiscal Year-End: December	1997	1998	1999	2000	2001	TTM
Revenue $Mil	6,778	8,027	9,116	9,815	9,802	10,311
Net Income $Mil	1,444	1,756	2,110	2,423	1,943	1,805
Earnings Per Share $	0.97	1.18	1.42	1.64	1.32	1.23
Shares Outstanding Mil	1,473	1,463	1,465	1,468	1,461	1,467
Return on Equity %	51.2	43.9	40.9	39.6	27.3	22.6
Net Margin %	21.3	21.9	23.1	24.7	19.8	17.5
Asset Turnover	1.0	1.0	1.0	0.9	0.8	0.8
Financial Leverage	2.3	2.0	1.8	1.8	1.7	1.7

Valuation Ratios	Stock	Rel to Industry	Rel to S&P 500
Price/Earnings	18.0	0.8	0.8
Price/Book	4.1	0.6	1.3
Price/Sales	3.2	0.8	1.6
Price/Cash Flow	14.5	0.7	1.1

Major Fund Holders	% of Fund Assets
American Capital Exchange	6.03
AIM Global Health Care A	5.25
Runkel Value	5.15
Vanguard Health Care	5.09

Morningstar's Take By Todd N. Lebor, 10-31-2002 Stock Price as of Analysis: $21.35

Schering-Plough's secretive management is a concern. If attitude or personnel changes aren't made soon, the company's ability to recover may be in danger. We would avoid the shares until the Securities and Exchange Commission concludes its investigation and management is no longer an issue.

Claritin, the blockbuster prescription antihistamine, drove Schering-Plough's sales growth and margins to a peak. But now that Claritin is on the verge of moving to the over-the-counter market, we think the company is headed for mediocrity. Its old margins simply aren't sustainable without prescription Claritin.

Mediocrity in the big pharma world isn't all that bad, though. Over the next five years, we expect gross margins to contract 4 percentage points, but operating margins should return, after a dip, to the low 30s as joint-venture income starts rolling in. The result is gross margins in the high 70s and operating margins in the high 20s to low 30s, right on par for a global pharmaceutical company.

It won't be easy for Schering-Plough, however. Although its Intron franchise has 90% share of the hepatitis C market, Roche is about to launch Pegasys, a similar treatment that has outperformed Intron drugs in clinical tests. That said, because of the high rate of persistent infection, a fourfold increase in the number of hepatitis C patients is expected over the next 15 years, so we think there's enough room for both drugs to grow 15%-20% annually over the next two years. Schering-Plough is also counting on Asmanex, a steroid treatment for asthma, to provide much-needed replacement revenue in its respiratory sector. But we expect GlaxoSmithKline to put up a serious fight to protect its leading position in the respiratory market.

Bringing Zetia, a novel cholesterol absorption inhibitor, to market is Schering-Plough's most vital task. Zetia works differently from statins like Lipitor, Zocor, and Pravachol, and will be marketed as a complementary treatment rather than an alternative. We view the market potential as enormous--statins currently bring in more than $19 billion a year worldwide. Merck, which markets Zocor, the number-two cholesterol-lowering drug, is comarketing Zetia, so we think its success is highly likely.

We question management's integrity, and think that investors should wait out the SEC storm on the sidelines. Only after our concerns about management are assuaged would we consider buying the stock at a 20%-30% discount to our fair value estimate.

MORNINGSTAR® Stocks 500

Schlumberger SLB

	Rating	Risk	Moat Size	Fair Value	Last Close	Yield %
	★	Med.	Narrow	$30.00	$42.09	1.8

Company Profile

New York City-based Schlumberger is one of the world's largest oil field services firms. The company provides services related to seismic surveys, drilling, well completion, and oil production optimization. Data and project management systems sold to oil and other industries are becoming an increasingly important part of Schlumberger after the company's 2001 acquisition of software firm Sema. Newly formed subsidiary SchlumbergerSema was responsible for the information technology systems that powered the Salt Lake City Olympic games.

Management

Chairman and CEO Euan Baird has been at the helm since 1986, but he will retire in February. Second in command is vice chairman Victor Grijalva, who also serves as chairman of offshore driller Transocean.

Strategy

Schlumberger aims to make finding and digging up oil and gas more profitable for its customers by using technology. The company is also hoping to improve its own growth and profitability by focusing more on non-capital-intensive businesses, namely information management services sold both in and outside the oil industry.

153 East 53 Street
New York, NY 10172
www.slb.com

Morningstar Grades

Growth [B]	1998	1999	2000	2001
Revenue %	1.3	-19.7	14.7	39.4
Earnings/Share %	-26.7	-64.1	95.4	-28.3
Book Value/Share %	10.0	-5.5	4.8	1.8
Dividends/Share %	0.0	0.0	0.0	0.3

Growth is erratic at Schlumberger because oil companies tend to vary their spending with cyclical and volatile commodity prices. Between internal growth and acquisitions, Schlumberger's long-term growth is in the low teens.

Profitability [B]	1999	2000	2001	TTM
Return on Assets %	2.4	4.3	2.3	3.2
Oper Cash Flow $Mil	1,704	1,645	1,568	2,027
- Cap Spending $Mil	792	1,323	2,053	1,586
= Free Cash Flow $Mil	912	322	-484	441

Profitability has been uninspiring in recent years. Returns on invested capital have been mired in the midsingle digits, below the firm's cost of capital. Schlumberger's long-term returns have been above its peers', however.

Financial Health [B]	1999	2000	2001	09-02
Long-term Debt $Mil	3,183	3,573	6,216	6,757
Total Equity $Mil	7,721	8,295	8,378	8,702
Debt/Equity Ratio	0.4	0.4	0.7	0.8

Schlumberger has cranked up leverage to pay for acquisitions, going from a long-term debt/equity ratio of 0.4 in 1998 to 0.8 currently. But debt is not a problem, with EBITDA covering interest expense 9 times.

Industry	Investment Style	Stock Type	Sector
Oil & Gas Services	▦ Large Growth	▦ Hard Assets	⬢ Energy

Competition	Market Cap $Mil	Debt/ Equity	12 Mo Trailing Sales $Mil	Price/Cash Flow	Return On Assets%	Total Return% 1 Yr	3 Yr
Schlumberger	24,440	0.8	13,553	12.1	3.2	-22.2	-6.9
Baker Hughes	10,840	0.4	5,227	14.0	4.5	-10.4	18.3
Electronic Data Systems	8,774	0.7	22,127	4.5	6.6	-72.6	-32.5

Price Volatility

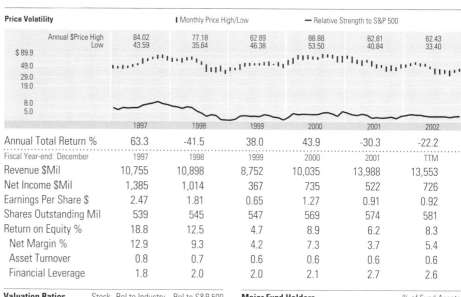

Annual $Price High	84.02	77.18	62.89	88.88	82.81	62.43
Low	43.59	35.64	46.38	53.50	40.84	33.40
	1997	1998	1999	2000	2001	2002
Annual Total Return %	63.3	-41.5	38.0	43.9	-30.3	-22.2

Fiscal Year-end: December	1997	1998	1999	2000	2001	TTM
Revenue $Mil	10,755	10,898	8,752	10,035	13,988	13,553
Net Income $Mil	1,385	1,014	367	735	522	726
Earnings Per Share $	2.47	1.81	0.65	1.27	0.91	0.92
Shares Outstanding Mil	539	545	547	569	574	581
Return on Equity %	18.8	12.5	4.7	8.9	6.2	8.3
Net Margin %	12.9	9.3	4.2	7.3	3.7	5.4
Asset Turnover	0.8	0.7	0.6	0.6	0.6	0.6
Financial Leverage	1.8	2.0	2.0	2.1	2.7	2.6

Valuation Ratios	Stock	Rel to Industry	Rel to S&P 500
Price/Earnings	45.8	1.4	1.9
Price/Book	2.8	1.1	0.9
Price/Sales	1.8	0.9	0.9
Price/Cash Flow	12.1	1.0	0.9

Major Fund Holders	% of Fund Assets
Rydex Energy Services Inv	17.47
Kelmoore Strategy C	4.81
UMB Scout Energy	4.60
Fidelity Select Energy	4.46

Morningstar's Take By Paul Larson, 11-18-2002 Stock Price as of Analysis: $41.75

Schlumberger is not your typical oil company. It is trying to bridge two very different industries--oil services and software. The jury remains out on whether its strategy will be a winning one, but the early results are encouraging. That said, we wouldn't buy the stock unless it were much cheaper.

The largest part of Schlumberger is oil services, a business that provides services to other firms exploring for and producing hydrocarbons. This includes traditional, capital-intensive services like well drilling and completion as well as newer ones like seismic surveys and information management. Thanks to natural field decline, oil companies will be forced to spend to optimize existing wells and drill in more remote places. Schlumberger's business is positioned to benefit from this need.

However, oil services tends to be cyclical, with demand varying drastically with commodity prices and the subsequent financial health of Schlumberger's clients. This is also a highly competitive industry. Schlumberger is one the largest firms in this field, though, and it has a technological edge in several areas. These advantages lead us to assign Schlumberger a narrow economic moat rating as opposed to the "none" we would apply to most of its competition.

In its quest to break out of the oil services mold, Schlumberger purchased software firm Sema. This advanced its goal of becoming a leading provider of information technology tailored for the energy industry, but it also gave the company lines of business totally unrelated to oil. For instance, Schlumberger is one of the largest providers of smart cards and cashless parking systems. Roughly one fourth of Schlumberger's revenue comes from SchlumbergerSema.

Schlumberger has done well cutting costs since the Sema merger. In the long run, we expect further profitability improvement as the integration of recent mergers and related cost-cutting continue. Revenue growth should be above industry norms as the proprietary data services the firm provides become even more critical to the industry's success.

Nevertheless, we wouldn't buy the stock at today's levels. The market has traditionally applied a generous valuation to the shares, and we think that is still the case. We don't think this makes sense, given the company's current level of profitability and growth potential. Our relatively low fair value estimate is a function of the company's high stock price, not any major problems with the firm. We'd look elsewhere to invest until the shares fell.

Scientific-Atlanta SFA

Data as of 12-31-02

	Rating	Risk	Moat Size	Fair Value	Last Close	Yield %
	★★	Med.	None	$13.00	$11.86	0.3

Company Profile

Scientific-Atlanta designs and manufactures networking equipment. The company produces signal-measurement and -monitoring equipment used by electronic manufacturers, telecommunication network operators, and military customers. In addition, Scientific-Atlanta manufactures spectrum analyzers and other testing devices for telecommunication equipment. The company sold its satellite networking operations to ViaSat in April 2000.

Management

James McDonald, who worked at IBM for 21 years before joining Scientific, is chairman as well as president and CEO. This may explain why he was able to cash in options of $85 million in 2001, despite a big drop in the shares.

Strategy

Scientific-Atlanta sells both the set-top cable boxes--featuring various applications, like video on demand, personal video recorders, and interactive TV--and the infrastructure gear that constitute a cable network. Recently the firm has ventured into supplying high-speed cable modems.

5030 Sugarloaf Parkway
Lawrenceville, GA 30044
www.scientificatlanta.com

Industry	Investment Style	Stock Type	Sector
Wireline Equipment	Mid Core	Slow Growth	Hardware

Competition

	Market Cap $Mil	Debt/ Equity	12 Mo Trailing Sales $Mil	Price/Cash Flow	Return On Assets%	Total Return% 1 Yr	3 Yr
Scientific-Atlanta	1,828	0.0	1,573	4.4	4.3	-50.3	-22.8
Sony ADR	38,122	0.4	60,413	6.5	0.2	-8.1	-32.4
Motorola	19,903	0.7	26,576	13.0	-12.9	-41.7	-42.2

Price Volatility

Monthly Price High/Low — Relative Strength to S&P 500

Annual $Price High / Low	12.47 / 7.13	13.97 / 5.88	33.25 / 11.06	94.00 / 24.41	65.80 / 15.75	28.18 / 10.30
	1997	1998	1999	2000	2001	2002
Annual Total Return %	12.0	36.6	145.3	16.6	-26.4	-50.3

Fiscal Year-End: June	1998	1999	2000	2001	2002	TTM
Revenue $Mil	1,181	1,243	1,715	2,512	1,671	1,573
Net Income $Mil	81	102	156	334	104	78
Earnings Per Share $	0.50	0.65	0.94	1.99	0.66	0.50
Shares Outstanding Mil	158	153	157	162	156	154
Return on Equity %	12.8	13.9	12.8	22.1	7.3	5.5
Net Margin %	6.8	8.2	9.1	13.3	6.2	5.0
Asset Turnover	1.3	1.2	1.0	1.3	0.9	0.9
Financial Leverage	1.5	1.4	1.5	1.3	1.3	1.3

Valuation Ratios

	Stock	Rel to Industry	Rel to S&P 500
Price/Earnings	23.7	1.8	1.0
Price/Book	1.3	0.8	0.4
Price/Sales	1.2	2.4	0.6
Price/Cash Flow	4.4	0.9	0.3

Major Fund Holders

	% of Fund Assets
Marketocracy Technology Plus Fund	7.74
Buffalo Science & Technology	3.00
Buffalo Large Cap	2.79
AFBA Five Star Equity	2.78

Morningstar Grades

Growth [C]	1999	2000	2001	2002
Revenue %	5.3	38.0	46.4	-33.5
Earnings/Share %	30.0	44.6	111.7	-66.8
Book Value/Share %	19.9	56.3	22.8	0.9
Dividends/Share %	0.0	16.7	14.3	0.0

The days of huge top-line growth are history; sales in the September quarter fell 24% from the year-ago period. Scientific's customers--the cable operators--are reducing capital spending in a quest for positive free cash flow.

Profitability [A+]	2000	2001	2002	TTM
Return on Assets %	8.8	16.7	5.5	4.3
Oper Cash Flow $Mil	222	259	358	417
- Cap Spending $Mil	83	105	36	37
= Free Cash Flow $Mil	139	154	322	380

Management has deftly offset a sales decline by consolidating facilities and reducing personnel. That said, profit growth is nonexistent and return on equity--now around 5%--continues to deteriorate.

Financial Health [A+]	2000	2001	2002	09-02
Long-term Debt $Mil	0	0	9	8
Total Equity $Mil	1,215	1,509	1,437	1,417
Debt/Equity Ratio	0.0	0.0	0.0	0.0

Sales growth may have disappeared, but Scientific runs a tight ship. The balance sheet is superb, with nearly no debt and $795 million in cash. Such strength has allowed the firm to repurchase its stock.

Morningstar's Take By Todd P. Bernier, 12-03-2002 Stock Price as of Analysis: $13.41

Scientific-Atlanta rode the digital wave up, and now it is riding it back down. We would be interested in Scientific, a company with no economic moat, only at a large discount to our fair value estimate.

Scientific was once a back-door play on the cable industry's upgrade cycle. Cable operators raced to deploy broadband services like digital cable and high-speed data, which meant lots of new orders for set-top boxes and network hardware. That hot sales growth is history, however.

Big Cable was always perceived as a safe haven, as operators enjoyed pseudomonopolies. But everything has changed over the past year thanks to nagging solvency concerns at Charter Communications and the bankruptcy of Adelphia, two of the nation's largest cable operators (and both significant Scientific customers). Cable valuations have plummeted.

To restore investors' confidence, cable execs have switched gears. Previously, cable firms borrowed copious amounts of money on the premise that cash flow would someday accelerate. Assuming debt payments were made as scheduled, free cash flow--operating cash flow minus capital spending and interest payments--was never a serious goal. That game is over, though, as skeptical lenders won't lend

and stock buyers won't buy. Now Big Cable worships at the altar of free cash flow. Unfortunately for vendors like Scientific, the simplest way to post free cash flow is to cut capital spending.

With the digital-upgrade process nearly finished, the only thing that will turn around Scientific's business is the launch of new services, like video on demand, that will force cable customers to buy a new digital box. This explains why the firm has frantically launched several new set-top models. Witness the recent unveiling of the Explorer 3100HD, designed for high-definition TV, and the Explorer 8000, which combines video on demand, e-mail, Web browsing, chat, and a personal video recorder. We don't buy the assertion that subscribers will lovingly embrace (and pay for) these advanced cable services, especially in a fragile economy. But it is guaranteed that viewing habits will change as a result of combining the storage capabilities of a personal computer with the functions of a cable box.

Being unavoidably cheap is the only reason to buy Scientific. We think investors should wait on the sidelines until the shares trade at a 40% discount to our fair value estimate.

MORNINGSTAR® Stocks 500

SCP Pool POOL

	Rating	Risk	Moat Size	Fair Value	Last Close	Yield %
	★★	Med.	None	$27.00	$29.20	0.0

Company Profile

SCP Pool distributes swimming pool supplies and related products. The company distributes more than 63,000 national-brand and private-label products to more than 34,000 customers. The products include nondiscretionary pool-maintenance products, like chemicals and replacement parts, as well as pool equipment, such as packaged pools (kits to build swimming pools), cleaners, filters, heaters, pumps, and lights. Customers include pool builders and remodelers, independent retail stores, and pool repair and service companies.

Management

CEO Manuel Perez de la Mesa has a thirst for acquisitions; the firm has made 20 since 1994. The management team collectively owns about 9% of the stock. Salaries seem conservative, considering SCP's tremendous growth over the years.

Strategy

SCP Pool is focused on maintaining high-quality service while capturing as much share as it can in the pool industry. The company is on the lookout for new acquisition targets, but is also conscious of its leverage. Positive cash flows may be used to pay down debt in the near future.

109 Northpark Boulevard   www.scppool.com
Covington, LA 70433-5001

Morningstar Grades

Growth [A+]	1998	1999	2000	2001
Revenue %	36.6	25.1	17.6	27.2
Earnings/Share %	61.2	54.6	34.2	25.5
Book Value/Share %	0.1	22.1	27.1	16.6
Dividends/Share %	NMF	NMF	NMF	NMF

Acquisitions have helped sales grow 26% annually since 1997. The nation's installed base of pools increases about 3% per year, adding to recurring revenue from maintenance and equipment, which makes up the majority of SCP's top line.

Profitability [A]	1999	2000	2001	TTM
Return on Assets %	10.9	11.1	10.2	10.2
Oper Cash Flow $Mil	37	18	27	23
- Cap Spending $Mil	3	4	6	7
= Free Cash Flow $Mil	34	14	20	16

Cost controls have helped increase operating margins from 4.7% in 1997 to 8.5% in 2001, excluding acquisitions. As a market leader in a high-end industry, SCP Pool should maintain its pricing power with distributors and end customers.

Financial Health [C-]	1999	2000	2001	09-02
Long-term Debt $Mil	23	35	85	147
Total Equity $Mil	98	123	145	147
Debt/Equity Ratio	0.2	0.3	0.6	1.0

The company is in good financial shape. Operating income covers interest expenses almost 20 times, leaving plenty of room to leverage the business to make additional acquisitions.

Industry	Investment Style	Stock Type	Sector
Recreation	Small Growth	Classic Growth	Consumer Goods

Competition	Market Cap $Mil	Debt/ Equity	12 Mo Trailing Sales $Mil	Price/Cash Flow	Return On Assets%	Total Return% 1 Yr	3 Yr
SCP Pool	682	1.0	958	29.6	10.2	6.4	36.5
Wal-Mart Stores	223,388	0.5	233,651	18.9	8.0	-11.8	-7.3
Home Depot	56,450	0.1	57,336	8.8	11.8	-52.7	-24.8

Price Volatility

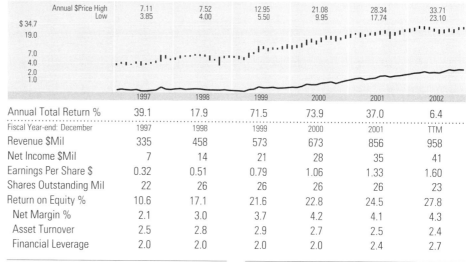

			Monthly Price High/Low		— Relative Strength to S&P 500	
Annual $Price High	7.11	7.52	12.95	21.08	28.34	33.71
Low	3.85	4.00	5.50	9.95	17.74	23.10

$34.7 / 19.0 / 7.0 / 4.0 / 2.0 / 1.0

	1997	1998	1999	2000	2001	2002
Annual Total Return %	39.1	17.9	71.5	73.9	37.0	6.4

Fiscal Year-end: December	1997	1998	1999	2000	2001	TTM
Revenue $Mil	335	458	573	673	856	958
Net Income $Mil	7	14	21	28	35	41
Earnings Per Share $	0.32	0.51	0.79	1.06	1.33	1.60
Shares Outstanding Mil	22	26	26	26	26	23
Return on Equity %	10.6	17.1	21.6	22.8	24.5	27.8
Net Margin %	2.1	3.0	3.7	4.2	4.1	4.3
Asset Turnover	2.5	2.8	2.9	2.7	2.5	2.4
Financial Leverage	2.0	2.0	2.0	2.0	2.4	2.7

Valuation Ratios	Stock	Rel to Industry	Rel to S&P 500
Price/Earnings	18.3	1.1	0.8
Price/Book	4.6	2.3	1.4
Price/Sales	0.7	0.2	0.4
Price/Cash Flow	29.6	2.6	2.2

Major Fund Holders	% of Fund Assets
Villere Balanced	3.98
Wilmington Small Cap Core Instl	2.95
CIGNA TimesSquare Small Cap Gr Instl	2.30
Wasatch Core Growth	2.23

Morningstar's Take By T.K. MacKay, 10-16-2002 Stock Price as of Analysis: $26.12

We like SCP Pool's splashy sales growth and dominant market share, but would consider investing in the stock only below $14.

SCP Pool has a lot more than its big toe dipped into the swimming pool supply industry. Through 20 acquisitions since 1994, SCP Pool has become the country's largest distributor of pool supplies and equipment. As the company has gained share over the years, its pricing power has increased: Gross margins on SCP's products climbed to 26% in 2002 from 22% in 1997. Because SCP is a wholesaler and not a manufacturer, it avoids having to shell out cash to build plants, thereby boosting profits even more. Returns on equity have been north of 20% over the past three years, and with about two thirds of sales coming from existing pools, additional pool installations just sweeten SCP's returns.

There are more than 7 million swimming pools in the United States, with 200,000 more being installed each year. Without acquisitions, we think SCP's revenue would grow in line with the growth in total pools nationwide, or about 3% annually. As the installed base of pools grows, more of SCP's revenue will be recurring. This revenue--from sales of algicide, bottom sweepers, and the like--is less discretionary than that associated with buying a new

pool, and is much less likely to be affected by a sour consumer climate or less-than-perfect summer days.

Growth beyond this depends on SCP's ability to acquire additional pool equipment distributors. We think the company can continue its acquisitive strategy and increase sales faster than the industry's growth rate. EBITDA (earnings before interest, taxes, depreciation, and amortization) covers interest expense 14 times, allowing the company plenty of room to issue additional debt to acquire new companies without having to tighten its belt. We expect future acquisitions to add 10% to revenue annually over the next several years.

In the short term, bad weather poses the greatest risk to SCP's product sales--and the stock price. A third of SCP's distribution centers are in California and Florida, and hurricanes and other nasty weather can spoil sales of chemicals and other pool equipment in these areas in a heartbeat. However, such events are short-term and not company-specific, and can lead to a buying opportunity for investors if the stock drops. We think SCP Pool is worth about $27 per share. We would strongly consider the shares if the market excessively punished them because of bad weather in SCP's primary markets and priced the stock at a 50% discount to our estimated fair value.

Sealed Air SEE

	Rating	Risk	Moat Size	Fair Value	Last Close	Yield %
	★	Med.	None	$33.00	$37.30	0.0

Company Profile

Sealed Air manufactures packaging materials, everything from polyethylene foam, plastic bubble wrap, and tear resistant mailing envelops to meat packing products. Sealed Air's Instapak packaging equipment is used by manufacturers of products like electronic equipment, furniture, office supplies, and cosmetics to produce custom-formed foam packing inserts. It operates and distributes to over 45 countries around the world.

Management

CEO William Hickey, a former Navy officer, took Sealed Air's rudder in March 2001 after serving in various managerial roles since 1980. Hickey holds degrees in engineering and management. In 2001, his cash compensation was valued at $700,000.

Strategy

Sealed Air relies on its 30 research and development labs to innovate and refine its lineup of protective packaging and shipping products. The company has become adept at acquiring and rapidly integrating companies in markets where it has little or no presence. Acquisition activity will probably be tempered as the firm digests the costs of its asbestos settlement.

Park 80 East
Saddle Brook, NJ 07663-5291   www.sealedair.com

Industry	Investment Style	Stock Type	Sector
Packaging	▦ Mid Growth	↻ Cyclical	🚗 Consumer Goods

Competition

	Market Cap $Mil	Debt/ Equity	12 Mo Trailing Sales $Mil	Price/Cash Flow	Return On Assets%	Total Return% 1 Yr	3 Yr
Sealed Air	3,131	0.9	3,140	7.5	4.6	-8.6	-11.7
Alcoa	19,232	0.7	20,631	11.4	1.7	-34.6	-16.1
Alcan	9,485	0.4	12,397	5.6	-0.1	-16.3	-9.0

Price Volatility

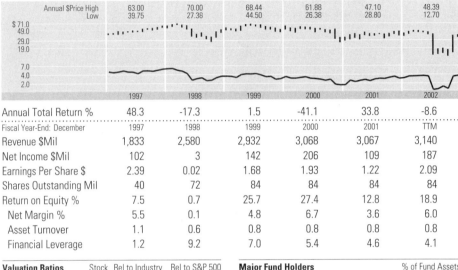

Annual $Price High	63.00	70.00	68.44	61.88	47.10	48.39
Low	39.75	27.38	44.50	26.38	28.80	12.70
	1997	1998	1999	2000	2001	2002

	1997	1998	1999	2000	2001	
Annual Total Return %	48.3	-17.3	1.5	-41.1	33.8	-8.6

Fiscal Year-End: December	1997	1998	1999	2000	2001	TTM
Revenue $Mil	1,833	2,580	2,932	3,068	3,067	3,140
Net Income $Mil	102	3	142	206	109	187
Earnings Per Share $	2.39	0.02	1.68	1.93	1.22	2.09
Shares Outstanding Mil	40	72	84	84	84	84
Return on Equity %	7.5	0.7	25.7	27.4	12.8	18.9
Net Margin %	5.5	0.1	4.8	6.7	3.6	6.0
Asset Turnover	1.1	0.6	0.8	0.8	0.8	0.8
Financial Leverage	1.2	9.2	7.0	5.4	4.6	4.1

Valuation Ratios	Stock	Rel to Industry	Rel to S&P 500
Price/Earnings	17.8	1.0	0.8
Price/Book	3.2	1.0	1.0
Price/Sales	1.0	1.2	0.5
Price/Cash Flow	7.5	1.0	0.6

Major Fund Holders	% of Fund Assets
Davis Financial A	2.94
AXP Partners Fundamental Value A	2.70
MassMutual Instl Large Cap Value S	2.51
John Hancock Mid Cap Growth A	2.38

Morningstar Grades

Growth [B]	1998	1999	2000	2001
Revenue %	40.8	13.6	4.6	0.0
Earnings/Share %	-99.2	EUB	14.9	-36.8
Book Value/Share %	-90.4	114.9	7.8	34.9
Dividends/Share %	NMF	NMF	NMF	NMF

Growth has averaged 14% annually over the past few years, driven by acquisitions. Packaging is a mature, competitive industry, and we expect long-term growth around 3%. Industrial and consumer spending are the primary drivers of growth.

Profitability [C+]	1999	2000	2001	TTM
Return on Assets %	3.7	5.0	2.8	4.6
Oper Cash Flow $Mil	430	329	579	417
- Cap Spending $Mil	75	114	146	95
= Free Cash Flow $Mil	355	215	432	322

Net margins over the long term have been very good, but earnings per share growth will be hurt by higher debt and the resulting interest expense.

Financial Health [C]	1999	2000	2001	09-02
Long-term Debt $Mil	665	944	788	861
Total Equity $Mil	551	753	850	987
Debt/Equity Ratio	1.2	1.3	0.9	0.9

The Cryovac deal added nearly $1 billion in debt to what was an otherwise pristine balance sheet, and the settlement will probably add another $500 million. However, the firm generates plenty of free cash, which should help it reduce debt.

Morningstar's Take By Daniel Quinn, 12-12-2002 Stock Price as of Analysis: $34.66

By resolving the asbestos issue, Sealed Air has removed a major risk hounding its shares. Taking into account the financial impact of the asbestos settlement, we think the stock is worth $33. We'd require a 30% margin of safety to this estimate before investing.

Sealed Air is a savvy innovator in the packaging industry. To bolster its top line, the firm has made a string of acquisitions--the biggest being Cryovac, the food packaging division of W.R. Grace. The Cryovac business accounts for about 60% of sales and provides stability to counter the firm's more cyclical businesses. But the acquisition came with a very expensive string attached--Sealed Air had to settle asbestos lawsuits brought against Grace and Cryovac. Sealed Air will pay $512 million and issue 9 million shares of common stock to a settlement fund. While the end result could have been much worse, the company will have to shuffle its priorities to meet the terms of the agreement.

Sealed Air will probably have to take on additional debt to pay some of the settlement. The company already has more than $860 million in debt, and sports a debt/equity ratio of 87%. Operations do throw off ample cash flow to meet additional interest costs, but the debt could limit Sealed Air's strategic

flexibility in an increasingly competitive industry. Alcoa and Alcan, for example, have recently made acquisitions in packaging, bringing the aluminum behemoths' resources to the industry.

But we don't think Sealed Air is in mortal danger. Its research and development platform has a long history of developing new, innovative products, and it owns several well-known and respected brands. The company's proven ability to generate solid cash flow from these products should allow it to reduce debt considerably over the next couple of years. However, packaging is a slow-growth industry. Coupled with increased competition, the lack of growth could lead to lower pricing power and margins. Further, Sealed Air may have to pull back on R&D as a result of the asbestos settlement, hurting its ability to compete.

Sealed Air has a record of generating solid margins and fantastic cash flows. The asbestos settlement and growing competition could keep the past from repeating, though, and we've attempted to factor slower growth and lower margins into our fair value estimate. Still, we'd wait until the shares fell to about $23 before investing. We think the margin of safety is great enough at that price, should the future prove worse than expected.

MORNINGSTAR® Stocks 500

Sears Roebuck S

	Rating	Risk	Moat Size	Fair Value	Last Close	Yield %
	★★★	High	None	$28.00	$23.95	3.8

Company Profile

Sears Roebuck conducts retail and credit card operations. Its Sears Merchandise Group subsidiary sells general merchandise and provides services through facilities in the United States, Canada, and Mexico. This subsidiary includes 867 full-line department stores and more than 1,300 specialty stores, including The Great Indoors. Sears Roebuck sells its proprietary Craftsman products as well as other brands.

Management

Sears is now legendary for its management shakeups. CEO Alan Lacy recently fired former credit head Kevin Keleghan, citing Keleghan's lack of credibility as the reason for a significant profit shortfall in the credit unit.

Strategy

Sears is rolling out Lands' End's merchandise in its stores in an effort to shore up its troubled apparel business. It hopes to attract more-affluent shoppers with branded and restyled merchandise. The company must also turn its attention to problems in its credit card unit.

3333 Beverly Road
Hoffman Estates, IL 60179
www.sears.com

Industry	Investment Style	Stock Type	Sector
Department Stores	Mid Value	High Yield	Consumer Services

Competition

	Market Cap $Mil	Debt/ Equity	12 Mo Trailing Sales $Mil	Price/Cash Flow	Return On Assets%	Total Return% 1 Yr	Total Return% 3 Yr
Sears Roebuck	7,576	3.3	41,156	—	2.1	-48.6	-6.5
Home Depot	56,450	0.1	57,336	8.8	11.8	-52.7	-24.8
Target	27,252	1.2	42,275	21.5	5.7	-26.5	-3.9

Price Volatility

I Monthly Price High/Low — Relative Strength to S&P 500

		1997	1998	1999	2000	2001	2002
Annual $Price High		65.25	65.00	53.19	43.50	48.93	59.90
Low		38.75	39.06	26.69	24.97	29.90	19.75

	1997	1998	1999	2000	2001	2002
Annual Total Return %	0.1	-4.5	-26.8	17.8	40.1	-48.6

Fiscal Year-end: December	1997	1998	1999	2000	2001	TTM
Revenue $Mil	39,837	39,953	39,484	40,937	41,078	41,156
Net Income $Mil	1,188	1,048	1,453	1,343	735	1,022
Earnings Per Share $	2.99	2.68	3.81	3.88	2.24	3.15
Shares Outstanding Mil	392	388	379	345	327	316
Return on Equity %	20.3	17.3	21.2	19.8	12.0	16.4
Net Margin %	3.0	2.6	3.7	3.3	1.8	2.5
Asset Turnover	1.0	1.1	1.1	1.1	0.9	0.9
Financial Leverage	6.6	6.2	5.4	5.5	7.2	7.7

Valuation Ratios	Stock	Rel to Industry	Rel to S&P 500
Price/Earnings	7.6	0.5	0.3
Price/Book	1.2	1.0	0.4
Price/Sales	0.2	0.6	0.1
Price/Cash Flow	—	—	—

Major Fund Holders	% of Fund Assets
MFS Strategic Value I	4.90
Hotchkis and Wiley Large Cap Value I	4.72
Leonetti Growth	4.33
Hillman Aggressive Equity	3.91

Morningstar Grades

Growth [C-]	1998	1999	2000	2001
Revenue %	0.3	-1.2	3.7	0.3
Earnings/Share %	-10.4	42.2	1.8	-42.3
Book Value/Share %	5.1	15.6	9.1	-4.6
Dividends/Share %	0.0	0.0	0.0	0.0

Sales growth has stagnated in recent years, as discount department store chains like Kohl's KSS have rapidly gained market share. The company hopes to spur retail growth with its Lands' End acquisition.

Profitability [B-]	1999	2000	2001	TTM
Return on Assets %	3.9	3.6	1.7	2.1
Oper Cash Flow $Mil	3,745	2,702	2,262	-318
- Cap Spending $Mil	1,033	1,084	1,126	898
= Free Cash Flow $Mil	2,712	1,618	1,136	-1,216

Sears' credit card business posts operating margins approaching 30%. But profitability is being weighed down by increasing charge-offs and poor performance in the company's retail division.

Financial Health [C]	1999	2000	2001	09-02
Long-term Debt $Mil	12,884	11,020	18,921	20,781
Total Equity $Mil	6,839	6,769	6,119	6,214
Debt/Equity Ratio	1.9	1.6	3.1	3.3

Sears' debt/equity ratio is high because of the liabilities associated with funding its credit card business, which generates the bulk of the company's ample cash flow. To finance the Lands' End acquisition, Sears added $1.5 billion in debt.

Morningstar's Take By Roz Bryant, 10-24-2002 Stock Price as of Analysis: $25.54

We think Sears has lost its retail identity, leaving it ill-equipped to win much market share. We also have serious concerns about its credit business, so we'd look for a 60% margin of safety to our fair value estimate before buying the shares.

We believe Sears' retail strategy will lead to anemic sales growth at best. The firm is keenly aware that its loyal, well-heeled appliance customers don't buy its apparel. In response, it's rolling out Lands' End merchandise and several new private-label brands in its stores. The company believes that items like $138 cashmere sweaters will attract the aforementioned customers to its clothing sections, but we think Sears' reputation for unfashionable clothing will be difficult to shake. At the same time, we think higher prices will alienate the stores' existing less-affluent base of apparel customers.

Missteps in Sears' credit card business also concern us. The unit, which earns wide margins on the spread between interest and fees charged to customer credit accounts and its borrowing and lending costs, delivers 60% of operating income. But successfully managing a credit card portfolio is no simple task.

A well-run credit card issuer sets realistic provisions for uncollectible accounts (receivables expected to go unpaid) and manages its portfolio in such a way that actual charge-off rates aren't likely to exceed provisions. Careful underwriting and ongoing account monitoring help screen out less creditworthy borrowers and catch problem accounts before they near charge-off status. Conversely, the closer a firm comes to offering cards indiscriminately, the more risk its portfolio is exposed to.

This is where Sears has fallen asleep at the wheel, and we believe its portfolio's performance could suffer even more. Sears introduced its gold MasterCard in 2000 to offset shrinking receivables from its proprietary Sears Card (which can be used only in Sears stores). Management loosened underwriting standards for the MasterCard in an effort to achieve overzealous growth targets, and riskier accounts now sit on Sears' books. The new card accounts constitute 37% of Sears' $31 billion receivables portfolio, and we estimate that nearly 50% of MasterCard accounts may be attributable to subprime borrowers. We think many more charge-offs may emerge.

Given a flawed retail strategy and a credit portfolio that's beginning to resemble Pandora's box, we'd avoid the shares unless they fell to $10-$12.

Sepracor SEPR

	Rating	Risk	Moat Size	Fair Value	Last Close	Yield %
	★	High	None	$0.00	$9.67	0.0

Industry	Investment Style	Stock Type	Sector
Drugs	Small Growth	Distressed	Healthcare

Company Profile

Sepracor is a specialty pharmaceutical company that develops improved versions--called improved chemical entities, or ICEs--of marketed drugs. It has several ICEs for the top-selling allergy drugs like Claritin, Allegra, and Zyrtec. The company also develops and markets drugs on its own. Its only marketed product is Xopenex, an asthma inhaler for patients 12 years and older. Sepracor also has drugs in various stages of clinical development for the treatment of respiratory, urology, and central nervous system disorders.

Management

CEO Timothy Barberich co-founded the company in 1984. Despite continuing losses and a troubled pipeline, all five top managers paid themselves hefty bonuses in 2001, equal to 30% or more of their salaries.

Strategy

Sepracor is trying to transition from a copycat drugmaker to a balanced pharmaceutical company. It has several royalty agreements with major pharmaceutical companies for allergy drugs, one asthma treatment on the market, and several new products in late-stage trials. Its success or failure will be determined by its next few products, because it has borrowed heavily to get where it is.

84 Waterford Drive   www.sepracor.com
Marlborough, MA 01752

Morningstar Grades

Growth [A+]	1998	1999	2000	2001
Revenue %	365.1	122.0	276.2	78.4
Earnings/Share %	NMF	NMF	NMF	NMF
Book Value/Share %	-64.8	NMF	NMF	NMF
Dividends/Share %	NMF	NMF	NMF	NMF

Sepracor's top line is growing nicely, thanks to Xopenex sales, but revenue is a long way from covering the escalating operating costs. Royalties are starting to pick up, contributing $23 million for the first six months of 2002.

Profitability [D]	1999	2000	2001	TTM
Return on Assets %	-45.0	-27.2	-20.5	-43.9
Oper Cash Flow $Mil	-164	-171	-208	-274
- Cap Spending $Mil	7	9	29	47
= Free Cash Flow $Mil	-171	-180	-237	-321

Sepracor is unprofitable and will most likely remain so until 2005. Selling and administrative costs as a percentage of revenue are extraordinarily high because the company expects several new product launches in the next few years.

Financial Health [F]	1999	2000	2001	09-02
Long-term Debt $Mil	491	854	1,261	999
Total Equity $Mil	-156	-215	-314	-354
Debt/Equity Ratio	ELB	ELB	ELB	NMF

Sepracor repurchased $131 million of its 7% convertible bonds in the third quarter, but still has about $1 billion in convertible bonds outstanding. It's not the $64 million in annual interest that bothers us; it's the possible shareholder dilution.

Competition

Competition	Market Cap $Mil	Debt/ Equity	12 Mo Trailing Sales $Mil	Price/Cash Flow	Return On Assets%	Total Return% 1 Yr	3 Yr
Sepracor	814	NMF	197	—	-43.9	-83.1	-41.1
King Pharmaceuticals	4,139	0.2	1,111	11.7	10.1	-59.2	-11.1
Biovail Corporation Inter	3,665	—	583	—	—	—	—

Price Volatility

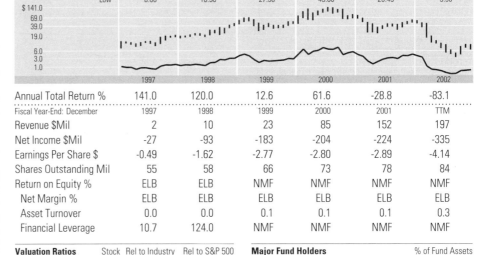

Annual $Price High	21.38	47.63	70.44	140.00	81.88	57.25
Low	8.00	16.50	27.50	45.06	23.45	3.90

	1997	1998	1999	2000	2001	2002
Annual Total Return %	141.0	120.0	12.6	61.6	-28.8	-83.1

Fiscal Year-End: December	1997	1998	1999	2000	2001	TTM
Revenue $Mil	2	10	23	85	152	197
Net Income $Mil	-27	-93	-183	-204	-224	-335
Earnings Per Share $	-0.49	-1.62	-2.77	-2.80	-2.89	-4.14
Shares Outstanding Mil	55	58	66	73	78	84
Return on Equity %	ELB	ELB	NMF	NMF	NMF	NMF
Net Margin %	ELB	ELB	ELB	ELB	ELB	ELB
Asset Turnover	0.0	0.0	0.1	0.1	0.1	0.3
Financial Leverage	10.7	124.0	NMF	NMF	NMF	NMF

Valuation Ratios	Stock	Rel to Industry	Rel to S&P 500
Price/Earnings	NMF	—	—
Price/Book	—	—	—
Price/Sales	4.1	1.0	2.1
Price/Cash Flow	—	—	—

Major Fund Holders	% of Fund Assets
GenomicsFund	3.75
Reserve Large-Cap Growth R	3.64
Amerindo Health & Biotechnology A	3.37
Phoenix-Engemann Small & MidCap Gr A	2.60

Morningstar's Take By Todd N. Lebor, 10-15-2002 Stock Price as of Analysis: $5.71

We don't see Sepracor's bet on the allergy market paying off, so we've dropped our fair value estimate to $0 and will be providing reduced coverage.

The copycat-turned-proprietary drugmaker has plenty of cash to survive for several more years, but with more than $1 billion in debt and only one product to support its bloated expenses, there's not much hope for Sepracor. After the Food and Drug Administration rejected allergy drug Soltara in March 2002, Sepracor's chances of success deteriorated.

Given its faster onset, Soltara was expected to give Schering-Plough's $3 billion-a-year allergy drug Claritin a run for its money. But now that Claritin is going over-the-counter, we believe growth for the entire prescription allergy market will dry up. Even if Soltara makes it to market, its financial reward to Sepracor will be peanuts compared with what was expected before Schering-Plough's announcement. Management still believes there will be a robust prescription allergy market after Claritin OTC. We think that's delusional.

A number of drug companies will be hurt by Schering-Plough's move, but none will suffer like Sepracor; besides counting on Soltara for the bulk of its revenue, it earns a small amount from royalties on the major prescription antihistamines.

Sepracor's one drug on the market, asthma inhaler Xopenex, is having moderate success, but its revenue stream cannot sustain the company's corporate structure. Operating expenses related to the anticipated launch of Soltara (management was preparing for a 2002 release) are adding up, placing additional strain on the company. Even though Sepracor is farming out its 450-person sales team to other companies that need help selling their allergy or asthma drugs, the staff is still a financial burden. Mothballing research projects isn't enough either. With its next product several years from producing sizable revenue (even if it's successful), Sepracor needs to do more than token cost-cutting.

Sepracor bet its future on the wrong sector. The outlook for the prescription allergy market is very questionable, and Soltara's success (which will determine Sepracor's success) becomes more unlikely with every passing day. Besides, the prescription allergy market is only going to get more competitive as Aventis, Schering-Plough, and Pfizer protect their turf. Ironically, Sepracor will gain (in the form of royalties) from competitors' success, but that also could lead to Sepracor's demise. We think betting on Sepracor is a losing proposition.

MORNINGSTAR® Stocks 500

ServiceMaster SVM

	Rating	Risk	Moat Size	Fair Value	Last Close	Yield %
	★★	Med.	Narrow	$10.00	$11.10	2.7

Company Profile

ServiceMaster provides services to 12 million residential customers. Its main services include lawn care and landscape maintenance, termite and pest control, plumbing, heating and air conditioning maintenance and repair, appliance maintenance and repair, cleaning, furniture maintenance, and home warranties. The firm counts Terminix, TruGreen ChemLawn, and Merry Maids among its brands.

Management

Jon Ward joined ServiceMaster from RR Donnelley in February 2001. He is the first CEO from outside the company since 1983. Going outside the firm is an indication of the difficult strategic decisions that had to be made.

Strategy

In 2001, ServiceMaster reviewed the businesses in its portfolio. It sold those with institutions as customers and retained its operations serving residential customers. Now the firm wants to improve the performance of the remaining businesses, de-emphasizing its past acquisitive nature.

2300 Warrenville Rd. www.servicemaster.com
Downers Grove, IL 60515-1700

Morningstar Grades

Growth [B]	1998	1999	2000	2001
Revenue %	23.2	40.1	11.4	3.3
Earnings/Share %	16.4	-14.1	3.6	-10.5
Book Value/Share %	82.6	18.6	-0.3	5.4
Dividends/Share %	6.1	9.1	5.6	5.3

In normal economic times, ServiceMaster has the potential to increase revenue at high-single-digit and earnings at low-double-digit rates. To meet this potential, the company is replicating the practices of its most successful service centers.

Profitability [B]	1999	2000	2001	TTM
Return on Assets %	4.5	4.4	4.2	3.5
Oper Cash Flow $Mil	174	314	363	297
- Cap Spending $Mil	56	57	40	47
= Free Cash Flow $Mil	118	257	323	250

After the firm sold its institutional businesses, its profitable consumer service operations became more visible. By instituting better practices and leveraging its scale, ServiceMaster should squeeze more profits from each dollar of revenue.

Financial Health [A]	1999	2000	2001	09-02
Long-term Debt $Mil	—	1,757	1,106	796
Total Equity $Mil	1,206	1,162	1,221	1,232
Debt/Equity Ratio	—	1.5	0.9	0.6

The proceeds from the sale of some businesses--more than $700 million--have been used to strengthen the balance sheet and ensure investment-grade marks from debt-rating firms like S&P.

Industry	Investment Style	Stock Type	Sector
Personal Services	▦ Mid Core	→ Slow Growth	▤ Consumer Services

Competition

	Market Cap $Mil	Debt/ Equity	12 Mo Trailing Sales $Mil	Price/Cash Flow	Return On Assets%	Total Return% 1 Yr	3 Yr
ServiceMaster	3,342	0.6	3,664	11.3	3.5	-17.5	0.9
Rollins	761	—	664				

Price Volatility

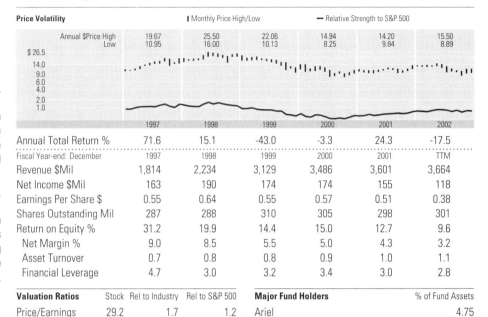

		1997	1998	1999	2000	2001	2002
Annual $Price High		19.67	25.50	22.06	14.94	14.20	15.50
Low		10.95	16.00	10.13	8.25	9.84	8.89
Annual Total Return %		71.6	15.1	-43.0	-3.3	24.3	-17.5

Fiscal Year-end: December	1997	1998	1999	2000	2001	TTM
Revenue $Mil	1,814	2,234	3,129	3,486	3,601	3,664
Net Income $Mil	163	190	174	174	155	118
Earnings Per Share $	0.55	0.64	0.55	0.57	0.51	0.38
Shares Outstanding Mil	287	288	310	305	298	301
Return on Equity %	31.2	19.9	14.4	15.0	12.7	9.6
Net Margin %	9.0	8.5	5.5	5.0	4.3	3.2
Asset Turnover	0.7	0.8	0.8	0.9	1.0	1.1
Financial Leverage	4.7	3.0	3.2	3.4	3.0	2.8

Valuation Ratios	Stock	Rel to Industry	Rel to S&P 500
Price/Earnings	29.2	1.7	1.2
Price/Book	2.7	0.8	0.8
Price/Sales	0.9	0.4	0.5
Price/Cash Flow	11.3	0.8	0.9

Major Fund Holders	% of Fund Assets
Ariel	4.75
Nicholas Equity Income	4.40
Transamerica Premier Aggr Grth Inv	3.27
Buffalo Large Cap	2.84

Morningstar's Take By Dan Schick, 10-21-2002 Stock Price as of Analysis: $9.55

ServiceMaster will never be the stock du jour. But given a stable portfolio of businesses that spew cash and a management team focused on making wise investments, we would consider buying the shares if they traded below $7, only a 30% discount to our $10 fair value estimate.

Any business that invests unwisely destroys the capital entrusted to it by shareholders. Because ServiceMaster is a holding company, its main goal is to funnel money to profitable opportunities in its current operating units as well as potential businesses. Therefore, one needs to watch especially closely where the firm puts its money. ServiceMaster has spent a lot on acquisitions. Some, like LandCare and American Residential Services, made sense because they strengthened existing businesses in ServiceMaster's portfolio. Others were mistakes. ServiceMaster never should have entered the professional employer organization business, for example. But after reviewing the moves the company made in 2001, we believe its capital allocation has improved.

CEO Jonathan Ward, who joined the company in 2001, oversaw a fairly radical change to the corporate portfolio. The firm rid itself of noncore, poor-performing businesses (like the professional employer organization business) and sold its lower-margin management services group that catered to institutions. The proceeds of these moves--more than $800 million--paid down debt, yielding a better balance sheet.

The firm's remaining units--the TruGreen lawn-care segment, the Terminix pest extermination business, and the home maintenance segment--are higher-return businesses focused on serving homeowners. In a further demonstration of better capital allocation, management is improving current operations, rather than buying more businesses.

On this front, ServiceMaster should have some low-hanging fruit to grab. For example, Terminix is installing an up-to-date management information system. By upgrading its information technology, Terminix should improve its productivity and customer satisfaction levels. ServiceMaster is also finally using its size to its advantage: A new fuel program buying gas from one supplier should yield savings of more than $4 million in 2002.

By improving its current operations, ServiceMaster should boost the returns it earns, providing more cash flow that it can then use to make small tuck-in purchases, buy back stock, and continue paying its generous dividend.

Shell Transport & Trading ADR SC

	Rating	Risk	Moat Size	Fair Value	Last Close	Yield %
	★★★	Low	Narrow	$41.00	$38.92	3.4

Company Profile

Shell Transport & Trading is a holding company whose primary asset is its 40% interest in Royal Dutch/Shell Group (Shell), a century-old Anglo-Dutch combination that is one of the world's three largest integrated oil and gas companies. Royal Dutch Petroleum owns the other 60% of Shell. With operations spanning all aspects of oil, Shell has 13.7 billion barrels of reserves, the capacity to refine 3 million barrels a day, and some 46,000 service stations around the globe.

Management

Royal Dutch and Shell Transport jointly appoint directors to the Shell board and rotate the chairmanship among representatives of the two parent firms. Industry vet Phil Watts runs the operations at Shell.

Strategy

Spurred by the 1998 global economic slump, Shell has focused on improving internal efficiency, chopping underperforming lines, and reducing capital employed. Forgoing the megamerger game played by its peers caused Shell to lose its spot as the world's largest energy company, but recent purchases of Pennzoil-Quaker State and Britain's Enterprise Oil indicate a new urge to merge.

Shell Centre
London, SE1 7NA
www.shell.com

Morningstar Grades

Growth [C-]	1998	1999	2000	2001
Revenue %	-26.9	12.5	41.6	-9.3
Earnings/Share %	-97.2	EUB	46.0	-11.9
Book Value/Share %	-44.4	80.2	0.1	1.6
Dividends/Share %	0.0	2.7	-2.7	-2.7

Sales grow and contract in spurts because of Shell's dependence on volatile commodity prices. Recent quarters saw commodity prices much lower than their 2000 peaks, and Shell's sales were down as a result. This is not a long-term concern.

Profitability [A]	1999	2000	2001	TTM
Return on Assets %	7.5	10.4	9.7	9.7
Oper Cash Flow $Mil	11,059	18,359	16,933	16,933
- Cap Spending $Mil	7,409	6,209	9,626	9,626
= Free Cash Flow $Mil	3,650	12,150	7,307	7,307

For years, Shell's been creating solid but unspectacular profitability. Recent efforts to cut costs and shed underperforming chemical units are aimed at bringing long-term returns on capital employed to 13%-15%.

Financial Health [A+]	1999	2000	2001	12-01
Long-term Debt $Mil	6,009	4,070	1,832	1,832
Total Equity $Mil	56,171	57,086	56,160	56,160
Debt/Equity Ratio	0.1	0.1	0.0	0.0

Sporting one of the healthiest balance sheets in the industry and an AAA credit rating, Shell has few liquidity concerns. Free cash flow has been reliably strong. Shell aims to leverage its financial health to acquire and shore up smaller firms.

	Industry	Investment Style	Stock Type	Sector
	Oil & Gas	▦ Large Value	▨ High Yield	◖ Energy

Competition	Market Cap $Mil	Debt/ Equity	12 Mo Trailing Sales $Mil	Price/Cash Flow	Return On Assets%	Total Return% 1 Yr	3 Yr
Shell Transport & Trading ADR	63,236	0.0	135,211	3.7	9.7	-3.2	-3.3
ExxonMobil	235,108	0.1	196,513	12.0	6.7	-8.9	-0.9
BP PLC ADR	152,063	0.2	175,389	6.8	5.7	-9.9	-9.2

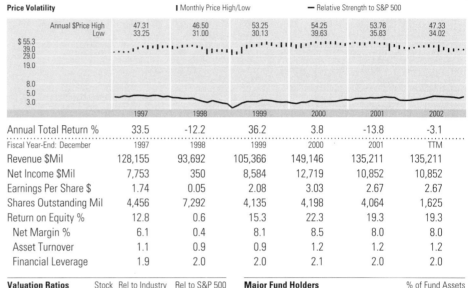

Price Volatility   I Monthly Price High/Low   — Relative Strength to S&P 500

Annual $Price High	47.31	46.50	53.25	54.25	53.76	47.33
Low	33.25	31.00	30.13	39.63	35.83	34.02
	1997	1998	1999	2000	2001	2002

Annual Total Return %	33.5	-12.2	36.2	3.8	-13.8	-3.1

Fiscal Year-End: December	1997	1998	1999	2000	2001	TTM
Revenue $Mil	128,155	93,692	105,366	149,146	135,211	135,211
Net Income $Mil	7,753	350	8,584	12,719	10,852	10,852
Earnings Per Share $	1.74	0.05	2.08	3.03	2.67	2.67
Shares Outstanding Mil	4,456	7,292	4,135	4,198	4,064	1,625
Return on Equity %	12.8	0.6	15.3	22.3	19.3	19.3
Net Margin %	6.1	0.4	8.1	8.5	8.0	8.0
Asset Turnover	1.1	0.9	0.9	1.2	1.2	1.2
Financial Leverage	1.9	2.0	2.0	2.1	2.0	2.0

Valuation Ratios	Stock	Rel to Industry	Rel to S&P 500	Major Fund Holders	% of Fund Assets
Price/Earnings	14.6	0.8	0.6	Saratoga International Equity I	4.93
Price/Book	1.1	0.5	0.4	Rydex Energy Inv	4.74
Price/Sales	0.5	0.4	0.2	CDC Nvest Large Cap Value A	3.41
Price/Cash Flow	3.7	0.6	0.3	Liberty European Thematic Equity Z	2.73

Morningstar's Take By Paul Larson, 12-06-2002 Stock Price as of Analysis: $38.15

Shell's integrated operations cover the entire spectrum in oil. Its upstream exploration and production business finds, digs up, transports, and sells crude oil and gas. When the prices of these commodities are above their costs to produce (typically in the low teens per barrel), Shell makes money. At the right price, Shell (and its twin Royal Dutch) is worth owning, in our opinion.

The OPEC cartel works to ensure profits for its member countries, which greatly benefits the entire oil patch. OPEC limits its members' production, which ends up raising oil prices. This action typically maintains a nice spread between the price and cost per barrel of oil. Though OPEC members tend to cheat when prices are high, the cartel's influence is still strong. The spread between the cost to produce and the price of a barrel of oil allows Shell to typically earn decent, though widely variable, margins in its exploration and production business.

Shell also has significant downstream refining and marketing operations. Its refineries get crude oil from the upstream business or on the open market and transform it into usable commodities, like heating oil and gasoline. Through the marketing business, Shell distributes these products to service stations around the globe, selling directly to consumers. Refining and marketing profit margins tend to remain healthy even when commodity prices are poor, providing a nice counterbalance to the upstream results that are so sensitive to commodity price swings.

Shell is highly profitable and has a long history of creating shareholder value. The company has not had an unprofitable year in decades and has enjoyed a healthy 13.0% return on its invested capital over the past three years. Free cash flow has also been strong, allowing the company to pare its debt to $20 billion, a comparatively small amount considering Shell's $146 billion base of hard assets.

Though volatile commodity prices make for a bumpy road, we expect Shell will continue to generate free cash flow for many years to come, enriching its shareholders in the process. Shell is one of the leaders in energy; we'd love to own it at the right price and receive a chunk of the robust dividends it pays. We'd wait for the shares to trade below $33 to provide an adequate margin of safety.

MORNINGSTAR® Stocks 500

Siebel Systems SEBL

	Rating	Risk	Moat Size	Fair Value	Last Close	Yield %
	★★★	Med.	Narrow	$9.00	$7.40	0.0

Company Profile

Siebel Systems provides sales and marketing information software systems. The company's Siebel Sales Enterprise combines client-server application products to allow corporations to deploy customer information systems, product information systems, competitive information systems, and decision support systems on a global basis. Siebel Systems' clients are in the transportation, financial services, securities brokerage, manufacturing, computer, communication, and chemical industries.

Management

CEO Tom Siebel spent six years at Oracle before starting Siebel Systems. He owns 36.2 million shares, or about 7% of the stock. Siebel's managerial bench is very deep, with years of tech experience.

Strategy

Siebel is using its position as the world's leading vendor of CRM software to grab share from fumbling rivals. Its strategy involves partnering with industry big shots like IBM or using its stock to buy other firms that round out its product portfolio. Siebel is obsessed with providing topnotch customer service.

2207 Bridgepointe Parkway   www.siebel.com
San Mateo, CA 94404

Morningstar Grades

Growth [B+]	1998	1999	2000	2001
Revenue %	84.7	94.7	120.7	14.1
Earnings/Share %	NMF	20.0	100.0	104.2
Book Value/Share %	NMF	90.7	83.4	41.7
Dividends/Share %	NMF	NMF	NMF	NMF

After years of eye-popping performance, growth has hit the wall as IT budgets have been pared. We now think Siebel's long-term sales growth will be no better than 15%-20%.

Profitability [A]	1999	2000	2001	TTM
Return on Assets %	4.5	5.7	9.3	2.3
Oper Cash Flow $Mil	90	439	593	471
- Cap Spending $Mil	46	162	251	88
= Free Cash Flow $Mil	44	276	342	383

Outstanding. Siebel generates returns on assets and equity in excess of 15%. But margins have suffered as licenses make up less of the sales mix.

Financial Health [A]	1999	2000	2001	09-02
Long-term Debt $Mil	300	300	300	318
Total Equity $Mil	645	1,280	1,836	1,982
Debt/Equity Ratio	0.5	0.2	0.2	0.2

The balance sheet is pristine; cash of $2 billion covers debt 6 times. The company continues to generate gobs of cash.

Industry	Investment Style	Stock Type	Sector
Business Applications	Mid Growth	Aggr. Growth	Software

Competition	Market Cap $Mil	Debt/ Equity	12 Mo Trailing Sales $Mil	Price/Cash Flow	Return On Assets%	Total Return% 1 Yr	3 Yr
Siebel Systems	3,539	0.2	1,692	7.5	2.3	-73.6	-42.2
Oracle	57,845	0.1	9,459	18.1	19.8	-21.8	-26.3
SAP AG ADR	24,556	0.0	6,546	27.8	9.5	-38.7	-25.0

Price Volatility

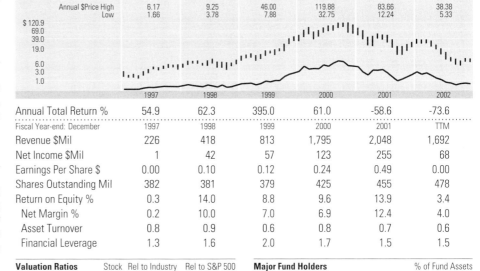

Annual $Price High Low	6.17 1.66	9.25 3.78	46.00 7.88	119.88 32.75	83.66 12.24	38.38 5.33

	1997	1998	1999	2000	2001	2002
Annual Total Return %	54.9	62.3	395.0	61.0	-58.6	-73.6
Fiscal Year-end: December	1997	1998	1999	2000	2001	TTM
Revenue $Mil	226	418	813	1,795	2,048	1,692
Net Income $Mil	1	42	57	123	255	68
Earnings Per Share $	0.00	0.10	0.12	0.24	0.49	0.00
Shares Outstanding Mil	382	381	379	425	455	478
Return on Equity %	0.3	14.0	8.8	9.6	13.9	3.4
Net Margin %	0.2	10.0	7.0	6.9	12.4	4.0
Asset Turnover	0.8	0.9	0.6	0.8	0.7	0.6
Financial Leverage	1.3	1.6	2.0	1.7	1.5	1.5

Valuation Ratios	Stock	Rel to Industry	Rel to S&P 500
Price/Earnings	15.1	0.5	0.6
Price/Book	1.8	0.3	0.6
Price/Sales	2.1	0.2	1.0
Price/Cash Flow	7.5	0.5	0.6

Major Fund Holders	% of Fund Assets
Reserve Blue Chip Growth R	2.58
Enterprise Equity B	2.35
TCW Galileo Select Equities I	2.32
Morgan Stanley Cap Opportunities B	2.22

Morningstar's Take By Mike Trigg, 10-21-2002 Stock Price as of Analysis: $6.47

We believe Siebel Systems is a stellar company, but uncertainty over IT spending makes us require a 25% discount to our fair value estimate before investing.

Siebel is the 800-pound gorilla of customer-relationship management (CRM) software. A CRM application can keep track of important client data, like purchasing histories, so promotional types can tailor specific product offerings to individual customers. This creates additional revenue opportunities and improves customer satisfaction.

We expect the CRM market to continue growing faster than the rest of the software industry as companies leverage the Internet as an efficient way to reach customers. Some say the CRM sector is maturing, as the enterprise resource planning (ERP) market did years ago. We disagree; ERP software can automate a finite number of back-office processes (like accounting), but there's no limit to how firms can interact more effectively with customers.

Siebel's competitive advantages are superior products and visionary leadership. No company can match Siebel's breadth of CRM software. Also, CEO Tom Siebel is the godfather of CRM. During his stint as the top salesman at Oracle, he practically founded the industry by developing an internal application to make the salesforce more efficient. When Oracle CEO

Larry Ellison balked at selling the product to customers, Siebel left and founded Siebel Systems.

Now the demand for CRM software has drawn a crowd, including Oracle, PeopleSoft, and SAP, all of which we expect will have success selling to their huge installed base of customers. Microsoft is currently avoiding Siebel by targeting smaller firms (less than $50 million in revenue), but we think it is simply a matter of time before the software giant targets larger ones. Salesforce.com, which sells CRM software over the Internet, is also making strides with small firms possessing smaller budgets.

Not only are Siebel's products the best, they are the most pricey. Hence, we expect rivals will take market share right now because many firms are willing to forgo a superior product for a cheaper alternative that meets their basic needs. And in some cases, companies like Oracle are practically giving away their CRM software to drive sales of other applications.

We think Siebel is worth $9 per share. But given increased competition and lackluster spending on IT, we wouldn't invest until the stock fell below $7.

Simon Property Group SPG

	Rating ★★★	Risk Low	Moat Size Narrow	Fair Value $36.00	Last Close $34.07	Yield % 6.4

Industry	Investment Style	Stock Type	Sector
REITS	Mid Value	Hard Assets	Financial Services

Company Profile

Simon Property Group owns, develops, manages, and leases regional shopping malls and community shopping centers. The company has an interest in more than 250 properties containing 187 million square feet of gross leasable area in 36 states. Simon is the largest publicly traded retail shopping center owner in the United States. It is the amalgamation of two family-controlled real estate empires that merged in 1996: Simon Properties of Indianapolis and the DeBartolo family of San Francisco.

Management

Brothers Melvin and Herbert Simon are cochairmen of the board. Melvin Simon's oldest son, David, is the chief executive officer. The Simons control the company and still own more than 15% of it.

Strategy

Simon Property's stated mission is to be the leading developer, owner, and manager of retail real estate in North America. Management wants to own the best malls in the best markets. Simon Property is an aggressive acquisitor, but also looks to increase the value of its existing malls by developing revenue-enhancing products and services.

National City Center   www.shopsimon.com
Indianapolis, IN 46204

Morningstar Grades

Growth [B-]	1998	1999	2000	2001
Revenue %	33.3	34.9	6.2	1.6
Earnings/Share %	-2.8	-8.6	15.6	-23.4
Book Value/Share %	73.1	-26.1	-6.8	-7.9
Dividends/Share %	-1.0	1.7	0.0	3.0

Although acquisitions have driven revenue growth of approximately 20% annually since the IPO, growth has dropped to the low single digits in the past few years.

Profitability [B]	1999	2000	2001	TTM
Return on Assets %	1.2	1.4	1.1	2.1
Oper Cash Flow $Mil	630	707	800	—
- Cap Spending $Mil	491	409	283	—
= Free Cash Flow $Mil	—	—	—	—

Simon Property's net operating margin (revenue less operating expenses, but excluding depreciation) has remained at about 65% for several years.

Financial Health [B]	1999	2000	2001	09-02
Long-term Debt $Mil	—	—	—	—
Total Equity $Mil	2,695	2,515	2,327	2,642
Debt/Equity Ratio	—	—	—	—

Simon Property's fixed-charge coverage ratio (operating income divided by interest expense and preferred stock dividends) of 2.4 is above the regional mall REIT average of 2.1. Debt/total market capitalization on September 30 was 56%.

Competition

Competition	Market Cap $Mil	Debt/ Equity	12 Mo Trailing Sales $Mil	Price/Cash Flow	Return On Assets%	Total Return% 1 Yr	3 Yr
Simon Property Group	6,384	—	2,130	—	2.1	24.0	23.9
General Growth Properties	3,242	—	899	—	—	—	—
Rouse	2,754	—	1,043	—	—	—	—

Price Volatility

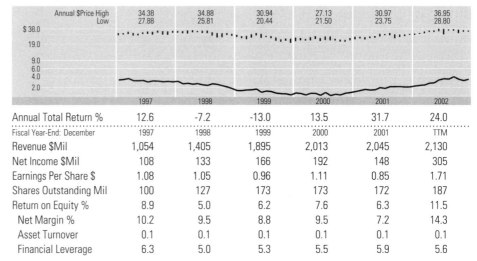

Annual $Price High/Low	34.38 27.88	34.88 25.81	30.94 20.44	27.13 21.50	30.97 23.75	36.95 28.80

	1997	1998	1999	2000	2001	2002
Annual Total Return %	12.6	-7.2	-13.0	13.5	31.7	24.0

Fiscal Year-End: December	1997	1998	1999	2000	2001	TTM
Revenue $Mil	1,054	1,405	1,895	2,013	2,045	2,130
Net Income $Mil	108	133	166	192	148	305
Earnings Per Share $	1.08	1.05	0.96	1.11	0.85	1.71
Shares Outstanding Mil	100	127	173	173	172	187
Return on Equity %	8.9	5.0	6.2	7.6	6.3	11.5
Net Margin %	10.2	9.5	8.8	9.5	7.2	14.3
Asset Turnover	0.1	0.1	0.1	0.1	0.1	0.1
Financial Leverage	6.3	5.0	5.3	5.5	5.9	5.6

Valuation Ratios	Stock	Rel to Industry	Rel to S&P 500
Price/Earnings	19.9	1.1	0.8
Price/Book	2.4	1.6	0.8
Price/Sales	3.0	0.9	1.5
Price/Cash Flow	—	—	—

Major Fund Holders	% of Fund Assets
Fremont Real Estate Securities	7.74
Scudder RREEF Real Estate Sec Instl	7.53
Morgan Stanley Real Estate A	7.27
Morgan Stanley Inst US Real Estate A	6.94

Morningstar's Take By Matthew Scholz, 12-16-2002 Stock Price as of Analysis: $33.75

There are clear scale advantages that come with being a mall colossus, but Simon Property's growth strategy makes us skeptical of the firm's prospects. Our net asset value is $36.

Just as the shopping mall has proved itself a resilient retailing concept--having survived such threats as catalog shopping, Wal-Mart, and e-commerce--the Simon family has proved that owning and running malls can be a lucrative business. Long leases (averaging seven to ten years), a diverse retailer base, and a relatively high occupancy level (90%-92% over the past three years) combine to produce a stable and predictable stream of leasing cash flows.

Recognizing the stability of this business, the market has elevated Simon Property's share price 14% over the past year. We're concerned, however, that this may be making too much of the firm's growth potential. The Simon empire includes roughly 30% of all malls in the United States with annual sales greater than $250 million. But with such a giant portfolio, it will be hard to obtain long-term growth in funds from operations above the 5%-10% that comes from gradually increasing rental rates and realizing greater operational efficiencies.

Through Simon Brand Ventures, the firm has

sought novel ways, like hosting product displays and promotions for Ford and Pepsi, to earn revenue from the 100 million people who traipse through its malls 2 billion times a year. This is a good idea, but the revenue generated via the venture and its sister program, Simon Business Network, will have a hard time growing fast enough to affect the massive stream of rental revenue.

A more fundamental issue is that Simon Property is so large that many of its malls are in secondary markets with lower population densities or lower average household income. These second-tier malls can generate only modest rental rates.

Also of concern is Simon Property's attempted hostile takeover of mall rival Taubman, which owns a desirable portfolio that generates sector-leading retail sales per square foot of $450. Even if Simon Property can purchase Taubman's attractive assets at a good price and without rancor, it still has to expand the firm via operational efficiencies.

Until the long-term direction of this company becomes clearer, the greatest benefits Simon Property can provide investors are exposure to the retail property sector and a stable 6%-plus dividend yield.

MORNINGSTAR® Stocks 500

SLM SLM

	Rating	Risk	Moat Size	Fair Value	Last Close	Yield %
	★★★	Low	Wide	$96.00	$103.86	0.8

Industry	Investment Style	Stock Type	Sector
Finance	Large Growth	→ Slow Growth	$ Financial Services

Company Profile

SLM Corporation is the parent of Sallie Mae, the Student Loan Marketing Association. It was formed in 1972 as a government-sponsored enterprise to provide affordable student loans, but will fully privatize by September 2008. The company funds education loans, most of which are federally guaranteed student loans. The majority of its revenue comes from interest payments, servicing, and securitizing loans it has originated. In 2001, Sallie Mae acquired two collection agencies to help it return uncollected loan dollars to the federal coffers.

Management

CEO Albert Lord's legacy so far is fomenting change. He became CEO in 1997 after leading a proxy battle. Now he must prove that he can implement his major strategic shift. At the same time, the firm must identify a successor to Lord.

Strategy

SLM aims to increase its share of the $200 billion student loan universe. The company has adopted a campus-based strategy in which it makes loans directly to students instead of acquiring loans, as it has in the past. Other sources of income like servicing, securitizing, and collections add necessary diversification.

11600 Sallie Mae Drive
Reston, VA 20193
www.salliemae.com

Competition

Competition	Market Cap $Mil	Debt/ Equity	12 Mo Trailing Sales $Mil	Price/Cash Flow	Return On Assets%	Total Return% 1 Yr	3 Yr
SLM	15,947	—	2,898	—	1.3	24.7	41.0
Bank of America	104,505	—	46,628	—	1.3	14.5	19.8
Wells Fargo	79,608	—	28,119	—	1.5	10.3	10.4

Price Volatility

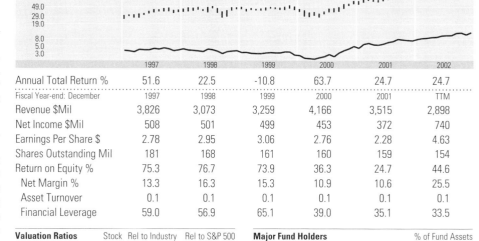

			I Monthly Price High/Low		— Relative Strength to S&P 500	
Annual $Price High	47.18	51.38	53.94	68.25	87.95	106.95
Low	25.43	27.50	38.56	27.81	55.88	77.00

$108.0 49.0 29.0 19.0 8.0 5.0 3.0

	1997	1998	1999	2000	2001	2002
Annual Total Return %	51.6	22.5	-10.8	63.7	24.7	24.7
Fiscal Year-end: December	1997	1998	1999	2000	2001	TTM
Revenue $Mil	3,826	3,073	3,259	4,166	3,515	2,898
Net Income $Mil	508	501	499	453	372	740
Earnings Per Share $	2.78	2.95	3.06	2.76	2.28	4.63
Shares Outstanding Mil	181	168	161	160	159	154
Return on Equity %	75.3	76.7	73.9	36.3	24.7	44.6
Net Margin %	13.3	16.3	15.3	10.9	10.6	25.5
Asset Turnover	0.1	0.1	0.1	0.1	0.1	0.1
Financial Leverage	59.0	56.9	65.1	39.0	35.1	33.5

Valuation Ratios	Stock	Rel to Industry	Rel to S&P 500
Price/Earnings	22.4	1.9	1.0
Price/Book	9.6	2.9	3.0
Price/Sales	5.5	2.8	2.7
Price/Cash Flow	—	—	—

Major Fund Holders	% of Fund Assets
SunAmerica Focused Large Cap Gr A	7.36
SunAmerica Focused Multi-Cap Gr A	7.06
Enterprise Capital Appreciation A	6.53
ASAF Marsico Capital Growth A	6.43

Morningstar Grades

Growth [D]	1998	1999	2000	2001
Revenue %	-19.7	6.1	27.8	-15.6
Earnings/Share %	6.1	3.7	-9.8	-17.4
Book Value/Share %	4.1	7.7	83.7	21.3
Dividends/Share %	10.2	7.0	7.4	10.7

Managed revenues grew 13.7% per year on average from 1997 through 2001, and were up 11.6% through the first three quarters of 2002. We've assumed compound annual topline growth of about 9% through 2006.

Profitability [C+]	1999	2000	2001	TTM
Return on Assets %	1.1	0.9	0.7	1.3
Oper Cash Flow $Mil	338	745	839	—
- Cap Spending $Mil	—	—	—	—
= Free Cash Flow $Mil	—	—	—	—

The student loan spread, the difference between borrowing and lending rates, drives profits. Because most loans are priced about 2%-3% above short-term Treasuries--and SLM borrows a hair above the Treasury rate--profits are very consistent.

Financial Health [B+]	1999	2000	2001	09-02
Long-term Debt $Mil	—	—	—	—
Total Equity $Mil	676	1,250	1,507	1,659
Debt/Equity Ratio	—	—	—	—

The company increased its provisioning for loan losses in 2001, though not as quickly as charge-offs mounted. Still, the firm writes off a minute portion of its loans and has a balance sheet allowance well in excess of its modest requirements.

Morningstar's Take By Craig Woker, 12-14-2002 Stock Price as of Analysis: $102.89

Picture this dream scenario: you're one of the biggest lenders in a fast-growing sector. The business is a structural oligopoly in which price competition is almost unheard of. Huge economies of scale prevent new rivals from touching you--they would lose money for so long to build critical mass that competing wouldn't be worth their while. And on top of everything else, you earn a virtually risk-free profit in your core business because the federal government subsidizes you.

That dream world belongs to SLM, a company that we think should be on almost every investor's radar screen. However, we wouldn't be buyers unless the stock took a tumble and traded at a reasonable discount to our $96 fair value estimate.

SLM--better known by its former name of Sallie Mae--is consistently one of the most profitable lenders in the world. On a cash income basis, its returns on equity have averaged in excess of 40% over the past five years, and we're forecasting that they trend down to about 30% over the next five.

The company owes a hefty thank-you to Uncle Sam for those super-sized profits. Because most student loans are backed by the federal government, SLM has phenomenally low levels of bad debt charge-offs, only about 0.1% of managed loans. So while net interest spreads are low--typically only about 2% versus about 5% for banks--the government's willingness to foot the tab for bad debt has sent net margins consistently above 30%.

Normally, big profits attract competition. However, Sallie Mae's customers have no incentive to throw their business elsewhere. After all, the government sets most student loan interest rates, thus limiting price competition. As a result, most schools work either with Sallie Mae and its bank partners or with the Federal Direct Loan Program, a government agency.

SLM doesn't come cheap, though. The stock trades close to 10 times book value, a surreal level for a finance company. Most big banks trade for about 2 or 2.5 times book so if the market ever caught a whiff out of Washington that the government's backing of college loans was going away, this stock could be in for a wild ride.

That said, we frankly doubt that a majority of legislators--for political reasons--would ever have the gall to vote "against education" by eliminating the federal backing of college loans. However, political scuttlebutt can create bargains in stocks like this, and if that ever happens, SLM would be worth pouncing on.

Smithfield Foods SFD

	Rating	Risk	Moat Size	Fair Value	Last Close	Yield %
	★★	Med.	None	$20.00	$19.84	0.0

Company Profile

Smithfield Foods produces meat products. Its products include smoked hams, boiled hams, bacon, sausage, hot dogs, deli meats, luncheon meats, pepperoni, dry salami, pork loins, pork chops, pork roasts, and pork ribs. The company markets its products to wholesale distributors, fast-food restaurants, restaurant chains, hotels, hospitals, and other institutional customers under brand names such as Smithfield, Luter's, Lykes, Great, Gwaltney, Esskay, Patrick Cudahy, John Morrell, Dinner Bell, Kretschmar, Peyton's, and Valleydale in the United States and overseas.

Management

Joseph Luter has been CEO for 26 years, during which he has built Smithfield into the largest hog farmer and pork processor in the United States. His family founded the business.

Strategy

Unlike most other meat processors, Smithfield owns and raises the hogs that go into its pork products, which in theory insulate it a bit from fluctuating hog prices. It tries to distinguish itself from its competitors by offering high-end, value-added pork products, a strategy it hopes to extend to beef through its recent acquisition of Packerland Holdings and several smaller beef producers.

200 Commerce Street   www.smithfieldfoods.com
Smithfield, VA 23430

Morningstar Grades

Growth [A+]	1999	2000	2001	2002
Revenue %	-2.4	36.4	14.6	24.7
Earnings/Share %	73.1	-34.5	167.1	-12.3
Book Value/Share %	46.4	37.8	4.7	28.8
Dividends/Share %	NMF	NMF	NMF	NMF

Sales increased 20% in the first half of fiscal 2003, but this growth was entirely due to acquisitions. Internal sales growth was hurt by sharply lower hog prices and a glut of meat in the marketplace.

Profitability [B]	2000	2001	2002	TTM
Return on Assets %	2.4	6.9	5.1	2.3
Oper Cash Flow $Mil	125	218	299	185
- Cap Spending $Mil	100	144	171	207
= Free Cash Flow $Mil	25	74	128	-21

Although a vertically integrated structure helps, Smithfield's profits are still strongly influenced by commodity prices. After several strong quarters, profits have plunged in the past three quarters after hog prices fell off a cliff.

Financial Health [C]	2000	2001	2002	10-02
Long-term Debt $Mil	1,188	1,146	1,387	1,493
Total Equity $Mil	903	1,053	1,363	1,362
Debt/Equity Ratio	1.3	1.1	1.0	1.1

Long-term debt has increased dramatically in recent years, but Smithfield's debt/equity ratio has grown only slightly. The firm has generated steady, albeit modest, free cash flows.

	Industry	Investment Style	Stock Type	Sector
	Food Mfg.	▦ Mid Core	↗ Classic Growth	🚗 Consumer Goods

Competition

	Market Cap $Mil	Debt/ Equity	12 Mo Trailing Sales $Mil	Price/Cash Flow	Return On Assets%	Total Return% 1 Yr	3 Yr
Smithfield Foods	2,170	1.1	8,008	11.7	2.3	-10.0	23.8
ConAgra Foods	13,431	—	27,085	—	—	—	—
Tyson Foods A	3,972	1.0	22,814	3.4	3.7	-1.6	-9.9

Price Volatility

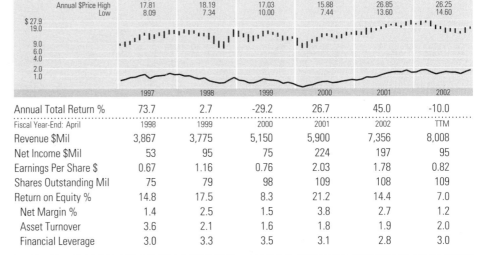

		Monthly Price High/Low			— Relative Strength to S&P 500	
Annual $Price High	17.81	18.19	17.03	15.88	26.85	26.25
Low	8.09	7.34	10.00	7.44	13.60	14.60
	1997	1998	1999	2000	2001	2002

Annual Total Return %	73.7	2.7	-29.2	26.7	45.0	-10.0

Fiscal Year-End: April	1998	1999	2000	2001	2002	TTM
Revenue $Mil	3,867	3,775	5,150	5,900	7,356	8,008
Net Income $Mil	53	95	75	224	197	95
Earnings Per Share $	0.67	1.16	0.76	2.03	1.78	0.82
Shares Outstanding Mil	75	79	98	109	108	109
Return on Equity %	14.8	17.5	8.3	21.2	14.4	7.0
Net Margin %	1.4	2.5	1.5	3.8	2.7	1.2
Asset Turnover	3.6	2.1	1.6	1.8	1.9	2.0
Financial Leverage	3.0	3.3	3.5	3.1	2.8	3.0

Valuation Ratios	Stock	Rel to Industry	Rel to S&P 500
Price/Earnings	24.2	1.2	1.0
Price/Book	1.6	0.4	0.5
Price/Sales	0.3	0.2	0.1
Price/Cash Flow	11.7	1.1	0.9

Major Fund Holders	% of Fund Assets
ING Midcap Value A	3.45
Queens Road Small Cap Value	2.13
Undiscovered Managers Hidden Val Inst	2.06
GE Small-Cap Value Equity B	2.00

Morningstar's Take   By David Kathman, 12-20-2002   Stock Price as of Analysis: $18.99

Smithfield has been hurt by the recent collapse in hog prices. But while the short-term effect will continue to be unpleasant, we still see Smithfield as a potentially good stock for the long term--as long as the price is right.

Smithfield differs from most of its peers in the meat-packing business because it's vertically integrated, raising and selling hogs as well as processing pork for the consumer market. In theory, this makes it less affected by volatile hog prices than its rivals: Rising hog prices help its hog-production business but hurt its meat-processing business, while falling hog prices have the opposite effect. In practice, though, the hog-production side of the business tends to dominate. When hog prices rose in 2000 and 2001, the profits of Smithfield's meat-processing business got squeezed, but this decline was more than offset by booming profits from hog production. However, when hog prices suddenly collapsed in the spring of 2002 and remained depressed for months, Smithfield's profits took a major hit.

To reduce its reliance on hog prices, Smithfield has been working to strengthen the meat-processing part of its business, emphasizing branded "value-added" pork products that tend to be more

profitable than traditional cuts of meat. It's had some success in this area, as processed-meat margins have increased over the past year from 1% in the first half of fiscal 2002 to 3% in the first half of fiscal 2003. But rivals Hormel and Tyson are pushing their own value-added meat products, making for a tough competitive environment.

Another way Smithfield has tried to reduce its reliance on hog prices is by diversifying into other meats. Its acquisitions of Packerland and American Foods made Smithfield the fourth-largest beef processor in the United States, with 9% market share, and profits at its beef-processing operations have been robust so far. Smithfield has also diversified geographically in recent years, buying meat processors in Canada, France, Poland, and Mexico.

All this diversification has helped to some degree, but Smithfield's short-term fortunes are still heavily influenced by the boom-and-bust cycle of hog prices. This means that it's not a stock for the faint of heart, but it also means that Smithfield sometimes becomes cheap for long-term investors willing to wait out the down times. If the stock dropped more than 40% below our estimated fair value of $20, we'd be inclined to snap it up.

M🌑RNINGSTAR® Stocks 500

Solectron SLR

	Rating	Risk	Moat Size	Fair Value	Last Close	Yield %
	★	High	None	$2.50	$3.55	0.0

Company Profile

Solectron provides customized manufacturing services. These include engineering, materials management, printed circuit board assembly, systems integration, testing, packaging, and product remanufacturing. Solectron provides its services to a diverse group of technology customers, like computer, cellular phone, and communication equipment manufacturers. The firm operates manufacturing facilities in the U.S., Latin America, Europe, and Asia. It purchased Asian competitor NatSteel Electronics in October 2001 for $2.4 billion in cash.

Management

CEO Koichi Nishimura joined Solectron in 1988 and is a pioneer in the EMS industry, but will retire to chair the board in 2003. Several executives have been with the firm for only a few years, while others are holdovers from various acquisitions.

Strategy

Solectron spreads its revenue stream fairly evenly across various tech industries, and uses its large scale to offer broad services and lower costs than rivals. A key to its strategy is acquiring the manufacturing assets of its customers and maintaining long-term partnerships with them. The firm is targeting Asia because of the region's strong growth prospects.

777 Gibraltar Drive   www.solectron.com
Milpitas, CA 95035

Morningstar Grades

Growth [C+]	1999	2000	2001	2002
Revenue %	58.5	46.2	32.2	-34.3
Earnings/Share %	29.8	31.1	NMF	NMF
Book Value/Share %	99.9	10.9	29.5	-22.9
Dividends/Share %	NMF	NMF	NMF	NMF

Fueled by acquisitions and EMS outsourcing, Solectron's sales have grown at a 27% annual compound rate over the past five years. We expect future revenue to grow 14%-15% per year, slightly less than the EMS industry as a whole.

Profitability [C]	2000	2001	2002	TTM
Return on Assets %	4.8	-0.9	-28.2	-28.2
Oper Cash Flow $Mil	-343	628	2,129	2,129
- Cap Spending $Mil	506	537	242	242
= Free Cash Flow $Mil	-849	91	1,888	1,888

EMS firms get low margins but turn over assets quickly. Because Solectron will be underinvesting in assets as it tries to reduce debt, we expect below-average gross margins (6%-7%).

Financial Health [D+]	2000	2001	2002	08-02
Long-term Debt $Mil	3,320	5,028	3,184	3,184
Total Equity $Mil	3,802	5,151	4,773	4,773
Debt/Equity Ratio	0.9	1.0	0.7	0.7

Solectron should have sufficient cash and operating cash flow to avoid insolvency or diluting equityholders with additional shares. After retiring $2 billion of convertible debt in 2003 and 2004, Solectron will be left with long-term debt of roughly $1.6-%1.8 billion.

Industry	Investment Style	Stock Type	Sector
Contract Manufacturers	▦ Mid Value	➡ Slow Growth	▣ Hardware

Competition	Market Cap $Mil	Debt/ Equity	12 Mo Trailing Sales $Mil	Price/Cash Flow	Return On Assets%	Total Return% 1 Yr	3 Yr
Solectron	2,928	0.7	12,276	1.4	-28.2	-68.5	-56.5
Flextronics International	4,239	0.2	13,217	5.1	-0.1	-65.9	-26.4
Jabil Circuit	3,542	0.2	3,545	6.4	1.4	-21.1	-17.8

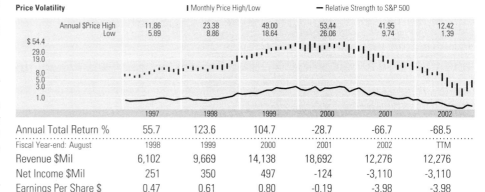

Price Volatility | Monthly Price High/Low   — Relative Strength to S&P 500

Annual $Price High Low	11.86 5.89	23.38 8.86	49.00 18.64	53.44 26.06	41.95 9.74	12.42 1.39
	1997	1998	1999	2000	2001	2002

Annual Total Return %	55.7	123.6	104.7	-28.7	-66.7	-68.5	
Fiscal Year-end: August	1998	1999	2000	2001	2002	TTM
Revenue $Mil	6,102	9,669	14,138	18,692	12,276	12,276
Net Income $Mil	251	350	497	-124	-3,110	-3,110
Earnings Per Share $	0.47	0.61	0.80	-0.19	-3.98	-3.98
Shares Outstanding Mil	513	539	599	650	781	825
Return on Equity %	17.0	11.1	13.1	-2.4	-65.2	-65.2
Net Margin %	4.1	3.6	3.5	-0.7	-25.3	-25.3
Asset Turnover	2.1	1.8	1.4	1.4	1.1	1.1
Financial Leverage	1.9	1.7	2.7	2.5	2.3	2.3

Valuation Ratios	Stock	Rel to Industry	Rel to S&P 500
Price/Earnings	NMF	—	—
Price/Book	0.6	0.6	0.2
Price/Sales	0.2	0.7	0.1
Price/Cash Flow	1.4	0.3	0.1

Major Fund Holders	% of Fund Assets
John Hancock Classic Value A	5.43
SunAmerica Focused Multi-Cap Gr A	4.88
ING Midcap Value A	3.40
Neuberger Berman Focus Inv	2.55

Morningstar's Take By Fritz Kaegi, 12-20-2002 Stock Price as of Analysis: $3.16

Solectron will probably avoid insolvency, but cost-cutting will put it at a competitive disadvantage in the electronics manufacturing services (EMS) industry.

Like other EMS firms, Solectron takes on production from original equipment manufacturers (OEMs) like Nortel. To differentiate itself from rivals, Solectron has been active in building activities complementary to core manufacturing, like design, component production, logistics, and customer service. Solectron plans to combine its product scope and operational scale to offer a bundled, integrated offering at the lowest cost to the OEM.

Yet OEMs also consider financial viability when selecting partners, since solvency directly affects whether a contract manufacturer can locate supplies on good terms to keep operations functioning smoothly. OEMs depend on EMS firms, so they want to avoid firms struggling with additional working capital requirements, cost-cutting measures, or battles with creditors. Solectron's large debt load, together with its use of exotic convertible securities and exposure to struggling telecom OEMs, has raised the specter of insolvency. One OEM we've met with says it won't use Solectron for this reason.

In our opinion, insolvency or serious equity dilution

are unlikely. Solectron has $2 billion in cash; given a 3% decline in sales and no change in gross margin in 2003, we expect cash burn of $250 million and retirement of convertible debt due in 2003 for $540 million. The company will probably enter 2004 breaking even and with $1.2 billion in available cash, giving it ample room to retire its remaining convertible debt of $590 million. In this scenario, Solectron would then have a very manageable $1.6-$1.8 billion in long-term debt.

However, Solectron's cost cuts will hurt competitiveness. Because it will need to conserve cash, Solectron can't fully replace equipment or buy attractive OEM plants. Underinvestment in plant and equipment could hurt the firm's margins and ability to grow, since Solectron would be using older equipment in an industry where gear rapidly matures. In 2002, Solectron couldn't bid on attractive deals that eventually went to Jabil Circuit and Flextronics. Given its lack of service or operating differentiation, Solectron is likely to continue to be at a competitive disadvantage. Until it becomes unavoidably cheap, Solectron isn't worth owning, in our opinion.

Sony ADR SNE

	Rating	Risk	Moat Size	Fair Value	Last Close	Yield %
	★★	Med.	None	$43.00	$41.31	0.4

Company Profile

Sony manufactures consumer electronics and has entertainment operations. Its electronic products include televisions, VCRs, camcorders, minidisc systems, CD and DVD players, video game consoles, CD-ROM drives, satellite broadcast reception systems, semiconductors, and computers. Sony's Columbia TriStar Motion Pictures Group includes Columbia Pictures and Sony Pictures Classics. The company's Sony Music Entertainment group produces and distributes recorded music under the Columbia and Epic brand names. Sales outside Japan account for about 72% of the company's revenue.

Management

CEO Nobuyuki Idei, a Sony employee for more than 30 years, recently reorganized the company to reduce bureaucracy and encourage creativity. He has quashed rumors that Sony might want to sell its erratic picture and music divisions.

Strategy

Sony has tried to shed money-losing projects in its core electronics division, and its PlayStation 2 video game console has fended off challenges from Nintendo and Microsoft. Sony hopes its PlayStation 2 and CLIE handheld computer will become gateways to multimedia Internet-based entertainment. The company has denied rumors that it wants to get rid of its entertainment divisions.

7-35, Kitashinagawa 6-Chome   www.sony.co.jp
Tokyo, 141-0001

Industry	Investment Style	Stock Type	Sector
Audio/Video Equipment	▦ Large Value	⊕ Cyclical	⬡ Consumer Goods

Competition

	Market Cap $Mil	Debt/ Equity	12 Mo Trailing Sales $Mil	Price/Cash Flow	Return On Assets%	Total Return% 1 Yr	3 Yr
Sony ADR	38,122	0.4	60,413	6.5	0.2	-8.1	-32.4
Philips Electronics NV AD	22,527	0.4	28,837	20.2	-6.8	-38.6	-18.3
Matsushita Electric Indus	19,964	—	70,299	—	—	—	—

Price Volatility

| Monthly Price High/Low   — Relative Strength to S&P 500

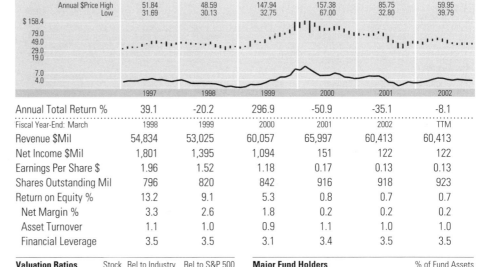

Annual $Price High / Low	51.84 / 31.69	48.59 / 30.13	147.94 / 32.75	157.38 / 67.00	85.75 / 32.80	59.95 / 39.79

	1997	1998	1999	2000	2001	2002
Annual Total Return %	39.1	-20.2	296.9	-50.9	-35.1	-8.1

Fiscal Year-End: March	1998	1999	2000	2001	2002	TTM
Revenue $Mil	54,834	53,025	60,057	65,997	60,413	60,413
Net Income $Mil	1,801	1,395	1,094	151	122	122
Earnings Per Share $	1.96	1.52	1.18	0.17	0.13	0.13
Shares Outstanding Mil	796	820	842	916	918	923
Return on Equity %	13.2	9.1	5.3	0.8	0.7	0.7
Net Margin %	3.3	2.6	1.8	0.2	0.2	0.2
Asset Turnover	1.1	1.0	0.9	1.1	1.0	1.0
Financial Leverage	3.5	3.5	3.1	3.4	3.5	3.5

Valuation Ratios	Stock	Rel to Industry	Rel to S&P 500
Price/Earnings	310.6	2.1	13.2
Price/Book	2.1	1.3	0.7
Price/Sales	0.6	1.0	0.3
Price/Cash Flow	6.5	0.9	0.5

Major Fund Holders	% of Fund Assets
IDEX Great Companies-Global A	4.88
Purisima Pure Foreign	3.68
Matthews Japan	3.50
Investec Wired Index	2.94

Morningstar Grades

Growth [B]	1999	2000	2001	2002
Revenue %	0.6	-1.7	9.4	3.6
Earnings/Share %	-19.1	-32.6	-85.4	-13.5
Book Value/Share %	0.8	18.5	12.9	-3.1
Dividends/Share %	-16.7	0.0	0.0	0.0

Sales growth has limped along in the low single digits the past couple of years, with strength in certain areas (like pictures) being offset by weakness in others (like electronics).

Profitability [C-]	2000	2001	2002	TTM
Return on Assets %	1.7	0.2	0.2	0.2
Oper Cash Flow $Mil	5,205	4,915	5,880	5,880
- Cap Spending $Mil	3,620	4,223	3,097	3,097
= Free Cash Flow $Mil	1,585	692	2,783	2,783

Sony's comparable net income in fiscal 2002 fell 9%, a figure that masks big quarter-to-quarter fluctuations. Even in its best years, Sony generates only single-digit returns on invested capital, which does not make it an appealing investment.

Financial Health [B]	2000	2001	2002	03-02
Long-term Debt $Mil	7,717	6,678	6,322	6,322
Total Equity $Mil	20,699	18,329	17,870	17,870
Debt/Equity Ratio	0.4	0.4	0.4	0.4

Sony has consistently maintained a conservative balance sheet. Financial leverage and the debt/equity ratio have shrunk since 1996, and are at reasonable levels.

Morningstar's Take   By David Kathman, 12-24-2002   Stock Price as of Analysis: $41.84

Every time Sony takes a step forward from its recent woes, it also seems to take a step back. We're frustrated by this stop-and-go progress, and we'd only be interested in the stock at a 40% discount to our fair value estimate.

At first glance, Sony seemed to have a great year in 2002. Led by the record-breaking box office performance of Spider-Man, Sony's movie division shattered its own annual box office record of $1.27 billion and challenged the all-time record of $2.68 billion, set in 1998 by 20th Century Fox. Revenue at its pictures business increased 27% for the six months ending September 30. But Spider-Man's positive influence won't last more than a couple of quarters, and to some extent its success masks question marks elsewhere in the company.

The core electronics business, accounting for two thirds of sales, has shown only sporadic signs of life. Sales of Sony's branded consumer electronics have held up remarkably well under tough economic conditions, but declines elsewhere in the division led to flat sales throughout most of 2002. The division is profitable again after the money-losing cell phone business was spun off into a joint venture with Ericsson, but just barely, with an operating margin of 2%. Sony's music division has continued to lose money on declining sales as the company struggles to combat the rise of online file-sharing and similar threats.

The game division has been a relative bright spot with the success of PlayStation 2, which has held off strong competition from Nintendo's GameCube and Microsoft's Xbox to remain entrenched at number one. Despite a price war that has cut into margins, profits in the division have slowly been growing; however, we're wary of a repeat of 2000-01, when delays in the rollout of PS2 caused the game division to gush red ink. Sony has been hoping that PS2 could become a broadband gateway to the Internet rather than just a game console, but any tangible benefits from this strategy are years off at best.

Sony has repeatedly raised and then lowered its profit and sales forecasts over the past year, making it difficult to get a handle on the company. Although its brand name in consumer electronics is valuable, the extreme volatility of all of Sony's businesses causes us to require a substantial margin of safety before investing in the shares. We would avoid Sony unless its price fell well below $30.

M⊙RNINGSTAR®   Stocks 500

Southern SO

	Rating ★★★	Risk Low	Moat Size Wide	Fair Value $26.00	Last Close $28.39	Yield % 4.8

Company Profile

Southern generates and distributes electricity and provides related services. The company owns five electric utilities in Alabama, Georgia, Florida, Maine, and Mississippi. It owns and operates 33 hydroelectric, 33 fossil fuel, and three nuclear power stations. About 76% of the company's electricity is generated at coal-fired stations. Its subsidiaries provide consulting services to consumers and other utility companies. The company spun off its entire Mirant stake in April 2001.

Management

Former COO Allen Franklin took over from CEO Bill Dahlberg, who retired in April 2000. Like Dahlberg, Franklin rose through the ranks to the top slot and has a long history with Southern.

Strategy

Southern's goal is to achieve modest growth and pay a healthy dividend as a low-cost producer. It plans to continue selling electricity from its substantial regulated utility operations in the Southeast to retail utility customers and the wholesale market.

270 Peachtree St., N.W. www.southerncompany.com
Atlanta, GA 30303

Morningstar Grades

Growth [D+]	1998	1999	2000	2001
Revenue %	-24.7	-1.9	8.0	0.9
Earnings/Share %	-1.4	32.9	8.1	-9.5
Book Value/Share %	-0.4	-4.4	22.0	-29.6
Dividends/Share %	3.1	0.0	0.0	0.0

Sales growth was roughly 1% through the first nine months of 2002, slowed by poor industrial demand in an anemic economy. We expect long-term growth to be 3%-4%, mirroring population and economic growth in the firm's service area.

Profitability [B+]	1999	2000	2001	TTM
Return on Assets %	4.4	4.2	4.2	4.0
Oper Cash Flow $Mil	2,219	2,376	2,384	2,829
- Cap Spending $Mil	1,881	2,225	2,617	2,672
= Free Cash Flow $Mil	338	151	-233	158

Southern has generated returns on invested capital of 5%-6% for years, and we do not expect this to change. Given the regulatory environment, we expect profit margins to stay relatively stable.

Financial Health [A]	1999	2000	2001	09-02
Long-term Debt $Mil	7,251	7,843	8,297	8,826
Total Equity $Mil	9,204	10,690	7,984	8,721
Debt/Equity Ratio	0.8	0.7	1.0	1.0

Southern's capital structure may appear to be highly leveraged with a debt/equity ratio of 1.0, but the debt load is acceptable, given the company's steady and dependable cash flow from regulated operations.

	Industry Electric Utilities	Investment Style ▦ Large Value	Stock Type ⚡ High Yield	Sector 🔋 Utilities

Competition

	Market Cap $Mil	Debt/ Equity	12 Mo Trailing Sales $Mil	Price/Cash Flow	Return On Assets%	Total Return% 1 Yr	3 Yr
Southern	20,256	1.0	10,252	7.2	4.0	17.6	35.0
Dominion Resources	16,867	—	10,018	—	—	—	—
Duke Energy	16,335	—	56,013	—	—	—	—

Price Volatility

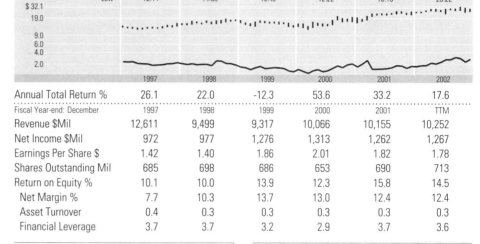

		Monthly Price High/Low		— Relative Strength to S&P 500		
Annual $Price High Low	15.99 12.11	19.22 14.58	18.05 13.43	21.32 12.22	26.00 16.10	31.14 23.22

	1997	1998	1999	2000	2001	2002
Annual Total Return %	26.1	22.0	-12.3	53.6	33.2	17.6

Fiscal Year-end: December	1997	1998	1999	2000	2001	TTM
Revenue $Mil	12,611	9,499	9,317	10,066	10,155	10,252
Net Income $Mil	972	977	1,276	1,313	1,262	1,267
Earnings Per Share $	1.42	1.40	1.86	2.01	1.82	1.78
Shares Outstanding Mil	685	698	686	653	690	713
Return on Equity %	10.1	10.0	13.9	12.3	15.8	14.5
Net Margin %	7.7	10.3	13.7	13.0	12.4	12.4
Asset Turnover	0.4	0.3	0.3	0.3	0.3	0.3
Financial Leverage	3.7	3.7	3.2	2.9	3.7	3.6

Valuation Ratios	Stock	Rel to Industry	Rel to S&P 500
Price/Earnings	15.9	1.3	0.7
Price/Book	2.3	1.6	0.7
Price/Sales	2.0	2.4	1.0
Price/Cash Flow	7.2	1.3	0.5

Major Fund Holders	% of Fund Assets
Liberty Utilities A	9.79
Rydex Utilities Inv	8.61
ProFunds Ultra Utilities Inv	5.89
Edgar Lomax Value	5.45

Morningstar's Take By Paul Larson, 12-18-2002 Stock Price as of Analysis: $28.23

We think Southern shares are fully valued. The firm operates in a stable, attractive business, though, so we wouldn't require a major fall in price to consider the stock.

Southern has been the picture of stability in a highly tumultuous energy sector. Revenue is up about 1% year to date, and consolidated net income is flat. While unexciting, these are solid results in a difficult environment. Southern offers investors something that few large electric utilities provide today: The firm is not involved in energy trading; it has a rock-solid balance sheet; its dividend is safe; and it has excellent relationships with regulators. Each of these traits enables Southern to deliver predictable results that can be easily understood, unlike much of the rest of the industry.

What's more, Southern's growth is tied to the population and economic growth in its service territories, not to electricity prices. This removes the risk of electricity price movements that heavily influence the results of the riskier independent power producers. Investors seeking a relative safe haven can find it in Southern. Today's Southern is much like utilities used to be--boring and slow-growing, yet safe with a nice dividend.

Even Southern's competitive operations, which

account for slightly more than 10% of revenue, are low-risk ventures because the firm doesn't try to sell power to any buyer on the transmission grid or trade energy contracts. Southern generates electricity for specific customers through long-term tolling contracts. In all of its deals, movements in fuel prices flow directly to its customers, leaving Southern with no exposure to fuel risk.

Management gets kudos for its timing of the Mirant spin-off. Southern issued Mirant shares to the public in October 2000 and distributed the rest of this high-risk, high-growth subsidiary to shareholders in April 2001, right when California's energy crisis had the energy sector overheating with enthusiasm. The market for unregulated wholesale electricity has since tanked, taking Mirant and a long list of its peers with it. In hindsight, separating Mirant from Southern was a good move.

Southern's stable, low-risk operations have not gone unnoticed by investors, and the stock is one of the very few among the electric utilities that has risen each of the past three years. As a result, the shares aren't cheap, but the stable nature of Southern's business coupled with a high dividend make them worth tracking.

Southtrust SOTR

	Rating ★★★	Risk Low	Moat Size Narrow	Fair Value $29.00	Last Close $24.85	Yield % 2.7

Company Profile

Southtrust is the holding company for Southtrust Bank and several bank-related affiliates. Southtrust has more than 700 banking offices and 850 ATMs in the Southeastern United States. The bank, which has $48.8 billion in assets, provides a range of financial services from checking accounts to trust services. It originates residential and commercial real-estate, business, and consumer loans. Real-estate loans account for about 54% of the bank's total loan portfolio. Southtrust's nonbank subsidiaries offer investment, mortgage, and insurance services.

Management

Chairman and CEO Wallace Malone Jr. started in the business at his family's bank in Dothan, Alabama. When this bank merged with three others in 1972 to form the nucleus of the current Southtrust, Malone became CEO. Other top Southtrust executives are also company veterans.

Strategy

Southtrust's operating strategy has been the same for quite a while: grow by concentrating on the burgeoning population centers of the Southeast. The growth is realized by internal sales efforts as well as acquisitions. The Texas triangle and Virginia are the areas of focus for growth.

420 North 20th Street   www.southtrust.com
Birmingham, AL 35203

Morningstar Grades

Growth [C-]	1998	1999	2000	2001
Revenue %	17.6	13.8	16.4	-4.1
Earnings/Share %	10.8	16.9	8.7	12.6
Book Value/Share %	15.1	3.9	14.4	15.8
Dividends/Share %	13.9	15.8	13.6	12.0

Southtrust's net income expanded at a compound annual rate of nearly 17% over the past five years. Internal growth, acquisitions, and expense controls have all contributed. Dividends grew at a compound annual rate of roughly 15% over the same period.

Profitability [C+]	1999	2000	2001	TTM
Return on Assets %	1.0	1.1	1.1	1.3
Oper Cash Flow $Mil	793	760	399	—
- Cap Spending $Mil	76	57	125	—
= Free Cash Flow $Mil	—	—	—	—

Return on equity in the third quarter was a respectable 14.7%. Considering that the bank has gradually reduced its leverage, these returns are fairly strong. Earnings have not been very volatile.

Financial Health [A]	1999	2000	2001	09-02
Long-term Debt $Mil	—	—	—	—
Total Equity $Mil	2,927	3,352	3,962	4,534
Debt/Equity Ratio	—	—	—	—

Because Southtrust has a loan portfolio composed mostly of relatively small loans and a long record of successfully minimizing credit risk, its credit profile is stable.

	Industry Regional Banks	Investment Style ▦ Large Value	Stock Type ▨ High Yield	Sector ⑤ Financial Services

Competition	Market Cap $Mil	Debt/ Equity	12 Mo Trailing Sales $Mil	Price/Cash Flow	Return On Assets%	Total Return% 1 Yr	 3 Yr
Southtrust	8,619	—	3,391	—	1.3	3.4	18.1
Wachovia	50,032	—	24,107	—	1.0	19.5	9.8
SunTrust Banks	16,225	—	7,631	—	1.2	-6.7	-0.4

Price Volatility

▮ Monthly Price High/Low   — Relative Strength to S&P 500

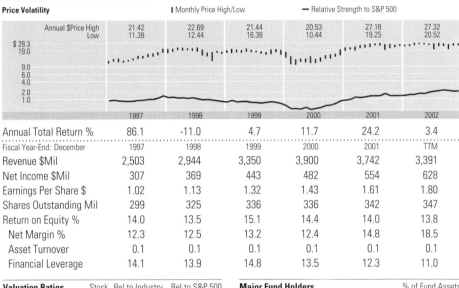

	1997	1998	1999	2000	2001	2002
Annual $Price High	21.42	22.69	21.44	20.53	27.18	27.32
Low	11.38	12.44	16.38	10.44	19.25	20.52

Annual Total Return %	86.1	-11.0	4.7	11.7	24.2	3.4

Fiscal Year-End: December	1997	1998	1999	2000	2001	TTM
Revenue $Mil	2,503	2,944	3,350	3,900	3,742	3,391
Net Income $Mil	307	369	443	482	554	628
Earnings Per Share $	1.02	1.13	1.32	1.43	1.61	1.80
Shares Outstanding Mil	299	325	336	336	342	347
Return on Equity %	14.0	13.5	15.1	14.4	14.0	13.8
Net Margin %	12.3	12.5	13.2	12.4	14.8	18.5
Asset Turnover	0.1	0.1	0.1	0.1	0.1	0.1
Financial Leverage	14.1	13.9	14.8	13.5	12.3	11.0

Valuation Ratios	Stock	Rel to Industry	Rel to S&P 500
Price/Earnings	13.8	1.0	0.6
Price/Book	1.9	0.9	0.6
Price/Sales	2.5	1.1	1.3
Price/Cash Flow	—	—	—

Major Fund Holders	% of Fund Assets
Navellier Large Cap Value	5.34
Henssler Equity	3.27
Harris Insight Equity Instl	3.10
Undiscovered Managers Hidden Val Inst	3.06

Morningstar's Take   By Matthew Scholz, 11-26-2002   Stock Price as of Analysis: $25.80

Southtrust is a premier regional bank. Our fair value estimate is $29 per share, and we would consider investing at a 20% discount to this.

Southtrust's success stands on several legs, one of which is that the bank promotes an energetic sales culture that seeks to maximize internal growth. An active sales philosophy is in vogue in contemporary banking, but the attitude has long been part of Southtrust. Top managers, including the CEO, spend much of their time contacting Southtrust's clients and prospects. At the branch level, the Cornerstone and Cornerstone Plus programs give branch employees direct sales responsibility. In the branches participating in these programs, 2001 loan volume was up 13% and referrals increased 27%. There are plans to roll these programs out to 250 branches.

Strong internal growth has been complemented by numerous successful small bank acquisitions. Southtrust has eschewed the cost and integration risk of large acquisitions in favor of a steady series of smaller purchases. This is how it built its initial presence in Florida, where the bank is now the state's fourth-largest deposit holder. Present expansion efforts center on the Texas triangle of Houston, Dallas, and San Antonio, as well as the populous areas of Virginia. These locations fit

Southtrust's simple formula for external growth: Focus exclusively on Southeastern population centers (broadly defined to include Texas) that enjoy above-average population and job growth.

To translate these revenue opportunities into consistent profits, Southtrust is vigilant about credit. For instance, every credit above $250,000 goes before senior management, and roughly 90% of the loan portfolio is secured by collateral. Many banks claim to have credit discipline, but Southtrust has a record that stretches over multiple credit cycles. As of September 30, net charge-offs were 0.32% of total loans, half the industry average. Over the past five years, net charge-offs have averaged a trim 0.28%.

Since Southtrust hasn't compromised its credit standards during the recession, it has built up capital. As of September 30, the bank's equity/assets ratio was roughly 9.1%, or 1 percentage point higher than a year ago. Southtrust will seek to loan a lot of these funds out as the economy and lending prospects improve.

Southtrust has solid management, a genuine sales culture, well-defined expansion plans in one of the fastest-growing regions in the country, and firm credit guidelines. We think Southtrust is one to buy and hang on to if it falls 20% below our fair value

MORNINGSTAR® Stocks 500

Southwest Airlines LUV

	Rating	Risk	Moat Size	Fair Value	Last Close	Yield %
	★★★	Med.	Narrow	$17.00	$13.90	0.1

Company Profile

Southwest Airlines is a commercial airline that provides passenger and freight transportation to nearly 60 cities in the United States. The airline specializes in short-haul routes and targets business commuters. The company's most-traveled routes are intrastate flights in California and Texas. Its fleet consists of about 310 Boeing 737 aircraft. Passenger transportation generates almost all revenue, accounting for more than 96% of the total.

Management

CEO Jim Parker has successfully led the company through one of the most challenging periods in airline history. He works closely with president and COO Colleen Barrett and chairman Herb Kelleher.

Strategy

Despite the industry downturn, Southwest is in growth mode; it is "connecting the dots" by adding routes to existing cities. Also, the company recently announced plans to offer transcontinental flights, a market that has until now been dominated by the major hub-and-spoke carriers.

2702 Love Field Drive   www.southwest.com
Dallas, TX 75235-1611

Morningstar Grades

Growth [C+]	1998	1999	2000	2001
Revenue %	9.1	13.7	19.3	-1.7
Earnings/Share %	31.8	8.5	28.1	-17.1
Book Value/Share %	15.3	17.3	22.6	13.8
Dividends/Share %	28.6	14.3	2.8	21.6

Southwest's sales have increased at a double-digit pace over the past twenty years. The downturn in the industry has slowed the airline down a bit, but we expect the firm's top line to grow nicely over the next five years.

Profitability [A]	1999	2000	2001	TTM
Return on Assets %	8.4	9.0	5.7	2.9
Oper Cash Flow $Mil	1,029	1,298	1,485	641
- Cap Spending $Mil	1,168	1,135	998	704
= Free Cash Flow $Mil	-138	164	487	-63

Southwest has generated a remarkably consistent record of profitability, while most of its rivals' earnings have been far more volatile. The company even managed a gain in 2001, when most rivals suffered huge losses.

Financial Health [A]	1999	2000	2001	09-02
Long-term Debt $Mil	872	761	1,327	1,661
Total Equity $Mil	2,836	3,451	4,014	4,323
Debt/Equity Ratio	0.3	0.2	0.3	0.4

This company has the best balance sheet in the business. Growth over the past few years has been financed internally. Consequently, financial leverage is far better than the industry average.

Industry	Investment Style	Stock Type	Sector
Air Transport	▦ Large Core	↗ Classic Growth	▤ Business Services

Competition	Market Cap $Mil	Debt/ Equity	12 Mo Trailing Sales $Mil	Price/Cash Flow	Return On Assets%	Total Return% 1 Yr	Total Return% 3 Yr
Southwest Airlines	10,768	0.4	5,359	16.8	2.9	-24.7	10.7
JetBlue Airways	1,706	1.3	543	8.6	3.3	—	—
Delta Air Lines	1,493	3.2	12,860	—	-6.9	-58.4	-37.0

Price Volatility

		Monthly Price High/Low			— Relative Strength to S&P 500	
Annual $Price High Low	7.78 4.20	10.56 6.81	15.72 9.58	23.33 10.00	23.32 11.25	21.99 10.90

	1997	1998	1999	2000	2001	2002
Annual Total Return %	68.2	38.4	6.7	108.1	-17.2	-24.7

Fiscal Year-end: December	1997	1998	1999	2000	2001	TTM
Revenue $Mil	3,817	4,164	4,736	5,650	5,555	5,359
Net Income $Mil	318	433	474	603	511	262
Earnings Per Share $	0.42	0.55	0.59	0.76	0.63	0.33
Shares Outstanding Mil	739	747	757	747	763	775
Return on Equity %	15.8	18.1	16.7	17.5	12.7	6.1
Net Margin %	8.3	10.4	10.0	10.7	9.2	4.9
Asset Turnover	0.9	0.9	0.8	0.8	0.6	0.6
Financial Leverage	2.1	2.0	2.0	1.9	2.2	2.1

Valuation Ratios	Stock	Rel to Industry	Rel to S&P 500	Major Fund Holders	% of Fund Assets
Price/Earnings	42.1	1.0	1.8	Fidelity Select Air Transportation	9.28
Price/Book	2.5	1.0	0.8	Fidelity Select Transportation	5.97
Price/Sales	2.0	1.0	1.0	Rydex Transportation Inv	4.34
Price/Cash Flow	16.8	1.0	1.3	Buffalo Large Cap	3.87

Morningstar's Take By Jonathan Schrader, 12-15-2002 Stock Price as of Analysis: $15.18

Regular readers know that we really like Southwest; the company "gets it." Both its management and its employees understand what it takes to be successful in the airline industry: keeping costs low. This is essential because of the large swings in demand that come with the business cycle. When travel demand ebbs with economic weakness, ticket prices inevitably fall; only the airlines with the lowest cost structures are able to avoid huge losses.

Southwest curbs costs by focusing on short-haul flights to second-tier airports. This means that Southwest gets a lot more use out of its aircraft than its rivals. Southwest also saves on pilot-training and maintenance costs by using just one aircraft type--the Boeing 737. Also, about 80% of its passengers fly ticketless, reducing the carrier's ticket-distribution expenses.

Most important, the company has very low compensation expenses compared with its peers. In aggregate, Southwest's employees are much more productive than those at other airlines, and the company has been able to capitalize on the excellent long-term performance of its stock by using it for compensation purposes.

Southwest's focus on minimizing costs--while others focused on maximizing revenue--has led to more than twenty straight years of profitability, an awesome achievement for an airline. This history of solid profitability and steady growth has meant excellent returns for its shareholders as well. Its shares sport an annualized total return of more than 25% since 1990, double the return of the stock market.

We think that Southwest has a bright future ahead of it as well. There are dozens of communities that are asking for service, and Southwest still has plenty of opportunity in just connecting all of the cities that it already serves. This includes transcontinental service, which the company has just initiated with its flights between Baltimore and L.A.

In all, we think that Southwest has significant advantages over its rivals. However, there are many outside factors, such as fluctuating fuel prices and economic conditions, that can have a negative impact on Southwest's results. And because competition is so fierce within the industry, profit margins aren't that great even in the good years. For these reasons, we think that Southwest deserves only a narrow moat rating. We'd want a 40% discount before buying shares of this airline.

Sovereign Bancorp SOV

	Rating ★★★	Risk Med.	Moat Size Narrow	Fair Value $16.00	Last Close $14.05	Yield % 0.7

Company Profile

Sovereign Bancorp is the third-largest bank in Pennsylvania as well as the third-largest in New England with 550 branches and more than 1,000 ATMs. The bank, which has been transitioning from a thrift to a retail bank, has assets of $35 billion.

Management

Jay Sidhu, Sovereign's ambitious CEO, has been with the thrift since 1986. He stopped the bank's sale in a famed brawl with Sovereign's former chairman. He's determined to prove the FleetBoston deal will reward shareholders.

Strategy

The Pennsylvania-based thrift is transforming itself into a post-Glass-Steagall financial services supermarket. (Glass-Steagall was the Depression-era law banning banks, brokers, and insurers from entering each others' businesses.) It has opened a trust company and a capital markets group, and broadened its commercial and consumer loan portfolio.

2000 Market Street   www.sovereignbank.com
Philadelphia, PA 19103

Morningstar Grades

Growth [A]	1998	1999	2000	2001
Revenue %	19.0	19.0	36.9	11.4
Earnings/Share %	28.8	18.8	NMF	NMF
Book Value/Share %	22.5	36.8	-18.4	1.3
Dividends/Share %	14.9	23.4	5.3	0.0

Acquisitions have boosted revenue, and fee income is helping the top line. Efforts to develop a strong sales culture are gaining speed. Sovereign now sells more than four products on average to each of its retail customers.

Profitability [D-]	1999	2000	2001	TTM
Return on Assets %	0.7	-0.1	0.3	0.8
Oper Cash Flow $Mil	-24	-189	-277	—
- Cap Spending $Mil	40	178	20	—
= Free Cash Flow $Mil	—	—	—	—

Merger-related expenses have pressured profits. While returns on equity and assets remain weak, the company is taking steps in the right direction.

Financial Health [B+]	1999	2000	2001	09-02
Long-term Debt $Mil	—	—	—	—
Total Equity $Mil	1,821	1,949	2,202	2,711
Debt/Equity Ratio	—	—	—	—

Financial leverage is high but improving. Average assets/equity dropped to 15.6 in the second quarter, its fourth consecutive quarterly decline.

Industry	Investment Style	Stock Type	Sector
Savings & Loans	Mid Value	Classic Growth	Financial Services

Competition	Market Cap $Mil	Debt/ Equity	12 Mo Trailing Sales $Mil	Price/Cash Flow	Return On Assets%	Total Return% 1 Yr	3 Yr
Sovereign Bancorp	3,725	—	2,481	—	0.8	15.6	26.2
FleetBoston Financial	25,459	—	16,036	—	0.2	-30.2	-4.6
PNC Financial Services Gr	11,900	—	6,095	—	0.7	-22.5	4.5

Price Volatility

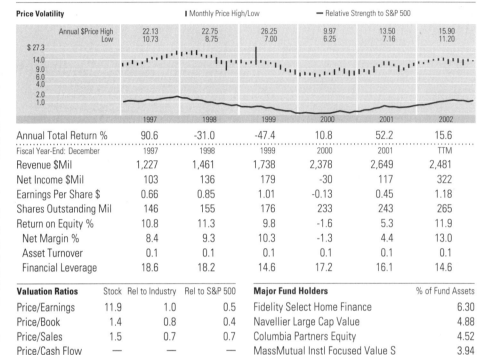

| | Monthly Price High/Low | | | | | — Relative Strength to S&P 500 |

Annual $Price High Low	22.13 10.73	22.75 8.75	26.25 7.00	9.97 6.25	13.50 7.16	15.90 11.20

	1997	1998	1999	2000	2001	2002
Annual Total Return %	90.6	-31.0	-47.4	10.8	52.2	15.6
Fiscal Year-End: December	1997	1998	1999	2000	2001	TTM
Revenue $Mil	1,227	1,461	1,738	2,378	2,649	2,481
Net Income $Mil	103	136	179	-30	117	322
Earnings Per Share $	0.66	0.85	1.01	-0.13	0.45	1.18
Shares Outstanding Mil	146	155	176	233	243	265
Return on Equity %	10.8	11.3	9.8	-1.6	5.3	11.9
Net Margin %	8.4	9.3	10.3	-1.3	4.4	13.0
Asset Turnover	0.1	0.1	0.1	0.1	0.1	0.1
Financial Leverage	18.6	18.2	14.6	17.2	16.1	14.6

Valuation Ratios	Stock	Rel to Industry	Rel to S&P 500
Price/Earnings	11.9	1.0	0.5
Price/Book	1.4	0.8	0.4
Price/Sales	1.5	0.7	0.7
Price/Cash Flow	—	—	—

Major Fund Holders	% of Fund Assets
Fidelity Select Home Finance	6.30
Navellier Large Cap Value	4.88
Columbia Partners Equity	4.52
MassMutual Instl Focused Value S	3.94

Morningstar's Take   By Richard McCaffery, 09-24-2002   Stock Price as of Analysis: $13.00

Sovereign is an increasingly well-run bank that's made good progress strengthening its balance sheet over the past year. While we see many trends headed in the right direction, the company is like a lot of big regional banks: It's well run, but not exceedingly so. It's showing nice signs of improvement, but doesn't trade at a steep enough discount to make it really compelling. The smart money bought Sovereign more than a year ago, when the stock traded at less than $10, and management had laid out a clear strategy for lowering debt, building capital, gathering deposits, and selling customers new products.

When the sun hits it just right, Sovereign has some of the best qualities of a thrift (its legacy) and of a commercial bank. Asset quality is strong, so charge-offs have remained relatively low throughout the latest downturn. Yet its low-cost funding base has grown quickly as the company has lured new customers with innovative deposit products.

On the downside, its cost structure remains out of line with the best competitors. Even if you ignore merger-related charges, the company's 52% efficiency ratio is higher than you see at the most efficient banks and thrifts. Management expects this to drop to the 46%-49% range over the coming years

(lower is better, since efficiency measures operating costs as a percentage of revenue), but we haven't built this much of an improvement into our model. We've already forecast net revenue growth of about 12% annually through 2006. The acceleration is warranted because management expects growth to increase once the company has built its capital base. But we'd have to see faster growth rates than this to drop the efficiency ratio sharply, and at this point we don't want to make that bet.

We do expect the company to perform well, now that it has worked through the toughest part of its integration of nearly 300 branches bought from FleetBoston in 1999. Sovereign has a nice focus on middle-market business, and should be able to gin up a lot of business making small loans to businesses that larger competitors wouldn't bother with. We look for the bank to become an increasingly important player in the Northeast.

Morningstar®   Stocks 500

Sprint FON

	Rating	Risk	Moat Size	Fair Value	Last Close	Yield %
	★★★	High	Narrow	$19.00	$14.48	3.5

Company Profile

Sprint provides telecommunication and information services. The company provides local phone service, with about 8.2 million phone lines in service. The company's long-distance services include voice, Internet access, Web hosting, and private line services. At the end of 2001, Sprint had 55,100 high-speed Internet access customers using DSL. The company also publishes directories in 20 states.

Management

CEO William Esrey, an industry veteran, has headed Sprint since 1985. Chief operating officer Ronald LeMay is often the executive most visible to investors.

Strategy

Cost-cutting is now the order of the day. Sprint discontinued ION, its attempt to provide phone and Internet service on a single connection, because the business wasn't generating much revenue relative to its cost. The company is trimming its workforce and reorganizing its long-distance division as sales fall.

P.O. Box 11315
Kansas City, MO 64112

www.sprint.com

Morningstar Grades

Growth [D]	1998	1999	2000	2001
Revenue %	—	NMF	3.1	-4.3
Earnings/Share %	—	NMF	24.2	NMF
Book Value/Share %	—	NMF	16.4	-3.4
Dividends/Share %	0.0	0.0	0.0	0.0

With long-distance prices falling sharply over the past couple of years, Sprint's total revenue has been shrinking. The local business offers much-needed stability, but this mature business offers little growth to offset long-distance's decline.

Profitability [B]	1999	2000	2001	TTM
Return on Assets %	7.1	8.2	-0.6	0.1
Oper Cash Flow $Mil	3,700	4,305	4,585	4,622
- Cap Spending $Mil	3,534	4,105	5,295	2,946
= Free Cash Flow $Mil	166	200	-710	1,676

The local phone business is Sprint's saving grace, generating virtually all of operating income. Long-distance profitability will remain weak as the unit struggles with sluggish demand. Cost-cutting has helped eliminate long-distance's drag.

Financial Health [A-]	1999	2000	2001	09-02
Long-term Debt $Mil	—	3,482	3,258	3,169
Total Equity $Mil	10,514	12,343	11,704	12,296
Debt/Equity Ratio	—	0.3	0.3	0.3

Sprint's balance sheet is solid and will be even stronger after the sale of the directory business. Sharply lower capital spending has brought free cash flow back into the black following last year's deficit. Growing Sprint PCS debt is a concern.

Industry	Investment Style	Stock Type	Sector
Telecommunication Services	▦ Large Value	⚡ High Yield	🖥 Telecom

Competition

	Market Cap $Mil	Debt/ Equity	12 Mo Trailing Sales $Mil	Price/Cash Flow	Return On Assets%	Total Return% 1 Yr	3 Yr
Sprint	12,953	0.3	15,951	2.8	0.1	-25.2	-37.5
WorldCom	—	—	—	—	—	—	—
AT&T	—	—	—	—	—	—	—

Price Volatility

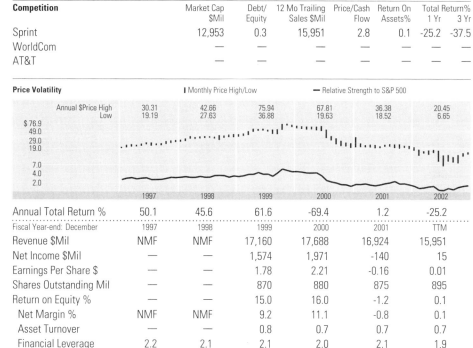

			1997	1998	1999	2000	2001	2002
Annual $Price High			30.31	42.66	75.94	67.81	36.38	20.45
Low			19.19	27.63	36.88	19.63	18.52	6.65

Annual Total Return %	50.1	45.6	61.6	-69.4	1.2	-25.2

Fiscal Year-end: December	1997	1998	1999	2000	2001	TTM
Revenue $Mil	NMF	NMF	17,160	17,688	16,924	15,951
Net Income $Mil	—	—	1,574	1,971	-140	15
Earnings Per Share $	—	—	1.78	2.21	-0.16	0.01
Shares Outstanding Mil	—	—	870	880	875	895
Return on Equity %	—	—	15.0	16.0	-1.2	0.1
Net Margin %	NMF	NMF	9.2	11.1	-0.8	0.1
Asset Turnover	—	—	0.8	0.7	0.7	0.7
Financial Leverage	2.2	2.1	2.1	2.0	2.1	1.9

Valuation Ratios	Stock	Rel to Industry	Rel to S&P 500
Price/Earnings	EUB	—	—
Price/Book	1.1	0.4	0.3
Price/Sales	0.8	0.5	0.4
Price/Cash Flow	2.8	0.5	0.2

Major Fund Holders	% of Fund Assets
John Hancock Communications A	3.82
IDEX Transamerica Value Balanced B	3.75
IDEX Transamerica Value Balanced A	3.75
Van Kampen Value Opportunities A	3.50

Morningstar's Take By Michael Hodel, 10-25-2002 Stock Price as of Analysis: $12.55

We believe the value of Sprint's local phone business supports a fair value in excess of $20 per share. However, the company's wireless division, Sprint PCS, operates in a very tough environment and has racked up a large debt load. We've knocked $3 off our fair value in an attempt to reflect the risk imposed by Sprint PCS. We've also bumped the FON group up to high risk, increasing the margin of safety we'd require to buy the stock. At $11 per share or less, we think Sprint would be an attractive investment.

Sprint's primary source of competitive advantage--and value for shareholders--rests in its local phone unit. Because wireline local phone service is provided over a network that is difficult to replicate and Sprint owns the only network well suited to this purpose, revenue is fairly steady. Competition is creeping into the local phone business, but many of Sprint's customers are in rural areas, which draw less interest from would-be rivals. Sprint has lost far fewer phone lines than its more urban Bell peers. Revenue growth has been weak lately in the local business, but tight cost controls have allowed Sprint to maintain operating margins above 30%, despite tough industry conditions.

Sprint is better known for its long-distance business, which has been hit hard by the telecom mess. A glut of competitors and the commoditylike nature of long-distance phone service have pushed revenue from this business sharply lower. Falling prices have also been a bugaboo on the data and Internet side of the business, with revenue from these services falling as well. The long-distance business generated $4 billion in operating income in 1999, but is only running near break-even today. We have been impressed with management's willingness to cut unprofitable operations in this unit, like ION, and recent cost-cutting and restructuring have reduced long-distance's drag on the firm.

Sprint's balance sheet is solid. Following the sale of the directory business, the FON group's allocated debt will total about $2 billion, an amount easily supported by the firm's operations. Sprint's PCS business, which is legally part of the same company as FON, has a huge debt load, though. We don't question that the assets of PCS have value (wireless analyst Todd Bernier pegs the stock's value at $3), but given the deterioration of the wireless market there are reasonable scenarios under which PCS won't be able to support its allocated debt load. To reflect the risk that FON cash flow is used to support PCS, we've lowered our fair value estimate.

Sprint PCS Group PCS

	Rating	Risk	Moat Size	Fair Value	Last Close	Yield %
	★	High	None	$3.00	$4.38	0.0

Company Profile

Sprint PCS Group is a tracking stock, representing the wireless assets of Sprint Corp. The company is the growth leader among the wireless carriers; it added 725,000 new subscribers in the March quarter and ended with 14.3 million customers. The company's wireless network, based on the code division multiple access (CDMA) technology pioneered by Qualcomm, covers roughly 192,000 million Americans.

Management

CEO William Esrey has been at Sprint's helm since 1985. However, there has been a lot of turmoil in PCS' executive suite: Chuck Levine, who spearheaded the troubled ClearPay program, was replaced as president by Len Lauer, and CFO William Gunter stepped aside.

Strategy

The firm uses a state-of-the-art all-digital CDMA network capable of reaching most Americans to offer big-bucket calling plans; this has made it the fastest-growing wireless operator (until recently) in the country. Sprint PCS has been at the technological forefront, being the first operator to launch third-generation service.

P.O. Box 11315
Kansas City, MO 64112
www.sprint.com

Morningstar Grades

Growth [A]	1998	1999	2000	2001
Revenue %	NMF	160.7	88.0	53.4
Earnings/Share %	NMF	NMF	NMF	NMF
Book Value/Share %	—	NMF	-53.4	-34.9
Dividends/Share %	NMF	NMF	NMF	NMF

Historically, PCS has set the pace of growth in the wireless industry; compounded annual growth was 53% from 1999-2002. But those days are over. In 2003, sales growth will slow to roughly 7%, the result mainly of weak subscriber growth.

Profitability [C-]	1999	2000	2001	TTM
Return on Assets %	-14.0	-9.5	-5.7	-2.8
Oper Cash Flow $Mil	-1,692	-8	106	1,364
- Cap Spending $Mil	2,580	3,047	3,751	2,968
= Free Cash Flow $Mil	-4,272	-3,055	-3,645	-1,604

Like other wireless carriers, PCS has been a money pit for a long time. Although it is benefiting from its large scale, PCS won't generate substantial shareholder returns for several more years.

Financial Health [F]	1999	2000	2001	09-02
Long-term Debt $Mil	—	14,136	13,243	16,264
Total Equity $Mil	2,794	1,366	912	751
Debt/Equity Ratio	—	10.3	14.5	21.7

PCS' balance sheet is brutal, with obligations exceeding $16 billion--more than 6 times 2002's projected EBITDA (earnings before interest, taxes, depreciation, and amortization). Heavy capital spending means PCS won't generate free cash flow until 2003.

Industry	Investment Style	Stock Type	Sector
Wireless Service	⊞ Mid Growth	◳ Distressed	▣ Telecom

Competition	Market Cap $Mil	Debt/ Equity	12 Mo Trailing Sales $Mil	Price/Cash Flow	Return On Assets%	Total Return% 1 Yr	3 Yr
Sprint PCS Group	4,376	21.7	11,782	3.2	-2.8	-82.1	-55.4
Verizon Communications	106,011	1.4	67,422	4.7	-0.1	-15.2	-9.8
AT&T Wireless Services	15,300	0.4	15,112	5.8	-7.5	-60.7	—

Price Volatility

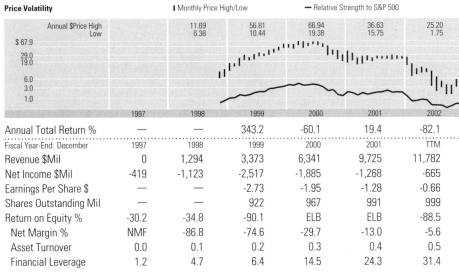

Annual $Price High Low		11.69 6.38	56.81 10.44	66.94 19.38	36.63 15.75	25.20 1.75
	1997	1998	1999	2000	2001	2002
Annual Total Return %	—	—	343.2	-60.1	19.4	-82.1

Fiscal Year-End: December	1997	1998	1999	2000	2001	TTM
Revenue $Mil	0	1,294	3,373	6,341	9,725	11,782
Net Income $Mil	-419	-1,123	-2,517	-1,885	-1,268	-665
Earnings Per Share $	—	—	-2.73	-1.95	-1.28	-0.66
Shares Outstanding Mil	—	—	922	967	991	999
Return on Equity %	-30.2	-34.8	-90.1	ELB	ELB	-88.5
Net Margin %	NMF	-86.8	-74.6	-29.7	-13.0	-5.6
Asset Turnover	0.0	0.1	0.2	0.3	0.4	0.5
Financial Leverage	1.2	4.7	6.4	14.5	24.3	31.4

Valuation Ratios	Stock	Rel to Industry	Rel to S&P 500
Price/Earnings	NMF	—	—
Price/Book	5.8	2.2	1.8
Price/Sales	0.4	0.1	0.2
Price/Cash Flow	3.2	0.3	0.2

Major Fund Holders	% of Fund Assets
Fidelity Select Wireless	4.52
ProFunds Ultra Wireless Inv	4.44
Fidelity Advisor Developing Comm A	4.13
Fidelity Select Developing Comm	3.25

Morningstar's Take By Todd P. Bernier, 12-17-2002 Stock Price as of Analysis: $5.10

We were once big fans of PCS, but a lack of competitive advantage and growing debt burden make this a stock to avoid now.

With perhaps the most advanced digital network and innovative calling plans, Sprint PCS was the wireless industry's pacesetter. It was the first carrier to add 1 million subscribers per quarter, a pace it sustained for all of 2001.

But that was then, and this is now.

Exceptional growth caused everyone--including us--to misjudge the impact the growing number of subprime users would have on Sprint. Credit-challenged people constitute an increasing percentage of PCS' growth, thanks primarily to the firm's ClearPay promotion, which was designed to mitigate credit concerns. If customers made a deposit, they were signed to a contract. But this strategy was destined to fail: These people shouldn't have qualified for credit in the first place.

Although subprime users fueled growth, they are the main reason Sprint's churn, already among the industry's worst, continues to deteriorate. Many ClearPay users have defaulted under the bright light of more stringent scoring requirements. An inability to hold on to customers is worrisome because it costs so much to find them in the first place. On average,

PCS retains its customers for roughly three years, a full year less than leader Nextel.

Sprint's problems are exacerbated by a competitive wireless industry. With six nationwide rivals scratching and clawing to add subscribers, per-minute prices have fallen more than 80% since the first George Bush was president. Although wireless executives don't want to admit it, little differentiates the major carriers; a consumer's purchase decision usually comes down to which carrier offers the best prices. Sprint has been among the most aggressive pricers, which explains why its finances are a mess.

The firm would be well along the path to bankruptcy without the implicit credit support of Sprint Corp. PCS has $18 billion in debt (including equity units) and continues to run a free cash flow deficit. PCS is a sinking ship springing new leaks. No one can predict whether Sprint will continue to shoulder the burden of its wireless subsidiary or allow it to fail. But one thing is certain: Unless PCS retains customers and reduces debt, the firm has no redeeming value. PCS has lost the one thing--torrid subscriber growth--that differentiated it. With no sustainable competitive advantage and very high risk, PCS has become the type of firm we'd avoid.

MORNINGSTAR® Stocks 500

SPX SPW

	Rating	Risk	Moat Size	Fair Value	Last Close	Yield %
	★★★	Med.	Narrow	$51.00	$37.45	0.0

Company Profile

SPX manufactures electrical products and automotive components. Its products include valves, fluid mixers, power transformers, electric motors, laboratory freezers and ovens, furnaces, and coal feeders. In addition, the company produces automatic fare-collection and fire-detection systems, networking equipment, broadcast antennas, and electronic engine diagnostic, emission-testing, and wheel service equipment.

Management

Chairman and CEO John Blystone, 48, was a rising star at GE before joining SPX in December 1995. He manages the company with a focus on shareholder value; the early results were great, but he is paid awfully well for a company this size.

Strategy

Having accumulated a sizable portfolio of industrial businesses, SPX has a policy of "fix, sell, or grow"--operating units will either be fixed by the company's Value Improvement Process, be sold if a different owner would find more value in the business, or grow through bolt-on acquisitions and market share gains. More large acquisitions are likely, with a blockbuster deal a possibility.

13515 Ballantyne Corporate Place   www.spx.com
Charlotte, NC 28277

Morningstar Grades

Growth [A+]	1998	1999	2000	2001
Revenue %	-6.6	48.6	-1.2	53.6
Earnings/Share %	NMF	NMF	82.6	-21.8
Book Value/Share %	-39.2	-2.1	7.7	141.7
Dividends/Share %	NMF	NMF	NMF	NMF

Despite a fivefold multiplication of SPX's top line since 1997, the underlying internal growth of the business portfolio is only slightly above average by industrial standards--perhaps midsingle-digit annual growth.

Profitability [B-]	1999	2000	2001	TTM
Return on Assets %	3.6	6.0	2.4	1.6
Oper Cash Flow $Mil	212	171	492	527
- Cap Spending $Mil	102	123	150	106
= Free Cash Flow $Mil	110	48	342	421

SPX has done a good job of improving the margins of its acquired businesses, though it's required massive restructuring to do so. Assuming acquisitions slow somewhat, we expect additional margin gains and fewer special charges.

Financial Health [B-]	1999	2000	2001	09-02
Long-term Debt $Mil	1,115	1,158	2,451	2,249
Total Equity $Mil	552	608	1,715	1,812
Debt/Equity Ratio	2.0	1.9	1.4	1.2

Unlike most of its peers, SPX garners only a high junk credit rating. With operating income relatively strong, the firm's $2.4 billion debt load has not posed a problem--but it could become a burden if SPX starts to succumb to weak end markets.

Industry	Investment Style	Stock Type	Sector
Electric Equipment	⊞ Mid Core	⭧ Cyclical	⚙ Industrial Mats

Competition

	Market Cap $Mil	Debt/ Equity	12 Mo Trailing Sales $Mil	Price/Cash Flow	Return On Assets%	Total Return% 1 Yr	3 Yr
SPX	3,016	1.2	4,981	5.7	1.6	-45.3	-0.7
Emerson Electric	21,411	0.5	13,838	11.8	0.8	-8.3	-1.1
Danaher	10,013	0.4	4,221	13.5	2.7	9.1	13.8

Price Volatility

| Monthly Price High/Low   — Relative Strength to S&P 500

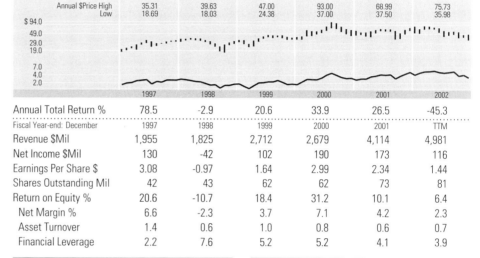

Annual $Price High Low	35.31 18.69	39.63 18.03	47.00 24.38	93.00 37.00	68.99 37.50	75.73 35.98
	1997	1998	1999	2000	2001	2002
Annual Total Return %	78.5	-2.9	20.6	33.9	26.5	-45.3

Fiscal Year-end: December	1997	1998	1999	2000	2001	TTM
Revenue $Mil	1,955	1,825	2,712	2,679	4,114	4,981
Net Income $Mil	130	-42	102	190	173	116
Earnings Per Share $	3.08	-0.97	1.64	2.99	2.34	1.44
Shares Outstanding Mil	42	43	62	62	73	81
Return on Equity %	20.6	-10.7	18.4	31.2	10.1	6.4
Net Margin %	6.6	-2.3	3.7	7.1	4.2	2.3
Asset Turnover	1.4	0.6	1.0	0.8	0.6	0.7
Financial Leverage	2.2	7.6	5.2	5.2	4.1	3.9

Valuation Ratios	Stock	Rel to Industry	Rel to S&P 500
Price/Earnings	26.1	1.6	1.1
Price/Book	1.7	0.4	0.5
Price/Sales	0.6	0.3	0.3
Price/Cash Flow	5.7	0.7	0.4

Major Fund Holders	% of Fund Assets
Fidelity Select Industrial Equipment	6.50
Croft-Leominster Value	5.48
Oppenheimer MidCap A	4.21
ICAP Select Equity	3.56

Morningstar's Take By Josh Peters, 12-20-2002 Stock Price as of Analysis: $37.26

Not long ago a minnow, SPX has managed to swallow a couple of whales. But there's still a fairly steep risk of indigestion, in our view: We'd require a 40% discount to our $51 fair value estimate before considering investment.

SPX isn't your ordinary industrial conglomerate: It's a conglomerate in a hurry. When CEO John Blystone (a General Electric alumnus) arrived in late 1995, SPX was a $1.1 billion supplier of original equipment manufacturer auto parts and vehicle diagnostic equipment. But after tripling itself with electrical grab bag General Signal in 1998 and doubling again with the 2001 acquisition of United Dominion, SPX has seen revenue growth of 24% since 1995, tops in our industrial coverage.

Amid this turmoil, operating profits--excluding charges--rose 3 times as fast as revenue. Credit the SPX Value Improvement Process, which seeks to maximize shareholder returns as measured by EVA (Economic Value Added, a set of analytical tools developed by consultants Stern Stewart). These techniques aim to reduce costs while cashing out of unnecessary assets (factories, inventories, and such). The compensation of Blystone and his lieutenants is tied to improvements as measured by EVA. Very GE of them, we must say.

Judging by the firm's pro forma return on tangible capital (that is, excluding goodwill) of nearly 20% in 2001, we believe SPX's overall portfolio of businesses has attractive economic characteristics, including domination of niche markets, technological superiority, and economies of scale.

But much of the value seems to have accrued to the sellers, not the buyers: Including restructuring and goodwill, we estimate 2001's return on investment at a meager 6.5%. We believe it will take still more restructuring, plus an uncertain rebound in SPX's industrial markets, to get true returns on investment above the firm's cost of capital.

In the meantime, we consider the shares considerably riskier than the average industrial. Debt is well above that of its peers at 57% of total capital. Goodwill is by far the company's largest asset--without this $2.6 billion accounting entry, equity is sharply negative. Furthermore, SPX has benefited from pension credits in recent years that will soon reverse into costs, and we think interest expense will be on the rise. These challenges, plus the head wind of the still weak industrial economy, merit a conservative approach to the shares.

St. Jude Medical STJ

	Rating	Risk	Moat Size	Fair Value	Last Close	Yield %
	★	Med.	Narrow	$30.00	$39.72	0.0

Company Profile

St. Jude Medical manufactures cardiovascular medical devices, including the world's most widely used replacement heart valve. Its products include tissue heart valves, catheters, intra-aortic balloon-pump systems and catheters, implantable cardioverter defibrillators, pacemakers, centrifugal pump systems, and other products related to cardiovascular surgery. St. Jude Medical sells its products to open-heart surgery centers in the United States and abroad. Foreign sales make up about 40% of the company's total sales.

Management

Terry L. Shepherd has been president and chief executive since 1999. He has more than 17 years of experience in sales and marketing of medical devices, which should help him lead the growth-oriented St. Jude.

Strategy

St. Jude is trying to keep sales and earnings growing by closing the technology gap with its main rivals, Guidant and Medtronic. To do so, it's spending aggressively on research and development. St. Jude is also trying to hold on to its dominant position in the heart valve market, with several new products on the way.

One Lillehei Plaza
St. Paul, MN 55117
www.sjm.com

Morningstar Grades

Growth [B-]	1998	1999	2000	2001
Revenue %	2.2	9.7	5.8	14.3
Earnings/Share %	158.6	-80.7	420.7	27.8
Book Value/Share %	-13.0	1.5	15.8	20.3
Dividends/Share %	NMF	NMF	NMF	NMF

St. Jude's three-year revenue growth rate of nearly 10% is much lower than the industry average of 17%. The company's emphasis on the fast-growing ICD business should help it keep this pace over the next several years.

Profitability [A]	1999	2000	2001	TTM
Return on Assets %	1.6	8.4	10.6	13.6
Oper Cash Flow $Mil	256	204	310	394
- Cap Spending $Mil	69	40	63	60
= Free Cash Flow $Mil	187	164	247	335

Since 1995, returns on equity have been spotty because of a series of one-time charges for in-process research and development. Removing the effects of these charges, returns would be healthy and in-line with the peer group.

Financial Health [A+]	1999	2000	2001	09-02
Long-term Debt $Mil	477	295	123	0
Total Equity $Mil	794	941	1,184	1,477
Debt/Equity Ratio	0.6	0.3	0.1	0.1

St. Jude is in excellent financial health. It has no long-term debt and generated $286 million in cash flow from operations during the first nine months of 2002.

Industry	Investment Style	Stock Type	Sector
Medical Equipment	▦ Mid Growth	↗ Classic Growth	◔ Healthcare

Competition	Market Cap $Mil	Debt/ Equity	12 Mo Trailing Sales $Mil	Price/Cash Flow	Return On Assets%	Total Return% 1 Yr	3 Yr
St. Jude Medical	7,053	0.1	1,529	17.9	13.6	2.3	39.0
Medtronic	55,399	0.3	6,669	34.6	11.4	-10.4	10.3
Guidant	9,458	0.2	3,063	9.3	18.6	-38.1	-11.7

Price Volatility

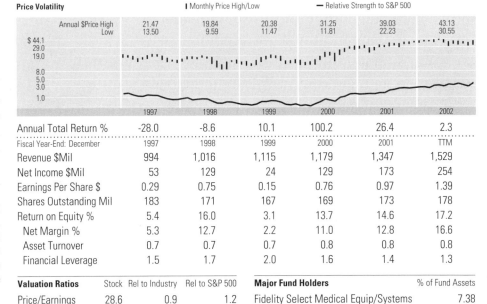

Annual $Price High Low	21.47 13.50	19.84 9.59	20.38 11.47	31.25 11.81	39.03 22.23	43.13 30.55	
	1997	1998	1999	2000	2001	2002	

Annual Total Return %	-28.0	-8.6	10.1	100.2	26.4	2.3
Fiscal Year-End: December	1997	1998	1999	2000	2001	TTM
Revenue $Mil	994	1,016	1,115	1,179	1,347	1,529
Net Income $Mil	53	129	24	129	173	254
Earnings Per Share $	0.29	0.75	0.15	0.76	0.97	1.39
Shares Outstanding Mil	183	171	167	169	173	178
Return on Equity %	5.4	16.0	3.1	13.7	14.6	17.2
Net Margin %	5.3	12.7	2.2	11.0	12.8	16.6
Asset Turnover	0.7	0.7	0.7	0.8	0.8	0.8
Financial Leverage	1.5	1.7	2.0	1.6	1.4	1.3

Valuation Ratios	Stock	Rel to Industry	Rel to S&P 500
Price/Earnings	28.6	0.9	1.2
Price/Book	4.8	0.7	1.5
Price/Sales	4.6	1.0	2.3
Price/Cash Flow	17.9	0.7	1.4

Major Fund Holders	% of Fund Assets
Fidelity Select Medical Equip/Systems	7.38
Chesapeake Growth Instl	5.10
INVESCO Advantage Glob Health Sci A	3.94
Lindner Large-Cap Growth Inv	3.83

Morningstar's Take By Travis Pascavis, 12-12-2002 Stock Price as of Analysis: $34.45

St. Jude has earned bragging rights for its results over the past couple of years, but we would only pick up shares at a 40% discount to our fair value.

The firm smartly emphasized treatments for heart problems in its research and development budget of more than 11% of sales. Indeed, St. Jude's efforts have paid off handsomely, and the firm has doubled its market share in implantable cardiac defibrillators, or ICDs. These devices automatically provide a sharp electrical shock directly to the ventricles of the heart if it starts to quiver, rather than just stimulating the heart beat by beat like a pacemaker does. With the ICD market at nearly $2.0 billion worldwide, St. Jude's share could be reach $300 million by the end of 2002.

Spending research dollars on areas neglected by rivals like Medtronic and Guidant is also paying off. For example, St. Jude has the first clinically proven algorithm to suppress atrial fibrillation--or very rapid, uncoordinated rhythm of the upper heart chambers. While this disease is progressive and can be treated with drug therapies or pacemakers, St. Jude's pacemakers combined with this algorithm offer better outcomes. This innovation has allowed the company to increase sales faster than its peers, which have largely focused on other heart ailments. Combining this algorithm with its ICD products is a logical next step, and this new product could be approved in early 2003.

Competition is still a threat, despite the past couple of years' successes. Both Medtronic and Guidant are market leaders, and both have launched new revolutionary products for heart failure. These resynchronization devices could crimp St. Jude's success in ICDs, despite St. Jude's attempt to get its own resynchronization device approved in the U.S.

Still, St. Jude is in excellent financial health with no long-term debt. Moreover, the company generates more cash from operations than is required to reinvest in the business, allowing the company to add to its cash on the balance sheet. This enviable financial position should help the company weather downturns should setbacks in product approvals occur.

MORNINGSTAR® Stocks 500

Stanley Works SWK

	Rating	Risk	Moat Size	Fair Value	Last Close	Yield %
	★★★	Med.	Narrow	$35.00	$34.58	2.9

Company Profile

Stanley Works produces tools and hardware for home-improvement, consumer, industrial, and professional use. Its tools division consists of consumer, industrial, and engineered tools. Consumer tools include hand tools such as hammers and saws. Industrial tools include air tools and tool boxes that are sold under the Stanley-Proto and Mac brand names. Engineered tools include air tools and Stanley-Bostitch fasteners. The company also makes hinges, residential door systems, power-operated doors, and other related items.

Management

CEO John Trani, 56, joined Stanley in 1996 after spending 18 years with General Electric, the last 10 as head of GE Medical Systems. He's been quick to deploy GE's aggressive practices--and been paid quite well despite muted results thus far.

Strategy

Stanley has become considerably leaner in recent years--closing inefficient plants, relocating production to low-cost areas, reducing redundant product offerings, and the like. Such initiatives will probably continue, but with much of the hardest cost-cutting behind the firm, accelerated new product development and acquisitions to expand the industrial tool lines are stepping to the forefront.

1000 Stanley Drive   www.stanleyworks.com
New Britain, CT 06053

Morningstar Grades

Growth [C]	1998	1999	2000	2001
Revenue %	2.2	0.8	-0.1	-4.5
Earnings/Share %	NMF	9.2	32.9	-18.5
Book Value/Share %	9.0	10.2	2.7	13.1
Dividends/Share %	7.8	4.8	3.4	4.4

Revenue has been essentially flat since 1996. Planned acquisition activity and a rebound in Stanley's industrial markets offer some hope for modest growth, but tools are likely to remain a slow-growing, hotly competitive industry.

Profitability [B+]	1999	2000	2001	TTM
Return on Assets %	7.9	10.3	7.7	8.3
Oper Cash Flow $Mil	222	236	222	326
- Cap Spending $Mil	103	64	73	59
= Free Cash Flow $Mil	119	172	149	267

Restructuring in recent years has boosted Stanley's financial performance, leading to improved margins and reduced fixed-asset intensity. Results have been penalized by the costs of this restructuring, however, which we expect to continue.

Financial Health [A+]	1999	2000	2001	09-02
Long-term Debt $Mil	290	249	197	205
Total Equity $Mil	735	737	832	975
Debt/Equity Ratio	0.4	0.3	0.2	0.2

Stanley can boast moderate use of debt (31% of total capital), healthy interest coverage, and strong free cash flows. As a result, the relatively conservative balance sheet has room for some cash-funded acquisitions.

Industry	Investment Style	Stock Type	Sector
Metal Products	Mid Core	High Yield	Industrial Mats

Competition	Market Cap $Mil	Debt/ Equity	12 Mo Trailing Sales $Mil	Price/Cash Flow	Return On Assets%	Total Return% 1 Yr	3 Yr
Stanley Works	3,064	0.2	2,577	9.4	8.3	-23.8	10.2
Masco	10,357	0.7	9,103	9.4	4.6	-12.1	-2.8
Danaher	10,013	0.4	4,221	13.5	2.7	9.1	13.8

Price Volatility

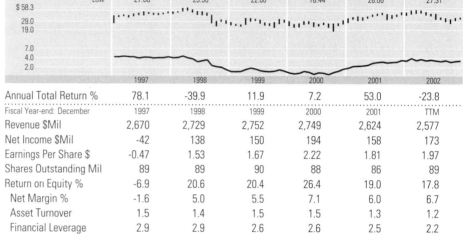

	Annual $Price High/Low					
	47.38 / 27.00	57.25 / 23.50	35.00 / 22.00	31.88 / 18.44	46.97 / 28.06	52.00 / 27.31
	1997	1998	1999	2000	2001	2002

	1997	1998	1999	2000	2001	2002
Annual Total Return %	78.1	-39.9	11.9	7.2	53.0	-23.8

Fiscal Year-end: December	1997	1998	1999	2000	2001	TTM
Revenue $Mil	2,670	2,729	2,752	2,749	2,624	2,577
Net Income $Mil	-42	138	150	194	158	173
Earnings Per Share $	-0.47	1.53	1.67	2.22	1.81	1.97
Shares Outstanding Mil	89	89	90	88	86	89
Return on Equity %	-6.9	20.6	20.4	26.4	19.0	17.8
Net Margin %	-1.6	5.0	5.5	7.1	6.0	6.7
Asset Turnover	1.5	1.4	1.5	1.5	1.3	1.2
Financial Leverage	2.9	2.9	2.6	2.6	2.5	2.2

Valuation Ratios	Stock	Rel to Industry	Rel to S&P 500
Price/Earnings	17.6	0.9	0.7
Price/Book	3.1	1.8	1.0
Price/Sales	1.2	1.9	0.6
Price/Cash Flow	9.4	1.3	0.7

Major Fund Holders	% of Fund Assets
Fidelity New Millennium	3.15
MassMutual Instl Fundamental Value S	2.72
Hartford Value A	2.65
Elite Growth & Income	2.22

Morningstar's Take By Josh Peters, 12-18-2002 Stock Price as of Analysis: $34.33

Although it leads in brand awareness, Stanley Works isn't the sharpest tool in the drawer. It's likely to benefit from an economic recovery in the next few years and it offers a healthy dividend, but we'd need a 30% discount to our $35 fair value estimate to call the stock a bargain.

In our view, the tool industry doesn't have attractive economic characteristics. Most hand tools and related hardware items are commodities exposed to low-cost foreign competition. Innovations, though crucial, are often easily copied. And though Stanley's yellow-on-black trademark can boast more than 150 years of customer satisfaction, the appeal of brand names is being diluted by the industry's increasingly powerful big-box retailers. Home Depot accounted for 18% of Stanley's top line in 2001, a proportion that is likely to rise in coming years.

As a result of these forces, toolmakers have lost much of their pricing power in the past decade. The business isn't as bad off as the domestic appliance or auto industries, but price increases have lagged manufacturers' rising costs.

Stanley, whose premium-priced offerings could prove especially vulnerable to low-cost foreign competition, has spent the past several years restructuring its manufacturing operations to reduce costs. Led by a former General Electric star, John Trani, Stanley has reduced manufacturing capacity and staff and attempted to rationalize the large, unwieldy catalog of products.

These cuts have brought improved profitability, though not without cost. Efficiency has improved, with plant productivity (measured by sales per dollar of plant and equipment) up 18% and a 40% gain in sales per employee since restructuring began in 1995. In fact, Stanley's operating margin of 12.6% in 2001--a recession year--reached heights not seen since the early 1980s. But these gains were bought with heavy restructuring: The firm recorded nonrecurring charges between 1995 and 2001 in every year but one, depressing earnings by more than a third.

We think Stanley will benefit from higher sales and still higher margins when the economy picks up. Revenue isn't much higher now than it was in the early 1990s, but a cyclical rebound in the company's industrial markets (40% of sales) and a selective eye toward acquisitions should get the top line moving again. While we're a bit cautious regarding additional restructuring, Stanley's long-running and well-funded dividend payment is attractive; at our $25 buy target, the shares would yield a nice 4%.

Staples SPLS

	Rating	Risk	Moat Size	Fair Value	Last Close	Yield %
	★★	Med.	None	$18.00	$18.30	0.0

Company Profile

Staples operates a chain of more than 1,300 superstores that sell deeply discounted, quality office products principally to small and medium-size businesses. The stores are located primarily in California, Florida, and the Northeastern United States. Staples also operates stores in Canada, the United Kingdom, the Netherlands, Portugal, and Germany. The company sells office supplies, business machines, computers and related products, office furniture, and other business-related products.

Management

Ron Sargent took over as president and CEO of Staples in 2002 from Thomas Stemberg, who guided the firm through a period of rapid growth during his tenure. Sargent is focused on profitable growth now that the company and industry are mature.

Strategy

After years spent trying to be all things to all people, Staples has sharpened its focus on its original and most profitable customers: small and medium-size companies. Growth will depend on satisfying the needs of those customers. Staples has also slowed its expansion by limiting the number of new stores and reducing their size.

500 Staples Drive
Framingham, MA 01702   www.staples.com

Morningstar Grades

Growth [B]	1999	2000	2001	2002
Revenue %	24.3	25.5	19.4	0.7
Earnings/Share %	5.1	0.0	NMF	NMF
Book Value/Share %	44.2	-35.0	NMF	NMF
Dividends/Share %	NMF	NMF	NMF	NMF

With square footage growth down and the office supply market basically mature, sales growth will be tough. We expect sales growth to average 6% over the next five years.

Profitability [B]	2000	2001	2002	TTM
Return on Assets %	8.2	1.5	6.5	7.0
Oper Cash Flow $Mil	300	692	685	909
- Cap Spending $Mil	355	450	340	274
= Free Cash Flow $Mil	-56	241	345	635

Staples outclasses its competitors in this department, as it has historically posted higher returns on assets and returns on equity. We think Staples will remain at the head of the class, given the new management team's focus on profitable growth.

Financial Health [A]	2000	2001	2002	10-02
Long-term Debt $Mil	562	514	436	827
Total Equity $Mil	1,829	1,749	2,054	2,440
Debt/Equity Ratio	0.3	0.3	0.2	0.3

The debt load is manageable. The company should be able to handle its store-remodeling project without adding to it significantly.

Industry	Investment Style	Stock Type	Sector
Specialty Retail	Large Growth	Classic Growth	Consumer Services

Competition

	Market Cap $Mil	Debt/ Equity	12 Mo Trailing Sales $Mil	Price/Cash Flow	Return On Assets%	Total Return% 1 Yr	Total Return% 3 Yr
Staples	8,608	0.3	11,190	9.5	7.0	-2.1	-4.1
Office Depot	4,554	0.2	11,369	6.0	6.3	-20.4	12.2
OfficeMax	674	—	4,653	—	—	—	—

Price Volatility

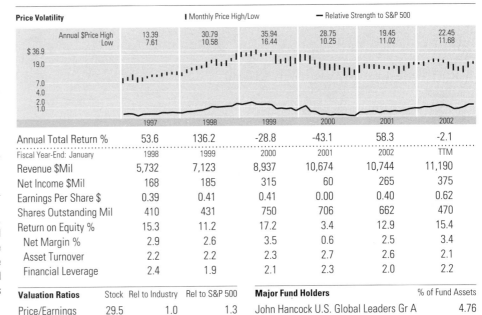

I Monthly Price High/Low   — Relative Strength to S&P 500

Annual $Price High / Low	13.39 / 7.61	30.79 / 10.58	35.94 / 16.44	28.75 / 10.25	19.45 / 11.02	22.45 / 11.68
	1997	1998	1999	2000	2001	2002

Annual Total Return %	53.6	136.2	-28.8	-43.1	58.3	-2.1
Fiscal Year-End: January	1998	1999	2000	2001	2002	TTM
Revenue $Mil	5,732	7,123	8,937	10,674	10,744	11,190
Net Income $Mil	168	185	315	60	265	375
Earnings Per Share $	0.39	0.41	0.41	0.00	0.40	0.62
Shares Outstanding Mil	410	431	750	706	662	470
Return on Equity %	15.3	11.2	17.2	3.4	12.9	15.4
Net Margin %	2.9	2.6	3.5	0.6	2.5	3.4
Asset Turnover	2.2	2.2	2.3	2.7	2.6	2.1
Financial Leverage	2.4	1.9	2.1	2.3	2.0	2.2

Valuation Ratios	Stock	Rel to Industry	Rel to S&P 500
Price/Earnings	29.5	1.0	1.3
Price/Book	3.5	1.0	1.1
Price/Sales	0.8	1.0	0.4
Price/Cash Flow	9.5	0.7	0.7

Major Fund Holders	% of Fund Assets
John Hancock U.S. Global Leaders Gr A	4.76
Bender Growth C	3.94
Phoenix-Seneca Mid-Cap Edge A	3.31
Seligman Capital A	3.07

Morningstar's Take By Tom Goetzinger, 12-05-2002 Stock Price as of Analysis: $18.98

We have reached the last couple of pages of Staples' big-growth story. The company is writing a new chapter on how it plans to succeed in a maturing industry, but we'd want a sizable discount to our fair value estimate in case revisions are needed.

Staples pioneered the office supply superstore concept more than 15 years ago, and explosive sales growth followed. Over the past decade, sales increased at a 33% clip compounded annually. Now, market saturation and competition have stifled Staples' fantastic growth. Sales growth averaged 48% per year in 1992-96, slowed to 24% in 1997-2000, and was just 1% in 2001. Sales have rebounded somewhat so far in 2002, but they're still up just 6% through the September quarter.

Staples is doing what it can to address weakness in its top and bottom lines. We're pleased with the company's target for improvements in the latter. New CEO Ron Sargent has a number of margin-boosting initiatives in place. For one thing, Staples is taking a cue from grocery chains and discount retailers and stocking more store-branded items. These items now represent 8.5% of sales, up from 7% a year ago. Staples will continue increasing the number of house-branded versions of basic office supplies that, while priced lower than name-brand items, are

actually more profitable for the store.

Margins should also benefit from Staples' renewed focus on its core business customers. Over the past few years the company has stocked more items geared toward nonbusiness customers, but wasn't making any money on them. While nonbusiness customers contributed 30% of the company's sales, they made up just 8% of profits. Selling a $700 computer appealed to consumers, but it wasn't helping Staples' bottom line. The elimination of these break-even products allows Staples to save cash by reducing the size of new stores being built and frees up space in existing stores that are being remodeled. Store productivity as measured by return on assets is up 9% in 2002.

Even so, it's still too early to call Staples' transition to a mature retailer a success. The company operates in a commoditylike industry with strong peers and small profit margins. Moreover, after a miserable 2001, Staples had relatively low hurdles to leap in 2002. The hurdles will be higher in 2003 and beyond. We'd wait for shares to fall to around $10-$12 before buying.

MORNINGSTAR® Stocks 500

Starbucks SBUX

	Rating	Risk	Moat Size	Fair Value	Last Close	Yield %
	★★	Med.	Narrow	$17.00	$20.38	0.0

Company Profile

Starbucks markets coffee products and operates more than 5,000 retail stores in the United States and overseas. Its stores sell coffee beans and beverages as well as coffee-making equipment, accessories, and pastries. Through its specialty sales group, Starbucks sells imported and roasted whole-bean coffees to wholesale clubs, specialty department-store chains, regional airlines, national bookstore chains, restaurants, and institutions.

Management

Chairman Howard Schultz bought the Starbucks chain in 1987, when it was just six stores, and has overseen its expansion into more than 5,500 stores. CEO Orin Smith focuses on U.S. operations while Schultz oversees international growth.

Strategy

Starbucks plans to increase sales more than 20% annually by almost doubling its store base to 10,000 by 2005. It targets an eventual store base of 25,000. About one fourth of the expansion has been abroad. Domestically, it clusters stores as a way of capturing share through market saturation. The firm is increasing its use of technology, like online ordering, to hasten service.

2401 Utah Avenue South
Seattle, WA 98134
www.starbucks.com

Morningstar Grades

Growth [A+]	1999	2000	2001	2002
Revenue %	28.9	29.1	21.6	24.2
Earnings/Share %	50.0	-11.1	91.7	17.4
Book Value/Share %	22.0	14.2	19.8	24.1
Dividends/Share %	NMF	NMF	NMF	NMF

Starbucks has plenty of room to expand, but we think 25% growth is a thing of the past. We expect growth to slow to 16% by 2006.

Profitability [A]	2000	2001	2002	TTM
Return on Assets %	6.3	9.8	9.4	9.4
Oper Cash Flow $Mil	319	456	478	478
- Cap Spending $Mil	316	384	375	375
= Free Cash Flow $Mil	2	72	102	102

Starbucks' profitability depends mightily on labor expense management and same-store sales growth. Its net profit margin should increase from an average of 5.6% over the past five years to 7.1% for the next five years.

Financial Health [A+]	2000	2001	2002	09-02
Long-term Debt $Mil	6	6	5	5
Total Equity $Mil	1,148	1,376	1,727	1,727
Debt/Equity Ratio	0.0	0.0	0.0	0.0

Starbucks has aggressively used off-balance-sheet financing in the form of store operating leases. Though no debt appears on the balance sheet, the leases have a similar effect as if the company used $1.3 billion in debt financing.

Industry	Investment Style	Stock Type	Sector
Restaurants	▦ Large Growth	↗ Classic Growth	▣ Consumer Services

Competition

	Market Cap $Mil	Debt/ Equity	12 Mo Trailing Sales $Mil	Price/Cash Flow	Return On Assets%	Total Return% 1 Yr	3 Yr
Starbucks	7,912	0.0	3,289	16.6	9.4	7.0	19.5
Krispy Kreme Doughnut	1,846	0.2	443	48.8	9.6	-23.6	—
Peet's Coffee & Tea	171	—	101	—	—	—	—

Price Volatility

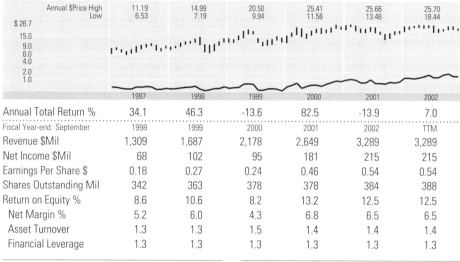

Annual Total Return %	34.1	46.3	-13.6	82.5	-13.9	7.0

Fiscal Year-end: September	1998	1999	2000	2001	2002	TTM
Revenue $Mil	1,309	1,687	2,178	2,649	3,289	3,289
Net Income $Mil	68	102	95	181	215	215
Earnings Per Share $	0.18	0.27	0.24	0.46	0.54	0.54
Shares Outstanding Mil	342	363	378	378	384	388
Return on Equity %	8.6	10.6	8.2	13.2	12.5	12.5
Net Margin %	5.2	6.0	4.3	6.8	6.5	6.5
Asset Turnover	1.3	1.3	1.5	1.4	1.4	1.4
Financial Leverage	1.3	1.3	1.3	1.3	1.3	1.3

Valuation Ratios	Stock	Rel to Industry	Rel to S&P 500
Price/Earnings	37.7	2.6	1.6
Price/Book	4.6	1.8	1.4
Price/Sales	2.4	1.8	1.2
Price/Cash Flow	16.6	2.3	1.3

Major Fund Holders	% of Fund Assets
John Hancock U.S. Global Leaders Gr A	4.62
Bender Growth C	4.13
Pitcairn Select Growth	4.08
Badgley Growth	4.07

Morningstar's Take By Carl Sibilski, 10-21-2002 Stock Price as of Analysis: $23.11

We're starting to see cracks in Starbucks' growth story. We still think the company has a good future, but we wouldn't buy the shares unless they fell to around $10.

We think Starbucks has made a successful transition from a faddish premium coffee to more of a staple in consumers' diets. Its continued success depends on snatching up convenient locations and ensuring consistent product quality. The company plans to achieve this by nearly doubling its current store base to 10,000 by 2005. Additionally, Starbucks has taken advantage of 30-year lows in coffee prices to strengthen relationships with suppliers--paying a premium now in hopes of securing good future sources for its exacting blends.

However, we think that rapid store expansion has put a financial strain on the company in the form of lease liabilities, which have been doubling each year for the past five years. As long as Starbucks maintains strong sales growth, we're confident that it will remain solvent. But it could run into trouble if it had to close stores and couldn't sublet store locations quick enough or at a reasonable rate.

This weaker financial condition is also evident in how Starbucks has chosen to expand internationally through licensing agreements. Licensing retailers to

sell coffee under the Starbucks brand is financially the least risky way to enter international markets. However, it also weakens the company's control over its brand because Starbucks doesn't control the store locations as it does in the United States. Other chains that have successfully expanded abroad have used different strategies, like wholly owned subsidiaries or joint ventures. Without enough cash on hand to fund alternative strategies, Starbucks has no choice but to license.

Considering the issues with international expansion, we think the company's expectations of 20%-25% annualized sales growth over the next five years depend too much on increases in same-store sales growth (sales from stores in operation at least a year) at U.S. locations. We think any hint of a slowdown in sales growth, particularly same-store growth, would send shares down in a hurry. We'd require at least a 30% margin of safety to our fair value estimate of $17 to buy in.

State Street STT

	Rating	Risk	Moat Size	Fair Value	Last Close	Yield %
	★★★★★	Med.	Wide	$50.00	$39.00	1.2

Company Profile

State Street provides back-office services for mutual fund companies and other investment managers, corporations, and public pensions. Clients look to State Street for custody and management of their assets, the firm's core product. The firm also sells additional services like foreign exchange, cash management, credit, and electronic trading services to help customers negotiate complex global financial markets efficiently.

Management

David Spina became chairman and CEO in 2001 after being at the firm for 33 years. He knows State Street inside and out after holding the posts of COO, CFO, and vice chairman.

Strategy

State Street has sold its corporate lending and trust operations and now focuses on two institutional businesses: providing back-office functions for asset managers and managing money through its State Street Global Advisors unit. The firm is targeting growth through selling ancillary services to its large stable of domestic clients and boosting its presence abroad.

225 Franklin Street
Boston, MA 02110
www.statestreet.com

Morningstar Grades

Growth [C]	1998	1999	2000	2001
Revenue %	23.5	17.5	19.0	-4.8
Earnings/Share %	14.7	42.1	-4.0	4.7
Book Value/Share %	15.8	14.9	22.9	16.9
Dividends/Share %	18.2	15.4	15.0	17.4

Fee income has grown at a compound annual rate of 16% over the past five years, an impressive record. Revenue growth has slowed to around 5% in 2002, but the firm has set an aggressive target of 15% growth through 2010.

Profitability [C]	1999	2000	2001	TTM
Return on Assets %	1.0	0.9	0.9	0.9
Oper Cash Flow $Mil	195	640	469	—
- Cap Spending $Mil	199	247	276	—
= Free Cash Flow $Mil	—	—	—	—

Return on assets has hovered consistently around 1% for years. Better expense controls would improve this, but the firm may feel too vulnerable amid the market turmoil to fiddle with the services it offers.

Financial Health [B]	1999	2000	2001	09-02
Long-term Debt $Mil	—	—	—	—
Total Equity $Mil	2,652	3,262	3,845	4,019
Debt/Equity Ratio	—	—	—	—

State Street maintains a large balance sheet and this is reflected in its high financial leverage compared with its peers. Most of the bank's assets are very liquid, however, so the risks are minimal.

	Industry	Investment Style	Stock Type	Sector
	Money Management	▦ Large Core	↗ Classic Growth	$ Financial Services

Competition

	Market Cap $Mil	Debt/ Equity	12 Mo Trailing Sales $Mil	Price/Cash Flow	Return On Assets%	Total Return% 1 Yr	Total Return% 3 Yr
State Street	12,649	—	4,947	—	0.9	-24.5	6.7
Bank of New York	17,396	—	6,017	—	1.4	-39.9	-11.1
Mellon Financial	11,252	—	4,350	—	3.8	-29.5	-2.6

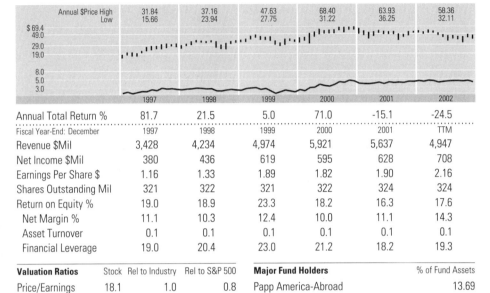

Price Volatility — Monthly Price High/Low — Relative Strength to S&P 500

Annual $Price High / Low	31.84 / 15.66	37.16 / 23.94	47.63 / 27.75	68.40 / 31.22	63.93 / 36.25	58.36 / 32.11
	1997	1998	1999	2000	2001	2002
Annual Total Return %	81.7	21.5	5.0	71.0	-15.1	-24.5

Fiscal Year-End: December	1997	1998	1999	2000	2001	TTM
Revenue $Mil	3,428	4,234	4,974	5,921	5,637	4,947
Net Income $Mil	380	436	619	595	628	708
Earnings Per Share $	1.16	1.33	1.89	1.82	1.90	2.16
Shares Outstanding Mil	321	322	321	322	324	324
Return on Equity %	19.0	18.9	23.3	18.2	16.3	17.6
Net Margin %	11.1	10.3	12.4	10.0	11.1	14.3
Asset Turnover	0.1	0.1	0.1	0.1	0.1	0.1
Financial Leverage	19.0	20.4	23.0	21.2	18.2	19.3

Valuation Ratios	Stock	Rel to Industry	Rel to S&P 500
Price/Earnings	18.1	1.0	0.8
Price/Book	3.1	1.2	1.0
Price/Sales	2.6	1.0	1.3
Price/Cash Flow	—	—	—

Major Fund Holders	% of Fund Assets
Papp America-Abroad	13.69
Papp Stock	10.96
Papp Focus	10.58
Jensen	6.28

Morningstar's Take By Rachel Barnard, 11-06-2002 Stock Price as of Analysis: $44.43

State Street's custody business has weathered the stormy equity markets relatively well and we think the shares are attractive below $40.

State Street's core businesses--global custody and asset management--are inextricably linked to investment markets because the company's fees are based on the level of assets it oversees. The downturn in the equity markets and the outflows of mutual fund assets have put a dent in State Street's revenue growth for 2002, although the firm is still expanding its top line at around 5%. The company continues to win new business, however, thanks to an outsourcing trend in the fund industry.

State Street has made a concerted effort to increase its dominance in custody and has rounded out its considerable suite of services by buying a separate accounts business and a hedge fund custodian. These are two of the fastest-growing areas of wealth management, and State Street is wise to step up for its share of the growing pie.

These added capabilities mean that State Street can offer one-stop shopping to its custody clients, many of whom manage a diverse menu of products. These clients can basically outsource their entire back office to State Street and expect the bank to keep track of their transactions, hang on to their securities, and provide a correct price for each portfolio at the end of the day.

In a further effort to focus its business, the bank announced that it is selling its corporate trust business to US Bancorp. State Street was only the number-six player in this industry and felt it had to fish or cut bait. The $725 million in proceeds will likely be used to pay for the acquisition of Deutsche Bank's custody business.

This acquisition is a large one for State Street, bringing in $2.2 trillion in assets under management and making it the world's largest custodian. At $1.5 billion (more than two times annual revenue), the deal seems a little pricey to us. However, the firm could maximize its purchase by making sharp staffing cuts and upselling its new clients on higher margin services. If this pans out, the deal could be more than worth the money.

With its dominant position in the global custody market, we think State Street can win a disproportionate share of new business and we expect the firm to continue buying up other back offices as the industry consolidates.

MORNINGSTAR® Stocks 500

Stilwell Financial SV

	Rating	Risk	Moat Size	Fair Value	Last Close	Yield %
	★★★	Med.	Narrow	$17.00	$0.00	0.4

Company Profile

Stilwell Financial is the parent company for several investment advisors. Its largest holding, bringing in 97% of its revenue, is Janus Capital. Stilwell owns nearly all of Janus, with the exception of equity stakes held by employees, which brings its stake to around 92%. Smaller holdings include Berger LLC and Nelson Money Managers. Stilwell also owns a third of DST Systems, a financial information processor focused on the mutual fund industry. Stilwell was spun off from Kansas City Southern Industries in mid-2000.

Management

Janus insider Mark Whiston will officially take over as CEO of Janus at the beginning of 2003 when Stilwell's subsidiaries merge under the Janus name. Whiston has been in charge of marketing for Janus and brings a focus on distribution and brand.

Strategy

Stilwell aims to leverage the strong Janus brand and the phenomenal fund growth records of the late 1990s while emphasizing its distinctive research process. Janus has focused on selling funds directly to retail investors, but the firm is adding additional advisor-class shares now that more investors are turning to professionals for mutual fund advice.

920 Main Street
Kansas City, MO 64105

www.stilwellfinancial.com

Morningstar Grades

Growth [B-]	1998	1999	2000	2001
Revenue %	38.3	80.7	85.4	-30.8
Earnings/Share %	NMF	NMF	NMF	NMF
Book Value/Share %	—	—	—	NMF
Dividends/Share %	NMF	NMF	NMF	100.0

Growth has been inconsistent and tied to the vagaries of the market. Revenue dropped 31% in 2001, a huge swing from the 85% increase in 2000. With assets under management down 28% as of September 30, we expect revenue to drop 23% in 2002.

Profitability [A]	1999	2000	2001	TTM
Return on Assets %	25.4	42.0	8.9	3.4
Oper Cash Flow $Mil	360	731	501	—
- Cap Spending $Mil	51	107	34	—
= Free Cash Flow $Mil	—	—	—	—

Return on assets has dropped because assets have ballooned with huge increases in goodwill and intangibles in 2001. An 8% ROA is still respectable, though--just slightly below Stilwell's asset-management peers.

Financial Health [A-]	1999	2000	2001	09-02
Long-term Debt $Mil	—	—	—	—
Total Equity $Mil	815	1,058	1,363	1,423
Debt/Equity Ratio	—	—	—	—

The company's $925 million debt gives it a debt/equity ratio of 60%, which is large for an asset manager. If cash flow continues to deteriorate, Stilwell could be forced to sell its stake in DST to maintain adequate interest coverage.

Industry	Investment Style	Stock Type	Sector
Money Management	▦ Mid Value	↑ Aggr. Growth	$ Financial Services

Competition	Market Cap $Mil	Debt/ Equity	12 Mo Trailing Sales $Mil	Price/Cash Flow	Return On Assets%	Total Return% 1 Yr	3 Yr
Stilwell Financial	2,907	—	1,231	—	3.4	-51.9	—
Amvescap PLC ADR	4,858	—	2,478	—	3.9	-55.8	-15.8
T Rowe Price Group	3,337	—	940	—	14.0	-19.8	-5.5

Price Volatility   ❙ Monthly Price High/Low   — Relative Strength to S&P 500

	54.50 30.75	46.63 18.20	29.22 8.97

Annual Total Return %	—	—	—	-30.9	-51.8	-51.9

Fiscal Year-end: December	1997	1998	1999	2000	2001	TTM
Revenue $Mil	485	671	1,212	2,248	1,556	1,231
Net Income $Mil	118	152	313	664	302	113
Earnings Per Share $	—	—	—	—	1.31	0.44
Shares Outstanding Mil	—	—	—	—	221	222
Return on Equity %	NMF	28.2	38.4	62.7	22.2	8.0
Net Margin %	24.3	22.7	25.8	29.5	19.4	9.2
Asset Turnover	0.7	0.8	1.0	1.4	0.5	0.4
Financial Leverage	—	1.5	1.5	1.5	2.5	2.3

Valuation Ratios	Stock	Rel to Industry	Rel to S&P 500
Price/Earnings	29.7	1.7	1.3
Price/Book	2.0	0.8	0.6
Price/Sales	2.4	0.9	1.2
Price/Cash Flow	—	—	—

Major Fund Holders	% of Fund Assets
Fidelity Select Brokerage & Investmnt	4.36
Regions Morgan Keegan Select Agg Gr B	3.09
Harbor Mid Cap Value	3.09
Permanent Portfolio Aggressive Growth	2.90

Morningstar's Take By Rachel Barnard, 11-05-2002 Stock Price as of Analysis: $13.21

As equity values sank, investors clamored to get some of their money back and Stilwell's assets under management have taken a beating. Third-quarter declines were particularly heavy. We think investors should seek a substantial discount to our $17 fair value estimate before buying, while being prepared for more volatility.

Stilwell Financial is learning the hard way not to put all of its eggs in one basket. Its Janus subsidiary accounts for more than 90% of assets under management. Janus is almost entirely invested in equities, and most of that is large-cap growth. Over the past 18 months, equity values have fallen, with growth stocks taking the worst of it.

Though many other asset managers have suffered in the market downturn, Stilwell is the hardest-hit among the publicly traded ones. Competitors like Fidelity and T. Rowe Price have large stables of diverse funds to attract investors in changing markets. Eaton Vance can sell both growth and value equity funds as well as bond funds, which have gained in popularity recently. Firms with deep benches tend to hold up well and even prosper as they rotate their starting lineups to meet demand.

Stilwell, in contrast, has almost no bench to go to, and with growth equities playing badly in a volatile market, investors have been leaving the stadium. The firm lost 680,000 accounts in the past year and recorded $11.3 billion in net outflows in the first six months of this year. Coupled with $25.4 billion in market depreciation, the blow to assets under management has been significant.

Through these turbulent times, however, Janus has maintained sound operating margins and many of its products boast excellent long-term records. When growth investing comes back, Stilwell should be one of the chief beneficiaries. But it will be a rocky ride until then.

In our opinion, Stilwell will continue to be a profitable company, but investors should recognize that its narrow focus makes it susceptible to wide swings in both assets under management and share price. For those with strong stomachs, we think the shares are a good buy below $10, and that Stilwell offers a fine opportunity to bet on the return of growth investments.

Stryker SYK

	Rating	Risk	Moat Size	Fair Value	Last Close	Yield %
	★★★	Med.	Wide	$64.00	$67.12	0.2

Company Profile

Stryker manufactures specialty surgical and medical products. The company's products include endoscopic systems like medical video cameras, light sources, and manual instruments; orthopedic and spinal implants; powered surgical instruments; and patient-handling equipment. Stryker markets its products to physicians and hospitals in the United States and abroad. It also operates about 230 physical therapy centers. Foreign sales account for approximately 42% of the company's total sales. Stryker operates manufacturing facilities in the United States and Europe.

Management

Chairman and chief executive John W. Brown has led Stryker since 1977. Brown, now 66, is known for his decentralized management style, so his yet-to-be-announced successor should be well prepared for the job.

Strategy

Stryker is grabbing as much of the joint-replacement market as it can to counter the effects of rapid consolidation of the hospital buying groups that are its customers. It hopes that its broad and deep product line will stanch pricing pressures from these buyers. The firm is also trying to boost margins by spreading its sales and marketing expenses over a larger revenue base.

P.O. Box 4085
Kalamazoo, MI 49003-4085
www.strykercorp.com

Morningstar Grades

Growth [B]	1998	1999	2000	2001
Revenue %	12.6	90.7	8.8	13.7
Earnings/Share %	-51.6	-67.7	1000.0	20.0
Book Value/Share %	11.0	-0.4	22.9	22.7
Dividends/Share %	9.1	8.3	23.1	25.0

Stryker's three-year average revenue growth of 32% is almost double the industry average. Much of this owes to acquisitions, however--recent growth has dropped to the mid-double digits.

Profitability [A]	1999	2000	2001	TTM
Return on Assets %	0.8	9.1	11.0	11.6
Oper Cash Flow $Mil	284	332	468	504
- Cap Spending $Mil	76	81	162	193
= Free Cash Flow $Mil	208	251	306	311

Returns on equity have been relatively stable over the past five years, although Stryker took charges in 1998 and 1999 for its acquisition of Howmedica. Net profit margins are increasing, and should be around 11.5% for all of 2002.

Financial Health [A]	1999	2000	2001	09-02
Long-term Debt $Mil	1,181	877	721	595
Total Equity $Mil	672	855	1,056	1,379
Debt/Equity Ratio	1.8	1.0	0.7	0.4

After the 1998 acquisition of Howmedica, Stryker's historically low debt/equity ratio rose to 2.2. The company has been reducing its debt since then, and debt/equity is now around 0.7.

Industry	Investment Style	Stock Type	Sector
Medical Equipment	▦ Large Growth	↑ Aggr. Growth	Healthcare

Competition	Market Cap $Mil	Debt/ Equity	12 Mo Trailing Sales $Mil	Price/Cash Flow	Return On Assets%	Total Return% 1 Yr	3 Yr
Stryker	13,276	0.4	2,892	26.3	11.6	15.2	25.9
Johnson & Johnson	159,452	0.1	35,120	18.0	16.3	-7.9	8.0
Zimmer Holdings	8,092	0.3	1,314	42.9	26.5	36.0	—

Price Volatility ‖ Monthly Price High/Low — Relative Strength to S&P 500

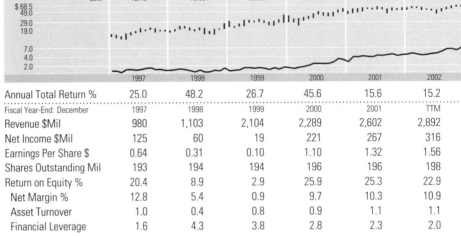

	1997	1998	1999	2000	2001	2002
Annual $Price High	22.66	27.88	42.50	57.75	63.20	67.45
Low	12.13	15.50	22.22	24.44	43.30	43.85
Annual Total Return %	25.0	48.2	26.7	45.6	15.6	15.2

Fiscal Year-End: December	1997	1998	1999	2000	2001	TTM
Revenue $Mil	980	1,103	2,104	2,289	2,602	2,892
Net Income $Mil	125	60	19	221	267	316
Earnings Per Share $	0.64	0.31	0.10	1.10	1.32	1.56
Shares Outstanding Mil	193	194	194	196	196	198
Return on Equity %	20.4	8.9	2.9	25.9	25.3	22.9
Net Margin %	12.8	5.4	0.9	9.7	10.3	10.9
Asset Turnover	1.0	0.4	0.8	0.9	1.1	1.1
Financial Leverage	1.6	4.3	3.8	2.8	2.3	2.0

Valuation Ratios	Stock	Rel to Industry	Rel to S&P 500
Price/Earnings	43.0	1.4	1.8
Price/Book	9.6	1.5	3.0
Price/Sales	4.6	1.0	2.3
Price/Cash Flow	26.3	1.1	2.0

Major Fund Holders	% of Fund Assets
Papp America-Pacific Rim	8.84
Jensen	5.46
Timothy Plan Large/Mid-cap Growth A	4.73
Alliance Health Care A	4.68

Morningstar's Take By Travis Pascavis, 12-14-2002 Stock Price as of Analysis: $64.59

Although we have underestimated Stryker's ability to increase sales in 2002 and we are raising our fair value estimate to $64--up from $56--the shares aren't attractive to us at current prices.

Unlike many other medical device procedures, joint replacements require major surgery with a long recovery time for the patient. In addition, once doctors get comfortable with Stryker's instrumentation and devices (about 65% of Stryker's sales), it is not easy for them to switch to another company's products. Given these factors, patients and their doctors want to use products that they absolutely know are safe and that the doctor knows how to use well. Thus, any new entrant would have to duplicate Stryker's long-term clinical history of about 30 years in some products. Also, because switching costs are so high for the doctor (many weeks of lost surgery time for retraining), market share is relatively stable in these devices.

This excellent competitive position is reflected in the company's financial performance. Excluding 1998, which included the Howmedica acquisition and its related restructuring charges, Stryker has a history of 20% or higher bottom-line growth for the past 20 years. We don't think much could keep the company from maintaining similar performance over the next five years.

The company's top line isn't too shabby, either. Joint replacement devices help people overcome debilitating diseases, like osteoporosis and osteoarthritis, that affect the middle-aged and the elderly--two growing demographics. Moreover, Stryker can increase sales by charging more for their products. Not many industries have pricing power, especially ones that have been around for as many years as the artificial joint industry. But Stryker has been able to hike prices by 2%-3% per year, and we see similar hikes for the next couple of years.

Stryker can also leverage its relationships with doctors to sell many of its other products, such as powered surgical instruments and spinal implants. In fact, it is already the market leader in powered surgical and number two in hospital beds and stretchers.

But all of this good news isn't enough for us to recommend the shares. By nearly any metric, including our fair value calculation, the company's shares are pricey. We have forecasted upper-teen earnings growth over the next five years for the company, but the shares still only seem about fairly valued.

MORNINGSTAR® Stocks 500

Student Loan STU

	Rating	Risk	Moat Size	Fair Value	Last Close	Yield %
	★★★★	Low	Narrow	$135.00	$97.80	2.9

Industry	Investment Style	Stock Type	Sector
Finance	▦ Mid Core	⚡ High Yield	$ Financial Services

Company Profile

Student Loan is a majority-owned subsidiary of Citigroup and was previously a division of Citibank, until it listed shares on the NYSE in 1992. Student Loan provides educational loans, principally government-backed, to students and parents; it is one of the largest originators and holders of government-backed student loans in the United States. The company began originating student loans in 1998 after two decades of buying loans on the secondary market. More than 95% of its revenue is derived from interest payments.

Management

Yiannis Zographakis, a Citibank alum, has been CEO since January 2001. Like Zographakis, most of Student Loan's board members have extensive ties to Citigroup, which owns 80% of the company.

Strategy

Student Loan is partnering with community banks and expanding geographically to reach new potential borrowers. In the first quarter of 2002, the firm began selling loans in asset-backed securitizations. This will help expand its revenue channels, and should drive higher growth rates. Student Loan has also invested in Web enhancements to attract new borrowers.

750 Washington Blvd.   www.studentloan.com
Stamford, CT 06901

Competition

	Market Cap $Mil	Debt/ Equity	12 Mo Trailing Sales $Mil	Price/Cash Flow	Return On Assets%	Total Return% 1 Yr	3 Yr
Student Loan	1,956	—	1,039	—	0.8	25.1	30.8
Bank of America	104,505	—	46,628	—	1.3	14.5	19.8
Wells Fargo	79,608	—	28,119	—	1.5	10.3	10.4

Price Volatility

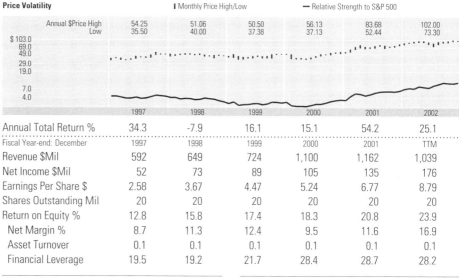

	1997	1998	1999	2000	2001	2002
Annual $Price High	54.25	51.06	50.50	56.13	83.68	102.00
Low	35.50	40.00	37.38	37.13	52.44	73.30
Annual Total Return %	34.3	-7.9	16.1	15.1	54.2	25.1

Fiscal Year-end: December	1997	1998	1999	2000	2001	TTM
Revenue $Mil	592	649	724	1,100	1,162	1,039
Net Income $Mil	52	73	89	105	135	176
Earnings Per Share $	2.58	3.67	4.47	5.24	6.77	8.79
Shares Outstanding Mil	20	20	20	20	20	20
Return on Equity %	12.8	15.8	17.4	18.3	20.8	23.9
Net Margin %	8.7	11.3	12.4	9.5	11.6	16.9
Asset Turnover	0.1	0.1	0.1	0.1	0.1	0.1
Financial Leverage	19.5	19.2	21.7	28.4	28.7	28.2

Valuation Ratios	Stock	Rel to Industry	Rel to S&P 500
Price/Earnings	11.1	0.9	0.5
Price/Book	2.7	0.8	0.8
Price/Sales	1.9	0.9	0.9
Price/Cash Flow	—	—	—

Major Fund Holders	% of Fund Assets
Artisan Mid Cap Value	3.87
Babson Value	3.67
DLB Value	3.29
Lazard Mid Cap Instl	1.56

Morningstar Grades

Growth [B+]	1998	1999	2000	2001
Revenue %	9.7	11.5	52.0	5.6
Earnings/Share %	42.2	21.8	17.2	29.2
Book Value/Share %	15.4	10.8	11.1	14.0
Dividends/Share %	11.1	225.0	23.1	16.7

Student Loan posted solid 16.5% average annual growth from 1996 to 2001, and revenue was up 35% in the first nine months of 2002. We're forecasting 10% compound annual revenue growth over the next five years.

Profitability [D+]	1999	2000	2001	TTM
Return on Assets %	0.8	0.6	0.7	0.8
Oper Cash Flow $Mil	-34	148	395	—
- Cap Spending $Mil	1	7	8	—
= Free Cash Flow $Mil	—	—	—	—

Education loans are low-risk, but federally mandated interest rate caps also prevent them from generating more than slim spreads. The net interest margin is typically about 2%, well below the spread earned by banks.

Financial Health [D]	1999	2000	2001	09-02
Long-term Debt $Mil	—	—	—	—
Total Equity $Mil	515	572	652	735
Debt/Equity Ratio	—	—	—	—

Student Loan has a high leverage ratio, but this is not a cause for concern. Instead of selling its loans, the firm holds most of them on its books, boosting assets. Plus, these government-secured loans carry little risk for the company.

Morningstar's Take By Craig Woker, 12-14-2002 Stock Price as of Analysis: $99.30

Student lending is one of the most attractive areas of consumer finance. The big two private lenders in this arena--Student Loan and SLM Corporation--benefit from economies of scale and a business structure that deters new competition. Demand for loans is noncyclical, steadily increasing during boom as well as bust times. Plus, the federal government subsidizes these lenders, almost ensuring they earn a healthy profit.

That said, Student Loan doesn't impress us quite as much as SLM, better known as Sallie Mae. Though we have a high degree of confidence that Student Loan's stock is undervalued--trading at only 2.7 times book value versus 9.5 times book for SLM--we feel there are reasons for this discrepancy that can't be explained away solely by the firm's weaker cash flows.

Namely, Student Loan is 80% owned by Citigroup, thus leaving a limited float that's unattractive to institutional investors, which could price the stock more efficiently but own only 3% of shares outstanding. Then there's always the threat that Citi could make another lowball run at the minority stake as it has in the past. Further, the ownership structure limits Student Loan's ability to partner with other big banks, an attractive market for SLM.

For investors willing to accept these limitations rather than wait for a healthy discount to buy SLM--a company with less baggage attached--Student Loan would be attractively priced at a level 20% below our fair value estimate of $135 per share.

Student Loan, by our estimate, has generated returns on capital that have averaged 22% over the past five years. The firm can thank the U.S. government for those profits. Because most college debt is backed by taxpayers, Student Loan has nearly no bad debt charge-offs. So while net interest spreads are low--typically only about 2% versus 5% for banks--the government's willingness to eat the bad debt has juiced net margins to nearly 40%.

Normally, big profits attract competition. But Student Loan's customers have no incentive to throw their business elsewhere. After all, the government sets student interest rates, thus limiting price competition. Plus, established lenders have long ties with colleges and banks, the two primary points of contact for students. They, in turn, work with SLM, the Federal Direct Loan Program, or Student Loan, which together command two-thirds of the market.

In sum, Student Loan is a phenomenal business, but to unleash its full value, it might need to cut ties to its parent.

Sun Microsystems SUNW

	Rating	Risk	Moat Size	Fair Value	Last Close	Yield %
	★★★★	High	None	$7.00	$3.11	0.0

Company Profile

Sun Microsystems manufactures computer equipment and software. Its products include network servers, workstations, peripheral equipment, operating software, accessories, and spare parts. The company markets its products under brand names like Solaris, Ultra, Sun Enterprise, Sun Ray, Sun StorEdge, and Gigaplane in the United States and abroad. Sun also produces its object-oriented Java and Jini software for use in Internet applications. Foreign sales account for approximately 47% of the company's revenue. Sun acquired Cobalt Networks in December 2000.

Management

CEO Scott McNealy has taken over for president and COO Ed Zander. The recent departures of Zander, CFO Michael Lehman, and a pair of executive vice presidents add to the numerous challenges facing Sun.

Strategy

The key to Sun's success has been its focus on the server market, which benefited enormously from the Internet explosion. Now that a large portion of its customer base has vanished with the death of many dot-coms and the capital-spending crunch at the telecom companies, Sun is reaching out to other markets.

901 San Antonio Road   www.sun.com
Palo Alto, CA 94303

Morningstar Grades

Growth [C]	1999	2000	2001	2002
Revenue %	19.7	33.2	16.1	-31.5
Earnings/Share %	31.9	77.4	-50.9	NMF
Book Value/Share %	NMF	48.0	42.2	-2.5
Dividends/Share %	NMF	NMF	NMF	NMF

Growth, which had been strong for several years, came to a screeching halt in early 2001. We expect no growth in fiscal 2003, but think long-term growth around 10% is still achievable, once IT spending rebounds.

Profitability [A-]	2000	2001	2002	TTM
Return on Assets %	13.1	5.1	-3.6	-3.4
Oper Cash Flow $Mil	3,754	2,089	880	729
- Cap Spending $Mil	982	1,292	559	429
= Free Cash Flow $Mil	2,772	797	321	300

Recent revenue shortfalls have hurt profitability, and the company is operating in the red. With some reluctance, management has finally embarked on an aggressive cost-control plan, and announced another round of job cuts in October.

Financial Health [A-]	2000	2001	2002	09-02
Long-term Debt $Mil	1,720	1,565	1,449	1,753
Total Equity $Mil	7,309	10,586	9,801	9,309
Debt/Equity Ratio	0.2	0.1	0.1	0.2

Although it deteriorated somewhat in 2001, the balance sheet remains strong. Sun carries $1.5 billion in long-term debt, but also has $2.6 billion in cash and another $2.6 billion of long-term investments.

Industry	Investment Style	Stock Type	Sector
Computer Equipment	▦ Large Core	◪ Distressed	▣ Hardware

Competition

	Market Cap $Mil	Debt/ Equity	12 Mo Trailing Sales $Mil	Price/Cash Flow	Return On Assets%	Total Return% 1 Yr	3 Yr
Sun Microsystems	9,687	0.2	12,382	13.3	-3.4	-74.7	-55.7
IBM	130,982	0.8	82,442	9.0	5.8	-35.5	-11.1
Dell Computer	69,252	0.1	32,054	20.1	13.4	-1.6	-16.9

Price Volatility

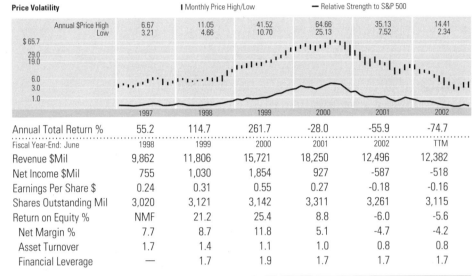

Annual $Price High Low	6.67 3.21	11.05 4.66	41.52 10.70	64.66 25.13	35.13 7.52	14.41 2.34
	1997	1998	1999	2000	2001	2002

Annual Total Return %	55.2	114.7	261.7	-28.0	-55.9	-74.7
Fiscal Year-End: June	1998	1999	2000	2001	2002	TTM
Revenue $Mil	9,862	11,806	15,721	18,250	12,496	12,382
Net Income $Mil	755	1,030	1,854	927	-587	-518
Earnings Per Share $	0.24	0.31	0.55	0.27	-0.18	-0.16
Shares Outstanding Mil	3,020	3,121	3,142	3,311	3,261	3,115
Return on Equity %	NMF	21.2	25.4	8.8	-6.0	-5.6
Net Margin %	7.7	8.7	11.8	5.1	-4.7	-4.2
Asset Turnover	1.7	1.4	1.1	1.0	0.8	0.8
Financial Leverage	—	1.7	1.9	1.7	1.7	1.7

Valuation Ratios	Stock	Rel to Industry	Rel to S&P 500
Price/Earnings	NMF	—	—
Price/Book	1.0	0.2	0.3
Price/Sales	0.8	0.5	0.4
Price/Cash Flow	13.3	1.5	1.0

Major Fund Holders	% of Fund Assets
Rydex Internet Inv	4.19
Hillman Aggressive Equity	3.81
Kelmoore Strategy Eagle A	3.44
FBR Technology	3.21

Morningstar's Take By Joseph Beaulieu, 10-25-2002 Stock Price as of Analysis: $2.88

After having chased Sun shares down by more than $20 over the course of the current IT spending downturn, we are reluctant to recommend them. However, we think that the stock's valuation already reflects an extremely pessimistic financial outlook for the company, and that the shares are a high-risk but potentially high-return investment.

While we believe Sun is undervalued, we are still concerned that the company's competitive position may be eroding. Competition for the few corporate IT dollars that are being spent is extremely intense, and IBM is a constant threat at the high end of the server market. Meanwhile, increasingly powerful Wintel boxes (computers running Windows on Intel processors) are nibbling at the bottom of the server market, as illustrated by the gains that Dell has been making. Recent management departures, including those of president and COO Ed Zander and CFO Michael Lehman, certainly don't boost our confidence that the company will be able to smoothly adjust to a rapidly shifting competitive landscape.

Sun has expanded its customer base beyond the telecom and dot-com companies that drove its heady growth in 1998-99, but it hasn't done so fast enough. Most of the dot-coms are gone, and the telecom companies have so much unused capacity that it could be at least a couple of years before they need to add more. This means that Sun is going to have to fight on less-friendly terrain to gain market share. While we think the company's products are still very competitive, this is going to be a customer-by-customer battle, and the outcome is far from certain.

Even though the forecasts that drive our discounted cash flow model are conservative, we would want a deep discount to our fair value estimate of $7 before we'd buy the shares, as we consider Sun a risky company that doesn't have a significant economic moat. The uncertain direction of IT spending, and the growing possibility that the company's midrange business may not be able to keep up with the squeeze at the high and low ends of the market, makes us wary.

MⓄRNINGSTAR® Stocks 500

SunTrust Banks STI

	Rating	Risk	Moat Size	Fair Value	Last Close	Yield %
	★★★	Low	Narrow	$64.00	$56.92	3.0

Company Profile

SunTrust Banks is the holding company for SunTrust Bank, which operates about 1,100 banking offices in Alabama, Florida, Georgia, Tennessee, Maryland, Virginia, and the District of Columbia. The bank provides savings, checking, money market, and individual retirement accounts. In addition, the bank offers trust, discount brokerage, corporate finance, credit-related insurance, and investment, computer, and mortgage-banking services. The bank also originates real-estate, business, and consumer loans. Real-estate loans make up about 45% of the bank's loan portfolio.

Management

Chairman and chief executive L. Phillip Humann has put a more aggressive stamp on this conservative organization by pursuing acquisitions and striving to lower its cost structure.

Strategy

SunTrust wants to jump-start its lackluster but key asset-management business. To do this, it has been piecing together a capital markets business through small acquisitions to offer higher-margin services to higher-net-worth individuals and institutional clients. Capital markets business will also expand lending relationships.

303 Peachtree Street N.E. www.suntrust.com
Atlanta, GA 30308

Morningstar Grades

Growth [C-]	1998	1999	2000	2001
Revenue %	11.2	3.5	13.6	-2.1
Earnings/Share %	0.0	35.7	2.9	9.8
Book Value/Share %	12.4	-7.4	13.9	4.8
Dividends/Share %	8.1	38.0	7.2	8.1

Slow revenue growth remains an issue for SunTrust in this weak environment. Net revenue grew just 2.3% over the past year.

Profitability [B]	1999	2000	2001	TTM
Return on Assets %	1.4	1.2	1.3	1.2
Oper Cash Flow $Mil	3,606	482	-1,291	—
- Cap Spending $Mil	257	146	89	—
= Free Cash Flow $Mil	—	—	—	—

Plunging interest costs and manageable charge-off levels have maintained profits even in the current environment.

Financial Health [B]	1999	2000	2001	09-02
Long-term Debt $Mil	—	—	—	—
Total Equity $Mil	7,627	8,239	8,360	8,848
Debt/Equity Ratio	—	—	—	—

Third-quarter charge-offs fell to 0.54% of average loans from 0.62% in the second quarter, though nonperforming assets ticked up, meaning it's too soon to assume credit quality has stabilized. Still, credit quality remains better than average.

Industry	Investment Style	Stock Type	Sector
Super Regional Banks	▦ Large Value	▨ High Yield	$ Financial Services

Competition

	Market Cap $Mil	Debt/ Equity	12 Mo Trailing Sales $Mil	Price/Cash Flow	Return On Assets%	Total Return% 1 Yr	3 Yr
SunTrust Banks	16,225	—	7,631	—	1.2	-6.7	-0.4
Bank of America	104,505	—	46,628	—	1.3	14.5	19.8
Wachovia	50,032	—	24,107	—	1.0	19.5	9.8

Price Volatility

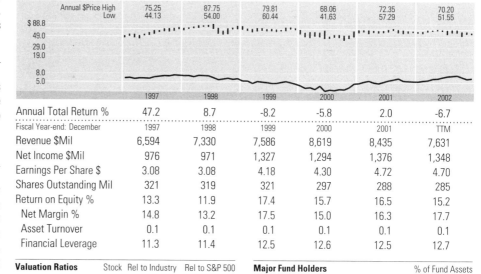

Annual $Price High	75.25	87.75	79.81	68.06	72.35	70.20
Low	44.13	54.00	60.44	41.63	57.29	51.55

	1997	1998	1999	2000	2001	2002
Annual Total Return %	47.2	8.7	-8.2	-5.8	2.0	-6.7

Fiscal Year-end: December	1997	1998	1999	2000	2001	TTM
Revenue $Mil	6,594	7,330	7,586	8,619	8,435	7,631
Net Income $Mil	976	971	1,327	1,294	1,376	1,348
Earnings Per Share $	3.08	3.08	4.18	4.30	4.72	4.70
Shares Outstanding Mil	321	319	321	297	288	285
Return on Equity %	13.3	11.9	17.4	15.7	16.5	15.2
Net Margin %	14.8	13.2	17.5	15.0	16.3	17.7
Asset Turnover	0.1	0.1	0.1	0.1	0.1	0.1
Financial Leverage	11.3	11.4	12.5	12.6	12.5	12.7

Valuation Ratios	Stock	Rel to Industry	Rel to S&P 500
Price/Earnings	12.1	0.8	0.5
Price/Book	1.8	0.9	0.6
Price/Sales	2.1	1.0	1.1
Price/Cash Flow	—	—	—

Major Fund Holders	% of Fund Assets
Banknorth Large Cap Value	6.63
FBR Financial Services	4.27
Commerce Core Equity Instl	3.30
Stonebridge Growth	3.20

Morningstar's Take By Richard McCaffery, 10-14-2002 Stock Price as of Analysis: $57.73

We think SunTrust should provide a decent return for minimal risk. The Atlanta-based company has more than 1,100 branches in attractive markets like Orlando, Atlanta, and Washington, D.C., and a growing ability to offer clients trust, investment banking, and trading account services. If it keeps underwriting smart loans, it will keep adding value. The company's strong point is its conservative lending philosophy, though it too has been stung by bad loans to cable and energy companies.

CEO Phillip Humann has given the company a more aggressive stance, pushing for acquisitions where they make sense and looking to sell additional products to depositors and mortgage customers. The company has deep roots and a well-established commercial banking business, which should help it compete with BB&T, Wachovia, Washington Mutual, and other punchy rivals. That said, the company isn't known for its aggressive sales culture. We expect a healthy portion of the growth investors will see over the next five years will come from stock repurchases.

With its vast branch network and strong commercial relationships, we see the SunTrust brand gaining strength in the Southeast. A recent push to cut costs and thereby improve efficiency is taking effect slowly, and we've built slightly improving cost ratios into our model to reflect the company's move to address its flabby cost structure. We believe the management team is honest and earnest, and that says a lot for a bank.

The strike against SunTrust is that it doesn't stand out, lacking the sales culture of a Washington Mutual, the acquisitive prowess of BB&T, or the efficiency of a Fifth Third.

Data as of 12-31-02

SuperValu SVU

	Rating	Risk	Moat Size	Fair Value	Last Close	Yield %
	★★★★	Low	None	$24.00	$16.51	3.4

Company Profile

SuperValu operates in two segments of the grocery industry: wholesale distribution and retail stores. Its wholesale distribution business, which is the largest in the United States, sells to more than 6,000 independent grocery stores, generating 60% of the company's revenue. The company also owns and licenses 1,194 retail stores, including Cub Foods, Shopper's Food Warehouse, Metro, bigg's and Shop 'n Save, as well low-price, limited-assortment Save-A-Lot. Supervalu acquired fellow grocery distributor Richfood Holdings in 1999.

Management

CEO Jeff Noddle is a 25-year company veteran with experience in virtually all of the company's operations. While we don't expect any dramatic changes in strategy, he is looking for new ways to leverage SuperValu's huge logistical resources.

Strategy

After a few years of strategic drift following its acquisition of Richfood Holdings, SuperValu aims to revive same-store sales growth by returning to its traditional low-price competitive strategy, symbolized by its Cub Foods and Save-A-Lot chains. The future of its wholesale business isn't as promising, but the firm is looking for ways to capitalize on its vast logistical network.

11840 Valley View Road   www.supervalu.com
Eden Prairie, MN 55344

Morningstar Grades

Growth [D]	1999	2000	2001	2002
Revenue %	1.3	16.8	14.0	-9.9
Earnings/Share %	-13.7	19.1	-66.8	146.8
Book Value/Share %	13.1	31.5	-3.2	5.2
Dividends/Share %	2.4	2.4	1.4	1.8

Although sales have fallen recently because of the loss of some big distribution customers, SuperValu can generate long-term growth if it successfully expands its retail operation. We don't expect top-line growth to exceed 3%.

Profitability [B-]	2000	2001	2002	TTM
Return on Assets %	3.7	1.3	3.5	3.8
Oper Cash Flow $Mil	341	651	787	678
- Cap Spending $Mil	408	398	293	371
= Free Cash Flow $Mil	-67	254	494	307

Margins are thin, but they've been improving as the company gets more of its revenue from retail stores.

Financial Health [B]	2000	2001	2002	08-02
Long-term Debt $Mil	1,954	2,008	1,876	2,011
Total Equity $Mil	1,821	1,793	1,917	1,996
Debt/Equity Ratio	1.1	1.1	1.0	1.0

SuperValu's debt levels are acceptable for the grocery trade, and despite weak sales, the firm is generating plenty of cash. Much of this cash should find its way into investors' pockets via dividends and stock buybacks.

Industry	Investment Style	Stock Type	Sector
Food Wholesale	▦ Mid Value	▨ High Yield	▣ Consumer Services

Competition	Market Cap $Mil	Debt/ Equity	12 Mo Trailing Sales $Mil	Price/Cash Flow	Return On Assets%	Total Return% 1 Yr	3 Yr
SuperValu	2,206	1.0	19,606	3.3	3.8	-23.5	-1.8
Safeway	13,376	1.5	34,757	6.3	3.4	-44.1	-12.2
Kroger	11,946	2.2	51,105	5.0	6.2	-26.0	-7.6

Price Volatility

| Monthly Price High/Low — Relative Strength to S&P 500

Annual $Price High Low	21.13 14.06	28.94 20.19	28.88 16.81	22.88 11.75	24.10 12.60	30.81 14.75

$ 31.8 / 19.0 / 9.0 / 6.0 / 4.0 / 2.0 / 1.0

	1997	1998	1999	2000	2001	2002
Annual Total Return %	51.9	36.8	-26.8	-28.4	64.5	-23.5

Fiscal Year-End: February	1998	1999	2000	2001	2002	TTM
Revenue $Mil	17,201	17,421	20,339	23,194	20,909	19,606
Net Income $Mil	231	191	243	82	206	234
Earnings Per Share $	1.82	1.57	1.87	0.62	1.53	1.74
Shares Outstanding Mil	125	120	129	132	134	134
Return on Equity %	19.3	14.7	13.3	4.6	10.7	11.7
Net Margin %	1.3	1.1	1.2	0.4	1.0	1.2
Asset Turnover	4.2	4.1	3.1	3.6	3.6	3.2
Financial Leverage	3.4	3.3	3.6	3.6	3.0	3.1

Valuation Ratios	Stock	Rel to Industry	Rel to S&P 500
Price/Earnings	9.5	0.3	0.4
Price/Book	1.1	0.1	0.3
Price/Sales	0.1	0.1	0.1
Price/Cash Flow	3.3	0.2	0.2

Major Fund Holders	% of Fund Assets
PIMCO NFJ Equity Income Admin	3.85
PIMCO NFJ Equity Income Instl	3.85
PIMCO NFJ Basic Value Instl	3.60
Valley Forge	3.48

Morningstar's Take   By David Kathman, 11-22-2002   Stock Price as of Analysis: $16.88

As SuperValu gradually moves from distribution toward grocery retailing, it faces a mix of tough challenges and promising opportunities. We'd consider buying the stock if it traded below $15.

As recently as five years ago, SuperValu got 75% of its revenue, and an even greater percentage of its profits, from distributing food to independent supermarkets. After some seismic shifts in the grocery industry that are still playing out, SuperValu now gets half its revenue and three fourths of its earnings from its growing network of retail grocery stores. We think this trend is a positive for SuperValu, despite the risks.

Though SuperValu is the leading grocery distributor in the United States, many of its customers (mainly independent grocers) are being squeezed by Wal-Mart and by the consolidation of the big grocery chains. SuperValu lost two big distribution customers in late 2001, Kmart and Genuardi's (bought by grocery giant Safeway), and as a result its distribution revenue has declined at double-digit rates in 2002. Even without those lost customers, sales are declining 2%-4% annually through attrition. The firm has been making its distribution centers more efficient and seeking out new channels like convenience stores, but we expect this segment to become an increasingly less important part of SuperValu's business.

The prospects are a bit better for SuperValu's retail grocery chains, though they've had a tough time in 2002 along with the rest of the grocery industry. Operating margins are higher than in distribution (4.5% in the first half of fiscal 2003 compared with 1.8% for the distribution segment), which should help overall margins as the firm continues to get more of its sales from retail. Its retail chains emphasize everyday low prices, which we see as the wave of the future in groceries, given Wal-Mart's increasing importance. Though comparable-store sales have been down slightly in recent quarters, customer traffic has remained steady; this means that customers are sticking around but switching to cheaper products, so sales should pick up again once the economy improves.

Though the outlook for grocers is not great, we think SuperValu has been positioning itself well for the long term and doing a good job in a tough environment. We think the stock is worth about $24 per share. We'd need a substantial discount to that estimate before buying, though SuperValu's 3%-plus dividend yield offers an additional attraction for income-oriented investors.

MORNINGSTAR® Stocks 500

Symantec SYMC

	Rating	Risk	Moat Size	Fair Value	Last Close	Yield %
	★	Med.	Narrow	$31.00	$40.45	0.0

Company Profile

Symantec is best known for its retail anti-virus software sold under the Norton brand. With the acquisition of Axent Technologies in December 2000, it launched a major shift toward serving the business customer. The company is trying to become a turnkey IT security solution shop with software and hardware appliances for anti-virus, intrusion detection and vulnerability assessment, firewall/virtual private network, and more. Symantec also has a small consulting business. Its products are sold worldwide. In 2000, 43% of total revenues were from outside North America.

Management

John Thompson was named president, CEO, and chairman in April 1999 after spending 28 years at IBM. Thompson owns a little over 1% of the stock.

Strategy

Symantec rules the retail shelf with its line of Norton antivirus software. But with this core market maturing, the firm wants to rule other high-growth areas as well and has acquired other companies to achieve this goal.

20330 Stevens Creek Blvd.   www.symantec.com
Cupertino, CA 95014-2132

Morningstar Grades

Growth [A]	1999	2000	2001	2002
Revenue %	11.2	25.8	14.5	25.5
Earnings/Share %	-39.4	218.6	-65.7	NMF
Book Value/Share %	11.6	68.3	103.4	-7.3
Dividends/Share %	NMF	NMF	NMF	NMF

The top line averaged 18% growth over the past five years. Although the antivirus market is maturing, new products like firewalls and intrusion detection should keep sales growing at roughly the same rate.

Profitability [A]	2000	2001	2002	TTM
Return on Assets %	20.1	3.6	-1.1	4.1
Oper Cash Flow $Mil	224	325	511	586
- Cap Spending $Mil	28	61	141	138
= Free Cash Flow $Mil	196	263	370	448

Symantec is very profitable. Excluding the impact of goodwill amortization, the company posts returns on invested capital above 40%.

Financial Health [A]	2000	2001	2002	09-02
Long-term Debt $Mil	2	2	604	605
Total Equity $Mil	618	1,377	1,320	1,437
Debt/Equity Ratio	0.0	0.0	0.5	0.4

Unlike most software vendors, Symantec carries debt. But financial health is excellent; cash is nearly double that of debt.

Industry	Investment Style	Stock Type	Sector
Systems & Security	▦ Mid Growth	↗ Classic Growth	▣ Software

Competition	Market Cap $Mil	Debt/ Equity	12 Mo Trailing Sales $Mil	Price/Cash Flow	Return On Assets%	Total Return% 1 Yr	3 Yr
Symantec	5,797	0.4	1,242	9.9	4.1	22.0	14.3
Infosys Technologies ADR	9,204	—	414	—	—	—	—
Computer Associates Inter	7,739	0.4	3,056	5.8	-5.3	-60.7	-41.5

Price Volatility   I Monthly Price High/Low   — Relative Strength to S&P 500

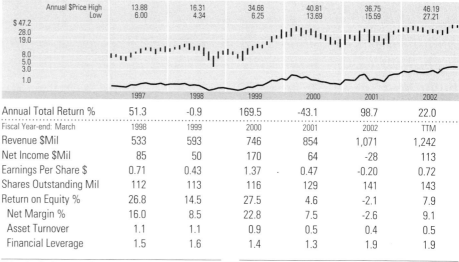

Annual $Price High Low	13.88 6.00	16.31 4.34	34.66 6.25	40.81 13.69	36.75 15.59	46.19 27.21

$47.2 / 28.0 / 19.0 / 8.0 / 5.0 / 3.0 / 1.0

1997   1998   1999   2000   2001   2002

Annual Total Return %	51.3	-0.9	169.5	-43.1	98.7	22.0
Fiscal Year-end: March	1998	1999	2000	2001	2002	TTM
Revenue $Mil	533	593	746	854	1,071	1,242
Net Income $Mil	85	50	170	64	-28	113
Earnings Per Share $	0.71	0.43	1.37	0.47	-0.20	0.72
Shares Outstanding Mil	112	113	116	129	141	143
Return on Equity %	26.8	14.5	27.5	4.6	-2.1	7.9
Net Margin %	16.0	8.5	22.8	7.5	-2.6	9.1
Asset Turnover	1.1	1.1	0.9	0.5	0.4	0.5
Financial Leverage	1.5	1.6	1.4	1.3	1.9	1.9

Valuation Ratios	Stock	Rel to Industry	Rel to S&P 500
Price/Earnings	56.2	0.9	2.4
Price/Book	4.0	1.8	1.3
Price/Sales	4.7	1.3	2.3
Price/Cash Flow	9.9	0.9	0.7

Major Fund Holders	% of Fund Assets
Berger Information Technology Instl	8.80
Berger Information Technology Inv	8.80
Permanent Portfolio	5.39
IPS New Frontier	5.28

Morningstar's Take By Mike Trigg, 11-18-2002 Stock Price as of Analysis: $42.13

Symantec's strategy of moving beyond the slow-growing antivirus market and into other areas of security is unproved. Thus, we wouldn't buy the stock until it traded at least 30% below our fair value estimate.

With its line of Norton software for personal computers, Symantec dominates the consumer antivirus market. It also has partnerships with all the major PC makers--including Dell, Hewlett-Packard, and Gateway--so its software comes preloaded on their PCs. The Norton brand combined with the ubiquity of the software has resulted in an economic moat that will make it difficult for a competitor to displace Symantec.

Symantec has expanded into the corporate antivirus market and stolen share from leader Network Associates. We credit this success to three factors: the Norton brand carries weight even among businesses, viruses like Code Red continue to cause damage and create demand, and Network Associates has had some internal problems that have hurt its credibility (an accounting-related inquiry by the Securities and Exchange Commission, for example).

However, the antivirus market is mature; most people already have some basic protection against viruses. This has forced Symantec into faster-growing areas of security like firewalls, virtual private networks, intrusion detection, and managed security services. Although we believe that the security market will eventually consolidate and that Symantec is ahead of the game, our enthusiasm is tempered because the firm is narrowing its moat by entering these markets.

The problem is that Symantec's brand has less cachet in the areas where heavyweights like Check Point Software Technologies, Internet Security Systems, and Cisco Systems have been competing for years. Outside of antivirus, these competitors also have superior products. Companies are willing to pay more for this superior technology, given the importance of security and protecting sensitive corporate data.

We think Symantec is a solid company. But given the maturation of the antivirus market and the risks related to the company's growth initiatives, we wouldn't buy the stock until it fell below $22.

Sysco SYY

	Rating	Risk	Moat Size	Fair Value	Last Close	Yield %
	★★★	Low	Narrow	$30.00	$29.79	1.6

Company Profile

Sysco distributes food and related products to the food-service industry. The company's traditional food-service customers include restaurants, hospitals, schools, hotels, and industrial caterers. Chain-restaurant customers include regional pizza and French-style bakery operations, and national hamburger chain operations. The company's SYGMA Network subsidiary specializes in customized service to chain restaurants.

Management

The management bench is very deep; most executives have been with Sysco for quite a while. Charles Cotros has been CEO since 1985. Management owns less than 2% of the company's stock.

Strategy

Sysco has steadily grown through expanding operations and acquisitions. Recent purchases were based on controlling "center of the plate" items (meat, seafood) and cross-selling secondary items. Sysco is increasing its presence with independent restaurant customers, where it can offer higher-margin services like menu planning and company-branded products.

1390 Enclave Pkwy.
Houston, TX 77077-2099
www.sysco.com

Morningstar Grades

Growth [B]	1999	2000	2001	2002
Revenue %	13.7	10.8	12.9	7.2
Earnings/Share %	25.6	24.1	31.3	14.8
Book Value/Share %	8.2	24.5	16.9	2.3
Dividends/Share %	-6.0	-12.8	52.9	23.1

Growth has been steady around 10% annually, but slipped to 7.2% in fiscal 2002, including 2.7% real sales growth. However, sales increased 10.2% in the first quarter of fiscal 2003 from the year-ago period, including 7% real sales growth.

Profitability [A]	2000	2001	2002	TTM
Return on Assets %	9.3	11.2	11.3	11.2
Oper Cash Flow $Mil	709	955	1,085	1,172
- Cap Spending $Mil	266	341	416	416
= Free Cash Flow $Mil	442	614	669	755

Rising net margins have lifted returns on equity. Despite razor-thin margins in the food wholesaling industry, Sysco is improving net margins through greater logistical efficiencies and increased emphasis on value-added products and services.

Financial Health [A-]	2000	2001	2002	09-02
Long-term Debt $Mil	1,024	961	1,176	1,266
Total Equity $Mil	1,762	2,101	2,133	2,194
Debt/Equity Ratio	0.6	0.5	0.6	0.6

The balance sheet is solid, with financial leverage below that of the average peer. Sysco is a cash cow, generating free cash flow (cash from operations minus capex) of $669 million in fiscal 2002, up nearly 9% from the year before.

Industry	Investment Style	Stock Type	Sector
Food Wholesale	▦ Large Growth	↗ Classic Growth	🗗 Consumer Services

Competition	Market Cap $Mil	Debt/ Equity	12 Mo Trailing Sales $Mil	Price/Cash Flow	Return On Assets%	Total Return% 1 Yr	3 Yr
Sysco	19,417	0.6	23,946	16.6	11.2	15.5	18.8
Royal Ahold ADR	10,398	—	48,745	—	—	—	—
Performance Food Group	1,534	—	4,155	—	—	—	—

Price Volatility

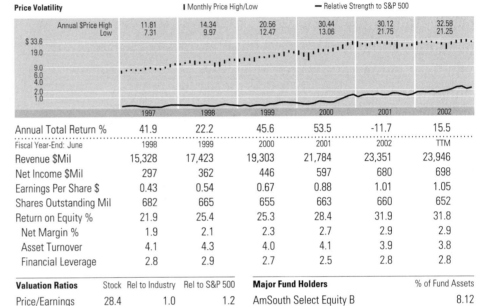

Annual $Price High	11.81	14.34	20.56	30.44	30.12	32.58
Low	7.31	9.97	12.47	13.06	21.75	21.25
	1997	1998	1999	2000	2001	2002

Annual Total Return %	41.9	22.2	45.6	53.5	-11.7	15.5
Fiscal Year-End: June	1998	1999	2000	2001	2002	TTM
Revenue $Mil	15,328	17,423	19,303	21,784	23,351	23,946
Net Income $Mil	297	362	446	597	680	698
Earnings Per Share $	0.43	0.54	0.67	0.88	1.01	1.05
Shares Outstanding Mil	682	665	655	663	660	652
Return on Equity %	21.9	25.4	25.3	28.4	31.9	31.8
Net Margin %	1.9	2.1	2.3	2.7	2.9	2.9
Asset Turnover	4.1	4.3	4.0	4.1	3.9	3.8
Financial Leverage	2.8	2.9	2.7	2.5	2.8	2.8

Valuation Ratios	Stock	Rel to Industry	Rel to S&P 500
Price/Earnings	28.4	1.0	1.2
Price/Book	8.9	1.0	2.8
Price/Sales	0.8	1.0	0.4
Price/Cash Flow	16.6	1.0	1.3

Major Fund Holders	% of Fund Assets
AmSouth Select Equity B	8.12
Huntington Growth Tr	6.41
W.P. Stewart & Co Growth	6.17
Sparrow Growth A	5.68

Morningstar's Take By David Kathman, 12-24-2002 Stock Price as of Analysis: $29.76

Size is only one of the competitive advantages Sysco enjoys in the cutthroat, low-margin food distribution business. We think it's an excellent company worth owning for the long haul--but only at the right price.

Though it may not have the name recognition of McDonald's or Coca-Cola, Sysco has built a formidable and profitable business as a middleman between manufacturers and the food-service industry. With $23 billion in annual sales and more than 400,000 customers spread across the United States and Canada, Sysco boasts economies of scale unparalleled in the highly fragmented food distribution field. This scale has allowed it to steadily improve gross margins, from 18.4% in 1998 to 19.8% in 2002, by improving efficiency and getting better prices from suppliers.

The only competitor with more than one fifth of Sysco's annual sales is Royal Ahold's U.S. Foodservice, at $17 billion. It reached that figure after swallowing number-three Alliant Foodservice, with $6 billion in sales, in an ill-advised attempt to catch up with Sysco; the result has been negative real sales growth and weakened profits caused by integration problems. Sysco has pursued a more deliberate acquisition strategy, buying much smaller distributors that fill a geographic or specialty niche,

like its recent purchases of Asian Foods and Buckhead Beef, a distributor of high-quality steaks. It has thus been able to maintain much steadier growth and solidify its number-one position.

Sysco has been developing other ways to set itself apart and stay on top. It's actively expanding its marketing associates program, which provides more individualized service to smaller customers. Such accounts generate higher margins than traditional broad-line sales, and are growing faster, now representing nearly half of all company sales. The firm also gets more than 40% of sales from its own Sysco-branded products, up from 36% four years ago; not only do these help margins because of the lower cost, but they encourage customer loyalty.

Sysco has been an amazingly steady performer over the past three decades, keeping sales and earnings rising through economic ups and downs. It's also been appealingly profitable, with returns on invested capital surpassing 20% in the past couple of years. The market recognizes these advantages, and the stock is seldom cheap. But if Sysco fell 20% below our $30 fair value estimate, we'd snap it up.

MRNINGSTAR® Stocks 500

T Rowe Price Group TROW

Rating ★★★	**Risk** Med.	**Moat Size** Narrow	**Fair Value** $30.00	**Last Close** $27.28	**Yield %** 2.4

Company Profile

T. Rowe Price Group manages assets for individuals through no-load mutual funds and for institutions in separate portfolios. The T. Rowe Price family of funds offers a wide spectrum of more than 80 stock, bond, and money market funds with low expenses. The firm also offers discount brokerage and trust services, retirement accounts, and specialized investment-management services. T. Rowe Price fund managers are guided by the company investment philosophy of controlling risk, resulting in relatively stable fund returns and measured growth for the company.

Management

Chairman George A. Roche joined the company in 1968 as an equity analyst and became the firm's president in 1997. T. Rowe Price traditionally has been run by a group of top officers who consult one another before making major decisions.

Strategy

T. Rowe Price gives the interest of its customers--individual investors--the highest priority. To that end, it has created a diversified offering of low-cost funds with an emphasis on risk control. To keep costs low, T. Rowe sells directly to customers and keeps a watchful eye on expenses. It has shunned all things flashy to focus on solid, cost-efficient investment returns.

100 East Pratt Street · · · · · · · · · · · www.troweprice.com
Baltimore, MD 21202

Morningstar Grades

Growth [D-]	1998	1999	2000	2001
Revenue %	17.4	17.0	17.0	-15.2
Earnings/Share %	18.6	38.1	12.4	-26.9
Book Value/Share %	24.1	25.9	28.7	9.2
Dividends/Share %	26.8	21.1	25.6	13.0

Revenue growth had been steady at 17% since 1998, but dropped 15% in 2001 with the stock market decline. Assets under management have slid 4% so far in 2002; this will probably lead to a similar decline in revenue for the year.

Profitability [A]	1999	2000	2001	TTM
Return on Assets %	24.0	18.3	14.9	14.0
Oper Cash Flow $Mil	297	323	290	—
- Cap Spending $Mil	77	86	41	—
= Free Cash Flow $Mil	—	—	—	—

T. Rowe Price lags the average asset manager's return on equity, but its 18% is still very respectable. The operating margin fell to 31% in 2001, but the 13% reduction in operating expenses should help margins rebound in 2002.

Financial Health [A+]	1999	2000	2001	09-02
Long-term Debt $Mil	—	—	—	—
Total Equity $Mil	770	991	1,078	1,100
Debt/Equity Ratio	—	—	—	—

The company used much of its cash flow to reduce its debt to $57 million from $312 million at the beginning of 2001. Long-term debt now is only 5% of equity and financial leverage is a low 1.2 times equity.

Industry	Investment Style	Stock Type	Sector
Money Management	▦ Mid Core	→ Slow Growth	$ Financial Services

Competition

	Market Cap $Mil	Debt/ Equity	12 Mo Trailing Sales $Mil	Price/Cash Flow	Return On Assets%	Total Return% 1 Yr	3 Yr
T Rowe Price Group	3,337	—	940	—	14.0	-19.8	-5.5
Franklin Resources	8,929	—	2,519	—	6.7	-2.6	3.8
Amvescap PLC ADR	4,858	—	2,478	—	3.9	-55.8	-15.8

Price Volatility

	▮ Monthly Price High/Low	― Relative Strength to S&P 500

Annual $Price High	36.88	42.88	43.25	49.94	43.94	42.69
Low	18.25	20.88	25.88	30.06	23.44	21.25

$ 50.9
29.0
19.0
7.0
5.0
3.0

	1997	1998	1999	2000	2001	2002
Annual Total Return %	46.1	10.1	9.2	15.9	-16.3	-19.8
Fiscal Year-end: December	1997	1998	1999	2000	2001	TTM
Revenue $Mil	755	886	1,036	1,212	1,027	940
Net Income $Mil	144	174	239	269	196	193
Earnings Per Share $	1.13	1.34	1.85	2.08	1.52	1.50
Shares Outstanding Mil	116	119	120	121	123	122
Return on Equity %	29.7	28.3	31.1	27.1	18.2	17.5
Net Margin %	19.1	19.7	23.1	22.2	19.1	20.5
Asset Turnover	1.2	1.1	1.0	0.8	0.8	0.7
Financial Leverage	1.3	1.3	1.3	1.5	1.2	1.3

Valuation Ratios	Stock	Rel to Industry	Rel to S&P 500
Price/Earnings	18.2	1.0	0.8
Price/Book	3.0	1.1	0.9
Price/Sales	3.6	1.3	1.8
Price/Cash Flow	—	—	—

Major Fund Holders	% of Fund Assets
Fidelity Select Brokerage & Investmnt	4.22
Fifth Third Mid Cap Growth Inv A	3.36
Managers AMG Rorer Mid Cap	3.35
Morgan Stanley Cap Opportunities B	2.85

Morningstar's Take By Rachel Barnard, 09-26-2002 Stock Price as of Analysis: $26.32

A tough equity market has handed this stock a disappointing year so far, but we have confidence in T. Rowe Price because of the consistently outstanding performance of its mutual fund products and its investor-friendly approach. We think the shares would be a good buy below $22.

Because the majority of its assets under management are in equity investments, T. Rowe Price has been buffeted by the stock market slide. Still, the firm is among the top 15 best-selling fund groups so far in 2002--a testament to the quality of its funds and the characteristic attention to valuation in selecting investments. We forecast a dip in revenue this year because of market depreciation, but we think the firm can easily make this up as the market recovers and we expect its conservative menu of funds to continue selling well.

The company has not been waiting around for a recovery. It has made significant expense cuts, trimming $23 million from operating expenses over the past year and reducing staff by 10%. This should pay off in higher operating margins by the end of 2002 and an increase in earnings over last year's levels.

T. Rowe Price is one of the most investor-friendly fund groups around and a favorite of Morningstar

fund analysts. Nearly all of its funds boast below-average expenses compared with other funds in the same categories and portfolio managers are meticulous about their investments, paying attention to valuation and not betting the farm on any one stock or sector. These are funds you would feel good about letting your granny invest in.

This approach has produced consistent results for T. Rowe and should continue to do so. The downside, however, is that not all investors are savvy enough to pick low-cost, low-risk funds, and many shun T. Rowe's conservative offerings for competitors' hot growth funds or hedge funds. Many financial advisors also avoid T. Rowe Price funds because they have no loads, meaning that the advisor doesn't get the hefty sales fee that other funds charge.

Given its particular niche, T. Rowe Price is destined to be a solid performer and not a growth superstar, but this is a company we would love to own for the long term--at the right price. The shares rarely go on sale, but we would find them attractive around $22, with a 25% margin of safety below our $30 fair value.

Taiwan Semiconductor ADR TSM

Rating	**Risk**	**Moat Size**	**Fair Value**	**Last Close**	**Yield %**
UR	UR	—	UR	$7.05	0.0

Company Profile

Taiwan Semiconductor Manufacturing is a dedicated semiconductor foundry. The firm provides chip manufacturing services to the semiconductor industry, mostly to chipmakers who don't have production facilities of their own. The company invests heavily in the most advanced chip manufacturing technologies and provides its services to chipmakers around the world. Domiciled in Taiwain, the firm has in place the ability to produce 332, 000 8-inch wafer equivalents per month.

Management

Chairman Morris Chang is one of the godfathers of the chip industry. A protege of his, F.C. Tseng, has been president since 1998. Through acquisition and internal development, the firm has built one of the most talented teams in the industry.

Strategy

As the world's largest chip foundry, Taiwan Semi has the scale to offer its customers an attractive mix of reliability, low price, and access to the best available manufacturing technologies. Because it's a pure foundry, Taiwan Semi remains noncompetitive with its customers, helping it to win more business. The firm has made heavy use of acquisitions to expand its production capacity.

No. 121 Park Ave III   www.tsmc.com
Hsinchu,

Industry	Investment Style	Stock Type	Sector
Semiconductors	▦ Large Growth	◆ Spec. Growth	▣ Hardware

Competition

	Market Cap $Mil	Debt/ Equity	12 Mo Trailing Sales $Mil	Price/Cash Flow	Return On Assets%	Total Return% 1 Yr	3 Yr
Taiwan Semiconductor Manufacturing ADR	25,567	0.1	3,709	12.1	4.5	-54.8	-33.7
CHRT	—	—	—	—	—	—	—
UMC	—	—	—	—	—	—	—

Price Volatility

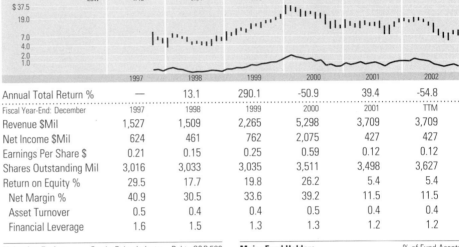

	1997	1998	1999	2000	2001	2002
Annual $Price High	9.42	8.64	23.21	36.53	17.71	19.08
Low	4.45	3.81	5.60	10.55	7.63	5.31
Annual Total Return %	—	13.1	290.1	-50.9	39.4	-54.8

Fiscal Year-End: December	1997	1998	1999	2000	2001	TTM
Revenue $Mil	1,527	1,509	2,265	5,298	3,709	3,709
Net Income $Mil	624	461	762	2,075	427	427
Earnings Per Share $	0.21	0.15	0.25	0.59	0.12	0.12
Shares Outstanding Mil	3,016	3,033	3,035	3,511	3,498	3,627
Return on Equity %	29.5	17.7	19.8	26.2	5.4	5.4
Net Margin %	40.9	30.5	33.6	39.2	11.5	11.5
Asset Turnover	0.5	0.4	0.4	0.5	0.4	0.4
Financial Leverage	1.6	1.5	1.3	1.3	1.2	1.2

Valuation Ratios	Stock	Rel to Industry	Rel to S&P 500
Price/Earnings	57.8	1.4	2.5
Price/Book	3.2	1.1	1.0
Price/Sales	6.9	1.8	3.4
Price/Cash Flow	12.1	1.0	0.9

Major Fund Holders	% of Fund Assets
Firsthand Global Technology	6.88
ING Emerging Countries A	6.72
TCW Galileo Asia Pacific Equity I	4.91
Firsthand Technology Leaders	4.37

Morningstar Grades

Growth [A+]	1998	1999	2000	2001
Revenue %	14.3	45.4	127.6	-24.3
Earnings/Share %	-14.8	59.6	129.3	-77.6
Book Value/Share %	20.9	43.5	87.5	6.6
Dividends/Share %	NMF	NMF	NMF	NMF

Relative to other chipmakers, Taiwan Semi's sales held up reasonably well in 2001 thanks to the rising trend of outsourced manufacturing in the sector. And 2002 sales look as though they may rise more than 20%.

Profitability [A+]	1999	2000	2001	TTM
Return on Assets %	14.8	20.1	4.5	4.5
Oper Cash Flow $Mil	1,396	2,798	2,111	2,111
- Cap Spending $Mil	926	2,526	2,004	2,004
= Free Cash Flow $Mil	470	272	108	108

High fixed costs, lower chip prices, and poor factory utilization continue to hurt short-term margins. But Taiwan Semi's size and scale allow it to generate decent margins; the firm even remained profitable on an operating basis in 2001.

Financial Health [A+]	1999	2000	2001	12-01
Long-term Debt $Mil	803	1,092	889	889
Total Equity $Mil	3,849	7,918	7,899	7,899
Debt/Equity Ratio	0.2	0.1	0.1	0.1

Taiwan Semi's balance sheet is in great shape. The firm has about a billion in debt but is well capitalized with almost $2 billion in cash and investments and a debt-to-equity of 0.1.

Morningstar's Take By Jeremy Lopez, 12-11-2002 Stock Price as of Analysis: $8.40

Taiwan Semi plays a crucial role in the chip industry as the world's largest foundry, but we're not convinced the stock should play a crucial role in investors' portfolios.

Taiwan Semi is a chipmaker's chipmaker, making chips for firms that want to farm out their manufacturing. Some customers like Broadcom and Nvidia depend entirely on outsourcing, while integrated firms (those that have chip plants) rely partially on foundries. Smaller chipmakers find outsourcing appealing because they gain access to new manufacturing technologies without the burden of building a pricey semiconductor plant. Integrated chipmakers are also increasingly adopting this model to make their operations more cost efficient. Taiwan's growth prospects look bright as these trends are likely to continue.

Being the world's largest foundry has its advantages. For one, the high switching costs inherent to this business protect Taiwan Semi from competition. Customers must work closely and exchange intellectual property with their foundry partner, meaning it would be difficult to change outsourcers. For Taiwan Semi's potential rivals, the cost of building and upgrading chip plants can be a large barrier to entry, especially since customers tend

to always want access to the latest technologies. In other words, large and well-capitalized foundries like Taiwan Semi are the most likely to succeed.

But Taiwan Semi is far from perfect. The firm carries much of the capital-spending burden of its customers, which crimps profits during chip downturns; fixed costs get spread across a smaller sales base. In the current slowdown, for example, Taiwan Semi's gross margins got hit worse than many of its customers', falling to 19%. Also, we're not fond of the firm's growth-through-acquisition strategy, because it runs the risk that Taiwan Semi may overpay in future transactions. Finally, the firm has unique risks being domiciled in Taiwan, such as touchy relations with mainland China and the threat of earthquakes.

There is little question Taiwan Semi is a good company given its growth prospects, strong balance sheet, and decent margins. But we concede that nailing down a reliable discounted cash flow value is difficult since Taiwan Semi reports in Republic of China GAAP. But in looking at traditional valuation metrics such as price/sales and price/earnings compared to the industry average, the shares aren't cheap. And without a clear margin of safety, we prefer to pass on the stock.

MORNINGSTAR® Stocks 500

Target TGT

	Rating	Risk	Moat Size	Fair Value	Last Close	Yield %
	★★★	Med.	Narrow	$40.00	$30.00	0.8

Company Profile

Through its subsidiaries, Target operates retail stores across the United States. Its Target division, which accounts for 80% of the company's revenue, is a discount merchandiser with 977 stores throughout the United States. Target features name-brand and private-label family apparel. The company's Mervyn's chain is a moderate-price department store emphasizing casual apparel at 266 stores in 14 states. The department store division operates 64 Marshall Field's stores in 8 states.

Management

Chairman and CEO Robert Ulrich has been with the company since 1967 and assumed his present position in 1987.

Strategy

Target Corp. is putting much of its financial resources into increasing the number of SuperTargets, which sell groceries as well as household items and provide a higher return on investment. Target aims to take share from department stores and small local stores by offering similar products at lower prices. The Target Visa rollout will make credit a larger part of profits.

....

1000 Nicollet Mall   www.target.com
Minneapolis, MN 55403

Morningstar Grades

Growth [A-]	1999	2000	2001	2002
Revenue %	11.6	9.9	9.5	8.1
Earnings/Share %	23.8	24.2	12.2	8.7
Book Value/Share %	19.9	18.0	12.9	21.1
Dividends/Share %	9.1	11.1	5.0	4.8

Target has averaged sales and operating income growth of 9.5% and 11.5%, respectively, over the past four years. Although top-line sales growth has been slowing, widening margins at Target stores have increased profits.

Profitability [B+]	2000	2001	2002	TTM
Return on Assets %	6.7	6.5	5.7	5.7
Oper Cash Flow $Mil	2,465	2,122	1,992	1,268
- Cap Spending $Mil	1,918	2,528	3,163	3,138
= Free Cash Flow $Mil	547	-406	-1,171	-1,870

The company's returns on assets have been in decline and will probably continue to drop, as credit becomes a higher percentage of overall profits.

Financial Health [C]	2000	2001	2002	10-02
Long-term Debt $Mil	4,521	5,634	8,088	10,559
Total Equity $Mil	5,862	6,519	7,860	8,756
Debt/Equity Ratio	0.8	0.9	1.0	1.2

Target has a substantial amount of debt, but generates enough free cash flow to service it.

Industry	Investment Style	Stock Type	Sector
Discount Stores	Large Core	Classic Growth	Consumer Services

Competition	Market Cap $Mil	Debt/ Equity	12 Mo Trailing Sales $Mil	Price/Cash Flow	Return On Assets%	Total Return% 1 Yr	3 Yr
Target	27,263	1.2	43,138	21.5	5.7	-26.5	-3.9
Wal-Mart Stores	223,388	0.5	233,651	18.9	8.0	-11.8	-7.3
Kohl's	18,851	0.4	8,277	31.0	9.8	-20.6	18.3

Price Volatility

	Annual $Price High / Low	18.50 8.97	27.13 15.72	38.50 25.03	40.00 21.63	41.74 26.00	46.15 24.90

	1997	1998	1999	2000	2001	2002
Annual Total Return %	74.2	62.1	36.2	-11.6	28.0	-26.5

Fiscal Year-end: January	1998	1999	2000	2001	2002	TTM
Revenue $Mil	27,487	30,662	33,702	36,903	39,888	43,138
Net Income $Mil	751	935	1,144	1,264	1,368	1,624
Earnings Per Share $	0.80	0.99	1.23	1.38	1.50	1.78
Shares Outstanding Mil	894	899	901	903	900	909
Return on Equity %	18.0	18.5	19.5	19.4	17.4	18.5
Net Margin %	2.7	3.0	3.4	3.4	3.4	3.8
Asset Turnover	1.9	2.0	2.0	1.9	1.7	1.5
Financial Leverage	3.4	3.1	2.9	3.0	3.1	3.3

Valuation Ratios	Stock	Rel to Industry	Rel to S&P 500
Price/Earnings	16.9	0.6	0.7
Price/Book	3.1	0.5	1.0
Price/Sales	0.6	0.7	0.3
Price/Cash Flow	21.5	1.1	1.6

Major Fund Holders	% of Fund Assets
Fidelity Select Retailing	5.69
PBHG Focused Value	5.66
Mairs & Power Growth	5.22
Sparrow Growth A	4.55

Morningstar's Take By Mike Porter, 12-13-2002 Stock Price as of Analysis: $30.96

Target has done excellent work in the discount-retailing arena. We'd consider purchasing the shares in the mid- to high-$20 range.

How can a discount retailer compete with Wal-Mart? It can't, at least not as an everyday-low-price retailer. To a large degree, Target of course competes with Wal-Mart, but it would be more accurate to say that it coexists with Wal-Mart. It sells lots of the same stuff, but also carries enough items that differentiate it from the biggest company in the world, so that it needn't compete primarily on price. The result has been, in our opinion, one of the great success stories in retail recently. Target's comparable-store sales numbers have been consistently strong, and earnings per share have grown 17% on average over the past four years.

Two things in Target's near future bear watching closely. The first is credit. Target has long offered an in-house credit card, and recently began offering a Target Visa card. Thanks to a successful rollout of that product, about 24% of the company's pretax earnings now come from credit sources, up from 15% a year ago. There's nothing inherently wrong with credit becoming a larger part of earnings--it's a very profitable way to make a buck--but it will push accounts receivable higher, lowering Target's returns

on assets. It also increases Target's exposure to consumer credit risk. Bad debt provisions are increasing at more than double the rate of credit revenues. This is acceptable for now, but not something we'd want to see continue for long.

The other development to watch is the company's increasing dependence on SuperTarget, the Target/grocery store combination. SuperTarget now makes up about 40% of the company's overall square-footage growth. On the surface, this sounds like a good thing; after all, bigger is better, and one-stop shopping is popular. But SuperTarget puts Target squarely in Wal-Mart territory, as Wal-Mart is the largest seller of groceries in the country. Target may find it more difficult to differentiate itself in groceries, where pricing is nearly all that matters to most people.

These developments have led us to be conservative in our earnings model. The company targets (bad pun intended) EPS growth around 15%. While we believe that is achievable, declining returns on assets give us a fair value on the company of $40 per share.

TCF Financial TCB

	Rating	Risk	Moat Size	Fair Value	Last Close	Yield %
	★★★	Med.	Narrow	$45.00	$43.69	2.6

Company Profile

TCF Financial is the holding company for bank subsidiaries that operate 351 banking offices and supermarket branches in Wisconsin, Illinois, Indiana, Michigan, and Colorado. The banks provide checking, savings, money-market, and individual retirement accounts, as well as certificates of deposit and computer-banking services. In addition, the banks originates residential and commercial real-estate, business, and consumer loans. Residential real-estate loans account for approximately 50% of the company's total loan portfolio.

Management

William Cooper, a certified public accountant, has been CEO of TCF since 1987. He's the driving force behind the bank's expansion strategy of opening new branches from scratch, its sales-focused approach, and its pursuit of middle-market customers.

Strategy

With 378 banks in six Midwest states and about 236 in supermarkets, TCF Financial strives to offer its middle-market customers convenience. Customers receive free checking, ATM cards, and debit cards at easy-to-reach branches that are open seven days a week, often 12 hours a day. The company focuses on gathering low-cost deposits and generating profits from fees and secured loans.

200 Lake Street East   www.tcfbank.com
Wayzata, MN 55391-1693

Morningstar Grades

Growth [C+]	1998	1999	2000	2001
Revenue %	13.3	3.0	9.4	4.1
Earnings/Share %	4.1	13.6	17.5	14.9
Book Value/Share %	NMF	-7.5	20.3	5.5
Dividends/Share %	30.6	18.4	13.8	21.2

TCF Financial has opened more than 200 new branches since 1998, driving strong internal growth. Checking deposits have increased almost 70% from 1998 to $2.6 billion. The company has 1.3 million checking accounts.

Profitability [A]	1999	2000	2001	TTM
Return on Assets %	1.6	1.7	1.8	1.9
Oper Cash Flow $Mil	400	202	145	—
- Cap Spending $Mil	—	—	—	—
= Free Cash Flow $Mil	—	—	—	—

Returns on average assets and equity increased steadily in the past six quarters as new branches reached break-even and delivered incremental profits to the bottom line. ROAA and ROAE of 2.03% and 25.5%, respectively, rank well above peers.

Financial Health [B]	1999	2000	2001	12-02
Long-term Debt $Mil	—	—	—	—
Total Equity $Mil	809	910	917	950
Debt/Equity Ratio	—	—	—	—

TCF employs a fair amount of leverage, though nothing unusual for a bank. Anyway, the high-quality nature of its assets allows the firm to be leveraged.

	Industry	Investment Style	Stock Type	Sector
	Savings & Loans	Mid Core	High Yield	Financial Services

Competition	Market Cap $Mil	Debt/ Equity	12 Mo Trailing Sales $Mil	Price/Cash Flow	Return On Assets%	Total Return% 1 Yr	3 Yr
TCF Financial	3,238	—	1,133	—	1.9	-6.7	27.1
Wells Fargo	79,608	—	28,119	—	1.5	10.3	10.4
Bank One	42,636	—	22,444	—	1.1	-4.4	9.4

Price Volatility

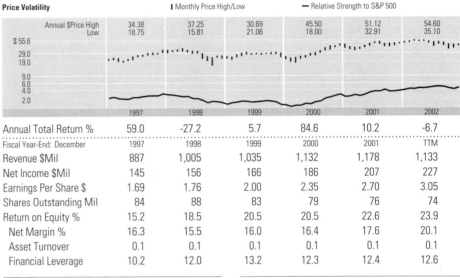

	Monthly Price High/Low		Relative Strength to S&P 500			
Annual $Price High	34.38	37.25	30.69	45.50	51.12	54.60
Low	18.75	15.81	21.06	18.00	32.91	35.10
	1997	1998	1999	2000	2001	2002

Annual Total Return %	59.0	-27.2	5.7	84.6	10.2	-6.7
Fiscal Year-End: December	1997	1998	1999	2000	2001	TTM
Revenue $Mil	887	1,005	1,035	1,132	1,178	1,133
Net Income $Mil	145	156	166	186	207	227
Earnings Per Share $	1.69	1.76	2.00	2.35	2.70	3.05
Shares Outstanding Mil	84	88	83	79	76	74
Return on Equity %	15.2	18.5	20.5	20.5	22.6	23.9
Net Margin %	16.3	15.5	16.0	16.4	17.6	20.1
Asset Turnover	0.1	0.1	0.1	0.1	0.1	0.1
Financial Leverage	10.2	12.0	13.2	12.3	12.4	12.6

Valuation Ratios	Stock	Rel to Industry	Rel to S&P 500
Price/Earnings	14.3	1.2	0.6
Price/Book	3.4	2.1	1.1
Price/Sales	2.9	1.3	1.4
Price/Cash Flow	—	—	—

Major Fund Holders	% of Fund Assets
Mairs & Power Growth	4.60
Sit Mid Cap Growth	3.38
INVESCO Financial Services Inv	3.22
Nations Financial Services Investor A	3.20

Morningstar's Take By Richard McCaffery, 12-16-2002 Stock Price as of Analysis: $42.27

We think TCF Financial is a first-class bank with a unique growth strategy, but the shares look fully valued. We've lowered the fair value estimate a bit, to $45 from $48, the result of putting the company into our new valuation model. But given the company's high returns and low-risk growth, we wouldn't need to see a huge discount. We'd get really excited about the shares around $30.

The company operates nearly 400 banks in the Midwest, more than half of which are in supermarkets. These branches offer customers convenience and give TCF the chance to gather deposits in high-traffic areas for a fraction of the cost of opening a typical bank.

We think the company has attractive growth opportunities. For example, in Illinois, where most of its branches are, TCF has just $2.2 billion in deposits--less than 1% market share. Fast-growing regions like Chicago offer attractive expansion opportunities. Even in Minnesota, where the company ranks third in deposits, its market share is around 4%, less than one fourth that of the number-two bank.

TCF focuses on getting customers in the door, using the deposits as a low-cost funding source, and selling fee-based products, which account for 45% of

its revenue. It has the fourth-largest supermarket banking chain in the country, and checking account balances have increased 70% since 1998 and are up 17% in the past year alone.

You can see the strategy's success in the company's results. Returns on assets and equity steadily improved as the company focused on lower-cost deposits and as new branches reached profitability, dropping profits to the bottom line.

The high returns on assets and equity are noteworthy, because the bank's cost efficiency is worse than average. Rather than cutting expenses to the bone to boost profits, TCF grows through branch expansions and low portfolio risk. Charge-offs in the third quarter were just 0.15% of average loans, far below average. TCF's risk-adjusted revenue margin is even higher than superstar Fifth Third's. Although it's fully valued now, TCF is worth watching closely.

MORNINGSTAR® Stocks 500

Tellabs TLAB

	Rating ★★★	Risk Med.	Moat Size Narrow	Fair Value $9.00	Last Close $7.27	Yield % 0.0

Company Profile

Tellabs manufactures digital cross-connect systems that telecom service providers use to manage voice and data communication traffic on their networks. In addition, the company manufactures broadband access equipment, voice quality enhancement products, and optical networking gear. Tellabs has a large installed base and a solid reputation with major telecom carriers. Foreign sales account for about 32% of the company's total sales.

Management

Past CEO and co-founder Michael Birck assumed command when Dick Notebaert left as CEO to run Qwest. Senior managers have long tenure, so succession should not be a major worry. Tellabs has a nimble, small-firm culture, unlike many rivals.

Strategy

Tellabs is looking to diversify sales from its hugely successful digital cross-connect gear. It has high hopes for several new products, like its next-generation cross-connect and other optical gear. Manufacturing remains in-house--for now--because Tellabs currently would get a poor price for its plants and demand is too uncertain to make outsourcing purchasing commitments.

One Tellabs Center   www.tellabs.com
Naperville, IL 60563

Industry	Investment Style	Stock Type	Sector
Wireline Equipment	▣ Mid Core	◪ Distressed	▦ Hardware

Competition

	Market Cap $Mil	Debt/ Equity	12 Mo Trailing Sales $Mil	Price/Cash Flow	Return On Assets%	Total Return% 1 Yr	3 Yr
Tellabs	2,995	0.0	1,474	9.8	-11.3	-51.4	-51.8
Nortel Networks	6,197	1.4	12,835	8.6	-29.6	-78.5	-67.5
Alcatel SA ADR A	5,615	1.0	17,080	1.7	-17.4	-72.9	-53.2

Price Volatility

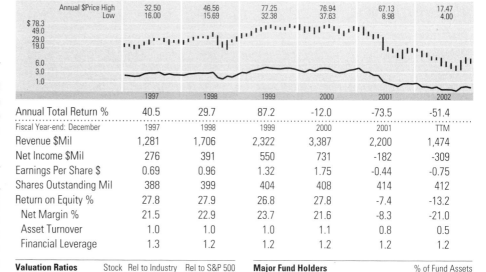

	1997	1998	1999	2000	2001	TTM
Annual Total Return %	40.5	29.7	87.2	-12.0	-73.5	-51.4
Fiscal Year-end: December	1997	1998	1999	2000	2001	TTM
Revenue $Mil	1,281	1,706	2,322	3,387	2,200	1,474
Net Income $Mil	276	391	550	731	-182	-309
Earnings Per Share $	0.69	0.96	1.32	1.75	-0.44	-0.75
Shares Outstanding Mil	388	399	404	408	414	412
Return on Equity %	27.8	27.9	26.8	27.8	-7.4	-13.2
Net Margin %	21.5	22.9	23.7	21.6	-8.3	-21.0
Asset Turnover	1.0	1.0	1.0	1.1	0.8	0.5
Financial Leverage	1.3	1.2	1.2	1.2	1.2	1.2

Valuation Ratios	Stock	Rel to Industry	Rel to S&P 500
Price/Earnings	NMF	—	—
Price/Book	1.3	0.8	0.4
Price/Sales	2.0	4.1	1.0
Price/Cash Flow	9.8	2.1	0.7

Major Fund Holders	% of Fund Assets
Ameristock Focused Value	19.98
ING MagnaCap A	3.28
ING Large Company Value A	3.25
Hotchkis and Wiley Mid-Cap Value I	2.97

Morningstar Grades

Growth [D]	1998	1999	2000	2001
Revenue %	33.2	36.1	45.9	-35.1
Earnings/Share %	39.1	37.5	32.6	NMF
Book Value/Share %	38.6	42.8	28.0	-5.3
Dividends/Share %	NMF	NMF	NMF	NMF

Sales, which surged during the 1990s, have plunged since 2001 because of the slump in carrier spending. We expect long-term sales growth of 10%-14%, though this will remain sensitive to the adoption of new products.

Profitability [A]	1999	2000	2001	TTM
Return on Assets %	23.3	23.8	-6.4	-11.3
Oper Cash Flow $Mil	452	426	419	306
- Cap Spending $Mil	99	208	208	68
= Free Cash Flow $Mil	353	219	211	238

The downturn has hurt profit margins, yet they remain higher than most peers' thanks to recurring add-on sales to existing Tellabs customers (like the Baby Bells). Margins will stay below former levels as Tellabs introduces new products.

Financial Health [A+]	1999	2000	2001	09-02
Long-term Debt $Mil	9	3	3	1
Total Equity $Mil	2,048	2,628	2,466	2,336
Debt/Equity Ratio	0.0	0.0	0.0	0.0

Tellabs has no debt, $1 billion in cash, and high-quality assets. Furthermore, management has mostly demonstrated restraint in capital spending and acquisitions.

Morningstar's Take By Fritz Kaegi, 12-19-2002 Stock Price as of Analysis: $7.02

Good judgment and skill as a niche player should put Tellabs in a position to do well over the next decade.

Tellabs' structure differs notably from rivals'. Its research and development focuses on a few key products that telecom carriers need to make their networks more efficient. Also, because it sells a few products to a few big customers, like Verizon and Sprint, Tellabs has a salesforce of only 360 people. It often sells products at a lower margin upon introduction, and then recoups years of high-margin add-on business, like cards that expand capacity. Finally, Tellabs manufactures products in-house, while others increasingly outsource.

The company often has a large share in specific niche markets, and relies on focused research, a small salesforce, and cachet with engineers to be successful. This strategy is conducive to carrier purchasing practices--different areas within a carrier choose vendors separately in separate projects. This allows niche specialists to pick their spots, and hinders bundling by large vendors.

Tellabs' key challenge is to make more operating costs variable with demand. While larger rivals have more discretionary areas to cut, Tellabs must lower production costs. Its current effort includes more logistics outsourcing and shifting more labor to a variable schedule. Tellabs is not outsourcing manufacturing for mostly short-term reasons: It would get a poor price for its manufacturing assets and demand is too uncertain to make multiyear purchasing commitments. Tellabs readily admits that costs would be lower and quality or service would not suffer with outsourcing, so we expect it to do more of this when these short-term conditions change.

Carriers' adoption of new products is key, since it drives both sales and margins. As we mentioned, new products are initially priced low. Over the long term, it's reasonable to expect Tellabs to successfully introduce new products, but changes in technology and greater competition to get initial sales probably spell shorter product cycles and lower margins. Tellabs will have to work particularly hard to sell more abroad, because the foreign salesforce is already spread thin. It may need to offer local distributors discounts to spur adoption in price-sensitive markets like China.

We think Tellabs is a fine company with a decent future. The stock would look attractive at a 40% discount to our fair value estimate.

Tenet Healthcare THC

	Rating	Risk	Moat Size	Fair Value	Last Close	Yield %
	UR	Med.	Narrow	$20.00	$16.40	0.0

Company Profile

Tenet Healthcare operates health-care facilities. The company wholly or partially owns 111 general hospitals, with about 27,000 beds. Most of its hospitals are in the Southern and Western United States and California. The company also owns long-term care facilities, physical rehabilitation hospitals, psychiatric facilities, and ancillary facilities connected with its general hospitals. The largest concentrations of the company's hospital beds are in California (26%), Texas (15%), and Florida (14%).

Management

Jeffrey Barbakow has been chairman and CEO since 1993. During his tenure, Tenet has grown from 35 hospitals generating $2.5 billion in revenue to more than 110 hospitals and related facilities with annual revenue approaching $13 billion.

Strategy

Tenet continues to use cash flow to expand existing facilities, acquire capital-starved hospitals, pay down debt, and repurchase shares. To beef up profitability and cash flow, the company has centralized many of its business operations and implemented a collection database to speed up its accounts receivable process and reduce bad debt.

3820 State Street   www.tenethealth.com
Santa Barbara, CA 93105

Morningstar Grades

Growth [B-]	1999	2000	2001	2002
Revenue %	10.0	4.9	5.6	15.4
Earnings/Share %	-5.9	21.5	105.2	18.8
Book Value/Share %	7.2	5.3	20.4	7.6
Dividends/Share %	NMF	NMF	NMF	NMF

After stripping out excess outlier payments, Tenet's revenue increased 14% in fiscal 2002 versus 2001. (It was originally reported as a 15% increase.) This is still significantly better than the 9% average growth between 1997 and 2001.

Profitability [B+]	2000	2001	2002	TTM
Return on Assets %	2.3	4.9	5.7	7.0
Oper Cash Flow $Mil	869	1,818	2,315	2,524
- Cap Spending $Mil	619	601	889	875
= Free Cash Flow $Mil	250	1,217	1,426	1,649

Excluding excess outlier payments, Tenet improved its operating margin from 8% to almost 12% over the past three years. Its shift toward high-acuity care should provide the leverage and profit growth needed to sustain this progress.

Financial Health [B+]	2000	2001	2002	08-02
Long-term Debt $Mil	5,668	4,202	3,919	3,551
Total Equity $Mil	4,066	5,079	5,619	5,881
Debt/Equity Ratio	1.4	0.8	0.7	0.6

Tenet has significantly reduced its debt over the past few years, and should not have any problem servicing its current balance of $3.5 billion. Cash flows would have to decrease dramatically for us to be concerned.

Industry	Investment Style	Stock Type	Sector
Hospitals	Large Core	Classic Growth	Healthcare

Competition	Market Cap $Mil	Debt/ Equity	12 Mo Trailing Sales $Mil	Price/Cash Flow	Return On Assets%	Total Return% 1 Yr	3 Yr
Tenet Healthcare	7,990	0.6	14,319	3.2	7.0	-58.1	1.0
HCA-The Healthcare Compan	21,270	1.2	19,243	8.3	5.0	7.9	13.4
Universal Health Services	2,726	0.7	3,148	9.0	5.9	5.4	35.2

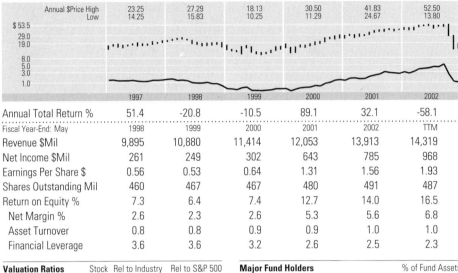

	23.25/14.25	27.29/15.83	18.13/10.25	30.50/11.29	41.83/24.67	52.50/13.80
Annual Total Return %	51.4	-20.8	-10.5	89.1	32.1	-58.1

Fiscal Year-End: May	1998	1999	2000	2001	2002	TTM
Revenue $Mil	9,895	10,880	11,414	12,053	13,913	14,319
Net Income $Mil	261	249	302	643	785	968
Earnings Per Share $	0.56	0.53	0.64	1.31	1.56	1.93
Shares Outstanding Mil	460	467	467	480	491	487
Return on Equity %	7.3	6.4	7.4	12.7	14.0	16.5
Net Margin %	2.6	2.3	2.6	5.3	5.6	6.8
Asset Turnover	0.8	0.8	0.9	0.9	1.0	1.0
Financial Leverage	3.6	3.6	3.2	2.6	2.5	2.3

Valuation Ratios	Stock	Rel to Industry	Rel to S&P 500
Price/Earnings	8.5	0.4	0.4
Price/Book	1.4	0.4	0.4
Price/Sales	0.6	0.5	0.3
Price/Cash Flow	3.2	0.4	0.2

Major Fund Holders	% of Fund Assets
Fidelity Select Medical Delivery	12.36
CDC Nvest Targeted Equity A	10.16
Nations Marsico Focused Eq Inv A	8.98
Marsico Focus	8.74

Morningstar's Take By Damon Ficklin, 11-12-2002 Stock Price as of Analysis: $14.98

Despite the deeply disappointing management of its pricing strategy, Tenet still has one of the best-run networks of hospitals. Some bad decisions at the executive level have shaken our confidence, but operations continue as usual at most of Tenet's hospitals. Although we now expect operations to yield lower returns than before, we stand by our fundamental evaluation of Tenet's strategic position.

Tenet has better scale and operating leverage than most of its competitors. With 116 hospitals under management (two thirds of which hold the number-one or -two position in their markets) and revenue growth in the middouble digits, Tenet's brawn is matched only by that of HCA. Size and leverage matter because hospitals have tremendous fixed costs. Because a hospital pays electric bills and purchases expensive patient-care equipment regardless of the number of patients it sees or procedures it performs, it helps to be as busy as possible and to spread expenses across a larger sales base. Tenet's occupancy rate is up 10% since 1999.

Tenet also has a significantly larger investment budget than most of its competitors do. While it may scale back investment a bit given recent events, it has invested billions to improve its facilities and expand profitable cardiology, neurology, orthopedic,

and intensive-care units. These are the backbone of Tenet's push to attract patients requiring greater (and more expensive) care, especially baby boomers. These significant investments will also help attract and retain employees. Everyone prefers to work in a state-of-the-art hospital; Tenet is investing billions toward this end while most hospitals are struggling to survive.

Tenet is focusing its expansion on high-acuity care, using its competitive advantages and positive demographic trends to increase its operating margins. Even after excluding excess outlier payments from past financial statements, Tenet has expanded its operating margin by 390 basis points during the last three years. While we are hesitant to project further improvements, we do expect Tenet will be able to hold on to that gain in profitability.

If Tenet can remain focused on operating its hospitals, we think that it will climb its way back out of the hole that it has dug. At a deep discount to our fair value estimate, the risks and rewards would be fairly balanced.

 Morningstar® Stocks 500

Teradyne TER

	Rating	Risk	Moat Size	Fair Value	Last Close	Yield %
	★	High	None	$11.00	$13.01	0.0

Company Profile

Teradyne manufactures semiconductor-testing equipment. It produces systems that test circuit boards and digital, analog, and mixed-signal integrated circuits. The company's systems are also used by telephone operating companies for the testing and maintenance of subscriber telephone lines and equipment. In addition, Teradyne makes backplaneconnector systems for use in electronic products, and also provides manufacturing services to its customers. Foreign sales account for about half of the firm's business.

Management

Chairman Alex d'Arbeloff is one of Teradyne's cofounders. Executives tend to be groomed internally, and turnover has been low. George Chamillard has been president and CEO since 1997, and has been with Teradyne since 1969.

Strategy

Although it's one of the industry's most diversified electronic-testing firms, Teradyne focuses on producing chip-testing gear. With a large direct sales and support team, Teradyne can expand its international footprint. The firm has also branched out into manufacturing services.

321 Harrison Avenue
Boston, MA 02118
www.teradyne.com

Morningstar Grades

Growth [D]	1998	1999	2000	2001
Revenue %	17.6	20.3	70.0	-52.7
Earnings/Share %	-19.6	79.8	134.6	NMF
Book Value/Share %	10.0	7.6	46.8	6.2
Dividends/Share %	NMF	NMF	NMF	NMF

Teradyne's revenue was roughly the same in 2001 as it was in 1998, thanks to a 53% decline last year. We expect sales weakness to continue well through 2002.

Profitability [B+]	1999	2000	2001	TTM
Return on Assets %	12.2	19.3	-8.0	-17.4
Oper Cash Flow $Mil	367	471	-79	-90
- Cap Spending $Mil	151	298	241	82
= Free Cash Flow $Mil	216	173	-320	-172

Profits can be volatile in such a cyclical industry. Operating margins are decent in an upcycle, ranging from the low teens to 20%. But on lower sales, operating margins will easily dip below zero (the case now).

Financial Health [B]	1999	2000	2001	09-02
Long-term Debt $Mil	9	8	452	451
Total Equity $Mil	1,153	1,707	1,764	1,518
Debt/Equity Ratio	0.0	0.0	0.3	0.3

The firm raised $400 million in a convertible debt offering several quarters ago, which explains why it has cash and investments of $340 million on its balance sheet. Despite the losses, Teradyne's cash burn hasn't been excessive.

Industry	Investment Style	Stock Type	Sector
Semiconductor Equipment	▦ Mid Growth	→ Slow Growth	▣ Hardware

Competition	Market Cap $Mil	Debt/ Equity	12 Mo Trailing Sales $Mil	Price/Cash Flow	Return On Assets%	Total Return% 1 Yr	3 Yr
Teradyne	2,382	0.3	1,109	—	-17.4	-56.8	-39.9
Schlumberger	24,304	0.8	13,942	12.1	3.2	-22.2	-6.9
Credence Systems	566	—	163	—	—		

Price Volatility | Monthly Price High/Low   — Relative Strength to S&P 500

Annual $Price High Low	29.59 11.81	24.22 7.50	66.00 20.63	115.44 23.06	47.21 18.43	39.99 7.10

	1997	1998	1999	2000	2001	2002
Annual Total Return %	31.3	32.4	211.5	-43.6	-19.1	-56.8

Fiscal Year-end: December	1997	1998	1999	2000	2001	TTM
Revenue $Mil	1,266	1,489	1,791	3,044	1,441	1,109
Net Income $Mil	128	102	192	454	-202	-407
Earnings Per Share $	0.74	0.60	1.07	2.51	-1.15	-2.25
Shares Outstanding Mil	167	167	171	173	176	183
Return on Equity %	13.6	9.9	16.6	26.6	-11.5	-26.8
Net Margin %	10.1	6.9	10.7	14.9	-14.0	-36.7
Asset Turnover	1.0	1.1	1.1	1.3	0.6	0.5
Financial Leverage	1.3	1.3	1.4	1.4	1.4	1.5

Valuation Ratios	Stock	Rel to Industry	Rel to S&P 500
Price/Earnings	NMF	—	—
Price/Book	1.6	0.6	0.5
Price/Sales	2.1	0.5	1.1
Price/Cash Flow	—	—	—

Major Fund Holders	% of Fund Assets
Fidelity Advisor Strategic Growth A	4.99
PIMCO PEA Value Instl	4.68
Schroder MidCap Value Inv	4.14
SunAmerica Focused Large Cap Value A	4.09

Morningstar's Take By Jeremy Lopez, 10-04-2002 Stock Price as of Analysis: $7.98

Teradyne might be one of the first firms to benefit from a chip sector recovery, but the stock won't look interesting until it trades at a significant discount to our fair value estimate.

Teradyne is well positioned in its chip equipment niche. Over the past four years, the firm has grown into a clear market share leader in the gear that chipmakers use to test the quality of their products. The firm has also picked its spots well in the testing market. It has avoided big exposure to memory chip testing, one of the most volatile segments of the market because of the unpredictability of demand and chip prices. Rather, it is best positioned in the mixed-signal and logic niches, which are more appealing from a long-term standpoint.

But Teradyne doesn't operate in one of the world's most attractive industries, especially during a cyclical downturn. Demand for testing gear is heavily tied to unit chip demand, often more so than so-called "front-end" suppliers that make gear for the early stages of chip production. As the industry struggles with overcapacity during a downcycle, demand for testing gear can dry up since chipmakers have plenty of testing gear to meet their own soft demand. And the firm's contract manufacturing business (about a third of sales) is also unappealing, in our view,

because of a dependency on a telecom sector that we don't see turning around soon.

It's not as if Teradyne makes up for its volatile sales with superior profitability, either. The firm's margins and returns on capital are historically no better than average relative to other front-end equipment makers like Applied Materials. In the current downturn, for example, the firm's operating margins have turned negative. In contrast, most of the major front-end companies have remained profitable so far.

Typically, test equipment makers are some of the first to feel the effects of a recovery in chip demand, since chip customers don't want to be caught flat-footed when their businesses improve. That recovery may be not be imminent, though, as capital spending remains weak and chipmakers manage anemic demand.

Given Teradyne's market leadership, we think the stock could be a decent long-term investment at the right price. But a history of volatile and middling fundamentals necessitates a significant margin of safety--about a 60% discount to our fair value estimate--before we'd find Teradyne attractive.

Teva Pharmaceutical Industries ADR TEVA

	Rating	Risk	Moat Size	Fair Value	Last Close	Yield %
	★	Med.	Narrow	$27.00	$38.61	0.4

Company Profile

Teva Pharmaceutical Industries develops and manufactures pharmaceuticals. The company produces generic drugs and also makes bulk pharmaceutical chemicals, veterinary products, and hospital supplies. Teva has one proprietary drug on the market, Copaxone, which treats multiple sclerosis. Strategic acquisitions and legal action against branded drugs also are essential competencies for the company. Teva is the largest generic manufacturer in the world with more than 150 generics in North America and 350 in Europe. In 2001, 64% of total revenue came from North America.

Management

Eli Hurvitz, Teva's president and CEO for 25 years, recently moved up to the chairman's office. Years ago, Hurvitz was convicted of tax fraud by an Israeli court, but the conviction was overturned. Former COO Israel Makov is now CEO.

Strategy

Teva Pharmaceutical Industries has made its name manufacturing generic drugs, but the success of Copaxone is the major factor behind expanding margins. Teva also uses its active pharmaceutical ingredient unit to supply its manufacturing units with a steady supply of low-cost chemicals. Acquisitions play a significant role in Teva's growth.

5 Basel St.
Petach Tikva, 49131
www.tevapharm.com

Morningstar Grades

Growth [A-]	1998	1999	2000	2001
Revenue %	-0.1	14.9	36.5	18.7
Earnings/Share %	-33.3	63.8	20.0	78.9
Book Value/Share %	8.4	11.6	45.5	14.5
Dividends/Share %	-9.8	-8.3	63.6	-13.7

Much of the company's top-line growth, which averaged 21% over the past four years, has come from acquisitions. Lately, sales from Copaxone have driven revenue growth, which is tracking to be around 15% for 2002.

Profitability [A]	1999	2000	2001	TTM
Return on Assets %	6.7	5.2	8.0	8.0
Oper Cash Flow $Mil	155	166	273	273
- Cap Spending $Mil	67	89	115	115
= Free Cash Flow $Mil	88	76	158	158

Margins have improved lately, and are slightly better than those of generic peers, thanks to efficient manufacturing and Copaxone. Third-quarter gross margins were up 2.2 percentage points from a year ago, but operating margins were flat around 19%.

Financial Health [B]	1999	2000	2001	12-01
Long-term Debt $Mil	—	550	910	910
Total Equity $Mil	747	1,151	1,381	1,381
Debt/Equity Ratio	—	0.5	0.7	0.7

Teva has $910 million in convertible debt that bears a low interest rate but could dilute shareholder value, if and when it's converted. Still, interest coverage is around 20 times, so we're not worried about debt.

Industry	Investment Style	Stock Type	Sector
Drugs	▦ Large Growth	↑ Aggr. Growth	◈ Healthcare

Competition	Market Cap $Mil	Debt/ Equity	12 Mo Trailing Sales $Mil	Price/Cash Flow	Return On Assets%	Total Return% 1 Yr	3 Yr
Teva Pharmaceutical Industries ADR	9,891	0.7	2,077	36.2	8.0	25.9	32.8
Biogen	5,972	0.0	1,128	26.6	11.5	-30.2	-18.2
Watson Pharmaceuticals	3,021	0.2	1,188	7.8	6.8	-9.9	-5.9

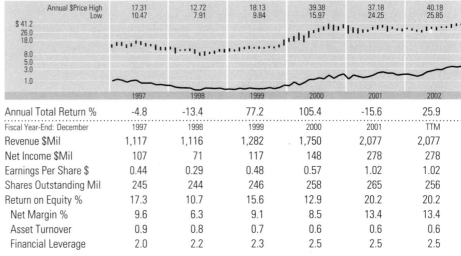

Price Volatility — Monthly Price High/Low — Relative Strength to S&P 500

Annual $Price High Low	17.31 10.47	12.72 7.91	18.13 9.84	39.38 15.97	37.18 24.25	40.18 25.85

	1997	1998	1999	2000	2001	2002
Annual Total Return %	-4.8	-13.4	77.2	105.4	-15.6	25.9
Fiscal Year-End: December	1997	1998	1999	2000	2001	TTM
Revenue $Mil	1,117	1,116	1,282	1,750	2,077	2,077
Net Income $Mil	107	71	117	148	278	278
Earnings Per Share $	0.44	0.29	0.48	0.57	1.02	1.02
Shares Outstanding Mil	245	244	246	258	265	256
Return on Equity %	17.3	10.7	15.6	12.9	20.2	20.2
Net Margin %	9.6	6.3	9.1	8.5	13.4	13.4
Asset Turnover	0.9	0.8	0.7	0.6	0.6	0.6
Financial Leverage	2.0	2.2	2.3	2.5	2.5	2.5

Valuation Ratios	Stock	Rel to Industry	Rel to S&P 500
Price/Earnings	37.9	1.6	1.6
Price/Book	7.2	1.0	2.2
Price/Sales	4.8	1.2	2.4
Price/Cash Flow	36.2	1.7	2.7

Major Fund Holders	% of Fund Assets
T. Rowe Price Em Eur & Mediterranean	9.38
Salomon Brothers International Eq B	7.05
Turner Healthcare & Biotechnology	5.73
Janus Aspen Global Life Sciences Inst	5.37

Morningstar's Take By Todd N. Lebor, 12-06-2002 Stock Price as of Analysis: $38.88

Advantages are hard to come by in the fiercely competitive, low-margin generic drug industry, but Teva has found one as the efficient manufacturer. On the other hand, Teva has a permanent handicap because it is based--and has 30% of its facilities--in war-torn Israel. For that reason, we'd demand a sizable margin of safety before investing.

Compared with the many firms that have visions of turning their fledgling generic operations into branded drug companies, Teva's focus on becoming the low-cost provider in the commoditylike generic drug industry is refreshing. Management has reaffirmed its commitment to this strategy a number of times and has set up the organization to do so. Teva has more than 20 plants scattered around the globe and is also one of the largest providers of active pharmaceutical ingredients (API). The API unit provides Teva with two competitive advantages: low-cost materials and uninterrupted supply.

Teva has another leg up with its access to Israeli universities and hospitals. Through knowledge-sharing arrangements, Teva has access to much of the pharma research in Israel. Teva also gets grants amounting to 20%-30% of its research budget from the Israeli government, for which it only has to reimburse the government in the form of 2%-3.5%

royalties. This keeps Teva's research and development costs low, allowing the firm to focus on improving the efficiency of its generic manufacturing and distribution network--the core business.

We also like the company's aggressive approach to Europe. Rather than shying away from the European market, where generic drug penetration averages a paltry 8%, Teva has been acquiring generic drug makers. (In comparison, 45% of prescription drugs sold in the United States are generic.) We think this strategy will pay off as the European Commission educates its citizens and doctors about the safety of generics and pushes for a more American-style generic drug approval process.

Copaxone is another ace in the hole for Teva. Even though the multiple sclerosis treatment faces competition, its sales are growing rapidly, and it doesn't lose U.S. patent protection until 2014. Copaxone sales are also pushing up Teva's margins.

Teva has managed to avoid any major interruption to its business, despite the terrorism and turmoil in and around Israel. Nonetheless, escalating conflicts in the Middle East force us to recommend a considerable margin of safety before investing. Stop the fighting in Israel, and Teva could be one of our favorite companies.

MORNINGSTAR® Stocks 500

Texas Instruments TXN

	Rating	Risk	Moat Size	Fair Value	Last Close	Yield %
	★★★	Med.	Narrow	$16.00	$15.01	0.6

Company Profile

Texas Instruments primarily manufactures semiconductors. It produces semiconductor products like analog integrated circuits, digital signal processors, reduced instruction set microprocessors, microcontrollers, digital imaging devices, and application-specific integrated circuits. The company also makes electrical controls and connectors, sensors, radio-frequency identification systems, and calculators. In addition, it develops high-speed Internet connections. Foreign sales account for about 67% of revenue. The company acquired Burr Brown in August 2000.

Management

Thomas Engibous took over as CEO in 1996. He is largely responsible for transforming Texas Instruments from a diversified electronics maker into a well-positioned and focused company.

Strategy

Texas Instruments has undergone a facelift over the past several years. It once had operations in many different industries, but now focuses on a few key areas, like digital signal processors, analog chips, and its steady calculator business. The firm uses large scale to its advantage, and also has a big influence in driving key industry technology standards.

12500 TI Boulevard   www.ti.com
Dallas, TX 75266-0199

Morningstar Grades

Growth [C]	1998	1999	2000	2001
Revenue %	-13.2	10.0	21.7	-30.9
Earnings/Share %	18.2	219.2	106.0	NMF
Book Value/Share %	7.2	35.9	28.5	0.8
Dividends/Share %	-24.8	33.3	0.0	0.0

This grade and the firm's negative 3% three-year average growth don't tell the whole story. TI has sold unappealing businesses since 1997, resulting in apples-to-oranges comparisons. Last year was horrible for TI, with sales falling 31%.

Profitability [B+]	1999	2000	2001	TTM
Return on Assets %	9.4	17.3	-1.3	0.9
Oper Cash Flow $Mil	2,357	2,185	1,819	2,028
- Cap Spending $Mil	1,398	2,762	1,790	802
= Free Cash Flow $Mil	959	-577	29	1,226

Return on equity was in the top 20% of the industry in 2000, thanks to TI's large size. But falling sales and high fixed costs--the opposite of what helped margins in 2000--hurt profits in 2001, with pro forma operating margins barely breaking even.

Financial Health [A]	1999	2000	2001	09-02
Long-term Debt $Mil	1,099	1,216	1,211	1,084
Total Equity $Mil	9,578	12,588	11,879	11,092
Debt/Equity Ratio	0.1	0.1	0.1	0.1

With a debt/equity ratio of 0.1, TI sports a strong balance sheet and modest debt. This financial health allows TI to invest heavily in chip equipment and R&D, giving it the strength to emerge from industry downturns in better shape than its peers.

Industry	Investment Style	Stock Type	Sector
Semiconductors	▦ Large Growth	➡ Slow Growth	◧ Hardware

Competition	Market Cap $Mil	Debt/ Equity	12 Mo Trailing Sales $Mil	Price/Cash Flow	Return On Assets%	Total Return% 1 Yr	3 Yr
Texas Instruments	25,982	0.1	8,024	12.8	0.9	-46.2	-32.5
Motorola	19,903	0.7	26,576	13.0	-12.9	-41.7	-42.2
Maxim Integrated Products	10,584	—	1,072	27.3	13.0	-37.0	-11.2

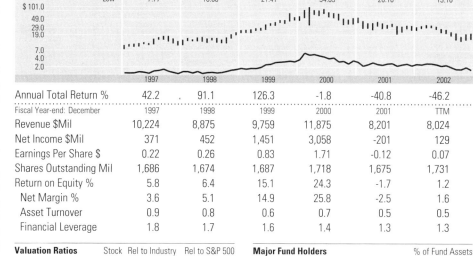

Price Volatility		I Monthly Price High/Low		— Relative Strength to S&P 500		
Annual $Price High Low	17.81 7.77	22.61 10.06	70.13 21.41	100.00 34.63	54.69 20.10	35.91 13.10

$ 101.0
49.0
29.0
19.0
7.0
4.0
2.0

	1997	1998	1999	2000	2001	2002
Annual Total Return %	42.2	91.1	126.3	-1.8	-40.8	-46.2
Fiscal Year-end: December	1997	1998	1999	2000	2001	TTM
Revenue $Mil	10,224	8,875	9,759	11,875	8,201	8,024
Net Income $Mil	371	452	1,451	3,058	-201	129
Earnings Per Share $	0.22	0.26	0.83	1.71	-0.12	0.07
Shares Outstanding Mil	1,686	1,674	1,687	1,718	1,675	1,731
Return on Equity %	5.8	6.4	15.1	24.3	-1.7	1.2
Net Margin %	3.6	5.1	14.9	25.8	-2.5	1.6
Asset Turnover	0.9	0.8	0.6	0.7	0.5	0.5
Financial Leverage	1.8	1.7	1.6	1.4	1.3	1.3

Valuation Ratios	Stock	Rel to Industry	Rel to S&P 500
Price/Earnings	214.4	5.2	9.1
Price/Book	2.3	0.8	0.7
Price/Sales	3.2	0.8	1.6
Price/Cash Flow	12.8	1.1	1.0

Major Fund Holders	% of Fund Assets
Rydex Electronics Inv	9.05
Fidelity Select Electronics	8.30
ProFunds Ultra Semiconductor Inv	8.03
Wireless	5.94

Morningstar's Take By Jeremy Lopez, 10-23-2002 Stock Price as of Analysis: $14.88

As one of the largest and most dominant firms in the chip sector, Texas Instruments would be one of our favorite semiconductor investment ideas at the right price.

With leading share in key semiconductor end markets, few chipmakers are better positioned than Texas Instruments. Whereas PC growth elevated the microprocessor into one of the most important chip segments during the 1980s and 1990s, the digital signal processor (DSP) has risen in sector importance most recently driven by the proliferation of digital technology and gadgets, like cell phones and digital cameras. TI rules the roost in DSPs with about 50% share. TI is also the world's largest producer of analog semiconductors--a market complementary to DSPs and also stable relative to most other chip niches. The firm's presence in broadband as a supplier of DSL and cable modem chips is also promising, although a small portion of sales. We think TI has a bright long-term growth opportunity, especially in DSP and analog.

TI has several key competitive advantages. The first is its large size. The firm can scale the fixed costs of its chip plants over a wide sales base, which is especially beneficial to margins when times are good. Also, TI has more resources than its peers to

reinvest in its business, whether it be research and development or capital spending. This is relevant during cyclical downturns: Recent investments in new manufacturing technology, for example, will extend TI's low-cost advantage. The firm's moat is widened by its industry prominence--TI is among the few influential companies that drive key wireless and chip standards. A huge network of engineers using its software makes TI's dominance all the harder to assail. Last, since DSPs and analog are complementary products, TI has ample cross-selling opportunities that its peers do not have.

As is the case for all chipmakers, TI continues to suffer from a weak technology market. Margins have been particularly weak largely because of fixed depreciation costs--the opposite effect of cost benefit in a good market. But by selling unattractive businesses in the late 1990s, focusing on proprietary areas like DSP and analog, and investing in manufacturing technology, TI's margins should improve from prior chip cycles.

We think TI's dominance, growth prospects, and product diversity make the stock one of the better investment ideas in the chip sector. We would find it appealing at a 40% discount to our fair value estimate.

Tiffany TIF

	Rating	Risk	Moat Size	Fair Value	Last Close	Yield %
	★★	Med.	Narrow	$21.00	$23.91	0.7

Industry	Investment Style	Stock Type	Sector
Jewelry/Accessories	Mid Growth	Classic Growth	Consumer Goods

Company Profile

Tiffany is an international jeweler and specialty retailer. The company designs fine jewelry constructed of gold, platinum, or sterling silver with or without precious gems and colored stones. It also sells sterling-silver merchandise, crystal tableware, fashion accessories, timepieces, fragrances, and gift items through more than 100 company retail stores in the United States and abroad. International retail operations include subsidiaries and affiliates with overseas locations. The company also has a direct-mail catalog business and online sales via tiffany.com.

Management

Chairman William Chaney has been with the company since 1980 and was CEO until 1999. Before joining Tiffany, he was an executive with Avon. CEO Michael Kowalski has been with the firm since 1983 and has a background in finance.

Strategy

After discontinuing its U.S. wholesale operations in 2001, Tiffany is seeking growth by expanding its retail presence. Management expects to open three to five new domestic stores annually. The company also renewed its contract with the Mitsukoshi department store chain, and plans to expand its reach in Japan.

727 Fifth Avenue
New York, NY 10022

www.tiffany.com

Morningstar Grades

Growth [B]	1999	2000	2001	2002
Revenue %	14.9	25.9	13.3	-3.7
Earnings/Share %	23.8	55.2	29.9	-8.7
Book Value/Share %	16.5	40.7	21.4	12.3
Dividends/Share %	30.8	32.4	33.3	6.7

Tiffany's popularity shows in its impressive growth history. But sales slump during economic weakness because of low consumer demand for luxury goods.

Profitability [A]	2000	2001	2002	TTM
Return on Assets %	10.8	12.2	10.7	9.8
Oper Cash Flow $Mil	230	111	242	255
- Cap Spending $Mil	171	108	171	210
= Free Cash Flow $Mil	59	2	71	44

Brand strength and premium prices afford Tiffany sizable gross margins. Because of its decent margins, we expect the company to post returns on invested capital above its cost of capital well into the future.

Financial Health [A]	2000	2001	2002	10-02
Long-term Debt $Mil	250	242	179	296
Total Equity $Mil	757	925	1,037	1,125
Debt/Equity Ratio	0.3	0.3	0.2	0.3

A conservative debt load and strong cash flows keep Tiffany in good financial health. It generates more than enough cash to fund its retail expansion internally.

Competition

Competition	Market Cap $Mil	Debt/ Equity	12 Mo Trailing Sales $Mil	Price/Cash Flow	Return On Assets%	Total Return% 1 Yr	3 Yr
Tiffany	3,471	0.3	1,653	13.6	9.8	-23.6	-16.1
Signet Group PLC ADR	1,818	—	1,707	—	—	—	—
Zale	1,058	—	2,192	—	—	—	—

Price Volatility

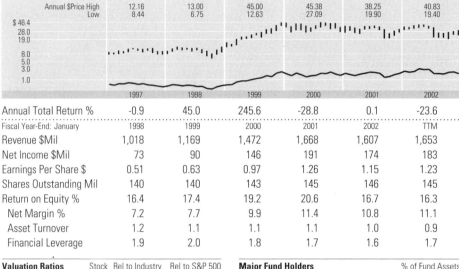

Annual $Price High Low	12.16 8.44	13.00 6.75	45.00 12.63	45.38 27.09	38.25 19.90	40.83 19.40

	1997	1998	1999	2000	2001	2002
Annual Total Return %	-0.9	45.0	245.6	-28.8	0.1	-23.6

Fiscal Year-End: January	1998	1999	2000	2001	2002	TTM
Revenue $Mil	1,018	1,169	1,472	1,668	1,607	1,653
Net Income $Mil	73	90	146	191	174	183
Earnings Per Share $	0.51	0.63	0.97	1.26	1.15	1.23
Shares Outstanding Mil	140	140	143	145	146	145
Return on Equity %	16.4	17.4	19.2	20.6	16.7	16.3
Net Margin %	7.2	7.7	9.9	11.4	10.8	11.1
Asset Turnover	1.2	1.1	1.1	1.1	1.0	0.9
Financial Leverage	1.9	2.0	1.8	1.7	1.6	1.7

Valuation Ratios	Stock	Rel to Industry	Rel to S&P 500
Price/Earnings	19.4	0.7	0.8
Price/Book	3.1	1.4	1.0
Price/Sales	2.1	0.6	1.0
Price/Cash Flow	13.6	0.7	1.0

Major Fund Holders	% of Fund Assets
SunAmerica Focused Large Cap Gr A	4.81
Selected Special	4.38
Marsico Focus	4.13
Nations Marsico Focused Eq Inv A	4.09

Morningstar's Take By Roz Bryant, 11-25-2002 Stock Price as of Analysis: $28.00

Tiffany's status as a legendary retailer wins its merchandise a hefty pricing premium, but economic weakness and a shifting tide in Japan challenge the firm's prospects. We'd look for a 30% margin of safety to our fair value estimate before investing.

After more than 150 years, shoppers are still enamored by Tiffany. Sales growth has averaged 12% annually over the past five years, which is better than most of its competitors. Because the retailer has a reputation for stylish and high-quality jewelry and accessories, its name conveys luxury and exclusivity. We expect steady sales growth over the next several years, as there is little indication that Tiffany's popularity is cooling. The company is opening new stores domestically and abroad to extend the brand's reach; management now plans to increase retail store square footage 5% annually.

Tiffany has exclusive agreements with several prominent jewelry designers. As a result, its merchandise commands higher prices relative to peers. Its gross margin, which is approaching 60%, trounces Zale's 51%. Both firms have similar overhead cost structures, so Tiffany's higher gross margin translates directly into bottom-line superiority.

We think the jeweler's efforts to boost

profitability should succeed. Tiffany negotiated fewer concessions when it renewed its contract with its Japanese distributor, Mitsukoshi, this past year. The retailer has also added more lower-price items with higher gross margins to its merchandise assortment. These items can be purchased inexpensively, but command a large markup just by wearing the Tiffany name. The company has raised prices on some select items as well.

Tiffany does face some challenges. Many people consider jewelry to be a luxury that they can live without in tough economic times. As domestic and international economies continue to struggle, Tiffany's top line may languish near-term. In addition, a cultural shift away from formal wedding engagements in Japan threatens to damp demand for diamond jewelry in that country on a long-term basis. Japan generated 28% of Tiffany's revenue in 2001, and year-to-date same-store sales in Japan (which exclude stores open less than one year) have fallen 7%.

We believe that Tiffany's competitive advantage is considerable and unlikely to fade. But given the firm's vulnerability to the macroeconomic climate and cultural trends, we'd look to invest only if the shares fell below $15.

MORNINGSTAR® Stocks 500

Timberland TBL

	Rating	Risk	Moat Size	Fair Value	Last Close	Yield %
	★★	Med.	Narrow	$30.00	$35.61	0.0

Company Profile

Timberland manufactures footwear, apparel, and accessories. The company's primary products are hiking boots and boating shoes for men and women. The company's other products include outerwear, sweaters, shirts, pants, and luggage. Timberland products are sold through department stores, retail specialty shops, and company-operated factory outlets and retail locations in the United States, South America, Europe, and Asia. The company also distributes its products through facilities in New Zealand and Australia.

Management

CEO Jeffrey Swartz is the third generation of his family to run the firm. The brand strategy rests with Frank Bifulco, who came aboard as chief marketing officer in January 2001 and has a lengthy record of building brand awareness.

Strategy

Timberland is focused on increasing its international presence, given the snail's pace of shoe sales growth in the United States. The firm is opening new stores in Asia and Europe with the hope of sustaining double-digit sales growth abroad over the next few years. Timberland is also extending its apparel line to capitalize on its brand name recognition in footwear.

200 Domain Drive
Stratham, NH 03885
www.timberland.com

Morningstar Grades

Growth [B+]	1998	1999	2000	2001
Revenue %	8.3	6.4	19.0	8.4
Earnings/Share %	24.8	34.9	68.2	-7.3
Book Value/Share %	23.6	8.5	20.7	20.1
Dividends/Share %	NMF	NMF	NMF	NMF

Though Timberland has struggled in 2002, its 12% average annual sales growth over the past five years trounced that of most large shoe companies. Given the firm's market saturation, we expect growth to slow considerably.

Profitability [A+]	1999	2000	2001	TTM
Return on Assets %	15.3	25.6	21.2	16.9
Oper Cash Flow $Mil	138	141	89	169
- Cap Spending $Mil	20	35	22	18
= Free Cash Flow $Mil	118	106	66	151

Timberland is struggling to maintain its excellent margins. Its operating margin has declined from 17% in 2000 and 14% in 2001 to 11% so far in 2002 because of higher leather costs, more advertising, and falling shoe prices.

Financial Health [A+]	1999	2000	2001	09-02
Long-term Debt $Mil	100	—	—	—
Total Equity $Mil	272	317	359	370
Debt/Equity Ratio	0.4	—	—	—

The balance sheet is in fine health, with no long-term debt. Even with stagnating profits and operating cash flow over the past couple of years, free cash flow (operating cash flow less capital expenditures) has been comfortably in the black.

Industry	Investment Style	Stock Type	Sector
Shoes	▦ Mid Core	↗ Classic Growth	Consumer Goods

Competition	Market Cap $Mil	Debt/ Equity	12 Mo Trailing Sales $Mil	Price/Cash Flow	Return On Assets%	Total Return% 1 Yr	3 Yr
Timberland	1,312	—	1,175	7.8	16.9	-4.0	12.9
VF	3,903	—	5,305	—	—	—	—
Columbia Sportswear	1,755	—	813	—	—	—	—

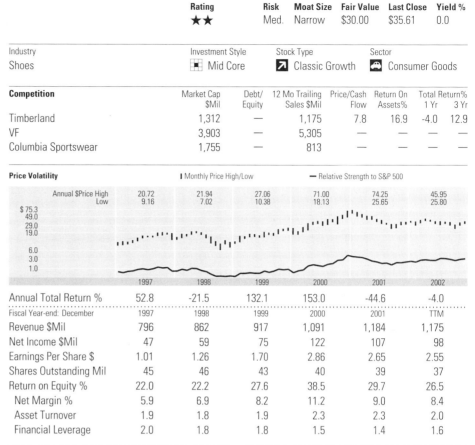

Price Volatility | Monthly Price High/Low — Relative Strength to S&P 500

Annual $Price High Low	20.72 9.16	21.94 7.02	27.06 10.38	71.00 18.13	74.25 25.65	45.95 25.80
	1997	1998	1999	2000	2001	2002

Annual Total Return %	52.8	-21.5	132.1	153.0	-44.6	-4.0
Fiscal Year-end: December	1997	1998	1999	2000	2001	TTM
Revenue $Mil	796	862	917	1,091	1,184	1,175
Net Income $Mil	47	59	75	122	107	98
Earnings Per Share $	1.01	1.26	1.70	2.86	2.65	2.55
Shares Outstanding Mil	45	46	43	40	39	37
Return on Equity %	22.0	22.2	27.6	38.5	29.7	26.5
Net Margin %	5.9	6.9	8.2	11.2	9.0	8.4
Asset Turnover	1.9	1.8	1.9	2.3	2.3	2.0
Financial Leverage	2.0	1.8	1.8	1.5	1.4	1.6

Valuation Ratios	Stock	Rel to Industry	Rel to S&P 500
Price/Earnings	14.0	0.5	0.6
Price/Book	3.5	1.1	1.1
Price/Sales	1.1	1.0	0.6
Price/Cash Flow	7.8	0.7	0.6

Major Fund Holders	% of Fund Assets
Lord Abbett Developing Growth A	2.16
Golden Oak Small Cap Value Instl	1.98
MainStay Small Cap Value A	1.72
Victory Small Company Opportunity G	1.64

Morningstar's Take By Tom Goetzinger, 11-15-2002 Stock Price as of Analysis: $34.34

The game plan for Timberland includes expanding its product line and geographic reach. Though we think these are the right moves, and we like the company's fundamentals, the stock just isn't cheap enough to buy. We'd stay on the sidelines for now.

Timberland isn't the type of company to panic or try something rash when the going gets tough. The firm made its name decades ago by producing high-quality boots and rugged wear, and has never strayed too far from what it knows best. When the brown-shoe boom was at its peak in the early to mid-1990s, Timberland averaged close to 40% annual sales growth; as demand has waned over the past five years, growth has averaged closer to 10% annually.

Timberland's reaction to the slower growth has been to focus on operational efficiency. Over the past five years, sales per employee have jumped 75%. The company has also doubled its inventory turnover and increased its accounts receivable turnover by nearly 50%. These methodical improvements to working capital decreased the short-term cash needed to run the business and allowed the firm to save more. The result is a pristine balance sheet with no long-term debt and a solid shareholder equity base.

Just because it's focusing on efficiency, though,

doesn't mean that Timberland has thrown in the towel on sales growth. Its segment of the footwear market is mature in the United States, where it holds a 20% share, so the company is looking abroad, where its share is around 5%. While domestic sales have been flat to slightly negative so far in 2002, Timberland's international business is growing at a double-digit clip. Its apparel business is also performing nicely, with a 10% increase in sales in the third quarter over the year-ago period.

Nonetheless, Timberland faces a number of challenges that will make sales growth an uphill battle. The U.S. economy continues to sputter, and prices for footwear and apparel are falling. In 2001, the consumer price index for apparel fell 3%, while footwear prices declined 2.5%. These numbers are in line with those of recent years. Plus, the intense competition among retailers for customer dollars has led to more promotions and discounts, further depressing prices. Given these challenges and our expectation of midsingle-digit growth at best for Timberland over the next couple of years, we'd wait for a price near $20 to buy in.

TJX Companies TJX

	Rating	Risk	Moat Size	Fair Value	Last Close	Yield %
	★★	Med.	Narrow	$18.00	$19.52	0.6

Company Profile

TJX is the largest off-price specialty apparel retailer in North America based on sales. It operates 662 T.J. Maxx stores and 536 Marshalls stores in the United States, as well as 117 Winners Apparel Ltd. stores in Canada, and 74 T.K. Maxx stores (in Europe) and 81 HomeGoods stores. The company also operates 25 A.J. Wright off-price family apparel stores. T.J. Maxx stores sell brand-name apparel and accessories, and are located in suburban shopping centers. Marshalls sells apparel, giftware, and accessories. Winners is an off-price family-apparel retailer.

Management

CEO Ted English took over from longtime chief Bernard Cammarata in April 2000. English knows off-price retail from the ground up; he started as a stock boy at Filene's Basement in 1969 and became a buyer there in 1976. He joined TJX in 1983.

Strategy

TJX's size provides the company tremendous leverage to buy closeout merchandise at favorable prices and pass savings on to consumers. It depends on high inventory turnover to offset lean gross margins. TJX hopes to offset slowing growth in its maturing core business through international expansion and investments in new store concepts like HomeGoods and A.J. Wright.

770 Cochituate Road
Framingham, MA 01701

www.tjx.com

Morningstar Grades

Growth [A-]

	1999	2000	2001	2002
Revenue %	7.6	10.6	8.9	11.8
Earnings/Share %	46.0	29.1	13.4	-3.2
Book Value/Share %	13.8	-4.5	19.7	14.5
Dividends/Share %	24.2	17.4	14.8	12.9

The more mature TJX has averaged slower growth than similar retailer Ross Stores. We expect the company's geographic expansion and product line diversification to drive top-line growth.

Profitability [A+]

	2000	2001	2002	TTM
Return on Assets %	18.6	18.4	13.9	14.6
Oper Cash Flow $Mil	595	557	912	1,007
- Cap Spending $Mil	239	257	449	433
= Free Cash Flow $Mil	357	300	463	574

As a discount retailer, TJX earns narrow gross margins. However, strong asset turnover has produced superior returns on assets averaging 26% over the past five years.

Financial Health [A]

	2000	2001	2002	10-02
Long-term Debt $Mil	319	319	702	678
Total Equity $Mil	1,119	1,219	1,341	1,362
Debt/Equity Ratio	0.3	0.3	0.5	0.5

TJX generates healthy cash flow, which covers interest payments several times over. Even with the accelerated rate of spending associated with new store openings, free cash flow (operating cash flow less capital spending) is positive.

Industry	Investment Style	Stock Type	Sector
Clothing Stores	▦ Large Core	↗ Classic Growth	▤ Consumer Services

Competition

	Market Cap $Mil	Debt/ Equity	12 Mo Trailing Sales $Mil	Price/Cash Flow	Return On Assets%	Total Return% 1 Yr	3 Yr
TJX Companies	10,250	0.5	11,684	10.2	14.6	-1.5	27.4
Wal-Mart Stores	223,388	0.5	233,651	18.9	8.0	-11.8	-7.3
Kohl's	18,851	0.4	8,277	31.0	9.8	-20.6	18.3

Price Volatility

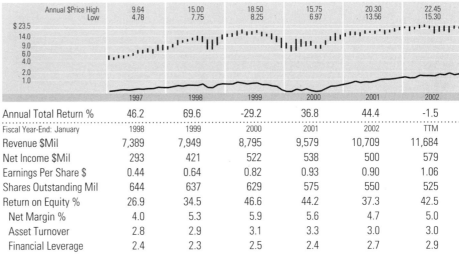

Annual $Price High	9.64	15.00	18.50	15.75	20.30	22.45
Low	4.78	7.75	8.25	6.97	13.56	15.30
	1997	1998	1999	2000	2001	2002
Annual Total Return %	46.2	69.6	-29.2	36.8	44.4	-1.5

Fiscal Year-End: January	1998	1999	2000	2001	2002	TTM
Revenue $Mil	7,389	7,949	8,795	9,579	10,709	11,684
Net Income $Mil	293	421	522	538	500	579
Earnings Per Share $	0.44	0.64	0.82	0.93	0.90	1.06
Shares Outstanding Mil	644	637	629	575	550	525
Return on Equity %	26.9	34.5	46.6	44.2	37.3	42.5
Net Margin %	4.0	5.3	5.9	5.6	4.7	5.0
Asset Turnover	2.8	2.9	3.1	3.3	3.0	3.0
Financial Leverage	2.4	2.3	2.5	2.4	2.7	2.9

Valuation Ratios	Stock	Rel to Industry	Rel to S&P 500
Price/Earnings	18.4	1.0	0.8
Price/Book	7.5	1.9	2.4
Price/Sales	0.9	1.0	0.4
Price/Cash Flow	10.2	1.0	0.8

Major Fund Holders	% of Fund Assets
Sequoia	7.40
Westcore Select	4.69
Neuberger Berman Focus Inv	4.49
Legg Mason American Leading Co Prim	3.94

Morningstar's Take By Roz Bryant, 10-07-2002 Stock Price as of Analysis: $16.58

At more than 3 times the size of rival Ross Stores, TJX is the 800-pound gorilla of off-price retailing. Thanks to the firm's proven off-price retail concept, we think the shares would be very attractive at a 40% discount to our fair value estimate.

TJX's Marmaxx division, which includes the U.S.-based T.J. Maxx and Marshalls chains, contributes more than 80% of the company's sales and has been the backbone of its strong past performance. Spurred by faster inventory turnover and wider margins than Ross Stores, the division averaged a 28% return on assets over the past three years. With increasing economies of scale from more than 1,300 stores, low prices, and a frequently changing merchandise selection, we think TJX can continue to attract value-conscious shoppers and boost margins.

Moreover, we think Marmaxx has expansion opportunities. Having a T.J. Maxx store near a Marshalls brings more traffic to both outlets because the proximity enables shoppers to choose from a wider selection. As only 20% of locations currently enjoy this advantage, we think the mature division is poised for further top-line expansion--albeit at a slower pace than in the past.

In addition, TJX is investing in new retail concepts

to stoke its slowing pace of growth, a smart strategy in our view. Its newest division, A.J. Wright, seeks to undercut discount store prices and helps the company reach lower-income customers. The chain posted 10% same-store sales growth (which measures revenue growth in stores open at least a year) during its most recent quarter, and is on track to expand its store base by 67% by the end of fiscal 2003.

TJX's international expansion has been a mixed bag. Winners--the Canadian version of the Marmaxx concept--has been a success. It has averaged a 30% return on assets and an 11% operating margin over the past three years thanks to a cost-efficient distribution system. Success in Europe has been elusive, though. Shoppers in the United Kingdom and Ireland haven't responded to the firm's T.K. Maxx stores. Despite being the only major European off-price retail presence, the chain's operating margins have remained below 3% over the past three years compared with an average of 9% for the company as a whole.

However, nearly 90% of TJX's revenue comes from the successful Marmaxx and Winners concepts. Given the strengths in these core businesses, we'd happily purchase TJX around $11.

M⌾RNINGSTAR® Stocks 500

Tommy Hilfiger TOM

	Rating	Risk	Moat Size	Fair Value	Last Close	Yield %
	★★★	Med.	None	$9.00	$6.95	0.0

Company Profile

Tommy Hilfiger designs, produces, and sources men's, women's, and children's casual and sports wear, footwear, and accessories, as well as fragrances and sunglasses. Its products are distributed mainly through in-store shops within department stores like Macy's, Bloomingdale's, and Lord & Taylor. Tommy Hilfiger has entered into licensing agreements with companies like Hartmarx, Jockey, Mountain High Hosiery, Aramis, Stride Rite, and Trafalgar. The company operates 100 outlet stores and 11 specialty retail stores in the United States and the United Kingdom.

Management

Hilfiger is looking for a new CEO to replace Joel Horowitz, who has led the company since 1994. Its strategy is likely to remain a little disjointed until new leadership is identified. Founder Tommy Hilfiger recently returned to the post of chairman.

Strategy

Tommy Hilfiger built up its brand with licensing agreements and high-profile celebrity endorsements, but increasing competition and the apparel maker's reliance on department stores is hurting revenue. The company recently announced its intention to abandon its plan for an aggressive retail store roll-out.

850-870 Lai Chi Kok Road   www.hilfiger.com
Kowloon,

Morningstar Grades

Growth [C+]	1999	2000	2001	2002
Revenue %	93.3	20.8	-4.9	-0.2
Earnings/Share %	24.8	-3.2	-20.6	4.2
Book Value/Share %	71.1	14.1	10.4	12.6
Dividends/Share %	NMF	NMF	NMF	NMF

The company's impressive historical growth appears to be a thing of the past, now that the brand has lost some of its popularity. With rivals stealing share in the menswear area, revenue growth has slowed dramatically.

Profitability [B]	2000	2001	2002	TTM
Return on Assets %	7.2	5.6	5.2	-13.4
Oper Cash Flow $Mil	231	191	353	321
- Cap Spending $Mil	152	74	97	97
= Free Cash Flow $Mil	79	117	256	224

Tommy's operating margins were once among the highest in the retail industry at 19%, thanks to the high prices its products commanded. But the margin slid below 10% in fiscal 2002 because of slack demand and lower prices.

Financial Health [A]	2000	2001	2002	09-02
Long-term Debt $Mil	579	529	575	351
Total Equity $Mil	1,278	1,349	1,497	1,152
Debt/Equity Ratio	0.5	0.4	0.4	0.3

Tommy has historically generated strong free cash flow, and inventory controls have been tightened to strengthen operating cash flows in response to slow sales. The firm's using its cash flow to repurchase debt.

	Industry	Investment Style	Stock Type	Sector
	Apparel Makers	⊞ Small Value	→ Slow Growth	🚗 Consumer Goods

Competition

	Market Cap $Mil	Debt/ Equity	12 Mo Trailing Sales $Mil	Price/Cash Flow	Return On Assets%	Total Return% 1 Yr	3 Yr
Tommy Hilfiger	630	0.3	1,887	2.0	-13.4	-49.5	-30.0
Jones Apparel Group	4,572	0.4	4,246	5.2	7.5	6.8	12.4
Polo Ralph Lauren	2,150	—	2,358	—	—	—	—

Price Volatility

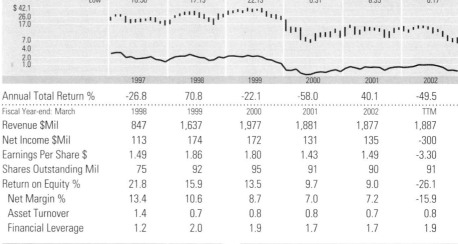

Annual $Price High Low	29.56 16.50	35.19 17.13	41.06 22.13	22.63 6.31	17.25 8.35	16.65 6.17

	1997	1998	1999	2000	2001	2002
Annual Total Return %	-26.8	70.8	-22.1	-58.0	40.1	-49.5

Fiscal Year-end: March	1998	1999	2000	2001	2002	TTM
Revenue $Mil	847	1,637	1,977	1,881	1,877	1,887
Net Income $Mil	113	174	172	131	135	-300
Earnings Per Share $	1.49	1.86	1.80	1.43	1.49	-3.30
Shares Outstanding Mil	75	92	95	91	90	91
Return on Equity %	21.8	15.9	13.5	9.7	9.0	-26.1
Net Margin %	13.4	10.6	8.7	7.0	7.2	-15.9
Asset Turnover	1.4	0.7	0.8	0.8	0.7	0.8
Financial Leverage	1.2	2.0	1.9	1.7	1.7	1.9

Valuation Ratios	Stock	Rel to Industry	Rel to S&P 500
Price/Earnings	NMF	—	—
Price/Book	0.5	0.3	0.2
Price/Sales	0.3	0.4	0.2
Price/Cash Flow	2.0	0.4	0.1

Major Fund Holders	% of Fund Assets
C&B Mid Cap Value	5.13
Capital Management Mid-Cap Instl	2.14
ING Smallcap Value A	2.09
Regions Morgan Keegan Select Agg Gr B	1.79

Morningstar's Take By Roz Bryant, 11-01-2002 Stock Price as of Analysis: $7.30

Tommy Hilfiger brand was once a hit, thanks to slick advertising and trendy designs. But the tide has turned, and we think the company's growth prospects have dimmed significantly. In our opinion, investors should look for a wide margin of safety before investing.

The fashion industry runs hot and cold in the mid- to late 1990s, Hilfiger was hot. Strong demand from young urban males drove sales growth that averaged 52% between 1996 and 1999. But the fever appears to have broken--at least among men. Hilfiger, which sold men's and boys' clothing exclusively at its inception, is now struggling to keep the male demographic interested in its brand. Privately held rivals like FUBU and Phat Farm have stolen much of its men's business, and have enjoyed more customer credibility than Hilfiger in recent years.

Future growth faces challenges, too. Menswear, which constitutes 28% of total sales, is likely to continue to struggle. Plus, its reliance on department stores hitches Hilfiger's growth to a slow-moving wagon. Many of these department store clients are also contending with market share losses (mainly to discounters like Kohl's). In response, many department stores are reserving more floor space for their own high-margin private-label brands, limiting Hilfiger's expansion possibilities.

In light of Hilfiger's failed foray into specialty retailing, we question its ability to find growth opportunities that enhance shareholder value. The firm spent $34 million to open 28 new specialty stores in fiscal 2002. Management has now decided to shutter all but seven of the stores due to poor financial performance. Because we never believed the stores would earn returns in excess of Hilfiger's cost of capital, we were relieved to hear that they would no longer be a drain on the company's resources. Still, the firm would be a lot better off now if management had recognized the stores' impending failure before spending so much to expand.

One bright spot for Hilfiger, however, is its fast-growing women's business, which it launched in the mid-1990s in an effort to begin diversifying its customer base. Sales have averaged better than 50% growth over the past five years, and the division is poised to deliver 34% of total revenue by the end of fiscal 2003.

Nonetheless, we fear that Hilfiger may be left with few attractive growth opportunities. Given our belief that U.S. expansion opportunities are limited, we'd happily leave the shares on the table until they fell to around $4.

Total Fina Elf SA ADR TOT

	Rating	Risk	Moat Size	Fair Value	Last Close	Yield %
	★★	Med.	Narrow	$71.00	$71.50	2.0

Company Profile

Total Fina Elf is one of the largest international companies in the oil patch. The company gained its heft when French firm Total merged with Belgian PetroFina in 1999. The two subsequently merged with fellow French company Elf Aquitaine in 2001. Total Fina Elf boasts 11.0 billion barrel equivalents of reserves, the ability to refine 2.6 million barrels a day, and 16,900 service stations under its three namesake brands. American depositary receipts of Total's shares trade on the NYSE.

Management

An engineer by trade, Thierry Desmarest has been CEO since 1995. He's credited with turning the French oil company into one of the largest international contenders, guiding the firm through several large acquisitions in the process.

Strategy

Total Fina Elf aims to cut costs and improve efficiency via economies of scale following the merger of Total, Petrofina, and Elf over the past three years. It aims to grow by investing in largely untapped areas, like West Africa, that have the potential for high returns. It also has access to resources in the Mideast that are politically untouchable for its rivals.

2, place de la Coupole
Courbevoie, 92400
www.totalfinaelf.com

Morningstar Grades

Growth [A+]	1998	1999	2000	2001
Revenue %	-16.5	73.3	171.6	-8.1
Earnings/Share %	-23.7	19.7	125.9	13.2
Book Value/Share %	1.8	86.5	-41.8	6.9
Dividends/Share %	1.0	17.5	40.4	15.2

Total's revenue growth has been above the industry norm, thanks to a steady stream of acquisitions. However, results remain at the whim of volatile commodity oil prices. Total was far from alone in reporting a sales decline in 2001.

Profitability [B+]	1999	2000	2001	TTM
Return on Assets %	2.1	8.0	8.7	8.7
Oper Cash Flow $Mil	3,634	12,438	10,971	10,971
- Cap Spending $Mil	3,988	6,123	6,703	6,703
= Free Cash Flow $Mil	-354	6,315	4,268	4,268

Total has done a tremendous job of improving profitability over the past two years. Merger-related cost efficiencies have greatly boosted returns on capital employed; even with oil prices down from 2000, Total achieved an ROIC of 12.9% last year.

Financial Health [A]	1999	2000	2001	12-01
Long-term Debt $Mil	10,172	10,858	9,881	9,881
Total Equity $Mil	27,669	30,567	30,028	30,028
Debt/Equity Ratio	0.4	0.4	0.3	0.3

Though slightly more leveraged than some of its competitors', Total's balance sheet is quite healthy, with debt/equity at a slim 0.3. Free cash flow has been robust in the past two years, allowing the company to buy back shares.

Industry	Investment Style	Stock Type	Sector
Oil & Gas	▦ Large Growth	▦ Hard Assets	◊ Energy

Competition	Market Cap $Mil	Debt/ Equity	12 Mo Trailing Sales $Mil	Price/Cash Flow	Return On Assets%	Total Return% 1 Yr	3 Yr
Total Fina Elf SA ADR	100,949	0.3	93,914	9.2	8.7	3.7	5.2
ExxonMobil	235,108	0.1	196,513	12.0	6.7	-8.9	-0.9
BP PLC ADR	152,063	0.2	175,389	6.8	5.7	-9.9	-9.2

Price Volatility

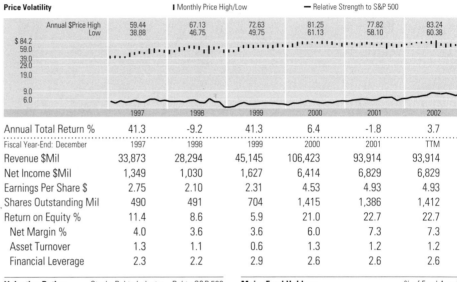

	Monthly Price High/Low		Relative Strength to S&P 500			
Annual $Price High Low	59.44 38.88	67.13 46.75	72.63 49.75	81.25 61.13	77.82 58.10	83.24 60.38
	1997	1998	1999	2000	2001	2002
Annual Total Return %	41.3	-9.2	41.3	6.4	-1.8	3.7

Fiscal Year-End: December	1997	1998	1999	2000	2001	TTM
Revenue $Mil	33,873	28,294	45,145	106,423	93,914	93,914
Net Income $Mil	1,349	1,030	1,627	6,414	6,829	6,829
Earnings Per Share $	2.75	2.10	2.31	4.53	4.93	4.93
Shares Outstanding Mil	490	491	704	1,415	1,386	1,412
Return on Equity %	11.4	8.6	5.9	21.0	22.7	22.7
Net Margin %	4.0	3.6	3.6	6.0	7.3	7.3
Asset Turnover	1.3	1.1	0.6	1.3	1.2	1.2
Financial Leverage	2.3	2.2	2.9	2.6	2.6	2.6

Valuation Ratios	Stock	Rel to Industry	Rel to S&P 500
Price/Earnings	14.5	0.8	0.6
Price/Book	3.4	1.5	1.1
Price/Sales	1.1	1.0	0.5
Price/Cash Flow	9.2	1.4	0.7

Major Fund Holders	% of Fund Assets
Nuveen European Value A	8.75
ICAP Euro Select Equity	7.44
Putnam Global Natural Resources A	6.64
Saratoga International Equity I	5.09

Morningstar's Take By Paul Larson, 10-04-2002 Stock Price as of Analysis: $66.69

We admire Total Fina Elf's impressive financial performance and improved position in the energy industry.

The oil patch has seen dramatic change in recent years, with companies madly merging in order to cut costs and generate economies of scale. Size is an advantage because bigger firms can find, dig up, and refine oil and gas cheaper than the small-fry can. Total Fina Elf is the French result of this trend; three midlevel European energy firms melded to create one of oil's new big five.

Even at this relatively early stage, the mergers that created the European giant have been a raging success. Total has been able to cut billions worth of redundant expenses and institute best practices from its component firms, and the results are evident on the income statement.

In 2001, even though sales were down 8% because of slumping oil prices, Total was able to largely maintain its operating margins and even increase its net profit margins. Return on invested capital has also been quite impressive, more than doubling since the company's premerger days. Last year, Total's ROIC was a robust 12.9%, well above its cost of capital and putting the company into the same rarified air of profitability as ExxonMobil and Royal Dutch.

Total has some characteristics that make it stick out. First, the company has some of the most aggressive production growth targets of its peer group, thanks largely to its investment in West Africa, namely Nigeria and Angola. Total is the most prolific producer in Africa, which holds large but mostly untapped reserves.

Total is also the second-largest producer in the Middle East, a politically volatile but lucrative area. Total has an edge over its Western peers when bidding for emerging projects in the area, since the French are much closer politically to the Arab states than the rest of the West. For instance, Total is now able to start producing in Libya, something no American company can come close to touching.

The oil and gas industry itself is attractive for investment, largely thanks to OPEC. The cartel's goal is to limit supply to keep commodity prices above costs, creating an environment in which the entire oil industry can profit. OPEC's influence remains strong enough that we believe profitability at Total Fina Elf and the rest of the industry will be sustained.

We would be interested in owning Total Fina Elf at the right price.

MORNINGSTAR® Stocks 500

Total System Services TSS

	Rating	Risk	Moat Size	Fair Value	Last Close	Yield %
	★★★	Med.	Wide	$13.00	$13.50	0.5

Company Profile

TSYS is a bank and private-label card-processing company. The company provides card-issuing institutions with a comprehensive online system of data-processing services. These services are provided through a nationwide data communication network. The company provides services like card production, international and domestic electronic clearing, statement preparation, customer-service support, and merchant accounting. Synovus Financial owns an 82% stake in Total System Services.

Management

Chairman and CEO Rick Ussery has led TSYS since the firm was formed from the data-processing department of Synovus in 1983. Synovus controls 81% of TSYS shares.

Strategy

TSYS uses its advanced processing system, TS2, and a focus on customer service to win business from card issuers that process accounts themselves. The flexibility of TS2 permits the company to diversify its business and target new markets, like processing student financial aid loans. TSYS also hopes to continue its international expansion.

1600 First Avenue   www.tsys.com
Columbus, GA 31902-2567

Industry	Investment Style	Stock Type	Sector
Data Processing	▦ Mid Growth	↗ Classic Growth	▤ Business Services

Competition

	Market Cap $Mil	Debt/ Equity	12 Mo Trailing Sales $Mil	Price/Cash Flow	Return On Assets%	Total Return% 1 Yr	3 Yr
Total System Services	2,660	0.0	693	15.8	15.8	-36.0	-5.3
First Data	26,633	0.8	7,118	16.5	4.6	-9.5	14.4
Concord EFS	8,007	0.1	2,045	10.7	9.6	-52.0	8.2

Price Volatility

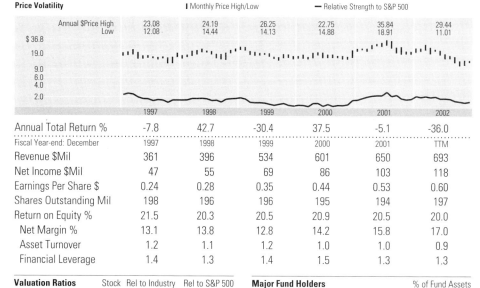

| | Monthly Price High/Low | — Relative Strength to S&P 500 |

	1997	1998	1999	2000	2001	2002
Annual $Price High	23.08	24.19	26.25	22.75	35.84	29.44
Low	12.08	14.44	14.13	14.88	18.91	11.01
Annual Total Return %	-7.8	42.7	-30.4	37.5	-5.1	-36.0

Fiscal Year-end: December	1997	1998	1999	2000	2001	TTM
Revenue $Mil	361	396	534	601	650	693
Net Income $Mil	47	55	69	86	103	118
Earnings Per Share $	0.24	0.28	0.35	0.44	0.53	0.60
Shares Outstanding Mil	198	196	196	195	194	197
Return on Equity %	21.5	20.3	20.5	20.9	20.5	20.0
Net Margin %	13.1	13.8	12.8	14.2	15.8	17.0
Asset Turnover	1.2	1.1	1.2	1.0	1.0	0.9
Financial Leverage	1.4	1.3	1.4	1.5	1.3	1.3

Valuation Ratios

	Stock	Rel to Industry	Rel to S&P 500
Price/Earnings	22.5	1.0	1.0
Price/Book	4.5	0.9	1.4
Price/Sales	3.8	1.1	1.9
Price/Cash Flow	15.8	1.0	1.2

Major Fund Holders

	% of Fund Assets
Fidelity Select Business Serv&Outsrcg	1.50

Morningstar Grades

Growth [A-]	1998	1999	2000	2001
Revenue %	9.6	34.8	12.6	8.2
Earnings/Share %	16.7	25.0	25.7	20.5
Book Value/Share %	23.4	23.6	23.2	22.8
Dividends/Share %	25.0	6.7	18.8	26.3

Solid trends support TSYS' revenue growth. However, because of the saturation of the credit card market, which should limit the growth rates of customers' card accounts, we don't believe the firm can grow as rapidly as before.

Profitability [A+]	1999	2000	2001	TTM
Return on Assets %	14.8	14.2	15.8	15.8
Oper Cash Flow $Mil	135	166	88	168
- Cap Spending $Mil	74	104	86	71
= Free Cash Flow $Mil	61	62	3	97

Like card-processing peers First Data and Concord EFS CEFT, TSYS is highly profitable. We believe the firm should be able to boost its operating margins as it leverages its fixed-cost structure.

Financial Health [A+]	1999	2000	2001	09-02
Long-term Debt $Mil	0	0	0	0
Total Equity $Mil	334	409	501	589
Debt/Equity Ratio	0.0	0.0	0.0	0.0

TSYS doesn't have significant liabilities. Robust operating cash flow and solid free cash flow in most years, even after big technology investments, mean the firm has little to worry about.

Morningstar's Take By Dan Schick, 12-16-2002 Stock Price as of Analysis: $13.46

TSYS boasts a good growth outlook, golden finances, experienced management, and a strong competitive position. We'd buy shares of this topnotch credit card processor at a 30% discount to our fair value estimate.

We believe the fundamental factors that drove TSYS' revenue to an 18%-plus compound annual growth rate during the past 11 years remain mostly in place. The trend for consumers to substitute plastic cards, both debit and credit, in place of cash and checks is not abating. For example, Visa reports that Visa card transactions are increasing at an 11% annual rate in the United States. While TSYS has historically experienced double-digit growth in accounts from current customers, the prevalence of cards causes us to assume slower growth than in the past, although there is no sign yet of a slowdown. Finally, the firm's advanced TS2 processing system should help TSYS increase share and win more business from card issuers that process accounts in-house.

In the early 1990s, TSYS foresaw rapid changes in the processing business and decided incremental improvements to its then-current system were unwise. The TS2 system, a "bet-the-company" project, was the result. The flexibility of the system is a key differentiator and point of attraction for potential clients; for example, it is the only third-party system able to service card accounts on more than one continent. The flexibility also gives TSYS access to markets beyond its origins as a bank card processor. In April, for instance, the company won a contract to process student financial aid loans for the Department of Education.

Thanks to the large investment in TS2 and TSYS' substantial share of the card-processing market, we believe the firm's impressive high-teens returns on capital should persist. Because the processing business is all about scale, the fact that TSYS and main competitor First Data control more than 40% of the card-issuer-processing market all but eliminates the potential for a new competitor to arise. Furthermore, TS2 differentiates TSYS services and allows it to command better pricing than First Data, which seems to have granted TSYS a technological checkmate.

With strong competitive advantages and good returns, TSYS is a buy at the right price, in our opinion.

Data as of 12-31-02

Toys R Us TOY

	Rating ★★★	Risk Med.	Moat Size None	Fair Value $14.00	Last Close $10.00	Yield % 0.0

Company Profile

Toys 'R' Us operates children's specialty retail stores. These stores include 708 U.S. and 494 international toy stores under the name Toys 'R' Us and 196 children's clothing stores under the name Kids 'R' Us. Toys 'R' Us stores sell products like children's and adult toys, games, bicycles and other wheel goods, electronic and video games, and infants' and children's clothing. Most Toys 'R' Us stores are about 46,000 square feet and are freestanding units. Kids 'R' Us feature brand-name children's clothing. It also owns 150 Babies 'R' Us and 40 Imaginarium stores.

Management

John Eyler came on board in 2000 from upscale toy retailer FAO Schwartz. He is the third CEO at Toys 'R' Us since founder Charles Lazarus retired in 1994. Eyler's store remodeling has done well so far, but it's still early.

Strategy

The company has remodeled stores to improve their appeal and merchandise mix. Most stores are now cleaner, and have wider aisles and better lighting; they're also selling more exclusive products, which have wider margins. Also, by bundling Toys 'R' Us stores with Kids 'R' Us and Babies 'R' Us stores in the same shopping centers, the company hopes to provide more selection and convenience.

461 From Road
Paramus, NJ 07652
www.toysrus.com

Morningstar Grades

Growth [D+]	1999	2000	2001	2002
Revenue %	1.2	6.2	-4.5	-2.8
Earnings/Share %	NMF	NMF	64.9	-82.4
Book Value/Share %	-10.6	9.5	5.8	5.7
Dividends/Share %	NMF	NMF	NMF	NMF

There hasn't been much growth--sales have been essentially flat over the past five years. The company is closing underperforming stores and renovating others, so sales growth will depend on healthy same-store sales increases.

Profitability [C]	2000	2001	2002	TTM
Return on Assets %	3.3	5.0	0.8	1.1
Oper Cash Flow $Mil	865	-151	504	386
- Cap Spending $Mil	533	402	705	541
= Free Cash Flow $Mil	332	-553	-201	-155

The operating margin has been halved since 1995, and currently stands around 5%. Not surprisingly, returns on invested capital have also fallen from the midteens to the midsingle digits over that span. We don't expect much of a rebound.

Financial Health [C]	2000	2001	2002	10-02
Long-term Debt $Mil	1,230	1,567	1,816	2,375
Total Equity $Mil	3,680	3,418	3,414	3,696
Debt/Equity Ratio	0.3	0.5	0.5	0.6

Toys 'R' Us is in decent financial shape, now that the heavy lifting is done on store renovation. The firm has $2.3 billion in real estate on the balance sheet, but this is offset by roughly the same amount in long-term debt.

Industry Specialty Retail	Investment Style Mid Value	Stock Type Distressed	Sector Consumer Services

Competition	Market Cap $Mil	Debt/ Equity	12 Mo Trailing Sales $Mil	Price/Cash Flow	Return On Assets%	Total Return% 1 Yr	3 Yr
Toys R Us	2,124	0.6	11,195	5.5	1.1	-51.8	-10.1
Wal-Mart Stores	223,388	0.5	233,651	18.9	8.0	-11.8	-7.3
Target	27,252	1.2	42,275	21.5	5.7	-26.5	-3.9

Price Volatility

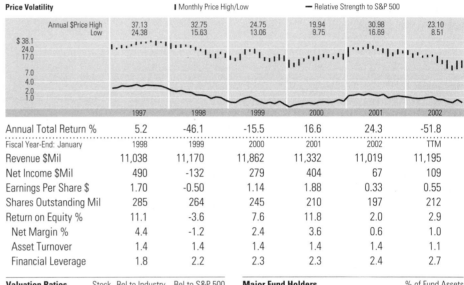

Annual $Price High Low	37.13 24.38	32.75 15.63	24.75 13.06	19.94 9.75	30.98 16.69	23.10 8.51
	1997	1998	1999	2000	2001	2002

Annual Total Return %	5.2	-46.1	-15.5	16.6	24.3	-51.8
Fiscal Year-End: January	1998	1999	2000	2001	2002	TTM
Revenue $Mil	11,038	11,170	11,862	11,332	11,019	11,195
Net Income $Mil	490	-132	279	404	67	109
Earnings Per Share $	1.70	-0.50	1.14	1.88	0.33	0.55
Shares Outstanding Mil	285	264	245	210	197	212
Return on Equity %	11.1	-3.6	7.6	11.8	2.0	2.9
Net Margin %	4.4	-1.2	2.4	3.6	0.6	1.0
Asset Turnover	1.4	1.4	1.4	1.4	1.4	1.1
Financial Leverage	1.8	2.2	2.3	2.3	2.4	2.7

Valuation Ratios	Stock	Rel to Industry	Rel to S&P 500
Price/Earnings	18.2	0.6	0.8
Price/Book	0.6	0.2	0.2
Price/Sales	0.2	0.2	0.1
Price/Cash Flow	5.5	0.4	0.4

Major Fund Holders	% of Fund Assets
ING Midcap Value A	4.08
Oakmark Select I	3.43
Ave Maria Catholic Values	2.85
Janus Adviser Strategic Value	2.81

Morningstar's Take By Tom Goetzinger, 12-20-2002 Stock Price as of Analysis: $11.49

Though visiting Toys 'R' Us may be a child's dream, parents seem to prefer to stop at giants like Wal-Mart and Target. With its market share fading, we'd pass on Toys 'R' Us unless the shares offer at least a 50% discount to our fair value estimate.

Toys 'R' Us has watched its share of the relatively mature $75 billion global toy market wither for the past decade. In the $35 billion U.S. market, the situation is even worse, according to Toy Industry Association surveys. Ten years ago Toys 'R' Us controlled 20% of the market--now, it's 16%.

When will the slide stop? Perhaps never. More consumers are choosing to make their toy purchases at discount stores, which offer low prices and the convenience of all-in-one shopping. Not surprisingly, Wal-Mart is now the leading seller of toys with 19% of the market, up from 13% a decade ago.

It's not just customers who are attracted to the discount chains. Vendors have also been happy to ship more merchandise to the likes of Wal-Mart and Target because those stores capture more of the nonholiday dollars spent on toys. Unless little Jimmy's birthday falls in December, his parents are more likely to pick up a gift on a routine visit to one of the discount chains than make an extra trip to the toy store. Time is more precious with both parents

working in a larger number of families.

To recoup interest, especially among adults, Toys 'R' Us has revamped its store base. The company spent more than $1 billion over the past two years to improve store layout and merchandise selection. The result has been cleaner stores with wider aisles, better displays, and more helpful customer service reps. The more important move, however, has been the push toward exclusive and private-label products. If a child absolutely must have the year's smash-hit toy or video game, and Toys 'R' Us has sole distributor rights, it's sitting in the catbird seat. Moreover, private-label offerings like Animal Planet now represent 20% of stores' merchandise mix, up from 5% in 1999. Toys 'R' Us can earn gross margins of 50%-60% on those items, compared with 10%-15% on a nationally advertised toy.

Still, this is the third time in the past decade that the company has tried to turn things around, and it's swung and missed twice already. In the past five years alone, sales haven't budged and the operating margin has swooned. While we think the right moves are in place, we're skeptical that they're enough for a sustainable turnaround.

500 ©2003 Morningstar, Inc. All rights reserved. Intended for United States residents only, this report is for information purposes and should not be considered a solicitation to buy or sell any security. Visit www.morningstar.com for your research.

MORNINGSTAR® Stocks 500

Transocean RIG

	Rating	Risk	Moat Size	Fair Value	Last Close	Yield %
	★	Med.	Narrow	$18.00	$23.20	0.3

Company Profile

Transocean is the largest underwater drilling company in the world. The company has 160 mobile offshore drilling units that include ships, jack-up rigs, and barges. Its rigs are used on a contract basis to drill and maintain wells. The current incarnation of the firm was formed by several large mergers; its predecessor companies include Sonat Offshore, Norwegian firm Transocean ASA, Schlumberger spin-off Sedco Forex, and American firm R&B Falcon. Transocean has its principal executive offices in Houston, but it's incorporated in the tax-friendly Cayman Islands.

Management

CEO Michael Talbert heads Transocean. Talbert was previously president of two predecessor companies, Transocean Offshore and Sonat. Current management has been key in executing the numerous mergers that created today's Transocean.

Strategy

In recent years, Transocean has been an industry consolidator, becoming the largest offshore driller in the process. The acquisition binge appears over, as the company is now planning on shedding some of its underperforming assets to focus on servicing the deep-water market. The goal is to increase profitability and reduce debt.

4 Greenway Plaza   www.deepwater.com
Houston, TX 77046

Morningstar Grades

Growth [A+]	1998	1999	2000	2001
Revenue %	22.3	-40.6	89.7	129.4
Earnings/Share %	31.1	-83.0	-3.8	56.9
Book Value/Share %	55.4	591.9	-47.3	83.7
Dividends/Share %	NMF	NMF	NMF	0.0

Transocean has roughly quadrupled its size in the past two years, thanks to mergers. But with asset sales and spin-offs, significant contraction is on the horizon. Internal sales growth over the long term should be in the high single digits.

Profitability [B+]	1999	2000	2001	TTM
Return on Assets %	0.9	1.7	1.5	-5.8
Oper Cash Flow $Mil	241	197	567	901
- Cap Spending $Mil	537	575	506	178
= Free Cash Flow $Mil	-296	-377	61	723

Transocean generated a paltry 3.2% return on its assets in 2001, even though it was a fairly good year in oil services. Profitability should improve as Transocean puts the merger-related turbulence and charges behind it.

Financial Health [A-]	1999	2000	2001	09-02
Long-term Debt $Mil	1,188	1,430	4,539	3,781
Total Equity $Mil	3,910	4,004	10,910	9,953
Debt/Equity Ratio	0.3	0.4	0.4	0.4

Transocean's debt is manageable, with debt of $4.9 billion against a tangible asset base of $9.8 billion. EBITDA covers interest expense 5 times. Reduced capital expenditures and proceeds from the proposed spin-off will also help pare debt.

	Industry	Investment Style	Stock Type	Sector
	Oil & Gas Services	▦ Mid Growth	▦ Hard Assets	◆ Energy

Competition	Market Cap $Mil	Debt/ Equity	12 Mo Trailing Sales $Mil	Price/Cash Flow	Return On Assets%	Total Return% 1 Yr	3 Yr
Transocean	7,406	0.4	2,757	8.2	-5.8	-31.3	-8.9
GlobalSantaFe	5,687	—	1,877	—	—	—	—
Noble	4,640	—	978	—	—	—	—

Price Volatility   ▌ Monthly Price High/Low   — Relative Strength to S&P 500

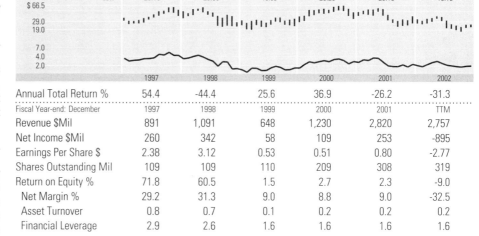

Annual $Price High / Low	60.50 / 26.13	59.94 / 23.00	36.50 / 19.63	65.50 / 29.25	57.64 / 23.10	39.33 / 18.10

	1997	1998	1999	2000	2001	2002
Annual Total Return %	54.4	-44.4	25.6	36.9	-26.2	-31.3
Fiscal Year-end: December	1997	1998	1999	2000	2001	TTM
Revenue $Mil	891	1,091	648	1,230	2,820	2,757
Net Income $Mil	260	342	58	109	253	-895
Earnings Per Share $	2.38	3.12	0.53	0.51	0.80	-2.77
Shares Outstanding Mil	109	109	110	209	308	319
Return on Equity %	71.8	60.5	1.5	2.7	2.3	-9.0
Net Margin %	29.2	31.3	9.0	8.8	9.0	-32.5
Asset Turnover	0.8	0.7	0.1	0.2	0.2	0.2
Financial Leverage	2.9	2.6	1.6	1.6	1.6	1.6

Valuation Ratios	Stock	Rel to Industry	Rel to S&P 500
Price/Earnings	NMF	—	—
Price/Book	0.7	0.3	0.2
Price/Sales	2.7	1.3	1.3
Price/Cash Flow	8.2	0.7	0.6

Major Fund Holders	% of Fund Assets
Rydex Energy Services Inv	8.54
Dean Large Cap Value A	4.23
Morgan Stanley Total Return B	4.21
Seligman Large Cap Value A	3.47

Morningstar's Take By Paul Larson, 12-18-2002 Stock Price as of Analysis: $24.23

We are not impressed with Transocean's financials and would not buy the stock unless it traded at least 30% below our fair value estimate.

One of the reasons we are not attracted to the stock is the company's low returns. Transocean has done an excellent job of destroying economic and shareholder value. Over the past decade, it has achieved a return on invested capital above its cost of capital in only one year. Excluding goodwill, its return on invested capital last year was a mere--and typical--3.6%. Poor profitability is one reason the stock sits at the same level it did in 1996.

Transocean is not alone in generating subpar returns. Nearly all of its peers make similarly anemic profits, which we take as proof that this is a highly competitive industry. We've given Transocean a narrow moat rating because it's the largest in the offshore drilling industry and should enjoy some minor cost and technological advantages, but even that rating is tenuous, given the nature of the industry.

Profitability will not improve when the books are closed on 2002. The company has already written off more than $1 billion of goodwill this year and plans on writing off another $5 billion before year-end. While these write-offs will not affect cash,

management clearly overpaid for past acquisitions, destroying value in the process.

We're also puzzled as to why Transocean is planning to spin off its shallow-water and inland drilling business. The company purchased these assets less than two years ago at a cyclical peak and is now trying to sell them at a cyclical low. We understand why Transocean wants to focus on deep-water drilling, where it is most profitable and has the greatest edge. But we wonder why, then, it went through the expensive merger with R&B Falcon. Perhaps management is merely admitting past mistakes, but those mistakes have been costly.

About the only bright spot we can see is that Transocean has done an excellent job of slashing capital expenditures to generate free cash flow this year. This cash has gone to reduce debt. Still, between the low returns and high cyclicality, we would not pay a premium valuation for Transocean shares. Unless the stock falls significantly below our fair value estimate, we see no reason to buy.

Data as of 12-31-02

Travelers Property Casualty TAP.A

	Rating	Risk	Moat Size	Fair Value	Last Close	Yield %
	★★★	Med.	None	$18.00	$14.65	0.0

Company Profile

Travelers offers personal and commercial property-casualty insurance through a network of 7,600 independent agencies. The firm's commercial lines, which include workers' compensation, disability, property, liability, specialty lines, surety bonds, and marine, contributed 58% of total net premiums written in 2001 and make Travelers the third-largest commercial insurer in the United States. Personal lines like homeowners and auto insurance generated 42% of 2001 net premiums written.

Management

Robert Lipp, Travelers' chairman and CEO, served in the same positions from 1993 to 2000. Several members of the executive team are Travelers veterans.

Strategy

Travelers will chase market share in the current favorable pricing environment by pitching its solid balance sheet along with its policy prices. Prospective policyholders are increasingly as concerned with an insurer's claims-paying ability as they are with the cost of the policy.

1 Tower Square   www.travelerspc.com
Hartford, CT 06183

Industry	Investment Style	Stock Type	Sector
Insurance (Property)	▦ Large Growth	→ Slow Growth	$ Financial Services

Competition

	Market Cap $Mil	Debt/ Equity	12 Mo Trailing Sales $Mil	Price/Cash Flow	Return On Assets%	Total Return% 1 Yr	3 Yr
Travelers Property Casualty	14,704	—	13,294	—	1.8	—	—
American International Gr	150,907	—	66,823	—	1.4	-26.9	-4.0
Berkshire Hathaway B	111,526	—	39,133	—	1.9	-4.0	12.5

Price Volatility

Monthly Price High/Low — Relative Strength to S&P 500

Annual $Price High 21.04 Low 11.75

$22.0 / 13.0 / 7.0 / 5.0 / 3.0 / 2.0

	1997	1998	1999	2000	2001	2002
Annual Total Return %	—	—	—	—	—	—

Fiscal Year-End: December	1997	1998	1999	2000	2001	TTM
Revenue $Mil	9,927	10,454	10,573	11,071	12,231	13,294
Net Income $Mil	1,034	1,104	1,024	1,312	1,065	1,069
Earnings Per Share $	—	—	—	—	—	—
Shares Outstanding Mil	—	—	—	—	—	1,004
Return on Equity %	15.7	19.1	15.9	14.2	10.0	9.6
Net Margin %	10.4	10.6	9.7	11.9	8.7	8.0
Asset Turnover	0.2	0.2	0.2	0.2	0.2	0.2
Financial Leverage	7.8	9.0	7.9	5.8	5.4	5.3

Valuation Ratios	Stock	Rel to Industry	Rel to S&P 500
Price/Earnings	—	—	—
Price/Book	1.3	0.7	0.4
Price/Sales	1.1	0.5	0.6
Price/Cash Flow	—	—	—

Major Fund Holders	% of Fund Assets
Fidelity Select Insurance	5.61
ICAP Select Equity	4.70
Cambiar Opportunity Inst	3.37
Schroder U.S. Large Cap Equity Inv	2.79

Morningstar Grades

Growth [B]	1998	1999	2000	2001
Revenue %	5.3	1.1	4.7	10.5
Earnings/Share %	NMF	NMF	NMF	NMF
Book Value/Share %	—	—	—	—
Dividends/Share %	NMF	NMF	NMF	NMF

Written premiums jumped 16% in the third quarter after growing in the midsingle digits in the late 1990s. Stronger demand for insurance after 9/11 and higher pricing should drive double-digit written premium gains at least through 2003.

Profitability [A]	1999	2000	2001	TTM
Return on Assets %	2.0	2.4	1.8	1.8
Oper Cash Flow $Mil	471	664	1,219	—
- Cap Spending $Mil	—	—	—	—
= Free Cash Flow $Mil	—	—	—	—

Heavy losses in the third quarter of 2001 pummeled Travelers' combined ratio, driving return on equity to an uncharacteristically low 10% in 2001. An average ROE in the midteens since 1997, however, shows that Travelers is generally very profitable.

Financial Health [A+]	1999	2000	2001	09-02
Long-term Debt $Mil	—	—	—	—
Total Equity $Mil	6,440	9,214	10,686	11,160
Debt/Equity Ratio	—	—	—	—

Travelers possesses disciplined underwriting and a healthy balance sheet--two traits critical for an insurer.

Morningstar's Take By Aaron Westrate, 12-17-2002 Stock Price as of Analysis: $15.24

Travelers is an above-average insurer, but we'd need a 40% discount to our fair value estimate--or a stock price of about $11--before we'd be interested. One of the best indicators of a standout insurer is a high return on equity, and on this score, Travelers is impressive. Travelers' average annual 14.4% ROE since 1997 has exceeded both the property-casualty industry's 6.9% and the 10.5% of four close rivals. Travelers' advantages are a low-cost operating platform and sharp underwriting skills. Loss trends across the property-casualty industry have deteriorated each year from 73% of earned premiums in 1997 to 83% in 2001. But Travelers' highest-loss year in the same period was 75%, from a base of 72% in 1997.

Travelers' double A rating has become another competitive advantage as independent agencies (Travelers' distribution channel) have begun directing more business to insurers with the strongest financial profiles, not just those offering the cheapest policies. The firm boasts a strong capital position and an investment portfolio exceeding $35 billion, of which all but 8% is composed of cash or fixed-income securities with an average credit quality of double A.

An ominous trend among property-casualty insurers has been the inexorable rise of asbestos claims, surprising at every turn nearly all insurers. In May 2002, three dozen insurers agreed to a $2.7 billion settlement for all pending and future asbestos claims against PPG Industries. Travelers' estimated share of the settlement amounts to about $370 million. Our main concern with this settlement is that the probable cost is 25% of Travelers' funds available to pay asbestos claims. Yet we do not believe this case represents merely one fourth of the firm's total asbestos exposure, raising the possibility that future reserve hikes will be required.

The primary way to counter the threat of runaway claims is to raise rates, and we believe premium hikes will be sustainable for at least the next year, primarily because rates in the 1990s were terribly inadequate. That said, we suspect that inadequate premiums will be the norm once again by 2004. The property-casualty business is filled with large rivals who have proved unable to resist the siren song of growth by lowering premiums in the past.

We think Travelers will go far, since it is an excellent insurer. But we won't recommend buying the shares until we are confident that asbestos claims won't continue to spiral out of control.

502 ©2003 Morningstar, Inc. All rights reserved. Intended for United States residents only, this report is for information purposes and should not be considered a solicitation to buy or sell any security. Visit www.morningstar.com for your research.

MORNINGSTAR® Stocks 500

Tribune TRB

	Rating	Risk	Moat Size	Fair Value	Last Close	Yield %
	★★★	Low	Narrow	$42.00	$45.46	1.0

Company Profile

Tribune provides information and entertainment services. Its newspapers include the Chicago Tribune, Los Angeles Times, and Newsday. The company also operates 22 network-affiliated television stations and 4 radio stations. In addition, Tribune produces and syndicates television and radio programming. The company owns the Chicago Cubs baseball team, has a stake in the WB television network, and acquired Times Mirror in June 2000.

Management

Dennis FitzSimons, a 20-year company veteran and product of the broadcasting group, was recently named to the CEO position. He was previously both COO and president. Outgoing CEO John Madigan will continue as board chairman until the end of 2003.

Strategy

Tribune is trying to gain scale in its two primary businesses: newspaper publishing and television broadcasting, with a particular emphasis now on the broadcasting segment. While this will only increase the company's exposure to advertising, it should also allow it to reduce expenses and boost profitability. Much of the expansion is being fueled by acquisition or swapping of assets.

435 North Michigan Avenue
Chicago, IL 60611   www.tribune.com

Morningstar Grades

Growth [B]	1998	1999	2000	2001
Revenue %	6.3	10.3	69.4	6.1
Earnings/Share %	7.1	270.7	-87.4	-60.0
Book Value/Share %	37.6	36.3	57.3	-8.3
Dividends/Share %	6.3	5.9	11.1	10.0

We think that the company has above-average growth prospects relative to peers, due to strong prospects for its WB stations and the company's presence in large markets like New York City, Chicago, and L.A.

Profitability [B]	1999	2000	2001	TTM
Return on Assets %	16.6	1.4	0.6	1.3
Oper Cash Flow $Mil	616	1,131	754	910
- Cap Spending $Mil	126	302	266	209
= Free Cash Flow $Mil	490	829	487	701

Historically, the company has had above-average profit margins, although these have taken a hit because of an advertising slump. We expect margins to recover in the next year or so, as the economy gets back on track.

Financial Health [B]	1999	2000	2001	09-02
Long-term Debt $Mil	2,694	4,007	3,685	3,378
Total Equity $Mil	3,178	5,513	5,294	5,516
Debt/Equity Ratio	0.8	0.7	0.7	0.6

The company has increased leverage to fund some important acquisitions. We're not too concerned at present, but we are watching the balance sheet closely; management has said that it is willing to sacrifice its credit rating in order to do deals.

Industry	Investment Style	Stock Type	Sector
Media Conglomerates	▦ Large Growth	❖ Spec. Growth	🎙 Media

Competition

	Market Cap $Mil	Debt/ Equity	12 Mo Trailing Sales $Mil	Price/Cash Flow	Return On Assets%	Total Return% 1 Yr	3 Yr
Tribune	13,856	0.6	5,273	15.2	1.3	22.7	-2.8
Gannett	19,190	0.7	6,354	16.2	8.1	8.1	-1.1
Washington Post	7,018	0.2	2,522	15.3	3.5	40.5	12.8

Price Volatility

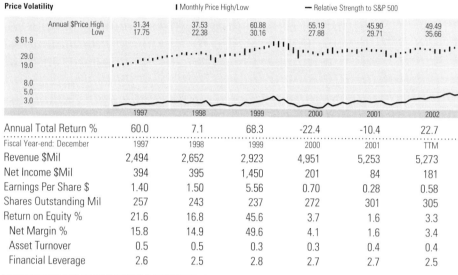

| | Monthly Price High/Low | — Relative Strength to S&P 500 |

	1997	1998	1999	2000	2001	2002
Annual $Price High	31.34	37.53	60.88	55.19	45.90	49.49
Low	17.75	22.38	30.16	27.88	29.71	35.66
Annual Total Return %	60.0	7.1	68.3	-22.4	-10.4	22.7

Fiscal Year-end: December	1997	1998	1999	2000	2001	TTM
Revenue $Mil	2,494	2,652	2,923	4,951	5,253	5,273
Net Income $Mil	394	395	1,450	201	84	181
Earnings Per Share $	1.40	1.50	5.56	0.70	0.28	0.58
Shares Outstanding Mil	257	243	237	272	301	305
Return on Equity %	21.6	16.8	45.6	3.7	1.6	3.3
Net Margin %	15.8	14.9	49.6	4.1	1.6	3.4
Asset Turnover	0.5	0.5	0.3	0.3	0.4	0.4
Financial Leverage	2.6	2.5	2.8	2.7	2.7	2.5

Valuation Ratios	Stock	Rel to Industry	Rel to S&P 500
Price/Earnings	78.4	2.9	3.3
Price/Book	2.5	1.8	0.8
Price/Sales	2.6	1.2	1.3
Price/Cash Flow	15.2	1.0	1.2

Major Fund Holders	% of Fund Assets
Torray	5.82
Torray Institutional	5.14
Pioneer Core Equity A	3.88
SSgA Aggressive Equity	3.40

Morningstar's Take By Jonathan Schrader, 12-10-2002 Stock Price as of Analysis: $45.04

Tribune has quickly become a major player in the media world. We'd buy the stock if it dropped below $30.

Tribune has a strong position in the most important media markets in the U.S.: New York City, Los Angeles, and Chicago. In each of these cities, Tribune owns both a major newspaper--Newsday, Times, and Tribune, respectively--and a television station. This cross-ownership allows the company to offer customized advertising packages while capturing a bigger share of the largest advertising markets in the country.

The company isn't stopping there. Tribune would like to increase its presence in the high-margin broadcasting market. First, the company would like to fill in the gaps in its system--especially in the top ten markets. Tribune would also like to add more stations in some existing markets so it could benefit from greater scale and shared resources. This would lead to even higher margins.

We like the company's strategy and believe that it will lead to higher future margins and generous free cash flow, as television stations have the potential to be even more profitable than newspaper publishing. We do see a couple of problems, though.

Most media companies are on the hunt for

television stations because of their excellent economics. This could easily drive up the price of these limited assets, and the high purchase prices may prompt Tribune to take on more debt than is prudent to finance its growth efforts. The firm's debt was recently downgraded by Moody's, but management doesn't seem to be bothered. Indeed, Tribune has said that it is willing to risk its credit rating in order to fund acquisitions. We will be watching the prices that the company pays and the impact on the balance sheet and cash flow.

As long as Tribune doesn't pay too dearly for acquisitions, its prospects are bright. We suspect that there are others out there who feel the same way, making Tribune an excellent takeover target. If one of the global media empires opted to bid for Tribune, the price would likely be much higher than our fair value, reflecting a control premium. However, we're making our buy decision based upon our estimate of the present value of the firm's future cash flows. If the stock were to trade at a 30% discount to our $42 estimate, then we'd be buying.

Triquint Semiconductor TQNT

	Rating	Risk	Moat Size	Fair Value	Last Close	Yield %
	★★★	High	None	$8.00	$4.24	0.0

Company Profile

Triquint Semiconductor designs and manufactures various analog and mixed-signal integrated circuits. The firm uses its proprietary gallium arsenide technology, which is intended to enable its products to overcome the performance barriers of silicon devices. Triquint's products are used in various industries, including wireless telecom, fiber-optic telecom, and military applications. Customers include Ericsson, Nokia, and Raytheon. Triquint acquired Sawtek in 2001.

Management

Steven Sharp has been president and CEO since 1991; he recently announced he will reduce his role with the firm over the next year. As of the last proxy statement (April 2002), management and directors closely held 3% of the firm.

Strategy

Triquint leverages its technology into several communication markets like wireless, telecom, and data-networking equipment. The firm uses specialized manufacturing techniques to produce both standardized and custom high-performance chips. Because Triquint has its own production facilities, it can offer manufacturing services to other chipmakers.

2300 N.E. Brookwood Parkway   www.tqs.com
Hillsboro, OR 97124

Morningstar Grades

Growth [C]	1998	1999	2000	2001
Revenue %	33.8	26.1	74.5	-27.3
Earnings/Share %	-25.9	125.0	144.4	NMF
Book Value/Share %	12.9	78.9	32.2	11.2
Dividends/Share %	NMF	NMF	NMF	NMF

Acquisitions (like Sawtek) mask the firm's underperformance relative to wireless peers like RF Micro. After sales rose 137% in 1999 and 75% in 2000, they declined 27% in 2001 and will probably fall around 20% this year.

Profitability [A-]	1999	2000	2001	TTM
Return on Assets %	10.5	13.9	-2.6	-6.9
Oper Cash Flow $Mil	77	167	147	40
- Cap Spending $Mil	27	195	109	12
= Free Cash Flow $Mil	50	-28	38	28

Operating margins peaked at 37% in 2000, but have since fallen to around break-even as a result of lower sales and acquisitions. But operating margins weren't great before their peak, ranging from below 0% into the single digits.

Financial Health [A-]	1999	2000	2001	09-02
Long-term Debt $Mil	—	347	297	269
Total Equity $Mil	460	674	683	682
Debt/Equity Ratio	—	0.5	0.4	0.4

The balance sheet is in very good shape: Cash and investments of roughly $450 million cover all of Triquint's liabilities. Moreover, the firm generated positive cash flow in 2001.

Industry	Investment Style	Stock Type	Sector
Semiconductors	▦ Small Core	➜ Slow Growth	▣ Hardware

Competition	Market Cap $Mil	Debt/ Equity	12 Mo Trailing Sales $Mil	Price/Cash Flow	Return On Assets%	Total Return% 1 Yr	3 Yr
Triquint Semiconductor	562	0.4	260	13.9	-6.9	-65.4	-46.7
RF Micro Devices	1,239	0.7	425	19.4	2.0	-61.9	-42.2
Vitesse Semiconductor	435	—	162	—	—		

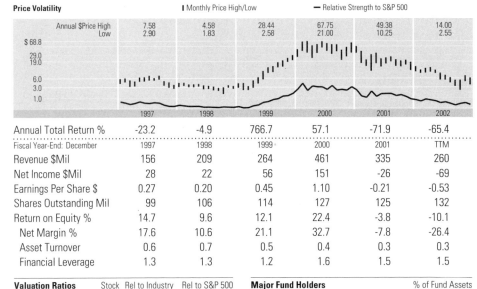

Price Volatility   I Monthly Price High/Low   — Relative Strength to S&P 500

Annual $Price High Low	7.58 2.90	4.58 1.83	28.44 2.58	67.75 21.00	49.38 10.25	14.00 2.55
	1997	1998	1999	2000	2001	2002

Annual Total Return %	-23.2	-4.9	766.7	57.1	-71.9	-65.4

Fiscal Year-End: December	1997	1998	1999	2000	2001	TTM
Revenue $Mil	156	209	264	461	335	260
Net Income $Mil	28	22	56	151	-26	-69
Earnings Per Share $	0.27	0.20	0.45	1.10	-0.21	-0.53
Shares Outstanding Mil	99	106	114	127	125	132
Return on Equity %	14.7	9.6	12.1	22.4	-3.8	-10.1
Net Margin %	17.6	10.6	21.1	32.7	-7.8	-26.4
Asset Turnover	0.6	0.7	0.5	0.4	0.3	0.3
Financial Leverage	1.3	1.3	1.2	1.6	1.5	1.5

Valuation Ratios	Stock	Rel to Industry	Rel to S&P 500
Price/Earnings	NMF	—	—
Price/Book	0.8	0.3	0.3
Price/Sales	2.2	0.6	1.1
Price/Cash Flow	13.9	1.2	1.1

Major Fund Holders	% of Fund Assets
IDEX Transamerica Growth Opport A	2.96
Choice Focus Fund	2.81
Transamerica Premier Growth Opp Inv	2.66
Choice Long-Short A	2.23

Morningstar's Take   By Jeremy Lopez, 12-17-2002   Stock Price as of Analysis: $4.59

While Triquint may not deliver much more than average performance, the market continues to take a much more pessimistic view.

Triquint is a niche player by virtue of its focus on less-used manufacturing processes like gallium arsenide. These processes tend to yield high-performance chips with certain physical attributes that make them particularly useful in various high-tech applications, like wireless, satellite, military, and telecom. Although the obscurity of the technology can lead to high entry barriers, these processes typically generate low margins, mostly because of high production costs and limited chip volume.

A look at Triquint's markets partially explains why the firm's recent financial performance has been disappointing. Although sales into the telecom infrastructure and satellite markets have been awful, Triquint's poor performance is primarily due to problems in the wireless sector, its largest end market. Because Triquint was late in developing power amplifier module products, it has lost share to firms like RF Micro Devices. Also, the acquisition of Sawtek has been disappointing; its products are losing market share. Triquint has not benefited much from demand in the wireless sector, one of the few bright spots in tech.

We still think Triquint can be a decent performer, but we don't expect a quick turnaround. The firm has been addressing some competitive issues by making a few small acquisitions and getting its products designed into new phones, but our sense is that it will take time for wireless sales to rebound, and no one knows when the state of telecom will improve.

Triquint is struggling with competitive issues, as well as tough industry conditions. But even in an ideal world, the company has only average growth and margin prospects. Lacking strong fundamentals, Triquint would need to get really cheap--roughly 50% below our fair value estimate--before we'd get excited about buying.

M◑RNINGSTAR® Stocks 500

Tuesday Morning TUES

	Rating	Risk	Moat Size	Fair Value	Last Close	Yield %
	★★★	High	Narrow	$26.00	$17.10	0.0

Company Profile

Tuesday Morning operates 431 deep-discount retail stores in 38 states under the Tuesday Morning name. The company purchases close-out merchandise at prices generally ranging from 10% to 50% of normal wholesale prices and sells the merchandise at prices that are 50% to 80% lower than retail prices charged by department and specialty stores. Merchandise includes dinnerware; silver serving pieces; gourmet housewares; bathroom, bedroom, and kitchen accessories and linens; luggage; toys; stationery; and silk pants.

Management

Tuesday Morning is controlled by Madison Dearborn Partners, an investment firm that took the retailer private in 1997 (and public again later) and that still owns more than 50% of the outstanding stock. Three of the six board members are from Madison.

Strategy

Tuesday Morning differentiates itself from other discounters by offering very-high-end luxury goods that are unavailable elsewhere except at full price. The firm keeps costs low by keeping stores open only about 250 days a year, and generates repeat customer traffic by heavily promoting several annual "sales events."

14621 Inwood Road   www.tuesdaymorning.com
Addison, TX 75001

Morningstar Grades

Growth [B]

	1998	1999	2000	2001
Revenue %	21.0	23.4	20.0	9.5
Earnings/Share %	NMF	NMF	NMF	24.6
Book Value/Share %	—	—	NMF	NMF
Dividends/Share %	NMF	NMF	NMF	NMF

Sales growth has generally been quite good, though the firm deliberately slowed down in 2001 as it revamped its distribution system. We're looking for midteen total sales growth and 4% same-store sales growth over the next few years.

Profitability [B]

	1999	2000	2001	TTM
Return on Assets %	8.4	10.1	11.9	14.2
Oper Cash Flow $Mil	8	2	91	76
- Cap Spending $Mil	14	11	10	28
= Free Cash Flow $Mil	-6	-9	82	48

Tuesday Morning's gross margins of 34% are very high for a retailer. Net margins have been depressed by high interest costs. We believe they will expand from their current 6% level to 7% over the next few years.

Financial Health [B]

	1999	2000	2001	09-02
Long-term Debt $Mil	162	166	113	108
Total Equity $Mil	-36	-11	20	36
Debt/Equity Ratio	ELB	ELB	5.6	3.0

This is the firm's weakest area. Tuesday Morning was taken private in 1997 and subsequently refloated publicly, which left it with a lot of debt. Interest coverage is about 3 times, which is tolerable but not great.

Industry	Investment Style	Stock Type	Sector
Department Stores	▦ Small Growth	↗ Classic Growth	🖬 Consumer Services

Competition

	Market Cap $Mil	Debt/ Equity	12 Mo Trailing Sales $Mil	Price/Cash Flow	Return On Assets%	Total Return% 1 Yr	3 Yr
Tuesday Morning	686	3.0	705	9.0	14.2	-5.5	0.2
Bed Bath & Beyond	10,104	—	3,318	28.6	13.7	1.9	30.7
Pier 1 Imports	1,748	0.0	1,661	10.5	13.4	10.3	48.5

Price Volatility

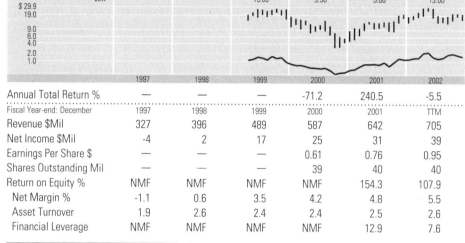

Annual $Price High / Low				26.75 / 15.00	18.22 / 3.50	20.80 / 5.06	28.88 / 13.00

	1997	1998	1999	2000	2001	TTM
Annual Total Return %	—	—	—	-71.2	240.5	-5.5
Fiscal Year-end: December	1997	1998	1999	2000	2001	TTM
Revenue $Mil	327	396	489	587	642	705
Net Income $Mil	-4	2	17	25	31	39
Earnings Per Share $	—	—	—	0.61	0.76	0.95
Shares Outstanding Mil	—	—	—	39	40	40
Return on Equity %	NMF	NMF	NMF	NMF	154.3	107.9
Net Margin %	-1.1	0.6	3.5	4.2	4.8	5.5
Asset Turnover	1.9	2.6	2.4	2.4	2.5	2.6
Financial Leverage	NMF	NMF	NMF	NMF	12.9	7.6

Valuation Ratios	Stock	Rel to Industry	Rel to S&P 500
Price/Earnings	18.0	1.1	0.8
Price/Book	19.0	15.6	6.0
Price/Sales	1.0	3.4	0.5
Price/Cash Flow	9.0	2.3	0.7

Major Fund Holders	% of Fund Assets
Monterey PIA Equity	3.80
Westcore Small-Cap Growth	2.99
Payden Small Cap Leaders R	1.90
Pioneer Small Company A	1.68

Morningstar's Take By Pat Dorsey, 12-15-2002 Stock Price as of Analysis: $19.49

Tuesday Morning has unique competitive advantages, and we think the stock would be worth buying at the right price.

The discount retailer sells closeout lots of high-end gifts and home furnishings from well-known brands like Wedgwood and Lalique. Brands of this quality are pretty difficult for a discounter to acquire; luxury-goods manufacturers hate to have their brand cheapened by selling through this channel. Tuesday Morning can get this type of merchandise when others can't because its business model minimizes the chance that goods will molder on the shelves.

By staying open only 250 days of the year for periodic "sales events" that last a few weeks, and by heavily promoting multiple "grand openings," Tuesday Morning is able to lure customers to its stores frequently. This gets merchandise off the shelves fast--about 40% of each event's total sales occur during the first five days, and the best merchandise is often gone on the first day. Speedy selling has also helped the firm's buyers forge strong relationships with suppliers that would be tough for competitors to replicate.

Tuesday Morning is very profitable as retailers go, with gross margins of around 34%. The high quality of the goods means high selling prices, while the

quick inventory turns mean goods are sold without multiple markdowns. Low costs also help. Only opening stores occasionally saves a lot of money on salaries, since part-time employees aren't paid when the stores aren't open. By locating stores in out-of-the-way locations, rent costs are minimized.

Despite these advantages, we'd need a significant discount to our fair value estimate to buy the stock. First, Tuesday Morning is quite leveraged for a retailer. Interest coverage is still reasonable, but its level of debt leverage decreases the company's margin of operational safety should it stumble.

Second, Tuesday Morning is still majority-controlled by Madison Dearborn, an investment firm that helped take the firm private years ago. So far Madison has done a good job, but minority shareholders wouldn't have much recourse if Madison took the firm in the wrong direction. Finally, Tuesday Morning--like many retailers--makes most of its money in the fourth quarter. A poor merchandise mix or distribution snafu near the holidays would disproportionately affect earnings, adding to the stock's risk level.

With these risks in mind, we'd wait until the shares hit $13 before considering them.

Tyco International TYC

	Rating	Risk	Moat Size	Fair Value	Last Close	Yield %
	★★★	High	None	$25.00	$17.08	0.3

Company Profile

Tyco International is a conglomerate with core annual sales of about $32 billion. It operates diverse businesses reported in four operating segments: electronics, health care, fire and security, and Tyco Capital, known as CIT. It plans to spin off CIT in the third fiscal quarter ending June 2002.

Industry	Investment Style	Stock Type	Sector
Electric Equipment	▦ Large Value	⚡ Cyclical	✪ Industrial Mats

Competition

	Market Cap $Mil	Debt/ Equity	12 Mo Trailing Sales $Mil	Price/Cash Flow	Return On Assets%	Total Return% 1 Yr	3 Yr
Tyco International	34,087	0.7	35,644	4.8	-14.2	-70.9	-22.1
Johnson & Johnson	159,452	0.1	35,120	18.0	16.3	-7.9	8.0
Honeywell International	19,705	0.5	22,272	8.7	5.6	-27.3	-22.9

Management

Ed Breen recently took over as chairman and CEO. He is very much admired by Wall Street and seems to be the right man for the job, given his strong performances at General Instrument and Motorola.

Price Volatility

| Monthly Price High/Low   — Relative Strength to S&P 500

Annual $Price High	22.75	39.59	53.88	59.19	63.21	58.90
Low	12.94	20.13	22.50	32.00	39.24	6.98

$ 64.2 29.0 19.0 7.0 4.0 2.0

	1997	1998	1999	2000	2001	2002
Annual Total Return %	70.9	67.7	3.5	42.4	6.2	-70.9

Fiscal Year-End: September	1998	1999	2000	2001	2002	TTM
Revenue $Mil	19,062	22,497	28,932	34,037	35,644	35,644
Net Income $Mil	1,166	1,022	4,520	3,971	-9,412	-9,412
Earnings Per Share $	0.72	0.61	2.64	2.17	-4.73	-4.73
Shares Outstanding Mil	1,576	1,648	1,687	1,805	1,990	1,996
Return on Equity %	11.8	8.3	26.5	12.5	-38.0	-38.0
Net Margin %	6.1	4.5	15.6	11.7	-26.4	-26.4
Asset Turnover	0.8	0.7	0.7	0.5	0.5	0.5
Financial Leverage	2.4	2.6	2.4	2.2	2.7	2.7

Strategy

Tyco is now focused on two things: improving its financial position and the performance of its various businesses. The acquisition machine has been turned off for now and it is possible that some businesses could be sold to improve cash flow or pay down debt.

The Zurich Center, Second Floor
Pembroke, HM 08   www.tycoint.com

Valuation Ratios	Stock	Rel to Industry	Rel to S&P 500	Major Fund Holders	% of Fund Assets
Price/Earnings	NMF	—	—	Clipper	9.93
Price/Book	1.4	0.4	0.4	PBHG Clipper Focus PBHG	9.27
Price/Sales	1.0	0.5	0.5	Yacktman Focused	9.00
Price/Cash Flow	4.8	0.6	0.4	Yacktman	7.99

Morningstar Grades

Growth [A]	1999	2000	2001	2002
Revenue %	18.0	28.6	17.6	4.7
Earnings/Share %	-15.3	332.8	-17.8	NMF
Book Value/Share %	20.8	34.8	74.3	-28.2
Dividends/Share %	0.0	0.0	0.0	0.0

Top-line growth was very strong over the past few years, thanks to acquisitions. Now that acquisitions are out of favor, we conservatively expect sales growth to slow to about 5% over the next five years.

Profitability [D+]	2000	2001	2002	TTM
Return on Assets %	11.2	5.6	-14.2	-14.2
Oper Cash Flow $Mil	5,275	6,665	7,158	7,158
- Cap Spending $Mil	1,704	1,798	1,709	1,709
= Free Cash Flow $Mil	3,571	4,868	5,450	5,450

While profit margins have expanded over the past few years, profitability has taken a big hit this year. We expect margins will increase substantially over the next five years, although they may be flat in 2003.

Financial Health [A]	2000	2001	2002	09-02
Long-term Debt $Mil	9,462	19,596	16,487	16,487
Total Equity $Mil	17,033	31,737	24,791	24,791
Debt/Equity Ratio	0.6	0.6	0.7	0.7

Tyco scores high because of its strong historical cash flow. However, this cash flow has weakened lately, as has the firm's balance sheet. Liquidity is a concern as well.

Morningstar's Take By Jonathan Schrader, 10-29-2002 Stock Price as of Analysis: $14.60

While we might buy Tyco if it fell into five-star territory, we don't see any reason to hold it as a long-term investment.

The firm is attractively positioned in two solid markets: disposable health-care products and security monitoring. But attractive positioning does not necessarily translate into an economic moat. Indeed, we have assigned a "no moat" rating to Tyco because we do not see how the company has any real sustainable advantages over its competitors. An analysis of the firm's financial performance--particularly its return on invested capital (ROIC)--supports our case.

A company with sustainable competitive advantages--an economic moat--tends to generate ROICs that are consistently or significantly above its cost of capital. We estimate that Tyco would need to boost its operating margin to 18% or so before it even matched its cost of capital. We reckon that the firm's margin--excluding a whole mess of charges--was below 14% in fiscal 2002. Granted, this past year was a challenging one for most companies, but we think Tyco will have a tough time getting to 18% even when the economy recovers.

This might seem like an odd thing to say, since margins were above 18% in both 2001 and 2000.

However, we don't have a lot of confidence in those reported results. Tyco recently restated its results for fiscal 2002, resulting in lower operating margins, and there may be more restatements in the future.

Perhaps as Tyco becomes an increasingly important player in its markets it will be able to push higher prices down to its customers, but it has some powerful rivals to deal with before it gets to that point. Or maybe the company will take even more charges against its goodwill account, which would reduce the amount of invested capital on its books, thus boosting ROIC. This appears to be the more likely option, although it would be an admission that the company overpaid for its previous acquisitions. It would also represent more destroyed shareholder wealth.

Either way, as we see it now, Tyco is a destroyer of wealth--it does not achieve economic profits above its cost of capital--and does not represent the type of company in which we would want to invest for the long run. However, below $12 the stock would be a solid bargain, which we'd be willing to hold until it reached our fair value estimate.

MORNINGSTAR® Stocks 500

Tyson Foods A TSN

	Rating	Risk	Moat Size	Fair Value	Last Close	Yield %
	★★★	Med.	None	$16.00	$11.22	1.4

Company Profile

Tyson Foods produces food products like value-enhanced poultry, fresh and frozen poultry, pork products, beef products, pasta products, flour and corn tortillas, and other Mexican food products. The company markets its products under brand names like Tyson, Holly Farms, Weaver, TastyBird, and Louis Kemp. Tyson Foods also has animal feed and pet food operations. The company's customers include grocery chains, grocery wholesalers, hospitals, restaurants, airlines, and military commissaries. It acquired beef and pork processor IBP in 2001.

Management

CEO John Tyson is the grandson of the company's founder and has held the top spot since April 2000. His father, Don Tyson, is senior chairman of the board and controls a majority of the company's voting stock.

Strategy

Tyson's focus lately has been on maintaining its excellent brand name and capitalizing on the increasing popularity of chicken. It's been working on integrating recently acquired IBP to create a one-stop source for protein products of all kinds (beef, chicken, pork), with particular emphasis on value-added products.

2210 West Oaklawn Drive   www.tysonfoodsinc.com
Springdale, AR 72762-6999

Morningstar Grades

Growth [A+]	1999	2000	2001	2002
Revenue %	2.8	-4.6	45.3	121.2
Earnings/Share %	809.1	-33.0	-40.3	170.0
Book Value/Share %	6.7	4.3	58.0	-32.3
Dividends/Share %	15.0	39.1	0.0	0.0

The IBP acquisition caused year-over-year revenue to spike in 2002, but that spike isn't sustainable. The chicken segment, which was not affected by the merger, saw sales increase 2.3% for the year despite a difficult environment.

Profitability [C]	2000	2001	2002	TTM
Return on Assets %	3.1	0.8	3.7	3.7
Oper Cash Flow $Mil	587	511	1,174	1,174
- Cap Spending $Mil	196	261	433	433
= Free Cash Flow $Mil	391	250	741	741

After a couple of quarters of encouraging post-merger earnings growth, Tyson lowered its profit forecasts twice in the second half of 2002. However, we expect margins to be more stable overall in the future.

Financial Health [C]	2000	2001	2002	09-02
Long-term Debt $Mil	1,357	4,016	3,733	3,733
Total Equity $Mil	2,175	3,354	3,662	3,662
Debt/Equity Ratio	0.6	1.2	1.0	1.0

The IBP merger raised debt significantly, but Tyson has already made good progress in working down that debt. It generates plenty of free cash flow, and liquidity isn't a problem.

	Industry	Investment Style	Stock Type	Sector
	Food Mfg.	▦ Mid Value	⬆ Aggr. Growth	🚗 Consumer Goods

Competition

	Market Cap $Mil	Debt/ Equity	12 Mo Trailing Sales $Mil	Price/Cash Flow	Return On Assets%	Total Return% 1 Yr	3 Yr
Tyson Foods A	3,959	1.0	23,367	3.4	3.7	-1.6	-9.9
ConAgra Foods	13,431	—	27,085	—	—	—	—
Hormel Foods	3,235	0.4	4,166	10.7	8.7	-11.8	7.5

Price Volatility

| Monthly Price High/Low   — Relative Strength to S&P 500

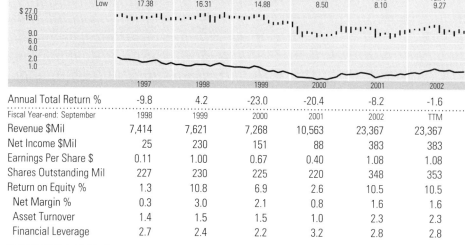

Annual $Price High Low	24.25 17.38	26.00 16.31	23.75 14.88	17.38 8.50	14.15 8.10	15.71 9.27

	1997	1998	1999	2000	2001	2002
Annual Total Return %	-9.8	4.2	-23.0	-20.4	-8.2	-1.6

Fiscal Year-end: September	1998	1999	2000	2001	2002	TTM
Revenue $Mil	7,414	7,621	7,268	10,563	23,367	23,367
Net Income $Mil	25	230	151	88	383	383
Earnings Per Share $	0.11	1.00	0.67	0.40	1.08	1.08
Shares Outstanding Mil	227	230	225	220	348	353
Return on Equity %	1.3	10.8	6.9	2.6	10.5	10.5
Net Margin %	0.3	3.0	2.1	0.8	1.6	1.6
Asset Turnover	1.4	1.5	1.5	1.0	2.3	2.3
Financial Leverage	2.7	2.4	2.2	3.2	2.8	2.8

Valuation Ratios	Stock	Rel to Industry	Rel to S&P 500
Price/Earnings	10.4	0.5	0.4
Price/Book	1.1	0.3	0.3
Price/Sales	0.2	0.1	0.1
Price/Cash Flow	3.4	0.3	0.3

Major Fund Holders	% of Fund Assets
PBHG Clipper Focus PBHG	2.75
Texas Capital Value & Growth	2.27
Kenwood Growth & Income	2.17
GE Mid-Cap Value Equity B	1.95

Morningstar's Take By David Kathman, 12-09-2002 Stock Price as of Analysis: $11.13

Despite going through a rough spell due to depressed meat prices, Tyson is doing a lot of things right. We'd gladly buy the stock if it dipped 40% below our fair value estimate.

Tyson's purchase of beef- and pork-processor IBP in 2001 was a risky move, but one that appears to be paying off. For one thing, the deal more than tripled Tyson's revenue base and gave it economies of scale unmatched among meat producers, an important factor in an industry with such notoriously thin margins. Tyson now has a single sales force pushing chicken, beef, and pork products, and it's been closing selected production facilities and eliminating underperforming product lines in an effort to make all its operations more efficient. So far, so good: The company is on track to meet its goal of $100 million in merger-related savings in fiscal 2003 and $200 million in 2004.

Another effect of the merger has been to diversify Tyson's product line and make it less dependent on any single commodity price. In an industry where meat prices tend to swing wildly and unpredictably, the relative stability of not having all its eggs in one basket should be a long-term positive for Tyson. True, the company's new pork segment was a hindrance in 2002 when pork prices plunged, but generally solid performance from beef and chicken mostly offset that.

Even before the IBP deal, Tyson was increasing its focus on value-added chicken products (like marinated chicken strips) as another way of lessening its dependence on chicken prices. Sales of these more-profitable high-end products increased 8% in 2002, faster than the rest of its chicken segment. Now Tyson is extending this value-added strategy to pork and beef, continuing what IBP started. IBP's Thomas E. Wilson precooked beef and pork lines have been quite successful against Hormel's similar products, but Tyson is phasing out that brand in order to put its own name on all of its value-added meat products. That makes sense to us, since Tyson already has excellent brand equity, and having one name across products will be simpler for consumers.

Tyson's size and its strong roster of value-added products give it some key advantages in the volatile meat industry. Even though the acquisition of IBP narrowed its gross margins (because beef is a lower-margin product than chicken or pork), we expect the new Tyson to be more stable than its rivals, with the potential for quite a bit of margin improvement. We'd be happy to buy the stock at the right price.

UAL UAL

	Rating	Risk	Moat Size	Fair Value	Last Close	Yield %
	UR	High	None	UR	$1.43	0.0

Company Profile

UAL is a holding company that has United Airlines as its principal subsidiary. United Airlines provides passenger and cargo transportation to 139 airports in 26 countries from hubs in Chicago, Los Angeles, Denver, San Francisco, Washington, D.C., London, and Tokyo. It also offers commuter service under the name United Express through partnerships with several regional carriers. UAL owns 277 and leases 317 aircraft. Mileage Plus, a subsidiary, administers frequent-flier bonus programs. The firm indirectly owns Air Wis Services.

Management

In September, Glenn Tilton joined UAL as chairman, president, and CEO. A career Texaco man, he rose to become chairman and CEO--vice chairman after the merger with Chevron--and briefly served as interim chairman of Dynegy before joining UAL.

Strategy

Right now, United is struggling to survive as a going concern. Declining revenue has brutalized cash flow, making it impossible for the company to pay the bills. Management's priority is to keep the business running during bankruptcy while deeply and permanently cutting costs.

1200 East Algonquin Road
Elk Grove Township, IL 60007
www.ual.com

Industry	Investment Style	Stock Type	Sector
Air Transport	Small Value	Distressed	Business Services

Competition	Market Cap $Mil	Debt/ Equity	12 Mo Trailing Sales $Mil	Price/Cash Flow	Return On Assets%	Total Return% 1 Yr	3 Yr
UAL	95	6.9	13,768	—	-8.5	-89.4	-73.1
Southwest Airlines	10,768	0.4	5,359	16.8	2.9	-24.7	10.7
Delta Air Lines	1,493	3.2	12,860	—	-6.9	-58.4	-37.0

Price Volatility

| Monthly Price High/Low — Relative Strength to S&P 500

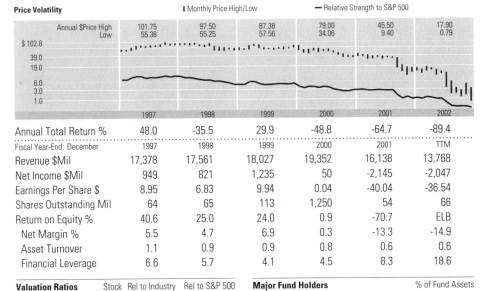

Annual $Price High / Low	101.75 / 55.38	97.50 / 55.25	87.38 / 57.56	79.00 / 34.06	45.50 / 9.40	17.90 / 0.79
	1997	1998	1999	2000	2001	2002

Annual Total Return %	48.0	-35.5	29.9	-48.8	-64.7	-89.4

Fiscal Year-End: December	1997	1998	1999	2000	2001	TTM
Revenue $Mil	17,378	17,561	18,027	19,352	16,138	13,768
Net Income $Mil	949	821	1,235	50	-2,145	-2,047
Earnings Per Share $	8.95	6.83	9.94	0.04	-40.04	-36.54
Shares Outstanding Mil	64	65	113	1,250	54	66
Return on Equity %	40.6	25.0	24.0	0.9	-70.7	ELB
Net Margin %	5.5	4.7	6.9	0.3	-13.3	-14.9
Asset Turnover	1.1	0.9	0.9	0.8	0.6	0.6
Financial Leverage	6.6	5.7	4.1	4.5	8.3	18.6

Valuation Ratios	Stock	Rel to Industry	Rel to S&P 500
Price/Earnings	NMF	—	—
Price/Book	0.1	0.0	0.0
Price/Sales	0.0	0.0	0.0
Price/Cash Flow	—	—	—

Major Fund Holders	% of Fund Assets
None	

Morningstar Grades

Growth [NA]	1998	1999	2000	2001
Revenue %	1.1	2.7	7.4	-16.6
Earnings/Share %	-23.7	45.5	-99.6	NMF
Book Value/Share %	23.8	51.9	-89.5	EUB
Dividends/Share %	NMF	NMF	NMF	-28.0

In the past few years, UAL's revenue growth has trailed that of peers. Because the airline has cut capacity significantly since 9/11 and overall ticket prices have fallen, revenue will probably remain very weak through 2003.

Profitability [NA]	1999	2000	2001	TTM
Return on Assets %	5.9	0.2	-8.5	-8.5
Oper Cash Flow $Mil	2,421	2,472	-160	-1,426
- Cap Spending $Mil	2,389	2,538	1,951	206
= Free Cash Flow $Mil	32	-66	-2,111	-1,632

In the first half of 2001, UAL lost $678 million. It lost an additional $3.2 billion through September 2002, and its billowing contrail of red ink will probably lead well into 2003.

Financial Health [NA]	1999	2000	2001	09-02
Long-term Debt $Mil	4,987	6,949	8,565	8,942
Total Equity $Mil	5,151	5,457	3,033	1,303
Debt/Equity Ratio	1.0	1.3	2.8	6.9

Soaring debt and continued losses make things worse for UAL every day. The company has significant bills that it cannot pay in the near term, and has sought bankruptcy protection as it restructures.

Morningstar's Take By Nicolas Owens, 12-09-2002 Stock Price as of Analysis: $0.93

Given the unsustainable nature of UAL's business model, we don't see any reason to invest in the shares.

One of our concerns is that UAL's strategy is not viable over the long term. Generally speaking, a company can pursue one of two strategies. The first is to offer a differentiated product for which customers are willing to pay a premium. The other approach is to be the low-cost provider in a particular market. However, UAL is the high-cost producer in a market that does not allow for much differentiation. Competition in the airline industry is largely based on price, making air travel a commodity. The success of Southwest over the years is based on its low cost structure, which allows it to charge less than its competition and turn a profit. The fact that UAL's unit costs are 61% higher than Southwest's--and 22% higher than the industry average--leaves the firm at a significant disadvantage.

Another issue that we have with UAL is the volatility of its operating results. Because the company depends on business travelers, UAL's earnings are very sensitive to the business cycle. In 1999, UAL made $1.2 billion in profit on $18 billion in sales. In 2000, it broke even, and last year it lost more than $2 billion on $16 billion in sales. This continues a pattern of large profits and losses that has persisted every decade since the 1940s. Since deregulation in 1978, the airline industry as a whole has lost $8.5 billion. Given the current structure of the industry, we don't see this pattern ending anytime soon.

The most pressing reason to avoid investing in UAL--and most of its rivals--is its significant leverage. UAL has a lot of operating leverage--which basically means that the company has high fixed costs--which is a very good thing when business is booming, but has the opposite effect when business is in the dumps. More important, the firm took on loads of debt to buy newer, more efficient aircraft. Recently, UAL has been using this debt to fund losses in its operations. The result of this financial leverage is to exacerbate the poor operating performance of the airline, resulting in enormous net losses.

Most airline stocks--including UAL--are bad long-term investments. Wild swings in share price can make for tempting speculative trades, but over the long haul airlines have a terrible record for shareholders, and that isn't about to change.

MORNINGSTAR® Stocks 500

United Parcel Service B UPS

	Rating	Risk	Moat Size	Fair Value	Last Close	Yield %
	★★★	Low	Wide	$55.00	$63.08	1.2

Company Profile

United Parcel Service provides time-definite delivery of packages in the United States and abroad. The company also provides logistics services, including integrated supply-chain management, for major businesses. Its fleet consists of about 150,000 delivery vehicles and more than 500 airplanes. The company delivers more than 12.9 million packages per day and about 80% of its deliveries are business-to-business. United Parcel Service has electronic-commerce alliance partnerships with companies such as AT&T. It agreed to acquire Fritz and First International Bancorp in 2001.

Management

Michael Eskew, a 30-year company veteran, recently replaced Jim Kelly as chairman and CEO. The management team is highly regarded for good reason; the organization is quite conservative and consistent in its results.

Strategy

UPS dominates the U.S. market for business-to-consumer package delivery. It is expanding its delivery business overseas and stepping up competition with rival FedEx in the overnight delivery market. UPS is also pushing into nonpackage businesses like financing and logistics to boost revenue growth.

55 Glenlake Parkway, NE
Atlanta, GA 30328
www.ups.com

Morningstar Grades

Growth [B]	1998	1999	2000	2001
Revenue %	10.4	9.1	10.1	2.9
Earnings/Share %	NMF	NMF	NMF	-16.0
Book Value/Share %	—	—	NMF	8.1
Dividends/Share %	NMF	NMF	126.7	11.8

Revenue growth has been better than the industry norm in recent years. UPS is aiming to maintain its growth rate by focusing on areas with more growth potential, like logistics management.

Profitability [A]	1999	2000	2001	TTM
Return on Assets %	3.8	13.5	9.7	9.2
Oper Cash Flow $Mil	2,259	2,742	3,900	3,683
- Cap Spending $Mil	1,476	2,147	2,372	1,687
= Free Cash Flow $Mil	783	595	1,528	1,996

Because of the weak business environment, operating profit margins have been soft. We expect improvement in profitability over the next few years as volume increases with economic recovery.

Financial Health [A]	1999	2000	2001	09-02
Long-term Debt $Mil	1,912	2,981	4,648	3,558
Total Equity $Mil	12,474	9,735	10,248	10,957
Debt/Equity Ratio	0.2	0.3	0.5	0.3

Years of solid operations have led to a strong balance sheet with relatively little debt.

	Industry	Investment Style	Stock Type	Sector
	Transportation - Misc	Large Growth	Classic Growth	Business Services

Competition	Market Cap $Mil	Debt/ Equity	12 Mo Trailing Sales $Mil	Price/Cash Flow	Return On Assets%	Total Return% 1 Yr	3 Yr
United Parcel Service B	70,397	0.3	31,337	19.1	9.2	17.2	0.3
FedEx	16,189	0.3	21,015	6.8	5.4	4.8	9.4
Airborne Freight	718	—	3,244	—	—	—	—

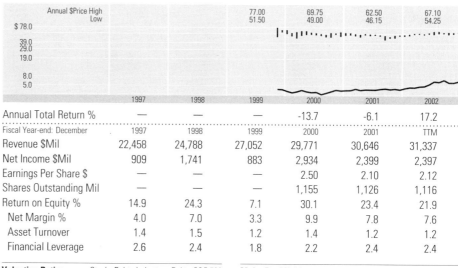

Price Volatility — Monthly Price High/Low — Relative Strength to S&P 500

	1997	1998	1999	2000	2001	2002
Annual $Price High			77.00	69.75	62.50	67.10
Low			51.50	49.00	46.15	54.25
Annual Total Return %	—	—	—	-13.7	-6.1	17.2

Fiscal Year-end: December	1997	1998	1999	2000	2001	TTM
Revenue $Mil	22,458	24,788	27,052	29,771	30,646	31,337
Net Income $Mil	909	1,741	883	2,934	2,399	2,397
Earnings Per Share $	—	—	—	2.50	2.10	2.12
Shares Outstanding Mil	—	—	—	1,155	1,126	1,116
Return on Equity %	14.9	24.3	7.1	30.1	23.4	21.9
Net Margin %	4.0	7.0	3.3	9.9	7.8	7.6
Asset Turnover	1.4	1.5	1.2	1.4	1.2	1.2
Financial Leverage	2.6	2.4	1.8	2.2	2.4	2.4

Valuation Ratios	Stock	Rel to Industry	Rel to S&P 500
Price/Earnings	29.8	1.0	1.3
Price/Book	6.4	1.0	2.0
Price/Sales	2.2	1.0	1.1
Price/Cash Flow	19.1	1.0	1.4

Major Fund Holders	% of Fund Assets
Rydex Transportation Inv	19.64
Fidelity Select Air Transportation	7.84
ProFunds UltraBull Inv	6.89
Pax World Growth	5.49

Morningstar's Take By Jonathan Schrader, 11-23-2002 Stock Price as of Analysis: $62.79

UPS is a world-class franchise. We'd happily hold the stock for the long term, but would buy only at the right price.

After almost 100 years of operations, UPS dominates the delivery of goods to American homes and businesses. Its delivery network--one of its competitive advantages--is unmatched, and its profit margins are superior to its rivals'. This is largely due to UPS' focus on deferred delivery. Since this delivery isn't time-sensitive, UPS can use methods of shipment, like trucks and trains, that are less costly to run than airplanes.

UPS' strongest competition in deferred delivery has traditionally been the U.S. Postal Service--not a very formidable competitor. Because competition has been weak, UPS' pricing power has been strong, allowing it to increase prices and margins. FedEx has recently been moving into these markets and giving UPS stiffer competition. FedEx is still a minor player in this area, but it is growing quickly. While we are concerned that the competition could diminish UPS' profitability, we think there is room enough for both of them.

It's not surprising that FedEx would encroach on UPS' turf; UPS has been aggressively pursuing FedEx's express delivery customers for years. UPS is using its established ground network to move into express delivery, where average shipping prices are more than triple ground shipment prices. Because much of its network has been in place for years, UPS' margins are superior to FedEx's and those of other rivals. This, in turn, leads to cash flow generation that is unmatched by peers.

The company has been using that generous cash flow to move into complementary lines of business, like customs brokerage and working-capital financing. We think this is a sound strategy, especially because it is backed by such a strong management team and a solid balance sheet.

We like the UPS story. We think the company has many years of profitable growth ahead of it, and we'd gladly buy the stock if it fell 20% below our fair value estimate.

United States Cellular USM

	Rating	Risk	Moat Size	Fair Value	Last Close	Yield %
	★★★	High	None	$32.00	$25.02	0.0

Company Profile

U.S. Cellular has 3.5 million wireless phone subscribers across 25 states. The company has focused on clustering its customers into eight regional zones, encompassing 142 cities, which allows it to provide cellular service without extensive roaming agreements in place. Parent company Telephone and Data Systems owns 81% of the company. Although U.S. Cellular predominantly uses TDMA technology, it is migrating to the third generation of rival platform CDMA.

Management

Jack Rooney, who became CEO in April 2000, has 10 years' experience in the telecom industry. Parent TDS owns 81% of the firm; through supermajority voting stock, it controls nearly all of it.

Strategy

U.S. Cellular focuses on the less-competitive rural markets, mainly in the Midwest. The firm's goal is to cluster as many users as possible in a relatively small geographic area, thus benefiting from cost efficiencies, and to provide excellent customer service. This explains why the company bought the Chicago-based assets--roughly 305,000 net subscribers--of PrimeCo Wireless in 2002.

8410 West Bryn Mawr
Chicago, IL 60631
www.uscellular.com

Morningstar Grades

Growth [C]	1998	1999	2000	2001
Revenue %	50.0	19.8	8.9	10.4
Earnings/Share %	85.3	37.2	-32.3	-10.4
Book Value/Share %	14.0	15.5	2.7	4.9
Dividends/Share %	NMF	NMF	NMF	NMF

The wireless industry was once fast growing, but not anymore; fierce competition is limiting subscriber gains. Excluding the PrimeCo acquisition, subscriber growth will be well below last year's level. We project single-digit long-term growth.

Profitability [A-]	1999	2000	2001	TTM
Return on Assets %	8.6	5.6	4.7	0.0
Oper Cash Flow $Mil	333	521	440	548
- Cap Spending $Mil	249	295	488	541
= Free Cash Flow $Mil	84	226	-47	7

The firm is profitable, an anomaly in the industry, but returns on invested capital are below the cost of capital. This suggests the company is destroying shareholder capital.

Financial Health [B+]	1999	2000	2001	09-02
Long-term Debt $Mil	546	449	403	849
Total Equity $Mil	2,275	2,215	2,336	2,390
Debt/Equity Ratio	0.2	0.2	0.2	0.4

The PrimeCo acquisition has put pressure on the balance sheet; debt/equity is 0.5, up from 0.3 at the end of 2001. Free cash flow is deeply negative, thanks to heavy capital spending.

Industry	Investment Style	Stock Type	Sector
Wireless Service	▦ Mid Core	↗ Classic Growth	▮ Telecom

Competition	Market Cap $Mil	Debt/ Equity	12 Mo Trailing Sales $Mil	Price/Cash Flow	Return On Assets%	Total Return% 1 Yr	3 Yr
United States Cellular	2,155	0.4	2,082	3.9	0.0	-44.7	-35.7
Verizon Communications	106,011	1.4	67,422	4.7	-0.1	-15.2	-9.8
AT&T Wireless Services	15,300	0.4	15,112	5.8	-7.5	-60.7	—

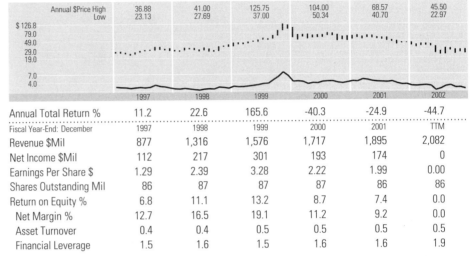

Price Volatility — Monthly Price High/Low — Relative Strength to S&P 500

Annual $Price High Low	36.88 23.13	41.00 27.69	125.75 37.00	104.00 50.34	68.57 40.70	45.50 22.97
	1997	1998	1999	2000	2001	2002
Annual Total Return %	11.2	22.6	165.6	-40.3	-24.9	-44.7

Fiscal Year-End: December	1997	1998	1999	2000	2001	TTM
Revenue $Mil	877	1,316	1,576	1,717	1,895	2,082
Net Income $Mil	112	217	301	193	174	0
Earnings Per Share $	1.29	2.39	3.28	2.22	1.99	0.00
Shares Outstanding Mil	86	87	87	87	86	86
Return on Equity %	6.8	11.1	13.2	8.7	7.4	0.0
Net Margin %	12.7	16.5	19.1	11.2	9.2	0.0
Asset Turnover	0.4	0.4	0.5	0.5	0.5	0.5
Financial Leverage	1.5	1.6	1.5	1.6	1.6	1.9

Valuation Ratios	Stock	Rel to Industry	Rel to S&P 500
Price/Earnings	NMF	—	—
Price/Book	0.9	0.3	0.3
Price/Sales	1.0	0.4	0.5
Price/Cash Flow	3.9	0.3	0.3

Major Fund Holders	% of Fund Assets
Fidelity Select Wireless	2.88
Lindner Communications Inv	2.84
FMC Select	1.71
Gabelli Global Telecommunications	1.44

Morningstar's Take By Todd P. Bernier, 11-27-2002 Stock Price as of Analysis: $30.20

U.S. Cellular is a small fish in a big pond, and that's enough to scare us away.

A wireless carrier with licenses covering 42 million Midwesterners, U.S. Cellular focuses on the less price-competitive rural markets. This regional positioning coupled with strong customer service is the firm's key attribute. To continue its growth, U.S. Cellular acquired the Chicago-based assets of PrimeCo Wireless, adding 305,000 net customers and 20 megahertz of spectrum (covering a population of 13 million). Although U.S. Cellular paid the dear sum of roughly $2,000 per subscriber, this acquisition vaults it into the big leagues.

Size is exactly what U.S. Cellular needs to compete in a competitive wireless industry. With six nationwide rivals slugging it out, per-minute prices have fallen more than 80% over the past decade. And although wireless execs don't want to admit it, little differentiates the major carriers; a consumer's purchase decision usually boils down to which carrier offers the best prices. Despite being near the top of the customer-service food chain, evidenced by the lowest rate of subscriber churn among the big carriers, U.S. Cellular does not offer the cheapest calling plans. The entry of national carriers into rural markets has made life difficult for U.S. Cellular,

because it cannot match the big boys' scale.

Another key disadvantage is the company's clientele. Although the PrimeCo acquisition will improve things, U.S. Cellular's typical customers are substandard; they tend to use only about five hours and spend less than $50 per month. Making matters worse, the nationwide carriers that once relied upon regional carriers to provide coverage are now expanding their own networks into less densely populated regions. This new competition leads to lower pricing for consumers and reduced roaming fees--the amount carriers charge each other for using its network--for U.S. Cellular. As a result, the trend in roaming revenue, which accounts for roughly 15% of U.S. Cellular's service revenue, continues to deteriorate.

U.S. Cellular has no fundamental competitive advantage. With subscriber growth slowing and price increasingly becoming a commodity, we have concerns about all wireless carriers, but especially the smaller players. With no defensible economic moat, U.S. Cellular stock would need to be very cheap--about 50% below our fair value estimate--before we'd get excited.

 M⌀RNINGSTAR® Stocks 500

United Technologies UTX

	Rating	Risk	Moat Size	Fair Value	Last Close	Yield %
	★★★★	Low	Wide	$70.00	$61.94	1.6

Company Profile

United Technologies produces aerospace, heating, and elevator products. The company's Pratt & Whitney, Sikorsky, and Hamilton Sundstrand subsidiaries manufacture helicopters, aircraft engines and parts, flight-control and radar systems, and rocket boosters. Its other products include Carrier heating, refrigeration, and air-conditioning equipment and Otis elevators and escalators. The company markets its products in the United States and overseas. United Technologies acquired Specialty Equipment in November 2000.

Management

CEO George David began his UTC career at Otis in 1975 and worked his way up to head the firm in 1994. He has brought strategic focus and financial discipline to UTC's diverse lines of business.

Strategy

UTC has thrived by building on its strengths rather than expanding into unrelated lines of business. The company continues to fine-tune its product portfolio and improve the efficiency of its major businesses. In 2002, the firm plans to spend at least $1 billion on acquisitions that bolster its existing businesses.

United Technologies Building   www.utc.com
Hartford, CT 06103

Morningstar Grades

Growth [B+]	1998	1999	2000	2001
Revenue %	-5.8	5.8	10.2	4.9
Earnings/Share %	20.5	19.0	17.9	7.9
Book Value/Share %	10.6	58.5	7.5	9.9
Dividends/Share %	12.1	9.4	8.6	9.1

Revenue increased 5% in 2001--not bad, given the U.S. recession and the sharp downturn in the airline industry. We expect minimal revenue growth in 2002.

Profitability [A]	1999	2000	2001	TTM
Return on Assets %	6.3	7.1	7.2	7.2
Oper Cash Flow $Mil	2,310	2,503	2,885	3,111
- Cap Spending $Mil	762	937	793	610
= Free Cash Flow $Mil	1,548	1,566	2,092	2,501

UTC has a consistent record of profitability, with return on equity averaging about 25% and return on assets averaging 6% over the past five years. We look for similar results over the next few years.

Financial Health [A]	1999	2000	2001	09-02
Long-term Debt $Mil	3,086	3,476	4,237	4,667
Total Equity $Mil	7,117	7,662	8,369	9,676
Debt/Equity Ratio	0.4	0.5	0.5	0.5

UTC has a solid balance sheet, with year-end net debt/total capitalization of 29%, an improvement from the 35% at the end of 2001.

Industry	Investment Style	Stock Type	Sector
Aerospace & Defense	Large Core	Cyclical	Industrial Mats

Competition

	Market Cap $Mil	Debt/ Equity	12 Mo Trailing Sales $Mil	Price/Cash Flow	Return On Assets%	Total Return% 1 Yr	3 Yr
United Technologies	29,339	0.5	27,971	9.4	7.2	-2.7	2.5
General Electric	242,308	2.2	130,295	8.2	2.7	-37.7	-18.9
Boeing	27,691	1.1	56,071	9.9	0.0	-13.4	-4.9

Price Volatility

| | Monthly Price High/Low   — Relative Strength to S&P 500 |

Annual $Price High	44.47	56.25	75.97	79.75	87.40	77.70
Low	32.56	33.50	51.63	46.50	40.10	48.83

	1997	1998	1999	2000	2001	2002
Annual Total Return %	11.7	51.6	21.0	22.6	-16.8	-2.7

Fiscal Year-end: December	1997	1998	1999	2000	2001	TTM
Revenue $Mil	24,222	22,809	24,127	26,583	27,897	27,971
Net Income $Mil	1,072	1,255	1,531	1,808	1,938	2,048
Earnings Per Share $	2.10	2.53	3.01	3.55	3.83	4.05
Shares Outstanding Mil	483	468	475	478	477	474
Return on Equity %	26.3	28.7	21.5	23.6	23.2	21.2
Net Margin %	4.4	5.5	6.3	6.8	6.9	7.3
Asset Turnover	1.5	1.3	1.0	1.0	1.0	1.0
Financial Leverage	4.0	4.1	3.4	3.3	3.2	2.9

Valuation Ratios	Stock	Rel to Industry	Rel to S&P 500
Price/Earnings	15.3	1.0	0.7
Price/Book	3.0	1.2	0.9
Price/Sales	1.0	1.2	0.5
Price/Cash Flow	9.4	1.0	0.7

Major Fund Holders	% of Fund Assets
IDEX Great Companies-America A	8.14
Fidelity Congress Street	7.15
IDEX Great Companies-Global A	5.67
Fidelity Select Defense & Aerospace	5.47

Morningstar's Take By Jonathan Schrader, 11-22-2002 Stock Price as of Analysis: $63.62

United Technologies (UTC) is a well-run firm with solid prospects. It has a relatively low level of risk and a wide economic moat, and so we'd be comfortable buying it at just a 20% discount to our fair value estimate.

We like this company. It's a well-diversified firm operating efficiently in several industrial markets. Building fighter jet engines is as sexy as this company gets. However, UTC generates loads of cash that it uses to pay dividends, repurchase shares, and make smart acquisitions. These prudent acquisitions--along with some effective cost-cutting--have enabled the firm to increase its earnings per share 16% annually over the past five years.

UTC operates in markets dominated by just a few big players, who usually recognize that they have a good thing and aren't interested in destroying each other's profit margins. Indeed, UTC's operating profit margins tend to be quite consistent and pretty juicy. The highest are in the Otis and Pratt & Whitney divisions; these also happen to be the most consolidated markets in which UTC operates.

Also, UTC's businesses demand relatively little in the way of capital spending. This is particularly true of Otis. Sure, Otis makes money from installing new elevators and escalators in commercial properties, but it also makes a lot of money from servicing the machines it has already installed. This makes the economics of the business very attractive. In 2001, this segment had an operating profit margin of almost 15%, generated more than $1 billion in cash flow (earnings before interest, taxes, depreciation, and amortization), and required only $80 million in capital investment.

Finally, UTC spends a lot of money on research and development. The firm regularly plows 5% of total sales back into research so it can continue to offer the most advanced products available. On top of this, UTC is a major beneficiary of R&D funds from the U.S. government, to the tune of $845 billion in 2001. This government-funded research often leads to advances that can be used to improve the firm's commercial product offerings, thus boosting overall sales.

We don't see any reason this company can't continue to flourish, while throwing off loads of cash to its shareholders. At the right price, we would be happy to become long-term investors in United Technologies.

UnitedHealth Group UNH

	Rating	Risk	Moat Size	Fair Value	Last Close	Yield %
	★★★★	Low	Wide	$94.00	$83.50	0.0

Company Profile

UnitedHealth Group provides health-care management and insurance products. The company has majority or minority ownership interest in health-maintenance organizations in all 50 states and Puerto Rico. These organizations contract with physician groups to provide health-care services at a fixed cost to the company's participants. UnitedHealth also has other businesses that focus on health-care networking, data analysis and research, and specialized services that address consumers' needs for mental health, vision, and dental services.

Management

William McGuire has been the company's chairman and CEO since 1991. He has overseen several acquisitions that transformed UnitedHealth from a small regional HMO into a national player with more than 21 million members.

Strategy

UnitedHealth's strategy is to maintain growth and improve margins by offering a larger and more flexible suite of health-care management products with more specialized care options (mental health, vision, dental). It is diversifying its businesses to reduce the risk of its future cash flows and driving growth to scale the benefits of its process and technology investments.

UnitedHealth Group Center   www.unitedheathgroup.com
Minnetonka, MN 55343

Morningstar Grades

Growth [C]	1998	1999	2000	2001
Revenue %	47.2	12.7	8.0	11.0
Earnings/Share %	NMF	NMF	36.9	27.4
Book Value/Share %	-0.1	3.0	0.8	8.4
Dividends/Share %	0.0	0.0	0.0	100.0

Second-quarter revenue increased almost 5% from the year-ago period because of membership gains and strong pricing. We expect overall revenue growth of 12% for 2002, driven by continued enrollment growth and the AmeriChoice acquisition.

Profitability [A-]	1999	2000	2001	TTM
Return on Assets %	5.5	6.7	7.3	8.9
Oper Cash Flow $Mil	1,189	1,521	1,844	2,024
- Cap Spending $Mil	196	245	425	380
= Free Cash Flow $Mil	993	1,276	1,419	1,644

The second-quarter operating margin was 8.6%, a 200-basis-point improvement from the year-ago quarter. Significant technology investments and the reduction of risk-based accounts should continue to drive improvements.

Financial Health [B+]	1999	2000	2001	09-02
Long-term Debt $Mil	400	650	900	1,300
Total Equity $Mil	3,863	3,688	3,891	4,361
Debt/Equity Ratio	0.1	0.2	0.2	0.3

While the debt/equity ratio has climbed in the past few years, this is not a real cause for concern. UnitedHealth generates enough operating cash flows to retire all of its current long-term debt within two years.

Industry	Investment Style	Stock Type	Sector
Managed Care	▦ Large Growth	↗ Classic Growth	✚ Healthcare

Competition

	Market Cap $Mil	Debt/ Equity	12 Mo Trailing Sales $Mil	Price/Cash Flow	Return On Assets%	Total Return% 1 Yr	3 Yr
UnitedHealth Group	25,235	0.3	24,358	12.5	8.9	18.0	46.6
WellPoint Health Networks	10,372	0.3	16,180	7.9	6.0	21.8	29.5
Anthem	8,884	—	11,954	—	3.8	27.1	—

Price Volatility

	1997	1998	1999	2000	2001	2002
Annual $Price High	30.06	36.97	35.00	63.44	72.80	101.00
Low	21.22	14.78	19.69	23.19	50.50	67.85

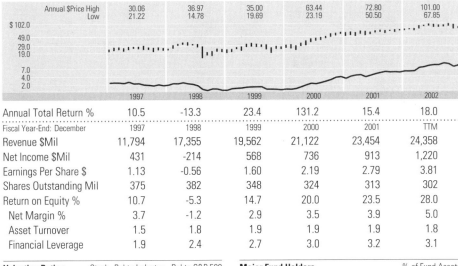

Annual Total Return %	10.5	-13.3	23.4	131.2	15.4	18.0
Fiscal Year-End: December	1997	1998	1999	2000	2001	TTM
Revenue $Mil	11,794	17,355	19,562	21,122	23,454	24,358
Net Income $Mil	431	-214	568	736	913	1,220
Earnings Per Share $	1.13	-0.56	1.60	2.19	2.79	3.81
Shares Outstanding Mil	375	382	348	324	313	302
Return on Equity %	10.7	-5.3	14.7	20.0	23.5	28.0
Net Margin %	3.7	-1.2	2.9	3.5	3.9	5.0
Asset Turnover	1.5	1.8	1.9	1.9	1.9	1.8
Financial Leverage	1.9	2.4	2.7	3.0	3.2	3.1

Valuation Ratios	Stock	Rel to Industry	Rel to S&P 500
Price/Earnings	21.9	1.0	0.9
Price/Book	5.8	1.0	1.8
Price/Sales	1.0	1.5	0.5
Price/Cash Flow	12.5	1.3	0.9

Major Fund Holders	% of Fund Assets
Fidelity Select Medical Delivery	14.49
Smith Barney Aggressive Growth A	9.35
PBHG Large Cap 20 PBHG	8.47
Legg Mason Value Prim	8.40

Morningstar's Take By Damon Ficklin, 12-23-2002 Stock Price as of Analysis: $83.72

UnitedHealth Group is an excellent company that has ascended to a dominant position in its industry. We believe it will remain dominant for the foreseeable future.

UnitedHealth has maintained strong sales growth while shifting its business mix to include a higher proportion of fee-based members (as opposed to risk-based members). This means that UnitedHealth is expanding its membership base faster than the average player in the industry while reducing its exposure to health-care cost inflation.

Fee-based members expanded to 62% of the total membership base in 2001, up from only 55% in 1999. Strong results in the second quarter of 2002 were underlined by further improvements in the mix, with fee-based members now accounting for 66% of the total membership base. This is a significantly higher proportion of fee-based members than most competitors have. For example, only about one third of WellPoint's membership base is fee-based.

Size is also an advantage for UnitedHealth. The size of its provider network and the breadth of its product offerings allow the company to create more combinations of comprehensive products to meet customers' increasing demand for alternatives (without investing in new capabilities). Furthermore,

the firm is able to spread its investments in technology and medical cost management across a larger sales base. The more than $1.7 billion that UnitedHealth has invested in technology over the past five years will support sales growth and margin improvement for years to come.

Unlike many of its competitors, UnitedHealth has not sacrificed margins or assumed additional risk to increase sales. In the short term, any company can increase enrollment by underpricing its products and assuming additional risk. UnitedHealth has actually been improving margins by increasing the proportion of revenue derived from more specialized care products, and has been reducing risk by decreasing the proportion of its risk-based accounts. This business mix shift is not only financially attractive, it also allows UnitedHealth to deliver the products that customers want.

UnitedHealth has a strong position, but this industry is intensely competitive. Therefore, we would look to invest only if the stock price provided a margin of safety of more than 20% to our fair value estimate.

M○RNINGSTAR® Stocks 500

Universal Health Services B UHS

	Rating	Risk	Moat Size	Fair Value	Last Close	Yield %
	★★★	Med.	Narrow	$46.00	$45.10	0.0

Company Profile

Universal Health Services owns and operates acute-care hospitals, behavioral health centers, ambulatory surgery centers, radiation oncology centers, and women's centers. Services provided by the company's hospitals include general surgery, internal medicine, obstetrics, cardiology, and pediatric care. Universal Health operates 24 acute-care hospitals and 37 behavioral health facilities, primarily in midsize cities.

Management

Alan B. Miller has been chairman, president, and CEO since Universal's inception in 1978. He has spearheaded the firm's steady admissions and revenue growth in its acute-care hospitals and behavioral health centers.

Strategy

Universal has switched from an acquisition-oriented growth strategy to internal expansion. The company is increasing investment in its existing core of hospitals to improve facilities and add higher-acuity services. These facilities are primarily in small to midsize markets that have favorable demographics and less competition.

....

Universal Corporate Center   www.uhsinc.com
King Of Prussia, PA 19406

Morningstar Grades

Growth [B]	1998	1999	2000	2001
Revenue %	29.9	9.0	9.8	26.7
Earnings/Share %	17.7	2.1	23.0	6.7
Book Value/Share %	18.5	6.9	14.4	12.6
Dividends/Share %	NMF	NMF	NMF	NMF

Strong pricing power, improved facilities, and favorable demographic trends should lead to revenue growth of 11%-13% over the next three years. This compares favorably with the 15% growth of the past three years, which was driven by acquisitions.

Profitability [A]	1999	2000	2001	TTM
Return on Assets %	5.2	5.4	4.7	5.9
Oper Cash Flow $Mil	176	182	312	304
- Cap Spending $Mil	68	114	153	198
= Free Cash Flow $Mil	108	69	159	106

Universal's operating margins have bounced around 8% for the past several years. We expect the firm will drive operating margins to about 10% over the next several years by expanding the services provided at existing facilities.

Financial Health [B]	1999	2000	2001	09-02
Long-term Debt $Mil	419	548	719	658
Total Equity $Mil	642	717	808	947
Debt/Equity Ratio	0.7	0.8	0.9	0.7

The debt/total capitalization ratio increased steadily from 0.35 in 1997 to 0.47 in 2001. But Universal has paid down more than $60 million in debt through the third quarter of 2002 and produces more than enough cash flow to manage what remains.

Industry	Investment Style	Stock Type	Sector
Hospitals	Mid Growth	Classic Growth	Healthcare

Competition

	Market Cap $Mil	Debt/ Equity	12 Mo Trailing Sales $Mil	Price/Cash Flow	Return On Assets%	Total Return% 1 Yr	3 Yr
Universal Health Services B	2,726	0.7	3,148	9.0	5.9	5.4	35.2
HCA-The Healthcare Compan	21,270	1.2	19,243	8.3	5.0	7.9	13.4
Tenet Healthcare	7,990	0.6	14,319	3.2	7.0	-58.1	1.0

Price Volatility

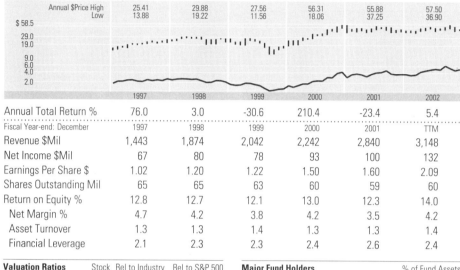

Annual $Price High Low	25.41 13.88	29.88 19.22	27.56 11.56	56.31 18.06	55.88 37.25	57.50 36.90

I Monthly Price High/Low   — Relative Strength to S&P 500

	1997	1998	1999	2000	2001	2002
Annual Total Return %	76.0	3.0	-30.6	210.4	-23.4	5.4
Fiscal Year-end: December	1997	1998	1999	2000	2001	TTM
Revenue $Mil	1,443	1,874	2,042	2,242	2,840	3,148
Net Income $Mil	67	80	78	93	100	132
Earnings Per Share $	1.02	1.20	1.22	1.50	1.60	2.09
Shares Outstanding Mil	65	65	63	60	59	60
Return on Equity %	12.8	12.7	12.1	13.0	12.3	14.0
Net Margin %	4.7	4.2	3.8	4.2	3.5	4.2
Asset Turnover	1.3	1.3	1.4	1.3	1.3	1.4
Financial Leverage	2.1	2.3	2.3	2.4	2.6	2.4

Valuation Ratios	Stock	Rel to Industry	Rel to S&P 500
Price/Earnings	21.6	0.9	0.9
Price/Book	2.9	0.8	0.9
Price/Sales	0.9	0.8	0.4
Price/Cash Flow	9.0	1.1	0.7

Major Fund Holders	% of Fund Assets
Turner Healthcare & Biotechnology	7.22
INVESCO Advantage Glob Health Sci A	5.03
Fidelity Select Medical Delivery	4.92
Westport R	4.58

Morningstar's Take By Damon Ficklin, 12-04-2002 Stock Price as of Analysis: $45.47

Universal Health Services is the leading hospital network focused on small to midsize markets. It has fortified its position in this attractive segment through acquisitions and by expanding the scope of services that it provides. We would buy shares of this niche leader at a 30% discount to our fair value estimate.

Universal has built an impressive portfolio of hospitals and a strong competitive position. With fewer hospitals, the smaller markets that the company serves are less competitive than large urban markets. The hospitals that Universal does compete with usually have only a fraction of the resources that Universal can bring to bear. Its facilities are concentrated in communities that have been growing twice as fast as the overall U.S. population and should continue to far outpace total U.S. population growth for many years to come. By carefully positioning itself and making good strategic investments, Universal has built competitive advantages that won't fade anytime soon.

Universal has slowed its acquisition pace recently and stepped up investment to expand and improve its existing facilities. It posted record capital expenditures of $153 million in 2001 and has increased investment another 50% in 2002. We

expect the company will continue to make substantial investments. By expanding the scope and increasing the quality of care provided in its hospitals, Universal is driving additional revenue growth and securing its dominant position in its communities.

The fruits of Universal's strategy are already apparent. By expanding services in its fast-growing communities, the company has realized strong admissions growth and consistently increased utilization rates at its acute-care and behavioral health facilities over the past several years. From 1997 to 2001, it increased the utilization rate for available beds from 57% to 68% at acute-care hospitals and from 52% to 73% at behavioral health facilities. This drives higher revenue against a highly fixed cost structure and has helped Universal maintain its margins despite acquisition and labor-shortage costs.

While we expect that Universal will continue to be opportunistically acquisitive, we look for it to invest heavily in its exiting facilities to drive strong internal growth. We would require a 30% margin of safety before investing, to guard against the risks inherent in the hospital industry.

Urban Outfitters URBN

	Rating	Risk	Moat Size	Fair Value	Last Close	Yield %
	★	Med.	None	$20.00	$23.57	0.0

Company Profile

Urban Outfitters is a specialty retailer and wholesaler. It sells fashion apparel, accessories, and household and gift merchandise. Its retail division includes 49 Urban Retail stores and 30 Anthropologie stores in North America and Europe. Urban Retail stores average about 10,000 selling square feet, average 60,000 stock-keeping units, and account for approximately 87% of net sales. Its wholesale subsidiary designs young women's casualwear, which it provides to the company and other stores under the Free People, Ecote, Anthropologie, and Co-Operative labels.

Management

President and chairman Richard A. Hayne co-founded Urban Outfitters in 1970. Its two operating units are run separately, with Glen Senk heading Anthropologie and Ted Marlow leading Urban Retail. Both have extensive retail experience.

Strategy

To maintain robust growth, Urban Outfitters is expanding its two retail formats and keeping abreast of the capricious preferences of fashion-conscious shoppers. Management focuses heavily on tailoring merchandise selection to serve young adults from 18 to 30 in its larger urban retail unit and women from 30 to 45 with its Anthropologie brand. The retailer is opening new stores under each concept.

1809 Walnut St · www.urbn.com
Philadelphia, PA 19103

Morningstar Grades

Growth [A-]	1999	2000	2001	2002
Revenue %	21.1	32.5	6.2	18.2
Earnings/Share %	12.8	19.3	-41.9	41.0
Book Value/Share %	15.4	15.6	10.8	11.0
Dividends/Share %	NMF	NMF	NMF	NMF

Urban Outfitters' tiny store base has delivered faster growth than most other clothing stores, thanks to new store openings and the popularity of its trendy merchandise. With fewer than 100 stores, the company has plenty of room to grow.

Profitability [A]	2000	2001	2002	TTM
Return on Assets %	12.2	6.2	7.7	9.1
Oper Cash Flow $Mil	26	23	33	48
- Cap Spending $Mil	38	37	22	23
= Free Cash Flow $Mil	-12	-14	10	25

Urban Outfitters' returns on assets have been impressive, particularly given that the retailer's size doesn't allow for the economies of scale that larger chains enjoy.

Financial Health [A-]	2000	2001	2002	10-02
Long-term Debt $Mil	—	—	—	—
Total Equity $Mil	121	130	146	213
Debt/Equity Ratio	—	—	—	—

The balance sheet is rock-solid. The company has no long-term debt and plenty of cash to fund expansion efforts. Its current assets (excluding inventories) are sufficient to cover its current liabilities more than 2 times.

Industry	Investment Style	Stock Type	Sector
Clothing Stores	▦ Small Growth	↗ Classic Growth	▭ Consumer Services

Competition	Market Cap $Mil	Debt/ Equity	12 Mo Trailing Sales $Mil	Price/Cash Flow	Return On Assets%	Total Return% 1 Yr	3 Yr
Urban Outfitters	454	—	409	9.4	9.1	-2.3	-3.2
Wet Seal A	361	—	631	—	—	—	—
bebe stores	343	—	317	—	—	—	—

Price Volatility

| Monthly Price High/Low — Relative Strength to S&P 500

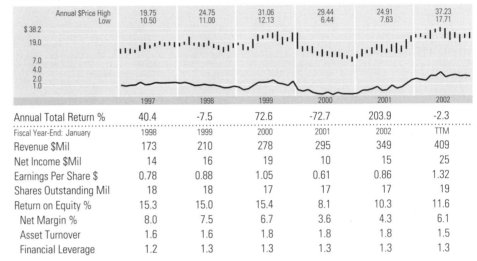

Annual $Price High / Low	19.75 / 10.50	24.75 / 11.00	31.06 / 12.13	29.44 / 6.44	24.91 / 7.63	37.23 / 17.71
	1997	1998	1999	2000	2001	2002
Annual Total Return %	40.4	-7.5	72.6	-72.7	203.9	-2.3

Fiscal Year-End: January	1998	1999	2000	2001	2002	TTM
Revenue $Mil	173	210	278	295	349	409
Net Income $Mil	14	16	19	10	15	25
Earnings Per Share $	0.78	0.88	1.05	0.61	0.86	1.32
Shares Outstanding Mil	18	18	17	17	17	19
Return on Equity %	15.3	15.0	15.4	8.1	10.3	11.6
Net Margin %	8.0	7.5	6.7	3.6	4.3	6.1
Asset Turnover	1.6	1.6	1.8	1.8	1.8	1.5
Financial Leverage	1.2	1.3	1.3	1.3	1.3	1.3

Valuation Ratios	Stock	Rel to Industry	Rel to S&P 500
Price/Earnings	17.9	1.0	0.8
Price/Book	2.1	0.5	0.7
Price/Sales	1.1	1.2	0.6
Price/Cash Flow	9.4	0.9	0.7

Major Fund Holders	% of Fund Assets
Seligman Small Cap Value A	3.22
Delaware American Services A	2.22
Mercantile Capital Opportunities I	2.20
Hennessy Cornerstone Growth	2.05

Morningstar's Take By Roz Bryant, 11-22-2002 Stock Price as of Analysis: $24.95

Urban Outfitters has an innovative retailing strategy and substantial growth opportunities, but its expansion plan holds its share of risks. We'd look for a 50% discount to our fair value estimate before investing.

Urban Outfitters has developed a retail strategy that has convinced customers to pay a premium to shop in its eye-catching street-front locations. Its core concept, after which the company is named, targets men and women between the ages of 18 and 30 with creative product displays and a frequently changing selection. In addition to popular national brands, Urban Outfitters sells merchandise from its own internally developed brands. However, the main draw seems to be the stores themselves, which showcase management's ability to attract customers by maintaining just the right product assortment and atmosphere. Revenue growth has averaged 18% over the past five years.

Anthropologie, its second retail concept, follows a similar strategy, but targets 30- to 45-year-old women. This demographic has responded with gusto; the chain's square footage has increased almost 50% annually since 1998. Anthropologie's clothing has a more bohemian feel than that of rival Chico's, so it appeals to a niche market of mature women who prefer whimsical styles.

With a combined 85 stores, both chains have plenty of room for expansion. Management is now eyeing malls as the fertile ground for new locations. Starting in 2003, the firm intends to average 20% annual square-footage growth. If the expansion proves successful, operating margins should return to double digits from closer to 7% in 2001 and 2002. As the retailer grows large enough to secure deeper volume discounts from its vendors, we expect per-unit buying costs to fall. Also, a larger store base would justify the expense of buying a West Coast distribution facility, which would lower handling and freight costs.

However, there's no guarantee that Urban Outfitters will reach critical mass smoothly, if at all. A small store base holds the promise of superior growth, but it also means the firm has a long way to go before it will win the economies of scale its larger rivals enjoy. Moreover, it's difficult to say with any certainty that its "urban hipster" image will thrive in traditional malls. While we like the growth prospects, the risks associated with investing in this small company would keep us on the sidelines until the stock fell to around $10.

MORNINGSTAR® Stocks 500

US Bancorp USB

	Rating	Risk	Moat Size	Fair Value	Last Close	Yield %
	★★★	Med.	Narrow	$28.00	$21.22	3.7

Company Profile

US Bancorp is the nation's eighth-largest bank by asset size. The firm serves more than 10 million customers in 24 states and has approximately 2,200 retail locations along with 5,000 ATMs. The bank provides typical services like savings, checking, money market, and individual retirement accounts, as well as products like trust services, asset management, and insurance. The firm's capital markets subsidiary, US Bancorp Piper Jaffray, offers investment banking and brokerage services.

Management

CEO Jerry Grundhofer, formerly the chief executive of Firstar, took the corporate reins of US Bancorp from his brother, John, at the beginning of this year. John, who had headed US Bancorp since 1990, has stayed on as chairman.

Strategy

US Bancorp, a Minneapolis-based superregional bank, intends to be the leading retail and commercial bank in the West and Midwest. It recently bought a transaction-processing unit, which handles ATM and card payment processing for merchants and other banks.

225 South Sixth Street
Minneapolis, MN 55402-4302
www.usbank.com

Morningstar Grades

Growth [C-]	1998	1999	2000	2001
Revenue %	12.4	5.7	14.0	-3.0
Earnings/Share %	29.4	11.8	22.0	-41.3
Book Value/Share %	6.3	11.1	9.9	7.3
Dividends/Share %	12.9	11.5	10.2	10.3

We expect US Bancorp to increase its balance sheet only modestly in 2003 as the firm attempts to build a bigger equity base relative to its asset size. In future years, we anticipate slightly above-average balance sheet growth.

Profitability [B]	1999	2000	2001	TTM
Return on Assets %	1.5	1.7	1.0	1.8
Oper Cash Flow $Mil	4,967	4,443	2,182	—
- Cap Spending $Mil	289	383	299	—
= Free Cash Flow $Mil	—	—	—	—

Profits have suffered recently because higher bad debt has prompted increased loan-loss provisioning. But the bank's efficiency ratio--a measure of profitability--has remained better than most rivals'.

Financial Health [A]	1999	2000	2001	09-02
Long-term Debt $Mil	—	—	—	—
Total Equity $Mil	13,947	15,168	16,461	17,518
Debt/Equity Ratio	—	—	—	—

US Bancorp has historically been one of the stronger financial services firms. However, the firm is now in a much more precarious situation with low capital levels and high bad-debt charge-offs.

Industry	Investment Style	Stock Type	Sector
Super Regional Banks	▦ Large Value	⬚ High Yield	$ Financial Services

Competition	Market Cap $Mil	Debt/ Equity	12 Mo Trailing Sales $Mil	Price/Cash Flow	Return On Assets%	Total Return% 1 Yr	3 Yr
US Bancorp	40,630	—	15,324	—	1.8	5.2	11.7
Bank of America	104,505	—	46,628	—	1.3	14.5	19.8
Wells Fargo	79,608	—	28,119	—	1.5	10.3	10.4

Price Volatility

| Monthly Price High/Low — Relative Strength to S&P 500

		1997	1998	1999	2000	2001	2002
Annual $Price High		30.73	37.50	30.09	24.11	25.89	24.50
Low		17.79	20.26	17.29	13.34	16.50	16.05

$ 38.5 19.0 9.0 6.0 4.0 2.0

	1997	1998	1999	2000	2001	2002
Annual Total Return %	67.5	-3.1	-31.3	27.4	-6.1	5.2

Fiscal Year-end: December	1997	1998	1999	2000	2001	TTM
Revenue $Mil	12,519	14,075	14,872	16,956	16,443	15,324
Net Income $Mil	1,588	2,133	2,382	2,876	1,707	3,135
Earnings Per Share $	0.85	1.10	1.23	1.50	0.88	1.63
Shares Outstanding Mil	1,847	1,904	1,905	1,904	1,917	1,915
Return on Equity %	13.9	17.0	17.1	19.0	10.4	17.9
Net Margin %	12.7	15.2	16.0	17.0	10.4	20.5
Asset Turnover	0.1	0.1	0.1	0.1	0.1	0.1
Financial Leverage	12.1	12.0	11.1	10.9	10.4	9.9

Valuation Ratios	Stock	Rel to Industry	Rel to S&P 500
Price/Earnings	13.0	0.9	0.6
Price/Book	2.3	1.1	0.7
Price/Sales	2.7	1.2	1.3
Price/Cash Flow	—	—	—

Major Fund Holders	% of Fund Assets
Cincinnati	5.09
Diamond Hill Bank & Financial A	4.97
Rydex Banking Inv	4.74
Diamond Hill Focus A	4.00

Morningstar's Take By Craig Woker, 12-05-2002 Stock Price as of Analysis: $21.16

US Bancorp is an anomaly. In an industry where mega-mergers have been the stumbling block for many once-proud companies, this firm not only is the successful offshoot of two big regional banks--the "old US Bancorp" and Firstar--but it also has fast become one of the most profitable large financial institutions. However, as much as the company's recent success depended on a trouble-free merger, US Bancorp's ability to deliver for shareholders will now depend on finding ways to grow internally.

We believe US Bancorp will succeed. This stock is worth $28 per share, in our view, and we would find it attractively priced at a 40% discount. The firm is targeting 10% earnings growth and returns on equity of at least 20%, goals we think are achievable.

Key to delivering solid results will be successfully boosting output from the legacy US Bancorp branches. The combined firm must implement Firstar's strong retail sales expertise to generate stronger results from these branches. Already, the company is showing results. For instance, the top 10 metro growth markets for small business loans are all legacy US Bancorp cities, and this was accomplished by offering products long available at Firstar.

Such results give us confidence that US Bancorp can meet its profitability targets and remain one of the best-run large banks. For instance, despite a tough banking environment, US Bancorp has delivered returns on equity in excess of 20% and an efficiency ratio in the low-40s, both at the top of the company's peer group of the nation's top 10 banks. Plus, while US Bancorp hasn't been immune from bad loans, the firm has an above-average level of operating earnings relative to charge-offs, and solid loan-loss reserves.

We also like the fact that US Bancorp is thinking long term. The firm's closed-loop card processing system, for instance, is a valuable asset in a fast-growing financial subsector. Plus, the firm has assembled a top-tier corporate trust business, a sector with good growth prospects and great economies of scale.

The one major challenge facing US Bancorp is the need to rebuild its relatively weak tangible capital base. The weak capital cushion, in our view, is the only major factor standing between US Bancorp and its goal of achieving an AA credit rating, up from A now. Though this adds risk if the economy nose-dives over the next year, we believe US Bancorp's solid long-term prospects more than make up for the risk, as long as the stock can be bought at a reasonable price.

USA Interactive USAI

Rating	Risk	Moat Size	Fair Value	Last Close	Yield %
★	Med.	None	$17.00	$22.92	0.0

Company Profile

USA Interactive is a diversified commerce and media company. The firm's Ticketmaster subsidiary provides automated-ticketing services. USA also operates Internet-based services and products through businesses including Expedia and Match.com. In early 2002, it completed the sale of USA Entertainment to Vivendi Universal. Upon completing that transaction, the company changed its name from USA Networks to USA Interactive.

Management

Charismatic chairman and CEO Barry Diller has been with the firm since 1995. His dozens of years in media management include stints with titans like Fox and Paramount Pictures.

Strategy

USA Interactive exploits various media to drive transactions with consumers. Assets like Home Shopping Network place the company in the sweet spot of televised direct marketing. It also has a rapidly growing presence in e-commerce with properties like Expedia and Match.com.

152 West 57th Street   www.usanetworks.com
New York, NY 10019

Industry	Investment Style	Stock Type	Sector
Media Conglomerates	▦ Large Growth	↑ Aggr. Growth	🎙 Media

Competition

	Market Cap $Mil	Debt/ Equity	12 Mo Trailing Sales $Mil	Price/Cash Flow	Return On Assets%	Total Return% 1 Yr	3 Yr
USA Interactive	10,290	0.1	4,231	37.7	11.8	-16.1	-2.9
AOL Time Warner	56,278	0.3	41,024	8.1	-34.6	-59.2	-44.6
Walt Disney	32,923	0.5	24,550	14.6	2.5	-20.3	-19.1

Price Volatility

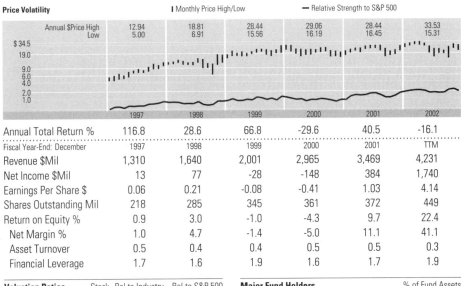

I Monthly Price High/Low   — Relative Strength to S&P 500

	1997	1998	1999	2000	2001	2002
Annual $Price High	12.94	18.81	28.44	29.06	28.44	33.53
Low	5.00	6.91	15.56	16.19	16.45	15.31
Annual Total Return %	116.8	28.6	66.8	-29.6	40.5	-16.1

Fiscal Year-End: December	1997	1998	1999	2000	2001	TTM
Revenue $Mil	1,310	1,640	2,001	2,965	3,469	4,231
Net Income $Mil	13	77	-28	-148	384	1,740
Earnings Per Share $	0.06	0.21	-0.08	-0.41	1.03	4.14
Shares Outstanding Mil	218	285	345	361	372	449
Return on Equity %	0.9	3.0	-1.0	-4.3	9.7	22.4
Net Margin %	1.0	4.7	-1.4	-5.0	11.1	41.1
Asset Turnover	0.5	0.4	0.4	0.5	0.5	0.3
Financial Leverage	1.7	1.6	1.9	1.6	1.7	1.9

Valuation Ratios	Stock	Rel to Industry	Rel to S&P 500
Price/Earnings	5.5	0.2	0.2
Price/Book	1.3	0.9	0.4
Price/Sales	2.4	1.1	1.2
Price/Cash Flow	37.7	2.5	2.8

Major Fund Holders	% of Fund Assets
Synovus Mid Cap Value C	5.41
Synovus Mid Cap Value Instl	5.41
Fidelity Select Multimedia	4.42
Legg Mason Focus	4.25

Morningstar Grades

Growth [A+]	1998	1999	2000	2001
Revenue %	25.2	22.0	48.1	17.0
Earnings/Share %	250.0	NMF	NMF	NMF
Book Value/Share %	5.6	14.2	18.8	11.2
Dividends/Share %	NMF	NMF	NMF	NMF

USA has experienced dramatic growth in recent years, boosted by successful acquisitions. Diller's plans for $9 billion in e-commerce acquisitions over the next three years have been scaled back.

Profitability [B-]	1999	2000	2001	TTM
Return on Assets %	-0.5	-2.6	5.9	11.8
Oper Cash Flow $Mil	78	87	298	273
- Cap Spending $Mil	102	160	131	141
= Free Cash Flow $Mil	-24	-73	168	132

USA Interactive's most profitable business segments, including Expedia and Match.com, are also the fastest-growing. Free cash flow has ballooned since the company switched to a more transaction-based model.

Financial Health [B]	1999	2000	2001	09-02
Long-term Debt $Mil	573	552	544	508
Total Equity $Mil	2,770	3,440	3,946	7,776
Debt/Equity Ratio	0.2	0.2	0.1	0.1

USA is among the healthiest companies in the media industry, enjoying a low debt/equity ratio and more than $2 billion in net cash and securities.

Morningstar's Take By T.K. MacKay, 12-15-2002 Stock Price as of Analysis: $24.95

Investing in USA Interactive places bets in a number of interesting businesses, but we'd only hand over our chips at the right price.

USA's consummation of its joint venture with Vivendi, Vivendi Universal Entertainment, did a lot more than score a huge return on investment. (CEO Barry Diller essentially sold $10 billion of assets that he'd bought for $4 billion four years earlier.) It removed second-rate, advertising-reliant cable channels SciFi and USA from USA's portfolio. By selling these ad-dependent entertainment assets, Diller focused USA Interactive on the lucrative niche that it now dominates--transaction-based media. In this area, USA has attained market leadership via HSN, Hotels.com, Expedia, Ticketmaster, and Match.com. We're much more comfortable with USA's business knowing that it depends less on advertising and is diversified in multiple industries.

However, we don't see evidence that any single unit besides Ticketmaster (which contributes just 15% of USA's total sales) has a substantial competitive advantage. Airfares and hotel rooms found on Expedia and Hotels.com may be found through other agents like Travelocity and Orbitz. HSN's alliances with chef Wolfgang Puck and designer Randolph Duke bode well for the cable channel, but Comcast's successful acquisition of AT&T Broadband opens the door to 13.5 million more potential households with QVC. Match.com, USA's online personals service, appears to be building a substantial "network effect" (a criterion for economic moats) through its quickly growing database of singles, which tops 5 million, but Yahoo Personals is in hot pursuit. We also believe that the market for personal ads is limited. While all of these businesses have met with relative success so far, whether they will be on top in five years (or even be owned by USA Interactive) is guesswork.

In addition to multiple businesses, investors in USA Interactive are buying a stake in Barry Diller's dealings. With the media industry changing almost daily and Diller at the helm, it is very likely that USA Interactive's portfolio of businesses will look different three to five years from now. Such changes make it difficult to predict USA Interactive's revenue and profits. Because of this, we would consider buying the stock only if it traded 40% or more below our estimated fair value.

MORNINGSTAR® Stocks 500

VeriSign VRSN

	Rating	Risk	Moat Size	Fair Value	Last Close	Yield %
	★★	High	None	$8.00	$8.02	0.0

Company Profile

VeriSign is a self-proclaimed Internet utility with technology that reaches nearly every corner of the Internet. It provides digital certificates and authentication services that protect digital data like credit card numbers and corporate communications. Such technology is key to virtual private networks and secure e-commerce applications. VeriSign also owns and operates the registry for the most popular domain names, like .com, .net, and .org. Plans are to cross-sell its ancillary services to the more than 30 million domain name registrants it manages.

Management

CEO Stratton Sclavos came on board in July 1995. D. James Bidzos, an industry hall of famer, has been chairman since VeriSign's founding in April 1995.

Strategy

VeriSign is building an Internet tollbooth. By amassing a portfolio of online commerce services including domain name registration, authentication services, and payments, the company has become a one-stop shop for anyone wanting to create a Web presence. VeriSign recently acquired Illuminet, which provides services like caller ID to telecom companies.

487 East Middlefield Road
Mountain View, CA 94043
www.verisign-grs.com

Industry	Investment Style	Stock Type	Sector
Systems & Security	Mid Growth	Spec. Growth	Software

Competition	Market Cap $Mil	Debt/ Equity	12 Mo Trailing Sales $Mil	Price/Cash Flow	Return On Assets%	Total Return% 1 Yr	3 Yr
VeriSign	1,902	0.0	1,230	8.8	ELB	-78.9	-65.1
RSA Security	341	—	234	—	—	—	—
Entrust	216	—	106	—	—	—	—

Price Volatility

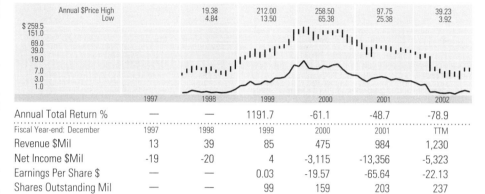

			1997	1998	1999	2000	2001	2002
Annual Total Return %			—	—	1191.7	-61.1	-48.7	-78.9

Fiscal Year-end: December	1997	1998	1999	2000	2001	TTM
Revenue $Mil	13	39	85	475	984	1,230
Net Income $Mil	-19	-20	4	-3,115	-13,356	-5,323
Earnings Per Share $	—	—	0.03	-19.57	-65.64	-22.13
Shares Outstanding Mil	—	—	99	159	203	237
Return on Equity %	ELB	-48.5	1.3	-16.9	ELB	ELB
Net Margin %	ELB	-50.7	4.7	ELB	ELB	ELB
Asset Turnover	0.5	0.6	0.2	0.0	0.1	0.5
Financial Leverage	2.0	1.6	1.1	1.0	1.2	1.6

Valuation Ratios	Stock	Rel to Industry	Rel to S&P 500
Price/Earnings	NMF	—	—
Price/Book	1.2	0.5	0.4
Price/Sales	1.5	0.4	0.8
Price/Cash Flow	8.8	0.8	0.7

Major Fund Holders	% of Fund Assets
SunAmerica Focused Technology A	5.26
Fairmont	4.59
ProFunds Ultra Internet Inv	3.16
Schroder MidCap Value Inv	3.00

Morningstar Grades

Growth [A+]	1998	1999	2000	2001
Revenue %	191.5	117.8	460.0	107.2
Earnings/Share %	NMF	NMF	NMF	NMF
Book Value/Share %	—	NMF	EUB	-72.4
Dividends/Share %	NMF	NMF	NMF	NMF

VeriSign was a prime beneficiary of the Internet boom, leading to average annual sales growth in the triple digits. However, those days are long gone; the dot-com halcyon days are history and slow-growing businesses have been added to the fold.

Profitability [C-]	1999	2000	2001	TTM
Return on Assets %	1.2	-16.2	ELB	ELB
Oper Cash Flow $Mil	15	192	228	217
- Cap Spending $Mil	6	59	380	466
= Free Cash Flow $Mil	9	133	-153	-249

Goodwill amortization has kept GAAP earnings in the red; that'll change now that amortization won't occur. However, we expect margins to get hurt as a result of the less-profitable firms VeriSign has added to its fold and domain name pricing pressure.

Financial Health [C]	1999	2000	2001	09-02
Long-term Debt $Mil	0	0	1	0
Total Equity $Mil	298	18,471	6,506	1,617
Debt/Equity Ratio	0.0	0.0	0.0	0.0

The balance sheet is getting worse; the cash balance has fallen more than 50% over the past year. Also, operating cash flow has declined significantly.

Morningstar's Take By Mike Trigg, 11-14-2002 Stock Price as of Analysis: $8.50

It's unclear in which direction VeriSign's sales and profits are heading. Given this uncertainty, we wouldn't buy the stock until it traded at least 50% below our fair value estimate.

All of VeriSign's businesses are struggling. The biggest problem is the registrar business. VeriSign receives money from registrants paying $35 annually to use Web addresses, like Morningstar paying for Morningstar.com. The firm benefited during the dot-com boom from people buying up names that could be resold for a profit, but business has slowed because the land grab is over and a growing number of competitors are chasing after fewer addresses.

But our concerns extend beyond the registrar business; we're skeptical of the firm's long-term strategy to handle all the boring (but necessary) transactions over the Internet. To realize its vision of being an Internet tollbooth, VeriSign has grown wildly through acquisition, beginning with the $21 billion Network Solutions deal in 2000. Now it's a one-stop shop for establishing e-commerce capabilities, from selling Web addresses to securing online transactions.

The problem is that VeriSign has yet to integrate many of its acquisitions, and the often-promised cross-selling opportunities are bearing little fruit. For instance, VeriSign's entrance into the struggling telecom industry seems misguided. The company bought Illuminet and H.O. Systems because it expects telephone numbers and Web addresses will converge. However, these businesses have struggled, hurting overall revenue growth and profitability.

Management's wild shopping spree boils down to poor capital allocation. VeriSign used a richly valued stock for acquisitions, but has essentially conceded that it overpaid, writing off nearly $15 billion of goodwill over the past year. Now, even with little goodwill remaining, we find it difficult to envision a scenario in our valuation model in which VeriSign can generate returns on capital in excess of the cost at which it can borrow (either debt or equity).

VeriSign has an array of businesses that could profit from the growth of the Internet. However, given its ambitious strategy of being an Internet tollbooth and management's dismal record of creating shareholder value (the stock is up only 25% since its 1998 initial public offering), we require a big margin of safety. We wouldn't buy the stock until it fell below $4.

Verizon Communications VZ

	Rating	Risk	Moat Size	Fair Value	Last Close	Yield %
	★★★	Med.	Narrow	$45.00	$38.75	4.0

Company Profile

Verizon is the product of the merger between Bell Atlantic and GTE. The company provides local phone and data services to more than one third of the U.S. population. Its local phone territory covers 13 states in the Northeast and several areas scattered across the rest of the country. It also offers long-distance services to customers where regulation permits. Verizon Wireless, the company's 55%-owned partnership with Vodafone, is the nation's largest wireless company. Verizon holds equity stakes in several other companies, giving it a presence in more than 40 countries.

Management

The former Bell Atlantic and GTE heads, Ivan Seidenberg and Charles Lee, share leadership duties, with Seidenberg as CEO and Lee as chairman. Lee will fully retire in 2004. Dennis Strigl, a wireless industry veteran, is CEO of Verizon Wireless.

Strategy

Verizon aims to use its financial and operational muscle to build a broad set of communication services. The firm offers customers bundles of wireless, local and long-distance phone, and Internet services where it has regulatory approval to do so. It is working to gain long-distance approval in three remaining states, cleaning house in its investment portfolio, and paying down debt.

1095 Avenue of the Americas www.verizon.com
New York, NY 10036

Morningstar Grades

Growth [C-]	1998	1999	2000	2001
Revenue %	6.5	2.0	11.2	3.8
Earnings/Share %	-5.3	65.9	45.1	-96.8
Book Value/Share %	3.0	22.3	33.3	-7.4
Dividends/Share %	2.7	0.0	-2.8	2.8

The weakening economy continues to take its toll on the number of phone lines in service, holding growth rates to very modest levels. Wireless and data revenue is picking up some of the slack, but solid growth won't return until the economy firms.

Profitability [B+]	1999	2000	2001	TTM
Return on Assets %	7.3	7.2	0.2	-0.1
Oper Cash Flow $Mil	17,017	15,827	19,773	22,755
- Cap Spending $Mil	13,013	17,633	17,371	13,002
= Free Cash Flow $Mil	4,004	-1,806	2,402	9,753

Investment losses and restructuring costs have pushed net income into the red. Verizon has cut costs aggressively, though, and the firm's businesses are solidly profitable. Pension credits contributed about 20% of earnings last year.

Financial Health [B]	1999	2000	2001	09-02
Long-term Debt $Mil	32,419	42,491	45,657	46,029
Total Equity $Mil	26,376	34,578	32,539	31,845
Debt/Equity Ratio	1.2	1.2	1.4	1.4

Verizon has used asset sales and cash flow to sharply reduce debt over the past year, and earnings easily cover interest payments. The debt load is still very large, which could limit strategic flexibility or hurt the company down the road.

Industry	Investment Style	Stock Type	Sector
Telecommunication Services	Large Value	High Yield	Telecom

Competition	Market Cap $Mil	Debt/ Equity	12 Mo Trailing Sales $Mil	Price/Cash Flow	Return On Assets%	Total Return% 1 Yr	3 Yr
Verizon Communications	106,011	1.4	67,422	4.7	-0.1	-15.2	-9.8
SBC Communications	90,011	0.6	43,824	6.1	5.1	-28.3	-12.8
BellSouth	48,170	0.7	22,961	5.9	3.3	-30.4	-14.8

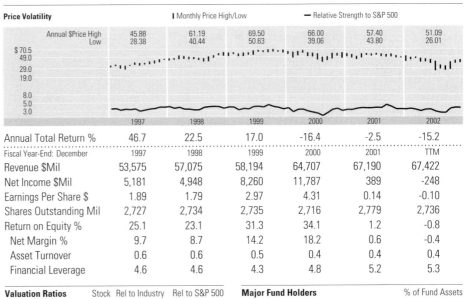

Price Volatility — Monthly Price High/Low — Relative Strength to S&P 500

		1997	1998	1999	2000	2001	2002
Annual $Price	High	45.88	61.19	69.50	66.00	57.40	51.09
	Low	28.38	40.44	50.63	39.06	43.80	26.01
Annual Total Return %		46.7	22.5	17.0	-16.4	-2.5	-15.2

Fiscal Year-End: December	1997	1998	1999	2000	2001	TTM
Revenue $Mil	53,575	57,075	58,194	64,707	67,190	67,422
Net Income $Mil	5,181	4,948	8,260	11,787	389	-248
Earnings Per Share $	1.89	1.79	2.97	4.31	0.14	-0.10
Shares Outstanding Mil	2,727	2,734	2,735	2,716	2,779	2,736
Return on Equity %	25.1	23.1	31.3	34.1	1.2	-0.8
Net Margin %	9.7	8.7	14.2	18.2	0.6	-0.4
Asset Turnover	0.6	0.6	0.5	0.4	0.4	0.4
Financial Leverage	4.6	4.6	4.3	4.8	5.2	5.3

Valuation Ratios	Stock	Rel to Industry	Rel to S&P 500
Price/Earnings	NMF	—	—
Price/Book	3.3	1.2	1.0
Price/Sales	1.6	1.0	0.8
Price/Cash Flow	4.7	0.9	0.4

Major Fund Holders	% of Fund Assets
Smith Barney Telecomm Income	23.66
ProFunds Ultra Telecommunications Inv	21.67
Rydex Telecommunications Inv	11.60
Schwab Communications Focus	10.82

Morningstar's Take By Michael Hodel, 12-05-2002 Stock Price as of Analysis: $39.07

Verizon enjoys several distinct advantages in today's telecom industry but faces several uncertainties. Despite the risks, we still think the Bells, including Verizon, are attractive investments, offering solid cash flow and the potential to lead the industry.

Verizon's competitive advantage stems from its control of the local phone networks in the markets it serves. The vastness of this network makes it extremely difficult to replicate, and the lack of a bona fide substitute has allowed Verizon to maintain prices and hold on to most of its customers, keeping cash flow strong. This network also gives Verizon an avenue to evolve its service offerings to meet the needs of customers down the road.

Competition is growing in the local market, though. A few long-distance carriers, including AT&T, aim to use local service to offset declines in long-distance revenue and slow customer loss. These firms' ability to offer local service depends largely on regulations that mandate the Bells lease parts of their network at wholesale rates. The Federal Communications Commission is debating changes to these rules. Cable companies are more of a threat, as many have upgraded their networks to offer high-speed Internet access and local phone service.

Verizon's push into wireless and long-distance has offset some of the impact of local competition. Verizon Wireless is well positioned in the industry, earning strong margins thanks to its massive scale while attracting new customers with its high-quality network. Verizon has also been a leader in winning regulatory approval to offer long-distance services. Adding long-distance to the service mix will help the company generate more revenue from smaller customers and offer comprehensive telecom service to large businesses. The latter is especially important, given the large number of national and multinational companies operating in the Northeast.

Despite growing competition and a weak economy, Verizon has greatly improved free cash flows. While cost-cutting has helped offset lower revenue, the biggest driver of this improvement has been capital spending cuts. While we don't think spending will return to levels seen during the telecom bubble, we also don't think current low levels are sustainable as the company's markets grow increasingly competitive. The ultimate level of spending required will have a big impact on the company's fair value--especially given Verizon's debt load. If operating cash flows shrink and capital needs escalate, the value of the stock will suffer.

 MORNINGSTAR® Stocks 500

Vertex Pharmaceuticals VRTX

| | Rating ★★★ | Risk High | Moat Size Narrow | Fair Value $22.00 | Last Close $15.85 | Yield % 0.0 |

Company Profile

Vertex Pharmaceuticals develops and manufactures drugs to treat diseases for which only limited treatments are available. The company produces its Agenerase protease inhibitor to treat HIV. It is developing treatments for AIDS, multidrug resistance in cancer, inflammatory diseases, and beta thalassemia, another genetic hemoglobin disorder. Vertex is collaborating with Novartis on eight drug candidates and with Aventis to develop anti-inflammatory treatments. Its recently acquired Aurora subsidiary sells platform technology and services to other drug-development firms.

Management

Joshua Boger heads the company. Previously the senior director of chemistry at pharmaceutical giant Merck, Boger is now using his expertise to shape Vertex's efforts in combining chemistry and biology in drug design.

Strategy

Although it takes a big-picture approach to drug development, Vertex focuses on families of proteins rather than broad-based gene discovery the way rival Millennium does. The technology aims to provide a large number of drug targets in less time than other processes. The company has several products in human trials, has a massive research alliance with Novartis, and seeks strategic acquisitions.

130 Waverly Street
Cambridge, MA 02139-4242
www.vrtx.com

Morningstar Grades

Growth [B-]	1998	1999	2000	2001
Revenue %	25.9	74.0	40.8	9.3
Earnings/Share %	NMF	NMF	NMF	NMF
Book Value/Share %	-22.5	-13.2	86.8	-15.4
Dividends/Share %	NMF	NMF	NMF	NMF

Because Vertex has only one product on the market from which it receives a small percentage of its sales, revenue growth is fairly erratic. The PanVera acquisition inflated sales growth in 2001 but will provide a steady revenue stream.

Profitability [C]	1999	2000	2001	TTM
Return on Assets %	-13.4	-3.7	-7.2	-9.6
Oper Cash Flow $Mil	-20	-14	-8	-25
- Cap Spending $Mil	18	18	54	42
= Free Cash Flow $Mil	-38	-32	-62	-67

Like many biotechnology companies, Vertex is still several years away from profitability. It will probably post losses at least through 2005.

Financial Health [D+]	1999	2000	2001	09-02
Long-term Debt $Mil	—	357	323	321
Total Equity $Mil	252	514	475	408
Debt/Equity Ratio	—	0.7	0.7	0.8

As of September 30, Vertex had a debt/equity ratio of 0.8, higher than most of its biotech rivals. But the firm has $651 million in cash to cover the debt and run operations for a couple of more years.

| | Industry Biotechnology | Investment Style Small Growth | Stock Type Spec. Growth | Sector Healthcare |

Competition

	Market Cap $Mil	Debt/ Equity	12 Mo Trailing Sales $Mil	Price/Cash Flow	Return On Assets%	Total Return% 1 Yr	3 Yr
Vertex Pharmaceuticals	1,206	0.8	169	—	-9.6	-35.5	-2.8
Genentech	17,067	0.0	2,541	28.3	0.2	-38.9	-19.2
Millennium Pharmaceutical	2,293	—	311	—	—	—	—

Price Volatility

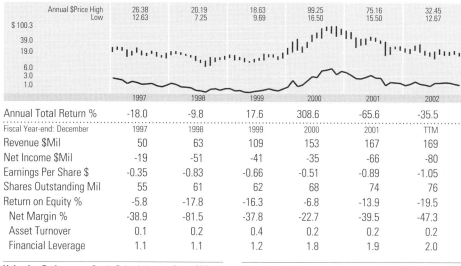

| Price Volatility | ❙ Monthly Price High/Low | — Relative Strength to S&P 500 |

Annual $Price High Low	26.38 12.63	20.19 7.25	18.63 9.69	99.25 16.50	75.16 15.50	32.45 12.67
	1997	1998	1999	2000	2001	2002
Annual Total Return %	-18.0	-9.8	17.6	308.6	-65.6	-35.5

Fiscal Year-end: December	1997	1998	1999	2000	2001	TTM
Revenue $Mil	50	63	109	153	167	169
Net Income $Mil	-19	-51	-41	-35	-66	-80
Earnings Per Share $	-0.35	-0.83	-0.66	-0.51	-0.89	-1.05
Shares Outstanding Mil	55	61	62	68	74	76
Return on Equity %	-5.8	-17.8	-16.3	-6.8	-13.9	-19.5
Net Margin %	-38.9	-81.5	-37.8	-22.7	-39.5	-47.3
Asset Turnover	0.1	0.2	0.4	0.2	0.2	0.2
Financial Leverage	1.1	1.1	1.2	1.8	1.9	2.0

Valuation Ratios	Stock	Rel to Industry	Rel to S&P 500
Price/Earnings	NMF	—	—
Price/Book	3.0	0.8	0.9
Price/Sales	7.1	0.6	3.6
Price/Cash Flow	—	—	—

Major Fund Holders	% of Fund Assets
Amerindo Health & Biotechnology A	8.59
Alliance Select Investor Biotech A	4.83
Scudder Global Biotechnology A	4.27
GenomicsFund	3.70

Morningstar's Take By Jill Kiersky, 12-09-2002 Stock Price as of Analysis: $16.65

Vertex has a few more years to profitability, and we think the shares will remain highly volatile. This stock is only for investors willing to hold a significant amount of risk.

Vertex has put itself on the biotechnology map with its chemogenomics platform, the firm's drug-discovery technology. While most firms search for a single disease target, chemogenomics uses supercomputers to target similar gene families. This allows the firm to simultaneously study clusters of genes rather than single gene targets. The anticipated result is cheaper, speedier design of multiple drugs. The approach appears to be working, with nine products in clinical trials. The company also hopes to patent-protect compounds arising from its research.

Meanwhile, revenue has increased at a compound annual rate of 80% since 1998, thanks to increasing revenue from subsidiary PanVera (formerly Aurora Biosciences) and cash payments from partnerships. Such collaborative research agreements are the means for coming-of-age biotech firms to stay afloat until they generate their own revenue. Vertex has convinced big drug firms and larger biotechs of its research value. To date, it has entered into partnerships that could provide $1.4 billion in

research funding and milestone payments, including an unprecedented $815 million pledge from Novartis, a substantial amount relative to other biotech partnerships.

Vertex also has a strong existing pipeline to augment Agenerase, a highly potent protease inhibitor that it brought to market with GlaxoSmithKline in 1999. Agenerase has captured 8% of the highly competitive HIV market with sales of $72 million. In addition to a second-generation protease inhibitor, the pipeline has eight drugs that target cancer and inflammatory and infectious diseases. Success with these compounds will give the company meaningful revenue growth in the long run. The probabilities indicate two or three will succeed.

Vertex has plenty of risks, including uncertainty about its ability to develop efficacious drugs and bring them to market, continued financial support from collaborations, and chemogenomics' development value. We've adjusted both our required return and our expectation for future cash flows to account for these risks. We believe that investors willing to make such a speculative investment should only do so at a 50% discount to our fair value estimate.

Viacom B VIA.B

	Rating	Risk	Moat Size	Fair Value	Last Close	Yield %
	★★	Low	Narrow	$40.00	$40.76	0.0

Company Profile

Viacom is a diversified entertainment company that owns or operates television networks, radio stations, billboards, theme parks, and publishing products. The firm's brand names include MTV, VH1, BET, CBS, and Paramount Pictures. Viacom also owns 81% of video rental retailer Blockbuster.

	Industry	Investment Style	Stock Type	Sector
	Broadcast TV	▦ Large Growth	✻ Spec. Growth	🎙 Media

Competition

Competition	Market Cap $Mil	Debt/ Equity	12 Mo Trailing Sales $Mil	Price/Cash Flow	Return On Assets%	Total Return% 1 Yr	Total Return% 3 Yr
Viacom B	71,391	0.2	23,868	20.3	0.0	-7.7	-8.8
General Electric	242,308	2.2	130,295	8.2	2.7	-37.7	-18.9
AOL Time Warner	56,278	0.3	41,024	8.1	-34.6	-59.2	-44.6

Price Volatility

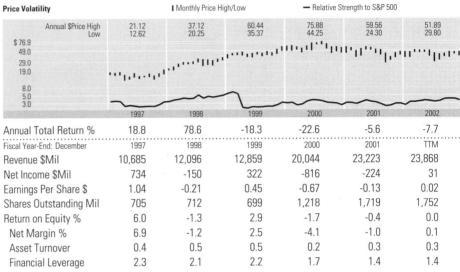

Annual $Price High Low	21.12 12.62	37.12 20.25	60.44 35.37	75.88 44.25	59.56 24.30	51.89 29.80
	1997	1998	1999	2000	2001	2002
Annual Total Return %	18.8	78.6	-18.3	-22.6	-5.6	-7.7

Fiscal Year-End: December	1997	1998	1999	2000	2001	TTM
Revenue $Mil	10,685	12,096	12,859	20,044	23,223	23,868
Net Income $Mil	734	-150	322	-816	-224	31
Earnings Per Share $	1.04	-0.21	0.45	-0.67	-0.13	0.02
Shares Outstanding Mil	705	712	699	1,218	1,719	1,752
Return on Equity %	6.0	-1.3	2.9	-1.7	-0.4	0.0
Net Margin %	6.9	-1.2	2.5	-4.1	-1.0	0.1
Asset Turnover	0.4	0.5	0.5	0.2	0.3	0.3
Financial Leverage	2.3	2.1	2.2	1.7	1.4	1.4

Management

CEO Sumner Redstone owns a controlling interest in Viacom, while former CBS head Mel Karmazin runs most of the day-to-day operations. Rumors of discord flare up occasionally, but Redstone has said that Karmazin's contract will be renewed in 2003.

Strategy

Viacom aims to be the most profitable and successful media company in the world. To get there, the company will continue to make acquisitions--using either cash or stock--that fit with its vertically integrated business model. Future acquisitions are likely to be in the area of cable programming, a high-margin business with excellent scale economics.

1515 Broadway
New York, NY 10036
www.viacom.com

Morningstar Grades

Growth [A-]	1998	1999	2000	2001
Revenue %	13.2	6.3	55.9	15.9
Earnings/Share %	NMF	NMF	NMF	NMF
Book Value/Share %	-6.9	-3.1	152.8	-7.4
Dividends/Share %	NMF	NMF	NMF	NMF

Thanks to acquisitions, Viacom's revenue is growing faster than that of most media conglomerates. But growth has slowed as a result of the ad industry's worst downturn in a decade.

Profitability [C]	1999	2000	2001	TTM
Return on Assets %	1.3	-1.0	-0.2	0.0
Oper Cash Flow $Mil	294	2,323	3,509	3,517
- Cap Spending $Mil	706	659	515	516
= Free Cash Flow $Mil	-412	1,664	2,994	3,002

Viacom's profit margins are quite good, and its cash flow margins are great. We expect margins to climb even higher over the next few years.

Financial Health [B-]	1999	2000	2001	09-02
Long-term Debt $Mil	5,698	12,474	10,824	10,464
Total Equity $Mil	11,132	47,967	62,717	62,570
Debt/Equity Ratio	0.5	0.3	0.2	0.2

Viacom's financial health is solid. The company generates loads of cash that it can use to pay down debt if needed. More likely, though, this free cash will be used for acquisitions.

Valuation Ratios

Valuation Ratios	Stock	Rel to Industry	Rel to S&P 500
Price/Earnings	EUB	—	—
Price/Book	1.1	1.0	0.4
Price/Sales	3.0	1.0	1.5
Price/Cash Flow	20.3	1.0	1.5

Major Fund Holders

Major Fund Holders	% of Fund Assets
ASAF Goldman Sachs Concentrated Gr A	9.85
IDEX Janus Growth A	9.28
Heritage Capital Appreciation A	8.91
Northern Global Communications	8.61

Morningstar's Take By Jonathan Schrader, 11-15-2002 Stock Price as of Analysis: $45.13

Viacom's narrow-moat qualities enable the firm to generate loads of cash, which always gets our attention. However, we'd only buy the stock at the right price: a 30% discount to our fair value estimate.

The company's competitive advantages lie primarily in intangible assets and economies of scale. Much like the Disney or Coca Cola brands, Viacom's brand names--including CBS, MTV, VH1, BET, and Nickelodeon--are wildly popular and highly regarded. Because of this, Viacom can charge a premium to those who wish to be associated with the brands. First, advertisers will pay up to get access to Viacom's audiences, especially those with excellent demographics like MTV and Nickelodeon. Second, cable service providers pay Viacom for the rights to carry its cable channels.

A second competitive advantage is the scale economics of Viacom's businesses. The marginal cost of adding cable channels or radio stations to Viacom's current holdings is small compared with the up-front costs associated with these businesses. Further, the programming costs that Viacom incurs can be spread over its various properties. For example, the popular CSI program can be run first on CBS, and then be shown again later on one of Viacom's cable channels, thus amortizing costs and improving margins.

There are other attractive aspects of Viacom's businesses. Unlike Disney's theme parks or AOL Time Warner's cable business, they do not require huge amounts of capital investment. This leaves even more money for shareholders, making Viacom's properties relatively more valuable than its peers'. Also, because the company is so involved in the advertising business, its fixed costs are larger than its variable costs, giving it operating leverage. This is a particularly great thing during strong economic times, because almost all marginal advertising revenue falls to the bottom line, boosting profits and cash flow.

Viacom has a great business model, and we are tempted to give the company a wide-moat standing. But even with its narrow moat, at the right price Viacom is still a relatively low-risk investment with great long-term prospects in the media sector.

MORNINGSTAR® Stocks 500

Vishay Intertechnology VSH

	Rating	Risk	Moat Size	Fair Value	Last Close	Yield %
	★★★	Med.	None	$16.00	$11.18	0.0

Company Profile

Vishay Intertechnology manufactures electronic components. Its products include resistors, which adjust and regulate levels of voltage and current, and capacitors, which perform energy storage, frequency control, timing, discrete semiconductor components, and filtering functions for electronic equipment. The company markets its products to original equipment manufacturers and government agencies in the United States and overseas. Sales generated outside the United States, which occur primarily in Europe, account for about 57% of the company's total sales.

Management

Felix Zandman is Vishay. He has been CEO since founding the company in 1962 and has been chairman since 1989. He has more than 41% voting control of the firm.

Strategy

Vishay has pursued an aggressive acquisition strategy, expanding from its origins as a resistor manufacturer to become a large producer of capacitors and semiconductors. The firm aims to gain efficiencies as it grows. Recent acquisition activity has been heavy, including the large purchases of General Semiconductor in 2001 and BCcomponents in 2002.

63 Lincoln Highway   www.vishay.com
Malvern, PA 19355-2120

Industry	Investment Style	Stock Type	Sector
Components	Mid Growth	→ Slow Growth	Hardware

Competition	Market Cap $Mil	Debt/ Equity	12 Mo Trailing Sales $Mil	Price/Cash Flow	Return On Assets%	Total Return% 1 Yr	3 Yr
Vishay Intertechnology	1,786	0.2	1,745	5.6	-0.6	-42.7	-16.7
AVX	1,708	—	1,170	11.8	-0.4	-58.0	-24.2
Fairchild Semiconductor I	1,076	—	1,383	—	—	—	—

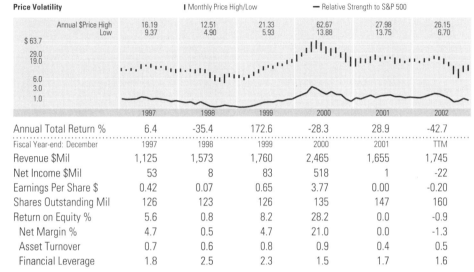

Price Volatility   I Monthly Price High/Low   — Relative Strength to S&P 500

Annual $Price High Low	16.19 9.37	12.51 4.90	21.33 5.93	62.67 13.88	27.98 13.75	26.15 6.70

	1997	1998	1999	2000	2001	2002
Annual Total Return %	6.4	-35.4	172.6	-28.3	28.9	-42.7
Fiscal Year-end: December	1997	1998	1999	2000	2001	TTM
Revenue $Mil	1,125	1,573	1,760	2,465	1,655	1,745
Net Income $Mil	53	8	83	518	1	-22
Earnings Per Share $	0.42	0.07	0.65	3.77	0.00	-0.20
Shares Outstanding Mil	126	123	126	135	147	160
Return on Equity %	5.6	0.8	8.2	28.2	0.0	-0.9
Net Margin %	4.7	0.5	4.7	21.0	0.0	-1.3
Asset Turnover	0.7	0.6	0.8	0.9	0.4	0.5
Financial Leverage	1.8	2.5	2.3	1.5	1.7	1.6

Valuation Ratios	Stock	Rel to Industry	Rel to S&P 500
Price/Earnings	NMF	—	—
Price/Book	0.7	0.4	0.2
Price/Sales	1.0	0.5	0.5
Price/Cash Flow	5.6	0.7	0.4

Major Fund Holders	% of Fund Assets
Fidelity Advisor Strategic Growth A	5.29
Manor Growth	4.10
Reserve Small-Cap Growth R	2.72
Meridian Growth	2.62

Morningstar Grades

Growth [C+]	1998	1999	2000	2001
Revenue %	39.8	11.9	40.1	-32.8
Earnings/Share %	-84.2	874.5	480.0	NMF
Book Value/Share %	7.3	-2.8	68.7	NMF
Dividends/Share %	NMF	NMF	NMF	NMF

Vishay has shown impressive growth, largely because of acquisitions. The firm recently suffered through one of the worst downturns in the history of the electronics business; revenue fell 33% in 2001, but should be up in 2002 thanks to acquisitions.

Profitability [B]	1999	2000	2001	TTM
Return on Assets %	3.6	18.6	0.0	-0.6
Oper Cash Flow $Mil	240	542	161	321
- Cap Spending $Mil	120	230	162	87
= Free Cash Flow $Mil	120	313	-1	234

Vishay is not as profitable as it could be. Continued integration of its acquired manufacturing and distribution infrastructure should help. Deriving a greater percentage of revenue from semiconductors should boost profits as well.

Financial Health [A-]	1999	2000	2001	09-02
Long-term Debt $Mil	657	140	605	486
Total Equity $Mil	1,014	1,834	2,367	2,443
Debt/Equity Ratio	0.6	0.1	0.3	0.2

Vishay entered this latest downturn with its strongest balance sheet in years. It used its financial strength to make several acquisitions. This increased debt, but the firm has been aggressively paying it off in 2002 and the current load is quite manageable.

Morningstar's Take By Dan Schick, 11-19-2002 Stock Price as of Analysis: $11.75

We believe the capacitor and discrete semiconductor industries should grow well over the long term. Vishay, along with fellow industry leaders AVX and Kemet, is positioned to benefit from this growth. While we think the shares of these companies are attractive when notoriously cyclical demand for their products is nearing a bottom--as it seems to be now--Vishay is our least favorite of the bunch. Although we would purchase Vishay at a 50% discount to our fair value, we would prefer AVX so long as it sold at a similar discount.

We prefer AVX for two main reasons. First, Vishay has been largely woven together through acquisitions. While CEO and chairman Zandman is a savvy buyer, stitching myriad acquisitions into a well-knit whole is never easy. Integrations can fail and purchase prices can turn out to be exorbitant, damaging shareholder value. AVX, on the other hand, has mainly built its business through internal growth, a less risky and more profitable strategy, in our opinion.

Second, Vishay focuses more on the niches and specialty areas of the electronics component market, whereas AVX targets higher-volume products. By doing this, Vishay benefits from better margins and more-stable sales because specialty products are less prone to swings in demand and pricing pressures.

However, nothing comes free; we believe Vishay makes two trade-offs. First, its inventory sits around longer before being sold. It takes an average of 144 days for Vishay to sell a component, while AVX carries inventory for 105 days. Second, a dollar of plant and equipment in Vishay's hands generates less revenue than the same dollar at AVX.

Because Vishay takes longer to sell its goods and needs more capital to produce its goods, margins must be sufficiently high to make the trade-off worthwhile. But we don't think margins are high enough. Vishay's poor returns on invested capital provide the evidence. Since 1995, Vishay has generated a double-digit return on capital only once, in the boom year of 2000.

Despite these problems, Vishay generates a lot of cash flow from operations. And thanks to a tremendous 2000 and the fact that the company has maintained profitability in the current downturn, it balance sheet is relatively strong. Taking advantage of this strength, Vishay has continued to expand with its recent purchase of BCcomponents, a Dutch manufacturer that will strengthen its passives business.

Visteon VC

	Rating	Risk	Moat Size	Fair Value	Last Close	Yield %
	★★★	Med.	None	$8.00	$6.96	3.4

Company Profile

Visteon manufactures automotive systems and components. Its operations include interiors (instrument panels, cockpits, interior trim), automotive chassis (steering systems, axles, exhaust systems), engine components, climate control systems, and auto glass. It has also been developing new technologies, notably voice-powered command systems. Visteon was spun off to Ford Motor shareholders in June 2000; sales to Ford accounted for 82% of the firm's revenue in 2001. North American business accounts for three fourths of sales.

Management

Chairman and CEO Peter Pestillo, formerly part of Ford's top brass, recruited Michael Johnston as president. Johnston comes to Visteon from Johnson Controls, a firm known for low costs, operating efficiencies, and product innovation.

Strategy

Visteon's first priority is to reduce its cost structure, which ranks among the highest in the parts industry. Lower costs should translate directly to higher profitability and allow the firm to become more price-competitive. That, combined with technical innovations, should help the firm expand its non-Ford business.

5500 Auto Club Drive
Dearborn, MI 48126
www.visteon.com

Morningstar Grades

Growth [C-]	1998	1999	2000	2001
Revenue %	3.1	9.0	0.5	-8.3
Earnings/Share %	NMF	NMF	NMF	NMF
Book Value/Share %	—	—	—	NMF
Dividends/Share %	NMF	NMF	NMF	100.0

Visteon is attempting to balance cost-cutting and growth. The firm expects its non-Ford business to double by 2007, which would otherwise drive midsingle-digit sales growth, but divestitures and declining market share will restrain progress.

Profitability [C]	1999	2000	2001	TTM
Return on Assets %	5.9	2.4	-1.1	-3.0
Oper Cash Flow $Mil	2,482	-526	436	787
- Cap Spending $Mil	876	793	752	697
= Free Cash Flow $Mil	1,606	-1,319	-316	90

The company's fixed-cost structure is hideous, leading to high operating leverage: Returns on invested capital fell to 2.2% in 2001 from a record 7.1% in 2000. Expense reductions are being offset in part by spending for new business programs.

Financial Health [C+]	1999	2000	2001	09-02
Long-term Debt $Mil	1,358	1,397	1,293	1,312
Total Equity $Mil	1,499	3,505	3,291	3,035
Debt/Equity Ratio	0.9	0.4	0.4	0.4

The balance sheet is fairly liquid but sluggish. It has $1.0 billion in cash and securities and net debt equal to 21% of capital, but poor asset efficiency, negative cash flow, and growing retirement liabilities are concerns.

Industry	Investment Style	Stock Type	Sector
Auto Parts	▦ Small Value	◪ High Yield	🏛 Consumer Goods

Competition	Market Cap $Mil	Debt/ Equity	12 Mo Trailing Sales $Mil	Price/Cash Flow	Return On Assets%	Total Return% 1 Yr	3 Yr
Visteon	912	0.4	18,345	1.2	-3.0	-52.7	—
Delphi	4,495	0.9	26,836	3.8	0.5	-39.6	-16.6
Dana	1,747	2.0	10,472	2.7	-4.7	-15.1	-23.1

Price Volatility

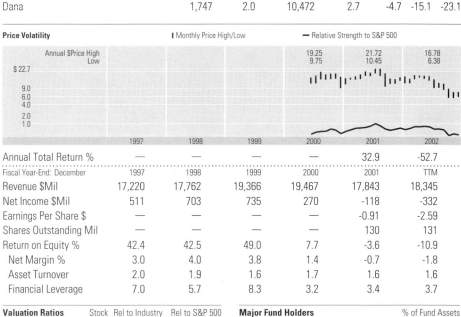

	Monthly Price High/Low	— Relative Strength to S&P 500

					19.25 9.75	21.72 10.45	16.78 6.38

	1997	1998	1999	2000	2001	2002
Annual Total Return %	—	—	—	—	32.9	-52.7

Fiscal Year-End: December	1997	1998	1999	2000	2001	TTM
Revenue $Mil	17,220	17,762	19,366	19,467	17,843	18,345
Net Income $Mil	511	703	735	270	-118	-332
Earnings Per Share $	—	—	—	—	-0.91	-2.59
Shares Outstanding Mil	—	—	—	—	130	131
Return on Equity %	42.4	42.5	49.0	7.7	-3.6	-10.9
Net Margin %	3.0	4.0	3.8	1.4	-0.7	-1.8
Asset Turnover	2.0	1.9	1.6	1.7	1.6	1.6
Financial Leverage	7.0	5.7	8.3	3.2	3.4	3.7

Valuation Ratios	Stock	Rel to Industry	Rel to S&P 500
Price/Earnings	NMF	—	—
Price/Book	0.3	0.0	0.1
Price/Sales	0.1	0.0	0.0
Price/Cash Flow	1.2	0.0	0.1

Major Fund Holders	% of Fund Assets
Runkel Value	4.52
Quaker Mid-Cap Value A	2.85
Impact Management Investment Retail	2.50
Putnam Capital Opportunities A	1.62

Morningstar's Take By Josh Peters, 11-01-2002 Stock Price as of Analysis: $6.87

We wouldn't find Visteon a worthwhile investment unless it were dirt-cheap.

In an industry increasingly dominated by lean, low-cost suppliers like Lear, Visteon bears the legacy of a mass-producing, high-cost assembler--former parent Ford. Visteon is built for volume, not flexibility. It made $3.14 per share in 2000, when Ford's North American production hit an all-time high, but a 14% drop in Ford's output in 2001 prompted an 89% drop in Visteon's operating income (before $192 million in restructuring charges).

The journey to a leaner future will be long and costly. First, Visteon must cope with Ford's declining market share, which makes sunk capital and engineering costs hard to recover. Second, it's stuck with the industry's worst labor situation. To gain UAW cooperation for the spin-off, Visteon's hourly U.S. workers remained Ford employees--which means they receive Ford's lucrative wage rates and benefits, reimbursed to Ford by Visteon. Then there's Ford's own cost-cutting, which will pressure Visteon to turn over much of its own cost improvements through price givebacks.

With Visteon and Ford tied this closely, it's hard to imagine Visteon achieving decent margins until Ford does--something we don't expect until 2005 or thereabouts. Until then, we expect restructuring to wipe out much of any Visteon profits.

In its defense, Visteon's enormous scale (the global industry's third-largest sales) partly offsets its high labor costs. Geographically, it's positioned to serve vehicle manufacturers most anywhere in the world. It also has proprietary technology in several product categories.

Management hopes to combine these assets into a role as a systems integrator. Visteon already has some noteworthy non-Ford program wins, like its contract to produce cockpits for Nissan's new truck plant in Mississippi. Also, we can't deny the restructuring potential here: With sales running at about $140 per share, even a 3% operating margin could generate impressive earnings. And until it does fix itself, Ford has a big reason to keep Visteon in at least a break-even state--those 23,000 UAW parts jobs are Ford's problem, too.

But however much potential it might have tomorrow, today's Visteon suffers a value-stifling relationship with Ford. We wouldn't have much interest unless the stock fell at least 50% below our fair value estimate.

MORNINGSTAR® Stocks 500

VISX EYE

	Rating	Risk	Moat Size	Fair Value	Last Close	Yield %
	★★★	Med.	Narrow	$13.00	$9.58	0.0

Company Profile

VISX develops and manufactures laser vision-correction systems. It produces excimer refractive surgical systems that treat eye disorders like nearsightedness, farsightedness, and astigmatism. The company's laser systems are used in procedures that reduce or eliminate the need for eyeglasses or contact lenses. VISX markets its laser vision-correction systems to health-care professionals in the United States and internationally. The United States accounts for approximately 88% of the company's revenue.

Management

Elizabeth Davila took the chairman and CEO reins in 2001. She owns 1.9% of the firm and successfully fended off an attempt by financier Carl Icahn to put the company up for sale.

Strategy

VISX's business model is similar to Gilette's razor blade business: Sell equipment at a thin margin and charge a premium for each use. Three fourths of the company's sales are from license and service fees to use and maintain its equipment. Technological advances should also fuel additional equipment sales.

3400 Central Expressway   www.visx.com
Santa Clara, CA 95051-0703

Morningstar Grades

Growth [D-]	1998	1999	2000	2001
Revenue %	94.9	102.8	-26.2	-15.3
Earnings/Share %	75.3	246.2	-59.3	-65.5
Book Value/Share %	21.7	120.0	-9.9	-26.8
Dividends/Share %	NMF	NMF	NMF	NMF

VISX's best days are behind it. The firm's 1998 and 1999 sales growth rates were above 100%, but sales have plummeted with the U.S. economy. Although sales growth will be erratic, we think a 10% average rate is easily achievable.

Profitability [A]	1999	2000	2001	TTM
Return on Assets %	25.3	11.0	5.0	10.6
Oper Cash Flow $Mil	135	76	6	36
- Cap Spending $Mil	4	3	3	3
= Free Cash Flow $Mil	131	73	4	32

VISX's margins were in a tailspin for more than two years, but seem to have settled. Gross margins are in the low to mid-60s, operating margins are averaging around 20%, and net margins are a healthy 14%-16%.

Financial Health [A+]	1999	2000	2001	09-02
Long-term Debt $Mil	—	—	—	—
Total Equity $Mil	317	269	176	158
Debt/Equity Ratio	—	—	—	—

VISX is in top financial condition. It has no debt and generates healthy free cash flows (cash flow from operations less capital expenditures). Free cash flow for the 12 months ended September 2002 was 28% of sales.

Industry	Investment Style	Stock Type	Sector
Medical Equipment	⊞ Small Core	→ Slow Growth	Healthcare

Competition	Market Cap $Mil	Debt/ Equity	12 Mo Trailing Sales $Mil	Price/Cash Flow	Return On Assets%	Total Return% 1 Yr	3 Yr
VISX	495	—	138	13.9	10.6	-27.7	-42.4
Alcon	11,835	0.5	2,748	22.4	7.8	—	—
Bausch & Lomb	1,942	0.5	1,828	9.1	1.1	-2.7	-16.3

Price Volatility   ‖ Monthly Price High/Low   — Relative Strength to S&P 500

		1997	1998	1999	2000	2001	2002
Annual $Price High		7.63	22.00	103.88	55.25	25.60	18.15
Low		4.47	4.88	21.50	8.75	10.13	6.90

Annual Total Return %	0.0	295.2	136.7	-79.8	26.9	-27.7
Fiscal Year-end: December	1997	1998	1999	2000	2001	TTM
Revenue $Mil	69	134	271	200	170	138
Net Income $Mil	14	26	92	35	11	21
Earnings Per Share $	0.22	0.39	1.35	0.55	0.19	0.39
Shares Outstanding Mil	62	61	63	62	57	52
Return on Equity %	12.8	18.4	29.0	13.1	6.2	13.4
Net Margin %	20.5	19.1	33.8	17.6	6.4	15.3
Asset Turnover	0.5	0.8	0.7	0.6	0.8	0.7
Financial Leverage	1.2	1.3	1.1	1.2	1.2	1.3

Valuation Ratios	Stock	Rel to Industry	Rel to S&P 500
Price/Earnings	24.6	0.8	1.0
Price/Book	3.1	0.5	1.0
Price/Sales	3.6	0.8	1.8
Price/Cash Flow	13.9	0.6	1.1

Major Fund Holders	% of Fund Assets
W&R Small Cap Growth C	1.97
Sterling Capital Small Cap Val Instl	1.78
Waddell & Reed Adv Small Cap A	1.74
MassMutual Instl Small Cap Gr Eq A	1.44

Morningstar's Take   By Todd N. Lebor, 12-14-2002   Stock Price as of Analysis: $9.56

VISX's heyday is over, but financial success is still in the cards.

VISX's success depends on the number of laser-correction surgeries performed, but as the U.S. economy--where VISX generates nearly 80% of its revenue--has suffered, so has VISX. Since LASIK surgery is an expensive, elective, and uninsured procedure, it is sensitive to the thickness of consumer wallets. With the drop in stock market wealth over the past few years, Americans feel poorer and unwilling to drop $3,000 on LASIK, when $300 will buy a nice pair of spectacles. Even so, we think the enormous untapped market of those who need vision correction makes VISX worth the gamble--at the right price.

In the late 1990s, VISX was in revenue growth bliss, but the honeymoon is over. VISX will never see 100% annual growth again, nor is it likely to sport operating margins over 50%. The pioneering company has also lost market share in the past few years. However, we think average revenue growth of 10% with operating margins in the high 30s is easily attainable, especially considering the current depressed base period. With an estimated 70 million Americans eligible for LASIK surgery and only 3%-4% of the market tapped, there's plenty of room to grow.

High margins and a huge market have drawn plenty of competition, leading to pricing pressure. In February 2000, VISX was forced to drop its per-procedure licensing fee from $250 to $100. Since VISX pulls in three fourths of its revenue from high-margin licenses and services, this was a painful move.

Competition in equipment (the other fourth of VISX's revenue) also played a role in our more conservative estimates. Alcon, the second-biggest player in the U.S. LASIK market, was the first company to win approval of wavefront-guided laser eye surgery system, an improved procedure with fewer side effects. But, as VISX has proved time and again, it is no slouch when it comes to the latest technology. Shortly after Alcon launched its system, VISX had a similar unit on the market.

Estimating precise revenue growth for VISX is futile, but we're confident that laser surgery eye procedures will increase once the U.S. economy recovers. VISX is still the market share leader and has the financial wherewithal to wait out the rough patches. We think it is a worthy purchase at a 40% discount to our fair value estimate.

Vivendi ADR V

	Rating	Risk	Moat Size	Fair Value	Last Close	Yield %
	UR	High	None	UR	$16.07	4.7

Company Profile

Vivendi Universal is a global conglomerate focusing on the media and communications sectors. The company, based in France, competes in markets that include print publishing, digital media, music, film production, amusement parks, and wireless communications. Vivendi's roots lie in water utilities, which still account for half of its total revenue. This segment was partially spun off in 2000 as Vivendi Environnement.

Management

Flamboyant CEO Jean-Marie Messier was forced to resign in July. New CEO Rene Fourtou embodies the clubby network of France's leading executives. He appears disinclined to continue his predecessor's effort to Americanize the firm.

Strategy

The company's strategy is up in the air right now. The priority at present is selling assets and reducing debt. Vivendi has started with the publishing business, and more asset sales will follow. The company has also discussed spinning off the U.S. entertainment assets, probably under the leadership of media mogul Barry Diller.

42, avenue de Friedland   www.vivendiuniversal.com
Paris, 75380

Industry	Investment Style	Stock Type	Sector
Media Conglomerates	▦ Large Value	💹 High Yield	🎤 Media

Competition	Market Cap $Mil	Debt/ Equity	12 Mo Trailing Sales $Mil	Price/Cash Flow	Return On Assets%	Total Return% 1 Yr	3 Yr
Vivendi ADR	17,500	0.8	51,149	4.4	-9.9	-69.3	-43.0
Sony ADR	38,122	0.4	60,413	6.5	0.2	-8.1	-32.4
Walt Disney	32,923	0.5	24,550	14.6	2.5	-20.3	-19.1

Price Volatility

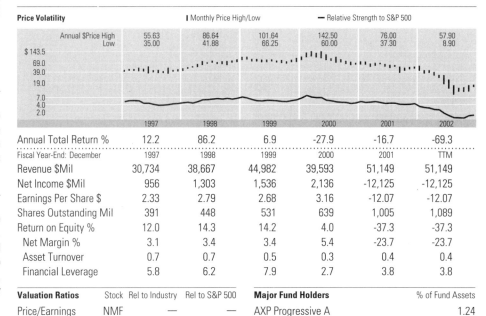

Annual $Price High	55.63	86.64	101.64	142.50	76.00	57.90
Low	35.00	41.88	66.25	60.00	37.30	8.90

	1997	1998	1999	2000	2001	2002
Annual Total Return %	12.2	86.2	6.9	-27.9	-16.7	-69.3
Fiscal Year-End: December	1997	1998	1999	2000	2001	TTM
Revenue $Mil	30,734	38,667	44,982	39,593	51,149	51,149
Net Income $Mil	956	1,303	1,536	2,136	-12,125	-12,125
Earnings Per Share $	2.33	2.79	2.68	3.16	-12.07	-12.07
Shares Outstanding Mil	391	448	531	639	1,005	1,089
Return on Equity %	12.0	14.3	14.2	4.0	-37.3	-37.3
Net Margin %	3.1	3.4	3.4	5.4	-23.7	-23.7
Asset Turnover	0.7	0.7	0.5	0.3	0.4	0.4
Financial Leverage	5.8	6.2	7.9	2.7	3.8	3.8

Valuation Ratios	Stock	Rel to Industry	Rel to S&P 500
Price/Earnings	NMF	—	—
Price/Book	0.5	0.4	0.2
Price/Sales	0.3	0.2	0.2
Price/Cash Flow	4.4	0.3	0.3

Major Fund Holders	% of Fund Assets
AXP Progressive A	1.24
Gabelli Value A	1.23
Longleaf Partners	1.08

Morningstar Grades

Growth [A+]	1998	1999	2000	2001
Revenue %	25.8	26.4	1.4	34.6
Earnings/Share %	20.0	4.2	36.0	NMF
Book Value/Share %	0.8	11.9	346.3	-56.4
Dividends/Share %	12.5	11.1	0.0	0.0

Revenue grew 38% last year, but this figure is overstated because of acquisitions. The firm's media and communication units are growing much faster than its water utility business.

Profitability [C-]	1999	2000	2001	TTM
Return on Assets %	1.8	1.5	-9.9	-9.9
Oper Cash Flow $Mil	826	2,336	4,013	4,013
- Cap Spending $Mil	5,415	5,388	4,760	4,760
= Free Cash Flow $Mil	-4,589	-3,053	-747	-747

Although the company has announced a number of EBITDA-positive quarters, its free cash flow has been negative for each of the past three years. Telecom and water utilities generate the bulk of its EBITDA growth.

Financial Health [D+]	1999	2000	2001	12-01
Long-term Debt $Mil	19,233	22,598	24,581	24,581
Total Equity $Mil	10,777	53,467	32,520	32,520
Debt/Equity Ratio	1.8	0.4	0.8	0.8

As a consequence of its acquisition binge, Vivendi shouldered a net debt load of $28.3 billion at the end of 2001. The firm is working frantically with bankers to address its liquidity crunch.

Morningstar's Take By Jonathan Schrader, 11-26-2002 Stock Price as of Analysis: $14.93

Investors should stay on the sidelines while Vivendi scrambles to address its liquidity crisis.

Most of Vivendi's woes are a direct result of the company's unfocused strategy. This debacle started years ago, when chief executive Jean-Marie Messier, unsatisfied with running a stodgy (but profitable) water utility business, took a stab at being a media mogul. Messier gobbled up a wide assortment of businesses and cobbled them together. The finished product: a company whose assets include a water utility, a movie studio, theme parks, telecom businesses, digital music acquisitions, cable networks, a publisher, and a pay-television business.

The buying spree saddled the company with nearly $30 billion in net debt by the end of 2001. Now, with limited cash on hand and stung by a wave of recent credit rating downgrades, the company is scrambling to sell pieces of the firm to raise funds. Vivendi paid top dollar for these businesses near the market peak and is now under pressure to dump them at fire-sale prices.

We're not totally writing off Vivendi. A source of encouragement is new CEO Rene Fourtou, who boasts a strong record from his days as vice chairman at successful pharmaceutical giant Aventis. Fourtou is doing the right things to rebuild the company's credibility--immediately after taking office, he admitted the firm faced a liquidity crunch and indicated major asset sales might be forthcoming. This is a refreshing improvement over his predecessor. Even in his last days in office, Messier vigorously denied there was a liquidity crisis and defiantly refused to sell parts of his bloated company.

We're expecting major changes (major asset sales, new financing arrangements), so the Vivendi of next year will look vastly different than the one of today. Among the options: a sale of its publishing unit or its Cegetel telecom stake (Vodafone appears to be interested in the latter). The magnitude of the forthcoming restructuring makes long-term financial projections a guessing game, and because the firm's financial reporting is being investigated by the Securities and Exchange Commission as well as French officials, we're not even guessing.

A new leader may help Vivendi regain its focus, but considering the great uncertainty and major changes ahead, we think investors should wait on the sidelines until the smoke clears.

M⊙RNINGSTAR® Stocks 500

Vodafone Group PLC ADR VOD

	Rating	Risk	Moat Size	Fair Value	Last Close	Yield %
	★	Med.	None	$16.00	$18.12	1.3

Company Profile

Vodafone Group is the world's largest provider of cellular radio network, voice mail, radio paging, and data communication services. Roughly three fourths of its 93 million subscribers are in Europe. Thanks to acquisitions, including that of Germany's Mannesmann in 2000, Vodafone now has operations in 29 countries.

Management

The savvy deal-making of the firm's pragmatic CEO, Chris Gent, is credited with transforming Vodafone into a wireless powerhouse.

Strategy

Vodafone is focusing on integrating its many acquisitions over the past few years, which have made it the world's largest wireless carrier, with more than 107 million subscribers, and given it global reach. The goal is to slow the pace of subscriber growth and derive as much profit as possible from existing customers by offering new data services in addition to voice.

The Courtyard, 2-4 London Road   www.vodafone.com
Berkshire, RG14 1JX

Morningstar Grades

Growth [A+]	1998	1999	2000	2001
Revenue %	41.3	36.0	134.3	90.6
Earnings/Share %	14.3	50.7	-56.1	NMF
Book Value/Share %	NMF	186.3	EUB	-40.7
Dividends/Share %	20.0	0.0	8.3	7.7

Vodafone is a growth machine, mainly thanks to acquisitions. It expects to add 10% more customers in fiscal 2003 (ending March 2003), or roughly 10 million users.

Profitability [B]	1999	2000	2001	TTM
Return on Assets %	17.9	0.3	-6.0	-6.0
Oper Cash Flow $Mil	1,726	4,034	6,824	6,824
- Cap Spending $Mil	1,216	2,970	5,502	5,502
= Free Cash Flow $Mil	509	1,064	1,323	1,323

The company's focus has shifted to wringing greater profits from existing customers instead of attracting new ones. The goal is to offset price declines with new data services, to maintain cash flow margins above 35%.

Financial Health [B-]	1999	2000	2001	03-01
Long-term Debt $Mil	10,281	17,833	18,476	18,476
Total Equity $Mil	1,314	223,544	204,779	204,779
Debt/Equity Ratio	7.8	0.1	0.1	0.1

Vodafone uses its free cash flow to repay debt and pay dividends, which explains why its debt rating remains investment-grade when most others in the wireless industry are on their knees.

Industry	Investment Style	Stock Type	Sector
Wireless Service	Large Growth	Spec. Growth	Telecom

Competition

	Market Cap $Mil	Debt/ Equity	12 Mo Trailing Sales $Mil	Price/Cash Flow	Return On Assets%	Total Return% 1 Yr	3 Yr
Vodafone Group PLC ADR	123,471	0.1	22,323	18.1	-6.0	-28.4	-27.1
Deutsche Telekom AG ADR	38,476	—	38,032	—	—	—	—
France Telecom SA ADR	20,504	—	31,283	—	—	—	—

Price Volatility

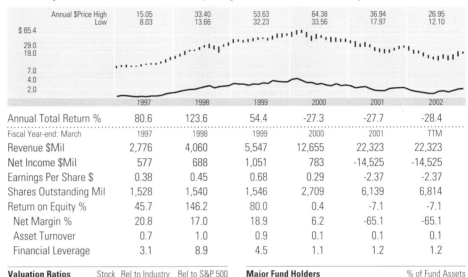

Annual $Price High	15.05	33.40	53.63	64.38	36.94	26.95
Low	8.03	13.66	32.23	33.56	17.97	12.10

	1997	1998	1999	2000	2001	2002
Annual Total Return %	80.6	123.6	54.4	-27.3	-27.7	-28.4

Fiscal Year-end: March	1997	1998	1999	2000	2001	TTM
Revenue $Mil	2,776	4,060	5,547	12,655	22,323	22,323
Net Income $Mil	577	688	1,051	783	-14,525	-14,525
Earnings Per Share $	0.38	0.45	0.68	0.29	-2.37	-2.37
Shares Outstanding Mil	1,528	1,540	1,546	2,709	6,139	6,814
Return on Equity %	45.7	146.2	80.0	0.4	-7.1	-7.1
Net Margin %	20.8	17.0	18.9	6.2	-65.1	-65.1
Asset Turnover	0.7	1.0	0.9	0.1	0.1	0.1
Financial Leverage	3.1	8.9	4.5	1.1	1.2	1.2

Valuation Ratios	Stock	Rel to Industry	Rel to S&P 500
Price/Earnings	NMF	—	—
Price/Book	0.7	0.2	0.2
Price/Sales	5.5	2.1	2.8
Price/Cash Flow	18.1	1.5	1.4

Major Fund Holders	% of Fund Assets
Smith Barney Telecomm Income	25.42
Rydex Telecommunications Inv	13.89
Fidelity Select Wireless	9.96
Fidelity Advisor Developing Comm A	6.98

Morningstar's Take By Todd P. Bernier, 11-19-2002   Stock Price as of Analysis: $18.65

Its heft makes Vodafone unique in a sea of wireless carriers. But a company with no economic moat, like Vodafone, is not the sort that catches our eye. We wouldn't buy the shares until they changed hands at least 40% below our fair value estimate.

Vodafone got its start in 1982 after winning a competitive tender to build and operate the second U.K. cellular telephone network. It launched service in 1985 under the Vodafone brand, and was fully spun off from Britain's Racal Electronics in 1991. Subscriber growth has been very strong; the company now claims more than 100 million users across 28 countries.

Vodafone's growth is the result of acquisitions orchestrated by CEO Chris Gent, who has been a member of the company's board since 1985. The firm usually takes a small stake in a carrier, accounted for as an equity interest, which it raises sufficiently over time to gain operational control. At this point Vodafone can book the revenue as its own, a practice that inflates sales and masks a bigger problem: Vodafone's organic growth is weak. Most of its primary markets, like Europe and the United States, are mature for wireless services. Anyone who wants a cell phone probably already has one, and those who do not get chased by a surplus of wireless carriers. It

is no surprise that pricing pressure, the byproduct of excessive competition, is steadily eroding average revenue per user.

The company's goal is to offset the decline of voice services by introducing new data services--for instance, text messaging, picture messaging, and mobile commerce--to encourage higher spending. Data now accounts for about 13% of service revenue, a figure Vodafone expects to raise to 20% by 2004. The firm is launching new high-speed networks to drive data usage; 2.5G networks, known as GPRS, are operational across all major markets and 3G should hit the mainstream in 2003.

From a financial perspective, Vodafone is in a class by itself. In addition to a rock-solid balance sheet, the firm generates substantial free cash flow. Vodafone is one of the few operators in the industry with the ability to buy wireless assets being liquidated. For example, Vivendi may be forced to pare debt by selling its 44% stake in France's Cegetel. Also, Vodafone still retains many of the assets inherited from Mannesmann that could yet be monetized along the lines of its sale of Orange PLC to France Telecom in 2000. No other wireless carrier can match Vodafone's balance sheet strength.

Wachovia WB

	Rating	Risk	Moat Size	Fair Value	Last Close	Yield %
	★★★	Med.	Narrow	$38.00	$36.44	2.7

Company Profile

Wachovia is the nation's fourth-largest bank holding company in terms of assets. It was created by the merger of First Union and Wachovia. A leading commercial lender in the United States, Wachovia also has investment banking and brokerage operations with a presence in 48 states and 30 offices abroad. Its consumer banking network extends throughout the Southeast and Mid-Atlantic and includes 4,700 automated teller machines. Besides brokerage and banking, Wachovia also provides treasury and asset-management services.

Management

Former Wachovia CEO L.M. "Bud" Baker is chairman of the merged firm; former First Union head Ken Thompson is CEO. The board is split equally between Wachovia and First Union members.

Strategy

Wachovia is targeting 10%-12% EPS growth on a cash basis. It intends to expand its high-net-worth client base through a wider array of financial services. In addition, it wants to gain more corporate clients via the greater distribution of a larger broker network.

One Wachovia Center
Charlotte, NC 28288-0013
www.wachovia.com

Morningstar Grades

Growth [D+]	1998	1999	2000	2001
Revenue %	14.7	3.1	9.8	-7.6
Earnings/Share %	5.4	12.9	-97.9	EUB
Book Value/Share %	10.2	0.1	-32.4	118.1
Dividends/Share %	29.5	19.0	2.1	-50.0

Revenue growth has been lackluster after an aggressive acquisition spree created enough disorganization to cause customer attrition. Competition from stronger rivals now may be the biggest roadblock to jump-starting growth.

Profitability [D]	1999	2000	2001	TTM
Return on Assets %	1.3	0.0	0.5	1.0
Oper Cash Flow $Mil	-345	7,897	7,287	—
- Cap Spending $Mil	957	884	523	—
= Free Cash Flow $Mil	—	—	—	—

First Union's returns on assets and equity plunged in the face of a spiraling loan-default rate and a bloated cost structure. The merger is expected to generate nearly $900 million in pretax cost savings, which should boost overall profits.

Financial Health [A+]	1999	2000	2001	09-02
Long-term Debt $Mil	—	—	—	—
Total Equity $Mil	16,709	15,347	28,438	32,103
Debt/Equity Ratio	—	—	—	—

First Union was suffering from rising loan defaults before the merger, and its loan-loss reserves were underfunded. The balance sheet is reserved against further losses, but Wachovia's capital position isn't great.

Industry	Investment Style	Stock Type	Sector
Super Regional Banks	▦ Large Value	⚡ High Yield	💲 Financial Services

Competition	Market Cap $Mil	Debt/ Equity	12 Mo Trailing Sales $Mil	Price/Cash Flow	Return On Assets%	Total Return% 1 Yr	3 Yr
Wachovia	50,032	—	24,107	—	1.0	19.5	9.8
Bank of America	104,505	—	46,628	—	1.3	14.5	19.8
J.P. Morgan Chase & Co.	47,901	—	42,911	—	0.2	-30.7	-17.5

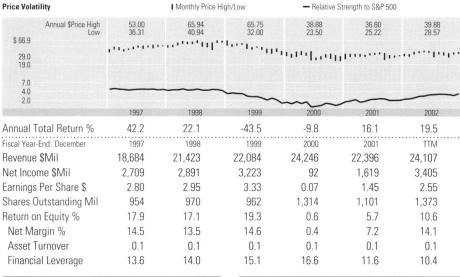

Price Volatility						
	▌Monthly Price High/Low			— Relative Strength to S&P 500		

Annual $Price High Low	53.00 36.31	65.94 40.94	65.75 32.00	38.88 23.50	36.60 25.22	39.88 28.57
	1997	1998	1999	2000	2001	2002

$66.9 / 29.0 / 19.0 / 7.0 / 4.0 / 2.0

	1997	1998	1999	2000	2001	TTM
Annual Total Return %	42.2	22.1	-43.5	-9.8	16.1	19.5
Fiscal Year-End: December	1997	1998	1999	2000	2001	TTM
Revenue $Mil	18,684	21,423	22,084	24,246	22,396	24,107
Net Income $Mil	2,709	2,891	3,223	92	1,619	3,405
Earnings Per Share $	2.80	2.95	3.33	0.07	1.45	2.55
Shares Outstanding Mil	954	970	962	1,314	1,101	1,373
Return on Equity %	17.9	17.1	19.3	0.6	5.7	10.6
Net Margin %	14.5	13.5	14.6	0.4	7.2	14.1
Asset Turnover	0.1	0.1	0.1	0.1	0.1	0.1
Financial Leverage	13.6	14.0	15.1	16.6	11.6	10.4

Valuation Ratios	Stock	Rel to Industry	Rel to S&P 500
Price/Earnings	14.3	1.0	0.6
Price/Book	1.6	0.8	0.5
Price/Sales	2.1	1.0	1.0
Price/Cash Flow	—	—	—

Major Fund Holders	% of Fund Assets
Senbanc	7.23
ProFunds UltraBull Inv	4.91
Rydex Banking Inv	4.85
Chicago Asset Management Value	4.43

Morningstar's Take By Craig Woker, 10-22-2002 Stock Price as of Analysis: $34.70

Wachovia has made progress in integrating last year's merger with First Union. However, we see little reason to pay close to our fair value estimate for a mediocre bank in turnaround mode.

We estimate this financial services firm to be worth $38 per share, just north of where the stock is trading. Though we believe the company has put many of the right pieces in place to improve its performance, the market has already factored that into the stock price. We would have to see the stock slip to $27 or lower before we'd start to find it attractive.

For investors to justify paying a higher price, Wachovia must become one of the better-performing banks, rather than just transforming itself into a C student, which is what we've assumed it will do. Wachovia's spotty record of integrating mergers and the fact that it competes in a slow-growth market give us no reason to think that it will do any better than that.

One of our concerns is that this firm has a history of getting bigger without using economies of scale to become more profitable. Wachovia's return on assets for 2001--calculated as though the two firms merged at the beginning of the year and backing out goodwill amortization--came in at a woeful 0.8%. This is pretty sad for a company with such a large, low-cost deposit base, especially considering the industry average has been above 1% for the past nine years.

The company argues that it should be evaluated on a pro forma basis, and it's not hard to see why. Since 1999, the new Wachovia or its predecessor, First Union, which was the acquisitor in the merger, have reported more than $2.5 billion in charges for severance and write-downs. But even if we strip out the charges the firm took in the first nine months of 2002, Wachovia still generated a return on equity of only about 14%, below most peer banks.

Plus, Wachovia's capital base is fairly weak compared with most large banks, and its earnings coverage to bad loans is only about average. Therefore, if credit quality suddenly takes a turn for the worse, Wachovia faces greater risk of a dividend cut or giving up on its goal of attaining an AA credit rating.

Wachovia has made a number of moves to improve operations. The firm sold its credit card portfolio, is cutting costs in other divisions, and has begun to sell more products like insurance and mutual funds. But most of the firm's potential for further improvement is already reflected in the share price, in our opinion.

MORNINGSTAR® Stocks 500

Wal-Mart Stores WMT

	Rating	Risk	Moat Size	Fair Value	Last Close	Yield %
	★★★	Low	Wide	$53.00	$50.51	0.6

Company Profile

Wal-Mart Stores is the largest retailer in the world, with more than 4,000 stores worldwide. The company operates 1,700 Wal-Mart discount stores, 486 Sam's Clubs, and 1000 Wal-Mart Supercenters (which combine supermarkets and discount stores) in the United States and Puerto Rico. In addition, it operates more than 1,080 stores internationally. The company sells merchandise under the Sam's American Choice, Popular Mechanics, Kathy Lee, and Better Homes & Gardens names.

Management

Former COO Lee Scott took the helm as CEO in February 2000. Scott's $1.1 million base salary and $1.8 million bonus seem reasonable for the leader of such a company. He also received $5 million in restricted stock in the most recent fiscal year.

Strategy

Wal-Mart has become the world's largest retailer by offering low prices and one-stop shopping. The firm's Supercenter stores, which combine groceries with general merchandise, have been the company's fastest-growing division over the past five years. Wal-Mart is also expanding overseas through acquisitions.

702 S.W. Eighth Street
Bentonville, AR 72716
www.wal-mart.com

Morningstar Grades

Growth [A]

	1999	2000	2001	2002
Revenue %	16.7	19.8	15.9	13.7
Earnings/Share %	26.9	21.2	16.7	6.4
Book Value/Share %	15.3	22.2	20.9	12.5
Dividends/Share %	14.8	29.0	20.0	16.7

Average annual sales growth of 16.5% over the past four fiscal years is remarkable, considering Wal-Mart's size. Sales grew 14% and earnings per share grew 6% for the fiscal year ending January 2002.

Profitability [A]

	2000	2001	2002	TTM
Return on Assets %	7.6	8.1	8.0	8.0
Oper Cash Flow $Mil	8,194	9,604	10,260	11,783
- Cap Spending $Mil	6,183	8,042	8,383	9,234
= Free Cash Flow $Mil	2,011	1,562	1,877	2,549

Wal-Mart executes its low-margin, high-turnover strategy flawlessly. It sports only 3% net margins, but efficient turnover of assets produces ample cash flow and profits.

Financial Health [B]

	2000	2001	2002	10-02
Long-term Debt $Mil	16,674	15,655	18,732	17,730
Total Equity $Mil	25,834	31,343	35,102	38,044
Debt/Equity Ratio	0.6	0.5	0.5	0.5

The company is solid as a rock and can easily cover such financial obligations as its debt and lease payments.

Industry	Investment Style	Stock Type	Sector
Discount Stores	Large Growth	Classic Growth	Consumer Services

Competition

	Market Cap $Mil	Debt/ Equity	12 Mo Trailing Sales $Mil	Price/Cash Flow	Return On Assets%	Total Return% 1 Yr	3 Yr
Wal-Mart Stores	222,949	0.5	241,163	18.9	8.0	-11.8	-7.3
Target	27,252	1.2	42,275	21.5	5.7	-26.5	-3.9
Safeway	13,376	1.5	34,757	6.3	3.4	-44.1	-12.2

Price Volatility — Monthly Price High/Low — Relative Strength to S&P 500

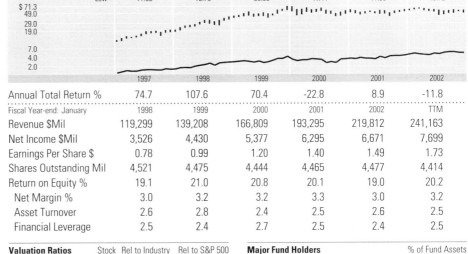

Annual $Price High Low	20.97 11.00	41.38 18.78	70.25 38.66	69.00 41.44	58.75 41.50	63.94 43.72

	1997	1998	1999	2000	2001	2002
Annual Total Return %	74.7	107.6	70.4	-22.8	8.9	-11.8

Fiscal Year-end: January	1998	1999	2000	2001	2002	TTM
Revenue $Mil	119,299	139,208	166,809	193,295	219,812	241,163
Net Income $Mil	3,526	4,430	5,377	6,295	6,671	7,699
Earnings Per Share $	0.78	0.99	1.20	1.40	1.49	1.73
Shares Outstanding Mil	4,521	4,475	4,444	4,465	4,477	4,414
Return on Equity %	19.1	21.0	20.8	20.1	19.0	20.2
Net Margin %	3.0	3.2	3.2	3.3	3.0	3.2
Asset Turnover	2.6	2.8	2.4	2.5	2.6	2.5
Financial Leverage	2.5	2.4	2.7	2.5	2.4	2.5

Valuation Ratios	Stock	Rel to Industry	Rel to S&P 500
Price/Earnings	29.2	1.0	1.2
Price/Book	5.9	1.0	1.8
Price/Sales	0.9	1.0	0.5
Price/Cash Flow	18.9	1.0	1.4

Major Fund Holders	% of Fund Assets
ProFunds UltraBull Inv	24.53
Rydex Retailing Inv	22.28
Noah	8.98
Wayne Hummer CorePortfolio	8.54

Morningstar's Take By Mike Porter, 12-11-2002 Stock Price as of Analysis: $52.00

There is a lot of solid evidence that the largest company in the world can become much larger--and at a pretty fast clip, too. Even so, like Wal-Mart shoppers, we're always looking for a bargain. We wouldn't need a huge discount to our fair value estimate to buy Wal-Mart shares, but certainly more than exists now.

The question has once again arisen: Can Wal-Mart keep expanding at a pace even close to historical levels? In the 1990s, when this was also a concern, Wal-Mart answered with a resounding "You bet," becoming the biggest grocery retailer in the country in less than 15 years. The Supercenter idea seems so obvious in hindsight: Put cheap groceries and general merchandise under one huge roof, and grocery shoppers, who tend to shop a lot more often than Wal-Mart shoppers, will meander into the clothing and housewares aisles and pick up a few things there too. Wal-Mart can accept a much lower margin on its groceries than a grocer like Albertson's because of the higher margins it gets on other goods.

Wal-Mart has a number of new frontiers left to go. For one, it's not done with this whole Supercenter thing just yet. It's only now getting to California with the concept--a rare untapped market for the company. We also expect Wal-Mart to continue to fill the gaps in areas where it has only standard Wal-Marts. A few years out, we expect the company's Neighborhood Markets concept to be its next big thing. So far, Wal-Mart has opened just a handful of the stores, which are essentially Supercenters scaled down in size by about 75%. The company is still tinkering with the concept and has not officially committed to it, but its plans to double food distribution centers over the next three years make it pretty clear where its priorities lie.

We have a long-term concern, though, and it's not a small one. Wal-Mart's main competitive advantage is its ability to beat everyone on price. One of the ways it does this is by pushing hard on its store managers to keep compensation costs low. Wal-Mart is still a nonunion shop, but it's becoming increasingly difficult to remain so. We believe the company will face some labor issues, and might even have pockets of unionization here and there. Wal-Mart's selling, general, and administrative line, which includes compensation, is around 16.5% of sales; Target's is a more typical 21%. If Wal-Mart is forced to cough up more money and the SG&A line rises, its low-cost-leader reputation could suffer.

We'd be happy picking up Wal-Mart shares in the mid-$40s or below.

Walgreen WAG

	Rating ★★★	Risk Med.	Moat Size Wide	Fair Value $32.00	Last Close $29.19	Yield % 0.5

Industry	Investment Style	Stock Type	Sector
Specialty Retail	▦ Large Growth	↗ Classic Growth	▣ Consumer Services

Company Profile

Measured by revenue, Walgreen is the nation's largest drugstore chain. As of November 30, 2001, the company operated 3,623 drugstores in 43 states and Puerto Rico. In recent years, Walgreen has converted many of its locations from strip-mall properties into free-standing corner locations, which offer greater convenience. Prescription drugs now account for nearly 60% of sales; Walgreen also provides full lines of nonprescription drugs, health and beauty items, toiletries, food, beverages, and general merchandise. The company plans to have 6,000 stores in operation by 2010.

Management

The firm prefers homegrown talent. President and CEO Dave Bernauer worked his way up the corporate ladder and has more than 35 years with Walgreen. Bernauer and chairman Daniel Jorndt (who will soon retire) both have large stakes in the company.

Strategy

Walgreen is writing the definitive guide to saturation strategy. Its own research indicates that most pharmacy patrons come from within one to two miles, meaning that the company can continue to open stores without cannibalizing its own sales. Walgreen aims to increase its store base from just under 4,000 now to more than 6,000 by the end of the decade.

200 Wilmot Road   www.walgreens.com
Deerfield, IL 60015

Morningstar Grades

Growth [A]	1999	2000	2001	2002
Revenue %	16.5	18.9	16.1	16.5
Earnings/Share %	21.6	22.6	13.2	15.1
Book Value/Share %	21.7	19.7	22.1	19.7
Dividends/Share %	3.8	3.9	3.6	2.9

Walgreen has averaged 16% sales and 18% earnings growth over the past five years. Though much of its sales growth comes from new stores, Walgreen still generates more sales per square foot than its rivals in existing stores.

Profitability [A+]	2000	2001	2002	TTM
Return on Assets %	10.9	10.0	10.3	10.3
Oper Cash Flow $Mil	972	719	1,474	1,474
- Cap Spending $Mil	1,119	1,237	934	934
= Free Cash Flow $Mil	-147	-518	539	539

Walgreen's net profit margin is much better than that of close competitor CVS CVS thanks to its strategy of opening primarily freestanding stores. These locations are typically larger and more lucrative than mall-based stores.

Financial Health [A]	2000	2001	2002	08-02
Long-term Debt $Mil	—	—	—	—
Total Equity $Mil	4,234	5,207	6,230	6,230
Debt/Equity Ratio	—	—	—	—

Walgreen's growth has historically been financed from strong operating cash flow. Even if we capitalized all of its operating leases (most have terms of more than 20 years), the firm could handle the higher debt load.

Competition

Competition	Market Cap $Mil	Debt/ Equity	12 Mo Trailing Sales $Mil	Price/Cash Flow	Return On Assets%	Total Return% 1 Yr	 3 Yr
Walgreen	29,917	—	28,681	20.3	10.3	-12.9	2.4
CVS	9,809	0.2	23,787	9.8	4.1	-15.0	-12.1
Rite Aid	1,262	—	15,551	—	—	—	—

Price Volatility

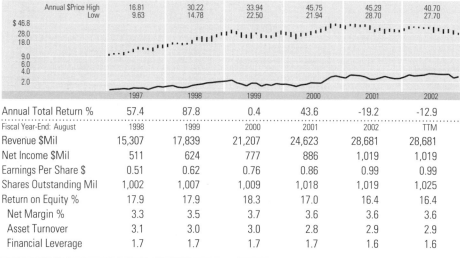

	1997	1998	1999	2000	2001	2002
Annual $Price High	16.81	30.22	33.94	45.75	45.29	40.70
Low	9.63	14.78	22.50	21.94	28.70	27.70
Annual Total Return %	57.4	87.8	0.4	43.6	-19.2	-12.9

Fiscal Year-End: August	1998	1999	2000	2001	2002	TTM
Revenue $Mil	15,307	17,839	21,207	24,623	28,681	28,681
Net Income $Mil	511	624	777	886	1,019	1,019
Earnings Per Share $	0.51	0.62	0.76	0.86	0.99	0.99
Shares Outstanding Mil	1,002	1,007	1,009	1,018	1,019	1,025
Return on Equity %	17.9	17.9	18.3	17.0	16.4	16.4
Net Margin %	3.3	3.5	3.7	3.6	3.6	3.6
Asset Turnover	3.1	3.0	3.0	2.8	2.9	2.9
Financial Leverage	1.7	1.7	1.7	1.7	1.6	1.6

Valuation Ratios	Stock	Rel to Industry	Rel to S&P 500
Price/Earnings	29.5	1.0	1.3
Price/Book	4.8	1.4	1.5
Price/Sales	1.0	1.4	0.5
Price/Cash Flow	20.3	1.5	1.5

Major Fund Holders	% of Fund Assets
Lutheran Brotherhood A	5.12
Papp Stock	4.64
Timothy Plan Large/Mid-cap Growth A	4.59
Liberty Young Investor Z	4.54

Morningstar's Take By Tom Goetzinger, 12-04-2002 Stock Price as of Analysis: $29.54

Walgreen has cemented its position as the drugstore industry leader with an aggressive internally financed expansion and consistent market share gains. Still, we recommend investors seek a margin of safety to account for the negative industry trends that are likely to crimp profit growth.

Few mature businesses of any kind can match Walgreen's steady and strong growth. The century-old chain has averaged 16% revenue and 18% earnings growth over the past five years. Careful selection of high-traffic, freestanding locations has enabled the firm to generate enough cash flow to double its store base over the past decade without making large acquisitions or taking on much debt.

We think expansion opportunities are still plentiful. Walgreen is the number-one player in 34 of the nation's top 100 markets, and it's building "fill-in" locations in many of its current markets while also entering new ones. We like this strategy because it minimizes the likelihood of a drastic profit or cash flow shortfall that could jeopardize the firm's mission of internally financed growth. Stores in new markets usually take three to four years to turn a profit, while those in existing markets might take only half that long.

Same-store sales growth (sales growth at stores open at least one year) has been impressive as well. The main reason is brisk prescription drug sales. U.S. drug spending has increased an average of 14% per year since 1995, and is expected to grow 12% annually through 2010. Walgreen filled 12% more prescriptions in fiscal 2002 than 2001. With baby boomers aging and preventive medicine through drugs becoming more popular, Walgreen's pharmacy business should continue to benefit.

Prescriptions are pressuring margins, however, even as they contribute to growth. Walgreen earns significantly lower margins on prescriptions than on front-of-store items like food and beauty products. Prescriptions represented 60% of total sales in 2002 (up from 52% in 1999), and we project them to reach 65% of sales by 2005. Moreover, 90% of Walgreen's prescriptions involve payments from formidable third-party sources like managed-care companies, which are looking to lower drug costs by squeezing drugstores.

Given the lack of pricing power on the pharmacy side and the intense competition from other retailers for customers in the high-margin front-of-store area, we'd seek a 20% discount to our fair value estimate before investing in this venerable company.

MORNINGSTAR® Stocks 500

Walt Disney DIS

	Rating	Risk	Moat Size	Fair Value	Last Close	Yield %
	★★★★	Low	Narrow	$21.00	$16.31	1.3

Company Profile

Walt Disney provides entertainment services. It operates Walt Disney World resort in Florida, as well as theme parks and hotels in California; earns royalties from the Tokyo Disneyland theme park; and holds a stake in Disneyland Paris. Walt Disney Pictures and Television produces films that are distributed under the Walt Disney Pictures, Touchstone Pictures, and Hollywood Pictures names, and is a distributor for Miramax Films. The company's ABC subsidiary provides television and radio broadcast and programming services.

Management

Management ranks have thinned after key departures--partly thanks to Michael Eisner's ego, according to reports. Eisner, CEO for nearly two decades, has vast experience but is in the hot seat because of Disney's problems.

Strategy

Disney sells fun. Its focus on entertainment takes the company into many industries, like television broadcasting, movie production, theme parks, and luxury cruises. Animated characters like Mickey Mouse form the heart of Disney. The media giant hopes to be the premier creator of engaging and enduring stories and characters that can be leveraged across all of its operating segments.

500 South Buena Vista Street   www.disney.com
Burbank, CA 91521

Morningstar Grades

Growth [C]

	1999	2000	2001	2002
Revenue %	2.0	8.4	-0.6	0.6
Earnings/Share %	-30.3	-8.1	NMF	NMF
Book Value/Share %	7.3	49.3	-80.8	296.6
Dividends/Share %	-72.5	296.2	0.0	0.0

The 20% annual sales growth that Disney once enjoyed is a distant memory. We expect the company's top line to grow at a single-digit pace over the next five years, largely driven by a recovery in the theme park business.

Profitability [B]

	2000	2001	2002	TTM
Return on Assets %	2.0	-0.4	2.5	2.5
Oper Cash Flow $Mil	3,755	3,048	2,286	2,286
- Cap Spending $Mil	2,013	1,795	1,086	1,086
= Free Cash Flow $Mil	1,742	1,253	1,200	1,200

Operating margins have been in decline over the past five years, thanks to weakness in all of the company's businesses. This has led to lower returns on equity and invested capital. We expect an improvement in profitability in the near future.

Financial Health [A-]

	2000	2001	2002	09-02
Long-term Debt $Mil	6,959	8,940	12,467	12,467
Total Equity $Mil	24,100	22,672	23,445	23,445
Debt/Equity Ratio	0.3	0.4	0.5	0.5

Disney's credit rating has been slashed a couple of times since late 2001, and we're wary of further deterioration. However, we expect that the firm's coverage ratios will expand over the next few years.

Industry	Investment Style	Stock Type	Sector
Media Conglomerates	⊞ Large Core	→ Slow Growth	🎤 Media

Competition

	Market Cap $Mil	Debt/ Equity	12 Mo Trailing Sales $Mil	Price/Cash Flow	Return On Assets%	Total Return% 1 Yr	3 Yr
Walt Disney	33,308	0.5	25,329	14.6	2.5	-20.3	-19.1
AOL Time Warner	56,278	0.3	41,024	8.1	-34.6	-59.2	-44.6
Vivendi ADR	17,447	0.8	39,593	4.4	-9.9	-69.3	-43.0

Price Volatility

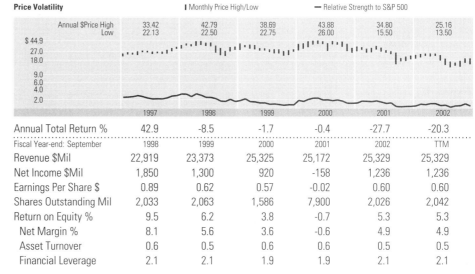

	I Monthly Price High/Low				— Relative Strength to S&P 500	
Annual $Price High	33.42	42.79	38.69	43.88	34.80	25.16
Low	22.13	22.50	22.75	26.00	15.50	13.50

	1997	1998	1999	2000	2001	2002
Annual Total Return %	42.9	-8.5	-1.7	-0.4	-27.7	-20.3

Fiscal Year-end: September	1998	1999	2000	2001	2002	TTM
Revenue $Mil	22,919	23,373	25,325	25,172	25,329	25,329
Net Income $Mil	1,850	1,300	920	-158	1,236	1,236
Earnings Per Share $	0.89	0.62	0.57	-0.02	0.60	0.60
Shares Outstanding Mil	2,033	2,063	1,586	7,900	2,026	2,042
Return on Equity %	9.5	6.2	3.8	-0.7	5.3	5.3
Net Margin %	8.1	5.6	3.6	-0.6	4.9	4.9
Asset Turnover	0.6	0.5	0.6	0.6	0.5	0.5
Financial Leverage	2.1	2.1	1.9	1.9	2.1	2.1

Valuation Ratios

	Stock	Rel to Industry	Rel to S&P 500
Price/Earnings	27.2	1.0	1.2
Price/Book	1.4	1.0	0.4
Price/Sales	1.3	0.6	0.7
Price/Cash Flow	14.6	1.0	1.1

Major Fund Holders

	% of Fund Assets
Longleaf Partners	6.58
PBHG Focused Value	5.85
Runkel Value	5.27
Fremont New Era Value	4.88

Morningstar's Take   By Jonathan Schrader, 11-27-2002   Stock Price as of Analysis: $19.88

The house that built Mickey has lost some of its magic. Despite its great entertainment properties, we don't think Disney merits a wide moat rating, so we'd look for a 30% discount to our fair value estimate before buying the stock.

Disney has been struggling over the past few years. While economic weakness is partly to blame, many of the company's issues predate the most recent downturn. Disney's ABC network has been languishing for years. Sales and profits at the company's consumer product unit have declined in each of the past five years.

The lone bright spot has been the studio entertainment business, but we don't have high hopes for it over the long term. The home video segment of this business has done well, but the most important element in its success has been Disney's partnership with Pixar. Although Disney's own efforts have failed to create an entertainment franchise since 1994's The Lion King, the company has split the profits from Pixar's lucrative offerings, including Monsters, Inc. and Toy Story. This partnership will come to an end in a few years, though, and any new deal would probably be less lucrative for Disney.

This points to one of the causes of Disney's lowly condition: an absence of creativity over the past few years. Many suggest that Michael Eisner's tendency to micromanage may be responsible. We're not sure, but our best measures of creative brilliance--sales and profits--tell us that something is amiss.

An increase in competition for the attention--and dollars--of America's children has also hurt Disney. Viacom's kid-focused Nickelodeon is one of the most popular channels on cable, and many of its characters, like the Rugrats and Jimmy Neutron, have also made it to the big screen.

Not all is gloom and doom at Disney. The company's theme parks should show strong results once happy economic times are here again. An improvement in the advertising market will also help results. However, we don't think the company enjoys the strong competitive advantages it once had, and we believe competition will continue to diminish its financial returns. We'd be willing to buy and hold the stock, but we'd want a sizable discount before doing so.

Washington Mutual WM

	Rating	Risk	Moat Size	Fair Value	Last Close	Yield %
	★★★	Med.	Narrow	$47.00	$34.53	3.1

Company Profile

Washington Mutual is the holding company for Washington Mutual Bank, which operates more than 1,000 banking offices in the Western United States and Florida. The bank provides savings, checking, money market, and individual retirement accounts, as well as certificates of deposit. Washington Mutual Bank also originates consumer, residential and commercial real-estate, and business loans. The company's nonbank subsidiaries offer brokerage, investment advisory, mortgage banking, consumer finance, and insurance services. It agreed to acquire Bank United in 2000.

Management

Chairman and CEO Kerry Killinger was the driver behind the recent acquisition spree and remains committed to the thrift's diversification effort.

Strategy

Washington Mutual, the nation's largest thrift, wants to be the premier consumer bank in the nation. The company is trying to move away from its savings and loan roots by developing fee-based products and services to make it less sensitive to interest rates. It is also growing through acquisitions, but thus far it has stuck with buying other thrifts.

1201 Third Avenue · · · · · · · · · · · www.wamu.com
Seattle, WA 98101

Morningstar Grades

Growth [A]	1998	1999	2000	2001
Revenue %	13.8	6.6	16.2	12.2
Earnings/Share %	68.4	23.6	11.8	52.1
Book Value/Share %	26.8	-3.0	20.2	27.7
Dividends/Share %	16.0	19.5	15.3	19.0

Washington Mutual continues its expansion into attractive markets. The company announced plans to open 70 branches in Chicago next year. The Chicago market is very competitive, but we think WaMu's alluring Ocasio branches will attract customers.

Profitability [C]	1999	2000	2001	TTM
Return on Assets %	1.0	1.0	1.3	1.4
Oper Cash Flow $Mil	5,270	3,022	-10,777	—
- Cap Spending $Mil	319	272	753	—
= Free Cash Flow $Mil	—	—	—	—

The efficiency ratio, a measure of operating costs, remains high as the company works to integrate five acquisitions over the past year and a half. Still, earnings are strong, and efficiency should improve.

Financial Health [A]	1999	2000	2001	09-02
Long-term Debt $Mil	—	—	—	—
Total Equity $Mil	9,053	10,166	13,961	20,161
Debt/Equity Ratio	—	—	—	—

Financial leverage is the only factor considered for a savings institution's financial health grade. Washington Mutual's current financial leverage is reasonable given the safety of its assets, which are primarily single-family mortgages.

Industry	Investment Style	Stock Type	Sector
Savings & Loans	Large Value	High Yield	Financial Services

Competition

	Market Cap $Mil	Debt/ Equity	12 Mo Trailing Sales $Mil	Price/Cash Flow	Return On Assets%	Total Return% 1 Yr	3 Yr
Washington Mutual	32,933	—	18,011	—	1.4	8.8	33.2
Bank of America	104,505	—	46,628	—	1.3	14.5	19.8
Wells Fargo	79,608	—	28,119	—	1.5	10.3	10.4

Price Volatility

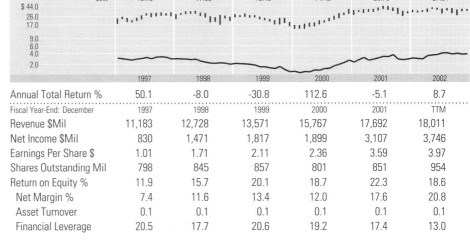

	Monthly Price High/Low	Relative Strength to S&P 500

Annual $Price High Low	32.28 18.78	34.45 17.83	30.50 16.46	37.29 14.42	42.98 26.70	39.98 27.84

	1997	1998	1999	2000	2001	2002
Annual Total Return %	50.1	-8.0	-30.8	112.6	-5.1	8.7

Fiscal Year-End: December	1997	1998	1999	2000	2001	TTM
Revenue $Mil	11,183	12,728	13,571	15,767	17,692	18,011
Net Income $Mil	830	1,471	1,817	1,899	3,107	3,746
Earnings Per Share $	1.01	1.71	2.11	2.36	3.59	3.97
Shares Outstanding Mil	798	845	857	801	851	954
Return on Equity %	11.9	15.7	20.1	18.7	22.3	18.6
Net Margin %	7.4	11.6	13.4	12.0	17.6	20.8
Asset Turnover	0.1	0.1	0.1	0.1	0.1	0.1
Financial Leverage	20.5	17.7	20.6	19.2	17.4	13.0

Valuation Ratios	Stock	Rel to Industry	Rel to S&P 500
Price/Earnings	8.7	0.7	0.4
Price/Book	1.6	1.0	0.5
Price/Sales	1.8	0.8	0.9
Price/Cash Flow	—	—	—

Major Fund Holders	% of Fund Assets
Oakmark Select I	17.84
CDC Nvest Select A	16.74
Sextant Growth	8.57
Scudder Dreman Financial Services A	7.29

Morningstar's Take By Richard McCaffery, 11-18-2002 Stock Price as of Analysis: $34.20

We put Washington Mutual into a class of banks with a strong operational advantage. Over the past five years, WaMu's efficiency, combined with an innovative sales culture, has allowed the company to increase revenue at a 20% compound annual rate, assets at 13%, and net income at better than 30%. Given our fair value estimate of $47, we think the shares remain attractive.

WaMu may not have the built-in kind of advantage that American Express does, but there's a lot to be said for a business that knows how to execute a well-articulated strategy. It's also not easy to put together a bank that knows how to sell financial products, which drive the top line, as well as lend conservatively, which protects the bottom line.

Despite this, the belief that WaMu is a bet on interest rates and fears about a housing bubble have depressed the stock. The company has shown the ability to add value in a variety of interest rate environments--in 2000, when rates rose, and in 2001 and 2002, when rates fell sharply. If the company didn't know how to hedge balance sheet risk, it would have blown up already. Consider that over the past nine months, WaMu has taken $2.9 billion in impairment charges on its mortgage-servicing asset,

a direct hit to the bottom line. Nevertheless, income has grown almost 30% over that period as a result of proper hedging.

When rates fall, WaMu originates fixed-rate mortgages, sells them into the secondary market, and makes a profit servicing them. Falling rates stimulate loan volume, lower the company's cost of borrowing, and expand margins. When rates rise, WaMu originates lots of adjustable-rate mortgages, which remain on the balance sheet and earn more than simply servicing the loans. Margins compress, but charge-offs usually decline. In addition, there's often a release of reserves from mortgage-servicing rights, which goes to the bottom line.

There has been much wailing and gnashing of teeth about housing bubbles. But given the growth rate of personal income, lean housing inventories, and weak growth in the early and mid-1990s, we think evidence of a national housing bubble is scarce.

WaMu management has incorporated a strong sales culture into a cost-efficient business model. It has an edge in execution that many banks lack, and one that's hard to recreate.

MORNINGSTAR® Stocks 500

Data as of 12-31-02

Washington Post WPO

	Rating	Risk	Moat Size	Fair Value	Last Close	Yield %
	★★	Low	Narrow	$650.00	$738.00	0.8

Company Profile

Washington Post publishes newspapers and operates media companies. The company publishes The Washington Post, which has a weekday daily circulation of about 800,000; Newsweek magazine, which has a circulation of more than 3 million; and 30 weekly community newspapers in Maryland. It also operates network television broadcast stations in five cities.

Management

Donald E. Graham became CEO in 1991 and chairman in 1993. Warren Buffett is on the board of directors and his Berkshire Hathaway owns 18% of total shares.

Strategy

Washington Post is best known for its eponymous newspaper, but the company is diversifying; it also has cable and TV stations. The firm's educational division is the growth engine.

1150 15th Street N.W.
Washington, DC 20071

www.washpostco.com

Morningstar Grades

Growth [C+]	1998	1999	2000	2001
Revenue %	7.9	5.0	8.9	0.2
Earnings/Share %	57.2	-45.7	-35.8	68.0
Book Value/Share %	42.1	-13.5	15.4	13.2
Dividends/Share %	4.2	4.0	3.8	3.7

While sales growth has remained fairly steady over the past five years, earnings growth has been slowed by the recession and large investments in cable and education.

Profitability [A-]	1999	2000	2001	TTM
Return on Assets %	7.5	4.2	6.4	3.5
Oper Cash Flow $Mil	291	369	349	458
- Cap Spending $Mil	130	172	224	174
= Free Cash Flow $Mil	161	196	125	285

The firm has maintained solid returns on assets and equity since 1995, but recent increases in expenses are cutting into what was a healthy profit margin.

Financial Health [A]	1999	2000	2001	09-02
Long-term Debt $Mil	398	873	883	405
Total Equity $Mil	1,368	1,481	1,683	1,743
Debt/Equity Ratio	0.3	0.6	0.5	0.2

We think the company is in very good financial shape. Cash flows are on the rise, and leverage is falling.

Industry	Investment Style	Stock Type	Sector
Media Conglomerates	▣ Mid Core	➜ Slow Growth	🎙 Media

Competition

	Market Cap $Mil	Debt/ Equity	12 Mo Trailing Sales $Mil	Price/Cash Flow	Return On Assets%	Total Return% 1 Yr	3 Yr
Washington Post	7,018	0.2	2,522	15.3	3.5	40.5	12.8
Gannett	19,190	0.7	6,354	16.2	8.1	8.1	-1.1
Tribune	13,856	0.6	5,273	15.2	1.3	22.7	-2.8

Price Volatility

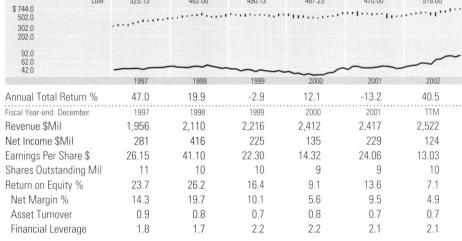

I Monthly Price High/Low			— Relative Strength to S&P 500			

Annual $Price High Low	491.06 325.13	605.50 462.00	594.50 490.13	628.75 467.25	651.50 470.00	743.00 516.00

	1997	1998	1999	2000	2001	2002
Annual Total Return %	47.0	19.9	-2.9	12.1	-13.2	40.5

Fiscal Year-end: December	1997	1998	1999	2000	2001	TTM
Revenue $Mil	1,956	2,110	2,216	2,412	2,417	2,522
Net Income $Mil	281	416	225	135	229	124
Earnings Per Share $	26.15	41.10	22.30	14.32	24.06	13.03
Shares Outstanding Mil	11	10	10	9	9	10
Return on Equity %	23.7	26.2	16.4	9.1	13.6	7.1
Net Margin %	14.3	19.7	10.1	5.6	9.5	4.9
Asset Turnover	0.9	0.8	0.7	0.8	0.7	0.7
Financial Leverage	1.8	1.7	2.2	2.2	2.1	2.1

Valuation Ratios	Stock	Rel to Industry	Rel to S&P 500
Price/Earnings	56.6	2.1	2.4
Price/Book	4.0	2.8	1.3
Price/Sales	2.8	1.3	1.4
Price/Cash Flow	15.3	1.0	1.2

Major Fund Holders	% of Fund Assets
Calamos Mid Cap Value A	3.80
Weitz Value	3.77
Weitz Partners Value	3.71
Citizens Emerging Growth Stndrd	2.64

Morningstar's Take By Jonathan Schrader, 11-22-2002 Stock Price as of Analysis: $722.00

Strong businesses and topnotch management make Washington Post a good stock to own at the right price.

Washington Post is best known for its flagship newspaper, which dominates the Washington, D.C., news scene. Its Newsweek is among the most popular news magazines in the country and generates excellent cash flow. Perhaps less well known is that the company also owns and operates several television stations, which normally throw off loads of cash thanks to operating margins of nearly 50%.

Recently, Washington Post has been seeking growth and diversification opportunities in other segments. Much of the company's attention over the past few years has been focused on its cable and education businesses. Several years of heavy investment in these businesses have depressed profit margins and returns on invested capital, making the stock look like a suspect investment at first glance. However, this investment is finally starting to pay off with strong top- and bottom-line growth. We expect the cable and education units to continue to drive earnings growth over the next five years.

As a result of these diversification efforts, cash flows should be less volatile. One problem with the

newspaper and magazine businesses is that they depend largely on advertising, which is in turn tied to the business cycle. Fortunately for Washington Post, profits at its newer businesses are relatively independent of the business cycle. In fact, by some measures, the profits of education services company Kaplan are countercyclical: Laid-off workers use its testing services on their way back to graduate school.

Beyond its solid line of businesses, one of Washington Post's greatest assets is its management. The executive team continually emphasizes long-term improvement over quarterly forecasts. Accounting practices are conservative, and the company doesn't take "one-time" charges on a frequent basis, in refreshing contrast to some of its peers. Moreover, the firm recently announced it would expense stock options.

Such corporate practices reflect the mind set of Warren Buffett, who is a large shareholder. Buffett bought at a steep discount to Washington Post's fair value; we'd suggest a 20% discount before buying as well.

Waste Management WMI

	Rating	Risk	Moat Size	Fair Value	Last Close	Yield %
	★★★★★	Low	Narrow	$35.00	$22.92	0.0

Company Profile

Waste Management provides nonhazardous solid-waste management services. The company collects, transfers, disposes, and recycles waste. It markets these services to municipal, commercial, industrial, and residential customers in North America and abroad. Waste Management has more than 27 million customers. About 58% of the company's revenue comes from collection and 38% is generated by transfer and disposal services.

Management

Maurice Myers, named chairman, CEO, and president in November 1999, is no greenhorn at turning around troubled companies. As the CEO of Yellow Corp., he guided the trucking firm through a difficult restructuring.

Strategy

With the sale of its international assets complete, Waste Management is focused on improving operating margins by running more-efficient trash-hauling routes, eliminating unprofitable contracts, and centralizing purchasing. The firm recognizes it has limited growth opportunities and intends to return free cash to shareholders via share repurchases and possibly dividends.

1001 Fannin Street   www.wmx.com
Houston, TX 77002

Morningstar Grades

Growth [C-]

	1998	1999	2000	2001
Revenue %	5.5	4.0	-4.8	-9.4
Earnings/Share %	NMF	NMF	NMF	NMF
Book Value/Share %	8.6	-3.9	10.0	8.3
Dividends/Share %	NMF	-50.0	0.0	0.0

Now that the company has curtailed its feverish acquisition pace, it must prove it can grow internally. Over the past year and a half, the sale of its international operations has stunted sales growth.

Profitability [C+]

	1999	2000	2001	TTM
Return on Assets %	-1.8	-0.5	2.6	3.7
Oper Cash Flow $Mil	1,690	2,125	2,355	2,374
- Cap Spending $Mil	1,327	1,313	1,328	1,399
= Free Cash Flow $Mil	363	812	1,027	975

Years of shoddy accounting resulted in massive earnings restatements, rendering the firm profitless from 1997 through 2000. New pricing software should enable the firm to negotiate more-profitable contracts, thus improving its return on assets.

Financial Health [D]

	1999	2000	2001	09-02
Long-term Debt $Mil	8,399	8,372	7,709	8,151
Total Equity $Mil	4,402	4,801	5,392	5,410
Debt/Equity Ratio	1.9	1.7	1.4	1.5

Having deleveraged its balance sheet significantly since 1999, Waste Management is now in a position to use its free cash flow to repurchase shares and increase its dividend. In 2001, operating income easily covered interest expense.

Industry	Investment Style	Stock Type	Sector
Waste Management	▦ Large Core	→ Slow Growth	▤ Business Services

Competition

	Market Cap $Mil	Debt/ Equity	12 Mo Trailing Sales $Mil	Price/Cash Flow	Return On Assets%	Total Return% 1 Yr	3 Yr
Waste Management	13,950	1.5	11,121	5.9	3.7	-28.1	9.9
Republic Services A	3,423	—	2,323	—	—	—	—
Allied Waste Industries	1,966	—	5,516	—	—	—	—

Price Volatility

     ▌ Monthly Price High/Low   — Relative Strength to S&P 500

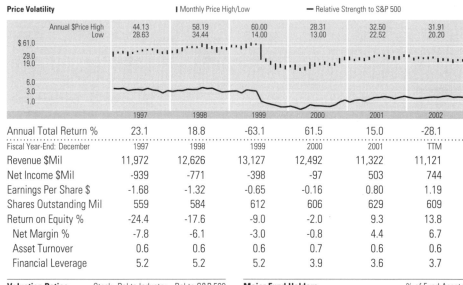

Annual $Price High Low	44.13 28.63	58.19 34.44	60.00 14.00	28.31 13.00	32.50 22.52	31.91 20.20
	1997	1998	1999	2000	2001	2002

	1997	1998	1999	2000	2001	TTM
Annual Total Return %	23.1	18.8	-63.1	61.5	15.0	-28.1
Fiscal Year-End: December	1997	1998	1999	2000	2001	TTM
Revenue $Mil	11,972	12,626	13,127	12,492	11,322	11,121
Net Income $Mil	-939	-771	-398	-97	503	744
Earnings Per Share $	-1.68	-1.32	-0.65	-0.16	0.80	1.19
Shares Outstanding Mil	559	584	612	606	629	609
Return on Equity %	-24.4	-17.6	-9.0	-2.0	9.3	13.8
Net Margin %	-7.8	-6.1	-3.0	-0.8	4.4	6.7
Asset Turnover	0.6	0.6	0.6	0.7	0.6	0.6
Financial Leverage	5.2	5.2	5.2	3.9	3.6	3.7

Valuation Ratios	Stock	Rel to Industry	Rel to S&P 500
Price/Earnings	19.3	1.0	0.8
Price/Book	2.6	1.0	0.8
Price/Sales	1.3	1.0	0.6
Price/Cash Flow	5.9	1.0	0.4

Major Fund Holders	% of Fund Assets
Legg Mason Value Prim	6.93
AmSouth Select Equity B	6.44
Runkel Value	5.34
Longleaf Partners	5.30

Morningstar's Take By Aaron Westrate, 12-16-2002   Stock Price as of Analysis: $24.12

We believe Waste Management is a compelling investment, given the competitive edge it gains from its irreplaceable disposal network. The firm is a low-risk investment, given the fairly steady demand for waste removal and because Waste Management generates lots of excess cash beyond its reinvestment needs. We'd open our pocketbooks to purchase the shares at a 30% discount to our fair value estimate of $35.

After several decades of consolidation, Waste Management possesses 302 landfills, which represents a remarkable 40% of the total disposal capacity in the United States. Combining these landfill assets with those of its top two competitors, Allied Waste and Republic Services, means that the three firms control 66% of total U.S. disposal capacity. Rounding out the firm's disposal network are 300 transfer stations and a fleet of 30,000 trucks.

The key disposal assets are clearly the landfills, since the NIMBY (Not In My Back Yard) principle has made it nearly impossible to construct new ones. We believe Waste Management's landfills will give the firm an ever-increasing measure of control in its markets as the number of landfills dwindles nationwide. At the same time, we recognize that competition will always exist on the collection side.

The scale of Waste Management's truck fleet does confer some negotiating power with suppliers, but it doesn't require a significant investment to compete against Waste Management on the collection side of the business at the local level.

Another key part of our thesis on Waste Management is that the firm has a lot of opportunity to boost operating margins despite the maturity of the waste industry. The firm was a serial acquirer in the past, but its ability to integrate those acquisitions in order to exploit any scale advantages was suspect. Since the end of 1999, new management has moved to reduce procurement costs, optimize collection routes, and improve customer service.

The firm's success in boosting its operating margins from 10% in 1999 to 15% in 2001 has contributed to a substantial improvement in free cash flow. In 1999, free cash flow was just $362 million compared with $1.03 billion in 2001. We anticipate Waste Management should be able to increase free cash flow at a midteen clip through 2006 and free cash flow on a per-share basis should rise even faster as a result of significant share repurchases. In February 2002, Waste Management announced a $1 billion share buyback program, which will result in the repurchase of about 6% of its outstanding shares.

     M⊙RNINGSTAR® Stocks 500

Waters WAT

	Rating	Risk	Moat Size	Fair Value	Last Close	Yield %
	★★★	Med.	Narrow	$30.00	$21.78	0.0

Company Profile

Waters is an analytical instrument maker with manufacturing and distribution expertise in three complementary technologies. The company is the world market leader in high-pressure liquid chromatography, mass spectrometry, and thermal analysis instruments. Its instruments are used in life sciences research including drug discovery, genomics and proteomics, and material synthesis.

Management

Douglas Berthiaume has been president and CEO since 1994; he became chairman in 1996. Berthiaume has successfully led efforts to expand Waters' industry expertise via acquisitions.

Strategy

The company is focusing on sales growth in its high-pressure liquid chromatography and mass spectrometry segments with product upgrades geared toward very profitable research in genomics and proteomics. By bundling these two product lines, Waters is increasing its average deal size and attracting new customers.

34 Maple Street   www.waters.com
Milford, MA 01757

Industry	Investment Style	Stock Type	Sector
Medical Equipment	Mid Growth	Cyclical	Healthcare

Competition

	Market Cap $Mil	Debt/ Equity	12 Mo Trailing Sales $Mil	Price/Cash Flow	Return On Assets%	Total Return% 1 Yr	3 Yr
Waters	2,824	0.0	882	12.1	10.7	-43.8	-3.9
Applied Biosystems Group	3,662	—	1,633	—	—	—	—
Millipore	1,645	—	687	—	—	—	—

Price Volatility

I Monthly Price High/Low   — Relative Strength to S&P 500

Annual $Price High Low	12.11 5.78	21.88 9.13	33.84 18.13	90.94 21.97	85.38 22.33	39.25 17.86
	1997	1998	1999	2000	2001	2002
Annual Total Return %	25.5	128.8	21.5	215.1	-53.6	-43.8

Fiscal Year-end: December	1997	1998	1999	2000	2001	TTM
Revenue $Mil	465	619	704	795	859	882
Net Income $Mil	-9	73	122	145	115	106
Earnings Per Share $	-0.08	0.57	0.92	1.06	0.83	0.78
Shares Outstanding Mil	115	120	123	127	130	130
Return on Equity %	-14.8	48.9	41.7	32.2	19.7	15.9
Net Margin %	-2.0	11.9	17.3	18.3	13.3	12.0
Asset Turnover	0.8	1.1	1.2	1.1	1.0	0.9
Financial Leverage	8.9	3.8	2.0	1.5	1.5	1.5

Valuation Ratios	Stock	Rel to Industry	Rel to S&P 500
Price/Earnings	27.9	0.9	1.2
Price/Book	4.2	0.6	1.3
Price/Sales	3.2	0.7	1.6
Price/Cash Flow	12.1	0.5	0.9

Major Fund Holders	% of Fund Assets
Pin Oak Aggressive Stock	7.03
Live Oak Health Sciences	5.76
MassMutual Instl Focused Value S	4.37
Buffalo USA Global	3.60

Morningstar Grades

Growth [C]	1998	1999	2000	2001
Revenue %	32.9	13.8	12.9	8.1
Earnings/Share %	NMF	61.4	15.2	-21.7
Book Value/Share %	115.8	89.3	49.4	27.9
Dividends/Share %	NMF	NMF	NMF	NMF

Sales growth slowed from 13% in 1999 and 2000 to 8% in 2001 and just 4% so far in 2002, as a result of market saturation and slowing pharmaceutical spending. Research in proteomics should produce better growth in 2003, in our opinion.

Profitability [A]	1999	2000	2001	TTM
Return on Assets %	20.8	21.0	12.9	10.7
Oper Cash Flow $Mil	151	151	189	233
- Cap Spending $Mil	24	35	42	36
= Free Cash Flow $Mil	126	115	147	197

Waters steadily increased its net profit margin from 17% in 1999 to 20% in 2001. Though the company has struggled through a difficult 2002, we think margins should improve again in 2003.

Financial Health [A+]	1999	2000	2001	09-02
Long-term Debt $Mil	81	0	0	0
Total Equity $Mil	292	452	582	667
Debt/Equity Ratio	0.3	0.0	0.0	0.0

Waters has a solid balance sheet with about $300 million in cash and no long-term debt. Impressive operating cash flow--now approaching $200 million per year--allows the firm to comfortably invest in research and development.

Morningstar's Take By Tom Goetzinger, 11-21-2002 Stock Price as of Analysis: $27.70

While its strategy of developing and manufacturing life sciences instruments for biotech and pharmaceutical firms isn't risk-free, Waters is immune to some of the volatility involved in the hit-or-miss business of drug discovery. Over the past five years, Waters has expanded its product line by acquiring market leaders in related instrumentation areas; the company now controls 20% of the $4 billion (and growing) analytical instrument market. We'd look to buy in at around $20.

Thanks to the mapping of the human genome, the market for advanced laboratory equipment looks ripe for growth. The genomics (study of gene sequences) market is expected to increase about 20% over the next couple of years, and the proteomics (study of proteins and disease interaction) market should see 15% growth. Waters is well positioned to benefit, as its mass spectrometry (MS) equipment--the central technology used in proteomics--has a 23% share of the market. Though it was forced to re-engineer some of its MS tools because of patent infringement earlier this year, Waters has a history of product innovation, and should overcome this setback.

Its steady stream of solid products has made Waters the market leader in all three of its complementary technologies: high-pressure liquid

chromatography, mass spectrometry, and thermal analysis. The company's diversified product lineup is also buffered by its wide set of customers, including academic institutions involved in research, biotechnology firms, pharmaceutical makers, and the government.

Waters is still subject to slowdowns in spending, however. The weak economy forced revenue growth down to 8% in 2001 and 4% so far in 2002, compared with the 19% average from 1997 to 2000. We expect sales to rebound in 2003, as pharmaceutical firms increase their capital spending from the depressed levels of 2001 and 2002 to spark somewhat stagnant drug-development pipelines.

With this in mind, we expect revenue growth to reach double digits again in 2003. Given management's penchant for cost control and profitable new product development, we also expect some margin expansion. We'd be buyers at a 30% discount to our fair value estimate of $30.

Watson Pharmaceuticals WPI

	Rating	Risk	Moat Size	Fair Value	Last Close	Yield %
	★★	Med.	Narrow	$27.00	$28.27	0.0

Company Profile

Watson Pharmaceuticals markets and produces generic and proprietary medications. It also develops advanced drug-delivery systems primarily designed to enhance the therapeutic benefits of drug compounds. It makes approximately 140 generic products, including analgesics and oral contraceptives. The company's main branded drugs are aimed at kidney-related disease and women's health. Watson acquired Schein Pharmaceutical in August 2000, which expanded its reach in treatments for iron deficiency and anemia. Approximately half of Watson's sales come from generics.

Management

The driving force behind the company is Allen Chao, who started Watson in 1984 after working for a major drug company for 10 years. The rest of his executive team is made up of MBAs and PhDs, most of whom have backgrounds in big pharma.

Strategy

Watson started off as a generic drug manufacturer specializing in complex chemistry, then began acquiring companies to establish proprietary brands. Now it has added drug-delivery technologies to its repertoire. Its generic division concentrates on drugs that are hard to formulate or manufacture and that complement Watson's existing product line.

311 Bonnie Circle   www.watsonpharm.com
Corona, CA 92880-2882

	Investment Style	Stock Type	Sector
Industry			
Drugs	Mid Growth	Spec. Growth	Healthcare

Competition

	Market Cap $Mil	Debt/ Equity	12 Mo Trailing Sales $Mil	Price/Cash Flow	Return On Assets%	Total Return% 1 Yr	3 Yr
Watson Pharmaceuticals	3,021	0.2	1,188	7.8	6.8	-9.9	-5.9
Pharmacia	54,044	—	13,943	—	—	—	—
Teva Pharmaceutical Indus	9,891	0.7	2,077	36.2	8.0	25.9	32.8

Price Volatility

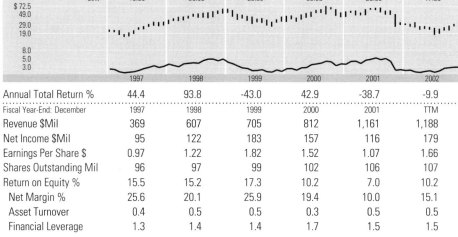

Annual $Price High Low	34.13 16.00	63.00 30.50	62.94 26.50	71.50 33.69	66.39 26.50	33.25 17.95

	1997	1998	1999	2000	2001	2002
Annual Total Return %	44.4	93.8	-43.0	42.9	-38.7	-9.9

Fiscal Year-End: December	1997	1998	1999	2000	2001	TTM
Revenue $Mil	369	607	705	812	1,161	1,188
Net Income $Mil	95	122	183	157	116	179
Earnings Per Share $	0.97	1.22	1.82	1.52	1.07	1.66
Shares Outstanding Mil	96	97	99	102	106	107
Return on Equity %	15.5	15.2	17.3	10.2	7.0	10.2
Net Margin %	25.6	20.1	25.9	19.4	10.0	15.1
Asset Turnover	0.4	0.5	0.5	0.3	0.5	0.5
Financial Leverage	1.3	1.4	1.4	1.7	1.5	1.5

Valuation Ratios	Stock	Rel to Industry	Rel to S&P 500
Price/Earnings	17.0	0.7	0.7
Price/Book	1.7	0.2	0.5
Price/Sales	2.5	0.6	1.3
Price/Cash Flow	7.8	0.4	0.6

Major Fund Holders	% of Fund Assets
Citizens Value	4.12
Stonebridge Growth	3.61
Stonebridge Aggressive Growth	3.44
IMS Capital Value	3.02

Morningstar Grades

Growth [B]	1998	1999	2000	2001
Revenue %	64.4	16.1	15.1	43.0
Earnings/Share %	25.8	49.2	-16.5	-29.6
Book Value/Share %	28.1	31.2	41.6	2.9
Dividends/Share %	NMF	NMF	NMF	NMF

Acquisitions have driven revenue growth; 2001 sales increased 43% thanks to the Schein acquisition in 2000. We expect low-single-digit revenue growth in 2002 and high-single-digit growth thereafter.

Profitability [A]	1999	2000	2001	TTM
Return on Assets %	12.5	6.1	4.6	6.8
Oper Cash Flow $Mil	128	-41	201	386
- Cap Spending $Mil	30	36	62	70
= Free Cash Flow $Mil	99	-76	139	316

Gross and operating margins in the mid-50s and mid-20s, respectively, are better than those of generic peers, but below those of pure-play pharmas. We expect gross margins to hit 60% by 2004 as branded drugs become a larger piece of the revenue pie.

Financial Health [A-]	1999	2000	2001	09-02
Long-term Debt $Mil	150	483	416	356
Total Equity $Mil	1,059	1,548	1,672	1,760
Debt/Equity Ratio	0.1	0.3	0.2	0.2

Watson's debt is manageable and its cash pile is plenty high. In June, total debt was $450 million, giving the firm a debt/equity ratio of 0.27 and interest coverage of 17 times. Both figures indicate a healthy balance sheet.

Morningstar's Take By Todd N. Lebor, 09-27-2002 Stock Price as of Analysis: $24.85

Watson holds a venerable position in the specialty/generic pharmaceutical world, but it's not a cash generator yet, so we'd demand a steep discount to our fair value estimate before buying the stock.

With half of its revenue from branded drugs and the other half from generic drugs, Watson has top-tier gross and operating margins relative to its peers. But, like many of its peers, Watson relies on others for many of its new products. From 1997 through 2001, the company spent more than $1 billion on acquisitions, which helped increase revenue from $380 million to $1.2 billion, but also drained operating cash. This strategy requires frequent visits to the capital markets to raise debt or issue new stock, neither of which is ideal for existing investors; Watson has used mostly debt, borrowing $500 million over the past five years. So far, Watson hasn't shown it can produce sustainable adjusted free cash flow (cash flow from operations less capital expenditures and acquisitions).

Also, many of Watson's branded drugs lack patent protection--one of the main competitive advantages for its larger cousins. Although sales generated from most of Watson's branded drugs are too small to draw competitive threats from the majors, Watson is more exposed nonetheless. Plus, Ferrlecit, the

company's only product with more than $100 million in annual revenue, loses U.S. market exclusivity in early 2004. Watson is also facing tough competition from Barr Labs in the oral contraceptive market.

We wouldn't dismiss Watson all together, though. It has Oxytrol, an incontinence drug that tested well against the competition and is under review with the Food and Drug Administration. The transdermal patch delivery method that distinguishes Watson's drug from the competition eases the common side effect of dry mouth. This in turn leads to less drinking, which is a tremendous help to those who suffer from incontinence. Breaking into this $1 billion market could help propel Watson into the big leagues, but that's not a given. Oxytrol's competitors are Pharmacia's Detrol and Johnson & Johnson's Ditropan. Taking on the big guys will be expensive: We anticipate Watson will spend nearly all its 2003 and 2004 profits from Oxytrol marketing the drug, if it's approved.

Watson's high concentration of branded drug revenue distinguishes it from its generic peers, but it isn't a competitive advantage, in our opinion.

MORNINGSTAR® Stocks 500

WellPoint Health Networks WLP

	Rating	Risk	Moat Size	Fair Value	Last Close	Yield %
	★★★	Low	Narrow	$69.00	$71.16	0.0

Company Profile

WellPoint Health Networks operates managed health-care networks under the Blue Cross Blue Shield name and a pharmacy benefit network. The company's networks include a health-maintenance organization, a preferred provider organization, and specialty managed-care networks. Members include large and small employers as well as individuals. WellPoint Health Networks' subsidiaries include CaliforniaCare Health Plans, WellPoint Dental Plan, WellPoint Pharmacy Plan, and Professional Claim Services.

Management

In 1986, chairman and CEO Leonard Schaeffer took over at Blue Cross of California, now a WellPoint subsidiary. He has successfully guided the company through its expansion into new states and transformed WellPoint into a national health-care firm.

Strategy

WellPoint plans to increase income through internal sales growth and tight cost controls. It will continue to drive internal growth by offering choice-oriented products in the targeted geographies that it dominates. While the string of recent acquisitions might suggest otherwise, WellPoint is only opportunistically acquisitive. It has simply found some great opportunities lately.

1 Wellpoint Way
Thousand Oaks, CA 91362
www.wellpoint.com

Morningstar Grades

Growth [A+]	1998	1999	2000	2001
Revenue %	14.8	15.5	23.3	34.7
Earnings/Share %	0.6	24.2	28.8	19.3
Book Value/Share %	6.4	3.0	31.3	27.7
Dividends/Share %	NMF	NMF	NMF	NMF

Acquisitions helped WellPoint increase membership and revenue 27% and 37%, respectively, in the second quarter from the year-ago period. The pending purchase of CareFirst should continue WellPoint's geographic expansion and spur sales growth.

Profitability [A]	1999	2000	2001	TTM
Return on Assets %	6.1	6.2	5.6	6.0
Oper Cash Flow $Mil	829	648	806	1,315
- Cap Spending $Mil	39	47	93	100
= Free Cash Flow $Mil	791	601	713	1,215

WellPoint has consistently posted a medical loss ratio of 80%-82% (better than the industry average of about 84%) and has decreased its administrative loss ratio from 18.0% in the second quarter of 2001 to 16.7% in the second quarter of 2002.

Financial Health [A-]	1999	2000	2001	09-02
Long-term Debt $Mil	348	401	838	1,156
Total Equity $Mil	1,313	1,644	2,133	3,773
Debt/Equity Ratio	0.3	0.2	0.4	0.3

Though WellPoint added $340 million in debt to finance the RightChoice acquisition, its financial health is still strong. The company generates enviable cash flow from operations and has plenty of cash to cover interest payments.

Industry	Investment Style	Stock Type	Sector
Managed Care	Large Growth	Aggr. Growth	Healthcare

Competition

	Market Cap $Mil	Debt/ Equity	12 Mo Trailing Sales $Mil	Price/Cash Flow	Return On Assets%	Total Return% 1 Yr	3 Yr
WellPoint Health Networks	10,372	0.3	16,180	7.9	6.0	21.8	29.5
UnitedHealth Group	25,235	0.3	24,358	12.5	8.9	18.0	46.6
Anthem	8,884	—	11,954	—	3.8	27.1	—

Price Volatility

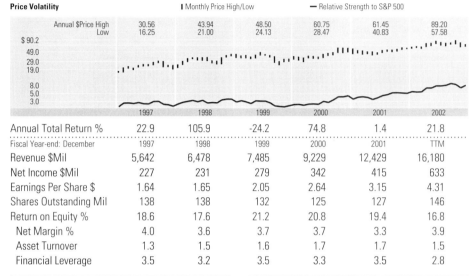

Annual $Price High / Low	30.56 / 16.25	43.94 / 21.00	48.50 / 24.13	60.75 / 28.47	61.45 / 40.83	89.20 / 57.58

I Monthly Price High/Low — Relative Strength to S&P 500

	1997	1998	1999	2000	2001	2002
Annual Total Return %	22.9	105.9	-24.2	74.8	1.4	21.8

Fiscal Year-end: December	1997	1998	1999	2000	2001	TTM
Revenue $Mil	5,642	6,478	7,485	9,229	12,429	16,180
Net Income $Mil	227	231	279	342	415	633
Earnings Per Share $	1.64	1.65	2.05	2.64	3.15	4.31
Shares Outstanding Mil	138	138	132	125	127	146
Return on Equity %	18.6	17.6	21.2	20.8	19.4	16.8
Net Margin %	4.0	3.6	3.7	3.7	3.3	3.9
Asset Turnover	1.3	1.5	1.6	1.7	1.7	1.5
Financial Leverage	3.5	3.2	3.5	3.3	3.5	2.8

Valuation Ratios	Stock	Rel to Industry	Rel to S&P 500
Price/Earnings	16.5	0.8	0.7
Price/Book	2.7	0.5	0.9
Price/Sales	0.6	0.9	0.3
Price/Cash Flow	7.9	0.8	0.6

Major Fund Holders	% of Fund Assets
Reserve Informed Investors Growth R	9.74
Legg Mason Special Investment Prim	6.57
IPS New Frontier	5.76
Fidelity Select Medical Delivery	4.76

Morningstar's Take By Damon Ficklin, 10-14-2002 Stock Price as of Analysis: $82.27

WellPoint Health Networks runs one of the tightest ships in the health insurance industry and we expect that it will continue to tack successfully.

WellPoint has posted impressive enrollment growth, even after adjusting for the string of acquisitions that it has made to transform itself from a regional Blue Cross Blue Shield provider in California into a leading national player.

Net of new acquisitions, it has delivered 8%-10% enrollment growth over the past couple of years, beating its long-term goal of 5% and the industry average of 3%-4%. Including acquisitions, WellPoint posted a 30% gain in membership in 2001, compared with 10% growth for industry bellwether UnitedHealth Group, flat growth for Cigna, and a 10% drop for struggling Aetna.

WellPoint has significant competitive advantages. It has some of the most flexible products in the industry and boasts leading share in each of the key markets in which it competes: California, Georgia, and Missouri. As health-care costs have escalated, the trend toward choice-oriented products has accelerated, and WellPoint has captured the lion's share of business in its markets. By offering a variety of tiered programs, with different levels of deductibles and co-pays, it has been able to meet customers' needs while limiting its exposure to medical cost increases.

WellPoint also uses its actuaries more strategically. Unlike most of its competitors, it pays its claims as fast as possible and closes its books monthly. This way its actuaries can run monthly projections with the most accurate data and identify changing trends faster than its competitors.

WellPoint can act on changes in actuarial estimates because it diversifies a larger portion of its business across small and midsize firms and individual plans. This allows it to reprice its products pretty evenly throughout the year while its competitors, which are more focused on large business accounts, can only reprice most products at the start of the year. WellPoint has produced one of the most consistent medical loss ratios (a key indicator of a firm's ability to price products accurately) in the industry with this strategy.

While we believe that strong underwriters like WellPoint will continue to gain share from the weaker players, the industry is intensely competitive. We would therefore look to buy only if the stock price provided a margin of safety of more than 20% to our fair value estimate.

Wells Fargo WFC

	Rating	Risk	Moat Size	Fair Value	Last Close	Yield %
	★★★	Med.	Wide	$50.00	$46.87	2.3

Company Profile

Wells Fargo operates more than 5,600 banking and mortgage-lending offices in the United States and abroad. The bank offers a robust line of consumer financial services, including online banking, trust, brokerage, credit card, and insurance. The bank also makes real estate, corporate, and consumer loans. After merging with Norwest in 1998, it became one of the top three mortgage providers in the nation. It remains highly acquisitive; it bought Utah's First Security, Texas' BankUnited, and Iowa's Brenton Banks in 2000.

Management

CEO Richard Kovacevich is one of the most highly regarded in the business. The recent departure of the firm's COO has stirred speculation that Wells might soon do a large acquisition, offering the number-two spot as bait to another firm's CEO.

Strategy

Wells Fargo wants to be the leading retail bank in its regional markets. It has a national presence in the small-business and other specialty lending segments. It is growing by cross-selling additional products to existing customers and by acquiring small banks and a broker-dealer. The bank's well-known name has enabled it to rapidly attract online banking customers at a lower cost.

420 Montgomery Street
San Francisco, CA 94163
www.wellsfargo.com

Morningstar Grades

Growth [C]

	1998	1999	2000	2001
Revenue %	46.2	6.9	15.3	-2.5
Earnings/Share %	-18.7	81.7	1.7	-15.5
Book Value/Share %	7.9	3.8	12.0	2.8
Dividends/Share %	13.8	12.1	14.7	11.1

Net revenue was up 26% in the first nine months of 2002, with mortgages and home equity loans serving as big drivers. Over the long term, the firm is targeting double-digit growth, which could be a bit of a stretch considering Wells Fargo's size.

Profitability [B-]

	1999	2000	2001	TTM
Return on Assets %	1.7	1.5	1.1	1.5
Oper Cash Flow $Mil	16,275	5,569	-11,226	—
- Cap Spending $Mil	—	—	—	—
= Free Cash Flow $Mil	—	—	—	—

Wells Fargo's return on assets is above the industry average, thanks in part to its sales of new and lucrative financial services. The firm has used derivatives to ensure it generates an adequate net interest margin this year.

Financial Health [B]

	1999	2000	2001	09-02
Long-term Debt $Mil	—	—	—	—
Total Equity $Mil	23,527	26,103	26,996	30,016
Debt/Equity Ratio	—	—	—	—

Wells Fargo's financial leverage is low, leading to this solid grade. While its loan default ratio is rising, it is still low compared with some peers. Moreover, it's conservatively reserved against future defaults.

Industry	Investment Style	Stock Type	Sector
Super Regional Banks	▦ Large Core	↗ Classic Growth	$ Financial Services

Competition

	Market Cap $Mil	Debt/ Equity	12 Mo Trailing Sales $Mil	Price/Cash Flow	Return On Assets%	Total Return% 1 Yr	3 Yr
Wells Fargo	79,608	—	28,119	—	1.5	10.3	10.4
Citigroup	177,948	—	106,096	—	1.6	-24.2	1.1
Bank of America	104,505	—	46,628	—	1.3	14.5	19.8

Price Volatility

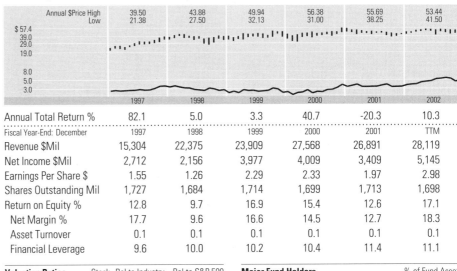

| | Monthly Price High/Low | — Relative Strength to S&P 500 |

Annual $Price High Low	39.50 21.38	43.88 27.50	49.94 32.13	56.38 31.00	55.69 38.25	53.44 41.50
	1997	1998	1999	2000	2001	2002
Annual Total Return %	82.1	5.0	3.3	40.7	-20.3	10.3

Fiscal Year-End: December	1997	1998	1999	2000	2001	TTM
Revenue $Mil	15,304	22,375	23,909	27,568	26,891	28,119
Net Income $Mil	2,712	2,156	3,977	4,009	3,409	5,145
Earnings Per Share $	1.55	1.26	2.29	2.33	1.97	2.98
Shares Outstanding Mil	1,727	1,684	1,714	1,699	1,713	1,698
Return on Equity %	12.8	9.7	16.9	15.4	12.6	17.1
Net Margin %	17.7	9.6	16.6	14.5	12.7	18.3
Asset Turnover	0.1	0.1	0.1	0.1	0.1	0.1
Financial Leverage	9.6	10.0	10.2	10.4	11.4	11.1

Valuation Ratios	Stock	Rel to Industry	Rel to S&P 500
Price/Earnings	15.7	1.1	0.7
Price/Book	2.7	1.3	0.8
Price/Sales	2.8	1.3	1.4
Price/Cash Flow	—	—	—

Major Fund Holders	% of Fund Assets
Rydex Banking Inv	9.73
ProFunds UltraBull Inv	8.84
Oppenheimer Quest Opportunity Value A	6.85
Profunds Ultra Banking Inv	6.81

Morningstar's Take By Craig Woker, 11-12-2002 Stock Price as of Analysis: $46.40

Wells Fargo's near-term outlook is much clearer than that of its troubled big bank peers. However, that clarity has already been priced into the stock. While this bank's performance is likely to continue to set the standard for its rivals, we'd demand a reasonable discount to our fair value estimate of $50 per share.

Wells Fargo has performed admirably in a tough environment, increasing revenue and profits at a double-digit pace so far this year. In addition, its solid capital base has provided the flexibility to expand its loan portfolio 11%. The secret for Wells has been solid underwriting. Unlike most banks, the firm hasn't been caught off-guard by rising corporate loan defaults, foreign debt exposure, or consumer bankruptcies. This isn't magic: Wells Fargo is well provisioned against loan losses, and its diverse business lineup has allowed strong sectors to pick up the slack for weaker performers.

Like other leading banks, Wells Fargo has established a strong sales culture and is focused on the right areas, in our opinion. To succeed in a mature industry, the best-performing banks focus on expanding revenue and keeping costs in line. Wells has some of the most aggressive sales targets in banking, hoping to sell eight products per household on average (up from four now) and increasing

revenue at a double-digit rate over the long term, though we've modeled a lower forecast.

We see two major opportunities for Wells to achieve this goal: (1) boost performance at the "old Wells Fargo" branches and (2) focus on fee income. Former managers of Norwest, which merged with Wells in 1998, are experts at selling additional products to existing customers. With the company continuing to add sales staff, we believe this will prove a driver of growth. The firm, which has traditionally derived close to 60% of its revenue from net interest income, is working to expand its fee businesses, particularly in areas like mutual funds, insurance, and trust banking.

The firm's close relationship with consumers also should keep funding costs in check over the long term and provide additional fee income. For instance, Wells' core deposits--the cheapest source of funding loans--are up about 8% this year. Fee income on deposit accounts also rose 18% in the first nine months of 2002 compared with a year earlier. Wells Fargo has a well-defined battle plan that should spell success for this company, but investors must wait patiently for the right price.

MORNINGSTAR® Stocks 500

Wendy's International WEN

	Rating	Risk	Moat Size	Fair Value	Last Close	Yield %
	★★★	Med.	Narrow	$34.00	$27.07	0.9

Company Profile

Wendy's International operates and franchises quick-serving restaurants. Each restaurant offers a standard menu featuring hamburgers and chicken sandwiches prepared to order, as well as pita wraps. At the end of 2001, there were 6,043 Wendy's restaurants in the United States and in 26 other countries. Of these restaurants, 1,228 were operated by the company, and 4,815 were operated by franchise owners. The company also operates approximately 2,163 Tim Hortons restaurants, primarily in Canada.

Management

CEO John Schuessler, 50, worked his way up through the ranks after joining the company in 1976. Schuessler has said the firm would consider making major acquisitions to ensure growth.

Strategy

Wendy's is focused on same-store sales growth and increasing profitability in its U.S. stores. Advertising spending will hit an all-time high this year, and the firm continues to spend heavily on technology to boost efficiency. Expansion efforts are conservative and reflect a slow build of franchise partnerships.

P.O. Box 256
Dublin, OH 43017-0256
www.wendys.com

Morningstar Grades

Growth [B]	1998	1999	2000	2001
Revenue %	-4.4	6.1	8.2	6.9
Earnings/Share %	-2.1	38.9	9.1	14.6
Book Value/Share %	-6.6	2.6	13.2	-8.2
Dividends/Share %	0.0	0.0	0.0	0.0

The growth grade reflects missteps made several years ago. We expect midsingle-digit growth, thanks to improvements at the domestic stores. Wendy's will have to try its hand again at foreign expansion to sustain a higher growth rate.

Profitability [A]	1999	2000	2001	TTM
Return on Assets %	8.8	8.7	9.3	8.4
Oper Cash Flow $Mil	291	302	305	403
- Cap Spending $Mil	248	276	301	322
= Free Cash Flow $Mil	43	27	4	81

Profitability is somewhat limited by the company's leasing agreements, which are partially based on a percentage of sales. We think margins can increase slightly because certain fixed store costs won't grow as fast as sales.

Financial Health [A]	1999	2000	2001	09-02
Long-term Debt $Mil	249	248	451	682
Total Equity $Mil	1,065	1,126	1,030	1,440
Debt/Equity Ratio	0.2	0.2	0.4	0.5

EBIT (earnings before interest and taxes) is 3 times the company's debt interest and capitalized lease obligations, a level similar to that of McDonald's. Overall, financial health has improved over the past few years.

	Industry	Investment Style	Stock Type	Sector
	Restaurants	Mid Core	Classic Growth	Consumer Services

Competition	Market Cap $Mil	Debt/ Equity	12 Mo Trailing Sales $Mil	Price/Cash Flow	Return On Assets%	Total Return% 1 Yr	3 Yr
Wendy's International	3,125	0.5	2,634	7.7	8.4	-6.5	11.2
McDonald's	20,411	0.9	15,278	7.2	6.4	-38.4	-24.8
Starbucks	7,914	0.0	3,113	16.6	9.4	7.0	19.5

Price Volatility

I Monthly Price High/Low — Relative Strength to S&P 500

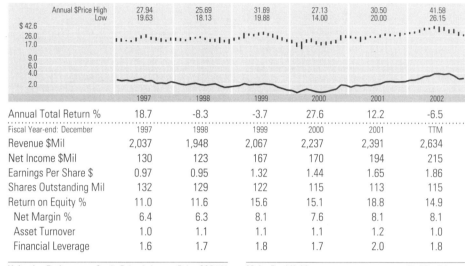

Annual $Price High / Low	27.94 / 19.63	25.69 / 18.13	31.69 / 19.88	27.13 / 14.00	30.50 / 20.00	41.58 / 26.15
	1997	1998	1999	2000	2001	2002

Annual Total Return %	18.7	-8.3	-3.7	27.6	12.2	-6.5

Fiscal Year-end: December	1997	1998	1999	2000	2001	TTM
Revenue $Mil	2,037	1,948	2,067	2,237	2,391	2,634
Net Income $Mil	130	123	167	170	194	215
Earnings Per Share $	0.97	0.95	1.32	1.44	1.65	1.86
Shares Outstanding Mil	132	129	122	115	113	115
Return on Equity %	11.0	11.6	15.6	15.1	18.8	14.9
Net Margin %	6.4	6.3	8.1	7.6	8.1	8.1
Asset Turnover	1.0	1.1	1.1	1.1	1.2	1.0
Financial Leverage	1.6	1.7	1.8	1.7	2.0	1.8

Valuation Ratios	Stock	Rel to Industry	Rel to S&P 500
Price/Earnings	14.6	1.0	0.6
Price/Book	2.2	0.8	0.7
Price/Sales	1.2	0.9	0.6
Price/Cash Flow	7.7	1.1	0.6

Major Fund Holders	% of Fund Assets
Homestead Value	5.92
Rydex Leisure Inv	3.31
W&R Large Cap Growth A	3.23
Waddell & Reed Adv Vanguard A	3.22

Morningstar's Take By Carl Sibilski, 10-16-2002 Stock Price as of Analysis: $32.79

Wendy's International has proved to be a solid restaurant operator, but we'd seek at least a 30% discount to our fair value estimate before buying the shares.

The firm's operations have improved markedly in the past few years. The stores, which used to be known for bad service, are now performing at the top of the quick-service restaurant industry group. Lately, Wendy's has been beating McDonald's in food quality and speed-of-service scores in U.S. consumer surveys. At just over two minutes, the average time to fill an order at Wendy's is 30% faster than at McDonald's.

While McDonald's has been focused on global expansion and Burger King hasn't been focused at all (with three owners in the past 10 years), Wendy's concentrated on improving its U.S. store operations. The company paid attention to details like menu offerings and coordinated marketing initiatives with its franchisees' ability to deliver the products. New stores were opened cautiously after checking into the prospects of new neighborhoods.

However, McDonald's and Burger King have regained their interest in the U.S. market. Wendy's, the number-three burger chain, will face substantially increased competition. We expect its sales growth

for the next couple years to slow to 6% from its 8% average since 1999.

To offset slowing domestic growth, the company will have to increase sales outside the U.S. burger business. However, we don't think its growth options are particularly exciting abroad. The company still remembers its botched efforts in Europe and Latin America in the mid-1990s, which resulted from poor planning for the cultural differences involved in operating under foreign governments. We expect Wendy's to try again, though very slowly.

The firm's Canadian coffee giant, Tim Hortons, seems like a reasonable concept to expand; there are just 145 locations in the United States compared with 2,048 in Canada. However, we'll wait and see. The stores have only shown success in border towns like Detroit and Buffalo. Just as Starbucks' premium brews have had difficulty entering Canada, we think Tim Hortons may have trouble gaining acceptance in the United States.

While we credit Wendy's for being a model restaurant operator, we think its growth options are bleak. The risk of increased industry competition limits the potential upside of the stock, which currently trades near our $34 fair value estimate.

Weyerhaeuser WY

	Rating	Risk	Moat Size	Fair Value	Last Close	Yield %
	★★	Med.	None	$50.00	$49.21	3.3

Company Profile

Weyerhaeuser is a diversified forest product company that also has real-estate operations. The company owns about 5.9 million acres of forestland in the Northwestern and Southern United States and holds licenses for about 39 million acres in Canada. Weyerhaeuser also makes building products (primarily lumber, plywood, and strand board) at 70 facilities, and paper goods (mainly packaging, containerboard, and pulp) at 111 others. The company's Weyerhaeuser Real Estate subsidiary develops commercial and residential lots.

Management

Steven Rogel is the first CEO to come from outside the company's ranks; he joined the firm in 1997 from rival Willamette, and spearheaded the acrimonious merger negotiations. His 2001 salary plus cash bonuses were valued at $2.1 million.

Strategy

Weyerhaeuser is seeking to improve its performance through acquisitions. Most notably, the firm acquired Canadian competitor MacMillan Bloedel in 1999 and Willamette Industries in 2002. The company is focusing on streamlining operations by selling noncore assets and reducing capacity via plant closures, as well as aggressively paring its large debt obligations to normal levels.

33663 Weyerhaeuser Way South   www.weyerhaeuser.com
Federal Way, WA 98063-9777

Morningstar Grades

Growth [A]	1998	1999	2000	2001
Revenue %	0.3	13.7	25.0	-9.0
Earnings/Share %	-14.0	73.5	45.9	-56.7
Book Value/Share %	-2.6	53.4	-12.8	0.6
Dividends/Share %	0.0	0.0	0.0	0.0

Weyerhaeuser operates in a mature, cyclical industry, which can make year-to-year growth volatile. Over the long term, we expect internal revenue growth of 2%-4%. Acquisitions would boost this figure.

Profitability [B-]	1999	2000	2001	TTM
Return on Assets %	2.9	4.6	1.9	0.3
Oper Cash Flow $Mil	1,501	1,454	1,118	1,038
- Cap Spending $Mil	548	929	791	990
= Free Cash Flow $Mil	953	525	327	48

Weyerhaeuser's past profitability has been decent, given the tough industry. The Willamette merger should boost profitability by providing additional scale, but higher interest expense will reduce earnings for the foreseeable future.

Financial Health [C-]	1999	2000	2001	09-02
Long-term Debt $Mil	5,100	5,093	6,073	13,160
Total Equity $Mil	7,173	6,832	6,695	6,469
Debt/Equity Ratio	0.7	0.7	0.9	2.0

Debt obligations more than doubled to $13 billion after the Willamette deal. While operations throw off solid free cash flow, Weyerhaeuser's strategic options will be limited in coming years as the company uses excess cash to pay down debt.

Industry	Investment Style	Stock Type	Sector
Forestry/Wood	Large Value	High Yield	Industrial Mats

Competition	Market Cap $Mil	Debt/ Equity	12 Mo Trailing Sales $Mil	Price/Cash Flow	Return On Assets%	Total Return% 1 Yr	3 Yr
Weyerhaeuser	10,774	2.0	17,267	10.4	0.3	-6.3	-2.1
International Paper	16,848	1.2	24,992	9.8	-0.4	-11.1	-11.3
MeadWestvaco	4,913	—	6,504	—	—	—	—

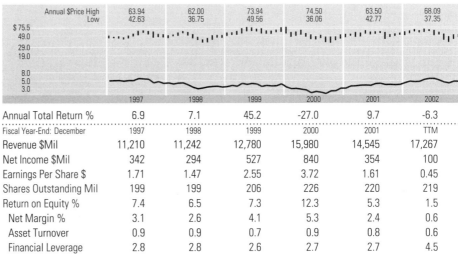

Price Volatility — Monthly Price High/Low — Relative Strength to S&P 500

Annual $Price High / Low	63.94 / 42.63	62.00 / 36.75	73.94 / 49.56	74.50 / 36.06	63.50 / 42.77	68.09 / 37.35
	1997	1998	1999	2000	2001	2002

Annual Total Return %	6.9	7.1	45.2	-27.0	9.7	-6.3

Fiscal Year-End: December	1997	1998	1999	2000	2001	TTM
Revenue $Mil	11,210	11,242	12,780	15,980	14,545	17,267
Net Income $Mil	342	294	527	840	354	100
Earnings Per Share $	1.71	1.47	2.55	3.72	1.61	0.45
Shares Outstanding Mil	199	199	206	226	220	219
Return on Equity %	7.4	6.5	7.3	12.3	5.3	1.5
Net Margin %	3.1	2.6	4.1	5.3	2.4	0.6
Asset Turnover	0.9	0.9	0.7	0.9	0.8	0.6
Financial Leverage	2.8	2.8	2.6	2.7	2.7	4.5

Valuation Ratios	Stock	Rel to Industry	Rel to S&P 500
Price/Earnings	109.4	1.0	4.6
Price/Book	1.7	0.1	0.5
Price/Sales	0.6	0.0	0.3
Price/Cash Flow	10.4	0.2	0.8

Major Fund Holders	% of Fund Assets
Fidelity Select Paper & Forest Prod	5.55
Rydex Basic Materials Inv	4.40
Edgar Lomax Value	3.87
Fidelity Select Industrial Materials	3.64

Morningstar's Take By Daniel Quinn, 12-20-2002 Stock Price as of Analysis: $49.20

We don't think the Willamette acquisition will generate sufficient value to justify its price tag. With the industry in a severe downturn, we'd avoid Weyerhaeuser stock unless it traded at a 40% or greater discount to our $50 fair value estimate.

Our concern with the merger has always been the cost, not the rationale. Neither Weyerhaeuser nor Willamette has earned its weighted average cost of capital in recent years--their respective operating profits relative to the resources used to generate them have been below what investors and lenders would typically require. Firms often try to combat this problem in mature, commodity businesses by merging to gain greater operational scale and efficiency. This was the reasoning for the Weyerhaeuser-Willamette deal.

Adding Willamette increased Weyerhaeuser's asset base 65% but increased revenue only about 30%. To overcome the hurdle this steep price imposes and to improve its already poor returns on assets, Weyerhaeuser must milk numerous synergies from the merger. It must keep capital spending needs to a minimum, manage working capital superbly, and rapidly repay debt. On top of this, growth must average about 3% per year and margins need to improve enough to boost earnings 15% annually.

Management's stated goals don't meet these requirements, so we think Weyerhaeuser's profitability will remain poor.

Another issue is poor industry fundamentals. The paper business suffers from chronic oversupply. Whenever demand slumps, prices tend to suffer and profitability plummets. A tariff dispute between the United States and Canada has worsened the situation. To forestall the dumping of cheap Canadian timber on the U.S. market, the U.S. government levies a duty of 27% on all softwood imports from Canada. In the six months after the duty was imposed, Weyerhaeuser paid nearly $47 million in duty fees (7% of its operating cash flow). Ironically, imports haven't slowed and prices are still low. Because the tariff is based on production cost, Canadian mills have been running at a higher rate to lower their per-unit cost. This cuts tax payments, but exacerbates the industry's oversupply problem.

With industry fundamentals in poor shape, and intransigent governments on both sides of the border, we would require a wide margin of safety to our fair value estimate before investing here.

MORNINGSTAR® Stocks 500

Whirlpool WHR

	Rating	Risk	Moat Size	Fair Value	Last Close	Yield %
	★★★	Med.	Narrow	$72.00	$52.22	2.6

Company Profile

Whirlpool produces appliances for consumer and industrial use. Its products include refrigerators, air conditioners, washers, dryers, coin-operated laundry machines, dehumidifiers, blenders, toasters, food processors, and trash compactors. In addition, the company makes products like refrigerators, dishwashers, and ranges for Sears Roebuck that are sold under the Kenmore and Sears trade names. Whirlpool also supplies home laundry appliances to Sears. The company sells its products under brand names like Whirlpool, KitchenAid, Estate, and Roper in the U.S. and abroad.

Management

David Whitwam, 60, has been with Whirlpool for three decades. In his last 15 years as CEO, he has led the firm's disappointing global expansion. Jeff Fettig, 45, helped build Whirlpool's foreign operations before becoming president and COO in 1999.

Strategy

Whirlpool wants to be the preferred consumer brand in major appliances worldwide. It already boasts number-one market share in the United States, which the company is reinforcing with appealing new products and strategies that strengthen its traditional retail channels. Operating costs are also being slashed; current restructuring initiatives call for overhead reductions of $225-$250 million.

2000 North M-63   www.whirlpoolcorp.com
Benton Harbor, MI 49022-2692

Morningstar Grades

Growth [C]	1998	1999	2000	2001
Revenue %	19.8	1.8	-1.8	0.2
Earnings/Share %	NMF	7.3	14.0	-94.0
Book Value/Share %	10.8	-6.2	-2.7	-9.8
Dividends/Share %	0.0	0.0	0.0	0.0

Appliance demand plods along with low-single-digit growth in most of Whirlpool's markets, and negative currency translation has hurt overall results. However, share gains made with new products have generated solid growth in the United States.

Profitability [C]	1999	2000	2001	TTM
Return on Assets %	5.1	5.3	0.3	1.2
Oper Cash Flow $Mil	801	445	1,024	612
- Cap Spending $Mil	437	375	378	387
= Free Cash Flow $Mil	364	70	646	225

Whirlpool's margins are disappointing compared with those of its peers, especially considering its leading market share. Heavy and frequent restructuring activity makes earnings quality an issue. However, we think recent improvements are sustainable.

Financial Health [B+]	1999	2000	2001	09-02
Long-term Debt $Mil	714	795	1,295	296
Total Equity $Mil	1,867	1,684	1,458	238
Debt/Equity Ratio	0.4	0.5	0.9	1.2

Following a goodwill write-off mandated by FAS 142, Whirlpool's debt/capital ratio is now 66%--much higher than we'd like. However, the company is a solid generator of free cash flow, which in turn has led to reduced borrowings.

Industry	Investment Style	Stock Type	Sector
Appliance & Furniture Makers	Mid Value	High Yield	Consumer Goods

Competition	Market Cap $Mil	Debt/ Equity	12 Mo Trailing Sales $Mil	Price/Cash Flow	Return On Assets%	Total Return% 1 Yr	3 Yr
Whirlpool	3,561	1.2	10,718	5.8	1.2	-27.3	-1.9
General Electric	242,308	2.2	130,295	8.2	2.7	-37.7	-18.9
Electrolux AB ADR	5,796	—	13,626	—	—	—	—

Price Volatility

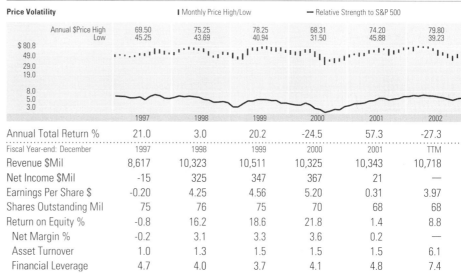

		1997	1998	1999	2000	2001	2002
Annual $Price High		69.50	75.25	78.25	68.31	74.20	79.80
Low		45.25	43.69	40.94	31.50	45.88	39.23

Annual Total Return %	21.0	3.0	20.2	-24.5	57.3	-27.3

Fiscal Year-end: December	1997	1998	1999	2000	2001	TTM
Revenue $Mil	8,617	10,323	10,511	10,325	10,343	10,718
Net Income $Mil	-15	325	347	367	21	—
Earnings Per Share $	-0.20	4.25	4.56	5.20	0.31	3.97
Shares Outstanding Mil	75	76	75	70	68	68
Return on Equity %	-0.8	16.2	18.6	21.8	1.4	8.8
Net Margin %	-0.2	3.1	3.3	3.6	0.2	—
Asset Turnover	1.0	1.3	1.5	1.5	1.5	6.1
Financial Leverage	4.7	4.0	3.7	4.1	4.8	7.4

Valuation Ratios	Stock	Rel to Industry	Rel to S&P 500
Price/Earnings	168.5	12.5	7.2
Price/Book	14.9	6.7	4.7
Price/Sales	0.3	0.7	0.2
Price/Cash Flow	5.8	0.7	0.4

Major Fund Holders	% of Fund Assets
Stratton Growth	2.99
Fidelity Select Construction&Housing	2.85
Elite Growth & Income	2.76
Muhlenkamp	2.22

Morningstar's Take By Josh Peters, 12-09-2002 Stock Price as of Analysis: $49.78

Still trying to prove its worldwide strategy can work, Whirlpool doesn't get much respect from investors. We like the company's turnaround prospects, though, and would find the stock attractive around $43.

In its core North American unit, Whirlpool has become a much stronger competitor in the past few years. It's long been the region's largest manufacturer, with number-one market share and strong relationships with Sears and other dominant appliance retailers. More recently, a focus on innovation has paid off with an improved image and higher profits. New products at the premium price points, like the Duet washer and dryer, have led to lucrative market share gains. Despite the investments required to keep its innovation pipeline full, Whirlpool North America today earns nearly double the operating margins of the mid-1990s.

The company is now in the midst of a two-year restructuring effort meant to export this strategy to its far-flung international operations. Earlier in 2002, the company wrote off nearly all the goodwill associated with these purchases. But European results are already starting to respond to restructuring initiatives, offering the prospect of EPS growth for an otherwise uninspiring 2003.

Despite these growing strengths, Whirlpool faces head winds. First among these would be a potential downturn in U.S. appliance demand, which could easily accompany a drop in housing activity or increase in interest rates. Other problems include higher pension expenses brought on by the bear market and the industry's persistent price deflation--both which will be difficult to offset with productivity gains. We're also concerned that the premium-price segment of the appliance market will encounter more competition from a rebounding Maytag and increasingly aggressive General Electric.

Earnings quality is another perennial sore spot. Whirlpool has recorded special charges in seven of the past eleven years that have consumed more than one fourth of total pretax income. Using North America's progress as a guide, we believe that most of these costs are in the rearview mirror. But since some repositioning expenses are unavoidable in the long term, we've adopted a margin forecast that uses Whirlpool's GAAP profit performance as a guide rather than pro forma views.

Though we'd demand a 40% discount to our $72 fair value estimate as insurance against future mediocrity, we maintain our view that Whirlpool is finally positioned to make a sustainable turn up.

White Mountains Insurance WTM

	Rating ★★★	Risk Med.	Moat Size Narrow	Fair Value $440.00	Last Close $323.00	Yield % 0.3

Company Profile

White Mountains Insurance offers property-casualty insurance and reinsurance. In June 2001, the firm acquired its OneBeacon subsidiary from British insurer CGNU, a move that more than quadrupled its investment base to $9.2 billion. The firm signed an agreement with Liberty Mutual in October 2001 that gives OneBeacon's business outside the Northeastern United States to Liberty, though White Mountains Insurance will reinsure the new business written by Liberty for five years.

Management

The executive team at White Mountains is one of the best. Industry legend Jack Byrne, 69, is chairman and owns 14% of the company. Nearly all top executives are industry veterans hailing either from GEICO or Fireman's Fund.

Strategy

Chairman Byrne calls White Mountains an "exit visa issuer," meaning that the firm likes to buy struggling insurance operations on the cheap. By raising underwriting standards, hiking premiums, eliminating unprofitable business, and giving unproductive agents the boot, the company can sell the improved business at a huge premium to the original purchase price.

28 Gates Street   www.whitemountains.com
White River Junction, VT 05001-7066

Morningstar Grades

Growth [A+]	1998	1999	2000	2001
Revenue %	33.0	48.4	46.4	281.2
Earnings/Share %	121.1	65.2	249.2	NMF
Book Value/Share %	18.0	-6.3	76.4	22.7
Dividends/Share %	100.0	0.0	-25.0	-16.7

The OneBeacon acquisition nearly quadrupled revenue in 2001, though about half of the new premiums will be transferred to Liberty Mutual. We expect strong internal revenue growth during the next several years, thanks to premium hikes.

Profitability [A]	1999	2000	2001	TTM
Return on Assets %	5.9	11.5	-3.4	3.3
Oper Cash Flow $Mil	-208	-114	-301	—
- Cap Spending $Mil	—	—	—	—
= Free Cash Flow $Mil	—	—	—	—

The strategy of buying struggling insurers means that newly acquired operations will post subpar results. Because of steps taken to fix OneBeacon and claims related to 9/11, the firm lost money in 2001.

Financial Health [NA]	1999	2000	2001	09-02
Long-term Debt $Mil	—	—	—	—
Total Equity $Mil	614	1,047	1,445	2,342
Debt/Equity Ratio	—	—	—	—

White Mountains sports a moderate debt load and a solid capital position of $2.3 billion. Further strengthening its financial position, the firm has boosted its loss reserves and increased its reinsurance coverage.

Industry	Investment Style	Stock Type	Sector
Insurance (Property)	Mid Growth	Aggr. Growth	Financial Services

Competition

	Market Cap $Mil	Debt/ Equity	12 Mo Trailing Sales $Mil	Price/Cash Flow	Return On Assets%	Total Return% 1 Yr	3 Yr
White Mountains Insurance	2,676	—	4,384	—	3.3	-6.9	41.2
American International Gr	150,907	—	66,823	—	1.4	-26.9	-4.0
Berkshire Hathaway B	111,526	—	39,133	—	1.9	-4.0	12.5

Price Volatility

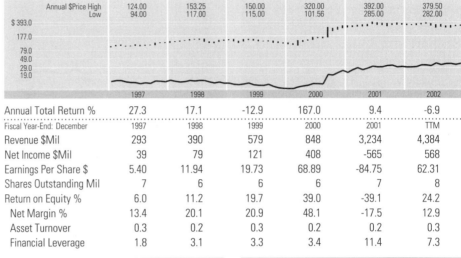

Annual $Price High Low	124.00 94.00	153.25 117.00	150.00 115.00	320.00 101.56	392.00 285.00	379.50 282.00
	1997	1998	1999	2000	2001	2002
Annual Total Return %	27.3	17.1	-12.9	167.0	9.4	-6.9

Fiscal Year-End: December	1997	1998	1999	2000	2001	TTM
Revenue $Mil	293	390	579	848	3,234	4,384
Net Income $Mil	39	79	121	408	-565	568
Earnings Per Share $	5.40	11.94	19.73	68.89	-84.75	62.31
Shares Outstanding Mil	7	6	6	6	7	8
Return on Equity %	6.0	11.2	19.7	39.0	-39.1	24.2
Net Margin %	13.4	20.1	20.9	48.1	-17.5	12.9
Asset Turnover	0.3	0.2	0.3	0.2	0.2	0.3
Financial Leverage	1.8	3.1	3.3	3.4	11.4	7.3

Valuation Ratios	Stock	Rel to Industry	Rel to S&P 500
Price/Earnings	5.2	0.3	0.2
Price/Book	1.1	0.6	0.4
Price/Sales	0.6	0.3	0.3
Price/Cash Flow	—	—	—

Major Fund Holders	% of Fund Assets
FAM Value	5.87
Mutual Shares Z	1.67

Morningstar's Take By Aaron Westrate, 12-16-2002 Stock Price as of Analysis: $320.00

If OneBeacon's improving results are any indication, White Mountains' legendary chairman, Jack Byrne, hasn't lost his touch. We'd be buyers at $300 or less.

In June 2001, White Mountains acquired the North American insurance operations of British insurer CGNU. This transformational deal more than quadrupled the firm's investment portfolio and expanded its equity base by 40%. Best of all, White Mountains paid just 75% of book value to take over the business (renamed OneBeacon), creating a buffer if repairing OneBeacon proved to be more difficult than anticipated.

But Byrne and his team appear to have the turnaround well in hand. OneBeacon's combined ratio (a measure of underwriting profitability in which lower is better) year to date is 109% compared with 120% for all of 2001. Upon closing the deal, management shored up OneBeacon's weak balance sheet by boosting loss reserves and buying additional reinsurance. The investment team also presciently pared the acquired investment portfolio's equity exposure from $1.7 billion to $272 million by the third quarter of 2002, deftly dodging declining equity markets.

Byrne struck a deal to transfer to Liberty Mutual all of OneBeacon's operations except for the Northeastern region and some select specialty lines of insurance. We like this move because the retained business carries much better combined ratios than the business being transferred to Liberty. Also, the disposition enables management to focus on improving a smaller operation, increasing the odds of success, in our view.

As capital flowed out of the insurance industry in the aftermath of the terrorist attacks, White Mountains shrewdly allocated capital to take advantage of the supply-demand imbalance. White Mountains infused $400 million of capital into its reinsurance operation, Folksamerica. This extra capital allows Folksamerica to write new business at the significantly higher premium rates reinsurers are now able to charge. White Mountains also raised $1 billion to form Montpelier Re to take advantage of higher premiums without any previous liabilities.

Our fair value remains $440 per share, though this assumes that White Mountains retains its current operations. Upside is possible if Byrne unloads OneBeacon in a year or two and reinvests the proceeds in undervalued insurance businesses, as is his modus operandi.

MORNINGSTAR® Stocks 500

Whole Foods Market WFMI

	Rating	Risk	Moat Size	Fair Value	Last Close	Yield %
	★★	Med.	Narrow	$52.00	$52.73	0.0

Company Profile

Whole Foods Market owns and operates 117 natural food supermarkets throughout the United States. The company's stores target customers interested in health, nutrition, food safety, and the environment. Its products include organically grown produce, grocery products, and environmentally safe household items; meat, poultry, and seafood free of growth hormones and antibiotics; bulk cereals; bakery goods, hot entrees, and sandwiches; and vitamins, homeopathic remedies, body-care products, and cosmetics.

Management

Co-founder John P. Mackey, 46, has been chairman and chief executive officer since 1980. His decentralized approach gives each store a large degree of autonomy.

Strategy

With twice the revenue of its closest competitor, Whole Foods has become the dominant natural food grocer by acquiring smaller operators, including Harry's Farmers Market, and aggressively opening new stores. Now the grocer intends to increase its market share primarily by building new stores in urban areas.

601 N. Lamar   www.wholefoods.com
Austin, TX 78703

Morningstar Grades

Growth [A+]	1999	2000	2001	2002
Revenue %	14.1	23.2	23.6	18.4
Earnings/Share %	-6.1	NMF	NMF	15.7
Book Value/Share %	13.5	0.7	27.5	33.8
Dividends/Share %	NMF	NMF	NMF	NMF

Whole Foods' revenue growth has handily outpaced that of traditional grocers, averaging more than 20% over the past three years. A combination of acquisitions, new store openings, and strong same-store sales growth is responsible.

Profitability [B+]	2000	2001	2002	TTM
Return on Assets %	-0.6	8.2	9.0	9.0
Oper Cash Flow $Mil	124	173	229	229
- Cap Spending $Mil	42	49	61	61
= Free Cash Flow $Mil	83	124	168	168

Whole Foods' products command higher gross margins than typical grocers, so its operations are more profitable than its peers'. We expect this gap to widen as the firm's store base grows.

Financial Health [A]	2000	2001	2002	09-02
Long-term Debt $Mil	298	251	162	162
Total Equity $Mil	307	409	589	589
Debt/Equity Ratio	1.0	0.6	0.3	0.3

Operating cash flows have grown steadily over the past five years, but the company has had to borrow to fund its aggressive expansion. As its store base matures, the firm should be able to reduce its leverage.

Industry	Investment Style	Stock Type	Sector
Groceries	Mid Growth	Classic Growth	Consumer Services

Competition	Market Cap $Mil	Debt/ Equity	12 Mo Trailing Sales $Mil	Price/Cash Flow	Return On Assets%	Total Return% 1 Yr	3 Yr
Whole Foods Market	3,045	0.3	2,690	13.3	9.0	21.1	34.4
Safeway	13,376	1.5	34,757	6.3	3.4	-44.1	-12.2
Kroger	11,946	2.2	51,105	5.0	6.2	-26.0	-7.6

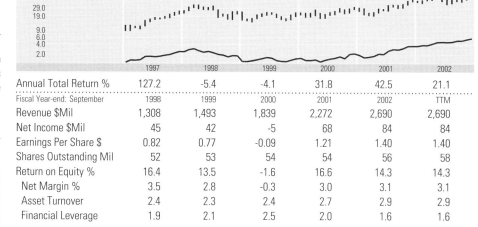

Price Volatility   ▎ Monthly Price High/Low   — Relative Strength to S&P 500

Annual $Price High Low	25.69 8.75	35.06 16.00	24.81 14.13	31.88 17.19	46.50 19.47	54.59 35.47

	1997	1998	1999	2000	2001	2002
Annual Total Return %	127.2	-5.4	-4.1	31.8	42.5	21.1

Fiscal Year-end: September	1998	1999	2000	2001	2002	TTM
Revenue $Mil	1,308	1,493	1,839	2,272	2,690	2,690
Net Income $Mil	45	42	-5	68	84	84
Earnings Per Share $	0.82	0.77	-0.09	1.21	1.40	1.40
Shares Outstanding Mil	52	53	54	54	56	58
Return on Equity %	16.4	13.5	-1.6	16.6	14.3	14.3
Net Margin %	3.5	2.8	-0.3	3.0	3.1	3.1
Asset Turnover	2.4	2.3	2.4	2.7	2.9	2.9
Financial Leverage	1.9	2.1	2.5	2.0	1.6	1.6

Valuation Ratios	Stock	Rel to Industry	Rel to S&P 500
Price/Earnings	37.7	1.9	1.6
Price/Book	5.2	1.7	1.6
Price/Sales	1.1	2.9	0.6
Price/Cash Flow	13.3	2.1	1.0

Major Fund Holders	% of Fund Assets
Fidelity Select Environmental	7.05
AXP Equity Select A	5.05
Pax World Growth	4.61
Winslow Green Growth	4.47

Morningstar's Take   By David Kathman, 12-13-2002   Stock Price as of Analysis: $53.21

Whole Foods Market has done a great job of dominating an affluent niche of the grocery world, but we're hesitant to project its blistering growth too far into the future. We'd only be inclined to buy the stock in the mid-$30s or below.

Whole Foods has become the category killer among grocers exploiting Americans' growing health-consciousness. It targets affluent consumers willing to pay a premium for organic foods and similar healthy products, and keeps them coming back with such attractions as cooking demonstrations and a large produce selection. The result has been 20% annualized sales growth while traditional grocers have struggled to retain customers.

Moreover, this growth has been remarkably broad-based. New store openings have been a factor--total square footage increased 16% in fiscal 2002--but comparable-store sales also increased 10% in a year that saw decreasing comps for Whole Foods' traditional rivals. The number of stores is steadily growing, but not at the expense of sales efficiency. Whole Foods generates around $700 in annual sales per square foot, far ahead of the $450 of Safeway, and that figure is up from $660 three years ago.

Whole Foods has leveraged this growth into

greater profitability. Operating cash flow has increased from 4.8% of revenue in 1997 to 8.5% in 2002, and there is every indication that margins can continue to expand as the store base matures. In the fourth quarter of 2002, stores open less than two years had average same-store sales growth of 33% and a cash return on invested capital of 9%; stores open more than five years had 7% same-store growth but significantly higher returns on capital. After up-front costs are out of the way, Whole Foods stores become cash cows that would be the envy of just about any other retailer.

The big question is how long Whole Foods can keep up this performance. With fewer than 150 stores heading into 2003, the firm appears to have plenty of room for expansion, but at some point growth will have to slow as it nears the limits of its core audience. Already, it's facing increased competition from traditional grocery stores, many of which are beefing up their service and selection of healthy foods. We think Whole Foods is well positioned to continue its outstanding recent performance for at least a few more years, but we're more cautious beyond that.

Williams Companies WMB

Rating	Risk	Moat Size	Fair Value	Last Close	Yield %
UR	High	Narrow	UR	$2.70	15.6

Company Profile

Williams transports and sells natural gas and petroleum products. The company has an interest in 26,000 miles of interstate natural gas pipelines across the United States. It also provides energy-related services like exploration, production, and storage of natural gas and petroleum. In addition, Williams is engaged in price risk management services (energy trading) and marketing of power, natural gas, natural gas liquids, and petroleum products. Williams owns 60% of Williams Energy Partners, a master limited partnership that operates petroleum terminals and pipelines.

Management

Steven Malcolm took over as chairman and CEO in May 2002. He was named president and COO in September 2001. He previously was president and CEO of the Williams Energy Services subsidiary.

Strategy

Management at Williams is focused on survival today. The company is selling assets at a rapid pace to raise cash and reduce debt. It is also looking to exit the energy trading business in order to free up liquidity. Williams aims to be a much smaller company with a stronger foundation.

One Williams Center   www.williams.com
Tulsa, OK 74172

Morningstar Grades

Growth [C]	1998	1999	2000	2001
Revenue %	-16.8	17.1	44.7	15.0
Earnings/Share %	-66.7	85.2	134.0	NMF
Book Value/Share %	-3.8	35.9	2.9	-8.6
Dividends/Share %	11.1	0.0	0.0	13.3

Williams is in full-throttle retrenchment, and revenue growth looks to be negative for several more quarters because of asset sales. Third-quarter revenue was down 23% year over year, and we expect similar declines in coming quarters.

Profitability [D+]	1999	2000	2001	TTM
Return on Assets %	1.0	1.5	-1.2	-5.2
Oper Cash Flow $Mil	1,534	594	1,783	-360
- Cap Spending $Mil	1,795	1,513	1,922	2,155
= Free Cash Flow $Mil	-261	-919	-140	-2,514

The core pipeline and gas production businesses at Williams are performing well with operating margins in excess of 45%, but massive asset write-downs and losses from energy trading obscure and erase this profitability.

Financial Health [C-]	1999	2000	2001	09-02
Long-term Debt $Mil	7,240	6,831	9,501	12,294
Total Equity $Mil	5,585	5,892	6,044	5,098
Debt/Equity Ratio	1.3	1.2	1.6	2.4

Williams' balance sheet is in dire straits, and the company is taking drastic measures to right its ship. The company has $14.7 billion of debt, some of it at egregiously high rates. It has $4.1 billion due before the first quarter of 2004.

Industry	Investment Style	Stock Type	Sector
Pipelines	▦ Mid Value	⚡ Distressed	◐ Energy

Competition	Market Cap $Mil	Debt/ Equity	12 Mo Trailing Sales $Mil	Price/Cash Flow	Return On Assets%	Total Return% 1 Yr	3 Yr
Williams Companies	1,395	2.4	8,895	—	-5.2	-89.0	-53.0
Kinder Morgan	5,145	1.1	1,014	12.4	3.1	-23.5	24.5
El Paso	4,160	1.6	12,207	8.6	1.3	-83.9	-41.2

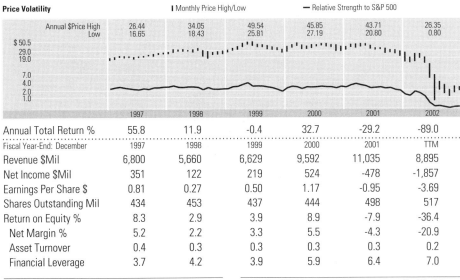

Price Volatility   ▮ Monthly Price High/Low   — Relative Strength to S&P 500

Annual $Price High Low	26.44 16.65	34.05 18.43	49.54 25.81	45.85 27.19	43.71 20.80	26.35 0.80
	1997	1998	1999	2000	2001	2002

Annual Total Return %	55.8	11.9	-0.4	32.7	-29.2	-89.0

Fiscal Year-End: December	1997	1998	1999	2000	2001	TTM
Revenue $Mil	6,800	5,660	6,629	9,592	11,035	8,895
Net Income $Mil	351	122	219	524	-478	-1,857
Earnings Per Share $	0.81	0.27	0.50	1.17	-0.95	-3.69
Shares Outstanding Mil	434	453	437	444	498	517
Return on Equity %	8.3	2.9	3.9	8.9	-7.9	-36.4
Net Margin %	5.2	2.2	3.3	5.5	-4.3	-20.9
Asset Turnover	0.4	0.3	0.3	0.3	0.3	0.2
Financial Leverage	3.7	4.2	3.9	5.9	6.4	7.0

Valuation Ratios	Stock	Rel to Industry	Rel to S&P 500
Price/Earnings	NMF	—	—
Price/Book	0.3	0.1	0.1
Price/Sales	0.2	0.1	0.1
Price/Cash Flow	—	—	—

Major Fund Holders	% of Fund Assets
AmSouth Value A	2.54
Pacific Capital Value B	1.91
Pacific Capital Value Y	1.91
Pacific Capital Growth & Income Y	1.69

Morningstar's Take   By Paul Larson, 12-19-2002   Stock Price as of Analysis: $2.35

Because of the great uncertainties surrounding Williams, we're not publishing a fair value estimate or star rating on the stock. It remains a highly speculative gamble, and the vast majority of investors should steer clear.

Williams is in a pickle. Its energy trading business melted down in the wake of Enron's collapse. When Williams and its energy trading partners saw their credit ratings downgraded to junk status, trading volume and profits quickly evaporated. While energy trading once made up more than half of Williams' operating profits, this business is now deeply in the red.

This trading implosion had a large impact on the company's liquidity. Williams found itself cut off from short-term debt financing, causing a liquidity crisis this past summer that almost put the firm into bankruptcy. It was saved from this fate only after taking out a $900 million secured loan from Lehman Brothers and a Berkshire Hathaway subsidiary at effective interest rates above 30%--loan terms telling of how desperate the situation was.

While near-term liquidity issues have passed, Williams still has a long road ahead. The firm is attempting to shutter its trading operations to free up resources, but this will not be cheap or easy, given

the long-term nature of its contracts. It is selling assets at a frenetic pace to raise cash to pay off debt coming due shortly. Williams has sold or announced the sale of nearly $6 billion in hard assets in 2002, a large amount considering the $15 billion in property, plant, and equipment it started the year with. Williams continues to sell assets at a rapid pace, greatly clouding the financial picture.

California is also a headache, as Williams is knee-deep in the controversy regarding the state's energy crisis two years ago. The firm has admitted reporting false trade data to an industry publication, raising the specter of market manipulation. While Williams has settled one lawsuit for $240 million and has refunds ordered by the Federal Energy Regulatory Commission of $192 million--liabilities far less than originally feared--we still aren't convinced the California problems are totally behind Williams.

For all of the liquidity problems, the company's core pipeline and natural gas businesses continue to perform well. There is definitely value in these businesses as they are relatively stable, cash flow positive, and have wide economic moats. However, it remains to be seen how much value will be eaten away by the major problems in other parts of the firm. We'd stay away for now.

    MORNINGSTAR® Stocks 500

Williams-Sonoma WSM

	Rating	Risk	Moat Size	Fair Value	Last Close	Yield %
	★	Med.	Narrow	$22.00	$27.15	0.0

Company Profile

Williams-Sonoma is a specialty retailer of cooking equipment, food products, furniture, and home and garden accessories. It sells its products through 425 retail stores, seven mail order catalogs, and four web sites. The company sells its products under the Williams-Sonoma, Pottery Barn, Pottery Barn Kids, Hold Everything, Chambers, and Pottery Barn Bed & Barn, and West Elm names.

Management

Howard Lester stepped down as CEO in 2001, ending a 20-year tenure. He picked as his replacement former Venator CEO Dale W. Hilpert, in the process losing merchandising whiz Gary Friedman.

Strategy

In an effort to boost overall and same-store sales growth, Williams-Sonoma is nurturing its existing brands and developing new ones. The company has introduced a well-received new product line in its core Pottery Barn business--Pottery Barn Kids--and is investing in newer concepts like its West Elm catalog.

3250 Van Ness Avenue   www.williams-sonoma.com
San Francisco, CA 94109

Morningstar Grades

Growth [A]	1999	2000	2001	2002
Revenue %	17.9	25.8	25.3	14.1
Earnings/Share %	28.0	20.8	-14.7	31.3
Book Value/Share %	50.7	23.6	14.1	23.7
Dividends/Share %	NMF	NMF	NMF	NMF

Thanks to new store openings, Williams-Sonoma's revenue growth has kept pace with that of its peers. We expect overall growth to remain solid given the expansion, but same-store sales growth is likely to fluctuate.

Profitability [A]	2000	2001	2002	TTM
Return on Assets %	9.2	6.4	7.5	9.9
Oper Cash Flow $Mil	108	181	205	328
- Cap Spending $Mil	128	235	156	155
= Free Cash Flow $Mil	-20	-54	49	173

Williams-Sonoma's returns on assets have lagged those of peers for years. However, the company has been revamping its distribution centers and improving inventory management, which should boost asset turnover and profitability.

Financial Health [A-]	2000	2001	2002	10-02
Long-term Debt $Mil	126	136	152	179
Total Equity $Mil	383	427	533	596
Debt/Equity Ratio	0.3	0.3	0.3	0.3

After two years of aggressive capital spending, Williams-Sonoma is free cash flow positive again. Operating cash flows are growing steadily, and we expect free cash flow to remain positive for the foreseeable future.

Industry	Investment Style	Stock Type	Sector
Furniture Retail	Mid Growth	Classic Growth	Consumer Services

Competition

	Market Cap $Mil	Debt/Equity	12 Mo Trailing Sales $Mil	Price/Cash Flow	Return On Assets%	Total Return% 1 Yr	3 Yr
Williams-Sonoma	3,154	0.3	2,280	9.6	9.9	26.6	8.7
Bed Bath & Beyond	10,104	—	3,318	28.6	13.7	1.9	30.7
Pier 1 Imports	1,748	0.0	1,661	10.5	13.4	10.3	48.5

Price Volatility

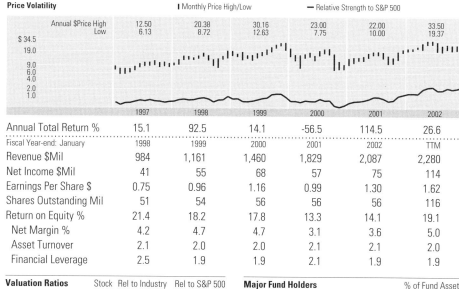

		12.50 / 6.13	20.38 / 8.72	30.16 / 12.63	23.00 / 7.75	22.00 / 10.00	33.50 / 19.37
Annual $Price High/Low		1997	1998	1999	2000	2001	2002

Annual Total Return %	15.1	92.5	14.1	-56.5	114.5	26.6
Fiscal Year-end: January	1998	1999	2000	2001	2002	TTM
Revenue $Mil	984	1,161	1,460	1,829	2,087	2,280
Net Income $Mil	41	55	68	57	75	114
Earnings Per Share $	0.75	0.96	1.16	0.99	1.30	1.62
Shares Outstanding Mil	51	54	56	56	56	116
Return on Equity %	21.4	18.2	17.8	13.3	14.1	19.1
Net Margin %	4.2	4.7	4.7	3.1	3.6	5.0
Asset Turnover	2.1	2.0	2.0	2.1	2.1	2.0
Financial Leverage	2.5	1.9	1.9	2.1	1.9	1.9

Valuation Ratios	Stock	Rel to Industry	Rel to S&P 500
Price/Earnings	16.8	0.4	0.7
Price/Book	5.3	0.6	1.7
Price/Sales	1.4	0.5	0.7
Price/Cash Flow	9.6	0.3	0.7

Major Fund Holders	% of Fund Assets
Reserve Small-Cap Growth R	6.82
Capital Advisors Growth	4.59
AXP Equity Select A	4.41
Seligman Capital A	2.90

Morningstar's Take By Roz Bryant, 11-11-2002 Stock Price as of Analysis: $21.25

Williams-Sonoma's ability to deliver "trend-right" home furnishings has led to brisk same-store sales growth and rapid expansion. But the retailer's products are relatively expensive and fashion-driven, so we'd seek a 30% margin of safety before purchasing the shares to insulate against future fashion missteps and weak economic times.

Over the years, Williams-Sonoma's trendy products (including those sold under the Pottery Barn name) have struck a chord with a growing number of middle- and upper-income shoppers seeking the latest designs in furniture and home accessories. Much of the retailer's merchandise is a twist on both classic and modern designs, so it fits in traditional as well as contemporary homes. As the store brands have become well known for such desirable offerings, customer traffic has grown, and Williams-Sonoma has aggressively opened new locations. The company has averaged 21% sales growth over the past five years.

Management remains focused on top-line growth and will plow cash into newer concepts while continuing to expand its core businesses. Pottery Barn Kids, its children's furniture concept, has nearly doubled its store base annually since the first store opened in 2000, and is set to do so again by the end of the current fiscal year. The company is also testing West Elm, a lower-price furniture and houseware catalog aimed at young professionals.

The firm's growth prospects are notable, but they do come with a degree of risk. Williams-Sonoma is mostly a high-end fashion retailer whose growth relies on the health of the economy and the firm's ability to accurately predict consumer tastes. During periods of prolonged economic weakness, customer traffic is likely to slow as shoppers rein in their spending. In the case of design missteps, steep price markdowns would probably be needed to move undesirable merchandise, which would hurt margins. The company lost its longtime merchandising guru, Gary Friedman, to Restoration Hardware in 2001, so the long-term fashion risk is a real one.

Given its ability to turn out well-received merchandise, rapidly expand its store base, and develop new brands to reach new customer segments, Williams-Sonoma has bright prospects, in our opinion, but they're not without risk. Past performance doesn't guarantee future results, and given the tendency for even the best retailers to occasionally have bad years, we wouldn't invest until the shares fell to the midteens.

Winn-Dixie Stores WIN

	Rating	Risk	Moat Size	Fair Value	Last Close	Yield %
	★★★	Med.	None	$20.00	$15.28	1.3

Company Profile

Winn-Dixie Stores operates a chain of approximately 1,100 retail grocery stores in 14 Southeastern states and the Bahamas. Its stores operate primarily under the names Winn-Dixie, Thriftway, Buddies, and Jitney Jungle. The company also operates several food manufacturing plants for private-label grocery items. It acquired 68 stores from the bankrupt Mississippi-based Jitney Jungle chain in early 2001.

Management

Winn-Dixie is 42% controlled by the founding Davis family. The firm hired Al Rowland (former CEO of Smith's Food and Drug) in late 1999. His extensive grocery experience, as well as the talent he's attracted, helps the chances for a turnaround.

Strategy

Stiff competition has whittled away at Winn-Dixie's profitability in recent years, prompting the grocer to embark on a major restructuring plan. The company is considerably less centralized than more-modern peers like Safeway. By improving its distribution system and closing unprofitable stores, the company hopes to revive depressed profit margins.

5050 Edgewood Court   www.winn-dixie.com
Jacksonville, FL 32254-3699

Industry	Investment Style	Stock Type	Sector
Groceries	▦ Mid Value	➡ Slow Growth	▤ Consumer Services

Competition

	Market Cap $Mil	Debt/ Equity	12 Mo Trailing Sales $Mil	Price/Cash Flow	Return On Assets%	Total Return% 1 Yr	3 Yr
Winn-Dixie Stores	2,151	0.6	12,359	6.0	3.6	8.7	-10.7
Wal-Mart Stores	223,388	0.5	233,651	18.9	8.0	-11.8	-7.3
Kroger	11,946	2.2	51,105	5.0	6.2	-26.0	-7.6

Price Volatility

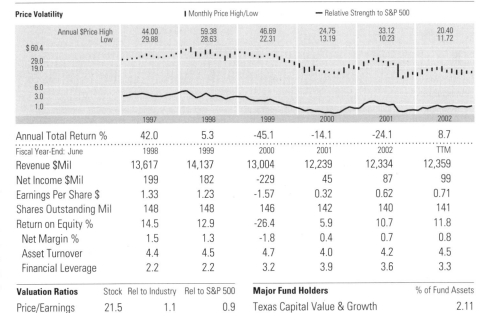

	1997	1998	1999	2000	2001	2002
Annual $Price High	44.00	59.38	46.69	24.75	33.12	20.40
Low	29.88	28.63	22.31	13.19	10.23	11.72
Annual Total Return %	42.0	5.3	-45.1	-14.1	-24.1	8.7

Fiscal Year-End: June	1998	1999	2000	2001	2002	TTM
Revenue $Mil	13,617	14,137	13,004	12,239	12,334	12,359
Net Income $Mil	199	182	-229	45	87	99
Earnings Per Share $	1.33	1.23	-1.57	0.32	0.62	0.71
Shares Outstanding Mil	148	148	146	142	140	141
Return on Equity %	14.5	12.9	-26.4	5.9	10.7	11.8
Net Margin %	1.5	1.3	-1.8	0.4	0.7	0.8
Asset Turnover	4.4	4.5	4.7	4.0	4.2	4.5
Financial Leverage	2.2	2.2	3.2	3.9	3.6	3.3

Valuation Ratios	Stock	Rel to Industry	Rel to S&P 500
Price/Earnings	21.5	1.1	0.9
Price/Book	2.6	0.8	0.8
Price/Sales	0.2	0.5	0.1
Price/Cash Flow	6.0	0.9	0.5

Major Fund Holders	% of Fund Assets
Texas Capital Value & Growth	2.11
Undiscovered Managers Behav Grth Inst	1.84
Monetta Mid-Cap Equity	1.09
Olstein Financial Alert C	1.04

Morningstar Grades

Growth [D+]	1999	2000	2001	2002
Revenue %	3.8	-8.0	-5.9	0.8
Earnings/Share %	-7.5	NMF	NMF	93.8
Book Value/Share %	3.8	-37.5	-8.4	6.4
Dividends/Share %	0.0	0.0	0.0	-65.2

Same-store sales finally started growing again in the June and September quarters after four years of declines. However, growth will be tough to maintain against increased competition, especially from Wal-Mart.

Profitability [C]	2000	2001	2002	TTM
Return on Assets %	-8.3	1.5	3.0	3.6
Oper Cash Flow $Mil	743	245	377	360
- Cap Spending $Mil	213	313	84	93
= Free Cash Flow $Mil	530	-68	293	267

The restructuring helped Winn-Dixie improve its gross margin to 28.2% in the September quarter from 26.8% a year earlier. However, operating expenses have not yet come down, and Winn-Dixie's margins are relatively thin.

Financial Health [B]	2000	2001	2002	09-02
Long-term Debt $Mil	32	726	565	465
Total Equity $Mil	868	772	812	843
Debt/Equity Ratio	0.0	0.9	0.7	0.6

Winn-Dixie's financials have deteriorated in the past few years, as it took on long-term debt at the same time its operations were faltering. A cut in the dividend has freed up cash, but it will take awhile to improve the balance sheet.

Morningstar's Take By David Kathman, 11-27-2002 Stock Price as of Analysis: $14.93

Winn-Dixie's recent improvements may be too little, too late for the struggling grocery chain. The long-term outlook remains doubtful, and we wouldn't buy the shares above $12.

Not too long ago, Winn-Dixie appeared to be a company on the slippery slope to oblivion. Same-store sales were declining at an alarming rate, often more than 5% a quarter, and the company slashed its dividend by 80% in late 2001 to conserve cash. A sale of the firm seemed like a real possibility.

Steps by management over the past year have stopped the bleeding, at least for now. The company shut down or sold its underperforming Texas and Oklahoma stores, and worked to improve efficiency and procurement costs. It introduced a customer reward card and converted dozens of stores to Save-Rite warehouse clubs, designed to appeal to price-conscious consumers who have been defecting to Wal-Mart and its ilk. The result has been two straight quarters of same-store sales growth in a tough environment, along with significant improvements in gross margin.

We're not celebrating yet, however. Winn-Dixie's 2% same-store sales growth in its fiscal first quarter wasn't as impressive as it seems, since it comes off a 5.2% decline in the year-ago period; compared with

two years ago, same-store sales still declined more than 3%. Costs related to the restructuring have pushed operating and administrative expenses to their highest level in three years, and it's still not clear how much improvement there will be once the benefits start coming in 2004.

Our bigger concerns are long-term, and they center on the formidable competition from Wal-Mart, which has become the largest grocery retailer in the United States through its SuperCenters, a disproportionate number of which are in Winn-Dixie's home turf of the Southeast. Wal-Mart will become an even more direct competitor once it starts rolling out its Neighborhood Markets, which are similar to traditional grocery stores. It will be tough for Winn-Dixie to match Wal-Mart's supply chain and cost structure, and its margins don't have a lot of wiggle room. Winn-Dixie's 3% operating margin is well below Wal-Mart's 5.5%, as well as those of rival grocers Albertson's and Kroger.

In our view, the best-case scenario is that Winn-Dixie maintains its current position against the Wal-Mart onslaught, but there's also a significant chance that it could go back into a downward spiral. We'd only consider the stock at $12 or below, and even then we'd be hesitant to buy for the long term.

MORNINGSTAR® Stocks 500

Wm. Wrigley Jr. WWY

	Rating	Risk	Moat Size	Fair Value	Last Close	Yield %
	★★	Med.	Wide	$45.00	$54.88	1.5

Company Profile

Wm. Wrigley Jr. manufactures chewing gum sold in more than 140 countries. Its brand names include Wrigley's Spearmint, Doublemint, Juicy Fruit, Big Red, Freedent, Winterfresh, and Extra chewing gum. The Amurol subsidiary makes chewing gum under the Big League Chew and Hubba Bubba brands, and individually wrapped hard roll candies under the Reed's name. In addition, Wm. Wrigley Jr. owns the Wrigley Building in Chicago. The company markets its products in the U.S. and abroad. Sales outside North America account for approximately 62% of the company's total sales.

Management

William Wrigley Jr. quickly hired his own team of top executives after succeeding his father as CEO in 1999. He has introduced edgy new advertising campaigns, started a health-care division, and made the company's first acquisition in 50 years.

Strategy

Wrigley is trying to juice up growth by introducing new products. In 1999, it introduced Eclipse, a gum with a hard mint coating, and more recently it introduced Orbit sugar-free gum and Eclipse Flash Strips. Its health-care division is trying to market antacid gums and dental-care gums in partnership with Procter & Gamble.

410 North Michigan Avenue   www.wrigley.com
Chicago, IL 60611

Morningstar Grades

Growth [A]	1998	1999	2000	2001
Revenue %	2.6	2.8	4.1	13.2
Earnings/Share %	12.4	1.1	9.0	11.0
Book Value/Share %	17.7	-1.6	1.6	13.3
Dividends/Share %	11.1	2.3	5.3	6.4

After several years of tepid revenue growth, Wrigley posted an impressive 13% increase in 2001, and maintained this momentum with 14% top-line growth in the first nine months of 2002.

Profitability [A+]	1999	2000	2001	TTM
Return on Assets %	19.9	20.9	20.6	19.0
Oper Cash Flow $Mil	358	448	390	438
- Cap Spending $Mil	128	125	182	215
= Free Cash Flow $Mil	230	323	209	222

Wrigley is highly profitable, with returns on equity consistently above 25%. Net margins have improved from a few years ago, but shrinking asset turnover has caused ROE to decline slightly.

Financial Health [A+]	1999	2000	2001	09-02
Long-term Debt $Mil	—	—	—	—
Total Equity $Mil	1,139	1,133	1,276	1,449
Debt/Equity Ratio	—	—	—	—

The firm consistently generates healthy free cash flows, and its financial leverage is excellent for a food company. It has no long-term debt.

Industry	Investment Style	Stock Type	Sector
Food Mfg.	Large Core	→ Slow Growth	Consumer Goods

Competition	Market Cap $Mil	Debt/ Equity	12 Mo Trailing Sales $Mil	Price/Cash Flow	Return On Assets%	Total Return% 1 Yr	3 Yr
Wm. Wrigley Jr.	12,360	—	2,673	28.2	19.0	8.5	13.4
Pfizer	188,377	0.2	34,407	21.1	18.3	-22.2	1.0
GlaxoSmithKline PLC ADR	116,607	0.3	27,512	6.2	13.9	-22.8	-9.3

Price Volatility

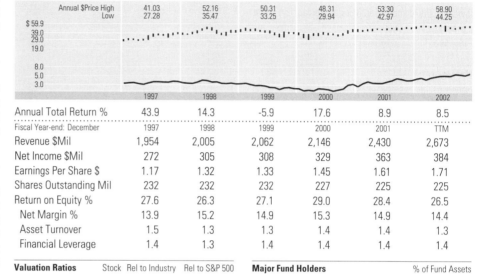

Annual $Price High Low	41.03 27.28	52.16 35.47	50.31 33.25	48.31 29.94	53.30 42.97	58.90 44.25

	1997	1998	1999	2000	2001	2002
Annual Total Return %	43.9	14.3	-5.9	17.6	8.9	8.5
Fiscal Year-end: December	1997	1998	1999	2000	2001	TTM
Revenue $Mil	1,954	2,005	2,062	2,146	2,430	2,673
Net Income $Mil	272	305	308	329	363	384
Earnings Per Share $	1.17	1.32	1.33	1.45	1.61	1.71
Shares Outstanding Mil	232	232	232	227	225	225
Return on Equity %	27.6	26.3	27.1	29.0	28.4	26.5
Net Margin %	13.9	15.2	14.9	15.3	14.9	14.4
Asset Turnover	1.5	1.3	1.3	1.4	1.4	1.3
Financial Leverage	1.4	1.3	1.4	1.4	1.4	1.4

Valuation Ratios	Stock	Rel to Industry	Rel to S&P 500
Price/Earnings	32.1	1.5	1.4
Price/Book	8.5	2.0	2.7
Price/Sales	4.6	3.2	2.3
Price/Cash Flow	28.2	2.6	2.1

Major Fund Holders	% of Fund Assets
W.P. Stewart & Co Growth	4.76
John Hancock U.S. Global Leaders Gr A	4.56
Smith Barney Large Cap Growth A	3.92
Institutional Investors Capital Appr	3.71

Morningstar's Take   By David Kathman, 11-11-2002   Stock Price as of Analysis: $52.59

A reinvigorated Wrigley is boosting its growth by venturing into new areas, but we wouldn't buy at this price.

Wrigley's offer to buy Hershey for $12.5 billion--an offer that fell through when the Milton Hershey Trust decided at the last minute not to sell the company--was the boldest of many recent bold moves by the company's youthful CEO. Since taking the reins in 1999, Bill Wrigley has shaken up the traditionally conservative company and boosted its formerly sluggish growth. Wrigley's sales grew 13% in 2001 and 14% in the first nine months of 2002, including an impressive 19% in the third quarter.

Wrigley's reinvigorated top line is the result of an increased emphasis on new products. The increased popularity of breath mints like Altoids led Wrigley to introduce Eclipse, a pellet gum with a hard mint coating, and to expand Orbit, a sugar-free breath-freshening gum formerly sold only in Europe, into the U.S. market. More recently, Wrigley introduced Eclipse Flash Strips, a breath freshener that dissolves on the tongue. These products are higher-priced than traditional gum, helping sales growth to run well ahead of volume growth. But new products also mean higher marketing expenses, and Wrigley's earnings have been growing only about

half as fast as its sales.

Innovation is particularly important now that Wrigley faces potentially tougher competition from number-two Adams Gum, which is being auctioned off by Pfizer. Potential suitors Nestle, Cadbury Schweppes, and Kraft could all bring considerable resources to the table to compete with Wrigley. But Wrigley has shown itself to be a tough competitor, so we're not too worried.

A riskier aspect of Wrigley's new direction is its health-care division. The division introduced its first product, antacid gum Surpass, in 2001, and is teaming up with Procter & Gamble to make and market dental gums. Such specialty health-care gums offer potentially higher margins and growth opportunities than regular gums. But sales of Surpass have been disappointing so far, and the health-care division continues to lose money because it's still mostly in the research and development phase.

Wrigley can afford to take some risks because it's a robustly profitable company with a dominant position in its field. We think the stock is worth about $45 per share, and we'd be happy to buy it if it dropped 10% or more below that level.

Wyeth WYE

	Rating	Risk	Moat Size	Fair Value	Last Close	Yield %
	★★★★	Low	Narrow	$52.00	$37.40	2.5

Industry	Investment Style	Stock Type	Sector
Drugs	Large Core	Classic Growth	Healthcare

Company Profile

Wyeth primarily manufactures and markets pharmaceuticals. It also sells consumer health-care products under brands like Advil, Robitussin, and Chap Stick. The company is also a major player in the global vaccine business. Approximately 5% of revenue comes from animal pharmaceuticals sold by its Fort Dodge division, another 15% from its consumer product division, and the remaining 80% from Wyeth-Ayerst, the human pharmaceutical division. The company sold its American Cyanamid agribusiness in 2000 and changed its name from American Home Products to Wyeth in 2002.

Management

Robert Essner replaced John Stafford as CEO in May 2001 and was elected as chairman in November 2002. Essner is thought of as a marketing expert and ran the pharmaceutical business prior to being promoted to COO in July 2000.

Strategy

With the diet-drug debacle behind it and failed merger attempts fading from memory, Wyeth is trying to generate a midteens earnings growth rate by maximizing the value of its pipeline, research efforts, and employees. The company is concentrating on its drug business and building strong franchises in vaccines and hormone-replacement therapies for women.

Five Giralda Farms www.wyeth.com
Madison, NJ 07940-0874

Morningstar Grades

Growth [C]	1998	1999	2000	2001
Revenue %	-6.7	4.9	11.8	6.9
Earnings/Share %	39.1	NMF	NMF	NMF
Book Value/Share %	15.5	-28.4	-54.8	42.5
Dividends/Share %	4.8	4.0	1.7	0.0

Revenue growth stems from a number of rapidly growing drugs such as Effexor, Protonix, Enbrel, and Prevnar. Revenue growth was 3.5% for the first nine months of 2002, and should average 9.5% for 2003 and 2004, based on our product growth forecasts.

Profitability [B]	1999	2000	2001	TTM
Return on Assets %	-5.3	-11.2	10.0	13.4
Oper Cash Flow $Mil	2,166	555	-4,447	597
- Cap Spending $Mil	937	1,682	1,924	1,951
= Free Cash Flow $Mil	1,228	-1,127	-6,371	-1,354

The huge drop in HRT product sales is wreaking havoc on gross margins (down to 71% in the third quarter from 76% for 2001). Operating margins are holding up in the low 20s, but are below industry averages in the mid- to high 20s.

Financial Health [C]	1999	2000	2001	09-02
Long-term Debt $Mil	3,606	2,395	7,357	7,558
Total Equity $Mil	6,215	2,818	4,073	6,731
Debt/Equity Ratio	0.6	0.9	1.8	1.1

More than half of Wyeth's $11 billion in debt is low-interest commercial paper, which we expect to be paid off soon with Amgen proceeds. Wyeth has $3 billion in cash and $4 billion in Amgen shares, so we're not worried about financial health.

Competition

	Market Cap $Mil	Debt/ Equity	12 Mo Trailing Sales $Mil	Price/Cash Flow	Return On Assets%	Total Return% 1 Yr	3 Yr
Wyeth	49,579	1.1	14,598	83.0	13.4	-37.9	-0.4
Merck	127,121	0.3	50,430	13.2	15.0	-1.3	-2.5
GlaxoSmithKline PLC ADR	116,607	0.3	27,512	6.2	13.9	-22.8	-9.3

Price Volatility

Monthly Price High/Low — Relative Strength to S&P 500

Annual $Price High Low	42.44 28.50	58.75 37.75	70.25 36.50	65.25 39.38	63.80 52.00	66.51 28.25

$71.3 / 49.0 / 29.0 / 19.0 / 8.0 / 5.0 / 3.0

	1997	1998	1999	2000	2001	2002
Annual Total Return %	33.5	50.1	-29.2	64.6	-1.9	-37.8

Fiscal Year-End: December	1997	1998	1999	2000	2001	TTM
Revenue $Mil	12,077	11,269	11,815	13,214	14,129	14,598
Net Income $Mil	1,748	2,474	-1,227	-2,371	2,285	3,696
Earnings Per Share $	1.33	1.85	-0.94	-1.81	1.72	2.77
Shares Outstanding Mil	1,314	1,316	1,305	1,310	1,313	1,326
Return on Equity %	23.1	27.8	-19.7	-84.1	56.1	54.9
Net Margin %	14.5	22.0	-10.4	-17.9	16.2	25.3
Asset Turnover	0.6	0.6	0.5	0.6	0.6	0.5
Financial Leverage	2.6	2.3	3.7	7.5	5.6	4.1

Valuation Ratios	Stock	Rel to Industry	Rel to S&P 500
Price/Earnings	13.5	0.6	0.6
Price/Book	7.4	1.0	2.3
Price/Sales	3.4	0.9	1.7
Price/Cash Flow	83.0	3.9	6.3

Major Fund Holders	% of Fund Assets
Eaton Vance Worldwide Health Sci A	6.25
Smith Barney Health Sciences B	6.22
AIM Global Health Care A	6.12
Fidelity Advisor Health Care A	5.95

Morningstar's Take By Todd N. Lebor, 12-11-2002 Stock Price as of Analysis: $37.59

Wyeth (formerly American Home Products) has shown its strength by surviving the fen-phen diet drug fiasco. We think the company has turned the corner and is in better shape than many of its peers.

Wyeth is a testament to the resilience and profitability of the big pharma business model. From 1998 through 2001, the company wiped out more than $6.5 billion in retained earnings, doubled its debt load, and paid or reserved more than $12 billion for fen-phen litigation. Yet today it holds an investment-grade credit rating, sits on plenty of cash, and most remarkably, is still in business. It's around because it generated more than $5 billion in free cash flow (cash flow from operations less capital expenditures) during those litigious years, and profited handsomely from its investment in Immunex made years earlier.

Over the past few years, Wyeth pocketed more than $3.4 billion in cash from its Immunex investment, and there's more to come. As a result of Amgen's acquisition of Immunex, Wyeth owns 7.7% of Amgen (worth $4 billion as of Dec. 10). Management plans to sell its holdings, which will go a long way toward paying down the debt incurred from fen-phen litigation. Wyeth should also benefit from rights to international sales from blockbuster

rheumatoid arthritis drug Enbrel, which it retained after the sale of Immunex. We expect international sales of Enbrel to top $1 billion by 2007.

Wyeth's near-term growth will come from depression med Effexor, ulcer treatment Protonix, child vaccine Prevnar, and synthetic blood substitute ReFacto. Although the late-stage pipeline isn't stacked, the aforementioned drugs don't face patent pressures until the second half of this decade, so we think the firm has plenty of time to develop or buy its next generation of growth drivers. We're expecting industry-beating sales growth of about 10% annually for Wyeth over the next five years.

The Premarin female hormone-replacement therapy franchise is Wyeth's wild card. The estrogen and progestin combination drug Prempro (40% of HRT franchise sales) has been questioned for safety concerns--specifically increased risks for breast cancer. Although news of the study results sent Prempro sales down 20%-30%, they have stabilized since. We believe that sales will level off, ending Premarin's growth but not drying up its $1.5-$2.0 billion annual revenue stream.

Wyeth has more going for it than its peers, and we think a 30% discount to our fair value estimate adequately accounts for the Premarin risk.

MORNINGSTAR® Stocks 500

Xerox XRX

	Rating	Risk	Moat Size	Fair Value	Last Close	Yield %
	★★★	High	None	$11.00	$8.05	0.0

Company Profile

Xerox produces document-processing machines and provides related services. The company manufactures products for black-and-white and color copying, digital publishing, and electronic printing. Xerox's products include photocopiers, duplicators, digital-publishing equipment, facsimile products, computer software, and ink-jet, laser, and electrostatic printers. The company's Xerox Credit subsidiary arranges financing for equipment purchases. Xerox markets its products in the United States and abroad. Foreign revenue accounts for approximately 46% of the company's revenue.

Management

In July 2001 Xerox named Anne Mulcahy, a 25-year company veteran, as its new CEO. She replaced Paul Allaire, the former CEO who returned after Rick Thoman resigned in May 2000.

Strategy

Xerox is in turnaround mode. The firm has sold assets, outsourced manufacturing and customer financing, exited businesses, and cut costs. To rejuvenate itself, Xerox is investing in digital printing and copying technology, concentrating on equipment that produces color documents. The firm also hopes to expand its services business.

800 Long Ridge Road
Stamford, CT 06904-1600
www.xerox.com

Morningstar Grades

Growth [C-]	1998	1999	2000	2001
Revenue %	7.6	1.2	-1.3	-9.3
Earnings/Share %	NMF	NMF	NMF	NMF
Book Value/Share %	15.8	-29.4	-22.6	-2.9
Dividends/Share %	12.5	11.1	-18.8	-92.3

Xerox is a mature, low-growth business. Revenue in 2002 will be about what it was in 1995. New products and a push into services should help boost growth to our forecast of 4% by 2005.

Profitability [C-]	1999	2000	2001	TTM
Return on Assets %	3.0	-1.0	-0.3	-0.1
Oper Cash Flow $Mil	551	207	1,566	1,841
- Cap Spending $Mil	594	452	219	169
= Free Cash Flow $Mil	-43	-245	1,347	1,672

Xerox used to be profitable, but internal mistakes and its failure to see changing competitive conditions led to steep losses. However, others in the industry make money and we see no reason Xerox can't approach average industry profitability.

Financial Health [C]	1999	2000	2001	09-02
Long-term Debt $Mil	11,521	15,557	10,128	10,470
Total Equity $Mil	2,953	1,801	1,820	1,943
Debt/Equity Ratio	3.9	8.6	5.6	5.4

Xerox's balance sheet isn't pretty. However, it is getting better, and liquidity worries have dissipated with the refinancing of its bank debt in June.

	Industry	Investment Style	Stock Type	Sector
	Office Equipment	Mid Value	Distressed	Industrial Mats

Competition	Market Cap $Mil	Debt/ Equity	12 Mo Trailing Sales $Mil	Price/Cash Flow	Return On Assets%	Total Return% 1 Yr	3 Yr
Xerox	5,909	5.4	15,985	3.2	-0.1	-22.7	-28.6
Hewlett-Packard	34,321	0.3	—	6.1	-3.5	-13.9	-24.7
Canon ADR	32,267	—	25,882	—	—	—	—

Price Volatility

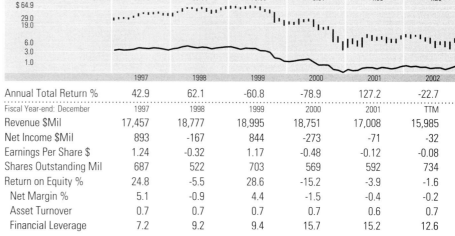

	1997	1998	1999	2000	2001	2002
Annual $Price High	44.00	60.81	63.94	29.31	11.35	11.45
Low	25.75	33.09	19.00	3.81	4.63	4.20
Annual Total Return %	42.9	62.1	-60.8	-78.9	127.2	-22.7

Fiscal Year-end: December	1997	1998	1999	2000	2001	TTM
Revenue $Mil	17,457	18,777	18,995	18,751	17,008	15,985
Net Income $Mil	893	-167	844	-273	-71	-32
Earnings Per Share $	1.24	-0.32	1.17	-0.48	-0.12	-0.08
Shares Outstanding Mil	687	522	703	569	592	734
Return on Equity %	24.8	-5.5	28.6	-15.2	-3.9	-1.6
Net Margin %	5.1	-0.9	4.4	-1.5	-0.4	-0.2
Asset Turnover	0.7	0.7	0.7	0.7	0.6	0.7
Financial Leverage	7.2	9.2	9.4	15.7	15.2	12.6

Valuation Ratios	Stock	Rel to Industry	Rel to S&P 500
Price/Earnings	NMF	—	—
Price/Book	3.0	1.0	1.0
Price/Sales	0.4	1.0	0.2
Price/Cash Flow	3.2	0.5	0.2

Major Fund Holders	% of Fund Assets
ING Midcap Value A	4.15
MainStay Research Value A	3.81
Fidelity Advisor Dynamic Cap App A	3.55
Oakmark Select I	2.83

Morningstar's Take By Dan Schick, 12-06-2002 Stock Price as of Analysis: $8.12

Xerox is convalescing from wounds suffered in the past few years. Because the firm faces stiff competition and is burdened by a debt-laden balance sheet, we would avoid the shares unless they traded at a 60% discount to our fair value estimate.

Xerox exemplifies the trouble that a firm with no economic moat can encounter. In 1999, a badly handled salesforce reorganization and a bout of poor customer service gave competitors a wide opening to steal business, which they did. Xerox failed to respond operationally, instead engaging in "accounting opportunities" to disguise the deterioration in its business.

Investors caught on to these shenanigans, locking the firm out of the capital markets. Without access to capital, which it needed both to finance its customers' purchases and meet its own obligations, Xerox teetered on the brink of ruin, facing looming debt maturities.

Since then, CEO Anne Mulcahy has led Xerox through a tough restructuring. The firm sold assets and securitized lease receivables, receiving billions in cash--enough to pay down some of the billions of maturing debt and refinance the rest. Xerox also stemmed losses in its emerging markets and hacked away at its cost structure. The company outsourced the manufacture of office products to Flextronics and has cut employment to fewer than 70,000 people from more than 94,000 in 1999. The resulting savings total more than $1 billion annually.

We think Mulcahy has done a brilliant job of restructuring Xerox, silencing doubts about the firm's viability. However, long-term vitality will not be won through cost-cutting and downsizing. Xerox must now find a way to increase revenue.

Though Xerox has recently released a bevy of new products that seem to be doing well, we urge caution. The slowdown in capital spending has damped demand for new equipment, and even when these cyclical factors swing back the other way, competition in Xerox's markets is intense. Canon and Ricoh give Xerox no breaks in the slow-growth office copier market, while Heidelberg and Hewlett-Packard are moving into the digital printing market. Since we doubt Xerox holds an enduring advantage over these rivals, we see a limit to the firm's ability to grow and deliver long-lasting value to shareholders.

Xilinx XLNX

	Rating	Risk	Moat Size	Fair Value	Last Close	Yield %
	★★★	Med.	Narrow	$22.00	$20.60	0.0

Company Profile

Xilinx develops programmable logic devices (PLDs) and related software products. These PLDs include advanced integrated circuits that may be client-programmed using the company's software. Xilinx's products also include field programmable gate arrays (FPGAs) Xilinx sells products in the United States and overseas, and outsources the production of PLD products to third-party semiconductor foundries.

Management

Chairman Bernard Vonderschmitt co-founded Xilinx in 1984. He appointed Wim Roelandts to take over as CEO in 1996. About 4% of Xilinx is owned by executives and directors.

Strategy

Xilinx aims to increase its market share in the programmable logic device industry, a specialized niche in the chip sector. The company seeks to create additional demand by expanding PLD use in nontraditional chip markets. Xilinx focuses on chip design and outsources production to other manufacturing companies.

2100 Logic Drive
San Jose, CA 95124
www.xilinx.com

Morningstar Grades

Growth [B-]	1999	2000	2001	2002
Revenue %	7.9	54.2	62.5	-38.8
Earnings/Share %	-17.5	475.8	-94.7	NMF
Book Value/Share %	62.7	82.9	5.2	4.7
Dividends/Share %	NMF	NMF	NMF	NMF

Xilinx's three-year average growth of 22% outpaces that of the broader chip sector and close peers like Altera. Sales fell 39% in fiscal 2002 because of the telecom industry downturn, but have trended up in recent quarters.

Profitability [A-]	2000	2001	2002	TTM
Return on Assets %	27.8	1.4	-4.9	5.3
Oper Cash Flow $Mil	341	377	281	341
- Cap Spending $Mil	144	223	95	64
= Free Cash Flow $Mil	197	155	186	277

Profitability is excellent. PLDs are high-margin products, so the firm typically generates returns on equity in excess of 20%, roughly equal to peers. Because Xilinx farms out its chip production, margins remain decent during downturns.

Financial Health [A+]	2000	2001	2002	09-02
Long-term Debt $Mil	0	0	0	0
Total Equity $Mil	1,777	1,918	1,904	1,904
Debt/Equity Ratio	0.0	0.0	0.0	0.0

Xilinx is in good health with no debt, decent cash flows, and almost $600 million in cash and short-term investments. In fact, the firm's cash position exceeds its total liabilities. Excess inventory is also no longer a big problem.

Industry	Investment Style	Stock Type	Sector
Semiconductors	Mid Growth	Slow Growth	Hardware

Competition	Market Cap $Mil	Debt/ Equity	12 Mo Trailing Sales $Mil	Price/Cash Flow	Return On Assets%	Total Return% 1 Yr	3 Yr
Xilinx	6,944	0.0	1,069	20.3	5.3	-47.3	-23.3
Altera	4,720	—	694	18.5	2.2	-41.9	-20.9
Atmel	1,038	—	1,174	—	—	—	—

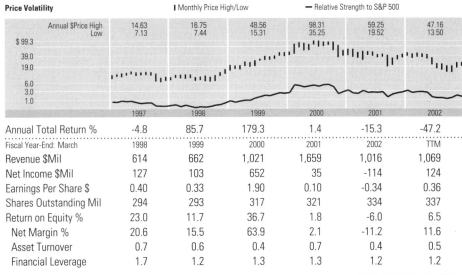

Price Volatility

Monthly Price High/Low	Relative Strength to S&P 500

Annual $Price High	14.63	16.75	48.56	98.31	59.25	47.16
Low	7.13	7.44	15.31	35.25	19.52	13.50

$ 99.3
39.0
19.0
6.0
3.0
1.0

	1997	1998	1999	2000	2001	2002
Annual Total Return %	-4.8	85.7	179.3	1.4	-15.3	-47.2

Fiscal Year-End: March	1998	1999	2000	2001	2002	TTM
Revenue $Mil	614	662	1,021	1,659	1,016	1,069
Net Income $Mil	127	103	652	35	-114	124
Earnings Per Share $	0.40	0.33	1.90	0.10	-0.34	0.36
Shares Outstanding Mil	294	293	317	321	334	337
Return on Equity %	23.0	11.7	36.7	1.8	-6.0	6.5
Net Margin %	20.6	15.5	63.9	2.1	-11.2	11.6
Asset Turnover	0.7	0.6	0.4	0.7	0.4	0.5
Financial Leverage	1.7	1.2	1.3	1.3	1.2	1.2

Valuation Ratios	Stock	Rel to Industry	Rel to S&P 500
Price/Earnings	57.2	1.4	2.4
Price/Book	3.6	1.2	1.1
Price/Sales	6.5	1.7	3.2
Price/Cash Flow	20.3	1.7	1.5

Major Fund Holders	% of Fund Assets
Pin Oak Aggressive Stock	5.14
Berger Information Technology Instl	3.37
Berger Information Technology Inv	3.37
Delaware Technology and Innovation A	2.98

Morningstar's Take By Jeremy Lopez, 10-31-2002 Stock Price as of Analysis: $18.99

Xilinx is well positioned in its semiconductor niche. Nonetheless, we would buy the shares only at a wide margin of safety--roughly 40%--to our fair value estimate.

As a producer of programmable logic devices (PLDs), Xilinx operates in one of the more attractive semiconductor niches. Since 1990, PLD growth has outpaced the chip industry's 10% average sales growth by about 6 percentage points. Part of this performance has been driven by the growth in end-market products that use PLDs, like consumer electronics, telecom/wireless infrastructure, and storage gear. Since PLDs are more customizable than preprogrammed ASIC (application-specific integrated circuit) chips, customers can save time designing their products with PLDs and release their products more quickly. This flexibility has resulted in PLDs gaining share on ASICs, a trend we expect to continue.

Xilinx and rival Altera control roughly three fourths of the PLD market. The rest of the niche consists of lower-end, marginal players like Lattice and Actel. Most recently, Xilinx has had a leg up on Altera, as its Virtex family of PLDs has resulted in better top-line growth over the past chip cycle. Given Xilinx's market leadership, we expect it to continue

outperforming the average PLD maker. But its lead on Altera may narrow in the coming cycle, as the latter has released a slew of new products over the past few quarters.

The main factor detracting from Xilinx's investment appeal is the huge downturn in technology spending in recent years. More than half of Xilinx's sales come from the communication sector, which has been the worst-hit in this slump. But one thing we like about the PLDs is how they are versatile and used in almost all major technology end markets. Xilinx also avoids the burden of capital spending by outsourcing its chip production. This "fabless" model, combined with limited rivalry in PLDs, contributes to relatively strong and stable profitability. Xilinx's gross margins are typically above 60% and it's not uncommon for operating margins to be around 30%.

We don't know when tech spending will rebound, but we think Xilinx's fundamentals will prove attractive when it does. For a company with only a narrow economic moat, Xilinx would make a nice investment at roughly a 40% discount to our fair value estimate.

MORNINGSTAR® Stocks 500

Yahoo! YHOO

	Rating	Risk	Moat Size	Fair Value	Last Close	Yield %
	★	High	Narrow	$8.00	$16.35	0.0

Company Profile

Yahoo offers navigational services that help users obtain information from the Internet's World Wide Web. The company's context-based directory is designed to allow users to search for information online. Yahoo also provides corporate-portal software and business services. Softbank owns a large stake in the company.

Management

Former Warner Bros. exec Terry Semel took the helm in April 2001. Semel has a valuable network of industry contacts, but his experience is largely limited to film rather than advertising.

Strategy

Yahoo wants to be the only place anyone in the world needs to go to find information, get connected to anyone, or buy anything. In light of the online ad industry meltdown, the company is renewing its focus on developing premium services and lessening its dependence on banner ads.

701 First Avenue
Sunnyvale, CA 94089   www.yahoo.com

Industry	Investment Style	Stock Type	Sector
Media Conglomerates	Large Growth	Spec. Growth	Media

Competition	Market Cap $Mil	Debt/ Equity	12 Mo Trailing Sales $Mil	Price/Cash Flow	Return On Assets%	Total Return% 1 Yr	3 Yr
Yahoo!	9,661	—	856	40.9	-0.4	-7.8	-58.1
Microsoft	276,411	0.0	29,985	16.0	13.2	-22.0	-22.9
AOL Time Warner	56,278	0.3	41,024	8.1	-34.6	-59.2	-44.6

Price Volatility | Monthly Price High/Low   — Relative Strength to S&P 500

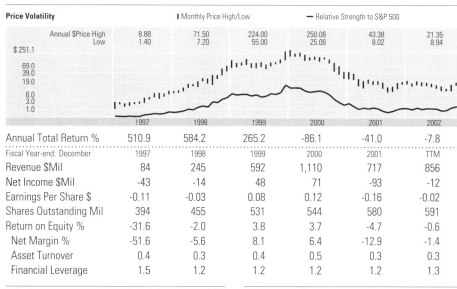

Annual $Price High / Low	8.88 / 1.40	71.50 / 7.20	224.00 / 55.00	250.06 / 25.06	43.38 / 8.02	21.35 / 8.94
	1997	1998	1999	2000	2001	2002
Annual Total Return %	510.9	584.2	265.2	-86.1	-41.0	-7.8

Fiscal Year-end: December	1997	1998	1999	2000	2001	TTM
Revenue $Mil	84	245	592	1,110	717	856
Net Income $Mil	-43	-14	48	71	-93	-12
Earnings Per Share $	-0.11	-0.03	0.08	0.12	-0.16	-0.02
Shares Outstanding Mil	394	455	531	544	580	591
Return on Equity %	-31.6	-2.0	3.8	3.7	-4.7	-0.6
Net Margin %	-51.6	-5.6	8.1	6.4	-12.9	-1.4
Asset Turnover	0.4	0.3	0.4	0.5	0.3	0.3
Financial Leverage	1.5	1.2	1.2	1.2	1.2	1.3

Valuation Ratios	Stock	Rel to Industry	Rel to S&P 500
Price/Earnings	NMF	—	—
Price/Book	4.5	3.2	1.4
Price/Sales	11.3	5.1	5.6
Price/Cash Flow	40.9	2.7	3.1

Major Fund Holders	% of Fund Assets
Fidelity Select Multimedia	9.96
ProFunds Ultra Internet Inv	9.86
IDEX Munder Net50 A	7.34
Fidelity Capital Appreciation	7.22

Morningstar Grades

Growth [B]	1998	1999	2000	2001
Revenue %	191.4	141.4	87.6	-35.4
Earnings/Share %	NMF	NMF	50.0	NMF
Book Value/Share %	327.4	40.8	53.6	5.5
Dividends/Share %	NMF	NMF	NMF	NMF

After a brief history of rapid growth, sales have dropped like a brick. New business lines, including listings and fee-based services, are filling the void left by advertising and we think revenue will expand 20% annually over the long term.

Profitability [C]	1999	2000	2001	TTM
Return on Assets %	3.1	3.1	-3.9	-0.4
Oper Cash Flow $Mil	204	510	107	236
- Cap Spending $Mil	52	94	86	49
= Free Cash Flow $Mil	152	415	21	187

Yahoo's profits have been all over the board in the past several quarters, but free cash flows have been strong, at more than $150 million over the past 12 months.

Financial Health [B+]	1999	2000	2001	09-02
Long-term Debt $Mil	—	—	—	—
Total Equity $Mil	1,252	1,897	1,967	2,156
Debt/Equity Ratio	—	—	—	—

While its income statement looks ugly, Yahoo boasts a rock-solid balance sheet. It is debt-free and has more than $1.5 billion in cash and equivalents.

Morningstar's Take   By T.K. MacKay, 10-30-2002 Stock Price as of Analysis: $14.99

We fear that as Yahoo changes its business model by entering areas like broadband access, games, and classifieds, its competitive advantage could deteriorate as a result of increased rivalry from the likes of AOL and Microsoft. We wouldn't touch Yahoo above $5 per share.

According to the Internet Advertising Bureau, the top 10 Web sites, including Yahoo.com, received 77% of the $7.2 billion spent on advertising in 2001. Yahoo derives its competitive advantage from a loyal user base of more than 200 million visitors a month. With this following comes lucrative advertising revenue, which tops $500 million on an annualized basis.

Advertising is cyclical, however, as evidenced by Yahoo's 35% drop in revenue in 2001. The company has made a big push to shield its top line from the ad market, which contributes just 59% of its revenue compared with more than 90% in 1998. New business lines like fees, listings, and transactions contribute 41% of revenue, up from less than 5% in 1998. Recent moves like the acquisition of HotJobs, a partnership with SBC Communications to deliver broadband access to consumers, and a push into subscription music and online games are distancing Yahoo's overall business from the ad market even

more.

In doing this, Yahoo is moving away from the business in which it has a big competitive advantage and stepping on rival turf. We believe that both AOL and MSN have created alliances (with Time Warner and Disney) that outpace Yahoo in terms of the content that they can deliver. We're skeptical about how many Yahoo users are willing to pay $14.95 a month to play online games or listen to music. We are also concerned that content from businesses like PressPlay and Yahoo Movies won't hold a candle to AOL Time Warner, once the latter delivers content to the Web in broadband style.

Historically, Yahoo's Web sites have provided content that earned the company a substantial economic moat and fat advertising fees. When this content moves behind a fee-based wall, however, Yahoo may lose its appeal to the average user. No matter how popular Yahoo may be to consumers today, the online media industry has one sustainable trait: There are plenty of goods that consumers can substitute, especially if these goods can be had for free. For these reasons, we would look for a substantial margin of safety--one of 50% or more--before considering the stock.

Yum Brands YUM

	Rating	Risk	Moat Size	Fair Value	Last Close	Yield %
	★★★	Med.	Narrow	$29.00	$24.22	0.0

Company Profile

Yum Brands owns, operates, licenses, or franchises restaurants in the United States and overseas, including more than 12,000 Pizza Hut restaurants, about 7,100 Taco Bell restaurants, and more than 10,800 KFC restaurants in 95 countries and territories. In addition, Yum Brands operates Pizza Hut, Taco Bell, and KFC kiosks and express units in locations such as airports, stadiums, amusement parks, colleges, service stations, and convenience stores. Foreign sales account for approximately 33% of the company's total sales.

Management

CEO David Novak has been president of the firm since its 1997 spin-off from PepsiCo. Yum already rewarded Novak for the mere beginnings of its turnaround, raising his bonus 40% in 2001.

Strategy

Yum is using its cash from operations to fund franchise-store expansions in high-growth regions like Asia, and to reduce long-term debt. In the United States, the firm is trying to revitalize sales by offering more than one brand per location. It has also been aggressively rolling out new menu items at Taco Bell and Pizza Hut.

1441 Gardiner Lane   www.yum.com
Louisville, KY 40213

Industry	Investment Style	Stock Type	Sector
Restaurants	▦ Mid Core	→ Slow Growth	▯ Consumer Services

Competition	Market Cap $Mil	Debt/ Equity	12 Mo Trailing Sales $Mil	Price/Cash Flow	Return On Assets%	Total Return% 1 Yr	3 Yr
Yum Brands	7,169	4.3	7,498	6.9	11.1	-1.5	9.8
McDonald's	20,411	0.9	15,278	7.2	6.4	-38.4	-24.8
AFC Enterprises	597	0.8	642	6.3	5.1	-26.0	—

Price Volatility

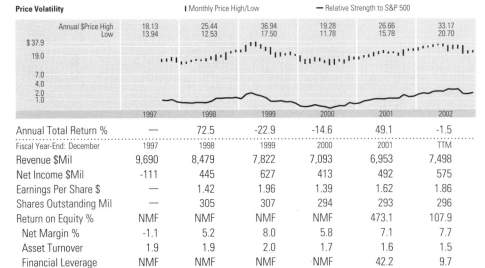

		18.13	25.44	36.94	19.28	26.66	33.17
Annual $Price High Low		13.94	12.53	17.50	11.78	15.78	20.70

	1997	1998	1999	2000	2001	2002
Annual Total Return %	—	72.5	-22.9	-14.6	49.1	-1.5

Fiscal Year-End: December	1997	1998	1999	2000	2001	TTM
Revenue $Mil	9,690	8,479	7,822	7,093	6,953	7,498
Net Income $Mil	-111	445	627	413	492	575
Earnings Per Share $	—	1.42	1.96	1.39	1.62	1.86
Shares Outstanding Mil		305	307	294	293	296
Return on Equity %	NMF	NMF	NMF	NMF	473.1	107.9
Net Margin %	-1.1	5.2	8.0	5.8	7.1	7.7
Asset Turnover	1.9	1.9	2.0	1.7	1.6	1.5
Financial Leverage	NMF	NMF	NMF	NMF	42.2	9.7

Valuation Ratios	Stock	Rel to Industry	Rel to S&P 500
Price/Earnings	13.0	0.9	0.6
Price/Book	13.5	5.3	4.2
Price/Sales	1.0	0.7	0.5
Price/Cash Flow	6.9	1.0	0.5

Major Fund Holders	% of Fund Assets
Longleaf Partners	6.24
Oakmark Select I	5.46
MassMutual Instl Focused Value S	4.87
Rydex Leisure Inv	4.77

Morningstar Grades

Growth [C-]	1998	1999	2000	2001
Revenue %	-12.5	-7.7	-9.3	-2.0
Earnings/Share %	NMF	38.0	-29.3	17.0
Book Value/Share %	NMF	NMF	NMF	NMF
Dividends/Share %	NMF	NMF	NMF	NMF

We expect the acquisition of Long John Silver's and A&W to help the company achieve a 10% increase in sales in 2002 and 2003, though our long-term sales growth expectations are closer to 5% annually for 2004-06.

Profitability [A]	1999	2000	2001	TTM
Return on Assets %	15.8	10.0	11.2	11.1
Oper Cash Flow $Mil	565	491	832	1,033
- Cap Spending $Mil	470	572	636	737
= Free Cash Flow $Mil	95	-81	196	296

Yum may be the largest fast-food organization in terms of number of restaurants, but its net profit margin significantly trails industry leader McDonald's at 12%.

Financial Health [B-]	1999	2000	2001	09-02
Long-term Debt $Mil	2,391	2,397	1,552	2,317
Total Equity $Mil	-560	-322	104	533
Debt/Equity Ratio	ELB	ELB	14.9	4.3

Earnings before interest and taxes is about 2.5 times interest expense, including the effect of capitalized operating leases. We'd like to see debt reduced.

Morningstar's Take   By Carl Sibilski, 12-13-2002   Stock Price as of Analysis: $23.25

Yum Brands has a winning game plan to generate steady sales and earnings growth. Still, the restaurant industry has a reputation for throwing curve balls, and we'd require a 40% discount to our fair value estimate before investing.

Yum Brands owns three of the most popular fast-food brands in the world--KFC, Pizza Hut, and Taco Bell--and has successfully packaged these brands under the same roof. Greater menu diversity drives higher traffic and extends it throughout the day, as one brand may attract more lunchtime traffic while another attracts the dinner crowd.

The company claims that multibrand conversions can add 30% more revenue per store, with lower overhead per brand resulting in greater asset efficiency and higher margins. Operating cash flow per conversion increases 30%-50%. Yum Brands expects to add 375 multibrand restaurants in 2002, and by acquiring brands Long John Silver's and A&W, the firm estimates that multibrand store concepts have long-term opportunities at about 13,000 U.S. locations. The company currently has 1,700 multibrand stores.

Yum Brands is also selling company stores to franchisees in order to achieve higher net profit margins. In recent years, this trend has resulted in

lower overall sales growth because the revenue mix has shifted toward more profitable royalty streams and away from restaurant operating-related revenue. Thus, we expect Yum's net profit margins over the next five years to average about 8%, up from a 6% average during the past five years.

We're confident in Yum's long-term prospects because each of its three major brands are leaders in their industry segments. Despite having a presence in almost 100 countries, the firm still has room to expand its footprint. For example, Yum Brands recently opened its 700th store in China. Yum stands to benefit substantially in the mainland as long as a business-friendly political climate continues to evolve. At the same time, Yum has a lot to lose if policy sours.

Nonetheless, we think Yum Brands' potential for sales and earnings growth make the stock a compelling buy under $17.

MORNINGSTAR® Stocks 500

Zimmer Holdings ZMH

	Rating ★★	Risk Med.	Moat Size Narrow	Fair Value $35.00	Last Close $41.52	Yield % 0.0

Company Profile

Zimmer Holdings is a spin-off from Bristol-Myers Squibb that designs, manufactures, and markets orthopedic reconstructive implants. The split was completed in mid-2001. Zimmer also manufactures and markets supplies and surgical equipment for orthopedic surgical procedures. Its products are distributed and sold to hospitals and clinics all over the world under brand names like NexGen, Zimmer, Pulsavac, VerSys, Trilogy, and TransFx. In 2001, Zimmer created the MIS Institute to educate and train surgeons on minimally invasive procedures.

Management

J. Raymond Elliott is Zimmer's chairman, president, and CEO. He climbed the ranks through sales and management positions at various firms and ran the division for Bristol-Myers Squibb beginning in 1997. Elliott is the only internal board member.

Strategy

Zimmer wants to increase its share of the orthopedic reconstructive implant market by offering innovative products and expanding its product line to include spinal and orthobiological products. Zimmer is at or near the top of the reconstructive market and wants be at the top in orthopedic devices too; management has said acquisitions may be a part of this strategy.

345 East Main Street   www.zimmer.com
Warsaw, IN 46580

Morningstar Grades

Growth [B-]	1998	1999	2000	2001
Revenue %	1.3	9.1	10.8	13.3
Earnings/Share %	NMF	NMF	NMF	NMF
Book Value/Share %	—	—	—	—
Dividends/Share %	NMF	NMF	NMF	NMF

Sales performance has been strong in 2002, and with hip and knee replacements as primary growth drivers, we expect full-year sales growth near the top of the industry at 14%-15%. Net income should also continue on a strong upward trend.

Profitability [A+]	1999	2000	2001	TTM
Return on Assets %	24.8	29.5	20.1	26.5
Oper Cash Flow $Mil	180	232	172	189
- Cap Spending $Mil	33	29	55	40
= Free Cash Flow $Mil	147	203	117	149

Excluding separation costs incurred in 2001, Zimmer's gross, operating, and net margins have been among the best in the pure-play orthopedic business. With selling and administration expenses declining, we expect operating margins to improve.

Financial Health [B+]	1999	2000	2001	09-02
Long-term Debt $Mil	0	0	214	99
Total Equity $Mil	391	261	79	286
Debt/Equity Ratio	0.0	0.0	2.7	0.3

Zimmer's debt has come down from the 4.6 debt/equity ratio immediately following the spin-off from Bristol. The company still has more than $250 million in debt, but it generates plenty of cash flow to cover its interest expense.

Industry Medical Equipment	Investment Style Large Growth	Stock Type Classic Growth	Sector Healthcare

Competition	Market Cap $Mil	Debt/ Equity	12 Mo Trailing Sales $Mil	Price/Cash Flow	Return On Assets%	Total Return% 1 Yr	3 Yr
Zimmer Holdings	8,092	0.3	1,314	42.9	26.5	36.0	—
Johnson & Johnson	159,452	0.1	35,120	18.0	16.3	-7.9	8.0
Stryker	13,276	0.4	2,892	26.3	11.6	15.2	25.9

Price Volatility

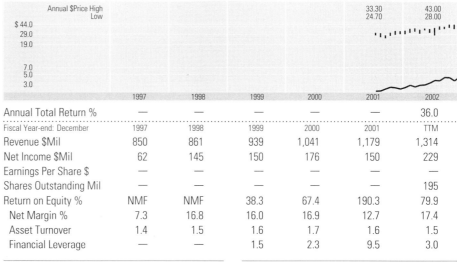

Monthly Price High/Low — Relative Strength to S&P 500

	1997	1998	1999	2000	2001	2002
Annual Total Return %	—	—	—	—	—	36.0

Fiscal Year-end: December	1997	1998	1999	2000	2001	TTM
Revenue $Mil	850	861	939	1,041	1,179	1,314
Net Income $Mil	62	145	150	176	150	229
Earnings Per Share $	—	—	—	—	—	—
Shares Outstanding Mil	—	—	—	—	—	195
Return on Equity %	NMF	NMF	38.3	67.4	190.3	79.9
Net Margin %	7.3	16.8	16.0	16.9	12.7	17.4
Asset Turnover	1.4	1.5	1.6	1.7	1.6	1.5
Financial Leverage	—	—	1.5	2.3	9.5	3.0

Valuation Ratios	Stock	Rel to Industry	Rel to S&P 500
Price/Earnings	—	—	—
Price/Book	28.3	4.3	8.8
Price/Sales	6.2	1.3	3.1
Price/Cash Flow	42.9	1.7	3.2

Major Fund Holders	% of Fund Assets
PF INVESCO Health Sciences A	3.46
Chesapeake Growth Instl	3.40
ASAF INVESCO Health Sciences A	3.13
Strong Advisor Technology A	2.95

Morningstar's Take By Jill Kiersky, 11-25-2002 Stock Price as of Analysis: $37.50

Since regaining its independence from Bristol-Myers Squibb, Zimmer is like a bird released from its cage. We would watch what we pay for its stock, though, because excitement over top- and bottom-line growth sent the price past our fair value estimate.

Zimmer competes in an attractive industry dominated by a handful of large orthopedic device firms. Growth prospects are good because of the aging population, technological innovations, and a more favorable reimbursement profile that leads to high prices and hefty margins. Since people continue to need hip and knee replacements and there's no real substitute for the full-blown procedure, device makers are somewhat shielded when the economy sours.

Zimmer's pricing power and shift to higher-margin products boosted sales 15.6% in the first nine months of 2002, compared with 13.2% in the year-ago period. Zimmer wavers between the number-two and number-one spot (which it shares with Johnson & Johnson's DePuy division) for total knee replacements with 27% share. Knee products represent the largest segment of the U.S. reconstructive device market at $1.6 billion, and demand is expected to increase 10%-12% annually. The company's minimally invasive knee surgery

products--which reduce operating and patient recovery time--strengthen its share of the market.

Without Bristol, Zimmer can plow its positive cash flow back into the company rather than have it snatched away for Bristol's drug development. It has the opportunity to expand its scope of products from mainstream devices like knees and hips to newer high-growth, high-margin areas like spinal devices, arthroscopy, and orthobiologics (combining medical devices with biologic drugs)--markets where its closest competitor, Biomet, already plays.

But since Zimmer hasn't proved its capabilities in these markets and its business is about to take on more risk, we can't give it the same credit in the form of higher margins that we give Biomet. Furthermore, Zimmer has to be smart in determining whether to acquire the capabilities or build them in-house. Either way, its investments will take on risks like possible development and regulatory failures or a costly acquisition that steals management's attention and focus.

While we believe Zimmer will remain a dominant player in the orthopedic device market, we'd like to see some margin of safety before we think the shares would be worth the risk.

Zions Bancorporation ZION

	Rating	Risk	Moat Size	Fair Value	Last Close	Yield %
	★★★	Med.	Narrow	$40.00	$39.35	2.0

Company Profile

Salt Lake City-based Zions Bancorporation is the holding company for bank subsidiaries that operate 362 banking offices in Utah, Idaho, Washington, Nevada, California, Arizona, New Mexico, and Colorado. The banks provide automated-teller, computer-banking, and trust services. The banks also make real-estate, business, and consumer loans. Real-estate loans account for approximately 67% of the company's loan portfolio. The company's nonbank subsidiaries provide mortgage-banking, discount-brokerage, and insurance services.

Management

President and CEO Harris Simmons has led Zions since 1990, when he took over from his father, who led the 1960 buyout of the bank from the Mormon Church. CFO Doyle Arnold recently joined the bank from Bank of America.

Strategy

Zions wants to be the premier banking company in the Western United States. It has grown by acquiring small community banks at reasonable prices. Although few purchases have taken place this year, growth by acquisition remains at the core of the bank's strategy. In addition to looking to expand its market share in its current states, the bank may enter other Western states.

One South Main
Salt Lake City, UT 84111   www.zionsbancorporation.com

Morningstar Grades

Growth [B]	1998	1999	2000	2001
Revenue %	43.3	31.5	16.7	4.8
Earnings/Share %	-8.9	29.1	-17.7	65.1
Book Value/Share %	41.6	9.0	5.8	20.9
Dividends/Share %	14.9	33.3	23.6	-10.1

Zions has used acquisitions to increase its net profits and assets by more than 20% annually over the past five years. We are modeling low-double-digit profit growth over the next few years.

Profitability [C]	1999	2000	2001	TTM
Return on Assets %	1.0	0.7	1.2	0.9
Oper Cash Flow $Mil	22	349	843	—
- Cap Spending $Mil	94	82	92	—
= Free Cash Flow $Mil	—	—	—	—

Zions' return on assets is lower than the peer average of 1.38%. For the quarter ended September 30, however, the bank's net interest margin was a respectable 4.53%.

Financial Health [A-]	1999	2000	2001	09-02
Long-term Debt $Mil	—	—	—	—
Total Equity $Mil	1,660	1,779	2,281	2,358
Debt/Equity Ratio	—	—	—	—

Zions' leverage is in line with its peer average, and its credit quality is above average. It depends heavily on commercial real estate loans, though, which constitute about 30% of the loan and lease portfolio.

Industry	Investment Style	Stock Type	Sector
Regional Banks	▦ Mid Core	↗ Classic Growth	$ Financial Services

Competition	Market Cap $Mil	Debt/ Equity	12 Mo Trailing Sales $Mil	Price/Cash Flow	Return On Assets%	Total Return% 1 Yr	3 Yr
Zions Bancorporation	3,587	—	1,837	—	0.9	-23.9	-7.9
Wells Fargo	79,608	—	28,119	—	1.5	10.3	10.4
Bank One	42,636	—	22,444	—	1.1	-4.4	9.4

Price Volatility

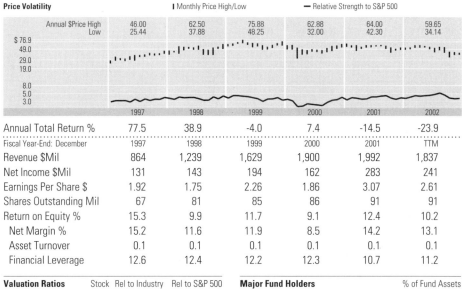

	Monthly Price High/Low		Relative Strength to S&P 500			
Annual $Price High / Low	46.00 / 25.44	62.50 / 37.88	75.88 / 48.25	62.88 / 32.00	64.00 / 42.30	59.65 / 34.14
	1997	1998	1999	2000	2001	2002
Annual Total Return %	77.5	38.9	-4.0	7.4	-14.5	-23.9

Fiscal Year-End: December	1997	1998	1999	2000	2001	TTM
Revenue $Mil	864	1,239	1,629	1,900	1,992	1,837
Net Income $Mil	131	143	194	162	283	241
Earnings Per Share $	1.92	1.75	2.26	1.86	3.07	2.61
Shares Outstanding Mil	67	81	85	86	91	91
Return on Equity %	15.3	9.9	11.7	9.1	12.4	10.2
Net Margin %	15.2	11.6	11.9	8.5	14.2	13.1
Asset Turnover	0.1	0.1	0.1	0.1	0.1	0.1
Financial Leverage	12.6	12.4	12.2	12.3	10.7	11.2

Valuation Ratios	Stock	Rel to Industry	Rel to S&P 500
Price/Earnings	15.1	1.1	0.6
Price/Book	1.5	0.7	0.5
Price/Sales	2.0	0.9	1.0
Price/Cash Flow	—	—	—

Major Fund Holders	% of Fund Assets
Rochdale Alpha	5.41
Barrett Growth	3.43
AIM Global Financial Services A	2.76
AIM Mid Cap Basic Value A	2.68

Morningstar's Take   By Matthew Scholz, 10-29-2002   Stock Price as of Analysis: $39.63

Zions is a broken growth story. Our fair value estimate is $40, about where the stock trades now.

The company and the stock grew at above-average rates during the 1990s, reflecting management's success in snapping up small community banks at reasonable prices. But trouble began in 2000, when Zions attempted to merge with its Utah rival, First Security. Another suitor--Western banking giant Wells Fargo--ultimately purchased First Security in a transaction that cost Zions not only an opportunity, but $97 million in a special impairment loss on First Security stock for fiscal 2001.

There are few bargains left among the small community banks that are Zions' traditional acquisition quarry. Not only has part of Zions' acquisition currency--its stock--declined in appeal, but the owners of many small banks still expect to bag the large acquisition premiums of 3-4 times book value that prevailed in 1997 and 1998.

The slowed rate of acquisitions highlights a crucial problem: Zions isn't an efficient operator. Asset turnover has averaged less than 5% over the past five years. Return on equity, which will be about 12% this year, is below the peer average of around 16%. The main cause of this low ROE is a high expense level that hinders bottom-line growth.

Management's investments in new businesses, like venture capital, have been a drag on earnings. Zions' goal of maintaining six separate regional bank subsidiaries has also inflated the company's cost structure. While a decentralized strategy has benefits, the duplicative layers of management and different technology systems that result have raised the cost of doing business. For the nine months ending September 30, Zions' efficiency ratio was about 60%, compared with 50%-55% for its regional banking peers. The firm has announced an initiative to curtail noninterest expenses by approximately $50 million per year, but since a majority of these cost savings will come from the sale or restructuring of its e-commerce ventures, we don't think this target is sufficiently aggressive.

Although we don't find Zions a compelling investment now, there are reasons to keep an eye on the firm. Besides its attractive footprint, the bank has a strong credit culture, and nearly 80% of the funding for Zions' loans and leases comes from the relatively stable and inexpensive deposits generated by its branch network.

MORNINGSTAR® Stocks 500

User's Guide

This section contains a glossary of investment terms. It explains how to use the data found in this publication to make better investment decisions.

User's Guide

% Annual Change
This number shows a company's year-on-year growth in a given measure, such as sales per quarter or earnings/share per quarter.

% Closely Held
see Closely Held %

% Fund Ownership
see Fund Ownership %

% of Fund Assets
In the context of the Major Fund Holders table, this number tells what percentage of each fund's assets is invested in this particular stock.

+/– Benchmark
The amount, in percentage points, by which a fund or stock has outperformed or under-performed a benchmark (such as the S&P 500) for a given time period. For example, 8% in the +/– Benchmark column means the stock has outperformed the benchmark by eight percentage points for that period.

12-Month Trailing Sales
A company's sales over the most recent four quarters.

1-Year Total Return
A stock's total return (including capital gains and dividends) from one year ago to the present.

3-Yr Avg Return %
see Average Return

52-Week High
The highest price the stock has reached over the trailing 52 weeks. If this price is much higher than the stock's current price, it generally means the stock has run into problems.

52-Week Low
The lowest price the stock has reached over the trailing 52 weeks. If this price is much lower than the stock's current price, it means that the stock has done very well recently.

5-Year High
The highest price the stock has reached over the past five years, adjusted for splits.

5-Year Low
The lowest price the stock has reached over the past five years, adjusted for splits.

5-Yr Avg Return %
see Average Return

90-Day Treasury Bill
see U.S. 90-Day Treasury Bill

A

Aggressive Growth
Aggressive-growth companies have shown very strong growth in both revenue and earnings. The requirement for high sales growth limits this type to companies that are garnering most of their earnings growth from increasing revenues, unlike the mixture of operational improvements and organic growth that drives most classic-growth companies.

Asset Turnover
Asset turnover is equal to total revenue divided by total assets. It measures a company's efficiency, or how many dollars of revenue it generates for each dollar of assets. Like most financial ratios, asset turnover can vary greatly across industries, so it's often more useful to compare a company to its peers than to the market as a whole. For example, grocery stores have high asset turnover, because they sell high volumes of low-priced goods.

Assets
All company-owned resources that are expected to provide benefits to that company's business. Total assets, as with other balance-sheet items, are shown in millions of dollars and are current as of the last day of the specified reporting period.

Average Daily Volume
Average daily volume is the average number of shares of a stock that have been traded per day over the previous 12 months. It's a rough gauge of a stock's popularity in the market.

Average Fund Rating

The weighted average Morningstar Rating (star rating) of mutual funds that have reported owning shares of the stock.

Average Fund Style Box

The weighted average style box of mutual funds that hold the stock.

Average Return

The annualized return of the stock, including both capital gains and dividends, over a multiyear period such as three or five years. This represents the annual return an investor would have received if the stock's returns were evenly spread across the time period.

Average Shares Outstanding

see Shares Outstanding

B

Balance Sheet

The purpose of a balance sheet is to tell how much a company owns (its assets), how much it owes (its liabilities), and the difference between the two (its equity), which represents the part of the company owned by shareholders. The basic equation underlying a balance sheet is:

Assets – Liabilities = Equity, which can also be expressed as:
Assets = Liabilities + Equity

Bear Market

A bear market is a period when stock prices fall and investors are pessimistic. Bear markets usually aren't labeled as such until stock prices have slipped by 15%. The opposite of a bear market is a bull market.

Book Value

Book value is another name for equity or net worth. It's equal to total assets minus total liabilities.

Book Value/Share

Book value/share is equal to book value (also known as equity or net worth) divided by shares outstanding. It's a handy way to see how much equity is represented by each share of stock.

Book Value/Share % Growth

Growth in book value per share (also known as equity per share) is one of the key variables in determining whether a company is increasing shareholder wealth over time. It typically comes from two sources: retained earnings (earnings the company does not pay out as dividends) and new share issuances. Young, capital-hungry companies typically achieve high equity/share growth through the second method by issuing shares.

Bull Market

A bull market is a period when stock prices rise and investors are optimistic. The opposite of a bull market is a bear market.

Business Risk

Business risk is the danger that a company you've invested in may run into trouble. Large, well-established companies (such as General Electric) tend to have less business risk than smaller, younger companies (such as Amazon.com).

C

Capital Gains

A capital gain is an investment gain resulting from a rise in a stock's price. (Conversely, capital losses result from a fall in a stock's price.) Capital gains (or losses) and dividend income are the two components of a stock's total return.

Capital Spending

Capital spending, also known as capital expenditures, is money invested in the future growth of a business. It includes spending on property, plants, and equipment, as well as on intellectual properties such as software, trademarks, and patents.

Cash Flow

Cash flow represents the amount of cash a company generates. It's similar to net income (earnings), except that cash flow excludes any noncash items. This can make a big difference in industries such as cable TV, where many companies have heavy depreciation charges that depress earnings but don't affect cash flow.

Cash Flow From Operations

Cash flow from operations is the cash flow a company generates from the day-to-day operation of its business. It can be found in a company's cash-flow statement. The other two types of cash flow found on this statement are cash flow from investing activities (such as capital spending) and from financing activities (such as issuing stock).

Cash Return %

Cash return equals free cash flow divided by the company's "enterprise value," or market capitalization plus net debt. It tells you how much free cash flow a company is generating for each dollar of the company's value, and is thus more directly useful than raw free cash flow. It can be directly compared with other return measures, such as the return on a 10-year Treasury bond or dividend yield.

Classic Growth

Classic-growth is one of the eight Morningstar stock types. Classic-growth companies have shown good but not spectacular growth in both revenue and earnings, and they usually pay a dividend. They're growing slower than aggressive-growth companies, but faster than slow-growth or high-yield companies.

Closely Held %

This number tells you what percentage of a stock's shares are held by individuals or corporations associated with the company, which can give you a good idea how volatile that stock is likely to be. If a large percentage of a company's stock is closely held (say, 80% to 90%), that means there isn't a big supply available for the public to buy. If demand outstrips this limited supply, the price can shoot up quickly; if that demand dries up, the price can plunge just as fast.

Common Size

A common-size balance sheet expresses each item as a percentage of assets, rather than as a raw number. Similarly, a common-size income statement expresses each item as a percentage of sales. This method allows two or more companies of very different sizes to be compared more easily.

Company Profile

This is a description of the company's main business operations. It is written using information taken from the company's annual reports, and updated as necessary by the analyst covering the company.

Company Name

A shortened version of the company's legal name.

Competition

This table lists a company's most important competitors.

Consumer Price Index

This index measures the price of a fixed basket of consumer goods in the U.S., and is commonly used to measure inflation. It is released monthly by the Bureau of Labor Statistics in the U.S. Department of Labor.

Credit Suisse First Boston High Yield Index

This index measures the value of a wide selection of high-yield bonds. It is often used as a benchmark for high-yield bonds and funds.

Current Assets

Current assets include cash plus any assets that a company expects to convert to cash within a year, such as short-term investments, accounts receivable, and inventories. It doesn't mean much in isolation, but in comparison with current liabilities (see Current Ratio) it's a good measure of a company's short-term liquidity.

Current Liabilities

Current liabilities are liabilities that a company expects to pay within a year, such as short-term debt, accounts payable, and interest payable. It doesn't mean much in isolation, but in comparison with current assets (see Current Ratio) it's a good measure of a company's short-term liquidity.

Current Ratio

Current ratio, equal to current assets divided by current liabilities, is a measure of a company's liquidity and ability to meet its short-term obligations. A high current ratio is generally good, because it means that the company has plenty of liquid assets to work with. However, companies with low inventories and reliable cash flow can afford to operate with lower current ratios than riskier companies can.

Cyclical

Cyclical is one of the eight Morningstar stock types. Companies of this type are in businesses that generally fluctuate in line with the overall economy, such as automakers and construction-equipment makers. In a booming economy, such companies often make fat profits, but in a recession, their growth stalls and they may even lose money.

D

Debt %

The percentage of the company's long-term capital that is composed of long-term debt. For nonfinancial companies, it is derived by dividing the total long-term debt by the sum of total shareholders' equity and total long-term debt and multiplying by 100. For financial companies, the calculation is:

[Total Assets - (Equity + Preferreds)]/Total Assets = Debt %

Debt Leverage

see Financial Leverage

Debt/Total Capital

Debt to total capitalization equals long-term debt divided by total capitalization (market cap plus long-term debt). It shows how much long-term debt the company uses as a percentage of its total long-term capital; the higher the number, the more a company has leveraged its capital structure with debt.

Debt/Equity Ratio

Debt/equity ratio equals long-term debt divided by shareholders' equity (also known as net worth or book value). A company with a high debt/equity ratio is riskier than one with a low debt/equity ratio, since interest on long-term debt is a fixed cost that must be paid regardless of how well the business is doing.

Depreciation & Amortization

Depreciation and amortization are noncash charges taken against a company's profits for the deterioration of an asset's value over its useful life. Depreciation refers to the reduction in value of a tangible asset (such as a factory), and amortization refers to the reduction in value of an intangible asset (such as goodwill).

Direct Investment

Some companies have direct investment plans which allow investors to purchase shares directly from the company, without a broker or other intermediary. Such plans are often combined with DRIPs (dividend reinvestment plans).

Distressed

Distressed is one of the eight Morningstar stock types. Companies of this type have run into significant operational problems, and often have negative earnings or cash flow. Companies that have filed for bankruptcy also fall into this type. However, companies whose revenues are growing faster than 50% are not considered distressed even if they're losing money; instead, they're classified as speculative growth.

Dividend

A dividend is a portion of a company's profit that it pays directly to shareholders, generally expressed in a per-share amount. The raw dollar amount of a company's dividend generally doesn't mean a lot except in comparison with its stock price (dividend yield) or its earnings per share (payout ratio). Many fast-growing companies pay no dividend, preferring to invest all of their profits back into the company.

Dividends/Share % Growth

Also known simply as dividend growth, this figure tells you the percentage change in a company's dividend for a given year (or the annualized change, for periods longer than one year). If a company's dividend has been growing steadily, that's generally a sign that the company is healthy and management has confidence in its prospects. Conversely, a falling dividend (indicated by a negative dividend growth rate) is usually a sign that the company is having financial troubles.

Dividend Yield

Dividend yield is a stock's dividend per share divided by price per share. Companies with a high dividend yield tend to be profitable but slow-growing, and they tend to be in such industries as tobacco and REITs. Companies that pay no dividend at all, including most technology companies, have a dividend yield of zero.

Dow Jones Industrial Average

The Dow Jones Industrial Average, or Dow, is the most widely known stock-market index. The 30 companies in the index are selected by the editors of *The Wall Street Journal*. Their prices are added together and divided by a divisor that changes when a new company replaces an old one in the index, or when any company in the index splits its stock. The Dow isn't as accurate a measure of the market as the S&P 500 or the Wilshire 5000, but it's still popular because it's been around so long and the companies in it are so well known.

Dow Jones Transportation Average

This index measures the value of 20 stocks in the airline, railroad, trucking, and shipping industries. Like the better-known Dow Jones Industrial Average, it is price-weighted, meaning it is based on the prices of the individual stocks, rather than their market capitalizations.

Dow Jones Utility Average

This index measures the value of 15 gas- and electric-utility stocks. Like the better-known Dow Jones Industrial Average, it is price-weighted, meaning it is based on the prices of the individual stocks, rather than their market capitalizations.

DRIP (Dividend Reinvestment Plan)

Dividend reinvestment plans, or DRIPs, allow stock investors to have their dividends automatically reinvested in shares of stock. Such plans can be handy for long-term investors who don't care about getting short-term income from dividends. Companies with DRIPs may also be good choices for beginning investors who are just starting to buy stocks, since they're generally well-established companies.

E

Earnings Per Share (EPS)

Earnings per share (EPS) tells you how much profit a company has made per share within a given period. It's a fairly arbitrary number by itself, since the company can control the number of shares outstanding through splits and buybacks. But comparing a company's most recent EPS to its EPS in previous years and quarters (adjusted for any splits) is one of the most common ways of telling how fast the company's profits are growing.

Earnings/Share Per Quarter

This shows a company's earnings per share (EPS) in each of the past four quarters, along with its year-on-year EPS growth in each of these quarters.

Earnings/Share % Growth

see EPS Growth

Earnings Growth

see Net Income Growth

EBITDA

EBITDA (earnings before interest, taxes, depreciation, and amortization) is often used instead of net income by companies with heavy depreciation charges on their income statement. Investors should always look at EBITDA with caution, because it's not officially sanctioned by the nation's accounting rules, and there's no standard way of figuring it. Still, it can be a useful number to know in conjunction with—but not in place of—reported net income.

ELB (Exceeds Lower Boundary)

If you see ELB in place of data, it means that the data that are available are too low to be meaningful.

EPS (Continuing Operations)

This number is the company's earnings per share from the day-to-day operations of its business, excluding discontinued operations, extraordinary items, and accounting changes.

EPS Growth

EPS growth represents the percentage growth in a company's earnings per share (EPS) over a certain period, usually a quarter or a year, compared to the same period a year earlier. EPS growth is more directly relevant for shareholders than net income growth because it expresses this growth on a per-share basis.

Equity

Sometimes "equity" means "stock", as in the term "equity mutual fund." In accounting terms, equity (also known as book value, net worth, or shareholders' equity) is equal to total assets minus total liabilities. It tells you what part of a company is owned by its shareholders, and represents (very roughly) the break-up value of the company: If the company were to sell off all its assets and use the money to pay off all its liabilities, total equity is the amount of cash that would be left over.

Equity %

The percentage of the company's long-term capital that is composed of equity, including retained earnings and total shareholder investment in the company.

Equity/Share % Growth

see Book Value/Share % Growth

EUB (Exceeds Upper Boundary)

If you see EUB in place of data, it means that the data that are available are too high to be meaningful.

Exchange

Most stocks are traded on an exchange, the two biggest being the New York Stock Exchange and the Nasdaq. The American Stock Exchange (AMEX) used to be the main alternative to the NYSE, but now it only lists small- and mid-cap stocks, and gets most of its business from trading options and similar financial instruments. Stocks that are not traded on any exchange are called "over-the-counter" stocks, and they tend to be much riskier and more volatile than listed stocks.

F

Fair Value

Morningstar analysts estimate a stock's fair value using a discounted cash flow model which takes into account their estimates of the company's growth, profitability, riskiness, and many other factors over the next five years. This fair value is then compared with the stock's market price to figure its Morningstar Rating.

Financial Health Grade

Financial health is one of the three grades that Morningstar assigns to each stock as a quick way to get a handle on its fundamentals. To get a good grade in this area, a company should have low financial leverage (assets/equity), high cash-flow coverage (total cash flow/long-term debt), and a high cash position (cash/assets) relative to its sector. Also, companies with improving financial health are rewarded, while those with deteriorating health are punished.

Financial Leverage

Financial leverage, equal to total assets divided by total equity, measures the extent to which a company's assets are financed by debt. A company with high financial leverage is generally risky, but industries vary in their average financial leverage, so it's a good idea to compare a company with its peers rather than the market as a whole. Financial companies, for example, inherently have much higher financial leverage than other companies.

First Boston High Yield Index

see Credit Suisse First Boston High Yield Index

Fiscal Year

A company's fiscal year (used for accounting purposes) is often, but not necessarily, the same as the calendar year. Some companies have fiscal years ending in March, June, or September rather than December, and many retailers have fiscal years ending in January, after the holiday season has ended.

Fiscal Year End

The month in which a company's fiscal year ends. This date can differ from December 31, the end of the calendar year.

Five-Year High

see 5-Year High

Five-Year Low

see 5-Year Low

Float

Float is the percentage of a stock's shares outstanding that are not held by individuals and corporations closely associated with the company. It can give you a good idea how volatile that stock is likely to be. If a company's float is small, say 10%-20%, that means there isn't a big supply available for the public to buy. If demand outstrips this limited supply, the price can shoot up quickly; if that demand dries up, the price can plunge just as fast.

Forward P/E

Forward P/E equals price divided by Wall Street analysts' average EPS estimate for the current fiscal year. A growing company's forward P/E will typically be lower than its trailing P/E, because its forecasted earnings for the current year are generally higher than its earnings for the previous year.

Free Cash Flow

Free cash flow is equal to operating cash flow minus capital spending, and it represents the cash a company has left over after investing in the growth of its business. Young, aggressive companies often have negative free cash flow, since they're investing heavily in their futures. As companies mature, though, they should start generating free cash flow.

Fund Ownership %

This number is the percentage of a stock's common shares owned by mutual funds. If a high percentage of a stock's shares are owned by mutual funds, this can indicate the market's overall belief in the value of the stock. Conversely, a low percentage of fund ownership can indicate that the stock hasn't yet proven itself with institutional investors, and is thus risky. Another reason this number is important is that mutual funds tend to purchase stock in large amounts, so if a significant chunk of a company's stock is owned by funds, there's less available for individual investors.

G

Goodwill

When one company buys another company, the difference between the purchase price and the book value of the company being purchased is called goodwill. Goodwill is listed as an asset on the purchasing company's balance sheet, and it generally must be depreciated, or subtracted from earnings, over a period of years.

Growth Grade

Growth is one of the three grades that Morningstar assigns to each stock as a quick way to get a handle on its fundamentals. To get a good grade in this area, a company's sales should be growing rapidly and consistently relative to its sector. Erratic or slowing growth detracts from a stock's growth grade.

H

Hard Asset

Hard asset is one of the eight Morningstar stock types. Companies of this type are in businesses that revolve around natural resources (such as metals and timber) or real estate. Such companies typically sport a low correlation with the overall stock market, and have traditionally been considered hedges against inflation.

High Yield

High yield is one of the eight Morningstar stock types. Companies of this type have dividend yields significantly higher than the average for large-cap stocks. They tend to be slow-growing companies with few opportunities for expansion, but they may be a good choice for conservative investors who want steady dividend income without a lot of risk.

I

Income

This is the portion of a stock's total return derived from dividends. Capital gains are the other component of total return.

Industry

A stock's industry tells you its primary area of business. Morningstar's industry classifications are more specific than sectors, and are useful for honing in on groups of companies that do the same thing. For example, within the hardware sector, there are such industries as optical equipment, wireless equipment, computer equipment, and semiconductors, each with its own ideosyncrasies.

Initial Public Offering (IPO)

When a company decides to sell stock in itself on the public markets, it has an initial public offering (IPO) in which its shares are sold on an exchange for the first time. Many IPOs received a lot of attention during the Internet bubble because of their stocks' rapid price appreciation. However, even in a bull market it's very difficult for ordinary investors to benefit from IPOs, because only well-placed insiders can generally buy shares at the IPO price.

Inventories

Roughly speaking, this figure represents the value of the goods that a company has manufactured (or bought wholesale) but not yet sold. Inventory growing at a faster rate than a company's assets may indicate that the firm is having trouble turning over that inventory.

Investment Style

see Style Box

IPO

see Initial Public Offering

J

JSE Gold (U.S. Dollars)
This index measures the market value of 13 gold-mining stocks traded on the Johannesburg Stock Exchange. It tends to track gold prices, and is commonly used as a benchmark for gold-related stocks and funds.

L

Last Close
The stock's most recent closing price.

Lehman Brothers Aggregate Index
This index measures the value of a wide variety of investment-grade government and corporate bonds, as well as asset-backed and mortgage-backed securities. It is widely used as a benchmark for the performance of bonds and bond funds.

Lehman Brothers Corporate Index
This index measures the value of a wide variety of U.S. corporate bonds. It is widely used as a benchmark for the performance of corporate bonds and bond funds.

Liabilities
All of a company's obligations to nonowners for cash, goods, or services in a given year. Total liabilities include current liabilities and long-term debt.

Long-Term Debt
Long-term debt is money that a company has borrowed for a period of time longer than a year. A company's long-term debt has little relevance as a raw number, but when compared with shareholders' equity (see debt/equity ratio), it's a good measure of how leveraged the company is. An excessive amount of long-term debt is dangerous, because the interest on that debt must be paid no matter how well the business is going. Also, rising long-term debt over time is a warning sign to watch out for.

M

Major Fund Holders
This table lists the mutual funds with the greatest percentage of their assets in a particular stock.

Management
A brief description of the background and experience of the company's top management.

Market Capitalization
A company's market capitalization (or market cap) is the total value of all the publicly traded stock in that company, equal to price per share times shares outstanding. It's a rough guide to a company's size, but some young companies without a lot of revenue have large market caps because the market expects them to grow rapidly. Market cap is used by Morningstar to classify stocks as small-cap, mid-cap, or large-cap.

Moat Size
An economic moat is a competitive barrier that gives a company an advantage over its rivals and allows it to generate above-average returns on invested capital. Four major types of economic moats are high customer switching costs, economies of scale, intangible assets such as brands or patents, and the network effect. Morningstar divides stocks into three categories according to moat size: wide moat (companies with the strongest competitive advantage), narrow moat (those with some competitive advantage), and no moat (those with no sustainable competitive advantage).

Morningstar Rating for Stocks
The Morningstar Rating for stocks is calculated by comparing Morningstar's assessment of a stock's fair value with the stock's current market price. The rating can range from 5 stars (for stocks trading at a substantial discount to their estimated fair value) down to 1 star (for stocks trading substantially above their fair value). The percentage discount or premium needed for a specific star rating depends on a company's moat size and risk. For example, a stock with a wide moat and low risk will get 5 stars if it's trading at a 20% discount to its fair value, but a stock with no moat and high risk would need a 60% discount to get 5 stars. On the other end, the wide-moat, low-risk stock will get 1 star if it's trading 30% or more above its fair value, while the no-moat, high-risk stock will get 1 star if it's only 10% above its fair value. Ratings can change because of a move in the stock's price, a change in the analyst's estimates of the stock's fair value, or a combination of both. If the price of a stock falls significantly below $5, we generally will not rate the stock, because the low price will make the Morningstar Rating too volatile to be meaningful.

Morningstar Risk for Stocks

Analysts score companies on each of seven different risk factors:

- How cyclical is the company's industry?
- How healthy is the company's balance sheet relative to other companies in its sector?
- How does the company's free cash flow compare with its sales?
- How sustainable is the company's operating cash flow?
- How big are the company's revenues relative to all other companies?
- How big is the company's economic moat?
- Is there some nonfinancial issue looming in the future that could materially affect the company's fortunes?

The scores are summed to produce a composite, which is translated into low, medium, and high risk. Answers to the first six questions are weighted equally, but the final question is given greater weight.

Morningstar Grades

The Morningstar stock-grading system consists of three grades, one each for growth, profitability, and financial health. They're meant to be a quick way to get a handle on a company's fundamentals. All grades are based on relative rankings of companies within their sector, based solely on the numbers. No Morningstar analyst makes a subjective call as to what grade a company should get. Within each sector for each of the three categories (growth, profitability, and financial health), we give equal numbers of companies As, Bs, Cs, and Ds, while the bottom 10% get Fs. The criteria for the individual grades are as follows:

Growth

To get a good grade in this area, a company's sales should be growing rapidly and consistently relative to its sector. Erratic or slowing growth detracts from a stock's growth grade.

Profitability

To get a good grade in this area, a company should have a high return on assets relative to its sector, and its ROA should be consistent and improving.

Financial Health

To get a good grade in this area, a company should have low financial leverage (assets/equity), high cash-flow coverage (total cash flow/long-term debt), and a high cash position (cash/assets) relative to its sector. Also, companies with improving financial health are rewarded, while those with deteriorating health are punished.

Morningstar Stock Type

Morningstar divides most stocks into eight types, each of which defines a broad category of investment characteristics. Stocks are assigned to a type based on objective financial criteria, so stocks of the same type have similar economic fundamentals. Every stock has individual idiosyncrasies, but in general, when evaluating investments, many of the same concerns and evaluation methods will apply across the stocks in one type. The eight Morningstar Stock Types are as follows:

Aggressive Growth:	These companies have shown very strong growth in both revenue and earnings.
Classic Growth:	These companies have shown good but not spectacular growth in both revenue and earnings, and they usually pay a dividend.
Cyclical:	Companies of this type are in businesses that generally fluctuate in line with the overall economy, such as automakers and construction-equipment makers.
Distressed:	Companies of this type have run into significant operational problems, and often have negative earnings and/or cash flow.
Hard Asset:	Companies of this type are in businesses that revolve around natural resources (such as metals and timber) or real estate, which typically have a low correlation with the overall stock market.
High Yield:	Companies of this type have dividend yields significantly higher than the average for large-cap stocks.
Slow Growth:	Companies of this type have shown slow revenue growth (slower than the general economy) and slow earnings growth over the past three years.
Speculative Growth:	Companies of this type have shown very strong revenue growth, but slower or spotty earnings growth; they tend to be young companies that haven't yet started generating consistent earnings.

Morningstar Style Box (Stocks)

Comparable with the equity style box found in Morningstar's mutual fund products, this is a visual tool that can give a general idea of a stock's size and riskiness. The nine-box matrix displays a stock's market capitalization in relation to its price multiples. Along the vertical axis of the box, Morningstar categorizes the stocks by market capitalization. Large-cap stocks make up the top 70% of the U.S. market's total market value, mid-cap stocks make up another 20%, and the rest are small-cap stocks. (Because some large-caps are so huge, there are actually many fewer large-caps than small-caps.) Along the horizontal axis, each stock is categorized as growth, core, or value. The category a given stock fall into depends on two components: a growth score, based partly on projected earnings growth and partly on historical growth in sales, earnings, cash flow, and book value; and a value score, based partly on the stock's P/E ratio and partly on its price/book, price/sales, and price/cash flow ratios. The value score is subtracted from the growth score to get an overall score, which determines the stock's category.

Morningstar's Take

Morningstar's Take gives our analyst's opinion of a stock, supported with an explanation of the company's strengths and weaknesses.

MSCI EAFE

Maintained by Morgan Stanley Capital International, this index measures the combined market value of a selected group of stocks from Europe, Australasia, and the Far East. It is one of the most commonly used benchmarks for international stocks.

MSCI Emerging Markets

Maintained by Morgan Stanley Capital International, this index measures the combined market value of a selected group of stocks from 26 emerging markets, including Latin America, Eastern Europe, and most of Asia except for Japan and Australia. It is commonly used as a benchmark for emerging-market funds and stocks.

MSCI Europe

Maintained by Morgan Stanley Capital International, this index measures the combined market value of a selected group of stocks from 16 West European countries. It is commonly used as a benchmark for European stocks.

MSCI Latin America

Maintained by Morgan Stanley Capital International, this index measures the combined market value of a selected group of stocks from seven Latin American countries. It is commonly used as a benchmark for Latin American stocks.

MSCI Pacific

Maintained by Morgan Stanley Capital International, this index measures the combined market value of a selected group of stocks from Pacific Rim countries, including Japan. It is commonly used as a benchmark for Pacific Rim stocks.

MSCI World

Maintained by Morgan Stanley Capital International, this index measures the combined market value of the stocks in all of MSCI's international indexes. It is commonly used as a benchmark for non-U.S. stocks.

N

Nasdaq Composite

The Nasdaq Composite measures the cumulative market cap of all the stocks traded on the Nasdaq stock market exchange. Since the Nasdaq exchange is heavily weighted with technology stocks, the Nasdaq Composite is often used as a proxy for the performance of the technology sector.

Net Income

Net income, also known as earnings, measures how much profit a company has earned within a given period. Declining net income is generally a sign of trouble, while rising net income is a sign of growth. Remember also that net income includes all charges and credits, including noncash charges such as depreciation and merger writeoffs. For companies in some industries, such as cable TV, EBITDA and operating income are used more often than net income.

Net Income Growth

Net income growth represents the percentage growth in a company's net income over a certain period, usually a quarter or a year, compared with the same period a year earlier. By comparing net income growth with revenue growth, you can see whether a company has been able to translate increased revenues into increase profits.

Net Margin

Net margin, equal to net income divided by revenue, is the most common measure of profitability. Be sure to look at it in context, though; some industries (such as grocery stores) inherently have low net margins, while others (such as software) have the potential for much bigger net margins.

Net Worth

Also known as shareholder's equity or book value, net worth is the difference between total assets and total liabilities.

NMF (Not Meaningful)

If you see NMF in place of data, it means that the data that are available are not meaningful.

Noncurrent Assets

Noncurrent assets are those that the company expects to keep for more than one year. They include plants and equipment, long-term investments, goodwill and other intangibles, and deferred costs. Noncurrent assets plus current assets equals total assets.

Noncurrent Liabilities

Noncurrent liabilities are the flip side of noncurrent assets; they represent money the company owes, but not until one year or more in the future. Though a variety of line items can appear under this heading, the most important one by far is long-term debt. In fact, noncurrent liabilities can be used in a pinch as a proxy for a company's long-term debt.

O

Operating Cash Flow

Operating cash flow adds depreciation and other noncash charges back into net income to tell you how much actual cash a company has generated from its day-to-day operations. It's similar to EBITDA, except that it includes interest and taxes. Like EBITDA, operating cash flow is favored by many companies with heavy depreciation charges, such as cable companies and many entertainment companies. However, cash flow should only be used as a supplement to net income, and not as a substitute for it.

Over-the-Counter Stocks

Over-the-counter stocks aren't traded on an exchange. Usually they are issued by smaller companies, are traded less often, and are riskier than other stocks. Brokers deal directly with other brokers to buy and sell over-the-counter stocks.

P

P/E Ratio

see Price/Earnings Ratio

Payout Ratio

Payout ratio is dividends per share divided by earnings per share, expressed as a percentage. The higher a company's payout ratio, the more of its earnings it pays out as dividends. Companies with high payout ratios tend to be mature, slow-growing companies without a lot of expansion opportunities, while those with low payout ratios tend to be younger companies with more growth potential.

PEG Payback

The PEG payback period represents the number of years it would take for a company's cumulative earnings to equal its stock price, given the company's earnings growth rate and its P/E. The longer the PEG payback period, the more expensive the stock is.

PEG Ratio

A stock's PEG ratio is its forward P/E divided by its projected five-year EPS growth. It tells how much investors are paying for a company's growth, and some people use PEG as a way to find growing companies that are undervalued by the market. However, PEG means little in isolation, so it's a good idea to compare a given company's PEG with those of similar companies in its industry.

Preferred Stock

Preferred stock is a class of stock that pays a set dividend that is often higher than the dividend of common stock. Preferred-stock shareholders are paid before common-stock shareholders if the company liquidates or declares bankruptcy, but they usually don't get to vote on company business decisions.

Price Range

The highest and lowest prices a stock has achieved during a certain period (such as a month, a year, or five years). A large range means that the stock has been volatile.

Price Volatility

The degree to which a stock's price has risen and fallen over a period of time. A price graph, such as those on Morningstar Stocks 500 pages, is a good way to get a quick idea of a stock's price volatility.

Price/Book Ratio

Price/book ratio is stock price divided by book value per share (or, alternately, market cap divided by total book value). It used to be one of the most popular valuation measures behind P/E, but it has lost some of that popularity recently. That's because book value only measures tangible assets that show up on a balance sheet, but the value of many technology companies comes primarily from their people and ideas.

Price/Cash Flow Ratio

Price/cash flow ratio equals stock price divided by annual operating cash flow per share (or, alternately, market cap divided by total annual operating cash flow). It can be an especially useful valuation measure for comparing stocks in industries that typically have a lot of depreciation charges, such as the cable industry, or for valuing foreign stocks, because cash flow minimizes the effect of accounting differences.

Price/Earnings Ratio (P/E)

Price/earnings ratio, or P/E, equals stock price divided by earnings per share (or, alternately, market cap divided by net income). It's the most common valuation measure for stocks, since it shows how much investors are willing to pay for a dollar of a company's earnings. However, like any valuation measure, P/E should be looked at in the context of a company's industry and the broader market.

Price/Sales Ratio

Price/sales ratio equals stock price divided by annual sales per share (or, alternately, market cap divided by total annual sales). It can often be a useful alternative to P/E when a company's earnings are negative or temporarily depressed; thus, it's commonly used to value younger companies with no earnings.

Profitability Grade

Profitability is one of the three grades that Morningstar assigns to each stock as a quick way to get a handle on its fundamentals. To get a good grade in this area, a company should have a high return on assets relative to its sector, and its ROA should be consistent and improving.

Projected Five-Year EPS Growth %

The average annualized earnings growth that Wall Street analysts are predicting for the company over the next five years. This number is used to calculate forward P/E.

Q

Quick Ratio

The quick ratio measures a company's balance-sheet liquidity, and is equal to current assets minus inventory, divided by current liabilities.

R

Rating

see Morningstar Rating for Stocks

Relative Strength

Relative strength measures the price return of a stock versus that of the S&P 500 index — the higher the relative-strength figure, the better the stock has performed versus the index. On a price graph, if the stock's line is above the index line, it indicates positive relative strength, while a line below the index line indicates negative relative strength.

Return on Equity

Return on equity (ROE) is a financial ratio that measures a firm's return on shareholder investment (the shareholder's equity or the net worth of the company). ROE is a useful gauge in determining how efficiently a company is using the shareholder's investment. Unlike return on assets, it considers the amount and cost of debt.

Return on Assets %

Return on assets (ROA), equal to net income divided by total assets, shows how much profit a company generates on its asset base. It differs from return on equity (ROE) in that a company can boost its ROE by taking on more debt, but the same strategy will not affect ROA. Another way to calculate ROA is net margin times asset turnover.

Revenue

Revenue is a measure of how much money a company has brought in within a given period. It's most useful in the context of revenue figures for previous years and quarters, but total revenue by itself is one common way to measure the size of a company. Remember, though, that just pulling in revenue is not enough for a company; it needs to make a profit in order to survive in the long term.

Revenue % Growth

Revenue growth represents the percentage growth in a company's revenue over a certain period, usually a quarter or a year, compared with the same period a year earlier. High growth is usually desirable, but if a rapidly growing company is losing lots of money (like many Internet companies), it can grow itself out of business.

Risk Measure

see Morningstar Risk for Stocks

ROA

see Return on Assets

ROE

see Return on Equity

Russell 2000

The Russell 2000, updated annually by the Frank Russell Company, is the most commonly used benchmark for measuring the performance of small-cap stocks. It consists of 1,001st through 3,000th largest companies in the U.S. in terms of market cap.

Russell 2000 Value

This index measures the performance of companies in the Russell 2000 with relatively low price/book ratios and projected growth rates. It is used as a benchmark for small-cap value stocks.

Russell 2000 Growth

This index measures the performance of companies in the Russell 2000 with relatively high price/book ratios and projected growth rates. It is used as a benchmark for small-cap growth stocks.

Russell Midcap Value

This index measures the performance of companies ranked 201st through 1,000th in terms of market cap, with relatively low price/book ratios and forecasted growth rates. It is used as a benchmark for mid-cap value stocks.

Russell Midcap Growth

This index measures the performance of companies ranked 201st through 1,000th in terms of market cap, with relatively high price/book ratios and forecasted growth rates. It is used as a benchmark for mid-cap growth stocks.

Russell Top 200 Value

This index measures the performance of the 200 largest U.S. companies in terms of market cap, with relatively low price/book ratios and forecasted growth rates. It is used as a benchmark for large-cap value stocks.

Russell Top 200 Growth

This index measures the performance of the 200 largest U.S. companies in terms of market cap, with relatively low price/book ratios and forecasted growth rates. It is used as a benchmark for large-cap value stocks.

S

Sales

Also known as revenue, this number includes all money a company has taken in from the sale of goods or services. With the exception of banks and some other financial companies, interest income is not included in sales.

Sales per Employee

This ratio is equal to sales over the trailing 12 months divided by the number of employees. It provides a rough guide to how efficiently a company is using its human capital.

Sales per Quarter

This table lists a company's sales in each of the past four quarters, with its year-on-year revenue growth in each of these quarters.

Sector

Morningstar divides stocks into 12 sectors according to their primary business, grouped into three larger "super-sectors". The Software, Hardware, Telecom, and Media sectors make up the Information group; Health Care, Consumer Services, Business Services, and Financial Services make up the Service group; and Consumer Goods, Industrial Materials, Energy, and Utilities make up the Manufacturing group. Since sectors can differ greatly in their characteristics, comparing a stock with its sector rather than the market as a whole is generally a better way of putting it in the proper context.

Sector Risk

The danger that the stock of many of the companies in one sector (like health care or technology) will fall in price at the same time because of an event that affects the entire industry.

Shareholder's Equity

Also known as net worth or book value, shareholder's equity is the difference between total assets and total liabilities.

Shares Outstanding

This number is the average number of shares a public company had on the market during a certain period of time, usually a quarter or a year. It's used to calculate earnings per share and other per-share numbers.

Slow Growth

Slow growth is one of the eight Morningstar stock types. Companies of this type have shown slow revenue growth (slower than the general economy) and slow earnings growth over the past three years. They tend to be older companies with few opportunities for expansion, but without the high dividend yields sported by high-yield companies.

Speculative Growth

Speculative growth is one of the eight Morningstar stock types. Companies of this type have shown very strong revenue growth, but slower or spotty earnings growth; they tend to be young companies that haven't yet started generating consistent earnings. Companies are also classified as speculative growth if they have only recently gone public or have annual revenue less than $5 million.

S&P 400 Index

The Standard & Poor's MidCap 400 (commonly known as the S&P 400 or the S&P Midcap 400) is one of the most common indexes used to measure the performance of midsize companies, or those with market caps between $1 billion and about $5 billion.

S&P 500 Index

The Standard & Poor's 500 (commonly known as the S&P 500, or simply the S&P) is one of the most common indexes used to represent the U.S. stock market. Contrary to popular belief, it doesn't just consist of the 500 biggest U.S. companies; the members of the index are selected by the Standard & Poor's Index Committee, and range in size from small caps to large caps. However, because it's a market-cap-weighted index, the largest companies have a disproportionate influence on it.

Stock

A piece of ownership in a company. You may buy stock hoping the company will pay you a portion of its profits, or a dividend. You also hope the company will increase its earnings so your stock will become more valuable. Some classes of stock let stockholders vote on company matters.

Stock Exchange

see Exchange

Stock Option

The right to buy specific amounts of a company's stock at a fixed price no matter how much the stock is selling for. If you had an option that let you buy at $5 and your company's stock was worth $7, you'd make $2 by exercising your option.

Stock Split

When a stock splits, the number of shares increases, while the price per share decreases in exact proportion. Contrary to popular belief, stock splits actually do nothing to benefit shareholders directly. If you own 100 shares of a stock that costs $50, and it splits 2-for-1, you're left with 200 shares of a stock that costs $25 — the total value is still $5,000. Still, some people believe that stock splits are a bullish sign, because they tend to indicate that management believes its share price will continue to rise.

Stock Type

see Morningstar Stock Type

Strategy

A brief description of what the company is doing to improve its business and set itself apart from its rivals. This description can include both long-term and short-term strategies.

Style Box

see Morningstar Style Box

Sustainable Growth Rate

Sustainable growth rate indicates how fast a company can theoretically grow without outside financing, given its current profitability, dividend policy, and debt levels. It's equal to return on equity (ROE) times (1 – payout ratio). A company whose sustainable growth rate is much lower than its EPS growth rate will have to find external sources of funding, either debt or equity.

T

Technical Analysis

A stock-picking method based on such things as price patterns and the trading volume in a stock. Technical analysis ignores fundamental factors such as the quality of a business or its management; as a result, it's not of much worth to long-term investors.

Ticker

Every publicly traded company is assigned a unique ticker that is used for identification. Tickers of stocks trading on the New York Stock Exchange contain one, two, or three letters; those trading on Nasdaq contain four letters; those trading over the counter contain four letters plus a Q at the end; and some foreign stocks contain four letters plus a Y at the end.

Total Cash Flow

This is all the cash a company generates, including noncash charges and credits. It is calculated by adding back depreciation and amortization, deferred taxes, and other sources of cash to net income in each year.

Total Equity

see Equity

Total Return %

Represents shareholders' gains from a stock over a given period of time. Total return includes both capital gains and losses (the increase or decrease in the stock price) and income (in the form of dividend payments). It is calculated by taking the change in the stock's price, assuming the reinvestment of all dividends, then dividing by the initial stock price, and expressing the result as a percentage.

Total Shares Mil

see Shares Outstanding

Trading Volume

see Average Daily Volume

TTM (Trailing 12 Months)

TTM, or trailing 12 months, refers to the most recent four quarters for which a company has reported financial results. Looking at a company's TTM results, rather than those for the most recent fiscal year, generally gives more up-to-date numbers. This is especially important for fast-growing companies.

Type

see Morningstar Stock Type

U

UR (Under Review)

If a given stock has UR for its Morningstar Rating or Fair Value, this means that the Morningstar analyst has placed the stock under review.

U.S. 90-Day Treasury Bill

These bills, issued by the U.S. government, are used as a common measure of short-term interest rates.

V

Valuation Ratios

These ratios measure how expensive a stock is. Beware, however—no single valuation ratio is perfect, and it's best to look at several different ratios in the appropriate context.

Volume

The number of shares traded during a given period. *see also Average Daily Volume*

W

Wilshire 4500

The Wilshire 4500 index consists of all the stocks in the Wilshire 5000 index minus the 500 stocks in the S&P 500 index. Like the Wilshire 5000, it measures the combined market value of these stocks, and is used as a benchmark for small- and mid-cap stocks.

Wilshire 5000

The Wilshire 5000 is one of the most common indexes for measuring the performance of the entire U.S. stock market, including companies of all sizes. Although it originally contained 5,000 stocks, the index now measures the combined market value of more than 6,500 stocks.

Wilshire REIT

The Wilshire REIT index measures the combined market value of equity real estate investment trusts (as opposed to mortgage REITs) with market caps above $1 billion. It is used as a benchmark for equity REIT performance.

Y

Yield

Also known as dividend yield, this number is equal to a stock's annual dividend per share divided by its price per share.

YTD

Year-to-date, or since the beginning of the current calendar or fiscal year. A stock's YTD total return is its return since January 1 of the current calendar year.